University Casebook Series

THE LAW AND FINANCE

OF

CORPORATE ACQUISITIONS

By

RONALD J. GILSON

Charles J. Meyers
Professor of Law and Business,
Stanford University
&
Marc & Eva Stern
Professor of Law and Business,
Columbia University

and

BERNARD S. BLACK

Professor of Law,
Columbia University

SECOND EDITION

Westbury, New York
THE FOUNDATION PRESS, INC.
1995

COPYRIGHT © 1986 THE FOUNDATION PRESS, INC.
COPYRIGHT © 1995 By THE FOUNDATION PRESS, INC.

        615 Merrick Ave.
        Westbury, N.Y. 11590–6607
        (516) 832–6950

Library of Congress Cataloging-in-Publication Data

Gilson, Ronald J., 1946–
   The law and finance of corporate acquisitions / by Ronald J.
  Gilson, Bernard S. Black. — 2nd ed.
     p.   cm. — (University casebook series)
  Includes index.
  ISBN 1–56662–067–8
   1. Consolidation and merger of corporations—United States—Cases.
  2. Corporations—Finance—Law and legislation—United States—Cases.
  I. Black, Bernard S., 1953–   . II. Title. III. Series.
  KF1477.A7G55   1995
  346.73'06626—dc20
  [347.3066626]   95–19904

TEXT IS PRINTED ON 10% POST CONSUMER RECYCLED PAPER

PRINTED WITH SOY INK

PREFACE TO THE SECOND EDITION

The field of corporate acquisitions has moved rapidly in the nine years since the first edition was written. The merger boom of the 1980s crested and broke. The stock market crashed in 1987, and took with it some extreme views on the efficiency of capital markets. New research casts doubt on whether we yet know how to measure the tradeoff between risk and return. The Supreme Court legitimated state antitakeover statutes, and the states responded with a vengeance. The poison pill, a nascent development in 1986, came to dominate takeover defenses, though the law on how it can be used is still developing. Proxy fights became important again, in response to the new vigor of tender offer defenses. Acquisitions of U.S. companies by foreign firms became more common. The empirical literature grew in scope and sophistication, as did the theoretical literature seeking to explain the empirical evidence and offering additional reasons for acquisitions. In response, the annual Supplements quickly swelled to unmanageable length. And that was without updating the by now obsolete chapter on the tax treatment of acquisitions, without a separate treatment of leveraged buyouts, without addressing the environmental law considerations that can make or break many transactions. A new edition was needed.

We tried in this edition to make the book more accessible both for students and for teachers. We reorganized and rewrote extensively in an effort to make the development of ideas and analysis more apparent. We edited virtually every page, looking to simplify and shorten the old, and make room for the new. Nonetheless, the second edition is not insignificantly longer than the first, reflecting the increased activity and complexity of the subjects covered. Below, we suggest alternatives for using this book, including proposed reading assignments for those who prefer to focus on friendly acquisitions, and for those who wish to skip or shorten some of the more technical discussions, including the chapters on event studies, taxation of acquisitions, and accounting for acquisitions.

Part I on finance theory is heavily rewritten, both for accessibility and to reflect new uncertainty about the validity of two central elements of finance theory -- the Capital Asset Pricing Model and the Efficient Capital Markets Hypothesis. Our approach to CAPM is to treat it as an example -- not necessarily correct -- of how assets *might* be priced, and to develop where possible the implications of diversification independent of any particular asset pricing model. Our approach to ECMH is to treat market efficiency as a matter of degree, rather than yes or no, as often a useful working assumption even if it isn't (and can't be) literally true. We also added problems to the end of each finance theory chapter, in the belief that finance is often best learned by solving problems. Solutions are available (to faculty only!) from the authors.

Part II on the motives for acquisitions now begins with the synergy and replacement of inefficient management explanations for acquisitions, rather than with the more technical and theoretically weaker financial alchemy and tax accounts. We have separated the discussion of hostile and friendly acquisitions in Part III. Teachers who lack the time to cover both can choose to emphasize the friendly deals that dominate corporate practice, even if hostile deals get a disproportionate share of the press. This separation also lets one focus on how, in friendly acquisitions, cooperative transaction planning can maximize the acquiring and target companies' joint value.

Part IV, covering non-corporate law planning considerations, has been expanded to include discussion of the Exon-Florio Amendment, in Chapter 25 and to include a review of successorship issues in connection with CERCLA environmental liability in Chapter 26.

We discovered to our surprise (and pleasure) that this book has been used about as often in business schools as in law schools. That led to a conscious effort to make this edition more accessible to business students. For this audience, the finance materials are less troublesome, but legal materials present a separate challenge -- how to explain legal materials to students who are skilled in finance but unskilled in law, without extending an already long book. We edited the old material and wrote new with a view to both a law and business school audience. The extra effort devoted to explaining legal concepts may also improve readability for a law school audience.

A new edition calls for thanks to new people. Special thanks go to Reinier Kraakman, who joined Ron on several supplements before deciding -- wisely, we're sure -- to devote more time to his newly enlarged family and less time to demands of a new edition. Michael Brown, Michael Dorf, Julie Grossman, Shuba Gosh, Arthur Haywoode, Julie Grossman, Sarkis Jebejian, Jennifer Olvey, Joseph Schohl and Collette Young also provided research assistance; Ann Alstott, Ian Ayres, Sanjai Bhagat, Marvin Chirelstein, Ron Daniels, Gerald Garvey, Noel Gaston, Victor Goldberg, Jeff Gordon, Claire Hill, David Ikenberry, Josef Lakonishok, Lou Lowenstein, Harold Mulherin, and Katherine Schipper commented on chapter drafts. Bernie thanks his wife, Brenda Hoy, for tolerating if not fully accepting his insistence on leaving the house at the crack of dawn to work on some project or other. Ron's family was used to it by now.

A word about mechanics. Citations in excerpted materials to cases, statutes, internal page or section references, items in a case record have been omitted or edited for style without so indicating. Equations, figures, and tables have been renumbered to correspond to the chapters in this book. Some variable names have been changed to provide greater consistency within this book. Complex tables have been edited, and footnotes have been deleted or shortened without so noting. The original footnote numbering has been retained; footnotes that we added to such materials are indicated by asterisks or letters. Deletions within a source are indicated by . . ., with no distinction between small and large deletions. Paragraph structure has sometimes been rearranged, and italics added, to improve the flow of edited material. Statute citations are idiosyncratic.

Selected securities laws and regulations are included in an appendix, as are selected sections of the Delaware corporate code. For those who want to use this book as a research tool, especially as a guide to the empirical literature on takeovers, we have expanded the index and added a list of cited articles, to complement the more customary list of cited cases.

We welcome comments, suggestions, corrections of typographical errors, etc.

Sections that Can be Omitted Due to Time Constraints

For those who find themselves unable to cover the entire textbook (indeed, we don't know of anyone who covers the whole thing, even in a 4-unit course), we offer below some suggestions for material, often the more technical and advanced material, that is relatively easy to omit without impairing the overall flow of the book.

Chapter 4: One can skip §§ C.3-4 on recent criticisms of CAPM, and § D on multi-factor asset pricing models.

Chapter 5: One can omit the Note on Noise Trading at the end of § C, and D on errors in human cognition.

Chapter 6: One can omit § A on the expected value of information and § E on variations and methodological issues in event studies.

Chapter 8: One can omit §§ B.3-4 on economies of scope and the managerial dimension, and §§ D.2-3 on empirical evidence on acquirer gains or losses from takeovers.

Chapter 9: Within the Note on the Failure of the Conglomerate Experiment in § C, one can omit points 3-4. In § D, one can omit the note on Evaluating Managerial Motives for Conglomerate Acquisitions. In § E, one can skip the Note on Post-merger Performance of Related Takeovers.

Chapter 10: One can skip the Herman & Lowenstein excerpt in § C and the note on the variety of takeover motives that follows this excerpt. One can omit the material from the Note on empirical tests of free cash flow theory in Chapter 10, through the end of the chapter.

Chapter 11: One can skip the Note on efficiency gains from leveraged buyouts in § C.1. One can also omit § C.2 on the semi-permanence of the LBO form and D.3 on the efficiency implications of overpriced LBOs.

Chapter 12: One can omit § A.2 on NOL, § A.3.a on basis step-up prior to 1986, § A.3 on taxation of highly leveraged transactions, § B.1.a on gains from basis step-up, and § B.3 on tax gains from transfer of NOLs.

Chapter 13: One can omit §§ A.2 and A.3 on accounting for partial and majority acquisitions, § A.5 on change in basis accounting, § D on a theory of choice of accounting method, and § E on how financial accounting standards should be set.

Chapter 15: One can omit § C on creation of market power.

Chapter 16: One can omit § D on Compulsory Share Exchanges and § E.2 on recharacterization of nonstatutory alternatives.

Chapter 17: If one is focusing the course on friendly transactions, one can omit § A.1.b and § B.1.b on shark repellant amendments and § C on the bidder's perspective.

Chapter 18: In light of the pervasive impact of poison pill, one can omit Wellman v. Dickinson, although we would retain the introduction to the case. One might also skip § C dealing with litigation under § 14 (e).

Chapter 21: This chapter can be omitted where sale of control has been covered in the basic corporations course, although we think that some effort by the instructor to put the doctrine in an acquisition context would be helpful.

Chapter 22: Singer v. Magnavox in § C.1, although interesting history, can be omitted and replaced with comment by the instructor.

Chapter 23: Edgar v. Mite in § A can be replaced with comment by the instructor on the antecedents to *CTS*. Section E on the valuation consequences of state takeover statutes can also be omitted.

Chapters 24-27: These chapters can all be omitted. Probably the first to go should be Chapter 25 on pre-acquisition review of takeovers and Chapter 26 on successor liability. A course that emphasizes friendly acquisitions will probably want to include Chapter 27; a course that includes full treatment of hostile acquisitions will probably want to include Chapter 24. Within Chapter 24, one can omit § D on ESOPs and other tainted votes, through the end of the chapter.

RONALD J. GILSON   BERNARD S. BLACK

December 1994

ACKNOWLEDGEMENTS

With appreciation, this acknowledgement is made for the publishers and authors who gave permission for the reproduction of excerpts from the following materials:

Accounting Review
> Hai Hong, Robert Kaplan & Gershon Mandelker, Pooling vs. Purchase: the Effects of Accounting for Mergers on Stock Prices

Addison-Wesley Publishing Company, Inc.
> Louis Lowenstein, Sense and Nonsense in Corporate Finance (1991)

American Bar Foundation Research Journal
> William Carney, Fundamental Corporate Changes, Minority Shareholders, and Business Purposes

American Institute of Certified Public Accountants
> APB Opinion No. 16, Business Combinations
> APB Opinion No. 18, The Equity Method of Accounting for Investments in Common Stock

American Law Institute
> Principles of Corporate Governance: Analysis and Recommendations

Bell Journal of Economics (RAND)
> Yakov Amihud & Baruch Lev, Risk Reduction as a Managerial Motive for Conglomerate Mergers

Warren Buffet
> Warren Buffett, 1989 Annual Report of Berkshire Hathaway Inc.

The Business Lawyer (ABA Section of Corporation, Banking and Business Law)
> Marshall Armstrong, The Work and Workings of the Financial Accounting Standards Board
> James Freund & Richard Easton, The Three-Piece Suitor: An Alternative Approach Negotiatied Corporate Acquisitions
> Charles Nathan & Marylin Sobel, Corporate Stock Repurchases in the Context of Unsolicited Takeover Bids
> James Tobin & James Maiwurm, Beachhead Acquisitions: Creating Waves in the Market Place and Uncertainty in the Regulatory Framework
> Herbert Wachtell, Special Tender Offer Litigation Tactics

Columbia University Press
> Reinier Kraakman, Taking Discounts Seriously: The Implications of "Discounted" Share Prices as an Acquisition Motive

Dow Jones & Company, Inc.
> Jay Palmer, Why This LBO Crashed: A Prescient Ananlysis of a Doomed Deal, Barron's, Oct. 30, 1989

Dow-Jones Irwin
Leveraged Management Buyouts (Yakov Amihud ed.1989)
James Lorie, Peter Dodd & Mary Kimpton, The Stock Market: Theories & Evidence (2d ed.1985)

The Dryden Press
Sidney Davidson, Clyde Stickney & Roman Weil, Financial Accounting (2d ed.1979)
Sidney Davidson, Clyde Stickney & Roman Weil, Financial Accounting (6th ed.1991)

Financial Accounting Standards Board
FASB Interpretation No. 35 -- Criteria for Applying the Equity Method of Accounting for Investments in Common Stock

Financial Analysts Journal (Financial Analysts Federation)
Franco Modigliani & Gerald Pogue, An Introduction to Risk and Retrun: Concepts and Evidence (Parts I & II)

Financial Analysts Journal (Association for Investment Management and Research)
Barrie Wigmore, The Decline in Credit Quality of New-Issue Junk Bonds

Forbes
Norm Alster, One Man's Poison . . ., Forbes, Oct. 16, 1989

The Free Press
Malcolm Salter & Wolf Weinhold, Diversification Through Acquisition (1979)

Joseph Grundfest
Job Losses and Takeovers (March 11, 1988)
Letter to the Honorable Mario M. Cuomo (June 6, 1989)

Harvard Law Review
William Andrews, The Stockholder's Right to Equal Opportunity in the Sale of Shares

Harvard Business Review
Michael Jensen, Eclipse of the Public Corporation

Houghton-Mifflin Company
F.M. Scherer & David Ross, Industrial Market Structure and Economic Performance (3d ed.1990)

Journal of Accountancy
William Beaver, What Should Be the FASB's Objectives?

Journal of Accounting and Economics
Robert Holthausen, Evidence on the Effect of Bond Covenants and Management Compensation Contracts on the Choice of Accounting Techniques: The Case of the Depreciation Switch-Back

Journal of Applied Corporate Finance
> Bernard Black & Joseph Grundfest, Shareholder Gains from Takeovers and Restructurings Between 1981 and 1986
> Steven Kaplan, The Staying Power of Leveraged Buyouts

Journal of Economic Behavior and Organization
> David Teece, Economies of Scope and the Scope of the Enterprise

Journal of Economic Literature
> R. Preston McAfee & John McMillan, Auctions and Bidding
> Oliver Williamson, The Modern Corporation: Origins, Evolution, Attributes

Journal of Economic Perspective
> Andrei Shleifer & Lawrence Summers, The Noise Trader Approach to Finance

Journal of Finance
> Eugene Fama & Kenneth French, The Cross-Section of Expected Stock Returns
> Haim Levy & Marshall Sarnat, Diversification, Portfolio Analysis and the Uneasy Case for Conglomerate Mergers
> R. Hal Mason & Maurice Goudzwaard, Performance of Conglomerate Firms: A Portfolio Approach

Journal of Financial Economics
> Michael Bradley, Anand Desai & E. Han Kim, The Rationale Behind Interfirm Tender Offers: Information or Synergy
> Michael Bradley, Anand Desai, & E. Han Kim, Synergistic Gains from Corporate Acquisitions and Their Division Between the Stockholders of Target and Acquiring Firms
> Steven Kaplan, The Effects of Management Buyouts on Operating Performance and Value

Journal of Portfolio Management
> Fischer Black, Beta and Return

Knight-Ridder Tribune News Service
> Bernie Shellum, Fruehauf Steers into Trouble: Management Cited in Decline of Truckmaker

Little, Brown and Company
> James Cox, Financial Information, Accounting and the Law (1980)
> Melvin Eisenberg, The Structure of the Corporation (1976)

McGraw-Hill, Inc.
> Richard Brealey & Stewart Myers, Principles of Corporate Finance (4th ed. 1991)

Mergers & Acquisitions
> Gary Haight, The Portfolio Merger: Finding the Company That Can Stabilize Your Earnings

The New York Times Company
    Seth Faison, Cigarette Ruling: Hour of Confusion

Oxford University Press
    Knights, Raiders & Targets: The Impact of the Hostile Takeover (John
        Coffee, Louis Lowenstein & Susan Rose-Ackerman eds.1988)

Prentice-Hall, Inc.
    Arthur Fleischer, Jr., Alexander Sussman & Henry Lesser, Takeover Defense
        (4th ed.1990)
    Charles Holloway, Decision Making Under Uncertainty (1979)
    James van Horne, Financial Management and Policy (7th ed.1986)

Science (American Association for the Advancement of Science)
    Andrei Shleifer & Robert Vishny, The Takeover Wave of the 1980's
    Amos Tversky & Daniel Kahneman, Judgment Under Uncertainty: Heuristics
        and Biases

Stanford Law Review
    Bernard Black, Bidder Overpayment in Takeovers
    Ronald Gilson, The Case Against Shark Repellent Amendments: Structural
        Limitations on the Enabling Concept
    Ronald Gilson, A Structural Approach to Corporations: The Case Against
        Defensive Tactics in Tender Offers

Time Inc.
    Bill Saporito, The Inside Story of Time Warner

University of Chicago Press
    Corporate Takeovers: Causes and Consequences (Alan Auerbach ed.1988)
    Benjamin Klein, Robert Crawford & Armen Alchian, Vertical Integration,
        Appropriable Rents, and the Competitive Contracting Process
    Mark Mitchell & Kenneth Lehn, Do Bad Bidders Become Good Targets?

University of Michigan Press
    Peter Steiner, Mergers: Motives, Effects, Policies (1975)

Virginia Law Review
    Ronald Gilson & Reinier Kraakman, The Mechanisms of Market Efficiency
    Note, Three-Party Mergers: The Fourth Form of Corporate Acquisition

Wachtell, Lipton, Rosen & Katz
    The Share Purchase Rights Plan (March 1994)

Warren, Gorham & Lamont, Inc.
    Encyclopedia of Investments (Marshall Blume & Jack Friedman eds.1982)

Yale Law Journal
    Frank Easterbrook & Daniel Fischel, Corporate Control Transactions
    Ronald Gilson, Value Creation by Business Lawyers

Bayless Manning, The Shareholder's Appraisal Remedy: An Essay for Frank
    Coker

SUMMARY OF CONTENTS

TABLE OF CONTENTS

TABLE OF CASES

Principal cases are in italic type. All other cases are in roman type.
References are to pages.

TABLE OF AUTHORITIES
References are to Pages.

THE LAW AND FINANCE
OF
CORPORATE ACQUISITIONS

CHAPTER 1: AN INTRODUCTION TO CORPORATE ACQUISITIONS AND TRANSACTION PLANNING

A. An Overview of This Book

This book is an effort to fuse several distinct innovations in corporate law scholarship and curriculum. The first, a transactional approach, treats as the focus of interest actual business activities that cut across several academic subject areas. This approach was pioneered by David Herwitz in his 1966 casebook *Business Planning: Materials on the Planning of Corporate Transactions*. Its insight lay in both its problem orientation and its integration of corporate, tax and securities law in a single book. The second innovation, pioneered by Victor Brudney and Marvin Chirelstein in their 1972 *Cases and Materials on Corporate Finance*, is the recognition that finance theory is centrally important to understanding corporate law issues. The third is the increasing importance of empirical evidence in corporate law scholarship. To assess the pros and cons of an active takeover market, for example, we must study the available evidence with a skeptical eye, and understand which questions the empirical evidence seems to answer and which it leaves open. This book builds on the premise that finance theory and empirical studies provide important insights not just for the familiar exercise of evaluating legal doctrine but, more importantly, for understanding the transactional process and, ultimately, for good lawyering.

Part I of the book (Chapters 2 through 7) provides the finance skills necessary to analyze corporate acquisitions. Chapter 2 introduces the idea of discounting and present value. Chapters 3 and 4 introduce the core of modern portfolio theory and capital asset pricing, including discussion of the Capital Asset Pricing Model's success in explaining how risk affects expected return. Chapter 5 examines the Efficient Capital Market Hypothesis with emphasis on the multiple meanings of market efficiency. It explores when we should, and should not, expect to find a reasonable level of market efficiency, the evidence for and against market efficiency, and the factors that lead toward or away from efficient pricing.

Chapter 6 introduces an important empirical technique for measuring whether a particular event alters the market value of a security -- the event study. This chapter is the most technically demanding in the book, but the payoff is large. Event studies form the core of much of the empirical literature examining whether corporate acquisitions result in gains to investors in the acquirer or the target. Understanding the event study technique is critical to evaluating the fit between theory and empirical evidence concerning gains from acquisitions. Moreover, students need to understand the uses and misuses of statistical data, independent of the value of that understanding for the particular subject of corporate acquisitions.

Part I ends with Chapter 7 on option pricing theory. Many common securities and business relationships can be characterized as options. Understanding what factors determine the value of an option can highlight the incentives of the parties to an acquisition or other business transaction.

The material in Part I should be understandable to readers who have had no prior exposure to finance theory. It requires no mathematical skills beyond high school algebra. Students need to understand the insights underlying each aspect of finance theory covered, but do not need to master the formal techniques in a computational sense. The book reflects the belief that lawyers must understand and, through advance planning, structure the incentives of the parties to the transaction. The finance theory covered in Part I can illuminate these incentives and suggest ways of dealing creatively with them. Using finance theory in this way requires conceptual understanding; it does not require mastery of the technical apparatus.

New to this edition are problems at the back of selected chapters. Our experience is that solving problems, even relatively simple ones, aids one in understanding the financial concepts developed in the text. Problems are also a good reality check -- does one really understand the concepts?

Building on the skills imparted in Part I, Part II (Chapters 8 through 15) evaluates in separate chapters the commonly offered explanations for acquisitions: operating synergy; financial synergy or anti-synergy from conglomerate acquisitions; replacing inefficient management; the management incentives, debt constraints, and concentrated ownership that characterize leveraged buyouts; tax savings; boosting financial statement earnings and thus share price through choice of accounting method; mispricing of the target company's stock that creates an opportunity for an acquirer to make a bargain purchase; and wealth transfers to shareholders from creditors or employees. For each explanation, the text describes why it might provide a motive for an acquisition, and evaluates its fit with the finance theory developed in Part I, and its consistency with the available empirical evidence. The chapters on financial accounting and tax motives for acquisitions also provide an opportunity to survey the financial accounting and tax aspects of acquisitions, with which *all* business lawyers need to be generally familiar.

We think it important to examine at length the alternative explanations for why acquisitions take place for several reasons. First, without a systematic analysis of the multifaceted phenomenon of takeovers, it is impossible to formulate sensible policy prescriptions. Second, lawyers need to understand how their clients expect to gain from a transaction. Third, the analysis of motives in Part II illustrates the importance of empirical evidence in formulating legal arguments and public policy. To evaluate the evidence, students must understand the empirical methodology well enough to evaluate the academic studies with an appropriate level of skepticism, something the original investigators sometimes have not done.

Part III (Chapters 16 through 24) considers corporate and securities law planning considerations in both hostile and friendly acquisitions. It begins our consideration of what can be called the public ordering role of the business lawyer: Structuring a transaction to minimize the cost of the potentially applicable regulatory apparatus. Chapter 16 examines, from the perspective of a planner, the alternative acquisition techniques available and such issues as what vote should be necessary to approve a negotiated acquisition, who should be allowed to vote, and the de facto merger doctrine. Chapter 17 addresses the corporate law concerns of the acquirer and the target in hostile acquisitions, especially the rules governing the actions of the target's board of directors in resisting an unwanted takeover. Chapter 18 addresses securities law concerns in hostile acquisitions, especially the Williams Act's regulation of tender offers and acquisitions of a 5% or greater stock interest.

Chapters 19-22 focus on friendly acquisitions. Chapters 19 and 20 discuss, respectively, corporate and securities law concerns in the standard context where a acquirer with no prior relationship with the target acquires 100% of a target company. Registration requirements under the Securities Act of 1933 for non-cash transactions are covered only briefly, on the assumption that they will be addressed in a securities regulation course. Chapter 21 addresses the corporate law issues that arise in the sale by a controlling shareholder or shareholder group of a controlling but less than 100% interest. Chapter 22 addresses corporate and securities law concerns in "freezeout" transactions, where an already controlling shareholder seeks to acquire the remainder of the target's stock.

Chapters 23 and 24 cover specialized topics in hostile acquisitions of control. Chapter 23 addresses state efforts to regulate hostile takeovers. Chapter 24 considers proxy fights for control, both as an alternative to a hostile takeover bid as a means to transfer corporate control, and as a complement to a hostile takeover bid.

Part IV (Chapters 25-26) covers other legal aspects of corporate acquisitions. Chapter 25 considers pre-acquisition governmental review under the Hart-Scott-Rodino Premerger Notification Act and, for takeovers by foreign acquirers, the Exon-Florio Amendment. Chapter 26 considers the acquiring company's ability to shed or limit its exposure to the target's preexisting liabilities, including hazardous waste cleanup liability, products liability, and collective bargaining and pension obligations.

Part V (Chapter 27) seeks to integrate the perspective of finance theory with the task of drafting an acquisition agreement. It illustrates how a "standard" form of acquisition agreement can solve a series of problems inherent in valuing a complex asset such as a business. Business value depends on expected cash flows and the riskiness of those expected returns. Standard finance theory values those assets under a set of perfect market assumptions, such as homogeneous expectations, common time horizons, and costless information, which are obviously not valid in the real world. Chapter 27 builds on this fact to develop two related ideas. The first is that part of the role of the business lawyer is to create a transactional structure which allows the parties to act more nearly *as if* the perfect market assumptions were valid. The second is that many elements of an acquisition agreement can be understood from this perspective.

The analysis presents the business lawyer as a transaction cost engineer whose task is to formulate the transaction structures as near to "perfect" as possible. Looking at the lawyer's role in an acquisition in terms of financial concepts can affect how lawyers negotiate acquisition agreements -- seeing representations as a means of reducing information asymmetry changes the lawyer's task from one of distributive bargaining to one of joint problem solving -- and improve their ability to respond creatively to new problems. Once one understands the transactional problems posed by asset pricing in an imperfect world, many seemingly new problems may turn out to be manifestations of the same problem in different contexts.

Having said something about the subjects the book covers, we should also say something about the manner in which those subjects are covered. This book does not hide the ball; our views on the issues considered are made apparent, sometimes insistently so. We have taken this approach, in contrast to the traditional agnosticism typified by a series of unanswered questions at the end of a section, for two reasons -- one pedagogic and one substantive. The pedagogic reason for giving the book an explicit point of view is that integrating different bodies of law, plus finance theory, plus an extensive empirical literature, is hard enough as it is. Our views are hardly the only ones possible (and we discuss alternatives) but they illustrate the way in which the various elements interact and what matters must be considered in reaching normative judgments. They can serve both as an example and as a target, each of which can be a useful pedagogic tool.

The substantive reason for the book's normative bent is the absence in the literature of an integrated treatment of the full range of legal issues raised by corporate acquisitions. The need for such a treatment is apparent in the performance of the Delaware Supreme Court and the state legislatures. The furious development in the 1980s of sophisticated hostile acquisition techniques and defensive tactics subjected the Delaware courts to a seemingly unending stream of difficult corporate law issues that left little time for contemplation, for stepping back to see how the individual problems fit together. Like a law professor launching a Socratic attack on a beleaguered corporations student, transaction planners almost immediately gave the courts back their own justifications, but now taken just another step forward.

Each new decision was reflected in the tactics of the next transaction; the Chancery Court often had to confront the "next case" on a motion for preliminary injunction soon after the initial decision. This drastic telescoping of the common law process makes careful reconsideration of prior doctrine quite difficult. The demands of individual cases for prompt resolution (lest delay alone resolve the outcome of a transaction) are also inconsistent with careful development of the common law. This book can hopefully provide some of the perspective, and perhaps a reconceptualization, that courts have not been able to undertake themselves.

As for the legislatures, their often frantic rush to enact a new statute to prevent a particular transaction is a caricature of how legislative policy should be made. Few academics think that all hostile takeovers are bad, or that corporate managers should be able unilaterally to decide whether a takeover bid may proceed, but that is the premise on which state legislatures often seem to act. We need to understand the special interest pressures that lead state legislatures to act this way, but we also need to criticize the legislative actions, in the hope that the tide may be stemmed in a calmer moment or in another forum.

B.   The Professional Setting: Value Creation by Business Lawyers[1]

We begin here an inquiry, set in the context of corporate acquisitions, into what business lawyers *really* do. By and large, critical study of the legal profession has displayed a myopic fixation with litigation -- its frequency, complexity, expense and unequal availability -- and what can be done to "improve" it: clinical training, methods of delivering legal services, procedural reforms.   Careful analysis of the function of the rest of the profession -- business lawyers -- has been absent.

Lawyers as a group are often criticized as non-productive actors in the economy.   Engineers, it is said, make the pie grow larger.   Lawyers only rearrange the slices, shrink the pie, and take some for themselves in the process.[2]   The criticism, though, doesn't distinguish among the tasks that lawyers do.   This book explores how business lawyers can add value as participants in corporate transactions.   Lawyers are necessary, but are they merely a necessary evil?   It is surprising and just a little embarrassing that there seems to be no coherent answer to the question of what business lawyers *really* do.[3]   That is not, of course, to say that answers have not been offered;   lawyers have offered a number of familiar responses at one time or another.   The problem is that none of them is very helpful.

Clients have their own, often quite uncharitable, view of what business lawyers do.   In an extreme version, business lawyers are perceived as evil sorcerers who use their special skills and professional magic to relieve clients of their possessions.   Kurt Vonnegut at least makes the point in an amusing way.   A law student is told by his favorite professor that, to get ahead in the practice of law, "a lawyer should be looking for situations where large amounts of money are about to change hands":

---

[1] This discussion draws heavily on Ronald Gilson, *Value Creation by Business Lawyers: Legal Skills and Asset Pricing*, 94 Yale L.J. 239 (1984).

[2] See, e.g., Kevin Murphy, Andrei Shleifer & Robert Vishny, *The Allocation of Talent: Implications for Growth*, 1991 Q.J.Econ. 503; Derek Bok, *The President's Report to the Board of Overseers of Harvard University for 1981-1982*, 33 J.Legal Educ. 570 (1983); Akio Morita, *Do Companies Need Lawyers? Sony's Experiences in the United States*, 30 Japan Q. 2 (Jan.-Mar.1983); Stephen Magee, *The Optimum Number of Lawyers: Cross-National Evidence*, (Univ. of Texas, Dept. of Fin., working paper, 1992).

[3] The work of William Klein is an important exception. In *Business Organization and Finance* (1980) and *The Modern Business Organization: Bargaining Under Constraints*, 91 Yale L.J. 1521 (1982), he has made a major effort to use finance theory to understand consensual business arrangements.

In every big transaction [the professor said], there is a magic moment during which a man has surrendered a treasure, and during which the man who is due to receive it has not yet done so. An alert lawyer will make that moment his own, possessing the treasure for a magic microsecond, taking a little of it, passing it on. If the man who is to receive the treasure is unused to wealth, has an inferiority complex and shapeless feelings of guilt, as most people do, the lawyer can often take as much as half the bundle, and still receive the recipient's blubbering thanks.[4]

Clients frequently advance another, more charitable but still quite negative view of the business lawyer that also should be familiar to practitioners. Business lawyers are just a transaction cost, part of a system of wealth redistribution from clients to lawyers; legal fees are a tax on business transactions. All too often, lawyers are also deal killers whose continual raising of obstacles, without a commensurate effort at finding solutions, kills otherwise viable transactions. A lawyer turned journalist has captured the criticism nicely:

What happens between lawyer and client today goes something like this: The lawyer sits at the elbow of the businessman while contracts are being negotiated, that is, while a deal is being made. Then, once the principals feel an agreement has been concluded, the lawyers assure them it has not. After further negotiation, the lawyers "draft a contract" -- *reduce the deal to written law* -- and pass it back and forth accompanied in each passage by increasingly minute argumentation (e.g., "We believe in all fairness that the law of Luxembourg should govern in the event of non-performance under Para. V(e)(ii)" etc., etc.). Once they have decided that neither party can be further hoodwinked or bullied, the typist prepares many copies to make "doubly sure" (making doubly sure in this special fashion is 28 per cent of law practice), and the clients sign all of them. Then they smile at each other and shake hands, while glancing sidelong at their lawyers, who are still scowling (it's part of the fee-action). This little drama, in numerous manifestations, is the beginning of law -- perhaps, even, the final heart of it as well.[5]

Lawyers, to be sure, do not share these harsh evaluations of their role. When this question -- what do business lawyers *really* do -- is put to business lawyers, the familiar response is that they "protect" their clients, get them the "best" deal. In the back of their minds is a sense that their clients neither perceive nor understand the risks that lawyers raise, and that, as a result, clients do not recognize that it is in their best interests when lawyers identify the myriad of subtle problems unavoidably present in a typical transaction.

The academic literature offers a more balanced view. Here the predominant approach is functional. The lawyer is presented as counselor,

---

[4] Kurt Vonnegut, *God Bless You, Mrs. Rosewater* 9 (Dell ed.1965).

[5] Bazelon, *Clients Against Lawyers: A Guide to the Real Joys of Legal Practice*, Harper's Mag. 104 (Sept.1967) (emphasis in original).

planner, drafter, negotiator, investigator, lobbyist, scapegoat, champion, and, most strikingly, even as friend. Certainly the list of functions identified rings true enough. An experienced practitioner can quickly recall playing each of these roles.

These characterizations of what business lawyers do share an important similarity and a common failure. The unfavorable view ascribed to clients reflects the belief that business lawyers *reduce* the value of a transaction, while both the favorable view held by business lawyers themselves, and the more neutral but still positive view offered by the academic literature, implicitly assume that business lawyers *increase* the value of a transaction. But both sides agree on the appropriate standard by which the performance of business lawyers should be judged: *Is the transaction worth more, net of legal fees, as a result of the lawyer's participation?* This same question can, of course, be asked for other professionals, including investment bankers and accountants, who participate in a business transaction. The critical failure of all of these views is not their differing conclusions. Rather, it is the absence of an explanation of *how* the activities of business lawyers and other professionals affect transaction value.

One goal of this book is to understand the relationship between what business lawyers do and transaction value, to develop analytical techniques that identify what activities can create value, and to explore approaches that make business lawyers better at achieving this potential. We will explore the two critical aspects of business lawyers' involvement with clients: the *public* ordering and *private* ordering aspects of business transactions. The public ordering aspect of business transactions arises because, in our mixed economy, complex business transactions are affected by multiple regulatory regimes. Tax law, corporate law, securities law, antitrust law, financial accounting rules, environmental law, tort law, labor law, and pension law all can affect the form of a particular acquisition. As a result, a transaction that is private, in the sense that the government is not a party, has important elements of public ordering resulting from the need to comply with regulatory requirements and emanating from the public policy concerns that gave rise to the regulations.

The most important part of the public ordering aspect of private transactions is not merely passive compliance -- structuring a business transaction to meet the terms of seemingly applicable regulations. Rather, business lawyers often must actively design the structure of the transaction to minimize the number of rules that apply and the cost of complying with those that do. Regulation determines the structure of the transaction but, for the client, the goal may be minimizing cost, not maximizing compliance. From this perspective, it is critical that most regulatory systems express the boundaries of their application and the detail of their requirements in formal terms: Transactions that take a particular outward form are covered. So, for example, Subchapter C of the Internal Revenue Code treats corporate acquisitions that take the form of a statutory merger differently from those that take the form of a sale of assets, and a similar distinction is drawn by many state corporation laws.

This approach to regulation invites a planning response. As will be developed in Part I, the subject of most acquisitions can be described as a collection of assets and people with a particular potential for generating future income and with a particular level of risk. If cash flows and risks are not altered, the formal trappings of the acquisition can be manipulated extensively without altering its financial substance. Thus, the parties can often structure transactions so that their form falls outside the terms of at least some otherwise applicable regulatory schemes. This regulatory eternal triangle is completed by the courts which, in the end, must determine whether to credit the form in which the parties cast a transaction, or to look beyond form to purpose and financial substance. This tension -- between voluntary selection of transactional form and regulatory purpose -- is a central dilemma for business law. The form versus substance and step transaction doctrines in tax law and the de facto merger doctrine in corporate law are among the familiar examples.

The opportunity thus exists for business lawyers to create value by structuring a transaction to minimize the cost to the client of the variety of complex, sometimes conflicting regulatory systems that might otherwise touch on the transaction. Much of this book is directed at this opportunity: to understand the regulatory systems that apply to corporate acquisitions and the public policy that gave rise to them, and to develop the facility to manipulate them to achieve a client's goals.

In addition to the public ordering aspects of business transactions, there are also important *private* ordering aspects: matters bearing on transactional structure that would be important even in a world with *no* regulation. To examine the lawyer's role with respect to these aspects of business transactions, however, it is important to be more specific about what it means to create value. Imagine that a client has the good fortune to retain a very talented business lawyer, while the other party to the transaction is represented by a dullard. This may alter the allocation of gains from the transaction between the parties. The transaction is worth more to the talented lawyer's client than if that lawyer had not participated.

One reaches a quite different conclusion, however, if the transaction is viewed from the perspective of *both* clients. Then the lawyers' participation doesn't increase the value of the transaction; rather, resources have been expended to alter the *distribution* of joint gains. And for purposes of evaluating whether business lawyers can increase transaction value, the appropriate perspective is not that of the client with the more talented lawyer, but the joint perspective of both clients.

As in many other areas, evaluating whether a practice is beneficial, in this case participation by business lawyers, depends on whether the issue is evaluated *ex ante* or *ex post*. If the evaluation is *ex post* -- that is, if it has already been determined that both sides will retain a lawyer -- then a business lawyer whose bargaining skill results in his client receiving a larger portion of the gain from the transaction has increased the transaction's value to *that* client. If, however, the evaluation is *ex ante* -- before either side has decided whether to retain a lawyer -- the result is quite different. Both clients would determine jointly whether to retain lawyers for the transaction, recognizing that if either retained a lawyer, so would the other to avoid being at a bargaining disadvantage. In this situation, if all business lawyers provide is skillful distributive bargaining, the clients' joint decision would be to hire *no* lawyers because, net of lawyers' fees, the surplus from the transaction to be divided between the clients would be *smaller* as a result of the participation of lawyers. Only a client who believed that its lawyer would systematically be better than the other party's, by enough so that the expected gain from better distributive bargaining exceeded the cost of *both* lawyers, would still use lawyers in the transaction. Given any reasonable assumption about the availability and distribution of legal talent among lawyers serving commercial clients, this disparity is unlikely to exist with any frequency.

Our focus with respect to the business lawyer's private ordering function thus will be on identifying how, regulation aside, a business lawyer can help private parties order their relationship in a way that increases the size of the entire pie, rather than merely increasing the size of one party's piece at the expense of the other's. This question is most prominent in Part II, where we examine motives for acquisitions; in Part III, where we consider friendly acquisitions; and in Part VI, where we examine a standard corporate acquisition agreement to see if it evidences techniques that hold the promise of creating value, and whether these techniques fit a general pattern that can help explain how business lawyers can create value through skill in designing the transaction structure.

The discussion thus far has focused on *value*. The central question is how business lawyers can increase the value of a transaction. But how can we determine whether a transaction would have been more valuable if a lawyer had participated or, conversely, would have been worth less had legal counsel not been hired? A truly empirical approach to measuring the impact of a business lawyer's participation seems impossible for a number of reasons. It is unlikely that we could find data covering both a sample of transactions in which a business lawyer did participate and a control group of equivalent transactions which were accomplished without a lawyer. Even if the data-collection problem could somehow be solved, serious methodological problems would remain. We might know the dollar value attached to particular transactions by the participants, but we would face overwhelming problems in determining whether the transactions were really comparable so that any difference in value could be ascribed to the business lawyer's participation.

There is, however, an alternative approach to determining the potential for business lawyers to add value to a transaction. The first step is to understand how a transaction is valued in the absence of a business lawyer's participation. If the factors that generally determine transaction value can be identified, the second step is relatively straightforward. By understanding the relationship between these factors and the business lawyer's activities, it should be possible to frame hypotheses that directly link the application of legal skills to transaction value.

We begin this analysis by recognizing that the subjects of business transactions are typically capital assets: assets whose value is determined solely by the income, whether in cash flow or appreciation, they are expected to earn.[6] A corporate acquisition can be seen as the transfer of a capital asset from one party to another. Characterizing transactions as transfers of capital assets is important because, over the last 30 years, financial economists have begun to develop a body of theory to explain how capital assets are valued or, as a financial economist would put it, "priced." If asset pricing theory can identify the factors that determine transaction value, then we can examine whether business lawyers can influence these factors in ways that alter transaction value. And if the systematic application of legal skills can affect transaction value, then two important results follow. First, we should be able to examine what business lawyers do and determine if their activities bear on transaction value. That is, it would be possible to inquire positively into the efficiency of the common business "lawyer." Second, and more important, we should be able to make normative statements about what business lawyers *should* do to increase the value of a transaction. Here the prospect is really quite exciting: Theory will have been brought to bear not merely to criticize doctrine or urge public policy reform, but as a tool to improve the quality of legal practice.

On a more prosaic level, corporate acquisitions are transactions where, as Vonnegut put it, "large amounts of money are about to change hands;" and large legal fees are hardly possible when *small* amounts of money change hands. Thus, corporate acquisitions are an important source of business for major law firms. Students aspiring to be business lawyers obviously can gain from an introduction to a significant area of their prospective employers' practice.

The effort to understand what business lawyers do, and to learn how better to do it, must begin with study of the modern theory of finance. Part I of the book introduces this theory. Part II applies the theory to evaluating the various reasons why clients might *think* corporate acquisitions are a useful activity. Understanding how the client hopes to gain from a transaction is a prerequisite to making the transaction more valuable (and to keeping the client happy). Moreover, if some reasons makes sense (e.g., synergy) and others (e.g., financial statement alchemy) do not, business lawyers can add value by structuring transactions so that the real values are

---

[6] This definition, while standard, is limited. Any asset that has consumption value -- i.e., its owner holds it for reasons other than (or in addition to) its potential for generating income -- falls outside the definition. For example, the psychic value of being your own boss may explain why many owners of small businesses continue in their vocation even though the businesses earn less than the market value of their owners' services plus a return on invested capital.

preserved, when these values come in conflict with less sensible reasons for acquisitions. Parts III through V review the various regulatory systems that bear on the opportunity to create value in connection with corporate acquisitions. We return to purely private ordering concerns in Part VI.

C.   The Historical Setting

With the potential for business lawyers to create value in mind, the next step is to explain the choice of corporate acquisitions as a context. It is, of course, critical to look at the value creation in context. Bringing theory to bear on practice requires its careful application in a *real* setting so that its relevance can be evaluated. In our case, the theory to be applied is modern finance theory, with special emphasis on how capital assets are valued. Corporate acquisitions are a particularly appropriate setting for applying this theory for three important reasons.

First, a corporate acquisition is centrally the transfer of a capital asset. Indeed, valuation of corporate securities -- the indicia of ownership of a corporation -- has dominated the empirical tests of modern finance theory. Moreover, a large body of empirical literature now exists that measures the impact of both corporate acquisitions generally, and of the techniques and alternatives associated with corporate acquisitions, on the security holders of both acquiring and target companies. Thus, there is a body of both theory *and* data against which both clients' beliefs about the private value of acquisitions, and public beliefs about the social impact of acquisitions can be assessed.

Second, despite extensive regulation, corporate acquisitions still provide substantial opportunity for private ordering. They thus allow examination of the potential for business lawyers to create value both by manipulating the regulatory regimes bearing on acquisition transactions and by structuring the private arrangement between the parties. And because the private ordering function is often difficult for outsiders to observe, acquisitions are a particularly useful setting in which to study what business lawyers do. A business lawyer's principal charge in the transaction is to negotiate and prepare the acquisition agreement. Thus, a fairly complete record of the lawyer's activity is created as a matter of course.

Third, corporate acquisitions are centrally important objects of study without regard to what they may tell us about how to be a business lawyer. In the 1980s, acquisition activity reshaped the structure of the American economy. Critics claim that takeovers exact a huge cost in jobs and financial stability. Others argue that corporate acquisitions are a critical element of the overall corporate governance structure, that helps to ensure corporate management keeps the goal of profit maximization firmly in mind. Moreover, corporate acquisitions may be a primary means by which changes in the economic environment affect the structure of individual companies and industries.[7] Numerous Congressional hearings have been held on the question of whether particular types of corporate acquisitions, or acquisitions generally, should be curtailed, and significant changes in the corporate income tax during the 1980s were motivated by concern over the level of acquisition activity, rather than issues of tax policy.[8] Developing a detailed understanding of so controversial an activity is thus justifiable in itself.

Despite the continued controversy, takeovers are not a new phenomenon. Apparent waves of acquisition activity, and controversy concerning them, have been a feature of the American economy since the late 1800s. But the character of the activity has changed dramatically over time, and understanding current transactional forms and legal rules is aided by understanding something of the history of corporate acquisitions in the United States.

Malcolm Salter & Wolf Weinhold
MERGER TRENDS AND PROSPECTS FOR THE 1980'S
2-27 (1980)

A Brief History of Corporate Mergers and Acquisitions in the U.S.

Economists and students of industrial organization have identified three major merger waves which swept the American economy between 1890 and 1975. Figure 1-1 . . . outlines the scope and magnitude of these cycles. Each cycle has been well documented with extensive economic literature and policy debate.[7] To help put current merger and acquisition activity into proper perspective, it is useful to briefly review these three waves.

The first peak in merger and acquisition activity just prior to 1900 was reached in a period of rapid economic expansion following two decades of economic stagnation (industrial production, for instance, grew 100%). The

---

[7] See Ronald Gilson, *The Political Ecology of Takeovers: Thoughts on Harmonizing the European Corporate Governance Environment*, 61 Ford.L.Rev. 161 (1992).

[8] For example, the original legislation concerning taxation of corporate acquisitions that became part of the Tax Equity and Fiscal Responsibility Act of 1982 was introduced by Representative Stark, in H.R. 6295, 97th Cong., 2d Sess. (1982), as The Corporate Takeover Tax Act of 1982. Martin Ginsburg describes the legislation as responding to the public impression "of a nation overwhelmed by a spreading rash of enormous corporate acquisitions motivated and financed in significant part by extraordinary tax avoidance." Martin Ginsburg, *Taxing Corporate Acquisitions*, 38 Tax L.Rev. 171, 216 (1983). With respect to the motives of the Tax Reform Act of 1986, see Myron Scholes & Mark Wolfson, *Taxes and Business Strategy: A Planning Approach* ch. 23 (1992).

[7] Jesse Markham, *Survey of the Evidence and Findings on Mergers*, in *Business Concentration and Price Policy* (NBER 1955); Peter Steiner, *Mergers: Motives, Effects, Policies* (1975); *The Corporate Merger* (William Alberts & Joel Segall eds.1966); F.M. Scherer & David Ross, *Industrial Market Structure and Economic Performance* (3d ed.1990); and Jesse Markham, *Conglomerate Enterprise and Public Policy* (1973), all provide excellent commentary on these merger waves.

wave of mergers between 1895 and 1905 involved an estimated 15% of all manufacturing assets and employees, and accompanied major changes in the nation's social and technological infrastructure. . . .

Figure 1-1
Number of Manufacturing and Mining Firms Acquired, 1895-1978

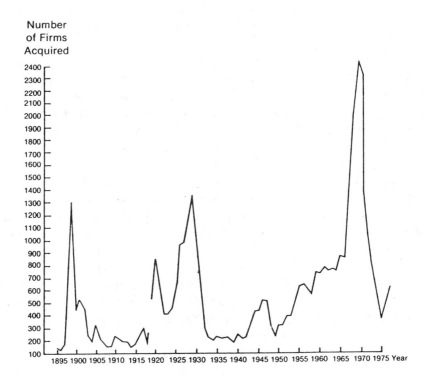

Source: Malcolm Salter & Wolf Weinhold, *Diversification Through Acquisition: Strategies for Creating Economic Value* (1979).

An important characteristic of this merger wave was the simultaneous consolidation of producers within numerous industries. These mergers, mostly horizontal integrations, were often made in search of market dominance. Many of today's industrial giants, including U.S. Steel, the several descendants of Standard Oil, General Electric, Westinghouse, United Fruit, Eastman Kodak, American Can, American Tobacco, U.S. Rubber, DuPont, PPG, International Harvester, and U.S. Gypsum, among others, trace their origins in this period. The tailend of this merger wave in 1903-1904 coincided with a severe economic recession and the *Northern Securities* decision which established that mergers could be successfully attacked under then existing antitrust law.

While George Stigler has characterized the first wave as "merging for monopoly," other economists have not been so bold. Many have noted that this merger wave accompanied a frenzied stock market and aggressive promotional activities by bankers and brokers. J.P. Morgan, for example, is estimated to have earned over $60 million for his efforts in the consolidation of U.S. Steel. Others have argued that many of the consolidations failed in the following recession and that others did not even lead to market dominance. Nevertheless, as Markham concluded, "The conversion of approximately 71 important oligopolistic or near-competitive industries into near monopolies by merger between 1890 and 1904 left an impact on the structure of the American economy that fifty years have not yet erased."

The two decades following the 1903-04 market crash were relatively quiet ones in terms of merger activity. Only two notable combinations arose, General Motors in 1909, and International Business Machines in 1911. Much more important, however, was a relatively wide scale legal attack on the trusts formed in the previous wave. The year 1911 was the landmark, with the Supreme Court ordering the breakups of the Standard Oil and American Tobacco Companies. Market monopolies were clearly established as illegal. However, further judicial decisions, such as the 1920 U.S. Steel Decision, established that dominant firms would be subject to antitrust attack only if they abused their market position through aggressive and predatory attacks on their rivals. Since the Sherman Act only addressed issues of substantial monopoly power, Congress passed the Clayton Act in 1914 whose stated purpose was "to arrest the creation of trusts, conspiracies and monopolies in their incipiency and before consummation."[12] The Federal Trade Commission was also established at this time to better control unrestrained corporate power. For the first time in antitrust history, specific business actions were declared illegal.

The second wave of merger and acquisition activity occurred during the 1920s and peaked in 1928. As with its predecessor, it too rode a period of economic growth and a stock market boom. All told, an estimated 12,000 firms disappeared during this period. Its impact on market structure, however, was much less noticeable for several reasons.

First, over one-third of this activity was in the banking and public utility sectors. Most significant was the rise of the giant utility holding company pyramids in the gas, electricity and water sectors, pyramids which were to collapse in the following depression. Since these sectors were already regulated, increased market concentration had little or no impact on economic power. Second, since the Clayton Act prevented large scale stock consolidations in search of market power, but not asset acquisitions, merger activity in the manufacturing sector was primarily limited to either small market share additions or to vertical integration. Worthy of special note, however, was the formation of strong "number two companies" in numerous industries previously dominated by one giant firm. The consolidations of

---

[12] S.Rep.No. 698, 63d Cong. 2d Sess. at 1 (1914).

Bethlehem Steel, Republic Steel and Continental Can all date from this era. This advent of oligopoly in many industrial sectors led George Stigler to characterize this period of merger activity as "merging for oligopoly."

It was outside the previously consolidated heavy manufacturing industrial sectors where much of the merger activity was occurring. Mergers in the still fragmented food processing, chemicals, and mining sectors comprised 60% of all merger activity in manufacturing. Extensive vertical integration (in mining) and product extension moves (in food processing and chemicals) led to many major industrial enterprises. Kennecott, Anaconda, and Phelps Dodge, Allied Chemical and DuPont (in chemicals outside explosives), and General Mills, General Foods, and Kraft all trace their emergence to this period.

While the merger wave of the 1920s was clearly as large or larger in absolute terms than the 1890-1904 wave, its relative impact was much less. In total, it apparently involved less than 10% of the economy's assets rather than the former wave's over 15%. Furthermore, in most industries, mergers embraced only a small proportion of the competing firms. Only in the food processing, metals, and chemicals sectors was industry structure substantially altered. . . .

The 1920s merger wave did, however, have several similarities with that of 1890-1905. Both occurred during a period of economic prosperity and a booming stock market. And, as before, it came to an end with a stock market crash and a severe economic slowdown. Internally, stock promoters once again seemed to have been a major driving force. Perhaps rightfully recognizing stock promotions as the principal avenue of abuse in this merger wave, legislation in the following years was aimed at securities regulation rather than at more rigorous antitrust controls.

The onset of a worldwide depression in 1929 brought merger activity to a halt. Throughout the 1930s and into World War II, acquisition activity remained at its lowest levels of the century. As the war ended, an upsurge in merger and acquisition activity began, once again accompanying economic prosperity and rising stock prices. The Federal Trade Commission, in its landmark 1948 report, concluded:

> No great stretch of the imagination is required to foresee that if nothing is done to check the growth in concentration, either giant corporations will ultimately take over the country, or the government will be impelled to step in and impose some form of direct regulation.[13]

Something was done, however, with the Celler-Kefauver Amendment substantially strengthening the anti-merger provisions of the Clayton Act in

---

[13] Federal Trade Commission, *The Merger Movement: A Summary Report* 25, 68 (1948). [Later studies challenge the FTC's conclusion that industrial concentration was increasing. See Philip Areeda, *Antitrust Analysis* 844 n.16 (2d ed.1981) (collecting studies showing industrial concentration roughly constant after 1909. Eds.]

1950. . . . [But by] the mid-1950s, a third merger and acquisition wave had begun. Table 1-1 . . . detail[s] this growth in acquisition activity. . . . This wave, which would prove to be longer and larger than either of the two preceding waves, was of an entirely new sort. This wave did not, in general, involve either large acquisitions or large acquirers. . . . What arose was a strategy of corporate diversification into new product markets.

Table 1-1
Acquisition Activity, 1950-1971

| Year | Number of Acquisitions | | | | Assets Acquired in Large M&M Acquisitions ($ millions) |
	Total Recorded	All Mfg. & Mining (M&M)	Large M&M*	Large M&M -- by 200 Largest Firms**	
1950	NA	219			186
1951	NA	235			204
1952	NA	288	15		361
1953	NA	295	26	16	839
1954	NA	387	38	16	1,465
1955	NA	683	69	33	2,179
1956	NA	673	59	25	2,076
1957	NA	585	50	23	1,363
1958	NA	589	45	22	1,242
1959	NA	835	62	30	1,947
1960	1,345	844	64	32	1,279
1961	1,724	954	60	25	2,356
1962	1,667	853	70	33	2,448
1963	1,479	861	83	41	3,148
1964	1,797	854	91	38	2,728
1965	1,893	1,008	91	29	3,845
1966	1,746	995	101	35	4,171
1967	2,384	1,496	168	73	9,091
1968	3,932	2,407	207	94	13,297
1969	4,542	2,307	155	52	11,353
1970	3,089	1,351	98	30	6,346
1971	2,633	1,011	66	19	2,544

* Acquired firms with assets of $10 million or more.
** Ranked by 1970 total assets.
NA = not available.
Source: Federal Trade Commission, Bureau of Economics, *Current Trends in Merger Activity, 1970 and 1971,* Statistical Rep. Nos. 8 (Mar.1971) & 10 (May 1972).

This concept of unrelated diversification was pioneered by Textron, Litton, and ITT, and led to high rates of corporate growth. These fast-growing firms, known as "conglomerates," [began as] small- to medium-sized companies that emphasized acquisition activity outside their traditional areas of interest. Furthermore, their acquisitions were also of typically small- to medium-sized firms operating in either fragmented industries or on the periphery of major industrial sectors. As the stock market soared in the mid-sixties, this concept became more and more popular with both investors and corporate executives. [Earnings per share] growth and synergy were the bywords of this period.

The dramatic increase in the number of companies following a diversification strategy during this period is seen in Figure 1-2, where "unrelated business" is roughly synonymous with conglomerate. Since this merger wave brought corporate growth but not increased market concentration, we have labeled this wave, to paraphrase George Stigler, "merging for growth."

Figure 1-2
Estimated Percentage of Fortune 500 Companies in Each Category

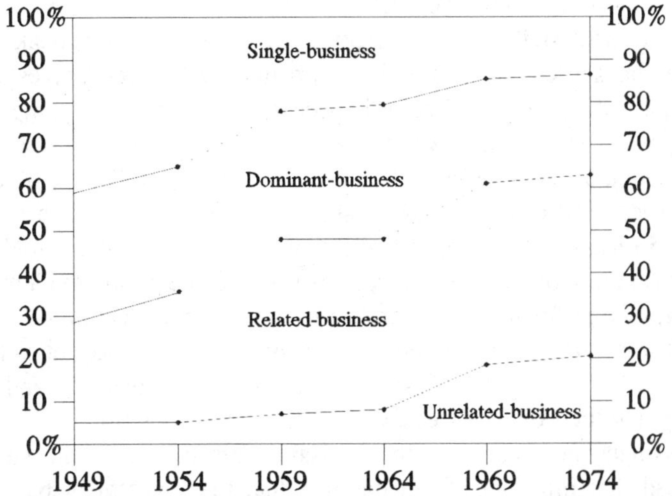

Source: Richard Rumelt, *Diversity and Profitability* (UCLA working paper 1977).

At its peak in 1967-1969, several conglomerates were selling at 100 times earnings and were using their stock to devour acquisitions, often at the rate of one per week. Over 10,000 independent companies were acquired in the 1967-69 peak (over 6,000 in mining and manufacturing alone) and over 25,000 firms disappeared over the course of the entire wave (1960-1971). . . . [A]t the wave's peak over 70% of these acquisitions were conglomerate in nature and over 30% [were] totally unrelated to the acquirer. Total assets acquired in the mining and manufacturing sectors exceeded $70 billion, or approximately 7-8% of all corporate manufacturing assets. . . . The 200 largest manufacturing firms accounted for approximately one-half of all acquired assets during this period and among these 200, the 25 most active acquirers accounted for 59% or a total of $20.2 billion. Of these 25, there were at least 17 companies actively following a strategy of unrelated diversification. . . .

As with the two previous merger waves, this wave was also accompanied by aggressive stock promotion and rose and fell with the stock market. For conglomerates, the wave ended with the collapse of their stock prices following lowered earnings in the mild 1969-70 recession. For other acquirers it came to an end in 1973 with the advent of the nation's severest economic recession and stock market collapse since the 1930s.

At this stage it is useful to review what we know about the three merger waves that have occurred so far in U.S. history. Four similarities, all previously identified by Jesse Markham in 1955, apply to each of the three waves.[14] Briefly stated, these similarities are:

1. Contrary to popular opinion, relatively few mergers seem to have had market monopolization as their goal. Market power was most evident in the first wave but declined in each of the next two. The conglomerate wave of the 1960s had virtually no effect on either market concentration or aggregate economic concentration;

2. The most striking single motive for merger at each peak seems to have been the search for promotional profits. All three waves occurred during sustained periods of economic prosperity and rapidly rising levels of stock prices. Each merger wave peaked with the stock market and then quickly receded as stock prices fell and each wave was followed by a serious economic recession (the 1903-04 crash, the 1929-37 Great Depression and the 1974-75 recession). As each wave progressed, speculative stock activity and the formation of less viable enterprises became more evident. Stock promotion, of one form or another, eclipsed economic reality as each wave peaked. Thorp's comment on the 1920s wave is just as relevant to the other two waves: " . . . one businessman regarded it as a loss of standing if he was not approached once a week with a merger proposition. . . . A group of businessmen and financiers in discussing this matter in the summer of 1928 agreed that nine out of ten mergers had the investment banker at its core;"[15]

3. Many mergers were simply ordinary business transactions among entrepreneurs. Mergers and acquisitions provide one of the best means for entrepreneurs to exit an industry while reaping the maximum benefits of their work; and

4. Many mergers accompanied or were stimulated by massive changes in the economy's infrastructure. Typically, these radical changes in the economy lead to new market definitions and/or new production and distribution technologies. For example, the first wave followed rapid rail building, the advent of electricity and the rise of coal. The second was accompanied by automotive transportation and the radio. The last wave was

---

[14] Markham (1955), *supra* note 7, at 180-82.

[15] Willard Thorp, *The Persistence of the Merger Movement,* Am.Econ.Rev. 86 (Supp.1931).

accompanied by aircraft, television, and the use of liquid hydrocarbons. Whether a cause-and-effect relationship exists or whether it is coincidence has not been established.

The differences between the waves are surprisingly few. In essence, they concern the relative impact of each wave on the economy and their primary focus. While each wave was larger than the ones before it in both the number of companies involved and assets acquired, they consumed increasingly smaller proportions of the total economy. Either the size and diversity of the economy outgrew the capacity of corporations to grow through merger or, as some cynics have suggested, fewer and fewer attractive assets were left to acquire. In either case, relatively effective antitrust measures changed the focus of corporate merger and acquisition activity from that of market domination in the first wave to one of product market diversity in the third. Nevertheless, the fear of unrestrained market power, established in the public's mind in earlier years, still continued to influence economic and political debate on corporate mergers and acquisitions.

Merger and Acquisition Activity Since 1975

Since 1975 the characteristics of merger and acquisition activity have continued to evolve. Table 1-2 . . . provide[s] a comparative profile of acquisition activity during this most recent period, based on data compiled by the Federal Trade Commission. . . . In contrast to the surge in small- to medium-sized acquisitions during the 1967-1973 period, the number of large and very large acquisitions has increased dramatically since 1975. This is even more striking in light of the fall in the rate of acquisition activity to one-half of its earlier level. . . . [The trend toward diversifying acquisitions has continued, and] many of the recent large and very large acquisitions have been unrelated diversification moves by the country's largest firms. . . .

Table 1-2
Trends in Acquisition Activity, 1951-1978

Year	All Acquisitions			Mining and Manufacturing Acquisitions		
	Number of Acquisitions	Number > $10 million	Number > $100 million	Number of Acquisitions	Number > $10 million	Number > $100 million
1951-55	NA	NA	NA	378/yr	30/yr	2/yr
1956-60	NA	NA	NA	705/yr	48/yr	1/yr
1961-66	1514/yr	NA	NA	920/yr	63/yr	5/yr
1967-69	3403/yr	NA	NA	2070/yr	150/yr	27/yr
1970	2854	NA	NA	1351	91	12
1971	2303	NA	NA	1011	59	5
1972	2758	NA	NA	NA	60	6
1973	1919	137	28	697	64	7
1974	1276	129	26	505	62	11
1975	889	112	16	355	59	11
1976	1081	159	23	461	81	14
1977	1182	195	38	619	99	19
1978	1350	260	45	NA	NA	31

Source: Salter & Weinhold (1979), *supra*.

Table 1-3 helps place the most recent upsurge in merger and acquisition activity in much broader perspective. While total acquired assets in 1977-1979 exceeded the 1967-1969 peak in book value terms, the amount of acquired assets relative to *existing assets* was just approaching the average acquisition rate for the 1960-1966 period and still far below that of the frenzied 1967-1969 period. In fact, background data suggests that 1955-1956 and 1963-1971 as having as high or higher rates of merger and acquisition activity, relative to either new investment or total existing assets, than the more current 1977-1979 period. . . .

The upswing in merger and acquisition activity beginning in 1975 has led many observers to announce a fourth wave of corporate marriages. This announcement reflects the fact that the aggregate annual value of all acquisitions in the late 1970s reached or exceeded the levels seen during the conglomerate wave of the late 1960s (though the total number of acquisitions was much lower). . . .

Table 1-3

Comparison of Large Acquired Assets to New and Existing Investments for Manufacturing and Mining Companies

Year	New Investment ($ billions)*	Acquired Assets ($ billions)*	Acquired Assets as % of New Investment	Acquired Assets as % of Existing Assets
1948-1953	$10.6/yr.	$0.3/yr.	2.8%	.18%
1954-1959	14.82/yr.	1.7/yr.	11.4	.80
1960-1966	20.2/yr.	2.9/yr.	14.5	.92
1967-1969	31.2/yr.	11.6/yr.	37.2	2.47
1970	33.8	6.6	19.5	1.14
1971	32.2	3.1	9.8	.51
1972	33.8	2.7	7.9	.41
1973	40.8	3.6	8.7	.50
1974	49.2	5.1	10.4	.69
1975	51.7	5.5	10.7	.68
1976	56.5	6.9	12.2	.79
1977	65.5	9.6	14.7	1.02
1978	73.2	12.3	16.8	1.19

* Total expenditures for new plant and equipment by manufacturing and mining firms.
** Acquired firms with assets of $10 million or more.
Source: Salter and Weinhold (1979), *supra*.

Whether or not another major merger movement was launched in the late 1970s will only become possible to determine with the passage of time. . . . [But] analysis based on gross comparisons between the total number of acquisitions made or the total asset values acquired will not be particularly enlightening. Both are static measures and fail to recognize the dynamic nature of the U.S. economy with its ever-growing size and complexity. . . . Furthermore, rapid rates of inflation (such as what the U.S. has experienced over the last 15 years) will further distort any comparisons of merger activity based upon asset or market values. To establish reasonably consistent and truly comparable comparisons between current merger activity and that of earlier periods, the data on merger activity normally reported must be refined. Two adjustments are especially important: (1) merger volume should be measured in terms of constant or inflation adjusted dollars; and (2) merger activity should be measured in terms of the assets acquired *relative* to the total assets of the economy. . . .

Table 1-4 looks at recent merger and acquisition activity on a constant dollar basis. . . . What this analysis shows is that a substantial portion of recent acquisition activity reflects the high rates of inflation that have occurred over the last decade. In real terms, current acquisition activity is only running at about two-thirds of the rate of the 1967-69 peak in conglomerate acquisitions.

Table 1-4
Inflation Adjusted Consideration Paid in Acquisitions, 1967-1979

Year	Total Consideration ($ billions)	GNP Implicit Price Deflator (1972 = 100)	Constant Dollar Consideration (1972 $ billions)
1967	18.0	$79.0	22.8
1968	43.0	82.6	52.1
1969	23.7	86.7	27.3
1970	16.4	91.4	16.9
1971	12.6	96.0	13.1
1972	16.7	106.0	16.7
1973	16.7	105.8	15.8
1974	12.5	116.0	10.8
1975	11.8	127.1	9.3
1976	20.0	133.7	15.0
1977	21.9	141.7	15.5
1978	34.2	152.1	22.5
1979	43.5	165.5	26.3

Source: *Mergerstat Review*

Table 1-5
Consideration Paid Relative to the Market Value of all U.S. Equities

Year	Consideration Paid ($ billions)	Total Market Value of all Equities ($ billions)	Consideration Paid as % of Market Value of all Firms
1967	$18.0 Est.	868	2.1%
1968	43.0	1,034	4.2
1969	23.7	914	2.6
1970	16.4	906	1.8
1971	12.6	1,060	1.2
1972	16.7	1,198	1.4
1973	16.7	947	1.8
1974	12.5	675	1.8
1975	11.8	891	1.3
1976	20.0	1,106	1.8
1977	21.9	1,039	2.1
1978	34.2	1,086	3.1
1979	43.5	1,244	3.5

Source: *Mergerstat Review*

Table 1-5 measures current acquisition activity . . . relative to all other assets in the economy. This approach recognizes that the U.S. economy is continuing to grow and that what might be a high level of merger activity at one period in time may amount to only a modest level of activity a decade or two later. This data suggests that despite the extremely high aggregate value of acquisition payments made during 1975-79, it was not as great as in the mid-1960s relative to the market value of all other corporations.

What we can see, then, is that merger activity in the 1975-79 period has indeed been significant when looked at in absolute terms. However, relative to the size of the economy or the level of merger activity during the 1960s, the size and magnitude of the current merger activity is much less impressive. The 1970s witnessed rapid inflation and a growing economy, both of which served to diminish dramatically the relative impact of a given level of merger and acquisition activity. Table 1-6 summarizes current acquisition activity in comparison to the previous three merger waves. When viewed in terms of constant dollars or as a percent of total assets, merger and acquisition activity within the mining and manufacturing sectors during the 1975-1979 period does not look as significant as that during earlier periods.

Table 1-6
Estimated Impact of Merger Activity on U.S. Mining and
Manufacturing: 1975-79 vs. the Three Previous Merger Waves

	1895-1902	1919-29	1960-70	1975-79[*]
Total Mining and Manufacturing Acquisitions	2,600+	8,000	12,000	3,100
Total Mining and Manufacturing Assets Acquired ($ billions)	6.4+	12-15	70+	50
Assets Acquired in constant dollars ($ billions)	26+	24-30	69	30
Assets Acquired as a % Total Mining & Manufacturing Assets	15+	7-9	10+	6

[*] The current merger wave is not yet over so these estimates will necessarily grow . . . .
Note: This table . . . does not reflect the increasing importance of service-based industries (and acquisitions within the service sector) in the post-WWII economy.

In addition to characteristics relating to the number, size, and diversity of transactions, other distinguishing characteristics of the current merger movement are emerging. Eight important ones stand out and are discussed below.

1. In contrast to the conglomerate buying spree of the 1960s, many of the acquiring companies in the late 1970s were well-established, conservative, old line giants. These acquirers typically had most of their assets concentrated in one or a few closely related businesses. More often than not, these conservative giants were also facing maturing product markets in their major lines of business. General Electric, Johns Mansville, Mobil,

Continental Group, Atlantic Richfield, R.J. Reynolds, Allied Chemical, United Technologies, and N.L. Industries all fall into this category.

This is not to say that these conservative giants were highly active acquirers during 1975-79, or that the conglomerates were not active acquirers. Both inferences are, in fact, misleading. . . . [T]he most active acquirers, in terms of the number of acquisitions made during the period, were companies following a strategy of either conglomerate diversification or companies within industries where environmental and competitive conditions were leading to substantial consolidation. On the other hand, the so-called conservative giants generally limited their merger activity to one or, at most, two acquisitions during this period. The important difference between these two groups, however, lies in the size of the acquisitions being made by the conservative giants. Despite little acquisition experience, they were the companies making the $300 million deals. . . . Ironically enough, in several instances, entire conglomerates (Eltra and Studebaker-Worthington) were themselves swallowed up by old line, conservative giants (Allied Chemical and McGraw Edison).

Virtually all of these large-scale acquisitions (outside continued consolidation within the petroleum sector) were unrelated to the acquirer in either classic economic or judicial senses. This pursuit of unrelated acquisitions undoubtedly reflects the antitrust constraints faced by most large U.S. companies. Their size and resource base virtually foreclosed either entry or expansion by acquisition in any market where they were a competitor or where they were perceived as a potential competitor. . . .

2. Unlike the conglomerate merger movement of the 1960s where virtually every sector of the economy was affected, merger and acquisition activity since 1975 has been more severe in certain sectors than in others. The most active sectors -- finance, bank, insurance, general services and wholesale and retail trade -- are all service industries. Together they encompass over 30% of all acquisition activity. This activity reflects the increasing importance of services in the U.S. economy as well as the fact that these industries have a history of fragmentation. . . .

3. The second sector where significant acquisition activity has occurred is the natural resources area. This sector has witnessed relatively few acquisitions, but acquisitions which often dwarfed those done in any other industry. In 1979, the 5 largest participants have been the large oil companies which have acquired both additional oil reserves as well as companies with other natural resources reserves. At the same time, many industrial companies have also acquired natural resources companies as a way of securing a known set of inflation resistant, irreplaceable assets. Perhaps the most dramatic example of this strategy was General Electric's $2.1 billion acquisition of Utah International, a major coal producer with smaller activities in copper, uranium and other metals. Similarly, International Telephone and Telegraph, a pioneer of the conglomerate movement (which had been quiet since the antitrust proceedings following its 1968 acquisition of Hartford Insurance), acquired both a coal and an oil company. It is worth

emphasizing that companies with their resource base in the United States or other safe, stable political environments have been those primarily sought after.

4.   Another distinct characteristic of 1975-79 merger and acquisition activity is the widespread use of cash as a principal means of payment. During the 1960s, by far the principal payment medium was common stock or equivalents such as convertible debt, convertible preferred, or debt plus warrants. The proliferation in the use of these common stock equivalents at the height of the conglomerate craze led many to call them "funny money" or "Chinese paper."   Only rarely was a cash payment used during this acquisition spree; when used, it was usually as a sweetener to an already complicated package of securities.

In contrast, cash or a package of cash and equivalents was the payment medium in over [50] transactions from the mid-1970s onward. Figure 1-3 shows how the relative importance of cash, common stock, or a package of securities as the payment medium has changed . . . . [T]he use of cash for payment has had an inverse relationship to the general level of stock prices. Cash usage surged in 1973-74 as stock prices fell by over 40%. . . .

Figure 1-3
Payment Medium Used in Corporate Acquisitions, 1964-1979

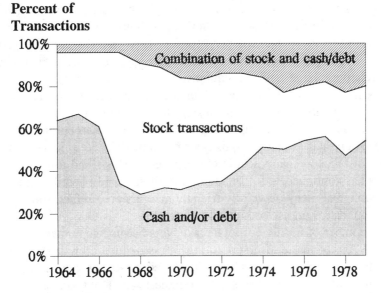

Source: *Mergerstat Review*

An additional observation about the "packaging" of acquisitions in 1975-79 is important. Since an acquisition may lead to a taxable transaction for both the buyer and the seller, tax considerations play an important part in structuring any deal. Marginal tax rates, the magnitude of capital gains, and the strength of the economy and the stock market are all significant forces in selecting an attractive securities package. Reflecting recent tax reforms and an unstable economy, many recent acquisitions have been structured to provide both taxable and tax free alternatives. In these cases, taxable cash payments are limited to less than half of the acquisition's purchase price. A package of common stock, preferred stock, convertible preferred, or debt instruments is then designed to preserve the transaction's tax status (generally tax-free or tax deferred to the seller) while meeting the acquirer's cash flow, tax and control requirements.

5. Closely linked to the use of cash as the primary payment medium for acquisitions during the 1975-79 period was the increase in the size of the average acquisition premium over market value. During the conglomerate merger wave of the 1960s, premiums on the order of 10% to 20% were common and only rarely did one exceed 40%.[20]

However, in the merger movement of the late 1970s, premiums of 100% or more were not uncommon. Acquisition offers which were successful had an average premium over market of about 50%. . . .

The relative magnitude of the premium in a successful acquisition has been inversely related to the level of stock prices over this time period. The highest average premiums occurred in 1973-74 as the stock market reached its lowest level in a decade. That successful offers have higher premiums during periods of relatively poor stock price performance is quite natural. In this environment, investors will remember the recently higher values of their holdings and tend to consider their stocks "temporarily depressed." For an acquisition offer to be successful in this psychological context it must be at a premium that more than compensates for the stock's currently depressed value. . . . It is also worth noting that large acquisitions have also tended to have relatively large tender premiums. . . .

6. One of the principal reasons for the increase in the average size of successful acquisition premiums during this period is that hostile or unwelcome takeovers have been much more common than before. Though there were only half as many acquisitions made in 1975/76 as in 1968, there were almost twice as many hostile tender offers. This trend toward hostile takeovers has continued. . . . In addition to these visibly hostile takeovers, it is probable that many outwardly friendly mergers are, in fact, the vestiges of, or reactions to, undisclosed hostile overtures.

The number of hostile corporate takeovers became so numerous during the late 1970s that an entire supporting infrastructure grew up around it. Specialists on each side, with well-developed strategies and competitive tactics, are brought in at the slightest indication of a takeover. If the unwanted suitor cannot be driven off through adverse publicity or exhaustive litigation, the goal then shifts to extract the maximum purchase price possible. Often the target's incumbent management brings in a "white

---

[20] Samuel Hayes & Russell Tausig, *Tactics of Cash Takeover Bids*, Harv.Bus.Rev. 135 (Mar.-Apr.1967); John Shad, *The Financial Realities of Mergers*, Harv.Bus.Rev. 133 (Nov.-Dec.1969).

knight," or a company that is more friendly to its interests. Bidding wars and legal battles between the unwelcome suitor and the "white knight" then decide who wins. A classic example of this intercorporate warfare was the attempted takeover of Babcock & Wilcox by United Technologies in 1977. Following United's opening bid, J. Ray McDermott acquired stock in the open market and became a second unwanted suitor. As events unfolded, Babcock & Wilcox decided that McDermott would be the lesser of two evils. In the ensuing bidding battle, won by McDermott, the final price of Babcock and Wilcox was driven up by $200 million over United's initial overture, a bid which was itself at a $100 million premium over market value. In several other instances, three or even four corporate bidders entered the fray for a particularly desirable property. The 1979 divestiture of oil rich General Crude by International Paper saw Gulf, Mobil, Tenneco and Southland Royalty as bidders. International Paper took its proceeds (over $800 million) and, in turn, won a bidding battle with Weyerhaeuser for timber rich, privately owned Bodcaw.

Other takeovers were even more hostile than the General Crude situation. Two offers, one in late 1978 and the other in early 1979, set new standards for unlimited corporate warfare. The first was Mead Corporation's rebuff of Occidental Petroleum. Mead's counterattack was so thorough and complete in its exposure of Occidental's business affairs that it led to an investigation and censure by the SEC. Failing in the acquisition attempt, Oxy's president resigned and Armand Hammer, Oxy's chairman, commented that "had we known of the bloodshed . . . we never would have gone into it." In early 1979, fireworks erupted with American Express' billion dollar offer for McGraw Hill. McGraw Hill's response spared no punches. Even the ethics and morals of American Express' top management were openly challenged in the business press. Leaving no stone unturned or word unsaid and implying self annihilation if unsuccessful in its defense, McGraw Hill's counterattack gave rise to what is now known in the trade as a "scorched earth" policy. . . . American Express backed down.

The exact level of hostility in merger and acquisition activity is impossible to measure. Still, the hottest topic in the business press as the 1970s ended was not how to do a takeover, but rather how to defend/protect yourself (and, consequently, your company) from one. Many of the most vocal supporters of legislation aimed at limiting large-scale corporate acquisitions were not economists nor consumer activists, but rather corporate executives of middle-sized, prosperous companies that were quickly becoming the most attractive targets. It is somewhat ironic that many of these vocal critics of corporate takeovers, 1979 style, were themselves aggressive acquirers a few years earlier.

7. A very distinctive and important characteristic of merger and acquisition activity in the late 1970s is that approximately one-half of all corporate acquisitions were also corporate divestitures. In contrast, during the conglomerate merger wave of the 1960s, divestitures made up only 10% to 15% of all acquisitions. Figure 1-4 details the ratio of divestments to

acquisition activity over this period. The significance of this increased divestment activity is that a substantial portion of acquisition activity merely resulted in the "swapping" of assets by different companies. . . .

The peak in divestment activity occurred in 1975-76 as many companies, both diversified and nondiversified, pruned their businesses following the severe 1974-75 recession. Product lines, operating units, and entire divisions were sold or shut down as companies attempted to rid themselves of weak or low potential units. N.L. Industries, for example, divested over 60 businesses . . . Many of these divestitures were businesses acquired during the conglomerate era of the 1960s, businesses that often had little relationship to the mainstream of the company's activities or whose financial and management needs were out of proportion with their performance. Others, such as General Motors' 1979 divestiture of Frigidaire, were of long-standing businesses that no longer fit the corporate image or which continued to absorb valuable assets. Finally, several companies such as W.R. Grace and Allegheny Ludlum, in a constant search for the "perfect" portfolio of businesses, developed divestiture programs that were almost as active as their acquisition programs.

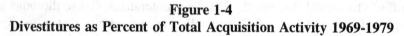

Figure 1-4

Divestitures as Percent of Total Acquisition Activity 1969-1979

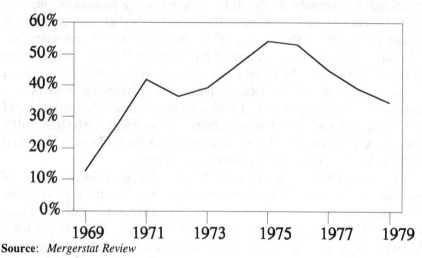

Source: *Mergerstat Review*

8. In contrast to the modest increase in the number of acquisitions in the 1975-1979 period, there was a noticeable increase in the number of acquisitions of publicly held companies. This is shown in Table 1-7. . . .

Table 1-7
Acquisitions of Publicly Held Companies, 1974-1979

Year	Public Companies		Total Announcements	Acquisitions of Public Cos. as % of all Acquisitions
	Announcements	Completed or Pending		
1974	133	68	2,861	4.7%
1975	174	130	2,297	7.6
1976	232	163	2,276	10.2
1977	267	193	2,224	12.0
1978	325	260	2,106	15.4
1979	343	248	2,128	16.1

Source: *Mergerstat Review*

There are three major links between the increased number of public acquisitions and the characteristics previously identified. First, publicly held companies tend to be several orders of magnitude larger than privately held companies and, therefore, it is only natural that the increasing number of public company acquisitions went hand in hand with the increasing size of acquisitions during the late 1970s. Second, since management and ownership are generally separated in public companies while closely linked in private companies, it was only natural that there were more tender offers involved in order to reach directly the public companies' owners. In addition, the so-called "hostility" surrounding these acquisitions was generally much higher since management had a limited ownership interest and any takeover would have severely affected its prerogatives. Third, since publicly held companies have a liquid market for their stock, their stockholders do not generally have as low a tax basis as shareholders in private companies for the stock. Payment packages for the acquisition of publicly held companies, therefore, tend to be biased toward the use of cash or cash equivalents, especially during periods of poor stock price performance, such as was the case during the 1970s.

Apart from these characteristics, an aspect of merger activity during the 1975-1979 period that has received considerable attention in the business press and in public policy debates is the purported preference of today's acquirers for "well-managed" companies. Corporate executives are often quoted as saying that they have neither the managerial resources nor the time to successfully undertake a turnaround. In contrast, many of the conglomerates of the 1960s argued that they brought new management talent and sophisticated management techniques to bear on poorly run companies. Whether or not this preference for well-managed companies is a real and distinctive characteristic of the current merger movement is not entirely clear.

It may be that the apparent emphasis on good management is merely coincidental with the increasing scale of many acquisitions being made today. Many large companies, by virtue of their age and experience, have often established themselves as market leaders. And while market leadership and good management often go hand in hand, they are often confused by outside observers. On the other hand, the high proportion of divestments and the fact that several conglomerates (such as Gulf + Western Industries and Tyco Labs) have continued to acquire low performing companies with underutilized assets suggests that substantial opportunities for "turnarounds" still exist. Thus, it is not at all clear that current acquisition activity is as sharply focused on well-managed companies as many commentators would lead us to believe. What is more clear is that many highly visible, large public companies have been acquired, that these companies are often leaders in one or more product markets, and that due to their age, size, and market position, many have well-established, solid managements. Yet, it is also apparent that a large proportion of current merger activity involves divestitures of unwanted divisional operations whose performance does not meet the standards of the divesting parent. Thus, in the presence of conflicting suppositions we feel that it is inappropriate to state that the acquisition of well-managed companies is a distinctive characteristic of current merger activity.

Note on Acquisitions in the 1980s: Characteristics of the Fourth Wave

Salter & Weinhold remark that "whether or not another major merger movement was launched in the late 1970s will only be possible to determine through the passage of time." By 1992 it was clear that the increased acquisition activity observed in the 1975-1979 period had begun a fourth wave of takeovers that lasted through the 1980s. It had four primary characteristics, three of which Salter & Weinhold noted with respect to the 1975-1979 period.

Table 1-8
Large Acquisitions, 1968-1992

Year	Number of acquisitions > $100 million	Number of acquisitions > $1 billion	Dollar value of acquisitions over $1 billion ($ billions)
1968	46	--	--
1969	24	--	--
1970	10	--	--
1971	7	--	--
1072	15	--	--
1973	28	0	--
1974	28	0	--
1975	14	1	--
1976	39	1	--
1977	41	0	--
1978	80	1	--
1979	83	3	--
1980	94	4	--
1981	113	12	--
1982	116	6	$19,440
1983	138	11	9,111
1984	200	18	55,179
1985	270	36	61,459
1986	346	27	67,932
1987	301	36	62,176
1988	369	45	96,399
1989	328	35	117,477
1990	181	21	48,211
1991	150	13	22,284
1992	200	18	30,982

Source: Merrill Lynch, *Mergerstat Review*; *Mergers and Acquisitions* 57 (May/June 1990).

First, the nominal size of transactions continued to grow, culminating in Kohlberg Kravis Roberts' 1989 acquisition of RJR Nabisco for $24.7 billion.   This can be seen in Table 1-8, which sets forth the number of acquisitions over $100 million from 1968 through 1992, and the number of acquisitions over $1 billion from 1973 through 1992.

Second, the trend toward hostile transactions continued, both directly and indirectly through friendly transactions undertaken in anticipation of a possible hostile transaction. Third, deconglomeration became a major theme of 1980s transactions. Fourth, a new transaction form, the leveraged buyout transaction form developed. More generally, many acquisitions and takeover defenses relied heavily on debt financing, often through high-yield or "junk" bonds.

Volume of Activity. Table 1-9 sets out, for each year from 1979 through 1992, the number of transactions, their nominal value and, to control for price changes and growth of the economy, the value of acquisitions as a percentage of real GNP. Table 1-10 restates Salter & Weinhold's Table 1-4 using 1982 (instead of 1972) to calculate constant dollar consideration and extends the period covered through 1992.

Table 1-9
Total Acquisition Activity, 1979-1992

Year	No. of Deals	Value ($bil)	Real GNP ($ bil; 1982 $)	Deals per $ billion real GNP	Value as % of real GNP
1979	2128	43.5	3192	0.67	1.4%
1980	1889	44.3	3187	0.59	1.4
1981	2395	82.6	3249	0.74	2.5
1982	2346	53.7	3166	0.74	1.7
1983	2533	73.1	3279	0.77	2.2
1984	2543	122.2	3501	0.73	3.5
1985	3001	179.9	3619	0.83	5.0
1986	3336	173.1	3722	0.90	4.7
1987	2302	163.7	3847	0.60	4.3
1988	2258	246.9	4024	0.56	6.1
1989	2366	221.1	4144	0.57	5.3
1990	2074	108.2	4188	0.50	2.6
1991	1877	71.0	4259	0.44	1.7
1992	2574	96.7	4330	0.59	2.2

Sources: *Mergerstat Review*; GNP data from Department of Commerce, Bureau of Economic Analysis, *Survey of Current Business*.

The continued growth in number of acquisitions appears from comparing where Salter and Weinhold's Table 1-2 ends and Table 1-9 begins. Table 1-2 shows the number of acquisitions rising from 1,081 in 1976 to 1,350 in 1978. Table 1-9 shows the number of acquisitions rising to a peak of 3,336 in 1986, and still at 2,074 in 1990 before dropping sharply in 1991. A similar pattern appears in Table 1-10. The total consideration paid in acquisition transactions increased dramatically over the 1980s, peaking in constant dollars in 1988 at almost four times the 1979 level.

Table 1-10
Inflation Adjusted Value of Acquisitions, 1967-1992

Year	Consideration ($ billions)	GNP Deflator (1982 = 100)	Consideration (1982 $ billions)
1967	18.0	35.9	50.1
1968	43.0	37.7	114.1
1969	23.7	39.8	59.6
1970	16.4	42.0	39.1
1971	12.6	44.4	28.4
1972	16.7	46.5	35.9
1973	16.7	49.5	33.7
1974	12.5	54.0	23.2
1975	11.8	59.3	19.9
1976	20.0	63.1	31.7
1977	21.9	67.3	32.5
1978	34.2	72.2	47.4
1979	43.5	78.6	55.3
1980	44.3	85.7	51.7
1981	82.6	94.0	87.8
1982	53.7	100.0	53.7
1983	73.1	103.9	70.4
1984	122.2	107.7	113.5
1985	179.8	110.9	162.1
1986	173.1	113.9	152.0
1987	163.7	117.7	139.1
1988	246.9	121.3	203.5
1989	221.1	126.3	175.1
1990	108.1	129.7	83.4
1991	71.2	133.7	53.3
1992	96.7	137.7	70.2

Source: *Mergerstat Review.* 1967-1979 data is identical to Salter & Weinhold.

   The data confirm the existence of a fourth merger wave that ran through the 1980s, and ended by 1991. To compare the size of this merger wave to that of the previous three, we must measure acquisition activity relative to the size of the economy. Figure 1-5 shows for 1895 through 1985 the value of assets transferred through acquisitions as a percentage of real GNP. Figure 1-6 shows for the same period the number of acquisitions per billion dollars of real GNP.

Figure 1-5

Value of Assets Acquired Relative to GNP, 1895-1985

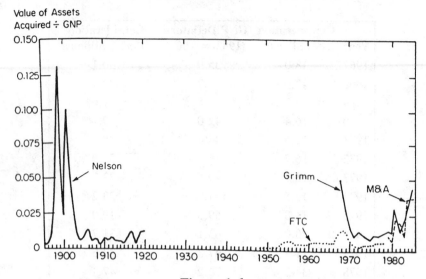

Figure 1-6

Number of Mergers per Billion Dollars of GNP, 1895-1985

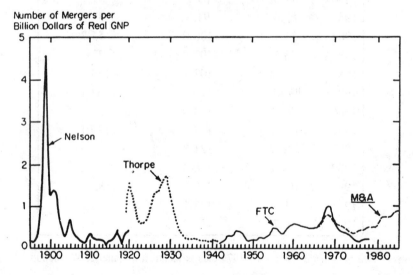

Source: Devra Golbe & Lawrence White, *A Time-Series Analysis of Mergers and Acquisitions in the U.S. Economy*, in *Corporate Takeovers: Causes and Consequences* 265 (Alan Auerbach ed.1988).

Both figures are extended through 1991 in the last two columns of Table 1-9. The data show that while the number and value of acquisitions in the 1980s were still relatively modest compared to the merger waves of the 1890s and 1920s, the 1980s wave was larger than that of the 1960s in dollars and comparable in number of transactions.

Deconglomeration. Table 1-11 shows, for each year from 1966 through 1993, the number of divestitures and the percentage of that year's acquisitions represented by divestitures.   Between 1965 and 1969, divestitures represented only 11-13% of all acquisitions. This percentage grew dramatically thereafter. Many of these divestitures reflect reversal of a prior acquisition.

Table 1-11
Divestitures, 1966-1993

Year	Number	Percent of Transactions	Year	Number	Percent of Transactions
1966	264	11%	1980	666	35%
1967	328	11	1981	830	35
1968	557	12	1982	875	37
1969	801	13	1983	932	37
1970	1,401	27	1984	900	36
1971	1,920	42	1985	1,218	41
1972	1,770	37	1986	1,259	38
1973	1,557	39	1987	807	40
1974	1,331	47	1988	894	40
1975	1,236	54	1989	1,005	45
1976	1,204	53	1990	940	45
1977	1,002	45	1991	849	45
1978	820	39	1992	1,026	40
1979	752	35	1993	1,134	43

Source: Merrill Lynch, *Mergerstat Review.*

The increased frequency of divestitures reflects an important shift in United States industrial organization. As we discuss in Chapter 9, after becoming more diversified during the 1960s and 1970s, American companies became less diversified in the 1980s. Divestitures were a principal means by which this shift in industrial organization took place.

Leverage. The deconglomeration of American industry that occurred over the 1980s was closely tied to another phenomenon: the increased role of leveraged buyouts ("LBOs") and other highly leveraged transactions.[9] The growth in LBOs is shown in Table 1-12. The table begins in 1984 because before that, LBOs were too new to be separately reported. The first leveraged buyout of a public company was Houdaille Industries in 1979. Five years later, deals of this type numbered in the hundreds, and were a significant percentage of all acquisition activity.

---

[9] Leveraged buyouts as a transactional form are considered in depth in Chapter 11, *infra.*

Leveraged transactions took several forms. The first form of leveraged buyout occurred when a large company voluntarily divested a division. The sale was often to the division's managers who lacked access to capital to finance the transaction. In that setting, the divesting company would loan the acquiring managers most of the purchase price, or provide enough equity financing to secure a loan from an outside lender.

Table 1-12
Leveraged Buyout Transactions, 1984-1992

Year	No. of Deals	Buyouts as % of All Deals	Value ($ million)	Value as % of Acq. Activity
1984	237	9.8%	$18,718	15.4%
1985	238	8.6	19,670	14.0
1986	330	8.7	45,160	22.5
1987	270	8.6	36,228	21.1
1988	378	11.4	47,100	20.2
1989	371	12.1	66,800	27.4
1990	241	7.6	15,900	9.7
1991	112	5.3	5,500	5.6
1992	199	5.7	7,207	5.8

Source: *Mergers & Acquisitions*.

The second form of leveraged transaction -- the hostile bust-up takeover -- arose following an innovation in the capital markets: the development of a public market for non-investment grade debt, called "high yield debt" or "junk bonds" depending on the orientation of the observer. This new form of debt provided financing to a new group of takeover entrepreneurs whose function was largely brokerage. Companies were acquired with borrowed funds and more or less broken up, the pieces being sold to pay down the debt with the acquirer keeping either the profits or the pieces of the business it thought it could most efficiently operate. A number of studies have directly linked this type of transaction to deconglomeration. For example, Randall Morck, Andrei Shleifer & Robert Vishny concluded "that the source of bust-up gains in the 1980s is the reversal of the unrelated diversification of the 1960s and 1970s."[10]

---

[10] Randall Morck, Andrei Shleifer & Robert Vishny, *Do Managerial Objectives Drive Bad Acquisitions*, 45 J.Fin. 31 (1990); see Sanjai Bhagat, Andrei Shleifer & Robert Vishny, *Hostile Takeovers in the 1980s: The Return to Corporate Specialization*, Brookings Papers on Econ. Activity, Microecon. 1 (1990) ("By and large, hostile takeovers represents the deconglomeration of American business and a return to corporate specialization."); Amar Bhide, *The Causes and Consequences of Hostile Takeovers*, J.Applied Corp.Fin. 36 (Summer 1989).

A closely related type of leveraged transaction was the management buyout or "MBO" of an entire company. These were largely friendly transactions, although often in response to an existing or anticipated hostile transaction. In an MBO, the "target's" management, often joined by an LBO firm -- a firm specializing in leveraged transactions like Kohlberg, Kravis, Roberts -- acquired the target. In addition to its leverage, this form of transaction was characterized by a large increase in management's equity investment in the company and the continuing oversight role played by the leveraged buyout firm. The combination was said to provide managers with both greater performance incentives than they previously had and more intense monitoring of management performance, by both the LBO firm and debt holders.

The End of the Fourth Wave. The fourth merger wave peaked in dollar value in 1988 and 1989, and was clearly over by 1991, when acquisition activity, measured by inflation adjusted dollars, receded to its lowest level since 1980, even though the overall level stock prices was several times higher in 1991 than in 1980. The trend clearly appears in Figure 1-7.

The full explanation for the end of the fourth merger wave remains speculative, although a number of factors seem relevant. The demise of the junk bond market, said to have resulted from the elimination of the central figures in junk bond financing, Michael Milken through criminal prosecution and his firm, Drexel Burnham, through bankruptcy, is one possible factor. One principal source of financing for acquisitions in the later part of the 1980s became less available.

A second explanation looks to a different external source: regulation. By the end of the 1980s, most states had adopted anti-takeover laws that made hostile acquisitions more difficult and, in some states, may have made them impossible.[11] With the diminished likelihood of a hostile takeover, the number of anticipatory friendly transactions also declined.

Others argue that the wave had simply run its course. From this perspective, the fourth merger wave, like earlier waves discussed by Salter & Weinhold, served an economic function. If the 1980s takeover wave was fueled by deconglomeration, as Morck, Shleifer & Vishny argue, then at some point deal makers would run out of companies that could be successfully broken up. By the end of the decade the best deals were said to have been done,[12] and acquisition activity accordingly dropped. An increase in acquisition activity then would have to wait for another idea, an explanation for why widespread ownership changes of capital assets would increase the assets' value.

---

[11] See Mark Roe, *Takeover Politics*, in *The Deal Decade: What Takeovers and Leveraged Buyouts Mean for Corporate Governance* 321 (Margaret Blair ed.1993).

[12] See William Long & David Ravenscraft, *Decade of Debt: Lessons from LBOS in the 1980s*, in *The Deal Decade: What Takeovers and Leveraged Buyouts Mean for Corporate Governance* 205 (Margaret Blair ed.1993).

The drop in both value and activity may also have reflected the 1990-1991 economic downturn. The recession, accompanied by economic uncertainty, poor consumer confidence and lack of job security, forced buyers and sellers to remain cautious when considering acquisitions.

Figure 1-7
Trends In Mergers And Acquisitions, 1972-1991

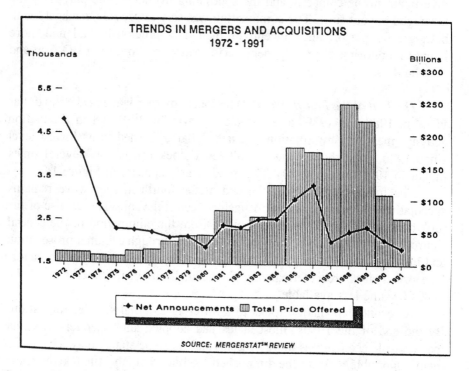

Source: *Mergerstat Review.*

D.   The Modern Transactional Setting

Until 1975, no major investment banking firm would participate in a hostile takeover attempt. But once Morgan Stanley, the most conservative of the leading firms, legitimized hostile takeovers by participating in a hostile tender offer for International Nickel in 1975, the conduct of parties to acquisitions moved farther and farther from the image of "gentlemen" conducting business in a restrained and courteous fashion. Increasingly, the dominant metaphor was war: "battle" replaced "transaction" as a description of the event; "sneak attacks" by an offerer and "scorched earth" tactics by a target replaced "negotiation" as a description of the parties' activities. Moreover, as the 1980s progressed, the parties grew ever more sophisticated in using the new techniques. The changed character of many transactions appears from the following account of one of the major deals of the decade:

Time Incorporated's successful friendly acquisition of Warner Communications in the face of Paramount Communications' hostile offer for Time. The account touches many of the subjects explored in this book, including important judicial opinions growing out of the Time-Paramount contest, that are considered later in this book. But the business story of the transaction -- its planning, the strategies forged and abandoned, and the role of lawyers and investment bankers -- gives a rich introduction to what corporate acquisitions have become.

Bill Saporito, THE INSIDE STORY OF TIME WARNER
Fortune, Nov. 20, 1989[*]

Around six o'clock on the evening of June 6, [1989,] Time Inc. CEO J. Richard Munro walked into the office of President N. J. "Nick" Nicholas Jr. holding a fax message in his hand and a blank stare of disbelief on his face. Munro is normally outgoing, excitable, and expressive, but his stunned look told Nicholas all he needed to know. "He did it," Munro said to his friend Nicholas. "Martin Davis did it."

Davis is the CEO of Paramount Communications. And what he did was waltz by Time's dream house with a pail of gasoline and a flame thrower, torching the company's long-planned merger with Warner Communications and touching off one of the most ferocious corporate clashes in a decade chock-full of them. The battle provoked tremendous controversy and touched every bare-wire business issue of the age: long-term vs. short-term value, shareholder rights, the significance of corporate culture, executive compensation, business ethics, management practice, and merger and acquisition tactics.

Paramount's offer to buy Time for $175 a share in cash hit barely two weeks before Time stockholders were set to vote on the planned merger with Warner, the diversified entertainment and media company run by Steven J. Ross. To hold off Davis and hold on to its independence, Time instead acquired Warner for $13.1 billion in cash and securities.

No one disputes that Time and Warner are an excellent fit. The combined company is an American giant in an age when global behemoths rule the media planet. Time Warner makes movies, television programs, records, tapes, books, and magazines, including this one, and can sell virtually all of these things around the world. It sells pay TV through Home Box Office and Cinemax to 23 million subscribers, and owns cable TV systems serving six million households across the U.S. "It is awesome how impressive this company will become," says Munro, now co-CEO of Time Warner with Ross. Sales in 1989 will approach $11 billion, and the underlying assets are worth some $25 billion. All that and Bugs Bunny, too. Awesome indeed.

But agreement about the combination ends there. Davis too wanted to walk in the land of the giants and saw a combination with Time as a perfect way to get there. In launching his bid Davis acknowledged Munro's logic but chose as a weapon a rather basic fact of arithmetic: $175 is more than $120. The first figure was Paramount's initial offer for each share of Time; the second was the maximum value Paramount and its investment adviser, Morgan Stanley, figured Time Warner's stock would reach if the original merger went through. Davis assumed that given the choice, shareholders would take the cash. He was probably right. They generally do. He was definitely wrong in assuming that they would get the choice.

Time and Warner managers view the acquisition as a perfect combination that would have sailed through in its original form had it not been for that spoilsport Davis. But he couldn't let it sail through, they say, arguing that the debt-free, tax-free merger would have left Paramount too small to compete with a media and entertainment powerhouse such as Time Warner. In this view Davis looked at a no-lose situation and jumped in: He might succeed in buying Time cheaply, or he might break up the deal, or he would at least saddle the new company with debt, making it less competitive. Davis says that notion is ridiculous.

Davis charged in the Paramount lawsuit to prevent Time from buying Warner that Munro and Nicholas sold the shareholders out to preserve their own empire. He said they did this on the pretense that Time's editorial independence and culture demanded it. Munro and Nicholas insist that notion is ridiculous. Says Munro, 58, who will retire as co-CEO next year after ten years of running Time: "This is my legacy. I did not work here 33 years to bust the company up." He and Nicholas, 50, own loads of company stock, he points out. If they had just wanted to get rich, they would have sold the company to Davis or the highest bidder -- and cleared many millions of dollars each.

Steve Ross, 62, Warner's affable, high-profile chairman and CEO, demonstrated once again that in the music of deals he has perfect pitch. Ross orchestrated a great short- and long-term bargain for his shareholders and flattened a persistent boardroom antagonist. He now will share the CEO's job for five years at a company twice the size of Warner. He also retains a compensation package so abundant in dollars that, should the oilman fail to show this winter, Ross can shovel money into his furnace and have plenty left over in the spring.

THE STRATEGY EMERGES

Publishing is a wonderfully profitable business. Basically it comprises a bunch of people and a bunch of trees that eventually run into each other at a printing press. The product of this union is sold to readers and to advertisers who wish to communicate with them. Publishing can offer a high return on assets and terrific margins. Time's magazines, which include Time, FORTUNE, Life, Sports Illustrated, Money, and People, plus a score more wholly or partly owned, are doing just swell, thank you.

But over the past decade Munro, Nicholas, and Time vice chairman Gerald M. Levin came to believe that the magazine division was not growing fast enough. Revenue gains in the division have averaged about 5.7% a year since 1985, and when the Warner deal was announced in March Time's investment bankers could not project anything beyond 6% for the future. Time already has about 22% of the U.S. magazine advertising business, more than twice the share of its nearest competitors, and 33% of magazine profits. Says Munro: "We have two huge engines that drive that division, People and Sports Illustrated. So I would say that the growth there is a little bit limited."   While Time's soul is in publishing, the company tried for decades to find another leg to hold up the financial body. Magazine publishing is a cyclical business hitched to the U.S. economy, and Time Inc. has suffered through several profit swings. The corporation has bought and sometimes sold newspapers, television stations, and forest-products companies in several unavailing efforts to diversify profitably.

Successful diversification did not come until the company happened on cable television and pay channels early in the game, and . . . they took off. Time had picked up a few cable systems in the Sixties, and in the early Seventies a free-spirited entrepreneur named Charles Dolan had briefly joined the company and started something called the Green Channel, soon renamed Home Box Office. By 1974, after years of losses and frustration, these ventures were about to start spouting money, and the executives in charge happened to be three young men named Munro, Nicholas, and Levin. With less than ten years' TV experience among them, they faced the best problem a manager can have: struggling to handle all the growth. Time's future was getting tuned in to a new channel. Today the video side and the magazine side are approximately the same size, $2.1 billion and $1.9 billion, respectively, in sales.

That was terrific, but as of the mid-Eighties Time's top executives still saw three large problems with the corporate structure.

Problem No. 1: Time didn't own any significant copyrights in the fastest-growing sector of the media business, video. Copyrights are a central concept in media. When a film, book, or magazine is produced, distributed, and sold, the copyright owner makes a big chunk of the money. With its cable and pay TV operations Time owned entertainment distribution channels, but it didn't own any entertainment. That stuff had to be bought on the open market, and prices were getting steep.

Problem No. 2: The media industry is increasingly diversified and global, and as Munro and Nicholas saw it, Time was sufficiently neither. While foreign companies such as Bertelsmann, Hachette, and Rupert Murdoch's News Corp. inhaled properties through the mid-Eighties, Time's management thought of these companies as collectors paying crazy prices.

Gradually, as prices continued to spiral and Time watched from the sidelines, another thought took hold.

Nicholas understood that not only would the prices continue to increase, but the very mass of these new empires also offered security from business risks. In addition, mass offered more protection from the appetites of the acquisitive. In a rapidly consolidating media industry, it was eat or be eaten -- and Time sincerely, intensely wished to avoid being eaten.

In pursuing this wish Time lacked a powerful weapon available to most of America's other great publishing enterprises: a separate class of nonvoting stock, which a company's founding family would sell to outside investors while retaining control of the voting stock. New York Times Co., Dow Jones, Washington Post Co., Times Mirror, all had created these two classes of stock, and all had remained independent. Failing to create such stock was, Nicholas says, one of founder Henry R. Luce's few big mistakes.

Besides being tough to take over, the newly forming media empires had another advantage, a capacity for laying off risk. Says Nicholas: "The idea is a very simple one. You get some businesses where you can spread your overhead. You've got to be able to control or have relationships with enough distribution channels to know you've got a great shot at amortizing the fixed costs." In other words, the $35 million price tag of a movie like Batman looks less chancy when a company knows it can get its money back by showing the movie in the U.S., then showing it abroad, selling the videocassette, selling the soundtrack on records, compact discs, and tapes, showing it on pay TV, and perhaps selling related books or producing related TV programs, all using the company's own resources. This year Warner's Batman opened the way for sales of videos, record albums, books, and even comic books (where the character originated) -- all owned by Warner.

Problem No. 3: Wall Street was not in love with Time Inc. and traded the stock at a fraction of its theoretical breakup value. Investors didn't like the variability of Time's earnings. With increasing frequency the stock would rise on rumors that Time was about to be taken over, but this was not Munro's idea of good news.

In the mid-Eighties Munro saw a way to attack all three problems: Hook up through merger or acquisition with another media giant. Allen Neuharth, chief of Gannett Co. and self-described S.O.B., came calling in 1985. Gannett's newspapers and broadcast division might have fit well with Time, but its management wouldn't. Munro had a cast-iron condition for any potential combination: Time Inc. would run the show or would share top-level authority equally. Neuharth scoffed at the idea.

CBS chief Tom Wyman also chatted with Munro about a merger in 1985, when Ted Turner was quixotically attacking CBS, but the talks led nowhere. In the fall of 1988, Warren Buffett came by with his friends from Capital Cities/ABC, in which he was a major investor. Munro and Nicholas met with Buffett and Cap Cities CEO Thomas Murphy and President Daniel Burke. The meetings continued into December, until, according to Nicholas, Murphy mentioned that in any deal there should be one or two more Cap

Cities directors than Time directors. Munro says he told Murphy, a good friend, thank you very much but Time Inc. is not for sale. A Cap Cities source says the two men couldn't agree on who would be boss.

Munro and Nicholas in 1987 began speculating about combining with a film and video producer. Disney had an excellent studio, but 60% of its revenues are from theme parks, a business in which Time had no expertise. Columbia Pictures, MCA, Fox -- each had charms but lacked size, strategic fit, or management. Only two companies looked right: Paramount (then called Gulf & Western) and Warner.

Warner was more profitable and a better strategic match than Paramount. Importantly, at a time when foreign markets offer the brightest growth opportunities, 40% of Warner's revenues come from overseas, vs. less than 10% of Time's (and only 16% of Paramount's). In movies and television both Warner and Paramount produced outstanding returns, but only Warner owned 100% of its movie distribution business. Additionally, Warner had 1.6 million cable subscribers who could combine nicely with the 4.3 million of Time's American Television & Communications, already America's No. 2 cable company (after Tele-Communications Inc.). Paramount's publishing division, Simon & Schuster, would also have fit well at Time, but the company wasn't looking to expand in book publishing. Instead Time got big eyes for Warner's wildly profitable record business, which accounts for about half the company's operating income.

NICK DROPS A DIME

One day in May 1987, Nick Nicholas found himself with an unexpected free afternoon. Citizen Nick had planned to spend the day on jury duty in state supreme court in Manhattan but was dismissed early. From the courthouse lobby he punched the digits for Warner Communications and asked for Steve Ross. Did Ross have some time that afternoon to discuss a couple of things? If Ross didn't have time, he soon made some available.

Nicholas knew Warner's cable operation well -- he had once negotiated, unsuccessfully, to sell Time's Manhattan Cable to it -- and he was interested in a joint cable venture. Ross was also interested because Warner was at a crossroads in cable -- "too big to be small and too small to be big," says Ross. In 1986 Warner had bought its partner American Express out of joint ownership in a cable television company that held systems Time coveted. A joint venture offered a way for Time to get co-ownership of those systems.

Ross took the idea one step further. During several subsequent meetings that summer he developed the notion that Time should throw in its HBO unit, while Warner would contribute its Warner Brothers studio. Such a combination would create a vertically integrated entertainment venture.

The egos in the media corporations that cluster around Manhattan's Sixth Avenue are as big as the buildings, and that was the problem the two sides grappled with in a sit-down at the Helmsley Palace Hotel on November 4, 1987. From Time came Munro, Nicholas, Levin, and HBO Chairman

Michael Fuchs. The Warner group included Ross, Deane F. Johnson from Warner's office of the president, and Warner Brothers studio bosses Robert A. Daly and Terry S. Semel. There were no Indians among these chiefs, making the subject of just who would report to whom a touchy one. Ross wanted Warner Brothers left alone; Time felt the same way about HBO. Both sides agreed the cable systems could be jointly run.

As the talks progressed a number of hurdles sprang up. There were questions of how much money each partner could take out of the venture, serious tax problems within the new company, and a need to develop a divorce agreement should the two parties, like those in so many other joint ventures, decide they didn't like each other after all. Against that formidable stack of problems a simple solution occurred to several of the people involved: Just merge the companies.

Nicholas, with Munro's agreement, popped that merger question in early June 1988, after a year of trying to work out a joint venture. Ross thought about it for a week and agreed to begin negotiating.

In the original joint venture proposal, Munro and Ross would have been co-CEOs of the enterprise, with HBO reporting to Munro, Warner Brothers reporting to Ross, and the cable companies reporting jointly. This structure carried over into the merger talks. The two sides spent the better part of the summer divvying up the reporting relationships and hammering out the roles of the chief executives.

The concept of a co-CEO is not foreign to Ross. He shared the title at Warner with William Frankel from 1967 until Frankel's death in 1972. At one meeting he brought along a FORTUNE article that discussed Unilever, invariably described as the "Anglo-Dutch consumer products company." Unilever is essentially two companies and has two CEOs, one in the Netherlands and one in Britain, who run what Ross called a staple corporation. The two are joined at the bottom line.

Without much debate, Ross and Munro agreed to make Nicholas their successor. Ross had no logical No. 2 to compete for the spot, and over the months of negotiations he had become increasingly impressed with Nicholas. Ross says, "If he weren't with Time I would have made overtures to have him with us. I think he is extremely capable and very knowledgeable. So we never had a problem."

A culture clash, however, has the makings of a problem.

THE CULTURE

Above all other considerations in any merger, Munro felt compelled to defend the Time culture. He sincerely believes, as do many employees, that working for Time isn't like working for, say, Amalgamated Spark Plugs. The executives and employees consider Time Inc. a kind of public institution and believe working for it confers special status.

The most famous feature of Time's culture is the separation, both psychic and structural, of church and state. Time founder Luce decreed that the editorial side of the business (church) would report directly to the editor-in-chief rather than to the publishing side (state), as it does in nearly every other journalistic enterprise in the world. The arrangement gives editors freedom to report and analyze the news without influence or interference from the business side and its advertisers.

The benefits of separating church and state are obvious: It attracts top journalists, it increases a magazine's value to readers, and it makes a magazine more valuable to advertisers, even though they may occasionally take their licks in the editorial pages. But the idea of dual hierarchies reaching all the way to the board is unknown at most companies, including Warner. Jason McManus, 55, Time Inc.'s editor-in-chief and church's high priest, took a philosophic view toward Warner. He was part of the tradition -- he had worked for Luce -- but believed that if Time didn't merge it would be taken over, with who-knows-what effect on the magazines' independence. "There was a nostalgia for Time Inc. as it was imagined to be," he says, "but the people who felt 'Gee, if we hadn't done anything we'd have been fine' were living in a dream world." . . .

To preserve the church-state structure, Warner acknowledged -- not that Time considered the matter negotiable -- the corporate hands-off policy regarding Time's magazines. Editorial operations would report only to editor-in-chief McManus, who is one of Time's four inside directors (the others: Munro, Nicholas, Levin). McManus reports only to the board. It exercises its responsibility for editorial operations through a committee of six outside directors, with four seats going to people who were on Time's board before the merger. Warner demanded the same protection for its creative output. Time agreed to an entertainment committee, controlled by directors who had been on Warner's board, to oversee Warner's movie and record businesses.

The Time directors came up with another method to ensure cultural survival: They authorized Levin, 50, to negotiate long-term contracts for Munro, Nicholas, and himself. Says Munro: "We told the board that we didn't want contracts, but they insisted."

Munro had long said that by age 60 he would step aside both as CEO and as a director. Working out the merger terms, he changed his mind in order to smooth the transition and be available should Ross be incapacitated. Munro's contract makes him co-CEO with Ross until he steps down next year. After that he will be chairman of the board's executive committee until 1994 and an adviser for five years more. He will be paid at least $1.5 million annually in salary and bonus as co-CEO. From 1990 until 1999 he will be paid at least $750,000 a year. He will later get another $4,275,000 in deferred compensation. Nicholas also signed a roughly comparable ten-year contract, making him co-CEO with Ross as soon as Munro resigns, and sole CEO in five years.

In theory the board could undo these arrangements, subject to restrictions in the contracts. But to the extent it was possible, Time had ensured that its cherished culture would have advocates at the top of Time

Warner for a decade. The contracts put Munro in the position of explaining to employees, including hundreds of journalists, that he and Nicholas accepted the extraordinarily handsome agreements to protect them. . . .

JERRY'S DEAL

The task of negotiating the merger's financial terms fell to Levin from Time and to Oded Aboodi for Warner. Aboodi, 48, is neither a Warner officer nor a director, nor an investment banker in the usual sense, though he is sometimes called one. But Ross wouldn't make a move without him. A Jerusalem-born accountant, Aboodi handled some Warner transactions while a partner at Arthur Young & Co. Technically astute, he loves the creative aspects of dealmaking, and in Steve Ross he found a soul mate. Says Levin: "He reads the psychological set of the people he deals with."

Levin, an attorney by training and Time's chief strategist and planner, insisted from the beginning of negotiations in early 1988 that Time had to be the acquiring entity. Says he: "There was never a discussion of the acquisition of Time by Warner. We were interested in an acquisition -- where the Time culture, the Time institution, the Time tradition prevails."

That was fine with Aboodi. He had an imperative of his own: Ross's demand that the deal be erected not as a cash buyout but as a merger in which only stock changed hands. Ross wanted Time to issue millions of new shares with which to buy Warner from its stockholders. Time executives had hoped to borrow billions in good old cash and buy Warner that way, preserving greater assets and earning power for each Time share. On this issue Time gave in early. Says Ross: "They threw in the sponge because they knew finally that I wasn't going to do anything but a stock deal."

One reason Ross insisted on this form of merger was that it would let the merged company treat the deal as a pooling of interests, a now rarely used accounting method that combines the assets of the merging enterprises as if they were never apart. Most mergers use purchase-price accounting, a technique with an insidious cost. Acquired companies are generally worth far more than the value of the hard assets shown on their balance sheets. The difference between the price paid and an acquired company's updated asset value is called goodwill. Under purchase-price accounting this amount is amortized over a long period, with the amount amortized each year deducted from reported profits, even though no cash loss is involved. In the Warner deal goodwill amounts to $10 billion to $12 billion, or something like $300 million to $400 million a year for 30 years. Ross did not want such a hit to earnings.

So the deal would be an exchange of stock -- but at what ratio? By the end of June 1988, the talks focused on that question. Aboodi was in the driver's seat because Warner had a better bottom line and a higher market value than Time. In 1988 Warner earned $423 million after taxes on sales of $4.2 billion. Although Time had sales of $4.5 billion, its net profit was

$289 million. Main reason: Warner enjoys a lower tax rate resulting from accumulated tax credits.

Warner's sales and earnings growth were outpacing Time's. Had the two companies remained independent, Warner's sales would have overtaken Time's this year. Aboodi argued further that Warner's stock price would rise faster and carry a higher earnings multiple because Wall Street liked its business mix better. He also noted that Time was supporting its own stock price, having bought back 10% of the shares, while Warner was not. Finally, and most important, Warner had to be accorded a takeover premium.

Time indicated it was willing to pay a premium for the right to take Warner out. The price of Warner's stock had been about 35% of Time's over the previous 12 months. Adding to that a premium of around 10 percentage points, Levin figured to get a deal at a ratio of 43% to 45% -- or, as the negotiators say, .43 to .45. He started at .40; Aboodi talked .50. They would not get any closer that year.

THE $193 MILLION MAN

A far more delicate challenge also awaited Levin, Munro, and Nicholas: how to sell Steve Ross to the Time board. Ross's contract was as lush as that of any CEO in America. In 1987, following a wild board meeting ending in a 9-to-6 vote, Ross took home a ten-year employment contract that guaranteed him base pay of $1.2 million a year. That's not unheard of, but the contract included a bonus that would pay an average $14 million a year for ten years if Warner stock appreciated 10% a year. It has.

Under his amended ten-year contract with Time Warner, Ross is due $193 million at the close of the deal for stock-based compensation he had coming at Warner: $70 million in cash and $123 million in deferred payments. He also gets the same $1.2 million annual salary and deferred compensation he did at Warner plus a minimum bonus of 0.4% of Time Warner's earnings before taxes and some amortization and depreciation. And he receives options on 1.8 million shares of stock at a minimum price of $150 a share. After 1999 he will collect $750,000 a year for five years as an adviser.

Time's management convinced the board that Ross's contract was his reward for founding the company in the 1960s and successfully nurturing it. Curiously, Ross owned only about 1% of his baby's stock, which is where most founders get their reward. Very few Time directors liked Ross's contract, but they viewed it as part of Warner's price. Says director Donald S. Perkins, a former CEO of Jewel Cos., a supermarket chain: "It just comes down to a cost of doing business. It was part of the price of the deal." Says another, who prefers to remain nameless: "I've made a lot of guys rich who didn't deserve it. The deal is what's important."

Ross patched Warner together initially by grafting a rental car business onto his father-in-law's funeral parlor business. He added parking lots and took the company public as Kinney National Service in 1962. In 1969, Kinney bought Warner Brothers-Seven Arts, then a broken-down relic of a Hollywood studio, for a reported $400 million in stock. But Warner also had real estate, a film library, a great record company, and good executives, such as Ahmet Ertegun of Atlantic Records. Warner is the ultimate people business, and it fit Ross's schmoozing style. A big guy's big guy, Ross lives the high life and makes no excuses for it. His longstanding friendships with Hollywood glitterati -- Clint Eastwood, Barbra Streisand, Steven Spielberg -- are counted as corporate assets.

Ross combined an uncanny sense of the future, a genial manner, and shrewd dealmaking skills to lift Warner onto the FORTUNE 500 in 1971. He put someone he could trust in charge of each business, left him alone, and paid handsomely if the division performed. The pay included stock appreciation rights. The deal with Time will enable about 700 Warner employees to cash in options totaling more than $600 million.

Retired Time president James Shepley, who died in November 1988, made no attempt to hide his belief that Ross and Warner were unsavory partners. In the early Eighties, Time lost three cable television franchise battles to Ross in Pittsburgh, Cincinnati, and the New York City borough of Queens, and Shepley was sure Warner had played dirty. Dick Munro had led the battle in Pittsburgh. He remembers: "We had the champagne all ready to pour. And then the word came that Warner had been picked. We couldn't believe we'd lost. They must have paid somebody off." Time sued Warner and the city of Pittsburgh, charging improper bidding procedures. The two sides eventually settled out of court.

TIME'S BOARD HOPS ON

Munro told Time's board in June 1988 that his team was talking to Warner about a merger, but he gave no details. . . . During the next few weeks Munro spoke with each director privately to explain his vision of Time Inc.'s future and ask for approval.

Events of the Eighties had affected several of Time's 12 outside directors in various ways that would directly influence their view of any deal. After he retired, Donald Perkins watched American Stores take over his Jewel Cos. and unhinge the organization he helped create. Edward S. Finkelstein, chairman of R.H. Macy & Co., had taken the retail merchandiser private when it became raider bait. James F. Bere, chairman of Borg-Warner, took his company private in a leveraged buyout to fend off raids by Irwin Jacobs and GAF.

A key player was director Michael D. Dingman, who [was] chairman of Henley Group. An astute shuffler of corporate assets, Dingman had done more deals in a few years than most executives do in a career. He knew leverage, he knew shareholder value, he sure as hell knew mergers and acquisitions -- and he knew as of late July 1988 that among Time directors

Munro's merger plan with Warner was dead. Says he: "It was damned controversial. If you ran a board vote on it, it would have failed."

Levin was also keeping score, and it wasn't looking good.   His handwritten notes revealed the tally: Bere was unenthusiastic, Perkins lukewarm, ditto Clifford J. Grum, CEO of Temple-Inland. Another director, Henry C. Goodrich, former chairman of Sonat, an Alabama energy company, was down as a flat no. John Opel, chairman of IBM's executive committee, was skeptical but open-minded. David T. Kearns, chairman and CEO of Xerox, was signed on, as was Finkelstein. Levin had no read on the board's two academics: Matina S. Horner, president of Radcliffe College, and Clifton R. Wharton Jr., former chancellor of the State University of New York and now chairman of Teachers Insurance & Annuity Association/College Retirement Equity Fund.

Director Arthur Temple's name did not appear on the list. Nor did that of director Henry Luce III, son of Time founder Henry R. Luce. There was no need. Arthur Temple would no sooner get in bed with Hollywood than he would climb a loblolly pine naked.

Director Henry Luce III wasn't wild about Hollywood either, but more fundamentally he did not yet buy the strategy. He had worked at Time for 30 years, including tours as publisher of FORTUNE and Time, then retired in 1981 to run the Henry Luce Foundation, which controls about 3.5% of Time's stock. For years he had approved company expansion into other media with mixed emotions. He accepted that Munro's strategy might be valid but felt it was not necessarily the only effective one. Says he: "I expressed disagreement to Dick and his colleagues. They made all their points that it was an important strategic move, but they left me unpersuaded." And like Temple, Luce was appalled by the rich employment contracts for Munro, Nicholas, and Ross.

Luce also believed that his father, Henry, would not have approved the Warner deal. In late July 1988, he sent Munro a note that quoted his father's will: "'Time Inc. is now, and is expected to continue to be, principally a journalistic enterprise, and, as such, an enterprise operated in the public interest.'" Luce III continued: "In the spirit of the above, and in view of many other specific factors, I don't believe I could vote for the proposition . . . ." Luce instead urged Munro to go after McGraw-Hill, the undermanaged publishing house two doors down Sixth Avenue from Time.
. . .

ROSS TAKES A HIKE

If anyone held fears of a boardroom showdown, they were dispelled on August 11, 1988, when Ross pulled out of the talks after an emotional meeting at his Park Avenue apartment with Munro, Levin, Nicholas, Aboodi, and attorneys. . . . Some Time directors felt relieved. Although many of the so-called governance issues had been worked out, the Time board had insisted that Ross accept a finite term as co-CEO and the assured succession of Nick Nicholas as sole chief. "We didn't want another Armand Hammer," explains one director. Lawyers for Time kept referring to Ross's tenure as transitional. The language grated on Ross. He felt unwanted and unloved by the Time board, and worse yet feared being locked into a lame duck status, which would undermine his authority.

The last thing Ross wanted was another contentious board. At Warner he was living with an archenemy in Herbert J. Siegel, the Chris-Craft Industries chief who as a director controlled 17% of Warner stock and who often clashed with Ross over strategy.[a] . . .

Once again Dingman stepped into the deal, this time to explain to Ross how things work in the Time & Life Building. Toward the end of 1988 the two met for dinner at Ross's apartment, and Dingman told Ross that he had put Munro and Nicholas in a bad position with the Time board over the governance issue. The Time executives had talked up Ross, but if the merger was ever to get back on track the Time directors needed to know that Ross had no designs on a power grab, and they needed it in writing.

Ross relented. He says, "I realized that I've got to decide what I want to do -- take off those deal blinders and say, Okay, Steve, you've been guiding the company, enjoying working with your people. You enjoy long range planning, you enjoy dreaming of tomorrow and seeing what you can do. But there's one thing you don't enjoy doing, and that's running a business on a day to day basis . . . So I said to myself, Maybe this is an opportunity." He told Dingman he would agree to retire as co-CEO in 1994 and retain the chairmanship another five years, through 1999, to give Nicholas whatever strategic help was necessary.

Dingman reported back to Munro that Ross was ready to deal again. Time's directors had viewed his reluctance to set a date for his retirement as the last roadblock to an agreement in principle. Levin and Aboodi resumed negotiations in January 1989, and over the next month closed the gap. On March 2 Ross was summoned from a Warner board meeting to a session with Aboodi, Levin, and Nicholas. They had a ratio: .465 shares of Time to be exchanged for each Warner share.

TIME FOR A COUNTERATTACK

Dick Munro felt certain that Martin Davis would not move against Time. He believed he had secured a firm promise that Davis would respect Time's independence. A few days before Davis announced his bid, Munro found out that Davis was to lunch with Joseph Flom, the famous M&A lawyer from Skadden Arps Slate Meagher & Flom who is a Time attorney. Munro, not exactly thrilled to learn that one of his attorneys was breaking bread with a potential enemy, sent word to Flom to feel Davis out one more time. According to depositions, Flom asked Davis if he knew anything about

---

[a] And Steve Ross's pay. Eds.

a raid on Time. Davis said something on the order of "Time? It's 12:30. I'll have the soup." Munro understood that the road to the deal wasn't mined.

Neither of Time's investment advisers, Bruce Wasserstein of Wasserstein Perella and J. Tomilson Hill of Shearson Lehman, was all that surprised by the Paramount raid. From the beginning they considered the all-stock merger a risky piece of dealmaking because it could be easily upset by a higher cash bid like Davis's. Neither Wasserstein nor Shearson was willing to recommend the deal without a commitment that Time would complete it for cash if the merger fell through.

Despite their concerns, Time's investment bankers had believed it was an auspicious time to try the merger. With the market set to digest the huge amounts of junk bonds being floated in early May in the RJR Nabisco takeover, buyers for newer issues might be scarcer, and the political environment was growing increasingly anti-buyout. These factors could discourage potential raiders, who might try to finance their attacks by issuing junk. Says one [Wasserstein Perella] staffer: "We thought the usual crazies would lie low. We went down the roster. We all knew these people and their predilections."

Still, Time's stock had begun to climb, from $110 in early March to about $135 by May 30, in anticipation of a raider's play. The investment bankers picked up Paramount's trail in late March, and it led to Morgan Stanley, the investment banking house. Morgan Stanley had marked Time for two years before the Warner merger, occasionally sharing its information with Paramount. Soon after Time and Warner announced their merger, Morgan sent Paramount a business-by-business analysis of Time Inc. with an estimate of what a potential acquirer might expect to pay for the company. And incidentally, if Paramount was interested, Morgan was ready and able to assist said potential acquirer to make the purchase. Morgan wasn't alone. Salomon Brothers smelled blood, too, and made a similar presentation to Paramount.

That Paramount was talking to Morgan Stanley did not seem all that threatening. Time's investment bankers assumed Davis was lining up a partner should someone else try to break the Time-Warner deal. He might then step in as a white knight, or buy one of the pieces. In fact, Paramount was getting calls from Bass and other interested parties about making a joint run at Time.

Davis, Munro, and Nicholas had circled one another for years. HBO signed a deal long ago to show Paramount movies and renewed the arrangement last year. The three men chatted occasionally, and several times they gathered for breakfast at the Ritz-Carlton Hotel on Central Park South, between Time's and Paramount's headquarters. Says Nicholas: "The discussions about doing things together probably lasted no more than five minutes, and they were initiated by Martin Davis, and he made comments like, 'You know, we're a great fit.' And then he would say, 'Gee Dick, you're retiring and then I can run it, and then Nick, you're younger and you can eventually run it.' That's about as substantive as it got." Davis also shared a lunch with Hollywood-hating Arthur Temple to get to know such an influential Time director a little better.

It is Munro's distinct recollection that Davis told him several times that Paramount would never attack Time. "I never asked Martin if he would make a hostile attempt to take over Time," says Munro. "He volunteered that on at least two or three occasions -- that he would never do anything hostile, period." In testimony for his lawsuit, Davis agrees with Munro on one point: They did meet. Memories diverge after that. Davis says Munro told him that Time Inc. was not interested in the motion picture business and wanted to remain just as it was.

By the end of May Paramount had hired Morgan Stanley to prepare for a raid on Time, with Paramount wheeling in the financial ammunition. Paramount paid Citibank to issue a "highly confident" letter stating that Paramount could secure the credit needed to take Time over.

Davis decided on Friday, June 2, that he would pull the trigger, and he sent relevant information to his directors so they could consider the matter over the weekend. He sounded out a small group of lieutenants but spent hours thinking by himself. Paramount's board met the following Tuesday, June 6, and Davis got the go-ahead then. The merger that had been all wrapped up and ready for delivery suddenly wasn't.

RAINMAKERS

The Time-Warner-Paramount battle brought together a monsoon's worth of Wall Street rainmakers. The Time lineup included Cravath Swaine & Moore, one of the company's law firms for more than 60 years, led by senior partner Samuel Butler and merger ace Allen Finkelson. Takeover titan Joe Flom was also on hand, as were Bruce Wasserstein, who has had a finger in nearly every big takeover pie, and Tom Hill, Shearson Lehman's top merger mogul.

Some of the bills were shocking. Cravath and other law firms jacked up their normally stiff hourly rates because of the difficulty of the assignment. Time's bill for Cravath and Skadden is $14 million and rising. Warner's fees, to be paid by Time Warner, include well over $25 million due the firm of Wachtell Lipton Rosen & Katz.

Warner's legal team included Arthur Liman of Paul Weiss Rifkind Wharton & Garrison. Liman, a legendary litigator, last made headlines as one of Ollie North's interrogators in the Senate's Iran-contra hearings. Warner also had Herbert Wachtell and Martin Lipton of Wachtell Lipton, the firm that virtually created all modern corporate defense strategies. As investment adviser, Ross had another old friend, Rohatyn of Lazard, assisted by three partners.

Paramount was outmanned but not outgunned. Davis's team included his inside counsel, Donald Oresman, a former partner at Simpson Thacher & Bartlett, Paramount's outside counsel and the law firm that represented Kohlberg Kravis Roberts in the RJR fight. Paramount often worked with

Lazard and Wasserstein, but their dance cards were obviously filled. So Davis went with Morgan Stanley. Stephen Waters, ex-Shearson merger specialist and no stranger to the takeover wars, led Morgan's group.

The M&A experts are like the Pharaohs: few, rich, powerful, and incestuous. They are also hired guns, and many of them had met a few months earlier at the battle for RJR, or in even more recent business. Rohatyn had worked for RJR's special committee of the board, prominently including Martin Davis. Shearson had banked Ross Johnson's losing hand in the RJR game. Wasserstein's was one of four banking houses employed by KKR; Morgan Stanley was another. Paramount retained Wasserstein for a year, until February, 1989, to review acquisition strategies. Lazard had represented Paramount in the recent sale of its Associates subsidiary; a Lazard partner sits on Paramount's board.

The sides chosen, the gang was ready to play again, and for big money: $16 million each for Shearson and Wasserella. Morgan signed on for pocket change, $2.5 million, but stood to gain more than $100 million in fees if Paramount's bid succeeded.

THE ACQUISITION SOLUTION

"We will not make a decision this week." Time's board convened on Thursday, June 8, to those words from Munro. The decision not to choose a response to Davis's hostile offer had several purposes, the first being to see if any other players were going to jump out of the wings. The second was to take some heat off the board and minimize the chance of committing a tactical error under pressure. The third and most important was to give the board time to carry out its strict legal duty of carefully deliberating over its next step.

Munro, livid and convinced that Davis had snookered him, sent the Paramount chief a so's-your-old-man letter flooded with invective and hyperbole. "You've changed the name of your corporation but not its character: it's still 'engulf and devour,'" he wrote. "Hostile takeovers are a little like wars: it's impossible to tell where they may end."

If Munro wanted the head of Martin Davis, an in-your-face, Pac-Man counterattack could deliver it. Just buy Paramount. Director John Opel asked the advisers for a detailed analysis of the pros and cons of Time making a counterbid for Paramount, the so-called Pac-Man defense. The company was, after all, No. 2 on Time's short list of merger-acquisition candidates, and it would be cheaper to buy than Warner.

The problem with Pac-Man attacks is that they seldom succeed, and the tactics are messy. There was, however, one intriguing potential outcome: Once Time turned the tables on Paramount, Davis might be amenable to a mutual disengagement. But then again he might not, and the strategy would be a step removed from the real goal of merging with Warner. So Time renounced Pac-Man.

Instead, Time attacked Paramount's bid on two fronts, price and conditions. Mack Rossoff of Wasserstein Perella appraised Time's value at $238 to $287 a share, a range some directors thought far too low. Later, however, Wasserstein lowered it a bit. Even by that measure, Paramount's $175-a-share offer didn't get into the ballpark. The Time board cited the low bid as a reason for refusing to negotiate with Paramount. The advisers figured that if Paramount owned Time, Paramount's stock price might double in a year. Wasserstein and Shearson's analysis of Paramount indicated that it could afford at least $225 a share.

Paramount attached a large number of conditions to the deal. Time had the usual poison pill defenses that Paramount wanted rescinded. As part of the original merger deal with Warner, the two companies had also agreed to exchange a small amount of each other's stock. Such a swap would increase the price Paramount would have to pay, and Davis wanted the obstacle removed.

Davis's offer had a standard "financing out" condition, a technical way of saying, "If we can't get the money, the deal's off." More important, the offer was contingent on Paramount's obtaining approvals from cities and towns across the U.S. for the transfer of cable television licenses from Time to Paramount. "If theirs was such a great offer," asks Ross, "why were there 27 conditions to it?"

Rossoff, Levin, and ATC Chairman Joseph J. Collins argued at one Time board meeting that Paramount's bid had to be discounted because the company needed at least three months and more likely a year to get approvals for the cable franchise transfers. Cable franchises generally carry a right to renewal, but Collins explained that it goes out the window in any change of ownership that is not first approved by the governing municipality. Furthermore, he said, no hostile acquirer had ever asked for franchise transfers; maybe some wouldn't be granted at all. Wasserstein noted that at a discount of 1% per month compounded -- the rate of return Time shareholders expect on their investment $175 four months down the road is worth $170 today. If the payoff is a year away, the present value is only $155.

In addition to the franchise transfers, Paramount also had to obtain license transfers from the Federal Communications Commission for such things as microwave relays and radio operating permits associated with cable transmission. That too would take a while. So Paramount asked the FCC to let it establish a voting trust, run by former Defense Secretary Donald Rumsfeld, that would hold Time shares while the company pursued the license transfers. Since Paramount's offer prevented the company from buying shares until it got FCC license and cable transfers, the company planned to have the trust pay Time's shareholders immediately. Collins told the Time board the trust was probably illegal.

In response, Time launched a guerrilla attack to delay the transfer approvals. Lawyers for Time and ATC told officials in many cities and towns that Paramount's plan to set up a trust for the shares violated franchise agreements. Should city fathers be as horrified as Time Inc. at this state of affairs, Time would help them sue Paramount for illegally interfering with the franchise. Time sent to officials of about a dozen large cities all the legal papers necessary to file suit -- just fill in the blanks -- and told a couple of cities it would even pay the legal costs and indemnify the plaintiffs against countersuits by Paramount. The company also challenged Paramount's application to the FCC to set up a voting trust. ATC sued Paramount in Connecticut for illegally interfering with its business.

Such civic-mindedness is hardly the type of behavior that usually characterized the preppies of Time Inc. This is big league, sharpen-your-spikes-and-slide-in-high type stuff. Asked by Paramount's lawyers if the legal ambush was an ethical business practice, Munro was clearly uneasy: "I would have a little trouble with that. I'm not sure it's right or it's wrong, but it's marginal." (Not to director Finkelstein. He says: "One pursues the tactics that one thinks are in one's own interest. Both sides do that.")

During meetings on June 8, 11, 15, and 16, the Time board debated options. It could do nothing and risk the shareholder vote on the Warner merger. It could take on debt and pay out a big dividend to the shareholders, enough to induce them to reject Paramount's bid. Or it could change the deal. Wasserstein told the board that by selling off 1.5 million cable subscribers (out of Time's 4.3 million) plus Scott Foresman, a Time textbook publishing subsidiary, and borrowing against the remaining assets, management could in theory raise enough cash to pay the stockholders $185 to $200 a share in a restructuring or leveraged buyout.

Only remotely did Time's board consider selling the company and delivering cash to the shareholders. The directors were convinced the Warner deal would pay off down the line. Only if the company lost Paramount's suit would they consider a sale. The lawyers assured the board there would be plenty of time to do that.

Having eliminated a sale, buying Paramount, or an LBO, the board focused on Warner. Says Finkelstein: "In looking at a variety of options that [the advisers] presented . . ., I came to the conclusion Time's a very valuable company, and it's my own judgment that the acquisition of Warner will magnify that value."

During the meeting on the 15th, advisers took the board through a variety of scenarios in which Time would buy Warner for $70 a share, either in cash or in combinations of cash and securities. The advisers favored a deal they had worked out with Warner: Time would tender for about 50% of Warner's stock in cash, with payment for the rest -- the so-called back end of the deal -- to be considered later.

Warner's stock was then selling for $55.63. Directors peppered the advisers with questions about why the back end was left so vague. The answer was straightforward: The back end was open because Warner negotiated it that way. Steve Ross was leaving himself some room to make a deal within a deal.

On the 16th the [Time] board voted unanimously to acquire about 50% of Warner for $70 a share in cash and to pick up the rest for cash or securities or some combination. The board then postponed the shareholders' meeting scheduled months earlier for June 23 to vote on the original merger.

The directors debated little whether to ask Time shareholders to approve the new proposal. Time executives later explained that it would take too long to mount the educational campaign to persuade them of the deal's long-term advantages. By that time Warner might have dropped out, and the overriding concern was getting the deal done. Even though most shareholders would have preferred to take Davis's cash, Time's board was persuaded that in the long run the Warner acquisition would be more valuable to them. Says Finkelstein: "Once you believe you are acting in the best interests of the shareholders, you can continue on until you have a better argument, and I don't think we were presented with a better argument."

When Munro explained the new deal to sometimes skeptical employee groups over the next couple of days, a number of them asked about the shareholder vote. He told them bluntly: "We are going by the law." Shareholder approval was not needed. It would not be asked for. . . .

After the [Warner board approved the revised deal], Ross told Time he was triggering the stock swap that the two companies negotiated as part of the original deal. The swap put 11% of Time's shares in Warner's hands and 9% of Warner's shares in Time's, an exchange that rendered a raid more costly and difficult to execute. Ross was playing defense: If Time did get taken over by Paramount, Warner would at least get a sweet going-away gift when Time's price rose.

On June 23 Davis turned up the pressure by increasing his bid to $200 a share, a maneuver the Time directors fully expected. They held firm.

DAVIS WOWS 'EM

Martin Davis won the media battle with startling ease. As a former movie publicist he understands how the press works. And as CEO of a once wide-ranging conglomerate he knows many industries and the reporters who cover them. Davis also happens to be a terrific source: knowledgeable, articulate, and unafraid to tackle tough questions.

On this issue Davis delivered a simple message: Here's the offer, it's cash, we don't plan to sell assets, and yes, we expect to have all the approvals we need just as quickly as we can get them. Clearly Paramount's deal was not that simple, but why complicate the issue?

Davis defused Munro's charge that Paramount would violate Time's editorial integrity. Why would he want to interfere with such great magazines? He told FORTUNE he would put in writing a pledge not to meddle with the magazines' editorial operations.

Munro told everyone who would listen that Paramount's offer was illusory, inadequate, and highly conditional, and that Davis was a lying so-and-so who would have to sell huge pieces of Time to finance his debt. His protestations did not get him far.

Some Time executives and Wall Street bankers had naively assumed the press would rally around a brother media company to repel such a raid. Instead, much of the press slammed Time. Davis framed the issue in black and white and left Munro to struggle with a dozen shades of gray. The media do not write much about gray.

[Time's directors] were disappointed by the cynicism shown their efforts to make an American institution into an international one. The cancellation of the shareholder vote, the rejection of a $200-a-share cash offer without negotiating, the high-paying, long-term contracts for top executives -- there were answers on all these issues, but explaining them took time and more willing ears, and Munro didn't find enough of either. Time could not even begin talking about Davis's bid until the board had fully considered all options -- and that took days. . . . [I]n a bizarre editorial the Wall Street Journal chastised Time for trampling shareholder rights -- bizarre because common shares of Dow Jones, the Journal's owner, have one vote, while the Class B shares, controlled mostly by insiders, have ten votes each. . . .

WAR IN DELAWARE

The day was July 11, and members of the Delaware bar said it was the damnedest thing they had ever seen. The 1989 Super Bowl of corporate litigation, Paramount Communications v. Time,[b] was under way. A mob of photographers and TV cameramen, reporters tethered to them by microphone cables, waited on the steps of the Court of Chancery in Wilmington. At 9 A.M. men and women began wheeling huge cartons of documents up the steps. The gang with the cameras followed en masse, a media mummers' parade capturing for posterity what appeared to be an office move.

About 85 stultifying degrees of thermal energy and twice that many lawyers, arbitragers, and reporters crammed into the corridor when courtroom 301 opened. An ugly scramble for seats forced the bailiffs to call for order. This being Wilmington in July the heat would have shown up anyway, but the crowd might have been thinner had everyone known what Robert D. Joffe knew.

Cravath's Joffe, lead counsel for Time, was going to argue before Chancellor William T. Allen. Joffe knew that Paramount's lawyers had deposed 13 Time and Warner executives, directors, and advisers. He knew they had copies of the minutes of board meetings, handwritten notes of phone conversations, and presentations made by Time's and Warner's bankers. And he knew they didn't have the case they went looking for.

. . . . Delaware law has always given directors wide latitude in determining corporate conduct. Only in recent years have the courts

---

[b] 565 A.2d 280 (Del.1990).

tightened the reins on them, and only in a few narrow cases. In Revlon v. MacAndrews & Forbes Holdings, a 1986 case now known as *Revlon*,[c] the Delaware Supreme Court ruled that if the directors decide to sell a company, they must sell it to the highest bidder. No favorites. In a 1985 case, Unocal Corp. v. Mesa Petroleum Co., called *Unocal*,[d] the court ruled that directors defending their company from a raider may respond only in a reasonable way. "Reasonable" did not necessarily mean "fair" to the raider. To prevail, Paramount would have to demonstrate clearly that Time had broken the Revlon or Unocal mode rules.

Paramount built its case on two foundations, the first being that Time put itself up for sale when it agreed to merge with Warner on March 3. The argument was largely technical: When Time acceded to a swap at a .465 ratio, 60% of its shares -- a majority -- would have gone to Warner stockholders, and Paramount said that's a sale. If it was, then Time was in the so-called Revlon mode and had to sell to the highest bidder. The second and more complex argument charged Time managers with entrenching themselves at shareholder expense and responding unreasonably to Paramount's bid, violating the *Unocal* rule. Time's plan to acquire Warner without shareholder approval was Exhibit A.

Paramount's attorney, Melvyn L. Cantor of Simpson Thacher, tried to string together a cohesive tale of entrenchment. In a calm though faintly sardonic voice he led Allen through the negotiation of the merger ratio, the management contracts, the governance provisions, the refusal to negotiate with Paramount, the cancellation of the shareholder vote, and the new plan to acquire Warner. He also suggested that Time didn't really believe that preserving the editorial culture is vital to the company. After all, he asked, "Who is going to preserve this culture, your honor? Nick Nicholas, a man who has worked 20 years in cable television."

The closest Paramount got to a smoking gun was a memo written by Time vice chairman Levin in August of 1987. Levin, Time's Big Thinker, outlined the logic for combining with Warner and Ted Turner's TBS. (Time then owned about 12% of TBS; Time Warner owns 18%.) He sketched what he believed would be the relative positions of Time's other businesses in the future. Levin also noted, "An overriding question would still be: Have we secured the company? Is sheer size sufficient protection, or will we still need a large block of stock in friendly hands?" To Paramount, the statement was direct evidence that Time's executives desired the company for themselves. But Levin closed the memo by saying, in effect, he was just thinking out loud, a postscript that may have been vital to Time's defense.

Cantor was terrific, but his argument didn't have much law behind it, and Joffe attacked it head on. Time's decision to merge with Warner was more than two years in the making, he pointed out. If that isn't thoughtful

---

[c] 506 A.2d 173 (Del.1986).

[d] 493 A.2d 946 (Del.1985).

corporate planning, what is? Warner attorney Herbert Wachtell asked the court: Had Paramount not appeared on the scene, would any court have prevented the original Time-Warner combination? The answer, as Wachtell knew, was no -- the proposed merger was clearly legal. Just because Paramount decided to make a bid for Time a day late and 50 bucks short, he argued, that was no reason for the court to stop the Time-Warner deal. Besides, for all Time had done, it had in no way prevented any future bids for the company. If Davis wanted to buy the new Time Warner, Wachtell noted, nobody was stopping him.

Chancellor Allen agreed wholeheartedly.

On appeal the Delaware Supreme Court upheld the decision unanimously. Justice Randy Holland asked Cantor, "Do you agree that Time and Warner is a good deal?" "Yes," Cantor agreed, but before he could add that Time Paramount was a better one, Holland shot back: "Then don't you lose?" You do.

The raid on Time cost Paramount more than $80 million pretax. But it resulted in Time's having to borrow $12 billion, an enormous debt load. As a result Time Warner paid $451 million in interest and financing fees in this year's third quarter and took a $40 million earnings hit for amortization of goodwill, contributing to a loss for the quarter of $176 million. The question is inevitable: Is this the reason Davis pulled the raid? "Just look at the depositions," says Davis. "You'll see that there isn't a shred of truth" to the charge.

A better question might be: Assuming Paramount really wanted to own Time, did it choose the right tactics? A lawyer involved on the Time side says, "Morgan Stanley had to know that Time was worth at least $225 a share. Why give the board a reason to reject you by coming in so low?" Court documents show Morgan Stanley valued Time at a minimum of $217 a share. Some investment bankers wonder why Davis didn't play the last card: bid for the merged Time Warner after prearranging a deal with some third party to take Warner off his hands. After losing in court Davis said he was not interested in further pursuit of Time Warner. He did not say he was not interested forever.

IS BIGGER BETTER?

Dick Munro, Nick Nicholas, and Steve Ross have their dream come true: Time Warner is the largest media empire on earth. Now these three men have some substantial promises to keep in the face of considerable uncertainty. They must show that an important premise of the deal was valid -- that the companies can enhance the value of print, video, and music and create new profit opportunities together. They must pay off at least some of Time Warner's $12 billion debt without divesting the core businesses of magazines, pay TV, cable systems, and film and record production -- though a rise in interest rates could poleax their repayment forecasts.

Munro must show that he was right to spend $13.1 billion for a company that depends enormously on one man. For now he acknowledges that "If I'm wrong about Steve Ross, it will be the biggest mistake I've ever made." Nicholas will eventually have to show that he was worth signing up as CEO five years in advance. All three executives will have to demonstrate that they merit their extraordinary long-term contracts.

Perhaps most important, Munro and Nicholas will have to show that their fundamental act of stewardship in this deal -- repulsing a highly conditional offer for Time shares in favor of a highly leveraged acquisition -- was sound. Remember that at one point they discounted the value of Paramount's offer by assuming Time investors demanded a 12% annual return. They also argued that their deal might not look as good as Paramount's in the short term but would be far more valuable in the long term. Fair enough. The $200 a share Time stockholders didn't get, at 12% a year, will be worth $352 in five years, $621 in ten years. The stock was recently around $140. The managers of Time Warner must now demonstrate that bigger is better. And in a big way.

Note on Post-Mortem of Time-Warner

No transaction turns out precisely as expected, but the period following Time's acquisition of Warner had some special surprises. First, the line of succession at Time-Warner turned out differently than had been expected. The co-CEO structure by which Nick Nicholas and Steve Ross would jointly run the combined company did not last. In 1992, Nicholas was fired and Ross took over the lead management role, elevating Gerald Levin to the lead Time role. Late that same year Ross died, leaving Levin as the sole CEO.

The second surprise -- at least for Time shareholders -- was in the post-transaction performance of Time-Warner stock. Recall that the Time directors thought the company was worth even more than Wasserstein Perella's estimate of $238 to $287. Recall too that the stock would have to be worth $352 a share after 5 years to equal a 12% return on the $200 a share that Paramount had offered. Figure 1-8 shows Time-Warner's actual stock price from 1988 through 1992 along with a line showing the value of Paramount's $200 per share offer if it had been received by Time's shareholders and invested at a more conservative 10% return.

Figure 1-8
TIME-WARNER STOCK PRICE, Jan. 4, 1988 - Sept. 10, 1992

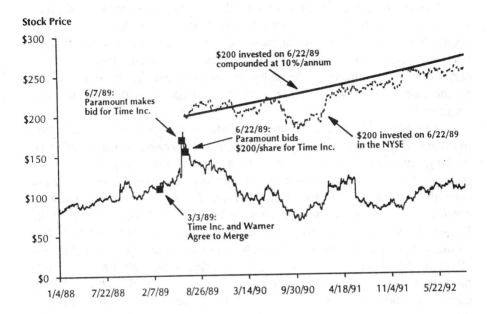

Source: Cornerstone Research.

PART I. MODERN FINANCE THEORY:
THE REQUIRED ANALYTICAL TOOLS

Modern financial theory is commonly treated as beginning in the late 1950s. Prior to that time, leading finance texts were rich in institutional detail, but offered little in the way of comprehensive theory.[1] Their normative statements on issues like the proper capital structure for a corporation were sometimes logically inconsistent and, in any event, could not be empirically tested. They were thus ad hoc both theoretically and empirically.

The late 1950s marked a shift in scholarly emphasis from description to theory, and finance began to change from a descriptive endeavor oriented in large measure to practitioners, to a specialized discipline with the theoretical rigor and mathematical complexity associated with academic economics. This shift was facilitated by the introduction in 1964 of computer tapes prepared by the Center for Research in Security Prices at the University of Chicago (CRSP). These tapes originally contained daily and monthly closing stock prices, dividends and changes in capital structure for all stocks listed on the New York and American Stock Exchanges. They have recently been extended to larger over-the-counter stocks. This database encouraged the development of statistical techniques that have made many of the theoretical statements of modern finance theory almost uniquely testable.[2]

This Part surveys the aspects of modern finance theory necessary to understand how business transactions are valued. It thus provides a foundation for later analysis of the motives for acquisitions and how business lawyers might increase transaction value. For example, it is commonly claimed that a company's publicly reported earnings are an important determinant of stock price, whether or not these earnings reflect actual cash flows. This assertion, in turn, has fueled a major controversy over the "right" way to account for acquisitions, with both sides taking seriously the idea that reported, as opposed to real earnings, influence share price. At bottom, this conflict is over what factors do or should determine the value of a capital asset -- in this case, do or should reported earnings influence the price of corporate stock, independent of the underlying cash flows? As a result, both finance theory and empirical tests of the theory are directly relevant.

Similarly, important elements of corporate law, such as when acquiring company and target company shareholders get to vote on an acquisition, depend on whether different transaction *forms* are substantively similar. If similarity is taken to mean "of equal value," then understanding the factors that determine value is central to understanding when different forms of

---

[1] See, e.g., Arthur Dewing, *The Financial Policy of Corporations* (2d ed.1953).

[2] For a more detailed history of modern financial theory, see Clifford Smith, *The Theory of Corporate Finance: An Historical Overview*, in *The Modern Theory of Corporate Finance* 3 (Clifford Smith ed., 2d ed.1990).

transactions should be subject to the same legal rules. Understanding the theory of asset valuation, and the techniques for testing the predictions of finance theory, is thus crucial to understanding and evaluating both the applicable law and the various motives for acquisitions.

A second point, less familiar but equally important, should also be stressed. Individuals often seek to maximize the value of their assets. As a result, understanding how assets are valued provides a useful way to predict, and to guide, private behavior. Suppose, for example, that you are negotiating the terms of a loan agreement on behalf of the lender. How do you anticipate what post-transaction behavior by the borrower the lender need to be protected against? Put differently, how might shareholders seek to increase their wealth at the creditors' expense? Finance theory, by specifying how the borrower's actions can shift value between shareholders and creditors, provides a coherent framework in which to address the problem. This will be particularly evident in our examination of option pricing in Chapter 7, and in our consideration of the private ordering aspects of corporate acquisitions in Part VI. Finance theory is thus important for both the public ordering and private ordering aspects of business transactions.

Chapters 2 and 3 lay the groundwork for the study of valuation. Chapter 2 examines valuation in a simple world where there is no risk -- the size and timely receipt of all future cash flows is certain. Chapters 3 and 4 introduce the concept of risk -- how should one value future cash flows when their size and eventual receipt are uncertain? We consider the uses and limits of the Capital Asset Pricing Model and alternative models of how assets should be priced under uncertainty. Chapter 5 examines the Efficient Capital Market Hypothesis, a central paradigm of modern finance theory. Here the issue is what mechanisms cause market prices to approach or depart from the "correct" values that asset pricing theory predicts. Chapter 6 then moves to a more practical perspective. How can we evaluate whether a transaction or other event has *changed* the value of a capital asset? Here the standard technique is regression analysis, especially cumulative abnormal returns analysis of stock price changes. Finally, Chapter 7 focuses on valuation of a different kind of asset -- an option -- and introduces a second paradigm of modern finance: option pricing theory. We will return to each of the concepts examined in this Part -- the time value of money, capital asset pricing, market efficiency, cumulative abnormal returns, and option pricing -- throughout our analysis of corporate acquisitions and the business lawyer's potential for creating value.

CHAPTER 2: VALUATION UNDER CERTAINTY

We begin learning how business transactions are valued by considering how assets would be valued in a world of complete certainty. In such a world, the only distinction between different assets is the quantity and timing of the future cash flows they generate. There is no risk (1) of not actually receiving the money, nor (2) of receiving a different amount than expected, nor (3) of receiving the money at a different time than expected.

This world of complete certainty, of course, is entirely artificial. Even so certain a cash flow as the interest payment on a short term Treasury bill is subject to the risk of change in the *inflation* rate -- the risk that the *real* amount received will purchase a different amount than expected, because inflation turns out to be higher or lower than expected over the investment period. A short-term Treasury bill is also subject to the risk of change in the *reinvestment* rate -- the risk that the rate of interest at which one can reinvest funds will change during the period of an investment.

In this simple world, value depends only on the *time value of money*. The concept of time value is equivalent to *opportunity cost*. A dollar now is worth more than one to be received in a year because a dollar received now can be swapped for goods that can be consumed now, rather than a year from now, or invested for a year at a positive rate of interest, so that it produces more than one dollar a year from now. Section A of this Chapter develops the mathematics of the time value of money. Section B applies the concept of time value to the task of valuing a stream of income across time.

A.   The Time Value of Money

James van Horne, FINANCIAL MANAGEMENT AND POLICY
13-24 (7th ed. 1986)[*]

In any economy in which time preferences of individuals, firms, and governments result in positive rates of interest, the time value of money is an important concept. For example, stockholders will place a higher value on an investment that promises returns over the next five years than on an investment that promises identical returns for years six through ten. Consequently, the timing of expected future cash flows is extremely important in the investment of funds. In essence, the methods proposed allow us to isolate differences in the timing of cash flows for various investments by discounting these cash flows to their present value.

Compound Interest and Terminal Values

The notion of compound interest is central to understanding the mathematics of finance. The term itself merely implies that interest paid on a loan or an investment is added to the principal. As a result, interest is earned on interest. This concept can be used [for] a class of problems illustrated in the following examples. To begin with, consider a person who has $100 in a savings account. If the interest rate is 8% compounded annually, how much will he have at the end of a year? Setting up the problem, we solve for the terminal value of the account at the end of the year (TV_1)

$$TV_1 = \$100(1 + .08) = \$108$$

[If left for a second year, the $108 earns 8% interest again, and] becomes $116.64, as $8 in interest is earned on the initial $100 and $0.64 is earned on the $8 interest paid at the end of the first year. In other words, interest is earned on previously earned interest, hence the name compound interest. Therefore the terminal value at the end of the second year is $100 times 1.08 *squared*, or times 1.1664. Thus,

$$TV_2 = \$100(1.08)^2 = \$116.64$$

At the end of three years, the depositor would have

$$TV_3 = \$100(1 + .08)^3 = \$125.97$$

Looked at in a different way, $100 grows to $108 at the end of the first year if the interest rate is 8%, and when we multiply this amount by 1.08 we obtain $116.64 at the end of the second year. Multiplying $116.64 by 1.08, we obtain $125.97 at the end of the third year.

Similarly, at the end of n years, the terminal value of a deposit is

$$TV_n = X_o \times (1 + r)^n \qquad \text{(2-1)}$$

where X_o = amount of savings at the beginning
          r = interest rate

. . . Table 2-1, showing the terminal values for our example problem at the end of years 1 through 10, illustrates the concept of interest being earned on interest. Equation 2-1 is our fundamental formula for calculating terminal values. Obviously, the greater the interest rate r, and the greater the number of periods n, the greater the terminal value.

Table 2-1
Compound Interest with $100 Initial Deposit and 8% Interest

Period	Beginning Value	Interest Earned During Period (8% of Beginning Value)	Terminal Value
1	$100.00	$ 8.00	$108.00
2	108.00	8.64	116.64
3	116.64	9.33	125.97
4	125.97	10.08	136.05
5	136.05	10.88	146.93
6	146.93	11.76	158.69
7	158.69	12.69	171.38
8	171.38	13.71	185.09
9	185.09	14.81	199.90
10	199.90	15.99	215.89

Although our concern has been with interest rates, the concept involved applies to compound growth of any sort. Suppose that the earnings of a firm are $100,000, but we expect them to grow at a 10% compound rate. At the end of years 1 through 5 they will be as follows . . .:

Year	Growth Factor	Expected Earnings
1	(1.10)	$110,000
2	$(1.10)^2$	121,000
3	$(1.10)^3$	133,100
4	$(1.10)^4$	146,410
5	$(1.10)^5$	161,051

Tables of Terminal Values. Using Equation 2-1, one can derive tables of terminal values (also known as future values). An example is shown in Table 2-2 for interest rates of 1 to [10%]. In the 8% column, we note that the terminal values shown for $1 invested at this compound rate correspond to our calculations for $100 in Table 2-1. Notice, too, that in rows involving two or more years, the proportional increase in terminal value becomes greater as the interest rate rises. This heightened growth is particularly impressive when we look a century ahead. A dollar deposited today will be worth only $2.70 if the interest rate is 1%, but it will fatten to [$13,780] if the interest rate is [10%]. Behold (or let your heirs behold) the wonders of compound interest!

Table 2-2
Terminal Value of One Dollar at the End of n Years

Year	1%	2%	3%	4%	5%	6%	7%	8%	9%	10%
1	1.010	1.020	1.030	1.040	1.050	1.060	1.070	1.080	1.090	1.100
2	1.020	1.040	1.061	1.082	1.103	1.124	1.145	1.166	1.188	1.210
3	1.030	1.061	1.093	1.125	1.158	1.191	1.225	1.260	1.295	1.331
4	1.041	1.082	1.126	1.170	1.216	1.263	1.311	1.361	1.412	1.464
5	1.051	1.104	1.159	1.217	1.276	1.338	1.403	1.469	1.539	1.611
6	1.062	1.126	1.194	1.265	1.340	1.419	1.508	1.587	1.677	1.772
7	1.072	1.149	1.230	1.316	1.407	1.504	1.606	1.714	1.828	1.949
8	1.083	1.172	1.267	1.369	1.478	1.594	1.718	1.851	1.993	2.144
9	1.094	1.195	1.305	1.423	1.551	1.690	1.839	1.999	2.172	2.358
10	1.104	1.219	1.344	1.480	1.629	1.791	1.967	2.159	2.367	2.594
11	1.116	1.243	1.384	1.540	1.710	1.898	2.105	2.332	2.580	2.853
12	1.127	1.268	1.426	1.601	1.796	2.012	2.252	2.518	2.813	3.138
13	1.138	1.294	1.469	1.665	1.886	2.133	2.410	2.720	3.066	3.452
14	1.150	1.320	1.513	1.732	1.980	2.261	2.579	2.937	3.342	3.798
15	1.161	1.346	1.558	1.801	2.079	2.397	2.759	3.172	3.643	4.177
20	1.220	1.486	1.806	2.191	2.653	3.207	3.870	4.661	5.604	6.728
25	1.282	1.641	2.094	2.666	3.386	4.292	5.427	6.849	8.623	10.84
50	1.645	2.692	4.384	7.107	11.47	18.42	29.46	46.90	74.36	117.4
100	2.705	7.245	19.22	50.51	131.5	339.3	867.7	2,200	5,529	13,780

* * *

Compounding More Than Once a Year

Up to now, we have assumed that interest was paid annually. Although this assumption is easiest to work with, we consider now the relationship between terminal value and interest rates for different periods of compounding. To begin, suppose that interest is paid semiannually, and $100 is deposited in a savings account at [an 8% annual rate of interest -- that is, 4% interest is paid every 6 months]. The terminal value at the end of six months will be

$$TV_{1/2} = \$100(1 + .08/2) = \$104.00$$

and at the end of a year it would be

$$TV_1 = \$100(1 + .08/2)^2 = \$108.16$$

This amount compares with $108.00 if interest were paid only once a year. The $0.16 difference is attributable to the fact that during the second 6 months, interest is earned on the $4.00 in interest paid at the end of the first 6 months. The more times during a year that interest is paid, the greater the terminal value at the end of a given year.

The general formula for solving for the terminal value at the end of year n where interest is paid m times a year [at an annual rate of r] is

$$TV_n = X_o \times (1 + r/m)^{mn} \qquad (2\text{-}2)$$

To illustrate, suppose that in our previous example interest were paid quarterly and that we wished again to know the terminal value at the end of one year. It would be

$$TV_1 = \$100(1 + .08/4)^4 = \$108.24$$

which, of course, is higher than that which occurs either with semiannual or annual compounding.

The terminal value at the end of 3 years for the above example with quarterly interest payments is

$$TV_3 = \$100(1 + .08/4)^{12} = \$126.82$$

Compared to a terminal value with semiannual compounding of

$$TV_3 = \$100(1 + .08/2)^6 = \$126.53$$

and [a terminal value with] annual compounding of

$$TV_3 = \$100(1 + .08/1)^3 = \$125.97$$

The greater the number of years, the greater the difference in terminal values arrived at by two different methods of compounding.

As m approaches infinity, the term $(1 + r/m)^{mn}$ approaches e^{rn}, where e is approximately 2.71828 and is defined as

$$e \quad = \quad \lim_{m \to \infty} \quad (1 + 1/m)^m \qquad (2\text{-}3)$$

with ∞ being the sign for infinity. . . . [C]ontinuous compounding results in the maximum possible terminal value at the end of n periods for a given rate of interest. As m is increased in Equation 2-2, the terminal value increases at a decreasing rate until ultimately it approaches the terminal value achieved with continuous compounding.

Present Values

Not all of us live by the credit card alone; some like to save now and buy later. For a $700 purchase one year from now, how much will you have to put aside in a bank paying 8% interest on one-year deposits? How much must you put aside in order to have $700 one year hence? If we let A_1

represent the amount of money you wish to have one year from now, *PV* the amount saved, and *k* the annual interest rate, we have

$$A_1 = PV(1 + k) \qquad \text{(2-4)}$$

For our example problem, this becomes

$$\$700 = PV(1.08)$$

Solving for *PV*, we obtain

$$PV = \$700/1.08 = \$648.15$$

Deposit $648.15 today and take home $700 one year hence. Stated another way, $648.15 is the *present value* of $700 to be received at the end of 1 year when the interest rate involved is 8%.

The present value of a sum to be received two years from now is

$$PV = A_2/(1 + k)^2 \qquad \text{(2-5)}$$

which for our example problem would be

$$PV = \$700/(1.08)^2 = \$700/1.1664 = \$600.14$$

Thus $700 two years from now has a lower present value than $700 one year from now. That is the whole idea of the time value of money.

In solving present-value problems, it is useful to express the interest factor separately from the amount to be received in the future. For example, our problem can be expressed as

$$PV = \$700 \times [1/(1.08)^2] = \$600.14$$

In this way we are able to isolate the interest factor, and this isolation facilitates present-value calculations. In such calculations, the interest rate is known as the *discount rate*, and henceforth we will refer to it as such.

So far we have considered present-value calculations for amounts of money to be received only 1 and 2 years in the future; however, the principles are the same for amounts to be received further in the future. The present value of $1 to be received at the end of *n* years is

$$PV = 1/(1 + k)^n \qquad \text{(2-6)}$$

The present value of $1 to be received five years from now when the discount rate is 10%, is [about 62 cents]:

$$\$1 \times [1/(1.10)^5] = \$.6209$$

. . . Fortunately, present-value tables [and calculators] relieve us of having to make these calculations every time we have a problem to solve. Table 2-3 . . . shows present values of $1, known as discount factors, for discount rates from 1% to [10%] and for periods 1 through 25 [years] in the future. We see in the table that for a 10% discount rate, the discount factor for five years in the future is .6209, just as we calculated. For 1 year, 2 years, and 3 years in the future, we see that the discount factors are .90909, .82645, and .7513, respectively. These discount factors are merely the result of the following calculations: $1/(1.10)$; $1/(1.10)^2$; and $1/(1.10)^3$.

Table 2-3
Present Value of One Dollar Due at the End of *n* Years

n	1%	2%	3%	4%	5%	6%	7%	8%	9%	10%
1	.9901	.9804	.9701	.9615	.9524	.9434	.9346	.9259	.9174	.9091
2	.9803	.9612	.9426	.9246	.9070	.8900	.8734	.8573	.8417	.8265
3	.9706	.9423	.9151	.8890	.8638	.8396	.8163	.7938	.7722	.7513
4	.9610	.9239	.8885	.8548	.8227	.7921	.7629	.7350	.7084	.6830
5	.9515	.9057	.8626	.8219	.7835	.7473	.7130	.6806	.6499	.6209
6	.9420	.8880	.8375	.7903	.7462	.7050	.6663	.6302	.5963	.5645
7	.9327	.8706	.8131	.7599	.7107	.6651	.6228	.5835	.5470	.5132
8	.9235	.8535	.7894	.7307	.6768	.6274	.5820	.5403	.5019	.4665
9	.9143	.8368	.7664	.7026	.6446	.5919	.5439	.5003	.4604	.4241
10	.9053	.8204	.7441	.6756	.6139	.5584	.5084	.4632	.4224	.3855
11	.8963	.8043	.7224	.6496	.5847	.5268	.4751	.4289	.3875	.3505
12	.8875	.7885	.7014	.6246	.5568	.4970	.4440	.3971	.3555	.3186
13	.8787	.7730	.6810	.6006	.5303	.4688	.4150	.3677	.32612	.2897
14	.8700	.7579	.6611	.5775	.5051	.4423	.3878	.3405	.2993	.2633
15	.8614	.7430	.6419	.5552	.4810	.4173	.3625	.3152	.2745	.2394
16	.8528	.7285	.6232	.5339	.4581	.3937	.3387	.2919	.2519	.2176
17	.8444	.7142	.6050	.5134	.4363	.3714	.3166	.2703	.2311	.1978
18	.8360	.7002	.5874	.4936	.4155	.3503	.2959	.2503	.2120	.1799
19	.8277	.6864	.5703	.4746	.3957	.3305	.2765	.2317	.1945	.1635
20	.8195	.6730	.5537	.4564	.3769	.3118	.2584	.2146	.1784	.1486
21	.8114	.6598	.5376	.4388	.3589	.2942	.2415	.1987	.1637	.1351
22	.8034	.6468	.5219	.4310	.3419	.2775	.2257	.1839	.1502	.1229
23	.7954	.6342	.5067	.4057	.3256	.2618	.2110	.1703	.1378	.1117
24	.7876	.6217	.4919	.3901	.3101	.2470	.1972	.1577	.1264	.1015
25	.7798	.6096	.4776	.3751	.2953	.2330	.1843	.1460	.1160	.0923

* * *

If we had an uneven series of cash flows -- $1 one year hence, $3 two years hence, and $2 three years from now -- the present value of this series, using a 10% discount rate, would be

PV of $1 received [in] 1 year	=	$1(0.9091)	=	0.9091
PV of $3 received [in] 2 years	=	$3(0.8265)	=	2.4795
PV of $2 received [in] 3 years	=	$2(0.7513)	=	1.5026
Present value of series			=	$4.8912

With a present-value table, we are able to calculate the present value for any series of future cash flows in this manner.

Present Value of an Annuity. The procedure can be simplified for a series of even cash flows. A series of this sort is known as an *annuity*. Suppose that $1 is to be received at the end of each of the next 3 years. The calculation of the present value of this stream, using a 10% discount rate, would be

PV of $1 received in 1 year	=	.9091
PV of $1 received in 2 years	=	.8265
PV of $1 received in 3 years	=	.7513
Present value of series	=	$2.4869

With an even series of future cash flows, it is unnecessary to go through these calculations. The discount factor, 2.4869, can be applied directly. Simply multiply $1 by 2.4869 to obtain $2.4869. [Annuity] tables . . . allow us to look up the appropriate [annuity] factor. . . .

If we trace across any of the rows in Table 2-3, we see that the higher the discount rate, the lower the discount factor. It is not a linear relationship because the discount factor decreases less and less as the discount rate increases. Therefore the present value of an amount of money to be received in the future decreases at a decreasing rate as the discount rate increases. The relationship is illustrated in Figure 2-1. At a zero rate of discount, the present value of $1 to be received in the future is $1. In other words, there is no time value of money. . . . As the discount rate approaches infinity, the present value of the future $1 approaches zero. . . .

Figure 2-1
Relationship Between Present Value and the Discount Rate

Present Value

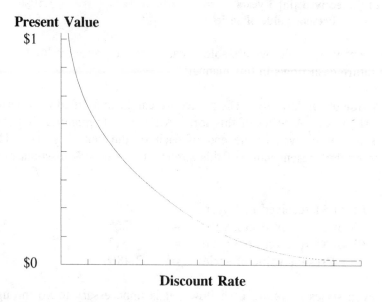

Discount Rate

Present Value When Interest Is Compounded More Then Once a Year

When interest is compounded more than once a year, the formula for calculating present values must be revised along the same lines as for the calculation of terminal value. Instead of dividing the future cash flow by $(1 + k)^n$ as we do when annual compounding is involved, the present value is determined by

$$PV = A_n/(1 + k/m)^{mn} \qquad (2\text{-}7)$$

where, as before, A_n is the cash flow at the end of year n, m is the number of times a year interest is compounded, and k is the discount rate. The present value of $100 to be received at the end of year 3, the discount rate being 10% compounded quarterly, is

$$PV = \$100/(1 + .10/4)^{4\times3} = \$74.36$$

. . . [T]he fewer times a year the discount rate is compounded, the greater the present value. This relationship is just the opposite of that for terminal values. To illustrate the relationship between present value and the number of times a year the discount rate is compounded, consider again our example involving $100 to be received at the end of 3 years with a discount rate of 10%. The following present values result from various compounding intervals. We see that the present value decreases but at a decreasing rate as the compounding interval shortens, the limit being continuous compounding.

Compounding	Present Value
Annual	$75.13
Semiannual	74.62
Quarterly	74.36
Monthly	74.17
Continuously	74.08

Internal Rate of Return or Yield

The internal rate of return or yield for an investment is the discount rate that equates the present value of the expected cash outflows with the present value of the expected inflows. Mathematically, it is represented by that rate, r, such that

$$\sum_{t=0}^{n} [A_t/(1 + r)^t] = 0 \qquad (2\text{-}8)$$

where A_t is the cash flow for period t, whether it be a net cash outflow or inflow, n is the last period in which a cash flow is expected, and the capital Greek sigma [Σ] denotes the sum of discounted cash flows at the end of periods 0 through n. If the initial cash outlay or cost occurs at time 0, Equation 2-8 can be expressed as

$$A_0 = A_1/(1+r) + A_2/(1+r)^2 + \ldots + A_n/(1+r)^n \qquad (2\text{-}9)$$

Thus r is the rate that discounts the stream of future cash flows (A_1 through A_n) to equal the initial outlay at time 0 -- A_0. [The higher the internal rate of return, the better the investment, other things equal.] We implicitly assume that the cash inflows received from the investment are reinvested to realize the same rate of return as r. . . .

To illustrate the use of Equation 2-9, suppose that we have an investment opportunity that calls for a cash outlay at time 0 of $18,000 and is expected to provide cash inflows of $5,600 at the end of each of the next five years. The problem can be expressed as

$$18,000 = \frac{5,600}{(1+r)} + \frac{5,600}{(1+r)^2} + \frac{5,600}{(1+r)^3} + \frac{5,600}{(1+r)^4} + \frac{5,600}{(1+r)^5}$$

Solving for the internal rate of return, r, involves an iterative procedure [commonly done using calculators or computer programs]. . . .

————————————

B.   Time Value in a Transactional Context: Project Choice

The discounting techniques developed in Section A reflect the impact of the time value of money on the value of a stream of income. In our assumed world of certainty, this offers a simple way to value an asset. The asset's value is the *present value* of the income it generates over its life. Present value is a summary statistic for the size of that income stream that takes into account when income will be received.

The *net present value* of an investment opportunity is the present value of the cash inflows that it generates, minus the present value of the cash outlays that it requires. Putting money in a bank at the market rate of interest has a net present value of zero -- the present value of the cash to be received just equals the present value of the cash deposited. Thus, net present value is a summary statistic for the desirability of an investment, compared to the alternative of putting money in a bank.

The next step in understanding how transactions are valued is to apply the discounting techniques to the choice among different investments -- typically called "capital budgeting." Put simply, capital budgeting is the analysis by which a firm or an individual decides how to invest resources. A number of different techniques are commonly used in capital budgeting, but all share the same three stages. First, the amount and timing of the income stream that an investment will generate is estimated. Second, net present value, internal rate of return, or another summary statistic for the income stream is calculated. Third, the summary statistic is compared to an acceptance criterion that represents the least favorable investment the firm will accept. Investments that meet or exceed the acceptance criterion are made, those that do not are rejected.

Because we are still working in a world of certainty, the first step in capital budgeting -- estimating the amount and timing of an investment's income stream -- can be passed over. We can assume that the amounts and timing of these cash flows are known. It is at the second stage -- computing a summary statistic for the income stream from an investment -- that different capital budgeting techniques diverge. Most importantly, the techniques differ fundamentally in the extent to which the summary statistic takes into account the time value of money.

1.   Average Rate of Return and Payback Period Methods

Two frequently used techniques, the average rate of return method and the payback method, do not adequately account for the time value of money. The average rate of return technique involves dividing the average annual accounting net profit from a project by the project's average book value. The result is a measure of the average return on the amount invested in the project. Suppose that Project X requires a $9,000 investment in a machine with a useful life of 3 years. The project will result in a cash flow of $4,500 in each of three years. If the up-front cost of the machine is taken into account prorata over the three years, through a $3,000 per year charge for *depreciation*, the annual net profit will be $1,500:

Project X	Year 1	Year 2	Year 3
Cash Flow	$4,500	$4,500	$4,500
Depreciation	3,000	3,000	3,000
Net Profit	$1,500	$1,500	$1,500

Average net profit = [$1,500 + $1,500 + $1,500]/3 = $1,500/year

The project's average book value is calculated as follows:

Project X	Year 1	Year 2	Year 3
Initial Investment	$9,000	$9,000	$9,000
Cumulative Depreciation	3,000	6,000	9,000
Net Book Value	$6,000	$3,000	$ 0

Average book value = [($6,000 + $3,000 + $0)/3] = $4,500

And average rate of return is:

[average net profit/average book value] = [$1,500/$4,500] = 33.3%

The project will be accepted if this average rate of return exceeds the minimum acceptance rate that the firm sets as part of its capital budgeting process.

The problem with the average rate of return technique is that it ignores the time value of money: all cash flows are treated equally whether they are received in the first year or in the last. This can be seen by comparing Project X with Project Y, which has the same cash flow, initial investment and depreciation schedule, and thus has the same average rate of return as Project X, but has a different cash flow pattern.

The average rate of return technique treats both cash flows as equivalent. If the time value of money is taken into account, even visual inspection of the cash flows shows that Project Y is preferable to Project X.

Net Profit from Projects With Different Cash Flow Patterns

	Project *X*	Project *Y*
Year 1	$1,500	$3,000
Year 2	$1,500	0
Year 3	$1,500	$1,500

The payback period approach is somewhat of an improvement in this regard. Here the idea is to calculate the number of periods necessary for the cash flows from a project to repay its initial investment. For example, the payback period for Project *X* -- the time necessary to recover the initial investment -- is two years. The cash flow, *before* depreciation, is $4,500 per year, so it takes two years to recover the initial $9,000 investment. The project will be accepted if this period is shorter than the maximum payback period that the firm sets as part of its capital budgeting process.

Other things equal, a project whose cash flows come sooner is preferable to one whose cash flows come later. Nonetheless, the method still fails to adequately account for the time value of money. It gives no value to cash flows that are received after the project's initial investment is repaid. As a result, projects with identical payback periods and identical returns *within* the payback period are deemed equivalent even if one has a large return in the year after the payback period ended while the other does not. In this sense, the payback period technique *over*-discounts payments outside the payback period.

The payback period technique also takes no account of differences in the timing of receipts during the payback period. For example, the payback period for Projects *X* and *Y* is the same -- two years -- so the payback technique, like the average rate of return technique, would treat the two projects as equivalent, despite the faster receipt of income from Project *Y*. In this sense, the payback period *under*-discounts payments within the payback period.

The average rate of return and the payback period techniques fail to provide appropriate guidance for capital budgeting decisions because they don't fully take into account the time value of money. We now turn to two techniques for evaluating potential investments that do fully consider time value.

2.   Internal Rate of Return and Net Present Value Methods

The mathematics of the internal rate of return and net present value techniques are described in the Van Horne excerpt in Section A of this Chapter. Both are discounted cash flow techniques that reduce future cash receipts to present value in determining the value of the asset giving rise to the payments. The internal rate of return technique solves for the discount rate -- the internal rate of return -- at which the net present value of the investment is zero: the present value of the cash invested equals in a project to the present value of the cash flows from the project. If the internal rate of return exceeds the minimum rate set by the firm as part of its capital budgeting process, the project is undertaken.

The net present value rule discounts to present value each cash outflow (including the original investment) and each cash inflow, using the rate of return available in the market for comparable investments as the discount rate. If net present value is positive, the project is undertaken.

Both techniques have substantial support in the financial community. Under most circumstances, the internal rate of return technique, with a minimum acceptable rate set equal to the rate of return available in the market for comparable investments, will yield the same results as the net present value technique. One important difference, however, is the discount rate each technique uses to reduce intermediate cash flows from a project to present value.[3] The internal rate of return technique assumes that all intermediate cash flows can be reinvested during the life of the project at the internal rate of return earned from the project. Thus, the actual rate of return achieved by a project will equal the internal rate of return calculated in the capital budgeting decision *only* if the intermediate cash flows generated by the project can be reinvested in an equally profitable investment. A similar problem exists with the net present value technique. Here the assumption is that all intermediate cash flows can be reinvested at the chosen discount rate. Again, the actual return will match the initial calculation *only* if opportunities for reinvestment at the discount rate exist when the cash flows are received.

It is often argued that the net present value technique is preferable because the discount rate chosen is presumably the external cost of capital, a market rate, while the discount rate implicit in the internal rate of return technique is the return associated with a particular project, which is less likely to be duplicable on reinvestment. However, both reinvestment rate assumptions highlight the artificiality of our assumed zero-risk world, and the difficulty associated with using these techniques in a world with uncertainty.

An example helps clarify the point. Suppose you are the Chief Financial Officer of an insurance company with $100,000 to invest. Your

---

[3] Among the difficulties with the use of the internal rate of return in contrast to net present value is the potential for a project to have multiple internal rates of return when cash flows change signs more than once over the life of the project. This can happen for a project that requires an initial investment, generates some cash, and then requires an additional mid-stream investment of capital. Problems also exist in taking into account the different scale of alternative projects. Because internal rate of return is a relative measure of return, while net present value is an absolute measure, project rankings will differ when the projects are of different size. A small project with a high internal rate of return may generate fewer dollars, and therefore have a lower net present value, than a large project. See Richard Brealey & Stewart Myers, *Principles of Corporate Finance* 79-88 (4th ed. 1991).

actuaries tell you that five years from now you will need $190,000 to pay anticipated life insurance claims. You have an opportunity to lend $100,000 for five years, with annual interest payments at 14% which is, we will assume, the current market rate of interest. The future value of $100,000 in five years at this rate of interest is:

$$TV_5 = \$100,000 \times (1.14)^5 = \$192,541$$

What keeps you in the office, and away from the beach, is the knowledge that, even if there is no *credit* risk -- no risk that the borrower won't make all payments in full and on time -- there is still a substantial risk that you won't earn enough over five years to meet the anticipated claims. The future value calculation assumes that the 14% annual interest payments can be reinvested at the same 14% rate. You still face *reinvestment risk*--the risk that this assumption will prove wrong. If interest rates drop during the five years, your actual reinvestment rate will be lower than 14% and your company may not have $190,000 on hand when the anticipated claims are presented for payment in five years. Present value and future value calculations ignore that risk.

Thus, if there is no credit risk, valuation techniques that are designed for a world without risk fail when reinvestment risk (or inflation risk) is introduced. This is not to say that the discounting techniques examined in this Chapter are not helpful. Rather, they are designed to deal with one aspect of valuation -- the time value of money. More complete valuation requires adding additional factors to take into account various kinds of risk.

Chapter 2 Problems

1. Assume that the market rate of interest is 6% per year, compounded annually. How much must you invest today to have $1 at the end of one year?

2. Assume that the market rate of interest is 6% per year, compounded annually. How much will you have in one year if you invest $1 today?

3.　Assume that the market rate of interest is 12% per year, compounded annually, and that:

    a. you have $162.53 in your bank account today
    b. you opened the account exactly one year ago
    c. your initial deposit was the only deposit you've made
    d. you've made no withdrawals
    e. the market rate of interest has not changed in the last year

How much was your initial deposit?

4. If you have $756,213 in your bank account today, and you opened the account one year ago with only $734,011, what rate of interest (to the nearest hundredth of a percentage point) did the bank pay you over the previous year?

5. You have two investment alternatives, investment 1 and investment 2. Both investments require the expenditure of $250,000, and both require that you wait one year to receive your return. Investment 1 will pay back $300,000 at the end of one year and investment 2 will pay back 400,000 at the end of one year. Which investment has a higher net present value?

6.　(a)　You have the opportunity to invest $75,000 today, for a payback of $100,000 in one year. What is the rate of return on this investment?

b) What is the net present value of this investment opportunity, if the discount rate is 10%?

7. You are advising Mortimer Bucks, who has a lot of money. He wants to put his money in the bank, but he cannot choose which bank to use. Banks A & B are both insured by the Federal Deposit Insurance Corporation, so a deposit in either has zero credit risk. Both offer attractive gifts to large depositors. In fact the two banks are as similar as two banks can be except for one thing. Bank A pays 6% interest compounded annually, and Bank B pays 5.8% interest compounded quarterly (1.45% interest every 3 months). Which bank would you advise Mortimer to use and why?

8.   Assume that the market rate of interest is 10% per year. Your rich and eccentric uncle offers to pay you $1,000,000 in 25 years in exchange for $100,000 today, or, if you prefer, to lend you $100,000 today in return for $1,000,000 in 25 years. Which offer should you accept?

9.   Assume that the market rate of interest is 10% per year. You have an opportunity to sell the old jalopy that you've been driving for the last decade for $375 cash.

a. Is this a better or worse deal than an opportunity to sell the car for five annual payments of $100 each, beginning one year from today, and why?

b. Is this a better or worse deal than an opportunity to sell the car for six annual payments of $50, $100, $100, $100, $100, and $100, beginning one year from today, and why?

10. All other things being equal, would you rather be paid weekly, biweekly or monthly?

11. You are looking for a loan and get quotes from three banks of 10% per annum interest. One bank wants interest paid every month (5/6 of 1% per month), another every quarter (2.5% per quarter) and the third every year. Which offers the lowest effective rate of interest?

12. Why would you expect the rate of interest to be greater than zero?

CHAPTER 3: VALUE UNDER UNCERTAINTY: RISK AND DIVERSIFICATION

Our next step is to relax the assumption of certainty. What happens to the net present value technique if we are not certain about the amount and timing of the cash flows that will flow from an asset? Suppose, for example, that the profit we expect from a proposed project depends on whether a particular technological problem can be solved. How do we express this uncertainty about future returns? How does that uncertainty affect the discount rate that one uses to account for the time value of money? This chapter and the next address these questions.

Different projects will involve both different *kinds* of risks, and different *degrees* of risk, about future returns. For example, a 30-year Treasury bond is usually assumed to have zero risk that payments will not be made in the amounts and at the times promised. After all, the government can simply print more money. But Treasury bonds still carry a substantial degree of *inflation risk* -- the risk that dollars to be received in the future will be worth more or less in *real* terms than investors now expect. A 10-year corporate bond carries some *default risk* -- the risk that the promised payments won't be made, or won't be made on time. But it carries less inflation risk than a 30-year Treasury bond because of its shorter duration. For common stocks, there isn't even a set of promised payments written down. Investors have to guess about future dividends and other cash payments. They might be right in their estimates, or they might be too high or too low. How does the value of risky assets reflect different kinds and degrees of risk, in a world in which investors are risk-averse, and insist on being paid for bearing risk through higher expected return?

It will turn out that all of these risks affect the *expected cash flows* from a risky investment. *Some* risks -- nondiversifiable risks -- also affect the expected *rate of return* that investors demand in order to make a risky investment. That is, *all* risks affect the numerator in a net present value calculation. Nondiversifiable risks also affect the discount rate that appears in the denominator. Which risks are diversifiable, and exactly how nondiversifiable risks affect the discount rate, though, are subject to active controversy in the finance literature.

Section A of this Chapter considers how to take uncertainty into account in expressing the expected cash flows from an asset. Section B considers how one can measure the extent of uncertainty associated with an asset's returns -- what financial economists mean when they use the term *risk*. Section C develops the value of diversifying one's investment portfolio, which can reduce risk without reducing expected cash flows. Finally, Section D considers how one can determine the residual, nondiversifiable risk associated with an investment. Chapter 4 will then introduce the Capital Asset Pricing Model as an example of how nondiversifiable risk might affect the expected rate of return demanded by risk-averse investors.

A. Expected Return Under Uncertainty

Elementary probability theory, familiar to many of you, offers guidance in expressing *expected return* when actual return is uncertain. Let's try an example:

Suppose that your good-natured grandmother makes you the following offer: You can flip a coin once, and she'll pay you $1000 if it lands on heads and nothing if it lands on tails. Or you can flip the coin twice, and she'll pay you $500 for each head, or three times, and you'll get $333 for each head, and so on. Your maximum gain is $1000 if you get all heads. You choose how many times to flip the coin.

If you flip the coin once, your expected return is $500. There is a 50% chance that you'll earn $1,000 and a 50% chance that you'll end up unhappy with your grandmother. In mathematical terms, the only possible outcomes are heads and tails. The *expected return* is:

> expected return =   (return on heads $\times$ probability of heads) +
> (return on tails $\times$ probability of tails)

In symbols, we can write this as:

$$ER_{1 \text{ flip}} = (ret_h \times p_h) + (ret_t \times p_t)$$

Where: ER = expected return
ret_h = return if you get heads   = $1,000
ret_t = return if you get tails   = $0
p_h = probability of getting heads = 0.5
p_t = probability of getting tails   = 0.5

Your expected return is then:

$$ER = (\$1{,}000 \times 0.5) + (\$0 \times 0.5) = \$500 + \$0 = \$500$$

Suppose that you instead choose to flip the coin twice, so that you will earn $500 for each head. The expected return is still $500, but getting there is a little more complicated. There are three possible outcomes: 2 heads (which we will denote **hh**); one head and one tail (which we will denote **ht**); and two tails (which we will denote **tt**). To compute expected return, we multiply the return in each possible state of the world by the probability that the state will occur. The formula for expected return now becomes:

$$ER_{2 \text{ flips}} = (ret_{hh} \times p_{hh}) + (ret_{ht} \times p_{ht}) + (ret_{tt} \times p_{tt})$$

The possible returns and associated probabilities are:

$$ret_{hh} = \$1000 \qquad p_{hh} = p_{tt} = 0.25^1$$
$$ret_{ht} = \$500 \qquad p_{ht} = 0.5$$
$$ret_{tt} = \$0$$

Thus, expected return is:

$$ER_{2 \text{ flips}} = (\$1000 \times .25) + (\$500 \times .5) + (\$0 \times .25)$$
$$= \$500$$

For three flips, each head is worth $333.33. The possible outcomes and associated probabilities are:

Expected Return for Three Coin Flips

Outcome	Conditional Return	Probability	Value x Prob.
hhh	$ 1000	.125	$125
hht	$ 666.67	.375	$250
htt	$ 333.33	.375	$125
ttt	$ 0	.125	$ 0
		Expected Return =	**$500**

The last column shows the calculation of expected return. The return for each possible outcome (called a *conditional return*) is computed, and multiplied by the probability of that outcome. These dollar amounts are then added together to get the expected return. For the coin flip example, the expected return is still $500. Indeed, expected return will continue to be $500 no matter how many coins you flip.

More formally, for any set of possible outcomes, expected return is defined as the sum over all outcomes of: (the conditional return if a particular outcome occurs) × (the probability of that outcome occurring). If we use the letter i to label the possible outcomes:

$$ER = \sum_i (ret_i \times p_i) \qquad \text{(3-1)}$$

So far, we have considered only the situation where all returns are received at the same time. If an investment has expected returns at several different times, we must compute the expected return for each time t at which a non-zero return is expected. We can write this formally by using

---

[1] The probability of getting two heads equals the .5 probability of getting a head on the first toss, multiplied by the .5 probability of getting a head on the second toss, for a total *compound* probability of .25. The probability of getting two tails is computed in similar fashion.

a subscript t to label both expected return at time t and the conditional returns and associated probabilities at time t:

$$ER_t \;=\; \sum_i (ret_{i,t} \times p_{i,t})$$

This section has discussed how we can compute expected return at particular points in time. But we don't yet know how to determine the risk-adjusted discount rate to be used to determine the *present value* of a stream of expected income. To do that, we must first learn how to express risk.

B.　Expressing Risk: Variance and Standard Deviation

For the coin flip example, the expected return is $500 no matter how many times you flip the coin. If so, one might ask, why bother to flip the coin more than once? The answer is risk. Flipping the coin once can be thought of as investing your entire *expected* wealth of $500 in a double or nothing gamble -- a single coin flip that will return either $1000 or $0. If you instead flip the coin ten times, that's like investing $50 in each of ten coin flips, each of which returns $100 or $0. On average, you'll get 5 heads. You're reasonably likely to get somewhere between 3 and 7 heads, and thus to end up with between $300 and $700. You could get 8, 9 or even 10 heads, or 0,1 or 2 heads, but that's less likely. With ten flips, you'll *probably* end up with between $300 and $700.[2]

Now suppose you flip the coin a hundred times. That's like investing $5 of your expected wealth in each of 100 coin flips, each of which returns $10 or 0. Once again, your expected return is $500, but now the possibility of an extreme return like zero becomes vanishingly small. You might throw ten tails in a row, but the chance of throwing a hundred in a row is almost zero. In fact, the probability of ending up with somewhere between 45 and 55 heads is pretty good (about 2 in 3) and the probability of ending up with between 40 and 60 heads is excellent, about 95%. If we repeat the experiment, and throw a hundred coins over and over again, the percentage of heads will fall along the familiar bell curve distribution, shown in Figure 3-1.

The more times you flip the coin, the narrower the bell curve distribution; the more tightly the actual outcomes will cluster around the expected or *mean* outcome of $500. So the difference between throwing a coin once and throwing it a hundred times is **risk**. The more throws, the more likely you are to come close to the expected return, and the less likely you are to be high or low by very much.

---

[2] The chance of ending up with between 3 and 7 heads is about 89%.

Figure 3-1
Bell Curve Distribution of Returns to 100 Coin Flips

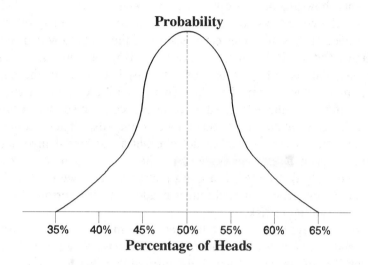

If you are like most investors, you are *risk-averse* where your investments are concerned. Given a choice between two investments with the same expected return and different levels of risk, you are likely to prefer the one with less risk. In the coin flip example, that means that you will probably flip the coin a substantial number of times, to reduce your risk. You will keep flipping up to the point where the nuisance value of flipping the coin more times exceeds the gains from further reduction in risk.

Put differently, suppose you were asked: How much would you *pay* for the opportunity to flip a coin *n* times for $1000/*n* per head? What is the *value* of the coin flip "investment" to you? Risk-aversion means that you will pay *less* than $500 for a chance to flip the coin once. It also means that you will pay more for two flips for $500 each than for a single $1000 flip; more for three flips than for two; and so on.

How much you will pay for a single flip, and how much extra you will pay for more flips, depends on your individual level of risk-aversion. The proposition that most investors are risk-averse is well-supported by empirical studies. But there is no theory to tell us *how* risk-averse investors ought to be, nor any reason to think that all investors have the same level of distaste for risk. Some may even be risk-preferring gamblers.

For symmetrical gambles like the coin flip, statisticians have developed a measure of risk, called *variance*, that treats risk as the extent to which possible outcomes depart from the expected return. Variance has some nice mathematical properties, which we develop below. But first two caveats. Variance, and its close relative, *standard deviation*, have useful mathematical properties. But that doesn't mean that they correspond to the risks to which investors are averse. Indeed, variance and standard deviation are somewhat counterintuitive measures of risk. They treat better-than-expected outcomes as adding as much to risk as worse-than-expected outcomes. Risk, in common parlance, means risk of *loss*. One would not commonly speak of the "risk" of getting heads and winning $1,000. Moreover, psychological experiments show that most people are *loss-averse* -- they are troubled more by a loss, relative to the status quo, than attracted by an equal dollar gain.[3]

Variance is thus an imperfect measure of the risks to which investors are averse. But we lack a better measure. Also, for important classes of investments, the risk of gain and loss are distributed, as in the coin flip example, more or less symmetrically. That is, an increase (decrease) in the likelihood of a better-than-expected outcome is accompanied by an equivalent increase (decrease) in the likelihood of a worse-than-expected outcome. This is especially true when one makes not one but a number of investments -- when one owns an investment *portfolio*. When risk of gain and risk of loss are symmetrically distributed, it doesn't matter whether we treat both good and bad deviations from expected return as adding to risk, or only count bad deviations as adding to risk.

A second caveat: Some of the desirable mathematical properties of variance and standard deviation hold in a strict sense only for certain types of distributions of returns, of which the *normal* distribution -- illustrated by the bell curve of returns to a large number of coin flips -- is the best known example. For other return distributions, variance is an incomplete measure of risk. To make matters worse, returns on actual investments often depart from normality. Fortunately, returns on investment *portfolios* come closer to normality than returns on individual investments. Moreover, many of the empirical tests of theories about finance, accounting, and related subjects rely on returns on publicly traded securities over relatively short time periods, for which portfolio returns come reasonably close to matching the "normal" distribution.

With these caveats in mind, we turn to how one calculates variance -- how one measures how far the possible outcomes depart from the expected return. First, one computes expected return. Each difference between a conditional return and the expected return is then *squared*, which gives heavier weight to large departures from the expected return. This is broadly consistent with intuitions about risk -- many people fear large losses much more than small ones. Squaring also results in counting positive and negative departures equally. Each squared departure is then weighted by the probability of that outcome, and the squared, weighted departures are summed:

$$Var = \sum_i p_i \times (ret_i - ER)^2 \qquad (3\text{-}2)$$

[3] See, e.g., Daniel Kahneman, Jack Knetsch & Richard Thaler, *Anomalies: The Endowment Effect, Loss Aversion, and Status Quo Bias*, 5 J.Econ.Persp. 193 (1991). We discuss loss aversion and other common cognitive biases in Chapter 5.

If there is only one possible return, with probability one, variance is zero, as it should be because whatever measure of risk we choose should go to zero when uncertainty is zero.

We can illustrate the concept of variance using the coin flip example. Consider a single flip, with a head worth $1,000 and a tail worth $0. The expected return is $500, so the variance is:

$$
\begin{aligned}
Var_{1\ flip} &= p_h \times (ret_h - ER)^2 & &+ p_t \times (ret_t - ER)^2 \\
&= .5 \times (\$1000 - \$500)^2 & &+ .5 \times (\$0 - \$500)^2 \\
&= .5 \times 250{,}000(\$^2) & &+ .5 \times 250{,}000(\$^2) \\
&= 250{,}000(\$^2) & &
\end{aligned}
$$

Notice that the good result adds as much to the variance as the bad result.

One problem with squaring the difference between each conditional return and the expected return is that it is hard to offer an intuitive interpretation of variance. What, after all, are dollars *squared*? The statistician's response is to introduce a third term, *standard deviation*, which is simply the square root of variance:

$$
Std\ Dev = Var^{1/2}
$$

For the coin flip example, we have:

$$
Std\ Dev_{1\ flip} = [250{,}000(\$^2)]^{1/2} = \$500
$$

Standard deviation, unlike variance, has an intuitive explanation. It is a rough measure of how far away from the expected outcome you will end up in a typical actual trial. If you flip the coin once, you will end up with either $1,000 or $0. In either case, that's $500 away from the expected return of $500. In a more complicated case, the correspondence is only rough because the procedure for computing variance gives heavy weight to outliers. Nonetheless, this qualitative explanation of standard deviation holds up reasonably well for a variety of return distributions.

If the conditional returns are normally distributed, then, as shown in Table 3-1, the odds are about 2 out of 3 that the actual return will be within one standard deviation of the expected return. The actual return will be within two standard deviations of the expected return about 95% of the time, and will be within three standard deviations of the expected return 99.7% of the time.

Table 3-1
The Normal Distribution

Departure from Expected Return (in standard deviations)	Probability that Actual Departure is Less than This
0.0	0%
0.5	38.3%
1.0	68.3%
1.5	86.6%
2.0	95.4%
2.5	98.8%
3.0	99.7%

Let's now flip a coin twice for $500 per head, to get a feel for how reduction in risk is reflected in variance and standard deviation. At the same time, we will introduce conventional notation for variance and standard deviation: standard deviation is denoted by the small Greek letter sigma [σ], and variance by σ^2. For two coin flips:

$$\sigma^2_{2\text{ flips}} = p_{hh} \cdot (ret_{hh} - ER)^2 + p_{ht} \cdot (ret_{ht} - ER)^2 + p_{tt} \cdot (ret_{tt} - ER)^2$$
$$= .25 \cdot 250{,}000(\$^2) + (.5 \times 0) + .25 \cdot 250{,}000(\$^2)$$
$$= 125{,}000(\$^2)$$

Variance is smaller, as expected. It is half as big as for one coin flip. For three coin flips, we have:

$$\sigma^2_{3\text{ flips}} = p_{hhh} \cdot (ret_{hhh} - ER)^2 + p_{hht} \cdot (ret_{hht} - ER)^2 + p_{htt} \cdot (ret_{htt} - ER)^2 + p_{tt} \cdot (ret_{tt} - ER)^2$$
$$= .125 \cdot (\$1000 - \$500)^2 + .375 \cdot (\$667 - \$500)^2 + .375 \cdot (\$333 - \$500)^2 + .125 \cdot (\$0 - \$500)^2$$
$$= 83{,}333(\$^2)$$

A pattern is emerging, where the variance of n coin flips equals the variance of one coin flip, 250,000, divided by the number of flips:

$$\sigma^2_{n\text{ flips}} = \sigma^2_{1\text{ flip}}/n$$

Since standard deviation equals the *square root* of variance, it declines more slowly as the number of flips increases -- as the *square root of n*:

$$\sigma_{n\text{ flips}} = \sigma_{1\text{ flip}}/n^{1/2}$$

This is illustrated in Table 3-2 and Figure 3-2 below:

Table 3-2
Expected Return, Variance, and Standard Deviation for Coin Flips

Number of Flips	Expected Return	Variance	Standard Deviation
1	$500	250,000(^{2})	$500
2	$500	125,000(^{2})	$353.55
3	$500	83,333(^{2})	$288.67
4	$500	62,500(^{2})	$250
. . .			
9	$500	27,778(^{2})	$166.67
16	$500	15,625(^{2})	$125
25	$500	10,000(^{2})	$100
. . .			
n	$500	250,000(^{2})/n	$500/n^{1/2}$

Figure 3-2
Reducing Risk Through Diversification: The Coin Flip Example

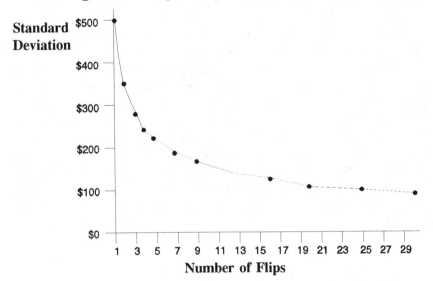

C.   The Value of Diversification

We have now quantified the reduction in risk from flipping a coin more times. You can see multiple coin flips as a form of diversification. You've decided to invest in coin flips. By flipping once, you earn $1000 for a head. If you flip twice, you earn $500 for each head. That's as if you invested $250 of your expected return in each of two coin flips, instead of investing

$500 in a single flip. By flipping three times, you invest one-third of your expected return in each of three flips, and so on.

Diversification, investing fewer dollars per flip in more flips, reduces the chance that you will earn less or more than $500. The statistical measures of risk -- variance and standard deviation -- reflect this. In a nutshell, this is why investors should diversify their investment portfolios. Investors can reduce risk, *without reducing expected return*, by splitting their investment dollars among a number of different investments. If investors are risk-averse, that makes the expected return *more valuable* -- investors will pay more for an investment with the same expected return but less risk.

For publicly traded investments, such as stocks and bonds, diversification is easy, so that others will diversify even if you do not. Having diversified, they are willing to pay a higher price for publicly traded stocks and bonds. If most investors are diversified, the market price will reflect the value that *diversified investors* place on risky securities. Undiversified investors will bear extra risk, *and will not be compensated for bearing that risk.*

There is, though, one critical difference between publicly traded investments such as stocks and our coin flip example. In the coin flip example, risk could be reduced *virtually to zero* by additional diversification. Flipping the coin 100 times instead of once will reduce variance by a factor of 100, and will reduce standard deviation by a factor of 10, from $500 to $50. Flipping the coin 1,000,000 times instead of once will reduce standard deviation by a factor of 1,000, to only $0.50.

In contrast, for stocks, diversifying by buying a large number of different stocks will reduce risk only to some irreducible minimum risk. Suppose that we run the following experiment: Take $1,000, divide it into *n* pieces of $1000/*n* each, and purchase *n* randomly selected stocks traded on the New York Stock Exchange. Then measure the percentage change in the value of the portfolio over a one-year period. The stock price database compiled by the Center for Research in Security Prices (CRSP) allows one to run this experiment for different time periods, and different stock portfolios. This experiment, run over and over, produces the results shown in Figure 3-3:

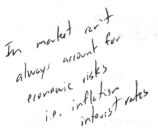

In market can't always account for economic risks i.e. inflation + rates interest

Figure 3-3
Reducing Risk Through Diversification: Stock Portfolios

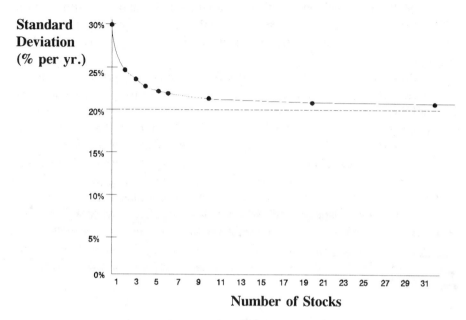

Why can diversification eliminate all risk in the coin flip example, but only *reduce* risk for common stocks? To answer these questions, we need to consider the types of risks that a particular firm faces.

Any firm is subject to two qualitatively different types of risk. Some risks are common to many firms across the stock market, though perhaps to differing degrees. The economy as a whole may do better or worse than expected, inflation may be higher or lower than expected, real interest rates may be higher or lower than expected, and so on. These risks affect the profits of all firms, so one cannot eliminate them by buying a portfolio of different stocks. We call the base level of stock market risk, which remains after full diversification, *systematic risk* or *market risk*. The systematic risk of a U.S. stock portfolio for a one-year holding period is a gain or loss of about 20%, relative to the average or expected return.

Each firm is also subject to various risks that are peculiar to it or to its industry. Maybe a plant burns down, or a competitor comes out with a great new product, or a competitor cuts prices and the firm must cut its own prices in response, or there's a strike, or the firm's managers do an unexpectedly good or bad job of running the business, or the firm makes a particular investment that turns out good or bad. These kinds of risks *can* be reduced by diversifying across firms and across industries. If one firm has a plant fire, another will not. If one firm is unexpectedly badly run, another will be unexpectedly well run. We call these company-specific or industry-specific risks *unsystematic risk* or *unique risk*. These risks fall above the dotted line in Figure 3-3; they decrease as the number of stocks in an investment portfolio increases.

The total percentage gain or loss from holding an average stock is about 30% per year. Thus, diversification reduces the overall risk of holding a stock portfolio, measured by standard deviation, by about one-third, from 30% per year to 20% per year. Diversification also greatly reduces the extreme outliers -- a diversified investor is far less likely to become rich or to go broke.

More formally, holding a portfolio of n stocks chosen from different industries reduces unsystematic variance by a factor of roughly $1/n$ compared to holding one stock. Holding 20 properly chosen stocks reduces unsystematic variance by roughly 95% and thus achieves most of the value of diversification. Holding 100 stocks reduces unsystematic variance by roughly 99%. This is shown in Table 3-3, which corresponds to Figure 3-3. In Table 3-3, we have assumed that each firm in the portfolio has a systematic standard deviation of 20% per year, and a total standard deviation of 30% per year. The pattern in Table 3-3 is the same as that shown for coin flips in Table 3-2, except that *total* variance and standard deviation decline toward the base established by systematic risk, rather than toward zero. *Only total variance and total standard deviation are directly measurable.*

Table 3-3
Reducing Unsystematic Risk By Holding a Diversified Portfolio

Number of Stocks	Total Variance (%^{2})	Total Standard Deviation (%)	Unsystematic Variance (%^{2})
1	900	30	500
2	650	25.5	250
3	567	23.8	167
4	525	22.9	125
. . .			
10	450	21.2	50
20	425	20.6	25
50	410	20.2	10
100	405	20.1	5
500	401	20.02	1
. . .			
n	$[400 + 500/n]$	$[400 + 500/n]^{1/2}$	$[500/n]$

The first central lesson of modern portfolio theory is: **Investors should hold a diversified portfolio to reduce unsystematic risk**. An immediate corollary: if diversification is easy, the market price -- the *value* -- of a stock, bond, or other capital asset **should depend only on systematic risk**.

How far investors should diversify depends on comparing the risk reduction benefits to the transaction costs of additional diversification, and to any other costs of greater diversification, such as reduced ability of shareholders to monitor the actions of corporate managers.

Example: Diversification in Law Firms[4]

Diversification can be important in contexts having nothing to do with stocks and bonds. Suppose that a lawyer is considering making the investment in human capital necessary to become either a securities lawyer, specializing in public offerings of securities, or a bankruptcy lawyer, specializing in reorganization of financially distressed companies. Further assume that the training for each of these specialties take the same amount of time, and are mutually exclusive. The lawyer believes that the expected return on an investment in becoming a securities or bankruptcy lawyer will depend on the performance of the economy. The expected return and its relationship to the strength of the economy are as follows:

Strength of Economy	Probability	Earnings as Securities Lawyer	Earnings as Bankruptcy Lawyer
Strong	1/3	$200,000	$0
So-so	1/3	$100,000	$100,000
Poor	1/3	$0	$200,000

Suppose, however, that two lawyers face this choice. They can go into partnership with each other, with profits evenly split. One will become a securities lawyer; the other a bankruptcy lawyer. The combined profits will now be $200,000 in all states of the world. The partnership lets both lawyers diversify the risk of a specialized investment in human capital.

In the real world, diversification will never be perfect. Sometimes, both bankruptcy and securities work will be booming; other times both specialties will be slow. Nonetheless, partial diversification is possible. Some scholars believe that diversification is an important, though not the only, reason for formation of professional partnerships.

As the stylized example of the lawyer's investment in specialization illustrates, the risk of a portfolio depends on the *covariance* of the returns on the investments in the portfolio -- the extent to which the returns vary together, rather than independently. If the returns move in exactly opposite directions in exactly the same amounts (*perfect negative covariance*), as in the example, all risk is eliminated; the portfolio return is always $200,000.

---

[4] This example is adapted from Ronald Gilson & Robert Mnookin, *Sharing Among the Human Capitalists: An Economic Inquiry into the Corporate Law Firm and How Partners Split Profits*, 37 Stan.L.Rev. 313, 327-28 (1985).

The value of diversification is not limited, though, to settings of perfect negative covariance. Two coin flips are independent of each other -- they have *zero covariance*. That is enough for diversification through multiple coin flips to eliminate risk. We must, however, flip often enough so that the independent risks can average out. Two flips won't do. Stocks generally have *positive* covariance -- they move up together in bull markets and down together in bear markets. Nonetheless, diversification will *partially* reduce the risk of investing in stocks. Diversification will reduce risk as long as the returns from two investments are not perfectly positively correlated.

D.   Measuring Systematic Risk: Beta

We have learned that diversification can reduce unsystematic risk, but not systematic risk. We don't yet know, though, how to measure these two separate components of risk. We loosely called the portion of the risk on an individual stock that is due to marketwide factors its systematic risk and the remainder of the risk its unsystematic risk. But it isn't obvious how one draws that distinction. A change in interest rates affects all stocks to some extent, but will have special significance for banks. A change in the price of oil affects all companies, but will have special significance for oil companies and airlines. And so on.

In the real world, all we can observe is *total* risk. How do we determine what part of a company's total risk is systematic and what part is unsystematic? The best available way is to run a regression analysis where we treat the return on each company's stock as a dependent variable, to be partially explained by one or more independent variables that are believed to contribute to systematic risk. Part of the return on a particular stock will correlate with the chosen risk factor(s), and part will not. The part that correlates with the risk factor(s) is treated as systematic risk; the remainder is treated as unsystematic risk.

Below, we explore how one measures systematic risk for a simple, commonly used model of stock price returns called the *market model*. In the market model, the only systematic risk factor is the return on the entire stock market. The market return is assumed to act as a proxy for the underlying economic factors that cause the market to rise or fall. We will return in the next chapter to the question of which risk factor(s) are best able to separate systematic from unsystematic risk, and how the market model might be improved on.

Graphically, the market model involves developing a scatter plot in which the daily or monthly returns on a firm's stock are plotted against the returns on a broad market index, such as the Standard & Poor's 500 Composite Stock Index (the S&P 500 Index). We then use least-squares statistical analysis to construct a "best fit" straight line that tells us how much the firm's stock will rise or fall, *on average*, when the market rises or falls

1%. Such a scatter plot is shown in Figure 3-4 for Host International, using monthly returns between 1975 and 1979.

The *slope* of the best-fit straight line is conventionally labelled by the Greek letter beta [β]. For Host International, the slope of the best-fit line is $\beta = 1.4$. This means that *on average*, when the market rises in price by 10%, Host International gains 14%. Similarly, on average, when the market drops in price by 10%, Host International drops 14%.

Beta is a measure of the *systematic risk* of a particular firm's stock, *relative* to the risk of the market as a whole. The market as a whole has only systematic risk; all unsystematic risk has been diversified away. If we know a stock's β, and we know the riskiness of the market as a whole, then we know how much of the variance of an individual stock is systematic, and can't be diversified away. The remaining risk is unsystematic, and can be diversified away.

Figure 3-4
Scatter Plot of Returns on Particular Stock Versus Market Returns

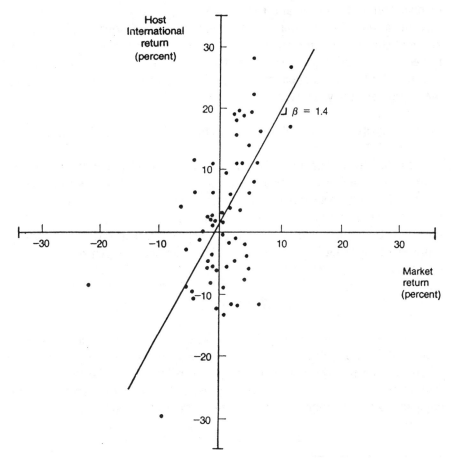

Source: James Lorie, Peter Dodd & Mary Kimpton, *The Stock Market: Theories & Evidence* 37 (2d ed.1985).

The average firm's stock cannot rise or fall faster or slower than the value of a well-constructed market index, since the purpose of the index is to reflect what is happening to the market as a whole. Thus, a firm with average systematic risk will have $\beta = 1$. Some firms will have $\beta > 1$, and others will have $\beta < 1$. Host International, with $\beta = 1.4$, has above-average sensitivity to market risk.

The next reading provides a more formal introduction to β as a measure of systematic risk, and extends the β measure to stock *portfolios*.

Franco Modigliani & Gerald Pogue, AN INTRODUCTION TO RISK AND RETURN: CONCEPTS AND EVIDENCE (Part I)
Fin. Analysts J. 68, 76-79 (Mar.-Apr.1974)[*]

[T]he systematic risk of an individual security is that portion of its total risk (standard deviation of return) which cannot be eliminated by combining it with other securities in a well diversified portfolio. We now need a way of quantifying the systematic risk of a security and relating the systematic risk of a portfolio to that of its component securities. This can be accomplished by dividing security return into two parts: one dependent (*i.e.*, perfectly correlated), and a second independent (*i.e.*, uncorrelated) of market return. The first component of return is usually referred to as "systematic," the second as "unsystematic" return. Thus we have

Security Return = Systematic Return + Unsystematic Return   **(3-3)**

Since the systematic return is perfectly correlated with the market return, it can be expressed as a factor, designated beta (β), times the market return, R_m. The beta factor is a market sensitivity index, indicating how sensitive the security return is to changes in the market level. The unsystematic return, which is independent of market returns, is usually represented by a factor epsilon (ϵ). Thus the security return, R, may be expressed

$$R = \beta R_m + \epsilon'$$ **(3-4)**

For example, if a security had a β factor of 2.0 (e.g., an airline stock), then a 10% market return would generate a systematic return for the stock of 20%. The [total] security return for the period would be the 20% plus [an] unsystematic component [which] depends on factors unique to the company, such as labor difficulties, higher than expected sales, etc.

The security returns model given by Equation 3-4 is usually written in a way such that the average value of the residual term, ϵ, is zero. This is accomplished by adding a factor, alpha (α), to the model to represent the average value of the unsystematic returns over time. That is, we set $\epsilon' = \alpha + \epsilon$ so that

$$R = \alpha + \beta R_m + \epsilon \tag{3-5}$$

where the average [of] ϵ over time is equal to zero.

The model for security returns given by Equation 3-5 is usually referred to as the "market model." Graphically, the model can be depicted as a line fitted to a plot of security returns against rates of return on the market index [as in Figure 3-3]. . . . The beta factor can be thought of as the slope of the line. It gives the expected increase in security return for a one per cent increase in market return. . . .

The alpha factor is represented by the intercept of the line on the vertical security return axis. It is equal to the average value over time of the unsystematic returns (ϵ') on the stock. For most stocks, the alpha factor tends to be small and unstable. . . .

The systematic risk of a security is equal to β times the standard deviation of the market return:

$$\text{Systematic Risk} = \beta \, \sigma_m \tag{3-6}$$

. . . Given measures of individual security systematic risk, we can now compute the systematic risk of [a] portfolio. It is equal to the beta factor for the portfolio, β_p, times the risk of the market index, σ_m:

$$\text{Portfolio Systematic Risk} = \beta_p \cdot \sigma_m \tag{3-7}$$

The portfolio beta factor in turn can be shown to be simply an average of the individual security betas, weighted by the proportion of each security in the portfolio, or

$$\beta_p = \sum_{j=1}^{n} X_j \cdot \beta_j \tag{3-8}$$

where: X_j = proportion of portfolio value represented by security j
          n = the number of securities.

Thus the systematic risk of the portfolio is simply a weighted average of the systematic risk of the individual securities. If the portfolio is composed of an equal dollar investment in each stock. . . , the β_p is simply an unweighted average of the component security betas. . . .

The implications of these results are substantial. First, we would expect realized rates of return over substantial periods of time to be related to the systematic as opposed to total risk of securities. Since the unsystematic risk is relatively easily eliminated, we should not expect the market to offer a risk premium for bearing it. Second, since security systematic risk is equal to the security beta times σ_m (which is common to all securities), beta is useful as a *relative* risk measure. The β gives the systematic risk of a security (or portfolio) relative to the risk of the market index. Thus it is often convenient to speak of systematic risk in relative terms (*i.e.*, in terms of beta rather than beta times σ_m).

Chapter 3 Problems

1. You are the chief asset manager at Monolithic Multinational Corp. One day, while you have your feet up on your desk in your spacious office, you get a call from your old schoolmate, Barney Straightarrow. Barney was the most honest person in your sixth-grade class, so you are surprised that he is now an institutional salesperson at the firm of Fast, Buck and Run. Barney's got some bonds to sell, and he'd love to tell you about them. The bonds are issued by the Irregular Company, and they come in two varieties, coupon bonds paying 10% annual interest and zero-coupon bonds. Both varieties have a face value of $1,000 and mature in 10 years. The zero coupon bonds sell for $370 (to yield 10.45% to maturity) and the coupon bonds sell for $1000 (and thus yield 10% to maturity). Why might the yields differ?

2. You're still with Monolithic-Multinational, and, on a fine Tuesday morning, one of your underlings bursts into your office claiming that she has found the fixed-income investment opportunity of the century. There's a new bond in town called an increasing rate note, being underwritten by Drexel Hutton Inc., and issued by Watcher Wallet Industries. The bond has a time to maturity of seven years, a face value of $1,000, and it makes a series of annual interest payments that grow (or compound) at a constant rate of 12%. The first interest payment will be made one year from today. The bond sells for $485.27 and its yield to maturity is 15.91%.

After citing these statistics, your underling gushes that a 12% growth opportunity is hard to find in the current economy. This must be a good bond. What's wrong with her reasoning? Explain briefly how she should analyze whether to buy this bond.

3. Jimmy Jumpshot, prized power forward of the Newark Vultures, has just signed a $20,000,000 contract with his team. He boasts to you that managing his new wealth is as easy as making layups. He simply chooses the stocks with the highest betas since these stocks offer the highest returns. Over the past year, during which the economy expanded rapidly, Jimmy achieved a return of 43%. What's wrong with Jimmy's reasoning?

4. An investment in Alpha Corp. has the following expected returns over a one-year period:

return (%)	probability (%)	$.1 * (.15-.13)^2$
-15	10	7.84
0	20	6.76
10	20	.36
20	20	1.96
25	20	5.76
35	10	+ 4.84

27.52 $\overline{ER} = 13\%$

a) What is the expected return on this investment? 13

b) What is the variance of this investment? 27.52

c) What is the standard deviation of this investment? 5.25

   5. Assume that there are 5 possible future states of the world, one year from today. The returns on Alpha Corp. and Gamma Inc. stock over the next year for each state of the world are set forth in the table below:

State of World	Probability (%)	Alpha Return (%)	Gamma Return (%)
1	10	-15	-10
2	20	0	-5
3	20	10	0
4	20	20	5
5	20	25	10
6	10	35	5

a) What is the variance of the expected returns for Gamma Inc.?

b) What is the expected return on a portfolio in which half of your money is invested in Alpha and half in Gamma?

c) What is the variance of the expected return on a portfolio in which half of your money is invested in Alpha and half in Gamma?

d) Why is this not the same as the equally weighted average of the variance of an investment solely in Alpha and the variance of an investment solely in Gamma? Why does it also not equal the sum of (i) the variance of putting half of your money in Alpha; plus (ii) the variance of putting half of your money in Gamma?

CHAPTER 4: THE RELATIONSHIP BETWEEN RISK AND RETURN: THE CAPITAL ASSET PRICING MODEL AND ALTERNATIVES

Most investors are risk-averse. In return for bearing more risk, they must be compensated with a higher expected return. In Chapter 3, we learned that the risk of an investment can be divided into systematic and unsystematic components, and that unsystematic risk can be diversified away. Since unsystematic risk can be shed through diversification, investors should hold diversified portfolios and should *not* require a higher expected return because an investment has unsystematic risk. Risk-averse investors *should* require a higher expected return for bearing systematic risk.

We do not yet know, though, the relationship between risk and expected return. How much extra expected return should investors receive for bearing various amounts of systematic risk? What kinds of systematic risk should investors be paid for bearing?

All asset pricing models share two common goals: (i) developing a framework for understanding how systematic risk affects security prices; and (ii) measuring the market price of various types of systematic risk. Our interest in this book is mostly in the first goal. Understanding what factors affect asset prices provides a necessary base for understanding how the purchase of a particular asset -- an ongoing business -- can affect the value of that asset. It also provides a base for understanding how the lawyer's efforts -- in structuring the transaction, drafting the contracts of sale and financing, and conducting a due diligence investigation of the target -- can enhance the value of the transaction to the buyer, the seller, or both.

In this Chapter, we develop a simple two-factor model of the relationship between risk and expected return, known as the *Capital Asset Pricing Model (CAPM)*. This model is related to the market model of systematic risk presented in Chapter 3. We then discuss the uses and limits of CAPM, including the equivocal empirical evidence supporting the model and theoretical questions about whether CAPM can properly be tested at all. We then introduce multifactor asset pricing models, such as Arbitrage Pricing Theory, that have been developed in response to the limitations of CAPM.

For a long time, CAPM was a central paradigm of modern finance theory. New doubts about how well it predicts stock price returns have weakened that status, but the model retains predictive value for the differences in the returns on broad asset classes, such as stocks, corporate bonds, and Treasury bills. CAPM also offers a theoretically attractive way to begin thinking about how risk and expected return *might* be related. And, despite CAPM's weaknesses, we lack, as yet, a better asset pricing model.

A.   The Capital Asset Pricing Model

The readings below describe the Capital Asset Pricing Model, with some assumptions explicitly stated and others left implicit. The Van Horne excerpt provides a qualitative introduction to CAPM. It is followed by a more formal development of the model by Modigliani and Pogue. Section B then explicitly states the assumptions underlying the model, and discusses some implications of relaxing various assumptions.

1.   A Qualitative Approach to CAPM

James van Horne, FINANCIAL MANAGEMENT AND POLICY
60-65 (7th ed. 1986)*

The best combination of expected value of return and standard deviation depends upon the investor's utility function. This function is derived [by asking the investor to rank order different combinations of expected return and risk]. If you are a risk-averse investor who [requires higher expected return to compensate you for an increase in the risk that actual return will diverge from expected return], your utility function might be that depicted graphically by Figure 4-1. The expected value of return is plotted on the vertical axis, while the standard deviation is along the horizontal. The curves are known as *indifference curves*; the investor is indifferent between any combination of expected value of return and standard deviation on a particular curve. In other words, [each indifference] curve is defined by those combinations of expected return and standard deviation that result in a fixed level of expected utility.[4] . . . [A]ll points on a specific indifference curve have the same certainty equivalent.

The greater the slope of the indifference curves, the more averse the investor is to risk. As we move to the left in Figure 4-1, each successive curve represents a higher level of expected utility. It is important to note that the exact shape of the indifference curves will not be the same for different investors. While the curves for all risk-averse investors will be upward-sloping, a variety of shapes are possible, depending on the risk preferences of the individual.

---

[4] For further discussion and proof that indifference curves for a risk-averse investor are concave [curve upward], see Eugene Fama & Merton Miller, *The Theory of Finance* 226-28 (1972).

Figure 4-1
Hypothetical Indifference Curves

Expected Return

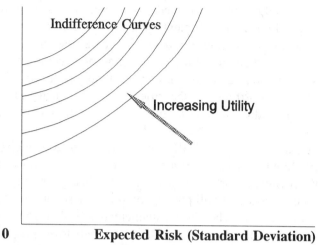

0   **Expected Risk (Standard Deviation)**

As an investor, you want to hold that portfolio of securities that places you on the highest indifference curve . . . . An example of an opportunity set, based upon the subjective probability beliefs of an individual investor, is shown in Figure 4-2. This opportunity set reflects all possible portfolios of securities as envisioned by the investor, every point in the shaded area representing a portfolio that is attainable. The dark line at the top of the set is the line of efficient combinations, or the efficient frontier. It depicts the tradeoff between risk and expected value of return. . . .

Figure 4-2
Hypothetical Opportunity Set

Expected Return

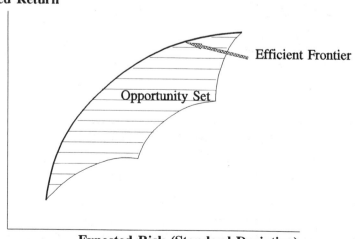

0   **Expected Risk (Standard Deviation)**

According to the Markowitz mean-variance maxim, an investor should seek a portfolio of securities that lies on the efficient frontier.[5] A portfolio is not efficient if there is another portfolio with a higher expected value of return and a lower standard deviation, a higher expected value and the same standard deviation, or the same expected value but a lower standard deviation. If your portfolio is not efficient, you can increase the expected value of return without increasing the risk, decrease the risk without decreasing the expected value of return, or obtain some combination of increased expected value and decreased risk by switching to a portfolio on the efficient frontier. . . . Portfolios of securities tend to dominate individual securities because of the reduction in risk obtainable through diversification. . . .

[Suppose that your personal tradeoff between risk and expected return is shown by the indifference curves in Figure 4-3. You should choose, from the efficient set of investment portfolios, shown by the heavy line in Figure 4-3, the particular portfolio x that will put you on the highest (furthest to the left) indifference curve. It can be shown mathematically that you should choose a portfolio where the efficient frontier is *tangent* to -- just barely touches at one point -- the highest reachable indifference curve.]

Figure 4-3
Choosing an Optimal Portfolio

Expected Return

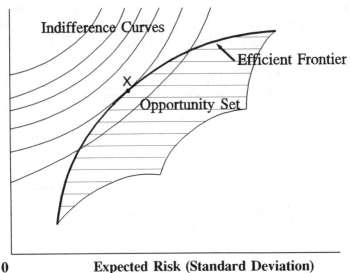

0   **Expected Risk (Standard Deviation)**

---

[5] Harry Markowitz, *Portfolio Selection: Efficient Diversification of Investments* chs. 7-8 (1959).

Presence of Risk-Free Security

Your objective is to choose the best portfolio from those that lie on the efficient frontier. In addition to the risky securities that fall in the opportunity set, you will usually be able to invest in a risk-free security that yields a certain future return. This security might be a U.S. Treasury security that is held to maturity. Although the expected return may be low, relative to other securities, there is complete certainty as to return. Suppose for now that you can not only lend at the risk-free rate but borrow at it as well. . . . To determine the optimal portfolio under these conditions, we first draw a line from the risk-free rate, r_f, through its point of tangency with the opportunity set of portfolio returns, as illustrated in Figure 4-4. This line then becomes the new efficient frontier. Note that only one portfolio of risky securities -- namely, m -- would be considered; it now dominates all others, including those on the efficient frontier of the opportunity set [of risky investments].

Figure 4-4
Selection of Optimal Portfolio When Risk-Free Asset Exists

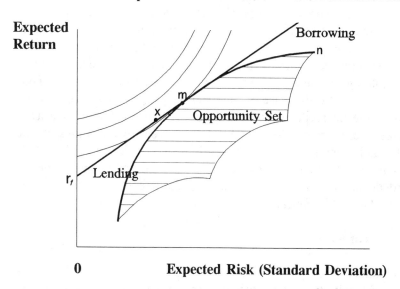

0   **Expected Risk (Standard Deviation)**

Any point on the straight line tells us the proportion [in your overall portfolio] of the risky portfolio, m, and the proportion of loans or borrowings at the risk-free rate. To the left of point m, you would [put a fraction of your total funds in] the risk-free security and [the remainder in] portfolio m. To the right, you would hold only portfolio m and would borrow funds, in addition to your initial investment funds, in order to invest further in it. The farther to the right in the figure, the greater borrowings will be. The overall investment return $= [w \times$ (expected return on risky portfolio)$] + [(1 - w) \times$ (risk-free rate)$]$, where w is the proportion of wealth invested in portfolio m, and $1 - w$ is the proportion invested in the risk-free asset. If lending were involved, w would be less than 1.0; if borrowing occurred, it would be greater than 1.0. The overall standard deviation is simply w times the standard deviation of the risky portfolio. No account is taken of the risk-free asset because its standard deviation is zero.

The optimal investment policy is determined by the point of tangency between the straight line in Figure 4-4 and the highest indifference curve. As shown in the figure, this point is portfolio x, and it consists of lending at the risk-free rate [which is the same thing as investing in the risk-free security] and investing in the risky security portfolio, m. If borrowing were prohibited, the efficient frontier would no longer be a straight line throughout but would consist of line r_f-m-n. . . .

If market participants have homogeneous expectations, in market equilibrium, point m represents a portfolio of all securities available in the market, weighted by their respective total market values. By definition, this weighted average portfolio is the *market portfolio*.

Capital Market Line

If both borrowing and lending are at the risk-free rate, the *capital market line* will be a straight line passing through the risk-free rate on the vertical axis and the expected return-standard deviation point for the market portfolio. The line is shown in Figure 4-4, but we illustrate it separately in Figure 4-5. This line describes the tradeoff between expected return and risk for various holdings of the risk-free security and the market portfolio. Thus two things are involved: the price of time and the price of risk. The former is depicted by the intercept of the capital market line and the vertical axis. The risk-free rate, then, can be thought of as the reward for waiting. The slope of the capital market line represents the market price of risk. It tells us the amount of additional expected return that is required for an increment in standard deviation. Thus the capital market line depicts the *ex ante* equilibrium relationship between return and risk.

Separation Theorem

In the context of the capital market line, the utility preferences of the individual affect only the amount that is borrowed or loaned. They do not affect the optimal portfolio of risky assets. Turning back to Figure 4-4, we would select portfolio m of risky assets no matter what the nature of our indifference curves. The reason is that when a risk-free security exists, and borrowing and lending are possible at that rate, the market portfolio dominates all others. As long as they can freely borrow and lend at the risk-free rate, two investors with very different preferences will both choose portfolio m.

Figure 4-5
The Capital Market Line

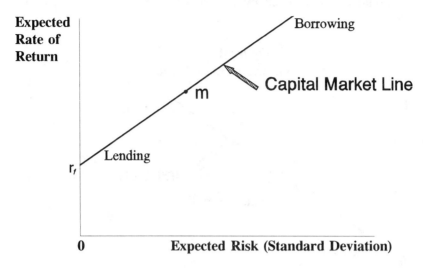

Thus the individual's utility preferences are independent or separate from the optimal portfolio of risky assets. This condition is known as the *separation theorem*. . . . In essence, the individual's approach to investing is two phased; first determine an optimal portfolio of risky assets; then determine the most desirable combination of the risk-free security and this portfolio. Only the second phase depends on [the individual's taste for risk]. The separation theorem . . . allows the management of a corporation to make decisions without reference to the utility preferences of individual owners.

---

2.   Relaxation to Equilibrium

The Van Horne excerpt above is misleading in one important respect. The opportunity set of risky portfolios shown in Figures 4-2 to 4-4 *cannot exist in equilibrium*. All investors will want to hold the same portfolio *m*, because this lets them reach the highest possible indifference curve. No one will want to hold a portfolio that lies below and to the right of the capital market line. The demand for portfolio *m* will cause its price to rise, which will reduce its expected rate of return. Similarly, the prices of portfolios that lie below and to the right of the capital market line will fall, which will increase their expected rates of return. This process will continue until, in equilibrium, *all diversified portfolios lie along the capital market line*.

Technically, any portfolio *except* the market portfolio is not fully diversified, and must lie at least infinitesimally to the right of the capital market line. But many diversified portfolios will, for all practical purposes, lie on the capital market line. Indeed, if one plots expected return not against *total risk*, as in Figures 4-2 to 4-5, but against *systematic risk*, then *all assets* should lie on the capital market line, or so close to it that the gains from further arbitrage (buying underpriced portfolios and selling overpriced portfolios) would be outweighed by transaction costs. This is shown in Figure 4-6.

Figure 4-6
Asset Pricing in Equilibrium

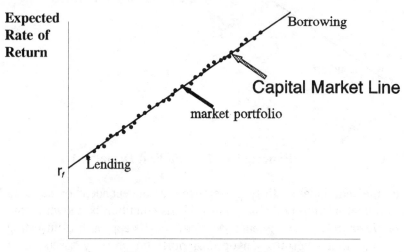

0   Expected *Systematic* Risk (Std. Dev.)

If many diversified portfolios with different levels of risk lie on the same capital market line, then investors can, over a broad range of risk, obtain their desired level of risk and expected return by directly buying a portfolio with that level of risk. They don't need to invest only in the market portfolio and the risk-free asset.

3.   A More Formal Development of CAPM

Franco Modigliani & Gerald Pogue, AN INTRODUCTION TO RISK AND RETURN: CONCEPTS AND EVIDENCE (Part II)
Fin. Analysts J. 69, 69-70 (May-June 1974)[*]

[We have] developed two measures of risk: one is a measure of total risk (standard deviation), the other a relative index of systematic or nondiversifiable risk (beta). The beta measure would appear to be the more relevant for the pricing of securities. Returns expected by investors should

---

logically be related to systematic as opposed to total risk. Securities with higher systematic risk should have higher expected returns.

The question to be considered now is the form of the relationship between risk and return. In this section we describe a relationship called the "Capital Asset Pricing Model" (CAPM), which is based on elementary logic and simple economic principles. The basic postulate underlying finance theory is that assets with the same risk should have the same expected rate of return. That is, the prices of assets in the capital markets should adjust until equivalent risk assets have identical expected returns.

To see the implications of this postulate, let us consider an investor who holds a risky portfolio with the same risk as the market portfolio (beta equal to 1.0). What return should he expect? Logically, he should expect the same return as that of the market portfolio.

Let us consider another investor who holds a riskless portfolio (beta equal to zero). The investor in this case should expect to earn the rate of return on riskless assets such as treasury bills. By taking no risk, he earns the riskless rate of return.

Now let us consider the case of an investor who holds a mixture of these two portfolios. Assuming he invests a proportion X of his money in the risky portfolio and $(1 - X)$ in the riskless portfolio, what risk does he bear and what return should he expect? The risk of the composite portfolio is easily computed when we recall that the beta of a portfolio is simply a weighted average of the component security betas, where the weights are the portfolio proportions. Thus the portfolio beta, β_p, is a weighted average of the beta of the market portfolio and the beta of the risk-free rate. However, the market beta is 1.0, and that of the risk-free rate is zero. Therefore

$$\beta_p \;=\; (1 - X) \cdot 0 \;+\; X \cdot 1 \;=\; X \qquad\qquad \textbf{(4-1)}$$

Thus, β_p is equal to the fraction of his money invested in the risky portfolio. If 100% or less of the investor's funds is invested in the risky portfolio, his portfolio beta will be between zero and 1.0. If he borrows at the risk-free rate and invests the proceeds in the risky portfolio, his portfolio beta will be greater than 1.0.

The expected return of the composite portfolio is also a weighted average of the expected returns on the two component portfolios; that is,

$$E(R_p) \;=\; (1 - X) \cdot R_f \;+\; X \cdot E(R_m) \qquad\qquad \textbf{(4-2)}$$

where $E(R_p)$, $E(R_m)$, and R_f are the expected returns on the portfolio, the market index, and the risk-free rate. Now, from Equation 4-1 we know that X is equal to β_p. Substituting into Equation 4-2, we have

$$E(R_p) \;=\; (1 - \beta_p) \cdot R_f \;+\; \beta_p \cdot E(R_m)$$

or

$$E(R_p) = R_f + \beta_p \cdot [E(\bar{R}_m) - \bar{R}_f] \qquad (4\text{-}3)$$

Equation 4-3 is the [equation for the capital market line shown in Figures 4-5 and 4-6 under the] Capital Asset Pricing Model (CAPM), an extremely important theoretical result. It says that the expected return on a portfolio should exceed the riskless rate of return by an amount which is proportional to the portfolio beta. That is, the relationship between return and risk should be linear. . . . We can illustrate the model by assuming that [the] short-term (risk-free) interest rate is 6% and the expected return on the market is 10%.

The expected risk premium for holding the market portfolio is just the difference between the 10% and the short-term interest rate of 6%, or 4%. Investors who hold the market portfolio expect to earn 10%, which is 4% greater than they could earn on a short-term market instrument for certain. In order to satisfy Equation 4-3, the expected return on securities or portfolios with different levels of risk must be:

Expected Return for Different Levels of Portfolio Beta

Beta	Expected Return
0.0	6%
0.5	8%
1.0	10%
1.5	12%
2.0	14%

The predictions of the model are inherently sensible. For safe investments ($\beta = 0$), the model predicts that investors would expect to earn the risk-free rate of interest. For a risky investment ($\beta > 0$) investors would expect a rate of return proportional to the market sensitivity (β) of the investment. Thus, stocks with lower than average market sensitivities (such as most utilities) would offer expected returns less than the expected market return. Stocks with above average values of beta (such as most airline securities) would offer expected returns in excess of the market.

B. The Assumptions Underlying CAPM

CAPM offers a simple and elegant model of how security prices ought to reflect different degrees of systematic risk. The model, though, depends on a series of strong assumptions. A set of assumptions that allow the model to be derived is listed below. Some of the assumptions can be relaxed without doing great damage to the model; others cannot be relaxed without making the model so complex that it becomes intractable. The assumptions are worth exploring in some detail, because many of the motives for corporate acquisitions, and many of the opportunities for lawyers to add value to an acquisition, involve departures from the simplifying assumptions underlying CAPM and other asset pricing models.

1. *Zero transaction costs*: Investors incur zero transaction costs to buy and sell assets. This assumption is reasonable for large institutions when they buy and sell publicly traded securities such as stocks and bonds. It fails for smaller investors, and for investments other than publicly traded securities. For example, the acquisition of a business, an investment of special concern in this book, is a complex and costly proposition.

The more important transaction costs are, the more asset prices will not fall exactly on the capital market line. Instead, some assets may be on one side of the line or the other because transaction costs outweigh the advantages of swapping a security that is slightly below the line for another security that is slightly above the line. The capital market line then becomes not a single line, but a band within which asset prices should lie. The greater transaction costs are, the wider the band.

When transaction costs are positive, it also no longer makes sense for investors to hold the entire market portfolio. At some point, the diversification gains from holding smaller and smaller pieces of more and more assets will be outweighed by the transaction costs of further diversification.

2. *Perfectly divisible assets*: All assets are infinitely divisible, so that an investor can buy a tiny fraction of each asset. This assumption is necessary if investors are to be able to purchase fully diversified portfolios. This assumption is reasonable for some assets, such as stocks and bonds; it is less reasonable for other assets, such as real estate and private businesses. Nondivisible assets also commonly involve higher transaction costs upon sale. Generally speaking, the less divisible an asset is, the more likely it is to lie outside the capital market band established by the transaction costs of trading highly divisible assets.

3. *Zero taxes*: The model assumes that no taxes are charged either on the sale of assets, or on the cash generated by an investment. In fact, taxes affect asset prices in a number of complex ways that can only be sketched here. First, taxes affect the expected return to a taxable investor, and thus affect the prices that taxable investors will pay. Second, capital gains taxes charged on the sale of a capital asset have much the same effect as transaction costs in allowing minor mispricing of assets, and thus spreading out the band within which asset prices will fall.

Third, if different assets are taxed differently (*e.g.*, if dividends are taxed at a higher effective rate than capital gains), then investors should hold higher proportions of those assets which are most tax-favorable *to them*. In theory, this *clientele effect* could lead to complete separation, with only tax-exempt investors holding assets of type *A*, and only taxable investors holding assets of type *B*. In practice, only partial separation occurs. The question of why firms pay tax-disfavored dividends, instead of the lower-tax alternative of occasionally repurchasing some of their shares, remains one of the unsolved mysteries of finance.[1]

4. *Homogeneous expectations*: Investors have the same beliefs about the expected returns and risks of all available investments. Thus, once a market price for risk is established, investors agree on the value of each investment. This is obviously a rough approximation. If all investors agreed on value, they would do far less swapping of stocks and bonds, and probably less buying and selling of businesses as well.

With heterogeneous expectations, asset prices depend on a complex mix of investor expectations and risk preferences. In essence, each investor has his own capital market line, and buys those assets which appear most favorably priced. Market prices reflect a blend of the expectations of different investors. Overall, the capital market line becomes fuzzy. If expectations are only moderately heterogeneous, rough estimates of the tradeoff between expected return and systematic risk can still be developed.

5. *Two-period world*: All available investments involve an investment at time $t = 0$, and a cash return at a known later time $t = 1$. This is a gross oversimplification of the complex returns on actual investments. It is possible to derive CAPM without this assumption, but only at the cost of making other equally strong assumptions. For example, one can relax the two-period assumption if the risk-free interest rate and the market price of risk: (i) are the same for all investment periods; and (ii) will not change over time, so that there is certainty about future reinvestment opportunities.

In a multi-period world, with different interest rates and risk premia for different time periods, we end up with a separate capital market line for each investment time horizon, plus some loose limits, established by the possibility of arbitrage between shorter and longer time periods, on interest rates and risk premia for different time periods.

6. *Known inflation rate*: CAPM can accommodate a nonzero inflation rate, but the inflation rate must be known at $t = 0$, when an investment is made. This assumption is reasonable for short periods of time, but becomes increasingly unrealistic as the investment horizon lengthens.

7. *Existence of a zero-risk security*: A zero-risk security must exist, in quantities large enough to satisfy the demand of all those who want to own

---

[1] See, e.g., Fischer Black, *The Dividend Puzzle*, J. Portfolio Mgmt. 5 (Winter 1976); Frank Easterbrook, *Two Agency-Cost Explanations of Dividends*, 74 Am.Econ.Rev. 650 (1984), both reprinted in *The Modern Theory of Corporate Finance* (Clifford Smith ed., 2d ed.1990).

it. In empirical tests of the model, short-term Treasury bills are commonly assumed to be zero-risk. If fact, even Treasury bills have reinvestment risk if one's investment time horizon extends beyond the T-bill maturity date, some inflation risk, and currency risk (the risk that changes in the purchasing power of different currencies will not track differences in inflation rates, which will affect one's ability to use funds received at $t = 1$ to purchase goods priced in other currencies). In the real world, it is not possible to construct a completely risk-free security.

One can relax this assumption by positing unlimited ability to sell assets *short* -- to sell an asset one doesn't own today, and buy it back later, thus profiting if the price goes down and losing money if the price goes up. Unlimited short selling allows investors to construct a *zero-β* portfolio, which can substitute for the zero-risk security. If a zero-β portfolio cannot be constructed, then security prices will still fall along a straight line, but only some portions of the line will be reachable through actual investment strategies.

8. *Purely passive investment*: Investors are purely passive. They purchase fractional interests in investments with known expected returns and risks. They cannot, by their actions, change an investment's expected return or risk. This assumption is reasonable for modestly sized investments in publicly traded stocks and bonds. It becomes less true as an investment becomes large enough to confer influence over future decisions by business managers. Indeed, the value of control, which carries with it the opportunity to affect future business decisions, is central to understanding many corporate acquisitions.

9. *Ability to borrow at risk-free rate*: Investors can lend money at the risk-free rate of interest by investing in the zero-risk security, assuming it exists. CAPM assumes that they can also *borrow* at the risk-free rate. This assumption is approximately true for large institutional investors who want to borrow an amount that is a modest fraction of their total assets. It is increasingly violated as investor size becomes smaller and as an investor's borrowing increases as a fraction of the investor's assets, thus increasing the risk of default.

If investors can borrow at the risk-free rate r_f plus an increment x which is the same for all investors, the capital market line becomes kinked, with one slope for $\beta < 1$, where investors are lending at the risk-free rate, and a lower slope for $\beta > 1$, where investors are borrowing. The lower slope reflects the higher cost of borrowed funds. If different investors have different borrowing rates, they each have their own kinked capital market line, and it becomes harder to generalize about asset prices for $\beta > 1$.

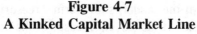

Figure 4-7
A Kinked Capital Market Line

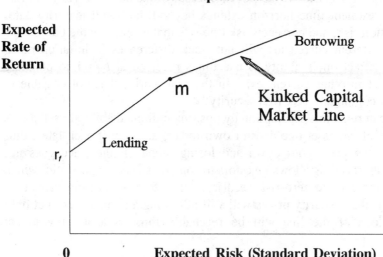

0   **Expected Risk (Standard Deviation)**

    10. *Beta is a complete measure of risk*: The standard deviation of an investment's systematic risk, measured relative to the standard deviation on the market as a whole, is assumed to be a complete measure of the risk for which investors must be compensated. In fact, while β is a plausible measure of a particular kind of risk, it does not fully capture some risks, such as inflation risk or liquidity risk (the risk of not being able to sell an asset quickly at the current market price, if your risk preferences change or you need funds).

    In addition, as we discussed in Chapter 3, standard deviation is a complete measure of risk only when the distribution of returns perfectly matches the normal, or bell-curve, distribution. Fluctuations in asset prices don't perfectly follow the normal distribution, especially over long periods of time. In particular, long-term returns show a long positive tail, reflecting the occasional firm -- like Microsoft or Walmart -- that becomes a spectacular success, and the many more firms that increase fivefold or tenfold in value. In contrast, no firm's stock can lose more than 100% of its starting value. Thus, standard deviation can't fully describe the systematic risks that investors face, and presumably must be compensated for.

C.   Empirical Tests of CAPM

    In light of the strong assumptions underlying CAPM, a key question is how well the model fit the facts. Is it valuable in explaining how security prices actually behave? Or is it only a theoretical construct that suggests how security prices ought to behave under highly artificial circumstances?

1.   Problems with Testing CAPM

Unfortunately, testing CAPM (or any other asset pricing model) is surprisingly difficult. One problem is that asset pricing theories predict a relationship between *expected* risk and *expected* return. All we can actually measure is *actual* risk and *actual* return. To test the connection between risk and return, we must hope that, on average and over time, actual returns will correlate with expected returns, and actual price fluctuations will correlate with expected risk.

Given actual patterns of asset price fluctuation, the time period needed to estimate the relationship between risk and return is very long. Over limited time periods, high-risk assets may -- and sometimes will -- produce *lower* returns than low-risk assets. That possibility is inherent in the concept of risk.

Estimating expected risk is also hard. A beta estimate depends on regression analysis of the returns on a particular stock versus the returns on the stock market as a whole. The regression is noisy, as you can see from the Host International example in Figure 3-3. Thus, even the historical β estimate isn't very accurate. Moreover, the riskiness of the market as a whole, and the riskiness of particular stocks relative to the market, change over time, especially over the long time periods needed to test the model. In practice, β estimates for particular companies are not very stable over time. CAPM tests are typically conducted on portfolios of 20 or more stocks, for which beta estimates are more stable, though with some tendency for *regression to the mean* -- high β values tend to decline over time, and low β values tend to increase.

A further problem for CAPM (but not some other asset pricing models) is that CAPM defines the market portfolio as a *complete* portfolio of risky assets, both liquid and illiquid. The complete market portfolio includes not only publicly traded common stocks but also bonds, real estate, oil wells, private companies, etc., on a *worldwide* basis. CAPM posits a relationship between expected risk and the expected return on this complete market portfolio. All one can measure, though, is the relationship between risk and return for publicly traded securities. Empirical tests typically use a proxy for the complete market portfolio, such as the S&P 500 Index or the New York Stock Exchange index. This makes the tests ambiguous. Observed returns may differ from those that CAPM predicts because we have used an incomplete market portfolio. Conversely, if observed returns match CAPM's predictions, that too may be an artifact resulting from use of an incomplete market portfolio.[2]

In practice, tests of CAPM are generally not sensitive to small changes in the proxy for the market portfolio, such as switching from the S&P 500 Index to the New York Stock Exchange index. But efforts to conduct asset

---

[2] See Richard Roll, *A Critique of Asset Pricing Theory's Tests, Part 1: On Past and Potential Testability of the Theory*, 4 J.Fin. 129 (1977).

pricing tests using a worldwide index of publicly traded stocks are still in their infancy.[3] And we are far from being able to construct a good proxy for the worldwide market portfolio.

Finally, all asset pricing models offer a *normative* theory of how assets *should* be priced. If assets are not priced as the theory predicts, that could mean that the theory is wrong. But it could also mean that assets are mispriced. In effect, every test of an asset pricing theory is a joint test of (i) the theory; and (ii) the efficiency of market pricing. To test the asset pricing theory, we must assume that assets are efficiently priced. Conversely, to test pricing efficiency, we must assume that a particular asset pricing theory, such as CAPM, describes how assets should be priced.

2.   Tests Using Broad Asset Classes

These practical problems aside, what do the tests show? Broad asset classes -- short-term Treasury bills, government bonds, corporate bonds, and common stocks -- show *roughly* the relationship that CAPM predicts. Over the period from 1926-1993 (1926 is as far back as we have good data), asset classes with higher levels of risk have produced higher returns. Table 4-1 shows the nominal and real (inflation adjusted) returns, assuming annual compounding, on different asset classes.

The risk premia shown in Table 4-1 are historical averages. The average estimated risk premium on large-company stocks (proxied by the S&P 500) *has been* 6.5%. The risk premium *today* may be lower or higher than this. In 1994, when this is written, many analysts believe that the risk premium on common stocks is lower than its historical mean, perhaps only 3-4%. Moreover, 6.5% is merely our best *estimate* of the average risk premium. The standard deviation of that estimate is about 2.5%. This means that there is about a 2/3 chance that the actual risk premium averaged between 4% and 9%, about a 1/6 chance that the actual risk premium was less than 4%, and a 1/6 chance that the actual premium was more than 9%.

Even over long time periods, greater risk does not ensure greater return. For example, short-term Treasury bills produced a *higher* total return from 1926-1981 than long-term Treasury bonds, because long-term bond prices are sensitive to inflation, which increased over much of the period. Long-term Treasuries performed much better than T-bills over the last decade, as interest rates generally fell. And, over the full 1926-1993 period, the cumulative return on long-term Treasury bonds has been slightly lower than the cumulative return on intermediate-term Treasuries, even though intermediate-term Treasuries have significantly lower risk.

---

[3] See, e.g., Campbell Harvey, *The World Price of Covariance Risk*, 46 J.Fin. 111 (1991); K.C. Chan, G. Andrew Karolyi & Rene Stulz, *Global Financial Markets and the Risk Premium on U.S. Equity* (Nat'l Bureau Econ.Res. Working Paper No. 4074, 1992).

Table 4-1
Annual Returns on Asset Classes: 1926-1993

Asset Class	Nominal Return	Real Return	Std. Dev. of Annual Returns	Risk Premium Over Treasury Bills
Short-Term Treasury Bills	3.7%	0.5%	3.3%	0%
Intermediate-Term Treasury Bonds	5.3	2.1	5.6	1.6
Long-Term Treasury Bonds	5.0	1.8	8.7	1.3
Corporate Bonds	5.6	2.4	8.4	1.9
Large-Company Stocks (S&P 500)	10.3	7.0	20.5	6.5
Small-Company Stocks	12.4	8.9	34.8	8.4

Source: Ibbotson Associates, *Stocks, Bonds, Bills and Inflation* (1994 Yearbook)

3.   Does CAPM Work?: The Critics

While CAPM has predictive power for the long-run relationship between risk and return for broad asset classes, its prediction that high-β stocks should produce higher returns than low-β stocks is not as well supported. At the least, β seems not to be a complete measure of the risks that are priced in securities markets. The next reading critically evaluates CAPM's ability to predict stock returns.

Eugene Fama & Kenneth French
THE CROSS-SECTION OF EXPECTED STOCK RETURNS
47 J.Fin. 427 (1992)

The [Capital Asset Pricing Model] has long shaped the way academics and practitioners think about average returns and risk. The central prediction of the model is that . . . (a) expected returns on securities are a positive linear function of their market βs (the slope in the regression of a security's return on the market's return), and (b) market βs suffice to describe the cross-section of expected returns.

There are several empirical contradictions of [CAPM]. The most prominent is the size effect of Banz (1981).[a] He finds that market equity, ME (a stock's price times shares outstanding), adds to the explanation of the cross-section of average returns provided by market βs. Average returns on small (low ME) stocks are too high given their β estimates, and average returns on large stocks are too low.

Another contradiction . . . is the positive relation between leverage and average return documented by Bhandari (1988).[b] It is plausible that leverage is associated with risk and expected return, but in [CAPM], leverage risk should be captured by market β. Bhandari finds, however, that leverage helps explain the cross-section of average stock returns in tests that include size (ME) as well as β.

Stattman (1980) and Rosenberg, Reid & Lanstein (1985) find that average returns on U.S stocks are positively related to the ratio of a firm's book value of common equity, BE, to its market value, ME.[c] Chan, Hamao & Lakonishok (1991) find that book-to-market equity, BE/ME, also has a strong role in explaining the cross-section of average returns on Japanese stocks.[d]

Finally, Basu (1983) shows that earnings-price ratios (E/P) help explain the cross-section of average returns on U.S stocks in tests that also include size and market β.[e] Ball (1978) argues that E/P is a catch-all proxy for unnamed factors in expected returns; E/P is likely to be higher (prices are lower relative to earnings) for stocks with higher risks and expected returns, whatever the unnamed sources of risk.[f]

Ball's proxy argument for E/P might also apply to size (ME), leverage, and book-to-market equity. All these variables can be regarded as different ways to scale stock prices, to extract the information in prices about risk and expected returns. Moreover, since E/P, ME, leverage, and BE/ME are all scaled versions of price, it is reasonable to expect that some of them are redundant for describing average returns. Our goal is to evaluate the joint roles of market β, size, E/P, leverage, and book-to-market equity in the cross-section of average returns on NYSE, AMEX, and NASDAQ stocks.

---

[a] Rolf Banz, *The Relationship Between Return and Market Value of Common Stocks*, 9 J.Fin.Econ. 3 (1981).

[b] Laxmi Bhandari, *Debt/Equity Ratio and Expected Common Stock Returns: Empirical Evidence*, 43 J.Fin. 507 (1988).

[c] Dennis Stattman, *Book Values and Stock Returns*, 4 Chi. MBA: J. Selected Papers 25 (1980); Barr Rosenberg, Kenneth Reid & Ronald Lanstein, *Persuasive Evidence of Market Inefficiency*, J. Portfolio Mgmt. 9 (Spr.1985).

[d] Louis Chan, Yasushi Hamao & Josef Lakonishok, *Fundamentals and Stock Returns in Japan*, 46 J.Fin. 1739 (1991).

[e] Sanjoy Basu, *The Relationship Between Earnings Yield, Market Value, and Return for NYSE Common Stocks: Further Evidence*, 12 J.Fin.Econ. 129 (1983).

[f] Ray Ball, *Anomalies in Relationships Between Securities' Yields and Yield-Surrogates*, 6 J.Fin.Econ. 103 (1978).

Black, Jensen & Scholes (1972) and Fama & MacBeth (1973) find that, as predicted by [CAPM], there is a positive simple relation between average stock returns and β during the pre-1969 period.[g] Like Reinganum (1981) and Lakonishok & Shapiro (1986), we find that the relation between β and average return disappears during the more recent 1963-1990 period, even when β is used alone to explain average returns.[h] The . . . simple relation between β and average return is also weak in the 50-year 1941-1990 period. In short, our tests do not support the most basic prediction of [CAPM], that average stock returns are positively related to market βs.

Unlike the simple relation between β and average return, the univariate relations between average return and size, leverage, E/P and book-to-market equity are strong.[i] In multivariate tests, the negative relation between size and average return is robust to the inclusion of other variables.[j] The positive relation between book-to-market equity and average return also persists in competition with other variables. Moreover, although the size effect has attracted more attention, book-to-market equity has a consistently stronger role in average returns. Our bottom-line results are: (a) β does not seem to help explain the cross-section of average stock returns, and (b) the combination of size and book-to-market equity seems to absorb the roles of leverage and E/P in average stock returns, at least during our 1963-1990 sample period.

---

[g] Fischer Black, Michael Jensen & Myron Scholes, *The Capital Asset Pricing Model: Some Empirical Tests*, in *Studies in the Theory of Capital Markets* 79 (Michael Jensen ed.1972); Eugene Fama & James MacBeth, *Risk, Return and Equilibrium: Empirical Tests*, 81 J.Pol.Econ. 607 (1973). These studies were key early studies that provided empirical support for CAPM, and led to its widespread acceptance.

[h] Marc Reinganum, *A New Empirical Perspective on the CAPM*, 16 J.Fin. & Quant.Anal. 439 (1981); Josef Lakonishok & Alan Shapiro, *Systematic Risk, Total Risk, and Size as Determinants of Stock Market Returns*, 10 J. Banking & Fin. 115 (1986).

[i] *Univariate* regression analysis involves asking whether one variable, called the *dependent* variable, correlates with a second variable, called the *independent* variable. For example, in the market model, $R = \alpha + \beta \cdot R_m + \epsilon$, we measure whether the daily returns R on a particular firm's stock correlate with the daily returns R_m on the stock market as a whole. Here R is the dependent variable, R_m is the independent variable, and β is a measure of how the two variables are related. In the market model, there is *one* independent variable (R_m) on the right hand side of the regression equation, hence the term *uni*variate analysis.

[j] *Multivariate* regression analysis involves asking whether a dependent variable, such as the daily returns R on a firm's stock, is simultaneously correlated with *two or more* independent variables. Sometimes, the dependent variable will correlate with a particular independent variable in a univariate analysis, but the correlation will disappear or become statistically insignificant when other independent variables are added to the regression. If the correlation between the dependent variable and a particular independent variable remains statistically significant when other independent variables are added to the regression, that makes it more likely that the independent variable explains part of the variation in the dependent variable. The correlation between the dependent variable and this independent variable is said to be *robust to* the inclusion of additional independent variables in the regression. We discuss the concept of statistical significance in Chapter 6.

If assets are priced rationally, our results suggest that stock risks are multidimensional. One dimension of risk is proxied by size, ME. Another dimension of risk is proxied by BE/ME, the ratio of the book value of common equity to its market value.

It is possible that the risk captured by BE/ME is the relative distress factor of Chan & Chen (1991).[k] They postulate that the earning prospects of firms are associated with a risk factor in returns. Firms that the market judges to have poor prospects, signalled here by low stock prices and high ratios of book-to-market equity, have higher expected stock returns (they are penalized with higher costs of capital) than firms with strong prospects. It is also possible, however, that BE/ME just captures the unraveling (regression toward the mean) of irrational market whims about the prospects of firms.

Whatever the underlying economic causes, our main result is straightforward. Two easily measured variables, size (ME) and book-to-market equity (BE/ME), provide a simple and powerful characterization of the cross-section of average stock returns for the 1963-1990 period. . . .

[W]hen common stock portfolios are formed on size alone . . ., average return is positively related to β. The βs of size portfolios are, however, almost perfectly correlated with size, so tests on size portfolios are unable to disentangle β and size effects in average returns. Allowing for variation in β that is unrelated to size breaks the logjam, but at the expense of β. Thus, when we subdivide size portfolios on the basis of preranking βs, we find a strong relation between average return and size, but no relation between average return and β. . . .

Can β Be Saved?

What explains the poor results for β? One possibility is that other explanatory variables are correlated with true βs, and this obscures the relation between average returns and measured βs. But this line of attack cannot explain why β has no power when used alone to explain average returns. Moreover, leverage, book-to-market equity, and E/P do not seem to be good proxies for β. The averages of the monthly cross-sectional correlations between β and the values of these variables for individual stocks are all within 0.15 of 0.

Another hypothesis is that . . . there is a positive relation between β and average return, but the relation is obscured by noise in the β estimates. However, our full-period post-ranking βs do not seem to be imprecise. Most of the standard errors of the βs are 0.05 or less, only 1 is greater than 0.1,

---

[k] K.C. Chan & Nai-fu Chen, *Structural and Return Characteristics of Small and Large Firms*, 46 J.Fin. 1467 (1991).

and the standard errors are small relative to the range of the βs (0.53 to 1.79).[1]. . . .

Our evidence on the robustness of the size effect and the absence of a relation between β and average return is so contrary to [CAPM] that it behooves us to examine whether the results are special to 1963-1990. . . . NYSE returns for 1941-1990 behave like the NYSE, AMEX, and NASDAQ returns for 1963-1990; there is a reliable size effect over the full 50-year period, but little relation between β and average return. Interestingly, there is a reliable simple relation between β and average return during the 1941-1965 period. These 25 years are a major part of the samples in the early studies of [CAPM]. Even for the 1941-1965 period, however, the relation between β and average return disappears when we control for size. . . .

β and the Market Factor: Caveats

Some caveats about the negative evidence on the role of β in average returns are in order. The average premiums for β, size, and book-to-market equity depend on the definitions of the variables used in the regressions. For example, suppose we replace [the logarithm of the ratio of book-to-market equity] (ln(BE/ME)) with [the logarithm of] book equity (ln(BE)].[m] As long as [the logarithm of] size (ln(ME)) is also in the regression, this change will not affect the intercept, the fitted values or the R^2.[n] But the change in variables increases the average slope (and the t-statistic) on ln(ME). In other words, it increases the risk premium associated with size. Other redefinitions of the β, size, and book-to-market variables will produce different regression slopes and perhaps different inferences about average premiums, including possible resuscitation of a role for β. And, of course, at the moment, we have no theoretical basis for choosing among different versions of the variables.

Moreover, the tests here are restricted to stocks. It is possible that including other assets will change the inferences about the average premiums for β, size, and book-to-market equity. . . . Extending the tests to bills and other bonds may well change our inferences about average risk premiums, including the revival of a role for market β.

---

[1] "Standard error" is another term for standard deviation.

[m] "Ln" is a commonly used abbreviation for natural logarithm. Fama and French work with the logarithms of variables like book equity and market equity because this improves the statistical properties of these variables.

[n] R^2 is a measure of how much of the variation in a dependent variable (here, stock price) is explained, in a regression analysis, by variation in the independent variables (here β, size, and book-to-market equity). A high R^2 (close to 1) indicates that the independent variables explain most of the variation in the dependent variable; a low R^2 (close to 0) indicates that the independent variables explain only a small fraction of the variation in the dependent variable. Most asset-pricing theories produce only modest values of R^2. See Richard Roll, R^2, 43 J.Fin. 541 (1988).

We emphasize, however, that different approaches to the tests are not likely to revive [CAPM]. Resuscitation of [CAPM] requires that a better proxy for the market portfolio (a) overturns our evidence that the simple relation between β and average stock returns is flat and (b) leaves β as the *only* variable relevant for explaining average returns. Such results seem unlikely, given Stambaugh's (1982) evidence that tests of [CAPM] do not seem to be sensitive to the choice of a market proxy.[o] Thus, if there is a role for β in average returns, it is likely to be found in a multi-factor model that transforms the flat simple relation between average return and β into a positively sloped conditional relation.

Rational Asset-Pricing Stories

. . . [Our results] are not economically satisfying. What is the economic explanation for the roles of size and book-to-market equity in average returns? We suggest several paths of inquiry.

. . . Examining the relations between the returns on [portfolios formed based on size and book-to-market equity] and economic variables that measure variation in business conditions might help expose the nature of the economic risks captured by size and book-to-market equity.

Chan, Chen & Hsieh (1985) argue that the relation between size and average return proxies for a more fundamental relation between expected returns and economic risk factors. Their most powerful factor in explaining the size effect is the difference between the monthly returns on low- and high-grade corporate bonds, which in principle captures a kind of default risk in returns that is priced.[p] It would be interesting to test whether loadings on this or other economic factors . . . can explain the roles of size and book-to-market equity in our tests. . . .

[I]f stock prices are rational, BE/ME, the ratio of the book value of a stock to the market's assessment of its value, should be a direct indicator of the relative prospects of firms. For example, we expect that high BE/ME firms have low earnings on assets relative to low BE/ME firms. Our work (in progress) suggests that there is indeed a clean separation between high and low BE/ME firms on various measures of economic fundamentals. Low BE/ME firms are persistently strong performers, while the economic performance of high BE/ME firms is persistently weak.

Irrational Asset-Pricing Stories

The discussion above assumes that the asset-pricing effects captured by size and book-to-market equity are rational. For BE/ME, our most powerful

---

[o] Robert Stambaugh, *On the Exclusion of Assets from Tests of the Two-Parameter Model: A Sensitivity Analysis*, 10 J.Fin.Econ. 237 (1982).

[p] K.C. Chan, Nai-fu Chen & David Hsieh, *An Exploratory Investigation of the Firm Size Effect*, 14 J.Fin.Econ. 451 (1985).

expected-return variable, there is an obvious alternative. The cross-section of book-to-market ratios might result from market overreaction to the relative prospects of firms. If overreaction tends to be corrected, BE/ME will predict the cross-section of stock returns. Simple tests do not confirm that the size and book-to-market effects in average returns are due to market overreaction, at least of the type posited by DeBondt & Thaler (1985).[q]. .

   If our results are more than chance, they have practical implications for portfolio formation and performance evaluation by investors whose primary concern is long-term average returns. If asset-pricing is rational, size and BE/ME must proxy for risk. Our results then imply that the performance of managed portfolios (e.g., pension funds and mutual funds) can be evaluated by comparing their average returns with the average returns of benchmark portfolios with similar size and BE/ME characteristics. Likewise, the expected returns for different portfolio strategies can be estimated from the historical average returns of portfolios with matching size and BE/ME properties.
   If asset-pricing is irrational and size and BE/ME do not proxy for risk, our results might still be used to evaluate portfolio performance and measure the expected returns from alternative investment strategies. If stock prices are irrational, however, the likely persistence of the results is more suspect.
. . .

---

4.   The Beta Backers Respond

Fischer Black, BETA AND RETURN
J. Portfolio Mgmt. 8 (Fall 1993)

   Eugene Fama says (according to Eric Berg of *The New York Times*, Feb. 18, 1992) "beta as the sole variable explaining returns on stocks is dead." He also says (according to Michael Peltz of *Institutional Investor*, June 1992) that the relation between average return and β is *completely* flat. In these interviews, I think that Fama is misstating the results in Fama & French (1992).[a] Indeed, I think Fama & French, in the text of that article, misinterpret their own data (and the findings of others).
   Black, Jensen & Scholes (1972)[b] and Miller & Scholes (1972)[c] find

---

   [q] Werner Debondt & Richard Thaler, *Does the Stock Market Overreact?*, 40 J.Fin. 557 (1985).

   [a] Eugene Fama & Kenneth French, *The Cross-Section of Expected Stock Returns*, 47 J.Fin. 427 (1992).

   [b] Fischer Black, Michael Jensen & Myron Scholes, *The Capital Pricing Model: Some Empirical Tests*, in *Studies in the Theories of Capital Markets* 79 (Michael Jensen ed.1972).

   [c] Merton Miller & Myron Scholes, *Rates of Return in Relation to Risk: A Re-examination*

that in the period from 1931-1965 low-β stocks in the United States did better than the capital asset pricing model (CAPM) predicts, while high-β stocks did worse. Several authors find that this pattern continued in subsequent years, at least through 1989. Fama & French extend it through 1990. All these authors find that the estimated slope of the [capital market] line relating [historical measured] *average* return and risk is lower than the slope of the line that the CAPM says relates *expected* return and risk. If we choose our starting and ending points carefully, we can find a period of more than two decades where the [estimated capital market] line is essentially flat. How can we interpret this? Why is the line so flat? Why have low-β stocks done so well relative to their expected returns under the CAPM? . . .

Fama & French say that their results "seem to contradict" the evidence that the slope of the line relating expected return and β is [even] *positive*. This is a misstatement, in my view. Even in the period they choose to highlight, they cannot rule out the hypothesis that the slope of the line is positive. . . . Moreover, if the line is really flat, that implies dramatic investment opportunities for those who use β. A person who normally holds both stocks and bonds or stocks and cash can shift to a portfolio of similar total risk but higher expected return by emphasizing low-β stocks.

Beta is a valuable investment tool if the line is as steep as the CAPM predicts. It is even more valuable if the line is flat. No matter how steep the line is, β is alive and well.

Data Mining

When a researcher tries many ways to do a study, including various combinations of explanatory factors, various periods, and various models, we often say he is "data mining." If he reports only the more successful runs, we have a hard time interpreting any statistical analysis he does. We worry that he selected, from the many models tried, only the ones that seem to support his conclusions. . . . Data mining is most severe when many people are studying related problems. Even when each person chooses his problem independently of the others, only a small fraction of research efforts result in published papers. By its nature, research involves many false starts and blind alleys. The results that lead to published papers are likely to be the most unusual or striking ones. But this means that any statistical tests of significance will be gravely biased.

The problem is worse when people build on one another's work. Each decides on a model closely related to the models that others use, learns from the others' blind alleys, and may even work with mostly the same data. Thus in the real world of research, conventional tests of significance seem almost worthless. In particular, most of the so-called anomalies that have plagued the literature on investments seem likely to be the result of data

of Some Recent Findings, in *Studies in the Theories of Capital Markets* 47 (Michael Jensen ed.1972).

mining. We have literally thousands of researchers looking for profit opportunities in securities. They are all looking at roughly the same data. Once in a while, just by chance, a strategy will seem to have worked consistently in the past. The researcher who finds it writes it up, and we have a new anomaly. But it generally vanishes as soon as it is discovered. . . .

The "size effect" may be in this category. Banz (1981)[d] finds that firms with little stock outstanding (at market value) had, up to that time, done well relative to other stocks with similar betas. Since his study was published, though, small firms have had mediocre and inconsistent performance. Fama & French continue studying the small-firm effect, and report similar results on a largely overlapping data sample. In the period since the Banz study (1981-1990), they find no size effect at all, whether or not they control for β. Yet they claim in their paper that size is one of the variables that "captures" the cross-sectional variation in average stock returns [while β does not].

Fama & French also give no reasons for a relation between size and expected return. They might argue that small firms are consistently underpriced because they are "neglected" in a world of large institutional investors. But they do not give us that reason or any other reason. Lack of theory is a tipoff: watch out for data mining!

Fama & French also find the ratio of book value to the market value of the firm's equity helps capture the cross-sectional variation in average stock returns. They favor the idea that this ratio captures some sort of rationally priced risk, rather than market overreaction to the relative prospects of firms. But they say nothing about what this risk might be, or why it is priced, or in what direction.

They mention the possibility that this result is due to "chance," which is another way to describe data mining, but they don't consider that plausible, because the result appears in both halves of their period, and because the ratio predicts a firm's accounting performance. I consider both those arguments weak. Given that an "effect" appears in a full period, we expect to find it in both halves of the period. . . . We know that when markets are somewhat efficient, stock prices react before accounting numbers to events affecting a firm's performance. Thus we [should not be] surprised when firms with high ratios of book-to-market equity show poor subsequent accounting performance. I don't think this is evidence of a priced risk factor at all.

Thus I think it is quite possible that even the book-to-market effect results from data mining, and will vanish in the future. But I also think it may result in part from irrational pricing. The ratio of book-to-market equity may pick up a divergence between value and price across any of a number of dimensions. . . .

---

[d] Rolf Banz, *The Relationship Between Return and Market Values of Common Stock*, 9 J.Fin.Econ. 3 (1981).

Beta Theory

I think most of the Fama & French results are attributable to data mining. . . . I especially attribute their results to data mining when they attribute them to unexplained "priced factors," or give no reason at all for the effects they find.

Strangely, the factor that seems most likely to be priced they don't discuss at all: the β factor [also called the zero-β portfolio]. We can construct the β factor by creating a diversified portfolio that is long in low-β stocks and short in smaller amounts of high-β stocks, so that its β is roughly zero. . . . [If the measured slope of the security market line is flatter than CAPM predicts, so that low-β stocks do better than predicted and high-β stocks do worse than predicted, then this zero-β portfolio should produce higher expected returns than simply investing in a conventional "zero-risk" asset such as short-term Treasury bills.]

The empirical evidence that the β factor [produced returns higher than the rate of interest available on short-term Treasury bills] is stronger than the corresponding evidence for the "small-stock" factor or the book-to-market equity factor. The first evidence was published in 1972, and the β factor has performed better since publication than it did prior to publication.

Moreover, we have some theory for the [good performance of the] β factor. Black (1972)[e] showed that borrowing restrictions might cause low-β stocks to have higher expected returns than the CAPM predicts. . . . Borrowing restrictions could include margin rules, bankruptcy laws that limit lender access to a borrower's future income, and tax rules that limit deductions for interest expense.

These restrictions have probably tightened in the United States in recent decades. Margin rules have remained in effect, bankruptcy laws seemed to have shifted against lenders, and deductions for interest expense have been tightened. Many countries outside the United States seem to have similar restrictions. . . . Moreover, many investors who can borrow, and who can deduct the interest they pay, are nonetheless reluctant to borrow. Those who want lots of market risk will bid up the prices of high-β stocks. This makes low-β stocks attractive and high-β stocks unattractive to investors who have low-risk portfolios or who are willing to borrow. . . .

Can't we do some tests on stock returns to sort out which of [the possible reasons for mispricing of β risk] is most important? I doubt that we have enough data to do that. We have lots of securities, but returns are highly correlated across securities, so these observations are far from independent. We have lots of days, but to estimate factor pricing [the extra return that investors receive for bearing a particular type of risk] what counts is the number of years for which we have data, not the number of distinct observations. If the factor prices are changing, even many years is not

---

[e] Fischer Black, *Capital Market Equilibrium with Restricted Borrowing*, 45 J.Bus. 444 (1972).

enough. By the time we have a reasonable estimate of how a factor was priced on average, it will be priced in a different way.

Moreover, if we try to use stock returns to distinguish among these explanations, we run a heavy risk of data mining. Tests designed to distinguish may accidentally favor one explanation over another in a given period. I don't know how to begin designing tests that escape the data mining trap. . . .

Send me your predictions! I'll record them, and in future decades we can see how many were right. My prediction is that the [measured security market] line will steepen, but that low-β stocks will continue to do better than the CAPM says they should.

Corporate Finance

Suppose you believe that the line relating expected returns to β will continue to be flat, or flatter than the CAPM suggests. What does that imply for a firm's investment and financing policy? . . .

The β of a corporation's stock depends on both its asset β [the riskiness of its underlying assets] and its leverage. [The higher the firm's leverage, the higher the β of its stock. If corporations can borrow more easily than individuals, then] a corporation will increase its stock price whenever it increases its leverage. . . .

If today's corporations do not face borrowing restrictions, and if a corporation makes its investment decisions to maximize its stock price, the market for corporate assets should be governed by the ordinary CAPM. A firm should use discount rates for its investments that depend on their betas in the usual way.

On the other hand, I think many corporations act as if they do face borrowing restrictions. They worry about an increase in leverage that may cause a downgrade from the rating agencies, and they carry over the investor psychology that makes individuals reluctant to borrow. This may mean that corporate assets are priced like common stocks. Low-β assets may be underpriced, while high-β assets are overpriced [compared to the theoretical value derived from CAPM]. . . .

No matter what the slope of the line, a rational corporation will evaluate an investment using the betas of that investment's cash flows. It will not use the betas of its other assets or the betas of its liabilities.

Announcements of the "death" of β seem premature. The evidence that prompts such statements implies more uses for β than ever. Rational investors who can borrow freely, whether individuals or firms, should continue to use the CAPM and β to value investments and to choose portfolio strategy.

Note on the Predictive Value of Beta

1. Kothari, Shanken & Sloan (1993) report that β values formed from *annual* returns have strong predictive value over the period from 1927-1990, in contrast to the *monthly* betas used by Fama & French. But they offer no theory for why the time interval used to measure β should be important. Like Fama & French, they find that β had no predictive value over the period from 1962-1990.[4]

2. Fama & French use a sample of firms for which accounting data was available on the *Compustat* computer database. Kothari, Shanken & Sloan report that this may introduce sample selection bias into their study: small firms with stock price data available on show much better stock price performance, on average, than firms *without* accounting data available on Compustat. A possible explanation: Compustat may pick more successful small firms for inclusion in its database. When Kothari, Shanken & Sloan correct (rather crudely) for this bias, the book-to-market-equity effect disappears.

3. The sensitivity of tests of CAPM to the period used to measure β, and the apparent sample selection bias from using Compustat data, strengthen Fischer Black's argument that the evidence for the size and book-to-market-equity effects, may reflect data mining rather than real differences in returns. But they bring us no closer to knowing how β-risk is priced.

D.   Multi-Factor Asset Pricing Models

Beta, as a measure of the risk that is priced in securities markets, has been weakened by studies such as Fama & French. The empirical doubts about CAPM also reinforce the theoretical objection discussed earlier: Because we lack a perfect proxy for the market portfolio, CAPM isn't really testable. Indeed, it is theoretically possible for CAPM would work perfectly, if we only could use the right proxy for the market portfolio, yet have no predictive value if we used even a moderately imperfect proxy such as the S&P 500.[5] CAPM would then be right in theory, but useless as a real world tool, much as quark theory is useless in predicting what will happen when a baseball collides with a baseball bat.

One approach that has both real-world promise and theoretical support is to develop a multi-factor asset pricing model that accounts for different types of risk. We also need to understand whether and how measurable quantities, like size or book-to-market equity, which don't directly measure risk, proxy for risk. Nothing intrinsic about size or BE/ME makes them

---

[4] S.P. Kothari, Jay Shanken & Richard Sloan, *Another Look at the Cross-section of Expected Stock Returns* (Bradley Pol'y Res.Ctr. working paper 93-01, 1993).

[5] See Shmuel Kandel & Robert Stambaugh, *Portfolio Inefficiency and the Cross-Section of Expected Returns* (NBER working paper No. 4702, 1994).

obvious surrogates for systematic risk, which is why Fama & French comment that their results are "not economically satisfying" and Fischer Black suggests that they result merely from "data mining." For size, one possibility is that liquidity, which is correlated with size, is an important underlying risk factor. Investor willingness to pay a premium for higher liquidity can potentially explain much of the size effect.

The leading alternative to CAPM is Arbitrage Pricing Theory (APT). APT posits that, rather than a single factor determining returns as in the CAPM, a number of risk factors interact to determine expected returns. An asset's expected return is determined by its sensitivity to each risk factor. Expected return is assumed to be linearly related to each risk factor. In effect, each risk factor has its own "beta." Empirical evidence that return is determined by factors in addition to β, so troublesome for CAPM, is expressly contemplated by APT. Indeed, CAPM can be seen as a special case of Arbitrage Pricing Theory where a single risk factor -- systematic risk -- determines returns.

Suppose that the expected return on a portfolio p depends on two factors -- say systematic risk (proxied by $\beta_p r_m$) and liquidity. APT predicts that the capital market line will become a *plane*, as shown in Figure 4-8. If expected return depends on three or more factors, the capital market plane will become a multidimensional hyperplane, which can't be shown visually.

Mathematically, APT predicts that the expected return on portfolio p is related to the various risk factors by:

$$ER_p = a + (b_1 \cdot RF_1) + (b_2 \cdot RF_2) + (b_3 \cdot RF_3) + \ldots \qquad \textbf{(4-4)}$$

For our example of two risk factors -- systematic risk and liquidity -- this becomes:

$$ER_p = a + (b_1 \cdot \beta_p r_m) + (b_2 \cdot L_p) \qquad \textbf{(4-5)}$$

where:

L_p = a measure of the liquidity of portfolio p
b_1 = the weighting factor for systematic risk
b_2 = the weighting factor for liquidity

Equation 4-5 is the equation of the plane shown in Figure 4-8. Since investors like more liquidity, the plane slopes *down* in the liquidity dimension.

Figure 4-8
A Possible Capital Market Plane

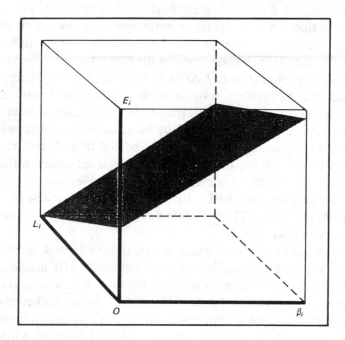

Source: William Sharpe, *Investments* 178 (3d ed.1985).

APT, like CAPM, requires a set of strong assumptions, similar but not identical to the CAPM assumptions. If these assumptions hold, then if an asset's price departs from the capital market hyperplane, investors will be able to engage in arbitrage transactions that will tend to push the security's price back towards the hyperplane.

The generality of APT comes at a price. CAPM makes the *normative* prediction that a particular risk factor -- β -- *should* affect asset prices. APT is agnostic on which risk factors count. Its usefulness will depend on whether future research allows us to determine which risk factors influence expected returns, and measure the sensitivity of expected returns to each factor. Empirical efforts to resolve these questions are still in a preliminary stage. There is evidence to support at least five risk factors: the level of industrial activity; the rate of inflation; the spread between short and long-term interest rates; the spread between the yields of low and high-risk corporate bonds (which is a measure of default risk); and liquidity (proxied by bid-asked spread).[6]

Given the uncertainties of asset-pricing theory, perhaps the most we can say is that systematic risks affect the expected returns demanded by risk-

---

[6] See Nai-fu Chen, Richard Roll & Stephen Ross, *Economic Forces and the Stock Market*, 59 J.Bus. 383 (1986); Yakov Amihud & Haim Mendelson, *Liquidity, Asset Prices and Financial Policy*, Fin. Analysts J. 56 (Nov.-Dec.1991).

averse investors.   But we lack, as yet, a solid understanding of *which systematic risks matter*, or *how much* they matter.   An investment in a venture capital startup is clearly riskier than an investment in a large, profitable firm, and venture capital investors should (and presumably do) demand a higher expected rate of return for to compensate for that risk. But we can only crudely estimate the extra risks that the venture capital investor is taking, or how much the investor should be paid for taking those risks. We must also keep in mind the possibility that *unsystematic risk* may affect prices, in a complex world where diversification is costly and no one is sure which risks are systematic and which aren't.

These uncertainties are less troublesome for our purposes than for stock traders. The potential for business combinations to affect risk will still be central in understanding how business combinations can increase the combined value of the merging firms. And the potential for the actions of lawyers and other professionals to reduce various risks will still be central in understanding their role in adding value. If lawyers can influence *any* factor bearing on asset value, the potential for value creation is present. Thus, the inability of financial theory to fully specify which risk factors affect asset values does not interfere with our project. (Though, to be sure, the more we know about the factors that determine value, the greater the potential for value creation.)

E.   Capital Budgeting Under Uncertainty

In Chapter 2, we discussed capital budgeting in a world without risk. There we stressed the need to take the time value of money into account in evaluating the returns from a prospective investment. In this Chapter and in Chapter 3, we introduced the concept of risk. In a risky world, the required return for a project is composed of two elements: a payment that reflects the time value of money; and a payment for bearing the risks associated with the project. It is now time to return to capital budgeting and ask how a firm should take risk into account in determining the appropriate discount rate for a project. The accepted approach to this question is developed in the excerpt below:

Richard Brealey & Stewart Myers
PRINCIPLES OF CORPORATE FINANCE
181-83 (4th ed. 1991)*

Long before the development of modern theories linking risk and expected return, smart financial managers adjusted for risk in capital budgeting. They realized intuitively that, other things being equal, risky

---

projects are less desirable than safe ones. Therefore they demanded a higher rate of return from risky projects or they based their decisions on conservative estimates of the cash flows.

Various rules of thumb are often used to make these risk adjustments. For example, many companies estimate the rate of return required by investors in its securities and use the *company cost of capital* to discount the cash flows on all new projects. Since investors require a higher rate of return from a very risky company, such a firm will have a higher company cost of capital and will set a higher discount rate for its new investment opportunities. . . .

This is a step in the right direction. Even though we can't measure risk or the expected return on risky securities with absolute precision, it is still reasonable to assert that [a computer company such as Digital Equipment Corp. (DEC) faces] more risk than the average firm and, therefore, should have demanded a higher rate of return from its capital investments.

But the company cost of capital rule can also get a firm into trouble if the new projects are more or less risky than its existing business. Each project should be evaluated at its *own* opportunity cost of capital. This is a clear implication of the value-additivity principle. For a firm composed of assets A and B, firm value is

$$\text{Firm value} \; = \; PV(AB) \; = \; PV(A) \; + \; PV(B)$$

. . . Here *PV(A)* and *PV(B)* are valued just as if they were mini-firms in which stockholders could invest directly. *Note:* Investors would value *A* by discounting its forecasted cash flows at a rate reflecting the risk of *A*. They would value *B* by discounting at a rate reflecting the risk of *B*. The two discount rates will, in general, be different.

If the firm considers investing in a third project *C*, it should also value *C* as if it were a mini-firm. That is, the firm should discount the cash flows of *C* at the expected rate of return investors would demand to make a separate investment in *C*. *The true cost of capital depends on the use to which the capital is put.*

[If a] project has a high risk, DEC needs a higher prospective return than if the project has a low risk. Now contrast this with the company cost of capital rule, which is to accept any project *regardless of its risk* as long as it offers a higher return than the *company's* cost of capital.

It is clearly silly to suggest that DEC should demand the same rate of return from a very safe project as from a very risky one. If DEC used the company cost of capital rule, it would reject many good low-risk projects and accept many poor high-risk projects. It is also silly to suggest that just because AT&T has a low company cost of capital, it is justified in accepting projects that DEC would reject. If you followed such a rule to its seemingly logical conclusion, you would think it possible to enlarge the company's investment opportunities by investing a large sum in Treasury bills. That would make the common stock safe and create a low company cost of capital.

The notion that each company has some individual discount rate or cost of capital is widespread, but far from universal. Many firms require different returns from different categories of investment. The following discount rates might be set . . .:

Category	Discount Rate(%)
Speculative ventures	30
New products	20
Expansion of existing business	15 (company cost of capital)
Cost improvement, known technology	10

Chapter 4 Problems

1.   Using the information in Table 4-1, use CAPM to estimate the expected rate of return on an investment with $\beta = 1.3$.   Assume that the S&P 500 Index has $\beta = 1$.

2. How would your answer to question 1 change if you were told that the current return on short-term Treasury bills was 6%, and that the estimated risk premium on a portfolio with $\beta=1$ was equal to 4%?

3. Assume that the S&P 500 Index has $\beta=1$, and that the return on the S&P 500 over the past five years has averaged 14% annually.   In contrast, the return on a portfolio of stocks with an estimated beta of .8 has been 11.5% annually over the same period.   Based on the information given, use CAPM to estimate the return on a portfolio of 90-day Treasury bills over the five year period.   Explain how you arrived at your estimate.

4. What are the principal sources of error in your estimate in problem 3?

5.   Assume that over the last 10 years, large-company stocks have produced an average return of 15% per year, while small-company stocks have produced an average return of only 12% per year.   Your stockbroker claims that this proves that the size effect is no longer valid, and large-company stocks are a better buy.   Do you agree or disagree, and why?

6. You are the CEO of Widget Corp. Your friendly (and fee-hungry) local investment banker, having read the Fama & French study, comes to visit you one day, and explains that this study proves that bigger is better. If a company is bigger, he explains, investors will demand a smaller expected rate of return. Thus, all you need to do to reduce the expected rate of return on Widget Corp. stock, and thus raise the stock price, is issue $5 billion in new stock, and use the proceeds to buy other companies. He has a few companies in mind.   What's wrong with the investment banker's reasoning?

CHAPTER 5: THE EFFICIENT CAPITAL MARKETS HYPOTHESIS

Chapters 2 through 4 surveyed the theory of how capital assets *should* be valued. In this chapter, we introduce a central paradigm of modern finance theory -- the *Efficient Capital Markets Hypothesis* -- the hypothesis that the prices of publicly traded assets, such as stocks and bonds, match the value that asset pricing theory says these assets should have. We will be interested principally in the *semistrong* form of the Efficient Capital Market Hypothesis (ECMH), which states that, at any point in time, market prices *are an unbiased forecast of future cash flows that fully reflects all publicly available information.* The semistrong form has considerable empirical support, at least for the common stock of large public companies.

In contrast, the *strong* form of ECMH states that market prices are an unbiased estimate of future cash flows that fully reflects *all* information, both public and private. The strong form of ECMH is an extreme hypothesis that is not satisfied in the real world. If it were, inside trading would not be a profitable activity. The *weak* form of ECMH states that investors can't earn an above-market return by relying on the past history of stock prices and stock trading. The weak form is subsumed in the semistrong form, since past prices and trading history are particular types of publicly available information.

Unfortunately, common usage of the phrase "market efficiency" often does not distinguish between different types of efficiency. For example, a statement that "the stock market is inefficient" might be a claim that the prices of publicly traded common stocks do not correctly reflect all information available to investors (semistrong inefficiency), or a claim that market prices differ from the price that a fully informed investor would pay (strong-form inefficiency). References in this book to "ECMH" or "market efficiency" mean semistrong efficiency, unless we explicitly state otherwise.

Semistrong market efficiency has far-reaching ramifications. At a practical level, semistrong efficiency implies that *new* information that bears on the expected risk or return of an asset is quickly reflected in the asset's price -- so quickly that no one can profit by being the first to trade on the new information. An immediate corollary: If you don't have better information than other investors, you can't consistently beat the market by picking particular stocks that *you think* are undervalued. All you can do is incur trading costs by trying. This has led to a popular strategy known as *indexing*. An index fund seeks to closely mirror the return on a stock market index such as the S&P 500. The index investor hopes that the buy-sell decisions of other, more active investors will keep prices efficient.

Understanding when assets are likely to be fairly valued in the market, and when they might be misvalued, is central to evaluating the motives for corporate acquisitions and the social value of an active takeover market. Consider takeover motives first. Profit opportunities can arise if assets aren't correctly priced. For example, an acquirer could gain by paying $75 per share for a target that is worth $100 per share, but is valued at $50 per share in the market.

Conversely, if market prices are semistrong efficient, buying a public company, at a premium to the target's market price, makes sense *only* if: (i) the acquisition will increase the combined cash flows to the shareholders of the bidder and target, or reduce the systematic risks associated with those cash flows; or (ii) the acquirer has private information about the target's expected cash flows or risks that the market lacks. To be sure, in any one case, the acquirer's forecast of future cash flows could be right and the consensus forecast of other investors, reflected in the market price, could be wrong. But on average and over time, the market price is more likely to be right than the value estimate, based on the same information set, of any one market participant. This is what it means for the market price to be an *unbiased* forecast of future cash flows.

With regard to the social value of takeovers, if markets are semistrong efficient, we can infer that the premium paid to the target's shareholders, unless offset by losses to other parties, reflects a real increase in social wealth. On the other hand, a takeover that reflects a smart bidder finding a bargain permits no such inference. The new owner, instead of the old shareholders, will receive the target's cash flows, but total social wealth hasn't increased.

Semistrong market efficiency has important implications for takeover policy. If shareholders are good at valuing public companies, that strengthens the case for a relatively free market in corporate control -- for letting shareholders decide whether a target should be sold. Conversely, if shareholders are prone to irrational fads, that strengthens the case for giving the target's board of directors some discretion to resist a takeover proposal that the shareholders would endorse.

Efficient market theory is also important outside the takeover context. For example, much regulation of public capital markets is intended to provide information to investors. The Securities Act of 1933 (the "Securities Act") requires an issuer of securities to distribute a prospectus -- a lengthy document filled with detailed information about the issuer -- before the issuer can sell its securities. Similarly, the Securities Exchange Act of 1934 (the "Exchange Act") requires public companies to issue periodic reports containing a wide range of information about their activities. Both acts assume that this disclosure is necessary if public investors are to pay a fair price for publicly traded securities.

Disclosure of *new* information can close the gap that might otherwise arise between the public price and the price that a fully informed investor would pay. In contrast, disclosure of information that investors already have is valuable only if capital markets are *not* semistrong efficient. This insight led the Securities and Exchange Commission, in the 1980s, to adopt an "integrated disclosure" system under which public companies, which already issue periodic financial reports under the Exchange Act, can omit most of this information from their Securities Act prospectuses. The theory is that investors already have the information contained in the financial reports. In contrast, new issuers must continue to prepare long-form prospectuses. For firms that qualify to use a short-form prospectus, integrated disclosure has greatly reduced the cost and increased the speed of issuing new securities to the public.

ECMH has also affected judicial doctrine on liability and damages in securities fraud cases. The "fraud on the market" doctrine, which presumes semistrong market efficiency, was endorsed by the Supreme Court in Basic, Inc. v. Levinson, 485 U.S. 224 (1988). The Court concluded that investors need not show that they actually read or relied on a statement by Basic, that falsely denied that Basic was engaged in merger negotiations. Instead, investors were entitled to assume that Basic's market price reflected the reaction of other investors to the misleading statement. This all but eliminates the reliance requirement from a securities fraud class action. The difference between the price under correct information and the actual market price becomes a measure of the damages suffered by an investor who buys at an artificially inflated price, or (as in *Basic*) sells at an artificially low price.

Section A of this Chapter reviews the history and empirical support for the different flavors of ECMH. Section B explores the factors that tend to lead asset prices to obey, or depart from, theoretically correct pricing. Section C examine recent research that chips away at the edges of efficient market theory, as well as recent "noise trading" theories, which combine theoretical claims about why prices might depart from true value with statistical claims that some departures from correct pricing can't be detected by the available tests. Finally, section D reviews the evidence on systematic biases in human cognition, which may underlie inefficient pricing.

A.   The Empirical Evidence Supporting ECMH

Development of the empirical evidence on ECMH must begin with a number of caveats. First, we don't know what the "right" price for an asset is. Thus, we can't test ECMH directly, by comparing the actual price to a theoretically correct price. This means that we can never prove that a market *is* efficient. All we can do is speculate about particular ways that prices might be *inefficient*, and test for evidence of those departures from efficiency. A study that fails to find evidence of a particular departure from efficient pricing is *consistent* with ECMH. Many such studies can give us confidence that ECMH is a useful theory. But no study can ever *prove* ECMH.

Second, even in its semistrong form, ECMH is an extreme null hypothesis that can't be strictly true. Prices can become and remain "right" only if investors, in a constant search for bargains, work at getting them that way. Investors will engage in this effort only if there is profit in it. The profit, though, must come from inefficiencies of one sort or another. Thus, there must be enough inefficiency to induce investors to search for and trade on mispricing -- an equilibrium level of inefficiency.[1] The interesting empirical question is how close public securities markets come to being semistrong efficient, not whether they are perfectly efficient.

Third, our ability to test ECMH is limited by the noisiness of stock prices. It is relatively easy to test whether today's stock price is an unbiased estimate of stock price tomorrow or next week. It is far harder to test whether today's stock price is an unbiased estimate of stock price in five years, or of the long-term future stream of dividends that a firm will pay. The few long-term tests that are available show some interesting departures from efficient market predictions. Unfortunately, these departures aren't statistically significant, so we don't know whether they are real or not.

Fourth, almost all tests of semistrong market efficiency involve asking whether particular investors, or particular investment strategies, can *beat the stock market as a whole*. They test whether Mobil is correctly priced *relative* to Exxon, or Ford is correctly priced *relative* to General Motors. It is very difficult to test whether the stock market as a whole is correctly priced in an *absolute* sense -- that is, would an all-knowing observer agree that the market value of all stocks equals the discounted present value of all expected corporate cash flows. It is also very hard to test whether stocks as a whole are correctly priced compared to other broad asset categories such as bonds or real estate.[2]

The stock market crash of 1987, when the Dow Jones Industrial Average fell 23% in a single day and 36% in two weeks, casts doubt on the absolute efficiency of stock market prices. Even in hindsight, scholars can't find any economic news that can explain the unprecedented one-day drop. This suggests that prices were too high before the crash, too low afterward,

---

[1] See Sanford Grossman & Joseph Stiglitz, *On the Impossibility of Informationally Efficient Markets*, 70 Am.Econ.Rev. 393, 393 (1980).

[2] Absolute and relative efficiency should be understood as rough endpoints along a continuum. The more that a test of pricing efficiency compares apples to apples (Mobil to Exxon, or Ford to GM), the stronger the statistical tests tend to be, and the stronger the qualitative reasons for believing that investors will do a reasonable job of comparing the value of *A* to the value of *B*. Conversely, the more a test of pricing efficiency compares apples to ice cream (stocks to bonds, or stocks to real estate), the weaker the statistical tests tend to be, and the more difficult the investor's task of valuation, because more variables are involved. An assessment of whether auto manufacturers are correctly priced relative to biotechnology firms would fall somewhere in between a relative test and an absolute test, both in terms of the analytical difficulty of the task, and in terms of our confidence in the statistical tests.

The terms *absolute* and *relative* efficiency are our own. Samuelson uses the terms *macro*-efficiency and *micro*-efficiency; Brealey & Myers use the terms *intrinsic* and *relative* efficiency. Paul Samuelson, *Foreword* to Marshall Blume & Jeremy Siegel, *The Theory of Security Pricing and Market Structure*, 1 Fin.Markets, Institutions & Instruments 1 (1992); Richard Brealey & Stewart Myers, *Principles of Corporate Finance* 299-300 (4th ed.1991). For discussion of the similar but not identical concepts of *allocative* and *speculative* efficiency, see Jeffrey Gordon & Lewis Kornhauser, *Efficient Markets, Costly Information and Securities Research*, 60 NYU L.Rev. 761 (1985).

or perhaps some of both. But it is as hard to disprove absolute pricing efficiency as to prove it. The price decline *could* be explained by a sudden change in investor expectations about future growth rates (a 1% change in expected growth rates would suffice). Perhaps there was some economic reason for such a change in expectations that we're not yet smart enough to understand.[3]

Still, after the 1987 market crash, many finance scholars are skeptical about absolute pricing efficiency. Some are also readier to believe that *relative* prices can be inefficient as well, though the market crash does not directly contradict the studies of relative pricing efficiency discussed below. Even skeptics about market efficiency, though, are generally also skeptical about whether investors, except perhaps a very few exceptional individuals, can regularly outperform the market as a whole. We will return in later chapters to the implications of absolute mispricing for takeover motives, and for regulatory policy toward takeovers.

A final difficulty with empirical tests of CAPM is the joint hypothesis problem. Recall from Chapter 4 that *every* test of market efficiency is also a test of the asset pricing model used to generate the prices against which market prices are compared. If observed prices differ from the prices predicted by the asset pricing model, that could mean that the market is inefficient, the asset pricing model is incorrect, or both. For example, Fama & French find a correlation between firm size and realized return. They interpret this as evidence against CAPM. But it could equally well be evidence against market efficiency.

Only by running many different tests for different types of inefficiency, using different asset pricing models, can we develop some sense for which is more robust -- ECMH or asset pricing theory. While definitive proof is (and will continue to be) unavailable, most financial economists believe that the evidence for relative pricing efficiency is stronger than the evidence for any particular asset pricing model. Thus, they interpret anomalies such as the size effect as indicating a need to rethink asset pricing theory, rather than a need to rethink efficient market theory.

With these caveats in mind, the next reading reviews the empirical tests supporting the semistrong efficiency of public securities markets. Section C will review evidence on various *departures* from efficient pricing. Consider, as you read, the extent to which the studies provide evidence for relative pricing efficiency of one stock relative to another, and the extent to which

---

[3] For a sampling of the literature on the implications of the market crash for ECMH, see Merton Miller, *Financial Innovations and Market Volatility* ch. 6 (1991); Richard Roll, *The International Crash of October 1987*, and Eugene Fama, *Perspectives on October 1987, or What Did We Learn from the Crash?*, both in Robert Barro, Eugene Fama, Daniel Fischel, Allan Meltzer, Richard Roll & Lester Telser, *Black Monday and the Future of Financial Markets* (1989); and Fischer Black, *An Equilibrium Model of the Crash*, Kenneth French, *Crash Testing the Efficient Market Hypothesis*, and Robert Shiller, *Portfolio Insurance and Other Investor Fashions as Factors in the 1987 Stock Market Crash*, all in *NBER Macroeconomics Annual 1988*.

they provide evidence for absolute pricing efficiency. How might one test for absolute pricing inefficiency?

James Lorie, Peter Dodd & Mary Kimpton
THE STOCK MARKET: THEORIES & EVIDENCE
55-75 (2d ed. 1985)[*]

During the 1960s, there was a curious and extremely important controversy about the process which determines common stock prices. Initially, the controversy focused on the extent to which successive changes in common stock prices were independent of each other. In more technical terms, the issue was whether or not common stock prices follow a random walk. If they do, knowledge of the past sequence of prices cannot be used to secure abnormally high rates of return. . . .

[Evidence that the walk is random] led to the theory of efficient markets. . . . [A useful definition of market efficiency] is from Jensen:

> A market is efficient with respect to a given information set if it is impossible to make profits by trading on the basis of that information set. By economic profits is meant the risk-adjusted returns net of all costs.[2]

. . . As the controversy and related work have progressed through the years, three forms of the efficient-market hypothesis have been distinguished: (1) the weak form; (2) the semistrong form; and (3) the strong form. The weak form asserts that current prices fully reflect the information implied by the historical sequence of prices. In other words, an investor cannot enhance his/her ability to select stocks by knowing the history of successive prices and the results of analyzing them in all possible ways. The semistrong form asserts that current prices fully reflect public knowledge about the underlying companies, and that efforts to acquire and analyze this knowledge cannot be expected to produce superior investment results. For example, one cannot expect to earn superior rates of return by analyzing annual reports, announcements of dividend changes, or stock splits. The strong form asserts that not even those with privileged information can make use of it to secure superior investment results. . . .

Early Beginnings

The term *random walk*, [first used in 1905, provides] the proper answer to a common, vexing problem: If one leaves a drunk in a vacant field and wishes to find him at some later time, what is the most efficient search

---

[*] Copyright © 1985. Reprinted by permission of Dow-Jones Irwin.

[2] Michael Jensen, *Some Anomalous Evidence Regarding Market Efficiency*, 6 J.Fin.Econ. 95 (1978).

pattern? It has been demonstrated that the best place to start is the point where the drunk was left. That position is an unbiased estimate of his future position, since the drunk will presumably wander without purpose or design in a random fashion.

Even before [1905], Louis Bachelier . . . presented convincing evidence that commodity speculation in France was a "fair game."[6] This meant that neither buyers nor sellers could expect to make profits. In other terms, the current price of a commodity was an unbiased estimate of its future price. . . .

Bachelier's earlier work was pregnant with meaning for investors, but the gestation period was one of the longest on record. . . . [In 1959], Roberts indicated that a series of numbers created by cumulating random numbers had the same appearance as a time series of stock prices. An observer with a predisposition to see familiar patterns in these wavy lines could detect the well-known head-and-shoulders formations and other patterns both in the stock price series and in the random series. . . . [Roberts' pictures are shown in Figures 5-1 and 5-2].

Early Tests of the Weak Form

[Random walk theory] was taken seriously only by a small group of academics at first. . . . Based on measurements of serial correlations between price changes, through investigation of successive changes of a given sign, and in other ways, these workers tested the statistical independence or the randomness of successive changes in stock prices. They uniformly found only insignificant departures from randomness. . . .

[Scholars also tested a trading rule with] the following form: Wait until stock prices have advanced by x percent from some trough and then buy stocks; next, hold those stocks until they have declined y percent from some subsequent peak, and then sell them or sell them short. Continue this process until bankrupt or satisfied. . . . Fama & Blume[17] demonstrated that filter schemes cannot, in general, provide returns larger than a naive policy of buying and holding stocks. Very small filters can generate larger profits before commissions, suggesting some persistence in short-term price movements. . . . However, the trends are so short that the profits are wiped out by commissions. The only ones to be enriched by using filter techniques to buy and sell stocks would be the brokers; the investors would be bankrupt.

All of these early investigations were tests of the so-called "weak form" of the random-walk hypothesis. That is, they tested the statistical properties of price changes themselves without reference to the relationship of these changes to other kinds of financial information. The evidence strongly

---

[6] Louis Bachelier, *Théorie de la Spéculation* (1900).

[17] Eugene Fama & Marshall Blume, *Filter Rules and Stock Market Trading*, 39 J.Bus. 226 (1966 Supp.).

supports the view that successive price changes are virtually independent. .

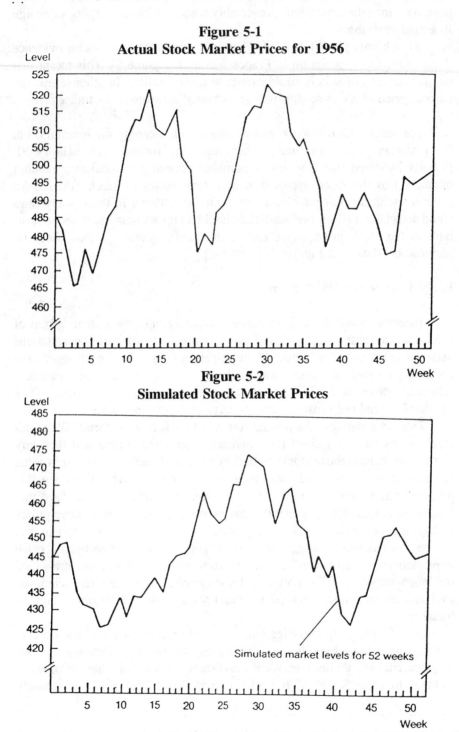

Figure 5-1
Actual Stock Market Prices for 1956

Figure 5-2
Simulated Stock Market Prices

Source: Harry Roberts, *Stock Market "Patterns" and Financial Analysis: Methodological Suggestions*, 14 J.Fin. 1 (1959).

Tests of the Semistrong Hypothesis

. . . Investigations of the semistrong form of the [efficient market] hypothesis are concerned with market efficiency and to what extent prices reflect public knowledge without bias. The focus of the empirical tests is the speed of adjustment to new information. Fama, Fisher, Jensen, & Roll[23] looked at the effect of stock splits on stock prices. The folklore about stock splits was that the total value of an issue of common stock was increased by increasing the number of shares. Efforts to explain this apparent irrationality were numerous and untested. . . .

[Fama, Fisher, Jensen & Roll's] hypothesis was that splits, which are usually accompanied by dividend increases, were interpreted by the market as a predictor of a dividend change. A dividend change can convey information about management's confidence about future earnings. In an efficient market, the only price effects of a split would be those associated with the information implied by a possible dividend change. . . . [They found that, *prior to the split*], the stocks earn higher returns than predicted by their historical relationship with the market. *After the split*, however, there is no evidence of abnormal returns.[a] . . .

After the split, stocks that did *not* have a subsequent dividend increase had relatively declining rates of return. The authors interpret these findings as an indication that the announcement of a stock split implies the strong likelihood of a subsequent increase in dividends. In fact, [71% of the stock splits] are followed by dividend increases. When it is disclosed, after the split, that the expected dividend increase will *not* eventuate, the stock price falls to reflect this unexpected bad news. For stocks that increase dividends as expected, the confirmation is reflected in higher prices. The fact that there is normal post-split stock price behavior for the sample of splits as a whole shows that the market makes an unbiased expectation of the dividend increase at the time of the split. . . .

Perhaps the transactions that best illustrate both the speed and unbiased nature of the efficient capital market are corporate takeovers. . . . [Figure 5-3 shows the stock price reaction to tender offer announcements]. The striking results include the magnitude of the stock price effect and the speed with which the market reacts. . . .

It is important to note that at the time of the first public announcement of the acquisition, the transaction's outcome is unknown. In many cases, the first offer is followed by higher competing offers from other bidders and higher revised offers by the same bidder. In other cases, the transaction

---

[23] Eugene Fama, Lawrence Fisher, Michael Jensen & Richard Roll, *The Adjustment of Stock Prices to New Information*, 10 Int'l Econ.Rev. 1 (1969).

[a] The term *abnormal return* refers to the return on a particular company's stock, *relative* to the stock market as a whole, after adjusting for risk. We discuss techniques for measuring abnormal returns in Chapter 6.

fails, and the stock price falls dramatically when the failure is announced. [The large returns to guessing the outcome have] attracted an industry of arbitrageurs who effectively bet on the outcomes of acquisition transactions. If the stock market is efficient, the returns from this arbitrage game should [equal the arbitrageur's cost of capital], on the average.

Figure 5-3
Abnormal Returns to Stockholders of Target Firms in Tender Offers

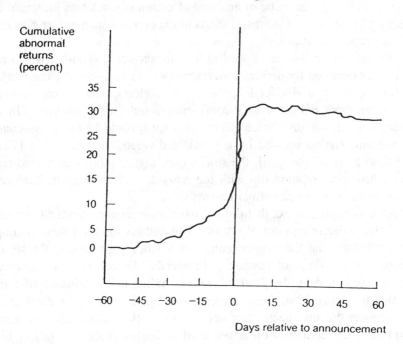

[Other studies examine] the performance of professionally managed portfolios. The argument is that the performance of professionally managed portfolios, [if] consistently superior to market performance as a whole or to relevant subsets of stocks in that market, would indicate an element of inefficiency in the price-setting process. . . .

[Michael Jensen[35]] compared the performance of [115] mutual funds [from 1955 to 1964] with the expected performance from randomly selected portfolios of equal riskiness [measured by β]. . . . [*Before expenses*], about half performed better and half performed worse than the control portfolios. [*After expenses*], only 43 of 115 mutual funds had superior performance. For the 10-year period, the average terminal value of mutual funds would have been about 9% less than the terminal value of the randomly selected portfolios.[b]. . .

---

[35] Michael Jensen, *The Performance of Mutual Funds in the Period 1945-64*, 23 J.Fin. 389 (1968).

[b] When first conducted, the tests of mutual fund performance were interpreted as providing support for the *strong form* of ECMH. The investigators assumed that professional

[Jensen also studied whether] some mutual funds *consistently* outperform randomly selected portfolios. . . . [A] mutual fund that was superior to a randomly selected portfolio in one period was superior to a randomly selected portfolio in a subsequent period about half the time. Jensen also sought to determine whether any fund was more often superior to randomly selected portfolios during the 10-year period than would be expected on the basis of chance alone. He found no evidence of such superiority. . . . One can readily imagine that [these findings] did not create strong euphoria in the mutual funds industry.

B.　How Markets Get to Be Efficient

The empirical evidence consistent with semistrong market efficiency begs the question of how markets get to be efficient. Semistrong efficiency can be explained under perfect market assumptions -- for example, that capital markets are complete, information is immediately and costlessly available to all investors, and all investors have homogeneous expectations and time horizons.[4]　But this explanation is, in the words of a joke commonly directed at both lawyers and economists, "absolutely accurate and totally useless."[5]　What makes ECMH non-trivial is its prediction that market prices will act *as if* information is immediately and costlessly available to all participants, and *as if* all investors have the same expectations about the future, even though these assumptions are obviously false. The next article explores the market processes that lead toward -- and limit -- market efficiency.

---

money managers had access to information that was not available to the general public. They sought to test whether these managers could beat the market by trading on this "nonpublic" information. Today, in light of evidence that corporate insiders *can* outperform the market, the inability of professional money managers to beat the market is generally interpreted as evidence that (i) securities markets are semistrong efficient; and (ii) money managers *do not* have valuable private information.

[4] See Paul Samuelson, *Proof that Properly Anticipated Prices Fluctuate Randomly*, 6 Indus.Mgmt.Rev. 41 (1965).

[5] The story usually begins with two people in a hot air balloon who have lost their way. They notice someone on the ground and call out, "Where are we?"

Unhesitatingly the ground observer responds, "You're in a balloon."

At this point one balloonist turns to the other and says, "He must be a lawyer (economist)."

"How can you tell?" the second passenger asks.

"It's easy," the first responds. "What he said was absolutely accurate and totally useless."

Ronald Gilson & Reinier Kraakman
THE MECHANISMS OF MARKET EFFICIENCY
70 Va.L.Rev. 549, 554-610 (1984)

The language of efficient capital market theory reveals its origins as a vocabulary of empirical description. The common definition of market efficiency, that "prices at any time 'fully reflect' all available information,"[22] is really a shorthand for the empirical claim that "available information" does not support profitable trading strategies or arbitrage opportunities. Similarly, . . . the now-familiar division of the ECMH into "weak," "semi-strong," and "strong" forms [began] as a device for classifying empirical *tests* of price behavior. . . .

Over time, however, scholars have pressed the weak, semi-strong, and strong form categories beyond their original service as a classification of empirical tests into more general duty as a classification of market responses to *particular kinds of information*. For example, prices might be said to incorporate efficiently one genre of information that is semi-strong or public, but fail to reflect another that is strong form, or non-public. Indeed, taken a step further, scholars sometimes describe markets themselves as weak, semi-strong, or strong form efficient. Without ever being quite explicit, this powerful shorthand implies that different market dynamics are involved in the reflection of different kinds of information into price, and that varying degrees of market efficiency might well be the consequence.

The recognition that different market mechanisms operate on different types of information is central to our analysis of market efficiency. But before we explore this conclusion in greater detail, it is first necessary that we define the key terms of the ECMH, and that we do so conceptually rather than operationally. . . . We need a concept of "relative efficiency" that distinguishes among and ranks the different market dynamics according to how closely they approximate the ideal of ensuring that prices *always* fully reflect all available information.

. . . Following Beaver's analysis, the requirement that prices "fully reflect" information means that prices must behave "*as if* everyone knows" the relevant information.[32] . . . By contrast, the second basic concept embodied in the operational definition of market efficiency, that prices mirror *all available information*, is less in need of reformulation than of expansion. The availability of information is a function of its distribution among traders in a given market. Different "bits" of information are more or less "available" depending on how many traders are aware of them. . . . [D]ifferent market mechanisms may be responsible for the reflection in price of differentially available categories of information. Differences among market mechanisms will matter, however, only if these mechanisms operate

---

[22] Eugene Fama, *Efficient Capital Markets: A Review of Theory and Empirical Work*, 24 J.Fin. 383, 383 (1970).

[32] William Beaver, *Market Efficiency*, 56 Acct.Rev. 23, 28 (1981).

with unequal results. We still require a measure of success -- a yardstick of "relative efficiency" -- in order to assess the importance of differences in the mechanisms of price formation. . . .

The operational definition of market efficiency tightly restricts the speed of the market's response to new information by requiring prices to reflect such information "always" -- i.e., very promptly. It is a short step from this emphasis on the rapidity of price response to a definition of "relative efficiency." The market, and the mechanisms that operate to reflect new information in price, are more or less efficient depending on how quickly they yield efficient equilibrium prices; relative efficiency is a measure of the *speed* with which new information is reflected in price. Similarly, the relative efficiency of market mechanisms determines the magnitude of arbitrage opportunities that new information creates for the fortunate traders who "know" it first. . . .

Mechanisms of Market Efficiency

Review of the basic vocabulary of efficient market theory reveals a missing link: an account of the mechanisms of market efficiency that its terms foreshadow but do not explicitly detail. . . . [These mechanisms] must be trading processes that, with more or less promptness (or "relative efficiency"), force prices to a new, fully informed equilibrium. Moreover, clarifying the meaning of informational "availability" also reveals the chief obstacle to any mechanism that serves to push prices toward a fully informed equilibrium. New information is "available" to the capital market under an extraordinary variety of circumstances, ranging from the extreme of near-universal initial distribution of information -- when everyone really does know the information -- to the opposite extreme of initial distribution to only a very few traders. A satisfactory account of the mechanisms of market efficiency must describe their operation over this entire continuum of availability, including those circumstances in which the initial distribution is extremely limited or incomplete. . . .

Over the past dozen years, financial economists have proposed four general forms of mechanisms, which may be termed "universally informed trading," "professionally informed trading," "derivatively informed trading," and "uninformed trading." . . . [We can] array the four market mechanisms on a continuum based on the initial distribution of information among traders, that is, on *how many* traders learn of the new information. Although all four mechanisms can ultimately lead to efficient equilibrium prices, the dynamics of equilibration will take longer as one moves from wide to narrow distribution. . . .

Universally Informed Trading

The simplest efficiency mechanism that causes prices to behave "as if" all traders knew of information is a market in which all traders are, in fact, costlessly and simultaneously informed. . . .   [S]everal varieties of price-relevant information at least approximate the ideal of universal dissemination.   "Old" information, embedded in securities prices, is one example.   Ongoing market activity assures its distribution to all interested traders, and precisely because all know it, we do not expect it to reveal arbitrage opportunities in the form of lucrative screens or trading rules that all alike could exploit.   Another example is important news items -- from presidential election results, which most citizens learn almost instantaneously, to changes in Federal Reserve Board policy, which are announced after trading hours precisely in order to ensure widespread dissemination.   Thus, the universally informed trading mechanism ranges over all "old" price information and much that is new.   It lumps together traditional "weak-form" information about price histories with information about current events into a single information set that prices reflect rapidly and with near perfect dynamic efficiency.

Professionally Informed Trading

In contrast to news about price and current events, however, much so-called "public" information is not universally disseminated among traders. Many traders are too unsophisticated to make full use of the technical accounting information contained in mandated disclosure reports;   much disclosure data is accessible in the first instance only through documents on file with government agencies;   and much information about a firm's prospects may be announced initially only to small groups of securities analysts and other market professionals.   How, then, do prices come to reflect this semi-public information?   The answer . . . is that rapid price equilibration does not require widespread dissemination of information, but only a minority of knowledgeable traders who control a critical volume of trading activity.   From this perspective, the universally informed trading mechanism is actually only a special case of price formation through the activity of traders who are direct recipients of information. . . .

The rapidity of such price adjustments depends on the volume of informed trading.   And although a precise account of that process has yet to be offered, it seems plausible that the relative efficiency of price adjustment to new information that proceeds through professionally informed trading declines only gradually as initial access to the information narrows to a threshold minority of traders, after which it declines rapidly.[67]

---

[67] This account still begs the question of exactly *how* informed minority trading can lead to the rapid price reflection of new information even when the minority is too small to dominate trading volume. If *un*informed traders held widely divergent beliefs about the value of a security, a short answer would be "price pressure": trading by informed investors that alters the demand or supply for particular securities, and raises or lowers their prices accordingly. This answer is almost certainly incomplete, however. It rejects wholesale the homogeneous expectations postulate of the Capital Asset Pricing Model, as well as the depiction of securities as fungible commodities with large numbers of near-perfect risk-return

In today's securities markets, the dominant minority of informed traders is the community of market professionals, such as arbitrageurs, researchers, brokers and portfolio managers, who devote their careers to acquiring information and honing evaluative skills.   The trading volume in most securities that these professionals control, directly or indirectly, seems sufficient to assure the market's rapid assimilation into price of most routine information.   Of course, the relative efficiency of the assimilation is never perfect.   Since informed trading is costly, market professionals must enjoy some informational advantage that permits them to earn a commensurate return.   But given competitive arbitrage and the market for analyst services, we would not expect the long-run returns of individual professionals to exceed the market average by very much, especially in exchange markets where professionals dominate trading.   This expectation is largely confirmed by empirical studies of mutual fund returns.

In sum, the professionally informed trading mechanism explains why any information that is accessible to significant portions of the analyst community is properly called "public," even though it manifestly is not. Such information is rapidly assimilated into price, with only minimal abnormal returns to its professional recipients.   And it is these characteristics, we submit, that largely convey the meaning of a "semi-strong form" market response.

Derivatively Informed Trading

Yet not all information is public, even within the narrow confines of the professional analyst community. Corporate insiders and exchange specialists, for example, enjoy easy access to information that would be prohibitively costly for anyone else to obtain,[73] while professional analysts conduct in-depth research that generates occasional informational monopolies.   In these and similar instances of monopolistic access, information first enters the market through a very small number of traders whose own resources are not

---

substitutes.   A far more plausible answer is that suggested by Myron Scholes, who demonstrated that secondary offerings affect securities prices primarily through the release of information rather than through price pressure. Myron Scholes, *The Market for Securities: Substitution versus Price Pressure and the Effects of Information on Share Prices*, 45 J.Bus. 179 (1972).   Similarly, intense trading by an informed minority will trigger temporary fluctuations in price and volume that may, in turn, alert an uninformed majority to the existence of new information. The ways in which uninformed traders may "learn" from price changes are discussed [below].

[73] The strong form efficiency tests amply document the systematic informational advantage enjoyed by corporate insiders and other "insider" groups. Indeed, if anything, these tests radically underestimate the magnitude of this advantage by relying on data about trades that are registered or otherwise public. Because trading on inside information is both unlawful and easily hidden, data limited only to publicly disclosed trading by insiders systematically excludes the trades most likely to reflect important informational advantages. See Arthur Keown & John Pinkerton, *Merger Announcements and Insider Trading Activity: An Empirical Investigation*, 36 J.Fin. 855, 856-57 (1981).

large enough to induce speedy price equilibration. But reflection of this information in price does not depend exclusively on the trading efforts of these insiders. Derivatively informed trading enhances relative efficiency and erodes the insider's advantage by capitalizing on the "informational leakage" associated with trading itself.

Informational leakage can assume many forms. Pure leakage -- inadvertent, direct communication of trading information to outsiders -- doubtlessly plays a significant role in rendering markets more efficient,[76] even if its effects remain erratic. But beyond such direct disclosure by accident or "theft," two forms of *indirect* leakage also contribute to market efficiency. These are trade decoding and price decoding.

Trade decoding occurs whenever uninformed traders glean trading information by directly observing the transactions of informed traders. Myron Scholes' classic study of secondary distributions documents a common example of this phenomenon by demonstrating that only *some* large block sales of stock lead to substantial, permanent declines in share price. The declines are especially pronounced when sellers are officers or other insiders of the issuer; moderate when sellers are investment companies and mutual funds (which act on the advice of research staffs); and barely noticeable when sellers are individuals, bank trust departments, and other traders who may liquidate their holding for reasons other than investment gain. The clear implication is that uninformed traders use the identities of large sellers to deduce whether the latter are likely to possess valuable information, and then proceed to trade accordingly.[80] . . .

[T]rade decoding remains limited by a significant constraint: uninformed traders must be able to identify informed traders individually and observe their trading activities directly. By contrast, the second form of indirect leakage, price decoding, does not require uninformed traders to discover the identity of their informed cohorts. It merely requires uninformed traders to observe and interpret anonymous data on price and trading volume against the backdrop of other information or expectations that these traders possess.

In theory, at least the logic of price decoding is simple. When trading on inside information is of sufficient volume to cause a change in price, this otherwise inexplicable change may itself signal the presence of new

---

[76] A professional in a major tender solicitation firm explains the "pure" informational leakage that precedes public announcement of tender offers as follows:

> You start with a handful of people, but when you get close to doing something the circle expands pretty quickly. . . . You have to bring in directors, two or three firms of lawyers, investment bankers, public-relations people, and financial printers, and everybody's got a secretary. If the deal is a big one, you might need a syndicate of banks to finance it. Every time you let in another person, the chance of a leak increases geometrically.

Klein, *Merger Leaks Abound, Causing Many Stocks To Rise Before the Fact*, Wall St.J., July 12, 1978, at 1, 31.

[80] Scholes (1972), *supra* note 67, at 202.

information to the uninformed. . . .   But beyond the "weak" learning involved in identifying the presence of new information, uninformed traders may also succeed in decoding the actual content of the information.   The trick here, and admittedly it is no mean feat, is the uninformed trader's ability to employ knowledge of the informational constituents of the old price to deduce which possible accretion of new information would successfully explain observed price changes.   Yet, probabilistically, such "strong" learning may be less difficult than it at first appears; consider, for example, how frequently increases in price signal the presence of inside information about impending tender offers.[86]. . .

Thus, the reflection of non-public information into price is a two-stage process; it is first triggered by initially informed "inside" trading, but, at a critical threshold, it rapidly accelerates as a result of reactive trades.   This much ensures that price reflects each "bit" of decoded information with a moderate degree of relative efficiency -- less, to be sure, than a wider initial distribution might provide, but far more than the trades of initially informed investors alone could produce. . . .   Derivatively informed trading thus explains how prices can come to reflect much information that is truly "non-public," even while suggesting the inevitable limits to the process.

Uninformed Trading

. . . [I]nformation is not limited to hard facts; it also includes soft information, the stuff of forecasts and predictions. . . . [In making forecasts, traders rely on] a wide variety of secondary facts, differing beliefs, and diverse levels of predictive skills. . . .   What is the mechanism by which the market comes to reflect the diverse and imperfect forecasts of individual traders into the aggregate forecast of price, and how well does this mechanism function as measured against the yardstick of optimal forecast data?

The final market efficiency mechanism, uninformed trading, permits prices, in some circumstances, to reflect aggregate -- or consensus -- forecasts that are more nearly optimal over the long run than those of any

---

[86] See Keown & Pinkerton (1981), *supra* note 73, who report not only accelerating price increases during the three weeks that precede tender offers, but also

> that 79, 60, and 64 *percent* of the acquired firms exhibited higher volume one, two and three weeks prior to the announcement date than they had three months earlier with the weekly average volume over this three week period 247, 112, and 102 percent higher than it was three months earlier.

Id. at 863.

It is impossible to determine how much such crescendos of trading activity owe to pure leakage, trade decoding, or price decoding, respectively.   The very strength of the incipient price and volume changes, however, suggests that "strong" price decoding plays a major role, especially as the other forms of informational leakage amplify the strength of the price signals.

individual trader. In this sense, prices can reflect information about which *all* traders are uninformed.[100] . . .

If each trader's forecast about the likelihood of a future event is informed in part by secondary facts and evaluations to which only he has access, then an aggregation of all forecasts draws on an information pool much larger than that possessed by any individual trader. Although each trader's own forecasts are skewed by the unique constraints on his or her judgment, other traders will have offsetting constraints. As trading proceeds, the random biases of individual forecasts will cancel one another out, leaving price to reflect a single, best-informed aggregate forecast. . . . In this respect, unsystematic bias "washes out" over trading in the same way that unsystematic risk "washes out" in a diversified portfolio. . . .

[Robert Verrecchia has modeled the conditions under which [the market price is the best available estimate of value.[105]] Verrecchia's model requires traders to make independent assessments of the value of risky securities based on their own facts and forecasts, which in the aggregate form a bounded, unbiased distribution around the hypothetical price that a fully informed trader would assign the security. The first of these conditions, that trader assessments be independent, requires an absence of collusion, "learning," or shared prejudice among traders that would render individual forecasting errors mutually reinforcing. . . .

The second condition of uninformed trading, that trader assessments be "bounded," merely requires that all such assessments fall in the same ball park. Traders with wildly-skewed personal assessments will impede price convergence -- reduce the relative efficiency of the uninformed trading mechanism -- and may even preclude it entirely in thinly-traded markets. [But] market discipline in the form of heavy trading losses will restrain idiosyncratic traders and may even eliminate them through a "Darwinian" process of natural selection.

. . . [The third, no-bias condition] embraces the preceding two requirements, since either widely-shared forecasting errors or idiosyncratic trading can bias the aggregate-level distribution of trader assessments. But, in addition, the "no-bias" condition carries implications for the acquisition of new [information]. . . . Once *any* trader acquires a new key fact that renders hitherto uncertain contingencies more (or less) likely, the consensus forecast of uninformed traders, as embodied in existing price, is biased relative to the newly-available information. Moreover, it remains so until the market fully incorporates the new key information into price, through one of the three "informed" trading mechanisms previously described. . . .

---

[100] Note, however, that uninformed trading *never* leads to prices that reflect wholly optimal forecast data. Rather, this mechanism can lead to prices that reflect a *better approximation*, over the long run, of such hypothetical optimal forecasts than can the parallel assessments made by individual traders.

[105] Robert Verrecchia, *Consensus Beliefs, Information Acquisition, and Market Information Efficiency*, 70 Am.Econ.Rev. 874 (1980).

[The uniformed and informed trading mechanisms are related]: traders themselves are acute observers of market behavior. If prices successfully aggregate all available information, including consensus forecasts and secondary facts, traders will begin to condition their trading activity on price as well as on their individual assessments of value. This conditioning on price adds "learning" to the basic aggregation mechanism of uninformed trading and is precisely the "weak learning" from price that we previously [discussed]. . . .

[Traders] only acquire an indication of whether the market disagrees with them, not of why it does. The force of such an indication depends on each trader's level of confidence. Individual estimates of value will move toward existing prices, and individual forecasts toward consensus predictions, in rough proportion to how highly each trader assesses the comparative quality of his or her own collection of information.[119] . . .

Summary

The uninformed trading mechanism completes the array of capital market mechanisms that [contribute to market efficiency]. . . . Moreover, the four efficiency mechanisms are complementary; each functions over a characteristic segment of the continuum of initial distributions of information among traders.

As Figure 5-4 illustrates, if the mechanisms are portrayed in this fashion, they parallel the criterion for partitioning information sets that implicitly informed Fama's trichotomy of weak/semi-strong/strong form tests of market efficiency. Universally informed trading extends over all widely-disseminated information, including the price-history information that underlies weak form tests. Professionally informed trading operates on all publicly available information, but it is particularly active where information is "semi-public" -- i.e., initially distributed or useful to only a minority of sophisticated trading professionals. . . . [D]erivatively informed trading acts most prominently on key trading facts over which very small numbers of traders exercise monopolistic access. . . . Finally uninformed trading acts on the "soft" information of forecasts and assessments that is not directly sampled by any of the other tests. . . .

---

[119] If traders rely on price in roughly inverse proportion to the quality of their independent assets, the most poorly informed traders will rely most on price, thereby reducing the number of wildly skewed "outlier" trades. . . . On the other hand, weak learning can also generate inefficiency in uninformed trading by amplifying any systematic bias reflected in price. Weak learning cannot *create* biased prices, but if the forecasts of confident investors who trade heavily on their independent assessment are already biased, weak learning by less confident traders may transmit the bias and "freeze" it into price.

Figure 5-4
Capital Market Efficiency Mechanisms

Traditional Categories of Efficiency	Weak Form	Semi-strong Form	Strong Form	
Relative Efficiency	**HIGH** ←———————————————→ **LOW**			
Initial Distribution of Information Among Traders	**BROAD** ←———————————————→ **NARROW**			
Capital Market Mechanisms	Universally Informed Trading	Professionally Informed Trading	Derivatively Informed Trading	Uninformed Trading

The Information Market

. . . Given the operative capital market mechanisms, the relative efficiency of the market's response to particular information depends on the initial distribution of that information among traders. The question now is, what determines that initial distribution? To answer that question, the focus of our analysis shifts to the operation of a different market: the market for information. . . .

The lower the cost of particular information, the wider will be its distribution, the more effective will be the capital market mechanism operating to reflect it in prices, and the more efficient will be the market with respect to it. Understanding market efficiency, then, requires detailed analysis of the nature and dynamics of information costs.

A Taxonomy of Information Costs

Information costs may be divided into three categories. . . . The first category is costs of *acquisition*. These costs will differ in character depending on whether one is the originator of the information or only its subsequent recipient. For the originator, acquisition costs are the costs of producing the information in the first place (as with a discovery or innovation). For the subsequent recipient, acquisition costs are those of securing access to information produced by someone else. This may be done either with the originator's cooperation, as through purchase, or despite the originator's efforts to prevent access, as, at the extreme, through industrial espionage.

The second category is the cost of *processing* information once it is acquired. For both the originator and a subsequent recipient, processing costs are best exemplified by investment in human capital. Evaluation of information, whether self-produced or acquired from others, requires special skills, such as a facility in accounting, finance, or securities analysis, that can ordinarily be obtained only through investment in expensive professional training. The cost of such training is reflected in the wages of the skilled employee or in the opportunity costs of his or her principal.

The third category of information costs arises from the problem of *verification*. Here the task is to determine the quality of information. . . . For the originator, verification costs take the form of further investments to determine the accuracy of the existing information by, for example, hiring an expert to evaluate it. A subsequent recipient may undertake similar efforts, but its principal verification cost is that of determining the veracity of the originator. . . . [V]erification costs may take the form of a direct investigation by the subsequent recipient, similar in character to the efforts undertaken by an originator, or of alternative verification techniques such as bonding or the use of third party experts.[135]

Market Responses to Information Costs

Market participants shape the cost structure of the information market by their efforts to reduce each category of information costs. . . . [E]conomizing on information costs, [in turn] pushes the capital market in the direction of greater efficiency. . . .

[We see] market efforts to economize on acquisition costs through collectivization at both the private and public levels. At the private level, for example, organizations of securities professionals hold cooperative programs in which high company officials speak to many analysts at once, thus reducing the cost of access for any individual analyst. Indeed, the very existence of information intermediaries such as financial and securities experts reflects, in part, the potential for economies of scale and scope in efforts to economize on information costs.

At the collective level, legislation such as the Securities Exchange Act of 1934, which requires continual disclosure of extensive current information by public companies, eliminates the repetitive cost of individual acquisition of information by each analyst. This form of mandatory disclosure collectivizes information acquisition by requiring the originators of information to distribute it and, in some cases, even requiring them to create it.

. . . [A] company that wishes to distribute information indicating favorable corporate prospects may do so at little cost merely by issuing a press release. The financial press as an institution functions to reduce the

---

[135] "Bonding" occurs when the originator of information puts at risk an asset that is forfeited if the information is less accurate than represented. . . . The general problem of verification costs, in relation to products as well as information, is surveyed in Yoram Barzel, *Measurement Cost and the Organization of Markets*, 25 J.L. & Econ. 27 (1982).

acquisition costs of information recipients, in large part by reducing the costs of voluntary distribution to the originators of information.

. . . [T]he specialized business of securities analysis . . . permits substantial economies of scale and scope in utilizing human capital. Similar economies are available in the use of the support equipment, such as computer hardware and software, that is increasingly necessary for performance of the analyst's task. As a result, there are specialists in information processing such as research firms and the research departments of brokerage firms, whose functional advantage is their ability to process information more cheaply than non-specialists.[152]

[Verification costs produce] the most interesting array of market techniques for reducing information costs. Consider the producer of a new financial product. The producer has an obvious incentive to supply the market with information indicating that the product is worth its asking price. . . . [But producers have incentives to exaggerate quality. If] the quality of the information is difficult to determine, its buyer has little choice but to assume that it, and the product it concerns, are of lower quality than represented. Only by discounting the information's accuracy can the buyer be certain that he or she has not unknowingly overpaid. The result is that sellers have too little incentive to provide better information, because "it won't be believed anyway." Poor quality information drives higher quality information from the market.[154] . . .

A broad range of market techniques has developed to deal with this problem by reducing verification costs. At the most costly end of the continuum are solutions that rely solely on buyer verification without the assistance of the originator. For example, buyers may employ experts, such as accountants, lawyers, or business consultants, to examine the offered information. . . .

[Verification costs are reduced if sellers can] "signal" in a believable fashion that they offer high quality information. . . . A typical but costly form of signaling is the investment by sellers in firm-specific capital, such as reputation and advertising, whose value would be reduced if the quality of the product were lower than represented. . . .

[In other situations], outside specialists acting as information intermediaries will offer their own reputation in lieu of the sellers' as a bond of quality. Examples of such specialists in the products market are the Underwriters Laboratory and the Good Housekeeping Seal; in the financial markets, the most obvious example is the role played by rating agencies such as *Standard & Poor's* and *Moody's*. A less obvious but similar role is also played by financial intermediaries, although the verification technique used by these information agents differs. Rather than demonstrating confidence

---

[152] The financial press plays a similar role, offering almost continual analysis of corporate and economic prospects.

[154] This is an example of the "lemon problem." E.g., George Akerlof, *The Market for "Lemons": Quality Uncertainty and the Market Mechanism*, 84 Q.J.Econ. 488 (1970).

in the accuracy of the seller's information by staking their reputation on it, these financial intermediaries signal their belief by purchasing the seller's offering for their *own* account, thereby staking *their* future directly on the accuracy of the seller's information.

A collective, and therefore potentially less expensive, solution to the problem is the legislative imposition of civil and criminal penalties on low quality producers. By imposing costs only on those producers who would exploit high buyer verification costs by falsely pretending to provide quality information, such legislation makes it more costly for producers of low quality goods to mimic the behavior of high quality producers. At the extreme, well-defined and energetically enforced legislation of this type turns the lemon problem on its head and drives low quality producers from the market. . . .

[In sum, from] the perspective of the capital market, market efficiency is a function of the initial distribution of information among traders; from the perspective of the information market, market efficiency is a function of the costs associated with particular information. The common factor is information costs. . . . As information costs decline, more -- and better -- information is available to more traders, and the market becomes more efficient, both because the information is better and because its wider distribution triggers a more effective capital market mechanism.

C.   The Limits of Market Efficiency

Writing in 1984, when there was strong evidence for semistrong market efficiency, Gilson & Kraakman took their principal task to be explaining how markets become efficient. They note but do not pursue the argument that uninformed trading, if *not* random, can push prices away from efficiency. Since then, however, the evidence for various anomalies has multiplied. The next article on *noise trading* complements the Gilson & Kraakman reading by exploring how markets can become *inefficient* and discussing the principal anomalies. Noise trading theory appears to have some explanatory power, but work on developing and testing the theory is still in its early stages.

The authors do not draw the distinction that we drew above between relative and absolute pricing efficiency. Consider as you read, though, which of the tests that they cite bear on relative efficiency, and which on the absolute level of stock prices.

Andrei Shleifer & Lawrence Summers
THE NOISE TRADER APPROACH TO FINANCE
4 J.Econ.Persp. 19 (1990)

If the efficient markets hypothesis was a publicly traded security, its price would be enormously volatile. . . . Michael Jensen was able to write in 1978 that "the efficient markets hypothesis is the best established fact in all of social sciences."[a] Such strong statements portend reversals, the efficient markets hypothesis itself notwithstanding. Stock in the efficient markets hypothesis lost ground rapidly following the publication of Shiller's (1981) and Leroy & Porter's (1981) volatility tests, both of which found stock market volatility to be far greater than could be justified by [subsequent] changes in dividends.[b] The stock snapped back following the papers of Kleidon (1986) and Marsh & Merton (1986) which challenged the statistical validity of volatility tests.[c] A choppy period then ensued, where conflicting econometric studies induced few of the changes of opinion that are necessary to move prices. But the stock in the efficient markets hypothesis -- at least as it has traditionally been formulated -- crashed along with the rest of the market on October 19, 1987. Its recovery has been less dramatic than that of the rest of the market.

This paper reviews an alternative to the efficient markets approach that we and others have recently pursued. Our approach rests on two assumptions. First, some investors are not fully rational and their demand for risky assets is affected by their beliefs or sentiments that are not fully justified by fundamental news. Second, arbitrage -- defined as trading by fully rational investors not subject to such sentiment -- is risky and therefore limited. The two assumptions together imply that changes in investor sentiment are not fully countered by arbitrageurs and so affect security returns. We argue that this approach to financial markets is in many ways superior to the efficient markets paradigm.

Our case for the noise trader approach is threefold. First, theoretical models with limited arbitrage are both tractable and more plausible than models with perfect arbitrage. The efficient markets hypothesis obtains only as an extreme case of perfect riskless arbitrage that is unlikely to apply in practice. Second, the investor sentiment/limited arbitrage approach yields a more accurate description of financial markets than the efficient markets

---

[a] Michael Jensen, *Some Anomalous Evidence Regarding Market Efficiency*, 6 J.Fin.Econ. 95 (1978).

[b] Robert Shiller, *Do Stock Prices Move Too Much to be Justified by Subsequent Changes in Dividends?*, 71 Am.Econ.Rev. 421 (1981); Stephen Leroy & Richard Porter, *Stock Price Volatility: Tests Based on Implied Variance Bounds*, 49 Econometrica 97 (1981). Shiller's work on market efficiency is collected in Robert Shiller, *Market Volatility* (1989).

[c] Allan Kleidon, *Anomalies in Financial Economics*, 59 J.Bus. S285 (1986); Terry Marsh & Robert Merton, *Dividend Variability and Variance Bounds Tests for the Rationality of Stock Market Prices*, 76 Am.Econ.Rev. 483 (1986).

paradigm. The approach not only explains the available anomalies, but also readily explains broad features of financial markets such as trading volume and actual investment strategies. Third, and most importantly, this approach yields new and testable implications about asset prices, some of which have been proved to be consistent with the data. . . .

The Limits of Arbitrage

We think of the market as consisting of two types of investors: "arbitrageurs" -- also called "smart money" and "rational speculators" -- and other investors. Arbitrageurs are defined as investors who form fully rational expectations about security returns. In contrast, the opinions and trading patterns of other investors -- also known as "noise traders" and "liquidity traders" -- may be subject to systematic biases. In practice, the line between arbitrageurs and other investors may be blurred, but for our argument it helps to draw a sharp distinction between them, since the arbitrageurs do the work of bringing prices toward fundamentals.

Arbitrageurs play a central role in standard finance. They trade to ensure that if a security has a perfect substitute -- a portfolio of other securities that yields the same returns -- then the price of the security equals the price of that substitute portfolio. If the price of the security falls below that of the substitute portfolio, arbitrageurs sell the portfolio and buy the security until the prices are equalized, and vice versa if the price of a security rises above that of the substitute portfolio. When the substitute is indeed perfect, this arbitrage is riskless. As a result, arbitrageurs have perfectly elastic demand for the security at the price of its substitute portfolio. . . .

Although riskless arbitrage ensures that relative prices are in line, it does not help to pin down price levels of, say, stocks or bonds as a whole. These classes of securities do not have close substitute portfolios, and therefore if for some reason they are mispriced, there is no riskless hedge for the arbitrageur. For example, an arbitrageur who thinks that stocks are underpriced cannot buy stocks and sell the substitute portfolio, since such a portfolio does not exist. The arbitrageur can instead simply buy stocks in hopes of an above-normal return, but this arbitrage is no longer riskless. If the arbitrageur is risk-averse, his demand for underpriced stocks will be limited. With a finite number of arbitrageurs, their combined demand curve is no longer perfectly elastic.

Two types of risk limit arbitrage. The first is fundamental risk. . . . Selling "overvalued" stocks is risky because there is always a chance that the market will do very well. Fear of such a loss limits the arbitrageur's original position, and keeps his short-selling from driving prices all the way down to fundamentals. The second source of risk that limits arbitrage comes from unpredictability of the future resale price. Suppose again that stocks are overpriced and an arbitrageur is selling them short. As long as the arbitrageur is thinking of liquidating his position in the future, he must bear the risk that at that time stocks will be *even more* overpriced than they are today. . . .

Japanese equities in the 1980s illustrate the limits of arbitrage. During this period, Japanese equities have sold at the price earnings multiples of between 20 and 60, and have continued to climb. Expected growth rates of dividends and risk premia required to justify such multiples seem unrealistic. Nonetheless, an investor who believes that Japanese equities are overvalued and wants to sell them short, must confront two types of risk. First, what if Japan actually does perform so well that these prices are justified? Second, how much more out of line can prices get, and for how long, before Japanese equities return to more realistic prices? Any investor who sold Japanese stocks short in 1985, when the price earnings multiple was 30, would have lost his shirt as the multiples rose to 60 in 1986.[d]

These arguments that risk makes arbitrage ineffective actually understate the limits of arbitrage. After all, they presume that the arbitrageur knows the fundamental value of the security. In fact, the arbitrageur might not exactly know what this value is, or be able to detect price changes that reflect deviations from fundamentals. . . . Are economists certain that Japanese stocks are overpriced at a price earnings ratio of 50?

Substantial evidence shows that, contrary to the efficient markets hypothesis, arbitrage does not completely counter responses of prices to fluctuations in uninformed demand. . . . Being added to the S&P 500 is not a plausible example of new information about the stock, since stocks are picked for their representativeness and not for performance potential. However, a stock added to the S&P 500 is subsequently acquired in large quantities by the so-called "index funds," whose holdings just represent the index. Both Harris & Gurel (1986) and Shleifer (1986) find that announcements of inclusions into the index are accompanied by share price increases of 2 to 3%. Moreover, the magnitude of these increases over time has risen, paralleling the growth of assets in index funds.[e] . . .

Further evidence on price pressure when no news is transmitted comes from Ritter's (1988) work on the January effect. The January effect is the name for the fact that small stocks have outperformed market indices by a significant percentage each January over the last 50 or so years. Ritter finds that small stocks are typically sold by individual investors in December -- often to realize capital losses -- and then bought back in January. These share shifts explain the January effect as long as arbitrage by institutions and

---

[d] See Kenneth French & James Poterba, *Are Japanese Stock Prices Too High*, 29 J.Fin.Econ. 337 (1991). American skepticism about Japanese stock prices in the late 1980s seems especially appropriate today, after the Nikkei 225 index dropped below 15,000 yen in 1992, down over 60% from a 1989 high of over 38,000 yen.

[e] Lawrence Harris & Eitan Gurel, *Price and Volume Effects Associated with Changes in the S&P 500: New Evidence for the Existence of Price Pressure*, 41 J.Fin. 851 (1986); Andrei Shleifer, *Do Demand Curves for Stocks Slope Down?*, 41 J.Fin. 579 (1986).

market insiders is ineffective, since aggressive arbitrage should eliminate the price effects of temporary trading patterns by individual investors.[f] . . .

French & Roll (1986) look at a period when the U.S. stock market was closed on Wednesdays and find that the market is less volatile on these days than on Wednesdays when it is open [even though the supply of fundamental news is presumably the same].[g] [Roll (1988)] finds that individual stocks exhibit significant price movements unrelated to the market on days when there are no public news about these stocks.[h] A similar and more dramatic result is obtained for the aggregate stock market by Cutler, Poterba, & Summers (1989), who find that the days of the largest aggregate market movements are not the days of most important fundamental news and vice versa.[i] The common conclusion of these studies is that news *alone* does not move stock prices; uninformed changes in demand move them too.

Investor Sentiment

Some shifts in investor demand for securities are completely rational. . . . [But] some seem to be a response to changes in expectations or sentiment that are not fully justified by information. Such changes can be a response to pseudo-signals that investors believe convey information about future returns but that would not convey such information in a fully rational model. An example of such pseudo-signals is advice of brokers or financial gurus. We use the term "noise traders" to describe such investors. . . . Changes in demand can also reflect investors' use of inflexible trading strategies or of "popular models." . . . One such strategy is trend chasing. Although these changes in demand are unwarranted by fundamentals, they can be related to fundamentals, as in the case of overreaction to news.

These demand shifts will only matter if they are correlated across noise traders. If all investors trade randomly, their trades cancel out and there are no aggregate shifts in demand. Undoubtedly, some trading in the market brings together noise traders with different models who cancel each other out. However, many trading strategies based on pseudo-signals, noise, and popular models are correlated, leading to aggregate demand shifts. The reason for this is that judgment biases afflicting investors in processing information tend to be the same. Subjects in psychological experiments tend to make the same mistake; they do not make random mistakes. . . .

Many of these persistent mistakes are relevant for financial markets. For example, experimental subjects tend to be overconfident, which makes

---

[f] Jay Ritter, *The Buying and Selling Behavior of Individual Investors and the Turn of the Year*, 43 J.Fin. 701 (1988).

[g] Kenneth French & Richard Roll, *Stock Return Variances: The Arrival of Information and the Reaction of Traders*, 17 J.Fin.Econ. 5 (1986).

[h] Richard Roll, R^2, 43 J.Fin. 541 (1988).

[i] David Cutler, James Poterba & Lawrence Summers, *What Moves Stock Prices?*, J. Portfolio Mgmt. 4 (Spr.1989).

them take on more risk. Experimental subjects also tend to extrapolate past time series, which can lead them to chase trends. Finally, in making inferences experimental subjects put too little weight on base rates and too much weight on new information, which might lead them to overreact to news. . . .

A look at how market participants behave provides perhaps the most convincing evidence that noise rather than information drives many of their decisions. Investors follow market gurus and forecasters, such as Joe Granville and "Wall Street Week." . . . So-called "technical analysis" is another example of demand shifts without a fundamental rationalization. Technical analysis typically calls for buying more stocks when stocks have risen (broke through a barrier), and selling stocks when they fall through a floor. . . .

There can be little doubt that these sorts of factors influence demand for securities, but can they be big enough to make a difference? The standard economist's reason for doubting the size of these effects has been to posit that investors trading on noise might lose their money to arbitrageurs, leading to a diminution of their wealth and effect on demand. Noise traders might also learn the error of their ways and reform into rational arbitrageurs.

However, the argument that noise traders lose money and eventually disappear is not self-evident. First, noise traders might be on average more aggressive than the arbitrageurs -- either because they are overoptimistic or because they are overconfident -- and so bear more risk. If risk-taking is rewarded in the market, noise traders can earn higher expected returns even despite buying high and selling low on average. The risk rewarded by the market need not even be fundamental; it can be the resale price risk arising from the unpredictability of future noise traders' opinions. With higher expected returns, noise traders as a group do not disappear from the market rapidly, if at all. . . .

Learning and imitation may not adversely affect noise traders either. When noise traders earn high average returns, many other investors might imitate them, ignoring the fact that they took more risk and just got lucky. Such imitation brings more money to follow noise trader strategies. Noise traders themselves might become even more cocky, attributing their investment success to skill rather than luck. As noise traders who do well become more aggressive, their effect on demand increases.

The case against the importance of noise traders also ignores the fact that new investors enter the market all the time, and old investors who have lost money come back. These investors are subject to the same judgment biases as the current survivors in the market, and so add to the effect of judgment biases on demand. . . .

Explaining the Puzzles

When arbitrage is limited, and investor demand for securities responds to noise and to predictions of popular models, security prices move in response to these changes in demand as well as to changes in fundamentals. Arbitrageurs counter the shifts in demand prompted by changes in investor sentiment, but do not eliminate the effects of such shifts on the price completely.

In this market, prices vary more than is warranted by changes in fundamentals, since they respond to shifts in investor sentiment as well as to news. Stock returns are predictably mean-reverting, meaning that high stock returns lead to lower expected stock returns. This prediction has in fact been documented for the United States as well as the foreign stock prices by Fama & French (1988) and Poterba & Summers (1988).[j] . . .

This approach fits very neatly with the conventional nonacademic view of financial markets. On that view, the key to investment success is not just predicting future fundamentals, but also predicting the movement of other active investors. Market professionals spend considerable resources tracking price trends, volume, short interest, odd lot volume, investor sentiment indexes and numerous other gauges of demand for equities. Tracking these possible indicators of demand makes no sense if prices responded only to fundamental news and not to investor demand. They make perfect sense, in contrast, in a world where investor sentiment moves prices and so predicting changes in this sentiment pays. The prevalence of investment strategies based on indicators of demand in financial markets suggests the recognition by arbitrageurs of the role of demand.

Not only do arbitrageurs spend time and money to predict noise trader moves, they also make active attempts to take advantage of these moves. When noise traders are optimistic about particular securities, it pays arbitrageurs to create more of them. These securities might be mutual funds, new share issues, penny oil stocks, or junk bonds: anything that is overpriced at the moment. . . .

When they bet against noise traders, arbitrageurs begin to look like noise traders themselves. They pick stocks instead of diversifying, because that is what betting against noise traders requires. They time the market to take advantage of noise trader mood swings. If these swings are temporary, arbitrageurs who cannot predict noise trader moves simply follow contrarian strategies. It becomes hard to tell the noise traders from the arbitrageurs. . . .

[Closed-end mutual fund discounts provide support for noise trading theories. An] investor who wants to liquidate his holdings of a closed-end fund must sell his shares to other investors; he cannot just redeem his shares as with an open-end fund. Closed-end funds present one of the most interesting puzzles in finance, because their fundamental value -- the value of the assets in their portfolios -- is observed, and tends to be systematically higher than the price at which these funds trade. The pervasiveness of

---

[j] Eugene Fama & Kenneth French, *Permanent and Temporary Components of Stock Market Prices*, 96 J.Pol.Econ. 246 (1988); James Poterba & Lawrence Summers, *Mean Reversion in Stock Prices: Evidence and Implications*, 22 J.Fin.Econ. 27 (1988).

discounts on closed-end funds is a problem for the efficient markets hypothesis: in the only case where value is observed, it is not equal to the price.

DeLong, Shleifer, Summers & Waldmann (1990) argue that investor sentiment about closed-end funds changes, and that this sentiment also affects other securities. When investors are bullish about closed-end funds, they drive up their prices relative to fundamental values, and discounts narrow or turn into premiums. When investors in contrast are bearish about closed-end funds, they drive down their prices and discounts widen. . . . [Arbitrage] does not effectively eliminate discounts on closed-end funds. An arbitrageur who buys a discounted fund and sells short its portfolio runs the risk that at the time he liquidates his position the discount widens and so his arbitrage results in a loss.[k] . . .

This theory of closed-end funds has a number of new empirical implications, investigated by Lee, Shleifer and Thaler (1991). First, it predicts that discounts on different closed-end funds fluctuate together, since they reflect changes in investor sentiment. This prediction is confirmed. Second, the theory predicts that new funds get started when investors are optimistic about funds, which is when old funds sell at a small discount or a premium. It is indeed the case that discounts on seasoned funds are much narrower in years when more new funds start. Perhaps most interestingly, the theory predicts that discounts on closed-end funds reflect the investor sentiment factor that also affects prices of other securities, which may have nothing to do with closed-end funds. Consistent with this prediction, Lee, Shleifer & Thaler find that when discounts on closed-end funds narrow, small stock portfolios tend to do well.[l] . . .

Implications of Positive Feedback Trading

One of the strongest investor tendencies documented in both experimental and survey evidence is the tendency to extrapolate or to chase the trend. Trend chasers buy stocks after they rise and sell stocks after they fall: they follow positive feedback strategies. Other strategies that depend on extrapolative expectations are "stop loss" orders, which prescribe selling after a certain level of losses, regardless of future prospects, and portfolio insurance, which involves buying more stocks (to raise exposure to risk) when prices rise and selling stocks (to cut exposure to risk) when prices fall.

When some investors follow positive feedback strategies -- buy when prices rise and sell when prices fall -- it need no longer be optimal for arbitrageurs to counter shifts in the demand of these investors. Instead, it may pay arbitrageurs to jump on the bandwagon themselves. Arbitrageurs

---

[k] J. Bradford DeLong, Andrei Shleifer, Lawrence Summers & Robert Waldmann, *Noise Trader Risk in Financial Markets*, 98 J.Pol.Econ. 703 (1990).

[l] Charles Lee, Andrei Shleifer & Richard Thaler, *Investor Sentiment and the Closed End Funds Puzzle*, 46 J.Fin. 75 (1991).

then optimally buy the stocks that positive feedback investors get interested in when their prices rise. When price increases feed the buying of other investors, arbitrageurs sell out near the top and take their profits. . . . Although eventually arbitrageurs sell out and help prices return to fundamentals, in the short run they feed the bubble rather than help it to dissolve.

Some speculators indeed believe that jumping on the bandwagon with the noise traders is the way to beat them. George Soros, the successful investor and author of *Alchemy of Finance* (1987), describes his strategy during the conglomerate boom in the 1960s and the Real Estate Investment Trust boom in the 1970s precisely in these terms. The key to success, says Soros, was not to counter the irrational wave of enthusiasm about conglomerates, but rather to ride this wave for awhile and sell out much later. . . .

Positive feedback trading reinforced by arbitrageurs' jumping on the bandwagon leads to a positive autocorrelation of returns at short horizons. Eventual return of prices to fundamentals, accelerated as well by arbitrage, entails a negative autocorrelation of returns at longer horizons. Since news results in price changes that are reinforced by positive feedback trading, stock prices overreact to news.[m]

These predictions have been documented in a number of empirical studies. Cutler, Poterba and Summers (1989) find evidence of a positive correlation of returns at horizons of a few weeks or months and a negative one at horizons of a few years for several stock, bond, foreign exchange, and gold markets. They report the average first order monthly serial correlation of more than .07 for 13 stock markets, and positive in every case.[n]. . .

The presence of positive feedback traders in financial markets also makes it easier to interpret historical episodes, such as the sharp market increase and the crash of 1987. According to standard finance, the market crash of October 1987 reflected either a large increase in risk premiums because the economy became a lot riskier, or a large decrease in expected future growth rate of dividends. These theories have the obvious problem that they do not explain what news prompted a 22% devaluation of the American corporate sector on October 19. Another problem is that there is no evidence that risk increased tremendously -- volatility indeed jumped up but came back rapidly as it usually does -- or that expected dividend growth has been revised sharply down. . . . Perhaps most strikingly, Seyhun (1990)

---

[m] *Autocorrelation* is a technical term that means that today's change in stock price predicts (correlates with) future stock price changes. *Positive* autocorrelation means that an increase today predicts a further increase in the future (bull markets tend to continue). *Negative* autocorrelation, also called *mean-reversion*, means that an increase in stock price today predicts a decrease in the future (bull markets tend to be followed by bear markets). Autocorrelation, whether positive or negative, is inconsistent with the weak form of ECMH, under which stock prices should follow a random walk.

[n] David Cutler, James Poterba & Lawrence Summers, *Speculative Dynamics*, 58 Rev.Econ.Stud. 529 (1991).

finds that corporate insiders bought stocks in record numbers during and after the crash, and moreover bought more of the stocks that later had a greater rebound. Insiders did not share the view that growth of dividends will slow or that risk will increase, *and they were right!*[o] Fully rational theories have a problem with the crash.

The crash is much easier to understand in a market with significant positive feedback trading. Positive feedback trading can rationalize the dramatic price increases during 1987, as more and more investors chase the trend. Positive feedback trading, exacerbated by possible frontrunning by investment banks, can also explain the depth of the crash once it has started. One still needs a theory of what broke the market on October 19, but the bad news during the previous week might have initiated the process, albeit with some lag.

Note on Noise Trading

1. *John Maynard Keynes on Investing as a Beauty Contest.* The Dean of the efficient market skeptics is John Maynard Keynes. In the book which laid the foundations for Keynesian economics, he stressed the difficulty of valuing securities from first principles, and argued that professional investors mostly didn't try. Keynes wrote:

> [Most professionals] are, in fact, largely concerned, not with making superior long-term forecasts of the probable yield of an investment over its whole life, but with foreseeing changes in the conventional basis of valuation a short time ahead of the general public. . . . For it is not sensible to pay 25 for an investment of which you believe the prospective yield to justify a value of 30, if you also believe that the market will value it at 20 three months hence. . .
>
> .
>
> [P]rofessional investment may be likened to those newspaper competitions in which the competitors have to pick the six prettiest faces from a hundred photographs, the prize being awarded to the competitor whose choice most nearly corresponds to the average preferences of the competitors as a whole; so that each competitor has to pick, not those faces which he himself finds prettiest, but those which he thinks likeliest to catch the fancy of the other competitors, all of whom are looking at the problem from the same point of view.[6]

---

[o] Nejat Seyhun, *Overreaction or Fundamentals: Some Lessons From Insiders' Response to the Market Crash of 1987*, 45 J.Fin. 1363 (1990).

[6] John Maynard Keynes, *The General Theory of Employment, Interest, and Money* 154-56 (1936). To similar effect, though less colorful, is the description by Benjamin Graham and David Dodd, the founders of the field of security analysis. They described the stock market as a "voting machine" in the short run, and a "weighing machine" only over the long term. Benjamin Graham & David Dodd, *Security Analysis* 23 (1st ed.1934).

2. *If Prices are Inefficient, Why Don't Professionals Beat the Market?* Among the more important tests of ECMH are the many studies that show that market professionals don't consistently outperform the market. The efficient markets explanation is that professionals, all trying to find undervalued stocks, compete away each other's profitable opportunities. Noise trading proponents respond that this is well and good, *if* that's what market professionals are trying to do. But if, as Keynes believed, most professionals are trying to outguess each other on short-term price movements, it's not surprising, nor very probative on whether prices are efficient, that the average professional achieves average results.[7]

3. *Herd Behavior Models.* Finance economists have recently developed models of "herd behavior" by investors, which can lead to departures from efficient pricing. In these models: (i) some investors make valuation mistakes; (ii) all investors recognize that their information may be outdated or their beliefs inaccurate; and (iii) accordingly, all investors pay some attention to the market price, as evidence of the information or beliefs of other investors. In such a world, if enough investors make a common mistake, the mistake will be reinforced by the efforts of other investors to learn from the (now incorrect) market price. Mistakes can be self-reinforcing, even if all investors are rationally trying to find bargains.[8] Empirical studies, though, have thus far found little evidence of herd behavior by institutional investors.[9]

4. *Rational Bubble Models.* Shleifer & Summers discuss the possibility that arbitrageurs may sometimes find it profitable to buy an already overpriced stock, in the belief that it will become still more overpriced, and they will be able to sell ahead of the crowd. Finance economists have recently developed theoretical models of "rational bubbles," in which once a price bubble forms, investors who expect the bubble to grow for a while, and then collapse at an unknown future time, will rationally act to reinforce the mispricing.[10]

Rational bubble models are analytically similar to herd behavior models. Either way, informed investors act to reinforce the pricing errors of other

---

[7] See Louis Lowenstein, *What's Wrong With Wall Street: Short-Term Gain and the Absentee Shareholder* 52-53 (1988).

[8] See, e.g., Abhijit Banerjee, *A Simple Model of Herd Behavior*, 107 Q.J.Econ. 797 (1992); David Scharfstein & Jeremy Stein, *Herd Behavior and Investment*, 80 Am.Econ.Rev. 465 (1990); David Romer, *Rational Asset Price Movements Without News* (NBER Working Paper No. 4121, 1992); Ivo Welch, *Sequential Sales, Learning & Cascades*, 47 J.Fin. 695 (1992).

[9] See Josef Lakonishok, Andrei Shleifer & Robert Vishny, *The Impact of Institutional Trading on Stock Prices*, 32 J.Fin.Econ. 23 (1992).

[10] See, e.g., J. Bradford DeLong, Andrei Shleifer, Lawrence Summers & Robert Waldman, *Positive Feedback Investment Strategies and Destabilizing Rational Speculation*, 45 J.Fin. 379 (1990).

investors.   In herd behavior models, informed investors *unknowingly* reinforce price bubbles because they aren't sure of the quality of their own information.   In rational bubble models, informed investors *knowingly* reinforce price bubbles because they believe that the bubble will persist for a while. The skill to succeed at buying into a bubble and getting out before the crowd on a consistent basis, though, is likely as rare as the skill to outperform the market by analyzing fundamentals.

5. *How Far From True Value Can Prices Go?* How far can noise trading push prices from fair value? Fischer Black, in the article that popularized the term *noise trading*, offers this suggestion:

> All estimates of value are noisy, so we can never know how far away price is from value. However, we might define an efficient market as one in which price is within a factor of 2 of value, i.e., the price is more than half of value and less than twice value. The factor of 2 is arbitrary, of course. Intuitively, though, it seems reasonable to me, in the light of sources of uncertainty about value and the strength of the forces tending to cause price to return to value. By this definition, I think almost all markets are efficient almost all of the time. "Almost all" means at least 90%.[11]

6. *Relative versus Absolute Efficiency.* We noted earlier in this chapter that the evidence for relative pricing efficiency of one stock relative to another is stronger than the evidence for absolute efficiency. Why might relative pricing be more efficient? Louis Lowenstein offers this explanation for the persistence of pricing errors, which has special force for the terribly difficult task of estimating the correct absolute level of stock prices:

> [Given] the overwhelming uncertainties affecting any long-term estimates of business and competition, given the lack of a sufficient basis for calculated mathematical projections, [we] take the next best course. We simply and conveniently assume that the current state of the world -- the economy, politics, war, climate, and so on -- represents a state of equilibrium and that the existing pattern or trend will continue indefinitely into the future until something happens to disturb it. Second, we assume that the stock market's valuations (and other markets' as well) reflect everything there is to know about business realities and prospects and that *they will change only as new information appears.*[12]

7. *Fads in the IPO market.* Discounts on closed-end mutual funds as one area where investor sentiment has predictive value: Closed-end fund discounts narrow in bull markets, and widen in bear markets. Initial public

---

[11] Fischer Black, *Noise*, 46 J.Fin. 529, 533 (1986).

[12] Louis Lowenstein, *Sense and Nonsense in Corporate Finance* 13 (1991) (emphasis in original) (citing John Keynes, *The General Theory of Employment, Interest and Money* (1936)).

offerings (IPOs) show similar swings. The annual volume of IPOs varies widely, typically soaring in bull markets, and almost disappearing in bear markets. Figure 5-5 shows this pattern:

Figure 5-5
Number of IPOs per Month, 1960-1992

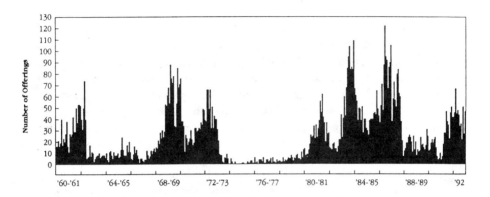

Source: Roger Ibbotson, Jody Sindelar & Jay Ritter, *The Market Problems with the Pricing of Initial Public Offerings*, J.Applied Corp.Fin. 66, fig. 2 (Spr.1994).

In addition, the short-run underpricing of IPOs (the tendency for stock price to rise above the offering price immediately after the offering) increases in IPO boom periods. At the same time, over the several years following the initial offering, IPOs seriously *underperform* the market, and this underperformance is stronger for offerings made during "hot" periods. These phenomena are not limited to the U.S.[13] This behavior is inconsistent with a semi-strong efficient IPO market, but fits the investor fad hypothesis nicely.

8. *Data Mining*. Recall the discussion by Fischer Black in Chapter 4 of the dangers of data mining. Concerns about data mining -- the tendency for studies that show inefficiencies to be published, while studies that find no evidence of inefficiency are relegated to the researcher's file cabinet -- apply with equal force to studies of market efficiency.

9. *How Strong is the Evidence for Noise Trading?* In addition to the ubiquitous problem of possible data mining, some of the evidence that seems to support noise trading theory can be questioned on statistical grounds, or

---

[13] See Jay Ritter, *The Long-Run Performance of Initial Public Offerings*, 46 J.Fin. 3 (1991); Tim Loughran & Jay Ritter, *The Timing and Subsequent Performance of IPOs: The U.S. and International Evidence* (working paper, 1993); Rajan Raghuuram & Henri Servaes, *The Effect of Market Conditions in Initial Public Offerings* (CRSP working paper no. 378, 1993).

interpreted in a way consistent with ECMH. To give a flavor for this problem, we consider below one piece of evidence that Shleifer & Summers cite: multi-year stock prices show *mean-reversion* -- bull markets tend to be followed by bear markets and vice versa. Shleifer & Summers interpret this as evidence that the market overreacts to fundamental news. Eugene Fama, though, in a recent review, calls the mean-reversion studies "a statistical power failure."[14] Fama explains:

> [Shiller (1984) and Summers (1986)] present simple models in which stock prices take large slowly decaying swings away from fundamental values (fads, or irrational bubbles), but short-horizon returns have little autocorrelation. In the Shiller-Summers model, the market is highly inefficient, but in a way that is missed in tests on short-horizon returns.[a]. . .
>
> The Shiller-Summers challenge spawned a series of papers on the predictability of long-horizon returns from past returns. The evidence at first seemed striking, but the tests turn out to be largely fruitless. Thus, Fama & French (1988) find that the autocorrelations of returns on diversified portfolios of NYSE stocks for the 1926-1985 period have the pattern predicted by the Shiller-Summers model. The autocorrelations are close to 0 at short horizons, but they become strongly negative, around -0.25 to -0.4, for 3- to 5-year returns. Even with 60 years of data, however, the [need for a long time window to conduct] tests on long-horizon returns imply [that the tests have] small sample sizes and low [statistical] power. More telling, when Fama & French delete the 1926-1940 period from the tests, the evidence of strong negative autocorrelation in 3- to 5-year returns disappears.[b]
>
> Similarly, Poterba & Summers (1988) find that, for *N* from 2 to 8 years, the variance of *N*-year returns on diversified portfolios grows much less than in proportion to *N*.[c] This is consistent with the hypothesis that there is negative autocorrelation in returns induced by temporary price swings. Even with 115 years (1871-1985) of data, however, the variance tests for long-horizon returns provide weak statistical evidence against the hypothesis that returns have no autocorrelation and prices are random walks.[15]

Fama also argues that mean-reversion, *if it exists*, could be consistent with market efficiency. Suppose that: (i) markets are efficient; (ii) the expected return that investors demand on stock portfolios varies randomly over time around a central value; and (iii) these fluctuations are unrelated to changes in investor expectations about future cash flows. In such a world,

---

[14] Eugene Fama, *Efficient Capital Markets: II*, 46 J.Fin. 1575, 1582 (1991).

[a] Robert Shiller, *Stock Prices and Social Dynamics*, 2 Brookings Papers on Econ. Activity 457 (1984), reprinted in Robert Shiller, *Market Volatility* ch. 1 (1989); Lawrence Summers, *Does the Stock Market Rationally Reflect Fundamental Values?*, 41 J.Fin. 591 (1986).

[b] Eugene Fama & Kenneth French, *Permanent and Temporary Components of Stock Market Prices*, 96 J.Pol.Econ. 246 (1988).

[c] James Poterba & Lawrence Summers, *Mean Reversion in Stock Prices: Evidence and Implications*, 22 J.Fin.Econ. 27 (1988).

[15] Fama (1991), *supra* note 14, at 1580-81.

an increase in the expected return demanded by investors will cause stock prices to decline, relative to a long-term trend line. The price decline will be gradually erased by the higher returns that investors will now receive. Similarly, a decrease in the expected return demanded by investors will cause stock prices to increase, but the increase will gradually be erased by the lower returns that investors will now receive. In such a world, we will observe mean reversion, but the mean-reversion does not imply that investors are overreacting. Fama concludes:

> [A] ubiquitous problem in time-series tests of market efficiency, with no clear solution, is that irrational bubbles in stock prices are indistinguishable from rational time-varying expected returns.[16]

Statistical attacks have also been launched against other observed anomalies, such as the tendency for a "contrarian" investment strategy of buying stocks that have dropped in price.[17] The disputes among scholars over whether or not the observed anomalies reflect real inefficiencies in the market are likely to continue for some time.

10. *When Do Investors Overreact or Underreact?* The challenge for noise trading theories, as they develop, will be to explain *when* investors overreact, when they don't, and *why*. There are literally hundreds of event studies of market reaction to specific news events. Most do not find evidence of investor overreaction. Examples are the stock split study by Fama, Fisher, Jensen & Roll, discussed in the Lorie, Dodd & Kimpton excerpt above, and the many studies, discussed later in this book, of the reaction of target stock prices to takeover announcements. These studies must be weighed against the studies that find evidence of overreaction.[18]

11. *Investor Underreaction.* Do investors sometimes *underreact* to new information? A recent study suggests -- contrary to the popular wisdom that investors overreact to bad earnings reports -- that stock prices do not fully impound the implication of a single earnings announcement for future earnings. Instead, "the three-day price reactions to announcements of earnings for quarters $t + 1$ through $t + 4$ are predictable, based on earnings of quarter t."[19]

---

[16] *Id.* at 1581.

[17] See, e.g., Ray Ball, S.P. Kothari & Jay Shanken, *Problems in Measuring Portfolio Performance: An Application to Contrarian Investment Strategies* (Bradley Pol'y Res.Ctr., working paper FR 93-07, 1993).

[18] See, e.g., Navin Chopra, Josef Lakonishok & Jay Ritter, *Measuring Abnormal Performance: Do Stocks Overreact?*, 31 J.Fin.Econ. 235 (1992).

[19] Victor Bernard & Jacob Thomas, *Evidence that Stock Prices Do Not Fully Reflect the Implications of Current Earnings for Future Earnings*, 13 J.Acct. & Econ. 305, 305 (1990); see also Claudia Mott & Daniel Coker, *Earnings Surprise in the Small-Cap World*, J.

12. *Cognitive Errors as a Cause of Market Inefficiency.* Shleifer &
Summers note that systematic human cognitive errors might lead to
mispricing. These errors are discussed in the next section.

D. Systematic Errors in Human Cognition

Research in cognitive psychology demonstrates that human beings make
a number of standard cognitive errors. Moreover, experimental subjects
often fail to fully correct these errors *even when told about them*. These
errors seem likely to affect the value assessments of *particular investors*,
perhaps even *most* investors, in public securities markets. Because the errors
are systematic, they won't average to zero across a large number of
investors. But cognitive errors, if reflected in price, will also give rise to
profitable arbitrage for investors who recognize them. The extent to which
cognitive biases affect equilibrium prices will depend on the relative strength
of the biases and of the correcting force of arbitrage.

Independent of their effect on security prices, cognitive errors may
infect the judgments of the CEOs and financial advisors who must decide
whether firm *A* should buy firm *B*, and at what price. These errors might
explain why firms act *as if* accounting earnings affect stock prices, despite
evidence to the contrary, or why bidders often overpay in acquisitions.

Amos Tversky & Daniel Kahneman, JUDGMENT UNDER
UNCERTAINTY: HEURISTICS AND BIASES
185 Sci. 1124 (1974)[*]

[P]eople rely on a limited number of heuristic principles which reduce
the complex tasks of assessing probabilities and predicting values to simpler
judgmental operations. In general, these heuristics are quite useful, but
sometimes they lead to severe and systematic errors. . . .

Representativeness

Many of the probabilistic questions with which people are concerned
belong to one of the following types: What is the probability that object *A*
belongs to class *B*? What is the probability that event *A* originates from
process *B*? What is the probability that process *B* will generate event *A*? In

---

Portfolio Mgmt. 64 (Fall 1993). Underreaction to earnings surprises can explain most of the
long-standing *Value Line anomaly* -- the tendency for the timeliness rankings published by the
Value Line Investment Survey (which depend in large part on earnings surprises) to predict
stock price returns. See John Affleck-Graves & Richard Mendenhall, *The Relation Between
the Value Line Enigma and Post-Earnings-Announcement Drift*, 31 J.Fin.Econ. 75 (1992).

answering such questions, people typically rely on the representativeness heuristic, in which probabilities are evaluated by the degree to which A is representative of B, that is, by the degree to which A resembles B. For example, when A is highly representative of B, the probability that A originates from B is judged to be high. On the other hand, if A is not similar to B, the probability that A originates from B is judged to be low. . . . This approach to the judgment of probability leads to serious errors, because similarity, or representativeness, is not influenced by several factors that should affect judgments of probability.

Insensitivity to Prior Probability of Outcomes

One of the factors that have no effect on representativeness but should have a major effect on probability is the prior probability, or base-rate frequency, of the outcomes. . . .   If people evaluate probability by representativeness, therefore, prior probabilities will be neglected.

This hypothesis was tested in an experiment where prior probabilities were manipulated. . . . Subjects were shown brief personality descriptions of several individuals, allegedly sampled at random from a group of 100 professionals -- engineers and lawyers. The subjects were asked to assess, for each description, the probability that it belonged to an engineer rather than to a lawyer. In one experimental condition, subjects were told that the group from which the descriptions had been drawn consisted of 70 engineers and 30 lawyers. In another condition, subjects were told that the group consisted of 30 engineers and 70 lawyers. The odds that any particular description belongs to an engineer rather than to a lawyer should be higher in the first condition, where there is a majority of engineers, than in the second condition, where there is a majority of lawyers. . . .   [In fact], subjects evaluated the likelihood that a particular description belonged to an engineer rather than to a lawyer by the degree to which this description was representative of the two stereotypes, with little or no regard for the prior probabilities of the categories.

   . . .   [P]rior probabilities were effectively ignored [even when the description] was totally uninformative. The responses to the following description illustrate this phenomenon:

> Dick is a 30 year old man. He is married with no children. A man of high ability and high motivation, he promises to be quite successful in his field. He is well liked by his colleagues.

This description was intended to convey no information relevant to the question of whether Dick is an engineer or a lawyer. Consequently, the probability that Dick is an engineer should equal the proportion of engineers in the group, as if no description had been given. The subjects, however, judged the probability of Dick being an engineer to be .5 regardless of whether the stated proportion of engineers in the group was .7 or .3. . . .

Insensitivity to Sample Size

. . . [I]f probabilities are assessed by representativeness, then the judged probability of a sample statistic will be essentially independent of sample size. Indeed, when subjects assessed the distributions of average height for samples of various sizes, they produced identical distributions. For example, the probability of obtaining an average height greater than 6 feet was assigned the same value for samples of 1000, 100, and 10 men. Moreover, subjects failed to appreciate the role of sample size even when it was emphasized in the formulation of the problem. . . .

Misconceptions of Chance

People expect that a sequence of events generated by a random process will *represent* the essential characteristics of that process even when the sequence is short. In considering tosses of a coin for heads or tails, for example, people regard the sequence H-T-H-T-T-H to be more likely than the sequence H-H-H-T-T-T, which does not appear random, and also more likely than the sequence H-H-H-H-T-H, which does not represent the fairness of the coin. Thus, people expect that the essential characteristics of the process will be represented, not only globally in the entire sequence, but also locally in each of its parts. A locally representative sequence, however, deviates systematically from chance expectation: it contains too many alternations and too few runs.

Another consequence of the belief in local representativeness is the well-known gambler's fallacy. After observing a long run of red on the roulette wheel, for example, most people erroneously believe that black is now due, presumably because the occurrence of black will result in a more representative sequence than the occurrence of an additional red. Chance is commonly viewed as a self-correcting process in which a deviation in one direction induces a deviation in the opposite direction to restore the equilibrium. In fact, deviations are not "corrected" as a chance process unfolds, they are merely diluted. . . .

Insensitivity to predictability

People are sometimes called upon to make such numerical predictions as the future value of a stock, the demand for a commodity, or the outcome of a football game. Such predictions are often made by representativeness. For example, suppose one is given a description of a company and is asked to predict its future profit. If the description of the company is very favorable, a very high profit will appear most representative of that description; if the description is mediocre, a mediocre performance will appear most representative. The degree to which the description is favorable is unaffected by the reliability of that description or by the degree to which it permits accurate prediction. . . .

[For example], subjects were presented with several paragraphs, each describing the performance of a student teacher during a particular practice lesson. Some subjects were asked to *evaluate* the quality of the *lesson* described in the paragraph in percentile scores, relative to a specified population. Other subjects were asked to *predict*, also in percentile scores, the standing of each student teacher 5 years after the practice lesson. . . . [T]he prediction of a remote criterion (success of a teacher after 5 years) was identical to the evaluation of the information on which the prediction was based (the quality of the practice lesson). The students who made these predictions were undoubtedly aware of the limited predictability of teaching competence on the basis of a single trial lesson 5 years earlier; nevertheless, their predictions were as extreme as their evaluations.

The illusion of validity

As we have seen, people often predict by selecting the outcome (for example, an occupation) that is most representative of the input (for example, the description of a person). The confidence they have in their prediction depends primarily on the degree of representativeness (that is, on the quality of the match between the selected outcome and the input) with little or no regard for the factors that limit predictive accuracy. Thus, people express great confidence in the prediction that a person is a librarian when given a description of his personality which matches the stereotype of librarians, even if [told that few people are librarians]. The unwarranted confidence [in predictions based on representativeness] may be called the illusion of validity. . . .

Misconceptions of regression

Suppose a large group of children has been examined on two equivalent versions of an aptitude test. If one selects ten children from among those who did best on one of the two versions, he will usually find their performance on the second version to be somewhat disappointing. Conversely, if one selects ten children from among those who did worst on one version, they will be found, on the average, to do somewhat better on the other version. . . . These observations illustrate a general phenomenon known as regression toward the mean. . . .

In the normal course of life, one encounters many instances of regression toward the mean, in the comparison of the height of fathers and sons, of the intelligence of husbands and wives, or of the performance of individuals on consecutive examinations. Nevertheless, people do not develop correct intuitions about this phenomenon. First, they do not expect regression in many contexts where it is bound to occur. Second, when they recognize the occurrence of regression, they often invent spurious causal explanations for it. We suggest that the phenomenon of regression remains elusive because it is incompatible with the [representativeness heuristic].

The failure to recognize the import of regression can have pernicious consequences, as illustrated by the following observation. In a discussion of flight training, experienced instructors noted that praise for an exceptionally smooth landing is typically followed by a poorer landing on the next try, while harsh criticism after a rough landing is usually followed by an improvement on the next try. The instructors concluded that verbal rewards are detrimental to learning, while verbal punishments are beneficial, contrary to accepted psychological doctrine. This conclusion is unwarranted because of the presence of regression toward the mean. . . .

Availability

There are situations in which people assess the frequency of a class or the probability of an event by the ease with which instances or occurrences can be brought to mind. For example, one may assess the risk of heart attack among middle-aged people by recalling such occurrences among one's acquaintances. Similarly, one may evaluate the probability that a given business venture will fail by imagining various difficulties it could encounter. This judgmental heuristic is called availability. . . .

When the size of a class is judged by the availability of its instances, a class whose instances are easily retrieved will appear more numerous than a class of equal frequency whose instances are less retrievable. In an elementary demonstration of this effect, subjects heard a list of well-known personalities of both sexes and were subsequently asked to judge whether the list contained more names of men than of women. Different lists were presented to different groups of subjects. In some of the lists the men were relatively more famous than the women, and in others the women were relatively more famous than the men. In each of the lists, the subjects erroneously judged that the class (sex) that had the more famous personalities was the more numerous.

In addition to familiarity, there are other factors, such as *salience* [also called *vividness*], which affect the retrievability of instances. For example, the impact of seeing a house burning on the subjective probability of such accidents is probably greater than the impact of reading about a fire in the local paper. Furthermore, recent occurrences are likely to be relatively more available than earlier occurrences. It is a common experience that the subjective probability of traffic accidents rises temporarily when one sees a car overturned by the side of the road. . . .

Adjustment and Anchoring

In many situations, people make estimates by starting from an initial value that is adjusted to yield the final answer. The initial value, or starting point, may be suggested by the formulation of the problem, or it may be the result of a partial computation. In either case, adjustments are typically insufficient. . . . We call this phenomenon *anchoring*.

Insufficient adjustment

In a demonstration of the anchoring effect, subjects were asked to estimate [the percentage of African countries in the U.N.   A] number between 0 and 100 was determined by spinning a wheel of fortune *in the subjects' presence*. The subjects were instructed to indicate first whether [the randomly chosen] number was higher or lower than the [true percentage], and then to estimate the [true percentage]. . . . [T]he median estimates of the percentage of African countries in the United Nations were 25 and 45 for groups that received 10 and 65, respectively, as [random] starting points. Payoffs for accuracy did not reduce the anchoring effect. . . .

In a recent study by Bar-Hillel, subjects were given the opportunity to bet on one of two events.   Three types of events were used: (i) *simple* events, such as drawing a red marble from a bag containing 50% red marbles and 50% white marbles;   (ii) *conjunctive* events, such as drawing a red marble seven times in succession, with replacement, from a bag containing 90% red marbles and 10% white marbles;   and (iii) *disjunctive* events, such as drawing a red marble at least once in seven successive tries, with replacement, from a bag containing 10% red marbles and 90% white marbles.   In this problem, a significant majority of subjects preferred to bet on the conjunctive event (the probability of which is .48) rather than on the simple event (the probability of which is .50).   Subjects also preferred to bet on the simple event rather than on the disjunctive event, which has a probability of .52.

[More generally], people tend to overestimate the probability of conjunctive events and to underestimate the probability of disjunctive events. These biases are readily explained as effects of anchoring.   The stated probability of the elementary event (success at any one stage) provides a natural starting point for the estimation of the probabilities of both conjunctive and disjunctive events.   Since adjustment from the starting point is typically insufficient, the final estimates remain too close to the probabilities of the elementary events in both cases.   Note that the overall probability of a conjunctive event is lower than the probability of each elementary event, whereas the overall probability of a disjunctive event is higher than the probability of each elementary event. . . .

Biases in the evaluation of compound events are particularly significant in the context of planning.   The successful completion of an undertaking, such as the development of a new product, typically has a conjunctive character: for the undertaking to succeed, each of a series of events must occur.   Even when each of these events is very likely, the overall probability of success can be quite low if the number of events is large.   The general tendency to overestimate the probability of conjunctive events leads to unwarranted optimism in the evaluation of the likelihood that a plan will succeed or that a project will be completed on time. . . .

Anchoring in the assessment of subjective probability distributions

[Suppose that a securities analyst is] asked to select a number, X_{90}, such that his subjective probability that this number will be higher than the value of the Dow-Jones average [at a specific future time] is .90. A subjective probability distribution for the value of the Dow-Jones average can be constructed from several such judgments corresponding to different percentiles. [If the analyst's judgment is sound], the true values should fall below X_{01} for 1% of the quantities and above X_{99} for 1% of the quantities. Thus, the true values should fall [below X_{01} or above X_{99} about 2% of the time].

[Investigators] have obtained probability distributions for [the Dow Jones average and many other] quantities from a large number of judges. These distributions indicated large and systematic departures from proper calibration. In most studies, the actual values of the assessed quantities are either smaller than X_{01} or greater than X_{99} for about 30% of the problems. That is, the subjects state overly narrow confidence intervals which reflect more certainty than is justified by their knowledge about the assessed quantities. This bias is common to naive and to sophisticated subjects. . . . [It] is attributable, at least in part, to anchoring.

To select X_{90} for the value of the Dow-Jones average, for example, it is natural to begin by thinking about one's best estimate of the Dow-Jones and to adjust this value upward. If this adjustment -- like most others -- is insufficient, then X_{90} will not be sufficiently extreme. A similar anchoring effect will occur in the selection of X_{10}, which is presumably obtained by adjusting one's best estimate downward. Consequently, the confidence interval between X_{10} and X_{90} will be too narrow, and the assessed probability distribution will be too tight. . . .

Note on Cognitive Biases

1. *Additional Cognitive Biases.* The literature on cognitive biases has exploded since Tversky & Kahneman wrote their review article in 1974. Additional biases documented in the literature that seem relevant to investor behavior include:

(i) *The endowment effect*:   People insist on a higher price to sell something they already own, than to buy the same item if they don't own it.

(ii) *Loss aversion*: Most people are risk averse for *profit* opportunities. They are indifferent, say, between $450 for sure and a 50% chance of gaining $1,000. Economic theory predicts that risk aversion should be roughly the same for gains and losses. Someone who is indifferent between a sure gain of $450 and a 50% chance of gaining $1,000 also ought to be indifferent between losing $550 for sure and a 50% chance of losing $1,000, as long as $1,000 is a small fraction of their total wealth. Either way, they would pay $50 in expected value to avoid uncertainty.

People don't act that way, though. Instead, they tend to be highly risk-averse for profit opportunities, and much less risk-averse, or even risk-preferrers, when they must take a chance to avoid a loss. Someone might, for example, be indifferent between $450 for sure and a 50% chance of gaining $1,000, yet willing to accept a 50% chance of losing $1,000, to avoid a sure loss of only $400. This willingness to gamble to avoid a loss is called *loss aversion*. One can readily imagine loss aversion affecting the relative prices of stocks (which carry a high probability of loss), and high-grade bonds (which carry a low probability of loss if held to maturity, at least in nominal dollars).[20]

(iii) *Insensitivity to small probabilities*:   People have trouble distinguishing between *different* small probabilities, and also tend to systematically overweight small probabilities, in choosing a course of action. For example, they will pay almost as much to avoid a 1% chance of loss as to avoid a 5% chance of the same loss.

(iv) *Cognitive dissonance*: Cognitive dissonance is a catchall phrase for the tendency of people to like to think about some things, and avoid thinking about others. For example, people don't like thinking about bad outcomes, or remembering their own mistakes. Thus, for example, investors whose stock picks have beaten the market half the time and done worse half the time will tend to remember the successes, and forget the failures.

(v) *Self-confidence*: People believe in their own skill. For example, surveys routinely show that 80% of automobile drivers believe that they are more skilled than the average. Investors show similar tendencies. They interpret their successes as reflecting their own skill, and ascribe the losses to bad luck.

How might various cognitive biases affect investor behavior? How might they lead to inefficient pricing, or acquisition mistakes?[21]

---

[20] See Amos Tversky & Daniel Kahneman, *Advances in Prospect Theory: Cumulative Representation of Uncertainty*, 5 J.Risk & Uncertainty 297 (1992).

[21] For a sampling of the literature on cognitive biases, see *Judgement Under Uncertainty: Heuristics and Biases* (Daniel Kahneman, Paul Slovic & Amos Tversky eds.1982); Richard Nisbett & Lee Ross, *Human Inference: Strategies and Shortcomings of Social Judgment* (1980); George Akerlof & William Dickens, *The Economic Consequences of Cognitive Dissonance*, 72 Am.Econ.Rev. 307 (1982); Daniel Kahneman, Jack Knetsch & Richard Thaler, *Anomalies: The Endowment Effect, Loss Aversion, and Status Quo Bias*, 5 J.Econ.Persp. 193 (1991).

2.   *Representativeness and Contrarian Investment Strategies*. Representativeness, including the tendency of people to put too much weight on recent experience, and too little on background probabilities, could explain why contrarian investment strategies (buying out-of-favor stocks) seem to outperform the market as a whole, while glamour stocks tend to underperform the market. Fama & French, in the article excerpted in chapter 3, speculate that out-of-favor stocks, proxied by a low ratio of market value to book value, are fundamentally riskier than other stocks, which would justify higher expected returns. But Josef Lakonishok, Robert Vishny & Andrei Shleifer find no evidence that out-of-favor stocks are riskier. On the contrary, out-of-favor stocks decline much less than glamour stocks in bear markets. These smaller declines are largely responsible for their higher long-term expected returns.[22]

E.   Summary

Thomas Kuhn argues that some scientific paradigms become so deeply embedded in scientific thought that scientists who grow up with a paradigm are often unable to discard it, even after its weakness becomes evident. A shift to a new paradigm must sometimes wait for a new generation of scholars, less wedded to old ways of thinking, to replace the old.[23] Is the efficient market hypothesis such a paradigm, already obsolete but surviving because today's scholars have grown up accepting it?[24]

Our judgment is no, especially if market efficiency is seen as a matter of *how much*, rather than yes or no. There is much evidence that stock prices are a good, even if not a perfect, estimate of value. And it seems unlikely that we will soon find another measure of value that works better, on average and over time, as a guide to investor behavior or legal policy.

In the words of an anonymous philosopher, "all things are difficult to predict, particularly the future." Investors in common stock face the incredibly difficult task of predicting dividends far into the future. The complexity of that task lays the seeds for departures from efficient pricing. But we cannot avoid the need to estimate value, and the difficulties do not disappear if we rely on other sources of value estimates. The consensus investor estimate of value reflected in price may sometimes reflect fads or other biases. But other plausible sources of value estimates -- such as judges in appraisal proceedings, regulators, or corporate managers, seem likely to produce even worse value estimates, on average.

---

[22] Josef Lakonishok, Robert Vishny & Andrei Shleifer, *Contrarian Investment, Extrapolation, and Risk* (NBER working paper no. 4360, May 1993).

[23] Thomas Kuhn, *The Structure of Scientific Revolutions* (1972).

[24] Donald Langevoort, *Theories, Assumptions, and Securities Regulation: Market Efficiency Revisited*, 140 U.Pa.L.Rev. 851 (1992), makes this argument.

In particular, regulators and corporate managers often have incentives to reach systematically biased answers. For example, the managers of a takeover target often claim, and may really believe, that their company is worth more than the bidder is offering. The managers' strong self-interest provides reason to distrust such estimates. Sometimes, the managers are right. But as we will see in Part II, the market's estimate of value seems better on average, even though the managers have superior information about their company.

Chapter 5 Problems

1. You're on vacation, and you take a wrong turn while touring the wine country in upstate New York. You ask a local farmer for directions and are surprised by the trappings of great wealth on the farm. There's a late model Mercedes-Benz sedan in the driveway. The farmer greets you wearing a gold Rolex watch. After getting directions, you comment that your host must produce an extraordinary wine. He answers with a polite "no," and explains that he never was any good at making wine and hasn't made any for twenty years. Instead, he plays the stock market. Once a month, he lets his prize rooster peck at the market reporting section of the Wall Street Journal. Wherever the rooster pecks a hole through the paper, he buys the stock. His return has averaged 20% per year over the last 20 years, and he's never had two down years in a row. He would be happy to manage your money for you. Assume that the farmer's claims are true. Would you let the farmer manage your money? Why or why not?

2. As a guest at the Wealthy Acres Country Club, you are excited at the prospect of getting to meet new people with interests so similar to your own. While you are watching the polo match, one of the members pulls you aside, and blurts out that he must tell you about the new account that his advertising agency just snagged away from another agency. He tells you that Dice Pizza is planning the greatest media blitz of all time. Everything is still in the planning stage now, but in three months time, when the campaign begins, he expects that pizza consumption around the world will increase dramatically, with Dice Pizza grabbing the lion's share of the global pizza market. You realize that the information you've just been given could be of great potential value to you. Dice Pizza is publicly held, and it would be easy to buy some stock, if you so choose. What factors should you consider in deciding whether or not to buy Dice stock based on this information?

3. The stock of Street Corner Auto Parts Corp. has risen fifteen percent in the last week since a rumor that a major auto manufacturer was looking to buy the company circulated on Wall Street. Such an acquisition would probably involve a premium of at least 50% over the pre-rumor market price. What are your thoughts on whether purchasing shares of Street Corner would be a good idea at this point?

4. Corporate officers must report their purchases and sales of their company's stock to the SEC on a monthly basis, where it is available in a public reference room. Several newsletters collect and publish this information. One of the newsletters claims that it has a system for analyzing these reports and generating buy or sell signals from them. Historical analysis shows that following their monthly recommendations by buying the recommended stocks at the closing price on the date when each

recommendation was made would have produced returns that exceed the market by an average of 3% per year, on a risk-adjusted basis.

a) If this pattern continues in the future, which form(s) of market efficiency would it call into question, and why?

b) Should you buy the newsletter? Why or why not?

5. *The Three Boxes*: You are asked to play the following two-stage game: There are 3 boxes on a table. One of them has a $100 bill under it; the others are empty. In stage 1, you must guess which box has the $100 bill. The game host, who knows which box has the bill, then opens the lid of *another* box (not the one you have chosen), and *always* opens an *empty* box. The host can always do this because at least one of the other boxes *must* be empty. At this point in the game, there are two closed boxes, one of which contains the $100 bill. In stage 2, you must decide whether to stick with your initial choice, or to switch and choose the other closed box.

a) Should you keep your initial choice or switch? What is the best strategy?

b) What is the chance that you will win, under the best available strategy?

6. *The AIDS Test*: Lifeco requires all applicants for life insurance to take an AIDS test. A particular applicant has a positive AIDS test. You have no other information about the applicant. You are told that:

- The test produces the correct result 87% of the time -- both for subjects with and without the disease.
- The incidence of the disease in the population is 1%.

(a) How likely is it that an applicant who tests positive really has AIDS?

(b) How likely is it that an applicant who tests negative really does not have AIDS?

7. *The Juror's Fallacy*: A cab was involved in a hit and run accident at night. Two cab companies, the Green and the Blue, operate in the city. You are told that:

- 85% of the cabs are Green and 15% are Blue.
- A witness identified the cab as Blue.

•   The witness can correctly identify the cab's color under the circumstances that existed on the night of the accident 80% of the time.

What is the probability that a Blue cab was involved in the accident? If you can't compute a precise answer, pick a range (0-20%; 20-40%; 40-60%; 60-80%; 80-100%).

$$\frac{.15 \times .80}{(.15 \times .80) + (.2 \div .85)} \approx 41\%$$

CHAPTER 6: EVENT STUDIES:
MEASURING THE IMPACT OF INFORMATION

In a semistrong efficient market, market prices provide an unbiased forecast of the present value of a firm's cash flows, based on all publicly available information. If new information becomes available, market prices respond rapidly and without bias to the new information. This leads to an important class of tests of semistrong efficiency called *event studies*. An event study involves identifying *when* information about a company is released and observing the stock price response. A rapid and unbiased response is consistent with semistrong efficiency.

In Figure 6-1, a particularly important piece of news about firm X is released on day 0, which is called the *announcement date* or the *event date*. This leads to an immediate stock price jump. The stock price fluctuates randomly, in response to other information, or perhaps due to noise trading, both before and after day 0. This response is consistent with semistrong market efficiency.

Figure 6-1
Efficient **Market Response to New Information**

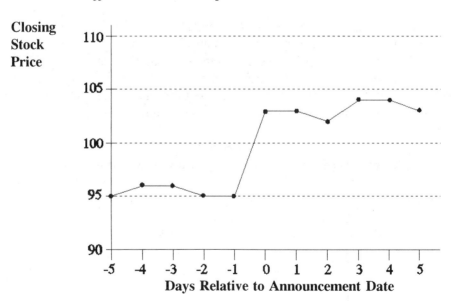

In contrast, the stock price response shown in Figure 6-2, is inconsistent with semistrong market efficiency because it is too *slow* -- it takes several days for the price to move from the old equilibrium price of $95 to the new price of $103. Arbitrageurs could buy firm X's stock right after the announcement and profit from the move to the new equilibrium price.

Figure 6-2
Slow (*Inefficient*) Market Response to New Information

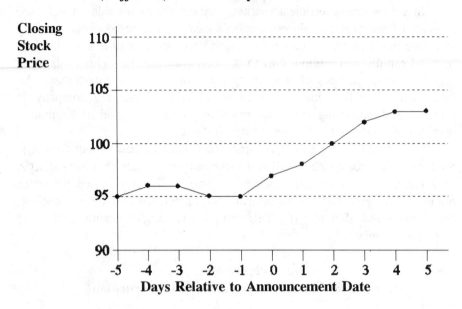

The stock price response shown in Figure 6-3 is also inconsistent with semistrong market efficiency. The response is fast, but it is not *unbiased*. Instead, firm X's stock price overshoots the new equilibrium value of $103, and then settles back to $103 over several days. Arbitrageurs could sell firm Z's stock short after it shoots up in response to the announcement and profit from the gradual decline back to the new equilibrium price.

Figure 6-3
Biased (*Inefficient*) Market Response to New Information

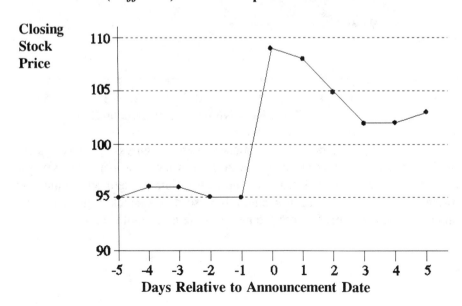

A second use of event studies *assumes* that the stock market is semistrong efficient. In an efficient market, the market price is an unbiased estimate of the present value of the firm's expected future cash flows, *given* a publicly available information set. This is true at all times, including just before and just after new information is released. Thus, the market's response to new information is an unbiased measure of *how important* the information is. A large response means that the information was important; a small change means that the information was unimportant.

For example, in Figure 6-1, investors value firm X at $95 before the announcement, and $100 after the announcement. The $5 per share increase measures how much more investors *think* firm X is worth after the announcement, relative to other firms. The announcement may involve a new event that increases the present value of firm X's expected cash flows by $5. Or the announcement may change investor *beliefs* about firm X's value, while actual value doesn't change at all. Or the price change may reflect a combination of (i) change in firm X's actual value, and (ii) change in investor beliefs about value, independent of actual change in value.

Some announcements appear mostly to affect actual value. For example, takeover bids appear not to change investor beliefs about the target's value as a stand-alone firm.[1] This suggests that the takeover premium reflects an increase in the target's value due to the takeover. Other announcements mostly affect investor beliefs about value. For example, the Fama, Fisher, Jensen & Roll study described in Chapter 5 suggests that stock split announcements affect price because they signal good news about the firm, not because investors value low-priced shares more highly.

Event studies can also provide information on *when* information is released to the market. For example, the target's stock price often creeps up *before* the formal announcement of a takeover bid. Examples of this are shown in Figures 5-3 and 6-8. This provides evidence of news leakage, perhaps through insider trading amplified by the trade and price decoding efforts of market professionals.[2]

Both uses of event studies -- as a *test* of semistrong market efficiency, and as a *measure* of the impact of new information -- are central to evaluating the motives for acquisitions, understanding how acquisitions affect the value of particular firms, and assessing legal policy toward takeovers. Section A of this Chapter introduces techniques for measuring the value of

---

[1] See Chapter 14.

[2] See Gregg Jarrell & Annette Poulsen, *Stock Trading Before the Announcement of Tender Offers: Insider Trading or Market Anticipation?*, 5 J.L.Econ. & Org. 225 (1989); John Pound & Richard Zeckhauser, *Clearly Heard on the Street: The Effect of Takeover Rumors on Stock Prices*, 63 J.Bus. 291 (1990). The statistical tests used to measure the significance of stock price returns require the investigator to first specify an announcement date, and then assess whether the announcement has significantly affected stock prices. One can work backwards -- inferring the release of information by observing a price runup -- only if prior studies clearly establish the importance of the information that has been released.

new information. Section B develops the statistical techniques underlying event studies. Section C provides an example of how event studies can be used to measure the impact of new information. Section D discusses the limits on what event studies can tell us, including the central problem of determining when information is *new*, and the often insoluble problem of determining *why* the market price has reacted to new information when there are competing explanations. Finally, section E discusses methodological issues in conducting event studies, and some common variations in the ways that event studies are conducted.

A.   The Expected Value of Information

Charles Holloway, DECISION MAKING UNDER UNCERTAINTY
348-359 (1979)*

What is the value of information in a particular setting? The basic principle is that *information only has value in a decision problem if it results in a change in some action to be taken by a decision maker*. . . . The value of information can be calculated using [decision tree techniques]. An *information alternative* is created and included in the decision diagram like any other alternative. The *cost* [of obtaining the information] that makes the information alternative equivalent to the *best alternative without the information* is called the *value* of the information. Two cases are usually considered. . . .

Expected Value of Perfect Information (EVPI)

Perfect information about a given event means complete elimination of all uncertainty about the event's outcomes. That is, *after* receiving the information, you will know exactly which outcome will occur. In some cases perfect information *is* obtainable. For instance, if the uncertain event involved the decision of a customer to [sign] a contract, it might be possible to find out what the decision is by offering the customer an incentive for telling you. In other cases perfect information is not possible but is a useful concept. It is useful because it provides an *upper bound* on the value of information in a particular decision, and because the calculations [of the value of perfect information] usually can be done easily.

> ### Expected Value of Perfect Information
> *Definition: Expected Value of Perfect Information (EVPI)* =
> (expected value if perfect information could be obtained) −
> (expected value of the best alternative without information)
>
> ### Expected Value of Sample Information
> *Definition: Expected Value of Imperfect or Sample Information (EVSI)* =
> (expected value of the information alternative) −
> (expected value of the best alternative without information)

There are several ways to visualize and calculate the EVPI. To illustrate the methods, consider the following example.

Example 6-1

A construction contract must be completed prior to [a specified date] to avoid a significant penalty. There are three different plans that can be used for the construction [and four different expected weather types: good (type n_1); hot (type n_2); cold (type n_3); and rainy (type n_4)]. The plans differ primarily in their ability to provide flexibility in the face of varying weather conditions. Plan 1 will be the most profitable if good weather exists during the construction period; however, it is the worst under other conditions. Plan 2 [does relatively well] under all conditions. Plan 3 is good [in good weather and adequate in cold weather] but poor under the other two possible weather types. The plans and their net [profit] in thousands of dollars for the four possible weather types are shown in Table 6-1 along with the assessed probabilities for the weather possibilities. . . .

Table 6-1
Profit Under Varying Weather Conditions

Weather	Plan 1	Plan 2	Plan 3	Probability
Good (n_1)	48	24	40	0.4
Hot (n_2)	16	24	16	0.2
Cold (n_3)	16	32	24	0.2
Rainy (n_4)	16	24	16	0.2
[Expected Profit]	28.8	25.6	27.2	1.0

In this example . . . the expected [profit if you have] *perfect advance information* is $35,200. [If the weather is good, you will choose Plan 1 and earn $48,000; otherwise you will choose Plan 2, and earn either $24,000 or $32,000. The calculation is shown in Table 6-2.] Note that the decision to obtain perfect information does *not* eliminate all uncertainty. You are still (until the perfect information is received) uncertain about what the information will reveal. Without perfect information Plan 1 will yield the maximum expected monetary value of $28,800. Therefore, the value of the perfect information must be the difference between $35,200 and $28,800, or $6,400. . . .

Table 6-2
Net Profit With Perfect Information

Weather	Choice with Perfect Information	[Profit]	Probability
Good (n_1)	Plan 1	48	0.4
Hot (n_2)	Plan 2	24	0.2
Cold (n_3)	Plan 2	32	0.2
Rainy (n_4)	Plan 2	24	0.2
[Expected Profit]		35.2	1.0

Another method of visualizing EVPI is to consider how much perfect information would be worth to you for each possible weather state. For instance, what if the information transmitted were that weather type n_1 would occur? Without this information you would choose Plan 1. With this information you would still choose Plan 1. Therefore, the information weather type n_1 would result in no change in your choice and it would not be worth anything to you. However, if the signal were weather type n_2, you would switch to Plan 2, increasing your payoff by $24,000 - $16,000 = $8,000. Table 6-3 displays your actions and the difference in payoff for each state of weather.

Table 6-3
Value of Information Under Varying Weather Conditions

Weather	Current Choice	[Perfectly Informed] Choice	Change in [Profit]	Probability
Good (n_1)	Plan 1	Plan 1	0	0.4
Hot (n_2)	Plan 1	Plan 2	8	0.2
Cold (n_3)	Plan 1	Plan 3	16	0.2
Rainy (n_4)	Plan 1	Plan 4	8	0.2
[Additional Profit			6.4	1.0

Now place yourself back at a point in time before the information on which weather state will occur has been transmitted, and ask: "How much would I be willing to pay for the information?" The amount clearly depends upon which signal (i.e., weather type) is transmitted. All you have available are the probabilities of various weather types, and therefore you can calculate the EVPI as $(0 \times 0.4) + (\$8,000 \times 0.2) + (\$16,000 \times 0.2) + (\$8,000 \times 0.2) = \$6,400$.

Expected Value of Imperfect or Sample Information

When the information available is not perfect but still offers the potential for reducing the uncertainty associated with a decision problem, its expected value can sometimes be calculated. . . .

Example 6-2

Faced with a difficult technological problem, the manager of an engineering and development laboratory was considering bringing in an outside expert to help determine whether the process under development would be a technological success. It was impossible to know for sure if the process would be a success until the research was completed. However, the expert he had in mind was more knowledgeable than anyone on his staff on the crucial part of the project. If the process turns out to be a success, the payoffs will be large -- approximately $10,000,000. On the other hand, a failure will result in a substantial loss, estimated to be $5,000,000. The manager currently assesses the chances of success at only 30%. When considering the expert, he feels confident the assessment provided after the investigation will be a probability of success of 60%, 40%, 20%, or 0%. Moreover, he feels that each possibility is equally likely. As a matter of fact, this assessment on the expert's response, which corresponds to an overall probability of success of 30% $[(.25)(.60) + (.25)(.40) + (.25)(.20) + (.25)(0) = .30]$, just confirms his opinion about the success of the project. . . .

[Without the expert's advice, the manager should terminate the project. Continuing would have an expected value of $(.30)(\$10,000,000) + (.70)(-\$5,000,000) = -\$500,000$. If the expert believes that the odds of success are 20% or 0%, the best option is still to terminate the project. But if the expert believes that the odds of success are 60%, the project has a positive expected value: $(.60)(\$10,000,000) + (.40)(-\$5,000,000) = \$4,000,000$. If the expert believes that the odds of success are 40%, the project also has positive expected value: $(.40)(\$10,000,000) + (.60)(-\$5,000,000) = \$1,000,000$. Thus, the best strategy -- proceed or stop -- depends on the expert's estimate.

Table 6-4 shows how the expert's opinion affects the choice of strategy, and the increased value from having the opinion available. The expected value of the expert's opinion, with the decision *proceed* if the expert predicts 60% or 40% chance of success and *stop* if the expert predicts 20% or 0% chance of success, is $1,250,000.]

Table 6-4
Value of Expert's Opinion About Project Success

Expert's Predicted Chance of Success	Current Choice	Choice with Expert's Imperfect Information	Change in Profit	Proba-bility
60%	Stop	Proceed	$4,000,000	0.25
40%	Stop	Proceed	$1,000,000	0.25
20%	Stop	Stop	0	0.25
0%	Stop	Stop	0	0.25
Additional Profit			**$1,250,000**	**1.0**

The Relationship Between Value of Information and Amount of Uncertainty

The value of information depends on both the amount of uncertainty [before the information is received] and the payoffs. To demonstrate, consider the following simplified example.

Example 6-3

As an investor you are convinced that XYZ Company's earnings have an equal chance to be either $2 per share or $2.50 per share for last year. Furthermore you believe the stock price will be 10 times last year's earnings per share (EPS) in either case. The stock is now selling for $22 per share and the earnings are to be reported in 1 month. . . . Although you are not sure if you can obtain "perfect" information, you realize that it would be possible to get close to perfect information by talking with company officials. Since this would be a time-consuming and expensive process, you want to get a feel for the value of the information. . . .

[Without the information, you expect a profit of $0.50 per share from the investment (a total of $500 if you buy 1,000 shares). Half the time, the earnings will be $2.50, and the stock will rise to $25, for a profit of $3 per share. The other half the time, the earnings will be $2.00, and the stock will drop to $20, for a loss of $2 per share. The expected per share profit is $(.50)(\$3) + (.50)(-\$2) = \$0.50$. Table 6-5 shows how your strategy changes if you can obtain perfect information about the expected earnings.

Table 6-5
Value of Information About Future Earnings

Actual Earnings	Current Choice	Choice with Perfect Information	Change in Profit	Probability
$2.50	Invest	Invest	0	0.50
$2.00	Invest	Don't Invest	$2,000	0.50
Additional Profit			**$1,000**	**1.0**

In this case, perfect information about XYZ's earnings is worth $1,000.] This value is based on the prior assessment $P_{EPS=\$2} = 0.5$, $P_{EPS=\$2.50} = 0.5$. If the prior probabilities were changed from 0.5, the EVPI would change. Figure 6-4 displays how EVPI changes for this particular problem as $P_{EPS=\$2.50}$ varies from 0 to 1.0. At either extreme the EVPI is low because the *amount* of uncertainty is not great. In the middle ranges the additional uncertainty is reflected in a higher EVPI.

Figure 6-4
Variation in EVPI with Prior Assessment of Probability

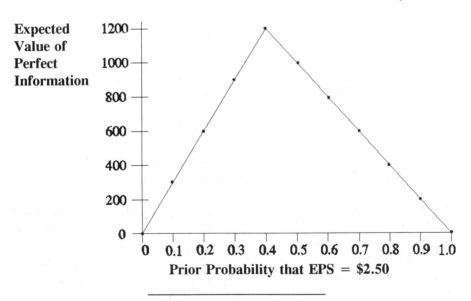

B.   The Event Study Methodology

An event study seeks to measure the impact of new information. A central problem is isolating a *single* release of information. Investors are constantly bombarded with information -- about particular companies, inflation, unemployment, interest rates, political decisions, and so on. If stock prices move, to which information have they reacted? We need a way to hold everything else constant, so that we can measure the impact on asset value of a single event, such as a takeover announcement.

Financial economists have developed a statistical technique -- *cumulative abnormal returns analysis* -- that, in appropriate circumstances, lets us do precisely that for publicly traded common stock. The idea is to predict the return from holding the stock in the absence of the information in question, so that we can compare the predicted return to the actual return. The difference is a measure of the impact of the information. In this section, we describe a common way to conduct an event study.

1.   Measuring Abnormal Returns

Cumulative abnormal returns analysis begins with the *market model* of stock returns that we developed in Chapter 3. The market model of the percentage return $R_{i,t}$ on an investment in the stock of firm i, on day t, is:

$$R_{i,t} = \alpha_i + \beta_i \cdot R_{m,t} + \epsilon_{i,t} \tag{6-1}$$

Where:

$R_{m,t}$ is the percentage return on the overall stock market on day t

β_i is the slope of the best fit straight line in a regression analysis of the relationship between the daily returns on firm i's stock and the returns on the stock market as a whole.

α_i is the intercept of the best fit regression line

$\epsilon_{i,t}$ is the residual portion of the change in Company i's stock price -- the part that *cannot* be explained by the change in the market price $R_{m,t}$

Equation 6-1 is identical to Equation 3-5, except that we have added subscripts to indicate that the equation applies to the returns on a particular stock, for a particular day.

In Chapters 3 and 4, we focused on β_i, which we interpreted as a measure of the *systematic risk* of Company i. The final term in the market model -- $\epsilon_{i,t}$ -- was unimportant. It was a measure of *unsystematic risk*. In a regression analysis intended to measure systematic risk, unsystematic risk merely adds *noise* (statisticians call $\epsilon_{i,t}$ an "error" term). Since unsystematic risk could be eliminated by holding a diversified portfolio, it didn't matter much how large the error term was for a particular firm on a particular day.

In an event study, in contrast, we care about unsystematic risk. We want to know how a news announcement that is specific to firm i affects firm i's stock price. $\epsilon_{i,t}$ is a measure of that effect. $\epsilon_{i,t}$ measures the change in the price of firm i's stock that is *independent* of what we would expect based on what happens to the rest of the market. An announcement that affects only firm i will affect $\epsilon_{i,t}$, but will not affect the other elements of the market model -- α_i or $\beta_i \cdot R_{m,t}$. Conversely, news that affects *all* stocks will be largely captured by $\beta_i \cdot R_{m,t}$, and will have only a limited effect on $\epsilon_{i,t}$.

Because of its importance to event studies, financial economists give $\epsilon_{i,t}$ a special name -- they call it the *abnormal return* on firm i's stock on day t. This is to distinguish $\epsilon_{i,t}$ from the *normal* return on firm i's stock, which is the return that is expected based on what happens to the rest of the market. From Equation 6-1, we have:

$$\text{Total Return} \quad = \quad \text{Normal Return} \quad + \quad \text{Abnormal Return}$$

$$\textbf{(6-2)}$$

$$R_{i,t} \quad = \quad [\alpha_i + \beta_i \cdot R_{m,t}] \quad + \quad \epsilon_{i,t}$$

Figure 6-5 shows Allied-Signal Corp.'s abnormal returns for a 21-day period in 1991. It appears that something important happened to cause the large positive abnormal return on the day labelled "day 0" (actually June 27, 1991). In fact, Allied-Signal announced on June 27 that its CEO, Edward Hennessy, had been forced to resign by the board of directors, and would be replaced by an outsider. Investors apparently didn't think much of Hennessy's ability, and reacted with glee to the news of his departure. The 12.5% abnormal return translates into a $500,000,000 increase in the value of Allied-Signal's shares.[3]

In Figure 6-5, the abnormal returns before and after the announcement date, though much less than 12.5%, *are not zero*. There are many possible reasons for this, including: (i) the division of total return into normal and abnormal components is based on an *estimate* of Allied-Signal's β, which may not equal the true β; (ii) as we learned in Chapter 4, there may be systematic factors that affect security prices which are not captured by β, and which therefore show up as part of the abnormal return $\epsilon_{i,t}$; (iii) other news bearing on the value of Allied-Signal stock may have been released on those days; (iv) some trades will occur at the *bid* price (the price at which market professionals stand ready to *buy* Allied-Signal stock), while other trades occur at the higher *asked* price (the price at which market professionals stand ready to *sell* Allied-Signal stock); and (v) possible noise trading.

In other words, $\epsilon_{i,t}$ is not a *clean* measure of the impact of a single piece of new information. Instead, it is contaminated by other sources of stock price fluctuations. How then do we tell whether a stock price change is a response to a *particular* piece of information, or a response to these other "background" sources?

---

[3] The Allied-Signal example is taken from Joseph Grundfest, *Just Vote No: A Minimalist Strategy for Dealing with Barbarians Inside the Gates*, 45 Stan.L.Rev. 857 (1993).

Figure 6-5
Allied-Signal Abnormal Returns: June 13 - July 12, 1991

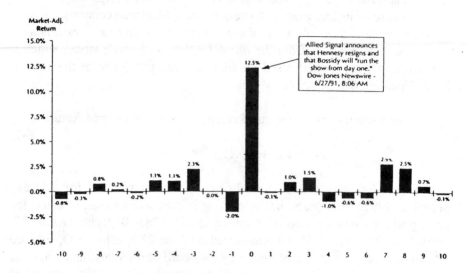

Days Relative to Announcement Date

Source: Cornerstone Research

2.   The Statistical Significance of Abnormal Returns

We can't ever know for sure what caused a stock price change, but standard statistical techniques let us ask *how likely* it is that the change was a response to particular event. One way to do this is as follows. As part of the regression analysis used to estimate β_i, we can also compute abnormal returns for each day in the time period used to estimate β_i. We can then compute the mean and the standard deviation of these abnormal returns.

The mean of the daily abnormal returns $\epsilon_{i,t}$ is uninteresting -- it equals zero. That is guaranteed by the regression procedure used to estimate β_i. The standard deviation, (which we will call σ_i) is important. It gives us a measure of how big $\epsilon_{i,t}$ is on an average day -- a day when nothing special is happening (at least nothing that we can identify).

We can also study the *distribution* of the daily abnormal returns around zero. Abnormal returns on common stocks *approximately* follow the *normal* or *bell curve* distribution discussed in Chapter 3. The terminology is confusing but the result is important: *abnormal* returns are *normally* distributed! This means that the abnormal returns fall within one standard deviation from zero about 68% of the time, and within two standard deviations from zero about 95% of the time (see Table 3-1). The standard deviation of Allied-Signal's daily abnormal returns is about 1.88%. This means that the 12.5% spike when Edward Hennessy was fired is 6.65

standard deviations from zero. The odds that this would happen by chance, on an ordinary day when there was no special news about Allied-Signal, are infinitesimal -- less than 1 in 10,000.

But suppose that the market response to Hennessy's firing was less clear-cut. When are we confident *enough* that the market response was not mere chance so that we can say that this new information caused Allied-Signal's stock price to increase? Statisticians use *confidence intervals* to express the likelihood that an event happened by chance. For abnormal returns, the 95% confidence interval runs from slightly less than two standard deviations below zero to slightly less than two standard deviations above zero (more precisely it runs from $-1.96\sigma_i$ to $+1.96\sigma_i$). In a large sample, 95% of the daily abnormal returns will fall inside the 95% confidence interval. Thus, if an abnormal return falls *outside* this confidence interval, we can be 95% confident that this was not by chance. For Allied-Signal, the 95% confidence interval runs from -3.7% to 3.7%.

Ninety-five percent confidence is a standard measure of *statistical significance*. If we are 95% confident that a stock price change didn't happen by chance, we say that the change is *statistically significant at the 95% confidence level*. Other common measures of statistical significance are the *90% confidence level* (returns falling outside the 90% confidence interval, which runs from $-1.65\sigma_i$ to $1.65\sigma_i$) and the *99% confidence level* (returns falling outside the 99% confidence interval, which runs from $-2.6\sigma_i$ to $2.6\sigma_i$). These confidence intervals are shown in Figure 6-6. The areas *outside* the confidence intervals shows the corresponding areas of statistical significance.

Figure 6-6
Statistical Significance: 90%, 95%, and 99% Confidence Levels

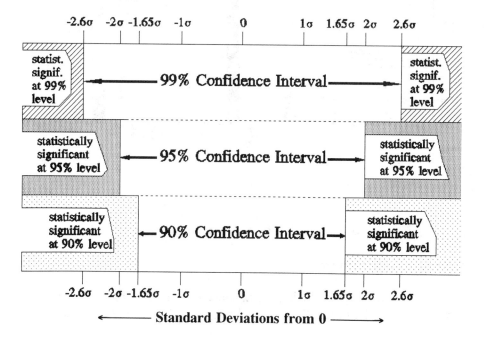

In this book, we will generally treat empirical results as statistically significant if they are significant at the 95% confidence level. We will generally treat all other empirical results as *statistically insignificant*. Sometimes, we will refer to results that are significant at the 90% confidence level as *marginally significant*.

To evaluate whether abnormal returns are statistically significant, researchers often convert them to a *standard normal* or z distribution, which is a normal distribution with mean $= 0$ and standard deviation $= 1$. To do this, we define a *standardized abnormal return (SAR)*, which is just the abnormal return divided by its standard deviation:

$$SAR_{i,t} = \epsilon_{i,t}/\sigma_i \qquad (6\text{-}3)$$

$SAR_{i,t}$ is a *test statistic* for the significance of the abnormal return $\epsilon_{i,t}$. Over the period used to estimate σ_i, the *SARs* are (approximately) normally distributed and have mean $= 0$ and standard deviation $= 1$. The *SAR* tells us if a result is statistically significant simply by inspection -- an *SAR* greater than about $+2$ or less than about -2 indicates statistical significance at the 95% confidence level. For example, the *SAR* for Allied-Signal on June 27, 1991 was 6.65 (12.5%/1.88%). This is clearly significant.

Figure 6-7

Allied-Signal Abnormal Returns and 95% Confidence Interval

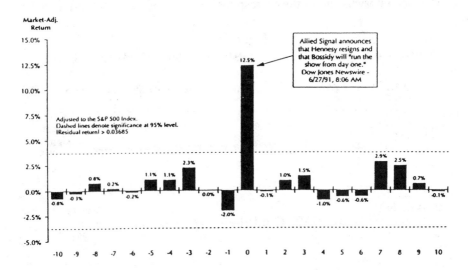

Days Relative to Announcement Date

Source: Cornerstone Research

To further illustrate the important concept of statistical significance, we have redrawn Allied-Signal's abnormal returns in Figure 6-7, together with dotted lines showing the 95% confidence interval. Over this 21-day period, the abnormal returns for all days except day 0 fell within the 95% confidence interval. Most of the abnormal returns *should* fall within the 95% confidence interval, but it wouldn't be surprising if one or two fell outside this confidence interval, *strictly by chance*.

3.   Cumulating and Averaging Abnormal Returns

Sometimes, information is released over a period of time. At other times, we aren't sure exactly when information was released. In both cases, we need to cumulate abnormal returns over time and test whether these *cumulative abnormal returns (CARs)* are statistically significant. We also often want to determine the response of a sample of firms that have received a similar announcement. For example, we may want to know how the market reacts, *on average*, to an announcement that a CEO has been fired, or that a firm has become a takeover target. Thus, we need to measure the *average abnormal return (AAR)* for a number of firms and test the statistical significance of the *AAR*. Finally, we often want to both average abnormal returns over a number of firms and cumulate them over time, and test the statistical significance of the *cumulative average abnormal return (CAAR)*.

This subsection develops the necessary statistical tools. Although the mathematical steps are complicated, each type of cumulation involves the same basic steps. First, we measure a desired quantity (either a *CAR*, or an *AAR*, or a *CAAR*). Second, we convert the measured quantity to the standard normal distribution. The standardized quantity is a *test statistic* that lets us measure statistical significance. Table 6-6, at the end of this subsection, summarizes the results and should help those who struggle with the mathematical details.

Cumulating Abnormal Returns Across Time.   We first consider cumulating returns across time for a single firm. To cumulate returns, we just add them up. The cumulative abnormal return on firm i's stock over a k trading day period (called an *event window*), running from day d_1 to day d_2, is:

$$CAR_i = \sum_{t=d_1}^{d_2} \epsilon_{i,t} \qquad\qquad (6\text{-}4)$$

To determine the statistical significance of the *CAR*, we first need to compute its standard deviation. Probability theory tells us that if k events are (i) *normally* distributed; (ii) *independent* of each other; and (iii) *identically* distributed with mean = 0 and standard deviation = σ, then the *sum* of the events is normally distributed with mean = 0 and standard deviation proportional to *the square root of the number of events*:

$$\sigma_{\text{sum of } k \text{ events}} = \sigma \cdot k^{1/2} \qquad\qquad (6\text{-}5)$$

Applying this general formula to the specific case of abnormal returns, the standard deviation of a k-day *CAR* is:

$$\sigma_{k\text{-day } CAR} = \sigma_i \cdot k^{1/2}$$

Once we know the k-day CAR and its standard deviation, we can define a *standardized CAR (SCAR)* as a test statistic for the statistical significance of the *CAR*. For 1-day returns, we divided the abnormal return by its standard deviation to obtain a standardized abnormal return (*SAR*). Similarly, the *SCAR* is just the *CAR* divided by its standard deviation:

$$SCAR_i = CAR_i / \sigma_{k\text{-day } CAR} = CAR_i / (\sigma_i \cdot k^{1/2}) \qquad (6\text{-}6)$$

Like the *SAR*, the *SCAR* has a standard normal or z distribution over the period used to estimate σ_i. An *SCAR* greater than about $+2$ (or less than -2) indicates statistical significance at the 95% confidence level.

The factor $k^{1/2}$ in the denominator of Equation 6-6, which does not appear in the definition of the 1-day *SAR* in Equation 6-3, means that a multiday *CAR* must be *larger* than a 1-day abnormal return to be statistically significant. Moreover, the longer the event window, the larger the *CAR* must be to be statistically significant. This is because each extra day adds more *noise* -- more sources of stock price movement in addition to the response to the information release that we're trying to study.

The extra noise introduced by using a long event window makes it important for researchers to measure as carefully as they can *when* information is released to the market. The narrower the event window, the easier it is to tell if and how investors have responded to the information release.

Averaging Abnormal Returns Across Firms. Often, we want to average abnormal returns across a sample of n firms that have experienced a similar event, such as a takeover bid, on *different* calendar days. Computing the average abnormal return is straightforward. For each firm, we use the market model to compute the abnormal return $\epsilon_{i,t}$ on the day of interest. Since the events occur on different calendar days, we measure t in *event time* -- *relative to that firm's announcement date*. It is common, as in the Allied-Signal example, to call the announcement date *day 0*. The *average abnormal return* for the sample for day t is:

$$AAR_t = (1/n) \cdot \sum_{i=1}^{n} \epsilon_{i,t} \qquad\qquad (6\text{-}7)$$

The next step is to assess statistical significance. Recall from Equation 6-5 that the *sum* of n normally distributed, independent, and identically distributed events (with mean $= 0$ and standard deviation $= \sigma$) is normally distributed with standard deviation proportional to the square root of the number of events. Similarly, the *average* of n such events is normally distributed with a standard deviation that is *inversely* proportional to the square root of the number of events:

$$\sigma_{\text{avg. of } n \text{ events}} = \sigma/n^{1/2} \tag{6-8}$$

This is because the average is simply the sum divided by n. Recall from Chapter 3 that the variance for the coin flip example decreased in proportion to $1/n$, and the standard deviation decreased in proportion to $1/n^{1/2}$. That was a specific instance of the general result shown in Equation 6-5.

Unfortunately, the abnormal returns for different firms are *not* identically distributed. Instead, each firm's abnormal returns have their own standard deviation σ_i. Fortunately, there is a cure for this problem. We can divide each firm's abnormal return $\epsilon_{i,t}$ by that firm's σ_i to obtain a standardized abnormal return ($SAR_{i,t} = \epsilon_{i,t}/\sigma_i$). The average SAR for the sample of n firms on day t is:

$$ASAR_t \quad = \quad (1/n) \quad \cdot \quad \sum_{i=1}^{n} \epsilon_{i,t}/\sigma_i$$

The SARs all have the same standard deviation ($\sigma = 1$). Thus, from Equation 6-8, the standard deviation of the average SAR is:

$$\sigma_{ASAR} \quad = \quad 1/n^{1/2}$$

We can now compute, as a test statistic for statistical significance, a *standardized average SAR (SASAR)*, which has the standard normal or z distribution. As usual, we divide the quantity of interest (here $ASAR_t$) by its standard deviation:

$$SASAR_t \quad = \quad ASAR_t/\sigma_{ASAR} \quad = \quad (1/n^{1/2}) \quad \cdot \quad \sum_{i=1}^{n} \epsilon_{i,t}/\sigma_i \tag{6-9}$$

The $SASAR$ has the usual interpretation in terms of statistical significance. If it is greater than about $+2$ (or less than -2), the event is statistically significant at the 95% level of confidence.

The most important feature of the $SASAR$ is that it *increases* as the number of firms in the sample increases. The sum in Equation 6-9 involves adding n abnormal returns. We then divide by $n^{1/2}$, so the $SASAR$ increases roughly in proportion to $n^{1/2}$. Thus, the *larger* the sample, the easier it is to assess whether an information release is statistically significant. For example, a 1-day abnormal return for Allied-Signal must be greater than 3.7% (or less than -3.7%) to be statistically significant at the 95% confidence level. In contrast, a 1-day return for a sample of 100 firms similar to Allied-Signal will be statistically significant if the average abnormal return is greater than about 0.4% (or less than -0.4%). *Event studies of a large sample of firms are much more powerful than event studies that focus on a single firm.*

The confidence interval gets narrower as *n* increases because factors that influence stock price, *other than the event of interest*, tend to average out. Good things will happen to some firms in the sample on the event date, but bad things will happen to other firms. The response to the event of interest is the only common influence on stock price. The factor $1/n^{1/2}$ tells us how fast this averaging process occurs as sample size increases.

The methodology for averaging returns across firms must be modified if the firms in the sample all have the *same* event date. This might be the case if we are studying the market response to new legislation -- for example, an antitakeover statute affecting all firms incorporated in New York. Because the firms have the same event date, their abnormal returns may not be *independent*. We can solve this problem by forming a portfolio consisting of the firms in the sample, and then estimating the market model and computing an abnormal return and standard deviation for the *portfolio*. In effect, we treat the portfolio as a single firm.[4]

Averaging Abnormal Returns Across Firms and Cumulating Them Across Time. Researchers doing event studies often want both to average abnormal returns over a sample of firms and cumulate them across time. This is straightforward. We first compute an average abnormal return AAR_t for the sample for each day *t* in the event window. As before, we measure *t relative* to each firm's announcement date. We also compute the associated $SASAR_t$, which measures the statistical significance of the average abnormal return.

Next, we add the daily *AAR*s to obtain a cumulative *AAR* for the sample over the full event window. Suppose, for example, that the event window runs for *k* days -- from day d_1 to day d_2. The cumulative *AAR* is:

$$CAAR \;=\; \sum_{t=d_1}^{d_2} AAR_t \;=\; \sum_{t=d_1}^{d_2} (1/n) \cdot \sum_{i=1}^{n} \epsilon_{i,t}$$

---

[4] See Stephen Brown & Jerold Warner, *Using Daily Stock Returns: The Case of Event Studies*, 14 J.Fin.Econ. 3 (1985). Many studies use this procedure -- forming a portfolio of all sample firms, and measuring the significance of the portfolio abnormal return -- even when event dates are not correlated. There is nothing wrong with this, but the resulting statistical tests are less powerful than tests that use firm-specific *SARs*, because the portfolio tests don't fully use the information in the firm-specific values of σ_i.

The common factor $(1/n)$ can be brought out of the sum to give:

$$CAAR = (1/n) \cdot \sum_{t=d_1}^{d_2} \sum_{i=1}^{n} \epsilon_{i,t} \qquad (6\text{-}10)$$

To measure whether the cumulative average abnormal return is statistically significant, we return to the *SASAR*s (which measure the statistical significance of the daily *AAR*s), and cumulate them over the k-day event window. Each daily *SASAR* is (approximately) normally distributed with mean $= 0$ and $\sigma = 1$. Thus, from Equation 6-5, the sum of k *SASAR*s is (approximately) normally distributed with mean $= 0$ and $\sigma = k^{1/2}$. To get back to a standard normal distribution with $\sigma = 1$, we divide by $k^{1/2}$. Thus, the test statistic (which we will call z) is:

$$z = (1/k^{1/2}) \cdot \sum_{t=d_1}^{d_2} SASAR_t = (1/n \cdot k)^{1/2} \cdot \sum_{t=d_1}^{d_2} \sum_{i=1}^{n} \epsilon_{i,t}/\sigma_i$$

As usual, a z value greater than about $+2$ (or less than -2) indicates statistical significance at the 95% confidence level. The *larger* the sample, and the *narrower* the event window, the larger z will be, and the more likely that the study will detect a statistically significant response to new information when such a response is present.

We developed the *CAAR* and the z test for the significance of *CAAR*s by first averaging daily abnormal returns across firms and then summing the average abnormal returns over time. But the measure of abnormal returns and the related test statistic would be exactly the same if we first cumulated abnormal returns over time for each firm, and then averaged those abnormal returns across firms.

And we're done! Table 6-6 summarizes the different measures of abnormal returns, and the test statistic for each. The names we have given to the various measures and test statistics are not important. In some cases, standard names have developed; in others, we have invented our own names. What matters is: (i) the different ways to sum and average abnormal returns; (ii) the *availability* of a test statistic for each; (iii) the *decrease* in noise as the number of firms increases; and (iv) the *increase* in noise as the number of days in the event window increases.

Table 6-6
Abnormal Returns and Test Statistics

Type of Return	Measure of Abnormal Returns	Test Statistic (standard normal or z distribution)
abnormal return: 1 firm, 1 day	$\epsilon_{i,t}$	$SAR_{i,t} = \epsilon_{i,t}/\sigma_i$
cumulative abnormal return: 1 firm, k days	$CAR_i = \displaystyle\sum_{t=d_1}^{d_2} \epsilon_{i,t}$	$SCAR_i = (1/k^{1/2}) \cdot \displaystyle\sum_{t=d_1}^{d_2} \epsilon_{i,t}/\sigma_i$
average abnormal return: n firms, 1 day	$AAR_t = (1/n) \cdot \displaystyle\sum_{i=1}^{n} \epsilon_{i,t}$	$SASAR_t = (1/n^{1/2}) \cdot \displaystyle\sum_{i=1}^{n} \epsilon_{i,t}/\sigma_i$
cumulative average abnormal return: n firms, k days	$CAAR = (1/n) \cdot \displaystyle\sum_{t=d_1}^{d_2} \sum_{i=1}^{n} \epsilon_{i,t}$	$z = (1/n \cdot k)^{1/2} \cdot \displaystyle\sum_{t=d_1}^{d_2} \sum_{i=1}^{n} \epsilon_{i,t}/\sigma_i$

C. An Event Study Example

The development of the statistical tools used in event studies was hard going for most readers, we suspect. It's time to see how these statistical techniques are used in an actual empirical study.

Michael Bradley, Anand Desai, & E. Han Kim
SYNERGISTIC GAINS FROM CORPORATE ACQUISITIONS AND THEIR DIVISION BETWEEN THE STOCKHOLDERS OF TARGET AND ACQUIRING FIRMS
21 J.Fin.Econ. 3 (1988)

Abstract: This paper documents that a successful tender offer increases the combined value of the target and acquiring firms by an average of 7.4%. We also provide . . . empirical evidence that competition among bidding firms increases the returns to targets and decreases the returns to acquirers . . . and that changes in the legal/institutional environment of tender offers have had no impact on the total (percentage) synergistic gains created but have significantly affected their division between the stockholders of the target and acquiring firms.

There is empirical evidence that corporate acquisitions effected through tender offers are wealth-increasing transactions for the stockholders of both the target and acquiring firms [Dodd & Ruback (1977) and Bradley (1980)].[a] Moreover, Bradley, Desai & Kim (1983) show that these gains are not due to the market's reassessment of previously undervalued securities. They document that the positive revaluation of the target's shares is permanent only if the offer is successful, i.e., only if the resources of the two firms are combined.[b] This evidence is consistent with the synergy theory of tender offers, which posits that the acquisition of control over the target enables the acquirer to redeploy the combined assets of the two firms toward higher-valued uses.

None of the above studies, however, documents the magnitude of the synergistic gains that result from successful acquisitions achieved through tender offers. Indeed, whether or not such acquisitions result in synergistic gains is still a contentious issue in the literature. For example, Roll (1986) has proposed the *Hubris Hypothesis*, which posits that the gains to target shareholders represent wealth transfers from acquiring firms' shareholders and not necessarily synergistic gains.[c] To test this hypothesis, it is necessary to measure synergistic gains using matched pairs of target and acquiring firms. None of the earlier studies impose this requirement on their samples.

In this paper, we estimate the magnitude of the synergistic gains [from successful tender offers], using the revaluation of the combined wealth of target-firm and acquiring-firm shareholders as a basis. We also examine the factors that determine the division of these gains between the stockholders of the two firms and document how the division and the total gains created have changed with the changing environment of the tender offer process. . . .

Synergistic Gains

. . . We define the total synergistic gain from a successful tender offer as the sum of the change in the wealth of the stockholders of the target and acquiring firms. . . . This definition assumes that corporate acquisitions effected through interfirm tender offers have no effect on the wealth of the senior claimants (e.g., bondholders and other creditors) of the firms involved. Kim & McConnell (1977) and Asquith & Kim (1982) provide evidence that is consistent with this assumption for a sample of firms involved in corporate mergers.[d]

---

[a] Peter Dodd & Richard Ruback, *Tender Offers and Stockholder Returns*, 5 J.Fin.Econ. 351 (1977); Michael Bradley, *Interfirm Tender Offers and the Market for Corporate Control*, 53 J.Bus. 345 (1980).

[b] Michael Bradley, Anand Desai & E. Han Kim, *The Rationale Behind Interfirm Tender Offers: Information or Synergy?*, 11 J.Fin.Econ. 183 (1983).

[c] Richard Roll, *The Hubris Hypothesis of Corporate Takeovers*, 59 J.Bus. 197 (1986).

[d] E. Han Kim & John McConnell, *Corporate Merger and the "Co-Insurance" of Corporate Debt*, 32 J.Fin. 349 (1977); Paul Asquith & E. Han Kim, *The Impact of Merger Bids on the Participating Firms' Security Holders*, 37 J.Fin. 1209 (1980).

[The sample for the study consists of 236 successful tender offers between 1963-1984 for which the shares of both the target and acquiring firms were traded on the New York or the American Stock Exchange]. Of the 236 acquiring firms, 155 held no target shares prior to the offer. The 236 acquiring firms sought, on average, 66.2% of the target shares. The mean as well as the median fraction of target shares ultimately purchased in our total sample is in excess of 50%. Thus the "typical" acquiring firm in our sample held no target shares prior to the offer but held a majority of the outstanding target shares upon successful execution of the offer.

Methodology

Our estimates of the gains created by tender offers are based on market model prediction errors. Under the assumption of multivariate normality [of stock price returns], the abnormal return (prediction error) to firm i on day t can be written as:

$$\epsilon_{i,t} = R_{i,t} - \alpha_i - \beta_i \cdot R_{m,t}$$

where:

$\epsilon_{i,t}$	=	abnormal return to firm i on day t
$R_{i,t}$	=	realized return to firm i on day t
α_i, β_i	=	market model parameter estimates
$R_{m,t}$	=	return to equally-weighted CRSP market portfolio on day t

The market model parameter estimates for each target firm are obtained using a maximum of 240 trading days of daily returns data beginning 300 days before the announcement of the first tender offer bid in the contest. Estimates for the acquiring firms are obtained using 240 trading days of returns data beginning 300 days before the first bid made for the target by this firm.

For each of the 472 firms in our sample, we cumulate the daily abnormal return over a contest-specific interval to obtain the cumulative abnormal return (*CAR*). The *CAR* is computed from five trading days before the announcement of the first bid through five days after the announcement of the ultimately successful bid. We begin to cumulate the *CAR* five days before the announcement of the initial bid in order to capture any anticipatory price behavior (leakage of information) that may occur before the actual public announcement.

Ideally, we would like to extend our *CAR* window until the day just before the offer is executed. Reliable execution dates are not available, however, for most of the offers in our sample. . . . We do not extend the *CAR* window through the execution of the offer because this would cause a downward bias in the measured returns to target shareholders. This downward bias stems from the necessary condition for a successful tender offer that the [tender] offer price, P_T, be greater than the expected postexecution price of the remaining target shares, P_E. [Otherwise, the target firm's shareholders will not tender their shares.][4]. . .

Our *CAR* algorithm generates an 11-day [event] window for all but 15 [of the 163] tender offers in which there is only one bidder. For tender offer contests in which there is more than one bidder, the window for targets varies, with a mean of 43 trading days and a standard deviation of 52 trading days. Using these variable-window *CAR*s, we estimate the dollar gain to the target and acquiring firms in each tender offer contest i as[e]

$$\delta W_{T,i} \; = \; W_{T,i} \cdot CAR_{T,i} \qquad\qquad \delta W_{A,i} \; = \; W_{A,i} \cdot CAR_{A,i}$$

where:

$W_{T,i}$ = market value of target equity as of six trading days prior to the first announcement for the target, minus the value of the target shares held by the acquirer

$CAR_{T,i}$ = cumulative abnormal return to the target firm . . .

$W_{A,i}$ = market value of acquiring firm as of six days prior to the first announcement made by the acquiring firm

$CAR_{A,i}$ = cumulative abnormal return to the acquiring firm . . .

. . . [O]ur estimate of the total percentage synergistic gains [$CAR_{C,i}$] is based on the *CAR* to a value-weighted portfolio of the ith target and the ith

---

[4] We recognize that our *CAR* statistic is but one measure of the increase in the wealth of target stockholders. An alternative measure has been proposed by Jensen (1985) and Comment & Jarrell (1987). These authors employ what has become known as the blended premium (*BP*), which is defined as:

$$BP = [f(P_T - P_O) + (1 - f)(P_E - P_O)]/P_O,$$

where [f = fraction of target shares purchased; P_T = tender offer price; P_O = pre-offer target stock price; and P_E = post-tender price of the shares that aren't purchased. Michael Jensen, *When Unocal Won Over Mesa, Shareholders and Society Lost*, 9 Financier 30 (1985); Robert Comment & Gregg Jarrell, *Two-Tier and Negotiated Tender Offers: The Imprisonment of the Free-Riding Shareholder*, 19 J.Fin.Econ. 283 (1987)].

[The mean *BP* for the 52 tender offers between 1981-1984 is 43.03%, compared to a *CAR* of 35.34%. There] are at least two computational reasons why *CAR* is systematically less than *BP*, and these explanations can easily account for the 7.7% difference. First, *CAR* is, by design, net of market movements, The average duration of the offers in this sample is 22 trading days or one trading month. The average monthly return to the CRSP equally-weighted market portfolio between 1981 and 1984 is roughly 1.7%. [Thus], 1.7% of the 7.7% difference between *BP* and *CAR* can be attributed to general market movements. [Second, *CAR*] is a sum of (abnormal) returns whereas [*BP*] is essentially a continuously compounded return. Given that the returns to the targets are predominantly positive over the tender offer period, it follows that the sum of the daily (abnormal) returns will be strictly less than a continuously compounded return. For example, the sum of 2% per day for 22 days is 44%, whereas the continuously compounded return of 2% [per day] for 22 days is 55%.

[e] In the equations below, the greek letter δ means *change in a quantity*. Thus, δW means "change in W."

acquiring firm, where the weights used are $W_{T,i}$ and $W_{A,i}$. . . . $CAR_{C,i}$ is measured by cumulating the abnormal returns to this portfolio from five trading days before the announcement of the first bid through five days after the announcement of the ultimately successful bid. Using this percentage measure, we estimate the total dollar synergistic gain, $\delta W_{C,i}$, as:

$$\delta W_{C,i} = W_{C,i} \cdot CAR_{C,i}$$

where:

$$W_{C,i} = W_{T,i} + W_{A,i}$$

Estimate of Synergistic Gains

Table 6-7 reports our measures of the synergistic gains created by tender offers, as well as the changes in the wealth of the stockholders of the target and acquiring firms. The data in the last column of the top panel of Table 6-7 (labeled *Combined Returns*) show that the combined value of the target and acquiring firms increased, on average, by 7.43%, with 75% of the combined revaluations being positive. Our estimate of this percentage synergistic gain is statistically greater than zero ($z = 19.95$).[5]

Table 6-7
Mean Percentage and Dollar Gains from Successful Tender Offers
(dollar figures in millions of 1984 dollars)

	Subperiod			Total
	7/63-6/68	7/68-12/80	1/81-12/84	7/63-12/84
Number of Contests	51	133	52	236
Combined Returns				
CAR_C (%)	7.78[a]	7.08[a]	8.00[a]	7.43[a]
δW_C ($)	91.1	87.5	218.5	117.1
% positive	78	74	73	75
Target Returns				
CAR_T (%)	18.92[a]	35.29[a]	35.34[a]	31.77[a]
δW_T ($)	70.7	71.6	233.5	107.1
% positive	94	98	90	95
Acquirer Returns				
CAR_A (%)	4.09[a]	1.30	-2.93[a]	0.97[a]
δW_A ($)	25.0	31.8	-27.3	17.3
% positive	59	48	35	47

[a] Significantly different from zero at the 0.01 level.

---

[5] This z-statistic is computed following [the techniques described in Section B of this Chapter].

The mean total dollar gain created by the acquisitions in our sample is $117 million (expressed in December 1984 dollars). Since the distribution of our dollar measure $\delta W_{C,i}$ is extremely leptokurtic and skewed to the right . . ., we conduct the nonparametric Wilcoxon Signed Rank test to test if the median $\delta W_{C,i}$ of $26.9 million for the total sample is statistically greater than zero.[f] This test yields a z-statistic of 9.30, which is significant at the 1% level.[g]

Table 6-7 also reports data for three subperiods: 1963-1968, 1968-1980, and 1981-1984. Although this division is somewhat arbitrary, there have been some dramatic changes in the tender offer process during the 22-year period under study, and these three subperiods correspond roughly to the three distinct regimes that have existed in the legal and institutional environment of tender offers since 1963.

The first period (1963-1968) is important because before 1968, cash tender offers were free of government regulation. They were considered private transactions between the acquiring firm and the stockholders of the target firm. In July 1968 Congress passed the Williams [Act], which brought the tender offer within the purview of the Securities and Exchange Commission (SEC). In the same year, Virginia enacted the first state antitakeover statute; by 1978, 36 states had enacted their own takeover regulations. By isolating the offers that occurred in the unregulated period, we can examine the effects of government regulation on the magnitude and division of the synergistic gains from tender offers.

The last period (1981-1984) is distinguished by three factors that have drastically changed the environment in which tender offers take place. First is the avowed laissez-faire attitude of the Reagan Administration toward corporate takeovers in general. Second is the development of sophisticated tactics to repel takeovers (poison pills, targeted share repurchases, lock-up provisions, and supermajority and fair-price amendments). The third factor is the advent of investment banking firms that specialize in raising funds to finance corporate takeovers. We are interested in how these recent developments in the market for corporate control have affected the gains created by tender offers.

The data in the top panel of Table 6-7 indicate that the percentage synergistic gains created by tender offers have remained remarkably constant, between 7% and 8%, over the three subperiods. The dollar gains, however, have increased dramatically from the first two subperiods to the third;

---

[f] Leptokurtosis and skewness are technical terms that indicate how a sample departs from the normal distribution, which has no leptokurtosis or skewness. If there is a large difference between the sample distribution and the normal distribution, statistical tests that assume that the sample is normally distributed are less reliable. Thus, for dollar returns, the authors use a "nonparametric" test that is not sensitive to whether the sample is normally distributed.

[g] The authors' references to statistical significance at the "1% level" or the "0.01 level" have the same meaning as what we called, in the text, the *99% confidence level*. Similarly, statistical significance at what we called the *95% confidence level* can also be called the 5% level or the 0.05 level.

expressed in December 1984 dollars, the average synergistic gain has grown from $91 million and $87 million in the first two subperiods to $219 million in the 1981-1984 subperiod. This increase in the dollar synergistic gains, but not in the percentage synergistic gains, is due to the increase in the size of target firms. . . . [This] may be due to the laissez-faire attitude of the Reagan Administration and innovative financing methods of investment banking firms. . . .

The overwhelming conclusion is that target stockholders capture the majority of the gains from tender offers. Ninety-five percent of the targets in the total sample experienced a positive abnormal return. The average abnormal return is 32% and the ratio of the mean dollar gain to targets to the mean dollar total gain ($\delta W_T / \delta W_C$) is 91%. In contrast, the average abnormal return to acquiring firms is 0.97%, only 47% of the observations are positive, and the ratio of the mean dollar gain [to acquirers] to the mean total gain ($\delta W_A / \delta W_C$) is 15%. Whether measured as rates of return or dollar gains, the lion's share of the gains from tender offers is captured by target shareholders.[h]

The data in Table 6-7 also indicate that the returns to acquiring firms have decreased over time, whereas the returns to targets have increased. The mean abnormal return to acquiring firms is 4.09% ($z = 5.88$) in the first period and -2.93% ($z = -2.79$) in the last. In contrast, the mean abnormal return to targets has increased from 18.92% ($z = 26.2$) to 35.34% ($z = 26.2$).

In sum, the data in Table 6-7 compel the following conclusions:

(1) Successful tender offers generate significant synergistic gains and lead to a more efficient allocation of corporate resources.[8]. . . .

(3) Both the rate of return and dollar gains to target stockholders have increased over time, whereas the returns to the stockholders of acquiring firms have decreased. In fact, in the most recent subperiod, acquiring firms actually suffered a significant abnormal loss. . . .

---

[h] The ratio of target dollar gains to total dollar gains (91%) and the ratio of acquirer dollar gains to total dollar gains (15%) do not sum to 100% because the event window for measuring total gains differs from the acquirer's event window for tender offers involving multiple bidders.

[8] We recognize that, theoretically, the gains from tender offers may stem from the creation of market power and not necessarily from increased allocative efficiency. However, the work of Eckbo (1983, 1985) and Stillman (1983) indicates that corporate acquisitions have no measurable effect on the degree of market power in the economy. [B. Espen Eckbo, *Horizontal Mergers, Collusion, and Stockholder Wealth*, 11 J.Fin.Econ. 241 (1983); B. Espen Eckbo, *Mergers and the Market Concentration Doctrine: Evidence from the Capital Market*, 58 J.Bus. 325 (1985); Robert Stillman, *Examining Antitrust Policy Towards Horizontal Mergers*, 11 J.Fin.Econ. 225 (1983).]

Empirical Evidence on the Determinants of the Division of the Gains from Tender Offers

[We examine] the time series of cumulative abnormal returns (*CARs*) to the portfolios of 236 targets and 236 acquiring firms, classified by the observed level of competition among bidding firms. . . . The time series of *CARs* are [plotted in Figure 6-8] for three portfolios of the target firms: 163 targets of single-bidder tender offers, 73 targets of multiple-bidder tender offer contests, and the total sample of 236 targets. . . .

Figure 6-8
CARs for *Targets* in Single and Multiple Bidder Tender Offers

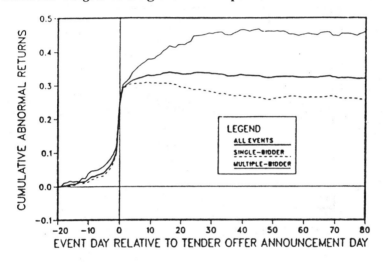

The *AR* and the *CAR* of the single-bidder subsample on day 0 (14.67% and 23.95%) are approximately equal to those of the multiple-bidder subsample (14.12% and 25.98%). Thus when a target receives an initial offer, the average value of this offer does not depend on whether it will be followed by other bids. Only when competing bids are actually announced do additional returns accrue to the targets of multiple-bidder contests. The additional returns are reflected in the gradual rise of the *CAR* series for the multiple-bidder sample. The difference in the *CAR* between the multiple-bidder and single-bidder subsamples reaches about 20% by day +40. Clearly, target shareholders earn greater returns from multiple-bidder contests than from single-bidder offers. These findings are not consistent with the alternative hypothesis that multiple-bidder contests arise because the initial bid was too low. . . .

The *CAR* series for the three portfolios of *acquiring* firms are plotted in Figure 6-9. Event day 0 is the day of the announcement of the first offer made by the acquiring firm. The *CAR* to the portfolio of all 236 acquiring firms from event day -5 through +5 is 0.79% with a *t*-statistic of 1.69. This is not significantly different from zero at the 5% level. However, the *CAR* from day -5 through day +20 is 1.70% ($t = 2.36$), which is significant at the 5% level. Thus, unlike for target firms, there is mixed evidence concerning the returns to acquiring firms.[i]

Classifying the portfolios of acquiring firms by the level of competition reveals that the *CAR* from day -5 through day +20 to the single-bidder portfolio is 2.8% ($t = 2.94$), whereas the return to the multiple-bidder portfolio is -0.70% ($t = -0.56$) over the same period. Thus, significant positive returns accrue to the stockholders of acquiring firms in single-bidder tender offers but not in multiple-bidder contests.

Figure 6-9

CARs for *Acquirers* in Single and Multiple Bidder Tender Offers

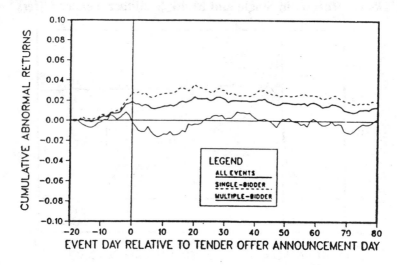

EVENT DAY RELATIVE TO TENDER OFFER ANNOUNCEMENT DAY

To examine the behavior of the *CARs* to the multiple-bidder portfolio more closely, we divide the sample into two groups: first-bidder, ultimately successful acquirers, and those acquirers who entered the contest after some other firm initiated the bidding process. Of the 73 acquirers in the multiple - bidder portfolio, 24 are first-bidder acquirers, and 49 are late-bidder acquirers. The *CAR* from day -5 to day +1 for the portfolio of first-bidder acquirers is 2.0%, whereas the *CAR* for the portfolio of late-bidder acquirers is -2.5% over the same interval. Apparently, the market's reaction to the first bid of first-bidder acquirers in multiple-bidder contests is similar to its reaction to bids made in single-bidder tender offers. Thus the negative *CAR*

---

[i] The t statistic has essentially the same interpretation as the z statistic for large samples. Technically, the t statistic is appropriate when the sample mean and standard deviation must be *estimated from the sample*, while the z statistic is appropriate when the sample mean and standard deviation are *already known*. The confidence intervals for the t statistic are somewhat larger for small samples. In section B of this Chapter, we used a z statistic because the mean and standard deviation of the abnormal returns *in the event window* were measured during the *separate* period used to estimate β, and thus were assumed to be known. It isn't clear why Bradley, Desai & Kim switch from z to t in mid-article.

from day -5 to day +1 to the portfolio of acquirers in multiple-bidder contests is due primarily to the negative returns to late-bidder acquirers, more commonly known as *white knights*. In other words, our data indicate that the average white knight pays 'too much' for the target it acquires.

In sum, our time-series analysis indicates that the net effect of multiple-bidder contests is to increase the returns to target firms and decrease the returns to acquiring firms. The market's average reaction to the bid that initiates a tender offer contest does not depend on whether the bid eventually leads to a multiple-bidder contest. This is true for both target and bidding firms. Only when competing bids are actually made do we observe greater returns to target shareholders and a dissipation of the initial gains to the stockholders of bidding firms. . . .

[To separate the] effects of regulation and competition on the returns to acquiring firms, we report the CAR_A by time period and our multiple/single-bidder classification in Table 6-8. The data show that acquiring firms gained most (4.62%, $z = 5.99$) in single-bidder contests effected during the unregulated period of 1963-1968; they lost the most (-5.10%, $z = -2.87$) in multiple-bidder contests effected in the most recent period (1981-1984).

Table 6-8

Acquirer *CAR*s: Time Period and Single vs. Multiple Bidder

	Subperiod			Total
	7/63-6/68	7/68-12/80	1/81-12/84	7/63-12/84
Number of Contests	51	133	52	236
Single Bidder	4.62[a]	1.74[b]	-1.08	2.00[a]
	($z = 5.99$)	($z = 2.04$)	($z = -1.14$)	($z = 4.11$)
	$n = 42$	$n = 93$	$n = 28$	$n = 163$
Multiple Bidder	1.62	0.27	-5.10[a]	-1.33
	($z = 1.05$)	($z = 0.22$)	($z = -2.87$)	($z = -1.44$)
	$n = 9$	$n = 40$	$n = 24$	$n = 73$
Total	4.09[a]	1.30	-2.93[a]	0.97[a]
	($z = 5.88$)	($z = 1.58$)	($z = -2.79$)	($z = 2.61$)
	$n = 51$	$n = 133$	$n = 52$	$n = 236$

[a] Significantly different from zero at the 0.01 level.
[b] Significantly different from zero at the 0.05 level.

Perhaps the most notable of the data reported in Table 6-8 is that the 52 acquiring firms in the most recent period (1981-1984) realized a significant abnormal loss of -2.93% ($z = -2.79$). This period is associated with an increase in the extent and degree of Congressional regulations, the tolerance of [the] Reagan Administration towards large-scale mergers, the advent of investment banking firms that specialize in raising funds to finance takeover battles, and the development of sophisticated defensive tactics. We believe that all of these factors have contributed to an increase in competition among bidding firms. Consistent with this conjecture, the data in the table indicate an increasing trend in the relative frequency of multiple-bidder contests over time; 18%, 30%, and 46%, in subperiods 1963-1968, 1968-1980, and 1981-1984, respectively. Obviously, an increase in competition among bidders does not explain *negative* returns to acquirers. However, if every successful bidder is pushed to its maximum valuation of the target, there is a greater probability that overvaluations will occur and the acquirer's shareholders will suffer a capital loss. . . .

Summary and Conclusions

This paper provides a theoretical and empirical analysis of interfirm tender offers. We analyze the mechanics of the tender offer process and demonstrate how this capital market transaction allocates corporate resources to their highest-valued use. Our empirical analysis documents the synergistic gains created by tender offers and how these gains are divided between the stockholders of the target and acquiring firms. . . .

We find that target stockholders have captured the lion's share of the gains from tender offers, and their share of the gains has increased significantly since the passage of the Williams [Act] in 1968. Acquiring firms, on the other hand, realized a significant positive gain only during the unregulated period 1963-1968 and, in fact, suffered a significant loss during the most recent subperiod, 1981-1984. We also find that the total percentage synergistic gains from tender offers have remained remarkably constant over time. Thus, government regulations and other changes that have occurred in the tender offer environment have been a zero sum game: the increase in the gains to the target stockholders has come at the expense of the stockholders of acquiring firms. . . .

We find that competition among bidding firms reduces the average gain to acquirers to a level that is not significantly different from zero. This adverse effect of competition is most severe for late-bidder acquirers, more commonly known as white knights. On average, the white knights in our sample pay 'too much' for the targets they acquire. . . .

In sum, our theoretical analysis implies that interfirm tender offers are efficient mechanisms to channel corporate resources to higher-valued uses. Our empirical results are consistent with this implication. We therefore see no justification for the continuing efforts by those in Washington to "reform" the tender offer process. Rather, we believe that public policy should be directed toward facilitating this capital market transaction.

Note on Interpreting Empirical Studies

1. We included the Bradley, Desai & Kim article at this point in this book primarily to illustrate the use of the event study methodology. We will consider in later chapters the implications of the evidence they develop for the sources of takeover gains, and for legal policy toward takeovers. Still, you should be skeptical about bold statements such as "[Our] data *compel*" the conclusion that "successful tender offers generate significant synergistic gains and lead to a more efficient allocation of corporate resources."

That conclusion may be right *on average*. But it is surely not true in every case, and it may not be true in every time period. As discussed in Chapter 9, there is reason to question the existence of efficiency gains for their 1963-1968 subperiod. Moreover, we can reach such a strong conclusion only after carefully winnowing out alternative explanations for the stock price gains. No one study can do that.

2. Bradley, Desai & Kim state that "competition among bidding firms reduces the average gain to acquirers to a level that is not significantly different from zero." This is technically true for their 21-year sample *as a whole*. But is it a fair summary of their results, when acquirers realized significant losses in the most recent period, 1981-1984, and those losses were concentrated in transactions where there was overt competition?

One reason to develop the ability to read event studies is so that you can assess the evidence yourself, and not just rely on what researchers *say* they found. Computing abnormal returns requires statistical skill. Interpreting them calls for analytical skill and openness to alternative explanations.

D.   Issues in Interpreting Event Studies

Event studies are a powerful tool for exploring the causes and consequences of takeovers. Otherwise, we wouldn't spend so much time on them. But event studies also have important limitations. This section discusses some recurring issues in interpreting event studies.

Absolute Versus Relative Pricing Efficiency. Event studies, *as a test of market efficiency*, are useful as a test of *relative* efficiency. They cannot test whether stock prices as a whole are too high or too low. This is inherent in a test that relies on *abnormal* returns -- returns measured relative to market returns.

Similarly, event studies, *as a measure of change in value*, are useful principally in measuring relative changes in value. Often, this limitation is not very important. If the market as a whole is 50% above true value, this may have little effect on the *percentage* change in value due to a particular event, and no effect on the *direction* of the change -- positive or negative. On the other hand, if we want to convert a percentage change in price into a change in *dollar value*, then absolute mispricing will affect our dollar estimates.

Gradual Release of Information. A second problem with interpreting event studies is that it is not always clear *when* information has been released to the market. Consider a tax bill that, *if adopted*, will reduce after-tax cash flows for some firms. Investors will react when they first learn of the bill -- say when it is first introduced into the House Ways and Means Committee. The stock price impact will be discounted by the probability that the bill will pass. If investors judge that the bill has a 10% chance of passage, and will reduce firm *X*'s cash flows by 10% (relative to other firms), firm *X*'s stock should immediately decline by 1% relative to the market (one-tenth of the 10% drop in relative value if the bill becomes law). If the Ways and Means Committee approves the bill, investors will increase their estimate of the likelihood that the bill will become law -- say to 30%. This will cause firm *X*'s stock price to drop a further 2%, relative to the market. If the provision is dropped in the Senate, the likelihood that it will become law may drop to 20% (it could be reintroduced in the Conference Committee). And so on.

In a situation like this, no single event date captures the full impact of the tax bill. There may be a few relatively clean dates on which important information about the bill's prospects is released. But investors will also revise their estimate that the provision will pass almost daily, as the bill is marked up, as important Representatives and Senators come out for or against it, as the President makes and withdraws veto threats. To measure the bill's impact, we can try to measure cumulative abnormal returns over the entire period when the bill is pending, but this will introduce a lot of noise into the *CAR* estimate.[5]

Anticipation. Investors do not always wait passively for news to be released. When important news is expected, investors will try to guess in advance what the announcement will say. If they guess right, stock prices will not move at the time of announcement, even if the announcement is very important.

A recent Supreme Court decision on the tort liability of tobacco companies illustrates both the speed of the market response to new information and the effect of anticipation. The U.S. Court of Appeals had found that tobacco companies were not liable *at all* to smokers for harm caused by cigarettes purchased after 1966, when federal law first required warning labels on cigarette packages. The federal warning law was deemed to preempt state tort law that might require a stronger warning. The Supreme Court granted certiorari to decide the preemption question.

---

[5] For an effort to measure the impact of tax legislation where it was possible to find a few reasonably clean event dates, see Mark Mitchell & Jeffry Netter, *Triggering the 1987 Stock Market Crash: Antitakeover Provisions in the Proposed House Ways and Means Tax Bill?*, 24 J.Fin.Econ. 37 (1989).

The stakes were huge. If the Supreme Court affirmed the Court of Appeals, this would drastically shrink the pool of potential plaintiffs. If the Supreme Court reversed, tobacco companies could be driven into bankruptcy by smoker lawsuits. Billions of dollars in value were riding on the decision. How were investors to value tobacco stocks?

Investors knew that the Supreme Court rarely grants certiorari simply to affirm a decision by a lower federal court. More likely, the Court was troubled by some aspect of the lower court opinion. Thus, complete affirmance was unlikely. Next, investors could analyze the case. They could hire legal experts to advise them on the likely outcome in light of the lower court opinion, the prior positions on preemption taken by individual Justices, and the questions asked at oral argument. Investors still had to guess, but they could at least make an educated guess.

The Supreme Court reversed the Court of Appeals, but only in part. The Court held that smokers could sue tobacco companies for fraud, but not (for cigarettes smoked after 1966) for failure to warn. The following story describes what happened next:

Seth Faison, CIGARETTE RULING: HOUR OF CONFUSION
N.Y. Times, June 26, 1992*

For a long hour on Wednesday morning, a big news event threw Wall Street into the kind of uncertainty that traders love and analysts hate. The first news of the Supreme Court's ruling on a case concerning cigarette makers' product liability was an eight-word electronic headline on the Bloomberg News Service that seemed to be bad news for tobacco stocks: *"High Court Says Smokers May Sue Tobacco Companies."*

As traders leaped into action, responding to an avalanche of sell orders in tobacco stocks, analysts who had tried to prepare for this moment for weeks were left grasping for more information. Was the ruling uniformly in favor of the plaintiffs, the analysts wondered, or was it split on different components?

Initial Response: Tumbling

The big tobacco stocks tumbled as soon as the news came at 10:20, except for the Philip Morris Companies, which was so overwhelmed with [sell] orders that trading was suspended at 10:21. Philip Morris was one of the companies sued; the others were the Loews Corporation and the Liggett Group. About an hour later, after analysts got copies of the decision, and were able to talk to big investors, the tobacco stocks rebounded.

It was a complex case concerning whether companies could be sued on the ground that they had withheld information about potential health dangers and whether they had responsibilities to disclose more than mandated by the 1966 Federal law requiring health warnings on cigarette packets. The Court in part reversed an appeals court ruling in a case brought by the family of Rose Cipollone, a Little Ferry, N.J., woman who died of lung cancer in 1984.

By the end of the day, most stocks closed only slightly down. Philip Morris was even up 62.5¢, to $73.75. "Millions were lost by people panicking on the news," said Max Holmes, director of bankruptcy research at Solomon Brothers. "And millions were made by people who caught it going back up." Mr. Holmes called the first headlines on news tickers "grossly misleading," and argued that subsequent flashes were little better, exaggerating the risk to tobacco companies. . . .

Lawrence Adelman, a tobacco analyst at Dean Witter Reynolds, lamented the way that a complex legal decision could be squeezed into a short news headline, provoking confusion. "We had explained to our traders and our retail operation that it could be a multilayered decision," he said. "This was definitely one of the most complex decisions on a business-related issue that I've ever seen."

Hired Two Lawyers

Rebecca Barfield, a tobacco analyst at First Boston, had gone to her firm's equities trading floor because she knew the decision might be announced Wednesday morning, and she wanted to be on hand when it came. She had already hired two lawyers to help her interpret court decisions, as well as a law student, who for the last month and a half went to the Supreme Court on each day that a decision might be announced.

When she first saw the news on the Bloomberg News Service, Ms. Barfield said, it appeared to signal that the Court had reached a split decision. But moments later, she saw what appeared to be a different message on the Dow Jones ticker, indicating that the Court had decided fully in favor of the plaintiffs. "It was total confusion," said Ms. Barfield, who was besieged with calls and requests for information. "Everybody was shouting and screaming." Only after she heard from the law student, who called and then faxed a copy of the decision, and from one of the legal experts she had hired, was she able to start telling clients that she thought the decision did not present a great new risk of liability.

First Boston convened a conference call with about 200 listeners at 1 P.M., and Morgan Stanley and Salomon Brothers held similar calls in the early afternoon. RJR Nabisco and American Brands had begun to recover shortly after 11 A.M., while Philip Morris remained suspended; it [reopened and] began its own tumble just before noon, and [then] rose gradually through the afternoon. . . .

Philip Morris ended Wednesday with a volume of 9.7 million shares traded. RJR Nabisco traded a whopping 14.7 million shares, closing down 12.5¢ at $9.375. American Brands ended down 12.5¢, to $45.375, on 1.5 million shares.

Figure 6-10 shows the intraday price changes to a portfolio consisting of the three tobacco companies discussed in the story above -- American Brands, Philip Morris, and RJR Nabisco. The figure shows the sharp impact of the initial, misleading headlines, and then the gradual rebound during the afternoon as investors digested the significance of the opinion. Between 10:20 and noon, Philip Morris stopped trading altogether because of an imbalance of buy and sell orders. For this period, Figure 6-10 shows the returns to Philip Morris and American Brands.

Figure 6-10
Value of $100 Invested Equally in American Brands, Philip Morris and RJR Nabisco at the Opening of Trading on June 24, 1992

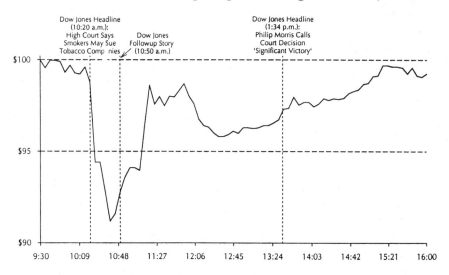

Source: Cornerstone Research

For the day as a whole, the three tobacco companies did not experience significant abnormal returns. Investors decided that their pre-decision guesses about the Court's ruling weren't far off. The next day, after investors had time to read the opinion more carefully, and reflect on its implications, most tobacco companies were down slightly, but again, not significantly.

Were investors wrong to dump tobacco stocks after the first misleading headline came out? Not in an efficient market. Instead, the initial price plunge probably reflected the sellers taking a calculated gamble that the headlines were mostly accurate, while buyers gambled that the news wasn't all bad. This time, the sellers lost their gamble. But if the full story had been as dismal for tobacco firms as the headlines, the sellers could profit by selling when they did, because tobacco stocks would probably have dropped even further.

Learning Over Time. A firm's stock price at any point in time reflects investor *estimates* of the firm's future cash flows, and the riskiness of those cash flows. In a semistrong efficient market, those estimates are *unbiased*, but they aren't necessarily *right*. In the tobacco example, the initial estimates were wrong, and were soon corrected.

Other mistakes aren't corrected as quickly. An example is the conglomerate merger wave of the 1960s. At the time, investors reacted favorably to conglomerate mergers -- the combined value of bidder and target increased sharply. The consensus view today is that most of these mergers were mistakes. In hindsight, the *estimate* was wrong.[6]

This is one reason to be skeptical about the claim by Bradley, Desai & Kim that the gains from tender offers didn't change between 1963 and 1984, and the only change was in the division of gains between bidders and targets. In hindsight, there wasn't much value added by the conglomerate acquisitions of the 1960s. Investors only *thought* there would be. By the 1980s, conglomerate acquisitions were out of favor, and many tender offers involved horizontal acquisitions (two firms in the same industry joining together). Some major takeovers involved busting up conglomerates that had been formed in the 1960s and 1970s.

Was investor enthusiasm for conglomerate firms an irrational fad, inconsistent with ECMH? Or was it just a garden variety mistake, albeit a large one? It's hard to say, even with the benefit of hindsight.

Did the Sample Firms Really Experience a Similar Event? Should an event study treat conglomerate and horizontal acquisitions as the same type of event, or as two different types of events? Should it treat mergers and tender offers, or friendly and hostile acquisitions, as the same type of event, or as two different types of events? There are almost limitless ways to subdivide samples based on various characteristics of the sample firms, and no clear answer as to when an event study should subdivide and when not. Researchers must use their best judgment, taking into account the questions the study is trying to answer, the loss of statistical power that comes from dividing a sample more finely, and -- most critically -- whether, *if the sample is divided*, there are significant differences between subsamples.

In interpreting an event study, one must always be sensitive to the possibility that the researcher has collapsed two different types of events into one (say, conglomerate and horizontal tender offers into an undifferentiated

---

[6] Chapter 9 discusses the evidence on conglomerate acquisitions.

pool of tender offers, or tender offers and mergers into an undifferentiated pool of acquisitions). If so, then the full sample results are really an average over distinct subclasses. A significant result for the full sample could reflect abnormal returns to only one subclass. Conversely, an insignificant result could reflect a mix of positive abnormal returns to one subclass and negative abnormal returns to another subclass.

The danger of unwittingly combining distinct subclasses is especially strong when an event study uses a sample collected over an extended period of time. The problem is that the nature of the event being studied may change over time. For example, most tender offers in the 1960s involved conglomerate acquisitions; this was no longer the case in the 1980s. This makes it important to subdivide the sample into shorter time periods, to see if the results are different in the subperiods. Bradley, Desai & Kim do this, but don't fully appreciate the implications of change over time in the nature of the acquisitions they are studying.

Multiple Explanations. An event study can tell us that something happened, but it can't tell us *why*. To explain positive or negative abnormal returns, we must closely examine the events and institutions involved. If the market's response was based on a strategy which the investigator does not understand, the *CAR* results, though technically accurate, will be used to support an inaccurate explanation of what occurred. The event study technique does not eliminate the need to assess cause through deductive reasoning; it only -- though this is substantial -- helps delineate what needs to be explained.

Sometimes, there will be two or more plausible explanations for why a firm's stock price changes in response to new information. For example, when firms raise cash by issuing additional common stock, their stock price usually drops.[7] One explanation is that firm value has not changed, but the stock issuance sends a *signal* to investors that the firm needs cash, and hence is in worse shape than investors had previously realized, or a signal that the managers think the firm's stock is overpriced, and hence think that this is an opportune time to sell some (overpriced) shares. An alternate explanation is that per share value declines *in fact* because cash-rich firms tend to waste cash, so existing shareholders won't get $1 of value for each $1 in funds raised.[8] An event study of stock issuances can't tell us which explanation is correct. Sometimes, other studies will indicate that one explanation is more likely, but in this case, both the *signalling* and the *free cash flow* explanation are supported by other studies. We simply don't know which is right; perhaps they both are.

---

[7] See Clifford Smith, *Investment Banking and the Capital Acquisition Process*, 15 J.Fin.Econ. 3 (1986).

[8] See Michael Jensen, *The Takeover Controversy: Analysis and Evidence*, in *Knights, Raiders & Targets: The Impact of the Hostile Takeover* 314 (John Coffee, Louis Lowenstein & Susan Rose-Ackerman eds.1988).

The Relationship Between CAPM and Event Studies. Event studies use the market model to separate abnormal from normal returns. CAPM is also related to the market model. Yet Chapter 4 suggested that CAPM doesn't predict expected returns very well. If CAPM fails, do event studies fail as well? To answer this question, we need to consider separately the two uses of event studies -- as a *measure of the impact of information*, and as a *test of market efficiency*.

Event studies as a measure of the impact of information survive largely intact. The abnormal returns procedure tests whether daily returns are *unusual* -- different than one would expect on a normal day. For that statistical test, it is perfectly appropriate to remove *usual* influences on stock prices. The market model does that. It's unfortunate that we lack a better model of stock prices. If we had such a model, we could do a better job of removing *systematic* factors that affect stock prices from the daily abnormal returns $\epsilon_{i,t}$. Noise would be lower, and statistical tests would be more powerful. But that doesn't mean that there is anything wrong with removing the influences we know about. And even if β_i doesn't predict the future rate of return on firm i's stock very well, it does predict how firm i's stock varies day to day with changes in overall stock market prices.

CAPM and the market model are also not identical. In CAPM, the return on firm i's stock can be written as:

$$R_{i,t} \; = \; (1 - \beta_i)R_f \; + \; \beta_i \cdot R_{m,t} \; + \; \epsilon_{i,t}$$

See Equation 4-3. Thus, CAPM requires that the constant term α_i in the market model equal $(1 - \beta_i)R_f$. The market model, in contrast, lets α_i take whatever firm-specific value emerges from the regression analysis used to determine β_i. Systematic factors other than β that affect asset prices will be partly reflected in α_i, and thus will have less effect on the residual term $\epsilon_{i,t}$ that we want to study.

For short-window event studies, we can take further comfort from the tendency for event study results not to be sensitive to the details of the model used to separate normal from abnormal stock price returns. Even simple techniques, such as techniques that don't use β to adjust for risk, work reasonably well.

For long-window studies, the situation is less clear. Long-window studies are often sensitive to the details of the underlying asset pricing model. We might reach different conclusions if we had a better asset pricing model. Thus, one should be cautious about relying heavily on long-window studies unless the degree of statistical significance is high.[9]

Short-window event studies *as tests of market efficiency* are probably also reliable. The studies are not sensitive to model specification, so it is

---

[9] For discussion of some methodological issues in long-horizon event studies, see John Campbell, *Why Long Horizons?: A Study of Power Against Persistent Alternatives* (NBER technical working paper no. 142, 1993).

unlikely that a better model would produce different results. This makes short-window event study tests of market efficiency *less subject* than other studies to the joint-hypothesis problem -- the need to always test market efficiency jointly with an asset pricing model. But long-window event studies, such as studies that test for overreaction or underreaction to news followed by gradual relaxation to true value, or studies that test the performance of takeover bidders and targets after a takeover bid, *are* sensitive to the particular model used to estimate abnormal returns. If we find an anomaly, such as early studies that showed that acquiring firms underperform the market after an acquisition, we don't know whether to attribute the anomaly to inefficient pricing or to use of an incorrect asset pricing model.[10]

Recently, some event studies have responded to the limitations of CAPM by using a multifactor asset pricing model (often using both β and size adjustments) to measure abnormal returns. Over time, we should learn which event study results are sensitive to model specification.

The Implications of Failure to Find a Significant Result. Suppose that an event study fails to find a statistically significant result. That does *not* mean that the announcement being studied had no effect, nor even that the announcement was unimportant. All it does is give us a *rough upper bound* on how important and unexpected the announcement was.

Lawyers and policymakers sometimes treat the absence of a *significant* change as equivalent to *no change in value*. This is simply wrong. The noise in stock prices can hide even important results. Recall, for example, the Allied-Signal example in Figure 6-7. Suppose that on the day when its CEO was fired, Allied-Signal's stock had climbed 3% relative to the market, instead of 12.5%. This would have been a change in value of $125 million, but it would not be statistically significant at the 95% confidence level.

Just as there can be multiple explanations for a statistically significant result, there can be multiple causes for the absence of a significant result. We noted earlier that investors react negatively to stock price issuances designed to raise cash. Consider now a stock-for-stock merger, in which the acquirer issues stock to buy another company. Suppose that the acquirer's stock price does not change significantly. This could reflect two offsetting effects -- a positive reaction to the merger, and a negative reaction to the issuance of stock. *If,* that is, investors react to the issuance of stock in a merger in the same way as to the issuance of stock to raise cash. We don't know whether they do or not, because we can't separate the multiple reasons why a stock-for-stock merger may affect the acquirer's stock price.

---

[10] See Julian Franks, Robert Harris & Sheridan Titman, *The Postmerger Share Price Performance of Acquiring Firms*, 29 J.Fin.Econ. 81 (1991).

E.   Variations and Methodological Issues

This Chapter has developed one common way to conduct an event study. The methodology we developed, though, is not the only possible one. This section discusses some variations in event study techniques, and some methodological issues in conducting event studies that drive the choice among the available techniques.[11]

1. *Event Studies for Preferred Stock and Debt.* The event study technique is used principally for common stock. It can be adapted for use with other securities, such as preferred stock and debt. This is important in assessing how takeovers affect creditors as well as stockholders. For leveraged buyouts and leveraged recapitalizations, which involve large increases in debt, we will want to ask whether stock price gains reflect net increases in firm value, or whether some of the stock price gains come at the expense of creditors. Other transactions may reduce firm-specific risk, and thus produce positive abnormal returns to creditors. If so, then the gains to common stockholders will understate the increase in firm value.[12]

2. *Event Studies Using Monthly Returns.* We have described the event study methodology for *daily returns*. Some event studies use *monthly returns*, especially for time periods prior to 1962, for which the CRSP data base contains only monthly returns. The methodology can be used for other time intervals as well, as long as stock price returns over the chosen interval are approximately normal.[13]

3. *Event Studies of Market-Wide Returns.* The event study methodology can be adapted to measure whether *market-wide* returns on a day when a news announcement is made -- say a discount rate cut by the Federal Reserve Board -- is made are significantly larger than on an average day. Such studies, though, are uncommon. The announcement must be important enough to move the whole market, and must be recurring for us to have much confidence that it was *this* announcement, rather than the many others on the same day, that moved prices. But important, recurring announcements are especially vulnerable to anticipation. Investors may approve of a discount rate cut, yet the market may drop because they had anticipated a larger cut.

---

[11] For a relatively nontechnical survey of event study methodology, see Glenn Henderson, *Problems and Solutions in Conducting Event Studies*, 57 J.Risk & Ins. 282 (1990).

[12] For an example of the use of event studies to measure returns to preferred stock and debt, see Debra Dennis & John McConnell, *Corporate Mergers and Security Returns*, 16 J.Fin.Econ. 143 (1986). Chapter 15 discusses the evidence on gains or losses to holders of preferred stock and debt from leveraged buyouts and other takeovers.

[13] For a careful discussion of event studies using monthly returns, see Stephen Brown & Jerold Warner, *Measuring Security Price Performance*, 8 J.Fin.Econ. 205 (1980).

4. *Abnormal Performance Index.* Bradley, Desai & Kim discuss one problem with *CARs* -- when positive returns are realized over a number of days in an event window, the *CAR* understates the total percentage gain over the event window, much as simple interest over a multi-year period will be less than compound interest. This can be avoided by an alternative measure called the *Abnormal Performance Index*, which is a *product* of the daily abnormal returns:

$$API = \prod_{t=d_1}^{d_2} (1 + \epsilon_{i,t})$$

Here the capital Greek letter Π means that one takes the product of the quantities $(1 + \epsilon_{i,t})$ over the indicated time period.[14] The API is a better measure than the CAR of the total economic gain (loss) to shareholders over the entire window period.

Yet a third measure of total shareholder gains involves estimating what the company's stock price *would have been* had it perfectly tracked the market model over the window period. If the price at the beginning of the window period is P_0, the predicted price at the end of the window period is:

$$\text{Predicted Price} = P_0 \cdot \prod_{t=d_1}^{d_2} (1 + \alpha_i + \beta_i \cdot r_{m,t})$$

The ratio of the actual market price at the end of the window period P_{d2} to this predicted price provides a measure of the shareholders' gain or loss as a result of the event being studied:

$$\text{Fractional Shareholder Gain (Loss)} = P_{d2}/(\text{Predicted Price}) - 1$$

This fraction will in general be slightly different than the comparable value provided by the API (API $-$ 1). Either is a respectable measure of the shareholders' compounded gain or loss over the window period.

5. *Sign tests and other nonparametric tests.* The z test for *CARs* developed in section B is a *parametric* test -- it depends on knowing a particular *parameter* -- the standard deviation σ_i. One way to reduce the problems caused by a variance shift (or other model misspecification) is to use a *nonparametric* test that does not depend on σ_i. One simple nonparametric test is the sign test: Is the percentage of positive abnormal returns significantly different from the (approximately) 50% positive abnormal returns we would expect when nothing special is happening?

---

[14] Steve Cantrell, Michael Maloney & Mark Mitchell, *On Estimating the Variance of Abnormal Stock Market Performance* (working paper, 1987) show that standard statistical tests for the API are at least as well specified as comparable tests for the significance of *CARs*.

For example, Bradley, Desai & Kim report in Table 6-7 that 75% of the completed tender offers in their sample produced positive combined bidder and target abnormal returns. We will use this result as an example of how a sign test can be used. For a large sample, the test statistic for the percentage of positive returns is:

$$z_{\text{sign test}} = (p - 0.5)/[p(1 - p)/n]^{1/2}$$

where:

p = fraction of positive returns

n = sample size

For the Bradley, Desai & Kim sample, $p = 0.75$, and $n = 236$, so:

$$z_{\text{sign test}} = (0.25)/[(0.75)(0.25)/236]^{1/2} = 8.87$$

Statistical significance is apparent.[15]

6.   *One-Tail Versus Two-Tail Tests.*   We have discussed statistical significance for the usual situation where we want to assess whether the response to information is *significantly different from zero*, against the null hypothesis that the response equals zero. In this situation, a so-called *two-tailed test* is appropriate.   Sometimes, we want to assess whether the response is significantly *greater than zero*, against the null hypothesis that the response is less than or equal to zero.   In this situation a *one-tailed* test must be used.   In a one-tailed test, the likelihood that the quantity being measured will be 2 or more standard deviations above zero is 2.5% -- exactly half as large as for a two-tailed test.

7.   *Correction for Finite Estimation Period.*   The market model parameters α_i and β_i, and the standard deviation of abnormal returns σ_i, are estimated over a finite measurement period and are then used to compute a test statistic for returns *outside* the estimation period.   Because of this, σ_i slightly underestimates the true standard deviation of the abnormal returns during the event period.   The correction factor is on the order of $2/n$, where n is the number of days in the estimation period.   Some event studies adjust σ_i to correct for the finite measurement period, but others do not.[16]

---

   [15] By way of comparison, the authors report a z statistic of 19.95 for their event study of the combined abnormal returns.   This reflects the greater power of the parametric test discussed in section B, compared to the nonparametric sign test, when abnormal returns are large.   This is because the parametric test uses information about *how far* the abnormal returns are from zero, while the sign test only uses the fact that an individual abnormal return is positive or negative.   It is also possible for the average abnormal return to be positive, even if more than half of the individual abnormal returns are negative.

   [16] James Patell, *Corporate Forecasts of Earnings Per Share and Stock Price Behavior: Empirical Tests*, 14 J.Acct.Res. 246 (1976), develops the correction factor.

8. *Choosing the Market Model Estimation Period.* Most event studies estimate the market model parameters α_i and β_i, and the standard deviation of the abnormal returns σ_i, over a period of 120-240 trading days *preceding* the event window. Some studies estimate these parameters both before and after the event window, and average the two, to take into account the possibility that the event being studied has changed either the market model parameters α_i and β_i, or the standard deviation of the abnormal returns σ_i. One can also estimate the market model over a time period that includes the event window, though this adds some statistical complexity. The choice of estimation period can be important for event study results that use long event windows, and in situations where the event being studied changes the variance of the abnormal returns.

9. *Dealing with Variance Shifts.* A general problem with event studies, including short-window studies, is that the event being studied may change the distribution of abnormal returns, either temporarily (while investors are absorbing the new information) or permanently. Suppose, for example, that the event causes a permanent increase in the standard deviation of a firm's abnormal returns. A test statistic, such as the *SAR*, that is computed by dividing daily abnormal returns by the *pre-event* standard deviation σ_i will make too many post-event returns appear to be statistically significant. There are techniques for measuring statistical significance that are less sensitive to a variance shift, or other forms of model misspecification, than the standard method we have described. The tradeoff is that these techniques generally have less power to detect statistical significance when a variance shift doesn't take place. These techniques are beyond the level of this book, but you should know that they exist.[17]

---

[17] For an event study involving a multi-firm sample and a multi-day event window, one fairly simple technique for handling variance shifts involves estimating the reduced model $R_{i,t} = \beta_i \cdot R_{m,t} + \epsilon_{i,t}$ *during* the event period. One measures the *average* variance σ^2 of the event period abnormal returns for all of the firms in the sample, and uses this average variance to compute a *t*-statistic. This method yields something of a hybrid of pre-event and post-event variance. One drawback of this method is that one can no longer factor the constant term α_i out of the daily returns, nor measure a firm-specific standard deviation of abnormal returns σ_i. This causes some loss of statistical power. In addition, the event being studied (or related events as in a protracted control contest) can cause large daily abnormal returns during the event period, which will bias the variance estimate upward, and cloak the presence of significant returns. This makes it critical to use this technique only for a multi-firm, multi-day study, which reduces the impact on the variance estimate of a particular firm's abnormal returns, and ensures that most of the firm-days in the measurement period are "normal" days. For a more sophisticated effort to deal with variance shift at the event date, see Sanjai Bhagat & Richard Jefferis, *Voting Power in the Proxy Process: The Case of Antitakeover Charter Amendments*, 30 J.Fin.Econ. 193 (1991). Tim Bollersev & Robert Hodrick, *Financial Market Efficiency Tests* (NBER Working Paper No. 4108, 1992), survey various statistical techniques for testing market efficiency.

10. *Nonnormality of Stock Price Returns.* The confidence intervals described in section B apply to returns that perfectly follow the normal distribution. Since abnormal returns are only approximately normal, the true confidence intervals are slightly larger (and theory doesn't tell us exactly what they are). The confidence intervals are also not perfectly symmetric around zero, due to skewness in the actual return distribution (slightly more than half of daily abnormal returns are negative, but there are more large positive than large negative abnormal returns). Departures from normality are important mostly for studies that use small samples. The *AAR*s for large samples come closer to following the normal distribution (this is a special case of a general result in probability theory called the Central Limit Theorem).[18]

---

[18] Brown & Warner (1985), *supra* note 4, discuss the statistical properties of daily abnormal returns, and their implications for event studies.

Chapter 6 Problems

1. Is the response of Allied-Signal's stock to the announcement that its CEO had been fired, shown in Figures 6-5 and 6-7, consistent with semistrong market efficiency? Why or why not?

2. Suppose that you are told that the average height of adult American males is 5'9", that approximately 95% of adult males in the United States are between 5'3" and 6'3" tall, and that the heights of adult males roughly follow a normal distribution.

    a.   What is the approximate standard deviation of the height of American males?

    b. What fraction of American males are taller than 6'6"?

3. For the 1981-1984 period, Bradley, Desai & Kim report that 35% of the tender offers in their sample produced positive abnormal returns for the acquiring firm. Is this result statistically significant, compared to the null hypothesis of 50% positive abnormal returns? If so, at what confidence level?

4.   (a) Suppose that news about a pending takeover comes out gradually over a 5-day period. In response, the target's stock price increases 5% per day relative to the market on each of the five days. What is the *CAR* for the five-day period?

    (b) What is the abnormal performance index (API) for the five-day period?

    (c) Which is a better measure of the increase in the value of the target's shares during the period, and why?

5. Sometimes, it is useful to compute results in a different way than the authors of a study. Based on Table 6-8 in the Bradley, Desai & Kim study, what is the average *CAR* to bidders in multiple bidder tender offers, for the period from July 1968 through December 1984 (their second and third subperiods)?

6. Buyback Corp. announces that it will conduct a self-tender offer, under which it will buy 25% of its outstanding shares at $150 per share. Each shareholder can tender some or all of her shares. If more than 25% of the shares are tendered, Buyback will buy stock prorata from each shareholder in proportion to the number of shares tendered. In response, the market price of Buyback stock jumps from $100 to $120 per share. Why

might Buyback's stock price have increased?   After all, the company's business has not changed. Suggest as many (reasonable) explanations as you can think of.

7. What value do investors expect Buyback's stock to have after the tender offer is completed? Ignore the time value of money for the time needed to complete the tender offer. Assume that all investors will tender their shares.

CHAPTER 7: THE OPTION PERSPECTIVE

Some of the most important recent developments in financial theory have concerned the valuation of *options* to acquire or dispose of other assets. The modern theory of option pricing begins with the development in 1973 of the Black-Scholes model of the value of an option to buy common stock. This model has become one of the major paradigms in modern financial theory.[1]

Our principal interest in option theory involves not the mathematical formula for determining an option's value, but instead the insight, also originating with Fischer Black and Myron Scholes, that much can be learned about various securities, including common stock and bonds, by seeing these securities as containing options, and exploring the factors that makes those options more or less valuable. Option theory tells us, for example, that in some circumstances common stock is really more like an option than like a fractional share in a business. Option theory also tells us that some corporate actions -- such as large, risky investments -- are good for stockholders but bad for creditors, because they increase the value of the stock (seen as an option) and decrease the wealth of the party that has sold the option (in this case, creditors).

If so, then stockholders can behave *strategically* or *opportunistically* -- for example, by making risky investments that benefit themselves at the expense of creditors -- even if those investments have a negative net present value for the company. Option theory also offers insight into when the stockholders' incentives to take such actions are especially strong.

Identifying incentives to act strategically is the first step in transaction planning. If you know when stockholders and creditor interests will diverge, you can structure a transaction to reduce the divergence, and write a contract that limits the other side's ability or incentive to act strategically. Such transaction planning can increase company value, with the gains split between shareholders and creditors. Anticipating and controlling strategic behavior is among the principal ways that advisors can add value when they participate in business transactions. And option theory is central to understanding how to anticipate strategic behavior.

With this brief introduction as motivation for why option theory is worth studying, we begin in Section A by introducing simple options on common stock in their standard context. Section B discusses the factors that affect option value. Section C applies the option perspective to two important situations: the conflict between shareholders and creditors over the firm's investment strategy; and efforts to develop compensation contracts that give managers the right risk-taking incentives.

---

[1] Fischer Black & Myron Scholes, *The Pricing of Options and Corporate Liabilities*, 81 J.Pol.Econ. 637 (1973); see also Robert Merton, *Theory of Rational Option Pricing*, 4 Bell J.Econ. 141 (1973).

A.   The Basics of Put and Call Options

A *call option* is a contract that gives the holder the right to *buy* an underlying asset -- for example, a share of common stock -- at a fixed price, on or before a specified date. A *put option* gives the holder the right to *sell* an underlying asset at a fixed price on or before a specified date. The fixed price for buying or selling the underlying asset is called the option *strike price* or *exercise price*. The last date when the option can be exercised is called its *maturity date* or *expiration date*. The seller of the option is also known as an *option writer*. The price that the option buyer pays to the option writer for the option is called the *option premium*.

If the price of the underlying security *exceeds* the exercise price of a call option, the call option is *in the money*. If this relationship still holds at expiration, the call option holder will exercise the option and make a profit. Suppose, for example, that you hold a call option to buy IBM stock at $70, and on the expiration date, IBM sells for $77 per share. You can make an immediate $7 profit by exercising your option to buy the stock for $70, and then selling the stock in the market for $77.

If the price of the underlying security is *less than* the call option exercise price, the call option is *out of the money*. If this relationship holds at expiration, the option holder will let the call option expire without exercising it. For example, if you hold a call option to buy IBM stock at $70, and on the expiration date, IBM sells for $63 per share, the call option is worthless. You would not exercise an option to buy IBM for $70 when you can buy IBM for $63 in the market.

If the price of the underlying security *exactly equals* the exercise price of a call option, the call option is *at the money*. If this relationship holds at expiration, you would be indifferent (before transaction costs) between exercising and not exercising. Either way, you make no profit and incur no loss.

Figure 7-1
Value of Call Option *at Expiration*

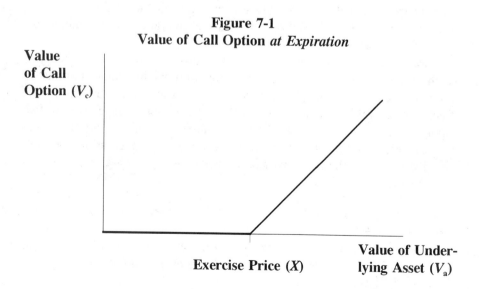

Value of Call Option (V_c)

Exercise Price (X)

Value of Under-lying Asset (V_a)

Figure 7-1 shows the relationship *at expiration* between the value of a call option V_c and the value of the underlying asset V_a. The call option is worth zero whenever the underlying asset is worth less than the exercise price X: that is, whenever $V_a < X$. As the value of the underlying asset increases above the exercise price X, the call option gains value dollar for dollar: Its value is $V_c = V_a - X$.

For a put option, these relationships are reversed. A put option is *in the money* if the price of the underlying security is *less than* the option exercise price. If this relationship still holds at expiration, the put option holder will exercise the option and make a profit by selling the underlying security for more than its market value. Suppose, for example, that you hold a put option to sell IBM stock at $70, and on the expiration date, IBM sells for $63 per share. You can make an immediate $7 profit by buying IBM for $63 in the market, and then using the put option to sell IBM to the option writer for $70.

If the price of the underlying security *exceeds* the put option exercise price, the put option is *out of the money*. If this relationship holds at expiration, the put option will expire worthless. You would not sell IBM stock for $70 using a put option if you can sell it for $77 in the market. Finally, if the price of the underlying security equals the put option exercise price, the put option is *at the money*. If this relationship holds at expiration, you would be indifferent (before transaction costs) between exercising and not exercising.

Figure 7-2 shows the relationship *at expiration* between the value of a put option (V_p) and the value of the underlying asset (V_a). The put option is worth zero whenever the underlying asset is worth *more* than the exercise price X: that is, whenever $V_a > X$. As the value of the underlying asset *decreases* below the exercise price X, the put option gains value dollar for dollar: Its value is $V_p = X - V_a$.

Figure 7-2
Value of Put Option *at Expiration*

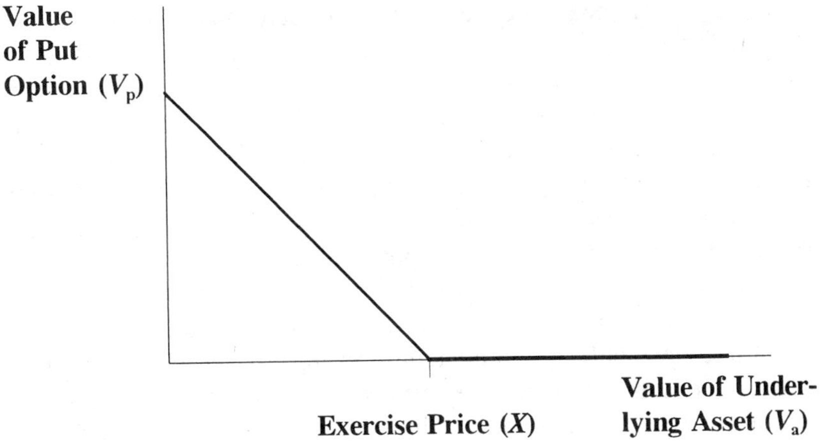

Value
of Put
Option (V_p)

Exercise Price (X) Value of Under-
                              lying Asset (V_a)

For both puts and calls, the option holder exercises if doing so is profitable, and lets the option expire otherwise. Before expiration, when the value of the underlying security at expiration is uncertain, the *expected value* of a call or put option is positive. In some states of the world, the holder gains by exercising the option; in all others, the holder throws the option away and breaks even. The option writer, in contrast, can only lose and never gain at expiration. The option writer's compensation comes up front, when the writer sells the option. In an efficient market, the sale price will equal the expected value of the option to the holder.

The next reading discusses how investors use publicly traded put and call options, as substitutes for or complements to investing in the underlying common stock.

Myron Scholes, OPTIONS -- PUTS AND CALLS
in *Encyclopedia of Investments*
559-578 (Marshall Blume & Jack Friedman eds. 1982)

Since 1973, call options and, more recently, put options have been trading on organized secondary markets. Investors have become familiar with the characteristics of these contracts, which are relatively simple contracts with set maturity dates and exercise prices. They may be unaware, however, that other commonly traded securities are first cousins to options. Warrants, executive stock options, and even the common stock and bonds of a corporation are examples of securities that are closely related to put and call options.

The common stock of a corporation with bonds in its capital structure is [a call] option because the shareholders have the right to buy back the assets of the firm from the bondholders by paying off the face amount of the debt (its fixed price) at the maturity of the bond (the expiration date of the contract). Since many financial instruments have characteristics similar to those of put and call options, a detailed knowledge of put and call options may be helpful in understanding these other contracts, and vice versa. . . .

[A put] option contract is similar to an insurance policy. The asset being insured is the underlying common stock. Investors insure against possible loss in return on the holdings of common stock by buying put options on their stock; a put option with the same exercise price as the current stock price insures against a decline in the stock price for the term of the put option. Loss . . . is limited to the premium paid for the put option; on a fall in price the investor puts the stock to the put seller, the insurer, and receives the exercise price in return. Naturally, if the stock increases in price, the put is not exercised; the insurance is not used. . . .

As an insurance policy on a home insures against the loss from a fire, holding put options on common stock insures against the loss from a drop in the price of the stock. Using options, investors can sell off part of the risk -- insure part of the risk of common stock investments. The sellers of options, like insurers generally, expect that the option premiums will cover the costs of the insurance they sell to the buyers of the options. If [the option price is] actuarially fair, neither the buyer nor the seller expects to earn an above-normal rate of return at the expense of the other side of the trade.

. . . [O]ptions have been confused with futures contracts and with forward contracts. The confusion arises because the terms are similar. Several concepts [first] used in the marketing of futures contracts were [adapted] for use in the trading of options. Buyers of futures [or forward] contracts for July wheat have *bought* the July wheat, although they will not take delivery until July. . . . Buyers of [call] options for July IBM, in contrast, have not bought IBM, but only the *right to buy* IBM at a fixed price. . . .

Since buyers match sellers and no new money is raised by corporations, [future and option] contracts have been compared to side bets and to gambling, contracts without an economic purpose. Futures and options both have economic purposes; they help investors with portfolio planning, thereby facilitating the functioning of the primary and secondary markets in the [underlying] commodities or securities.[a] . . .

Reduction of Risk in Investment Portfolios

The attractive characteristics of options become evident when options are combined with other securities. Combining options with other securities transforms the returns and risks of an option into the returns and risks of an investment strategy: options combine with other investments to produce patterns of returns for a portfolio of investments.

There are several important ways to limit the risk of investing in securities. Diversification is one of the main ways to limit the risk of holding securities. The larger the number of assets held in a portfolio, the smaller will be an investor's exposure to the risks of any one of the securities within the portfolio; the risk of the portfolio approaches the risk of the market portfolio. Another approach to limiting the risk of holding securities is to invest a percentage of the assets in bonds. By holding a larger fraction of the portfolio in bonds or money market funds, the investor unlevers the

---

[a] The critics of option trading, to whom Scholes is responding, argue that options *can* be used to insure a stock portfolio against loss, but they don't *have to* be used this way. For example, one can buy a put option without owning the underlying stock. In contrast, you can't buy fire insurance on a house you don't own. Buying a put option on stock you don't own can be seen as a side bet on the future performance of the stock, in which the option buyer wagers against the option seller. Transaction costs aside, the wager is a zero-sum game. Once we include transactions costs, the wager is negative sum. Critics of options trading believe that most trading involves this sort of negative-sum gamble. In contrast, supporters like Scholes believe that most options trading involves investor efforts to adjust the risk and return characteristics of an investment portfolio, with the potential for net gains in *risk-adjusted* value.

portfolio. The percentage changes in the value of the total portfolio will be less than the percentage changes in the value of the risky securities. With options, investors can limit risk by insuring against adverse changes in the prices of their holdings of securities, or against adverse changes in the value of a portfolio of assets. . . .

Use as Investment Insurance

Put options as insurance. A put option is like a term insurance policy in which the term or maturity is the length of time between the purchase of the put and its expiration date; the item being insured is the value of the underlying stock. The face value of the policy, or the maximum claim that is paid in the event that the underlying stock becomes worthless, is equal to the number of shares specified in the contract times the exercise price. For partial losses, the amount received is equal to the number of shares times the difference between the exercise price and the market price of the underlying security at the time that the put is exercised.

Moreover, depending upon the relation between the strik[e] price and the price of the underlying stock when the put is purchased, the put option will have features quite similar to an insurance policy with a deductible amount. If investors own 100 shares of stock with a market value of $100 per share, and if they buy a put with a strik[e] price of $100, they insure totally against any decline in the price of the stock during the life of the option. If, however, investors buy instead a put on the stock with an exercise price of $90 per share, they are not insured against the first 10 point decline (i.e., the first $1,000 in losses), although they are covered against any additional losses resulting from a decline below $90; therefore, the put has a $1,000 deductible. It is even possible to buy the insurance with a negative deductible: The investor purchases a put option with an exercise price of $110, thereby insuring against the event that the stock price does not appreciate by at least 10 percent. Unlike traditional insurance, however, the investor can buy the insurance without owning the asset.

Call options as insurance. Call options are also akin to insurance policies. Consider the following investment strategy: (1) Buy one share of a non-dividend-paying security; (2) take out a [loan under which you must] pay $X, the strik[e] price, at the maturity of the option, *t* months in the future. The loan, if prepaid, is prepayable at face value; (3) buy a put option on one share of the stock with a strik[e] price of $X and an expiration date *t* months in the future. If, at the end of *t* months, the stock [is worth] V_a per share, the value of the position would be as follows. If V_a were less than X, the put would be exercised [and] the stock delivered, for $X. The face amount of the loan, $X, however, must be repaid. The net value of the position is zero. On the other hand, if V_a were greater than X, the put would expire, the stock would be sold for V_a, and the loan [would be] repaid from the sale of the stock. The net value of the position would be $(V_a - X)$. . .

Suppose the investment strategy [instead] consisted of buying a call option on one share of the stock with an exercise price of X and an expiration date t months in the future. If, at the end of t months, the stock were selling for V_a per share, with V_a less than X, the call would expire unexercised; the value of the position would be zero. If V_a, however, were larger than X, the call would be exercised, paying X for the stock, [and then] selling the stock for V_a; the value of the position would be $(V_a - X)$. [The payoff is exactly the same].

Since the payoffs to both strategies are the same for every possible price of the underlying security at the maturity of the contracts, the two are functionally equivalent: *Call options are equivalent to [(i) owning] the underlying security; [(ii) being obligated to repay] a term loan with a face value of X; plus [(iii) owning] an insurance policy against declines in the stock price below $X per share.* While the leverage component of a call option is its most commonly known characteristic, the insurance characteristic distinguishes call-option strategies from simple stock strategies such as buying stocks on margin. . . .

[Selected] Glossary

Black-Scholes	Pricing model for options used by practitioners.
call option	Right to buy a security for a fixed price on or before a given date.
exercise value	Value of the option if it was to be exercised.
expiration date	Last day on which the option can be exercised.
fully covered	Writing an option on stock held by the writer.
futures contract	Buying an asset today for delivery in the future.
hedging	Reducing risk by selling an asset similar to the one held.
in-the-money call	Stock price is above the strik[e] price of the option.
in-the-money put	Stock price is below the strik[e] price of the option.
leverage	Borrowing money to buy an asset.
naked option	Writing an option to deliver a security that is not owned.
option buyer	One who has the right to exercise the option.
option writer	Person who sells the right of exercise to the buyer of the option.
out-of-the-money	For a call option, the stock price is below the strik[e] price; for a put option, the stock price is above the strik[e] price.
premium	Price paid for the option to the writer by the buyer.
put option	Right to sell a security for a fixed price on or before a given date.
strik[e] price	Price at which the option can be exercised.

B.　Factors that Determine Option Value

The Scholes reading describes some of the investment strategies that can be pursued using options. We turn next to the factors that determine the value of an option. We will consider only call options, but the same factors determine the value of put options. For simplicity, we assume that all cash flows from the underlying asset will be received after the option expires. Thus, the call option holder can capture all the cash flows from the underlying asset at expiration, and has no reason to exercise before the expiration date.

At expiration, valuing a call option is easy. The value of an in-the-money call option equals the value of the underlying asset V_a minus the exercise price X. The value of an out-of-the-money call option is zero. Valuing the option become complex, though, when there is time remaining until expiration, and the value of the underlying asset *at expiration* is uncertain. Before expiration, an out-of-the-money option has value because the option *may* become in-the-money by the time it expires.

Five fundamental factors determine call option value:

(1) The *current* value V_a of the underlying asset;

(2) The exercise price X;

(3) The risk-free rate of interest r_f, which tells us the time value of money;

(4) The variability in the value of the underlying asset, measured by the standard deviation of price σ_a; and

(5) The time t remaining until the option expires.

We will consider each factor in turn.

1.　Current Value of Underlying Asset

Other things equal, the value of a call option increases with an increase in the current value V_a of the underlying asset. In an efficient market, the higher today's asset price is, the higher the *expected* price at expiration. And the higher the asset price at expiration, the more the *option* will be worth. Today's value and the value at expiration are linked, *for both the option and the underlying asset*, by the time value of money.

An increase in current asset value V_a will make a call option worth more even if the option is out of the money. An increase in current value makes it more likely that the option will be in the money at expiration. *How much* more likely the option is to be in the money, and how far in the money it is likely to be, depends on how far out of the money the option currently is, the time t remaining until expiration, and the standard deviation σ_a of the asset's value.

2. Exercise Price

The lower the exercise price X, the more likely a call option is to be in the money at expiration, and the further in the money it will be. Thus, an option with a *lower* exercise price is worth more than an otherwise identical option with a higher exercise price. Option value depends largely not on current value alone, nor exercise price alone, but the difference between the two: $V_a - X$. If $V_a < X$, the option is out of the money. The further out of the money the option is, the less it is worth. If $V_a > X$, the option is in the money. The further in the money the option is, the more it is worth.

3. Time Value of Money

To exercise a call option, the option holder must pay the option writer the exercise price $X on the expiration date. To have $X available at expiration, the option holder today needs only a smaller amount, which can be invested to return $X on the expiration date. That amount is simply the present value of $X:

$$PV(\$X \text{ at time } t) = \$X/(1 + r_f)^t$$

The longer the time until expiration, and the higher the interest rate r_f, the more valuable the option, because the holder needs less money today to be able to exercise the option at expiration.[2] The size of the discounting effect depends on the likelihood that the option will be exercised, since only then is the exercise price paid. The more likely an option is to be exercised, the more important the factors -- r_f and t -- that determine the present value of the exercise price.

4. Variance in Value of Underlying Asset

A central factor in valuing an option is the variance in value of the underlying asset. The *greater* the variance in the value of the underlying asset, *holding constant the value of the asset*, the more the option is worth. At first glance, this seems counterintuitive. For the asset itself, higher systematic risk means that investors demand a higher expected rate of return. Thus, an increase in systematic risk, *holding constant the expected cash flows from the asset*, means that those cash flows have a lower *discounted present value*. But when an option on that asset is being sold, an increase in variance *increases* the value of the option.

---

[2] The present value formula works for any time period -- day, week, month, or year. If the time period is measured in, say, months, then the risk-free interest rate is the *monthly* rate.

This is due to the differences between the payoff to the holder of a call option and the payoff to the holder of the underlying asset. Consider first an option which is *at the money in present value terms*. The two curves in Figure 7-3 show the probability distributions of the value *at expiration* of the stock of two companies, Stableco and Variableco. Each has an expected value at expiration of $X. The heavy black line shows the payoff at expiration to a call option with an exercise price of $X -- the gain on exercise of the option and sale of the underlying common stock.

By "at the money *in present value terms*" we mean that the expected value of each company's stock *at expiration* equals the option exercise price. The Stableco and Variableco options illustrated in Figure 7-3 are slightly out-of-money giving the term its usual meaning, which ignores the time value of money. If an asset's expected value is $X sometime in the future, its current value must be less than $X.

To keep the example simple, we will assume that the extra variance in Variableco stock results solely from *unsystematic* risk. Thus, Stableco and Variableco stock will sell at the same price in an efficient market.

Variableco stock has both greater upside and greater downside than Stableco stock. A call option holder, though, only cares about the upside. In bad states of the world, the option holder will let the option expire worthless. The holder *cannot do worse than zero*, no matter how badly the stock performs. Holding a Variableco option, rather than Variableco stock, preserves the extra upside and eliminates the extra downside. This makes the Variableco option worth more than a Stableco option, even though the stocks are worth the same and the options have the same exercise price and expiration date.

Figure 7-3
Effect of Variance in Asset Value on Option Value

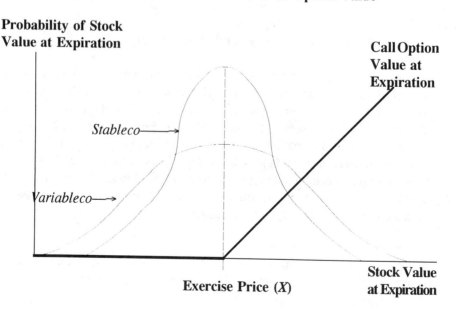

In Figure 7-3, the option holder neither gains nor loses if the share price is below the exercise price. The only part of the probability distribution that matters is the part where the share price at expiration exceeds the exercise price. Greater variance in the value of the underlying common stock shifts *that portion of the distribution* to the right. This increases the probability of a high stock price and, therefore, of a high option value.

Figure 7-4 shows the probability distribution of value at expiration *for the option holder*. The left half of the bell curves in Figure 7-3 has been collapsed to the heavy black line at a value of zero, because zero is the option holder's outcome whenever the stock price at expiration is less than or equal to the exercise price $X. In Figure 7-4, the mean of the option holder's probability distribution curve is greater for Variableco than for Stableco. The striped area under the Stableco curve and the dotted area under the Variableco curve are equal in size -- they represent equal probabilities. But the dotted area is at a higher price than the striped area. Thus, the Variableco option has a higher expected value than the Stableco option.

Figure 7-4
Option Value Probability Distribution

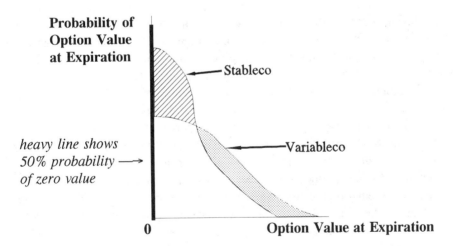

The same result -- greater stock price means greater option value -- holds *even more strongly* for an option that is out of the money in present value terms. It also holds, *though less strongly*, for an option that is in the money in present value terms. The holder of such an option sees all of the increased upside, and *only some* of the increased downside. Thus, the Variableco option is still worth more than the Stableco option. But as we steadily reduce the exercise price toward zero, the difference in value becomes less and less. In the extreme case where the option is so deep in the money that it is almost certain to be exercised, the option value will equal the stock value V_a minus the present value of the exercise price $PV(\$X)$.

Since Stableco and Variableco have the same stock price, their options will also have the same value in this extreme case. In effect, as an option becomes deeper and deeper in the money, its return characteristics approach those of the underlying asset.

The effect of increased variance on option value is more complex if the increased variance results from *systematic*, rather than unsystematic, risk. For an option that is at the money or out of the money in present value terms, the same analysis applies. Investors will now pay less for Variableco stock than for Stableco stock, because Variableco promises the same expected return but has higher systematic risk. But investors will still pay more for a Variableco option, because the option holder sees only the greater upside. The positive effect on value of the greater upside potential outweighs the negative effect of the increase in systematic risk.

For an option that is *in the money* in present value terms, we need more information to know how option value changes as systematic risk increases. The increase in systematic risk will make the option worth less; the increase in total variance will make the option worth more. The sign of the change in value will depend on which effect is larger. The deeper in the money the option is, the more stock-like the return on the option, and thus the weaker the second, value-increasing factor will be.

Finally, if the systematic variance of the underlying asset increases and expected return also increases just enough so that the *value* of the underlying asset doesn't change, the value of a call option on the asset increases, *even if* the option is in the money. This is the situation considered in the Black-Scholes option pricing model, which gives option value as a function of the variance of the underlying asset, holding asset value constant.

To summarize: An increase in variance, *holding asset value constant*, increases call option value. If we instead hold *expected return* constant, then: (i) an increase in *unsystematic risk* increases option value; (ii) an increase in systematic risk increases the value of an option that is *at the money* or *out of the money* in present value terms; and (iii) an increase in systematic risk has an uncertain effect on the value of an option that is *in the money* in present value terms. The further out of the money a call option is, the stronger the effect of asset value variance on option value. Conversely, the deeper in the money an option is, the weaker the variance effect. The value of a deep-in-the-money option tracks the value of the underlying asset, nearly dollar for dollar.

This relationship between variance and option value yields an insight that will be of substantial value. Suppose you are a Stableco shareholder and have to decide whether it will make a major acquisition. After studying the issue, you decide not to make the acquisition because the expected return is insufficient to compensate Stableco for the associated risk. Your conclusion might change if you held an option on Stableco's stock rather than the stock itself? A change in risk has a very different impact on an option holder than it does on the holder of the underlying security.

5.   Time Remaining Until Expiration

The last factor that affects call option value is time remaining until expiration. Time to expiration affects option value in two ways. The first, considered in subsection 3, involves the need to discount the exercise price to present value. The second effect involves variability in the value of the underlying asset. The longer the time remaining until expiration, the more time there is for the value of the underlying asset to change.

If asset values follow a random walk over time, the variance in expected value on a future date is proportional to the time between today and the future date. The standard deviation is proportional to the *square root* of the time remaining. All that is needed to change the distribution of expected future returns for Stableco into a distribution more like Variableco is to increase the time remaining until expiration.

Figure 7-5 shows the effect of time to expiration on the distribution of expected value of the underlying asset *at expiration*. If the option expires in a week, the probability distribution is very narrow. There isn't enough time for much to happen to change asset value. Thus, a deep out-of-the-money option will be nearly worthless. As the time to expiration increases, the probability distribution flattens out more and more. This makes an option, especially an out-of-the-money option, worth more. More specifically, in the Black-Scholes option pricing formula, the standard deviation of the return on the underlying asset σ_a is estimated for a specified time period (such as one month or one year), and then multiplied by $t^{1/2}$.

Figure 7-5
Effect of Time to Expiration on Option Value

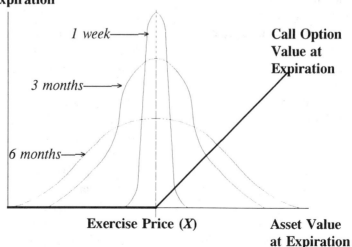

**Probability of Asset
Value at Expiration**

1 week⟶

3 months⟶

6 months⟶

**Call Option
Value at
Expiration**

Exercise Price (*X*)

**Asset Value
at Expiration**

C. Applying the Option Perspective

Understanding the factors that affect option value, can help in understanding a broad range of events. Many common relationships can be recharacterized as involving the grant and receipt of an option. This can provide insight into the factors that bear on the value of the interests held by each party to the relationship and, as a result, each party's incentives. We will use this perspective often in later chapters. Here we offer two examples: (i) the conflict between bondholders and stockholders; and (ii) the conflict between management and stockholders.

1. The Conflict Between Debt and Equity

Assume that Firm X has a capital structure made up of only debt and equity, and that the debt has a specified face value and is repayable on a specified date in a single lump sum. The value of the equity then equals the firm's total value minus the value of the debt. If the debt is not repaid when due, the firm will go into bankruptcy, with the result (we will assume for simplicity) that the stockholders are wiped out and the debtholders become the owners of the firm. Thus, the value of the debt on the repayment date is either: (i) its face value if it is repaid; or (ii) the value of Firm X's assets if the debt is not repaid and the debtholders take over the firm.

This arrangement can be recharacterized as an option. The stockholders can be seen as having sold an *unlevered* firm X to the debtholders in return for: (i) the proceeds from issuing the debt; (ii) a management contract; and (iii) most importantly, a call option to repurchase the unlevered firm by paying off the debt (face value plus interest). On the repayment date, if the firm's assets are worth more than the repayment price, the stockholders will "exercise their option" to repurchase the unlevered firm by repaying the debt. If the firm's assets are worth less than the repayment price, the equity holders won't exercise their option. They do this by defaulting on the debt.

Given this recharacterization of the relationship between debtholders and equity holders as involving a call option, how do the factors that determine option value affect the incentives of both parties? We would expect the debtholders to negotiate an interest rate that reflects their view of the risk of default at the time the terms of the debt are negotiated. But now consider the stockholders' incentives once the debt has been sold. The stockholders hold, in effect, a call option on an unlevered firm X. A major determinant of the value of that option is the variance in the future value of firm X. The stockholders thus have an incentive to cause firm X to make *riskier* investments than would be optimal for an unlevered firm.

Stockholders in a highly levered firm (say a firm worth $100, with outstanding debt with a face value of $90) hold a slightly in-the-money call option. The stockholders get all of the increased upside potential from taking a large risk. Much of the increased downside is borne by the debtholders, who suffer all losses that drop the firm's value below $90. A highly risky project that has zero net present value, and thus doesn't change the value of the firm as a whole, will increase the value of the stock and decrease the value of the debt.

This can be shown with a simple numerical example. Suppose that Firm X has assets of $100, all invested in Treasury bills, and outstanding debt of $90. If the firm keeps its funds in Treasury bills, it will be able to pay the debt for sure, so the debt will be worth $90 and the stock will be worth $10. Suppose though, that the stockholders find a project that requires a $100 investment, and has a 50% chance of returning $200 and a 50% chance of returning $0. The expected return on the $100 investment is $100.

The expected payoff to the stockholders from this investment is strongly positive. If the investment pays off, they repay the debt and are left with stock worth $110. If the investment doesn't pay off, the stockholders default on the debt and are left with $0. Since both outcomes are equally likely, the expected payoff is $55. This is shown in Table 7-1:

Table 7-1

Effect of Risky Investment on Levered Firm's Stock and Debt

	Before Risky Investment	After Risky Investment
Stock Value	$ 10	(.50 × $110) + (.50 × $0) = $ 55
Debt Value	$ 90	(.50 × $90) + (.50 × $0) = $ 45
Firm Value	$100	(.50 × $200) + (.50 × $0) = $100

The stockholders' gain, though, is the debtholders' loss. If the investment pays off, the debtholders receive $90. If the investment doesn't pay off, they are left with a claim on a worthless firm, worth $0. Since both outcomes are equally likely, the expected payoff is $45. This is also shown in Table 7-1.

Bond Covenants. The debtholders will anticipate such risk-increasing behavior when the terms of the debt were negotiated. They will demand some combination of (i) covenants that limit the stockholders' ability to make risky gambles, and (ii) an interest rate that reflects the anticipated increase in risk (taking the covenants into account). If the stockholders want to limit the interest rate they must pay, they will agree to covenants that prohibit the firm from, for example, substantially altering its investment portfolio, incurring additional debt, or taking other actions that would increase the risk of default. The more highly levered the firm, the more important such covenants will be.

The option perspective focuses attention on the importance of variance in the value of the underlying asset. Thus, it highlights the stockholders' incentives to take risks, and hence the debtholders' need for protection, by contract, a higher interest rate, or some of both.[3] A similar analysis is possible with respect to the conflict between preferred and common stockholders.

One might think that, if the debtholders are compensated through a higher interest rate for risk-increasing behavior by stockholders, the two parties would be indifferent between a high interest rate loan that allowed such strategic behavior, or a lower interest rate loan plus strong covenants. In fact, the problem is not zero sum. Often, an option holder can gain from a risky investment even if the investment has a negative net present value. Thus, viewed *ex ante*, covenants that limit strategic behavior can increase the total value of the firm. Stockholders benefit from this increase in firm value. The lower interest rate on the firm's debt more than offsets the lost opportunity to act strategically once debt has been issued.

Many terms in debt contracts are standardized, but opportunities for innovation remain. For example, the growth in leveraged buyouts and leveraged recapitalizations in the 1980s led to the development of "event risk" covenants, which give bondholders the right to "put" their bonds back to the issuing firm if the firm takes one of the leverage-increasing actions described in the covenant.[4] But many early event risk covenants were not very effective, perhaps because the legal and financial advisors who developed them did not fully understand the stockholders' incentives to increase leverage. Identifying the options implicit in the relationship, and how those implicit options affect the parties' incentives, could have offered a systematic way to identify the actions that an event-risk covenant should cover.

Strategic Behavior in Bankruptcy. The option perspective on the conflict between debt and equity is especially important when a firm is in or near bankruptcy. In a bankrupt firm, there are conflicts not only between stockholders and debtholders, but also between senior creditors, who are entitled to be paid first, and junior creditors, who get what's left over after the senior creditors are paid. Often, the common stock and one or more classes of junior debt may be worthless, or nearly so, if the firm were

---

[3] Option-sensitive efforts to analyze bond covenants include Clifford Smith & Jerold Warner, *On Financial Contracting: An Analysis of Bond Covenants*, 7 J.Fin.Econ. 117 (1979), reprinted in *The Modern Theory of Corporate Finance* 167 (Clifford Smith ed. 2d ed.1990); Kose John & Avner Kalay, *Costly Contracting and Optimal Payout Constraints*, 37 J.Fin. 457 (1982); Avner Kalay, *Stockholder-Bondholder Conflict and Dividend Constraints*, 10 J.Fin.Econ. 211 (1982) (evaluating American Bar Foundation, *Corporate Debt Financing Project: Commentaries on Model Debenture Indenture Provisions* (1971)).

[4] See, e.g., Leland Crabbe, *Event Risk: An Analysis of Losses to Bondholders and "Super Poison Put" Bond Covenants*, 46 J.Fin. 689 (1991); Steven Zimmer, *Event Risk Premia and Bond Market Incentives for Corporate Leverage*, Fed. Reserve Bank N.Y.Q.Rev. 15 (Spr.1990). These covenants are also called "poison put" covenants because they can be structured to increase the cost of a hostile takeover, whether or not accompanied by an increase in leverage.

liquidated or sold today. This gives them strong incentives to delay a liquidation or sale, in the hope that the firm's prospects will improve. In effect, stockholders and junior debtholders hold an out-of-the-money call option on the firm's assets, and want to stretch out the time to maturity of their option.

The incentives for some classes of claimants to delay do much to explain why bankruptcy is often a costly and protracted process. In most cases, the value of the *firm* is maximized by a quick restructuring and exit from bankruptcy. But that might wipe out stockholders and junior creditors. As a result, they may litigate (or threaten to litigate) every issue in order to delay the resolution of the bankruptcy. Unfortunately, bankruptcy law leaves ample room for protracted litigation. Scholars have argued that society would be better served by a bankruptcy process that emphasized speed, and limited the parties' ability to delay the needed financial restructuring. *Ex ante*, shareholders and creditors would be better off under such a system because bankruptcy costs would be lower.[5]

Fiduciary Duty and Conflicts of Interest. Option analysis can also illustrate when particular actions involve a conflict of interest. For example, a risky investment, normally a matter of unreviewable business judgment, may take on a different light when a company's ability to pay its debt is uncertain. By increasing the risk of default, the investment benefits stockholders at the expense of debtholders.

Judges have begun to appreciate the implications of option theory for the fiduciary duties of the directors. In a recent case, Delaware Chancellor William Allen explicitly used option theory to argue that directors of a firm at or near insolvency should maximize the value of the firm as a whole, rather than the value of its stock.

CREDIT LYONNAIS BANK NEDERLAND, N.V. v. PATHE COMMUNICATIONS CORP.
1991 WL 277613, at n.55 (Del.Ch.1991)

The possibility of insolvency can do curious things to incentives, exposing creditors to risks of opportunistic behavior and creating complexities for directors. Consider, for example, a solvent corporation having a single asset, a judgment for $51 million against a solvent debtor. The judgment is on appeal and thus subject to modification or reversal. Assume that the only liabilities of the company are to bondholders in the

---

[5] See, e.g., Mark Roe, *Bankruptcy and Debt: A New Model for Corporate Reorganization*, 83 Colum.L.Rev. 527 (1983).

amount of $12 million. Assume that the array of probable outcomes of the appeal is as follows:

[Outcome]	Expected Value
25% chance of affirmance ($51mm)	$12.75 million
70% chance of modification ($4mm)	$ 2.8 million
5% chance of reversal ($0)	$ 0
Expected Value of Judgment on Appeal	$15.55 million

Thus, the best evaluation is that the current value of the equity is $3.55 million. ($15.55 million expected value of judgment on appeal − $12 million liability to bondholders). Now assume an offer to settle at . . . $17.5 million. By what standard do the directors of the company evaluate the fairness of [this offer]?

The creditors of this solvent company would be in favor of accepting . . . [the offer to] avoid the 75% risk of insolvency and default. The stockholders, however, . . . very well may be opposed to acceptance of the $17.5 million offer [even though] the residual value of the corporation would increase from $3.5 to $5.5 million. This is so because the litigation alternative, with its 25% probability of a $39 million outcome to them ($51 millon − $12 million = $39 million) has an expected value to the residual risk bearer of $9.75 million ($39 million × 25% chance of affirmance), substantially greater than the $5.5 million available to them in the settlement. . . .

[I]t seems apparent that one should in this hypothetical accept the best settlement offer available providing it is greater than $15.55 million, and one below that amount should be rejected. But that result will not be reached by a director who thinks he owes duties directly to shareholders only. It will be reached by directors who are capable of conceiving of the corporation as a legal and economic entity. Such directors will recognize that in managing the business affairs of a solvent corporation in the vicinity of insolvency, circumstances may arise when the right (both the efficient and the fair) course to follow for the corporation may diverge from the choice that the stockholders (or the creditors, or the employees, or any single group interested in the corporation) would make if given the opportunity to act. Thus, the option perspective can support a rule that gives directors' fiduciary duties to debtholders when a firm approaches insolvency.

A subsequent case, Geyer v. Ingersoll Publications Co., 1992 WL 136473 (Del.Ch.1992), relies on *Lyonnais Bank* in holding that directors owe fiduciary duties to creditors as soon as a firm becomes insolvent, even if the firm has not yet filed for bankruptcy. This, though, doesn't fully resolve the tension between maximizing value to the corporation, and maximizing value to the shareholders. Chancellor Allen's hypothetical, after all, involved a solvent corporation.

2. Management Incentive Compensation

An option perspective can also be useful in examining the conflict between managers and stockholders. It is commonplace to recognize that managers and stockholders have different incentives with respect to some firm decisions. Stockholders desire profit maximization. Managers, however, desire that combination of salary, perquisites, and profit maximization that yields *them* the most value. Absent corrective forces, managers will engage in less profit maximization than the stockholders would prefer.

Managers are also often more risk-averse than diversified shareholders. There are two principal reasons. First, managers typically have a large investment in firm-specific human capital. Taking more risk exposes this human capital to greater risk, since the managers are more likely to lose their jobs if the company gets into financial trouble. Second, managers' financial assets are often concentrated in the firm they manage. Thus, managers may be more risk averse than stockholders would prefer. The concentration of human and financial capital in a single firm also makes the managers averse to both systematic and firm-specific risk, while diversified stockholders care only about systematic risk.[6]

One way to make managers more interested in profits is to give them stock in the firm. Too little stock, and managers won't care enough about profits. Too much stock, though, will make the managers less financially diversified and may make them too risk averse.

Firms can also offer managers stock options, instead of or in addition to stock. Options will also enhance the profit incentive, and can make the managers more willing to accept risk. Too many options, though, and the managers may develop too great an affinity for risk. This may partly explain why management stock options are often issued with an exercise price equal to the current market price, and a long time (often 10 years) until expiration, so the options are deep in the money in present value terms. This gives managers incentives that are something of a hybrid between stock and an out of the money option.

A further possibility is leveraging the firm, say through a leveraged buyout. This makes stock take on more of the characteristics of a call option. By reducing the fraction of invested capital that is in the form of equity, leverage also makes it feasible to give managers a larger percentage stake in the residual value of the firm.

---

[6] See Eugene Fama, *Agency Problems in the Theory of the Firm*, 88 J.Pol.Econ. 288 (1980).

　　　Complexities like these make designing a good management compensation package a difficult task. *No* compensation system can produce perfect incentives.[7] But understanding the option characteristics of stock, and how options can be used as part of the compensation mix is an essential tool. Option theory is central to understanding managers' attitudes toward risk, and how manager and shareholder interests may diverge.[8]

---

[7] See Carlos Meeo-e-Souza, *Mortal Managers and Long-Term Goals: An Impossibility Result*, 24 Rand J.Econ. 313 (1993).

[8] For a recent effort to incorporate some of these complications into the theory of managerial compensation, see M.P. Narayanan, *Compensation Contracts and Managerial Myopia* (U.Mich.Bus.Sch. working paper 92-10, 1992).

Chapter 7 Problems

1. Figure 7-1 shows the return at expiration to the *holder* of a call option on common stock, as a function of the value of the stock at expiration. Draw the return at expiration to the *seller* of a call option on common stock, with an exercise price of $X, as a function of the value of the stock at expiration.

2. Draw the return at expiration to the seller of a put option on common stock, with an exercise price of $X, as a function of the value of the stock at expiration.

3. In order to get your feet wet in the world of option finance you have decided to buy both a call and a put on the same stock. The stock sells for $40 per share. The call option has an exercise price of $45 and the put has an exercise price of $35. Both expire in 6 months. Draw a graph of the value at expiration of this package of options, as a function of the value of the stock at expiration. Label as many points as you can.

4. What beliefs about future changes in the price of the underlying common stock would lead an investor to adopt the strategy described in problem 3?

5. Draw the return at expiration to an investor who both (i) holds a call option on an asset with an exercise price of $X, and (ii) has sold a put option on the same asset, with the same exercise price and expiration date, as a function of the value at expiration of the underlying asset.

6. Explain why holding the option position described in problem 5, and also having on hand enough money to pay the exercise price at expiration, is *equivalent* to owning the underlying asset, if there are no cash distributions on the underlying asset between now and the expiration date.

7. Alpha Company common stock currently sells for $40 per share. Alpha has just issued $100 million of 8% convertible debentures due in ten years at a price equal to their principal value of $1000. The debentures pay interest annually. Each debenture is convertible, on the maturity date of the debentures, into 20 shares of Alpha common stock. Describe the Alpha convertible debentures as a combination of nonconvertible debentures and a call option on Alpha common stock. Specify the exercise price and expiration date of the option.

8. You are a consultant to the Ministry of Finance of the newly democratized nation of Freedonia. The government is anxious to implement its new privatization program. Privatization of state owned companies will

be conducted by distributing 20% of the shares in each company to its current employees, and selling the remaining 80% to the highest bidders. To attract investor interest, the shares will carry, for 10 years after issuance, a guaranteed minimum annual dividend of 4.5% of the initial price of the shares. There may also be a bonus dividend which will be set by the board of directors based on the success of each company and its need for new funds to invest in the business. Each share will be entitled to one vote on the election of directors and other matters on which shareholders are entitled to vote. To prevent disparities in personal wealth from appearing too quickly, the government will have the right to repurchase the shares within 10 years after issuance for three times the initial sale price. Holders of these "Freedonia shares" will have a claim on the firm's assets which is junior to that of all other creditors.

Break the Freedonia shares into two or more component parts, so that each part resembles a simple security -- common stock, preferred stock, debt, or option -- that is commonly traded in the U.S. That is, construct a bundle of component securities that offer the same expected payoff as the Freedonia shares.

9. Suppose, in Table 7-1, that the risky investment being considered by Firm X has a 30% chance of returning $250, and a 70% chance of being a total loss.

a) What is the expected return from this investment?

b) What is the expected gain for the stockholders of Firm X from making this investment?

c) What is the expected loss to the debtholders of Firm X from making this investment?

d) What is the expected value of Firm X if it makes this investment?

PART II. MOTIVES FOR ACQUISITIONS

In this Part, we survey the major explanations for why corporate acquisitions take place. The core questions we will ask are:

- Do these transactions add value? In other words, does the transaction increase the combined value of the acquirer and the target?
- Most critically, *where does the value added come from?*
- If there is value added in only some transactions, which ones?
- How are the gains split between the acquiring and target firms?
- Are there identifiable losers from takeovers?
- How are firms that are not themselves takeover targets affected -- positively or negatively -- by an active takeover market?

In asking these questions, it is critical to separate *market value* -- the value that investors place on a firm's debt and equity -- from the firm's underlying *business value* -- the present value of the expected cash flows from the firm's assets. If shareholders were perfectly informed about a firm's business prospects, and perfectly rational in assessing those prospects, then market value would equal business value. In the real world of imperfect information and possible investor irrationality, the two can diverge.

More precisely, let:

total market value = the combined market value of the firm's outstanding debt, preferred stock, and common stock

shareholder market value = market value of the firm's outstanding common stock (market price × number of shares outstanding)

Total market value is often hard to measure, even for public companies, because much of their debt is not publicly traded. However, often we care about the *change* in market value as the result of an acquisition or other event, rather than the absolute level of market value. Moreover, the value of common stock is much more sensitive to various corporate events than the value of more senior securities. If an event causes only negligible changes in the market value of senior securities, then the change in shareholder market value (which is readily observable for public companies) will equal the change in total market value.

For business value, let:

total business value = present value of the expected cash flows accruing to all security holders from the business

shareholder business value = total business value - present value of expected cash flows accruing to senior claimants

Business value is often what we really want to know, but it isn't directly observable. A key question will be whether we can infer that an acquisition has increased (unobservable) business value because we observe that it has increased (observable) shareholder market value.

If (i) the acquirer's and target's shares trade in a semi-strong efficient market, in which public information is promptly reflected in each company's share price (the *semi-strong efficiency assumption*); and (ii) all information about the expected cash flows of both firms, both before and after the acquisition, is publicly available (the *full information assumption*), then changes in shareholder *market* value when an acquisition is announced will reflect investors' unbiased estimate of how the acquisition will change shareholder *business* value. If, in addition, the transaction does not transfer wealth between shareholders and holders of other securities, then changes in shareholder market value when an acquisition is announced will reflect investors' best estimate of changes in *total* business value.

These assumptions, though, require empirical testing. Moreover, value estimates are only that. Investors will surely make mistakes, especially when evaluating a new form of transaction. For example, it appears in hindsight that investors overestimated the value of conglomerate acquisitions when they were in vogue in the 1960s, and overestimated the ability of many highly leveraged firms to repay their debts in the late 1980s.

For the target company, the source of added shareholder market value is straightforward. A typical acquirer pays a large premium above the market price for the target company's stock. That premium is a measure of the target shareholders' market value gains.

Whether the acquiring firm's shareholder market value also increases as a result of a takeover is less obvious. The acquirer's shares will increase in market value only if the post-transaction market value of the combined companies increases by *more than* the sum of: (i) the premium paid to target shareholders; plus (ii) the transaction costs associated with the acquisition.

In some cases, market value and business value are unduly narrow concepts. If a transaction increases cash flows to shareholders, but only by reducing cash flows to others with claims on the acquirer or target (principally employees, customers, and the U.S. Treasury), then the increase in shareholder market value and total business value will not reflect a corresponding increase in the firm's total contribution to social wealth.

The chapters that follow systematically canvass the principal explanations for increases in combined (acquirer and target) shareholder market value as a result of acquisitions. In each chapter, we first assess the theoretical strength of the explanation. Why is it claimed that the acquisition increases shareholder market value? Is the claim consistent with what we learned in Part I about financial theory and the functioning of capital markets? Does the increase in shareholder market value reflect an increase in *total business value* and *total social value*, or merely a wealth transfer from some other group to shareholders? We then evaluate, for each claimed source of market value gains, whether the empirical evidence is consistent with the theory.

The starting point for evaluating the motives for acquisitions is the principle of *value additivity*.[1] Value additivity means that if we have two streams of cash flow, *A* and *B*, then the present value of *A* + *B* is equal to the present value of *A* plus the present value of *B*. Unless cash flows change, combining two corporations cannot result in a business value for the combined entity greater than the sum of the pre-combination values of the separate firms.

In a semi-strong efficient and fully informed market, the market value of the acquirer's and target's stock will equal business value both before and after the transaction.[2] Value additivity means that, absent wealth transfers from non-shareholder claimants, the market value of the merged firm should equal the sum of the market values of the separate firms. In the language of game theory, the acquisition is a zero-sum game; the premium that the acquirer pays for the target's stock comes out of the pockets of the acquirer's shareholders. Once we add in the transaction costs incurred by both sides, the transaction is a negative-sum game -- the acquirer's shareholders lose more than the target's shareholders gain.

If investors were *not* fully informed about expected cash flows before the acquisition, the *market* value of the combined firms may change even if cash flows don't, because the announcement of the transaction conveys information to investors about the pre-existing cash flows of the two firms. But actual cash flows, which are the touchstone of *business* value, won't change. The game is still zero-sum before transaction costs, and negative-sum after transaction costs.

Each acquisition motive considered below is an effort to identify circumstances where the shareholder market value of the combined firm can exceed the pre-transaction shareholder market value of the component parts. The many explanations can be divided into four broad classes.

Cash-flow-improvement (chapters 8-11): First, the acquisition may lead to changes in the underlying cash flows. For example, combining two firms in related industries can lead to efficiencies of scale or scope in running the combined enterprise. Or the acquirer's managers may be more skilled than the target's managers at running the target's business. Or a leveraged buyout, by providing a different capital structure, stronger incentive compensation, and stronger shareholder oversight, may let the same firm, run by the same managers, generate more cash than it did before the buyout. Under these explanations, the gains in shareholder market value reflect gains in total business value and total social value. The gains in shareholder market value can be split between acquiring and target firms, they can accrue

---

[1] This principle was developed qualitatively in Chapter 4, and is considered further in Chapter 9.

[2] Note that the semi-strong efficiency assumption, coupled with the full information assumption, is equivalent to strong-form market efficiency.

entirely to the target firm, or the acquiring firm's shareholders can even realize losses, with the target's shareholders reaping more than 100% of the market value gains.

Tax savings and other wealth transfers (chapters 12 & 15): A second family of potential acquisition motives involves wealth transfers to acquiring and target firm shareholders from others -- creditors, employees, customers, or taxing authorities -- who also have an interest in the corporate cash flow, or in competitive pricing of the firm's products. Chapter 12 focuses on tax motives for acquisitions. It explains the basic tax rules governing corporate acquisitions, as a predicate for evaluating how acquisitions can change the combined tax burden of the acquirer and target, at either the corporate or the shareholder level. Chapter 15 considers the potential for, and evidence on, wealth transfers from creditors, customers, and employees. Under these explanations, the gains in shareholder market value do not reflect gains in total social wealth.

Informational explanations (chapters 13-14): A third broad possibility is that the gains to shareholders arise because market values don't (or by financial wizardry can be made not to) match the present value of the underlying cash flows. Chapter 13 considers the accounting rules that govern acquisitions, how an acquisition will change reported earnings, book value, and return on equity or total assets, and whether these accounting changes do or should affect market values. Chapter 14 considers other situations where market price may deviate from business value, and the possibility that some acquisitions reflect the acquirer's effort to buy an undervalued target. Under these explanations, the gains in shareholder market value may or may not (depending on the explanation) reflect gains in shareholder and total business value.

Managerialist explanations: Finally, some acquisitions may reflect the separation of ownership and control of the acquiring firm -- they make sense for the acquirer's managers, but not for the acquirer's shareholders. This explanation has special force in the common situation where the market value of the acquirer's shares decreases. Several chapters, especially 9 and 15, evaluate the possibility that many acquirers overpay for targets (which provides a motive on the target side, but calls for explanation on the acquirer's side).

Close study of the multiple reasons why acquisitions take place is important for purposes of both public policy and private lawyering. Although public policy toward corporate acquisitions might also take into account noneconomic considerations, such as the desirability of concentration of economic power in a democracy, a critical influence on that policy will be whether corporate acquisitions improve economic performance. If acquisitions motivated by some theories hold out promise of increases in total social wealth, while those motivated by other theories do not, the regulatory question is whether we can encourage the value-increasing transactions, and discourage others. If some types of acquisitions produce both gains in total social wealth and identifiable losers, the regulatory question is whether the losers should be compensated.

From the private lawyering perspective, it is critical to understand how both sides seek to gain from an acquisition. Whatever your client's motivation, the structure of the transaction must be designed to facilitate it. Moreover, in choosing among alternative structures, it is critical to understand which structures promise real value added, and which do not. For example, opportunities may arise to trade style (higher reported earnings for the acquirer) for substance (a higher price for the target), when the acquirer cares about reported earnings.

CHAPTER 8: OPERATING SYNERGY

Synergies of various sorts -- operating, financial, or managerial -- are the most common explanation offered by the acquirer's managers for an acquisition. The concept of synergy is the flip side of value additivity. Value additivity asserts that two plus two equal four; synergy exists when the answer is five or more. Without more, however, synergy is less a theory than a tautology; it posits the fact of value creation but offers no hint of what caused it.

To be helpful in explaining acquisitions, the concept of synergy must be expanded from an after-the-fact description of a result, to a predictive theory that offers guidance on how and where that result can be achieved. For this purpose, it is useful to divide the concept into two parts: operating synergy (this chapter), and financial synergy (Chapter 9). Operating synergy involves the prospect of improvements in the productive activities of the two companies. From this perspective, displacement of inefficient management, while warranting separate treatment in Chapter 10 because of its prominence in the legal and economic literature, is simply one variant of operating synergy. Financial synergy concerns the potential value of reducing the variance of a company's earnings by diversifying at the firm level, or replacing the external capital market with an internal market.

We begin in section A by collecting the overall evidence on gains from takeovers, which suggests that synergy -- or some other source of value -- is at work in at least some transactions. Section B examines a range of factors that are claimed to have the potential to produce operating synergy. Section C discusses the consistency of the claims with the financial theory developed in Part I. Section D then reviews the empirical evidence that bears on whether operating synergy is realized in practice.

A. The General Evidence on Value Creation in Takeovers

The Bradley, Desai & Kim study of tender offers reproduced in Chapter 6 is representative of many studies that find that takeovers are very, very good for target shareholders.[1] The aggregate dollar gains are enormous, as Grundfest & Black suggest in the article excerpted below. This aggregate data establishes the challenge for this part of the book -- to understand where these large gains to target shareholders come from, and whether they reflect real increases in economic performance.

---

[1] For reviews, see Michael Jensen & Richard Ruback, *The Market for Corporate Control: The Evidence*, 11 J.Fin.Econ. 5 (1983); Gregg Jarrell, James Brickley & Jeffry Netter, *The Market for Corporate Control: The Empirical Evidence Since 1980*, 2 J.Econ.Persp. 49 (1988).

Bernard Black & Joseph Grundfest
SHAREHOLDER GAINS FROM TAKEOVERS AND
RESTRUCTURINGS BETWEEN 1981 AND 1986
J. Applied Corp.Fin. 5 (Spr.1988)

Back in 1789 Benjamin Franklin claimed that nothing was certain in life but death and taxes. If Franklin were alive and paying taxes today he might add a third immutable constant to his list: shareholders gain from takeovers. . . . There is no shortage of research demonstrating takeover premiums averaging 30-50%. However, these percentage premiums have not been translated into estimates of the billions of dollars by which takeover activity has increases shareholder wealth. This paper is an initial attempt to fill that gap. . . . [As shown in Table 8-1, we] estimate that between 1981 and 1986, [three categories of takeover-related transactions -- takeovers of public companies, including leveraged buyouts (LBOs); divestitures by public companies; and leveraged recapitalizations --] increased shareholder wealth by at least $162 billion. . . .

Table 8-1
Estimated Shareholder Gains: Takeovers
and Restructurings, 1981-1986
($ billions)

Transaction Type	Nominal Dollars	1987 Dollars	If reinvested in T-bills thru Dec. 1987
Takeovers of Public Companies (including LBOs)	$134.4	$148.5	$174.6
Divestitures by Public Companies (*excluding* spinoffs)	21.9	23.9	27.6
Leveraged Recapitalizations	5.3	5.6	6.0
TOTAL	**$161.6**	**$178.0**	**$208.2**

[Our estimate] substantially understates the true gain from takeover activity because it excludes gains from "the more important impact of the takeover, [which] may well be on those firms and managers who are not taken over, but who change their behavior as a result of the general deterrent threat of a takeover."[4]

Why are Shareholder Gains Important?

Shareholder gains from takeovers are important because they reflect the market's expectation that these transactions will increase the value to

---

[4] John Coffee, *Shareholders Versus Managers: The Strain in the Corporate Web*, 85 Mich.L.Rev. 1 (1986).

investors of the operations being sold. The gains reflect in substantial part investor expectations that the new owners will run the acquired businesses more efficiently. The amount of the gains measures the market's best estimate of the present value of the future improvements in the target's financial performance.

Opponents of takeover activity often criticize the focus on shareholder gains as overly narrow and excessively dependent on the assumption that stock market profits accurately measure efficiency gains in the economy. One need not, however, be a firm believer in the efficient market hypothesis to agree that aggregate measures of shareholder gains are highly relevant to the policy debate about takeovers.

To begin with, takeover gains are neither shredded nor burned. The proceeds to investors from takeover activity are recycled in the economy and become available for investment in other stocks, bonds, and financial instruments. To the extent that these proceeds are reinvested, takeovers do not deplete the pool of capital available for investment in real assets. Takeover activity can thereby promote the reallocation of capital to higher-valued activities.

Second, acquirers in takeover transactions have powerful incentives to operate the target companies as efficiently as possible. Having paid a large premium for a target's shares, an acquirer can hardly afford to let his new investment lie fallow. By the same token, an acquirer has no rational reason to cut back on research and development or capital expenditures that would increase the acquired company's value.

Therefore, it is probably no accident that the high level of takeover activity in manufacturing in the 1980s has coincided with rapid growth in manufacturing productivity. U.S. manufacturing productivity has grown at an annual rate of 3.4% in the 1980s, faster than any other decade for which data are available. During this period, manufacturing represented about 22% of GNP, but accounted for over 40% of takeover activity. Moreover, productivity growth was particularly strong in industries that experienced substantial takeover activity.[6]

The efficiency and productivity gains from takeovers may also have positive implications for American labor. While individual takeovers may lead to local job loss, efficiency gains can also preserve jobs at plants that otherwise would have closed, and can lead to faster long-term growth, and thus to greater employment. Indeed, while further research would be valuable, the available academic evidence sharply disputes the popular perception that takeovers cause unemployment and tends to support the view that takeovers often save existing jobs and enhance formation of new jobs.

Thus, Charles Brown and James Medoff report that, "Contrary to the tenor of public press coverage of acquisitions, we find that wages generally

---

[6] John Paulus & Robert Gay, *Is America Helping Herself: Corporate Restructuring and Global Competitiveness* (Morgan Stanley & Co.1987); see also Frank Lichtenberg, *Corporate Takeovers and Productivity* ch. 3 (1992).

grow faster following acquisitions. . . . We also find employment grows faster.[8]   Similarly, Steven Kaplan finds that employment increases, on average, after a leveraged buyout,[9] and Glenn Yago and Gelvin Stevenson conclude that takeovers "could well be considered an *alternative* to plant closings.   Non-acquired firms were more likely to close [plants] than acquired firms."[10]. . .

Moreover, when one considers a universe broader than just target companies, the potential for takeover activity to increase job opportunities is even stronger.   As the additional capital made available by takeover-related efficiency gains is reinvested, new growth opportunities are realized throughout the economy and new jobs are created.   Thus, just as productivity growth in the 1980s may partly reflect efficiency gains from takeovers, strong U.S. job growth in the 1980s may also partly reflect the indirect benefits of an active market for corporate control.

Finally, as noted above, the efficiency gains from takeover activity are likely to go far beyond those companies that are taken over.   To ward off a real or perceived threat of a takeover, companies may restructure operations, cut costs, return excess cash to shareholders through dividends or stock repurchases, and take other efficiency enhancing steps.   As an executive at Manufacturers Hanover described the bank's recent restructuring: "We did what we thought an outsider would do to us.   We think we did enough, but maybe someone out there thinks we haven't and will take a run at us." These spillover gains from takeover active cannot be readily quantified, but they are certainly large, and may well exceed the directly observable gains.[12]

Shareholder gains are not, of course, a perfect measure of future efficiency gains from takeovers, for several reasons.   First, if investors already expect that a particular company may become a target or a bidder, the stock price reaction to the announcement of an actual transaction will capture only part of the gain to the target, and only part of the gain or loss to the bidder.

Second, the market's estimates of expected gains may be low in some cases and high in others.   If, however, the anticipated gains are not realized

---

[8] Charles Brown & James Medoff, *The Impact of Firm Acquisitions on Labor*, in *Corporate Takeovers: Causes and Consequences* 9 (Alan Auerbach ed.1988).

[9] Steven Kaplan, *The Effects of Management Buyouts on Operating Performance and Value*, 24 J.Fin.Econ. 217 (1989).

[10] Glenn Yago & Gelvin Stevenson, *Mergers and Acquisitions in the New Jersey Economy* (Econ.Res. Bureau, State Univ. of N.Y. at Stony Brook, 1986) (emphasis in original).

[12] Managers, out of fear of a takeover, may also take actions that involve economic costs. Steps like adoption of poison pills and antitakeover charter amendments are likely to he relatively inexpensive.   However, managers who believe that the market is myopic and undervalues long-term investments may try to maximize short-term profits, even if the academic evidence shows that their beliefs are misguided. The costs of such efforts may be substantial.   Nevertheless, the benefits of efficiency-increasing ways to avoid takeovers seem likely to far exceed the costs of efficiency-decreasing efforts.

on average, then investors should learn from prior experience and bid down the price of acquirers to reflect the investors' revised expectations. In turn, acquirers may also reduce the premiums they are willing to pay. The observed stock price gains should therefore reflect an unbiased estimate, informed by the market's prior experience with takeovers, of the expected increases in value.

Third, investors value the returns to their contingent claims on a company's assets and earnings capacity, and not efficiency as such. For example, tax benefits from a takeover would produce stock price gains that do not reflect efficiency gains. Several studies, however, conclude that tax savings are not a significant source of gain for most takeovers.[14] . . .

Finally, the stock market crash of October 1987 has raised questions about the validity of the efficient capital markets hypothesis, on which the link between stock price gains and future cash flow gains depends. The market crash has reinforced the doubts of some about the proposition that . . . the overall level of stock prices is neither too high nor too low. [This type of] efficiency, however, is of limited importance to our study. Instead, our estimates rely primarily on the market's [relative efficiency] -- its ability to establish *relative* values among securities by incorporating publicly available information into securities prices. That proposition has survived the [market crash] largely unscathed.

To he sure, if the market as a whole is too high (or too low), then measured shareholder gains may overstate (or understate) the increases in value likely to be realized in the future. But that merely confirms that stock price increases reflect only investor *estimates* of increases in future cash flow. The stock price data still reflect the market's best expectation of future gains, measured for each transaction at the time the transaction occurs.

In sum, while there may not be a dollar-for-dollar match between gains to shareholders and increased efficiency, there is surely a strong correlation between the two.

Takeovers of Publicly Traded Companies

Returns to Target Shareholders

Studies of takeovers from the early 1960s through the present uniformly find large percentage gains to target company shareholders. . . . [T]hese gains, on average, do not come at the expense of the bidder's shareholders,

---

[14] See, e.g., Alan Auerbach & David Reishus, *The Impact of Taxation on Mergers and Acquisitions*, in *Mergers and Acquisitions* 69 (Alan Auerbach ed.1988); Ronald Gilson, Myron Scholes & Mark Wolfson, *Taxation and the Dynamics of Corporate Control: The Uncertain Case for Tax-Motivated Acquisitions*, in *Knights, Raiders and Targets: The Impact of the Hostile Takeover* 271 (John Coffee, Louis Lowenstein & Susan Rose-Ackerman, eds.1988).

nor at the expense of holders of debt or preferred stock of the target or the bidder. They therefore represent net gains to all investors as a class.[a]

The most comprehensive single source on takeovers of U.S. companies is the *Mergerstat Review*, [formerly published by W.T. Grimm & Co. and currently published by Merrill Lynch]. W.T. Grimm reports the total dollar value paid for common stock of public U.S. companies involved in takeovers (including LBOs), as well as the average percentage premium paid for those shares. The premium is measured relative to the market price five days prior to the first public announcement of the transaction. The average percentage premium is computed by assigning equal weight to each transaction.

Using the W.T. Grimm data, we can estimate the total dollar premiums paid to target shareholders in takeovers of public U.S. companies between 1981 and 1986. We construct the estimate in two steps. First, we treat all takeovers in each year as a single transaction with a percentage premium equal to the average percentage premium for that year reported by W.T. Grimm. The resulting estimate is shown in the third column of Table 8-2.

This estimate is biased downward because the W.T. Grimm data do not capture any increases in stock prices that occur more than five days before the initial public announcement. This omission is substantial. For tender offers between 1980 and 1985, [Gregg Jarrell and Annette Poulsen report] that the average cumulative abnormal return ("CAR") to targets from day −20 [20 days before the initial announcement] through day −6 equaled 24.7% of the mean CAR from day −5 through day +5.[24]. . .

Table 8-2
Target Shareholder Gains, Takeovers of Public Companies, 1981-1986
($ millions)

| Year | Consideration Paid | Average Percentage Premium | Estimated Dollar Premium | Run-up Adjusted | |
				Average Percentage Premium	Estimated Dollar Premium
1981	$56,569	48.0%	$18,347	57.6%	$20,675
1982	31,502	47.4	10,130	56.9	11,422
1983	39,471	37.7	10,807	45.2	12,294
1984	82,731	37.9	22,738	45.5	25,863
1985	116,676	37.1	31,573	44.5	35,943
1986	89,866	38.2	24,840	45.8	28,246
Total	$416,815	39.8%	$118,435	47.8%	$134,443

[a] More recent studies, discussed in section D, find stock price losses to acquiring firms from takeovers in the 1980s, though the losses are only a fraction of the gains to target shareholders. Eds.

[24] Gregg Jarrell & Annette Poulsen, *Stock Trading Before the Announcement of Tender Offers: Insider Trading or Market Anticipation?*, 5 J.L.Econ. & Org. 225 (1989).

To adjust for runup prior to day -5, we estimated conservatively that the actual percentage gains equaled 120% of the percentage gains reported by W.T. Grimm. As shown in Table 8-2, after adjusting for runup effects, we estimate that shareholder gains from the 1,471 takeovers of public companies between 1981 and 1986 totalled $134.4 billion. The weighted average takeover premium was 47.8%. . . .

Sources of Conservatism in the Estimate

The total gain to shareholders of $134.4 billion, estimated above, is conservative and likely to understate the total profits earned by shareholders from takeover activity, for several reasons.

First, the W.T. Grimm data exclude any gains to target shareholders from partial tender offers in which the bidder acquires less than a 50% interest in the target. Such offers are typically at a significant premium to market. Also, shares not acquired in a partial tender offer (with no second-step merger) usually continue to trade at a premium to the pre-offer price. Any resulting gains to target shareholders are not included in the total reported above.[30]

Second, W.T. Grimm's data exclude payments by bidders in acquiring a "toehold" stake in the target company. Many toehold acquisitions will affect market price, and thus will involve payment by the bidder of a premium over the unaffected market price.[31]

[The $134 billion figure also excludes gains from corporate divestitures, which are discussed below, and gains from] corporate restructurings undertaken in response to takeover attempts. In these defensive restructurings, targets frequently implement the same types of changes that a successful bidder would make. One class of such restructurings, leveraged recapitalizations, is discussed [below].

Divestitures

Percentage Gains

Sales of divisions or subsidiaries by U.S. companies have increased substantially recent years. Such "divestitures" catalogued by W.T. Grimm totaled $192 billion between 1981 and 1986. . . . This total does not include "spinoffs" of a division or subsidiary to the public.

---

[30] See Robert Comment & Gregg Jarrell, *Two-Tier and Negotiated Tender Offers: The Imprisonment of the Free-Riding Shareholder*, 19 J.Fin.Econ. 283 (1987) (pure partial tender offers between 1981 and 1984 involved a mean front-end premium of 35.4% and a mean back-end premium of 14.5%).

[31] Jarrell & Poulsen (1989), *supra* note 24, found that 95 of 167 tender offers were preceded by toehold acquisitions, averaging 10.9% of the target's outstanding shares. The study did not determine the amount of any premium paid in the toehold acquisitions.

Many of these divestitures involve publicly traded U.S. sellers, buyers or both. By examining net-of-market price movements for the common stock of the sellers and buyers around the dates of divestiture announcements, we can determine whether investors value these companies more or less highly after a divestiture is announced.

Prior academic studies of divestiture sellers find positive and statistically significant CARs ranging from 0.7% to 3% for transactions where the price is stated. These gains do not come at the expense of holders of the seller's debt or preferred stock. However, none of these studies reports data sufficient to enable us to estimate aggregate dollar gains from divestitures.[34]

To develop such data, we used a standard risk-adjusted cumulative abnormal returns technique to study stock price movements for several window periods around the announcement date for the 50 largest divestitures for each of 1985 and 1986, as reported by W.T. Grimm. After excluding (1) companies without stock price data available in the Center for Research in Security Prices database, (2) companies with confounding events (for example, a simultaneous announcement by the seller of a divestiture and a stock repurchase program), and (3) sellers in government-mandated divestitures (which may have different return characteristics than voluntary divestitures), we obtained a sample of 57 sellers whose divestitures totaled $34.2 billion and 43 buyers whose purchases totaled $22.9 billion. . . .

As shown in Table 8-3, the CARs for sellers were positive and statistically significant for all window periods. They averaged 3.04% for the narrow $(-1, +1)$ window. Seventy-four percent of the sellers also showed positive CARs over the $(-1, +1)$ window. The sign tests are significant for all but one of the window periods.

For buyers, the CARs were positive but insignificant for all window periods. Sign tests also generally were not statistically significant, and in two of the six window periods, more than half of the buyers showed negative returns. These results should be contrasted with the significant positive CARs, ranging from 0.3% to 2.1%, found in several prior studies of divestiture buyers. Our results are consistent, however, with the generally small or zero returns observed for bidders in acquisitions of entire companies. They suggest that the market for divested operations is relatively competitive, so that buyers find it difficult to earn abnormal returns.

---

[34] See April Klein, *The Timing and Substance of Divestiture Announcements: Individual, Simultaneous and Cumulative Effects*, 41 J.Fin. 685 (1986); James Rosenfeld, *Additional Evidence on the Relation Between Divestiture Announcements and Shareholder Wealth*, 39 J.Fin. 1437 (1984); Scott Linn & Michael Rozeff, *The Corporate Sell-Off*, Midland Corp.Fin.J. 17 (Summer 1984); Gailen Hite, James Owers & Ronald Rogers, *The Market for Interfirm Asset Sales: Partial Selloffs and Total Liquidations*, 18 J.Fin.Econ. 229 (1987); Prem Jain, *The Effect of Voluntary Sell-Off Announcements on Shareholder Wealth*, 40 J.Fin. 209 (1985); Gailen Hite & Michael Vetsuypens, *Management Buyouts of Divisions and Shareholder Wealth*, 44 J.Fin. 953 (1989).

Table 8-3

Cumulative Abnormal Returns from Divestiture Announcements[b]

Time Window (days)	Sellers (n = 57)		Buyers (n = 43)	
	Average CAR	Percent Positive	Average CAR	Percent Positive
(−1, +1)	3.04%	74%	0.74%	47%
	(t=4.48)	(z=4.06)	(t=0.81)	(z=−0.46)
(−20, +20)	3.69%	65%	1.03%	53%
	(t=2.28)	(z=2.36)	(t=0.65)	(z=0.46)

Dollar Gains

The CAR for each company in our sample can be multiplied by the company's market value, and the results summed, to estimate dollar gains. As Table 8-4 shows, dollar gains to sellers are statistically significant for all window periods and total $5.0 billion over the narrow (−1, +1) window. For purposes of this study, we will use the $5.9 billion figure because the narrow window minimizes the effects of noise and potential confounding events. . . . [N]o significant runup prior to day −1 was observed.

Dollar returns to buyers, although positive for all window periods, are statistically insignificant. For purposes of this paper, we will conservatively assume that dollar returns to buyers are zero.

Table 8-4

Shareholder Gains from Selected Divestitures, 1985-1986

Time Window (days)	Sellers (n = 57)		Buyers (n = 43)	
	Stock Price Gains ($ millions)	Gains as % of Divestiture Value	Stock Price Gains ($ millions)	Gains as % of Divestiture Value
(−1, +1)	$5,871	17.2%	$310	1.4%
	(t=3.01)		(t=0.23)	
(−20, +20)	$7,233	21.1%	$2,755	12.0%
	(t=2.02)		(t=0.98)	

The dollar gains to sellers reported in Table 8-4 could, in theory, be skewed by random variations in the stock prices of a few large capitalization sellers. We take some comfort, however, in three observations. First, the high percentage of positive price changes (74% positive) for sellers over the (−1, +1) window period suggests that the divestiture announcements were,

---

[b] The authors also report data for (-5, +1), (-10, +1), (-5, +5), and (-10, +10) window periods. These window periods are omitted in Tables 8-3 and 8-4.

in most cases, the principal news over the window period. Second, the ratio of the seller's stock price gain to divestiture size showed few outliers (max = 1.18; min = −0.70). Third, [the dollar total for each window period] is an unbiased estimate of the actual gain, and the $5.9 billion estimate for the (−1, +1) window was the smallest gain observed for any of the window periods. . . .

The observed stock price gains [suggest] an increase in value for the divested operations as a result of the divestiture transaction. . . . For the relatively large buyers, sellers, and divestitures that we studied, analysts are not likely systematically to underestimate or overestimate the value of the divested operations to the seller. Thus, price signalling effects are unlikely to explain much, if any, of the observed price movements.

Sources of Conservatism in the Estimate

. . . [O]ur estimate is likely to understate substantially aggregate gains from divestitures. . . . First, the divestitures in our sample represent only 17.8% of the total dollar value of divestitures in the 1981-1986 period as reported by W.T. Grimm. If one assumes that (1) for all divestitures, the gains to sellers equal 15% of the dollar value of the transactions (this percentage is 17.2% for the sample), and (2) the percentage of divestitures by dollar value involving public U.S. sellers equals the percentage of 76% observed [for] the sample, then the total gains to the sellers' shareholders for all divestitures by public U.S. companies between 1981 and 1986 would equal at least $21.9 billion. . . .

Second, in some cases, a company announces a planned divestiture (or a divestiture program) some time before it announces its actual divestiture transaction or transactions. The first announcement will cause investors to revalue the seller's shares based on their estimates of the sale price, but discounted to reflect uncertainty over whether, when, and at what price a sale will take place. The subsequent announcement of an actual transaction is also likely to have a price impact because the divestiture becomes more certain and the price becomes known. Thus, neither event date will fully capture the gain to the seller. Also, in the common case where a divestiture is announced prior to completion, stock price gains around the announcement date will understate the total gains because investors will discount the seller's stock price to reflect the risk that the transaction will not be completed, or will be completed at a lower price.

Leveraged Recapitalizations

Corporations often undertake restructurings of various types in response to an actual or perceived threat of a takeover. Such restructurings frequently involve the same types of changes that a successful bidder would make after a takeover. These defensive actions often produce stock price gains that are excluded from the estimates of gains from takeovers and divestitures developed above.

. . . A leveraged recapitalization of a public company involves the payment to shareholders, in cash, debt securities or preferred stock, of a large percentage of the pre-transaction market value of the company's common equity. After the recapitalization, the shareholders continue to own common stock in the company but the market value of that equity is substantially reduced. . . .

We define a transaction as a leveraged recapitalization if it involved payment to shareholders (whether by extraordinary dividend, self-tender, or merger with a shell corporation) of value equal to or greater than the residual value of the company's shares after the transaction. Using this restrictive definition, which excludes many defensive recapitalizations, we were able to identify eight public companies that successfully undertook leveraged recapitalizations in the 1985-1986 period. . . . The average percentage premium for these recapitalizations was 31.2%, and the aggregate dollar gain to shareholders was $5.3 billion.

Total Shareholder Gains

. . . A conservative estimate of gains from takeovers of public companies [between 1981 and 1986] is $134.4 billion. A conservative estimate of shareholder gains from divestitures is $21.9 billion. Finally, we estimate shareholder gains from eight leveraged recapitalizations in 1985 and 1986 at $5.3 billion. Overall, we conservatively estimate total shareholder gains from these three sources at $162 billion.

We do not purport in this paper to conduct a full cost-benefit analysis of takeover activity. We believe, however, that the gains for shareholders are of such magnitude that they must be considered as a major factor in the policy debate over takeovers. One hundred and sixty-two billion dollars, by any reasonable standard, is a lot of money.

B. The Theoretical Sources of Operating Synergy

It is common to classify acquisitions based on the fit between the acquirer's and the target's core business. If the acquirer and target are in the same business, the acquisition is *horizontal*. U.S. Steel, for example, was formed in the early 1900s through the merger of several steel manufacturers. If acquirer and target have a supplier-customer relationship with each other, the acquisition is *vertical*. For example, coal is an input into steel manufacturing, and several steel companies have acquired coal companies. More generally, if acquirer and target are in similar businesses, the acquisition is said to be *related*. Relatedness is obviously a matter of degree. A horizontal acquisition involves a close relationship between the acquirer's and the target's businesses; a vertical acquisition is one type of non-horizontal relationship.

Finally, acquisitions with little or no overlap between the acquirer's and target's businesses are called *unrelated* or *conglomerate*. In this chapter, we explore how related acquisitions may add value; unrelated acquisitions are considered in Chapter 9.[2]

1. Horizontal Acquisitions: Economies of Scale

F.M. Scherer & David Ross, INDUSTRIAL MARKET STRUCTURE AND ECONOMIC PERFORMANCE
97-106, 111-125 (3d ed. 1990)

Concentrated market structures could stem from persistent scale economies, permitting relatively large producers to manufacture and market their products at lower average cost per unit than relatively small producers. Economies of scale are best analyzed in terms of three categories: product-specific economies, associated with the volume of any single product made and sold; plant-specific economies, associated with the total output (possibly encompassing many products) of an entire plant or plant complex; and multiplant economies, associated with a firm's operation of multiple plants. . . .

Ball bearing manufacturing provides a good illustration of several *product-specific* economies. If only a few bearings are to be custom-made, the ring machining will be done on general-purpose lathes by a skilled operator who hand-positions the stock and tools and makes measurements for each cut. With this method, machining a single ring requires from five minutes to more than an hour, depending upon the part's size and complexity and the operator's skill.

If a sizeable batch is to be produced, a more specialized automatic screw machine will be used instead. . . . [This machine will produce] from 80 to 140 parts per hour . . . but setting up the screw machine to perform these operations takes about eight hours. If only 100 bearing rings are to be made, setup time greatly exceeds total running time, and it may be cheaper to do the job on an ordinary lathe. . . . The larger the batch, the lower the average cost (i.e., setup *plus* running time per unit) will be. . . .

---

[2] In antitrust analysis, the terms horizontal, vertical, and conglomerate are used with somewhat different meanings. The Federal Trade Commission, which together with the Department of Justice is responsible for federal antitrust enforcement, classifies a merger between two competitors as horizontal, a merger between supplier and customer as vertical; and all other mergers as conglomerate. Conglomerate acquisitions are then subdivided into *product line extension* (which we would classify as related acquisitions), *market extension* involving two firms that operate in the same industry but *in different geographic markets* (which we would classify as horizontal acquisitions), and *pure conglomerate* (coextensive with our conglomerate category).

If very large quantities (say, a million per year) of a single bearing design can be sold . . ., even more specialized higher-speed machines are used, and parts are transferred automatically to the next processing stage in a straight-line flow. . . . [U]nit costs may be 30 to 50% lower than with medium-volume batch methods. But in order to realize these savings, the production line must be kept running without changeover two shifts per day, and this requires a large and continuous volume. . . .

Product-specific economies of scale also have an important dynamic dimension. When intricate labor operations must be performed, as in shoe stitching and aircraft or computer assembly . . ., unit costs fall as workers and operators learn by doing. . . .   [For example, in integrated circuit production, *learning curve* cost] reductions of 25 to 30% with each doubling of cumulative output are common. Thus, if the tenth good chip will cost approximately $1,000 . . ., the 10,000th chip [will cost about] $42, and the millionth chip $6. . . .

[T]he most important economies of scale at the *plant-specific* level come from expanding the size of individual processing units. The output of a processing unit tends within certain physical limits to be roughly proportional to the volume of the unit, other things being equal, while the amount of materials and fabrication effort (and hence investment cost) required to construct the unit is proportional to the surface area of the unit's reaction chambers, storage tanks, connecting pipes, and the like. Since the area of a sphere or cylinder varies as the two-thirds power of volume, the cost of constructing process industry plants can be expected to rise as the two-thirds power of their output capacity, at least up to the point where the units become so large that extra structural reinforcement and special fabrication techniques are required. . . .

What Checks the Realization of Scale Economies?

It is clear that economies of scale exist and that unit costs fall with increases in product volume, plant size, and firm size, at least within limits. Does this decline in average costs continue indefinitely? There are many reasons for believing that it does not.

In nearly all production and distribution operations, the realization of scale economies appears to be subject to diminishing returns. With a large enough volume, setup costs dwindle to insignificance. Learning curves flatten out as very large cumulative output volumes are attained. . . . [S]caled-up process vessels and machines become unwieldy or require special structural reinforcement beyond some point, increasing unit costs rather than reducing them. . . . Workers and machines become so specialized that they cannot adapt or be adapted to change. And so on. . . .

Psychological surveys show that for reasons still imperfectly understood, workers express less satisfaction with their jobs, and especially with the challenge their jobs offer, in large plants than in small plants. To attract a work force in the face of such alienating job conditions, large plants must in effect buy off their workers with a wage premium -- one that has apparently been growing over time. . . . . [I]ncreasing the size of a plant's work force may require expanding the geographic radius from which workers are drawn, which in turn implies higher worker commuting costs and higher offsetting wages. . . . [M]aterials flows lengthen and become more complex as plant scales increase. . . . [T]he risks of fire, explosion, and wildcat strikes are at a maximum when all production is concentrated at a single plant site, so firms enjoying sufficient sales volume generally prefer to expand at other locations once they have achieved the minimum efficient scale (and sometimes even before) at one site. Finally, it is much harder to manage a big plant than a small one, all else being equal. . . .

[At the *firm* level], as enterprises increase in size, their chief executives are confronted with more and more decisions, and are removed farther and farther from the reality of front-line production and marketing operations. Their ability to make sound decisions is attenuated, with a consequent rise in costs and/or fall in revenues. The problem is aggravated when the firm operates in a complex or rapidly changing environment. . . .

Few if any [large firms] have succeeded completely in overcoming the problems of large-scale bureaucracy. Interviews with 125 North American and European companies revealed a virtually unanimous consensus that decision-making in the large multiplant firm is slower and that top executives' remoteness from operational details often (but not always) impaired the quality of decisionmaking. . . .

Figure 8-1
A Typical Long-Run Average Cost Curve

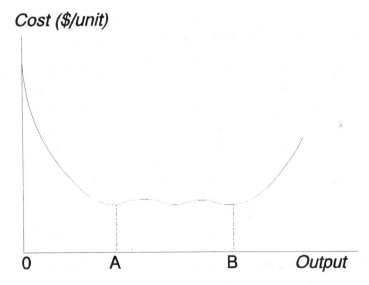

We conclude then that the long-run average cost function of industrial firms has a shape something like that shown . . . in Figure 8-1. Up to some minimum efficient scale *OA*, economies of scale lead to reductions in unit cost as capacity and output rise.   Through decentralization and other organizational techniques, it is possible to increase the firm size considerably beyond *OA* at more or less constant costs per unit.   But if the enterprise expands too far -- that is, beyond scale *OB* -- managerial diseconomies of scale intrude [and average cost per unit begins to increase].

The Measurement of Cost-Scale Relationships

We have proposed viewing economies of scale in terms of the minimum efficient scale [MES] at which all attainable unit cost savings are realized. The crucial question remains: Is the MES large or small in relation to the demand for an industry's output? Whether there is room for many firms in the market, each large enough to enjoy all scale economies, for only one firm (a *natural monopoly* situation), or for just a few (*natural oligopoly*) depends upon the relevant technology and the size of the market. . . .

[Notwithstanding the differences across industries in efficient scale, is there a systematic relationship between profitability and size?] Table 8-5 arrays the average after-tax returns on stockholders' equity for all manufacturing corporations in six size classes during six time intervals characterized by widely varying macroeconomic conditions. . . . In all six periods the billion-dollar-plus corporations exhibit the highest returns. The differential is . . . prominent in the recessions of 1969-1971 and 1979-1982. [But in the most recent time period, there was little overall correlation between size and profitability, with the smallest firms being almost as profitable (11.1% average return on equity) as the largest (11.7% average return on equity).] . . .

Table 8-5
Average Return on Equity for U.S. Manufacturing Firms, 1963-1987

Asset Size ($ millions)	1963-1965	1966-1969	1969-1971	1975-1977	1979-1982	1984-1987
Over $1,000	13.5%	12.7%	10.3%	13.2%	13.1%	11.7%
$250 - $1,000	11.0	12.1	10.4	13.0	10.8	9.0
$100 - $250	11.2	12.0	9.7	12.1	10.5	9.7
$50 - $100	10.4	11.2	8.6	12.0	10.2	10.4
$25 - $50	10.0	11.4	8.2	11.9	9.2	10.4
$10 - $25	9.9	11.0	7.9	12.4	9.9	11.1

Source: Federal Trade Commission and (after 1981) U.S. Bureau of the Census.

The Impact of Technological Change and Market Growth

How high seller concentration must be to secure production efficiency depends upon the balance between technology and market size. Both of these variables change over time. In the early 1950s, Joe S. Bain found that a least-cost flat-rolled steel products plant had a capacity of from 1.0 to 2.5 million tons per year. By 1965, the MES capacity had risen to 4.0 million tons. Further advances in . . . continuous casting technology raised the optimum further by the late 1970s -- most likely to a capacity of about 12 million tons per year. For simpler steel products such as reinforcing bars . . ., the trend was in the opposite direction as least-cost production shifted from large integrated works to "mini-mills" using electric arc furnaces to process scrap at capacities of 750,000 tons per year or less. . . .

Economies of Multiplant Operation

. . . [T]he need to operate [efficiently sized] plants . . . is not the only, or perhaps even the main, cause of high concentration. That other influences are at work is shown by the fact that the leading firms in most industries operate multiple plants supplying a similar array of products. . . . [In a careful 1963 survey of 417 industries], the leading sellers averaged 3.25 plants each. The leaders operated a single plant each in only 22 industries, or 5% of all industries. Evidently, the preeminent position of most leading firms can be attributed not merely to maintaining large plants, but to operating *many* of them. . . .

The crucial remaining question is, does this multi-plant operation by leading firms confer economies above and beyond those associated with operating a single plant of optimal scale? And, if so, how significant are they? Or to reverse the focus, how seriously disadvantaged are firms operating only a single MES plant, compared to the larger multiplant enterprises?

We shall [consider here] three main categories -- economies of multiplant production, investment, and physical distribution; economies of risk spreading and finance; and advantages of sales promotion on a multiplant scale. As we shall see, these have varying performance implications, some entailing clear-cut efficiency gains, some redistributions of income, and some a blend of efficiency, redistributive, and monopolistic effects. . . .

[In addition to these three categories], economies of scale in conducting research and development may persist into a size range embracing multiple least-cost plants. . . . [Also], a multiplant enterprise may be able to economize on management services by having a common central pool of financial planners, accountants, market researchers, labor relations specialists, purchasing agents, lawyers, and the like. There is statistical evidence that size, both absolute and relative, does yield overhead cost savings. . . .

[One situation where] multiplant operation affects the costs of production, investment, and physical distribution . . . [is where] a market of considerable geographic expanse is served, and outbound transportation costs are appreciable. Then the firm's least-cost strategy is likely to entail operating multiple geographically dispersed plants, each supplying for the most part only the customers nearest its location. The operating patterns of sizeable firms in the cement, petroleum refining, beer, and glass bottle industries provide relatively pure examples. [A second case is] firms with low shipping costs . . . but complex product lines. Then each plant of a multiplant enterprise may specialize in some narrow segment of the product array -- for example, one plant in women's cemented-sole fashion shoes, another in women's casuals, a third in men's Goodyear welts, a fourth in work shoes, and so on. . . .

If delivery costs are substantial, as they are for beer or cement or steel reinforcing bars, it is obviously more economical, if one is to serve a large market like the continental United States or the European Community, to have multiple dispersed plants than to ship everything from one giant, centrally located installation. But this begs the fundamental question: Why does a firm have to serve the entire geographic expanse? Are there production, investment, and/or distribution cost differences between the situation in which a single company operates five least-cost, geographically dispersed plants and the one in which five independent geographically dispersed firms operate a single MES plant each?

There may be. When demand grows over time and when scale economies can be realized by expanding capacity in large indivisible chunks, excess capacity carrying costs can be reduced, and the scale economy opportunities can be exploited more fully, by playing a kind of investment whipsaw game. First a large investment is made at location A, with other plants reducing their shipping radii to satisfy growing nearby demand more fully and letting plant A serve what would normally be their peripherally located customers. Later, plant B expands and territories are readjusted to utilize its new capacity, and so on. . . .

Economies may also result from the operation of multiple geographically dispersed plants as an integrated system. For instance, the demand for automobile batteries peaks during the winter months in the northern United States and during the summer in the South. A firm with plants in both areas might be able to maintain less peak-load capacity by shipping north in the winter and south in the summer. [This will not be done, though, if] the costs of carrying additional capacity [are] less than cross-shipping costs. . . .

The other main interesting mode of multiplant operation occurs when plants specialize in some narrow slice of a product array -- for example, small mass-produced ball bearings at one plant, other small ball bearings at a second, large ball bearings at a third, tapered bearings at a fourth, and so on. Plants with a narrow line of products are easier to manage. . . . The key interpretive questions are, can the same degree of plant specialization be achieved by single-plant firms choosing to offer only a narrow line of products? And are the plants of multiplant sellers in fact more narrowly specialized than those of single-plant firms?

In answer to the first question, it appears that at least in some industries, there are marketing advantages to being a broad-line supplier.

This in turn argues for multiplant operation unless one's product line can be rounded out through purchases from other manufacturers. . . . The second question in effect asks whether single-plant producers in multi-product industries incur not only a marketing disadvantage by failing to offer a broad line, but also cram relatively more low-volume products into the production plans of their only plant and therefore sacrifice product-specific economies as well. Some single-plant firms do experience shorter production runs than their multiplant rivals. However, many exceptions exist, and the shorter runs of some relatively small firms may signify nothing more than deliberate specialization on the low-volume items in which the larger companies have no interest -- for example, because their management structures are too hierarchical to cope with the challenges of small-lot production. . . . [T]here is insufficient hard evidence on this important dimension of multiplant scale economies.

Note on Economies of Scale

1. *Merging to Grow.* Economies of scale imply that firms can improve performance by increasing the level of production. Acquiring a competitor is an obvious way to add new capacity. The capital budgeting problem for the acquiring firm will often be *buy or build*. The acquirer must assess whether building its own new plant is cheaper than acquiring a competitor's plant(s).

In some industries, regulation or market structure is such that building is not viable, which leaves buying as the only option. Examples include television broadcasting, where the number of stations in a particular geographic area is fixed; banking, where state law may bar an out-of-state bank from opening a branch, but permit the out-of-state bank to buy a local bank; and passenger airlines, where a shortage of airport gates effectively bars new entry in some markets. It should not be surprising that these industries have all experienced substantial takeover activity in recent years.

2. *Merging to Shrink.* Horizontal acquisitions take on special importance in mature industries where the number of efficient-scale plants is declining, because demand for the product is declining or simply not keeping pace with increases in minimum efficient scale. It may be cheaper in the long run for firm A to buy firm B and close down some of B's capacity, than for A and B to both incur losses until one of them unilaterally cuts capacity. Recent examples include automobile tires, steel, and airlines.

3. *Managerial Economies.* Scale economies can exist both for direct production efficiencies and for non-tangible assets, such as management. Suppose, for example, that the best managers prefer to work for large companies. If so, then larger firms can attract more talented executives.

From this perspective, acquisitions where the gains depend in replacing the target company's inefficient managers (considered in Chapter 10) may also based on economies of scale. This will be possible only if the acquirer has unused managerial capacity, either because the senior managers' time is not fully occupied with the acquirer's existing business, or because junior managers have the ability to undertake more responsible positions, but lack opportunities within the acquiring firm. Such economies are likely to be strongest when the acquirer and target are in the same line of business, because the acquirer's managers are more likely to have transferable skills.

2.　　Vertical Integration:　Defining the Boundaries of the Firm

A buyer-seller relationship prompts many acquisitions. Most commonly, a "downstream" firm that relies on an "upstream" firm for a good or service buys the upstream firm, thus gaining an assured source of supply. Less commonly, an upstream firm buys a downstream firm, thus gaining an assured customer.

Vertical integration has obvious costs. The enterprise becomes more complex, and may suffer the diseconomies of size that Scherer & Ross discuss. Integration can also cause the upstream firm to lose other customers. For example, McDonalds is likely to purchase cola syrup from Coca-Cola rather than Pepsi because Pepsi owns Kentucky Fried Chicken and Taco Bell, which compete with McDonalds. Also, because the upstream firm has an assured customer, it is somewhat insulated from market forces, and may become a technological laggard.

Why then integrate? The next two readings discuss advantages of vertical integration that may, in some settings, more than offset these costs.

F.M. Scherer & David Ross, INDUSTRIAL MARKET STRUCTURE AND ECONOMIC PERFORMANCE
109-111 (3d ed. 1990)

The typical large manufacturing corporation carries out a bewilderingly complex array of activities. Yet . . . it spends more than half its sales dollar purchasing raw materials, components, machines, special services, and the like from other firms. What determines which operations a firm will perform internally and which it will farm out to others? And how does this choice affect the scale of operation?

Of particular interest here are activities entailing minimum efficient scales (MES) large in relation to other facets of the firm's operations. For example, the most costly component of a refrigerator or a windowsill air conditioner is its compressor. In the early 1970s, economies of scale in compressor manufacturing persisted out to outputs of 2 to 3 million units per year, not necessarily all of the same design. Scale economies in refrigerator box fabrication and assembly, on the other hand, were exhausted at a plant output of roughly 800,000 units per year. Must the refrigerator assembler be large enough to produce its own compressors at minimum unit cost, or could it buy its compressors from outside specialists and operate efficiently at the smaller assembly-only MES? Similarly, a minimum-cost automobile assembly plant produced only about 200,000 vehicles per year on double-shift operation. But stamping body parts and machining automatic transmissions required larger annual volumes -- for example, from 250,000 to 400,000 units per year for each line. Is an auto firm of efficient size one that merely assembles other firms' high-scale-economy parts efficiently, or must it be large enough to span the full range of component manufacturing activities at minimum unit cost? In short, how vertically integrated must the firm be, or obversely, to what extent can it satisfy its needs through outside procurement of high-scale-economy components, perhaps avoiding thereby some diseconomies of managing a large organization?

There are several related answers to these questions. In a seminal article, [Ronald] Coase observed that the distinguishing mark of a "firm" is the "suppression of the price mechanism."[27] Resource allocation *in the market* is normally guided through prices, but *within the firm* the job is done through the conscious decisions and commands of management. Activities are collected in what we call a firm, Coase argues, when transaction costs incurred in using the price mechanism exceed the cost of organizing those activities through direct managerial controls. One reason why market transaction costs may be appreciable is that price shopping, the communication of work specifications, and contract negotiation take time and effort. Especially when goods or services would have to be contracted for repeatedly in small quantities or when designs are changing in complex ways, it may be cheaper to bring them under the firm's direct span of internal managerial control.

For components, materials, and services whose provision entails compelling scale economies, the choice between integration and disintegration has an important additional dimension. . . . [O]ne might expect the rewards from vertical disintegration to be especially great. . . . But precisely because scale economies are so compelling, the number of nonintegrated suppliers is likely to be small. For example, the total U.S. market for household and analogous refrigerators, freezers, and air conditioners in 1972 was large enough to support only five or six least-cost compressor manufacturers. Similar conditions hold with respect to the supply of automobile and truck transmissions, diesel truck and bus engines, specialized paint pigments, and many other intermediate goods. From limited supply sources may follow monopolistic pricing of components bought outside. Even if the monopolistic supplier chooses not to exercise fully its power to elevate prices, buyers recognize their dependence upon the supplier's restraint and fear, naturally

---

[27] Ronald Coase, *The Nature of the Firm,* 4 Economica n.s. 386, 389 (1937), reprinted in Ronald Coase, *The Firm, the Market and the Law* (1988).

enough, that they may not always be so fortunate. To avoid actual or feared monopolistic exploitation, users of high-scale-economy materials or components often decide to undertake production, even though they may incur a cost penalty in doing so. In effect, they view the higher cost of vertically integrated production, sacrificing some scale economies, as a less onerous burden than the risk of being gouged by a more efficient but monopolistic outside supplier.

Nor does the story end there. If several firms reason in this way and integrate vertically, the independent supply market will become thinner or even disappear. To be sure, nonintegrated firms may obtain their needed supplies from firms that have chosen to integrate. But although being dependent upon a single independent supply source for some critical raw material or component is unnerving, it is even worse when the supplier is also one's main-line competitor. The situation is unstable. When vertical integration induced by the fewness of supply sources thins the market further, other buyers may be stampeded into integrating too even though they must accept appreciable scale economy sacrifices.

Quite generally, the more prone markets are to a breakdown of competitive supply conditions, either because scale economies limit the number of suppliers or because buyer and seller are locked together in complex coordinating relationships, the stronger is the buyer's incentive to protect itself by integrating upstream. An extreme illustration of this generalization can be seen by comparing the shoe industries of the United States and the Soviet Union. In the United States, more or less workably competitive sources of supply exist for glues, shoe finishing chemicals, sole rubber compounds, paperboard containers, lasts, and special shoe-making machines. U.S. shoe manufacturers are therefore willing to rely upon independent specialists to meet their needs. In the Soviet Union, markets were virtually nonexistent, at least before reforms were initiated in the mid-1980s, and independent suppliers often failed to meet plan requirements, thereby disrupting downstream operations. To avoid such supply problems, Soviet shoe-making firms undertook extensive vertical integration to satisfy their requirements internally. . . .

Benjamin Klein, Robert Crawford & Armen Alchian
VERTICAL INTEGRATION, APPROPRIABLE RENTS,
AND THE COMPETITIVE CONTRACTING PROCESS
21 J.L. & Econ. 297, 297-306 (1978)˙

More than forty years have passed since Coase's fundamental insight that transaction, coordination, and contracting costs must be considered

---

explicitly in explaining the extent of vertical integration. Starting from the truism that profit-maximizing firms will undertake those activities that they find cheaper to administer internally than to purchase in the market, Coase forced economists to begin looking for previously neglected constraints on the trading process that might efficiently lead to an intrafirm rather than an interfirm transaction. This paper . . . explor[es] one particular cost of using the market system -- the possibility of postcontractual opportunistic behavior.

Opportunistic behavior has been identified and discussed in the modern analysis of the organization of economic activity. . . . [David] Teece has elaborated:

> Even when all of the relevant contingencies can be specified in a contract, contracts are still open to serious risks since they are not always honored. The 1970's are replete with examples of the risks associated with relying on contracts . . . [O]pen displays of opportunism are not infrequent and very often litigation turns out to be costly and ineffectual.[3]

The particular circumstance we emphasize as likely to produce a serious threat of this type of reneging on contracts is the presence of appropriable specialized quasi rents. After a specific investment is made and such quasi rents are created, the possibility of opportunistic behavior is very real. Following Coase's framework, this problem can be solved in two possible ways: vertical integration or contracts. . . . [A]s assets become more specific and more appropriable quasi rents are created (and therefore the possible gains from opportunistic behavior increases), the costs of contracting will generally increase more than the costs of vertical integration. Hence, *ceteris paribus*, we are more likely to observe vertical integration.[a]

Appropriable Quasi Rents of Specialized Assets

Assume an asset is owned by one individual and rented to another individual. The *quasi-rent value* of the asset is the excess of its value [to the owner in its current use] over its salvage value, that is, its value in its next best *use* to another renter [at another location]. The potentially *appropriable specialized portion of the quasi rent* is that portion, if any, in excess of its value [in its current location] to the second highest-valuing *user*. If this seems like a distinction without a difference, consider the following example.

Imagine a printing press owned and operated by party *A*. Publisher *B* buys printing services from party *A* by leasing his press at a contracted rate of $5,500 per day. The amortized fixed cost of the printing press is $4,000 per day and it has a current salvageable value if moved elsewhere of $1,000 (daily rental equivalent). Operating costs are $1,500 and are paid by the printing-press owner, who prints final printed pages for the publisher.

---

[3] David Teece, *Vertical Integration and Divestiture in the U.S. Oil Industry* 31 (1976).

[a] "Ceteris paribus" means "holding other things constant."

Assume also that a second publisher C is willing to offer at most $3,500 for daily service. The current quasi rent on the installed machine is $3,000 [actual rent of $5,500 - operating costs of $1,500 - salvage value of $1,000].

However, the daily quasi rent [that A receives] from publisher B relative to use of the machine for publisher C is only $2,000 [the rent of $5,500 paid by B - the rent of $3,500 that C is willing to pay]. At $5,500 revenue daily from publisher B the press owner would break even on his investment [because operating costs of $1,500 plus amortization of fixed cost of $4,000 just equals rental payment of $5,500]. If [publisher B] were then able to cut his offer for the press from $5,500 down to almost $3,500, he would still have the press service available to him. He would be appropriating $2,000 of the quasi rent from the press owner. . . . If no second party were available at the present site, the entire quasi rent [of $3,000] would be subject to threat of appropriation by an unscrupulous or opportunistic publisher.

Our primary interest concerns the means whereby this risk [of appropriation] can be reduced or avoided. In particular, vertical integration is examined as a means of economizing on the costs of avoiding risks of appropriation of quasi rents in specialized assets by opportunistic individuals. This advantage of [vertical integration] must of course be weighed against the costs of administering a broader range of assets within the firm.

An appropriable quasi rent is not a monopoly rent in the usual sense, that is, the increased value of an asset protected from market entry over the value it would have had in an open market. An appropriable quasi rent can occur with no market closure or restrictions placed on rival assets. . . . [E]ven if there were free and open competition for entry to the market, the specialization of the installed asset to a particular user (or more accurately the high costs of making it available to others) creates a quasi rent, but no "monopoly" rent. At the other extreme, an asset may be costlessly transferable to some other user at no reduction in value, while at the same time, entry of similar assets is restricted. In this case, monopoly rent would exist, but no quasi rent. . . .

We maintain that if an asset has a substantial portion of quasi rent which is strongly dependent upon some other particular asset, both assets will tend to be owned by one party. For example, reconsider our printing press example. Knowing that the press would exist and be operated even if its owner got as little as [$3,500], publisher B could seek excuses to renege on his initial contract to get the weekly rental down from $5,500 to close to $3,500 (the potential offer from publisher C, the next highest-valuing user at its present site). If publisher B could effectively announce he was not going to pay more than, say, $4,000 per week, the press owner would seem to be stuck. This unanticipated action would be opportunistic behavior . . . . if the press owner had installed the press at a competitive rental price of $5,500 anticipating (possibly naively) good faith by the publisher. The publisher, for example, might plead that his newspaper business is depressed and he will be unable to continue unless rental terms are revised.

Alternatively, and maybe more realistically, because the press owner may have bargaining power due to the large losses that he can easily impose on the publisher (if [the publisher] has no other source of press services quickly available), the press owner might suddenly seek to get a higher rental price than $5,500 to capture some newly perceived increase in the publisher's profits. . . .

[T]he costs of contractually specifying all important elements of quality varies considerably by type of asset. For some assets it may be essentially impossible to effectively specify all elements of quality and therefore vertical integration is more likely. But even for those assets used in situations where all relevant quality dimensions can be unambiguously specified in a contract, the threat of production delay during litigation may be an effective bargaining device. A contract therefore may be clearly enforceable but still subject to postcontractual opportunistic behavior. For example, the threat by the press owner to break its contract by pulling out its press is credible even though illegal and possibly subject to injunctive action. This is because such an action, even in the very short run, can impose substantial costs on the newspaper publisher.[6]

This more subtle form of opportunistic behavior is likely to result in a loss of efficiency and not just a wealth-distribution effect. For example, the publisher may decide, given this possibility, to hold or seek standby facilities otherwise not worthwhile. . . . [L]ess specific investments will be made to avoid being "locked in." In addition, the increased uncertainty of quality and quantity leads to larger optimum inventories and other increased real costs of production.

Contractual Solutions

The primary alternative to vertical integration as a solution to the general problem of opportunistic behavior is some form of economically enforceable long-term contract. Clearly a short-term (for example, one transaction, nonrepeat sale) contract will not solve the problem. . . .

Long-term contracts used as alternatives to vertical integration can be assumed to take two forms: (1) an explicitly stated contractual guarantee legally enforced by the government or some other outside institution, or (2) an implicit contractual guarantee enforced by the market mechanism of withdrawing future business if opportunistic behavior occurs. Explicit long-term contracts can, in principle, solve opportunistic problems, but . . . . [t]hey entail costs of specifying possible contingencies and the policing and

---

[6] While newspaper publishers generally own their own presses, book publishers generally do not. One possible reason book publishers are less integrated may be because a book is planned further ahead in time and can economically be released with less haste. Presses located in any area of the United States can be used. No press is specialized to one publisher, in part because speed in publication and distribution to readers are generally far less important for books than newspapers, and therefore appropriable quasi rents are not created.

litigation costs of detecting violations and enforcing the contract in the courts.[14]. . .

Since every contingency cannot be cheaply specified in a contract or even known and because legal redress is expensive, transactors will generally also rely on an implicit type of long-term contract that employs a market rather than legal enforcement mechanism, namely, the imposition of a capital loss by the withdrawal of expected future business. This goodwill market-enforcement mechanism undoubtedly is a major element of the contractual alternative to vertical integration. . . .

One way in which this market mechanism of contract enforcement may operate is by offering to the potential cheater a future "premium," more precisely, a price sufficiently greater than average variable (that is, avoidable) cost to assure a quasi-rent stream that will exceed the potential gain from cheating. The present-discounted value of this future premium stream must be greater than any increase in wealth that could be obtained by the potential cheater if he, in fact, cheated. . . .

The larger the potential one-time "theft" by cheating (the longer and more costly to detect a violation, enforce the contract, switch suppliers, and so forth) and the shorter the expected continuing business relationship, the higher this premium will [need to be to create] a nondeceiving equilibrium. This may therefore partially explain both the reliance by firms on long-term implicit contracts with particular suppliers and the existence of reciprocity agreements among firms. The premium can be paid in seemingly unrelated profitable reciprocal business. The threat of termination of this relationship mutually suppresses opportunistic behavior. . . .

The firms collecting the premium payments necessary to assure fulfillment of contractual agreements in a costly information world may appear to be earning equilibrium "profits" although they are in a competitive market. That is, there may be many, possibly identical, firms available to supply the services of nonopportunistic performance of contractual obligations yet the premium will not be competed away if transactors cannot costlessly guarantee contractual performance. . . .

[Any] fixed (sunk) costs of supplying credibility of future performance are repaid or covered by future sales on which a premium is earned. In equilibrium, the premium stream is then merely a normal rate of return on the "reputation," or "brand-name" capital created by the firm by these initial expenditures. This brand-name capital, the value of which is highly specific

---

[14] The recent Westinghouse case dealing with failure to fulfill uranium-supply contracts on grounds of "commercial impossibility" vividly illustrates these enforcement costs. Nearly three years after outright cancellation by Westinghouse of their contractual commitment, the lawsuits have not been adjudicated and those firms that have settled with Westinghouse have accepted substantially less than the original contracts would have entitled them to. A recent article by Paul Joskow, *Commercial Impossibility, the Uranium Market, and the Westinghouse Case*, 6 J.Legal Stud. 119 (1977), analyzes the Westinghouse decision to renege on the contract as anticipated risk sharing and therefore, using our definition, would not be opportunistic behavior.

to contract fulfillment by the firm, is analytically equivalent to a forfeitable collateral bond put up by the firm which is anticipated to face an opportunity to take advantage of appropriable quasi rents in specialized assets.

. . . [T]he larger the appropriable specialized quasi rents (and therefore the larger the potential short-run gain from opportunistic behavior) and the larger the premium payments necessary to prevent contractual reneging, the more costly this implicit contractual solution will be. We can also expect the explicit contract costs to be positively related to the level of appropriable quasi rents since it will pay to use more resources (including legal services) to specify precisely more contingencies when potential opportunities for lucrative contractual reneging exist.

Although implicit and explicit contracting and policing costs are positively related to the extent of appropriable specialized quasi rents, it is reasonable to assume, on the other hand, that any internal coordination or other ownership costs are not systematically related to the extent of the appropriable specialized quasi rent of the physical asset owned. Hence we can reasonably expect the following general empirical regularity to be true:

. . . integration by common or joint ownership is more likely [and a contractual relationship less likely], the higher the appropriable specialized quasi rents of the assets involved.

Note on Alternatives to Vertical Integration

Scherer & Ross develop the possibility that vertical integration is a response to market power (the ability to set prices at above competitive levels and thus earn *monopoly rents*) on one or both ends of the buyer-seller relationship. Klein, Crawford & Alchian note that vertical integration can also be a response to what they call *quasi rents* -- pricing power that arises in a long-term contractual relationship because the parties are interdependent, even if neither had pricing power before the contract was signed.

Vertical integration, though, is only one possible response to the possibility of pricing power. Alternatives include *long-term contracts*, where legal remedies or the potential for reprisal constrains opportunistic behavior; the ability of firms to develop over time a *reputation* for not behaving opportunistically, which has value because it facilitates business dealings, value that would be lost if the firm misbehaves in any one transaction; *joint ventures*, where the central contract describes how the residual profits from the relationship are divided, rather than specifying what the relationship will be; and *partial cross-ownership*, which mutes (but doesn't eliminate) incentives to behave strategically.

We still know relatively little about the circumstances under which each of these alternatives will dominate. Indeed, one often observes different firms different approaches to handle the same type of relationship. For example, Albert Chandler reports that early factories in the United States exhibited low degrees of vertical integration. Instead, one observed a symbiotic relationship between separately owned businesses *within a single plant*, each of which occupied a different stage in the production of the product. The efficiency gains from a common production location were achieved by contract rather than by common ownership.[3]

In Japan, keiretsu groups make extensive use of cross-ownership. They also typically have less detailed contracts and less vertical integration than comparable American firms. These elements of Japanese industrial organization may be related. Cross-ownership reduces the risk of opportunism. Thus, it may permit group members to engage in complex business relationships without resort to either vertical integration or complex contracts.[4]

3. Related Diversification: Economies of Scope

The problem posed by horizontal and vertical integration is to define the efficient boundary of the firm with respect to the production of a *single* product. The same problem also arises with respect to the range of *different* products produced by a single firm. Why do firms produce more than one product or participate in more than one industry? One possible answer is economies of *scope*: not the savings from increased production of the same product that we call economies of scale, but rather the savings from joint production of a number of different products.

One source of scope economies involves products where the production processes are sufficiently similar so that cost reductions can be achieved with respect to the common inputs. Or the products can be sold through the same distribution channel, permitting economies of distribution or marketing. Analysis of the availability of these scope economies depends heavily on the technical details of particular industries, and resembles the Scherer & Ross discussion of scale economies.

A second source of scope economies is closely related to vertical integration. Suppose that two products require a common input. The two products could be produced by separate firms, each of which purchases the input from a third firm in market transactions. Or, the two products could be produced by the same firm, which would open up the possibility of vertical integration -- of also owning the supplier of the common input. When the shared input is tangible, whether least-cost production is best achieved through interfirm transactions, or within a single firm, depends on a market power and transaction cost analysis similar to that developed above

---

[3] Alfred Chandler, *The Visible Hand: The Management Revolution in American Business* ch. 2 (1977).

[4] See Ronald Gilson & Mark Roe, *Understanding the Japanese Keiretsu: Overlaps Between Corporate Governance and Industrial Organization*, 102 Yale L.J. 871 (1993); W. Carl Kester, *Japanese Takeovers: The Global Contest for Corporate Control* ch. 3 (1991).

for vertical integration.[5]   When the shared input is intangible, like technological know-how and other forms of knowledge, though, special difficulties arise in gaining access to the shared input by contract. These difficulties, and the resulting potential for economies of scope, are considered in the following article.

David Teece
ECONOMIES OF SCOPE AND THE SCOPE OF THE ENTERPRISE
1 J.Econ.Behav. & Org. 223, 223-30 (1980)

[T]he received theory of industrial organization is unable to explain why General Motors is not a dominant factor in the coal business, or why A&P does not manufacture airplanes. Nor does the received theory explain why aircraft manufacturers are now producing missiles and space vehicles, why Union Oil is producing energy from geothermal sources, or why Exxon is looking for uranium. One reason for this neglect is suggested by [the] observation that microeconomic analysis [has long viewed] the enterprise as little more than a black box. . . .

Economies of Scope and Diversification

Efforts have recently been made to formulate an efficiency-based theory of the multiproduct firm. These endeavors rest upon specifying cost functions which exhibit economies of scope. Economies of scope exist when for [two] outputs y_1 and y_2, the cost of joint production is less than the cost of producing each output separately. . . .

[But even] if the technology displays scope economies the joint production of two goods by two firms need not be more costly than production of the two goods by one enterprise. This can be readily established by counterexample.[3] . . . Just as technological interdependency between successive stages of a production process [alone does] not explain vertical integration nor do scope economies explain the multiproduct firm.
. . .

---

[5] For a overview of economies of scope arising from shared tangible assets, see Elizabeth Bailey & Ann Friedlaender, *Market Structure and Multiproduct Industries,* 20 J.Econ.Lit. 1024 (1982).

[3] Consider mixed farming. Orchardists must have space between fruit trees in order to facilitate adequate growth of the trees and the movement of farm machinery between the trees. This land can, however, be planted in grass, and sheep may graze to advantage in the intervening pasture. Economies of scope are clearly realized (land is the common input) but . . . [r]ather than producing both fruit and sheep, the orchardist can lease the pasture to a sheep farmer. The scope economies in sheep farming and fruit production are realized, but the single product focus of the sheep farmer and the orchardist are preserved. Clearly, market contracts can be used to undo the organization implications [of] the cost function.

As a general matter, "economies of scope arise from inputs that are shared. . . . The shared factor may be imperfectly divisible, so that the manufacture of a subset of the goods leaves excess capacity in some stage of production, or some human or physical capital . . ., when purchased for use in one production process, is then freely available to another."[a] I submit that the facility with which the common input or its services can be traded across markets will determine whether economies of scope will require the enterprise to be multiproduct in its scope. Where such trading is difficult, and intrafirm governance is superior, then . . . [a multiproduct firm will be efficient. Two classes of common inputs where this market failure appears to hold] are knowhow and specialized and indivisible physical assets. Yet even here, market processes are often sustained. The remainder of this paper seeks to identify the circumstances under which markets for these inputs may break down and where intrafirm transfer is called for. . . .

Knowhow

A principal feature of the modern business enterprise is that it is an organizational entity possessing knowhow. To the extent that knowhow has generic attributes, it represents a shared input which can find a variety of end product applications. Knowhow may also display some of the characteristics of a public good in that it can sometimes be used in many different non-competing applications without its value in any one application being substantially impaired. Furthermore, the marginal cost of employing knowhow in a different endeavor is likely to be much less than its average cost of production and dissemination (transfer). Accordingly, although knowhow is not a pure public good, the transfer of proprietary information to alternative activities is likely to generate scope economies if organizational modes can be discovered to conduct the transfer at low cost. In this regard, the relative efficiency properties of markets and internal organization need to be assessed. If reliance on market processes is surrounded by special difficulties -- and hence costs -- internal organization, and in particular multiproduct enterprise, may be preferred.

An examination of the properties of information markets readily leads to the identification of several difficulties. They can be summarized in terms of (1) recognition, (2) disclosure and (3) team organization. Thus consider a firm which has accumulated knowhow which can potentially find application in fields of industrial activity beyond its existing markets. If there are other firms in the economy which can apply this knowhow with profit, then according to received microtheory, trading will ensue until Pareto Optimality conditions are satisfied. . . . However, one cannot in general expect this happy result in the market for proprietary knowhow. . . .

---

[a] Robert Willig, *Multiproduct Technology and Market Structure*, 69 Am.Econ.Rev. 346 (1979).

In order to carry out a market transaction it is necessary to discover who it is that one wishes to deal with, to inform people that one wishes to deal and on what terms, to conduct negotiations leading up to the bargain, to draw up the contract, to undertake the inspection needed to make sure that the terms of the contract are being observed, and so on. Furthermore, the opportunity for trading must be identified. As Kirzner has explained:

> for an exchange transaction to be completed it is not sufficient merely that the conditions for exchange which prospectively will be mutually beneficial be present; it is necessary also that each participant be aware of his opportunity to gain through exchange. . . . It is usually assumed . . . that where scope for (mutually beneficial) exchange is present, exchange will in fact occur. . . . In fact of course exchange may fail to occur because knowledge is imperfect, in spite of conditions for mutually profitable exchange.[b]

The transactional difficulties identified by Kirzner are especially compelling when the commodity in question is proprietary information, be it of a technological or managerial kind. This is because the protection of the ownership of technological knowhow often requires suppressing information on exchange possibilities. By its very nature, industrial R&D requires disguising and concealing the activities and outcomes of the R&D establishment. . . .

Even where the possessor of the technology recognizes the opportunity [to sell knowhow], market exchange may break down because of the problems of disclosing value to buyers in a way that is both convincing and does not destroy the basis for exchange. A very severe information impactedness[c] problem exists, on which account the less informed party (in this instance the buyer) must be wary of opportunistic representations by the seller. . . . [T]he "fundamental paradox" of information arises: "its value for the purchaser is not known until he has the information, but then he has in effect acquired it without cost."[d]

Suppose that recognition is no problem, that buyers concede value, and are prepared to pay for information in the seller's possession. Occasionally that may suffice. The formula for a chemical compound or the blue prints for a special device may be all that is needed to effect the transfer. However, more is frequently needed. Knowhow has a strong learning-by-doing character, and it may be essential that human capital in an effective team configuration accompany the transfer. Sometimes this can be effected through a one-time contract (a knowhow agreement) to provide a "consulting team" to assist start-up. Although such contracts will be highly incomplete, and the failure to reach a comprehensive agreement may give

---

[b] Israel Kirzner, *Competition and Entrepreneurship* 215-16 (1973).

[c] "Information impactedness" exists when all of the facts relating to a transaction are known to one party but cannot be costlessly discovered by the other.

[d] Kenneth Arrow, *Essays on the Theory of Risk-Bearing* 152 (1971).

rise to dissatisfaction during execution . . ., integration (diversification) is an extreme response to the needs of a one-time exchange. . . .

Where a succession of proprietary exchanges seems desirable, reliance on repeated contracting is less clearly warranted. Unfettered two-way communication is needed not only to promote the recognition and disclosure of opportunities for information transfer but also to facilitate the execution of the actual transfer itself. . . . [C]ontracting may be shot through with hazards for both parties. The seller is exposed to hazards such as the possibility that the buyer will employ the knowhow in subtle ways not covered by the contract, or the buyer might "leap frog" the licensor's technology and become an unexpected competitive threat in third markets. The buyer is exposed to hazards such as the seller asserting that the technology has superior performance or cost reducing characteristics than is actually the case; or the seller might render promised transfer assistance in a perfunctory fashion. While bonding or the execution of performance guarantees can minimize these hazards, they need not be eliminated since costly haggling might ensue when measurement of the performance characteristics of the technology is open to some ambiguity. . . .

Hence, when the continuous exchange of proprietary knowhow between the transferor and transferee is needed, and where the end use application of the knowledge is idiosyncratic in the sense that it has not been accomplished previously by the transferor, it appears that something more than a classical market contracting structure is required. As Williamson notes, "The nonstandardized nature of (these) transactions makes primary reliance on market governance hazardous, while their recurrent nature permits the cost of the specialized governance structure to be recovered."[e] . . . [T]his can take the form of bilateral governance [through a long-term "relational" contract], where the autonomy of the parties is maintained; or unified structures, where the transaction is removed from the market and organized within the firm subject to an authority relation. . . .

Exchange [can be] conducted between independent firms . . . where both parties realize the paramount importance of maintaining an amicable relationship as overriding any possible short-run gains either might be able to achieve. But as transactions become progressively more idiosyncratic, [relational] contracting may also fail, and internal organization (intrafirm transfer) is the more efficient organizational mode. The intrafirm transfer of knowhow avoids the need for repeated negotiations and ameliorates the hazards of opportunism. Better disclosure, easier agreement, better governance, and therefore more effective execution of knowhow transfer are likely to result. Here lies an incentive for enterprise diversification.

The above arguments are quite general and extend to the transfer of many different kinds of proprietary knowhow. Besides technological knowhow, the transfer of managerial (including organizational) knowhow,

---

[e] Oliver Williamson, *Transaction-Cost Economics: The Governance of Contractual Relations*, 22 J.L. & Econ. 233, 250 (1979).

and goodwill (including brand loyalty) represent types of assets for which market transfer mechanisms may falter, and for which the relative efficiency of intrafirm as against interfirm trading is indicated.

---

4.   Related Acquisitions: The Management Dimension

David Teece, writing in the economics literature, offers one perspective on the potential for an acquisition to increase the combined value of the two firms by facilitating ongoing transfer of knowhow.   A company with transferable skills can acquire another company and boost its performance; a company in need of a skill infusion can acquire those skills by acquiring (or being acquired by) another firm that already has them.   The excerpt below, from the managerial literature, provides a different perspective on the potential for transfer of special skills, especially managerial skills, through related acquisitions.

Malcolm Salter & Wolf Weinhold
DIVERSIFICATION THROUGH ACQUISITION: STRATEGIES FOR CREATING ECONOMIC VALUE
49-63 (1979)*

According to the *strategy model*, a company's special competences are defined in terms of a set of core skills -- that is, what the company is good at.   In one case, this might mean the manufacture of high-volume, low-value-added metal assemblies; in another, the mass distribution of frequently purchased consumer products. This set of core skills is not just what the company does well, but what it does particularly well. . . .

Implications for the Diversification Decision

The strategy model provides specific guidelines within which managers are to approach the diversifying acquisition. The key issue to be considered in the evaluation of an acquisition candidate is the fit it provides with the company's resources. . . .   [U]sers of the strategy model favor closely related diversification. The underlying theory is both simple and intuitively appealing: Really successful results in business require the development of a distinctive competence or competitive advantage and the ability to anticipate trends in markets and technology.   The ability to maintain a distinctive competence and to anticipate is greatly enhanced by a knowledge of the industry and its environment.   Thus, where diversification is related to a

---

company's current industrial environment, the advantages of special competence and industry knowledge can create more opportunity for above-average results than unrelated diversification can.

It is not surprising that, seen in this light, questions relevant to the diversification decision posed by the model stress the notions of strategic fit and operating compatibility. These questions can be summarized as follows:

1. What opportunities and risks does the potential acquisition present?

2. What is the basis of competition in the acquisition candidate's industrial environment? What must he do well to succeed there?

3. Can we assist the acquisition candidate in any way? Do our resources and skills fit the needs of the acquisition candidate? Which of our resources are transferable?

4. Quite apart from assisting the acquisition candidate, do we understand the strategic logic, or key success factors, of this new business sufficiently well to make intelligent resource allocation decisions?

. . . Where the resource requirements are similar for each company and where the diversifying company's strengths can be reinforced or extended and/or its weaknesses minimized or eliminated, the elements of strategic fit will be present and a diversifying acquisition will represent an attractive strategic option. . . .

How, then, can an assessment of corporate resources be systematically pursued so that a company's conclusions about its strengths and weaknesses are sufficiently detailed and objective to serve as the basis for serious diversification planning? Such an assessment requires, first, that a company develop a profile of its principal resources and skills. These tend to cluster around three dimensions:

1. *financial dimension*, including such resources as cash flow, debt capacity, and the ability to attract new capital;

2. *operating dimension*, including tangible assets, such as office buildings, manufacturing plant and equipment, warehouses, inventories, and service and distribution facilities, and more intangible resources, such as high-quality products, low-cost production methods, and high brand loyalty; and

3. *management and organization dimension*, including such resources as scientists, engineers, sales personnel, financial analysts, general managers, and bureaucratic traditions embodied in quality assurance systems, cash-management systems, and management-control systems.

Once such a profile has been developed, a company then should compare the strength of its resources with those factors critical to the company's success in its relevant product markets to see what characteristics make the company uniquely qualified to carry out its key tasks or inhibit the company's ability to fulfill its purpose. This step in the analysis yields what is called a capability or competence profile. The final step in the process is to compare this capability profile with that of major competitors in order to identify those areas where the company may be able to build a competitive advantage in the marketplace.

      . . . [For example], McCord Corporation was one of the first companies to start supplying the automotive industry. As the automotive market grew to maturity, McCord become a major supplier of gaskets, radiators, and other automotive equipment. By 1963 the company was a well-established manufacturer selling most of its production in the original equipment (O/E) market. The consolidated 1963 sales of $45 million and profits of $1.8 million had some fluctuations but little real change over the previous five years.

In 1963 management attention was focused on growth and diversification through acquisition and internal development. The company was dependent on three major auto makers in the O/E market for over half its total corporate sales.   Previous efforts of internally generated diversification and recent attempts at acquisition had borne no fruits. The question facing McCord was how could the company build on its strengths and compensate for or eliminate its weaknesses? This question needed to be answered in the context of the company's four principal objectives:

- to minimize the pressure of the cyclical O/E market
- to find more productive uses for the company's financial resources
- to grow at a more rapid pace
- to generate a greater level of public interest and confidence in the company. . . .

A merger in 1964 with the Davidson Rubber Corporation, a manufacturer of padded trim products for the automotive industry, provided a certain degree of fit from a marketing, financial, and manufacturing point of view even though the company was not able to build a strong hedge against the market power of the "Big Three" automakers. As it turned out, many of each company's resource requirements were similar, and Davidson offered McCord a broader product line, a position in the emerging safety market, more modern plants, and a younger middle-level management experienced in the auto supply market. But in the final analysis, the extent to which Davidson fit McCord's strategic needs can only be judged in light of McCord's strengths and weaknesses in the automotive supply market and the overall attractiveness of that market or industry. As depicted in Figure 8-2, both business position (defined in terms of relative market share, relative product quality, price, marketing strength, new product activity, manufacturing scale, and overall experience) and industry or market attractiveness (defined in terms of market size and growth, number and size of competitors, position in the product life cycle, rate of technological change, and industry profitability) can help define appropriate related diversification strategies for companies like McCord. Without going into all the details of McCord's situation in 1963-1964, we can show that while Davidson offered McCord some benefits of related-supplementary diversification, the company's real needs, based on an analysis of its strengths and weaknesses and industry attractiveness, lay more in the direction of related-complementary diversification. Let's look first at this argument in conceptual terms and then return to the McCord case.

Figure 8-2
Framework for Selecting Appropriate
Related Diversification Strategy

		Business Position		
		High	Medium	Low
Industry Attractive- ness	High	No Diversification	Related- Complementary Diversification	Related- Complementary Diversification
	Medium	Related- Supplementary Diversification	No Diversification	Related- Complementary Diversification
	Low	Related- Supplementary Diversification	Related- Supplementary Diversification	No Diversification

    . . . *[R]elated-complementary diversification* involves expanding a business by adding new functional activities and skills to its existing set without substantially changing its product-market orientation. *Related-supplementary diversification* involves expanding a business by entering new product markets requiring functional skills similar to those already possessed by the company. Figure 8-2 suggests the following guidelines regarding related-complementary and related-supplementary diversification:

    1. *No diversification.* First, where a company has a strong position in an attractive industry, diversification is usually unnecessary from an economic perspective. Second, where a company possesses few unique strengths but operates in an industry of average or medium attractiveness, it may make sense to work at developing existing skills and improving its business position before considering any diversification. Finally, a weak company in an unattractive industry is

clearly in a desperate situation, unlikely to be able to afford diversification or to present itself as an attractive merger partner.

2.　*Related-Complementary Diversification.*　Where a company participates in a highly attractive industry but possesses only average or even below-average skills, related-complementary diversification can help that company add functional skills critical to improving its overall business position.　Even where a company finds itself as a weak competitor in an industry of average or medium attractiveness, some benefits can accrue from improving its competitive position through related-complementary diversification.

3.　*Related-Supplementary diversification.*　Where a company has a strong business position but participates in a market of only average attractiveness or low attractiveness, there is the obvious potential to increase rates of growth and profitability by committing existing functional skills and resources to new, more attractive markets.　Where a company qualifies as only an average competitor in a specific industry or market, but where that market has become relatively unattractive, there are potential benefits of using existing skills and resources to enter more attractive, related product markets.

Using the related diversification grid [shown in Figure 8-2] requires a healthy dose of judgment since there is no simple, useful system for assessing relative business position or relative industry attractiveness.　Nevertheless, the grid does suggest some crude propositions that can channel thinking along the lines of the strategy model.　More specifically, the grid can help companies study their related diversification options in the light of corporate strengths and weaknesses as well as industry or market characteristics.

Returning to the case of the McCord Corporation, the company can be characterized as having "low to medium" business position in an industry of "medium" attractiveness.　The automotive equipment industry has two major segments, the O/E market and the replacement market, commonly referred to as the aftermarket.　McCord participated in both segments.　As indicated above, the O/E market experienced severe cyclical swings, while overall growth was more or less on a par with that of the economy as a whole.　This market was also dominated by a powerful oligopoly who posed a continuous threat of backward integration into McCord's lines.　Any failure of McCord to meet preestablished product specifications, delivery schedules, or price expectations would cause a punitive shift of purchases away from McCord.　The aftermarket, supplied by chains such as Sears and independent wholesale distributors who sold to service stations and the public, was more fragmented, less price-sensitive, and less cyclical.　On balance, however, the automotive equipment industry was not a "growth" industry, nor was it characterized by above-average returns to automotive-equipment suppliers.　In addition, while McCord was a competitive participant in the industry, the company was not a leader either in terms of market-share position, product quality, new-product activity, or manufacturing efficiency.

Viewed from the perspective of the related-diversification grid, McCord appeared to be in a position to benefit either from reinforcing its current strategic posture or, possibly, from pursuing related-complementary diversification. . . . [T]he company could have improved its business position and performance by acquiring companies with the ability to place McCord in a stronger market-share position in the aftermarket or a stronger technological position in the O/E market. . . . While the Davidson acquisition clearly offered McCord the opportunity to exploit a new technology and a new market segment, it is less clear that the attendant economic advantages were superior to those offered by a complementary diversifying acquisition.

---

5. The Risks of Acquisitions

Our survey of the potential for horizontal, vertical, and other related acquisitions to *add* value would be incomplete if we did not also consider the potential for these acquisitions to *subtract* value -- for the combined enterprise to be worth less than the separate parts. We know from experience that many acquisitions fail. The high rate of divestitures is one indication of acquisition failure.

If failures were only occasional, we might simply chalk that up to the difficulty of the task. It is not easy to assess whether the economies of scale or scope that can flow from further expansion outweigh the difficulties of managing a larger venture, or whether vertical integration is preferable to a long-term "relational" contract. It can be extraordinarily difficult for managers to assess *honestly* what they are good at, and not so good at, as Salter & Weinhold suggest. Indeed, we don't know which is less plausible -- Salter & Weinhold's suggestion that a firm with a "low" business position, deriving from weak managerial skills, should go out *and buy another firm*, or their implicit assumption that some managers will rate themselves as below average.

Failure is more than occasional, though. Ravenscraft and Scherer, writing in a "managerialist" tradition, in which managers, for their own reasons, often pursue takeovers that have little promise for adding value, offer cautionary words:

> [It does not] suffice to laud, however accurately, sell-offs as an effective means of undoing the acquisitions "that did not work out as planned." When the roads are strewn with wrecks, government officials cannot rest content because the tow trucks, ambulances, and hearses are doing a good job of removing the remnants and clearing the right-of-way. They must also inquire whether there might be something wrong with driver training, traffic engineering, and the rules of the road.

> We are convinced that the driver training does need significant improvement. Thousands of would-be managers and middle managers pour from the business administration schools each year imbued with naive views of merger-making as a quick, easy road to wealth creation. . . . [B]usiness school professors . . . [must] find ways to impress upon their students that making mergers while drunk with power greatly increases the risk of mishap, that merger trips should be planned carefully, with adequate attention to the known hazards, and that double-bottom, 18-wheeler conglomerates should be operated only by the extraordinarily skilled.[6]

The frustratingly vague advice that Professors Salter & Weinhold of the Harvard Business School offer seems to us to illustrate the weak driver training that Ravenscraft & Scherer lament. The root problem may be that the potential savings from acquisitions are highly industry-specific, and hard to generalize about. The next reading develops several reasons why acquisitions often don't work out as planned.

Bernard Black, BIDDER OVERPAYMENT IN TAKEOVERS
41 Stan.L.Rev. 597, 623-628 (1989)[*]

Much of the theoretical basis for expected overpayment comes from divergence between manager and shareholder interests. However, even if managers were faithful servants of the shareholders, some of them would overpay because of habitual overoptimism and ignorance of 'winner's curse' theory. In most cases, the overpayment is likely to be unintentional -- the bidder's managers believe wrongly that the deal is a good one.

Manager Optimism and Uncertainty about Value

Ex ante, a target's true value is unknown, and each potential bidder must estimate that value based on the information available to it. Only those potential bidders who believe that the target's value exceeds the expected price of a successful takeover will bid. Managers, like the rest of us, differ in their degree of optimism or pessimism. Some managers, surely, are habitually optimistic and therefore likely to overestimate a target's value. Moreover, pessimists will be less likely to make takeover bids. Managers who are successful in one business may be especially prone to overestimate their ability to run another business. [Consistent with this hypothesis], Varaiya reports that bidders who are successful in their own businesses (as

---

[6] David Ravenscraft & F.M. Scherer, *Mergers, Sell-Offs and Economic Efficiency* 217 (1987); see also Robin Marris, *The Economic Theory of Managerial Capitalism* (1964); Dennis Mueller, *Profits in the Long Run* (1986); Randall Morck, Andrei Shleifer & Robert Vishny, *Do Managerial Objectives Drive Bad Acquisitions*, 45 J.Fin. 31 (1990); Richard Roll, *The Hubris Hypothesis of Corporate Takeovers*, 59 J.Bus. 197 (1986).

measured by positive preannouncement abnormal returns) are *more* likely [than other bidders] to suffer stock price declines in acquisitions.[63]   And Nielsen & Melicher report that premiums paid for targets correlate with the *bidder's* accounting profitability.[64]   In addition, the structure of some large corporations, in which managers who are visibly successful are more likely to be promoted, may overselect for optimists who are lucky enough to be proven right.

Optimism can creep into value estimates in a number of ways.   To mention only some of the possibilities, the bidder may err in assessing the attainable level of operating income as a percentage of sales, the target's future sales growth rate, or the proper discount rate. A manager who makes a relatively small error in any of these estimates can substantially overestimate a target's value. . . .

Manager Ignorance and the Winner's Curse

A second source of expected overpayment, in addition to managers' optimism, is their ignorance about bidding theory.   In an auction of an asset of uncertain value, bidders are vulnerable to the 'winner's curse': Even if they estimate value accurately on average, they win the bidding primarily when they overestimate an asset's true value, and thus tend to overpay on average.   The auction need not be explicit;   it is enough that there are potential bidders waiting in the wings to make a higher offer if the first bid is too low.

If uncertainty is high, a bidder that takes the apparently conservative approach of offering a little less than its best estimate of value will still overpay, on average.   Winner's curse theory dictates that bidders must offer substantially less than they think an asset is worth, and be prepared to have only a fraction of their bids succeed.   Winner's curse problems apply, however, only to an asset whose value is "common" to all bidders.   Thus, a bidder who has unique synergy with a target faces a winner's curse risk only to the extent of the target's value to other bidders.

I know of no evidence that the investment bankers who advise managers on takeover bids, let alone the corporate managers themselves, know anything about winner's curse theory.   My personal experience as a takeover lawyer is that they do not.   Also, experiments show that "avoiding the winner's curse is not easy.   Even experienced subjects who are given significant learning opportunities fail to solve the buy-a-firm problem and fail to understand the need to become more conservative when the number of bidders increases."[69]. . .

---

[63] Nikhil Varaiya, *The 'Winner's Curse' Hypothesis and Corporate Takeovers*, 9 Managerial & Decision Econ. 209 (1988).

[64] James Nielsen & Ronald Melicher, *A Financial Analysis of Acquisition and Merger Premiums*, 8 J.Fin. & Quant.Anal. 139 (1973).

[69] Richard Thaler, *Anomalies: The Winner's Curse*, 2 J.Econ.Persp. 191, 196 (1988).

Learning from prior mistakes will tend to limit the bidding errors of repeat bidders (whether due to optimism or to the winner's curse). However, success or failure may not be obvious for a number of years. This is ample time for the old CEO to make more mistakes or a new CEO to be appointed. Moreover, acquisitions can fail or be only marginally successful for many reasons. An overpayment can be hidden by, or wrongly ascribed to, changes in economic conditions, unforeseen new technology, lack of due diligence (presumably correctable the next time), mistakes in integrating the two businesses (also presumably correctable), or other factors. Thus, learning from past overpayment is, at best, a weak cure for future overpayment. . . .

Investment bankers, as repeat players, have better opportunities than most corporate managers to learn from prior mistakes. However, investment bankers are usually paid only for completed transactions. This discourages nay-saying advice. . . . Bankers may advise clients (rightly) that a "low-ball" bid (of the type that winner's curse theory would suggest) is unlikely to win. Reputational constraints [on such advice] are imperfect because the target's true value is unobservable and takeovers can fail for many reasons. Moreover, the seemingly reasonable advice to bid slightly less than your value estimate may both preserve the banker's reputation and lead to an overbid. . . .

Principal-Agent Conflicts

. . . [M]anagers and shareholders often have different incentives. Indeed, agency theory tells us that some divergence is inevitable, given the costs of shareholder monitoring of managers. In particular, managers may want to increase the size of their firms and to diversify, even if this reduces the return on the shareholders' investment. Baumol's model of the firm as maximizing sales subject to a profit constraint[76] and Donaldson's description of the "deep, almost instinctive, need for organizational growth"[77] are especially suggestive. . . .

Incentives to increase size include managers' desire for greater prestige and visibility, the desire of the chief executive officer to leave a legacy and not be a mere caretaker, and compensation structures that reward growth in sales and profits. These incentives for growth may lead managers to overinvest, either by expanding their own business or by buying a new business.

Incentives to diversify the firm include the incentives for growth noted above, plus risk-aversion by managers whose human or financial capital is

---

[76] William Baumol, *Business Behavior, Value and Growth* ch. 6 (rev.ed.1967).

[77] Gordon Donaldson, *Managing Corporate Wealth: The Operation of a Comprehensive Financial Goals System* 37 (1984); see also *GE Chairman Welch, Though Much Praised, Starts to Draw Critics*, Wall St.J., Aug. 4, 1988, at 1 (General Electric CEO Welch quoted as exclaiming, "The more value this company has, the more things we can buy!").

concentrated in a single firm. The desire for growth and the desire to diversify may combine to produce diversification, especially into high growth areas, by companies with limited growth prospects in their own industries. . . .

Moreover, once a target is selected and a bid is made, managers may stay in the bidding too long because others will perceive dropping out as failure. This is especially true if the bidding contest is public. What manager wants to be branded in the Wall Street Journal as the "loser" of a takeover battle? Managers with such incentives may be willing to "pay for the benefits of the acquisitions that they care about but shareholders do not."[81]

C.   Evaluation: Consistency With Analytic Tools

The financial theory considered in Part I provides a frame of reference for evaluating claims that certain types of corporate acquisitions result in operating synergy. Asset pricing theory tells us that a firm's value is determined by its return (dividends plus appreciation) and its systematic risk (the variation in return that cannot be reduced by diversification). This suggests two possible ways that synergistic acquisitions can increase firm value. Return may be increased without an offsetting increase in systematic risk, or systematic risk may be reduced without an offsetting reduction in return. Each source of synergy considered in this chapter can be evaluated as an effort to alter either risk or return.

The strategies for increasing return through acquisitions are most straightforward. Consider, for example, the impact of economies of scale. An acquisition that allows an acquiring company to expand production to a more efficient portion of its average cost curve can increase profits more than proportionately because of higher margins on the new sales. The return on the capital invested in the combined corporation will exceed the weighted average of the pre-acquisition returns for the parties to the acquisition.

While this example may seem self-evident, the result is less clear than may appear. In our analytic model, a greater return is preferable to a lesser return *only* if the level of systematic risk is held constant. Even for economies of scale, the assumption of constant risk may be troublesome. For example, different segments of industry demand may respond quite differently to changes in general economic conditions -- a critical element of systematic risk. Consider an extreme example: Assume that an acquiring company and a target company manufacture essentially the same products, but that the acquiring company is principally a defense contractor, the demand for whose product is less responsive to overall economic conditions

---

[81] Andrei Shleifer & Robert Vishny, *Value Maximization and the Acquisition Process*, 2 J.Econ.Persp. 7, 14 (1988).

than that of the target company, whose market is largely civilian. The acquiring company may believe that expanding production to accommodate civilian demand will offer economies of scale (or scope), resulting in an increase in return and, therefore, an increase in the value of the combined company over its constituent parts. The problem, however, is that the systematic risk of the combined company is greater than that of the pre-transaction acquiring corporation alone. The greater risk of the civilian market should require an increase in return simply to *maintain* value. What other sources of increased systematic risk might exist?

A focus on expected return alone makes for misleading project choices. The attractiveness of increased return depends on the level of systematic risk associated with the increase. As Brealey & Myers stress in their discussion of capital budgeting at the end of Chapter 4, the expected return on each project must be evaluated relative to *that project's* required rate of return, not relative to the acquirer's existing return on equity.

Each explanation for synergy thus requires analysis of the implications for *both* return and systematic risk. As an exercise, think through the explanations for synergy provided by economies of vertical integration and scope in terms of risk and return. Which primarily focus on risk and which on return? Does this perspective alter your evaluation of the likelihood of successfully achieving synergy?

D.   Evaluation: Consistency with Empirical Evidence

How might we test for the presence of operating synergy? If one or more sources of synergy are operative, and investors realize this, the post-acquisition shareholder market value of the combined firm should exceed the sum of the pre-acquisition values of the individual corporations. An *event study* of stock price response to the announcement of a planned acquisition should result in positive cumulative abnormal returns taking into account both the acquiring and target companies. This approach -- inferring business value gains from stock price gains -- is taken by Bradley, Desai & Kim, in the article excerpted in Chapter 6, and by Black & Grundfest earlier in this chapter.

But the event study methodology, without more, offers no clue as to *why* stock prices have increased. Bradley, Desai & Kim and Black & Grundfest address this problem in the standard way, by seeking to exclude *non-efficiency* sources of stock price gains, such as wealth transfers from employees, creditors, or the U.S. Treasury. They then infer that the resulting stock price gains most likely reflect efficiency gains.

We will evaluate the potential for wealth transfers in takeovers at length in later chapters. But even if wealth transfers are small, event studies that report *average* gains from a large, undifferentiated pool of takeovers remain unsatisfying, in several respects. First, we would like to understand the distribution of gains between the target and acquiring firm. Why does it appear that, at least on average, essentially all of the gains go to the target's shareholders, and none to the acquirer's shareholders? Second, we don't know *which* of the multiple possible sources of efficiency gains is operating. Third, stock price changes when a transaction is announced reflect only changes in investor *beliefs* about future cash flows. We would like to know whether those *ex ante* beliefs turn out, *ex post*, to correspond to actual increases in cash flow. Below, we consider each of these issues in turn.

1. Gains or Losses to Acquiring Firms

Takeovers increase the shareholder market value of the target both on average and in almost every individual case. Otherwise, the transaction wouldn't be completed. The target's shareholders would vote against the transaction (if a shareholder vote was required) or refuse to sell their shares (if the acquirer sought to complete the transaction through a tender offer for the target's stock).[7]

The returns to acquiring companies are both less favorable and more variable. In a 1983 review, Jensen & Ruback calculate that acquiring companies making successful *tender offers* earn positive average abnormal returns of 3.8% when the tender offer is announced. In contrast, acquirers making successful acquisitions by *merger* earned neither positive nor negative abnormal returns, on average. Jensen & Ruback could not explain the difference between these two types of transactions.[8]

The studies collected by Jensen & Ruback mostly used takeovers in the 1960s and 1970s. More recent studies cast acquirer returns in a less favorable light. The Bradley, Desai & Kim study in chapter 6 is representative of a number of studies that show that acquirers in the 1980s suffered stock price *losses*, both on average and in more than half of all transactions. These losses were observed in both tender offers and mergers. Studies that find significant negative returns to acquirers in the 1980s, significantly fewer than 50% positive returns, or both, are collected in Table 8-6. Recall from chapter 6 that a *t* or *z* statistic greater than about +2, or less than about −2, indicates statistical significance at the 95% confidence level.

---

[7] We discuss the mechanics of a tender offer in Part III. In essence, the acquirer offers to purchase stock directly from the target's shareholders, at a stated price. If the price is attractive, target shareholders will tender their shares and the acquisition will succeed.

[8] Jensen & Ruback (1983), *supra* note 1.

Table 8-6
Acquirer Returns in the 1980s

(t or z statistic or confidence level in parentheses)[9]

Study	Sample Period	Sample Size	Event Window	Average Acquirer CAR	Positive Acquirer CARs - %
Asquith, Bruner & Mullins (1987)	1973-83	343	$(-1,0)$	-0.85% $(t = -8.42)$	41% $(z = -3.35)$
Banerjee & Owers (1992)	1978-87	57 white knights	$(-1,0)$	-3.3% $(z = -11.75)$	21% $(z = -5.36)$
Bradley, Desai & Kim (1988)	1981-84	52	$(-5,+5)$	-2.9% $(z = -2.79)$	35% $(z = -2.33)$
Byrd & Hickman (1993)	1980-87	128	$(-1,0)$	-1.2% $(z = -6.78)$	33% $(z = -4.14)$
Jennings & Mazzeo (1991)	1979-85	352	day 0	-0.8% $(z = -8.11)$	37% $(z = -5.08)$
Morck, Shleifer & Vishny (1990)	1980-87	172	$(-1,+1)$	n.a.	37% $(z = -2.12)$
Servaes (1991)	1981-87	366	0 thru closing	-3.35% (96% conf.)	n.a.
Varaiya & Ferris (1987)	1974-83	96	$(-1,0)$	-2.15% $(z = -8.67)$	n.a.
You, Caves, Smith & Henry (1986)	1975-84	133	$(-1,+1)$	-1.5% (n.a.)	33% $(z = -4.15)$

---

[9] The studies reported in the table are: Paul Asquith, Robert Bruner & David Mullins, *Merger Returns and the Form of Financing* (working paper 1987); Ajeyo Banerjee & James Owers, *Wealth Reduction in White Knight Bids*, Fin.Mgmt. 48 (Autumn 1992) (study limited to second "white knight" bidders); Michael Bradley, Anand Desai & E. Han Kim, *Synergistic Gains from Corporate Acquisitions and Their Division Between the Stockholders of Target and Acquiring Firms*, 21 J.Fin.Econ. 3 (1988); John Byrd & Kent Hickman, *Do Outside Directors Monitor Managers?: Evidence from Tender Offer Bids*, 32 J.Fin.Econ. 195 (1992); Robert Jennings & Michael Mazzeo, *Stock Price Movements around Acquisition Announcements and Management's Response*, 64 J.Bus. 139 (1991); Morck, Shleifer & Vishny (1990), *supra* note 6; Henri Servaes, *Tobin's Q and the Gains from Takeovers*, 46 J.Fin. 409 (1991); Nikhil Varaiya & Kenneth Ferris, *Overpayment in Corporate Takeovers: The Winner's Curse*, Fin. Analysts' J. 64 (May-June 1987); Victor You, Richard Caves, Michael Smith & James Henry, *Mergers and Bidders' Wealth: Managerial and Strategic Factors*, in *The Economics of Strategic Planning: Essays in Honor of Joel Dean* 201 (Lacy Thomas ed.1986). Where the authors report results for more than one time period, only results for the 1980s are reported. Where the authors report results for more than one event window, only results for the narrowest window are reported. The z-statistic for the sign test was constructed where the authors did not report it using the standard formula $z = (p - 0.5)/[p(1 - p)/n]^{1/2}$, where $p =$ fraction of positive returns.

In addition to the studies in table 8-6, Sanjai Bhagat & David Hirschleifer report evidence that bidders overpay on average in tender offers between 1963 and 1984, in a complex study that attempts to control for the fact that the announcement of a tender offer conveys information about the bidder's financial strength.[10]

These results raise an important puzzle: If there is synergy from combining acquirer and target, *why don't acquirers earn a share of the gains from trade?* At least three approaches to this central question can be isolated.

The first explanation posits a competitive market for corporate control. If there are many fungible bidders competing for any one target, the gains to the bidder will be competed away, so that targets earn all of the gains and bidders earn zero abnormal returns. This explanation is consistent with studies that show positive abnormal returns to acquirers in the 1960s, and roughly zero returns in the 1970s, after new tender offer regulation (the Williams Act, adopted in 1968) promoted greater competition for takeover targets.[11] Table 8-7 collects studies showing the trend over time toward lower acquirer returns.

Table 8-7
Trends Over Time in Acquirer Returns[12]
(*t* or *z* statistics in parentheses)

Study	Transaction Type	Average Acquirer CARs		
		1960s	1970s	1980s
Asquith, Bruner & Mullins (1983)	mergers	4.6% (n.a.)	1.7% (n.a.)	n.a.
Bradley, Desai & Kim (1988)	tender offers	4.1% ($z = 5.88$)	1.3% ($z = 1.58$)	−2.93% ($z = -2.79$)
Jarrell, Brickley & Netter (1988)	tender offers	4.4% ($t = 4.02$)	1.2 ($t = 2.12$)	−1.10 ($t = -1.54$)
Loderer & Martin (1990)	tender offers and mergers	1.7% ($z = 8.73$)	0.6% ($z = 5.49$)	−0.07% ($z = -0.34$)

---

[10] Sanjai Bhagat & David Hirschleifer, *Market-Based Estimates of Value Gains from Takeovers: An Intervention Approach* (Univ. of Colo.-Boulder working paper, March 1993).

[11] We discuss the Williams Act in Chapter 18.

[12] The studies reported in the table are: Paul Asquith, Robert Bruner & David Mullins, *The Gains to Bidding Firms from Merger*, 11 J.Fin.Econ. 121 (1983); Bradley, Desai & Kim (1988), *supra* note 9; Jarrell, Brickley & Netter (1988), *supra* note 1 (reporting results from an early version of Gregg Jarrell & Annette Poulsen, *The Returns to Acquiring Firms in Tender Offers: Evidence from Three Decades*, Fin.Mgmt. 12 (Autumn 1989), that are not reported in the published version); Claudio Loderer & Kenneth Martin, *Corporate Acquisitions by Listed Firms: The Experience of a Comprehensive Sample*, Fin.Mgmt. 17 (Winter 1990). Some studies provide time breakdowns that only roughly coincide with calendar decades; these details are omitted from Table 8-7.

This *competitive market* explanation for roughly zero acquirer returns has problems, though.   The corporate control market has become more competitive over time, but still seems a long way from being perfectly competitive.   Target managers often go to extreme lengths to avoid an auction (recall the Time-Warner example from Chapter 1), and most takeovers do not involve an explicit auction.   Moreover, targets and bidders aren't always fungible.   Indeed, most of the explanations for operating synergy depend on the fit between the acquirer and the target.   Yet where the target is uniquely valuable to a particular bidder, auction theory predicts that the bidder and target should share the gains from trade, though the theory cannot predict the precise division of gains.

In addition, in a perfectly competitive market, bidder abnormal returns should cluster closely around zero.   To be sure, *ex post*, some transactions will turn out to be winners and others will prove to be mistakes.   But *ex ante*, the value estimates of the bidder's managers, which determine the amount that the bidder will pay, shouldn't diverge greatly from the value estimates of shareholders, which drive the stock price response to the takeover announcement.   Thus, bidder returns ought to be sometimes negative and sometimes positive, but generally close to zero.   This is not observed.   Instead, there is a lot of scatter -- many cases in which the bidder's stock price rises, suggesting positive expected returns that were not competed away, and many others in which the bidder's stock price falls by 5% or more, suggesting that investors believe that the acquirer has grossly overpaid.   There are also many anecdotal examples of apparent overpayment -- cases in which investors sharply marked down the bidder's stock when the deal was announced, and the acquisition later proved to have major problems.

But the most central problem with the competitive market explanation is that competition among value-maximizing bidders ought to drive returns to zero, *but no further*.   Competition, without more, cannot explain average returns that are negative.   In particular, it can't explain the sharply negative returns to "white-knight" acquirers -- second, nominally friendly bidders who attempt to outbid another firm that has made an initial unfriendly bid.   In Table 8-6, the study by Banerjee & Owers, which is limited to white knights, shows average acquirer losses of 3.3%. And an astonishing 81% of white knight acquirers sufferer negative abnormal returns.[13]   More generally, several studies confirm that overt competition between two or more bidders correlates with lower acquirer returns.   Since average acquirer returns in the 1980s are already negative; returns in multiple-bidder transactions must be even worse.[14]

---

[13] See also Bradley, Desai & Kim (1988), *supra* note 9 (excerpted in Chapter 6 (finding that negative returns to acquirers in the 1980s are driven by losses to white knights)).

[14] See Byrd & Hickman (1992), *supra* note 9 (in regression analysis, presence of multiple bidders reduces acquirer returns by 2.3%; $t = -2.30$); Steven Kaplan & Michael Weisbach,

A second approach, implicitly adopted by Bradley, Desai & Kim, stresses the high percentage of transactions that involve combined bidder and target gains, and downplays the importance of bidder losses. In this *joint gains* approach, the existence of combined gains is strong evidence of synergy (once other sources of shareholder market value gains are ruled out). That more than 100% of the gains accrue to targets is a minor detail.

But negative returns to acquirers remain troubling, even if the target's shareholders gain more than the acquirer's shareholders lose. Finding potential synergies, and realizing that potential once an acquisition is made, is difficult and heavily dependent on managerial skill. If acquirers make valuation mistakes and thus overpay, that casts some doubt on their ability to achieve operating synergy. And there are still the transactions where the dollar losses to acquirers exceed the dollar gains to targets. These are only 27% of the tender offers in the Bradley, Desai & Kim sample, but (as discussed below) are a substantially higher percentage for other types of transactions.

A third explanation for the observed acquirer returns stresses not the return to an average acquirer, but rather the scatter around the mean. Perhaps there are some "good" bidders who maximize firm value and some "bad" bidders who pursue other goals, such as greater managerial power or perquisites. The good bidders engage in transactions involving joint gains. Their shareholders either receive some of these gains or at worst do not lose. In contrast, the bad bidders either pursue transactions with no joint gains, or pay too much for whatever joint gains exist. This *good bidder/bad bidder* explanation is consistent with transactions where combined value increases and acquirer value either increases or remains constant, and with transactions where combined value decreases. It is less successful in explaining the sources of joint gains in transactions where the acquirer's stock price drops, but the target's gains outweigh the acquirer's losses.

Most likely, all three of these explanations are *partly* right. Competition will tend to drive bidder returns toward zero, so it isn't surprising that targets capture much of the joint gains. Some transactions involve both synergy *and* benefits to managers but not shareholders. That could explain the juxtaposition of combined acquirer and target gains with acquirer losses. And some transactions are simply mistakes, perhaps driven by benefits to the acquiring firm's managers. More generally, a recurring theme in our survey of acquisition motives is that takeovers are a multifaceted phenomenon, which no single explanation can hope to capture.

The Success of Acquisitions: Evidence from Divestitures, 47 J.Fin. 107 (1992) (in regression analysis, presence of multiple bidders reduces acquirer returns by 2.5%; $t = -2.3$); Servaes (1991), *supra* note 9 (acquirers suffer losses of 3.0% in multiple-bidder transactions between 1972 and 1987, compared to 0.35% in single-bidder transactions, measured from day -1 through completion; difference is not statistically significant for this long window, but regression analysis using a 2-day window indicates significance at 99% confidence level).

2.   Event Studies: Partitioning the Data Set

To gain further insight into the importance of synergy in explaining combined acquirer and target stock price gains, as well as the relative importance of the competitive market, joint gains, and good bidder/bad bidder explanations for negative average acquirer returns, we must go beyond average returns to all acquirers, or all targets, and attempt to understand *which* acquirers, and *which* transactions, hold the promise of business value gains, and which do not. We thus turn in this section to studies that partition their data sets based on various characteristics that suggest synergy or overpayment, or larger or smaller acquirer returns.

Partitioning Based on Relatedness of Acquirer and Target. How might one predict, *ex ante*, whether an acquisition holds out the promise of synergy? The theoretical sources of synergy depend on the relatedness of the acquirer's and the target's businesses. Thus, the synergy explanation for takeover gains implies that related acquisitions will produce higher joint gains. Those gains will be reflected in higher target returns, higher acquirer returns, or both. Most studies find no significant difference in *target* returns for related versus unrelated acquisitions; thus, we can focus on acquirer returns. Table 8-8 and footnote 15 collect studies that find significantly higher acquirer returns in related acquisitions.[15]

---

[15] The studies reported in the table are: Espen Eckbo, *Mergers and the Market Concentration Doctrine: Evidence from the Capital Market*, 58 J.Bus. 325 (1985) (comparing horizontal to nonhorizontal mergers); Kevin Scanlon, Jack Trifts & Richard Pettway, *Impacts of Relative Size and Industrial Relatedness on Returns to Shareholders of Acquiring Firms*, 12 J.Fin.Res. 103 (1989) (an acquisition is related if the acquirer and target share the same 2-digit SIC code); Neil Sicherman & Richard Pettway, *Acquisition of Divested Assets and Shareholders' Wealth*, 42 J.Fin. 1261 (1987) (same definition of relatedness) (studying divestitures). In addition, Doug Wakeman & John Stewart, *The Empirical Determinants of Merger Returns* (working paper 1987), report a *t*-statistic of 5.85 for a relatedness variable in a regression analysis, but the variable is defined in a way that does not permit calculation of the percentage difference in related versus unrelated acquisitions; and Morck, Shleifer & Vishny (1990), *supra* note 6, at 45-46, report that the return to bidders was significantly higher for related acquisitions in the 1980s. The much more positive investor reaction to unrelated acquisitions in the early days of the conglomerate movement is discussed in Chapter 9.

Table 8-8
Acquirer Returns in Related Versus Unrelated Acquisitions
(confidence level in parentheses)

Study	Sample Period	Window Period	Difference in Acquirer CARs: Related vs. Unrelated Acquisitions
Eckbo (1985)	1963-81	(−20, +10)	2.0% (approx. 95% confidence)
Scanlon, Trifts & Pettway (1989)	1968-85	(−20, +20)	4.2% (99% confidence)
Sicherman & Pettway (1987)	1983-85	(−10, +10)	4.0% (99% confidence)

Espen Eckbo and Doug Wakeman & John Stewart also find higher *combined* abnormal returns to bidder and target from related acquisitions, with acquirer and target weighted by their pre-transaction market value.[16] The higher combined returns suggest that operating synergy is an important source of shareholder market value gains. At the same time, the positive combined returns in unrelated transactions suggest that operating synergy is not the *only* source of gains.

Partitioning based on relative size of acquirer and target. Acquiring firms are generally significantly larger than their targets. This makes it hard to measure abnormal returns both to the acquirer and to the acquirer and target combined. To take an extreme example, suppose that McDonald's Corp. acquires a single store from the franchise holder and pays a substantial premium. The seller should earn positive abnormal returns as a result of the transaction. But the transaction is so small that any gain or loss to McDonald's shareholders will be buried in the noise resulting from normal variation in McDonald's stock price. This is true whether there are joint gains, shared in some fashion by the franchisee and McDonald's, or no joint gains, so that the premium reflects overpayment by McDonald's.

In a less extreme case, even if the acquirer earns a significant fraction of the joint gains, the target's stock price may move much further in percentage terms. Suppose, for example, that the acquirer has a pre-transaction market value of $100 million, while the target's pre-transaction market value is $20 million (a 5:1 ratio is about the average for acquisitions of public companies); that the acquisition produces joint gains of $8 million, and that 75% of these gains accrue to the target's shareholders. The target's market value will jump by 30%, from $20 million to $26 million. In contrast, the acquirer's stock price will increase by only 2%, from $100,000,000 to $102 million. This problem of relative size helps to explain why many studies find no significant returns to acquirers, either positive or

---

[16] Eckbo (1985), *supra* note 15; Wakeman & Stewart (1987), *supra* note 15.

negative. Differences in relative size also complicate efforts to measure combined gains to matched acquirer-target pairs; indeed, only in the last few years were researchers able to convincingly document that joint gains even *existed* on average.

There are two distinct ways that researchers try to find significant returns to acquirers -- positive or negative -- despite the noise of daily stock price movements. The first involves large sample sizes, to take advantage of the tendency of z or t statistics to increase in proportion to $n^{1/2}$, where n is the number of firms in the sample. It is no accident that the studies reported in Table 8-6, which report significant negative acquirer returns, mostly use samples of 100 or more transactions. In contrast, many other studies, especially studies that rely on smaller samples, fail to find significant positive or negative abnormal returns to acquirers.

The need for large sample sizes becomes problematic, though, when we need to go beyond average returns to an undifferentiated group of acquiring firms, and partition the data set in various ways. The finer the partitioning, the smaller the effective sample size, and thus the harder it is to find statistically significant results.

The second response to the relative size problem is to focus on transactions where the target is large *relative* to the acquirer. This should make it easier to observe a large percentage change in the acquirer's stock price in response to a takeover announcement. Unfortunately, the results from such studies are mixed. Asquith, Bruner & Mullins divide a sample of mergers between 1963 and 1979 into two groups: mergers where the pre-transaction equity value of the target is at least 10% of the equity value of the acquiring company; and mergers where the equity value of the target company is less than 10% of that of the acquiring company. Companies that acquired relatively large targets earned significant positive abnormal returns, while that acquired smaller targets earned only insignificant returns.[17] This suggests that acquirers earning positive abnormal returns, but those returns are buried in the noise when the target is small. Jarrell & Poulsen find a similar tendency in a regression analysis of tender offers -- acquirer returns increase with the *relative* size of the target; this pattern persists into the 1980s.[18] But Scanlon, Trifts & Pettway find the opposite result for a sample of mergers between 1968 and 1985: acquirers do *worse* in relatively large transactions.[19]

These conflicting results may reflect the tendency for both positive and negative acquirer returns to show up with greater clarity for relatively large acquisitions. If the transactions in a sample, on the whole, produce positive acquirer returns, those positive returns will be larger if the target is large

---

[17] Asquith, Bruner & Mullins (1983), *supra* note 12.

[18] Jarrell & Poulsen (1989), *supra* note 12. Loderer & Martin (1990), *supra* note 12, also find a significant positive correlation between relative target size and acquirer returns in a regression analysis that separately controls for *absolute* target size.

[19] Scanlon, Trifts & Pettway (1989), *supra* note 15.

relative to the acquirer. Conversely, if the sample transactions, on the whole, provide negative returns to acquirers, those negative returns will be larger if the target is large relative to the acquirer. Taken as a whole, these results confirm the obvious -- significant abnormal returns to acquirers are more likely in relatively large transactions, while acquirer gains or losses are obscured by stock price noise in smaller acquisitions. But they do not tell us what the source of the gains or losses might be. Moreover, acquisitions of relatively large targets might be more (or less) profitable than smaller deals for other reasons. For example, transactions that are large *for the acquirer* may be more carefully thought out than smaller transactions. Relatively large transactions may also be subject to greater capital market discipline, since the acquirer is more likely to need financing, and greater scrutiny from outside directors. Conversely, relatively large targets may be more difficult for the acquirer to successfully integrate into its existing business, and may be more likely to involve overt competition.

Partitioning Based on the Prior Performance of Acquirer and Target. Acquiring firm managers who are doing a good job of running their own business are probably better able to overcome the problems of skill transfer and integration that accompany any merger, and thus realize whatever synergies are available. If we could isolate transactions where the acquirer's are skilled, we could better isolate the sources of gains or losses from takeovers. Unfortunately, there is no direct way to measure manager quality, so empirical studies must rely on proxies -- other variables that are believed to correlate with manager quality. A commonly used proxy is *Tobin's q*, defined as the ratio of the firm's market value to the estimated replacement value of its tangible assets. If firm A has skilled managers, and otherwise similar firm B does not, then firm A should have a higher Tobin's q, because its managers can extract higher earnings from the same tangible assets.

The available studies suggest that synergy gains depend on the quality of both the acquirer's and the target's managers. Larry Lang, Rene Stulz & Ralph Walkling partition acquiring and target companies in a sample of 209 tender offers between 1968 and 1986 into high-q and low-q subsamples. They find that high-q (presumably well-managed) acquirers earn positive abnormal returns of approximately 10% when they acquire low-q (presumably mismanaged) targets. In contrast, low-q acquirers suffer losses averaging 4.9% when they acquire high-q targets. The difference between the two subsamples is significant ($t = 2.99$). The gains to high-q acquirers seem to reflect greater total gains to acquirer and target combined, rather than the acquirer receiving a larger share of the joint gains.[20]

Henri Servaes extends the Lang, Stulz & Walking study. He uses a larger sample (704 targets and 384 acquirers between 1972 and 1987), and

---

[20] Larry Lang, Rene Stulz & Ralph Walkling, *Managerial Performance, Tobin's q and the Gains from Successful Tender Offers*, 24 J.Fin.Econ. 137 (1989).

computes *industry-adjusted* Tobin's q's, with consistent results.[21] Servaes also finds that the *target's q* is an important determinant of takeover gains. Target abnormal returns, and combined acquirer and target returns, are significantly *higher* if the target has a *low* Tobin's q. This suggests that less value can be created by taking over a well-managed firm.[22] In the least-promising category -- acquisition of a high-q target by a low-q acquirer -- Servaes finds *negative* combined acquirer and target returns, suggesting no joint gains. These results also suggest the importance of management quality, and the potential for gains to come from the displacement of inefficient management, a topic taken up in Chapter 10.

Randall Morck, Andrei Shleifer & Robert Vishny also provide evidence that returns to acquiring companies depend on the quality of acquiring and target company management. They study 326 acquisitions between 1975 and 1986, using the firm's industry-adjusted income growth rate over the previous three years as a proxy for management quality. Well-managed acquirers (those with growth above the mean of the sample) earn positive abnormal returns equal to 3% of the target's pre-transaction market value, while poorly-managed acquirers (those with relative growth below the sample mean) suffer losses averaging 5% of the target's pre-transaction market value. The difference between the two groups is statistically significant ($t = 2.67$). A regression analysis shows that acquirers also earn higher returns when they buy poorly-managed targets.[23]

3. Post-Acquisition Returns to Acquiring Firms

Taken as a whole, the empirical evidence discussed in the last subsection supports the conclusion that, on average, corporate acquisitions increase the combined shareholder market value of the acquiring and target companies, and that synergy is a likely explanation for at least some and perhaps most of the gains. But they also yield a puzzle: Why do so many acquirers overpay?

Moreover, there is a further puzzle in the data on long-term returns to acquiring firms. Acquiring firms appear to suffer negative abnormal returns in the several years following the transaction. These long-term losses are potentially large enough to outweigh the combined gains at the time of the announcement.[24] This could be caused by misspecification of the asset

---

[21] Servaes (1991), *supra* note 9.

[22] Consistent with this, Larry Lang, Rene Stulz & Ralph Walkling, *A Test of the Free Cash Flow Hypothesis: The Case of Bidder Returns*, 29 J.Fin.Econ. 315 (1991), report that acquirer returns are lower when the *target* has a high Tobin's q.

[23] Morck, Shleifer & Vishny (1990), *supra* note 6.

[24] See, e.g., Anup Agrawal, Jeffrey Jaffe & Gershon Mandelker, *The Post-Merger Performance of Acquiring Firms: A Re-examination of an Anomaly*, 47 J.Fin. 1605 (1992); Paul Asquith, *Merger Bids, Uncertainty, and Stockholder Returns*, 11 J.Fin.Econ. 51 (1983);

pricing model. Recall from Chapter 6 that model misspecification is a serious problem for long-term event studies. But the anomaly has proven to be reasonably robust to changes in model specification, at least in some time periods.[25] If real, these long-term stock price losses suggest that shareholders have been too optimistic about the prospects for takeover gains, and have only gradually learned the error of their ways. Long-term joint gains in business value may have been less than the announcement period returns suggest, perhaps even nonexistent.

Such investor errors, *if never corrected*, would call into question the efficiency of the initial response. They would offer a profitable trading strategy: Sell acquiring companies' stock short on the announcement date. On the other hand, investor errors, *confined to particular time periods*, can be consistent with market efficiency. Market efficiency doesn't require that investor value estimates be right, only that the estimates be unbiased, based on the best available information at the time. In the 1960s, for example, the conglomerate merger was a new transaction form, to which investors reacted with enthusiasm. As we discuss in Chapter 9, it appears, in hindsight, that this enthusiasm was misplaced. The negative long-term returns to acquirers in the 1960s could reflect investors gradually learning that these new transactions weren't delivering on their initial promise.

In the 1980s, the new transaction form was the highly leveraged takeover, to which investors also reacted with enthusiasm. As we discuss in Chapter 11, it appears in hindsight that *some* enthusiasm was warranted, but perhaps not as much as investors showed, especially for the higher-priced transaction of the late 1980s. This too, could be consistent with efficient capital markets, in which investors initially guess about the future profitability of a class of transactions, and turn out to guess wrong.

Terence Langetieg, *An Application of a Three-Factor Performance Index to Measure Stockholder Gains from Merger*, 6 J.Fin.Econ. 365 (1978); Claudio Loderer & Kenneth Martin, *Postacquisition Performance of Acquiring Firms*, Fin.Mgmt. 69 (Autumn 1992); Ellen Magenheim & Dennis Mueller, *Are Acquiring Firm Shareholders Better Off After an Acquisition*, in *Knights, Raiders & Targets: The Impact of the Hostile Takeover* 171 (John Coffee, Louis Lowenstein & Susan Rose-Ackerman eds.1988) (finding negative abnormal returns to acquirers averaging 42% over the three years following an acquisition).

[25] Compare Michael Bradley & Gregg Jarrell, *Comment*, in *Knights, Raiders & Targets: The Impact of the Hostile Takeover* 253 (John Coffee, Louis Lowenstein & Susan Rose-Ackerman eds.1988) (model respecification reduces estimated 3-year post-acquisition losses to the Magenheim & Mueller sample to a statistically insignificant 16%); and Julian Franks, Robert Harris & Sheridan Titman, *The Postmerger Share Price Performance of Acquiring Firms*, 29 J.Fin.Econ. 81 (1991) (anomaly disappears for sample of takeovers between 1975 and 1984, if one uses a multifactor asset pricing model); with Agrawal, Jaffe & Mandelker (1992), *supra* note 24 (anomaly is robust to model specification in 1950s, 1960s, and 1980s (through 1987)); and Loderer & Martin (1992), *supra* note 24 (acquiring firm losses robust to model specification for 3 and 5-year periods following an acquisition in the 1960s; over a 3-year period but not a 5-year period following an acquisition in the 1970s; no post-acquisition losses for 1980s acquisitions (through 1986)).

Efficient market skeptics, on the other hand, point to episodes like these, where investors were overenthusiastic, as evidence that investors are prone to fads. Why is it, they might ask, that investors have been habitually too optimistic about takeovers, rather than sometimes optimistic and sometimes pessimistic, as efficient market theory would predict?

Both groups ought to agree on the need to test whether actual realized gains match investor expectations at the time of the transaction. Stock price studies are one way to do this, but the high degree of noise in long-term studies makes it difficult to draw firm conclusions. Thus, there is need for other types of studies of the long-term outcomes of corporate acquisitions, such as studies that rely on accounting data, or on subsequent reversal of the acquisition through a later divestiture. A few such studies have been performed; we discuss these studies more carefully in later chapters. In brief, they find evidence of improved operating performance from takeovers in the 1980s, including leveraged buyouts, but little evidence of improved performance from the conglomerate acquisitions that dominated in the 1960s. Thus, they are broadly consistent with operating synergy as a potential source of takeover gains. But the accounting data on which these *ex post* studies rely is too uncertain for us to be able to assess whether the observed operating improvements in the 1980s are large enough to justify the shareholder market value gains when the transactions were announced.

For now, synergy must stand as a plausible, but not a *proven*, source of joint gains from acquisitions.

CHAPTER 9: DIVERSIFICATION
AND FINANCIAL SYNERGY

Operating synergy is a central theoretical explanation for how corporate acquisitions can increase value. But many acquisitions don't involve a close fit between acquirer and target. Mergers between unrelated companies were the dominant transaction form in the "conglomerate" merger wave of the 1960s. Conglomerate mergers were less fashionable in the 1980s, but even so, only 1/3 of large acquisitions between 1980 and 1987 involved companies in the same industry,[1] as measured by a commonly used government classification scheme called SIC (Standard Industrial Classification).[2]

In this chapter, we explore the theoretical rationale for why combining two unrelated businesses might produce a combined value that is greater than the sum of their separate values. Sections A and B develop theoretical explanations for why conglomerate mergers might increase the value of the combined firm, and assess each explanation for consistency with the financial tools we developed in Part I. Section C then reviews the empirical evidence on whether conglomerate acquisitions increase value. In light of the strong evidence that many conglomerate acquisitions *decrease* value, we consider in Section D an *agency cost* explanation for why these transactions take place. In this explanation, firms pursue diversifying acquisitions because they have value not to shareholders, but to the managers of the acquiring firm. Finally, in Section E, we evaluate whether "bust-up" takeovers, where an acquirer breaks up a conglomerate into its component parts, can recover some of the value lost through conglomeration.

A. Diversification at the Firm Level

1. The Theory

Diversification can reduce the fluctuations in a firm's earnings stream. The next excerpt develops the claim that this makes the firm worth more to shareholders.

---

[1] Randall Morck, Andrei Shleifer & Robert Vishny, *Do Managerial Objectives Drive Bad Acquisitions?*, 45 J.Fin. 31 (1990); accord, John Byrd & Kent Hickman, *Do Outside Directors Monitor Managers?: Evidence from Tender Offer Bids*, 32 J.Fin.Econ. 195 (1992) (24% of sample of tender offers between 1980 and 1987 involved bidder and target with the same 4-digit SIC code).

[2] The SIC system assigns a 4-digit code to each industry. Closely related industries will share the same first three digits, generally related industries will share the same first 2 digits. For example, men's and boy's shirts (SIC code 2321) is within the 3-digit code 232 (men's and boy's clothing), which is within the 2-digit code 23 (apparel). For discussion of the defects in the SIC system, see Richard Clarke, *SICs as Delineators of Economic Markets*, 62 J.Bus. 17 (1989).

Gary Haight, THE PORTFOLIO MERGER: FINDING
THE COMPANY THAT CAN STABILIZE YOUR EARNINGS
Mergers & Acquisitions 33-34 (Summer 1981)

The pricing of an acquisition is a difficult task which often requires that buyers predict future performance in risky areas. In making this assessment, buyers must consider the candidate's strategic fit, the effect of both financial and operating leverage on their income stream, and the acquisition's impact on their overall earnings growth rate. However, there is another kind of acquisition benefit, one which is often overlooked: the "portfolio" effect.

Although as individual investors [mergers & acquisitions (M&A)] practitioners are likely to seek the benefits of portfolio diversification, few, if any, have incorporated the classic portfolio diversification model into their merger decisions by considering the earnings stability that the diversification-motivated merger can bring. . . . The technical portfolio model can allow the buyer to estimate earnings flow from potential acquisition, then select the flow which will achieve the greatest earnings stability. It can also be applied to divestiture decisions.

The basic balance sheet elements of the portfolio model are: earnings before depreciation, interest, and taxes (EBDIT), and adjusted gross assets (AGA). The "EBDIT/AGA" approach can help identify the acquisition which will bring the greatest -- or, in the case of a spin-off candidate, the least -- earnings stability. This will depend not only upon the degree of correlation between the two firms' sales, but also on the relative mix and correlation of *fixed* and *variable* costs in their respective operating cost structures. Firms in capital-intensive industries, for example, have a higher percentage of fixed (vs. variable) costs. In such cases, changes in sales will contribute to greater variability in return on real assets due to operating leverage. To determine the degree of diversification effect, the buyer should ask if the merged firms' operating cost structures are compatible in these ways. . . .

To measure return on assets (ROA) in terms of its operational impact, you can set the ROA of the combined entities equal to their EBDIT divided by their combined AGA. This EBDIT/AGA approach adds back depreciation expense to operating income, and accumulated depreciation to net asset value. To apply this same principle to divestiture decisions, simply *subtract* contributions of the spin-off candidate from your calculations. . . .

If you are considering the purchase of a manufacturing or mining firm, you should recognize that a large portion of their fixed costs comes in the form of depreciation and/or depletion expenses. By eliminating the noncash portion of fixed costs in the return measure, you can increase the proportion of variable to total costs in your firm's operating cost structure. The larger the proportion of variable to total costs, the less pronounced will be changes in operating profits resulting from revenue fluctuation. As a result, the measures you take will be more representative of the operating environment.

To calculate what your return on real assets will be after a merger, average the premerger returns of both the acquiring and acquired firms. The weights to be applied to each firm's return should be a function of each one's contribution to the total assets at the time the merger is consummated. In addition, you should calculate the "coefficient of correlation" for the combined earnings of the two merged firms.

Every dealsmaker knows that there is a gray area in earnings estimates. You don't really know exactly what will happen to your earnings when you merge, only the range of likely results -- plus or minus what the statisticians call the "standard deviation." The postmerger standard deviation is a function of the standard deviation of each firm's premerger return and the degree to which these returns are correlated -- technically, a "coefficient of correlation." *The lower the correlation between these two streams, the greater the stabilizing effect of the merger. . . .*

This calculation, along with the others the AGA/EBDIT approach suggests, can predict post-acquisition or divestiture earnings results for even the most complex transactions. For example, given only 1979 information, according to the model, the 1980 post-merger returns of Dart & Kraft should have been 15.8449 percent $\pm$ .77 percent. The actual 1980 combined results were 16.1659 percent, well within the forecasted amount. The coefficient of correlation was negative ($-.82118$), indicating that the two firms were a good fit for diversification purposes.

Remember, the portfolio approach does *not* apply to mergers where synergy, whether positive or negative, is expected to add or detract from the earnings picture. But despite the vogue of synergy, many firms do choose to make acquisitions or divestitures for the purpose of financial diversification. If you contemplate making such a deal, the EBDIT/AGA "portfolio" approach can help you predict the future firm's earnings stability.

---

2.   Evaluation: Consistency with Analytic Tools

Haim Levy & Marshall Sarnat, DIVERSIFICATION, PORTFOLIO ANALYSIS AND THE UNEASY CASE FOR CONGLOMERATE MERGERS
25 J.Fin. 795 (1970)

That horizontal and vertical mergers potentially can produce real economic gains is nowhere denied, but the economic case for a conglomerate merger is somewhat less clear. Much of the traditional analysis relating to the possible creation of economies of scale in production, research, distribution and management is not relevant for the pure conglomerate in which there are no discernible economic relationships between the parties to the merger. Recognizing the need for an alternative approach to conglomerate growth, [a number of authors] have analyzed the diversification inherent in a conglomerate acquisition as a special case of the general theory of diversification and portfolio selection. . . . Such an approach identifies the reduction in standard error engendered by the combination of statistically independent or negatively correlated income streams as a "conglomerate effect" produced by the merger of firms whose economic activities are unrelated, and the purely conglomerate type of merger, as one in which profits are not increased, "but only stabilized by bringing together centers with zero or negative correlations."[a]

It would seem to follow that even in the absence of economies of scale and complimentaries (synergism), the stabilization of the profit stream, induced by the merger, should still produce a clear-cut economic gain. But despite the plausibility of this argument, it can be shown that in a perfect capital market an economic advantage cannot be achieved by a purely conglomerate merger.

I

Let us assume such a merger between two completely unrelated companies. In the absence of synergistic effects, the postmerger return to shareholders in the new firm will be the weighted average of the returns of each of the individual firms making up the merger:

$$z = w{\cdot}x_1 + (1 - w){\cdot}x_2$$

where:

z	$=$	a random variable denoting the postmerger return to shareholders of the new firm
x_1, x_2	$=$	random variables denoting the return to shareholders of the two individual firms, in the absence of the merger
w	$=$	the relative size of the first firm [expressed as a fraction of the size of the combined firm]
$1-w$	$=$	the relative size of the second firm

. . . [This same relationship holds for the *expected* postmerger return to the combined firm, u_z.] Since we are assuming the absence of perfect correlation between the returns of the individual firms, the total postmerger variance [σ_z^2] is lower than the simple sum of the individual variances.[3] And as we have also assumed that the expected return after the merger is a weighted average of the individual returns . . ., total risk has been reduced with no change in the level of return. It would appear to follow that the

---

[a] M.A. Adelman, *The Antimerger Act, 1950-60*, 51 Am.Econ.Rev. 236, 242 (1961).

[3] Throughout this paper, the analysis is carried out within the framework of [CAPM]; i.e., reduction of the variance (or standard deviation) of returns serves as a measure of risk diversification, and optimal portfolio selection is a function solely of the mean and variance of the distribution of returns.

shares of the new firm should sell at a premium *vis-a-vis* the weighted sum of the premerger prices of the individual firms. However, such a premium will not be forthcoming in a perfect capital market because the superior risk-return combination (σ_z^2, u_z) could have been achieved by investors, even in the absence of the merger, by combining the individual shares in a portfolio in the proportions w and $1-w$.

Thus, despite the stabilizing diversification effect, a conglomerate merger *per se* does not necessarily create opportunities for risk diversification over and beyond what was possible to individual (and institutional) investors prior to the merger. In a perfect capital market, the premerger equilibrium prices of the shares would reflect the possibility of all such combinations. Therefore, after the merger has been effected, no increase in the combined market value of the two firms is to be expected or, in fact, is even possible.
. . .

[T]he optimal proportion of [an investor's total portfolio that should be invested in the combined firm] after the merger is simply the sum of the proportions which were invested in the individual companies prior to the merger. Thus, the merger *per se* calls forth no market forces to change the equilibrium share prices which existed prior to the change and, therefore, we may conclude that the stabilizing diversification effected by pure conglomerate merger cannot produce an economic gain in a perfect capital market. . . .

II

Given the neutrality of a pure conglomerate merger in a perfect capital market, we now turn to the possible influence of market imperfections on the economic effects of such mergers. In practice investors do not include all security issues in their portfolios because of indivisibilities, differential transactions costs, cost of acquiring information, and the difficulties of keeping track of numerous investments. For simplicity we assume that for all, or some, of the above reasons, an investor restricts his portfolio to two shares only, A and B. . . .

[T]he investor, following a merger of companies B and C, can invest in . . . the new merger $(B + C)$ and in company A. . . . Thus, unlike the case of the perfect market, the conglomerate merger in an imperfect market does allow a degree of additional diversification which the investor hitherto could not effect for himself owing to the two share constraint, and this added degree of freedom may [produce] an economic gain for the investor.[8] But upon reflection, it is equally clear that the investor may not gain, and in fact may even lose, from this type of merger -- for while gaining the additional degree of freedom to invest *indirectly* in the shares of company C, he has lost the option of investing *directly* in the shares of B.

---

[8] By permitting a greater degree of diversification to the small investor, the conglomerate merger serves as a sort of substitute for a mutual fund or closed-end investment company.

Note: Firm Versus Shareholder Diversification

1. *Diversification as a Problem in Comparative Transaction Costs.* The central message of Chapter 3 was that there was value in diversification. The issue posed by diversification as an acquisition motive is whether diversification *at the firm level* adds value. As long as the shareholders of the acquiring company can diversify their own portfolios, the price of the acquiring firm's stock will already reflect the value of diversification in reducing unsystematic risk. If transaction costs are zero, as Levy & Sarnat implicitly assume in relying on CAPM, there should be no value added (or value lost) from diversification at the firm level.

In the real world of positive transaction costs, the value of firm-level diversification depends on who can diversify more cheaply -- the firm or its shareholders.   Firm-level diversification will add value if the firm can diversify more cheaply than the shareholders.   Conversely, firm-level diversification will *subtract* value if shareholder can diversify more cheaply than firms.

It seems likely that the transaction costs of diversification are lower for shareholders than for firms. Small shareholders pay brokerage commissions to buy stock that depend in part on the number of transactions: It costs more to buy 100 shares in each of 10 firms than to buy 1000 shares in a single firm. But the differences in commissions are small. Small investors can also diversify by buying a mutual fund, at the cost of paying the fund's fees. No-load funds with annual fees of about 1% of assets are widely available.

For large institutional investors, the transaction cost disadvantage of diversification disappears; the commission is the same (only a few pennies a share) to buy 10,000 shares in each of 10 firms as to buy 100,000 shares in a single firm. Large institutions also face *market impact costs* when they buy or sell stocks -- the tendency for a large buy (sell) order to increase (decrease) the market price.   Moderate diversification may well *reduce* market impact costs for large investors.

In contrast, the acquisition of another company typically involves substantial transaction costs *and* takes place at a substantial premium over the pretakeover market price. For example, if shareholders of U.S. Steel had thought it wise in 1982 to diversify their portfolios by acquiring stock in Marathon Oil, they could have done so (many had *already* done so) at the pretakeover market price of about $60 per share. U.S. Steel paid an average price of about $100 per share to acquire Marathon, plus transaction costs (legal, investment banking, and accounting fees, borrowing costs, management time, etc.) of several dollars per Marathon share. It is hard to see how this zero-synergy acquisition benefitted U.S. Steel's shareholders, though much of the premium was a wealth transfer to Marathon shareholders, rather than a net social loss.

2. *Diversification by Closely Held Firms*. Diversification by public firms doesn't add value because it can be replicated more cheaply, and tailored more carefully to individual preferences, if undertaken by the shareholders themselves. But what if the firm is owned by a single individual or by a family that views itself as a single economic unit? In this setting there is only a formal distinction between diversification at the shareholder level and diversification at the company level. Tax-based motives (a subject we defer until Chapter 12) aside, there is no reason to prefer one to another.[3]

If a close corporation is owned by more than a single individual, the problem of diversification is more complicated. In an efficient market, the stock price of a publicly traded company doesn't depend on the risk preferences or personal tastes of its shareholders. Shareholders can arrange their individual portfolios to reflect their own tastes for risk and diversification without regard to the firm's investment decisions. A shareholder who wants to diversify can do so. If the company's systematic risk is too high for a shareholder's tastes, the shareholder can sell some of its stock and purchase lower-risk assets. A shareholder with a taste for additional risk can buy more shares using borrowed funds, or buy stock in higher-risk firms. Firms can ignore the personal tastes of shareholders for risk, diversification, and other investment characteristics. The shareholders' care only that the firm's decisions maximize the market value of its stock and, hence, the resources available to shareholders to pursue their individual tastes.

The situation in a close corporation is drastically different. By definition, the shares of a close corporation are not publicly traded; the market for its stock is at best thin and often all but nonexistent. Moreover, the close corporation form is particularly suited to businesses where individuals must have substantial authority to make decisions and where those decisions are difficult for others to monitor. In this setting, a common way to encourage decision makers to perform well is to make them the owners, so that they bear the consequences of poor decisions.[4] A correspondence between decision makers and shareholders, however, makes the identity of each shareholder important to the others. As a result, many close corporations prohibit shareholders from transferring their shares without the approval of the other shareholders. (For similar reasons, partnerships often restrict the transferability of partnership interests.)

---

[3] There remains a question as to why a closely held firm would choose to diversify by buying *all*, rather than only part, of another firm or firms, since buying all usually costs more per share than buying a fractional stake. A *diversification* motive cannot explain this, though tax or other advantages of buying an entire firm might.

[4] See Armen Alchian & Harold Demsetz, *Production, Information Costs, and Economic Organization*, 62 Am.Econ.Rev. 777 (1972); Eugene Fama & Michael Jensen, *Organizational Form and Investment Decisions*, 14 J.Fin.Econ. 101 (1985).

Since the shareholders of a close corporation cannot alter corporate investment decisions by rearranging their individual portfolios, they may favor diversification at the firm level. But different shareholders may have different preferences and, as a result, different ideas about what investment policy the corporation should pursue. Two conclusions flow from this reasoning. First, close corporations should not necessarily make only those investments that would maximize the firm's value if its stock were publicly traded. Instead, the close corporation's investment decisions will also be partly based on the personal tastes of the shareholders for diversification, risk, and liquidity. Second, the need to take shareholder preferences into account in making corporate investment decisions reinforces the incentive to maintain control over who the shareholders are. Put simply, the shareholders (or the partners in a law firm) are better off if they all have the same tastes.

The failure of close corporations to maximize profit puts them at a competitive disadvantage in the product market vis-a-vis publicly traded corporations. However, the continued survival of this organizational form suggests the existence of offsetting advantages in other areas. Close corporations may survive in businesses where central decision making is cheaper and more efficient than the diffuse decision making systems associated with larger firms. This savings may outweigh the costs -- like the inability of shareholders to fully diversify -- that result from the absence of a public market for the corporation's shares.

3. *Bankruptcy Costs as a Motive for Firm Diversification.* The academic search for a motive for conglomerate acquisitions has included close attention to the impact of merger on the risk of bankruptcy or financial distress.[5] Bankruptcy typically results in substantial transaction and business disruption costs; financial distress can have similar effects even if resolved without a formal bankruptcy filing. These costs are "transaction costs" in the broad sense of the term. They would not exist if capital markets worked costlessly, because capital providers would quietly and quickly adjust their claims to match the reduced value of the troubled firm.

Diversification can reduce a firm's inherent business risk, and thus reduce the expected costs of financial distress. There may, however, be offsetting costs. For a firm with heavy exposure to future tort claims, the lower risk of bankruptcy increases the expected value of those claims, since the firm is more likely to be able to pay them. And, in a world where shareholders have limited ability to monitor managers, the risk of financial distress is an important constraint on the ability of managers to depart from profit maximization.

Firm-specific risk is centrally affected by two factors: the inherent riskiness of the business, and the proportion of debt in a firm's capital

---

[5] See, e.g., James Scott, *On the Theory of Conglomerate Mergers*, 32 J.Fin. 1235 (1977); Robert Higgins & Lawrence Schall, *Corporate Bankruptcy and Conglomerate Merger*, 30 J.Fin. 93 (1975).

structure. The two are interrelated. A firm with a high degree of business risk will often choose a less leveraged capital structure, and vice versa. Because firm-level diversification and leveraging have opposing effects on firm-specific risk, the arguments for (against) leverage correspond closely to the bankruptcy-related arguments against (for) firm-level diversification. Of the two, leverage has by far the larger effect on bankruptcy risk. For that reason, we defer further consideration of the interaction among bankruptcy costs, monitoring costs, and firm-specific risk to Chapter 11 on leveraged buyouts and recapitalizations.

B.   The Conglomerate Firm as an Internal Capital Market

1.   The Theory

A more promising argument for firm-level diversification is not that conglomerate firms can diversify more cheaply than shareholders, but that conglomerate managers can pick better investments. The next two readings develop the claim that conglomerate managers can allocate capital to promising new projects more effectively than investors in the capital markets.

Malcolm Salter & Wolf Weinhold
DIVERSIFICATION THROUGH ACQUISITION
65-78 (1979)˜

[T]he several variants of the *product/market-portfolio model* focus on the overall economic characteristics of a company's business or portfolio of businesses. One of the early expressions of the product/market-portfolio model was developed by the Boston Consulting Group (BCG) and emphasizes a matrix of relative market share and market growth. This framework has been used widely during the past decade as a way of analyzing the competitive position of a business and the business portfolios of multiproduct, multimarket companies. . . .

Product/market-portfolio models focus on the strengths of a company's portfolio of products or businesses, such strengths being defined in terms of market position and market attractiveness. The key relationship stressed by the BCG variant is the relationship between the cash flow of a business and its market-share/market-growth characteristics. These characteristics are used as key indicators of a company's market position and the attractiveness of its market commitments. The model tells managers to . . . balanc[e] the generation and use of cash within the company. . . . The advantage of internally generated cash is that it has greater reliability than external funding. . . .

Propositions of the Product/Market-Portfolio Model

[T]he product/market-portfolio model holds that in most competitive environments relative market share and market growth determine the cash-generation or cash-usage characteristics of businesses. The logic of this proposition can be explained as follows.

When companies pursue marketing and pricing strategies geared to increasing production volume faster than their competitors, cost advantages relative to competitors will normally follow. This relationship between the accumulated experience associated with increased production volume and declining costs is referred to by BCG as the "experience-curve" effect. The experience curve relationship, as described by BCG, states that unit costs decline by approximately 20 to 30% (in constant dollars) with each doubling of accumulated production. While similar to the well-known and documented learning-curve phenomenon, BCG has found this effect to extend to most elements of value added, including capital, labor, and overhead. The . . . underlying forces are believed to include (1) labor efficiency, (2) new processes and improved methods, (3) product redesign that conserves material, allows greater efficiency in manufacture, and takes advantage of less costly resources, (4) product standardization, and (5) scale effects. Each of these forces is related to growth in accumulated production experience and provides opportunities that alert managements can exploit. The experience-curve relationship is often shown in a [logarithmic] graph of unit costs (or prices if a constant profit margin is assumed) versus total production, such as those shown for . . . Integrated Circuits in Figure 9-1.

Figure 9-1
The Experience Curve for Integrated Circuits

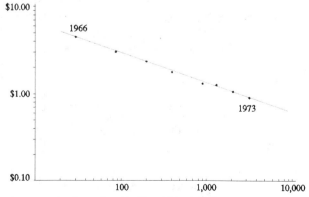

Source: Texas Instruments, Inc., *Stockholders' Meeting Report* (1973)

As is the case with accumulated experience, market share can have enormous value. Indeed, according to the model, a company's accumulated experience can best be measured by relative market share. When competitors follow similar experience curves, the dominant producer in an industry will have the greatest accumulated experience and the lowest unit costs. Assuming a single industrywide price, he will therefore have the highest profit margins. . . . [The dominant producer can] generate a significantly larger cash flow than its competitors because of both its greater volume and a greater [profit] contribution per unit sold.

While cash generation is a function of accumulated experience, best summarized through relative market share, cash use or investment, according to the model, is a function of market growth. To maintain market share in a growing market requires the infusion of cash for both working capital and capacity expansion. Attempting to gain additional market share further increases the business unit's growth rate and [cash use]. . . .

Based on the general proposition outlined above, the product market-portfolio model isolates businesses into four categories reflecting their cash-use and cash-generation characteristics. Market growth is separated into high or low by an arbitrary dividing line, usually 10%, and cash use is depicted as high or low accordingly. Market share is viewed in terms of relative share -- that is, company sales in that business divided by the sales of the company's leading competitor. Since only one competitor can have a relative market share greater than 1.0, this figure is used to identify companies within an industry with high or low relative market shares and, therefore, high or low levels of relative cash generation. These four business categories are portrayed by BCG in a portfolio chart depicted in Figure 9-2.

Figure 9-2
Market-Share/Market-Growth Portfolio Chart

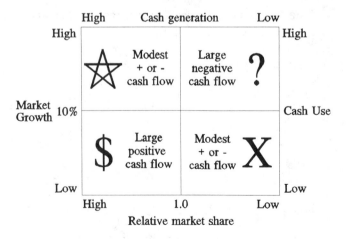

Each quadrant in Figure 9-2 has its own pattern of cash generation and use, and BCG has given each its own name to reflect these characteristics.

- *Stars* in the upper left quadrant are the investment opportunities. With high cash use and cash generation (due to a favorable cost position in its industry), they are relatively self-sufficient.
- *Cash Cows* in the lower-left quadrant generate high cash flows yet use little in their low-growth market. These are net providers of cash.
- *Dogs* in the lower-right quadrant are cash traps in that additional cash investments cannot be recovered. Increasing market share in a stable market is futile because no one can afford to increase capacity any more than they can afford to run at much less than full capacity. Dogs are candidates for liquidation.
- *Question Marks* in the upper-right quadrant are the real risks. Left alone they will become dogs as market growth slows, and their profit margins contract relative to those of the industry's dominant competitors. To make stars of them requires a great deal of cash for investment in increased market share and, therefore, accumulated experience.

. . . So far we have only described the static situation as viewed by the product/market-portfolio model. The dynamics of the product life cycle yield the model's prescriptions for developing a balanced portfolio of businesses. As market growth slows, stars become cash cows. The throw-off from the cash cows must be either distributed to investors or reinvested in new assets. According to this model, the most rewarding investment is in market share to turn question marks into stars before their market growth slows. The underlying logic for this investment sequence is that the highest cash returns (and profits) occur when a dominant market share position can be obtained. . . . [T]his dominant position can be most easily achieved during the early phases of rapid market growth, when competitive positions and purchasing patterns have not yet been firmly established. . . . Such a successful sequence is depicted in Figure 9-3. . . .

Figure 9-3
Successful Portfolio Dynamics

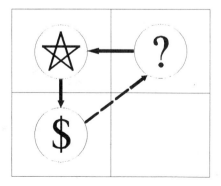

The solid line connotes product movement over time. The dotted line connotes the optimal cash flow pattern.

Implications for the Diversification Decision

The focus of the product/market-portfolio model is on the cash-flow characteristics of a business. A high-potential business is one with the opportunity to stake out a leadership position in a growing industry. If this business can maintain or expand its market share position before industry growth slows, it will subsequently be in the best position to "harvest" the investments it made during the market's period of growth. The product/market-portfolio model argues and empirical evidence supports the notion that higher market share leads to higher cash flow and return on investment. Evidence, presented in Figure 9-4, indicates that, on the average, a 5% increase in ROI typically accompanies every 10% increase in market share. Experience also shows that the market-share investments with the highest incremental returns are those made during a business' growth phase. Since stars are relatively self-sufficient and already have dominant market share positions, such investments are best made for businesses that are question marks.

These observations on market-share investments and cash-flow returns reveal the benefits of constructing a portfolio of businesses through unrelated diversifying acquisitions. A company with a balanced portfolio of cash cows feeding question marks and stars is in a position both to reap the current benefits of its high market share and advantageous cost position and to develop sources of future cash flow. Sustained growth is thus ensured by investing surplus cash from mature businesses in less mature, high-potential businesses.

Figure 9-4
Relationship Between Market Share and Profitability

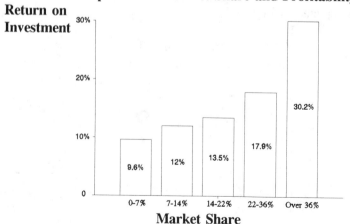

Source: Sidney Shoeffler, Robert Buzzell & Donald Heany, *Impact of Strategic Planning on Profit Performance*, Harv.Bus.Rev. 141 (Mar.-Apr.1974).

The benefits of a balanced product/market-portfolio suggest a set of criteria by which to evaluate a potential diversifying acquisition. The key criterion is the fit of the target company's cash flow characteristics with those of the existing portfolio. The degree of fit will be governed by the target company's competitive position, the expected growth of its market, the cost of retaining or improving its competitive position, and the cash-flow characteristics of the acquiring company's existing portfolio of businesses. . . .

According to the logic of the model, changes in the business portfolio are intended to fill in financial weak spots or build upon financial strengths. For example, a company in a high-growth industry may feel that access to a secure (and inexpensive) cash-flow source would enable it to maintain its present growth and possibly improve its market share position. This situation is similar to that faced by Tyco Labs, a manufacturer of high-technology products, in the mid-1970s. To fund both its rapid growth and its research-and-development programs, Tyco acquired (at a price equivalent to only four times cash flow) the Grinnel Co. from ITT. Grinnel was a major competitor in the low-growth, low-capital-intensity business of fire protection. The cash flow from Grinnel was able to fuel Tyco's internal growth as well as its active acquisition program.

Alternatively, a mature company generating substantial cash flows may see an opportunity to nourish emerging growth companies or to convert a so-called question mark into a star. This was the situation in which Philip Morris found itself in the late 1960s with its tobacco business. The question mark Philip Morris acquired was Miller High Life, at the time number five in the brewing industry. With an infusion of over $500 million in production facilities and Philip Morris's marketing talent, Miller's growth exploded. By 1978 Miller was second in the industry with strong prospects of becoming number one. . . .

Philip Morris's acquisition of Miller High Life provides an interesting insight into the product/market-portfolio model and its implications for the diversification decision. Philip Morris brought to Miller not only a large, surplus cash flow but also a formidable marketing talent that had established Philip Morris as the strongest competitor in the cigarette market. Prior to Philip Morris's entry, the brewing business was production oriented; brewmasters brewed beer and let the beer sell itself. Philip Morris's enormous cash flow enabled Miller to compete on this basis by building large, low-cost breweries; but Philip Morris's marketing skills also introduced a new competitive tactic into the industry. Miller High Life was both brewed and marketed. Caught between Miller's low-cost production and high marketing expenditures, the brewing industry underwent a major strategic and competitive transition in the mid-1970s.

Note: Who Decides What Projects to Fund?

In the product/market-portfolio model, market share serves as a proxy both for cumulative experience -- the greater the market share, the greater the cumulative experience -- and for competitive advantage -- the company with the greatest market share is further down the experience curve and, therefore, has a cost advantage. A conglomerate firm can use the cash flow of a "cash cow" to boost the market share (and thus the future profitability) of a "question mark."

The advantages of moving down the experience curve are clear enough. But not all question marks can become stars. The difficult business question is whether an investment in buying market share today will return sufficient profit down the road so that the investment will have positive net present value.   In the conglomerate, that judgment is made by the firm's top managers. But there is another possibility. Mature firms with surplus cash could distribute their cash flow to shareholders and let the shareholders reinvest it.   Growing firms in need of cash would then raise funds in the capital markets, rather than from a rich corporate parent. Investors in the capital markets, rather than conglomerate managers, would decide which projects to fund.   Some firms (banks, for example) would specialize in providing capital to growing firms.

For the conglomerate firm to add value, its top managers must have special competence in selecting the best "question marks" in which to invest or, perhaps, access to investments not available to other investors. The BCG approach requires that the acquiring firm's managers have greater ability to identify which investment opportunities deserve funding than the outside investors who participate in the capital markets by buying stocks and bonds, or the banks, insurance companies, venture capitalists and private investors who provide loans and equity financing outside the public securities markets. The claim must be that capital allocation decisions *within the firm* (which we can call an *internal capital market*) are better than those made in the external capital markets.

The premise that internal capital markets can function more effectively than external capital markets is made explicit in the work of Oliver Williamson. For Williamson, the central attribute of the conglomerate firm is its multidivisional or *M-form* organization. The business units of a pure conglomerate firm have neither shared inputs, related outputs, nor a customer-supplier relationship.   All that they share is a common organization. Williamson focuses on this shared factor to explain the growth of the conglomerate firm.

**Oliver Williamson, THE MODERN CORPORATION:
ORIGINS, EVOLUTION, ATTRIBUTES**
19 J.Econ.Lit. 1537, 1555-60 (1981)

The Multidivisional Structure

The most significant organizational innovation of the 20th century was the development in the 1920s of the multidivisional structure. Surprisingly, this development was little noted or widely appreciated as late as 1960. Leading management texts extolled the virtues of "basic departmentation" and "line and staff authority relationships," but the special importance of multidivisionalization went unremarked. . . .

The leading figures in the creation of the multidivisional (or M-form) structure were Pierre S. du Pont and Alfred P. Sloan; the period was the early 1920s; the firms were Du Pont and General Motors; and the organizational strain of trying to cope with economic adversity under the old structure was the occasion to innovate in both. The structures of the two companies, however, were different.

Du Pont was operating under the centralized, functionally departmentalized or unitary (U-form) structure. General Motors, by contrast, had been operated more like a holding company by William Durant -- whose genius in perceiving market opportunities in the automobile industry evidently did not extend to organization. Chandler summarizes the defects of the large U-form enterprise in the following way:

> The inherent weakness in the centralized, functionally departmentalized operating company . . . became critical only when the administrative load on the senior executives increased to such an extent that they were unable to handle their entrepreneurial responsibilities efficiently. This situation arose when the operations of the enterprise became too complex and the problems of coordination, appraisal, and policy formulation too intricate for a small number of top officers to handle both long-run, entrepreneurial, and short-run, operational administrative activities.[a]

The ability of the management to handle the volume and complexity of the demands placed upon it became strained and even collapsed. Unable meaningfully to identify with or contribute to the realization of global goals, managers in each of the functional parts attended to what they perceived to be operational subgoals instead. In the language of transaction cost economics, bounds on rationality[b] were reached as the U-form structure

---

[a] Alfred Chandler, *Strategy and Structure: Chapters in the History of the Industrial Enterprise* 382-83 (1966).

[b] "Bounded rationality" is the limit on human ability to solve complicated problems and in utilizing (receiving, storing, retrieving and transmitting) information. See Oliver Williamson, *Markets and Hierarchies: Analysis and Antitrust Implications* 21-24 (1975). The comparable popular term might be "informational overload."

labored under a communication overload while the pursuit of subgoals by the functional parts (sales, engineering, production) was partly a manifestation of opportunism.

The M-form structure fashioned by du Pont and Sloan involved the creation of semi-autonomous operating divisions (mainly profit centers) organized along product, brand, or geographic lines. The operating affairs of each were managed separately. More than a change in decomposition rules were needed, however, for the M-form to be fully effective. Du Pont and Sloan also created a general office "consisting of a number of powerful general executives and large advisory and financial staffs" to monitor divisional performance, allocate resources among divisions, and engage in strategic planning. The reasons for the success of the M-form innovation are summarized by Chandler as follows:

> The basic reason for its success was simply that it clearly removed the executives responsible for the destiny of the entire enterprise from the more routine operational activities, and so gave them the time, information, and even psychological commitment for long-term planning and appraisal. . . .
>
> [The] new structure left the broad strategic decisions as to the allocation of existing resources and the acquisition of new ones in the hands of a top team of generalists. Relieved of operating duties and tactical decisions, a general executive was less likely to reflect the position of just one part of the whole.[c]

In contrast with the holding company -- which is also a divisionalized form but has little general office capability and hence is little more than a corporate shell -- the M-form organization adds (1) a strategic planning and resource allocation capability and (2) monitoring and control apparatus. As a consequence, cash flows are reallocated among divisions to favor high yield uses, and internal incentive and control instruments are exercised in a discriminating way. In short, the M-form corporation takes on many of the properties of (and is usefully regarded as) a miniature capital market, which is a much more ambitious concept of the corporation than the term holding company contemplates.

Although the structure was imitated very slowly at first, adoption by U.S. firms proceeded rapidly during the period 1945 to 1960. . . . As compared with the U-form organization of the same activities, the M-form organization of the large, complex corporation served both to economize on bounded rationality and attenuate opportunism. Specifically:

> Operating decisions were no longer forced to the top but were resolved at the divisional level, which relieved the communication load. Strategic decisions were reserved for the general office, which reduced partisan political input into the resource allocation process. And the internal auditing and control techniques which the general office had access to served to overcome

---

[c] Chandler (1966), *supra* note a, at 382-83.

information impactedness conditions and permit fine timing controls to be exercised over the operating parts.[d]

The Conglomerate

Chandler's studies of organizational innovation do not include the conglomerate form of corporate enterprise. These are more recent developments, the appearance of which would not have been feasible but for the prior development of the M-form structure. . . .

[T]he conglomerate is essentially a post World War II phenomenon. To be sure, General Electric's profit centers number in the hundreds and GE has been referred to as the world's most diversified firm. Until recently, however, General Electric's emphasis has been the manufacture and distribution of electrical appliances and machinery. Similarly, although General Motors was more than an automobile company, it took care to limit its portfolio. Thus Sloan remarked that "tetraethyl lead was clearly a misfit for GM. It was a chemical product, rather than a mechanical one. And it had to go to market as part of the gasoline and thus required a gasoline distribution system." Accordingly, although GM retained an investment position, the Ethyl Corporation became a free-standing entity rather than an operating division. Similarly, although Durant had acquired Frigidaire, and Frigidaire's market share of refrigerators exceeded 50% in the 1920s, the position was allowed to deteriorate as rivals developed market positions in other major appliances (radios, ranges, washers, etc.) while Frigidaire concentrated on refrigerators. . . .

The conglomerate form of organization, whereby the corporation consciously took on a diversified character and nurtured its various parts, evidently required a conceptual break in the mind-set of Sloan and other prewar business leaders. This occurred gradually, more by evolution than by grand design and it involved a new group of organizational innovators -- of which Royal Little [of Textron] was one. The natural growth of conglomerates, which would occur as the techniques for managing diverse assets were refined, was accelerated as antitrust enforcement against horizontal and vertical mergers became progressively more severe. Conglomerate acquisitions -- in terms of numbers, assets acquired, and as a proportion of total acquisitions -- grew rapidly with the result that "pure" conglomerate mergers, which in the period 1948-1953 constituted only 3% of the assets acquired by merger, had grown to 49% by 1973-1977. . . .

[T]he conglomerate is best understood as a logical outgrowth of the M-form mode for organizing complex economic affairs. Thus once the merits of the M-form structure for managing separable, albeit related, lines of business (e.g., a series of automobile or a series of chemical divisions) were recognized and digested, its extension to manage less closely related activities was natural. This is not to say that the management of product

---

[d] Williamson (1975), *supra* note b, at 137-38.

variety is without problems of its own. But the basic M-form logic, whereby strategic and operating decisions are distinguished and responsibilities are separated, carried over. The conglomerates in which M-form principles of organization are respected are usefully thought of as internal capital markets whereby cash flows from diverse sources are concentrated and directed to high yield uses. . . .

Viewed in contractual terms, the M-form conglomerate can be thought of as substituting an administrative interface between an operating division and the stockholders where a market interface had existed previously. Subject to the condition that the conglomerate does not diversify to excess, in the sense that it cannot competently evaluate and allocate funds among the diverse activities in which it is engaged, the substitution of internal organization can have beneficial effects in goal pursuit, monitoring, staffing, and resource allocation respects. The goal-pursuit advantage is that which accrues to M-form organizations in general: since the general management of an M-form conglomerate is disengaged from operating matters, a presumption that the general office favors profits over functional goals is warranted. Relatedly, the general office can be regarded as an agent of the stockholders whose purpose is to monitor the operations of the constituent parts. Monitoring benefits are realized in the degree to which internal monitors enjoy advantages over external monitors in access to information -- which they arguably do. The differential ease with which the general office can change managers and reassign duties where performance failures or distortions are detected is responsible for the staffing advantage. Resource-allocation benefits are realized because cash flows no longer return automatically to their origins but instead revert to the center, thereafter to be allocated among competing uses in accordance with prospective yields.[36]

This has a bearing on the problem of separation of ownership from control, noted by Adolph Berle and Gardiner C. Means in 1932.[e] Thus they inquired, "have we any justification for assuming that those in control of a modern corporation will also choose to operate it in the interests of the stockholders." The answer, then as now, is almost certainly no. . . .

There are important differences, however, between the U-form structure, which was the prevailing organization form at the time Berle and Means were writing, and the M-form structure, which in the U.S. was substantially in place by the 1960s. For one thing, as argued above, U-form managers identified more strongly with functional interests and hence were

---

[36] To be sure, this substitution of internal organization for the capital market is subject to tradeoffs and diminishing returns. Breadth -- that is, access to the widest range of alternatives -- is traded off for depth -- that is, more intimate knowledge of a narrower range of possible investment outlets -- where the general office may be presumed to have the advantage in the latter respect. The diminishing returns feature suggests that the net benefits of increased diversity eventually become negative. Were further diversification thereafter to be attempted, effective control would pass back into the hands of the operating divisions with problematic performance consequences.

[e] Adolph Berle & Gardiner Means, *The Modern Corporation and Private Property* (1932).

more given to subgoal pursuit. Secondly, and related, there was a confusion between strategic and operating goals in the U-form structure which the M-form served to rectify -- with the result that the general office was more fully concerned with enterprise goals, of which profit is the leading element. Third, the market for corporate control, which remained ineffectual so long as the proxy contest was the only way to challenge incumbent managements, was activated as conglomerates recognized that tender offers could be used to effect corporate takeovers. As a consequence, managements that were otherwise secure and would have permitted managerial preferences to prevail were brought under scrutiny and induced to self-correct against egregious managerial distortions.

To be sure, managerial preferences (for salary and perquisites) and stockholder preferences for profits do not become perfectly consonant as a result of conglomerate organization and the associated activation of the capital market. The continuing tension between management and stockholder interests is evident in the numerous efforts that incumbent managements have taken to protect target firms against takeover. Changes in internal organization have nevertheless relieved these concerns. A study of capitalist enterprises which makes no allowance for organization form changes and their capital market ramifications will naturally overlook the possibility that the corporate control dilemma posed by Berle and Means has since been alleviated more by *internal* than it has by regulatory or external organizational reforms.

---

2.   Evaluation: Consistency with Analytic Tools

Internal Capital Markets as a Problem in Comparative Transaction Costs. Recall from Chapter 8 Ronald Coase's central insight that the optimal boundaries of the firm can only be determined by close study of the *relative* transaction costs of carrying out activities administratively within the firm, or through interfirm market transactions. Williamson's argument that internal capital markets, overseen by the top managers of the conglomerate firm, are an improvement over external capital markets is a particular example of Coase's more general theory. External capital markets involve costs and imperfections, but so too do internal capital markets administered by the "large advisory and financial staffs" that Williamson thinks central to the conglomerate's success. Which is cheaper cannot be determined by resort to pure financial theory. Rather, we need to study the success of actual conglomerate firms, a study that we undertake in section C.

We may begin, though, with some skepticism about the claim that the internal capital market adds *enough* value to justify the transaction costs of a takeover, plus the premium that the acquirer typically pays for the target's shares. The evidence developed in Chapter 5 on the relative efficiency of stock prices suggests that it is no easy task to improve on the investor consensus about the merits of a particular business, reflected in its stock price.

To be sure, efficiency is always defined *relative to an information set*, and the conglomerate manager is operating with a *different* information set than that available to outside investors. But different isn't necessarily better. The conglomerate manager has access to more detailed accounting information than a stand-alone public company typically discloses to its shareholders. But outside investors in private companies also typically receive highly detailed financial information before they invest, as do banks and insurers when they make loans. And outside investors in public companies have access to stock prices that reflect other investors' beliefs about value. The conglomerate manager lacks that information. He cannot check his value estimate against those of others, and reconsider if his estimate is much higher or lower than the mean. This increases the chance that the manager will err in evaluating the prospects of a business unit. Moreover, outside investors can specialize. One investor, or analyst, or bank loan officer, can focus on auto parts suppliers, another on specialty chemicals, another on computers. In contrast, the conglomerate manager probably oversees only one firm in any one industry, and must divide his attention among a number of disparate businesses. Once again, the conglomerate manager lacks information available to the outside investor; in this case, the background knowledge that comes from specialization.

The Conglomerate Firm as an Internal Labor Market. A second claimed advantage of the conglomerate firm, closely related to its value as an internal *capital* market, is that top managers can do a better job of choosing and replacing divisional managers than can the board of directors of a stand-alone firm. But, as with the internal capital market, intermediaries (call them "executive search firms") can develop that specialize in finding good managers, and the intensive oversight that characterizes the conglomerate is hardly costless. Moreover, the extent to which the conglomerate can rely on internal candidates will depend on the extent to which managerial skills are transferable from one business to another.

The claim that the internal labor market works better than the external market, like the parallel claim about the internal capital market, is neither provable nor disprovable as a theoretical matter. The question is again one of comparative transaction costs, and of whether any advantage that the conglomerate firm has outweighs the transaction costs of the acquisition, plus the premium price paid for the target.

Organizational Form and Agency Costs. One transaction cost of particular importance for the success of the conglomerate form is the agency costs that arise because shareholders can only imperfectly monitor the actions of corporate managers. Williamson argues that the conglomerate firm partly solves this problem, because top managers can monitor divisional managers more carefully than outside investors. But his argument is incomplete. The

M-form firm does little to constrain the discretion of the top-level strategists who make the financial decisions. They continue to be monitored only loosely by the board of directors and by shareholders. The cash cows in their stable of businesses ensure that they face little discipline from external capital markets. The top managers in a conglomerate are also freed of the discipline that comes, in a single business firm, from having to run that one business well. If a business unit fails, the top managers find new divisional management, or arrange a divestiture. Either way, they escape direct blame for the failure, and can go on to make future mistakes.

While an anecdote is no substitute for quantitative data, the 15-year reign of James Robinson as CEO of American Express, enlivened every year or two by a business disaster at some business unit or other, is suggestive. Until the Amex board, prodded by restive shareholders, finally replaced Robinson in 1993, he was known in some cynical circles as the "Teflon CEO": All these problems, and nothing ever stuck.

Louis Lowenstein
SENSE AND NONSENSE IN CORPORATE FINANCE
161-66 (1991)*

Charles R. Sitter, [Chief Financial Officer] at Exxon, rightly fears, as he has said, that companies with strong cash flows will "let the money burn a hole in [their] pockets" if they don't distribute the excess. Diversification is a seductive trap. The fact that you can run one type of business well, he explained, doesn't prove that you can also run something else -- or, he might have added, overcome the burden of having paid too high an entry price.

Sitter did not name any companies that had embarked on misguided diversification programs, but one that fits the description marvelously well is American Express, a company that dissipated more than half of its likely value in this fashion. American Express owned a great business, better than Exxon's, called Travel Related Services (TRS), which included the company's credit card and traveler's check operations. The American Express credit card was the prestige card in the industry and commanded a loyal following despite its higher charges. Traveler's checks were an even more attractive operation because customers received no interest for depositing large amounts of money with the company -- $24 billion of checks were issued in 1989 -- which the company could then lend out at high rates. During the 1980s, TRS's net income (after taxes) grew at a 20% compounded annual rate -- from $177 million in 1980 to $830 million in 1989. TRS consistently earned 27% or more on shareholders' equity. Exxon, on the other hand, deals in a commodity, whose pricing is erratic and subject to political and other factors over which Exxon has no control.

In a sense, the success at TRS may have been the problem because it emboldened management to suppose that it could repeat it elsewhere. The company used the entire stream of profits from TRS, and much more, to stitch together the pieces of what became Shearson Lehman Hutton, hoping to make of it the keystone of a diversified financial services supermarket, a global one at that. American Express bought other businesses, too, but the Shearson operation was by far the largest and most grandiose. As of June 30, 1990, the company had invested about $4 billion in Shearson, not including capital raised directly by Shearson itself. It began with the purchase of Shearson for $1 billion in shares of American Express in 1981 and concluded with [a cash infusion of] more than $1 billion . . . in late 1989 and early 1990 to staunch the hemorrhaging at Shearson. To put that $4 billion in scale, at the beginning of 1981, the year the first segment of Shearson was acquired, American Express's entire net worth was $2.2 billion, and the total stock market value of the company was $2.9 billion. Shearson built lavish offices around the world, including a $25 million conference center-ski resort in Colorado, but the so-called synergy from a global financial services business was never more than a mirage; it shone brightly in the prose of American Express's annual reports but then disappeared on a closer look. Even in the salad years 1987-1988, Shearson failed to earn a return of more than 6% on equity. From 1981 through mid-1990, taken as a whole, and after allocating corporate overhead expenses, the business did not make so much as a single dollar. In the language of an Exxon, it was a dry hole.

American Express bought a variety of other businesses, and on some of them it made money, but overall the results there too were mixed at best. In 1987 and 1988, for example, a banking subsidiary, Trade Development Bank (now merged with American Express Bank), took huge losses on $1.6 billion of Third World country loans, and half again as much remained on the books. At the end of the 1980s, of all the major businesses it had bought under the incumbent management, only one was still there and *profitable:* IDS Financial Services, a business that was earning about 14% on shareholders' equity but which will always be for American Express a relatively small one. It would be difficult to unravel all of these bold moves to see what American Express would have looked like today if it had possessed the discipline of an Exxon, except, of course, that it would have been a great company. But it is not too difficult to do so just with Shearson, to see what American Express might have looked like in June 1990 if it had reinvested the TRS profits back into the well managed TRS business by buying back stock, instead of ploughing money into a [troubled business] in pursuit of an imperial dream.

The company began the decade with 285 million shares outstanding. Using the Shearson monies to buy back stock would have reduced that to perhaps as little as 188 million. Instead, management allowed the outstanding shares to balloon to 445 million by mid-1990. James D. Robinson III, the chairman, seemed oblivious to the fact that each newly issued share represented a dilution of the shareholders' stake in its existing businesses, including the wonderful TRS. Almost all those shares, including the 27 million sold in June 1990 to make good the losses at Shearson, were sold at low multiples of earnings. It was little short of criminal. American Express, which owned the outstanding TRS business, was selling parts of it on the cheap. (Peter Lynch, who ran the Fidelity Magellan fund, has coined a crude but apt term for such acquisition programs, *diworseification.*)

It is true that Wall Street, at least, applauded the purchase of the first segments of Shearson Lehman Hutton. And it is surely possible that if American Express had not been so taken with the ambitious model of a financial supermarket and if Shearson had continued to be run in the same penny-pinching, prudent style as before the acquisition, the outcome would have been acceptable. But as much as half of the ultimate investment in the Shearson financial supermarket came as part of, or in the wake of, the purchase of Hutton, and by then the applause had dried up.

More telling than any cheers or boos from the gallery was an incident that took place in the summer of 1985. Sanford I. Weill had been the CEO of Shearson when it was acquired in 1981, and in 1983 he became the president of American Express itself. By 1985, having left the company, he offered to buy its [money-losing] insurance subsidiary, Fireman's Fund. At a meeting of the American Express board of directors to consider his offer, Weill appeared and so, too, did Warren Buffett, the chairman of Berkshire Hathaway, who was to have provided some of Weill's capital. Buffett had once been a substantial investor in American Express and knew the company well. He was sitting on Weill's side of the table but, even so, offered the board some advice. Regardless of whether they sold Fireman's Fund to Weill, he said, they should sell it to someone. Buffett described TRS as an exquisite franchise, which to him meant that TRS operated in a market and with products that, like few others, did not have to compete primarily on price. American Express should sell all its other businesses, because, he said, they were fuzzying up this great franchise. According to one of the participants, Buffett's comments had an "electric impact" on the board, particularly on Howard L. Clark, Sr., the retired CEO of American Express. It might have been hoped that these comments would stimulate some reexamination of the American Express diversification program. . . . But by 1987 Robinson was back on the diworseification trail in a serious way, throwing the ill-fated Hutton log on the Shearson pile.

Table 9-1 gives values for American Express -- both actual and as it might have looked had it never heard of Shearson. Let's assume that American Express had not issued the 85 million shares of stock (adjusted for stock splits) used to buy Shearson in 1981. Assume, too, that using the $3 billion in cash it later invested in Shearson, it had retired stock at a price equal to the highest price in each of the years those monies were disbursed. Valued at the same multiple of twelve times current earnings at which it was actually selling in mid-1990, the stock of this "what if" American Express would have traded at over twice the price at which it was in fact trading.

. . . [Another measure of the cost of diversification: Between 1981 and 1989], the company's long-term debt had mushroomed from $1.1 billion to $11.7 billion, more than half of which -- precisely how much more is unclear -- had been incurred to finance diworseification. Long-term debt, once modest, now far exceeded shareholders' equity. This company, which should have been awash in the earnings and (except to finance credit card receivables) the cash flow from TRS, was instead forced to issue new shares in June 1990 to bolster its weakened credit.

Table 9-1
American Express: What Was and What If

	Actual	What If
Earnings per share		
1990	$2.49	$5.74
Average for 1987-1989	$2.11	$3.82
TRS contribution (three-year average) to		
Revenues	45%	65%
Earnings	79%	85%
Shares outstanding (millions)		
1980	285	285
1990	445	188
Stock price at June 30, 1990 (at 12 × earnings)	$30-¾	$68-⅞

C. Evaluation: Consistency with Empirical Evidence

The American Express anecdote suggests the problems that *can* arise with a diversification program, but it does not tell us whether such problems are the norm or the exception. To assess the likely outcome of a diversification program, we turn in this subsection to the quantitative evidence on the long-term success of conglomerate firms.

R. Hal Mason & Maurice Goudzwaard, PERFORMANCE OF CONGLOMERATE FIRMS: A PORTFOLIO APPROACH
31 J.Fin. 39 (1976)

Several authors have recently attempted to evaluate the performance of mergers. Most have dealt with highly diversified firms or those which have been heavily involved in conglomerate mergers and acquisitions. Methodological approaches have differed, as have the conclusions regarding the benefits (or lack thereof) accompanying mergers and acquisitions.

Controversy continues particularly with respect to the benefits of the conglomerate merger. While we cannot expect to settle the controversy, our methodological approach is different and our results indicate that conglomeration may not provide positive economic benefits to either the firm or its shareholders. Our contribution to the understanding of the conglomerate phenomenon centers around our method of measuring relative performance, i.e., the use of simulated portfolios which mirror the asset structures of conglomerate firms. Our results indicate that randomly selected portfolios offered superior earnings performance and shareholder returns than did the conglomerates in our sample. . . .

Methodology

Given knowledge of the composition of the asset base for each [of the 22 conglomerates in the sample], it was possible to construct matching portfolios for 1962 and 1967. The population of candidate firms to be included in a particular portfolio consisted of those listed in *Newsfront's Directory* of 25,000 U.S. Firms. Twenty-two portfolios were constructed -- one for each conglomerate. To test the hypothesis that conglomerate firms should outperform a portfolio of the same asset content, the rules of construction were as follows:

1. Assign random numbers to each *Newsfront* firm participating in each SIC classification identified by the conglomerate as an area of participation. Firms in the population had to exist in both 1962 and 1967. From this group of firms select at random five firms in each of these SIC classifications and assign weights to each firm for 1962 and 1967.

2. Calculate the ratio of net earnings (before interest, taxes and dividends) to total assets for each firm in the portfolio.

3. Using the weights, arrive at an aggregate rate of return to the portfolio for both 1962 and 1967.

To test the hypothesis that stockholders in the conglomerate should fare better than those holding a portfolio, we used the 1962 and 1967 lists of firms developed above. We assumed that an investor in 1962 had the option of investing either in the conglomerate of his choice or a portfolio approximating the asset composition of the conglomerate. Furthermore he could adopt one of three portfolio strategies.

1. He could manage the portfolio himself and buy and sell stocks in order to maintain the portfolio in the exact composition of the conglomerate, i.e., when the conglomerate's composition changed he would sell off stock in those SIC classifications which shrank and buy stock in those SIC classifications which grew. He would also reinvest all dividends, pay brokerage fees and pay income and capital gains taxes at an average rate of 25%. Also he would

confine his portfolio to the list of firms chosen above in the construction of the portfolios.

2. He could employ a mutual fund manager who would follow strategy one and in so doing pay any brokerage fees at standard rates and pay income and capital gain taxes at the rate of 25%. In addition the fund manager received an annual fee of 0.75% of average assets.

3. He could buy and hold, i.e., not emulate the conglomerate but maintain the 1962 portfolio composition. Because the stock prices in his portfolio changed relative to one another over time and because he received dividends, there were some adjustments necessary between 1962-1967. The same rules of brokerage fees and taxation used in strategy one (1) were applied.

On November 15, 1962, the investor would buy in, and regardless of the strategy chosen . . . the investor would sell his entire holding of stock plus reinvested dividends on November 15, 1967. . . .

Results of the Simulation

We can look upon the conglomerates and their counterpart portfolios as two samples receiving different treatments. One receives the treatment of management control while the other does not. . . .

Table 9-2
Performance of Conglomerate versus Simulated Portfolios

a) *Rate of Return [on] Total Assets*   *Direction of Difference*

a.1) Conglomerates vs. Portfolios: 1962	No difference
a.2) Conglomerates vs. Portfolios: 1967	Portfolio superior
a.3) Conglomerates: 1962 vs. 1967	1962 superior
a.4) Portfolios: 1962 vs. 1967	No difference

b) *Rate of Return to Stockholders*

b.1) Conglomerates vs. Self-managed portfolio	Portfolio superior
b.2) Conglomerates vs. Mutual-fund portfolio	Portfolio superior
b.3) Conglomerates vs. Buy and hold portfolio	Portfolio superior

We had neither hypothesized nor expected the results reported in Table 9-2. We had expected the sample of conglomerate firms to either significantly outperform or at least perform as well as a set of randomly selected portfolios -- simply because operating control should confer certain advantages to a diversified portfolio of assets. We find quite the opposite from the data at hand. The statistical tests indicate that the portfolios outperformed the conglomerates in terms of both rates of return on assets and accumulated stockholder wealth over the 1962 to 1967 period. . . . [The difference is due to] the deterioration in rate of return for the conglomerates between 1962 and 1967 while the earnings performance of our portfolios were not significantly different between the two years. In the case of stockholder wealth, portfolios demonstrated superior performance despite the fact that our hypothetical stockholder was forced to incur transactions costs, taxes and fees associated with buying and selling stocks. . . .

One dollar invested in the conglomerate cross-section in 1962 and held along with reinvested dividends, until 1967 would have yielded a rate of return of 7.46% over the five year period. This is not inconsiderable. Yet the portfolio cross-sections yielded rates of return of 12.75%, 11.82%, and 13.99% depending on the strategy followed, i.e., self-managed, mutual fund, and buy-and-hold respectively.

Note: The Failure of the Conglomerate Experiment

Mason & Goudzwaard is representative of a large number of studies that reach the consistent conclusion that firm-level diversification reduces firm value. We briefly review here the principal results.[6]

1. *Ex Post Accounting Studies.* Especially noteworthy is a massive study by David Ravenscraft & F.M. Scherer, who used Federal Trade Commission data to measure the performance of business units acquired between 1950 and 1977, a period that covers the conglomerate merger wave that peaked in the late 1960s.[7] They found that the typical target firm was highly profitable (compared to industry norms) before being acquired, but this above-average profitability faded after the acquisition. The deterioration was greatest for unrelated acquisitions.

The regression equations reported below give a flavor for Ravenscraft & Scherer's results. In each, the *dependent* variable is the operating income of a line of business, as a percentage of assets, which we will call $OPERINCOME_{year}/A$, where the subscript indicates the time period over which profits are measured. The regression analysis tests whether various *independent* variables, such as whether the business unit was acquired between 1950 and 1977, correlate with profitability. The statistical significance of each correlation is measured by a *t*-statistic, shown in

---

[6] See also Ronald Melicher & David Rush, *The Performance of Conglomerate Firms: Recent Risk and Return Experience*, 28 J.Fin. 381 (1973); Ronald Melicher & David Rush, *Evidence on the Acquisition-Related Performance of Conglomerate Firms*, 29 J.Fin. 141 (1974).

[7] David Ravenscraft & F.M. Scherer, *Mergers, Sell-Offs & Economic Efficiency* (1987). The regressions in text are adapted from their tables 4-2(2), 4-2(7), and 4-4(2), respectively.

parentheses.　As usual, a *t*-statistic greater than about 2, or less than -2, indicates statistical significance at the 95% confidence level.

Regression 9-1

$$\text{OPERINCOME}_{1977}/A \quad = \quad \text{[industry intercept]}$$
$$- (2.35 \cdot \text{MERGERSHARE}) \quad (t = -2.50)$$

MERGERSHARE $\quad = \quad$ the fraction of the assets of the line of business obtained through acquisitions

Regression 9-1 implies that by 1977, business units that had been obtained through acquisition had below-average profitability. Their operating income as a percentage of assets was 2.35% below the industry average, even though these businesses had above-average profitability *when acquired*. This picture is complicated, however, by differences in the accounting treatment of acquisitions.　As Chapter 13 discusses in detail, some acquisitions are accounted for in the same way as the purchase of any other asset (*purchase* accounting), while others are accounted for *as if* the acquired business had been bought at its historical book value (*pooling* accounting). Since most acquisitions take place at a premium over book value, the pooling method overstates the profitability of the acquisition to the acquiring firm. *From the perspective of the acquiring firm*, the implication of pooling treatment for *some* acquisitions is that the negative coefficient on *MERGERSHARE* in Regression 9-1 is *too small*; the actual performance was worse than the regression suggests.

On the other hand, if the target had not been acquired, it would have continued to report operating income and assets on a historical basis. *From the perspective of the target firm*, the implication of purchase treatment for *some* acquisitions is that the negative coefficient on *MERGERSHARE* is *too large*; actual post-acquisition performance, relative to non-acquired firms, was not as bad as Regression 9-1 suggests.

Ravenscraft & Scherer were sensitive to the impact of purchase versus pooling accounting. They control for accounting treatment in various ways; Regression 9-2 is representative of their results.　In Regression 9-2, the insignificant coefficient on *POOLINGSHARE* suggests that businesses acquired through pooling transactions exhibited average profitability over the 1975-1977 period. They had lost the special spark that made them above-average performers (and attractive targets), but had not dropped below average. The significant negative coefficient on *PURCHASESHARE* suggests that acquirers earned a below-normal return on the purchase price of the businesses they acquired.[8]　Ravenscraft & Scherer control for the strong

---

[8] In additional regressions, Ravenscraft & Scherer find that the greater profitability of pooling persists when one controls for the effects of different accounting methods. One is left to speculate as to why the *form* of accounting treatment should correlate with a *substantive*

positive correlation between profitability and market share, shown by the large positive coefficient on *MARKETSHARE*. Since unrelated acquisitions do not increase market share, and most unrelated acquisitions involved targets with small market shares, the average acquisition would have looked worse without this adjustment.

Regression 9-2

$$\text{OPERINCOME}_{1975\text{-}77}/\text{A} = [\text{industry intercept}] + \ldots$$

$$+ (0.36 \cdot \text{POOLINGSHARE}) \quad (t = 0.32)$$
$$- (3.84 \cdot \text{PURCHASESHARE}) \quad (t = -3.26)$$
$$+ (30.16 \cdot \text{MARKETSHARE}) \quad (t = 5.67)$$

POOLINGSHARE	=	fraction of assets of the line of business obtained through acquisitions treated as poolings
PURCHASESHARE	=	fraction of assets of the line of business obtained through acquisitions treated as purchases
MARKETSHARE	=	market share of the line of business in its industry

The next step is to see whether post-merger profitability depends on the type of acquisition -- horizontal, vertical, related but not horizontal, or unrelated. Regression 9-3 shows that for poolings, post-acquisition profitability is greatest for horizontal and related acquisitions, and lowest for conglomerate acquisitions. The coefficient on horizontal acquisitions would have been larger if the regression had not included the *MARKETSHARE* variable, since horizontal acquisitions, by definition, increase market share.[9]

---

difference in profitability.

[9] Oddly, Ravenscraft & Scherer found significant differences between acquisition types only for poolings, not for purchases. Again, there is no obvious reason why the difference in accounting treatment should be important.

Regression 9-3

$$\text{OPERINCOME}_{1977}/\text{A} \quad = \quad \text{[industry intercept]} + \ldots$$

$+ (4.18 \cdot \text{HORIZONT} \cdot \text{POOL})$	$(t = 1.73)$
$+ (5.61 \cdot \text{RELATED} \cdot \text{POOL})$	$(t = 2.74)$
$+ (1.77 \cdot \text{VERTICAL} \cdot \text{POOL})$	$(t = 0.42)$
$+ (1.18 \cdot \text{CONGLOM} \cdot \text{POOL})$	$(t = 0.42)$
$- (3.74 \cdot \text{PURCHASESHARE})$	$(t = 3.06)$
$+ (39.12 \cdot \text{MARKETSHARE})$	$(t = 6.31)$

HORIZONT·POOL	=	fraction of assets of the line of business obtained through *horizontal* acquisitions treated as poolings
RELATED·POOL	=	fraction of assets of the line of business obtained through *related* acquisitions treated as poolings
VERTICAL·POOL	=	fraction of assets of the line of business obtained through *vertical* acquisitions treated as poolings
CONGLOM·POOL	=	fraction of assets of the line of business obtained through *unrelated* acquisitions treated as poolings

These results are troubling. The *best* one can say is that there is no evidence of the value added that is needed to justify the acquirer paying a premium for the target. If anything, the evidence suggests that conglomerates turn 2 + 2 into a little bit less than 4, on average.

2. *Evidence from Subsequent Divestitures*. The Ravenscraft & Scherer results become much more troubling when one recognizes that they are biased upward by strong survivorship effects. By 1977, many acquisitions made between 1950 and 1977 had already been sold off. Ravenscraft & Scherer estimate that about 1/3 of all acquired units had been sold, with unrelated units especially likely to be divested. Other studies confirm that acquirers divest a high percentage of their unrelated acquisitions (an astonishing 74% in one study; 60% in another), and that unrelated acquisitions are especially likely to end in divestiture.[10]

The sold-off businesses were highly troubled, on average. Thus, acquired business units that were not sold, and hence were included in the regressions above, *were the more successful ones*. The typical acquisition performed substantially *worse* than the regressions suggest. Table 9-3 reports the dismal pre-selloff performance found by Ravenscraft & Scherer

---

[10] See Ravenscraft & Scherer (1987), *supra* note 7, at 166 & table 6-7; Michael Porter, *From Competitive Advantage to Corporate Strategy*, Harv.Bus.Rev. 43 (May-June 1987) (74% of unrelated units bought by sample of 33 active acquirers between 1950 and 1980 had been sold off by 1986); Steven Kaplan & Michael Weisbach, *The Success of Acquisitions: Evidence from Divestitures*, 47 J.Fin. 107 (1992) (60% of unrelated large acquisitions between 1971 and 1982 had been divested by 1989).

for lines of business that were fully divested by 1977 (they find similar, though weaker results for lines of business that were partly divested).

Table 9-3
Industry-Adjusted Profitability of Divested Units Before Selloff
(*t*-statistics in parentheses)

Years Before Selloff	Number of Selloffs	Operating Income/Assets, Relative to Industry Average
7	58	-1.5% $(t = -0.51)$
6	110	-3.5% $(t = -1.68)$
5	155	-3.7% $(t = -2.58)$
4	191	-6.4% $(t = -4.71)$
3	204	-9.9% $(t = -8.20)$
2	201	-10.6% $(t = -8.69)$
1	210	-13.5% $(t = -8.41)$
0	121	-12.7% $(t = -5.92)$

Source: Ravenscraft & Scherer (1987), *supra* note 7.

To provide a feel for the strong correlation between the relatedness of an acquisition and the likelihood of later divestiture, Table 9-4 reports data from a study by Steven Kaplan & Michael Weisbach. They computed the fraction of a sample of large acquisitions between 1971 and 1982 that had been divested by 1989. They classified the acquisitions by the closeness of the SIC codes of acquirer and target. The percentage of acquisitions that were later divested was significantly higher (99% confidence level) for loosely related and unrelated acquisitions than for closely related or horizontal acquisitions.[11]

---

[11] Kaplan & Weisbach (1992), *supra* note 10, stress that a subsequent divestiture does not mean that the acquisition was a mistake, and report some evidence of divestitures even when the initial acquisition appears successful. But on the whole, their data is consistent with the Ravenscraft & Scherer picture of most unrelated divestitures as reflecting failed acquisitions. For their sample, the median divestiture price is 100% of book value during a period when most public companies traded at a multiple of book; resale of an acquired company resulted in a median 23% loss in value from purchase through divestiture, relative to the S&P 500, and 38% of unrelated divestitures were accompanied by visible indicia of failure, compared with 13% of related divestitures.

Table 9-4
Likelihood of Divestiture Based on Acquisition Relatedness

Relatedness of Acquirer and Target	Number of Acquisitions	Percent Divested
Horizontal (same 4-digit SIC code)	75	13%
Closely related (same 3-digit SIC code)	19	26%
Loosely related (same 2-digit SIC code)	54	56%
Unrelated (different 2-digit SIC code)	123	60%
All acquisitions	**271**	**44%**

Source: Kaplan & Weisbach (1992), *supra* note 10.

3. *Evidence on the Relationship between Firm Performance and Degree of Firm Diversification.* A further source of evidence on the success of conglomerate acquisitions are studies that relate firm performance to the firm's level of diversification, without regard to whether the diversification resulted from an acquisition or from internal growth. These studies also cast a dim light on the wisdom of firm-level diversification. For example, Richard Caves and David Barton, in an extensive study of factors that affect manufacturing productivity, report that diversification is "seriously hostile" to efficiency.[12] The number of industries in which a company operates also correlates with lower Tobin's q (the ratio of market capitalization to estimated replacement value of a company's tangible assets, which is often used as a rough measure of performance),[13] with lower stock prices than comparable single-line companies,[14] and with lower return on equity.[15] One might expect that the deep pockets of the conglomerate parent would permit its business units to invest more heavily than their industry peers in R&D, but this is not the case either; conglomerates spend *less* on R&D.[16]

---

[12] Richard Caves & David Barton, *Efficiency in U.S. Manufacturing Industries* 7, 89-91 (1990). Frank Lichtenberg, *Corporate Takeovers and Productivity* ch. 7 (1992), reaches a similar conclusion.

[13] See Birger Wernerfelt & Cynthia Montgomery, *Tobin's q and the Importance of Focus in Firm Performance*, 78 Am.Econ.Rev. 246 (1988); Larry Lang & Rene Stulz, *Tobin's Q, Corporate Diversification and Firm Performance* (NBER working paper No. 4376, 1993).

[14] Dean LeBaron & Lawrence Speidell, *Why Are the Parts Worth More than the Sum? "Chop Shop," A Corporate Valuation Model*, in *The Merger Boom* 78 (Lynn Browne & Eric Rosengren eds.1987).

[15] See Winson Lee & Elizabeth Cooperman, *Conglomerates in the 1980s: A Performance Appraisal*, Fin.Mgmt. 45 (Spr.1989) (studying conglomerate performance from 1980 through 1985, and citing earlier studies).

[16] David Ravenscraft & Curtis Wagner, *The Role of the FTC's Line of Business Data in Testing and Expanding the Theory of the Firm*, 34 J.L. & Econ. 703, 721-22 (1991); Ravenscraft & Scherer (1987), *supra* note 7, table 4-8.

4. *The Anomalous Evidence: Event Studies of Early Transactions.* One piece of evidence runs counter to the gloomy picture of conglomerate acquisitions developed above. In the 1960s, investors liked these transactions. Event studies show positive abnormal returns to acquiring firms, when the transaction are announced. Recall from Table 8-7 that acquirers earned significant abnormal returns in the 1960s, when conglomerate acquisitions were in vogue. Also, firms that announced acquisition programs between 1952 and 1968, and virtually all such programs involved diversifying acquisitions, earned positive abnormal returns at the time of the announcement.[17]

Not only did investors applaud conglomerate acquisitions, they liked them better, on average, than related acquisitions! For example, John Matsusaka reports that over the 1968-1974 period, related acquirers earned roughly zero returns, while unrelated acquirers earned significant positive abnormal returns.[18] Only in the late 1970s and 1980s did the investor preference for unrelated acquisitions turn to a preference for related acquisitions (more recent studies are collected in Table 8-8).

The puzzling question is why did investors react so favorably, and with the benefit of hindsight, so wrongly, to the conglomerate movement? What does that error tell us about the value of event studies? There are two plausible answers to the "why" question, with very different implications for the value of event studies.

Scholars sympathetic to the efficiency of capital markets can explain that there is no inconsistency between investor errors and market efficiency. The positive reaction to conglomeration was simply a mistake, albeit a large one, about the likely success of this new organizational form. Presumably investors made their best estimates about the value added by conglomerate management, based on incomplete information. As new information came out, investors revised their views. That investors made a mistake does not mean that their *ex ante* value estimates were biased. The value estimates made by investors when transactions are announced remain the best available estimate of actual value.

Scholars sympathetic to claims of market inefficiency will say it isn't that easy. For them, the positive reaction to conglomerates looks very much like a fad. Smart investors might have known better early on, but there were too few of them, too many faddish investors, and too much risk involved, for smart investors to bet heavily against the success of conglomerates. Andrei Shleifer and Robert Vishny write:

---

[17] Katherine Schipper & Rex Thompson, *Evidence on the Capitalized Value of Merger Activity for Acquiring Firms*, 11 J.Fin.Econ. 85 (1983); see also Paul Malatesta & Rex Thompson, *Partially Anticipated Events: A Model of Stock Price Reactions with an Application to Corporate Acquisitions*, 14 J.Fin.Econ. 237 (1985).

[18] John Matsusaka, *Takeover Motives During the Conglomerate Merger Wave*, 24 Rand J.Econ. 357 (1993); see also Pieter Elgers & John Clark, *Merger Types and Shareholder Returns: Additional Evidence*, Fin.Mgmt. 66 (Summer 1980).

Stock market participants had a model in mind -- scientific management or internal capital allocation -- that was the source of their optimism about diversification. This was not a model that could have been refuted by prior experience, since unrelated diversification was a new phenomenon. . . . The [time] horizon of reversals was far too long for whatever smart money was available to try to take advantage of [this mistaken optimism]. It did not pay to sell stocks of conglomerates short on the expectation that, in the long run, their stock prices will fall, and with the risk that, in the meantime, they could rise enormously. As a result, the incorrect "popular model" of scientific management carried the day. . . .

[T]his interpretation of the evidence is quite in line with recent research on market inefficiency. According to this research, fads or popular models can influence stock prices for prolonged period of time. Arbitrage by smart investors will be weak and will not undo these influences, because arbitrage over several year horizons, as would be required in the case of conglomerates, is very costly and risky. Betting against the conglomerates would have proven to be a mistake for all but the longest horizon investors with access to cheap capital.[19]

The skeptics can also point to studies like Mason & Goudzevaard that show that early conglomerate acquisitions did not work out well. Why, they will ask, were investors still applauding diversification in the late 1960s, in the face of negative evidence, available to be gathered?

Which of these views comes closer to your own?

D.   Agency Costs: Does Diversification Benefit Corporate Managers?

The evidence in section C strongly suggests that in most cases, diversification at the firm level does not benefit the acquiring company's shareholders. A few conglomerate managers may have unique skill at allocating capital within the firm, just as a few money managers may have unique skill at picking stocks. Most conglomerate managers, though, have succeeded largely in wasting large amounts of other peoples' (the shareholders') money. If their motive was profit maximization, they were peculiarly inept.

What happens, however, if we change the point of the inquiry? Shareholders may not benefit from firm-level diversification, but it is managers, not shareholders, who make the decision to diversify. We thus ought to ask whether firm-level diversification can make *management* better off, regardless of its impact on shareholders. If so, then we have found a motive for conglomerate acquisitions, even if it is not one that maximizes shareholder wealth.

---

[19] Andrei Shleifer & Robert Vishny, *Takeovers in the '60s and the '80s: Evidence and Implications*, 12 Strategic Mgmt.J. 51 (Winter 1991).

This possibility -- that management, when given the opportunity, will maximize their own interests at the expense of the shareholders' -- is a classic agency problem.   The managers are in theory the agents of the shareholders, bound by contract and fiduciary duty to serve the shareholders' interests. But when self-interest points in one direction, and duty as an agent in another, it should come as no surprise that corporate managers, like other agents, sometimes depart from strict adherence to duty. Sometimes this may be intentional, but we suspect that it more often results from the remarkable ability of the human animal to convince oneself that what is in one's self-interest is good for others as well, in situations where the latter proposition is dubious.

In the following excerpt, Professors Amihud and Lev develop and empirically test the hypothesis that conglomerate mergers are motivated by managers' desire to diversify their own portfolios.

Yakov Amihud & Baruch Lev, RISK REDUCTION AS A MANAGERIAL MOTIVE FOR CONGLOMERATE MERGERS
12 Bell J.Econ. 605 (1981)*

Despite extensive research, the motives for conglomerate mergers are still largely unknown: What drives a substantial number of firms to engage in conglomerate mergers, given that *a priori* no real economic benefit (synergism) is expected from the combination of such functionally unrelated parties? . . . [T]he risk-reduction benefits of conglomerate mergers from the stockholders' point of view seem highly questionable, given the relatively low cost of portfolio diversification in the capital market. Moreover, [option theory] suggests that adoption of projects which reduce the variance of the firm's income distribution (i.e., diversification) may adversely affect equity holders by inducing a wealth transfer from stockholders to bondholders. How, then, can the widespread and persisting phenomenon of conglomerate mergers be explained?

It is argued below that the fast growing literature on "managerialism," and in particular the agency cost models, provide a possible explanation for the conglomerate merger phenomenon. In essence, such mergers may be viewed as a form of management perquisite intended to decrease the risk associated with managerial human capital. Accordingly, the consequences of such mergers may be regarded as an agency cost. The validity of this hypothesis is empirically examined below and found to be consistent with the data.

Conglomerate Mergers and Agency Cost

Managers' income from employment constitutes, in general, a major portion of their total income. Employment income is closely related to the firm's performance through profit-sharing schemes, bonuses, and the value of stock options held by managers. Hence, the risk associated with managers' income is closely related to the firm's risk. Quite often, a firm's failure to achieve predetermined performance targets, or in the extreme case the occurrence of bankruptcy, will result in managers' losing their current employment and seriously hurting their future employment and earnings potential. Such "employment risk" cannot be effectively diversified by managers in their personal portfolios, since unlike many other sources of income such as stocks, human capital cannot be traded in competitive markets. Risk-averse managers can therefore be expected to diversify this employment risk by other means, such as engaging their firms in conglomerate mergers, which generally stabilize the firm's income stream and may even be used to avoid the disastrous effects bankruptcy has on managers. Thus, conglomerate mergers, while not of obvious benefit to investors, may benefit managers by reducing their employment risk, which is largely undiversifiable in capital or other markets.

Managers' efforts to engage their firms in conglomerate mergers may be viewed as an agency problem. The parties to the agency relationship (managers vs. stockholders) can be assumed to be expected utility maximizers and therefore "there is good reason to believe that the agent [manager] will not always act in the best interests of the principal."[a] . . .

Consider a fully equity-financed firm facing two alternative projects, X_1 and X_2, which are identical with respect to both expected return and *systematic* risk. However, the unsystematic risk associated with X_1 is smaller than that of X_2. (X_1 may be considered a pure conglomerate merger or any other activity which increases the diversification of the firm). Under the assumption that assets are priced according to the capital asset pricing model, the value of the firm will be independent of the project adopted. However, the manager will prefer X_1, since its adoption will increase [the value of his human capital by decreasing the variance associated with its value.] In this case, stockholders will be indifferent to the diversifying activities undertaken by the manager, and therefore no conflict arises.

Now let the expected return of X_1 be smaller than that of X_2. Thus, X_1 is equivalent to undertaking a costly merger for the sake of reducing unsystematic risk. This situation may produce a conflict between stockholders and the manager: The [stockholders] will prefer X_2 over X_1, since $V_2 > V_1$ (where V is the value of the firm with project X), while the manager's choice is unclear, since he is faced with a tradeoff between risk and return. The manager may choose X_1 when the increase in [the value of

---

[a] Michael Jensen & William Meckling, *Theory of the Firm: Managerial Behavior, Agency Costs, and Ownership Structure*, 3 J.Fin.Econ. 305 (1976).

his human capital] due to risk reduction outweighs the reduction in his . . . income due to the smaller expected return of project X_1. This is a classical agency problem.

Assume further that the firm is partially financed by debt. If the two projects have identical expected return and systematic risk (but differ in the unsystematic risk), there is again a possible conflict between stockholders and the manager. While (under the CAPM) the *total* value of the firm is independent of the project adopted, . . . adoption of the project with the smaller unsystematic risk, X_1, will induce a wealth transfer from equity holders to existing bondholders. . . .

The Hypothesis

It has been suggested above that conglomerate mergers may be motivated by managers' own preferences. Testing the validity of this argument is obviously not an easy task, since all firms are run by managers. However, the discretion managers can exercise in following their own preferences differs across firms. . . . In [*manager-controlled firms*], where ownership is widely dispersed across stockholders, managers are relatively free to exercise their discretion and pursue their own preferences, while in [*owner-controlled firms*], where ownership is concentrated, the owners-stockholders are generally able to exert rather tight control on managers' decisions and to see to it that owners' interests are not compromised. . . .

We can therefore expect more intensive risk-reduction activities in manager-controlled firms than in owner-controlled firms. This then constitutes a basis for testing the hypothesis that when allowed to pursue their own preferences, managers of management-controlled firms will engage in risk-reduction activities, such as conglomerate mergers, to a greater extent than managers of owner-controlled firms.

Test Procedures and Results

. . . [We use] the actual number of mergers performed by each firm as a measure of the propensity to diversify. This test is aimed at finding whether the intensity of conglomerate mergers is associated with the type of control of firms. . . . Formally, the following cross sectional relationship is [tested using conventional regression analysis]:

$$M_{ij} = \beta_o + \beta_1 \cdot D_{mi} + \beta_2 \cdot D_{wi} + \beta_3 \cdot S_i + u_i \qquad \textbf{(9-1)}$$

where:

$M_{ij} =$ the number of corporate acquisitions made by firm i within the ten-year period, 1961-1970. The index j denotes the type of acquisition according to the following well-known categorization:

$j = 1$:   *horizontal mergers*; between companies producing one or more of the same, or closely related, products

$j = 2$:   *vertical mergers*; between companies having a buyer-seller relationship before the merger

$j = 3$:   *conglomerate mergers -- product extension*; when products of the acquiring/acquired companies are functionally related in production or distribution, but do not compete with one another

$j = 4$:   *conglomerate mergers -- market extension*; when the acquiring and acquired companies manufacture the same products, but sell them in different geographic markets

$j = 5$:   *pure conglomerate mergers*; between firms that are functionally unrelated

$D =$ a dummy variable, indicating the type of control exercised in firm i: D_m [$=1$ for *management control* (no single party holds 10% or more of the outstanding stock); $D_w = 1$ for *weak owner control* (a single party holds between 10% and 29.9% of the stock); the residual category is *strong owner control* (one party or a specific group owns at least 30% of the outstanding common stock)

$S_i =$ the size of firm i, measured by total sales in 1961

Equation 9-1 can be estimated cross sectionally for each of the five types of acquisitions . . . [and] for a meaningfully aggregated group of acquisitions, such as all conglomerate mergers. . . .

If our hypothesis is valid, we expect to find both β_1 and β_2 positive for conglomerate mergers, thus implying that the weaker the owner control (as we move from strong owner through weak owner to management control), the stronger the firm's propensity to engage in conglomerate acquisitions. . . . In addition, we would expect $\beta_1 > \beta_2$, implying that the propensity of firms to engage in conglomerate mergers is monotonically increasing as we move from strong owner through weak owner to manager control.

Since the number of acquisitions might also be affected by firm size, we [control for this possibility with] an explicit size variable (S_i). . . . Of course, size not only may affect the number of acquisitions, but also is affected by acquisitions. Hence, to distinguish between these two effects, we measured size at the *beginning* of the examined period, 1961.

[We classified the *Fortune* 500 largest industrial U.S. firms by type of control for 1965], the mid-point of the period examined. Standard and Poor's Compustat tape had the required data on sales, income, and equity for the entire period examined for 309 of these 500 firms. These 309 firms constitute our sample. The sampled firms were then checked against the FTC *Statistical Report on Mergers and Acquisitions* (1976) to determine the number and type of acquisitions carried out during the period 1961-1970.

Not all sampled firms had acquisitions during that period.   Since the acquiring firms in the sample were the largest in the U.S., and since very small acquisitions cannot be expected to result from risk-reduction motives nor will their impact be detected by our statistical tools, we concentrated in this study on relatively large acquisitions for which the total asset size of the acquired firm was at least ten million dollars.

A general indication of the propensity of firms to merge is provided in Table 9-5, which presents the average number of acquisitions per firm by type of merger and control. For [horizontal and vertical mergers], for which risk reduction does not appear to be the primary motive, there is no clear pattern for the average number of acquisitions as we move from "management control" to "strong owner control." On the other hand, for the conglomerate types of acquisitions, the pattern is clear and consistent with our hypothesis: The average number of acquisitions per firm decreases as we move from "management control" to "strong owner control.". . .

Table 9-5
Acquisitions Per Firm Based on Type of Control

Type of Merger	Type of Control		
	Management	Weak Owner	Strong Owner
Horizontal	.099	.061	.098
Vertical	.153	.182	.049
Conglomerate Product Extension	.748	.576	.293
Conglomerate Market Extension	.059	.030	.000
Pure Conglomerate	.297	.167	.073
All Conglomerates	1.104	.773	.360

Our [regression] estimates, presented in Table 9-6, are consistent with our hypothesis. Consider first [horizontal and vertical acquisitions], for which risk reduction does not appear to be a primary motive.   The type-of-control coefficients, β_1 and β_2, are not significantly different from zero (at the 5% level), indicating that for these kinds of mergers, there appears to be no difference in the propensity to acquire between manager- and owner-controlled firms. On the other hand, the β_1 and β_2, coefficients are statistically significant for conglomerate acquisitions. This indicates that [manager-controlled and weak owner-controlled firms undertake more] conglomerate mergers, where diversification is generally considered to be a primary motive. . . .   Further, the sizes of β_1 and β_2 for conglomerate mergers are consistent with our hypothesis, namely β_1 is larger than β_2. Finally, firm size does not appear to be associated with the number of acquisitions, since in most cases β_3 is insignificantly different from zero.

Table 9-6
Estimated Regression Coefficients

	Type of Acquisition		
Coefficient	**Horizontal**	**Vertical**	**Conglomerate**
β_1	.0004	1.29	1.93
	(t = .001)	(t = 1.52)	(t = 3.72)
β_2	−.45	1.43	1.26
	(t = .69)	(t = 1.54)	(t = 2.16)
β_3	.00008	.0003	−.0001
	(t = .53)	(t = 1.69)	(t = .75)

Note: Evaluating Managerial Motives for Conglomerate Acquisitions

1. *Subsequent Studies on Diversification by Manager Controlled Firms.* Lloyd, Hand & Modani confirm Amihud & Lev's central result -- manager controlled firms make more diversifying acquisitions, controlling for firm size -- for 1971 to 1980. They also find that the stock price returns of manager-controlled firms more closely track market returns, a result consistent with greater diversification (whether from acquisitions or internal growth) between 1976 and 1980.[20]

Davis, Diekmann & Tinsley find a significant negative correlation between ownership concentration and frequency of unrelated acquisitions by Fortune 500 firms between 1986 and 1990. But they also find that few firms made *any* unrelated acquisitions in this period. One reason for this, they suggest, is that unrelated acquisitions no longer served managers' interests in risk-reduction. On the contrary, hostile bust-up takeovers directed at conglomerate firms made an unrelated acquisition seem an invitation to a future hostile bid.[21]

2. *The Incentives of Controlling Shareholders.* Consider whether Amihud & Lev fully capture the incentives facing the owners of

---

[20] William Lloyd, John Hand & Naval Modani, *The Effect of the Degree of Ownership Control on Firm Diversification, Market Value, and Merger Activity*, 15 J.Bus.Res. 303 (1987); accord, Yakov Amihud, Jacob Kamin & Joshua Ronen, *"Managerialism," "Ownerism" and Risk*, 7 J. Banking & Fin. 189 (1983); Julia Liebeskind & Tim Opler, *Corporate Diversification and Agency Costs: Evidence from Privately Held Firms*, ___ J.Fin.Econ. ___ (forthcoming 1994) (private firms are less diversified than publicly owned firms, controlling for number of employees).

[21] Gerald Davis, Kristina Diekmann & Catherine Tinsley, *The Decline and Fall of the Conglomerate Firm in the 1980s: A Study in the De-Institutionalization of an Organizational Form*, 59 Am.Soc.Rev. 547 (1994).

owner-controlled firms. If these incentives are misspecified, then their data are subject to alternative explanations. Amihud & Lev implicitly assume that owners can diversify their portfolios outside the company. Otherwise, owners would share management's incentive to diversify at the firm level. It seems likely that many owners *cannot* diversify their portfolios through investments outside the company because their investment in the company represents too large a percentage of their total portfolio.

We then need a more subtle hypothesis to explain why manager-controlled firms diversify more than owner-controlled firms. We suggest the following alternative hypothesis: A non-diversified owner, faced with the opportunity to make a negative-NPV diversifying acquisition, faces a conflict between the incentive to diversify, and the incentive to make only positive NPV investments. Sometimes this tension is resolved in favor of diversification, sometimes not. Managers, in contrast, face no such conflict. Thus, manager-controlled firms will make *more* diversifying acquisitions, consistent with Amihud & Lev's data. This refined hypothesis also explains why owner-controlled firms make *some* diversifying acquisitions.

This perspective on the conflicting incentives of owners suggests a further way to test whether self-interest drives managers' decisions to diversify. The more stock a manager owns, the more the manager faces the same conflict as a non-diversified owner between diversifying and maximizing value. Thus top managers who own more stock should make fewer diversifying acquisitions. Consistent with this hypothesis, Hermalin & Weisbach report, for a sample of 142 NYSE-traded firms in 1977, a significant negative correlation between the ownership stake of the CEO (and former CEOs still on the board), and the number of industries in which the firm operates.[22]

3. *Management Stock Ownership and Acquirer Stock Price Returns.* Another approach to assessing whether managers undertake acquisitions partly out of their own self-interest is to see whether the abnormal return to the acquiring firm correlates with management stock ownership. The agency cost perspective yields the prediction that managers who own large stakes will make better acquisitions than managers who own little stock. Thus, we should find a positive correlation between management stock ownership and stock returns. Several studies confirm this prediction.[23]

---

[22] Benjamin Hermalin & Michael Weisbach, *The Determinants of Board Composition*, 19 Rand J.Econ. 589, 594 (1988).

[23] See Yakov Amihud, Baruch Lev & Nickolaos Travlos, *Corporate Control and the Choice of Investment Financing: The Case of Corporate Acquisitions*, 45 J.Fin. 603 (1990); Wilbur Lewellen, Claudio Loderer & Ahron Rosenfeld, *Merger Decisions and Executive Stock Ownership in Acquiring Firms*, 7 J.Acct. & Econ. 209 (1985); Michael Maloney, R. McCormick & Mark Mitchell, *Managerial Decision Making and Capital Structure* (CRSP working paper, 1992); Victor You, Richard Caves, Michael Smith & James Henry, *Mergers and Bidders' Wealth: Managerial and Strategic Factors*, in *The Economics of Strategic Planning: Essays in Honor of Joel Dean* 201 (Lacy Thomas ed.1986).

4. *Acquisitions with Mixed Motives.* A further question concerning the Amihud & Lev study is definitional. The authors assume that diversification cannot increase the value of a publicly held company because shareholders can accomplish this result for themselves. But what if acquisitions can increase firm value for reasons other than increased diversification? Amihud & Lev include within the category of conglomerate mergers both product extension acquisitions, where the products of both companies are related but do not compete, and market extension acquisitions, where the products of both companies are the same but are sold in different geographic markets. In both situations there may be significant opportunities for synergy. In addition, many acquisitions don't neatly fall into a single category. This is particularly true where the acquirer or the target is already diversified. Consider the mix of business overlaps present in the Time-Warner combination discussed in Chapter 1. How would you classify this combination, among the five alternatives used by Amihud & Lev? What would be the impact on the analysis and interpretation of the Amihud & Lev data if, as appears to be the case, the conglomerate category includes many transactions that have the potential for diversification *and* synergy?

5. *The "Managerialist" Tradition and Incentives for Growth.* The Amihud & Lev study, and the other studies cited above, provide empirical support for the approach of "managerialist" writers, who argue that managers for a variety of reasons, prefer to see their firm grow.[24] For example, managers have been said to prefer growth because: (i) compensation is a function of firm size;[25] (ii) size provides protection against hostile takeovers; (iii) because the personal prestige of managers is a function of firm size; and (iv) because growth increases the opportunity for promotion within the firm.[26] If antitrust rules make growth through horizontal or vertical acquisitions difficult, as they did in the 1960s, managers of mature firms may diversify because this is the only avenue of growth left to them. This tradition, though it preceded the formal development of agency theory that began in the 1970s, is entirely consistent with the agency cost approach. The principal self-interested objective of managers is growth rather than, as Amihud & Lev suggest, risk-reduction. But the strategy (diversification) is the same, as is the conflict with the shareholder interest in value maximization.

---

[24] See, e.g., William Baumol, *Business Behavior, Value and Growth* (rev.ed.1967); Oliver Williamson, *The Economics of Discretionary Behavior: Managerial Objectives in a Theory of the Firm* (1964); Robin Marris, *The Economic Theory of Managerial Capitalism* (1964).

[25] See, e.g., Ajay Khorana & Marc Zenner, *Does the Relation Between Executive Compensation and Firm Size Explain the Large Takeovers of the 1980s?* (Kenan-Flagler Bus.Sch. working paper 1993) (large acquisitions tend to be followed by an increase in the cash compensation of the acquiring firm's CEO).

[26] See John Coffee, *Regulating the Market for Corporate Control: A Critical Assessment of the Tender Offer's Role in Corporate Governance*, 84 Colum.L.Rev. 1145, 1167-69 (1984).

How might we distinguish between growth and risk-reduction as acquisition motives? One way is to see whether managers take steps to reduce risk without altering firm size. A simple step is to use more equity and less debt financing. This would reduce the systematic and unsystematic risk associated with the firm's equity, and also reduce the chance of bankruptcy. Amihud, Kamin & Ronen finds only an insignificant difference in the systematic risk of manager-controlled and owner-controlled firms (albeit with the predicted sign).[27] Moreover, the most active conglomerate acquirers in the 1960s were typically highly leveraged; most had β's well over one. This suggests that growth was a more central motive for diversification than risk-reduction (though both could well be present).

Larry Lang & Rene Stulz report further evidence in favor of growth as a motive for diversification. They report that firms that choose to diversify have lower industry-adjusted Tobin's q's that non-diversified firms. Tobin's q correlates both with managerial skill (the same tangible assets are worth more in the hands of good managers) and with the presence of growth opportunities (a firm with strong growth opportunities will have a higher ratio of market value to tangible asset value). This suggests that firms are more prone to diversify when they exhaust (or when their managers cannot find) growth opportunities within their own industry. The tendency for poor performers to diversify, in turn, can do much to explain why diversification often turns out poorly.[28]

6.   *Interaction Between Investor and Manager Beliefs.*   Should managers rely on investor reactions to tell them whether they are pursuing a good business strategy? Standard finance texts say yes. For example, Brealey & Myers state that "TRUST MARKET PRICES" is a central "lesson of market efficiency."[29] The problem with this advice is information asymmetry: Managers should trust market prices only if investors have full information. Still, if managers pay attention to investor beliefs, could that explain part of the manager enthusiasm for conglomerate mergers in the 1960s? Investors loved conglomerates, at least for a while. That would surely provide strong reinforcement to acquisition-minded managers.

Managers listening to the market cannot fully explain the conglomerate merger boom. After all, as Amihud & Lev point out, owner-controlled firms didn't make the same mistakes. But it is easy to imagine managers' preference for growth and diversification, buttressed by investor enthusiasm for diversifying acquisitions, producing a managerial culture that encouraged diversification. Similarly, investor distaste for unrelated acquisitions in the

---

[27] Amihud, Kamin & Ronen (1983), *supra* note 20 (manager controlled firms had average β values 0.11 lower than owner-controlled firms, but difference is statistically insignificant ($t = 1.28$)).

[28] Lang & Stulz (1993), *supra* note 13.

[29] Richard Brealey & Stewart Myers, *Principles of Corporate Finance* 300 (4th ed.1991) (emphasis in original).

1980s helps to explain why they have become less common. Many managers still have the discretionary power to pursue this strategy if they choose, but it is no longer a legitimate, respected strategy within American corporate culture.[30]

7. *The Uses and Limits of Management Stock Options.* Consider finally how one might modify the incentives of the managers of a manager-controlled company. What happens if we consider their position from an option perspective? If managers have substantial numbers of out-of-the-money stock options, are they made better off by an increase or a decrease in the variability of the company's future value? Can out-of-the-money options be used to balance management's incentives so that they are closer to those of the shareholders?

Note, however, that managers have historically controlled the decision as to the form that their compensation will take, including what kinds of options they will receive. A typical management stock option is issued with an exercise price equal to the current market price, and ten years to expiration. Such an option, although nominally at-the-money, is deep-in-the-money in economic terms, once we take the time value of money into account. It will be in the money at expiration, because of expected growth in firm value, unless the firm does unusually poorly over the next ten years. This means that the expected return on the option looks more stock-like than option-like.

The studies cited above suggest that managers who own more stock make fewer diversifying acquisitions, *despite* the risk reduction benefits from doing so. A similar conclusion ought to follow for increased ownership of in-the-money options. But we have not solved the problem of managerial aversion to risk. Indeed, in-the-money options may *strengthen* managers' aversion to risk. A large option grant means that not only the managers' human capital, but much of their financial capital as well, will be invested in company stock or in stock-like options.

Thus, even if out-of-the-money stock options theoretically could reduce managers' incentives to diversify at the shareholders' expense, the shareholders may be unable to insist that firms use these options, in precisely the situation (manager-controlled firms) where they are most needed. Unfortunately, the burgeoning literature on optimal incentive contracts generally assumes that these contracts can be imposed by shareholder fiat.[31]

---

[30] Matsusaka (1993), *supra* note 18, offers an investor-reinforcement explanation for the conglomerate mergers boom in the 1960s. Davis, Diekmann & Tinsley (1994), *supra* note 21, stress the cultural aspects of the legitimation of diversifying acquisitions in the 1960s, and their delegitimation in the 1980s.

[31] Recent overviews include Paul Milgrom & John Roberts, *Economics, Organization and Management* chs. 7 (Risk Sharing and Incentive Contracts), 13 (Executive and Managerial Compensation) (1992); Myron Scholes, *Stock and Compensation*, 46 J.Fin. 803 (1991); George Baker, Michael Jensen & Kevin Murphy, *Compensation and Incentives: Theory and*

The deeper problem, with no obvious solution, is developing incentive contracts that give managers both good incentives *and* incentives to adopt the contracts.

8. *Corporate Law Implications.* Should the conflict faced by managers between their own self-interest and their fiduciary duties to shareholders when considering a diversifying acquisitions lead to heightened judicial scrutiny of these transaction?[32]

E.   Bust-Up Takeovers and Deconglomeration

During the 1980s merger boom, the most reviled of all transactions in the public press was the "two-tier, junk bond, bust-up takeover," where a corporate raider, often using mostly borrowed money, launched a hostile tender offer for a diversified firm, with the intent promptly to sell off most of the pieces of the target and fire the unproductive headquarters staff. Probably nowhere was the gap between popular and academic opinion larger than for bust-up takeovers. For many academics, conglomerates were the problem, and bust-ups were the market's painful but necessary solution.

Andrei Shleifer & Robert Vishny
THE TAKEOVER WAVE OF THE 1980's
249 Sci. 745, 746-47 (1990)

As did all merger waves, the 1980s saw rising stock prices and rising corporate cash reserves stimulating the usual demand for expansion through acquisitions. However, in the 1980s the Reagan Administration consciously eased up on antitrust enforcement in an effort to leave the market alone. As a consequence, intraindustry acquisitions became possible on a large scale for the first time in 30 years. The easy availability of internal and external funds for investment coupled with the negative experience with the diversification of the 1960s and the first laissez-faire antitrust policy in decades shaped the takeover wave of the 1980s.

The return to expansion in core businesses is evident in the prevalence of two types of deals in the 1980s. In the first type, a large firm with most of its assets in a particular industry bought another large firm in the same industry. Some peripheral businesses were divested, but most of the acquired assets were kept. Such deals were common in gas pipelines, food,

---

Practice, 43 J.Fin. 593 (1988). For a survey of the legal standards governing management compensation, see Detlev Vagts, *Challenges to Executive Compensation: For the Markets or the Courts,* 8 J.Corp.L. 231 (1983).

[32] See Note, *The Conflict Between Managers and Shareholders in Diversifying Acquisitions,* 88 Yale L.J. 1238 (1979).

banking, airlines, and oil. In the second type of deal, a "bustup," the acquired firm was typically a conglomerate. Placing its assets in specialists' hands required a sale of many divisions to separate buyers. Our [research with Sanjai Bhagat shows] that in 62 hostile takeover contests between 1984 and 1986, 30% of the assets were on average sold off within 3 years.[a] In 17 cases more than half the assets were sold. Roughly 70% of the selloffs were to buyers in the same line of business.

In the face of the hostile pressure to divest, some managers realized that they themselves could profit from bustups, by taking the company private and then selling peripheral business to specialized acquirers. This realization explains a significant number of leveraged buyouts of the 1980s followed by large-scale divestitures. For leveraged buyouts in our 1984 to 1986 sample, selloffs are even higher than for takeovers as a whole, amounting to 44% of total assets.

In the 1980s takeover wave, the so-called "corporate raiders" and many leveraged buyout (LBO) specialists played the critical role of brokers. They acquired conglomerates, busted them up, and sold off most business segments to large corporations in the same businesses. Michael Jensen has argued that takeovers by raiders and by leveraged buyout funds move us toward a new incentive-infused organizational form that will permanently deliver shareholders from the wasteful ways of public corporations.[b] The evidence does not support his view. First, most takeovers do not involve raiders or LBO funds. Second, many raider and LBO-controlled firms are temporary organizations designed to last only as long as it takes to sell off the pieces of the acquired firm to other public corporations. The remaining pieces are often reoffered to the public, especially when their value has been enhanced by some operating changes.

A takeover that illustrates some of the features of the 1980s wave is the acquisition of cosmetics giant Revlon by the raider Ronald Perelman. This fiercely hostile takeover took place in 1985, at the price of $2.3 billion. Before the takeover, Revlon acquired many businesses outside cosmetics, particularly in health care. The top management of Revlon thought that health care offered better growth opportunities than cosmetics, and so reduced the investment and advertising budget of cosmetics to support the growth of the health care business. After the takeover, Perelman sold off $2.06 billion of Revlon's health care and other noncosmetics businesses. Perelman had an offer to sell the cosmetics business for $905 million. About 60% of asset selloffs were to other companies in the health care field, but some were to management buyout groups. After the selloffs, Revlon substantially revamped the cosmetics business and tripled its advertising

---

[a] Sanjai Bhagat, Andrei Shleifer & Robert Vishny, *Hostile Takeovers in the 1980s: The Return to Corporate Specialization,"* in Brookings Papers on Econ. Activity, Microecon. 1 (1990).

[b] Michael Jensen, *The Eclipse of the Public Corporation,* Harv.Bus.Rev. 61 (Sept.-Oct.1989).

budget. ("Some of the most beautiful women in the world wear Revlon.") Headquarters staff was also reduced, although there is no evidence of blue-collar layoffs or of investment cuts. Revlon's profits increased substantially.

Table 9-7 summarizes more systematically the eventual allocation of assets induced by the hostile takeovers of 1984 to 1986. Combining direct acquisition of related assets with acquisitions of divested assets, we find that 72% of all assets that changed hands as a result of hostile takeovers were sold to public corporations in closely related businesses within 3 years. Only 15% of the assets ended up in private firms, such as those formed when management and leveraged buyout specialists take divisions private (MBOs). And only 4.5% of the assets was bought by public corporations acquiring outside of their core businesses. This last number clearly illustrates the move away from conglomerates.

Has deconglomeration and expansion in core businesses raised efficiency and U.S. competitiveness? Some economists have taken the increase in stock prices of the acquired firms -- which is not nearly offset by the modest stock price declines of acquiring firms -- to be by itself incontrovertible evidence that efficiency must have improved. We do not take this position, since much evidence shows that the stock market can make large valuation mistakes. The possibility that the stock market is overly enthusiastic about the takeovers of the 1980s should not be dismissed. After all, the market greeted the conglomerate mergers of the 1960s with share price increases, and most of these mergers failed. Nonetheless, there are reasons to expect the takeovers of the 1980s to raise long-term efficiency.

Table 9-7

Hostile Takeovers and Movement of Corporate Assets, 1984 to 1986

	$ millions	Percent
Assets that changed hands:	**$68,743**	**100%**
Assets that went to strategic buyers:	49,660	72
Strategic acquisitions net of selloffs	*26,010*	*38*
Selloffs to strategic buyers	*23,650*	*34*
Assets that went to MBOs:	10,234	15
Direct MBOs net of selloffs	*4,834*	*7*
Selloffs to MBOs	*5,400*	*8*
Assets that stayed with nonstrategic bidders:	3,810	5.5
Assets that went to unrelated acquisitions:	3,154	4.5
Direct unrelated bidders	*373*	*0.5*
Selloffs to unrelated bidders	*2,781*	*4*
Selloffs of headquarters & stockholdings:	667	1
Not identified selloffs:	1,219	2

The fact that many takeovers dismantle conglomerates and allocate divisions to specialists creates a presumption that performance should improve. There is, in fact, evidence that divisions are more productive when they are part of less diversified companies, although this evidence does not establish the link specifically for divested divisions.[c] There is also evidence that acquired firms [in the 1980s] are less profitable than the firms buying them.[d] This suggests that more assets in an industry are being allocated to the organizations that can better manage them. Overall, the evidence recommends cautious optimism about the efficiency of takeovers in the 1980s.

Note: Evidence on the Value of Bust-Up Takeovers

1. *An Anecdote: The Revlon Bust-Up.* Shleifer & Vishny use Ronald Perelman's acquisition of Revlon in 1985 as an example of the potential value of a bust-up acquisition. Before Perelman appeared on the scene, Revlon's stock traded in the low-30's, for a total market value of about $1.2 billion. It's CEO, taking a page from the BCG manual, had announced an intent to milk the cosmetics business for cash to support an expansion into pharmaceuticals and health care. Perelman eventually acquired Revlon for $58 per share, a total of $2.3 billion. Even so, he made a huge profit. Counting the $2.06 billion that Perelman received for Revlon's pharmaceutical, health care, film, and other subsidiaries, plus the $905 million offer that he turned down for the cosmetics business, the busted up Revlon was worth $75 per share -- almost 2-½ times its pretakeover market value!

2. *The 1980s Trend Toward Less Diversification.* In the 1980s, the 1960s and 1970s trend for large companies to become more diversified, was reversed. For example, Robert Comment & Gregg Jarrell report that between 1978 and 1988, the percentage of firms that had only a single business segment increased from 36% in 1978 to 54% in 1988.[33] The dediversification trend was welcomed by shareholders. Comment & Jarrell report that

> the trend toward increasing focus has been associated with significant positive abnormal returns to shareholders controlling for market and industry stock returns and for various accounting measures of firm performance. . . . The

---

[c] Lichtenberg (1992), *supra* note 12.

[d] Henri Servaes, *Tobin's Q and the Gains from Takeovers*, 46 J.Fin. 409 (1991).

[33] See also Liebeskind & Opler (1994), *supra* note 20 (from 1980-1989, percentage of a firm's workers employed in its largest industry, measured using 4-digit Standard Industrial Classification (SIC) codes, increased on average by 10.6%; percentage of a firm's workers employed in its 2-digit industry group increased by 16.8%); Lichtenberg (1992), *supra* note 12, ch. 7.

economic magnitude of this empirical relation is small but not trivial -- a 10% increase in focus is associated with [abnormal returns of] 2.3% just over the year of the focus increase.[34]

3. *Conglomerates as Attractive Takeover Targets.* Davis, Diekmann & Tinsley offer further evidence that takeovers were an important cause of the dediversification in the 1980s. They use a logarithmic measure of diversification, $D = \Sigma f_i \cdot \ln(1/f_i)$, where f_i is the fraction of a firm's sales in business segment i. Under this measure, a single-line firm has $D = 0$. The average diversification level of the Fortune 500 dropped from $D = 1.00$ in 1980, to $D = 0.90$, in 1985, and $D = 0.67$ in 1990. A major impetus for this drop was the greater likelihood that a diversified firm would be acquired. For example, firms at the 75% percentile in degree of diversification were 2.3 times as likely as single-line firms to be acquired during the decade, after controlling for firm size.[35]

Note: Post-Merger Performance of Related Takeovers

Ravenscraft & Scherer report evidence of poor post-acquisition performance after conglomerate acquisitions. For related acquisitions, there is limited evidence that the stock price gains from related acquisitions anticipate improved accounting profitability, but work in this area is still in its early stages. We discuss here the principal studies of takeovers in general. Chapter 11 reviews studies of the post-transaction performance of firms that undergo leveraged buyouts.

Ravenscraft & Scherer. One indirect source is Ravenscraft & Scherer. Their regressions show a strong positive correlation between profitability and market share. See Regressions 9-2 and 9-3. This suggests that related acquisitions, which increase market share, might also increase profitability.

Healy, Palepu & Ruback. Paul Healy, Krishna Palepu & Richard Ruback test post-acquisition performance more directly. They measure industry-adjusted, pretax cash flow, as a percentage of the market value of assets, for the 50 largest acquisitions between 1979 and 1984. On average, industry-adjusted cash flow increases from 2.1% for the 5 years preceding the acquisition to 3.2% for the 5 years following the acquisition, which is statistically significant at the 5% level. Moreover, these gains appear to be concentrated in firms with a high degree of relatedness. A dummy variable for high relatedness predicts an increase of 5.1% in post-acquisition industry adjusted cash flow once two outliers are excluded (though this result is significant only at the 10% level). A dummy variable for moderate

---

[34] Robert Comment & Gregg Jarrell, *Corporate Focus and Stock Returns* (Bradley Pol'y Res. Center, Univ. of Rochester working paper MR 91-01, 1991).

[35] Davis, Diekmann & Tinsley (1994), *supra* note 21.

relatedness also has the predicted (positive) sign, but is not statistically significant.[36]

An important caveat, however: *All* of the cash flow gains are realized in the first two years after merger. By post-merger year 3, the gains have disappeared, and in years 4 and 5, the merged firm is doing less well than the separate firms did before the merger. This makes one wonder if the early gains are real, or instead reflect the efforts of the acquirer's managers to boost accounting earnings or cash flow in order to make the acquisition look better than it really is.[37]

Jarrell. Sherry Jarrell compares post-merger net income as a percentage of sales for merged firms to a control sample of similar non-merged firms, for takeovers between 1973 and 1985. The merged firms perform worse than the control firms in post-merger year 1, but better than the control firms in years 2-6. In years 4-6, the median merged firm has net income/sales that is 8.7% higher than the control sample. But she finds no significant difference between horizontal and vertical mergers, on the one hand, and conglomerate mergers, on the other. Jarrell also reports that announcement period stock returns correlate with increases in net income/sales, suggesting some investor ability to discriminate between good and bad takeover.[38]

Banking. There have been several studies of the profitability of bank mergers. Banking is an attractive industry to study because good post-merger financial data is available and because banking laws allow only banks to own banks, so that all acquisitions are related. The general conclusion is that post-merger expenses, as a fraction of interest income, do not decline. Generally, the anticipated savings either are not realized or are offset by a decline in market share.[39]

---

[36] Paul Healy, Krishna Palepu & Richard Ruback, *Does Corporate Performance Improve After Mergers?*, 31 J.Fin.Econ. 135 (1992).

[37] See also Edward Herman & Louis Lowenstein, *The Efficiency Effects of Hostile Takeovers,* in *Knights, Raiders & Targets: The Impact of the Hostile Takeover* 211 (John Coffee, Louis Lowenstein & Susan Rose-Ackerman eds.1988). Herman & Lowenstein measure return on equity (a less useful measure of performance than cash flow based measures) and don't control for the acquirer's or target's industry. They find evidence that the bidder's post-acquisition return on equity increases for hostile takeovers in the late 1970s, but decreases for hostile takeovers in the early 1980s. Their 1980s sample overlaps the Healy, Palepu & Ruback sample, which suggests the importance of careful methodology.

[38] Sherry Jarrell, *Do Takeovers Generate Value?: Evidence on the Capital Market's Ability to Assess Takeovers* (Southern Methodist U. working paper 1991). Jarrell normalizes net income/sales by comparing it to analyst projections. The value of doing this is unclear, since analyst forecasts have negligible predictive value this far in the future. But there is no obvious reason why this should bias her results. A more important concern is that Jarrell often finds significance only for differences in medians and not for differences in means.

[39] See, e.g., Stephen Rhoades, *The Operating Performance of Acquiring Firms in Banking Before and After Acquisition* (Staff Study No. 149, Board of Governors of the Federal Reserve System, 1986); Aruna Srinivasan & Larry Wall, *Cost Savings Associated with Bank Mergers* (Fed. Reserve Bank of Atlanta working paper 92-2, 1992).

CHAPTER 10: REPLACING INEFFICIENT MANAGEMENT

Quality of management is widely recognized as a critical element of firm performance. If a firm performs poorly because it is badly managed, an acquirer can substitute good management for bad and thereby increase the target's post-acquisition value. Recall from Chapter 6 and Figures 6-5 and 6-7 the sharp increase in Allied-Signal's stock price when its board unexpectedly replaced Edward Hennessy as CEO. In cases where the board does not act, the potential for similar gains can become a motive for an outside acquirer.

A.   Motivating the Inquiry

Bernie Shellum, FRUEHAUF STEERS INTO TROUBLE: MANAGEMENT CITED IN DECLINE OF TRUCKMAKER
Chi.Trib., Feb, 27, 1989, at C1[*]

In the macho world of highway trucking, no name conveyed more muscle in the 1950s, '60s and '70s than Fruehauf, the emblem that adorned the mud flaps of more big rigs than any other. Detroit-based Fruehauf Corp. was the biggest and best truck-trailer manufacturer, the IBM of its industry.

Today, Fruehauf is awash in debt from a 1986 leveraged buyout, and its future is in doubt. It has lost money at a rate of nearly $1 million a week the last three years. . . . [In] 1988, Fruehauf lost $56.5 million, compared to $41.5 million in 1987, on a 7% increase in revenue to $2.09 billion from $1.96 billion in 1987.

To stay afloat, Fruehauf has sold $775 million in assets and shrunk its worldwide work force to 15,000 from 26,100 in 1986. The company is talking to possible buyers, including Varity Corp., Allied-Signal Inc. and Robert Bosch G.m.b.H. of West Germany. Investors are so skittish about its future that they demand, and get, 20% interest on the money they provide to keep the company afloat. One bond research firm puts odds at 50-50 of a Fruehauf debt default in the next five years. If that happens, Fruehauf would become the biggest leveraged buyout debacle [to date], surpassing the $1.3 billion Revco drug chain bankruptcy filing in July.[a]

What happened here? Fruehauf's decline is commonly attributed to corporate raider Asher Edelman, whose hostile takeover attempt in 1986 prompted Fruehauf management to engineer the buyout that thwarted Edelman but left the company $1.4 billion in debt. But many former

---

[*] Reprinted by permission of Knight-Ridder Tribune News Service.

[a] In May, 1989, Fruehauf sold its business units and liquidated. Shareholders received a small interest in Varity Corp., the buyer of the largest unit; bondholders exchanged their Fruehauf bonds for cash and Varity subordinated debt worth substantially less than the principal amount of their bonds. See Stan Hinden, *The LBO That Failed: Debt-Ridden Fruehauf Sells Its Last Unit*, Wash. Post, May 9, 1989, at B1.

Fruehauf executives and advisers dismiss the Edelman explanation as too simplistic. Fruehauf is failing, they say, because Chairman Robert Rowan and other company brass fostered a culture that prized golf and yachting over attention to business in the early 1980s, a period of radical change in the economics of trucking.

"Rowan was a member at Oakland Hills, and I know they spent a lot of time in Florida and around the country on the golf course," said John Blunt, a longtime Fruehauf consultant. "In any business where they spend too much time on the golf course, it says they're not minding the store." A former high-ranking Fruehauf executive was more outspoken. "Nothing interfered with tee times," he said. "When tee times came, the top guys disappeared on you. Usually, by noon on a nice day, you couldn't find anybody." . . .

For this report, more than a dozen current and former Fruehauf executives, advisers and employees, most of whom requested anonymity, were interviewed. In some cases, they are still receiving income from Fruehauf and fear it might be cut off. If Edelman hadn't pounced, they say, another raider would have, because Fruehauf's sagging sales and profits had dragged its stock to $20.25 a share from the mid-30s in 1984. That was too tempting to resist. . . .

Rowan also aroused dismay among Fruehauf workers and managers, the former Fruehauf executives say, by his personal use of the corporate yacht, the Mallard. Rowan, 66, remains Fruehauf's $295,485-a-year chairman, but relinquished the chief executive's post in May to T. Neal Combs. . . .

By the 1950s, almost half of the rigs on U.S. roads bore the company's nameplate. Fruehauf wasn't only the biggest, but the best, in its field. Spending heavily on research, its engineers regularly secured new patents for design innovations that later filtered through the industry. Competitors bestowed on Fruehauf the kind of unspoken flattery that clone-computer manufacturers once accorded to International Business Machines Corp. They bought the new Fruehauf trailers, took them apart and tried to devise improvements in price or quality. Those who succeeded held on to tiny niches in the trailer business, and Fruehauf rolled on unchallenged as the industry leader.

Through the 1950s, the company was run by Fruehauf family members, though not always in harmony. In the early 1950s, for instance, the founder's youngest son, Roy Fruehauf, borrowed $1 million from Dave Beck, the corrupt Teamsters union president, to finance a proxy fight against his oldest brother, Harvey Fruehauf.

Roy Fruehauf won the battle, ending what some Fruehauf veterans regard as the only period of sound management in recent decades. . . . Roy Fruehauf turned out to be an erratic manager who quickly steered the company into deep difficulty. The board sought fresh blood in the late 1950s by acquiring a Ft. Worth tanker-trailer manufacturer, obtaining the services of William Grace, a Texan who had saved the firm from bankruptcy. Grace also was a high 70s, low 80s golfer -- a sign of things to come.

Fruehauf flourished under Grace, but in 1970 he and Rowan, then vice president for finance, were indicted on charges of criminal tax fraud. They were convicted in 1975 of conspiring to evade $12.3 million in corporate excise taxes from 1956 until 1965, and were sentenced to six months in prison and $10,000 fines. The sentences were reduced to four months of community service. In late 1978, after exhausting all appeals, Grace resigned the chairmanship and Rowan resigned as president and chief executive.

Their absence was temporary, however. They returned to Fruehauf in mid-1979. . . . Rowan returned to Fruehauf a changed man, according to one-time associates. The tax case "had a profound effect on the man," one said of Rowan. "He lost interest in the company. His perspective changed. He began to surround himself with people who would only agree with him."

In the new corporate culture, the critics say, research and development that had once been the company's lifeblood lost vitality, strategic planning all but stopped and the work ethic withered. Golf replaced business sessions at the company's annual overseas management meetings, according to some who participated in the excursions for many years. In the 1970s, they said, those meetings were held in such places as Mexico, Brazil and South Africa, where Fruehauf rented or sold trailers. But, in the early 1980s, they said, the meetings shifted to more hospitable locales such as Hawaii, and came to include "rented trains and extravagant extras." . . .

The latest tumultuous chapter in Fruehauf's history began early in 1986, when Edelman launched his takeover bid. To fend him off, Fruehauf's management joined Merrill Lynch & Co., the investment firm, in a $1.4 billion leveraged buyout so laden with debt that it crippled the company. . . .

According to the former Fruehauf men, Edelman's role in the company's misfortunes was incidental rather than pivotal. If Edelman hadn't taken a run at Fruehauf, they say, someone else would have. Ultimately, Fruehauf's board cut a deal to make Edelman go away, giving him $30 million to $40 million for his efforts. The old stockholders also made out, getting $49.50 a share. But those who bought stock or bonds in the new Fruehauf have taken a licking and remaining employees are left wondering who will sign their paychecks in six months.

B.   The Theory: Separation of Ownership and Control

Ronald Gilson, A STRUCTURAL APPROACH TO CORPORATIONS: THE CASE AGAINST DEFENSIVE TACTICS IN TENDER OFFERS
33 Stan.L.Rev. 819, 933-44 (1981)[*]

The Structure of the Corporation and the Theory of the Firm

All corporate statutes define the corporate skeleton in essentially identical terms. Owners of freely transferable voting securities elect a board of directors which, in turn, selects executive officers who, with the help of lesser employees, manage the business of the corporation. The remainder of the corporate structure and the behavioral characteristics exhibited by the various participants depend heavily on matters not the subject of statutory concern. For the publicly held corporation, the markets in which the corporation participates -- product, managerial, and capital -- are the central determinants of that structure and behavior. To understand the role these markets play in the structure of public corporations, we must begin at what was the beginning of modern corporate analysis -- the separation of ownership and management.

That the identity of the nominal owners of a public corporation -- the shareholders -- and those managing it diverged resulted inevitably from industry's capital needs in an expanding economy. The founder of a business, lacking the personal resources to exploit available opportunities, turned to outside sources of capital to finance expansion. As capital flowed into the corporation from nonmanagement sources, so did overall ownership of the corporation flow to the providers of capital. As Berle and Means stressed in their classic work, "[i]t is precisely this separation of control from ownership which makes possible tremendous aggregations of property."[56]

As the number of shareholders increased, separating the management function from the function of providing capital also became affirmatively desirable. . . . [S]uccessful management of a large corporation requires specialized skills which individual shareholders are unlikely to possess. It is therefore beneficial for those having capital but lacking managerial expertise to hire those with expertise at managing capital but lacking the capital to manage. . . .

---

[*] Copyright © 1981 by the Board of Trustees of the Leland Stanford Junior University.

[56] Adolph Berle & Gardiner Means, *The Modern Corporation and Private Property* 5 (1932). . . . My description of shareholders as the "owners" of the corporation does not suggest that the role described for them in the following pages flows, normatively, from their "ownership." It derives, rather, from the need for those holding the residual interest in corporate profits to have the means to displace management which performs poorly. As will be apparent, this position is based on matters other than a preconception of the rights associated with "ownership"; indeed, if the statute did not provide for shareholders we would have to invent them.

The advantages of centralized, specialized management, however, are not without cost. Management monitors the performance of components of the enterprise in order to achieve efficient production. But a mechanism is necessary to ensure that management carries out its monitoring function efficiently; the performance of management must also be monitored, and hiring yet another team of monitors merely recreates the problem one level removed.[61]. . .

The costs resulting from delegating the monitoring responsibility to professional management have been more precisely developed by Jensen and Meckling.[64] Management acts as agents of the shareholders. They can be expected, if otherwise unconstrained, to maximize their own welfare rather than the shareholders'. As a result, it is in the owners' interests to incur "monitoring" costs: expenditures, like third-party audits, designed to make it more difficult for management to prefer itself at the expense of the shareholders. But even third-party monitoring cannot be fully effective, and it will also be in the owners' interests to provide profit-sharing incentives

---

[61] Alchian and Demsetz ask: "But who will monitor the monitor?" Armen Alchian & Harold Demsetz, *Production, Information Costs and Economic Organization,* 62 Am.Econ.Rev. 777, 782 (1972). The best description of the problem I have discovered is that in Theodore Geissel (Dr. Seuss), *Did I Ever Tell You How Lucky You Are?* 26-29 (1973) (emphasis in original):

> Oh, the jobs people work at!
> Out west, near Hawtch-Hawtch,
> there's a Hawtch-Hawtcher Bee-Watcher.
> His job is to watch . . .
> is to keep both his eyes on the lazy town bee.
> A bee that is watched will work harder, you see.
> Well . . . he watched and he watched.
> But, in spite of his watch,
> that bee didn't work any harder. Not mawtch.
> So then somebody said,
> "Our old bee-watching man
> just isn't bee-watching as hard as he can.
> *He* ought to be watched by *another* Hawtch-Hawtcher.
> The thing that we need
> is a Bee-Watcher-Watcher."
> 　　　WELL . . .
> The Bee-Watcher-Watcher watched the Bee-Watcher.
> He didn't watch well. So another Hawtch-Hawtcher
> had to come in as a Watch-Watcher-Watcher.
> and today all the Hawtchers who live in Hawtch-Hawtch
> are watching on Watch-Watcher-Watchering-Watch,
> Watch-Watching the Watcher who's watching that bee.
> *You're* not a Hawtch-Hawtcher. You're lucky, you see.

I am grateful to Catherine Hillary Gilson and Rebecca Ann Gilson for calling this source to my attention.

[64] Michael Jensen & William Meckling, *Theory of the Firm: Managerial Behavior, Agency Costs and Ownership Structure,* 3 J.Fin.Econ. 305 (1976).

designed to reduce the divergence of interests between management and shareholders.[66]

The sum of these costs -- of efforts to prevent management from favoring itself and to positively motivate management to operate in the shareholders' interests -- together with the loss in potential value of the enterprise resulting from the inability to entirely prevent divergence of management and shareholder interest, "are the costs of 'separation of ownership and control'" in the public corporation.[67]

Constraints on Management Discretion

. . . The opportunities for management to favor itself at the expense of shareholders fall into two broad categories. First, management may be inefficient -- if the managers worked harder, or were more careful, or were smarter, the shareholders' return might increase. This inefficiency affects shareholders by reducing production and therefore the amount of the corporation's income. Second, management may appropriate part of the corporation's income stream. For example, management may engage in transactions with the corporation which are unfair to the corporation, may provide itself luxurious office facilities or other perquisites, or in some other fashion may retain for itself more than a competitive return for managerial services. These two forms of managerial discretion are limited by several mechanisms, important aspects of which are market rather than legal.

Management's self-interest should constrain significant deviation from efficient operation. The viability of the corporation, critical to both the shareholders' investment and management's continued employment, depends on the corporation's success in the market for the good or service it provides. Competition in the product market will penalize a company with inefficient management. Ultimately, the corporation will fail, so that management lose their jobs and the shareholders lose their capital. The market for managerial talent also provides incentives for management efficiency. The corporation's performance is commonly treated as a measure of a manager's skills, and hence is a central determinant of the future value of the manager's services.[72] Finally, managerial inefficiency is constrained

---

[66] Incentive plans are also never fully effective. It is difficult to design a plan which measures only the performance of a single manager undiluted by the efforts of others. Moreover, once the performance measures are specified, strategic behavior is possible which manipulates the system in a fashion which favors participants without achieving the productivity gains intended. See, e.g., Alfred Rappaport, *Executive Incentives vs. Corporate Growth,* Harv.Bus.Rev. 81 (July/Aug.1978).

[67] Jensen & Meckling (1976), *supra* note 64, at 327; see Eugene Fama, *Agency Problems and the Theory of the Firm,* 88 J.Pol.Econ. 288, 296 (1980).

[72] The role of the managerial market as a mechanism for constraining managerial discretion to deviate from profit maximization is considered in detail in Fama (1980), *supra* note 67. . . . As developed by Professor Fama, this mechanism operates both within the

by the capital market. A corporation's poor performance in its product market is reflected in the market price of the corporation's stock. Where poor performance is due to management inefficiency, the potential for gain exists through purchasing the corporation's shares at the depressed price and then installing efficient management. . . .

Where incentive mechanisms created by one part of the corporate structure -- the various markets in which the corporation and its managers function -- constrain managerial discretion to perform inefficiently, one would not expect a different part of that structure to provide redundant controls. As we have seen, the legal elements of the corporate structure are consistent with this conclusion. The typical corporate statute assigns management responsibility to the board of directors. The business judgment rule measures the discharge of that responsibility. The rule operates to bar courts from providing additional, and unnecessary, constraints on management discretion through judicial review of operating decisions.

The role of low-cost market mechanisms in restraining managerial discretion is more limited with respect to management's incentive to allocate to itself an excessive portion of the corporation's income. Incentives to succeed in the product market are less likely to constrain managerial self-dealing, since what is of concern is management's ability to allocate to itself income generated through *successful* operation of the corporation's business. Nor will the capital market provide a substantial constraint. Although a lower rate of return to shareholders may increase the corporation's cost of new equity capital by decreasing the value of the corporation's shares, this constraint operates only to the extent the corporation cannot finance its activities through retained earnings and debt. In any event, the cost is borne by existing shareholders through dilution of their interests.

The managerial services market is also less likely to constrain self-dealing than to constrain inefficiency. The buyers of managers for public corporations are, realistically, other managers. There is no reason to believe that an efficient manager's penchant for high pay or perquisites will be negatively viewed. Thus, except for the potential constraint imposed by the market for corporate control, the market component of the corporate structure is not likely to impose substantial limits on management's ability to self-deal. In contrast to its function with respect to managerial inefficiency, the legal component of the corporate structure has a significant role in constraining management's self-dealing.

---

firm, powered by the ambition of lower managers, and through external forces such as the price of the corporation's stock as a measure of managerial talent. Ultimately, however, the extent of the constraint on top management depends on the extent to which top management can be policed. So long as these managers control their own tenure, the constraint imposed by a potential reduction in the market value of their services if they were forced to change jobs is reduced. . . .

Consistent with this conclusion, the courts (and some statutes) require that management demonstrate the fairness of its dealings with the corporation. But while a judicially enforced fairness standard may reduce management discretion to self-deal in many settings, there are important situations where the potential for management's favoring itself at the expense of shareholders cannot be limited by reference to fairness. For example, where corporate income is diverted to acquiring new businesses rather than being distributed to the shareholders, the question of fairness, as measured by the price paid for the business, is beside the point. Judicially determining whether a particular acquisition was "fair," or whether the funds should instead have been returned to the shareholders by way of dividends, is impossible. . . . [T]he same problem exists when management's self-dealing takes the form of resisting changes in corporate control.

Thus far, the structure of the corporation -- market constraints and a judicially enforced fiduciary duty -- does not effectively limit management's ability to self-deal by protecting its control position. The market for corporate control is the remaining potential source of constraint.

The Market for Corporate Control

Owing to the groundbreaking work of Henry Manne,[a] it is now commonly acknowledged that the market for corporate control is an important mechanism by which management's discretion to favor itself at the expense of shareholders may be constrained. Indeed, where that favoritism is expressed in subtle ways, the market for corporate control may be the only potentially serious force for limiting management discretion. Thus, the fit of this constraint within the legal and market structure of the corporation is of central importance.

The theory of a corporate control market posits that a decrease in corporate profits, whether because of inefficient management or because efficient but self-dealing management has diverted too much income to itself, causes the price of the corporation's stock to decline to a level consistent with the corporation's reduced profitability. This creates an opportunity for entrepreneurial profit. If shares representing control can be purchased at a price which, together with the associated transaction costs, is less than the shares' value following displacement of existing management, then everyone -- other than the management to be displaced -- benefits from the transaction. Selling shareholders receive more for their stock than its value under previous management; new management receives an entrepreneurial reward through the increased value of acquired shares; and society benefits from more efficiently used resources.

Two important conditions are necessary for this happy concurrence of results. First, the market price of the corporation's stock must accurately

---

[a] The original work was Henry Manne, *Mergers and the Market for Corporate Control,* 73 J.Pol.Econ. 110 (1965). Eds.

reflect incumbent management's inefficiency or greed. Second, there must be mechanisms available for displacing incumbent management.

Note on the Causes of Managerial Inefficiency

In the excerpt above, Gilson distinguishes between inefficient management and efficient but self-dealing management. But a somewhat different classification can be useful in assessing the need for *new* management, as opposed to better policing of the current managers. If the managers are simply dumb, or unwilling to work hard, the only available solution is new management. But if the managers are competent, and willing to work, but left on their own will deliver suboptimal effort or divert income to themselves, there is the potential for retaining management, while reducing their discretion and improving their incentives. In this chapter, we focus on replacing management through takeover. Chapter 11 considers an important acquisition form, the leveraged buyout, that attacks the twin problems of discretion and incentives.

In both situations, a takeover is an extreme response to management failure. Board action to replace a poor CEO, or provide better incentives, is quicker, cheaper, and less disruptive than a takeover. Takeovers should thus be regarded as a fall-back mechanism when the board does not act, perhaps because the board has been coopted by the CEO.

Below, we examine the empirical and theoretical support for the management-replacement motive for takeovers. We also consider the factors that affect whether managerial inefficiency is likely to lead to a takeover, or simply to internal management change.

C.   Evaluation: Preacquisition Performance of Bidders and Targets

A role for corporate acquisitions in facilitating the transfer of control over productive assets from inefficient to efficient managers is perfectly compatible with the financial theory discussed in Part I. Superior management generates greater return for equivalent amounts of systematic risk, therefore supporting a higher value for the firm.

This explanation yields a number of testable hypotheses. As James Ellert explains, "[i]f the function of the market for corporate control is to transfer assets from poorly managed firms to well managed ones, then it would not be surprising to observe positive abnormal returns for acquiring firms in periods preceding merger activity."[1] Similarly, if acquisitions are motivated by the opportunity to displace poorly performing management, we

---

[1] James Ellert, *Mergers, Antitrust Law Enforcement and Stockholder Returns*, 31 J.Fin. 715, 723 (1976).

would expect target companies to underperform the market prior to being acquired. The event study methodology can be used to test both hypotheses.

Table 10-1 collect the principal studies of pre-announcement abnormal returns to *target* firms. The overall picture is consistent with the hypothesis that targets are poorly managed, on average.[2]

The general pattern of negative abnormal returns to targets in the preacquisition period is reversed in the months immediately preceding announcement of the transaction, when targets earn *positive* abnormal returns. These positive returns may reflect investor anticipation (sometimes fueled by insider trading) that the target will be acquired, with a premium paid to its shareholders.

Table 10-1
Pretakeover Abnormal Returns to Target Firms
(results are statistically significant at 95% confidence level, except as noted)

Study	Sample Period	Sample Size	Window (months)	CAR
Asquith (1983)	1962-1976	211	$(-16, -3)$	-13.8%
Dodd & Ruback (1977)	1958-1976	136	$(-60, -8)$	2.1% (not signif.)
Ellert (1976)	1950-1970	311	$(-100, -8)$	-11.7%
Langetieg (1978)	1941-1962	149	$(-72, -19)$	-12.6%
Malatesta (1983)	1969-1974	85	$(-60, -25)$	12.6%
			$(-24, -4)$	-8.5% (not signif.)
Mandelker (1974)	1941-1962	252	$(-40, -9)$	-3.0%
Martin & McConnell (1991)	1958-1984	253	$(-48, -3)$	4.3% (not signif.)
				-6.6% industry-adjusted (not signif.)

Table 10-2 collects studies of pretakeover abnormal returns to *acquiring* firms. These studies are also generally consistent with replacement of inefficient management as a takeover motive. Acquirers earn positive pretakeover returns, suggesting that they possess above average management.

---

[2] The studies reported in the table are: Paul Asquith, *Merger Bids, Uncertainty and Stockholder Returns*, 11 J.Fin.Econ. 51 (1983); Peter Dodd & Richard Ruback, *Tender Offers and Stockholder Returns: An Empirical Analysis*, 5 J.Fin.Econ. 351 (1977); Ellert (1976), *supra* note 1; Terence Langetieg, *An Application of a Three-Factor Performance Index to Measure Stockholder Gains from Merger*, 6 J.Fin.Econ. 365 (1978) (window period measured relative to date of merger *completion*); Paul Malatesta, *The Wealth Effect of Merger Activity and the Objective Functions of Merging Firms*, 11 J.Fin.Econ. 155 (1983); Gershon Mandelker, *Risk and Return: The Case of Merging Firms*, 1 J.Fin.Econ. 303 (1974).

Table 10-2

Pretakeover Abnormal Returns to Acquiring Firms

(results are statistically significant at 95% confidence level, except as noted)

Study	Sample Period	Sample Size	Window (months)	CAR
Asquith (1983)	1962-1976	196	$(-16, -3)$	13.4%
Dodd & Ruback (1978)	1958-1976	124	$(-60, -8)$	3.2% (not signif.)
Ellert (1976)	1950-1970	772	$(-100, -8)$	18.5%
Langetieg (1978)	1941-1962	149	$(-72, -7)$	11.1%
Malatesta (1983)	1969-1974	256	$(-60, -25)$	3.9%
			$(-24, -4)$	-1.6% (not signif.)
Mandelker (1974)	1941-1962	241	$(-40, -9)$	3.1%

Some pieces of evidence don't fit, however. On the acquirer's side, recall from Chapter 8 that in the 1980s, the average acquirer earned negative abnormal returns from a takeover. This hardly suggests good management. The failure of conglomerate mergers, discussed in Chapter 9, tells a similar story.

On the target side, there is anecdotal evidence that many targets are well-managed. A representative opinion:

> [I]f you look at the businesses which have been target companies in recent years, you'll find that, by and large, they're successful companies except in limited instances. One doesn't normally buy a company that has a history of losses.[3]

Similarly, in a survey of corporate directors, 84% of the respondents listed "excellent management" as a "major attraction" in selecting a target company for acquisition.[4]

Moreover, if we turn from stock price data to accounting data, we find much weaker support for the claim that targets are less well managed than bidders. A number of studies fail to find a significant correlation between various measures of financial performance and the probability that a firm will become a takeover target. The next article is by two authors who are skeptical about the efficiency gains from hostile takeovers. They surmised that replacement of inefficient managers should be a more important motive in hostile than in friendly takeovers. If so, then hostile takeover targets should show especially poor pretakeover performance. Accordingly, the

---

[3] Raymond Troubh, *Characteristics of Target Companies*, 32 Bus.Law. 1301, 1302 (1977); accord, William Steinbrink, *Management's Response to the Takeover Attempt*, 28 Case W.Res.L.Rev. 882, 892 (1978) ("the common belief is that the typical target companies today are successful participants in their particular fields and are managed by able personnel").

[4] Touche Ross & Co., *The Effect of Mergers, Acquisitions and Tender Offers on American Business: A Touche Ross Survey of Corporate Directors' Opinions* 12 (1981).

authors examined the financial performance of 56 targets of successful hostile takeover bids between 1975 and 1983. The results reinforced their initial doubts about the value of hostile takeovers.[5]

Edward Herman & Louis Lowenstein
THE EFFICIENCY EFFECTS OF HOSTILE TAKEOVERS
in *Knights, Raiders & Targets: The Impact of the Hostile Takeover* 211, 225-27
(John Coffee, Louis Lowenstein & Susan Rose-Ackerman eds.1988)

[I]f takeovers are to impose discipline on a discriminating basis -- otherwise, it is not discipline at all -- the targets should as a group show the significantly inadequate rates of return on capital that would justify such heavy-handed and costly intervention. In short, even before the bid the targets' published results of operations should reveal the existence of these possibilities. Since hostile bidders do not have access to inside information -- they are no better off than we -- there is in fact no better place to begin. . . .

Table 10-3 shows the [average return on equity (ROE)] for all targets for the years $B-5$ to $B-1$ [where B is the year of the takeover bid] on a weighted and also on an unweighted basis. On a weighted basis, the one that best measures the overall economic impact of these tender offers, the targets' ROE is remarkably good. American nonfinancial firms earn on average about 13% on total equity, preferred as well as common. The targets as a group earned about that much, or slightly better, on common equity in the early years before the bid announcement, and then in $B-2$ and $B-1$ they earned 16 to 17% on equity. Those last are "gee whiz" numbers. Returns that high are earned by very few companies -- a fact known, of course, to the bidders.

Table 10-3
Hostile Takeover Target Return on Equity, 1975-1983

Year	$B-5$	$B-4$	$B-3$	$B-2$	$B-1$
Weighted Average	13.1%	11.5%	13.5%	17.2%	16.4%
Unweighted Average	12.2%	11.8%	11.9%	13.0%	12.5%

---

[5] Other studies include Krishna Palepu, *Predicting Takeover Targets: A Methodological and Empirical Analysis*, 8 J.Acct. & Econ. 3 (1986) (studying takeover targets generally between 1971 and 1979; criticizing methodology of earlier studies that found predictive value in financial data); Gerald Davis & Suzanne Stout, *Organizations Theory and the Market for Corporate Control: A Dynamic Analysis of the Characteristics of Large Takeover Targets*, 37 Admin.Sci.Q. 605, 624 (1992) (studying Fortune 500 firms between 1980 and 1990); Timothy Hannan & Stephen Rhoades, *Acquisition Targets and Motives: The Case of the Banking Industry*, 69 Rev.Econ. & Stat. 67, 72 (1987).

We cannot be sure that these 56 targets were not engaged in activities that were especially profitable. In that case, bidders might yet have seen opportunities for substantial improvement, and the disciplinary-synergy thesis of takeovers might yet be validated by the data. We are inclined to doubt any such striking congruence of factors, however, for several reasons. First, our sample is quite large; it covers nine years of bidding; and there is no apparent indication that it is skewed in such a fashion. Second, we have data for five full fiscal years before the bids, a period usually considered sufficient by security analysts to compensate for cyclical factors. Third, on a weighted basis the earnings of the group rose dramatically in the years immediately before the bid, and that is not typical of firms that are underutilizing their resources.

[Boone Pickens, a prominent corporate raider of the early 1980s,] and his academic supporters tell us that potential targets are much in need of restructuring -- a concept that often entails the sale of cyclically depressed businesses, at of course cyclically depressed prices. What we found, however, when we looked first at the early bids, those announced in the years 1975-1978, and then the later ones, those announced in 1981-1983, was a very non-Pickensian pattern. The ROE data in Table 10-4 suggest that there existed targets appropriately ripe for picking a decade ago . . . but that the takeover game greatly changed thereafter. For 21 targets of bids first announced in 1975-1978, the mean return on equity on a weighted basis was a not-very-good 8.8% for the five years ending $B-1$. The two latest years, it is true, showed markedly better results, but the returns for the period as a whole suggest that some of these targets may have offered meaningful opportunities. Calculated on a similar basis, the mean ROE for 25 targets of hostile bids in the years 1981-1983, however, was 15.9%, almost twice as high. And again, the two latest years showed the highest returns, averaging over 18%. These are once again remarkable numbers. . . . [T]hese are not toads but ready-made, off-the-shelf princes, and kissing them [at a typical takeover premium of 80%] would appear to have required little skill but may have run large risks.

Table 10-4
Target Return on Equity, 1975-1978 versus 1981-1983

Year	$B-5$	$B-4$	$B-3$	$B-2$	$B-1$
1975-1978 Bids					
Weighted Average	8.7%	6.0%	7.8%	10.0%	11.5%
Unweighted Average	9.5%	8.8%	10.1%	11.5%	12.8%
1981-1983 Bids					
Weighted Average	14.5%	13.1%	15.3%	19.0%	17.4%
Unweighted Average	13.8%	14.7%	14.7%	14.3%	11.5%

These figures, in short, are scarcely the results one would expect from the better-resource-utilization thesis. Instead, it appears that the supply of promising targets having dried up, the game continued and even accelerated but with much larger, more profitable targets brought into play. . . . The weighted data for the later 1981-1983 bids is perhaps influenced by the presence in the group of four large oil companies that had shown excellent rates of return. Applying industry controls . . . will help to deal with such concerns. But the likely benefits of such controls should not be overstated. Assuming even a modest degree of efficiency in product and capital markets, the consistently high operating returns over a five-year period enjoyed by the 1981-1983 targets make it unlikely that the bidders could have found major sources of real gains. The targets' particularly strong showing in the years $B-2$ and $B-1$ makes it even more unlikely.

[Herman & Lowenstein go on to document that bidders also had above average return on equity. Out of 56 transactions, the bidder had a higher return on equity than its target for the two years ending in $B-1$ in 37 cases (66%). For early takeovers, return on assets increased after the takeover, suggesting gains from the acquisition (whether from synergy, improved management, or other factors). But, for takeovers between 1981 and 1983, the bidder's profitability dropped sharply in the two years after the acquisition, presumably reflecting inability to improve performance sufficiency to justify the high price paid for the target.]

Note: The Variety of Takeover Motives

1. *General Deterrence*. One strength of the Herman & Lowenstein study, as compared to the event studies reported in Tables 10-1 and 10-2, is their explicit effort to consider whether the nature of takeovers has changed over time.

It is certainly plausible that the increased frequency of hostile takeovers, beginning around 1975 and continuing through the 1980s, discouraged managerial shirking, and thus reduced the profit available from displacing the target's managers. If so, manager replacement should have become less important as an acquisition motive over time, in comparison to other motives. This could explain why the only study in Table 10-1 that extends beyond 1976, by Martin & McConnell, finds *positive*, albeit statistically insignificant, pretakeover returns to targets, before industry adjustment.

Christopher James reports evidence from the banking industry consistent with takeover serving a general deterrence role. He compared banks in states whose banking laws severely restricted bank acquisitions with banks in states with fewer restrictions. "[C]onsistent with the hypothesis that the market for corporate control serves to enforce managerial efficiency," James found that "[s]alary expenses, occupancy expenses, and total employment are . . . higher *ceteris paribus* for banks located in states prohibiting acquisitions than for banks in states which do not restrict acquisitions."[6] Similarly, Mary Schranz reports that banks are less profitable in states that severely restrict bank acquisitions.[7] The general deterrence imposed by the threat of a bust-up takeover may also have contributed to the trend toward dediversification in the 1980s, discussed in Chapter 9.[8]

If general deterrence is important, one might expect managerial shirking to increase again in the 1990s, with the apparent demise of hostile takeovers as a significant threat to corporate managers, unless shirking is constrained by other sources of deterrence, such as increased oversight by boards of directors.

2. *Multiple Takeover Motives.* Neither the Herman & Lowenstein study nor the aggregate data reported in Tables 10-1 and 10-2 address the possibility that at any given point in time, some takeovers may be motivated by synergy, while others are motivated by the target's poor management (including unwillingness to engage in a synergistic transaction that might displace the target's managers), and still others reflect misjudgment or empire building by the acquiring firm's managers. The relative weights of these different motives will determine whether targets, *on average*, perform better or worse than the stock market as a whole, or than acquiring firms. Yet all three could be present regardless of the outcome of aggregate studies.[9]

3. *Weighed vs. Unweighted Averages.* A second problem is Herman & Lowenstein's reliance on *weighted* average profitability. This approach gives heavy weight to the largest targets, and may submerge interesting results for smaller targets. Consider, for example, their conclusion, based

---

[6] Christopher James, *An Analysis of the Effect of State Acquisition Laws on Managerial Efficiency: The Case of the Bank Holding Company Acquisitions*, 27 J.L. & Econ. 211, 226 (1984).

[7] Mary Schranz, *Takeovers Improve Firm Performance: Evidence from the Banking Industry*, 101 J.Pol.Econ. 299 (1993).

[8] See generally John Coffee, *Shareholders versus Managers: The Strain in the Corporate Web*, 85 Mich.L.Rev. 1 (1986).

[9] John McConnell & Timothy Nantell, *Corporate Combinations and Common Stock Returns: The Case of Joint Ventures,* 40 J.Fin. 519 (1985), provide indirect evidence that some acquisitions are motivated by synergy rather than displacement of inefficient management. McConnell & Nantell argue that any gains from joint ventures must result from synergy because neither participant's management is displaced. They find that joint venture participants earn positive abnormal returns, similar in magnitude to the returns earned by the parties to an acquisition. This does not mean, however, that all acquisitions have a synergy motive. Joint ventures and *some* acquisitions could be motivated by synergy, while other acquisitions are motivated by displacement of inefficient management. Also, is it clear that a joint venture cannot displace management? Suppose that the joint venture will be managed by personnel from only one of the venturers, or by newly hired personnel. The transaction could then be described as shifting control over corporate resources from one set of managers to another.

on a weighted average, that targets performed unusually well in the 1981-1983 period, especially in last two years before the takeover. The *unweighted* data tell a different story. The profitability of the average target declines from 14.7% in year B−3 to 11.5% in year B−1. Moreover, the sharp difference in year B−1 between the weighted average ROE of 17.4% and the unweighted average of 11.5% suggests that the averages must conceal some real dogs, with ROE's well below the 11.5% average.

4. *The Problem of Researcher Bias.* There is an important lesson here about the need to scrutinize the way in which empirical data is packaged. Authors of all persuasions, whether they be takeover proponents like Bradley, Desai & Kim, whose study we excerpted in Chapter 6, or skeptics like Herman & Lowenstein, often interpret their data in ways consistent with their prior beliefs, when alternative interpretations are possible. If they are intellectually honest, they will present enough data so that readers can draw their own conclusions. Herman & Lowenstein, for example, report both weighted and unweighted data. But authors will not always realize the different ways in which their data could have been reported. And in an advocacy context, such as a lawsuit, one cannot expect candor in presenting data that might undercut the presenter's desired conclusions.

5. *Does High Return on Equity Mean Good Management?* A limitation of the Herman & Lowenstein study, which the authors acknowledge, is their failure to measure profitability on an industry-adjusted basis. The oil industry, for example, saw some of the largest hostile takeovers of the early 1980s. The 1979 jump in the price of oil greatly increased the market value of oil reserves, and the cash flow from those reserves, without affecting book value. Thus, almost all oil companies showed high returns on equity in the early 1980s. Indeed, oil company takeovers may well drive the high *weighted* returns on target equity in Table 10-3 and the 1981-1983 panel of Table 10-4. This does not mean that oil companies were well managed at the time. We must ask instead whether they were earning a good return on the *market value* of their assets.

We must also ask whether oil companies were investing their huge cash flows in new projects with positive NPV. Overall ROE principally reflects past investment decisions. Thus, high ROE can mask poor current investment decisions. The next section addresses the claim that excess cash often burns a hole in managers' pockets. Unless disciplined by the corporate control market or other outside forces, many managers will waste free cash flows on bad investments (such as oil wells in locations with poor prospects), rather than return the surplus to shareholders.

D.   Takeovers and Free Cash Flow: Theory and Evidence

1.   Free Cash Flow Theory

Michael Jensen
THE TAKEOVER CONTROVERSY: ANALYSIS AND EVIDENCE
in *Knights Raiders & Targets: The Impact of the Hostile Takeover* 314, 329-37
(John Coffee, Louis Lowenstein & Susan Rose-Ackerman eds.1988)

The oil industry is large and visible. It is also an industry in which the importance of takeovers in motivating change and efficiency is particularly clear. Therefore, detailed analysis of it provides an understanding of how the market for corporate control helps motivate more efficient use of resources in the corporate sector.

Radical changes in the energy market from 1973 to the late 1970s imply that a major restructuring of the petroleum industry had to occur. These changes include the following:

- A tenfold increase in the price of crude oil from 1973 to 1979.
- Reduced annual consumption of oil in the United States. . . .
- Increased exploration and development costs.
- Increased real interest rates.

. . .   Price increases created large cash flows in the industry. For example, 1984 cash flows of the ten largest [U.S.] oil companies were $48.5 billion, 28% of the total cash flows of the top 200 [public] firms. Consistent with the agency costs of free cash flow, management did not pay out the excess resources to shareholders. Instead, the industry continued to spend heavily on exploration and development even though average returns on these expenditures were below the cost of capital. . . .

The hypothesis that oil industry exploration and development expenditures were too high during this period is consistent with the findings of a study by McConnell & Muscarella.[35] Their evidence indicates that announcements of increases in exploration and development expenditures by oil companies in the period 1975-1981 were associated with systematic decreases in the announcing firm's stock price. Moreover, announcements of decreases in exploration and development expenditures were associated with increases in stock prices. These results are striking in comparison with their evidence that exactly the opposite market reaction occurs with increases and decreases in [capital] expenditures by industrial firms, and SEC evidence that increases in research and development expenditures are associated with increased stock prices.

Additional evidence of the uneconomic nature of the oil industry's exploration and development expenditures is contained in a study by Bernard Picchi of Salomon Brothers (1985). His study of the rates of return on

---

[35] John McConnell & Chris Muscarella, *Corporate Capital Expenditure Decisions and the Market Value of the Firm*, 14 J.Fin.Econ. 399 (1985).

exploration and development expenditures for 30 large oil firms indicated that on average the industry . . . did not earn "even a 10% return on its pretax outlays" in the period 1982-1984. . . . [T]aking the cost of capital to be only 10% on a pretax basis, the industry was realizing on average only 60¢ to 90¢ on every dollar invested in these activities. Picchi concludes:

> For 23 of the companies in our survey, we would recommend *immediate* cuts of perhaps 25-30% in exploration and production spending. It is clear that much of the money that these firms spent last year on petroleum exploration and development yielded subpar financial returns -- even at $30 per barrel, let alone today's $26-$27 per barrel price structure."[38]

The waste associated with excessive exploration and development expenditures explains why buying oil on Wall Street was considerably cheaper than obtaining it by drilling holes in the ground. . . . [Investors were] correctly valuing the wasted expenditures on exploration and development that oil companies were making. When these managerially imposed "taxes" on the reserves were taken into account, the net price of oil on Wall Street was very low. . . .

The fact that oil industry managers tried to invest funds outside the industry is also evidence that they could not find enough profitable projects within the industry to use the huge inflow of resources efficiently. Unfortunately, these efforts failed. The diversification programs involved purchases of companies in retailing (Marcor by Mobil), manufacturing (Reliance Electric by Exxon), office equipment (Vydec by Exxon), and mining (Kennecott by Sohio, Anaconda Minerals by ARCO, Cyprus Mines by Amoco). These acquisitions turned out to be among the least successful of the last decade, partly because of bad luck (e.g., the collapse of the minerals industry) and partly because of a lack of managerial expertise outside the oil industry.

The Effects of Takeovers

Ultimately, the capital markets, through the takeover market, have begun to force managers to respond to the new market conditions. Unfortunately, there is widespread confusion about the important role of takeovers in bringing about the difficult but necessary organizational changes required in the retrenchment. Managers, quite naturally, want large amounts of resources under their control to insulate them from the uncertainties of markets. Retrenchment requires cancellation or delay of ongoing and planned projects. This adjustment affects the careers of the people involved, and the resulting resistance means such changes frequently do not get made without the major pressures often associated with a crisis. A takeover

---

[38] Bernard Picchi, *The Structure of the U.S. Oil Industry: Past and Future* (Salomon Bros.1985) (emphasis in original).

attempt can create the crisis that brings about action where none would otherwise occur.

T. Boone Pickens of Mesa Petroleum perceived early that the oil industry must be restructured. Partly as a result of Mesa's efforts, firms in the industry were led to merge, and in the merging process they paid out large amounts of capital to shareholders, reduced excess expenditures on exploration and development, and reduced excess capacity in refining and distribution. The result has been large gains in efficiency. Total gains to the shareholders in the Gulf/Chevron, Getty/Texaco and DuPont/Conoco mergers, for example, were over $17 billion. . . .

Free Cash Flow Theory of Takeovers

Free cash flow is only one of approximately a dozen theories to explain takeovers, all of which are of some relevance in explaining the numerous forces motivating merger and acquisition activity. The agency cost of free cash flow is consistent with a wide range of data for which there has been no consistent explanation. Here I sketch some empirical predictions of the free cash flow theory for takeovers and mergers and what I believe are the facts that lend it credence.

      . . .   [T]he theory implies that managers of firms with unused borrowing power and large free cash flows are more likely to undertake low-benefit or even value-destroying mergers. Diversification programs generally fit this category, and the theory predicts that they will generate lower total gains. The major benefit of such transactions may be that they involve less waste of resources than if the funds had been invested internally in unprofitable projects.

Acquisitions made with cash or securities other than stock involve payout of resources to (target) shareholders, and this can create net benefits even if the merger creates operating inefficiencies. To illustrate the point, consider an acquiring firm, *A*, with substantial free cash flow that the market expects will be invested in low-return projects with a negative net present value of $100 million. If Firm *A* makes an acquisition of Firm *B* that generates zero synergies but uses up all of Firm *A*'s free cash flow (and thereby prevents its waste), the combined market value of the two firms will rise by $100 million. . . . Extending the argument, we see that acquisitions that have negative synergies of up to $100 million in current value will still increase the combined market value of the two firms. Such negative synergy mergers will also increase social welfare and aggregate productivity . . . . Because the bidding firms are using funds that would otherwise have been spent on low or negative-return projects . . ., they will tend to overpay for the acquisition and thereby transfer most, if not all, of the gains to the target firm's shareholders. In extreme cases they may pay so much that the bidding firm's share price falls, in effect giving the target shareholders more than 100% of the gains. These predictions are consistent with the evidence.

Low-return mergers are more likely to occur in industries with large cash flows whose economics dictate retrenchment. Horizontal mergers (where cash or debt is the form of payment) within declining industries will tend to create value because they facilitate exit -- the cash or debt payments to shareholders of the target firm cause resources to leave the industry directly. Mergers outside the industry are more likely to have low or even negative returns because managers are likely to know less about managing such firms. Oil fits this description, and so does tobacco. Tobacco firms face declining demand as a result of changing smoking habits but generate large free cash flow and have been involved in major diversifying acquisitions recently -- for example, the $5.6 billion purchase of General Foods by Philip Morris. The theory predicts that these acquisition in nonrelated industries are more likely to create negative productivity effects, although these appear to be outweighed by the reductions in waste from [less] internal expansion.

Forest products is another industry with excess capacity and acquisition activity, including the acquisition of St. Regis by Champion International and Crown Zellerbach by Sir James Goldsmith. Horizontal mergers for cash or debt in such an industry generate gains by encouraging exit of resources (through payout) and by substituting existing capacity for investment in new facilities by firms that are short of capacity. Food industry mergers also appear to reflect the expenditure of free cash flow. The industry apparently generates large cash flows with few growth opportunities. It is therefore a good candidate for leveraged buyouts, and these are now occurring; the $6.3 billion Beatrice LBO is the largest ever.

The broadcasting industry generates rents in the form of large cash flows on its licenses and also fits the theory. Regulation limits the overall supply of licenses and the number owned by a single entity. Thus, profitable internal investments are limited, and the industry's free cash flow has been spent on organizational inefficiencies and diversification programs, making the firms takeover targets. The CBS debt for stock exchange and restructuring as a defense against the hostile bid by [Ted] Turner fits the theory, and so does the $3.5 billion purchase of American Broadcasting Company by Capital Cities Communications. Completed cable systems also create agency problems from free cash flows in the form of rents on their franchises and quasi rents on their investment and are likely targets for acquisition and leveraged buyouts. Large cash flows earned by motion picture companies on their film libraries also represent quasi rents and are likely to generate free cash flow problems. The attempted takeover of Disney and its subsequent reorganization is also consistent with the theory. Drug companies with large cash flows from previous successful discoveries and few potential future prospects are also likely candidates for large agency costs of free cash flow.

The theory predicts that value-increasing takeovers occur in response to breakdowns of internal control processes in firms with substantial free cash flow and organizational policies (including diversification programs) that are wasting resources. It predicts hostile takeovers, large increases in leverage, the dismantling of empires with few economies of scale or scope to give them economic purpose (e.g.. conglomerates), and much controversy as current managers object to loss of their jobs or changes in organizational policies forced on them by threat of takeover. . . .

Consistent with the data, free cash flow theory predicts that many acquirers will tend to perform exceptionally well prior to acquisition. This exceptional stock price performance will often be associated with increased free cash flow, which is then used for acquisition programs. . . . Targets will be of two kinds: firms with poor management that have done poorly before the merger, and firms that have done exceptionally well and have large free cash flow, that they refuse to pay out to shareholders. Both kinds of targets seem to exist, but more careful study is required. . . .

The theory predicts that takeovers financed with cash and debt will create larger benefits than those accomplished through exchange of stock. Stock acquisitions do nothing to take up the organizations' financial slack and are therefore unlikely to motivate managers to use resources more efficiently. The recent evidence on takeover premiums is consistent with this prediction.[42]. . .

Palepu (1986), in the best study to date of the determinants of takeover, finds strong evidence consistent with the free cash flow theory of mergers. He studied a sample of 163 [mining and manufacturing] firms that were acquired in the period 1971-1979 and a random sample of 256 firms that were not acquired. . . . [He] finds that poor prior [stock market] performance . . . is significantly related to the probability of takeover and, interestingly, that accounting measures of past performance such as return on equity are unrelated to the probability of takeover. He also finds that firms with a mismatch between growth and resources are more likely to be taken over. These are firms with high growth (measured by average sales growth), low liquidity (measured by the ratio of liquid assets to total assets), and high leverage, and firms with low growth, high liquidity, and low leverage.[a]. . .

The McConnell & Muscarella (1985) findings of positive average market response to announcements of increase in capital expenditure programs in all industries except oil is inconsistent with free cash flow theory. The inconsistency . . . could occur because firms that announce changes in capital expenditure programs tend not to have free cash flow. Resolution of these issues awaits more explicit tests.[b]

---

[42] See James Wansley, William Lane & Ho Yang, *Abnormal Returns to Acquired Firms by Type of Acquisition and Method of Payment*, Fin.Mgmt. 16 (Autumn 1983); James Wansley, William Lane & Ho Yang, *Gains to Bidder Firms in Cash and Securities Transactions*, 22 Fin.Rev. 403 (1987), who find higher returns to targets and to bidders in cash transactions.

[a] Palepu (1986), *supra* note 5.

[b] We consider in Chapter 11 a separate aspect of Jensen's free cash flow model -- his claim that the high debt, such as that incurred in a leveraged buyout, can increase firm value

2.   Evidence: Do Bad Takeovers Beget Good Takeovers?

Jensen theorizes that hostile takeovers displace corporate managers who would otherwise waste free cash flow.   But at the same time, the conglomerate phenomenon suggests that misguided acquisitions are a major way in which cash-rich firms waste cash. The next article is an ingenious effort to reconcile these two effects. The authors develop evidence that an important motive for value-enhancing takeovers is undoing prior value-decreasing takeovers (and replacing the target's managers before they can undertake future value-decreasing takeovers).

Mark Mitchell & Kenneth Lehn
DO BAD BIDDERS BECOME GOOD TARGETS?
98 J.Pol.Econ. 372, 374-86 (1990)*

Anecdotal evidence suggests that the *raison d'etre* of some takeovers is the poor acquisition record of target firms. For example, one stated motive of Sir James Goldsmith's unsuccessful hostile takeover attempt of Goodyear Tire and Rubber Company in October 1986 was his desire to sell Goodyear's petroleum and aerospace divisions and concentrate Goodyear's attention on its tire and rubber operations. Goldsmith offered a premium of approximately $1.13 billion (roughly 30% of the preoffer equity value of Goodyear).

. . . [Goodyear's] 1983 purchase of Celeron Oil for approximately $800 million was its first major petroleum acquisition. On the day of the acquisition announcement, February 8, 1983, Goodyear's stock price suffered an abnormal decline of 10.04%, resulting in a loss of $249 million for Goodyear stockholders. . . . The premium offered by Goldsmith may have recouped losses sustained by Goodyear shareholders 3 years earlier when Goodyear began its diversification into the oil industry.   Goodyear successfully defeated Goldsmith's takeover attempt, but its stock price did not fall to the preoffer level since [Goodyear] instituted a major restructuring program that . . . included the sale of Celeron Oil.

To determine whether the Goodyear case generalizes to a large sample of takeovers, we examine the stock price reactions to acquisitions made by two sets of firms during 1982-86: firms that become targets of takeover attempts after their acquisitions ("targets") and a control group of [acquiring] firms that do not receive takeover bids during the sample period ("nontargets"). Within the sample of targets, we estimate the stock price

---

by reducing managers' discretion over cash flow.

effects associated with acquisitions [by] firms that later receive hostile bids ("hostile targets") and acquisitions [by] firms that later receive friendly bids ("friendly targets"). The following results are revealed.

1. For the entire sample, the average stock price effect associated with acquisition announcements is not significantly different from zero. . . .

2. . . . The stock prices of targets *decline* significantly when they announce acquisitions (-1.27% over the $[-5, 1]$ window and -3.38% over the $[-5, 40]$ window), and the stock prices of nontargets *increase* significantly when they announce acquisitions (0.82% and 3.32%, respectively). Within the sample of targets, this stock price effect is similar in magnitude for hostile targets and friendly targets.

3. For the entire sample of acquisitions, the average stock price effect associated with acquisitions that subsequently are divested is significantly lower (-1.53% and -4.01%, respectively) than the corresponding stock price effect associated with acquisitions that are not subsequently divested (0.56% and 1.89%, respectively). This difference is especially striking for the sample of acquisitions by target firms. The average stock price effect associated with acquisitions made by targets that subsequently are divested following the reception of their bids, either by their acquiring firms or by themselves, is -2.07% and -7.04%, respectively. . . .

4. . . . [W]ith equity value and the percentage of equity held by management held constant, the probability that a firm is a target, especially a hostile target, during 1982-88 is inversely and significantly related to the stock price effects associated with announcements of the firm's acquisitions: The more negative these effects, the higher the likelihood of a subsequent takeover attempt.

These results suggest that one source of value in many corporate takeovers, especially hostile takeovers, is recoupment of target equity value that had been lost because of the targets' poor acquisition strategies . . . . Additionally, the divestiture findings suggest that when companies announce acquisitions, the stock market provides an unbiased forecast of the likelihood that the assets will be ultimately divested.

Description of Data

The sample for this study consists of 1,158 public corporations in 51 industries covered by *Value Line* during the fourth quarter of calendar year 1981. . . . The sample includes 64.4% of the companies in the 1981 S&P 500 index and 75.2% of the companies in the 1981 *Fortune* 500. Each of the 1,158 firms was classified into one of four groups on the basis of whether the firm was a takeover target during January 1980-July 1988: (1) nontargets; (2) hostile targets; (3) friendly targets; and (4) miscellaneous firms. The 600 nontarget firms (51.8% of the sample) did not receive friendly or hostile bids, pay greenmail, file bankruptcy, significantly restructure, or become subject to large unsolicited open-market purchases. The hostile target group consists of 228 firms (19.7%) that were targets of successful and unsuccessful hostile tender offers, proxy contests (in which the dissenting shareholder sought control) and large unsolicited open-market purchases in which the purchaser attempted to secure control. The friendly target group contains 240 firms (20.7% of the sample) that were targets of successful and unsuccessful friendly tender offers, mergers, and leveraged buy-outs. . . .

The Dow Jones Broadtape was then examined for announcements of acquisitions by the 1,158 firms during 1982-86, including acquisitions of private companies, and purchases of assets, divisions, subsidiaries, and stock of other companies. We limit the sample to acquisitions in which the disclosed purchased price was at least 5% of the market value of the acquiring firm's common equity. . . .

[M]ost firms in the sample did not make acquisitions of an amount that was at least 5% of their equity value during 1982-86. During this period, 280 firms (24% of the sample) made 401 acquisitions, [including]: (1) 232 acquisitions by 166 nontargets (28% of all nontargets); (2) 113 acquisitions by 77 targets (16% of all targets); (3) 70 acquisitions by 48 hostile targets (21% of all hostile targets); (4) 43 acquisitions by 29 friendly targets (12% of all friendly targets); and (5) 56 acquisitions by 38 miscellaneous firms (42% of all miscellaneous firms). Although these data might appear to indicate that nontarget firms make acquisitions more often than targets, it is inappropriate to compare these frequencies directly since the sample period is effectively longer for nontargets than for targets. . . .

Since 79% of the hostile targets did not make a large acquisition during the period preceding the reception of their bids, at best, the bad bidder explanation of hostile takeovers can explain only part of the reason for these transactions. . . .

Stock Market Analysis of Acquisitions

We employ event-study methodology to measure the stock price effects associated with announcement of acquisitions. Using the [CRSP] daily returns tapes, we estimate the abnormal return (ϵ_{it}) for each acquiring firm during the period 20 days preceding the event date through 40 days following the event date. Abnormal returns are computed as

$$\epsilon_{it} \quad = \quad R_{it} - \alpha_i - \beta_i \cdot R_{mt}$$

where R_{it} is the return to firm i at time t, R_{mt} is the return to the CRSP value-weighted index of NYSE and AMEX stocks, and α_i and β_i are market model parameter estimates from the period 170 through 21 trading days preceding the event date.[a]

---

[a] This is the standard event study methodology reviewed in Chapter 6.

The event date for each acquisition is the first date on which the Dow Jones Broadtape reports a story about the acquisition. These initial stories range from reports that the acquiring firm is rumored to be interested in making the acquisition, often with no price disclosed, to reports that both the bidder and the target definitively agreed to the acquisition. We then average the daily abnormal returns across firms in each group to obtain the portfolio abnormal return,

$$AAR_t \quad = \quad [\sum_{i=1}^{n} \epsilon_{it}]/n$$

where n is the number of firms in each portfolio of interest, and cumulate over various windows to obtain the cumulative abnormal return,

$$CAAR \quad = \quad \sum_{t=1}^{T} AAR_t$$

where T is the length of the event window. In the absence of abnormal performance, the expected value of the *AAR* and *CAAR* equals zero.[3]

Stock Price Performance of Acquiring Firms

Table 10-5 displays the announcement day *AAR* and corresponding *CAAR*s associated with the announcements of acquisitions made by each [group] of firms [for three different window periods].[b]. . .

. . . [T]he stock price effects associated with announcements of acquisitions made by target firms differs significantly from the stock price effects associated with announcements of acquisitions made by nontarget firms. The announcement day *AAR* associated with 113 acquisitions made by all target firms is −0.78% [and is statistically significant at the 1% level]. The [multiday CARs are also negative and] statistically significant at the 1% level. Furthermore, the CAR becomes significantly more negative when the event window extends beyond the acquisition announcements. These data indicate that the market reacted negatively to the initial announcements of these acquisitions and suggest that as the market learned more about these

---

[3] We construct standardized test statistics to assess the statistical significance of stock market abnormal performance. We divide each abnormal return by the square root of its forecast variance . . . to form a standardized abnormal return, $sar_{it} = \epsilon_{it}/\sigma_i$. The test statistic for the AR . . . [and] the CAR is [a z-statistic constructed as described in Chapter 6]. We also conduct nonparametric tests to test the robustness of the results reported. These tests include a test for the percentage of the abnormal returns that are positive and the Wilcoxon signed rank test. The statistical significance of the results reported throughout the text is robust with respect to these nonparametric tests.

[b] The authors also report results for [−1,1] and [−20,40] windows, and for the miscellaneous category of firms, which are omitted below.

acquisitions during the succeeding weeks (e.g., purchase price, definitiveness of the acquisition, and resulting synergy), the market further devalued the acquiring firms.

[T]he results are especially significant for hostile targets.   The announcement day *AAR* associated with 70 acquisitions made by hostile targets is −0.95%, and the *CAAR* ranges from −3.37% [−5,40] to −1.3% ([−5,1]). All the estimates are significant at the 5% level or higher. These results compare with the corresponding results for acquisitions by friendly targets.   The *AAR* on the announcement day for 43 acquisitions made by friendly targets is −0.50% and is significant [only] at the 10% level. . . .

The abnormal stock price performance associated with 232 acquisitions made by nontarget firms contrasts sharply with the results for target firms. The announcement day *AAR* for nontarget firms is 0.09%. . . . The *CAAR* for nontargets increases and [is] statistically significant when the event window extends beyond the day after the announcement of the acquisitions, a result that contrasts sharply with the corresponding result for target firms.
. . .

Table 10-5

Abnormal Returns to Firms Announcing Acquisitions, 1982-86

(z statistics in parentheses; % positive returns listed below z-statistics)

(* = significant at 5% level; ** = significant at 1% level)

Category	Sample	Event Window [days]		
		[0]	[−5, 1]	[−5, 40]
Entire Sample	401	−0.21%* ($z = -2.18$) 42% pos.	0.14% ($z = .53$) 50% pos.	0.70% ($z = 1.05$) 54% pos.
Nontargets	232	0.09% ($z = .66$) 45% pos.	0.82%* ($z = 2.42$) 56% pos.	3.32%* ($z = 3.80$) 63% pos.
All targets	113	−0.78%** ($z = -4.59$) 40% pos.	−1.27%** ($z = -2.82$) 38% pos.	−3.38%** ($z = -2.93$) 38% pos.
Hostile targets	70	−0.95%** ($z = -4.64$) 39% pos.	−1.34%* ($z = -2.46$) 36% pos.	−3.37%* ($z = -2.42$) 39% pos.
Friendly targets	43	−.50 ($z = -1.68$) 42% pos.	−1.17% ($z = -1.47$) 42% pos.	−3.39 ($z = -1.67$) 37% pos.

The empirical results from Table 10-5 indicate that the stock market negatively values acquisitions by firms that become takeover targets, especially hostile targets, whereas it positively values acquisitions by firms that never did become takeover targets during the sample period. Figure 10-

1 graphically depicts the difference in the serial pattern of *CAAR*s for hostile targets, friendly targets, nontargets, miscellaneous firms, and the entire sample for the [−5, 40] window. . . .

Figure 10-1
Stock Price Reactions to Acquisition Announcements, 1982-86

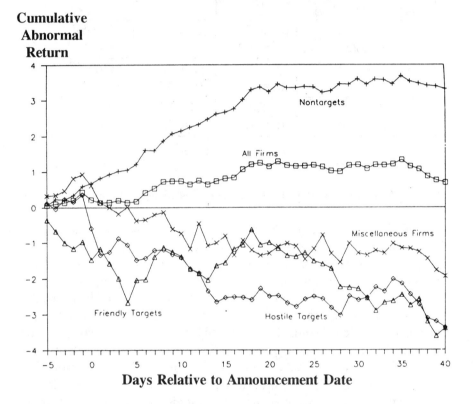

Days Relative to Announcement Date

The . . . *difference* in abnormal stock returns associated with acquisitions by targets and nontargets also is significant. Table 10-6 lists the differences in the announcement day *AAR* and corresponding *CAAR*s associated with acquisitions made by *(a)* all targets and nontargets, *(b)* hostile targets and nontargets, and *(c)* friendly targets and nontargets. The difference in stock price abnormal performance is statistically significant at the .01 level for the comparisons involving all targets and nontargets, and hostile targets and nontargets. . . . The difference is significant for friendly targets and nontargets at the [.05 level or higher for the longer event windows].

Table 10-6
Differences in Abnormal Returns,
Acquisition Announcements, 1982-86

(z-statistics in parentheses; * = signif. at 5% level; ** = signif. at 1% level)

Comparison Groups	Event Window		
	[0]	[−5,1]	[−5,40]
All targets v. nontargets	0.87%** ($z = 3.99$)	2.09%** ($z = 3.71$)	6.70%** ($z = 4.63$)
Hostile targets v. nontargets	1.04%** ($z = 4.23$)	2.16%** ($z = 3.37$)	6.69%** ($z = 4.07$)
Friendly targets v. nontargets	0.59% ($z = 1.80$)	1.99%* ($z = 2.30$)	6.71%** ($z = 3.04$)

Note: Empirical Tests of Free Cash Flow Theory

1. *Can Takeover Losses Be Recouped?* A takeover of a bad bidder, and divestiture of its misguided acquisitions, can recoup some but not all of the acquirer's losses. The amounts paid in those acquisitions have been irrevocably transferred to the shareholders of the original targets. Sometimes, those amounts will exceed the sale price available in a later divestiture. Moreover, bad business decisions by the original acquirer can create unrecoverable economic losses. Goodyear, for example, compounded the error of acquiring Celeron Oil by building a $1.7 billion oil pipeline that was designed to take Alaskan and offshore California oil from California to Texas refineries. California lawmakers put the kibosh on those plans by persuading the federal government not to permit oil drilling off the California coast, and forbidding tankers from unloading Alaskan oil off the California coast. Goodyear has been unable to find a buyer for the largely empty (and destined to remain so) pipeline.[10]

2. *The Use of an Extended Window Period.* Mitchell & Lehn's results become much stronger when they extend the event window beyond the initial announcement date. What might explain this? Is it consistent with the efficient capital markets hypothesis?

3. *Evidence from Tobin's q Studies.* Reread the discussion in Chapter 8.D.2 of event studies that measure announcement period gains to acquirers and targets for samples partitioned based on the prior performance of the

---

[10] See, e.g., Jonathan Hicks, *At Goodyear, A Turnaround of Spirits and Well as Profits*, N.Y.Times, Aug. 9, 1992, § 3, at 4.

acquirer and the target. These studies provide evidence that gains are highest if acquirers with high Tobin's q (the ratio of market value to replacement value of tangible assets) buy low-q targets, and lowest if low-q targets acquire high-q targets. Other things equal, a lower Tobin's q suggests that managers are producing less value from the same level of assets, which suggests managerial inefficiency. These studies do not measure whether the target's management is replaced. But they are consistent with replacing poor target managers as a motive in some takeovers, and empire building by poor acquiring firm managers as an explanation for other takeovers.

Tobin's q can also proxy for poor reinvestment opportunities (and thus more free cash flow), since, other things equal, a firm with more profitable reinvestment opportunities will have a higher q. Thus, these studies are also consistent with the free cash flow hypothesis that firms with high cash flow will tend to waste it through misguided acquisitions, and will also be good takeover targets.[11]

4. *Which Firms Waste Cash?* Lang, Stulz & Walkling take the further step of stratifying their sample of tender offers both by Tobin's q and by a measure of free cash flow.[12] They find that bidder stock price losses are concentrated in firms with *both* industry-adjusted Tobin's $q < 1$ and free cash flow above the median for their sample. These bidders suffer average announcement period stock price losses of 5.9%. For bidders with Tobin's q above the industry average, there was no significant difference in bidder returns between low cash flow and high cash flow firms, and the sign of the difference was the opposite of that predicted by free cash flow theory: high cash flow, high-q firms earn average returns of 5.4%, while low cash flow, high-q returns averaged 0.5% returns. This suggests that high-q firms do not waste cash, either because they are well-managed, or because they have profitable internal investment opportunities.

5. *Evidence from Cash Windfalls.* Blanchard, Lopez-de-Silanes & Shleifer study a small sample of 11 firms that received cash windfalls through litigation. The firms used the cash principally to diversify (typically with poor results), increase management compensation, and make targeted repurchases of shares from large shareholders (who might threaten the managers' control). Dividend increases were trivial and only one firm engaged in a large nontargeted share repurchase. Moreover:

---

[11] The principal studies are Larry Lang, Rene Stulz & Ralph Walkling, *Managerial Performance, Tobin's q and the Gains from Successful Tender Offers*, 24 J.Fin.Econ. 137 (1989); Larry Lang, Rene Stulz & Ralph Walkling, *A Test of the Free Cash Flow Hypothesis: The Case of Bidder Returns*, 29 J.Fin.Econ. 315 (1991); Randall Morck, Andrei Shleifer & Robert Vishny, *Do Managerial Objectives Drive Bad Acquisitions?*, 45 J.Fin. 31 (1990); Henri Servaes, *Tobin's Q and the Gains from Takeovers*, 46 J.Fin. 409 (1991).

[12] Lang, Stulz & Walkling (1991), *supra* note 11. The cash flow measure is the ratio of net income plus depreciation minus dividends to the book value of total assets.

[The four] firms which sat on the cash and did not waste it themselves were acquired within a few years. This finding suggests that the only equilibrium strategy for managerial firms [that do not want to return cash to shareholders] is to waste the cash, for if they do not, another managerial firm will buy them and waste the cash for them. Diversification makes the firm less attractive to these acquirers than holding cash.[13]

6. *Do Managers Knowingly Overpay?* The rhetoric of empire building and managerial shirking can leave the impression that cash-rich managers deliberately embark on a strategy of making acquisitions (and overpaying to do so if necessary) instead of returning cash to shareholders. It seems more likely that managers convince themselves that they are making good acquisitions, when they are not. Ekkehart Boehmer & Jeffry Netter provide evidence consistent with this more charitable view of managerial motives.[14] It is well established that managers generally outperform the market when they trade their own company's stock.[15] Boehmer & Netter study inside purchases and sales by acquirers and report that:

> [M]anagers of [acquiring] firms that were later subject to hostile bids . . . tend to be more optimistic and less successful (in terms of the stock performance after their trades) than insiders in [acquiring] firms that were not [later] subject to a hostile bid.[16]

More specifically, inside purchases by managers of acquiring firms that did not later become targets produced positive abnormal returns averaging 4.5% ($t = 3.80$) over the next 50 trading days, while inside purchases by managers of acquiring firms that later became hostile targets produced average abnormal returns of -1.4% ($t = -1.41$).[17]

Similarly, Nejat Seyhun reports that bidder managers increase their purchases of their own firm's stock prior to making acquisitions. This effect is strongest when the subsequent acquisition increases the bidder's stock price. But it is also present for a subsample of 42 firms whose subsequent acquisition led to a 5% or greater *decrease* in the bidder's stock price. Seyhun concludes that his evidence supports hubris rather than deliberate overpayment by acquiring firm managers.[18]

---

[13] Olivier Blanchard, Florencio Lopez-de-Silanes & Andrei Shleifer, *What Do Firms Do with Cash Windfalls?* (NBER working paper No. 4258, 1993). To be sure, the authors' rhetoric goes beyond their data. We don't know why these four firms were acquired, or by whom, nor that diversification would have "saved" them.

[14] Ekkehart Boehmer & Jeffry Netter, *Market vs. Insider Perceptions of Corporate Acquisitions: Evidence from Insider Trading* (U.Ga. working paper, June 1992).

[15] See, e.g., Joseph Finnerty, *Insiders and Market Efficiency*, 31 J.Fin. 1141 (1976); Nejat Seyhun, *Insiders' Profits, Cost of Trading, and Market Efficiency*, 16 J.Fin.Econ. 189 (1986).

[16] Boehmer & Netter (1992), *supra* note 14, at 1.

[17] *Id.* table 6.

[18] H. Nejat Seyhun, *Do Bidder Managers Knowingly Pay too Much for Target Firms*, 63

E.   Synergy vs. Manager Replacement as Takeover Motives

The discussion thus far should make it clear that distinguishing between synergy, management replacement, and other takeover motives is a difficult task, especially since multiple motives may be present in the same transaction, and one form of poor management is resisting (or not seeking out) a synergistic business combination. The studies below shed additional light on this question. They also take the important step of measuring *industry-adjusted* performance.

Martin & McConnell: Kenneth Martin & John McConnell take the management displacement concept literally: Acquisitions where the target's CEO was replaced within two years after the transaction are treated as displacement motivated; all other acquisitions are treated as synergy motivated. The results support the hypothesis that displacement of inefficient management is an important (but hardly exclusive) motive for takeovers. Over a long preacquisition window period (-48 months, -3 months), *displacement* targets suffer cumulative industry-adjusted losses of 15.4%, while *non-displacement* targets realize industry-adjusted gains of 4.4%. The losses by displacement targets, and the difference between displacement and non-displacement targets, were significant ($p < .01$).[19]

Moreover, *industry-adjusted* performance for both types of targets were significantly worse than non-adjusted performance. Average CARs to the full sample over this window are 4.3% without industry adjustment, compared to -6.6% with industry adjustment, with large differences in both the displacement and non-displacement subsamples. This suggests that takeovers tend to be aimed at laggards within a given industry, but are not necessarily concentrated in poorly performing industries.

With respect to the importance of management displacement as an acquisition motive, the authors found that in 56% of tender offers occurring between 1958 and 1984, the target's most senior executive was replaced within two years after the acquisition, an annual turnover rate about four times that of the five-year period prior to the acquisition. Surprisingly, CEO replacement was as common in friendly as in hostile takeovers.[20]

Morck, Shleifer & Vishny: Morck, Shleifer & Vishny take a different approach to identifying which acquisitions are motivated by the opportunity to displace inefficient management. They hypothesize that hostile

---

J.Bus. 439 (1990).

[19] Kenneth Martin & John McConnell, *Corporate Performance, Corporate Takeovers, and Managerial Turnover*, 46 J.Fin. 671 (1991).

[20] In contrast, Julian Franks & Colin Mayer, *Hostile Takeovers in the UK and the Correction of Managerial Failure* (London Bus.Sch. working paper, 1992), report a much higher rate of target CEO turnover in hostile than in friendly takeovers in the UK.

acquisitions are likely to be displacement motivated, since target managers are likely to resist displacement, while friendly acquisitions are more likely to be synergy motivated.[21] They study the 82 members of the 1980 Fortune 500 that were acquired between 1981 and 1985, 40 in hostile and 42 in friendly transactions. Martin & McConnell's finding of similar rates of CEO replacement casts doubt on whether bid hostility is a good proxy for a management replacement motive, but it is nonetheless interesting to examine how friendly and hostile takeovers differ.

Morck, Shleifer & Vishny's data support the proposition that displacement of inefficient management is an important motive for hostile takeovers. Firms that were subject to hostile takeovers had a significantly lower Tobin's q than either firms who were subject to friendly takeovers or members of the 1980 Fortune 500 who were not acquired during the sample period. On average, targets of hostile takeovers had lower Tobin's q than the average firm in their industry *and* were concentrated in low-q industries.[22]

In a later article, the authors compare the characteristics of the 93 companies within their Fortune 500 sample that underwent a complete turnover of management between 1981 and 1985 *without* being subject to a takeover, to the characteristics of firms that were taken over.[23] They report interesting differences between firms whose managers are displaced through a hostile takeover and firms where managers are replaced by board of directors:

> The board of directors looks at other firms in the same industry to evaluate the performance of its firm's managers, and replaces top managers when the firm underperforms its industry, that is, when the managers can be blamed with some confidence. On the other hand, when the whole industry is suffering, the board is reluctant to make changes. . . . In these cases, a hostile bidder often buys the firm and implements profit-increasing changes. . . . More generally, takeovers come to play a role in replacing managers who the board is unable or unwilling to discipline, as in firms with one-man management teams.[24]

---

[21] Morck, Randall, Andrei Shleifer & Robert Vishny, *Characteristics of Targets of Hostile and Friendly Takeovers*, in *Corporate Takeovers: Causes and Consequences* 101 (Alan Auerbach ed.1988).

[22] The industry's low q had more predictive power than the company's low industry-adjusted q.

[23] Randall Morck, Andrei Shleifer & Robert Vishny, *Alternative Mechanisms for Corporate Control*, 79 Am.Econ.Rev. 842 (1989). A complete turnover of management occurs if "none of the corporate officers who signed the annual report in 1980 also signs in 1985." *Id.* at 843.

[24] *Id.* at 842. A caveat to this conclusion: Martin & McConnell report that replacement of the target's CEO is as common in friendly as in hostile takeovers. Martin & McConnell (1991), *supra* note 19, at 684. This casts doubt on the assumption that hostile takeovers are necessarily more disciplinary in nature than friendly takeovers.

Industry-Specific Studies.   Allen & Sirmans find significant positive abnormal returns, averaging 5.8% over a (−1, 0) window, to Real Estate Investment Trusts (REITs) that acquire other REITs between 1977 and 1983. They argue that these gains most likely reflect improved management of the target, because the nature of the REIT industry makes significant synergy implausible.[25]

F.   Post-Acquisition Performance of Takeover Targets

The studies discussed above share a common deficiency: They assess whether displacing poor managers is an important takeover *motive*, but do not assess whether the new managers *in fact* do any better than the old managers. One can answer this question only by studying the *post-takeover* performance of targets in acquisitions where management replacement is a likely takeover motive.

This, however, is a difficult task. Acquirers are typically much larger than targets. Thus examining the post-takeover performance of the acquirer as a whole will shed little light on the performance of the *target's* business. In most cases, the target will have no post-acquisition stock price performance to measure, and accounting data on the performance of a segment of the acquiring firm is generally sparse.

It is possible to examine the stock price behavior of *targets* for *partial* takeovers, when the acquirer acquires control, *but a minority interest remains in public hands.*   The market value of these minority shares can then be measured.   Moreover, such takeovers are relatively unlikely to involve synergy, which would normally require integration of the acquirer's and target's business in a manner that is difficult when the target remains as a separate company with separate shareholders.

If the motivation of a successful tender offer is to increase the efficiency of the target firm, the value of the target firm should increase substantially following the acquisition. The data are consistent with this hypothesis. For example, Michael Bradley finds an average revaluation of the target's shares of 36% following a partial tender offer.[26] However, this revaluation may partly reflect anticipation of a subsequent freezeout transaction, in which the tender offeror buys the minority shares at a premium.

Consistent with post-tender-offer revaluation of the target's stock, Larry Lang, Rene Stulz & Ralph Walkling report that Tobin's q also increases, for a small sample of about a dozen targets that remain public after a tender offer.   This effect persists for 5 years after the acquisition,

---

[25] Paul Allen & C.F. Sirmans, *An Analysis of Gains to Acquiring Firm's Shareholders: The Special Case of REITs*, 18 J.Fin.Econ. 175 (1987).

[26] Michael Bradley, *Interim Tender Offers and the Market for Corporate Control*, 53 J.Bus. 345, 364 (1980); see also Gregg Jarrell & Michael Bradley, *The Economic Effects of Federal and State Regulations of Cash Tender Offers*, 23 J.L. & Econ. 371, 392-93 (1980).

suggesting that the expectation of a freezeout transaction is not a full explanation. They explain:

> [This] result is consistent with the view that the bidder's equity stake improves target management and/or creates valuable synergies, [but] the effect of market movements on a small . . . sample cannot be ruled out as an explanation.[27]

A puzzle in the stock price data is that the post-takeover value of the target's shares is less than the price paid by the acquirer in the tender offer. This could be consistent either with overpayment, or with anticipation by the minority shareholders that the new majority shareholder will use its controlling stake to appropriate more than its prorata share of the benefits from the takeover.[28]

Concluding Notes

1. One tends to take for granted that when managerial replacement is a takeover motive, it is the *target's* managers who are slated for replacement. But this need not always be so. For example, an expressed motive in AT&T's $7 billion hostile acquisition of NCR in 1991 was the desire to have NCR's managers run AT&T's money-losing computer operations.[29]

2. We have thus far focused on stock price performance as a measure of the pretakeover performance of acquirers and targets. An alternate measure of performance, that has produced some interesting results, is Tobin's q. Larry Lang, Rene Stulz & Ralph Walkling report that both bidders and targets in a sample of tender offers between 1968 and 1986 had *below-average* Tobin's q's, and had declining q ratios in the 5 years preceding the acquisition, with the decline greater for targets. These results suggest poor management of both acquirers and targets. They are consistent with the stock price evidence for targets, but are unexpected for bidders, and deserve further exploration.[30]

---

[27] Lang, Stulz & Walkling (1989), *supra* note 11, at 144.

[28] "The checks on unfair dealing by the parent are few. In theory, of course, the fairness of the parent's behavior is subject to the check of judicial review; but in practice such review is difficult even where the courts have the will to engage in it, and they often lack the will." Melvin Eisenberg, *The Structure of the Corporation* 309 (1976) (citations omitted).

[29] See L.J. Davis, *When A.T.&T. Plays Hardball*, N.Y. Times Mag., June 9, 1991, pt. II, at 14. See also Bryan Burrough & John Heylar, *Barbarians at the Gate: The Fall of RJR Nabisco* (1990) (recounting the rise of Ross Johnson to become head first of Standard Brands, then of Nabisco after Nabisco bought Standard Brands, then of RJR Nabisco after RJ Reynolds bought Nabisco). See generally Walter Novaes & Luigi Zingales, *Buying versus Hiring: A New Theory of Mergers* (CRSP working paper 372, 1992).

[30] Lang, Stulz & Walkling (1989), *supra* note 11, at 143. Davis & Stout (1992), *supra* note 5, at 624, find that during the 1980-1990 period, a low market-to-book ratio (which is highly correlated with low Tobin's q) significantly increased the likelihood that Fortune 500

3. Joseph Grundfest collects anecdotal evidence of the inefficiencies caused by poor management at RJR Nabisco, Goodyear, Allied-Signal, Tenneco, and General Motors, buttressed by one-company event studies showing statistically significant price jumps when a CEO is unexpectedly replaced. These case studies indicate the potential for gains, at least at some firms, from replacing incumbent management.[31]

---

firms would become takeover targets. They found no significant difference between friendly and hostile targets.

[31] Joseph Grundfest, *Just Vote No: A Minimalist Strategy for Dealing with Barbarians Inside the Gates*, 45 Stan.L.Rev. 857, 873-901 (1993). See also George Baker, *Beatrice: A Study in the Creation and Destruction of Value*, 47 J.Fin. 1081 (1992).

CHAPTER 11: LEVERAGED BUYOUTS AND RECAPITALIZATIONS

The 1980s saw the emergence of a new transaction form -- the leveraged buyout or LBO. Leveraged buyouts, essentially nonexistent before 1980, grew to involve total consideration of almost $50 billion per year between 1986 and 1989.[1] For their supporters, LBOs were more than just a new way to finance an acquisition -- they were a new and improved form of corporate organization. Michael Jensen, for example, christened the new entity an "LBO Association," and argued that "[t]he publicly held corporation . . . has outlived its usefulness in many sectors of the economy and is being eclipsed."[2]

For their detractors, LBOs and other highly leveraged "junk-bond, bust-up" takeovers symbolized everything that was wrong with takeovers in the 1980s -- the "greed decade." For them, leveraged acquisitions were a "speculative binge" that enriched investment bankers and financial raiders, but stripped companies of the cash that they need to invest in long-term growth.[3]

The detractors predicted that the wave of leveraged buyouts was a bubble that would soon burst, and they were right. The dollar volume of leveraged acquisitions plummeted from a peak of $67 billion in 1989 to only $5.5 billion in 1991 and $7 billion in 1992. Many companies that underwent LBOs in the late 1980s went bankrupt, or went through financial restructurings outside of the bankruptcy courts.

The collapse of the LBO bubble does not, however, end the debate on the value of LBOs as a transaction form. There were many spectacularly successful LBOs, especially in the early 1980s. Perhaps the LBO structure is sensible, but only (i) for some firms, and (ii) at the right price. As the 1980s progressed, and investors watched the early successes, perhaps lenders relaxed their standards too far, and the LBO form was simply applied to unsuitable companies at unrealistic prices.

The goal of this chapter is to evaluate critically the LBO as a form of corporate organization and assess how much truth lies behind the bold rhetoric of the supporters and opponents of leveraged acquisitions. Section A begins by explaining how a leveraged buyout, and its close cousin, the leveraged recapitalization, works. Section B develops the theory for why LBOs might lead to efficiency gains, even though they have little or no potential for operating synergy. Section C reviews the empirical evidence on whether LBOs have produced the efficiency gains that the theory predicts are possible. Section D then returns to theory -- this time the theory of why LBOs can be economic mistakes. It reviews the collapse of the LBO form

---

[1] See Table 1-12.

[2] Michael Jensen, *Eclipse of the Public Corporation*, Harv.Bus.Rev. 61, 68 (Sept./Oct.1989) (excerpted later in this chapter).

[3] Martin Lipton, *Is This the End of Takeovers?* (Wachtell, Lipton, Rosen & Katz letter to clients, Oct. 28, 1988).

after 1989, the most likely causes of the collapse, and the implications of the collapse for the future viability of LBOs.

A.   What is a Leveraged Buyout?

1.   Conventional Leveraged Buyouts

In a traditional corporate acquisition, one operating company buys another. A central feature of a leveraged buyouts is that the acquirer is a *shell* company -- a company with no prior operating history, formed solely to conduct this acquisition. A second central feature of the leveraged buyout is *high leverage* -- the shell company borrows most of the purchase price.

A typical leveraged buyout works as follows. A merchant bank -- the best known is Kohlberg, Kravis, Roberts & Co. (KKR) -- agrees to acquire Targetco for $100 million. The merchant bank forms a new company, Shellco, which will actually make the acquisition. The merchant bank, has previously raised funds from investors for the purpose of making acquisitions like this. It draws on this "LBO equity fund" to invest $10 million in Shellco stock. Shellco then borrows the rest of the funds it needs to complete the transaction.

Targetco can be either a stand-alone company, or a subsidiary or division of a larger company. If Targetco is a subsidiary or division, the transaction is sometimes called a *divisional buyout*. In a divisional buyout, the selling parent company will sometimes invest in Shellco's debt or equity, either to facilitate completion of the transaction, or because it wants to retain an equity interest in the division that is being sold.

Typically, the merchant bank that arranges the LBO invites Targetco's managers to purchase some of the stock of Shellco. A leveraged buyout in which the target's management participates is often called a *management buyout (MBO)*: most *LBOs* are also *MBOs*. The high leverage that Shellco uses to buy Targetco reduces the dollar cost to buy a given percentage of Shellco's stock. Thus, even if Targetco's managers have limited wealth, they still can buy a significant fraction of Shellco's stock. Sometimes, the merchant bank will bring in its own management team, but here too the new managers will usually buy a substantial fraction of Shellco's stock.

LBOs are generally friendly transactions, although whole-company LBOs are often undertaken in response to a hostile takeover bid, or a perceived threat of a hostile bid. Sometimes, especially for defensive LBOs, Targetco's management takes the initiative in proposing an MBO, and finds an investment bank that can assist in arranging financing.

Typically some of Shellco's debt will be in the form of bank loans. The remainder will come from private placements of debt with other lenders, often insurance companies, or from sale of debt securities to the public. The banks will generally hold the most senior debt, with the remaining debt subordinated in priority of payment to the bank loans. Shellco's subordinated debt will have a substantial risk of default and a correspondingly high interest rate. If sold to the public and therefore rated by debt rating agencies, it won't qualify for an *investment grade* rating from the major debt rating agencies (AAA, AA, A, or BBB in the Standard & Poor's rating system). Instead, Shellco's public debt will be non-investment grade (BB or below in the Standard & Poor's system) -- commonly called *junk bonds*.

LBO acquirers' interest in issuing debt to the public helped to fuel the growth of the junk bond market in the 1980s. The junk bond market's growth, in turn, made it easier for LBO acquirers to sell to the public the low-rated debt that they needed as part of their capital structure. But junk bonds and LBOs are not synonymous. The first LBO to be partly financed with publicly issued junk bonds (Kelso's 1985 acquisition of Blue Bell) took place only after LBOs had become a well-established part of the takeover landscape.

In sum, the characteristic features of a leveraged buyout are: (i) a shell company as acquirer; (ii) a highly leveraged, multilayered capital structure; (iii) concentrated equity ownership, with the merchant bank that structures the transaction often controlling an absolute majority of Shellco's stock; and (iv) substantial ownership of Shellco's equity by operating management.

Figure 11-1
Sources of Funds: Leveraged Buyout of O.M. Scott
($ millions)

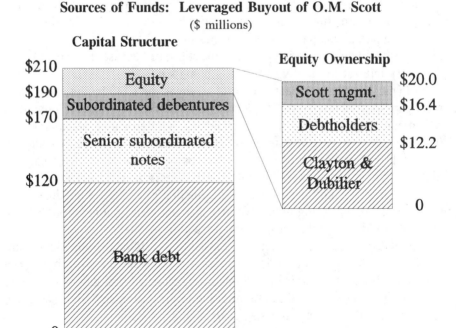

Figure 11-1 shows the capital structure for the 1986 leveraged buyout of O.M. Scott, formerly a subsidiary of ITT, by Clayton & Dubilier (now called Clayton, Dubilier & Rice).[4] The total cost of the acquisition was around $210 million, of which $190 million was borrowed. The bar chart on the left shows the debt in order of seniority, with the most senior debt, the bank loans, at the bottom. The bar chart on the right shows the post-buyout owners of Scott's equity. In Scott, as in many LBOs, the lenders acquired a minority equity position in the LBO company.

2.   Leveraged Recapitalizations

An important variation on the leveraged buyout is the *leveraged recapitalization*. In a leveraged recapitalization, a company (usually a public company) borrows money and uses the money to pay a large special dividend to its shareholders. After the dividend, the company will be highly leveraged. Often, the managers use the dividends they receive on their own shares to buy more shares, so that management's percentage ownership increases.

A company can also undergo a leveraged recapitalization by using borrowed funds to repurchase a large fraction of its shares. The company's capital structure will be the same as if it had paid a special dividend, except that its remaining equity will be divided into fewer outstanding shares. The choice between a dividend and a stock repurchase often turns on the different tax treatment of the two means of recapitalizing. Chapter 12 discusses generally the impact of federal income taxation on the choice among alternative transaction forms.

The principal difference between a leveraged buyout and a leveraged recapitalization is in who owns the equity after the transaction. In a leveraged buyout, the investors in Shellco own all of the equity in Targetco's business after the buyout. Targetco's managers often invest in Shellco, but the other Targetco shareholders are cashed out. If Targetco undergoes a leveraged recapitalization, its shareholders, as a group, will continue as shareholders. If Targetco was publicly held before the leveraged recapitalization, it will still be a public company after the recapitalization. In a leveraged buyout, control usually passes to the merchant bank that arranges the buyout. In a leveraged recapitalization, in contrast, the company's management usually retains control. Indeed, management often strengthens its control by increasing its percentage ownership.

Figure 11-2 shows the capital structure of Holiday Corp. after its 1987 leveraged recapitalization, in which Holiday paid a special dividend of approximately $1.6 billion to its public shareholders. Holiday's capital structure, shown in the bar on the left, is a typical LBO capital structure, with multiple layers of debt and a small amount of equity. But Holiday's

---

[4] The description of the O.M. Scott buyout in this chapter is based on George Baker & Karen Wruck, *Organizational Changes and Value Creation in Leveraged Buyouts: The Case of the O.M. Scott & Sons Company*, 25 J.Fin.Econ. 163 (1989).

equity ownership, shown in the bar on the right, is very different from the LBO pattern shown in Figure 11-1. Before the recapitalization, management had owned 2.1% of Holiday and employees had owned another 0.6% through an employee stock ownership plan (ESOP). These percentages soared in the recapitalization, because management and the ESOP received additional Holiday shares instead of the cash dividend, and Holiday made a large grant of restricted stock to a small group of top managers.

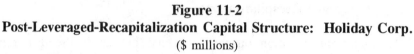

Figure 11-2
Post-Leveraged-Recapitalization Capital Structure: Holiday Corp.
($ millions)

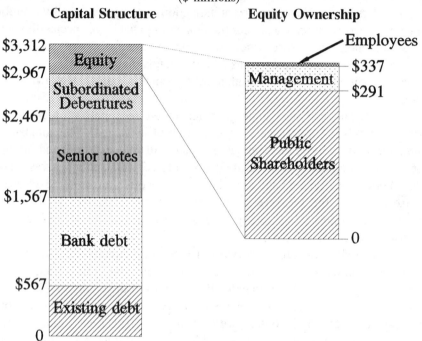

Figure 11-2 is based on an assumed $13 per share value for Holiday's common stock after the recapitalization. The actual market value of this "stub" equity -- so called because most of the common stock's value was contained in the special dividend -- would not be known until the recapitalization was completed.[5]

Most leveraged recapitalizations have been defensive -- entered into as a way for the target to defeat a hostile takeover bid by offering the same or greater value, or to preempt a possible hostile takeover. Holiday, for example, began actively to consider a leveraged recapitalization after Donald Trump indicated interest in buying Holiday, and reportedly acquired close to 5% of Holiday's stock.

---

[5] The description of the Holiday leveraged recapitalization is based on Holiday's proxy statement (Jan. 29, 1987) and on news stories about the transaction.

3. Which Companies Are Good LBO Candidates?

The ideal candidate for an LBO (or leveraged recapitalization) is a mature, slowly growing company, that generates more cash than it can profitably reinvest in its business -- a *cash cow* in the BCG terminology of Chapter 9. Instead of using this cash to fund other businesses, the LBO company will use the cash to repay its debt. Conversely, a fast-growing company is unsuitable for a leveraged buyout, because it needs all its available cash to reinvest in its business.

In addition, the ideal LBO candidate should have *predictable* cash flow. The company should be able to cover all of its interest payments, and at least some of its principal payments, even in a recession.

O.M. Scott was a stable cash cow, and thus was a good LBO candidate. Its principal business is selling brand-name grass seed and lawn fertilizer to homeowners -- a thoroughly mature business. Moreover, Scott's business was predictable -- homeowners buy pretty much the same amount of seed and fertilizer year after year. If the buyout went as planned, Scott's cash flow, in excess of its modest capital expenditures, would let Scott pay down most of its debt over an 8-10 year time period. Scott's equity would increase sharply in value, even if the value of Scott's business did not change.

Conversely, some LBOs got into trouble because LBO promoters ignored these ground rules. For example, the two principal producers of gypsum wallboard, USG and National Gypsum, underwent LBOs in the late 1980s. Gypsum wallboard is a highly cyclical commodity, used in building construction. When the 1990 recession hit, both the quantity and price of the wallboard that USG and National Gypsum could sell dropped sharply, and their cash flow shriveled. National Gypsum declared bankruptcy, and USG reorganized outside of bankruptcy by giving its principal lenders an 81% stake in the company's equity in return for debt forgiveness.

Holiday was a risky candidate for an LBO. Some of its income -- from Harrah's casinos and management fees for its franchised hotels -- was stable. But Holiday's also owned many hotels, and hotel ownership is a highly cyclical business. In a recession, fewer rooms are filled and room rates drop as hotels compete for customers by lowering their prices. Holiday planned to sell off its owned hotels, and continue as a casino operator and hotel management company. As things turned out, Holiday was able to sell most of its hotels, and use the proceeds to repay its debt, before the value of hotel properties crashed in the 1990 recession. If the recession had hit a couple of years earlier, Holiday might also have become a "busted LBO," like National Gypsum and USG.

4.　LBOs and Asset Sales

In a divisional buyout, such as O.M. Scott, the acquirer usually buys only a single business (or several related businesses) that it plans to keep. An acquirer of a whole company cannot always be so picky. LBO promoters who buy multidivisional companies often plan to keep some of the businesses, sell the remainder, and use the sale proceeds to repay debt. Leveraged recapitalizations are also often followed by substantial asset sales. LBOs and leveraged recapitalizations thus formed part of the 1980s trend, discussed in Chapter 9, toward companies becoming less diversified.

The Holiday Corp. leveraged recapitalization illustrates this. Holiday projected that in the first 3 years after its recapitalization, it would sell assets with a present value, measured at the time of the recapitalization, of around $900 million -- over half the amount of its special dividend. These assets were principally owned hotels, which were cyclical assets that were unsuitable for a highly leveraged company, undeveloped land, and a fleet of early 20th century airplanes collected by William Harrah, that Holiday had acquired when it bought Harrah's casinos from Mr. Harrah. The airplane collection was valued at around $100 million, and obviously generated no cash flow. (One can only wonder why Holiday's managers hadn't sold the airplane collection long before the recapitalization. Maybe they liked old airplanes too.)

Bust-up takeovers, where the acquirer plans to profit by selling off the target in pieces, also usually rely on heavy leverage. A leveraged buyout coupled with large asset sales can look very similar to a bust-up takeover. The *Revlon* case that you will read in Part IV is a good example. It involved a leveraged acquisition of Revlon by Pantry Pride, a shell company controlled by Ronald Perelman. Perelman planned to buy Revlon and then sell all of Revlon's businesses *except* the cosmetics business. The businesses that Perelman planned to sell comprised about 75% of Revlon's value. As it turned out, the sale prices for Revlon's divisions roughly equalled the takeover price -- Perelman ended up with Revlon's cosmetics business for free. Is Pantry Pride's acquisition of Revlon better described as a bust-up or as a leveraged buyout?

B.　The Theory:　Where Do LBOs Premiums Come From?

1.　The Puzzle of LBO Premiums

The gains to target shareholders in leveraged buyouts and leveraged recapitalizations are comparable to those in other types of acquisitions.[6]

---

[6] See, e.g., Steven Kaplan, *The Effects of Management Buyouts on Operating Performance and Value*, 24 J.Fin.Econ. 217 (1989) (excerpted later in this chapter); Bernard Black & Joseph Grundfest, *Shareholder Gains from Takeovers and Restructurings Between 1981 and*

This raises a puzzle: The principal sources of value creation that we have discussed thus far -- operating synergy and replacement of inefficient management -- are not present in a classic leveraged buyout. There is no operating synergy between acquirer and target, because the acquirer is a shell. And there can't be gains from replacing the target's management if management isn't replaced. Where then do the gains come from?

Synergy-Related Explanations. If the conglomerate form produces inefficiencies, then the deconglomeration that results from a divisional buyout, or a whole company buyout followed by asset sales, can produce a kind of financial synergy -- the reversal of conglomerate *anti*synergy.

The gains to target shareholders from LBOs that are followed by asset sales could also reflect some indirect operating synergy. Many post-LBO asset sales are to *strategic buyers* -- companies that are already in the same or related businesses. The price that the LBO promoter expects to sell these assets for should reflect some of the ultimate buyer's operating synergy. In a reasonably competitive acquisition market, that expected sale price will, in turn, affect the price that the LBO promoter pays for the target.

But many LBOs don't involve significant asset sales. And even for LBOs that do, it would take implausibly large premiums on the asset sales to explain the hefty premium that is typically paid for the whole company. Suppose, for example, that an LBO promoter expects to sell assets representing 25% of the target's pretakeover value, at a 50% premium to their current value. Even if that value is fully passed through to the target shareholders in the initial LBO, it can justify only a 12% premium for the entire target company -- even less after transaction costs.

Moreover, neither reversal of conglomerate antisynergy, nor indirect operating synergy from asset sales, can explain the characteristic features of LBOs: high leverage, concentrated ownership, and high management ownership. A number of other general explanations for acquisitions that we will consider in later chapters, including accounting tricks (Chapter 13), mispricing of the target's stock (Chapter 14), and wealth transfers from employees (Chapter 15), share this basic flaw. Whether or not these explanations are empirically plausible as a source of takeover gains, they are not specific to LBOs, and thus cannot explain the features that make LBOs a distinct transaction form.

Leverage-Related Explanations. Two additional explanations for LBO premiums relate the high leverage that characterizes LBOs. The first involves the tax advantages of debt financing, compared to equity financing. We will consider tax motives for acquisitions in Chapter 12. The available empirical evidence suggests that tax savings are an important but only partial explanation for LBOs premiums.

1986, J.Applied Corp.Fin. 5 (Spr.1988) (excerpted in Chapter 6) (reporting data on leveraged recapitalizations).

The second leverage-related explanation for LBO premiums involves wealth transfers from creditors to shareholders. Consider the Holiday recapitalization, for example. Before its recapitalization, Holiday Corp. had about $1.3 billion in outstanding debt. It repaid more than half of that debt at the time of the recapitalization, but $567 million in old debt remained outstanding. The recapitalization substantially increased the default risk associated with those old loans, and thus the market rate of interest appropriate to that level of risk. Thus, the recapitalization decreased the market value of Holiday's outstanding debt -- a decrease that inured to the benefit of Holiday's shareholders.

We will defer until Chapter 15 consideration of wealth transfers from creditors as an acquisition motive. But the available empirical evidence suggests that wealth transfers from creditors are only a minor explanation for shareholder gains from LBOs and leveraged recapitalizations *even* when a significant amount of old debt remains outstanding. Moreover, in many LBOs, little or no old debt remains outstanding.

In addition, tax savings and wealth transfers from creditors, while they can explain high leverage, cannot explain the concentrated ownership and high management ownership that also characterize LBOs. In the O.M. Scott buyout, for example, Clayton & Dubilier, having bought 79% of the equity in the Scott buyout, sold 18% of Scott's common stock to Scott management, at Clayton & Dubilier's cost. Clayton & Dubilier is not a charitable institution. It must have believed that the expected profits from owning roughly 60% of Scott, with managers owning roughly 20%, were higher than the profits from keeping almost 80% of the equity for itself, as it could have. None of the explanations for LBOs considered thus far can explain this behavior.

2.   The Incentive Effects of the LBO Structure

Michael Jensen, ECLIPSE OF THE PUBLIC CORPORATION
Harv.Bus.Rev. 61 (Sept./Oct.1989)

The publicly held corporation, the main engine of economic progress in the United States for a century, has outlived its usefulness in many sectors of the economy, and is being eclipsed. New organizations are emerging in its place -- organizations that are corporate in form but have no public shareholders and are not listed or traded on organized exchanges. These organizations use public and private debt, rather than public equity, as their major source of capital. . . . By resolving the central weakness of the public corporation -- the conflict between owners and managers over the control and use of corporate resources -- these new organizations are making remarkable gains in operating efficiency, employee productivity, and shareholder value.

. . .

The current trends do not imply that the public corporation has no future. The conventional twentieth-century model of corporate governance -- dispersed public ownership, professional managers without substantial equity holdings, a board of directors dominated by management-appointed outsiders -- remains a viable option in some areas of the economy, particularly for growth companies whose profitable investment opportunities exceed the cash they generate internally. . . .   The public corporation is not suitable in industries where long-term growth is slow, where internally generated funds outstrip the opportunities to invest them profitably, or where downsizing is the most productive long-term strategy.

In the tire industry, the shift to radials, which last three times longer than bias-ply tires, meant that manufacturers needed less capacity to meet world demand. Overcapacity inevitably forced a restructuring. The tenfold increase in oil prices from 1973 to 1981, which triggered worldwide conservation measures, forced oil producers into a similar retrenchment. Industries under similar pressure today include steel, chemicals, brewing, tobacco, television and radio broadcasting, wood and paper products. In these and other cash-rich, low-growth or declining sectors, the pressures on management to waste cash flow through organizational slack or investments in unsound projects is often irresistible. It is in precisely these sectors that the publicly held corporation has declined most rapidly. . . .

The public corporation is a social invention of vast historical importance. Its genius is rooted in its capacity to spread financial risk over the diversified portfolios of millions of individuals and institutions and to allow investors to customize risk to their unique circumstances and predilections.   By diversifying risks that would otherwise be borne by owner-entrepreneurs and by facilitating the creation of a liquid market for exchanging risk, the public corporation lowered the cost of capital. . . .

From the beginning, though, these risk-bearing benefits came at a cost. Tradable ownership claims create fundamental conflicts of interest between those who bear risk (the shareholders) and those who manage risk (the executives). The genius of the new organizations is that they eliminate much of the loss created by conflicts between owners and managers, without eliminating the vital functions of risk diversification and liquidity once performed exclusively by the public equity markets. . . .

[T]he fact that takeover and LBO premiums average 50% above [the pretakeover] market price illustrates how much value public-company managers can destroy before they face a serious threat of disturbance. Takeovers and buyouts both create new value and unlock value destroyed by management through misguided policies. . . .

The widespread waste and inefficiency of the public corporation and its inability to adapt to changing economic circumstances have generated a wave of organizational innovation over the last 15 years -- innovation driven by the rebirth of "active investors." By active investors I mean investors who hold large equity or debt positions, sit on boards of directors, monitor and sometimes dismiss management, are involved with the long-term strategic direction of the companies they invest in, and sometimes manage the companies themselves.

Active investors are creating a new model of general management. These investors include LBO partnerships such as Kohlberg Kravis Roberts and Clayton & Dubilier; entrepreneurs such as Carl Icahn, Ronald Perelman, Laurence Tisch, Robert Bass, William Simon, Irwin Jacobs, and Warren Buffett; the merchant banking arms of Wall Street houses such as Morgan Stanley, Lazard Freres, and Merrill Lynch; and family funds such as those controlled by the Pritzkers and the Bronfmans. Their model is built around highly leveraged financial structures, pay-for-performance compensation systems, substantial equity ownership by managers and directors, and contracts with owners and creditors that limit both cross-subsidization among business units and the waste of free cash flow. . . . More than any other factor, these organizations' resolution of the owner-manager conflict explains how they can motivate the same people, managing the same resources, to perform so much more effectively under private ownership than in the publicly held corporate form.

In effect, LBO partnerships and the merchant banks are rediscovering the role played by active investors prior to 1940, when Wall Street banks such as J.P. Morgan & Company were directly involved in the strategy and governance of the public companies they helped create. . . . Morgan's model of investor activism disappeared largely as a result of populist laws and regulations approved in the wake of the Great Depression.

These laws and regulations -- including the Glass-Steagall Banking Act of 1933, the Securities Act of 1933, the Securities Exchange Act of 1934, the Chandler Bankruptcy Revision Act of 1938, and the Investment Company Act of 1940 -- . . . created an intricate web of restrictions on company "insiders" (corporate officers, directors, or investors with more than a 10% ownership interest), restrictions on bank involvement in corporate reorganizations, court precedents, and business practices that raised the cost of being an active investor. Their long-term effect has been to insulate management from effective monitoring and to set the stage for the eclipse of the public corporation. . . .

The absence of effective monitoring led to such large inefficiencies that the new generation of active investors arose to recapture the lost value. These investors overcome the costs of the outmoded legal constraints by purchasing entire companies -- and using debt and high equity ownership to force effective self-monitoring.

A central weakness and source of waste in the public corporation is the conflict between shareholders and managers over the payout of free cash flow -- that is, cash flow in excess of that required to fund all investment projects with positive net present values. . . . [S]enior management has few incentives to distribute the funds, and there exist few mechanisms to compel distribution.

A vivid example is the senior management of Ford Motor Company, which sits on nearly $15 billion in cash and marketable securities in an industry with excess capacity. Ford's management has been deliberating about acquiring financial service companies, aerospace companies, or making some other multibillion-dollar diversification move -- rather than deliberating about effectively distributing Ford's excess cash to its owners so they can decide how to reinvest it. . . .

The struggle over free cash flow is at the heart of the role of debt in the . . . [new] going-private transactions. . . . This perceived "leveraging of corporate America" is perhaps the central source of anxiety among defenders of the public corporation and critics of the new organizational forms. But most critics miss three important points. First, the trebling of the market value of public-company equity over the last decade means that corporate borrowing had to increase to avoid a major deleveraging.

Second, debt creation without retention of the proceeds of the issue helps limit the waste of free cash flow by compelling managers to pay out funds they would otherwise retain. Debt is . . . a mechanism to force managers to disgorge cash rather than spend it on empire-building projects with low or negative returns, bloated staffs, indulgent perquisites, and organizational inefficiencies.

By issuing debt in exchange for stock, companies bond their managers' promise to pay out future cash flows in a way that simple dividend increases do not. . . . Companies whose managers fail to make promised interest and principal payments can be declared insolvent and possibly hauled into bankruptcy court. In the imagery of G. Bennett Stewart and David M. Glassman, "Equity is soft, debt hard. Equity is forgiving, debt insistent. Equity is a pillow, debt a sword." Some may find it curious that a company's creditors wield far more power over managers than its public shareholders, but it is also undeniable.

Third . . ., "overleveraging" can be desirable and effective when it makes economic sense to break up a company, sell off parts of the business, and refocus its energies on a few core operations. Companies that assume so much debt they cannot meet the debt service payments out of operating cash flow force themselves to rethink their entire strategy and structure. Overleveraging creates the crisis atmosphere managers require to slash unsound investment programs, shrink overhead, and dispose of assets that are more valuable outside the company. . . .

The case of Revco . . . makes the point well. Critics cite Revco's bankruptcy petition, filed in July 1988, as an example of the financial perils associated with LBO debt. I take a different view. The $1.25 billion buyout, announced in December 1986, did dramatically increase Revco's annual interest charges. But several other factors contributed to its troubles, including management's decision to overhaul pricing, stocking, and merchandise layout in the company's drugstore chain. This mistaken strategic redirection left customers confused and dissatisfied, and Revco's performance suffered. Before the buyout, and without the burden of interest payments, management could have pursued these policies for a long period of time, destroying much of the company's value in the process. Within six months, however, debt served as a brake on management's mistakes, motivating the board and creditors to reorganize the company before even more value was lost. . . .

What explains [the] vehement opposition to a trend that clearly benefits shareholders and the economy? One important factor . . . [is that] Wall Street can allocate capital among competing businesses and monitor and discipline management more effectively than the CEO and headquarters staff of the typical diversified company. KKR's New York offices . . . are direct substitutes for corporate headquarters in Akron or Peoria. CEOs worry that they and their staffs will lose lucrative jobs in favor of competing organizations. Many are right to worry; the performance of active investors versus the public corporation leaves little doubt as to which is superior.

Active investors are creating new models of general management, the most widespread of which I call the LBO Association. A typical LBO Association consists of three main constituencies: an LBO partnership that sponsors going-private transactions and counsels and monitors management in an ongoing cooperative relationship; company managers who hold substantial equity stakes in an LBO division and stay on after the buyout; and institutional investors (insurance companies, pension funds, and money management firms) that fund the limited partnerships that purchase equity and lend money (along with banks) to finance the transactions.

Much like a traditional conglomerate, LBO Associations have many divisions or business units, companies they have taken private at different points in time. KKR, for example, controls a diverse collection of 19 businesses including all or part of Beatrice, Duracell, Motel 6, Owens-Illinois, RJR Nabisco, and Safeway. But LBO Associations differ from publicly held conglomerates in at least four important respects. See Figure 11-3: *Public Company vs. LBO Association.*

Figure 11-3
[Multidivisional] Public Company vs. LBO Association

Typical [Multidivisional] Public Company

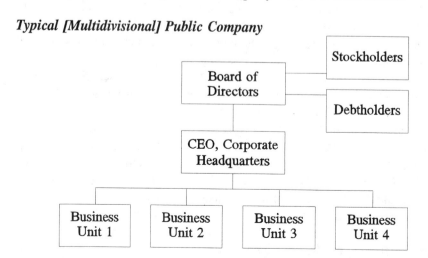

Typical LBO Association

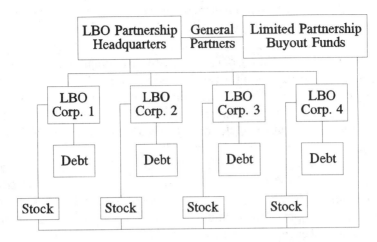

Management incentives are built around a strong relationship between pay and performance. Compensation systems in LBO Associations usually have higher upper bounds than do public companies (or no upper bounds at all), tie bonuses much more closely to cash flow and debt retirement than to accounting earnings, and otherwise closely link management pay to divisional performance. . . .

Steven Kaplan studied all public-company buyouts from 1979 through 1985 with a purchase price of at least $50 million. Business-unit chiefs hold a median equity position of 6.4% in their unit.[a] Even without considering bonus and incentive plans, a $1,000 increase in shareholder value triggers a $64 increase in the personal wealth of business-unit chiefs. The median public-company CEO holds only 0.25% of the company's equity. Counting all sources of compensation -- including salary, bonus, deferred compensation, stock options, and dismissal penalties -- the personal wealth of the median public-company CEO increases by only $3.25 for a $1,000 increase in shareholder value.[b]

Thus the salary of the typical LBO business-unit manager is almost 20 times more sensitive to performance than that of the typical public-company manager. This comparison understates the true differences in compensation. The personal wealth of managing partners in an LBO partnership (in effect, the CEOs of the LBO Associations) is tied almost exclusively to the performance of the companies they control. The general partners in an LBO Association typically receive (through overrides and direct equity holdings) 20% or more of the gains in the value of the divisions they help manage. This implies a pay-for-performance sensitivity of $200 for every $1,000 in

---

[a] Steven Kaplan, *The Effects of Management Buyouts on Operating Performance and Value*, 24 J.Fin.Econ. 217 (1989) (excerpted later in this chapter).

[b] See Michael Jensen & Kevin Murphy, *Performance Pay and Top-Management Incentives*, 98 J.Pol.Econ. 225 (1990).

added shareholder value. It's not hard to understand why an executive who receives $200 for every $1,000 increase in shareholder value will unlock more value than an executive who receives $3.25.

LBO Associations are more decentralized than publicly held conglomerates. The LBO Association substitutes compensation incentives and ownership for direct monitoring by headquarters. The headquarters of KKR, the world's largest LBO partnership, has only 16 professionals and 44 additional employees. In contrast, the Atlanta headquarters of RJR Nabisco employed 470 people when KKR took it private last year in a $25 billion transaction. . . .

It is physically impossible for KKR and other LBO partnerships to become intimately involved in the day-to-day decisions of their operating units. They rely instead on stock ownership, incentive pay that rewards cash flow, and other compensation techniques to motivate managers to maximize value without bureaucratic oversight. My survey of 7 LBO partnerships found an average headquarters staff of 13 professionals and 19 nonprofessionals that oversees almost 24 business units with total annual sales of more than $11 billion. See Table 11-1, *LBO Partnerships Keep Staff Lean*.

LBO Associations rely heavily on leverage. The average debt ratio (long-term debt as a percentage of debt plus equity) for public companies prior to a buyout is about 20%. The Kaplan study shows the average debt ratio for an LBO is 85% on completion of the buyout.

Table 11-1
LBO Partnerships Keep Staff Lean

LBO Partnership	Year Started	Profes- sionals	Nonprofes- sionals	Business Units	Annual Revenues ($ billions)
Berkshire Partners	1986	14	6	15	$1
Butler Capital	1979	8	14	33	2.3
Clayton & Dubilier	1976	10	11	8	4.8
Gibbons Green van Amerongen	1969	6	7	12	5.3
Kohlberg Kravis Roberts	1976	16	44	19	58.7
Thomas H. Lee Co.	1974	15	12	25	8
Odyssey Partners	1950	19	39	53	N.A.

Intensive use of debt dramatically shrinks the amount of equity in a company. This allows the LBO general partners and divisional managers to control a large fraction of the total ownership without requiring huge investments they would be unable to make or large grants of free equity [to management]. For example, in a company with $1 billion in assets and a debt ratio of 20%, management would have to raise $80 million to buy 10% of the equity. If that same company had a debt ratio of 90%, management would have to raise only $10 million to control a 10% stake. By concentrating equity holdings among managers and LBO partners, debt intensifies the ownership incentives that are so important to efficiency.

High debt also allows LBO Associations and other private organizations to tap the benefits of risk diversification once provided only by the public equity market. . . . [Much LBO debt is] in the form of public, high-yield, noninvestment-grade securities, better known as junk bonds. This debt, which was pioneered by Drexel Burnham Lambert, [carries a level of risk similar to that] borne by shareholders in the typical public company. Placing this public debt in the well-diversified portfolios of large financial institutions spreads equity-like risk among millions of investors, who are the ultimate beneficiaries of mutual funds and pension funds -- without requiring those risks to be held as equity. . . .

The limited partnership agreement [for an LBO Association] denies the general partner the right to transfer cash or other resources from one LBO division to another. That is, all returns from a business must be distributed to the limited partners and other equity holders of that business. Such binding agreements reduce the risk of unproductive reinvestment by prohibiting cross-subsidization among LBO units. . . .

To be sure, this [model] is not without its tensions. The fact that LBO partnerships and divisional managers control the LBO Association's small equity base but hold little of the debt creates incentives for them to take high-risk management gambles. If their gambles succeed, they reap large rewards by increasing their equity value; if their gambles fail, creditors bear much of the cost. But the reputational consequences of such reckless behavior can be large. As long as creditors behave rationally, an LBO partnership that tries to profit at the expense of its creditors or walks away from a deal gone sour will not be able to raise funds for future investments.

. . .

Public companies can learn from LBO Associations and emulate many of their characteristics. But this requires major changes in corporate structure, philosophy, and focus. They can reduce the waste of free cash flow by borrowing to repurchase stock or pay large dividends. . . . Some corporations are experimenting with such changes -- FMC, Holiday, and Owens-Corning -- and the results have been impressive.[c] But only a coordinated attack on the status quo will halt the eclipse of the public company. It is unlikely such an attack will proceed fast enough or go far enough. . . .

The relationship between debt and insolvency is perhaps the least understood aspect of this entire organizational evolution. . . . Critics of leverage . . . fail to appreciate that insolvency in and of itself is not always something to avoid -- and that the costs of becoming insolvent are likely to be much smaller in the new world of high leverage than in the old world of

---

[c] These companies all underwent leveraged recapitalizations. Eds.

equity-dominated balance sheets. The proliferation of takeovers, LBOs, and other going-private transactions has inspired innovations in the reorganization and workout process. I refer to these innovations as "the privatization of bankruptcy." LBOs do get in financial trouble more frequently than public companies do. But few LBOs ever enter formal bankruptcy. They are reorganized quickly (a few months is common), often under new management, and at much lower costs than under a court-supervised process.
. . .

The evolving U.S. system of corporate governance and finance exhibits many characteristics of the postwar Japanese system. LBO partnerships act much like the main banks (the real power center) in Japan's keiretsu business groupings. The keiretsu make extensive use of leverage and intercorporate holdings of debt and equity. Banks commonly hold substantial equity in their client companies and have their own executives help them out of difficulty. (For years, Nissan has been run by an alumnus of the Industrial Bank of Japan, who became CEO as part of the bank's effort to keep the company out of bankruptcy.) Other personnel, including CFOs, move frequently between banks and companies as part of an ongoing relationship that involves training, consulting, and monitoring. Japanese banks allow companies to enter formal bankruptcy only when liquidation makes economic sense -- that is, when a company is worth more dead than alive. . . .

Ironically, even as more U.S. companies come to resemble Japanese companies, Japan's public companies are becoming more like U.S. companies of 15 years ago. . . . Many of Japan's public companies are flooded with free cash flow far in excess of their opportunities to invest in profitable internal growth. In 1987, more than 40% of Japan's large public companies had no net bank borrowings -- that is, cash balances larger than their short- and long-term borrowings. Toyota, with a cash hoard of $10.4 billion, more than 25% of its total assets, is commonly referred to as the Toyota Bank. . . . Unless shareholders and creditors discover ways to prohibit their managers from behaving like U.S. managers, Japanese companies will make uneconomic acquisitions and diversification moves, generate internal waste, and engage in other value-destroying activities. . .
.

Meanwhile, in the United States, the organizational changes revitalizing the corporate sector will create more nimble enterprises and help reverse our losses in world product markets. As this profound innovation continues, however, people will make mistakes. To learn, we have to push new policies to the margin. It will be natural to see more failed deals.

There are already some worrisome structural issues. I look with discomfort on the dangerous tendency of LBO partnerships, bolstered by their success, to take more of their compensation in front-end fees rather than in back-end profits earned through increased equity value. As management fees and the fees for completing deals get larger, the incentives to do deals, rather than *good* deals, also increases. Institutional investors (and the economy as a whole) are best served when the LBO partnership is the last member of the LBO Association to get paid and when the LBO partnership gets paid as a fraction of the back-end value of the deals, including losses.

Moreover, we have yet to fully understand the limitations on the size of this new organizational form. LBO partnerships are understandably tempted to increase the reach of their talented monitors by reconfiguring divisions as acquisition vehicles. This will be difficult to accomplish successfully. . . .

These and other problems should not cloud the remarkable benefits associated with the eclipse of the large public corporation. What surprises me is how few mistakes have occurred thus far in an organizational change as profound as any since World War II.

C. Evaluation: LBO Efficiency Gains and Longevity

In Jensen's view, the LBO Association has three distinctive characteristics, each of which leads to greater productive efficiency. First, each company controlled by the LBO Association is highly leveraged. This capital structure requires that the organization's free cash flow be paid out as mandatory interest payments rather than discretionary dividends. It also gives managers an important incentive: unpaid debtholders can quickly displace management through bankruptcy. Second, managers own a substantial portion of the organization's equity. Again, management's incentive to perform is increased. Finally, the intensity of the monitoring of management goes up sharply after an LBO. The partners in the LBO fund control the company, both through stockholdings and through seats on the board of directors. They have an enormous financial stake in the company's success, and the power to act if they are unhappy with management or with major strategic decisions.

Jensen's analysis suggests two hypotheses:

(i) because of improved managerial incentives and monitoring, a company's performance will improve following an LBO; and

(ii) because of the efficiency characteristics of this organizational form, companies that undergo LBOs will retain this form over time.

Data are beginning to accumulate with respect to each.

1. Efficiency Gains from Leveraged Buyouts

Steven Kaplan, THE EFFECTS OF MANAGEMENT BUYOUTS ON OPERATING PERFORMANCE AND VALUE
24 J.Fin.Econ. 217 (1989)

In the typical [management buyout (MBO)], investors, including some of the firm's current managers, pay pre-buyout shareholders a premium of more than 40% above the prevailing market price to take the company private (see DeAngelo, DeAngelo & Rice (1984), Marais, Schipper & Smith (1989)), and my results which follow).[a] Several sources of wealth increases to shareholders and buyout investors are frequently mentioned: reduced agency costs and new incentives, wealth transfers from employees and public bondholders to the investor group, information held by managers that is not known by public shareholders that results in a bargain purchase, and tax advantages. The first three of these nonmutually exclusive explanations for buyout gains predict that operating cash flows increase after the buyout.

. . . According to Jensen's reduced-agency-cost or new-incentive hypothesis, the new incentives lead to increases in operating income and operating margins as well as reductions in wasteful capital expenditures. Shleifer and Summers (1988) suggest that buyouts and takeovers transfer wealth to investors by laying off employees or reducing their wages. This employee-wealth-transfer hypothesis argues that operating income increases after the buyout at the expense of employee layoffs and wage reductions.[b] Lowenstein (1985) argues that managers have information about the company that is not available to other bidders. For example, at the time of the buyout announcement, managers may know that cash flows will be higher than the market expects. Because they have private information, managers can buy the company for less than a similarly informed bidder would be willing to pay.[c] . . .

This paper analyzes a sample of 76 management buyouts completed between 1980 and 1986 for evidence on whether the operating changes predicted by these hypotheses occur. . . . The 48 buyout companies with post-buyout financial data experience increases in operating income (before depreciation) and net cash flow as well as reductions in capital expenditures. Operating income, measured net of industry changes, is essentially unchanged in the first two post-buyout years and 24% higher in the third year. The change in operating income, however, does not control for post-buyout divestitures, which may lead the measured change in operating income to underestimate the true change. I [also] measure operating income in relation to both assets and sales to control for post-buyout asset divestitures and acquisitions. The increases in both ratios are significantly greater than the industry changes, by approximately 20%.[d] The median net cash flow (the difference between operating income and capital expenditures),

---

[a] Harry DeAngelo, Linda DeAngelo & Edward Rice, *Going Private: Minority Freezeouts and Stockholder Wealth*, 27 J.L. & Econ. 367 (1984); Laurentius Marais, Katherine Schipper & Abbie Smith, *Wealth Effects of Going Private on Senior Securities*, 23 J.Fin.Econ. 155 (1989).

[b] Andrei Shleifer & Lawrence Summers, *Breach of Trust in Hostile Takeovers*, in *Corporate Takeovers: Causes and Consequences* 33 (Alan Auerbach ed.1988).

[c] Louis Lowenstein, *Management Buyouts*, 85 Colum.L.Rev. 730 (1985).

[d] Below we omit Kaplan's data on operating performance relative to sales, which is generally similar to his data on operating performance relative to assets. Eds.

net of industry changes, in the first three post-buyout years is 22.0%, 43.1%, and 80.5% larger than in the last pre-buyout year. . . .

Consistent with the results for operating changes, pre-buyout and post-buyout investors earn a median total market-adjusted return of 77.0% (mean = 96.0%). Pre-buyout public shareholders earn a median market-adjusted return of 37.2% (mean = 37.9%) and investors in post-buyout capital earn a median market-adjusted return of 28.0% (mean = 41.9%). . . .

In general, the results in this paper favor the reduced-agency-cost or new-incentive hypothesis over the employee-wealth-transfer and information-advantage hypotheses as explanations for post-buyout operating changes and wealth increases. . . .

Evidence on Post-buyout Operating Cash Flows

. . . The analyses [below] focus on changes in three-cash flow variables:

(1) *Operating income (before depreciation)* . . . measures the cash generated from buyout company operations before depreciation, interest, or taxes . . . [and before] gains or losses from sales of divisions or assets. All three hypotheses described [above] suggest that buyout companies experience increases in operating income.

(2) *Capital expenditures* (including capitalized leases), which measures new investment by the buyout company. It does not include acquisitions or receipts from divestitures. . . . The reduced-agency-cost hypothesis argues that buyout companies previously were investing in negative net present value projects. According to this hypothesis, reductions in capital expenditures increase company profitability and value.

(3) *Net (operating) cash flow,* which equals operating income before depreciation minus capital expenditures. . . . Net cash flow would be the primary component of the numerator in a net present value analysis to value a buyout company. A permanent increase in net cash flow, therefore, should lead to an increase in value.

The three cash-flow variables are all measured before taxes. . . . Managerial operating decisions, not taxes or financial decisions, affect the three cash-flow variables analyzed in this section.

The analyses measure the percentage differences or changes in the cash flow variables in the first three full years after the buyout (years +1, +2, and +3) compared to the last fiscal year before the buyout (year −1). Results for year 0, the fiscal year that includes both pre- and post-buyout operations, are not presented here because they are difficult to interpret as pre- or post-buyout performance. . . . To control for economy-wide and industry effects, the analyses also present an industry-adjusted percentage change in the cash flows. . . .

I measure each cash flow variable [both] in levels [and] as a fraction of end-of-period total assets. . . . Each of these measures is imperfect. If the post-buyout companies pursue the same growth, divestiture, and acquisition strategies as the control firms, the industry-adjusted change in levels would be the appropriate measure of abnormal performance. . . .

I partially control for divestitures by using restated financial information [for the 5 companies whose] post-buyout financial statements provide pre-buyout financial data restated for divestitures. . . . [But] at least 20 of the 48 buyouts divest operations valued at more than 5% of the value of the going-private transaction.[10] . . . Dividing the annual cash flow variables by year-end total assets (adjusted for buyout accounting changes) [also] partially controls for divestitures and differences in growth. . . .

Even measuring the variables as a fraction of total assets . . ., however, is subject to criticism. For example, if MBOs tend to sell unprofitable divisions, measured operating income and net cash flow divided by total assets . . . may increase without any real change having taken place.

The results for medians (and Wilcoxon signed rank tests) are presented rather than for means (and t-tests) to control for outliers that dominate the means in some of the small samples analyzed. The results for means are similar, and usually larger in absolute value. All significance levels are based on two-tailed tests. . . .

Operating income

Table 11-2 summarizes the changes in operating income (before depreciation). Panel A shows that the median increases are 15.6%, 30.7%, and 42.0%, in years +1, +2, and +3 in comparison with year −1. Measured net of industry changes, operating income is essentially unchanged in the first two post-buyout years and 24.1% higher in the third year. However, as discussed above the change [in operating income] for many buyout companies will be downward biased because many observations are not restated to take account of post-buyout divestitures. Similarly, it is likely that the change in operating income for many control firms is upward biased because control company observations are not restated to take account of acquisitions. . . . Consistent with this, I find (but do not present in the table) that the industry-adjusted percentage changes in sales of the buyout companies are −7.7%, −6.0%, and 2.7% in years +1, +2, and +3. The decreases in years +1 and +2 are significant at the 1% level. The buyout companies grow slower at first than the industry controls.

---

[10] The results that follow are similar for the subsample of buyouts that [excludes these] 20 firms. . . .

Table 11-2

Effect of Management Buyouts on Operating Income

(* = significant at 5% level; ** = significant at 1% level)

	From year i to year j			
Cash-flow measure	-2 to -1	-1 to $+1$	-1 to $+2$	-1 to $+3$
A. *Operating Income*	n=48	n=39	n=32	n=14
Percentage change	11.4%**	15.6%**	30.7%**	42.0%**
Industry-adjusted % change	-1.2%	-2.7%	0.7	24.1%
B. *Operating Income/Assets*	n=46	n=42	n=34	n=15
Percentage change	5.9%	13.7%**	20.1%**	14.6%*
Industry-adjusted % change	5.0%	16.6**	36.1%**	21.3%*
Median at year -1: 13.1%				

Changes in operating income as a percentage of assets . . . partially control for differences in divestitures and acquisitions [between] the buyout and control companies. Panel B shows that industry-adjusted increases in operating income to assets are 16.6%, 36.1%, and 21.3% in years $+1$, $+2$, and $+3$ relative to year -1. . . .

The results in Table 11-2 are consistent with better post-buyout operating performance. The increases would also occur, however, if buyout company managers use accounting slack to [artificially] reduce measured operating income before the buyout . . . [so they can] purchase the company for less than its true value . . . . DeAngelo (1986) examines a sample of management buyouts and finds no evidence of unusually negative earnings [changes] in the year before the buyout.[d] Similarly, Table 11-2 shows that the buyout companies experience small and statistically insignificant changes in . . . industry-adjusted operating income from year -2 to year -1. . . .

Capital expenditures

Table 11-3 reports changes in capital expenditures. Panel A finds that the buyout companies reduce their level of capital expenditures in years $+1$, $+2$, and $+3$ relative to year -1. None of these reductions, however, is significant. The industry-adjusted changes in capital expenditures, however, are very negative, equal to -35.9%, -32.6%, and -64.4% for years $+1$, $+2$ and $+3$ compared with year -1. These results are significant in years $+1$ and $+2$. As with operating income, the large decreases in [industry-adjusted] capital expenditures may be caused by a failure to take divestitures [by buyout companies] and acquisitions [by nonbuyout companies] fully into account. . . .

---

[d] Linda DeAngelo, *Accounting Numbers as Market Valuation Substitutes: A Study of Management Buyouts of Public Stockholders*, 61 Acct.Rev. 400 (1986).

Table 11-3
Effect of Management Buyouts on Capital Expenditures
(* = significant at 5% level; ** = significant at 1% level)

Cash-flow measure	From year i to year j			
	−2 to −1	−1 to +1	−1 to +2	−1 to +3
A. *Capital expenditures*	n=48	n=39	n=32	n=14
Percentage change	−1.5%	−21.1%	−21.4%	−6.9%
Industry-adjusted % change	−7.9%*	−35.9%**	−32.6%*	−64.4%
B. *Capital expenditures/Assets*	n=46	n=42	n=34	n=15
Percentage change	−8.5%	−11.9%*	−25.4%*	−24.5%
Industry-adjusted % change	−3.5%	−6.1%	−5.7%	−19.3%
Median at year −1: 4.1%				

Negative industry-adjusted capital expenditures are consistent with reduced agency costs and increased efficiency if the pre-buyout companies have large amounts of free cash flow and were investing in negative net present value projects. Low capital expenditures are also consistent with the hypotheses that buyout companies are cash-constrained and underinvest after the buyout. . . . The accounting evidence presented here cannot determine whether reductions in capital expenditures are value-increasing or value-decreasing. . . .

Net cash flow

The results for operating income and capital expenditures suggest that the buyout companies are successful in generating cash after the buyout. This section examines net cash flow, the difference between operating income and capital expenditures.

The industry-adjusted changes in net cash flow . . . are all positive and significant. Panel A [of Table 11-4] shows that the net cash flow of the buyout [companies] increases 22.0%, 43.1%, and 80.5% more than that of other companies in the same industry in years +1, +2, and +3 compared with year −1. Similarly, panel B shows that the increase in net cash flow to assets for the buyout companies in those three years are 50.5%, 85.4%, and 64.3%. . . .

If the increases in net cash flow are permanent, then, in the absence of tax and financing effects, the value of the buyouts should rise by the same percentage. The large increases in net cash flow are consistent with large increases in values. In fact, the changes in net cash flow are of the same rough magnitude as the premiums or excess returns paid to pre-buyout shareholders to take the company private. . . .

Table 11-4

Effect of Management Buyouts on Net Cash Flow

(* = significant at 5% level; ** = significant at 1% level)

Cash-flow measure	From year *i* to year *j*			
	−2 to −1	−1 to +1	−1 to +1	−1 to +2
A. *Net cash flow*	n=47	n=37	n=30	n=14
Percentage change	11.2%	41.1%**	59.3%**	95.6%**
Industry-adjusted % change	2.5%	22.0%*	43.1%**	80.5%*
B. *Net cash flow/Assets*	n=45	n=39	n=33	n=13
Percentage change	5.3%	43.4%**	66.3%**	79.4%**
Industry-adjusted % change	4.3%	50.5%**	85.4%**	64.3%**
Median at year −1: 7.8%				

Potential selection bias

The [subsample of firms with available post-buyout financial information] analyzed here is subject to a selection bias if buyout specialists and managers in the more successful buyouts [are especially likely to] sell their shares in an initial public offering (IPO) or sell the company to another buyer. . . .

Although I cannot examine those companies for which data are unavailable, I can divide the sample of companies with post-buyout data into those for which post-buyout filings are required [by SEC rules (10-K companies)] and those for which such filings [result from voluntary actions such as an IPO or sale (IPO/sale companies)], and, therefore, may be related to post-buyout performance. . . . If there is a selection bias, the IPO/sale companies will perform differently than the 10-K companies. . . .

[T]he IPO/sale companies experience larger increases in operating income than the 10-K companies. In general, these differences are significant. . . . At the same time, however, the industry-adjusted changes in operating income to assets and to sales for the 10-K companies are all positive. Three of the six are significant at the 10% level or better. This is consistent with the hypothesis that the 10-K companies are using their assets more efficiently than the industry controls.

[T]he industry-adjusted changes in net cash flow for both groups are still large and, in most cases, still significant. The 10-K companies obtain industry-adjusted increases in net cash flow of 17.8%, 39.2%, and 99.5%, although only the result for year +2 is significant at the 5% level. The 10-K companies also obtain large and significant industry-adjusted increases in net cash flow to assets and to sales. . . . [These results] suggest that if a selection bias is present, it is small. . . .

Wealth Increases to Investors in Management Buyouts

This section considers whether the accounting changes identified [above] represent real, that is, valuable, economic changes. To do so, I estimate the total market-adjusted returns earned by investors in a subsample of the management buyouts. Positive market-adjusted returns would be consistent with the existence of valuable operating changes. . . .

I was able to find a market value for the post-buyout equity of 25 buyout companies at some date after the buyout. I refer to the date that a market value is first available as the post-buyout valuation date. Eleven of the 25 companies sold equity to the public through an IPO; six companies borrowed money in the public debt markets to purchase post-buyout equity and releverage themselves; and eight companies were sold to public companies or liquidated. The average time from the going-private date to the post-buyout valuation date was 2.68 years. For these 25 companies, I estimate the nominal and market-adjusted returns to pre-buyout shareholders, to post-buyout investors, and to the two groups combined. . . .

Consistent with management buyouts generating large value increases, the median market-adjusted return to pre-buyout shareholders and post-buyout investors [shown in Panel A of Table 11-5] is 77.0% (average = 96.0%). This measure is positive in all but one case. . . .

Table 11-5
Returns to Pre- and Post-buyout Investors in Management Buyouts
(from 2 months before buyout announcement to post-buyout valuation date)

(n = 25)	Median	Mean	% > 0
A. Total returns to pre-buyout shareholders and post-buyout investors			
Nominal return	220.3%	235.0%	100.0%
Market-adjusted return	77.0%	96.0%	96.0%
B. Returns to pre-buyout shareholders			
Nominal return	42.3	46.7	100.0
Market-adjusted return	37.2	37.9	100.0
C. Returns to post-buyout investors			
All post--buyout investors			
Nominal return	111.3%	127.9%	100.0%
Market-adjusted return	28.0%	41.9%	88.0%
Investors in post-buyout equity	785.6%	4,274.6%	100.0%
Length of time from going-private date to post-buyout valuation date	2.60 yrs	2.68 yrs	

The nominal return on capital earned by the post-buyout investors from the going-private date until the [post-buyout] valuation date for the buyouts is a median 111.3% (average = 127.9%). The median market-adjusted or excess return earned by post-buyout investors is 28.0% (average = 41.9%). Post-buyout investors in 22 of the 25 companies earn positive market-adjusted returns during this period. . . .

The evidence in Table 11-5 that the buyouts earned a large and significant market-adjusted returns is consistent with the evidence from the accounting data on changes in operating cash flows. As with the operating changes, these valuation results will be biased upward if the buyouts that can be valued are the better performers. . . .

Evidence on Changes in Employment

Shleifer and Summers (1988) argue that hostile takeovers and other control transactions can transfer value to shareholders from employees by breaking implicit contracts with those employees. Implicit contracts are broken by firing workers and/or reducing their wages. This section considers whether post-buyout decreases in employment accompany the operating changes.

Forty-two of the 48 buyout companies with post-buyout financial data also have post-buyout employment data. Table 11-6 presents the percentage change in employees at the end of the first full post-buyout year, year 1*, in which employment numbers are reported, in relation to the number of employees in the year before the buyout. In some cases, year 1* is the third or fourth year after the buyout. Table 11-6 then compares these changes in employment with the median industry change over the same period to obtain a measure of unexpected change in employees.

. . . [T]he median change in employment for [all] buyout companies is 0.9%. Employment increases in 50% of the companies. At the same time, employment has grown 12.0% less in these buyout companies than in other companies in the same industry (which is significant at the 1% level). This industry-adjusted result is consistent with the industry-adjusted decreases in sales experienced by the buyout companies.

Table 11-6
Effect of Management Buyouts on Employment
(from year −1 to first post-buyout year with employment data available)
(* = significant at 5% level; ** = significant at 1% level)

	Percentage change			Industry-adjusted change	
	N	Median	% pos.	Median	% pos.
Total sample	42	0.9%	50.0%	−12.0%**	30.9%*
Companies without significant divestitures or acquisitions	26	4.9%	61.5%	−6.2%	38.5%

. . . If a buyout company sells a division, its measured employment drops by the number of employees in the division. Unless the purchaser fires all of the division's employees, the measured change in employment overstates the true reduction in employment.   [I control] for this over-statement by [considering a subsample of 26 companies without large post-buyout acquisitions or divestiture]. More than three-fifths (61.5%) of these companies increase employment, with a median increase of 4.9%.   The industry-adjusted change is again negative (−6.2%), but is not significant.

In interpreting these results, the reader should note that the Shleifer and Summers argument pertains to actual employment changes rather than industry-adjusted changes.   The results here do not support the view that buyout gains come from firing a large number of employees. . . .

Evidence on Information Advantages and Incentive Changes

The information-advantage or underpricing hypothesis suggests that buyout investors and managers have information about potential operating changes or value increases that public shareholders do not have. . . . According to this view, operating changes would have occurred without the buyouts. . . .   The primary issue in distinguishing between the underpricing and reduced-agency-cost hypotheses is whether public shareholders (and other potential bidders) have the same information as buyout investors and managers. . . .

Pre-buyout equity ownership

This section examines the shareholdings of managers and directors of the buyout company as well as other informed players who do *not* invest in post-buyout equity (referred to collectively as informed nonparticipants). According to the underpricing view, these informed nonparticipants know that the true value of the buyout company (even without the buyout) exceeds the buyout price. In this case, it would be irrational for them to approve the buyout by selling their shares and [not] participating in the MBO.   The reduced-agency-cost hypothesis, on the other hand, has no such implications.

. . . [Members of the board of directors] who sell their shares into the buyout transaction and do not invest in equity of the post-buyout company are classified as management nonparticipants. . . .   [H]ostile parties that purchase at least 5% of the target's stock before the buyout, but do not invest in post-buyout equity . . ., are considered [to be informed nonparticipants] because they may have private information [about the company's value] that leads them to invest in the pre-buyout equity of the buyout company. . . .

Table 11-7 presents the shareholdings of informed management participants in the MBO and informed nonparticipants. The results document the existence of significant informed nonparticipants. Table 11-7 shows that management nonparticipants control a median 5.50% (average 9.66%) of the buyout company. In addition, hostile nonparticipants have stakes in 20 of 76 companies. The average stake of hostile parties in these 20 companies is 9.78%. The holdings of all informed nonparticipants equal a median of

10.00% (average 12.92%). These holdings are large, exceeding [the pre-buyout holdings] of the management participants. . . . This evidence is not supportive of the underpricing hypothesis. . . .

Table 11-7

**Pre-buyout Shareholdings of Informed Parties
in Management Buyouts**

	N	Percentage of shares of pre-buyout company		Value of shares held ($millions)	
		Median	Mean	Median	Mean
Management-MBO participants	74	4.67%	12.05%	$12.15	$39.80
All informed nonparticipants	75	10.00%	12.92%	$16.97	$32.56
Management nonparticipants	75	5.50%	9.66%	$ 8.30	$22.46
Hostile nonparticipants	75	0.00%	3.26%	$ 0.00	$10.11

Post-buyout equity ownership

Both underpricing and incentive considerations predict that the percentage of equity held by management increases after a MBO. . . . Table 11-8 presents the [difference between the] pre- and post-buyout equity ownership held by [the post-buyout] managers, both as a percentage of total equity and in dollars. . . . [T]he post-buyout managers increase their equity stakes by a median of 16.03%. . . .

In transactions involving a buyout specialist, at least one member of the buyout specialist sits on the board of directors. These specialists both own post-buyout equity and manage limited partnerships that buy post-buyout equity. In 62 transactions for which data are available, managers, directors, and buyout specialists together own or control a median 99.00% (average 83.10%) of post-buyout equity.

Table 11-8

Post- minus Pre-buyout Management Equity Ownership

	Percentage of total shares			Value ($ millions)		
	Median	Mean	N	Median	Mean	N
Chief executive officer	3.57	8.11	65	−1.55	−6.27	65
Two top managers	4.41	10.23	68	−1.55	−9.22	67
All other managers	9.96	10.79	68	−0.43	−1.50	67
All post-buyout managers	16.03	21.02	68	−3.69	−10.7	67

The distribution of the equity ownership . . . favors an efficiency or incentive interpretation over one of underpricing. Table 11-8 shows that the percentage of equity owned by the two top managers increases by a median of 4.41% whereas the percentage owned by all other managers increases by

9.96%. . . . This is a puzzling result if the buyout participants know that the buyout price is low [because then the top managers would want to keep a large fraction of the bargain-priced shares for themselves]. On the other hand, the results suggest that new incentives for junior managers play an important role in buyouts.

The smaller increase in percentage equity for the two top managers [is not] caused by a liquidity constraint. . . . Table 11-8 shows that the two top post-buyout managers reduce the dollar amount of their equity holdings by a median $1.55 million.

Hostile or competing bids

. . . During the sample period, 46 companies made unsuccessful MBO proposals valued at $50 million or more. . . . Management lost control . . . . in 34 of the 46 unsuccessful MBO bids. . . . This suggests that managers and investors who propose a buyout face an active market for corporate control that limits the degree of underpricing that can occur. . . .

Management turnover at the time of the buyout

The information-advantage hypothesis implies that the same managers run the company before and after the buyout. It would be irrational for a manager who knows the value of the company is higher than the buyout price to leave the company without investing in the new company. Alternatively, high management turnover would be consistent with the replacement of bad managers by good ones.

. . . [I]n 19 of 76 buyouts (25%), either the chairman, the CEO, or both do not join the new management team. In all of these cases, the departing executives approve the buyout either by tendering their shares or by voting for the buyout as members of the board of directors. . . . The unusually high top-executive turnover in buyout companies at the time of the buyout does not support a large role for superior managerial information.

Note on the Efficiency Gains from Leveraged Buyouts

1. *Other Studies of Post-LBO Performance.* Abbie Smith reports results that are qualitatively similar to Kaplan's for a sample of 58 management buyouts between 1977 and 1986. For her sample, the ratio of operating cash flow to operating assets increased from the year before the buyout (year -1) to the year after the buyout (year $+1$) by a statistically significant 6.3%. For the 20 firms with data available for year $+2$, the

change in operating returns from year -1 to year $+2$ was a statistically significant 9.8%.[7]

Frank Lichtenberg & Donald Siegel investigated the effects of LBOs between 1981 and 1986 on productivity using a plant-level database that included 1132 plants that were involved in leveraged buyouts. Their sample includes divisional buyouts as well as buyouts of entire firms, and includes both private and public companies. Lichtenberg and Siegel report statistically significant post-buyout increases in total factor productivity at LBO plants, compared to non-LBO plants, in the three years following the buyout. But they don't find productivity gains in the fourth and fifth post-buyout years; indeed the point estimates of productivity, although insignificant, are *lower* than non-LBO firms.[8] One possible explanation: cutbacks in capital expenditures may increase productivity in the near-term, but not in the long-term.

2. *Manager Conflicts of Interest.* Managers who plan to remain with the company after an MBO often face a conflict of interest. If they will own a higher percentage of Shellco than of Targetco, a *lower* acquisition price makes them better off. Moreover, the managers will strongly prefer that Shellco succeed in acquiring Targetco, rather than another bidder who may not want their services, nor offer them the same opportunity to get seriously rich.

These conflicts, coupled with managers' possibly superior information about the target's true value, have led some scholars to worry that public shareholders may lose from some MBOs because the company's true value, known to managers but not to shareholders, exceeds the takeover price. This *information asymmetry* explanation for MBOs, like the improved incentives explanation, predicts that MBO firms will show improved operating performance after the LBO -- but, without regard to improved incentives. It also predicts that target managers will receive too large a share of any efficiency gains compared to the public shareholders.

Kaplan doesn't find evidence that MBOs are systematically underpriced. Moreover, if managers conceal good news prior to an MBO, operating results should improve even when the LBO fails to close. Eli Ofek, however, finds no evidence of operating improvements after failed LBOs.[9]

---

[7] Abbie Smith, *Corporate Ownership Structure and Performance: The Case of Management Buyouts*, 27 J.Fin.Econ. 143 (1990). Other studies of post-LBO performance that reach results consistent with Kaplan's and Smith's include Ivan Bull, *Management Performance in Leveraged Buyouts: An Empirical Analysis*, in *Leveraged Management Buyouts: Causes and Consequences* 69 (Yakov Amihud ed.1989); Chris Muscarella & Michael Vetsuypens, *Efficiency and Organizational Structure: A Study of Reverse LBOs*, 45 J.Fin. 1389 (1990).

[8] Frank Lichtenberg & Donald Siegel, *The Effect of Leveraged Buyouts on Productivity and Related Aspects of Firm Behavior*, 27 J.Fin.Econ. 165 (1990).

[9] Eli Ofek, *Efficiency Gains in Unsuccessful Management Buyouts*, 49 J.Fin. 637 (1994).

Consistent with the accounting evidence, when the target of a failed is *not* subsequently acquired, its stock price returns to the pre-buyout level.[10]

But the evidence against the information asymmetry hypothesis is only suggestive, not definitive. A minority of LBOs could be underpriced, and this would not show up in the aggregate data. Moreover, in takeovers involving public acquirers, acquirers earn *at best* zero abnormal returns. Kaplan's finds large market-adjusted gains to LBO investors. This comparison suggests that LBOs may be underpriced in the sense that the acquirer keeps a large fraction of the total gains. From this perspective, the puzzle to be explained is not why LBO premiums are so high, but why aren't they even higher.[11]

3. *LBOs and Layoffs.* The evidence is mixed on whether LBOs lead to significant layoffs. Some studies, including Kaplan's and Smith's, find little evidence of layoffs. Others find significant cutbacks in employment.[12] Evidence on layoffs, like evidence on cutbacks in capital expenditures, is ambiguous. The layoffs could involve wealth transfers from employees to shareholders. But they could also be an important element of LBO-induced productivity gains.

4. *Sample Selection Bias.* In reading an empirical study, you should *always* be alert to the possibility of sample selection bias. Whenever the researcher has data for only *some* of the population of interest, the sample for which data is available may differ systematically from the remainder of the population, for which data is unavailable. This limits the extent to which we can infer that results for the sample for which data was available will also hold for the larger population from which the sample was drawn. Some researchers are careful to discuss possible sample selection biases. But other researchers are less careful, and even a careful researcher like Kaplan may not think of all of the possible biases that may infect a study.

Kaplan's LBO study is subject to at least three different types of sample selection bias. One is that he has financial data only for LBOs with publicly held debt or equity. But LBOs that voluntarily return to public equity ownership may perform better than LBOs whose equity remains privately held. Kaplan finds evidence of this by comparing the performance of a

---

[10] See *id.*; D. Scott Lee, *Management Buyout Proposals and Inside Information*, 47 J.Fin. 1061 (1992).

[11] See Ronald Gilson, *Market Review of Interested Transactions: The American Law Institute's Proposal on Management Buyouts*, in *Leveraged Management Buyouts: Causes and Consequences* 217 (Yakov Amihud ed.1989).

[12] See, e.g., Julia Liebeskind, Margarethe Wiersema & Gary Hansen, *LBOs, Corporate Restructuring, and the Incentive-Intensity Hypothesis*, Fin.Mgmt. 73 (Spr.1992); Krishna Palepu & Karen Wruck, *Consequences of Leveraged Shareholder Payouts: Defensive versus Voluntary Recapitalizations* (Harv.Bus.Sch. working paper 93-006, 1992). Chapter 15 discusses wealth transfers from employees at greater length.

subsample that is subject to this bias with a subsample -- firms with publicly held debt -- that should not show this bias. This result is confirmed by Francois DeGeorge & Richard Zeckhauser.[13]

A second source of sample selection bias is that many LBO companies are acquired by other companies, or otherwise drop out of the sample for which accounting data is available. This is a large part of the reason why the sample size in Kaplan's study drops to about 15 by post-buyout year $+3$, and why he could not extend his study beyond year $+3$. The sample with continuing public financial data may differ systematically from other LBO firms, in ways that are difficult to measure.

A third problem is that many LBO firms divest some businesses soon after the LBO. Kaplan can't measure how the divested businesses perform, nor tell for sure how the divestitures affect the pre-LBO versus post-LBO comparison of operating performance. How does he try to control for this problem?

5. *Puffing in Reverse LBOs*. A problem that is closely related to sample selection bias is that *reverse LBOs* -- LBOs that return to public ownership -- have an incentive to inflate their accounting results for the period *before* they go public, to increase the public offering price. Francois DeGeorge & Richard Zeckhauser find that after going public, reverse LBOs suffer a partial dropoff in performance (measured by operating income as a percentage of assets). To the authors, this suggests puffing in the pre-IPO financial data, though the LBO firms continue to outperform control firms. But it is also consistent with the common phenomenon of *reversion to the mean* -- the tendency of very good performance to deteriorate *overtime and* of very bad performance to improve in a wide variety of contexts.

These performance reversals do not cause reverse LBOs to underperform the market. If anything, reverse LBOs outperform other companies, which suggests that investors anticipate that LBO firms' accounting numbers at the time of a public offering are somewhat soft.[14]

2.   The Semi-Permanence of the LBO Organizational Form

If LBOs are truly a more efficient form of industrial organization, one would expect LBO companies to retain this organizational form, rather than return to public ownership. Many LBOs, however, soon return to public ownership and reduce their debt.

---

[13] Francois DeGeorge & Richard Zeckhauser, *The Reverse LBO Decision and Firm Performance: Theory and Evidence*, 48 J.Fin. 1323 (1993).

[14] See DeGeorge & Zeckhauser (1993), *supra* note 13; Shehzad Mian & James Rosenfeld, *Takeover Activity and the Long-Run Performance of Reverse Leveraged Buyouts*, Fin.Mgmt. 46 (Winter 1993).

Steven Kaplan
THE STAYING POWER OF LEVERAGED BUYOUTS
J.Applied Corp.Fin. 15 (Spr.1993)

Shortly after the publication of Jensen's *The Eclipse of the Public Corporation*, the *Harvard Business Review* published a response by Alfred Rappaport called *The Staying Power of the Public Corporation.*[2] Rappaport's principal objection to Jensen's argument was that high debt and concentrated ownership impose costs in the form of reduced managerial flexibility in responding to competition and change. Compounding the pressure for near-term results exerted by the heavy debt load, the typical LBO sponsor invests funds provided by outside investors who expect to be repaid in five to ten years. For these two reasons, Rappaport maintained, buyouts are inherently unstable and short-lived organizations.

There is another important source of instability in even the most successful LBOs -- one that Rappaport did not mention. As the value of the controlling investors' and managers' equity stakes increases over time, both groups bear an increasing amount of undiversified risk. One way to reduce or diversify this risk is to return the company to public ownership.[a]

Although Rappaport does not say so explicitly, his position is consistent with a view of buyouts as a form of "shock therapy." According to this view, buyout incentives lead managers to focus directly on increasing operating cash flow, curbing unprofitable investment, and selling unproductive assets. Many of these changes are one-time events. Once they have been accomplished, the benefits of the buyout become steadily less important over time. At some point, the costs arising from inflexibility [caused by the high debt], illiquidity, and excessive risk-bearing begin to outweigh the continuing benefits of buyout incentives, thus driving LBO companies to return to public ownership [and lower leverage]. . . .

[To assess the permanence of the LBO form, Kaplan studied a sample of 170 large LBOs completed between 1979 and 1986. As of December 1992, 41% of the sample remained privately owned. For the entire sample, the estimated median time spent in private ownership was 5.5 years. LBOs that returned to public ownership substantially reduced their debt. Their median ratio of interest expense to operating income dropped to .276 (with further declines possible over time), not much higher than the median of .235 for a comparison group of non-LBO companies.]

---

[2] Harv.Bus.Rev. 96 (Jan./Feb.1990).

[a] Kaplan suggests that insiders sell their shares to the public to reduce their exposure to the company's *unsystematic* risk. This point can be broadened. The high leverage that characterizes LBOs magnifies both the systematic and unsystematic risk borne by equity investors. This may be more total risk than managers care to bear over the long term. Deleveraging the company by having it sell shares to the public reduces the insiders' exposure to total risk. Eds.

[For the 18 companies that returned to public ownership by 1989 and had stock ownership data available, i]nsiders (buyout sponsors and managers) held a median of 39% (and an average of 42%) of post-IPO equity in these 18 companies. By contrast, the median inside ownership of over 1,000 nonfinancial companies tracked by the Value Line Investment Survey in 1986 was reported to be 5% (with an average of 12%). The much larger insider ownership percentages of post-IPO equity suggest that significant incentives to maximize shareholder value are still present in LBOs that return [to public ownership]. . . .

My evidence is consistent with the existence of two distinct kinds of LBOs: those [(probably a majority)] in which the process of going private functions as a kind of shock therapy for accomplishing one-time changes, and those in which the LBO is an inherently more efficient form of organization. . . .

Finally, my study also finds a moderate role for LBOs in transferring assets to strategic buyers through post-LBO divestitures. Just under 30% of the LBO companies and roughly a third of the original LBO assets end up being sold to companies with other operating assets.

Note on the Long-Run Competitive Strength of LBO Firms

1. High debt makes firms less flexible. The article below suggests how this can lead to long-run costs.

Norm Alster, ONE MAN'S POISON . . .
Forbes, Oct. 16, 1989, at 38

What do you do if one of your major competitors gets LBO'd? You smile viciously and go in and take market share away from him. . . . "It's a good position to be in," nods Gary Michael, vice chairman of retail food and drug chain giant Albertson's Inc. Based in Boise, Idaho, Albertson's is a well-heeled, conservatively financed company in an industry recently transformed by blockbuster mergers and LBOs. How does Albertson's (1988 revenues, $6.8 billion) capitalize on its competitors' financial fragility?

To find out, let's look at southern California. There Albertson's competes against debt-laden American Stores, which took over Lucky Stores in 1988 for $2.6 billion. Also in southern California is Vons, [an LBO] whose debt approaches 80% of capitalization; and Ralphs, which was bought in 1988 [in a leveraged acquisition] by Campeau Corp. With long-term debt just above 10% of total assets, Albertson's intends to use its financial power to expand at its leveraged rivals' expense. . . . In the southern California market, it is doubling its rate of expansion from four or five new stores a year to nine or ten. Where its rivals will need to use much of their available cash flow to cover interest and debt repayment, Albertson's will use its own internally generated funds to cover [most of its] capital expenditures over the period.

"[Rival chains] have to cut back on capital expenditures," says Albertson's Michael. "There are more sites available to us." . . . "We own the land, we own the stores," explains Michael. "With the leveraged buyouts, the developers own the land, and the developers are extracting premiums for leases." Some retail chains, Michael marvels, are leasing their equipment to hoard cash. "We don't have to pay interest on meat saws," says Michael. "I think our overall occupancy costs are about 20% cheaper. . . . As the low-cost operator, we're going to end up getting market share. That's our game plan."

Albertson's is not alone in taking advantage of leveraged rivals. James Moody Jr., chairman and chief executive officer of Hannaford Brothers Co. . . ., has been able to expand aggressively against such leveraged chains as Supermarkets General (a 1987 leveraged buyout). In recent months, says Moody, he's been surprised at how many times Hannaford has been chosen over rivals by prime shopping-site developers.

Why the good fortune? The most likely explanation, Moody reckons, is that a developer lowers his own borrowing costs by securing financially stable tenants. "He uses the leases with major tenants to go to an insurance company for financing. The insurance company looks at the strength of the tenants." Albertson's Michael agrees. "The developer," he says, "is charging for the risk."

The sharp blade of pricing can also be effective against leveraged rivals. The ink was not yet dry on Safeway's 1986 LBO when Giant Food Inc. of Landover, Md., slashed prices on more than 400 items in its Washington-area outlets. Safeway responded with its own cuts, but Giant has been able to sustain pricing pressure. David Sykes, senior vice president of finance at Giant, contends that his chain has the cash to do a better job in maintaining service and remodeling stores. The result: major market share shifts. Giant's share in the Washington area has climbed from 43% to 48% since 1986, while Safeway's share has declined from 34% to 30%, reports Kimberly K. Walin, senior retail trade analyst with Prudential-Bache securities.

This competitive advantage for the relatively unleveraged extends well beyond the grocery business. Take paper products giant Fort Howard Corp. It was taken private in a $3.6 billion deal. . . . Largely because of the costs of servicing its debt, explains Ross, Fort Howard began running losses at a rate of $100 million a year. This forced it to delay expansion of a Georgia tissue paper plant temporarily. With less industry capacity, prices have firmed and rivals have [gained market share].

When more than one industry leader is leveraged, normal market dynamics are unbalanced to the benefit of more conservative rivals. This shows up clearly in the prices of gypsum wallboard. With the housing market weak, wallboard prices have come down, says Jonathan Goldfarb, building analyst with Merrill Lynch Capital Markets. But they have come down much less sharply than in previous downturns. No one has taken the lead in cutting prices because no one can afford to, says Goldfarb. Neither National Gypsum (an LBO) nor USG Corp. (which took on heavy debt to escape a takeover) is ready to sacrifice precious cash flow for market share. Who wins? According to Goldfarb, the chief beneficiary may be the number three producer, the relatively unleveraged Georgia-Pacific. It can go after market share without having to worry about rivals cutting prices to stop it.

. . . James F. Nordstrom, cochairman of retailer Nordstrom, Inc. in Seattle, says he may become more aggressive against leveraged rivals. "They pay a lot more interest than we do as a percent of their sales," says Nordstrom. "We should have an advantage. Whether we use it or not is up to us." Nordstrom sees potential advantages in pricing its merchandise and in store maintenance. "They don't seem to be remodeling their stores as quickly as they used to," he says of leveraged competitors. Nordstrom says he is sure of one competitive advantage: retaining and motivating employees through profit sharing. Many of his leveraged competitors, he notes, "don't have any profits. It's hard to have profit sharing when you don't have profits."

––––––––––

2. The anecdotal evidence of competitive weakness in the story above is confirmed by a case study of the supermarket industry by Judith Chevalier. The study reports that (i) *non-LBO* firms experience positive abnormal returns when their competitors undergo LBOs; (ii) the non-LBO firms gain market share at the expense of LBO firms; and (iii) market share correlates strongly with profitability. Chevalier interprets these results as suggesting that LBOs can make supermarket firms weaker competitors.[15]

D.   What Made the LBO Boom Go Bust?

Sometime in 1989, the merger boom of the 1980s came to an end. By 1991, the inflation-adjusted dollar value of merger activity had dropped by more than 50% from the 1988 peak. Leveraged buyouts shrank even faster, with dollar volume declining by about 90%. Moreover, the nature of buyouts changed. Smaller transactions still took place, but the megabuyouts of the late 1980s all but disappeared. Defaults on LBO debt soared soon afterward, in the recession that began in 1990.

––––––––––

[15] Judith Chevalier, *Debt and Product Market Competition: An Event Study of Supermarket LBOs* (MIT Dept. of Econ. working paper 1992); Judith Chevalier, *Debt and Product Market Competition: Local Market Entry, Exit, and Expansion Decisions of Supermarket Chains* (MIT Dept. of Econ. working paper 1992).

1.   The Buyout Bubble

An anecdote: The UAL Buyout that Almost Happened: Perhaps the surprise failure to close of the United Airlines LBO in October 1989 was the pin that pricked the buyout bubble. The failure announcement, at 3:30 P.M. on October 13, 1989, sent the Dow Jones Industrial Average tumbling 190 points (about 8%) by the 4:00 close of trading. Or perhaps it was the Federated bankruptcy in 1990. But whatever the proximate cause, it appears in hindsight that takeover prices escalated in the late 1980s well beyond the value of the underlying businesses. When the takeover was financed almost entirely with debt, the result was default, bankruptcy, and often poor operating performance as well.

UAL Corp., the parent of United Airlines, was trading at around 120 in mid-1989 before Marvin Davis made a takeover bid. Management responded with an $300 per share LBO, which came within a whisker of completion. How, if investors valued UAL at $120, did management almost borrow the funds to buy it at a premium of 150% over the prior price?

The answer isn't obvious. UAL was generally thought to be well-run already. Moreover, it had undergone a leveraged recapitalization in 1987. As part of the leveraged recapitalization, UAL had sold off its hotel and car-rental businesses, so deconglomerating wasn't a source of value. And the leveraged recapitalization should have already forced UAL to do the easy things that it could do to increase cash flow. UAL was already fairly highly leveraged, so there weren't large tax savings available from further leveraging. And UAL was in a cyclical business, hardly ideal for an LBO.

The projections that UAL management furnished to bankers to justify the takeover made highly optimistic assumptions, and even then showed UAL losing money for years and barely repaying its loans. UAL's CEO, Stephen Wolf, would have walked away from the deal with $76 million in cash (plus a large equity stake in the LBO company). He certainly wasn't putting his money where his projections were. Why did the lenders (almost) lend?

Jay Palmer, WHY THIS LBO CRASHED: A PRESCIENT ANALYSIS OF A DOOMED DEAL
Barron's, Oct. 30, 1989, at 13

The bad news from UAL . . . did not shock . . . Anthony Low-Beer, a money manager and former airline analyst who . . . saw the UAL deal as flawed from the start and said so in no uncertain terms in a report released the week before the buyout came apart. . . . "The projections backing the [LBO] proposal suggests an unrealistic level of optimism," contends Low-Beer in his report. . . . [A] real risk exists of a downward spiral from which the airline may never recover. UAL employees and the banks stand to lose large sums of money."

Low-Beer's objections to the buyout began with the substantial benefits it provided for management and directors. Under the terms proposed, UAL's top two executives -- CEO Stephen Wolf and Chief Financial Officer John Pope -- were to invest only $15 million in the new company. Yet, if the deal went through according to the buyout prospectus,they would take home an exceptionally generous windfall profit of $114 million from the exercise of stock options. At the same time, UAL's independent directors and their entire families would be given free [first-class] travel for life on United, a perk valued at $800,000.

Though the banking fees that Citicorp, Chase Manhattan and others were to earn from the deal were by some accounts on the low side compared with those thrown off by other LBOs, they were hardly peanuts. . . . All told, [investment banking, legal, accounting, and other] fees and pre-paid interest expenses would aggregate $400 million, nearly double the $220 million that the pilot-management group proposed to invest in the enterprise.

. . .

The lead commercial bankers were Citicorp and Chase, while First Boston, Lazard Freres and Salomon Brothers acted as investment advisers to the deal. These financial powers apparently raised no serious challenge to management's extravagantly bullish forecasts for the decade through 1999, forecasts that formed the foundation of the buyout but were based on nothing in the airline's actual operating experience. . . .

The projections prepared by UAL management showed the airline enjoying friendly skies during bad times as well as good. Revenues were supposed to climb from $8.89 billion in 1988 to $11 billion in '90, $12.8 billion in '91, $14.8 billion in '92 and then uninterruptedly to $25.1 billion in 1999. Between 1990 and '99, operating profits were expected to rise [even more rapidly], from $488 million to $1.66 billion. . . .

The problem, Low-Beer pointed out, is that these projections were based largely on wishful thinking. UAL . . . figured that its load factor (the percentage of available seats occupied by paying passengers) would [average] 66.9% over the decade. By historical standards, this sort of performance would be nothing short of remarkable. It would represent a vast improvement over the 63.3% average load factor enjoyed by the airline in the past decade.

. . .

Low-Beer's report also questioned UAL's estimate that its yield (the average revenue earned per paying passenger mile) would rise from 12.8¢ in '90 to 17.4¢ in '99, a jump of 35.9%. . . . He pointed out that . . . in 1988, the airline's 11.3¢ yield was no higher than it had been in 1981.

. . . Low-Beer calculated that a 1% drop in the load factor [compared to the projections] would cut earnings by close to $130 million in 1990 . . . . [and] a 0.1¢ fall in yield would cut 1990 net income by $76 million . . . . If the [1990] load factor were to fall from the projected 66.7% to [a still respectable] 64% and if the yield were to drop to 12.5¢ from 12.8¢, the net loss [for 1990] would rise to $900 million from the projected $435 million deficit. If the load factor were to slide to 63% and the yield drop to 12.2¢, the loss could be as great as $1.26 billion.

In hindsight, the only question, had the United Airlines LBO closed, is how soon UAL would have defaulted on its debt, not if. Scholars may never untangle why or when the LBO boom became a bubble, or even demonstrate for sure that a bubble existed, but stories like UAL are suggestive, especially when supported by quantitative evidence on pricing. The next article, on the decline in junk-bond quality, reflects the increase in takeover prices, because takeover financing represented at least 75% of junk bond dollar volume for each year from 1985-1989.

Barrie Wigmore, THE DECLINE IN CREDIT QUALITY OF NEW-ISSUE JUNK BONDS
Fin. Analysts' J. 53 (Sept.-Oct. 1990)[*]

Credit ratio averages for new junk bond issuers in 1986-88 declined by 27-69% (depending on the ratio selected) compared with 1983-85 averages. This decline in credit quality reflects that over 75% of junk bond issues in 1986-88 were incurred to finance merger-related transactions at prices and capitalization ratios that entailed interest coverage ratios well below one.

The decline in credit quality was partially reflected in a decline in the percentage of new-issue junk bonds rated [BB (the highest non-investment grade rating)] from over 40% in 1982 to under 10% in 1988. But this decline understates the true decline in credit quality, because credit ratios for issuers of new bonds rated B by Moody's or Standard & Poor's declined 30-50% between 1983-85 and 1986-88. . . .

Table 11-9

Pro Forma Credit Ratios for Junk Bond Issuers, 1980-1988

(weighted by principal)

Year	EBIT Coverage of Interest[1]	Debt as % of Net Tangible Assets[2]	Cash Flow as % of Debt[3]	Common Equity as % of Capital	Volume Issued ($ bil)	Merger-Related as % of Total Volume
1980	1.99	60%	17%	39%	0.9	11%
1981	1.96	62	22	35	1.2	5
1982	2.07	65	18	35	1.5	13
1983	0.78	72	13	35	3.6	22
1984	1.14	175	7	21	7.4	45
1985	1.35	100	9	22	8.1	75
1986	0.77	123	5	16	24.4	75
1987	0.69	151	2	3	25.9	82
1988	0.71	202	3	4	27.0	93

1. *[P]ro forma* earnings before interest and taxes [(EBIT)] divided by *pro forma* interest.

2. *Pro forma* total debt divided by *pro forma* total assets minus goodwill, other intangibles, and current liabilities excluding current debt.

3. Net income plus depreciation and amortization divided by total debt.

---

2.   An Agency Cost Explanation for Overpricing

1. Wigmore's data show the dramatic decline in the ability of LBO companies to service their debt as the 1980s progressed. Early 1980s LBOs could prosper with no improvements in cash flow after the buyout. But by 1986, a typical LBO needed to increase its operating income by 50% simply to cover its interest, with nothing left over for repayment of principal.

One would expect, as takeover prices climbed as a multiple of operating income, that more of the capital structure would be in the form of equity, on which dividends could be deferred until the hoped for operating improvements were realized. Instead, the opposite occurred. Equity fell dramatically as a percentage of total capital, reaching the trivial level of 3-4% of capital in 1987 and 1988. After paying upfront fees and expenses, which were typically 4-6% of the buyout price, late 1980s LBOs began their new life with essentially zero equity.

2. Wigmore suggests one possible reason why a bubble may have developed. Investors may have relied on safety ratings by Standard & Poor's and Moody's, and not realized that S&P and Moody's were lowering their rating standards as the decade progressed. But that can be only a partial explanation, because institutional investors ought to be doing their own credit analysis, not just relying on published ratings.

3. A second explanation involves the structure of the junk bond market. Many junk bonds were sold to high yield mutual funds, which were created by the mutual fund industry for the express purpose of chasing the high yields promised by junk bonds. High-yield mutual funds were marketed to (often unsophisticated) individual investors on the basis of yield. Having promised to buy junk bonds, the mutual fund managers had to do so regardless of quality. Indeed, the higher interest rates on low-rated junk bonds let mutual fund managers advertise higher yield -- whether or not the higher yield would translate into a higher return after the higher defaults that one would expect on these bonds. The defaults would affect total return, but not yield.

Indeed, mutual funds were allowed to advertise, as yield, the accrual of interest on zero coupon and pay-in-kind bonds, which paid no current cash interest. This might be reasonable if the company were earning enough money to cover the accrued interest. But in many cases, as Wigmore documents, LBO company weren't earning their interest accruals, which cast doubt on whether the interest would ever be paid.[16]

Some savings and loans were also substantial junk bond buyers. They too, may have cared more about the ability to report "earnings" today, in order to boost their net worth and keep regulators at bay for a while longer, than about the ultimate return on their investment.

4. Legendary investor Warren Buffett was among the early skeptics about lending practices that became common in the late 1980s, especially the use of zero-coupon bonds to finance acquisitions at prices so high that the projected cash flow couldn't cover interest payments.

Warren Buffett
1989 ANNUAL REPORT OF BERKSHIRE HATHAWAY INC.

A zero-coupon bond . . . requires no current interest payments; instead, the investor receives his yield by purchasing the security at a significant discount from maturity value. The effective interest rate is determined by the original issue price, the maturity value, and the amount of time between issuance and maturity. . . .

As happens in Wall Street all too often, what the wise do in the beginning, fools do in the end. In the last few years, zero-coupon bonds

---

[16] See Louis Lowenstein, *Ignorance Isn't Bliss: Lack of Disclosure by Junk-Bond Funds is Shameful*, Barron's, May 29, 1989.

(and their functional equivalent, pay-in-kind [PIK] bonds, which distribute additional PIK bonds semi-annually as interest instead of paying cash) have been issued in enormous quantities by ever-junkier credits. To these issuers, zero (or PIK) bonds offer one overwhelming advantage: It is impossible to default on a promise to pay nothing. . . .

This principle at work -- that you need not default for a long time if you solemnly promise to pay nothing for a long time -- has not been lost on promoters and investment bankers seeking to finance ever-shakier deals. But its acceptance by lenders took a while: When the leveraged buyout craze began some years back, purchasers could borrow only on a reasonably sound basis, in which conservatively-estimated *free* cash flow -- that is, operating earnings plus depreciation and amortization less normalized capital expenditures -- was adequate to cover both interest and modest reductions in debt.

Later, as the adrenalin of deal-makers surged, businesses began to be purchased at prices so high that all free cash flow necessarily had to be allocated to the payment of interest. That left nothing for the paydown of debt. . . . Debt now became something to be refinanced rather than repaid. The change brings to mind a New Yorker cartoon in which the grateful borrower rises to shake the hand of the bank's lending officer and gushes: "I don't know how I'll ever repay you."

Soon borrowers found even the new, lax standards intolerably binding. To induce lenders to finance even sillier transactions, they introduced an abomination, EBDIT -- Earnings Before Depreciation, Interest and Taxes -- as the test of a company's ability to pay interest. Using this sawed-off yardstick, the borrower ignored depreciation as an expense on the theory that it did not require a current cash outlay.

Such an attitude is clearly delusional. At 95% of American businesses, capital expenditures that over time roughly approximate depreciation are a necessity and are every bit as real an expense as labor or utility costs. . . . Capital outlays at a business can be skipped, of course, in any given month, just as a human can skip a day and even a week of eating. But if the skipping becomes routine and is not made up, the body weakens and eventually dies. Furthermore, a start and stop feeding policy will over time produce a less healthy organism, human or corporate, than that produced by a steady diet. . . .

You might think that waving away a major expense such as depreciation in an attempt to make a terrible deal look like a good one hits the limits of Wall Street's ingenuity. If so, you haven't been paying attention during the past few years. Promoters needed to find a way to justify even pricier acquisitions. Otherwise, they risked -- Heaven forbid! -- losing deals to other promoters with more "imagination."

So, stepping through the Looking Glass, promoters and their investment bankers proclaimed that EBDIT should now be measured against cash interest only, which meant that interest accruing on zero-coupon or PIK bonds could be ignored when the financial feasibility of a transaction was being assessed.

. . . Under this new standard, a business earning, say, $100 million pre-tax and having debt on which $90 million of interest must be paid currently, might use a zero-coupon or PIK issue to incur another $60 million of annual interest that would accrue and compound but not come due for some years. The rate on these issues would typically be very high, which means that the situation in year 2 might be $90 million cash interest plus $69 million accrued interest, and so on as the compounding proceeds. Such high-rate reborrowing schemes, which a few years ago were appropriately confined to the waterfront, soon became models of modern finance at virtually all major investment banking houses.

When they make these offerings, investment bankers display their humorous side: They dispense income and balance sheet projections extending five or more years into the future for companies they barely had heard of a few months earlier. If you are shown such schedules, I suggest that you join in the fun: Ask the investment banker for the one-year budgets that his own firm prepared as the last few years began and than compare these with what actually happened. . . .

With zeros, one party to a contract can experience "income" without his opposite experiencing the pain of expenditure. In our illustration, a company capable of earning only $100 million annually -- and therefore capable of paying only that much in interest -- magically creates "earnings" for bondholders of $150 million. Here, finally, was an instrument that would let Wall Street make deals at prices no longer limited by actual earning power. . . .

The zero-coupon or PIK bond possesses one additional attraction for the promoter and investment banker, which is that the time elapsing between folly and failure can be stretched out. This is no small benefit. If the period before all costs must be faced is long, promoters can create a string of foolish deals -- and take in lots of fees -- before any chickens come home to roost from their earlier ventures. . . .

Our advice: Whenever an investment banker starts talking about EBDIT -- or whenever someone creates a capital structure that does not allow all interest, both payable and accrued, to be comfortably met out of current cash flow net of *ample capital expenditures* -- zip up your wallet. Turn the tables by suggesting that the promoter and his high-priced entourage accept zero-coupon fees, deferring their take until the zero-coupon bonds have been paid in full. . . .

---

5. Even if one can explain why mutual funds and S&L's bought overpriced junk bonds, why were banks willing to lend ever higher amounts as senior debt? Several answers are plausible: First, the banks did exercise some restraint: Bank loans as a percentage of total LBO debt declined as the 1980s progressed, while subordinated debt increased. Second, the banks may have relied, to some degree, on the willingness of junior lenders to invest.

As long as someone else put up half of the money in the form of subordinated debt or equity, the banks were willing to put up 50% in senior debt, trusting that the junior lenders and equity investors, with their money at greater risk, knew what they were doing. Meanwhile, the junior lenders may have returned this dubious favor by relying on the credit analysis that they expected the banks to be doing.

A further possibility: commercial banking had become an unprofitable business, and the banks were forced to chase yield wherever they could find it. From this perspective, the bad loans that banks made to leveraged companies are similar to the developing country loans, energy loans, and real estate loans that also produced much grief for banks in the 1980s. Indeed, the more loan losses the banks suffered in other areas, the more they needed profits from takeover loans to offset those losses. It surely helped that takeover loans carried hefty upfront fees, that (under applicable accounting rules) could be booked as income right away. Indeed, the issue that reportedly killed the UAL buyout was not the $300 per share takeover price, but UAL's relative stinginess with upfront fees on its bank loans.

Bank regulators might have clamped down, and later did, but at the time they were chasing a new phenomenon. They hadn't yet put loans for highly leveraged transactions (HLTs) into a separate classification so they could assess the risks that such loans posed to bank solvency.

6. If we can explain why lenders would lend to overpriced acquisitions, explaining why equity investors would invest is relatively simple. The equity investors were, in substance, buying an option that would pay off if the company did well. Even if the acquisition price exceeded company value -- that is, the option was out of the money -- the option would still have value because the company *might* do better than expected. From this perspective, the use of zero coupon and PIK bonds made the option more valuable by lengthening its term.

In addition, it became common, as equity investments shrank as a percentage of total capital, for managers to be paid much more for their pre-buyout stock and options than they reinvested for the post-buyout equity. The $76 million payday that UAL CEO Stephen Wolf stood to receive in the UAL buyout is an extreme example of this trend. Similarly, LBO promoters often earned more in upfront fees than they reinvested in post-buyout equity. Thus, the post-buyout equity was akin to a valuable option that the managers and LBO promoters received for free.

Some junk bond buyers were, like equity investors, effectively buying options. The S&L's, for example, some of whom bought junk bonds and made LBO loans, were operating with close to 100% government financing, through deposit insurance. If takeover loans and junk bonds did well, great; if not, the deposit insurance fund would pick up the tab.

7. Another partial explanation for overpricing: many leveraged buyouts in the late 1980s were sponsored, not by the established LBO promoters, who had reputational capital at stake if a deal went bust, but by investment banks who were trying desperately to enter this hugely profitable

business. They created LBO departments, and staffed them with relatively young investment bankers who were hired to do deals and earn fees, had never experienced a bust period, and could find themselves looking for another job if they went for too long saying, time and again, "No thanks, the price is too high."

8. For LBOs and leveraged recapitalizations that were undertaken in response to hostile bids, the target's managers also had a strong incentive to promote a transaction that kept them in control, almost regardless of price or the company's suitability for an LBO. This might lead the managers to make unreasonably aggressive projections of future performance, or downplay business risks, when seeking financing for a defensive transaction. If lenders were insufficiently sensitive to this incentive, they might finance bad transactions.

Consistent with this view, Krishna Palepu and Karen Wruck report that profitability improvements for firms undergoing leveraged recapitalizations are concentrated in firms that recapitalized without a hostile bid having been publicly announced. In contrast, defensive recapitalizations, undertaken in response to a hostile bid, produce smaller, statistically insignificant increases in operating income as a percentage of assets. These poor results were apparently not anticipated by investors -- on average, defensive recapitalizations show large negative abnormal stock returns after the recapitalization. This is consistent with some defensive recapitalizations being driven more the desire of the target's managers to avoid a takeover than by their intent (or ability) to use the crisis of high debt to improve operations.[17]

9. These explanations have in common the need to go beyond the efficient markets hypothesis, in which institutional investors never systematically pay more for a security than it's worth or make imprudent loans, and investigate the incentives of the people who work at financial institutions. Perhaps mutual fund managers realized that the junk bonds they were buying were, well, junk, but bought them anyway, because of the need to show high yield in order to market the fund to investors. Perhaps bank loan officers had doubts about LBO pricing, but suppressed them because the upfront fees were attractive. After all, last year's loans were still current. And so on.

10. Steven Kaplan & Jeremy Stein report evidence consistent with an agency cost explanation of overpriced LBOs. They studied the financial characteristics of 124 large LBOs between 1980 and 1989 to explain the dramatic increase in defaults they document: none of the 19 pre-1983 LBOs, 4 of the 39 LBOs between 1983 and 1985, and 14 of the 66 LBOs between 1986 and 1988. Over the 1980-89 period, the price paid in LBOs rose relative to current cash flows with no evidence of lower risk or higher expected growth. At the same time, public subordinated debt replaced

---

[17] Palepu & Wruck (1992), *supra* note 12.

private subordinated debt, making a restructuring in the event of financial distress more difficult. Finally, management and LBO sponsors took more of their compensation up front, which gave them incentives to close the transaction regardless of price.[18]

3.   The Efficiency Implications of Overpriced LBOs

Does it matter that some LBOs are overpriced, or lead to defaults? Jensen argues that defaults are of little importance; perhaps even beneficial. Both leveraged and unleveraged businesses sometimes fall in value. When an unleveraged business loses value, the stockholders suffer the loss. When a leveraged business loses value, debtholders suffer losses too. There's nothing wrong with that, as long as the debtholders are compensated for that risk through a higher interest rate. Defaults can be valuable if they cause the firm to respond more quickly to the cause of the cash shortfall. They will be harmful if they cause the value of the company's business to fall. Jensen argues that workouts will be quick and cheap in the new world of high leverage. So why worry?

The countervailing view is that while some workouts are quick and cheap, many others are slow and costly, and cause substantial harm to the underlying business, as customers and valued employees flee the apparently sinking business, and creditors squabble over the remains. Moreover, company managers may take steps in an effort to avoid default, such as cutting back on positive NPV projects, that reduce the company's long-term value.[19]

The Operating Performance of Late 1980s LBOs. Research on the benefits and costs of financial distress is in its early stages, and the available empirical studies on whether overleveraging is a cause for serious concern is mixed. William Long & David Ravenscraft divide a sample of 198 LBOs between 1981 and 1987 into 91 early (1981-1984) and 107 late (1985-1987) LBOs. They find that early LBOs led to a significant 1.99% increase in cash flow as a percentage of sales, while later, higher priced LBOs did not (the average change was an insignificant −0.15%). In other words, early LBOs, which could pay their debts even if their cash flow didn't grow, increased their operating margins. In contrast, later LBOs, which desperately needed

---

[18] Steven Kaplan & Jeremy Stein, *The Evolution of Buyout Pricing and Financial Structure (Or, What Went Wrong) in the 1980s*, 108 Q.J.Econ. 313 (1993); see also Martin Fridson, *What Went Wrong with the Highly Leveraged Deals? (Or, All Variety of Agency Costs)*, J.Applied Corp.Fin. 57 (Spring 1993).

[19] For a case study that outlines the complex and conflicting incentives of different LBO investors when the LBO firm encounters financial distress, see Karen Wruck, *What Really Went Wrong at Revco?*, J.Applied Corp.Fin. 79 (Summer 1991).

operating improvements to pay their debt, failed to achieve them.[20] The implicit verdict: debt can be a valuable corporate medicine, but not if administered in oversized doses.

On the other hand, Tim Opler finds very different results for a sample of 44 very large LBOs between 1985-1989: median industry-adjusted operating cash flow was roughly flat from year -1 to year $+2$, but operating cash flow/sales increased by a statistically significant 11.6%.[21] David and Diane Denis find significant improvements in the ratio of operating income to total assets in year $+1$ for a sample of leveraged recapitalizations between 1984 and 1988. However, the improvements tail off and become statistically insignificant in year $+2$.[22]

Capital Expenditures. Several studies find sharp reductions in capital expenditures after late-1980s LBOs and leveraged recapitalizations. These spending cuts could be value increasing, but they could also impair the firm's long-run competitive position, in ways not captured by the 2-3 years of post-buyout accounting data that are available in the published studies.[23]

The Costs of Financial Distress. David Brown, Christopher James & Michael Ryngaert study whether highly leveraged firms respond differently to earnings shocks than less leveraged firms. They find that the operating returns of leveraged firms rebound faster in post-shock year $+1$, but the differences are negligible in post-shock year $+2$. They also find that highly leveraged firms are about twice as likely to go bankrupt, be acquired, or change CEOs, in the two years after the earnings shock.[24]

On their face, these results tend to support the optimistic view that highly leveraged firms respond faster to financial distress. But the data conceal some worrisome trends. The high leverage firms already have lower capital expenditures than low leverage firms, yet both groups cut capital spending by similar amounts (as a percentage of assets) in response to an earnings shock. If the high leverage firms have already trimmed their capital spending, one wonders whether these further cuts will harm their long-run competitiveness.

---

[20] William Long & David Ravenscraft, *Decade of Debt: Lessons from LBOs in the 1980s*, in *The Deal Decade: What Takeovers and Leveraged Buyouts Mean for Corporate Governance* 205 (Margaret Blair ed.1993).

[21] Tim Opler, *Operating Performance in Leveraged Buyouts: Evidence from 1985-1989*, Fin.Mgmt. 27 (Spr.1992).

[22] David Denis & Diane Denis, *Managerial Discretion, Organizational Structure, and Corporate Performance*, 16 J.Acct. & Econ. 209 (1993).

[23] See, e.g., Denis & Denis (1993), *supra* note 22; Opler (1992), *supra* note 21.

[24] David Brown, Christopher James & Mike Ryngaert, *Does Leverage Impede Recovery from an Earnings Shock? An Analysis of Firms' Responses to Poor Performance* (U.Fla.Grad.Sch. of Bus. working paper 1992).

Also, the highly leveraged firms quickly cut employment, while low leverage firms do not. Employment at high leverage firms declines by almost 14% in the shock year, compared to a 3% increase at low leveraged firms. That might be good strategy in the short run, but the highly leveraged firms may lose valuable employees that cannot be easily replaced. One wonders too about the quality of employees that a firm that fires workers so quickly will attract in the future.

In sharp contrast to Brown, James & Ryngaert, Tim Opler & Sheridan Titman find evidence that leveraged firms fare worse than their competitors when the industry gets into trouble. Highly leveraged firms in troubled industries underperform their industry peers across a wide variety of performance measures, including market share, operating income, and stock price. For example, the most highly leveraged 10% of firms have sales declines 26% greater than the least leveraged 10%.[25]

4.   Can an LBO that Ends in Bankruptcy Add Value?: A Case Study of Federated

It is possible for an LBO to increase value, compared to the pre-LBO company, and still go bankrupt because the new higher value is not enough to let the LBO firm pay its debts. The bankruptcy process will result in direct and indirect costs, but the overall transaction could still add value in the sense that the market-adjusted post-bankruptcy value of the firm exceeds its pre-LBO value. Robert Campeau's acquisition of Federated Department Stores offers a lovely laboratory to test this hypothesis, because it has been studied by two researchers, one sympathetic to LBOs and the other an opponent of high leverage, using very different methodologies.

On the optimistic side, Steven Kaplan reports evidence that convinces him that Campeau's acquisition of Federated added value, even though it ended in bankruptcy court. Kaplan reports that the acquisition increased Federated's value by roughly $1.8 billion, but led to bankruptcy because Campeau paid a premium of $3.4 billion over Federated's pre-bankruptcy market price. In particular, Campeau was able to resell 9 of Federated's 15 operating divisions for proceeds, discounted back to the date of the acquisition, of $3.77 billion -- 89% of Federated's pretakeover value. Yet the retained divisions accounted for only 44% of Federated's pretakeover operating income. Kaplan also finds little evidence that the costs of the bankruptcy process were significant.[26]

---

[25] Tim Opler & Sheridan Titman, *Financial Distress and Corporate Performance*, 49 J.Fin. 1015 (1994).

[26] Steven Kaplan, *Campeau's Acquisition of Federated: Value Destroyed or Value Added*, 25 J.Fin.Econ. 191 (1989); Steven Kaplan, *Campeau's Acquisition of Federated: Post-Bankruptcy Results*, 35 J.Fin.Econ. 123 (1994).

Louis Lowenstein, on the other hand, sees the excessive leverage imposed by the acquisition as an unmitigated disaster.

Louis Lowenstein
SENSE AND NONSENSE IN CORPORATE FINANCE
30-46 (1991)*

The Perils of Debt

Let's do some comparison shopping at Bloomingdale's . . . and Lord & Taylor. . . . Their respective owners -- Federated Department Stores . . . and May Department Stores -- had once looked very much alike: strong department store franchises, each earning about the same profit on a dollar of sales, [with] conservative balance sheets. Sooner than they could have guessed, however, the resemblances would all but disappear.

After having been acquired by Robert Campeau in 1988, Federated was utterly awash in debt. Cash shortages and other financial distractions took management's eye off customers and the stores, and the company soon foundered. . . . May Department Stores, [which remained] soundly financed, was . . . able to keep its attention where it belonged. Better yet, the turmoil in the industry created unusual opportunities for May to seize market share from now-troubled competitors and to make opportunistic acquisitions.

Campeau put Federated Department Stores into play in January 1988. . . . When the bruising [bidding war] was over, the Federated shareholders, who only a few weeks before had owned a stock that traded at $33 a share, received over $73 a share from Campeau. For the shareholders, it was a triumph. They received $6.5 billion, or over 20 times the company's $313 million of net earnings in its most recent year.

But Campeau had borrowed virtually the entire purchase price and now was forced to sell off large pieces of the Federated business. He sold to Macy two West Coast divisions, Bullock's and I. Magnin, as part of the settlement of the bidding contest. Then he sold to May two others, Filene's and Foley's. Following the same script he had used with some initial success at Allied Stores in 1987, he then sold off or transferred elsewhere a few other divisions. Even so, the new LBO enterprise, Federated/Campeau, ended up with a highly attractive group of stores: Abraham & Straus, Bloomingdale's, Burdines, Lazarus, and Rich's/Goldsmith's. These divisions accounted for about 41% of the sales of the old company in the year ended January 30, 1988 (fiscal 1987), and 56% of total divisional profits. If the company had been financially viable, Robert Campeau would have bought a good business. . . .

The Summer of 1985 -- Before the Fall

[Federated and May both] operated in the same, traditional, full-service segment of the department store business. They competed in many of the same markets, with roughly similar merchandise and expense structures. Table 11-10 contains some comparative numbers for [fiscal 1985]. . . . The similarities [in financial performance are] striking. . . .

Table 11-10
May and Federated -- Before Campeau
(in $ millions, except sales per square foot)

Financial Data	May [fiscal 1985]	Federated [fiscal 1985]
Department Stores Only		
Sales	$3,327	$6,685
Divisional operating profit	$345	$662
Divisional profit margin	10.4%	9.3%
Sales per square foot	$121	$152
Company-wide totals		
Earnings before interest and taxes (EBIT)	$485	$655
Interest expense	$51	$86
Ratio of EBIT to interest expense	9.5×	7.6×
Capital expenditures	$225	$364
Bond rating	AA	AA
Return on assets	8.1%	6.3%
Return on total capital	11.8%	8.5%
Long-term debt as of total capital	30%	22%

[However, Federated's performance had been slipping. Its] CEO, Howard Goldfeder . . ., was known as someone who, fearing mistakes, would study a problem endlessly -- "analysis/paralysis," a colleague would later describe it. . . . Same-store sale increases -- a key figure in retailing -- were a skimpy 2.5% percent in 1987. Over time, the impact of such slow growth is chilling. . . .

After the Fall

By 1988, Federated was ripe for a shake-up. There had been only slow progress in adopting a program similar to the one unfolding at May: spinning off the unrelated operations, buying back a major amount of stock, refocusing and centralizing operations, and improving returns to shareholders. . . . [O]ne could have rightly said in 1988 that Federated was a candidate for an LBO -- at least an LBO of the more prudent kind that had been done earlier in the decade.

But Federated was an abominable choice for an LBO of the high-leverage sort that was in vogue in 1988. . . . Strong companies will stagger under a heavy debt load, but those that are already slipping, need to change or realign management, need to make quick asset sales, must reinvest in the business the cash flow from depreciation simply to maintain market position, must soon refinance a large amount of short-term debt, and for good measure, do not have owners with deep pockets standing on the sideline, will almost certainly collapse. That was Federated. It collapsed.

Managers, particularly newly arrived ones, need time to make changes in an orderly and efficient way, and with scalpels, not meat cleavers. They need time to make some mistakes. In short, they need a margin of safety, and in a thinly capitalized LBO, such as Federated . . ., there is only a margin of peril. Instead of producing success, a push-to-the-limit LBO is likely to produce trauma, unnecessary costs, and, far too often, failure.

How else can we explain why Federated, which had consistently earned over $600 million before interest and taxes before the LBO, was bankrupt within 18 months after? The popular explanation was that Campeau was a loon, but as every retailer and creditor in and around Federated with whom I talked agreed, this mountain of debt would have buried almost anyone. It just might have taken a little longer.

By 1990, when Federated filed for bankruptcy . . ., a retailer who studied [its] financial statements would have been unable to identify them as belonging to the same compan[y] . . ., not simply because [Federated] had assumed so much debt but because [its] operations had been so badly shaken. Table 11-11 summarizes the changes at [May and Federated].

May Department Stores -- Right on Course

May Department Stores had also changed considerably during the four years since fiscal 1985 (the year reflected in Table 11-10). . . . May bought the poorly performing Associated Dry Goods [for $2.4 billion in stock] in 1986 believing that it would improve the stores, which it soon did. . . . Then in 1988 it acquired the two Federated divisions, Filene's and Foley's, for $1.5 billion in cash and notes. May also sold off several non-core businesses for over $600 million, and [sold] much of its real estate, whose value had not been reflected in the stock price. In 1989, the company bought back almost 20% of its outstanding stock. In all, the company's long-term debt jumped by $2.4 billion, and its credit rating slipped from AA to A+.

Table 11-11

The Sequel to Campeau

(in $ millions, except sales per square foot)

Financial Data	May [fiscal 1989]	Federated [fiscal 1989]
Sales per square foot	$159	$162
Earnings before interest and taxes (EBIT)	$1,032	$151
Interest expense	$233	$516
Ratio of EBIT to interest expense	4.4×	0.3×
Interest as a % of total sales	2.4%	10.6%
Capital expenditures	$427	$111
Debt rating	A+	D
Return on assets*	8.1%	0.9%
Return on total capital*	9.2%	-10.8%
Long term-debt as % of total capital	56%	134%

* Excludes bankruptcy-related charges at Federated. Federated's return on assets is positive, even though return on capital is negative, because return on assets is calculated by adding back to net income the after-tax cost of interest expense, then dividing by average assets.

Remarkably, however, four years later, after all these changes, it was still pretty much business as usual at May. The company was operating on a far larger scale but at the same high level of performance. Return on assets was precisely the same 8.1% it had been in 1985. While return on equity in fiscal 1989 had increased, from 16.7% to an even better 18.5%, that was largely a reflection of the additional leverage. Return on total capital declined, from 11.8 to 9.2%.

May is a marvelous yardstick for measuring [what Federated might] have looked like if [it] had not been so distracted by financial concerns. Figure 11-4 tracks three revealing ratios, year by year, for May from fiscal 1984 to fiscal 1989: capital expenditures, interest expense, and earnings before interest and taxes (EBIT), each as a percentage of sales. (By looking at earnings before interest charges, rather than after, we can see more readily how the underlying business was doing, apart from changes in financial structure.) The results are clear. Business was good, and there were no great surprises over the six years. . . .

Figure 11-4
May Company
Capital Expenditures, Interest Expense, Operating Profit
(As a Percent of Sales)

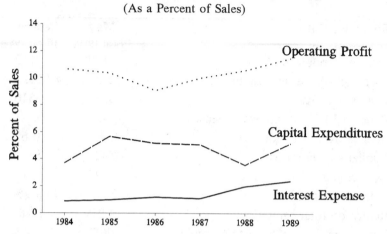

Federated -- Debt is Destiny

The story on Federated is painfully simple (as well as simply painful). In a mere 18 months between the buyout and bankruptcy, there were 8,000 layoffs in the five divisions of Federated/Campeau [that weren't sold off] -- more than half of them in the first few weeks. Robert Campeau visited each of the divisional chiefs and, depending on the size of the operation, told them that he wanted $40 million, $50 million, a year in savings, with none of it from the sales force -- and no discussion, please. He got them. Some of the cuts were appropriate, but many were not. And for what? Given the company's Humpty Dumpty financial structure, the odds that Federated/Campeau would have a great fall were close to 100%. The company began life with interest charges that would, on a pro forma basis, consume 11.9% of every dollar of sales. No retailer can do that and expect to survive without divine intervention. Everything has to go just right, and that's not the way retailing is.

. . . The pro forma EBITDA [earnings before interest, taxes, depreciation and amortization] at the time of the LBO was about $700 million. One senior official at Federated said [later] that the annual level of capital expenditures required just to maintain market position, without growth, was about $200 million, and that an additional $75-90 million a year was required to fund the additional working capital for same-store growth in accounts receivable and inventories. Even EBITDA would not be enough to cover those outlays and also $600 million of [annual] interest charges. . . .

Much of the real story for Federated/Campeau is captured by Figure 11-5, but this one tells a very different tale from the one for May.

Figure 11-5
Federated Department Stores
Capital Expenditures, Interest Expense, Operating Profit
(As a Percent of Sales)

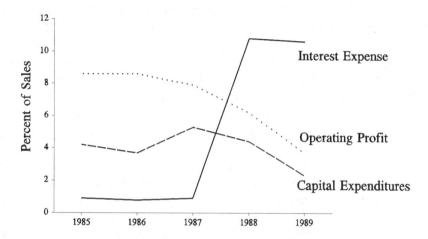

Beginning in 1988 . . ., both capital expenditures and earnings -- even earnings *before* interest and taxes -- plummeted. The drop in capital expenditures was predictable. A company that is overtaxed by interest payments has little money left for investments. Even if the will is there, developers begin to look for other chains to anchor their malls.

The explanation for the other drop-off, the one in earnings, is only slightly more complicated. As the chart shows, Federated/Campeau's interest charges exceeded its earnings by a wide margin from the day of the takeover. Such a company will survive only if it runs swifter than the rest of us, and with no time for a warmup. . . . Retailers like to talk about having momentum; although they mean momentum on the upside, it works in both directions, and for Federated it was all downhill. Federated's suppliers became discouraged, many of them reluctant to make goods, say, in the Far East, where lead times were long [with no assurance that the goods would be bought or they would be paid]. . . .

By the fall of 1989, Bloomingdale's and its sister stores were being run for cash, not profit. Discounting was heavy. The traditional Thanksgiving sales were extended right through Christmas. The Federated management was distracted. Financial issues took time from business issues. A veritable army of suppliers and lenders were increasingly nervous and would have to be stroked. There were also errors of execution, reflecting the pressures of the LBO itself, the excessive leverage and, to a lesser degree, Campeau's destabilizing personality. Underlying many of the errors, said [Federated CEO Zimmerman], was the simple fact of too much change all at once. In [a mature] industry with no tail wind, one where execution and implementation were everything, management's attention was continually diverted. . . .

The Inevitability of Bankruptcy

At a company that is troubled financially but sound at the business level, the CEO knows that it would be foolish to allow it to slide into bankruptcy. The direct costs alone are enormous. According to an informed estimate, the out-of-pocket fees and similar expenses for the Allied Stores/Federated bankruptcy proceedings were going to average $60 million *annually.* . . . Beyond them, the costs were more difficult to quantify but also significant. Management would have to be segmented so that the Chapter 11 process and the development of a plan of reorganization did not intrude (too much) into the day-to-day running of the business. And, of course, bankruptcy proceedings often damage a business permanently, some more than others.

Logic would also tell our CEO that he or she should, as a resourceful executive, be able to negotiate an informal, out-of-bankruptcy reorganization with the creditors, who, after all, also know how costly and disruptive bankruptcy can be. During the 1980s, while the Great LBO Bubble was still building, it was repeatedly said by Michael Milken, and his numerous, sometimes subsidized, and often sycophantic followers, that bankruptcy would be the exceptional case, rather than the usual one. Reorganizations would now be accomplished speedily and informally. . . .

The theory didn't hold up at Federated, but not for want of trying. Working with Merrill Lynch, the company tried diligently to put together a package that would avoid a filing. But the issues, the capital structure and the personalities were too complex for a plan to be worked out in a few months time. Vince Lombardi used to say that his Green Bay Packers never lost a game, it was just that the clock ran out. The clock, said Zimmerman, also ran out on Federated.

[The] capital structure of Federated was anything but simple. Claims against the subsidiary operating companies were effectively senior to parent company obligations. The bank debt was secured. There were "temporary" bridge loans in three different flavors, with different security protections. The long-term debt of the pre-LBO company had not been paid off, and was held by quite different interests from the newly issued junk debt. In short, with 80,000 vendors, 150 or so banks, and other creditors as well, their creditors alone would require 450 chairs in a meeting hall. Where the boosters had spoken of LBOs as if the investors and lenders were a choir group singing in harmony, this crowd would sound more like the Tower of Babel. . . .

In a mature but competitive business, such as department stores . . ., [m]anagement needs to devote its energies to merchandising and to stores and people. May Department Stores could do that, and indeed the chaos at Allied, Federated and elsewhere gave it openings to move into new markets and to seize additional market share in existing ones. Meanwhile, at Federated . . ., financial pressures seriously distracted management from its normal, day-to-day, operations. The stability and the strength that are essential for a company to work effectively with people, and for people to respect the leadership, were either damaged or destroyed.

Note: Postscript on Federated

1. Can Kaplan's and Lowenstein's accounts be reconciled? How can Campeau's acquisition have added value if operating income plummeted? A glimmer of an answer appears by inspecting the sources of the gain that Kaplan reports. Much of the gain came from the post-LBO sale of some of Federated's divisions at high prices. Lowenstein doesn't analyze these sales, but he would probably contend that the high sale prices reflect not value added by Campeau, but rather that Campeau wasn't the only fool willing to overpay for department stores at the time.

2. To value the divisions that Federated retained, Kaplan relies not on a multiple of operating income, but on projected sale prices prepared by Federated's investment bankers. Those valuations were probably based on Federated's historic performance, not its depressed performance at the time the projections were prepared, which was hopefully only temporary. And indeed, Federated did later emerge from bankruptcy as a reasonably healthy company. By 1994, it emerged as the winning bidder for R.H. Macy, which had also made the downhill journey from LBO to bankruptcy court.

CHAPTER 12: TAX INCENTIVES FAVORING
(OR DISFAVORING) ACQUISITIONS

A common explanation for acquisitions is that the federal income tax system, both individual and corporate, creates incentives which favor them.[1] This explanation involves a form of wealth transfer: *Business* value doesn't change, but the combined firm has a higher *market* value than the sum of the pre-acquisition constituent companies' market values because the present value of expected tax payments declines.

Congress has repeatedly acted on the belief that the tax code favors acquisitions. For example, significant portions of the corporate income tax changes enacted by the Tax Equity and Fiscal Responsibility Act of 1982 (TEFRA) were first introduced as the Corporate Takeover Tax Act of 1982.[2] Professor Ginsburg describes TEFRA as responding to the public impression "of a nation overwhelmed by a spreading rash of enormous corporate acquisitions motivated and financed in significant part by extraordinary tax avoidance."[3] Similarly, the repeal of the *General Utilities* doctrine in the Tax Reform Act of 1986, discussed below, was designed to restrict one purported tax benefit from acquisitions: a step-up in basis that increased future depreciation.

But the accuracy of the claim that a significant number of acquisitions are tax-motivated -- are undertaken to achieve favorable tax treatment -- has remained hard to assess. Those asserting that the tax system favors acquisitions have never clearly stated just what tax favoritism means in this context.[4] The first step in evaluating whether (and how) the tax system encourages *or discourages* acquisitions is to more precisely define the concept of tax favoritism.

Three different meanings can be ascribed to the claim that the tax system favors acquisitions, each of which reflects a different belief about the importance of the tax system in determining the level of acquisition activity.

The first sense in which the tax system might favor acquisitions is that acquisitions can result in "pure" tax gains that are not achievable in other

---

[1] See, e.g., Federal Trade Commission, *Economic Report on Corporate Mergers* 142-58 (1969); Walter Hellerstein, *Mergers, Taxes, and Realism,* 71 Harv.L.Rev. 254 (1957); John Lintner, *Expectations, Mergers and Equilibrium in Purely Competitive Securities Markets,* 61 Am.Econ.Rev. 101, 107 (Papers & Proceedings, 1971); Lucian Bebchuk, *The Case for Facilitating Competing Tender Offers: A Reply and Extension,* 35 Stan.L.Rev. 23 (1982); Fred Weston, Kwang Chung & Susan Hoag, *Mergers, Restructuring and Corporate Control* 208-12 (1990); F.M. Scherer, Testimony before the Subcomm. on Telecomm., Consumer Protection & Fin., House Comm. on Energy & Commerce 15 (Mar.12, 1984).

[2] H.R. 6295, 97th Cong., 2d Sess. (1982).

[3] Martin Ginsburg, *Taxing Corporate Acquisitions,* 38 Tax L.Rev. 171, 216 (1983).

[4] The discussion of the different meanings of the statement that the tax system favors acquisitions draws heavily on Ronald Gilson, Myron Scholes & Mark Wolfson, *Taxation and the Dynamics of Corporate Control: The Uncertain Case for Tax-Motivated Acquisitions,* in *Knights, Raiders and Targets: The Impact of the Hostile Takeover* 271 (John Coffee, Louis Lowenstein & Susan Rose-Ackerman eds.1988).

ways. This claim is that an acquisition will increase the aftertax cash flows from a group of assets without any change in pretax cash flows. Such a transaction would produce no synergy, only a wealth transfer from the Treasury to the shareholders of the constituent firms.[5] A familiar example is the claim that the acquirer can step-up the basis of the target company's assets, thereby increasing future depreciation deductions associated with the assets and thereby decreasing taxable income.

The second possible meaning of tax favoritism reflects a claim that the tax gain in question, while also achievable by other means, is *best* achieved by an acquisition. One must then explain why an acquisition is the preferred means of achieving the tax gain in question.

The first two claims involve the *existence* of different levels of tax favoritism. A third, stronger, claim involves the *importance* of tax favoritism, relative to other takeover motives. Tax gains are said to be the principal cause of some acquisitions. This claim can be stated in terms of *but for* causation: But for the prospect of tax gains, an acquisition would not have occurred. Or it can be stated in terms of acquisition pricing: Tax gains are said to explain the size of premiums observed in acquisitions.

The claim of but for causation is not directly testable. Researchers cannot observe *why* a particular transaction took place. Causation can be inferred, however, if estimated tax gains are a large fraction of the increase in shareholder market value from an acquisition. Conversely, if estimated tax gains (or losses) are a small fraction of the increase in shareholder market value, it is more likely that changes in expected tax payments are an incidental element of a transaction undertaken for other purposes.

This Chapter has two principal goals. The first is to evaluate these claims concerning the importance of taxes as an acquisition motive. To do so requires some familiarity with the federal tax treatment of corporate acquisitions, a domain of enormous complexity. Section A provides a simple overview of those aspects of the subject necessary for the project. However, the discussion must come with a disclaimer and a warning. First, the disclaimer: Even the leading corporate tax treatise[6] provides no more than an overview of acquisition taxation; a more detailed understanding requires recourse to the voluminous professional literature.[7] The warning: We discuss a good deal of tax history, involving rules since repealed. This history is necessary because most empirical studies of the importance of taxes as an acquisition motive concern tax rules in place before the Tax Reform

---

[5] The point of the definition is to eliminate the possibility that the acquisition results in any operational efficiencies or cost savings. If these were present, pre-tax cash flows would also increase.

[6] Boris Bittker & James Eustice, *Federal Income Taxation of Corporations and Shareholders* (5th ed.1987).

[7] The best place to start is Martin Ginsburg & Jack Levin, *Mergers, Acquisitions and Leveraged Buyouts* (updated annually).

Act of 1986. In addition, it is easier to understand the present rules if you know how they evolved.

Following this overview of the tax treatment of acquisitions, Section B sets out the theory underlying the different claims concerning the impact of taxes on acquisition activity in light of the applicable tax rules both before and after 1986. Section C then surveys the available empirical evidence.

The Chapter's second goal is to introduce students to *transactional planning*: The effort to choose among functionally similar acquisition techniques in order to achieve a particular goal, here the deferral or reduction of tax payments. The tax overview is designed to highlight the ways in which transaction *form* affects tax *substance*.

A. An Overview of Federal Income Taxation of Corporate Acquisitions

To assess the transactional incentives created by the federal income tax system, it is useful to examine separately the principal tax concerns of the target shareholders on the one hand, and the acquiring company on the other. The target shareholders' principal concern is whether they must recognize gain or loss when they exchange their shares in the target for the consideration offered by the acquirer. The acquiring company's principal concern is how the tax attributes of the target company change as a result of the transaction -- especially the tax basis to be used for depreciation or subsequent sale of its assets, whether recapture of previous depreciation will be required, and the continued availability of the target's net operating loss, if any. The resolution of these concerns depends, in the first instance, on whether the transaction is a "reorganization" within the meaning of the highly technical definition of that term in Internal Revenue Code (hereinafter IRC or Code) § 368. If so, the transaction is a *tax-free reorganization*; if not the transaction is *taxable*.

1. Tax-Free Reorganizations

The Code provisions dealing with the consequences of the disposal of property build on the proposition that taxation is only appropriate when a gain or loss is "realized." The taxpayer realizes gain or loss by substantially altering the form in which wealth is held, for example by selling stock for cash. A mere increase in the market value of the stock will not result in tax. The concept of a tax-free reorganization reflects the policy judgment that, when specified conditions are met, changes in the identity or business of a corporation in which the shareholder holds stock will not trigger realization, and recognition of gain or loss at either the corporate or shareholder level will be deferred.[8] No tax is due, and there is no change in the shareholder's basis in the corporation's stock, nor in the corporation's basis in its assets.

a.   *Which Transactions are Tax-Free Reorganizations?*

IRC § 368(a)(1) defines three basic types of acquisitive reorganizations. In general terms, an *A* reorganization (so termed because it is defined in § 368(a)(1)(A)), is a statutory merger, a *B* reorganization is an exchange offer in which the acquiring company buys enough target stock from the target company's shareholders so that the acquirer owns at least 80% after the transaction, and a *C* reorganization is a transaction in which the acquiring company purchases substantially all of the assets of the target and the target thereafter liquidates. The underlying concept is that these three transaction forms are functionally equivalent ways to make a corporate acquisition, and thus should receive roughly equivalent tax treatment.
Even at the definitional level, however, this concept is imperfectly executed; the transactions are *not* defined in equivalent terms. The type of consideration that may be used in each of the three forms of the transaction is different. The statute does not restrict the type of consideration that can be received by target shareholders in an *A* reorganization. Judicial gloss on the statute, through the "continuity of interest" doctrine, requires that a substantial portion of the consideration received by target shareholders be *stock* of the acquiring company (which can be voting or nonvoting) and that most of the target shareholders hold the acquiring firm's stock for a period of time.[9] The IRS generally requires that stock constitute 50% of the consideration in a merger before it will rule in advance that a planned transaction meets the *A* reorganization definition.[10] In contrast, in a *B* reorganization, the *only* consideration that can be used to acquire the target's stock is *voting stock of the acquiring company*. The *C* reorganization fits somewhere between these extremes. Voting stock is the only consideration

---

[8] Treas.Reg. § 1.1002-1(c) states that "[t]he underlying assumption of the [nonrecognition] provisions is that the new property is substantially a continuation of the old investment still unliquidated; and in the case of reorganizations, that the new enterprise, the new corporate structure, and the new property are substantially continuations of the old still unliquidated."

[9] The continuity of interest doctrine, reflected in Treas.Reg. §1.368-1(b), is part of the effort to distinguish reorganizations, where there has been a change in the form of an investment but not substance, from sales. See generally, Bittker & Eustice (1987), *supra* note 6, at ¶ 14.11; Ginsburg & Levin, *supra* note 7, ¶ 610 *et seq.*

[10] Rev.Proc. 77-37, § 3.02, 1977-2 C.B. 568. The courts have been more lenient, having approved transactions where as much as 62%, Nelson v. Helvering, 296 U.S. 374 (1935), and 75%, Miller v. Commissioner, 84 F.2d 415 (6th Cir.1936), of the total consideration was cash. Experienced practitioners are said to treat 40% stock as a rough cut-off point. Ginsburg & Levin, *supra* note 7, ¶ 610.03.

that can be paid for the target's assets, but the acquirer's assumption of the target's liabilities doesn't count as consideration.[11]

The Code also allows, subject to greater or fewer restrictions, *triangular* and *reverse triangular* variations of the three standard reorganization formats. A triangular acquisition involves the acquirer's use of a wholly-owned subsidiary to effect the acquisition. The non-tax aspects of triangular acquisitions are considered in Chapter 16. Examination of the tax treatment is not necessary to evaluate whether the tax system provides a motive for acquisitions, and is omitted here.

Section 368 only defines when a reorganization exists.[12]   Other sections of the Code, to which we turn next, specify the consequences if a transaction is a reorganization. In this Chapter, the term "reorganization" means a reorganization as defined in IRC § 368.

b.   *Treatment of Target Shareholders in a Reorganization*

If target shareholders exchange their stock for stock of the acquiring company in a reorganization, they recognize no gain or loss, on the theory that the essential character of their investment hasn't changed. This is accomplished by IRC § 354, which provides (with qualifications) that gain or loss is not recognized when stock or securities of a party to a reorganization are exchanged solely for stock or securities in another

---

[11] A *C* reorganization typically involves the acquirer assuming the liabilities of the target because the consideration for the transaction is voting stock and the target otherwise would have no way to meet its obligations after selling substantially all its assets. In a mirage-like exception, the *C* reorganization definition allows up to 20% non-stock consideration, but if *any* non-stock consideration is used, assumed liabilities then count against the 20% cap. Because assumed liabilities usually represent more than 20% of the total consideration in the transaction, this exception is of little practical significance.

[12] In addition to the matters specified in § 368(a), a transaction must meet two judicially created requirements to constitute a reorganization -- the business purpose doctrine and the continuity of business enterprise doctrine. The former requires that the transaction have a non-tax purpose, although whether that purpose must be the transaction's primary purpose remains ambiguous. See Ginsburg & Levin, *supra* note 7, ¶ 609. The latter requires that the transaction contemplate "a continuity of the [target's] business enterprise under the modified corporate form." Treas.Reg. § 1.368-1(b). This can be satisfied either by continuing the target's historic business or by using a significant portion of the target's assets in the acquirer's business (or a new business). *Id.* § 1.368-1(d)(2).

corporation that is a party to the reorganization.[13] This accounts for the popular description of reorganizations as "tax-free."

The tax freedom is not permanent, however. Recognition of gain or loss is merely deferred, not foregone. Deferral is accomplished by § 358, which provides that target shareholders "carry over" their basis in the target's stock to the stock or securities of the acquiring company that they receive. If the market value of the acquiring company stock received exceeds a shareholder's basis in the target stock given up, the carryover basis retains this potential gain, which will be recognized when the new securities are sold. For example, suppose a target shareholder receives in a reorganization acquiring company stock worth $100 in exchange for target stock in which the shareholder has a $50 basis. No gain or loss would be recognized on the exchange pursuant to § 354. However, the shareholder's basis in the acquiring company's stock would be $50, a carryover of the previous basis in the target company's stock. This preserves the unrecognized gain that existed at the time of the exchange. If the shareholder later sells the acquirer's stock for $100, the deferred $50 gain is recognized.[14]

From the perspective of a target shareholder, deferral of gain is desirable because of the time value of money. In the previous example, putting off $50 of gain for two years, assuming a 40% marginal tax rate, a pretax discount rate of 10% and an after tax discount rate of 6%, reduces the present value of the tax from $20 to $20/(1.06)^2 = $17.80 -- a savings of $2.20 in present value. Put differently, the $20 tax that would have been paid can be reinvested at an aftertax rate of 10%, and will grow in two years to $20 × (1.06)^2 = $22.47. The present value of the extra $2.47 is $2.20.

The incentives are reversed when the target shareholder would recognize a loss, were it not for reorganization treatment -- that is, when the shareholder's basis in the target's stock *exceeds* the value of the consideration offered by the acquiring corporation, the shareholder's incentives are reversed. This tax loss could otherwise be used to offset other taxable income, and thus reduce the total tax that is due. The present value of this offset is reduced by deferral.

---

[13] The qualifier "solely" in § 354 serves a very different purpose than in the definitions *B* and *C* reorganizations in § 368. In § 368, "solely" is jurisdictional in character. If other than voting stock is used as consideration in a *B* or *C* transaction, the transaction does not qualify as a reorganization. In § 354 the term deals with the situation, generally in an *A* reorganization, where a shareholder receives some cash or other nonqualifying consideration in a transaction that qualifies as a reorganization. Gain is recognized as to this portion of the consideration, and is deferred for qualifying consideration. The character of the gain (ordinary income or capital gain) is determined under the § 302(b) dividend equivalency tests applied as if the non-qualifying consideration were received in a redemption occurring after the reorganization. Clark v. Commissioner, 489 U.S. 726 (1989).

[14] If the shareholder dies before disposing of the stock in the acquiring company, the deferral becomes forgiveness of *income tax* because IRC § 1014 provides for a step-up in basis to market value at the time of death. *Estate tax* may still be due based on market value at the time of death.

While whether target shareholders prefer reorganization treatment depends on whether the value of the offered consideration exceeds their basis in their target stock, the intensity of their preference is unlikely to be symmetrical. Deferral can be achieved *only* by structuring the entire transaction to fall within § 368. Individual shareholders generally cannot achieve deferral through their own tax planning.[15] But if particular target shareholders prefer to recognize gain, they can simply sell the securities of the acquiring company received in the transaction.[16]

The importance to the target shareholders of whether the transaction qualifies as a reorganization is also attenuated for tax-exempt shareholders, such as pension funds, who qualify for tax deferral for all transactions. This is of increasing importance as such entities come to hold a large percentage of the stock of publicly held companies.

c. *Vehicles for Shareholder Choice*

When the takeover consideration is stock of a publicly held acquirer, the ability of target shareholders to recognize loss by selling their shares if the transaction qualifies as a reorganization reduces the extent to which the tax treatment of the transaction affects the value of the transaction to shareholders. If some shareholders desire recognition, while others desire nonrecognition, the desires of both can be satisfied by structuring the *transaction* as a reorganization. But while structuring an acquisition as a reorganization should satisfy most target shareholders' interest in flexibility, the acquiring company may also care about the form of the transaction.

---

[15] Deferral can sometimes be accomplished in a nonreorganization transaction by giving shareholders who desire deferral an interest only installment note. See generally Theodore Ness & William Indoe, *Tax Planning for Dispositions of Business Interests* ¶ 6.01[1][a] at 6-3 to 6-4 (1985). If the interest rate equals the market rate, the result is essentially the same as receiving cash, except that capital gain (but after 1984 not recapture, if any) is deferred until the note's principal is paid. The attractiveness of this alternative depends on the risk associated with the acquiring company's promise to make the balloon principal payment, and the shareholder's willingness to defer receipt of the cash. In general, reducing default risk through bank or other third party guarantees of the installment note will not prevent installment sale treatment. See Ginsburg & Levin, *supra* note 7, ¶ 203.042. But installment treatment is not available if the installment note is readily tradeable, nor if the shareholder "monetizes" the note by using it as security for a loan. IRC § 453A.

[16] Shareholders will incur brokerage fees and other transactions costs if they sell the acquirer's securities after a reorganization transaction. Also, the election is available as a practical matter only if (i) there is a public market for the acquiring company securities received; (ii) the shareholder doesn't want to remain as a shareholder of the acquiring company, or is willing to accept the price risk involved in selling the acquirer's stock, and buying it back only after waiting long enough to avoid a claim that the sale and repurchase was a sham. Shareholders who are affiliates of the acquirer (or become affiliates in the transaction) also face securities law restrictions on how and when they can resell the acquirer's stock.

Most important, the acquiring company may want to use cash or debt securities as the sole or principal form of consideration.

An acquiring company may prefer using cash as consideration for several reasons. One often-stated reason is that use of cash can reduce or avoid the dilution in earnings per share (EPS) that would result if stock were used. Suppose that the acquirer and the target have the same number of shares outstanding, and each earned $3.00 per share in the year prior to the acquisition. If the acquiring company exchanges more than one of its shares for each share of the target company's stock, the acquisition will *reduce* the earnings per share of the acquiring company. For example, if the acquirer exchanges 1.5 of its shares for each target share, the acquirer's post-acquisition earnings of the acquiring company will be only $2.40 per share.[17] In contrast, paying in cash, presumably borrowed at a market rate of interest or currently invested and earning interest, will often, depending on the price-earnings ratio of the acquirer and the market rate of interest, produce less or even no dilution in EPS.

Note, however, that the higher EPS will be earned by a more highly leveraged, and hence riskier, company. Other things equal, the acquirer's stock should trade at a lower P/E ratio, to reflect this higher risk. This raises the question of whether the higher EPS will result in the acquirer's stock trading for a higher price in the market. Why might paying with $50 worth of stock result in a lower market valuation of the acquirer's stock than paying with $50 in cash? (Hint: recall the discussion of free cash flow theory in the last two chapters.) Could part of the concern be not with earnings per share as such, but with whether the acquiring firm has overpaid, with dilution in EPS serving as a signal of possible overpayment?

The acquiring company may also prefer to use cash to avoid regulatory delays under federal (and some state) securities laws. Under federal securities law, if stock is used as consideration, its offer and sale must be registered under the Securities Act of 1933, which can entail substantial delay between announcement of the proposed transaction covering the shares to be offered and the date the Securities and Exchange Commission declares the registration statement effective and the offer can be completed. During this delay period, various unfavorable events may occur, including the appearance of a competing bidder, a decline in the acquirer's stock price, and defensive action by the target if the offer is unwelcome. Cash tender offers, in contrast, although also requiring substantial disclosure of information, involve a shorter delay before the offer can be completed.[18]

Taking the needs of the target shareholders and those of the acquiring company together, there will be situations where the goal is to devise an

---

[17] Earnings will have increased by 100% while the number of outstanding shares has increased by 150%.

[18] A cash transaction may also reduce delay resulting from the Hart-Scott-Rodino Premerger Notification Act, under which the waiting period for cash offers can be shorter than for stock transactions. See Chapter 25, *infra*.

acquisition technique that: 1) gives target shareholders the option of tax deferral; 2) lets the acquiring firm use a substantial amount of cash as consideration; and 3) where speed is important, lets the acquiring firm avoid the regulatory delays associated with the use of stock as consideration.

For this purpose, an *A* reorganization is the only possibility, because *B* and *C* reorganizations permit only voting stock to be used as consideration. An *A* reorganization, it will be recalled, requires only that the acquirer use enough stock to satisfy the "continuity of interest" doctrine (50% stock consideration will suffice to obtain a private letter ruling confirming reorganization treatment from the IRS; a somewhat lower percentage appears to satisfy the courts).[19] This flexibility in type of consideration allows an acquisition technique called a *cash-election merger*. In this form of transaction the target is merged into the acquiring company[20] and each target shareholder can elect whether to receive cash or acquiring company stock. To insure that enough target shareholders choose stock to satisfy the continuity of interest doctrine, the cash option is typically limited to no more than 49% of the target's stock, with a provision for proration if cash elections exceed the ceiling.

This "one-step" cash-election merger does not meet the acquiring company's need for speed because the transaction involves issuing the acquiring company's securities in addition to cash, so registration under the Securities Act of 1933 is still required. This problem of delay can be solved if the two aspects of the transaction -- cash and stock -- can be segregated. In the *two-step cash-election merger,* the first step is a cash tender offer, typically for 45-49% of the target's stock. This can be made without the delay of registration or the need for a shareholder vote on a merger. If the acquirer wants to obtain absolute voting control, it can buy 51% of the target's shares from target shareholders without appreciable tax risk. Also, in a friendly transaction, the acquirer can assure absolute control by obtaining a "leg up" option to buy additional shares for cash or stock *directly from the target*. If the option is exercised, these shares do not count for the continuity of interest requirement, which turn on whether enough of the target's shareholders will hold the acquirer's stock after the transaction.

Once the first-step tender offer has been completed, the threat of defensive tactics or competing bids is minimal, and the remaining shares can be acquired on a more leisurely timetable in a second-step merger using stock as consideration.[21] For tax purposes, the two steps will presumably be

---

[19] See note 10, *supra.*

[20] Cash-election mergers can also be structured in triangular and reverse triangular variations.

[21] See generally James Freund & Richard Easton, *The Three-Piece Suitor: An Alternative Approach to Negotiated Corporate Acquisitions,* 34 Bus.Law. 1679 (1979).

integrated under the familiar step transaction doctrine and *A* reorganization treatment is available.[22]

d.   *Treatment of the Acquiring Company in a Reorganization*

The concept underlying the reorganization provisions of the Internal Revenue Code -- that only the form but not the substance of the shareholders' investment has changed -- carries over to the treatment of the acquiring company in a reorganization. Just as the transaction is disregarded at the shareholder level through nonrecognition of gain or loss and carryover of basis, it is also disregarded at the corporate level. Two aspects of corporate level nonrecognition are critical: (1) carryover of the target company's basis in its assets, and (2) survival of the target's other tax attributes, particularly its net operating loss.

Basis Determination.   In an *A* or *C* reorganization, the acquiring company succeeds directly to ownership of the target company's assets. Consistent with the notion that only a formal shift in ownership has occurred, § 362(b) provides that the acquiring company retains the target company's basis in the assets acquired: a carryover basis. The acquirer's tax incentives then depend on whether the target's basis in its assets exceeds the consideration to be paid. If so, reorganization treatment is desirable so that the target's higher basis, and resulting higher depreciation, can be maintained. In the more common case where the value of the consideration exceeds the target's basis, taxable treatment -- which produces a new basis that reflects the acquirer's cost -- would be preferable if no other tax consequences turned on this *step-up* in basis.

In a *B* reorganization, the acquiring company merely acquires the target company's stock. Title to the target's assets has not changed hands, so there is no occasion for changing their basis in the target's hands. The target retains its original basis in its assets unless a further step is taken: the liquidation or merger of the target, now a controlled or wholly-owned subsidiary, into the parent. If a liquidation follows as part of a prearranged plan, the step transaction doctrine is applied and the transaction is recharacterized as if the end result of both steps, the target's assets coming to rest inside the parent, had been accomplished in a single step. The entire transaction is then treated as a *C* reorganization and tested under those rules.[23] If the assets of the target become directly owned by the parent

---

[22] See King Enterprises, Inc. v. U.S., 418 F.2d 511 (Cl.Ct.1969); see generally Jack Levin & Stephen Bowen, *Taxable and Tax-Free Two-Step Acquisitions and Minority Squeeze-Outs,* 33 Tax L.Rev. 425 (1978).

[23] See, e.g., Rev.Rul. 67-274, 1967-2 C.B. 141. Because the requirements of *B* and *C* reorganizations differ somewhat -- for example, a "creeping *B*" reorganization, where the acquiring company has a previous position in the target's stock before making the acquisition,

through a subsequent merger, the stock purchase and the merger are collapsed and treated as a single *A* reorganization under the step transaction doctrine.[24] Either way, the acquiring company takes a carryover basis.

Survival of Other Tax Attributes. The Code's nonrecognition concept has implications at the corporate level beyond determining the acquiring company's basis in the target's assets. Do the other tax attributes of the target company disappear, as merely part of the target company's formal structure that has been shed, like the shell of a hermit crab in pursuit of larger quarters; or do they become part of the target company's genetic heritage which follow its substance to the acquiring company?

The survival of tax attributes other than asset basis is the province of IRC § 381. Twenty-three tax attributes of the target company -- including historical earnings and profits, tax accounting methods, investment tax credits, and most important, net operating losses -- are specified to carry over to the acquiring company, in each case subject to quite extensive statutory and regulatory detail.

The tax attributes of the target company carry over in *A* and *C* reorganizations as both transactions result in the acquiring company holding the assets of the target company directly. These tax attributes also carry over following the liquidation of a controlled subsidiary under § 332. Such a liquidation is common at some point after a *B* reorganization (exchange offer), for the purpose of freezing out the remaining minority.[25] When a *B* reorganization is not followed by a second step freezeout, the target remains as a separate entity and the problem of "survival" of tax attributes does not arise, except with respect to the filing of consolidated returns[26] and the use of its net operating loss, to which we now turn.

---

is acceptable while a "creeping *C*" reorganization is not -- integration of formally separate steps (the stock purchase and the subsequent liquidation) through the step transaction doctrine can disqualify an otherwise qualifying transaction. See Bittker & Eustice (1987), *supra* note 6, at 14-148 to -152; Ginsburg & Levin, *supra* note 7, ¶ 702.071, 074. If the liquidation occurs long enough after the original stock purchase so as not to be integrated with the stock purchase, carryover treatment is generally still required under IRC § 332, governing the liquidation of 80%-owned subsidiaries.

[24] *King Enterprises, supra* note 23; Ginsburg & Levin, *supra* note 7, ¶ 702.073, 075.

[25] Where the second step liquidation was part of the original plan, the entire transaction would be treated as a single step *C* reorganization, as discussed above.

[26] IRC § 1501 allows an affiliated group of corporations, affiliation being defined, in essence, as 80% common ownership, to file a single return that treats the group as a single taxable entity. The rules governing eligibility to file a consolidated return and the method of computing consolidated taxable income are extraordinarily complex and tax even the clarifying power of Professor Bittker. See Bittker & Eustice (1987), *supra* note 6, ch. 15.

2. Survival and Transfer of Net Operating Losses

The target company's net operating loss carryforward (NOL) is an important element of our overall concern with tax savings as a motive for acquisitions. One can easily imagine circumstances where a company's net operating loss, because it is too large to be fully used to offset income during the carryforward period, because it is uncertain whether the company will ever become profitable, or merely because the number of years needed to use up the carry forward reduces its value, would be worth more to another company. If that extra value can be captured by selling the company to another company that can use the loss, and if the loss cannot be readily transferred to a profit-making company in other ways, a potentially substantial acquisition motive is provided. An anecdote: Professor Bittker reports a 1943 New York Times advertisement offering: "For sale. Stock of corporation having 1943 tax loss deduction $120,000. Sole assets are $80,000 in cash and equivalent."[27]

Congressional efforts to restrict "traffic" in net operating losses date back to the Revenue Act of 1924.[28] Thereafter, the ongoing game between Congress and taxpayers, with taxpayers responding to Congress' efforts with ever more clever transactions, and Congress responding with ever more complex statutory provisions, has produced some of the most arcane tax rules of all.

a. *Pre-1986 Limits on the Survival and Transfer of NOLs*

Our review of limits on the use of NOLs following an acquisition starts with the governing rules in the early 1980s, prior to the Tax Reform Act of 1986. These rules both set the stage for the substantial changes made in 1986 and, because the empirical studies of NOLs as an acquisition motive concern the pre-1986 period, will be important in Section C when we evaluate the claim that NOLs are (or at least were) an important acquisition motive.

We need at the outset to distinguish two different issues concerning the impact of an acquisition on a target's NOLs. The first is *survival*: does the acquisition eliminate the NOLs? The second is *transfer*: can the target's NOLs be used to offset the acquiring company's income?

The treatment of acquisitions that did not qualify as reorganizations was simple. The NOL died with the target. For *A* and *C* reorganizations, the primary limit on survival of the target's NOLs was in § 382(b): If target

---

[27] Bittker & Eustice (1987), *supra* note 6, ¶16.21 n.67.

[28] The Revenue Act of 1924 enacted the predecessor of § 482, which authorized the IRS to reallocate income and deductions among related taxpayers to discourage tax avoidance. Bittker & Eustice (1987), *supra* note 6, ¶ 16.02, trace the history of anti-NOL trafficking efforts.

shareholders received less than 20% of the acquiring company's voting stock, the target's NOLs were reduced by 5% for each percentage point below 20%. Thus, if a large profitable company acquired a small company with NOLs, and the target's shareholders received only 10% of the acquiring company's stock, the target company's NOLs were reduced by 50% (5% for each percentage point below 20% received by target shareholders).

NOLs that survived the § 382(b) test were also limited in their transferability. The application of § 381(a) and the nonapplication of § 382(b) assured that the target's NOLs could be used against the acquiring company's income, but that privilege did not extend to the acquirer's affiliates, even affiliates within a group that together filed a consolidated tax return. In effect, the consolidation privilege was withheld to the extent that consolidation would be used to shield income other than that earned by the specific company that acquired the NOL company's assets.[29]

In a *B* reorganization, the target company remains a separate taxable entity and its NOLs survive for its own use. However, under the consolidated return regulations, the target's NOLs could be used only to offset the target's own post-acquisition income.[30]

An avoidance strategy was available, however. An acquirer could use a *B* reorganization to acquire a small target (whose NOLs would largely die in an *A* or *C* reorganization because its shareholders would receive a small percentage of the acquirer's voting stock). The acquiring company would then hold the target's stock for long enough so that the step transaction doctrine was unlikely to apply and then liquidate the now subsidiary under § 332. The NOLs of the liquidated target would survive (assuming the step-transaction doctrine didn't apply), and could be used by the acquiring company.[31]

Thus far, we have assumed that a company with income to offset seeks to acquire a target with NOLs. Suppose instead that an acquirer with NOLs buys a profitable target. The goal of the transaction would be the same as where a profitable company acquires a loss company: to increase the value of the NOLs. However, here pre-1986 restrictions on both survival and transferability essentially disappeared. Sections 381 and 382 and the

---

[29] The relevant consolidated return regulations are extremely complex. For a introduction, see Bittker & Eustice (1987), *supra* note 6, ¶ 15.24.

[30] In effect, the rules for stock acquisitions (*B* reorganizations) were more generous than for asset acquisitions (*A* and *C* reorganizations) as to *survival* of the NOL, but more restrictive as to *transfer* of the surviving NOL to the acquiring company. In an *A* or *C* reorganization, the target's NOLs might be partly extinguished by the ownership requirements of § 382, but NOLs that survived this test could be used against the acquiring company's income without additional restriction. In contrast, in a *B* reorganization, the acquiring company could not directly use the target's NOLs to offset the acquiring company's future income.

[31] See Bittker & Eustice (1987), *supra* note 6, ¶ 16.26.

consolidated return regulations limited the survival and transfer only of the *target's* NOLs.[32]

b.   *Post-1986 Limits on the Survival and Use of NOLs*

The 1986 amendments to § 382 took a different approach to regulating the sale of NOLs in acquisitions. A 1983 Senate Finance Committee report that initiated the legislative process argued that the existing restrictions were both too harsh and too loose.[33] Section 382 sought to specify circumstances where a risk of NOL sales existed, and then eliminate all or part of the NOLs. Planners put continual pressure on the triggering definitions by adjusting the form of their transactions. The 1986 Act sought instead to eliminate the incentive to traffic in NOLs in the first place.

NOLs provide an incentive for acquisitions only if the NOLs are worth more to the transferee than the transferor. The 1986 Act sought to eliminate the inequality. Where the triggering conditions of new § 382 are met, NOLs generally survive a reorganization, but their annual use is limited to a formula amount that approximates the amount that could have been used by the loss company had the acquisition not taken place. Thus, the value of the NOLs cannot be increased by transferring them, and the incentive to traffic is eliminated.

Under new § 382, the annual limit on the use of NOLs is triggered if within a three-year measuring period there occurs both an "ownership change" with respect to the loss company, which generally means a combined increase in the stock ownership of all 5% shareholders of greater than 50 percentage points. All under-5% shareholders are treated as a single 5% shareholder. The annual limit equals the equity value of the loss corporation at the time of the transaction multiplied by the "long-term tax-exempt interest rate." This limit reflects one possible use that the company could have made of its NOLs -- selling its assets and investing the proceeds in tax-exempt bonds. While the mechanics of determining when an ownership change occurs are complex, the NOL limits catch virtually any transaction that can fairly be called an "acquisition," and many others besides.

---

[32] The consolidated return regulations did address efforts to avoid the restrictions on NOL transfers by having the target become the putative acquirer. The regulations provided that if the target shareholders received more than 50% of the acquiring company's stock, the putative acquirer would be treated as the target instead.

[33] Bittker & Eustice (1987), *supra* note 6, ¶ 16.23.

CONFERENCE COMMITTEE REPORT
H.R.Conf.Rep.No.841, 99th Cong., 2d Sess. II-172 to -191 (1986)

Ownership change

The special limitations [on the use of NOLs] apply after any ownership change. An ownership change occurs, in general, if the percentage of stock of the new loss corporation owned by any one or more 5% shareholders (described below) has increased by more than 50 percentage points relative to the lowest percentage of stock of the old loss corporation owned by those 5% shareholders at any time during the testing period (generally a three-year period). . . . For this purpose, all stock owned by persons who own less than five percent of a loss corporation's stock is generally treated as stock owned by a single 5% shareholder. The determination of whether an ownership change has occurred is made after any *owner shift* involving a 5% shareholder or any *equity structure shift*. . . .

Owner shift involving a 5-percent shareholder

[A]n owner shift involving a 5% shareholder includes (but is not limited to) [situations in which (a) the percentage ownership of a person who previously owned at least 5% of the voting stock of a loss corporation increases or decreases by any amount, or (b) a person not previously a 5% shareholder becomes a 5% shareholder through a taxable purchase of stock].

Example 1 -- The stock of *L* corporation is publicly traded; no shareholder holds 5% or more of *L* stock. During the three-year period between January 1, 1987 and January 1, 1990, there are numerous trades involving *L* stock. No ownership change will occur as a result of such purchases, provided that no person (or persons) becomes a 5% shareholder, either directly or indirectly, and increases his (or their) ownership of *L* stock by more than 50 percentage points.

Example 2 -- On January 1, 1987, the stock of *L* corporation is publicly traded; no shareholder holds 5% or more of *L* stock. On September 1, 1987, individuals *A*, *B*, and *C*, who were not previously *L* shareholders and are unrelated to each other or any *L* shareholders, each acquired one-third of *L* stock. . . . [A]n ownership change has occurred, because the percentage of *L* stock owned by the three 5% shareholders after the owner shift (100%) has increased by more than 50 percentage points over the lowest percentage of *L* stock owned by *A*, *B*, and *C* at any time during the testing period (0% prior to September 1, 1987). . . .

Example 4 -- *L* corporation is closely held by four unrelated individuals, *A*, *B*, *C*, and *D*. On January 1, 1987, [*A*, *B*, *C*, and *D* sell 80% of the outstanding *L* shares in a public offering]. No person who acquires stock in a public offering acquires 5% or more . . . . The percentage of stock owned by the less-than-5% shareholders [as a group] after the owner shift (80%) has increased by more than 50 percentage points over the lowest percentage of stock owned by those shareholders at any time during the testing period (0% prior to January 1, 1987). Thus, an ownership change has occurred. . . .

Example 6 -- The stock of *L* corporation is publicly traded; no shareholder owns 5% or more. On January 1, 1987, there is a stock offering as a result of which stock representing 60% of *L*'s value is acquired by an investor group consisting of 12 unrelated individuals, each of whom acquires 5% of *L* stock. Based on these facts, there has been an ownership change, because the percentage of *L* stock owned after the owner shift by the 12 5% shareholders in the investor group (60%) has increased by more than 50 percentage points over the lowest percentage of stock owned by those shareholders at any time during the testing period (0% prior to January 1, 1987). . . .

Equity structure shift

An equity structure shift is defined under the conference agreement as any tax-free reorganization within the meaning of § 368, other than a divisive reorganization or an *F* reorganization. In addition, to the extent provided in regulations, the term equity structure shift will include other transactions, such as public offerings not involving a 5% shareholder or taxable reorganization-type transactions (*e.g.*, mergers or other reorganization-type transactions that do not qualify for tax-free treatment due to the nature of the consideration or the failure to satisfy any of the other requirements for a tax-free transaction). . . .

Under the conference agreement, for purposes of determining whether an ownership change has occurred following an equity structure shift, the less-than-5% shareholders of each corporation that was a party to the reorganization will be segregated and treated as a single, separate 5% shareholder. . . .

Example 8 -- On January 1, 1988, *L* corporation (a loss corporation) is merged in [an *A* reorganization] into *P* corporation (not a loss corporation), with *P* surviving. Both *L* and *P* are publicly traded corporations with no shareholder owning 5% or more of either corporation or the surviving corporation. In the merger, *L* shareholders receive 30% of the stock of *P*. There has been an ownership change of *L*, because the percentage of *P* stock owned by the former *P* shareholders (all of whom are less-than-5% shareholders who are treated as a separate single 5% shareholder) after the equity structure shift (70%) has increased by more than 50 percentage points over the lowest percentage of *L* stock owned by such shareholders at any time during the testing period (0% prior to the merger). If, however, the former shareholders of *L* had received at least 50% of the stock of *P* in the merger, there would not have been an ownership change of *L*.

It is anticipated that the same results would apply in a taxable merger in which the loss corporation [and thus its NOLs] survives, under facts as described above, pursuant to regulations treating taxable reorganization-type transactions as equity structure shifts. . . .

Example 10 -- *L* corporation stock is widely held; no shareholder owns as much as 5% of *L* stock. On January 1, 1988, *L* corporation, which has a value of $1 million, directly issues stock with a value of $2 million to the public; no one person acquired as much as 5% in the public offering. . . . [N]o ownership change has occurred, because a public offering in which no person acquires as much as 5% of the corporation's stock, however large, by a corporation that has no 5% shareholder before the offering would not affect the percentage of stock owned by a 5% shareholder.[a]. . .

. . . [However, under regulations to be adopted by the Treasury], the group of less-than-5% shareholders prior to the offering and the new group of less-than-5% shareholders that acquire stock pursuant to the offering could be segregated and treated as a separate 5% shareholder. Thus, an ownership change may result from the public offering described above, because the percentage of stock owned by the group of less-than-5% shareholders who acquire stock in the public offering, who are treated as a separate 5% shareholder (66.67%) has increased by more than 50 percentage points over the lowest percentage of *L* stock owned by such shareholders at any time during the testing period (0% prior to the public offering). . . .

Example 13 -- The stock of *L* corporation is widely held by the public; no single shareholder owns 5% or more of *L* stock. *G* corporation also is widely held with no shareholder owning 5% or more. On January 1, 1988, *L* corporation and *G* corporation merge (in a tax-free transaction), with *L* surviving, and *G* shareholders receive 49% of *L* stock. On July 1, 1988, *B*, an individual who has never owned stock in *L* or *G*, purchases 5% of *L* stock in a transaction on a public stock exchange.

The merger of *L* and *G* is not an ownership change of *L*, because the percentage of stock owned by the less-than-5% shareholders of *G* (who are aggregated and treated as a single 5% shareholder) (49%) has not increased by more than 50 percentage points over the lowest percentage of *L* stock owned by such shareholders during the testing period (0% prior to the merger). The purchase of *L* stock by *B* is an owner shift involving a 5% shareholder, which is presumed (unless otherwise established) to have been made proportionately from the groups of former *G* and *L* shareholders (49% from the *G* shareholders and 51% from the *L* shareholders). There is an ownership change of *L* because, immediately after the owner shift involving *B*, the percentage of stock owned by the *G* shareholders (presumed to be 46.55 -- 49% actually acquired in the merger less 2.45% presumed sold to

---

[a] A different result would occur if the public offering were performed by an underwriter on a "firm commitment" basis, because the underwriter would be a 5% shareholder whose percentage of stock (66.67%) has increased by more than 50 percentage points over the lowest percentage of stock owned by the underwriter at any time during the testing period (0% prior to public offering). See Rev.Rul. 78-294, 1978-2 C.B. 141. [This result seems silly; in a firm commitment underwriting, the underwriter is no more than a conduit. It can also be easily avoided by forming a large syndicate of underwriters, each of whom buys and resells less than 5% of the issuer's stock. Eds.]

B) and *B* (5%) has increased by more than 50 percentage points over the lowest percentage of *L* stock owned by those shareholders at any time during the testing period (0% prior to the merger).

Example 14 -- The stock of *L* corporation and *G* corporation is widely held by the public; neither corporation has any shareholder owning as much as 5% of its stock. On January 1, 1988, *B* purchases 10% of *L* stock. On July 1, 1988, *L* and *G* merge (in a tax-free transaction), with *L* surviving, and *G* shareholders receiving 49% of *L* stock. The merger of *L* and *G* is an ownership change because, immediately after the merger, the percentage of stock owned by *G* shareholders (49%) and *B* (5.1%) has increased by more than 50 percentage points over the lowest percentage of *L* stock owned by such shareholders at any time during the testing period (0% prior to the stock purchase by *B*). . . .

3-year testing period

In general, the relevant testing period for determining whether an ownership change has occurred is the three-year period preceding any owner shift involving a 5% shareholder or any equity structure shift. Thus, a series of unrelated transactions occurring during a three-year period may constitute an ownership change. . . .

Effect of ownership change

Section 382 limitation

For any taxable year ending after the [ownership] change date . . ., the amount of a loss corporation's taxable income that can be offset by a pre-change loss (described below) cannot exceed the § 382 limitation for such year. The § 382 limitation for any taxable year is generally the amount equal to the value of the loss corporation immediately before the ownership change multiplied by the long-term tax-exempt rate [to be published monthly by the Treasury]. . . . [I]f the § 382 limitation for a taxable year exceeds the taxable income for the year, the § 382 limitation for the next taxable year is increased by such excess. If two or more loss corporations are merged or otherwise reorganized into a single entity, separate § 382 limitations are determined and applied to each loss corporation that experiences an ownership change.

Example 22 -- *X* corporation is wholly owned by individual *A* and its stock has a value of $3,000; *X* has NOL carryforwards of $10,000. *Y* corporation is wholly owned by individual *B* and its stock has a value of $9,000; *Y* has NOL carryforwards of $100. *Z* corporation is owned by individual *C* and its stock has a value of $18,000; *Z* has no NOL carryforwards. On July 22, 1988, *X*, *Y* and *Z* consolidate into W corporation in a transaction that qualifies as [an A reorganization]. The applicable long-term tax-exempt rate on such date is 10%. As a result of the consolidation, *A* receives 10% of W stock, *B* receives 30% and *C* receives 60%.

The consolidation of *X*, *Y* and *Z* results in an ownership change for old loss corporations *X* and *Y*. . . . Therefore, the annual limitation on *X*'s NOL carryforwards is $300 [the long-term tax-exempt rate of 10% multiplied by *X*'s equity value of $3,000] and the annual limitation on *Y*'s NOL carryforwards is $900 [the long-term tax-exempt rate of 10% multiplied by *Y*'s equity value of $9,000].

For *W*'s taxable year ending on December 31, 1989, *W*'s taxable income before any reduction for its NOLs is $400. The amount of taxable income of W that may be offset by *X* and *Y*'s pre-change losses (without regard to any unused § 382 limitation) is $400 (the $300 § 382 limitation for *X*'s NOL carryforwards and all $100 of *Y*'s NOL carryforwards because that amount is less than *Y*'s $900 § 382 limitation). The unused portion of *Y*'s § 382 limitation may not be used to augment *X*'s § 382 limitation for 1989 or in any subsequent year. . . .

Value of loss corporation

The value of a loss corporation is generally the fair market value of the corporation's stock (including preferred stock described in section 1504(a)(4) immediately before the ownership change. . . . In determining value, the conferees intend that the price at which loss corporation stock changes hands in an arms-length transaction would be evidence, but not conclusive evidence, of the value of the stock. . . .

Example 23 -- All of the outstanding stock of *L* corporation is owned by individual *A* and has a value of $1,000. On June 15, 1988, *A* sells 51% of his stock in *L* to unrelated individual *B*. On January 1, 1989, *L* and *A* enter into a 15-year management contract and *L* redeems *A*'s remaining stock interest in such corporation. The latter transactions were contemplated in connection with *B*'s earlier acquisition of stock in 1988.

The acquisition of 51% of the stock of *L* on June 15, 1988, constituted an ownership change. The value of *L* for purposes of computing the § 382 limitation is the value of the stock of such corporation immediately before the ownership change. Although the value of such stock was $1,000 at that time, the value must be reduced by the value of *A*'s stock that was subsequently redeemed in connection with the ownership change.

Long-term tax-exempt rate

. . . The use of a rate lower than the long-term Federal rate is necessary to ensure that the value of NOL carryforwards to the buying corporation is not more than their value to the loss corporation. Otherwise there would be a tax incentive for acquiring loss corporations. If the loss corporation were to sell its assets and invest in long-term Treasury obligations, it could absorb its NOL carryforwards at a rate equal to the yield on long-term government obligations. Since the price paid by the buyer is larger than the value of the loss company's assets (because of [sic] the value of NOL carryforwards are taken into account), applying the long-term Treasury rate to the purchase price would result in faster utilization of NOL carryforwards by the buying corporation. The long-term tax-exempt rate normally will fall between 66 (1 minus the corporate tax rate of 34%) and 100% of the long-term Federal rate. . . .

Continuity of business enterprise requirements

Following an ownership change, a loss corporation's NOL carryforwards . . . are subject to complete disallowance, except to the extent of any recognized . . . § 338 gain [due to an election to step-up a target corporation's basis], unless the loss corporation's business enterprise is continued at all times during the two-year period following the ownership change. . . . This continuity of business enterprise requirement is the same requirement that must be satisfied to qualify a transaction as a tax-free reorganization under § 368. (See Treas. Reg. § 1.368-1(d).) Under these continuity of business enterprise requirements, a loss corporation (or a successor corporation) must either continue the old loss corporation's historic business or use a significant portion of the old loss corporation's assets in a business. . . .

Reduction in loss corporation's value for certain capital contributions

Any capital contribution (including a § 351 transfer) that is made to a loss corporation [during the 2-year period ending on the ownership change date] shall not be taken into account for any purpose under § 382. . . . The application of this rule will result in a reduction of a loss corporation's value for purposes of determining the § 382 limitation.[b]. . .

---

3.   Taxable Transactions: Basis Step-up and Corporate Level Tax

In some circumstances, target shareholders may not want the deferral associated with reorganization treatment because the transaction would otherwise result in a loss that they would like to recognize immediately. In others, reorganization treatment may be undesirable to the acquiring

---

[b] This limitation is designed to frustrate schemes of the following type. Assume *L* corporation has a value of $1,000 and an NOL of $200, and that the long-term tax-exempt rate is 10%. If *L* is then acquired, the annual NOL limit will be $100. If, instead, *A*, the sole shareholder of *L*, contributes $1,000 to *L*'s capital immediately before the acquisition, *L*'s value increases to $2,000. *A* recovers the contribution by selling *L* for $2,000, and the annual NOL limit is now $200, despite the absence of any substantive change. Eds.

company.   If the consideration exceeds the target company's basis in its assets, the acquiring company might prefer that the excess be reflected in a higher basis for the target's depreciable assets.

Under the Code, nonreorganization treatment of an asset purchase or stock purchase transaction is easy to achieve; the acquirer need merely buy the target company's stock or assets using a small percentage of cash, thereby violating the solely for voting stock requirement of the *B* and *C* reorganization definitions.[34]   For a transaction structured as a merger, taxable treatment is more difficult to achieve: The acquirer must buy enough of the target's stock for cash to violate the judicial continuity of interest test for an *A* reorganization.

Once taxable treatment is selected, the parties' major concerns, at least in a setting where the transaction will result in gain to the target shareholders, are clear. The target shareholders want to insure that they pay only capital gains tax at the shareholder level. The acquiring company wants to secure a step-up in basis in the target's assets to reflect the purchase price, without the target paying corporate level tax. The acquiring company also cares about the survival of the target's net operating losses.

a.   *Basis Step-up Without Corporate Level Tax Before 1986*

Before 1986, an acquirer could generally to obtain a basis step-up in an acquisition structured as a merger or a stock purchase, *without* the target paying corporate level tax on the amount of the step-up. The target avoided tax by adapting a *plan of complete liquidation* under provisions of § 337 which were repealed in 1986. The target recognized gain to *recapture* the benefits of prior *accelerated* depreciation (tax depreciation in excess of straight line depreciation), but often the present value of the higher future depreciation deductions outweighed the recapture tax. The acquirer could also obtain a carryover basis if desired.[35]

In an asset purchase, in contrast, a basis step-up was unavoidable. Once again, the target could avoid corporate level tax by adopting a plan of complete liquidation under § 337.

The *incidence* of the recapture tax depended on the transaction form. In a merger or stock purchase, the acquirer paid the recapture tax when the target was merged or liquidated into the acquirer (or a subsidiary of the

---

[34] This is an example of a peculiar characteristic of Subchapter C of the IRC. Many of its provisions are elective, but only transactionally, rather than formally. That is to say, the election is made by selecting the appropriate formal structure for the transaction from among substantive equivalents, rather than by checking a box on a tax return. Such transactional elections create tax "traps for the unwary." See Ginsburg (1983), *supra* note 3, at 196.

[35] Before 1982, this election depended on transaction form, but was simple to achieve. Since 1982, the election independent of transaction form. The acquirer simply elects under § 338 to step up basis or not in a stock purchase or merger.

acquirer). In an asset acquisition the target company owed the recapture tax, which had to be paid when it liquidated under § 337. But the parties presumably could anticipate the incidence of the recapture tax, and adjust the purchase price accordingly.

Indeed, while we have referred in this chapter to the interests of the target shareholders and the acquirer as if they were separate, from a planning perspective the interests merge: The better the tax treatment available to the acquirer, the more the company is worth. Tax savings are a source of joint gains. In general, these gains will be split between the acquirer and the target's shareholders. In a fully competitive acquisition market, the acquirer's share of these gains will be competed away, and they will accrue entirely to the target's shareholders.

The complete liquidation required to avoid corporate level tax of the target had an unfortunate side effect: It destroyed the target's NOL, if any. However, ingenious tax planners devised methods by which, prior to 1982, the acquirer company could have at least some of its cake -- survival of the target company's NOL and other tax attributes -- and eat it too -- obtain a basis step-up.

This result was achieved by two variations on a theme. In the first, the acquirer would first buy the depreciable assets of the target company, resulting in a basis step-up, as for any asset purchase, under § 1012. The target would recognize gain, but the target's NOL could be used to offset the gain. Thereafter, the acquirer would buy the target's stock, but not liquidate it. This allowed the target's NOLs to survive and offset the target's future income. In the second variation, the target transferred the depreciable assets to related companies before the acquisition. The acquiring company then acquired both the original target and the related companies, and liquidated only the related companies. The overall result was the same as in the first variation -- a step-up in basis for the target's depreciable assets *and* survival of the target's tax attributes. This result was contrary to the underlying structure of the Code. An acquisition that results in basis adjustments to the target's assets should not also result in survival of its tax attributes.

In 1982, Congress, in new § 338, forced acquirers to choose either a step-up in basis and the survival of the target company's tax attributes, as to *all* of the target's pre-acquisition assets. Under § 338, an acquiring company which makes a "qualified stock purchase" can elect to have the transaction treated *as if* the target company had sold all of its assets to a new corporation and then liquidated. The target company's new basis in its assets would be based on the acquiring company's basis in the stock of the target. Thus, the basis step-up can be accomplished (and recapture triggered) without a formal liquidation, a desirable elimination of a formality that had been required for a basis step-up, but frequently had significant non-tax consequences.[36]

---

[36] A liquidation, or a transaction initially structured as an asset acquisition, can cause termination of, for example, franchise rights, leases, and government licenses, because of non-assignability clauses in the original grant. See Chapter 16, *infra*.

The post-acquisition target company is treated as a new company which had purchased the assets of the pre-acquisition company on the day after the acquisition date. The target's pre-acquisition tax attributes, including any NOLs, are eliminated. If no § 338 election is made, no step-up basis is possible because, a parent company's basis in the assets received upon the liquidation of a subsidiary is a carryover as specified in § 334(a). In that case, the target company's tax attributes survive pursuant to § 381.[37]

b.   *Basis Step-up and Corporate Level Tax after 1986*

The conceptual framework for taxation of taxable (nonreorganization) transactions is symmetry in the treatment of asset and stock acquisitions. Prior to 1986, a central feature of that symmetry was that gain resulting from an increase in the value of the target's assets could be avoided at the corporate level when the entire company was sold, and thus recognized only once, at the shareholder level.

Assume that a target corporation has a single nondepreciable asset with basis of $100, and that the stockholders also have a $100 basis in their stock. Over time, the asset's value increases to $200. Assume that the corporation sells the asset to a third party for $200 and then liquidates or, alternatively, that the shareholders sold their stock for $200 and the acquiring company then liquidates its then wholly-owned subsidiary. Until 1986, the asset's basis could be increased to $200 through a taxable acquisition without the target paying corporate level tax on the increase in the asset's value. If the transaction took the form of an asset sale, § 337 provided for nonrecognition of gain by the target if the sale was pursuant to a plan of complete liquidation and the proceeds were distributed to shareholders within twelve months after the plan's adoption. If the transaction took the form of a stock sale by the shareholders (directly or through a merger) and the acquirer made a § 338 election to step-up basis, § 338(a)(1) provided that the deemed asset sale resulting from the election would be treated as if it had occurred under § 337. Either way, only a shareholder level tax was imposed.[38] . . .

The Tax Reform Act of 1986 retained the symmetric treatment of taxable asset and stock acquisitions, but imposed a corporate level tax on both transactional forms. This is accomplished for an asset acquisition by

---

[37] If the acquiring company, in addition to purchasing the target company's stock, also separately acquires any of the target's assets, § 338(e)(1) generally treats the acquiring company *as if* it had made a § 338 election to step-up basis with respect to the stock acquisition. If the acquiring company acquires the target and other companies affiliated with the target, the election decision made with respect to the first acquisition is binding with respect to all subsequent acquisitions of affiliated companies. In both cases, consistent treatment is achieved, and the acquiring company must choose between a basis step-up and survival of the target's tax attributes.

[38] A corporate level tax was imposed on any accelerated depreciation, investment tax credit, or prior tax benefits that had reduced the asset's basis in the target's hands.

amending §§ 336 and 337.   The nonrecognition language of § 337 was eliminated so that a sale of assets at the corporate level calls for gain or loss recognition even if made pursuant to a plan of complete liquidation.[39] Thus, gain is now recognized at both the corporate level and at the shareholder level whenever a basis step-up occurs.

The same result -- tax at both corporate and shareholder levels -- occurs if the transaction takes the form of a stock acquisition. The Act amends § 338(a)(1) to eliminate the statement that the deemed sale (the imaginary sale that steps up the basis of the target company's assets) is to be treated as having occurred under § 337. The deemed sale thus becomes taxable at the corporate level. And a shareholder level tax was already imposed when the target company shareholders sold their shares.

c.   *Restricting the Use of NOLs*

The NOL amendments to § 382 contained in the Tax Reform Act of 1986, discussed above, were primarily forward looking. Their goal was to ensure that an acquiring company could shelter no more of its future income with a target company's NOLs than the target company could have done itself. In the highly leveraged buyouts and recapitalizations of the late 1980s, interest expense often exceeded operating income, resulting in taxable losses after the buyout.   The buyout company would *carryback* these post-acquisition losses to secure refunds of taxes paid in pre-acquisition years.

The Revenue Reconciliation Act of 1989 added §§ 172(b)(1)(E) and 172(h), which bar carryback of losses that result from interest expense associated with leveraged acquisitions or leveraged restructurings, referred to as corporate equity reduction transactions ("CERT"). The limitation is triggered if a company participates in a CERT -- essentially an acquisition of at least 50% of the voting power or value of the stock of another corporation, or a distribution (including redemptions) to shareholders in excess of 150% of the average distribution over the prior three years and representing in excess of 10% of the value of the corporation. Once the limitation is triggered, the company cannot carry back that portion of a subsequent loss that is the lesser of (i) the interest cost resulting from the CERT, or (ii) the amount by which interest cost in the particular year exceeds the company's average interest cost for the three prior years.[40]

---

[39] To avoid a return to the *Court Holding Company* era when taxpayers could avoid a corporate level tax on appreciated assets by first distributing the assets in liquidation, after which they would be sold by the shareholders, the 1986 Act amends § 336 to provide that the distribution of assets by a corporation to its shareholders in liquidation will be treated as if the corporation sold the assets to the shareholders at fair market value.

[40] The limit does not apply if it would reduce the carryback by less than $1 million. For a discussion of these provisions, see Martin Ginsburg, Jack Levin, William Welke & Richard Wolfe, *CERTS: The New Limitations on NOL Carrybacks*, 46 Tax Notes 1315 (1990).

B. The Theory: Claims that the Tax System Favors Acquisitions

Four characteristics of the tax treatment of acquisitions are typically said to provide an incentive for acquisitions: (i) the tax deferral granted to target shareholders in tax-free reorganization acquisitions; (ii) the step-up in basis allowed the acquiring company in taxable acquisitions; (iii) the ability to transfer a target company's net operating loss; and (iv) the deductibility of interest on debt incurred to make the acquisition.

Unfortunately, the debate concerning the influence of taxes on acquisition activity has been largely ad hoc, as can be seen from the fact that the tax treatment of both tax-free and taxable transactions is said to encourage acquisitions. In this section, we examine critically the claim that the tax system favors acquisitions with respect to each of these four features of acquisition taxation. We will ask in each case: (i) whether the characteristic yields a tax gain; (ii) whether that tax gain can best be achieved by an acquisition as opposed to other available alternatives; and (iii) how large the tax gain is, relative to typical takeover premia. Section C reviews the available empirical evidence.

Some preliminary comments are necessary with respect to what circumstances would satisfy each of the claims of tax favoritism. The claim of a tax gain asserts that the tax treatment of an acquisition increases the target company's aftertax cash flows without altering its pretax cash flows. For example, the step-up in the basis of the target's assets in a taxable acquisition is said to accomplish this by allowing an increase in post-acquisition depreciation deductions. But a step-up alone is not sufficient to demonstrate a tax gain. The target's shareholders and the constituent companies pay for those future tax savings through a immediate shareholder level capital gains tax, a recapture tax, and (after 1986) a corporate level tax. Moreover, the present value of the basis step-up depends on how much of the increased basis is allocable to depreciable, depletable or amortizable assets, the useful life of those assets, and the discount rate applied to future tax savings. A tax gain exists only if there are *net* tax savings, after taking into account the tax costs incurred by the target company, the acquiring company, and the target shareholders.

Even if net tax gains exist, they provide a complete acquisition motive only if they exceed the transaction and information costs associated with the acquisition. These consist of more than just the legal, accounting and investment banking costs associated with making the deal. More important, there are substantial information asymmetries that create the potential for moral hazard and adverse selection problems.

The conditions necessary for the second claim of tax favoritism -- that an available tax gain can better be achieved by an acquisition than by alternatives -- also presents a specification problem. Too often the discussion assumes that an acquisition is the *only* method by which the tax gain can be achieved. This focus on acquisitions may be explainable; if tax professionals are brought into the transaction only after the principals have determined that an acquisition will take place, the professionals may be restricted to viewing the optimization problem as maximizing the tax gains available by means of an acquisition, rather than considering other methods of achieving the gains. For example, the tax gains (if any) from a step-up in basis might be better achieved by a sale and leaseback of some of the target company's assets because fewer information asymmetry problems are associated with this method of achieving the gain.

The testable form of the third claim of tax favoritism -- that tax gains explain a large fraction of the premiums paid in acquisitions -- also requires specification. For tax gains to result in a premium -- an acquisition price higher than the market price of the target's stock -- they must be unanticipated. Otherwise their availability already would have been incorporated into the price of the target's stock. And much of the data necessary to calculate the potential tax gains from the target's acquisition are publicly available. To be sure, anticipated tax gains must be discounted to reflect the likelihood and timing of an acquisition, and the potential that target management might block the acquisition despite the gain, but the problem of explaining the magnitude of observable premiums remains.

1. Tax Favoritism from Basis Step-Up in Taxable Acquisitions

a. *Net Tax Gains from Basis Step-up Prior to 1986*

Prior to 1986, the potential for net tax gains from a step-up in the basis of the target's assets resulted from a combination of three factors: a higher basis for the target company's assets; a short time period over which assets were depreciated, depleted, or amortized for tax purposes; and no corporate level tax on the step-up. (Below, for convenience, we generally use "depreciation" as shorthand for depreciation, depletion, and amortization -- the three ways to write off the value of assets for tax purposes over a period of time.) When the acquiring company elected a step-up, its basis in the acquired assets equaled the fair market value of the assets. The total purchase price was allocated among the target's assets in proportion to their fair market value. If the purchase price exceeded the fair market value of the target's assets, the balance was treated as nondepreciable goodwill. If the new basis for the target's depreciable assets exceeded the target company's basis in those assets, the higher basis would yield larger tax deductions after the acquisition than before. Fair market value greater than tax basis was a common result, because allowable tax depreciation is typically faster than economic depreciation, because of inflation, and because many amortizable intangible assets (copyrights, computer software, drug patents, etc.) have low or zero basis in the hands of the company that created them.

The increased deductions, however, are spread over the useful life of the assets. The present value of the increased deductions then depends on the discount rate and on how quickly depreciation can be taken. This led to the second factor creating the potential for a tax gain from a basis step-up in a taxable acquisition. Assets acquired after 1981 can be depreciated under the Accelerated Cost Recovery System (ACRS), which dramatically shortened the depreciation period for most assets. Because ACRS applies to used as well as new assets, an acquisition could shorten the period over which depreciation could be taken for assets that were acquired prior to 1981.

These two factors -- (i) increased depreciation over (ii) a shorter period -- are not, however, enough to establish the potential for an equilibrium tax gain from an acquisition. Tax costs that the transaction imposes on the target company must also be taken into account.

These costs were significant even prior to 1986. First, the target shareholders would likely incur immediate capital gains taxes. This tax liability alone would not eliminate the potential of an equilibrium tax gain from the acquisition. Prior to 1986, each dollar of increased depreciation deduction resulting from the acquisition was worth up to 46¢ (assuming a maximum corporate tax rate of 46%), but the cost was only a 20¢ capital gains tax (assuming a maximum capital gains tax of 20% at the shareholder level). Second, there was corporate level tax to recapture prior accelerated depreciation under §§ 1245 or 1250. In the extreme case where the full amount of the basis step-up was subject to recapture, this alone would produce a net tax *loss* from the acquisition because the recapture tax would be due immediately, but the higher depreciation deductions would be available only over the assets' useful lives.

An example illustrates the complex trade-offs. Assume that an acquisition will result in (1) a $100 increase in basis, $90 of which is allocable to depreciable assets and $18 of which is subject to recapture at the corporate level; (2) a remaining useful life for the target's depreciable assets of five years; (3) straight-line depreciation, with tax benefits realized beginning one year from today; (4) a $120 gain to the target's shareholders, 75% of whom are taxable (the rest are tax-exempt); (5) a shareholder capital gains tax rate of 20% (versus 0% in present-value terms if this gain were deferred) and an ordinary corporate income tax rate on recapture and other income of 46%; and (5) an aftertax discount rate of 8%. The net tax gain from this transaction is shown in Table 12-1.

The point of the illustration is that a net tax gain is *possible*, not that a net tax gain will be present in every acquisition. For example, increasing the useful life of the asset in the example from five years to ten years will reduce the annual depreciation charge to $9.00, the annual aftertax value to $4.14, and the present value of the tax benefit to $27.78, while assuming that all shareholders are taxable will increase the current tax to $32.68, with the result that the basis step-up increases the present value of expected income tax payments, holding constant operating cash flows.

Table 12-1

Pre-1986 Computation of Net Tax Gain (Loss) in Taxable Acquisition

Benefit of Increased Depreciation to Acquirer		Tax Cost to Target, Acquirer, and Target's Shareholders	
Increase in basis	$90.00	Shareholder-level capital gain tax on $90 gain at 20%	$18.00
Increase in annual depreciation	$18.00	Corporate-level tax on $18 of recapture at 46%	$ 8.28
Annual tax savings at 46%	$8.28		
Present value ($r=.08$)	$33.06	Total tax	$26.28
Net tax gain from basis step-up = $6.78			

b.   *Net Tax Losses from Basis Step-up After 1986*

The Tax Reform Act of 1986 quite unfavorably altered the tax gain calculus associated with a taxable acquisition. Two changes effected by the 1986 Act -- the change in corporate and individual rates and the addition of a corporate level tax -- bear on the tradeoff between increased future depreciation and current taxes paid to achieve it. Consider first just the rate changes. What drove the pre-1986 Act tax gain argument was the difference between the 46% corporate rate and the 20% capital gains rate: The acquiring company could purchase a deduction worth 46¢ (before discounting to present value) at the cost of a 20¢ capital gains tax and some recapture tax. The change in corporate and individual rates by the 1986 Act reduced that 26% spread to 6%: a 34% corporate tax rate and a 28% individual capital gains rate (based on 1994 income tax rates).

The difference is substantial. For example, under the pre-86 Act tax rates and assuming a 10% discount rate, an increase in basis of $100 purchased at a cost of a 20% shareholder level tax is a positive net present value project for all useful lives up to 19 years. Under the Act's reduced tax rate spread, the increase in basis is a positive net present value project only if the asset has a useful life of three years or less.

Thus, the Act's change in rates alone would have been sufficient to greatly weaken the claim that taxable transactions provide an opportunity for tax gains through a step-up in basis. The addition of a corporate level tax on appreciation of the target company's assets is sufficient to bury the claim. To see this, we return to the numerical example in Table 12-1. The new tradeoff between increased depreciation and current tax appears in Table 12-2:

Table 12-2

Post-1986 Computation of Net Tax *Loss* in Taxable Acquisitions

Benefit of Increased Depreciation to Acquirer		Tax Cost to Target, Acquirer, and Target's Shareholders	
Increase in basis	$90.00	Shareholder-level capital gain tax on $90 gain at 20%	$25.20
Increase in annual depreciation	$18.00	Corporate-level tax on $100 gain at 34%	$34.00
Annual tax savings at 34%	$6.12		
Present value (*r*=.08)	$24.44	Total tax	$59.20
Net tax *loss* from basis step-up = $34.76			

The 1986 Act effectively eliminates the claim that taxable acquisitions can yield a net tax gain through a step-up in the basis of the target company's assets. The step-up promises increased depreciation deductions which are worth 34¢ on the dollar *before* discounting to present value. The step-up costs, *at the corporate level alone*, an immediate 34% tax on the amount of the step-up. The present value of the depreciation deductions will always be less than the tax on the step-up. Barring unusual circumstances (such as an about-to-expire NOL carryforward that can be used to shield the tax on the step-up), no acquirer will ever elect a basis step-up, if a carryover basis is an available option, as it often is.

Even when a basis step-up can be avoided, there remains the need to pay shareholder level tax on the target shareholders' gains. Thus, after 1986, the problem that need to be explained is why companies choose a taxable transaction form, which increases the present value of the tax payments to be made by the target's shareholders, when a tax-free alternative is available.

c. *Acquisitions as the **Best** Way to Achieve Tax Gains from Step-up in Asset Basis.*

Even before 1986, when a basis step-up could produce net tax gains in some transactions, there was an alternative way to obtain a basis step-up for a company's depreciable assets -- sell those assets and only those assets. The relative tax savings from these alternative transactions was quite context specific. Because of rapid change in tax rules, the dominance of one technique over another depends importantly on when a particular transaction took place. Just between 1980 and 1986, the Economic Recovery Tax Act of 1981, the Tax Equity and Fiscal Responsibility Tax Act of 1982, and the Tax Reform Acts of 1984 and 1986 all changed the relative attractiveness of the alternatives. Moreover, an acquisition's relative tax efficiency had to be offset by associated transaction and information costs. For example, selling an entire business changes the economic ownership of the business, which can result in either new people managing those assets or an agency cost problem. If pre-acquisition managers were good, any tax gains could be offset by the costs of having the assets managed either by less skilled replacement managers or of continued management by the pre-acquisition managers who, having sold the assets, then had different (and often worse) incentives than before.[41]

Piecemeal sales of assets held by an ongoing business can also result in less efficient use of the assets, plus severance costs if the assets are an integral part of the seller's production process. But if the assets were then leased back by the seller -- a sale-leaseback transaction -- both the severance costs and the costs of changed management or changed managerial incentives are avoided. Yet many of the tax benefits available from selling the entire company could be preserved.[42]

To see this we can compare, assuming the pre-1986 tax regime, an acquisition with a sale of only a company's depreciable assets. The primary advantage of acquiring the entire business was the target's ability to avoid a corporate level capital gains tax by adopting a plan of complete liquidation pursuant to § 337. However, installment sales treatment of the pure asset sale also deferred payment of the capital gains tax and, prior to the Tax Reform Act of 1984, also deferred recapture tax, a deferral not possible in an acquisition. Suppose the buyer paid for the assets with an interest only installment note. The longer the time to the balloon payment, the longer the deferral and the lower the present value of the capital gains tax that ultimately would be due. For example, if the tax on a transaction were $25,000, but the seller received a fifteen year interest only note and reported on the installment basis, the present value of the tax (assuming an aftertax discount rate of 7%) is $9,061 -- 36% of the amount due if the tax were paid immediately. Moreover, the sale at the corporate level permitted shareholders to defer payment of shareholder level tax on the increase in the company's value.

To be sure, deferring payment of principal by taking an installment note subjects that payment to risk and thereby reduces an asset's risk-adjusted sale price. But that risk can be monetized by obtaining a third party guarantee of the note without jeopardizing installment sale treatment. Moreover,

---

[41] See Gilson, Scholes & Wolfson (1988), *supra* note 4.

[42] At their high point, the safe harbor leasing rules would have allowed a step-up in basis on a sale and leaseback transaction without the lessor bearing any residual risk with respect to the asset -- that is, without any element of a change in ownership. See Alvin Warren & Alan Auerbach, *The Transferability of Tax Incentives and the Fiction of Safe Harbor Leasing*, 95 Harv.L.Rev. 1752 (1982). Under present law, the lessor must bear some residual risk, but agency and information asymmetry costs are minimized because the bulk of the residual risk can remains with the operator. See Alvin Warren & Alan Auerbach, *Tax Policy and Equipment Leasing after TEFRA*, 96 Harv.L.Rev. 1579 (1983).

before 1987, a seller who needed immediate cash could pledge the installment note as a security for a loan.[43]

A similar comparison can be made between an acquisition and a sale and leaseback of depreciable assets. Sales and leasebacks were not perfect substitutes for the tax treatment of acquisitions and asset sales. For example, assets placed in service prior to 1981 were not eligible for ACRS treatment following a sale and leaseback. But a sale and leaseback, because primarily a financing transaction, could achieve a step-up in basis with lower transaction costs, without a change in management or effective ownership of the assets and without the information asymmetry associated with either an acquisition or a partial asset sale without leaseback.

In sum, even prior to 1986, there was reason to question how often the tax gains available from a basis step-up were a but-for cause of acquisitions, given the availability of alternative transactions that could also achieve tax gains from a basis step-up by arbitraging the difference between ordinary income and capital gains rates, with fewer non-tax ramifications.

d. Tax Gains from Basis Step-up and Acquisition Premiums

A separate claim from the claim that tax favoritism motivates acquisitions is that tax gains determine the size of the acquisition premium. As discussed earlier, the fact that tax gains can be achieved by an acquisition is not sufficient for a premium to result. If investors are aware of the potential for tax gains from an acquisition, those gains, as with any other sources of increase in expected future cash flows, will already be incorporated into the target company's stock price. For a tax-related premium to exist, the tax-related increase in cash flows from an acquisition must have been previously *unanticipated*.

A premium that reflected potential tax gains form an acquisition might not be anticipated if the acquiring company has nonpublic information concerning potential tax gains from the target's acquisition (e.g., the tax basis of the target's assets, potential recapture amounts, and remaining depreciable life of the assets). An example where the public financial statements were *not* adequate to estimate the tax savings from an acquisition is the 1984 acquisition of Electronic Data Systems (EDS), a computer service firm, by General Motors. EDS owned millions of lines of proprietary computer software code, carried on its books at zero value. GM (or another acquirer) could write up this code to its estimated fair market value and then depreciate it over 5 years. If EDS had enough useful lines of code so that the entire $2.5 billion purchase price could be ascribed to software, the present value of $500 million in annual depreciation deductions for 5 years would be $943 million, at an aftertax discount rate of 7%, and a corporate

---

[43] See Ginsburg & Levin, *supra* note 7, ¶ 302.02.

income tax rate of 46%.[44]   This could go far to explain why EDS was worth more to General Motors than EDS's public market price. If EDS had only enough lines of code to support $1.25 billion in ascribed value, the tax savings would be only half this amount. Yet no one outside EDS could know how many lines of software code EDS had.

Often, however, tax gains from a step-up in basis (or from the other sources of potential tax gains that have been the center of policy debate) can be roughly computed based on the target's publicly disclosed financial statements. To explain a tax-related premium, one must invoke the role of target management. Suppose that investors expect the target's managers to resist relinquishing control to achieve a tax gain from selling the company. The tax gains from a successful offer would then be unanticipated, although what is unanticipated is not the potential for tax gains but that target management can be displaced. Even here, however, shareholders could anticipate that the target would probably avail itself of tax savings from strategies, such as a sale-leaseback, that did not threaten a change of control. Thus, the tax-related *acquisition* premium in this case would be only the difference between: (i) the actual tax gain from the acquisition; and (ii) the greater of (a) the expected tax gain from an acquisition multiplied by the expected probability that a change in control will occur; or (b) the tax gain achievable through the most effective technique that does not require a change in control, multiplied by the probability that this gain will be realized.

In sum, there is only an indirect connection between tax gains achievable only (or best) by an acquisition and the size of takeover premiums. Tax gains can *exceed* the observed premium if they are partially anticipated. In the end, however, the claim that tax gains produce takeover premia is empirical. It depends on the size of the available tax gains and the size of premiums in particular transactions, a relationship considered in Section C, *infra*.

2.   Tax Favoritism Arising from Shareholder Tax Deferral in Reorganizations

a.   *The Claim of Net Tax Gains*

The argument that the tax system favors *taxable* acquisitions does not rule out making a similar argument with respect to acquisitions treated as reorganizations. Indeed, the deferral of gain for target shareholders in a reorganization has been the most familiar basis for the claim that the tax system motivates acquisitions.[45]

---

[44] The depreciation deduction is a 5-year annuity, with annual payments of $500 million x .46 = $230 million. At a 7% discount rate, this annuity's present value is $943 million.

[45] The Federal Trade Commission once stated that the "[t]ax exemption of corporate reorganizations has the most pervasive impact of all tax provisions favoring mergers."

At one level, the claim of tax favoritism is a tautology. Taxable and tax-free acquisitions have *different* tax consequences. When the tax-free form produces less tax in present value than a taxable alternative, one can say that the tax system favors tax-free over taxable acquisitions; when the tax-free form produces higher tax than a taxable alternative, one can say that the tax system favors taxable acquisitions over tax-free acquisitions. One will *always* be preferable to the other, in any given transaction. After 1986, a tax-free reorganization, which leaves the prior level of expected tax payment unchanged, is (almost) always the preferred outcome, on a net basis.

Moreover, from the target shareholders' perspective, the value of deferral of gain is straightforward: Each year of deferral reduces the present value of the tax. At the limit, if a individual shareholder retains the acquirer's shares received in a reorganization until death, the tax is forgiven because the basis of the stock in the hands of the shareholder's heirs is stepped up to market value on the shareholder's death, though estate tax will be based on the stock's fair market value at the time of death.

But if the claim of tax favoritism is that the tax system provides an incentive for an acquisition structured as a reorganization over the no-acquisition alternative, the claim of favored treatment for tax-free reorganizations evaporates. Leaving NOLs aside for the moment, the tax consequences of a reorganization are identical to doing nothing. Target shareholders do not need a reorganization to secure nonrecognition of the appreciation in value of their stock. All they need to do is *not sell* one's shares. One is left without a tax-based explanation for why the target shareholders chose to dispose of their interest in the target, at least without further specifying the goals that the target's shareholders might have sought to achieve.

b.   *Reorganizations as the **Best** Way for Shareholders to Diversify without Taxation*

The most common goal said to be achieved by the target company's sale is the potential for target shareholders to diversify their portfolios without the imposition of a tax. If this is the goal, the relevant comparison for purposes of determining the tax incentives for acquisitions is not how the sale transaction might otherwise be taxed, but the tax treatment of alternative means by which target shareholders can increase their diversification. So understood, this claim that reorganizations are the best way to diversify is problematic.

The claimed benefit is tenuous if the target company is publicly held. There is no barrier to diversification at the shareholder level, as might be the

---

Federal Trade Commission (1969), *supra* note 1, at 143.

case were the target closely held. Thus, no obvious reason appears why target shareholders as a group would need further diversification. Nor will the simple swap of one company's stock for another's materially affect the level of diversification.

If the target company is privately held and diversification therefore is, we will presume, not available at the shareholder level, the claim of risk reduction benefits to the target's shareholders is plausible. But the risk reduction benefits are quite limited. The target's shareholders still own stock in a single company. That scarcely constitutes adequate diversification. Even if the acquiring firm is diversified, it remains vulnerable to the mistakes of a single top management team. Moreover, the acquirer may offset the lower risk from diversification by incurring more debt. Indeed, given the tax advantages of debt financing, discussed below, the acquirer would arguably be mismanaged if it did not do so.

Moreover, if the target shareholders desire diversification, we must compare a tax-free acquisition with the tax treatment of alternative means by which target shareholders can diversify. Most directly, the target can diversify at the company level. This alternative requires that the target's shareholders agree on the desirability of making diversifying acquisitions, which impose some efficiency costs because the company's investment decisions will depend on a factor other than profit maximization. But it also holds the potential for more effective diversification than by swapping one company's shares for another's in a reorganization.

A final possible benefit to close corporation shareholders from an acquisitive reorganization is that they gain access to a previously unavailable public market, and to the value of that enhanced liquidity. Still, however, one must explain why access to a public market is best secured by selling the target company rather than through an obvious alternative that has the same (that is, zero) tax consequences as an acquisition structured as a reorganization, without the control consequences -- a public offering of the target company's stock. The most plausible reasons involve the relative transaction and information costs of going public versus being acquired. But then the incentive for an acquisition no longer arises from the tax system.

In short, achieving deferral of gain seems an unlikely reason for target shareholders to sell the company. Rather, the sale will most likely be motivated by other considerations, such as gains from synergy. The more favorable tax treatment of reorganizations, compared to taxable acquisitions, can then explain why tax planners, in their efforts to secure the most favorable tax treatment for an acquisition that has been entered into for other reasons, choose this structure.

In addition, some acquisitions that promise non-tax benefits will be entered into, that would not have been entered into if reorganization treatment were unavailable, because the net tax *cost* of the taxable acquisition exceeds the acquisition's expected non-tax benefits. This, in turn, reflects not tax favoritism toward tax-free acquisitions, but rather the current tax-*disfavored* status of taxable acquisitions.

If a claim of tax favoritism toward tax-free reorganizations has content, it must be premised on a shift in the baseline of what constitutes tax neutrality. In a sense, *all* asset transfers for value are tax-disfavored in a tax system that taxes accretions to wealth, but only when realized. From that perspective, the ability to achieve zero tax consequences in a tax-free reorganization can be seen as favored treatment of a particular form of asset transfer, within a tax system that generally disfavors asset transfers, and thereby inhibits the movement of assets from their current owners to higher-valuing users. The degree of favored treatment depends on the availability of other ways to transfer assets, such as an installment sale, that also produce tax treatment more favorable than immediate realization of gain.

c. *Shareholder Tax Deferral and Acquisition Premiums*

Even if deferral of tax on the target shareholders' gain cannot explain why an acquisition structured as a tax-free reorganization takes place, tax-free treatment can affect the size of the acquisition premium. Assume first that the synergy between acquirer and target is relatively unique, so that the purchase price can be modelled as the outcome of bilateral bargaining. The tax deferral available to the target's shareholders may then lead to a *lower* purchase price, which lets the acquirer and the target's shareholders split the tax savings.

If, alternatively, the gains from the acquisition are available to a number of potential acquirers, then competitive bidding should enable the target's shareholders to realize the same percentage premium as in a taxable transaction, since the target shareholders' benefit does not come at the acquirer's expense. Prior to 1986, when acquirers often preferred a basis step-up, which is not available in a reorganization, the target shareholders' tax deferral thus did cost the acquirer the opportunity to achieve that step-up, and that cost would presumably have been reflected in a lower premium.

3. Tax Favoritism Arising from Transfer of NOLs

For NOLs, as for basis step-up, we must consider the various possible claims of tax favoritism separately before and after the changes made in the Tax Reform Act of 1986. We begin with the pre-1986 period.

a. *Net Tax Gains from NOL Transfers before 1986*

For a tax gain to result from transferring NOLs by means of an acquisition, the NOLs must be worth more to the acquiring company than to the target company. The current value of a target's NOLs depends on several factors, including existing and anticipated future tax rates, the likelihood that the company will earn enough income in the future to use its NOLs before they expire, and discount factors to reflect the timing and the probabilities of *when* the NOLs might be used. Assume, for example, that a potential target company has fallen on hard times and has accumulated NOLs of $50,000. Further assume that there is only a 50% chance that the company will return to profitability so that the NOLs can be used. Ignoring for the moment the discount factor relating to *when* the NOLs would be used, the value of the NOLs to the company would be

$$\$50,000 \times 46\% \times 0.5 = \$11,500$$

In contrast, if an acquiring company is certain of at least $50,000 in earnings, the last term of the calculation becomes 1, and the value of the NOLs would increase to $23,000.

The potential tax gain increases when timing considerations are taken into account. Assume that the target company will break even for 3 years and has a 50% chance of earning $50,000 or nothing in the fourth year, while the acquiring company is certain of having at least $50,000 in earnings this year that the NOLs can be used to offset. At an 8% aftertax discount rate, the no-acquisition value of the target's NOLs would be

$$\$50,000 \times 46\% \times 0.5 \times [1/(1/08)^3 = \$9,129$$

Recall that the tax gain from transferring NOLs by acquisition requires that the NOLs not only survive, but are transferable to reduce the post-acquisition income of the acquiring company. For example, suppose that the tax law allowed the loss company's NOLs to survive an acquisition, but that the NOLs could only be used to offset the future earnings of the loss company's pre-acquisition business.[46] In this situation, no tax gain results from the acquisition. The probability and timing of income that could be offset by the NOLs remain the same after the acquisition as before, *unless* one assumes that the acquiring company's management is more skillful at operations or can take other steps to increase the loss company's near-term earnings. This, however, is in essence a bad-management argument. The ability to shield income through NOLs increases the returns available from improving the target's management.

Apart from this tax-related boost for operating efficiencies created by acquiring NOL firms, the existence of an NOL *tax* gain depends on whether the acquiring company can use the transferred NOLs against its *own* income. This use of NOLs, in turn, depends on tax law restrictions which were

---

[46] This would be the case in a taxable stock acquisition where no §338 election was made whether or not the acquirer filed returns on a consolidated basis.

canvassed earlier in this Chapter. In fact, tax law often allowed this result prior to 1986, although with costly restrictions.[47]

These restrictions imposed two general constraints on an acquiring company's ability to use a loss company's NOLs to offset its own income. The first required that it continue to operate the target company's pre-acquisition business. For an acquisition to qualify as a reorganization, which was a prerequisite for survival of the target's NOLs, Treas. Reg. § 1.368-1(b) requires that the acquirer either "(i) continue the [loss company's] historic business or (ii) use a significant portion of [the loss company's] historic business assets in a business." The business continuity requirement would reduce the value of the NOLs to the acquiring company whenever the acquirer would otherwise have done something different with the target's assets.[48] This requirement could explain why, for example, Chrysler was not an attractive takeover candidate in the early 1980s, when it had billions of dollars in NOLs.

The second constraint on transfer of the target's NOLs to the acquirer was that the acquirer had to take a carryover basis in the target's assets even if the transaction was taxable to target stockholders. Under §§ 332 and 362, the acquiring company had to take a carryover basis in the assets acquired in any transaction covered by § 381. Thus, the acquirer had to choose between the possible tax gain from a basis step-up and the gain from preserving and transferring the target's NOLs.

Prior to the 1982 enactment of § 338, however, tax planners had developed techniques to acquire assets that allowed some of the target's assets to be acquired in a taxable transaction with a basis step-up, while the rest of the target, and most of its NOLs, were acquired in a second transaction that let the acquirer use the target's remaining NOLs.[49]

Both constraints also applied only to a transaction in which a profitable company acquired a loss company. If the loss company was the acquirer, its

---

[47] One should be cautious about the policy implications of the fact that NOLs may be worth more to an acquiring company. Congress has repeatedly sought to discourage transfers by making NOLs *less* valuable to the *acquiring* company. But many scholars favor making them *more* valuable to the *target* company by making tax losses fully refundable when incurred. Limiting the refundability of net operating losses creates a tax incentive in favor of diversification at the company rather than the shareholder level, and in favor of existing as opposed to new firms, because a diversified firm is less likely to lose money, and an existing firm can obtain a partial refund through the rules allowing carryback of losses to offset taxable income during the previous three years. In effect, a profitable firm shares both the project's gains and losses with the tax collector, while the start-up firm shares its gains, and bears all of its losses. See, e.g., John Campisano & Roberta Romano, *Recouping Losses: The Case for Full Loss Offsets*, 76 Nw.U.L.Rev. 709 (1981).

[48] The continuity-of-business-enterprise doctrine under § 368 could be avoided by an acquirer first purchasing the loss company's stock in a taxable transaction, and then merging its profitable business into the loss company in a separate transaction, but § 382(a) imposed a similar restriction. If more than 50% of the ownership of a company with NOLs changed hands in a year, the NOLs were lost unless the company's business was continued.

[49] See Section A.2, *supra*.

tax attributes survived, and could be used to offset the target's income, because nothing had happened to alter the acquirer's tax status.

Thus, pre-1986 Act tax rules governing the treatment of a loss company's NOLs following its acquisition created the potential for a net tax gain from the transfer of NOLs by acquisition. This outcome changed radically after 1986. The critical changes were the increased difficulty in avoiding the impact of § 382's anti-trafficking rules and the limitation on post-acquisition use of the target company's NOLs.

After 1986, the principal remaining way that NOLs can produce net tax gains is for a loss company to acquire other profitable businesses (without issuing so many new shares that it undergoes an ownership change itself). But even then, the loss company could have instead issued shares and invested the proceeds in taxable bonds, tax on which would be sheltered by the NOLs. Thus, the *net* tax gain equals the tax savings from sheltering the income of the acquired businesses, minus the tax savings from sheltering interest income.

b.   *Acquisitions as the **Best** Way to Capture NOL Tax Gains*

Stated generically, an acquisition can increase the value of a target company's NOLs by increasing the likelihood of income against which to offset the NOLs. In a world without information and transaction costs, however, a company with NOLs but without the future income from its current business to use them has a broad range of alternatives that accomplish this result without selling the company and without the costly restrictions on acquiring a company with NOLs that existed even before the 1986 Act. In such a world, a loss company could use its NOLs fully and immediately without being acquired or acquiring other businesses.

In this perfect-market setting, assume that the returns to assets are such that tax-exempt assets bear an implicit tax at the full corporate tax rate -- that is, tax-exempt assets carry a lower pretax return so that taxable and tax-exempt assets yield the same aftertax return.[50] For example, if the maximum marginal tax rate on corporate income is 46% (as was the case before 1986), and fully taxable assets (e.g., corporate bonds) return 10%, then tax-exempt assets (e.g., municipal bonds) with the same risk would return 5.4%. Assume also that a firm's operations will give rise to $10 of NOLs at the end of the year and that the firm has $1000 in funds to invest.

If the loss company acquires $100 in taxable bonds and $900 in municipal bonds, it will earn $10 on the fully taxable bonds, thereby eliminating its NOLs, and $48.60 on the municipal bonds for a total aftertax return of $58.60. At the end of the year, the loss company's aftertax earnings on the $1000 investment would be $4.60 greater than those of a

---

[50] Arbitrage would ensure this equivalency. See Myron Scholes & Mark Wolfson, *Taxes and Business Strategy* 83-99 (1992).

fully taxable company ($58.60 - $54.00). On the other hand, if a fully taxable company were to bid for the loss company, it would pay $4.60 (at the end of the period) for the NOLs (0.46 x $10) and then use the NOLs to offset its own taxable income. If the acquiring firm's offer was accepted, the shareholders of the loss company would earn $54.00 (0.054 x $1000) plus the NOL value of $4.60, or a total of $58.60, exactly the same as if the firm had used up its NOLs by buying taxable bonds. In this setting, it makes no difference whether the loss company buys taxable bonds, buys a combination of taxable and municipal bonds with taxable bonds sufficient to use up its NOLs, or sells its NOLs to another fully taxable company through a merger.

Once we consider implicit taxes, additional nonacquisition alternatives are available for securing value for NOLs by rearranging the company's assets and liabilities. If the company lacks sufficient income to use up its NOLs in the next year, it is a low-marginal tax rate taxpayer.[51] Consider first the asset side of the balance sheet. Suppose that the loss company holds as assets either common stock or municipal bonds. These assets are tax-favored. They bear low *explicit* taxes. As a result, their market prices are bid up to reflect the assets' tax advantages, producing an *implicit* tax. The low-bracket loss company is in the wrong tax clientele to hold these implicitly taxed assets. For NOL companies, selling tax-favored assets and purchasing tax-disfavored assets can reduce the total (implicit plus explicit) tax burden, at the same time that it uses up the company's NOLs, by generating taxable income.

In addition, the loss company cannot use the depreciation deductions from its depreciable assets as effectively as can fully taxable firms. A sale and leaseback of these assets -- in effect a sale of the depreciation deductions -- is a substitute for selling part of the loss company's NOLs. The loss company can then invest the proceeds of the sale in taxable bonds, thereby increasing income at the same time that deductions are reduced. Between 1981 and 1984, tax rules allowed sale-and-leaseback transactions that amounted to a simple sale of depreciation deductions; the lessor bore no risk concerning the residual value of the investment. Although the lessor must now bear some investment risk, a sale and leaseback remains an attractive way to increase the value of NOLs.

The same type of restructuring is possible on the equity side of the balance sheet. The interest rate on taxable debt reflects its tax-disfavored status to investors, relative to equity -- interest is fully taxable. Just as a loss company should hold debt and not equity, it should *owe* -- have in its capital structure -- equity and not debt. Under our perfect market assumptions, the loss company can simply replace its debt with lower-cost equity. The resulting increase in taxable income will increase the value of its NOLs.

---

[51] If the company expects never to use all its NOLs, its effective marginal tax rate is zero. If it expects to use them in future years, its effective marginal tax rate is reduced because of the time value of money.

A loss company could also issue equity and use the proceeds to buy taxable bonds. This strategy is functionally identical to sale of NOLs through an acquisition of the loss company by a profitable company. In one case the loss company's shareholders' equity in the NOLs is sold to the public, and the proceeds are used to enhance the value of the NOLs by increasing taxable income in the form of taxable bonds. In the other case, equity in the NOLs is sold directly to a profitable company, and the NOLs are used to shelter the acquiring company's future income. This approach simply generalizes the technique of having the loss company make an acquisition, rather than be acquired, as a way to avoid Internal Revenue Code restrictions on the sale of NOLs. The generalization is important, however, because buying taxable bonds is easier than buying another business, which the acquirer may lack the expertise to run.

If we now lift the assumption of no information and transaction costs, the case for tax motivated acquisitions as the best way to use up NOLs is further weakened. We have already noted that an acquisition involves potentially severe agency problems. When these costs are high, some acquisitions will not take place, and tax gains -- in the form of observable NOLs -- will be left on the table. By the same token, some methods of using up NOLs internally (i.e., without an acquisition) will also prove too costly. For example, issuing stock to purchase fully taxable bonds suffers from the same sort of adverse selection costs as the sale of the company in an acquisition.

This result is consistent with empirical observation -- we observe companies with nontrivial NOLs (hundreds of millions of dollars for some companies). For example, start-up companies commonly accumulate NOLs. In the absence of information and agency costs, we would not see these losses; indeed, the higher value of the expected early losses to a profitable company would make every start-up project more valuable to an existing profitable company than to a start-up company. Start-up companies could avoid the wasteful existence of early-stage NOLs by issuing larger quantities of stock and using the proceeds to purchase ordinary income-generating assets. That this strategy is not exploited is prima facie evidence of the importance of adverse selection and moral hazard problems.

But many nonacquisition strategies involve lower information and transaction costs than acquisitions. Restructuring the asset side of a loss company's balance sheet by altering its passive investments, if any, in favor of tax-disfavored assets involves low costs beyond brokerage fees, early recognition of capital gains tax (shielded by the NOLs) or the costs of negotiating installment sales. Adverse-selection-related costs specific to these transactions should be minimal. When a loss company's operating assets are sold and leased back, information and transaction costs should also be relatively small compared with those that arise in an acquisition of an entire business.

The information and transaction cost advantages of nonacquisition alternatives also extend to more active strategies such as issuing equity to acquire tax-disfavored assets. NOLs of a loss company can be transferred by an acquisition only if the consideration includes a substantial amount of voting stock. Thus, adverse selection and other information-related costs appear on *both* sides of the acquisition: The acquiring company must worry about the price it pays for the loss company, and the loss company shareholders must worry about the value of the acquiring company shares they receive. In contrast, the issuance of stock by the loss company and the purchase of taxable bonds with the proceeds of that issuance largely eliminates one layer of adverse selection problems. The costs, however, could be so great in either situation that the NOLs remain unused.

Thus, even before 1986, the claim that acquisitions were the best way to increase the value of a company's NOLs seems significantly overstated. Even when we observe that substantial NOLs were transferred through an acquisition, the primary motive is more likely something other than the attempt to achieve the tax gain (although given the acquisition, the parties will seek to capture the tax gain). One possible motive is efficiency gains from better management: companies with significant NOLs are often candidates for improved performance through external intervention. After 1986, the claim that acquisitions are the best way to use NOLs essentially evaporates.

c. Tax Gains from NOL Transfers and Acquisition Premiums

The claim that tax gains from NOL transfers form a large fraction of observed acquisition premiums is also tenuous. The existence of NOLs is easily observable by investors; gains from the use of the NOLs -- whether through sale of the business or the alternatives discussed above -- are likely to be anticipated.

4. Tax Favoritism Arising from the Tax Treatment of Debt

Recently, the tax treatment of debt has been prominently featured in the policy debate over the influence of the tax system on the level of acquisition activity. In particular, the deductibility of interest is said to motivate debt financed acquisitions. This argument first surfaced prominently in the 1960s, when many conglomerates issued convertible subordinated debt in acquisitions. Congress responded in 1969 by adding § 279 to the IRC, which denies a deduction for interest payments in excess of $5 million on acquisition-related indebtedness that has an equity feature such as convertability and is issued by a highly leveraged company. It surfaced again, with greater force, in the last half of the 1980s, with the surge in leveraged buyouts and leveraged recapitalizations, and other debt-financed acquisitions (many ordinary acquisitions involve the buyer borrowing cash to pay for the seller's shares).

Congress again responded, in the Revenue Reconciliation Act of 1989, which limited two leveraging techniques that were common in leveraged buyouts and leveraged recapitalizations. First, new §§ 172(b)(1)(E) and 172(h) limit the carryback to pre-acquisition years of post-acquisition losses that result from interest expense incurred in a corporate equity reduction transaction.[52] Second, new §§ 163(e)(5) and (i) restrict deductibility of interest on high-yield zero-coupon and pay-in-kind (PIK) debt, both of which were commonly used in highly leveraged transactions.[53] Zero-coupon and PIK debt share the feature that the issuer obtains interest deductions without corresponding cash payments. The result was the best kind of tax deduction, one that preceded the cash outflow that ultimately justified the deduction. (Of course, the holder, if taxable, would recognize income without receiving any cash.) Interest on high-yield zero-coupon and PIK debt is now allowed only when cash payments are made.

Despite the attention the subject has received both in the press and in Congress, the claim that the deductibility of interest is a motive for acquisitions is troublesome at a number of levels.

a.   *The Claim of Net Tax Gains from Increased Leverage*

The leverage variant of the claim that acquisitions result in tax gains is no more complicated than that interest paid on debt is deductible while dividends paid on equity are not. The aftertax cost of financing the purchase of assets with debt is therefore cheaper than the aftertax cost of financing the purchase of the same assets with equity. This claim raises, in a different framework, the debate initiated by Merton Miller and Franco Modigliani more than 20 years ago over the existence of an optimal capital structure.[54] The first response to their claim that in a perfect capital market with no taxes, capital structure would not affect firm value, was that the structure of the corporate tax system -- the deductibility of interest on debt and nondeductibility of dividends on stock -- made a difference. The debate over the extent of the difference continues.[55] It remains unclear whether the

---

[52] See Section A.3.c, *supra*.

[53] These instruments are described in Chapter 11D, *supra*. These provisions apply to any original issue debt, in order to pick up bonds issued at a discount to face value that pay some interest currently, but not at the full market rate.

[54] See Merton Miller & Franco Modigliani, *The Costs of Capital, Corporate Finance, and the Theory of Investment*, 48 Am.Econ.Rev. 261 (1958).

[55] Miller and Modigliani first responded in 1963. Merton Miller & Franco Modigliani, *Corporate Income Taxes and the Cost of Capital: A Correction*, 53 Am.Econ.Rev. 433 (1963). The debate's continuation is evidenced by their continued contributions. See, e.g., Merton Miller, *Debt and Taxes*, 32 J.Fin. 261 (1977); Merton Miller & Myron Scholes, *Dividends and Taxes*, 6 J.Fin.Econ. 333 (1978); Franco Modigliani, *Debt, Dividends Policy, Taxes Inflation and Market Valuation*, 38 J.Fin. 255 (1973); Merton Miller, *The Miller-Modigliani Propositions after Thirty Years*, 2 J.Econ.Persp. 99 (1988); Franco Modigliani,

apparent tax advantages of debt remain in equilibrium, taking into account the tax treatment of shareholders and the shareholders' ability to alter their own tax positions by altering the composition of their own portfolios. While pursuing that debate would take us too far afield, it should be apparent that the claim has nothing to do with acquisitions.

Let us assume that there are tax advantages, in equilibrium, in using debt rather than equity financing. The problem is that the interest on debt incurred to buy *any* asset, whether another corporation or a manufacturing plant, is deductible. A debt-financed acquisition can result in tax gains, but an acquisition is hardly necessary to achieve those gains.

A different formulation of the claim focuses not on the benefits of using debt to finance the purchase of *new* assets, but on the role of acquisitions solely with respect to the refinancing of *existing* assets. If replacing equity with debt on the balance sheets of existing firms is tax advantageous, the claim may be that acquisitions are an especially attractive way to accomplish that recapitalization. Management buyout transactions seem a good example for this claim, since the acquisition drastically alters the target company's capital structure by replacing equity with debt.

But again, one must look at alternatives. Instead of leveraging up all at once, the company could have leveraged up over time, by systematically paying large dividends, and financing its growth with debt rather than equity. Thus, the puzzle remains. Debt financing may have tax advantages. But acquisitions, or one-time equity reduction transactions like leveraged recapitalizations, are manifestly not the only way to achieve those tax advantages.

b.   *Acquisitions as the **Best** Way to Capture Tax Gains from Increased Leverage*

If leveraged buyouts are not the only way to achieve the tax gains from high leverage, might they nonetheless be the *best* way? To examine this claim, we need to consider more closely the differences between alternative ways of leveraging a firm. Recall from Chapter 11 that high leverage is only one of the distinguishing characteristics of an LBO. LBOs also typically involve a change of control, highly concentrated equity ownership, and high management ownership of equity.

The tax gains available from an LBO can also be secured through a leveraged recapitalization, where a company replaces equity with debt but is not acquired. Indeed, Congress recognized this in part in 1989 by denying deductibility of interest not paid in cash that resulted from a "corporate equity reduction transaction" (or CERT) -- a term that was intended to capture both LBOs and leveraged recapitalizations. But while the leveraged recapitalization produces the same tax gains, it does not produce a change in control, nor concentrated equity ownership.

The question then becomes whether these *non-tax* differences can explain why LBOs could be a preferable means of capturing the tax gains from high leverage. Suppose that a company can obtain a tax gain by leveraging the company. Management may not pursue this strategy even if doing so is favorable to shareholders. The increase in leverage increases the risk to which management's firm-specific human capital investment in the company is subject, increases the risk to which management's financial investment in the firm is subject, and decreases the managers' discretion over how to spend the company's cash flow. The managers may prefer the somewhat easier life that a less leveraged company can provide.

The managers' preference for low leverage would also explain why most leveraged recapitalizations -- leveragings without a change of control -- have been defensive responses to a threatened change in control. If the managers' first choice -- running a lightly leveraged firm -- is no longer available, they may prefer running a leveraged company to the alternative, which often involves no longer running the company at all. From this perspective, an acquisition may be the best, and an acquisition or the threat thereof may be the *only*, practical way of inducing management to capture available tax gains.

Further pursuit of this line of analysis suggests that type of acquisition matters. A hostile acquisition, in which management is replaced, may not be the best way to capture the gains from increased leverage. The problem is not that management cannot capture the tax gains, but that they have the wrong incentives because they are not compensated for the costs *to them* resulting from higher leverage. A hostile acquisition overcomes the incentive problem by replacing management, but at the substantial cost of turning operation of the company's business over to possibly less qualified managers.[56]

The need to provide incentives can explain why management buyouts (MBOs) typically involve a large increase in management's ownership interest in the company. The higher ownership interest can overcome management's reluctance to leverage the firm. This permits capture of the tax gains from leverage without the cost of replacing the managers who have the most experience running the company. The increase in management's ownership that is common in leveraged recapitalizations may serve a similar function.

That leaves one remaining difference between MBOs and leveraged recapitalizations: many MBOs transfer ultimate control to the LBO promoter while leveraged recapitalizations leave control where it was, presumably with management. So understood, the question is simply whether the LBO Association lives up to Michael Jensen's claim that it more effectively

---

[56] See Ian Ayres & Peter Cramton, *An Agency Perspective on Relational Investing* (Stanford Law Sch. Olin Program in L. & Econ., Working Paper No. 105, 1993).

reduces agency costs than the techniques available to a public corporation.[57]

This question should be susceptible to empirical testing: the post-transaction performance of companies that were subject to MBOs could be compared with the post-transaction performance of companies that were subject to leveraged recapitalizations. If the LBO Association successfully plays the role claimed for it, the MBO sample should display better performance. We know of no such test.

c. *Tax Gains from Increased Leverage as a Determinant of Acquisition Premiums*

Evaluating the importance of the tax system in determining the level of acquisition activity is relatively easy in the case of tax gains from increased leverage. As with the transfer of net operating losses, the information necessary to determine the size of the tax gains from increased leverage is publicly available. Also as with the transfer of NOLs, there are non-acquisition alternative ways to capture the tax gain. Thus, the tax gain from increased leverage should be incorporated into stock price prior to public announcement of an offer intended to capture that gain, but discounted to reflect the likelihood that management will act to capture the gain. If, for example, investors' assigned a 20% probability to the likelihood that managers would capture the tax gains from leverage, the takeover premium would reflect the tax gains multiplied by the prior 80% probability that management would *not* capture these gains.

C. Empirical Evidence on Taxes as an Acquisition Motive

1. Acquisitions Generally

Because the claim that taxes motivate acquisition has been central to the public policy debate, the dearth of empirical evidence concerning the relationship is surprising. Prior to 1987, the literature typically was either analytical or anecdotal, foregoing empirical verification completely or relying on inadequate samples. In this section, we will review the small empirical literature that has emerged since 1987. However, two cautionary notes are appropriate at the outset. First, the dates of the transactions covered by each study are critical. The Internal Revenue Code provisions relevant to the potential for tax gains from acquisitions (and acquisition substitutes) have been amended repeatedly. Thus, the role of taxes may differ from period to period. Additionally, the dominant non-tax motives for acquisitions likely also changed over time, further complicating the effort to empirically isolate

---

[57] See Michael Jensen, *Eclipse of the Public Corporation*, Harv.Bus.Rev. 61 (Sept./Oct.1989) (excerpted in Chapter 11).

particular motives. Second, *all* the empirical studies involve transactions prior to 1986. Thus, they explore whether taxes *were* an important acquisition motive, not whether they *are* an important motive for acquisitions (or, perhaps more likely, an important deterrent to acquisitions) today.

Three studies by Alan Auerbach & David Reishus estimate the size of acquisition-related tax gains, compared to overall acquisition premia, for three of the sources considered in this chapter: NOL transfer, basis step-up, and increased leverage.[58] As discussed above, the fourth source, the availability of a tax-free reorganization, produces no net tax gains compared to the no-acquisition alternative. Their sample consisted of 318 acquisitions between 1968 and 1983 (75% of which occurred between 1976 and 1982).

For NOL transfers, in only 20% of the sample did one party have NOLs to begin with. In the subsample where tax gains from NOL transfer were possible, the gains from NOL transfer had an average value of approximately 10% of the target's market value in the year prior to the acquisition. On this basis, the tax benefit could account for a premium of no more than 10%, a nontrivial but relatively small fraction of the average takeover premium during this period. As discussed above, if investors partially anticipate the capture of NOL-related tax gains, the actual capture will not be reflected in transaction premiums.[59]

Auerbach & Reishus found even smaller tax gains from a step-up in basis but the date covered by the sample is important in evaluating this result. Recall that the Economic Recovery Tax Act of 1981 increased the value of a basis step-up by shortening the period over which depreciation could be taken, thus increasing the potential value of a basis step-up.

Auerbach & Reishus also failed to find large gains from increased leverage. The ratio of long-term debt to long-term debt plus equity in their sample increased only 1.3% as a result of the acquisition -- from an average of 25.4% to one of 26.7%. Where the target company was relatively large (25-50% of the size of the acquiring company) the average debt-equity ratio *declined*, presumably because many of these transactions were financed with equity.

Auerbach & Reishus sought to examine the relative importance of tax gains for their sample by creating a parallel sample of "pseudo mergers." For each actual merger, a "pseudotarget" of the same size as the actual target, and a "pseudoparent" of the same size as the actual acquirer, were

---

[58] Alan Auerbach & David Reishus, *Taxes and the Merger Decision*, in *Knights, Raiders and Targets: The Impact of the Hostile Takeover* 300 (John Coffee, Louis Lowenstein & Susan Rose-Ackerman eds.1988); Alan Auerbach & David Reishus, *The Impact of Taxes on Mergers and Acquisitions*, in *Mergers and Acquisitions* 69 (Alan Auerbach ed.1988); Alan Auerbach & David Reishus, *The Effects of Taxation on the Merger Decision*, in *Corporate Takeovers: Causes and Consequences* 157 (Alan Auerbach ed.1988).

[59] Norman Moore & Stephen Pruitt, *The Market Pricing of Net Operating Loss Carryforwards: Implications of the Tax Motivations of Mergers*, 10 J.Fin.Res. 153 (1987), present weak evidence that the gain from capturing the value of NOLs (through an acquisition or otherwise) is partially priced without an acquisition.

selected at random from a universe of public industrial firms. The idea is that if taxes are an important acquisition motive, then actual mergers should show higher tax benefits than the pseudo mergers. This was not observed. Actual mergers were no more likely than pseudo mergers to produce tax benefits. This suggests that even if acquisitions sometimes result in tax gains, the gains are not large enough, compared to other factors that affect takeover activity, to significantly affect the level of acquisition activity. The parties to an acquisition will capture the available tax gains, but the acquisition would have taken place even in their absence.

2.   Tax Gains in Leveraged Buyouts

Management buyouts are a transaction type that is reputed to be particularly tax motivated, in part because two important non-tax motives for acquisition -- operating synergy and replacement of inefficient management -- are largely absent. Two recent studies, by Katherine Schipper & Abbie Smith[60] and Steven Kaplan[61] examine the importance of increased depreciation from a step-up in basis and increased interest deductions from debt used to finance the transaction in a large sample of pre-1986 MBOs.

Schipper & Smith express skepticism concerning the importance of basis step-up as a motive for significant numbers of MBOs. Of the 93 transactions in their sample, fewer than one-third of the acquirers elected under § 338 to step-up the basis of the target's assets. In the 30 transactions where the acquirer did elect a basis step-up, the median estimated tax savings was only 29% of the premium paid. But this greatly overstates the net tax gains from a basis step-up, because it ignores recapture taxes and the capital gains tax paid by target shareholders. LBOs, by their nature, involve payment of cash for the target's shares, so the target's shareholders will pay capital gains tax, whatever the acquirer does. The acquirer's tax calculus, in deciding whether to step-up basis, is simple: A basis step-up is desirable if the present value of higher future depreciation deductions exceeds the recapture tax. Thus, recapture taxes are the *only* plausible reason why an acquirer would *not* elect a basis step-up, yet 2/3 of Schipper & Smith's sample took no step-up. Kaplan reports similar results. In his sample of 76 MBOs completed in the 1980-1986 period, only about half of the acquirers elected to step-up the target's basis. In those transactions, the average gains from higher depreciations, *before* payment of recapture tax, represented 25% of the premium paid. Since recapture taxes should be similar in magnitude in LBO and non-LBO transactions, these studies are consistent with Auerbach &

---

[60] Katherine Schipper & Abbie Smith, *Effects of Management Buyouts on Corporate Interest and Tax Deductions*, 34 J.L. & Econ. 295 (1991).

[61] Steven Kaplan, *Management Buyouts: Evidence on Taxes as a Source of Value*, 44 J.Fin. 611 (1989).

Reishus's finding on the unimportance of basis step-up as a motive in acquisitions generally.

Both Schipper & Smith and Kaplan reach more complicated conclusions with respect to gains from increased interest deductions. In estimating increased interest costs, one must make assumptions about how fast the LBO debt will be repaid. Schipper & Smith assume that debt incurred in the LBO will be repaid according to its stated maturity. They report that in the median transaction involving (not involving) an asset writeup, tax savings from interest deductions can explain roughly 91% (65%) of the premium paid to target shareholders. Kaplan reports results of similar magnitude. During the time period covered by their sample, LBO debt was typically retired much faster than Schipper & Smith assumed, often through the LBO company issuing equity and returning to public ownership. This would translate into lower interest deductions, but even so, interest deductions are a substantial fraction of overall LBO premia.

Interest deductions do not, however, translate dollar for dollar into tax gains. As Schipper & Smith note, the tax gains to the issuer from increased leverage do not take into account the higher pretax cost of debt compared to equity because of the unfavorable tax treatment of interest income to the recipient.

Kaplan argues that the increased post-MBO interest deductions appear to result from the buyout structure, because companies that are subject to MBOs did not have lower leverage than other firms in their industry, from which he infers that they did not have unused debt capacity prior to the MBO. But this data is also consistent with an industry-wide pattern of unused debt capacity that is only corrected when a firm is the subject of an MBO (or of a hostile offer -- companies that were the subject of a successful third party acquisition were apparently excluded from the industry control group). On this analysis, the puzzle is what prompts the change in leverage for the MBO firms. The explanation may be that the change in management incentives in an MBO makes a leverage increase to secure a tax gain a more palatable strategy for management.

MBOs were also the object of an effort by Michael Jensen, Steven Kaplan & Laura Stiglin to test whether a typical MBO yields net losses to the U.S. Treasury.[62] A net tax gain for the participants in the transaction would roughly correspond to an offsetting tax loss for the Treasury. Looking at buyouts over the period from 1979 through 1985, the authors compared the average revenue costs of MBOs -- increased interest deduction on the debt incurred in the acquisition and lower tax revenues from a decrease in dividends paid -- with five sources of revenue gains from LBOs: (1) capital gains taxes paid by target shareholders; (2) income taxes payable on the interest received by holders of the debt incurred in the acquisition; (3) corporate income taxes payable on post-transaction disposition of target

---

[62] Michael Jensen, Steven Kaplan & Laura Stiglin, *Effects of LBOs on Tax Revenues of the U.S. Treasury*, Tax Notes 727 (Feb. 6, 1989).

assets; (4) increased income taxes payable as a result of more efficient post-transaction use of capital; and (5) increased income taxes resulting from post-transaction improvement in the target's operations and, hence operating income. They conclude that "at a total dollar volume of LBO transactions of $75 billion per year, the Treasury *gains* about $9 billion in the first year and about $16.5 billion in present value of future net tax receipts."[63] The calculation is shown in Table 12-4. Applying the same analysis to the projections for post-buyout performance for the $25 billion buyout of RJR-Nabisco by Kohlberg, Kravis and Roberts, the authors find a similar result: an increase in the present value of net future tax revenues of $3.76 billion.[64]

Table 12-4[65]
Federal Income Tax Implications of Typical ($500 million) LBO
($ millions)

Typical LBO Features

Pre-buyout market value of equity	$360
Buyout purchase price	500
Incremental debt	400
Tax basis of selling shareholder's stock	290
Post-buyout value of firm (in 5 years)	750
Taxable capital gain to pre-buyout shareholders (500−290)	210
Capital gain to buyout investors (750−500)	250

---

[63] *Id.* at 727.

[64] Gerard Cahill & Camille Castorina, *Did the Treasury Win or Lose in the RJR Buyout*, Mergers & Acquisitions 47 (March/April 1990), estimated a somewhat higher benefit to the Treasury. In contrast, Haynes Leland, *LBOs and Taxes: No One to Blame but Ourselves*, Cal.Mgmt.Rev. 19 (Fall 1989), finds a net tax *loss* to the Treasury of $1.7 to $6.6 billion. Among the reasons for the difference is that Jensen, Kaplan & Stiglin include in their calculation of incremental tax revenues to the Treasury, $2.25 billion in taxes on increased operating income that results from the transaction, $1.09 billion in taxes on increased capital efficiency, and $1.16 billion in taxes on post-acquisition asset sales, none of which are included in Leland's calculation. Additionally, Leland assumed that all of the increased debt was permanent while Jensen, Kaplan & Stiglin assumed that 40% would be retired after the first year.

[65] The table format is adapted from Scholes & Wolfson (1992), *supra* note 57, at 519.

Incremental Tax Revenues

Capital gains taxes:

At buyout: $\$210 \times .70^a \times .28^b$	$\$41.2$
At subsequent restructuring: $\$250 \times .30^c \times .28^b \times .62^d$	13.0

Taxes on increased operating income:

$\$100^e \times .25^f \times .34^g \times 10^h$ 85.0

Taxes on LBO creditor's income: $\$400 \times .6^i \times .5^j \times .34^g$ 40.8

Taxes from increased capital efficiency: 29.9
$\$44^k \times .20^l \times .10^m \times 10^n \times 10^h \times .34^g$

Taxes to selling corporation on subsequent sale of assets: $\underline{17.0}$
$\$500 \times .20^o \times .50^p \times .34^g$

                                                   $\$226.9$

Incremental Tax Losses

Tax deductibility of interest payments on debt: -81.6
$-\$400 \times .60^i \times .34^g$

Taxes on foregoing dividend payments: $\underline{-35.3}$
$-.05^q \times \$360 \times .70^a \times .28^b \times 10^h$

Net Incremental Tax Revenues to U.S. Treasury   **$110.0**

---

[a] Percent of stock owned by taxable shareholders.

[b] Capital gains tax rate.

[c] Percent of stock owned by taxable shareholders at post-buyout sale.

[d] Present value factor for cash flows in 5 years discounted at 10% per year.

[e] Typical operating income pre-buyout.

[f] Incremental operating income of 25% post-buyout due to increased efficiency.

[g] Corporate tax rate.

[h] Present value of a perpetuity of one dollar discounted at 10% per year.

[i] Percent of incremental debt deemed to be permanent.

[j] Percent of debt held by taxable investors.

[k] Typical annual capital expenditure by pre-buyout firm.

[l] Typical percentage reduction in annual capital expenditures post-buyout.

[m] Reduced capital expenditures are assumed to be returned to investors where they earn this rate (10% per year before tax), whereas the capital expenditure would have been a waste (earning 0%).

[n] The capital expenditure savings are expected to recur in perpetuity. This is the present value factor at a discount rate of 10%.

[o] Assumes sale of 20% of the $500 million of LBO assets within a year after the LBO.

[p] The basis of the assets sold within a year of the LBO is assumed to equal half the sales price, so the other half is taxable gain.

[q] Elimination of 5% dividend on $360 million worth of equity.

Unfortunately, Jensen, Kaplan & Stiglin do not measure tax gains from an acquisition in the sense that we have used the term -- that is, whether the acquisition can increase aftertax earnings with no increase in pretax earnings. To accomplish this requires eliminating several sources of revenue to the Treasury: the taxes on increased income from greater operating efficiency; the taxes on increased income from greater capital efficiency; taxes on subsequent sale of assets by the MBO firm (for which the authors neither compute offsetting tax costs to the Treasury, nor account for a then-available tax-avoidance strategy known as mirroring, nor allow for the possibility that some assets would have been sold without the LBO); and taxes on the assumed post-buyout sale of equity in the buyout firm (once again, a complete tax calculus is not offered). With these corrections, their typical LBO shows a net tax gain of about $35 million, which is an appreciable fraction of the $140 million premium.

To understand the difference between the revenue gains to the Treasury reported in the study, and the likely tax gains to shareholders as we have used the term, one must define the baseline of tax neutrality with greater precision. The Treasury generally shares in the revenue from economic activity that increases wealth. If LBOs achieve wealth increases, tax revenue will increase. Jensen, Kaplan & Stiglin's central result is that the revenue gains that flow from LBO efficiency gains exceed the revenue losses that flow from the tax consequences associated with the transaction itself. The LBO form can still be tax favored, in the sense that *less* of the wealth increase produced by LBOs is shared with the tax collector than is the case for wealth created by corporations generally.

The result also may be affected by a failure to include in the calculation the Treasury's opportunity cost. A significant fraction of the increased tax revenues from MBOs in the Jensen, Kaplan & Stiglin analysis results from taxes paid on interest received by the holders of the debt incurred in the transaction. However, the funds used to purchase the debt presumably were invested in income producing assets prior to the transaction. Thus, the net increase in tax revenues from this source is only the tax on the amount by which the interest paid on the new debt exceeds the income that had been earned on the funds in their pre-transaction investment.

3.   Do Tax Law Changes Affect the Incidence of Takeover Activity

A final study takes a different approach to assessing how the tax system influences acquisition activity. Rather than trying to measure the potential tax gains from acquisitions, Myron Scholes & Mark Wolfson look at the impact of important changes in the tax treatment of acquisitions on the aggregate level of acquisition activity.[66] They observe that the Tax Reform

---

[66] Myron Scholes & Mark Wolfson, *The Effects of Changes in Tax Laws on Corporate Reorganization Activity*, 63 J.Bus. S141 (1990).

Act of 1986 "put nails in the tax-induced asset-sales-and-mergers coffin along *all* of the tax dimensions that are important in motivating mergers and acquisitions.[67] That leads to two hypotheses. If tax motives are a major determinant of acquisition activity, then the number of acquisitions should (1) increase markedly in the quarter preceding the effectiveness of the 1986 Act, as planners rush to complete transactions before the effective date of the new law; and (2) decrease markedly and permanently following its effectiveness.

Table 12-5 presents the quarterly data developed by Scholes & Wolfson to test these hypotheses.

Table 12-5
Acquisitions from 4th Quarter 1985 through Fourth Quarter 1987
(transactions between U.S. companies only, in $ billions)

Quarter	Nominal Dollars	Constant Dollars	Adjusted for Changes in S&P 500 Index
1984-5	45.93	48.60	57.26
1986-1	29.97	31.65	32.75
1986-2	44.55	47.15	45.97
1986-3	34.86	36.65	38.76
Sum	**155.31**	**164.05**	**174.65**
Average	**38.83**	**41.01**	**43.66**
1986-4	64.65	67.44	68.03
1987-1	21.66	22.38	18.78
1987-2	32.97	33.63	27.20
1987-3	33.66	33.96	26.04
1987-4	35.82	35.82	35.82
Sum	**188.76**	**193.23**	**175.87**
Average	**37.75**	**38.65**	**35.17**

Table 12-5 confirms that acquisition activity increased substantially in the fourth quarter of 1986. Scholes & Wolfson report that the dollar volume of transactions in this quarter represents a record, whether in nominal or real terms, over the last 50 years. It exceeds the average volume of the eight quarters surrounding it by 85% in nominal dollars, 86% in constant dollars, and by 93% adjusted for changes in the S&P 500 Index. The table also confirms that acquisition activity decreased substantially in the first quarter of 1987, following the 1986 Act's effective date. Indeed, acquisition activity during all of 1987 represented a decrease from 1986 levels of 20% in

---

[67] *Id.* at S142-43.

nominal dollars, 23% in constant dollars, and 38% in S&P 500 adjusted dollars.

The data presented in Table 12-5 are consistent with planners making a concerted effort to fall within the more favorable tax environment available before the end of 1986. But the data do not tell us whether this is because the tax code favored acquisitions before 1986, disfavored them after 1986, or some of both. Nor do they tell us how important a determinant tax impacts are in whether an acquisition takes place. The increased number of transactions during the fourth quarter of 1986 and the decline during 1987 could reflect either a permanent change in the level of acquisition activity, or simply planners' efforts to move transactions originally planned for 1987 into 1986 to secure desirable but not make-or-break tax gains.

Scholes & Wolfson recognize this alternative explanation, and note that levels of acquisition activity for a longer period of time can help resolve the ambiguity. Table 12-6 presents annual acquisition data for 1984 through 1991 in nominal and constant 1986 dollars.

Table 12-6
Merger and Acquisition Values for 1984-1991
($ billions)

Year	Nominal Dollars	Constant Dollars
1984	122.2	129.0
1985	179.9	183.2
1986	201.4	201.4
1987	175.0	168.8
1988	232.4	215.3
1989	244.1	215.8
1990	164.3	137.8
1991	98.0	78.9

The data in Table 12-6 on their face value support a bunching phenomenon. The value of acquisitions in both 1988 and 1989 exceeded the value of acquisitions in 1986. Meanwhile, large drops occurred in 1990 and 1991 without major changes in the tax laws. This suggests that tax gains are a second-order explanation for the overall level of acquisition activity.

D.   Conclusion

The survey presented in this Chapter is consistent with the possibility that over different periods of time, especially prior to 1986, acquisitions could sometimes produce net tax gains not otherwise available and that acquisitions could sometimes be a preferred way to capture tax gains that could be captured in other ways as well. But neither theory nor data support the claim that the opportunity to capture tax gains significantly affects acquisition premiums or the level of acquisition activity.

A closing note is appropriate about the role for the tax system in influencing the level of acquisition activity. Among its other functions, the tax system serves as a regulatory regime designed to influence the level of particular activities. Some favored activities are subsidized through the use of tax credits, as is the case from for low-income housing. Other disfavored activities are penalized with the goal not of raising revenue, but of reducing their incidence. That the tax system may not have contributed greatly to the level of acquisition activity before 1986 does not mean that it does not discourage acquisitions *at the margin* today, or cannot be used to discourage them even more strongly in the future.

CHAPTER 13: FINANCIAL ACCOUNTING
TREATMENT OF ACQUISITIONS

A prominent acquisition motive involves how the acquisition will be reflected in the acquiring company's financial statements. The logic of this theory of acquisitions, at first glance, is straightforward. If the acquiring company has a choice of how to account for an acquisition or other transaction, it will usually choose the method that produces the highest earnings per share. The higher the current earnings that the company reports, the higher the future earnings that investors will expect and the higher the company's market value. It would then follow that if an accounting method that generates high reported earnings is available only for transactions with particular characteristics, we would observe acquiring firms structuring transactions to qualify for the favorable accounting method.

At second glance, however, the logic behind this theory of acquisitions is less clear. Suppose two acquisitions are identical in substance, but one can be accounted for by a method that lets the acquirer report higher earnings than the other. Will higher reported earnings, without a difference in actual cash flow, result in the acquiring firm having a higher post-transaction stock market value? Or will investors see through the accounting rules, and pay attention only to actual cash flows?

The controversy over the appropriate method of accounting for corporate acquisitions squarely presents this issue. Two different methods of accounting for acquisitions are available and, depending on the circumstances, one method or the other will predictably result in higher reported earnings. By carefully structuring the transaction, including using stock as consideration when it might otherwise have used cash, an acquiring company can choose, albeit at some cost, which accounting method will be used. Do such accounting choices affect the company's value? If so, then accounting rules have important policy implications because they influence real economic activity. Accounting rules should then presumably be chosen to reflect the substance of the transaction as accurately as possible. And lawyers must be able to use whatever flexibility remains within the accounting rules to structure a transaction that creates the most *stock market value*.

If, on the other hand, investors see through differences in accounting treatment, then it becomes less important for policymakers to choose the "right" accounting rule, and more important to choose rules that make it easy for investors to determine underlying cash flows, and to compare similarly situated companies. The lawyer's role then becomes one of choosing a structure that maximizes *business value*, even if that means forgoing the most favorable accounting treatment.

The conventional wisdom on accounting for acquisitions assumes that there is a relationship between how an acquirer accounts for an acquisition and the acquirer's post-transaction stock market value. In the taxonomy of acquisition motives set out in the Introduction to Part II, this is an information-based theory of acquisitions. *Stock market value* increases not because of changes in real economic performance, but because changes in the manner in which information about economic performance is disclosed. *Business value*, obviously, is unaffected.

This Chapter explores the link between accounting method and post-acquisition value and, more generally, the relationship between financial accounting methods and firm value. Parts A–C examine the methods of accounting for acquisitions and when each is available. Part D then considers the theory that links the choice of accounting method to firm value. Part E considers the consistency of this theory with the financial theory discussed in Part I and the available empirical evidence. In particular, we take up an apparent conflict between the belief that the choice of accounting method affects firm value and market efficiency. If ECMH holds, then firm value should be independent of accounting method used. Yet sophisticated participants often take a different view. For example, in AT&T's 1991 acquisition of NCR, AT&T reportedly increased its offering price by some $650 million in return for NCR's cooperation in securing pooling of interest accounting for the transaction.[1] From AT&T's perspective, was this simply a mistake? Part F then examines efforts to develop a theory of choice of accounting method. Finally, Part G describes how financial accounting standards are set and the insights that financial theory offers for that process.

A. Accounting for Complete Acquisitions: Purchase Versus Pooling

In the U.S., there have historically been two available methods of accounting for the acquisition of a business: as a *purchase* (just like the purchase of any other asset) and as a *pooling of interests*. Purchase accounting was the only available method for acquisitions involving primarily cash as consideration. Both methods were available for acquisitions involving primarily stock as consideration.

The debate over the merits of the purchase and pooling methods of acquisitions accounting historically took the form of a search for a Platonic ideal. One ideal transaction form involves a company buying an asset. Standard principles of historical cost accounting require recording the asset on the acquirer's books at cost. This is the core of the purchase method of accounting for acquisitions: a corporate acquisition is just the purchase of an aggregation of assets, each of which should be recorded at its cost.

The other ideal form of transaction was thought to occur when two companies combined, or "pooled" their operations through a merger, but the shareholders remained the same and neither company could be said to have acquired the other. In this case, the argument goes, there is no reason to alter the historical cost of either company's assets. This is the core of the pooling of interests method.

---

[1] See Eben Shapiro, *AT&T Buying Computer Maker in Stock Deal Worth $7.4 Billion*, N.Y.Times, May 7, 1991, at A5.

The problem was how to tell which ideal form a particular acquisition most resembled. In the common case where the purchase price exceeded the target's book value, pooling of interests treatment would result in lower depreciation and other charges against income, and thus higher reported income. Thus, acquirers almost always wanted pooling treatment.

The principal actors in the line drawing exercise were public accountants and, to a lesser degree, lawyers, both of whom wanted to facilitate their clients' goals. Lawyers will hardly be surprised at how this standard setting worked out over time. Transaction planners stretched the pooling concept further and further by making each transaction sufficiently like a previous transaction so that the desired outcome could be justified. The end result was that the choice of purchase or pooling in stock-for-stock acquisitions came to turn on the virtually unlimited discretion of the acquiring company. This led, to a regulatory response -- the adoption in 1970 of Accounting Principles Board (APB) Opinion 16 -- which restricted but did not eliminate the availability of pooling treatment.[2]

The excerpts below, from an accounting textbook and from APB 16, describe the mechanics of both methods of accounting for complete acquisitions (in essence, the stakes of the debate), the terms in which the debate was carried out, and how the debate was resolved.

1.   The Mechanics of Purchase and Pooling Accounting

Sidney Davidson, Clyde Stickney & Roman Weil
FINANCIAL ACCOUNTING
477-87 (2d ed. 1979)[*]

Purchase Method -- Central Concepts

The purchase method follows normal historical-cost accounting principles for recording acquisitions of assets and issuances of stock. Three particular principles are central to the purchase method.

First, assets acquired under historical costing are recorded at their cost. Cost is generally the amount of cash given in exchange for the asset acquired. If a firm acquires a building for $100,000, the entry is

Building	100,000	
Cash		100,000

---

[2] The Accounting Principles Board was, at the time, the authoritative accounting standards setting body. Section F of this Chapter discusses how accounting standards are set.

[*] Copyright © 1979 by The Dryden Press. Reprinted by permission of CBS College Publishing.

Second, cost is measured by the fair market value of any noncash consideration given in exchange for an asset acquired. If a firm gives 5,000 shares of its $2-par-value common stock for a building and the common stock currently sells for $20 a share, the cash-equivalent value of the shares given is $100,000 (= 5,000 shares × $20 per share). The entry is

Building	100,000	
Common Stock -- $2 Par Value		10,000
Additional Paid-in Capital		90,000

. . . Third, when more than one asset is acquired in a single transaction, the total cost must be allocated to each of the assets acquired according to their market value. . . . Assume the preceding transaction involved the acquisition of land with a market value of $25,000 and of a building with a market value of $75,000. The entry is

Land	25,000	
Building	75,000	
Common Stock -- $2 Par Value		10,000
Additional Paid-in Capital		90,000

The purchase method may require two extensions of the historical-cost model. In most business combinations, the amount of the consideration given by the acquiring company exceeds the sum of the market values of the identifiable assets acquired. This excess generally represents items not shown in the balance sheet such as a good reputation with customers, a well-trained labor force, superior managerial talent, or the fruits of internal research and development efforts. . . . Under the purchase method, the excess of cost over the fair market value of the identifiable net assets acquired is called "goodwill."

Assume that the preceding transaction involved the acquisition of land with a market value of $25,000 and a building having a market value of $75,000, and that these were the only assets of the firm acquired. Now assume that 6,000 (rather than 5,000 as before) shares are required to persuade the previous owner to sell. The value of the shares given up is $120,000 (= 6,000 shares × $20 per share). The market value of the identifiable assets acquired is $100,000 (= $25,000 + $75,000). The goodwill is $20,000 (= $120,000 − $100,000). The entry would be

Land	25,000	
Building	75,000	
Goodwill	20,000	
Common Stock -- $2 Par Value		12,000
Additional Paid-in Capital		108,000

. . . The second extension of the historical-cost model occurs when liabilities of an acquired company are assumed by the acquiring company. The liabilities assumed will be stated at the present value of the future cash payments at the date of acquisition. The payments are discounted at a *current* rate of interest appropriate for the risk of the borrowing company. This present value is the current market value of the liabilities. Assume in the preceding transaction that liabilities having a present value of $20,000 were assumed by the acquiring company but still 6,000 shares were given up. The entry would be

Land	25,000
Building	75,000
Goodwill	40,000
Liabilities	20,000
Common Stock -- $2 Par Value	12,000
Additional Paid-in Capital	108,000

. . .

Example -- Merger

To illustrate the application of the purchase method, consider the balance sheet amounts for *P* Company [the acquirer] and *S* Company [the seller] shown in Table 13-1.

Table 13-1
Illustration Data for *P* Company and *S* Company

Assets	P Company Book Value	S Company Book Value	S Company Market Value
Current Assets	$ 500,000	$200,000	$250,000
Property, Plant & Equipment (net)	$2,000,000	500,000	600,000
Patent	0	0	50,000
Total Assets	**$2,500,000**	**$700,000**	--
Equities			
Current Liabilities	$ 300,000	$ 80,000	$ 80,000
Long-Term Liabilities	400,000	100,000	90,000
Common Stock - $5 Par Value	1,000,000	100,000	--
Additional Paid-in Capital	200,000	200,000	--
Retained Earnings	600,000	220,000	--
Total Equities	**$2,500,000**	**$700,000**	--

P Company and *S* Company have agreed to merge. *P* Company will give 40,000 shares of its $5 par-value common stock for all of the outstanding common shares of *S* Company. The *S* Company shares will then be canceled and *S* Company will be legally dissolved. The current market price of *P* Company stock is $20 per share. The market value of the shares given is $800,000 (= 40,000 shares × $20 per share). . . . Table 13-2 shows the effects of recording the merger on the books of *P* Company. Note the following aspects of the purchase method:

1. All assets are recorded on *P* Company's books at their cost. *P* Company gave consideration for the patent and goodwill and these assets are therefore recorded, even though they did not appear on the records of *S* Company. (Recall that costs incurred for internally developed patents are expensed.)

2. The book value of *P* Company, after the merger, exceeds the sum of the book values of *P* Company and *S* Company before the merger. This is caused by the fact that the recorded assets and liabilities of *S* Company were restated to current market values and the patent and goodwill were recognized.

3. The goodwill arising from a purchase is a long-lived asset, and generally accepted accounting principles require that this asset be amortized over a period of no more than 40 years.[7]. . .

Table 13-2
Effects on *P* Company's Books of Recording the Merger of
S Company Under the Purchase Method

Assets	Before Merger	Debit	Credit	After Merger
Current Assets	$ 500,000	$250,000		$ 750,000
Fixed Assets (net)	2,000,000	600,000		2,600,000
Patent	0	50,000		50,000
Goodwill	0	70,000		70,000
Total Assets	**$2,500,000**			**$3,470,000**
Equities				
Current Liabilities	$ 300,000		$ 80,000	$ 380,000
Long-Term Liabilities	400,000		90,000	490,000
Common Stock - $5 Par Value	1,000,000		200,000	1,200,000
Additional Paid-in Capital	200,000		600,000	800,000
Retained Earnings	600,000			600,000
Total Adjustments		**$970,000**	**$970,000**	
Total Equities	**$2,500,000**			**$3,470,000**

---

[7] *Accounting Principles Board Opinion No. 17* (1970).

Pooling of Interests -- Central Concepts

. . . In a pooling of interests, the *form* in which the entities conduct their operations has changed (that is, a new combined firm replaces the previously separate firms) but the *substance* has not -- each business entity has the same assets and liabilities and carries out the same business activities as before. . . .   Since no acquisition has taken place, no new basis of accounting arises. The book values of the assets and liabilities of the former companies are carried over to the new combined company. . . .   Current market values are ignored. . . .

Illustration of the Pooling-of-Interests Method

The balance sheet data for *S* Company and *P* Company, as presented in Table 13-1, will be used to illustrate the pooling-of-interests method. [As before, *P* Company exchanges 40,000 shares of its common stock, worth $20 per share, for all of the outstanding common shares of *S* Company. Table 13-3 shows the entries to record the acquisition. From the standpoint of the combined firm, the shares of *P* Company merely replace the shares of *S* Company. *S* Company's contributed capital of $300,000 (= $100,000 + $200,000) is carried over to *P* Company, and is] allocated to common stock and additional paid-in capital of *P* Company based on the par value of the shares issued. (That is, 40,000 shares × $5 par value = $200,000. This amount is allocated to common stock at par value. The remainder is allocated to Additional Paid-in Capital.) . . .

Table 13-3
Effects on *P* Company's Books of Recording the Merger
of *S* Company Under the Pooling-of-Interests Method

Assets	Before Merger	Debit	Credit	After Merger
Current Assets	$ 500,000	$200,000		$700,000
Fixed Assets (net)	2,000,000	500,000		2,500,000
Total Assets	**$2,500,000**			**$3,200,000**
Equities				
Current Liabilities	$ 300,000		$80,000	$380,000
Long-Term Liabilities	400,000		100,000	500,000
Common Stock-$5 Par Value	1,000,000		200,000	1,200,000
Additional Paid-in Capital	200,000		100,000	300,000
Retained Earnings	600,000		220,000	820,000
Total Adjustments		**$700,000**	**$700,000**	
Total Equities	**$2,500,000**			**3,200,000**

Note the following aspects of the pooling-of-interests method:

1. The amounts for the individual assets and liabilities after the merger are merely the sum of the amounts for each firm before the merger.

2. The total contributed capital after the merger ($1,200,000 + $300,000) is equal to the sum of the contributed capital accounts of the two companies before the merger.

3. Retained earnings after the merger is the sum of the retained earnings of the two firms before the merger.

Effect of Purchase and Pooling of Interests on Net Income

The asset amounts recorded under the purchase method in Table 13-2 exceed the corresponding amounts under the pooling-of-interests method in Table 13-3. Such an excess usually occurs. The market values of assets acquired usually exceed their book values. What are the effects of these two methods of recording the business combination on net income of subsequent years?

Net income under the purchase method will be lower than under pooling. The higher amounts for inventory, buildings, and equipment recorded in a purchase lead to larger amounts for cost of goods sold and depreciation. In addition, any previously unrecorded assets that are recognized in a purchase, such as patents and goodwill, must be amortized. The extra amortization expense after a purchase lowers the income as compared to that after a pooling.

To illustrate the effects of these methods on net income subsequent to the combination, assume that the $50,000 excess of market value over book value of S Company's current assets is attributable to an undervaluation of inventory . . . [and that S Company's] fixed assets and patents have a 10-year life remaining on the date of the combination. The goodwill is to be amortized over 40 years, the longest period allowed in generally accepted accounting principles. The straight-line method of depreciation (for fixed assets) and amortization (for patents) is to be used.

Table 13-4 shows the calculation of net income for the first year after the merger assuming that the levels of income for the two firms before the merger are maintained afterwards. . . . The pretax net income under the pooling method of $650,000 is higher than under the purchase method, since the additional cost of goods sold, depreciation, and amortization expense are not recognized after a pooling. Coupling this higher net income with the lower book value of assets and owners' equity under pooling leads to significant differences in the rates of return on both assets and owners' equity. . . .

Pooling of interests not only keeps reported income from decreasing after the merger, it may also allow management of the pooled companies to manage the reported earnings in an arbitrary way. Suppose, as has happened, that Company *P* merges with an old, established firm, Company *F*, which has produced commercial movie films. . . . [T]he book value of these films is zero or close to zero. But the market value of the films is much larger than zero, because television stations find that old movies please their audiences. If Company *P* purchases Company *F*, then the old films will be shown on the consolidated balance sheet at the films' current fair market value. If Company *P* merges with Company *F* using the pooling-of-interests method, the films will be shown on the consolidated balance sheet at their near-zero book values. Then, when Company *P* wants to bolster reported earnings for the year, all it need do is sell some old movies to a television network, and a handsome gain can be reported. Actually, of course, the owners of Company *F* enjoyed this gain when their stock was "sold to" (or exchanged with) Company *P* for current asset values, not the obsolete book values.

Table 13-4
Effects of Purchase and Pooling-of-Interests Methods on Net Income

	Before Combination		Combined Operations After Merger	
	P Company	*S* Company	Purchase	Pooling
Sales	$2,000,000 +	$400,000 =	$2,400,000	$2,400,000
Cost of Goods Sold	(1,200,000) +	(200,000) =	(1,400,000)	(1,400,000)
Selling and Administrative Expenses	(300,000) +	(50,000) =	(350,000)	(350,000)
Additional Cost of Goods Sold			(50,000)	--
Additional Depreciation ($100,000/10 years)			(10,000)	--
Patent Amortization ($50,000/10 years)			(5,000)	--
Goodwill Amortization ($70,000/40 years)			(1,750)	--
Net Income Before Taxes	$ 500,000	$150,000	$ 583,250	$ 650,000
Income Taxes at 40%	(200,000)	(60,000)	(260,000)	(260,000)
Net Income	$ 300,000	$ 90,000	$ 323,250	$ 390,000
Total Assets on Merger Date			**$3,470,000**	**$3,200,000**
All Capital Earnings Rate			9.3%	12.2%
Owners' Equity at Merger Date			$2,600,000	$2,320,000
Return on Owners' Equity			12.4%	16.8%

2.   Determinants of the Choice Between Purchase and Pooling

The debate leading up to the adoption of APB No. 16 was lengthy and controversial. As early as 1963, Wyatt (1963)[3] recommended eliminating or severely curtailing the availability of pooling treatment. An SEC official testified before Congress that the SEC would establish accounting standards for business combinations unless the Accounting Principles Board acted. This led to an initial APB proposal that would have effectively prohibited pooling. In response to negative reaction from the business community, the regulatory effort shifted to setting conditions for when pooling would be available. These conditions were also hotly contested. For example, a proposal to prohibit pooling if the acquiring firm was more than three times the size of the target was dropped in the final draft.[4]

Accounting Principles Board
OPINION NO. 16, BUSINESS COMBINATIONS
(1970)*

Appraisal of Accepted Methods of Accounting

15. The pooling of interests method of accounting is applied only to business combinations effected by an exchange of stock and not to those involving primarily cash, other assets, or liabilities. Applying the purchase method of accounting to business combinations effected by paying cash, distributing other assets, or incurring liabilities is not challenged. Thus, those business combinations effected primarily by an exchange of equity securities present a question of choice between the two accounting methods.

16. The significantly different results of applying the purchase and pooling of interests methods of accounting to a combination effected by an exchange of stock stem from distinct views of the nature of the transaction itself. Those who endorse the pooling of interests method believe that an exchange of stock to effect a business combination is in substance a transaction between the combining stockholder groups and does not involve the corporate entities. The transaction therefore neither requires nor justifies establishing a new basis of accountability for the assets of the combined corporation. Those who endorse the purchase method believe that the transaction is an issue of stock by a corporation for consideration received from those who become stockholders by the transaction. The consideration

---

[3] Arthur Wyatt, *Accounting Research Study No. 5: A Critical Study of Accounting for Business Transactions* (1963).

[4] See Richard Leftwich, *Evidence on the Impact of Mandatory Changes in Accounting Principles on Corporate Loan Agreements,* 3 J.Acct. & Econ. 3, 15-16 (1981).

* Copyright © 1970 by the American Institute of Certified Public Accountants, Inc.

received is established by bargaining between independent parties, and the acquiring corporation accounts for the additional assets at their bargained -- that is, current -- values.

Purchase Method

... 19. *A bargained transaction.* Proponents of purchase accounting hold that a business combination is a significant economic event which results from bargaining between independent parties. Each party bargains on the basis of his assessment of the current status and future prospects of each constituent as a separate enterprise and as a contributor to the proposed combined enterprise. The agreed terms of combination recognize primarily the bargained values. . . .

20. Accounting by the purchase method is essentially the same whether the business combination is effected by distributing assets, incurring liabilities, or issuing stock because issuing stock is considered an economic event as significant as distributing assets or incurring liabilities. A corporation must ascertain that the consideration it receives for stock issued is fair, just as it must ascertain that fair value is received for cash disbursed. Recipients of the stock similarly appraise the fairness of the transaction. Thus, a business combination is a bargained transaction regardless of the nature of the consideration.

21. *Reporting economic substance.* The purchase method adheres to traditional principles of accounting for the acquisition of assets. Those who support the purchase method of accounting for business combinations effected by issuing stock believe that an acquiring corporation accounts for the economic substance of the transaction by applying those principles and by recording:

a. All assets and liabilities which comprise the bargained cost of an acquired company, not merely those items previously shown in the financial statements of an acquired company.

b. The bargained costs of assets acquired less liabilities assumed, not the costs to a previous owner.

c. The fair value of the consideration received for stock issued, not the equity shown in the financial statements of an acquired company.

d. Retained earnings from its operations, not a fusion of its retained earnings and previous earnings of an acquired company.

e. Expenses and net income after an acquisition computed [based] on the bargained cost of acquired assets less assumed liabilities, not on the costs to a previous owner.

22. *Defects attributed to purchase method.* Applying the purchase method to business combinations effected primarily by issuing stock may entail difficulties in measuring the cost of an acquired company if neither the

fair value of the consideration given nor the fair value of the property acquired is clearly evident. Measuring fair values of assets acquired is complicated by the presence of intangible assets or other assets which do not have discernible market prices. Goodwill and other unidentifiable intangible assets are difficult to value directly, and measuring assets acquired for stock is easier if the fair value of the stock issued is determinable. . . .

23. However, the fair value of stock issued is not always objectively determinable. A market price may not be available for a newly issued security or for securities of a closely held corporation. Even an available quoted market price may not always be a reliable indicator of fair value of consideration received because the number of shares issued is relatively large, [the stock is restricted stock under the securities laws], the market for the security is thin, the stock price is volatile, or other uncertainties influence the quoted price. . . .

24. Those who oppose applying the purchase method to some or most business combinations effected by stock also challenge the theoretical merits of the method. They contend that the goodwill acquired is stated only by coincidence at the value which would be determined by direct valuation. The weakness is attributed not to measurement difficulties (direct valuation of goodwill is assumed) but to the basis underlying an exchange of shares of stock. Bargaining in that type of transaction is normally based on the market prices of the equity securities. Market prices of the securities exchanged are more likely to be influenced by anticipated earning capacities of the companies than by evaluations of individual assets. The number of shares of stock issued in a business combination is thus influenced by values attributed to goodwill of the acquirer as well as goodwill of the acquired company. Since the terms are based on the market prices of both stocks exchanged, measuring the cost of an acquired company by the market price of the stock issued may result in recording acquired goodwill at more or less than its value determined directly.

25. A related argument is that the purchase method is improper accounting for a business combination in which a relatively large number of shares of stock is issued because it records the goodwill and fair values of only the acquired company. Critics of purchase accounting say that each group of stockholders of two publicly held and actively traded companies evaluates the other stock, and the exchange ratio for stock issued is often predicated on relative market values. The stockholders and management of each company evaluate the goodwill and fair values of the other. Purchase accounting is thus viewed as illogical because it records goodwill and values of only one side of the transaction. Those who support this view prefer that assets and liabilities of both companies be combined at existing recorded amounts, but if one side is to be stated at fair values, they believe that both sides should be recorded at fair values. . . .

Pooling of Interests Method

. . . 28. *Validity of the concept.* Those who support the pooling of interests method believe that a business combination effected by issuing common stock is different from a purchase in that no corporate assets are disbursed to stockholders and the net assets of the issuing corporation are enlarged by the net assets of the corporation whose stockholders accept common stock of the combined corporation. There is no newly invested capital nor have owners withdrawn assets from the group since the stock of a corporation is not one of its assets. Accordingly, the net assets of the constituents remain intact but combined; the stockholder groups remain intact but combined. Aggregate income is not changed since the total resources are not changed. Consequently, the historical costs and earnings of the separate corporations are appropriately combined. . . . By pooling equity interests, each group continues to maintain risk elements of its former investment and they mutually exchange risks and benefits. . . .

30. Each stockholder group in a pooling of interests gives up its interests in assets formerly held but receives an interest in a portion of the assets formerly held in addition to an interest in the assets of the other. The clearest example of this type of combination is one in which both groups surrender their stock and receive in exchange stock of a new corporation. The fact that one of the corporations usually issues its stock in exchange for that of the other does not alter the substance of the transaction. . . .

31. *Consistency with other concepts.* Proponents of pooling of interests accounting point out that the pooling concept was developed within the boundaries of the historical-cost system and is compatible with it. . . . Accounting recognizes the bargaining [between the two firms] by means of the new number of shares outstanding distributed in accordance with the bargained ratio, which has a direct effect on earnings per share after the combination. . . .

34. Some proponents of pooling of interests accounting support a restriction on the difference in size of combining interests because a significant sharing of risk cannot occur if one combining interest is minor or because a meaningful mutual exchange does not occur if the combination involves a relatively small number of shares. Most, however, believe that there is no conceptual basis for a size restriction. . . .

36. [M]any opponents of the pooling of interests method of accounting believe that effective criteria [distinguishing a pooling from a purchase] cannot be found. The concept of a uniting or fusing of stockholder groups on which pooling of interests accounting is based implies a broad application of the method because every combination effected by issuing stock rather than by disbursing cash or incurring debt is potentially a pooling of interests

unless the combination significantly changes the relative equity interests. However, so broad an application without effective criteria results in applying the pooling of interests method to numerous business combinations which are clearly in economic substance the acquisition of one company by another. . . .

39. The most serious defect attributed to pooling of interests accounting by those who oppose it is that it does not accurately reflect the economic substance of the business combination transaction. They believe that the method ignores the bargaining which results in the combination by accounting only for the amounts previously shown in [the] accounts of the combining companies. . . .

Applicability of Accounting Methods

42. The Board finds merit in both the purchase and pooling of interests methods of accounting for business combinations and accepts neither method to the exclusion of the other. The arguments in favor of the purchase method of accounting are more persuasive if cash or other assets are distributed or liabilities are incurred to effect a combination, but arguments in favor of the pooling of interests method of accounting are more persuasive if voting common stock is issued to effect a combination of common stock interests. Therefore, the Board concludes that some business combinations should be accounted for by the purchase method and other combinations should be accounted for by the pooling of interests method.

43. The Board also concludes that the two methods are not alternatives in accounting for the same business combination. . . .

Conditions for Pooling of Interests Method

45. . . . A business combination which meets *all* of the conditions specified and explained in paragraphs 46 to 48 should be accounted for by the pooling of interests method. The conditions are classified by (1) attributes of the combining companies, (2) manner of combining interests, and (3) absence of planned transactions.

46. *Combining companies.* Certain attributes of combining companies indicate that independent ownership interests are combined in their entirety to continue previously separate operations. . . .

    a. Each of the combining companies is autonomous and has not been a subsidiary or division of another corporation within two years before the plan of combination is initiated.

A plan of combination is initiated on the earlier of (1) the date that the major terms of a plan, including the ratio of exchange of stock, are announced publicly or otherwise formally made known to the stockholders of any one of the combining companies or (2) the date that stockholders of a combining company are notified in writing of an exchange offer. . . .

A wholly owned subsidiary company which distributes voting common stock of its parent corporation to effect the combination is also considered an autonomous company provided the parent corporation would have met all conditions in paragraphs 46 to 48 had the parent corporation issued its stock directly to effect the combination. . . .

> b. Each of the combining companies is independent of the other combining companies.

This condition means that at the dates the plan of combination is initiated and consummated the combining companies hold as intercorporate investments no more than 10% in total of the outstanding voting common stock of any combining company. . . .

47. *Combining of interests.* The combining of existing voting common stock interests by the exchange of stock is the essence of a business combination accounted for by the pooling of interests method. The separate stockholder interests lose their identities and all share mutually in the combined risks and rights. Exchanges of common stock that alter relative voting rights, that result in preferential claims to distributions of profits or assets for some common stockholder groups, or that leave significant minority interests in combining companies are incompatible with the idea of mutual sharing. Similarly, acquisitions of common stock for assets or debt, reacquisitions of outstanding stock for the purpose of exchanging it in a business combination, and other transactions that reduce the common stock interests are contrary to the idea of combining existing stockholder interests. The seven conditions in this paragraph relate to the exchange to effect the combination.

> a. The combination is effected in a single transaction or is completed in accordance with a specific plan within one year after the plan is initiated.

Altering the terms of exchange of stock constitutes initiation of a new plan of combination unless earlier exchanges of stock are adjusted to the new terms.

A business combination completed in more than one year from the date the plan is initiated meets this condition if the delay is beyond the control of the combining companies because proceedings of a governmental authority or litigation prevent completing the combination.

b. A corporation offers and issues only common stock with rights identical to those of the majority of its outstanding voting common stock in exchange for substantially all of the voting common stock interest of another company at the date the plan of combination is consummated.

The plan to issue voting common stock in exchange for voting common stock may include, within limits, provisions to distribute cash or other consideration for fractional shares, for shares held by dissenting stockholders, and the like but may not include a pro rata distribution of cash or other consideration. Substantially all of the voting common stock means 90% or more for this condition. . . .

A *transfer of the net assets of a combining company* to effect a business combination satisfies condition 47-b provided all net assets of the company at the date the plan is consummated are transferred in exchange for stock of the issuing corporation. However, the combining company may retain temporarily cash, receivables, or marketable securities to settle liabilities, contingencies, or items in dispute if the plan provides that the assets remaining after settlement are to be transferred to the corporation issuing the stock to effect the combination.

Only voting common stock may be issued to effect the combination unless both voting common stock and other stock of the other combining company are outstanding at the date the plan is consummated. The combination may then be effected by issuing all voting common stock or by issuing voting common and other stock in the same proportions as the outstanding voting common and other stock of the other combining company. . . .

c. None of the combining companies changes the equity interest of the voting common stock in contemplation of effecting the combination either within two years before the plan of combination is initiated or between the dates the combination is initiated and consummated; changes in contemplation of effecting the combination may include distributions to stockholders and additional issuances, exchanges, and retirements of securities.

Distributions to stockholders which are no greater than normal dividends are not changes for this conditions. Normality of dividends is determined in relation to earnings during the period and to the previous dividend policy and record. Dividend distributions on stock of a combining company that are equivalent to normal dividends on the stock to be issued in exchange in the combination are considered normal for this condition.

d. Each of the combining companies reacquires shares of voting common stock only for purposes other than business combinations, and no company reacquires more than a normal number of shares between the dates the plan of combination is initiated and consummated.

Treasury stock acquired for purposes other than business combinations includes shares for stock option and compensation plans and other recurring distributions provided a systematic pattern of reacquisitions is established at least two years before the plan of combination is initiated. A systematic pattern of reacquisitions may be established for less than two years if it coincides with the adoption of a new stock option or compensation plan. The normal number of shares of voting common stock reacquired is determined by the pattern of reacquisitions of stock before the plan of combination is initiated.

Acquisitions by other combining companies of voting common stock of the issuing corporation after the date the plan of combination is initiated are essentially the same as if the issuing corporation reacquired its own common stock.

 e. The ratio of the interest of an individual common stockholder to those of other common stockholders in a combining company remains the same as a result of the exchange of stock to effect the combination.

This condition means that each individual common stockholder who exchanges his stock receives a voting common stock interest exactly in proportion to his relative voting common stock interest before the combination is effected. Thus no common stockholder is denied or surrenders his potential share of a voting common stock interest in a combined corporation.

 f. The voting rights to which the common stock ownership interests in the resulting combined corporation are entitled are exercisable by the stockholders; the stockholders are neither deprived of nor restricted in exercising those rights for a period.

This condition is not met, for example, if shares of common stock issued to effect the combination are transferred to a voting trust.

 g. The combination is resolved at the date the plan is consummated and no provisions of the plan relating to the issue of securities or other consideration are pending.

This condition means that (1) the combined corporation does not agree to contingently issue additional shares of stock or distribute other consideration at a later date to the former stockholders of a combining company [in, for example, an earnout transaction] or (2) the combined corporation does not issue or distribute to an escrow agent common stock or other consideration which is to be either transferred to common stockholders or returned to the corporation at the time the contingency is resolved.

An agreement may provide, however, that the number of shares of common stock issued to effect the combination may be revised for the later settlement of a contingency at a different amount than that recorded by a combining company.

48. *Absence of planned transactions.* Some transactions after a combination is consummated are inconsistent with the combining of entire existing interests of common stockholders. Including those transactions in the negotiations and terms of the combination, either explicitly or by intent, counteracts the effect of combining stockholder interests. The three conditions in this paragraph relate to certain future transactions.

a. The combined corporation does not agree directly or indirectly to retire or reacquire all or part of the common stock issued to effect the combination.

b. The combined corporation does not enter into other financial arrangements for the benefit of the former stockholders of a combining company, such as a guaranty of loans secured by stock issued in the combination, which in effect negates the exchange of equity securities.

c. The combined corporation does not intend or plan to dispose of a significant part of the assets of the combining companies within two years after the combination other than disposals in the ordinary course of business of the formerly separate companies and to eliminate duplicate facilities or excess capacity.

Subsidiary Corporation

49. Dissolution of a combining company is not a condition for applying the pooling of interests method of accounting for a business combination. One or more combining companies may be subsidiaries of the issuing corporation after the combination is consummated if the other conditions are met. . . .

Application of Purchase Method

. . . 87. An acquiring corporation should allocate the cost of an acquired company to the assets acquired and liabilities assumed. . . . First, all identifiable assets acquired, either individually or by type, and liabilities assumed in a business combination, whether or not shown in the financial statements of the acquired company, should be assigned a portion of the cost of the acquired company, normally equal to their fair values at date of acquisition.

Second, the excess of the cost of the acquired company over the sum of the amounts assigned to identifiable assets acquired less liabilities assumed should be recorded as goodwill. The sum of the market or appraisal values of identifiable assets acquired less liabilities assumed may sometimes exceed the cost of the acquired company. If so, the values otherwise assignable to noncurrent assets acquired (except long-term investments in marketable securities) should be reduced by a proportionate part of the excess to determine the assigned values. A deferred credit for an excess of assigned value of identifiable assets over cost of an acquired company (sometimes called "negative goodwill") should not be recorded unless those assets are reduced to zero value. . . .

Excess of Acquired Net Assets Over Cost

91. The value assigned to net assets acquired should not exceed the cost of an acquired company. . . . An excess [of the apparent fair market value of identifiable assets] over cost should be allocated to reduce proportionately the values assigned to noncurrent assets (except long-term investments in marketable securities in determining their fair values [for accounting purposes] (paragraph 87). . . .

92. No part of the excess of acquired net assets over cost should be added directly to stockholders' equity at the date of acquisition. . . .

The Opinion entitled "Business Combinations" was adopted by the assenting votes of twelve members of the Board. Messrs. Broeker, Burger, Davidson, Horngren, Seidman, and Weston dissented.

Messrs. Broeker, Burger, and Weston dissent to issuance of this Opinion because they believe that it is not a sound or logical solution of the problem of accounting for business combinations. They believe that, except for combinations of companies whose relative size is such as to indicate a significant sharing of ownership risks and benefits, business combinations represent the acquisition or purchase of one company by another and that accounting should reflect that fact. . . .

Messrs. Davidson, Horngren, and Seidman dissent to the Opinion because it seeks to patch up some of the abuses of pooling. The real abuse is pooling itself. On that, the only answer is to eliminate pooling. . . . The fundamental [defect] is that pooling ignores the asset values on which the parties have traded, and substitutes a wholly irrelevant figure -- the amount on the seller's books. Such nonaccounting for bargained acquisition values permits the reporting of profits upon subsequent disposition of such assets when there really may be less profit or perhaps a loss. Had the assets been acquired from the seller for cash, the buyer's cost would be the amount of the cash. Acquisition for stock should make no difference. The accounting essence is the amount of consideration, not its nature. Payment in cash or stock can be a matter of form, not substance. Suppose the seller wants cash. The buyer can first sell stock and turn over the proceeds to the seller, or the seller can take stock and promptly sell the stock for cash.

The following deal with some arguments made in the Opinion for pooling: (1) Pooling is described in paragraph 28 as a fusion resulting from "pooling equity interests." But it is the sort of fusion where a significant exchange transaction takes place. The seller parts with control over its assets and operations. In return the buyer issues stock representing an interest in its assets and operations. That interest has value and is a measure of the cost of the acquisition to the buyer. (2) [Paragraph 16] declares that pooling is really a transaction among the stockholders. That just is not the fact. The buyer is always a company. (3) Paragraph 25 decries purchase accounting because it results in a write-up of only seller's assets. There is no write-up. There is only a recording of cost to the buyer. That cost is measured by the value of the assets acquired from the seller. (4) Pooling is said to avoid the difficulty of valuing assets or stock (paragraph 22). Difficulty of valuation should not be permitted to defeat fair presentation. Besides, the parties do determine values in their bargaining for the amount of stock to be issued.

Some say that to eliminate pooling will impede mergers. Mergers were prevalent before pooling, and will continue after. Accounting does not exist to aid or discourage mergers, but to account for them fairly. Elimination of pooling will remove the confusion that comes from the coexistence of pooling and purchase accounting. Above all, the elimination of pooling would remove an aberration in historical-cost accounting that permits an acquisition to be accounted for on the basis of the seller's cost rather than the buyer's cost of the assets obtained in a bargained exchange.

---

3. Purchase Accounting in a Down Market

At this point, it is important to return to the acquirer's goal in selecting among alternative accounting methods. The acquirer wants to account for an acquisition by the method that maximizes reported earnings. The controversy at which APB 16 was primarily directed was the use of pooling to avoid the earnings reduction caused by write-up of assets under the purchase method. Therefore, APB 16, adopted in 1970, focused on restricting the use of pooling because of fears of artificially inflated earnings. During the 1970s, however, the stock of many companies traded at prices substantially below book value. For example, in the transaction giving rise to the Singer v. Magnavox case discussed later in this book,[4] the book value

---

[4] 380 A.2d 969 (Del.1977) (discussed in Chapter 18, *infra*).

of Magnavox's net assets exceeded the consideration paid by North American Phillips by almost $22 million.[5]

This condition presents a strikingly different accounting problem than that which gave rise to APB 16. If Phillips accounted for the Magnavox acquisition as a pooling, Magnavox's assets would be added to Phillips' books at the value at which they were carried on Magnavox's books. But what if purchase accounting were used? Under purchase accounting, when the price paid *exceeds* book value, the excess increases the value of the assets acquired and, perhaps, creates goodwill. This in turn, reduces net income. In Phillips-Magnavox there was a deficiency -- book value exceeded the purchase price. What happens to this amount?

Under Paragraph 91 of APB 16, Phillips could write *down* Magnavox's assets by $22 million. This would reduce future depreciation and other charges against income, and thus *increase* reported income. (In the unlikely case where noncurrent assets are written down to zero, the acquirer creates a *negative goodwill* account that is amortized, which means it is *added* to income, over an appropriate period of time, compared to the result if pooling was used. In fact, Phillips was able to increase its reported income by $3.5 million, or 12.5%, solely because it could write down Magnavox's assets to reflect the below-book-value purchase price.

Thus, neither the pooling nor purchase method consistently results in higher earnings; it depends on economic conditions. Acquirers prefer pooling treatment in a strong stock market, and purchase accounting when the market is low. (Though it would take a huge plunge from current stock prices to again produce a situation where many U.S. companies trade for less than book value.)

That leaves us with the question of which accounting method is "right"? The academic members of the Accounting Principles Board dissented from the adoption of APB 16 because:

> it seeks to patch up some of the abuses of pooling. The real abuse is pooling itself. . . . The fundamental [defect] is that pooling ignores the asset values on which the parties have traded, and substitutes a wholly irrelevant figure -- the amount on the seller's books. . . . Had the assets been acquired from the seller for cash, the buyer's cost would be the amount of the cash. Acquisition for stock should make no difference.

Viewed this way, pooling is simply inconsistent with economic reality; the cost of an asset should reflect the amount paid for it.

Others, however, levied precisely the same criticism at purchase accounting. Writing in 1975, Phillip Defliese, a former chair of the Accounting Principles Board and a vigorous critic of APB 16's restriction on the use of pooling, complained about the outcome of using purchase accounting in a down market:

---

[5] North American Phillips Corp., *1975 Annual Report*, Note 2 to Financial Statements.

At present, the stocks of many companies are being traded at values far below book value. A good example is American Airlines, which at December 31, 1972, had a book value of about $21 per share. In December 1973, it was trading in the neighborhood of $8 per share. An aggressive and enterprising company could [acquire American for $10-11 per share, a premium of 25-38%.] Under the purchase method, the net assets of American Airlines would have to be written down approximately 50% (about $290 million) and future earnings would be raised by a consequent reduction of about $25 million in depreciation. Thus, a losing company might suddenly become a profitable company! This is unrealistic from either an accounting or an economic standpoint.[6]

So which side is right?

From one perspective, the critics of pooling seem to have the best of the debate. The price paid for an asset reflects current economic reality. The price at which American Airlines could be acquired reflected the cash flow that the company was expected to generate in the airline business. The principal assets of the company -- passenger aircraft -- would be written down after the acquisition because the value of capital assets depends on the stream of income the assets are expected to earn. If the amounts that can be made in the airline business goes down, so does the value of airplanes. The airplanes would be written down for the same reason the price of the stock was down -- both were worth less. Put somewhat differently, wouldn't the acquirer's return on investment properly be higher because it would receive the same cash flow as before the acquisition, but had invested less to obtain that cash flow?

From a different perspective, both methods are wrong, because they respond to the wrong question. APB 16 addresses a narrow question -- what kinds of acquisitions establish a new cost basis for the target company's assets. The broader problem is to identify what forms of external valuation, of which an arm's length acquisition is only one example, warrant restating the value of a company's assets. For example, if acquiring a target company with stock is a valuation event sufficient to warrant restating the cost basis of the target company's assets, shouldn't the same exchange also serve to revalue the acquiring company's assets?

Conversely, if the mere fact that a company's stock is trading in the market for, say, $20 per share, when its book value is $10 per share, does not warrant revaluing the company's assets, why should those assets be revalued because someone has purchased *all* of the company's shares for $20 per share, rather than just a few? One cannot sensibly answer these questions by Platonic reasoning about whether a "purchase" has taken place. Instead, one must return to first principles: for what purposes are accounting

---

[6] Phillip Defliese, *Business Combinations Revisited: A Temporary Defense of the Status Quo*, 35 Ohio St.L.J. 393, 394 (1974).

statements used; and what are the risks of error in marking assets to market under various circumstances?

In all events, APB 16 remains in effect, and is subject to continuing and complex interpretations. We discuss the broader issues involved in deciding when to mark assets to market later in this Chapter.

4.   How Strong a Constraint is APB 16:   Transaction Planning and the AT&T-NCR Precedent

APB 16 sought to constrain an acquiring company's choice of how to account for an acquisition. The critical issue from the perspective of both public policy and private lawyering is whether it succeeds. APB 16 specifies circumstances which if present dictate that the acquisition *must* be treated as a pooling and whose absence dictates purchase treatment. But rather than restricting the choice of accounting method, the listing of conditions may only give planers an explicit road map of how to structure their transaction so that it can be accounted for by whichever method is preferable for the particular transaction. How tightly APB 16 constrains a planner's choice of accounting methods depends on three inquiries. First, can the structure of a transaction be modified to meet or not meet APB 16's conditions, as the acquirer chooses? Second, if the transaction can be so modified, how costly are the necessary changes? Finally, because APB 16's conditions cover both the acquiring and target company, the results of the first two inquiries depend importantly on whether the two companies cooperate.

Planning to Assure Purchase Accounting. Because pooling of interests accounting was viewed as the more controversial alternative, APB 16 is structured so that purchase accounting is the default method: Unless each condition is met, an acquisition must be accounted for a purchase. That greatly simplifies the task of a planner whose client prefers purchase accounting. For example, condition 47(a) requires that the acquiring company hold no more than 10% of the target company's stock prior to the transaction. A purchase of more than 10% of the target's stock prior to the transaction's consummation, either in the open market or from the target, assures purchase accounting. Similarly, condition 47(b) requires that the acquiring company acquire at least 90% of the target's stock in exchange for its own voting stock. Thus, a part cash, part stock acquisition also would assure purchase accounting, as long as the cash is paid for more than 10% of the target's shares.

Planning a transaction to assure purchase accounting can be achieved without the target's cooperation, an important element in a transactional environment in which hostile takeovers are important. The acquiring company in a hostile acquisition controls pre-transaction purchases and the form of consideration to be used.

Planning to Assure Pooling of Interests Accounting. The structure of APB 16 makes planning for pooling of interests accounting difficult for the same reason it makes planning for purchase accounting easy. An acquisition must satisfy each of APB 16's conditions to achieve pooling, but must fail only one to achieve purchase. Moreover, several conditions go back two years in time, so that actions taken before the acquisition was contemplated can block pooling of interest accounting. For example, condition 47(c) makes pooling unavailable if a special dividend is paid or a recapitalization that alters voting rights is undertaken within two years prior to the acquisition. Similarly, condition 47(d) requires that neither the acquirer nor the target has reacquired its own voting stock other than pursuant to a systematic pattern of reacquisition established two years before the acquisition.

That action by the target prior to the acquisition can prevent the acquirer from using pooling of interests accounting makes the target's cooperation critical, and may provide the target of a hostile takeover an important defense. Unilateral action by the target company, like paying a special dividend, can block pooling of interest accounting.

Finally, it may be costly for the acquiring company to satisfy even some of the conditions for pooling that are entirely in its control. For example, condition 47(b) prohibits pooling unless the acquiring company uses only voting stock as consideration. As we will see in Part III, a hostile takeover is far more difficult to complete using stock rather than cash consideration. Indeed, complying with APB 16 may be costly even in a negotiated transaction. Condition 47(g) prohibits the use of earnouts -- an acquisition price that depends on the post-acquisition performance of the target company -- in a transaction to be accounted for as a pooling. An earnout can be very useful tool in solving problems of information asymmetry in acquisition negotiations.

A number of these planning considerations were presented by AT&T's 1991 acquisition of NCR.[7] First, the transaction demonstrates that, some acquirers are willing to pay a great deal to obtain pooling of interests accounting. Second, AT&T-NCR illustrates the opportunity that APB 16 creates for the target of a hostile offer to take actions that block the use of pooling, as part of its takeover defense. Finally and most important, the transaction highlights the extent to which barriers to pooling -- whether

---

[7] Our discussion of this acquisition is based on Alison Cowan, *NCR Accounting Could Hurt Any Merger*, N.Y.Times, March 22, 1991, at D2; Alison Cowan, *AT&T Alters Merger to Win Audit Ruling*, N.Y.Times, July 4, 1991, at D2; Peter Coy, *NCR's 'Nancy Reagan' Defense May Not Work Much Longer*, Business Week, Apr. 1, 1991, at 25; John Keller, *AT&T Believes Merger to be Called a Pooling of Interest*, Wall St.J., July 2, 1991, at 8; Shapiro (1991), *supra* note 1; Randall Smith, *AT&T to Sell NCR Shares for $650 Million*, Wall St.J., Aug. 30, 1991; and on the Unaudited Pro Forma Combined Financial Statements in NCR's proxy statement for the AT&T merger (Aug.13, 1991).

inadvertent or intentionally defensive -- can be dismantled if the acquiring and target companies cooperate.

AT&T's hostile offer for NCR commenced in December, 1990, with an offer of $90 per share when NCR shares were trading at $56. From the beginning, NCR vigorously resisted the takeover, and from the beginning AT&T treated as critical the issue of whether it could account for the acquisition as a pooling. By March 1991, AT&T's offer had risen to $100 per share if NCR would drop its opposition, and AT&T's managers had indicated willingness to pay an even higher price if pooling treatment could be achieved. On March 27, AT&T turned down an NCR counteroffer for a $110 per share takeover price. On April 22nd, AT&T offered $110 per share if the transaction could be accounted for as a pooling -- an increase of $685 million over AT&T's previous $100 per share offer. After some skirmishing over whether NCR shareholders would be protected against a drop in the price of AT&T stock before the merger was consummated, an agreement was reached.

Even with pooling treatment, the acquisition would dilute AT&T's earnings per share in the near term. Moreover, the $7.4 billion purchase price exceeded NCR's net assets by approximately $5.5 billion. Whether that excess was translated into increased asset values resulting in higher depreciation or into goodwill that could have to be amortized, AT&T's post-transaction earnings would be reduced by $5.5 billion over the relevant period. There were no offsetting tax benefits since AT&T would elect a carryover basis in NCR's assets for tax purposes regardless of the accounting treatment. Analysts estimated that AT&T's 1991 earnings would be 5% lower if the transaction had to be accounted for as a purchase.

The availability of pooling turned on two actions that had been taken by NCR during the two years preceding the merger. On the day that a federal court struck down a leveraged ESOP that NCR had established as a defensive measure (and that itself might have blocked pooling treatment),[8] NCR announced a $1 per share special dividend that was paid on March 20, 1991. APB 16's condition 47(c) generally bans special dividends within two years prior to a pooling, and NCR apparently declared this dividend to kill AT&T's hopes of achieving pooling treatment.

AT&T's second problem was that during the years preceding the transaction, NCR had repurchased 19.5 million shares of its own stock on the open market. These repurchases violated condition 47(d), which prohibits pooling if either company has repurchased its stock within the preceding two years, other than pursuant to a systematic pattern of repurchases.

---

[8] See NCR Corp. v. American Telephone and Telegraph Co., 761 F.Supp. 475 (W.D. Ohio 1991) (excerpted in Chapter 24). Had it not been invalidated, the ESOP, which involved the issuance of shares representing 8% of NCR's common stock, would have conflicted with APB 16 condition 47(c), which prohibits pooling if the target has issued stock within two years prior to the pooling transaction.

AT&T nonetheless convinced its own accountants to permit pooling treatment, and launched a major campaign to persuade the SEC to allow it to account for the transaction as a pooling.[9] Professor John Burton, a former SEC Chief Accountant, was outspoken in the view that pooling should not be allowed. "[This has been] an area where the accounting profession and the SEC have stood very firm. And if that's been the case, I'd hate to see them, once they get a big one, say, 'Now we're going to waffle.'"[10]

In the end, AT&T successfully persuaded the SEC to allow it to account for the NCR acquisition as a pooling of interests on the theory that both offending actions -- NCR's special dividend and share repurchases -- could be undone before the merger closed. With respect to the special dividend, the SEC approved a plan by which NCR withheld two quarterly dividends of 37¢ each prior to closing, thus offsetting most of the $1 per share special dividend. However, the change was purely cosmetic. To make up for the foregone dividends, AT&T increased the consideration paid for the NCR shares by an equivalent amount.

NCR's repurchases of its common stock were undone by an agreement to sell an equivalent amount of NCR treasury shares in a private placement that would close shortly before the merger closed. The purchaser retained the right to rescind the purchase if the merger did not go forward. Thus, in substance, the purchaser was agreeing to acquire the AT&T stock into which the NCR would be converted in the merger.

From a planning perspective, AT&T's success in dismantling barriers to pooling posed by prior actions by reversing them dramatically expands the availability of pooling. APB 16's conditions fall into two categories: conditions dealing with prior actions, such as those AT&T confronted; and conditions dealing with the structure of the transaction whose accounting treatment is in question, such as the requirement of at least 90% voting stock consideration and the ban on earnouts. The SEC's approval of AT&T's efforts to undo prior NCR actions greatly reduces the importance of the first category of conditions. Moreover, planners contemplating actions which would prevent a future pooling transaction, such as a stock repurchase, can now largely ignore that potential future cost, since the cost of undoing the earlier act, if necessary to achieve a pooling, will often be small.

APB 16 retains value as a defensive tactic. To be sure, certain actions, like issuing stock, will no longer act as accounting doomsday devices that

---

[9] SEC approval was required because AT&T's registration statement under the Securities Act of 1933 covering the shares to be issued in the NCR transaction, and its post-transaction periodic filings under the Securities Exchange Act of 1934 would include AT&T pro-forma or actual financial statements. The SEC has review authority over these filings.

[10] Cowan (1991), *supra* note 7. Not all observers opposed allowing AT&T the opportunity to pool. David Hawkins, an accounting professor at the Harvard Business School, favored loosening of the barriers to pooling to move U.S. acquisition accounting closer to the more favorable rules in other countries. *Id.*

prevent the acquisition from ever being accounted for as a pooling. But a large special dividend will still be hard to reverse. Also, a target company bent on negotiating a higher price, rather than independence at all costs, facing an acquirer who prefers pooling treatment, can use its ability to erect barriers to pooling -- that can be subsequently dismantled with the target's cooperation if the price is right (as in the AT&T-NCR transaction) -- as a bargaining chip.

B.   Accounting for Partial Acquisitions

Not all acquisitions are accomplished in one or even two steps. Frequently an acquiring company purchases a small stake in a target company as an initial step. This lets the potential acquirer retain substantial flexibility concerning whether, when, and how to proceed with an acquisition. Frequently too, an acquirer will have business reasons for acquiring less than 100% of the target, such as the desire to sell a minority stake to management.[11]

As with complete acquisitions, alternative methods of accounting for partial acquisitions are available that have significantly different effects on the acquirer's balance sheet and reported earnings. Here, however, the accounting treatment turns not on the form of the acquisition, but (for the most part) on the percentage stake in the target that the acquirer holds. The principal breakpoints are:

(i) less than 20% ownership, which generally means that the acquirer must use the *lower-of-cost-or-market* method to account for its equity interest in the target;

(ii) 20% or more but less than 50% ownership, which generally means that the acquirer must use the *equity* method to account for its equity interest in the target; and

(iii) 50% or greater ownership, which generally means that the acquirer must *consolidate* the target's balance sheet and income statement with its own (*accounting* consolidation is different than federal income *tax* consolidation, which generally occurs at 80% ownership).

From a planning perspective, an acquirer can choose among these accounting treatments by varying its percentage ownership in the target. The business cost of exercising accounting choice in this manner is that the acquirer will own a different percentage of the target than the acquirer would

---

[11] The non-accounting advantages of partial acquisitions and the problems they present under a variety of regulatory systems are canvassed in James Maiwurm & James Tobin, *Beachhead Acquisitions: Creating Waves in the Marketplace and Uncertainty in the Regulatory Framework,* 38 Bus.Law. 419 (1983).

otherwise have chosen to acquire. As with purchase vs. pooling, a central policy question raised by acquirers' willingness to accept business costs to alter accounting form is whether the accounting differences affect the acquirer's stock market value, or whether investors see through the differences in financial reporting.

1.   Accounting for Minority Interests: Equity vs. Lower-of-Cost-or-Market

There are two basic methods of accounting for a minority investment in another company -- the *equity* method and the *lower-of-cost-or-market* method -- often simply called the *cost* method. The equity method lets the acquirer include in its income statement the same percentage of the target company's income as it owns of the target company's stock. The cost method lets the acquirer report as income from a continuing investment only the dividends paid by the target company.

In the common case where the target company earns more than it pays out in dividends, the acquirer will show higher earnings using the equity method than the cost method. Thus, for the same reasons that the choice between pooling and purchase accounting for complete acquisitions was controversial, so too were the standards governing the choice between equity and cost accounting for minority acquisitions.

The excerpts below describe the mechanics of both methods of accounting for minority investments and the standards governing their availability.

a.   *The Mechanics of Accounting for Minority Investments*

Sidney Davidson, Clyde Stickney & Roman Weil
FINANCIAL ACCOUNTING
454-59 (2d ed. 1979)*

When a firm owns less than 50% of the voting shares of another company, the firm is called a *minority* investor. Investors account for minority investments using one of two methods, depending on the fraction of shares owned. These two methods are the *lower-of-cost-or-market method* and the *equity method.*

Lower-of-Cost-or-Market Method

When a corporation, *P*, holds less than 20% of the stock of another corporation, *S*, *P* [typically] will use the lower-of-cost-or-market method to account for its investment under current generally accepted accounting principles. . . . Suppose that *P* acquires 1,000 shares of *S* for $40,000. This is P's only investment in an equity security, so the single investment is its "portfolio" for purposes of applying the lower-of-cost-or-market method. The entry to record the acquisition would be

Investment in Equity Securities	40,000	
Cash		40,000

. . . If the purpose of the purchase were merely a short-term investment to use idle cash, the debit would be to Marketable Securities [instead of Investment in Equity Securities].

If, while *P* holds this stock, *S* declares a dividend of $2 per share, *P* would make the following entry:

Dividends Receivable	2,000	
Dividend Revenue		2,000

. . . When the dividend is collected, *P* will debit Cash and credit Dividends Receivable.

If, at the end of the period, the market value of the investment has dropped to $30,000, the journal entry would be:

Unrealized Loss on Investment in Equity Securities	10,000	
Allowance for Excess of Cost of Investment in Equity Securities over Market Value		10,000

. . . The credit is to a contra account, known as a *valuation account*. . . . The Unrealized Loss account does not appear on the income statement for the period, but appears in the owners' equity section of the balance sheet as an amount reducing owners' equity.

If, at the end of the next period, the market value of the investment has increased to $36,000, the entry would be

Allowance for Excess of Cost of Investment in Equity Securities over Market Value	6,000	
Unrealized Loss on Investment in Equity Securities		6,000

. . . This entry [also] does not affect reported income for the period. . . . The Allowance [for Excess of Cost of Investment in Equity Securities over Market Value] account can never have a debit [(negative)] balance. That is, [the investment can never be carried at more than] original cost.

When the investment is sold, or otherwise disposed of, a realized gain or loss is recognized in an amount equal to the difference between selling price and the *original cost* (not current book value) of the securities. Assume that the investment is sold at the end of the third period for $39,000. Then the holding loss during the time the investment is held is $1,000 (= $40,000 − $39,000). The entire loss is recognized in the period when the investment is sold:

Cash	39,000	
Realized Loss on Investment in Equity		
Securities	1,000	
Investment in Equity Securities		40,000

. . . Suppose that the investment were [instead] sold for $42,000. The [entry] would be

Cash	42,000	
Investment in Equity Securities		40,000
Realized Gain on Investment in Equity		
Securities		2,000

. . . To summarize, when Company *P* accounts for its long-term investment in Company *S* using the lower-of-cost-or-market method:

1. Company *P* reports as income each period its share of the dividends declared by Company *S*.

2. Company *P* reports on the balance sheet the lower-of-cost-or-market value of the shares in Company *S*.

   a. Declines in market value below cost are debited directly to an owners' equity account such as "Unrealized Losses on Investments" and credited to an asset contra account.

   b. Subsequent increases in price up to, but not exceeding, the original cost of the investment are debited to the asset contra [account] and credited to the balance sheet account for unrealized losses.

3. Company *P* recognizes gains or losses on the income statement from holding the stock of Company *S* only at the time the shares are sold. The gain or loss is the difference between selling price and original cost.

Equity Method: Rationale

Under the lower-of-cost-or-market method, P recognizes income or loss on the income statement only when it becomes entitled to receive a dividend or sells all or part of the investment. Suppose, as often happens, that S follows a policy of financing its own growing operations through retention of earnings and consistently declares dividends substantially less than its net income. The market price of S's shares may increase. Under the lower-of-cost-or-market method, P will continue to show the investment at original cost and P's income from the investment will be only the modest dividends it receives. If P holds a substantial fraction of the shares of S, then P can influence the dividend policy of S. Under these conditions, the lower-of-cost-or-market method may not reasonably reflect the earnings of S generated under P's control. The equity method is designed to provide a better measure of P's earnings and its assets for investments where it can control the operations of S because of substantial holdings.

When Company P can exercise significant influence over operating and financial policies of Company S, generally accepted accounting principles require that the investment by P in S be reported using the *equity method*. To determine when significant influence can be exercised involves judgment. For the sake of objectivity, generally accepted accounting principles *presume* that P can influence S and should use the equity method when P owns 20% or more of the common stock of S, but not more than 50% of it. It may be required even when less than 20% is owned, but in those cases management and accountants must agree on whether or not Company P exercises significant influence over Company S. (The equity method is also required when more than 50% of the shares are owned and consolidated statements are not issued.)

Equity Method: Procedure

Under the equity method, the initial purchase of an investment is recorded at cost, the same as under the lower-of-cost-or-market method. Company P treats as income (or revenue) each period its proportionate share of the periodic *earnings*, not the *dividends*, of Company S. Dividends declared by S are then treated by P as a reduction in its Investment in S.

Suppose that P acquires 30% of the outstanding shares of S for $600,000. The entry to record the acquisition would be

(1) Investment in S	600,000	
Cash		600,000

. . . Between the time of the acquisition and the end of P's next accounting period, S reports income of $80,000. P, using the equity method, would record [income equal to 30% of $80,000]:

(2)	Investment in *S*	24,000	
	Revenue from Investments		24,000

. . . *[The revenue account] often used in practice is Equity in Income of Unconsolidated Affiliates.*

If *S* declares a dividend of $30,000 to holders of common stock, *P* would be entitled to receive [30% of $30,000 =] $9,000 and would record

(3)	Dividends Receivable	9,000	
	Investment in *S*		9,000

Notice that the credit is to the Investment in *S* account. *P* records income earned by *S* as an *increase* in investment. The dividend becomes a return of capital or a *decrease* in investment.

Suppose that *S* subsequently reports earnings of $100,000 and also declares dividends of $40,000. *P*'s entries would [reflect its 30% interest in *S*'s earnings and dividends]:

(4)	Investment in *S*	30,000	
	Revenue from Investments		30,000
(5)	Dividends Receivable	12,000	
	Investment in *S*		12,000

. . . *P*'s Investment in *S* account now has a balance of $633,000 as follows:

Investment in S

Debits		Credits	
(1)	600,000	9,000	(3)
(2)	24,000	12,000	(5)
(4)	30,000		
Balance	633,000		

If *P* now sells one-fourth of its shares for $152,000, *P*'s entry to record the sale would [reflect a loss of $6,250, since *P* was carrying these shares at a value of ¼ × $633,000 = $158,250]:

(6)	Cash	152,000	
	Loss on Sale of Investment in *S*	6,250	
	Investment in *S*		158,250

. . . [A] complication in using the equity method arises when the [purchase price for the shares that P acquires] exceeds P's proportionate share of the book value of the net assets (= assets − liabilities), or stockholders' equity of S, at the date of acquisition. For example, assume that P acquires 25% of the stock of S for $400,000 when the total stockholders' equity of S is $1 million. The excess of P's cost over book value acquired is $150,000 (= $400,000 − (.25 × $1,000,000)) and is called *goodwill*. Goodwill must be amortized over a period not greater than forty years. . . .

On the balance sheet, an investment accounted for on the equity method is shown in the Investments section. The amount shown will generally be equal to the acquisition cost of the shares plus P's share of S's undistributed earnings since the date the shares were acquired [minus any amortization of goodwill arising from the purchase]. On the income statement, P shows its share of S's income as [revenue]. (The financial statements of the investee, S, are not affected by the accounting method used by the investor, P.)

---

b.   *Determinants of the Choice Between Cost and Equity Accounting*

Shortly after it adopted APB 16 covering complete acquisitions, the Accounting Principles Board turned its attention to when the equity or cost methods of accounting should be used for minority acquisitions. APB 18 and FASB Interpretation 35 set out the standards governing the choice.

Accounting Principles Board
OPINION NO. 18, THE EQUITY METHOD OF
ACCOUNTING FOR INVESTMENTS IN COMMON STOCK
(1971)*

7. Under the cost method of accounting for investments in common stock, dividends are the basis for recognition by an investor of earnings from an investment. Financial statements of an investor prepared under the cost method may not reflect substantial changes in the affairs of an investee. Dividends included in income of an investor for a period may be unrelated to the earnings (or losses) of an investee for that period. For example, an investee may pay no dividends for several periods and then pay dividends substantially in excess of the earnings of a period. Losses of an investee of one period may be offset against earnings of another period because the investor reports neither in [the investor's] results of operations at the time they are reported by the investee. Some dividends received from an investee

---

do not cover the carrying costs of an investment whereas the investor's share of the investee's earnings more than covers those costs. Those characteristics of the cost method may prevent an investor from reflecting adequately the earnings related to an investment in common stock -- either cumulatively or in the appropriate periods. . . .

10. Under the equity method, an investor recognizes its share of the earnings or losses of an investee in the periods for which they are reported by the investee in its financial statements rather than in the period in which an investee declares a dividend. An investor adjusts the carrying amount of an investment for its share of the earnings or losses of the investee subsequent to the date of investment and reports the recognized earnings or losses in income. Dividends received from an investee reduce the carrying amount of the investment. Thus, the equity method is an appropriate means of recognizing increases or decreases measured by generally accepted accounting principles in the economic resources underlying the investments. Furthermore, the equity method of accounting more closely meets the objectives of accrual accounting than does the cost method since the investor recognizes its share of the earnings and losses of the investee in the periods in which they are reflected in the accounts of the investee. . . .

12. The equity method tends to be most appropriate if an investment enables the investor to influence the operating or financial decisions of the investee. The investor then has a degree of responsibility for the return on its investment, and it is appropriate to include in the results of operations of the investor its share of the earnings or losses of the investee. Influence tends to be more effective as the investor's percent of ownership in the voting stock of the investee increases. Investments of relatively small percentages of voting stock of an investee tend to be passive in nature and enable the investor to have little or no influence on the operations of the investee.

13. Some hold the view that . . . the equity method is [not] appropriate accounting for investments in common stock where the investor holds less than majority ownership of the voting stock. They would account for such investments at cost. Under that view the investor is not entitled to recognize earnings on its investment until a right to claim the earnings arises, and that claim arises only to the extent dividends are declared. The investor is considered to have no earnings on its investment unless it is in a position to control the distribution of earnings. Likewise, an investment or an investor's operations are not affected by losses of an investee unless those losses indicate a loss in value of the investment that should be recognized.

OPINION

... 17. The Board concludes that the equity method of accounting for an investment in common stock should [be used by an investor who owns a majority of a company's voting stock and] by an investor whose investment in voting stock gives it the ability to exercise significant influence over operating and financial policies of an investee even though the investor holds 50% or less of the voting stock. Ability to exercise that influence may be indicated in several ways, such as representation on the board of directors, participation in policy making processes, material intercompany transactions, interchange of managerial personnel, or technological dependency. Another important consideration is the extent of ownership by an investor in relation to the concentration of other shareholdings, but substantial or majority ownership of the voting stock of an investee by another investor does not necessarily preclude the ability to exercise significant influence by the investor. The Board recognizes that determining the ability of an investor to exercise such influence is not always clear and applying judgment is necessary to assess the status of each investment. In order to achieve a reasonable degree of uniformity in application, the Board concludes that an investment (direct or indirect) of 20% or more of the voting stock of an investee should lead to a presumption that in the absence of evidence to the contrary an investor has the ability to exercise significant influence over an investee. Conversely, an investment of less than 20% of the voting stock of an investee should lead to a presumption that an investor does not have the ability to exercise significant influence unless such ability can be demonstrated.

Financial Accounting Standards Board
INTERPRETATION NO. 35:
CRITERIA FOR APPLYING THE EQUITY METHOD OF
ACCOUNTING FOR INVESTMENTS IN COMMON STOCK
An Interpretation of APB Opinion No. 18
(1981)[*]

1. The Board has been asked to clarify the provisions of APB Opinion No. 18, *The Equity Method of Accounting for Investments in Common Stock,* regarding application of that method to investments of 50% or less of the voting stock of an investee enterprise (other than a corporate joint venture).

Interpretation

2.   Opinion 18 requires that the equity method of accounting be followed by an investor whose investment in voting stock gives it the ability to exercise significant influence over operating and financial policies of an investee. The presumptions in paragraph 17 of Opinion 18 are intended to provide a reasonable degree of uniformity in applying the equity method. The presumptions can be overcome by predominant evidence to the contrary.

3.   [Determining whether there is predominant e]vidence that an investor owning 20% or more of the voting stock of an investee [is] unable to exercise significant influence over the investee's operating and financial policies requires an evaluation of all the facts and circumstances relating to the investment. . . .

4. Examples of indications that an investor may be unable to exercise significant influence over the operating and financial policies of an investee include:

a. Opposition by the investee, such as litigation or complaints to governmental regulatory authorities, challenges the investor's ability to exercise significant influence.

b.   The investor and investee sign an agreement under which the investor surrenders significant rights as a shareholder.

c. Majority ownership of the investee is concentrated among a small group of shareholders who operate the investee without regard to the views of the investor.

d. The investor needs or wants more financial information to apply the equity method than is available to the investee's other shareholders (for example, the investor wants quarterly financial information from an investee that publicly reports only annually), tries to obtain that information, and fails.

e. The investor tries and fails to obtain representation on the investee's board of directors.

This list is illustrative and is not all-inclusive. None of the individual circumstances is necessarily conclusive that the investor is unable to exercise significant influence over the investee's operating and financial policies. However, if any of these or similar circumstances exists, an investor with ownership of 20% or more shall evaluate all facts and circumstances relating to the investment to reach a judgment about whether the presumption that the investor has the ability to exercise significant influence over the investee's operating and financial policies is overcome. . . .

9. [A "standstill agreement" between an investor and investee] under which the investor agrees to limit its shareholding in the investee . . . [is] commonly used to compromise disputes when an investee is fighting against a takeover attempt or an increase in an investor's percentage ownership. Depending on their provisions, the agreements may modify an investor's rights or may increase certain rights and restrict others compared with the situation of an investor without such an agreement. If the investor surrenders significant rights as a shareholder under the provisions of such an agreement, this Interpretation clarifies that the investor shall assess all the facts and circumstances of the investment to determine whether they are sufficient to overcome the presumption. . . .

12. Some [commenters] suggested that the Interpretation would strengthen investees relative to investors in takeover disputes by making it more difficult for the investor to use the equity method to account for its investment. The Board disagrees with that suggestion for two reasons. First, the Board believes this Interpretation is a faithful interpretation of Opinion 18. The Board has not attempted to favor either investors or investees and does not believe that its role is to do so. The Board's role on this project is to faithfully interpret Opinion 18. Second, the Board notes that the actual cash returns on an investment and the income taxes that would be paid are unaffected by the method of accounting for the investment. Therefore, a decision not to proceed with an otherwise attractive investment simply because the equity method of accounting cannot be used would seem to be unlikely for the vast majority of companies. Conversely, an investment that is not otherwise attractive does not become so simply because the equity method will be used to account for that investment in the investor's financial statements.[a]

---

2. Planning Considerations for Minority Investments

The mechanical character of APB 18's 20% test makes the planner's job relatively easy. The general view is that an investor company which acquires a 20% interest in an investee company can use the equity method without inquiry as to whether *in fact*, in the words of APB 18, "the investor has the ability to exercise significant influence over an investee." This is based on the Opinion's statement that 20% ownership creates a "presumption" of influence "in the absence of evidence to the contrary." It is hardly in the interest of an investor seeking to use the equity method to disclose such evidence to their auditors, and auditors have not interpreted the Opinion as requiring them to search it out.

---

[a] If this is correct, why would the Financial Accounting Standards Board care which method was used as long as the choice was disclosed? Eds.

Conversely, suppose that an acquirer wants to avoid equity treatment, say because it is investing in a startup company that will incur losses for a number of years. If the acquirer is willing to keep its investment below 20%, this result is readily achievable. The acquirer will not volunteer, and auditors are not required to ask about, whether the presumption against the equity method is overcome in this case, even if, as is common, the acquirer receives a board seat and is able to block major corporate actions. How can the acquirer cause the accounting result to change after the high tech company became profitable?

The advantage of the equity method to an investor company that holds minority stakes in profitable companies and wants to show higher earnings can be substantial. Table 13-5 contains examples of the differences in earnings per share that would be reported by some public companies depending on whether they were to use the equity or cost method of accounting.

Table 13-5
Net Income of Firms Having 20-50% Common Stock Investments
(\$ per share, after extraordinary items)

	1971 Net Income		1970 Net Income	
Investor	Equity Method	Cost Method	Equity Method	Cost Method
Hercules	\$2.78	\$2.67	\$2.61	\$2.51
Kaiser Industries	.14	.02	.94	.82
Marathon Oil	2.28	2.18	2.90	2.83
Penn Virginia Corp.	2.65	1.18	6.01	2.65
Phillips Petroleum	1.78	1.67	1.58	1.50
Sifco Industries	(.20)	(.55)	.91	.52
St. Regis Paper	1.34	1.26	2.56	2.50

Source: Thomas Lynch, *Accounting for Investments by the Equity and Market Value Methods,* 31 Fin.Analysts' J. 62 (Jan.-Feb.1975).

While FASB Interpretation 35 describes some circumstances -- such as litigation by the investee against the investor -- that *might* indicate the absence of the requisite influence, the presumption arising from 20% ownership remains sufficient in itself to justify use of the equity method "until overcome by predominant evidence to the contrary." Does the Interpretation impose any obligation on the investor or its auditor to investigate whether the presumption is overcome?

3.   Accounting for Majority Investments: Consolidation

When an acquirer's ownership crosses from minority to majority status, the accounting method required by GAAP changes as well, from the equity method to consolidation. These two methods produce the same reported earnings and stockholders' equity, but arrive at this result in different ways. Under the equity method, acquirer *P*'s investment in Company *S* is shown as a single item in the balance sheet -- Investment in *S*. Similarly, the acquirer's proportionate share of *S*'s earnings are shown as a single item -- Revenue from Investments. Under consolidation, *P*'s and *S*'s full assets and results of operations are combined, as described below. Why might an acquirer care about this difference in the manner of reaching the same bottom line results for earnings and stockholders' equity?

Sidney Davidson, Clyde Stickney & Roman Weil
FINANCIAL ACCOUNTING
529-35 (6th ed. 1991)[*]

When one firm, *P*, owns more than 50% of the voting stock of another company, *S*, *P* can control the activities of *S*. This control can be both at a broad policy-making level and at a day-to-day operational level. The majority investor in this case is the parent and the majority-owned company is the subsidiary. Generally accepted accounting principles require the parent to combine, or consolidate, the financial statements of majority-owned companies with those of the parent.

Purpose of Consolidated Statements

For a variety of reasons . . . a single economic entity may exist in the form of a parent and several legally separate subsidiaries. (The General Electric company, for example, comprises about 150 legally separate companies.) A consolidation of the financial statements of the parent and each of its subsidiaries presents the results of operations, financial position, and cash flows of an affiliated group of companies under the control of a parent, essentially as if the group of companies were a single entity. . . .

Consolidation Policy

An investor generally consolidates a subsidiary when the investment meets the two following criteria:

1. The parent owns more than 50% of the voting stock of the subsidiary.
2. The parent can exercise control over the subsidiary.

Ownership of more than 50% of the subsidiary's voting stock [ordinarily] implies an ability to exert control over the activities of the subsidiary. For example, the parent can control the subsidiary's corporate

---

policies and dividend declarations. There may be situations, however, where the parent cannot effectively control the subsidiary's activities, despite owning a majority of the voting stock. For example, the subsidiary may be located in a foreign country that has restricted the withdrawal of funds from that country. Or the subsidiary may be in bankruptcy and under the control of a court-appointed group of trustees. In these cases, the parent will probably not consolidate the financial statements of the subsidiary. When the parent owns more than 50% of the shares but cannot exercise control, so that it does not prepare consolidated statements, it uses the lower-of-cost-or-market method.

> **Example 1** General Motors, General Electric, and Westinghouse, among others, have wholly-owned finance subsidiaries. These subsidiaries make a portion of their loans to customers who wish to purchase the products of the parent company. The parent company consolidates the financial statements of these subsidiaries. The assets of these subsidiaries are largely receivables. Statement readers may misunderstand the relative liquidity of firms preparing consolidated statements, which combine the assets of the parent -- largely noncurrent manufacturing plant and equipment -- with the more liquid assets of the finance subsidiary. The counter-argument is that these entities operate as a single integrated unit so that consolidated financial statements depict more accurately the nature of their operating relationships.[a]

> **Example 2** A major mining company owns a mining subsidiary in South America. The government of the country enforces stringent control over cash payments outside the country. The company cannot control the use of all the assets, despite owning a majority of the voting shares. Therefore, it does not prepare consolidated statements with the subsidiary. . . .

Understanding Consolidated Statements

This section discusses three concepts essential for understanding consolidated financial statements:

1. The need for intercompany eliminations.
2. The meaning of consolidated net income.
3. The nature of the external minority interest. . . .

Need for Intercompany Eliminations

    . . . [T]he accounting records of each corporation will record transactions of that entity with all other entities (both affiliated and

---

[a] Prior to the adoption of FASB Statement No. 94 in 1987, companies could elect whether to use consolidation or the equity method to account for the operations of subsidiaries that were in substantially different businesses than the parent. Most industrial companies chose not to consolidate the financial statements of their finance subsidiaries. Eds.

nonaffiliated). At the end of the period, each corporation will prepare its own financial statements. The consolidation of these financial statements basically involves summing the amounts for various financial statement items across the separate company statements.

The accountant must adjust the amounts resulting from the summation, however, to eliminate double counting resulting for intercompany transactions. [Otherwise, an item that was sold from *S* to *P*, and then resold by *P* to an outside customer, would be counted in revenue twice -- once on *S*'s books to reflect its sale by *S* to *P*, and again on *P*'s books to reflect its sale by *P* to the outside customer. Similarly, an intercompany transaction might cause similar assets to appear twice on the balance sheet. For example, *S* might record an account receivable for the sale of an item to *P*, while *P* also records an account receivable for the resale of the item to an outside customer.]

Consolidated financial statements will reflect the reported results that would appear if the affiliated group of companies were a single company. Consolidated financial statements reflect the transactions between the consolidated entity and others outside the entity. . . .

If either company holds bonds or long-term notes of the other, the consolidation process would eliminate the investment and related liability in the consolidated balance sheet. It would also eliminate the "borrower's" interest expense and the "lender's" interest revenue from the consolidated income statement. . . .

Consolidated Income

The amount of consolidated net income for a period exactly equals the amount that the parent would show on its separate company books if it used the equity method. . . . A consolidated income statement differs from an income statement using the equity method only in the *components* presented. Under the equity method for an unconsolidated subsidiary, the parent's share of the subsidiary's net income minus gain (or plus loss) on intercompany transactions appears on a single line, Equity in Earnings of Unconsolidated Subsidiary. A consolidated income statement combines the individual revenues and expenses of the subsidiary (less intercompany adjustments) with those of the parent. The consolidation process eliminates the account, Equity in Earnings of Unconsolidated Subsidiary.

External Minority Interest in Consolidated Subsidiary

In many cases, the parent does not own 100% of the voting stock of a consolidated subsidiary. The owners of the remaining shares of voting stock are the *external minority shareholders* or the minority interest. These shareholders own a proportionate interest in the net assets (= total assets − total liabilities) of the subsidiary as shown on the subsidiary's separate corporate records. They also have a proportionate interest in the earnings of the subsidiary.

. . . The parent, with its controlling voting interest, can effectively direct the use of all the subsidiary's assets and liabilities, not merely an amount equal to the parent's percentage of ownership. The generally accepted accounting principle is, therefore, to show all of the assets and liabilities of the subsidiary. The consolidated balance sheet and income statement will [also] disclose the interest of the minority shareholders in the consolidated, but less-than-wholly-owned, subsidiary.

The amount of the minority interest appearing in the balance sheet generally results from multiplying the common shareholders' equity of the subsidiary by the minority's percentage of ownership. For example, if the common shareholders' equity (= assets − liabilities) of a consolidated subsidiary totals $500,000, and the minority owns 20% of the common stock, the minority interest appearing on the consolidated balance sheet is $100,000 (= .20 × $500,000). . . .

[The minority interest reduces the parent's shareholders' equity. Similarly,] the minority interest in the subsidiary's income appears as a deduction in calculating consolidated net income.

---

4.   Summary of Accounting Treatment

Figure 13-1
Illustration of Accounting for Partial and Complete Acquisitions

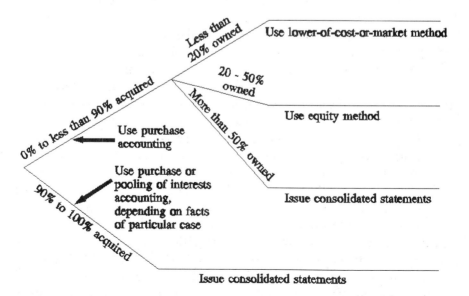

Source: Adapted from Sidney Davidson, Clyde Stickney & Roman Weil, *Financial Accounting* ex. 12-1 (2d ed.1979).

C.   Change in Basis Accounting: LBOs and Push Down Accounting

The expansion of leveraged acquisitions and other complex acquisition structures during the 1980s generated problems of acquisition accounting that were not contemplated in the simple taxonomy of complete acquisitions, minority investments, and majority investments around which the accounting framework established by the APB was organized. We consider below the two principal problems: how the acquirer accounts for a leveraged buyout; and more generally how one accounts for a cash acquisition of a holding company, whose principal assets are the shares of operating subsidiaries.

1.   Accounting for LBOs

In a standard LBO transaction, a newly formed holding company with no previous operations (which we will call Newco) acquires all of the outstanding stock of an operating company (which we will call Oldco) for cash using the proceeds from large borrowings. Typically this is accomplished through the merger between Oldco and a subsidiary of Newco. After the merger, Newco owns 100% of the stock of Oldco. Under APB 16, accounting for the transaction is straightforward. Newco uses purchase accounting, and writes up the carrying value of Oldco's assets to fair market value.

The problem becomes more complicated, however, when some Newco shareholders are also Oldco shareholders. At the extreme, if the shareholders in both companies are identical, the transaction could be a sham designed merely to inflate the value of the company's assets to market value -- or even to more than market value, since the shareholders of Newco are paying themselves. In response to the potential for sham transactions of this sort, American Institute of Certified Public Accountants, *Accounting Interpretation 39 of APB 16, Transfers and Exchanges between Companies Under Common Control* (1973), bars a change in basis if the transfer is between entities that are under common control.

Standard LBO patterns often present intermediate cases. In a typical management buyout, Oldco's managers both own some Oldco equity and participate in the buyout by buying equity in Newco -- often in exchange for their Oldco stock. Similarly, in a divisional buyout, the selling parent company may take an equity interest in Newco either to help finance the sale or to retain an interest in the future performance of the business. In either case, the carryover of shareholders distinguishes the transaction from the standard acquisition form contemplated by APB 16. The question is whether Newco takes a carryover basis in Oldco's assets, as contemplated by AICPA Interpretation 39, or a fair market value basis, as contemplated by plain vanilla purchase accounting.

The example below illustrates the difference between the two accounting alternatives and the stakes involved in determining how to account for the transaction.[12] Oldco has 1,000 shares outstanding, and is owned 10% by management and 90% by the public. Oldco's balance sheet, with total assets of $4,300 and shareholder's equity of $4,000, is shown in Table 13-6.

Table 13-6
Oldco's Pre-LBO Balance Sheet

Assets		
Current assets		$1,500
Fixed assets	$4,000	
Less accumulated depreciation	1,200	
Net fixed assets		2,800
Total assets		**$4,300**
Liabilities		
Current Liabilities		$ 300
Long-term debt		--
Shareholders' equity		4,000
Total liabilities and shareholders' equity		**$4,300**

Now assume that Newco, owned 100% by Oldco management, acquires Oldco for $20 per share (a total of $20,000). Newco borrows 90% of the purchase price. Assume that the excess of Oldco's market value ($20,000) over its book value is attributable entirely to appreciation in Oldco's fixed assets. Figure 13-7 shows Newco's balance sheet with purchase accounting and with carryover basis accounting. If Newco can use purchase accounting, it will have shareholders' equity of $2,000 after the transaction. If Newco must take a carryover basis in Oldco's assets, it will have a large deficit in shareholders' equity. The $18,000 increase in long-term debt, with (by assumption) no change in assets, turns Oldco's $4,000 in shareholders' equity into a $14,000 *deficit* in shareholders' equity on Newco's books.

---

[12] The example is adapted from Jerry Gorman, *How Accounting Rules Shook Up LBO Dealmaking*, Mergers & Acquisitions 45 (July/Aug.1990).

Table 13-7
Newco's Post-LBO Balance Sheet With and Without Basis Step-up

	Carryover Basis		Basis Step-up	
Assets				
Current assets		$1,500		$1,500
Fixed assets	$4,000		$18,800	
Less accumulated depreciation	1,200		--	
Net fixed assets		2,800		18,800
Total assets		$4,300		$20,300
Liabilities				
Current Liabilities		$ 300		$ 300
Long-term debt		18,000		18,000
Shareholders' equity		(14,000)		2,000
Total liabilities and shareholders' equity		$4,300		$20,300

The accounting outcome desired by an LBO acquirer is the opposite of what a traditional acquirer wants. The LBO acquirer is essentially uninterested in earnings per share, but would like to avoid a deficit in shareholders' equity. In California for example, restrictions on corporate actions such as paying dividends or repurchasing shares are keyed to generally accepted accounting principles (GAAP).[13] In addition, financial covenants in outstanding debt contracts may also be measured by reference to GAAP. Carryover basis accounting may result in a breach of existing covenants.[14]

The Financial Accounting Standards Board, Emerging Issues Task Force (EITF) addressed the proper accounting treatment for LBOs in 1989.[15] The EITF's consensus allows a change in Oldco's accounting basis following the transaction only if the transaction results in a change in control of Oldco. The rules for determining whether a change in control has taken place are extremely complex. Absent a change in control, Newco takes a carryover basis in Oldco's assets.

Where there is a change in control, but some Oldco shareholders also become Newco shareholders, the post-transaction consolidated balance sheet reflects a hybrid basis: fair market value except that if former Oldco shareholders are part of the new control group, Oldco's basis carries over to the extent of their proportional ownership of Oldco.[16]

---

[13] See, e.g., Cal.Corp. Code §§ 114, 500.

[14] We consider the interaction between accounting standards and debt covenants in Section E of this Chapter.

[15] Financial Accounting Standards Board, Emerging Issues Tax Force, Issue No. 88-16, *Basis in Leveraged Buyout Transactions* (1989).

[16] In addition, if more than 20% of the total consideration received by Oldco shareholders consists of Newco equity, an equivalent percentage of Oldco's assets take a carryover basis.

Table 13-8 shows how the EITF consensus would apply to the foregoing example, in which the new control group formerly held 10% of Oldco's shares. Newco's balance sheet will reflect a 90% basis step-up, plus a 10% carryover basis. For the example, the EITF consensus results in positive shareholders' equity of $400, but this result depends on the relative proportion of basis step-up and carryover basis.

The overall result reminds us of the old joke that a camel is a horse drafted by a committee, with the EITF acting as the committee, and the hybrid basis approach being the relevant camel. It is hard to see this hybrid basis approach serving the needs of users for information about the company's assets or earnings. Users who want information about fair market value don't get that; users who want comparability with the LBO company's prior performance or with non-LBO competitors don't get that; and it takes complex calculations to turn the hybrid balance sheet and income statement into a form that either group can use.

Table 13-8
Newco's Post-LBO Balance Sheet: Hybrid Basis Under EITF 88-16

Assets		
Current assets		$1,500
Fixed assets	$17,320[a]	
Less accumulated depreciation	120[a]	
Net fixed assets		17,200[a]
Total assets		**$18,700**
Liabilities		
Current Liabilities		$ 300
Long-term debt		18,000
Shareholders' equity		400
Total liabilities and shareholders' equity		**$18,700**

[a] The values for fixed assets, accumulated depreciation, and net fixed assets equal the sum of (i) 90% of the values shown in Table 13-7 for full basis step-up; plus (2) 10% of the values shown in Table 13-7 for carryover basis.

2.   Push Down Accounting

In many acquisitions, the target becomes a subsidiary of the acquirer. In some cases, the new subsidiary will continue to file its own public financial statements -- as when the target has publicly held debt that remains outstanding after the acquisition.   When the acquirer accounts for the acquisition as a purchase, or as a hybrid under EITF 88-16, the question then arises as to whether the acquirer's new basis for post-transaction accounting, which will be reflected on the *acquirer's* consolidated financial statements, must be reflected -- *pushed down* -- to the separate financial statements of its new subsidiary. In this circumstance, the Securities and Exchange Commission staff encourages, but does not require, the acquirer to push down the new basis to its subsidiary.[17]

This result -- different accounting bases for the same assets depending on whether one is looking at the consolidated financial statements of the parent, or at the subsidiary's separate financials -- may seem anomalous, especially in an LBO where the parent's only asset is the stock of its operating subsidiary, and where the decision to use a holding company structure, with Newco owning Oldco, has no bearing on the actual value of Oldco's assets. But the same result -- different accounting bases for parent and subsidiary -- follows automatically if the acquirer buys less than 100% of the target, because there is no occasion for the now majority-owned subsidiary to change the basis of its assets.

3. The Conceptual Problem: Change in Basis Accounting v. Current Value Accounting

The broader question raised by LBO accounting and push-down accounting, which is also at the heart of the purchase vs. pooling debate, is how to draw meaningful lines that identify what changes in a company's ownership or financial condition should require or permit a new basis for accounting. These questions are the subject of an ongoing FASB Project on Consolidations and Related Matters.[18]

The problem of when to change accounting basis is inherent in an historical cost accounting model. Since asset values change over time, the question necessarily arises: what discrete events should result in bringing asset values up to date? The difficult line-drawing problems that question presents are avoided in a current value accounting model because in a current value model, assets are continuously revalued. At least for the present time, however, the Financial Accounting Standards Board is committed to historical accounting, and to drawing lines that address when assets should

---

[17] Securities and Exchange Commission, Staff Accounting Bulletin No. 54, *Application of "Push Down" Basis of Accounting in Financial Statements of Subsidiaries Acquired by Purchase* 48 FR 51769 (1983). Similar issues arise when, for example, OLDCO makes a public offering of stock following its acquisition by NEWCO. In this circumstance the SEC staff requires push down accounting with respect to debt incurred for the purpose of OLDCO's acquisition. See Securities and Exchange Commission, Staff Accounting Bulletin No. 55, *"Push Down" Basis of Accounting for Parent Company Debt Related to Subsidiary Acquisitions* 48 FR 54810 (1983).

[18] The status of the portion of the project dealing with change in basis accounting is reported in Financial Accounting Standards Board, Discussion Memorandum, *New Basis Accounting*, Financial Accounting Series No. 110-C (1991).

be revalued at current market value.   The recent FASB Discussion
Memorandum for FASB's change in basis project states:

> This project does not debate the relative merits of the historical cost and
> current value accounting models because the Board does not propose a
> fundamental change to the present historical cost model.   An essential
> characteristic of the current value accounting model is a series of continual
> revaluations to maintain the carrying amounts of an entity's assets and
> liabilities at their current fair values.   In contrast, [under historical cost
> accounting] a new basis of accountability results from a single revaluation to
> current value of assets and liabilities, [which] is triggered by the occurrence
> of one or more requisite events. A key objective of this project is to identify
> those events.[19]

The Discussion Memorandum does not confront the problems of line-
drawing in a transactional environment where planners respond to a given set
of rules with clever transactional structures that achieve accounting results
not contemplated by the accounting rulemakers, to which the rulemakers
must respond with more complex rules, and so on, in the kind of never-
ending spiral we saw in Chapter 12 for trafficking in NOLs. Its discussion,
for example, of which of 13 different stock purchase scenarios should trigger
a change in basis suggests that complexity is the shape of the future.

D.   The Theory: Gain in Stock Market Value as a Result of Choice of Accounting Methods

The common explanation for acquirers' interest in how an acquisition
is accounted for assumes a link between reported earnings and share price.
Higher reported earnings per share results in a higher market value for the
acquiring company, even if the higher earnings are merely a result of choice
of accounting method and reflect no change in actual cash flow.   In this
view, the ability to account for an acquisition as a pooling of interests rather
than as a purchase has real economic consequences for the acquiring
company.   However, the explanation for the linkage between earnings per
share reported for financial accounting purposes and firm value is typically
not discussed. What is needed is an explanation of why altering reported,
but not real, earnings alters stock market value. In the terminology of the
introduction to this Part II, changing accounting method does not directly
change *business value* -- the present value of expected future cash flows.
Why then should it change *stock market value*? The excerpt below offers a
careful exposition of the purported link between accounting method and firm
value.

---

[19] *Id.* at 1.

Peter Steiner, MERGERS: MOTIVES, EFFECTS, POLICIES
103-19 (1975)*

The PE Ratio, the PE Game, and the Incentive to Merge

The Price-Earnings Relationship

. . . [O]ne might expect a dollar's worth of present expected value of an annual earnings stream to command a value that is some well-defined multiple of the annual expected earnings, just as the present value of an annuity is some multiple of the annual payment. In a world of perfect knowledge of the future one might expect the price of every security to be the *same* multiple of the annual certainty-equivalent income stream. . . .

Unfortunately a company's future income stream is not known. Suppose instead that what is known are the earnings of the company in the years past, rather than the years ahead. We can still treat today's price as a multiple of present or past earnings. But now quite rationally the multiples (the price-earnings ratios) will not be the same for different companies because a dollar of past or current earnings may not be the same predictor of future earnings for different companies. . . . The PE ratio is a perfectly reasonable summary concept for the whole congeries of things that lead to variable expectations of future events. The price of a company's stock at time t is by definition the product of its PE ratio at time t, and its earnings per share at time t.

Behavioral Assumptions Underlying the PE Theory of Incentives to Merge

The definitional identity just stated can be transformed into a *theory* of behavior that plays an important role in conglomerate acquisitions by the following assumptions:

1. The PE ratio of a particular company tends to become an established parameter and to change but slowly over time. Because of this, anything that increases earnings per share of the company tends to increase the price of its stock.

2. When a Company B acquires a Company S with a different historic PE ratio from its own, Company B's PE ratio becomes applicable to Company S's earnings per share.

3. The PE ratio tends to increase secularly if the rate of growth of earnings increases and if the profits per dollar of net assets increase.

These assumptions may make it possible and profitable to transfer by merger one company's PE ratio to another company's earnings, and thus create an incentive to merge.

A fourth assumption -- that the relevant "earnings" to which the PE ratio applies are those as reported in the accounting statements of the firm -- creates the role for accounting conventions and changes therein in affecting behavior.

The Pure PE Game

It may be intuitively obvious that otherwise unattractive mergers may be eagerly sought if a company with a high PE rating can by merger transfer this ratio to the earnings of a company with a lower one. Table 13-9 illustrates this possibility by an example that provides a useful benchmark for less obvious matters that follow. . . . Company *B* is assumed to have a price per share of $1 and earnings per share of $.05; its PE ratio is thus 20. Company *S*'s stock also sells for $1 per share, but it has earnings per share of $.10 and a PE ratio of 10. A simple combination of these companies into *B* + *S*, column (3), would show earnings per share of $.0667. One might expect [the combined company's] stock, absent any synergy, to have a price per share of $1, and a PE ratio of 15. In every way *B* + *S* is the weighted average of Company *B* and Company *S*.

Table 13-9
Example: The PE Game

	Company B (1)	Company S (2)	B + S weighted average k = 1 (3)	B acquires S k = 1 (4)	B acquires S k = 1.20 (5)
Net assets	$2,000	$1,000	$3,000	$3,000	$3,000
Net equity	$2,000	$1,000	$3,000	$3,000	$3,000
(Number of shares)	[2,000]	[1,000]	[3,000]	[3,000]	[3,200]
Earnings	$ 100	$ 100	$ 200	$ 200	$ 200
Earnings per share	$ .05	$ .10	$ .0667	$.0667	$.0625
Price per share	$ 1.00	$ 1.00	$ 1.00	$1.333	$1.250
PE ratio	20:1	10:1	15:1 avg	20:1	20:1
Market value	$2,000	$1,000	$3,000	$4,000	$4,000
Earnings/Net assets	.05	10	.0667	.0667	.0667
Earnings/Equity	.05	10	.0667	.0667	.0667

Now, however, assume Company *B* acquires Company *S* on a share for share exchange (*k* = 1) as shown in column (4). Earnings per share are $.0667, as just above, but now these earnings are converted by the stock market into a price per share *using B's PE ratio of 20:1*. The price of [*B*]'s stock is $1.33 per share instead of $1.00 and everyone is a winner! The same 3,000 shares of stock as in (A + B) now command a third more on the market.[6]

But the advantages are not yet exhausted. . . . *B*'s earnings per share have risen from $.05 before the merger to $.0667 after it; moreover, its stock price has risen, and so have its earnings per dollar of net assets. Each of these changes is viewed as "favorable" by the market and may lead to an upward revision of *B*'s PE ratio. If it rises to 25 (after all, investors may reason, this is a company showing good growth in profits and in stock prices), its price per share rises to 25 × $.0667 = $1.67.

This rise is of a different kind from that of the previous paragraph. The earlier one (the rise in earnings per share of *B* due to the acquisition) is real enough and will continue as long as the two companies' earnings continue at the levels pertaining at the time of acquisition. In contrast, the rate of increase in earnings per share (that may lead to an inflation of the PE ratio) will not be maintained into the following years (absent a real gain somewhere) unless the company makes subsequent acquisitions of companies with positive earnings but relatively low PE's. Thus arises one source of the alleged inexorable search by so-called go-go firms for more and more merger partners: to maintain an upward rate of growth in earnings per share. This would work (by assumption) as long as the investing public continued to assign an appropriate PE ratio by the identity of the acquiring firm, not the source of the earnings. . . .

This example depended primarily on the willingness of investors to transfer an acquiring company's PE ratio to acquired earnings. To the incentives for merger so created, additional incentives existed in the opportunities to manipulate nominal earnings and the other determinants of PE ratios. Here was the role of imaginative accounting.

Merger Accounting and Incentives to Merge

The Role of Accounting

To the economist, although not to the businessman, the first question requiring an answer is why accounting conventions matter. . . . The explanation . . . lies in the multiplicity and complexity of the measures of performance of huge corporations. Investors, potentially overwhelmed by a flood of measures of corporate performance, have come to rely upon

---

[6] All of the above assumed $k = 1$, and thus avoided any problem of accounting for payments to *S* in excess of book value. . . . Column (5) shows how the example works out if the exchange of stock occurred at a 20% premium to *S*'s stockholders. Because there are more shares (3,200) the earnings per share rises only to .0625 and price per share (at a PE of 20:1) to $1.25 instead of to $1.33. The pie is divided somewhat differently. *S*'s new shareholders get half (rather than one-third) of the gain from applying *B*'s PE ratio to *S*'s earnings.

accounting measures sanctioned by the APB and condoned by the Securities and Exchange Commission (SEC). This reliance creates the incentive and the opportunity to creative accountants to operate within the existing rules to achieve unintended ends. Such behavior in turn generates changes in the rules, but often with a sizable lag. Precisely such a period of discovered opportunities and lagged response occurred during the [conglomerate] merger wave [of the 1960s].

Pooling Versus Purchase Accounting

. . . In most acquisitions, the effective purchase price for assets is well above their *book* value, both because of the premium characteristically paid for stock and because in our economy average book values tend to be well below market values of assets. This is partly due to inflation and the use of original cost, and partly to various forms of accelerated depreciation in use. For present purposes the two sources have the same effect, and I will thus continue to assume the acquisition occurs without a premium being paid [$k = 1$ in the example].

Suppose, with no real changes, Company *S* in our example carries its assets (which are "worth" $1,000) at only $200 in its balance sheet. Table 13-10, column (4'), recomputes the pooled balance sheet. Comparison with column (4) (repeated from table 13-9) shows that this has no effect on earnings per share or price but does inflate the rate of earnings on assets and equity. This may . . . [persuade] the market to raise the PE ratio appropriate to the company.

Table 13-10
Example: Pooling with Market Value Above Book Value

	Company B (from Table 13-9) (1)	B acquires S (from Table 13-9) (4)	Company S understated book values (2')	B acquires S (pooling) (4')
Net assets	$2,000	$3,000	$ 200	$2,200
Net equity	$2,000	$3,000	$ 200	$2,200
[Number of shares]	[2,000]	[3,000]	[1,000]	[3,000]
Earnings	$ .05	$.0667	$ .10	$.0667
Price per share	$ 1.00	$1.333	$ 1.00	$1.333
PE ratio	20:1	20:1	10:1	20:1
Market value	$2,000	$4,000	$1,000	$4,000
Earnings/Net assets	.05	.0667	.50	.091
Earnings Equity	.05	.0667	.50	.091

The main advantage of pooling undervalued assets is that it creates the opportunity for "instant earnings" in any year that they are required. Suppose Company [B] now sells all the assets of Company S (worth $1,000, but carried at $200) to another party for $500. It forgoes thereby the $100 per year that those assets earn. *But on the books of Company [B] this transaction will appear to realize a gain of $300 not a loss of $500.*

The effect on Company [B]'s earnings per share *in the year of the sale* may be spectacular as is illustrated in column (8) of table 13-11, and if the market continues to play the PE game the price of the stock can shoot up. Of course, the following year, things become less attractive: the company has lost the income stream the assets produced yet still has S's former shareholders among its owners, see column (9). But if another acquisition and another sale can be concluded, the effect on Company [B]'s earnings per share may be counteracted, at least for another year. Once started on this track, the company must continue to acquire companies at an increasing rate if it is not to have its past conversion of future earnings into instant income catch up to it. The best analogy is to the chain letter.

Table 13-11
Example: Sale of Undervalued Assets to Create "Instant Income"

	B acquires S (from table 13-10) (4)	Company B after sale of S's assets for $500 (8)	Company B next year after sale (9)
Net assets	$2,000	$2,500	$2,500
Net equity	$2,200	$2,500	$2,500
[Number of shares]	[3,000]	[3,000]	[3,000]
Earnings	$ 200	$ 400	$ 100
Earnings per share	$.0667	$.1333	$.0333
Price per share	$1.333	$2.667	$ .667
PE ratio	20:1	20:1	20:1
Market value	$4,000	$8,000	$2,000
Earnings/Net assets	.091	.16	.04
Earnings/Equity	.091	.16	.04

Although Professor Steiner focuses on the pooling versus purchase choice, a minority investment accounted for using the equity method fits the theoretical framework just as well. An acquirer with a high PE ratio can buy a 20% or greater stake in a target with a low P/E at a price reflecting that lower PE ratio. The acquirer's shareholders capitalize those acquired earnings at the acquirer's higher PE ratio. If the acquirer finances the acquisition by selling shares to the public, its earnings per share will increase. The same assumption is critical to the argument in both the complete and partial acquisition situations: that the acquisition not change the acquiring company's PE ratio.

E. Evaluation: Consistency With Analytic Tools and Empirical Evidence

The mechanistic relationship between reported earnings per share and firm value described by Professor Steiner depends critically on his fourth assumption -- that the market considers *only* a company's financial accounting data in valuing the company's securities and, as a necessary but unstated corollary, that the market accepts that data at face value without discriminating among accounting data produced by different accounting methods. This assumption is in obvious tension with the Efficient Capital Market Hypothesis considered in Chapter 5.

From the perspective of ECMH, investors will acquire the additional information necessary to discriminate between earnings generated by Company *B*'s original business and earnings acquired through *B*'s acquisition of *S*, and the additional information needed to recognize that additional earnings generated through pooling accounting are worth less -- should carry a lower PE ratio -- if the value of the information exceeds the cost of acquiring it. Moreover, the value to long-term investors of accurate valuation of the acquirer's expected future cash flows is quite high. If there are sources of low cost information concerning the quality of the acquirer's earnings, and if reconstruction of the company's performance assuming purchase accounting is not unduly costly, then the company's choice among accounting methods should not alter the value of the company's stock.

The proposition that accounting results affect stock price can be empirically tested by means of the event study methodology considered in Chapter 6. If investors take an acquirer's earnings at face value, then acquirers using the pooling of interests method of accounting for acquisitions should experience greater abnormal returns than acquirers using purchase accounting, after controlling for other factors that could affect the acquirer's returns. The following study reports the results of such an empirical test.

Hai Hong, Robert Kaplan & Gershon Mandelker
POOLING VS. PURCHASE: THE EFFECTS
OF ACCOUNTING FOR MERGERS ON STOCK PRICES
53 Acct.Rev. 31 (1978)[*]

[S]everal recent studies have looked at the informational content of alternative accounting methods and their effects on stock prices. Accounting changes or manipulations not accompanied by real economic impacts seem to have no statistically significant effects on stock prices. Apparently, the presence of alternative and more timely sources of information on corporate performance enables investors to look beyond simple income numbers in valuing equity securities.

Accounting for business combinations has been an especially troublesome issue for accountants. Up until APB 16 was issued in October 1970, business combinations which were accomplished by means of an exchange of securities could have been accounted for either by the "purchase" method or the "pooling-of-interests" method. . . . [T]here is no difference in the cash flows associated with using one method or the other. . . . Since the method of accounting for the combination is usually fully disclosed in the proxy statement, an efficient market should be able to respond to the real economic consequences of the combination and not be affected by the particular accounting method used.

In this article, we will examine whether the use of the pooling of interests method does tend to increase the stock prices of acquiring companies. Our null hypothesis is that the market is efficient and thus able to distinguish between higher earnings caused by using pooling-of-interests from higher earnings caused by real economic events of the firm. If the use of pooling-of-interests in a merger were associated with an increased valuation of a firm, the market may be inefficient with respect to this accounting convention. . . .

Data and Sample

. . . Studies indicate that merger accounting was confused before Accounting Research Bulletin No. 43 was issued in 1953. Pooling-of-interests, as a well defined method of accounting for business combinations, became more widespread after 1954, and increased in popularity to become the predominant option in the latter half of the sixties. The period 1954-64 was chosen, therefore, as one in which purchase and pooling existed as distinct and practical alternative forms of accounting. Post-1964 mergers were not considered because securities returns data were available only up to June, 1968, in our CRSP file and also because the low incidence of purchase accounting in the late sixties would have led to a highly unbalanced sample in that time period.

To be admitted into the sample, a merger had to satisfy the following criteria:

1. The merger must be significantly large relative to the acquiring firm. This criterion was adopted to avoid admitting the very large number of small and insignificant acquisitions whose inclusion in the sample would tend to dilute the impact, if any, of the merger events on average residuals. A relative size of 3% in net asset value was used as the rough cutoff point. . . .

2. There should be no other major mergers close in time to the one under consideration. This criterion was necessary to avoid confounding the effect of two or more mergers in the same time period. . . .

3. The acquiring firms must be listed on the NYSE and their returns data available for at least 24 months on each side of the merger date.

4. The mergers must take place by exchange of shares. This means that each merger would have been a candidate for either pooling or purchase accounting given the great flexibility that accounting practice provided in the period under consideration. This criterion rules out cash acquisitions, which cannot be accounted for as poolings. It also virtually rules out taxable mergers. . . .

[Of the mergers in the sample,] 138 used pooling-of-interests [and] 62 used purchase accounting. . . . Of the 62 purchases, only 37 amortized positive goodwill; the rest either did not amortize [goodwill], had negative goodwill, or involved an unknown amount and sign of goodwill. . . . Of the 138 pooling firms, 122 involved an acquisition price in excess of book value [so that the acquirer would report higher earnings under pooling than under the purchase method]. . . .

Methodology

. . . In order to evaluate the performance of stocks around the merger dates, it is necessary to abstract from general market conditions which affect stock returns and isolate any specific effects that the merger event might have. The [event study method model developed in Chapter 6] has been used in a number of similar studies of stock prices performance associated with accounting or financial events. . . .

Shifts in Parameters σ_y and β_y

Since a merger may lead to important changes in the riskiness of a firm, it would seem reasonable to allow for different risk parameters in pre-merger and post-merger periods. Changes in [the acquiring firm's unsystematic risk, which is reflected in the standard deviation of its residual returns σ_y, and in the acquirer's systematic risk, reflected in its sensitivity to marketwide movements] β_y, would come about by the addition of the acquired firm's assets to those of the surviving firm and also by a change in the debt-equity ratio of the acquiring firm which has issued new securities for its acquisition. Accordingly, one set of parameters is estimated for the pre-merger period and another for the post-merger period for each firm. . . .

Selection of Critical Date

In this and similar studies, we look for abnormal behavior in months surrounding a critical event, such as the first earnings announcement when using a new accounting procedure. For this study, one might also identify the critical event as the merger itself. We will initially describe and present results with data centered about two earnings announcement dates: the month of the first annual earnings announcement after the merger and the month of the first earnings announcement, interim or annual, after the merger. If investors are to be "fooled" by the higher earnings reported because the pooling-of-interests method is used, the largest impact should show up in the earnings announcement immediately after the merger. Subsequently, we will also present the abnormal residuals centered on the month of the merger itself.

Define month 0 as the month of the critical event (e.g., post-merger earnings announcement); month 1 is then the month immediately following the event, and month −1 is the month immediately preceding it. . . .

Figure 13-2 displays the [average Cumulative abnormal return to the 122 firms in the sample that used pooling accounting and paid more than book value to acquire their targets], centered on the [month of] the first earnings announcement, quarterly or annual, after the merger. . . .

The results displayed in Figure 13-2 suggest that there is no abnormal price behavior associated with earnings announcements subsequent to a pooling-of-interests merger. While the level of cumulative abnormal returns appears high around the first earnings announcement in Figure 13-2, this is caused by positive residuals ten to fifteen months prior to this event. . . .

Figure 13-2
CARs to Acquirers Using Pooling-of-Interests Accounting
(month relative to first post-merger earnings announcement)

CAR

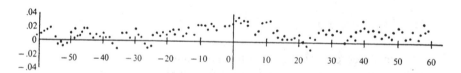

The preceding analysis was replicated using the merger date as the critical date for centering the study of abnormal residuals. A merger is accompanied with analysis of proxy statements, tender offers, and pro forma financial statements. Thus, a merger accomplished under "favorable" accounting practices (i.e., pooling-of-interests) could be associated with unusual price behavior around the time of the merger. For purposes of comparison, we also present the results for our much smaller sample of firms who used purchase accounting for mergers with amortization of positive goodwill even though the conditions of the merger would have permitted the pooling method.

Plots of the cumulative abnormal residuals (see Figure 13-3) for the pooling-of-interests firms are analogous to those displayed in Figure 13-2 with no abnormal price movement for the two years centered on the merger date. The purchase firms, however, show a strong positive price movement in the year prior to the merger date. The [average] CAR [was] 8.8% during these 12 months and this increase was maintained for 8 subsequent months.

Figure 13-3
Acquirer CARs at Merger Date
(month relative to merger date)

*122 Acquirers Paying More than Book Value and Using **Pooling** Accounting*

CAR

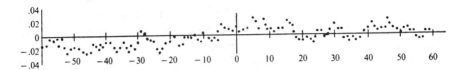

*37 Acquirers Paying More than Book Value and Using **Purchase** Accounting*

CAR

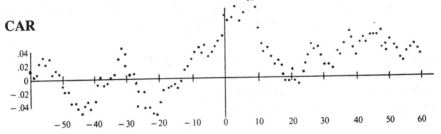

Statistical tests on these two samples . . . show the insignificant residuals for the pooling firms. [None of the monthly t-statistics for the sample of pooling firms are significant. The results also show] the strong positive movement [during the year before the merger] for the small sample of purchase firms. . . . Apparently, firms who opt to use the more conservative purchase method have been doing well in the year prior to the merger. Perhaps a self-selection bias is operating, as has been suggested in previous studies . . . in that firms who choose the purchase method can "afford" to report the lower earnings caused by use of this method. The small sample of firms who used the purchase method in our sample, however, cautions as against drawing too strong an inference from this peculiar price behavior. . . .

Finally, the importance of using different pre-merger and post-merger estimates of a firm's β was highlighted by a CAR analysis when the parameters of the market model were estimated from observations running from months -40 to -13 and $+12$ to $+39$. The cumulative residuals and the portfolio t-statistics were much higher than those previously displayed. Thus, if we had not captured the nonstationarity in relative risk of merging firms by estimating separate pre- and post-merger betas, our t-statistics would have been biased upward toward significance.

Discussion of Results

There is a clear lack of evidence to support the hypothesis that using the pooling-of-interests method raises the stock prices of acquiring firms around the time or in the year after the merger. Investors do not seem to have been fooled by this accounting convention into paying higher stock prices . . . .

People who wish to continue to believe that "dirty pooling" raises the stock prices of acquiring firms may raise the following objections to our study. First, they could argue that the market is fooled by the pooling method but that the difference in earnings caused by pooling and the "proper" alternative of purchase accounting with a 40-year amortization of goodwill is too small to cause a change in stock prices that would be detected by our empirical procedures. This is certainly possible. But if the effect is so small that it is undetectable using what we consider to be fairly sophisticated and sensitive procedures, it would not be a very important effect, almost surely below the threshold of materiality. . . .

Finally, one could argue that our procedure of excluding firms with multiple mergers within a two-year period excluded firms from whom the potential distortion was largest. Advocates of this position must then believe that the market is efficient with respect to one merger per year but somehow becomes inefficient when more than one merger per year occurs, an argument which we find less than convincing.

A variant of this position would claim that the real excesses in the use of poolings in mergers occurred in the late 1960s with the boom in conglomerate mergers, and this period was excluded from our study. Again, supporters of this criticism must then argue that while the market appeared efficient with respect to merger accounting in the 1954-1964 time period, [investors] somehow forgot how to adjust for pooling-of-interests accounting [as poolings became more common] in the 1965-1970 time period. . . .

No single empirical study is ever completely convincing on settling a controversy. Problems in sample selection, financial and statistical models, and interpretation of results are inherent in all empirical work. We believe, however, the effect of this study is to shift the burden of proof to those who claim that the stock price of acquiring firms is raised when the pooling-of-interests method is used in a merger. . . . In the absence of future studies that would demonstrate such an effect, we must believe that fully disclosed accounting policies are properly reflected in the stock prices of firms.

Note: Interpreting Event Studies of Accounting Changes

1. *The Choice of Event Date.* As we stressed in Chapter 6, one must interpret event studies with caution. Calculating the relevant abnormal returns requires only knowledge of statistics; understanding the meaning of the resulting numbers requires careful analysis and a good sense of the institutional setting in which the events under study took place. The Hong, Kaplan & Mandelker study's methodology contains a potentially serious problem concerning the choice of an event date. The authors recognized that the date of the first earnings announcement after the acquisition, on which they initially focused, may be too late to capture the effect they are looking for. The proxy statement delivered to shareholders to secure their approval of the transaction (which is thus available to investors at low cost) contains pro forma financial statements which detail how the transaction will be accounted for. Thus, investors will understand the impact, if any, of pooling accounting long before the first post-transaction earnings report is released.

To meet this concern, the authors also calculated the acquiring company's abnormal returns for the month in which the transaction actually occurred. The authors found no abnormal results at this earlier time either But is even the merger date early enough? The proxy statement containing pro forma financial statements that restate the two companies' prior year's financial statements on a consolidated basis is mailed to shareholders at least a month before the shareholders' meeting at which the transaction is voted upon. Moreover, there is often a several month delay between the announcement of the transaction and the date when the proxy statement comes out. The initial announcement will often contain enough information for investors to infer the likely effects of the transaction on the acquirer's earnings.

Can one determine from the presentation of the data whether the authors' conclusion would have changed had they considered the correct event date? The lack of positive abnormal returns in the months preceding mergers accounted for as poolings, shown in Figure 13-3, indicates that the authors' conclusions would not have changed had they used an earlier, and probably more appropriate, event date.

2. *Purchase vs. Pooling: The Impact of the Adoption of APB 16.* An alternative approach to studying the importance of the pooling versus purchase choice, which contains its own difficulty in isolating an event date, would be to examine how the adoption of APB 16 affected companies with announced acquisition programs. If the ability to use the pooling of interest method did result in increased value, then APB 16's restriction on the use of pooling should have caused negative abnormal returns for acquisition-minded companies.

Here again, however, the date of APB 16's adoption is probably too late to fully capture any abnormal returns associated with restricting the use of pooling. The adoption of APB 16 was preceded by a number of events, including newspaper reports of internal APB drafts and the issuance of public exposure drafts even more restrictive than the opinion ultimately adopted. In an efficient market, investors should have anticipated the likely adoption of APB No. 16. From this perspective, abnormal returns would occur when the final opinion was actually adopted only if (i) the rule affected firms' stock market values; and (ii) its final form differed from the market's expectation.

Katherine Schipper & Rex Thompson, studied the events leading up to APB 16 to assess the market's reaction, if any, to the anticipated adoption of APB 16. They authors conclude, consistent with Hong, Kaplan & Mandelker, that "[e]vidence on the significance of . . . APB Opinions 16 and 17 is comparatively weak and suggest an overall insignificant impact for these regulations."[20]

3. *Equity vs. Lower-of-Cost-or-Market: The Impact of the Adoption of APB 18.* There has been no study, comparable to Schipper & Thompson's, of how the adoption of APB 18 affected the stock prices of firms with large minority investments in other companies. However, one study by Barrett sought to examine the claim of a link between accounting method and stock price by looking at the personification of the link: financial analysts. If analysts are fooled by choice of accounting method, then they and other professional traders will presumably cause the misinformation to be reflected in stock price.

Barrett compared the value that financial analysts placed on hypothetical companies where one group of analysts was given financial statements prepared using the cost method and a second group was given identical statements except using the equity method. The results led the author to conclude that a switch from the cost to the equity method in response to the greater availability of the equity method after the adoption of APB 18 "will probably have little, if any, direct effect upon the price of the firm's common stock."[21] However, valuations did differ when the cost method was used with insufficient footnote disclosure to allow reconstruction of the results as if the equity method were used. Is this result consistent with the Efficient Capital Market Hypothesis?[22]

---

[20] Katherine Schipper & Rex Thompson, *The Impact of Merger-Related Regulations on the Shareholders of Acquiring Firms,* 21 J.Acct.Res. 184, 216 (1983). Leftwich (1981), *supra* note 4, conducted a similar study, but found negative abnormal returns associated with some events foretelling the ultimate adoption of APB 16. Schipper & Thompson, however, stress that other regulatory activity that could be expected to make acquisitions less profitable -- especially the enactment of the Williams Act in 1968 and the Tax Reform Act of 1969 (restricting debt financed acquisitions) -- occurred at the same time, thereby causing a problem of confounding events. Schipper & Thompson attempted to control for this; Leftwich did not.

[21] M. Edgar Barrett, *APB Opinion Number 18: A Move Toward Preference of Users,* Fin.Analysts' J. 47, 53 (July-Aug. 1972).

[22] George Foster, *Valuation Parameters of Property-Liability Companies,* 32 J.Fin. 823 (1977), studied a problem similar to that posed by APB 18. Pursuant to standard accounting

4. *Do Firms Pay Higher Premiums in Pooling Transactions?* A final approach to determining whether acquisition accounting affects has a valuation effect shifts the object of inquiry. Hong, Kaplan & Mandelker asked whether the market valued pooling and purchase transactions differently. This implicitly assumes that the transactions are otherwise similar. Nathan reasoned that satisfying APB 16's conditions to the availability of pooling required the target's cooperation, as we observed in the AT&T-NCR transaction. If pooling was important to the acquirer, APB 16 would give the target company increased bargaining power which, in turn, would cause the price paid in transactions accounted for as a pooling to increase. Recall that AT&T offered to pay $110 per share for NCR if pooling could be achieved, but only $100 per share otherwise.[23]

Using a sample of 461 acquisitions between 1963 and 1978, including 261 poolings and 200 purchases, Nathan found no evidence that accounting for an acquisition as a pooling caused an increase in the price. Acquirers did not have to pay for pooling. However, the study may be based on a false premise. Prior to 1978 (the ending date for the study), hostile acquisitions were rare. Does APB 16 really add to the target company's bargaining power if target management can veto *any* acquisition, without significant fear of a hostile takeover?

F.　Toward a Theory of Choice of Accounting Method

The problem posed by accounting for acquisitions is hardly unique. A company can choose among alternative accounting methods for reporting the same transaction in numerous areas where the alternatives can have very different impact on the company's reported earnings, assets and liabilities, but no effect on the company's actual cash flows. Thus, it is important to know whether the results canvassed in Section C can be generalized: Does the market "see through" accounting choices in valuing a company? Studies have shown, for example, that the choice among different methods of depreciation for financial accounting purposes,[24] and the choice of whether to expense or capitalize research and development costs do not significantly

---

practice, the financial statements of property-liability insurance companies do not reflect unrealized gains and losses on their stock portfolios, even though these portfolios represented roughly a quarter of the companies' total assets during the period studied. Foster found that total earnings, including unrealized gains, was a much better predictor of stock price than only realized earnings. The implication is that the market takes unrealized gains and losses into account even if they are not formally disclosed.

[23] Kevin Nathan, *Do Firms Pay to Pool?: Some Empirical Evidence*, 7 J.Acct. & Pub.Pol. 185 (1988).

[24] See, e.g., William Beaver & Ronald Dukes, *Interperiod Tax Allocation and Delta-Depreciation Methods: Some Empirical Results*, 48 Acct.Rev. 549 (1973); David Cassidy, *Investor Evaluation of Accounting Information: Some Additional Empirical Evidence*, 14 J.Acct.Res. 212 (1976).

affect a company's stock price.[25] These and other studies consistently support the proposition that the capital market is efficient with respect to choice of financial accounting methods -- as long as financial disclosure is complete enough so that investors can compare financial statements prepared using different accounting methods.[26]

These results are troubling because, while they paint a consistent picture of how *investors* behave, they do not seem to reflect the way *managers* behave. Many major companies still seem to select among alternative accounting techniques based on which technique maximizes reported earnings even if that choice has real costs; that is, the companies accept reduced cash flow as the price of increased accounting earnings. In terms of cash flow per share, AT&T's investors were demonstrably worse off if, in fact, AT&T paid extra to account for its acquisition of NCR as a pooling. Nor is the apparent willingness of AT&T's managers to forego real cash gains for favorable accounting treatment unique. Consider the following statement by the Head of Arthur Andersen & Co.'s Corporate Reorganization Tax Speciality Team, made at a time (1982) when a basis step-up could, in theory, offer joint tax gains to the acquirer and the target's shareholders:

> [F]rom a practical standpoint, a major consideration in an acquisition is the impact the acquisition will have on the acquiring corporation's financial statements. This is due to the fact that the accounting rules are, in some measure, different from the tax rules dealing with corporate acquisitions. *Often, an acquiring corporation has foregone a tax basis step-up in the target corporation's assets where to do so would have had an adverse impact on its earnings for financial reporting purposes.*[27]

Similarly, Arthur Wyatt, a former member of the Financial Accounting Standards Board, reports that the abandonment of an otherwise desirable acquisition because it could not be accounted for as a pooling "isn't atypical."[28]

---

[25] Ronald Dukes, *An Investigation of the Effects of Expensing Research and Development Costs on Security Prices*, in *Proceedings of the Conference on Topical Research in Accounting* 147 (Michael Schiff & George Sorter eds.1975).

[26] For surveys, see, e.g., George Foster, *Financial Statement Analysis* (1978); Paul Griffin, *Usefulness to Investors and Creditors of Information Provided by Financial Reporting: A Review of Empirical Accounting Research* (1981); Robert Kaplan, *The Information Content of Financial Accounting Numbers: A Survey of Empirical Evidence*, in *The Impact of Accounting Research on Practice and Disclosure* 134 (A. Rashad Abdel-Khalik & Thomas Keller eds.1978).

[27] Statement of Earl C. Brown, Arthur Andersen & Co., on Proposed "Corporate Takeover Tax Act of 1982" (H.R. 6295) before the Subcomm. on Select Revenue Measures of the House Comm. on Ways and Means (May 24, 1982) (emphasis added).

[28] Arthur Wyatt, *Efficient Market Theory: Its Impact on Accounting*, 155 J.Acct. 56, 60 (1983). Takeover lawyers report the same result. For example, James Freund states that the use of earnouts or contingent price arrangements in acquisitions, a potentially valuable contractual technique that is considered in Chapter 27, *infra*, declined sharply following the

Why do corporate managers behave this way?   Knowledge of the Efficient Capital Market Hypothesis is no longer limited to academics. Indeed, often it is the former MBA students of the academics who conducted the relevant ECMH studies who proceed to ignore the studies' results. This suggests that factors other than a desire to increase stock price must underlie the preference for favorable accounting treatment. What factors are these? And what is the tie between accounting choices and real economic results?

A growing literature in accounting research seeks to identify the link between the choice of accounting method and real economic results *given that markets are efficient*. The goal is to explain how an accounting change that doesn't directly affect cash flows can nonetheless either (i) indirectly impact the *firm's* cash flow; or (ii) impact the *manager's* expected future income.

The following study is illustrative of this literature. It seeks to explain why companies switch from accelerated depreciation to straight line depreciation for financial accounting purposes.

Robert Holthausen
EVIDENCE ON THE EFFECT OF BOND COVENANTS AND MANAGEMENT COMPENSATION CONTRACTS ON THE CHOICE OF ACCOUNTING TECHNIQUES: THE CASE OF THE DEPRECIATION SWITCH-BACK
3 J.Acct. & Econ. 73 (1981)

The accounting literature at present has no fully developed theory which is capable of explaining how firms select accounting techniques. Recently, however, researchers have begun to examine management's incentives to influence the menu of accepted accounting techniques and to choose among available alternatives. [Some commentators] hypothesize that management considers the effects of reported accounting numbers on taxes, regulation, political costs, management compensation, information production costs and restrictions found in bond indenture provisions. These advances differ from most earlier attempts to explain the demand for alternative accounting techniques because the incentives of the parties involved in the process are explicitly considered and the efficiency of the capital markets in processing publicly available information is assumed. . . .

Recent research in economics has modeled the firm as a set of contracts among individuals, which are factors of team production. These factors are all motivated to maximize their own welfare which is in part determined by the performance of the entire team or firm.   However, because the compensation of these individuals is determined differentially, conflicts of interest arise. [Below], I review the potential conflicts between stockholders

---

adoption of APB 16 because that opinion prohibits pooling if a transaction has an earnout. James Freund, *Anatomy of a Merger: Strategies and Techniques for Negotiating Corporate Acquisitions* 205 (1975).

and bondholders and managers as well as the contractual agreements that have been hypothesized to reduce those conflicts. The [contractual] agreements which utilize accounting numbers are examined to yield predictions on the choice of accounting techniques by managers. Specific hypotheses are developed on the effects of a switch from accelerated to straight-line depreciation. These hypotheses are contrasted with two alternative hypotheses which have appeared in the literature, the no effects hypothesis and the mechanistic hypothesis. . . .

The stockholder-bondholder conflict of interests and predictions arising from bond indentures

The potential conflict of interests between stockholders and bondholders has been investigated extensively in the finance literature. In summary, this literature identifies actions that can transfer wealth between bondholders and stockholders. For example, if the manager chooses a higher variance project than anticipated by the bondholders, wealth is transferred from the holders of risky debt to the stockholders. Wealth can also be transferred from the bondholders to the stockholders by reducing planned investments and paying out the saved outlays as a dividend.

Temporarily, it is assumed that managers follow a decision rule to maximize the value of the common shares. If the bondholders have rational expectations concerning the potential wealth transfers resulting from maximizing shareholder wealth, they price the bonds such that they are compensated for the managers' expected actions. . . . [If] the bondholders' loss from a wealth transfer is larger in absolute value than the stockholders' gain, then the stockholders are not indifferent to the form of the contract since the bondholders charge for those expected losses in setting the price of the bonds.[6] In the latter case, the stockholders' wealth is affected by the contractual arrangement and they will seek to reduce the costs associated with the conflict of interests.

[I]ndenture . . . covenants which rely on accounting numbers commonly use minimum working capital and maximum leverage constraints. For example, the firm is not permitted to merge, issue new debt, or pay a dividend if leverage is about the specified maximum and/or working capital is below the stated minimum. If the firm violates the required working capital and leverage constraints, the firm is in 'technical default' which gives the bondholders the discretion to accelerate the maturity of the debt or renegotiate the contract. In addition to using leverage and working capital to constrain dividend payments, the direct dividend constraint defines the maximum dividend which can be paid in any period as a positive function of cumulative earnings and proceeds from new stock issues and a negative

---

[6] Examples of negative sum games would include switching to higher variance but lower present value projects than were expected to be taken. Another example would be dropping planned *positive* net present value projects to increase dividends.

function of cumulative dividends paid and funds used for share repurchase.
. . .

The contractual definitions of accounting variables specified in the covenants use generally accepted accounting principles (GAAP) as a benchmark. Some covenants, particularly in private placements, then make adjustments to GAAP which are designed to reduce management discretion. Aside from these requirements, firms are not prohibited from changing accounting techniques. . . .

Thus, the choice of an accounting method for financial reporting purposes generally affects the contractual constraints in bond covenants. Managers of firms which face these constraints on production, investment and financing decisions have incentives to relax those constraints if the value of the stock or stock options held by the manager can be increased by relaxing the restrictions. Since the empirical work to be performed in this paper concerns the switch from accelerated to straight-line depreciation for financial reporting purposes only, the analysis that follows, while quite general, is framed within that depreciation choice.

The switch to straight-line (SL) from accelerated (ACC) decreases the book value of leverage because it increases both net tangible assets and stockholders' equity. The decreased leverage affects the firm's ability to issue new debt, pay dividends, merge, lease or be construed to be in default through the leverage restriction in bond indentures. The switch also increases the amount of dividends that can be paid as measured by the direct dividends constraint.

Consider a firm which is using ACC for book purposes and which is facing some bond covenant restrictions which are imposing costs given the firm's current opportunity sets. If switching to SL is less costly than the costs of renegotiating the covenants, repurchasing the debt, or operating within the constraints without alteration, then firms have an incentive to change their depreciation method (or any other accounting technique) to relax those constraints.

Ceteris paribus [Other things equal], the potential wealth transfers to the stockholders from the bondholders increase as the firm's leverage rises. Of course, bondholders are aware of this, and price the bonds accordingly. If the management wishes to avoid this reduction in the price the bondholders are willing to pay, they write more restrictive constraints. Kalay presents cross-sectional evidence consistent with the joint hypothesis that firms write more restrictive dividend constraints as leverage increases, and that the cost of deviations from the constraint increases with leverage. He finds that more highly levered firms are closer to their dividend constraint. Thus, *ceteris paribus*, the market value of the common stock increases more as a result of an accounting change for firms with higher leverage and for firms which are closer to their constraints. In addition, the greater the impact of the accounting change on the restrictiveness of the covenants, *ceteris paribus*, the greater the increase in the market value of the equity. This analysis suggests the following hypotheses:

Hypothesis 1. The common stock of firms changing to straight-line depreciation for financial reporting purposes only, experiences positive abnormal performance at the time of the announcement of the change, which is, *ceteris paribus,* an increasing function of the impact of the change in depreciation method on earnings.

Hypothesis 2. The positive abnormal performance of the stockholders' claims at the time of the announcement of a switch to straight-line depreciation for book purposes only, is, *ceteris paribus,* an increasing function of the firm's leverage.

Hypothesis 3. The positive abnormal performance of the common stock at the time of a firm's announcement of a switch to straight-line depreciation for book purposes only, is, *ceteris paribus,* a decreasing function of the firm's inventory of payable funds.

An alternative to relaxing bond covenant constraints by choice of accounting techniques is to renegotiate the bond covenants. Since the owners of publicly placed debt are more diffuse than the holders of private placements, it is likely that renegotiation costs are much higher for public issues. . . . This suggests the following:

Hypothesis 4. The positive abnormal performance of the common stock at the time of a firm's announcement of a switch to straight-line depreciation for book purposes only, is, *ceteris paribus,* greater for firms as the relative proportion of public debt leverage to private debt leverage increases.

The stockholder-manager conflict of interests and a prediction arising from management compensation contracts

In the previous discussion of the stockholder-bondholder conflict of interests, it is assumed that the manager's self-interest is best served by maximizing the market value of stockholders' equity. . . . Conflicts also exist between managers and non-manager equity owners. . . . What is of interest for the topic at hand is . . . whether any of the components of the [management] compensation package gives managers an incentive to change accounting techniques.

One form of compensation observed is incentive plans which determine bonuses as a function of accounting earnings. These plans typically provide that a management compensation committee, which is ineligible to participate in the plans, is authorized by the stockholders to award a total bonus not to exceed an amount which is a positive function of accounting earnings and a negative function of capitalization. . . . [E]arnings often have to be above a minimum, a specified percentage of capitalization, before the manager receives any bonus.

The plans state that the accounting numbers used in the plans must agree with the equivalent numbers in the financial statements, and that the statements must be prepared in accordance with generally accepted accounting principles. The choice of accounting principles within the set of GAAP is not constrained, which may be due to the costs of writing such a contract and the benefits of potentially renegotiating the compensation agreements with the managers through accounting technique changes at a relatively low cost. . . .

The manager's incentive to increase earnings by changing accounting techniques, which arises from these contracts, does not exist in all periods. If accounting earnings, both before and after the change, are below the minimum or above the maximum bounds of the compensation scheme, the change has no impact on compensation paid. In these cases, the manager has an incentive to decrease reported earnings and use the 'saved' earnings in future periods when they can affect his compensation. . . .

[E]mpirical evidence of a suggestive nature exists [on whether managers change accounting method to increase their bonuses]. Zmijewski & Hagerman[a] find evidence that managers choose income increasing techniques more often in firms with accounting based compensation plans than in those firms without them. If managers can *appreciably* affect their bonus by changing to income increasing techniques, abnormal performance of the common stock should be negatively related to the existence of a management compensation plan which is based on accounting net income at the time of the announcement of an unanticipated change. The following hypothesis concerning the switch to SL depreciation is suggested:

> *Hypothesis 5.* The abnormal performance of the common equity of firms switching to straight-line depreciation from accelerated depreciation is, *ceteris paribus*, negatively related to the existence of a management compensation plan which defines management bonuses as a function of accounting income.

Thus, Hypotheses 1 to 5 are derived from the form of bond indenture agreements and management compensation contracts which use accounting numbers to define the rights of the parties in the contracts. . . .

Two alternative hypotheses

Previous research on changes in accounting techniques provides two alternative hypotheses that have consistently appeared in the literature. The two hypotheses are the Mechanistic Hypothesis and the No Effects Hypothesis.

The Mechanistic Hypothesis states that increases (decreases) in earnings necessarily lead to increases (decreases) in the prices of the outstanding claims of the firm regardless of the source of the earnings. Thus, the Mechanistic Hypothesis implies that changes in accounting techniques which increase (decrease) earnings should be associated with increases (decreases)

---

[a] Mark Zmijewski & Robert Hagerman, *An Income Strategy Approach to the Positive Theory of Accounting Standard Setting/Choice,* 3 J.Acct. & Econ. 129 (1981).

in the value of the common stock of the firm. The assumption is that the market is not efficient in processing the information content of publicly available accounting information. The formal statement of the Mechanistic Hypothesis for this study is:

> *Mechanistic Hypothesis.* The common stock of firms changing to straight-line depreciation for reporting purposes only, experience positive abnormal performance at the time of the announcement of the change, which is, *ceteris paribus*, an increasing function of the impact of the change in depreciation methods on earnings. . . .

Another alternative hypothesis is . . . the No Effects Hypothesis. Under the No Effects Hypothesis, it is assumed that there are no real cash flow effects associated with changes in accounting techniques and that the market is efficient with respect to publicly available information. Thus, under the No Effects Hypothesis, changes in accounting techniques [do not affect stock prices]. . . . The No Effects Hypothesis serves as the Null Hypothesis for this paper. . . .

Summary and Interpretation

The results presented in the paper can be summarized as follows:

(i) The average abnormal performance of switch-back firms is negative but insignificantly different from zero in the period immediately surrounding the announcement of the switch. . . .

(iii) The abnormal performance of the switch-back firms . . . is positively related to the unexpected earnings [at the time of the accounting change] and negatively related to leverage over the period day −3 to day +2. . . .

(iv) The abnormal performance of the firms is not systematically related to the existence of a management compensation plan, the impact of the depreciation change on reported earnings, the firm's deviation from its dividend constraint or the size of the firm. . . .

In attempting to interpret the evidence presented, . . . the . . . question to address is why do managers change accounting techniques? This is an especially important question given that the results indicate the market value of the common stock of highly levered firms is adversely impacted. Since the change is voluntary, it is reasonable to assume that someone benefits. Perhaps the managers gain at the expense of the stockholders, but if this is true, the tests used in this paper are not powerful enough to measure the economic significance of the management's gain. . . . Perhaps the market value of the common stock would have fallen more if the change in depreciation methods had not been made because of binding dividend or new debt issue constraints. If this is true, however, either the tests used to measure the deviation from the dividend constraint are not well enough specified to detect closeness to the constraint or the leverage constraint is more important for this sample of firms. What is lacking is a theory of the optimal deviation from the constraint as a function of variables which are endogenous to the firm.

The evidence in this paper concerning abnormal performance may be weak for several reasons. . . . [R]esults which support the hypotheses may not be obtained because of variation in the market's assessed probability of a firm making an accounting change and failure to isolate the period in which market expectations are revised. Second, the effects of other events must be eliminated in order to measure the stock price impact of the accounting change. To the extent that firms changing accounting techniques are not a random selection of firms, the other events may be confounding the results, even though an attempt has been made to control for them by adjusting for the effects of [unexpected] earnings announcements [that coincide with the accounting change] and eliminating firms with other significant announcements. Third, the hypotheses developed may be based on incorrect assumptions about relative costs [of accounting change versus contract renegotiation] which lead to incorrect predictions . . . [of why managers change accounting method]. Fourth, the change in the value of the common stock from accounting changes may be too small . . . [to be measured] using presently available techniques. . . . The evidence in this paper is not conclusive enough to allow a determination of which of these factors contributes to the lack of more definitive results.

Note: Alternative Links Between Accounting Method and Economic Performance

1.   The Holthausen study focuses on whether bond covenants and management compensation plans that are drafted to allow change in accounting method can explain accounting method choices. Other studies have considered additional potential links between accounting choice and economic performance. One such link is the role of governmental regulation. Quite commonly, a regulation is written in terms of financial accounting numbers. Examples include the capital adequacy tests and reserve requirements of federal and state banking and insurance authorities, cost recovery in defense contracts, and most rate setting in public utility regulation. In these situations, one would expect companies to choose accounting standards that respond to the regulatory structure.

For example, a public utility would be expected to seek to use -- at least for rate-setting purposes -- accounting methods that increase the value of the assets in its rate base and decrease the reported return on those assets. Utility regulators, meanwhile, would seek to require the utility to do the opposite -- keep assets out of the rate base, and defer recognizing costs. The accounting methods actually adopted by utilities would reflect a mix of these opposing interests.

2.   An additional potential link between accounting numbers and economic involves concern over political visibility. In some circumstances, high earnings might be politically undesirable. For example, companies in the oil industry might be embarrassed to report high earnings during an oil shortage, or companies in the steel industry might think it politically disadvantageous to report high earnings while lobbying for domestic protection from foreign competition. More recently, pharmaceutical companies might wish to change accounting methods to reduce their reported earnings in the face of political attacks on excess drug industry profits.

3.   On balance, the empirical results from the studies that have examined whether reasons like these can explain why companies choose particular financial accounting methods are consistently and disappointingly less compelling than the logic of the agency approach to accounting choice.[29] Holthausen & Leftwich explain the problem as follows:

> Economic consequence theories are based on contracting and monitoring costs, and those costs place an upper limit on the wealth effect of any accounting choice. Our priors are that accounting choice is not a major determinant of firm values, relative to other decisions a manager makes, such as investment decisions. Likewise, we expect that accounting choice has only a small impact on managers' wealth through compensation plans, although the relative effect is probably larger than for firm values.
>
> If accounting choice has relatively small wealth effects, powerful tests are required to detect economic consequences. . . .   [C]urrent techniques for measuring firm-specific stock price performance are probably not sufficiently powerful to detect [the] hypothesized economic consequences, given that the magnitude of the economic impact of most accounting choices is unlikely to be large relative to the variability of the value of the common equity.[30]

G.   How Are Financial Accounting Standards Set?

The body of theory and empirical evidence examined in the previous sections has important implications for how financial accounting standards should be set. Recently, for example, the Financial Accounting Standards Board has moved toward a policy of eliminating the availability of alternative accounting methods for the same transaction in favor of a single mandatory standard. The Efficient Capital Market Hypothesis suggests that, so long as

---

[29] For a survey, see Robert Holthausen & Richard Leftwich, *The Economic Consequences of Accounting Choice: Implications of Costly Contracting and Monitoring,* 5 J.Acct. & Econ. 77 (1983).

[30] *Id.* at 108-09.

there is sufficient footnote disclosure provided in the financial statements to allow their reconstruction to reflect alternative methods, the imposition of one or another mandatory standard should have no impact on stock price. In contrast, the costly contracting and monitoring approach exemplified by the Holthausen study suggests that imposition of a particular mandatory accounting rule may have a real impact because accounting information is used for purposes where form does affect substance. In sum, there is at least surface conflict over how important it is to set mandatory financial accounting standards at all. The traditional approach to standard setting -- for example, the search for the Platonic ideal of a pooling transaction -- assumes that the standard selected makes a difference because investors accept the accounting results at face value. The ECMH implies that the standard chosen doesn't matter because investors, if given the information to do so, can see through the accounting rule to the cash flow substance underneath it. The costly contracting and monitoring approach suggests that standard selection may matter after all, albeit for reasons very different from those underlying the traditional approach.

In the face of this apparent conflict, it is important to know how financial accounting standards are actually set, and to evaluate, in light of the three conflicting approaches, how they should be set.

1.   The Formal Structure

James Cox
FINANCIAL INFORMATION, ACCOUNTING AND THE LAW
6-12 (1980)

A business' financial statements, the primary source of financial information, are prepared in accordance with an established body of assumptions and standards designed to fulfill the objective of disclosing relevant financial information. This body, called *generally accepted accounting principles* defines the accepted accounting practices of a particular time.[2] These principles, largely established by both private and public

---

[2] A principle or practice of accounting is deemed part of the body of generally accepted accounting principles if there is substantial authoritative support for the principle or practice. Paul Grady, *Inventory of Generally Accepted Accounting Principles for Business Enterprises* 52-53 (AICPA, Acct.Res. Study No. 7, 1965) identifies the bases for such support:

1. In the practices commonly found in business. This does not follow from the mere fact that a practice exists, but from the fact that experience of the business has demonstrated that the practice produces dependable results for the guidance of management and for the information of investors and others.

2. The requirements and views of stock exchanges as leaders in the financial community; similarly the views and opinions of commercial and investment bankers would be entitled to weight.

organizations, also arise from practices in businesses and opinions held by practicing and academic accountants.

The important professional organization for accountants is the American Institute of Certified Public Accountants (AICPA), whose membership primarily comprises accountants performing independent audits of their client's financial statements. In 1938, within the AICPA, the Committee on Accounting Procedures was created with the purpose of promulgating accounting principles. . . . The Committee on Accounting Procedures was the profession's first attempt to institutionalize and therefore regularize the consideration and adoption of accounting standards in the private sector. Over the next 20 years, it issued 51 Accounting Research Bulletins (ARB). . . .

The bulletins were in the form of *recommendations* of acceptable accounting practices for treating a range of unrelated accounting issues. Compliance with these positions, however, was not mandatory. In fact, the Committee, in recommending accounting methods for specific topics, did not list a number of methods deemed included in the generally accepted accounting principles. Accountants could opine that financial statements were in compliance with these principles as long as the method used had some acceptance in practice or theory. Thus, the authority of the Accounting Research Bulletins depended upon the independent accountants' and their clients' broad acceptance of the methods recommended.

Dissatisfaction with the development of the ARBs arose because the Committee did not conduct any research prior to releasing a bulletin but based its decisions on its members' notions of what was desirable. In 1959, as a result of this dissatisfaction, the Accounting Principles Board (APB) was created to replace the Committee on Accounting Procedures.

The APB initially had 18 members (later 21) selected mainly from the large accounting firms with a few from business, academia, or government,

---

3. The regulatory commissions' uniform systems of accounts and accounting rulings exercise a dominant influence on the accounting practices of the industries subject to their jurisdiction. . . .

4. The regulations and accounting opinions of the Securities and Exchange Commission have the controlling authority over reports filed with the Commission. The Commission and its chief accountants have demonstrated a high degree of objectivity, restraint and expertness in dealing with accounting matters. The regulations and opinions issued to date are entitled to acceptance by their merit as well as on the basis of the statutory authority of the Commission.

5. The affirmative opinions of practicing and academic certified public accountants constitute authoritative support for accounting principles or practices. These may be found in oral or written opinions, expert testimony, textbooks and articles.

6. Published opinions by committees of the American Accounting Association and of the American Institute of CPAs.

To the last category must be added the Financial Accounting Standards Board, which as later material will make clear, is currently the leading body in the private sector concerned with the establishment of accounting principles and procedures.

all of whom served in a part-time capacity. The APB had a small, albeit permanent, research staff to provide input on subjects which were under consideration. Small project advisory committees were formed from time to time for specific accounting problems, and, frequently, research reports, called Accounting Research Studies, prepared by leading academicians or practitioners, preceded APB actions. During its existence, the APB issued 31 opinions and 4 statements.

The APB opinions posed the same question as the pronouncements of its predecessor: Could financial statements prepared using an accounting method which differed substantially from that adopted by the APB be viewed as complying with generally accepted accounting principles? The answer, a qualified yes, was not provided by the AICPA until 1964. . . . The use of methods other than those embraced by the APB could . . . qualify as generally accepted accounting principles, provided they had substantial authoritative support, such as "practices commonly found in business," "requirements and views of stock exchanges," "the views of commercial and investment bankers," "regulatory commissions' uniform systems of accounts and accounting rules," "the regulations and accounting opinions of the Securities Exchange Commission," and finally, "affirmative opinions of practicing and academic . . . accountants."

Throughout its existence, the APB encountered a seemingly endless flow of criticism: it produced an insufficient amount of work, it failed to concern itself with broad statements on the objective of financial statements and the underlying principles of accounting, and its opinions fed the ever-present disquiet over the ability of the accounting profession to establish standards adverse to the interest of its clients. Also, there was the concern that the procedures and organization did not insure participation on the APB or its advisory committee by nonaccountants, such as security analysts and financial executives, whose concern for meaningful accounting standards was at least equal to that of the independent public accountants.

In response to such criticism . . ., the APB was disbanded and the Financial Accounting Standards Board (FASB) came into existence in July 1973 as the leading body in the private sector for establishing accounting standards. [The FASB] comprises seven members who are required to sever all ties with their former employers to assure their independence, with a maximum of only four members being certified public accountants drawn from private practice. The FASB receives extensive research and technical support from a substantial permanent staff which is frequently augmented by leading academicians who prepare studies for it in areas of concern. The FASB's procedures for identifying pressing accounting issues, obtaining input necessary for their resolution, and considering the action to be taken are much more systematic than those of the APB.

Marshall Armstrong, THE WORK AND WORKINGS OF THE FINANCIAL ACCOUNTING STANDARDS BOARD
29 Bus.Law. 145, 147-48 (Supp.1974)

The standard setting process begins with the placing of a question on the Board's technical agenda. For advice in this regard, FASB looks to all segments of the economic community, and particularly to the 28-member Financial Accounting Standards Advisory Council which [meets quarterly]. Decisions on adopting agenda items are made by the Board itself. After a topic has been placed on the agenda, a Board member is assigned to prepare with staff assistance, a preliminary definition of the problem and a bibliography of significant literature on the subject.

When the preliminary definition of the problem has been completed and reviewed by the FASB, a task force normally is appointed. Task forces include at least one member of the Board, who serves as Chairman, as well as members of the Advisory Council and other persons who are aware of the responsibilities of preparers and the needs of users of financial statements, or who possess an expertise or viewpoint particularly relevant to the project. The task force is responsible for refining the definition of the problem and its financial accounting and reporting issues, and for preparing a neutral and comprehensive discussion memorandum which outlines alternative solutions to the problem and the arguments and implications relative to each alternative solution. . . . Upon completion of research and preparation of the discussion memorandum, the Board normally will seek the views of all interested parties by holding a public hearing [on the discussion memorandum]. . . .

After the public hearing, the Board will begin its evaluation of the information at hand, and on the basis of this evaluation an exposure draft of a proposed Statement of financial accounting standards will be prepared. . . . The public comment exposure period normally will be 60 days -- after which the Board will review the exposure comments, and if new and persuasive information has been received, it may make revisions in the proposed Statement. When a final draft is completed, an affirmative vote by at least five of the seven members of the Board is required before a Statement of Financial Accounting Standards is issued. . . .

To insure the FASB's financial independence from the accounting profession, the Financial Accounting Foundation (FAF) was established to raise funds from all sectors of the financial community. The nine trustees of the FAF include five public accountants, three representatives from the finance-corporate sector (financial analysts, business executives, bankers, etc.), and one accounting educator. Also, the FAF trustees appoint members to vacancies on the FASB.

Today, Rule 203 of the AICPA Code of Professional Ethics governs the FASB's pronouncements, as well as the effectiveness of the earlier Accounting Research Bulletins and Opinions of the Accounting Principles Board.

Rule 203 -- Accounting Principles. A member shall not express an opinion that financial statements are presented in conformity with generally accepted accounting principles if such statements contain any departure from an accounting principle promulgated by the body designated by [the AICPA] Council to establish such principles which has a material effect on the statements taken as a whole, unless the member can demonstrate that due to unusual circumstances the financial statements would otherwise have been misleading.   In such cases his report must describe the departure, the approximate effects thereof, if practicable, and the reasons why compliance with the principle would result in a misleading statement.

Rule 203, through its requirement that the auditor's opinions "demonstrate that due to unusual circumstances" departure from the accounting method prescribed in official bulletins is necessary, reduces the freedom of accountants and their clients to choose nonofficial accounting methods. . . .

The Public Sector -- The SEC

. . . Among the many governmental regulatory agencies which influence business accounting and reporting practices, the SEC's impact is the most pervasive. Its power is derived from provisions in the acts it enforces; the most important are the Securities Act of 1933 and the Securities Exchange Act of 1934.

The Securities Act requires the registration of a public offering of new securities and the filing of the related financial statements audited by independent public accountants. The SEC is empowered to establish the precise content and form of financial statements filed with it.[8] Implicit in this authority is the power to prescribe the accounting principles and practices to be used in registering securities.

The Securities Exchange Act also confers equal power upon the SEC to regulate the accounting principles and practices used in preparing periodic financial reports such as those required for companies whose shares are traded on national stock exchanges or whose total assets and number of shareholders exceed a certain level. . . .

The SEC has deferred to the private sector as the primary standard setter but continues to guide the form and substance of disclosure of financial information in important ways. Examples include the issuance of Regulation S-X, an extensive, detailed description of the form and content of financial statements required to be filed; the issuance of its Accounting Series Releases (ASR's) dealing with accounting matters not specifically dealt with by any of the private sector's bulletins, opinions, or statements; and beginning in 1975, the issuance of Staff Accounting Bulletins, which do not

---

[8] Section 19(a) of the Securities Exchange Act further confers authority upon the SEC to define accounting terms, the form in which financial information is to be set forth, the items and details to be reflected in financial statements, and the accounting methods to be used in connection with statements subject to the SEC's jurisdiction.

have the official sanction of the SEC, but represent the accounting approach, interpretation, and practices of the staff in administering the disclosure requirements.[10] Occasionally, however, the SEC has prescribed in its ASRs a different accounting method than that established by the private sector.[11]

2.　Choice of Accounting Standards With Efficient Markets

William Beaver, WHAT SHOULD BE THE FASB'S OBJECTIVES?
136 J.Acct. 49 (1973)*

Was the acrimony arising out of the investment tax credit much ado about nothing? Does it matter whether special gains and losses are reported in the ordinary income or in the extraordinary item section? When firms switch from accelerated to straight-line depreciation, what is the effect upon investors? Did the Accounting Principles Board allocate its resources in an appropriate manner? If its priorities needed reordering, where should the emphasis have been shifted? What objectives should be adopted for financial accounting standards? . . . [N]ow is an appropriate time to take stock of the current body of knowledge [concerning market efficiency] and assess its implications for the setting of financial accounting standards. . . . The findings have a direct bearing on the questions raised at the outset and suggest that our traditional views of the role of policy-making bodies, such as the APB, SEC and FASB, may have to be substantially altered. . . . There are at least four major implications.

First. Many reporting issues are trivial and do not warrant an expenditure of FASB resources. The properties of such issues are twofold: (1) There is essentially no difference in cost to the firm of reporting either method. (2) There is essentially no cost to statement users in adjusting from one method to the other. In such cases, there is a simple solution. Report one method, with sufficient footnote disclosure to permit adjustment to the other, and let the market interpret implications of the data for security prices. . . .

Second. The role of financial statement data is essentially a preemptive one -- that is, to prevent abnormal returns accruing to individuals by trading upon inside information. This purpose leads to the following disclosure policy: If there are no additional costs of disclosure to the firm, there is prima facie evidence that the item in question ought to be disclosed. . . .

---

[10] See ASR No. 180 (Nov. 4, 1975).

[11] For a more extensive discussion of the SEC powers over accounting and auditing standards and practice, see James Strother, *The Establishment of Generally Accepted Accounting Principles and Generally Accepted Auditing Standards,* 28 Vand.L.Rev. 201 (1975).

Third. The FASB must reconsider the nature of its traditional concern for the naive investor. If the investor, no matter how naive, is in effect facing a fair game, can he still get harmed? If so, how? The naive investor can still get harmed, but not in the ways traditionally thought. For example, the potential harm is not likely to occur because firms use flow-through v. deferral for accounting for the investment credit. Rather, the harm is more likely to occur because firms are following policies of less than full disclosure and insiders are potentially earning monopoly returns from access to inside information. Harm is also likely to occur when investors assume speculative positions with excessive transactions costs, improper diversification and improper risk levels in the erroneous belief that they will be able to "beat the market" [by analyzing] published accounting information. . . .

Fourth. Accountants must stop acting as if they are the only suppliers of information about the firm. Instead, the FASB should strive to minimize the total cost of providing information to investors. In an efficient market, security prices may be essentially the same under a variety of financial accounting standards, because, if an item is not reported in the financial statements, it may be provided by alternative sources. Under this view . . ., the market uses a broad information set, and the accountant is one -- and only one -- supplier of information. One objective is to provide the information to investors by the most economical means. In order to accomplish this objective, several questions must be addressed: What are the alternative sources of information to financial statements? What are the costs of providing a given piece of information via the alternative source vis-a-vis the financial statements? Most importantly, do financial statement data have a comparative advantage in providing any portion of the total information used by the market, and, if so, what portion?

The nature of the costs has already been alluded to. One set of costs is the "cost" of abnormal returns being earned by insiders because of monopolistic access to information. A second set of costs is excessive information costs. They can occur in two situations:

1. When the accountant fails to report an item that must be conveyed to the investing public through some other, more expensive source.

2. When the FASB requires firms to report an item that has a "value" less than its cost or items that could have been reported through other, less expensive sources of information. . . .

Erroneous interpretations

The implications of market efficiency for accounting are frequently misunderstood. There are at least two common misinterpretations.

The first belief is that, in an efficient market world, there are no reporting issues of substance because of the "all-knowing" efficient market. Taken to its extreme, this error takes the form of asserting that accounting data have no value and hence the certification process is of no value. The efficient market in no way leads to such implications. It may very well be that the publishing of financial statements data is precisely what makes the market as efficient as it is. . . . [M]erely because the market is efficient with respect to published data does not imply that market prices are also efficient with respect to nonpublished information. Disclosure is a substantive issue.

A second erroneous implication is, simply find out what [accounting] method is most highly associated with security prices and report that method in the financial statements. As it stands, it is incorrect for several reasons. One major reason is that such a simplified decision rule fails to consider the costs of providing information. For example, a nonreported method may be less associated with security prices than the reported method because the cost of obtaining the nonreported numbers via alternative sources is too high. Yet such information [could] be provided via financial statements at substantially lower costs [and the numbers reported under the method might strongly correlate with stock prices]. In another context, suppose the nonreported method showed the higher association with security prices; does it follow that the nonreported method should be reported? No, not necessarily. Perhaps the market is obtaining the information at lower cost via the alternative sources.

Note: Incorporating the Costly Contracting Approach into Setting Financial Accounting Standards

While Beaver's recommendations take account of the implications of the Efficient Capital Market Hypothesis for how financial accounting standards should be set, they do not consider the implications of the costly contracting and monitoring approach. For this purpose, we need to take into account the role of self-help. Can the parties themselves deal with the problem of management manipulation of the terms of a bond contract?

Richard Leftwich examined a sample of lending agreements obtained from five major private lenders and the terms of the American Bar Foundation's *Commentaries on Model Debenture Indenture Provisions* (1971). He found that although the agreements generally specified that references to accounting information referred to within the agreement meant accounting information calculated in accordance with GAAP, a substantial number also contractually specified deviations from GAAP. For example, the loan agreements typically mitigated the impact of the accounting method used for acquisitions by prescribing rules that minimized the manipulative potential inherent in both pooling and purchase methods.[31]

---

[31] Richard Leftwich, *Accounting Information in Private Markets: Evidence from Private Lending Agreements,* 58 Acct.Rev. 23 (1983).

When the ability of private parties to contract out of GAAP is taken into account, the implications of the ECMH and the costly contracting and monitoring approach for how financial accounting standards should be set begin to converge.   Beaver suggests choosing standards that facilitate reconstruction by users who have different preferences. Leftwich's analysis reinforces this suggestion by demonstrating that private parties will alter GAAP when necessary to achieve their own purposes.   The more easily financial statements prepared in accordance with GAAP can be reconstructed, the more effective will be the private contracting. Additionally, the Leftwich analysis suggests that GAAP should be set to reflect the needs of those who are not in a position to negotiate directly with the company. Those who can negotiate directly with the company would be able to alter these accounting rules, if they chose.

From the perspective of this synthesis, both the ECMH and the costly contracting and monitoring approach counsel that the critical determinant of financial accounting standards should be reduction in information costs. First, standards should reflect the needs of those users not in a contractual relation with the company. Second, standards should minimize the costs of reconstructing financial statement information by those who need the information in a format different from that specified in the standards. Third, the primary reporting method should be reasonably consistent across users, to reduce the costs to users of reconstructing financial statements that were originally prepared in a wide variety of different formats.[32]

---

[32] For an effort to evaluate the importance of financial accounting standards in light of both the ECMH and the costly contracting and monitoring approach, see Joshua Ronen, *The Dual Role of Accounting: A Financial Economic Perspective,* in *Handbook of Financial Economics* (James Bicksler ed.1979).

Chapter 13 Problems

The table below shows the balance sheets of Adams Corp. and Wood Corp. at December 31, 1994. Assume that Adams acquires Wood by merger, on terms providing that a) holders of Wood debentures will receive similar debentures of Adams; b) preferred stockholders of Wood will receive seven shares of Adams common stock for each share of Wood preferred; and c) common stockholders of Wood will receive one share of Adams common stock for each five shares of Wood common stock. Further assume that the stock of both companies is publicly traded on the over-the-counter market, with Adams common selling at $4-½ bid, $5 asked; Wood preferred trading at $30 bid, $32 asked, and Wood common at ¾ bid, $1 asked.

ADAMS CORPORATION

Assets		Liabilities	
Cash	$ 75,000	Current Liabilities	$ 200,000
U.S. Government Bonds	150,000	Mortg. Note Payable	300,000
Accounts Receivable	175,000	Capital Stock (400,000	
		shs. $1 par common)	400,000
Inventory	450,000	Earned Surplus	600,000
Plant	650,000		
	$1,500,000		**$1,500,000**

WOOD CORPORATION

Assets		Liabilities	
Cash	$ 50,000	Current Liabilities	$ 250,000
		Debentures Payable	300,000
Accounts Receivable	160,000	Preferred Stock	
		(6000 shs. $50 par)	300,000
	200,00	Common stock	
Inventory		(100,000 shs. $5 par)	500,000
Plant	840,000	Earnings (Deficit)	(100,000)
	$1,250,000		**$1,250,000**

1. Prepare post-transaction balance sheets for Adams accounting for the transaction (a) as a pooling and (b) as a purchase. Assume that the carrying value of all assets shown for both Adams and Wood reflect fair market value except for their plants.

2. Which accounting method would Adams consider most favorable, and why?

3. Given the description of the transaction, which accounting method is required by APB 16? How would you alter the transaction to achieve a different result?

CHAPTER 14: MISPRICING OF THE TARGET COMPANY'S STOCK

The motives for acquisitions we have considered thus far fall into two different categories, based on how value additivity is said to be overcome. Some motives contemplate that the gain from the transaction results from improvements in the constituent companies' real economic performance. Operating synergy (Chapter 8), replacement of inefficient management (Chapter 10), and improved management incentives (Chapter 11) fall into this category. Other motives contemplate no change in the companies' economic performance, but only a change in the information the market is provided about that performance. The ability to select a favorable accounting method considered in Chapter 13 falls into this category. In this Chapter we consider the most familiar information-based motive for acquisitions: the market's mispricing of the target company's stock. The acquirer offers to pay a premium for the target not because it can improve the target's operation, but because it believes that the market has undervalued the target's stock, by enough so that the acquirer can pay a substantial premium and still make a positive (or at least a zero) net present value investment. Similarly, the target's management, in opposing a hostile bid, will almost invariably claim that the target's true value exceeds the takeover price. Like the accounting motive for acquisitions, the mispricing claim, whether used to justify or defend against an acquisition, implicates the efficient capital market hypothesis.

Two explanations are possible for the asserted undervaluation, one which is consistent with the semi-strong form of the efficient capital market hypothesis, and one which contradicts it. First, the market might undervalue the target company's stock because it has incomplete information about the target's real value. The acquirer may have private information about value not available to investors generally. This new information explanation is consistent with semi-strong market efficiency. The second explanation, in contrast, asserts that the market systematically undervalues at least certain kinds of companies -- in effect, investors inefficiently discount to the present the target's expected future cash flows. This market inefficiency explanation underlies the familiar managerial lament: the market undervalues our stock.

The two explanations for mispricing share one common characteristic. Unlike acquisition motives that anticipate improved post-transaction economic performance, an information-based motive anticipates only more accurate pricing and therefore better allocation of capital. In first instance, the acquirer's gain from acquiring an underpriced target is merely a wealth transfer from the target's future shareholders (who would otherwise have benefitted from the target's actual cash flows as received) to the acquirer's. The social benefit from information-based acquisitions is limited.

Section A considers the new information variant of the mispricing explanation for acquisitions. Section B considers the market inefficiency explanation.

A.   New Information

The empirical evidence summarized in Chapter 8 -- that acquisitions, on average, increase the market value of the combined companies -- is consistent with a synergistic explanation for acquisitions. An alternative explanation for the higher post-transaction market value of the combined companies' involves new information resulting from the acquisition bid itself. When an acquirer offers a premium for the target, investors revise their estimates of the target's value to reflect this new information. If investors judge that the acquirer's bid is motivated by private information about the target's value, they will increase their own estimates of the target's value; thus, the combined value of acquirer and target will increase.

If the takeover bid succeeds, we can observe investors' post-takeover valuations only for the combined firm. Thus, we cannot determine whether investors have revised their beliefs about the target's stand-alone value, or whether the combined acquirer and target stock market gains come from other sources, such as synergy. Suppose, however, that the acquisition attempt fails? The target remains publicly held, and its stock price offers a guide to investors' revised beliefs about the target's stand-alone value. In the following article, Michael Bradley, Anand Desai & Han Kim seek to distinguish between synergy and new information as explanations for acquisition gains by investigating what happens to the target's stock price following an *unsuccessful* tender offer.

Michael Bradley, Anand Desai & E. Han Kim
THE RATIONALE BEHIND INTERFIRM TENDER OFFERS:
INFORMATION OR SYNERGY
11 J.Fin.Econ. 193 (1983)

There is empirical evidence that corporate acquisitions by tender offers provide significant and positive abnormal returns to the stockholders of both the target and the acquiring firms. This finding is consistent with the hypothesis that tender offers are an attempt by the bidding firm to exploit some specialized resource by gaining control of the target and implementing a higher-valued operating strategy. . . . The specific nature of the [strategy] is not important to this "synergy" theory of tender offers. Rather, the critical aspect of the hypothesis is that the increase in the value of the target shares derives from the transfer of control of the target resources and their [different use] subsequent to the acquisition.

An alternative hypothesis, which is also consistent with the existing empirical evidence, posits that the revaluation of the target shares is due to new information that is generated during the tender offer process. . . . [T]he information hypothesis posits that the revaluation of the target shares is generated by actions of the market or the target managers in response to new information. That is, the positive revaluation does not require a successful acquisition of the target resources. . . .

There is empirical evidence that is consistent with the information hypothesis of tender offers. Dodd & Ruback[a] and Bradley[b] find that firms that are the targets of unsuccessful tender offers experience significant and permanent increases in their share prices. Furthermore, Bradley finds that in unsuccessful tender offers, this permanent revaluation of the target shares exceeds the per share premium of the rejected bid. In other words, after the announcement of the to-be-rejected offer, the market price of the target shares on average is greater than the amount target stockholders would have received had they tendered their shares.

The apparently permanent revaluation of the shares of targets of unsuccessful tender offers seems to contradict the synergy theory of tender offers. The results suggest that it is the announcement of a tender offer per se (or, more precisely, the information contained therein) that precipitates the revaluation of the target shares, not the transfer of control of the target resources that accompanies the execution of a successful offer. That is, the mere announcement of a tender offer, whether successful or not, appears to release positive information regarding the value of the target shares.

While the revaluation of the shares of targets of unsuccessful tender offers is consistent with the information hypothesis, it is not sufficient evidence to reject the synergy hypothesis. The positive returns to unsuccessful targets may be due to the anticipation of a future, higher-valued bid. . . . [If so, then in] those instances where the target stockholders turn out to be correct and a subsequent, higher-valued, successful offer does materialize, they will experience an additional increase in wealth. In those instances where the target stockholders turn out to be incorrect and a subsequent successful bid fails to materialize, the price of the target shares will gradually fall back to the pre-offer level, as the uncertainty about the [likelihood of a] subsequent bid is resolved over time.

In contrast, the information hypothesis states that it is the information contained in the tender offer that generates the positive revaluation of the target shares. Since there is no reason to expect that the positive information will vanish simply because there is no subsequent bid, the information hypothesis does not predict that the shares of targets that receive no subsequent bid will fall back to their pre-offer level.

We test the competing implications of the synergy and information hypotheses by examining the returns realized by the stockholders of firms that are the targets of unsuccessful tender offers. The unsuccessful targets are separated into two groups: those that became the targets of a subsequent successful bid and those that did not. Consistent with previous research, we

---

[a] Peter Dodd & Richard Ruback, *Tender Offers and Stockholder Returns*, 5 J.Fin.Econ. 351 (1977).

[b] Michael Bradley, *Interfirm Tender Offers and the Market for Corporate Control*, 53 J.Bus. 345 (1980).

find that target stockholders realize a significant positive return on the announcement of a tender offer and the return is not dissipated subsequent to the rejection of the offer by the target shareholders. However, closer examination reveals that this revaluation is due primarily to the emergence of and/or the anticipation of another acquisition bid. The share prices of the target firms that are not targets of subsequent, successful acquisition attempts within five years of an unsuccessful offer fall back to their pre-offer level. The share prices of those targets that receive a successful subsequent bid experience an additional significant positive revaluation.

The evidence suggests that a *permanent* revaluation of the target shares requires that the target resources be combined with those of an acquiring firm. That is, the gains to the stockholders of unsuccessful targets stem from the anticipation of a future successful acquisition and not simply from the revelation of new information regarding the "true" value of the target resources. On the basis of these findings we conclude that the synergy hypothesis is more consistent with the evidence than the information hypothesis. . . .

Sample characteristics

The empirical tests of this paper are based on the returns realized by the stockholders of firms that either received or made an unsuccessful, control-oriented tender offer during the period 1963-1980. We define a control-oriented tender offer as one in which the bidding firm holds less than 70% of the target shares outstanding and is attempting to increase its holdings by a least 15%. We classify a tender offer as being successful if the bidding firm increases its holding of the target shares by 15% or more.

The primary data base of this study consists of 697 interfirm tender offers that were made during the period October 1958 to December 1980 where either the target or bidding firm was listed on either the NYSE or AMEX at the time of the offer. . . . The primary data base contains 371 unique target firms that received one or more control-oriented offers, [of which 112 both] . . . received an unsuccessful, first-time control-oriented offer, [and had] CRSP data available. . . .

The returns to the shares of targets of unsuccessful tender offers

. . . To examine the impact of an unsuccessful offer on the wealth of the target stockholders, we perform a Cumulative Abnormal Return (CAR) analysis on the shares of the firms in the sample. For each firm in the sample, we calculate monthly cum-dividend stock returns for 72 months prior to the announcement of the initial offer through 60 months thereafter. . . . The CAR analyses are based on a monthly time-frame because we are interested in the long-term effects of a unsuccessful tender offer, i.e., the post-offer price behavior of the target shares over the next five years.

In event time, month 0 is the announcement month. Thus, event time runs from −72 to +60. Data from the event months −72 to −13 are used to estimate the parameters of the market model.[c]

Table 14-1 reports the Abnormal Returns (AR) and the Cumulative Abnormal Returns (CAR) starting in month -6 for three different portfolios of unsuccessful target firms: the entire sample of unsuccessful targets (columns 3 and 4); the subsample of firms that are subsequently taken over within five years following the end of an unsuccessful tender offer (columns 6 and 7); and the subsample of firms that are not taken over within the same five-year period. The CAR's in Table 14-1 are plotted in Figure 14-1 and are summarized for various holding periods in Table 14-2.

Table 14-1
Percentage Abnormal Returns (AR) and Cumulative Abnormal Returns (CAR) to Targets of Unsuccessful Takeover Bids (1963-1980)

Event month	Total sample			Subsequently taken over			Not taken over		
	N	AR	CAR	N	AR	CAR	N	AR	CAR
−6	112	−0.95	−0.95	86	−0.92	−0.92	26	−1.05	−1.05
. . .									
−3	112	−0.13	−1.41	86	−0.41	−0.76	26	0.80	−3.57
−2	112	−0.32	−1.74	86	−0.43	−1.19	26	0.03	−3.53
−1	112	3.56	1.83	86	2.99	1.80	26	5.46	1.93
0	112	35.55	37.38	86	39.06	40.86	26	23.94	25.87
1	111	1.09	38.47	85	4.25	45.10	26	−9.24	16.63
2	108	−0.80	37.66	82	0.02	45.13	26	−3.41	13.22
3	96	−0.73	36.93	70	−0.66	44.47	26	−0.93	12.30
. . .									
6	70	0.784	35.84	45	0.61	44.74	25	1.10	8.37
. . .									
12	50	1.84	40.42	27	4.86	55.73	23	−1.71	3.43
. . .									
24	36	−1.38	39.15	13	0.45	58.99	23	−2.41	−1.60
. . .									
36	30	−1.55	35.04	11	−1.59	61.38	19	−1.53	−9.8
. . .									
48	24	0.62	47.93	10	−0.03	81.69	14	1.08	−1.51
. . .									
60	23	2.96	40.93	9	6.52	68.80	14	0.67	−4.6
Std. error of monthly % abnormal return	0.971			1.101			1.952		

Consistent with [prior studies], the data show that target shareholders, on average, realize significant positive abnormal returns surrounding the

---

[c] The authors used the standard market model set out in Chapter 6. Eds.

month of the announcement of a tender offer. The AR and CAR for the total sample of unsuccessful targets (columns 3 and 4 in Table 14-1 and the dotted line in Figure 14-1) show a positive revaluation of the target shares which does not dissipate subsequent to the rejection of the offer by the target shareholders. As reported in Table 14-2, the percentage CAR statistic from one month before the announcement of the offer through six months thereafter (-1 to $+6$) is 37.57 with a t-statistic of 11.61. These results for the total sample suggest that it is the announcement of a tender offer per se (or, more precisely, the information contained therein) that precipitates the revaluation of the target shares, not necessarily the transfer of control of the target resources that accompanies the execution of a successful offer. In other words, while the acquisition of a target by a bidding firm may be sufficient to effect a revaluation of the target resources, it does not appear to be a necessary condition.

Figure 14-1
Cumulative Abnormal Returns to Unsuccessful
Target Firms (1963-1980)

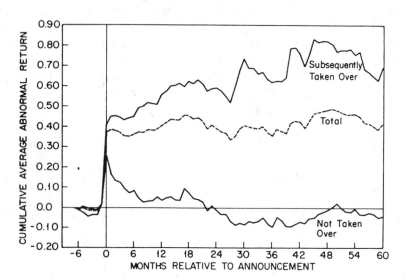

Table 14-2
Percentage Cumulative Abnormal Returns
for Unsuccessful Targets (1963-1980)
(*t*-statistics in parenthesis)*

Event time period (months)	Total sample (N=112)	Subsequently taken over (N=86)	Not taken over (N=26)
−1 to 0	39.29 (28.64)	42.05 (27.03)	29.40 (10.66)
−1 to +1	40.20 (23.93)	46.30 (24.30)	20.16 (5.97)
−1 to +6	37.57 (13.69)	45.03 (14.76)	11.19 (2.16)
−1 to +12	42.15 (11.61)	56.92 (13.83)	6.96 (0.95)
−1 to +24	40.89 (8.27)	60.18 (10.73	1.93 (0.19)
−1 to +48	42.66 (6.22)	69.99 (9.00)	−1.07 (0.08)
+1 to +12	3.04 (0.90)	15.63 (4.10)	−22.44 (3.32)
+1 to +24	1.78 (0.37)	17.35 (3.22)	−27.47 (2.87)
Std. error of monthly abnormal return	0.97	1.10	1.95

* The *t*-statistics is this table are based on the assumption of serially uncorrelated standard errors of the monthly abnormal returns to the indicated portfolio.

As discussed earlier, however, in an informationally efficient capital market, the post-expiration price of unsuccessful target shares will reflect an unbiased estimate of the probability that the firm will receive a subsequent higher-valued acquisition bid. We test this hypothesis by dividing the sample of unsuccessful offers into two groups. The first group consists of those firms that received a subsequent successful acquisition bid within five years following the end of an unsuccessful tender offer. The second group consists of those firms that received no subsequent successful acquisition bid either within the same five-year period or before December 1981 (the end of the CRSP data base). The Abnormal Returns (AR) and the Cumulative Abnormal Returns (CAR) to these two subsamples are also reported in Tables 14-1 and 14-2 and Figure 14-1. . . .

The abnormal returns to the 86 firms in the "subsequently taken over" subsample show a further positive revaluation over the one-year period *following* the announcement of an unsuccessful offer. The CAR from +1 to +12 is 15.3% with a t-statistic of 4.10; and the two year CAR from +1 to +24 is 17.34% with a t-statistic of 3.22.

In contrast, the CAR to the 26 firms in the "not taken over" sample is negative over the one-year period *following* the announcement of an unsuccessful offer. The one-year CAR from +1 to +12 is −22.44% with a t-statistic of −3.32; and the two year CAR from +1 to +24 is −27.47% with a t-statistic of −2.87. Further more, the CAR from −1 to +48 is −1.07% with a t-statistic of −0.08. This shows that whatever abnormal gains the target shareholders realized with the announcement of the offer are completely wiped out over the ensuing two-year period.

The striking contrast between the returns to the shares of targets that are subsequently taken over and those that are not suggests an obvious interpretation of unsuccessful tender offer events. The announcement of a tender offer causes an immediate increase in the value of the target shares. If the target stockholders believe that the present value of an expected future acquisition bid is greater than the value of the current bid, they will reject the offer. If a subsequent bid does materialize, they realize a greater positive abnormal return. If, however, another bid does not materialize, the entire positive abnormal returns earned from the announcement of the initial offer are dissipated over the following two years.

These results are consistent with the hypothesis that a successful acquisition (change in control) of the target resources is required in order to effect a permanent positive revaluation of the target shares. That is, the revaluation requires some specialized resource that is not possessed by the target firm. Since according to the information hypothesis the revaluation does not require a successful acquisition, the synergy hypothesis appears to be more consistent with the evidence than the information hypothesis. . . .

Summary and conclusions

In this paper we attempt to provide evidence that discriminates between the information and synergy hypotheses of tender offers. Both hypotheses predict that a successful tender offer will have a positive impact on the wealth of the target firm's stockholders. Thus, both are consistent with the empirical evidence documented in the literature on the returns to the stockholders of targets of *successful* offers. However, the two hypotheses have contradictory predictions concerning the returns to the stockholders of *unsuccessful* tender offers.

The information hypothesis assumes that the rationale behind interfirm tender offers is the bidding firm's discovery of undervalued or underutilized assets owned by the target firm. Moreover, the hypothesis assumes that this new information becomes a public good subsequent to the announcement of the offer and, thus, exploiting the information does not require a specialized resource. Therefore, the hypothesis predicts that the target stockholders will realize a significant positive abnormal return with the announcement of a tender offer and that the return will not dissipate even if the offer is rejected by the target shareholders. In contrast, the synergy hypothesis predicts that target stockholders will experience an increase in wealth only if control of their firm is transferred to another firm. Thus, the hypothesis predicts that the stockholders of targets of unsuccessful tender offers will not realize a permanent increase in wealth.

Consistent with the information hypothesis, we find that target stockholders, on average, realize a significant positive abnormal return with the announcement of an offer and that these returns do not dissipate subsequent to the rejection of the offer. However, in contrast to this hypothesis, we find that the revaluation is due primarily to the anticipation of a future successful acquisition bid. The entire abnormal returns to the shareholders of the target firms that are not subsequently taken over within five years of an unsuccessful offer dissipate within two years of the initial unsuccessful bid. The shareholders of those targets that are subsequently taken over experience an additional positive and significant abnormal return.

The evidence suggests that a *permanent* revaluation of the target shares requires the combination of the target resources with those of an acquiring firm. That is, the gains to the target stockholders stem from a synergy effect and not simply the revelation of new information regarding the "true" value of the target resources. On the basis of these findings we conclude that the synergy hypothesis is a better description of the nature of tender offers than the information hypothesis.

Note: Additional Empirical Evidence

More recent empirical studies are consistent with the proposition that new but private information held by the acquiring company is an unlikely motive for acquisitions. Fabozzi, Ferri, Fabozzi & Tucker replicate the Bradley, Desai & Kim study but with a more carefully selected and more recent sample: 21 target companies that were the object of failed tender offers occurring between 1977 and 1983 (over half occurring after 1979) where the target received no other bid during the 12 months following the offer's withdrawal.[1] The results are consistent with the basic conclusion: An offer conveys no new information about the stand-alone value of the target company; all offer-related returns disappear when the prospect of an offer disappears. The Fabozzi study results, however, reflect a more

---

[1] Frank Fabozzi, Michael Ferri, T. Dessa Fabozzi & Julia Tucker, *A Note on Unsuccessful Tender Offers and Stockholder Returns* 43 J.Fin. 1275 (1988). Recall that the Bradley, Desai & Kim sample was drawn from the 1966-1980 period, with most failed offers occurring before 1974.

informationally efficient market than do those of Bradley, Desai & Kim. The Bradley study found that a portion of the gains associated with the offer's announcement persisted for up to two years after the offer's withdrawal. In contrast, the Fabozzi study reports that all announcement associated target company gains disappear by the time of the withdrawal of the offer, with average abnormal returns in the year after withdrawal staying close to zero. The Fabozzi study explains the difference in the persistence of post-withdrawal gains in the two studies by reference to the particular reasons why the offers in their study failed. The Bradley study explains the lingering post-withdrawal gains as reflecting the market's estimate of the likelihood of a future offer. Fabozzi et al. examined the actual causes of withdrawal of offers in their sample, finding that "most offers fail because of either vigorous and effective opposition by the target's management or intervention by regulatory agencies. Because of such strong barriers to a takeover, investors would not expect other bidders to step forward soon. Hence, when the offers are terminated, no offer-related gain remains and the target shareholders quickly revert to their pre-offer levels.[2] . . . Note that this explanation necessarily assumes that an offer's failure reveals something special about the particular target company. Over the Fabozzi sample period, 83% of all tender offers were successful.[3] For the prospect of a future offer to entirely disappear, when the initial offer fails, the successful defense must reveal that the target can repeat its success should another offer appear.

John Pound provides additional empirical evidence for the proposition that acquisitions are not motivated by private information concerning the target company's "real" value using a very different methodology.[4] While the Bradley and Fabozzi studies sought evidence of the information content of an acquisition bid in the performance of the target's stock following the bid's withdrawal, Pound instead looked at the impact of the bid's initial announcement on financial analysts' estimate of the target's future earnings. Pound reasons that if the bidder's motivation was to capitalize on a better estimate of the target's stand-alone value, the fact of the bid should cause analysts to increase their earnings predictions of the target as an independent entity. Using a compilation of analysts' earnings predictions for a sample of the 94 target companies between 1979 and 1984 which were included in the compilation, Pound found that analysts did not increase their estimates of the target's future earnings as a result of a takeover bid. Thus, the fact of a bid appeared to convey, at least to this class of market professionals, no new information concerning the target's future stand-alone earnings. Interestingly, analysts did revise their earnings predictions downwards for

---

[2] *Id.* at 1282.

[3] *Id.* at 1276.

[4] John Pound, *The Information Effects of Takeover Effects and Resistance*, 22 J.Fin.Econ. 207 (1988).

those target companies that resisted an offer, apparently reflecting the belief that earnings would decline if the company's resistance was successful.

B.   Market Inefficiency: Discount Theories of Acquisitions.

The most familiar response of a target company's management to an unwanted takeover bid strikes directly at the bidder's claim that the offered price represents a premium and at the empirical claim that acquisitions result in an increase in the combined value of the bidder and target companies. Management argues that because the market undervalues the target company's stock, the premium is illusory; while higher than market price, the bid is lower than the stock's "real value." The transaction results only in a more accurate price, not an increase in value.

The typical academic response to the claim that the market "discounts" the target company's real value is scornful, conditioned in part by the routine incantation by target companies' investment bankers that any unwanted offer is inadequate, and in part because of a belief in market efficiency. Yet there is striking empirical evidence of the existence of such market discounts in the persistent discounting of the prices of shares in closed-end investment funds from their net asset values.[5] These investment companies issue publicly traded shares which are quoted in national securities exchange. The assets of many closed-end funds consist entirely of portfolios of publicly-traded, exchange listed stocks. The puzzle is that for periods of five years or more, many seasoned closed-end funds trade at discounts of 20% or more,[6] despite the fact that their net asset values and the resulting discounts can be measured exactly and are regularly reported in the financial press.

The existence of these discounts is treated as an "anomaly" by financial economists,[7] an exception to the market efficiency dictated general rule that the market price of a company's stock accurately reflects the value of its underlying assets. But one might just as readily argue that the label of anomaly is misplaced. Typically the value of a company's underlying assets cannot be directly observed; the asserted equivalence is driven more by theory than by data. In the one case where asset value can be directly observed -- closed-end funds -- discounts appear. Which is the anomaly? To be sure, target management claims of market undervaluation are self-serving, but they cannot be dismissed as only self-serving.

---

[5] Seth Anderson & Jeffrey Born, *Closed-End Investment Companies: Issues and Answers* (1992), provide an excellent review of the closed-end fund phenomenon and the related literature.

[6] Reinier Kraakman, *Taking Discounts Seriously: The Implications of "Discounted" Share Prices as an Acquisition Motive*, 88 Colum.L.Rev. 891, 903 (1988) (excerpted below).

[7] See, e.g., Burton Malkiel, *The Valuation of Closed-End Investment-Company Shares*, 32 J.Fin. 847, 847 (1977); Rex Thompson, *The Informational Context of Discounts and Premiums on Closed-End Fund Shares*, 6 J.Fin.Econ. 151, 151-52 (1978).

In the following article, Reinier Kraakman develops the case for market inefficiency as an acquisition motive.

Reinier Kraakman
TAKING DISCOUNTS SERIOUSLY: THE IMPLICATIONS OF "DISCOUNTED" SHARE PRICES AS AN ACQUISITION MOTIVE,
88 Colum.L.Rev. 891 (1988)

Assume that the Acme Oil Company has 100,000 shares of stock trading at $10 per share, no debt, and a proven oil well as its only asset; how much should an identical firm pay to acquire Acme's oil well? Businessmen might fail the quiz, but finance students would probably answer: "Not more than $1,000,000 ($10 x 100,000), excluding synergy gains or tax savings."

This answer echoes a common presumption in the finance literature that informed securities prices credibly estimate the underlying value of corporate assets. . . . As the Acme hypothetical suggests, the presumption that share prices fully value corporate assets carries a basic implication for acquisition premia. If share prices already reflect the value of targets' assets, then takeover premia, which now average over 50% of prebid share prices, must reflect something else of value that bidders bring to acquisitions: for example, better management or synergy gains. An astute acquirer would never pay $1,500,000 for Acme's shares unless it could earn at least $500,000, on a present value basis, more than what Acme already expects to earn. By contrast, on the view that share prices may discount asset values, takeover premia have an alternative source in the *existing* value of targets' assets. Acme's acquirer might pay $1,500,000 simply because Acme's oil well was reliably appraised at, say, $1,700,000. In this case, the "premium" received by Acme's shareholders might be more accurately described as a recaptured discount.

The discount claim conforms to an intuition, deeply rooted in corporate law and business practice, that share prices often diverge from asset values.[4]

Discount Hypotheses

True discount hypotheses rely on neither private information nor a traditional inquiry into how acquirers might extract larger net cash flows from target assets. The discount claim assumes that acquisition premia reflect the existing value of target assets, a value that may be much higher than the pre-bid market value of target shares. A discount hypothesis must explain why these values differ. . . .

---

[4] See, e.g., Smith v. Van Gorkom, 448 A.2d 858, 875-76 (Del.1985) (large premium, or spread between offer price and market price, may still undervalue corporate assets). . . .

The . . . market [discount] hypothesis fits [un]easily with standard accounts of the securities market. In this view, share prices may discount asset values for reasons endogenous to the formation of market prices. Financial economics conventionally assumes that share prices are best estimates, given available information, of the present value of expected corporate cash flows available for distribution to shareholders. Thus, share prices should fully capitalize the value of corporate assets in the hands of existing managers. In real markets, this assumption is an approximation; it is unlikely to be either precisely correct or, given the sensitivity of share prices to new information, wholly misguided. It is a very good approximation in the standard view. By contrast, the market hypothesis asserts that discounts arise because share prices are sometimes very poor estimates of the expected value of corporate assets.

Modern objections to identifying share prices with asset values typically fall into two classes. The first class includes "valuation" challenges that question whether a single valuation model can apply across the markets for shares and firms or within the share market itself. Even if traders in both the asset and share markets value corporate assets similarly, share prices might nonetheless discount asset values simply because assets and shares differ in ways that matter to traders.[23]

The second and more prominent class of objections to equating share prices with asset values challenges the price setting role of informed traders. Thus, there is a growing theoretical literature on "mispricing" behavior, which argues that uninformed traders may introduce persistent biases or cumulative noise into share prices or that speculative trading might lead to positive or negative price "bubbles".[26] Large-scale noise trading -- arising from misconceived strategies, erroneous valuation assumptions, fashion and fads, or simple pleasure in trading -- might distort share prices and generate discounts or premia through the sheer pressure of trading. In addition, some commentators suggest that noise trading further distorts share prices by encouraging informed traders to speculate on noise and by imposing "noise trader risk" on all traders in a noisy market. Finally, noise theorists find evidence of mispricing in the long-term price behavior of both individual firms and the entire market.[a]

---

[23] Professors Louis Lowenstein and Martin Shubik vigorously urge this point as part of their broader advocacy of the market hypothesis. See, e.g., Louis Lowenstein, *Pruning Deadwood in Hostile Takeovers: A Proposal for Legislation*, 83 Colum.L.Rev. 294 (1983); Martin Shubik, *Corporate Control, Efficient Markets, The Public Good, and Economic Theory and Advice*, in *Knights, Raiders and Targets: The Impact of the Hostile Takeover* 31 (John Coffee, Louis Lowenstein, Susan Rose-Ackerman eds.1988).

[26] E.g., Fisher Black, *Noise*, 41 J.Fin. 529 (1986) (cumulative noise in price following uninformed trading); Oliver Blanchard & Mark Watson, *Bubbles, Rational Expectations, and Financial Markets*, in *Crises in Economic and Financial Structure* 295-315 (Paul Wachtel ed.1982) (modeling the formation of "rational" bubbles); Jean Tirole, *On the Possibility of Speculation Under Rational Expectations*, 59 Econometrica 1162 (1982) (same).

[a] The noise trader model is set out in Chapter 5. Eds.

For present purposes, however, the important point does not involve a particular model of noisy prices, but rather the uncertainty, generated by a wide range of recent research, about the extent and persistence of mispricing behavior. Few observers would assert that mispricing never occurs, just as few would deny that share prices rapidly reflect information bearing on future corporate prospects. What remains uncertain is how effectively share prices estimate the full present value of corporate cash flows, as distinct from predicting near-term share prices, and how large residual mispricing effects are likely to be. The market hypothesis simply asserts that recurrent discrepancies between share prices and asset values can explain major portions of at least some acquisition premia.

The Case for Discounts

Market discounts must satisfy three conditions to be meaningful. First, potential acquirers and market professionals must be able to form reliable asset or break up values for the firm "as is"; that is, as its component assets are already managed and deployed. Asset values in this sense are particularly credible when assets can be separated from the functions of top management. Thus, natural resources or established corporate divisions may lend themselves to reliable valuation, while start-up projects or undeveloped investment opportunities might be impossible to value with confidence. Second, share prices must fall significantly below asset values. And third, potential acquirers must accept appraisals within the consensus range as useful -- perhaps as minimal -- estimates of what target assets will be worth to themselves and competing bidders.

Although these conditions are difficult to test, the case for discounts is nonetheless persuasive. Certain specialized firms that hold easily priced assets provide direct evidence of discounting. In addition, pervasive discounting can explain much recent acquisition behavior, including breakup acquisitions, management buyouts, and the sheer size of takeover premia. Finally, support for discounts can be found in many forms of corporate restructuring, including the wave of share repurchases and recapitalizations that swept American corporations during the mid 1980s.

Discounts on Specialized Firms

Specialized firms whose shares clearly trade below the value of their assets provide direct evidence of discounting. Because these firms hold fungible assets that trade in separate markets and require little active management, even casual observers can locate discounts by comparing share prices with asset values. The closed-end investment fund is the best example of such a firm, and discounts on closed-end funds have long been viewed as important anomalies by financial economists. Yet discounts appear to be common among holding companies and natural resource companies, which are also firms that possess easily accessible and seemingly reliable asset values. Thus, even though reliable appraisals are not readily available for most firms, the suggestion is clear: If discounts appear wherever we are able to detect them, we have good reason to suspect that they may occur elsewhere. . . .

Although there have been numerous investigations of discounts on closed-end funds, none has satisfactorily accounted for their origins. Discounts are certainly not due to misinformation about the value of fund assets, nor are they attributable to management expenses or trading costs, which are generally modest. Tax liabilities may explain some discounting behavior, but even this is uncertain.[41] Thus, the larger portion of the variance in discounts is fair game for informed conjecture. . . .

Regardless of the origins of discounts, however, the market demonstrates a rational if uneven response to the existence of large discounts. Discounts rapidly disappear when closed-end funds announce plans to liquidate or merge with mutual funds.[46] Further, funds with larger discounts are more likely to liquidate or "open" than those with smaller discounts, whether openings occur on management's initiative or in response to threats of proxy contests or takeovers. . . .

For present purposes, the key issue is how far discounting behavior extends beyond closed-end funds. Here, there is direct evidence for at least two categories of firms. The first includes holding companies with large investments in marketable securities. Two familiar examples from the late 1970s, Kaiser Industries and the American Manufacturing Company, suggest that these firms behave much like closed-end funds.[50] At least in the case of Kaiser Industries, moreover, the announcement of a liquidation and spin-off plan immediately raised the share value of the parent company and eventually eliminated any discount, just as the analysis of closed-end funds would suggest.[b]

The other category of firms that are frequently cited as examples of discounting are natural resource companies. For much of the past decade, oil and timber stocks have traded at less than half of industry appraisal values

---

[41] Because investors are taxed directly when funds realize capital gains, discounts might arise form tax liability on unrealized capital gains. Professor Malkiel found that unrealized capital gains and distribution policy were among the few variables that correlated with discount levels. Even so, they "explain only a small part of the discounts that exist." Burton Malkiel, *The Valuation of Closed-End Investment Company Shares*, 32 J.Fin. 847, 857 (1977). . . .

[46] Gregory Brauer, *"Open-Ending" Closed-End Funds*, 13 J.Fin.Econ. 491, 503-06 (1984).

[50] More recent examples include Chris-Craft Industries, a holding company with a large stake in Warner Communications, and the Seagram Company Ltd., which currently holds 22.7% of E.I. DuPont de Nemours and Co. Chris-Craft, in particular, has traded at prices below the pro rata market value of its holdings in Warner throughout much of 1988, although it holds significant broadcasting assets in addition to stock holdings. See J. Tinker, *Morgan Stanley Research Comment* (Feb. 10, 1988).

[b] See Chapter 17 for an analysis of the Kaiser Industries liquidation. Eds.

of their holdings. Even allowing for appraisal errors, such dramatic numbers are difficult to dismiss. They are especially hard to ignore for the oil industry, which witnessed numerous major acquisitions during the same period and accounted for 26% of all acquisition activity between 1981 and 1984.[55] In addition, Professor Jensen has argued, recent-event studies strongly suggest that discounts in the oil industry may have been linked to investor disapproval of corporate investments in costly exploration and development projects. . . .

Acquisition Behavior

Given a basic presumption in favor of discounts, the discount claim becomes an intuitively attractive explanation over a broad spectrum of corporate activity. In particular, it accords well with at least two aspects of acquisition behavior where traditional hypotheses falter. One is the sheer size of premia in hostile acquisitions and management buyouts. The other is the recent prominence of break up acquisitions that exploit perceived differences between the share prices and asset values of conglomerate firms.

Consider first the size of acquisition premia. In recent years, premia have averaged about 50% of share value in management buyouts and 50% or more in hostile acquisitions. Most studies suggest that acquisitions of all kinds are approximately zero net present value transactions on average [for acquirers]. Thus, assuming that most acquirers reasonably expect to recover their premia costs, the obvious question is: How can they be so sure? Apart from possible tax gains, which few commentators believe to dominate premia, we are left to choose among market discounts and the usual suspects including the displacement of inefficient management, synergy gains, or the exploitation of private information. The fact that these various sources of premia and gain are not mutually exclusive makes this choice more difficult. Yet we can learn which sources of gain dominate in which transactions and, in particular, whether discounts yield significant gains at all. Absent better information, our only handle is the plausibility of the assumptions underlying each source of gain.

An evaluation of these assumptions shows the superiority of the discount claim. Large premia are easily explained if reliable appraisals of large firms can reveal the existence of market discounts. Under these circumstances, acquirers can calculate discounts with standard appraisal techniques and thereby learn, within the limits of appraisal error, whether the bulk of their premia costs are a simple purchase of assets at their existing values. That is, acquirers learn that their premia costs largely pay for assets that are worth the price if they merely continue to perform as they have in the past. By contrast, the synergy and better management hypotheses require acquirers to

---

[55] Michael Jensen, *The Takeover Controversy: Analysis and Evidence* in *Knights, Raiders and Targets: The Impact of the Hostile Takeover* 314, 317 (John Coffee, Louis Lowenstein & Susan Rose-Ackerman, eds.1988).

value novel and still hypothetical changes in targets' operating assets, while the information hypothesis demands that acquirers routinely discover dramatic good news relative to market expectation about targets.

This comparison becomes more pointed for particular transactions. In the hostile bids for large firms, for example, a purely private information theory is generally weak. Acquirers lack any unique informational edge over the market, and the incumbent managers, who know their firms best, have every incentive to reduce takeover risks by keeping the market informed.

In addition, informational disabilities undermine efforts to explain hostile bids solely in terms of synergy or management gains. Without detailed information about operating assets, novel management or synergy strategies must often be very obvious or very large to be valued -- or even formulated -- with confidence before control changes hands. For example, risk-neutral acquirers who are only 50% certain of realizing operational gains from hostile bids must expect gains exceeding 100% of target pre-bid market value to justify 50% premia. Thus, even when operating changes might yield generous returns, acquirers who wish to rely on these changes to justify 50% premia may face an exceptionally difficult challenge. Either they must be able to value hypothetical changes reliably, or they must discover opportunities so lucrative that the uncertainties of planning and valuing wholesale changes in target assets simply cease to matter.

The key intuition, then, turns on the informational constraints confronting hostile acquirers. Generally, these acquirers need much less information to evaluate discounts than to appraise opportunities for management of synergy gains. Rough appraisals of the value of assets "as is" may be generated from aggregate financial data, reporting documents, analyst reports, and general familiarity with an industry. By contrast, valuing operational changes often requires familiarity with existing projects that can only come from close study and internal records. The exchanges of information and warranties that characterize friendly acquisitions highlight the uncertainties facing hostile acquirers.[69]

Many commentators implicitly recognize the difficulty of valuing hypothetical changes by surmising that the cost of searching for opportunities to extract operating gains is a principal determinant of takeover activity.[70]

---

[69] See James Freund, *Anatomy of a Merger: Strategies and Techniques for Negotiating Corporate Acquisitions* (1975) (discussing friendly acquisitions). Apart from this informational point, moreover, operational accounts of takeover premia also face other anomalies. For example, the better management hypothesis runs afoul of survey data suggesting that acquirers prefer well-managed targets. See John Coffee, *Regulating the Market for Corporate Control: A Critical Assessment of the Tender Offer's Role in Corporate Governance*, 84 Colum.L.Rev. 1145, 1212 (1984). In addition, neither management efficiencies nor synergy gains can easily explain why tender offers by controlling shareholders (who lack obvious synergy prospects) should reward target shareholders as generously as offers from outsiders.

[70] See, e.g., Frank Easterbrook & Daniel Fischel, *The Proper Role of a Target's Management in Responding to a Tender Offer*, 94 Harv.Rev. 1161 (1981); Alan Schwartz,

But this assumption encounters institutional difficulties. Casual evidence of several kinds suggests that acquirers rely heavily upon routine appraisals of the existing value of target assets rather than farsighted assessments of their potential value.[71]. . .

Conversion Behavior

In addition to acquisitions behavior, the discount claim can also comfortably accommodate a broad class of what might be termed "conversion behavior." The most prominent examples are shareholder distributions financed by debt of the sale of assets, which managers often initiate to raise share prices. Since virtually any form of discounting would imply that these redemptions must indeed raise share prices, their success lends support to the discount claim.

Consider first the intuitive relationship between discounts and distributions to shareholders financed by sales of corporate assets. By hypothesis, shareholders must capture all discounts net of transaction costs when discounted firms are liquidated at their asset values. It follows that expected distributions from partial liquidations are also likely to raise share prices. If shareholders forecast constant market discounts relative to the value of corporate assets before and after partial liquidations, then shareholders will merely expect to capture discounts on those corporate assets that are actually sold at prices reflecting "true" asset values. On the more plausible assumption that distributions may disproportionately affect discounts, fractional liquidations might even lower discount levels on assets that remain in the hands of discounted firms. This is why, presumably, discounted investment funds often liquidate securities to finance periodic redemptions of limited numbers of shares.[72]

Search Theory and the Tender Offer Auction, 2 J.L.Econ. & Org. 229 (1986).

[71] Like most generalizations, this contrast between the informational requisites for evaluating operational and discount gains should not be overstated. Clearly, there are occasions when large synergy or operational gains can be estimated relatively accurately, as, for example, when discrete departments of administrative units are simply disbanded, or when assets with relatively fixed costs and revenues, such as airline route structures, are integrated. Such detailed valuations of potential operating gains do occur and may be critical, even in hostile acquisitions. The question is: How often do they occur and how much do they contribute to total premia in hostile takeovers?

[72] Recall that asset values here are the going concern -- or discounted cash flow -- values of assets in the hands of incumbent managers. Absent synergies, market imperfections, or unique managerial skills, however, these values should also approximate what third parties will pay for a wide range of proven corporate assets.

Note: Evaluating the Discount Hypothesis

1. As Kraakman acknowledges, the free cash flow theory explored in Chapter 10 also explains why the market price of a company's stock may reflect a discount from the stand-alone value of the underlying assets. In this account, the discount reflects the market's distrust of management's future investment decisions. If managers can be expected to invest the cash flows from the company's assets in negative present value investments, the market will rationally price companies at below accurate appraisals of their asset values. Is this a discount in a Kraakman sense -- that is, an undervaluation of the company -- or simply an accurate appraisal of the value of the assets under existing management?

The Delaware Supreme Court's opinion in Smith v. Van Gorkom[8] illustrates the confusion that can result from failing to distinguish between a mispricing and a mismanagement explanation for why shares trade at a discount. In that case, the court held that Trans Union Corporation's directors had breached their duty of care by approving the company's acquisition at a large premium above market price without sufficient investigation into the company's real value. Early in the opinion the court describes Trans Union's problem: "During the period here involved, the Company had a cash flow of hundred of millions of dollars annually. However, the Company had difficulty in generating sufficient taxable income to offset the increasingly large investment tax credits (ITCs). . . ."[9]

The court then went on to assess the impact of Trans Union's difficulty in fully utilizing its valuable tax attributes on the company's market and real value:

> The record is clear that before [the board meeting approving the Pritzker offer] . . . members of Trans Union's Board knew that the market had consistently undervalued the worth of Trans Union's stock, despite the steady increases in the Company's operating income. . . . The Board related this occurrence in large part to Trans Union's inability to use its ITCs. . . . Van Gorkom testified that he did not believe the market price accurately reflected Trans Union's true worth; and several of the directors testified that, as a general rule, most chief executive officers think that the market undervalues their companies' stock. Yet, on September 20, Trans Union's Board apparently believed that the market price accurately reflected the value of the Company for the purpose of determining the adequacy of the premium for its sale.[10]

Which type of discount did the court have in mind? Did the court believe that the market irrationally discounted the value of Trans Union's assets, and that the failure of the Board to take that discount into account in setting the

---

[8] 488 A.2d 858 (1985).

[9] 488 A.2d at 864.

[10] 488 A.2d at 876.

acquisition price breached their duty of care? Or was the court pointing to the valuation consequences of Trans Union's inability to fully exploit its assets, in particular, its ITCs? From this perspective, Trans Union was like a manufacturing company that has a lower market value if operating at 70% of capacity than at 100%. But if the market valued Trans Union stock at a discount only compared to its hypothetical value if the company could use its ITCs effectively, which value should the Board have used in evaluating the takeover bid?

2. The discounts from the value of their publicly traded stock portfolios at which the shares of closed-end investment companies commonly trade are the primary empirical support for the proposition that the stock market prices some companies at a discount to the fundamental value of their assets. But whether it is appropriate to infer the existence of unobservable discounts in the market's valuation of operating companies from the existence of observable closed-end fund discounts depends on understanding why closed-end funds trade at a discount. Rejecting rational explanations such as agency costs, taxes and illiquidity, Charles Lee, Andrei Shleifer & Richard Thaler recently proposed a market inefficiency explanation for the discount that has interesting implications for corporate acquisitions.[11]

Any market inefficiency explanation requires one irrational player.[12] Lee, Shleifer & Thaler posit that individual investors are noise traders; that is, in different periods they randomly overestimate and underestimate expected returns. Securities prices are set by the trades of both rational and noise traders, with the rational investors acting as arbitragers by trading against the noise traders' irrational sentiment. The discount results from an assumption that rational traders have short horizons (because of the cost of holding securities and performance expectations). The existence of noise traders means that at the time rational traders wish to sell, a risk exists that irrationally pessimistic noise traders will have driven down a company's stock price below its fundamental value. Rational traders will require an additional return to hold assets that impose this noise trader risk, which will be reflected in a lower price -- a discount -- for such assets than their fundamental value.

The final step in the model is that individual investors are more likely to hold and trade closed-end funds than to directly hold and trade the assets in the funds' portfolios. In that event, holding the underlying assets imposes less noise trader risk than holding the shares of the closed-end funds. The result is the closed-end fund discount; an indirect interest in an asset by means of an investment in a vehicle disproportionately held by noise traders is worth less than a direct interest in the asset itself. Lee, Shleifer & Thaler

---

[11] Charles Lee, Andrei Shleifer & Richard Thaler, *Investor Sentiment and the Closed-End Fund Puzzle*, 46 J.Fin. 75 (1991).

[12] If all traders are rational, the market will be efficient conditional on the level of information costs. See Ronald Gilson & Reinier Kraakman, *The Mechanisms of Market Efficiency*, 70 Va.L.Rev. 549 (1984) (excerpted in Chapter 5).

close the circle by offering evidence that closed-end funds are disproportionally held by individual investors.

For purposes of acquisitions, a noise trader discount model focuses attention on circumstances where particular companies are disproportionately held by individual investors. There is evidence that small companies meet this criterion, although increased institutional interest in this part of the market has narrowed the difference of late.[13] Thus, small company stocks may also be underpriced relative to their fundamentals, and an opportunity for discount motivated acquisitions therefore may exist. Similarly, investors in publicly traded real estate companies and master limited partnerships are primarily individuals, and the securities in such entities also reportedly trade at a discount.[14] Again, there may be an opportunity for discount motivated acquisitions.[15]

3. Kraakman notes an additional explanation for why the market price of a company's stock may be lower than the acquisition price that also involves a form of discount. Here the idea is that what is traded in the stock market and what is traded in the market for corporate control are simply different. The stock market trades and therefore values non-controlling shares; the market for corporate control trades and therefore values control. The market price thus reflects a discount from the value of the target to someone with control. But is this different from saying that any company trades at a discount from its value if someone could put its assets to better use? If so, then all motivations for acquisitions are discount theories.

Alternatively, the control premium may depend not on putting the company's assets to better use, but on using control to take a disproportionate share of the company's income. Put this way, the issue raised is the familiar corporate law problem of whether a shareholder who sells control must share any premium received with other shareholders. This issue is taken up in Chapter 21.

---

[13] Lee, Shleifer & Thaler (1991), *supra* note 11, at 96-99.

[14] See Deborah DeMott, *Rollups of Limited Partnerships: Questions of Regulation and Fairness*, 70 Wash.U.L.Q. 617 (1992). The existence of the discount is less observable in the case of real estate companies than closed-end funds because the value of the underlying real estate is typically determined by appraisal. Particularly in a declining market, commercial real estate appraisals may lag market prices because the market will reflect expected occupancy and rent levels, while appraisals will be more heavily influenced by existing conditions.

[15] The Lee, Shleifer & Thaler claim to have solved the closed-end discount puzzle has not gone unchallenged. For an unusually pointed (at least for financial economists) exchange concerning the robustness of the Lee, Shleifer & Thaler empirical support for their noise trader model of discounts, see Nai-Fu Chen, Raymond Kan & Merton Miller, *Are the Discounts on Closed-End Funds a Sentiment Index?*, 48 J.Fin. 795 (1993); Navin Copra, Charles Lee, Andrei Shleifer & Richard Thaler, *Yes, Discounts on Closed-End Funds are a Sentiment Index*, 48 J.Fin. 801 (1993); Nai-Fu Chen, Raymond Kan & Merton Miller, *A Rejoinder*, 48 J.Fin. 809 (1993); Navin Copra, Charles Lee, Andrei Shleifer & Richard Thaler, *Summing Up*, 48 J.Fin. 811 (1993).

CHAPTER 15: WEALTH TRANSFERS
AS AN ACQUISITION MOTIVE

A controversial explanation for why acquisitions take place challenges a central premise of much of the empirical literature surveyed in this Part. That target shareholders earn substantial positive abnormal returns and, more powerfully, that on average the *net* returns to target and acquiring shareholders are positive, typically are taken as demonstrating the efficiency of the transaction. As Michael Jensen has put it: "Positive stock price changes indicate a rise in the profitability of the merged companies."[1] But this need not be the case. Premia reflect only the extent to which target shareholders are better off after acquisitions, and calculation of net abnormal returns adds in the experience of acquiring company shareholders. Yet target shareholder gains may reflect not expectations of greater efficiency, but simply too high an acquisition price, in effect a wealth transfer from acquiring company shareholders to target company shareholders. And even positive net returns to both acquiring company and target company shareholders may reflect only wealth transfers from corporate stakeholders, like employees, to shareholders. Thus, the absolute magnitude of acquisition premia or the fact of positive net abnormal returns earned jointly by acquirer and target shareholders bear *no necessary relationship* to the efficiency gains created by takeovers if takeovers can also have a negative impact on non-shareholder groups.

This Chapter reviews three such wealth transfer explanations for acquisitions. Section A considers the possibility that shareholder gains represent a wealth transfer from non-shareholder corporate participants to target shareholders. Section B considers the additional possibility that target shareholder gains result from overbidding by acquirers, a wealth transfer from acquiring company shareholders to target shareholders. Finally, Section C considers the possibility that shareholder gains result from the creation of market power, thereby allowing the post-acquisition firm to earn monopoly rents -- in effect a wealth transfer from consumers to target shareholders.

A. Breach of Implicit Contracts: Wealth Transfers from Stakeholders to Shareholders

The claim that shareholder acquisition gains represent only redistributions from stakeholders -- non-shareholder participants in the corporate enterprise -- to shareholders has two implications for the debate over the efficiency of acquisitions, especially hostile acquisitions. The first sets the upper limit on the efficiency of acquisitions. If shareholder gains

---

[1] Michael Jensen, *Takeovers: Folklore and Science*, Harv.Bus.Rev. 61, 109-121 (Nov.-Dec.1984).

result only from wealth transfers, then acquisitions are at best neutral with respect to efficiency, and may have undesirable distributional consequences. The second suggests that such wealth transfers may even result in a net reduction in efficiency. Suppose the threat of a wealth transferring hostile takeover reduces the willingness of stakeholders to make company specific investments unless they are protected by written contracts. Then hostile takeovers can reduce the value of the company by increasing its contracting costs -- expensive written contracts must be used instead of relying on trust and good faith -- and can reduce the level of investment to the extent that written contracts are an imperfect substitute. These implications can be evaluated both conceptually and empirically.

1.   The Theory

Andrei Shleifer & Lawrence Summers
BREACH OF TRUST IN HOSTILE TAKEOVERS
in *Corporate Takeovers: Causes and Consequences* 33-56
(Alan Auerbach ed.1988)

Introduction

Corporate restructurings through hostile takeover, merger, or management buyout are wealth enhancing in the sense that the combined market value of the acquiring and the acquired companies usually rises. Many economists . . . point to the increase in market value created by takeovers as evidence of the magnitude of these efficiency gains. And they suggest that the effect on the market value serves as a touchstone for evaluating the social desirability of various tactics for launching and defending against hostile takeovers. . . .

Many business leaders and some academic commentators have dissented sharply from this view, arguing that takeovers create private value by capturing rents but create little or no social value. Their argument is that shareholder gains come from the exploitation of financial market misvaluations, from the use of tax benefits, and from rent expropriation from workers, suppliers, and other corporate stakeholders. The dissenters suggest that the disruption costs of at least some hostile takeovers may well exceed their social benefits.

This [discussion considers] the elements of truth in the claims that improved management and redistributed wealth are the sources of takeover premia. We show how hostile takeovers can be privately beneficial and take place even when they are not socially desirable. Our argument does not invoke tax, financial markets, or monopoly power considerations. . . .

Value Creation and Value Redistribution

Consider three scenarios. In scenario A, T. Boone Pickens takes over Plateau Petroleum and immediately lays off 10,000 workers, who immediately find work elsewhere at the same wage. Pickens also stops purchasing from numerous suppliers, who find that they can sell their output without any price reduction to other customers. The stock of Plateau Petroleum rises by 25%.

In scenario B, Frank Lorenzo takes over Direction Airlines and immediately stares down the union so that the wages of the existing workers are reduced by 30% and 10% of the work force is laid off and unable to fund subsequent employment at more than 50% of their previous wage. Lorenzo does not change the airline's route structure or flight frequency. The stock of Direction Airlines rises by 25%.

In scenario C, Carl Icahn takes over USZ. He closes down the corporate headquarters and lays off thousands of highly paid, senior employees, who had previously been promised lifetime employment by the now-displaced managers. Icahn also shuts down factories that dominate the economies of several small towns. As a consequence numerous local stores, restaurants, and bars go bankrupt. The stock of USZ goes up by 25%.

All three takeovers yield equal private benefits to the shareholders of the target firms. Yet their social consequences are very different. In scenario A society is better off because resources are diverted from less productive to more productive uses. The increased value of Plateau Petroleum approximately reflects the value of this gain. In scenario B society is about equally well off. The gains to Direction shareholders are approximately offset by the losses to the human wealth of Direction employees. The redistribution is probably antiegalitarian. On the other hand, it may ultimately lead to advantages for customers of the airline. In scenario C society is worse off. The gains to USZ shareholders are offset by the losses incurred by the laid-off employees and by the firms with immobile capital whose viability depended on the factories' remaining open. And other firms find that once their workers see what happened at USZ, they become less loyal and require higher wages to compensate them for a reduction in their perceived security. These firms also have a harder time inducing their suppliers to make fixed investments on their behalf.

These three examples make it clear that increases in share values in hostile takeovers in no way measure or demonstrate their social benefits. Scenario A is the only one in which share price increases capture the elimination of waste and the gains in social welfare. In contrast, shareholder gains in scenarios B and C to a large extent come from losses of the value of employees' human capital. Even if some efficiency is realized from wages coming more into line with marginal products, the efficiency is only a second order effect relative to the transfer from employees to shareholders. Scenario C has additional external effects of the acquisition which, while not resulting in gains to the acquirer, should enter the social calculation. The claim that the 25% takeover premium in scenarios B and C measures social gains is simply incorrect.

In [what follows] we develop issues raised by scenarios B and C. Why are there implicit contracts it pays to breach? Why are raiders willing but incumbents unwilling to breach contracts? What are the transfers accompanying such a breach? What are the social costs of the breach of implicit contracts? Before taking up these questions, however, we must stress an a priori consideration suggesting that scenarios B and C have much more to do with observed takeover premia than does scenario A.

Consider a rather stylized firm that has a capital stock worth $100, hires 14 workers at $5 a year, purchases $20 worth of materials, and has sales of $100 a year. Its profits are $10 a year and its cost of capital is .10, and so its market value will be $100. The ratios of market value, earnings, and payroll are roughly accurate as representations of typical firms in the U.S. economy. Imagine that the firm is in steady state. Suppose the firm, because of an excess of free cash flow, starts to invest excessively rather than keeping its capital stock constant, to the point that it invests half of its profits in projects with a present value of .5. If the market expects this practice to continue indefinitely, the firm's value will fall by 25%. Eliminating this rather disastrous policy of excessive reinvestment in terrible projects could presumably produce a takeover gain of about 25%.

Now suppose that the firm invests rationally but, because of agency problems involving management's greater loyalty to the employees than to the shareholders, overpays the work force by 5%. To put this figure in perspective, note that unions typically raise labor costs by about 15% and that firms in the same industry in the same city typically pay wages to workers in the same detailed occupational category that differ by 50% or more. This overpayment to labor, if expected to endure, will reduce profits by $3.50 a year, leading to a reduction in market value of 35%. To the extent that the cash flows obtainable by cutting wages are safer than the firm's profit stream, this figure is an underestimate.

The point of these examples is simple. Since firms' labor costs far exceed their profits and since even poor capital investments yield some returns, very small differences in firms' success in extracting rents from workers and other corporate stakeholders are likely to be much more important in determining market value than the differences in corporate waste associated with differences in firms' volume of reinvestment. An intermediate case is provided by changes in the level of employment. Here the reduction in payroll is likely to be offset by some loss of product, so that it is more difficult to raise value by increasing efficiency in this way. Moreover, some rent extraction is involved since the appropriate opportunity cost for laid-off labor is likely to be less than its wage.

These considerations suggest that takeovers that limit managerial discretion increase the acquired firm's market value primarily by redistributing wealth from corporate stakeholders to share owners. To this extent, the existence and magnitude of takeover premia is not probative regarding the social costs and benefits of takeovers. Rather, the social valuation of hostile takeovers must turn on the impact of these redistributions on economic efficiency, which will obviously vary from case to case. . . .

The Value of Implicit Contracts

A corporation is a nexus of long-term contracts between shareholders and stakeholders. Because the future contingencies are hard to describe, complete contracting is costly. As a result, many of these contracts are implicit, and the corporation must be trusted to deliver on the implicit contracts even without enforcement by courts. To the extent that long-term contracts reduce costs, such trustworthiness is a valuable asset of the corporation. Shareholders own this asset and are therefore able to hire stakeholders using implicit long-term contracts.

The principal reason why long-term contracts between shareholders and stakeholders are needed is to promote relationship-specific capital investments by the stakeholders. An employee will spend time and effort to learn how to do his job well only if he knows that his increased productivity will be subsequently rewarded. A subcontractor exploring for oil will buy site-specific new equipment only if he believes that the contracting oil firm will not try to squeeze his profits once he sinks the cost. . . . In these and other cases it is important to the shareholders that the stakeholders do a good job, but shareholders may be unable to describe what specific actions this calls for, let alone to contract for them.

The necessary arrangement to ensure appropriate investment by stakeholders is a long-term contract, which allows them to collect some of the rewards of doing good work over the time. The expense of writing a complete contingent contract ensures that these long-term contracts are implicit. . . .

The Importance of Trust

Although both shareholders and stakeholders benefit ex ante from implicit long-term contracts, ex post it might pay shareholders to renege. For example, it will pay shareholders to fire old workers whose wage exceeds their marginal product in a contract that, for incentive reasons, underpaid them when they were young. Or shareholders might profit from getting rid of workers whom they insured against uncertain ability and who turned out to be inept. Or shareholders might gain from refusing to compensate a supplier for investing in the buyer-specific plant, after this plant is built. . . . In all these cases implicit contracts specify actions that ex post reduce the firm's value, even though agreeing to these actions is ex ante value maximizing. Breach of contract can therefore raise shareholder wealth, and the more so the greater is the burden of fulfilling past implicit contracts. . . .

To take advantage of implicit contracts, shareholders must be trusted by potential stakeholders. Otherwise, stakeholders would expect breach whenever it raises the firm's value and would never enter into implicit contracts. To convince stakeholders that implicit contracts are good, shareholders must be trusted not to breach contracts even when it is value maximizing to do so.

A standard solution to the problem of how implicit contracts are maintained is the theory of rational reputation formation, described most notably by Kreps.[a] In this theory managers adhere to implicit contracts because their adherence enables them to develop a reputation for trustworthiness, and thus to benefit from future implicit contracts. If violating an implicit contract today would make the managers untrustworthy in the future, they will uphold the contract as long as the option of entering into future contracts is valuable enough. Conversely, if it is not important for the managers to be trusted in the future, that is, if a reputation is not valuable, they will violate the implicit contract. Formally, a rational reputation is modeled as a small probability that the manager is irrationally honest, sustained by honest behavior on the part of the manager. . . .

To dispel the fear of breach on the part of stakeholders, shareholders find it value maximizing to *seek out* or *train* individuals who are capable of commitment to stakeholders, *elevate* them to management, and *entrench* them. To such managers, stakeholder claims, once agreed to, are prior to shareholder claims. Even when a rational reputation is not of high enough value to shareholders to uphold the implicit contracts with stakeholders, as would be the case if the company suffered a large permanent decline in demand, trustworthy managers will still respect stakeholder claims. From the ex ante viewpoint, such dedication to stakeholders might be a value-maximizing managerial *attribute* (not choice!). In a world without takeovers, potential stakeholders counting on such managers to respect their claims will enter into contracts with the firm. . . .

Breach of Trust in Hostile Takeovers

In some circumstances upholding the implicit contracts with stakeholders becomes a liability to shareholders. The incumbent managers are nonetheless committed to upholding stakeholder claims. In these cases ousting the managers is a prerequisite to realizing the gains from the breach. This is precisely what hostile takeovers can accomplish. As the incumbent managers are removed after the takeover, control reverts to the bidder, who is not committed to upholding the implicit contracts with stakeholders. Shareholders can then renege on the contracts and expropriate rents from the stakeholders. The resulting wealth gains show up as the takeover premia.

---

[a] David Kreps, *Corporate Culture and Economic Theory*, in *Perspectives on Positive Political Economy* 90 (James Alt & Kenneth Shepsle eds.1990).

Hostile takeovers thus enable shareholders to redistribute wealth from stakeholders to themselves.

Managers committed to upholding stakeholder claims will not concede to the redistribution. They will resist it, even though the shareholders at this point will withdraw their support from the managers to realize the ex post gain. Not surprisingly, then, takeovers that transfer wealth from stakeholders to shareholders must be hostile. . . .

For breach to be an important source of gains, hostile takeovers must come as a surprise to stakeholders, who entered into implicit contracts expecting the firm to be run by trustworthy managers. For if the stakeholders anticipate a hostile takeover, they will realize the trustworthiness of the incumbent managers is worthless, since they will be duly removed when shareholder interest so demands. Implicit contracts based on trust are feasible only insofar as the managers upholding them are entrenched enough to retain their jobs in the face of a hostile threat.

The elements of the story now fall into place. In a world without takeovers, shareholders hire or train trustworthy managers, who on their behalf enter into implicit contracts with the stakeholders. Subsequently, some or many of these contracts become a liability to shareholders, who cannot default on them without replacing the incumbent managers. Managers are hard to replace internally because to a large extent they control the board of directors, their own compensation scheme, and the proxy voting mechanism. This failure of internal controls may in fact be in shareholders' ex ante interest, since it may be the only way to assure commitment by shareholders to stakeholders in the absence of takeovers.

Hostile takeovers are external means of removing managers who uphold stakeholder claims. Takeovers then allow shareholders to appropriate stakeholders' ex post rents in the implicit contracts. The gains are split between the shareholders of the acquired and the acquiring firms. At least in part, therefore, the gains are wealth redistributing and not wealth creating.
. . .

Empirical Evidence

In evaluating the importance of transfers from stakeholders to shareholders, we always compare them to efficiency gains, whose significance has been emphasized in much of the literature. We proceed in four steps. First, we show that the presence of large redistributions is consistent with established statistical generalizations about takeovers. Second, we study a special case -- Carl Icahn's takeover of TWA -- to determine how much of the takeover premium can be accounted for by the expropriation of rents from corporate stakeholders. . . .

Basic Facts

In this section we note that the stylized facts of takeovers are consistent both with the prevalence of efficiency gains and with the prevalence of transfers of wealth. In reviewing the evidence, we return to calling the first case scenario A and the second scenario B or C.

Our theory clearly explains the takeover premia since some portion of stakeholder wealth is transferred to shareholders. More subtly, it explains why most of the wealth gains accrue to the acquired firm's shareholders. If it takes little skill to break implicit contracts, the market for corporate control is essentially a common values auction. In such a competitive auction all the gains accrue to the seller, namely, the target's shareholders.[b]

Managers would resist takeovers both if the gains come purely from eliminating their incompetence, as in scenario A, and if they come from transfers from stakeholders, as in scenarios B and C. In the former case poor managers ar reluctant to be exposed and lose control. In the case of breach managers are reluctant to let stakeholders' claims be ignored. . . .

Patterns of reorganization following a takeover can also be understood using either scenario A or scenarios B and C. Either efficient cost cutting or breach can justify employee dismissals, plant closings, project curtailment, divestments, and subcontractor removals. To see whether the parties that lose association with the acquired firm suffer wealth losses, one must trace their subsequent employment. This is necessary, but not sufficient, to establish breach, and it is hard to do empirically. Otherwise such separations could be efficient, as in scenario A.

One striking fact militating in favor of the importance of wealth transfer as opposed to pure efficiency gains is that a significant fraction of hostile acquisitions are initiated and executed by only a few raiders. It is hard to believe that Carl Icahn has a comparative advantage in running simultaneously a railcar leasing company (ACF), an airline (TWA) and a textile mill (Dan River). It is more plausible that his comparative advantage is tough bargaining and a willingness to transfer value away from those who expect to have it. In fact, those who describe him (including he himself) point to this as his special skill. The industrial diversity of many raiders' holdings suggests that their particular skill is value redistribution rather than value creation. It is not at all surprising, in this context, that many of these raiders have hardly any employees of their own.

It is important to emphasize at this point that our discussion of efficiency gains and of transfers concerns *hostile* takeovers. [T]hese are

---

[b] A common value auction is one in which although there is ex ante uncertainty about the value of the asset being sold, the ex post value is the same to all bidders. A private value auction, in contrast, is one in which the value of the asset will be different for different bidders. See Preston McAfee & John McMillan, *Auctions and Bidding*, 25 J.Econ.Lit. 699 (1987). For example, competing bids to acquire a target company by bidders with different potential for synergy would be a private value auction. Eds.

disciplinary acquisitions designed to change the operations of the firm. They should be contrasted with synergistic acquisitions, which are usually friendly and motivated by market power, diversification, or tax considerations. [T]he two types of deals are targeted at very different companies and hence should not be treated as examples of the same economic process. . . .

Case Study: Carl Icahn and TWA

Carl Icahn's takeover of TWA in 1985 has attracted enough attention and commentary to provide us with sufficient data to assess stakeholder losses. In particular, Icahn's gain of control was accompanied by changes in compensation for members of the three major unions at TWA. By looking at changes in the wages and benefits of TWA's workers, we can gauge stakeholder losses. At the same time, we acknowledge from the start that the case of TWA does not strictly fit out model. Wages for union members at TWA were determined under governmental regulation. The pre-Icahn management had not been successful (or competent) in renegotiating wages; for a variety of reasons TWA had bad labor relations. It is, therefore, not the case that TWA management resisted the acquisition to avoid a breach of contract. All the evidence suggests that the managers wanted to keep their jobs and resisted acquisition for that reason. Nonetheless, the main observation of this paper--that takeover premia are often paid for by stakeholders--is much more general than the particular model of managerial behavior we develop.

Before Icahn began investing in TWA on the open market, its 33 million shares traded at $8. Icahn eventually bought 40% of the airline through open market purchases and the rest through a (hotly contested) tender offer. Although his cost per share on the open market varied from $8 to $24, the offer was completed at $24 per share. At most, then, Icahn's premium was $500 million. There is evidence, however, that he bought 20% of the stock at an average price of $12 and another 20% at the average price of $16 to $18. Icahn's overall average price therefore was $20, putting the premium in the range between $300 million and $400 million. This figure is consistent with estimates made in the popular press.

TWA's three major unions represented its pilots, flight attendants, and machinists. Contracts signed between the pilots and Icahn basically prohibited significant trimming down of TWA operations and, in particular, pilot layoffs or significant airplane sales. In fact, leases on three Boeing 747s were not renewed, and one was sold. There were also some, though not major, layoffs at TWA's St. Louis headquarters. Most of the action by far came from wage reductions for the "production" workers, calculated below.

Before Icahn took control TWA paid its 3,000 pilots an average salary of $90,000 per year, including benefits. The agreement with Icahn cut this around 30%, for an annual savings of approximately $100 million. The company employed about 9,000 machinists at an average cost of $38,000.

They agreed to a 15% cut, saving TWA around $50 million per year. The story with flight attendants is more complicated, since no agreement was reached. On average, a TWA flight attendant made $35,000 a year. Some of the attendants (around 2,500 out of 6,000 within 3 months) were replaced by rookies and paid an average of $18,000 per year. This is essentially a transfer of wealth from the existing flight attendants, who could presumably take entry-level jobs, to Icahn. In fact, some of them accepted wage cuts, and it appears that, over time, most who did not were replaced. Assuming conservatively that the average saving was $10,000 per flight attendant, the total annual saving adds up to $60 million. . . .

This brief analysis indicates that the average annual transfer from TWA's unionized employees amounted to at least $200 million under Icahn. Since TWA was a very risky investment (and Icahn was not diversified), the appropriate discount rate for these savings could be as high as 25%. This yields a present value for the transfer of $800 million. In return for these wage concessions, employees received a profit share and an ownership stake in TWA, which together amounted to about one-third of the company. Immediately after the takeover, market value of these shares was under $200 million, which reduces the value of the transfer from unions to $600 million. By these very conservative estimates, then, the transfer from members of the three unions to Icahn amounted to one and a half times the takeover premium.

It is hard to gauge the efficiency consequences of Icahn's acquisition. There appears to be a consensus that the previous TWA management was awful. If the airline went bankrupt, some of the valuable assets of TWA (such as its name and goodwill) might have lost value, which is a social cost. Moreover, TWA can probably make better investment decisions now than in the past, since its labor costs more accurately reflect shadow prices. On the other hand, some inefficiencies might have resulted from the replacement of well-trained flight attendants by rookies. In addition, large time costs of Icahn and others as well as large transaction costs were incurred. Overall, we suspect efficiency has been gained. This is not the main point, though. The point is that at least one and a half times the premium can be explained by transfers, which in this case were an *explicit* part of the justification for the acquisition. Shareholders gained primarily because stakeholders lost. . . .

---

2. Evaluation

Evaluating the stakeholder wealth transfer explanation for acquisitions has both conceptual and empirical elements. At the conceptual level, the explanation poses questions of causation and construction. Assuming a transfer of wealth from stakeholders to shareholders in fact occurs and breaches an implicit contract,[2] is it accurate to assume that the acquisition actually caused the breach? In turn, if there is uncertainty as to cause, can we reliably specify the ex ante contract's actual terms? That is, can we tell if the observed behavior was actually a breach?

At the empirical level, inquiry shifts from the possible to the observable. Do we actually observe wealth transfers? Do the results Shleifer and Summers describe with respect to the Icahn takeover of TWA generalize? At this point, the causation issue reemerges. Are such transfers as we do observe the result of acquisitions? For example, stakeholders in non-target companies in the same industries as targets also experience a redistribution of wealth? Here there are two sources of empirical evidence: following Shleifer and Summers, the impact of takeovers on levels of employment and wages; and the impact of leveraged buyouts on the value of outstanding debt.

1. *Conceptual Problems with the Wealth Transfer Explanation.* Shleifer and Summer's argument that takeovers transfer wealth from stakeholders to shareholders in breach of implicit contracts rests on three claims: that wealth transfers can be observed following a takeover; that takeovers cause the transfers; and that the transfers violate the terms of preexisting implicit contracts. The conceptual foundations of each of these claims can be examined in terms of Shleifer and Summer's focus on the airline industry.

Assume that prior to the CAB's deregulation of airline routes and ticket prices, an implicit contract existed between United States airlines and their unions that wage increases would not be seriously contested because the cost could be passed on to consumers through CAB approved fare increases.

---

[2] It may be helpful at this point to expand somewhat on the concept of an implicit contract. In a tradition pioneered by labor economists, voluntary relations, the terms of which are not governed by an enforceable legal agreement, are called *implicit* contracts. See Sherwin Rosen, *Implicit Contracts: A Survey*, 23 J.Econ.Lit. 1144 (1985). The simple intuition underlying the phrase is that the terms of the bargain are not stated explicitly in a detailed written agreement, but are reflected implicitly in the substance of the continuing voluntary interaction between the parties. The reason for the absence of an explicit contract is the difficulty of specifying the full range of contingencies that might require the parties to alter their arrangement and the appropriate response to each such contingency. With an implicit contract the parties accommodate these changes in an ongoing incremental way, in light of actual circumstances. In this setting, enforcement is also implicit rather than explicit. For the same reason that an explicit contract is not possible, explicit enforcement -- that is, judicial enforcement -- is also not possible. Just as the parties could not fully specify the consequences of each possible future state, neither can a court. Rather, enforcement of an implicit contract is also implicit, through market mechanisms like reputation. We thus observe a symmetry between the form of the relationship and the method of enforcement: explicit contract/explicit remedy; implicit contract/implicit remedy. David Charny, *Nonlegal Sanctions in Commercial Relations*, 104 Harv.L.Rev. 373 (1990), carefully develops this distinction. Given this symmetry, the notion that "some courts have found implicit promises to be enforceable," Katherine Stone, *Policing Employment Contracts Within the Nexus-of-Contracts Firm*, 43 U.Toronto L.J. 353, 369 (1993), conflates two radically different ideas.

Deregulation dramatically changed that world. New low-wage airlines entered the market with lower employment levels and wages, and charged correspondingly lower fares. At this point, the value of established high-wage airlines dropped. If the employment and wage structure of the high-wage airlines remained in place but competition required them to match the low-wage airline prices, the incidence of deregulation would fall on capital: the price of the high-wage airlines' stock would decline to reflect decreased post-deregulation profitability.

Alternatively, the high-wage airline's wage and employment structure could be changed. This is where the takeover comes in. A post-acquisition change in labor structure to match that of the low-wage airlines shifts the incidence of some of the deregulation loss from capital to labor. A portion of the wealth transfer goes to target shareholders in the form of a premium; and a portion goes to the acquirer in the form of increased post-acquisition profitability. However, these are unlikely to be the only transfers involved. The gains to the target shareholders (who receive a premium only compared to the post-deregulation stock price, not compared to the airline's stock price prior to deregulation) and the acquirer would not completely offset the combined losses suffered by target shareholders and employees due to the loss of regulatory rents. The difference presumably is passed on to consumers through lower air fares as a result of competition with the low-wage airlines. Thus, the story is one of a net wealth transfer from high-wage airline shareholders *and* employees to consumers. This loss is caused not by the takeover, but by deregulation.[3] Shleifer and Summer's analysis concerns the allocation of that loss between capital and labor.

This is where the implicit contract argument enters the analysis. The problem is how to specify the terms of the implicit contract. What did the pre-deregulation implicit contract say about changes in employment structure in response to deregulation? Shleifer and Summers' argument assumes that the implicit contract allocated the risk of deregulation to capital, and that employees could rely on management to perform the contract because unexpected breach would diminish the value of management's reputation for trustworthiness, an asset with future value to managers and shareholders. According to Shleifer and Summers, only raiders, who presumably do not care about their reputations, would breach the implicit contract.

The soft spot in the argument is the claim that existing management would respect the implicit contract while a raider would not. This result depends on target management and the raider having different incentives with

---

[3] See Ronald Gilson, *The Political Ecology of Takeovers: Thoughts on Harmonizing the European Corporate Governance Environment*, 61 Ford.L.Rev. 161, 189-91 (1992). A similar story could be told with respect to changes in wages and employment in the automobile industry in response to Japanese competition, although in that industry incumbent management (although not without some shareholder prodding) rather than a takeover effected the shift. Oliver Williamson develops a similar point in his comments on the Shleifer & Summers article. Oliver Williamson, *Comment*, in *Corporate Takeovers: Causes and Consequences* 61 (Alan Auerbach ed.1988).

respect to breaching the implicit contract. Management is said to have an incentive to forgo the gains from breaching the implicit contract because the loss of a reputation for trustworthiness will result in even larger losses in connection with future dealings with stakeholders. If trust has long-term value, that value will be capitalized in the price of the company's stock; breaching the contract would *reduce* the value of the company. But then why would the raider's incentives be any different? Having purchased the airline, the raider looks forward to precisely the same future dealings with stakeholders as target management. If a reputation for trustworthiness is more valuable that the gains from breach, the raider will have no more incentive to breach the implicit contract than target management because to do so would decrease the company's value.[4] Conversely, if the post-deregulation competitive structure of the industry has so devalued labor's contribution that a raider would have an incentive to breach the implicit contract, *so too will target management.* And in that case, an implicit contract term that allocates the risk of deregulation to capital will not be credible ex ante because in precisely the circumstance in which it would be relied upon, the gains from breach will exceed the cost of lost reputation.[5] Thus, on a conceptual level the implicit contract term on which Shleifer and Summers base their argument seems unlikely to exist.

This analysis suggests that implicit contracts -- by definition enforceable only by reputation and other market mechanisms rather than by legal sanction -- will provide employees little protection against large unexpected changes that permanently devalue their future participation. From this perspective, the efficiency loss Shleifer and Summers assign to takeover implemented opportunism is caused not by takeovers, but by the parties' inability to effectively contract over the unexpected. And this perspective suggests a different regulatory approach. Unexpected external changes that result in increases in efficiency can also result in wealth transfers. Risk averse groups like labor can benefit from risk sharing arrangements that protect their firm specific investments, with the resulting increase in investment pointed to by Shleifer and Summers. The difficulties with implicit contracting suggest that firm level risk sharing may not work in times of substantial change. The alternative might be government provided risk sharing, premised on both the barriers to contractual resolution and the public good associated with efficient levels of employee investment.[6]

---

[4] That the raider does not yet have a reputation for trustworthiness should not alter the analysis. The very act of not breaching the implicit contract following the acquisition would credibly establish one. Indeed, under these circumstances simply acquiring the airline should credibly establish the raider's intention to honor the implicit contract.

[5] See Ronald Gilson & Mark Roe, *Understanding the Japanese Keiretsu: Overlaps Between Corporate Governance and Industrial Organization*, 102 Yale L.J. 871, 901 (1993).

[6] Ronald Daniels, *Stakeholders and Takeovers: Can Contractarianism be Compassionate*, 43 U. Toronto L.J. 315 (1993), develops this theme.

   2. *Empirical Evidence Bearing on the Wealth Transfer Hypothesis.*
Arguments that takeovers were fueled by wealth transfers from stakeholders,
especially labor, to shareholders have played an important political role.
When both management groups and organized labor came to oppose
takeovers, the combination was a formidable force in state legislatures.[7] The
difficulty with the debate, however, has been the quality of the data, and the
care with which the wealth transfer hypothesis has been formulated.

   With respect to the data, the problem has been its largely anecdotal
character. Shleifer and Summers stress the impact on labor of Carl Icahn's
acquisition of TWA, but in a later article Shleifer dismisses TWA as no more
than "one famous case."[8] In turn, the labor movement claims the loss of
80,000 union jobs[9] and 500,000 jobs overall from takeovers,[10] and
bondholders are said to have suffered "possibly the largest expropriation of
investors in American business history."[11] However, the figures are either
simply asserted or are based on particular cases rather than aggregate data.

   With respect to the formulation of the hypothesis the data are said to
support, the observation of job loss or a bond price drop following an
acquisition is typically taken as sufficient to prove the hypothesis. In fact,
the wealth transfer hypothesis requires three steps, each of which is capable
of empirical investigation: 1) Is there a transfer, that is, did labor or
bondholders actually lose something? 2) Did the takeover cause the loss, or
were the loss and the takeover responsive to the same outside forces? 3) If
a takeover caused loss occurred, did it breach an implicit contract? The
remainder of this section describes the empirical evidence concerning these
three questions with respect to claims that acquisitions effect transfers from
labor and bondholders. To anticipate the results of the survey, some
aggregate data exists with respect to the first question; just a little exists

---

   [7] See Mark Roe, *Takeover Politics,* in *The Deal Decade: What Takeovers and Leveraged
Buyouts Mean for Corporate Governance* 321 (Margaret Blair ed.1993). For example, the
coalition behind the Pennsylvania antitakeover statute, the nation's most restrictive, was
described as follows: "Behind the debate in Pennsylvania is a power struggle between the
shareholders . . . and the directors and managers. . . . Pennsylvania business groups
supporting the bill are aligned with unions seeking to protect the jobs of their members."
Leslie Wayne, *Takeovers Face New Obstacles,* N.Y. Times, April 19, 1990, p.D1.

   [8] Sanjai Bhagat, Andrei Shleifer & Robert Vishny, *Hostile Takeovers in the 1980s: The
Return to Corporate Specialization,* Brookings Papers on Economic Activity, Microecon. 1,
6 (1990). KKR's acquisition of Safeway Stores, Inc., is another common example, See, e.g.,
Susan Faludi, *The Reckoning: Safeway LBO Yields Vast Profits but Exacts a Heavy Human
Toll,* Wall St.J., May 16, 1990, at A8, col.2.

   [9] Oversight Hearing before the House Subcom. on Economic Stabilization and Urban
Affairs on Effects of Corporate Mergers and Acquisitions on the Economy of the United
States, 100th Cong., 1st Sess. (1987) (testimony of Henry Schectner, Deputy Director,
Econ.Res.Dept., AFL-CIO).

   [10] Hostile Takeovers: Hearings before the Senate Committee on Banking, Housing and
Urban Affairs, 100th Cong., 1st Sess. 262 (1987) (Statement of Thomas Donahue, Secretary-
Treasurer, AFL-CIO).

   [11] Morey McDaniel, *Bondholders and Stockholders,* 13 J.Corp.L. 205 (1988).

with respect to the second; and almost none exists with respect to the third. Taken together, however, the data offers little support for the proposition that anticipated wealth transfers explain significant amounts of acquisition activity.

    a.   *Are There Transfers?*

    For purposes of this question, a wealth transfer occurs when we observe, with respect to labor, a post-transaction drop in wages or employment, and with respect to bondholders, post-announcement negative abnormal returns. Keep in mind, however, that the mere presence of transfers, like the mere presence of premia, does not demonstrate inefficiency. Absent distributional concerns, a redistribution of rents has no efficiency consequences unless it negatively affects an implicit contract regime or positively affects the utilization of resources.

    Transfers from Labor. The available data concerning wage and job loss following takeovers provides little support for the claim that 1980s takeovers effected significant wealth transfers from labor to shareholders. Steven Kaplan examined the impact of leveraged management buyouts on employment levels for a sample of 76 transactions completed between 1980 and 1986.[12] He found that the median change in employment associated with a buyout was +0.9%, treating post-transaction divestitures as decreases in employment.[13] For a subsample of buyouts following which large divestitures did not occur, the median change in employment was +4.9%, an increase of approximately the same magnitude as experienced by other companies in the buyout firm's industry.

    Frank Lichtenberg and Donald Siegel report similar results using plant level employment data for more than 19,000 U.S. manufacturing plants.[14] Plants that underwent ownership changes experienced lower employment growth than non-change plants in the period *before* the control change. However, the gap disappeared *after* the control change, indicating a comparatively higher rate of employment growth in plants that had been the subject of a takeover. This result is inconsistent with a wealth transfer from employees to shareholders through a post-transaction reduction in employment levels.

---

    [12] Steven Kaplan, *The Effect of Management Buyouts on Operations and Value*, 24 J.Fin.Econ. 217 (1989).

    [13] Treating divestitures as decreases in employment overstates the number of jobs lost. Typically divestitures are of a going business which continues to provide employment. The effect of treating divestitures as decreases in employment improperly assumes that all employees of divested operations lose their jobs.

    [14] Frank Lichtenberg & Donald Siegel, *Productivity and Changes in Ownership of Manufacturing Plants*, Brookings Papers on Econ. Activity 643 (1987).

A later study by the same authors focuses on the precise character of post-transaction employment loss.   As in the prior study, wages and employment of blue collar workers in plants subject to takeovers declined relative to non-takeover plants prior to the takeover, but grew more quickly after the takeover.   However, employment and wages of white collar employees declined significantly after takeovers.[15]   Thus, the only empirical evidence of wealth transfers from labor in connection with takeovers concerns more highly compensated white collar employees, and even then do not appear to be of a magnitude to provide a significant motivation for takeovers.[16]

A final study directly investigated the presence of wealth transfers from labor to shareholders by comparing union wage contracts before and after takeovers.[17]   The wealth transfer hypothesis predicts a post-transaction reduction in wage rates. Using a sample of some 5,000 contracts covering over 1,000 companies -- roughly 25% of all New York and American Stock Exchange companies and 25% of private unionized labor -- Joshua Rosett found a small post-transaction increase in union wages following hostile takeovers. While the results displayed significant variance, they offer no support for the wealth transfer hypothesis.

The careful empirical studies of the effect of acquisitions on wages and employment thus tell a consistent story: no evidence appears of significant wealth transfers.[18] Nonetheless, a puzzle remains: the anecdotal evidence still persuades some observers, including some familiar with the empirical evidence, that takeovers "left devastation for employees."[19] To understand this conflict -- between an empirical finding of little impact on average, and the observation that particular takeovers have left target employees either with lower pay or without jobs -- remember that the mean describes only part of a distribution. As developed in Chapter 3, the second characteristic of a

---

[15] Frank Lichtenberg & Donald Siegel, *The Effect of Ownership Changes on the Employment and Wages of Central Office and Other Personnel*, 33 J.L. & Econ. 383 (1990).

[16] See Bhagat, Shleifer & Vishny (1990), *supra* note 8, at 6, 7; Amar Bhide, *The Causes and Consequences of Hostile Takeovers*, J.Applied Corp.Fin. 36, 48 (Summer 1989). Consistent with the impact of takeovers being concentrated on middle management rather than production workers, Blackwell, Marr and Spivey find that in a sample of 286 plant closings, only 48 were announced by companies that either were or became the target of an acquisition, and only 22 were announced by targets of a hostile acquisition. David Blackwell, Wayne Marr & Michael Spivey, *Plant-closing Decisions and the Market Value of the Firm*, 26 J.Fin.Econ. 277, 287 (1990) ("[F]ew of the plant-closing announcements in our sample were made by firms that were targets of takeover attempts.").

[17] Joshua Rosett, *Do Union Wealth Concessions Explain Takeover Premiums?   The Evidence on Contract Wages*, 27 J.Fin.Econ. 263 (1990).

[18] Frank Lichtenberg states flatly: "The gains realized by both acquiring and target shareholders appear to be social gains, not merely private ones. We found no evidence that ownership change is usually accompanied by the abrogation of implicit contracts with workers or suppliers." Frank Lichtenberg, *Corporate Takeovers and Productivity* 43 (1992).

[19] Stone (1993), *supra* note 2, at 353.

distribution is its variance -- the extent to which outcomes differ from the mean. All of the studies described in this section report high variance. This means that, despite the fact that on average workers are not made worse off by takeovers, the experience of some workers is far from average; consistent with the average, some transactions may inflict a good deal of pain on labor. The policy implication of a high variance sample concerns the distributive consequences of the activity in question. The mean speaks to the efficiency of the activity; the variance speaks to who bears the costs. The studies surveyed here do not counsel against programs that seek to spread the social cost of acquisitions more widely.

Transfers from Bondholders. The data concerning the effect of takeovers on bondholders tell a more complex story. Here the redistribution hypothesis is that a highly leveraged transaction increases the risk of the company. Recall from Chapter 7 that shareholders in a company with risky debt can be characterized as holding an option. Increasing the risk associated with the asset underlying the option increases the value of the option. Thus, increasing the risk of the outstanding debt by issuing large amounts of new debt should decrease the value of the outstanding debt and increase the value of the outstanding stock. The puzzle is that at least the early studies of leveraged takeovers did not find a decrease in the value of outstanding bonds following takeovers that substantially increased the target company's overall leverage. Marais, Schipper and Smith found that for a sample of 290 leveraged buyout announcements between 1974 and 1985, the mean and median abnormal return to nonconvertible debt were approximately zero, with half the abnormal returns falling between -2% and $+1\%$, despite the fact that leverage ratio on average tripled as a result of the transactions.[20] In the absence of bondholder losses, there is nothing to transfer to shareholders.

The authors also approach the wealth transfer hypothesis from the opposite direction. If a wealth transfer from bondholders is an important source of shareholder gains from leveraged buyouts, then the larger the amount of debt outstanding before the transaction, the greater the pool of wealth to be transferred to shareholders and, presumably, the larger the shareholders' gains. The data disclose, however, that the size of shareholder gains is not correlated with the amount of pre-transaction outstanding debt.[21]

There is a possible explanation for the conflict between the data and the predictions of both the wealth transfer hypothesis and option theory: Leveraged buyouts can have conflicting effects on the value of outstanding

---

[20] Laurentius Marais, Katherine Schipper & Abbie Smith, *Wealth Effects of Going Private for Senior Securities*, 23 J.Fin.Econ. 155 (1989).

[21] Kenneth Lehn & Annette Poulsen, *Leveraged Buyouts: Wealth Created of Wealth Distributed, in Public Policy Towards Corporate Takeovers* 46 (Murray Weidenbaum & Kenneth Chilton eds.1988), also report minimal price changes for a smaller sample of outstanding nonconvertible bonds over approximately the same period.

debt. Increases in operating income and cash flow that appear to result from leveraged buyouts work to the advantage of shareholders and bondholders alike. But presumably the disciplinary advantages of increased debt decrease at the margin, while the valuation consequences of the additional risk associated with increased debt increases at the margin. Thus, as the amount of new debt increases, the curves at some point will cross, the valuation consequences of the increased risk will come to override the increased efficiency, and negative abnormal returns to bondholders should result.

The curves appear to have crossed in connection with the larger, more heavily leveraged buyouts of the post-1985 period, transactions which were not included in the Marais, Schipper and Smith sample. Studies by Kaplan and Stein,[22] and Long and Ravenscraft[23] show a marked change in the structure of buyouts in the pre- and post-1985 periods. Among other characteristics, the extent of leverage increased significantly in post-1985 transactions, and the extent of post-transaction operating improvement decreased, resulting in a significant increase in the effective price paid relative to cash flow increase. Put differently, during the post-1985 period, the risk imposed on outstanding bonds as a result of buyouts increased and the benefits from improved performance decreased. As a result, bondholders in post-1985 transactions should have had a more negative experience. A study by Warga and Welch reports results consistent with this analysis.[24] In a sample of 43 public bonds issued by 16 companies that underwent leveraged buyouts between 1985 and 1989, bondholders experienced returns of −2.4% over a period from two months before to one month after the transaction's announcement. When adjusted for bond risk and duration, the negative return increased to −7.0%.

While the data for the 1985-1989 period are consistent with a wealth transfer from bondholders to stockholders, the size of the transfer was not sufficient to explain the size of the premia. Even in this period, the losses suffered by bondholders were "an order of magnitude smaller than shareholder gains."[25] Moreover, consistent with the results reported by Marais, Schipper and Smith for the earlier period, the magnitude of the bondholder losses were not correlated with the magnitude of the shareholder gains.

---

[22] Steven Kaplan & Jeremy Stein, *The Evolution of Buyout Pricing and Financial Structure in the 1980s*, 108 Q.J.Econ. 313 (1993).

[23] William Long and David Ravenscraft, *Decade of Debt: Lessons from LBOs in the 1980s*, in *The Deal Decade: What Takeovers and Leveraged Buyouts Mean for Corporate Governance* 205 (Margaret Blair ed.1993).

[24] Arthur Warga & Ivo Welch, *Bondholder Losses in Leveraged Buyouts* (Working Paper, 1990).

[25] *Id.*

b.   *Do Takeovers Cause the Transfers?*

The second level of empirical inquiry concerns causation: Assuming a transfer took place, did a takeover cause it, or was the transfer triggered by an external shock, such as deregulation of the airline industry or Japanese competition in the automobile industry? Here the point is to distinguish between takeovers as merely redistributive, and takeovers as an equilibrating mechanism by which the economic system responds to real changes in the environment.[26]

Transfers from Labor. With respect to claims that takeovers cause transfers from labor, the key is to compare the experience of target companies with that of comparable companies that remain independent. The following analysis by Joseph Grundfest illustrates the point with respect to the takeover of Gulf Oil.

Joseph Grundfest
JOB LOSSES AND TAKEOVERS
(March 11, 1988)[27]

If a company lays off 5,000 workers shortly after a takeover, there is an urge to claim that 5,000 people lost their jobs because of takeovers. Any such conclusion could well be incorrect because it is entirely possible that these 5,000 workers would have been laid off regardless of the takeover. [T]wo . . . examples . . . help illustrate this point.

The battle for Gulf Oil was one of the largest and most bitter takeover contests in history. Much has been written about the takeover's adverse consequences on Gulf's Pittsburgh employees. . . . Generally overlooked, however, is the fact that Gulf was firing people by the trainload before any takeover threat was announced. Gulf employed 58,000 people in 1981. By 1983, the number of Gulf employees was 42,700 and falling.[12] The relevant question is what would have happened to employment at Gulf Oil had there been no takeover.

For purposes of comparison, Exxon, the largest U.S. oil producer, and presumably the oil company with the least to fear from takeovers, has steadily reduced its worldwide employment from its 1981 peak of 182,000 to a current level of about 102,000.[13] This decline constitutes a 44%

---

[26] See Gilson (1992), *supra* note 3.

[27] Address to the University of Toledo College of Law, Third Annual Colloquium on Corporate Law and Social Policy (March 11, 1988).

[12] See L.J. Davis, *The Biggest Knockover: T. Boone Pickens and the End of Gulf Oil,* Harper's, Jan. 1985, at 53, 63.

[13] Tanner, *Lean Exxon Tiger, Still a Giant, Has a Smaller Appetite,* Wall St.J., Mar. 16, 1987, at 6.

reduction from 1981 workforce levels. Had Gulf remained independent and reduced its 1981 workforce at the same pace as Exxon, it would today have about 32,480 employees. Gulf would therefore have had to lay off another 10,000 workers, or about a quarter of its 1983 workforce, had it remained independent, to keep pace with employment changes at its least takeover-vulnerable competitor.

In 1984, Chevron acquired Gulf in a white-knight transaction designed to avoid a Pickens-led takeover attempt. Now suppose that following the Chevron-Gulf merger Chevron laid off 10,000 Gulf workers. Would it be possible to claim that all those jobs were "lost" because of a takeover? Hardly, because many, if not all, of those jobs would likely have been cut even if there were no Pickens-led battle for control of Gulf, and even if Chevron never engaged in the merger. This simple example illustrates the fallacy of counting the number of layoffs after a takeover and blaming all those dismissals on takeover activity.

As a second example, consider Chemical Bank's recent announcement that it intends to "trim about 10% of its 21,000 employees and sell several subsidiaries to strengthen the bank's financial performance."[14]   Now, suppose a competitor announces a takeover of Chemical Bank and stated its intention to continue with management's plan to trim employment and sell some subsidiaries. Would it then be reasonable to claim a takeover caused 10% of Chemical's workforce to lose its jobs? No, but that's just the way the calculation would be done by some takeover opponents.

Comparisons like this show why one cannot conclude that jobs lost *after* a takeover were lost *because of* the takeover. Rather, job gains or losses must be measured relative to industrywide trends. Takeover critics have overlooked this important adjustment and have therefore overstated the job loss consequences of takeover activity.

While Grundfest's analysis, like that of Summers and Shleifer's, relies on a single case, the limited aggregate data is consistent with the claim that takeovers are primarily an equilibrating mechanism and that such post-transaction job losses as occur are a response to real changes in the economic environment. As discussed above, Kaplan found that in leveraged buyouts that did not involve significant divestitures, the median change in target company post-transaction employment was both positive (+4.9%) and of approximately the same magnitude as other companies in the industry.[28] Similarly, Lichtenberg and Siegel found lower pre-transaction employment growth in plants that were later the subject of an ownership change, but

---

[14] Wayne, *Chemical to Cut Jobs and Sell Units*, N.Y. Times, Sept. 15, 1987, at D1.

[28] Kaplan (1989), *supra* note 12.

higher post-transaction growth;[29] that is, employment growth was higher in plants after a buyout than in plants that did not experience an ownership change. Neither result supports characterizing the ownership change as negatively influencing employment.

Transfers from Bondholders. Identifying the counter-factual alternative to an acquisition with respect to transfers from bondholders is more difficult. The central characteristic of a leveraged buyout is that control is transferred from public shareholders to a private partnership. But a change in control is not the only way to increase a company's leverage. The same result can be achieved without a change in control by means of a leveraged recapitalization. In this version, the company (rather than the acquiring entity as in a leveraged buyout) borrows the money and uses the proceeds to pay a large dividend to shareholders. The impact on the company's capital structure is the same as a leveraged buyout: debt replaces equity by the amount of the dividend.[30] Moreover, the impact of the two forms of transactions on both shareholder value and corporate performance is similar to leveraged buyouts.[31] Thus, at first glance, it is hard to blame takeovers for increasing debt since the same phenomenon is also observed in the absence of takeovers; something must have occurred to alter the optimal capital structure of companies the subject of either leveraged buyouts or leveraged recapitalizations. The difference is only whether incumbent management seizes the opportunity itself.

On further consideration, the causation issue becomes less clear. Many of the firms that undertook a leveraged recapitalization did so in response to a threatened hostile takeover.[32] From this perspective, takeovers reappear as a cause of increased leverage: leveraged recapitalizations might not have occurred absent the threat of takeover. This ambiguity concerning causation serves to highlight the importance of the implicit contract argument. Absent such a claim, whether a takeover is the cause or just the means is unimportant: market transactions are assumed efficient. Thus, the next step in the analysis becomes critical.

---

[29] Lichtenberg & Siegel (1987), *supra* note 14.

[30] This form of transaction is discussed in greater detail in Chapter 11. For examples of leveraged recapitalization structures, see Robert M. Bass Group, Inc. v. Evans, 552 A.2d 1227 (Del.Ch.1988); Black & Decker Corp. v. American Standard, Inc., 682 F.Supp. 772 (D.Del.1988).

[31] David Denis & Diane Denis, *Managerial Discretion, Organizational Structure, and Corporate Performance*, 16 J.Acct. & Econ. 209 (1993); Robert Kleiman, *The Shareholder Gains from Leveraged Cash-outs: Some Preliminary Evidence*, in *Corporate Restructuring and Executive Compensation* (Joel Stern, Bennett Stewart, & Donald Chew, eds.1989); Puneet Handa & A. Radhakrishnan, *An Empirical Investigation of Leveraged Recapitalizations: A New Takeover Defense Strategy* (Working Paper, Stern Sch. of Management, N.Y.U., No. 480, 1988).

[32] Larry Dann, *Highly Leveraged Transactions and Managerial Discretion over Investment Policy*, 16 J.Acct. & Econ. 237 (1993); Handa & Radhakrishnan (1989), *supra* note 31.

c.   *Do Takeovers Breach Implicit Contracts?*

The final level of analysis is whether takeovers breach implicit contracts even if such wealth transfers as occur are initially triggered by exogenous events. For example, even if employee human capital has been devalued by increased foreign competition, a takeover that causes the incidence of that devaluation to fall on labor could breach an implicit contract by which the company undertook to bear that risk.

Transfers from Labor.   The claim that takeovers breach implicit contracts with employees necessarily assume that employees are being paid more than their marginal products; otherwise, they could secure identical positions after a takeover. These extramarginal payments could appear in two ways: either through generally higher wages compared to other firms; or through higher wages to more senior employees as an incentive to perform earlier in their tenure.[33] The promise of continued extramarginal wages then might constitute an implicit contract, and their termination after a takeover might constitute a breach.

Gokhale, Groshen and Neumark test both formulations of how takeovers may breach implicit contracts using salary survey data from 133 employers in Cleveland, Cincinnati, and Pittsburgh, some of which had been subject to a hostile takeover.[34] Whether takeovers reduce extramarginal wages generally is tested by determining the relationship between a company's relative wage levels and the likelihood of becoming a takeover target. If the takeover motive is to eliminate extramarginal wages, then companies that have relatively higher wages should have a higher probability of becoming a takeover target. The authors found that higher wage levels were not positively related to likelihood of takeover, a result inconsistent with a breach of implicit contract motive for takeovers.

The hypothesis that takeovers breach an implicit contract by reducing extramarginal wages to senior workers is tested by examining post-takeover changes in wage patterns. Here the authors find some support for the wealth transfer hypothesis: for takeover targets that have high concentrations of

---

[33] Suppose firms can only imperfectly monitor workers. In this setting, a wage structure by which workers earn less than their marginal products early in their careers and more than their marginal products later in their careers reduces workers incentives to take advantage of imperfect monitoring by shirking. The deferred compensation serves, in effect, as a bond that is forfeit if the worker is caught shirking and dismissed. In effect, reduced likelihood of being caught shirking is offset by the increased penalty of loss of deferred compensation. This explanation for a rising wage profile originates with Edward Lazear, *Why is There Mandatory Retirement?*, 87 J.Pol.Econ. 1261 (1979).

[34] Jagadeesh Gokhale, Erica Groshen & David Neumark, *Do Hostile Takeovers Reduce Extramarginal Wage Payments?* (Nat'l Bureau of Econ. Working Paper No. 4346, Apr.1993).

senior workers, the extramarginal returns to senior workers are reduced.[35] Interestingly, this result is consistent with Lichtenberg and Siegel's finding that white collar employees -- in contrast to production workers those employees whose performance is most difficult to observe and whose wage profile is therefore likely to be the steepest -- do suffer significant wage and employment cuts.

Transfers from Bondholders. The hypothesis that takeovers breach an implicit contract with bondholders is particularly interesting because bondholders already have an explicit contract with the company: the bond indenture that contains more or less detailed limits on company behavior.[36] Thus, the argument for the existence of a supplementary implicit contract must be that the contracting parties could not anticipate all actions that shareholders could take that would adversely affect bondholders. The events that could be anticipated were included in the explicit contract; the supplementary implicit contract would then prohibit the company from taking any other action that unfairly affected the bondholders.[37]

The history of debt covenants puts the argument in context. As William Bratton notes, bond covenants routinely restricted post issuance substantial increases in indebtedness for most of this century, and also restricted dividend payments in a fashion that would have blocked significant payouts to shareholders after a recapitalization. Even the most creditworthy borrowers were at least subject to a debt restriction.[38] This apparently changed in the mid-1970s, leaving bondholders largely unprotected against leveraged buyouts and recapitalizations. The reasons that have been offered for the change are interesting. Commentators argue that bondholders were willing to forgo covenant protections for precisely the same reasons that ultimately gave rise to LBOs and recapitalization. Managers' self interest lay with reducing the risk of their human capital by growth and by diversification financed with retained earnings; retaining free cash flow protected both managers and bondholders. Thus, bondholders came to rely

---

[35] The authors also report a positive relationship between high wages to senior employees coupled with a high concentration of senior employees on the one hand, and the likelihood of hostile takeover on the other. However, this relationship is not statistically significant.

[36] See Chapter 7.

[37] Victor Brudney, *Corporate Bondholders and Debtor Opportunism: In Bad Times and Good*, 105 Harv.L.Rev. 1821 (1992), and William Bratton, *Corporate Debt Relationships: Legal Theory in a Time of Restructuring*, 1989 Duke L.J. 92, argue that courts can impose restrictions based on an implied obligation of good faith with respect to unanticipated borrower behavior. McDaniel (1988), *supra* note 11, Morey McDaniel, *Bondholders and Corporate Governance*, 41 Bus.Law. 413 (1986), advocate reaching the same result by treating directors as under a fiduciary duty to bondholders as well as shareholders. Metropolitan Life Ins. Co. v. RJR Nabisco, Inc., 716 F.Supp. 1504 (S.D.N.Y.1989), rejects the implied covenant argument in the context of the RJR Nabisco leveraged buyout. Simons v. Cogan, 549 A.2d 300 (Del.1988), rejects the fiduciary claim.

[38] Bratton (1989), *supra* note 37.

not on covenants, but on the absence of constraints on the self-interested exercise of managerial discretion.[39]

In all events, following the RJR Nabisco transaction some relatively restrictive forms of covenants have come into use. The protection of the covenant is triggered by specified events, such as an LBO, takeover, or a leveraged recapitalization that leads to a S&P or Moody's ratings downgrade of a sufficient magnitude. The consequence of trigger is either an option to put the bond back to the borrower at par (a "poison put"), or an interest rate reset that seeks to assure that the bond will trade at par by increasing the interest rate to match the borrower's new risk level.[40] By 1989, 32.1% of nonconvertible bonds sold to the public had such event risk covenants, up from only 3.1% in 1986.[41] And it seemed that the market valued these protections: Estimates indicate that bonds with event risk covenants yielded 24 basis points less than comparable unprotected bonds.[42] Finally, following the sharp drop in buyout activity in 1990,[43] event risk covenants became less common.[44]

How can the implicit contract argument be assessed in light of this history? A first take might be that an implicit contract was breached because leverage increasing transactions could not be anticipated. Once understood, transaction planners could and did devise effective covenant protection. The implicit contract protected against the one time wealth transfer that occurred because of the imperfect foresight of indenture drafters.

---

[39] *Id.*; John Coffee, *Stockholders Versus Managers: The Strain in Corporate Web*, 85 Mich.L.Rev. 1, 68-69 (1986). LBOs and recapitalizations, however, were not entirely unanticipated. In *RJR Nabisco*, the court pointed out that Metropolitan Life agreed to eliminate protective covenants in certain RJR Nabisco obligations after it had already begun internal discussions of the need for protection against leveraged transactions. The internal memorandum stated: "Questions have . . . been raised about our ability to force payouts in similar situations, particularly when we would not be participating in the buyout financing. . . . A method of closing this apparent loophole would be through a covenant dealing with a change in ownership. Such a covenant is standard in financings with privately-held companies. . . . It provides the lender with . . . some type of special redemption." Metropolitan Life Ins. Co. v. RJR Nabisco, Inc., 716 F.Supp. 1504, 1510-11 (S.D.N.Y.1989).

[40] See Marcel Kahane & Michael Klausner, *Antitakeover Provisions in Bonds: Bondholder Protection or Management Retrenchment*, 40 UCLA L.Rev. 931 (1993); Kenneth Scott, *Are the Barbarians After the Bondholders? Event Risk in Law, Fact and Fiction* (Working Paper, Aug.1991); Richard Steinwurtzel & Janice Gardner, *Super Poison Puts as a Protection Against Event Risk*, 3 Insights 1 (Oct.1989).

[41] Kenneth Lehn & Annette Poulsen, *Contractual Resolution of Bondholder-Stockholder Conflicts in Leveraged Buyouts*, 34 J.L. & Econ. 645, 663 (1991). Leland Crabbe, *Event Risk: An Analysis of Losses to Bondholders and "Super Poison Put" Bond Covenants*, 46 J.Fin. 689 (1991), puts the figure for recent issuances at 40%.

[42] Crabbe (1991), *supra* note 41.

[43] The statistics are recounted in Chapter 1.

[44] Kahane & Klausner (1993), *supra* note 40.

The problem with this analysis is the facts; neither prescience nor super poison put covenants were necessary to protect outstanding bonds against LBOs and leveraged recapitalizations. Using a sample of 214 bonds representing all outstanding publicly traded debt securities issued by the targets of 65 large LBOs proposed between 1980 and 1988,[45] Asquith and Wizman found that the effect of an LBO on bondholder wealth depended on the existence of traditional covenant protection on subsequent debt and dividends.[46] In the 47 successful transactions, representing 149 bond issues, bondholders on average experienced negative abnormal returns of −2.8%. The average, however, masks sharp differences in the impact on bonds with covenants that limited total debt, bonds with covenants that limited only dividend payments, and bonds without either form of covenant. Bonds with total debt limits experienced *positive* abnormal returns of 2.1%, bonds with only dividend restrictions experienced negative returns of −2.0%, and bonds with no protection experienced negative returns of −5.3%.[47]

Thus, even before the advent of highly leveraged transactions, some bondholders negotiated for protection against increased leverage and others did not, a result that did not change after the post-LBO invention of event risk covenants. The next level of inquiry is then why some bondholders required covenant protection and some did not. The answer is that covenant protection is not free. For example, debt restrictions can prevent issuers from undertaking positive net present value projects without first amending the covenants,[48] a procedure that is at best time consuming and may be infeasible with publicly traded bonds.[49] And this brings us back to the original transaction cost based implicit contract argument: explicit covenants cannot distinguish ex ante between good debt increasing transactions and bad debt increasing transactions; implicit covenants can. But here we again encounter the symmetry between contract and remedy: implicit contracts are linked to implicit remedies. For the same reasons transaction planners cannot draft an explicit contract ex ante, a court will have difficulty determining the terms of the implicit contract ex post. Efforts like the RJR Nabisco bond litigation seek to make the implicit contract they assert explicitly enforceable.

---

[45] The 1988 cutoff for the sample assures a significant number of the more highly leveraged post-1985 transactions.

[46] Paul Asquith & Thierry Wizman, *Event Risk, Covenants, and Bondholder Returns in Leveraged Buyouts*, 27 J.Fin.Econ. 195 (1990).

[47] Douglas Cook, John Easterwood & John Martin, *Bondholder Wealth Effects of Management Buyouts*, Fin. Management 102 (Spring 1992) report similar results with a sample covering the same period.

[48] Stewart Myers, *Determinants of Corporate Borrowing*, 5 J.Fin.Econ. 147 (1977).

[49] For this reason, privately placed debt typically has more expansive covenant protection because the cost of subsequent renegotiation is low.

B. Overbidding by Acquirers: Wealth Transfers from Acquiring Shareholders to Target Shareholders

Overbidding is the second genre of explanation for the size of acquisition premia that is fundamentally agnostic on the issue of social gains.[50] In its strongest form, the notion is that the positive returns experienced by target shareholders simply represent a wealth transfer from acquiring company shareholders to target company shareholders; target shareholder gains are offset by acquiring shareholder losses. Even where the acquisition results in net positive abnormal returns, a result consistent with social efficiency, the fact that the returns to acquiring company shareholders are either zero or mildly negative[51] still leave room for significant wealth transfers in favor of target shareholders.

Overbidding hypotheses must include several major elements. One is an explanation of why acquirers might be willing to overpay in the first instance. Here, there are several possible explanations on which to draw, and the explanations are not necessarily mutually exclusive. The most familiar is a variation on the familiar agency problem, this time viewed from the acquirer's side of the equation. Acquisitions may reflect a kind of agency cost, not for target shareholders but for the shareholders of acquiring firms. For example, managers may misuse free cash flow to make diversifying acquisitions.[52] A second explanation for why acquirers might be willing to overpay is purely psychological: Managers (or at least some managers) may be habitually overoptimistic or vulnerable to "hubris".[53] Finally, a third account of overpayment is the so-called "winner's curse":

> Even if [acquirers] estimate accurately on average, they win the bidding primarily when they overestimate an asset's value, and thus tend to overpay on average. The auction need not be explicit; it is enough that there are potential bidders waiting in the wings to make a higher offer if the bid is too low.[54]

However, suggesting why acquirers might be willing to pay too much is just one aspect of constructing an overbidding hypothesis. A more delicate aspect of the analysis is making the case that acquirers do, in fact, overpay. And evidence that acquiring company shareholders earn zero or small negative abnormal returns from hostile acquisitions would seem to cut against

---

[50] This discussion draws heavily on Bernard Black, *Bidder Overpayment in Takeovers*, 41 Stan.L.Rev. 597 (1989).

[51] These results are summarized in Chapter 8D.

[52] See, e.g., Robert Morck, Andrei Shleifer & Robert Vishny, *Do Managerial Objectives Drive Bad Acquisitions?*, 45 J.Fin. 31 (1990); Mark Mitchell & Kenneth Lehn, *Do Bad Bidders Become Good Targets*, 98 J.Pol.Econ. 372 (1990).

[53] Richard Roll, *The Hubris Hypothesis of Corporate Takeovers*, 59 J.Bus. 197 (1986).

[54] Black (1989), *supra* note 50, at 625.

an overbidding explanation. After all, if on average acquirers lose little if anything from acquisitions, how can they be bidding too much?

Bernard Black has explained this conundrum by combining a free cash flow theory of managerially motivated acquisitions with a rational expectations perspective that builds on market efficiency. In Professor Black's view, a poorly managed (from the shareholders' perspective) acquirer can overbid for a target without its own share price falling precisely because the market already anticipates that it will misinvest its free cash flow and has incorporated that expectation in the acquirer's current stock price. Thus, as long as the acquirer's overpayment does not exceed what the market already expects, its share price will remain unchanged despite overpayment. Indeed, the rational expectations phenomenon may actually exacerbate the problem. If managers use stock price reaction as a metric of the efficiency of an announced transaction, the worse the bidder, the more likely it is to win. Announcement of a bid reflecting the same level of overpayment will result in negative abnormal returns for a bidder of whom the market thought better, and positive abnormal returns for a bidder of whom the market thought worse -- a result that encourages the worst bidders to increase their bids.[55]

If bidder overpayment is a problem, what can be done about it? Professor Black's suggestions treat the problem as a manifestation of the general need to enhance the effectiveness of mechanisms that align the interests of managers and shareholders:

> [T]he Overbidding Hypothesis counsels us to look for ways to enhance the various market constraints on overpayment and to improve managers incentives. Friction in the market for corporate control should be reduced, but we must also review management compensation schemes and board of director oversight, and recognize that for some companies, high leverage can play a positive role.[56]

C.   Creation of Market Power: Transfers from Consumers to Target Shareholders

Creation of market power is the final wealth transfer explanation for acquisitions. Through market power resulting from an acquisition, the acquiring company is said to be able to earn monopoly rents at the expense of consumers. A portion of the anticipated monopoly rents are passed on to target shareholders through the premium paid in the acquisition. While this explanation has motivated most legislative restrictions on acquisitions, notably § 7 of the Clayton Act,[57] it is of lesser note with respect to more

---

[55] *Id.* at 613-21.

[56] *Id.* at 653.

[57] 15 U.S.C. § 18 (1993). Section 7 Provides that no corporation "shall acquire . . . the whole or any part of the stock . . . [or] the whole or any part of the assets of another

recent acquisition activity because completed acquisitions have been determined either by enforcement agencies or the courts not to have an anticompetitive effect. Nonetheless, the proper level of antitrust enforcement can be controversial; the possibility therefore remains that unchallenged acquisitions still result in market power.

Empirical tests of the market power hypothesis have focused on the returns to *competitors* of parties to horizontal acquisitions at the time of an acquisition's announcement, and at the time the acquisition is challenged under the antitrust laws. If market power is created by the acquisition, the result will be increased prices for the products sold by the combined firm and its competitors. Thus the hypothesis predicts positive abnormal returns for the combining companies and their competitors at the time the acquisition is announced and, conversely, negative abnormal returns if the acquisition is challenged. Robert Stillman finds positive abnormal returns for competitors associated with only one of the eleven acquisitions in his sample, a result inconsistent with the market power hypothesis.[58] Espen Eckbo's study of a much larger sample reports positive abnormal returns for rivals of the combining companies on the transaction's announcement, a result consistent with the market power hypothesis.[59] However, Eckbo also reports that competitors do not experience negative abnormal returns when the acquisition is challenged, a result inconsistent with the market power hypothesis and which leads Eckbo to reject it.[60]

A second body of evidence also may bear on the market power hypothesis. Chapter 9 recounted the studies showing that conglomerate acquisitions -- by definition unlikely to create market power -- produced lower returns than related acquisitions, and that most of the more successful acquisitions of the 1980s resulted in shifting assets to buyers who already were in the relevant industry. The better performance of the related acquisitions may result from gains in operating efficiency, as some of the

---

corporation . . ., where in any line of commerce in any section of the country, the effect of such acquisition may be substantially to lessen competition, or to tend to create a monopoly."

[58] Robert Stillman, *Examining Antitrust Policy Toward Horizontal Mergers*, 11 J.Fin.Econ. 225 (1983).

[59] B. Espen Eckbo, *Horizontal Mergers, Collusion and Stockholder Wealth*, 11 J.Fin.Econ. 241 (1983); see B. Espen Eckbo & Peggy Wier, *Antimerger Policy Under the Hart-Scott-Rodino Act: A Reexamination of the Market Power Hypothesis*, 28 J.L. & Econ. 119 (1985).

[60] But why is not the fact that competitors earn abnormal returns on the acquisition's announcement date sufficient to lend support to the market power hypothesis regardless of what happens when the acquisition is challenged? If the gains to the parties to the acquisition resulted from anticipation of improved efficiency, then the transaction would make their competitors worse off, and they should experience negative abnormal returns. How might an improvement in the combining companies' efficiency result in gains to their competitors? Eckbo argues that the method by which the combining firms achieve the efficiency gains is somehow disclosed to competitors, who can then match their combining rivals' increased efficiency by adopting the same method.

studies suggest, or they may result from anticipated market power.[61] Post-takeover evidence of productivity improvement at the plant level, discussed earlier in this Chapter, provides support for the efficiency explanation.[62]

---

[61] Roberta Romano, *A Guide to Takeovers: Theory, Evidence and Regulation*, 9 Yale J.Reg. 119, 143 (1992), makes this point.

[62] Healy, Palepu & Ruback argue that the gains result from increased efficiency rather than market power because they find no post-transaction increase in sales margins. Paul Healy, Krishna Palepu & Richard Ruback, *Does Corporate Performance Improve After Mergers*, 31 J.Fin.Econ. 135 (1992).

PART III. CORPORATE AND SECURITIES
LAW PLANNING CONCERNS

The examination in Part II of possible explanations for why companies make acquisitions did not, for the most part, require drawing distinctions between different methods by which corporate acquisitions can be carried out. Our attention centered on the preconditions for and subsequent impact of the transaction; the mechanics of the acquisition itself were treated essentially as a black box. The focus of Part III, dealing with corporate law planning considerations in friendly and hostile transactions, and Part IV, dealing with non-corporate law concerns, is on understanding what determines the size and shape of the box. These matters loom particularly large for business lawyers because determining the box's architectural specifications is traditionally considered a business lawyer's major role.

If there were but a single technique by which an acquisition could be accomplished, the inquiry would be trivial. Only the existence of a choice creates the opportunity to *plan* -- to select among future alternatives in order to maximize predetermined goals. But choice alone is insufficient to justify expenditures for planning. As should be clear from Parts I and II, the desirability of an acquisition should not turn on the mechanical form chosen to accomplish it *unless* collateral consequences attach to the selection of the form. The planner's task then is to choose the form which imposes the fewest undesirable collateral consequences but that otherwise leaves unaltered the substance of the transaction. And it is precisely because the substance of a commercial transaction can be cast in a myriad of forms without altering its economic reality, that most regulatory systems -- whose jurisdictional boundaries and actual requirements are commonly expressed in terms of transactional form rather than substantive effect -- act as an invitation to the business lawyer to maximize the client's interests by selecting a transactional form that minimizes regulatory intrusion.[1] The inevitable result is a regulatory eternal triangle. Efforts by the objects of regulation to structure transactions so that their form falls outside the literal terms of the regulation, and responsive efforts by regulators to cast a wider net,[2] are mediated by

---

[1] Cf. Jan Deutsch, *The Mysteries of Corporate Law: A Response to Brudney and Chirelstein*, 88 Yale L.J. 235, 237 (1978) (correspondence) ("[T]he clearer and more uniform a rule is, the more likely it is to be regarded as a formality that can justifiably be manipulated so long as compliance with its explicit formulation is maintained!").

[2] A good example of the length to which regulators occasionally go is IRC § 338(i), added by the Tax Reform and Fiscal Responsibility Act of 1984, which is intended to back up § 338's effort to prevent selectivity with respect to basis step up and recapture recognition in non-reorganization acquisitions:

> The Secretary [of Treasury] shall prescribe such regulations . . . as may be necessary . . . to ensure that the purpose of this section to require consistency of treatment of stock and asset purchases with respect to a target corporation and its target affiliates (whether by treating all of them as stock purchases and all of them as asset purchases) may not be circumvented through the use of any provision of law or regulations (including the consolidated return regulations).

courts which, applying such tools as the form versus substance and step transaction doctrines in tax law[3] and the de facto merger doctrine in acquisitions,[4] must determine whether to credit the form in which the planner has cast the transaction, or to vindicate the public policy reflected in the regulation by expanding its reach beyond its language.[5]

This is the public ordering aspect of private transactions[6] in which the business lawyer's role is to cast a transaction in the form that minimizes the cost to the client of the variety of complex and conflicting regulatory systems that may touch on the transaction. In this Part we begin a survey of the regulatory influences on the structure of corporate acquisitions by examining the corporate law considerations bearing on transaction structure and conduct. Part III (Chapters 16 through 24) considers corporate and securities law planning considerations in both hostile and friendly acquisitions. Chapter 16 examines the alternative acquisition techniques available and such issues as what vote should be necessary to approve a negotiated acquisition, who should be allowed to vote, and the de facto merger doctrine. Chapter 17 addresses the corporate law concerns of the acquirer and the target in hostile acquisitions, especially the rules governing the actions of the target's board of directors in resisting an unwanted takeover. Chapter 18 addresses securities law concerns in hostile acquisitions, especially the Williams Act's regulation of tender offers and acquisitions of a 5% or greater stock interest.

Chapters 19-22 focus on friendly acquisitions. Chapters 19 and 20 discuss, respectively, corporate and securities law concerns in the standard context where a acquirer with no prior relationship with the target acquires 100% of a target company. Chapter 21 addresses the corporate law issues that arise in the sale by a controlling shareholder or shareholder group of a controlling but less than 100% interest. Chapter 22 addresses corporate and securities law concerns in "freezeout" transactions, where an already controlling shareholder seeks to acquire the remainder of the target's stock.

Chapters 23 and 24 cover specialized topics in hostile acquisitions of control. Chapter 23 surveys state securities regulation of hostile transactions through a generational analysis and consideration of the valuation consequences of state takeover statutes. Chapter 24 examines the alternative tactics used by management in proxy fights and how they affect shareholders.

. . .

[3] See, e.g., Joseph Isenbergh, *Musings on Form and Substance in Taxation*, 49 U.Chi.L.Rev. 859 (1982); Marvin Chirelstein, *Learned Hand's Contribution to the Law of Tax Avoidance*, 77 Yale L.J. 440 (1968); Randolph Paul & Philip Zimet, *Step Transactions*, in *Selected Studies in Federal Taxation* 200 (2d Ser.1938).

[4] See Chapter 16E.

[5] For an excellent effort at linking substantive policy to the decision whether to disregard the form in which planners have cast a transaction, see Marvin Chirelstein & Benjamin Lopata, *Recent Developments in the Step Transaction Doctrine*, 60 Taxes 970 (1982).

[6] See Chapter 1A for differentiation of the public and private ordering aspects of private transactions.

CHAPTER 16: THE MECHANICS OF ALTERNATIVE ACQUISITION TECHNIQUES

In this Chapter we examine the menu of alternative acquisition techniques from which the transaction planner may choose and the mechanics -- of voting rights, appraisal rights and the like -- associated with each. What shapes the planner's problem is that each of the alternatives has different requirements and different burdens despite the fact that, absent those differences in process, the outcome of all the alternatives is essentially the same. The result of this tension between form and substance has been a continuing debate concerning when the planner's selection of the form of the transaction will be disregarded in favor of a recharacterization which triggers requirements the court thinks somehow more appropriate.

In the acquisition area, the terms of this debate have centered on the idea of equivalence. Once past the initial barrier of statutory language, the theory is that like transactions should be treated alike. The task is then to identify those characteristics that identify whether transactions which differ in form are equivalent in substance. In the materials that follow, the alternative techniques provided by typical statutes, and their corporate law collateral consequences are described. The judicial and scholarly debate concerning equivalency is next considered and an effort made to apply the analysis developed in Parts I and II to determining both the bases on which equivalence might be determined, and the limits of the concept itself.

A. Merger

1. The Statute

[Read closely the following provisions of the Delaware corporation law, which are reproduced in Appendix B:

§ 251. *Merger or consolidation of domestic corporations*: subsections (a)-(d), (f)

§ 259. *Status, rights, liabilities, etc., of constituent and surviving or resulting corporations following merger or consolidation*: subsection (a)

§ 261. *Effect of merger upon pending actions*

§ 262. *Appraisal rights*: subsections (a)-(d)(1)]

2. Variations in Who Votes, How Many Votes Are Needed, How the Votes Are Counted, and Who Gets to Complain

The Delaware statute is typical of the merger provisions of all jurisdictions in the character of the transaction contemplated. Following approval by the boards of directors and shareholders of the affected corporations, the actual combination -- the act of "merger" -- occurs instantaneously upon the filing of a document with the designated state official.[1] At one moment two corporations exist; at the next, the acquiring corporation has enveloped the target, like an amoeba engulfing its prey, and has succeeded to all of its properties, rights and other attributes. The technique has significant advantages in reducing the transaction costs associated with the mechanical aspects of accomplishing an acquisition. If all of a target company's assets and liabilities had to be separately transferred to or assumed by the acquiring company, each (or at least each class) would require a separate document of transfer or assumption and, for example, multiple filings for different recording systems (e.g., U.C.C., real property records, the F.A.A. Aircraft Records Branch) would be necessary. The effect of statutory provisions like Delaware § 259 is to substitute a single document, the merger agreement, for the flood of paper that would otherwise be required to effect the transaction.

Despite the similarity of the transaction contemplated by the statutory provisions in each state, there is substantial variation among jurisdictions as to the precise steps necessary to authorize the statutory transfer. Of principal interest are differences in the percentage vote necessary to authorize the transaction, which corporate constituents are allowed to vote, how the votes are counted, and who gets to complain.

How many votes are needed? As late as 1886 the leading corporate law treatise stated unequivocally that business combinations required the *unanimous* consent of shareholders.[2] But by the close of the first third of the 20th century, allowing such a fundamental change by less than unanimous vote had become the norm.[3] The precise percentage required still varies substantially among jurisdictions. Prior to the 1960s, the great majority of states required a two-thirds vote. This pattern was broken in 1962 when the Model Business Corporation Act reduced the required percentage approval to a majority.[4] Many of the major commercial jurisdictions then followed suit, Delaware reducing the vote requirement in its statute from two-thirds

---

[1] See Del.Gen.Corp. Code § 259(a); see generally Byron Fox & Eleanor Fox, *Corporate Acquisitions and Mergers* § 24.02 (1981) (exhaustive survey of jurisdictions).

[2] 2V. Victor Morawetz, *A Treatise on the Law of Private Corporations* 908-9 (2d ed.1886). The history of the shift from unanimous consent to approval by a specified percentage of shareholders is traced in detail in William Carney, *Fundamental Corporate Changes, Minority Shareholders, and Business Purposes,* 1980 Am.B.Found.Res.J. 69 (excerpted later in this chapter).

[3] Id. at 94.

[4] 2 ABA-ALI Model Bus.Corp. Act Ann.2d. § 73, ¶ 2 (1971).

to a majority in 1967.[5] New York, however, still maintains a two-thirds requirement.[6]

The balance of interests reflected in the reduction of the percentage approval required to authorize a merger to a majority was described by the American Bar Association's Committee on Corporate Laws, the group responsible for ongoing revision of the Model Act, as follows:

> Because of the fundamental change in corporate existence that may result from a merger or consolidation, it was thought that sound reasons exist for requiring more than a mere majority of voting shares for the imposition of such an alteration on the minority. The extent to which the margin may be increased above that point involves a balancing with the need to prevent a small minority from arbitrarily blocking the wishes of a substantial majority. Accordingly, the Model Act originally adopted two-thirds as a point for attaining reasonable balance. However, in 1969 an amendment reduced the required vote from two-thirds to a majority in recognition of the generally prevailing view that . . . a minority should not be permitted to block the wishes of the majority.[7]

The concept underlying the balance struck in the Model Act seems fairly straightforward. Stated generally, the percentage chosen should be one that facilitates a transaction that, although perhaps not beneficial to *all* shareholders, represents an overall *net* gain (taking all shareholder gains and losses into account). A majority requirement satisfies this concern based on the simple assumption that if more shareholders favor a transaction than oppose it, the gains to those favoring it will exceed the losses to those opposing it and, therefore, the transaction will result in a net gain.

This shift from unanimity to a majority requirement, motivated by a desire to prevent a minority from blocking otherwise beneficial transactions, has a parallel in economic theory. Stated more generally, the problem is to specify a test which, if satisfied, would guarantee that we would be better off as a result of taking a particular action rather than not taking it. Two formulations of such a standard are relevant here. One, Pareto Optimality,

---

[5] Ernest Folk, *The Delaware General Corporation Law* 318 (1972). See Cal.Corp. Code §§ 152, 1201; Mich.Comp. Laws Ann. §§ 450.173; and N.J.Stat.Ann. § 14A:10-3.

[6] N.Y.Bus.Corp. Law § 903. A compilation of the voting requirements of different jurisdictions can be found in Fox & Fox (1981), *supra* note 1, at § 24.02. See also Stephen Schulman & Alan Schenk, *Shareholders' Voting and Appraisal Rights in Corporate Acquisition Transactions,* 38 Bus.Law. 1529 (1983).

In recent years a number of states have amended their corporate statutes to require a higher percentage approval when the acquiring company already holds a substantial percentage of the target's stock. Because these provisions were uniformly enacted as a response to judicial invalidation of state efforts at strengthening target management's hand in a hostile takeover, they will be considered in Chapter 23 concerning state securities law regulation of tender offers.

[7] 2 ABA-ALI Model Bus.Corp. Act Ann.2d § 73 ¶ 2 (1971). Note that the drafters had already lost sight of the direction of historical change. It seems quite clear that the movement was from unanimity down rather than from a majority up.

states that we can be certain an action will improve our collective well-being if no one is made worse off by it, but at least one person's position is improved. An alternative, Kaldor-Hicks Efficiency, asserts that an action is beneficial, even if some individuals are made worse off, so long as those who are made better off gain enough that they could (although they are not required to) compensate the losers and still end up ahead.[8]

The shift from unanimity to majority rule for approval of corporate combinations can be seen as a shift from a rule requiring Pareto Optimality to one requiring only Kaldor-Hicks Efficiency. If unanimity is required, we can be relatively certain that anyone whom the transaction would make worse off would object, thereby assuring that any transaction which received unanimous approval was Pareto Optimal. A majority rule, in contrast, requires only that the winners outnumber the losers, thereby, at least on the surface, satisfying the Kaldor-Hicks criteria. The move to a majority rule is thus justified as one which allows transactions which increase the overall welfare even though a minority is injured as a result.[9]

While he does not disagree with using the Kaldor-Hicks measure of efficiency, Professor Carney takes issue with the assertion that a majority requirement for corporate combinations really assures that the Kaldor-Hicks standard is satisfied:

William Carney, FUNDAMENTAL CORPORATE CHANGES, MINORITY SHAREHOLDERS, AND BUSINESS PURPOSES
1980 Am.B.Found.Res.J. 69, 110-18

The long and painful development of the law of fundamental corporate changes . . . has been designed to assure majority rule and to provide methods for bringing the minority along or at least making certain that they do not frustrate the desires of the majority. To conclude that these transactions, accomplished over the objections of some minority stockholders, have all of the benefits of freely bargained exchanges involves an unwarranted leap.

What is true of individual welfare may not be true of group welfare where exchanges are between groups rather than individuals. . . .

When a group makes a collective decision binding all its members to engage in an exchange, and does so by majority rule, it is possible that large

---

[8] The distinctions between Pareto Optimality and Kaldor-Hicks Efficiency are discussed in an accessible fashion in Jules Coleman, *Markets, Morals and the Law* (1988).

[9] This formulation assumes that shareholders are acting in good faith. If, however, some shareholders act strategically, that is, hold out their vote unless they receive more than a proportionate share of the benefit, then a reduction in the percentage necessary for action also reduces the costs of the decision-making process itself. See generally James Buchanan & Gordon Tullock, *The Calculus of Consent* 43-62 (1965).

losses to the minority may exceed, in the aggregate, the gains to the majority. . . .

Any test that attempts to weigh costs and benefits in a fundamental corporate change or to assure that some benefits of substance do exist faces a difficult if not impossible task. To determine whether a fundamental change is "efficient" in the sense of enhancing aggregate welfare, we must determine aggregate shareholder gains and losses. In voluntary transactions, where control is transferred entirely through stock purchases, we can be certain that both sides agree that there are gains involved. In a successful tender offer for control, we can be certain that there are gains to the new controlling shareholder or that gains are anticipated after completion of the squeeze-out merger. In a competitive market, these gains should produce a competitive rate of return for the acquiring corporation. If it were possible to draw an accurate supply curve for the selling shareholders . . . it would be possible to measure the gains of this group by determining the difference between the tender offer price, which is normally at a premium over the market, and the supply curve. Some approximation of this is possible, since we do know the terminal points on the segment of the supply curve represented by the shares tendered.[183] The premium paid to this group of

---

[183] If, for example, the acquiring corporation begins owning no shares of the target, the point of zero supply or at least of a minimal supply (in the short run) is represented by the current market price: (It is possible that a gradual process might lead to an accumulation of a significant number of shares through market transactions carefully disguised, but this is a longer run view of the supply curve.) The other end of the segment of the supply curve we can chart is represented by the percentage of shares tendered in response to the invitation for tenders at what is presumably a premium over the market price that prevailed prior to the tender offer regardless of whether the acquiring corporation accepts all of them. If not all are accepted at that price, a surplus exists. Diagrammed below are two supply curves, illustrating the premium paid, represented by the difference between the supply curve and the tender offer price. In the second example (Figure 1b) where not all shares are taken, we know something about the supply curve beyond the number of shares purchased.

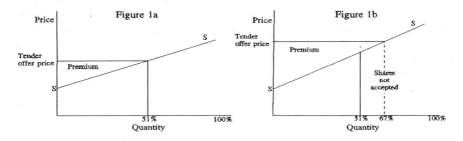

Thus, in Figure 1a, we know the share of the curve SS up to the tender offer price but not beyond: the rest is merely an extension of the earlier segment. We do not, of course, know the precise slope of the curve between these points. In Figure 1b, we know the general shape of the curve SS up to the tender offer price, even though the acquiring corporation did not take all of the shares tendered, but took only 51% of the total shares. This suggests either a miscalculation of the supply curve by the acquiring corporation or intervening events that caused a greater tender than required by the acquiring corporation. The latter could be the

shareholders represents the identifiable benefit to this group over the marginal benefit that otherwise would have persuaded them to sell their shares.

Against these gains to the majority who have tendered we must balance the losses suffered by the minority who declined to tender at the offering price. In many cases they may be squeezed out at the tender offer price.[184] Since no market transactions are involved, any measure of the magnitude of their losses, based on the supply curve, is purely speculative. These shareholders suffer a loss when their shares are taken at a price they did not freely consent to. We can only speculate about the slope of the supply curve beyond the point of the last voluntary transaction and thus cannot measure the magnitude of the difference between the price demanded by these shareholders in the aggregate and the price received, which would determine the amount of the losses to be balanced against the gains to other participants in the exchange, both sellers and buyers. Supply curves can be determined only by revealed behavior of market participants. To the extent that the curve involves persons unwilling to sell at current market prices, descriptions of such curves are speculation, albeit more or less informed.

In a situation where a minority's shares are acquired in involuntary transactions, such as those involved in squeeze-outs, whether aggregate gains exceed aggregate losses depends on (1) whether the slope of the supply curve is relatively less elastic beyond the point of the last voluntary sale than over the balance of its length and (2) the relative length of each section.[185] Put

---

endorsement of the offer by target management, adverse business developments for the target in the interim, or a failure of target management to mount an effective defense against the tender offer.

[184] See, e.g., Singer v. Magnavox Co., 380 A.2d 969 (Del.1977).

[185] This can be illustrated in two ways. First, we must look at the slope of the supply curve. To the extent it slopes more steeply upward as we reach higher quantities of stock, the potential losses to dissenters will be greater. In Figure 1a below, constant elasticity of supply at all levels, illustrated arbitrarily here by a constant slope of the supply curve, indicates that a 51% approval of a squeeze-out merger will result in benefits only slightly exceeding costs. Put another way, the premium to voluntary sellers slightly exceeds the losses to forced sellers. In Figure 1b, the supply curve slopes more steeply at higher quantities and illustrates that the losses to forced sellers will be greater at the same price, and losses will exceed gains to sellers.

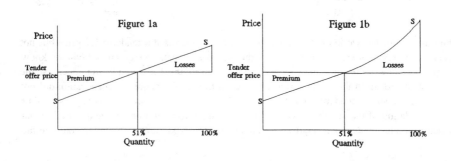

another way, if the last dissenters exhibit a high degree of inelasticity in their behavior, and if they hold a relatively large number of shares (say 49%), their losses may exceed the gains of a great many willing sellers who are relatively indifferent about whether to hold this particular stock.

. . . [Thus,] the only certain guarantee of efficient mergers[191] is unanimous consent of the shareholders, but this has been rejected as impractical or impossible. The higher the percentage vote required, the more certain we are that aggregate shareholder gains are likely to exceed losses. The English Company Act's requirement of approval by holders of 90% of the shares within a limited time provides far greater assurance than our own system that only efficient acquisitions will proceed.

The problem that Professor Carney describes is one that students of the branch of microeconomics known as "public choice" have long recognized as inherent in any voting system that requires less than unanimous approval but does not account for different intensities among voters. Carney sets that problem in an acquisition context by questioning the relative slope of the supply curve for a target's shares above the acquisition price. The problem is that if 49% of the voters feel more strongly about an issue than the remaining 51%, there will be a net loss in welfare as a result of the transaction if a majority rule applies.[10]

The second factor is the length of each segment of the supply curve, which reflects the percentage voting requirement of state law for fundamental changes. Thus a rule of simple majority approval for fundamental changes increases the number of shares whose holders may suffer losses, which is illustrated by Figure 2. . . .

The heavily cross-hatched area represents the smaller losses that would be incurred under a rule of two-thirds consent to fundamental changes, while the larger lightly shaded area represents the losses under a rule of simple majority approval.

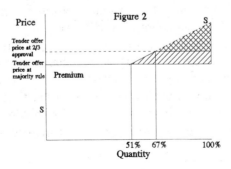

Figure 2

[191] It should be emphasized that an efficient merger is one in which there is gain for the aggregate of all shareholders, when the gain and loss of each shareholder is measured individually.

[10] See generally Dennis Mueller, *Public Choice: A Survey,* 14 J.Econ.Lit. 395 (1976), Buchanan & Tullock (1965), *supra* note 9.

One approach to this problem would be to allow vote buying or selling, so that those who feel strongly about the result can acquire enough votes to match their intensity. If capital markets were perfect, the existence of a market for the corporation's shares might serve this purpose and eliminate Professor Carney's concern. Then a minority who valued the corporation's shares at a price sufficiently greater than the majority that a transaction favored by the majority would result in a net overall loss would simply purchase the shares held by the majority (or a sufficient number to block the transaction under the applicable decision rule).[11] The difficulty, however, is that transaction costs and problems associated with collective action by the minority, such as free riding, make it quite unlikely that this corrective action would occur with sufficient frequency to ease Professor Carney's concern. The question is then whether any other forces operate to minimize the problem.

Some guidance on this point can be derived from the financial theory considered in Part I. The capital asset pricing model states that all shareholders will value the target's stock based only on the systematic risk associated with its return. Individual circumstances will not enter into the determination of stock price, the separation theorem relegating such concerns to a determination of the content of the individual's portfolio.[12] If that is correct, i.e., that the shareholders view a corporation's stock as only a fungible stream of income with a particular risk, then under the assumptions on which the CAPM is based there is no reason to expect that different shareholders will value the target's stock differently. Therefore, the problem posed by Professor Carney will not exist. In other words, the supply curve will be horizontal. Cast in terms of public choice, the implication is that all voters hold their views with equal intensity, in which event public choice theorists have demonstrated that a majority decision rule is Kaldor-Hicks efficient.[13]

The persuasiveness of this response to Professor Carney diminishes, however, when it is recalled that one of the assumptions on which the CAPM is based is that there are homogeneous expectations, i.e., that all stockholders have the same beliefs about the future risk and return characteristics of the corporation.[14] What if shareholders have *different* expectations about the future? How does this alter analysis of a majority requirement in mergers?

The answer seems to depend on whether a shareholder can expect his or her beliefs about the future to be systematically more accurate than those of other shareholders. Only in that event does a greater than majority rule, which reduces below 50% the likelihood that a shareholder will be in the minority, seem desirable. Put differently, only if a shareholder's views are

---

[11] See Eugene Fama, *The Effect of a Firm's Investment and Financing Decisions on the Welfare of its Security Holders,* 68 Am.Econ.Rev. 272, 282-83 (1978).

[12] See Chapter 4, *supra.*

[13] Mueller (1976), *supra* note 10, at 402-03.

[14] See Chapter 4, *supra.*

systematically more accurate than the majority's will a greater than majority rule make the shareholder better off.[15] At this point, data concerning the Efficient Capital Market Hypothesis become relevant. The semi-strong form of the ECMH suggests that none of us can expect to outperform the majority over time; hence, we should all prefer a majority voting requirement.

However, there are circumstances where capital market theory fails to justify the efficiency of a majority vote requirement. For example, what happens to reliance on the separation theorem to eliminate the problem of different intensities if there are shareholders who do not hold their shares as a pure investment -- when proposed corporate action may affect the shareholders' wealth otherwise than through the value of their stock.[16] Traditional corporate law analysis recognizes that there are circumstances when a shareholder is "interested" in the subject of a shareholder vote. For present purposes, the term "interested" is a shorthand for the fact that the shareholder is disproportionately affected by the proposed action. Consider, for example, when approval is sought from the shareholders of one of a group of affiliated corporations for a transaction with the group's parent. Although the wealth of the affiliated corporation's stockholders will be affected only by the impact of the proposed transaction on the value of their affiliated corporation stock, the impact on the parent's wealth will be determined by the effect of the proposed action on the value of the entire affiliated group. In this circumstance, a majority vote of the *disinterested* shareholders is typically required.[17]

A more complicated exercise in using the separation theorem to understand corporate voting rules is identifying when those forming a

---

[15] See Ronald Gilson, *The Case Against Shark Repellant Amendments: Structural Limitations on the Enabling Concept,* 34 Stan.L.Rev. 775, 822-31 (1982); Mueller (1976), *supra* note 10, at 402.

[16] See Gilson (1982), *supra* note 15, at 833-34. This formulation raises the problem of under what circumstances a shareholder would prefer to have the firm deviate from profit-maximization. More generally, if some shareholders' welfare is affected in their nonshareholder capacities, because the firm's decisions alter consumer prices or because some shareholders are subject to externalities produced by the firm, there will not be unanimity concerning the firm's investment decisions even with homogeneous expectations, because different shareholders will be affected differently. See Frank Milne, *The Firm's Objective Function as a Collective Choice Problem,* 37 Public Choice 473 (1981). For more detailed development of the circumstances formally necessary for unanimity, see Harry DeAngelo, *Competition and Unanimity,* 71 Am.Econ.Rev. 18 (1981); Sanford Grossman & Joseph Stiglitz, *Stockholder Unanimity in Making Production and Financial Decisions,* 94 Q.J.Econ. 543 (1980); David Baron, *Investment Policy, Optimality, and the Mean-Variance Model,* 34 J.Fin. 207 (1979) (review article). For discussions of the impact on corporate voting rules of the absence of unanimity because of the failure of separation, see Jeffrey Gordon, *Shareholder Initiative: A Social and Game Theoretic Approach to Corporate Law,* 60 U.Cin.L.Rev. 347 (1991); Peter Letsou, *Shareholder Voice and the Market for Corporate Control,* 70 Wash.U.L.Q. 755 (1992); David Skeel, *The Nature and Effect of Corporate Voting in Chapter 11 Reorganization Cases,* 78 Va.L.Rev. 461 (1992).

[17] See, e.g., Fleiger v. Lawrence, 361 A.2d 218 (Del.1976); Cal.Corp. Code § 310(a).

corporation whose stock is to be sold to the public would select other than a majority decision rule. Suppose the founders wished to maintain control despite the proposed public offering. In this setting, specifying a particular decision rule would not solve the founders' problem unless they retained a majority of the stock. And retaining control by this technique is costly. It limits the extent to which the founders can diversify their portfolios -- they would have to retain a majority of the stock -- and limits the availability of future equity financing because that would dilute the founders' control. An alternative approach to maintaining control would be to create a class of nonvoting or limited voting stock and sell that to the public. This approach would allow the founders to sell off as much of their equity as they wanted because they would still retain all of the superior voting stock.[18] Also, future equity offerings of the nonvoting or limited voting stock could be made without significantly diluting the founders' continuing control.

A first reaction to this solution to the founders' problem is that it does not work. If voting rights have value, as the founders clearly believe,[19] establish that the founders will bear the cost of retaining the ability to approve self-dealing transactions and engage in other abuses of control, the public will pay less for the shares, and the founders will end up no better off for their effort to separate ownership and control. Indeed, if the founders had not intended to engage in self-serving behavior, they may end up worse off.

A second look at the issue suggests a different result. Suppose that the reason the founders want to maintain control is that they have a great deal of human capital invested in the company. In this situation, separation will not apply because a corporate action will impact the founders not only through its effect on the value of the corporation's stock, but also through its impact on the value of the founders' human capital. Thus, because separation does not apply, control has a *private* value to the founders that it does not have to the public. In this situation, the founders may gain by going public with a nonvoting or limited voting class of stock because the public, for whom separation *does* apply, will not value control as highly as do the founders.[20]

---

[18] The mechanics of the transaction would take the form of a pre-offering recapitalization in which the founders would exchange their shares of the pre-transaction single class of voting stock for shares of a new class of voting stock and shares of a new class of nonvoting or limited voting stock. The nonvoting or limited voting stock would then be sold to the public.

[19] Michael Jensen & William Meckling, *Theory of the Firm, Managerial Behavior, Agency Costs and Ownership Structure*, 3 J.Fin.Econ. 305 (1976).

[20] For efforts at developing a framework for determining efficient allocations of voting rights, on which the preceding discussion draws, see Jean-Francois Dreyfus, *Should We Agree? Unanimity and the Value of Control*, (N.Y.U.Grad.Sch. of Bus.Admin. Working Paper No.426, June 1986); Sanford Grossman & Oliver Hart, *One Share-One Vote and the Market for Corporate Control*, 20 J.Fin. 175 (1987); Milton Harris & Arthur Raviv, *Corporate Governance: Voting Rights and Majority Rules*, 20 J.Fin. 203 (1988); Douglas Blair, Devra Golbe & James Gerard, *Unbundling the Voting Rights and Profit Claims of Common Shares*, 97 J.Pol.Econ. 420 (1989).

Who gets to vote? Whatever the percentage approval required by the particular statute, the question of who gets to vote on the issue remains. Do shares that are nonvoting for other matters, as is commonly the case with preferred stock, nonetheless get to vote on a merger? The major commercial jurisdictions do not allow preferred or other nonvoting shares to vote on a merger, although there are notable exceptions.[21] Other states do provide the right to vote if the effect of the transaction is to change the rights, preferences or privileges of preferred shares in a way that would require their approval if attempted by means other than a merger. For example, if the effect of a merger will be to reduce the priorities of the preferred stock because of differences between the terms of the stock to be received and that held before the merger, the preferred stockholders will be allowed to vote.[22]

The assumption underlying this approach is that so long as the terms of the preferred are not altered, the transaction will not affect holders of preferred and, therefore, they do not need voting rights to protect themselves. But while this assures that the preferred's position will not be nominally altered, might they nonetheless be adversely affected? The value of the preferred depends not only on its return -- presumably the preferred dividend rate is protected by the statute from alteration without consent -- but also on the systematic risk associated with those returns. If the effect of the merger is to cause the preferred stockholders to receive identical stock, but in a corporation having greater systematic risk, then the value of what they have received is lower than that which they have given up, a danger not protected against by the typical corporate statute.

The problem may be seen more clearly when posed in terms of the strategic considerations bearing on how to divide the price to be paid for the target company between common and preferred stockholders. If the amount that the acquiring company will pay for the entire company is fixed, then it is to the advantage of the common to negotiate the terms of the transaction so that the value of the preferred is reduced, and, to that extent, the value of the common is increased. If this transfer of value from the preferred to the common is accomplished by increasing the systematic risk associated with the preferred, under typical statutes the *nominally* equivalent terms of the consideration given the preferred vest exclusive voting power in the common. Ironically, this gives the sole approval right to precisely those who have an incentive to favor themselves at the expense of the preferred.[23]

This problem is identical to that facing debenture holders of the target company who also have no statutory right to vote on the transaction.[24] To protect themselves against the risk that the common stockholders will

---

[21] E.g., Cal.Corp. Code §§ 152, 1201; Conn.Gen.Stat. § 33-366(b).

[22] ABA-ALI Model Bus.Corp. Act Ann.2d § 73(b); Wis.Stat.Ann. § 180.64(2).

[23] Cf. Dalton v. American Investment Co., 490 A.2d 574 (Del.Ch.1985) (transaction structured to avoid sharing premium with preferred shareholders).

[24] No state affirmatively grants debt holders the right to vote, and only a few states even allow such a provision as an option. See, e.g., Cal.Corp. Code § 204(a)(7).

structure the transaction to their own advantage, debt holders typically secure a contractual right to prior approval of an acquisition -- in substance a contractual class vote.[25] Similarly, in the majority of states where preferred stockholders do not have a statutory right to vote on a merger, the preferred stock contract typically grants a class vote in an acquisition.[26]

A recent statutory trend extends to common shareholders the approach of eliminating the requirement of a shareholder vote when the transaction does not alter the shareholders' position. California pioneered this extension; Cal.Corp. Code § 1201(b) and (d) eliminate the need for a vote of acquiring company shareholders in a merger if the rights, preferences and privileges of the shareholders are not changed and if those shareholders own immediately after the transaction shares of the acquiring company representing more than five-sixths of the voting power of the acquiring company.[27] The California pattern was followed in the Revised Model Business Corporation Act and in Delaware, except that the trigger for eliminating voting rights is that the acquiring company not issue in the merger shares amounting to more than 20% of the number of shares outstanding before the merger.[28]

How the votes are counted. Once otherwise nonvoting shares are given the right to vote on a proposed merger, a question arises as to how to count their votes. Are their votes simply added to the total of common stockholder votes in determining whether the statutory percentage is met or, as the preceding discussion assumed, are they given a class vote? That is, in addition to approval by the common, must the statutory percentage of preferred stockholders also approve the transaction? Typically, if nonvoting shares are allowed to vote on a merger transaction, the vote contemplated is a class vote, although in New York, for example, preferred stockholders are both given a class vote and have their votes counted along with the common in determining whether the overall statutory percentage is required.[29]

The discussion in the preceding paragraph focused on the numerator in determining whether the statutory fraction for approval is satisfied. Another question concerning the manner in which the votes are counted is how to determine the proper denominator. In a majority approval jurisdiction, for example, is the required number of shares 51% of the shares represented and

---

[25] See Clifford Smith & Jerold Warner, *On Financial Contracting: An Analysis of Bond Covenants,* 7 J.Fin.Econ. 117 (1979).

[26] See Richard Buxbaum, *Preferred Stock -- Law and Draftsmanship,* 42 Cal.L.Rev. 243 (1954).

[27] The California statute was patterned after the New York Stock Exchange requirement of a shareholder vote as a prerequisite to listing shares issued in an acquisition if the issued shares represent an increase in outstanding shares of approximately 18.5% or more. *New York Stock Exchange Company Manual* A-283-284 (1978).

[28] Rev. Model Bus.Corp. Act § 11.03(g) (1984); Del.Gen.Corp. Law § 251(f).

[29] N.Y.Bus.Corp.L. § 903.

voting at the meeting, or the almost certainly higher number, 51% of all outstanding shares eligible to vote whether actually voting or not? This distinction is drawn in the California Corporations Code where some actions, like mergers, require the "approval of the outstanding shares," defined in § 152 as a "majority of the outstanding shares entitled to vote," while other actions, such as election of directors, require only "approval of the shareholders," defined in § 153 as a "majority of the shares represented and voting at a duly held meeting." Typically, the higher number is required for mergers.[30]

Who gets to complain? Except where voting rights are eliminated for all acquiring company shareholders (as in California or New Jersey when fewer than a specified number of shares are issued in the merger), or for all target company shareholders (as in a short form merger, see Chapter 15, *supra*), appraisal rights are typically limited to those having voting rights. If one's interests are sufficiently affected to require a vote, then it seems to be assumed that those on the losing end of the vote may require appraisal rights. Conversely, if voting is unnecessary to protect a particular class of stockholders, then so are appraisal rights. The wisdom of this assumption, which extends beyond mergers to other acquisition techniques, is also considered in Chapter 15.

B.   Sale of Substantially All Assets

1.   The Statutes

DELAWARE GENERAL CORPORATION LAW

§ 271. Sale, lease or exchange of assets; consideration; procedure

(a) Every corporation may at any meeting of its board of directors or governing body sell, lease, or exchange all or substantially all of its property and assets, including its goodwill and its corporate franchises, upon such terms and conditions and for such consideration, which may consist in whole or in part of money or other property, including shares of stock in, and/or other securities of, any other corporation or corporations, as its board of directors or governing body deems expedient and for the best interests of the corporation, when and as authorized by a resolution adopted by a majority of the outstanding stock of the corporation entitled to vote thereon . . . at a meeting thereof duly called upon at least 20 days notice. The notice of the meeting shall state that such a resolution will be considered.

---

[30] See Del.Gen.Corp. Law § 251(c).

(b) Notwithstanding authorization or consent to a proposed sale, lease or exchange of a corporation's property and assets by the stockholders or members, the board of directors or governing body may abandon such proposed sale, lease or exchange without further action by the stockholders or members, subject to the rights, if any of third parties under any contract relating thereto.

MODEL BUSINESS CORPORATION ACT
(Revised through 1991)

§ 12.02. Sale of Assets Other Than in Regular Course of Business

(a) A corporation may sell, lease, exchange, or otherwise dispose of all, or substantially all, of its property (with or without the good will), otherwise than in the usual and regular course of business, on the terms and conditions and for the consideration determined by the corporation's board of directors, if the board of directors proposes and its shareholders approve the proposed transaction.

(b) For a transaction to be authorized:

(1)   the board of directors must recommend the proposed transaction to the shareholders unless the board of directors determines that because of conflict of interest or other special circumstances it should make no recommendation and communicates the basis for its determination to the shareholders with the submission of the proposed transaction; and

(2) the shareholders entitled to vote must approve the transaction.

(c) The board of directors may condition its submission of the proposed transaction on any basis.

(d)   The corporation shall notify each shareholder, whether or not entitled to vote, of the proposed shareholders' meeting. . . . The notice must also state that the purpose, or one of the purposes, of the meeting is to consider the sale, lease, exchange, or other disposition of all, or substantially all, the property of the corporation and contain or be accompanied by a description of the transaction.

(e) Unless the articles of incorporation or the board of directors (acting pursuant to subsection (c)) require a greater vote or a vote by voting groups, the transaction to be authorized must be approved by a majority of all the votes entitled to be cast on the transaction.

(f) After a sale, lease, exchange, or other disposition of property is authorized, the transaction may be abandoned (subject to any contractual rights) without further shareholder action. . . .

§ 13.02 Right to Dissent

(a) A shareholder is entitled to dissent from, and obtain payment of the fair value of his shares in the event of, any of the following corporate actions: . . .

> (3) Consummation of a sale or exchange of all, or substantially all, of the property of the corporation other than in the usual and regular course of business, if the shareholder is entitled to vote on the sale or exchange, including a sale in dissolution, but not including a sale pursuant to court order or a sale for cash pursuant to a plan by which all or substantially all of the net proceeds of the sale will be distributed to the shareholders within one year after the date of sale. . . .

---

2.   What Is "Substantially All"?

GIMBEL v. SIGNAL COMPANIES, INC.
316 A.2d 599 (Del.Ch.1974)

QUILLEN, Chancellor. This action was commenced on December 24, 1973 by plaintiff, a stockholder of the Signal Companies, Inc. ("Signal"). The complaint seeks, among other things, injunctive relief to prevent the consummation of the pending sale by Signal to Burmah Oil Incorporated ("Burmah") of all of the outstanding capital stock of Signal Oil and Gas Company ("Signal Oil"), a wholly-owned subsidiary of Signal. The effective sale price exceeds 480 million dollars.[1] The sale was approved at a special meeting of the Board of Directors of Signal held on December 21, 1973.

. . . It should be noted that the plaintiff is part of an investment group which has some 2,400,000 shares representing 12% of the outstanding stock of Signal. . . .

Count 1 of the complaint asserts that . . . the proposed sale requires authorization by the majority of the outstanding stock of Signal pursuant to 8 Del.C. § 271(a). . . .

A sale of less than all or substantially all assets is not covered by negative implication from the statute.[3]

---

[1] The purchase price consists of 420 million dollars cash to be paid by Burmah at the closing, the cancellation of approximately 60 million dollars in indebtedness of Signal to Signal Oil, and the transfer by Signal Oil to Signal of a 4-¾% net profits interest in the unexplored portion of Block 211/18 in the North Sea.

[3] . . . The predecessor statute was evidently originally enacted in 1916 in response to Chancellor Curtis' statement of the common law rule in Butler v. New Keystone Copper Co., 93 A. 380, 383 (Del.Ch.1915):

> The general rule as to commercial corporations seems to be settled that neither the directors nor the stockholders of a prosperous, going concern have the power to sell all,

It is important to note in the first instance that the statute does not speak of a requirement of shareholder approval simply because an independent, important branch of a corporate business is being sold. The plaintiff cites several non-Delaware cases for the proposition that shareholder approval of such a sale is required. But that is not the language of our statute. Similarly, it is not our law that shareholder approval is required upon every "major" restructuring of the corporation. Again, it is not necessary to go beyond the statute. The statute requires shareholder approval upon the sale of "all or substantially all" of the corporation's assets. That is the sole test to be applied. While it is true that test does not lend itself to a strict mathematical standard to be applied in every case, the qualitative factor can be defined to some degree notwithstanding the limited Delaware authority. But the definition must begin with and ultimately necessarily relate to our statutory language.

In interpreting the statute the plaintiff relies on Philadelphia National Bank v. B.S.F. Co., 199 A.2d 557 (Del.Ch.1964), *rev'd on other grounds*, 204 A.2d 746 (Del.1964). In that case, B.S.F. Company owned stock in two corporations. It sold its stock in one of the corporations, and retained the stock in the other corporation. The Court found that the stock sold was the principal asset B.S.F. Company had available for sale and that the value of the stock retained was declining. The Court rejected the defendant's contention that the stock sold represented only 47.4% of consolidated assets, and looked to the actual value of the stock sold. On this basis, the Court held that the stock constituted at least 75% of the total assets and the sale of the stock was a sale of substantially all assets.

But two things must be noted about the *Philadelphia National Bank* case. First, even though shareholder approval was obtained under § 271, the case did not arise under § 271 but under an Indenture limiting the activities of B.S.F. for creditor financial security purposes. On appeal, Chief Justice Wolcott was careful to state the following:

> We are of the opinion that this question is not necessarily to be answered by references to the general law concerning the sale of assets by a corporation. The question before us is the narrow one of what particular language of a contract means and is to be answered in terms of what the parties were intending to guard against or to insure.

204 A.2d at 750.

Secondly, the *Philadelphia National Bank* case dealt with the sale of the company's only substantial income producing asset.

The key language in the Court of Chancery opinion in *Philadelphia National Bank* is the suggestion that "the critical factor in determining the character of a sale of assets is generally considered not the amount of property sold but whether the sale is in fact an unusual transaction or one

---

or substantially all, the property of the company if the holder of a single share dissent.

made in the regular course of business of the seller." (199 A.2d at 561). Professor Folk suggests from the opinion that "the statute would be inapplicable if the assets sale is 'one made in furtherance of express corporate objects in the ordinary and regular course of the business'" (referring to language in 199 A.2d at 561).

But any "ordinary and regular course of the business" test in this context obviously is not intended to limit the directors to customary daily business activities. Indeed, a question concerning the statute would not arise unless the transaction was somewhat out of the ordinary. While it is true that a transaction in the ordinary course of business does not require shareholder approval, the converse is not true. Every transaction out of normal routine does not necessarily require shareholder approval. The unusual nature of the transaction must strike at the heart of the corporate existence and purpose.

. . . It is in this sense that the "unusual transaction" judgment is to be made and the statute's applicability determined. If the sale is of assets quantitatively vital to the operation of the corporation and is out of the ordinary and substantially affects the existence and purpose of the corporation, then it is beyond the power of the Board of Directors. With these guidelines, I turn to Signal and the transaction in this case.

Signal or its predecessor was incorporated in the oil business in 1922. But, beginning in 1952, Signal diversified its interests. In 1952, Signal acquired a substantial stock interest in American President lines. From 1957 to 1962 Signal was the sole owner of Laura Scudders, a nationwide snack food business. In 1964, Signal acquired Garrett Corporation which is engaged in the aircraft, aerospace, and uranium enrichment business. In 1967, Signal acquired Mack Trucks, Inc., which is engaged in the manufacture and sale of trucks and related equipment. Also in 1968, the oil and gas business was transferred to a separate division and later in 1970 to the Signal Oil subsidiary. Since 1967, Signal has made acquisition of or formed substantial companies none of which are involved or related with the oil and gas industry. . . . As indicated previously, the oil and gas production development of Signal's business is now carried on by Signal Oil, the sale of the stock of which is an issue in this lawsuit.

According to figures published in Signal's last annual report (1972) and the latest quarterly report (September 30, 1973) and certain other internal financial information, the following tables can be constructed.

SIGNAL'S REVENUES (in millions)

	9 Mos. Ended Sept. 30, 1973	December 31, 1972	1971
Truck manufacturing	$655.9	$712.7	$552.5
Aerospace & industrial	407.1	478.2	448.0
Oil & gas	185.8	267.2	314.1
Other	16.4	14.4	14.0

SIGNAL'S PRE-TAX EARNINGS (in millions)

	9 Mos. Ended Sept. 30, 1973	December 31, 1972	1971
Truck manufacturing	$55.8	$65.5	$36.4
Aerospace & industrial	20.7	21.5	19.5
Oil & gas	10.1	12.8	9.9

SIGNAL'S ASSETS (in millions)

	9 Mos. Ended Sept. 30, 1973	December 31, 1972	1971
Truck manufacturing	$581.4	$506.5	$450.4
Aerospace & industrial	365.2	351.1	331.5
Oil & gas	376.2	368.3	369.9
Other	113.1	102.0	121.6

SIGNAL'S NET WORTH (in millions)

	9 Mos. Ended Sept. 30, 1973	December 31, 1972	1971
Truck manufacturing	$295.0	$269.7	$234.6
Aerospace & industrial	163.5	152.2	139.6
Oil & gas	280.5	273.2	254.4
Other	(55.7)	(42.1)	(2.0)

Based on the company's figures, Signal Oil represents only about 26% of the total assets of Signal. While Signal Oil represents 41% of Signal's total net worth, it produces only about 15% of Signal's revenues and earnings. Moreover, the additional tables shown in Signal's brief . . . are also interesting in demonstrating the low rate of return which has been realized recently from the oil and gas operation.

PRE-TAX DOLLAR RETURN ON VALUE OF ASSETS			
	9 Mos. Ended Sept, 30, 1973	1972	1971
Truck manufacturing	12.8%	12.9%	8.1%
Aerospace & industrial	7.5	6.1	5.9
Oil & gas	3.6	3.5	2.7
PRE-TAX DOLLAR RETURN ON NET WORTH			
	9 Mos. Ended Sept. 30, 1973	1972	1971
Truck manufacturing	25.1%	24.2%	15.5%
Aerospace & industrial	16.8	14.1	14.0
Oil & gas	4.8	4.7	3.9

While it is true, based on the experience of the Signal-Burmah transaction and the record in this lawsuit, that Signal Oil is more valuable than shown by the company's books, even if, as plaintiff suggests in his brief, the $761,000,000 value attached to Signal Oil's properties by the plaintiff's expert Paul V. Keyser, Jr., were substituted as the asset figure, the oil and gas properties would still constitute less than half the value of Signal's total assets. Thus, from a straight quantitative approach, I agree with Signal's position that the sale to Burmah does not constitute a sale of "all or substantially all" of Signal's assets.

In addition, if the character of the transaction is examined, the plaintiff's position is also weak. While it is true that Signal's original purpose was oil and gas and while oil and gas is still listed first in the certificate of incorporation, the simple fact is that Signal is now a conglomerate engaged in the aircraft and aerospace business, the manufacture and sale of trucks and related equipment, and other businesses besides oil and gas. The very nature of its business, as it now in fact exists, contemplates the acquisition and disposal of independent branches of its corporate business. Indeed, given the operations since 1952, it can be said that such acquisitions and dispositions have become part of the ordinary course of business. The facts that the oil and gas business was historically first and that authorization for such operations are listed first in the certificate do not prohibit disposal of such interest. . . .

It is perhaps true, as plaintiff has argued, that the advent of multi-business corporations has in one sense emasculated § 271 since one business may be sold without shareholder approval when other substantial businesses are retained. But it is one thing for a corporation to evolve over a period of years into a multi-business corporation, the operations of which include the purchase and sale of whole businesses, and another for a single business corporation by a one transaction revolution to sell the entire means of operating its business in exchange for money or a separate business. In the former situation, the processes of corporate democracy customarily have had the opportunity to restrain or otherwise control over a period of years.

Thus, there is a chance for some shareholder participation. The Signal development illustrates the difference. For example, when Signal, itself formerly called Signal Oil and Gas Company, changed its name in 1968, it was for the announced "need for a new name appropriate to the broadly diversified activities of Signal's multi-industry complex." . . .

The situation is also dramatically illustrated financially in this very case. Independent of the contract with Burmah, the affidavit of Signal's Board Chairman shows that over $200,000,000 of Signal Oil's refining and marketing assets have been sold in the past five years. This activity, prior to the sale at issue here, in itself constitutes a major restructuring of the corporate structure.

I conclude that measured quantitatively and qualitatively, the sale of the stock of Signal Oil by Signal to Burmah does not constitute a sale of "all or substantially all" of Signal's assets. . . .

KATZ v. BREGMAN
431 A.2d 1274 (Del.Ch.1981)

MARVEL, Chancellor. The complaint herein seeks the entry of an order preliminarily enjoining the proposed sale of the Canadian assets of Plant Industries, Inc. to Vulcan Industrial Packaging, Ltd., the plaintiff Hyman Katz allegedly being the owner of approximately 170,000 shares of common stock of the defendant Plant Industries, Inc. . . .

The complaint alleges that during the last six months of 1980 the board of directors of Plant Industries, Inc., under the guidance of the individual defendant Robert B. Bregman, the present chief executive officer of such corporation, embarked on a course of action which resulted in the disposal of several unprofitable subsidiaries of the corporate defendant located in the United States, namely Louisiana Foliage Inc., a horticultural business, Sunaid Food Products, Inc., a Florida packaging business, and Plant Industries (Texas), Inc., a business concerned with the manufacture of woven synthetic cloth. As a result of these sales Plant Industries, Inc. by the end of 1980 had disposed of a significant part of its unprofitable assets.

. . . Mr. Bregman thereupon proceeded on a course of action designed to dispose of a subsidiary of the corporate defendant known as Plant National (Quebec) Ltd., a business which constitutes Plant Industries, Inc.'s entire business operation in Canada and has allegedly constituted Plant's only income producing facility during the past four years. The professed principal purpose of such proposed sale is to raise needed cash and thus improve Plant's balance sheets. And while interest in purchasing the corporate defendant's Canadian plant was thereafter evinced not only by Vulcan Industrial Packaging, Ltd. but also by Universal Drum Reconditioning Co., which latter corporation originally undertook to match or approximate and recently to top Vulcan's bid, a formal contract was entered into between

Plant Industries, Inc. and Vulcan on April 2, 1981 for the purchase and sale of Plant National (Quebec) despite the constantly increasing bids for the same property being made by Universal.   One reason advanced by Plant's management for declining to negotiate with Universal is that a firm undertaking having been entered into with Vulcan that the board of directors of Plant may not legally or ethically negotiate with Universal. . . .

In seeking injunctive relief, . . . plaintiff relies on . . . 8 Del.C. § 271 to the effect that a decision of a Delaware corporation to sell "all or substantially all of its property and assets . . ." requires not only the approval of such corporation's board of directors but also a resolution adopted by a majority of the outstanding stockholders of the corporation. . . .

Turning to the possible application of 8 Del.C. § 271 to the proposed sale of substantial corporate assets of National to Vulcan, it is stated in Gimbel v. Signal Companies, Inc., as follows:

> If the sale is of assets quantitatively vital to the operation of the corporation and is out of the ordinary and substantially affects the existence and purpose of the corporation then it is beyond the power of the Board of Directors.

According to Plant's 1980 10K form, it appears that at the end of 1980, Plant's Canadian operations represented 51% of Plant's remaining assets. Defendants also concede that National represents 44.9% of Plant's sales' revenues and 52.4% of its pre-tax net operating income. Furthermore, such report by Plant discloses, in rough figures, that while National made a profit in 1978 of $2,900,000, the profit from the United States businesses in that year was only $770,000.   In 1979, the Canadian business profit was $3,500,000 while the loss of the United States businesses was $344,000. Furthermore, in 1980, while the Canadian business profit was $5,300,000, the corporate loss in the United States was $4,500,000. And while these figures may be somewhat distorted by the allocation of overhead expenses and taxes, they are significant. In any event, defendants concede that ". . . National accounted for 34.9% of Plant's pretax income in 1976, 36.9% in 1977, 42% in 1978, 51% in 1979 and 52.4% in 1980."

While in the case of Philadelphia National Bank v. B.S.F. Co., the question of whether or not there had been a proposed sale of substantially all corporate assets was tested by provisions of an indenture agreement covering subordinated debentures, the result was the same as if the provisions of 8 Del.C. § 271 had been applicable, the trial Court stating:

> While no pertinent Pennsylvania case is cited, the critical factor in determining the character of a sale of assets is generally considered not the amount of property sold but whether the sale is in fact an unusual transaction or one made in the regular course of business of the seller. . . .

In the case at bar, I am first of all satisfied that historically the principal business of Plant Industries, Inc. has not been to buy and sell industrial facilities but rather to manufacture steel drums for use in bulk shipping as well as for the storage of petroleum products, chemicals, food, paint, adhesives and cleaning agents, a business which has been profitably performed by National of Quebec. Furthermore, the proposal, after the sale of National, to embark on the manufacture of plastic drums represents a radical departure from Plant's historically successful line of business, namely steel drums. I therefore conclude that the proposed sale of Plant's Canadian operations, which constitute over 51% of Plant's total assets and in which are generated approximately 45% of Plant's 1980 net sales, would, if consummated, constitute a sale of substantially all of Plant's assets. By way of contrast, the proposed sale of Signal Oil in Gimbel v. Signal Companies, Inc., *supra*, represented only about 26% of the total assets of Signal Companies, Inc. And while Signal Oil represented 41% of Signal Companies, Inc. total net worth, it generated only about 15% of Signal Companies, Inc. revenue and earnings.

I conclude that because the proposed sale of Plant National (Quebec) Ltd. would, if consummated, constitute a sale of substantially all of the assets of Plant Industries, Inc., as presently constituted, that an injunction should issue preventing the consummation of such sale at least until it has been approved by a majority of the outstanding stockholders of Plant Industries, Inc., entitled to vote at a meeting duly called on at least twenty days' notice.
. . .

Note: Qualitative Gloss on a Quantitative Statute

The problem posed by the construction of statutes like Del.C. § 271 and Model Act § 12.02 has both quantitative and qualitative dimensions. Consider first the purely quantitative side. Assuming the statutory phrase "substantially all" is to be given its commonplace meaning -- that a specified large percentage, say 75%, 85% or 90% of the company's assets must be sold to trigger the requirement of a shareholder vote -- how is the percentage to be calculated? At the most obvious level, is book value the measure, which certainly makes the calculation process easier, or must market value be taken into consideration? Certainly it must have been market value which management had in mind when it determined that the transaction was attractive. At the same time, however, the computational problems associated with a market value determination are potentially substantial. While the arms-length sales price for the assets may make determination of the numerator, the market value of the assets being sold, straightforward, how is the denominator, the market value of the remaining assets (and liabilities), to be determined? The task essentially involves the reconstruction of the target company's entire balance sheet without the application of the historical cost convention, a problem similar to that presented by efforts to alter financial accounting standards to take into account inflation and changing prices.[31]   Which figures were used in Gimbel v. Signal Companies, Inc., and Katz v. Bregman? In this regard, how do you evaluate the following advice offered by three experienced practitioners:

> [A] guideline derived from the Delaware cases on the subject, which gives some useful information, is that if the sale involves more than 75% of the balance sheet assets, at market value, then a court probably would consider the sale to be of substantially all the assets, but if the sale involves less than 26% of the assets, courts probably would not consider the sale to be of substantially all of the assets, notwithstanding qualitative significance. In between these quantitative limits a careful analysis of the qualitative significance of the sale to the corporation must be made.[32]

That advice raises the second problem of construction, which, as the quoted passage suggests, covers all the interesting cases.   Whatever percentage is chosen to correspond to the statutory phrase "substantially all," and however asset values are measured in determining whether the chosen percentage has been met, the much more difficult problem posed by the statute remains. Is there a qualitative aspect to the inquiry?[33] Suppose that a company sold substantially all of its operating assets but retained sufficient liquid assets so that a strictly quantitative measure was not met.[34]

Is the question any easier when a multidivision company sells a division? To be sure, Gimbel v. Signal Companies, Inc., speaks to the sale of one division among many in a situation where the company has become a conglomerate. What of the sale of one of two divisions? While 50% is certainly not "substantially all" in commonplace quantitative terms, Professor Melvin Eisenberg has argued, in effect, that this language reflects not a legislative determination of the primacy of the quantitative measure, but merely the historical fact that, at the time this type of statutory provision was first enacted, single-purpose corporations were the rule.[35]   But if the quantitative aspect of the statute is the result of historical coincidence, what is the statute's real concern? The task then becomes one of identifying the

---

[31] For a sense of the extreme complexity of the issues presented and the range of possible solutions, see Stanley Siegel, *Accounting and Inflation: An Analysis and a Proposal*, 29 UCLA L.Rev. 271 (1981).

[32] Leo Herzel, Timothy Sherck & Dale Colling, *Sales and Acquisitions of Divisions*, 5 Corp.L.Rev. 3, 25 (1982).

[33] In Gimbel v. Signal Companies, Inc., the court stressed that the definition of "all or substantially all" must "begin with and ultimately relate to our statutory language." How does the court in Katz v. Bregman deal with the fact that the assets sold represented only 51% of the company's assets? Isn't there a major linguistic difference between "substantially all" and "a majority"?

[34] See Stiles v. Aluminum Products Co., 86 N.E.2d 887 (Ill.App.1949) (retention of liquid assets amounting to approximately 35% of total assets); Campbell v. Vose, 515 F.2d 256 (10th Cir.1975) (retention of liquid assets amounting to approximately 66% of total assets).

[35] Melvin Eisenberg, *The Structure of the Corporation* 259 n.15 (1976).

qualitative circumstances which make shareholder approval a necessary protection. And posing the question in this way pushes the issue back yet another step: Against what must shareholders be protected? At what problem is the statute really directed?

Professor Eisenberg has recently approached this issue by trying to identify the appropriate allocation of responsibilities between shareholders and the board of directors. If the function of the board of directors is to "manage the business" of the corporation, as the typical corporations statute provides,[36] then dispositions of significant corporate businesses

> should be shareholder matters: they work a significant change in the structure of the enterprise; they involve investment rather than purely business skills -- an evaluation of whether the business in question is worth the offering price; they occur relatively infrequently in the life of the corporation; and they are likely to take a relatively long time to consummate in any event.[37]

The thrust of Professor Eisenberg's distinction is that a corporate divestiture is an investment rather than a business decision and, thus, appropriately a shareholder rather than purely a director determination. The dichotomy suggested -- business decisions for directors, investment decisions for shareholders -- has an appealing logic and simplicity. Shareholders, after all, are by definition investors; directors, in contrast, are selected by shareholders to supervise the running of the business. Nevertheless, the explanation seems flawed in two critical aspects. Most important, the assumption that one can meaningfully distinguish between business skills and investment skills, or business decisions and investment decisions, in an acquisition context simply seems wrong. To be sure, selling a business is like selling stock in that it involves a determination of the value of what is sold. But the sale of an entire business also involves, for example, determination of the synergy to be lost, the cost of restructuring existing businesses, and the tax treatment of the sale at the corporate level, all of which seem much more like business decisions than investment decisions. In any event, they are matters which we hardly believe shareholders are *better* at evaluating than managers. This is not to say, at least as yet, that shareholders should not vote on them, but only that one cannot base a determination to allow them to vote on the premise that these decisions are inherently ones belonging to shareholders because of their special competence.

The second difficulty with Professor Eisenberg's business skills/investment skills dichotomy is that the statute itself belies the construction. The entire quotation applies with equal force to *acquisitions* of a significant corporate business as it does to dispositions. But the typical

---

[36] E.g., Del.Bus.Corp.Law § 141; Rev. Model Bus.Corp. Act Ann. § 8.01; N.Y.Bus.Corp.Law § 701; Cal.Corp.Code § 300.

[37] Eisenberg (1976), *supra* note 35, at 260.

corporate statute does not require shareholder approval of the cash acquisition of a substantial business even if approval would be required for disposition of the same business thereafter.

Ultimately the problem with Professor Eisenberg's construction is that it never offers an explanation of the function that the shareholders' vote is intended to serve. As a result, it no more provides a way of determining which transactions, although not meeting a purely quantitative measure of "substantially all," still should have shareholder approval than does the simple fiat of the court in Katz v. Bregman.[38] Considered in this way, it should not be surprising that construction of the phrase "substantially all" in the sale of assets section raises precisely the same problem as the de facto merger doctrine raises with respect to a broader range of transactions. That is, by what principle can we identify those transactions whose substantive characteristics should require a shareholder vote even though their formal terms, because too small a percentage of all assets are to be sold or because not cast in the form of a statutory merger, fall outside the language of the statute? Consideration of potential solutions to the broader problem must await discussion of the de facto merger doctrine in Section E of this Chapter.

3.   Variations on Who Votes, How Many Votes Are Needed, How the Votes Are Counted, and Who Gets to Complain

The advantage of a statutory merger is its reduction in transaction costs. By the filing of a single document, all assets of the target are transferred to the acquiring company, which simultaneously assumes all of the target company's liabilities, and the target company itself blinks out of existence at the same time and without further ado. While the same result can be accomplished by means of an asset acquisition, each step must be separately accomplished. Documents of transfer must be prepared for all assets; written assumptions must cover all liabilities; and, following these transfers, the target company typically must be formally dissolved pursuant to the dissolution procedures specified in the corporate statute, and its remaining

---

[38] The court in Katz v. Bregman seems to conclude that the shift in the company's business from manufacturing steel drums to manufacturing plastic drums was what made the sale "quantitatively vital" as required by Gimbel v. Signal Companies, Inc. Is the notion that the drum business differs so significantly depending on the material from which the drum is manufactured, or was it that, because the company was moving out of its only profitable business into a related, but untried one, the decision was a very risky one? If the latter is the critical element, then what happens to the quantitative side of the test? After all, it is not difficult to imagine that business changes as significant as that in Katz v. Bregman could be implemented by borrowing funds and retrofitting existing manufacturing machinery, thereby requiring the sale of a much smaller percentage of assets. Is the sale still "quantitatively vital"? If so, is there a trade-off between the riskiness of the business decision and the percentage of assets that must be sold?

assets -- the consideration received in the transaction and any assets not sold in the transaction -- distributed to its shareholders.

Thus far a statutory merger seems vastly more desirable than an asset acquisition. Why go through the multiple steps required in an asset acquisition when a statutory merger accomplishes the same result with so much less effort? When the desired results of the transactions are the same, the merger is preferable; however, the attractiveness of an asset acquisition becomes more apparent when the desired result is *not* the same as a merger.

The ease with which assets are transferred, liabilities assumed, and the target company eliminated in a statutory merger comes at the price of flexibility. Only if it is desired that *all* assets be transferred, *all* liabilities assumed, *and* the target company dissolved, does a statutory merger provide the intended result. An asset acquisition, in contrast, provides the flexibility to alter each of these aspects, albeit at the cost of increased transaction costs. If the acquisition of less than all of the assets is desirable, or if certain liabilities, like contingent or as yet unasserted claims, are not to be assumed, or if, perhaps for tax reasons, it is desirable to keep the target in existence, an asset acquisition may be preferable.[39] Indeed, it is precisely this flexibility -- to transfer assets *not* subject to liabilities -- that results in asset acquisitions being scrutinized under such doctrines as successor liability in tort or labor law.[40]

As with mergers, there is substantial variation among the states with respect to the statutory procedure for authorizing asset acquisitions. Additionally, the statutory requirements for asset acquisitions typically vary in significant respects from those for mergers.

How many votes are needed? As a general rule, the shareholder vote required to approve the sale of substantially all of a company's assets is the same as required for approval of a statutory merger, although Delaware required only a majority vote for an asset sale even prior to the 1967 amendment which reduced the approval required for mergers from two-thirds to a majority. As with mergers, such transactions at common law required unanimous consent.[41]

Who gets to vote and how the votes are counted. The issues raised by participation by nonvoting shares and the need for class voting in asset

---

[39] That is not to say that pre-merger planning may not allow similar results to be achieved even though the final step will be a statutory merger. For example, if certain assets are not to be acquired, they can be transferred to another corporation in anticipation of the merger. See generally Martin Ginsburg & Jack Levin, *Mergers, Acquisitions and Leveraged Buyouts* ch.10 (updated annually). Note, however, that not all flexibility can be recovered and, in any event, the machinations necessary quickly begin to erode the transaction cost advantage of the merger technique.

[40] See Chapter 26, *infra*.

[41] See Carney (1980), *supra* note 2; Gimbel v. Signal Companies, Inc., *supra*, at n.3.

acquisitions are virtually identical to those raised in the context of a statutory merger. A distinction drawn by the California Corporations Code, however, is worth noting. While class voting for all shares, voting and nonvoting, is generally required,[42] the requirement of a class vote and the enfranchising of otherwise nonvoting shares is eliminated when the consideration to be received is cash or debt securities which are adequately secured and which have a maturity date of five years or less.[43] Why should the form of consideration alter the need for protection against a decision made solely by the common? To be sure, because they receive cash or short-term debt, the nonvoting shareholders are not forced to become shareholders in a different enterprise as would be the case if the consideration in the transaction were stock in the acquiring corporation, but the danger of a transfer of wealth from nonvoting shareholders to common shareholders remains, particularly since, as discussed *infra*, appraisal rights are also eliminated. Moreover, if the concern is only with nonvoting shareholders being locked in, rather than with their being ripped off, could not the exception be extended to stock consideration so long as a public market for it existed?

Despite the substantial similarities in approach, statutory treatment of an asset acquisition raises one critical question about the relevant electorate not posed by the treatment of mergers. In most jurisdictions, shareholder approval of an asset acquisition is required only for the selling corporation. Unlike in a merger, there is no involvement of the acquiring corporation's shareholders.[44] This distinction prompts much of the controversy over the de facto merger doctrine considered in Section E of this Chapter.

Who gets to object? As with mergers, the typical statutory pattern allows dissenter's rights in asset acquisitions only to those who have the right to vote on the transaction. The result, however, is quite different than in mergers; because shareholders of the acquiring company have no vote, they also lose the appraisal rights they would have had in the merger. Additionally, there are some significant differences in the way asset acquisitions are treated. Most important, the Delaware General Corporation Law does not grant appraisal rights even to shareholders of the target company in an asset acquisition, another distinction between mergers and sales of assets which has fueled controversy over the de facto merger doctrine.[45] The Model Act also restricts appraisal rights in asset acquisitions. Section 13.02(a)(3) eliminates appraisal rights -- but not voting rights -- in connection with a sale of assets where the consideration is cash

---

[42] Cal.Corp.Code § 1201

[43] Cal.Corp.Code §§ 181, 1001. These sections of the California Corporations Code are reproduced in Section E.3 of this Chapter, *infra*.

[44] Cal.Corp.Code § 1200(a) and *New York Stock Exchange Company Manual* A-284 are the principal exceptions and are discussed in Section E.3 of this Chapter, *infra*.

[45] A few other states follow Delaware's example. See D.C.Code Ann. §§ 29-373, -375 (1981); Kan.Stat.Ann. 17-6712, -6801 (1981); Nev.Rev.Stat. 78.481 (1979).

and the net proceeds are required to be distributed within one year, and some states provide similar exceptions.[46] The California Corporations Code goes somewhat further in this direction by eliminating appraisal rights where the consideration is either cash *or* adequately secured debt securities with maturities of five years or less, and imposes no requirement that the proceeds be distributed. The elimination of appraisal rights seems even more puzzling than the elimination of voting rights because appraisal rights directly concern whether the amount received is fair.

C. Triangular Transactions

Note, THREE-PARTY MERGERS: THE FOURTH FORM OF CORPORATE ACQUISITION
57 Va.L.Rev. 1242 (1971)

. . . A straight three-party merger involves a parent corporation, the acquirer; its subsidiary, which may be a shell formed for the purpose of completing the acquisition, and capitalized solely with the stock of the parent; and a target corporation, the corporation to be acquired. Using the stock of the parent as consideration the basic merger is consummated between the subsidiary and the target, with the subsidiary surviving.

The 1967 revision of the Delaware Corporation Law greatly facilitated the use of the three-party merger. An amendment to § 251(b) permitted a party to a merger to use the stock or securities of a corporation not a party to the merger as consideration. Other states have followed suit. . . . The effect of these revisions is to allow a subsidiary to participate in a statutory merger using the stock of its parent as consideration. . . .

Traditional Forms of Acquisition v. Three-Party Mergers

Two-party Merger v. Three-party Merger

For purposes of avoiding recognition of taxable gain, the statutory merger, or *A* reorganization, is the most advantageous form of corporate acquisition. As long as continuity of interest requirements are satisfied, the [Internal Revenue] Code places few limits on the types of consideration that may be used in a tax free merger. In contrast, the Code places severe restrictions on the types of consideration that the parties may give in stock or asset acquisitions. Only in *A* reorganizations (statutory mergers) can the parties give appreciable amounts of [nonvoting stock] in consideration for the acquisition.

---

[46] See, e.g., Ariz.Rev.Stat.Ann. § 10-080.A.2 (1977); N.Y.Bus.Corp.Law § 910(a)(1)(B) (McKinney Supp.1983).

Beyond tax considerations, there are other advantages of the merger form. In a merger, the surviving corporation obtains 100% control of the acquired corporation. There is no problem with continuing minority interest. The directors of the survivor are thus given greater flexibility in their actions vis-a-vis the acquired corporation.

The transfer of assets by operation of law is perhaps the most advantageous aspect of the merger form, but the concurrent transfer of liabilities can be very dangerous, especially if the acquired company has unknown or contingent liabilities. In traditional two-party mergers, there is no way for the acquiring, or surviving corporation to avoid assuming these liabilities. Therefore, before the advent of the three-party merger, when the acquiring corporation felt behooved to protect itself from potential liability, it had to abandon the merger form and resort to stock or asset acquisitions which were treated more harshly by the Internal Revenue Code.

If, however, a statutory merger can be consummated between a wholly owned subsidiary of an acquirer-parent and a target, the acquirer-parent can gain control of the target without incurring separate liability for its debts. Thus, by utilizing the three-party merger technique, the acquirer can avoid a major disadvantage of the traditional merger form, while maintaining the favorable tax treatment accorded mergers.

A more important problem with the traditional merger form is that statutes normally require that proposed mergers be approved by vote of the [acquiring company's] shareholders, and that those who oppose the plan be given appraisal rights. The necessity of submitting a plan to shareholders for approval is always inconvenient, but rarely fatal to an acquisition. The prospect of having to buy out shareholders who oppose the acquisition, on the other hand, can cause the entire transaction to be aborted. Especially when the merging corporations are illiquid, the opposition of even a small minority of one party's shareholders may have a profound effect. In order to avoid this unpleasant aspect of the traditional merger form, parties were often forced into stock acquisitions . . . or asset acquisitions.[a] . . . Now, by using the three-party merger technique, the impact of voting and appraisal requirements can be substantially mitigated in a merger, thus obviating the need to resort to stock or asset acquisitions. In a three-party merger, the shareholders of the acquirer-parent are denied voting and appraisal rights, since the parent-acquirer is the only shareholder of the merging subsidiary capable of voting and dissenting. The parent-acquirer's shareholders have no voice in the merger transaction.

Of course, the shareholders of the acquired corporation still have to approve the merger and may demand appraisal rights if they dissent. But the use of the three-party form will effectively deny voting and appraisal rights to the shareholders of one of the substantive parties to the acquisition. . . .

---

[a] Recall that no vote of the acquiring company's shareholders is necessary to authorize the acquisition of either the stock or assets of a target company. Eds.

A final possible disadvantage of the traditional merger form is that the acquired corporation must disappear. Only one of the two corporations can continue to exist. The amalgamation of corporate entities may foster such unpleasant results as demands for new labor contracts, lowered management and employee morale, and impaired customer relations. By utilizing the three-party merger technique, these problems may be avoided, since the subsidiary may be kept in existence. Moreover, as will be seen below, when it is desirable to maintain the corporate existence of the target corporation, a reverse three-party merger may be used. Of course, the parties might have chosen another acquisition form, the stock acquisition (*B* reorganization) to achieve the desired result -- continued separate existence of the acquiring and acquired corporations -- but the tax limitations on the type of consideration which can be used in a stock acquisition would impair management's flexibility in working out the plan. The three-party merger is thus the superior acquisition form.

Stock Acquisition v. Reverse Three-party Merger

. . . . Several of the disadvantages of the merger form can be avoided by the use of the stock acquisition . . . technique. For example, no shareholder vote is required when the acquiring corporation goes directly to the shareholders of the target corporation to buy their stock. [T]hose shareholders will effectively have voting rights [through deciding whether to sell their stock]. But the shareholders of neither corporation will have appraisal rights. Another advantage of the stock acquisition technique is that the target corporation may remain in existence. A final advantage is that the acquiring corporation generally will not assume the liabilities of the acquired corporation.

But the stock acquisition technique is not without substantial disadvantages, the foremost of which are the inflexible consideration requirements imposed by the Internal Revenue Code, if tax free status is to be maintained. To qualify for non-recognition treatment as a *B* reorganization, the acquirer must receive an 80% or more controlling stock interest in the acquired corporation. Consideration is limited to voting stock, and extreme care must be taken to avoid boot in any form; otherwise, the reorganization may be disqualified. The strict requirements of the *B* reorganization contrast sharply with the flexibility available in *A* reorganizations. Thus, where tax considerations prevail, the stock acquisition runs a poor second to mergers.

Another important disadvantage of the stock acquisition technique is that complete control is nearly impossible to obtain, since at least a few of the acquired corporation's shareholders are likely not to sell out. At best, it may take an unjustified premium to induce the recalcitrant minority to sell. When there is a minority interest in a subsidiary, the parent must deal at arm's length with the subsidiary in intercorporate matters. Here again, the merger form is superior, since no minority remains after a merger.

By reversing the three-party merger technique, all the disadvantages of the stock acquisition technique may be avoided, and most of the advantages may be maintained. In a reverse three-party merger, the subsidiary merely merges into the target. Subsidiary stock held by the parent is converted into target stock, and the parent stock which was funneled through the subsidiary is distributed to the target's shareholders in exchange for their target stock.

After completion of the reverse three-party merger, the parent has complete control of the target. The effect of the transaction is a forced 100% stock acquisition, a forced *B* reorganization. The parent will not be hobbled by fiduciary duty to the subsidiary, since there is no minority interest to affront. . . .

Asset Acquisition v. Three-party Merger

If substantially all of the assets of the selling corporation are exchanged for voting stock of the acquirer, the acquisition will qualify for tax-deferred treatment as a *C* reorganization. The consideration that may be exchanged for assets in a *C* reorganization, however, is limited to voting stock and small amounts of cash and other consideration. While an asset acquisition may be used to achieve a merger result, the more stringent requirements of a *C* reorganization do not allow the federal tax flexibility permitted by the *A* reorganization merger or consolidation.

Under state law, a sale of substantially all the assets of a corporation normally requires approval by the seller's shareholders. Several states do not provide appraisal rights for the shareholders of the selling corporation, and voting or appraisal rights for shareholders of an acquiring corporation are rare. The principal disadvantage of the asset acquisition is its cumbersome form. Deeds, contract assignments, and other similar instruments must be executed. If any rights and privileges are nonassignable, the acquisition cannot be completed without consent, and amalgamation via the asset acquisition route may be impossible. Thus, in many situations the transfer of assets by operation of law in a merger may be a practical necessity if the acquisition is to be completed. In these situations the three-party merger technique is the obvious choice, since it avoids many of the problems of the traditional merger.

D.   Compulsory Share Exchange

The most recently devised acquisition technique is the compulsory share exchange, added to the Model Business Corporation Act in 1976.[47]

----

[47] Model Bus.Corp.Act.Ann. § 72A (1982). See Committee on Corporate Laws, *Final Changes in the Model Business Corporation Act Revising Sections 63, 74, 76, 77, 80 and Adding a New Section -- 72-A,* 31 Bus.Law. 1747 (1976). This technique is now reflected

Although the Model Act's lead has been followed in a number of jurisdictions,[48] this technique has not been adopted by any major commercial jurisdiction.[49] Professors Schulman and Schenk describe the technique as a simplified alternative to the reverse triangular merger:

> Under this form of acquisition, all shareholders (or shareholders of a particular class of shares) of the acquired company must transfer their shares to the acquiring corporation for the consideration set forth in the plan of exchange. Thus, assuming that the exchange involves all classes of target shares, the target remains alive as a wholly owned subsidiary of the acquiror -- precisely the result obtained by a reverse triangular merger. Although the Act requires approval of the plan by the boards of both corporations and grants voting and dissenters' rights to the shareholders of the target, it provides no rights for the acquiror's shareholders.[50]

One possible explanation for the apparent lack of success of an innovative effort to develop a new acquisition technique illustrates a serious problem confronting drafters of corporation statutes. While the drafters control only the corporation statute, the planners' choice among available acquisition techniques depends on a balance of all regulatory regimes bearing on the transaction. For tax purposes, within which of the definitions of reorganization in IRC § 368(a) would a compulsory share exchange fall? While it seems closest to a *B* reorganization, it does seem more like a merger in that it is compulsory with respect to the target company shareholders rather than voluntary as in the typical *B* reorganization. To be sure, there would seem to be little risk that the transaction would be found to fall outside all of the reorganization definitions, but even a very small amount of uncertainty must be balanced against the gains from a less complicated alternative to a reverse triangular merger. How large a saving in transaction costs does the compulsory share exchange really offer? If the savings are not large, and if new techniques carry with them some uncertainty, successful

---

in the Rev. Model Bus.Corp.l Act § 11.02.

[48] Schulman & Schenk (1983), *supra* note 6, at 1532 n.13, report that the compulsory share exchange has been included in the corporate statutes of the following jurisdictions: Colo.Rev.Stat. 7-7-102.5 (Supp.1982); Idaho Code § 30-1-72A (1980); Md.Corps & Ass'ns Code Ann. § 3-105 (Supp.1982); Mont.Code Ann. 35-1-801(3) (1981); Neb.Rev.Stat. § 21-2071.01 (Cum.Supp.1982); N.H.Rev.Stat.Ann. 293-A: 73 (Supp.1981); Or.Rev.Stat. 57.462 (1981); S.C.Code Ann. § 33-17-25 (Law.Co-op.Supp.1982); Va.Code § 13.1-69.1 (Supp.1982); Wash.Rev.Code Ann. 23A.20.025 (West Supp.1982); Wyo.Stat.Ann. § 17-1-402.1 (Supp.1982).

[49] Although California Corporations Code § 181 defines an "exchange reorganization," unlike the Model Act technique shareholders of the target company are not bound and the definition serves only to grant shareholders of the *acquiring* company voting and appraisal rights if the number of shares issued in the transaction exceeds one-sixth of the company's outstanding shares prior to the transaction. Cal.Corp.Code §§ 1200, 1201.

[50] Schulman & Schenk (1983), *supra* note 6, at 1532-33.

reform -- successful in the sense that planners choose to use the technique -- may be very difficult to accomplish.

E.   The De Facto Merger Doctrine

Viewing the choice among alternative acquisition techniques from the perspective of the corporate planner, the assertion of something akin to what has come to be called the de facto merger doctrine was inevitable.   A statutory merger provides the most protection to both shareholders and creditors.   From the shareholders' point of view, it requires a vote by the shareholders of the acquiring and target companies and grants appraisal rights to both.   From the point of view of the creditors of the target company, all of the liabilities of the target company, including those which are unknown, or have not yet accrued, at the time of the transaction, are assumed by the acquiring company as a matter of law.   It was predictable that in particular circumstances such protection would be viewed as undesirable by those planning an acquisition transaction, and that if alternative techniques -- such as a sale of assets or triangular merger -- were available which both avoided them and did not alter the substance of the transaction, an alternative would be chosen.   It was equally predictable that in precisely those circumstances when the planners thought it advantageous to eliminate the protection given shareholders and creditors under a statutory merger, those denied the protection would complain.   The assertion by creditors that the acquiring company should be deemed to have assumed their claims, as would have occurred in a statutory merger but did not under the arguably functionally equivalent technique actually chosen by the planners, is considered in Chapter 18, *infra*.   The claim by shareholders that they are entitled to the very statutory protections which the planners sought to avoid by their selection of the acquisition technique is the traditional province of the de facto merger doctrine and is the subject of our attention here.   Invariably the claim reflects an effort made by those disadvantaged by a transaction to recast it in a form, usually a statutory merger, which would have afforded them greater protection, even though the transaction as carried out did not formally fall within the statutory definition of the more protective alternative form.

1. Recharacterization of Statutory Alternatives

a. *Sale of Substantially All Assets*

FARRIS v. GLEN ALDEN CORP.
143 A.2d 25 (Pa.1958)

COHEN, Justice. We are required to determine on this appeal whether, as a result of a "Reorganization Agreement" executed by the officers of Glen Alden Corporation and List Industries Corporation, and approved by the shareholders of the former company, the rights and remedies of a dissenting shareholder accrue to the plaintiff.

Glen Alden is a Pennsylvania corporation engaged principally in the mining of anthracite coal and lately in the manufacture of air conditioning units and fire-fighting equipment. In recent years the company's operating revenue has declined substantially, and in fact, its coal operations have resulted in tax loss carryovers of approximately $14,000,000. In October 1957, List, a Delaware holding company owning interests in motion picture theaters, textile companies and real estate, and to a lesser extent, in oil and gas operations, warehouses and aluminum piston manufacturing, purchased through a wholly owned subsidiary 38.5% of Glen Alden's outstanding stock.[1] This acquisition enabled List to place three of its directors on the Glen Alden board.

On March 20, 1958, the two corporations entered into a "reorganization agreement," subject to stockholder approval, which contemplated the following actions:

1. Glen Alden is to acquire all of the assets of List, excepting a small amount of cash reserved for the payment of List's expenses in connection with the transaction. These assets include over $8,000,000 in cash held chiefly in the treasuries of List's wholly owned subsidiaries.

2. In consideration of the transfer, Glen Alden is to issue 3,621,703 shares of stock to List. List in turn is to distribute the stock to its shareholders at a ratio of five shares of Glen Alden stock for each six shares of List stock. In order to accomplish the necessary distribution, Glen Alden is to increase the authorized number of its shares of capital stock from 2,500,000 shares to 7,500,000 shares without according preemptive rights to the present shareholders upon the issuance of any such shares.

3. Further, Glen Alden is to assume all of List's liabilities including a $5,000,000 note incurred by List in order to purchase Glen Alden stock in 1957, outstanding stock options, incentive stock options plans, and pension obligations.

4. Glen Alden is to change its corporate name from Glen Alden Corporation to List Alden Corporation.

---

[1] Of the purchase price of $8,719,109, $5,000,000 was borrowed.

5. The present directors of both corporations are to become directors of List Alden.

6. List is to be dissolved and List Alden is to then carry on the operations of both former corporations.

Two days after the agreement was executed notice of the annual meeting of Glen Alden to be held on April 11, 1958, was mailed to the shareholders together with a proxy statement analyzing the reorganization agreement and recommending its approval as well as approval of certain amendments to Glen Alden's articles of incorporation and bylaws necessary to implement the agreement.   At this meeting the holders of a majority of the outstanding shares, (not including those owned by List), voted in favor of a resolution approving the reorganization agreement.

On the day of the shareholders' meeting, plaintiff, a shareholder of Glen Alden, filed a complaint in equity against the corporation and its officers seeking to enjoin them temporarily until final hearing, and perpetually thereafter, from executing and carrying out the agreement.[2]

The gravamen of the complaint was that the notice of the annual shareholders' meeting did not conform to the requirements of the Business Corporation Law, 15 P.S. § 2852-1 *et seq.*, in three respects: (1) It did not give notice to the shareholders that the true intent and purpose of the meeting was to effect a merger or consolidation of Glen Alden and List; (2) It failed to give notice to the shareholders of their right to dissent to the plan of merger or consolidation and claim fair value for their shares, and (3) It did not contain copies of the text of certain sections of the Business Corporation Law as required.[3]

By reason of these omissions, plaintiff contended that the approval of the reorganization agreement by the shareholders at the annual meeting was invalid and unless the carrying out of the plan were enjoined, he would suffer irreparable loss by being deprived of substantial property rights.

The defendants answered admitting the material allegations of fact in the complaint but denying that they gave rise to a cause of action because the transaction complained of was a purchase of corporate assets as to which shareholders had no rights of dissent or appraisal. For these reasons the defendants then moved for judgment on the pleadings.[5]

---

[2] The plaintiff also sought to enjoin the shareholders of Glen Alden from approving the reorganization agreement and from adopting amendments to Glen Alden's articles of incorporation, certificate of incorporation and bylaws in implementation of the agreement. However, apparently because of the shortness of time, this prayer was refused by the court.

[3] The proxy statement included the following declaration:

Appraisal Rights. In the opinion of counsel, the shareholders of neither Glen Alden nor List Industries will have any rights of appraisal or similar rights of dissenters with respect to any matter to be acted upon at their respective meetings.

[5] Counsel for the defendants concedes that if the corporation is required to pay the dissenting shareholders the appraised fair value of their shares, the resultant drain of cash would prevent Glen Alden from carrying out the agreement. On the other hand, plaintiff contends that if the shareholders had been told of their rights as dissenters, rather than

The court below concluded that the reorganization agreement entered into between the two corporations was a plan for a *de facto* merger, and that therefore the failure of the notice of the annual meeting to conform to the pertinent requirements of the merger provisions of the Business Corporation Law rendered the notice defective and all proceedings in furtherance of the agreement void. . . .

This appeal followed.

When use of the corporate form of business organization first became widespread, it was relatively easy for courts to define a "merger" or a "sale of assets" and to label a particular transaction as one or the other. . . . But prompted by the desire to avoid the impact of adverse, and to obtain the benefits of favorable, government regulations, particularly federal tax laws, new accounting and legal techniques were developed by lawyers and accountants which interwove the elements characteristic of each, thereby creating hybrid forms of corporate amalgamation. Thus, it is no longer helpful to consider an individual transaction in the abstract and solely by reference to the various elements therein determine whether it is a "merger" or a "sale". Instead, to determine properly the nature of a corporate transaction, we must refer not only to all the provisions of the agreement, but also to the consequences of the transaction and to the purposes of the provisions of the corporation law said to be applicable. We shall apply this principle to the instant case.

Section 908A of the Pennsylvania Business Corporation Law provides: "If any shareholder of a domestic corporation which becomes a party to a plan of merger or consolidation shall object to such plan of merger or consolidation . . . such shareholder shall be entitled to . . . [the fair value of his shares upon surrender of the share certificate or certificates representing his shares]."

This provision had its origin in the early decision of this Court in Lauman v. Lebanon Valley R.R. Co., 30 Pa. 42 (1858). There a shareholder who objected to the consolidation of his company with another was held to have a right in the absence of statute to treat the consolidation as a dissolution of his company and to receive the value of his shares upon their surrender.

The rationale of the Lauman case, and of the present section of the Business Corporation Law based thereon, is that when a corporation combines with another so as to lose its essential nature and alter the original fundamental relationships of the shareholders among themselves and to the corporation, a shareholder who does not wish to continue his membership therein may treat his membership in the original corporation as terminated and have the value of his shares paid to him. . . .

Does the combination outlined in the present "reorganization" agreement so fundamentally change the corporate character of Glen Alden

---

specifically advised that they had no such rights, the resolution approving the reorganization agreement would have been defeated.

and the interest of the plaintiff as a shareholder therein, that to refuse him the rights and remedies of a dissenting shareholder would in reality force him to give up his stock in one corporation and against his will accept shares in another? If so, the combination is a merger within the meaning of § 908A of the corporation law. . . .

If the reorganization agreement were consummated plaintiff would find that the "List Alden" resulting from the amalgamation would be quite a different corporation than the "Glen Alden" in which he is now a shareholder. Instead of continuing primarily as a coal mining company, Glen Alden would be transformed, after amendment of its articles of incorporation, into a diversified holding company whose interests would range from motion picture theaters to textile companies, plaintiff would find himself a member of a company with assets of $169,000,000 and a long-term debt of $38,000,000 in lieu of a company one-half that size and with but one-seventh the long-term debt.

While the administration of the operations and properties of Glen Alden as well as List would be in the hands of management common to both companies, since all executives of List would be retained in List Alden, the control of Glen Alden would pass to the directors of List; for List would hold eleven of the seventeen directorships on the new board of directors.

As an aftermath of the transaction plaintiff's proportionate interest in Glen Alden would have been reduced to only two-fifths of what it presently is because of the issuance of an additional 3,621,703 shares to List which would not be subject to pre-emptive rights. In fact, ownership of Glen Alden would pass to the stockholders of List who would hold 76.5% of the outstanding shares as compared with but 23.5% retained by the present Glen Alden shareholders.

Perhaps the most important consequence to the plaintiff, if he were denied the right to have his shares redeemed at their fair value, would be the serious financial loss suffered upon consummation of the agreement. While the present book value of his stock is $38 a share after combination it would be worth only $21 a share. In contrast, the shareholders of List who presently hold stock with a total book value of $33,000,000 or $7.50 a share, would receive stock with a book value of $76,000,000 or $21 a share.

Under these circumstances it may well be said that if the proposed combination is allowed to take place without right of dissent, plaintiff would have his stock in Glen Alden taken away from him and the stock of a new company thrust upon him in its place. He would be projected against his will into a new enterprise under terms not of his own choosing. It was to protect dissident shareholders against just such a result that this Court one hundred years ago in the Lauman case, and the legislature thereafter in § 908A granted the right of dissent. And it is to accord that protection to the plaintiff that we conclude that the combination proposed in the case at hand is a merger within the intendment of § 908A.

Nevertheless, defendants contend that the 1957 amendments to §§ 311 and 908 of the corporation law preclude us from reaching this result and require the entry of judgment in their favor. Subsection F of § 311 dealing with the voluntary transfer of corporate assets provides: "The shareholders of a business corporation which acquires by sale, lease or exchange all or substantially all of the property of another corporation by the issuance of stock, securities or otherwise shall not be entitled to the rights and remedies of dissenting shareholders. . . ."

And the amendment to § 908 reads as follows: "The right of dissenting shareholders . . . shall not apply to the purchase by a corporation of assets whether or not the consideration therefor be money or property, real or personal, including shares or bonds or other evidences of indebtedness of such corporation. The shareholders of such corporation shall have no right to dissent from any such purchase."

Defendants view these amendments as abridging the right of shareholders to dissent to a transaction between two corporations which involves a transfer of assets for a consideration even though the transfer has all the legal incidents of a merger. They claim that only if the merger is accomplished in accordance with the prescribed statutory procedure does the right of dissent accrue. In support of this position they cite to us the comment on the amendments by the Committee on Corporation Law of the Pennsylvania Bar Association, the committee which originally drafted these provisions. The comment states that the provisions were intended to overrule cases which granted shareholders the right to dissent to a sale of assets when accompanied by the legal incidents of a merger. See 61 Ann.Rep.Pa.Bar Ass'n 277, 284 (1957).[7] Whatever may have been the intent of the *committee,* there is no evidence to indicate that the *legislature* intended the 1957 amendments to have the effect contended for. But furthermore, the language of these two provisions does not support the opinion of the committee and is inapt to achieve any such purpose. The amendments of 1957 do not provide that a transaction between two corporations which has the effect of a merger but which includes a transfer of assets for consideration is to be exempt from the protective provisions of §§ 908A and 515. They provide only that the shareholders of a corporation which

---

[7] "The amendment to § 311 expressly provides that a sale, lease or exchange of substantially all corporate assets in connection with its liquidation or dissolution is subject to the provisions of Article XI of the Act, and that no consent or authorization of shareholders other than what is required by Article XI is necessary. The recent decision in Marks v. Autocar Co., D.C.E.D.Pa., Civil Action No. 16075 [153 F.Supp. 768] is to the contrary. This amendment, together with the proposed amendment to § 1104 expressly permitting the directors in liquidating the corporation to sell only such assets as may be required to pay its debts and distribute any assets remaining among shareholders (§ 1108B now so provides in the case of receivers) have the effect of overruling Marks v. Autocar Co., . . . which permits a shareholder dissenting from such a sale to obtain the fair value of his shares. The Marks case relies substantially on Bloch v. Baldwin Locomotive Works, 75 [Pa.] Dist. & Co.R. 24, also believed to be an undesirable decision. That case permitted a holder of stock in a corporation which *purchased* for stock all the assets of another corporation to obtain the fair value of his shares. That case is also in effect overruled by the new §§ 311F and 908C." 61 Ann.Rep.Pa. Bar Ass'n, 277, 284 (1957).

acquires the property or purchases the assets of another corporation, *without more,* are not entitled to the right to dissent from the transaction. So, as in the present case, when as part of a transaction between two corporations, one corporation dissolves, its liabilities are assumed by the survivor, its executives and directors take over the management and control of the survivor, and, as consideration for the transfer, its stockholders acquire a majority of the shares of stock of the survivor, then the transaction is no longer simply a purchase of assets or acquisition of property to which §§ 311F and 908C apply, but a merger governed by § 908A of the corporation law. To divest shareholders of their right of dissent under such circumstances would require express language which is absent from the 1957 amendments.

Even were we to assume that the combination provided for in the reorganization agreement is a "sale of assets" to which § 908A does not apply, it would avail the defendants nothing; we will not blind our eyes to the realities of the transaction. Despite the designation of the parties and the form employed, Glen Alden does not in fact acquire List, rather, List acquires Glen Alden, and under § 311D[8] the right of dissent would remain with the shareholders of Glen Alden.

We hold that the combination contemplated by the reorganization agreement, although consummated by contract rather than in accordance with the statutory procedure, is a merger within the protective purview of §§ 908A and 515 of the corporation law. The shareholders of Glen Alden should have been notified accordingly and advised of their statutory rights of dissent and appraisal. The failure of the corporate officers to take these steps renders the stockholder approval of the agreement at the 1958 shareholders' meeting invalid. The lower court did not err in enjoining the officers and directors of Glen Alden from carrying out this agreement.[9]

Decree affirmed at appellants' cost.

HARITON v. ARCO ELECTRONICS, INC.
188 A.2d 123 (Del.1963)

SOUTHERLAND, Chief Justice. This case involves a sale of assets under § 271 of the corporation law, 8 Del.C. It presents for decision the

---

[8] "If any shareholder of a business corporation which sells, leases or exchanges all or substantially all of its property and assets otherwise than (1) in the usual and regular course of its business, (2) for the purpose of relocating its business, or (3) in connection with its dissolution and liquidation, shall object to such sale, lease or exchange and comply with the provisions of § 515 of this act, such shareholder shall be entitled to the rights and remedies of dissenting shareholders as therein provided."

[9] Because of our disposition of this appeal, it is unnecessary for us to consider . . . whether amended §§ 908C and 311F of the corporation law may constitutionally be applied to the present transaction to divest the plaintiff of his dissenter's rights.

question presented, but not decided, in Heilbrunn v. Sun Chemical Corporation, 150 A.2d 755 (Del.1959).[a] It may be stated as follows:

A sale of assets is effected under § 271 in consideration of shares of stock of the purchasing corporation. The agreement of sale embodies also a plan to dissolve the selling corporation and distribute the shares so received to the stockholders of the seller, so as to accomplish the same result as would be accomplished by a merger of the seller into the purchaser. Is the sale legal?

The facts are these:

The defendant Arco and Loral Electronics Corporation, a New York corporation, are both engaged, in somewhat different forms, in the electronic equipment business. In the summer of 1961 they negotiated for an amalgamation of the companies. As of October 27, 1961, they entered into a "Reorganization Agreement and Plan." The provisions of this Plan pertinent here are in substance as follows:

1. Arco agrees to sell all its assets to Loral in consideration (inter alia) of the issuance to it of 283,000 shares of Loral.

2. Arco agrees to call a stockholders meeting for the purpose of approving the Plan and the voluntary dissolution.

3. Arco agrees to distribute to its stockholders all the Loral shares received by it as a part of the complete liquidation of Arco.

At the Arco meeting all the stockholders voting (about 80%) approved the Plan. It was thereafter consummated.

Plaintiff, a stockholder who did not vote at the meeting, sued to enjoin the consummation of the Plan on the grounds (1) that it was illegal, and (2) that it was unfair. The second ground was abandoned. Affidavits and documentary evidence were filed, and defendant moved for summary judgment and dismissal of the complaint. The Vice Chancellor granted the motion and plaintiff appeals.

The question before us we have stated above. Plaintiff's argument that the sale is illegal runs as follows:

The several steps taken here accomplish the same result as a merger of Arco into Loral.[b] In a "true" sale of assets, the stockholder of the seller retains the right to elect whether the selling company shall continue as a holding company. Moreover, the stockholder of the selling company is

---

[a] In *Heilbrunn* a shareholder of the *acquiring* company, Sun Chemical, objected to the loss of appraisal rights resulting from casting the transaction as a sale of assets rather than a merger. The Court did not reach the de facto merger claim because it "fail[ed] to see how any injury has been inflicted upon the [shareholders of the acquiring company.] Their corporation has simply acquired property and paid for it in shares of stock. The business of Sun will go on as before, with additional assets. The Sun stockholder is not forced to accept stock in another corporation. Nor has the reorganization changed the essential nature of the purchasing corporation." Eds.

[b] The plan also specified that Loral would assume all of Arco's liabilities and required Arco's prompt liquidation following the closing of the transaction. See the Vice Chancellor's opinion below, 182 A.2d 22 (Del.Ch.1962). Eds.

forced to accept an investment in a new enterprise without the right of appraisal granted under the merger statute. Section 271 cannot therefore be legally combined with a dissolution proceeding under § 275 and a consequent distribution of the purchaser's stock. Such a proceeding is a misuse of the power granted under § 271, and a *de facto* merger results. . . .

Plaintiff's contention that this sale has achieved the same result as a merger is plainly correct. The same contention was made to us in Heilbrunn v. Sun Chemical Corporation, 150 A.2d 755 (Del.1959). Accepting it as correct, we noted that this result is made possible by the overlapping scope of the merger statute and § 271. . . .

We also adverted to the increased use, in connection with corporate reorganization plans, of § 271 instead of the merger statute. Further, we observed that no Delaware case has held such procedure to be improper, and that two cases appear to assume its legality. Finch v. Warrior Cement Corp., 141 A. 54 (Del.Ch.1928), and Argenbright v. Phoenix Finance Co., 187 A. 124 (Del.Ch.1936). But we were not required in the Heilbrunn case to decide the point.

We now hold that the reorganization here accomplished through § 271 and a mandatory plan of dissolution and distribution is legal. This is so because the sale-of-assets statute and the merger statute are independent of each other. They are, so to speak, of equal dignity, and the framers of a reorganization plan may resort to either type of corporate mechanics to achieve the desired end. This is not an anomalous result in our corporation law. As the Vice Chancellor pointed out, the elimination of accrued dividends, though forbidden under a charter amendment (Keller v. Wilson & Co., 190 A. 115 (Del.Ch.1936)) may be accomplished by a merger. Federal United Corp. v. Havender, 11 A.2d 331 (Del.Ch.1940).

In Langfelder v. Universal Laboratories, D.C., 68 F.Supp. 209 (D.Del.1946), Judge Leahy commented upon "the general theory of the Delaware Corporation Law that action taken pursuant to the authority of the various sections of that law constitute acts of independent legal significance and their validity is not dependent on other sections of the Act." 68 F.Supp. 211, footnote. . . .

Plaintiff concedes, as we read his brief, that if the several steps taken in this case had been taken separately they would have been legal. That is, he concedes that a sale of assets, followed by a separate proceeding to dissolve and distribute, would be legal, even though the same result would follow. This concession exposes the weakness of his contention. To attempt to make any such distinction between sales under § 271 would be to create uncertainty in the law and invite litigation.

We are in accord with the Vice Chancellor's ruling, and the judgment below is affirmed.

The Delaware Supreme Court's approach to the corporate statute in *Hariton* seems strikingly at odds with the approach taken in Gimbel v. Signal Companies, Inc., and Katz v. Bregman, *supra*. Although *Hariton* dealt with an effort to turn a sale of assets into a merger, while *Signal Companies* and *Katz* dealt with whether there had been a sale of substantially all the target company's assets, in a critical respect all three cases presented precisely the same issue. Could a transaction whose formal terms fell outside the literal language of the statute be recharacterized in light of its alleged substance to fall within the statute? In *Hariton,* the court read the language of the statute as a Fundamentalist reads the Bible; each passage was "of equal dignity" even though, as in Genesis for example, different passages describe exactly the same events quite differently. In contrast, the court in *Signal Companies* and *Katz* treated the statutory language with far less reverence. Why did the court in either case go beyond the language of the statute? A *Hariton*-like approach would simply have concluded that the sale of somewhere between 26% and 50% of total assets in *Signal Companies,* and 51% of total assets in *Katz,* did not constitute the sale of "all or substantially all" of the target company's assets. The puzzle is then to explain why a form of statutory interpretation that looks to substance rather than form is appropriate in determining whether shareholders require the protection associated with the sale of assets provisions rather than no protection at all, but not in determining whether shareholders require the protection associated with the merger provisions rather than the lesser protection associated with the sale of asset provisions.

b.   *Triangular Transactions*

TERRY v. PENN CENTRAL CORP.
668 F.2d 188 (3d Cir.1981)

ADAMS, Circuit Judge.   The Penn Central Corporation ("Penn Central"), an appellee in this case, has sought to acquire Colt Industries Inc. ("Colt"), also an appellee, by merging Colt with PCC Holdings, Inc. ("Holdings"), a wholly-owned subsidiary of Penn Central. Howard L. Terry and W.H. Hunt, the appellants, are shareholders of Penn Central who objected to the transaction. In a diversity action before the United States District Court for the Eastern District of Pennsylvania, appellants sought injunctive and declaratory relief to enforce voting and dissenters' rights to which appellants asserted they were entitled. Appellants further sought to enjoin Holdings from proceeding with the proposed merger, and in particular moved to enjoin a vote on the transaction, scheduled for October 29, 1981, by the shareholders of Penn Central. In an opinion issued on October 22, 1981, Judge Pollak denied appellants' requests. Appellants thereupon filed an appeal in this Court. . . .

The shareholders of Penn Central voted, as scheduled, on October 29. . . . After argument on appeal, the shareholders disapproved of the merger in that vote, and the corporations thereafter publicly announced their abandonment of this particular merger.   Penn Central, however, has not abandoned its proposed series of acquisitions, of which the Colt acquisition was merely one instance.

I

Penn Central is the successor to the Penn Central Transportation Corporation, which underwent a reorganization under the bankruptcy laws that was completed in 1978. No longer involved in the railroading business, Penn Central, since 1978, has had the advantage, for tax purposes, of a large loss carry-forward. In order to put that loss carry-forward to its best use, Penn Central has embarked on a program of acquiring corporations whose profits could be sheltered. To this end Penn Central created Holdings, a wholly-owned subsidiary which was to acquire the businesses that Penn Central desired. The first acquisition under the plan was Marathon Manufacturing Company ("Marathon"), in 1979. In the Marathon acquisition, a class of preferred Penn Central stock was created, and 30 million shares of "First Series Preference Stock" was issued to the owners of Marathon stock. Appellants were shareholders of Marathon who thereby acquired shares of this First Series Preference Stock. Terry was promptly elected to the Penn Central board of directors.

In 1981, Penn Central decided upon a second acquisition: Colt. The management and directors of Colt and Penn Central agreed upon a merger of Colt into Holdings, compensated for by issuance of a second series of Penn Central preference stock to Colt shareholders. Terry opposed the merger at the directors' meeting, and now seeks to preclude the consummation of the transaction.

. . . [A]ppellants argue that under Pennsylvania's corporate law, they are entitled to dissent and appraisal rights if the merger is adopted over their opposition. . . . The district court held that [the claim was incorrect] as a matter of law. . . .

Because Colt and Penn Central have now announced their abandonment of the proposed merger, the request for injunctive relief considered by the district court is now conceded by all parties to be moot. However, the appellants' request for declaratory relief, which the appellants now contend is moot as well, involves legal questions that go to Penn Central's plan of acquisitions, rather than to the Colt transaction alone, and these questions appear likely to recur in future disputes between the parties here. It is clear from the record that the Colt merger was one in a series of similar acquisitions by Penn Central. The appellants, one of whom has now objected to each of the last two proposed mergers by Penn Central, will continue to have a lively interest in challenging any future acquisitions structured in roughly the same manner as the transaction before us now. The declaratory relief requested here thus arises from a genuine and continuing controversy, and involves adverse parties who have diligently presented their cases to this Court. The continuing threat of legal action creates some present injury, and not merely a speculative future injury, to Penn Central: without a judgment on the merits of this appeal, Penn Central's present ability to negotiate other acquisitions will be severely impaired by the desire of companies to avoid the legal complications faced by Penn Central and Colt. In a case such as this, a voluntary termination by the parties of the specific activity challenged in the lawsuit -- in this case, the proposed treatment of the dissenting preferred shareholders in the Colt-PCC plan -- does not render the case moot because there is "a reasonable likelihood that the parties or those in privity with them will be involved in a suit on the same issues in the future." American Bible Society v. Blount, 446 F.2d 588, 595 (3d Cir.1971); Marshall v. Whittaker Corp., 610 F.2d 1141, 1147 (3d Cir.1979). . . .

III

Terry and Hunt contend that under Pennsylvania law they are entitled to dissent and appraisal rights if a merger is approved by the Penn Central shareholders. . . .

Briefly, appellants' argument is that the proposed merger between Holdings and Colt constitutes a *de facto* merger between Colt and Penn Central, and that the Penn Central shareholders are therefore entitled to the protections for dissenting shareholders that Pennsylvania corporate law provides for shareholders of parties to a merger. Although this reasoning, with its emphasis on the substance of the transaction rather than its formal trappings, may be attractive as a matter of policy, it contravenes the language used by the Pennsylvania legislature in setting out the rights of shareholders.

Section 908 of the Pennsylvania Business Corporation Law (PBCL) provides that shareholders of corporations that are parties to a plan of merger are entitled to dissent and appraisal rights, but adds that for any acquisition other than such a merger, the only rights are those provided for in § 311 of the PBCL. Section 311, in turn, provides for dissent and appraisal rights only when an acquisition has been accomplished by "the issuance of voting shares of such corporation to be outstanding immediately after the acquisition sufficient to elect a majority of the directors of the corporation." In this case the shares of Penn Central stock to be issued in the Colt transaction do not exceed the number of shares already existing, and thus the transaction is not covered by § 311. Any statutory dissent and appraisal rights for Penn Central shareholders are therefore contingent upon Penn Central's status as a party to the merger within the meaning of § 908. And as the district court points out, the PBCL describes the parties to a merger as those entities that are *actually* combined into a single corporation. Section 907 states that:

> Upon the merger or consolidation becoming effective, the several corporations
> parties to the plan of merger or consolidation shall be a single corporation
> which, in the case of a merger, shall be that corporation designated in the plan
> of merger as the surviving corporation. . . .

At the end of the proposed merger plan here, both Holdings and Penn Central would survive as separate entities, and it would therefore appear that Penn Central is not a party within the meaning of § 907. We can discern no reason to infer that the legislature intended the word "party" to have different meanings in §§ 907 and 908, and accordingly conclude that Penn Central is not a party to the merger.

Appellants argue that Penn Central is nevertheless brought into the amalgamation by the *de facto* merger doctrine as set out in Pennsylvania law in Farris v. Glen Alden Corp., 143 A.2d 25 (Pa.1958). *Farris* was the penultimate step in a *pas de deux* involving the Pennsylvania courts and the Pennsylvania legislature regarding the proper treatment for transactions that reached the same practical result as a merger but avoided the legal form of merger and the concomitant legal obligations. In the 1950s the Pennsylvania courts advanced the doctrine that a transaction having the effect of an amalgamation would be treated as a *de facto* merger. See, e.g., Bloch v. The Baldwin Locomotive Works, 75 Pa.D. & C. 24 (1950). The legislature responded with efforts to constrict the *de facto* merger doctrine. *Farris,* addressing those efforts, held that the doctrine still covered a reorganization agreement that had the effect of merging a large corporation into a smaller corporation. In a 1959 response to *Farris,* the legislature made explicit its objection to earlier cases that found certain transactions to be *de facto* mergers. The legislature enacted a law, modifying *inter alia* §§ 311 and 908, entitled in part:

> An Act . . . changing the law as to . . . the acquisition or transfer of corporate
> assets, the rights of dissenting shareholders, . . . abolishing the doctrine of de
> facto mergers or consolidation and reversing the rules laid down in Bloch v.
> Baldwin Locomotive Works, 75 D & C 24, and Marks v. The Autocar Co.,
> 153 F.Supp. 786. . . .

Act of November 10, 1959 (P.L. 1406, No. 502).[a]

Following this explicit statement, the *de facto* merger doctrine has rarely been invoked by the Pennsylvania courts. Only once has the Pennsylvania Supreme Court made reference to it, in In re Jones & Laughlin Steel Corp., 412 A.2d 1099 (Pa.1980). Even there, the Court's reference was oblique. It merely cited *Farris* for the proposition that shareholders have the right to enjoin "proposed unfair or fraudulent corporate actions." 412 A.2d at 1104. This Court, sitting in diversity in Knapp v. North

---

[a] This Act added the language in § 311 concerning issuance of shares sufficient to elect a majority of directors quoted in the text, *supra*. Eds.

American Rockwell Corp., 506 F.2d 361 (3d Cir.1974), *cert. denied*, 421 U.S. 965 (1975), invoked the *de facto* merger doctrine to hold that a transaction structured as a sale of assets could nevertheless be deemed a merger for purposes of requiring the merging corporation to assume the acquired corporation's liability for damages to a worker who was injured by a faulty piece of equipment manufactured by the acquired company. Perhaps the broadest application of the doctrine was made in In re Penn Central Securities Litigation, 367 F.Supp. 1158 (E.D.Pa.1973), in which the district court held that the doctrine provided the plaintiffs in that case with standing for a 10b-5 lawsuit alleging *fraud* and also gave rise to dissent and appraisal rights in a triangular merger situation.

None of these cases persuades us that a Pennsylvania court would apply the *de facto* merger doctrine to the situation before us. Although *Jones & Laughlin Steel* suggests that dissent and appraisal rights might be available if fraud or fraudulent unfairness were shown, we are not faced with such a situation. No allegation of fraud has been advanced, and the only allegation of fundamental unfairness is that the appellants will, if the merger is consummated, be forced into what they consider a poor investment on the part of Penn Central without the opportunity to receive an appraised value for their stock. Even if appellants' evaluation of the merits of the proposed merger is accurate, poor business judgment on the part of management would not be enough to constitute unfairness cognizable by a court. And the denial of appraisal rights to dissenters cannot constitute fundamental unfairness, or the *de facto* merger doctrine would apply in every instance in which dissenters' rights were sought and the 1959 amendments by the legislature would be rendered nugatory.[7]

The two federal cases invoking the doctrine, *Knapp* and *Penn Central Securities,* are not persuasive as to the applicability of the *de facto* merger to the present situation. *Knapp* was not concerned with the rights of shareholders as the Pennsylvania legislature was in 1959. Although *Penn Central Securities* did hold, in part, that the triangular merger in that case constituted a *de facto* merger, it is clear from the briefs submitted to the district court in that case that the court was not made aware of the post-*Farris* 1959 amendments or the legislative statement of intent to limit the *de facto* merger doctrine.

In the absence of any explicit guidance to the contrary by the Pennsylvania courts, we conclude that the language of the legislature in 1959 precludes a decision that the transaction in this case constitutes a *de facto* merger sufficient to entitle Penn Central shareholders to dissent and appraisal

---

[7] A different result might be reached if here, as in *Farris,* the acquiring corporation were significantly smaller than the acquired corporation such that the acquisition greatly transformed the nature of the successor corporation. But in this situation we do not have such a case; after the merger Penn Central would remain a major, diversified corporation, and would continue on the course of acquiring other corporations.

rights. We therefore hold that appellant does not possess such rights if a transaction such as the one involved here is consummated.

---

2. Recharacterization of Nonstatutory Alternatives

Up to this point, we have focused on the judicial response to efforts by planners to eliminate some of the rights granted shareholders under a statutory merger -- the most restrictive statutory technique -- by choosing among alternative acquisition techniques also authorized by the corporate statute. What happens, however, when planners accomplish what is claimed to be the functional equivalent of a statutory technique by an alternative which, rather than providing *fewer* protections than other statutory techniques, is not, at least in form, covered by the statute at all and, therefore, provides *no* protection?

A sense of the opportunity for creative planning this approach provides can be obtained by recalling the perspective on the corporation offered by the Klein, Crawford & Alchian, and Teece and Williamson articles in Chapter 8. In this view, any function necessary to the corporation's business can be accomplished either within the corporation or through a market transaction by means of contract. For example, a corporation engaged in manufacturing a consumer product needs to sell that product to the public. This can be accomplished either by contract with a third party, a distribution agreement is a common approach, or by having the company vertically integrate by engaging in retailing itself. One means by which this integration can be achieved, of course, is by acquisition. And the availability of a contractual alternative to acquisition is not limited to vertical integration. Where horizontal expansion is sought, either to acquire additional capacity or to allow the pursuit of a cooperative rather than a competitive strategy, a joint venture (contractual) approach is a functional alternative to acquisition.[51]

The question then becomes what factors influence a corporation to choose between an acquisition and a contractual solution: What determines the economic boundary of the firm? More general answers to this question were considered in Chapter 8, but in particular cases one factor may be the cost of protections for shareholders and others imposed by the corporate statute on the acquisition alternative. Is the de facto approach still available if the need for a shareholder vote or appraisal rights increases the costs of an acquisition and, thus, causes the planner to choose a contractual alternative rather than merely a less restrictive statutory alternative?

---

[51] See John McConnell & Timothy Nantell, *Corporate Combinations and Common Stock Returns: The Case of Joint Ventures,* 40 J.Fin. 519 (1985).

PRATT v. BALLMAN-CUMMINGS FURNITURE CO.
495 S.W.2d 509 (Ark.1973)

BROWN, Justice. The appellants are minority stockholders of Ballman-Cummings Furniture Company of Ft. Smith. They claim that by a vote of the majority stockholders of Baldwin-Cummings, the corporation, under the pretext of forming a partnership with Ft. Smith Chair Company, Inc., accomplished a de facto merger or consolidation of the two corporations. If the arrangement is in fact a partnership it is authorized by Ark.Stat.Ann. § 64-104 (B.6) (Repl.1966); if the arrangement constitutes a merger then the appellants, protesting minority stockholders, are entitled to be paid by the succeeding corporation, the fair value of their stock. Ark.Stat.Ann. § 64-707 (Repl.1966). . . .

The Ayers family of Ft. Smith, by virtue of its stock holdings, is in control of both corporations and the corporations have interlocking directors.

The partnership agreement was executed in November 1967. It provided that the partnership would consist of two partners, naming the two corporations. The name of the partnership was designated Ayers Furniture Industries. Each partner would contribute $1500 to the initial capital of the partnership. It was agreed that each corporation would sell its merchandise to the partnership. The partnership would be responsible for all merchandising functions in connection with the promotion and sale of furniture. It would also handle billing and collection of accounts receivable. The partnership would also assume the responsibility for the delivery of furniture to customers. (It was explained by witness John Ayers, ownership of the furniture by the partnership made it possible to load furniture produced by both factories in a single trailer which otherwise was not permitted by ICC regulations.) It was also explained by the same witness that the partnership would eliminate the duplication of expenses of billing and collections. It was also provided that the partners would designate one individual as a general manager of the partnership who would be fully authorized to conduct the business and affairs of the partnership.

It would be most difficult to say that the partnership arrangement, as exemplified by the agreement which we have briefly described, constituted in and of itself a merger of the two corporations. . . .

On the other hand, there are well recognized in the law, de facto mergers -- an association under the guise of a partnership whereby one of the corporations loses its identity as such and is actually controlled by the management of the partnership. When a particular corporate combination "is in legal effect a merger or a consolidation, even though the transaction may be otherwise labeled by the parties, the courts treat the transaction as a de facto merger or consolidation so as to confer upon dissenting stockholders the right to receive cash payment for their shares." 15 Fletcher Cyclopedia Corporations § 7165.5.

Mr. John Ayers is the chief officer of Ballman-Cummings, of Ft. Smith Chair, and of the partnership. It is the position of appellants, while asserting that they do not accuse Mr. Ayers of fraud, that under his executive direction, Ballman-Cummings has lost its long standing identity in the market place. That development, so they say, has resulted in consistent annual losses by the corporation of thousands of dollars, while the profits of Ft. Smith Chair remained stable. The evidence shows that Ballman-Cummings is in the process of liquidation. . . .

According to appellants the events which brought about the alleged destruction of Ballman-Cummings are summarized in their brief and their argument, and absent any other explanation, are persuasive:

> Not only is the separate identity of the merging corporations as marketing entities replaced by the image of a separate and new entity, but Art. 2, § 5 (Articles of Partnership) provides: "The partners shall designate one individual as a General Manager of the partnership who will be fully authorized to conduct the business and affairs of the partnership".
>
> Furthermore, the management, sales and bookkeeping functions of the two corporations were entirely merged together, with a single officer, not the one elected by the directors of each corporation, in charge of each function. John Ayers became the General Manager of both corporations and the partnership, or more properly of both corporations in the partnership. Prior to the merger each corporation had a sales manager, after the merger Gene Rapley who had been sales manager for Ballman-Cummings became sales manager for the combined operations, while Tom Condren who had been sales manager for Chair Company became the designer for the combined operations. The controller for one corporation, Mr. Layman, was placed in charge of the accounting processes for the combined operations, while the controller for the other corporation, Mr. Thompson, took over the credit collection and customer service activities of the combined operation. Dale Keller, who had been purchasing agent for Ballman-Cummings, became purchasing agent for the combined operations, while Mr. Keller who had been with Chair Company became the chief assistant in the purchasing department.

Whether there is a correlation between the shifting of the described responsibilities and the resultant folding of Ballman-Cummings is not the question; the question is whether a prima facie case was made. We think it was. We might add that no solid reason was given by Mr. Ayers for Ballman-Cummings' collapse. There was only a general statement that it was due to economic reasons. Mr. Ayers said he had no explanation why the loss of Ballman-Cummings rose so severely except "apparently loss cycles that we had been experiencing, the problems we had been experiencing in production were pyramiding on us during that year". Appellees are also burdened by the fact that the partnership was proposed on the basis that it would increase profits, which of course it did not do.

[The Court concluded that the facts established a prima facie case for the application of de facto merger doctrine.]

Reversed and remanded.

GOOD v. LACKAWANNA LEATHER CO.

233 A.2d 201 (N.J.Super.1967)

MINTZ, J.S.C. Plaintiffs Donald A. Good and Marjean M. Good are minority stockholders of defendants Good Bros. Leather Co. (hereinafter referred to as Good Bros.) and Lackawanna Leather Co. (hereinafter referred to as Lackawanna). They seek an appraisal of the value of their shares in accordance with N.J.S.A. 14:12-6 and 7 and N.J.S.A. 14:3-5. Alternatively, they seek an appraisal of their shares in both corporations in accordance with alleged common law rights. Plaintiffs specifically charge that Lackawanna and Good Bros. have been merged without the stockholder approval of either corporation required by N.J.S.A. 14:12-3, despite a rejection of the proposed merger by the majority of the stockholders of Good Bros. . . .

Defendant corporations have enjoyed a close relationship over the years. The predecessor to both corporations was a partnership between Herman B. Good and his brother Robert C. Good formed in 1896. This partnership engaged in various phases of the leather processing business. In 1903 the partners arranged for the incorporation of Lackawanna, which corporation chrome-tanned leather for the automobile trade. The plant was located in Hackettstown, N.J., where it still exists. In 1914 Herman and Robert Good organized Good Bros., Inc., which established a plant in Newark. Herman B. Good was president and general manager. Robert's son, Donald S. Good, entered the employ of Lackawanna in about 1920, and upon the death of his father in 1944 became president of the company. Donald's son, Donald A. Good, is one of the plaintiffs in the within cause of action. Carl F. Good, one of the defendants, is the son of the late Herman B. Good.

Since 1957 Carl F. Good, Ross L. Dimm, Jr., Gerard K. Lind and Dale McKnight have been the majority shareholders and have controlled the boards of directors of both Good Bros. and Lackawanna. Carl F. Good is the president of Good Bros. and the chairman of the board of Lackawanna. Ross L. Dimm, Jr. is the president of Lackawanna and vice-president of Good Bros.

Almost since its inception Lackawanna has engaged in the business of finishing and selling fine leather for use by furniture and automobile manufacturers. It worked closely with Good Bros. purchasing much of its russet leather from it. Lackawanna was Good Bros.' principal customer for russet-tanned top grains. However, in 1956 Lackawanna acquired additional facilities in Hackettstown where it could accomplish the russet-tanning [1] of top grains cheaper than it would cost it to purchase the russet leather from Good Bros. Thus when in 1956 Lackawanna was able to russet-tan its own

---

[1] Russet-tanning is the first tanning operation taken to start the hides on their way toward a finished product. Beaming is the operation of soaking, defurring and defleshing green salted hides after they are received from the slaughter house. Splitting is the longitudinal splitting of the hides into component parts; the top section is the top grain and the lower section is referred to as the split. Splitting of the whole hide is part of the beam house operation.

hides, Good Bros. went out of this phase of hide processing. The only tanning operations in which it thereafter engaged was on the splits, which it conducted for a period of approximately three years.

In 1956 Donald S. Good, who was then president of Lackawanna, offered to buy the majority interest in that company. The offer was rejected by the majority stockholders. He thereupon resigned, as did the executive vice-president and several other key employees. They immediately went to work for the Good-McCree Leather Company, a competitor, in Hackettstown, of which plaintiff Donald A. Good was president. In the fall of 1956, as a consequence of these resignations, Carl F. Good was elected president of Lackawanna, Ross L. Dimm, Jr. executive vice-president and Dale McKnight vice-president in charge of sales. Lackawanna was in poor condition. Its building, machinery and equipment had received little maintenance. The credit of the company was limited. Its customer relations were impaired and it had no inventory.

In the 1950s "lime splitting," a technological advance in the industry, was adopted in various tanneries. Theretofore, tanneries were unable to produce all the russet leather which they required. They looked to beam house processors, such as Good Bros., to supplement their needs for russet leather. With the advent of lime splitting they were able, with their current facilities, to produce all the russet leather needed. Thus, this new process seriously affected Good Bros. business. Lackawanna, however, did not become a fully integrated plant. Sewage problems at its Hackettstown plant would not permit the beam house operation. Hence, Good Bros. remained a source of supply of beamed hides.

In the light of this situation the boards of directors of Lackawanna and Good Bros. considered merger proposals. In December 1957 a memorandum proposing the merger of Good Bros. and Lackawanna was circulated among the directors, assigning the following reasons for the merger:

> The largest and most important leather finishing companies now have their own tanning departments which can supply all of their needs and, therefore, Good is dependent upon Lackawanna for the disposal of a major portion of its products. Obviously it would not be wise for Lackawanna to be dependent upon its competitors for its supply of partially processed hides. Under present conditions, probably neither Good nor Lackawanna could successfully operate independently of the other. Obviously, it is important for both companies and for the stockholders of both companies that the company producing the finished product and offering it in the competitive market be in the strongest position possible to meet its competition.

The merger memorandum recommended that about one-third of the machinery and tools of Good Bros. be disposed of at salvage value, the Newark property of Good Bros. be sold, and the beaming operations of the merged companies be moved to a new location. The memorandum also called for the exchange and distribution of 1.85 shares of Lackawanna for each share of Good Bros. It further indicated that if dissents were filed, the proposed merger would not be effectuated because the appraisal rights attaching to the shares of the dissenters would cause a cash drain upon the affected companies which they could ill afford.

A formal merger agreement was approved by the boards of directors of both Good Bros. and Lackawanna. On April 26, 1958 said merger agreement was submitted to the stockholders of Lackawanna, at which time a resolution adopting the agreement of merger was passed by the two-thirds vote of the stockholders, as required by N.J.S.A. 14:12-3. However, the shares held or controlled by plaintiffs, comprising approximately 20% of the outstanding shares, were voted against the merger, thereby entitling them to receive the appraisal value of their stock.

On May 24, 1958 Carl F. Good, as president of both corporations, advised the stockholders as follows:

> This is to advise you that the proposed merger of Good Bros. Leather Co. into The Lackawanna Leather Company dated as of March 31, 1958, will not be consummated. The holders of 1345-½ shares of stock of The Lackawanna Leather Company and the holders of 75 shares of stock of Good Bros. Leather Co. have given the respective corporations written notice of their dissent. Consequently if the merger were consummated the surviving corporation would be obliged to purchase the share of these dissenting stockholders at the appraised market value of such shares. . . . Accordingly, at the adjourned meeting of the stockholders of Good Bros. Leather . . . a vote on the merger will be taken, but the shares owned by members of the Board of Directors and their families will be voted to reject the proposed merger.

On June 7, 1958, the proposed merger was rejected by a majority of the stockholders of Good Bros. Plaintiffs allege, however, that defendants achieved the very objectives sought by the statutory merger plan notwithstanding the rejection, and thus actually accomplished a *de facto* merger as of about December 31, 1960. Plaintiffs also contend that by the end of 1961 Good Bros. sold substantially all of its assets without the stockholder authorization required by N.J.S.A. 14:3-5. It is asserted that the subsequent course of conduct on the part of the respective corporations confirms and establishes the *de facto* merger and alleged unauthorized sale of all the assets of Good Bros.

Plaintiffs point to the marked change and curtailment in the nature of Good Bros. operations after 1959. Good Bros. faltering business is evidenced by the fact that at the end of 1959 it had but one remaining customer, namely, Lackawanna for whom it beamed hides. The sales pattern also manifests a business decline. In 1958 its gross sales amounted to $1,291,524. Although in 1959 its gross sales increased to $2,192,395, this substantial increase was in some measure attributable to the sale in December of its entire hide inventory to Lackawanna, and a temporary increase in demand and price for its beamed products. However, in 1960 sales totalled only $260,544. In 1961 sales totalled $267,360, and in 1964 $306,893.

On December 1, 1960 Good Bros. sold its land, buildings and improvements in Newark to the Remis Trust Fund. At the same time it entered into a contract with H. Remis & Co. to perform such beaming operations as Good Bros. should require for a period of five years. Good Bros. tried to sell its beaming equipment to Remis but Remis would not purchase it. For the following five years Good Bros. was able to do the beaming required by Lackawanna and to make a profit by charging Lackawanna a competitive price which was in excess of the price under its subcontract with Remis. In addition to the beaming for Good Bros., Remis did some beaming for its own account for which it paid Good Bros. for the use of the latter's machinery.

In 1961 all personnel at the Newark plant were transferred to the Remis payroll except for a supervisor and Carl F. Good. Remis performed the beaming of hides owned by Lackawanna under its subcontract with Good Bros. This arrangement continued until August 1, 1966. As a consequence of the change in the Good Bros. operation after 1959, there was little need for the fixed assets, which accordingly were sold, scrapped or abandoned. There was a gradual disposal of the operating assets, such as inventories which were sold to Lackawanna, and accounts receivable which were converted into cash or its equivalent.

In the 1960s the net worth of Good Bros. averaged about $400,000. By 1964, when 94% of its assets were reduced to cash or its equivalent, the only equipment included in the net worth figure was the beaming machinery being used by Remis, having a book value of $25,900.

As early as June 1, 1960, and perhaps prior thereto, the officers and directors of Good Bros. made known to its stockholders its plan, if possible, to sell its Newark property and relocate its beaming and pickling operations in another area. The testimony indicates that substantial freight as well as other charges could be eliminated by the relocation of the beam house in close proximity to the raw hide market.

During the period 1960-1966 the risk of purchasing hides in a highly volatile and fluctuating market was borne by Lackawanna. During this period, green hides when purchased by Good Bros., were billed to Lackawanna at cost. Good Bros. from time to time loaned funds to Lackawanna to finance the purchase of hides by Lackawanna which were beamed by Good Bros. under its subcontract with Remis. On such borrowings Good Bros. was paid interest at current bank rates. Resolutions were adopted from time to time by Lackawanna and Good Bros. authorizing the loans. The first such resolution was adopted by the directors of Lackawanna on December 23, 1959. This resolution authorized the corporation to borrow approximately $100,000 from Good Bros. at current interest rates. The funds were to be used to purchase green hides and to pay for the processing of the hides by Good Bros. in Newark.

Good Bros. likewise on December 23, 1959 adopted a resolution authorizing said corporation to loan up to $100,000 to Lackawanna at current interest rates to enable Lackawanna to purchase the hide inventory required for its business.   Subsequently, this loan authorization was increased to $200,000.   On September 12, 1961, at a special meeting of the board of directors of Lackawanna, its officers were authorized to borrow an additional $50,000 in excess of the $200,000 then permitted from Good Bros. as a temporary measure until October 2, 1961.   Apparently on that date Lackawanna was unable to repay the $50,000 to Good Bros.   There is a journal entry under date of October 2, 1961 for the purchase of green hides by Good from Lackawanna in the amount of $49,715.66 and a charge to interest income on the Good Bros. books in the sum of $284.34.   A credit in favor of Lackawanna was entered on the notes receivable account for $50,000, thereby reducing the loan account to $200,000.   Good Bros. subsequently resold the green hides to Lackawanna for $50,123.   In other words, as an accommodation to Lackawanna, Good Bros. temporarily carried the green hides on its books as an asset.   It also appears that God [sic] Bros. occasionally purchased hides for its own account which were later resold to Lackawanna at cost.

In 1965 the directors of Good Bros. and Lackawanna were apprised of an available location in Omaha, Nebraska, on which to erect a tannery. Apparently it was agreed between the corporations that Good Bros. purchase the site and erect a building thereon in which beaming operations would be conducted by a corporation to be formed, in which Good Bros. and Lackawanna would be the stockholders. Accordingly, Good Bros. purchased the property and erected a building thereon. The two corporations organized Lackawanna of Omaha, a Delaware corporation, two-thirds of the stock being subscribed to by Lackawanna and one-third by Good Bros.   The invested capital of Good Bros. in Lackawanna of Omaha was $10,000. Good Bros. erected a building on the property which it, in turn, leased to Lackawanna of Omaha.   The land and building cost Good Bros. approximately $200,000. The lease with Lackawanna of Omaha was for a period of 20 years, with Good Bros. receiving as rent a 12% return upon its investment.   The beam house equipment was apparently installed by Lackawanna of Omaha. In August 1966 Lackawanna of Omaha commenced beaming hides under contracts for Lackawanna.   At about this time Good Bros. disposed of its machinery then used for beaming in the Newark plant.

It is anticipated that the new beam house operations in Omaha will prove mutually beneficial to Good Bros. and Lackawanna.   As already observed, Lackawanna cannot operate a beam house at its Hackettstown plant because of sewage problems.   It now has an assured and advantageously located source of beamed hides in Omaha. Good Bros. has an advantageous real estate investment under lease to Lackawanna of Omaha. It will also participate, by virtue of its one-third interest in Lackawanna of Omaha, in the profits that are expected to be earned by it in the beaming operation. And as already observed, Good Bros. is relieved from the risk of dealing in the volatile green hides market.

I

It is plaintiffs' theory that the close working relationship existing between Good Bros. and Lackawanna is tantamount to a merger of the two companies. Plaintiffs assert that Good Bros. assets are fully at the disposal of Lackawanna and that Good Bros. is, in effect, a private bank to be utilized in accordance with the whims of the directors of Lackawanna. It is argued that although Good Bros. was not liquidated, it had no active business or tanning function to perform after December 31, 1960, and that by December 31, 1964, 94% of its plant and equipment was converted into money or investment securities.

Plaintiffs allege that the gross sales appearing on Good Bros. records for the year 1961 and thereafter are really not gross sales at all. For example, the gross sales for 1964 reflect sales in hide processing and sales of green hides. Actually, the only hide processing Good Bros. performed was for Lackawanna through its arrangement with Remis. The sales of green hides were billed to Lackawanna at cost. It is thus contended that all the objectives of the proposed merger stated in the merger resolutions were in fact accomplished.

Initially, it may be noted that this is not a stockholder's derivative action. There is no charge of mismanagement or fraud to the detriment of either corporation. There is no charge that Good Bros. has been unfairly treated. True, the net worth of Good Bros. has not increased since 1959. However, this was in good measure due to loss of business because of changes in the industry and the obsolescence of its operation. The fact remains that since 1959 dividends have been paid annually to the stockholders of Good Bros.

A merger is defined in the leading New Jersey case dealing with the doctrine of *de facto* merger as the absorption by one corporation of one or more usually smaller corporations, which latter corporations lose their identity by becoming part of the larger enterprise. Applestein v. United Board & Carton Corp., 342, 159 A.2d 146 (N.J.Super.Ch.Div.1960), *aff'd* 161 A.2d 474 (N.J.1960). The court in *Applestein* made the following findings, which it held spelled out a *de facto* merger of the two companies:

> Thus, every factor present in a corporate merger is found in this corporate plan, except, perhaps, a formal designation of the transaction as a 'merger.' There is proposed: (1) a transfer of all the shares and all the assets of Interstate to United; (2) an assumption by United of Interstate's liabilities; (3) a 'pooling of interests' of the two corporations; (4) the absorption of Interstate by United, and the dissolution of Interstate; (5) a joinder of officers and directors from both corporations on an enlarged board of directors; (6) the present executive and operating personnel of Interstate will be retained in the employ of United; and (7) the shareholders of the absorbed corporation, Interstate, as represented by the sole stockholder, Epstein, will surrender his 1,250 shares in Interstate for 160,000 newly issued shares in United, the amalgamated enterprise.

Although every element found by the court in *Applestein* may not be essential in determining the existence of a *de facto* merger, there are certain key elements existing therein which are not present in the case at bar. Significantly, there has been no exchange or transfer of shares between Good Bros. and Lackawanna. A consolidation or merger always involves a transfer of the assets and business of one corporation to another in exchange for its securities. Ballantine on Corporations, § 280, p. 664. The leading cases discussing the applicability of the *de facto* merger doctrine all concern situations where there is a transfer of assets by one corporation in exchange for shares of the purchasing corporation. Applestein v. United Board & Carton Corp., *supra*; . . . Hariton v. Arco Electronics, Inc., 182 A.2d 22 (Del.Ch.1962), *aff'd* 188 A.2d 123 (Del.1963); Farris v. Glen Alden Corp., 143 A.2d 25 (Pa.1958). The issue common to all of the cited cases was whether the sale of assets in exchange for the shares of the purchasing corporation actually comprised a *de facto* merger of the corporations, thus making available dissenters' rights under the respective merger statutes. A concomitant of all the cases was that the corporation disposing of its assets terminated all business functions and virtually went out of existence.

This is not the factual pattern presented in the case at bar. There has not been a transfer of assets by Good Bros. to Lackawanna in exchange for shares as called for in the rejected merger agreement. Good Bros. has not ceased its corporate functions in furtherance of its charter. It earned interest on its loans to Lackawanna, and made an annual profit on the hide processing performed for Lackawanna through Remis. Good Bros. is very much alive and is enjoying profitable operations. It owns a building and land in Omaha from which it expects a 12% return on its investment. It also owns a one-third interest in Lackawanna of Omaha, Inc., a beaming operation, which corporation leases the aforementioned Omaha land and building. Good Bros. thus indirectly maintains its interest in the hopefully profitable phase of the hide processing industry. Lackawanna and Good Bros. always maintained and continue to maintain separate boards of directors and officers who hold regular meetings. Each corporation has its own accountant and files its separate tax returns. Each maintains its own bank accounts and investments.

Also lacking in the instant case, and of key importance, is the fact that Good Bros. has not assumed any of the liabilities of Lackawanna. True, Good Bros. has loaned working capital to Lackawanna, but in no instance has Good Bros. guaranteed the debts of Lackawanna. It has no liability to the creditors of Lackawanna and has not directed that the borrowed funds be utilized in any particular manner. Furthermore, Lackawanna has repaid its entire obligation to Good Bros., and the loan account was closed as of September 30, 1966.

Thus, it may be seen that virtually all of the elements which comprised a *de facto* merger in *Applestein* and the other cited decisions are lacking. There does exist a close working relationship between the two companies and there is an interlocking of directors and officers. However, the presence of these factors do not *per se* constitute a merger. The definition of merger in *Applestein* has not been satisfied. There has been no absorption of one corporation of the other, with the absorbed corporation losing its identity. This finding is illustrated by the fact that if appraisal rights were to be granted, it would be impossible to decide which corporation, Good Bros. or Lackawanna, would be responsible for paying the value of the shares. N.J.S.A. 14:12-7, incorporating N.J.S.A. 14:12-6, provides for court-appointed appraisers to value the shares of the dissenters. N.J.S.A. 14:12-6 specifically provides that the "*consolidated* corporation shall pay to such stockholder the value of his stock . . . " (emphasis supplied). The existence of two functioning corporate entities, each owning respective assets and carrying on distinct business functions, makes the statute impossible to apply. There is no consolidated corporation that may be called upon to pay the dissenters the value of their shares.

Although many of the economic objectives sought to be accomplished under the proposed and rejected statutory merger in fact have been achieved, this without more does not constitute a *de facto* merger.

If the facts in Pratt v. Ballman-Cummings Furniture Co. and Good v. Lackawanna Leather Co. are viewed most favorably to the planners of the transaction in each, their strategy is entirely understandable. The potential for synergy seemed to exist -- in *Ballman-Cummings* because of ICC regulations concerning the availability of truck load shipping rates,[52] and in *Lackawanna* because of gains from vertical integration -- if the operations of the two companies could be combined. The cost of doing so by one of the statutory techniques was to provide appraisal rights to minority shareholders who, apparently, had no other way to liquidate their investment. Not wanting the loss of capital that would have resulted from appraisal and, perhaps, because of the unavoidable uncertainty associated with judicial valuation, the planners in each case devised an extra-statutory technique to accomplish their ends. Is either the Delaware "equal dignity" approach or the Pennsylvania approach to statutory interpretation helpful in identifying where the line ought to be drawn?

---

[52] Even though the two furniture companies were controlled by the same families and had interlocking directorates, ICC regulations apparently respected the formality of their separate existence. As a result, the lower shipping rates available when one company hired an entire truck were not available if the two companies shared a truck. This suggests a motivation for merger not directly considered in Part II: regulatory failure.

3.   The Concept of Equivalency

It takes no great insight to conclude that what is troubling about the differing statutory treatment of alternative acquisition techniques is the sense that functionally equivalent transactions are treated differently. The motive for applying the de facto merger doctrine is then to prevent the elevation of form over substance and its goal is to cause functionally equivalent transactions to be treated alike. It would follow that a measure of the quality of the judicial response to the planner's ingenuity would be the extent to which planners were thereafter indifferent to transactional form.

But the ease with which this goal can be achieved and, perhaps, the wisdom of its pursuit, turn on our ability to clearly delineate the basis on which two forms of acquisitions can be said to be functionally equivalent. The difficulty of this inquiry is considered by Bayless Manning in an excerpt from a well known evaluation of the desirability of one of the consequences of the application of the de facto merger doctrine, the availability of appraisal rights. This is followed by a recent effort by Professor Melvin Eisenberg, the current Chief Reporter of the American Law Institute project on corporate governance and a major influence on the relevant portions of the California Corporations Code, to describe how the lines of equivalency should be drawn.

Bayless Manning, THE SHAREHOLDER'S APPRAISAL REMEDY: AN ESSAY FOR FRANK COKER
72 Yale L.J. 223, 239-44 (1962)[*]

Triggering Transactions

. . . When, under what circumstances, should . . . shareholders be given a statutory appraisal remedy so they can jump clear of the corporate enterprise if they do not like its course? One possible reply would be: "Under all circumstances." . . .

In earlier pages, the point was made that the appraisal statutes, where applicable, pose a difficulty for the corporation because of the drain on the company's liquidity and because of procedural difficulties. Every extension of the appraisal remedy increases the burdens on the going enterprise. Indiscriminate extension of the remedy is pernicious. The remedy should apply only where the risks to the shareholder are great. And the remedy should not be made applicable to a class of transactions unless the benefits to the minority shareholders outweigh the consequent burden imposed upon the enterprise.

---

[*] Reprinted by permission of *The Yale Law Journal* Company and Fred B. Rothman & Company.

We must be selective. To help us to be selective it is useful to consider and compare a series of candidates. Following and on succeeding pages are three lists of events that may occur in the normal life course of an incorporated enterprise. The reader is asked to read over the lists with some deliberation. The question is: Should objecting shareholders be given the appraisal remedy in some, all, or none of the listed transactions or events -- and why?

List I

-- A rise in the United States balance of payments deficit
-- An Antitrust suit brought by the Justice Department against the company
-- A Presidential heart attack[35]
-- Introduction of a promising new product by a competitor
-- A declining stock market
-- Nationalization of some of the company's foreign assets
-- Large scale disarmament

In each of the cases in List I the shareholder may suddenly find his investment in the company threatened with extinction. He would be delighted to have the appraisal option open to him. But despite his desires in the matter and despite the economic fate about to overtake him, the appraisal statutes are, as every lawyer knows, not available to him. It is said that risks of the kind just listed are "assumed" by the investor. This answer is no more satisfactory here than it ever is, for the question is: Why are these risks imposed upon the investor while others are not?

All the events listed above have one feature in common. They are all, in a manner of speaking, external to the corporate enterprise -- that is, they are events that were not, in a direct sense, brought about any of the constituencies of the corporation. One may say, and it is usually said, that the "reason" these transactions are not triggering transactions under the appraisal statutes is that they are not transactions brought about by the will of the majority and objected to by the minority. This statement may be accepted as descriptively accurate. But it is hardly a satisfactory "explanation," for it leaves open the question: Why are we interested in protecting the investor against internal risks only? Let us leave that one with the answer that we are interested in internal risks because we are, and move on.

Here then is a second list of events out of a corporate biography. To meet the criterion just set, each of these transactions is internal to the constituent structure of the corporation, and not imposed by outside forces:

---

[35] On the day following President Eisenhower's first heart attack the aggregate market value of all securities listed on the New York Stock Exchange dropped fourteen billion dollars. N.Y.Times, Sept. 28, 1955, p. 1, col. 6.

List II

-- Mass resignation by the management
-- An involuntary petition in bankruptcy for the corporation
-- A demand by the relevant union for higher wages, accompanied by strike threat
-- The refusal by a majority of the debenture holders to approve an indenture amendment considered by the shareholders to be vital to the continued successful operation of the enterprise
-- A buyers' strike
-- A refusal by important suppliers to continue to supply the company

Each of these events is fraught with danger to the shareholder's investment. And each is precipitated by a group that is in some sense "internal" to the enterprise, is in some degree committed to its fortunes, and is in a position to affect those fortunes directly. Yet the appraisal statutes do nothing to protect the shareholder against the decisions of his fellow constituents in any of these instances. Creditors, workers, officers, customers, suppliers -- all may whip things about as they will, and the shareholder will have to hold on to his seat and ride it out. When these people rock his world, the dissenter may not order it stopped for him to get off. He is never given that option unless the transaction was brought on by his fellow shareholders, or, very occasionally, by the directors. No one else counts.

The significance of this evident fact is seldom observed. To limit statutory concern to shareholders' and directors' acts is wholly arbitrary. The dissenters' investment can be as much threatened by acts of bondholders as by acts of shareholders, as much by wage paid workers and salary paid officers as by fee paid directors. It is circular and meaningless to say that the remedy is available in transaction X but not in transaction Y, "because" shareholders decide transaction X while transaction Y is brought on by non-shareholders.

To limit our concern to acts of shareholders makes it now apparent that we are not dealing with an economic problem or with economic solutions. The economic risk to the shareholder does not turn on the question of who was responsible for the event giving rise to the risk; and when the statutes undertake to differentiate among those effectively causing the event, they do not make the differentiation in economic categories, but in lawyer's categories. We may say of an operating business enterprise that a variety of economic constituencies play important parts, and we can to some extent isolate and describe these. In statements of this kind we are seeking to make operational statements about economic phenomena. But when we say that we are interested only in those events that are brought about immediately by "shareholders" and "directors" we are no longer in the world of the economist or political scientist -- we have reconfirmed our disinterest in economics and climbed onto a level of unadulterated legal categories. . . . We have fled the brassy realm of practical effects and entered upon the golden realm of lawyers' abstraction where the din of the market place can scarcely be heard.

Just *why* we should have proceeded in this way is not at all clear. But accepting as given that no shareholder will be accorded the appraisal remedy except in events or transactions brought about by other shareholders or directors, we should now look at a third list of transactions, all of which meet this condition. This list is somewhat more detailed and, for ease of comparison, the events have been arranged into crude groupings. Which, if any, of the following events should give what shareholders a statutory out?

List III

-- The shareholders vote out the board. Ninety-eight percent of the shareholders mark their proxies "da" on a resolution of confidence in the management currently languishing in jail under Sherman Act convictions. A majority interest in the corporation's stock or other securities changes hands.

-- In 1962, the company shifts from the manufacture of buggy whips to the manufacture of seat belts. The company shifts from the manufacture of seat belts to the manufacture of buggy whips. The company plunges into, or pulls out of, European operations. The company buys 100,000 shares of New Haven Railroad stock. The company files a voluntary petition in bankruptcy.

-- The shareholders amend the purpose clause in the charter. They amend the charter to: change the corporate name; change the home office; change the number of directors; scrap cumulative voting; change the par value of a class of stock.

-- The company pays a large dividend. The company refuses to pay any dividends. The company makes a large distribution of assets to junior security holders. The company makes periodic distributions of cash or of other assets, looking forward to a distribution of all assets. The corporation donates a million dollars to charity.

-- The corporation dissolves.

-- The company enters into a long term labor contract under which all foreseeable profits will go to the union. The company enters into a long term labor contract under which, by prevailing standards, the workers are grossly underpaid. The company enters into long term executive employment contracts calling for astronomical salaries and lavish perquisites.

-- The company issues senior stock. It issues . . . junior stock. It issues stock for cash. It issues stock for securities or other noncash assets. It issues stock for cash or assets at less than the "market." It grants stock options to a management group at less than "market." It grants stock options to others at less than "market."

-- Corporation *A* merges with Corporation *B*, the latter "surviving." Corporation *A* merges with Corporation *B*, the former "surviving." Corporation *A* consolidates with Corporation *B*, Corporation *C* resulting. Corporation *A* acquires all the stock of Corporation *B*. Corporation *B*, a 100% subsidiary of Corporation *A*, is eliminated by merger with Corporation *A*, by dissolving and handing over its assets as a liquidating distribution, by distributing its assets without dissolving, by buying up and cancelling all the *B* securities held by *A*.

-- Corporation *A* buys $1 million of assets from Corporation *B*. *A* sells $1 million in assets to *B*. *A* sells all its assets to *B* for $1 million. *A* buys *B*'s blast furnace for cash; *B* buys *A*'s cash for a blast furnace. *A* sells real estate to *B* with a lease back to *A*. *A* buys real estate from *B* with a lease back to *B*. *A* buys assets, paying for them by issuing its securities -- equity and debt. *A* translates its fixed assets into cash or securities in one transaction. *A* translates its fixed assets into cash or securities in a series of transactions.

-- Corporation *A* buys all the assets of Corporation *B* for *A* securities, and after X months, *B* distributes the *A* securities to its shareholders; sells the *A* securities on the market and distributes the cash to the *B* shareholders; dissolves and distributes the *A* securities; dissolves and sells the *A* securities.

-- The corporation lists or delists on the New York Stock Exchange.

If a man from Mars were to read over this list of events, how would he assess their significance to the objecting shareholder and pick out those transactions so direful as to call for the extraordinary measures of the appraisal remedy? Only the most highly sophisticated Martian -- or the most unsophisticated -- would be able to guess what our statutes have done.

Melvin Eisenberg, THE STRUCTURE OF THE CORPORATION
224-35, 250-51 (1976)

**Stock-For-Assets Combinations Under the Traditional
Corporate Statutes -- A Problem in Statutory Ambiguity**

The Delaware position, although a minority view, has generally received the commentators' approbation.[1] Thus, the *Farris* result has been

---

[1] See, e.g., Ernest Folk, *De Facto Mergers in Delaware: Hariton v. Arco Electronics, Inc.*, 49 Va.L.Rev. 1261 (1963); Bayless Manning, *The Shareholder's Appraisal Remedy:*

described as a "blaze of Platonism," because it is based upon finding "a 'true and real merger' that exists beyond, and is merely reflected in, the merger statutes,"[2] whereas the Delaware cases are praised for "requiring only adherence to form," thereby affording an objective test and avoiding "the inherent complexities of a judicial test which seeks a 'real' merger beyond the form of the transaction."[3] Is this analysis just?

Let us begin with the typical stock-for-assets combination, in which the survivor assumes all of the transferor's rights and obligations, and the transferor dissolves pursuant to the underlying agreement. The first question to be determined in such a case, obviously, is whether the transaction constitutes a "merger" or a "sale" within the meaning of the statute. The Delaware court has dealt with this question by invoking its equal-dignity theory -- that the validity of "action taken under one section of [the Delaware corporation] law . . . is not dependent upon, nor to be tested by the requirements of other unrelated sections." Applied to combination cases, this theory apparently means that the validity of action taken under sale-of-substantially-all-assets provisions is not to be tested by the requirements of the merger provisions. But such an answer is virtually irrelevant to the question it purports to address. The question in these cases is whether a given combination *is* a sale. It is in no way responsive to that question for the court to say, as Delaware says, that *if* a combination is a sale, it need not meet the requirements laid down for mergers. In applying its so-called equal-dignity theory to cases like *Hariton,* all the Delaware court has done is assume its own conclusion.

What led Delaware into this logical dead end? Pretty clearly, two implicit assumptions: (1) that the terms "merger" and "sale," as used in the corporate statutes, are unambiguous; and (2) that the combinations before the court were sales, and not mergers, within the meaning of those unambiguous terms. The first assumption, at least, is also reflected in the work of those commentators who have criticized cases like *Farris* for platonically finding "a 'true and real merger' that exists beyond, and is merely reflected in, the merger statutes." To a certain extent this assumption is implicit even in *Farris, . . .* since the combinations in those cases were held to be mergers de facto rather than mergers within the meaning of the statutes.

A close examination of the statutes, however, reveals that the terms "merger" and "sale," rather than being unambiguous, are marked by nothing so much as by ambiguity. Take for example the New York statute, which is typical in this regard. Mergers between domestic corporations (other than short-form, parent-subsidiary mergers) are governed by §§ 901-904, 906,

---

An Essay for Frank Coker, 72 Yale L.J. 223, 257 (1962). . . .

[2] Manning (1962), *supra* note 1, at 257. See also Folk (1963), *supra* note 1, at 1277.

[3] Folk (1963), *supra* note 1, at 1277.

and 910.[4] Section 901(a)(1) provides that "[t]wo or more domestic corporations . . . may [m]erge into a single corporation which shall be one of the constituent corporations." Section 901(b)(1) provides that "[w]henever used in this article . . . '[m]erger' means a procedure of the character described in subparagraph (a)(1)." Section 902 provides that to consummate a merger, the board of each constituent shall first adopt a plan of merger setting forth the name of each constituent, its capitalization, and the terms of the proposed merger, including the manner of converting the shares of each constituent into shares or other securities of the survivor, or the cash or other consideration to be paid, a statement of any amendments to the survivor's certificate, and such other provisions as the board considers necessary or desirable. Section 903 provides that the plan shall then be submitted to the shareholders of the constituents for their approval. Section 904 provides for the filing of a certificate of merger. Section 906 provides that upon the filing of such a certificate, the surviving corporation shall succeed to the assets, rights, and liabilities of each constituent. Section 910 provides for appraisal rights.

And that is all. The statute (and to repeat, the New York statute is typical in this regard) lays down the procedures to *effect* a merger, and it lays down the operative *results* of a merger, but it nowhere defines a merger. We know that if a merger is effected, two corporations become one. We know little more -- at least from the statute. Why not? Probably because the legislature thought that a merger was a well-understood business transaction, no more in need of definition than a mare. In other words, a merger is *precisely* something that "exists beyond, and is merely reflected in, the merger statutes." A merger is a real-live-flesh-and-blood thing that businessmen do and legislators regulate. The platonist is one who thinks that mergers are created by Caesar rather than Crassus.

But then what is the business transaction which the legislature contemplated? In common usage, as evidenced by *Webster's,* "merger" means the "absorption by a corporation of one or more others. . . ."[6] Similarly, *Black's Law Dictionary* defines a corporate merger as "the union of two or more corporations by the transfer of property of all to one of them, which continues in existence, the others being swallowed up or merged therein."[7] Economic and financial usage tends to subsume under the term "merger" any business combination involving the issuance of stock.

All this, and the statutory scheme itself, points in one direction: the prototypical transaction contemplated by the legislature when it used the term "merger" is a combination of two corporations, effected through the issuance of consideration -- normally stock -- by one in exchange for shares of the other, and resulting in a fusion of the constituents and the consequent

---

[4] N.Y.Bus.Corp.Law §§ 901-904, 906, 910 (McKinney 1963 & Supp.1974).

[6] *Webster's New International Dictionary of the English Language* 1414 (3d ed.1961).

[7] *Black's Law Dictionary* 1140 (4th rev.ed.1968). . . .

disappearance of the transferor as a going enterprise. In fact, once it is understood that the statutes do not define a merger, it is difficult to see how the term can be construed so as not to include such combinations. The only alternative would be to construe the statutes to cover only combinations which the board *labels* a merger. But such a construction seems impermissible. First, it would render almost meaningless the legislative prescription that a merger requires shareholder approval and gives rise to appraisal rights. This prescription is intended to protect shareholders. Unless the legislature clearly so indicates, therefore, it cannot be presumed to . intend that management could nullify these rights through the mere expedient of labeling. . . .

Thus at least some stock-for-assets combinations seem to constitute mergers within the meaning of the corporate statutes -- not "de facto," but de jure. But this still leaves a second question: Are such transactions also sales? Based on common usage, a strong argument can be made that they are not. For example, suppose *A* and *B* organize a partnership, *AB,* and each contributes to the partnership a going business. Generally speaking, neither lawyers nor laymen would say that *A* has "sold" his business (or that *AB* has "purchased" it). The reason *A*'s transfer would not normally be called a "sale" is that the term "sale usually refers to a transaction in which a transferor *disposes* of his interest in the thing transferred, whereas in the hypothetical *A* retains an interest in the transferred business. Now suppose that *AB* is not a partnership, but a corporation? Again, generally speaking neither lawyers nor laymen would call *A*'s transfer of his business to *AB* in exchange for *AB* stock a "sale" by *A* (or a "purchase" by *AB*), and for the same reason. . . .

But then suppose *A* transfers his business to *AB* in exchange for *AB* stock when *AB* is an existing corporation, wholly owned by *B* ? Here too the transaction would not normally be described as a "sale" of his business by *A* (or a "purchase" by *AB*), again for the same reason: *A*'s continuity of interest in the transferred business. But this last transaction is, of course, a stock-for-assets combination.

It therefore appears that many stock-for-assets transactions could be deemed *either* mergers or sales under the corporate statutes. Which characterization should be applied must then depend on which would best reconcile the overlapping merger and sale provisions, and best effectuate the apparent statutory purpose. For reasons already reviewed, the label given the transaction cannot be dispositive. However, there are several other techniques, consistent with the statutory schemes, which may be employed to segregate sales and mergers. Thus, a distinction could be drawn between those stock-for-assets transactions which do not involve any other indicia of a merger -- "without more," to use the language of *Farris* -- and those which are accompanied by some such indicia; for example, a requirement that the transferor dissolve and an assumption by the survivor of the transferor's liabilities.[16]   Alternatively, those transactions in which the survivor issues principally common or other voting stock could be distinguished from those in which it issues principally nonvoting securities -- treating the former as a merger and the latter as a sale. . . .

Still a third possibility would be to draw a distinction on the basis of the relative size of the two constituents. Reverting to the hypothetical transfer of a business by *A* to the existing corporation *AB,* if *AB*'s business is so much larger than *A*'s that *A* receives only a negligible interest in *AB* -- for example, if *A*'s business consists of several small supermarkets and *AB* is a national chain of supermarkets -- both laymen and lawyers probably would say that *A* had "sold" his business. This is so because while *A* retains a continuity of interest in his former assets, his stake in those assets and in *AB* as a whole is so small that for all practical purposes *A* has parted with substantially all of that interest.   What constitutes a substantial stake? Although the corporate cases have not addressed themselves to this question, the courts are nevertheless not without guidelines; as will be shown below, several statutes and the rules of the American and New York stock exchanges have recognized 15-20% as a cutoff for closely related purposes. Under this line of analysis, if the transferor's shareholders receive less than a 15-20% stake in the reconstituted enterprise the transaction would be deemed a sale within the meaning of the statute; if more, a merger.

A Modern Statutory Treatment of Stock-For-Assets Combinations (Including Classical Mergers)

If we put aside the problems raised by the traditional statutes, and consider instead the optimal legislative treatment of stock-for-assets combinations and classical mergers, three things seem clear: (1) A classical merger (that is, a merger so denominated) is simply a special case of a stock-for-assets transaction;   (2) Shareholder rights in such transactions should depend on the real impact of the transaction (which may of course include significant changes in legal rights), not on how the transaction is labeled;   and (3) The impact of such a transaction on shareholders of a transferor may differ from the impact on shareholders of a survivor, so that the rights of each body of shareholders must be considered separately.

---

[16] Such an approach has been criticized on the ground that an assumption of the transferor's liabilities merely constitutes additional consideration for the assets received, while dissolution of the transferor is "frequently, if not usually" an incident of a stock-for-assets transaction. [*Intercorporate Sale of Assets Unifying Stockholder Interests Held De Facto Merger and Enjoined for Failure to Notify of Appraisal Rights Under Merger Statute,*] 59 Colum.L.Rev. 366, 370 (1959). But if such requirements are "frequently, if not usually" an incident of stock-for-assets transactions, that may simply indicate that such transactions are "frequently, if not usually" mergers within the meaning of the statutes.

The Transferor's Shareholders

On the transferor's side, the issues are relatively straight-forward. If one corporation transfers substantially all of its assets to a second in exchange for stock in the latter (or indeed for any consideration other than cash), from the perspective of the transferor's shareholders the result is a radical reconstitution of the enterprise -- so radical that it should not only require approval by the transferor's shareholders, but give rise to appraisal rights for those of the transferor's shareholders who do not choose to participate; and this is true whether the transaction is denominated a merger, or not.

The Survivor's Shareholders

On the survivor's side, the picture is somewhat more complex. If a stock-for-assets combination has a significant economic or legal impact on the survivor's shareholders it should certainly require approval by those shareholders, and give rise to appraisal rights on their part, for much the same reasons that apply to shareholders of the transferor. But if the amount of stock issued by the survivor is not significant in terms of its previously outstanding stock, and no significant change is made in the control structure of the legal entity in which the survivor's corporate enterprise is enveloped, the combination is unlikely to have a significant economic impact on the survivor's shareholders. Such a transaction, therefore, should neither require approval of the survivor's shareholders nor give such shareholders appraisal rights; and this is true even if the combination is denominated a merger. . . .

[Such an approach is] taken by the New York . . . Stock Exchange, which require[s] shareholder approval as a condition to listing new stock issued by listed companies to effect business combinations, "[w]here the present or potential issuance [to the transferor] of common stock or securities convertible into common stock could result in an increase in outstanding common shares approximating 20% or more. . . ."[32] [Professor Eisenberg goes on to point out that the New York Stock Exchange provision also covers the acquisition of assets other than by means of a business combination and recommends that approach as well.]

Cash-For-Assets Combinations

1. The transferor's shareholders. Under the traditional statutes, a sale of substantially all assets for cash requires the approval of the transferor's shareholders. This is as it should be: such a transaction constitutes a radical reconstruction of the enterprise from the transferor's perspective. There is,

---

[32] *New York Stock Exchange Company Manual* at A-284. . . .

however, an important difference between a stock-for-assets and a cash-for assets transaction. Where the transfer is for stock, the result is not only a radically restructured but a continuing enterprise; but where the transfer is for cash and the transferor is immediately liquidated (as is typically the case), the transferor's shareholders are not being brought along in a continuing enterprise, and appraisal rights may therefore be unnecessary, except perhaps as a check on the fairness of price in a self-dealing situation.

2. *The survivor's shareholders.* A cash-for-assets transaction looks much different from the perspective of the survivor's shareholders. An initial question from this perspective is whether such transactions are mergers within the meaning of the traditional statutes. At one time it would have been fairly clear they were not, since a classical merger involved the issuance of stock by the survivor. Today, however, it is common for merger provisions to contemplate the issuance of cash,[34] and it seems likely that, properly or improperly, these provisions will be interpreted to permit the issuance solely of cash. Under such an interpretation, a cash-for-assets transaction could be viewed as a merger within the meaning of the traditional statutes. On the other hand, such transactions could also be viewed as purchases, and which view should be taken may properly depend on underlying policy considerations. Unlike stock-for-assets combinations, an acquisition of substantially all of a transferor's assets by a survivor for cash may involve neither an increase in the size of the survivor's assets (but instead only a reshuffling of liquid into fixed assets), nor a reallocation of ownership interests. From the survivor's perspective cash-for-assets combinations will therefore frequently be difficult to distinguish from internal expansion; that is, they will frequently not rise to the level of a structural change. Therefore, such transactions should not normally require approval by the survivor's shareholders nor give rise to appraisal rights for such shareholders.

Unlike most academics who must passively wait for others to implement their recommendations, Professor Eisenberg had the opportunity to take up that burden himself as a participant in the revision process that led up to the California Corporations Code that became effective January 1, 1977. The following are the principal provisions of the California Corporations Code bearing on acquisitions.

---

[34] Del.Code Ann. tit. 8, § 251(b) (1974).

CALIFORNIA CORPORATIONS CODE:
SECTIONS BEARING ON ACQUISITIONS

Chapter 1. General Provisions and Definitions

§ 152. Approved by (or Approval of) the Outstanding Shares

"Approved by (or approval of) the outstanding shares" means approved by the affirmative vote of a majority of the outstanding shares entitled to vote. Such approval shall include the affirmative vote of a majority of the outstanding shares of each class or series entitled, by any provision of the articles or of this division, to vote as a class or series on the subject matter being voted upon and shall also include the affirmative vote of such greater proportion (including all) of the outstanding shares of any class or series if such greater proportion is required by the articles or this division.

§ 153. Approved by (or Approval of) the Shareholders

"Approved by (or approval of) the shareholders" means approved or ratified by the affirmative vote of a majority of the shares represented and voting at a duly held meeting at which a quorum is present (which shares voting affirmatively also constitute at least a majority of the required quorum) or by the written consent of shareholders (§ 603) or by the affirmative vote or written consent of such greater proportion (including all) of the shares of any class or series as may be provided in the articles or in this division for all or any specified shareholder action.

§ 160. Control

(a)   Except as provided in subdivision (b), "control" means the possession, direct or indirect, of the power to direct or cause the direction of the management and policies of a corporation.

(b)   "Control" in §§ 181, 1001 and 1200 means the ownership directly or indirectly of shares possessing more than 50% of the voting power.

§ 161. Constituent Corporation

"Constituent corporation" means a corporation which is merged with one or more other corporations, or one or more limited partnerships, and includes the surviving corporation.

§ 175. Parent

Except as used in §§ 1001, 1101 and 1200, a "parent" of a specified corporation is an affiliate controlling such corporation directly or indirectly through one or more intermediaries. In §§ 1001 and 1101, "parent" means a person in control of a corporation as defined in subdivision (b) of § 160.

§ 181. Reorganization

"Reorganization" means:

(a) A merger pursuant to Chapter 11 (commencing with § 1100) other than a short-form merger (a "merger reorganization");

(b) The acquisition by one corporation in exchange in whole or in part for its equity securities (or the equity securities of a corporation which is in control of the acquiring corporation) of shares of another corporation if, immediately after the acquisition, the acquiring corporation has control of such other corporation (an "exchange reorganization"); or

(c) The acquisition by one corporation in exchange in whole or in part for its equity securities (or the equity securities of a corporation which is in control of the acquiring corporation) or for its debt securities (or debt securities of a corporation which is in control of the acquiring corporation) which are not adequately secured and which have a maturity date in excess of five years after the consummation of the reorganization, or both, of all or substantially all of the assets of another corporation (a "sale-of-assets reorganization").

§ 190. Surviving Corporation

"Surviving corporation" means a corporation into which one or more other corporations are merged.

§ 1001. Sale, Lease, Exchange, etc.; of Property or Assets; Approval; Abandonment; Terms, Conditions and Consideration

(a) A corporation may sell, lease, convey, exchange, transfer or otherwise dispose of all or substantially all of its assets when the principal terms are

(1) Approved by the board, and

(2) Unless the transaction is in the usual and regular course of its business, approved by the outstanding shares (§ 152), either before or after approval by the board and before or after the transaction.

A transaction constituting a reorganization (§ 181) is subject to the provisions of Chapter 12 (commencing with § 1200) and not this section (other than subdivision (d) hereof). . . .

(d) If the buyer in a sale of assets pursuant to subdivision (a) of this section or subdivision (g) of § 2001 is in control of or under common control with the seller, the principal terms of the sale must be approved by at least 90% of the voting power unless the sale is to a domestic or foreign corporation in consideration of the nonredeemable common shares of the purchasing corporation or its parent. . . .

Chapter 12. Reorganizations

§ 1200. Approval by Board

A reorganization (§ 181) or a share exchange tender offer (§ 183.5) shall be approved by the board of:

(a) Each constituent corporation in a merger reorganization;

(b) The acquiring corporation in an exchange reorganization;

(c) The acquiring corporation and the corporation whose property and assets are acquired in a sale-of-assets reorganization;

(d) The acquiring corporation in a share exchange tender offer (§ 183.5); and

(e) The corporation in control of any constituent or acquiring corporation under subdivision (a), (b) or (c) and whose equity securities are issued or transferred in the reorganization (a "parent party").

§ 1201. Approval of Shareholders; Abandonment by Board; Actions to Attack Validity of Party Directly or Indirectly Controlled by Other Party

(a) The principal terms of a reorganization shall be approved by the outstanding shares (§ 152) of each class of each corporation the approval of whose board is required under § 1200, except as provided in subdivision (b) and except that (unless otherwise provided in the articles) no approval of any class of outstanding preferred shares of the surviving or acquiring corporation or parent party shall be required if the rights, preferences, privileges and restrictions granted to or imposed upon such class of shares remain unchanged (subject to the provisions of subdivision (c)). For the purpose of this subdivision, two classes of common shares differing only as to voting rights shall be considered as a single class of shares.

(b) No approval of the outstanding shares (§ 152) is required by subdivision (a) in the case of any corporation if such corporation, or its shareholders immediately before the reorganization, or both, shall own (immediately after the reorganization) equity securities, other than any warrant or right to subscribe to or purchase such equity securities, of the surviving or acquiring corporation or a parent party (subdivision (e) of § 1200) possessing more than five-sixths of the voting power of the surviving or acquiring corporation or parent party. In making the determination of ownership by the shareholders of a corporation, immediately after the reorganization, of equity securities pursuant to the preceding sentence, equity securities which they owned immediately before the reorganization as shareholders of another party to the transaction shall be disregarded. For the purpose of this section only, the voting power of a corporation shall be calculated by assuming the conversion of all equity securities convertible (immediately or at some future time) into shares entitled to vote but not assuming the exercise of any warrant or right to subscribe to or purchase such shares.

(c) Notwithstanding the provisions of subdivision (b), a reorganization shall be approved by the outstanding shares (§ 152) of the surviving corporation in a merger reorganization if any amendment is made to its articles which would otherwise require such approval.

(d) Notwithstanding the provisions of subdivision (b), a reorganization shall be approved by the outstanding shares (§ 152) of any class of a corporation which is a party to a merger or sale-of-assets reorganization if holders of shares of that class receive shares of the surviving or acquiring corporation or parent party having different rights, preferences, privileges or restrictions than those surrendered. Shares in a foreign corporation received in exchange for shares in a domestic corporation have different rights, preferences, privileges and restrictions within the meaning of the preceding sentence.

(e) Notwithstanding the provisions of subdivisions (a) and (b), a reorganization shall be approved by the affirmative vote of at least two-thirds of each class of the outstanding shares of any close corporation if the reorganization would result in their receiving shares of a corporation which is not a close corporation; provided, however, that the articles may provide for a lesser vote, but not less than a majority of the outstanding shares of each class.

(f) Notwithstanding the provisions of subdivisions (a) and (b), a reorganization shall be approved by the outstanding shares (§ 152) of any class of a corporation which is a party to a merger reorganization if holders of shares of that class receive interests of a surviving limited partnership in the merger.

(g) Any approval required by this section may be given before or after the approval by the board. Notwithstanding approval required by this section, the board may abandon the proposed reorganization without further action by the shareholders, subject to the contractual rights, if any, of third parties.

§ 1300. Reorganization or Short-form Merger; Dissenting Shares; Corporate Purchase at Fair Market Value; Definitions

(a) If the approval of the outstanding shares (§ 152) of a corporation is required for a reorganization under subdivisions (a) and (b) or subdivision (e) of § 1201, each shareholder of such corporation entitled to vote on the transaction and each shareholder of a disappearing corporation in a short-form merger may, by complying with this chapter, require the corporation in which the shareholder holds shares to purchase for cash at their fair market value the shares owned by the shareholder which are dissenting shares as defined in subdivision (b). The fair market value shall be determined as of the day before the first announcement of the terms of the proposed reorganization or short-form merger, excluding any appreciation or depreciation in consequence of the proposed action, but adjusted for any stock split, reverse stock split or share dividend which becomes effective thereafter.

(b) As used in this chapter, "dissenting shares" means shares which come within all of the following descriptions:

(1) Which were not immediately prior to the reorganization or short-form merger either (A) listed on any national securities exchange certified by the Commissioner of Corporations under subdivision (*o*) of § 25100 or (B) listed on the list of OTC margin stocks issued by the Board of Governors of the Federal Reserve System, and the notice of meeting of shareholders to act upon the reorganization summarizes the provisions of this section and §§ 1301, 1302, 1303 and 1304; provided, however, that this provision does not apply to any shares with respect to which there exists any restriction on transfer imposed by the corporation or by any law or regulation; and provided, further, that this provision does not apply to any class of shares described in subparagraph (A) or (B) if demands for payment are filed with respect to 5% or more of the outstanding shares of that class.

(2) Which were outstanding on the date for the determination of shareholders entitled to vote on the reorganization and (A) were not voted in favor of the reorganization or, (B) if described in subparagraph (A) or (B) of paragraph (1) (without regard to the provisos in that paragraph), were voted against the reorganization, or which were held of record on the effective date of a short-form merger; provided, however, that subparagraph (A) rather than subparagraph (B) of this paragraph applies in any case where the approval required by § 1201 is sought by written consent rather than at a meeting.

(3) Which the dissenting shareholder has demanded that the corporation purchase at their fair market value, in accordance with § 1301.

(4) Which the dissenting shareholder has submitted for endorsement, in accordance with § 1302.

(c) As used in this chapter, "dissenting shareholder" means the recordholder of dissenting shares and includes a transferee of record.

The present California Corporations Code represents the most thorough response to Professor Eisenberg's call for a modern approach that focuses on the impact upon shareholders rather than the boundaries of assertedly ambiguous statutory terms. As described by a prominent practitioner, its distinctive structure -- defining the term "reorganization" to include each common acquisition technique, and then specifying the statutory requirements for "reorganization" generally rather than for each technique -- was intended "to create a statutory framework under which both the form of the transaction and the entity chosen to be the acquiring or surviving corporation are determined by considerations other than avoidance of stockholders' voting and appraisal rights."[53] As an exercise, work through how the transactions described in *Farris* and *Penn Central* would have been treated under the California statute. Also note, as was pointed out earlier, that the California statute, following Professor Eisenberg's recommendation, treats shareholders of corporations selling substantially all of their assets for cash or cash equivalents differently than if the consideration was securities of the purchaser; appraisal rights are not available in the former situation.[54] Although it is true that the distinction may reflect the fact that shareholders receiving cash are not forced to become shareholders in a different corporation, which is an argument believed to originally explain the development of appraisal rights,[55] the point then should also extend to shareholders of the target corporation in a cash merger. How does the California statute treat the latter transaction? Also keep in mind that the California statute does not require the approval of, or grant appraisal rights to, the shareholders of the acquiring company in an asset acquisition if the consideration is cash or cash equivalents. In this regard, the statute is consistent in that no vote of the acquiring company shareholders is required in a stock transaction if they retain five-sixths of the voting power of the surviving corporation.

California is not the only state which has updated its corporate statute to acknowledge the equivalence of alternative statutory techniques. See, e.g., Ohio Rev.Code Ann. §§ 1701.01(Q), 1701.83(A), 1701.84(D); N.J.Stat.Ann. 14A:10-3, 14A:10-12; Pa.Stat.Ann. tit. 15, § 1311(F).

Note: The Scope of the Inquiry

The goal of the de facto merger doctrine is to cause functionally equivalent transactions to be treated alike. The problem, however, is in specifying the touchstone against which functional equivalence should be measured. In its most straightforward application the doctrine asserts that statutory acquisition techniques which are functionally equivalent to a merger should provide shareholders of the constituent corporations the same protections as are provided in a merger. Professor Eisenberg clearly adopts this approach in concluding that the statutory terms "merger" and "sale" are ambiguous and then resolving that ambiguity by reference to functional equivalence. Certainly recommendations for a modern statutory approach, triggering equivalent protections in connection with any of the statutory

---

[53] Marshall Small, *Corporate Combinations Under the New California General Corporation Law,* 23 UCLA L.Rev. 1190, 1191 (1976).

[54] This is accomplished by excluding such transactions from the definition of a reorganization in § 181(c). Under § 1300, appraisal rights are available only in a reorganization.

[55] See Eisenberg (1976), *supra* note 35, at 75 and sources there cited.

transactional forms, reflects the notion that the protections given shareholders in a merger should be the measure.

But why limit the inquiry concerning the existence of equivalence to statutory alternatives? If all transactions which are functionally equivalent to mergers should offer shareholders the same protections, then the de facto merger doctrine should also apply to efforts by planners to achieve the results of a merger by nonstatutory techniques. This problem may be seen more clearly with an example. Recall that Professor Eisenberg recommends that a modern statute should require approval by the acquiring company's shareholders where the consideration used is stock, but not when the consideration is cash. This is accomplished in the new California Corporations Code for cash asset acquisitions by excluding them from the definition of "reorganizations," in § 181 and thereby from the requirements of §§ 1200 and 1300 dealing with shareholder approval and appraisal rights. The same result is accomplished for cash mergers by § 1201(b) which eliminates voting and appraisal rights if a constituent corporation "or its shareholders immediately before the reorganization, or both, shall own (immediately after the reorganization) equity securities . . . possessing more than five-sixths of the voting power" of the acquiring corporation. Because no shares are issued in a cash merger, shareholders of the acquiring company obviously meet the five-sixths requirement. But what happens when the planner goes to work? Can approval of the shareholders of the acquiring company be avoided by making a public offering of new stock, representing one-sixth of the company's voting power, and then, after more or less time has passed, using the cash proceeds from that offering to acquire substantially all of the assets of another corporation or to effect a cash merger? Similarly, should transactions be aggregated for the purposes of the five-sixths calculation? Suppose an acquiring company contemplates a series of transactions as in Terry v. Penn Central Corporation, no one of which will involve issuance of shares representing one-sixth of the company's voting power, but which fairly can be expected to exceed that figure in the aggregate?

The issue posed is how broadly the de facto merger doctrine extends. Even if the claimed ambiguity concerning the words "merger" and "sale" in traditional statutes is eliminated,[56] what of a transaction which, in the

---

[56] How persuasive is Professor Eisenberg's argument that the statutory terms "merger" and "sale" are, in fact, ambiguous? His point is essentially that the typical statute does not define either word in terms of their result, but only in terms of the mechanism by which a common result is accomplished. This distinction is then rejected as merely involving "labels" and a construction giving substance to it is therefore deemed "impermissible." But the type of distinction drawn by the statute can be described in a more favorable light. What the statute actually does is define two different processes, both of which reach the same result but by quite different means. Viewed in this way, it is not unusual to distinguish between different means to a common result. It is, for example, hardly persuasive to argue that natural childbirth and caesarian section are really the same thing because their results, a child, are indistinguishable; the difference in the processes is itself significant. Similarly, the

absence of a de facto analysis clearly falls outside of the statute entirely? The issue is particularly important with respect to statutes like that of California whose legislative history indicates that its approach was selected "for the purpose of codifying the 'de facto merger' doctrine."[57] Does the doctrine survive the enactment of such a statute or will the response to efforts to apply it to non-statutory alternatives meet an analysis of the sort found in Terry v. Penn Central Corporation?

That the problem at which the de facto merger doctrine was directed was not eliminated in California by enactment of a modern statutory approach was demonstrated by Woods v. Natomas Co., No. 811-238 (Cal.Super.Ct., Aug. 1, 1983). That case involved Diamond Shamrock's acquisition of Natomas Company by merging Natomas with a Diamond-Shamrock subsidiary created for that purpose,[58] and the issue posed was whether Natomas' preferred shareholders were entitled to a class vote on the transaction under Cal.Corp.Code § 1201(a). If the transaction had been structured as a typical triangular merger, in which Natomas was merged into the newly formed Diamond Shamrock subsidiary, the transaction clearly would have required the approval of the Natomas preferred shareholders voting as a class. However, the transaction planners were clever indeed. Section 1201(a) eliminates the requirement of a class vote for the preferred shareholders of the "surviving corporation," as defined in § 190, so long as the rights, preferences, privileges and restrictions of the preferred shares are not altered in the transaction. The planners' solution, then, was to structure the transaction not as a forward triangular merger in which Natomas would be merged into the new subsidiary (and a class vote would have been required), but as a *reverse* triangular merger in which the new subsidiary would be merged into Natomas. By reversing the transaction, Natomas became the "surviving corporation" and § 1201(a) then operated to eliminate the preferred shareholders' class vote.

Not surprisingly, the preferred shareholders made a de facto merger type argument. Regardless of the literal language of the statute, the effect

---

difference in the processes by which the same result is achieved in a merger and in a sale of assets is also very important. The planner is given the option of trading efficiency for flexibility and the result of that decision with respect to such things as contingent liabilities and union contracts can be critical. The question of whether the *unambiguous* differences in processes justify the difference in shareholder voting and appraisal rights of course still remains; however, that question must be considered directly rather than avoided by treating the differences as if they did not exist.

[57] *Report of the Assembly Select Committee on the Revision of the Corporations Code* 93 (1975).

[58] The facts have been simplified for ease of presentation. In the actual transaction, a new holding company was created and both Natomas and the pre-transaction Diamond Shamrock were merged with the holding company's newly formed subsidiary. The analysis in the text is not affected by this complication. Richard Buxbaum, *The Internal Division of Powers in Corporate Governance*, 73 Cal.L.Rev. 1671, 1687-93 (1985), provides a careful analysis of the case.

of either a forward or a reverse triangular merger on the Natomas preferred shareholders was the same -- they would become minority shareholders in a Diamond Shamrock subsidiary for which there was no public market. If a class vote is necessary to protect preferred shareholders in a forward triangular merger, nothing but form is changed by casting the transaction as a reverse triangular merger. The court disagreed. Despite a statute designed explicitly to cause shareholder protection in acquisitions to depend on substance, the court credited the form in which the planners cast the transaction, and the preferred shareholders were denied their class vote.

In short, the problem to which the de facto merger doctrine responds has proven difficult to eliminate by statute even when the drafters were trying and, in all events, the problem is more complicated than simply determining which acquisition transactions, statutory or not, are the functional equivalent of a merger. The choice of merger as a touchstone may be only a contextual shorthand for a set of circumstances that presents special risks and thus requires special protections in the form of voting and appraisal rights for shareholders. Should not then the de facto doctrine also extend to those events which are functionally equivalent to mergers not because they are acquisition transactions but, more fundamentally, because they pose the same special risks as mergers?

This seems to be Manning's point in creating his three different lists of events, that no meaningful distinction separates the three categories of events from the perspective of their impact on shareholders. The implication is that appraisal rights are appropriate in all of the situations described or in none. If we are unwilling to extend appraisal rights to all equivalent events, they should be eliminated where they do exist. Put in the context of the de facto merger doctrine, the question becomes not how far the equivalence argument carries in extending protection, but how far it forces us to roll back the protection that already exists.

The challenge that Manning articulates -- to either distinguish among his lists in a manner that intelligently identifies when additional protection is appropriate or, as it seems he expects, admit our inability to do so and accept the implications of our failure -- is, in fact, more easily met than he believed.

A sensible approach to drawing the distinctions of whose existence Manning seems so skeptical begins with evaluating his lists in terms of whether the events they contain represent systematic or unsystematic (diversifiable) risk. Consider first List I, containing occurrences like a rise in the United States balance of payments deficit or a Presidential heart attack. Manning asks with respect to these: "Why are these risks imposed upon the investor [without additional protections] while others are not?" The question, however, is not difficult and the answer is not, as Manning puts it, "because [they] are."

Examination of the risks described in List I discloses that they are essentially all systematic in character.[59] They are assumed by the shareholder because under the capital asset pricing model it is *only* for bearing these risks that the shareholders receive more than a risk-free return. Since the shareholders receive a return that is strictly proportionate to how susceptible the security is to systematic risk, the shareholder is paid to assume *precisely* the kinds of risk exemplified in List I and additional protections are thus hardly necessary.

Does this analysis then suggest that special protections should be provided in connection with events of the sort comprising Manning's List II, resignations of executives or labor strife, because shareholders are *not* paid to assume these? Here again finance theory provides an answer, also in the negative. List II risks are entirely unsystematic which, portfolio theory teaches us, can be entirely diversified away by the shareholder. The shareholders are not paid to assume unsystematic risks because they do not bear them; *a fortiori,* they do not need protection from them.

The problem, however, cannot be made to disappear entirely. Financial theory does identify one kind of risk that can be imposed on shareholders and for which they may not be otherwise compensated. This point focuses attention on the kinds of events described in Manning's List III. The price of a company's stock depends on the responsiveness of its return to systematic risk, its beta. From the shareholder's perspective, a corporation's stock represents only a future income stream with a particular sensitivity to systematic risk. As a result, the most important changes are ones that alter that sensitivity. The common link between the events comprising List III is the ability of those events, by altering the asset makeup or leverage of the company, or the businesses in which the company is engaged, to alter the company's beta in a fashion that the shareholders could not have anticipated. Thus, putting feasibility aside for the moment, could we completely respond to Manning's challenge by ignoring the risks on Lists I and II and selecting as candidates for additional protection those voluntary events on List III that alter the beta of the company's stock by more than, say, 25 percent? This approach is, in fact, similar to that taken under current law, although our theoretical statement of the kinds of transactions which require additional protection is very different in formulation than the present statutory alternatives backstopped by a poorly delineated de facto merger doctrine.

Coming back to the effort to develop a satisfactory solution, the suggested theoretical criterion for additional protection is, to be sure, hopelessly unworkable; measurement of beta is hardly an exact science and there is also a question concerning the stability of betas over time. But it does suggest an approach that is feasible, draws definable distinctions between different types of transactions, and provides an answer to the

---

[59] The filing of an antitrust suit against the company, as well as a competitor's new product and expropriation of some of the company's property, are exceptions. From this perspective they belong in List II.

question with which we began: How broadly should the inquiry concerning functional equivalence, the de facto merger doctrine, extend?

We require a technique that can realistically distinguish transactions that are likely to present real risks of change in the systematic risk of the company without reliance on what are, as yet, statistical techniques that cannot bear up to the strain.   The effort to develop one begins with recognition that it is not all changes in beta which present a risk to shareholders. As the discussion of capital budgeting in Chapter 4E indicated, a project with a different risk than the company as a whole still will be desirable so long as the project's return is commensurate with its particular risk. From this perspective, there is no difference in terms of the relevant impact on shareholders between the acquisition of assets and their disposition;   both have the capacity of affecting the shareholders of the transacting corporation in the same way.   And although Manning put it differently, it was the fact that the typical statutory and doctrinal approach draws precisely this distinction between acquiring and target companies without attempting a justification, that provides the basis of Manning's criticism. The justification for the particular distinction and a framework for a workable solution appears when it is recognized that statutory language and judicial doctrine are not the only sources of shareholder protection.

The Gilson excerpt in Chapter 10 presented the corporate structure as an interplay of statutory, judicial and market elements that mesh to provide a coherent check on the discretion necessarily associated with specialized management.   Both Manning's difficulty in distinguishing between acquisitions and non-acquisitions, and the inherent strain in Eisenberg's effort to distinguish between business decisions and investment decisions based on whether the corporation is a buyer or a seller, seem to result from too narrow a view of the corporate structure.   Just because one form of transaction receives statutory protection does not mean that the other is unprotected;   it may only be protected in a different manner.

The first step in putting the problem in a structural perspective is to recognize that in most situations management provides the best (and cheapest) protection for shareholders against an uncompensated alteration in the company's beta.   Put most simply, a transaction that results in an uncompensated alteration in beta is just a bad deal. Normally, however, we do not require that shareholders approve *all* transactions to protect themselves against a bad deal; instead we rely on the business judgment of management for that purpose. Under ordinary circumstances management has precisely the same orientation as the shareholders in evaluating prospective transactions, that is, to maximize risk-adjusted return. And we recognize our inability to devise any better judicial or statutory protective device by insulating management from after-the-fact challenge of their efforts by the virtually absolute barrier created by the business judgment rule. The shareholders are thus saved the cost of judicial intervention and, because the risk of management bad judgment can be diversified, suffer little harm when it occurs. In order for a category of transactions to be a candidate for additional protection, there must be a danger of management self-dealing. In this situation management can no longer be relied upon to protect shareholders and, because all managers can be expected to favor themselves if given the opportunity, the risk *cannot* be diversified away. It is for precisely this reason that the traditional business judgment rule does not apply to self-dealing transactions, and it is for precisely this reason that it makes sense to distinguish between the treatment of acquiring company shareholders and target company shareholders in an acquisition transaction.

Consider first the acquiring company. In an acquisition setting its management is subject to a variety of constraints limiting their freedom to make both bad judgments and self-interested ones. If the acquisition is a poor one for either reason, then all of the constraints on managerial inefficiency and self-dealing discussed in Chapter 10 -- the product market, the capital market, the market for managers, and the market for corporate control -- remain operative to penalize the offending management and, thus, create a substantial *ex ante* incentive for management to avoid uncompensated alterations in beta. The critical point is that this may well *not* be the case for target company management. And recognition of why these market constraints may not operate with respect to target company management provides an explanation for the general statutory pattern of requiring a shareholder vote only for the target company[60] and, in turn, suggests a workable principle for determining when the de facto merger doctrine should apply to nonstatutory transactions.

The expectation of acquiring company management that after the acquisition they will continue to operate the company and remain subject to the discipline of the various markets in which they and the company operate serves to constrain management's self-interest in evaluating the acquisition. In contrast, when the company is instead the object of the acquisition, the constraint imposed by anticipation of post-transaction market penalties on self-dealing management is severely reduced by what economists call "final period problems."

Simply put, in a situation where parties expect to have repeated transactions, the recognition that a party who cheats in one transaction will be penalized by the other party in subsequent transactions reduces the incentive to cheat. However, when a transaction is the last (or only) in a series -- that is, the final period -- the incentive to cheat reappears because, by definition, the penalty for doing so has disappeared.[61] In the context of

---

    [60] See Schulman & Schenk (1983), *supra* note 6, at 1533.

    [61] Analysis of the differences in the incentives of parties to a transaction depending on whether the transaction is the last (or only) one contemplated also has been used, for example, to determine the optimum compensation arrangements for law enforcers, Gary Becker & George Stigler, *Law Enforcement, Malfeasance, and Compensation of Enforcers*, 3 J.Legal Stud. 1 (1974); to understand the incentives for performing contractual obligations even if performance is purely voluntary, Lester Telser, *A Theory of Self-Enforcing Agreements*, 53 J.Bus. 27 (1980); and to evaluate market mechanisms developed to deal with final period

an acquisition nothing stops target management from selling out the shareholders in return for side payments from the acquiring company because target management, by definition, will no longer be subject to the constraints of the product, capital and control markets after the acquisition. Perhaps more importantly, if the remaining professional careers of target management are getting short, the size of the side payment may more than compensate them for any *ex post* penalty imposed by the market for managers.

In a structural approach to corporate law, it is precisely when market constraints on managerial misbehavior fail that legal constraints play a central role. The typical corporate structure reflects this in the historical distinction between the protections given the shareholders of acquiring and target companies. It is only the latter who are subject to final period problems and therefore cannot rely on their management for protection, and require, instead, the barrier of a shareholder vote as a protection against management. It is recognition of this problem that prompts the statutory and judicial concern for the situation in which the form of the transaction is cast as a minnow swallowing a whale in order to circumvent statutory protection against final period problems given target shareholders. And it is precisely the principle derived from understanding the problem -- transactions which present final period problems require additional mechanisms for shareholder protection -- that should govern determination of the breadth of application of the de facto merger doctrine.[62] In this regard, it is interesting that Professor Fischel's treatment of the economic function of appraisal rights,[63] as a means of protecting minority shareholders against opportunism, a danger created by the anticipation of a final period, is directly consistent with this analysis of the de facto merger doctrine.[64]

Statutory literalism -- the province of the Delaware equal dignity approach and the apparent explanation for an otherwise inexplicable result in Woods v. Natomas Co. -- should prove no barrier to resolving the problem in this fashion. Professor Eisenberg has recognized that "American corporate statutes . . . are 'in no sense a code of company law. . . .'"[65]

---

problems, Benjamin Klein & Keith Leffler, *The Role of Market Forces in Assuring Contractual Performance,* 89 J.Pol.Econ. 615 (1981).

[62] From this perspective, the typical de facto merger analysis with respect to acquiring company shareholders is turned on its head. The issue is no longer whether acquiring shareholders should receive the same protections with respect to other acquisition techniques as they do in mergers, but why the protections should be provided in mergers in the first place. If, as appears, the only answer is historical, then the use of protections accorded in mergers as a touchstone is clearly misplaced. The issue is the presence of particular risks, not the form of the transaction.

[63] Daniel Fischel, *The Appraisal Remedy in Corporate Law,* 1983 Am.B.Found.Res.J. 875

[64] See also Hideki Kanda & Saul Levmore, *The Appraisal Remedy and the Goals of Corporate Law,* 32 UCLA L.Rev. 429 (1985) (a "discovery" goal, in order to constrain management self-dealing, best explains the need for an appraisal remedy).

[65] Eisenberg (1976), *supra* note 35, at 86 (quoting, in part, Laurence Gower, *The Principles of Modern Company Law* 8 (2d ed.1957)).

Extrastatutory principles, like the de facto merger doctrine, are required to flesh out the statutory skeleton and their shape is discernible only through an understanding of the entire corporate structure in its statutory, judicial and market elements.

At this point we can come back to an issue that we raised earlier in Section B.2. of this Chapter, but deferred. If determination of whether a sale of substantially all of the assets of a target company includes a qualitative as well as a quantitative element, for what quality are we to look? The answer again should be the final period principle. In the context of an asset sale, the appropriate inquiry concerns whether the assets of the target company remaining after the transaction will be operated in a manner so that target management can expect to remain subject to market constraints.[66]

That leaves for consideration the final form of acquisition, the tender offer, which raises quite different problems in explaining both its typical statutory treatment and the application of the non-statutory de facto merger doctrine to it.

F. Tender Offers: Limits on the Equivalency Concept

While the state and federal securities law treatment of tender offers can be quite complex,[67] their corporate law treatment is very simple indeed. The essence of a tender offer is that the proposal for business combination is made directly to the shareholders without the necessity of prior approval by the board of directors of the target company.[68] Moreover, because the

---

[66] The American Institute Corporate Governance Project moves in the direction of a final period based definition of sales of control that warrant shareholder approval. Section 1.38 defines "transaction in control." Like the California Corporations Code, this definition then serves as the trigger for shareholder approval requirements. Section 1.38(a)(2) includes within the definition "a sale of assets that would leave the corporation without a significant continuing business." 1 American Law Institute, *Principles of Corporate Governance*, §1.38 (1994). While this formulation captures one aspect of the final period analysis, it notably ignores whether management will remain with the target company. If target management can leave the company a "significant continuing business" but exit themselves, the final period problem that creates a conflict of interest remains. The justification for ignoring whether target management will remain in place may be that whoever will run the post-transaction target management will have an incentive to negotiate on behalf of the target shareholders. However, if these negotiators lack the experience and knowledge of those who actually have been running the company, the need for special approval procedures remain. Section 1.38 offers at least nodding recognition of this problem in the commentary to the section, noting that "where doubt exists concerning whether the assets that remain constitute a 'significant continuing business,' the courts may properly consider whether most of the corporation's principal senior executives will continue in their positions with the corporation after the transactions. *Id.* at 49.

[67] See Chapter 18, *infra*.

[68] Thus, the American Law Institute's Corporate Governance Project limits the requirement for shareholder approval to transactions in control "to which the corporation is a party. . . ." American Law Institute (1994), *supra* note 66, at § 6.01(b).

offer is addressed to the shareholders in their individual capacities, no action by shareholders as a group is necessary either.   At this formal level, corporate law treats the technique as if a separate, unrelated offer has been made to purchase the stock of each target shareholder without acknowledging that the effect of aggregating these individual purchases is the transfer of control of the target company, i.e., a corporate acquisition.[69]

Viewed in this fashion, the tender offer poses the most difficult challenge for traditional analysis, both in understanding why its statutory treatment differs so greatly from that of mergers and sales of assets and why, despite that difference, the de facto merger doctrine has not been applied to it.   Not only are the shareholder voting and appraisal rights associated with mergers eliminated, but so is the formal role of the target company's board of directors, a role that is required not only in mergers, but in any other acquisition technique, statutory or non-statutory.   Moreover, the final period principle that governs the application of the de facto merger doctrine should also be operative in the context of tender offers.   While the absence of a requirement of management approval may ease the problem somewhat, the importance of a favorable recommendation by management leaves substantial room for its existence.

What explains this disparity in statutory shareholder protection, and, perhaps even more puzzling, what explains the failure to apply the de facto merger doctrine to a statutory disparity in shareholder protection substantially more significant than that between merger and sale of assets in *Farris?* And to complete the statement of the puzzle, what accounts for the fact that even a firm proponent of functional equivalence like Professor Eisenberg concludes that less protection is appropriate for tender offers:

> Under traditional statutes . . . the nontransferring shareholders would have neither voting nor appraisal rights. Nor would voting rights seem desirable in such cases. For one thing, by its very mechanics the transaction requires shareholder approval of sorts, because the combination cannot take place unless a sufficient number of the transferor's shareholders agree to exchange their shares. . . . More important, it would be unwise to give the shareholders as a body a right to vote on whether some shareholders can sell their stock, and it would seem virtually impossible to develop a mechanism pitched to that objective without placing an inordinate restriction on the normally free alienability of shares.[70]

Clearly something distinguishes tender offers from other acquisition techniques. The following develops a structural basis for the distinction.

---

[69] In recent years, a number of states have amended their corporate statutes to require a vote of target shareholders, or approval of the target company's board of directors, before a tender offer can be made. Because these provisions were uniformly enacted as a response to judicial invalidation of state antitakeover statutes, they will be considered in Chapter 23, *infra*, dealing with state securities law regulation of tender offers.

[70] Eisenberg (1976), *supra* note 35, at 239.

Note: The Structural Role of Tender Offers

The argument that a particular acquisition technique is really like a merger and, thus, that shareholders should have the same protections as accorded in a merger, has a flip side in connection with tender offers. Not only do target shareholders get no statutory protection when the acquisition transaction takes the form of a tender offer, but the statutory role accorded target management in this acquisition form is critically different from that accorded them in mergers and sales of assets. While both mergers and sales of assets *require* approval by the target company's board of directors, the corporate statute makes no express provision for any management role in tender offers. Not surprisingly, management has claimed a role in tender offers similar to that accorded them in mergers and sales of assets and the argument advanced by them is strikingly similar to that on which the de facto merger doctrine is traditionally based. In the following excerpt, limits on target management's functional equivalence argument are developed by reference to the fit of particular acquisition techniques in the overall corporate structure.

Ronald Gilson
A STRUCTURAL APPROACH TO CORPORATIONS:
THE CASE AGAINST DEFENSIVE TACTICS IN TENDER OFFERS
33 Stan.L.Rev. 819, 846-51 (1981)*

Corporate statutes properly place the ultimate responsibility for evaluating proposals for merger or sale of assets with management. These complicated transactions require substantial time investments for shareholders to understand them.[101] Assuming loyal management, a rational shareholder would not invest time considering a merger or sale of assets unless management, through application of its specialized skills, had already approved it. The problem is ensuring, within reasonable limits, that management's determination -- for example, to reject an offer -- is motivated

---

[101] Where the transaction involves the issuance of the offeror's securities, the offer must be registered with the Securities and Exchange Commission pursuant to the Securities Act of 1933 unless an exemption from registration is available. See generally Richard Jennings & Harold Marsh, *Securities Regulation: Cases and Materials* 464-95 (4th ed.1977). Until recently, such a transaction would be registered on Form S-14, 17 C.F.R. § 239.23 (1980), which has been described as generating "some of the longest and most complex disclosure documents presented to investors," with an average length of 110 pages, and some exceeding 200 pages. House Comm. on Interstate and Foreign Commerce, 95th Cong., 1st Sess., Report of the Advisory Comm. on Corporate Disclosure to the Securities and Exchange Commission 440 (Comm. Print 1977) [hereinafter cited as Report on Corporate Disclosure].

. . .

by the shareholders', rather than management's, best interests. . . . The solution is the check and balance of the tender offer. If management, in rejecting merger or sale of assets proposals, gives priority to its own interests rather than those of the shareholders, the spurned suitor can make a tender offer to the shareholders.[103] Should management become too recalcitrant, an alternative is available.

This system of check and balance, of management control of some mechanisms by which control may be shifted but with unfettered access to shareholders through another, is precisely the structure reflected in the typical corporation statute. While control of the merger and sale of asset mechanisms is firmly ensconced in management, the tender offer mechanism generally is not even mentioned in the statute, let alone placed within management's control.[104] . . .

The most common argument supporting managerial discretion to block a tender offer asserts that a tender offer is functionally no different from any other acquisition technique.[105] If management has effectively complete

---

[103] Where management favors itself by accepting an offer -- perhaps because of favorable side payments in the form of employment contracts or stock options -- the statute provides an explicit . . . check through the statutory requirement of shareholder approval. . . . The constraint of shareholder approval, however, is buttressed by the operation of the market for corporate control. Between the public announcement of board of director approval of the transaction and the date of the shareholder meeting, competing offers -- via tender offers -- may be made if the transaction negotiated by management was too favorable to the offeror or to management. [Thus, protection against final period problems in tender offers, as in mergers or sales of assets, comes from shareholder action, although in tender offers the shareholders do not act by a statutory process. Note that the availability of shareholder action in response to a tender offer made in competition with an acquisition approved by target management adds a level of market protection to the statutory protection against final period problems existing with respect to mergers and sales of assets. Eds.]

[104] Where the tender offer is explicitly mentioned, it is in an effort to provide a statutory solution to the de facto merger problem. For example, Cal.Corp.Code § 181 (West 1977) defines three types of reorganizations, including an "exchange reorganization" which amounts to an acquisition by means of a tender offer where the consideration is the offeror's stock. Section 1201 requires a vote of the shareholders of the offeror if, following the transaction, these shareholders will own shares of the offeror representing less than five-sixths of the voting power. No role at all is created for the target board. See generally Marshall Small, *Corporate Combinations Under the New California General Corporation Law*, 23 UCLA L.Rev. 1190 (1976).

That the statute does not assign management a role in traditional tender offers is underscored by the addition in 1976 of Model Business Corporation Act § 72A. ABA-ALI Model Bus.Corp.Act Ann. 2d § 72A (Supp.1977). This section creates a mechanism by which an exchange offer can be made binding on target shareholders if both the board of directors and the shareholders approve the transaction by the same procedures required for mergers and sales of assets. While management is given a role where the transaction is made binding, the statute expressly preserves the option of a traditional tender offer, and in that setting no role is accorded target management. . . .

[105] See, e.g., . . . Martin Lipton, *Takeover Bids in the Target's Boardroom*, 35 Bus.Law. 101, 104, 116 (1979); Pearlmutter, *Shareholders vs. The Corporation*, N.Y. Times, Mar. 9, 1980, § 3, at 18, col.3 (Mr. Pearlmutter is a general partner of Lazard Freres & Co., a major

discretion over whether shareholders will be given the opportunity to vote on a merger or sale of assets, then it should have a comparable role with respect to tender offers. Certainly, the argument continues, the mere form chosen for substantively equivalent transactions should not determine management's role.[106]

The argument extrapolates the typical statutory terms dealing with mergers and asset sales to a form of transaction -- the tender offer -- rarely mentioned in the typical statute. A nonstructural response is that a technical construction of the statute -- contrasting the pivotal role assigned management with respect to mergers and asset sales with the absence of any statutory role with respect to tender offers -- favors a more limited tender offer role for management. The statutory silence regarding tender offers may simply reflect a legislative assumption that free alienation of property is the norm, so that management's affirmative role in mergers and asset sales needs to be stated, while its nonrole in tender offers need not. And while functional equivalence advocates argue that the earlier statutes were silent because they were adopted prior to the time when hostile tender offers became popular acquisition techniques, even a vigorous proponent of management discretion acknowledges that "continuation of [the statutory silence] in recently adopted statutes is disquieting."[110]

One need not, however, limit response to the language of the statute. Under a structural view, functional equivalence among acquisition techniques is important, but this view favors a nonequivalent, much more limited, role for management in tender offers. The management monopoly of the market

---

investment banking firm); William Steinbrink, *Management's Response to The Takeover Attempt,* 28 Case W.Res.L.Rev. 882, 892 (1978). When the transaction is friendly -- i.e., target management has approved the acquisition -- a tender offer *is* the equivalent of the alternative acquisition techniques and the choice among them is made on the basis of criteria other than the need to avoid a management veto.

[106] Some commentators have taken the point a good deal further by pointing to the statutory award of the duty to manage the corporation to the board of directors, and then arguing that a tender offer presents a policy decision no different from others -- like plant investment -- which no one disputes should be made solely by management. E.g., Pearlmutter (1980), *supra* note 105, at 18, col.3 ("is a takeover bid of such a different nature from other important business decisions, such as hiring a new chief executive officer or approving a large capital expenditure program, that the shareholders should decide the issue themselves?"); see Lipton (1979), *supra* note 105, at 120.

The broader position proves too much. The basic equivalence argument asserts that a tender offer is the same as a merger or sale of assets. But in those decisions, the typical corporation statute clearly gives the shareholders a role different from that given with respect to other "important" policy decisions: Actions which involve direct sales of the corporation, like mergers and sales of assets, require shareholder approval, while the supposedly analogous policy decisions do not. See Eisenberg (1976), *supra* note 663, at 213-51; William Carney, *Fundamental Corporate Changes, Minority Shareholders, and Business Purposes,* 1980 Am.B.Found.Res.J. 69. Therefore, the analogy between takeover bids and other policy decisions, given the equivalence argument, should also apply to mergers and sales of assets, which is inconsistent with the structure of the statute.

[110] Steinbrink (1978), *supra* note 105, at 890 (citations omitted).

for corporate control which would result from extending management autonomy to tender offers eliminates the discipline imposed on management by that same market. Restricting management's role in a tender offer does not deny the value of management's expertise in evaluating and negotiating complex corporate transactions, but rather validates the unfettered discretion given management with respect to mergers and sales of assets.

For this purpose, the crucial distinction is not between different acquisition techniques, but between negotiated and hostile transactions. In a negotiated transaction, the acquisition terms result from bargaining between the offeror and target management, and shareholders benefit from management's skill and experience. The problem, however, is that target management may elect not to negotiate, or not to negotiate in good faith. Management's interest in remaining in office creates a conflict which the traditional standards of care and loyalty are incapable of policing. In this setting, the tender offer provides a self-executing check on management's discharge of its responsibility as holder of primary control over the acquisition process. "If negotiations break down, it is still possible for the acquiring company or someone else to go forward with a tender offer. The existence of this safety valve against the directors' conflict of interest is an important justification for giving the directors unfettered discretion in the process of negotiating acquisitions."[111]

Moreover, offerors should not prefer to use a tender offer to side-step target management and thereby deprive target shareholders of management's guidance and bargaining. The negotiation process typically involves transferring to the offeror substantial amounts of nonpublic information concerning the target.[112] This information reduces uncertainty about the

---

[111] Leo Herzel, John Schmidt & Scott Davis, *Why Corporate Directors Have a Right to Resist a Tender Offer,* [3 Corp.L.Rev. 107 (1980)].

[112] While substantial consideration will have been given to the selection of an acquisition candidate prior to the point at which actual negotiations begin, it is commonly recognized that the negotiation process itself generates large amounts of information concerning the target which is available through no other source. . . . Consider, for example, the process of negotiating the representations and warranties contained in a typical acquisition agreement. The target will be asked to warrant, *inter alia,* the accuracy of financial statements and the absence of significant change since the date of the most recent audited statement; the absence of any liabilities for taxes or other matters not disclosed in the agreement including, most importantly, the absence of contingent liabilities; the condition of various assets believed to be of importance to the operation of the target's business; the existence of litigation against the target, whether actual or threatened; and the extent to which various elements of the target's work force are unionized or with respect to which organization efforts are underway. . . . Freund, a prominent practitioner in the acquisition area, stresses the information-producing role of such contractual provisions and the negotiation process generally:

There are no known statistics on the subject, but I'm willing to bet my briefcase that lawyers spend more time negotiating 'Representations of the Seller' than any other single article in the typical acquisition agreement. . . .

From the purchaser's viewpoint, representations serve [several] distinct, although overlapping, purposes. First, they are useful as a device to obtain the maximum degree

future return on the acquisition and hence increases the value of the investment to the offeror.[113] Even though target management may drive a hard bargain on behalf of the shareholders, the offeror has an incentive to negotiate, because resort to a hostile tender offer eliminates access to valuable information.[114]

How would a structural approach limit the argument that a tender offer is the functional equivalent of a merger not from the perspective of target

---

of disclosure about the acquired business prior to the purchaser undertaking a binding commitment to make the acquisition. In other words, representations constitute a systematic smoke-out of the data about the seller which the buyer feels is important.

. . . This focusing aspect of representations can often alert the purchaser to questionable areas for more detailed investigation, and may even provide ammunition for use in renegotiating the price or other terms of the deal.

The second general purpose of representations, from the purchaser's viewpoint, is to set the stage for the purchaser to walk away from the deal if the facts develop that make it unwise to consummate the acquisition. Although in most cases the purchaser has been able to make a preliminary investigation prior to signing the agreement and has relied on certain data supplied to him by the seller, purchaser's *definitive* investigation -- the opening up of all seller's doors and drawers -- usually takes place *after* the agreement has been signed."

James Freund, *Anatomy of a Merger: Strategies and Techniques for Negotiating Corporate Acquisitions* 229-31 (1975) (emphasis in the original).

A similar point was made recently by the investment banker for St. Joe Minerals Corp. in explaining Seagram Co.'s loss to Fluor Corp., the white knight, in the contest for St. Joe: "Seagram 'underbid' for St. Joe because the Montreal-based distiller apparently had access only to public information on St. Joe's asset value and earning power. 'Seagram was fighting from the outside. It's like a guy fighting blind against a guy with clear vision.'" *Seagrams Ends $2.13 Billion Bid for St. Joe,* Wall St.J., Apr. 8, 1981, at 3, col.1.

[113] Assuming the offeror is risk-averse, the additional information can increase the value of the acquisition even if it does not affect the expected return on the investment. See William Sharpe, *Portfolio Theory and Capital Markets* 20-33 (1970); Franco Modigliani & Gerald Pogue, *An Introduction to Risk and Return,* 30 Fin. Analysts J. 68 (1974). Moreover, because the information disclosed may eliminate some risks which the offeror had considered in determining an initial offering price, such as particular contingent liabilities, or may disclose assets, such as favorable lease renewal terms, of which the offeror had not known, the expected return on the transaction may increase as well.

[114] Existing empirical data provide indirect support for the information value of the negotiation process. Peter Dodd, *Merger Proposals, Management Discretion and Stockholder Wealth,* 8 J.Fin.Econ. 105 (1980) compared the market response to the cancellation of previously announced nonhostile acquisitions when the cancellation was due to target management veto and when the cancellation was due to the offeror backing away from the transaction. When management vetoed the deal, the market price of the target shares, although it dropped from the offer price, remained some 10% above the pre-announcement price. *Id.* at 131. When the transaction was terminated by the offeror, the market value of the target shares dropped, on average, to their pre-announcement price. *Id.* This suggests that the market interprets offeror termination as signalling the discovery of negative information concerning the target *during* the negotiating process.

management but, rather, from the perspective of a shareholder of the target? This, of course, is not quite the traditional de facto merger argument where target management will have already approved the transaction and it is protection against their self-interest that is sought. In the tender offer context, might not a shareholder still want protection against a transaction which, whatever management's role and even though imposed by a majority through a sale of their stock, is involuntary with respect to the shareholder who does not approve the transaction?

In this regard, it is helpful to consider what rule a shareholder would choose to govern the application of the de facto merger doctrine to tender offers if the choice had to be made before the shareholder knew whether he would favor or oppose a particular transaction.[115] Given the role of tender offers in the corporate structure, a rule that encouraged them would benefit all stockholders of potential target companies by increasing the market constraints on managerial discretion and, presumably, increasing shareholder return as a result. To be balanced against this benefit is the chance that a tender offer will occur concerning which the shareholder will find himself in the minority which opposes it and who, in that event, would benefit from more restrictive rules. In evaluating the costs associated with the latter situation, the shareholder must consider whether his view of a prospective transaction can be expected to be better than that of the majority, an analysis which should be similar to that undertaken in Section A.2 of this Chapter with respect to how high a vote should be required to approve a merger. The shareholder must also estimate the costs associated with being a minority shareholder in an enterprise controlled by someone else. This estimate, and the legal rules bearing on the manner of estimation, is taken up in connection with the problem of freeze-outs and freeze-ins in Chapter 22. Because the application of the de facto merger doctrine to tender offers also focuses on the position of the minority shareholder after a successful transaction, evaluation of it is deferred until Chapter 22.

---

[115] This is an approach suggested by Professors Easterbrook and Fischel in two important articles: Frank Easterbrook & Daniel Fischel, *The Proper Role of a Target's Management in Responding to a Tender Offer*, 94 Harv.L.Rev. 1161 (1981); Frank Easterbrook & Daniel Fischel, *Corporate Control Transactions*, 91 Yale L.J. 698 (1982).

CHAPTER 17: CORPORATE LAW CONSIDERATIONS IN HOSTILE TRANSACTIONS

Some of the motivations for acquisitions considered in Part II can only be implemented through a hostile transaction. In some circumstances, value creation requires changes that will make managers worse off, who then can be expected to oppose them. Acquisitions designed to break up conglomerates (Chapter 9E) or to reduce free cash flow (Chapter 10D) may have this characteristic. In other circumstances, managers believe the market undervalues the target company (Chapter 14B), and resist an offer to protect shareholders from selling for less than the company's intrinsic value. In either event, an acquisition must be in the form of a hostile tender offer because, as we saw in Chapter 16, only this acquisition technique does not require the approval of the target company's board of directors.

Once a bidder makes a hostile tender offer, a difficult set of issues arise concerning the appropriate role for target management. Defenses can be deployed for both good and bad reasons. An effective defense can work to the advantage of shareholders by allowing management to act as a central bargaining agent who can secure the highest price for the company either by negotiating effectively with a single bidder or by soliciting competitive bids. A survey of 275 unsolicited bids between 1980 and 1989 shows that less than 20% of the targets were acquired at the price initially offered.[1] But an effective defense can also block an offer, and thereby protect managers' positions at the cost of depriving shareholders of the opportunity to accept a favorable bid. The same study reports that some 23% of targets successfully defended against a hostile offer and remained independent.[2] Moreover, if effective defenses are available, bidders may be discouraged from making a bid at all.

With respect to any particular bid, determining which reason motivates management resistance may be difficult, since a hostile bid's success can be consistent with either loyal negotiating by management or ineffective defensive tactics, and a bid's failure can be consistent with either self-interested management entrenchment or a well-intentioned negotiating strategy that failed. The problem is to design rules that maximize the opportunity for managers to act on behalf of shareholder but minimize managers' opportunity to misuse that discretion for their own benefit.

In this Chapter, we consider the corporate law considerations bearing on target and acquiring company planning in a hostile transaction. Section A reviews the range of defensive techniques available to defensive planners and Section B evaluates the empirical evidence concerning their effectiveness. Section C considers the principal concern of the acquiring company:

---

[1] Arthur Fleischer, Jr., Alexander Sussman & Henry Lesser, *Takeover Defense* 3 (4th ed.1990) (reporting Mergerstat Review data as adjusted by the authors).

[2] *Id.* A post-hostile offer independence rate of approximately 20% seems consistent over time. See Douglas Austin, *Tender Offer Update: 1978-1979*, Mergers & Acquisitions 12, 16 (Summer 1980) (1956-1979 data).

discouraging competing bidders from entering the contest. Section D then presents one of the most interesting bodies of corporate law -- the development of legal standards concerning the appropriate deployment of defensive tactics.

A. The Defensive Arsenal

Defensive tactics can be deployed at two different stages in the acquisition process. Some defenses can be undertaken in anticipation of a hostile offer, the goal being either to deter an offer from being made at all, or to assure that defenses are already in place should a hostile bid actually be made. Others, like litigation and greenmail, can be deployed only after a potential bidder has surfaced.

1. Pre-Offer

a. *Preparation*

Arthur Fleischer, Jr., Alexander Sussman & Henry Lesser
TAKEOVER DEFENSE
17-20 (4th ed.1990)

A "team" should be organized in order to provide an effective mechanism for making decisions; that is, day-to-day decision-making should be delegated to a small group which is able to take prompt action. The group should consist of key members of management, and legal, public relations, investment banking, auditing, and shareholder relations advisors. Generally, it is useful to develop a briefing manual that may cover various organizational and procedural matters such as: (i) a list with telephone numbers of key personnel including counsel, investment bankers and financial public relations personnel; (ii) procedures for discussions with the press and others, such as analysts, respecting an unsolicited bid; (iii) methods for calling a "emergency" board meeting; (iv) a checklist of items for an agenda at a board meeting to consider an unsolicited bid; and (v) routines for the prompt contacting of shareholders.[1]

The shareholder population should be reviewed for a variety of purposes, including a determination of its geographic location. This is important because local shareholders are more likely to support the continued

---

[1] For a detailed discussion of the role that public relations can play during the course of a takeover contest, see Richard Cheney, *What Directors Should Know About Public Relations in Takeovers* (Mar. 5, 1986) (speech given to the National Association of Corporate Directors).

existence of an independent company. Geographic concentration will also indicate the possible applicability of state blue sky laws or takeover statutes.

Moreover, the type of shareholder should be ascertained by differentiating among individuals, institutions, employees of the company, customers, and other pertinent groups. This analysis may assist in estimating the likelihood of shareholder loyalty and will indicate to a company where its soliciting efforts should be concentrated. In addition, the extent to which shares are held by trustees, executors or other fiduciaries, who might be viewed as more susceptible to a premium offer, might be ascertained. The company's outside proxy solicitors can contribute to this process and can provide advice and assistance in shareholder relations.

An analysis of turnover among shareholders as well as an effort to estimate the tax basis of their shares should also be conducted. A company whose shares show a high turnover rate may have a less "loyal" group of shareholders. In addition, shareholders with a low cost basis may be more easily discouraged from selling in a taxable transaction. The larger shareholders should be identified and their probable reaction to an unnegotiated tender offer estimated. In all of these procedures the target's stockholder list must be kept secure.

A potential target should initiate a "stock watch" program through the monitoring of daily trading. This effort should include: a periodic review of stock transfer sheets for unusual movements in Cede[2] which might reveal the acquisition of the corporation's stock in preparation for a tender offer; a regular review of Schedule 13D filings to detect large accumulations; and a check of significant holdings held in various "street names." The potential target should keep in contact with its specialist or key market-makers, who may be able to promptly inform the target about unusual market activity. Unusual trading should be checked out.

A mechanism should be established to ensure prompt mailings to shareholders. Thus, an effort should be made to secure the names of the beneficial owners of shares held in "street names," which the company is generally entitled to do under the "NOBO" rule, Rules 14b-1(c) and 14b-1(e) under the Securities Exchange Act of 1934.

The ability to call a board meeting on short notice should be assured. Thus, meetings could be called, for example, on twenty-four hours advance notice by telephone or on such shorter notice as is set forth by the person calling the meeting.

In order to be in a position to capitalize on the increasingly popular restructuring defenses, several issues should be explored by management well in advance of any actual takeover attempt. Debt instruments of the company may contain restrictive covenants which prohibit certain restructuring plans such as a sale of assets or a repurchase of shares. Unless these covenants are defeasible or the instruments are presently redeemable, a company will be

---

[2] Cede & Co. is the nominee name used for certificates deposited with the Depository Trust Company.

limited in its ability to engage in these types of defenses. Consequently, before a company publicly offers debt instruments, attention should be given to the types of financial covenants.

A company's ability to spin-off or sell assets is greatly enhanced if it has current financial data on its operations and has obtained, if material and practical, appraisals of undervalued assets and off-balance sheet items. This type of information will also be helpful in any white knight negotiations, as it can be used to illustrate the value of the company. Additionally, a company wishing to spin-off or sell business as a takeover defense can encounter problems if the operations to be sold are intertwined with the company's other business (if, for example, the disposed of business shares office space or other facilities with the retained operation, or has a customer or supplier relationship with the continuing business.

Prudent advance planning dictates that the company consider these matters. Thus, if otherwise sensible, separate divisions could be incorporated. Furthermore, attention could be focussed on how to split-off operations using, for example, common computer or accounting services or participating in one pension plan. Resolving these issues is time consuming, and hence more difficult, in the short period of time available once a hostile bid has commenced, unless some form of preplanning has occurred. Finally, a target may be able to respond more flexibly to an unsolicited offer if it has credit lines available. These might enable it to consider such options as stock repurchases . . . or a leveraged buyout.

The company's directors and officers liability insurance policy should be reviewed from the standpoint of its coverage of potential takeover-related litigation costs and liabilities. Consideration should be given to modifying the policy or seeking new or additional coverage, if available.[3] Corporations should also consider entering into indemnification agreements with their directors and should determine whether their charter and by-laws permit indemnification to the full extent authorized by the law of the state in which they are incorporated.

Finally, the retention of a law firm with experience in the area is generally thought advisable. This caution has been thought advisable, whether or not a takeover threat appears imminent, in that "[s]uch a course . . . would have permitted the crucial time devoted to recruiting and briefing attorneys to have been spent more productively in responding to the takeover bid."[5] Working along with the company's investment bankers, the law firm can assist the target in formulating structural defenses, maintaining a state-of-the-art poison pill, and advising management and the board on recent developments in takeover defense law and tactics as well as on useful business and financial strategies. It is highly desirable for the outside

---

[3] At one time Lloyd's offered so-called "tender offer defense expense" insurance.

[5] Peter Davey, *Defenses Against Unnegotiated Cash Tender Offers*, Rep.No.726 (The Conference Board, Inc.1977).

financial and legal advisors to become familiar with both company management and its business to assure more effective and comfortable defensive coordination in the event of an actual takeover threat or bid.

Depending upon the particular situation, it is often advisable for the target to familiarize antitrust counsel with its lines of business and markets as well as any expansion or acquisition plans it may have. Where a prospective hostile bidder has been identified, an antitrust evaluation should be undertaken. In some circumstances, it may be advisable to retain an economist to assist counsel. Once a hostile bid commences, time is precious for the target. Advance antitrust preparation will enable counsel quickly to provide sound advice to the target's board and to implement an effective antitrust strategy, including litigation if it is authorized by the board.

---

b.   *Deterrence: Shark Repellent Amendments*

If all a professional adviser can present to a concerned chief executive officer is the ability to know in advance that an offer is coming, or to assure that a team will be in place to respond, little in the way of gratitude should be expected. The real issue in the pre-offer stage is whether a potential hostile bidder can be deterred, that is, convinced never to make the offer at all.

Ronald Gilson
THE CASE AGAINST SHARK REPELLENT AMENDMENTS: STRUCTURAL LIMITATIONS ON THE ENABLING CONCEPT
34 Stan.L.Rev. 775-90 (1982)*

The tactical history of the tender offer movement resembles an unrestrained arms race. Faced with offeror assaults in the form of Saturday night specials, various types of bear-hugs, godfather offers, and block purchases,[2] target management responded with equally intriguing defensive

---

[2] A *Saturday night special* is an offer made without prior consultation with the target and left open for only the minimum offering period. The technique is intended to minimize the target's response time and to maximize the pressure on target shareholders. A conflict exists as to the origin of the term. Compare Raymond Troubh, *Purchased Affection: A Primer on Cash Tender Offers,* Harv.Bus.Rev. 79, 86 (July-Aug.1976) (term arose out of General Cable Corporation's attempt to acquire Microdot, Inc.), with Larry Gurwin, *The Scorched Earth Policy,* The Institutional Investor 33, 34 (June 1979) (term attributed to public relations man Richard Cheney as an effort to convey the impression that an offer by Colt Industries was "cheap and that it went off quickly" (quoting Cheney)).

There are at least three variants of the *bear-hug.* In a classic bear-hug, the target is notified of the offeror's intention to make a tender offer at a specified price but without a

tactics: the black book, reverse bear-hug, sandbag, show stopper, white knight, and, drawing directly on military jargon, the scorched earth.[3]   But however varied the labels given particular defensive strategies, they share the common characteristic of being responsive: They are available only after an offer is made and the battle for the target's independence joined.   From the target's perspective, what was missing from the defensive arsenal was a deterrent -- a tactic that would convince a potential offeror not even to attempt the attack, thereby not only saving the target the substantial costs associated with tender offer conflicts but, more importantly, eliminating the not insubstantial risk that all defenses would fail and the offer prove successful.

Shark repellent amendments are intended to fill this gap in a prospective target's defenses.   The idea is to amend the target's articles of incorporation to make it a less desirable or more difficult acquisition, and thereby to

---

concurrent public announcement.   The strong bear-hug contemplates a simultaneous public announcement of the offer and attempts to negotiate for the target's cooperation.   The super strong bear-hug adds to this the threat that opposition or delay by the target will result in a decrease in the offering price.   E.g., Arthur Fleischer, *Tender Offers: Defenses, Responses, and Planning* 57-59 (1981); Robert Greenhill, *Structuring an Offer,* 32 Bus.Law. 1305, 1308 (1977).

A *godfather offer* is a "cash offer so rich that . . . the directors do not believe . . . they can reasonably refuse it."   Fleischer (1981), *supra,* at 103 n.291. . . .   A *block purchase* is the pre-offer accumulation of a significant position in the target's stock, meant both to exert leverage over the target and to prevent others from joining the bidding.   E.g., James Freund & Charles Easton, *The Three-Piece Suitor: An Alternative Approach to Negotiated Corporate Acquisitions,* 34 Bus.Law. 1679, 1683 (1979).   A pre-offer accumulation of target stock also allows an unsuccessful offeror to recover at least some of the costs incurred in connection with the offer if a competing bidder is ultimately successful.   See Ronald Gilson, *A Structural Approach to Corporations: The Case Against Defensive Tactics in Tender Offers,* 33 Stan.L.Rev. 819, 871-72 (1981).

[3] A *black book* is an outline of the actions to be taken if a tender offer should occur. E.g., Peter Davey, *Defenses Against Unnegotiated Cash Tender Offers* 2 (1977). . . .   In a *reverse bear-hug,* a target responds to an offer by expressing a willingness to negotiate a friendly acquisition but at a price far in excess of that proposed by the offeror.   Fleischer (1981), *supra* note 2, at 63-64. . . .   A *sandbag* is intended to delay the making of a tender offer following a bear-hug.   The target agrees to negotiate, but draws out the negotiations as long as possible.   Don Reuben & Gary Elden, *How to be a Target Company,* 23 N.Y.L.Sch.L.Rev. 423, 441 (1978).

A *show stopper* is a lawsuit by the target seeking a permanent injunction barring the offer.   The most common claim is that the acquisition of the target will violate the antitrust laws.   E.g., Pargas, Inc. v. Empire Gas Corp., 423 F.Supp. 199 (D.Md.), *aff'd per curiam,* 546 F.2d 25 (4th Cir.1976). . . .   A *white knight* is a third party to whom the target turns for a friendly acquisition as an alternative to the tender offer. . . .   A *scorched earth* defense seeks to convince the offeror that the target's defense will be so vigorous as to reduce its value to the offeror.   Gurwin (1979), *supra* note 2.   One example of this approach was Houghton Mifflin's success in causing its authors to advise an offeror that they would sever their relationships with the target if the offer was successful.   *Id.* at 37.

encourage the "shark" to seek a more appetizing or more easily digested alternative. . . .

A Survey of the Phenomenon

Shark repellent amendments and the theories behind their asserted deterrent effect fall into three general categories. A first group of amendments is directed at impeding a successful offeror from taking control of the target's board of directors by protecting the incumbency of existing management. A second group is directed at making more difficult a second-step freezeout merger which eliminates any nontendering shareholders. The third group is intended to deprive the offeror of control over the total cost of the acquisition by specifying the price to be paid nontendering shareholders in a freezeout transaction or, at the extreme, by allowing nontendering shareholders to require the offeror to purchase their shares at a formula price even if the offeror does not initiate a freezeout transaction. All three categories of amendment will usually share a further provision -- the requirement of a supermajority shareholder vote for further amendment or repeal. . . .

The Three Categories of Shark Repellent Amendments

1. Impeding transfer of control of the board of directors

Under a typical corporation statute, an offeror, having successfully tendered for a majority of a target's shares, will encounter little delay in replacing the target's board of directors. Most corporations elect their board of directors annually, without cumulative voting. A new majority shareholder who is unwilling to wait until the next annual meeting of shareholders to install his designees may remove the incumbent directors without cause and select their replacements, either by written consent or at a special shareholders' meeting called pursuant to the majority holder's request.

Shark repellent amendments in theory can delay this process substantially. The initial step is to classify the board into, for example, three classes of which only one is elected annually.[24] The effect, of course, is to require up to two annual meetings for a successful offeror to select a majority of the board through the normal election process.

But classification alone will not prevent a majority shareholder from removing and replacing incumbent directors or, if the particular state statute

---

[24] While the corporate laws of some states allow creation of more than three classes, e.g., Fla.Stat.Ann. § 607.114(4) (West 1977) (not more than four); N.Y.Bus.Corp.Law § 704(a) (McKinney 1963) (two, three, or four), both Delaware, Del.Code Ann. tit.8, § 141(d) (Supp.1980), and the New York Stock Exchange, New York Stock Exchange Company Manual § A-15, at A-280 (Aug. 1, 1977), limit the number of classes to three.

bars removal of directors without cause or bars such removal where the board is classified, from "packing" the board of directors by amending the charter or bylaws so that directors elected by the offeror to fill new vacancies will constitute a majority. Therefore, a complete set of amendments to protect the tenure and majority of pre-offer board members must go beyond classification and reserve to the board the sole right to determine the number of directors and to fill any vacancies created by resignation or increase in the number of directors. Amendments may also limit the mechanics of "flanking" action -- the call of special meetings of shareholders and shareholders' ability to act by written consent -- as well as restrict removal of directors to instances of "cause" narrowly defined.

Even a full complement of these amendments, however, can only delay the transfer of control. If the offeror is content to wait the period necessary to secure control of the target's board of directors, the protective amendments will achieve little, save for distinguishing the target from other corporations that may not have adopted similar measures. However, delay in the shift in control of the target's board of directors may be a significant deterrent to making an offer.

2. Barriers to second-step transactions

Often a tender offer represents only the first step in a plan for the complete acquisition of the target. The second step is commonly a merger in which any remaining minority shareholders are frozen out of the new subsidiary. The second group of shark repellent amendments is intended to make this second-step transaction more difficult.

All corporate statutes require that shareholders approve a statutory merger, and most allow the articles of incorporation to impose a greater-than-majority vote requirement with respect to particular transactions. The typical defensive amendment package can therefore impose a barrier to second-step transactions through a supermajority shareholder vote requirement -- generally from two-thirds to as high as 95% -- for a freezeout merger or comparable transaction with a "related person" -- an intricately defined term which will always include a successful tender offeror. The percentage required for approval is often chosen to approximate the average number of shares represented at the past few annual meetings, in effect requiring an offeror to procure a virtually unanimous vote. Since the combined shareholdings of incumbent directors, officers, and their affiliates often approach or exceed the number of shares necessary to block the requisite supermajority, these provisions may present a significant barrier to a second-step transaction by a successful tender offeror.

Anti-freezeout amendments, however, usually do not impede all transactions falling within their complex definitions. Having broadly defined the covered "transactions" in order to avoid circumvention, the amendments usually include exceptions to the supermajority requirement to permit transactions *favored* by management, such as a friendly takeover or other transaction not motivated by an impending tender offer. These exceptions allow transactions that are approved by a supermajority of "continuing" directors -- those who were in office at the time the related party initially acquired any substantial interest in the corporation. The purpose of that formulation, of course, is to prevent recourse to the exception by a board of directors "packed" or otherwise controlled by the "related person."

3. *Fair price and compulsory redemption provisions*

Fair price amendments are a variation on the supermajority theme. They provide another exception to a supermajority vote requirement for a second-step transaction where the price to be paid minority shareholders exceeds a specified amount which may be greater than the price paid in the initial tender offer.[49]

In an important sense, fair price provisions are inconsistent with the approach reflected in the standard supermajority provision. Rather than strengthening the barriers to second-step transactions, a fair price exception instead provides a way to effect the second-step transaction, albeit at a share price that may be higher than that paid in the initial tender offer. Further, it can be said that a fair price provision, rather than reflecting management self-interest, recognizes the potential danger to minority shareholders in second-step transactions by tying the application of the supermajority requirement to "fairness" to minority shareholders.

The position of minority shareholders following a tender offer is also emphasized in right of redemption provisions, the newest and, so far, least popular variety of shark repellent amendment. This amendment, seemingly borrowed in concept from § 209(2) of the English Companies Act, allows any minority shareholder, following a successful offer for more than a specified percentage of the target's outstanding shares, to require the target company to purchase the remaining shares at a formula price that equals or may even exceed the price paid in the tender offer.

While a right of redemption provision focuses on the position of the minority shareholder who does not tender, it may be a more substantial deterrent to an offeror than a fair price provision in certain circumstances. If a potential offeror contemplates an offer for less than 100% of a target's stock, a right of redemption provision may remove control over the size of an offeror's total investment from its hands. Because shareholders may in

---

[49] A typical formulation waives the supermajority requirement if the price to be paid is equal to or greater than the highest of: (1) the highest price paid by the offeror for any shares acquired during the offer; (2) a price which reflects the same percentage premium (based on the price of the target's stock at the time the second-step transaction was announced) as the initial offer (based on the price of the target stock at the commencement of the initial offer); and (3) an amount determined by multiplying the *target's* average earnings per share over the previous four years by the *offeror's* price-earnings ratio over that time.

effect force a second-step transaction by exercising their right to require redemption, they, and not the offeror, have the last word on the number of shares ultimately acquired and, if the provision's pricing formula could yield a price higher than the offer, on the price to be paid. Indeed, a fair price provision may even deter an offeror who is willing and financially able to tender for all the outstanding shares. If the pricing formula assures holdouts a price no lower than the tender offer and provides the potential of a higher price, target shareholders will be given an incentive *not* to tender in the original offer.[54]

Lock-up Amendments

While not themselves shark repellents, lock-up amendments are probably the most important . . . of the amendments a potential target commonly adopts to deter unwanted tender offers. Consider a potential offeror's evaluation of a target draped with the full panoply of protective amendments. While a 95% vote may be required for a second-step transaction, unless the target's charter also has been amended to require a supermajority to further amend the charter itself, a successful offeror can eliminate the supermajority provision by the vote for charter amendment specified in the statute -- typically a simple majority. The carefully plotted defensive measures would then be left, like the Maginot Line, with their guns pointing in the wrong direction. To avoid this result, virtually all shark repellent amendments also require a supermajority vote for repeal or further amendment. . . . Lock-up amendments are thus the key to whatever potential for deterrence any of the shark repellent amendments may possess. . . .

---

[54] . . . Although not shark repellent amendments in that they are not intended to pose a deterrent to an offeror, social justice amendments, pioneered by Control Data, see Proxy Statement of Control Data Corp., reprinted in Fleischer (1981), *supra* note 2, at 448-11 (extract), and more recently adopted by McDonald's, see Proxy Statement of McDonald's Corp., reprinted in Fleischer (1981), *supra* note 2, at 448-13 (extract), warrant comment. These amendments, purportedly offered "in the spirit of social responsibility and justice," Proxy Statement of Control Data Corp., *supra*, at 448-11, direct the board of directors, in their evaluation of an acquisition offer, to "give due consideration to all relevant factors, including without limitation the social and economic effects on the employees, customers, suppliers and other constituents of the Corporation and its subsidiaries and on the communities in which the Corporation and its subsidiaries operate or are located." *Id*. at 448-12.

Social justice amendments do not provide a deterrent to a potential offeror, but rather attempt to protect management from subsequent shareholder claims based on management's rejection of an offer. Indeed, the McDonald's Corporation proxy statement proposing such an amendment was explicit in stating that the provision was not intended "to create any rights on behalf of franchisees, employees, suppliers, customers or any other persons." Proxy Statement of McDonald's Corp., *supra*, at 448-13. While an offeror might conceivably be deterred by the potential increase in discretion the board of directors may gain from a social justice provision, the likelihood of deterrence seems remote at best. . . .

Shark repellent amendments proved to be quite popular among large companies. The Investor Responsibility Research Center, Inc., reported that as of mid-1989, 54% of the approximately 1,500 largest public corporations had adopted staggered terms for directors, 32% had adopted fair price amendments, and 17% had adopted supermajority requirements for second-step mergers.[3] Nonetheless, they proved to have one flaw as a defensive tactic: they required shareholder approval. The very act of proposing the amendments might signal management's concerns and thereby call the company to the attention of potential bidders.

More important, significant shareholder resistance to management's proposal would inform potential bidders that shareholders might be receptive to an offer. While the large number of adoptions indicate that shareholders were willing to approve them much of the time, by the mid-1980s two factors called their use into question. First, the percentage of stock held by institutional investors had dramatically increased. In 1955, institutions, including pension funds, mutual funds, insurers and bank trust departments held 23% of the outstanding stock of U.S. corporations. By 1989, institutional investors held 50% of the equity of the fifty largest U.S. corporations, 53.2% of the largest 100, and 48.1% of the largest 1,000.[4] Second, by the late 1980s, institutions, particularly the large public pension plans, had come to object to efforts to shelter companies from hostile takeovers, and increasingly opposed them.[5] Putting aside until Section B.1.a., *infra*, evaluation of the effectiveness of shark repellent amendments at actually deterring hostile bids, managers of a potential target needed a pre-offer planning technique that did not require shareholder approval. The poison pill filled that need.

c.   *Deterrence: The Poison Pill*

The poison pill is an innovation in defensive tactics that has become one of the most popular techniques. By 1990, 50% of all Fortune 500 corporations, and 43% of all U.S. exchange listed companies had adopted

---

[3] Investor Responsibility Research Center, Inc., *Corporate Takeover Defenses 1989* (June 1989).

[4] Carolyn Brancato, *The Pivotal Role of Institutional Investors in Capital Markets* (June 1989) (table 7).

[5] See, e.g., Bernard Black, *Agents Watching Agents: The Promise of Institutional Investor Voice*, 39 UCLA L.Rev. 811 (1992); Bernard Black, *The Value of Institutional Investor Monitoring: The Empirical Evidence*, 39 UCLA L.Rev. 895 (1992); Ronald Gilson & Reinier Kraakman, *Reinventing the Outside Director: An Agenda for Institutional Investors*, 43 Stan.L.Rev. 863, 867-71 (1991).

such a plan.[6] The operation of this technique is described in a memorandum prepared by Wachtell, Lipton, Rosen & Katz, the law firm that originally devised it.[7]

Wachtell, Lipton, Rosen & Katz
THE SHARE PURCHASE RIGHTS PLAN
(March 1994)

. . . Our recommended plan includes a "flip-in" feature designed to deter creeping accumulations of a company's stock. The "flip-in" feature is structured to be available from a 10% to a 20% ownership threshold. The plan also has the "flip-over" feature which provides shareholders protection against squeezeout. Appendix A contains a summary of the terms of our recommended plan. . . .

The basic objectives of the rights plan are to deter abusive takeover tactics by making them unacceptably expensive to the raider and to encourage prospective acquirors to negotiate with the board of directors of the target by making the rights issued pursuant to the plan redeemable for a nominal amount prior to a change of effective control through the acquisition of a large block of the target's shares. The plan was designed not to interfere, and has not interfered, with the day-to-day operations of the companies that have adopted it. Prior to its being activated by an acquisition of a large block of the target company's shares, it has no effect on a company's balance sheet or income statement and it is not taxable to the company or the shareholders. Companies have split their stock, issued stock dividends and combined their stock without interference from the plan. While the plan requires special care in such transactions, it has not hindered public offerings of common stock (including associated rights) or SEC clearance of pooling of interests mergers.

The plan was first developed to deal with the then current two-tier, front-end loaded tender offer and related techniques. The "flip-over" provision of the plan stopped the two-tier, the partial and the creeping tender offers that were intended to be followed by a second-step merger. It accomplished this by giving the target's shareholders rights [upon the raider crossing the triggering threshold, typically 20% but often as low as 10%],

---

[6] Robert Bruner, *The Poison Pill Anti-takeover Defense: The Price of Strategic Deterrence* 1 (1991).

[7] We are grateful to Wachtell, Lipton, Rosen & Katz for allowing us to present excerpts from their memorandum. We should note that in a portion of the memorandum not reprinted here, the firm objects to the common characterization of the rights plan as a poison pill: "Despite . . . substantial evidence of the beneficial effects of rights plans, they will still be called 'poison pills.' This is a most unfortunate misnomer. A rights plan is neither a pill nor poisonous."

that would have to be assumed by a raider in a second-step merger, to buy the raider's common stock at half of its market price. The raider was faced with unacceptable dilution unless it either offered a price that was sufficient to attract the tender of substantially all of the shares and the rights, or negotiated a merger at a price acceptable to the target's board of directors so that the rights were redeemed and thereby removed as an impediment to the acquisition. . . . The effectiveness of the flip-in, unlike the flip-over, is dependent upon its discriminatory feature, without which the flip-in would not result in dilution to the raider since the raider would be able to buy additional shares on the same basis as the other shareholders. The flip-in feature provides greater protection against the takeover abuses described above. . . .

Our recommended plan combines the flip-over with a flip-in that is triggered by an acquisition at the 20% level. The flip-in at a 20% threshold will provide greater protection against current takeover abuses involving partial and creeping accumulations. The plan also allows the board of directors to lower the threshold to not less than 10% if appropriate in light of specific circumstances.

If the flip-in is triggered, each holder of rights (other than the raider, whose rights become void) will be able to exercise such rights for common stock of the target having a market value, at the time the raider crosses the 20% threshold, of twice the right's exercise price. This would result in dilution to the raider both economically and in terms of its percentage ownership of the target's shares. The exact level of the dilution would depend on the market value of the target's common stock in relation to the exercise price of the rights.

Our recommended plan also contains a feature that gives the board of directors the option, after the flip-in is triggered by an acquisition at the 20% level (or such lower threshold down to 10% as shall have been set by the board) but before there has been a 50% acquisition, to exchange one new share of common stock of the corporation for each then valid right (which would exclude rights held by the raider that have become void). This provision will have an economically dilutive effect on the acquiror, and provide a corresponding benefit to the remaining rightsholders, that is comparable to the flip-in without requiring rightsholders to go through the process and expense of exercising their rights. . . .

Appendix A

Terms of Flip-in Rights Plan[*]

Issuance: One right to buy one one-hundredth of a share of a new series of preferred stock as a dividend on each outstanding share of common stock of the company   Until the rights become exercisable, all further issuances of common stock, including common stock issuable upon exercise of outstanding options, would include issuances of rights.

Term: 10 years.

Exercise price: An amount per one one-hundredth of a share of the preferred stock which approximates the board's view of the long-term value of the company's common stock. Factors to be considered in setting the exercise price include the company's business and prospects, its long-term plans and market conditions. For most companies that have adopted rights plans, the exercise price has been between three and five times current market price. The exercise price is subject to certain anti-dilution adjustments. For illustration only, assume an exercise price of $150 per one one-hundredth of a share.

Rights detach and become exercisable: The rights are not exercisable and are not transferable apart from the company's common stock until the tenth day after such time as a person or group acquires beneficial ownership of 20% or more of the company's common stock or the tenth business day (or such later time as the board of directors may determine) after a person or group announces its intention to commence or commences a tender or exchange offer the consummation of which would result in beneficial ownership by a person or group of 20% or more of the company's common stock. As soon as practicable after the rights become exercisable, separate right certificates would be issued and the rights would become transferable apart from the company's common stock.

Protection against squeezeout: If, after the rights have been triggered, an acquiring company were to merge or otherwise combine with the company, or the company were to sell 50% or more of its assets or earning power, each right then outstanding would "flip over" and thereby would become a right to buy that number of shares of common stock of the acquiring company which at the time of such transaction would have a market value of two times the exercise price of the rights. Thus, if the acquiring company's

---

[*] These terms are as they would be set by a company that uses authorized blank check preferred stock, with terms that make 1/100th of a share of the preferred stock the economic equivalent of one share of common stock, as the security for which the rights are exercisable.

common stock at the time of such transaction were trading at $75 per share and the exercise price of the rights at such time were $150, each right would thereafter be exercisable at $150 for four shares (*i.e.*, the number of shares that could be purchased for $300, or two times the exercise price of the rights) of the acquiring company's common stock.

Protection against creeping acquisition/open market purchases: In the event a person or group were to acquire a 20% or greater position in the company, each right then outstanding would "flip in" and become a right to buy that number of shares of common stock of the company which at the time of such acquisition would have a market value of two times the exercise price of the rights. The acquiror who triggered the rights would be excluded from the "flip-in" because his rights would have become null and void upon his triggering acquisition. Thus, if the company's common stock at the time of the "flip-in" were trading at $75 per share and the exercise price of the rights at such time were $150, each right would thereafter be exercisable for $150 for four shares of the company's common stock. As described below, the amendment provision of the Rights Agreement provides that the 20% threshold can be lowered to not less than 10%. The board can utilize this provision to provide additional protection against creeping accumulations.

Exchange: At any time after the acquisition by a person or group of affiliated or associated persons of beneficial ownership of 20% or more of the outstanding common stock of the company and before the acquisition by a person or group of 50% or more of the outstanding common stock of the company, the board of directors may exchange the rights (other than rights owned by such person or group which have become void), in whole or in part, at an exchange ratio of one share of the company's common stock (or one one-hundredth of a share of junior participating preferred stock) per right, subject to adjustment.

Redemption: The rights are redeemable by the company's board of directors at a price of $.01 per right at any time prior to the acquisition by a person or group of beneficial ownership of 20% or more of the company's common stock. The redemption of the rights may be made effective at such time on such basis and with such conditions as the board of directors in its sole discretion may establish. Thus, the rights would not interfere with a negotiated merger or a white knight transaction, even after a hostile tender offer has been commenced. The rights may prevent a white knight transaction after a 20% acquisition.

Voting: The rights would not have any voting rights.

Terms of preferred stock: The preferred stock issuable upon exercise of the rights would be non-redeemable and rank junior to all other series of the company's preferred stock. The dividend, liquidation and voting rights, and the non-redemption feature, of the preferred stock are designed so that the value of one one-hundredth interest in a share of the new preferred stock purchasable with each right will approximate the value of one share of common stock. Each whole share of preferred stock would be entitled to receive a quarterly preferential dividend of $1 per share but would be entitled to receive, in the aggregate, a dividend of 100 times the dividend declared on the common stock. In the event of liquidation, the holders of the new preferred stock would be entitled to receive a preferential liquidation payment of $100 per share but would be entitled to receive, in the aggregate, a liquidation payment equal to 100 times the payment made per share of common stock. Each share of preferred stock would have 100 votes, voting together with the common stock. Finally, in the event of any merger, consolidation or other transaction in which shares of common stock are exchanged for or changed into other stock or securities, cash and/or other property, each share of preferred stock would be entitled to receive 100 times the amount received per share of common stock. The foregoing rights are protected against dilution in the event additional shares of common stock are issued. Since the "out of the money" rights would not be exercisable immediately, registration of the preferred issuable upon exercise of the rights with the Securities and Exchange Commission need not be effective until the rights become exercisable and are "in the money" or are so close to being "in the money" so as to make exercise economically possible.

Federal income tax consequences: The Internal Revenue Service has published a revenue ruling holding that the adoption of a rights plan is not a taxable event for the company or its shareholders under the federal income tax laws. The physical distribution of rights certificates upon the rights becoming exercisable should not result in any tax. After such physical distribution, the rights would be treated for tax purposes as capital assets in the hands of most shareholders, the tax basis of each right would be zero in most cases (or, in certain cases, an allocable part of the tax basis of the stock with respect to which the right was issued) and the holding period of each right would include the holding period of the stock with respect to which such right was issued. Upon the rights becoming rights to purchase an acquiror's common stock, holders of rights probably would be taxed even if the rights were not exercised. Upon the rights becoming rights to purchase additional common stock of the company, holders of rights probably would not have a taxable event. The redemption of the rights for cash and, most likely, the acquisition of the rights by the company for its stock would each be taxable events. The use of company stock (with the rights attached) will not interfere with the company's ability to engage in tax-free acquisitions nor will it affect any net operating losses of the company.

Accounting consequences: The initial issuance of the rights has no accounting or financial reporting impact. Since the rights would be "out of the money" when issued, they would not dilute earnings per share. Because the redemption date of the rights is neither fixed nor determinable, the accounting guidelines do not require the redemption amount to be accounted for as a long-term obligation of the company. The rights do raise certain issues with respect to pooling of interests transactions, but several national accounting firms have advised that the rights should not interfere with a company's ability to consummate a pooling transaction so long as the transaction is properly structured.

Miscellaneous: The Rights Agreement provides that the company may not enter into any transaction of the sort which would give rise to the "flip-over" right if in connection therewith there are outstanding securities or there are agreements or arrangements intended to counteract the protective provisions of the rights. The Rights Agreement may be amended from time to time in any manner prior to the acquisition of a 20% position.

COMPARISON OF RIGHTS PLANS

	"Flip-Over" Rights Plan	**"Flip-in" Rights Plan**
Prior to 20% Acquisition or Tender Offer	Rights "trade with" common	Rights "trade with" common
"flip-over"	On merger or sale of assets	On merger or sale of assets
"flip-in"	In some plans, in the event of self dealing transactions by a 20% holder -- no status flip-in	Status flip-in if 20% acquired (threshold can be reduced to 10% by amendment)
Redeemable	By the Board prior to 20% acquisition	By the Board prior to 20% acquisition
Exchange	None	After 20% acquisition (but before 50% acquisition), the Board may exchange each Right (other than Rights held by the 20% acquiror) for one newly issued common share of the Company or 1/100 of a share or junior participating preferred

The explanation for the addition of flip-in provisions to the standard poison pill package appears when one considers what happens when only a flip-over pill is in place and the hostile bidder is content to acquire control and thereby render the pill nonredeemable. By not proceeding with a second-step merger, target shareholders are frozen in, and the pill can serve to restrict the company's ability to undertake other transactions. This was the strategy followed by Sir James Goldsmith in his 1985 takeover of Crown Zellerbach. Following his acquisition of 51% of Crown Zellerbach's stock despite the company's flip-over pill, a takeover was negotiated, although on terms arguably more favorable to shareholders than his initial offer.

A central characteristic of a poison pill plan is that shareholder approval is not required for adoption. As a result, management can avoid increasing institutional investor disfavor of shark repellent amendments. Statutes like Delaware General Corporation Law § 151(a) authorize the issuance of what is called blank check preferred stock: preferred stock which the corporate charter authorizes to be issued with such "designations, preferences . . . or other special rights . . . as shall be stated . . . in the resolution . . . providing for the issuance of such stock adopted by the board of directors. . . ." So long as the corporate charter authorizes such stock, the board alone can adopt the poisonous characteristics when it decides to issue the stock.

Two empirical studies support the proposition that the absence of a shareholder approval requirement is an important element of the attractiveness of the poison pill. The Office of the Chief Economist[8] found that for a sample of 245 firms, the average inside ownership was approximately 5%. In contrast, the average inside ownership for 624 firms adopting shark repellent charter amendments, which do require shareholder approval, was 13.6%.[9] Paul Malatesta and Robert Walking[10] came at the same problem somewhat differently, but found strikingly similar results. They hypothesized that managers who have smaller ownership stake in their firms would gain less from a premium takeover than managers who had a greater ownership stake (because they would receive less of the premium), and thus would be more likely to cause their companies to adopt defensive measures like poison pills. Their data supported this hypothesis: Managerial ownership in firms that adopted poison pill plans was less than half that of other companies in the same industries. Inside ownership in their sample of 122 firms that adopted poison pill plans through March 1986 averaged 9.39%. In contrast, managerial ownership of other firms in the same

---

[8] Office of the Chief Economist, *The Effects of Poison Pills on the Wealth of Target Shareholders* (Oct. 23, 1986).

[9] *Id.* at 36-37.

[10] Paul Malatesta & Robert Walking, *Poison Pill Securities: Stockholder Wealth, Profitability, and Ownership Structure*, 20 J.Fin.Econ. 347 (1988).

industries averaged 23.12%, a statistically significant difference of 13.78%.[11]

These data -- that the less stock management owns, the more likely they are to select defensive tactics that do not require shareholder approval -- support the hypothesis that the lower the managerial ownership, the more difficult shareholder approval will be to secure, and the more likely managers will select a tactic that does not require approval.

With the increase in institutional investor shareholdings and increased institutional opposition to defensive tactics,[12] the importance of the fact that a poison pill can be adopted without shareholder approval may be somewhat overstated. Beginning in 1987, institutional investors began offering precatory shareholder resolutions urging that poison pill plans be redeemed, submitted for shareholder approval, or subjected to sunset provisions. In 1987, the average vote for the anti-pill proposals was 29.4%,[13] increasing to 38.2% in 1988, 39.5% in 1989, and 42.8% in 1990. To be sure, the resolutions did not bind the board of directors even in the few cases in which a majority of shareholders voted in favor. However, a high vote in favor certainly signalled that shareholders would entertain a hostile offer.[14]

d.   Deterrence: Dual Class Common Stock

The most effective deterrent to a hostile tender offer is for management to have voting control of the company. In that setting no takeover is possible without management approval. For management of existing public companies, however, the problem is how to achieve that control if a majority of stock is already in public hands. A leveraged buyout is possible, but this technique requires paying a substantial premium to the existing public shareholders,[15] with the result of a substantial increase in debt and, hence, in the risk of the company and of management's human capital. An alternative that generated a great deal of attention and controversy is a dual class common stock recapitalization in which management (or an existing dominant shareholder group) ends up with a class of common stock that

---

[11] *Id.* at 369, Table 6.

[12] See note 5, *supra*.

[13] This compared to an average vote of 12.4% in favor of proposals urging companies to cease doing business in South Africa. Although no proposal received a majority of the votes cast, four received more than 40%.

[14] Another interpretation of these voting results is possible. The companies selected by institutional investors for anti-pill proposals had especially high institutional ownership and were thought to be particularly vulnerable. For example, of the 32 companies subject to anti-pill shareholder proposals in 1987, institutional ownership varied form a low of 36% to a high of 78%, with an average of 56.5%. Thus, the proposals failed to garner support from a substantial number of institutional investors.

[15] Empirical studies of leveraged buyouts report average premiums over market of 40 to 60% over substantial samples of transactions. See Chapter 11, *supra*.

confers voting control, and public shareholders end up with a class of non-voting common stock or common stock with reduced voting rights.[16] While stock exchange rules now bar such alterations in the voting power of outstanding common stock, itself an interesting story, the concept remains viable for companies that either adopt such a capital structure on formation or prior to an initial public offering.

This shift in control was accomplished by three different techniques. The most common was an exchange recapitalization. In the first step of such a transaction shareholders approve a new class of common stock that carries multiple votes per share -- ten is a common figure -- but typically with dividend rights pegged at 10% lower than the pre-existing class of common stock. The terms of the new class of multiple vote stock provide that if the stock is transferred outside the shareholder's immediate family, it automatically converts to the lower vote pre-existing common. In the second step, shareholders can exchange their pre-existing common stock for the new multiple vote common stock. Because of the dividend differential, only management (or the group seeking to establish control) is expected to exchange. If a 10 to 1 voting differential is used, management will acquire voting control so long as they held more than 9% of the pre-existing common before the recapitalization.

The second technique consists of a special stock dividend in which shares of a new class of common stock, with terms similar to those of the new class of stock used in an exchange recapitalization, are distributed to holders of the pre-existing class of common stock. When public shareholders transfer these shares in the course of normal portfolio transactions, the special voting rights are eliminated. As a result, management ends up with increased control simply by retaining their dividend shares.

The final technique operates by distinguishing between the voting rights of different holders of the same class of common stock, rather than by creating a second class of stock. This is accomplished by a charter amendment that increases the voting rights of shares that have been held for a substantial period of time; however, the shares lose their special voting rights if they are transferred. If management retains their shares, normal portfolio turnover among public shareholders will result in increased management control.[17]

The attractiveness of this tactic -- that it works -- presented problems for the New York Stock Exchange (NYSE) and opportunities for its competitors, the American Stock Exchange (AMEX) and the National Association of Securities Dealers Automatic Quotation System (NASDAQ). Because the NYSE had a long standing rule prohibiting the listing of the stock of a company with either non-voting stock or with more than one class

---

[16] See Ronald Gilson, *Evaluating Dual Class Common Stock: The Relevance of Substitutes*, 73 Va.L.Rev. 807 (1987).

[17] See Gilson (1987), *supra* note 16, at 813 & n.13.

of common stock having unequal voting rights, while the AMEX had much more limited restrictions and NASDAQ had none at all, the NYSE feared it would lose the listings of companies that wanted to take advantage of this tactic.[18]

The NYSE responded by proposing to amend its prohibition on dual class common stock to require only that limited voting rights created by a modification of the voting rights of existing shareholders be approved by a majority of both independent directors and public shareholders.[19] As a self regulatory organization under § 19 of the Securities Exchange Act, any change in NYSE rules requires SEC approval. Following the NYSE's request for approval, the SEC held public hearings in December 1986.

There followed SEC sponsored negotiations among the NYSE, AMEX and NASDAQ toward the end of the exchanges voluntarily adopting a uniform rule that protected the voting rights of existing shareholders. When these negotiations failed, the SEC adopted Rule 19c-4 which prohibited the listing of the securities of an issuer who "issues any class of security or takes any other corporate action that would have the effect of nullifying, restricting, or disparately reducing the per share voting rights of holders of an outstanding class of common stock."[20]

The rule thus carves out from its prohibition initial or subsequent public offerings of lesser vote common stock because these actions, unlike the techniques discussed above, do not reduce the voting rights of existing shareholders. This distinction between new issues of non-voting or limited voting stock and the alteration of the voting rights of existing stock is developed in Gilson (1987), *supra*. The considerations bearing on choice of an optimal voting structure by a corporation's founders in anticipation of an initial public offering are discussed in Chapter 13.

Shortly after Rule 19c-4 was adopted, the Business Roundtable sought review by the D.C. Circuit claiming that the Rule exceeded the SEC's jurisdiction. In Business Roundtable v. SEC, 905 F.2d 406 (D.C.Cir.1990), the court invalidated the Rule as an improper incursion into matters of corporate governance left by Congress to the states.

---

[18] There was some cause for concern. Thirty seven companies had adopted dual class voting structures between 1980 and 1984, Megan Partch, *The Creation of a Class of Limited Voting Common Stock and Shareholder Wealth*, 18 J.Fin.Econ. 313 (1987); and another 45 companies did so in 1985 and 1986. Gregg Jarrell & Annette Poulsen, *The Effects of Recapitalization with Dual Classes of Common Stock on the Wealth of Shareholders*, 20 J.Fin.Econ. 129, 135 (Table 1) (1988). A compilation of all NYSE, AMEX and NASDAQ companies with dual class common stock is found in Pamepinto, *Dual Class Capitalization and Unequal Voting Rights Plans*, at A13-A15 (Investor Responsibility Research Center Inc.) (Jan.1987).

[19] See NYSE's *Proposed Rule Change on Disparate Voting Rights*, 18 Sec.Reg. & L.Rep. (BNA) no.37, at 1389-92 (Sept. 19, 1986) (text of NYSE proposal).

[20] Exchange Act Release No. 34-25891, Voting Rights Listing Standards -- Disenfranchisement Rule (July 7, 1988) [1987-1988 Trans. Binder] Fed.Sec.L.Rep (CCH) ¶ 84,247.

Following a period of competitive skirmishing among the exchanges and regulatory negotiation, the New York Stock Exchange, the American Stock Exchange, and NASDAQ have proposed a common listing standard that largely follows Rule 19c-4:

> Voting rights of the existing shareholders of publicly traded common stock registered under § 12 of the Exchange Act cannot be reduced or restricted through any corporate action or issuance. Examples of such corporate action or issuance include, but are not limited to, the adoption of time-phased voting plans, the adoption of capped voting rights plans, the issuance of supervoting stock, or the issuance of stock with voting rights less than the per share voting rights of the existing common stock through an exchange offer.[21]

Because the language of the common standard was proposed by the Chairman of the SEC,[22] it is fair to assume the new listing standard will be approved.

The policy reflected by Rule 19c-4 and the proposed common listing standard -- allowing issuances of new classes of low or nonvoting stock but prohibiting the reduction of the voting rights of already outstanding voting stock -- has a number of components: that shifts in control should be paid for whether effected through an LBO or dual class recapitalization,[23] that dual class recapitalizations are inherently coercive,[24] and that the transfer of voting rights should be mediated by a market as opposed to an electoral mechanism.[25]

The alternative approach, reflected in post-*Business Roundtable* proposals by both the New York and American Stock Exchanges, allowed dual class recapitalizations if approved by independent directors and disinterested shareholders.[26]

---

[21] Proposed Rule Change by New York Stock Exchange, Inc. (June 1, 1994); *Exchanges Seek Approval of Voting-Rights Policy*, Wall St.J.,July 27, 1994, at C3.

[22] Stephen Bainbridge, *Revisiting the One Share/One Vote Controversy: The Exchanges' Uniform Voting Rights Policy*, 22 Sec.Reg.L.J. 175, 176 (1994).

[23] See Ronald Gilson, *Regulating the Equity Component of Capital Structure: The SEC's Response to the One Share, One Vote Controversy*, in *Modernizing U.S. Securities Regulation* 211 (Kenneth Lehn & Robert Kamphuis eds.1992); Gilson (1987), *supra* note 16.

[24] Jeffrey Gordon, *Ties that Bond: Dual Class Common Stock and the Problem of Shareholder Choice*, 76 Cal.L.Rev. 1 (1988); Richard Ruback, *Coercive Dual-Class Exchange Offers*, 20 J.Fin.Econ. 153 (1988).

[25] Exchange Act Release, *supra* note 20, at ¶ 89,216 (Grundfest, C., concurring).

[26] See Gilson (1992), *supra* note 23, at 220-21. For a rigorous defense of independent directors as a sufficient check on dual class recapitalizations, see Bainbridge (1994), *supra* note 22.

2. Post-Offer

The variety of possible defensive tactics after a hostile offer has been made is substantial and has spawned a voluminous literature. The material which follows describes the most important categories of defensive tactics and provides a context in which to develop a general approach both to determining when a familiar tactic has the potential to be effective and to designing new tactics that hold the promise of being effective.[27]

a. *Litigation*

The single most common response to an unwanted offer is litigation. If one thinks about that response for a moment, it really has two components. First, litigation is a means by which a substantive claim is vindicated. It is merely a transaction cost necessarily incurred to vindicate the claim and has no value independent of the substantive claim being pursued. From this perspective, if the litigation ultimately is unsuccessful, it will have been a waste of time and money. Second, litigation is a means of inflicting additional costs on someone else's transaction, where the goal sought is not vindication of a substantive claim, but merely the creation of an impediment to someone else's activities. In the latter case, the creation of transaction costs is not an undesirable, but unavoidable, byproduct of the exercise, but its very point. In considering the following excerpt by a senior partner in one of the prominent law firms specializing in takeovers, think about which function is being discussed at which point.

Herbert Wachtell
SPECIAL TENDER OFFER LITIGATION TACTICS
32 Bus.Law. 1433 (1977)*

Takeover litigation is a unique area. . . . You are operating at what is essentially an interface of big case litigation, in the very highly sophisticated and specialized areas of securities law, financing law, margin requirements and antitrust law. It is not the place to have on-the-job training.

---

[27] For more exhaustive surveys of the extensive range of tactics which have at one time or another been suggested, see, e.g., Edward Aranow, Herbert Einhorn & George Berlstine, *Developments in Tender Offers for Corporate Control* (1977); Peter Davey, *Defenses Against Unnegotiated Cash Tender Offers* (1977); Fleischer, Sussman & Lesser (1990), *supra* note 1; Simon Lorne & Joy Bryan, *Acquisitions and Mergers: Negotiated and Contested Transactions* (1994).

You are operating in a pressure atmosphere where you have constant surprise. You have very little turnaround time. The company goes running for counsel: help us. You have to commence litigation immediately. You have to get out your deposition notices. You have to get out your discovery notices. You have to make your motions for expedited discovery. You have to set up your teams for taking what could be two or three sets of simultaneous depositions, often in different cities. You have to be prepared to flow all the information you're getting from depositions and documents into affidavits and briefs almost simultaneously with the taking of the depositions and the review of the documents. You have to be scheduling your applications for temporary restraining orders, stays, preliminary injunctions and the like. You are essentially compressing into a span of four, five or six days what would normally be months and months, if not years, of typical big case litigation, including analysis of antitrust ramifications, industry studies, competitive lines of product and the like. . . .

[T]he tender is made. Now, it used to be thought that at this point counsel for the tendering company really didn't have very much to do except to sit back and wait for the inevitable lawsuit to be brought for an injunction against the offer. But in recent times a nuance has been added to the litigating tactics in tender offer cases. This sometimes is referred to as the preemptive lawsuit and sometimes as the "one-two punch."

First, a surprise tender offer is made for a target company. Then, before the target company has caught its breath from that body blow, the company making the tender sues the target. Well, the question is: why bother? What's to be gained? Why has this become a tactic?. . .

There are a couple of sound reasons why in certain cases this may be a very good litigating tactic. The first has to do with choice of forum. If the target is left to its own devices, it is going to choose to bring the suit for an injunction in what it would deem to be a favorable forum. Often this will be its own home District where it can invoke perhaps a general feeling against outside predators coming in and preying on local industry. In certain instances, this could be a real problem. It can very largely color what is going to happen in the litigation.

By having the bidder bring the initial lawsuit against the target, the bidder can essentially choose a forum of its own liking and then, by invoking the mystique that anything the target now wants to do really lies under the compulsory counterclaim rule, can effectively preclude the target from litigating in any jurisdiction other than the jurisdiction of the bidder's choice. . . .

A second advantage which can be gained by the bidder's actually commencing the litigation is a very real psychological one, both in the general marketplace of the tender offer and in the courthouse as well. What is being done here is: the target company essentially is coming in and is saying to the world at large, including the arbitrageurs, "we are not afraid of litigation here. We welcome it. We are going to court. These fellows are the wrongdoers. We have nothing to fear here." And by seizing this initiative and by staking out a position of plaintiff before the court, one almost makes that inevitable counterclaim, when it comes, anticlimactic both in the courthouse and in the marketplace. So there is a tactical advantage to be gained as well as a forum advantage.

Now, having said that, someone might ask the question, "what do you sue them for?"

I mean, here's this company that's peacefully minding its own business with this weak management that we've all heard about. It gets hit by a "Saturday night special." What conceivable cause of action can now exist for the bidder to sue the target?

Well, actually, it really isn't hard at all because of what oftentimes happens in this kind of situation: a surprise tender is made. The executives of the target company hurriedly caucus. Panic reigns supreme. Someone comes up with a bright idea: "Hey, we had better get out a press release and we had better get it out fast and we ought to say that the price which is being offered is inadequate and besides our lawyers tell us that there are some very serious antitrust problems here."

And so they do. And you now have your lawsuit. The first cause of action will recite that management is engaged in illegal opposition and solicitation in opposition to a lawful tender offer in violation of the Williams Act without having filed the requisite Schedule 14D setting forth that they are opposing; and the second cause of action will set forth that they are engaged in making false and misleading statements in violation of the antifraud provisions of § 14(e), because when they said that the offer was inadequate, they failed to point out that the offer was 20% in excess of any price that the stock has traded for in the last five years, and they also failed to point out that six months ago they themselves bought some of the stock cheaper. So how could the present offer be inadequate?[2] That's a material omission. And besides, when they say it violates the antitrust laws, that really isn't true, so that's a material misstatement. You now have your lawsuit. There's usually three or four other causes of action. You could throw in, for good measure, allegations such as manipulating the market and engaging in a conspiracy to entrench themselves in their management positions in violation of the interests of everybody in sight. You're in. You're home. You're in court. . . .

Let's turn now to the job of unhappy counsel for the target company. He brings a lawsuit. We all agree about that. And he brings it fast. Now, one of the questions you might ask is: Why? What's the purpose of the lawsuit -- except that it's obviously something that always gets done and it's axiomatic that he bring it.

Well, of course, one purpose is to seek to obtain an injunction to bar the offer from going forward. However, in many of these cases a close

---

[2] See, e.g., Emhart Corp. v. USM Corp., 403 F.Supp. 660 (D.Mass.1975).

observer can detect that there are other consequences of the lawsuit than merely the attempt to obtain an injunction, and it behooves counsel for the target company to be aware of the ramifications and consequences of his lawsuit in the marketplace outside of the courthouse because there are very real consequences in a tender offer context.

For example, one of the consequences of lawsuits in takeover situations is to chill the arbitrage. It was pointed out . . . that if the arbitraguers go into the market and buy heavily in the stock, they in essence are going to be the owners of that company. They have a very short-term interest in their investment which means a 99% chance that that company is going to get owned by *someone* in the end -- be it the original bidder or someone else -- but it is not in all likelihood going to remain independent.

So, one might be very interested, if one is representing the target company, in chilling the arbitrage, and chilling it fast, which means that a complaint has to get out very quickly. There's no point saying: "Well, gee, I have ten days to get a preliminary injunction. I can afford to go into court on the eighth day," because by the eighth day the battle is going to be all over.

So, it is important to get in very fast and it is important to get in with a complaint that is not only a sound legal document, but which also sounds terribly legal. Then when the arbitrageurs' counsel read it, they are going to be impressed. The arbitrageurs are going to be weighing the likelihood of the success of the offer. If they read the complaint and if the legal theories are spelled out in a way that is impressive, understandable and "good sounding," the arbitrageurs' counsel are going to say to the arbitrageurs, "I would be careful on this one. It sounds like these fellows might have a chance of getting an injunction." And that heavy arbitrage buying may well not develop.

Another thing that sometimes happens as a result of a lawsuit is that there can be delay. The offer can be ordered to be extended by the court and, of course, the investment bankers can scurry around looking for some other marriage partner which might be more preferable to the target than the original bidder. And that is a possible consequence of the lawsuit that very much has to be kept in mind.

Another function or consequence of the lawsuit, and one that should not be underestimated, is a very simple moral-building psychological one. A "Saturday night special" has a traumatic effect upon the executives of a target company, particularly if they have not done their homework in advance and are not prepared. It can be shattering and demoralizing, and they can for all practical purposes virtually stop functioning.

A lawsuit becomes a focal point for rallying the troops. Everyone can feel good -- "we're doing something. We're hitting back. Boy, we really have got something there to protect us." And people will then start to function again in a real way to see what actually can be done to defend against this tender, which defense may not be in the courthouse at all.

Now, by the same token, you can't let your clients overrate the likelihood of success in that lawsuit or they may just blindly assume that they have this Maginot Line of the lawsuit and that they really don't have to do anything else. That would be extremely foolhardy.

Of course, ultimately one may even get an injunction in one of these lawsuits. Now, I've heard a lot about the antitrust laws as a basis for injunctive relief in these suits and I must say I do not share the general feeling I detected -- and maybe I'm overstating it -- that the antitrust laws are a sound defense in these tender offer cases. The leading case on the subject, which is the *Missouri Portland/Cargill* case in this Circuit,[3] basically told the District Courts: never grant a preliminary injunction on antitrust grounds because such a preliminary injunction, where you're going to have a three-year trial, is the equivalent of a permanent injunction. And the only case that I'm aware of since then where a preliminary injunction has issued -- maybe there are others -- on an antitrust ground is *Pargas/Empire*[4] where there were other grounds as well and where it was essentially a very specialized case. Everyone throws up the antitrust defense, but the likelihood of getting relief on it is really not very good except in a terribly aggravated kind of case.

Securities disclosure grounds are obvious: the offer omits this or that material fact -- but the trouble with that is the courts increasingly have taken the position of permitting amendment and it is rare now that a court will say that the defect is not curable. Sometimes, however, you can come up with a disclosure problem which is more than merely a disclosure problem, and which really shows that there's something wrong. For example, if you can come up with something that's terribly wrong with the financing or if you can come up with a margin violation or something of that nature, then the injunction may actually bar the offer in pragmatic terms forever.

In any event, getting a preliminary injunction has a major psychological effect. It throws the bidder off stride. It scares the arbitrageurs and it is a very great victory in litigation of this nature.

Now, as I say, speed is essential in getting out a complaint, and the question is, what kinds of things do you do? How do you know what you're going to sue for? What kinds of defenses can you throw up against the tender offer?

Well, what you have to do is to make a very fast canvass of every possible theory you can think of where the offer may be lacking. Look for pragmatic pressure points. Zero in on the financing. Read the offer through a microscope. Is there anything queasy about the financing? Does it sound peculiar? Is it close to the line on margin? Does it look conditional? Does it sound as if there's an "if" there? Is there any other language in the offer -- be it with respect to financing, plans, intent or whatever -- that sounds

---

[3] Missouri Portland Cement Co. v. Cargill, Inc., 498 F.2d 851 (2d Cir.1974), *cert. denied*, 419 U.S. 883 (1974).

[4] Pargas, Inc. v. Empire Gas Corp., 423 F.Supp. 199 (D.Md.1976).

unusual? Is there any peculiar choice of language which may indicate that someone was doing a clever drafting job to conceal an iceberg, of which the peculiar choice of language in the offer may be the tip, and which may be the signal that there's something there to look at.

What are some of the obvious causes of action, the ones that get thrown up every day in cases of this nature? "They fail to make adequate disclosure of their plans. In other words, they really intend to have a two-step merger." That's one thing to look for. Is the financing such or are the finances of the bidder such that in pragmatic terms it is inevitable that it's going to have to use the assets of the target in order to handle the debt service and repayment that it's taking on? Is it inevitable that this has to be the first step of a two-step transaction and it has not adequately disclosed the second step -- or possible complications of the second step -- such as if it acquires less then 50% by tender, maybe it then will have an investment security. Maybe you can stake out an argument that the bidder will be an investment company under the Investment Company Act. That would be an impediment to the second step.

"They fail to disclose material information regarding the value of the target." That can come into play sometimes where there have been preliminary discussions between the parties and you can utilize the theory that a lot of information about value has been disclosed to the bidder and it has failed to disclose it in its offer.

Antitrust. The question comes up. Why bother to put antitrust in if it can't win anyway? Also, there's another possible complication with antitrust: when the bidder raises its price $3 a share, your management may decide to give the offer a blessing, and there you are on record about this terrible, horrible offer that's violating § 7 of the Clayton Act and which should not conceivably be permitted to go ahead. Or the investment bankers may come up with another company for a marriage where the antitrust problems on their face may be far more serious than those you've already damned in your complaint attacking the first offer. These are pragmatic considerations. Nonetheless, you usually come up with the point of view: "I'll argue the antitrust defense today and I'll worry about the complications tomorrow. I need every argument I can get." Besides, there's a lot of discovery you can do with people on antitrust grounds. You can ask them a great many questions; you can get numerous executives and can ask for a great many documents. . . .

Now, from the target company's lawyer's point of view, speed is of essence in the litigation. Keep in mind that no matter how many counterclaims may be thrown up against you and no matter how many theories the other fellow may come up with, don't be diverted. You are the one who needs relief. He doesn't. So, keep your eye on the ball. You want to get into court. You want to set up the timetable in such a way that if you're going to get relief from the court, you're going to get that relief before the offer is over and the game is finished. This which means that if you want to have any prayer whatsoever of getting an injunction, you have to have *evidence,* and the way you're going to get evidence means you have to fire out immediate notices of deposition and immediate document demands. And immediately, I mean within hours (24 hours at the outside), you have to file your complaint. You have to be in court with the notices of deposition, the demands for document production and your motion for expedited discovery: "What was said at the Board meeting? What documents were given to the bankers? What documents were given to the investment bankers? How was the $50,000,000 loan justified to the bank in order to get this loan commitment? What did you say you were going to do with the company when you got it?" These are the areas where gold is to be mined, but you have to be in there doing it by asking the right questions and demanding the right documents.

You have to press very hard on this question of document discovery and depositions, which means you need great availability of experienced man-power in order to mount one of these litigations. You cannot afford to take a leisurely course of depositions. You want to be taking the depositions of the principal executive officer of the tendering company. You want to be taking the deposition of the financial officer. You want to be taking depositions of anyone in the acquisition program. You want to be taking depositions of the banks that they went to. You want to be taking depositions of the investment bankers -- in certain extraordinary situations where that might really be crucial -- and all of this has to be done not *seriatim,* but rather on two or three tracks simultaneously. And in the meantime they're going to be taking the depositions of your people. You also have depositions on the antitrust grounds which mean you may well be taking all the operating officials of the bidder in order to develop the requisite facts for an antitrust defense.

The manpower that must be brought into play -- and sometimes in many different cities because you can't necessarily haul people around -- really becomes extraordinary. At the same time, you need a team which will be collating all the information as it's developed on depositions, reviewing the documents, pulling it all in, writing affidavits and briefs, going to court, seeking scheduling orders and asking the court when it's going to hear the temporary restraining order and preliminary injunction applications. And that is a whole subject in and of itself, which is: when do you seek to ask the court for a temporary restraining order? Do you do it early? Do you do it late? The considerations can vary from case to case.

Also, there are numerous practical matters to be kept in mind. You need local counsel in many jurisdictions. That's already been referred to, but also keep your eye on some mundane mechanics which can easily be lost sight of given the pressures. You need court reporters for all of those depositions. They have to be lined up for daily copy. You may need airline reservations to get all your people to the right places. You need hotel reservations. You must make arrangements to type all the papers and get them across country, perhaps to a court in a different jurisdiction. There are very practical considerations, all of which have to mesh at the same time.

Note: Purely Tactical Litigation

Do issues of professional responsibility arise when litigation is pursued for purposes of delay, psychological advantage or to influence the behavior of non-litigants such as arbitrageurs? The relevant portions of the American Bar Association's Model Rules of Professional Responsibility provide as follows:

MODEL RULES OF PROFESSIONAL RESPONSIBILITY RULE 3.1 MERITORIOUS CLAIMS AND CONTENTIONS

A lawyer shall not bring or defend a proceeding, or assert or controvert an issue therein, unless there is a basis for doing so that is not frivolous, which includes a good faith argument for an extension, modification or reversal of existing law. A lawyer for the defendant in a criminal proceeding, or the respondent in a proceeding that could result in incarceration, may nevertheless so defend the proceeding as to require that every element of the case be established.

Comment

The advocate has a duty to use legal procedure for the fullest benefit of the client's cause, but also a duty not to abuse legal procedure. The law, both procedural and substantive, establishes the limits within which an advocate may proceed. However, the law is not always clear and never is static. Accordingly, in determining the proper scope of advocacy, account must be taken of the law's ambiguities and potential for change.

The filing of an action or defense or similar action taken for a client is not frivolous merely because the facts have not first been fully substantiated or because the lawyer expects to develop vital evidence only by discovery. Such action is not frivolous even though the lawyer believes that the client's position ultimately will not prevail. The action is frivolous, however, if the client desires to have the action taken primarily for the purpose of harassing or maliciously injuring a person or if the lawyer is unable either to make a good faith argument on the merits of the action taken or to support the action taken by a good faith argument for an extension, modification or reversal of existing law.

Model Code Comparison

DR 7-102(A)(1) provided that a lawyer may not "[f]ile a suit, assert a position, conduct a defense, delay a trial, or take other action on behalf of his client when he knows or when it is obvious that such action would serve merely to harass or maliciously injure another." Rule 3.1 is to the same general effect as DR 7-102(A)(1), with three qualifications. First, the test of improper conduct is changed from "merely to harass or maliciously injure another" to the requirement that there be a basis for the litigation measure involved that is "not frivolous." This includes the concept stated in DR 7-102(A)(2) that a lawyer may advance a claim or defense unwarranted by existing law if "it can be supported by good faith argument for an extension, modification, or reversal of existing law." Second, the test in Rule 3.1 is an objective test, whereas DR 7-102(A)(1) applied only if the lawyer "knows or when it is obvious" that the litigation is frivolous. Third, Rule 3.1 has an exception that in a criminal case, or a case in which incarceration of the client may result (for example, certain juvenile proceedings), the lawyer may put the prosecution to its proof even if there is no nonfrivolous basis for defense.

RULE 3.2 EXPEDITING LITIGATION

A lawyer shall make reasonable efforts to expedite litigation consistent with the interests of the client.

Comment

Dilatory practices bring the administration of justice into disrepute. Delay should not be indulged merely for the convenience of the advocates, or for the purpose of frustrating an opposing party's attempt to obtain rightful redress or repose. It is not a justification that similar conduct is often tolerated by the bench and bar. The question is whether a competent lawyer acting in good faith would regard the course of action as having some substantial purpose other than delay. Realizing financial or other benefit from otherwise improper delay in litigation is not a legitimate interest of the client.

Model Code Comparison

DR 7-101(A)(1) stated that a lawyer does not violate the duty to represent a client zealously "by being punctual in fulfilling all professional commitments." DR 7-102(A)(1) provided that a lawyer "shall not . . . file a suit, assert a position, conduct a defense [or] delay a trial . . . when he knows or when it is obvious that such action would serve merely to harass or maliciously injure another."

Note particularly the comment to Rule 3.2 which states that "[r]ealizing financial or other benefit from otherwise improper delay in litigation is not a legitimate interest of the client."

The discrepancy between the reality described by Wachtell and the standards set forth by the Model Rules of Professional Responsibility is substantial. A possible explanation for the discrepancy is that standards like those of the Model Rules and their predecessors[28] have never been enforced by the bar; the principal enforcement agent has been a lawyer's conscience. Moreover, self-enforcement is particularly likely to be unsuccessful when those who are asked to exercise self-restraint must sell their services in a competitive market. Imagine that a client asks her lawyer to file a lawsuit against a hostile offerer merely to buy the time necessary for the client to find a more desirable purchaser. The benefit from the lawyer exercising self-restraint by refusing to initiate litigation in violation of the Model Rules of Professional Conduct accrues to the profession as a whole and, in the end, to society in general. The lawyer, however, bears all the costs. Analysis of this situation in terms of the free rider problem suggests that there may be little self-enforcement in a competitive market.[29]

b.　*Stock Repurchases*

Charles Nathan & Marylin Sobel
CORPORATE STOCK REPURCHASES IN THE CONTEXT
OF UNSOLICITED TAKEOVER BIDS
35 Bus.Law. 1545 (1981)*

. . .STRATEGIC, LEGAL AND RELATED IMPLICATIONS
OF DEFENSIVE STOCK ACQUISITION PROGRAMS

Introduction

In contrast to the "preventive" use of a stock acquisition program as a general means of reducing an issuer's vulnerability to unsolicited acquisition

---

[28] See, e.g., American Bar Association, *Model Rules of Professional Responsibility*, Disciplinary Rule 7-102(A)(1) (1978); State Bar of California, *Rules of Professional Conduct*, Rule 2-110(1) (1977).

[29] For a discussion of the barriers to professional self-enforcement of prohibitions on strategic litigation, see Ronald Gilson, *The Devolution of the Legal Profession*, 49 Md.L.Rev. 860 (1990).

bids, the "defensive" stock acquisition program is a response to a particular imminent or already pending takeover bid. The defensive stock repurchase program may serve several, often complementary, purposes:

(a) To increase the percentage of the issuer's stock held by a control group that has decided not to tender to a point which will, or it is hoped will, defeat the "hostile" tender offer;

(b) To thwart the pending acquisition proposal by raising the bidding price beyond the level the bidder is willing or able to pay or, at the least, to cause the bidder to raise its price;

(c) To deny the bidder access to a significant block of stock held by a dissident or "weak" shareholder; and/or

(d) To "settle" out with a potential bidder by buying its stock at a profit to the bidder.

The Stock Acquisition Program as a Means of Enhancing the Strength of an Existing Control Position or Raising the Bidder's Price

Business Analysis

Where a strong control block already exists, this tactical move has the [objective of increasing the percentage ownership of the control group by buying in the public's stock. Where supermajority provisions exist, the ability to block a transaction may arise at less than majority ownership.] In the absence of such an existing control block, the strategy is simply one of pricing the acquisition out of the third party bidder's reach or, at the least, increasing the third party's bidding price.

Because the stock must be purchased quickly if either variant of this strategy is to succeed, the stock acquisition program almost certainly has to be accomplished through an issuer cash tender offer under SEC Rule 13e-4.[26] The only other possibly viable alternative from a timing point of view would be through negotiated block purchases. However, the success of a negotiated purchase program would depend upon the ability of the issuer and its financial advisors to locate large blocks of stock the holders of which can be persuaded to sell. The negotiated purchase technique, moreover, might leave the issuer vulnerable to a claim that it has engaged in an illegal "unconventional" tender offer not in compliance with Rule 13e-4, particularly if the blocks are purchased at a premium over current market and the total amount of the stock involved represents a substantial percentage of the

---

[26] SEC Rule 13e-4 under the Securities and Exchange Act of 1934 (the "1934 Act") and related Schedule 13e-4, SEC, Sec.Ex. Act Rel.No. 16112 (Aug. 16, 1979), regulating issuer tender offers, became effective on September 21, 1979. The rule applies to all tender offers by an issuer for its own equity securities if the issuer has a class of equity securities registered pursuant to § 12 of the 1934 Act, is required to file periodic reports under § 15(d) of the 1934 Act, or is a closed-end investment company registered under the Investment Company Act of 1940. [The Williams Act Rules concerning issuer tender offers are considered in Chapter 18, *infra*. Eds.]

issuer's outstanding capitalization.[a] There is also the practical problem of making sure the potential sellers are fully apprised of the pending bid, if it has not yet been publicly announced (as well as any other material non-public information concerning the issuer), and persuading the sellers to give up the potential profits of any bidding war.

Assuming the issuer chooses the cash tender offer route, a number of tactical questions would be presented. The first is whether the issuer should try to strike first by announcing its cash offer before the bidder announces its offer. There is always something to be said for seizing the initiative in a takeover contest. For example, an issuer self-tender at a substantial premium over market may well confuse the bidder, disrupt its planning and timing and cause it to reassess the desirability of the acquisition.

However, it must be recognized that more often than not the bidder will have more pricing flexibility and frequently more pricing capability than the issuer. Many issuers are subject to financial covenants that depend upon maintaining certain debt/equity ratios, and, more fundamentally, even the most strongly capitalized issuer can only buy back so much of its stock within the limits of sound financial planning. . . . Finally, if the issuer's purpose is to increase the ultimate tender offer price and/or to give at least some of its shareholders the opportunity to sell at a better price than the bidder is offering, it can more certainly achieve that goal by responding to a third party bid than by initiating the bidding itself. The question ultimately reduces to one of bidding strategy. If the analysis is that the issuer has more limited resources and less flexibility to participate in several rounds of competing bids, saving its first bid for use as a response is probably a better tactic.

A second and more fundamental question is whether an issuer tender offer that, by definition, will be only for a portion (usually a minority) of its outstanding stock makes sense in competition with an any and all third party tender offer. The answer is probably yes, as long as there is a sufficiently large group of insider shareholders so that, in combination with a successful partial tender offer by the issuer, the control group would own at least a veto block against major corporate actions (such as a merger or sale of the issuer's assets) and ideally a majority of the issuer's outstanding stock. An issuer tender offer under these circumstances should force the bidder to the choice of raising its price sufficiently to defeat the issuer's tender offer or abandoning the hostile tender offer.

An example of this strategy is illustrated by MITE Corp. v. Dixon. In *MITE*, MITE Corporation made a tender offer to purchase any and all of Chicago Rivet & Machine Company's outstanding shares for cash at $28 per share. Chicago Rivet's board of directors determined that MITE's offer was inadequate, and, in response to that offer, announced a tender offer to

---

[a] What types of transactions are "tender offers" within the meaning of the Williams Act is considered in Chapter 18, *infra*. Eds.

purchase, with corporate funds, 350,000 (approximately 40%) of Chicago Rivet's outstanding shares at $30 per share. Chicago Rivet's offer stated that all of the officers and directors and certain other shareholders who owned, in the aggregate, approximately 285,000 shares of Chicago Rivet did not intend to tender their shares in response to MITE's tender offer. Chicago Rivet had 866,264 shares outstanding; hence, if its offer were successful, the officers, directors, and other key shareholders holding 285,000 shares would be in effective control. MITE raised its offering price in response to Chicago Rivet's offer, but for various reasons later withdrew its bid for Chicago Rivet.

On the other hand, absent a strong and loyal control block, the issuer's self-tender, standing alone, almost certainly would not defeat a hostile bid. As is the case for all preventive and defensive stock acquisition programs, the issuer is working for the bidder to the extent it reduces its outstanding capitalization and lowering the number of shares the bidder must acquire in order to achieve control. Absent some other goal, such as causing the bidder to raise its price, self-tender by an issuer as a defensive technique has no rational purpose. Indeed, there is a real question whether an issuer self-tender standing alone (that is to say, without an inside control group whose position will be enhanced) will be able to achieve even the goal of causing the bidder to raise its price. The "hostile" bidder may conclude that its original price is high enough to attract a majority of the issuer's outstanding stock, notwithstanding the higher partial offer by the issuer. The question, then, would be whether the issuer tender offer is worth the time, expense and litigating risk it would almost certainly entail.

The issuer's tactical position in this context should be enhanced if the "hostile" bid is for less than all of the issuer's stock. Now both the issuer and the "hostile" bidder would be asking the public to assume a prorationing risk. This presumably would cool the ardor of the arbitrageurs and might lead a number of other shareholders to forego the opportunity of tendering to both parties. Even if this does not occur, the issuer would not face the pricing disadvantage inherent in matching its partial bid against an any and all third party bid -- that is, the pricing differential necessary to overcome the prorationing risk inherent in the issuer's partial offer.

In sum, although not without its attractions in some situations, the fact that so few issuers have adopted a strategy of self-tender as a response to a hostile bid strongly suggests that the device is of limited utility and rarely will be ultimately successful. For example, in the MITE-Chicago Rivet situation, MITE was able to defuse this defense merely by raising its tender offer price from $28 to $31. . . .

The Stock Acquisition Program as a Means of "Settling" Out with a Potential Bidder

Business Analysis

This strategy presents a scenario that has been played out with some regularity in recent years. An issuer becomes aware that another company, usually with a reputation as an aggressive acquiror, has accumulated a threateningly large block of its stock. Sometimes the issuer's awareness comes through the filing of a Schedule 13D or a Hart-Scott-Rodino Notification and Report Form. Not infrequently, however, the acquiring company overtly or covertly makes this fact known to the issuer before any such reports are due. In an ensuing conversation, the issuer will usually reject any overture for an acquisition and take a determinedly "hostile" stance. The acquiror then suggests, or signals in a more subtle way, that it would be amenable to selling the block to the issuer at what often turns out to be a very handsome profit. The issuer accepts, usually not without trepidation, and the repurchase is consummated.

This chain of events, of course, has its variations. Sometimes, the issuer extracts a promise from the acquiror not to engage in a "hostile" tender offer against the issuer, or a similar form of "standstill" arrangement. Sometimes, the issuer tries various forms of leverage on the acquiror such as suggesting that a combination of the two companies does indeed make some sense, but, from a financial point of view, the issuer should be the acquiring company and to this end it has just happened to prepare a Schedule 14D-1 and Hart-Scott-Rodino filing for the issuer's tender offer for the acquiror.

Variations notwithstanding, an observer is left with the strong impression that often the acquiror wanted the result. By playing the role of a tough acquisition minded company, the acquiror achieves something close to a "no lose" situation. If the issuer "rolls over" and "plays dead", the acquiror gets a friendly acquisition without a great risk of a bidding war; if the issuer fights by promoting a bidding war, the acquiror can always sell out to the white knight, usually at a large profit; if the issuer is willing to discuss a stock repurchase, again the acquiror can win financially. In effect, the acquiror is counting on the fact that if it can assemble its block at a relatively low price and then stimulate the dynamics of the acquisition game, it is almost certainly going to come out with a favorable transaction.

Note: Greenmail

Perhaps more than any other defensive tactic, "greenmail" -- the practice of a target company repurchasing at a premium the shares held by a potential or actual hostile bidder in order to eliminate the threat of an offer -- has engaged the public's attention and approbation. The SEC's Advisory Committee on Tender Offers recommended prohibiting the practice, and the Chairman of the SEC has stated that the SEC agrees with the Advisory Committee's recommendation.[30] It is worth recalling that although the furor over the technique is of recent origin, its use is not.[31] However, the frequency with which the tactic is used, and the magnitude of the payments made, changed substantially from the 1960s to the 1980s. The Office of the Chief Economist of the Securities and Exchange Commission has reported that between January 1979 and March 1984 $5.5 billion was paid in greenmail, representing a premium over market price of over $1 billion.[32]

The result has been the adoption of a number of barriers to the payment of greenmail, including a federal excise tax on the gain realized from the receipt of greenmail,[33] state statutes prohibiting its payment,[34] and company charter amendments that restrict payment by the particular corporation.[35] However, greenmail has not been without its defenders. The basic claim is that greenmail has the potential to result in gains to target shareholders by drawing additional bidders into the contest for the target, thereby resulting in a higher price.[36] While the effectiveness of greenmail as a defensive tactic is considered in Section B of this Chapter, *infra*, we should note that, even if effective, this function of greenmail does not meet the needs of a defensive planner whose goal is not to generate a higher price, but to keep the target company independent.

---

[30] Statement of John S.R. Shad, Chairman of the Securities and Exchange Commission, before *Hearings of the House Subcommittee on Telecommunications, Consumer Protection, and Finance* (March 28, 1984), reprinted in CCH Fed.Sec.L.Rep. ¶ 83,511 (Current Vol.).

[31] See, e.g., Cheff v. Mathes, 199 A.2d 548 (Del.Ch.1964) (reprinted in Section D.1 of this Chapter, *infra*).

[32] Office of the Chief Economist, *The Impact of Targeted Share Repurchases (Greenmail) on Stock Prices* 1 (September 11, 1984).

[33] Internal Revenue Code § 5881 (50% non-deductible excise tax on any gain realized upon the receipt of greenmail as defined).

[34] See, e.g., Ariz. Rev.Stat.Ann. § 10-1204; Minn.Stat.Ann. § 302A.553, subdivision 3; N.Y.Bus.Corp.Law § 513(e).

[35] Between 1984 and 1987, some 70 publicly traded corporations, including, for example, Alcoa, Anheuser-Busch, B.F. Goodrich, Mobile, and NYNEX, amended their articles of incorporation to add a prohibition of greenmail. Jaenicke, *Greenmail: Background Report B*, Investor Responsibility Research Center, Corporate Governance Service B-12 (Feb.1987). Ronald Gilson, *Drafting an Effective Greenmail Prohibition*, 88 Colum.L.Rev. 329 (1988), argues that the standard definition of greenmail in corporate charters, as well as state legislation and federal tax law, is very underinclusive.

[36] Andrei Shleifer & Robert Vishny, *Greenmail, White Knights and Shareholder Interest*, 17 Rand J.Econ. 293 (1986), make the argument most effectively.

c.   *Miscellaneous Tactics*

In addition to the tactics already described, a number of other approaches merit mention.

1. *Scorched Earth*. Here the notion is to cause the game not to be worth the candle by reducing the post-acquisition value of the target company.[37] The most effective variant of this approach is selective destruction in which value is reduced only if the takeover is successful. An examples of this approach is said to be publisher Houghton Mifflin's successful effort to convince a hostile bidder that its authors would change publishers if the takeover was successful.[38] Less effective is a reduction in the value of the target company that survives a successful defense, for example, the sale of the asset motivating the hostile offer at a less than market price.

2. *Defensive Acquisitions*. Once a hostile bid has been made, carefully selected acquisitions by the target company can create antitrust or regulatory barriers for the bidder. The clearest example is where the bidder is a foreign national. A number of federal statutes restrict foreign control of companies in certain strategic industries such as coastal shipping, civilian aviation and certain aspects of the defense industry. Others impose approval requirements for changes in the control of regulated companies such as broadcasters and savings and loan associations. State regulations impose similar requirements with respect to insurers, state chartered banks and savings and loan associations and public utilities.[39]

3. *Control Clauses*. It has been suggested that an offerer may be deterred if the target company's loan agreements or other material contracts allow, or are amended to allow, the lender or other party to accelerate the loan or terminate the contract in the event of a change of control.[40] The option analysis in Chapter 7 makes it easy to understand why a creditor would like the opportunity to accelerate or terminate. It serves as a check on opportunistic behavior by preventing the company from increasing the risk associated with the loan or contract by transferring control to a more risky party. Additionally, it allows the creditor to accelerate the loan or terminate the contract when the transfer of control coincides with an unrelated event, like an increase in interest rates or a decrease in the market price of the goods to be delivered under the contract, that causes it to be to that party's

---

[37] See Gurwin (1979), *supra* note 2.

[38] *Id.*

[39] See Fleischer, Sussman & Lesser (1990), *supra* note 1, at Ch. IX.

[40] See Richard Clemens, *Poison Debt: The New Takeover Defense*, 42 Bus.Law. 747 (1987); Harry Kamen, *Special Problems of Institutional Lenders*, 32 Bus.Law. 1423 (1977).

advantage to accelerate or terminate regardless of a change in control.[41] Although this explains why a creditor would want a control clause, it does not explain why a target company would be willing to agree to one. The advantage to the creditor, at least with respect to amending existing loans and contracts, comes at the expense of the target unless the terms of the loan or contract are otherwise adjusted to compensate the target for the reduction in risk. If the only benefit to the target is the ability to defend against an unwanted takeover by making the target less valuable, the technique is only another manifestation of the "scorched earth" tactic.

4. *Golden Parachutes.* A very popular tactic involves the target company awarding very favorable employment contracts to its senior management which become effective only in the event of a change in control. Once effective, the employee is either given the unilateral right to terminate employment and receive a substantial lump sum payment ("single trigger" parachutes) or, if the right is not entirely unilateral, to do so if the employee's situation -- e.g., duties, benefits, employment location, etc. -- is changed ("double trigger" parachutes). In an extreme example, Conoco, Inc., awarded new employment contracts to senior management following expression of interest by suitors such as Seagrams, Cities Services Co., and Texaco, Inc. The contract given the Chairman of the Board, for example, granted him the right to quit and receive a $5 million lump sum payment if Conoco were taken over.[42]

Categorizing golden parachutes as a defensive tactic is subject to debate. First, if limited to senior employees, it is unlikely that the total payments called for will be large enough to affect the acquiring company's decision in a major transaction.[43] Second, golden parachutes are commonly justified not as a defensive tactic, but as a means of *eliminating* the conflict of interest between target management and target shareholders with respect to a takeover. One way this can be described is by reference to portfolio diversification. In this analysis, target management starts with a one asset portfolio -- its investment of firm specific human capital in the target -- which is subject to the risk of a hostile takeover. Without more, target management will try to reduce that risk (and protect the value of its human

---

[41] See the discussion of event risk provisions in Chapter 15, *supra.*

[42] See generally Wendy Cooper, *The Spread of Golden Parachutes,* Institutional Investor 65 (Aug.1982) (collecting examples).

[43] Some golden parachute arrangements, however, do reach a magnitude that would affect an acquiring company's decision. A recent analysis of a sample of 90 firms that had adopted golden parachute programs disclosed that the maximum payout under the contracts averaged only 1.73% of the market value of the company's equity and only 12.13% of annual earnings. Although the averages are low, they mask a large variation within the sample. The payout under one plan was approximately 11.23% of the market value of the company's equity. Similarly, the payout as a percentage of annual earnings was as high as 65% and this excluded companies that had losses. Richard Lambert & David Larker, *Golden Parachutes, Executive Decision-Making, and Shareholder Wealth,* 7 J.Acct. & Econ. 179 (1985).

capital investment) by resisting takeovers. Awarding management golden parachutes adds a second asset to management's portfolio: the expectation of a large termination payment which can be realized only if a takeover actually occurs. The result, it is argued, is a portfolio the value of which is invariant to the risk of a takeover. As a result, management will consider a proposed offer solely from the perspective of what is best for shareholders because management's personal positions are protected either way.[44]

Aligning the interests of managers and shareholders may not be quite that easy. Indeed, the result may be only to bias decision making in the opposite direction. If the payout under the golden parachute is greater than the amount by which the present value of a manager's future earnings with the target (including the psychic value of control) exceeds the present value of the manager's future earnings in alternative employment, the manager will have a financial incentive *to cause* the target to be taken over and accept the next most remunerative position, even if that result is *not* in the shareholders' best interests. The perverse incentive to facilitate a takeover may be even stronger for older executives whose future earnings will be smaller because of their shorter remaining worklife, but whose lump sum payment under a golden parachute award is likely higher due to greater seniority and current earnings. In this setting something akin to a final period problem is created.[45]

A variant on this theme is the "tin" parachute in which a much greater number of employees are covered, albeit for individually smaller amounts, based on arguments similar to the implicit contract analysis discussed in Chapter 15.

As a practical matter, the stakes involved in the golden parachute controversy have at least been limited by the 1984 addition of IRC § 280G,[46] which limits, following a change in control, the deductibility by the target company of termination payments to senior management to three times a manager's average annual gross income from the company over the previous five years. Additionally, the manager would be subject to a 20% excise tax on amounts in excess of the limit.[47]

---

[44] See Michael Jensen, *Takeovers: Their Causes and Consequences*, 2 J.Econ.Persp. 21 (1988); Charles Kroeber, *Golden Parachutes, Shark Repellents, and Hostile Tender Offers*, 76 Am.Econ.Rev. 155 (1986).

[45] Empirical evidence supports the proposition that the presence of golden parachutes increases the likelihood of a successful takeover, the likelihood of multiple bids, and the magnitude of the premium. See Judith Machlin, Hyuk Choe & James Miles, *The Effects of Golden Parachutes on Takeover Activity*, 36 J.L. & Econ. 861 (1993).

[46] Deficit Reduction Act of 1984, P.L. 98-369, 988 Stat. 494 (codified at IRC §§ 280, 4999).

[47] A second regulatory barrier to both golden and tin parachutes is the possibility that ERISA will apply. See Pane v. RCA Corp., 868 F.2d 631 (3rd Cir.1989).

5. *Placing Securities in Friendly Hands.* Where the acquiring company intends a complete acquisition, the target may create some deterrence by issuing a substantial block of the target's stock to a friendly party. This tactic should be distinguished, however, from a similar issuance intended to facilitate the acquisition of the target by another company whom the target prefers to the offerer. The latter tactic, commonly called a "lock-up," is simply part of an effort to seek out a more attractive competing bid and is not intended to keep the target company independent. As such, it is more accurately a negotiated surrender rather than a defensive tactic.[48] In the purely defensive setting, the friendly party is typically prevented from becoming less friendly once it is a target shareholder through the use of a "standstill" agreement which (i) limits future purchases on the part of the friendly purchaser, (ii) prohibits the purchaser from attempting to exercise control or otherwise influence the conduct of the target's business, (iii) grants the target a right of first refusal should the purchaser determine to sell the shares, and (iv) requires the purchaser to vote its stock as target management directs or, in some cases, in the same proportion as all shares are voted. In return, the purchaser is commonly given board representation and registration rights.[49]

Whether standstill agreements should be categorized as a defensive tactic depends in large measure on when the stock acquisition to which the standstill agreement relates is made and the purpose of the acquisition. At one extreme is a standstill agreement that accompanies a stock purchase by a party with whom the target expects to have important future dealings.[50] In this situation, the investment is not made in anticipation of an acquisition and the restrictions might be justified as an effort to prevent the target from inadvertently facilitating a later acquisition at a price lower than could have been negotiated in the absence of the pre-existing purchase. This use of a standstill agreement does not seem to operate as a defensive tactic.

At the other extreme, standstill agreements are also entered into *after* a purchaser has unilaterally acquired its shareholdings in the target, and seem clearly designed to neutralize a party whom target management perceives might launch a hostile takeover. This use of standstill agreements does seem to operate as a defensive tactic since it serves to eliminate an important potential bidder for the target.[51]

---

[48] Problems associated with lock-ups and avoiding competing bids are considered in Chapter 19, *infra*.

[49] See, e.g., Joseph Bartlett & Christopher Andrews, *The Standstill Agreement: Legal and Business Considerations Underlying a Corporate Peace Treaty,* 62 B.U.L.Rev. 143 (1982); Kenneth Bialkin, *The Use of Standstill Agreements in Corporate Transactions,* in *Thirteenth Annual Institute on Securities Regulation* 91 (PLI 1981); Note, *The Standstill Agreement: A Case of Illegal Vote Selling and a Breach of Fiduciary Duty,* 93 Yale L.J. 1093 (1984).

[50] Because of the difficulties involved in technology transfers, for example, such purchases may be particularly useful when the future dealings contemplate such transfers.

[51] A broadly drafted confidentiality agreement, intended to protect the target company against the would-be acquiring company's later use of proprietary information of the target

6. *The "Pac-Man" Defense.* In a number of hostile takeover battles in the early 1980s, including Cities Service-Mesa Petroleum and Martin Marietta-Bendix, the target company resorted to a tactic playfully styled the "Pac-Man strategy" by participants. As described by a merger specialist at a major investment banking firm, "[t]hat's where my client eats yours before yours eats mine."[52] In the Martin Marietta-Bendix transaction, for example, Martin Marietta responded to Bendix's tender offer for all outstanding Martin Marietta stock by making a tender offer for all outstanding Bendix stock. Despite the public controversy surrounding the transaction and the dire predictions of what might happen if both offers were successful so that the ownership of the two parties became a loop -- Bendix owned a majority of Martin Marietta which owned a majority of Bendix which owned a majority of Martin Marietta and so on -- neither of the parties was willing to admit defeat and both offers went forward. The original Bendix offer drew over 70% of Martin Marietta's outstanding stock and the Martin Marietta counter offer drew 75% of Bendix's outstanding stock.[53]

This looped ownership raised a number of unusual issues of corporate law. For example:

(1) Where a statute like Del. Gen. Corp. Act § 160(c) prohibits a corporation that owns a majority of the stock in another corporation from voting that stock, who then could exercise control over either Martin Marietta or Bendix?

(2) How should the rules governing the mechanics of noticing and holding shareholders meeting be applied when their application -- which corporation's shareholders can meet first to remove the original directors -- may determine the outcome of the battle?

(3) To whom do the directors of each corporation owe their fiduciary duty? If the answer is that the duty is owed to the majority shareholder, is another loop created?[54]

---

disclosed during friendly negotiations that failed, may serve the same function as a standstill agreement. In General Portland, Inc. v. LaFarge Coppee S.A., [1981 Transfer Binder] Fed.Sec.L.Rep. (CCH) ¶ 99,148 (N.D.Tex.1981), the would-be acquirer agreed, as a condition to friendly negotiations, that it would not purchase target shares without consent so long as it was "in possession of confidential information." When the friendly negotiations failed and the acquirer threatened a hostile tender offer, the tender offer was enjoined on the ground that the acquirer was prohibited from acting by the confidentiality agreement "so long as information furnished by [the target] to [the acquirer] remains competitively sensitive and confidential."

[52] Metz & Inman, *Martin Marietta Spurns Bendix Offer as 'Inadequate,' Countering with $75-a-Share Bid for Control of Suitor,* Wall St.J., Aug. 31, 1982, p.3, c.1.

[53] The tangled histories of the Martin Marietta-Bendix battle and other transactions in which the Pac-Man technique was used are traced in Morris Kramer, *Other Current Developments in Acquisition Techniques,* in 1 *Fourteenth Annual Institute on Securities Regulation* 821 (PLI 1982).

[54] For a discussion of these issues, see Deborah DeMott, *Pac-Man Tender Offers,* 1983

In the end, none of these issues were resolved in the Martin Marietta-Bendix transaction because the legal conflict was cut short by the acquisition of Bendix by Allied Corporation in a transaction in which Allied purchased all of Bendix's stock (paying for Martin Marietta's block with part of Bendix's block of Martin Marietta stock) and retained a 39% in Marietta stock subject to a standstill agreement. Thus, when the smoke cleared, the two participants in the reciprocal control battle ended up in a very different position from where they started. Rather than making an acquisition, Bendix was itself acquired. Martin Marietta remained independent, but with a new 39% shareholder and with a vast amount of new debt that was incurred to finance the original acquisition of Bendix stock.

Beyond the arcane legal issues, the economics of the conflicting tender offers pose an interesting situation from the perspective of the shareholders of Martin Marietta and Bendix. Although it was clear that the managements of the two companies viewed the offers as competing, considering the interests of the shareholders of both companies as a group suggests a different analysis. If we consider the two corporations as one, hardly unreasonable in light of the dual acquisition efforts, the entire transaction can be recharacterized as a massive recapitalization. The combined corporation simply borrowed substantial sums from banks (the financing secured by both companies in order to fund their respective tender offers) which was then used to repurchase at a substantial premium more than 70% of the combined company's outstanding shares (through the tender offers). The net result, then, was simply a large shift in the combined company's capital structure from equity to debt. What belief about the future income of the combined company would be necessary to justify paying a substantial premium for the privilege of substituting high interest debt financing for existing equity?

A final question about this most peculiar transaction concerns identification of the winners and the losers. The empirical results described in Part II indicate that target shareholders gain substantially from acquisitions, but that acquiring company shareholders earn, at best, returns in the normal range. In the Martin Marietta-Bendix transaction, who would have been, in effect, the target company shareholders and who the acquiring company shareholders (assuming Allied never appeared)? If this phenomenon can be generalized by the statement that the losers will be the providers of capital to the surviving entity, who would have played that role in Martin Marietta-Bendix?

B.   The Effectiveness of the Arsenal

Evaluating the effectiveness of particular defensive tactics confronts the same problem with which we began this Chapter. Defensive tactics may be

---

motivated by quite different goals: target management may deploy defensive tactics to remain independent for their own purposes; or to increase the value of the corporation either by staying independent or by securing time to attract another bidder. We will consider both goals in this section -- whether a particular tactic has the promise of keeping the target company independent, and whether shareholders are well served by that outcome. In general, the empirical evidence is consistent. Defensive tactics sometimes succeed in keeping the target company independent -- over time the success rate is approximately 20%[55] -- but on average shareholders benefit only if the defeat of one offer leads to the target's acquisition in a subsequent offer.

1. Pre-Offer

a.   *Deterrence: Shark Repellent Amendments*

Ronald Gilson
THE CASE AGAINST SHARK REPELLENT AMENDMENTS: STRUCTURAL LIMITATIONS ON THE ENABLING CONCEPT
34 Stan.L.Rev. 775, 792-804 (1982)[*]

Efficacy of the Deterrent

Despite the logic underlying the expectation that shark repellent amendments will deter potential offerors, . . . some prominent practitioners have asserted that such provisions do not fulfill their promise.[67] An examination of the three categories of amendments I have considered suggests that there is substantial basis for questioning the extent of their deterrence. While there are circumstances where shark repellent amendments will have some effect, it seems clear that their potential for deterrence has been substantially exaggerated.

1. Impeding transfer of control of the board of directors

The deterrent effect of an incumbency amendment is premised on the belief that immediate control of the target's board of directors is so important to the offeror that the prospect of substantial delay in achieving it will make a particular acquisition less attractive. Still, the extent of any deterrence ultimately depends on how effective the delaying mechanism is.

---

[55] See notes 1 and 2, *supra*, and accompanying text.

[*] Copyright © 1982 by the Board of Trustees of the Leland Stanford Junior University.

[67] Indeed, Joseph Flom has characterized the approach as a "total waste of time." Transcript, *Tenth Annual Institute on Securities Regulation* 443 (1978). And Martin Lipton has concluded that shark repellent amendments' "efficacy is open to debate."

Amendments seeking to delay transfer of board control necessarily assume that the incumbent directors will choose to remain in office and exercise the authority given them by the shark repellent amendments to control board size and name successor directors in a manner inconsistent with the desires of the successful offeror. This central assumption about the behavior of incumbent directors is open to serious question. It depends, in the final analysis, on the potential offeror believing that even after the offer is successful, members of the incumbent board will act in a fashion inconsistent with their own self-interest.

Consider the position of a target company's incumbent directors following a successful tender offer. A new majority shareholder now exists who wishes to control the target's board. The incumbent board will consist of some combination of owner-managers, professional managers, and, increasingly, independent directors. Analysis suggests that none of the incumbents in these three categories has an incentive to continue the defense by delaying the inevitable shift in board control. An independent director should certainly recognize the potential for time-consuming and expensive litigation brought by a successful offeror intent on securing board control. Free of the ties that may encumber other categories of directors, an independent director has no reason to fight a fall-back action in the face of both inevitable defeat and the ideology of majority rule.

Professional management would also have little reason to go down with the ship. Their behavior during and after a tender offer can be expected to have a significant impact both on the likelihood of continued employment with the target following a shift in control of the board and on employment prospects with other firms. While loyalty and a commitment to a tenacious takeover defense could make a manager an attractive employee to other potential targets, one must wonder whether this extends to activity occurring after the defense has failed. Moreover, professional managers remain in a position to sell their future services to the offeror, just as shareholders sell their shares, and thereby secure a portion of the benefits of the transaction. Because any payment for resignation from the board would be difficult if not impossible to distinguish from a legitimate payment for future services, the rational reaction by professional management would be surrender, albeit at a price. In this sense, the potential for delay may operate more as a means to allocate the pie between target management and target shareholders than as a way to discourage an offeror.

The only directors who might have an interest in holding out "to the last man" are owner-managers -- substantial shareholders and often founders of the concern -- who likely draw substantial nonmonetary benefits from their controlling positions in an independent concern, and who simply do not look forward to evaluation of the quality of their performance by a different owner. Even here, however, one must doubt the wisdom and, hence, the likelihood of recourse to the mechanisms provided by incumbency amendments. While there is an incentive to successfully defend the target's independence, there is no reason to continue the fight -- to the individual's financial disadvantage -- when it has already been lost. Thus, while a target bristling with hostility before the offer may deter even if the individual quills are not alarming, once the offer succeeds one would expect rational owners to secure whatever compensation they can for their cooperation.[77] . . .

2. *Barriers to second-step transactions*

Effectiveness in preventing freezeout mergers. Because its effectiveness does not depend on the behavior of individuals whose self-interest is inconsistent with the desired result, an amendment preventing second-step transactions has more promise as a deterrent than one directed at maintaining the incumbent board of directors. If a supermajority requirement for a second-step transaction is waivable only by "continuing directors" -- effectively the pre-offer board -- the resignation or replacement of the incumbent board will not render the amendment ineffective. In that event the supermajority requirement may not be waivable at all.

Because the goal of an offeror to whom a second-step transaction is important is, by definition, to acquire all of the target's stock, the initial impact of a supermajority amendment -- to cause the offeror to increase the number of shares sought by tender to an amount in excess of the supermajority required -- is not itself a serious burden. The potential for deterrence arises, however, from the possible increase in the total cost of the transaction even if the offeror had intended to pay the same price in the second-step transaction. If the supply curve for the target's stock is upward-sloping, the need to acquire a greater number of shares will result in an increased price not only for the marginal shares acquired due to the supermajority requirement, but, because the Williams Act requires the same price to be paid for all shares tendered,[80] for the original shares as well.[81]

---

[77] The common phenomenon of target management turning to a white knight following an initial offer, and the fact that a company that is a raider in one transaction may be a white knight in the next, suggest the accuracy of this prediction.

[80] See Securities Act Release No. 6159, Securities Exchange Act Release No. 16,385 . . . (interpreting Exchange Act § 14(d)(7), 15 U.S.C. § 78n(d)(7) (1976), to require the same price be paid for all shares).

[81] The notion of an upward-sloping supply curve for the target's stock is not inconsistent with existing empirical evidence suggesting that because shares of stock represent only a right to a future income stream with a particular risk-return relationship, as to which a multitude of substitutes exist, more or less of a security can be purchased without a resulting change in price. Myron Scholes, *The Market for Securities: Substitution versus Price Pressure and the Effects of Information on Share Prices*, 45 J.Bus. 179 (1972). Professor Scholes points out that particular purchases or sales may reflect new information concerning the issuer which warrants alteration in the price of its shares relative to substitutes. A tender offer may be the most extreme example since the offer to purchase reflects information that, for at least one buyer, there are no substitutes for the security, thus allowing a much greater role for price as opposed to substitution effects.

The alteration in offeror strategy required by a supermajority provision may also increase the cost of the total transaction through its impact on the type of consideration used and the amount of financing necessary for the complete acquisition of the target. It is not uncommon for an offeror to make an initial cash tender offer for a bare majority of the target's outstanding shares, expecting that its securities will be the consideration in the second-step transaction. This approach reduces the cash cost of the acquisition to the offeror and benefits the target shareholders by providing them the option of a tax-free exchange. Increasing the number of shares that must be acquired in the initial offer to satisfy the supermajority requirement raises the cash cost of the acquisition and, necessarily, the cost of the financing necessary to complete it. It may also reduce the opportunity to offer target shareholders the choice between a taxable and tax-free exchange, a benefit which presumably must be replaced if the transaction is to remain equally attractive to shareholders.

The deterrent potential of supermajority amendments obviously increases where target management itself owns or controls enough shares to block the supermajority vote even if the offeror tenders for all the outstanding shares. However, as with the efficacy of shark repellent amendments protecting the incumbent board of directors, the deterrent effect of management power to block a second-step transaction depends not only on the existence of the power, but also on the offeror's evaluation of management's will to use it in the face of a successful tender offer for a controlling, but not supermajority, interest. From this perspective, it must be kept in mind that target management pays a substantial price by exercising its power to block the second-step transaction. While such an action prevents the offeror from securing the potential benefits from eliminating minority shareholders, members of management will then remain minority shareholders with sharply reduced opportunities to liquidate their investment. . . . Indeed, if one assumes that management's investment in the shares used to block the supermajority vote represents a significant portion of each manager's assets -- a not unreasonable assumption with respect to professional management -- the behavior necessary for the provision to operate as an effective deterrent is even more irrational than for incumbency amendments.

Importance of second-step transactions. Evaluation of the deterrence created by supermajority requirements thus far has assumed that the availability of second-step transactions is critical to the offeror. To the extent this assumption overstates the importance of these transactions to the offeror, the potential deterrence of even a perfectly effective amendment[85]

---

[85] One can imagine a form of shark repellent that could be effective at blocking a second-step transaction. A very high vote requirement together with a requirement for approval by a majority of nontendering shareholders, . . . and with no exceptions other than approval by the target board prior to the offeror's acquisition of a significant percentage of target shares . . . might make a second-step transaction impossible even if target management

is reduced. In fact, on examination the reasons commonly offered for the desirability of a second-step transaction, although real, hardly seem compelling. The constraints on a parent's discretion in allocating synergistic benefits between itself and its subsidiary with public shareholders do not appear to be substantial. The administrative costs associated with public shareholders, while nontrivial, are hardly large enough to affect a transaction of significant size. Finally, the available empirical evidence strongly suggests that the offeror's return comes from the right "to control . . . the target's resources,"[89] not from a postoffer increase in the value of the target's shares. This, of course, would counsel against a second-step transaction, because once the offeror achieves control, its rate of return on the investment may well *decrease* with the purchase of additional shares.[a] .

. .

In sum, shark repellent amendments creating a barrier to second-step transactions have more promise as a deterrent than incumbency amendments. The significance of this barrier is attenuated by the reality facing target management when an offeror secures majority, but not supermajority, control, and by doubts about the overall importance of the second-step transaction to the offeror. Still, to the extent that a second-step transaction is desirable, these provisions retain the potential, because of Williams Act requirements, for disproportionately increasing the cost of the offer by increasing the number of shares an offeror must acquire to accomplish it.

3. *Fair price and compulsory redemption provisions*

Fair price amendments act as a backstop to supermajority barriers to second-step transactions. Although they can help the overall package of amendments to appear more balanced by providing a means to avoid the supermajority requirement, the formulas contained in these amendments may increase the price required to be paid in the second-step transaction, perhaps to a level above the initial tender price, so that the option is illusory. Because fair price amendments focus only on second-step transactions, their effectiveness as a deterrent, like that of supermajority requirements generally, depends on the belief that target management will choose to enforce the requirements, on the size of the resulting increase in total acquisition cost, and ultimately on the overall importance of a second-step transaction to the offeror.

Right of redemption provisions, in contrast, promise greater deterrence than either supermajority or fair price amendments. Like fair price

---

conceded after the success of the initial offer.

   [89] Gregg Jarrell & Michael Bradley, *The Economic Effects of Federal and State Regulations of Cash Tender Offers*, 23 J.L. & Econ. 371, 381-82 (1980).

   [a] The full range of reasons why an acquiring corporation may pursue a second-step merger are evaluated in Chapter 22A, *infra*.

amendments, right of redemption provisions make the entire acquisition more expensive by increasing the price of the second-step transaction. But they go a step further by removing the offeror's alternative of *not* proceeding with a second-step transaction if its cost appears too great or its benefits too small. Right of redemption provisions thereby institutionalize the free-rider problem that I argued was not significant with respect to second-step transactions alone. If shareholders understand that a successful tender offer will give them the *right* to demand a higher price for their shares -- a fact target management might be expected to disseminate with enthusiasm -- there is no avoiding the incentive to hold out in the hope that other shareholders will tender and the offer will succeed.[98]

Thus, of the categories of shark repellent amendments, right of redemption provisions, the type least frequently adopted, present the greatest potential for deterring an offeror.

Note: Empirical Evidence

Consistent with the potentially conflicting goals of defensive tactics, the empirical evidence on the effects of shark repellent amendments is somewhat ambiguous. In general, studies have examined samples of companies that had adopted shark repellent amendments to test competing explanations for why the amendments were proposed. One explanation -- the managerial entrenchment hypothesis -- posits that shark repellent amendments are efforts by management to protect their positions. Because this is achieved by reducing the likelihood of future tender offers at a premium, and because managers are thereby shielded from the discipline of the capital market on their performance, their increased security comes at the expense of shareholders. If this hypothesis is correct, one would expect *negative* abnormal returns on proposal and adoption because the amendments reduce the expected value of the company. The alternative explanation -- the stockholder interests hypothesis -- claims that shark repellent amendments benefit shareholders because they facilitate effective bargaining by target management over the division of gains and do little to reduce overall market

---

[98] The classic example is that of a closed-end, mutual fund. Although the only assets held by the fund are the securities of other companies, so that net asset value and liquidation value are virtually identical, the securities of many of them, for significant periods of time, have traded at a price below net asset value. See generally Kenneth Boudreaux, *Discounts and Premiums on Close-End Mutual Funds: A Study in Valuation,* 28 J.Fin. 515 (1973); Burton Malkiel, *The Valuation of Closed-End Investment-Company Shares,* 32 J.Fin. 847 (1977); Morris Mendelson, *Closed-End Fund Discounts Revisited,* 13 Fin.Rev. 48 (1978). Thus, one acquiring control of the fund at market price and liquidating it would profit by the amount of the pre-existing discount from net asset value. But a shareholder who believed that the offer would be successful would refuse to sell for a premium less than the full discount since, on liquidation, the shareholder would receive the full benefit. . . .

discipline on managerial performance. If this hypothesis is correct, one would expect *positive* CARs as a result of the amendments because the resulting increase in expected premium would outweigh any decrease in the likelihood of future offers.

Early empirical studies lumped together all types of shark repellent amendments and all types of adopting companies, and found little in the way of results. Harry DeAngelo and Edward Rice[56] found small, but statistically insignificant, negative abnormal returns associated with shark repellent amendments. Nonetheless, the authors tentatively, and somewhat reluctantly, treat the data as supportive of the managerial entrenchment hypothesis: "If forced to choose between the managerial entrenchment and stockholder interest hypothesis, we conclude that the preponderance of observed negative returns at the time of amendment proposal can be viewed as weak preliminary support for the managerial entrenchment hypothesis."[57] Scott Linn and John McConnell[58] reach a different, albeit also tentative, conclusion. Like DeAngelo & Rice, they found that the CAR for their sample was not significantly different from zero around the *date* (i) when the companies' boards of directors approved the shark repellent amendments; (ii) when the proxy statements concerning the amendments were mailed to shareholders; and (iii) of the stockholder meetings concerning the amendments. Looking at the *periods* between the proxy mailing date and the shareholders' meeting date, and over the 90 days following the shareholders' meeting, however, they found small but statistically significant, positive abnormal returns. On this basis they concluded that:

> Although the results are not unambiguous, the overall impression yielded by the analysis is that the introduction and adoption of antitakeover amendments is associated with an increase in common stock prices. . . . From the perspective of individual firms, the implication is that antitakeover amendments are proposed by managers who seek to enhance shareholder wealth.[59] . . .

One important problem in evaluating these results and abnormal return studies of all other pre-offer defensive tactics should be noted. What if the proposal of shark repellent amendments also transmits to the market private information previously held only by company management? From this perspective, management's proposal of shark repellent amendments might signal that management believes that there is a higher likelihood of a hostile tender offer than the market previously had believed. If this causes the

---

[56] Harry DeAngelo & Edward Rice, *Antitakeover Charter Amendments and Stockholder Wealth*, 11 J.Fin.Econ. 329 (1983).

[57] *Id*. at 40.

[58] Scott Linn & John McConnell, *An Empirical Investigation of the Impact of "Antitakeover" Amendments on Common Stock Prices*, 11 J.Fin.Econ. 361 (1983).

[59] *Id*. at 397.

market to increase its assessment of the likelihood of a premium tender offer, then the result of the proposal would be a positive CAR. This possibility may make the empirical results reported by both articles quite ambiguous: Any abnormal return reported can be explained by a number of different combinations of the signalling effect and either the managerial entrenchment hypothesis or the stockholder interests hypothesis.[60]

Even if the data reported are taken at face value, the predominant result -- no abnormal returns -- seems more consistent with the no-effects hypothesis offered by Gilson in the previous excerpt: that because shark repellent amendments are unlikely to be effective, their proposal and adoption should not result in positive or negative abnormal returns. This, in fact, is the predominant empirical result reported by the two studies.[61]

More recent empirical studies have broken down the samples both by type of shark repellent amendment and by type of adopting company. Gregg Jarrell and Annette Poulsen[62] found no abnormal returns associated with adoption of fair price or classified board amendments, but found statistically negative abnormal returns of 4.86% for supermajority amendments that allowed directors to waive the supermajority requirement. Interestingly, the firms that adopted such amendments had large blocks of stock held by insiders, averaging 19.2%, but as high as 23.8% for non-exchange listed public firms. Because most supermajority amendments specify 80% as the necessary supermajority, the combination of the amendment and the size of the insiders' holdings gave the insiders an absolute veto over a second-step transaction.

Anup Agrawal and Gershon Mandelker[63] focus on the relation between ownership distribution in the firm and the effect of shark repellent amendments on shareholder wealth. They find a statistically significant positive relation between changes in shareholder wealth as a result of shark repellent amendments and the percentage of institutional ownership. Shareholders of the one-third of the sample of companies with the lowest institutional ownership experienced statistically significant negative returns of 6.4% on announcement, while the stockholders in the remainder of the sample companies experienced no abnormal returns.

Overall, the most interesting thing about these empirical results is that they seem to track the conflict inherent in defensive tactics: when defensive

---

[60] For example, a positive abnormal return might reflect the combination of a negative abnormal return resulting from the adoption of the shark repellent amendment (the managerial entrenchment hypothesis) that is more than outweighed by a positive signalling effect.

[61] Of course, the possibility that shark repellant amendments may have a signalling effect confounds this interpretation of the empirical results as well.

[62] Gregg Jarrell & Annette Poulsen, *Shark Repellents and Stock Prices: The Effects of Antitakeover Amendments Since 1980*, 19 J.Fin.Econ. 127 (1987).

[63] Anup Agrawal & Gershon Mandelker, *Large Shareholders and the Monitoring of Managers: The Case of Antitakeover Charter Amendments*, 25 J.Fin. & Quant.Anal. 143 (1990).

tactics are deployed in circumstances that restrict managers' ability to misuse them (in the Agrawal & Mandelker study when large institutional holders monitor managers' post-adoption behavior), no abnormal returns result; when defensive tactics are deployed in circumstances that give managers control over their use (in the Jarrell & Poulsen study when insiders control sufficient shares to themselves block a supermajority vote), negative abnormal returns result.

A final difficulty in evaluating the empirical studies of the effectiveness of shark repellent amendments will affect studies of all pre-offer defensive tactics. Most companies that undertake defensive planning deploy more than one defensive device. As result, the effect of the adoption of one device will depend on what other devices are already in place; the abnormal return observed on adoption will measure only the marginal effect of the new device. This appears most clearly with respect to the interaction of shark repellent amendments and state antitakeover legislation because of the overlap in their substantive content.[64]　Jonathan Karpoff and Paul Malatesta[65] found that adoption of state antitakeover legislation had no effect on the companies that already had firm level shark repellents in place, but a statistically significant negative effect on companies without firm level defenses. The converse should also be true, so that further cross-sectional analysis of the shark repellent amendment samples, to control for the presence of state antitakeover legislation and other defensive devices, would be necessary to fully isolate the impact of the amendments.

b.　*Deterrence: The Poison Pill*

As with shark repellent amendments, evaluating the effectiveness of poison pills requires that we be clear about what we mean by effectiveness: a poison pill may be effective in the sense that it gives target management the power to block a hostile bid; or it may be effective in the sense that management actually utilizes that power to bargain effectively on behalf of shareholders. The mechanics of a poison pill starkly reveal the potential for either outcome. Unlike shark repellent amendments, a poison pill can be effective in blocking an offer; no bidder will complete a hostile offer if the target has an unredeemed poison pill in place. But for the very same reason, a poison pill can be equally effective in forcing a bidder to negotiate with target management over the size of the premium. Both possibilities are apparent in an early study of the impact of poison pill plans.[66]　Looking at

---

[64] State antitakeover legislation is considered in Chapter 23, *infra*.

[65] Jonathan Karpoff & Paul Malatesta, *The Wealth Effects of Second Generation State Takeover Legislation*, 25 J.Fin.Econ. 291 (1989).

[66] Office of the Chief Economist, Securities and Exchange Commission, *The Effects of Poison Pills on the Wealth of Target Shareholders* (Oct.1986).

a sample 30 hostile takeovers in which the target company had a poison pill in place, the SEC's Office of the Chief Economist found that the target company successfully defeated the hostile offer in 14 cases (46%). For a defensive planner, this compares favorably to the historical successful defense rate of approximately 20%.[67] In 13 cases, however, competitive bidding facilitated by target management's ability to stave off the initial bidder by means of a poison pill resulted in the ultimate sale of the target at a higher price.[68] Poison pills thus have the potential to be effective in both senses of the terms: facilitating management entrenchment or serving shareholder interests.

For this and other reasons, empirical evaluation of the overall effect of poison pill adoption on target shareholders is difficult. Studies whose samples were drawn from firms adopting poison pill plans through 1986 (roughly the first one-fifth of firms that came to adopt poison pill plans through 1991), reported only very small negative abnormal returns on announcement of a company's adoption of a poison pill. In one study, adoption of a poison pill plan by a company not subject to an existing takeover threat resulted in a statistically significant (barely) negative abnormal return of 0.34%. Even when the poison pill was adopted at a time when takeover speculation already existed, the negative abnormal return increased to only 1.51%, and when that subsample was further restricted to companies that had adopted the more effective form of poison pill, the negative abnormal return reached only 2.12%.[69] A second study covering the same period reported similar results: a statistically significant negative return of 0.915% for the entire sample and a negative return of 2.3% for companies already subject to takeover speculation.[70] Expanding the sample to include all companies adopting poison pills through 1991 does not really alter the magnitude of the results: the entire sample of adopting companies earned non-significant negative returns of 0.06% and a subsample limited to control contests earned statistically significant negative returns of 2.4 %.[71]

The puzzle presented by this data is why the negative returns are so small given the potential for poison pill plans to allow target management to

---

[67] See note 1 and accompanying text, *supra*. Breaking the sample down based on the type of plan magnifies the potential effectiveness of a poison pill to block a hostile bid. Companies with flip-in and back-end plans, which were developed to overcome the defensive flaws of flip-over plans, remained independent two-thirds of the time, while companies with flip-over plans remained independent only one-third of the time. Office of the Chief Economist (1986), *supra* note 66, at 25-26.

[68] *Id*. at 27.

[69] Michael Ryngaert, *The Effect of Poison Pill Securities on Shareholder Wealth*, 20 J.Fin.Econ. 377 (1988).

[70] Paul Malatesta & Ralph Walkling, *Poison Pill Securities: Stockholder Wealth, Profitability, and Ownership Structure*, 20 J.Fin.Econ. 347 (1988).

[71] Robert Comment & William Schwert, *Poison or Placebo: Evidence on the Deterrent and Wealth Effects of Modern Antitakeover Measures*, (Simon Grad.Sch. of Bus.Admin., Univ. of Rochester Working Paper FR 93-04, March 1993).

effectively block an offer. "If the probability of a takeover typically decreases by 10% with the adoption of an antitakeover measure, and if a 50% gain is deterred, then the wealth decline on adoption should be about 5%."[72] A number of explanations of poison pill plans' modest stock price effect come to mind. Like shark repellent amendments, the response of share prices to the announcement of a poison pill may reflect the balance of the negative effect of the pill and the positive effect of the new information concerning the likelihood of a takeover bid. The fact that the deterrent and information effects of a poison pill offsetting each other is apparent in the data: larger negative returns result when pills are adopted at a time when takeover speculation already exists and therefore when the offsetting information effect should be negligible. However, the offsetting effects explanation is at best only partial. The negative returns are relatively small even when a poison pill plan is adopted in the face of existing takeover speculation, a result inconsistent with the poison pill's potential to block an offer.

A second explanation for the small stock price effect questions the actual, not the potential, effectiveness of a poison pill. Whether target management can rely on the mechanical terms of a poison pill to block a hostile bid depends on the legal rules governing its use. Suppose that the applicable legal rule allows target management to use a poison pill plan to delay a hostile bid while it searches for a more favorable offer, but ultimately requires that the pill be redeemed and shareholders be allowed to decide whether to accept the hostile offer. In that event, the poison pill would be the perfect defensive tactic: it could be used to increase shareholders' range of alternatives, but not to maintain the target company's independence over the objection of shareholders. As we will see in Section D of this Chapter, Delaware law (which covers a large proportion of the samples of all the studies) governing target directors' obligations in the face of a hostile bid was subject to just this interpretation (albeit with substantial uncertainty) over a three year period -- 1986 through 1989 -- which covered approximately one-half of all pill adoptions between 1983 and 1991.[73] To return to the earlier calculation of the likely effect of a poison pill, the possibility that the applicable legal rule limited the use of a pill to block an offer as opposed to securing a better alternative, may help account for the small negative returns reported by the empirical studies. Thus, the ultimate effectiveness of poison pill plans in either the entrenchment or shareholder interest sense depends on the terms of their legal regulation.

---

[72] *Id.* at 5.

[73] Comment & Schwert (1993), *supra* note 71, at 2 (Figure 1).

c.   *Deterrence: Dual Class Common Stock*

Dual class recapitalizations (prior to their prohibition by the SEC's adoption of Rule 19c-4) present the same empirical puzzle as poison pill plans: a conflict between the potential effectiveness of their deterrent and the absence of substantial negative abnormal returns associated with their announcement or adoption. Three studies have measured the stock price impact of the announcement and adoption of dual class transactions; all report no statistically significant abnormal returns.[74] An explanation for the absence of negative returns as a result of a transaction that gives target management (or a controlling shareholder block) the absolute power to block a hostile bid lies in the characteristics of the companies that effected such transactions; in some companies gains from fixing control in management offset the costs of eliminating the possibility of a hostile takeover.

Consider a company that suffers from a capital shortage because they are in an earlier stage of development, both in terms of the market in which they participate and in terms of their own organization.[75] Such companies are in markets that are growing quickly, so substantial additional capital investments are necessary to maintain or increase market share. Markets in the growth portion of their life cycles are also characterized by entrepreneurial companies which have only recently gone public (to raise expansion capital), the founding entrepreneurs of which still retain a controlling ownership stake. To use the jargon of the managerial literature surveyed in Chapter 9, companies in growing markets with large additional working capital needs are called "question marks."

Dominant shareholders of question mark companies face a dilemma. If they finance growth by further sales of an existing class of common stock, their control of the firm is diluted. But if they avoid dilution by purchasing enough new shares themselves to maintain their percentage ownership, they suffer an uncompensated increase in the unsystematic risk of their investment portfolio. In either event, financing growth imposes a cost on existing dominant shareholders that is not shared by public shareholders.

Engaging in a dual class transaction prior to raising additional equity allows a dominant shareholder group to secure capital for the company for positive net present value investments without forcing them to bear a disproportionate part of the cost. Such transactions would be approved by public shareholders not only because the dominant shareholder group already controls a large portion of the vote, but, more interestingly, also because at the question mark stage of a company's development the interests of the controlling and public shareholders are reasonably well aligned. The need

---

[74] Gregg Jarrell & Annette Poulsen, *Dual-Class Recapitalizations as Antitakeover Mechanisms*, 20 J.Fin.Econ. 129 (1988); Gordon (1988), *supra* note 24; Partch (1987), *supra* note 18.

[75] This analysis draws on Gilson (1987), *supra* note 16, at 816-32.

to maintain or increase market share in an expanding market gives target management sufficient incentive to run the firm efficiently.[76]

The question mark concept nicely explains the patterns reported for companies that undertake dual class capital recapitalizations. The companies typically already have a dominant shareholder group. Megan Partch reports that the companies in her sample of proposed dual class transactions were relatively young: half of the companies had been traded on an exchange or over-the-counter for less that 10 years, and some 27% had been traded for less that 5 years.[77] Consistent with the question mark concept, virtually all companies announced that a main purpose of the dual class transactions was to raise additional equity capital without diluting the dominant shareholder group's control. Moreover, the justification appears to be more than boilerplate. Partch reports that in the two years following the dual class transactions, 38.6% of the sample companies made public equity offerings of the class of stock with limited voting rights (or securities convertible into limited voting stock).

Finally, the question mark concept also explains the absence of positive abnormal returns when recapitalization transactions are announced. Gains from other changes in capital structure that result from concentrating ownership in a small group, particularly LBOs where the concentration of ownership is in the LBO association, result from eliminating the conflict of interest between managers and shareholders over the use of free cash flow.[78] In question mark companies, no such conflict is likely to exist because the market demands of the competitive environment already serve to align the interests of management and shareholders: they suffer from a capital deficit, not free cash flow, necessitated by the need to increase market share in a growing market. The gain from the dual class transaction -- the ability of the company to secure new capital without the dominant shareholder group having to bear a disproportionate amount of the costs --

---

[76] Although this explanation is also consistent with a management entrenchment motivation for the dual class capital structure, the role of the market for corporate control as a means by which management is disciplined is substantially reduced for question mark companies because a different market -- the product market for the good or service that the company produces -- provides an equivalent discipline. Thus, when the product market operates to align the interests of management and shareholders, the role of the market for corporate control is correspondingly reduced. This suggests that the market for corporate control operates as a last ditch means for disciplining management. Only when other market disciplines fail is the market for corporate control triggered.

[77] Partch (1987), *supra* note 18. Partch's data and that of Jarrell & Poulsen (1988), *supra* note 18, also suggest that the companies in their samples were relatively successful. Companies in Partch's samples earned positive abnormal returns of 6.243% over the 90 days prior to their announcement of the dual class transactions. Measured over the entire year prior to 20 trading days before the recapitalization transaction, companies in the Jarrell and Poulsen sample earned abnormal returns of 44.6%.

[78] See Chapter 11, *supra*.

should be reflected in an increase in the value of control shares, not public shares. The market price of the preexisting single class of common stock, however, reflects the value of non-controlling shares,[79] so that, consistent with the data, the dual class transaction should have little impact on the trading value of public shares.[80]

2.   After the Offer

The empirical evidence bearing on the effectiveness of post-offer defensive tactics presents the same conflict as pre-offer tactics. Defensive tactics that frustrate an initial hostile offer but are followed by a successful second offer are effective in increasing the price shareholders receive. However, when a first offer is defeated and no second offer follows, defensive tactics are effective in maintaining target management in control, but at the cost of substantial losses (relative to the value of the defeated initial bid) to target shareholders.

a.   *Greenmail*

Greenmail -- target management paying a potential bidder to go away by repurchasing his shares at a premium -- is typically seen as the archetypal entrenching defensive tactic: management uses corporate funds to ensure that shareholders will not have the opportunity to receive a premium offer. However, other analyses suggest that greenmail can be effective in the alternative sense of increasing the price shareholders will receive in an offer. Andrei Shleifer and Robert Vishny develop a model in which the elimination of an initial bidder works to the advantage of shareholders by encouraging other bidders to incur the costs of investigating whether to make a bid.[81] The encouragement comes either by eliminating the initial bidder who would be seen by potential bidders as having an advantage over later entrants, or by signalling that target management's private information shows that the target will be worth more to other bidders.

Shleifer and Vishny's model does not, however, take into account the basic agency conflict between management and shareholders and, as a result, assumes away the basic quandary in evaluating the effectiveness of defensive tactics: Even if loyal management can use greenmail can serve to attract a

---

[79] See Ronald Lease, John McConnell & Wayne Mikkelson, *The Market Value of Differential Voting Rights in Closely Held Corporations*, 57 J.Bus. 443, 458, 466 (1984).

[80] For an empirical confirmation of this analysis of dual class recapitalizations, see Kenneth Lehn, Jeffry Netter & Annette Poulsen, *Consolidating Corporate Control: The Choice Between Dual-Class Recapitalizations and Leveraged Buyouts*, 27 J.Fin.Econ. 557 (1990).

[81] Shleifer & Vishny (1986), *supra* note 36.

competitive bid, less loyal management can still use it for entrenchment.[82] Which effect is dominant is an empirical question.

The initial round of greenmail studies supported the position that greenmail was predominantly an entrenching device. The first two studies found that target companies who repurchase the shares of potential offerers experience statistically significant *negative* abnormal returns of 2.37% in one study[83] and 2.85% in the other[84] over the three days surrounding announcement of the repurchase. A third study found statistically significant negative abnormal returns of 5.2% over the ten days surrounding repurchase.[85] In contrast, studies of the impact of general stock repurchase programs on a company's stock show substantial *positive* abnormal returns.[86] That the control issue puts target management in a position where its interests and those of the shareholders conflict is apparent; that management succumbs to the conflict when it engages in greenmail seemed supported by the empirical data.

This pattern was upset by a second generation of studies which call into question the conclusion that greenmail harms target shareholders. Clifford Holderness and Dennis Sheehan[87] and Wayne Mikkelson and Richard Ruback[88] both measured the abnormal returns associated with the greenmail process not just on the days surrounding announcement of the greenmail payment, but over the entire period from the date an investor announces that it has made a significant purchase of target company stock through the date the target company repurchases the stock. Both studies confirm the results of earlier studies in one respect: Target companies earn negative abnormal returns when they announce the payment of greenmail. A surprising result appears, however, when one examines the net returns over the entire period

---

[82] Other models of this sort make the same simplifying assumption. See, e.g., Elazar Berkovitch & Naveen Khanna, *How Target Shareholders Benefit from Value-Reducing Defensive Strategies in Takeovers*, 45 J.Fin. 137 (1990).

[83] Larry Dann & Harry DeAngelo, *Standstill Agreements, Privately Negotiated Stock Purchases, and the Market for Corporate Control*, 11 J.Fin.Econ. 275, 294 (1983).

[84] Michael Bradley & Larry Wakefield, *The Wealth Effect of Target Share Repurchases*, 11 J.Fin.Econ. 301, 308 (1983). The negative abnormal return increased to 5.51% when the sample was limited to repurchases that terminated a control contest. *Id.* at 311.

[85] Office of the Chief Economist, *The Impact of Targeted Share Repurchases (Greenmail) on Stock Prices* (Sept. 11, 1984) (Table 1). As did Bradley & Wakefield (1983), *supra* note 84, this study also reported that negative returns increased, to 6.8%, when the sample was limited to control contests.

[86] See, e.g., Ronald Masulis, *Stock Repurchase by Tender Offer: An Analysis of the Causes of Common Stock Price Changes*, 35 J.Fin. 305 (1981); Theo Vermaelen, *Common Stock Repurchases and Market Signalling: An Empirical Study*, 9 J.Fin.Econ. 139 (1981).

[87] Clifford Holderness & Dennis Sheehan, *Raiders or Saviors? The Evidence on Six Controversial Investors*, 14 J.Fin.Econ. 555 (1985).

[88] Wayne Mikkelson & Richard Ruback, *Corporate Investments in Common Stock*, (Sloan Sch. of Management, Working Paper No.1633-85, Mass.Inst. of Tech., Feb.1985).

from announcement of the investor's acquisition of target company stock to announcement of the repurchase.

Event	Holderness & Sheehan Abnormal Returns	Mikkelson & Ruback Abnormal Returns
Initial Stock Purchase	+4.1%[*]	+4.64%[*]
Intermediate Period	-0.4%	-1.40%
Greenmail Announcement	<u>-1.3%[*]</u>	<u>-2.29%[*]</u>
Net Return Over Period	+3.2%[*]	+1.69%[*]

[*] Statistically significant

These results seem to show that the negative abnormal returns associated with the payment of greenmail are more than offset by the positive abnormal returns associated with announcement of the initial investment. From this perspective, greenmail is effective in the sense of increasing the value of target company shares. However, the stability of these gains was questionable. Studies of target companies that successfully defeated hostile bids by any means showed that similar net gains were subsequently lost over the two years following the hostile bid's defeat if the company was not the subject of a successful takeover.[89] Why should greenmail, only one of a number of defensive tactics, show different results?

A third generation of greenmail studies confirm that greenmail has the same effect as other successful defensive tactics. If the defeated bid is not followed by a successful acquisition, the net gain that remains after the greenmail payment disappears.[90] Thus, some greenmail payments benefit shareholders (if they lead to a subsequent offer) and some greenmail payments entrench management (if they do not). One may argue that this result counsels against a blanket restriction of greenmail unless a way exists of distinguishing "good" greenmail from "bad" greenmail.[91] From this perspective, recall that Shleifer and Vishny's pro-greenmail argument is that

---

[89] Michael Bradley, Anand Desai & Han Kim, *The Rationale Behind Interfirm Tender Offers: Information or Synergy*, 11 J.Fin.Econ. 183 (1983).

[90] James Ang & Alan Tucker, *The Shareholder Wealth Effects of Corporate Greenmail*, 11 J.Fin.Res. 265 (1988); Wayne Mikkelson & Richard Ruback, *Targeted Repurchases and Common Stock*, (Working Paper, Univ. of Oregon, 1988); Sanjai Bhagat & Richard Jefferis, *Why Good Managers Pay Greenmail: The Economics of Target Share Repurchases*, (Univ. of Utah Sch. of Bus. Working Paper, Sept.1986).

[91] See Fred McChesney, *Transaction Costs and Corporate Greenmail: Theory, Empirics and Mickey Mouse Case Study*, 14 Management & Decision Econ. 131 (1993); John Macey & Fred McChesney, *A Theoretical Analysis of Corporate Greenmail*, 95 Yale L.J. 12 (1985).

greenmail can be an effective form of signal concerning target management's information. Could an alternative form of signalling, such as the use of the poison pill to buy time and the use of an investment bank to disseminate management's private information, serve the same purpose without providing disloyal management the opportunity to camouflage self-interested greenmail as a beneficial signal?

b.　*Litigation*

The limited empirical evidence concerning the effectiveness of litigation as a defensive tactic parallels that with respect to greenmail. Gregg Jarrell studied a sample of 89 targets of hostile bids who, following Herbert Wachtell's advice,[92] responded to the bid by filing suit against the bidder.[93] By now the empirical results should be predictable. In the approximately 80% of the time when the litigation resulted in a competitive bid, the final price received by shareholders was 17% higher than the initial bid. However, in the 20% of the time when the litigation resulted in the target remaining independent, the consequences to target shareholders were "disastrous."[94] Shareholders lose the average premium of 32% represented by the initial bid as well as the costs of the litigation.

Evaluating litigation as a defensive tactic would seem to depend on how it operates to attract a competitive bid. The most obvious effect is delay; this gives target management the opportunity to search out a white knight. As with greenmail, however, litigation runs the risk of misuse; target management also can use litigation to remain independent. After looking at the particular offers in which the target company remained independent, Jarrell concluded that it was "hard to justify management's actions" in terms of shareholder welfare, but cautioned against judging the tactic too harshly because the benefits to shareholders when litigation led to competitive bidding were so significant.[95] The problem, then, is whether one could achieve the benefits of delay without running the risk that management would use the opportunity to defeat all offers. Again, the poison pill presents an opportunity to distinguish between efforts to secure a competitive bid and to remain independent. So long as the pill is redeemed after an appropriate period of time, the chance of misuse is minimized.

---

[92] See Section A.2.a, *supra*.

[93] Gregg Jarrell, *The Wealth Effects of Litigation By Targets: Do Interests Diverge in a Merger?*, 28 J.L. & Econ. 151 (1985).

[94] *Id.* at 171.

[95] *Id.* at 172.

c.   *What Makes a Defensive Tactic Effective?*

Given the wide range of defensive tactics that have been proposed, the puzzle that remains is their general ineffectiveness: on average, only one out of five targets of hostile bids remain independent. From the perspective of a defensive planner, this persistent statistic focuses attention on what makes a defensive tactic effective, understanding effectiveness to mean success in keeping the target company independent.

Approaching the problem from this perspective necessitates shifting our attention from the target company's choice of tactics to the acquiring company's decision to proceed with the offer. An effective defensive tactic from target management's narrow perspective is, by definition, one that persuades the acquirer to change its mind. The key, then, is to somehow change the balance of factors bearing on the acquiring company's decision from one favoring proceeding with the transaction to one favoring retreat. And this, in turn, requires understanding why the offer was made in the first place.

We canvassed a variety of potential motivations for an acquisition in Part II; however, for present purposes a much more general formulation will suffice. Consider the following: A tender offer is made when the value to the acquiring company of the shares acquired exceeds the price paid plus transaction costs. Put in terms of a formula, a necessary condition for a hostile offer is that $V > P + TC$, where V = post transaction value to the acquiring company, P = price paid, and TC = transaction cost.[96] The benefit of this approach is clearly not its ability to predict when takeover bids will be made. Part II demonstrated the complexity of that subject and, in any event, the formula offers no explanation for *why* post-transaction value may be greater than the cost of the acquisition. Rather, its benefit is to provide a systematic way of thinking about what might make a defensive tactic effective. Unless the tactic in question can change the value of one of the components of the formula in the appropriate direction -- reduce V, or increase P or TC -- it should have no effect on the acquiring company's decision to proceed with the offer.

This approach to devising effective defensive tactics can best be understood by examining each component of the formula and the types of defensive tactics each suggests.

Post-transaction Value.   What kinds of defensive tactics have the potential for decreasing the post-transaction value of the target company to the acquiring company? Suppose the target knew that the acquiring company was relying upon a particular opportunity for synergy in its forecast of post-transaction value. If the target could demonstrate that the acquiring

---

[96] This is the condition commonly considered necessary to induce a takeover bid. See, e.g., Sanford Grossman & Oliver Hart, *Takeover Bids, the Free-Rider Problem, and the Theory of the Corporation*, 11 Bell J.Econ. 42 (1980).

company would not be able to capitalize on that opportunity after the transaction, the acquiring company's forecast of post-transaction value would decrease. If the decrease was sufficient to entirely eliminate the inequality necessary to induce the acquiring company to proceed with the transaction, the defensive tactic should then be successful.

A rather extreme defensive strategy of this sort was successfully used by Brunswick Corporation in fending off an unwanted takeover by Whittaker Corporation. Determining that the principle motivation for the Whittaker offer was to acquire Brunswick's Sherwood Medical Industries subsidiary, Brunswick simply sold Sherwood to another company.[97] Although the tactic was successful, it was not without cost to Brunswick. In the Brunswick Annual Report to Shareholders for the year immediately preceding that in which the Whittaker offer occurred, the Chairman of Brunswick's Board of Directors described the company's business plan as using its recreational business "as a source of cash flow to fund the growth of our medical [Sherwood Medical Industries] and technical operations." Thus, in order to remain independent, Brunswick was forced to sell, in terms of Chapter 9's product/market portfolio analysis, its "star."[98]

A less extreme version of this approach is usually credited to McGraw-Hill in its defense against an unwanted bid from American Express. There the idea was that McGraw-Hill was unusually dependent on its employees for profitability. In the publishing business, one commentator remarked, the assets go home very night at 5:00 P.M. Apparently with this in mind, McGraw-Hill unleashed a public relations campaign intended to demonstrate that American Express was unfit to operate the McGraw-Hill business by claiming that editorial responsibility would be eliminated, and that the integrity of McGraw-Hill publications would be compromised for the benefit of American Express. The target of the campaign was less McGraw-Hill shareholders than McGraw-Hill employees, and its object was to persuade American Express that, if it persisted with the offer, the number of employees who would quit as a result would substantially reduce McGraw-Hill's post-transaction value.[99]

In evaluating tactics intended to reduce the target's post-transaction value, a particular difficulty, bordering on a paradox, must be kept in mind. For the defensive tactic really to be effective, the reduction in post-transaction value must be permanent. The acquiring company would

---

[97] See Whittaker Corp. v. Edgar, 535 F.Supp. 933 (N.D.Ill.), *aff'd mem.* (7th Cir.1982).

[98] For detailed histories of the Brunswick-Whittaker battle, see Arthur Fleischer & Raymond, *Developments in Defensive Tactics to Tender Offers: A Study of the Whittaker-Brunswick Bid,* 5 J.Comp.Bus. & Cap.Mkt.L. 97 (1983); John Thackray, *The Battle of Brunswick,* Institutional Investor 73 (June 1982).

[99] For example, one of the McGraw-Hill businesses rated the credit worthiness of municipal bonds while American Express was a major investor in such bonds (employing the "float" generated by its traveler's checks operations). See Gurwin (1979), *supra* note 2.

have no reason to adjust downward the post-transaction value component of its decision calculus as a result of a defensive tactic if the tactic could be reversed, and the original post-transaction value restored, once the acquiring company obtained control of the target. To be effective, the decline in value must therefore be irreversible. The problem with an irreversible tactic, however, is that unless its effect is specific to the acquiring company, the value of the target company will remain reduced even if the acquiring company is successfully deterred. In this regard, was the defensive tactic used by Brunswick or by McGraw-Hill more successful?

Transaction Costs. Put simply, a defensive tactic that increases the acquiring company's transaction costs causes the acquiring company to expend more money, thereby decreasing the potential for gain from the transaction. Litigation by the target company is a good example. It was reported that the total costs associated with Occidental Petroleum's unsuccessful offer for Mead Corp. were in excess of $15 million. Similarly, the professional fees alone -- for lawyers, accountants, investment bankers, proxy solicitors and public relations representatives -- incurred by the three parties in the battle between McDermott, Inc. and Wheelabrator-Frye, Inc. for Pullman, Inc., amounted to $17 million.[100] Putting a value on the time acquiring company management is forced to spend on the litigation -- having their depositions taken, conferring with their own lawyers, distracting them from daily operations -- would substantially increase the totals.

It should be noted, however, that litigation, as with most defensive efforts to interpose third party regulators like courts and administrative agencies as a barrier to the takeover, is likely to cost the target company at least as much as the acquiring company. This suggests that the cost-benefit analysis undertaken by the target company in its decision whether to pursue the tactic must be somewhat skewed. If the tactic proves unsuccessful there is no cost to the target; in that event, the takeover succeeds and the acquiring company ends up paying the bill.[101] Only if the tactic is successful is the cost borne by the target company and the question then is whether the benefits of remaining independent are worth the costs. Here the question gets sticky, however, because the answer may be quite different depending on *whose* costs and benefits are considered. If management is allowed to take into account only its own costs and benefits, the analysis and the resulting decisions will be predictably biased: Management gets the benefits of remaining independent while shareholders bear the cost. Thus,

---

[100] *Outside Professionals Play an Increasing Role in Corporate Takeovers,* Wall St.J., Dec. 2, 1980, at 1, col.6.

[101] If the acquiring company really was willing to spend more to acquire the target, the additional amounts paid as transaction costs could have gone to target shareholders. Although from the acquiring company's perspective the two types of costs -- P and TC -- are fungible, from the target shareholders' perspective there is a critical difference in that increases in P go to the shareholders while increases in TC go to the lawyers and investment bankers.

whether target management must include shareholders' concern in its decision making is critical to what decision will be made. This issue, which depends heavily on the legal standards governing target management conduct in hostile takeovers, is considered in detail later in Section D of this Chapter.

In thinking about how to impose additional transaction costs on the acquiring company, it is important to recognize that the impact of some of the most significant, and therefore potentially most destructive, transaction costs are not necessarily easy to quantify in dollar terms. For example, it is widely believed that a court decision -- requiring Anderson Clayton to make detailed disclosure concerning questionable foreign payments before it would be allowed to proceed with its offer for Gerber Products Company -- was the reason the offer was withdrawn.[102]   If disclosure would interfere with the conduct of Anderson Clayton's foreign business, or open it to prosecution in foreign jurisdictions for the disclosed activities, the transaction costs of the takeover would be substantially increased.[103]   Similarly, embarrassment, particularly of acquiring company management, can also be a significant transaction cost. The continued disclosure of unfavorable information about Armand Hammer, the Chairman of Occidental Petroleum, is often credited with that company's decision to withdraw its offer for Mead Petroleum.[104]

Price. The effect of a tactic that increases the market price of the target company's shares relative to the tender offer price is to reduce the premium offered target shareholders. This will decrease the attractiveness of the transaction to target shareholders and might require an increase in the offered price for the takeover to succeed. An increased price, of course, would unfavorably alter the acquiring company's offering calculus.

Commentators have made a number of suggestions as to how target companies might act to increase their stock price.[105]   One is for the target company to repurchase its own stock. On closer inspection, however, the tactic seems to have a substantial possibility of backfiring. Although a reduction in the number of outstanding shares by repurchase should increase the price of the remaining shares, the total cost of the acquisition should not change because the number of shares outstanding has decreased. Indeed, if the acquiring company has a pre-existing investment in the target company, the tactic likely *reduces* the total cost of the transaction. Assume that a target company has one million shares outstanding which trade at $10 per share, and that the acquiring company already owns 100,000 shares and would like to acquire 400,000 more (a 50% position). If the additional

---

[102] See Berman v. Gerber Products Co., 454 F.Supp. 1310 (W.D.Mich.1978).

[103] Put differently, the post-transaction value of Anderson Clayton's existing business would be reduced.

[104] See Gurwin (1979), *supra* note 2.

[105] If there were easy ways to increase the price of the target's stock, why would a hostile offer be required before they were implemented?

shares could be purchased at the $10 market price, the total cost to raise the acquiring company's position to 50% would be $400,000. Now assume that target management decides to raise its share price to discourage the offer and, to accomplish this, repurchases half its outstanding stock. In that event, the market price of the remaining shares presumably would double. The total cost of the acquisition, however, would *fall*. As a result of the repurchase, the number of shares the acquiring company must purchase to secure the desired 50% has been reduced from 400,000 to 150,000 (assuming the acquiring company did not sell any of its pre-existing holdings). Although the per share price of these shares has doubled, the number of shares that must be purchased has been reduced by more than one-half, resulting in a decrease in the total cost of acquiring control from $400,000 to $300,000. The target company has simply helped finance its own acquisition.[106]

Overview. The lesson to be learned from this discussion is that there are *not* generally available, easily implemented, off-the-rack defensive tactics that have the promise of success. In order for a defensive tactic to have a significant chance of working, it must be carefully created with a view to the particular motivation of the acquiring company in making the offer. And it must be recognized that there is a substantial danger that any tactic capable of significantly influencing the offerer's decision calculus also will have a substantial, if not identical, impact on the target. In sum, the statistics concerning the success of defensive tactics described at the outset of this section are surprising only in two unanticipated respects: first, that the number of successful defenses is as high as 20%; and second, that defensive tactics remain so common despite their low probability of success. Evaluation of the latter point requires an understanding of the legal standards governing management conduct in hostile takeovers. If, for example, the costs of defense were borne by target shareholders, but the benefits of a successful defense reaped only by target management, the frequency to which defensive tactics were resorted might not be surprising even though the effort is not often successful.

C.   The Bidder's Perspective: Discouraging Competitive Bids

From the hostile bidder's perspective, the target company's defensive effort to remain independent is only one of the two bad things that can

---

[106] As pointed out by Nathan & Sobel (1981), *supra*, a defensive repurchase may be effective when management already owns a sufficient number of shares that, after the repurchase, they can themselves prevent the hostile offer's success. In the example in the text, if management held 250,001 shares at the outset and did not sell any of their shares in repurchase, they would own one share more than 50% of the outstanding shares after the offer, just enough to prevent the offer from ever being made.

happen in response to its offer. The second is the appearance of a competitive bidder, either on its own accord or in response to the target company's active efforts to find a higher bid or a more compatible acquirer -- a white knight in takeover parlance. This section considers the difficult position of a hostile bidder who seeks to reduce the likelihood of a competing bid that, at worst, will capture the prize and, in any event, will surely raise the price.

Precisely because the bidder is hostile, the only element of the transaction that is under its sole control is the structure of its bid. The problem is to identify what elements of a bid most effectively reduce the likelihood that a competing bid could be successful and, therefore, most effectively reduce the likelihood that one will be made.

From the hostile bidder's perspective, the most critical strategic element -- in contrast to substantive matters such as the price offered and the number of shares sought -- is speed. A competitive bid takes time to develop. However willing the target company may be to entertain an alternative transaction, a white knight must first be found, some investigation of the target by that company will still be necessary, some negotiation with the target (even if only over the terms of a lock-up) must still take place, and financing for the transaction must still be arranged. If the hostile bidder can structure its offer so that target shareholders must decide to tender *before* a competitive bid can be arranged, a substantial advantage will be secured. This is not to say that, in evaluating the hostile bid, target shareholders will not take into account the possibility that a more favorable bid may be forthcoming if the hostile bid is rejected. Indeed, in such a situation target company management likely will have disclosed that it is actively soliciting an alternative transaction. But for target shareholders, the difference between the *certainty* of a competitive bid and only the *possibility* of one is substantial.

Suppose a hostile bid has been made at a price of $25 per share when the target company's stock is trading at $15 per share. All other things equal, if a competing bid over $25 per share is made before the target shareholders must respond to the initial hostile bid, the competing bid will succeed. More is simply more. But the nature of the target shareholders' decision changes markedly if they have to respond to the initial hostile bid before they know with certainty whether and on what terms a competitive bid will be made. If the target shareholders believe there is only a 50% probability that a competitive bid ultimately will be made, at what price would they have to believe the uncertain competitive bid would be made, if in fact it was made, to be more attractive than the certain hostile offer?

If for ease of exposition we ignore complications like the time value of money over the presumably longer period before payment would be made pursuant to the anticipated competing bid and whether target shareholders are risk averse, the expected value of not tendering in the hostile offer can be expressed as

Expected Value of
Not Tendering $= (\text{Prob}_{NB} \cdot P_{NB}) + (\text{Prob}_{CB} \cdot P_{CB})$

where

Prob_{NB}	= the probability that no competitive bid will be made.
P_{NB}	= the original market price of target company stock.[107]
Prob_{CB}	= the probability that a competitive bid will be made.
P_{CB}	= the expected price of the competitive bid.

Since we are interested in knowing the price at which a competitive bid would have to be made for the expected value of not tendering to exceed the $25 value of the hostile bid, we can set the expected value at $26 and solve the equation for P_{CB}:

$$\$26 = (\text{Prob}_{NB} \cdot P_{NB}) + (\text{Prob}_{CB} \cdot P_{CB})$$
$$\$26 = (.5 \times \$15) + (.5 \times P_{CB})$$
$$\$26 = \$7.50 + .5\, P_{CB}$$
$$\$18.50 = .5\, P_{CB}$$
$$\$37 = P_{CB}$$

Thus, in our example, target shareholders would have to believe that a competitive bid, *if made,* would be at a price of at least $37 per share before they would be better off by rejecting the hostile bid on the 50% probability that a competitive bid would be made. Sensitivity analysis[108] can be used to understand the impact on the calculation of changes in the probability assigned to the competitive bid.

Individual target shareholders need not, however, undertake the difficult and time-consuming process of gathering the information and developing the skills necessary to make such detailed predictions concerning the likelihood and price of a potential competitive bid. Sophisticated investors, such as arbitrageurs and institutions, would make these forecasts which would then be reflected in the price of the target's stock by means of the professionally informed trading mechanism discussed in Chapter 5.[109]   All an

---

[107] The assumption is that the value of the target's stock will drop back to its pre-offer price if the hostile offer is defeated and no competitive offer arises. This is consistent with existing empirical studies that find unsuccessful offers result in no permanent revaluation of the target company. See Chapter 14, *supra*. For ease of exposition, the hypothetical assumes that this happens quite quickly, although this assumption is not consistent with the data.

[108] See Chapter 6A, *supra*.

[109] Examples of circumstances where the market's anticipation of a competitive bid was reflected in the price of the target company's stock prior to its being made are commonplace. For example, on March 11, 1981, Seagram's made a $45 per share tender offer for St. Joe Minerals, which had traded at $28 a share immediately prior to announcement of the Seagram bid. The day after the Seagram's bid, the price of St. Joe stock rose to $49, which was attributed to arbitrageurs' belief that a competitive bid would be forthcoming. N.Y.Times, Mar. 12, 1981, at D1, col.6; *id.*, Mar. 13, 1981, at D3, col.5.

unsophisticated shareholder has to know is whether the market price of the target's shares is higher than the hostile bid.

The upshot is that speed is the hostile bidder's greatest ally. In the absence of any regulation, the hostile bidder would structure its offer so that it was open for only the minimum length of time necessary to secure the required number of target shares. Not surprisingly, this was precisely the type of offer typically made when, prior to the passage of the Williams Act, there was no regulation of the terms of the offerer's bid. After the passage of the Williams Act, however, the problem of structuring the hostile bidder's offer so as to minimize the likelihood of a competitive bid became more complicated.

The Williams Act, which will be the subject of our attention in Chapter 18, imposes significant restrictions on a hostile bidder's freedom to structure its offer in a manner designed to minimize the likelihood of a competitive bid. In addition to requiring that the hostile bidder make significant disclosure concerning its offer, the Williams Act also tries to reduce the pressure on target shareholders to make up their minds, the idea being that the information required to be disclosed is of little value if shareholders do not have the time to evaluate it. This regulatory goal is currently reflected in restrictions on three important elements of a bid's structure. First, SEC Rule 14e-1(a) requires that an offer remain open a minimum of 20 business days. Second, in the case of an offer for less than all of a target company's outstanding shares, Rule 14d-8 requires that when more shares are tendered than will be purchased, they must be taken up pro rata rather than, for example, on a first-come, first-served basis. Third, Rule 14d-7(a)(1) allows shareholders to withdraw their tenders during the first 15 business days of the offer. All time periods are extended by 10 business days if a competing bid is made. These restrictions are ostensibly designed to give target shareholders an opportunity to evaluate the information concerning the offer disclosed by the hostile bidder. This function, however, is discharged quite quickly in an efficient market and the evaluation is reflected in the price of the target's stock. More important, the restrictions also give the target company the time to seek out a competing bid, and, as a result, make formulating a bidding strategy a quite complex task.

Lawrence Lederman[110] provides an example that illustrates the problem. Assume that on June 1st an acquiring company ("Acquirer") makes a two-step, front-end loaded offer for a target company ("Target") whose shares, prior to the offer, were trading at $15 per share. Further assume that Target's management holds 15% of Target's shares, and that Acquirer has purchased 5% of Target's shares in market transactions before the offer. The offer's first step seeks 1,500,000 of the Target's 3,000,000 outstanding shares (50%) at $30 per share. The second step will be a freeze-out merger

---

[110] Lawrence Lederman, *Tender Offer Bidding Strategy,* 17 Rev.Sec.Reg. 917 (1984). Some of the numbers in the Lederman example have been altered here.

in which the remaining target shareholders will receive securities valued at $20 per share. The average price of both steps of the offer is thus $25 per share. The importance of the two-tier structure of Acquirer's offer for our purposes becomes apparent when we consider its impact on a potential white knight.

Assume, not unrealistically, that it takes 15 calendar days for Target to locate a company ("White Knight") willing to make a competitive bid and an additional 5 days to work out the details of the bid. So, on June 20th, White Knight bids $27 per share for all of Target's outstanding stock. The competitive bid exceeds the average price of Acquirer's two-tier bid by $2 per share and, it seems, should win. However, despite the fact that it is only the SEC rules restricting the structure of Acquirer's bid that allow the time for a competitive bid to be made at all, the actual operation of these rules leaves open the possibility that Acquirer may still prevail even in the face of White Knight's higher bid.

Under the rules, Acquirer can purchase shares under its hostile offer six days before White Knight can purchase shares under its competing offer.[111] This creates an interesting situation if arbitrageurs and other sophisticated investors have come to hold a substantial percentage of Target's shares.

For sophisticated investors, the critical issue in evaluating the competing bids is not the average price under Acquirer's two-step offer, which is computed on the assumption that all shares are tendered in the first-step and taken up pro-rata, but the price they can actually expect to receive in the first-step based on the particular facts of the transaction. In our hypothetical, it can be assumed that Target management's 15%, Acquirer's 5%, and -- because of ignorance or inertia -- at least 10% of the remaining outstanding shares, will not be tendered in the first-step offer. The impact of the fact that each of these categories of shares will not be tendered on the price paid to those who do tender and, as a result, on the *real* average price of the transaction, is shown in the table below.

If sophisticated investors believe that only 2,100,000 shares will be tendered in the first-step transaction -- that is, in addition to Acquirer and Target Management, holders of 10% of Target's outstanding shares also will not tender -- then the relevant price to be compared with White Knight's competitive bid changes. For this purpose, the value of Acquirer's offer is not $25 per share, but $27.14 per share. The result is that Acquirer's offer will succeed even though it yields less in total than White Knight's offer.

---

[111] The effect of White Knight's offer was to extend Acquirer's withdrawal date (and the expiration and proration dates) until July 5th, which allows Acquirer to begin purchasing shares under its offer on July 6th. White Knight, however, cannot begin to purchase shares under its offer until its withdrawal period -- 15 business days -- ends on July 12th. Note that because the proration period for a partial offer extends for the entire period of the offer, a minimum of 20 days, an offer for all shares normally has a time advantage over a partial offer. Purchasing can commence under an offer for all outstanding shares as soon as the withdrawal period ends, a minimum of 5 days before the proration period ends in a partial offer.

How could White Knight overcome Acquirer's advantage? The easiest approach would be to structure its competitive bid on a two-tier basis as well. If White Knight offered $34 per share for half of Target's shares in the first round, and $20 per share for the remainder in the second round, the relevant comparison for sophisticated investors would then be between the real values of both first steps. For White Knight's competitive bid, that value would be $28.23, assuming that Target management does tender in the first-step and that, consistent with our analysis of Acquirer's bid, Acquirer and the holders of an additional 10% of Target's stock do not tender their shares. Moreover, White Knight's first-step transaction could be made even more attractive to sophisticated investors if Target management agreed to sell its shares to White Knight directly at $27 per share, the hypothetical average value of the offer. This would have the result of reducing the number of shares tendered in the first-step by an additional 450,000 and increasing the real average value to $30 per share.

Number of Shares Tendered in First-Step Transaction	Shares not Tendered	Pro-Rata Percent-age	Per Share Value of First-Step Transaction ($30 x (3))	Per Share Value of Second-Step Transaction ($20 x 1-(3))	Real Average Per Share Price (4 + 5)
3,000,000	0	50%	$15.00	$10.00	$25.00
2,850,000	150,000 (Acquirer's Shares)	52.63%	$15.79	$9.47	$25.26
2,400,000	600,000 (Acquirer and Manage-ment's Shares)	62.5%	$18.75	$7.50	$26.35
2,100,000	900,000 (Acquirer and Manage-ment's Shares plus 10% non-tendering)	71.43%	$21.43	$5.71	$27.14

At this point it is useful to examine the two critical elements of the front-end loaded, two-tier structure that makes it effective in a competitive bidding situation. First, in the case of an initial bid, it increases the time pressure by increasing the risk associated with waiting for a competitive offer to develop. If both ends of the offer were at the same price, waiting to see if a competitive bid developed would be virtually costless;[112]   if a competitive bid was not forthcoming, the shareholder would still receive the same price as if he had tendered in the first round. Second, the technique operates to allow the bidder to favor sophisticated investors over unsophisticated investors. In our examples, the front-end loaded, two-tier structure did not change the total value of the offer. Rather, it merely transferred a portion of the first-step premium from those who did not tender, presumably through ignorance or lack of time, to sophisticated investors who did tender.

Three developments have significantly limited a hostile bidder's ability to speed up its offer to reduce the likelihood of a competitive bid. First, market infrastructure developed to support the market for corporate control that greatly reduced the time necessary to find and secure financing for a competitive bid. Investment banks, commercial banks and potential bidders all developed the expertise to act much more quickly.

Second, the SEC eliminated one of the benefits of speed. Prior to December 1982, only those shares tendered in the first 10 days of a partial offer were required to be taken up pro-rata. The SEC then amended Rule 14d-8 to require pro-rata purchases of shares tendered in a partial offer for the entire period the offer is open -- a minimum of 20 days. Thus, the period during which a target shareholder could costlessly wait to see if a competitive bid developed was extended to 20 days, a length that, given the development of sophisticated control market infrastructure, substantially limited the advantages available from bid structure.[113]

Finally, and most important, the popularity of poison pills essentially eliminated a bidder's ability to influence the speed with which target shareholders had to respond to its bid. As we will see in the next section, the law is clear that a target company can keep its poison pill in place for a substantial period -- far longer than SEC rules required the bidder to leave open its offer -- while it searches for a higher bid.

That leaves only one other element of the bid structure that can influence the likelihood of a competitive bid: price. Here the issue is whether a higher initial bid can make it less attractive for a potential bidder. The idea is that the price of the initial bidder's offer signals something about its valuation of the target to potential bidders. Assume that making a bid is

---

[112] There would be a cost associated with waiting to be paid until the second-step transaction occurs if a competitive bid were not forthcoming.

[113] The impact of the change seemed to be immediate. As part of the SEC's study of the Advisory Committee on Tender Offer's 1984 recommendations, the Office of the Chief Economist studied the relative premia on 91 any-or-all offers, two-tier offers and partial offers occurring in the 1981-1983 period. For the sample as a whole, the data suggested that two-tier and partial bids were successful at discouraging competition, with premiums highest in any-or-all bids (63.4%), followed by two-tier bids (55.1%) and partial offers (31.3%). However, if one looks only at 1983 offers -- those occurring after the SEC lengthened the proration period -- the relationship disappears: two-tier premia averaged 66.4%; any-or-all offers averaged 49.6%; and partial offers averaged 49.4%.

costly. Further assume that a potential bidder believes the target could be acquired at a premium between 10% and 40%, and that both the initial and the potential bidder would be willing to pay a 25% premium. If the initial bid is at a 10% premium, the potential bidder would think that the initial bidder had a relatively low valuation of the target, so that the likelihood of the potential bidder entering and winning was high enough to cover the costs of bidding. If the initial bid is instead at 20%, the potential bidder has to assess the likelihood that the bid would be as high as 20 if the initial bidder did not value the target at more than 25. The higher the initial bid, the more likely the initial bidder's valuation is higher than that of the potential bidder, and the more likely that the expected return on the potential bidder's cost is negative.[114]

D. Legal Standards Governing the Use of Defensive Tactics

Courts have struggled with a standard for reviewing management efforts to block a hostile tender offer since takeovers appeared in their modern incarnation in the 1960s. Corporate law provided two general standards of review of management conduct: the business judgment rule which applied to claims that management violated its duty of care; and the intrinsic fairness test which applied to claims that management violated its duty of loyalty. Neither traditional standard easily fit behavior that implicates both management's business acumen and its loyalty. On the one hand, evaluating the desirability of a proposed transaction, mapping out the best negotiating strategy, and calculating the transaction's likely tax effects on different groups of shareholders, are just the kind of decisions that the business judgment rule should largely protect from judicial review. But application of the business judgment rule would sanction virtually all defensive conduct. On the other hand, target management faces an inherent conflict of interest in evaluating a proposed change in control. While the hostile bid may be favorable to shareholders, blocking it may serve to maintain management in their positions. The decision to deploy defensive tactics thus resembles an interested transaction that calls for review under the intrinsic fairness standard. But invoking this rigorous standard would condemn virtually all defensive tactics. Thus, from the outset, judicial review of defensive tactics posed questions concerning the respective roles of management, shareholders and courts that the traditional structure of corporate law did not easily accommodate.

---

[114] See Michael Fishman, *A Theory of Pre-emptive Takeover Bidding*, 19 Rand J.Econ. 88 (1988); Michael Fishman, *Preemptive Bidding and the Role of the Medium of Exchange in Acquisitions*, 44 J.Fin. 41 (1989).

1.   The Early Doctrine: Policy Conflict/Primary Purpose

CHEFF v. MATHES
199 A.2d 548 (Del.1964)

CAREY, Justice.   This is an appeal from the decision of the Vice-Chancellor in a derivative suit holding certain directors of Holland Furnace Company liable for loss allegedly resulting from improper use of corporate funds to purchase shares of the company. . . .

Holland Furnace Company, a corporation of the State of Delaware, manufactures warm air furnaces, air conditioning equipment, and other home heating equipment. At the time of the relevant transactions, the board of directors was composed of the seven individual defendants. Mr. Cheff had been Holland's Chief Executive Officer since 1933, received an annual salary of $77,400, and personally owned 6,000 shares of the company. He was also a director. Mrs. Cheff, the wife of Mr. Cheff, was a daughter of the founder of Holland and had served as a director since 1922. She personally owned 5,804 shares of Holland and owned 47.9% of Hazelbank United Interest, Inc. Hazelbank is an investment vehicle for Mrs. Cheff and members of the Cheff-Landwehr family group, which owned 164,950 shares of the 883,585 outstanding shares of Holland. As a director, Mrs. Cheff received a compensation of $200.00 for each monthly board meeting, whether or not she attended the meeting.

The third director, Edgar P. Landwehr, is the nephew of Mrs. Cheff and personally owned 24,010 shares of Holland and 8.6% of the outstanding shares of Hazelbank. He received no compensation from Holland other than the monthly director's fee.

Robert H. Trenkamp is an attorney who first represented Holland in 1946. In May 1953, he became a director of Holland and acted as general counsel for the company. During the period in question, he received no retainer from the company, but did receive substantial sums for legal services rendered the company. Apart from the above-described payments, he received no compensation from Holland other than the monthly director's fee. He owned 200 shares of Holland Furnace stock. Although he owned no shares of Hazelbank, at the time relevant to this controversy, he was serving as a director and counsel of Hazelbank.

John D. Ames was then a partner in the Chicago investment firm of Bacon, Whipple & Co. and joined the board at the request of Mr. Cheff. During the periods in question, his stock ownership varied between ownership of no shares to ownership of 300 shares. He was considered by the other members of the Holland board to be the financial advisor to the board. He received no compensation from Holland other than the normal director's fee.

Mr. Ralph G. Boalt was the Vice President of J.R. Watkins Company, a manufacturer and distributor of cosmetics. In 1953, at the request of Mr. Cheff, he became a member of the board of directors. Apart from the normal director's fee, he received no compensation from Holland for his services.

Mr. George Spatta was the President of Clark Equipment Company, a large manufacturer of earth moving equipment. In 1951, at the request of Mr. Cheff, he joined the board of directors of Holland. Apart from the normal director's fee, he received no compensation from the company.

The board of directors of Hazelbank included the five principal shareholders: Mrs. Cheff; Leona Kolb, who was Mrs. Cheff's daughter; Mr. Landwehr; Mrs. Bowles, who was Mr. Landwehr's sister; Mrs. Putnam, who was also Mr. Landwehr's sister; Mr. Trenkamp; and Mr. William DeLong, an accountant.

Prior to the events in question, Holland employed approximately 8,500 persons and maintained 400 branch sales offices located in 43 states. The volume of sales had declined from over $41,000,000 in 1948 to less than $32,000,000 in 1956. Defendants contend that the decline in earnings is attributable to the artificial post-war demand generated in the 1946-1948 period. In order to stabilize the condition of the company, the sales department apparently was reorganized and certain unprofitable branch offices were closed. By 1957 this reorganization had been completed and the management was convinced that the changes were manifesting beneficial results. The practice of the company was to directly employ the retail salesman, and the management considered that practice -- unique in the furnace business -- to be a vital factor in the company's success.

During the first five months of 1957, the monthly trading volume of Holland's stock on the New York Stock Exchange ranged between 10,300 shares to 24,200 shares. In the last week of June 1957, however, the trading increased to 37,800 shares, with a corresponding increase in the market price. In June of 1957, Mr. Cheff met with Mr. Arnold H. Maremont, who was President of Maremont Automotive Products, Inc. and Chairman of the boards of Motor Products Corporation and Allied Paper Corporation. Mr. Cheff testified, on deposition, that Maremont generally inquired about the feasibility of merger between Motor Products and Holland. Mr. Cheff testified that, in view of the difference in sales practices between the two companies, he informed Mr. Maremont that a merger did not seem feasible. In reply, Mr. Maremont stated that, in the light of Mr. Cheff's decision, he had no further interest in Holland nor did he wish to buy any of the stock of Holland.

None of the members of the board apparently connected the interest of Mr. Maremont with the increased activity of Holland stock. However, Mr. Trenkamp and Mr. Staal, the Treasurer of Holland, unsuccessfully made an informal investigation in order to ascertain the identity of the purchaser or purchasers. The mystery was resolved, however, when Maremont called Ames in July of 1957 to inform the latter that Maremont then owned 55,000 shares of Holland stock. At this juncture, no requests for change in corporate policy were made, and Maremont made no demand to be made a member of the board of Holland.

Ames reported the above information to the board at its July 30, 1957 meeting. Because of the position now occupied by Maremont, the board elected to investigate the financial and business history of Maremont and corporations controlled by him. Apart from the documentary evidence produced by this investigation, which will be considered infra, Staal testified, on deposition, that "leading bank officials" had indicated that Maremont "had been a participant, or had attempted to be, in the liquidation of a number of companies." Staal specifically mentioned only one individual giving such advice, the Vice President of the First National Bank of Chicago. Mr. Cheff testified, at trial, of Maremont's alleged participation in liquidation activities. Mr. Cheff testified that: "Throughout the whole of the Kalamazoo-Battle Creek area, and Detroit too, where I spent considerable time, he is well known and not highly regarded by any stretch." This information was communicated to the board.

On August 23, 1957, at the request of Maremont, a meeting was held between Mr. Maremont and Cheff. At this meeting, Cheff was informed that Motor Products then owned approximately 100,000 shares of Holland stock. Maremont then made a demand that he be named to the board of directors, but Cheff refused to consider it. Since considerable controversy has been generated by Maremont's alleged threat to liquidate the company or substantially alter the sales force of Holland, we believe it desirable to set forth the testimony of Cheff on this point: "Now we have 8,500 men, direct employees, so the problem is entirely different. He indicated immediately that he had no interest in that type of distribution, that he didn't think it was modern, that he felt furnaces could be sold as he sold mufflers, through half a dozen salesmen in a wholesale way."

Testimony was introduced by the defendants tending to show that substantial unrest was present among the employees of Holland as a result of the threat of Maremont to seek control of Holland. Thus, Mr. Cheff testified that the field organization was considering leaving in large numbers because of a fear of the consequences of a Maremont acquisition; he further testified that approximately "25 of our key men" were lost as the result of the unrest engendered by the Maremont proposal. Staal, corroborating Cheff's version, stated that a number of branch managers approached him for reassurances that Maremont was not going to be allowed to successfully gain control. Moreover, at approximately this time, the company was furnished with a Dun and Bradstreet report, which indicated the practice of Maremont to achieve quick profits by sales or liquidations of companies acquired by him. The defendants were also supplied with an income statement of Motor Products, Inc., showing a loss of $336,121.00 for the period in 1957.

On August 30, 1957, the board was informed by Cheff of Maremont's demand to be placed upon the board and of Maremont's belief that the retail sales organization of Holland was obsolete. The board was also informed of the results of the investigation by Cheff and Staal. Predicated upon this

information, the board authorized the purchase of company stock on the market with corporate funds, ostensibly for use in a stock option plan.

Subsequent to this meeting, substantial numbers of shares were purchased and, in addition, Mrs. Cheff made alternate personal purchase of Holland stock. As a result of purchases by Maremont, Holland and Mrs. Cheff, the market price rose. On September 13, 1957, Maremont wrote to each of the directors of Holland and requested a broad engineering survey to be made for the benefit of all stockholders. During September, Motor Products released its annual report, which indicated that the investment in Holland was a "special situation" as opposed to the normal policy of placing the funds of Motor Products into "an active company". On September 4th, Maremont proposed to sell his current holdings of Holland to the corporation for $14.00 a share. However, because of delay in responding to this offer, Maremont withdrew the offer. At this time, Mrs. Cheff was obviously quite concerned over the prospect of a Maremont acquisition, and had stated her willingness to expend her personal resources to prevent it.

On September 30, 1957, Motor Products Corporation, by letter to Mrs. Bowles, made a buy-sell offer to Hazelbank. At the Hazelbank meeting of October 3, 1957, Mrs Bowles presented the letter to the board. The board took no action, but referred the proposal to its finance committee. Although Mrs. Bowles and Mrs. Putnam were opposed to any acquisition of Holland stock by Hazelbank, Mr. Landwehr conceded that a majority of the board were in favor of the purchase. Despite this fact, the finance committee elected to refer the offer to the Holland board on the grounds that it was the primary concern of Holland.

Thereafter, Mr. Trenkamp arranged for a meeting with Maremont, which occurred on October 14-15, 1957, in Chicago. Prior to this meeting, Trenkamp was aware of the intentions of Hazelbank and Mrs. Cheff to purchase all or portions of the stock then owned by Motor Products if Holland did not so act. As a result of the meeting, there was a tentative agreement on the part of Motor Products to sell its 155,000 shares at $14.40 per share. On October 23, 1957, at a special meeting of the Holland board, the purchase was considered. All directors, except Spatta,[1] were present. The dangers allegedly posed by Maremont were again reviewed by the board. Trenkamp and Mrs. Cheff agreed that the latter informed the board that either she or Hazelbank would purchase part or all of the block of Holland stock owned by Motor Products if the Holland board did not so act. The board was also informed that in order for the corporation to finance the purchase, substantial sums would have to be borrowed from commercial lending institutions. A resolution authorizing the purchase of 155,000 shares from Motor Products was adopted by the board. The price paid was in excess of the market price prevailing at the time, and the book value of the

---

[1] Spatta agreed by telephone.

stock was approximately $20.00 as compared to approximately $14.00 for the net quick asset value. The transaction was subsequently consummated. The stock option plan mentioned in the minutes has never been implemented. In 1959, Holland stock reached a high of $15.25 a share.

On February 6, 1958, plaintiffs, owners of 60 shares of Holland stock, filed a derivative suit in the court below naming all of the individual directors of Holland, Holland itself and Motor Products Corporation as defendants. The complaint alleged that all of the purchases of stock by Holland in 1957 were for the purpose of insuring the perpetuation of control by the incumbent directors. The complaint requested that the transaction between Motor Products and Holland be rescinded and, secondly, that the individual defendants account to Holland for the alleged damages. Since Motor Products was never served with process, the initial remedy became inapplicable. Ames was never served nor did he enter an appearance.

After trial, the Vice Chancellor found the following facts: (a) Holland directly sells to retail consumers by means of numerous branch offices. There were no intermediate dealers. (b) Immediately prior to the complained-of transactions, the sales and earnings of Holland had declined and its marketing practices were under investigation by the Federal Trade Commission. (c) Mr. Cheff and Trenkamp had received substantial sums as Chief Executive and attorney of the company, respectively. (d) Maremont, on August 23rd, 1957, demanded a place on the board. (e) At the October 14th meeting between Trenkamp, Staal and Maremont, Trenkamp and Staal were authorized to speak for Hazelbank and Mrs. Cheff as well as Holland. Only Mr. Cheff, Mrs. Cheff, Mr. Landwehr, and Mr. Trenkamp clearly understood, prior to the October 23rd meeting, that either Hazelbank or Mrs. Cheff would have utilized their funds to purchase the Holland stock if Holland had not acted. (g) There was no real threat posed by Maremont and no substantial evidence of intention by Maremont to liquidate Holland. (h) Any employee unrest could have been caused by factors other than Maremont's intrusion and "only one important employee was shown to have left, and his motive for leaving is not clear." (i) The Court rejected the stock option plan as a meaningful rationale for the purchase from Maremont or the prior open market purchases.

The Court then found that the actual purpose behind the purchase was the desire to perpetuate control, but because of its finding that only the four above-named directors knew of the "alternative", the remaining directors were exonerated. No appeal was taken by plaintiffs from that decision.

An examination of the record indicates that a substantial portion of the evidence presented to the Vice Chancellor consisted of deposition testimony and documentary evidence. The only individuals who testified personally (aside from a financial expert) were Mr. Cheff, Trenkamp and Staal. Depositions of the other directors were introduced, but no deposition was taken from Maremont. The standard of review governing this court in such cases was established in Blish v. Thompson Automatic Arms Corp., 64 A.2d 581 (Del. 1948), wherein we stated:

. . . regardless of the state of the evidence below, if there be sufficient oral testimony in the record to support the findings of fact below, such findings should not be disturbed by this Court. (64 A.2d at 604).

Under the provisions of 8 Del.C. § 160, a corporation is granted statutory power to purchase and sell shares of its own stock. Such a right, as embodied in the statute, has long been recognized in this State. The charge here is not one of violation of statute, but the allegation is that the true motives behind such purchases were improperly centered upon perpetuation of control. In an analogous field, courts have sustained the use of proxy funds to inform stockholders of management's views upon the policy questions inherent in an election to a board of directors, but have not sanctioned the use of corporate funds to advance the selfish desires of directors to perpetuate themselves in office. See Hall v. Trans-Lux Daylight Picture Screen Corp., 171 A. 226 (Del.Ch.1934). Similarly, if the actions of the board were motivated by a sincere belief that the buying out of the dissident stockholder was necessary to maintain what the board believed to be proper business practices, the board will not be held liable for such decision, even though hindsight indicates the decision was not the wisest course. See Kors v. Carey, 158 A.2d 136 (Del.Ch.1960). On the other hand, if the board has acted solely or primarily because of the desire to perpetuate themselves in office, the use of corporate funds for such purposes is improper. See Bennett v. Propp, 187 A.2d 405 (Del.1960), and Yasik v. Wachtel, 17 A.2d 309 (Del.Ch.1957).

Our first problem is the allocation of the burden of proof to show the presence or lack of good faith on the part of the board in authorizing the purchase of shares. Initially, the decision of the board of directors in authorizing a purchase was presumed to be in good faith and could be overturned only by a conclusive showing by plaintiffs of fraud or other misconduct. . . .

In *Kors*, cited *supra*, the court merely indicated that the directors are presumed to act in good faith and the burden of proof to show to the contrary falls upon the plaintiff. However, in Bennett v. Propp, *supra*, we stated:

> We must bear in mind the inherent danger in the purchase of shares with corporate funds to remove a threat to corporate policy when a threat to control is involved. The directors are of necessity confronted with a conflict of interest, and an objective decision is difficult. . . . Hence, in our opinion, the burden should be on the directors to justify such a purchase as one primarily in the corporate interest. (187 A.2d 409, at 409).

The case of Martin v. American Potash and Chemical Corp., 92 A.2d 295 (Del.1952) relied upon by defendants to support their contention that the burden of proof should be on plaintiffs, is inapposite. As noted in Bennett,

Martin was concerned with a statutory reduction of capital, which has the additional safeguards of notice to stockholders and shareholder approval.

To say that the burden of proof is upon the defendants is not to indicate, however, that the directors have the same "self-dealing interest" as is present, for example, when a director sells property to the corporation. The only clear pecuniary interest shown on the record was held by Mr. Cheff, as an executive of the corporation, and Trenkamp, as its attorney. The mere fact that some of the other directors were substantial shareholders does not create a personal pecuniary interest in the decisions made by the board of directors, since all shareholders would presumably share the benefit flowing to the substantial shareholder. See Smith v. Good Music Station, Inc., 129 A.2d 242 (Del.Ch.1957). Accordingly, these directors other than Trenkamp and Cheff, while called upon to justify their actions, will not be held to the same standard of proof required of those directors having personal and pecuniary interest in the transaction.

As noted above, the Vice Chancellor found that the stock option plan, mentioned in the minutes as a justification for the purchases, was not a motivating reason for the purchases. This finding we accept, since there is evidence to support it; in fact, Trenkamp admitted that the stock option plan was not the motivating reason. The minutes of October 23, 1957 dealing with the purchase from Maremont do not, in fact, mention the option plan as a reason for the purchase. While the minutes of the October 1, 1957 meeting only indicated the stock option plan as the motivating reason, the defendants are not bound by such statements and may supplement the minutes by oral testimony to show that the motivating reason was genuine fear of an acquisition by Maremont. See Bennett v. Propp, cited *supra*.

Plaintiffs urge that the sale price was unfair in view of the fact that the price was in excess of that prevailing on the open market. However, as conceded by all parties, a substantial block of stock will normally sell at a higher price than that prevailing on the open market, the increment being attributable to a "control premium". Plaintiffs argue that it is inappropriate to require the defendant corporation to pay a control premium, since control is meaningless to an acquisition by a corporation of its own shares. However, it is elementary that a holder of a substantial number of shares would expect to receive the control premium, as part of his selling price, and if the corporation desired to obtain the stock, it is unreasonable to expect that the corporation could avoid paying what any other purchaser would be required to pay for the stock. In any event, the financial expert produced by defendant at trial indicated that the price paid was fair and there was no rebuttal. Ames, the financial man on the board, was strongly of the opinion that the purchase was a good deal for the corporation. The Vice Chancellor made no finding as to the fairness of the price other than to indicate the obvious fact that the market price was increasing as a result of open market purchases by Maremont, Mrs. Cheff and Holland.

The question then presented is whether or not defendants satisfied the burden of proof of showing reasonable grounds to believe a danger to corporate policy and effectiveness existed by the presence of the Maremont stock ownership. It is important to remember that the directors satisfy their burden by showing good faith and reasonable investigation; the directors will not be penalized for an honest mistake of judgment, if the judgment appeared reasonable at the time the decision was made.

In holding that employee unrest could as well be attributed to a condition of Holland's business affairs as to the possibility of Maremont's intrusion, the Vice Chancellor must have had in mind one or both of two matters: (1) the pending proceedings before the Federal Trade Commission concerning certain sales practices of Holland; (2) the decrease in sales and profits during the preceding several years. Any other possible reason would be pure speculation. In the first place, the adverse decision of the F.T.C. was not announced until *after* the complained-of transaction. Secondly, the evidence clearly shows that the downward trend of sales and profits had reversed itself, presumably because of the reorganization which had then been completed. Thirdly, everyone who testified on the point said that the unrest was due to the possible threat presented by Maremont's purchases of stock. There was, in fact, no *testimony* whatever of any connection between the unrest and either the F.T.C. proceedings or the business picture.

The Vice Chancellor found that there was no substantial evidence of a liquidation posed by Maremont. This holding overlooks an important contention. The fear of the defendants, according to their testimony, was not limited to the possibility of liquidation; it included the alternate possibility of a material change in Holland's sales policies, which the board considered vital to its future success. The *unrebutted* testimony before the court indicated:

(1) Maremont had deceived Cheff as to his original intentions, since his open market purchases were contemporaneous with his disclaimer of interest in Holland; (2) Maremont had given Cheff some reason to believe that he intended to eliminate the retail sales force of Holland; (3) Maremont demanded a place on the board; (4) Maremont substantially increased his purchases after having been refused a place on the board; (5) the directors had good reason to believe that unrest among key employees had been engendered by the Maremont threat; (6) the board had received advice from Dun and Bradstreet indicating the past liquidation or quick sale activities of Motor Products; (7) the board had received professional advice from the firm of Merrill Lynch, Fenner & Beane, who recommended that the purchase from Motor Products be carried out; (8) the board had received competent advice that the corporation was over-capitalized; (9) Staal and Cheff had made informal personal investigations from contacts in the business and financial community and had reported to the board of the alleged poor reputation of Maremont. The board was within its rights in relying upon that investigation, since 8 Del.C. § 141(f) allows the directors to reasonably rely upon a report provided by corporate officers.

Accordingly, we are of the opinion that the evidence presented in the court below leads inevitably to the conclusion that the board of directors, based upon direct investigation, receipt of professional advice, and personal observations of the contradictory action of Maremont and his explanation of corporate purpose, believed, with justification, that there was a reasonable threat to the continued existence of Holland, or at least existence in its present form, by the plan of Maremont to continue building up his stock holdings. We find no evidence in the record sufficient to justify a contrary conclusion. The opinion of the Vice Chancellor that employee unrest may have been engendered by other factors or that the board had no grounds to suspect Maremont is not supported in any manner by the evidence.

As noted above, the Vice-Chancellor found that the purpose of the acquisition was the improper desire to maintain control, but, at the same time, he exonerated those individual directors whom he believed to be unaware of the possibility of using non-corporate funds to accomplish this purpose. Such a decision is inconsistent with his finding that the motive was improper, within the rule enunciated in Bennett. If the actions were in fact improper because of a desire to maintain control, then the presence or absence of a non-corporate alternative is irrelevant, as corporate funds may not be used to advance an improper purpose even if there is no non-corporate alternative available. Conversely, if the actions were proper because of a decision by the board made in good faith that the corporate interest was served thereby, they are not rendered improper by the fact that some individual directors were willing to advance personal funds if the corporation did not. It is conceivable that the Vice Chancellor considered this feature of the case to be of significance because of his apparent belief that any excess corporate funds should have been used to finance a subsidiary corporation. That action would not have solved the problem of Holland's over-capitalization. In any event, this question was a matter of business judgment, which furnishes no justification for holding the directors personally responsible in this case.

Accordingly, the judgment of the court below is reversed and remanded with instruction to enter judgment for the defendants.

---

2.   Criticism of the Traditional Approach

Ronald Gilson
A STRUCTURAL APPROACH TO CORPORATIONS:
THE CASE AGAINST DEFENSIVE TACTICS IN TENDER OFFERS
33 Stan.L.Rev. 819, 821-31 (1981)*

The Traditional Approach to Management's Role in Takeovers: Applying the Fiduciary Principle in Control Settings

In traditional terms, the question posed by management's implementing defensive tactics in response to a tender offer is whether management has acted in its own self-interest at the expense of the shareholders. Cast in doctrinal terms, the attack on such activities would be framed in terms of management's violating its fiduciary duty. Examining the development and content of traditional fiduciary analysis, however, demonstrates that it is incapable of resolving the problem posed by defensive tactics. Under prevailing legal standards, the common measure of fiduciary obligation is virtually without content where the conflict of interest triggering its application concerns maintaining control.

The scope of management's fiduciary responsibility and the measure of its discharge are traditionally described by the content of and interplay between two statements of obligation -- the duty of care and the duty of loyalty -- and the corresponding standards by which courts measure discharge of those obligations -- the business judgment rule and the fairness test. The statements of obligation are in themselves unremarkable. The duty of care states that management owes the corporation reasonable diligence described by a traditional negligence formula: "A director shall perform his duties . . . with such care as an ordinarily prudent person in a like position would use under similar circumstances."[6] The duty of loyalty requires only that the director's dealings with the corporation be consistent with the "fiduciary" position held. In both cases, the standards by which the discharge of these obligations is measured are of real significance.

Duty of Care: The Business Judgment Rule

The substance of the duty of care is contained in the measure of its discharge, the business judgment rule: "Absent bad faith or some other corrupt motive, directors are normally not liable to the corporation for mistakes of judgment, whether those mistakes are classified as mistakes of

---

[6] ABA-ALI Model Bus.Corp. Act Ann.2d § 35 (Supp.1977). . . .

fact or mistakes of law."[8] In practice, however, the rule functions less as a standard of management conduct than as a statement of judicial restraint: "[T]he liability aspect of the rule may well have been incidental to its principal function. The rule is more likely to have survived because it functioned as a quasi-jurisdictional barrier to prevent courts . . . from exercising regulatory powers over the activities of corporate managers."[9] Put this way, the business judgment rule does not express the measure by which a court determines whether management has discharged its duty of care; rather, its application reflects a conclusion that the management action in question will not be reviewed at all.

The courts' abdication of regulatory authority through the business judgment rule may well be the most significant common law contribution to corporate governance. Although critics have complained that the "[d]irectors' duty of due care has almost been interpreted out of existence,"[11] a broader judicial role is difficult to justify. First, courts are ill-suited to review the wisdom of complex business judgments;[12] it is, for example, almost impossible to distinguish between acts of corporate social responsibility and acts of long-term profit maximization. Second, even if such a review were possible, it seems virtually certain that the game would not be worth playing.

By definition, the issue of managerial performance arises only after a decision has turned out badly, and a court could accomplish little at this stage. The impact of the court's decision on future management does not justify judicial review. A general directive to be wise rather than foolish is of little help. More specific remarks concerning the wisdom of the competing alternatives and the manner in which they might better have been evaluated, even if correct, are unlikely to prove a source of guidance for future managers. And, in any event, litigation is an unjustifiably expensive way to develop a case study to aid in future business decisions.

Finally, judicial review, and the resulting potential for personal liability, cannot be justified as a necessary incentive for managers to behave responsibly. It is now widely recognized that a variety of markets -- product, employment, capital, and corporate control -- constrain inefficient management performance without the enormous transaction costs associated

---

[8] Cramer v. General Tel. & Elec. Corp., 582 F.2d 259, 274 (3d Cir.1978), *cert. denied*, 439 U.S. 1129 (1979).

[9] Henry Manne, *Our Two Corporation Systems: Law and Economics*, 53 Va.L.Rev. 259, 271 (1967).

[11] Elliott Weiss, *Disclosure and Corporate Accountability*, 34 Bus.Law. 575, 587 (1979); see William Cary, *Federalism and Corporate Law: Reflections Upon Delaware*, 83 Yale L.J. 663 (1974).

[12] On occasion this point is acknowledged by a court asked to consider applying the business judgment rule. E.g., Auerbach v. Bennett, 393 N.E.2d 994, 1000 (N.Y.1979) ("It appears to us that the business judgment doctrine, at least in part, is grounded in the prudent recognition that courts are ill equipped and infrequently called on to evaluate what are and must be essentially business judgments.").

with litigation.[16] In short, the business judgment rule's wisdom -- its declination to provide judicial regulation when other forces more cheaply accomplish the same end -- is precisely what generates its most persistent criticism. It also, however, identifies the limits of its application.

Duty of Loyalty: The Policy Conflict/Primary Purpose Test

While the business judgment rule acts as a jurisdictional barrier to review of most managerial decisions, the common law also recognizes that regulation of management conduct is appropriate where management has a conflict of interest. Drawing on trust law doctrine by analogy, the duty of loyalty originally prohibited transactions between a corporation and its management.[17] This restriction, however, was bent over time to reflect commercial necessity. Prohibition gave way to an overriding emphasis on the substantive fairness of the transaction. In contrast to judicial restraint under the business judgment rule, courts adopted an active regulatory posture with respect to transactions posing conflicts of interest: A court would "review such a contract and subject it to rigid and careful scrutiny, and would invalidate the contract if it was found to be unfair to the corporation."[19] To be sure, fairness did not offer talismanic precision. A "fair" price is no more than one set somewhere between the lowest price a seller will accept and the highest price a buyer will pay. But the concept does offer an objective measure; recourse to comparable market transactions is possible and appraisals, although inexact, are available. This allows the structuring of beneficial transactions with some certainty of their consequences and without enormous regulatory costs. In short, the fairness standard is a thoroughly respectable rule of law as applied to the area of its original application.

The fairness standard, however, has been an inadequate measure of management's discharge of its duty of loyalty in the area of particular concern here -- its application in the context of change of control. Indeed, it was never tried. There is little question that management is subject to a conflict of interest when confronted with a proposal for the corporation's acquisition. As Harold Marsh has commented, "It is impossible to command the directors in this situation to avoid any conflict of interest, since it has been unavoidably thrust upon them." Because corporate statutes commonly require the approval of the target's board of directors before a proposed

---

[16] Among recent works by lawyers, see, e.g., Richard Posner, *Economic Analysis of Law* 300-13 (2d ed.1977); Ralph Winter, *Government and the Corporation* 5-46 (1978); Alison Anderson, *Conflicts of Interest: Efficiency, Fairness and Corporate Structure*, 25 UCLA L.Rev. 738, 784-87 (1978); Walter Werner, *Management, Stock Market and Corporate Reform: Berle and Means Reconsidered*, 77 Colum.L.Rev. 388, 389 (1977).

[17] See generally Harold Marsh, *Are Directors Trustees?*, 22 Bus.Law. 35 (1966).

[19] Marsh (1966), *supra* note 17, at 43.

merger or sale of assets can even be put to the shareholders, most acquisitions cannot be undertaken without management consent. As a result, management can reject offers beneficial to shareholders to retain the emoluments, both pecuniary and nonpecuniary, that flow from a position of high authority in a public corporation. Alternatively, control over access to shareholders gives management the power to "sell" that access to an offeror for such things as favorable employment contracts and attractive treatment of existing fringe benefits like stock options. Thus, it is impossible to identify at the outset any path management might take which would eliminate the inherent conflict of interest; any action, whether rejection or approval, reflects the potential for diversion of benefit to management and away from shareholders.

A potential acquisition thus seems the paradigmatic setting for judicial regulation of management conduct. While the absence of judicial review was sensible in nonconflict settings because other constraints protected shareholders, the conflict of interest inherent in a potential change in control called for "rigid and careful scrutiny" of the fairness of management conduct. But while doctrinal logic demanded such a review, it did not occur. Faced with the problem of attempting to police management behavior in this setting, the courts abdicated, albeit, I will suggest, in an inventive manner.

The difficulty in policing management conduct in connection with changes of control, and the devices by which the courts chose to avoid the task, can best be seen by considering two common defensive tactics. In the first, a third party acquires a significant minority of shares and seeks either to acquire the remainder of the target's shares or to make substantial changes in the target's operations. Target management opposes either course and, after more or less conflict, the target corporation resolves the issue by repurchasing the dissident's shares at a price higher than market. In the second, an offeror announces its intent to tender for control and target management takes action -- like placing a significant amount of the target's common stock in hands sympathetic to management's desire to remain independent -- which prevents the change in control from occurring.

In the first setting, where the management action taken -- repurchase of the outsider's stock -- has as its announced purpose preventing a shift in control of the corporation, the conflict of interest is apparent. Reviewing management's action under the fairness standard, however, presents substantial difficulties. Inquiry could be made concerning whether the price paid by the company was fair, but in that sense, the transaction was arm's length; management had no interest in paying more for the shares than was necessary to convince the holder to sell. Moreover, that the price was "fair" only demonstrates the irrelevancy of the inquiry. Management's conflict of interest was not in the price paid, but in the decision to acquire the shares at all. Applying a fairness standard to this decision, however, requires a court to determine whether it was "fair" for control to remain with management rather than shift to the offeror. And this inquiry must necessarily focus on whether the shareholders would be better off with existing management or by selling their shares. But this is an investment decision, made continually by shareholders in deciding whether to sell their shares, and raises the same issue of judicial competence which justifies a restrictive judicial role with respect to the duty of care.

In the second setting, where the management action taken -- a sale of target shares to a friendly party -- has the effect of blocking a potential change in control, a court could also evaluate whether the price received for the shares was fair. As in the first setting, however, inquiry into the fairness of the price is beside the point; management's conflict of interest goes not to the commercial reasonableness of the defensive action's terms, but to the decision to block a change in control. As in the first setting, a fairness review of the relevant conflict forces the court to consider precisely the factors which the business judgment rule excludes from consideration.

The manner in which the courts sidestepped this dilemma is a marvel of doctrinal development. The first setting is recognizable as Cheff v. Mathes, where the Delaware Supreme Court avoided the problem by shifting the focus of the inquiry. If the court was ill-equipped to review the fairness of management's belief that it was the better repository for future control of the corporation, it was at least competent to engage in an inquiry with which it *was* familiar, a review of motive:

> [T]he allegation is that the true motives behind such purchases were improperly centered upon perpetuation of control. . . . [I]f the actions of the board were motivated by a sincere belief that the buying out of the dissident stockholder was necessary to maintain what the board believed to be proper business practices, the board will not be held liable for such decision. . . . On the other hand, if the board has acted solely or primarily because of the desire to perpetuate themselves in office, the use of corporate funds for such purposes is improper.[30]

Recognizing that inventive counsel could always discover a conflict over policy between management and an insurgent, the court required an additional showing: that the board's determination that a policy conflict existed was based on "reasonable investigation."[31]

While the Cheff decision has been extensively criticized, note how neatly the court avoided the fairness dilemma. A conflict of interest existed which, in the court's view and, I think, in fact, was not subject to a traditional fairness review. An analysis of management's motives then served as a surrogate for a fairness review to validate the transaction: Where management's investigation demonstrates that a policy difference was the motivation for the transaction, then the conflict of interest has been exorcised. Absent a conflict of interest, the business judgment rule is the

---

[30] 199 A.2d at 554.

[31] *Id.* at 555.

appropriate standard of review, precisely the standard applied by the court in *Cheff:*

> [T]he directors satisfy their burden by showing good faith and reasonable investigation; the directors will not be penalized for an honest mistake of judgment, if the judgment appeared reasonable at the time the decision was made. 199 A.2d at 555.[33]

Since management can almost always find a conflict over policy between itself and an insurgent, the motive analysis collapses into the business judgment standard. And while this approach neither solved nor addressed management's conflict of interest, it did eliminate substantive review of questions which the court was institutionally incompetent to resolve.

The second setting arose in Northwest Industries v. B.F. Goodrich Co.[35] Goodrich was a participant with Gulf Oil in a joint venture which both had concluded would be more valuable if owned entirely by either. Despite extensive negotiations, the parties could not agree upon a price at which Goodrich would acquire Gulf's interest, and so the matter stood for some four years. Then, ten days after the announcement of a tender offer for Goodrich by Northwest, negotiations reopened and, in a single day, without further study, Goodrich management agreed to acquire Gulf's interest in exchange for 700,000 shares of authorized but unissued Goodrich common stock.[36] The Goodrich board approved the transaction the following day on the basis of "a hastily prepared two page memorandum and a one page statistical analysis of the transaction."[37] Northwest sued to block the transaction, claiming that the stock issuance was a mechanism to defeat the Northwest tender.[38]

While the price paid for the joint venture could be reviewed in traditional fairness terms,[39] the court also had to deal with the claim that the transaction should not have taken place at any price. And this inquiry was

---

[33] 199 A.2d at 555.

[35] 301 F.Supp. 706 (N.D.Ill.1969).

[36] The court noted that "[w]hile Gulf's officers had updated their 1965 studies of Chemicals [the joint venture], the only Goodrich documents were a brief, handwritten memorandum of possible valuations of Gulf's one-half interest and a sheet of paper containing longhand calculations." *Id.* at 709 n.3.

[37] *Id.* at 709.

[38] Although the court's opinion considers only the Gulf transaction, it was not the only defensive tactic undertaken by Goodrich. The Goodrich defense included litigation claiming violation by Northwest of the federal securities laws, political pressure, an additional defensive acquisition designed to create an antitrust barrier, and the proposal of shark repellant amendments. See Oliver Williamson, *Corporate Control and Business Behavior* 100-02 (1970).

[39] 301 F.Supp. at 710. Among Northwest's claims was an assertion that the price paid by Goodrich for the Gulf joint venture interest was too high.

particularly difficult because the court had to acknowledge that it was the Northwest tender offer which triggered the transaction.[40] Nonetheless, the court avoided reviewing the "fairness" of Goodrich's resistance by analyzing motive instead. While acknowledging that one of Goodrich's motives was to defeat the offer, the court expressly rejected the contention that "'where a board of directors has as one of its motives manipulation for control the transaction is invalid, regardless of fairness, and regardless of whether a legitimate corporate purpose is also being served.'"[41] Only if "Goodrich officials' desire to remain in office was the sole or the primary motive for their decisions"[42] would resistance breach the duty of loyalty. Where dual motives are present -- maintaining control *and* furthering a legitimate corporate interest -- the conflict of interest is eliminated and the appropriate standard, as in *Cheff,* is the business judgment rule: "Goodrich's officers and directors appear to have been exercising their honest business judgment, so that their decision is conclusive."[43]

Despite the doctrinal ingenuity by which the policy conflict/primary purpose test avoids the impossible task of substantive judicial review of the merits of conflicting claimants for corporate control, the central problem still remains: Blocking a change in control may reflect management's self-interest regardless of policy differences with a rival for control, and regardless of whether the defensive tactic chosen also serves an unrelated corporate purpose. This approach converts the issue from one of duty of loyalty to one of duty of care, with the consequent "incongruity of applying a standard designed to vindicate the exercise of business judgment in non-conflict-of-interest situations as a measure of compliance with the duty of loyalty, which arises only in conflict-of-interest situations." So long as the policy conflict/primary purpose test is applied, management's conflict of interest cannot be and, I have argued, was not intended to be, confronted.

The courts were led to this impasse because they concentrated narrowly on the appropriateness of management conduct in the case at hand, an inquiry which, unless limited, would necessarily involve the court in an exercise resembling fundamental security analysis, rather than approaching the problem through a broader examination of the appropriate allocation of responsibility between management and shareholders with respect to change in control.

---

[40] *Id.* at 712 ("Northwest's tender offer announcement galvanized Goodrich and Gulf to complete the purchase at this time.").

[41] *Id.* (quoting Cummings v. United Artists Theatre Circuit, Inc., 204 A.2d 795, 805 (Md.1964)).

[42] *Id.*

[43] *Id.*

3.   The Adoption of Proportionality Review

The clever doctrinal manipulation by which the Delaware courts opted for the business judgment rule under the guise of the policy conflict/primary purpose standard framed by *Cheff* survived unchanged only as long as its implication -- blanket protection of defensive tactics -- remained at least partly submerged. By the early 1980s, this implication was fully visible. Novel financing techniques and a dramatic rise in takeover activity stimulated demand for improved takeover defenses. New defenses, in turn, prompted new litigation and a long string of victories for targets that soon revealed the full scope of management's discretion to block takeovers under *Cheff*'s motive analysis.[115] Inevitably, top takeover lawyers began to pass *Cheff*'s implicit message on to their clients: If target managers, in good faith and after reasonable investigation, could locate a policy conflict with a would-be acquirer, any defensive response would be protected under the business judgment rule.[116]

As *Cheff*'s implications became clearly visible, however, they attracted hostile notice from other corners. An outpouring of academic commentary called for constraints on defensive tactics, and it even appeared possible that Congress might act to displace state law -- and especially Delaware law -- that was thought to be unduly favorable to target management. The political situation thus recalled an earlier period prior to the Delaware Supreme Court's decision in Singer v. Magnavox.[117] Then the sensitive issue was the dearth of standards governing the freezeout of minority shareholders by majority or controlling shareholders. And when the outcry became too loud, the Delaware Supreme Court announced a new, seemingly more stringent standard of review that promised to constrain management's discretion to force out minority shareholders.[118] Thus, there was an historical basis for predicting that political pressure might eventually prompt the Delaware courts to tighten the lax standard of review implicit in *Cheff*'s policy conflict/primary purpose test.

In principle, the Delaware courts had three quite different doctrinal options for reforming the *Cheff* standard. On the one hand, the courts could have restricted defensive tactics by emphasizing the primacy of shareholder choice to accept or reject a hostile offer that follows from the role of the

---

[115] This expansion in management discretion to take actions to deflect hostile offers probably hit its apogee in Panter v. Marshall Field & Co., 646 F.2d 271, *cert. denied*, 454 U.S. 1092 (1981).

[116] Martin Lipton put the matter as follows: "Where the directors have made a reasonable good-faith decision to reject the takeover on one or more of the bases set forth above, the business judgment rule should apply equally to any and all defensive tactics." Martin Lipton, *Takeover Bids in the Target's Boardroom*, 35 Bus.Law. 101, 124 (1979).

[117] 380 A.2d 969 (1977) (excerpted in Chapter 22, *infra*).

[118] For the suggestion that the Delaware Court's decision in *Singer* was influenced by political consideration, see Chapter 22, *infra*.

tender offer in the structure of the corporation. Precisely because target management can unilaterally block a merger or sale of assets, a takeover can occur without management approval only through a tender offer made directly to target shareholders. Thus, management enjoys a monopoly over corporate control unless it is restrained from preventing shareholders from tendering to a hostile offeror.[119] The following represents this general position, which had wide support from academics.

Ronald Gilson
A STRUCTURAL APPROACH TO CORPORATIONS:
THE CASE AGAINST DEFENSIVE TACTICS IN TENDER OFFERS
33 Stan.L.Rev. 819, 845-48, 875-81 (1981)[*]

The General Principle: Shareholders Must Make the Decision

The argument thus far presented is that other elements of the structure of the corporation, having statutory, judicial and market components, serve to constrain the managerial discretion unavoidably resulting from the modern corporation's need for specialized managerial skills and capital. The tender offer is the critical mechanism through which the corporate structure imposes constraints on certain forms of managerial self-dealing. It is in this context that a structural approach to corporate law considers the validity of defensive tactics.

The result of management adopting successful defensive tactics is to make impossible a tender offer which management has not blessed. For example, the post-offer acquisition by the target of a business which creates an antitrust barrier to the offer causes access to shareholders through a tender offer to be conditioned in the same manner that the corporate statute conditions access to shareholders in a merger of sale of assets. Absent approval of incumbent management, a tender offer, like a merger or sale of assets, is impossible.

This result, however, is flatly inconsistent with the structure of the corporation. The market for corporate control is crucial to the corporate structure because neither other markets nor a fiduciary "fairness" standard effectively constrains some forms of management self-dealing. Moreover, the control market allows a final constraint on management inefficiency short of business failure. In turn, the tender offer is crucial because no other displacement mechanism is available without management cooperation. If management can use defensive tactics to obtain a degree of control over tender offers similar to that given it over mergers and sales of assets, then

---

[119] See Chapter 16, *supra*.

the corporate structure is fundamentally altered in a fashion which allows management effective monopoly power over corporate control. Rather than displacement occurring when the gains from displacement (the benefits of synergy or the elimination of inefficiency or self-dealing) exceed the price to be paid (including transaction costs), transfer of control will occur only when the benefits to incumbent management from the transaction exceed the capitalized value to management of its existing discretion. In short, defensive tactics, if successful, circumvent the mechanism by which the corporate structure constrains managerial discretion and, therefore, are improper.

The structural argument establishing the invalidity of defensive tactics, generally based on the interplay between statute, courts, and markets,[a] is perfectly consistent with a construction of the statutory terms dealing directly with displacement mechanisms. Not surprisingly, this construction is based on analysis of the relationships created by the statute itself; coming full circle, this is precisely the form of argument by which the courts initially developed the fiduciary duty concept.

Corporate statutes properly place the ultimate responsibility for evaluating proposals for merger or sale of assets with management. These complicated transactions require substantial time investments for shareholders to understand them.[101] Assuming loyal management, a rational shareholder would not invest time considering a merger or sale of assets unless management, through application of its specialized skills, had already approved it. The problem is ensuring, within reasonable limits, that management's determination -- for example, to reject an offer -- is motivated by the shareholders', rather than management's, best interests. And it was precisely the difficulty of making such a determination which forced courts to sidestep the problem by applying the business judgment rule to management's fiduciary role in changes of control. The solution is the check and balance of the tender offer. If management, in rejecting merger or sale of assets proposals, gives priority to its own interests rather than those of the shareholders, the spurned suitor can make a tender offer to the shareholders. Should management become too recalcitrant, an alternative is available.

---

[a] See Chapter 16, *supra*.

[101] Where the transaction involves the issuance of the offeror's securities, the offer must be registered with the Securities and Exchange Commission pursuant to the Securities Act of 1933 unless an exemption from registration is available. See generally Richard Jennings & Harold Marsh, *Securities Regulation: Cases and Materials* 464-95 (4th ed.1977). Until recently, such a transaction would be registered on Form S-14, 17 C.F.R. § 239.23 (1980), which has been described as generating "some of the longest and most complex disclosure documents presented to investors," with an average length of 110 pages, and some exceeding 200 pages. House Comm. on Interstate and Foreign Commerce, 95th Cong., 1st Sess., *Report of the Advisory Comm. on Corporate Disclosure to the Securities and Exchange Commission* 440 (Comm. Print 1977) [hereinafter cited as *Report on Corporate Disclosure*].

. . .

This system of check and balance, of management control of some mechanisms by which control may be shifted but with unfettered access to shareholders through another, is precisely the structure reflected in the typical corporation statute. While control of the merger and sale of asset mechanisms is firmly ensconced in management, the tender offer mechanism generally is not even mentioned in the statute, let alone placed within management's control. Thus, to reiterate my basic point from a somewhat different perspective, all components of the structure of the modern corporation -- market, judicial, and statutory -- combine to establish a critical role for the tender offer: as the principal displacement mechanism by which the capital market may police the performance of management and thereby justify the central role accorded management in other displacement mechanisms. Defensive tactics, because they alter the allocation of tender offer responsibility between management and shareholders contemplated by this structure, are inappropriate. . . .

Reducing the Structural Principle to a Rule

In an important sense, my argument has come full circle. There has never been significant judicial debate over the principle that self-perpetuating action by target management is invalid. The difficulty, I have argued, has been the courts' inability to distinguish defensive tactics from neutral corporate action, particularly where dual effects are present. The traditional solution -- an inquiry into motive -- fails not in principle, but in implementation, in reducing the principle to a form which meaningfully separates management conduct into valid and invalid categories. This task still remains.

The effort, however, can now begin from a substantially different position. Unlike courts confronting the matter originally, we now understand the tender offer's role in the corporate structure and the relationship between management and shareholders dictated by that role. We have seen that the tender offer is centrally important to the structure of the corporation because it is the key displacement mechanism through which the market for corporate control constrains management behavior and because it is a critical safety valve against management's misuse of its controlling role in all other displacement mechanisms. Its success depends on independent shareholder action; shareholders tendering their shares transfer control to better management, and it is the potential for such shareholder action which constrains self-interested behavior by management in connection with mergers and asset sales. A structural approach to allocating responsibility between management and shareholders with respect to tender offers thus yields a straightforward principle: Shareholders must make tender offer decisions.

Before formulating a rule implementing that principle, it is worth pausing to identify the benefits which derive from a structural approach. The major pitfalls facing courts in reviewing management action under traditional standards are no longer present. It is simply no longer relevant to inquire whether management action was in the best interests of the shareholders, a question which, if confronted rather than avoided through the subterfuge of motive, requires judicial review of the alternative futures presented by the contestants for control. The structural principle focuses on how management action affects the role assigned to shareholders, a factual inquiry which ought not to pose special difficulties to courts. This question is one which the court is institutionally competent to answer. . . .

We can now formulate a rule which reflects the structurally defined roles for management and shareholders by describing the effect to be avoided -- interfering with shareholder decision -- rather than specifying the particular techniques likely to have that effect. Recognizing that the desired generality lessens the demand upon the drafter, the following is a workable solution:

> During the period commencing with the date on which target management has reason to believe that a tender offer may be made for part or all of a target company's equity securities, and ending at such time thereafter that the offeror shall have had a reasonable period in which to present the offer to target shareholders, no action shall be taken by the target company which could interfere with the success of the offer or result in the shareholders of the target company being denied the opportunity to tender their shares, *except* that the target company (1) may disclose to the public or its shareholders information bearing on the value or the attractiveness of the offer, and (2) may seek out alternative transactions which it believes may be more favorable to target shareholders.

Limiting target management conduct by focusing on its effect on shareholder decision highlights the most important manner in which the rule differs from the traditional inquiry. The central difficulty with the policy conflict/primary purpose test is that it assigns management an important discretionary role in the tender offer process. So long as management "genuinely" concludes that an offeror's policy differs from its own, or otherwise determines that an offer is "not in the best interest of the corporation or its shareholders," traditional doctrine validates defensive action. Subject only to the effectiveness of the defensive tactic selected, target management is, in effect, authorized to act instead of the shareholders. So understood, the common criticism of traditional doctrine -- that the tests are indeterminate because it is impossible to differentiate situations where there *really* are policy differences, or where management *really* believes it is acting in the best interests of the corporation or shareholders, from situations where such assertions are only a ploy -- is beside the point. Under a structural approach the issue is not the wisdom or good faith of particular action, but simply whether, and what kind of, action has been taken. In other words, the approach has the flavor of *ultra vires* -- certain actions are simply outside management's authority.

Thus, the first alternative to *Cheff* available to the Delaware courts was simply to prohibit defensive tactics other than those that developed alternatives for shareholders. The decision whether to accept a hostile offer would belong solely to target shareholders.

The second available alternative was to make explicit *Cheff*'s implicit application of the business judgment rule. This position was championed by defenders of incumbent management, and expressed succinctly by Martin Lipton: "Where the directors have made a reasonable good-faith decision to reject the takeover . . . the business judgment rule should apply equally to any and all defensive tactics."[120] Given the broad protection the business judgment rule provides, the decision whether to accept a hostile offer would belong largely to target management.

While these two alternatives have strikingly different prescriptions, they share one important commonality: Shareholders decide in one case, target management in the other, but neither contemplate a significant evaluative role for courts. The third available alternative, in contrast, places courts at the center of it all. The Delaware courts could have moved from the *Cheff* standard to an intermediate standard of judicial review that contemplated a genuine effort to distinguish defensive tactics that would benefit shareholders from suspect tactics designed to entrench management. If this alternative were adopted, it was predictable that defensive tactics would be challenged as entrenching in every hostile bid, and that the ultimate success of a takeover would be determined not in the marketplace, but in the courthouse.

Not surprisingly, the Delaware Supreme Court opted for an active judicial role of review. Unocal v. Mesa Petroleum and Moran v. Household International, Inc., announced an explicitly intermediate standard that sought to differentiate good and bad defensive tactics.

UNOCAL CORP. v. MESA PETROLEUM CO.
493 A.2d 946 (Del.1985)

Before McNEILLY and MOORE, J.J., and TAYLOR, J. (Sitting by designation pursuant to Del. Const., Art. 4, § 12.)

MOORE, Justice. We confront an issue of first impression in Delaware -- the validity of a corporation's self-tender for its own shares which excludes from participation a stockholder making a hostile tender offer for the company's stock.

The Court of Chancery granted a preliminary injunction to the plaintiffs, Mesa Petroleum Co., Mesa Asset Co., Mesa Partners II, and Mesa

---

[120] Lipton (1979), *supra* note 116, at 124.

Eastern, Inc. (collectively "Mesa"),[1] enjoining an exchange offer of the defendant, Unocal Corporation (Unocal) for its own stock. The trial court concluded that a selective exchange offer, excluding Mesa, was legally impermissible. We cannot agree with such a blanket rule. The factual findings of the Vice Chancellor, fully supported by the record, establish that Unocal's board, consisting of a majority of independent directors, acted in good faith, and after reasonable investigation found that Mesa's tender offer was both inadequate and coercive. Under the circumstances the board had both the power and duty to oppose a bid it perceived to be harmful to the corporate enterprise. On this record we are satisfied that the device Unocal adopted is reasonable in relation to the threat posed, and that the board acted in the proper exercise of sound business judgment. We will not substitute our views for those of the board if the latter's decision can be "attributed to any rational business purpose." Sinclair Oil Corp. v. Levien, 280 A.2d 717, 720 (Del.1971). Accordingly, we reverse the decision of the Court of Chancery and order the preliminary injunction vacated.

I

The factual background of this matter bears a significant relationship to its ultimate outcome.

On April 8, 1985, Mesa, the owner of approximately 13% of Unocal's stock, commenced a two-tier "front loaded" cash tender offer for 64 million shares, or approximately 37%, of Unocal's outstanding stock at a price of $54 per share. The "back-end" was designed to eliminate the remaining publicly held shares by an exchange of securities purportedly worth $54 per share. However, pursuant to an order entered by the United States District Court for the Central District of California on April 26, 1985, Mesa issued a supplemental proxy statement to Unocal's stockholders disclosing that the securities offered in the second-step merger would be highly subordinated, and that Unocal's capitalization would differ significantly from its present structure. Unocal has rather aptly termed such securities "junk bonds".[3]

---

[1] T. Boone Pickens, Jr., is President and Chairman of the Board of Mesa Petroleum and President of Mesa Asset and controls the related Mesa entities.

[3] Mesa's May 3, 1985 supplement to its proxy statement states:

(i) following the Offer, the Purchasers would seek to effect a merger of Unocal and Mesa Eastern or an affiliate of Mesa Eastern (the "Merger") in which the remaining Shares would be acquired for a combination of subordinated debt securities and preferred stock; (ii) the securities to be received by Unocal shareholders in the Merger would be subordinated to $2,400 million of debt securities of Mesa Eastern, indebtedness incurred to refinance up to $1,000 million of bank debt which was incurred by affiliates of Mesa partners II to purchase Shares and to pay related interest and expenses and all then-existing debt of Unocal; (iii) the corporation surviving the Merger would be responsible for the payment of all securities of Mesa Eastern (including any such securities issued pursuant to the Merger) and the indebtedness referred to in item (ii) above, and such securities and indebtedness would be repaid out

Unocal's board consists of eight independent outside directors and six insiders. It met on April 13, 1985, to consider the Mesa tender offer. Thirteen directors were present, and the meeting lasted nine and one-half hours. The directors were given no agenda or written materials prior to the session. However, detailed presentations were made by legal counsel regarding the board's obligations under both Delaware corporate law and the federal securities laws. The board then received a presentation from Peter Sachs on behalf of Goldman Sachs & Co. (Goldman Sachs) and Dillon, Read & Co. (Dillon Read) discussing the bases for their opinions that the Mesa proposal was wholly inadequate. Mr. Sachs opined that the minimum cash value that could be expected from a sale or orderly liquidation for 100% of Unocal's stock was in excess of $60 per share. In making his presentation, Mr. Sachs showed slides outlining the valuation techniques used by the financial advisors, and others, depicting recent business combinations in the oil and gas industry. The Court of Chancery found that the Sachs presentation was designed to apprise the directors of the scope of the analyses performed rather than the facts and numbers used in reaching the conclusion that Mesa's tender offer price was inadequate.

Mr. Sachs also presented various defensive strategies available to the board if it concluded that Mesa's two-step tender offer was inadequate and should be opposed. One of the devices outlined was a self-tender by Unocal for its own stock with a reasonable price range of $70 to $75 per share. The cost of such a proposal would cause the company to incur $6.1-6.5 billion of additional debt, and a presentation was made informing the board of Unocal's ability to handle it. The directors were told that the primary effect of this obligation would be to reduce exploratory drilling, but that the company would nonetheless remain a viable entity.

The eight outside directors, comprising a clear majority of the thirteen members present, then met separately with Unocal's financial advisors and attorneys. Thereafter, they unanimously agreed to advise the board that it should reject Mesa's tender offer as inadequate, and that Unocal should pursue a self-tender to provide the stockholders with a fairly priced alternative to the Mesa proposal. The board then reconvened and unanimously adopted a resolution rejecting as grossly inadequate Mesa's tender offer. Despite the nine and one-half hour length of the meeting, no formal decision was made on the proposed defensive self-tender.

---

of funds generated by the operations of Unocal; (iv) the indebtedness incurred in the Offer and the Merger would result in Unocal being much more highly leveraged, and the capitalization of the corporation surviving the Merger would differ significantly from that of Unocal at present; and (v) in their analysis of cash flows provided by operations of Unocal which would be available to service and repay securities and other obligations of the corporation surviving the Merger, the Purchasers assumed that the capital expenditures and expenditures for exploration of such corporation would be significantly reduced.

On April 15, the board met again with four of the directors present by telephone and one member still absent. This session lasted two hours. Unocal's Vice President of Finance and its Assistant General Counsel made a detailed presentation of the proposed terms of the exchange offer. A price range between $70 and $80 per share was considered, and ultimately the directors agreed upon $72. The board was also advised about the debt securities that would be issued, and the necessity of placing restrictive covenants upon certain corporate activities until the obligations were paid. The board's decisions were made in reliance on the advice of its investment bankers, including the terms and conditions upon which the securities were to be issued. Based upon this advice, and the board's own deliberations, the directors unanimously approved the exchange offer. Their resolution provided that if Mesa acquired 64 million shares of Unocal stock through its own offer (the Mesa Purchase Condition), Unocal would buy the remaining 49% outstanding for an exchange of debt securities having an aggregate par value of $72 per share. The board resolution also stated that the offer would be subject to other conditions that had been described to the board at the meeting, or which were deemed necessary by Unocal's officers, including the exclusion of Mesa from the proposal (the Mesa exclusion). Any such conditions were required to be in accordance with the "purport and intent" of the offer.

Unocal's exchange offer was commenced on April 17, 1985, and Mesa promptly challenged it by filing this suit in the Court of Chancery. On April 22, the Unocal board met again and was advised by Goldman Sachs and Dillon Read to waive the Mesa Purchase Condition as to 50 million shares. This recommendation was in response to a perceived concern of the shareholders that, if shares were tendered to Unocal, no shares would be purchased by either offeror. The directors were also advised that they should tender their own Unocal stock into the exchange offer as a mark of their confidence in it.

Another focus of the board was the Mesa exclusion. Legal counsel advised that under Delaware law Mesa could only be excluded for what the directors reasonably believed to be a valid corporate purpose. The directors' discussion centered on the objective of adequately compensating shareholders at the "back-end" of Mesa's proposal, which the latter would finance with "junk bonds". To include Mesa would defeat that goal, because under the proration aspect of the exchange offer (49%) every Mesa share accepted by Unocal would displace one held by another stockholder. Further, if Mesa were permitted to tender to Unocal, the latter would in effect be financing Mesa's own inadequate proposal.

On April 24, 1985, Unocal issued a supplement to the exchange offer describing the partial waiver of the Mesa Purchase Condition. On May 1, 1985, in another supplement, Unocal extended the withdrawal, proration and expiration dates of its exchange offer to May 17, 1985.

Meanwhile, on April 22, 1985, Mesa amended its complaint in this action to challenge the Mesa exclusion. A preliminary injunction hearing was scheduled for May 8, 1985. However, on April 23, 1985, Mesa moved for a temporary restraining order in response to Unocal's announcement that it was partially waiving the Mesa Purchase Condition. After expedited briefing, the Court of Chancery heard Mesa's motion on April 26.

On April 29, 1985, the Vice Chancellor temporarily restrained Unocal from proceeding with the exchange offer unless it included Mesa. The trial court recognized that directors could oppose, and attempt to defeat, a hostile takeover which they considered adverse to the best interests of the corporation. However, the Vice Chancellor decided that in a selective purchase of the company's stock, the corporation bears the burden of showing: (1) a valid corporate purpose, and (2) that the transaction was fair to all of the stockholders, including those excluded.

Unocal immediately sought certification of an interlocutory appeal to this Court pursuant to Supreme Curt Rule 42(b). On May 1, 1985, the Vice Chancellor declined to certify the appeal on the grounds that the decision granting a temporary restraining order did not decide a legal issue of first impression, and was not a matter to which the decisions of the Court of Chancery were in conflict.

However, in an Order dated May 2, 1985, this Court ruled that the Chancery decision was clearly determinative of substantive rights of the parties, and in fact decided the main question of law before the Vice Chancellor, which was indeed a question of first impression. We therefore concluded that the temporary restraining order was an appealable decision. However, because the Court of Chancery was scheduled to hold a preliminary injunction hearing on May 8 at which there would be an enlarged record on the various issues, action on the interlocutory appeal was deferred pending an outcome of those proceedings.

In deferring action on the interlocutory appeal, we noted that on the record before us we could not determine whether the parties had articulated certain issues which the Vice Chancellor should have an opportunity to consider in the first instance. These included the following:

a) Does the directors' duty of care to the corporation extend to protecting the corporate enterprise in good faith from perceived depredations of others, including persons who may own stock in the company?

b) Have one or more of the plaintiffs, their affiliates, or persons acting in concert with them, either in dealing with Unocal or others, demonstrated a pattern of conduct sufficient to justify a reasonable inference by defendants that a principle objective of the plaintiffs is to achieve selective treatment for themselves by the repurchase of their Unocal shares at a substantial premium.

c) If so, may the directors of Unocal in the proper exercise of business judgment employ the exchange offer to protect the corporation and its shareholders from such tactics? See Pogostin v. Rice, 480 A.2d 619 (Del.1984).

d) If it is determined that the purpose of the exchange offer was not illegal as a matter of law, have the directors of Unocal carried their burden of showing that they acted in good faith? See Martin v. American Potash & Chemical Corp., 92 A.2d 295, 302 (Del.1952).

After the May 8 hearing the Vice Chancellor issued an unreported opinion on May 13, 1985 granting Mesa a preliminary injunction. Specifically, the trial court noted that "[t]he parties basically agree that the directors' duty of care extends to protecting the corporation from perceived harm wither it be from third parties or shareholders." The trial court also concluded in response to the second inquiry in the Supreme Court's May 2 order, that "[a]lthough the facts, . . . do not appear to be sufficient to prove that Mesa's principal objective is to be bought off at a substantial premium, they do justify a reasonable inference to the same effect."

As to the third and fourth questions posed by this Court, the Vice Chancellor stated that they "appear to raise the more fundamental issue of whether directors owe fiduciary duties to shareholders who they perceive to be acting contrary to the best interests of the corporation as a whole." While determining that the directors' decision to oppose Mesa's tender offer was made in good faith belief that the Mesa proposal was inadequate, the court stated that the business judgment rule does not apply to a selective exchange offer such as this.

On May 13, 1985 the Court of Chancery certified this interlocutory appeal to us as a question of first impression, and we accepted it on May 14. The entire matter was scheduled on an expedited basis.[5]

II

The issues we address involve these fundamental questions: Did the Unocal board have the power and duty to oppose a takeover threat it reasonably perceived to be harmful to the corporate enterprise, and if so, is its action here entitled to the protection of the business judgment rule?

Mesa contends that the discriminatory exchange offer violates the fiduciary duties Unocal owes it. Mesa argues that because of the Mesa exclusion the business judgment rule is inapplicable, because the directors by tendering their own shares will derive a financial benefit that is not available to *all* Unocal stockholders. Thus, it is Mesa's ultimate contention that Unocal cannot establish that the exchange offer is fair to *all* shareholders, and argues that the Court of Chancery was correct in concluding that Unocal was unable to meet this burden.

Unocal answers that it does not owe a duty of "fairness" to Mesa, given the facts here. Specifically, Unocal contends that its board of directors reasonably and in good faith concluded that Mesa's $54 two-tier tender offer

---

[5] Such expedition was required by the fact that if Unocal's exchange offer was permitted to proceed, the proration date for the shares entitled to be exchanged was May 17, 1985, while Mesa's tender offer expired on May 23. After acceptance of this appeal on May 14, we received excellent briefs from the parties, heard argument on May 16 and announced our oral ruling in open court at 9:00 a.m. on May 17.

was coercive and inadequate, and that Mesa sought selective treatment for itself. Furthermore, Unocal argues that the board's approval of the exchange offer was made in good faith, on an informed basis, and in the exercise of due care. Under these circumstances, Unocal contends that its directors properly employed this device to protect the company and its stockholders from Mesa's harmful tactics.

III

We begin with the basic issue of the power of a board of directors of a Delaware corporation to adopt a defensive measure of this type. Absent such authority, all other questions are moot. Neither issues of fairness nor business judgment are pertinent without the basic underpinning of a board's legal power to act.

The board has a large reservoir of authority upon which to draw. Its duties and responsibilities proceed from the inherent powers conferred by 8 Del.C. § 141(a), respecting management of the corporation's "business and affairs".[6] Additionally, the powers here being exercised derive from 8 Del.C. § 160(a), conferring broad authority upon a corporation to deal in its own stock.[7] From this it is now well established that in the acquisition of its shares a Delaware corporation may deal selectively with its stockholders, provided the directors have not acted out of a sole or primary purpose to entrench themselves in office. Cheff v. Mathes, 199 A.2d 548, 554 (Del.1964).

Finally, the board's power to act derives from its fundamental duty and obligation to protect the corporate enterprise, which includes stockholders, from harm reasonably perceived, irrespective of its source. See, e.g., Panter v. Marshall Field & Co., 646 F.2d 271, 297 (7th Cir.1981); Northwest Industries v. B.F. Goodrich Co., 301 F.Supp. 706, 712 (N.D.Ill.1969). Thus, we are satisfied that in the broad context of corporate governance,

---

[6] The general grant of power to a board of directors is conferred by 8 Del.C. § 141(a), which provides:

> (a) The business *and affairs* of every corporation organized under this chapter shall be managed by or under the direction of a board of directors, except as may be otherwise provided in this chapter or in its certificate of incorporation. If any such provision is made in the certificate of incorporation, the powers and duties conferred or imposed upon the board of directors by this chapter shall be exercised or performed to such extent and by such person or persons as shall be provided in the certificate of incorporation. (Emphasis added)

[7] This power under 8 Del.C. § 160(a), with certain exceptions not pertinent here, is as follows:

> (a) Every corporation may purchase, redeem, receive, take or otherwise acquire, own and hold, sell, lend, exchange, transfer or otherwise dispose of, pledge, use and otherwise deal in and with its own shares; . . .

including issues of fundamental corporate change, a board of directors is not a passive instrumentality.[8]

Given the foregoing principles, we turn to the standards by which director action is to be measured. In Pogostin v. Rice, 480 A.2d 619 (Del.1984), we held that the business judgment rule, including standards by which director conduct is judged, is applicable in the context of a takeover. *Id.* at 627. The business judgment rule is a "presumption that in making a business decision the directors of a corporation acted on an informed basis, in good faith and in the honest belief that the action taken was in the best interests of the company." Aronson v. Lewis, 473 A.2d 805, 812 (Del.1984) (citations omitted). A hallmark of the business judgment rule is that a court will not substitute its judgment for that of the board if the latter's decision can be "attributed to any rational business purpose." Sinclair Oil Corp. v. Levien, 280 A.2d 717, 720 (Del.1971).

When a board addresses a pending takeover bid it has an obligation to determine whether the offer is in the best interests of the corporation and its shareholders. In that respect a board's duty is no different from any other responsibility it shoulders, and its decisions should be no less entitled to the respect they otherwise would be accorded in the realm of business judgment.[9] See also Johnson v. Trueblood, 629 F.2d 287, 292-293 (3d Cir.1980). There are, however, certain caveats to a proper exercise of this function. Because of the omnipresent specter that a board may be acting primarily in its own interests, rather than those of the corporation and its shareholders, there is an enhanced duty which calls for judicial examination at the threshold before the protections of the business judgment rule may be conferred.

This Court has long recognized that:

> We must bear in mind the inherent danger in the purchase of shares with corporate funds to remove a threat to corporate policy when a threat to control is involved. The directors are of necessity confronted with a conflict of interest, and an objective decision is difficult.

---

[8] Even in the traditional areas of fundamental corporate change, i.e., charter, amendments [8 Del.C. § 242(b)], mergers [8 Del.C. §§ 251(b), 252(c), 253(a), and 254(d)], sale of assets [8 Del.C. § 271(a)], and dissolution [8 Del.C. § 275(a)], director action is a prerequisite to the ultimate disposition of such matters. See also Smith v. Van Gorkom, 488 A.2d 858, 888 (Del.1985).

[9] This is a subject of intense debate among practicing members of the bar and legal scholars. Excellent examples of these contending views are: Dennis Block & Yvette Miller, *The Responsibilities and Obligations of Corporate Directors in Takeover Contests,* 11 Sec.Reg.L.J. 44 (1983); Frank Easterbrook & Daniel Fischel, *Takeover Bids, Defensive Tactics, and Shareholders' Welfare,* 36 Bus.Law. 1733 (1981); Frank Easterbrook & Daniel Fischel, *The Proper Role of a Target's Management in Responding to a Tender Offer,* 94 Harv.L.Rev. 1161 (1981). Leo Herzel, John Schmidt & Scott Davis, *Why Corporate Directors Have a Right to Resist Tender Offers,* 3 Corp.L.Rev. 107 (1980); Martin Lipton, *Takeover Bids in the Target's Boardroom,* 35 Bus.Law. 101 (1979).

Bennett v. Propp, 187 A.2d 405, 409 (Del.1962). In the face of this inherent conflict directors must show that they had reasonable grounds for believing that a danger to corporate policy and effectiveness existed because of another person's stock ownership. Cheff v. Mathes, 199 A.2d at 554-55. However, they satisfy that burden "by showing good faith and reasonable investigation. . . ." *Id.* at 555. Furthermore, such proof is materially enhanced, as here, by the approval of a board comprised of a majority of outside independent directors who have acted in accordance with the foregoing standards. See Aronson v. Lewis, 473 A.2d at 812, 815; Puma v. Marriott, 283 A.2d 693, 695 (Del.Ch.1971); Panter v. Marshall Field & Co., 646 F.2d 271, 295 (7th Cir.1981).

IV

A

In the board's exercise of corporate power to forestall a takeover bid our analysis begins with the basic principle that corporate directors have a fiduciary duty to act in the best interests of the corporation's stockholders. Guth v. Loft, Inc., 5 A.2d 503, 510 (Del.1939). As we have noted, their duty of care extends to protecting the corporation and its owners from perceived harm whether a threat originates from third parties or other shareholders.[10] But such powers are not absolute. A corporation does not have unbridled discretion to defeat any perceived threat by any Draconian means available.

The restriction placed upon a selective stock repurchase is that the directors may not have acted solely or primarily out of a desire to perpetuate themselves in office. See Cheff v. Mathes, 199 A.2d at 556; Kors v. Carey, 158 A.2d at 140. Of course, to this is added the further caveat that inequitable action may not be taken under the guise of law. Schnell v. Chris-Craft Industries, 285 A.2d 437, 439 (Del.1971). The standard of proof established in Cheff v. Mathes . . . is designed to ensure that a defensive measure to thwart or impede a takeover is indeed motivated by a good faith concern for the welfare of the corporation and its stockholders, which in all circumstances must be free of any fraud or other misconduct. Cheff v. Mathes, 199 A.2d at 554-55. However, this does not end the inquiry.

---

[10] It has been suggested that a board's response to a takeover threat should be a passive one. Easterbrook & Fischel *supra*, 36 Bus.Law. at 1750. However, that clearly is not the law of Delaware, and as the proponents of this rule of passivity readily concede, it has not been adopted either by courts or state legislatures. Easterbrook & Fischel, *supra*, 94 Harv.L.Rev. at 1194.

B

A further aspect is the element of balance. If a defensive measure is to come within the ambit of the business judgment rule, it must be reasonable in relation to the threat posed. This entails an analysis by the directors of the nature of the takeover bid and its effect on the corporate enterprise. Examples of such concerns may include: inadequacy of the price offered, nature and timing of the offer, questions of illegality, the impact on "constituencies" other than shareholders (i.e., creditors, customers, employees, and perhaps even the community generally), the risk of nonconsummation, and the quality of securities being offered in the exchange.   See Lipton and Brownstein, *Takeover Responsibilities and Directors' Responsibilities: An Update*, p. 7, ABA National Institute on the Dynamics of Corporate Control (December 8, 1983).   While not a controlling factor, it also seems to us that a board may reasonably consider the basic stockholder interests at stake, including those of short term speculators, whose actions may have fueled the coercive aspect of the offer at the expense of the long term investor.[11] Here the threat posed was viewed by the Unocal board as a grossly inadequate two-tier coercive tender offer coupled with the threat of greenmail.

Specifically, the Unocal directors had concluded that the value of Unocal was substantially above the $54 per share offered in cash at the front end. Furthermore, they determined that the subordinated securities to be exchanged in Mesa's announced squeeze out of the remaining shareholders in the "back-end" merger were "junk bonds" worth far less than $54. It is now well recognized that such offers are a classic coercive measure designed to stampede shareholders into tendering at the first tier, even if the price is inadequate, out of fear of what they will receive at the back end of the transaction.[12] Wholly beyond the coercive aspect of an inadequate two-tier

---

[11] There has been much debate respecting such stockholder interests. One rather impressive study indicates that the stock of over 50% of target companies, who resisted hostile takeovers, later traded at higher market prices than the rejected offer price, or were acquired after the tender offer was defeated by another company at a price higher than the offer price. See Lipton (1979), *supra* note 9, at 106-109, 132-133. Moreover, an update by Kidder Peabody & Company of this study, involving the stock prices of target companies that have defeated hostile tender offers during the period from 1973 to 1982 demonstrates that in a majority of cases the target's shareholders benefited from the defeat. The stock of 81% of the targets studies has, since the tender offer, sold at prices higher than the tender offer price. When adjusted for the time value of money, the figure is 64%. See Lipton & Brownstein, *supra* ABA Institute at 10. The thesis being that this strongly supports application of the business judgment rule in response to takeover threats. There is, however, a rather vehement contrary view. See Easterbrook & Fischel, *supra* 36 Bus.Law. at 1739-1745.

[12] For a discussion of the coercive nature of a two-tier tender offer, see, e.g., Victor Brudney & Marvin Chirelstein, *Fair Shares in Corporate Mergers and Takeovers*, 88 Harv.L.Rev. 297, 337 (1974); Jesse Finkelstein, *Antitakeover Protection Against Two-Tier and Partial Tender Offers: The Validity of Fair Price, Mandatory Bid, and Flip-Over Provisions Under Delaware Law*, 11 Sec.Reg.L.J. 291, 293 (1984); Lipton (1979), *supra*, 35

tender offer, the threat was posed by a corporate raider with a national reputation as a "greenmailer".[13]

In adopting the selective exchange offer, the board stated that its objective was either to defeat the inadequate Mesa offer or, should the offer still succeed, provide the 49% of its stockholders, who would otherwise be forced to accept "junk bonds", with $72 worth of senior debt. We find that both purposes are valid.

However, such efforts would have been thwarted by Mesa's participation in the exchange offer. First, if Mesa could tender its shares, Unocal would effectively be subsidizing the former's continuing effort to buy Unocal stock at $54 per share. Second, Mesa could not, by definition, fit within the class of shareholders being protected from its own coercive and inadequate tender offer.

Thus, we are satisfied that the selective exchange offer is reasonably related to the threats posed. It is consistent with the principle that "the minority stockholder shall receive the substantial equivalent in value of what he had before." Sterling v. Mayflower Hotel Corp., 93 A.2d 107, 114 (Del.1952). See also Rosenblatt v. Getty Oil Co., 493 A.2d 929, 940 (Del.1985). This concept of fairness, while stated in the merger context, is also relevant in the area of tender offer law. Thus, the board's decision to offer what it determined to be the fair value of the corporation to the 49% of its shareholders, who would otherwise be forced to accept highly subordinated "junk bonds", is reasonable and consistent with the directors' duty to ensure that the minority stockholders receive equal value for their shares.

V

Mesa contends that it is unlawful, and the trial court agreed, for a corporation to discriminate in this fashion against one shareholder. It argues correctly that no case has ever sanctioned a device that precludes a raider from sharing in a benefit available to all other stockholders. However, as we have noted earlier, the principle of selective stock repurchases by a Delaware corporation is neither unknown nor unauthorized. Cheff v. Mathes, 199 A.2d at 554. The only difference is that heretofore the approved transaction was the payment of "greenmail" to a raider or dissident posing a threat to the

---

Bus.Law. at 113-14; Note, *Protecting Shareholders Against Partial and Two-Tiered Takeovers: The Poison Pill Preferred*, 97 Harv.L.Rev. 1964, 1966 (1984).

[13] The term "greenmail" refers to the practice of buying out a takeover bidder's stock at a premium that is not available to other shareholders in order to prevent the takeover. The Chancery Court noted that "Mesa has made tremendous profits from its takeover activities although in the past few years it has not been successful in acquiring any of the target companies on an unfriendly basis." Moreover, the trial court specifically found that the actions of the Unocal board were taken in good faith to eliminate both the inadequacies of the tender offer and to forestall the payment of "greenmail".

corporate enterprise. All other stockholders were denied such favored treatment, and given Mesa's past history of greenmail, its claims here are rather ironic.

However, our corporate law is not static. It must grow and develop in response to, indeed in anticipation of, evolving concepts and needs. Merely because the General Corporation Law is silent as to a specific matter does not mean that it is prohibited. See Providence and Worcester Co. v. Baker, 378 A.2d 121, 123-124 (Del.1977). In the days when *Cheff, Bennett, Martin* and *Kors* were decided, the tender offer, while not an unknown device, was virtually unused, and little was known of such methods as two-tier "front-end" loaded offers with their coercive effects. Then, the favored attack of a raider was stock acquisition followed by a proxy contest. Various defensive tactics, which provided no benefit whatever to the raider, evolved. Thus, the use of corporate funds by management to counter a proxy battle was approved. Hall v. Trans-Lux Daylight Picture Screen Corp., 171 A.2d 226 (Del.1934); Hibbert v. Hollywood Park, Inc., 457 A.2d 339 (Del.1983). Litigation, supported by corporate funds, aimed at the raider has long been a popular device.

More recently, as the sophistication of both raiders and targets has developed, a host of other defensive measures to counter such ever mounting threats has evolved and received judicial sanction. These include defensive charter amendments and other devices bearing some rather exotic, but apt, names: Crown Jewel, White Knight, Pac Man, and Golden Parachute. Each has highly selective features, the object of which is to deter or defeat the raider.

Thus, while the exchange offer is a form of selective treatment, given the nature of the threat posed here the response is neither unlawful nor unreasonable. If the board of directors is disinterested, has acted in good faith and with due care, its decision in the absence of an abuse of discretion will be upheld as a proper exercise of business judgment.

To this Mesa responds that the board is not disinterested, because the directors are receiving a benefit from the tender of their own shares, which because of the Mesa exclusion, does not devolve upon *all* stockholders equally. See Aronson v. Lewis, 473 A.2d 805, 812 (Del.1984). However, Mesa concedes that if the exclusion is valid, then the directors and all other stockholders share the same benefit. The answer of course is that the exclusion is valid, and the directors' participation in the exchange offer does not rise to the level of a disqualifying interest. The excellent discussion in Johnson v. Trueblood, 620 F.2d at 292-293, of the use of the business judgment rule in takeover contests also seems pertinent here.

Nor does this become an "interested" director transaction merely because certain board members are large stockholders. As this Court has previously noted, that fact alone does not create a disqualifying "personal pecuniary interest" to defeat the operation of the business judgment rule. Cheff v. Mathes, 199 A.2d at 554.

Mesa also argues that the exclusion permits the directors to abdicate the fiduciary duties they owe it. However, that is not so. The board continues to owe Mesa the duties of due care and loyalty. But in the face of the destructive threat Mesa's tender offer was perceived to pose, the board had a supervening duty to protect the corporate enterprise, which includes the other shareholders, from threatened harm.

Mesa contends that the basis of this action is punitive, and solely in response to the exercise of its rights of corporate democracy.[14] Nothing precludes Mesa, as a stockholder, from acting in its own self-interest. See e.g., DuPont v. DuPont, 251 F. 937 (D.Del.1918), *aff'd*, 256 F. 129 (3d Cir.1918); Ringling Bros.-Barnum & Bailey Combined Shows, Inc., v. Ringling, 53 A.2d 441, 447 (Del.1947); Heil v. Standard Gas & Electric Co., 151 A. 303, 304 (Del.Ch.1930). But see, Allied Chemical & Dye Corp. v. Steel & Tube Co. of America, 120 A. 486, 491 (Del.Ch.1923) (majority shareholder owes a fiduciary duty to the minority shareholders). However, Mesa, while pursuing its own interests, has acted in a manner which a board consisting of a majority of independent directors has reasonably determined to be contrary to the best interests of Unocal and its other shareholders. In this situation, there is no support in Delaware law for the proposition that, when responding to a perceived harm, a corporation must guarantee a benefit to a stockholder who is deliberately provoking the danger being addressed. There is no obligation of self-sacrifice by a corporation and its shareholders in the face of such a challenge.

Here, the Court of Chancery specifically found that the "directors' decision [to oppose the Mesa tender offer] was made in the good faith belief that the Mesa tender offer is inadequate." Given our standard of review under Levitt v. Bouvier, 287 A.2d 671, 673 (Del.1972), and Application of Delaware Racing Association, 213 A.2d 203, 207 (Del.1965), we are satisfied that Unocal's board has met its burden of proof. Cheff v. Mathes, 199 A.2d at 555.

VI

In conclusion, there was directorial power to oppose the Mesa tender offer, and to undertake a selective stock exchange made in good faith and upon a reasonable investigation pursuant to a clear duty to protect the corporate enterprise. Further, the selective stock repurchase plan chosen by

---

[14] This seems to be the underlying basis of the trial court's principal reliance on the unreported Chancery decision of Fisher v. Moltz, Del.Ch. No. 6068 (1979), published in 5 Del.J.Corp.L. 530 (1980). However, the facts in *Fisher* are thoroughly distinguishable. There, a corporation offered to repurchase the shares of its former employees, except those of the plaintiffs, merely because the latter were then engaged in lawful competition with the company. No threat to the enterprise was posed, and at best it can be said that the exclusion was motivated by pique instead of a rational corporate purpose.

Unocal is reasonable in relation to the threat that the board rationally and reasonably believed was posed by Mesa's inadequate and coercive two-tier tender offer. Under those circumstances the board's action is entitled to be measured by the standards of the business judgment rule. Thus, unless it is shown by a preponderance of the evidence that the directors' decisions were primarily based on perpetuating themselves in office, or some other breach of fiduciary duty such as fraud, overreaching, lack of good faith, or being uninformed, a Court will not substitute its judgment for that of the board.

In this case that protection is not lost merely because Unocal's directors have tendered their shares in the exchange offer. Given the validity of the Mesa exclusion, they are receiving a benefit shares generally by all other stockholders except Mesa. In this circumstance the test of Aronson v. Lewis, 473 A.2d at 812, is satisfied. See also Cheff v. Mathes, 199 A.2d at 554. If the stockholders are displeased with the action of their elected representatives, the powers of corporate democracy are at their disposal to turn the board out. Aronson v. Lewis, 473 A.2d 805, 811 (Del.1984). See also 8 Del.C. §§ 141(k) and 211(b).

With the Court of Chancery's findings that the exchange offer was based on the board's good faith belief that the Mesa offer was inadequate, that the board's action was informed and taken with due care, that Mesa's prior activities justify a reasonable inference that its principal objective was greenmail, and implicitly, that the substance of the offer itself was reasonable and fair to the corporation and its stockholders if Mesa were included, we cannot say that the Unocal directors have acted in such a manner as to have passed an "unintelligent and unadvised judgment". Mitchell v. Highland-Western Glass Co., 167 A. 831, 833 (Del.Ch.1933). The decision of the Court of Chancery is therefore REVERSED, and the preliminary injunction is VACATED.

MORAN v. HOUSEHOLD INTERNATIONAL, INC.
500 A.2d 1346 (Del.1985)

Before CHRISTIE, Chief Justice, and McNEILLY and MOORE, J.J.

McNEILLY, Justice. This case presents to this Court for review the most recent defensive mechanism in the arsenal of corporate takeover weaponry -- the Preferred Share purchase Rights Plan ("Rights Plan" or "Plan"). The validity of this mechanism has attracted national attention. *Amici curiae* briefs have been filed in support of appellants by the Security and Exchange Commission ("SEC")[1] and the Investment Company Institute.

---

[1] The SEC split 3-2 on whether to intervene in this case. The two dissenting Commissioners have publicly disagreed with the other three as to the merits of the Rights

An *amicus curiae* brief has been filed in support of appellees ("Household") by the United Food and Commercial Workers International Union.

In a detailed opinion, the Court of Chancery upheld the Rights Plan as a legitimate exercise of business judgment by Household. Moran v. Household International, Inc., 490 A.2d 1059 (Del.Ch.1985). We agree, and therefore, affirm the judgment below.

I

The facts giving rise to this case have been carefully delineated in the Court of Chancery's opinion. A review of the basic facts is necessary for a complete understanding of the issues.

On August 14, 1984, the Board of Directors of Household International, Inc. adopted the Rights Plan by a fourteen to two vote.[2] The intricacies of the Rights Plan are contained in a 48-page document entitled "Rights Agreement". Basically, the Plan provides that Household common stockholders are entitled to the issuance of one Right per common share under certain triggering conditions. There are two triggering events that can activate the Rights. The first is the announcement of a tender offer for 30% of Household's shares ("30% trigger") and the second is the acquisition of 20% of Household's shares by any single entity or group ("20% trigger").

If an announcement of a tender offer for 30% of Household's shares is made, the Rights are issued and are immediately exercisable to purchase 1/100 share of new preferred stock for $100 and are redeemable by the Board for $.50 per Right. If 20% of Household's shares are acquired by anyone, the Rights are issued and become non-redeemable and are exercisable to purchase 1/100 of a share of preferred. If a Right is not exercised for preferred, and thereafter, a merger or consolidation occurs, the Rights holder can exercise each Right to purchase $200 of the common stock of the tender offeror for $100. This "flip-over" provision of the Rights Plan is at the heart of this controversy.

Household is a diversified holding company with its principal subsidiaries engaged in financial services, transportation and merchandising. HFC, National Car Rental and Vons Grocery are three of its wholly-owned entities.

Household did not adopt its Rights Plan during a battle with a corporate raider, but as a preventive mechanism to ward off future advances. The Vice-Chancellor found that as early as February 1984, Household's management became concerned about the company's vulnerability as a

---

Plan. 17 Sec.Reg. & Law Report 400; Wall St.J., March 20, 1985, at 6.

[2] Household's Board has ten outside directors and six who are members of management. Messrs. Moran (appellant) and Whitehead voted against the Plan. The record reflects that Whitehead voted against the Plan not on its substance but because he thought it was novel and would bring unwanted publicity to Household.

takeover target and began considering amending its charter to render a takeover more difficult. After considering the matter, Household decided not to pursue a fair price amendment.[3]

In the meantime, appellant Moran, one of Household's own Directors and also Chairman of the Dyson-Kissner-Moran Corporation, ("D-K-M") which is the largest single stockholder of Household, began discussions concerning a possible leveraged buy-out of Household by D-K-M. D-K-M's financial studies showed that Household's stock was significantly undervalued in relation to the company's break-up value. It is uncontradicted that Moran's suggestion of a leveraged buy-out never progressed beyond the discussion stage.

Concerned about Household's vulnerability to a raider in light of the current takeover climate, Household secured the services of Wachtell, Lipton, Rosen and Katz ("Wachtell, Lipton") and Goldman, Sachs & Co. ("Goldman, Sachs") to formulate a takeover policy for recommendation to the Household Board at its August 14 meeting. After a July 31 meeting with a Household Board member and a pre-meeting distribution of material on the potential takeover problem and the proposed Rights Plan, the Board met on August 14, 1984.

Representatives of Wachtell, Lipton and Goldman, Sachs attended the August 14 meeting. The minutes reflect that Mr. Lipton explained to the Board that his recommendation of the Plan was based on his understanding that the Board was concerned about the increasing frequency of "bust-up"[4] takeovers, the increasing takeover activity in the financial service industry, such as Leucadia's attempt to take over Arco, and the possible adverse effect this type of activity could have on employees and others concerned with and vital to the continuing successful operation of Household even in the absence of any actual bust-up takeover attempt. Against this factual background, the Plan was approved.

Thereafter, Moran and the company of which he is Chairman, D-K-M, filed this suit. On the eve of trial, Gretl Golter, the holder of 500 shares of Household, was permitted to intervene as an additional plaintiff. The trial was held, and the Court of Chancery ruled in favor of Household. Appellants now appeal from that ruling to this Court.

II

The primary issue here is the applicability of the business judgment rule as the standard by which the adoption of the Rights Plan should be reviewed. Much of this issue has been decided by our recent decision in Unocal Corp. v. Mesa Petroleum Co., 493 A.2d 946 (Del.1985). In *Unocal*, we applied

---

[3] A fair price amendment to a corporate charter generally requires supermajority approval for certain business combinations and sets minimum price criteria for mergers.

[4] "Bust-up" takeover generally refers to a situation in which one seeks to finance an acquisition by selling off pieces of the acquired company.

the business judgment rule to analyze Unocal's discriminatory self-tender. We explained:

> When a board addresses a pending takeover bid it has an obligation to determine whether the offer is in the best interests of the corporation and its shareholders. In that respect a board's duty is no different from any other responsibility it shoulders, and its decisions should be no less entitled to the respect they otherwise would be accorded in the realm of business judgment.

Id. at 954 (citation and footnote omitted).

Other jurisdictions have also applied the business judgment rule to actions by which target companies have sought to forestall takeover activity they considered undesirable. See Gearhart Industries v. Smith International, 741 F.2d 707 (5th Cir.1984) (sale of discounted subordinate debentures containing springing warrants); Treco, Inc. v. Land of Lincoln Savings and Loan, 749 F.2d 374 (7th Cir.1984) (amendment to by-laws); Panter v. Marshall Field, 646 F.2d 271 (7th Cir.1981) (acquisitions to create antitrust problems); Johnson v. Trueblood, 629 F.2d 287 (3d Cir.1980), *cert. denied*, 450 U.S. 999 (1981) (refusal to tender); Crouse-Hinds Co. v. InterNorth, Inc., 634 F.2d 690 (2d Cir.1980) (sale of stock to favored party); Treadway v. Cane Corp., 638 F.2d 357 (2d Cir.1980) (sale to White Knight); Enterra Corp. v. SGS Associated, 600 F.Supp. 678 (E.D.Pa.1985) (standstill agreement); Buffalo Forge Co. v. Ogden Corp., 555 F.Supp. 892 (W.D.N.Y.), *aff'd* 717 F.2d 757 (2d Cir.), *cert. denied*, 464 U.S. 1018 (1983) (sale of treasury shares and grant of stock option to White Knight); Whittaker Corp. v. Edgar, 535 F.Supp. 933 (N.D.Ill.1982) (disposal of valuable assets); Martin Marietta Corp. v. Bendix Corp., 549 F.Supp. 623 (D.Md.1982) (Pac-Man defense).[6]

This case is distinguishable from the ones cited, since here we have a defensive mechanism adopted to ward off possible future advances and not a mechanism adopted in reaction to a specific threat. This distinguishing factor does not result in the Directors losing the protection of the business judgment rule. To the contrary, pre-planning for the contingency of a hostile takeover might reduce the risk that, under the pressure of a takeover bid, management will fail to exercise reasonable judgment. Therefore, in reviewing a pre-planned defensive mechanism it seems even more appropriate to apply the business judgment rule. See Warner Communications v. Murdock, 581 F.Supp. 1482, 1491 (D.Del.1984).

Of course, the business judgment rule can only sustain corporate decision making or transactions that are within the power or authority of the

---

[6] The "Pac-Man" defense is generally a target company countering an unwanted tender offer by making its own tender offer for stock of the would-be acquirer. Dennis Block & Yvette Miller, *The Responsibilities and Obligations of Corporate Directors in Takeover Contests*, 11 Sec.Reg.L.J. 44, 64 (1983).

Board. Therefore, before the business judgment rule can be applied it must be determined whether the Directors were authorized to adopt the Rights Plan.

III

Appellants vehemently contend that the Board of Directors was unauthorized to adopt the Rights Plan. First, appellants contend that no provision of the Delaware General Corporation Law authorizes the issuance of such Rights. Secondly, appellants, along with the SEC, contend that the Board is unauthorized to usurp stockholders' rights to receive hostile tender offers. Third, appellants and the SEC also contend that the Board is unauthorized to fundamentally restrict stockholders' rights to conduct a proxy contest. We address each of these contentions in turn.

A

While appellants contend that no provision of the Delaware General Corporation Law authorizes the Rights Plan, Household contends that the Rights Plan was issued pursuant to 8 Del.C. §§ 151(g) and 157. It explains that the Rights are authorized by § 157[7] and the issue of preferred stock underlying the Rights is authorized by § 151.[8] Appellants respond by making several attacks upon the authority to issue the Rights pursuant to § 157.

Appellants begin by contending that § 157 cannot authorize the Rights Plan since § 157 has never served the purpose of authorizing a takeover

---

[7] The power to issue rights to purchase shares is conferred by 8 Del.C. § 157 which provides in relevant part:

> Subject to any provisions in the certificate of incorporation, every corporation may create and issue, whether or not in connection with the issue and sale of any shares of stock or other securities of the corporation, rights or options entitling the holders thereof to purchase from the corporation any shares of its capital stock of any class or classes, such rights or options to be evidenced by or in such instrument or instruments as shall be approved by the board of directors.

[8] 8 Del.C. § 151(g) provides in relevant part:

> When any corporation desires to issue any shares of stock of any class or of any series of any class of which the voting powers, designations, preferences and relative, participating, optional or other rights, if any, or the qualifications, limitations or restrictions thereof, if any, shall not have been set forth in the certificate of incorporation or in any amendment thereto but shall be provided for in a resolution or resolutions adopted by the board of directors pursuant to authority expressly vested in it by the provisions of the certificate of incorporation or any amendment thereto, a certificate setting forth a copy of such resolution or resolutions and the number of shares of stock of such class or series shall be executed, acknowledged, filed, recorded, and shall become effective, in accordance with § 103 of this title.

defense. Appellants contend that § 157 is a corporate financing statute, and that nothing in its legislative history suggests a purpose that has anything to do with corporate control or a takeover defense. Appellants are unable to demonstrate that the legislature, in its adoption of § 157, meant to limit the applicability of § 157 to only the issuance of Rights for the purposes of corporate financing. Without such affirmative evidence, we decline to impose such a limitation upon the section that the legislature has not. Compare Providence & Worchester Co. v. Baker, 378 A.2d 121, 124 (Del.1977) (refusal to read a bar to protective voting provisions into 8 Del.C. § 212(a)).

As we noted in *Unocal*:

> [O]ur corporate law is not static. It must grow and develop in response to, indeed in anticipation of, evolving concepts and needs. Merely because the General Corporation Law is silent as to a specific matter does not mean that it is prohibited.

493 A.2d at 957. See also Cheff v. Mathes, 199 A.2d 548 (Del.1964).

Secondly, appellants contend that § 157 does not authorize the issuance of sham rights such as the Rights Plan. They contend that the Rights were designed never to be exercised, and that the Plan has no economic value. In addition, they contend the preferred stock made subject to the Rights if also illusory, citing Telvest, Inc. v. Olson, C.A. No. 5798 (Del.Ch.1979).

Appellants' sham contention fails in both regards. As to the Rights, they can and will be exercised upon the happening of a triggering mechanism, as we have observed during the current struggle of Sir James Goldsmith to take control of Crown Zellerbach. See Wall St.J., July 26, 1985, at 3, 12. As to the preferred shares, we agree with the Court of Chancery that they are distinguishable from sham securities invalidated in *Telvest, supra*. The Household preferred issuable upon the happening of a triggering event, have superior dividend and liquidation rights.

Third, appellants contend that § 157 authorizes the issuance of Rights "entitling holders thereof to purchase from the corporation any shares of *its* capital stock of any class. . ." (emphasis added). Therefore, their contention continues, the plain language of the statute does not authorize Household to issue rights to purchase another's capital stock upon a merger or consolidation.

Household contends, *inter alia*, that the Rights Plan is analogous to "anti-destruction" or "anti-dilution" provisions which are customary features of a wide variety of corporate securities. While appellants seem to concede that "anti-destruction" provisions are valid under Delaware corporate law, they seek to distinguish the Rights Plan as not being incidental, as are most "anti-destruction" provisions, to a corporation's statutory power to finance itself. We find no merit to such a distinction. We have already rejected appellants' similar contention that § 157 could only be used for financing purposes. We also reject that distinction here.

"Anti-destruction" clauses generally ensure holders of certain securities of the protection of their right of conversion in the event of a merger by giving them the right to convert their securities into whatever securities are to replace the stock of their company. The fact that the rights here have as their purpose the prevention of coercive two-tier tender offers does not invalidate them.

Fourth, appellants contend that Household's reliance upon § 157 is contradictory to 8 Del.C. § 203.[9] Section 203 is a "notice" statute which generally requires that timely notice be given to a target of an offeror's intention to make a tender offer. Appellants contend that the lack of stronger regulation by the State indicates a legislative intent to reject anything which would impose an impediment to the tender offer process. Such a contention is a *non sequitur*. The desire to have little state regulation of tender offers cannot be said to also indicate a desire to also have little private regulation. Furthermore, as we explain *infra*, we do not view the Rights Plan as much of an impediment on the tender offer process.[a] . . .

Having concluded that sufficient authority for the Rights Plan exists in 8 Del.C. § 157, we note the inherent powers of the Board conferred by 8

---

[9] 8 Del.C. § 203 provides in relevant part:

(a) No offeror shall make a tender offer unless:

(1) Not less than 20 nor more than 60 days before the date the tender offer is to be made, the offeror shall deliver personally or by registered or certified mail to the corporation whose equity securities are to be subject to the tender offer, at its registered office in this State or at its principal place of business, a written statement of the offeror's intention to make the tender offer. . . .

(2) The tender offer shall remain open for a period of at least 20 days after it is first made to the holders of the equity securities, during which period any stockholder may withdraw any of the equity securities tendered to the offeror, and any revised or amended tender offer which changes the amount or type of consideration offered or the number of equity securities for which the offer is made shall remain open at least 10 days following the amendment; and

(3) The offeror and any associate of the offeror will not purchase or pay for any tendered equity security for a period of at least 20 days after the tender offer is first made to the holders of the equity securities, and no such purchase or payment shall be made within 10 days after an amended or revised tender offer if the amendment or revision changes the amount or type of consideration offered or the number of equity securities for which the offer is made. If during the period the tender offer must remain open pursuant to this section, a greater number of equity securities is tendered than the offeror is bound or willing to purchase, the equity securities shall be purchased pro rata, as nearly as may be, according to the number of shares tendered during such period by each equity security holder.

---

[a] The court also held that a poison pill plan adopted pursuant to State law did not violate the Commerce Clause. Following the decision of the United States Supreme Court in CTS Corp. v. Dynamics Corp. of America, 481 U.S. 69 (1987), upholding an Indiana second-generation state anti-takeover statute, this issue is no longer central. The *CTS* case is excerpted in Chapter 23, *infra*. Eds.

Del.C. § 141(a),[11] concerning the management of the corporation's "business and *affairs*" (emphasis added), also provides the Board additional authority upon which to enact the Rights Plan. *Unocal*, 493 A.2d at 953.

B

Appellants contend that the Board is authorized to usurp stockholders' rights to receive tender offers by changing Household's fundamental structure. We conclude that the Rights Plan does not prevent stockholders from receiving tender offers, and that the change of Household's structure was less than that which results from the implementation of other defensive mechanisms upheld by various courts.

Appellants' contention that stockholders will lose their right to receive and accept tender offers seems to be premised upon an understanding of the Rights Plan which is illustrated by the SEC *amicus* brief which states: "The Chancery Court's decision seriously understates the impact of this plan. In fact, as we discuss below, the Rights Plan will deter not only two-tier offers, but virtually all hostile tender offers."

The fallacy of that contention is apparent when we look at the recent takeover of Crown Zellerbach, which has a similar Rights Plan, by Sir James Goldsmith. Wall St.J., July 26, 1985, at 3, 12. The evidence at trial also evidenced many methods around the Plan ranging from tendering with a condition that the Board redeem the Rights, tendering with a high minimum condition of shares and Rights, tendering and soliciting consents to remove the Board and redeem the Rights, to acquiring 50% of the shares and causing Household to self-tender for the Rights. One could also form a group of up to 19.9% and solicit proxies for consents to remove the Board and redeem the Rights. These are but a few of the methods by which Household can still be acquired by a hostile tender offer.

In addition, the Rights Plan is not absolute. When the Household Board of Directors is faced with a tender offer and a request to redeem the Rights, they will not be able to arbitrarily reject the offer. They will be held to the same fiduciary standards any other board of directors would be held to in deciding to adopt a defensive mechanism, the same standard as they were held to in originally approving the Rights Plan. See *Unocal*, 493 A.2d at 954-55, 958.

---

[11] 8 Del.C. § 141(a) provides:

(a) The business and affairs of every corporation organized under this chapter shall be managed by or under the direction of a board of directors, except as may be otherwise provided in this chapter or in its certificate of incorporation. If any such provision is made in the certificate of incorporation, the powers and duties conferred or imposed upon the board of directors by this chapter shall be exercised or performed to such extent and by such person or persons as shall be provided in the certificate of incorporation.

In addition, appellants contend that the deterrence of tender offers will be accomplished by what they label "a fundamental transfer of power from the stockholders to the directors." They contend that this transfer of power, in itself, is unauthorized.

The Rights Plan will result in no more of a structural change than any other defensive mechanism adopted by a board of directors. The Rights Plan does not destroy the assets of the corporation. The implementation of the Plan neither results in any outflow of money from the corporation nor impairs its financial flexibility. It does not dilute earnings per share and does not have any adverse tax consequences for the corporation or its stockholders. The Plan has not adversely affected the market price of Household's stock.

Comparing the Rights Plan with other defensive mechanisms, it does less harm to the value structure of the corporation than do the other mechanisms. Other mechanisms result in increased debt of the corporation. See Whittaker Corp. v. Edgar, *supra* (sale of "prize asset"), Cheff v. Mathes, *supra*, (paying greenmail to eliminate a threat), Unocal Corp. v. Mesa Petroleum Co., *supra*, (discriminatory self-tender).

There is little change in the governance structure as a result of the adoption of the Rights Plan. The Board does not now have unfettered discretion in refusing to redeem the Rights. The Board has no more discretion in refusing to redeem the Rights than it does in enacting any defensive mechanism.

The contention that the Rights Plan alters the structure more than do other defensive mechanisms because it is so effective as to make the corporation completely safe from hostile tender offers is likewise without merit. As explained above, there are numerous methods to successfully launch a hostile tender offer[b]

C

Appellants' third contention is that the Board was unauthorized to fundamentally restrict stockholders' rights to conduct a proxy contest. Appellants contend that the "20% trigger" effectively prevents any stockholder from first acquiring 20% or more shares before conducting a proxy contest and further, it prevents stockholders from banding together into a group to solicit proxies if, collectively, they own 20% or more of the stock.[12] In addition, at trial, appellants contended that read literally, the Rights Agreement triggers the Rights upon the mere acquisition of the right

---

[b] How would a back-end or flip-in plan fare under this analysis? Eds.

[12] Appellants explain that the acquisition of 20% of the shares trigger the Rights, making them non-redeemable, and thereby would prevent even a future friendly offer for the ten-year life of the Rights.

to vote 20% or more of the shares through a proxy solicitation, and thereby precludes any proxy contest from being waged.[13]

Appellants seem to have conceded this last contention in light of Household's response that the receipt of a proxy does not make the recipient the "beneficial owner" of the shares involved which would trigger the Rights. In essence, the Rights Agreement provides that the Rights are triggered when someone becomes the "beneficial owner" of 20% or more of Household stock. Although a literal reading of the Rights Agreement definition of "beneficial owner" would seem to include those shares which one has the right to vote, it has long been recognized that the relationship between grantor and recipient of a proxy is one of agency, and the agency is revocable by the grantor at any time. Henn, *Corporations* § 196, at 518. Therefore, the holder of a proxy is not the "beneficial owner" of the stock. As a result, the mere acquisition of the right to vote 20% of the shares does not trigger the Rights.

The issue, then, is whether the restriction upon individuals or groups from first acquiring 20% of shares before waging a proxy contest fundamentally restricts stockholders' right to conduct a proxy contest. Regarding this issue the Court of Chancery found:

> Thus, while the Rights Plan does deter the formation of proxy efforts of a certain magnitude, it does not limit the voting power of individual shares. On the evidence presented it is highly conjectural to assume that a particular effort to assert shareholder views in the election of directors or revisions of corporate policy will be frustrated by the proxy feature of the Plan. Household's witnesses, Troubh and Higgins, described recent corporate takeover battles in which insurgents holding less than 10% stock ownership were able to secure corporate control through a proxy contest or the threat of one.

Moran, 490 A.2d at 1080.

We conclude that there was sufficient evidence at trial to support the Vice-Chancellor's finding that the effect upon proxy contests will be minimal. Evidence at trial established that many proxy contests are won with an insurgent ownership of less than 20%, and that very large holdings are no guarantee of success. There was also testimony that the key variable in proxy contest success is the merit of an insurgent's issues, not the size of his holdings.

---

[13] The SEC still contends that the mere acquisition of the right to vote 20% of the shares through a proxy solicitation triggers the rights. We do not interpret the Rights Agreement in that manner.

IV

Having concluded that the adoption of the Rights Plan was within the authority of the Directors, we now look to whether the Directors have met their burden under the business judgment rule.

The business judgment rule is a "presumption that in making a business decision the directors of a corporation acted on an informed basis, in good faith and in the honest belief that the action taken was in the best interests of the company." Aronson v. Lewis, 473 A.2d 805, 812 (Del.1984) (citations omitted). Notwithstanding, in *Unocal* we held that when the business judgment rule applies to adoption of a defensive mechanism, the initial burden will lie with the directors. The "directors must show that they had reasonable grounds for believing that a danger to corporate policy and effectiveness existed. . . . [T]hey satisfy that burden 'by showing good faith and reasonable investigation. . . .'" *Unocal*, 493 A.2d at 955 (citing Cheff v. Mathes, 199 A.2d at 554-55). In addition, the directors must show that the defensive mechanism was "reasonable in relation to the threat posed." *Unocal*, 493 A.2d at 955. Moreover, that proof is materially enhanced, as we noted in *Unocal*, where, as here, a majority of the board favoring the proposal consisted of outside independent directors who have acted in accordance with the foregoing standards. *Unocal*, 493 A.2d at 955; *Aronson*, 473 A.2d at 815. Then, the burden shifts back to the plaintiffs who have the ultimate burden of persuasion to show a breach of the directors' fiduciary duties. *Unocal*, 493 A.2d at 958.

There are no allegations here of any bad faith on the part of the Directors' action in the adoption of the Rights Plan. There is no allegation that the Directors' action was taken for entrenchment purposes. Household has adequately demonstrated, as explained above, that the adoption of the Rights Plan was in reaction to what it perceived to be the threat in the market place of coercive two-tier tender offers. Appellants do contend, however, that the Board did not exercise informed business judgment in its adoption of the Plan.

Appellants contend that the Household Board was uninformed since they were, *inter alia*, told the Plan would not inhibit a proxy contest, were not told the plan would preclude all hostile acquisitions of Household, and were told that Delaware counsel opined that the plan was within the business judgment of the Board.

As to the first two contentions, as we explained above, the Rights Plan will not have a severe impact upon proxy contests and it will not preclude all hostile acquisitions of Household. Therefore, the Directors were not misinformed or uninformed on these facts.

Appellants contend the Delaware counsel did not express an opinion on the flip-over provision of the Rights, rather only that the Rights would constitute validly issued and outstanding rights to subscribe to the preferred stock of the company.

To determine whether a business judgment reached by a board of directors was an informed one, we determine whether the directors were grossly negligent. *Smith v. Van Gorkom*, 488 A.2d 858 (Del.1985). Upon a review of this record, we conclude the Directors were not grossly negligent. The information supplied to the Board on August 14 provided the essentials of the Plan. The Directors were given beforehand a notebook which included a three-page summary of the Plan along with articles on the current takeover environment. The extended discussion between the Board and representatives of Wachtell, Lipton and Goldman, Sachs before approval of the Plan reflected a full and candid evaluation of the Plan. Moran's expression of his views at the meeting served to place before the Board a knowledgeable critique of the Plan. The factual happenings here are clearly distinguishable from the actions of the directors of Trans Union Corporation who displayed gross negligence in approving a cash-out merger. *Id.*

In addition, to meet their burden, the Directors must show that the defensive mechanism was "reasonable in relation to the threat posed." The record reflects a concern on the part of the Directors over the increasing frequency in the financial services industry of "bootstrap" and "bust-up" takeovers. The Directors were also concerned that such takeovers may take the form of two-tier offers.[14] In addition, on August 14, the Household Board was aware of Moran's overture on behalf of D-K-M. In sum, the Directors reasonably believed Household was vulnerable to coercive acquisition techniques and adopted a reasonable defensive mechanism to protect itself.

V

In conclusion, the Household Directors receive the benefit of the business judgment rule in their adoption of the Rights Plan.

The Directors adopted the Plan pursuant to statutory authority in 8 Del.C. §§ 141, 151, 157. We reject appellants' contentions that the Rights Plan strips stockholders of their rights to receive tender offers, and that the Rights Plan fundamentally restricts proxy contests.

The Directors adopted the Plan in the good faith belief that it was necessary to protect Household from coercive acquisition techniques. The Board was informed as to the details of the Plan. In addition, Household has demonstrated that the Plan is reasonable in relation to the threat posed. Appellants, on the other hand, have failed to convince us that the Directors breached any fiduciary duty in their adoption of the Rights Plan.

While we conclude for present purposes that the Household Directors are protected by the business judgment rule, that does not end the matter.

---

[14] We have discussed the coercive nature of two-tier tender offers in *Unocal*, 493 A.2d at 956, n.12. We explained in *Unocal* that a discriminatory self-tender was reasonably related to the threat of two-tier tender offers and possible greenmail.

The ultimate response to an actual takeover bid must be judged by the Directors' actions at that time, and nothing we say here relieves them of their basic fundamental duties to the corporation and its stockholders. *Unocal*, 493 A.2d at 954-55, 958; Smith v. Van Gorkom, 488 A.2d at 872-73; *Aronson*, 473 A.2d at 812-13; Pogostin v. Rice, 480 A.2d 619, 627 (Del.1984). Their use of the Plan will be evaluated when and if the issue arises.

AFFIRMED.

Unocal and *Moran* announced an intermediate level of review that applies to director action bearing on corporate control. An enhanced business judgment standard is first applied as a condition to the availability of traditional business judgment protection. A board whose conduct fails this enhanced standard loses the protection of the business judgment rule and must face judicial scrutiny under the intrinsic (or entire) fairness test.

As *Unocal* explicitly states, the need for an intermediate standard of review in a takeover setting results from "the omnipresent specter that a board may be acting primarily in its own interests, rather than those of the corporation and its shareholders." *Unocal* and *Moran* lay a framework for approaching the range of conflicts that are presented by the drama of a takeover proposal. *Unocal* itself scripts a main act for the drama by prescribing the standard against which director conduct will be evaluated in what has been the most familiar story line -- management efforts to defeat an unwanted offer. *Moran* writes a prologue by allowing management to acquire, before a hostile offer is made, the means necessary to defeat one if that proves appropriate. However, *Unocal* cautions that reliance on the poison pill will be resolved at the time of the offer: a decision not to redeem the pill in the face of a hostile bid will be tested as a defensive tactic at that time. *Moran* merely allows putting the poison pill in place.[121]

But whether *Unocal* contemplates more than a drama, substance rather than a *Cheff*-like script, requires further inquiry: is the new standard is intended to be a substantive constraint on defensive tactics or merely another formal justification for defensive tactics that corporate planners must recite to succeed. If the standard is substantive, two further questions follow from the requirement that defensive tactics be "reasonable" in relation to a "threat." First, does the new standard regulate defensive responses or merely pose a threshold test: that is, supposing some threat is shown, how far does the new standard nonetheless constrain the range of permissible

---

[121] A third case, Revlon v. MacAndrews & Forbes Holdings, 506 A.2d 173 (Del.1986), supplies an epilogue for occasions when defense fails, and target management seeks to effect the company's sale to a favored bidder. Chapter 19 considers the legal standards governing the friendly sale of the target company, albeit as a way to avoid a forced sale to a less favorable bidder.

tactics? Second, and closely related, what forms of hostile offers -- if any -- might fail to qualify as "threats", and so preclude *any* defensive tactics under the proportionality test?

4. Is There Substance to Proportionality Review?

Unocal and *Moran* can be read to suggest that proportionality review is primarily a formal, rhetorical instruction rather than a substantive standard of review.[122] On this view, the new standard, like the old policy conflict/primary purpose test, serves chiefly to signal judicial concern and to invite planners to proceed with their defenses only after constructing a record that demonstrates reasonableness and articulates a "threat". The best evidence for this construction is how little effort the Delaware Supreme Court devoted to justifying the discriminatory repurchase in *Unocal* and the poison pill in *Moran* as "proportional" to the threats posed by two-tier, front-end loaded offers and offers financed by junk bonds (or any offers made by T. Boone Pickens).[123]

The difficulty with construing proportionality review as simple rhetoric, however, is the care that the Delaware Court took to announce and reiterate the new standard. Surely, there are less confusing ways to demonstrate rhetorical concern than to articulate a new and potentially far-reaching standard of review. A more prudent reading of the cases takes proportionality review seriously. The cases introducing the new standard point to the significance of concrete threats.[124] The Mesa offer in *Unocal* was at least potentially coercive, and the poison pill in *Moran*, because it could be redeemed by the board, did not foreclose a particular offer. Indeed, the Court in *Moran* stressed that should the board determine not to redeem the pill when an actual offer was made, its decision could then be reviewed under the two-step test. Not redeeming the pill would itself qualify as a defensive tactic that management would have to justify as reasonable in relation to the threat posed by the particular offer.[125]

---

[122] See, e.g., Jennifer Johnson & Mary Siegel, *Corporate Mergers: Redefining the Role of Target Directors*, 136 U.Pa.L.Rev. 315, 332-37 (1987).

[123] In *Unocal*, the Court seems to have held that the very fact that the offer was made by Pickens constituted a sufficient threat: "Wholly beyond the coercive aspect of an inadequate two-tier tender offer, the threat was posed by a corporate raider with a national reputation as 'greenmailer'." 493 A.2d at 956. The Court expressed a similar view of Pickens in Ivanhoe Partners v. Newmont Mining Corp., 535 A.2d 1334, 1342 (Del.1987).

[124] As the Delaware Chancery Court has recently observed: "Takeover bids found to be a threat have typically involved a coercively structured proposal, such as a two-tier hostile tender offer. (citation omitted)" Robert M. Bass Group, Inc. v. Evans, 552 A.2d 1227 (Del.Ch.1988).

[125] 500 A.2d at 1354.

Yet, concluding that *Unocal* and *Moran* are likely to contemplate a form of substantive review by the courts only begins the inquiry. The more difficult questions concern how rigorous a fully developed standard of proportionality review is likely to become.

a.   *Is the New Standard More than a Threshold Test?*

One question is whether the proportionality standard is a threshold test or a form of regulatory review. To see this distinction clearly, consider the ambiguous holdings of *Unocal* and *Moran*, which establish that potentially coercive bids justify *some* forms of defensive action without indicating the range of permissible forms. If the proportionality standard is a threshold test, any hostile offer that is arguably coercive would give management a free hand without further scrutiny by the courts. By contrast, if the standard is a regulatory test, management would be forced to justify its choice of defensive actions by reference to the amount of coercion associated with a particular bid. This difference is significant because any bid, apart from an any-or-all cash bid with a commitment to freeze out non-tendering shareholders at the bid price, may have *some* coercive effect on target shareholders.[126]   Thus, unless the "proportionality element in the new standard has regulatory import, second-step review will have very little meaning for most offers as they are now framed."

The Delaware Court of Chancery's decision in AC Acquisitions Corp. v. Anderson, Clayton & Co.[127] provides strong support for the view that

---

[126] Consider an offer that may seem non-coercive on its face: a 100% cash offer at a significant premium, but without any commitment to buy out non-tendering shareholders at a fixed price. A shareholder who believes that the stock is worth more than the offer, perhaps because he expects a higher offer in the future, would prefer not to tender. However, if he does not tender while other shareholders do tender, he will be left holding minority shares in a controlled corporation with a market value that is likely to be well below the tender offer price. Thus any partial offer, including an any-or-all offer without a freezeout commitment, is potentially coercive. See Lucian Bebchuk, *Toward Undistorted Choice and Equal Treatment in Corporate Takeovers*, 98 Harv.L.Rev. 1693, 1717-35 (1985). How much shareholders are actually coerced in practice, however, is open to debate. The risk of competing bidders limits the opportunity for initially coercive bids. Thus, the evidence suggests that the creation of an informal auction period under the Williams Act by Rule 14d-8's extension of the minimum offering period in partial (including two-tier) offers from 10 to 20 days eliminated the difference in premia between two-tier and any-or-all bids. See Robert Comment & Gregg Jarrell, *Two-Tier and Negotiated Tender Offers: The Imprisonment of the Free-riding Shareholder*, 19 J.Fin.Econ. 310 (1987) (over 1981-84, differences in premiums in two-tier and any-or-all offers statistically insignificant). This may explain the recent dramatic decline in the use of two-tier bids in third-party offers. While in 1982 and 1983 there were 35 third-party two-tier bids amounting to about 20% of all tender offers, in 1985 and 1986 there were only 11 such bids amounting to only about 3% of all tender offers, and in the first five months of 1987 there were none. See Joseph Grundfest, *Two-Tier Tender Offers: A Mythectomy* (June 15, 1987) (Address to the United Shareholders Association).

[127] 519 A.2d 103 (Del.1986).

the proportionality test is more than a threshold standard. For our purposes, the facts of the case can be stated simply. A cash tender offer was made for a minimum of 5% of Anderson, Clayton's common stock at $56 per share, with the announced intention of a second-step freezeout cash merger also at $56 per share. Thus, the hostile offer was not coercive. A shareholder who viewed the $56 price as too low could decline to tender without fear of being disadvantaged; if other shareholders tendered and the offer succeeded, the non-tendering shareholder would still receive the same price.

Anderson, Clayton responded by offering an alternative transaction that the company believed would result in greater value for its shareholders: an issuer self-tender for 65% of its common stock at $60 per share.[128] The company's offer, however, had one wrinkle. Because it had to be accepted before the hostile offer was completed, shareholders were coerced into accepting it. A shareholder who did not tender to the company because he preferred the hostile offer would run a major risk. If other shareholders tendered to the company, the hostile offer would be withdrawn and the non-tendering shareholder would be left with, in effect, the back-end of the company's two-tier offer: the reduced value of the remaining company shares after the repurchase of 65% of its stock at a premium.[129]

In reviewing a challenge to this transaction, the *Anderson, Clayton* court easily approved the company's offer under the traditional first step of the two-step review: providing shareholders with a competitive alternative to a hostile offer is self-evidently a valid corporate purpose. Yet, the court's analysis at the second step of the review was far from routine. The court might have reasoned, tautologically, that the company's offer should be considered "reasonably related" to the hostile offer by definition, merely because providing an alternative to this offer was an appropriate corporate purpose. But the court did not take this tack; instead, it carefully examined the alternative that the company actually provided:

---

[128] The court described the calculation by Anderson, Clayton's investment banker of the value of the company's offer as follows: "$60 cash price x 65.5% (proration figure) = $39.34 cash + the per share value of the remaining 34.5% equity interest ($13 to $18 per remaining share) or in total a range of $52.34 to $57.34 per existing share." 519 A.2d at 108 n.6.

[129] Michael Bradley & Michael Rosenzweig, *Defensive Stock Repurchases*, 99 Harv.L.Rev. 1378 (1986), demonstrate that any repurchase by a target of less than the number of shares sought by the hostile bidder has the potential to be coercive in this way. Perhaps for this reason, two-tier offers have been most frequently used in recent years in support of management buyouts or, as in *Anderson, Clayton*, by management defending against a single tier hostile offer. See Grundfest (1987), *supra* note 126.

In *Anderson, Clayton*, the coercive effect was magnified because the company's investment banker declined to give an opinion on the expected value of Anderson, Clayton shares after the repurchase, estimating only a range of $13 to $18. At all but the top end of this range, the hostile offer was more valuable.

The fatal defect with the Company Transaction, . . . becomes apparent when one attempts to apply the second leg of the *Unocal* test and ask whether the defensive step is "reasonable in relation to the threat posed." The [hostile] offer poses a "threat" of any kind (other than a threat to the incumbency of the Board) only in a special sense and on the assumption that a majority of the Company's shareholders might prefer an alternative to the [hostile] offer. On this assumption, it is reasonable to create an option that would permit shareholders to keep an equity interest in the firm, but, in my opinion, it is not reasonable in relation to such a "threat" to structure such an option so as to preclude as a practical matter shareholders from accepting the [hostile] offer.[130]

Thus, *Anderson, Clayton* clearly indicates that proportionality review, unlike *Cheff*'s policy conflict/primary purpose test, is not an empty threshold test: defensive tactics must be justified in relationship to the particular terms of hostile offers.[131] This is an important result in its own right, even if it still leaves open the basic issue of how the Delaware courts will balance defensive tactics against the terms of hostile offers in other contexts.

b.   *What Constitutes a Threat?*

Thus far, it appears, the proportionality test limits the range of permissible defensive tactics according to the nature of the threat associated with a particular hostile offer. It is a short step from this observation to the next question: What, then, constitutes a "threat" under the proportionality test? If "threat" means that a takeover bid must pose a demonstrable risk of injury to target shareholders, might some takeover bids arguably not threaten at all? The most serious aspect of developing the likely content of the proportionality test is that, in such cases, it might reasonably be construed to bar target management from initiating any significant defensive measures at all.

Unocal, Moran, and *Anderson, Clayton* illustrate easy circumstances under the proportionality test for locating a threat that might reasonably seem to warrant a defensive response of some kind. In *Unocal* and *Moran*, the structure of the hostile offers threatened to coerce shareholders into tendering on unfavorable terms. In *Anderson, Clayton*, a hostile offer threatened to deprive shareholders of access to management's alternative offer. Leeway to respond to these threats under the proportionality test, however, will give little comfort to defensive planners who wish to keep their companies

---

[130] 519 A.2d at 112-3.

[131] *Anderson, Clayton*'s analysis is developed even more pointedly in the recent *Robert M. Bass Group* decision, where the Delaware Court of Chancery observes that a reasonable response to an alleged underpriced offer is to "develop a more valuable economic alternative" for shareholders. 552 A.2d at 1241-2 (Del.Ch.1988).

independent.[132] Indeed, a broad reading of *Anderson, Clayton* leads to a kind of safe harbor for hostile acquirers: In response to a hostile bid that is *not* coercive on its face, management can do no more than offer a genuine alternative.   Although this reading admittedly represents a significant narrowing of pre-*Unocal* Delaware law, it accords with *Anderson, Clayton*'s holding that a hostile offer may be non-coercive when it promises to cash out non-tendering shareholders at an equal price.[133]   As the court explicitly states, tactics that preclude shareholders from accepting a hostile offer are not, without more, reasonably related to the "threat" that shareholders will accept the offer.[134]   Thus, the case may support the proposition that the proportionality test bars preclusive defensive action whenever non-coercive takeover bids offer equal treatment to non-tendering shareholders. Such a rule would dramatically restrict the flexibility of defensive planners in a market where hostile bidders can easily raise cash financing.

Similarly, defensive planners cannot take great comfort in *Anderson, Clayton*'s invitation to offer shareholders a non-coercive alternative. Inherent in *Anderson, Clayton*'s conception of providing shareholders with a choice is that they may choose to accept the hostile offer. Considered from this perspective, moreover, management's proposal for keeping a target company independent is simply an alternative to a hostile offer rather than a presumptively favored outcome. After all, if shareholders had selected Anderson, Clayton's self-tender offer, the company would have remained independent. *Anderson, Clayton* clearly allows management to offer the alternative of independence, but the logic of the opinion would seem to foreclose preclusive tactics that *force* shareholders to accept the independence option (or prevent shareholders from choosing at all).[135]

---

[132] A fair reading of *Anderson, Clayton* suggests that maintaining independence was management's real motive.

[133] 519 A.2d at 112.

[134] *Id.*

[135] Accord Robert M. Bass Group, Inc. v. Evans, 552 A.2d 1227 (Del.Ch.1988). The Delaware Supreme Court's decision in Ivanhoe Partners v. Newmont Mining Corp., 535 A.2d 1334 (Del.1987), demonstrates that the road to doctrinal clarity in Delaware is neither straight nor straightforward. There Newmont management believed the company to be caught between two potentially coercive offers. On the one hand, Ivanhoe Partners, a T. Boone Pickens acquisition vehicle, had announced a hostile offer for 42% of Newmont's outstanding stock. Although the Ivanhoe offer stated that it intended to acquire all remaining shares for cash at the same price of the initial offer, its offer also stated, in contrast to the hostile offer in *Anderson, Clayton*, "that no specific second step transaction had been devised, and that there was no firm commitment to do so." 535 A.2d at 1139. As a result, the Court concluded that the Ivanhoe offer was a two-tier offer "fit[ting] perfectly the mold of . . . a coercive device." *Id.* at 1324.

On the other hand, Newmont management believed that Consolidated Gold Fields, Newmont's largest shareholder with 26% of the outstanding stock, also posed a threat of coercion. Gold Fields held its shares subject to a 1983 standstill agreement that limited Gold Fields to a maximum holding of 33-1/3%, but that terminated if any other party acquired

From the perspective of defensive planners who want to keep a target independent (and "un-restructured"), then, the critical issue in evaluating Delaware's two-step proportionality review is what "threats" from hostile bidders, apart from unequal treatment for non-tendering shareholders, are sufficiently grave to justify preclusive defensive tactics without offering any transactional alternative at all? To take an obvious candidate, suppose that management honestly believes that the price of a non-coercive hostile offer is inadequate: in management's view, the securities market undervalues the target company's assets by more than the premium offered by the acquirer. Would a preclusive defense be "reasonably related" to the "threat" that shareholders might accept what management deems to be an inadequate price?[136]

In *Unocal*, where the proportionality test was first unveiled, the Delaware Supreme Court provided a litany of factors that might bear on the existence of a threat:

> If a defensive measure is to come within the ambit of the business judgment rule, it must be reasonable in relation to the threat posed. This entails an analysis by the directors of the nature of the takeover bid and its effect on the corporate enterprise. Examples of such concerns may include: inadequacy of

---

more than 9.9%. When Ivanhoe intentionally increased its holding to 9.95%, Gold Fields became free to "cancel the 1983 standstill agreement and acquire control of the company [presumably through market purchases], thus leaving the remaining shareholders without protection on the "back end." *Id*.

As such, Newmont's defensive tactic -- financing a Gold Fields street sweep with a $33 per share special dividend that gave Gold Fields 49.7% of the outstanding stock but subject to a revised standstill agreement that limited Gold Fields' board membership to 40% -- could be justified as a careful effort to steer a path between the coercion threatened, explicitly or implicitly, by *both Ivanhoe and Gold Fields*.

Analysis is complicated, however, by the fact that the Court also refers to Newmont's desire to remain independent: "The Newmont board acted to maintain the company's independence and not merely to preserve its own control." *Id*. at 1344. A preferred interpretation of the Court's opinion treats its discussion of independence as simply loose language occurring in a context in which coercion was the dominant consideration, rather than as a statement that any hostile offer is a threat to a company's independence (and that any defense is therefore reasonably related to that threat), thereby reducing the proportionality test to rhetoric.

In Mills Acquisition Co. v. Macmillan, 559 A.2d 1261 (Del.1989) (excerpted in Chapter 19) the Delaware Supreme Court seems to distinguish *Ivanhoe Partners* in precisely the fashion suggested in this Note. *Id*. at n.36.

[136] *Anderson, Clayton* itself avoids the issue by noting that the case presented an unusual circumstance in which target management did not claim that the price offered by the hostile bidder was inadequate:

> Unlike most of our cases treating defensive tactics, the Board does not seek to justify the Company Transaction as necessary to fend off an offer that is inherently unfair. . . . The Board recognizes that the [hostile] offer -- being for all shares and offering cash consideration that the Board's expert advisor could not call unfair -- is one that a rational shareholder might prefer.

519 A.2d at 112.

the price offered, nature and timing of the offer, questions of illegality, the impact on "constituencies" (i.e., creditors, customers, employees, and perhaps even the community generally), the risk of nonconsummation, and the quality of the securities being offered in the exchange. While not a controlling factor, it also seems to us that a board may reasonably consider the basic stockholder interests at stake, including those of short term speculators, whose actions may have fueled the coercive aspect of the offer at the expense of the long term investor.

493 A.2d at 955-6.

How might these factors rise to the threshold of "threats" able to justify a preclusive defense against a non-coercive takeover bid? The answer, clearly, is that these factors can be threats only if a target's directors' believe that shareholders will *mistakenly* accept a non-coercive offer. And this returns us to our starting point: the options open to the Delaware Supreme Court after determining that defensive tactics required a more rigorous standard of review. The Court might have proceeded directly by vesting *shareholders* with a qualified right to choose whether to accept a hostile offer without interference by target management. Instead, it opted to proceed indirectly by adopting an intermediate standard of review to screen when *directors* might unilaterally block shareholders from choosing at all. As the analysis thus far reveals, however, this intermediate standard can only lead back to the core issue underlying defensive tactics: If takeover bids are not coercive, why shouldn't shareholders make up their own minds about how to respond?

CITY CAPITAL ASSOCIATES v. INTERCO INC.
551 A.2d 787 (Del.Ch.1988)

ALLEN, Chancellor. This case, before the court on an application for a preliminary injunction, involves the question whether the directors of Interco Corporation are breaching their fiduciary duties to the stockholders of that company in failing to now redeem certain stock rights originally distributed as part of a defense against unsolicited attempts to take control of the company. In electing to leave Interco's "poison pill" in effect, the board of Interco seeks to defeat a tender offer for all of the shares of Interco for $74 per share cash, extended by plaintiff Cardinal Acquisition Corporation. The $74 offer is for all shares and the offeror expresses an intent to do a back-end merger at the same price promptly if its offer is accepted, Thus, plaintiffs' offer must be regarded as noncoercive.

As an alternative to the current tender offer, the board is endeavoring to implement a major restructuring of Interco that was formulated only recently. The board has grounds to conclude that the alternative restructuring transaction may have a value to shareholders of at least $76 per share. The restructuring does not involve a Company self-tender, a merger or other corporate action requiring shareholder action or approval.

It is significant that the question of the board's responsibility to redeem or not to redeem the stock rights in this instance arises at what I will call the end-stage of this takeover contest. That is, the negotiating leverage that a poison pill confers upon this company's board will, it is clear, not be further utilized by the board to increase the options available to shareholders or to improve the terms of those options. Rather, at this stage of this contest, the pill now serves the principal purpose of "protecting the restructuring" --that is, precluding the shareholders from choosing an alternative to the restructuring that the board finds less valuable to shareholders.

Accordingly, this case involves a further judicial effort to pick out the contours of a director's fiduciary duty to the corporation and its shareholders when the board has deployed the recently innovated and powerful antitakeover device of flip-in or flip-over stock rights. That inquiry is, of course, necessarily a highly particularized one.

In Moran v. Household International, Inc., 500 A.2d 1346 (Del.1985), our Supreme Court acknowledged that a board of directors of a Delaware corporation has legal power to issue corporate securities that serve primarily not to raise capital for the firm, but to create a powerful financial disincentive to accumulate shares of the firm's stock. Involved in that case was a board "reaction to what [it] perceived to be the threat in the market place of coercive two-tier tender offers." 500 A.2d at 1356. In upholding the board's power under §§ 157 and 141 of our corporation law to issue such securities or rights, the court, however, noted that:

> When the Household Board of Directors is faced with a tender offer and a request to redeem rights, they will not be able to arbitrarily reject the offer. They will be held to the same fiduciary standards any other board of directors would be held to in deciding to adopt a defensive mechanism, the same standard they were held to in originally approving the Rights Plan. See *Unocal*, 493 A.2d at 954-55, 958.

Moran v. Household International, Inc., 500 A.2d at 1354. Thus, the Supreme Court in *Moran* has directed us specifically to its decision in Unocal Corp. v. Mesa Petroleum Co., 493 A.2d 846 (Del.1985) as supplying the appropriate legal framework for evaluation of the principal question posed by this case.[1]

---

[1] In saying that *Unocal* supplies the framework for decision of this aspect of the case, I reject plaintiffs' argument that the board bears a burden to demonstrate the entire fairness of its decision to keep the pill in place while its recapitalization is effectuated. Ivanhoe Partners v. Newmont Mining Corp., 535 A.2d 1334, 1341 (Del.1987). While the recapitalization does represent a transaction in which the 13 person board (and most intensely, its seven inside members) has an interest -- in the sense referred to in *Unocal* -- it does not represent a self-dealing transaction in the sense necessary to place upon the board the heavy burden of the intrinsic fairness test. See Weinberger v. UOP, Inc., 457 A.2d 701 (Del.1983); Sinclair Oil

In addition to seeking an order requiring the Interco board to now redeem the Company's outstanding stock rights, plaintiffs seek an order restraining any steps to implement the Company's alternative restructuring transaction.

For the reasons that follow, I hold that the board's determination to leave the stock rights in effect is a defensive step that, in the circumstances of this offer and at this stage of the contest for control of Interco, cannot be justified as reasonable in relationship to a threat to the corporation or its shareholders posed by the offer; [and] that the restructuring itself does represent a reasonable response to the perception that the offering price is "inadequate." . . .

I turn first to a description of the general background facts. The facts necessary for a determination of the issue relating to the stock rights are, however, set forth later with particularity.

I

Interco Incorporated.

Interco is a diversified Delaware holding company that comprises 21 subsidiary corporations in four major business areas: furniture and home furnishings, footwear, apparel and general retail merchandising. Its principal offices are located in St. Louis, Missouri. The Company's nationally recognized brand names include London Fog raincoats; Ethan Allen, Lane and Broyhill furniture; Converse All Star athletic shoes and Le Tigre and Christian Dior sportswear. The Company's sales for fiscal 1988 were $3.34 billion, with earnings of $3.50 a share. It has approximately 36 million shares of common stock outstanding.[2]

The Company's subsidiaries operate as autonomous units. Rather than seeing the subsidiaries as parts of an integrated whole, the constituent companies are viewed by Interco management as "a portfolio of assets whose investment merits have to be periodically reviewed." Owing to the lack of integration between its operating divisions, the Company is, in management's opinion, particularly vulnerable to a highly leveraged "bust-up" takeover of the kind that has become prevalent in recent years. To combat this perceived

---

Corp. v. Levien, 280 A.2d 717 (Del.1971).

[2] Plaintiff City Capital Associates Limited Partnership ("CCA: or "City Capital") is a Delaware limited partnership. The partnership is owned by two limited partners, Patrick W. Allender and Michael G. Ryan, each of whom owns a 1% interest, and two general partners, City GP I, Inc. and City GP II, Inc., each of which owns a 49% interest in City Capital. Steven M. Rales is the sole shareholder of GP I, and his brother, Mitchell P. Rales, is the sole shareholder of GP II. Moving down the business structure, City Capital owns 100% of Cardinal Holdings Corporation which, in turn, owns 100% of Cardinal Acquisition Corporation. Cardinal Acquisition is the entity extending the offer to purchase. Unless otherwise noted, references to CCA are meant to include the offeror.

danger, the Company adopted a common stock rights plan, or poison pill, in late 1985, which included a "flip-in" provision.

The board of directors of interco is comprised of 14 members, seven of whom are officers of the Company or its subsidiaries.

The Rales Brothers' Accumulation of Interco Stock; The Interco Board's Response.

In May, 1988, Steven and Mitchell Rales began acquiring Interco stock through CCA. The stock had been trading in the low 40's during that period. Alerted to the unusual trading activity taking place in the Company's stock, the Interco board met on July 11, 1988 to consider the implications of that news. At that meeting, the board redeemed the rights issued pursuant to the 1985 rights plan and adopted a new rights plan that contemplated both "flip-in" and "flip-over" rights.

In broad outline, the "flip-in" provision contained in the rights plan adopted on July 11 provides that, if a person reaches a threshold shareholding of 30% of Interco's outstanding common stock, rights will be exercisable entitling each holder of a right to purchase from the Company that number of shares per right as, at the triggering time, have a market value of twice the exercise price of each right.[3] The "flip-over" feature of the rights plan provides that, in the event of a merger of the Company or the acquisition of 50% or more of the Company's assets or earning power, the rights may be exercised to acquire common stock of the acquiring company having a value of twice the exercise price of the right. The exercise price of each right is $160. The redemption price if $.01 per share.

On July 15, 1988, soon after the adoption of the new rights plan, a press release was issued announcing that the Chairman of the Company's board, Mr. Harvey Saligman, intended to recommend a major restructuring of Interco to the board at its next meeting.

On July 27, 1988, the Rales brothers filed a Schedule 13D with the Securities and Exchange Commission disclosing that, as of July 11, they owned, directly or indirectly, 3,140,300 shares, or 8.7% of Interco's common stock. On that day, CCA offered to acquire the Company by merger for a price of $64 per share in cash, conditioned upon the availability of financing. On August 8, before the Interco board had responded to this offer, CCA increased its offering price to $70 per share, still contingent upon receipt of the necessary financing.

At the Interco board's regularly scheduled meeting on August 8, Wasserstein Perella, Interco's investment banker, informed the board that, in its view, the $70 CCA offer was inadequate and not in the best interests of the Company and its shareholders. This opinion was based on a series of

---

[3] Rights, however, will not be exercisable in the event that an acquiror who holds 20% or less of Interco's common stock acquires not less than 80% of its outstanding stock in a single transaction.

analyses, including discounted cash flow, comparable transaction analysis, and an analysis of premiums paid over existing stock prices for selected tender offers during early 1988. Wasserstein Perella also performed an analysis based upon selling certain Interco businesses and retaining and operating others. This analysis generated a "reference range" for the Company of $68-$80 per share. Based on all of these analyses, Wasserstein Perella concluded the offer was inadequate. The board then resolved to reject the proposal. Also at that meeting, the board voted to decrease the threshold percentage needed to trigger the flip-in provision of the rights plan from 30% to 15% and elected to explore a restructuring plan for the Company.

The Initial Tender Offer for Interco Stock.

On August 15, the Rales brothers announced a public tender offer for all of the outstanding stock of Interco at $70 cash per share. The offer was conditioned upon (1) receipt of financing, (2) the tender of sufficient shares to give the offeror a total holding of at least 75% of the Company's common stock on a fully diluted basis at the close of the offer, (3) the redemption of the rights plan, and (4) a determination as to the inapplicability of 8 Del.C. § 203.[4]

The board met to consider the tender offer at a special meeting a week later on August 22. Wasserstein Perella had engaged in further studies since the meeting two weeks earlier. It was prepared to give a further view about Interco's value. Now the studies showed a "reference range" for the whole Company of $74-$87. The so-called reference ranges do not purport to be a range of fair value; but just what they purport to be is (deliberately, one imagines) rather unclear.

In all events, after hearing the banker's opinion, the Interco board resolved to recommend against the tender offer. In rejecting the offer, the board also declined to redeem the rights plan or to render 9 Del.C. § 203 inapplicable to the offer. Finally, the board refused to disclose confidential information requested by CCA in connection with its tender offer unless and until CCA indicated a willingness to enter into a confidentiality and standstill agreement with the Company.[5]

The remainder of the meeting was devoted to an exploration of strategic alternatives to the CCA proposal. Wasserstein Perella presented the board with a detailed valuation of each operating component of the Company. The

---

[4] CCA sued Interco in the federal district court for a determination that § 203 was an invalid enactment under the federal Constitution. It was unsuccessful in that attempt. See City Capital Associates LP v. Interco Inc., 696 F.Supp. 1551 (D.Del.1988).

[5] The standstill agreement would commit CCA not to make any tender offer for three years unless asked to do so by the Company; it apparently does not have an out should CCA seek to make an offer for all shares at a price higher than an offer endorsed by the board.

board adopted a resolution empowering management ". . . to explore all appropriate alternatives to the CCA offer, including, without limitation, the recapitalization, restructuring or other reorganization of the company, the sale of assets of the company in addition to the Apparel Manufacturing Group, and other extraordinary transactions, to maximize the value of the company to the stockholders. . . ." Minutes of Meeting, August 22, 1988.

On August 23, 1988, a letter was sent to CCA informing it that Interco intended to explore alternatives to the offer and planned to make confidential information available to third parties in connection with that endeavor. Interco informed CCA that it would not disclose information to it absent compliance with a confidentiality agreement and a standstill agreement. (See fn.5). Interco's proposal was met with an August 26, 1988 counterproposal by CCA suggesting an alternative confidentiality agreement -- without standstill provisions.

Apart from the exchange of letters, there were no communications between CCA and Interco between the time the $70 offer was made on August 22 and a later, higher offer at $72 per share was made on September 10. There is some dispute as to why this occurred; one side claims that CCA did place a phone call to Mr. Saligman on September 7 that was never returned. Mr. Saligman asserts that the call was returned by him and that there was no response from CCA.

In all events, on September 10, the Rales brothers did amend their offer, increasing the price offered to $72 per share. The Interco board did not consider that offer until September 19 when its investment banker was ready to report on a proposed restructuring. At that meeting, the board rejected the $72 offer on grounds of financial inadequacy and adopted the restructuring proposal.

The Proposed Restructuring.

Under the terms of the restructuring designed by Wasserstein Perella, Interco would sell assets that generate approximately one-half of its gross sales and would borrow $2.025 billion. It would make very substantial distributions to shareholders, by means of a dividend, amounting to a stated aggregate value of $66 per share. The $66 amount would consist of (1) a $25 dividend payable November 7 to shareholders of record on October 13, consisting of $14 in cash and $11 in face amount of senior subordinated debentures, and (2) a second dividend, payable no earlier than November 29, which was declared on October 19, of (a) $24.15 in cash, (b) $6.80 principal amount of subordinated discount debentures, (c) $5.44 principal amount of junior subordinated debentures, (d) convertible preferred stock with a liquidation value of $4.76, and (e) a remaining equity interest or stub that Wasserstein Perella estimates (based on projected earnings of the then remaining businesses) will trade at a price of at least $10 per share. Thus, the total value of the restructuring to shareholders would, in the opinion of Wasserstein Perella, be at least $76 per share on a fully distributed basis.

The board had agreed to a compensation arrangement with Wasserstein Perella that gives that firm substantial contingency pay if its restructuring is successfully completed. Thus, Wasserstein Perella has a rather straightforward and conventional conflict of interest when it opines that the inherently disputable value of its restructuring is greater than the all cash alternative offered by plaintiffs. The market has not, for whatever reason, thought the prospects of the Company quite so bright. It has, in recent weeks, consistently valued Interco stock at about $70 a share. (The value at which Drexel Burnham has valued the restructuring in this litigation).[6]

Steps have not been taken to effectuate the restructuring. On September 15, the Company announced its plans to sell the Ethan Allen furniture division, which is said by the plaintiffs to be the Company's "crown jewel." Ethan Allen, the Company maintains, has a unique marketing approach which is not conducive to integration of that business with Interco's other furniture businesses, Lane and Broyhill. Moreover, the Company says that Ethan Allen is not a suitable candidate for the cost cutting measures which must be undertaken in connection with the proposed restructuring.

Since Interco announced the terms of the restructuring on September 20, it has made two changes with respect to it. It announced on September 27 first that the dividend declared on October 13, 1988 would accrue interest at 12% per annum from that date to the payment date; and second, that the second phase dividend would similarly accrue interest (currently expected to be at a rate of 13-3/4% per annum) from the date of its declaration.

The Present CCA Offer and the Interco Board's Reaction.

In its third supplemental Offer to Purchase dated October 18, 1988, CCA raised its bid to $74. Like the preceding bid, the proposal is an all cash offer for all shares with a contemplated back-end merger for the same consideration.

At its October 19, 1988 board meeting, the board rejected the $74 offer as inadequate and agreed to recommend that shareholders reject the offer. The board based its rejection both on its apparent view that the price was inadequate and on its belief that the proposed restructuring will yield shareholder value of at least $76 per share.

II

This case was filed on July 27, 1988. Following extensive discovery, it was presented on plaintiffs' application for a preliminary injunction on October 24, 1988. As indicated above, the relief now sought has two

---

[6] Interco refers to the risks that this litigation poses to the restructuring and the resulting risk that perhaps the shareholders might have an opportunity to accept that $74 in cash that CCA offers, as accounting for the market's $70 valuation.

principal elements. First, CCA seeks an order requiring the Interco board to redeem the defensive stock rights and effectively give the Interco shareholders the opportunity to choose as a practical matter. Second, it seeks an order restraining further steps to implement the restructuring, including any steps to sell Ethan Allen.

In order to justify that relief, plaintiffs offer several theories. First, it is their position that this case involves an interested board which has acted to entrench itself at the expense of the stockholders of the Company. Second, because they assert that the board comprises interested directors, plaintiffs also assert that the proposed restructuring transaction involves self-dealing, and that the board is therefore obligated, under Weinberger v. UOP, Inc., 457 A.2d 701 (Del.1983), to establish the entire fairness of the restructuring and its refusal to rescind the stock rights, which plaintiffs assert it cannot do. Third, plaintiffs urge that under the approach first adopted by the Delaware Supreme Court in *Unocal*, the board's action is said *not* to be reasonable in relation to any threat posed by the plaintiffs because, they say, their noncoercive, all cash offer does not pose a threat. . . .

Interco answers that only the *Unocal* standard applies in this case. Defendants urge that the *Weinberger* entire fairness test is inapposite because there has been no self-dealing. (See n.1, *supra*). Similarly, defendants claim that no *Revlon* duties have arisen because the restructuring does not amount to a sale of the Company and the Company is not, in fact, for sale. See Ivanhoe Partners v. Newmont Mining Corp., *supra*. Defendants state that the Interco board is proceeding in good faith to protect the best interests of the Company's stockholders. The board believes that CCA's offer is inadequate, and therefore constitutes a threat to the Company's stockholders; it is their position that the restructuring and the poison pill are, therefore, reasonable reactions to the threat posed. Moreover, defendants assert that leaving the pill in place to protect the restructuring is reasonable because the restructuring will achieve better value for stockholders than will be garnered by shareholders' acceptance of the plaintiffs' inadequate offer.

III

The pending motion purports to seek a preliminary injunction. The test for the issuance of such a provisional remedy is well established. It is necessary for the applicant to demonstrate both a reasonable probability of ultimate success on the claims asserted and, most importantly, the threat of an injury that will occur before trial which is not remediable by an award of damages or the later shaping of equitable relief. Beyond that, it is essential for the court to consider the offsetting equities, if any, including the interests of the public and other innocent third parties, as well as defendants. See generally Ivanhoe Partners v. Newmont Mining Corp., 535 A.2d 1334 (Del.1987).

With respect to plaintiffs' request that steps in furtherance of the restructuring transaction be enjoined *pendente lite*, the relief now sought is classically awarded on such a motion where the elements of this test are satisfied. The relief now sought with respect to the board's decision not to redeem the stock rights, however, is another matter. That relief, if awarded now, would constitute affirmative relief. Steiner v. Simmons, 111 A.2d 574 (Del.1955). Moreover, if it is awarded (and if a majority of shares are tendered into plaintiff's offer thereafter), it would, in effect, constitute relief that could not later effectively be reversed following trial. It would in that event, in effect, constitute final relief. Therefore, in my opinion, that relief ought not be awarded at this time unless plaintiffs can show that it is warranted based upon facts that are not legitimately in dispute.

It is appropriate, therefore, before subjecting the board's decision not to redeem the pill to the form of analysis mandated by *Unocal*, to identify what relevant facts are not contested or contestable, and what relevant facts may appropriately be assumed against the party prevailing on this point. They are as follows:

First. The value of the Interco restructuring is inherently a debatable proposition, most importantly (but not solely) because the future value of the stub share is unknowable with reasonable certainty.

Second. The board of Interco believes in good faith that the restructuring has a value of "at least" $76 per share.

Third. The City Capital offer is for $74 per share cash.

Fourth. The board of Interco has acted prudently to inform itself of the value of the Company.

Fifth. The board believes in good faith that the City Capital offer is for a price that is "inadequate."

Sixth. City Capital cannot, as a practical matter, close its tender offer while the rights exist; to do so would be to self-inflict an enormous financial injury that no reasonable buyer would do.

Seventh. Shareholders of Interco have differing liquidity preferences and different expectations about likely future economic events.

Eighth. A reasonable shareholder could prefer the restructuring to the sale of his stock for $74 in cash now, but a reasonable shareholder could prefer the reverse.

Ninth. The City Capital tender offer is in no respect coercive. It is for all shares, not for only a portion of shares. It contemplates a prompt follow-up merger, if it succeeds, not an indefinite term as a minority shareholder. It proposes identical consideration in a follow-up merger, not securities or less money.

Tenth. While the existence of the stock rights has conferred time on the board to consider the City Capital proposals and to arrange the restructuring, the utility of those rights as a defensive technique has, given the time lines for the restructuring and the board's actions to date, now been effectively exhausted except in one respect: the effect of those rights continues to "protect the restructuring."

IV

I turn then to the analysis contemplated by *Unocal*, the most innovative and promising case in our recent corporation law. That case, of course, recognized that in defending against unsolicited takeovers, there is an "omnipresent specter that a board may be acting primarily in its own interest." 493 A.2d at 954. That fact distinguishes takeover defense measures from other acts of a board which, when subject to judicial review, are customarily upheld once the court finds the board acted in good faith and after an appropriate investigation. E.g., Aronson v. Lewis, 473 A.2d 805 (Del.1984). *Unocal* recognizes that human nature may incline *even one acting in subjective good faith* to rationalize as right that which is merely personally beneficial. Thus, it created a new intermediate form of judicial review to be employed when a transaction is neither self-dealing nor wholly disinterested. That test has been helpfully referred to as the "proportionality test."[8]

The test is easy to state. Where it is employed, it requires a threshold examination "before the protections of the business judgment rule may be conferred." 493 A.2d 954. That threshold requirement is in two parts. First, directors claiming the protections of the rule "must show that they had reasonable grounds for believing that a danger to corporate policy and effectiveness existed." The second element of the test is the element of balance. "If a defensive measure is to come within the ambit of the business judgment rule, it must be reasonable in relationship to the threat posed." 493 A.2d 955.

Delaware courts have employed the *Unocal* precedent cautiously.[9] The promise of that innovation is the promise of a more realistic, flexible and, ultimately, more responsible corporation law. See generally Ronald Gilson & Reinier Kraakman, n.8, *supra*. The danger that it poses is, of course, that courts -- in exercising some element of substantive judgment -- will too readily seek to assert the primacy of their own view on a question upon which reasonable, completely disinterested minds might differ. Thus, inartfully applied, the *Unocal* form of analysis could permit an unraveling of the well-made fabric of the business judgment rule in this important context. Accordingly, whenever, as in this case, this court is required to apply the *Unocal* form of review, it should do so cautiously, with a clear appreciation for the risks and special responsibility this approach entails.

---

[8] See Ronald Gilson & Reinier Kraakman, *Delaware's Intermediate Standard for Defensive Tactics: Is There Substance To The Proportionality Review?*, 44 Bus.Law. 247 (1989). Professors Gilson and Kraakman offer a helpful structure for reviewing problems of this type and conclude with a perceptive observation concerning the beneficial impact upon corporate culture that the *Unocal* test might come to have.

[9] Only two cases have found defensive steps disproportionate to a threat posed by a takeover attempt. See AC Acquisitions Corp. v. Anderson, Clayton & Co., 519 A.2d 103 (Del.Ch.1986); Robert M. Bass Group, Inc. v. Evans, [1988 WL 73744] (Del.Ch.1988).

A

Turning to the first element of the *Unocal* form of analysis, it is appropriate to note that, in the special case of a tender offer for all shares, the threat posed, if any, is not importantly to corporate policies (as may well be the case in a stock buyback case such as Cheff v. Mathes, 199 A.2d 548 (Del.1964) or a partial tender offer case such as *Unocal* itself), but rather the threat, if any, is most directly to shareholder interests. Broadly speaking, threats to shareholders in that context may be of two types: threats to the voluntariness of the choice offered by the offer, and threats to the substantive, economic interest represented by the stockholding.

1. *Threats to voluntariness.* It is now universally acknowledged that the structure of an offer can render mandatory in substance that which is voluntary in form. The so-called "front-end" loaded partial offer -- already a largely vanished breed -- is the most extreme example of this phenomenon. An offer may, however, be structured to have a coercive effect on a rational shareholder in any number of different ways. Whenever a tender offer is so structured, a board may, or perhaps should, perceive a threat to a stockholder's interest in exercising choice to remain a stockholder in the firm. The threat posed by structurally coercive offers is typically amplified by an offering price that the target board responsibly concludes is substantially below a fair price.[10]

Each of the cases in which our Supreme Court has addressed a defensive corporate measure under the *Unocal* test involved the sharp and palpable threat to shareholders posed by a coercive offer. See Unocal Corp. v. Mesa Petroleum Co., 493 A.2d 946 (Del.1985); Moran v. Household International, 500 A.2d 1346 (Del.1985); Ivanhoe Partners v. Newmont Mining Corp., 535 A.2d 1334 (Del.1987).

2. *Threats from "inadequate" but noncoercive offers.* The second broad classification of threats to shareholder interests that might be posed by a tender offer for all shares relates to the "fairness" or "adequacy" of the price.[11] It would not be surprising or unreasonable to claim that where an offer is not coercive or deceptive (and, therefore, what is in issue is essentially whether the consideration it offers is attractive or not), a board -- even though it may expend corporate funds to arrange alternatives or to inform shareholders of its view of fair value -- is not authorized to take

---

[10] A different form of threat relating to the voluntariness of the shareholder's choice would arise in a structurally noncoercive offer that contained false or misleading material information.

[11] Timing questions may be seen as simply a special case of price inadequacy. That is, the price offered is seen as inadequate because the firm's prospects will appear better later; thus, a fair price now would be higher than that offered.

preclusive action. By preclusive action I mean action that, as a practical matter, withdraws from the shareholders the option to choose between the offer and the status quo or some other board sponsored alternative.

Our law, however, has not adopted that view and experience has demonstrated the wisdom of that choice. We have held that a board is not required simply by reason of the existence of a noncoercive offer to redeem outstanding poison pill rights. See Facet Enterprises, Inc. v. Prospect Group, Inc., [1988 WL 36140] (Del.Ch.1988); Nomad Acquisition Corp. v. Damon Corp., [1988 WL 96192] (Del.Ch.1988); Doskocil Companies v. Griggy, [1988 WL 105751] (Del.Ch.1988).[12] The reason is simple. Even where an offer is noncoercive, it may represent a "threat" to shareholder interests in the special sense that an active negotiator with power, in effect, to refuse the proposal may be able to extract a higher or otherwise more valuable proposal, or may be able to arrange an alternative transaction or a modified business plan that will present a more valuable option to shareholders. See, e.g., In re J.P. Stevens & Co. Shareholders Litigation, 542 A.2d 770 (Del.Ch.1988) and CFRT v. Federated Department Stores, Inc., 693 F.Supp. 422 (S.D.N.Y.1988) where defensive stock rights were used precisely in this way. See also Gilson & Kraakman, *supra* n.8 at 26-30. Our cases, however, also indicate that in the setting of a noncoercive offer, absent unusual facts, there may come a time when a board's fiduciary duty will require it to redeem the rights and to permit the shareholders to choose. See Doskocil Companies Inc. v. Griggy, *supra*, slip op. at 11; Mills Acquisition Co. v. Macmillan, Inc., [1988 WL 108332] (Del.Ch.1988), slip op. at 49-50.

B

In this instance, there is no threat of shareholder coercion. The threat is to shareholders' economic interests posed by an offer the board has concluded is "inadequate." If this determination is made in good faith (as I assume it is here), it alone will justify leaving a poison pill in place, even in the setting of a noncoercive offer, for a period while the board exercises its good faith business judgment to take such steps as it deems appropriate to protect and advance shareholder interests in light of the significant development that such an offer doubtless is. That action may entail negotiation on behalf of shareholders with the offeror, the institution of a *Revlon*-style auction for the Company, a recapitalization or restructuring designed as an alternative to the offer, or other action.[13]

---

[12] See also CFRT v. Federated Department Stores, Inc., 683 F.Supp. 422 (S.D.N.Y.1988); BNS, Inc. v. Koppers Co., 683 F.Supp. 458 (D.Del.1988) (both of which apply Delaware law).

[13] I leave aside the rare but occasionally encountered instance in which the board elects to do nothing at all with respect to an any and all tender offer.

Once that period has closed, and it is apparent that . . . [the board] has taken such time as it required in good faith to arrange an alternative value-maximizing transaction, then, in most instances, the legitimate role of the poison pill in the context of a noncoercive offer will have been fully satisfied. The only function then left for the pill at this end-stage is to preclude the shareholders from exercising a judgment about their own interests that differs from the judgment of the directors, who will have some interest in the question. What then is the "threat" in this instance that might justify such a result? Stating that "threat" at this stage of the process most specifically, it is this: *Wasserstein Perella may be correct in their respective valuations of the offer and the restructuring but a majority of the Interco shareholders may not accept that fact and may be injured as a consequence.*

C

Perhaps there is a case in which it is appropriate for a board of directors to in effect permanently foreclose their shareholders from accepting a noncoercive offer for their stock by utilization of the recent innovation of "poison pill" rights. If such a case might exist by reason of some special circumstance, a review of the facts here show this not to be it. The "threat" here, when viewed with particularity, is far too mild to justify such a step in this instance.

Even assuming Wasserstein Perella is correct that when received (and following a period in which full distribution can occur), each of the debt securities to be issued in the restructuring will trade at par, that the preferred stock will trade at its liquidation value, and that the stub will trade initially at $10 a share, the difference in the values of these two offers is only 3%, and the lower offer is all cash and sooner. Thus, the threat, at this stage of the contest, cannot be regarded as very great even on the assumption that Wasserstein Perella is correct.

More importantly, it is incontestable that the Wasserstein Perella value is itself a highly debatable proposition. Their prediction of the likely trading range of the stub share represents one obviously educated guess. Here, the projections used in that process were especially prepared for use in the restructuring. Plaintiffs claim they are rosy to a fault, citing, for example, a $75 million cost reduction from remaining operations once the restructuring is fully implemented. This cost reduction itself is $2 per share; 20% of the predicted value of the stub. The Drexel Burnham analysis, which offers no greater claim to correctness, estimates the stub will trade at between $4.53 and $5.45. Moreover, Drexel opines that the whole package of restructure consideration has a value between $68.28 and $70.37 a share, which, for whatever reason, is quite consistent with the stock market price of a share of Interco stock during recent weeks.[16]

The point here is not that, in exercising some restrained substantive review of the board's decision to leave the pill in place, the court finds Drexel's opinion more persuasive than Wasserstein Perella's. I make no such judgment. What is apparent -- indeed inarguable -- is that one could do so. More importantly, without access to Drexel Burnham's particular analysis, a shareholder could prefer a $74 cash payment now to the complex future consideration offered through the restructuring. The defendants understand this; it is evident.

The information statement sent to Interco shareholders to inform them of the terms of the restructuring accurately states and repeats the admonition:

> There can be no assurances as to actual trading values of [the stub shares]. . . . It should be noted that the value of securities, including newly-issued securities and equity securities in highly leveraged companies, are subject to uncertainties and contingencies, all of which are difficult to predict and therefore any valuation [of them] may not necessarily be indicative of the price at which such securities will actually trade.

October 1, 1988 Interco Information Statement, at 3.

Yet, recognizing the relative closeness of the values and the impossibility of knowing what the stub share will trade at, the board, having arranged a value maximizing restructuring, elected to preclude shareholder choice. It did so not to buy time in order to negotiate or arrange possible alternatives, but asserting in effect a right and duty to save shareholders from the consequences of the choice they might make, if permitted to choose.

Without wishing to cast any shadow upon the subjective motivation of the individual defendants, I conclude that reasonable minds not affected by an inherent, entrenched interest in the matter, could not reasonably differ with respect to the conclusion that the CCA $74 cash offer did not represent a threat to shareholder interests sufficient in the circumstances to justify, in effect, foreclosing shareholders from electing to accept that offer.

Our corporation law exists, not as an isolated body of rules and principles, but rather in a historical setting and as a part of a larger body of law premised upon shared values. To acknowledge that directors may employ the recent innovation of "poison pills" to deprive shareholders of the ability effectively to choose to accept a noncoercive offer, after the board has had a reasonable opportunity to explore or create alternatives, or attempt to negotiate on the shareholders' behalf, would, it seems to me, be so inconsistent with widely shared notions of appropriate corporate governance as to threaten to diminish the legitimacy and authority of our corporation law.

---

[16] See n.6, *supra*.

I thus conclude that the board's decision not to redeem the rights following the amendment of the offer to $74 per share cannot be justified in the way *Unocal* requires.[17] This determination does not rest upon disputed facts and I conclude that affirmative relief is therefore permissible at this stage. . . .

VI

Plaintiffs also seek an order enjoining any act in furtherance of the restructuring *pendente lite*. Specifically, they seek to stop the shopping of Ethan Allen Company (or *a fortiori* its sale) and the dividend distribution of cash and securities to be accomplished no sooner than November 7. The theory offered is essentially the same as that put forward in support of the poison pill relief: these actions are defensive; they are taken by a board that is interested (recall that half of the board members are officers of the Company, or its subsidiaries); that the board is motivated to entrench itself for selfish reasons; it cannot demonstrate the fairness of these acts and, even if it need not, they cannot be justified under *Unocal* as reasonable in relation to any threat posed by the CCA offer.

I take up the specific acts sought to be preliminarily enjoined separately. Before doing so, I refer to note 1 above. Here too, the appropriate test to determine whether these steps qualify for the deferential business judgment form of review is set forth in *Unocal*. Each of the steps quite clearly was taken defensively as part of a reaction to the Rales brothers' efforts to buy Interco, but neither is a self-dealing transaction of the classic sort.

As to the sale of Ethan Allen, I conclude that step does appear clearly to be reasonable in relation to the threat posed by the CCA offer. Above I indicated that it was the case that one could regard either of these alternatives as the more desirable, depending upon one's liquidity preference, expectation about future events, etc. The board itself was, of course, supplied with specific expert advice that stated that the CCA offer was inadequate. I assumed that the board acted in good faith in adopting that view.

I make some additional assumptions about the effort to sell the Ethan Allen business. First, the business is being competently shopped. The record suggests that. Second, the board will not sell it for less than the best available price. Third, the board will not sell it for less than a fair price (i.e., there will be no fire sale price). In the absence of indications by plaintiffs to the contrary, the board is entitled to these assumptions.

The question of reasonableness in this setting seems rather easy. Of course, a board acts reasonably in relation to an offer, albeit a noncoercive offer, it believes to be inadequate when it seeks to realize the full, market

---

[17] By that point, it was apparent that the board sought, by leaving the rights in place, only to "protect the restructuring"; and while not utterly clear, it by then appeared that CCA's frustrated, self-induced successive bids had come to about the top of their range.

value of an important asset. Moreover, here the board puts forth sensible reasons why Ethan Allen should be sold under its new business plan. Finally, as a defensive measure, the sale of Ethan Allen is not a "show stopper" insofar as this offer is concerned. This is not a "crown jewel" sale to a favored bidder; it is a public sale. On my assumption that the price will be a fair price, the corporation will come out no worse from a financial point of view. Moreover, the Rales' interests are being supplied the same information as others concerning Ethan Allen and they may bid for it. I do understand that this step complicates their life and indeed might imperil CCA's ability to complete its transaction. CCA, however, has no right to demand that its chosen target remain in status quo while its offer is formulated, gradually increased and, perhaps, accepted. I therefore conclude that the proposed sale of Ethan Allen Company is a defensive step that is reasonable in relation to the mild threat posed by this noncoercive $74 cash offer.

As to the dividend question, I will reserve judgment. It is, however, difficult for me to imagine how a pro rata distribution of cash to shareholders could itself ever constitute an unreasonable response to a bid believed to be inadequate. (Collateral agreements respecting use of such cash would raise a more litigable issue). Cf. Ivanhoe Partners v. Newmont Mining Corp., *supra*. I reserve judgment here, however, because I have not found in the record, and thus have not studied, the covenants contained in the various debt securities. They perhaps have not yet been drafted. Those covenants may contain provisions offering antitakeover protection. In the event they do, the question whether distribution of such securities was a reasonable step in reaction to the threat of an inadequate offer (of the specific proportions involved here) will be one that should be reviewed with particularity. The efficient adjudication of this case, however, warrants issuing an order on what has been decided. Should plaintiffs want a ruling on this issue, they will have to submit a written statement outlining any antitakeover effect the securities proposed to be dividended may contain. . . .

Interco issued a clear statement of the importance of shareholder choice in assessing defensive tactics. However, *Interco* also affirmed an important role for target management. While requiring the company to redeem its pill, the court declined to enjoin the sale of its Ethan Allen division. Here the court concluded that, unlike the preclusive effect of the poison pill, the sale of the business in an effort to secure better terms for shareholders was reasonably related to the threat of an inadequate offer: "Of course, a board acts reasonably in relation to an offer, albeit a noncoercive offer, it believes to be inadequate, when it seeks to realize the full, market value of an important asset. . . . I do understand that [the sale] complicated [the hostile bidder's] life and indeed might imperil [its] ability to complete its transaction. [The hostile bidder], however, has no right to demand that its chosen target remain in status quo while its offer is formulated, increased and, perhaps, accepted." Thus, the shareholders choose whether to accept a hostile offer and management manages the day-to-day operations of the business.

In fact, the Chancellor correctly anticipated that the company's substantive defensive actions might doom the hostile bid even if the poison pill were redeemed. Note what this implies concerning the planning of a defense. So long as shareholders ultimately get to decide, the poison pill will only buy time. As in *Interco*, it may take scorched earth tactics to be preclusive.

5.   The "Just Say No Defense" Under *Unocal*

After *Interco* and a number of Chancery Court cases that followed its lead, price inadequacy alone seemed unlikely to justify a target company's refusal to redeem its poison pill in the face of a noncoercive offer.[18]   In effect, *Interco* could be read as establishing a safe harbor for hostile bidders: While target management could take time to look for and pursue a more favorable alternative, in the end a court would order the pill redeemed, leaving the target company's future in the hands of its shareholders.[19]

However, proponents of a greater role for target management nonetheless saw in *Interco* and *Pillsbury* an important distinction. In both cases, target management was attempting to implement without shareholder approval a substantive alternative to the hostile offer that worked a change in the company comparable to the offer itself. If the two cases are read as limiting management's ability to impose an alternative on shareholders, then what remained open was management's declination to respond at all. Management would simply announce that the offer was not in the company's best interest, and decline to redeem its poison pill. In takeover parlance, management would just say no. Chancellor Allen's opinion in TW Services, Inc. v. SWT Acquisition Corp.,[20] provided encouragement by taking seriously target management's claim that in the face of an unsound offer, it could decline to redeem its pill without the need to present the shareholders an alternative or otherwise alter the conduct of the company's business. Although the case ultimately was resolved on other grounds, to management

---

[18] Grand Metropolitan Public Limited Co. v. The Pillsbury Co., [1988-1989 Trans. Binder] Fed.Sec.L.Rep. (CCH) ¶ 94,104 (Del.Ch.1988); Shamrock Holdings, Inc. v. Polaroid Corp., 559 A.2d 278 (Del.Ch.1989).

[19] This reading closely resembled the pre-*Unocal* position of the academics: no defensive tactics except, perhaps, to secure a better price. See Section C.3 of this Chapter, *supra*.

[20] Fed.Sec.L.Rep. ¶94,334 (CCH) (Del.Ch.1989).

supporters *TW Services* resurrected the issue of the viability of the just say no defense.[21]

So matters stood when the Paramount Communication, Inc.'s hostile disruption of a friendly merger between Time Incorporated and Warner Communications, Inc., gave the Delaware Supreme Court its first opportunity to consider the Chancery Court's *Unocal* doctrine.

PARAMOUNT COMMUNICATIONS, INC. v. TIME INC.
Fed.Sec.L.Rep. (CCH) ¶ 94,514 (Del.Ch.1989)[*]

ALLEN, Chancellor. Pending are motions in several related lawsuits seeking, principally, a preliminary injunction restraining Time Incorporated from buying stock under a June 16, 1989, offer to purchase 100 million shares of common stock (comprising 51% of the outstanding common stock) of Warner Communications Inc. at $70 per share cash. . . .

Plaintiffs in these lawsuits include Paramount Communications Inc. and its KDS Acquisition Corp. subsidiary, which is itself currently extending an offer to purchase up to all shares of Time at $200 per share; various holders of modest amounts of Time common stock, who purport to represent Time shareholders as a class; and several very substantial Time shareholders who sue on their own behalf. Defendants are Time Incorporated, all 12 of its current and three recently resigned directors, as well as Warner Communications Inc.

On this motion, the court is required to express an opinion on the question whether the directors of Time, who plainly have been granted the legal power to complete a public tender offer transaction that would be the first stage in accomplishing a thoughtfully planned consolidation of the business of Time with that of Warner Communications, have a supervening fiduciary obligation to desist from doing so in order that it be made more likely that the shareholders of Time will be afforded an opportunity to accept the public tender offer for all shares extended by Paramount's KDS subsidiary. The record in this case indicates . . . that it is very unlikely that the market price of Time stock immediately following consummation of the now planned two-stage Warner transaction will equal the initial $175 price offered by Paramount.

---

[21] See Theodore Mirvis, *TW Services: Just Another Brick in the Wall?: The Return of "Just Say No"*, N.Y.L.J. 5 (March 30, 1989). This reading closely resembled the pre-*Unocal* position of management defenders: defensive tactics should be subject only to business judgment review. See Section C.3 of this Chapter, *supra*.

[*] Paramount Communications, Inc. v. Time Inc. also involved important issues concerning the obligations of the target company board in connection with the target's friendly sale under Revlon Inc. v. MacAndrews & Forbes Holdings, 506 A.2d 183 (Del.1986). This aspect of *Time* is taken up in Chapter 19, *infra*.

It is the gist of the plaintiff's position . . . that Time's board of directors does have such a supervening fiduciary duty and has failed to understand or, more accurately, has chosen to ignore that fact, in order to force the Warner transaction upon the corporation and its shareholders -- a transaction that, plaintiffs assert, the shareholders would not approve, if given the opportunity to vote on the matter. The board of Time is doing this, it is urged, not for any legitimate reason, but because it prefers that transaction which secures and entrenches the power of those in whose hands management of the corporation has been placed.

It is the gist of the position of the directors of Time that they have no fiduciary duty to desist from accomplishing the transaction in question in these circumstances. They contend, quite broadly speaking, that their duty is to exercise their judgment prudently (i.e., deliberately, in an informed manner) in the good faith pursuit of legitimate corporate goals. This, they say, the record shows they have done. Moreover, they assert that the result of that judgment is a proposed transaction of extraordinary benefit and promise to Time and its shareholders. It is quite reasonable, they contend, for the board to prefer it, on behalf of the corporation and its shareholders, to the sale of the company presently for $200 per share cash, which sale is plainly inconsistent with accomplishment of the proposed Warner transaction. In short, the directors say the question whether the Warner transaction in its current form should be pursued or not in the corporation's interest is for them to decide, not the shareholders; that they have addressed it deliberately and in good faith; and that while some shareholders, even a majority of shareholders, may disagree with the wisdom of their choice, that fact provides no reason for this court to force them, under the guise of a fiduciary obligation, to take another, more popular course of action. . . .

I

A.   Time Incorporated and the composition of its board of directors

Time Incorporated is a Delaware corporation with its principal offices in New York City. . . . Time's board presently is composed of 12 directors. It includes . . . four officers of the company [and 8 outside directors]. . . .

B.   The genesis of the March 3, 1989 Time-Warner merger agreement

1.   *Strategic planning and management's commitment to maintaining Time as an independent enterprise*

Over the years, Time's business appears to have evolved from one completely dominated by its publishing activities to one in which to an increasingly important degree, video supplies the medium in which its products reach consumers. Simultaneously, the firm has tended to reinterpret its mission from one of supplying information to a relatively educated market segment to one in which entertainment of a mass audience plays an important role. Time was, of course, founded as a journalistic enterprise. That meant most importantly that its writers created the material that it offered for sale. Publishing continues to be vitally important to it.[4] As Time has in this decade become importantly dependent upon video media for its income and growth, however, it has recognized a need to create for itself and thus own the video or film products that it delivers through its cable network (HBO) and cable franchises. To fail to develop this capacity would, it was apparently feared, leave the firm at the mercy of others (both as to quality and to price) with respect to the element most critical to success in the video entertainment business. Thus, for some time, management of the corporation has reviewed ways in which the firm might address this need.

Another large-scale consideration that has played a role in the strategic thinking of Time's management and its outside directors is the emergence of a deeply interrelated global economy. Recognition of this fact . . . led management and the company's outside directors to perceive the expansion of Time into international markets in a more substantial way, as an important long-term goal for the company.

Neither the goal of establishing a vertically integrated entertainment organization, nor the goal of becoming a more global enterprise, was a transcendent aim of Time management or its board. More important to both, apparently, has been a desire to maintain an independent Time Incorporated that reflected a continuation of what management and the board regarded as distinctive and important "Time culture." This culture appears in part to be pride in the history of the firm -- notably *Time* magazine and its role in American life -- and in part a managerial philosophy and distinctive structure that is intended to protect journalistic integrity from pressures from the business side of the enterprise.

I note parenthetically that plaintiffs in this suit dismiss this claim of "culture" as being nothing more than a desire to perpetuate or entrench existing management disguised in a pompous, highfalutin' claim. I understand the argument and recognize the risk of cheap deception that would be entailed in a broad and indiscriminate recognition of "corporate culture" as a valid interest that would justify a board in taking steps to defeat a non-coercive tender offer. Every reconfiguration of assets, every fundamental threat to the status quo, represents a threat to an existing corporate culture. But I am not persuaded that there may not be instances in which the law might recognize as valid a perceived threat to a "corporate culture" that is shown to be palpable (for lack of a better word), distinctive and advantageous. In any event, for now it is enough to note that the management and the outside board members of Time from early in this process did, in any transaction that might satisfy the perceived need to

---

[4] Time's magazines earn about 20% of the revenues generated in the United States magazine industry and more than a third of the profits.

acquire better access to video production and to global markets, seek to maintain a distinctive Time organization, in part at least in order to maintain a distinctive Time corporate culture. There has never been the slightest subjective interest in selling to or submerging Time into another entity.

2. *Anti-takeover protections*

Management and the outside board of Time have been concerned for some while that the company have in place certain of the protections against uninvited acquisition attempts. In fact, Time seems to have equipped itself with a full armory of defenses including, among other things, a staggered board, restriction on shareholder action by consent or to call a meeting, rather long (50-day) notice of shareholder motions at meetings, and a poison pill preferred stock rights plan, which was recently (1988) amended to reduce its trigger to acquisition of a 15% stake in the company.

3. *Exploration of possible opportunities to meet strategic goals*

Time's management appears to have been alert to opportunities to meet the goal of providing the corporation with a video production capacity. In the spring of 1987, senior management . . . advised members of the board that, upon the initiative of Steven Ross, chief executive officer of Warner, management was pursuing conversations with Warner in order to explore the mutual advantages of a joint venture involving at least each company's cable television franchises and perhaps HBO and Warner Brothers Studios. . . . Those discussions, however, encountered tax and other impediments and did not lead to a definitive proposal. Warner by that time had become the focus of Time's strategic thinking. . . .

At the Time board meeting of July 21, 1988, the board heard reports from management concerning the possibility of a Warner merger. Management reported that it had reviewed other "studios" -- including Disney, Paramount (then Gulf & Western), MCA-Universal, Columbia and Twentieth Century Fox, and had concluded that Warner was the most desirable prospect for achieving the corporation's goals. . . .

4. *Outside directors informally approve the pursuit of a Warner combination but express conditions*

No resolution was adopted by the July 1988 board meeting but the record is without contradiction that the board at that meeting approved the negotiations of a merger agreement with Warner if . . . "corporate governance" issues [were] resolved in a way that assured that Time's senior management would ultimately come to control the combined entity. . . . Time has developed a unique structure (in which the senior writer -- the editor-in-chief -- reports directly to a special committee of the board of directors) in order to protect the "culture" or value of journalistic independence which the corporation had found, historically, to have been economically advantageous. . . .

There may be at work here a force more subtle than a desire to maintain a title or office in order to assure continued salary or prerequisites. Many people commit a huge portion of their lives to a single large-scale business organization. They derive their identity in part from that organization and feel that they contribute to the identity of the firm. The mission of the firm is not seen by those involved with it as wholly economic, nor the continued existence of its distinctive identity as a matter of indifference. . . .

Thus, while the record suggests that the "Time culture" importantly includes directors' concerns for the larger role of the enterprise in society, there is insufficient basis to suppose at this juncture that such concerns have caused the directors to sacrifice or ignore their duty to seek to maximize in the long run financial returns to the corporation and its stockholders.

In all events, in July 1988, the governance agenda included a plan for co-CEO's (initially Munro and Ross, then Nicholas and Ross to be followed by a sole CEO, Nicholas). It also provided for a board equally divided between 12 former Time directors and 12 former Warner directors and required a supermajority board vote (2/3) to modify the structure that established the board committee to whom the editor-in-chief would report. . . .

C. Negotiation of the Time-Warner March 3, 1989, agreement of merger

Negotiation of a possible transaction seemed to fall to the ground promptly when the parties were unable to agree to a management structure of a combined entity that satisfied Time's expressed need to assure continuation of its "culture" by assuring the ultimate succession of Time executives to the senior executive positions in the new firm. . . .

The rub came in agreeing to a plan for a chief executive officer. Mr. Munro was set to retire in 1990. Mr. Nicholas was to succeed him. The prospect of co-CEO's had been discussed and agreed upon in principle: Munro and Ross until Munro's retirement, then Nicholas and Ross until such time as Ross was to retire. At that time, it was proposed that Nicholas would succeed as sole CEO. Time, however, insisted that Mr. Ross should set a retirement date at the outset, to be agreed upon, and Mr. Ross did not find this appealing. Discussions broke off in August.

Negotiations were reopened in January 1989. . . . The agreement reached was that Ross would retire five years after the merger and that Nicholas would then become the sole CEO of Time-Warner. . . .

The exchange ratio was the last item agreed upon. It was agreed at a fixed rate (rather than a formula that would work off future data) of .465 of a Time share for each share of Warner's common stock. The ratio of market value of Warner's stock to Time's was about .38. The deal struck represented about a 12% premium for Warner shareholders. Should this merger have been effectuated, the shareholders of Warner would have owned approximately 62% of the common stock (and the voting power) of Time-Warner. In terms of market capitalization and 1988 net income, Warner was the larger of the two companies.

D.　The initial Time-Warner merger agreement

On March 3, 1989, the boards of both companies authorized entering into the merger agreement, which was done also on that day. Both corporations have a majority of outside directors. . . .

As a technical matter, the merger agreement contemplated the merger of Warner into a wholly-owned Time subsidiary (TW Sub Inc.) with Warner as the surviving corporation. The common stock of Warner would be converted into common stock of Time Incorporated at the agreed upon ratio. The name of Time would then be changed to Time-Warner. In such circumstances, the Delaware General Corporation Law requires for the effectuation of a merger an affirmative vote of a majority of the shareholders of Warner (since its stock is being converted into something else in the merger), but does not require a vote of the shareholders of Time (since its stock will remain unaffected by the merger and the issuance of additional shares did not require amendment of Time's certificate of incorporation). See 8 Del.C. § 251. The merger agreement, however, contemplated a stockholder vote by both corporations since under New York Stock Exchange rules, issuance of the number of Time shares contemplated required such a vote.

E.　Steps to protect the merger

1.　*The Share Exchange Agreement*

At the same time that they authorized entering into the merger agreement, each board authorized execution of a Share Exchange Agreement. This agreement gave each party the option to trigger an exchange of shares in which event if triggered, Warner would acquire . . . 11.1% of Time, and Time would acquire . . . 9.4% of Warner's outstanding stock. These blocks of stock would have had approximately equal value if calculated on average closing prices of Time and Warner stock for the five business days preceding the announcement of the merger. This agreement is said to have served several purposes including giving each part an investment in the other should the merger fail to be completed for any reason. For present purposes, I assume its principal purpose was to discourage any effort to upset the transaction. . . .

2. *Restriction on information and "dry-up" agreements*

Everyone involved in this negotiation realized that the transaction contemplated might be perceived as putting Time and Warner "in play." Realizing that the corporation might be deemed "in play," management sought and paid for commitments from various banks that they would not finance an attempt to take over Time. In this litigation they are cited by plaintiffs as wrongful attempts by the "target" corporation to interfere with the ability of an offeror to present the shareholders with the best available price. In all events, these "dry-up" fees appear to be a dubious, futile innovation at this point when the global economy seems awash in cash available to finance takeovers.

An additional attempt to secure the closing of the merger may be reflected in a provision of the merger agreement that severely limits the ability of Time to enter into any takeover negotiations prior to the closing of the merger. "Time may not solicit or encourage or take any other action to facilitate any inquiries on the making of any proposal which constitutes or may . . . lead to, any takeover proposal." The only exception to such provision would occur if a hostile tender offer for 25% or more of Time's stock is announced (or 10% of its stock is purchased), at which time Time may, after consultation with Warner, communicate with the offeror (or stockholder). In all events, such an occurrence would not excuse Time's performance under the merger agreement, but would give Warner an out.

F.   **Paramount announces a $175 cash offer on June 7**

The Time board had fixed June 23 as the date for the annual shareholders meeting of the company at which the Time-Warner merger was to be presented for shareholder approval. On June 7, Paramount announced that it was extending an offer to purchase all of the outstanding common stock of Time at $175 per share cash. . . . Paramount's offer was subject to a number of conditions, the most pertinent of which were the following:

1. termination of the Time-Warner merger agreement (or the agreement being left subject to a vote in which Paramount controlled 51% of the vote);

2. termination or invalidation of the Share Exchange Agreement under circumstances in which there would be no liability to Time;

3. Paramount to be satisfied in its sole discretion that all material approvals, consents and franchise transfers relating to Time's programming and cable television business had been obtained on terms satisfactory to Paramount;

4. removal of a number of Time-created or Time-controlled impediments to closing of the offer (e.g., redemption of a "poison pill" preferred rights purchase plan) or effectuation of a second-stage merger (e.g., supermajority voting requirements of 8 Del.C. § 205 and

supermajority voting provisions of Time's certificate of incorporation); and

    5. financing and majority acceptance of the offer.

G. Market reaction to the Paramount offer

The Time-Warner merger had been warmly received. The stock for both companies rose on the market, although perhaps that only reflected that both began to receive attention from arbitrageurs. In any event, Time stock which had been traded in a $103-5/8 - $113-3/4 range in February, rose to $105 - $122-5/8 in March and April; Warner stock, which had been trading in a range of $38-7/8 - $43-3/4 in February, prior to the announcement of the merger agreement, traded in a $42-7/8 - $50-1/2 range in March and April.

The prospect of immediate $175 cash payment, however, excited the market even more. Following the announcement of the Paramount offer, Time stock jumped 44 points in one day to $170; it hit a high of $182-3/4 on June 13 whence it relaxed to close at $146-1/4 on the day of presentation of this motion. . . .

H. Time and Warner react to the demand to terminate their negotiated contract

Time's management immediately responded to Paramount's announcement, aggressively sending to Mr. Davis of Paramount a biting letter attacking his "integrity and motives," and calling the offer "smoke and mirrors." . . . Management also appears to have sought to cause delay in the process that Paramount would engage in to secure necessary governmental approvals for the transfer of cable franchises. . . .

The board resolved on June 16 after further negotiations with Warner to reject the implicit demands of Paramount and to recast the Warner transaction in a form (a cash acquisition of a majority stake in Warner to be followed by a merger for cash or securities, or a combination of both) that would not require shareholder approval, which now, of course, was problematic.

While plaintiffs in these lawsuits interpret these actions as those of directors determined to ignore shareholder rights and interests in the pursuit of a transaction that assures them continued access to the salaries and prerequisites of a powerful corporation, the Time board purports to have been motivated on June 16 chiefly by two considerations: (1) a reasonable belief that the $175 per share offer was inadequate *if* Time were to be sold, and (2) a reasonable belief that if Time were not to be sold, which was the board's determination, then Warner was a far more appealing partner with whom to have ongoing business consolidation than was Paramount.

1.   *The Time board's purported conclusion that the $175 offer was inadequate*

. . . With respect to the question of the adequacy of the $175 price offered, the board was advised by its investment bankers that if it elected to sell the company, a substantial premium over the current values to be achieved otherwise would be realized. Several techniques to estimate this control market value were employed. The board was told that "the price [in such a transaction] would likely be in the mid to high end of the pre-tax segment value range," which is to say that the price would likely be greater than $250 per share. This analysis was premised upon a pre-tax valuation of each segment (i.e., did not contemplate a "bust-up" acquiror). The board was also presented with valuation ranges for a strategic acquiror; a leveraged buyout range (on various assumptions) and recapitalization ranges, both of which ranged from levels somewhat above the $175 price to prices higher than the now current offer. . . .

2.   *What the board was advised with respect to (a) likely short-term stock price following a revised Time-Warner merger, and (b) likely longer-term stock price*

It was the view of Wasserstein, Perella that the stock of Time-Warner would trade at around $150 per share. They noted as well that the range might also be higher, citing a range of $160 to $175 per share. In the written presentation given to the board on June 16, the trading range given for the year 1990 is $106 - $188, based on both cash flow and earnings per share analysis.[8]

In the longer term, Time's advisors have predicted trading ranges of $159 - $247 for 1991, $230 - $332 for 1992 and $208 - $402 for 1993. The latter being a range that a Texan might feel at home on.

3.   *Purported consideration of non-price terms*

In addition to price, the board considered that the $175 offer was itself subject to conditions that would delay its effectuation for, at a minimum, some months or as much as a year, to get the approvals for the transfer of

---

[8] Dillon, Read & Co., Inc. was retained by Paramount's counsel as an independent financial analyst to evaluate Time's financial data. Mr. Phillips of that firm opined that the common stock of the combined Time-Warner entities would trade in a range between $90 and $140 per share. Time's investment banker takes issue with Mr. Phillips' cash flow multiples, stating that they are inappropriately low for a company such as the proposed Time-Warner. Several other outside analysts have produced the following trading estimates:

David J. Londoner of Wertheim Schroder	-- $155
Kendrick Nobel of Paine Webber Group	-- $173
Jeffrey Russell of Drexel Burnham Lambert	-- $145-$160
Richard MacDonald of First Boston	-- $120-$150

control of local cable television franchises, which approvals Paramount had made a condition to its closing. In fact, it appears that this point was seen less as a problem than as an opportunity. Time has been active in trying to impede Paramount's ability to satisfy this condition.

The board considered that the terms of the offer (Paramount to be satisfied in its sole discretion, etc.) gave Paramount great flexibility and that in a sense the offer would be viewed as a "request" to terminate the Warner deal and to grant Paramount a free option on the company for some period necessary to see if the transfer of all material franchises could be arranged. . . .

4. *Recasting the merger transaction*

With the determination to decline Paramount's invitation to negotiate the sale of Time and to continue to pursue the Warner transactions, the directors faced the fact that it was problematic whether the Time shareholders would share the board's expressed view that $175 cash now should be rejected in order to afford the company's management some additional years to manage the trading value of Time shares to levels materially higher than the future value of $175 now. The annual meeting had been set for June 23. Time's shares are held largely by institutional investors. While some of these investors could be expected to continue, despite the emergence of a cash option, to support what had been widely supported as a fine transaction, it is reasonable to suppose that most such money managers would be tempted by the cash now. . . .

Thus, the "return" to a cash acquisition format must be seen as a reaction to the effect that emergence of the Paramount offer could be expected to have on the shareholder vote. . . . With respect to an appropriate price for Warner in a cash deal, the investment bankers advised that a $70 cash price would be fair from Time's point of view. Warner had been trading at around $45 prior to the announcement of the merger so the price represented about a 56% premium. . . .

At meetings on June 15 and 16, Warner's board approved the restructured proposal. That same day, Warner caused the exchange of shares contemplated by the Share Exchange Agreement to be triggered.

I. **Paramount's $200 offer and Time's rejection of it on June 26**

On June 22, Paramount, not having been able to induce Time to engage in negotiations, unilaterally increased the cash price of its offer to $200. That subject was addressed at a June 26 meeting of the Time board. The factors that had earlier led to the decision not to pursue a sale transaction with Paramount apparently continued to dominate the board's thinking. The increase in price did not overcome the factors earlier relied upon: the continued possibility of delay, the presence of possible Paramount outs in the cable franchise approval process and the comparison of the new price with the ranges of sale values earlier discussed. . . .

III

On June 16, the board of directors of Time, upon what would appear competent advice, resolved that it would commit the corporation to the revised Warner transaction [and forgo the $175 per share offered by Paramount with the understanding] that immediately following the effectuation of a Warner merger, the stock market price of Time stock was likely to be materially lower than the $175 then "on the table," perhaps $150, but more likely, within the wide range of $106 - $188.

. . . This is the heart of the matter: the board chose less current value in the hope (assuming that good faith existed, and the record contains no evidence to support a supposition that it does not) the greater value would make that implicit sacrifice beneficial in the future. . . .

The question raised by the decision of June 16 is this: who, under the evolving law of fiduciary obligations is, or should be, the agency for making such a choice in circumstances of the sort presented here -- the board or the shareholders? . . . Where legally (an easy question) and equitably (more subtle problem) [should] the locus of decision-making power . . . reside in circumstances of this kind. The argument of plaintiffs is that the directors' duty of loyalty to shareholders requires them at such a time to afford to the shareholders the power and opportunity to designate whether the company should now be sold. . . .

The . . . more difficult doctrinal setting for the question of whose choice is it, is presented by Unocal Corp. v. Mesa Petroleum Co. and a string of Chancery opinions construing its test to require, in certain circumstances, the taking of action -- typically the redemption of a so-called poison pill -- to permit shareholders to choose between two functionally equivalent alternative transactions. Grand Metropolitan PLC v. The Pillsbury Company, C.A. No. 10319 (Del.Ch.1988); City Capital Associates Limited v. Interco, Inc., 551 A.2d 787 (Del.Ch.1988); Robert M. Bass Group, Inc. v. Edward P. Evans, 552 A.2d 1227 (Del.Ch.1988); AC Acquisition Corp. v. Anderson, Clayton & Co., 519 A.2d 103 (Del.Ch.1986). . . .

The claim that the Warner tender offer is a disproportionate response to a non-coercive Paramount offer that threatens no cognizable injury to Time of its shareholders

1.   *Does Unocal apply?*

Powerful circumstances in this case include the fact that the original Time-Warner merger agreement was, or appears at this stage to have been, chiefly motivated by strategic business concerns; that it was an arm's-length transaction; and, that while its likely effect on reducing vulnerability to unsolicited takeovers may not have been an altogether collateral fact, such effect does not appear to be predominating.[20] Time urges that judicial review of the propriety of the Warner tender offer should involve the same business judgment form of review as would have been utilized in a challenge to the authorization of the original merger agreement. . . . [A] rather lengthy list of cases from this court has construed *Unocal* to mean that its form of review applies, at the least, to all actions taken after a hostile takeover attempt has emerged that are found to be defensive in character. See e.g., AC Acquisition Corp. v. Anderson, Clayton & Co., 519 A.2d 103, (Del.Ch.1986); Robert M. Bass Group, Inc. v. Edward P. Evans, 552 A.2d 1227 (Del.Ch.1988); The Henley Group, Inc. v. Santa Fe Southern Pacific Corp. (Del.Ch.1988); Doskocil Companies Inc. v. Griggs, (Del.Ch.1988). Thus, while the preexistence of a potential transaction may have pertinence in evaluating whether implementing it or a modified version of it after the board is under attack is a reasonable step in the circumstances, that fact has not been thought in this court to authorize dispensing with the *Unocal* form of analysis. The risks that *Unocal* was shaped to protect against are equally present in such instances.

Factually it is plain . . . that the reformatting of the stock for stock merger into a leveraged purchase transaction was in reaction to the emergence of the Paramount offer and its likely effect on the proposed Warner transaction.

2. *Does the Paramount all cash, all shares offer represent a threat to an interest the board has an obligation or a right to protect by defensive action?*

Unocal involved a partial offer for cash; consideration in the second-step merger was to be highly subordinated securities. Equally significant, the facts there justified "a reasonable inference" that the "principal objective [of the offeror was] to be bought off." Thus, the case presented dramatically and plainly a threat to both the shareholders and the corporation.

In two cases decided during the last year, this court has held under similar circumstances that an all cash, all shares offer falling within a range of value that a shareholder might reasonably prefer, to be followed by a prompt second-step merger for cash, could not, so long as it involved no deception, be construed as a sufficient threat to shareholder interests to justify as reasonable board action that would permanently foreclose

---

[20] This fact distinguishes in a material way the case of AC Acquisition Corp. v. Anderson, Clayton & Co., 519 A.2d 103 (Del.Ch.1986), which originated from a threat to the existing control arrangement. Other material distinctions are that the two transactions there involved were competing versions of a "bust-up" plan for the corporation as it had existed and the board could not determine that either was inadequate.

shareholder choice to accept that offer. See Grand Metropolitan PLC v. The Pillsbury Company, C.A. No. 10319 (Del.Ch.1988); City Capital Associates v. Interco Inc., 551 A.2d 787 (Del.Ch.1988). Cf. Shamrock Holdings, Inc. v. Polaroid Corp., (Del.Ch.1989). Those cases held that in the circumstances presented, "whatever danger there is relates to shareholders and that concerns price only." *Pillsbury, supra,* or that "in the special case of a tender offer for all shares, the threat posed, if any, is not importantly to corporate policies . . . but rather . . . is most directly to shareholder interests." *Interco,* 551 A.2d at 796.

Plaintiffs argue from these cases that since the Paramount offer is also for all shares for cash, with a promised second-step merger offering the same consideration, the only interests the board may legitimately seek to protect are the interests of shareholders in having the option to accept the best available price in a sale of their stock. Plaintiffs admit that this interest would justify defensive action at this stage. The board may leave its stock rights plan in place to provide it time to conduct an auction or to arrange any other alternative that might be thought preferable to the shareholders. But, they say, this stockholder interest cannot justify defensive action (the revised merger) that is totally unrelated to a threat to shareholders.

In my opinion, the authorities relied upon do not establish that Time has no legally cognizable interest that the Paramount offer endangers. In each of those cases, the board sought to assure continued control by compelling a transaction that itself would have involved the sale of substantial assets, an enormous increase in debt and a large cash distribution to shareholders. In other words, in those cases, management was presenting and seeking to "cram down" a transaction that was the functional equivalent of the very leveraged "bust-up" transaction that management was claiming presented a threat to the corporation.

Here, in sharp contrast, the revised transaction, even though "reactive" in important respects, has its origin and central purpose in *bona fide* strategic business planning, and not in questions of corporate control. Compare *AC Acquisition Corp., supra* (recapitalization had its genesis in a threat to corporate control posed by the imminent termination of trusts that had exercised effective control for years); Robert M. Bass Group v. Evans, *supra* (recapitalization under consideration prior to acquisition proposal would have shifted control to management group of a substantial portion of corporation's assets). To be sure, Time's management and its board had, at all times, one eye on the takeover market, considered that market in all they did, and took steps to afford themselves the conventional defenses. But I do not regard that fact as darkly as do plaintiffs. It is inevitable today for businessmen to be mindful of this factor. At this stage, I do not regard the record as establishing, as was done in *AC Acquisitions, Bass, Interco* or *Pillsbury,* that there is a reasonable likelihood that such concern provided the primary motivation for the corporate transaction. Nor is this transaction an alternative to the sale Paramount proposes (i.e., the functional equivalent) in the way the enjoined transactions in the cited cases can be said to be equivalents of sales. . . .

. . . I conclude that the achievement of the long-term strategic plan of the Time-Warner consolidation is plainly a most important corporate policy; while the transaction effectuating that policy is reactive in important respects (and thus must withstand a *Unocal* analysis), the policy itself has, in a most concrete way, its origin in non-defensive, *bona fide* business considerations. . . .

In my opinion, where the board has not elected explicitly or implicitly to assume the special burdens recognized by *Revlon*, but continued to manage the corporation for long-term profit pursuant to a preexisting business plan that itself is not primarily a control device or scheme, the corporation has a legally cognizable interest in achieving that plan. Whether steps taken to protect transactions contemplated by such plan are reasonable in all of the circumstances is another matter, to which I now turn.

3.　*Is the Warner tender offer a reasonable step in the circumstances?*

This step requires an evaluation of the importance of the corporate objective threatened; alternative methods for protecting that objective; impacts of the "defensive" action and other relevant factors. In this effort it is prudent to keep in mind that the innovative and constructive rule of *Unocal* must be cautiously applied lest the important benefits of the business judgment rule (including designation of authority to make business and financial decisions to agencies, i.e., boards of directors, with substantive expertise) be eroded or lost by slow degrees. See *Interco*, 551 A.2d at 796.

In this instance, the objective -- realization of the company's major strategic plan -- is reasonably seen as of unquestionably great importance by the board. Moreover, the reactive step taken was effective but not overly broad. The board did only what was necessary to carry forward a preexisting transaction in an altered form. That "defensive" step does not legally preclude the successful prosecution of a hostile tender offer. And while effectuation of the Warner merger may practically impact the likelihood of a successful takeover of the merged company, it is not established in this record that that is foreclosed as a practical matter. Recent experience suggests it may be otherwise. In Re RJR Nabisco, Inc. Shareholders Litigation, Del.Ch. (January 31, 1989).

I therefore conclude that the re　 ٬ merger agreement and the Warner tender offer do represent actions that are reasonable in relation to the specific threat posed to the Warner merger by the Paramount offer. . . .

Reasonable persons can and do disagree as to whether it is the better course from the shareholders' point of view collectively to cash out their stake in the company now at this (or a higher) premium cash price. However, there is no persuasive evidence that the board of Time has a corrupt or venal motivation in electing to continue with its long-term plan even in the face of the cost that that course will no doubt entail for the company's shareholders in the short run. In doing so, it is exercising perfectly conventional powers to cause the corporation to buy assets for use in its business. Because of the timing involved, the board has no need here to rely upon a self-created power designed to assure a veto on all changes in control.[22]

The value of a shareholder's investment, over time, rises or falls chiefly because of the skill, judgment and perhaps luck -- for it is present in all human affairs -- of the management and directors of the enterprise. When they exercise sound or brilliant judgment, shareholders are likely to profit; when they fail to do so, share values likely will fail to appreciate. In either event, the financial vitality of the corporation and the value of the company's shares is in the hands of the directors and managers of the firm. The corporation law does not operate on the theory that directors, in exercising their powers to manage the firm, are obligated to follow the wishes of a majority of shares. In fact, directors, not shareholders, are charged with the duty to manage the firm.

In the decision they have reached here, the Time board may be proven in time to have been brilliantly prescient or dismayingly wrong. In this decision, as in other decisions affecting the financial value of their investment, the shareholders will bear the effects for good or ill. That many, presumably most, shareholders would prefer the board to do otherwise than it has done does not, in the circumstances of a challenge to this type of transaction, in my opinion, afford a basis to interfere with the effectuation of the board's business judgment.

Chancellor Allen's opinion in *Time* can be read either to vindicate the just say no defense, or to cabin its application to a very narrow category of cases. Doctrinally, a just say no defense required two extensions: one must imagine the possibility of a threat to the company that is not a threat to its shareholders, and one must imagine a response that, despite disfavoring shareholders by denying them access to a premium offer, is reasonable in relation to that threat. Read favorably to the just say no position, the Chancery Court opinion can provide both of the necessary doctrinal extensions.

The existence of a threat is the most difficult step. Establishing that the company has an interest that can be threatened by a hostile offer independently of the interest of its shareholders inevitably requires some sleight of hand because, in the end, the ultimate impact of any interest of the

---

[22] Thus, in my view, a decision not to redeem a poison pill, which by definition is a control mechanism and not a device with independent business purposes, may present distinctive considerations than those presented in this case.

entity is on the value of the shareholders' investment. Allen finds that interest in the company's desire to achieve its long-term business plan.

> In my opinion, the authorities [*Interco* and *Pillsbury*] do not establish that Time has no legally cognizable interest that the Paramount offer endangers. . . . [T]he revised transaction, even though "reactive" in important respects, has its origin and central purpose in *bona fide* strategic business planning, and not in questions of corporate control. . . .
>
> I conclude here that the achievement of the long-term strategic plan of the Time-Warner consolidation is plainly a most important corporate policy. . . . In my opinion, where the board has not elected explicitly or implicitly to assume the special burdens recognized by *Revlon*, but continues to manage the corporation for long-term profit pursuant to a preexisting business plan that itself is not primarily a control device or scheme, the corporation has a legally cognizable interest in achieving the plan.[137]

That left the second doctrinal step: proportionality. Again, Chancellor Allen looked favorably on Time's long-term planning: "[T]he reactive step taken was effective but not overly broad. The board did only what was necessary to carry forward a preexisting transaction in altered form. That 'defensive' step did not legally preclude the successful prosecution of a hostile tender offer."

Thus, from the perspective of pro-management forces, *Time* appears as a great victory: effectuation of a long-term business plan can be protected from a hostile takeover. However, another reading of Chancellor Allen's opinion suggests a much narrower interpretation. On this reading, the just say no defense may not have received a death sentence, but it has been confined for life to a very small cell.

Central to the narrow reading are the peculiarities of transactional timing that shaped the Time/Warner/Paramount contest. Allen repeatedly stresses that the defensive action taken by Time was only the effectuation of its long-term business plan. Because of the business exigencies, Paramount could not complete its tender offer for Time prior to Time completing its offer for Warner. Thus, so long as Paramount was not prepared to tender for the combined Time-Warner entity, effectuating Time's business plan was itself a complete defense.

---

[137] Here is the sleight of hand. Chancellor Allen's phrasing is ambiguous. The reference to "long-term profit" may merely indicate that the corporation has a legally cognizable interest in protecting the "long-term" financial interests of its shareholders and that, based on the record, the court is disinclined to dispute the board's judgment that the long-term value of the Warner transaction exceeded Paramount's offer -- however much Time's shareholders may have felt differently. If this is all that *Time* held, however, it might be objected that the decision made remarkably little effort to scrutinize the merits of the board's decision, in contrast to *Interco* or *Anderson, Clayton*. Indeed, Allen suggests elsewhere in the opinion that such scrutiny would be inappropriate.

This may be a unique result. The continued implementation of most business plans, however carefully created, will not preclude a hostile offer. If the plan is sound, the bidder will continue it after the offer. If unsound, the bidder will reverse it after the offer. And if the plan resulted in some reduction in the target's value, the bidder will reduce the price offered to reflect it. In these situations, presumably the most common setting in which the issue will arise, recognition of the target company's interest in a long-term business plan will be a hollow victory for pro-management forces unless there is some, necessarily artificial, way to protect that plan.

That means the poison pill. And that is where Chancellor Allen's opinion in *Time* sharply narrows. In concluding that recasting the Warner acquisition as a cash tender offer was reasonable in relation to the threat to Time's long-term business plan, Allen highlights the fact that the defensive effect of the plan was self-implementing: "Because of the timing involved, the board has no need here to rely upon a self-created power designed to assure a veto on all changes in control." And to eliminate any possibility that the point would not be understood, footnote 22, relating to this sentence, states explicitly: "Thus, in my view a decision not to redeem a poison pill, which by definition is a control mechanism and not a device with independent business purposes, may represent distinctive considerations than those presented in this case."

If this narrowed reading of *Time* is correct, the just say no defense survives, but in weakened form indeed. Unless the target company is in the midst of an acquisition whose consequences would make the target so unattractive as to defeat the offer -- a scorched earth defense -- the fact that a hostile offer may constitute a threat to the target under the proportionality test will make no difference. The only tactic that would succeed -- declining to redeem a poison pill -- would not be proportional to the threat. Interestingly, this outcome precisely parallels Chancellor Allen's resolution of the *Interco* contest. Recall that in *Interco* Allen declined to enjoin the target's sale of its largest divisions, finding their sale to be a reasonable response to a claim that the divisions were undervalued by the market. However, Allen nonetheless ordered Interco to redeem its poison pill, an outcome that left Interco's pursuit of its plan for the company without protection against the hostile offer. From this perspective, any long-term plan can be threatened by a hostile offer; but the only response that would be reasonable would be to stay the course. If implementing the plan did not itself defeat the offer, the shareholders ultimately would be allowed to choose.

The future of the just say no defense thus rested on whether the Delaware Supreme Court adopted a broad or narrow reading of *Time*.

PARAMOUNT COMMUNICATIONS, INC. v. TIME INC.
571 A.2d 1140 (Del.1990)

HORSEY, Justice. . . . Paramount asserts only a *Unocal* claim in which the shareholders join. Paramount contends that the Chancellor, in applying the first part of the *Unocal* test, erred in finding that Time's board had reasonable grounds to believe that Paramount posed both a legally cognizable threat to Time shareholders and a danger to Time's corporate policy and effectiveness. Paramount also contests the court's finding that Time's board made a reasonable and objective investigation of Paramount's offer so as to be informed before rejecting it. Paramount further claims that the court erred in applying *Unocal*'s second part in finding Time's response to be "reasonable." Paramount points primarily to the preclusive effect of the revised agreement which denied Time shareholders the opportunity both to vote on the agreement and to respond to Paramount's tender offer. Paramount argues that the underlying motivation of Time's board in adopting these defensive measures was management's desire to perpetuate itself in office. . . .

We turn now to plaintiffs' *Unocal* claim. We begin by noting, as did the Chancellor, that our decision does not require us to pass on the wisdom of the board's decision to enter into the original Time-Warner agreement. That is not a court's task. Our task is simply to review the record to determine whether there is sufficient evidence to support the Chancellor's conclusion that the initial Time-Warner agreement was the product of a proper exercise of business judgment.

We have purposely detailed the evidence of the Time board's deliberative approach, beginning in 1983-84, to expand itself. Time's decision in 1988 to combine with Warner was made only after what could be fairly characterized as an exhaustive appraisal of Time's future as a corporation. After concluding in 1983-84 that the corporation must expand to survive, and beyond journalism into entertainment, the board combed the field of available entertainment companies. By 1987 Time had focused upon Warner; by late July 1988 Time's board was convinced that Warner would provide the best "fit" for Time to achieve its strategic objectives. The record attests to the zealousness of Time's executives, fully supported by their directors, in seeing to the preservation of Time's "culture," i.e., its perceived editorial integrity in journalism. We find ample evidence in the record to support the Chancellor's conclusion that the Time board's decision to expand the business of the company through its March 3 merger with Warner was entitled to the protection of the business judgment rule.

The Chancellor reached a different conclusion in addressing the Time-Warner transaction as revised three months later. He found that the revised agreement was defense-motivated and designed to avoid the potentially disruptive effect that Paramount's offer would have had on consummation of the proposed merger were it put to a shareholder vote. Thus, the court declined to apply the traditional business judgment rule to the revised transaction and instead analyzed the Time board's June 16 decision under *Unocal*. The court ruled that *Unocal* applied to all director actions taken, following receipt of Paramount's hostile tender offer, that were reasonably determined to be defensive. Clearly that was a correct ruling and no party disputes that ruling.

In *Unocal*, we held that before the business judgment rule is applied to a board's adoption of a defensive measure, the burden will lie with the board to prove (a) reasonable grounds for believing that a danger to corporate policy and effectiveness existed; and (b) that the defensive measure adopted was reasonable in relation to the threat posed. Directors satisfy the first part of the *Unocal* test by demonstrating good faith and reasonable investigation. We have repeatedly stated that the refusal to entertain an offer may comport with a valid exercise of a board's business judgment.

Unocal involved a two-tier, highly coercive tender offer. In such a case, the threat is obvious: shareholders may be compelled to tender to avoid being treated adversely in the second stage of the transaction. In subsequent cases, the Court of Chancery has suggested that an all-cash, all-shares offer, falling within a range of values that a shareholder might reasonably prefer, cannot constitute a legally recognized "threat" to shareholder interests sufficient to withstand a *Unocal* analysis. AC Acquisitions Corp. v. Anderson, Clayton & Co., 519 A.2d 103 (Del.Ch.1986); see Grand Metropolitan, PLC v. Pillsbury Co., C.A. No. 10319 (Del.Ch.1988); City Capital Associates v. Interco, Inc., 551 A.2d 787 (Del.Ch.1988). In those cases, the Court of Chancery determined that whatever danger existed related only to the shareholders and only to price and not to the corporation.

From those decisions by our Court of Chancery, Paramount and the individual plaintiffs extrapolate a rule of law that an all-cash, all-shares offer with values reasonably in the range of acceptable price cannot pose any objective threat to a corporation or its shareholders. Thus, Paramount would have us hold that only if the value of Paramount's offer were determined to be clearly inferior to the value created by management's plan to merge with Warner could the offer be viewed -- objectively -- as a threat.

Implicit in the plaintiffs' argument is the view that a hostile tender offer can pose only two types of threats: the threat of coercion that results from a two-tier offer promising unequal treatment for nontendering shareholders; and the threat of inadequate value from an all-shares, all-cash offer at a price below what a target board in good faith deems to be the present value of its shares. See, e.g., *Interco*. Since Paramount's offer was all-cash, the only conceivable "threat," plaintiffs argue, was inadequate value. We disapprove of such a narrow and rigid construction of *Unocal*, for the reasons which follow.

Plaintiffs' position represents a fundamental misconception of our standard of review under *Unocal* principally because it would involve the court in substituting its judgment for what is a "better" deal for that of a corporation's board of directors. To the extent that the Court of Chancery has recently done so in certain of its opinions, we hereby reject such approach as not in keeping with a proper *Unocal* analysis. See e.g., *Interco* and its progeny; but see TW Services, Inc. v. SWT Acquisition Corp., (Del.Ch.1989).

The usefulness of *Unocal* as an analytical tool is precisely its flexibility in the face of a variety of fact scenarios. *Unocal* is not intended as an abstract standard; neither is it a structured and mechanistic procedure of appraisal. Thus, we have said that directors may consider, when evaluating the threat posed by a takeover bid, the "inadequacy of the price offered, nature and timing of the offer, questions of illegality, the impact on contingencies other than shareholders, the risk of nonconsummation and the quality of securities being offered in the exchange." 493 A.2d at 955. The open-ended analysis mandated by *Unocal* is not intended to lead to a simple mathematical exercise; that is, of comparing the discounted value of Time-Warner's expected trading price at some future date with Paramount's offer and determining which is the higher. Indeed, in our view, precepts underlying the business judgment rule mitigate against a court's engaging in the process of attempting to appraise and evaluate the relative merits of a long-term versus a short-term investment goal for shareholders. To engage in such an exercise is a distortion of the *Unocal* process and, in particular, the application of the second part of *Unocal*'s test, discussed below.

In this case, the Time board reasonably determined that inadequate value was not the only legally cognizable threat that Paramount's all-cash, all-shares offer could present. Time's board concluded that Paramount's eleventh hour offer posed other threats. One concern was that Time shareholders might elect to tender into Paramount's cash offer in ignorance or a mistaken belief of the strategic benefit which a business combination with Warner might produce. Moreover, Time viewed the conditions attached to Paramount's offer as introducing a degree of uncertainty that skewed a comparative analysis. Further, the timing of Paramount's offer to follow issuance of Time's proxy notice was viewed as arguably designed to upset, if not confuse, the Time stockholders' vote. Given this record evidence, we cannot conclude that the Time board's decision of June 6 that Paramount's offer posed a threat to corporate policy and effectiveness was lacking in good faith or dominated by motives of either entrenchment or self-interest. . . .

We turn to the second part of the *Unocal* analysis. The obvious requisite to determining the reasonableness of a defensive action is a clear identification of the nature of the threat. As the Chancellor correctly noted, this "requires an evaluation of the importance of the corporate objective threatened; alternative methods of protecting that objective; impacts of the 'defensive' action, and other relevant factors." It is not until both parts of the *Unocal* inquiry have been satisfied that the business judgment rule attaches to defensive actions of a board of directors.[18] As applied to the facts of this case, the question is whether the record evidence supports the Court of Chancery's conclusion that the restructuring of the Time-Warner transaction, including the adoption of several preclusive defensive measures, was a *reasonable response* in relation to a perceived threat.

Paramount argues that, assuming its tender offer posed a threat, Time's response was unreasonable in precluding Time's shareholders from accepting the tender offer or receiving a control premium in the immediately foreseeable future. Once again, the contention stems, we believe, from a fundamental misunderstanding of where the power of corporate governance lies. Delaware law confers the management of the corporate enterprise to the stockholders' duly elected board representatives. 8 Del.C. § 141(a). The fiduciary duty to manage a corporate enterprise includes the selection of a time frame for achievement of corporate goals. That duty may not be delegated to the stockholders. Directors are not obliged to abandon a deliberately conceived corporate plan for a short-term shareholder profit unless there is clearly no basis to sustain the corporate strategy.

Although the Chancellor blurred somewhat the discrete analyses required under *Unocal*, he did conclude that Time's board reasonably perceived Paramount's offer to be a significant threat to the planned Time-Warner merger and that Time's response was not "overly broad." We have found that even in light of a valid threat, management actions that are coercive in nature or force upon shareholders a management-sponsored alternative to a hostile offer may be struck down as unreasonable and nonproportionate responses.

Here, on the record facts, the Chancellor found that Time's responsive action to Paramount's tender offer was not aimed at "cramming down" on its shareholders a management-sponsored alternative, but rather had as its goal the carrying forward of a pre-existing transaction in an altered form.[19] Thus, the response was reasonably related to the threat. The Chancellor noted that the revised agreement and its accompanying safety devices did not preclude Paramount from making an offer for the combined Time-Warner company or from changing the conditions of its offer so as not to make the

---

[18] Some commentators have criticized *Unocal* by arguing that once the board's deliberative process has been analyzed and found not to be wanting in objectivity, good faith or deliberateness, the so-called "enhanced" business judgment rule has been satisfied and no further inquiry is undertaken. See generally, Jennifer Johnson & Mary Siegel, *Corporate Mergers: Redefining the Role of Target Directors*, 136 U.Pa.L.Rev. 315 (1987). We reject such views.

[19] The Chancellor cited Shamrock Holdings, Inc. v. Polaroid Corp., 559 A.2d 257 (Del.Ch.1989), as a closely analogous case. In that case, the Court of Chancery upheld, in the face of a takeover bid, the establishment of an employee stock ownership plan that had a significant antitakeover effect. The Court of Chancery upheld the board's action largely because the ESOP had been adopted *prior* to any contest for control and was reasonably determined to increase productivity and enhance profits. The ESOP did not appear to be primarily a device to affect or secure corporate control.

offer dependent upon the nullification of the Time-Warner agreement. Thus, the response was proportionate. We affirm the Chancellor's rulings as clearly supported by the record. . . .

Applying the test for grant or denial of preliminary injunctive relief, we find plaintiffs failed to establish a reasonable likelihood of ultimate success on the merits. Therefore, we affirm.

The *Unocal* test involves two steps: threat analysis -- did the offer pose a threat to corporate policy and effectiveness? -- and, if a threat is established, proportionality analysis -- was the response reasonable in relation to the threat? The difficulty confronting the Chancery Court in *Time* was the threat analysis: Could there be a threat to the corporation that was not also a threat to the shareholders? While Chancellor Allen dealt with the problem by verbal sleight of hand, the Delaware Supreme Court dealt with the problem directly by eviscerating the threat aspect of the *Unocal* test. The Supreme Court first takes a swipe at *Interco*, construing that case (and the plaintiffs' argument in *Time*) as "involv[ing] the court in substituting its judgment for what would be a 'better' deal for that of a corporation's board of directors" and then "reject[ing] such approach as not in keeping with a proper *Unocal* analysis." Query: Does *Interco* involve the court's substituting its judgment of a better deal for that of the board's, or does it involve preventing the board from substituting its judgment for that of the shareholders when the only issue is the attractiveness of the offer?

The Supreme Court then goes on to state its approach to determining whether an offer presents a threat: "Given [the] record evidence, we cannot conclude that the Time board's decision . . . that Paramount's offer posed a threat . . . was lacking in good faith or dominated by motives of either entrenchment or self-interest." Mirroring the court's approach in Cheff v. Mathes, the threat analysis seems to reduce simply to the board's business judgment.

Given that prelude, the Supreme Court's analysis of the proportionality aspect of the *Unocal* test was unexpected. Chancellor Allen had rested his conclusion that Time's response was proportional on the fact that the action did not entirely foreclose shareholder choice -- Paramount remained free to make a post-transaction offer for the combined entity. It was precisely this analysis that left open a narrow reading of his opinion which confined the just say no defense to the unusual circumstance when merely pursuing a business plan -- rather than relying on a poison pill -- would defeat an offer. Surprisingly, the Supreme Court essentially adopted the Chancellor's proportionality analysis: "The Chancellor noted that the revised agreement and its accompanying safety devices did not preclude Paramount from making an offer for the combined Time-Warner company or from changing the conditions of its offer so as not to make the offer dependent upon the nullification of the Time-Warner agreement. Thus, the response was proportionate. We affirm the Chancellor's rulings as clearly supported by the record."

So where does the just say no defense stand after the Supreme Court had its shot in *Time*? We are left, it appears, just where we stood after the Chancery Court's opinion -- in doubt. One analysis builds on an allocation of responsibilities between target management and target shareholders: the board runs the business and affairs of the corporation and the shareholders make decisions about selling their shares. The fact that an offer is made cannot prevent the board from pursuing its business plans but, at the same time, the board cannot use a control oriented device like a poison pill to prevent the bidder from pursuing its bid and thereby deny target shareholders the opportunity to decide whether to sell their shares.

However, a second analysis, more favorable to the "just say no" defense, is also possible. Building less on the Supreme Court's words, than on the music, the argument is that the key to *Time* is whether the target corporation should be able to protect its business plan. If so, then the particular manner in which it does so should be beside the point; if merely pursuing the business plan will not be effective, then reliance on a poison pill should be equally appropriate.

Does the second analysis completely eviscerate *Unocal*? The Supreme Court's opinion reduces to a business judgment inquiry judicial review of the target board's determination that an offer presents a threat to the company's business plans. If a poison pill is always a reasonable response to such a threat, then the *Unocal* intermediate standard has become just another incantation of the business judgment rule.[138]

Further confusion was added in Unitrin, Inc. v. American General Corp., 1995 WL 12461 (Del.). In a response to an unwanted bid, Unitrin announced an issuer repurchase offer that would increase the shareholdings of directors who were not participating from 23% to 28%. The increase was important because Unitrin's charter required a 75% shareholder vote for a freezeout merger without the approval of continuing directors.[139] Thus, after the repurchase a second step transaction would require first replacing the Unitrin board through a proxy fight whose likely success was also reduced by the directors' increased holdings. The Chancery Court enjoined the repurchase, finding it disproportionate to the threat because an already existing poison pill meant that the repurchase was not "necessary." The

---

[138] One thoughtful commentator saw the question as already answered:

> The net effect appears to be the collapse of the Delaware Supreme Court's five-year-old effort to erect and sustain an intermediate standard of review for takeover defense tactics. We may be back to the earlier era of simple business judgment review of defensive measures. That restraint is no restraint at all to a well-advised board. . . . Indeed, because of the preclusive effect of current defense technology, a board may now be in a position to refuse an unwanted bid.

Jeffrey Gordon, *Corporations, Markets, and Courts*, 91 Colum.L.Rev. 1931, 1994-45 (1991).

[139] See Section A.1.b. of this Chapter, *supra*.

Delaware Supreme Court reversed, holding that *Unocal* requires only reasonableness, not necessity; a defensive tactic need only be in "a range of reasonableness," taking into account such factors as whether the particular defense "was limited and corresponded in degree or magnitude to the degree or magnitude of the threat (i.e., assuming the threat was relatively 'mild,' was the response relatively 'mild'?). . . ." However, the court appeared to add a preliminary inquiry to the *Unocal* test. Before inquiring as to proportionality, the court must ask whether a tactic is "draconian" -- that is, whether it is "coercive or preclusive." Draconian tactics fail *Unocal*. But is not the point of a poison pill that the target board's refusal to redeem it is preclusive? Put differently, does it do a target board any good to just say not if target shareholders cannot be prevented from saying yes? Perhaps the Supreme Court meant that a defensive tactic would be preclusive only if it also blocked a proxy contest to replace the target board with individuals who would redeem the pill, but this qualification does not appear in the opinion.

In all events, we began this inquiry into the nature of the Delaware Supreme Court's *Unocal* experiment with a question: Is there likely to be a substance to proportionality review? It seems we now end the inquiry on the same note.

CHAPTER 18: FEDERAL SECURITIES REGULATION OF HOSTILE ACQUISITIONS: THE WILLIAMS ACT

Virtually any hostile acquisition of a target company large enough (or, more accurately, small enough) to have a class of securities registered under the Securities Exchange Act of 1934,[1] will be subject to one or more aspects of federal securities laws. If, as is typical, the acquisition is structured as a cash tender offer, the Williams Act will be applicable; and if the acquisition is structured as an exchange offer, a tender offer in which the consideration is the acquiring company's securities, both the Williams Act and the Securities Act of 1933 will be applicable. In this Chapter we focus on the Williams Act. Federal regulation of exchange offers under the Securities Act of 1933, most commonly a friendly transaction, is taken up in Chapter 19. State regulation of corporate acquisitions, an area of increasing activity, is the subject of Chapter 23.

Prior to July 29, 1967, cash tender offers were essentially unregulated. This was of little moment for most of the country's business history because, as Salter & Weinhold describe in Chapter 1, there were very few such transactions. Things began to change in the early 1960s. Although in 1960 there were only eight cash tender offers for exchange listed companies, by 1966 the number had increased to 107.[2] Moreover, the technique was increasingly being used to displace target management who had no desire to give up the reins. Thus, concerned observers saw two challenges to the existing regulatory regime. First, those interested in the coherence of federal regulation of tender offers saw a critical gap in coverage. Tender offers in which the consideration was the offeror's securities -- exchange offers -- were subject to the disclosure and anti-fraud rules of the Securities Act of 1933; tender offers in which the consideration was cash were not. Thus, transaction planners could avoid existing disclosure rules by selecting the "right" consideration. This "gap" in the coverage of the federal securities law led to efforts, supported by the Securities and Exchange Commission, to fill it by legislation. Second, those whose interest was somewhat less academic noted that incumbent management were subject to challenge in a new and more threatening way. This "gap" in the ability of target management to protect themselves also fueled legislative efforts at gap-filling. In October, 1965, Senator Harrison Williams introduced legislation which he saw as responding directly to target management's problem:

> In recent years we have seen proud old companies reduced to corporate shells after white-collar pirates have seized control with funds from sources which

---

[1] Under § 12(g) of the Exchange Act, a company with total (*not* net) assets exceeding $1 million must register any class of equity securities held of record by more than 500 persons. These limits were raised by SEC rule to $3 million in 1982 and to $5 million in 1986 by the SEC's adoption of Rule 12g-1.

[2] 111 Cong.Rec. 24,662 (Aug. 30, 1967).

are unknown in many cases, then sold or traded away the best assets, later to split up most of the loot among themselves.[3]

Senator Williams' initial legislative effort failed. However, a second effort in 1967 proved successful; the Williams Act, in the form of various amendments to the Securities Exchange Act of 1934, was enacted on July 29, 1968.[4] The Act was amended in 1970 to extend the Commission's rule-making authority and to expand the types of offers covered.[5]

The regulatory structure established by the Williams Act has four principal components. The first, expressed in Exchange Act § 13(d), is an early warning system designed to alert target management and the market of any concentration in shareholdings that might foretell a future change in control by any method. The second, expressed in Exchange Act § 14(d)(1) and the regulations adopted thereunder, requires extensive disclosure concerning any tender offer and the offeror's plans for the target company if the offer is successful, to assist target shareholders in deciding whether to tender their shares. The third, expressed in Exchange Act §§ 14(d)(4)-(7) and substantially expanded by SEC regulation, regulates the substantive terms of a tender offer, including the length of time an offer must be left open, the right of a shareholder to withdraw previously tendered shares, the manner in which tendered shares must be purchased if more shares are tendered than the offeror is committed to purchase, and the effect of the offeror changing the terms of the offer during its pendency.[6] The fourth, expressed in Exchange Act § 14(e), prohibits misrepresentation, nondisclosure or "any fraudulent, deceptive, or manipulative acts or practices" in connection with a tender offer.

We begin our review of the regulatory structure created by the Williams Act with the first three components. Then, having developed an understanding of the consequences of a transaction being subject to the Williams Act, we turn to the Act's jurisdictional limits: What is a "tender offer" for purposes of the Williams Act? Finally, we consider the scope of the anti-fraud rule in § 14(e), and the elements of a cause of action under that section.

---

[3] 111 Cong.Rec. 28,257 (Oct. 22, 1965).

[4] Act of July 29, 1968, Pub.L. No. 90-439, 82 Stat. 454.

[5] Most important, the 1970 Amendments reduced the percentage ownership that triggered a reporting obligation under § 13(d) from 10% to 5%.

[6] The Williams Act also added Exchange Act § 14(f) which requires disclosure equivalent to that called for by the proxy rules if, in connection with a transaction covered by § 13(d) or 14(d), there is an arrangement or understanding pursuant to which any persons would be elected as directors of the target company other than at a meeting of shareholders if those persons would constitute a majority of the board of directors. See generally David Ratner, *Section 14(f): A New Approach to Transfers of Corporate Control*, 54 Cornell L.Q. 65 (1968).

A.   Disclosure and Remedies Under Section 13(d)

1.   Introduction: The Statute and Regulations

[Read Securities Exchange Act § 13(d) and Regulation 13D-G in Appendix A.]

Although § 13(d) was added to the Williams Act as something of an afterthought, it is the first part of federal securities law regulation of tender offers that an acquirer encounters. Indeed, because the section's purpose is to provide information about any concentration of shareholdings, even an investor making just a significant passive investment, one *really* made only for investment and not for the purpose of acquiring control, will have to deal with its requirements.[7] Nonetheless, the disclosure obligation imposed by § 13(d) has particular significance for a would-be acquirer.

From the perspective of an acquiring company, maintaining the secrecy of its acquisition plans, especially the identity of the target, is critically important. In Chapter 17C, we considered how secrecy limited the target company's opportunity to seek a competitive bid. Here the concern is the acquiring company's ability to purchase the target company's stock at the

---

[7] The Commission has made special provision for one group of passive investors: institutional investors. Under Rule 13d-1(b) a person who would otherwise be required to file a Schedule 13D can instead file the much less burdensome Schedule 13G if (i) the securities were acquired in the ordinary course of business "and not with the propose nor with the effect of changing or influencing the control of the issuer, nor as a participant in any transaction having such purpose or effect . . . "; and (ii) the person is a registered broker or dealer, a bank, an insurance company, a registered investment company, a registered investment adviser, an employee benefit or pension fund subject to the Employee Retirement Security Act of 1974, or an endowment fund. If the person's eligibility under Rule 13d-1(b) terminates, a Schedule 13D must be filed within ten days and, for ten days after filing, the person cannot vote its shares or acquire more. *Query:* Is a bank that finances a tender offer a "participant" in the transaction for purposes of determining the eligibility of its trust department to file Schedule 13G?

Section 13(g) itself, pursuant to which Schedule 13G was promulgated by the Commission, provides simply that anyone who is the beneficial owner of more than 5% of a class of securities must file more limited information than that listed in § 13(d)(1). Although its terms at first glance seem similar to those of § 13(d)(1), note that it picks up those persons who are exempt from filing under § 13(d)(1) because Rule 13d-6 excludes from the definition of acquisition any transaction or series of transactions which involve less than 2% of any class of equity securities within the previous twelve months. This allows a shareholder who proceeds slowly, at a rate of no more than 2% a year, to accumulate a substantial amount of stock without having to file under the Williams Act. Section 13(g) was added by § 203 of the Domestic and Foreign Investment Improved Disclosure Act of 1977, 91 Stat. 1499, to fill this gap.

Section 13(f), a final aspect of the Williams Act dealing with passive investors, was added in 1975. Any institutional investment manager which holds at least $100 million in exchange listed or NASDAQ quoted securities at the end of the year must file Form 13F describing the number of shares and market value of each security held, and the managers' discretion with respect to the security, including its voting.

then market price, before disclosure of the acquiring company's plans causes the price of target company stock to increase significantly. Empirical evidence indicates that the stock of target companies experiences an average abnormal return of 7.74% when an acquiring company files a Schedule 13D disclosing that it is only *considering* making an acquisition.[8] Thus, the operation of § 13(d) takes on importance because it sets the boundaries on an acquiring company's ability to secretly purchase target company stock at the lower, pre-announcement price.

Section 13(d)(1) sets forth the elements of the regulatory structure. A Schedule 13D must be filed within ten days by

(1) any *person* who,
(2) after *acquiring*
(3) any *equity security* registered under § 12 of the Exchange Act,
(4) becomes the *beneficial owner*
(5) of more than 5% of such security.

The surface simplicity of the § 13(d)'s operative language masks very substantial ambiguity; none of its central terms, italicized above, really mean what they say. Thus, some examination of these ambiguities and how the courts and the SEC have dealt with them is necessary in order to understand § 13(d)'s operation. But how much effort we should invest in that task, and how much care an acquiring company might invest in compliance, is at least in part a function of what happens if an acquiring company runs afoul of the section's terms. After all, in the absence of an effective penalty, the opportunity to purchase target company stock at lower prices may sing a siren's song. Thus, it is useful to defer more detailed consideration of § 13(d)(1)'s operation until after we examine the potential for noncompliance.

---

[8] Wayne Mikkelson & Richard Ruback, *Corporate Investments in Common Stock* 16 (Mass.Inst. of Tech., Sloan Sch. of Management Working Paper No. 1633-85, Feb.1985) (Table 4).

2. Standing and Remedies

James Tobin & James Maiwurm
BEACHHEAD ACQUISITIONS: CREATING WAVES IN THE MARKET PLACE AND UNCERTAINTY IN THE REGULATORY FRAMEWORK
38 Bus.Law. 419, 445-52 (1983)*

ENFORCEMENT OF THE ACCUMULATOR'S DISCLOSURE

The confrontation between the beachhead accumulator* and the target usually comes to a head in litigation initiated by the target. The litigation may be triggered by a proxy contest, a tender offer, or even the accumulation of the beachhead itself. The target has a number of possible claims in such litigation, including allegations of disclosure violations, claims under federal and state legislation regulating takeovers, and charges that the accumulator has unlawfully manipulated the market for the target's securities. The first wave of litigation normally involves allegations of inadequate compliance with § 13(d). . . .

Relief Under Section 13(d)

[Most federal courts have recognized an implied private right of action for violations of § 13(d) that can be invoked by the target company.[b] Such] an action challenging the adequacy of the beachhead holder's schedule 13D disclosures or alleging a failure to file a schedule 13D or a required amendment thereto. False and misleading statements as to the acquiring party's financial position or the source of funds for an offer, its formation of an offering "group", and its intentions and purposes have all been successfully alleged by targets. Frequently, when a tender offer follows on the heels of a schedule 13D filing, the target will allege that the bidder made a material omission in its 13D filing by not stating an intent to acquire a particular percentage interest in the target or to acquire control of, or make a tender offer for, the target.

The results of this type of litigation have varied with the specific facts of each case, but the most common remedy for a § 13(d) violation has been an order requiring amended disclosure and prohibiting further purchases until

---

* Copyright © 1983, by the American Bar Association. All rights reserved. Reprinted with the permission of the American Bar Association and its Section of Corporate, Banking and Business Law.

[a] A "beachhead accumulator" is one who acquires a significant block of target company stock -- a beachhead -- in anticipation of an effort to acquire control. Eds.

[b] See, e.g., Florida Commercial Banks v. Culverhouse, 772 F.2d 1513 (11th Cir.1985); Gearhart Industries v. Smith Int'l Inc., 741 F.2d 707 (5th Cir.1984).

corrective disclosure, in the form of an amendment to the defective schedule 13D, is made.

If the most recent filing is accurate, i.e., amended vis-a-vis the prior filing complained of, the courts generally will not enjoin further purchases or grant other extraordinary relief. If material disclosure defects are found at the time of the hearing or trial, the courts have sometimes restrained further stock purchases until curative amendments are filed. If equitable relief is granted, however, the courts rarely extend injunctions beyond the time needed to file a properly amended statement.[161] In the most extreme such case, the court upheld a thirty-day cooling-off period, during which the reporting person's right to acquire the stock in question was suspended in order to "give the market an opportunity to 'settle'."[162]

Courts have generally been reluctant to issue orders requiring divestiture by the acquiring party or suspension of voting rights or solicitation of proxies with respect to shares purchased while § 13(d) was not complied with, reasoning that such extraordinary relief is warranted only upon a showing of irreparable harm. Thus, § 13(d) has been of little use to targets in ultimately forestalling a tender offer. However, several recent district court decisions indicate that a more expansive view of the range of remedies available in § 13(d) cases may be in the offing.

The Recent Expansion of Section 13(d) Remedies

In framing its request for relief under § 13(d), a target may seek an order enjoining further purchases and the making of a tender offer, rescission rights for shareholders who sold their target securities during the accumulation, divestiture of shares acquired unlawfully, and suspension of the right to solicit proxies and vote such shares. One or more of such remedies have been granted to targets in appropriate circumstances, primarily in the early years of the Williams Act,[166] and the recent trend appears to favor expanding the scope of equitable relief under § 13(d) in ways that could be effective against beachhead accumulators.

---

[161] The rationale is that revisions are quickly digested by the marketplace. . . .

[162] Kirsch Co. v. Bliss Loughlin Industries, 495 F.Supp. 488, 507 (W.D.Mich.1980).

[166] Bath Industries v. Blot, 427 F.2d 97 (7th Cir.1970) (injunction against calling special shareholders' meeting); Graphic Sciences, Inc. v. International Mogul Mines, Ltd., 397 F.Supp. 112 (D.D.C.1974) (injunction against further acquisitions, soliciting proxies, and proceeding with tender offer); Water & Wall Assoc., Inc. v. American Consumer Industries, [1973 Transfer Binder] Fed.Sec.L.Rep. (CCH) ¶ 93,943 (D.N.J.1973) (injunction against voting shares and certifying election if defendants were successful); Committee for New Management of Butler Aviation v. Widmark, 335 F.Supp. 146 (E.D.N.Y.1971) (injunction against voting in proxy context shares acquired after 13D should have been filed). See also Ozark Airlines, Inc. v. Cox, 326 F.Supp. 1113 (E.D.Mo.1971) at 1119-20 (court "would have considered" disenfranchisement if there had been no 13(d) filing before litigation commenced).

General Steel Industries v. Walco National Corp.[167] awarded a target almost all of the above-mentioned remedies. The plaintiff General Steel Industries (GSI) moved for a preliminary injunction enjoining Walco's tender offer for 750,000 shares of GSI common stock. The district court granted the motion and enjoined Walco from doing anything to advance its tender offer or influence GSI until corrective disclosures were approved by the court. Furthermore, Walco was ordered to rescind the purchases or otherwise divest itself of the shares acquired by it while its "false and misleading" schedule 13D was effective. The order was eventually vacated pursuant to a court-approved settlement between the parties.

More recently, the Northern District of Ohio went beyond the result in *Walco* and granted broad remedial relief to a target company where the acquiring party purchased an 8.8% beachhead, filed a schedule 13D that stated an investment purpose, made no further purchases for a number of months, announced a tender offer, and then filed a 13D amendment stating its intent was to obtain control.[169] In contrast to *Walco*, where the far-reaching relief described above was applied to those shares purchased *after* an allegedly misleading schedule 13D was filed, the district court in Hanna Mining Co. v. Norcen Energy Resources Ltd. issued an expansive preliminary injunction affecting shares that had been acquired *prior* to the filing of a schedule 13D. Specifically, the court enjoined the beachhead holder from acquiring additional shares, publicly announcing or commencing a tender offer, exercising influence, directly or indirectly, on target management, selling or disposing of any shares already acquired, or engaging in any step to further its plan to obtain control. As in *Walco* the SEC filed an amicus curiae brief in the appellate court generally supporting the power of federal district courts to fashion remedies beyond amended disclosure for violations of § 13(d).[171]

These decisions and others like them may enhance the effectiveness of § 13(d) as a defensive weapon, particularly where a postviolation purchase or an intentional violation can be shown. The SEC amicus briefs dealing

---

[167] [1981-82 Transfer Binder] Fed.Sec.L.Rep. (CCH) ¶ 98,402 (E.D.Mo.1981).

[169] Hanna Mining Co. v. Norcen Energy Resources, Ltd., No. C82-959 (N.D.Ohio 1982).

[171] The thrust of the SEC's brief in *Hanna Mining Co.* and *Walco* was summarized in SEC Litigation Release No. 9533, [1981-82 Transfer Binder] Fed.Sec.L.Rep. (CCH) ¶ 98,387 at 92,344:

> The Commission urged in its brief that the district court's equitable jurisdiction to remedy § 13(d) violations includes the authority to enter any relief appropriate under the circumstances. The Commission expressed the view that equitable remedies in addition to corrective disclosures, such as rescission and divestiture, may be necessary or appropriate to remedy violations of the Williams Act, particularly in cases where the defendant deliberately violated § 13(d) and the illegal conduct has permitted the defendant to obtain a sufficient number of shares to inhibit competing tender offers or merger proposals. In such cases, absent rescission or divestiture or other remedy removing the wrongfully obtained blocking position, shareholders could be irreparably harmed and the defendant would be permitted to benefit from its wrongful conduct.

with § 13(d) . . . may foreshadow new regulatory or legislative proposals involving § 13(d).

The authors may have been overly optimistic with respect to the availability of a remedy. In Liberty Nat'l Insurance Holding Co. v. Charter Co., 734 F.2d 454 (11th Cir.1984), the court held that an issuer did not have an implied right of action to force a bidder to divest issuer stock acquired after a § 13(d) violation.

In one important respect, the cases discussed miss the most critical advantage of avoiding § 13(d), something even divestment does not remedy. If the Schedule 13D states that the purchase is only for investment, target stock earns positive abnormal returns of 3.24%. If, however, the Schedule 13D states that additional purchases are being contemplated, the abnormal returns increase to 7.74%.[9] By downplaying its intentions, the acquirer limits the rise in the price of the target's stock, thereby minimizing the price at which additional shares can be purchased in the period between the Schedule 13D filing and the subsequent tender offer. Divesting does not eliminate the profit from the § 13(d) violation because stock prices retain the gain on announcement for a period after the initial bidder withdraws. This gain is reflected in the price the acquirer receives when it sells the stock.[10]

An even greater advantage can be secured if the acquirer does not file a Schedule 13D at all. Then, so long as its buying is done carefully, the price of the target's stock may not rise at all. The practice of attempting to avoid filing a Schedule 13D by having someone else purchase shares on the acquirer's behalf has come to be known as "parking."

What is interesting about the parking setting is not the standards governing its legality -- Rule 13d-3's definition of "beneficial ownership" as having voting or investment power held "directly or indirectly, through any contract, arrangement, understanding, relationship, or otherwise" is broad enough to pick up any parking arrangement. The interesting questions concern the remedial aspects of parking violations.

Suppose that the party engaging in a parking arrangement subsequently terminates its effort to secure control of the target because greenmail is paid. In this case, enjoining the tender offer and ordering divestiture is irrelevant because the offer already will have been withdrawn and the shares sold to the target at a profit augmented by the § 13(d) violation itself. For § 13(d) to deter parking violations, a disgorgement remedy is necessary: the violator must give up the tainted profits.

---

[9] Mikkelson & Ruback (1985), *supra* note 8, (Table 4).

[10] See Ronald Gilson, *Drafting an Effective Greenmail Prohibition*, 88 Colum.L.Rev. 329 (1988).

In the following case, the SEC secured a disgorgement remedy for the first time in a parking setting that ended in greenmail.

SEC v. FIRST CITY FINANCIAL CORP., LTD.
890 F.2d 1215 (D.C.Cir.1989)

Before EDWARDS, GINSBURG and SILBERMAN, Circuit Judges.

SILBERMAN, Circuit Judge. Section 13(d) of the Securities Exchange Act of 1934 requires any person who has directly or indirectly obtained the beneficial ownership of more than 5% of any registered equity security to disclose within 10 days certain information to the issuer, the exchanges on which the security trades, and to the Securities and Exchange Commission ("SEC"). The SEC charged appellants, First City Financial Corporation, Ltd., ("First City") and Marc Belzberg, with deliberately evading § 13(d) and its accompanying regulations in their attempted hostile takeover of Ashland Oil Company ("Ashland") by filing the required disclosure statement after the 10 day period. The district court concluded that appellants had violated the statute; it then enjoined them from further violations of § 13(d) and ordered them to disgorge all profits derived from the violation. See SEC v. First City Financial Corp., et al., 688 F.Supp. 705 (D.D.C.1998). . . .

I

The SEC's case is based on its contention that on March 4, 1986, Marc Belzberg, a vice-president of First City, telephoned Alan ("Ace") Greenberg, the Chief Executive Officer of Bear Stearns, a large Wall Street brokerage firm, and asked Greenberg to buy substantial shares of Ashland for First City's account. Appellants claim that Greenberg "misunderstood" Belzberg: the latter intended only to recommend that Bear Stearns buy Ashland for its own account. . . .

[Prior to that date, Belzberg had determined that Ashland Oil was a "sensational business opportunity" and began accumulating Ashland stock. By February 28, 1986, First City held just over 4.9% of Ashland's common stock.]

[O]n March 4, Marc Belzberg telephoned Greenberg and engaged him in a short conversation that would be the centerpiece of this litigation. At his disposition, Greenberg described the conversation in the following manner:

> [Marc Belzberg] called me and said something to the effect that -- something like, "It wouldn't be a bad idea if you bought Ashland Oil here," or something like that. And I took that to mean that we were going to do another put and

call arrangement that we had done in the past. . . . . I was absolutely under the impression I was buying at their risk and I was going to do a put and call.[4]

While Greenberg interpreted Marc Belzberg's call as an order to purchase Ashland stock on behalf of First City, Marc Belzberg later claimed that intended only to recommend that Greenberg buy the stock for himself, that is, for Bear Stearns, and that Greenberg apparently misunderstood Belzberg. Immediately after the phone call, Greenberg purchased 20,500 Ashland shares. If purchased for First City, those shares would have pushed First City's Ashland holdings above 5% and triggered the beginning of the 10 day filing period of § 13(d). In that event, First City would have been obliged to file a Schedule 13D disclosure statement on March 14 with the SEC.

Between March 4 and 14, Greenberg purchased an additional 330,700 shares of Ashland stock for First City costing more than $14 million. Greenberg called Marc Belzberg periodically during those ten days to discuss various securities, including Ashland. In these conversations, Greenberg reported to Marc Belzberg the increasing number of Ashland shares Greenberg had accumulated. According to Greenberg, Belzberg replied to these reports by saying, "'Fine, keep going,' or something to that effect." Greenberg also characterized Belzberg's response as "grunt[ing]" approvingly. Belzberg did not squarely deny that testimony; he testified that he, Belzberg, said "uh-huh, I think it's cheap." Over the March 15-16 weekend, Marc Belzberg met with his father and uncles in Los Angeles to discuss Ashland. On Sunday, March 16, Samuel Belzberg decided that First City should continue to buy Ashland stock. Marc Belzberg then advised his father that Greenberg had accumulated a block of Ashland shares that "First City could acquire quickly." Samuel Belzberg later testified that he had no prior knowledge of the Greenberg purchases.

Returning to New York the next morning, March 17, Marc Belzberg called Greenberg and arranged a written put and call agreement for the 330,700 shares Bear Stearns had accumulated. During that conversation, Marc Belzberg did not mention a price to Greenberg. Several days later, Marc Belzberg received the written agreement with a "strike price," or the price Bear Stearns was charging First City, or $43.37; thus, the total March 17 put and call price was almost $500,000 below market. Marc Belzberg apparently expressed no surprise that Bear Stearns was charging almost half

---

[4] Large investors sometimes purchase stock through "put and call agreements." Under these agreements, a broker such as Bear Stearns would purchase the stock subject to the agreement and place it in its own account. The agreement entitles the investor to "call" or purchase the shares from the broker for an agreed upon period at an agreed upon price, the cost to the broker plus interest and a small commission. At the same time, the broker has the right to "put" or sell the shares to the investor at the same price. As a result, the investor rather than the broker bears all of the market risks in buying the stock. The put and call agreements were developed apparently in response to the pre-merger notification requirements of the Hart-Scott-Rodino Act.

a million dollars less than market value. He later testified that he believed that Bear Stearns was acting as a "Santa Claus" and that Greenberg was giving him "a bit of a break" to gain more business from First City in the future.

When Blumenstein, the officer responsible for ensuring First City's compliance with the federal securities laws, noticed the strike price, he immediately met with Marc Belzberg. Blumenstein recognized that the computation of the price reflected only the cost to Bear Stearns of acquiring the stock over the two week period before the written agreement (plus interest and commission), thus creating an inference that First City was the beneficial owner of the securities before March 17. After Blumenstein outlined the problem to Belzberg, the two men called Greenberg on a speakerphone. Belzberg later testified, "I informed Mr. Greenberg [during that conversation] that the letter [the written agreement] was incorrect, that I didn't care what the price of the stock was that he bought for himself, I didn't care what day he made the trades for himself, that I was buying stock from him as of today." Belzberg then testified that Greenberg said, "[Y]ou're right, the letter's wrong, I didn't read it before it went out, throw it out and I will send you a corrected copy." Greenberg, however, testified that Belzberg referred only to an error in the calculation of interest and not to the date on which First City acquired the stock. At the end of the conversation, Belzberg suggested he pay $44.00 per share, 4 cents per share higher than the original strike price but still $1.36, or a total of nearly $450,000, below the market price. At trial, Belzberg admitted to picking the $44 figure "out of the air" and that he "did not want the price [he] was paying to relate to [Greenberg's] cost." Between March 17 and 25, on Marc Belzberg's instructions, Greenberg bought another 890,100 Ashland shares on behalf of First City using several put and call agreements.

After these purchases, Samuel Belzberg sent a letter to Ashland's management, informing them of First City's holdings in their stock and proposing a friendly takeover of the company. Ashland rejected the offer, and on the morning of March 25 the company issued a press release disclosing that First City held between 8 and 9% of Ashland's stock. Almost immediately, the price of Ashland stock rose 10% to $52.25. The next day, on March 26, First City filed the Schedule 13D disclosure statement required by § 13(d). The statement indicated that First City had accumulated 9% of Ashland stock and intended to launch a tender offer for the remaining shares at $60 per share. The market price of Ashland stock then rose to $55, peaking at $55.75 per share the next day.

. . . On March 31, Ashland agreed to buy back First City's shares for $51 per share, or $134.1 million, resulting in a $15.4 million profit for First City. In return, First City agreed not to purchase any Ashland shares for the next 10 years.

. . . [T]he SEC filed a civil complaint against Marc Belzberg and First City, alleging that they crossed the 5% threshold on March 4 but filed the required disclosure statement on March 26, twelve days past the § 13(d) deadline.

The district court found that Marc Belzberg and First City entered into an informal put and call agreement on March 4 and then deliberately violated the 10 day filing requirement of § 13(d). The district court, in an extensive opinion, relied primarily on First City's acknowledged ultimate purpose to take over Ashland, Greenberg's understanding of his March 4 telephone conversation with Marc Belzberg, the subsequent conversations between Belzberg and Greenberg, and the suspicious price of the March 17 written agreement. The court discounted Marc Belzberg's "misunderstanding" explanation as "self-serving, inconsistent with his later actions and [not] squar[ing] with the objective evidence." 688 F.Supp. at 712. Belzberg, to put it bluntly, was not credited. The court also refused to consider Greenberg's later testimony that there might have been an "honest misunderstanding" since Greenberg reached that conclusion based only on Belzberg's suggestions and statements. See *id.* at 720.

The district court permanently enjoined appellants from future violations of § 13(d) because they violated the statute deliberately, showed no "remorse," and were engaged in a business which presented opportunities to violate the statute in the future. See *id.* at 725-26. The court also ordered appellants to disgorge approximately $2.7 million, representing their profits on the 890,000 shares of Ashland stock acquired between March 14 and 15. The court reasoned that appellants were able to purchase these shares at an artificially low price due to their failure to make the § 13(d) disclosure on March 14. See *id.* at 726-28. Appellants appeal the district court's finding of violation as unsupported by the evidence and a product of judicial bias. They further contend that the district court abused its discretion in ordering the injunction and disgorgement remedies.

II

A shareholder must comply with the § 13(d) disclosure law if he beneficially owns 5% of a public company's equity securities. Under Commission Rule 13d-3(a), whenever a person possesses investment or voting power through any agreement or understanding, he enjoys beneficial ownership. Rule 13d-3 is crafted broadly enough to sweep within its purview informal, oral arrangements that confer upon a person voting or investment power. See SEC v. Savoy Indus., Inc., 587 F.2d 1149, 1163 (D.C.Cir.1978), *cert. denied*, 440 U.S. 913 (1979); see also Wellman v. Dickinson, 682 F.2d 355, 363-67 (2d Cir.1982), *cert. denied*, 460 U.S. 1069 (1983). Appellants concede that a put and call agreement even if informal, constitutes beneficial ownership to the investor of the stock subject to the agreement.

The case before the district court turned on the question whether the put and call agreement between First City and Bear Stearns was entered into on

March 4, as the SEC claims, or not until March 17 as First City argues. That issue, of course, is a question of fact (or of mixed fact and law), the district court's answer to which normally may not be overturned on appeal unless clearly erroneous. . . .

IV

The district court directed disgorgement of profits, and appellants' challenge to this aspect of the order presents an issue of first impression -- whether federal courts have the authority to employ that remedy with respect to § 13(d) violations and whether it is appropriate in this sort of case. Appellants also claim that the amount ordered disgorged is excessive. We reject both arguments and affirm the district court's order on these issues as well.

Appellants, by claiming that Congress did not explicitly authorize a monetary remedy for § 13(d) violations, misapprehend the source of the court's authority. Disgorgement is an equitable remedy designed to deprive a wrongdoer of his unjust enrichment and to deter others from violating the securities laws. See SEC v. Tome, 833 F.2d 1086, 1096 (2d Cir.1987), *cert. denied*, 486 U.S.1014 (1988); SEC v. Blavin, 760 F.2d 706, 713 (6th Cir.1985); SEC v. Texas Gulf Sulphur Co., 446 F.2d 1301, 1307 (2d Cir.), *cert. denied*, 404 U.S. 1005 (1971). "Unless otherwise provided by statute, all the inherent equitable powers of the District Court are available for the proper and complete exercise of that jurisdiction." Porter v. Warner Holding Co., 328 U.S. 395 (1946); see also Mitchell v. Robert DeMario Jewelry, Inc., 361 U.S. 288, 291-92 (1960). We see no indication in the language or the legislative history of the 1934 Act that even implies a restriction on the equitable remedies of the district courts. See Mills v. Electric Auto-Lite Co., 396 U.S. 375, 391 (1970). Disgorgement, then, is available simply because the relevant provisions of the Securities Exchange Act of 1934, §§ 21(d) and (e), vest jurisdiction in the federal courts.

Indeed, appellants concede that disgorgement is rather routinely ordered for insider trading violations despite a similar lack of specific authorizations for that remedy under the securities law. See, e.g., SEC v. Tome, 833 F.2d at 1096; SEC v. Materia, 745 F.2d 197, 201 (2d Cir.1984); see generally Louis Loss, *Fundamentals of Securities Regulation* 1004-11 (1988). But they seek to distinguish § 13(d) violations as a "technical" transgression of reporting rules that really do not cause injury. In contrast, they argue, insider trading under modern theory is tantamount to theft; an actual injury is inflicted on the individual or institution entitled to confidentiality. Section 13(d), however, is the pivot of the entire Williams Act regulation of tender offers. To be sure, some may doubt the usefulness of that statute generally or the § 13(d) requirement specifically, but it is hardly up to the judiciary to second-guess the wisdom of Congress' approach to regulating takeovers. Suffice it for us to note that § 13(d) is a crucial requirement in the congressional scheme, and a violator, it is legislatively assumed, improperly benefits by purchasing stocks at an artificially low price because of a breach of the duty Congress imposed to disclose his investment position. The disclosure of that position -- a holding in excess of 5% of another company's stock -- suggests to the rest of the market a likely takeover and therefore may increase the price of the stock. Appellants circumvented that scheme, and the theory of the statute, by which we are bound, is that the circumventions caused injury to other market participants who sold stock without knowledge of First City's holdings. We therefore see no relevant distinction between disgorgement of inside trading profits and disgorgement of post-section 13(d) violation profits.

There remains, of course, the question of how the court measures those illegal profits. Appellants vigorously dispute the $2.7 million figure that the district court arrived at by simply calculating all of the profits First City realized (in its eventual sale back to Ashland) on the 890,000 shares First City purchased between March 14 and 25. See 638 F.Supp. at 728 n.24. The SEC's claim to disgorgement, which the district court accepted, is predicated on the assumption that had First City made its § 13(d) disclosure on March 14, at the end of the statutory 10 day period, the stock it purchased during the March 14-25 period would have been purchased in a quite different and presumably more expensive market. That hypothetical market would have been affected by the disclosure that the Belzbergs had taken a greater than 5% stake in Ashland and would soon propose a tender offer.

Since disgorgement primarily serves to prevent unjust enrichment, the court may exercise its equitable power only over property causally related to the wrongdoing. The remedy may well be a key to the SEC's efforts to deter others from violating the securities laws, but disgorgement may not be used punitively. See SEC v. Blatt, 583 F.2d 1325, 1335 (5th Cir.1978); SEC v. Manor Nursing Centers, Inc., 458 F.2d 1082, 1104 (2d Cir.1972). Therefore, the SEC generally must distinguish between legally and illegally obtained profits. See CFTC v. British Am. Commodity Options Corp., 788 F.2d 92, 93 (2d Cir.), *cert. denied*, 479 U.S. 853 (1986). Appellants assert that the hypothetical market between March 14-15 that the SEC urged and the district court accepted was simplistic, quite unrealistic, and so *de facto* punitive. It did not take into account other variables -- besides the § 13(d) disclosure -- which caused the post-March 25 price of the stock to rise above that which prevailed during the March 14-25 period. At trial appellants' expert witness testified that four independent factors combined to increase the stock price to the level it reached on March 25 and that these factors were not present on March 14, when the defendants should have disclosed. He identified these factors as: (1) the Belzbergs by the 25th held between 8 and 9% of Ashland, (2) the Belzbergs had prior to the 25th communicated to Ashland the size of their holdings, (3) Ashland publicly disclosed the Belzbergs' position on the 25th before the 13(d) disclosure, and (4) by the 25th, rumors swirled of an imminent takeover bid at $55 per share. In an attempt to hypothesize how the Belzbergs would have acted -- had they disclosed on March 14 -- and how the market would have responded to those actions, the witness presented three alternative scenarios that in his view more accurately measured the impact of the nondisclosure and which yielded disgorgement figures of zero, $496,050, and $864,588. Perhaps not surprisingly, appellants' witness testified that the most realistic scenario required no disgorgement at all.[23]

If exact information were obtainable at negligible cost, we would not hesitate to impose upon the government a strict burden to produce that data to measure the precise amount of the ill-gotten gains. Unfortunately, we encounter imprecision and imperfect information. Despite sophisticated econometric modelling, predicting stock market responses to alternative variables is, as the district court found, at best speculative. Rules for calculating disgorgement must recognize that separating legal from illegal profits exactly may at times be a near-impossible task. See, e.g., Elkind v. Liggett & Myers, Inc., 635 F.2d 156, 171 (2d Cir.1980).

Accordingly, disgorgement need only be a reasonable approximation of profits causally connected to the violation. In the insider trading context, courts typically require the violator to return all profits made on the illegal trades, see, e.g., SEC v. Texas Gulf Sulphur Co., 446 F.2d 1301, 1307 (2d Cir.), *cert. denied*, 404 U.S. 1005 (1971), and have rejected calls to restrict the disgorgement to the precise impact of the illegal trading on the market price. See *Elkind*, 635 F.2d at 171; cf. CFTC v. British Am. Commodity Options Corp., 788 F.2d 92 (2d Cir.) (concluding that a nexus between the unlawful conduct and the disgorgement figure need not be shown because of the pervasiveness of the fraud), *cert. denied*, 479 U.S. 853 (1986).

Although the SEC bears the ultimate burden of persuasion that its disgorgement figure reasonably approximates the amount of unjust enrichment, we believe the government's showing of appellants' actual profits on the tainted transactions at least presumptively satisfied that burden. Appellants, to whom the burden of going forward shifted, were then obliged clearly to demonstrate that the disgorgement figure was not a reasonable approximation. Defendants in such cases may make such a showing, for instance, by pointing to intervening events form the time of the violation. In SEC v. MacDonald, 699 F.2d 47 (1st Cir.1983) (en banc), the First Circuit reversed a district court order requiring the defendant to disgorge all profits from an illegal insider trade when the defendant had held on to the

---

[23] The expert witness concluded that disgorgement was unnecessary because if First City had disclosed on March 14, as the SEC claims it should have, we should assume that the 890,000 shares actually bought in the March 17-25 period (the 10-day window in Belzberg's view) would have been purchased in the lawful March 4-14 10-day window. Since Ashland prices were lower in the March 4-14 period than during March 17-25, the witness believed that no disgorgement was appropriate. This analysis, however, does not consider the impact of buying these 890,000 shares within this 10-day period -- in addition to the 330,000 shares the Belzbergs actually purchased then -- which presumably would have itself pushed up the price.

stock for more than a year. The court restricted the amount to a figure based on the price of the stock "a reasonable time after public dissemination of the inside information." *Id.* at 55. Similarly, the Second Circuit in SEC v. Manor Nursing Centers, Inc., 458 F.2d 1082 (2d Cir.1972), refused to extend the disgorgement remedy to income subsequently earned on the initial illegal profits. In those cases, the defendant demonstrated a clear break in or considerable attenuation of the causal connection between the illegality and the ultimate profits.

Here, appellants took a different approach using a sophisticated expert witness. As we noted, they maintained that the post-March 25 price was influenced by four other independent factors besides the belated § 13(d) disclosure, so even if First City had disclosed on March 14, the price would not have run up then to the extent it did after March 25. The difficulty we see with appellants' argument is that none of the four factors are independent of the § 13(d) disclosure determination. Thus, although by March 25 First City had accumulated 8-9% of Ashland, whereas on March 14 it had slightly over 5% (and although the market might react more strongly to the higher figure), we do not see why we should not assume that First City would have acquired 8-9% before March 14 -- if they knew they had to disclose on the earlier date. Second, it seems likely that First City would have notified Ashland's management on March 13 if they had planned to disclose on the next day, just as they did on March 25. Third, Ashland's premature disclosure of First City's holdings (prior to the § 13(d) notice) would likely have also occurred. And finally, the March 25 market takeover rumors were probably associated with all of the above activity, which is inextricably linked with the impending § 13(d) notice. We therefore agree with the district court that appellants' efforts to hypothesize both the takeover efforts of a First City that complied with § 13(d) and the market reaction to that are impossibly speculative.

Placing the burden on the defendants of rebutting the SEC's showing of actual profits, we recognize, may result, as it has in the insider trader context, in actual profits becoming the typical disgorgement measure. But the line between restitution and penalty is unfortunately blurred, and the risk of uncertainty should fall on the wrongdoer whose illegal conduct created that uncertainty. See SEC v. MacDonald, 699 F.2d 47, 55 (1st Cir.1983) (en banc); Elkind v. Liggett & Myers, Inc., 635 F.2d 156, 171 (2d Cir.1980); cf. Bigelow v. RKO Radio Pictures, 327 U.S. 251, 265 (1946) (placing the risk of uncertainty on the wrongdoer in the antitrust context). . . .

Suppose First City had actually completed the tender offer for Ashland Oil. How would you calculate profit for purposes of disgorgement then?

3.   The Triggers to Disclosure

Person and Beneficial Owner. The first step in construing the terms governing § 13(d)'s operation is specifying whose acquisitions and stock ownership are to be counted in determining whether the obligation to file a Schedule 13D has been triggered. Two statutory terms are implicated in this inquiry: "person" and "beneficial owner."

With respect to the term "person," § 13(d)(3) provides that a group formed "for the purpose of acquiring, holding, or disposing of securities of an issuer" will be treated as a single person in determining whether a filing obligation has been triggered. The need for such a provision is obvious; in its absence, a planner could avoid § 13(d)(1)'s 5% trigger at will simply by splitting stock acquisitions among a number of individuals who had agreed to act in concert. However, it would be very difficult to draw a brightline rule that would determine whether a group exists. If the group concept were limited to combinations held together by formal agreement, it could be avoided by individuals whose existing relationship -- as family members or co-venturers in other projects -- assured the performance of informal obligations undertaken in connection with a new project. Thus, it was predictable that determining whether a group existed would depend on examination of the detailed facts and circumstances of each case,[11] and that, much as with respect to the existence of a conspiracy under the Sherman Act, circumstantial evidence alone would support a finding that a group exists.

This, however, does not end the matter of line drawing. Even informal agreements to act in concert do not spring to life full blown; preliminary discussion necessarily proceeds the formation of a group and § 13(d)(1) can hardly require a filing with respect to a group that has not yet been formed. As the court stated in Pantry Pride, Inc. v. Rooney, 598 F.Supp. 891, 900 (S.D.N.Y.1984): "Section 13(d) allows individuals broad freedom to discuss the possibilities of future agreements without filing under securities laws." The resulting conflict -- between the need for a general standard to prevent avoidance and the need to avoid imposing a filing obligation too early in the process of negotiating the formation of the group -- may help explain the courts' reluctance, as discussed in the previous section and exemplified by the Supreme Court in Rondeau v. Mosinee Paper Co.,[12] to impose meaningful sanctions for violations of § 13(d)(1). Given the inherent uncertainty in distinguishing between, on the one hand, the informal formation of a group and, on the other, nonbinding discussions preliminary to forming a group, it would be difficult to justify a significant penalty if the penalty's application depended upon the inevitably somewhat random

---

[11] See, e.g., Jacobs v. Pabst Brewing Co., 549 F.Supp. 1050 (D.Del.1982); Financial General Bankshares, Inc. v. Lance, 80 F.R.D. 22 (D.D.C.1978); Jewelcor, Inc. v. Pearlman, 397 F.Supp. 221 (S.D.N.Y.1975).

[12] 422 U.S. 49 (1975). In *Rondeau* the Supreme Court required a showing of irreparable injury before injunctive relief would be granted for a violation of § 13(d)(1).

resolution of that uncertainty. Yet this can be precisely the case in some §
13(d) settings; where a group is involved, the filing obligation often accrues
10 days after the group is formed even though the date from which one
begins the count is unclear.[13]

The chilling effect of the uncertainty in determining when a group is
formed for purposes of § 13(d)(1) was increased by the terms of Rule
13(d)(5). While the statute imposes a filing requirement only on a group
formed "for the purpose of acquiring, holding or disposing of securities of
an issuer,"[14] the rule extends that requirement to groups formed for the
purpose of "voting" such securities. The result is to erect an additional
barrier to shareholder activity designed to monitor management rather than
influence control.[15]

The same type of issue arises with respect to the term "beneficial
owner." Individuals own some equity securities formally: They are the
record owners of the securities. They own other securities informally: Even
though others are the record owners, the securities *really* belong to them.
Here Rule 13d-3 does provide some certainty, although the potential for
ambiguity still remains. Note, for example, that subsection (a) of Rule 13d-3
speaks in terms of voting or investment power held "directly or indirectly,
through any contract, arrangement, understanding, relationship, or otherwise.
. . ." Thus, the same problem that created the uncertainty in connection with
the term "group" reappears in connection with the term "beneficial owner."

Acquiring. On its face, § 13(d)(1) seem to require that, to trigger a
filing obligation, a person or group actually must make an acquisition of
stock. If this were correct, the uncertainty concerning precisely when a
group was formed would be substantially ameliorated. So long as all
potential group members did not acquire stock while the terms of their
relationship were being negotiated, there would be no danger of unknowingly

---

[13] Where the members of the group together own 5% of the issuer's stock, the filing of
a Schedule 13D would be required 10 days after the date on which the group was formed.
This result follows from the construction of the term "acquiring" in § 13(d)(1) considered,
infra.

Do the facts in *First City Financial Corp.* present the kind of uncertainty discussed in
the Text? If a disgorgement remedy is available only to the SEC, prosecutorial discretion can
limit its application to cases where the existence of the group is clear.

[14] § 13(d)(3).

[15] See Bernard Black, *Shareholder Passivity Reexamined*, 89 Mich.L.Rev. 520 (1990);
Bernard Black, *Next Steps in Corporate Governance Reform: 13(d) Rules and Control Person
Liability*, in *Modernizing U.S. Securities Regulation: Economic and Legal Perspectives* 197
(Kenneth Lehn & Robert Kamphuis eds.1993). Commentators differ about how extensively
Rule 13d-5 restricts shareholder activity -- compare Ronald Gilson & Reinier Kraakman,
Reinventing the Outside Director: An Agenda for Institutional Investors, 43 Stan.L.Rev. 863
(1991) with John Coffee, *Liquidity versus Control: The Institutional Investor as Corporate
Monitor*, 81 Colum.L.Rev. 1277 (1991) -- but there is little academic dispute concerning the
need to roll back its application to institutional shareholder activity.

triggering a filing obligation. The ten days would run only from a discernible event: an actual acquisition of securities. Thus, a brightline rule with respect to "acquiring" largely would make irrelevant the ambiguity with respect to "group."

It did not work out that way. Although an early case adopted this construction of the statute for the explicit purpose of providing some certainty,[16] later cases did not follow it.[17] In any event, the SEC resolved the matter in 1977 by the adoption of Rule 13d-5 which expressly provides that a group is deemed to acquire the securities of its members on the date the group is formed.

Equity Security and 5%. Here the issues are ones of calculation. How are convertible securities counted? What if a person has an option to acquire securities? These issues are addressed in the context of the beneficial ownership provisions in Rule 13d-3.

Problems

What are the parties' § 13(d) filing obligations in the following circumstances?

1. Susan Reynolds, a 22 year old law student, owns 3% ($150,000 face value) of the outstanding convertible subordinated debentures of GSSB, Inc., and 4% (40,000 shares) of its outstanding common stock. Both classes of securities are traded on a national securities exchange. The debentures are convertible into common stock at the rate of one share per $10 face value of debenture. Reynold's father, the original source of her GSSB holdings, owns 22% of GSSB's outstanding common stock and 10% of its outstanding debentures. As a Valentine Day's present Reynold's father presents her with an additional $150,000 face value of GSSB convertible debentures. All of Reynold's securities are held in street name by the family broker.

2. Ronald Davis is the President of TD, Inc., whose common stock is traded on a national securities exchange. One million shares are outstanding. Davis owns 25,000 shares of common stock and holds options to purchase 15,000 shares under the company's stock option plan. Davis also is (i) the beneficiary of a pledge of 7,500 shares of the company's common stock given as security for his loan of their purchase price to a company vice president; (ii) the trustee of an irrevocable trust for the benefit of his children (established by the children's grandfather) which holds 3,500 shares of the company's common stock.

---

[16] Bath Industries v. Blot, 427 F.2d 97, 110 (7th Cir.1970).

[17] See, e.g., GAF Corp. v. Milstein, 453 F.2d 709 (2d Cir.1971), *cert. denied*, 406 U.S. 910 (1972).

4.   The Content of Required Disclosure

[*Read Schedule 13D in Appendix A.*]

For an acquirer, Item 4 of Schedule 13D poses the central § 13(d) disclosure dilemma. Suppose that two acquirers each make a 5% acquisition that triggers the obligation to file a Schedule 13D -- one a straightforward company that desires only to comply with applicable legal requirements, and one with a more strategic orientation that would like to minimize the extent to which disclosure interferes with achieving its aims. Item 4 requires disclosure of whether the offeror intends to seek control of the issuer.[18] Now suppose that the straightforward company genuinely made its acquisition only as an investment and has no intention of seeking control. The problem with simply so stating in its Schedule 13D is twofold. First, some courts have viewed a substantial acquisition as itself evidence that the acquirer had an intent to seek control.[19] Second, circumstances change. If the company later seeks control, the accuracy of its original statement of intent unavoidably will be determined in light of the fact that it turned out to be an inaccurate prediction.[20]

One approach to resolving this dilemma is what has been called "waffling"[21] or "kitchen sink" disclosure: Disclosure that covers all possibilities without disclosing the acquirer's estimate of their relative likelihood. Jewelcor's disclosure in connection with its acquisition of Lafayette stock is an example of this approach that passed judicial muster:

> Item 4: The Common Stock of Lafayette to which this statement relates was purchased by Jewelcor for the purpose of investment. Although Jewelcor has considered the possibility of a future acquisition of control of the business of Lafayette, whether by means of a tender offer, merger or other business combination, open market purchases, private transactions, or otherwise, Jewelcor has not made any definitive plans to attempt to acquire control of

---

[18] Although item 4 does not by its terms explicitly require this disclosure, the courts have consistently held that it is required. James Tobin & James Maiwurm, *Beachhead Acquisitions: Creating Waves in the Marketplace and Uncertainty in the Regulatory Framework*, 38 Bus.Law. 419, 430 (1983).

[19] See, e.g., Dan River, Inc. v. Unitex Ltd., 624 F.2d 1216 (4th Cir.1980), *cert. denied*, 449 U.S. 1101 (1981); Saunders Leasing System, Inc. v. Societe Holding Gray D'Albion, 507 F.Supp. 627 (N.D.Ala.1981); General Steel Industries v. Walco National Corp., 529 F.Supp. 305 (E.D.Mo.), *vacated per stipulation*, 676 F.2d 704 (8th Cir.1981).

[20] Martin Lipton & Erica Steinberger, *Takeovers and Freezeouts* 85 (1978), reports that the SEC staff has stated informally that it "is inclining to a strict integration approach whereby later action taken by the acquirer with respect to the target company will be rebuttably presumed to have been intended at the time of the earlier filing."

[21] Tobin & Maiwurm (1983), *supra* note 18, at 434.

Lafayette, nor has Jewelcor entered into any contracts, arrangements or understandings with Lafayette or its affiliates for this purpose.[22] . . .

While the analysis is somewhat different in the case of the strategic acquirer, it may well lead to the same conclusion. Suppose that this acquirer is seriously considering seeking control of the target company, but would like to do so as cheaply as possible. To this end, the acquirer would like its Schedule 13D to have as little impact on the price of target company stock as possible consistent with disclosure that has a reasonable probability of being sustained if challenged. It knows that Schedule 13D disclosures which state that the acquirer is considering additional investments in the target company's stock are associated with an average abnormal return of 7.74%, while Schedule 13D disclosures which state that the acquisition was only for investment are associated with an average abnormal return of 3.24%.[23] Would not the same form of disclosure that was best for the straightforward acquirer then also be best for the strategic acquirer?[24] How sensible is a system that leads to the same disclosure in situations that are so different? Although the content of mandatory disclosure warrants more careful consideration, it will be deferred until we take up the same issues in connection with § 14(d) in the following section.

---

[22] Jewelcor, Inc., v. Pearlman, 397 F.Supp. 221, 228 (S.D.N.Y.1975). A more extreme example is set forth in Lipton & Steinberger (1978), *supra* note 20, at 80-81:

Raider purchased the shares of Target's common stock presently owned by Raider to acquire an equity interest in Target. Raider has also considered, but has not decided whether or not to pursue, other possible courses of action with respect to Target, including (i) seeking control of Target by purchasing additional shares in brokerage transactions on the New York Stock Exchange, in private transactions, in a tender offer or exchange offer, or otherwise; (ii) proposing a merger or other form of combination between Raider and Target; and (iii) seeking representation on Target's Board of Directors. . . .

Raider intends to review, from time to time, the possible courses of action referred to above and to take such action with respect to Target as Raider considers desirable in the light of the circumstances then prevailing. Pending Raider's decision whether or not to pursue any of such possible courses of action, and depending on market conditions and other factors, Raider presently intends to continue to purchase shares of Target's common stock in brokerage transactions on the New York Stock Exchange or in private transactions, if appropriate opportunities to do so are available, on such terms and at such times as Raider considers desirable. Raider also may determine to continue to hold its shares of Target's common stock or to dispose of all or a portion of such shares.

Although the possibilities referred to above do exist, Raider has no plans or proposals to liquidate Target to sell its assets, to merge it with any other person or to make any other major change in its business or corporate structure.

[23] Mikkelson & Ruback (1985), *supra* note 8, Table 4.

[24] Ambiguous disclosure in the Schedule 13D, however, might be clarified by the identity of the purchaser. Would the market believe a statement by T. Boone Pickens that a purchase was made for investment?

B.　Disclosure and Substantive Regulation of Tender Offers

Although an acquiring company's first encounter with the Williams Act likely will be with § 13(d) following its predisclosure acquisition of target company stock, the disclosure required of both the acquiring company and the target company in connection with the tender offer, and the substantive terms of the tender offer itself, will be controlled by §§ 14(d) and (e).　This combination of disclosure and substantive regulation is virtually unique in the universe of federal securities regulation.　Other sections of the Securities Exchange Act of 1934 focus mainly on either requiring disclosure, as with registration under § 12 and periodic reporting under § 13(a), or on forbidding misleading disclosure as under § 10(b).　Similarly, the Securities Act of 1933 requires only disclosure of material facts bearing on whatever security the issuer proposes to offer to the public.　Only the Williams Act seems to cross the boundary separating regulatory regimes that leave informed parties free to make whatever deal they choose, from those that limit the range of permissible deals available even to informed parties.　As we will see, controversy over whether the Williams Act in fact crosses the boundary between disclosure regulation and substantive regulation has shaped debate over one of the statute's major jurisdictional limits.[25]

The general shape of §§ 14(d) and (e) is straightforward.　Section 14(d)(1) prohibits making a tender offer that would result in the offeror holding more than 5% of a class of the target company's equity securities without filing a disclosure statement.　Sections 14(d)(5)-(7) specify the minimum period that tender offers must be left open, the extent of a shareholder's right to withdraw shares after tender, the effect of over-subscription in a partial offer, and the effect of an offeror increasing the price during the pendency of a tender offer.　Section 14(e) prohibits misrepresentation, nondisclosure and fraudulent, deceptive or manipulative acts or practices in connection with tender offers.

Note that all three aspects of the regulatory structure of §§ 14(d) and (e) share a common jurisdictional limit: They apply only to a "tender offer." This term, however, is nowhere defined in the statute or regulations.　Thus, a natural place to begin our examination of the transactional aspects of the Williams Act would seem to be with the definition of the covered transactions:　What is a tender offer?　What kinds of transactions trigger the regulatory apparatus?　For our purposes, however, this inquiry is a more fitting end than a beginning.　A conventional tender offer is hardly difficult to recognize; the problem is with unconventional transactions -- typically the work of planners whose very purpose is to avoid the impact of §§ 14(d) and

---

[25] This debate is posed in terms of whether the prohibition of "fraudulent, deceptive, or manipulative acts" in § 14(e) extends to target company defensive tactics such as lock-ups, or is limited to acts of misrepresentation or nondisclosure.　The subject is considered in Section C.1 of this Chapter, *infra*.

(e). As a result, it is necessary to understand the stakes for which the planners are playing -- the collateral consequences of calling a transaction a tender offer -- before evaluating the efforts of the courts and the SEC at defining a tender offer. Moreover, as we saw in Chapter 17, the principal advantage of avoiding the application of the Williams Act is speed -- the ability close an offer before a competitive bid can surface. The widespread adoption of poison pills and the clear judicial sanction of their use to obtain time to secure a competitive bid, serves to significantly reduce the incentive to design transactional alternatives that fall outside the boundaries of §§ 14(d) and (e).

1. Disclosure Under Sections 14(d) and (e)

a. *Introduction: The Statute and Regulations*

[Read Securities Exchange Act §§ 14(d) and (e), and Regulations 14D and 14E in Appendix A.]

Prior to January 7, 1980, the Williams Act's requirement of mandatory disclosure in connection with a tender offer extended only to the offeror; the target company remained free to stone wall it. To be sure, if target management elected to comment on an offer or to make a recommendation to target shareholders, Rule 14d-9 required the filing of Schedule 14D-9, and § 14(e) would apply to the content of the communication; however, there was no *requirement* that target management say anything. The January 7, 1980 effective date of Rule 14e-2 changed this imbalance. The Commission explained the reason for imposing a mandatory disclosure obligation on the target company as follows:

> The subject company's position with respect to a tender offer can have a determinative effect on the outcome of a tender offer and thus is material to security holders. The subject company therefore should not be permitted to state its position when it maximizes its tactical advantage and to remain silent when it does not. Such complete discretion increases the likelihood for hasty, ill-considered decision-making by security holders and the possibility for fraudulent, deceptive or manipulative acts or practices by a subject company and others.[26]

Is the case for the imposition of mandatory disclosure quite so easy? Suppose a tender offer were made and the target company did not comment. Would not the market infer that the failure of the target company to recommend against the offer meant that the target did not object to the offer?

---

[26] Exchange Act Release No. 16384 (Nov. 29, 1979), reprinted in [1979-1980 Transfer Binder] Fed.Sec.L.Rep. (CCH) ¶ 82,373.

If that were the case, mandatory disclosure of a sort already existed in that the target company could not keep the market in doubt as to its view of the offer; silence would be read as tacit acceptance. Moreover, how significant a change does Rule 14e-2 effect? If the target company can limit its comment, as permitted by Rule 14e-2, to a statement that "it is unable to take a position with respect to the bidder's tender offer", and can explain the reasons for its inability by boilerplate,[27] has there been any gain over silence?

b.　　*Standing and Remedies*

PIPER v. CHRIS-CRAFT INDUSTRIES
430 U.S. 1 (1977)

Mr. Chief Justice BURGER delivered the opinion of the Court.

We granted certiorari in these cases to consider, among other issues, whether an unsuccessful tender offeror in a contest for control of a corporation has an implied cause of action for damages under § 14(e) of the Securities Exchange Act of 1934, as added by § 3 of the Williams Act of 1968, . . . based on alleged antifraud violations by the successful competitor, its investment adviser, and individuals constituting the management of the target corporation.

Result encourages seeking white knight and drawing SH if necessary about offer values.

I

Background

The factual background of this complex contest for control, including the protracted litigation culminating in the cases now before us, is essential to a full understanding of the contending parties' claims.

The three petitions present questions of first impression, arising out of a "sophisticated and hard fought contest" for control of Piper Aircraft Corp., a Pennsylvania-based manufacturer of light aircraft. Piper's management consisted principally of members of the Piper family, who owned 31% of Piper's outstanding stock. Chris-Craft Industries, Inc., a diversified manufacturer of recreational products, attempted to secure voting control of Piper through cash and exchange tender offers for Piper common stock. Chris-Craft's takeover attempt failed, and Bangor Punta Corp. (Bangor or Bangor Punta), with the support of the Piper family, obtained control of

---

[27] For example, could the target company decline to take a position because it believes that target management has an inherent conflict of interest concerning any tender offer and therefore believes that the decision is appropriately one for shareholders?

Piper in September 1969.   Chris-Craft brought suit under § 14(e) of the
Securities Exchange Act of 1934 . . . alleging that Bangor Punta achieved
control of the target corporation as a result of violations of the federal
securities laws by the Piper family, Bangor Punta, and Bangor Punta's
underwriter, First Boston Corp., who together had successfully repelled
Chris-Craft's takeover attempt.

The struggle for control of Piper began in December 1968.   At that
time, Chris-Craft began making cash purchases of Piper common stock.   By
January 22, 1969, Chris-Craft had acquired 203,700 shares, or
approximately 13% of Piper's 1,644,790 outstanding shares.   On the next
day, following unsuccessful preliminary overtures to Piper by Chris-Craft's
president, Herbert Siegel, Chris-Craft publicly announced a cash tender offer
for up to 300,000 Piper shares at $65 per share, which was approximately
$12 above the then-current market price.   Responding promptly to
Chris-Craft's bid, Piper's management met on the same day with the
company's investment banker, First Boston, and other advisers.   On January
24, the Piper family decided to oppose Chris-Craft's tender offer.   As part
of its resistance to Chris-Craft's takeover campaign, Piper management sent
several letters to the company's stockholders during January 25-27, arguing
against acceptance of Chris-Craft's offer.   On January 27, a letter to
shareholders from W.T. Piper, Jr., president of the company, stated that the
Piper Board "has carefully studied this offer and is convinced that it is
inadequate and not in the best interests of Piper's shareholders."

In addition to communicating with shareholders, Piper entered into an
agreement with Grumman Aircraft Corp. on January 29, whereby Grumman
agreed to purchase 300,000 authorized but unissued Piper shares at $65 per
share.   The agreement increased the amount of stock necessary for
Chris-Craft to secure control and thus rendered Piper less vulnerable to
Chris-Craft's attack.   A Piper press release and letter to shareholders
announced the Grumman transaction but failed to state either that Grumman
had a "put" or option to sell the shares back to Piper at cost, plus interest,
or that Piper was required to maintain the proceeds of the transaction in a
separate fund free from liens.

Despite Piper's opposition, Chris-Craft succeeded in acquiring 304,606
shares by the time its cash tender offer expired on February 3.   To obtain the
additional 17% of Piper stock needed for control, Chris-Craft decided to
make an exchange offer of Chris-Craft securities for Piper stock.   Although
Chris-Craft filed a registration statement and preliminary prospectus with the
SEC in late February 1969, the exchange offer did not go into effect until
May 15, 1969.

In the meantime, Chris-Craft made cash purchases of Piper stock on the
open market until Mr. Siegel, the company's president, was expressly
warned by SEC officials that such purchases, when made during the
pendency of an exchange offer, violated SEC Rule 10b-6.   At Mr. Siegel's
direction, Chris-Craft immediately complied with the SEC's directive and
canceled all outstanding orders for purchases of Piper stock.

While Chris-Craft's exchange offer was in registration, Piper in March 1969 terminated the agreement with Grumman and entered into negotiations with Bangor Punta. Bangor had initially been contacted by First Boston about the possibility of a Piper takeover in the wake of Chris-Craft's initial cash tender offer in January. With Grumman out of the picture, the Piper family agreed on May 8, 1969, to exchange their 31% stockholdings in Piper for Bangor Punta securities. Bangor also agreed to use its best efforts to achieve control of Piper by means of an exchange offer of Bangor securities for Piper common stock. A press release issued the same day announced the terms of the agreement, including a provision that the forthcoming exchange offer would involve Bangor securities to be valued, in the judgment of First Boston, "at not less than $80 per Piper share."

While awaiting the effective date of its exchange offer, Bangor in mid-May 1969 purchased 120,200 shares of Piper stock in privately negotiated, off-exchange transactions from three large institutional investors.

. . .

With these three block purchases, amounting to 7% of Piper stock, Bangor Punta in mid-May took the lead in the takeover contest. The contest then centered upon the competing exchange offers. Chris-Craft's first exchange offer, which began in mid-May 1969, failed to produce tenders of the specified minimum number of Piper shares (80,000). Meanwhile, Bangor Punta's exchange offer, which had been announced on May 8, became effective on July 18. The registration materials which Bangor filed with the SEC in connection with the exchange offer included financial statements, reviewed by First Boston, representing that one of Bangor's subsidiaries, the Bangor & Aroostock Railroad (BAR), had a value of $18.4 million. This valuation was based upon a 1965 appraisal by investment bankers after a proposed sale of the BAR failed to materialize. The financial statements did not indicate that Bangor was considering the sale of the BAR or that an offer to purchase the railroad for $5 million had been received.[5]

In the final phase of the see-saw of competing offers, Chris-Craft modified the terms of its previously unsuccessful exchange offer to make it more attractive. The revised offer succeeded in attracting 112,089 additional Piper shares, while Bangor's exchange offer, which terminated on July 29, resulted in the tendering of 110,802 shares. By August 4, 1969, at the conclusion of both offers, Bangor Punta owned a total of 44.5%, while Chris-Craft owned 40.6% of Piper stock. The remainder of Piper stock, 14.9%, remained in the hands of the public.

After completion of their respective exchange offers, both companies renewed market purchases of Piper stock, but Chris-Craft, after purchasing 29,200 shares for cash in mid-August, withdrew from competition. Bangor Punta continued making cash purchases until September 5, by which time it

---

[5] Shortly after the contest for control was completed, Bangor entered into an agreement to sell the BAR for $5 million, thereby resulting in a $13.8 million book loss.

had acquired a majority interest in Piper. The final tally in the nine-month takeover battle showed that Bangor Punta held over 50% and Chris-Craft held 42% of Piper stock.

II

Before either side had achieved control, the contest moved from the marketplace to the courts. Then began more than seven years of complex litigation growing out of the contest for control of Piper Aircraft. . . .

III

. . . The threshold issue in these cases is whether tender offerors such as Chris-Craft, whose activities are regulated by the Williams Act, have a cause of action for damages against other regulated parties under the statute on a claim that anti-fraud violations by other parties have frustrated the bidder's efforts to obtain control of the target corporation. . . .

IV

Our analysis begins, of course, with the statute itself. Section 14(e), like § 10(b), makes no provision whatever for a private cause of action, such as those explicitly provided in other sections of the 1933 and 1934 Acts. E.g., §§ 11, 12, 15 of the 1933 Act; §§ 9, 16, 18, 20 of the 1934 Act. This Court has nonetheless held that in some circumstances a private cause of action can be implied with respect to the 1934 Act's antifraud provisions, even though the relevant provisions are silent as to remedies. J.I. Case Co. v. Borak, 377 U.S. 426 (1964) (§ 14(a)); Superintendent of Ins. v. Bankers Life & Cas. Co., 404 U.S. 6, 13 n.9 (1971) (§ 10(b)).

The reasoning of these holdings is that, where congressional purposes are likely to be undermined absent private enforcement, private remedies may be implied in favor of the particular class intended to be protected by the statute. . . .

Against this background we must consider whether § 14(e), which is entirely silent as to private remedies, permits this Court to read into the statute a damages remedy for unsuccessful tender offerors. To resolve that question we turn to the legislative history to discern the congressional purpose underlying the specific statutory prohibition in § 14(e). Once we identify the legislative purpose, we must then determine whether the creation by judicial interpretation of the implied cause of action asserted by Chris-Craft is necessary to effectuate Congress' goals.

A

Reliance on legislative history in divining the intent of Congress is, as has often been observed, a step to be taken cautiously. Department of Air

Force v. Rose, 425 U.S. 352, 388-389 (1976) (Blackmun, J., dissenting); United States v. Public Utilities Comm'n, 345 U.S. 295, 319 (1953) (Jackson, J., concurring); Scripps-Howard Radio v. FCC, 316 U.S. 4, 11 (1942). In this case both sides press legislative history on the Court not so much to explain the meaning of the language of a statute as to explain the absence of any express provision for a private cause of action for damages. As Mr. Justice Frankfurter reminded us: "We must be wary against interpolating our notions of policy in the interstices of legislative provisions." *Ibid.* With that caveat, we turn to the legislative history of the Williams Act.

In introducing the legislation on the Senate floor, the sponsor, Senator Williams, stated:

> This legislation will close a significant gap in *investor protection* under the Federal securities laws by requiring the disclosure of pertinent information *to stockholders* when persons seek to obtain control of a corporation by a cash tender offer or through open market or privately negotiated purchases of securities. 113 Cong.Rec. 854 (1967). (Emphasis supplied.)

. . . The legislative history thus shows that Congress was intent upon regulating takeover bidders, theretofore operating covertly, in order to protect the shareholders of target companies. That tender offerors were not the intended beneficiaries of the bill was graphically illustrated by the statements of Senator Kuchel, cosponsor of the legislation, in support of requiring takeover bidders, whom he described as "corporate raiders" and "takeover pirates," to disclose their activities.

> Today there are those individuals in our financial community who seek to reduce our proudest businesses into nothing but corporate shells. They seize control of the corporation with unknown sources, sell or trade away the best assets, and later split up the remains among themselves. The tragedy of such collusion is that the corporation can be financially raped without management *or shareholders* having any knowledge of the acquisitions. . . . The corporate raider may thus act under a cloak of secrecy while obtaining the shares needed to put him on the road to a successful capture of the company. 113 Cong.Rec. 857-858 (1967). (Emphasis supplied.)

. . . The sponsors of this legislation were plainly sensitive to the suggestion that the measure would favor one side or the other in control contests; however, they made it clear that the legislation was designed solely to get needed information to the investor, the constant focal point of the committee hearings. Senator Williams articulated this singleness of purpose, even while advocating neutrality:

> We have taken extreme care to avoid tipping the scales either in favor of management or in favor of the person making the takeover bids. *S.510 is*

designed solely to require full and fair disclosure for the benefit of investors.
113 Cong.Rec. 24664 (1967). (Emphasis supplied.)

Accordingly, the congressional policy of "evenhandedness" is nonprobative of the quite disparate proposition that the Williams Act was intended to confer rights for money damages upon an injured takeover bidder.

Besides the policy of evenhandedness, Chris-Craft emphasizes that the matter of implied private causes of action was raised in written submissions to the Senate Subcommittee. Specifically, Chris-Craft points to the written statements of Professors Israels and Painter, who made reference to J.I. Case Co. v. Borak, 377 U.S. 426 (1964). Chris-Craft contends, therefore, that Congress was aware that private actions were implicit in § 14(e).

But this conclusion places more weight on the passing reference to *Borak* than can reasonably be carried. Even accepting the value of written statements received without comment by the committee and without cross-examination, the statements do not refer to implied private actions by *offeror-bidders.* . . .

The legislative history thus shows that the sole purpose of the Williams Act was the protection of investors who are confronted with a tender offer. As we stated in Rondeau v. Mosinee Paper Corp., 422 U.S. at 58: "The purpose of the Williams Act is to insure that public shareholders who are confronted by a cash tender offer for their stock will not be required to respond without adequate information. . . ." We find no hint in the legislative history, on which respondent so heavily relies, that Congress contemplated a private cause of action for damages by one of several contending offerors against a successful bidder or by a losing contender against the target corporation. . . .

B

Our conclusion as to the legislative history is confirmed by the analysis in Cort v. Ash, 422 U.S. 66 (1975). There, the Court identified four factors as "relevant" in determining whether a private remedy is implicit in a statute not expressly providing one. The first is whether the plaintiff is " 'one of the class for whose *especial* benefit the statute was enacted. . . .' " *Id.* at 78. (Emphasis in original.) As previously indicated, examination of the statute and its genesis shows that Chris-Craft is not an intended beneficiary of the Williams Act, and surely is not one "for whose *especial* benefit the statute was enacted." *Ibid.* To the contrary, Chris-Craft is a member of the class whose activities Congress intended to regulate for the protection and benefit of an entirely distinct class, shareholder-offerees. As a party whose previously unregulated conduct was purposefully brought under federal control by the statute, Chris-Craft can scarcely lay claim to the status of "beneficiary" whom Congress considered in need of protection.

Second, in Cort v. Ash we inquired whether there was "any indication of legislative intent, explicit or implicit, either to create such a remedy or to deny one." *Ibid.* Although the historical materials are barren of any express intent to deny a damages remedy to tender offerors as a class, there is, as we have noted, no indication that Congress intended to create a damages remedy in favor of the loser in a contest for control. Fairly read, we think the legislative documents evince the narrow intent to curb the unregulated activities of tender offerors. The expression of this purpose, which pervades the legislative history, negates the claim that tender offerors were intended to have additional weapons in the form of an implied cause of action for damages, particularly if a private damages action confers no advantage on the expressly protected class of shareholder-offerees, a matter we discuss later.

Chris-Craft argues, however, that Congress intended standing under § 14(e) to encompass tender offerors since the statute, unlike § 10(b), does not contain the limiting language, "in connection with the purchase or sale" of securities. Instead, in § 14(e), Congress broadly proscribed fraudulent activities "in connection with any tender offer . . . or any solicitation . . . in opposition to or in favor of any such offer. . . . "

The omission of the purchaser-seller requirement does not mean, however, that Chris-Craft has standing to sue for damages under § 14(e) in its capacity as a takeover bidder. It may well be that Congress desired to protect, among others, shareholder-offerees who decided not to tender their stock due to fraudulent misrepresentations by persons opposed to a takeover attempt. See generally 1 A. Bromberg, *Securities Law: Fraud* § 6.3 (1021), p.122.17 (1969). See also Senate Report 2; House Report 3. These shareholders, who might not enjoy the protection of § 10(b) under Blue Chip Stamps v. Manor Drug Stores, 421 U.S. 723 (1975), could perhaps state a claim under § 14(e), even though they did not tender their securities.[25] But increased protection, if any, conferred upon the class of shareholder-offerees by the elimination of the purchaser-seller restriction can scarcely be interpreted as giving protection to the entirely separate and unrelated class of persons whose conduct the statute is designed to regulate.

Third, Cort v. Ash tells us that we must ascertain whether it is "consistent with the underlying purposes of the legislative scheme to imply such a remedy for the plaintiff." 422 U.S. at 78. We conclude that it is not. As a disclosure mechanism aimed especially at protecting shareholders of target corporations, the Williams Act cannot consistently be interpreted as conferring a monetary remedy upon regulated parties, particularly where the award would not redound to the direct benefit of the protected class. Although it is correct to say that the $36 million damages award indirectly benefits those Piper shareholders who became Chris-Craft shareholders when they accepted Chris-Craft's exchange offer, it is equally true that the

---

[25] These cases, of course, do not present that issue, and we express no view on it.

damages award injures those Piper shareholders who exchanged their shares for Bangor Punta's stock and who, as Bangor Punta shareholders, would necessarily bear a large part of the burden of any judgment against Bangor Punta. The class sought to be protected by the Williams Act are the shareholders of the *target* corporation; hence it can hardly be said that their interests as a class are served by a judgment in favor of Chris-Craft and against Bangor Punta. Moreover, the damages are awarded to the very party whose activities Congress intended to curb; Chris-Craft did not sue in the capacity of an injured Piper shareholder, but as a defeated tender offeror.

Nor can we agree that an ever-present threat of damages against a successful contestant in a battle for control will provide significant additional protection for shareholders in general. The deterrent value, if any, of such awards can never be ascertained with precision. More likely, however, is the prospect that shareholders may be prejudiced because some tender offers may never be made if there is a possibility of massive damages claims for what courts subsequently hold to be an actionable violation of § 14(e).[26] Even a contestant who "wins the battle" for control may well wind up exposed to a costly "war" in a later and successful defense of its victory. Or at worst -- on Chris-Craft's damages theory -- the victorious tender offeror or the target corporation might be subject to a large substantive judgment, plus high costs of litigation.

In short, we conclude that shareholder protection, if enhanced at all by damages awards such as Chris-Craft contends for, can more directly be achieved with other, less drastic means more closely tailored to the precise congressional goal underlying the Williams Act.

Fourth, under the Cort v. Ash analysis, we must decide whether "the cause of action [is] one traditionally relegated to state law. . . ." 422 U.S. at 78. Despite the pervasiveness of federal securities regulation, the Court of Appeals concluded in these cases that Chris-Craft's complaint would give rise to a cause of action under common-law principles of interference with a prospective commercial advantage. Although Congress is, of course, free to create a remedial scheme in favor of contestants in tender offers, we conclude, as we did in Cort v. Ash, that "it is entirely appropriate in this instance to relegate [the offeror-bidder] and others in [that] situation to whatever remedy is created by state law," *id.* at 84, at least to the extent that

---

[26] The liability of the Piper family petitioners is instructive in this regard. Several able federal judges, including District Judges Tenney and Pollack and Chief Judge Lumbard of the Second Circuit, have expressly concluded that the Piper defendants did *not* violate the securities laws in their efforts to defeat Chris-Craft's bid. Judge Mansfield, while of the view that the Pipers had violated § 14(e), was convinced that their violations had not caused injury to Chris-Craft. The legal uncertainties that inevitably pervade this area of the law call into question whether "deterrence" of § 14(e) violations is a meaningful goal, except possibly with respect to the most flagrant sort of violations which no reasonable person could consider lawful. Such cases of flagrant misconduct, however, are not apt to occur with frequency, and to the extent that the violations are obvious and serious, injunctive relief at an earlier stage of the contest is apt to be the most efficacious form of remedy.

the offeror seeks damages for having been wrongfully denied a "fair opportunity" to compete for control of another corporation.

C

What we have said thus far suggests that, unlike J.I. Case Co. v. Borak, *supra*, judicially creating a damages action in favor of Chris-Craft is unnecessary to ensure the fulfillment of Congress' purposes in adopting the Williams Act. Even though the SEC operates in this context under the same practical restraints recognized by the Court in *Borak*, institutional limitations alone do not lead to the conclusion that any party interested in a tender offer should have a cause of action for damages against a competing bidder. First, as Judge Friendly observed in Electronic Specialty Co. v. International Controls Corp., 409 F.2d 937, 947 (2nd Cir.1969), in corporate control contests the stage of preliminary injunctive relief, rather than post-contest lawsuits, "is the time when relief can best be given." Furthermore, awarding damages to parties other than the protected class of shareholders has only a remote, if any, bearing upon implementing the congressional policy of protecting shareholders who must decide whether to tender or retain their stock.[28] Indeed, as we suggested earlier, a damages award of this nature may well be inconsistent with the interests of many members of the protected class and of only indirect value to shareholders who accepted the exchange offer of the defeated takeover contestant.

We therefore conclude that Chris-Craft, as a defeated tender offeror, has no implied case of action for damages under § 14(e). . . . Accordingly, the judgment of the Court of Appeals is Reversed.[*]

Piper resolved one important issue concerning the remedies available under §§ 14(d) and 14(e) and the parties who are authorized to pursue them: Offerors do not have standing to pursue a damage remedy. The Court explicitly reserved the questions of whether target shareholders have an implied right of action, and the standing of the target company. 430 U.S. at 42 n.28, 47 n.33. In the context of transactional planning, however, the most critical question is who has standing to seek *injunctive relief* during the period in which the fate of the offer is being determined in the market place.

---

[28] Our holding is a limited one. Whether shareholder-offerees, the class protected by § 14(e), have an implied cause of action under § 14(e) is not before us, and we intimate no view on the matter. Nor is the target corporation's standing to sue an issue in this case. We hold only that a tender offeror, suing in its capacity as a takeover bidder, does not have standing to sue for damages under § 14(e). . . .

[*] Mr. Justice Blackmun concurred in the result. Mr. Justice Stevens, joined by Mr. Justice Brennan, dissented. [Eds.]

For this purpose, *Piper* has not deterred the courts from taking an expansive view of the standing requirements. In contrast to an action for damages, the courts have consistently held that both the offeror and the target company have standing to seek injunctive relief for violations of § 14(e).[28]

This resolution -- giving standing to both "contestants" in a hostile tender offer battle -- is clearly correct even in light of the Supreme Court's insistence in *Piper* that the class protected by § 14(e) was limited to target shareholders. While the contest is going on, target shareholders simply are in no position to assert their rights under the Williams Act. As the court stated in Mobil Corp. v. Marathon Oil with respect to the offeror:

> In a tender offer battle, events occur with explosive speed and require immediate response by a party seeking to enjoin illegal conduct. Issues such as incomplete disclosure and manipulative practices can only be effectively spotted and argued by parties with complete knowledge of the target, its business, and others in the industry. The tender offerer has frequently made intensive investigations before deciding to commence its offer and may often be the only party with enough knowledge and awareness to identify nondisclosure or manipulative practices in time to obtain a preliminary injunction.[29]

The situation is no different with respect to the target company's standing; no one else is in as good a position to monitor the offeror's compliance with § 14(e). In this view, both the offeror and the target have standing, in effect, as surrogates for the target shareholders, rather than to protect their own interests.

What does this analysis suggest about the nature of the appropriate remedies for violations? The interests of neither surrogate completely correspond to those of the target shareholders; the offeror will be committed to the success of the transaction regardless of the benefits to the target shareholders, while target management may be committed to defeating the offer to protect their own positions regardless of the attractiveness of the offer to target shareholders. Thus, although it is helpful to rely upon surrogates to raise the issues, any remedy for violations discovered and pursued by a surrogate should be fashioned with an eye only to giving the target shareholders the opportunity to make an intelligent decision concerning the offer and without concern for the interests of the particular surrogate. This approach would counsel in favor of heavy use of preliminary relief requiring amendment of previous disclosure, but little in the way of permanent relief -- such as requiring an offeror either to divest stock

---

[28] See, e.g., Mobil Corp. v. Marathon Oil Co., 669 F.2d 366 (6th Cir.1981), *cert. denied*, 455 U.S. 982 (1982) (offeror); Whittaker Corp. v. Edgar, 535 F.Supp. 933 (N.D.Ill.1982) (offeror); Gearhart Industries v. Smith International, Inc., 741 F.2d 707 (5th Cir.1984) (target); Wellman v. Dickinson, 475 F.Supp. 783 (S.D.N.Y.1979), *aff'd*, 682 F.2d 355 (2d Cir.1982), *cert. denied sub nom.*, Dickinson v. SEC, 460 U.S. 1069 (1983) (target).

[29] 669 F.2d at 370-73.

acquired, or not to vote it, or to delay the offer for some "cooling off" period -- that seriously would interfere with the offeror's ability, in the end, to put its offer before the shareholders.[30]

c.　*The Triggers to Disclosure*

The triggers of the filing and disclosure requirements under §^F^F 14(d)(1) and regulation 14D substantially overlap those encountered in connection with § 13D. Thus, the terms *person, equity security*, and *beneficial owner*, and the manner of calculating whether the tender offer would result in more than 5% ownership, are treated for purposes of § 14(d) in the same way they are treated for purposes of § 13(d). One triggering concept, however, is unique to § 14(d):[31] The concept of when a tender offer commences. As well, the consequences of the trigger under § 14(d) are also unique. Not only does the commencement of a tender offer trigger disclosure obligations, as does any acquisition that results in a person's holdings crossing the 5% threshold under § 13(d), but it also serves as a critical benchmark for §§ 14(d) and 14(e)'s regulation of the substantive terms of tender offers: The various time periods governing the minimum length of the offer, and the withdrawal and proration periods, are measured from the commencement of the offer; and the obligations of equal treatment of target shareholders thereafter apply.

Prior to the effectiveness of present Rule 14d-2 in 1980, neither the statute nor the regulations defined the term "commencement of a tender offer." The principal drawback to this state of affairs was uncertainty; there was no bright line rule which allowed a planner to conform a transaction to the requirements of the statute. This problem is now addressed in Rule 14d-2(a). A tender offer commences on the day that the tender offer is first published or sent to shareholders in one of the specified ways. Thus, a

---

[30] Judge Friendly's opinion in Electronic Specialty Co. v. International Controls Corp., 409 F.2d 937, 948 (2d Cir.1969), nicely captures this approach:

> The likeness of tender offers to proxy contests is not limited to the feature of standing. They are alike in the fundamental feature that they generally are contests. This means that the participants on both sides act, not "in the peace of a quiet chamber," but under the stresses of the market place. They act quickly, sometimes impulsively, often in angry response to what they consider, whether rightly or wrongly, to be low blows by the other side. Probably there will no more be a perfect tender offer than a perfect trial. Congress intended to assure basic honesty and fair dealing, not to impose an unrealistic requirement of laboratory conditions that might make the statute a potent tool for incumbent management to protect its own interests against the desires and welfare of the stockholders. These are the considerations to be applied in testing conduct -- of both sides. . . .

[31] We continue to defer discussion of the definition of a tender offer, conceptually, but no longer practically, the most significant and difficult triggering concept, until Section B.2.c. of this Chapter, *infra*.

planner now can achieve certainty simply by selecting one of the designated ways to announce its offer.

The adoption of a bright-line rule, however, does more than simply provide a guide for compliance; it also provides a blueprint for avoidance. By publicly announcing the terms of a tender offer, the bidder can trigger arbitrage and other market activity before the offer's formal commencement.

Rule 14d-2(b) was adopted to deal with this problem. Under its terms, any public statement by an offeror which discloses the offeror's identity, the identity of the target company, the class of equity security the object of the offer, and the price or range of prices to be offered, constitutes the commencement of an offer. As a result the disclosure obligation is triggered and all time periods begin running.

There are two exceptions to this automatic commencement rule. First, an offer will be deemed never to have commenced if, within five business days after the public announcement triggering automatic commencement, the offeror announces that it will not proceed with the offer. Second, if within the same five day period the offeror files a Schedule 14D as required by Rule 14d-3 and contemporaneously with the filing disseminates to shareholders the information required by Rule 14d-6, the tender offer will be deemed to have commenced on the filing date, rather than on the date of automatic commencement.

Although the automatic commencement trigger was designed to prevent offerors from delaying compliance with the filing and disclosure requirements of the Williams Act, the nature of the solution has the potential to take from an offeror some of its control over when to commence its offer. Suppose, for example, that an enterprising analyst discovers that a company intends to make an offer and discloses that fact to the public along with the identity of the target company, the number of shares sought, and the price to be paid. Will the analyst's announcement -- which contains all of the information specified in Rule 14d-2(c) -- trigger the commencement of the offer? The SEC has taken the position, consistent with the language of the Rule, that the triggering announcement must be made by the offeror.[32] However, it remains the case that third parties can force the offeror's hand, the SEC having noted that, "[a]s a practical matter . . . if a bidder's intention becomes generally known, the bidder may be unable to deny its intentions, and any affirmation of the information referred to in Rule 14d-2(c) by or on behalf of the bidder would cause the tender offer to start under Rule 14d-2(b)."[33]

A second problem with the operation of Rule 14d-2(b)'s automatic commencement trigger results from its interaction with other regulatory regimes. Suppose that the Federal Communications Commission must

---

[32] Exchange Act Rel. No. 16623, Interpretative Release Relating to Tender Offer Rules (March 5, 1980), 3 Fed.Sec.L.Rep. (CCH) ¶ 24,281. The same result would hold if the announcement were made by the target company in an effort to upset the offeror's plans. *Id.*

[33] *Id.*

approve the transfer of control of any company that has a broadcast license. If the application for approval requires disclosure of the information that would automatically trigger the commencement of an offer, the offeror confronts a Catch 22: It would be required to commence an offer under one body of regulation that would be illegal under another. Could this problem be avoided by making the offer, but conditioning it on FCC approval?[34] The same kind of conflict can arise with other securities law disclosure requirements. What if an offeror discloses in Item 4 of its Schedule 13D that it intends to make an any or all offer at a designated price? Does accurate disclosure under § 13(d) eliminate the offeror's discretion over when to commence an offer under § 14(d)? See Ludlow Corp. v. Tyco Laboratories, Inc., 529 F.Supp. 62 (D.Mass.1981). Similarly, what if one party to a proxy contest discloses that if it is successful it will cause a tender offer to be made at a designated price? See Pabst Brewing Co. v. Jacobs, 549 F.Supp. 1068 (D.Del.1982).

How well does the SEC's concern with premature disclosure hold up to analysis? If an offeror is competently advised, it can avoid the automatic commencement trigger simply by delaying release of any information concerning the likelihood of its making an offer, thereby recapturing control over the timing of its offer. Why would this make target shareholders better off? Information concerning the offeror's intentions is clearly material, yet the SEC seems to take the position that the shareholders are better off without it. The trade-off seems to be between the interests of two potential groups of target shareholders: (i) those target shareholders who for other reasons have determined to sell their shares at the time disclosure would have been made in the absence of an automatic disclosure rule and who, with an automatic commencement rule, end up selling their shares in the market at a lower price because the rule results in the offeror delaying release of information concerning the prospective offer, and (ii) those target shareholders who, in the absence of an automatic commencement rule, would make one investment decision after public announcement of partial information, but would make a better decision had they been fully informed. In evaluating this trade-off, keep in mind that the automatic commencement rule does not really protect target shareholders from having to make an investment decision with only partial information concerning the prospective offer. Market rumors, or announcements of the imminence of the offer by third parties or the target company itself, cause precisely the same market activity and the same likelihood of shareholders making investment decisions "on the basis of incomplete information" that motivated the SEC's adoption of the automatic commencement rule, yet do not operate as an automatic trigger. Disclosure by the offeror, in response to third party statements, only makes *more* complete the information available to shareholders, but the effect

---

[34] See *id.*

of the automatic commencement rule denies shareholders access to information from the one party who actually knows the truth.

d.   *The Content of Required Disclosure*

The disclosure philosophy reflected in §§ 14(d) and (e), and the unique aspects of the disclosure issues raised under these sections, differ in two critical respects from the more familiar disclosure pattern associated with the Securities Act of 1933 and with Rule 10b-5. First, mandatory disclosure is imposed not on the seller of securities, as under the Securities Act, nor with respect to nonpublic information originating with the issuer of the securities, as is commonly the case under Rule 10b-5. Rather, the Williams Act requires the *offeror* to disclose, and the particular information Schedule 14D requires largely concerns not the current status of the target's business, the issuer of the securities in question, but the intentions of the offeror. Second, disclosure is required in the context of an ongoing transaction to which the target company is a party. As a result, the question of when disclosure must be made takes on unusual significance. Required early disclosure will benefit those shareholders who would have traded at that time in any event; however, the disclosure itself, coming during the course of complex negotiations, may have the effect of reducing the likelihood that the negotiations will succeed. The common thread joining the two special characteristics of Williams Act disclosure is the tendency of courts to cloak their analysis under the guise of a traditional "materiality" inquiry.

Offeror Disclosure. Suppose that an offeror, Alpha Corp., has extensively analyzed the business of a potential target company, the industry in which the target operates, and the potential for synergistic gains from combining the two companies. Further suppose that this analysis persuades Alpha that if the target company could be acquired for no more than $20 per share above the then current market price, the acquisition would have a positive net present value. The question posed by the Williams Act is why Alpha should be required to disclose this information to target shareholders.

The short answer to this question is that disclosure "protects" the target shareholder; as the Supreme Court put it in Piper v. Chris-Craft Industries, 430 U.S. 1, 35 (1977): "The purpose of the Williams Act is to insure that public shareholders who are confronted by a cash tender offer for their stock will not be required to respond without adequate information. . . . "[35] This formulation, however, begs the real questions. From what must target shareholders be protected? What information must be disclosed to provide the appropriate protection?

---

[35] Quoting Rondeau v. Mosinee Paper Corp., 422 U.S. 49, 58 (1975).

Continuing the hypothetical, suppose that Alpha makes a tender offer for any or all of the target company's stock at $10 per share above the market price immediately before the offer, and also announces that any shares not tendered would be acquired in a freezeout merger at the same price paid in the tender offer.   What information is relevant to a target shareholder in deciding whether to tender?   In particular, why would disclosure of Alpha's analysis of the target company's value, or of Alpha's plans to achieve synergistic gains following the acquisition, protect the target shareholders?   From one perspective, information of this sort is of no value to target shareholders.   Target shareholders need to compare the value of the two alternatives open to them: Either to accept the tender price or to continue to hold the target stock.   Information about Alpha's plans for the transaction, or about Alpha's estimates of the value of the target after the transaction, is irrelevant because the announced freezeout cuts off a potential third alternative: remaining shareholders in the target after Alpha's offer has been successful.

Target shareholders, however, might not be quite so willing to concede the irrelevance of this information.   For them, disclosure of the information, although irrelevant to deciding between the two alternatives posed by the offer, does open up additional alternatives.   The target company may use the information disclosed by Alpha to attract a competing bid at a higher price or use it by simply implementing some of the plans and ideas generated by Alpha's analysis.   In either event, the result may be to increase the value of the target company either by altering (because of competitive bidding) the division of the synergistic gain in favor of the target, or by the target's independent adoption of some of Alpha's value enhancing ideas.   From this perspective, however, it is somewhat difficult to describe offeror disclosure as serving to "protect" target shareholders.   Rather, mandatory disclosure serves to benefit target shareholders by transferring to them a portion of the value of the offeror's investment in information.

When mandatory disclosure is analyzed in this way, judicial resolution of some difficult disclosure issues may seem more intelligible.   Consider whether an offeror must disclose information -- such as appraisals of the value of the target's assets or estimates of liquidation value -- that it commissioned or otherwise acquired in making its decision to proceed with the offer.   The manner in which the courts have approached this issue is described in the following case.

FLYNN v. BASS BROTHERS ENTERPRISES, INC.
744 F.2d 978 (3rd Cir. 1984)

Before SEITZ, ADAMS and HAYNSWORTH, Circuit Judges.

ADAMS, Circuit Judge. This appeal concerns the adequacy under federal securities law of disclosure in a tender offer by defendant Bass Brothers Enterprises, Inc. (Bass Brothers) for the outstanding shares of defendant National Alfalfa Dehydrating and Milling Company (National Alfalfa). . . .

I

The essential facts of the case are undisputed. Bass Brothers is a closely held Texas corporation. At the time of the tender offer its principal business was oil exploration with subsidiary interests in hydrocarbon production, radio, television, ranching and cattle-raising. In 1974 Bass Brothers was approached by the president of Prochemco, Inc. (Prochemco), a Texas corporation engaged in ranching and cattle-feeding, as a possible source of financing for a purchase by Prochemco of a large block of National Alfalfa's stock. National Alfalfa, a Delaware corporation whose stock was traded on the American Stock Exchange, was engaged in farming, farm supply operations and the sale of animal feed. Its former president, Charles Peterson, was seeking to sell his controlling interest in the company in order to raise sufficient capital to repay a large personal debt. To present its proposal to Bass Brothers and other potential sources of funding, Prochemco prepared two reports on National Alfalfa's history and operations, including an appraisal of its assets based in alternative hypothetical valuations.

Although Bass Brothers declined to finance such a purchase by Prochemco, it indicated that it might consider proceeding as a principal should Prochemco fail to obtain the necessary funding. In late 1975 Prochemco informed Bass Brothers that it had been unable to obtain financing and that Peterson's block of National Alfalfa stock was still available. In return for providing the detailed information about National Alfalfa contained in the Prochemco reports and for assistance in analyzing National Alfalfa's current and potential performance, Bass Brothers agreed to pay Prochemco a $130,000 finders fee.

In December 1975 Bass Brothers entered into an option agreement for the purchase of Peterson's 52% share of National Alfalfa's outstanding common stock. Thereafter, Bass Brothers exercised its option and bought the approximately 1.3 million shares from Peterson for a price of $8.44 million or $6.47 per share. A short time later, in a private sale, Bass Brothers was able to acquire an additional 226,673 shares of National Alfalfa, representing 9.1% of the outstanding shares, at $6.45 per share. This acquisition increased Bass Brothers' holding to 61.2% of the outstanding shares of National Alfalfa.

On March 2, 1976, Bass Brothers made public its tender offer for "any and all" outstanding shares of National Alfalfa at $6.45 per share. The reports prepared by Prochemco for Bass Brothers were not appended to the tender offer, nor did the tender offer refer to Prochemco's appraisal of the overall values per share of National Alfalfa which stated that:

> $6.40 could be realized through "liquidation [of National Alfalfa] under stress conditions";

> $12.40 could be realized through "liquidation in an orderly fashion over a reasonable period of time";

> $16.40 represented National Alfalfa's value "as [an] ongoing venture."

Further, the tender offer did not refer to a second report prepared by Prochemco which gave two additional valuations: $17.28 representing the "Value per Peterson"; $7.60 representing the "Value per Prochemco." To the contrary, the tender offer stated in bold letters that

> Offeror did not receive any material non-public information [National Alfalfa] with respect to its prior acquisitions of shares nor . . . does it believe it presently possesses any such information. Offeror has not been able to verify independently the accuracy or completeness of the information contained in Appendices A through E [furnished by National Alfalfa] and assumes no responsibility therefor.

On March 15, 1976, Bass Brothers did, however, issue a supplement to the tender offer describing the book value of "certain land owned or leased by" National Alfalfa and advising the shareholders that:

> While the Offeror has made no independent appraisal of the value of the Company's land and makes no representation with respect thereto, in view of the foregoing factors the aggregate current fair market value of the Company's agricultural land may be substantially higher than its original cost as reflected on the books of the Company. Depending upon the respective market values for such land, stockholders could receive, upon liquidation of the Company, an amount per share significantly higher than the current book value and possibly higher than the price of $6.45 per Share offered by Offeror in the Offer. The amount received by stockholders upon liquidation of the Company would also be dependent upon, among other things, the market value of the Company's other assets and the length of time allowed for such liquidation. The Offeror has no reason to believe that the Company's management has any present intention of liquidating the Company. As noted on page 8 of the Offer to Purchase under "Purpose of This Offer: Present Relationship of Company and Offeror". Offeror does not currently intend to liquidate the Company.

The supplement also extended the duration of the offer by one week "to afford stockholders an opportunity to evaluate" the new information. While the offer was in effect, the named plaintiffs tendered their shares to Bass Brothers for $6.45 per share. At the expiration of the extended offer, Bass Brothers owned more than 92% of the outstanding shares of National Alfalfa and took control of the company by removing the board of directors and electing a new board of directors. Shortly thereafter, a Delaware "short-form merger" was effected between National Alfalfa and Bass Brothers Farming Company, a wholly owned subsidiary of Bass Brothers. Emerging as the surviving entity, National Alfalfa became a wholly owned subsidiary of Bass Brothers.

On June 21, 1976, a group of former shareholders of National Alfalfa filed this class action for damages in the district court charging that the information disclosed in the tender offer was insufficient under federal and state securities law. Cross motions for summary judgment were denied. Flynn v. Bass Brothers Enterprises, Inc., 456 F.Supp. 484 (E.D.Pa.1978). . . . On September 15, 1983, at the close of plaintiffs' case, defendants moved for a directed verdict. The district judge concluded that "the information that was provided by the tender offeror was not materially misleading in any way" particularly because "the information that was contained in the Prochemco report is the kind that is not permitted to be disclosed to shareholders because it is not based on sufficient information. . . . [T]he people who prepared it were interested in whatever transaction they were preparing it for at that time." . . . The district judge, determining that plaintiffs had not presented sufficient evidence of fraud under federal or state law to warrant sending the case to the jury, granted defendants' motion for a directed verdict. . . .

III

Plaintiffs allege that Bass Brothers and the management of National Alfalfa violated §§ 10(b) and 14(e) of the 1934 Act and Rule 10b-5 of the Securities and Exchange Commission (SEC) by not disclosing certain information with the tender offer. Specifically, plaintiffs maintain that defendants had a duty to disclose certain asset appraisal values because such information would have aided National Alfalfa's shareholders in deciding whether or not to accept Bass Brothers' tender offer. We must determine whether the district judge committed reversible error when he ruled that defendants had no duty to disclose the asset appraisal values they possessed.

In 1968, Congress enacted the Williams Act as an amendment to the Securities and Exchange Act of 1934. The purpose of the Williams Act was to protect investors confronted by a tender offer for their stock. See Piper v. Chris-Craft Industries, 430 U.S. 1, 22-27 (1977). Presenting the bill to the Senate, Senator Williams, its sponsor, stated:

[t]his legislation will close a significant gap in investor protection under the Federal securities laws by requiring the disclosure of pertinent information to stockholders when persons seek to obtain control of a corporation by a cash tender offer or through open market or privately negotiated purchases of securities.

113 Cong.Rec. 854 (1967); see also *id*. at 664.

Congress sought to ensure that public shareholders who are suddenly faced with a tender offer will not be forced to respond without adequate information regarding the qualifications and intentions of the offering party. See Rondeau v. Mosinee Paper Corp., 422 U.S. 49, 58 (1975). To that end, § 14(e) of the Williams Act prohibits the making of untrue statements of material fact or the omission of material facts in tender offers that could mislead the shareholders of a target company. Similar in thrust to rule 10b-5, this broadly worded anti-fraud provision protects target shareholders by subjecting tender offerors to advance disclosure requirements. See *Piper*, 430 U.S. at 22-27.

Where a "duty to speak" exists, therefore, federal securities law requires the disclosure of any "material fact" in connection with the purchase or sale of a security under rule 10b-5 or the tendering of an offer under § 14(e). Bass Brothers does not deny that at the time of the tender offer it was under a duty to make certain disclosures in its capacity as a majority shareholder of National Alfalfa as well as in its capacity as a tender offeror. Similarly, the management of National Alfalfa does not deny that it owed a duty of disclosure to its shareholders. Our task, then, is to determine whether the alleged nondisclosures were material omissions, and thus breached the duty to disclose.

This Court has previously noted that § 14(e) of the Williams Act makes unlawful the failure to disclose any "material fact" in connection with a tender offer. Rule 10b-5 similarly prohibits such omissions with regard to the purchase or sale of a security. The Supreme Court defined materiality in the context of an alleged violation of rule 14a-9, which governs disclosure requirements for proxy statements, in the following manner:

An omitted fact is material if there is a substantial likelihood that a reasonable shareholder would consider it important in deciding how to vote. This standard is fully consistent with [Mills v. Electric Auto-Lite Co., 396 U.S. 375 (1970)] general description of materiality as a requirement that "the defect have a significant *propensity* to affect the voting process." It does not require proof of a substantial likelihood that disclosure of the omitted fact would have caused the reasonable investor to change his vote. What the standard does contemplate is a showing of a substantial likelihood that, under all the circumstances, the omitted fact would have assumed actual significance in the deliberations of the reasonable shareholder. Put another way, there must be a substantial likelihood that the disclosure of the omitted fact would have been viewed by the reasonable investor as having significantly altered the "total mix" of information made available.

TSC Industries, Inc. v. Northway, Inc., 426 U.S. 438, 449 (1976). This definition of "material" has been adopted for cases involving rule 10b-5 and we see no reason not to utilize the same formulation for evaluating materiality in the context of a tender offer.

As a matter of public policy, the SEC and the courts generally have not required the inclusion of appraised asset valuations, projects, and other "soft" information in proxy materials or tender offers. See e.g., South Coast Services Corp. v. Santa Ana Valley Irrigation Co., 669 F.2d 1265, 1271 (9th Cir.1982); Panter v. Marshall Field & Co., 646 F.2d 271 (7th Cir.), *cert. denied*, 454 U.S. 1092 (1982); Gerstle v. Gamble-Skogmo, Inc., 478 F.2d 1281, 1292-94 (2d Cir.1973); Kohn v. American Metal Climax, Inc., 458 F.2d 255, 265 (3d Cir.), *cert. denied*, 409 U.S. 874 (1972); Resource Exploration v. Yankee Oil and Gas, 566 F.Supp. 54 (N.D.Ohio 1983); Alaska Interstate Co. v. McMillian, 402 F.Supp. 532 (D.Del.1975); Denison Mines Ltd. v. Fibreboard Corp., 388 F.Supp. 812 (D.Del.1974). The reasons underpinning the SEC's longstanding policy against disclosure of soft information stem from its concern about the reliability of appraisals, its fear that investors might give greater credence to the appraisals or projections than would be warranted, and the impracticability of the SEC's examining such appraisals on a case by case basis to determine whether they are sufficiently reliable to merit disclosure. See *Gerstle*, 478 F.2d at 1294; see also 17 C.F.R. § 240.14a-9 (note following rule 14a-9) (1976).

Although the disclosure of soft information has not been prohibited as a matter of law, this Court in the past has followed the "general rule" that "presentations of future earnings, appraised asset valuations and other hypothetical data" are to be discouraged. *Kohn*, 458 F.2d at 265. In failing to require disclosure, courts have relied on a perceived SEC policy favoring nondisclosure of soft information, the lack of reliability of such information, and the reluctance to impose potentially huge liability for nondisclosure, even if desirable as a matter of public policy, because the law discouraged nondisclosure at the time of the alleged violation.

In assessing the need to disclose an appraised asset valuation courts have considered several indicia of reliability: the qualifications of those who prepared or compiled the appraisal; the degree of certainty of the data on which it was based; the purpose for which it was prepared; and evidence of reliance on the appraisal.

South Coast, for example, involved a shareholders' challenge to the adequacy of disclosure in a proxy statement. The board of directors of SAVI received several offers to sell all of the company's assets for cash. During negotiations, the SAVI board hired an expert appraiser to value two of SAVI's properties; the board prepared internal valuations for the remainder of the company's property. *South Coast*, 669 F.2d at 1267-69. In its proxy statement issued with the intent to elicit shareholder approval of a sale of

SAVI's assets, the board revealed the expert's valuations with an appropriate disclaimer. The internal valuations for the remaining properties were not revealed, however, A divided panel of the Ninth Circuit held that the trial judge did not commit reversible error in determining that SAVI had no duty to disclose its internal appraisals. The court reasoned that none of the directors were expert appraisers and that no satisfactory basis upon which the estimates were made had been established. *Id*. at 1272.

At the time Bass Brothers was making its tender offer, although courts did not generally require the disclosure of asset valuations, such disclosure was not prohibited. In *Alaska Interstate*, the acquiring company, over the objection of the target management, included, with proper cautionary remarks, a range of hypothetic liquidation values made by the target management. The court approved the release of the valuations in spite of the "general rule" discouraging such disclosure which this Court announced in *Kohn*, *Alaska Interstate*, 402 F.Supp. at 572.

Recently, there have been indications that the law, in response to developing corporate trends, such as the increase in mergers, has begun to favor more disclosure of soft information. In this regard, we note that SEC policy -- a primary reason courts in the past have not required the disclosure of soft information -- has begun to change. With respect to disclosure of projections of future earnings, the SEC in 1976 deleted future earnings from the list of examples of potentially misleading disclosures in the note which follows rule 14a-9.[15]

More important, in 1978 the SEC issued a safe harbor rule for "forward-looking" statements, such as future earnings, made in good faith, 17 C.F.R. § 230.175 (1983). And with respect to asset valuations, the SEC in 1980 authorized disclosure of good faith appraisals made on a reasonable basis in proxy contests in which a principal issue is the liquidation of all or a portion of a target company's assets. See SEC Release No. 34-16833, Fed.Sec.L.Rep. (CCH) ¶ 24,117 (1980), codified at 17 C.F.R. § 241.16833 (1983). While SEC policy has not yet explicitly approved the disclosure of appraisal values when the target is to continue as a going concern rather than being liquidated, recent SEC promulgations herald a new view, more favorably disposed towards disclosure.

Part of the reason for this shift in policy is recognition of shareholders' need for such information. One rationale for the initial prohibition of soft information was the fear that potential *purchasers* of securities would be misled by overly optimistic claims by management. See *Gerstle*, 428 F.2d at 1294. An unintended by-product of such concern, however, was to keep valuable information from those shareholders who had to decide, within the context of a tender offer or merger, whether or not to *sell* their securities. See Kripke, *Rule 10b-5 Liability and "Material Facts,"* 46 N.Y.U.L. Rev.

---

[15] See Securities Act Release No. 5,699. Notice of Adoption of an Amendment to Rule 14a-9, etc., [1975-1976 Transfer Binder] CCH Fed.Sec.L.Rep. ¶ 80,461 (1976).

1061, 1071 (1971). The present spate of proxy contests and tender offers was not anticipated when the SEC initially formulated its policy of nondisclosure of soft information.

At least one court has recognized that disclosure of asset valuations may be required. In *Radol*, plaintiffs challenged, among other things, the adequacy of disclosure in United States Steel's successful tender offer for Marathon Oil Company's stock in 1981. Rejecting the notion that "asset valuations are, as a matter of law, not material," the court held that such a determination was a matter for the jury to resolve in light of all the circumstances. *Radol*, 556 F.Supp. at 594; see also Weinberger v. UOP, Inc., 457 A.2d 701 (Del.1983).

The time lag between when a challenged tender offer or proxy statement is issued and when a trial or appellate court finally renders a decision on its sufficiency often can be considerable. This time lag has caused an unexpected side effect; it has retarded the evaluation of the law concerning disclosure. For example, the Second Circuit decided *Gerstle* in 1973, yet the challenged proxy statement had been issued in 1963.

In *Gerstle*, the SEC filed an amicus brief which set forth the view that notwithstanding the Commission's longstanding position that "in financial statements filed with the Commission, fixed assets should be carried at historical cost (less any depreciation)" and that "appraisals generally cannot be disclosed because they may be misleading," existing appraisals of current liquidating value must be disclosed if they have been made by a qualified expert and have a sufficient basis in fact. *Gerstle*, 478 F.2d at 1291, 1292. The Second Circuit stated, however, that in 1963 it had "long been an article of faith among lawyers specializing in the securities field that appraisals of assets could not be included in a proxy statement." Id. at 1293. The court also added that "[h]owever desirable such a policy may be, we do not believe this is what it was in 1963." *Id*. Holding that defendant Skogmo was not liable for its failure to disclose appraisals of the current market value of the merged company's plants which remained unsold at the time of the merger, the court candidly admitted that it "would be loath to impose a huge liability on Skogmo" because the law had evolved in the interim. *Id*. at 1294.

The Second Circuit's holding in 1973, admittedly influenced by the ten year time lapse between the proxy statement and the culmination of the litigation, became one basis for the Ninth Circuit's decision in *South Coast* in 1982. Once again, a court deciding a case a substantial time after the challenged acts felt compelled not to give full weight to changes in SEC policy and scholarly debate on disclosure. See *South Coast*, 669 F.2d at 1271-73.

In order to give full effect to the evolution in the law of disclosure, and to avoid in the future, at least in the Third Circuit, the problem caused by the time lag between challenged acts and judicial resolution, today we set forth the law for disclosure of soft information as it is to be applied from this date on. Henceforth, the law is not that asset appraisals are, as a matter of law, immaterial. Rather, in appropriate cases, such information must be disclosed. Courts should ascertain the duty to disclose asset valuations and other soft information on a case by case basis, by weighing the potential aid such information will give a shareholder against the potential harm, such as undue reliance, if the information is released with a proper cautionary note.

The factors a court must consider in making such a determination are: the facts upon which the information is based; the qualifications of those who prepared or compiled it; the purpose for which the information was originally intended; its relevance to the stockholders' impending decision; the degree of subjectivity or bias reflected in its preparation; the degree to which the information is unique; and the availability to the investor of other more reliable sources of information.

IV

It is against the background set forth in Part III, *supra*, that we must determine whether the trial judge erred in ruling that Bass Brothers and the management of National Alfalfa had no duty to disclose the asset valuations at issue in this case. We note that despite our formulation of the current law applicable to corporate disclosure, we are constrained by the significant development in disclosure law since 1976 not to apply the announced standard retroactively,[19] but to evaluate defendants' conduct by the standards which prevailed in 1976.

Plaintiffs point to three sources of information that they believe should have been disclosed in the tender offer; the Prochemco reports; a report allegedly commissioned by Bass Brothers to corroborate the appraisals in the Prochemco reports; and an internal valuation prepared by National Alfalfa's accountant and vice-president, Carl Schweitzer.

A

The shareholders contend that the Prochemco reports were material and should have been disclosed. However, employing the approach commonly followed by courts when Bass Brothers made its tender offer in early 1976, we do not find the Prochemco reports had sufficient indicia of reliability to require disclosure. Plaintiffs did not adequately establish that the reports were prepared by experts. Although Prochemco did have experience in acquisitions, there was scant evidence of the company's expertise in appraising the type of land involved in the present case. Moreover, plaintiffs did not establish that the reports had sufficient basis in fact to be reliable. Evidence introduced at trial demonstrated only that the first Prochemco report was based on a report prepared by one of the company's employees,

---

[19] Our reluctance to apply the new standard for disclosure retroactively is confined to the facts of this case. We do not intend to imply that in other cases based on actions occurring before the date of this opinion, the new standard necessarily is inapplicable.

but no basis for the reliability of this foundation report was established. The first Prochemco report itself merely stated that it "is our opinion, based on an evaluation by our staff as well as local interviews with those knowledgeable in farm real estate and with the Soil Conservation Service." No basis was established for the second report.

The purpose for which the Prochemco reports were prepared -- to attract financing for its proposed purchase of Peterson's controlling block of National Alfalfa shares -- also diminishes the reliability of the reports. Further, at the time of the tender offer the valuations in the Prochemco reports were outdated.

Plaintiffs assert that the reliability of the reports was amply demonstrated by Bass Brothers' reliance on them and by the payment of $130,000 to Prochemco for them. The shareholders reason that "if the Prochemco reports were reliable and accurate enough for Bass Brothers to use . . . in deciding to [purchase Peterson's stock] then the existence of and valuations in the Prochemco reports were material and should have been shared with National Alfalfa's shareholders" through the tender offer. To bolster their argument, the shareholders note that after buying Peterson's stock, Bass Brothers chose not to examine any of National Alfalfa's internal asset valuations before making the tender offer.

Although it is not inconceivable that Bass Brothers may have relied on the Prochemco valuations, plaintiffs did not advance sufficient evidence to establish the point. Moreover, even if there had been some reliance on the reports, that alone would be insufficient to mandate disclosure in this case. The reports were not prepared by experts, had no adequately demonstrated basis in fact and were prepared to encourage financing to purchase Peterson's share. In light of the record before us, we cannot say that the district court erred in concluding that at the time of the tender offer Bass Brothers had no duty to disclose the Prochemco reports.

B

Plaintiffs assert that Bass Brothers also should have disclosed its own internal valuations. To substantiate their belief that Bass Brothers commissioned a report to corroborate the information in the Prochemco report, the shareholders point to an informal typewritten list of "Items for Investigation" drawn up by Rusty Rose, a Bass Brothers consultant. The list sets forth a number of assignments to be performed by Rose. Item 2(a) states: "Have expert appraise farm land and equipment." A handwritten notation after this item states "Done -- values confirmed." At trial it was revealed that Richard Rainwater, a Bass Brothers officer, had written the notation, although no evidence was produced concerning the circumstances under which the notation was made. The shareholders contend that this cryptic notation, without more, "confirms that Bass Brothers had obtained an 'expert' appraisal." Plaintiffs had ample opportunity during discovery to pursue this lead yet failed to turn up any additional evidence of a corroborating study. Presentation of this handwritten notation, alone, to the jury simply could not support a finding of fraudulent and material nondisclosure of information.

C

The third piece of information that the shareholders claim should have been disclosed was a study prepared by Carl Schweitzer, a vice president of National Alfalfa, using various assumptions, such as the projected appreciation of National Alfalfa's land holdings, to arrive at a value per share of $12.95. At trial, Schweitzer's unrefuted testimony indicated that such a figure was, in fact, hypothetical because of the nature of the assumptions used in the calculation. Schweitzer stated that he used land values supplied by Peterson and some "unnamed people within or without of the company." Thus, plaintiffs have not established a sufficient factual basis for the valuations. Moreover, the purpose of some of these calculations was to help Peterson find a buyer for his stock. Schweitzer testified that the land values were inflated, or optimistic, so as to present the company in the best possible light to future investors. Moreover, Schweitzer admitted that neither he nor members of National Alfalfa's accounting staff had expertise with regard to land appraisal. Thus, plaintiffs were unable to produce evidence that the Schweitzer reports were sufficiently reliable to be material for shareholders confronted with the tender offer. . . .

Concluding that appraisals need not be disclosed because they are not "material" hardly seems convincing. What facts would be more likely to "have assumed actual significance in the deliberations of the reasonable investor" than the offeror's private information concerning the target's value? Nor does concern over the unreliability of appraisals provide a more persuasive rationale. Even if unsophisticated investors would systematically "give greater significance to the appraisals . . . than would be warranted," the arbitrage activity of sophisticated investors would cause the market price of the target's stock to reflect the actual value of the information.[36] Whatever justification there might be in restricting the use of appraisals and

---

[36] The claim of unreliability with respect to an appraisal may be particularly unpersuasive in *Flynn*. In many cases, the unreliability of an appraisal is based on the fact that it was prepared by an interested party. In *Flynn* the appraisal in question was the work of a third party.

projections in the offer of securities under the Securities Act of 1933,[37] it does not seem to extend to the tender offer situation.

A different explanation for judicial reluctance to require disclosure of offeror estimates of target company value, such as appraisals, focuses not on materiality, but on the propriety character of the information at issue. To require disclosure of this offeror information is simply to transfer value from the offeror to target shareholders, and as a result to reduce the incentives for potential offerors to create it in the first place.[38] The target company, of course, could commission and disclose its own appraisals, but then it would have to pay for them. Thus, the issue is not materiality -- target shareholders would like to know what the offeror thinks the target company is worth just as any negotiator would like to know the other side's reservation price -- and not the protection of target shareholders. Rather, the issue is distributional: Is it appropriate to cause the transfer of wealth from the acquiring company to target shareholders?[39] If this analysis is followed, is Judge Adam's balancing test an improvement?[40]

Thus, all in all, offeror disclosure may be of value to target shareholders in the context of a particular transaction. There is, however, serious question as to whether it improves the lot of potential target shareholders as a class. What should happen to the frequency and price of

---

[37] Frank Easterbrook & Daniel Fischel, *Mandatory Disclosure and the Protection of Investors*, 70 Va.L.Rev. 669, 702-3 (1984), argue that because of the difficulty of verifying projections, fraud rules are more difficult to apply to them. This leads the authors to recommend that disclosure of projections be permissible but not mandatory, thereby allowing a seller to disclose projections only when it thinks the resulting increase in the value of the security it seeks to sell exceeds the risk of liability from the difficulty of demonstrating that projections which proved to be wrong (or else there would be no suit) were nevertheless reasonable when disclosed. This approach does not extend to the tender offer situation because there the party with respect to which mandatory disclosure is at issue is the buyer, not the seller; its incentives are to keep the value of the securities low, not high.

In Starkman v. Marathon Oil Co., 772 F.2d 231 (6th Cir.1985), the court rejected *Flynn*'s balancing approach in favor of a rule requiring disclosure of "projections and asset appraisals based upon predictions regarding future economic and corporate events only if the predictions underlying the appraisal or prediction are substantially certain to hold."

[38] See, e.g., Anthony Kronman, *Mistake, Disclosure, Information, and the Law of Contracts*, 7 J.Legal Stud. 1, 11-18 (1978).

[39] Where the offeror owes target shareholders some level of fiduciary duty, the result, though not the issue, may change. Compare Weinberger v. UOP, Inc., 457 A.2d 701 (Del.1983) with Rosenblatt v. Getty Oil Co., 493 A.2d 929 (Del.1985), with respect to whether the acquiring company in a freezeout transaction must disclose its reservation price.

[40] Another way to pose the issue is as a conflict between informational efficiency and allocational efficiency. Disclosure increases informational efficiency but, by reducing the incentives to engage in the transaction at all, may reduce allocational efficiency. In this sense, the issue is identical to whether an issuer has an affirmative duty to disclose under Rule 10b-5, even in the absence of insider trading, where disclosure would interfere with the substantive operations of the company. The familiar example of this conflict is a mining company that has made a significant strike but wishes to withhold disclosure while it purchases land in the vicinity of the strike.

premium offers if disclosure of appraisals and the like is mandated? The average premium in successful offers should go up (reflecting the impact of competitive bidding and the target company's opportunity to implement some of the offeror's plans itself). The number of offers, however, might decline. The other side of an increase in the premium is a decrease in the return to the offeror on its investment in information concerning potential targets; a decrease in return should result in a decrease in investment. If the reduced frequency effect exceeds the increased premium effect, mandatory disclosure has not protected target shareholders.[41]

Some tentative empirical evidence is available concerning the impact of the Williams Act's imposition of mandatory offeror disclosure. Gregg Jarrell & Michael Bradley (1980)[42] report that tender offer premiums were 20% higher in a sample of offers completed after the adoption of the Williams Act than in a sample of pre-Williams Act offers.[43] They also found some evidence of a decrease in frequency of offers, although the decrease became apparent only after the extension of the Williams Act to exchange offers in 1970. Both of these results, however, are subject to alternative explanations. With respect to the post-Williams Act increase in premium, what would be the impact of the parallel increase in the respectability of hostile tender offers, and the participation of major companies as acquirers in the market for corporate control? With respect to the decrease in frequency of offers following the 1970 Amendments to the Williams Act, why would the extension of Williams Act mandatory disclosure to exchange offers change anything in light of the fact that exchange offers always had been subject to the mandatory disclosure obligations of the Securities Act of 1933?

At this point in the discussion it is useful to recall that our analysis of mandatory offeror disclosure thus far has been limited to an any and all offer in which there is a commitment to freeze out any nontendering shareholders at the tender offer price. As was pointed out, under this circumstance target

---

[41] See Frank Easterbrook & Daniel Fischel, *Auctions and Sunk Costs in Tender Offers*, 35 Stan.L.Rev. 1 (1982). This analysis may not hold generally with respect to whether encouraging competitive bidding decreases the return to potential bidders because different kinds of information producers are better with and without competitive bidding. Ronald Gilson, *Seeking Competitive Bids Versus Pure Passivity in Tender Offer Defense*, 35 Stan.L.Rev. 51 (1982). However, the potential benefit to some information producers does not warrant mandating all offerors to disclose their information about the target. The point of Gilson's argument is that some information producers would be better off with competitive bidding and others would not; leaving target management free to seek competitive bids allows each information producer to exploit its information in whatever manner it finds most profitable. Mandatory disclosure, in contrast, eliminates producer choice about how to proceed.

[42] Gregg Jarrell & Michael Bradley, *The Economic Effects of Federal and State Regulations of Cash Tender Offers*, 23 J.L. & Econ. 371 (1980).

[43] To isolate only the influence of the adoption of the Williams Act, the samples excluded offers which were also subject to state tender offer regulation.

shareholders have only two alternatives -- either (i) take the offer, or (ii) keep their target stock and, if the offer is unsuccessful, be left in the same position they were prior to the offer being made, or if the offer is successful, be frozen out and left in the same position they would have been had they taken the offer.   As to both of these alternatives, much of the offeror disclosure required by Schedule 14D, dealing with the offeror's post-acquisition plans, is irrelevant. The analysis changes, however, if the terms of the hypothetical transaction are changed. Suppose now that the offer in question is instead only a partial offer intended simply to secure control, or even an any and all offer, but without a representation that non-tendering target shareholders will be frozen out.   Under these circumstances shareholders have a third alternative: Keep their target stock but, if the offer is successful, in a company that is now controlled by the offeror. In fact, it was this situation that provided a major justification for mandatory offeror disclosure in the first place. As part of the campaign to pass the Williams Act in the first place, Manuel Cohen, then Chairman of the SEC, noted that "the shareholder to whom even a cash offer is made is, in a sense, a purchaser as well as a seller of a security. A change in control can result in what amounts to a new, or at least vastly changed, company. A decision not to accept the offer amounts to a decision to buy into that new Company."[44]   If this is the real justification for mandatory offeror disclosure, then two results follow. First, what first appears as unique offeror disclosure is in fact best understood as run of the mill seller disclosure; the offeror is really selling, and the target shareholder is really buying, a share in a corporation controlled by the offeror. Second, it follows that information like the offeror's post-acquisition plans for the company is important for target shareholders because the transaction consists, in part, of the target shareholders exchanging their old stock in the target for stock in the "new" target that will exist if the offeror achieves control of the target. Which parts of Schedule 14D can be supported on this basis?

2.   Substantive Regulation of Tender Offers Under Sections 14(d) and (e) and Section 10(b)

[Read Securities Exchange Act §§ 14(d)(5), (6) and (7) and Rules 14d-7, 14d-8, and 14e-1 in Appendix A.]

a.   *Sections 14(d) and (e)*

The most unusual feature of the Williams Act is that it is not limited to disclosure. Under the Securities Act of 1933, it is at least technically true that an issuer can offer and sell a security with whatever substantive terms

---

[44] Manuel Cohen, *A Note on Takeover Bids and Corporate Purchases of Stock*, 22 Bus.Law. 149, 152 (1966).

it can dream up as long as, in effect, it discloses that it does not own the Golden Gate Bridge and, in all events, is offering only a quit claim deed.[45] In contrast to this pure disclosure approach to the sale of securities, the Williams Act explicitly regulates the substantive terms under which securities can be purchased by tender offer. As originally enacted, the Williams Act's substantive regulation was contained in §§ 14(d)(5), (6) and (7). Section 14(d)(5) permits shareholders to withdraw their tendered securities within a tender offer's first seven calendar days and again after 60 calendar days from the offer's commencement. Section 14(d)(6) provides that when a partial offer -- one for less than all of the outstanding securities of the class sought in the offer -- is oversubscribed, shares tendered within the first ten calendar days must be purchased pro rata, rather than in the order they were tendered. Taken together, these two sections effectively established a minimum tender offer period: Seven days for any and all offers and ten days for partial offers. Finally, § 14(d)(7) requires that any increase in price during a tender offer has to be paid with respect to all shares purchased, regardless of whether the shares are taken up prior to the price increase. This "best price" rule is supported by Rule 14d-10 that requires that a tender offer be open to all holders of the class of securities sought in the offer, and by Rule 10b-13, considered *infra*, that prohibits a bidder from purchasing any securities of the class sought during the pendency of the offer other than pursuant to the offer.[46]

The Williams Act's substantive reach was significantly expanded in 1979 when the Securities and Exchange Commission took up the invitation to adopt regulations that always was contained in § 14(d)(5), and that was added to § 14(e) by the 1970 Amendments to the Williams Act, substantially expanding target shareholder withdrawal rights and more than doubling the minimum length of a tender offer. Rule 14d-7 extends the initial withdrawal period from ten calendar days to fifteen business days and creates a new withdrawal period -- the ten business days following the commencement of a competing bid. Rule 14e-1 prohibits any tender offer of less than twenty business days duration as well as any increase in the consideration to be paid to target shareholders (or an increase in the dealer's soliciting fee) unless the offer remains open for ten business days after the increase. This expansion

---

[45] This point easily can be overstated; the Securities and Exchange Commission has broad enough discretion in its administration of the disclosure system under the Securities Act of 1933 to accommodate a wide range of arm-twisting with respect to substantive matters. For example, the Commission has discretion whether to grant acceleration of the effectiveness of a registration statement. It has used this discretion, for example, to press its view that indemnification against statutory liabilities is unenforceable in certain situations by requiring, as a condition to acceleration, that the issuer undertake to present any claim for indemnification for judicial review prior to honoring it. See Louis Loss, *Fundamentals of Securities Regulation* 131-36 (1983).

[46] The cluster of Williams Act equal treatment requirements -- § 14d-7 and Rules 14d-10 and 10b-13 -- are discussed in Chapter 21A, *infra*.

in the scope of substantive regulation continued in 1982 when the Commission revised Rule 14d-8 to extend the ten day proration period specified in § 14(d)(6) of the statute to the entire period of the offer.[47]

Both Congress and the Commission have been consistent in their explanation for the presence of these substantive aberrations in the Williams Act's otherwise pristinely disclosure-oriented structure. In its explanation for the adoption of a twenty business day minimum tender offer period in Rule 14e-1, the Commission stated: "Tender offers which do not stay open for a reasonable length of time increase the likelihood of hasty, ill-considered decision making on the basis of inadequate or incomplete information. . . ."[48]   From this perspective, these provisions are less substantive than supplementary. The idea is that disclosure of information about a tender offer is of little value if target shareholders lack the time to evaluate the information. The movement toward a longer minimum tender offer period, and especially the extension of the pro rata period, serves to minimize pressure on shareholders either to tender promptly or miss out and, therefore, facilitates the shareholders' use of the information disclosed.[49]

---

[47] The conflict between the plain language of the Williams Act and the regulations -- seven day withdrawal and ten day proration in the Act and fifteen day withdrawal and twenty day proration in the regulations -- raises questions about the limits of the SEC's rule making authority. The SEC has relied largely on its rulemaking authority under § 14(e) to justify the adoption of rules flatly inconsistent with the statute. For example, see Securities Exchange Act Release No. 19,336, reprinted in [1982-83 Transfer Binder] Fed.Sec.L.Rep. (CCH) ¶ 83,306 (1982), with respect to the conflict between § 14(d)(6) and Rule 14d-8. Note, *SEC Tender Offer Timing Rules: Upsetting a Congressionally Selected Balance*, 68 Cornell L.Rev. 914 (1983), effectively presents the position, expressed by Commissioners Shad and Treadway in their dissent from the adoption of Rule 14d-8, that the Commission lacks the statutory authority to alter § 14(d)(6)'s proration period. In Schrieber v. Burlington Northern, Inc., 472 U.S. 1 (1985), reproduced later in this Chapter, the Supreme Court held that § 14(e) prohibits manipulation only in connection with a material misrepresentation or omission. What does extending various statutory periods have to do with misrepresentations or omissions? Nonetheless, Polaroid Corp. v. Disney, 862 F.2d 987 (3rd Cir.1988), upheld the SEC's authority under § 14(e) to adopt Rule 14d-10 requiring that a tender offer be open to all holders of the targeted class.

[48] Securities Exchange Act Release No. 16,384, [1979-80 Transfer Binder] Fed.Sec.L.Rep. (CCH) ¶ 82,373 (1979), at 82,596. Similarly, the requirement that an offer remain open for at least ten business days following an increase in consideration was supported by the Commission's belief "that this provision will facilitate communication during tender offers and provide a reasonable time frame for security holders to evaluate certain increases before making an investment decision." *Id.*

[49] A different justification for longer minimum tender offer and proration periods -- to help provide all shareholders an equal opportunity to participate -- has also been advanced. Small shareholders, especially unsophisticated individuals, are said to be peculiarly disadvantaged by short time periods because it takes them longer to receive their tender offer disclosure material, longer to evaluate the material, and longer simply to get their shares to the tender offer depository should they decide to tender. Extending the time periods reduce their disadvantage as against sophisticated investors. See SEC Advisory Committee on Tender Offers, Report Recommendations 27-8, [Extra Addition No. 1028 (July 15, 1983)] Fed.Sec.L. Rep. (CCH). If this were the concern, however, why also extend the time periods for

As discussed in Chapter 17, it is in the interest of the offeror to design the terms of an offer to create pressure on a target shareholder to tender. The problem with the Commission's justification is the link it establishes between time and information. Because of the existence of a sophisticated arbitrage community, very little time is necessary for the market to evaluate an offer and for that evaluation to be reflected in the market price of the security sought. Thus, the concern about time pressure resulting in ill-informed decisions seems somewhat attenuated. What is really at stake with respect to the length of various tender offer periods appears when one considers the impact on the bidder of longer minimum periods, longer withdrawal periods, longer proration periods, and especially the extension of all periods when a competing offer is made or there is an increase in the offered compensation. From this perspective, every increase in the various periods increases the likelihood of a competing bid. Giving the target company more time to solicit another offer, giving the target shareholders the confidence that they can withdraw their shares if there is another offer, and giving additional time for a competitive response each time one competing bidder increases its offer, all serve to facilitate an auction market for target companies. Thus, the central issue with respect to the "substantive" elements of the Williams Act seems to be resolution of the debate over the desirability of competitive bidding, not concern over giving target shareholders the opportunity to thoughtfully evaluate the offeror's disclosure.[50]

What might explain the fixation of the Commission's rhetoric on the purported linkage between information and time periods? If Congress thought the Williams Act was *solely* a disclosure statute, the Commission's rulemaking authority would be similarly limited; it would then be difficult to find statutory justification for a preference for competitive bidding. Whether the reach of the Williams Act extends beyond disclosure was considered by the United States Supreme Court in a somewhat different context in Schreiber v. Burlington Northern, Inc., 472 U.S. 1 (1985), and will be discussed in Section C.1 of this Chapter, *infra*.

Whatever underlying purpose the Commission has in mind for its substantive regulations, they do have one significant effect that has not yet been considered. It is quite easy to understand how the regulations are to be complied within the context of a traditional tender offer. But what if the term "tender offer" is defined broadly? If, for example, a publicly

---

institutions and other sophisticated investors? One way to differentiate between sophisticated and unsophisticated investors might be by the size of their holdings; under this approach, only small investors would get more time. Although there may be large investors who also are unsophisticated, they are in a position -- and by definition have the means -- to retain sophisticated advice.

[50] Lucian Bebchuk, for example, treats the principal function of the Williams Act as providing the time necessary for an auction market to develop. See Lucian Bebchuk, *The Case for Facilitating Tender Offers*, 95 Harv.L.Rev. 1028 (1982); Lucian Bebchuk, *The Case for Facilitating Tender Offers: A Reply and Extension*, 35 Stan.L.Rev. 23 (1982).

announced series of open market purchases constitutes a tender offer, then the substantive regulations operate not as a means of regulating the transaction, but as a means of prohibiting it. How can the proration requirements of § 14(d)(6) and Rule 14d-8 be met in the context of open market purchases? We will consider this issue in Section B.2.c. of this Chapter where we confront the Williams Act's central, but entirely undefined, jurisdictional boundary: What is a tender offer?

b.   *Section 10(b): Rules 10b-13 and 10b-4*

In addition to direct regulation of the terms of tender offers under the Williams Act, the Securities and Exchange Commission in Rule 10b-13 has restricted the ability of offerors to acquire target shares other than pursuant to the offer, and in Rule 10b-4 has restricted the practice of short tendering through which sophisticated shareholders could avoid some of the impact of the proration requirements in partial offers. These rules, together with Rule 14d-10 (the "all holders" rule requiring that any tender offer be available to all holders of the designated class of securities), protect the equal opportunity principle reflected in § 14(d)(7)'s requirement that all shareholders receive the best price paid to any shareholder in the tender offer. The operation of these rules is explained in the Releases announcing their adoption.

SECURITIES EXCHANGE ACT RELEASE NO. 8712
October 8, 1969

The Securities and Exchange Commission today announced the adoption of Rule 10b-13 under the Securities Exchange Act of 1934 ("the Act") to prohibit a person who makes a cash tender offer or exchange offer for an equity security from purchasing that security (or any other security immediately convertible into or exchangeable for that security) otherwise than pursuant to the tender or exchange offer, during the period beginning with the public announcement or other commencement of the offering, whichever is earlier, and the time when the offer must by its terms be accepted or rejected. . . .

Where securities are purchased for a consideration greater than that of the tender offer price, this operates to the disadvantage of the security holders who have already deposited their securities and who are unable to withdraw them in order to obtain the advantage of possible resulting higher market prices. Additionally, irrespective of the price at which such purchases are made, they are often fraudulent or manipulative in nature and they can deceive the investing public as to the true state of affairs. Their consequences can be various, depending upon conditions in the market and the nature of the purchases. They could defeat the tender offer, either by driving the market price above the offer price or by otherwise reducing the number of shares tendered below the stated minimum. Alternatively, they could further the tender offer by raising the market price to the point where ordinary investors sell in the market to arbitrageurs, who in turn tender. Accordingly, by prohibiting a person who makes a cash tender offer or exchange offer from purchasing equity securities of the same class during the tender offer period otherwise than pursuant to the offer itself, the rule accomplishes the objective of safeguarding the interests of the persons who have tendered their securities in response to a cash tender offer or exchange offer; moreover once the offer has been made, the rule removes any incentive on the part of holders of substantial blocks of securities to demand from the person making a tender offer or exchange offer a consideration greater than or different from that currently offered to public investors.

[*Persons Affected*] . . . The rule deals with purchases or arrangements to purchase, directly or indirectly, which are made from the time of public announcement or initiation of the tender offer or exchange offer, until the person making the offer is required either to accept or reject the tendered securities. . . . Moreover, any understanding or arrangement during the tender offer period, whether or not the terms and conditions thereof have been agreed upon, to make or negotiate such a purchase after the expiration of that period would be prohibited by the rule. Purchases made prior to the inception of that period are not specifically prohibited under the rule, although disclosure of such purchases within a specific prior period is required to be filed in schedules filed under §§ 13(d) and 14(d) of the Act. Of course, the general anti-fraud and anti-manipulation provisions could apply to such pre-tender purchases. The prohibition of Rule 10b-13 applies to exchange offers when publicly announced even though they cannot be made until the happening of a future event, such as the effectiveness of a registration statement under the Securities Act of 1933. . . .

Since Rule 10b-13 applies to a cash tender offer or an offer of an exchange by an issuer to its own security holders of one class of its securities for another, if repurchase of the other security is subject to the prohibitions of Rule 10b-6, the issuer would have to obtain an exemption under paragraph (f) of that rule. Rule 10b-13 does, however, exempt from its prohibitions purchases if otherwise lawful, under specified conditions pursuant to "qualified stock options" or "employee stock purchase plans" as defined in §§ 422 and 423 of the Internal Revenue Code of 1954 as amended, or "restricted stock options" as defined in § 424(b) of the Internal Revenue Code of 1954 as amended, as well as purchases under specified types of employee plans.

In addition, Rule 10b-13 contains a provision that the Commission may, unconditionally or on terms and conditions, exempt any transaction from the operation of the rule, if the Commission finds that the exemption would not result in the use of a manipulative or deceptive device or contrivance or of a fraudulent, deceptive or manipulative act or practice comprehended within the purpose of the rule. It is contemplated that this exemptive provision would be narrowly construed and that an exemption would be granted by the Commission only in cases involving very special circumstances. . . .

By the Commission.

SECURITIES EXCHANGE ACT RELEASE NO. 20,799
March 29, 1984

I. BACKGROUND

In making a tender offer for securities of the corporation that is the subject of the offer, the bidder usually offers as consideration either cash, its own securities, or a combination of both. Tender offers can be for all the outstanding securities of the subject company or for a lesser amount.

Offers for less than all of the outstanding shares involve a risk to the securityholder of the subject company that not all of the securities that the securityholder tenders will be accepted.[3] Before the adoption of Rule 10b-4, certain securityholders tendered more securities than they owned in order to diminish this risk. By tendering a greater number of securities than they owned, and by guaranteeing their own tenders, market professionals were able to secure acceptance of a disproportionately larger number of the securities owned and tendered by them than could be secured by other persons who tendered only securities that they owned. Accordingly, the Commission adopted Rule 10b-4 in May 1968 for the specific purpose of prohibiting short tendering. Rule 10b-4 makes it a "manipulative or deceptive device or contrivance," as used in § 10(b) of the Act, for any person, in response to an offer or invitation for tenders of any security, to tender securities that he does not own. Ownership is defined in paragraph (b) of the Rule. The Rule applies to all tender offers whether made by a third party or by the issuer of the securities sought.

II. NEED FOR THE AMENDMENTS

By prohibiting short tendering, Rule 10b-4 was designed to promote equality of opportunity and risk for all tendering securityholders. In the years since the Rule's adoption, it has become apparent that simply requiring a tendering person to tender from a long position does not reach certain conduct that has the same purpose and effect as short tendering. Under the Rule, arbitrageurs are able to tender to an offer involving prorationing or selection by lot and then sell into a market that reflects the offer the portion

---

[3] When tendered securities are accepted on a *pro rata* basis, the offeror accepts only a percentage of the securities tendered by each securityholder. The percentage is calculated from a fraction whose numerator represents the total number of securities accepted and whose denominator represents the total number of securities tendered.

of shares that they estimate will be returned unaccepted by the bidder. The shares sold may, in turn, be bought and tendered by another arbitrageur who may also hedge his tender by selling a portion of the shares. As a result, the same shares are effectively tendered by two (or more) shareholders and those shareholders who tender and do not engage in any hedging continue to experience the same dilution of their *pro rata* acceptance that occurred before the Rule was adopted.[7]

To address this concern, the Commission on August 21, 1981, published for comment a proposal to amend Rule 10b-4 to require that a tendering person own the tendered securities not only when they are tendered, but also at the end of the proration period. Since consistent treatment of short tendering and hedged tendering could also be achieved by deregulation and because it has been argued that deregulation might result in broader economic benefits, the Commission also requested comment on the effects, costs and benefits that would result from a deregulation of short tendering.

More recently, the Commission formed an Advisory Committee on Tender Offers ("Advisory Committee"). The Advisory Committee considered a wide range of matters relating to the regulation of tender offers, including the appropriate regulatory treatment of short and hedged tendering. The Advisory Committee recommended that both short and hedged tendering should be prohibited. . . .

A majority of the commentators believed that hedged tendering should be proscribed. A substantial minority of commentators argued that hedged tendering should not be curtailed. They asserted that hedged tendering enables arbitrageurs to minimize prorationing risks and therefore to bid higher for securities during a tender offer. This, in turn, benefits those securityholders who wish to avoid proration risk by selling all of their shares in the market at a known price.

The benefits to such securityholders, however, come at the expense of those shareholders who tender without hedging and thereby suffer from the

---

[7] For example, assume there is a tender offer for less than all the outstanding securities of the target and that A and B each own 200 shares of the subject security and expect that the offeror will accept on a *pro rata* basis 60% of the securities tendered. If A tenders his 200 shares, and then sells 80 shares, he will (assuming the 601 expectation proves correct) have 120 shares accepted by the offeror, or 100% of the securities that he owns at the time the proration period ends. In contrast, if B simply tenders his 200 shares and does not engage in any hedging (possibly because he cannot borrow the subject security), he will have only 120 of his shares accepted and 80 shares will be returned unaccepted to him.

It seems anomalous that A, who would have engaged in a prohibited short tender if he had sold the 80 shares immediately before tendering 200 shares, can accomplish precisely the same result under the current Rule by waiting to sell the 80 shares until a moment after tendering. Furthermore, the 80 shares A tendered and then sold may be bought by an arbitrageur or other purchaser who will tender the same shares to the bidder and thereby increase the likelihood or degree of prorationing. If that occurred, it would reduce the number of tendered securities that would be accepted from other securityholders.

expansion of the proration pool. The Commission believes that the impact of hedged tendering is unfair because, as a practical matter, hedged tendering is not available to most shareholders. . . .

The Commission recognizes that hedged tendering and short tendering may be distinguished, largely because the hedged tenderer owns the tendered securities at the moment of tender. The Commission believes, however, that the two practices are closely analogous in terms of their purpose, availability, and effect on other shareholders who tender, and that hedged tendering should therefore be proscribed for essentially the same reasons that support the prohibition of short tendering.

III. SUMMARY OF AMENDED RULE

The amended Rule is designed to prohibit hedged tendering by the additional requirement that all tendering securityholders be "net long" the amount of securities tendered at the end of the proration period, or on the last day securities may be tendered in order to be accepted by lot where that method of acceptance is used. . . . The provisions of the rule are discussed below.

Paragraph (a)(1) sets forth the definition of ownership, which is essentially unchanged from current Rule 10b-4(2)(b), except for a revision to reflect the use of "equivalent security" as a defined term in paragraph (a)(2). The ownership definition has been refined to provide that a person who might otherwise tender securities will be deemed not to own the securities, and thus will be prohibited from tendering them, if he has entered into any arrangement or agreement (other than stock loans or the writing of exchange-traded call options) whereby another person can tender those securities under the Rule. Thus, for example, a person who has title to subject securities would not be permitted to tender them if he has (i) entered into an unconditional contract to sell them or (ii) written an over-the-counter call option on them and caused the holder to have the reasonable belief set forth in paragraph (a)(2) of the Rule.

Paragraph (a)(2) defines equivalent security to include (1) options, warrants, and rights issued by the person whose securities are the subject of the offer and (2) any other option to acquire the subject security, but only if the holder reasonably believes that the maker or writer of the option has title to and possession of the subject security and upon exercise will promptly deliver the subject security. This language tracks in all significant respects the proviso in existing Rule 10b-4(a)(1). An option traded on a national securities exchange would not be included within the definition of equivalent security since the holder of such an option cannot know that the maker or writer of the option has "title to and possession of" the underlying security within the meaning of the Rule. Since an unlimited number of options can be written on an uncovered basis, Rule 10b-4 does not permit listed options holders to tender unless they have exercised those options. The exclusion of options that are traded on a national securities exchange from the definition of equivalent securities represents a codification of prior staff interpretations of Rule 10b-4.

The term "tender" is defined in paragraph (a)(4) to encompass all methods by which a person can affirmatively respond to a request or invitation for tenders. Current Rule 10b-4(a)(1) refers to tendering for a person's own account; paragraph (a)(2) refers to tenders or guarantees on behalf of others. It has thus been possible to read Rule 10b-4 as prohibiting guarantees of delivery for a person's own account, although it is the Commission's understanding that market professionals routinely have employed so-called "self-guarantees" as a method of tendering securities purchased but not yet received. The definition of "tender" in paragraph (a)(4) specifically includes "guarantee" and thus eliminates any implication in the current Rule that self-guarantees are improper.[14]

Paragraph (b) of the Rule limits the substantive provisions to partial offers. In addition, new paragraph (c) would expressly exclude any partial offer where acceptance of tenders is not primarily by lot or on a *pro rata* basis for a specified period.[15]

Paragraph (b) of the amended Rule contains the substantive provisions of the Rule and covers acts by "any person acting alone or in concert with others, directly or indirectly." The phrase "directly or indirectly," together with the "in concert" language, is intended to make it clear that persons may not do indirectly what they may not do directly, and thereby to emphasize that indirect forms of short tendering are prohibited. This does not, however, effect a substantive change in the Rule, in view of the provisions of § 20(b) of the Act.[16]

Paragraph (b)(1) incorporates the ownership provisions of current Rule 10b-4(a)(1), considerably abbreviated through the use of defined terms. In addition, paragraph (b)(1) makes it unlawful for any person to tender any security unless he owns the securities tendered both at the time of tender and at the end of the proration acceptance period. This provision assures that the *pro rata* determination more fairly and accurately reflects actual ownership

---

[14] If broker-dealers were unable to utilize self-guarantees, they could not tender securities purchased "regular-way" in the last five days of a partial offer, unless they secured the guarantee of another broker-dealer. There would not appear to be any regulatory rationale for imposing such a requirement.

[15] Incidental prorationing would not bring an offer within the coverage of the Rule. Such incidental prorationing might occur, for example, when some, but not all, securities at the highest acceptable price were accepted in an offer conducted on a "lowest price first" basis. Thus, Rule 10b-4, as amended, does not apply to most tender offers for municipal and corporate debt securities. Each of the commentators addressing the issue favored limiting the application of Rule 10b-4 to partial offers.

[16] Section 20(b) of the Act [15 U.S.C. § 78t(b)] makes it unlawful for "any person, directly or indirectly, to do any act or thing which it would be unlawful for such person to do under the provisions of [the Act] or any rule or regulation thereunder through or by means of any other person."

of tendered securities at that time. Securityholders who tender and do not thereafter sell the securities are unaffected by this amendment. A securityholder who tenders the subject security, and thereafter during the proration period sells all or a portion of the subject securities that constituted his net long position is required by this provision either to repurchase sufficient shares, or to withdraw shares from his tender, in order to comply with the net long proviso at the end of the proration period. The "end of the proration period" is the time after which securities would not be accepted by the bidder on a *pro rata* basis. Sales of subject securities occurring after the proration period are not prohibited since they do not affect the *pro rata* calculation.

In the case of a tender based upon ownership of an equivalent security, the Rule, as amended, clarifies the intent of the current Rule that equivalent securities need be converted, exchanged, or exercised only to the extent required by the bidder's terms of acceptance.

Paragraph (b)(2), which covers guarantees of tender, is largely comparable to current Rule 10b-4(a)(2), again simplified through the use of defined terms. The current standard of inquiry imposed upon guarantors by Rule 10b-4 remains unchanged. A guarantor must have "a reasonable belief that, upon information furnished by the person on whose behalf the tender is made," the person could tender in accordance with the provisions of the Rule.

Paragraph (b)(3) prohibits a tendering securityholder from tendering the same securities to more than one partial offer at the same time, i.e., multiple tendering. Some commentators believed that allowing multiple tendering would allow investors to have greater flexibility in choosing the best offer. The Advisory Committee, however, specifically recommended that multiple tendering be prohibited. The Commission agrees with the Advisory Committee and with the majority of commentators that prohibiting multiple tendering will prevent the confusion and possible deception to the market and to bidders that could otherwise arise, as well as the potential unfairness to certain securityholders for whom this practice may not be available. . . .

DISSENT OF COMMISSIONER COX

I respectfully dissent. From the standpoint of investor protection, I cannot agree to prohibit hedged tendering. My analysis leads me to conclude that a prohibition of hedged tendering arbitrarily favors one group of investors over another.

The Division of Market Regulation's ("Division") action memorandum recognizes the argument that the practice of hedged tendering benefits target shareholders who sell their shares rather than tender them during the interim period between announcement and execution of a tender offer. Unfortunately, the Division's analysis of that argument does not go far enough. Taken to its logical conclusion the analysis shows that hedged tendering merely transfers wealth between two groups of target shareholders.

The Commission has no good reason, on the basis of investor protection, to say that one of these groups of target shareholders is more deserving than the other.

As it stands, the Division's analysis concludes that the benefits from hedged tendering accruing to target shareholders who sell into the market are at the expense of target shareholders who tender shares to the bidder without hedging those tenders. This is because hedged tendering expands the proration pool and thereby decreases the fraction of the tendered shares accepted. Let us briefly consider this redistribution of wealth from tenderers to sellers.

It is useful to divide target shareholders into three groups: (1) those who tender shares to the bidder but do not hedge the tenders, (2) those who sell shares into the market where the shares may be purchased and tendered by a market professional, a risk arbitrageur, who finds it worthwhile to hedge his tender, and (3) those who neither tender nor sell, that is, a group that does nothing. To understand the effect of hedged tendering, consider first the case of an oversubscribed partial tender offer when there is no hedged tendering. In this case, the larger is the group that does nothing, the better off are the shareholders who tender because a larger fraction of their shares is accepted by the bidder. This is to say that the inaction of those who do not tender benefits those who do tender.

Next, add the practice of hedged tendering to the market. This means adding a group of risk arbitrageurs who buy shares in the market, tender those shares, and then sell short the fraction of shares they estimate will be returned under prorationing. Note that the arbitrageurs buy these shares from target shareholders who prefer to sell at the interim price rather than go through the process of tendering the shares. The demand for shares by arbitrageurs who engage in hedged tendering bids up the market price, the price becomes closer to the tender premium offered by the bidder, and this benefits the target shareholders who sell into the market.

In order to accomplish hedged tendering, the arbitrageurs have to borrow shares to cover their short sales. Who will tend shares to these arbitrageurs without charging a premium, since the shares used to pay back the lender will be worth less than the shares lent? The answer is that target shareholders who neither tender nor sell their shares and who hold the shares in street name or a similar type of account "lend" the shares to the arbitrageurs. Arbitrageurs can borrow shares from these accounts as long as they stand ready to replace the shares immediately if the beneficial owner decides to tender or sell his shares.

Besides bidding up the interim price of shares, hedged tendering enlarges the proration pool and thereby decreases the fraction of shares accepted from target shareholders who tender. Now, however, the ultimate source of the wealth transfer is clear. When there is no hedged tendering, inaction by target shareholders who neither tender nor sell transfers wealth to target shareholders who tender their shares. This is to say, there is a redistribution of wealth from inactive target shareholders to those who tender. With hedged tendering, some of that wealth is redistributed away from the target shareholders who tender to the target shareholders who sell into the market. Put another way, target shareholders who tendered without hedged tendering gained greater benefits at the "expense" of those target shareholders who neither tendered nor sold. Hedged tendering allows target shareholders who sell to avail themselves of some of the gains otherwise enjoyed by the target shareholders who tendered.

The fact that some shareholders choose neither to tender nor to sell their shares creates a potential gain for target shareholders who tender or sell. There is no objective basis on which to judge that the group of shareholders that tenders is more worthy of the gains than the group of shareholders that sells into the market. To me, shareholder protection implies that both groups of target shareholders are equally worthy and the precise division of the tender premium is best left to market processes.

A helpful analogy is the sale of used cars. Is there any basis for deciding that people who choose to sell used cars to ultimate buyers by using such methods as newspaper advertisements (analogous to target shareholders who tender) are more deserving than people who choose to sell used cars to used car dealers (analogous to target shareholders who sell into the market)? I think not.

What about the risk arbitrageurs, the market professionals who have the ability to engage in hedged tendering? They supply a service to target shareholders who decide to sell at the interim price rather than bear the risk and go through the process of tendering. The professionals bear risk and provide other services to target shareholders who sell. In a competitive market they are compensated at a competitive rate. This is to say, they benefit the target shareholders who sell and they are compensated for it. There is neither reason to think nor evidence to show that they are compensated at a supracompetitive rate.

In summary, hedged tendering is a market practice that developed in response to a demand by target shareholders who do not want to bear the burdens of tendering shares. There is no basis for the Commission to judge these target shareholders less worthy of a share of the tender premium than target shareholders who choose to tender their shares. Prohibiting hedged tendering benefits target shareholders who tender and harms target shareholders who sell. Overall investor protection is not increased by this change.

For a planner, the most important impact of Rule 10b-13 is that it presents a further barrier to paying a control premium to a large shareholder. From this perspective, the Rule's critical feature is that it does not apply to purchases made before the commencement of a tender offer. Thus, so long as the acquisition of the controlling shares is made prior to the offer, neither

§ 14(d)(7) nor Rule 10d-13 prevent paying a controlling shareholder a higher price than will be paid in a subsequent tender offer.[51]

c. *What is a Tender Offer?*

The foregoing survey of the regulatory structure of the Williams Act framed what was for a significant period a central challenge for those planning a hostile acquisition. The overall impact of the Williams Act is delay,[52] which increases both the likelihood of a competitive bid and the opportunity for the target company to take defensive actions. The planner's task, then, was to structure a transaction that falls outside the jurisdictional boundary of the Williams Act -- one that is not a statutory "tender offer" -- while giving up as little as possible of the benefits of a tender offer's transactional form. To put the problem more concretely, one critical benefit of a tender offer is that it bypasses target company management; a hostile acquisition simply cannot be accomplished without bypassing target management. The Williams Act operates, in effect, to impose a tax -- the delay necessitated by the substantive aspects of the Williams Act -- on bypassing target management. Can a transaction be designed that tiptoes past target management without awakening the regulatory guardian? The effort to add content to the statutory term "tender offer" thus represents a strategic game between transaction planner and regulator. The following case describes the development of the current rules of the game in the context of a transaction which was explicitly planned to fall outside what was perceived to be the definition of a "tender offer." In reading the case, consider how the hostile bidder's strategy would have been affected if the target had a poison pill in place.

WELLMAN v. DICKINSON
475 F.Supp. 783 (S.D.N.Y.1979),
aff'd, 682 F.2d 355 (2d Cir.1982),
cert. denied sub nom., Dickinson v. SEC, 460 U.S. 1069 (1983)

ROBERT L. CARTER, District Judge.

I

. . . This litigation stems from the acquisition by Sun Company, Inc. ("Sun"), a Pennsylvania corporation whose principal business is oil and gas,

---

[51] This subject is also considered in Chapter 21.

[52] The combination of an extended minimum offering period and an extended proration period largely eliminates any pressure on target shareholders to tender their shares quickly.

of roughly 34% of the stock of Becton, Dickinson & Company ("BD"), a New Jersey corporation which manufactures health care products and medical testing and research equipment. Sun's brilliantly designed, lightning strike took place in January, 1978, and gave rise to seven separate actions which were consolidated for trial. In 78 Civ. 1055, the Securities and Exchange Commission ("Commission") brings an enforcement action against Sun, L.H.I.W., Inc. (an acronym for *Lets Hope It Works*), the corporation Sun formed to receive the BD shares; Salomon Brothers ("Salomon"), a New York limited partnership engaged in the investment banking and brokerage business; F. Eberstadt & Co., Inc., ("Eberstadt"), a Delaware corporation engaged in investment banking, institutional stock brokerage and the management of pension funds and advisory accounts and which, along with Salomon, handled the Sun acquisition; F. Eberstadt & Co. Managers & Distributors, Inc. ("M & D"), a Delaware company 75% owned by Eberstadt and 25% owned by the estate of Ferdinand Eberstadt, which manages the two Eberstadt mutual funds involved in this proceeding; Robert Zeller, chief executive officer of Eberstadt and vice chairman of M & D; Fairleigh S. Dickinson, Jr., former chairman of BD and one of its principal stockholders; J.H. Fitzgerald Dunning, a former director and large stockholder in BD; and Kenneth Lipper, a partner in Salomon. The Commission charges the defendants with violating or aiding and abetting the violation of §§ 10(b), 13(d), 14(d) and 14(e) of the Securities Exchange Act of 1934; Rules 10b-5 and 10b-13 and Regulation 14D, promulgated thereunder.

In 78 Civ. 539, BD, its officers and several of its shareholders individually and derivatively sue Sun, L.H.I.W., Dickinson, Dunning, Salomon, Eberstadt, Chemical Fund, Inc., and Surveyor Fund, Inc., alleging violations of the Exchange Act similar to those charged in the Commission's case. . . .

II

. . . The background and governing facts in this complex drama embrace personality conflicts, animosity, distrust, and corporate politics, as well as a display of ingenuity and sophistication by brokers, investment bankers and corporate counsel.

Fairleigh S. Dickinson, Jr. was the son of one of the founders of BD. He held the reins of the company from 1948 until 1973. When he became BD chief in 1948, BD was a private family enterprise with gross sales of 10 million dollars annually. When he released the reins of the company in 1973, it was a public company with gross sales of $300 million annually. Dickinson loosened his hold on the helm but did not entirely let go. In 1974, he stepped upstairs to become Chairman of the Board, while Wesley Howe became Chief Executive and Marvin Asnes became Chief Operating Officer. Differences between the management team and the chairman became evident in late 1976 when Dickinson threatened to fire Asnes.

Sometime prior to January, 1977, Howe became interested in the acquisition by BD of National Medical Care Corp. Negotiations went well, and BD announced a proposed merger with the company in January, 1977. Without advising the board or management, Dickinson engaged the services of Salomon and Eberstadt to look into the proposal and advise him about it. Dickinson was a personal friend of William Salomon, a senior partner of Salomon, and Eberstadt had been BD's investment banker. . . . Both Salomon and Eberstadt filed negative reports on the National Medical Care proposal. Dickinson sent the Salomon report to BD board members in February, and on March 3 at a meeting of the Executive Committee, the proposal was abandoned.

Intrigue deepened at BD. Howe's secretary, Dorothy Matonti, began listening to telephone conversations that Dickinson's administrative assistant, Adele Piela, had with Jerome Lipper, Dickinson's attorney, and Board members. Matonti copied Piela's shorthand notes and material from Dickinson's appointment book, and Piela's secretary and Dickinson's driver kept Matonti informed of Dickinson's activities. This surveillance was duly recorded in memoranda given to Howe. On March 27, Dickinson held a meeting with Salomon attended by Kenneth Lipper, his brother Jerome Lipper, Dr. Edwards, an employee of BD, and several BD directors. At the meeting the participants discussed the financial community's reaction to changes in BD that Dickinson was contemplating. Dickinson apparently felt he had sufficient power in the company to bring about a change in management. Events, however, were soon to prove him wrong.

In early April, Dickinson, Howe, and Asnes met, presumably to bring their differences into the open and to resolve them. The meeting settled nothing. Howe and Asnes then decided on a show of strength. They canvassed the board, found enough votes to get rid of Dickinson, and on April 18 sent out notices for an April 20 meeting. Jerome Lipper knew the purpose of the meeting but Dickinson did not attend. . . . Dickinson was deposed as chairman and nudged out the back door with the title of Honorary Chairman.[16]

    . . . On April 21, Dickinson had a meeting at Salomon to secure advice on how to proceed. Richard Rosenthal, John Gutfreund, and Kenneth Lipper of Salomon, two BD directors, Kane and Thompkins, Jerome Lipper and Salomon Brothers counsel, Martin Lipton were in attendance. The meeting centered on BD's trouble and the possibility of restoring Dickinson to power. A lawsuit based on procedural irregularities at the board meeting was ruled out. Nor was a proxy fight considered a viable option when the small percentage of total BD shares Dickinson held was revealed. Although Dickinson and members of his family still held the largest segment of stock

---

[16] In September, 1977, Dickinson was terminated as a BD employee, and in December, 1977 he was dropped from the list of directors to be elected at the BD annual meeting in February.

in the company, acquisitions, public offerings and the sale of some of their holdings had caused their aggregate portion to be reduced to approximately 5% of BD's outstanding shares. Discussion then turned to more practical solutions, e.g., for Dickinson to sell his shares on the open market to BD or to a third party, or to bring pressure on management through the outside directors. Dickinson . . . accepted two remaining options -- to vote with outside directors to bring pressure on management and to sell his stock to a company interested in a takeover of BD -- and engaged Salomon for the latter purpose. . . .

[By summer 1977, Howe became] aware that Dickinson was seeking a takeover of BD by another company. Joseph Flom, BD counsel, called Lipton and threatened a lawsuit if Dickinson continued to try to secure a buyer for a large percentage of BD stock. Lipton suggested to Salomon that it secure an indemnification from Dickinson. . . . [Such a letter was signed on] October 12, 1977, and it confirms Dickinson's engagement of Salomon "in connection with seeking an offer for [his] shares" of BD stock. Dickinson agrees to indemnify Salomon against all claims relating to or arising out of the firm's acting on his behalf in securing a buyer for his stock.

From the spring of 1977 forward, Salomon and Eberstadt, particularly Lipper and Zeller, worked zealously to interest a company in acquiring a minority interest or in buying 100% of BD. Between April 25 and December, 1977, Salomon and Eberstadt arranged meetings with Avon, AHP, Monsanto Corp., ("Monsanto"), Hoffman-LaRoche, Inc. ("Hoffman-LaRoche"), Shering-Plough Corp. ("Shering-Plough"), Squibb Corp. ("Squibb"), and Sun in an effort to interest those institutions in acquiring a position in BD. Dickinson himself participated in these activities until late December when he was hospitalized for about one month. In part, these efforts failed to bear fruit before Sun Company came on the scene because most of the other corporations were not interested in a takeover attempt in the face of hostile management. Since Sun's strategy was to move as quickly as possible, without public notice, the hostility of management was no deterrent. . . .

Harry Sharbaugh, Sun's chief executive, had determined in 1977 that Sun needed to diversify by investing in institutions outside the energy field. Sun sought the acquisition of no less than a 20% interest and not more than a 50% interest in 3 or 4 companies over the succeeding two or three years by investing some 300-400 million dollars in each organization. Sun's corporate development committee was given responsibility for developing major acquisition opportunities for Sun. In August, Salomon was engaged to undertake some studies in connection with Sun's diversification program and Horace Kephart, a senior vice president concerned with corporate development and diversification, was given responsibility for dealing with Salomon. Kenneth Lipper was one of the Salomon partners in charge of the Sun account. Thus, the stage was now set for the main event.

Kephart discussed Sun's diversification program with Lipper, and in late November the two met at Salomon. Kephart was given a copy of BD's annual report, and Lipper suggested that Sun might consider BD as an acquisition possibility in its corporate development program. After studying the report, Kephart had further conversations with Lipper about BD. He learned about the rift between Dickinson and management, and about Salomon and Eberstadt's connection to Dickinson. In these discussions Kephart was told that a block of roughly 15% of BD shares was available, and that this included 1.2 million shares owned by Dickinson, 400,000 shares owned by Lufkin, 500,000 shares owned by Chemical Fund and 300-400,000 shares owned by Dunning. He was also informed that BD was attempting to buy back Dickinson's stock, and that Dickinson had refused but would be willing to sell his shares to a major company. Kephart further learned that BD had publicly announced in June its desire to remain independent and had hired special counsel to assist it in resisting any takeover efforts. . . .

On December 22, Kephart assembled a study team of Sun executives . . . to provide top executives with necessary information to enable them to make an informed determination on whether to acquire an interest in BD. On December 27, there was a meeting in New York attended by Sun's study team, Salomon, Eberstadt, Arthur Andersen and James Fogelson of Wachtell, Lipton (Salomon counsel), at which possible strategies for acquiring BD were discussed. Partial tender was dismissed as having a limited chance of success, and a friendly takeover bid was ruled out. . . . By this time [Kephart] knew that a large percentage of BD shares were held by institutions, and he was assured that the Chemical Fund's 500,000 shares were available to Sun. Rosenthal proposed a two tier price -- a higher price with no recourse and a lower figure with a guaranty to make up the difference between the lower price and the highest price eventually paid for any shares acquired. This was the so-called most favored nation clause, and the idea was accepted in principle. It was understood that a premium over the market was a prerequisite.

There was further discussion at Radnor, Pennsylvania on January 3 and 4 by the study team, Sun officials, Salomon, Eberstadt and Fogelson, all of whom were brought together by Kephart in preparation for a presentation on January 5 to Sun's board. . . . The board heard the presentation. It was not asked to vote, but [t]he consensus was that the matter should go forward. On the next day Wachtell, Lipton was employed as Sun's counsel and thereafter, Cleary, Gottlieb, Steen & Hamilton ("Cleary, Gottlieb") was employed by Salomon.

On January 9, there was a meeting of lawyers at Salomon. The lawyers indicated that the law regarding tender offers was still murky and that the concept of a tender offer had not been precisely defined. The lawyers wanted to structure a "privately negotiated" transaction. Fogelson and Charles Nathan of Cleary, Gottlieb felt this required that those solicited be limited in number. One felt that up to 60 solicitees was safe; the other argued for an upper limit of 40, but within those limits the lawyers felt there would be no problem.

Between December 22 and January 13 (when the executive committee authorized the acquisition and the expenditure of up to 350 million dollars), the study group was engaged in the examination of a myriad of alternatives. The study team knew that 10-13% of BD shares were held by non-management individuals who were willing to sell and that a large percentage of BD stock was in the hands of institutions. The study team concluded that the optimum percentage level for Sun to reach was over 33-1/3%. At that level, Sun could utilize equity accounting and would have sufficient holdings to have a significant voice in BD's future direction. Even if BD increased the number of authorized shares, Sun's strength could not be diluted enough to frustrate these two objectives. The study team considered it acceptable for Sun to hold 20-30% of the stock for a short time, but a percentage in excess of 33-1/3% was the basic objective.

On January 10 and 11, Kephart and the study team, augmented by Salomon . . . Eberstadt . . . Fogelson, Howard Blum, Sun's staff counsel, and Nathan met in Sun's headquarters to devise final recommendations to present to the Sun Board. There was an extended discussion of strategy. Kephart led the discussion, considering (1) open market purchases, (2) a conventional tender offer, and (3) private purchases. In the face of a hostile target, a conventional tender offer was not considered attractive. It was felt that it would lead to competitive bidding which would make the desired acquisition more expensive, and there was certain to be time consuming legal maneuvering to try to thwart the acquisition effort. What was needed was a procedure that would enable the acquisition to be effectuated quickly and put Sun in physical possession of the shares in the shortest possible time. There was a discussion of legal risk, but this was not a concern about the risk of litigation itself since everyone accepted that as inevitable. Rather, the participants were concerned with the chance that Sun's objective would be thwarted in mid-stream by legal maneuvers.

Four possible strategies were listed by Kephart on a blackboard and rated in terms of legal risk, quick control and price: (1) to seek shares sequentially first from individuals, then from institutions; (2) to seek shares simultaneously from these two groups; (3) to tender immediately; and (4) to contact management.

Simultaneous acquisition was considered the most desirable in terms of quick control and price, although there was a measurable legal risk that the effort would be aborted. Sun was advised by its lawyers that the exact boundary line between a private purchase and a tender offer had not been defined in the law. Nonetheless, the lawyers believed simultaneous purchases from large individual and institutional shareholders, carried out off the market after the New York Stock Exchange had closed and with as much secrecy as possible, constituted the strategy best suited to meet Sun's needs. The tender offer approach was rated best in terms of legal risk, but disadvantageous in terms of price. It would also give BD a wide opportunity to make counter moves. The lawyers felt it necessary to keep the solicitees limited in number in order for the acquisition to be considered a private transaction. There were discussions of the possibility of attaining the objective with purchases from 4 individuals and 6 institutions, but approaching as many as 40 solicitees was discussed. . . .

On January 11, these recommendations were presented to Sun senior officials. On January 13, the executive committee approved the "private transaction" proposal and authorized a $350 million expenditure for a 34% acquisition. . . .

On January 11, Fogelson, Nathan and Blum carefully considered the approach to be made to solicitees. When they learned that the strategy envisioned approaches to a number of individuals and institutions, they initially wanted Rosenthal to make all the solicitations. When he said that was impossible because there were too many solicitees, the lawyers decided on preparing two scripts: one for those soliciting individuals and a second one for those soliciting institutions.[19] The instructions stressed

---

[19] *OUTLINE FOR MAJOR INDIVIDUAL INVESTORS*

1. Stress Need for Absolute Confidentiality
    (a) To make transaction possible.
    (b) To avoid liability under securities laws.

2. Provide outline of proposed transaction. . . .

3. Determine *precise* details of investor's shareholders and those of his family, including how registered, where securities located, whose approval needed for sale. Way shares held may affect ability to buy. . . .

4. Terms of Offer
    (a) Purchaser not able to make absolute commitment until minimum investment is assured. Thus final commitment from Purchaser must await results of institutional contacts.

    (b) Price being offered and "most favored nation clause" [N.B. If raised by seller, no discussion of any kind concerning installment notes. Have lawyers work out all details]. . . .

    (d) To avoid any possible breach of confidentiality, *no* offer to trust or other holdings where action or approval by a co-trustee or other party is required.

    (e) Offer initially limited to 950,000 shares to avoid technical § 13(d) questions re formation of family group. This not clear and lawyers still considering.

    (f) Depending on reaction of friend and further evaluation by lawyers, may come back for additional shares, including trust shares.

    (g) Goal of Purchaser is to acquire as many shares from investor and family as possible, consistent with law and interests of friend. . . .

OUTLINE FOR INSTITUTIONS
I. *MANDATORY SELLING POINTS*

1. Emphasize that transaction cannot proceed unless absolute confidentiality is maintained by all parties. Also warn of risk of seller becoming member of a Williams Act group with filing responsibility if talks to others.

2. Emphasize that your principal will not finally commit to purchase until a block meeting its minimum requirements is assembled.

II. *PERMISSIBLE SELLING POINTS*

confidentiality and it was agreed that a lawyer would be at the side of each solicitor to monitor the latter's side of the conversation.

Rosenthal's two tiered price offer with a most favored nation clause was agreed upon. At his suggestion, solicitees were to be offered a top price of $45 per share with no recourse or $40 per share with the right to receive the highest price subsequently paid to any other solicitee. It was the understanding of Salomon, Sun and Eberstadt that all solicitees would get the benefit of the highest price paid. . . .

Kephart advised Lipper on January 13 that the executive committee had given the go ahead sign. . . . At 4:00 P.M. [on January 16] all the persons assigned to do the solicitation met in the trading room of Salomon. Each solicitor had a script from which to read, and a lawyer was teamed up with each caller. Shortly after 4:00 P.M. the telephoning began. Some 30 institutions were contacted. The following institutions accepted the offer and sold their BD shares at $45 per share: American Security and Trust Co. sold 180,700 shares, Bank of America in California sold 143,400 shares, First National Bank of Boston sold 778,731 shares, First Wisconsin Trust Co. sold 96,625 shares, Hartford Fire Insurance Co. in Connecticut sold 99,300 shares, Home Indemnity Co. sold 10,000 shares, Home Insurance Company sold 28,600 shares, Investors Mutual Fund of Minnesota sold 200,000

---

1. If institution expresses reluctance to agree because of future expectations, you may point out that its refusal to sell may preclude reaching minimum target and that your principal has no intention of going forward in such event. If this transaction is not consummated because principal can't assemble block, institution's expectations will be defeated.

2. As is customary in block transactions, you may state both the minimum size requirements for the block and the status of sellers' commitments at the time.

III. *DON'TS*

1. Do not characterize the price as a "take it or leave it" proposition. Be appropriately responsive to negotiating initiative by institution.

2. Do not impose a time constraint or institution's response shorter than is customary for institutional block purchases.

3. Do not disclose identity of principal unless absolutely necessary to consummate the transaction and, in any event, not before the minimum size requirement for the block has been reached. If identity of principal is disclosed, make clear that purchase contract will be executed by subsidiary of principal.

4. Do not go beyond language in draft purchase agreement prefacing the "most favored nation" provision in response to questions regarding the intent of your principal.

IV. *POST-COMMITMENT INSTRUCTIONS*

1. If transaction with institution is *without* most favored nation clause, point out that contract will be amended by deleting last paragraph.

2. *Execution of Contract.* A representative of your principal will present a completed purchase contract (in form already submitted to institution with blanks filled in) for signature by the institution at the institution's office at the opening of business on the following morning. Determine whom the representative should ask to see.

3. *Proxy.* A form of proxy will be presented for signature by the institution together with the purchase contract.

4. *Settlement procedures.* Settlement will be C.O.D. as soon as possible. If institution willing to settle next day simultaneously with execution of purchase contract, arrange mechanics and form of payment (check, wire transfer, other). . . .

shares, Investors Variable Fund of Minnesota sold 250,000 shares, Lincoln First Bank of Rochester sold 127,200 shares, Madison Fund sold 135,000 shares, Massachusetts Investors Growth Stock Fund sold 100,000 shares, Central Pension Fund of Massachusetts sold 15,000 shares, Seaboard Surety Co. sold 15,000 shares, State Street Research and Management Corp. of Massachusetts sold 508,300 shares, T. Rowe Price Growth Stock Fund of Maryland sold 461,000 shares, T. Rowe Price New Era Fund of Maryland sold 68,000 shares, T. Rowe Price Investment Counsel Account of Maryland sold 672,612 shares, Travellers Fund A for Variable Annuities of Connecticut sold 35,000 shares, the Massachusetts Fund sold 35,000 shares, Union Bank of California sold 1,100 shares, and the State of Wisconsin Investment Board sold 413,700 shares.

The following rejected the offer for various reasons: United States Trust Co. held 38,930 shares, North Carolina National Bank held 129,800 shares, Bankers Trust Co. held 394,880 shares, First National Bank of Chicago held 2,000 shares, First National Bank of Minneapolis held 2,000 shares. Morgan Guaranty Trust Co. was one of the institutions alerted to have someone available at 4:00 P.M., but it manifested no interest unless the offer was available to all of its accounts.

The calls from Boston were made only to the Massachusetts institutions, but the calls from Salomon's office in New York were made to cities throughout the United States.

The callers followed the script. There were slight variations, but each solicitee was told that a non-disclosed purchaser, sometimes identified as in the top fifty of Fortune Magazine's 500, was looking for 20% of BD stock; that no transaction would be final unless 20% of the shares were acquired; that the $45 option was a top final price and the $40 option could be accepted with protection in the event shares were later bought at a higher figure; and that the desired 20% goal was within reach or that the order was filling up fast and a hurried response was essential. Each solicitee was asked to respond within one hour or less, although some were given until the next day. Sun was identified to a few institutions, but to most the purchaser's specific identity was not revealed.

The institutions solicited had to consult with their in-house officials hurriedly. By 4:45 Kephart advised Burtis that verbal commitments for 3.1 million shares had been obtained. At 5:35 P.M. the total had reached 20%, and Kephart was given authorization to seal the bargain with these institutions that had committed their shares. Those institutions were called again, and Kephart was put on the phone. He identified himself, and after confirming that the solicitees were interested in selling at $45 a share, he accepted on behalf of Sun's subsidiary L.H.I.W. The project had gone so well that Kephart was concerned that the total might far exceed 34%, and he called Sharbaugh and asked whether he was to pro rate the shares if the 34% figure was exceeded. Sharbaugh replied that there would be no problem unless the figure was over 50%. Before retiring for the night on January 16,

Sun officials knew that they had obtained their objective in that there were verbal commitments for at least 30% of BD's outstanding shares. Indeed, there was some concern that they might have overreached their goal by a wide margin. . . .

Success had been achieved, but the lawyers were now concerned that the legal risks of the transaction were not entirely past. The solicitors had been in communication with a goodly number of individuals. To a few of these, Sun had been identified, and the solicitees had consulted with others in their organization to determine the institution's reaction to the offer. Thus, there was the likelihood that the transaction had already been traced to Sun, and the news would spread. Sun wanted to have physical possession of the stock certificates it had purchased before its identity was generally revealed. Blum feared that verbal commitments were not binding. The lawyers debated whether it was wiser to adopt a wait and see approach and react to the unfolding events or to seek to halt trading in BD stock on the NYSE. Fogelson and Nathan wanted trading halted.

The latter course was approved, but Sun executives forbade disclosure of Sun's identity to NYSE officials. At 9:20 on the morning of January 17, Fogelson called the NYSE and spoke to Richard Grasso, vice president for corporate services. Fogelson identified himself as a "partner of Wachtell, Lipton," said that "a client would be making a Williams Act filing with respect to [BD] by approximately noon the next day," and asked that trading be halted in BD. Grasso asked Fogelson to identify the client and reveal the purpose of the Williams Act filing, but Fogelson refused to give that information. Grasso told him that the NYSE could not order a halt in trading without further data. Some 15 minutes later Grasso received a second call from Fogelson. The latter said that rumors had come to his attention concerning BD. He repeated his earlier statement about a Williams Act filing the next day and requested that Grasso reconsider his trading halt request. Again Grasso asked Fogelson to identify the client and the nature of the Williams Act filing, and again Fogelson refused to provide the requested response. Grasso said trading could not be halted without further information and that he would have to communicate with BD. Fogelson suggested that he could confirm the rumors by speaking to Rosenthal, and Grasso said he would call him. Grasso then called Rosenthal and told the latter that the information Fogelson supplied him with was insufficient to warrant a halt in trading. Rosenthal said that there would be a material development announced upon the Williams Act filing and recommended that trading be halted.

Grasso reported the substance of the telephone conversations to the floor governor. Grasso again called Rosenthal, this time from the trading floor, and requested that he be given additional information. Rosenthal gave no additional information but repeated his request that trading be halted pending announcement of a Williams Act filing. Rosenthal told Grasso that "he and [the] senior partners in his firm were staking their credibility on the request that in fact a material development would be announced and therefore their recommendation was that we not trade in the stock." Rosenthal named Gutfreund and Salomon as the senior partners to whom he was referring. Grasso talked to the floor manager again, and the opening in trading was delayed. Trading in BD was officially halted at about 10:40 A.M. At 11:00 A.M., Leonard Quigley representing BD called Grasso to ascertain the reason for the halt in trading. BD at first wanted the trading halt lifted but then acquiesced, and on January 19 it requested the trading halt remain in effect. The halt continued until January 23.

Instead of the next day as promised, Sun's Williams Act filing did not take place until January 19 when its 13(d) was filed. Jerome Lipper, after discussion with his partner and Fogelson, advised Dickinson and Turner to file 13(d) statements. The statements were prepared and filed on January 19, the same day Sun's statements were filed. Dunning made a 13(d) filing on January 24. . . .

III

. . . The next threshold inquiry concerns whether this was a privately negotiated transaction or series of such transactions or a public offering. There can be no disagreement that a purely private transaction is not subject to the pre-filing strictures under § 14. . . . These activities are covered by § 13(d) when 5% of a company's shares are acquired.

Although the difference between a privately negotiated transaction and a tender offer was alluded to on several occasions in the course of the debate on the Williams Act, the distinction was never articulated. As Judge Frankel said in Heine v. The Signal Companies, [1976-77 Transfer Binder] (CCH) Fed.Sec.L.Rep. ¶ 95,898 at 91,320 (S.D.N.Y.1977), the "exact line of demarcation between a privately negotiated transaction and a public tender offer has not been . . . identified." Our first responsibility is therefore to distinguish a privately negotiated transaction, which is outside the scope of § 14 of the Williams Act, from a public transaction, which may not be. While no differentiation between private and public has been spelled out in the Williams Act or the debates leading to its enactment, we have not been cast totally adrift. Some guidelines developed in defining a private offering exemption under § 4(1) of the Securities Act of 1933 should be of aid in determining whether this transaction may properly be classified as one privately negotiated or publicly offered.

Arms-length negotiations between two persons epitomize a private transaction. As the number of actors increases, the identifiable characteristics of a private activity become blurred. In S.E.C. v. Ralston Purina Co., 346 U.S. 119 (1953), the Court held that the proper way to interpret the private offering exemption provided under § 4(1) of the Securities Act of 1933, was in the light of the statutory purpose. "Since exempt transactions are those as to which 'there is no practical need for . . . [the bill's] application,' the applicability of § 4(1) should turn on whether the particular class of persons affected need the protection of the Act. An offering to those who are shown to be able to fend for themselves is a transaction 'not involving any public offering.'" S.E.C. v. Ralston Purina Co., *supra*, 346 U.S. at 125. The Court held that the statute applied to a public offering whether "few or many," and while it concluded the Commission could rightfully use a "numerical test in deciding when to investigate particular exemption claims," *ibid*, the Court did not favor embellishing the statute with the addition of a quantitative test as a means for defining a private offering. Finally, the Court stated that those claiming the private offering exemption properly have the burden of persuasion. . . .

Gloss has been added by case law developments since *Ralston Purina*. The number and relationship of the offers and the size and manner of the offering are all relevant in determining whether an offering qualifies for private exemption under the 1933 Act. See Doran v. Petroleum Management Corp., 545 F.2d 893, 900 (5th Cir.1977). An offering to a "diverse and unrelated group . . . would have the appearance of being public," Hill York Corp. v. American International Franchises, Inc., 448 F.2d 680, 688 (5th Cir.1971), and each offeree in a private transaction must be afforded the same information that would have been afforded a prospective investor in a public offering, or the offeree must be shown otherwise to have had such information or ready access to it. Woolf v. Cohn, 521 F.2d 591, 613 (5th Cir.1975). Nor does the "high degree of business or legal sophistication" of the offerees suffice to render a transaction private. Doran v. Petroleum Management Corp., *supra*, 545 F.2d at 902. Sophistication is not a substitute for access to the kind of information the 1933 Act requires. See Hill York Corp. v. American International Franchises, Inc., *supra*, 448 F.2d 680, 691. "[T]here must be a sufficient basis of accurate information upon which the sophisticated investor may exercise his skills." Doran v. Petroleum Management Corp., *supra*, 545 F.2d at 903. As in *Ralston Purina*, all the above cases place the burden of persuasion on the party who claims that it should not be subjected to the statute's pinch because the activity engaged in was private in nature. With these guidelines in mind, we now turn to the instant case.

Here, there were face to face transactions with four persons -- Dickinson, Dunning, Turner and Lufkin. A total of 39 individuals and institutions were solicited with holdings involving a variety of discretionary accounts. There was no common characteristic binding the solicitees together except that they were uniformly shareholders with substantial BD holdings. Among those approached were highly knowledgeable individuals like Lufkin as well as unsophisticated investors like Smith, Willock and Drake. There were insurance companies, mutual funds, banks, a state entity, partnerships and corporations. The solicitation was nationwide. Some institutions held shares in their own account; others held shares in discretionary and non-discretionary accounts. While the Sun solicitors had been instructed by their lawyers to limit their offer to discretionary accounts, some institutions sold shares in non-discretionary accounts when faced with the demand to respond quickly to the offer lest the opportunity be lost, while others overlooked some of their shares held in discretionary accounts.

Defendants contend that here, unlike *Ralston Purina*, the private nature of the transaction cannot be determined by the solicitees' access to information because the distinction between 13(d) and 14(d) turns not on access to information, but on "which types of acquisition transactions should require prior, and which types subsequent, disclosure." They argue that a private offering in the 1933 Act and privately negotiated purchases in the Williams Act are not analogous.

It is true that a private or a public offering of an issuer concerns matters not relevant to considerations which would inform the boundaries separating a tender offer from a privately negotiated transaction. However, the present exercise is not yet an attempt to define a tender offer. Indeed that question need not be reached if what Sun did constituted a "privately negotiated" transaction. In determining the narrow threshold issue under consideration, it is submitted that *Ralston Purina* and cognate cases provide at least some rough guidance. . . .

Since these were undoubtedly not "privately negotiated" transactions in which there was a mutual desire to avoid premature disclosure, the "access to information standard" derived from *Ralston Purina* and its cognate cases becomes even more relevant. The cases indicate that the supposed sophistication of the solicitees will not suffice to render the transaction private if they are given no information on which to exercise their skills. The procedure employed in this case required a hurried response on the basis of little information other than the price offered. The solicitors had no authorization to engage in negotiations with those they called. Their job was to obtain quick, oral commitments.

Plaintiffs argued in summation that the defendants chose from the list of shareholders "the ones they knew, they had done business with, hoped to do business with in the future, people they had reason to believe might not have challenged what they were doing." Defendants agree.

However, it is clear on this record that some solicitees were not previously known to defendants. *Vickers Guide* or some comparable publication was used to identify the institutional holders of BD shares. The information gleaned from these sources, not from Eberstadt or Salomon's private listing, determined who the solicitees were to be.

Defendants contend that the factors which decide whether a transaction is a "privately negotiated" purchase are the number of shareholders solicited, the way they are located, the publicity or lack thereof before the purchases are consummated and the procedures by which the sales terms are agreed upon and executed. They point to similarities between this transaction and those in Kennecott Copper Corp. v. Curtiss Wright Corp., *supra. Kennecott*, however, does not support defendants' definitional distinctions. The opinion never uses the phrase privately negotiated transaction and never attempts to distinguish a private from a public offering. Moreover, the transactions in

Kennecott were in large part effectuated on the floor of the Exchange and it is clear that open market purchases are not subject to § 14's pre-acquisition filing requirements. That certainly was not the case here.

This was a well structured, brilliantly conceived, and well executed project. The acquisition itself commenced Saturday, January 14 with the offer to Dickinson and Turner in confidence. Then Sunday, January 15, Dunning was approached, again with a pledge of confidentiality. On Monday morning, January 16, Lufkin was brought in as an insider. On Monday afternoon before the close of the NYSE, calls were made to institutions around the country believed to possess large holdings in BD stock asking each to have someone available to receive an offer after 4:00 P.M., E.S.T., when the NYSE closes for trading. Some of these institutions had been sent earlier in the week a draft of the substance of the two tiered price agreement to be used (without the actual dollar figures). Shortly after 4:00 P.M., calls were made from Boston to Massachusetts based institutions and from New York to other solicitees around the country offering to purchase from each its holdings of BD stock. The solicitees were not told the name of the purchaser, except that it was in the top 50 of Fortune's 500, and the two tiered price was stated as $45 with no recourse or $40 with protection. The solicitees were told that the offer was contingent on the purchaser securing 20% of all the stock, and each was told that a response must be received within half an hour or an hour, although some were given until the next day. Additional pressure was placed on some who were told that acceptances were coming in very fast, inferring that the solicitee had better act quickly or be left out.

Based on the decided case law distinguishing "public" from "private" transactions, defendants have failed to carry their burden of showing that Sun's acquisition was "privately negotiated." Nor were these agreements a series of separate, independent contracts. This was a single integrated project, planned and executed to secure for Sun some 33-1/3% of outstanding BD shares, secretly and quickly so that the acquisition could not be aborted or halted at mid-point by legal action or other countermoves by BD. The institutions were solicited on the 4th market which, as I understand it, is the designation given transactions effectuated during the hours when the NYSE is not operating. Except for Turner and Dickinson, the same offer was made to each solicitee. There were no individual features to distinguish one confirmed solicitation from another except that the number of shares held by each institution varied. Nor, of course, is there any contention that these were open market purchases. Accordingly, the transaction fits neither of the traditional exceptions to § 14.

This is not the end but merely the beginning of the inquiry. The conclusion that this was a public solicitation does not necessarily mean that the pre-acquisition filing requirements of the Williams Act apply. We now proceed to consider that issue.

Section 14(d) Claims

The Senate subcommittee introduced its report on the proposed Williams Act with a brief description of a typical tender offer:

> The offer normally consists of a bid by an individual or group to buy shares of a company -- usually at a price above the market price. Those accepting the offer are said to tender their stock for purchase. The person making the offer obligates himself to purchase all or a specified portion of the tendered shares if certain specified conditions are met.

S.Rep.No. 550, 90th Cong., 1st Sess. 2 (1967). Thus, the Senate report identified as attributes of a tender offer a bid, a premium price, tender by the solicitees, and the conditional nature of the buyer's obligation. The House subcommittee's definition of a tender offer was identical to that adopted by its Senate counterpart. H.Rep.No. 1,711, 90th Cong., 2d Sess. 2 (1968), U.S.C.C. & A.N. 1968, p.2811.

The committee reports reflected statements made during the earlier committee hearings. For example, Commission Chairman, Manuel F. Cohen, had testified that a tender offer typically involved the solicitation by the buyer of options to purchase. The option would only be exercised up to the maximum number of shares desired and would not be exercised at all unless some minimum number of shares had been tendered. *Full Disclosure of Corporate Equity Ownership and in Corporate Takeover Bids: Hearings on S. 510 Before the Subcomm. on Securities of the Comm. on Banking and Currency*, 90th Cong., 1st Sess., 17 (1967). Chairman Cohen further indicated that the buyer usually gave the impression that an immediate response was necessary but did not disclose either what its intentions were with respect to the target company or what the consequences might be for the investor who failed to tender if the acquisition was successful. *Ibid*. Commission General Counsel Phillip Loomis added to this definition his observation that buyers frequently hurried the decision of the solicitees by indicating that shares would be taken up on a first come, first served basis. *Id*. at 207. This general outline of the nature of a tender offer was reiterated by Senator Kuchel, co-sponsor of the Williams Act. *Id*. at 72. Finally, in opening the floor debate on the bill, Senator Williams alluded to many of these same characteristics and added that buyers often hired investment bankers and took out newspaper advertisements to facilitate the transactions. 113 Cong.Rec. 858 (1967). . . .

One of the chief concerns of Congress in enacting the Williams Act provisions was to remove the secrecy which had heretofore cloaked transactions involving a shift in corporate control. Defendants concede this purpose but contend that the transaction at issue here requires a post-acquisition § 13(d) filing rather than a pre-acquisition § 14(d) filing.

Senator Williams noted in the floor debate that the tender offer provisions were designed to remove the element of secrecy from transfers of control. 113 Cong.Rec. 855. According to the Senate report, no law prior to the Williams Act required that the person seeking control "disclose his identity, the source of his funds, who his associates are, or what he intends to do if he gains control of the corporation." S.Rep. No. 550, *supra* at 2. Congress was also concerned that investors would choose to sell without the information necessary for a reasoned decision for fear that if they failed to tender quickly their shares would not be taken up at all. *Ibid.*

All of these elements -- bid, premium price, obligation to purchase all or a specified portion of the tendered shares if certain specified conditions are met (in this instance, if 20% of the outstanding shares are acquired) -- are present here. The above definition is set forth in *Kennecott, supra*, 584 F.2d at 1206, a case on which defendants rely as the "definition of a conventional tender offer [that] has received general recognition in the courts" (citations omitted). Defendants also assert, however, that publicity, the widespread solicitation of the general body of shareholders, and placement of the tendered shares in a depository are requisites for a conventional tender offer. However, there is no mention in *Kennecott* of these factors. The court there appeared to be concerned that the position taken by some courts and commentators would create an overlap between open market purchases and tender offers, thereby rendering § 14(d)(5)-(d)(7) unworkable. See Gulf & Western Industries v. Great Atlantic & Pacific Tea Co., 356 F.Supp. 1066, 1073-74 (S.D.N.Y.) (Duffy, J.), *aff'd*, 476 F.2d 687 (2d Cir.1973). But there were open and off-the-market purchases involved in both *Kennecott* and *Gulf & Western Industries*, while there are no open market purchases involved in this case. This was a single cohesive transaction involving face to face transactions with Turner, Dickinson, Lufkin and Dunning, and 4th market telephone communication with institutional holders in which Sun received in hand roughly 6-1/2 million shares and paid out 290 million dollars in about 5 days.

What is probably more important than the fact that this transaction has all the characteristics of a tender offer that were identified by Congress in the debates on consideration of the Williams Act is that Sun's acquisition is infected with the basic evil which Congress sought to cure by enacting the law. This purchase was designed in intent, purpose and effect to effectuate a transfer of at least a 20% controlling interest in BD to Sun in a swift, masked maneuver. It would surely undermine the remedial purposes of the Act to hold that this secret operation, which in all germane respects meets the accepted definition of a tender offer, is not covered by § 14(d)'s pre-acquisition filing requirements because Sun's coup was not heralded by widespread publicity and because no shares were placed in a depository. Sun wanted no publicity. It deliberately chose to keep its moves hidden because as Kephart stated, Sun executives were fearful that they might have large sums of corporate funds committed before having in hand shares and proxies representing a 33-1/3% controlling interest in BD. Nor did Sun put trust in a depository. It wanted to have physical possession of the stock certificates purchased as quickly as possible.

The argument that the solicitees were sophisticated investors and therefore did not need § 14 disclosure is no more convincing in this connection than it was in relation to the issue of whether this was merely a private transaction. Sophistication serves no purpose unless it can be applied to the particulars of an investment or sale decision. Therefore, sophistication and expertise cannot be relied on here to exempt this transaction from the reach of § 14(d). See Aranow, Einhorn & Berlstein, *Developments in Tender Offers For Corporate Control* 8 (1977). . . .

Even if this transaction were not seen as a *conventional* tender offer, it would not necessarily fall outside the ambit of § 14(d). As discussed above, the concept of a tender offer has never been precisely defined either in the Williams Act itself or by the Commission. Congress left to the Commission the task of providing through its experience concrete meaning to the term. The Commission has not yet created an exact definition, but in this case and in others, it suggests some seven elements as being characteristic of a tender offer: (1) active and widespread solicitation of public shareholders for the shares of an issuer; (2) solicitation made for a substantial percentage of the issuer's stock; (3) offer to purchase made at a premium over the prevailing market price; (4) terms of the offer are firm rather than negotiable; (5) offer contingent on the tender of a fixed number of shares, often subject to a fixed maximum number to be purchased; (6) offer open only a limited period of time; (7) offeree subjected to pressure to sell his stock. These characteristics were recently accepted as appropriately describing the nature of a tender offer. See Hoover v. Fuqua Industries, C. 79-1062A (N.D.Ohio 1979). In that case, the Commission also had listed an 8th characteristic not included here -- whether the public announcements of a purchasing program concerning the target company precede or accompany rapid accumulation of large amounts of the target company's securities. The reason this last characteristic was left out undoubtedly was because publicity was not a feature of this transaction.

At any rate, it seems to me that the list of characteristics stressed by the Commission are the qualities that set a tender offer apart from open market purchases, privately negotiated transactions or other kinds of public solicitations. With the exception of publicity, all the characteristics of a tender offer, as that term is understood, are present in this transaction. The absence of one particular factor, however, is not necessarily fatal to the Commission's argument because depending upon the circumstances involved in the particular case, one or more of the above features may be more compelling and determinative than the others.

There was certainly "active and widespread solicitation" involved. Defendants contend that there was no widespread public solicitation of the general body of shareholders. But institutional holdings accounted for roughly 40% of all BD's outstanding shares as of January 16, and there was surely widespread solicitation of this class of shareholders. In addition, there was solicitation of individual shareholders holding a considerable percentage of BD shares. Measured by the size of the holdings solicited (34%), the geographic dimensions of the effort (from New York to California and from Massachusetts to North Carolina) and by the number of solicitees approached (30 institutions and 9 individuals, not including 3 institutions that were approached earlier and either indicated no interest, as did Morgan Guaranty Co., or were forgotten, as was Allendale Insurance Co.), there was widespread solicitation of BD's shareholders. See Hoover v. Fuqua Industries, *supra*; Cattlemen's Investment Co. v. Fears, 343 F.Supp. 1248, 1251-52 (W.D.Okl.1972).

The second characteristic, substantial percentage, does not move us very far, for unless the solicitation embraces at least 5% of the issuer's stock, the Act would not be called into play. The third element, premium over market, is regarded as one of the typical indicia of a conventional tender offer and was certainly present here. See Kennecott Copper Corp. v. Curtiss-Wright Corp., *supra*, 584 F.2d at 1206.

The fourth element -- the firm terms of the offer and the absence of opportunity for negotiation -- is stressed by the Commission. Defendants argue that the solicitees were not told that negotiations were barred, but the price was so attractive that none sought to negotiate. No negotiation took place and indeed if any had occurred, the whole project would have been derailed. It is undisputed that the solicitors could not barter about the terms of the offer. Any desire by a solicitee to deviate from the proffered terms had to be referred to Kephart. He, in turn, had to call Radnor to obtain permission to accept such a variation. That time-consuming process would have slowed the project and increased the legal risk of BD's being able to abort the acquisition. This project was structured so that there would be no individualized negotiations. The hope and expectation were that the price would be so attractive that negotiation would be unnecessary.

The fifth, sixth, and seventh elements were also present. The offer was contingent on Sun's achieving a stated percentage of BD shares -- another characteristic of a typical tender offer. See Kennecott Copper Corp. v. Curtiss-Wright Corp., *supra*, 584 F.2d at 1206; Smallwood v. Pearl Brewing Co., *supra*, 489 F.2d at 597 n.22. Time constraints were placed on each solicitee, and although some were given additional time to respond, most felt that they had to reply within the time constraints imposed. See Great Western United Corp. v. Kidwell, 577 F.2d 1256, 1261 n.2 (5th Cir.1978), *rev'd on other grounds*, 443 U.S. 173 (1979). The solicitors tried to exert a maximum amount of pressure on the solicitees they contacted. The latter were told that favorable responses were coming in fast, and it was implied that either they had better make a hurried acceptance of this attractive offer or their chance would be gone.

The one element missing is publicity. Lack of publicity, however, should be no deterrent to classifying this transaction as a tender offer since, as has been stated, a principal objective of the Williams Act was to prevent secret corporate takeovers. Congress intended the Williams Act "to be construed . . . not technically and restrictively, but flexibly to effectuate its remedial purposes," SEC v. Capital Gains Research Bureau, *supra*, 375 U.S. at 195. . . .

Defendants contend, in effect, that acceptance of the Commission's characterization of this transaction as a tender offer would offend due process. That argument is devoid of merit in any event, but coming from counsel in this case, it is particularly disingenuous. Sun wanted to achieve a 33% holding without being cut off in mid-stream. The pre-filing requirements of § 14(d) would have given BD warning and insured its interference with Sun's objective. Defendants' lawyers simply sought to devise a strategy to meet Sun's needs and those of the investment bankers whose fee was contingent on a successful acquisition. The strategy was purposed to avoid the pitfalls which compliance with the Act mandated. There is nothing necessarily wrong with creating a *sui generis* approach to suit the particular needs of a client. But, when knowledgeable lawyers advise their clients to take an action which falls within the periphery of the law's proscriptions, due process considerations do not come into play simply because of miscalculation. . . .

There are, therefore, no due process constraints barring the court from holding that the Sun transaction was a tender offer within the meaning of the Williams Act. None of the cases in which it was held that there had been no tender offer, e.g., *Kennecott, supra*; *Brascan, supra*, has all the definitional features that courts have traditionally used to describe a tender offer. As noted above, however, the important elements are present here. Accordingly, in acquiring 34% of BD stock in the transaction at issue here, Sun made a tender offer for BD stock without a pre-acquisition filing in violation of § 14(d) of the Williams Act. . . .

As the *Wellman* court recognized, some forms of "private" purchases had to be excluded from the definition of a tender offer. In the absence of such an exclusion, a simple negotiated sale between a purchaser and a controlling shareholder would be drawn into the statute's regulatory orbit. The result, through the application of the statute's best price and proration requirements, would be to impose an equal opportunity resolution of the Perlman v. Feldmann issue[53] as a matter of federal law. The more difficult problem is to identify the exclusion's breadth.

The *Wellman* court approached this problem in a traditional way; it used the statute's purpose to define the limits of its application. An important purpose of the Williams Act was to provide information to target

---

[53] See Chapter 21, *supra*.

shareholders. Relying on a line of Fifth Circuit cases defining the scope of the private offering exemption in § 4(2) of the Securities Act of 1933, the court held that the mere sophistication of the offerees did not eliminate the need for the information that compliance with the Williams Act would have provided. But why not? A sophisticated investor should know what information she needs to make a decision and whether or not she has it. Is there any reason to deny that investor the opportunity to make her decision with less information if she thinks the return is worth the extra risk? Interestingly, the Securities and Exchange Commission in its rulemaking has not interpreted the scope of the private offering exemption in the same way as the Fifth Circuit. Regulation D under the Securities Act of 1933 defines a safe harbor that, if met, assures the availability of the private offering exemption from registration under § 4(2). There is no requirement that particular information be given investors so long as the offer is made only to "accredited investors,"[54] defined, *inter alia*, to include specified institutional investors, any person who purchases at least $150,000 of the offered securities so long as the total price does not exceed 20% of the person's net worth, and any individual whose net worth exceeds $1 million or whose income has been in excess of $200,000 for the two previous years.[55] If the analogy to the Securities Act of 1933 carries the weight the *Wellman* court gave it, and if the offerees would have been accredited investors under the terms of Regulation D, then was the case incorrectly decided? Keep in mind that the thrust of the Fifth Circuit cases as the *Wellman* court read them -- "that the supposed sophistication of the solicitees will not suffice to render the transaction private if they are given no information on which to exercise their skills" -- was rejected by the Commission in drafting Regulation D.[56]

This, in turn, leads to a different question. If the Commission had rejected the Fifth Circuit's absolute information requirement in Regulation D, why did it bring an enforcement action against Sun Co. in the first place? One answer might be that disclosure of information has an additional function under the Williams Act that it does not have under the Securities Act of 1933. Not only does it inform the offerees about the transaction, it also informs the market. The problem with this explanation, however, is that it runs headlong into the structure of the statute. The filing required by § 13(d), whether the transaction is a tender offer or not, serves to inform the market -- albeit only 10 days *after* the transaction, but that is all Congress

---

[54] Rule 502(b)(1).

[55] Rule 501(a).

[56] That large scale private purchases can fall outside the definition of a tender offer was again demonstrated by Hanson Trust PLC v. SCM Corp., 774 F.2d 47 (2d Cir.1985). There Hanson Trust terminated a conventional tender offer and immediately thereafter purchased 25% of the target company's outstanding stock from five sophisticated institutional investors and in one open market transaction. The Second Circuit held that the purchases did not constitute a tender offer.

required -- while § 14(d) is concerned with informing the offeree *prior* to the transaction.

That leaves as a source of Commission motivation not lack of offeree information, but lack of fairness. In February 1980, the Commission responded to an inquiry by Senator Proxmire and others concerning the operation of the Williams Act with a series of memoranda and a proposed revision of the Williams Act that would have defined the Act's jurisdictional boundary not by reference to a tender offer, but by reference to a "statutory offer": Any offer by a person who could thereby become the owner of more than 10% of the class of securities subject to the offer.[57] The Commission explained the need for the revision as follows:

MEMORANDUM OF THE SECURITIES AND EXCHANGE COMMISSION TO THE SENATE COMMITTEE ON BANKING, HOUSING AND URBAN AFFAIRS PROPOSING AMENDMENTS TO THE WILLIAMS ACT

. . . At the time § 14(d) was enacted, the prevailing business practice was for public acquisitions of controlling stock interests in contested situations to be conducted as tender offers. Therefore the legislation, which was written to respond to the abuses associated with that prevailing practice, was drafted in terms of regulation of tender offers. . . . Whereas the conventional tender offer was the preferred method of acquisition in the 1960s and early 1970s, new techniques have evolved which are designed to avoid the literal application of § 14(d). If successful, these techniques deprive investors, confronted with a takeover bid, of the protections afforded by the provisions of § 14(d).

. . . In light of the Commission's experience in the tender offer area, it is our conclusion that the most suitable and workable alternative to § 14(d) would be a provision whose application was triggered by the acquisition in the aggregate of a fixed percentage of the voting securities of a company, which represents the ability to exert or influence control . . . .

The overall effect of a statute based upon the acquisition of a fixed percentage of securities would be to channel stock purchase programs into a regulatory mold similar to that now used to govern "tender offers." As a policy matter, such a statute would further the goal of providing all security holders an equal opportunity to participate in the sale of controlling interests in public issuers. . . .

---

[57] The Commission's response to Senator Proxmire appears in Securities Regulation & Law Report (BNA), No. 542 (Special Supp.) (Feb. 27, 1980). Under the Commission's proposal, acquisitions from no more than 10 persons in any twelve month period would have been exempted.

Where in the Williams Act does the Commission find an equal opportunity goal?[58]   Section 14(d)(6) does require proration, but says nothing about whether the offer must be made to all offerees. Moreover, the proration requirement is typically treated as a means of diminishing time pressure on target shareholders to the end of making disclosure more effective, not as an independent goal in itself.   Of course, if equal opportunity is an independent goal, then the statute is not limited to disclosure and careful (and creative) inspection might uncover other policy goals.[59]

The private solicitation exclusion is not the only significant judicial exclusion from the concept of a tender offer. There is also substantial support for the proposition that open market purchases are not tender offers subject to the Williams Act.[60] As with the private solicitation exclusion, the problem is to define the breadth of the exclusion, rather than to justify the concept. At one extreme, it seems clear that simply purchasing shares on a securities exchange in normal market transactions without publicity or solicitations is not a tender offer. If it were, the statute would operate not as a regulation but as a prohibition; there is no way in which market purchases can be made to comply with the withdrawal, proration and best price rules of §§ 14(d)(5), (6) and (7), let alone their expansion by Commission rules. The other extreme seems equally clear. Suppose that after the exchange closed one evening an offeror publicly announced that it would place a buy order the next morning to purchase 30% of the target company's outstanding stock at a 50% premium over that evening's closing price. It is hardly persuasive to argue that the transaction is not a tender offer because it is impossible to satisfy the terms of the statute in connection with market purchases. There is simply no reason to use the exchange as a means to effect the purchases in preference to the use of a depository as in the typical tender offer. Between the extremes, however, is a substantial expanse of gray.

There have been a number of efforts to spell out in greater detail the definition of a tender offer so as to eliminate the uncertainty concerning the scope of the private solicitation and open market exclusions, as well as to

---

[58] That the Commission was serious about an equal opportunity regime was clear from its adoption of Rule 14d-10 which provides that third-party tender offers must be open to all holders of the class of securities sought, thus imposing the Perlman v. Feldmann rule on acquisitions cast in the form of tender offers. Securities Exchange Release No. 22,198 (1985), reprinted in [1985-86 Transfer Binder] Fed.Sec.L.Rep. (CCH) ¶83,797. In the release announcing the proposal, the Commission reiterated its view, held "since the Williams Act was enacted," that "the Williams Act . . . [contains] an implicit requirement for equal treatment of security holders." *Id*. at 87,562.

[59] The viability of this enterprise turns on the Supreme Court's interpretation of the scope of the Williams Act, which we consider in Section C.1 of this Chapter.

[60] See, e.g., Kennecott Copper Corp. v. Curtiss-Wright Corp., 584 F.2d 1195 (2d Cir.1978); Brascan v. Edper Equities, Ltd., 477 F.Supp. 773 (S.D.N.Y.1979).

delineate more precisely the application of the Williams Act to a varied range of unconventional transactions such as block purchases.[61] Although the Commission at one time proposed a rule defining a tender offer,[62] the Commission's eight factor analysis, discussed in *Wellman* has been the most prominent effort at clarification. This factor analysis hardly provides certainty because, as *Wellman* emphasizes, it is apparent that all of the factors need not be met in any single case;[63] indeed, some of the factors may be redundant. For example, if factor 8 -- public announcements of a purchasing program -- is present, what does factor 1 -- active and widespread solicitation of public shareholders -- add? It may be that factor 8 is concerned with open market purchases while factor 1 is concerned with

---

[61] See In the Matter of Paine Webber Jackson & Curtis, Inc., [1982-83 Transfer Binder] Fed.Sec.L.Rep. (CCH) ¶83,310 (1982).

[62] In Securities Exchange Act Rel. No. 16,385, [1979-80 Transfer Binder] Fed.Sec.L.Rep. (CCH) ¶ 82,374 (1979), the Commission proposed to add the following definition of a tender offer to Regulation 14D:

> (1) The term 'tender offer' includes a 'request or invitation for tenders' and means one or more offers to purchase or solicitations of offers to sell securities of a single class, whether or not all or any portion of the securities sought are purchased, which

>> (i) during any 45-day period are directed to more than 10 persons and seek the acquisition of more than 5% of the class of securities, except that offers by a broker (and its customer) or by a dealer made on a national securities exchange at the then current market or made in the over-the-counter market at the then current market shall be excluded if in connection with such offers neither the person making the offers nor such broker or dealer solicits or arranges for the solicitation of any order to sell such securities and such broker or dealer performs only the customary functions of a broker or dealer and receives no more than the broker's usual and customary commission or the dealer's usual and customary mark-up; or

>> (ii) are not otherwise a tender offer under paragraph (1)(i) of this section, but which (A) are disseminated in a widespread manner, (B) provide for a price which represents a premium in excess of the greater of 5% or $2 above the current market price and (C) do not provide for a meaningful opportunity to negotiate the price and terms.

The American Law Institute, Federal Securities Code § 202 (166) (Official Draft, 1980) made a similar effort:

> (A) GENERAL. -- 'Tender offer' means an offer to buy a security, or a solicitation of an offer to sell a security, that is directed to more than 35 persons, unless

>> (i) it (I) is incidental to the execution of a buy order by a broker, or to a purchase by a dealer, who performs no more than the usual function of a broker or dealer, or (II) does no more than state an intention to make such an offer or solicitation; and

>> (ii) it satisfies any additional conditions that the Commission imposes by rule.

What explains the Commission's emphasis on solicitation and premium?

[63] See SEC v. Carter Hawley Hale Stores, Inc., 760 F.2d 945 (9th Cir.1985); Zuckerman v. Franz, 573 F.Supp. 351 (S.D.Fla.1983); Hoover Co. v. Fuqua Industries, [1979-80 Transfer Binder] Fed.Sec.L.Rep. (CCH) ¶ 97,107 (N.D.Ohio 1979).

private solicitations, but the general problem remains: There is no guidance concerning either the number of factors necessary for there to be a tender offer or the relative importance of the individual factors. Additionally, many of the factors are ambiguous. Some of the ambiguity is obvious: Is an offer firm or negotiable if the offeror provides the opportunity to negotiate but then elects not to make concessions?[64] Other ambiguity is less obvious but more complex.

In SEC v. Carter Hawley Hale Stores, Inc., 760 F.2d 945 (9th Cir.1985), The Limited had made a cash tender offer for some 55% of Carter Hawley Hale (CHH) common stock at $30 per share at a time when CHH stock was trading at $23.78 per share. After the offer was announced, CHH stock rose to $29.25 per share. CHH did not favor the offer and, in response, took a number of defensive actions including an announcement that it would repurchase 15 million of its outstanding shares in market purchases.[65] Thereafter, the price of CHH stock fell, reflecting the reduced likelihood that The Limited's offer would be successful. CHH then carried out its repurchase, succeeding in repurchasing some 17.5 million shares -- over 50% of its outstanding stock -- in market transactions at prices between $25 and $26 per share. The Limited ultimately withdrew its offer and the price of CHH stock fell to $20.62 per share, slightly more than $3.00 per share below the pre-tender price.

The SEC then filed an action against CHH alleging that the repurchases were an illegal tender offer in violation of § 13(e)(1) of the Securities Exchange Act of 1934[66] and Rule 13e-4 promulgated thereunder. Under Rule 13e-1, a target company is allowed to make open market repurchases in response to a hostile tender offer subject only to filing with the Commission a Rule 13e-1 Transaction Statement describing the relevant facts.[67] Under Rule 13e-4, however, an issuer *tender offer* is subject to withdrawal, proration and minimum length requirements that are similar to those governing third party tender offers. CHH had complied with Rule 13e-1, but not with Rule 13e-4; the legality of its repurchase program thus turned on whether it was a tender offer.[68]

---

[64] For example, the *Wellman* script could be altered to have the solicitor recite that the offer was negotiable but remain unwilling to alter the offer more than a minimal amount. Some negotiations prove unsuccessful although meaningful discussions actually take place; others are a charade despite all the talking. No bright line rule distinguishes between the two.

[65] CHH also sold to General Cinema Corporation one million shares of convertible preferred stock representing 22% of the CHH voting securities then outstanding. The effect of the CHH repurchase was to raise General Cinema's voting power to 38%. Additionally, CHH granted General Cinema an option to buy its Walden Book subsidiary.

[66] Section 13(e)(1) prohibits issuer repurchases in contravention of rules and regulations adopted by the Securities and Exchange Commission.

[67] These include the amount of securities purchased, from whom purchased, and the purpose of the purchase.

[68] The regulatory pattern reflected in the Commission's issuer repurchase rules is rather bizarre. The acquirer, seeking control of the target company, is subject to the restraints

In determining whether the CHH repurchases were a tender offer, both the district court[69] and the Court of Appeals applied the 8 factor analysis described in *Wellman*. Among other factors determined not to be present in the CHH repurchases, both courts found that the repurchases did not take place at a premium price.[70] The ambiguity concerning this factor was whether the existence of a premium was to be measured by comparison with the market price at the time CHH began its market purchases, or by comparison with the pre-tender offer price. Rejecting the Commission's argument that the relevant comparison was the pre-tender price, the Court of Appeals held that the proper measure of a premium was by comparison with the market price at the time of the repurchase, even if it had increased as a result of the hostile offer.[71] Because the market price of a target's stock always increases after a premium third party offer, the Court of Appeals reasoned that to adopt the pre-tender comparison would eliminate "consideration of this *Wellman* factor in the context of issuer repurchases during a tender offer"[72] because it would always be met.[73]

Is the court's reliance on the determinist character of a pre-tender price comparison persuasive? Market purchases are by definition at the then market price; in the absence of a complicated theory about the influence of the issuer's purchases on the market price,[74] a market price comparison is no less tautological. Perhaps the court felt more troubled by one tautology than the other because the existence of Rule 13e-1 holds out the potential that some open market repurchases are not tender offers; however, the issue should have been less the coherence of the SEC's regulatory pattern, than what the statutory term meant.

There is a fourth approach to defining a tender offer that also has drawn some attention. In S-G Securities Inc. v. Fuqua Investment Co., 466 F.Supp. 1114 (D.Mass.1978), the court held that a tender offer is present if there is "(1) a publicly announced intention by the purchaser to acquire a

---

imposed by Regulation 14D. Target management, who by adopting defensive tactics like repurchases is also competing for control of the target company, is subject to no effective restraints so long as Rule 13e-1 applies. The result is to give target management an important strategic advantage. Indeed, Bradley & Rosenzweig persuasively argue that an issuer repurchase not subject to the requirements of Rule 13e-4 will dominate even a value increasing third party offer. Michael Bradley & Michael Rosenzweig, *Defensive Stock Repurchases*, 99 Harv.L.Rev. 1377 (1986).

[69] 587 F.Supp. 1248 (C.D.Cal.1984).

[70] 587 F.Supp. at 1254; 760 F.2d at 951.

[71] Is it clear which comparison the Commission had in mind in its proposed Rule defining a tender offer?

[72] 760 F.2d at 951.

[73] Accord, LTV v. Grumman Corp., 526 F.Supp. 106 (E.D.N.Y.1981).

[74] Should it matter whether this influence is a result of the increase in market demand resulting only from the issuer's purchases or whether the price was also affected by the derivatively derived trading mechanism?

block of the stock of the target company for purposes of acquiring control thereof, and (2) a subsequent rapid acquisition by the purchaser of large blocks of stock through open market and privately negotiated purchases."[75] Interestingly, the Commission urged the application of this definition in *Carter Hawley Hale* in preference to the 8 factor test it had itself developed. The reason for the Commission's preference is clear enough; CHH's repurchase program could hardly fail to satisfy the *S-G Securities* test in light of the clear intention to move control of CHH to a coalition composed of CHH management and General Cinema. The Court of Appeals rejected this test, finding that it offered little guidance to the issuer in determining whether Rule 13e-4 or Rule 13e-1 governed its conduct.[76]

In 1987, the SEC proposed, but never adopted, a rule to deal with open market purchases following a terminated tender offer, so-called "street sweeps."[77] The proposed rule provided that following the termination of a tender offer a bidder could not increase its beneficial ownership of the target by 10% or more for 30 days. The SEC did, however, adopt Rule 13-5(f)(6) for issuer self-tenders which prohibits an issuer from acquiring any additional shares for 10 days following the termination of an offer.[78]

The SEC's memorandum to the Senate Banking Committee, *supra*, proposed a statutory specification of the boundaries of the Williams Act because development of new bidder tactics, like street sweeps, threatened to make the statute irrelevant. Ironically, the development of new target defensive tactics has eliminated the principal advantage to the bidder of avoiding the Williams Act by devising unconventional offer structures. As a result, the task of more specifically defining a tender offer no longer seems so pressing. Bidders sought to avoid the Williams Act to avoid the delay that gave targets the opportunity to undertake defensive action and seek competitive bids. The development and widespread deployment of poison pills, and the courts' explicit sanction of a target's refusal to redeem a poison pill while the target sought a competitive transaction,[79] make it impossible for a bidder to avoid delay regardless of how the transaction is structured. In this respect, the poison pill solves the problem of defining the transactional technique by focusing instead on the outcome to be avoided: the pill is triggered when the bidder's holding of target stock crosses the ownership threshold, regardless of the manner of acquisition. If Becton, Dickinson had adopted a pill, the transaction so carefully devised by the lawyers and investment bankers would never have been attempted.

---

[75] 466 F.Supp. at 1126-27.

[76] 760 F.2d at 953.

[77] Securities Exchange Act Rel. No. 24,976 (proposed Rule 14a-11).

[78] See Dale Osterle, *The Rise and Fall of Street Sweep Takeovers*, 1989 Duke L.J. 202 for a general treatment of the area.

[79] See Chapter 17, *supra*.

C.   Litigation Under Section 14(e)

Litigation is a central element of hostile tender offer practice. As we have already seen in Chapter 17, a target's first step typically will be to commence an action against the hostile bidder.[80]   Claims under Williams Act § 14(e) are certain to figure prominently in the litigation.

Section 14(e) makes it unlawful "in connection with any tender offer" to make any untrue statement of a material fact or omit to state any material fact necessary in order to make the statements made, in the light of the circumstances under which they are made, not misleading, or to engage in any fraudulent, deceptive, or manipulative acts or practices.[81]

Rather obviously, this language is patterned after Rule 10b-5 which makes it unlawful, "in connection with the purchase or sale of any security"

> (a) to employ any device, scheme, or artifice to defraud,
>
> (b) to make any untrue statement of a material fact or omit to state a material fact necessary in order to make the statements made, in the light of circumstances under which they were made, not misleading, or
>
> (c) to engage in any act, practice, or course of business which operates or would operate as a fraud or deceit upon any person. . . .

Because of this commonality of language, and because of the federal courts' vast store of precedents concerning the scope and elements of a Rule 10b-5 cause of action, it is hardly surprising that Rule 10-5 solutions have been applied to § 14(e) problems.   Although understandable, this transposition nonetheless merits careful consideration.   Issues under Rule 10b-5 arise in a wide variety of contexts; the only common thread is a purchase or sale of securities.   In contrast, Rule 14(e) clearly eliminates the purchase or sale requirement, and issues under § 14(e) arise only in the context of a special transaction: a tender offer.   How much reliance should be placed on Rule 10b-5 precedent when, despite the similarity in language between Rule 10b-5 and § 14(e), there is a substantial transactional difference?

We focus on two inquiries that may best be characterized as jurisdictional. First, what type of misconduct is covered by § 14(e)? Does it, like Rule 10b-5, reach only misrepresentation and nondisclosure, or does it extend more broadly, perhaps to encompass such matters as defensive tactics or lock-ups? Second, assuming the particular misconduct is covered, how far must the transaction have progressed before that misconduct is "in connection with any tender offer?"   Thereafter we consider the treatment of

---

[80] Describing the job of counsel for the target company following a hostile tender offer, Herbert Wachtell states: "He brings a lawsuit. We all agree about that. And he brings it fast." Herbert Wachtell, *Special Tender Offer Litigation Tactics*, 32 Bus.Law. 1433, 1437 (1977).

[81] Section 14(e), goes on to authorize the Securities and Exchange Commission to adopt regulations "reasonably designed to prevent such practices as are fraudulent, deceptive, or manipulative."

another possible element of a cause of action under § 14(e), scienter, that also has figured prominently in the development of Rule 10b-5.

1.   What Types of Misconduct are Covered by Section 14(e)?

The parallel development of Rule 10b-5 and § 14(e) has been especially striking with respect to the range of misconduct each provision has been held to encompass. In the early 1970s, the failure of state law litigation efforts to restrain minority freezeouts led plaintiffs to what was, for a time at least, a more sympathetic forum. Reaching its apogee in the opinion of the Second Circuit in Santa Fe Industries v. Green,[82] Rule 10b-5 was held to cover "breaches of fiduciary duty by majority against minority shareholders without any charge of misrepresentation or lack of disclosure."[83] At the same time, state courts were equally unreceptive to efforts to restrict a target company's use of defensive tactics to defeat a tender offer.[84] As with freezeouts, plaintiffs moved to federal court and their early success with § 14(e) matched that experienced with Rule 10b-5. Expressly relying on the Second Circuit decision in *Santa Fe*, the court in Applied Digital Data Systems v. Milgo Electronic[85] held that the issuance of a large block of stock to a friendly suitor to block a hostile offer may violate § 14(e).[86]

The bubble burst for Rule 10b-5 when the Supreme Court reversed the Second Circuit in Santa Fe Industries v. Green, 430 U.S. 462 (1979).

The Court interpreted the language of § 10(b) of the Securities Exchange Act as prohibiting only conduct involving manipulation or deception, and held that Rule 10b-5 could extend no further than the statutory provision that authorized its adoption. The Court then went on to conclude that the term manipulation did not extend to "instances of corporate mismanagement [such as an undervalued freezeout] in which the essence of the complaint is that shareholders were treated unfairly by a fiduciary." In support of its conclusion, the Court raised federalism concerns:

> The reasoning behind a holding that the complaint in this case alleged fraud under Rule 10b-5 could not be easily contained. It is difficult to imagine how a court could distinguish, for purposes of Rule 10b-5 fraud, between a majority

---

[82] 533 F.2d 1283 (2d Cir.1976), *rev'd*, 430 U.S. 462 (1977).

[83] 533 F.2d at 1287. The history of state law efforts to restrict freezeouts is traced in Chapter 22, *supra*.

[84] See Chapter 23B.3, *infra*.

[85] 425 F.Supp. 1145 (S.D.N.Y.1977). The court stated that "Section 14(e) was intended to make Rule 10b-5 applicable to the tender offer or exchange offer situation." *Id*. at 1157.

[86] Accord, Royal Industries v. Monogram Industries, [1976-1977 Transfer Binder] Fed.Sec.L.Rep. (CCH) ¶95,863 (C.D.Cal.1976) (acquisition of a corporation solely to defeat a hostile tender offer violated § 14(e); Crane Co. v. Anaconda Co., 411 F.Supp. 1208 (S.D.N.Y.1975) (complaint that sole purpose of acquisition by target was to defeat tender offer would state cause of action).

stockholder's use of a short-form merger to eliminate the minority at an unfair price and the use of some other device, such as a long-form merger, tender offer, or liquidation, to achieve the same result; or indeed how a court could distinguish the alleged abuses in these going private transactions from other types of fiduciary self-dealing involving transactions in securities. The result would be to bring within the Rule a wide variety of corporate conduct traditionally left to state regulation. . . . Federal courts applying a "federal fiduciary principle" under Rule 10b-5 could be expected to depart from state fiduciary standards at least to the extent necessary to ensure uniformity within the federal system. Absent a clear indication of congressional intent, we are reluctant to federalize the substantial portion of the law of corporations that deals with transactions in securities, particularly where established state policies of corporate regulation would be overridden.

The lower federal courts responded to the Supreme Court's decision in *Santa Fe* by continuing their simple application of Rule 10b-5 precedent to the interpretation of § 14(e), only now with the effect of restricting the scope of the Section; claims that target company defensive tactics violated § 14(e) were routinely rejected by simple reference to *Santa Fe*.[87] So matters stood until the decision of the Sixth Circuit in Mobil Corp. v. Marathon Oil Co.

MOBIL CORP. v. MARATHON OIL CO.
669 F.2d 366 (6th Cir.1981), *cert. denied*, 455 U.S. 982 (1982)

Before EDWARDS, Chief Judge and ENGEL and MERRITT, Circuit Judges.

ENGEL, Circuit Judge. On October 30, 1981, Mobil Corporation ("Mobil") announced its intention to purchase up to 40 million outstanding common shares of stock in Marathon Oil Company ("Marathon") for $85 per share in cash. Mobil conditioned that purchase upon receipt of at least 30 million shares, just over one-half of the outstanding shares. It further stated its intention to acquire the balance of Marathon by merger following its purchase of those shares.

Marathon directors were concerned about the effects of a merger with Mobil, and they immediately held a board meeting. The directors

---

[87] E.g., In re Sunshine Mining Securities Litigation, 496 F.Supp. 9, 11 (S.D.N.Y.1979) ("In order for the plaintiff's complaint to withstand this motion to dismiss, we must find that the wrongful withholding of support for a proposed tender offer amounts to a fraudulent, deceptive, or manipulative act or practice. After Santa Fe v. Green, such a finding is untenable."); Altman v. Knight, 431 F.Supp. 309, 313-14 (S.D.N.Y.1977) ("After the United States Supreme Court's decision in Santa Fe v. Green, it is clear that Anaconda's acquisition of Walworth, even if for no valid business purpose, does not alone constitute a manipulative or deceptive device, as is necessary to state a claim under § 14(e) of the Act.")

determined that, together with consideration of other alternatives, they would seek a "white knight" -- a more attractive candidate for merger.

Negotiations developed between Marathon and several companies. . . . United States Steel Corporation ("U.S. Steel") indicated its interest, and on November 18, 1981, offered what it termed a "final proposal" to be acted upon that day. By that proposal U.S. Steel offered $125 per share for 30 million shares of Marathon stock, with a plan for a follow-up merger with its subsidiary, U.S.S. Corporation ("USS").

The Marathon directors voted to recommend the U.S. Steel offer to the shareholders on November 18, 1981. Marathon, U.S. Steel and USS executed a formal merger agreement on that day. USS made its tender offer on November 19, 1981. Both USS and Marathon filed the appropriate documents with the Securities Exchange Commission.

The USS offer, and subsequently the merger agreement, had two significant conditions. First, they required a present, irrevocable option to purchase ten million authorized but unissued shares of Marathon common stock for $90 per share ("stock option"). These shares equalled approximately 17% of Marathon's outstanding shares. Next, they required an option to purchase Marathon's 48% interest in oil and mineral rights in the Yates Field for $2.8 billion. ("Yates Field option"). The latter option could be exercised only if USS's offer did not succeed and if a third party gained control of Marathon. Thus, in effect, a potential competing tender offeror could not acquire Yates Field upon a merger with Marathon.

The value of Yates Field to Marathon and to potential buyers is significant; Marathon has referred to the field as its "crown jewel."

> One of the world's most remarkable oil fields is the Yates Field in Pecos County (of the Permian basin province of West Texas). Producing from an unusually prolific and highly permeable reservoir rock, under natural hydraulic pressure, the potential production of 313 wells distributed over 17,000 acres in this field was in 1929 estimated to be in excess of 5 million bbl. per day. This was more than the total daily production of all United States fields; however, production has been drastically curtailed. (Footnote omitted.)

. . . The importance of Yates to a potential tender offeror is illustrated by the fact that both Gulf Oil and Allied indicated that they would propose a tender offer only upon assurances that they would have an option to buy Marathon's interest in the Yates Field. Such requests are a recent but recurring phenomenon in connection with tender offers.

Following this agreement, Mobil filed suit in the United States District Court for the Southern District of Ohio, seeking to enjoin the exercise of the options and any purchase of shares in accordance with the tender offer. . . . Mobil alleged that the options granted to USS served as a "lock-up" arrangement to defeat any competitive offers of Mobil or third parties, thereby constituting a "manipulative" practice "in connection with a tender offer," in violation of § 14(e) of the Williams Act. . . .

[W]e now consider Mobil's claim that the Yates Field and stock options granted by Marathon to USS, the wholly owned subsidiary of U.S. Steel, constitute a "manipulative act or practice" in connection with the USS tender offer of November 19, 1981, in violation of § 14(e). . . . The district court found no substantial likelihood of success by Mobil on the merits of this claim, holding that it "amounts to no more than a claim that the Marathon directors acted unfairly and breached their fiduciary [duty] to Marathon and its shareholders," and as such fails to state a cause of action under § 14(e). The district court relied on Santa Fe Industries v. Green, 430 U.S. 462 (1977), in which the Supreme Court held that a mere breach of corporate fiduciary duty does not violate § 10(b) of the Securities Exchange Act of 1934. We believe the district court's interpretation of the *Santa Fe* case and its characterization of Mobil's claim as nothing more than a breach of fiduciary duty were erroneous.

Santa Fe involved a claim under § 10(b) of the Securities Exchange Act of 1934 and SEC Rule 10b-5. Section 10(b) concerns the sale and purchase of securities rather than tender offers, but its anti-manipulation language is similar to that of § 14(e), and provides:

> It shall be unlawful for any person . . . [t]o use or employ, in connection with the purchase or sale of any security, any manipulative or deceptive device or contrivance in contravention of such rules and regulations as the Commission may prescribe as necessary or appropriate in the public interest or for the protection of investors.

Santa Fe held that a mere allegation of unfair treatment of minority shareholders, corporate mismanagement, or breach of corporate fiduciary duty by majority shareholders or corporate directors does not state a cause of action under § 10(b), and particularly that such conduct, standing alone, does not constitute a "manipulative device or contrivance" under the statute. 430 U.S. at 474-77. . . . We . . . conclude that the Yates Field option and the stock option individually and together are "manipulative" as that term is used in § 14(e).

The term "manipulative" is not defined in either the Securities Exchange Act or the Williams Act. "Manipulation" in securities markets can take many forms, see, e.g., 15 U.S.C. §§ 78i, 78j (proscribing certain forms of manipulation), but the Supreme Court has recently indicated that manipulation is an affecting of the market for, or price of, securities by *artificial* means, i.e., means unrelated to the natural forces of supply and demand.

> Use of the word "manipulative" is especially significant. It is and was virtually a term of art when used in connection with securities markets. It connotes intentional or willful conduct designed to deceive or defraud investors by controlling or artificially affecting the price of securities.

Ernst & Ernst v. Hochfelder, 425 U.S. 185, 199 (1976) (footnote omitted).

> "Manipulation" is "virtually a term of art when used in connection with securities markets." *Ernst & Ernst*, 425 U.S. at 199. The term refers generally to practices, such as wash sales, matched orders, or rigged prices, that are intended to mislead investors by artificially affecting market activity.

Santa Fe Industries v. Green, 430 U.S. 462, 476 (1977). In our view, it is difficult to conceive of a more effective and manipulative device than the "lock-up" options employed here, options which not only artificially affect, but for all practical purposes completely block, normal healthy market activity and, in fact, could be construed as expressly designed solely for that purpose.

The types of options demanded and received by USS in this case are relatively new to the world of tender offer takeover contests, and we are unaware of any Supreme Court or Court of Appeals case confronting the question of whether these particular techniques are "manipulative" within the meaning of § 14(e) of the Williams Act. However, courts have recognized that the term "manipulative" must remain flexible in the face of new techniques which artificially affect securities markets. "No doubt Congress meant to prohibit the full range of ingenious devices that might be used to manipulate securities prices." Santa Fe Industries v. Green, *supra*, 430 U.S. at 477 (§ 10(b)). . . .

We are of the opinion that under the circumstances of this particular case, Mobil has shown a sufficient likelihood of ultimately establishing that the Yates Field option and the stock option had the effect of creating an artificial price ceiling in the tender offer market for Marathon common shares, and that the options therefore are "manipulative acts or practices" in connection with a tender offer in violation of § 14(e) of the Williams Act. . . .

The Yates Field option is exercisable if, and only if, control of Marathon is obtained by a third party. The only effect of this option can be to deter Mobil and any other potential tender offerors from competing with USS in an auction for control of Marathon. Others cannot compete on a par with USS; its bid of $125 per share thus amounts to an artificial ceiling on the value Marathon shareholders can receive for their shares. Therefore, there is a substantial likelihood that the option is manipulative under § 14(e) of the Williams Act.

The particular facts before us also indicate that the stock option that USS demanded and received in connection with its tender offer prevents all others from competing on a par with USS for control of Marathon. In our opinion, the stock option was large enough in this takeover contest to serve as an artificial and significant deterrent to competitive bidding for a controlling block of Marathon shares. . . .

The Yates Field option and the stock option, both individually and in combination, have the effect of circumventing the natural forces of market demand in this tender offer contest. Were this contest a straight price-per-share auction, tender offers well in excess of the USS offer of $125 per share may have been forthcoming. Of course, Mobil itself has offered $126 per share, conditional on the judicial removal of the options. Our task under the Williams Act is not to speculate about what price the Marathon shareholders might have been offered if the natural market forces existed in this tender offer contest, but rather to enforce the mandate of § 14(e) against manipulation of the market. The purpose of the Williams Act, protection of the target shareholders, requires that Mobil and any other interested bidder be permitted an equal opportunity to compete in the marketplace and persuade the Marathon shareholders to sell their shares to them.

The defendants argue that § 14(e) requires full disclosure and nothing more. They point to the following language in the Supreme Court's opinion in *Santa Fe*, concerning § 10(b):

> [T]he Court repeatedly has described the "fundamental purpose" of the [Securities Exchange] Act as implementing a "philosophy of full disclosure"; once full and fair disclosure has occurred, the fairness of the terms of the transaction is at most a tangential concern of the statute.

430 U.S. at 477-78. The defendants read too much into this language. *Santa Fe* held that mere allegations of unfairness and breach of fiduciary duty by majority shareholders to the minority did not violate § 10(b). It did not find that nondisclosure was the only ground upon which to base a 10(b) claim. Instead, the Court expressly made a factual determination that "the conduct . . . alleged in the complaint was not 'manipulative'. . . ." 430 U.S. at 476. *Santa Fe* thus cannot be taken to mean that conduct that falls within the special meaning of the term "manipulation" is legal so long as it is fully disclosed. "[N]ondisclosure is usually essential to the success of a manipulative scheme," *id*. at 477, but this case illustrates that disclosure alone does not always mean that there is no manipulation. It may be that the Marathon shareholders in this case have now been fully informed that their management granted USS the Yates Field option and the stock option. They may now understand fully how these options deter any tender offers higher than $125 per share. Yet, they have had no real alternative to accepting the USS offer, because Mobil's offer of $126 is conditional upon the invalidity of the options, and there is and could be no other comparable tender offer as long as the "lock-up" options remain in effect. The artificial ceiling on the price of their shares at $125 is manipulation to which they must submit whether it is disclosed to them or not, since in not tendering their shares to USS they risk being relegated to the "back end" of USS's takeover proposal and receiving only $90 per share.

In short, to find compliance with § 14(e) solely by the full disclosure of a manipulative device as a *fait accompli* would be to read the "manipulative acts and practices" language completely out of the Williams Act. . . ."*

The holding in *Mobil* attracted no following in other circuits.[88] Yet, its underlying premise -- that, whatever the result reached, determination of the breadth of misconduct covered by § 14(e) could not be resolved by simple reference to Rule 10b-5 precedent -- had an inviting logic. Although the cases remained almost unanimously opposed to the proposition that § 14(e) extended to substantive conduct, the first round of academic comment largely favored the *Mobil* result, if not its rationale.[89] The resulting uncertainty meant that the scope of § 14(e) would be litigated in every contested tender offer until the issue was definitively resolved. The Supreme Court undertook this effort in the following case.

SCHREIBER v. BURLINGTON NORTHERN, INC.
472 U.S. 1 (1985)

Chief Justice BURGER delivered the opinion of the Court.

We granted certiorari to resolve a conflict in the Circuits over whether misrepresentation or nondisclosure is a necessary element of a violation of § 14(e) of the Securities Exchange Act of 1934, 15 U.S.C. § 78n(e).

I

On December 21, 1982, Burlington Northern, Inc., made a hostile tender offer for El Paso Gas Co. Through a wholly owned subsidiary, Burlington proposed to purchase 25.1 million El Paso shares at $24 per share. Burlington reserved the right to terminate the offer if any of several specified events occurred. El Paso management initially opposed the

---

* Judge Merritt dissented on the grounds that the Sixth Circuit's separate decision against Mobil on an antitrust issue made the case moot. Eds.

[88] See, e.g., Feldbaum v. Avon Products, Inc., 741 F.2d 234 (8th Cir.1984); Data Probe Acquisition Corp. v. Datatab, Inc., 722 F.2d 1 (2d Cir.1983), *cert. denied*, 465 U.S. 1052 (1984); Buffalo Forge Co. v. Ogden Corp., 717 F.2d 757 (2d Cir.1983), *cert. denied*, 464 U.S. 1018 (1983); Schreiber v. Burlington Northern Inc., 731 F.2d 163 (3d Cir.1984), *rev'd*, 472 U.S. 1 (1985); Pin v. Texaco, Inc., 793 F.2d 1448 (5th Cir.1986).

[89] See James Junewicz, *The Appropriate Limits of Section 14(e) of the Securities Exchange Act of 1934*, 62 Texas L.Rev. 1171 (1984); Note, *Target Defensive Tactics as Manipulative under Section 14(e)*, 84 Colum.L.Rev. 228 (1984); Mark Loewenstein, *Section 14(e) of the Williams Act and the Rule 10b-5 Comparisons*, 71 Geo.L.J. 1311 (1983); Elliott Weiss, *Defensive Responses to Tender Offers and the Williams Act's Prohibition Against Manipulation*, 35 Vand.L.Rev. 1087 (1982).

takeover, but its shareholders responded favorably, fully subscribing the offer by the December 30, 1982 deadline.

Burlington did not accept those tendered shares; instead, after negotiations with El Paso management, Burlington announced on January 10, 1983, the terms of a new and friendly takeover agreement. Pursuant to the new agreement, Burlington undertook, *inter alia*, to (1) rescind the December tender offer, (2) purchase 4,166,667 shares from El Paso at $24 per share, (3) substitute a new tender offer for only 21 million shares at $24 per share, (4) provide procedural protections against a squeeze-out merger of the remaining El Paso shareholders, and (5) recognize "golden parachute" contracts between El Paso and four of its senior officers. By February 8, more than 40 million shares were tendered in response to Burlington's January offer, and the takeover was completed.

The rescission of the first tender offer caused a diminished payment to those shareholders who had tendered during the first offer. The January offer was greatly oversubscribed and consequently those shareholders who retendered were subject to substantial proration. Petitioner Barbara Schreiber filed suit on behalf of herself and similarly situated shareholders, alleging that Burlington, El Paso, and members of El Paso's board violated § 14(e)'s prohibition of "fraudulent, deceptive or manipulative acts or practices . . . in connection with any tender offer." She claimed that Burlington's withdrawal of the December tender offer coupled with the substitution of the January tender offer was a "manipulative" distortion of the market for El Paso stock. . . .

The District Court dismissed the suit for failure to state a claim. 568 F.Supp. 197 (Del.1983). The District Court reasoned that the alleged manipulation did not involve a misrepresentation, and so did not violate § 14(e). The District Court relied on the fact that in cases involving alleged violations of § 10(b) of the Securities Exchange Act, 15 U.S.C. § 78j(b), this Court has required misrepresentation for there to be a "manipulative" violation of the section. 568 F.Supp. at 202.

The Court of Appeals for the Third Circuit affirmed. 731 F.2d 163 (1984). The Court of Appeals held that the acts alleged did not violate the Williams Act, because "§ 14(e) was not intended to create a federal cause of action for all harms suffered because of the proffering or the withdrawal of tender offers." *Id.* at 165. The Court of Appeals reasoned that § 14(e) was "enacted principally as a disclosure statute, designed to insure that fully-informed investors could intelligently decide how to respond to a tender offer." *Id.* at 165-166. It concluded that the "arguable breach of contract" alleged by petitioner was not a "manipulative act" under § 14(e).

We granted certiorari to resolve the conflict, 469 U.S. 815 (1984). We affirm.

II

A

We are asked in this case to interpret § 14(e) of the Securities Exchange Act. . . . The starting point is the language of the statute. Section 14(e) provides:

> It shall be unlawful for any person to make any untrue statement of a material fact or omit to state any material fact necessary in order to make the statements made, in the light of the circumstances under which they are made, not misleading, or to engage in any fraudulent, deceptive or manipulative acts or practices, in connection with any tender offer or request or invitation for tenders, or any solicitation of security holders in opposition to or in favor of any such offer, request, or invitation. The Commission shall, for the purposes of this subsection, by rules and regulations define, and prescribe means reasonably designed to prevent, such acts and practices as are fraudulent, deceptive, or manipulative.

Petitioner relies on a construction of the phrase, "fraudulent, deceptive or manipulative acts or practices." Petitioner reads the phrase "fraudulent, deceptive or manipulative acts or practices" to include acts which, although fully disclosed, "artificially" affect the price of the takeover target's stock. Petitioner's interpretation relies on the belief that § 14(e) is directed at purposes broader than providing full and true information to investors.

Petitioner's reading of the term "manipulative" conflicts with the normal meaning of the term. We have held in the context of an alleged violation of § 10(b) of the Securities Exchange Act:

> Use of the word 'manipulative' is especially significant. It is and was virtually a term of art when used in connection with the securities markets. It connotes intentional or willful conduct *designed to deceive or defraud* investors by controlling or artificially affecting the price of securities. Ernst & Ernst v. Hochfelder, 425 U.S. 185, 199 (1976) (emphasis added).

Other cases interpreting the term reflect its use as a general term comprising a range of misleading practices:

> The term refers generally to practices, such as wash sales, matched orders, or rigged prices, that are intended to mislead investors by artificially affecting market activity. . . . Section 10(b)'s general prohibition of practices deemed by the SEC to be 'manipulative' -- in this technical sense of artificially affecting market activity in order to mislead investors -- is fully consistent with the fundamental purpose of the 1934 Act 'to substitute a philosophy of full disclosure for the philosophy of *caveat emptor*. . . .' Indeed, nondisclosure is usually essential to the success of a manipulative scheme. . . . No doubt Congress meant to prohibit the full range of ingenious devices that might be used to manipulate securities prices. But we do not think it would have chosen

this 'term of art' if it had meant to bring within the scope of § 10(b) instances of corporate mismanagement such as this, in which the essence of the complaint is that shareholders were treated unfairly by a fiduciary. Santa Fe Industries v. Green, 430 U.S. 462, 476-477 (1977).

The meaning the Court has given the term "manipulative" is consistent with the use of the term at common law,[3] and with its traditional dictionary definition.[4]

She argues, however, that the term manipulative takes on a meaning in § 14(e) that is different from the meaning it has in § 10(b). Petitioner claims that the use of the disjunctive "or" in § 14(e) implied that acts need not be deceptive or fraudulent to be manipulative. But Congress used the phrase "manipulative or deceptive" in § 10(b) as well, and we have interpreted "manipulative" in that context to require misrepresentation. Moreover, it is a "'familiar principle of statutory construction that words grouped in a list should be given related meaning.'" Securities Indus. Assn. v. Board of Governors, 468 U.S. 207, 218 (1984). All three species of misconduct, i.e., "fraudulent, deceptive or manipulative," listed by Congress are directed at failures to disclose. The use of the term "manipulative" provides emphasis and guidance to those who must determine which types of acts are reached by the statute; it does not suggest a deviation from the section's facial and primary concern with disclosure or Congressional concern with disclosure which is the core of the Act.

B

Our conclusion that "manipulative" acts under § 14(e) require misrepresentation or nondisclosure is buttressed by the purpose and legislative history of the provision. Section 14(e) was originally added to the Securities Exchange Act as part of the Williams Act. "The purpose of the Williams Act is to insure that public shareholders who are confronted by a cash tender offer for their stock will not be required to respond without adequate information." Rondeau v. Mosinee Paper Corp., 422 U.S. 49, 58 (1975).

---

[3] See generally, Louis Loss, *Securities Regulation* 984-989 (3d ed.1983). For example, the seminal English case of Scott v. Brown, Doering, McNab & Co., [1892] 2 Q.B. 724, 724 (C.A.), which broke new ground in recognizing that manipulation could occur without the dissemination of false statements, nonetheless placed emphasis on the presence of deception. As Lord Lopes stated in that case, "I can see no substantial distinction between false rumours and false and fictitious acts." *Id.* at 730. See also, United States v. Brown, 5 F.Supp. 81, 85 (S.D.N.Y.1933) ("[E]ven a speculator is entitled not to have any present fact involving the subject matter of his speculative purchase or the price thereof misrepresented by word or act").

[4] See Webster's *Third New International Dictionary* 1376 (1971) (Manipulation is "management with use of unfair, scheming, or underhanded methods").

It is clear that Congress relied primarily on disclosure to implement the purpose of the Williams Act. Senator Williams, the Bill's Senate sponsor, stated in the debate:

> Today, the public shareholder in deciding whether to accept or reject a tender offer possesses limited information. No matter what he does, he acts without adequate knowledge to enable him to decide rationally what is the best course of action. This is precisely the dilemma which our securities laws are designed to prevent. 113 Cong.Rec. 24,664 (1967) (Remarks of Sen. Williams).

The expressed legislative intent was to preserve a neutral setting in which the contenders could fully present their arguments. The Senate sponsor went on to say:

> We have taken extreme care to avoid tipping the scales either in favor of management or in favor of the person making the takeover bids. S. 510 is designed solely to require full and fair disclosure for the benefit of investors. The bill will at the same time provide the offeror and management equal opportunity to present their case. *Ibid.*

To implement this objective, the Williams Act added §§ 13(d), 13(e), 14(d), 14(e), and 14(f) to the Securities Exchange Act. Some relate to disclosure; §§ 13(d), 14(d) and 14(f) all add specific registration and disclosure provisions. Others -- §§ 13(e) and 14(d) -- require or prohibit certain acts so that investors will possess additional time within which to take advantage of the disclosed information.

Section 14(e) adds a "broad antifraud prohibition," Piper v. Chris Craft Industries, 430 U.S. 1, 24 (1977), modeled on the antifraud provisions of § 10(b) of the Act and Rule 10b-5.[8] It supplements the more precise disclosure provisions found elsewhere in the Williams Act, while requiring disclosure more explicitly addressed to the tender offer context than that required by § 10(b).

While legislative history specifically concerning § 14(e) is sparse, the House and Senate Reports discuss the role of § 14(e). Describing § 14(e) as regulating "fraudulent transactions," and stating the thrust of the section:

> This provision would affirm the fact that persons engaged in making or opposing tender offers or otherwise seeking to influence the decision of

---

[8] . . . Because of the textual similarities, it is often assumed that § 14(e) was modeled on § 10(b) and Rule 10b-5. See, e.g., Panter v. Marshall Field & Co., 646 F.2d 271, 283 (7th Cir.), *cert. denied*, 454 U.S. 1092 (1981). For the purpose of interpreting the term "manipulative," the most significant changes from the language of § 10(b) were the addition of the term "fraudulent," and the reference to "acts" rather than "devices." Neither change bears in any obvious way on the meaning to be given to "manipulative."

Similar terminology is also found in § 15(c) of the Securities Exchange Act, 15 U.S.C. § 780(c), § 17(a) of the Securities Act of 1933, 15 U.S.C. § 77q, and § 206 of the Investment Advisers Act of 1940, 15 U.S.C. § 80b-6.

investors or the outcome of the tender offer are under an obligation to make *full disclosure* of material information to those with whom they deal. H.R.Rep. No. 1,711, 90th Cong., 2d Sess., 11 (1968) (emphasis added); S.R.Rep. No. 550, 90th Cong., 1st Sess., 11 (1967) (emphasis added).

Nowhere in the legislative history is there the slightest suggestion that § 14(e) serves any purpose other than disclosure,[9] or that the term "manipulative" should be read as an invitation to the courts to oversee the substantive fairness of tender offers; the quality of any offer is a matter for the marketplace.

To adopt the reading of the term "manipulative" urged by petitioner would not only be unwarranted in light of the legislative purpose but would be at odds with it. Inviting judges to read the term "manipulative" with their own sense of what constitutes "unfair" or "artificial" conduct would inject uncertainty into the tender offer process. An essential piece of information -- whether the court would deem the fully disclosed actions of one side or the other to be "manipulative" -- would not be available until after the tender offer had closed. This uncertainty would directly contradict the expressed Congressional desire to give investors full information.

Congress' consistent emphasis on disclosure persuades us that it intended takeover contest to be addressed to shareholders. In pursuit of this goal, Congress, consistent with the core mechanism of the Securities Exchange Act, created sweeping disclosure requirements and narrow substantive safeguards. The same Congress that placed such emphasis on shareholder choice would not at the same time have required judges to oversee tender offers for substantive fairness. It is even less likely that a Congress implementing that intention would express it only through the use of a single word placed in the middle of a provision otherwise devoted to disclosure.

C

We hold that the term "manipulative" as used in § 14(e) requires misrepresentation or nondisclosure. It connotes "conduct designed to deceive

---

[9] The Act was amended in 1970, and Congress added to § 14(e) the sentence, "The Commission shall, for the purposes of this subsection, by rules and regulations define, and prescribe means reasonably designed to prevent, such acts and practices as are fraudulent, deceptive, or manipulative." Petitioner argues that this phrase would be pointless if § 14(e) was concerned with disclosure only.

We disagree. In adding the 1970 amendment, Congress simply provided a mechanism for defining and guarding against those acts and practices which involve material misrepresentation or nondisclosure. The amendment gives the Securities and Exchange Commission latitude to regulate nondeceptive activities as a "reasonably designed" means of preventing manipulative acts, without suggesting any change in the meaning of the term "manipulative" itself.

or defraud investors by controlling or artificially affecting the price of securities." Ernst & Ernst v. Hochfelder, 425 U.S. at 199. Without misrepresentation or nondisclosure, § 14(e) has not been violated.

Applying that definition to this case, we hold that the actions of respondents were not manipulative. The amended complaint fails to allege that the cancellation of the first tender offer was accompanied by any misrepresentation, nondisclosure or deception. The District Court correctly found, "All activity of the defendants that could have conceivably affected the price of El Paso shares was done openly." 568 F.Supp. at 203. . . .

The judgment of the Court of Appeals is affirmed.

The Supreme Court's resolution of the breadth of § 14(e) is clear enough: "We hold that the term 'manipulative' as used in § 14(e) requires misrepresentation or nondisclosure." But is it clear why the Court came out the way that it did?

The bulk of the Court's analysis is a parsing of the precise language chosen by Congress for § 14(e). Yet while the Court's treatment of the statutory language is a possible interpretation, it is hardly the only interpretation or even the most persuasive. For example, the operative part of § 14(e) breaks down into two components: The first prohibiting untrue statements and material omissions; and the second prohibiting fraudulent, deceptive, or manipulative acts or practices. Does the Supreme Court's holding that manipulative acts require misrepresentation or nondisclosure make § 14(e)'s second component redundant? Would not any manipulative act that violated the second component because it involved misrepresentation or nondisclosure also violate the first component?[90] Additionally, the phrase "fraudulent, deceptive or manipulative" in § 14(e)'s second component is in the disjunctive. The implication is that an act need not be deceptive or fraudulent -- and therefore need not involve misrepresentation and nondisclosure -- to be manipulative.[91] To be sure, there is nothing in the phrase that is inconsistent with the Court's rejection of a disjunctive construction in favor of treating the phrase as simply a legal litany of synonyms whose juxtaposition indicates a similarity rather than a difference in meaning, much as a traditional form of bill of sale would "sell, grant, and devise" some piece of personal property. But there is also nothing in the Court's opinion that explains *why* it chose its interpretation from among the possible alternatives.[92]

---

[90] See Junewicz (1984), *supra* note 89, at 1174-74.

[91] See Weiss (1982), *supra* note 89, at 1096.

[92] The Court does briefly argue that the legislative history of the Williams Act supports its statutory construction. A more detailed review of the legislative history leads to the same conclusion as the linguistic analysis: The Court's interpretation of the statute's legislative history is plausible, but is neither compelled nor even the most convincing of the alternatives.

Some sense of what may have motivated the Court's narrow construction of the breadth of § 14(e) comes from more careful examination of *Santa Fe* whose holding -- that Rule 10b-5 requires misrepresentation or nondisclosure -- *Schreiber* extended to § 14(e). The concern that the Second Circuit was creating a federal law of fiduciary duty seems well placed. For about a fifteen year period from 1960 to 1975, Rule 10b-5 seemed increasingly "like the medieval alchemist's 'universal solvent' which was so potent that it dissolved every container employed to hold it."[93] The Second Circuit decision in *Santa Fe* seemed a natural extension of prior case law. But then the tide turned. The unifying theme of the Supreme Court's securities law decisions of the mid-1970s was to reverse the trend and more narrowly confine the application of federal securities law.[94] The significance of the Supreme Court's linguistic analysis of § 10(b) in *Santa Fe* can be understood only in that context.

Recall that *Santa Fe* explicitly raised federalism concerns. The Court stressed that a broad reading of Rule 10b-5 would "bring within the Rule a wide variety of corporate conduct traditionally left to state regulation. . . . Absent a clear indication of congressional intent, we are reluctant to federalize the substantial portion of the law of corporations that deals with transactions in securities, particularly where established state policies of corporate regulation would be overridden." Does § 14(e) present the same federalism concerns that seem to have motivated the Court's linguistic analysis in *Santa Fe*? Section 10(b) concerns trading in securities generally; the Court is thus correct that a broad reading of it "could not be easily contained." The range of activities covered by § 14(e), however, is self-limiting: It concerns only tender offers. Moreover, the imposition on state prerogatives by a broader construction of § 14(e) is similarly limited; it extends to but a narrow slice of state corporate law. Finally, in Edgar v. Mite, 457 U.S. 624 (1982), the Supreme Court held that the Williams Act preempted state antitakeover statutes, hardly an indication that behavior in hostile takeovers was one traditionally governed by state law. Perhaps *Schreiber* presaged the Court's subsequent decision in CTS Corp. v. Dynamics Corp. of America, 481 U.S. 69 (1987), which upheld a second generation state antitakeover statute against preemption challenges based in

---

As with its linguistic analysis, the Court offers no explanation for its choice among competing histories.

[93] Stanley Kaplan, *Fiduciary Responsibility in the Management of the Corporation*, 31 Bus.Law. 883, 885 (1976).

[94] See Blue Chip Stamps v. Manor Drug Stores, 421 U.S. 723 (1975) (standing under Rule 10b-5 requires actual purchase or sale of securities); Rondeau v. Mosinee Paper Corp., 422 U.S. 49 (1975) (narrowed availability of injunctive relief under § 13(d)); Ernst & Ernst v. Hochfelder, 425 U.S. 185 (1976) (proof of scienter required under Rule 10b-5); Piper v. Chris-Craft Industries, 430 U.S. 1 (1977) (tender offeror lacks standing to recover damages under § 14(e)); Santa Fe Industries v. Green, *supra* (misrepresentation or nondisclosure required under Rule 10b-5).

part on federalism grounds.[95] *Schrieber* may simply have signalled the direction the Court was going.[96]

The upshot of this analysis is that the Court's decision in *Schreiber* seems curiously unexplained; deprived of the support provided by the federalism analysis in *Santa Fe*, the opinion amounts to mere fiat. What, then, was going on?

An explanation for both the *Schreiber* result and the opinion's lack of explicit justification for it may come from recognizing the difficulty of articulating a broader construction of § 14(e). Among the alternatives suggested by commentators who support a broader reach for the Section are:

(1) Section 14(e) is violated by "[c]onduct by the target that interferes with the shareholders' right to decide the fate of the offer or with the bidder's opportunity to present its case. . . ."[97]

(2) Section 14(e) is violated by "any arrangements that artificially impair the tender offer market for a company's shares."[98]

(3) Section 14(e) is violated when target "management breaches its fiduciary duty to its shareholders and the effect of that breach is to thwart the offeror's efforts."[99]

2.   "In Connection With Any Tender Offer": The Problem of Causation in an Aborted Offer

Sometimes target management successfully defeats a tender offer. Suppose that a hostile bidder carries an offer through to completion, but the offer fails because target management's misrepresentations convince too many of its shareholders not to tender. In this situation it is clear that target management's misrepresentations were "in connection with" a tender offer as required by § 14(e) and that target shareholders could bring a § 14(e) action against their management. A more common situation, however, is one in which a bidder announces a tender offer, but target management's defensive activity -- again assume it consists at least in part of misrepresentations -- causes the bidder to withdraw the offer *before* target shareholders are able to tender. In this situation two barriers confront target shareholders who wish to sue their management under § 14(e) to recover the now lost premium. First, were target management's misrepresentation's "in connection with" a tender offer? Put differently, what is the temporal limit

---

[95] Edgar v. Mite and CTS Corp. v. Dynamics Corp. of America are considered in Chapter 23, *infra*.

[96] The federalism issue arises again in connection with the claim that the Williams Act pre-empts state takeover litigation. See Chapter 23, *infra*.

[97] Note, *Target Defensive Tactics as Manipulative Under Section 14(e)*, *supra* note 89, at 253.

[98] Weiss (1982), *supra* note 89, at 1100.

[99] Loewenstein (1983), *supra* note 89, at 1352.

of § 14(e)'s jurisdiction? Second, assuming that the transaction had gone far enough to meet jurisdictional requirements, how can target shareholders prove reliance on the misrepresentations when the tender offer's withdrawal prevented them from acting with respect to them at all?

PANTER v. MARSHALL FIELD & CO.
646 F.2d 271 (7th Cir.1981), *cert. denied*, 454 U.S. 1092 (1981)

[Carter Hawley Hale (CHH)] announced its intention to make an exchange offer of $42.00 per share in cash and CHH stock for each share of Marshall Field & Co.'s stock tendered, conditioned on the satisfaction of some twenty conditions. Three weeks later, after Field's had engaged in a variety of defensive maneuvers, CHH withdrew its proposed offer before it became effective. None of the events that conditioned CHH's offer had occurred by the date of the withdrawal. Following the withdrawal, Field stock traded at $19.00 per share. Field shareholders then sued the company and its directors.]

Before PELL and CUDAHY, Circuit Judges, and DUMBAULD, Senior District Judge.

PELL, Circuit Judge. . . .

III. THE FEDERAL SECURITIES LAW CLAIMS

The plaintiffs . . . claim the defendants violated § 14(e) of the Williams Act, which prohibits deception "in connection with any tender offer." . . . [§ 14(e) and Rule 10b-5] are coextensive in their antifraud prohibitions, and are therefore construed *in pari materia* by courts. . . . However, . . . the "in connection with any tender offer" language of the Williams Act provision presents special concerns not present in analysis under Rule 10b-5. . . .

A. *The Williams Act Claims*

Section 14(e) of the Williams Act is a broad antifraud provision . . . is designed to insure that shareholders confronted with a tender offer have adequate and accurate information on which to base the decision whether or not to tender their shares. Piper v. Chris-Craft Industries, 430 U.S. 1, 35 (1977); Rondeau v. Mosinee Paper Corp., 422 U.S. 49, 58 (1975); Lewis v. McGraw, 619 F.2d 192 (2d Cir.), *cert. denied*, 449 U.S. 941 (1980).

Upon the announcement of a tender offer proposal a target company shareholder is presented with three options: he may retain his shares; he may tender them to the tender offeror if the offer becomes effective; or he may dispose of them in the securities market for his shares, which generally rises on the announcement of a tender offer. The plaintiffs have alleged that the defendants violated § 14(e) both by depriving them of their opportunity to tender their shares to CHH, the tender offeror, and by deceiving them as to the attractiveness of disposing of their shares in the rising market.

1. The Lost Tender Offer Opportunity

By denying the plaintiffs the opportunity to tender their shares to CHH, the plaintiffs claim the defendants deprived them of the difference between $42.00, the amount of the CHH offer, and $19.76, the amount at which Field's shares traded in the market after withdrawal of the CHH proposal. Total damages under this theory would exceed $200 [million].

Because § 14(e) is intended to protect shareholders from making a tender offer decision on inaccurate or inadequate information, among the elements of § 14(e) plaintiff must establish is "that there was a misrepresentation upon which the target corporation shareholders relied. . . ." Chris-Craft Industries v. Piper Aircraft Corp., 480 F.2d 341, 373 (2d Cir.), *cert. denied*, 414 U.S. 910 (1973). Because the CHH tender offer was withdrawn before the plaintiffs had the opportunity to decide whether or not to tender their shares, it was impossible for the plaintiffs to rely on any alleged deception in making the decision to tender or not. Because the plaintiffs were never presented with that critical decision and therefore never relied on the defendants' alleged misrepresentations, they fail to establish a vital element of a § 14(e) claim as regards the CHH $42.00 offer.

In the recent case of Lewis v. McGraw, 619 F.2d 192 (2d Cir.), *cert. denied*, 449 U.S. 941 (1980), the Second Circuit similarly held that when a proposed tender offer fails to become effective, shareholders of the target company cannot state a cause of action for alleged misstatements under § 14(e) because of the absence of this crucial element of reliance. *Id*. at 195-96.

It is difficult indeed to imagine a case more directly to the point here than the *Lewis* decision. In that case the American Express Company proposed a "friendly business combination" with McGraw-Hill. McGraw-Hill's directors rejected the offer in a public letter as reckless, illegal, and improper. American Express then filed a proposed tender offer with the SEC, revealing its intention to make a second offer for the McGraw-Hill stock. The offer would not become effective unless McGraw-Hill agreed not to oppose it. McGraw-Hill's directors rejected the second offer, however, which therefore expired before becoming effective. McGraw-Hill shareholders sued for damages under § 14(e) of the Williams Act. In affirming the district court's dismissal for failure to state a cause of action, the court noted that "[i]n the instant case, the target's shareholders simply could not have relied upon McGraw-Hill's statements, whether true or false, since they were never given an opportunity to tender their shares." *Id*. at 195. The plaintiffs here seek to distinguish *Lewis* on its "unique facts." The two cases, however, are the same in all material aspects: both involve shareholders' allegations that incumbent management and directors prevented the plaintiffs from accepting a tender offer by issuing false and misleading statements or by breaching the fiduciary duties owed to the shareholders. In both cases the requisite element of reliance is absent.

The plaintiffs seek to establish that reliance is presumed from materiality in a case involving primarily a failure to disclose, relying on a line of cases culminating in Affiliated Ute Citizens v. United States, 406 U.S. 128, 153-54 (1972). As the court pointed out, however, in *Lewis*, neither Mills v. Electric Auto-Lite Co., 396 U.S. 375 (1970), nor *Affiliated Ute* abolished the reliance requirement, but "[r]ather . . . held that in cases in which reliance is possible, and even likely, but is unduly burdensome to prove, the resulting doubt would be resolved in favor of the class the statute was designed to protect." *Lewis* at 195.

The *Mills-Ute* presumption is essentially a rule of judicial economy and convenience, designed to avoid the impracticality of requiring that each plaintiff shareholder testify concerning the reliance element. However, when the logical basis on which the presumption rests is absent, it would be highly inappropriate to apply the *Mills-Ute* presumption. "[W]here no reliance [is] possible under any imaginable set of facts, such a presumption would be illogical in the extreme." *Lewis* at 195.

The plaintiffs here pose two additional arguments to application of the *Lewis* holding; first, that it allows a target company management to profit by their own wrong if they are successful in driving off a tender offeror with misrepresentations or omissions otherwise violative of the Act.

Courts seeking to construe the provisions of the Williams Act have also noted that its protections are required by the peculiar nature of a tender offer, which forces a shareholder to decide whether to dispose of his shares at some premium over the market, or retain them with knowledge that the offeror may alter the management of the target company to its detriment. See Piper v. Chris-Craft Industries, 430 U.S. at 35.

In another context, courts seeking to determine whether unconventional means of acquisition of controlling blocks of shares constitute a "tender offer" within the meaning of the Williams Act (which leaves the term undefined) have determined that the distinguishing characteristic of the activity the Williams Act seeks to regulate is the exertion of pressure on the shareholders to make a hasty, ill-considered decision to sell their shares. See, e.g., Wellman v. Dickinson, 475 F.Supp. 783 (S.D.N.Y.1979) (intensive private solicitation plus premium plus strict time constraints on acceptance created tender offer); S-G Securities, Inc. v. Fuqua Investment Co., 466 F.Supp. 1114 (D.Mass.1978) (widespread publicity campaign plus massive open market purchases created tender offer pressures). Here there was no deadline by which shareholders were forced to tender, and by hypothesis when we are discussing market transactions, no premium over the market. Therefore Field's shareholders were simply not subjected to the proscribed pressures the Williams Act was designed to alleviate. See

Kennecott Copper Corp. v. Curtiss-Wright Corp., 584 F.2d 1195, 1207 (2d Cir.1978) (solicitations to sell on national exchange where shareholders were offered no premium over the market and given no deadline by which to make their decision created "no pressure . . . on sellers other than the normal pressure of the marketplace," although the purchaser sought to obtain and exercise control of the company). . . .

We hold that § 14(e) of the Williams Act does not give a damages remedy for alleged misrepresentations or omissions of material fact when the proposed tender offer never becomes effective. The brief filed by the SEC as *amicus curiae* contends that failure to afford investors a damages remedy under § 14(e) in situations where a tender offer proposal is withdrawn before it becomes effective might lead to abuses. It poses the hypothetical situation "where a person announces a proposed tender offer that he never intends to make in order to dispose of securities of the subject company at artificially inflated prices. . . ." We note that such conduct would fall within the ambit of the prohibitions of Rule 10b-5. . . .

The SEC also suggests that without such a remedy, persons could announce tender offers, again without intending to make them, to put pressure on management to consider merger proposals. Although the present case does not present such a situation, we believe that preliminary injunctive relief would be the appropriate remedy for such conduct. . . . The rule urged by the SEC would only serve to intensify the pressure such spurious offers would exert on incumbent management, by confronting them with the spectre of shareholder damage suits which could result from the withdrawal of even a sham tender offer. . . .

CUDAHY, Circuit Judge (concurring in part and dissenting in part). . . . I disagree with the majority's view that misleading and deceptive representations about an offeror's proposal are immunized from the proscriptions of § 14(e) if the offer is withdrawn before the shareholders have an opportunity to tender. . . . The type of rule which the majority advocates is simply an invitation to incumbent management to make whatever claims and assertions may be expedient to force withdrawal of an offer. Management could speak without restraint knowing that once withdrawal is forced there is no Securities Act liability for deception practiced before withdrawal took place. Such a rule provides a major loophole for escaping the provisions of § 14(e) and obviously frustrates the remedial purpose of the Act. . . . The management of a company subject to a tender offer proposal is in a unique position to take steps and make representations that may have a significant impact on the likelihood that the proposal will be frustrated. For example, in the instant case, Field's undertook a hasty acquisition program which may have made Field's significantly less attractive and contributed to the withdrawal of the proposal. Admittedly, this was a course of action rather than primarily a course of representation -- but the effect of the latter could be the same.

Compelled by the logic of its position that § 14(e) provides no protection with respect to offers which are withdrawn before stockholders have an opportunity to tender, the majority also concludes that § 14(e) does not apply to decisions not to sell into markets which are rising on news of a tender offer announcement. But in [Berman v. Gerber Products Co., 454 F.Supp. 1310 (W.D.Mich.1978)] the court said that claims based on the interim market price of stock were actionable even where a proposed tender offer is withdrawn without becoming effective:

> The requisite causation does exist, however, to the extent that [shareholders] were misled into retaining their holdings when they could have sold them on the market at a higher price. The legislative history of the Williams Act indicates that the legislation was intended to reach such transactions as well as those involving the actual tender of a stockholder's shares. . . . If [the board of directors] misrepresented or omitted material facts in connection with their opposition to the [tender offer] proposal so that [the shareholders] were induced to retain their shares in reliance upon the integrity and good judgment of the board of directors, but had they known the truth they would have sold their stock in the rising market, a direct causative link exists between [the board of directors'] acts and [the shareholders'] investment decision.

Berman, 454 F.Supp. at 1325.

The majority places heavy reliance on Lewis v. McGraw, 619 F.2d 192 (2d Cir.) (per curiam), *cert. denied*, 449 U.S. 941 (1980), where the Court of Appeals for the Second Circuit dismissed the stockholders' § 14(e) claim for failure to establish reliance or causation. There a tender offer, conditioned on the approval of target management, never became effective because the board of the target corporation rejected the proposal. The district court in *Lewis* concluded that the complaint sufficiently alleged deception "in connection with the tender offer" because "the prospective offeror [had] made a public announcement of a proposed tender offer and [plaintiff had alleged] a clear and definite intent to make a tender offer." Lewis v. McGraw, [1979-1980 Transfer Binder] Fed.Sec.L.Rep. (CCH) ¶ 97,195, 96,568 (S.D.N.Y.1979). Although the complaint was dismissed for failure to allege causation and reliance, the district court emphasized that "it would be inconsistent with the purpose of § 14(e) to preclude an action for damages relating to pre-tender offer violations in cases where no tender offer was in fact made. Such [a rule] would have the effect of providing a safe harbor for target companies who were successful in their use of misstatements or deception to discourage the making of tender offers." *Id.* at 96,568. I find the district court's mode of analysis reflective of the economic realities of the situation and consistent with the thrust of prior case law. See Berman v. Gerber Products Co., *supra*; Applied Digital Data Systems, Inc. v. Milgo Electronic Corp., 425 F.Supp. 1145

(S.D.N.Y.1977).[34] If, therefore, *Lewis* is to be construed as the majority would have it here, I am quite unpersuaded by what would seem to be the Second Circuit's unexplained and summary departure from a well-established line of analysis.

. . . From the perspective of a public shareholder, once announcement of a tender offer proposal is made, it matters little whether fraud occurs before or after shareholders are given the opportunity to tender to the bidder, or whether they are ever given that opportunity. A shareholder, who, in the face of a proposed tender offer elects not to sell into the market in reliance on management's misleading statements, is in a position similar to that of a shareholder who elects not to tender to the bidder in reliance upon such statements. Congress clearly protected the latter, as well as, I believe, the former. . . .

As Judge Cudahy's dissent stresses, the majority opinion in *Panter* conflates two quite different issues. First, a tender offer may have been aborted so early that the misconduct complained of was not "in connection with any tender offer." Here the issue is jurisdictional; regardless of what plaintiffs prove about the materiality of any misrepresentation or their reliance upon it, § 14(e) simply does not apply. Second, even if the temporal jurisdiction requirement of § 14(e) is met, plaintiffs may not have proven that the misrepresentations by the target company caused their damage. Here the issue is factual; the plaintiffs have the opportunity to offer proof on the issue of causation.

With respect to the jurisdictional issue, the District Court's formulation in Lewis v. McGraw that Judge Cudahy relied upon seems clearly correct. To exclude from the scope of § 14(e) misrepresentations made after a tender offer's announcement, but before its effectiveness, would provide antifraud immunity for misrepresentations that are serious enough -- and made early enough -- to cause the offer's withdrawal. The *Panter* majority responds to a similar argument by suggesting that an action under Rule 10b-5 might still be available. Would a Rule 10b-5 action be available when the misrepresentation prevented the target shareholders from selling their shares? What transaction would satisfy the *Blue Chip* purchase or sale requirement?

Does the majority opinion really hold that Field's misrepresentations were not in connection with a tender offer? In its *amicus* brief in *Panter* the Securities and Exchange Commission expressed its fear that a narrow construction of § 14(e)'s temporal jurisdiction would allow acquirers to pressure target companies into friendly transactions by announcing tender

---

[34] "When . . . a public announcement of a proposed offer has been made, the very dangers that the Act was intended to guard against come into play, and the application of section . . . 14(e) is thus appropriate." *Applied Digital*, 425 F.Supp. at 1155 (footnote omitted).

offers that they never intended to pursue. The majority responded to this fear by suggesting that preliminary injunctive relief, although not damages, would be available in that situation. But the availability of any relief under § 14(e) requires that the claim be within the statute's jurisdiction. Perhaps the court did not mean to rest its decision on the jurisdictional ground at all.

In any event, the jurisdictional issue effectively may have been resolved by the Commission's 1979 adoption of the automatic commencement trigger in Rule 14d-2(b). Can misrepresentations made after the offeror publicly announces the identity of the target company, the securities sought and the price to be paid, and thereby triggers the commencement of a tender offer, not be "in connection with" a tender offer?

That leaves the issue of causation. Plaintiffs made two claims: That the withdrawal of the tender offer prevented them from receiving the offered premium; and that Field's misrepresentations deceived plaintiffs into not selling their shares in the market when the market price of Field's stock still reflected the pendency of the CHH offer. The court resolved the first claim against plaintiffs on the absence of a showing of reliance. Plaintiffs could not show that they relied upon Field's misrepresentations because they never had the opportunity to rely on the misrepresentations; the offer was withdrawn before the plaintiffs could act at all. Does this analysis misunderstand the function of the reliance requirement? Is the real issue causation -- whether the misrepresentation caused plaintiffs' injury? Where the injury requires that the plaintiffs take some affirmative action, as will always be the case in a Rule 10b-5 action because of the *Blue Chip* purchase or sale requirement, the reliance requirement causally links the defendant's misrepresentations to the plaintiffs' actions -- in a Rule 10b-5 case the purchase or sale of the security -- that caused the damage. In the case of an aborted tender offer, however, the damage is inflicted by the withdrawal of the offer without any action by plaintiffs. There is simply no causal link that reliance by plaintiffs must provide.[100]

That does not mean that the issue of cause is without difficulty. The critical causal issue is whether defendant's misrepresentations caused the tender offer to be withdrawn: Did the *offeror* rely on the misrepresentations? To be sure, the court notes that it was Field's defensive actions, not its misrepresentations, that caused CCH to withdraw the tender offer, and that this form of misconduct is not covered by § 14(e). But that just indicates that plaintiffs did not prove their case. Suppose that in Lewis v. McGraw plaintiffs could prove that American Express withdrew its tender offer for McGraw-Hill because McGraw-Hill falsely represented that all of its editorial

---

[100] See Loewenstein (1983), *supra* note 89, at 1343. In the case of a suit by a non-tendering shareholder in connection with a successful offer, the fact that other shareholders relied upon the misrepresentation in tendering was sufficient to provide the necessary causal connection between the bidder's misrepresentation and the plaintiff's injury, even though the plaintiff did not rely. See Plaine v. McCabe, 797 F.2d 713 (9th Cir.1986).

employees would quit if the offer were successful.   Why is plaintiffs' inaction relevant to the issue of causation?

The court's treatment of the reliance issue in connection with plaintiffs' claim that Field's misrepresentations dissuaded them from selling their shares into the market prior to the offer's withdrawal is even more puzzling. Here there is no question that plaintiffs relied on the misrepresentations. At best the court's argument seems to be that such reliance was inadequate as a matter of law because it was not "in connection with any tender offer." Referring to the statutory language, the court states "[t]he language is not unambiguous, but it does seem to contemplate the existence of an offer capable of acceptance by the shareholders." Is this argument plausible after the adoption of Rule 14d-2(b)?

3.   Is Scienter Required Under § 14(e)?

In Ernst & Ernst v. Hochfelder, 425 U.S. 185 (1976), the Supreme Court held that Rule 10b-5 requires proof of scienter. Consistent with the lower courts' pattern of incorporating Rule 10b-5 concepts directly into the jurisprudence of § 14(e), scienter quickly was treated as a necessary element of a § 14(e) cause of action.[101]   Rule 10b-5, however, is not the only possible analogy. Rule 14a-9 prohibits proxy statements "which are false or misleading with respect to any material fact, or which omits to state any material fact necessary in order to make the statements therein not false or misleading. . . ." In Gerstle v. Gamble-Skogmo, Inc.,[102] Judge Friendly held that scienter was not required under Rule 14a-9. Moreover, that the language of § 14(e) so closely tracks that of § 17 of the Securities Act of 1933, which does not require scienter, suggests that negligent misrepresentations or omissions would be sufficient for § 14(e).[103]   The issue seems to have been resolved in favor of requiring scienter.[104]   The resulting difference in standards between § 14(e) and Rule 14a-9 is particularly puzzling since both have a common transactional focus -- a contest for control. Indeed, the two forms of transactions -- tender offers and proxy fights -- are alternative means of achieving the same goal. Should the standard of liability for misstatements depend on the form in which the transaction is cast?

---

[101] E.g., Bell v. Cameron Land Co., 669 F.2d 1278 (9th Cir.1982); see Edward Aranow, Herbert Einhorn & George Bernstein, *Developments in Tender Offers for Corporate Control* 118-22 (1977).

[102] 478 F.2d 1281 (2d Cir.1973).

[103] For the argument that § 14(e) should be construed similarly to Rule 14a-9, see Lowenstein (1983), *supra* note 89.

[104] See Connecticut Nat'l Bank v. Fluor Corp., 808 F.2d 957 (2nd Cir.1987).

CHAPTER 19: CORPORATE LAW CONCERNS IN FRIENDLY ACQUISITIONS

Despite the sharp increase in the number of hostile takeovers since 1975,[1] most acquisitions are friendly. However, the emergence of hostile bids did change the character of friendly transactions. Planning for a friendly transaction had been a cooperative effort by the acquiring and target companies whose primary goal was shaping the transaction's form to secure the desired corporate law consequences[2] and to minimize future claims on the revenues of the combined entity by taxing authorities,[3] labor unions and future creditors.[4] Planners could ignore the prospect of a competing bid because the major investment banking firms were reluctant to represent a hostile bidder, and few potential competitors had ready enough access to sufficient capital that a bid could be marshalled in time to challenge an ongoing friendly transaction.

By the 1980s, the acquisition environment had changed radically. In response to the increased frequency of hostile bids, a sophisticated transactional infrastructure developed that supported competitive bidding. New types of bidders such as leveraged buyout associations emerged.[5] Investment bankers no longer resisted participating in hostile offers. Rather, the announcement of a friendly acquisition would trigger an aggressive search by investment banks not otherwise involved in the transaction for a client willing to make a competitive bid. Most important, a world wide market for high yield debt evolved to finance competitive bids. Legal and financial documents became routinized, transactional structure took on familiar patterns, and large amounts of capital stood at the ready. Thus, lack of time or a supporting infrastructure no longer protected a friendly transaction from unwanted competition. By 1989 frictions in the market for corporate control had been so reduced that the leveraged buyout firm of Kohlberg, Kravis & Roberts needed only four days to respond to a management led group's announcement of a $15 billion dollar bid for RJR Nabisco, with a $20 billion competing bid.[6]

The central planning problem in a friendly acquisition thus became whether the acquiring and target companies can cooperate to protect the transaction from competition. The problem arises in two different situations.

---

[1] See Chapter 1C, *supra*.

[2] See Chapter 16, *supra*.

[3] See Chapter 12, *supra*.

[4] See Chapter 26, *supra*. Where the friendly acquisition took the form of a tender offer, planners also had to consider the need to eliminate non-tendering target shareholders in a second-step freeze out merger. This subject is taken up in Chapter 22, *infra*.

[5] See Chapter 11, *supra*.

[6] See In re RJR Nabisco, Inc. Shareholders Litigation, 1989 WL 7036 (Del.Ch. 1989). For a colorful account of the transactional infrastructure supporting hostile bids in general and the RJR Nabisco transaction in particular, see Bryan Burrough & John Helyar, *Barbarians at the Gate: The Fall of RJR Nabisco* (1990).

The first is a strategic transaction -- a negotiated acquisition that is friendly from the outset, undertaken without outside pressure and where target management's goal is the company's acquisition by the particular acquirer. In this situation, the acquiring company may want assurances that the transaction will succeed before beginning. In turn, the target company may have decided to go forward only with the particular acquirer, not simply to sell the company to the highest bidder. Can planners discourage a competing bid from being made at all? The second situation arises in response to an initial hostile bid that target management opposes. Can the target company and an alternative preferred suitor -- called a *white knight* -- cooperate to protect their responsive transaction against further competition from the original hostile bidder or anyone else?

This chapter takes up the corporate law concerns arising in friendly transactions. Section A surveys the variety of techniques that can be used to favor a particular bidder or protect a friendly transaction from competitive bids. Section B then turns to the legal standards governing friendly acquisitions: what standards apply to target management actions to protect a favored transaction against competitors. Section C then surveys what we know about how a target management seeking to secure the best price for its shareholders should go about selling the company.

A.   Acquisition Techniques in Friendly Transactions

James Freund & Richard Easton
THE THREE-PIECE SUITOR: AN ALTERNATIVE APPROACH
NEGOTIATED CORPORATE ACQUISITIONS
34 Bus.Law. 1679, 1680-95 (1979)[*]

Aardvark Corp., a public company looking to be acquired, has a number of potential suitors. Your large corporate client is one of them. You are concerned, however, that the public announcement of an agreement in principle on a merger will signal one or more other interested companies to make a competing bid during the lengthy period prior to the time the deal closes. You are also conscious of the risk that the market price of Aardvark stock will run up toward the proposed premium while negotiations for the agreement in principle are underway. Aardvark's two principal stockholders own 55 [percent] of its outstanding stock.

[This situation] represents [an] instance where a fresh approach to negotiated corporate acquisitions had been successfully utilized -- [an] instance in which, had the conventional format been followed, the acquiring company might have lost out on the deal or wound up paying a higher price.

The new approach, which might be termed the multistep acquisition (and its architect, the three-piece suitor), begins with a cash private purchase (generally from an insider) of a substantial block of the target's stock; is followed by a cash tender offer to public stockholders at the same price; and concludes with a cash merger of the target and a subsidiary of the acquiring company at the same price. When the dust clears, the acquiring company owns 100 [percent] of the target. In recent years, more and more deals involving public target companies are being done this way. The purpose of this article is to analyze this important and relatively new acquisition technique.

I. THE EMERGENCE OF THE MULTISTEP ACQUISITION

The Business Framework

In order to understand the increasing popularity of the multistep acquisition, some brief business background is in order. In the old black-and-white days, there used to exist a real dichotomy between negotiated (or "friendly") acquisitions on the one hand, and hostile takeovers on the other. In recent years, however, this dichotomy has evolved into more of a continuum, with the absolutely friendly deal (lacking even covert pressures) at one end of the spectrum; the absolutely unfriendly takeover (with no lines of communication open between the parties) at the other; and most deals falling somewhere between the poles, not uncommonly possessing characteristics of each.

So, for example, a vulnerable target, lacking confidence in its ability to thwart a potential acquirer's hostile approach, may turn from discouraging the acquirer to negotiating a higher price for an uncontested deal -- or may seek a more tranquil haven with a willing third party. A tart rebuff to the relatively friendly approach of an unwanted suitor may lead to hostile maneuverings down the road. . . .

Just as the *substance* of acquisitions may vacillate on the friendly-unfriendly scale, we are also witnessing the use of *methodologies* formerly associated with unfriendly deals to accomplish friendly ones. In the hostile situation, where the target's management and board spurn an approach, the acquirer is forced to go over their heads to deal directly with the target's stockholders by way of a tender offer -- in effect, to tempt them (with a substantial premium) to overrule management. But, with the growing respectability of unfriendly acquisitions . . . the tender offer, having proved its effectiveness as a potent tool in accomplishing hostile takeovers, is now an accepted technique for use in friendly acquisitions, with little trace of the opprobrium formerly attending its deployment. Put another way, even in a transaction where matters can be dealt with at the corporate level -- with the target's management and board fully involved and supportive -- acquisition strategists are handling the initial stages at the stockholder level. . . .

But the real impetus to the multistep acquisition has been the recognition that we are in the midst of an era of intense competition for desirable acquisition candidates -- where auctions and bidding contests are very much the "in" thing.   Just as third parties invade hostile takeover territory -- either invited in by the beleaguered target or simply attracted by the noise of the scuffle -- uninvited acquirers are likely to barge in on friendly situations.

Observe, e.g., Upforgrabs Inc. and Synergy Ltd., which have just agreed in principle that Synergy will acquire Upforgrabs.   They announce their intentions. Pickemoff Corp., which has long had its eye on Upforgrabs (or whose interest is piqued by the announcement) decides to come in with a better offer than the one Synergy has made.   Even if Pickemoff's intrusion is not warmly received, it must be dealt with by the Upforgrabs board.   And Upforgrab's stockholders, whose concern may be less with management's feeling comfy in a new home than with the amount of money being paid for their shares, are likely to react favorably to the higher price.   Synergy either has to quit or to fight (which presumably will entail upping its bid) -- in the one case, losing the Upforgrabs deal;   in the other, making it on less favorable terms.

So this is the context in which the multistep transaction has emerged as a highly practical alternative to the conventional one-step merger transaction for negotiated acquisitions of public companies -- utilizing various tools of the acquisition trade formerly considered appropriate only in hostile or overreaching situations.

Synopsis of the Three Stages

[T]he "classic" multistep acquisition is accomplished in three consecutive stages, as follows:

1. The Block Purchase

The first step is a negotiated private purchase by the acquiring company (the "purchaser" or the "bidder"), usually for cash, of a substantial block of stock of the company being acquired (the "target") from a controlling stockholder or group if one exists, or from a large but noncontrolling holder (often institutional).   The purchase agreement is generally quite short and simple.[19]   Optimally, the parties provide for a simultaneous signing and closing;   if delay is required,[20] it should be minimal with no substantial

---

[19] An exception to this occurs where an employment contract is simultaneously negotiated.
. . .

[20] In addition to any delay required in order to obtain necessary regulatory approvals, it may be necessary to defer the closing (or at least the closing of the purchase of a portion of the shares) in order to comply with the notification and waiting period requirements of the Hart-Scott-Rodino Antitrust Improvements Act of 1976, § 7A of the Clayton Act, 15 U.S.C.

conditions to closing -- just the passage of time. The principal collateral obligation contained in the agreement is the purchaser's undertaking to use its best efforts to make a cash offer to all other stockholders of the target, for any and all shares tendered, at the same price the blockholder is receiving. Upon signing of the agreement, a press release is issued -- the first notice of the deal -- announcing that the bidder has acquired (or, if the closing is not simultaneous, has signed a binding agreement to acquire) the block and has undertaken to make a tender offer on comparable terms to all other stockholders in the very near future.

2. The Tender Offer

The second step is the "friendly" tender offer itself, directed to all the stockholders of the target, for any and all of their shares, at the same price as was paid for the block. This should commence as soon as practicable after the signing and/or closing of the block purchase, subject to any delays required in order to obtain any necessary regulatory approvals. . . . Ideally, the target's board of directors should recommend acceptance of the offer to stockholders -- or at least not oppose it and cooperate in its implementation (e.g., by furnishing a list of stockholders to facilitate mailing of the offer).

3. The Cash Merger

The third step is a merger transaction between the target and the bidder (or, more commonly, between the target and a subsidiary of the bidder), as a result of which the bidder ends up owning 100 [percent] of the target. In this transaction, once the requisite stockholder vote is cast (with the presumption being that the bidder has acquired sufficient shares through the block purchase and tender to approve the merger), the target's remaining stockholders are involuntarily eliminated. In exchange for their shares, they receive a cash payment, which is generally equal to that received by the blockholder and tendering stockholders. In almost all cases, they have appraisal rights. Depending on the percentage of outstanding target shares owned by the bidder upon completion of the tender offer, a so-called short-form merger under applicable state corporate law may be utilized;[26] if not, regular statutory merger procedures apply, but with little suspense over the ultimate vote. . . .

---

§ 18a [hereinafter referred to as the "HSR Act"].

[26] A short-form merger is a merger between a parent corporation and its subsidiary which does not require a vote of the subsidiary's minority stockholders where the parent owns at least a specified percentage (usually 90%) of the subsidiary's stock. Not all states permit short-form mergers.

II. COMPARISON OF MULTISTEP ACQUISITION AND TRADITIONAL SINGLE-STEP MERGER

Review of Traditional Merger Phases

The variance in acquisition procedure and relative advantages and disadvantages of the three-piece suitor can best be examined if we turn for a moment to review the scenario for a traditional single-step merger.

The courtship begins with a period of preliminary negotiations between the parties -- feeling each other out, trying to decide whether they can live together -- with the principal emphasis on arriving at a mutually satisfactory price. If a meeting of the minds occurs, the parties are said to have reached an "agreement in principle" on the transaction. This might be oral, or it can be reduced to writing in a "letter of intent" or memorandum of understanding. This document reiterates the parties' mutual intent to merge at a stated (or formula) price, which is made expressly subject to the negotiation and execution of a definitive acquisition agreement, the approval of their respective boards of directors and at least the target's stockholders, and the obtaining of needed consents from major creditors and perhaps regulatory authorities. In other words, pending the signing and approval of the definitive agreement, the agreement in principle has no binding effect.

Nevertheless -- and this is true whether it is written or oral -- the agreement in principle is considered sufficient evidence of the parties' seriousness toward the transaction that a press release is invariably issued at this point, describing the basic terms of the deal.[41] As a result, the world is put on notice that the target is up for sale at a time when the parties are *not* contractually obligated to each other. There is nothing to stop any other company interested in acquiring the target from entering the fray.[42] Contrast this with the three-piece suitor's first public announcement, stating that it has *already* purchased (or at least entered into a firm agreement to purchase) the key block and that it is about to commence a tender offer for the balance of the target's shares.

The period following agreement in principle in a conventional acquisition is one of three-fold activity: intense investigation of the target's affairs by the purchaser;[43] negotiation of the definitive merger agreement, with preparation of detailed schedules and lists concerning the target's structure and business; and preparation of a full-blown proxy statement containing detailed prospectus-style information about the deal, the target,

---

[41] With respect to the legal obligation to make an announcement at this point, cf. SEC v. Geon Industries, Inc., 531 F.2d 39 (2d Cir.1976); NYSE Company Manual § A-2 at A-18; ASE Manual § 402 at 101; (2d Cir.1976) [sic]; SEC Securities Act Release No. 5092 (Oct. 15, 1970).

[42] This is true even where a definitive merger agreement has been signed. . . .

[43] This is less likely to be *vice versa* if the deal is for cash; but if securities of the purchaser are to be issued, then the target has to investigate the purchaser also.

and perhaps (if the purchaser will be issuing its securities) the purchaser, with full financial information including pro-forma statements. All this can easily take more than a month to complete. During the comparable period, a three-piece suitor is holding (or at least getting started on) its tender offer for any and all of the target's remaining shares. By the time the parties are ready to sign a binding agreement in a traditional acquisition, the three-piece suitor may well own a substantial majority of the target's shares -- without any worries over preparing and clearing a detailed proxy statement at this stage.

Let's assume that all the information has been gathered and analyzed to everyone's satisfaction, the companies' respective boards of directors have met and approved the final form of the traditional merger agreement, and it is then signed by their designated officers. The agreement will invariably provide for a deferred closing, because prior to the deal being consummated some events have to occur which cannot even get underway until the agreement is signed -- most notably, the proxy solicitation of the target's stockholders. Moreover, a number of other conditions have to be satisfied in order for the parties to be obligated to close; put another way, even with careful drafting, each party may have several "escape valves" were it to consider wriggling out of the agreement.

If the target is an attractive one, "grey knights" -- dripping with cash or proffering attractive securities -- can be expected to enter the picture. The obligations of the target's board of directors in the event a better offer materializes after an agreement of merger has been signed is the subject of some controversy[44] and a cautious target may want to provide specifically in the merger agreement that its board is free to accept -- if not to solicit -- a better offer.[45]

Even where the merger agreement itself contains no usable "out", the target's board is going to have to consider any higher third party proposals seriously -- and would be hard-pressed to recommend the purchaser's lesser offer. And, as a practical matter, since approval by the target's stockholders is always requisite, and since they can't be expected to vote for the negotiated deal if a better competing offer materializes, the existence of a signed contract by no means assures the purchaser of ultimate success. Even if the third party were spurned by the target, it could go over the heads of the target's board directly to the stockholders -- attempting to buy enough shares through a tender offer to defeat the merger. The chances are pretty

---

[44] See generally David Ward, *The Legal Effect of Merger and Asset Sale Agreements Before Shareholder Approval,* 18 Case W.Res.L.Rev. 780 (1967).

[45] See, e.g., Agreement and Plan of Reorganization among Johns-Manville Corporation, JM Capital Corporation and Olinkraft, Inc., attached to Joint Proxy Statement of Johns-Manville Corporation and Olinkraft, Inc., dated Dec. 1, 1978, containing one version of the so-called "law firm out" -- which provides that the target's board of directors will not approve or recommend to stockholders any business combination or similar transaction with a company other than the bidder unless in the opinion of the target's counsel the directors' fiduciary duties require them to do so. . . .

good that, if the purchaser wants to preserve its deal, it will have to jack up the price to meet the competition. In contrast, by the time a three-piece suitor gets around to signing a merger agreement, it already owns sufficient shares to approve the transaction -- and more than enough shares to discourage outside intervention by third party predators.

Once the traditional merger agreement has been signed, the proxy statement is filed with the SEC.[49] Processing by the staff can easily take a month before final clearance, at which time the material is mailed to stockholders with a solicitation period of another month before the meeting takes place.[50] Once the meeting has been held and the deal approved, it can close immediately -- provided that all other conditions have been satisfied; and some, such as the receipt of tax rulings from the Internal Revenue Service, can take quite a while to come through.

If you add up the time -- a month here, a month there -- at best it will take three or four months from the time the deal is first announced until closing. In today's environment, that's a long time for the purchaser to own nothing except some tenuous contractual rights.

Advantages of the Multistep Technique

As must be obvious by now, the principal advantage of the multistep approach is to lessen the likelihood of a competing bid -- to more effectively freeze out the competition. . . . In a multistep transaction, at the point when the world discovers what's up, the bidder already owns, or has locked up, a substantial chunk of the target's stock, and is about to launch its tender offer. Possession may not be nine-tenths of the law, but it is clear that any potential competitor is *not* starting from a point of equality -- as it would be had the purchaser and target merely initialed a letter of intent, lacking contractual obligations, and with their mutual willingness to go forward subject to a variety of specified conditions.

---

[49] Actually, there's no reason why the proxy materials cannot be filed prior to the time the agreement is executed, if the parties want to expedite the transaction. However, since much of the disclosure contained in the proxy statement consists of a description of the terms of the merger, it is advisable to wait before filing until a fully negotiated (albeit unsigned) agreement is produced.

[50] Most states require that notice of a meeting generally be given at least ten but not more than 50 or 60 days prior to the meeting. See, e.g., Del.Gen.Corp.Law § 222 (not less than ten nor more than 60 days); N.Y.Bus.Corp.Law § 605 (not less than ten nor more than 50 days). Some states have specific notice provisions applicable to mergers. See, e.g., Del.Gen.Corp.Law § 251(c) (at least 20 days' advance notice). Although the rules of the New York Stock Exchange do not specify a minimum advance notice requirement, the Exchange recommends that a minimum of 30 days be allowed between the record date and the meeting date. See NYSE Company Manual § A-8 at A-132. The rules of the American Stock Exchange require that at least ten days' written notice be given in advance of all stockholders' meetings, and the Exchange recommends that at least 20 days' advance notice be given. See ASE Company Guide § 703 at 181.

Thus, in the first situation [noted at the outset of this article], since the announcement identified the bidder as now owning 55 [percent] of Aardvark Corp., no competition was allowed to develop -- although there were later indications that, had the deal proceeded in traditional fashion, there may have been a competing bid at a higher price.

Second, the multistep method helps assure the bidder of success in consummating the deal. In a conventional merger, where either a majority or two-thirds vote of the target's outstanding shares is usually required to approve the transaction, the purchaser cannot be certain of achieving the requisite vote; after all, the purchaser itself is not voting, since it does not own any of the target's shares. The three-piece suitor, on the other hand, is likely to end up -- through the block purchase and a successful tender offer -- with the requisite stock ownership to authorize the final-step merger single-handedly, thereby lessening the risk that the deal will abort.

A third advantage of the multistep transaction relates to the stock market's significant role in acquisitions. It's quite typical today, no matter what form the deal takes, for bidders to pay significant premiums over the current market value of the target's stock. Where extended negotiations between the companies occur prior to an announcement -- neither side wanting to make premature disclosure before reaching an agreement in principle[54] -- rumors of an impending deal almost inevitably leak out. The rumors propel the stock price upward toward the bidder's anticipated premium. When the announcement finally comes, the merger price makes less of a splash than it would have prior to the market run-up.

Assume that the target's stock has been selling for around $10. The purchaser proposes to offer $15. Rumors inflate the market price to $12.50. Instead of a 50 [percent] premium, the spread is only 20 [percent] when the announcement is finally made. Stockholders, who have notoriously short memories, forget that the stock was selling at $10 only a few short days ago; the purchaser gets no credit for the run-up. The smaller premium makes it more likely that the target's board will become huffy about price (even to the point of trying to retrade the deal), more likely that other bidders will step up to the plate and, assuming the transaction is submitted to stockholders, less certain that they will vote in favor of the deal. More than once, this kind of involuntary market action has caused a purchaser to increase its initial price, in order to preserve the premium at a respectable level. So, one of the real advantages of the multistep transaction is the reduced chances of a leak, since the target itself may not be directly involved in the early stages. With a little luck, the target's stock will still be selling at $10 when the

---

[54] The New York Stock Exchange has expressed the view that once the negotiations have broadened in scope to include persons other than top management, and the risk of a leak or the misuse of inside information necessarily becomes greater, an announcement of the existence of negotiations should be made. See NYSE Company Manual § A-2 at A-19. . .

announcement is made, and the bidder (and, indirectly, the target's management and board) will get credit for the entire five-point premium.

A fourth advantage of the multistep deal -- which is perhaps more psychological than substantive, but definitely not to be discounted -- is the sense of moving a lot faster than in traditional terms. With a conventional merger, nothing really definitive happens (such as shares or money actually changing hands) until three or four months pass. Contrast the three-piece suitor, who on the *first day* owns a substantial block of the target; a month or so later, it owns at least a majority (and maybe much more) with its first purchases under the tender offer. Corporate executives react favorably to the speed with which a multistep deal is implemented. Lawyers who suggest this format tend to be looked upon as expediters -- makers of deals rather than authors of complexities. This is particularly true if the businessman has been considering the deal in traditional terms; imagine the reaction when you tell him: "I can get you a controlling interest in the target a lot faster, while minimizing the risks of being outbid or forced to raise the ante."

Disadvantages of the Multistep Technique

Nothing is perfect; there are also disadvantages inherent in multistep deals. For example, at the time the bidder buys the blockholder's stock, it cannot know for sure whether it will be able to successfully complete the balance of the transaction and achieve 100 [percent] ownership. Multistep deals are definitely not for the faint-hearted. If the tender offer is unsuccessful and the initial block is insufficient for working control, the bidder could be left with a substantial investment, purchased at a premium (which the market may not support), and yet not be in control of the target. If the size of the block isn't large enough to preempt a competing bid (and the bidder is not prepared to increase its price), the bidder could lose out to another suitor. (This is not necessarily a disaster, however, since the losing bidder can usually sell its block into the competing tender, presumably at a profit, thereby at least recouping its expenses -- and generally without liability under section 16(b) of the Exchange Act even though the block exceeds 10 [percent] of the outstanding shares.)[58]

---

[58] Section 16(b) provides that any profits realized by, among others, a beneficial owner of more than 10% of a class of an issuer's registered equity securities from any purchase and sale or any sale and purchase of any of the issuer's equity securities within a period of less than six months are recoverable by or on behalf of the issuer. But since there can be no § 16(b) liability unless the person was a greater than 10% beneficial owner *prior* to *both* the purchase and the subsequent sale, there is no § 16(b) liability in respect of the initial purchase which makes the bidder a greater than 10% shareholder. See Foremost-McKesson, Inc. v. Provident Securities Co., 423 U.S. 232 (1976). Even if the purchaser has made additional purchases after becoming a greater than 10% stockholder and then sells its entire holdings within six months of its initial purchases, its liability will be limited to the profit realized on the purchases made after becoming a 10% stockholder. Cf. Reliance Elec. Co. v. Emerson Elec. Co., 404 U.S. 418 (1972).

Perhaps the most significant disadvantage of the three-step transaction is that the bidder has no chance to perform the extensive business and legal review that occurs in a traditional acquisition *before* the purchaser is bound. In the period between agreement in principle and execution of a definitive agreement, the one-step purchaser has its people swarming all over the target, collecting data on a great variety of matters. At the same time, the target is compiling reams of information about itself into formal schedules and lists which are usually attached to the contract and which -- together with other business, financial and legal facts concerning the target -- become the subject of elaborate representations and warranties. In the period between signing and closing the purchaser monitors the accuracy of these representations, which are deemed reiterated at the closing for purposes of a condition to the purchaser's obligation to close. All of this tends to insure that by the time the purchaser actually puts its money or securities on the line, it knows exactly what it's getting into; the risks based on ignorance of the facts are few and far between.

The three-piece suitor, however, is unlikely to have the same opportunities for investigation and verification, for extensive warranties and correlative conditions. As a matter of fact, the bidder would probably prefer not to know too much about the target's business at the time of the tender, since any significant nonpublic information in the bidder's possession (such as the target's favorable financial projections) would have to be disclosed in the bidder's offering materials. So, the bidder usually proceeds on the basis of the target's audited financial statements and other SEC filings, hoping that any shortfall will not be material, and forced into greater reliance on the honesty and candor of the selling blockholder.

Another disadvantage is that the multistep approach does not lend itself so well to noncash transactions -- at least during the first two stages. Although securities could presumably be issued to the blockholder without a registration statement in reliance on section 4(2) of the Securities Act of 1933 or [R]ule 146 thereunder, the blockholder may be unwilling to accept them because of the resale limitations under [R]ule 144. If the second-step offer to the target's stockholders were to consist of the bidder's securities (rather than cash), a registration statement and prospectus would have to be filed and cleared with the SEC prior to commencing the offer, thereby causing considerable delay -- which detracts from the preemptive nature of the multistep approach.

Unless a fixed maximum number of shares is built into the tender offer, exclusive use of cash at the first two stages will normally make it difficult, if not impossible, to structure the final-step merger as a tax-free reorganization -- since the bidder will probably purchase so much of the target's stock for cash that the continuity of interest rules applicable to tax-free reorganizations will not be satisfied. A sizeable use of cash will also preclude accounting for the acquisition as a pooling of interests.

The multistep acquisition is more prone to litigation than a conventional transaction, particularly in connection with the final-step cash merger. In large part this is due to the recent flurry of "going private" cases, and the apparent resemblance of the final stage of the multistep transaction to freezeouts of minority stockholders (the bidder having sufficient votes to force only the target's remaining stockholders).[*]

Note: Expanding the Concept: Lock-ups

Both the problem and the solution identified by Freund & Easton can be generalized. If bidding is costly, a potential acquirer's decision to invest in making a bid depends on the likelihood that the investment will be profitable. Before the advent of competitive bidding, the profitability of a friendly acquisition depended only on the post-transaction performance of the combined entity. Competitive bidding adds a new risk: that the investment in making a bid will be lost because a competitive bid will be successful. The planning problem is then how to encourage a favored acquirer to go forward by reducing that risk. Note that the problem is not simply assuring the favored acquirer that it will win. Rather, the favored acquirer must be assured that its investment in bidding will have a positive net present value even if it loses the competition.

Four types of techniques have been used to protect the favored acquirer's investment.[7] These can be arrayed along a continuum of likely effectiveness.

At the least effective pole of the continuum is a *no shop* agreement by the target company. Such a provision prohibits the target company from seeking competitive bids, or negotiating with or providing non-public information to third parties. A companion obligation commits target management to use its best efforts to secure shareholder approval of the transaction. Both are typically subject to a *fiduciary out* pursuant to which the target's obligations terminate upon receipt of an opinion of counsel that the fiduciary duty of the target board of directors requires it to consider competitive bids.[8] Because in an efficient control market the public announcement of the transaction will serve to alert potential competitors, the real impact of a no shop agreement depends on the importance of non-public information in valuing the company and on the scope of the fiduciary out.[9]

---

[*] These issues are considered in Chapter 22, *infra.* [Ed.]

[7] See generally Stephen Fraidin & Joseph Franco, *Lock-Up Arrangements,* 14 Rev.Sec.Reg. 821 (1981).

[8] The necessity and impact of a fiduciary out depends on the legal standards governing efforts to favor a preferred bidder considered in the remainder of this Chapter.

[9] Where the acquisition is of a smaller company, announcement of the transaction may not attract the attention of investment bankers whose independent solicitation of competitive bids serves to make the control market efficient. In that setting, a no-shop agreement can have a significant impact.

More effective in protecting the favored acquirer's investment in making a bid are target company commitments to reimburse the favored acquirer's expenses, typically expressed as a fixed amount, and to pay a *breakup or termination fee*, if the target is ultimately acquired by a competitive bidder.[10] Both amounts can be quite substantial, reflecting not only out of pocket expenses and the executive time associated with making the bid, but also the opportunity of costs of forgoing other investments.[11]

Still further along the effectiveness continuum is a *stock lockup* -- the sale of newly issued target stock to the favored bidder, or the grant of an option to buy newly issued target stock on the occurrence of the same events that trigger the payment of a termination fee, typically at the same price as the favored acquirer's initial bid. This arrangement directly hedges the risk of the favored acquirer's investment in bidding costs from a competitive bid. When a competitive bidder makes a higher offer, the value of the option increases at the same time as the expected value of the favored acquirer's investment in the transaction decreases. If the competitive bidder ultimately wins the contest, the favored acquirer exercises the option and sells the shares to the competitive bidder, thereby earning a profit on its investment in bidding. Indeed, at some point the value of the option exceeds the expected value of the acquisition to the favored acquirer, and the initial bidder will prefer losing the contest to completing the acquisition.[12]

This technique was used in the acquisition of Marathon Oil Co. by United States Steel ("USS") to induce USS to make a bid competing with an initial hostile bid by Mobil Oil. At the time the USS option was granted, Mobil had offered to acquire 68% of Marathon's common stock for $85 per share in cash, with the remainder to be acquired in a second-step merger where the consideration would be Mobil debentures with a principal amount of $85 per share. The terms of the option gave USS the right to purchase ten million newly issued Marathon shares (approximately 17% of Marathon's outstanding stock) for $90 per share -- the price at which USS made a competing offer. If Mobil subsequently won the contest, the option would have a value equal to ten million times the difference between the winning bid and USS's offer.

Does a stock lockup also influence who wins the bidding contest in addition to hedging the recipient against losing it? The option can be seen as giving USS a substantial "leg up" in a subsequent bidding contest with Mobil. If Mobil increased its bid, it would have to purchase all shares at the increased price. In contrast, if USS increased its bid, it still would be able

---

[10] The termination fee may also be triggered if the transaction is structured to require shareholder approval and target shareholders reject it.

[11] As an extreme example, the termination fee in Paramount Communications, Inc. v. QVC Network, Inc., 637 A.2d 34 (Del.1994), was $100 million. This case is reprinted later in this Chapter.

[12] See Ronald Gilson, *Seeking Competitive Bids Versus Pure Passivity in Tender Offer Defense*, 35 Stan.L.Rev. 51 (1982).

to purchase 17% of Marathon's stock at the lower option price, thereby insuring that it would always pay a lower price than Mobil for the same number of shares. As stated in the court's opinion that considered the validity of the option, its effect was "that every dollar raise in the bid by USS would cost USS $30 million while each such dollar raise would cost Mobil $47 million."[13]

Does the option actually change the likelihood that the bidder that most highly values the target will win? Ian Ayres points out that USS incurs an offsetting cost when it increases its bid -- the foregone profit that it would have received from its option if it had allowed Mobil to win.[14] Thus, USS's reservation price -- the highest amount that USS would be willing to bid for Marathon -- is reduced by each increase in Mobil's bid because the alternative of losing the contest and taking the value of the option rather than the expected profits form the acquisition becomes increasingly more valuable.

Does the analysis change if USS cares about its reputation as an aggressive acquirer? If potential competitive bidders in future USS transactions will be deterred from bidding by USS's aggressive behavior in past transactions, USS may not treat the profits from the option as offsetting the costs of losing. Then the grant of the option can allow USS to bid more than Mobil even if Mobil values Marathon more highly.[15]

Moving even further in the direction of effectiveness is another type of option, a *crown jewels* lockup that covers target company assets instead of target company stock. Suppose you could identify the particular target assets that were critical to a competitive bidder -- its crown jewels in takeover parlance. Giving the favored acquirer an option to purchase those assets exercisable only if the contest is lost to a competitive bid would have a substantial impact on the bidders' conduct. Again, the USS/Marathon transaction illustrates the technique.

In addition to a stock option, USS was also granted an option to purchase for $2.8 billion Marathon's 48% interest in the oil and mineral rights in the Yates Field in West Texas, one of the most productive domestic

---

[13] Marathon Oil Co. v. Mobil Corp., 669 F.2d 366, 375 (11th Cir.1981).

[14] Ian Ayres, *Analyzing Stock Lock-ups: Do Target Treasury Sales Foreclose or Facilitate Takeover Auctions?*, 90 Colum.L.Rev. 682 (1990). See Stephen Fraidin & Jon Hanson, *Toward Unlocking Lockups*, 103 Yale L.J. 1739 (1994).

[15] Fraidin & Hanson (1994), *supra* note 14, argue that the reputation concern will not cause potential bidders to credibly commit to a pro-management position to secure a lockup. *Id.* at 1795-1801. They argue that favoring management would cause the bidder to place a lower value on the target than those free to fire management. At least in one setting, however, their argument is counter-factual. In management buyouts, financial buyers who need target management to run the target after the transaction often outbid competitors of the target who would have displaced target management. See Chapter 11, *supra*. Moreover, in the case of KKR, one of the leading MBO promoters, their pro-management inclination had to have been established by reputation because they would not contractually commit to the terms of the target management's participation until after the price and terms of the target's acquisition were set.

sources of oil ever discovered. The option was exercisable only if USS's offer was unsuccessful and a third party acquired control of Marathon. In the court's terms, the effect of the option was that "a potential competing tender offeror could not acquire Yates Field upon a merger with Marathon."[16] Stressing the importance of the Yates Field, the court pointed out that it had been referred to by Marathon as the company's "crown jewel," and that other companies had indicated that they would have no interest in Marathon in the absence of the Yates Field.

A crown jewels lockup can serve to hedge the favored acquirer's investment in bidding costs if the assets covered are independently attractive to the favored acquirer or if the option price is below market so the assets can be resold at a profit. In this case, however, the principal effect of the lockup may not be to hedge the favored acquirer's bidding costs, but to reduce the value of the target to competing bidders. In this respect, a crown jewel option is less a lockup technique than simply the deployment of the scorched earth defense, considered in Chapter 17, to the end of facilitating a friendly transaction rather than remaining independent. As a result, it has the clear potential of causing the target company to be acquired by other than the highest bidder.

Can a crown jewels lockup be used in situations where the target does not have unique tangible assets? For example, could contingent employment contracts with key employees serve a similar purpose in high technology companies?

B.   Legal Standards Governing Friendly Acquisitions

The change in the transaction environment effected by the emergence of hostile transactions also focused attention on the legal standards governing friendly acquisitions. Like hostile transactions, friendly transactions also pose a conflict of interest for target management. A transaction with a favored acquirer may have been encouraged -- and competing bids discouraged -- not because the transaction provides shareholders the best price, but because it provides target management the best post-contractual arrangements, like favorable employment contracts and increased equity participation. But like defensive tactics in hostile transactions, the impact on target shareholders of efforts to favor a particular bidder in a friendly transaction are difficult to evaluate. These tactics may be invoked in favor of self-interest, but they also may reflect target management's belief that a preferred transaction is best for shareholders and that favoring a bidder is necessary to induce the bid in the first place.

Traditionally, target management behavior in friendly transactions was protected by the business judgment rule. This is reflected in § 6.01 of the

---

[16] 669 F.2d at 367.

American Law Institute's *Principles of Corporate Governance: Analysis and Recommendations*: "The board of directors, in the exercise of its business judgment, may approve, reject, or decline to consider a proposal to the corporation to engage in a transaction in control."[17] From this perspective, shareholders rather than courts are the best monitor of management self-interest in friendly transactions because any friendly transaction requires approval by target shareholders.[18] If a management-favored transaction is too sympathetic to the acquirer (and target management), target shareholders simply will turn it down. However, the problem is whether shareholders can effectively exercise their approval right. The best measure of the value of a transaction is the price offered by competitors. If target management can deter competing bids by the use of lockups, then target shareholders may approve a management-favored transaction not because it is the best possible, but because it is better than remaining independent.[19]

Just as the demand for protection from hostile offers combined with a permissive standard of judicial review to give rise to more extreme forms of defensive tactics and, ultimately, to a reconsideration of the applicable legal standard, so too did the demand for protection for friendly transactions combine with permissive judicial review to give rise to more extreme forms of lockups and, ultimately, to a similar judicial reconsideration. The first effort at reconsideration took place in context of the traditional business judgment rule.

1.   Application of the Business Judgment Rule to Selling the Company

In conventional analysis, the target board of directors' duty of care in a friendly acquisition commands that the board use reasonable diligence to secure the best available transaction on behalf of its shareholders. The board's discharge of its obligation is protected by the business judgment rule.

---

[17] Section 6.01 does not, however, authorize directors to deploy defensive tactics against a hostile takeover. A tender offer is made directly to the shareholders and is, therefore, not a "proposal to the corporation." As a result, it falls outside the ambit of § 6.01. Defensive tactics fall within § 6.02: "Action of Directors That Was the Foreseeable Effect of Blocking Unsolicited Tender Offers."

[18] See Chapter 16, *supra*.

[19] In the early stages of the Corporate Governance Project, the Reporters recognized this problem with the application of the business judgment rule to lockups, and recommended that lockups be subject to shareholder approval. American Law Institute, *Principles of Corporate Governance: Analysis and Recommendations*, Reporters' Study No. 1 -- Transactions in Control (Feb.22, 1985). However, this recommendation did not meet the approval of the Council of the American Law Institute and did not go forward. In its final version, the Project "took no position on lockups," 1 Principles of Corporate Governance at 393 (Commentary to § 6.01), other than to prohibit their grant to a bidder with whom management was participating. *Id*. at 369 (Commentary to § 5.15).

However, the advent of an environment of competitive bids put considerable pressure on this pattern of judicial deference. Defending a lockup in favor of a preferred acquirer was more problematic in the face of a competing bidder who sought to offer target shareholders a higher price. Moreover, in the absence of a competitive bid, how did the target's board of directors in a friendly transaction know that it had secured the best available transaction? The Delaware Supreme Court first confronted the application of the business judgment rule in the new acquisition environment in the following case.

SMITH v. VAN GORKOM
488 A.2d 858 (Del.1985)

Before HERRMANN, C.J., and McNEILLY, HORSEY, MOORE and CHRISTIE, JJ., constituting the Court en banc.

HORSEY, Justice. . . . This appeal from the Court of Chancery involves a class action brought by shareholders of the defendant Trans Union Corporation ("Trans Union" or "the Company"), originally seeking rescission of a cash-out merger of Trans Union into the defendant New T Company ("New T"), a wholly-owned subsidiary of the defendant, Marmon Group, Inc. ("Marmon"). Alternate relief in the form of damages is sought against the defendant members of the Board of Directors of Trans Union, New T, and Jay A. Pritzker and Robert A. Pritzker, owners of Marmon.[1]

Following trial, the former Chancellor granted judgment for the defendant directors by unreported letter opinion. Judgment was based on two findings: (1) that the Board of Directors had acted in an informed manner so as to be entitled to protection of the business judgment rule in approving the cash-out merger; and (2) that the shareholder vote approving the merger should not be set aside because the stockholders had been "fairly informed" by the Board of Directors before voting thereon. The plaintiffs appeal.

Speaking for the majority of the Court, we conclude that both rulings of the Court of Chancery are clearly erroneous. Therefore, we reverse and direct that judgment be entered in favor of the plaintiffs and against the defendant directors for the fair value of the plaintiffs' stockholdings in Trans Union, in accordance with Weinberger v. UOP, Inc., 457 A.2d 701 (Del.1983).

We hold: (1) that the Board's decision, reached September 20, 1980, to approve the proposed cash-out merger was not the product of an informed business judgment; (2) that the Board's subsequent efforts to amend the

---

[1] The plaintiff, Alden Smith, originally sought to enjoin the merger; but, following extensive discovery, the Trial Court denied the plaintiff's motion for preliminary injunction by unreported letter opinion dated February 3, 1981. On February 10, 1981, the proposed merger was approved by Trans Union's stockholders at a special meeting and the merger became effective on that date. . . .

Merger Agreement and take other curative action were ineffectual, both legally and factually; and (3) that the Board did not deal with complete candor with the stockholders by failing to disclose all material facts, which they knew or should have known, before securing the stockholders' approval of the merger.

I

The nature of this case requires a detailed factual statement. The following facts are essentially uncontradicted:

A

Trans Union was a publicly-traded, diversified holding company, the principal earnings of which were generated by its railcar leasing business. During the period here involved, the Company had a cash flow of hundreds of millions of dollars annually. However, the Company had difficulty in generating sufficient taxable income to offset increasingly large investment tax credits (ITCs). Accelerated depreciation deductions had decreased available taxable income against which to offset accumulating ITCs. The Company took these deductions, despite their effect on usable ITCs, because the rental price in the railcar leasing market had already impounded the purported tax savings. . . .

Beginning in the late 1960's, and continuing through the 1970's, Trans Union pursued a program of acquiring small companies in order to increase available taxable income. In July 1980, Trans Union Management prepared the annual revision of the Company's Five Year Forecast. This report was presented to the Board of Directors at its July, 1980 meeting. The report projected an annual income growth of about 20%. The report also concluded that Trans Union would have about $195 million in spare cash between 1980 and 1985, "with the surplus growing rapidly from 1982 onward." The report referred to the ITC situation as a "nagging problem" and, given that problem, the leasing company "would still appear to be constrained to a tax breakeven." The report then listed four alternative uses of the projected 1982-1985 equity surplus: (1) stock repurchase; (2) dividend increases; (3) a major acquisition program; and (4) combinations of the above. The sale of Trans Union was not among the alternatives.[*] . . .

B

On August 27, 1980, Van Gorkom met with Senior Management of Trans Union. . . . Various alternatives were suggested and discussed

---

[*] What if Trans Union used its positive cash flow to purchase taxable bonds the interest on which would generate taxable earnings against which the ITCs could be applied? See Chapter 11, *supra*. [Eds.]

preliminarily, including the sale of Trans Union to a company with a large amount of taxable income.

Donald Romans, Chief Financial Officer of Trans Union, stated that his department had done a "very brief bit of work on the possibility of a leveraged buy-out." This work had been prompted by a media article which Romans had seen regarding a leveraged buy-out by management. The work consisted of a "preliminary study" of the cash which could be generated by the Company if it participated in a leveraged buy-out. As Romans stated, this analysis "was very first and rough cut at seeing whether a cash flow would support what might be considered a high price for this type of transaction."

On September 5, at another Senior Management meeting which Van Gorkom attended, Romans again brought up the idea of a leveraged buy-out as a "possible strategic alternative" to the Company's acquisition program. Romans and Bruce S. Chelberg, President and Chief Operating Officer of Trans Union, had been working on the matter in preparation for the meeting. According to Romans: They did not "come up" with a price for the Company. They merely "ran the numbers" at $50 a share and at $60 a share with the "rough form" of their cash figures at the time. Their "figures indicated that $50 would be very easy to do but $60 would be very difficult to do under those figures." This work did not purport to establish a fair price for either the Company or 100% of the stock. It was intended to determine the cash flow needed to service the debt that would "probably" be incurred in a leveraged buy-out, based on "rough calculations" without "any benefit of experts to identify what the limits were to that, and so forth." These computations were not considered extensive and no conclusion was reached.

At this meeting, Van Gorkom stated that he would be willing to take $55 per share for his own 75,000 shares. He vetoed the suggestion of a leveraged buy-out by Management, however, as involving a potential conflict of interest for Management. Van Gorkom, a certified public accountant and lawyer, had been an officer of Trans Union for 24 years, its Chief Executive Officer for more than 17 years, and Chairman of its Board for 2 years. It is noteworthy in this connection that he was then approaching 65 years of age and mandatory retirement.

For several days following the September 5 meeting, Van Gorkom pondered the idea of a sale. He had participated in many acquisitions as a manager and director of Trans Union and as a director of other companies. He was familiar with acquisition procedures, valuation methods, and negotiations; and he privately considered the pros and cons of whether Trans Union should seek a privately or publicly-held purchaser.

Van Gorkom decided to meet with Jay A. Pritzker, a well-known corporate takeover specialist and a social acquaintance. However, rather than approaching Pritzker simply to determine his interest in acquiring Trans Union, Van Gorkom assembled a proposed per share price for sale of the Company and a financing structure by which to accomplish the sale. Van

Gorkom did so without consulting either his Board or any members of Senior Management except one: Carl Peterson, Trans Union's Controller. Telling Peterson that he wanted no other person on his staff to know what he was doing, but without telling him why, Van Gorkom directed Peterson to calculate the feasibility of a leveraged buy-out at an assumed price per share of $55. Apart from the Company's historic stock market price,[5] and Van Gorkom's long association with Trans Union, the record is devoid of any competent evidence that $55 represented the per share intrinsic value of the Company.

Having thus chosen the $55 figure, based solely on the availability of a leveraged buy-out, Van Gorkom multiplied the price per share by the number of shares outstanding to reach a total value of the Company of $690 million. Van Gorkom told Peterson to use this $690 million figure and to assume a $200 million equity contribution by the buyer. Based on these assumptions, Van Gorkom directed Peterson to determine whether the debt portion of the purchase price could be paid off in five years or less if financed by Trans Union's cash flow as projected in the Five Year Forecast, and by the sale of certain weaker divisions identified in a study done for Trans Union by the Boston Consulting Group ("BCG study"). Peterson reported that, of the purchase price, approximately $50-80 million would remain outstanding after five years. Van Gorkom was disappointed, but decided to meet with Pritzker nevertheless.

Van Gorkom arranged a meeting with Pritzker at the latter's home on Saturday, September 13, 1980. Van Gorkom prefaced his presentation by stating to Pritzker: "Now as far as you are concerned, I can, I think, show how you can pay a substantial premium over the present stock price and pay off most of the loan in the first five years. . . . If you could pay $55 for this Company, here is a way in which I think it can be financed."

Van Gorkom then reviewed with Pritzker his calculations based upon his proposed price of $55 per share. Although Pritzker mentioned $50 as a more attractive figure, no other price was mentioned. However, Van Gorkom stated that to be sure that $55 was the best price obtainable, Trans Union should be free to accept any better offer. Pritzker demurred, stating that his organization would serve as a "stalking horse" for an "auction contest" only if Trans Union would permit Pritzker to buy 1,750,000 shares of Trans Union stock at market price which Pritzker could then sell to any higher bidder. After further discussion on this point, Pritzker told Van Gorkom that he would give him a more definite reaction soon.

On Monday, September 15, Pritzker advised Van Gorkom that he was interested in the $55 cash-out merger proposal and requested more

---

[5] The common stock of Trans Union was traded on the New York Stock Exchange. Over the five year period from 1975 through 1979, Trans Union's stock had traded within a range of a high of $39-1/2 and a low of $24-1/4. Its high and low range for 1980 through September 19 (the last trading day before announcement of the merger) was $38-1/4 - $29-1/2.

information on Trans Union. Van Gorkom agreed to meet privately with Pritzker, accompanied by Peterson, Chelberg, and Michael Carpenter, Trans Union's consultant from the Boston Consulting Group. The meetings took place on September 16 and 17. Van Gorkom was "astounded that events were moving with such amazing rapidity."

On Thursday, September 18, Van Gorkom met again with Pritzker. At that time, Van Gorkom knew that Pritzker intended to make a cash-out merger offer at Van Gorkom's proposed $55 per share. Pritzker instructed his attorney, a merger and acquisition specialist, to begin drafting merger documents. There was no further discussion of the $55 price. However, the number of shares of Trans Union's treasury stock to be offered to Pritzker was negotiated down to one million shares; the price was set at $38 -- 75 cents above the per share price at the close of the market on September 19. At this point, Pritzker insisted that the Trans Union Board act on his merger proposal within the next three days, stating to Van Gorkom: "We have to have a decision by no later than Sunday [evening, September 21] before the opening of the English stock exchange on Monday morning." Pritzker's lawyer was then instructed to draft the merger documents, to be reviewed by Van Gorkom's lawyer, "sometimes with discussion and sometimes not, in the haste to get it finished."

On Friday, September 19, Van Gorkom, Chelberg, and Pritzker consulted with Trans Union's lead bank regarding the financing of Pritzker's purchase of Trans Union. The bank indicated that it could form a syndicate of banks that would finance the transaction. On the same day, Van Gorkom retained James Brennan, Esquire, to advise Trans Union on the legal aspects of the merger. Van Gorkom did not consult with William Browder, a Vice-President and director of Trans Union and former head of its legal department, or with William Moore, then the head of Trans Union's legal staff.

On Friday, September 19, Van Gorkom called a special meeting of the Trans Union Board for noon the following day. He also called a meeting of the Company's Senior Management to convene at 11:00 a.m., prior to the meeting of the Board. No one, except Chelberg and Peterson, was told the purpose of the meetings. Van Gorkom did not invite Trans Union's investment banker, Salomon Brothers or its Chicago-based partner, to attend.

Of those present at the Senior Management meeting on September 20, only Chelberg and Peterson had prior knowledge of Pritzker's offer. Van Gorkom disclosed the offer and described its terms, but he furnished no copies of the proposed Merger Agreement. Romans announced that his department had done a second study which showed that, for a leveraged buy-out, the price range for Trans Union stock was between $55 and $65 per share. Van Gorkom neither saw the study nor asked Romans to make it available for the Board meeting.

Senior Management's reaction to the Pritzker proposal was completely negative. No member of Management, except Chelberg and Peterson, supported the proposal. Romans objected to the price as being too low;[6] he was critical of the timing and suggested that consideration should be given to the adverse tax consequences of an all-cash deal for low-basis shareholders; and he took the position that the agreement to sell Pritzker one million newly-issued shares at market price would inhibit other offers, as would the prohibitions against soliciting bids and furnishing inside information to other bidders. Romans argued that the Pritzker proposal was a "lock up" and amounted to "an agreed merger as opposed to an offer." Nevertheless, Van Gorkom proceeded to the Board meeting as scheduled without further delay.

Ten directors served on the Trans Union Board, five inside . . . and five outside. . . .   Of the outside directors, four were corporate chief executive officers and one was the former Dean of the University of Chicago Business School.   None was an investment banker or trained financial analyst. All members of the Board were well informed about the Company and its operations as a going concern. They were familiar with the current financial condition of the Company, as well as operating and earnings projections reported in the recent Five Year Forecast. The Board generally received regular and detailed reports and was kept abreast of the accumulated investment tax credit and accelerated depreciation problem.

Van Gorkom began the Special Meeting of the Board with a twenty-minute oral presentation. Copies of the proposed Merger Agreement were delivered too late for study before or during the meeting.[7]   He reviewed the Company's ITC and depreciation problems and the efforts theretofore made to solve them.   He discussed his initial meeting with Pritzker and his motivation in arranging that meeting. Van Gorkom did not disclose to the Board, however, the methodology by which he alone had arrived at the $55 figure, or the fact that he first proposed the $55 price in his negotiations with Pritzker.

Van Gorkom outlined the terms of the Pritzker offer as follows: Pritzker would pay $55 in cash for all outstanding shares of Trans Union stock upon completion of which Trans Union would be merged into New T Company, a subsidiary wholly-owned by Pritzker and formed to implement the merger; for a period of 90 days, Trans Union could receive, but could not actively solicit, competing offers; the offer had to be acted on by the next evening, Sunday, September 21; Trans Union could only furnish to competing bidders published information, and not proprietary information;

---

[6] Van Gorkom asked Romans to express his opinion as to the $55 price. Romans stated that he "thought the price was too low in relation to what he could derive for the company in a cash sale, particularly one which enabled us to realize the values of certain subsidiaries and independent entities."

[7] The record is not clear as to the terms of the Merger Agreement. The Agreement, as originally presented to the Board on September 20, was never produced by defendants despite demands by the plaintiffs. Nor is it clear that the directors were given an opportunity to study the Merger Agreement before voting on it. All that can be said is that Brennan had the Agreement before him during the meeting.

the offer was subject to Pritzker obtaining the necessary financing by October 10, 1980; if the financing contingency were met or waived by Pritzker, Trans Union was required to sell to Pritzker one million newly-issued shares of Trans Union at $38 per share.

Van Gorkom took the position that putting Trans Union "up for auction" through a 90-day market test would validate a decision by the Board that $55 was a fair price. He told the Board that the "free market will have an opportunity to judge whether $55 is a fair price." Van Gorkom framed the decision before the Board not as whether $55 per share was the highest price that could be obtained, but as whether the $55 price was a fair price that the stockholders should be given the opportunity to accept or reject.[8]

Attorney Brennan advised the members of the Board that they might be sued if they failed to accept the offer and that a fairness opinion was not required as a matter of law.

Romans attended the meeting as chief financial officer of the Company. He told the Board that he had not been involved in the negotiations with Pritzker and knew nothing about the merger proposal until the morning of the meeting; that his studies did not indicate either a fair price for the stock or a valuation of the Company; that he did not see his role as directly addressing the fairness issue; and that he and his people "were trying to search for ways to justify a price in connection with such a [leveraged buy-out] transaction, rather than to say what the shares are worth." Romans testified:

> I told the Board that the study ran the numbers at 50 and 60, and then the subsequent study at 55 and 65, and that was not the same thing as saying that I have a valuation of the company at X dollars. But it was a way -- a first step towards reaching that conclusion.

Romans told the Board that, in his opinion, $55 was "in the range of a fair price," but "at the beginning of the range." . . .

The Board meeting of September 20 lasted about two hours. Based solely upon Van Gorkom's oral presentation, Chelberg's supporting representations, Romans' oral statement Brennan's legal advice, and their knowledge of the market history of the Company's stock,[9] the directors approved the proposed Merger Agreement. However, the Board later claimed to have attached two conditions to its acceptance: (1) that Trans

---

[8] In Van Gorkom's words: The "real decision" is whether to "let the stockholders decide it" which is "all you are being asked to decide today."

[9] The Trial Court stated the premium relationship of the $55 price to the market history of the Company's stock as follows:

     . . . the merger price offered to the stockholders of Trans Union represented a premium of 62% over the average of the high and low prices at which Trans Union stock had traded in 1980, a premium of 48% over the last closing price, and a premium of 39% over the highest price at which the stock of Trans Union had traded any time during the prior six years.

Union reserved the right to accept any better offer that was made during the market test period; and (2) that Trans Union could share its proprietary information with any other potential bidders. While the Board now claims to have reserved the right to accept any better offer received after the announcement of the Pritzker agreement (even though the minutes of the meeting do not reflect this), it is undisputed that the Board did not reserve the right to actively solicit alternate offers.

The Merger Agreement was executed by Van Gorkom during the evening of September 20 at a formal social event that he hosted for the opening of the Chicago Lyric Opera. Neither he nor any other director read the agreement prior to its signing and delivery to Pritzker. . . .

On Monday, September 22, the Company issued a press release announcing that Trans Union had entered into a "definitive" Merger Agreement with an affiliate of the Marmon Group, Inc., a Pritzker holding company. Within 10 days of the public announcement, dissent among Senior Management over the merger had become widespread. Faced with threatened resignations of key officers, Van Gorkom met with Pritzker who agreed to several modifications of the Agreement. Pritzker was willing to do so provided that Van Gorkom could persuade the dissidents to remain on the Company payroll for at least six months after consummation of the merger.

Van Gorkom reconvened the Board on October 8 and secured the directors' approval of the proposed amendments -- sight unseen. The Board also authorized the employment of Salomon Brothers, its investment banker, to solicit other offers for Trans Union during the proposed "market test" period.

The next day, October 9, Trans Union issued a press release announcing: (1) that Pritzker had obtained "the financing commitments necessary to consummate" the merger with Trans Union; (2) that Pritzker had acquired one million shares of Trans Union common stock at $38 per share; (3) that Trans Union was now permitted to actively seek other offers and had retained Salomon Brothers for that purpose; and (4) that if a more favorable offer were not received before February 1, 1981, Trans Union's shareholders would thereafter meet to vote on the Pritzker proposal.

It was not until the following day, October 10, that the actual amendments to the Merger Agreement were prepared by Pritzker and delivered to Van Gorkom for execution. As will be seen, the amendments were considerably at variance with Van Gorkom's representations of the amendments to the Board on October 8; and the amendments placed serious constraints on Trans Union's ability to negotiate a better deal and withdraw from the Pritzker agreement. Nevertheless, Van Gorkom proceeded to execute what became the October 10 amendments to the Merger Agreement without conferring further with the Board members and apparently without comprehending the actual implications of the amendments. . . .

Salomon Brothers' efforts over a three-month period from October 21 to January 21 produced only one serious suitor for Trans Union -- General

Electric Credit Corporation ("GE Credit"), a subsidiary of the General Electric Company. However, GE Credit was unwilling to make an offer for Trans Union unless Trans Union first rescinded its Merger Agreement with Pritzker. When Pritzker refused, GE Credit terminated further discussions with Trans Union in early January.

In the meantime, in early December, the investment firm of Kohlberg, Kravis, Roberts & Co. ("KKR"), the only other concern to make a firm offer for Trans Union, withdrew its offer under circumstances hereinafter detailed.

On December 19, this litigation was commenced and, within four weeks, the plaintiffs had deposed eight of the ten directors of Trans Union, including Van Gorkom, Chelberg and Romans, its Chief Financial Officer. On January 21, Management's Proxy Statement for the February 10 shareholder meeting was mailed to Trans Union's stockholders. On January 26, Trans Union's Board met and, after a lengthy meeting, voted to proceed with the Pritzker merger. The Board also approved for mailing, "on or about January 27," a Supplement to its Proxy Statement. The Supplement purportedly set forth all information relevant to the Pritzker Merger Agreement, which had not been divulged in the first Proxy Statement. . . .

On February 10, the stockholders of Trans Union approved the Pritzker merger proposal. Of the outstanding shares, 69.9% were voted in favor of the merger; 7.25% were voted against the merger; and 22.85% were not voted.

II

We turn to the issue of the application of the business judgment rule to the September 20 meeting of the Board.

The Court of Chancery concluded from the evidence that the Board of Directors' approval of the Pritzker merger proposal fell within the protection of the business judgment rule. The Court found that the Board had given sufficient time and attention to the transaction, since the directors had considered the Pritzker proposal on three different occasions, on September 20, and on October 8, 1980 and finally on January 26, 1981. On that basis, the Court reasoned that the Board had acquired, over the four-month period, sufficient information to reach an informed business judgment on the cash-out merger proposal. The Court ruled:

> . . . that given the market value of Trans Union's stock, the business acumen of the members of the board of Trans Union, the substantial premium over market offered by the Pritzkers and the ultimate effect on the merger price provided by the prospect of other bids for the stock in question, that the board of directors of Trans Union did not act recklessly or improvidently in determining on a course of action which they believed to be in the best interest of the stockholders of Trans Union.

The Court of Chancery made but one finding; i.e., that the Board's conduct over the entire period from September 20 through January 26, 1981 was not reckless or improvident, but informed.   This ultimate conclusion was premised upon three subordinate findings, one explicit and two implied. The Court's explicit finding was that Trans Union's Board was "free to turn down the Pritzker proposal" not only on September 20 but also on October 8, 1980 and on January 26, 1981. The Court's implied, subordinate findings were: (1) that no legally binding agreement was reached by the parties until January 26; and (2) that if a higher offer were to be forthcoming, the market test would have produced it, and Trans Union would have been contractually free to accept such higher offer. However, the Court offered no factual basis or legal support for any of these findings; and the record compels contrary conclusions.

This Court's standard of review of the findings of fact reached by the Trial Court following full evidentiary hearing is as stated in Levitt v. Bouvier, 287 A.2d 671, 673 (Del.1972):

> [In an appeal of this nature] this court has the authority to review the entire record and to make its own findings of fact in a proper case. . . . We do not, however, ignore the findings made by the trial judge. If they are sufficiently supported by the record and are the product of an orderly and logical deductive process, in the exercise of judicial restraint we accept them, even though independently we might have reached opposite conclusions. It is only when the findings below are clearly wrong and the doing of justice requires their overturn that we are free to make contradictory findings of fact.

Applying that standard . . ., we conclude that the Court's ultimate finding that the Board's conduct was not "reckless or imprudent" is contrary to the record and not the product of a logical and deductive reasoning process.

The plaintiffs contend that the Court of Chancery erred as a matter of law by exonerating the defendant directors under the business judgment rule without first determining whether the rule's threshold condition of "due care and prudence" was satisfied: The defendants . . . submit that their decision to accept $55 per share was informed because: (1) they were "highly qualified;" (2) they were "well-informed;" and (3) they deliberated over the "proposal" not once but three times. On essentially this evidence and under our standard of review, the defendants assert that affirmance is required. We must disagree.

Under Delaware law, the business judgment rule is the offspring of the fundamental principle, codified in 8 Del.C. § 141(a), that the business and affairs of a Delaware corporation are managed by or under its board of directors. . . . The business judgment rule exists to protect and promote the full and free exercise of the managerial power granted to Delaware directors. The rule itself "is a presumption that in making a business decision, the directors of a corporation acted on an informed basis, in good faith and in the honest belief that the action taken was in the best interests of the company." Aronson v. Lewis, 473 A.2d 805, 812 (Del.1984). Thus, the party attacking a board decision as uninformed must rebut the presumption that its business judgment was an informed one. *Id.*

The determination of whether a business judgment is an informed one turns on whether the directors have informed themselves "prior to making a business decision, of all material information reasonably available to them." *Id.*

Under the business judgment rule there is no protection for directors who have made "an unintelligent or unadvised judgment." Mitchell v. Highland-Western Glass, 167 A. 831, 833 (Del.Ch.1933). A director's duty to inform himself in preparation for a decision derives from the fiduciary capacity in which he serves the corporation and its stockholders.

Since a director is vested with the responsibility for the management of the affairs of the corporation, he must execute that duty with the recognition that he acts on behalf of others. Such obligation does not tolerate faithlessness or self-dealing. But fulfillment of the fiduciary function requires more than the mere absence of bad faith or fraud. Representation of the financial interests of others imposes on a director an affirmative duty to protect those interests and to proceed with a critical eye in assessing information of the type and under the circumstances present here.

Thus, a director's duty to exercise an informed business judgment is in the nature of a duty of care, as distinguished from a duty of loyalty. Here, there were no allegations of fraud, bad faith, or self-dealing, or proof thereof. Hence, it is presumed that the directors reached their business judgment in good faith, and considerations of motive are irrelevant to the issue before us.

The standard of care applicable to a director's duty of care has also been recently restated by this Court. In *Aronson, supra*, we stated:

> While the Delaware cases use a variety of terms to describe the applicable standard of care, our analysis satisfies us that under the business judgment rule director liability is predicated upon concepts of gross negligence. (footnote omitted)

473 A.2d at 812.

We again confirm that view. We think the concept of gross negligence is also the proper standard for determining whether a business judgment reached by a board of directors was an informed one.

In the specific context of a proposed merger of domestic corporations, a director has a duty under 8 Del.C. § 251(b), along with his fellow directors, to act in an informed and deliberate manner in determining whether to approve an agreement of merger before submitting the proposal to the stockholders. Certainly in the merger context, a director may not abdicate that duty by leaving to the shareholders alone the decision to approve or disapprove the agreement. Only an agreement of merger satisfying the requirements of 8 Del.C. § 251(b) may be submitted to the shareholders under § 251(c).

It is against those standards that the conduct of the directors of Trans Union must be tested, as a matter of law and as a matter of fact, regarding their exercise of an informed business judgment in voting to approve the Pritzker merger proposal.

III

The defendants argue that the determination of whether their decision to accept $55 per share for Trans Union represented an informed business judgment requires consideration, not only of that which they knew and learned on September 20, but also of that which they subsequently learned and did over the following four-month period before the shareholders met to vote on the proposal in February, 1981. The defendants thereby seek to reduce the significance of their action on September 20 and to widen the time frame for determining whether their decision to accept the Pritzker proposal was an informed one. Thus, the defendants contend that what the directors did and learned subsequent to September 20 and through January 26, 1981, was properly taken into account by the Trial Court in determining whether the Board's judgment was an informed one. We disagree with this *post hoc* approach.

The issue of whether the directors reached an informed decision to "sell" the Company on September 20, 1980 must be determined only upon the basis of the information then reasonably available to the directors and relevant to their decision to accept the Pritzker merger proposal. This is not to say that the directors were precluded from altering their original plan of action, had they done so in an informed manner. What we do say is that the question of whether the directors reached an informed business judgment in agreeing to sell the Company, pursuant to the terms of the September 20 Agreement presents, in reality, two questions: (A) whether the directors reached an informed business judgment on September 20, 1980; and (B) if they did not, whether the directors' actions taken subsequent to September 20 were adequate to cure any infirmity in their action taken on September 20. We first consider the directors' September 20 action in terms of their reaching an informed business judgment.

A

On the record before us, we must conclude that the Board of Directors did not reach an informed business judgment on September 20, 1980 in voting to "sell" the Company for $55 per share pursuant to the Pritzker cash-out merger proposal. Our reasons, in summary, are as follows:

The directors (1) did not adequately inform themselves as to Van Gorkom's role in forcing the "sale" of the Company and in establishing the per share purchase price; (2) were uninformed as to the intrinsic value of the Company; and (3) given these circumstances, at a minimum, were grossly negligent in approving the "sale" of the Company upon two hours' consideration, without prior notice, and without the exigency of a crisis or emergency.

As has been noted, the Board based its September 20 decision to approve the cash-out merger primarily on Van Gorkom's representations. None of the directors, other than Van Gorkom and Chelberg, had any prior knowledge that the purpose of the meeting was to propose a cash-out merger of Trans Union. No members of Senior Management were present, other than Chelberg, Romans and Peterson; and the latter two had only learned of the proposed sale an hour earlier. Both general counsel Moore and former general counsel Browder attended the meeting, but were equally uninformed as to the purpose of the meeting and the documents to be acted upon.

Without any documents before them concerning the proposed transaction, the members of the Board were required to rely entirely upon Van Gorkom's 20-minute oral presentation of the proposal. No written summary of the terms of the merger was presented; the directors were given no documentation to support the adequacy of $55 price per share for sale of the Company; and the Board had before it nothing more than Van Gorkom's statement of his understanding of the substance of an agreement which he admittedly had never read, nor which any member of the Board had ever seen.

Under 8 Del.C. § 141(e),[15] "directors are fully protected in relying in good faith on reports made by officers." Michelson v. Duncan, 386 A.2d 1144, 1156 (Del.Ch.1978), *aff'd in part and rev'd in part on other grounds*, 407 A.2d 211 (Del.1979). The term "report" has been liberally construed to include reports of informal personal investigations by corporate officers. However, there is no evidence that any "report," as defined under § 141(e), concerning the Pritzker proposal, was presented to the Board on September 20.[16] Van Gorkom's oral presentation of his understanding of the terms of the proposed Merger Agreement, which he had not seen, and Romans' brief oral statement of his preliminary study regarding the feasibility of a leveraged buy-out of Trans Union do not qualify as § 141(e) "reports" for these reasons: The former lacked substance because Van Gorkom was basically uninformed as to the essential provisions of the very document about which he was talking. Romans' statement was irrelevant to the issues before the Board since it did not purport to be a valuation study. At a

---

[15] Section 141(e) provides in pertinent part:
> A member of the board of directors . . . shall, in the performance of his duties, be fully protected in relying in good faith upon the books of accounts or reports made to the corporation by any of its officers, or by an independent certified public accountant, or by an appraiser selected with reasonable care by the board of directors . . ., or in relying in good faith upon other records of the corporation.

[16] In support of the defendants' argument that their judgment as to the adequacy of $55 per share was an informed one, the directors rely on the BCG study and the Five Year Forecast. However, no one even referred to either of these studies at the September 20 meeting; and it is conceded that these materials do not represent valuation studies. Hence, these documents do not constitute evidence as to whether the directors reached an informed judgment on September 20 that $55 per share was a fair value for sale of the Company.

minimum for a report to enjoy the status conferred by § 141(e), it must be pertinent to the subject matter upon which a board is called to act, and otherwise be entitled to good faith, not blind, reliance. Considering all of the surrounding circumstances -- hastily calling the meeting without prior notice of its subject matter, the proposed sale of the Company without any prior consideration of the issue or necessity therefor, the urgent time constraints imposed by Pritzker, and the total absence of any documentation whatsoever -- the directors were duty bound to make reasonable inquiry of Van Gorkom and Romans, and if they had done so, the inadequacy of that upon which they now claim to have relied would have been apparent.

The defendants rely on the following factors to sustain the Trial Court's finding that the Board's decision was an informed one: (1) the magnitude of the premium or spread between the $55 Pritzker offering price and Trans Union's current market price of $38 per share; (2) the amendment of the Agreement as submitted on September 20 to permit the Board to accept any better offer during the "market test" period; (3) the collective experience and expertise of the Board's "inside" and "outside" directors; and (4) their reliance on Brennan's legal advice that the directors might be sued if they rejected the Pritzker proposal. We discuss each of these grounds *seriatim:*

(1)

A substantial premium may provide one reason to recommend a merger, but in the absence of other sound valuation information, the fact of a premium alone does not provide an adequate basis upon which to assess the fairness of an offering price. Here, the judgment reached as to the adequacy of the premium was based on a comparison between the historically depressed Trans Union market price and the amount of the Pritzker offer. Using market price as a basis for concluding that the premium adequately reflected the true value of the Company was a clearly faulty, indeed fallacious, premise, as the defendants' own evidence demonstrates.

The record is clear that before September 20, Van Gorkom and other members of Trans Union's Board knew that the market had consistently undervalued the worth of Trans Union's stock, despite steady increases in the Company's operating income in the seven years preceding the merger. The Board related this occurrence in large part to Trans Union's inability to use its ITCs as previously noted. Van Gorkom testified that he did not believe the market price accurately reflected Trans Union's true worth; and several of the directors testified that, as a general rule, most chief executives think that the market undervalues their companies' stock. Yet, on September 20, Trans Union's Board apparently believed that the market stock price accurately reflected the value of the Company for the purpose of determining the adequacy of the premium for its sale.

In the Proxy Statement, however, the directors reversed their position. There, they stated that, although the earnings prospects for Trans Union were "excellent," they found no basis for believing that this would be reflected in future stock prices. With regard to past trading, the Board stated that the prices at which the Company's common stock had traded in recent years did not reflect the "inherent" value of the Company. But having referred to the "inherent" value of Trans Union, the directors ascribed no number to it. Moreover, nowhere did they disclose that they had no basis on which to fix "inherent" worth beyond an impressionistic reaction to the premium over market and an unsubstantiated belief that the value of the assets was "significantly greater" than book value. By their own admission they could not rely on the stock price as an accurate measure of value. Yet, also by their own admission, the Board members assumed that Trans Union's market price was adequate to serve as a basis upon which to assess the adequacy of the premium for purposes of the September 20 meeting.

The parties do not dispute that a publicly-traded stock price is solely a measure of the value of a minority position and, thus, market price represents only the value of a single share. Nevertheless, on September 20, the Board assessed the adequacy of the premium over market, offered by Pritzker, solely by comparing it with Trans Union's current and historical stock price.

Indeed, as of September 20, the Board had no other information on which to base a determination of the intrinsic value of Trans Union as a going concern. As of September 20, the Board had made no evaluation of the Company designed to value the entire enterprise, nor had the Board ever previously considered selling the Company or consenting to a buy-out merger. Thus, the adequacy of a premium is indeterminate unless it is assessed in terms of other competent and sound valuation information that reflects the value of the particular business.

Despite the foregoing facts and circumstances, there was no call by the Board, either on September 20 or thereafter, for any valuation study or documentation of the $55 price per share as a measure of the fair value of the Company in a cash-out context. It is undisputed that the major asset of Trans Union was its cash flow. Yet, at no time did the Board call for a valuation study taking into account that highly significant element of the Company's assets.

We do not imply that an outside valuation study is essential to support an informed business judgment; nor do we state that fairness opinions by independent investment bankers are required as a matter of law. Often insiders familiar with the business of a going concern are in a better position than are outsiders to gather relevant information; and under appropriate circumstances, such directors may be fully protected in relying in good faith upon the valuation reports of their management. See 8 Del.C. § 141(e).

Here, the record establishes that the Board did not request its Chief Financial Officer, Romans, to make any valuation study or review of the proposal to determine the adequacy of $55 per share for sale of the Company. On the record before us: The Board rested on Romans' elicited response that the $55 figure was within a "fair price range" within the context of a leveraged buy-out. No director sought any further information from Romans. No director asked him why he put $55 at the bottom of his range. No director asked Romans for any details as to his study, the reason why it had been undertaken or its depth. No director asked to see the study; and no director asked Romans whether Trans Union's finance department could do a fairness study within the remaining 36-hour[18] period available under the Pritzker offer.

Had the Board, or any member, made an inquiry of Romans, he presumably would have responded as he testified: that his calculations were rough and preliminary; and, that the study was not designed to determine the fair value of the Company, but rather to assess the feasibility of a leveraged buy-out financed by the Company's projected cash flow, making certain assumptions as to the purchaser's borrowing needs. Romans would have presumably also informed the Board of his view, and the widespread view of Senior Management, that the timing of the offer was wrong and the offer inadequate.

The record also establishes that the Board accepted without scrutiny Van Gorkom's representation as to the fairness of the $55 price per share for sale of the Company -- a subject that the Board had never previously considered. The Board thereby failed to discover that Van Gorkom had suggested the $55 price to Pritzker and, most crucially, that Van Gorkom had arrived at the $55 figure based on calculations designed solely to determine the feasibility of a leveraged buy-out.[19] No questions were raised either as to the tax implications of a cash-out merger or how the price for the one million share option granted Pritzker was calculated.

We do not say that the Board of Directors was not entitled to give some credence to Van Gorkom's representation that $55 was an adequate or fair price. Under § 141(e), the directors were entitled to rely upon their chairman's opinion of value and adequacy, provided that such opinion was reached on a sound basis. Here, the issue is whether the directors informed themselves as to all information that was reasonably available to them. Had they done so, they would have learned of the source and derivation of the $55 price and could not reasonably have relied thereupon in good faith.

---

[18] Romans' department study was not made available to the Board until circulation of Trans Union's Supplementary Proxy Statement and the Board's meeting of January 26, 1981, on the eve of the shareholder meeting; and, as has been noted, the study has never been produced for inclusion in the record in this case.

[19] As of September 20 the directors did not know: that Van Gorkom had arrived at the $55 figure alone, and subjectively, as the figure to be used by Controller Peterson in creating a feasible structure for a leveraged buy-out by a prospective purchaser; that Van Gorkom had not sought advice, information or assistance from either inside or outside Trans Union directors as to the value of the Company as an entity or the fair price per share for 100% of its stock; that Van Gorkom had not consulted with the Company's investment bankers or other financial analysts; that Van Gorkom had not consulted with or confided in any officer or director of the Company except Chelberg; and that Van Gorkom had deliberately chosen to ignore the advice and opinion of the members of his Senior Management group regarding the adequacy of the $55 price.

None of the directors, Management or outside, were investment bankers or financial analysts. Yet the Board did not consider recessing the meeting until a later hour that day (or requesting an extension of Pritzker's Sunday evening deadline) to give it time to elicit more information as to the sufficiency of the offer, either from inside Management (in particular Romans) or from Trans Union's own investment banker, Salomon Brothers, whose Chicago specialist in merger and acquisitions was known to the Board and familiar with Trans Union's affairs.

Thus, the record compels the conclusion that on September 20 the Board lacked valuation information adequate to reach an informed business judgment as to the fairness of $55 per share for sale of the Company.

(2)

This brings us to the post-September 20 "market test" upon which the defendants ultimately rely to confirm the reasonableness of their September 20 decision to accept the Pritzker proposal. In this connection, the directors present a two-part argument: (a) that by making a "market test" of Pritzker's $55 per share offer a condition of their September 20 decision to accept his offer, they cannot be found to have acted impulsively or in an uninformed manner on September 20; and (b) that the adequacy of the $17 premium for sale of the Company was conclusively established over the following 90 to 120 days by the most reliable evidence available -- the marketplace. Thus, the defendants impliedly contend that the "market test" eliminated the need for the Board to perform any other form of fairness test either on September 20, or thereafter.

Again, the facts of record do not support the defendants' argument. There is no evidence: (a) that the Merger Agreement was effectively amended to give the Board freedom to put Trans Union up for auction sale to the highest bidder; or (b) that a public auction was in fact permitted to occur. The minutes of the Board meeting make no reference to any of this. Indeed, the record compels the conclusion that the directors had no rational basis for expecting that a market test was attainable, given the terms of the Agreement as executed during the evening of September 20. We rely upon the following facts which are essentially uncontradicted:

The Merger Agreement, specifically identified as that originally presented to the Board on September 20, has never been produced by the defendants, notwithstanding the plaintiffs' several demands for production before as well as during trial. No acceptable explanation of this failure to produce documents has been given to either the Trial Court or this Court. Significantly, neither the defendants nor their counsel have made the affirmative representation that this critical document has been produced. Thus, the Court is deprived of the best evidence on which to judge the merits of the defendants' position as to the care and attention which they gave to the terms of the Agreement on September 20.

Van Gorkom states that the Agreement as submitted incorporated the ingredients for a market test by authorizing Trans Union to receive competing offers over the next 90-day period. However, he concedes that the Agreement barred Trans Union from actively soliciting such offers and from furnishing to interested parties any information about the Company other than that already in the public domain. Whether the original Agreement of September 20 went so far as to authorize Trans Union to receive competitive proposals is arguable. The defendants' unexplained failure to produce and identify the original Merger Agreement permits the logical inference that the instrument would not support their assertions in this regard. Van Gorkom, conceding that he never read the Agreement, stated that he was relying upon his understanding that, under corporate law, directors always have an inherent right, as well as a fiduciary duty, to accept a better offer notwithstanding an existing contractual commitment by the Board.

The defendant directors assert that they "insisted" upon including two amendments to the Agreement, thereby permitting a market test: (1) to give Trans Union the right to accept a better offer; and (2) to reserve to Trans Union the right to distribute proprietary information on the Company to alternative bidders. Yet, the defendants concede that they did not seek to amend the Agreement to permit Trans Union to solicit competing offers.

Several of Trans Union's outside directors resolutely maintained that the Agreement as submitted was approved on the understanding that, "if we got a better deal, we had a right to take it." Director Johnson so testified; but he then added, "And if they didn't put that in the agreement, then the management did not carry out the conclusion of the Board. And I just don't know whether they did or not." The only clause in the Agreement as finally executed to which the defendants can point as "keeping the door open" is the following underlined statement found in subparagraph (a) of section 2.03 of the Merger Agreement as executed:

> The Board of Directors shall recommend to the stockholders of Trans Union that they approve and adopt the Merger Agreement ('the stockholders' approval') and to use its best efforts to obtain the requisite votes therefor. *GL acknowledges that Trans Union directors may have a competing fiduciary obligation to the shareholders under certain circumstances.*

Clearly, this language on its face cannot be construed as incorporating either of the two "conditions" described above: either the right to accept a better offer or the right to distribute proprietary information to third parties. The logical witness for the defendants to call to confirm their construction of this clause of the Agreement would have been Trans Union's outside attorney, James Brennan. The defendants' failure, without explanation, to call this witness again permits the logical inference that his testimony would not have been helpful to them. The further fact that the directors adjourned, rather than recessed, the meeting without incorporating in the Agreement these important "conditions" further weakens the defendants' position. As has been noted, nothing in the Board's Minutes supports these claims. No reference to either of the so-called "conditions" or of Trans Union's reserved right to test the market appears in any notes of the Board meeting or in the Board Resolution accepting the Pritzker offer or in the Minutes of the meeting itself. That evening, in the midst of a formal party which he hosted for the opening of the Chicago Lyric Opera, Van Gorkom executed the Merger Agreement without he or any other member of the Board having read the instruments.

The defendants attempt to downplay the significance of the prohibition against Trans Union's actively soliciting competing offers by arguing that the directors "understood that the entire financial community would know that Trans Union was for sale upon the announcement of the Pritzker offer, and anyone desiring to make a better offer was free to do so." Yet, the press release issued on September 22, with the authorization of the Board, stated that Trans Union had entered into "definitive agreements" with the Pritzkers; and the press release did not even disclose Trans Union's limited right to receive and accept higher offers. Accompanying this press release was a further public announcement that Pritzker had been granted an option to purchase at any time one million shares of Trans Union's capital stock at 75 cents above the then-current price per share.

Thus, notwithstanding what several of the outside directors later claimed to have "thought" occurred at the meeting, the record compels the conclusion that Trans Union's Board had no rational basis to conclude on September 20 or in the days immediately following, that the Board's acceptance of Pritzker's offer was conditioned on (1) a "market test" of the offer; and (2) the Board's right to withdraw from the Pritzker Agreement and accept any higher offer received before the shareholder meeting.

(3)

The directors' unfounded reliance on both the premium and the market test as the basis for accepting the Pritzker proposal undermines the defendants' remaining contention that the Board's collective experience and sophistication was a sufficient basis for finding that it reached its September 20 decision with informed, reasonable deliberation.[21] Compare Gimbel v. Signal Cos., Inc., 316 A.2d 599 (Del.Ch.1974), *aff'd per curiam*, 316 A.2d

---

[21] Trans Union's five "inside" directors had backgrounds in law and accounting, 116 years of collective employment by the Company and 68 years of combined experience on its Board. Trans Union's five "outside" directors included four chief executives of major corporations and an economist who was a former dean of a major school of business and chancellor of a university. The "outside" directors had 78 years of combined experience as chief executive officers of major corporations and 50 years of cumulative experience as directors of Trans Union. Thus, defendants argue that the Board was eminently qualified to reach an informed judgment on the proposed "sale" of Trans Union notwithstanding their lack of any advance notice of the proposal, the shortness of their deliberation, and their determination not to consult with their investment banker or to obtain a fairness opinion.

619 (Del.1974). There, the Court of Chancery preliminarily enjoined a board's sale of stock of its wholly-owned subsidiary for an alleged grossly inadequate price. It did so based on a finding that the business judgment rule had been pierced for failure of management to give its board "the opportunity to make a reasonable and reasoned decision." 316 A.2d at 615. The Court there reached this result notwithstanding the board's sophistication and experience; the company's need of immediate cash; and the board's need to act promptly due to the impact of an energy crisis on the value of the underlying assets being sold -- all of its subsidiary's oil and gas interests. The Court found those factors denoting competence to be outweighed by evidence of gross negligence; that management in effect sprang the deal on the board by negotiating the asset sale without informing the board; that the buyer intended to "force a quick decision" by the board; that the board meeting was called on only one-and-a-half days' notice; that its outside directors were not notified of the meeting's purpose; that during a meeting spanning "a couple of hours" a sale of assets worth $480 million was approved; and that the Board failed to obtain a *current* appraisal of its oil and gas interests. The analogy of *Signal* to the case at bar is significant. . . .

B

We now examine the Board's post-September 20 conduct for the purpose of determining first, whether it was informed and not grossly negligent; and second, if informed, whether it was sufficient to legally rectify and cure the Board's derelictions of September 20.[23]

(1)

First, as to the Board meeting of October 8: Its purpose arose in the aftermath of the September 20 meeting: (1) the September 22 press release announcing that Trans Union "had entered into definitive agreements to merge with an affiliate of Marmon Group, Inc.;" and (2) Senior Management's ensuing revolt.

Trans Union's press release stated:

FOR IMMEDIATE RELEASE:

CHICAGO, IL -- Trans Union Corporation announced today that it had entered into definitive agreements to merge with an affiliate of The Marmon Group, Inc. in a transaction whereby Trans Union stockholders would receive $55 per share in cash for each Trans Union share held. The Marmon Group, Inc. is controlled by the Pritzker family of Chicago.

---

[23] As will be seen, we do not reach the second question.

The merger is subject to approval by the stockholders of Trans Union at a special meeting expected to be held sometime during December or early January.

Until October 10, 1980, the purchaser has the right to terminate the merger if financing that is satisfactory to the purchaser has not been obtained, but after that date there is no such right.

In a related transaction, Trans Union has agreed to sell to a designee of the purchaser one million newly-issued shares of Trans Union common stock at a cash price of $38 per share. Such shares will be issued only if the merger financing has been committed for no later than October 10, 1980, or if the purchaser elects to waive the merger financing condition. In addition, the New York Stock Exchange will be asked to approve the listing of the new shares pursuant to a listing application which Trans Union intends to file shortly.

Completing of the transaction is also subject to the preparation of a definitive proxy statement and making various filings and obtaining the approvals or consents of government agencies.

The press release made no reference to provisions allegedly reserving to the Board the rights to perform a "market test" and to withdraw from the Pritzker Agreement if Trans Union received a better offer before the shareholder meeting. The defendants also concede that Trans Union never made a subsequent public announcement stating that it had in fact reserved the right to accept alternate offers, the Agreement notwithstanding.

The public announcement of the Pritzker merger resulted in an "en masse" revolt of Trans Union's Senior Management. The head of Trans Union's tank car operations (its most profitable division) informed Van Gorkom that unless the merger were called off, fifteen key personnel would resign.

Instead of reconvening the Board, Van Gorkom again privately met with Pritzker, informed him of the developments, and sought his advice. Pritzker then made the following suggestions for overcoming Management's dissatisfaction: (1) that the Agreement be amended to permit Trans Union to solicit, as well as receive, higher offers; and (2) that the shareholder meeting be postponed from early January to February 10, 1981. In return, Pritzker asked Van Gorkom to obtain a commitment from Senior Management to remain at Trans Union for at least six months after the merger was consummated.

Van Gorkom then advised Senior Management that the Agreement would be amended to give Trans Union the right to solicit competing offers through January, 1981, if they would agree to remain with Trans Union. Senior Management was temporarily mollified; and Van Gorkom then called a special meeting of Trans Union's Board for October 8.

Thus, the primary purpose of the October 8 Board meeting was to amend the Merger Agreement, in a manner agreeable to Pritzker, to permit

Trans Union to conduct a "market test."[24] Van Gorkom understood that the proposed amendments were intended to give the Company an unfettered "right to openly solicit offers down through January 31." Van Gorkom presumably so represented the amendments to Trans Union's Board members on October 8. In a brief session, the directors approved Van Gorkom's oral presentation of the substance of the proposed amendments, the terms of which were not reduced to writing until October 10. But rather than waiting to review the amendments, the Board again approved them sight unseen and adjourned, giving Van Gorkom authority to execute the papers when he received them.[25]

Thus, the Court of Chancery's finding that the October 8 Board meeting was convened to *reconsider* the Pritzker "proposal" is clearly erroneous. Further, the consequence of the Board's faulty conduct on October 8, in approving amendments to the Agreement which had not even been drafted, will become apparent when the actual amendments to the Agreement are hereafter examined.

The next day, October 9, and before the Agreement was amended, Pritzker moved swiftly to off-set the proposed market test amendment. First, Pritzker informed Trans Union that he had completed arrangements for financing its acquisition and that the parties were thereby mutually bound to a firm purchase and sale arrangement. Second, Pritzker announced the exercise of his option to purchase one million shares of Trans Union's treasury stock at $38 per share -- 75 cents above the current market price. Trans Union's Management responded the same day by issuing a press release announcing: (1) that all financing arrangements for Pritzer's acquisition of Trans Union had been completed; and (2) Pritzker's purchase of one million shares of Trans Union's treasury stock at $38 per share.

The next day, October 10, Pritzker delivered to Trans Union the proposed amendments to the September 20 Merger Agreement. Van Gorkom promptly proceeded to countersign all the instruments on behalf of Trans Union without reviewing the instruments to determine if they were consistent

---

[24] As previously noted, the Board mistakenly thought that it had amended the September 20 draft agreement to include a market test.

A secondary purpose of the October meeting was to obtain the Board's approval for Trans Union to employ its investment advisor, Salomon Brothers, for the limited purpose of assisting Management in the solicitation of other offers. Neither Management nor the Board then or thereafter requested Salomon Brothers to submit its opinion as to the fairness of Pritzker's $55 cash-out merger proposal or to value Trans Union as an entity.

There is no evidence of record that the October 8 meeting had any other purpose; and we also note that the Minutes of the October 8 Board meeting, including any notice of the meeting, are not part of the voluminous records of this case.

[25] We do not suggest that a board must read *in haec verba* every contract or legal document which it approves, but if it is to successfully absolve itself from charges of the type made here, there must be some credible contemporary evidence demonstrating that the directors knew what they were doing, and ensured that their purported action was given effect. That is the consistent failure which cast this Board upon its unredeemable course.

with the authority previously granted him by the Board. The amending documents were apparently not approved by Trans Union's Board until a much later date, December 2. The record does not affirmatively establish that Trans Union's directors ever read the October 10 amendments.[26]

The October 10 amendments to the Merger Agreement did authorize Trans Union to solicit competing offers, but the amendments had more far-reaching effects. The most significant change was in the definition of the third-party "offer" available to Trans Union as a possible basis for withdrawal from its Merger Agreement with Pritzker. Under the October 10 amendments, a better *offer* was no longer sufficient to permit Trans Union's withdrawal. Trans Union was now permitted to terminate the Pritzker Agreement and abandon the merger only if, prior to February 10, 1981, Trans Union had either consummated a merger (or sale of assets) with a third party or had entered into a "definitive" merger agreement more favorable than Pritzker's and for a greater consideration -- subject only to stockholder approval. Further, the "extension" of the market test period to February 10, 1981 was circumscribed by other amendments which required Trans Union to file its preliminary proxy statement on the Pritzker merger proposal by December 5, 1980 and use its best efforts to mail the statement to its shareholders by January 5, 1981. Thus, the market test period was effectively reduced, not extended.

In our view, the record compels the conclusion that the directors' conduct on October 8 exhibited the same deficiencies as did their conduct on September 20. The Board permitted its Merger Agreement with Pritzker to be amended in a manner it had neither authorized nor intended. . . .

(2)

Next, as to the "curative" effects of the Board's post-September 20 conduct, we review in more detail the reaction of Van Gorkom to the KKR proposal and the results of the Board-sponsored "market test."

The KKR proposal was the first and only offer received subsequent to the Pritzker Merger Agreement. The offer resulted primarily from the efforts of Romans and other senior officers to propose an alternative to Pritzker's acquisition of Trans Union. In late September, Romans' group contacted KKR about the possibility of a leveraged buy-out by all members of Management, except Van Gorkom. By early October, Henry R. Kravis of KKR gave Romans written notice of KKR's "interest in making an offer to purchase 100%" of Trans Union's common stock.

Thereafter, and until early December, Romans' group worked with KKR to develop a proposal. It did so with Van Gorkom's knowledge and apparently grudging consent. On December 2, Kravis and Romans

---

[26] There is no evidence of record that Trans Union's directors ever raised any objections, procedural or substantive, to the October 10 amendments or that any of them, including Van Gorkom, understood the opposite result of their intended effect -- until it was too late.

hand-delivered to Van Gorkom a formal letter-offer to purchase all of Trans Union's assets and to assume all of its liabilities for an aggregate cash consideration equivalent to $60 per share. The offer was contingent upon completing equity and bank financing of $650 million, which Kravis represented as 80% complete. The KKR letter made reference to discussions with major banks regarding the loan portion of the buy-out cost and stated that KKR was "confident that commitments for the bank financing . . . can be obtained within two or three weeks." The purchasing group was to include certain named key members of Trans Union's Senior Management, excluding Van Gorkom, and a major Canadian company. Kravis stated that they were willing to enter into a "definitive agreement" under terms and conditions "substantially the same" as those contained in Trans Union's agreement with Pritzker. The offer was addressed to Trans Union's Board of Directors and a meeting with the Board, scheduled for that afternoon, was requested.

Van Gorkom's reaction to the KKR proposal was completely negative; he did not view the offer as being firm because of its financing condition. It was pointed out, to no avail, that Pritzker's offer had not only been similarly conditioned, but accepted on an expedited basis. Van Gorkom refused Kravis' request that Trans Union issue a press release announcing KKR's offer, on the ground that it might "chill" any other offer.[27] Romans and Kravis left with the understanding that their proposal would be presented to Trans Union's Board that afternoon.

Within a matter of hours and shortly before the scheduled Board meeting, Kravis withdrew his letter-offer. He gave as his reason a sudden decision by the Chief Officer of Trans Union's rail car leasing operation to withdraw from the KKR purchasing group. Van Gorkom had spoken to that officer about his participation in the KKR proposal immediately after his meeting with Romans and Kravis. However, Van Gorkom denied any responsibility for the officer's change of mind.

At the Board meeting later that afternoon, Van Gorkom did not inform the directors of the KKR proposal because he considered it "dead." Van Gorkom did not contact KKR again until January 20, when faced with the realities of this lawsuit, he then attempted to reopen negotiations. KKR declined due to the imminence of the February 10 stockholder meeting.

GE Credit Corporation's interest in Trans Union did not develop until November; and it made no written proposal until mid-January. Even then, its proposal was not in the form of an offer. Had there been time to do so, GE Credit was prepared to offer between $2 and $5 per share above the $55 per share price which Pritzker offered. But GE Credit needed an additional 60 to 90 days; and it was unwilling to make a formal offer without a concession from Pritzker extending the February 10 "deadline" for Trans

---

[27] This was inconsistent with Van Gorkom's espousal of the September 22 press release following Trans Union's acceptance of Pritzker's proposal. Van Gorkom had then justified a press release as encouraging rather than chilling later offers.

Union's stockholder meeting. As previously stated, Pritzker refused to grant such extension; and on January 21, GE Credit terminated further negotiations with Trans Union. Its stated reasons, among others, were its "unwillingness to become involved in a bidding contest with Pritzker in the absence of the willingness of [the Pritzker interests] to terminate the proposed $55 cash merger." . . .

In the absence of any explicit finding by the Trial Court as to the reasonableness of Trans Union's directors' reliance on a market test and its feasibility, we may make our own findings based on the record. Our review of the record compels a finding that confirmation of the appropriateness of the Pritzker offer by an unfettered or free market test was virtually meaningless in the face of the terms and time limitations of Trans Union's Merger Agreement with Pritzker as amended October 10, 1980.

(3)

Finally, we turn to the Board's meeting of January 26, 1981. The defendant directors rely upon the action there taken to refute the contention that they did not reach an informed business judgment in approving the Pritzker merger. The defendants contend that the Trial Court correctly concluded that Trans Union's directors were, in effect, as "free to turn down the Pritzker proposal" on January 26, as they were on September 20. . . .

The Board's January 26 meeting was the first meeting following the filing of the plaintiffs' suit in mid-December and the last meeting before the previously-noticed shareholder meeting of February 10. All ten members of the Board and three outside attorneys attended the meeting. At that meeting the following facts, among other aspects of the Merger Agreement, were discussed:

(a) The fact that prior to September 20, 1980, no Board member or member of Senior Management, except Chelberg and Peterson, knew that Van Gorkom has discussed a possible merger with Pritzker;

(b) The fact that the price of $55 per share had been suggested initially to Pritzker by Van Gorkom;

(c) The fact that the Board had not sought an independent fairness opinion;

(d) The fact that, at the September 20 Senior Management meeting, Romans and several members of Senior Management indicated both concern that the $55 per share price was inadequate and a belief that a higher price should and could be obtained;

(e) The fact that Romans had advised the Board at its meeting on September 20, that he and his department had prepared a study which indicated that the Company had a value in the range of $55 to $65 per share, and that he could not advise the Board that the $55 per share offer made by Pritzker was unfair.

The defendants characterize the Board's Minutes of the January 26 meeting as a "review" of the "entire sequence of events" from Van Gorkom's initiation of the negotiations on September 13 forward. The defendants also rely on the testimony of several of the Board members at trial as confirming the Minutes. On the basis of this evidence, the defendants argue that whatever information the Board lacked to make a deliberate and informed judgment on September 20, or on October 8, was fully divulged to the entire Board on January 26. Hence, the argument goes, the Board's vote on January 26 to again "approve" the Pritzker merger must be found to have been an informed and deliberate judgment.

On the basis of this evidence, the defendants assert: (1) that the Trial Court was legally correct in widening the time frame for determining whether the defendants' approval of the Pritzker merger represented an informed business judgment to include the entire four-month period during which the Board considered the matter from September 20 through January 26; and (2) that, given this extensive evidence of the Board's further review and deliberations on January 26, this Court must affirm the Trial Court's conclusion that the Board's action was not reckless or improvident.

We cannot agree. We find the Trial Court to have erred, both as a matter of fact and as a matter of law, in relying on the action on January 26 to bring the defendants' conduct within the protection of the business judgment rule.

Johnson's testimony and the Board Minutes of January 26 are remarkably consistent. Both clearly indicate recognition that the question of the alternative courses of action, available to the Board on January 26 with respect to the Pritzker merger, was a legal question, presenting to the Board (*after* its review of the full record developed through pre-trial discovery) *three* options: (1) to "continue to recommend" the Pritzker merger; (2) to "recommend that the stockholders vote against" the Pritzker merger; or (3) to take a noncommittal position on the merger and "simply leave the decision to [the] shareholders."

We must conclude from the foregoing that the Board was mistaken as a matter of law regarding its available courses of action on January 26, 1981. Options (2) and (3) were not viable or legally available to the Board under 8 Del.C. § 251(b). The Board could not remain committed to the Pritzker merger and yet recommend that its stockholders vote it down; nor could it take a neutral position and delegate to the stockholders the unadvised decision as to whether to accept or reject the merger. Under § 251(v), the Board had but two options: (1) to proceed with the merger and the stockholder meeting, with the Board's recommendation of approval; *or* (2) to rescind its agreement with Pritzker, withdraw its approval of the merger, and notify its stockholders that the proposed shareholder meeting was cancelled. There is no evidence that the Board gave any consideration to these, its only legally viable alternative courses of action.

But the second course of action would have clearly involved a substantial risk -- that the Board would be faced with suit by Pritzker for breach of contract based on its September 20 agreement as amended October 10. As previously noted, under the terms of the October 10 amendment, the

Board's only ground for release from its agreement with Pritzker was its entry into a more favorable definitive agreement to sell the Company to a third party. Thus, in reality, the Board was not "free to turn down the Pritzker proposal" as the Trial Court found. Indeed, short of negotiating a better agreement with a third party, the Board's only basis for release from the Pritzker Agreement without liability would have been to establish fundamental wrongdoing by Pritzker. Clearly, the Board was not "free" to withdraw from its agreement with Pritzker on January 26 by simply relying on its self-induced failure to have reached an informed business judgment at the time of its original agreement.

Therefore, the Trial Court's conclusion that the Board reached an informed business judgment on January 26 in determining whether to turn down the Pritzker "proposal" on that day cannot be sustained. The Court's conclusion is not supported by the record; it is contrary to the provisions of § 251(b) and basic principles of contract law; and it is not the product of a logical and deductive reasoning process. . . .

Upon the basis of the foregoing, we hold that the defendants' post-September conduct did not cure the deficiencies of their September 20 conduct; and that, accordingly, the Trial Court erred in according to the defendants the benefits of the business judgment rule. . . .

V

The defendants ultimately rely on the stockholder vote of February 10 for exoneration. The defendants contend that the stockholders' "overwhelming" vote approving the Pritzker Merger Agreement had the legal effect of curing any failure of the Board to reach an informed business judgment in its approval of the merger.

The parties tacitly agree that a discovered failure of the Board to reach an informed business judgment in approving the merger constitutes a voidable, rather than a void, act. Hence, the merger can be sustained, notwithstanding the infirmity of the Board's action, if its approval by majority vote of the shareholders is found to have been based on an informed electorate.

The disagreement between the parties arises over: (1) the Board's burden of disclosing to the shareholders all relevant and material information; and (2) the sufficiency of the evidence as to whether the Board satisfied that burden.

On this issue the Trial Court summarily concluded "that the stockholders of Trans Union were fairly informed as to the pending merger. . . ." The Court provided no supportive reasoning nor did the Court make any reference to the evidence of record.

. . . In Lynch v. Vickers Energy Corp., *supra*, this Court held that corporate directors owe to their stockholders a fiduciary duty to disclose all facts germane to the transaction at issue in an atmosphere of complete candor. We defined "germane" in the tender offer context as all "information such as a reasonable shareholder would consider important in deciding whether to sell or retain stock." *Id.* at 281.

Applying this standard to the record before us, we find that Trans Union's stockholders were not fully informed of all facts material to their vote on the Pritzker Merger and that the Trial Court's ruling to the contrary is clearly erroneous. We list the material deficiencies in the proxy materials:

(1) The fact that the Board had no reasonably adequate information indicative of the intrinsic value of the Company, other than a concededly depressed market price, was without question material to the shareholders voting on the merger.

Accordingly, the Board's lack of valuation information should have been disclosed. Instead, the directors cloaked the absence of such information in both the Proxy Statement and the Supplemental Proxy Statement. Through artful drafting, noticeably absent at the September 20 meeting, both documents create the impression that the Board knew the intrinsic worth of the Company. In particular, the Original Proxy Statement contained the following:

> [a]lthough the Board of Directors regards the intrinsic value of the Company's assets to be significantly greater than their book value . . ., systematic liquidation of such a large and complex entity as Trans Union is simply not regarded as a feasible method of realizing its inherent value. Therefore, a business combination such as the merger would seem to be the only practicable way in which the stockholders could realize the value of the Company.

The Proxy stated further that "[i]n the view of the Board of Directors . . ., the prices at which the Company's common stock has traded in recent years have not reflected the inherent value of the company." What the Board failed to disclose to its stockholders was that the Board had not made any study of the intrinsic or inherent worth of the Company; nor had the Board even discussed the inherent value of the Company prior to approving the merger on September 20, or at either of the subsequent meetings on October 8 or January 26. Neither in its Original Proxy Statement nor in its Supplemental Proxy did the Board disclose that it had no information before it, beyond the premium-over-market and the price/earnings ratio, on which to determine the fair value of the Company as a whole.

(2) We find false and misleading the Board's characterization of the Romans report in the Supplemental Proxy Statement. The Supplemental Proxy stated:

> At the September 20, 1980 meeting of the Board of Directors of Trans Union, Mr. Romans indicated that while he could not say that $55.00 per share was an unfair price, he had prepared a preliminary report which reflected that the value of the Company was in the range of $55.00 to $65.00 per share.

Nowhere does the Board disclose that Romans stated to the Board that his calculations were made in a "search for ways to justify a price in connection with" a leveraged buy-out transaction, "rather than to say what the shares are worth," and that he stated to the Board that his conclusion thus arrived at "was not the same thing as saying that I have a valuation of the Company at X dollars." Such information would have been material to a reasonable shareholder because it tended to invalidate the fairness of the merger price of $55. Furthermore, defendants again failed to disclose the absence of valuation information, but still made repeated reference to the "substantial premium."

(3) We find misleading the Board's references to the "substantial" premium offered. The Board gave us their primary reason in support of the merger the "substantial premium" shareholders would receive. But the Board did not disclose its failure to assess the premium offered in terms of other relevant valuation techniques, thereby rendering questionable its determination as to the substantiality of the premium over an admittedly depressed stock market price.

(4) We find the Board's recital in the Supplemental Proxy of certain events preceding the September 20 meeting to be incomplete and misleading. It is beyond dispute that a reasonable stockholder would have considered material the fact that Van Gorkom not only suggested the $55 price to Pritzker, but also that he chose the figure because it made feasible a leveraged buy-out. The directors disclosed that Van Gorkom suggested the $55 price to Pritzker. But the Board misled the shareholders when they described the basis of Van Gorkom's suggestion as follows:

> Such suggestion was based, at least in part, on Mr. Van Gorkom's belief that loans could be obtained from institutional lenders (together with about a $200 million equity contribution) which would justify the payment of such price. .
> . .

Although by January 26, the directors knew the basis of the $55 figure, they did not disclose that Van Gorkom chose the $55 price because that figure would enable Pritzker to both finance the purchase of Trans Union through a leveraged buy-out and, within five years, substantially repay the loan out of the cash flow generated by the Company's operations. . . .

VI

To summarize: we hold that the directors of Trans Union breached their fiduciary duty to their stockholders (1) by their failure to inform themselves of all information reasonably available to them and relevant to their decision to recommend the Pritzker merger; and (2) by their failure to disclose all material information such as a reasonable stockholder would consider important in deciding whether to approve the Pritzker offer.

We hold, therefore, that the Trial Court committed reversible error in applying the business judgment rule in favor of the director defendants in this case.

On remand, the Court of Chancery shall conduct an evidentiary hearing to determine the fair value of the shares represented by the plaintiffs' class, based on the intrinsic value of Trans Union on September 20, 1980. Such valuation shall be made in accordance with Weinberger v. UOP, Inc., *supra*, at 712-715. Thereafter, an award of damages may be entered to the extent that the fair value of Trans Union exceeds $55 per share. . . .

REVERSED and REMANDED for proceedings consistent herewith.[*]

Note: The Business Judgment Rule in Acquisitions

The Delaware Supreme Court's decision in *Trans Union* was met by astonishment in the corporate bar. Professor Fischel, in a representative comment, described it as "one of the worst decisions in the history of corporate law. . . ."[20] If the case is stated most simply, the vigorous reaction is understandable: Independent directors were held personally liable for a potentially enormous amount -- the court's measure of damages was the amount by which "the fair value of transaction exceeds $55 per share" and the case was subsequently settled for approximately $23.5 million[21] -- for approving a transaction reflecting a premium of some 60% over market. From a transactional perspective, the central issue is what, precisely, the Trans Union directors did wrong. If that can be identified, then business lawyers can help clients avoid liability in the future. The result of that inquiry, in turn, is central to evaluating the case from a doctrinal perspective. If the protective steps developed in response to *Trans Union* are improvements in transactional conduct, the case was correctly decided. If not, then we will still have the same question: What, precisely, did the Trans Union directors do wrong?

Although the court does not say so explicitly, the clear implication of the opinion is that Van Gorkom was looking out for his own interests rather than those of Trans Union. As in most cases finding a violation of the business judgment rule, there are strong hints of breach of the duty of loyalty. Why would Van Gorkom have wanted the Pritzker deal so badly? After all, he owned 75,000 shares and would have benefitted along with other shareholders from any increase in price that resulted from better

---

[*] Dissenting opinions of Justices McNeilly and Christie omitted. [Eds.]

[20] Daniel Fischel, *The Business Judgment Rule and the Trans Union Case*, 40 Bus.Law. 1437, 1455 (1985).

[21] *Trans Union Corp's Ex-directors to Settle Suit for $23.5 Million*, Wall St.J., Aug. 2, 1985, p.10, col.5. The settlement exceeded Trans Union's director and officer liability insurance by $13.5 million. The Pritzker family voluntarily assumed the outside directors' (but not Van Gorkom's) personal liability. Why might they have done so? If the Pritzker family intended to be a repeat player in the market for corporate control, what did this action signal to the directors of potential target companies?

information about the company's intrinsic value. The court does single out for comment the fact that Van Gorkom was approaching mandatory retirement; a $20 per share premium would have represented a $1.5 million additional retirement fund for him. Perhaps other alternatives the board had considered, such as an acquisition program to use up Trans Union's tax benefits, also might have raised the price of Trans Union stock. Compared to the Pritzker deal, however, all other alternatives involved substantially more risk. And if Van Gorkom had doubts that another offer could be obtained -- after all, the company was not deluged by bidders as a result of Salomon Brothers' efforts -- then his impending retirement might have caused him to be more risk averse than the court would have preferred.

That Van Gorkom may have put his own interests above those of the shareholders (although the record apparently would not support that conclusion) would explain his liability. But why include the outside directors? The court treats the issue as one of the directors failing to inform themselves. It was not sufficient to rely on the judgment of the company's chief executive officer of 17 years; the outside directors should have kept him honest. One could respond by reference to the price premium offered -- the CEO is trustworthy and the price is good so why go any further -- but the court also did not like the price.

If Van Gorkom's motives are the first mystery in the case, the court's treatment of value is the second. The court seemed to believe statements made by Trans Union management that its shares were undervalued because it could not use all the tax benefits thrown off by its leasing activities. But that is only to say that Trans Union was accurately valued as it then existed, unable to fully utilize some of its assets. From this perspective, most American steel companies also are undervalued compared to what their value would be if only demand were sufficient to warrant using all of their production capacity. Nonetheless, the court concluded that market value was insufficient evidence of what the company was really worth.

Perhaps part of the puzzle is whether *Trans Union* really is a business judgment case at all. The same year as it decided *Trans Union*, the Delaware Supreme Court also decided *Unocal*, which held that because of the "omnipresent specter of self-interest," an intermediate standard, not the business judgment rule, applied to defensive action taken by target directors in a hostile transaction. An alternative reading of *Trans Union* is that it was a takeover case and that, as in *Unocal*, the court applied a higher standard of care than the business judgment rule.[22] From this perspective, *Trans Union* may be the Delaware Supreme Court's first attempt at counseling directors about the right way to sell the corporation.[23] Recall that Pritzker

---

[22] See Jon Macey & Geofrey Miller, *Trans Union Reconsidered*, 98 Yale L.J. 127 (1988); Ronald Gilson, *The Law and Finance of the Business Judgment Rule*, in *Corporate Governance, Restructuring, and the Market for Corporate Control* (J. Bicksler & A. Sametz eds. 1989).

[23] Some interesting data suggest that *Trans Union* may not have been interpreted as a

had given the Trans Union board only three days to accept the offer and had demanded a stock lockup and a no shop clause. The court held that the directors violated whatever was the applicable standard of care by acceding to these demands without seeking investment banking advice or otherwise determining the corporation's "intrinsic" value. Thus, *Trans Union* may teach that in selling the company, target directors must act with deliberation and make a careful determination of the right price, perhaps by soliciting competing bids, even at the risk of losing the initial bid. Under *Trans Union*, when could a target company protect a transaction by granting a favored suitor a lockup?

That *Trans Union* is difficult to interpret does not mean it is unimportant. Sometimes cases have their principal impact not through their doctrinal significance, but through their impact on transactional practice. Recall the importance the court attached to the Trans Union board's not having obtained a fairness opinion from an investment banker. To be sure, the court noted that it had not "state[d] that fairness opinions by independent investment bankers are required as a matter of law." But as counsel to a target company that is a party to a friendly transaction after *Trans Union*, would not you strongly recommend that a fairness opinion be secured? Professor Fischel concluded that the principal transactional change after *Trans Union* "will be that no firm considering a fundamental corporate change will do so without obtaining a fairness letter . . . [from an investment banker]. . . . Firms will have no difficulty finding an 'expert' who is willing to state that a price at a significant premium over the market price in an arm's-length transaction is 'fair.' (I wish someone would pay me several hundred thousand dollars to state that $55 is greater than $35)."[24] In reading

---

business judgment rule case by important segments of the affected community. When the case was decided, the corporate legal community publicly derided the outcome, counseling that public companies would have difficulty attracting outside directors in the face of an increased risk of personal liability. Given that corporate counsel trumpeted that the risk of director liability had substantially increased, it is hardly surprising that the insurers who wrote directors and officer liability policies took the opportunity to increase premiums. An index measuring the general level of D&O premiums rose more than ten-fold between 1984 and 1986. Indeed, premiums increased by 252% relative to their year earlier level in the quarter *Trans Union* was decided. Michael Bradley & Cindy Schipani, *The Relevance of the Duty of Care Standard in Corporate Governance*, 75 Iowa L.Rev. 1 (1989). If the increase in premiums merely matched an increase in expected claims due to *Trans Union*'s weakening of the business judgment rule's protection, then the value of D&O issuers' stock should not have been affected. In fact, D&O issuers' stock earned substantial abnormal returns over the same period, suggesting that premium increases exceeded expected claims increases. *Id.* This is consistent with treating *Trans Union* as a takeover case that could be dealt with through excluding, for example, hostile takeovers, from coverage, rather than as effecting a broad reduction in business judgment rule protection.

[24] Fischel (1985), *supra* note 20, at 1453. By this analysis, the big winners in *Trans Union* were the professional advisers, especially investment bankers. Lawyers, however, also did not fare badly. It is notable how small a role Trans Union's lawyers seemed to play in the transaction, the court's emphasis on the process of the board's decision-making went a

the cases that appear in the remainder of this Chapter, think about the role investment bankers came to play in friendly transactions (and the court's ultimate view of the value of their valuation opinions). Which perspective on investment bankers -- the *Trans Union* court's respectful view or Professor Fischel's quite cynical one -- came out on top? Independent of whether *Trans Union* made good law, did it lead to good transaction practice?

　　Trans Union also raised, but gave less guidance concerning, other areas of acquisition practice. What room was left for lockups to a favored bidder? Must a target company in a friendly transaction solicit competing bids, or even hold an auction, to be sure the best price has been obtained? Alternatively, can the target company rely on negotiations with the acquirer, perhaps supported by valuation opinions?

Note: Statutory Responses to *Trans Union*

　　In addition to convincing the D&O insurance carriers that *Trans Union* had created a director liability crisis, the corporate bar also convinced the Delaware legislature. Within a few months after the decision in *Trans Union* was decided, the Delaware legislature amended Del.Gen.Corp.Law §102(b) to add subsection (7) to the litany of permissible provisions that may be placed in a corporation's certificate of incorporation:

> (7) A provision eliminating or limiting the personal liability of a director to the corporation or its stockholders for monetary damages for breach of fiduciary duty as a director, provided that such provision shall not eliminate or limit the liability of a director (i) for any breach of the director's duty of loyalty to the corporation or its stockholders' (ii) for acts or omissions not in good faith or which involve intentional misconduct or a knowing violation of law; (iii) under section 174 of this title [improper distributions], or (iv) for any transaction for which the director derived an improper personal benefit. . . [25]

　　Delaware's action evoked a favorable response both from other states and from companies. Since the amendment of § 102(b), more than 41 states have amended their corporate statutes to provide directors additional protection from liability that matched or exceeded the Delaware provision.[26] Moreover, of the 593 Delaware companies followed by the Investor

---

long way toward seeing that would not happen again.

　　[25] At the same time, the Delaware legislature also amended § 145 to expand a corporation's ability to provide broader indemnification by contract or by-law than provided in the statute.

　　[26] See James Hanks, *Evaluating Recent State Legislation on Director and Officer Liability Limitation and Indemnification*, 43 Bus.Law. 1207 (1988).

Responsibility Research Center, 94% have amended their charters in accordance with § 102(b)(7), the vast majority of which amendments occurred at the company's first annual meeting following the adoption of § 102(b)(7).[27]

Because of Delaware's dominance as an incorporation state, its response to *Trans Union* warrants careful attention. For our purposes, the major concern is the application of exculpatory charter amendment to a decision either to defeat a hostile takeover through defensive tactics or to favor a particular bidder through the grant of a lock-up. Two of the statutory limitations on exculpation are especially relevant, those barring exculpation for violations of the duty of loyalty and in situations where the director derived an improper personal benefit.

With respect to the duty of loyalty limitation, the issue is whether the Delaware Supreme Court's new intermediate standard of review for defensive tactics measures compliance with the duty of care or the duty of loyalty. As the court noted in AC Acquisitions Corp. v. Anderson, Clayton & Co., 519 A.2d 103 (Del.Ch.1986), the new standard is neither the traditional business judgment rule measure of the duty of care, nor the traditional entire fairness measure of the duty of loyalty:

> Because the effect of the proper invocation of the business judgment rule is so powerful and the standard of entire fairness so exacting, the determination of the appropriate standard of judicial review frequently is determinative of the outcome of derivative litigation.
>
> Perhaps for that reason, the Delaware Supreme Court recognized in Unocal Corp. v. Mesa Petroleum Co. that where a board takes action designed to defeat a threatened change in control of the company, a more flexible, intermediate form of judicial review is appropriate.

529 A.2d at 111 (citations omitted). If this intermediate, enhanced business judgment standard is violated, have the directors violated their duty of care or their duty of loyalty? The consequences of the answer to this question are enormous. If the violation is of the duty of care, directors of companies that have invoked § 102(b)(7) have no personal liability; if it is of the duty of loyalty, however, the directors remain personally liable.

Which duty is measured by the intermediate standard is not immediately clear from the case law. In *Unocal*, the Delaware Supreme Court explained the need for a special standard of review in cases involving defensive tactics by reference to the "omnipresent specter that a board may be acting primarily in its own interest."[28] This suggests that what is really involved is the duty of loyalty. While directors may not have given in to a conflict of interest in

---

[27] Bradley & Schipani (1989), *supra* note 23.

[28] 559 A.2d 1261 (Del.1989) (reproduced in Chapter 17, *supra*). Note that in addressing its earlier decision in *Revlon*, the Macmillan Court explicitly observed that Revlon's directors had violated *both* their duties of care and loyalty. 559 A.2d 1284, n.32.

electing to pursue a particular defensive tactic, it is also the case that not all interested transactions are on unfair terms; in both cases, the argument runs, it is merely the increased possibility of unfairness caused by the conflict of interest that warrants a more detailed duty of loyalty review.

Pointing in the same direction is the nature of the test that is applied if the directors fail the intermediate test, the entire fairness test. This test is typically applied to measure violations of the duty of loyalty. Conduct that would violate its tenets, the argument goes, is hardly a mere violation of the duty of care.

What kind of self-interest should be necessary to deprive a director of the protection of § 1021(b)(7)? Might one distinguish between an interest in retaining one's position as a director and a direct financial interest in the transaction, as in a director's participation in a leveraged buyout? Section 6.02 of the American Law Institute's Principles of Corporate Governance deals with the personal liability issues in connection with a heightened standard of review in takeover cases in a different way. Recognizing that acquisition transactions typically are challenged in an injunction proceeding, § 6.02 applies an intermediate standard with respect to the validity of the transaction, but applies the business judgment rule to determination of directors' personal liability.

The ambiguity in characterizing the new Delaware "intermediate" review of defensive conduct as raising duty of care or duty of loyalty issues is not the only interpretive problem in construing the coverage of § 102(b)(7).[29] For defensive planners, however, it is the most important problem.

2. Application of the Intermediate Standard to Selling the Company: *Revlon, Inc. v. MacAndrews & Forbes Holdings, Inc.*

Less than a year after *Trans Union*, the Delaware Supreme Court revisited the subject of target board conduct in selling the company to a favored suitor. In the interim, however, the court had decided *Unocal*, establishing an intermediate standard of review -- between business judgment and entire fairness -- for defensive tactics in response to a hostile takeover attempt.[30] In Revlon, Inc. v. MacAndrews & Forbes Holdings, Inc., the

---

[29] For example, would a § 102(b)(7) provision protect from personal liability reckless conduct, or only negligent (or grossly negligent) conduct? Unfortunately, the duty of care/duty of loyalty dichotomy does not resolve the question. To be sure, reckless conduct would violate the duty of care, but did the Delaware legislature really intend to protect reckless, as opposed to negligent, directors? In this regard, note that other state exculpatory statutes, which do not base the scope of permissible protection on the duty of care/duty of loyalty dichotomy, explicitly exclude recklessness. See, e.g., Ind. Code Ann. §23-1-35-1(a) (Burns Supp.1986).

[30] See Chapter 17, *supra*.

court took up the application of the intermediate standard to friendly transactions.

REVLON, INC. v. MacANDREWS & FORBES HOLDINGS, INC.
506 A.2d 173 (Del.1986)

Before McNEILLY and MOORE, J.J., and BALICK, Judge (Sitting by designation pursuant to Del. Const., Art. IV, § 12.).

MOORE, Justice. In this battle for corporate control of Revlon, Inc. (Revlon), the Court of Chancery enjoined certain transactions designed to thwart the efforts of Pantry Pride, Inc. (Pantry Pride) to acquire Revlon.[1] The defendants are Revlon, its board of directors, and Forstmann Little & Co. and the latter's affiliated limited partnership (collectively, Forstmann). The injunction barred consummation of an option granted Forstmann to purchase certain Revlon assets (the lock-up option), a promise by Revlon to deal exclusively with Forstmann in the face of a takeover (the no-shop provision), and the payment of a $25 million cancellation fee to Forstmann if the transaction was aborted. The Court of Chancery found that the Revlon directors had breached their duty of care by entering into the foregoing transactions and effectively ending an active auction for the company. The trial court ruled that such arrangements are not illegal *per se* under Delaware law, but that their use under the circumstances here was impermissible. We agree. Thus, we granted this expedited interlocutory appeal to consider for the first time the validity of such defensive measures in the face of an active bidding contest for corporate control. Additionally, we address for the first time the extent to which a corporation may consider the impact of a takeover threat on constituencies other than shareholders. See Unocal Corp. v. Mesa Petroleum Co., 493 A.2d 955 (Del.1985).

In our view, lock-ups and related agreements are permitted under Delaware law where their adoption is untainted by director interest or other breaches of fiduciary duty. The actions taken by the Revlon directors, however, did not meet this standard. Moreover, while concern for various corporate constituencies is proper when addressing a takeover threat, that principle is limited by the requirement that there be some rationally related benefit accruing to the stockholders. We find no such benefit here.

Thus, under all the circumstances we must agree with the Court of Chancery that the enjoined Revlon defensive measures were inconsistent with the directors' duties to the stockholders. Accordingly, we affirm.

---

[1] The nominal plaintiff, MacAndrews & Forbes Holdings, Inc., is the controlling stockholder of Pantry Pride. For all practical purposes their interests in this litigation are virtually identical, and we hereafter will refer to Pantry Pride as the plaintiff.

I

The somewhat complex maneuvers of the parties necessitate a rather detailed examination of the facts. The prelude to this controversy began in June 1985, when Ronald O. Perelman, chairman of the board and chief executive officer of Pantry Pride, met with his counterpart at Revlon, Michel C. Bergerac, to discuss a friendly acquisition of Revlon by Pantry Pride. Perelman suggested a price in the range of $40-50 per share, but the meeting ended with Bergerac dismissing those figures as considerably below Revlon's intrinsic value. All subsequent Pantry Pride overtures were rebuffed, perhaps in part based on Mr. Bergerac's strong personal antipathy to Mr. Perelman.

Thus, on August 14, Pantry Pride's board authorized Perelman to acquire Revlon, either through negotiation in the $42-43 per share range, or by making a hostile tender offer at $45. Perelman then met with Bergerac and outlined Pantry Pride's alternate approaches. Bergerac remained adamantly opposed to such schemes and conditioned any further discussions of the matter on Pantry Pride executing a stand-still agreement prohibiting it from acquiring Revlon without the latter's prior approval.

On August 19, the Revlon board met specially to consider the impending threat of a hostile bid by Pantry Pride.[3] At the meeting, Lazard Freres, Revlon's investment banker, advised the directors that $45 per share was a grossly inadequate price for the company. Felix Rohatyn and William Loomis of Lazard Freres explained to the board that Pantry Pride's financial strategy for acquiring Revlon would be through "junk bond" financing followed by a break-up of Revlon and the disposition of its assets. With proper timing, according to the experts, such transactions could produce a return to Pantry Pride of $60 to $70 per share, while a sale of the company as a whole would be in the "mid 50" dollar range. Martin Lipton, special counsel for Revlon, recommended two defensive measures: first, that the company repurchase up to 5 million of its nearly 30 million outstanding shares; and second, that it adopt a Note Purchase Rights Plan. Under this plan, each Revlon shareholder would receive as a dividend one Note Purchase Right (the Rights) for each share of common stock, with the Rights entitling the holder to exchange one common share for a $65 principal Revlon note at 12% interest with a one-year maturity. The Rights would become effective whenever anyone acquired beneficial ownership of 20% or more of Revlon's shares, unless the purchaser acquired all the company's stock for cash at $65 or more per share. In addition, the Rights would not

---

[3] There were 14 directors on the Revlon board. Six of them held senior management positions with the company, and two others held significant blocks of its stock. Four of the remaining six directors were associated at some point with entities that had various business relationships with Revlon. On the basis of this limited record, however, we cannot conclude that this board is entitled to certain presumptions that generally attach to the decisions of a board whose majority consists of truly outside independent directors.

be available to the acquiror, and prior to the 20% triggering event the Revlon board could redeem the rights for 10 cents each. Both proposals were unanimously adopted.

Pantry Pride made its first hostile move on August 23 with a cash tender offer for any and all shares of Revlon at $47.50 per common share and $26.67 per preferred share, subject to (1) Pantry Pride's obtaining financing for the purchase, and (2) the Rights being redeemed, rescinded or voided.

The Revlon board met again on August 26. The directors advised the stockholders to reject the offer. Further defensive measures also were planned. On August 29, Revlon commenced its own offer for up to 10 million shares, exchanging for each share of common stock tendered one Senior Subordinated Note (the Notes) of $47.50 principal at 11.75% interest, due 1995, and one-tenth of a share of $9.00 Cumulative Convertible Exchangeable Preferred Stock valued at $100 per share. Lazard Freres opined that the notes would trade at their face value on a fully distributed basis. Revlon stockholders tendered 87 percent of the outstanding shares (approximately 33 million), and the company accepted the full 10 million shares on a pro rata basis. The new Notes contained covenants which limited Revlon's ability to incur additional debt, sell assets, or pay dividends unless otherwise approved by the "independent" (non-management) members of the board.

At this point, both the Rights and the Note covenants stymied Pantry Pride's attempted takeover. The next move came on September 16, when Pantry Pride announced a new tender offer at $42 per share, conditioned upon receiving at least 90% of the outstanding stock. Pantry Pride also indicated that it would consider buying less than 90%, and at an increased price, if Revlon removed the impeding Rights. While this offer was lower on its face than the earlier $47.50 proposal, Revlon's investment banker, Lazard Freres, described the two bids as essentially equal in view of the completed exchange offer.

The Revlon board held a regularly scheduled meeting on September 24. The directors rejected the latest Pantry Pride offer and authorized management to negotiate with other parties interested in acquiring Revlon. Pantry Pride remained determined in its efforts and continued to make cash bids for the company, offering $50 per share on September 27, and raising its bid to $53 on October 1, and then to $56.25 on October 7.

In the meantime, Revlon's negotiations with Forstmann and the investment group Adler & Shaykin had produced results. The Revlon directors met on October 3 to consider Pantry Pride's $53 bid and to examine possible alternatives to the offer. Both Forstmann and Adler & Shaykin made certain proposals to the board. As a result, the directors unanimously agreed to a leveraged buyout by Forstmann. The terms of this accord were as follows: each stockholder would get $56 cash per share; management would purchase stock in the new company by the exercise of their Revlon "golden parachutes";[5] Forstmann would assume Revlon's $475 million debt incurred by the issuance of the Notes; and Revlon would redeem the Rights and waive the Notes covenants for Forstmann or in connection with any other offer superior to Forstmann's. The board did not actually remove the covenants at the October 3 meeting, because Forstmann then lacked a firm commitment on its financing, but accepted the Forstmann capital structure, and indicated that the outside directors would waive the covenants in due course. Part of Forstmann's plan was to sell Revlon's Norcliff Thayer and Reheis divisions to American Home Products for $335 million. Before the merger, Revlon was to sell its cosmetics and fragrance division to Adler & Shaykin for $905 million. These transactions would facilitate the purchase by Forstmann or any other acquiror of Revlon.

When the merger, and thus the waiver of the Notes covenants, was announced, the market value of these securities began to fall. The Notes, which originally traded near par, around 100, dropped to 87.50 by October 8. One director later reported (at the October 12 meeting) a "deluge" of telephone calls from irate noteholders, and on October 10 the Wall Street Journal reported threats of litigation by these creditors.

Pantry Pride countered with a new proposal on October 7, raising its $53 offer to $56.25, subject to nullification of the Rights, a waiver of the Notes covenants, and the election of three Pantry Pride directors to the Revlon board. On October 9, representatives of Pantry Pride, Forstmann and Revlon conferred in an attempt to negotiate the fate of Revlon, but could not reach agreement. At this meeting Pantry Pride announced that it would engage in fractional bidding and top any Forstmann offer by a slightly higher one. It is also significant that Forstmann, to Pantry Pride's exclusion, had been made privy to certain Revlon Financial data. Thus, the parties were not negotiating on equal terms.

Again privately armed with Revlon data, Forstmann met on October 11 with Revlon's special counsel and investment banker. On October 12, Forstmann made a new $57.25 per share offer, based on several conditions.[6] The principal demand was a lock-up option to purchase Revlon's Vision Care and National Health Laboratories divisions for $525 million, some $100-$175 million below the value ascribed to them by Lazard Freres, if another acquiror got 40% of Revlon's shares. Revlon also was required to accept a no-shop provision. The Rights and Notes covenants had to be removed as in the October 3 agreement. There would be a $25 million cancellation fee

---

[5] In the takeover context "golden parachutes" generally are understood to be termination agreements providing substantial bonuses and other benefits for managers and certain directors upon a change in control of a company.

[6] Forstmann's $57.25 offer ostensibly is worth $1 more than Pantry Pride's $56.25 bid. However, the Pantry Pride offer was immediate, while the Forstmann proposal must be discounted for the time value of money because of the delay in approving the merger and consummating the transaction. The exact difference between the two bids was an unsettled point of contention even at oral argument.

to be placed in escrow, and released to Forstmann if the new agreement terminated or if another acquiror got more than 19.9% of Revlon's stock. Finally, there would be no participation by Revlon management in the merger. In return, Forstmann agreed to support the par value of the Notes, which has faltered in the market, by an exchange of new notes. Forstmann also demanded immediate acceptance of its offer, or it would be withdrawn. The board unanimously approved Forstmann's proposal because: (1) it was for a higher price than the Pantry Pride bid, (2) it protected the noteholders, and (3) Forstmann's financing was firmly in place.[7] The board further agreed to redeem the rights and waive the covenants on the preferred stock in response to any offer above $57 cash per share. The covenants were waived, contingent upon receipt of an investment banking opinion that the Notes would trade near par value once the offer was consummated.

Pantry Pride, which had initially sought injunctive relief from the Rights plan on August 22, filed an amended complaint on October 14 challenging the lock-up, the cancellation fee, and the exercise of the Rights and the Notes covenants. Pantry Pride also sought a temporary restraining order to prevent Revlon from placing any assets in escrow or transferring them to Forstmann. Moreover, on October 22, Pantry Pride again raised its bid, with a cash offer of $58 per share conditioned upon nullification of the Rights, waiver of the covenants, and an injunction of the Forstmann lock-up.

On October 15, the Court of Chancery prohibited the further transfer of assets, and eight days later enjoined the lock-up, no-shop, and cancellation fee provisions of the agreement. The trial court concluded that the Revlon directors has breached their duty of loyalty by making concessions to Forstmann, out of concern for their liability to the noteholders, rather than maximizing the sale price of the company for the stockholders' benefit.

II

To obtain a preliminary injunction, a plaintiff must demonstrate both a reasonable probability of success on the merits and some irreparable harm which will occur absent the injunction. *Gimbel v. Signal Cos.*, 316 A.2d 599, 602 (Del.Ch.1974), *aff'd*, 316 A.2d 610 (Del.1974). Additionally, the Court shall balance the conveniences of and possible injuries to the parties. *Id*.

---

[7] Actually, at this time about $400 million of Forstmann's funding was still subject to two investment banks using their "best efforts" to organize an syndicate to provide the balance. Pantry Pride's entire financing was not firmly committed at this point either, although Pantry Pride represented in an October 11 letter to Lazard Freres that its investment banker, Drexel Burnham Lambert, was highly confident of its ability to raise the balance of $350 million. Drexel Burnham had a firm commitment for this sum by October 18.

A

We turn first to Pantry Pride's probability of success on the merits. The ultimate responsibility for managing the business and affairs of a corporation falls on its board of directors. 8 Del.C. § 141(a). In discharging this function the directors owe fiduciary duties of care and loyalty to the corporation and its shareholders. Guth v. Loft, Inc., 5 A.2d 503, 510 (Del.1939); Aronson v. Lewis, 473 A.2d 805, 811 (Del.1984). These principles apply with equal force when a board approves a corporate merger pursuant to 8 Del.C. § 251(b); Smith v. Van Gorkom, 488 A.2d 858, 873 (Del.1985); and of course they are the bedrock of our law regarding corporate takeover issues. Pogostin v. Rice, 480 A.2d 619, 624 (Del.1984); Unocal v. Mesa Petroleum Co., 493 A.2d 946, 953, 955 (Del.1985); Moran v. Household International, Inc., 500 A.2d 1345, 1350 (Del.1985). While the business judgment rule may be applicable to the actions of corporate directors responding to takeover threats, the principles upon which it is founded -- care, loyalty and independence -- must first be satisfied. Aronson v. Lewis, 473 A.2d at 812.

If the business judgment rule applies, there is a "presumption that in making a business decision the directors of a corporation acted on an informed basis, in good faith and in the honest belief that the action taken was in the best interests of the company." Aronson v. Lewis, 473 A.2d at 812. However, when a board implements anti-takeover measures there arises "the omnipresent specter that a board may be acting primarily in its own interests, rather than those of the corporation and its shareholders . . .." Unocal Corp. v. Mesa Petroleum Co., 493 A.2d at 954. This potential for conflict places upon the directors the burden of proving that they had reasonable grounds for believing there was a danger to corporate policy and effectiveness, a burden satisfied by a showing of good faith and reasonable investigation. Id. at 955. In addition, the directors must analyze the nature of the takeover and its effect on the corporation in order to ensure balance -- that the responsive action taken is reasonable in relation to the threat posed. Id.

B

The first relevant defensive measure adopted by the Revlon board was the Rights Plan, which would be considered a "poison pill" in current language of corporate takeovers -- a plan by which shareholders receive the right to be bought out by the corporation at a substantial premium on the occurrence of a stated triggering event. See generally Moran v. Household International, Inc., 500 A.2d 1346 (Del.1985). By 8 Del.C. §§ 141 and 122(13),[11] the board clearly had the power to adopt the measure. See

---

[11] The relevant provision of Section 122 is:

Every corporation created under this chapter shall have power to:

Moran v. Household International, Inc., 500 A.2d at 1351. Thus, the focus becomes one of reasonableness and purpose.

The Revlon board approved the Rights Plan in the face of an impending hostile takeover bid by Pantry Pride at $45 per share, a price which Revlon reasonably concluded was grossly inadequate. Lazard Freres had so advised the directors, and had also informed than that Pantry Pride was a small, highly leveraged company bent on a "bust-up" takeover by using "junk bond" financing to buy Revlon cheaply, sell the acquired assets to pay the debts incurred, and retain the profit for itself.[12] In adopting the Plan, the board protected the shareholders from a hostile takeover at a price below the company's intrinsic value, while retaining sufficient flexibility to address any proposal deemed to be in the stockholders' best interests.

To that extent the board acted in good faith and upon reasonable investigation. Under the circumstances it cannot be said that the Rights Plan as employed was unreasonable, considering the threat posed. Indeed, the Plan was a factor in causing Pantry Pride to raise its bids from a low of $42 to an eventual high of $58. At the time of its adoption the Rights Plan afforded a measure of protection consistent with the directors' fiduciary duty in facing a takeover threat perceived as detrimental to corporate interests. *Unocal*, 493 A.2d at 954-55. Far from being a "show-stopper," as the plaintiffs had contended in *Moran*, the measure spurred the bidding to new heights, a proper result of its implementation. See *Moran*, 500 A.2d at 1354, 1356-67.

Although we consider adoption of the Plan to have been valid under the circumstances, its continued usefulness was rendered moot by the directors' actions on October 3 and October 12. At the October 3 meeting the board redeemed the Rights conditioned upon consummation of a merger with Forstmann, but further acknowledged that they would also be redeemed to facilitate any more favorable offer. On October 12, the board unanimously passed a resolution redeeming the Rights in connection with any cash proposal of $57.25 or more per share. Because all the pertinent offers eventually equalled or surpassed that amount, the Rights clearly were no longer any impediment in the contest for Revlon. This mooted any question of their propriety under *Moran*, or *Unocal*.

---

(13) Make contracts, including contracts of guaranty and suretyship, incur liabilities, borrow money at such rates of interest as the corporation may determine, issue its notes, bonds and other obligations, and secure any of its obligations by mortgage, pledge or other encumbrance of all or any of its property, franchises and income. . . ." 8 Del.C. § 122(13).

[12] As we noted in *Moran*, a "bust-up" takeover generally refers to a situation in which one seeks to finance an acquisition by selling off pieces of the acquired company, presumably at a substantial profit. See *Moran*, 500 A.2d at 1349, n.4.

C

The second defensive measure adopted by Revlon to thwart a Pantry Pride takeover was the company's own exchange offer for 10 million of its shares. The directors' general broad powers to manage the business and affairs of the corporation are augmented by the specific authority conferred under 8 Del.C. § 160(a), permitting the company to deal in its own stock.[13] *Unocal*, 493 A.2d at 953-54; *Cheff v, Mathes*, 100 A.2d 548, 554 (Del.1964); *Kors v. Carey*, 158 A.2d 136, 140 (Del.Ch.1960). However, when exercising that power in an effort to forestall a hostile takeover, the board's actions are strictly held to the fiduciary standards outlined in *Unocal*. These standards require the directors to determine the best interests of the corporation and its stockholders, and impose an enhanced duty to abjure any action that is motivated by considerations other than a good faith concern for such interests. *Unocal*, 493 A.2d at 954-55; see *Bennett v. Propp*, 187 A.2d 405, 409 (Del.1962).

The Revlon directors concluded that Pantry Pride's $47.50 offer was grossly inadequate. In that regard the board acted in good faith, and on an informed basis, with reasonable grounds to believe that there existed a harmful threat to the corporate enterprise. The adoption of a defensive measure, reasonable in relation to the threat posed, was proper and fully accorded with the powers, duties, and responsibilities conferred upon directors under our law. *Unocal*, 493 A.2d at 954; *Pogostin v. Rice*, 480 A.2d at 627.

D

However, when Pantry Pride increased its offer to $50 per share, and then to $53, it became apparent to all that the break-up of the company was inevitable. The Revlon board's authorization permitting management to negotiate a merger or buyout with a third party was a recognition that the company was for sale. The duty of the board had thus changed from the preservation of Revlon as a corporate entity to the maximization of the company's value at a sale for the stockholders' benefit. This significantly altered the board's responsibilities under the *Unocal* standards. It no longer faced threats to corporate policy and effectiveness, or to the stockholders' interests, from a grossly inadequate bid. The whole question of defensive measures became moot. The directors' role changed from defenders of the corporate bastion to auctioneers charged with getting the best price for the stockholders at a sale of the company.

---

[13] The pertinent provision of this statute is:

(a) Every corporation may purchase, redeem, receive, take or otherwise acquire, own and hold, sell, lend, exchange, transfer or otherwise dispose of, pledge, use and otherwise deal in and with its own shares. 8 Del.C. § 160(a).

III

This brings us to the lock-up with Forstmann and its emphasis on shoring up the sagging market value of the Notes in the face of threatened litigation by their holders. Such a focus was inconsistent with the changed concept of the directors' responsibilities at this stage of the developments. The impending waiver of the Notes covenants had caused the value of the Notes to fall, and the board was aware of the noteholders' ire as well as their subsequent threats of suit. The directors thus made support of the Notes an integral part of the company's dealings with Forstmann, even though their primary responsibility at this stage was to the equity owners.

The original threat posed by Pantry Pride -- the break-up of the company -- had become a reality which even the directors embraced. Selective dealing to fend off a hostile but determined bidder was no longer a proper objective. Instead, obtaining the highest price for the benefit of the stockholders should have been the central theme guiding director action. Thus, the Revlon board could not make the requisite showing of good faith by preferring the noteholders and ignoring its duty of loyalty to the shareholders. The rights of the former already were fixed by contract. Wolfensohn v. Madison Fund, Inc., 253 A.2d 72, 75 (Del.1969); Harff v. Kerkorian, 324 A.2d 215 (Del.Ch.1974). The noteholders required no further protection, and when the Revlon board entered into an auction-ending lock-up agreement with Forstmann on the basis of impermissible considerations at the expense of the shareholders, the directors breached their primary duty of loyalty.

The Revlon board argued that it acted in good faith in protecting the noteholders because *Unocal* permits consideration of other corporate constituencies. Although such considerations may be permissible, there are fundamental limitations upon that prerogative. A board may have regard for various constituencies in discharging its responsibilities, provided there are rationally related benefits accruing to the stockholders. *Unocal*, 493 A.2d at 955. However, such concern for non-stockholder interests is inappropriate when an auction among active bidders is in progress, and the object no longer is to protect or maintain the corporate enterprise but to sell it to the highest bidder.

Revlon also contended that by Gilbert v. El Paso Co., 490 A.2d 1050, 1054-55 (Del.Ch.1984), it has contractual and good faith obligations to consider the noteholders. However, any such duties are limited to the principle that one may not interfere with contractual relationship by improper actions. Here, the rights of the noteholders were fixed by agreement, and there is nothing of substance to suggest that any of those terms were violated. The Notes covenants specifically contemplated a waiver to permit sale of the company at a fair price. The Notes were accepted by the holders on that basis, including the risk of an adverse market effect stemming from a waiver. Thus, nothing remained for Revlon to legitimately protect, and no rationally related benefit thereby accrued to the stockholders. Under such circumstances we must conclude that the merger agreement with Forstmann was unreasonable in relation to the threat posed.

A lock-up is not *per se* illegal under Delaware law. Its use has been approved in an earlier case. Thompson v. Enstar Corp., 509 A.2d 518 (Del.Ch.1984). Such options can entice other bidders to enter a contest for control of the corporation creating an auction for the company and maximizing shareholder profit. Current economic conditions in the takeover market are such that a "white knight" like Forstmann might only enter the bidding for the target company if it received some form of compensation to cover the risks and costs involved. However, while those lock-ups which draw bidders into the battle benefit shareholders, similar measures which end an active auction and foreclose further bidding operate to the shareholders' detriment.

Recently, the United States Court of Appeals for the Second Circuit invalidated a lock-up on fiduciary duty grounds similar to those here. Hanson Trust PLC, et al. v. ML SCM Acquisition Inc., et al., 781 F.2d 264 (2nd Cir.1986). Citing Thompson v. Enstar Corp., *supra*, with approval, the court stated:

> In this regard, we are especially mindful that some lock-up options may be beneficial to the shareholders, such as those that induce a bidder to compete for control of a corporation, while others may be harmful, such as those that effectively preclude bidders from competing with the optionee bidder. 781 F.2d at 274.

In *Hanson Trust*, the bidder, Hanson, sought control of SCM by a hostile cash tender offer. SCM management joined with Merrill Lynch to propose a leveraged buy-out of the company at a higher price, and Hanson in turn increased its offer. Then, despite very little improvement in it subsequent bid, the management group sought a lock-up option to purchase SCM's two main assets at a substantial discount. The SCM directors granted the lock-up without adequate information as to the size of the discount or the effect the transaction would have on the company. Their action effectively ended a competitive bidding situation. The Hanson Court invalidated the lock-up because the directors failed to fully inform themselves about the value of a transaction in which management had a strong self-interest. "In short, the Board appears to have failed to ensure that negotiations for alternative bids were conducted by those whose only loyalty was to the shareholders." *Id*. at 277.

The Forstmann option had a similar destructive effect on the auction process. Forstmann had already been drawn into the contest on a preferred basis, so the result of the lock-up was not to foster bidding, but to destroy it. The board's stated reasons for approving the transactions were: (1) better financing, (2) noteholder protection, and (3) higher price. As the Court of Chancery found, and we agree, any distinctions between the rival bidders' methods of financing the proposal were nominal at best, and such a consideration has little or no significance in a cash offer for any and all shares. The principal object, contrary to the board's duty of care, appears to have been protection of the noteholders over the shareholders' interests.

While Forstmann's $57.25 offer was objectively higher than Pantry Pride's $56.25 bid, the margin of superiority is less when the Forstmann price is adjusted for the time value of money. In reality, the Revlon board ended the auction in return for very little actual improvement in the final bid. The principal benefit went to the directors, who avoided personal liability to a class of creditors to whom the board owed no further duty under the circumstances. Thus, when a board ends an intense bidding contest on an insubstantial basis, and where a significant by-product of that action is to protect the directors against a perceived threat of personal liability for consequences stemming from the adoption of previous defensive measures, the action cannot withstand the enhanced scrutiny which *Unocal* requires of director conduct. See *Unocal*, 493 A.2d at 954-55.

In addition to the lock-up option, the Court of Chancery enjoined the no-shop provision as part of the attempt to foreclose further bidding by Pantry Pride. MacAndrews & Forbes Holdings, Inc. v. Revlon, Inc., 501 A.2d at 1251. The no-shop provision, like the lock-up option, while not *per se* illegal, is impermissible under the *Unocal* standards when a board's primary duty becomes that of an auctioneer responsible for selling the company to the highest bidder. The agreement to negotiate only with Forstmann ended rather than intensified the board's involvement in the bidding contest.

It is ironic that the parties even considered a no-shop agreement when Revlon had dealt preferentially, and almost exclusively, with Forstmann throughout the contest. After the directors authorized management to negotiate with other parties, Forstmann was given every negotiating advantage that Pantry Pride had been denied: cooperation from management, access to financial data, and the exclusive opportunity to present merger proposals directly to the board of directors. Favoritism for a white knight to the total exclusion of a hostile bidder might be justifiable when the latter's offer adversely affects shareholder interests, but when bidders make relatively similar offers, or dissolution of the company becomes inevitable, the directors cannot fulfill their enhanced *Unocal* duties by playing favorites with the contending factions. Market forces must be allowed to operate freely to bring the target's shareholders the best price available for their equity.[15] Thus, as the trial court ruled, the shareholders' interests necessitated that the board remain free to negotiate in the fulfillment of that duty.

---

[15] By this we do not embrace the "passivity" thesis rejected in *Unocal*. See 493 A.2d at 954-55, nn.8-10. The directors' role remains an active one, changed only in the respect that they are charged with the duty of selling the company at the highest price attainable for the stockholders' benefit.

The court below similarly enjoined the payment of the cancellation fee, pending a resolution of the merits, because the fee was part of the overall plan to thwart Pantry Pride's efforts. We find no abuse of discretion in that ruling.

IV

Having concluded that Pantry Pride has shown a reasonable probability of success on the merits, we address the issue of irreparable harm. The Court of Chancery ruled that unless the lock-up and other aspects of the agreement were enjoined, Pantry Pride's opportunity to bid for Revlon was lost. The court also held that the need for both bidders to compete in the marketplace outweighed any injury to Forstmann. Given the complexity of the proposed transaction between Revlon and Forstmann, the obstacles to Pantry Pride obtaining a meaningful legal remedy are immense. We are satisfied that the plaintiff has shown the need for an injunction to protect it from irreparable harm, which need outweighs any harm to the defendant.

V

In conclusion, the Revlon board was confronted with a situation not uncommon in the current wave of corporate takeovers. A hostile and determined bidder sought the company at a price the board was convinced was inadequate. The initial defensive tactics worked to the benefit of the shareholders, and thus the board was able to sustain its *Unocal* burdens in justifying those measures. However, in granting an asset option lock-up to Forstmann, we must conclude that under all the circumstances the directors allowed considerations other than the maximization of shareholder profit to affect their judgment, and followed a course that ended the auction for Revlon, absent court intervention, to the ultimate detriment of its shareholders. No such defensive measure can be sustained when it represents a breach of the directors' fundamental duty of care. See Smith v. Van Gorkom, 488 A.2d 858, 874 (Del.1985). In that context the board's action is not entitled to the deference accorded it by the business judgment rule. The measures were properly enjoined. The decision of the Court of Chancery, therefore, is AFFIRMED.

Revlon extends the application of the intermediate standard of review announced in *Unocal* from target company defensive tactics to efforts by a target company to protect a favored acquirer. Like *Unocal*, *Revlon* left much about the intermediate standard uncertain. As framed in *Revlon*, much turns on identifying when the new standard's application is triggered: the point at which the board's duty "change[s] from the preservation of Revlon as a corporate entity to the maximization of the company's value at a sale for the stockholders' benefit."[31] From a defensive planner's perspective, the prize of an independent -- and perhaps even an "unrestructured" -- company will always remain within reach, at least in theory, as long as the board's actions are governed by *Unocal*'s proportionality test: successful defensive tactics may still be found proportional to the threat. By contrast, after *Revlon* is triggered, the board may no longer be able to select the company's buyer or even dictate the form of the transaction in which it is sold. Thus, planners will search for defensive transactions that can block a pending hostile bid without triggering management's *Revlon* duties. Here the issue is locating the doctrinal boundary between *Revlon* and *Unocal*.

Revlon's trigger is equally important in a friendly acquisition, although the doctrinal boundary that must be located is different. Suppose two companies determine that combining their assets will result in synergy. May the companies restrict their shareholders' choice to the favored strategic alliance or remaining independent? More extreme, can the board cut off even the option of remaining independent by approving a lockup arrangement that is extremely favorable to the other party and which becomes operative if target shareholders' reject the acquisition? If another bidder offers more, can the target company decline to consider it? Here the relevant doctrinal boundary is that between *Revlon* and the business judgment rule. In light of *Trans Union*, how much difference does it make on which side of the boundary the planner finds herself?

Once the nature of *Revlon*'s trigger has been identified, the substance of the target board's new obligations must be clarified. *Revlon* speaks of the board's obligation to secure the best price and of the board's role as "auctioneers." Does *Revlon* require that a formal auction be held in every case, with each side having the opportunity to counter the other's bid until only one bidder is left? The analysis can be broken down into three categories. First, how can the target board determine the company's value? An auction is one way, but not the only one. An asset's value is sometimes determined by negotiating with a single bidder,[32] and the target board may be assisted by the expert advice of investment bankers as the court stressed in *Trans Union*.

Second, how does the target board go about securing the highest price? An auction may be the right technique in some circumstances, but in others favoring a particular bidder may secure the highest bid. However, favoring a bidder may also reflect management's self-interest. *Revlon* presented both sides of the issue. The court clearly thought Revlon management favored Forstmann Little, presumably because management would be given an equity stake in the transaction and would run the post-acquisition company. Thus, the court was unable to imagine why Revlon would give Forstmann Little a

---

[31] See Ronald Gilson & Reinier Kraakman, *What Triggers Revlon?*, 25 Wake Forest L.Rev. 37 (1990).

[32] See Peter Cramton & Alan Schwartz, *Using Auction Theory to Inform Takeover Regulation*, 7 J.L.Econ. & Org. 27 (1991).

lockup in return for only a $1 per share bid increase at a time when Pantry Pride had announced it would beat any Forstmann bid. But $1.00 per share may have been significant as the bidders approached their limits. Recall the bidding. After Pantry Pride initially made a $47.50 hostile offer, Revlon and Forstmann announced a friendly LBO at $56 per share. Pantry Pride countered by increasing its bid by 25 cents per share and announcing that it would beat any subsequent Forstmann bid by 5 cents per share. What if Forstmann would not have further increased its bid without a lockup? If Forstmann did not receive a lockup, the highest bid would have been $56.25 from Pantry Pride. With a lockup, the highest bid was $57 from Forstmann. It was irrelevant that Pantry Pride would have offered $57.05 in the absence of a lockup; in that event Pantry Pride would have won the auction at $56.25.[33] The availability of another alternative to Revlon at this point highlights the difficulty of assessing which depiction of the process -- self-serving or value maximizing -- is correct. Suppose instead of giving Forstmann a lockup, Revlon had announced a final, one-round, sealed bid auction with a lockup being given to the highest bidder. Might that approach have forced Pantry Pride to bid 5 cents more than it thought Revlon was worth to Forstmann?

Third, by what standard of review does the court evaluate target management's conduct?

In the remainder of this Chapter we first consider *Revlon*'s trigger in the context of a hostile offer. We then assess *Revlon*'s substantive obligations, and then turn to *Revlon*'s application in a friendly transaction. Finally, we assess *Revlon*'s standards in light of the teachings of auction theory.

3. *Revlon*'s Trigger in the Setting of a Hostile Bid: The Boundary Between *Revlon* and *Unocal*

We turn first to *Revlon*'s application in the setting familiar from Chapter 17: mounting a defense against a hostile takeover bid. *Revlon* itself reviewed a board's decision to frustrate a hostile bidder by agreeing to a leveraged buyout by the company's managers and an affiliated investment group. Approval of the leveraged buyout resulted in an inevitable "sale" of the company, in the terms used by the Delaware Supreme Court, because the transaction *was* a formal sale. For precisely this reason, however, defensive planners immediately sought to avoid *Revlon* by means of transactions, termed here "management recapitalizations," that would transfer control to management without requiring public shareholders to dispose of their shares. Although these transactions were functionally equivalent to management buyouts, it was possible to argue that they merited review under *Unocal*'s

---

[33] See Fraidin & Hanson (1994), *supra* note 14, at 1754-55.

proportionality test, rather than under the higher standard of the *Revlon* auctioneering duty, because they were not formal sales. The equivalence of management buyouts and management recapitalizations thus became a critical planning issue that highlights the importance of linking *Revlon*'s application to a transfer of control.

a.   *Management Recapitalizations*

The practical equivalence of management recapitalizations and management buyouts was never a secret. Their financial impact on shareholders was similar: Both transactions yielded shareholder gains of approximately the same order of magnitude.[34] Even more telling, it was always apparent that management recapitalizations were carefully crafted to shift a controlling interest to incumbent managers and their allies.[35] What was not apparent, however, was how the Delaware courts would deal with this effort to avoid *Revlon*'s trigger through the device of formal recharacterization. The Delaware Supreme Court ultimately concluded, in Mills Acquisition Co. v. Macmillan, Inc.,[36] that *Revlon* applies to a defensive recapitalization which transfers control to management. Because the *Macmillan* Court's treatment of this issue was brief, and because of the importance of the role of a control change in defining *Revlon*'s trigger, it is useful to review the history that preceded it before presenting the opinion.

Ivanhoe Partners v. Newmont Mining Corp.[37] was the Delaware Supreme Court's first attempt at construing *Revlon*'s scope. Although *Ivanhoe Partners* seemed to support a narrow and formalistic construction of *Revlon*'s critical criterion of an impending sale, its significance was clouded by an idiosyncratic fact pattern. Among other peculiarities, the transaction at issue in *Ivanhoe Partners* was not an ordinary management recapitalization, since Newmont -- the target company in the case -- did not attempt to increase the equity stake of its own management. Instead, Newmont defeated a T. Boone Pickens offer by agreeing with Consolidated

---

[34] See Robert Kleiman, *The Shareholder Gains from Leveraged Cash-Outs: Some Preliminary Evidence*, 1 J.Applied Corp.Fin. 46 (1988); Puneet Handa & A. Radhakrishnan, *An Empirical Investigation of Leveraged Recapitalizations: A New Takeover Defense Strategy*, (Working Paper No.480, Salomon Brothers Center the Study of Financial Institutions, Grad.Sch. of Bus.Admin., NYU, July 1988).

[35] If the amount of stock owned by management prior to the transaction was insufficient to provide management the desired level of equity given the expected post-dividend value of the stock, management control nonetheless might be assured by selling post-dividend shares to an ESOP whose trustees were members of management. See Black & Decker v. American Standard, Inc., 682 F.Supp. 772 (D.Del.1988). Alternatively, management's stake might be increased by a pre-dividend grant of stock options that could be exchanged for post-dividend stock. See Robert M. Bass Group, Inc. v. Evans, 552 A.2d 1227 (Del.Ch.1988).

[36] 559 A.2d 1261 (Del.1989) (reproduced later in this section).

[37] 535 A.2d 1334 (Del.1987).

Gold Fields PLC, Newmont's largest shareholder, to pay a cash dividend that permitted Gold Fields to increase its ownership to 49.7% by purchasing shares in the open market (a "street sweep"). Although this agreement did not increase management's equity stake, control was nonetheless effectively transferred to management by a standstill commitment that obligated Gold Fields to limit its ownership to 49.9%, to limit its board representation to 40%, to support management's nominees for the remaining board positions, and to refrain from transferring its stock to any third party who refused to be bound by the standstill commitment.[38] Because management and Gold Fields together held a majority of Newmont's outstanding stock, and because Gold Fields could neither tender to a hostile acquirer nor initiate a proxy contest on its own, the transaction was no less effective than a management buyout or recapitalization in guaranteeing management's continued control.

The Delaware Supreme Court quickly disposed of the claim that Newmont's recapitalization should have triggered a *Revlon* obligation to entertain Pickens' bid with an opaque comment:

> *Revlon* applies here only if it was apparent that the sale of Newmont was "inevitable." The record, however, does not support such a finding for two reasons.
>
> First, Newmont was never for sale. During the short period in which these events occurred, the Newmont Board held fast to its decision to keep the company independent. Ultimately, this goal was achieved by the standstill agreement and related defensive measures. Second, there was neither a bidding contest, nor a sale. The only bidder for Newmont was Ivanhoe. Gold Fields was not a bidder, but wished to protect its already substantial interest in the company. It did so through the street sweep. Thus, the Newmont board did not "sell" the company to Gold Fields. The latter's purchases were from private sellers. . . . Even though Newmont's declaration of the dividend facilitated the street sweep, it did not constitute a "sale" of the company by Newmont.[39]

While the court's conclusion is clear, its reasoning is not. Newmont was kept "independent" only in the sense that control was not transferred to a third party; from the perspective of the public shareholders, a shift in control did take place: control was effectively transferred to management. From this perspective, the chief distinction between the Newmont device and

---

[38] 535 A.2d at 1340. In response to a finding by the Chancery Court that the standstill agreement was a breach of the target directors' fiduciary duty, the agreement was amended to allow Gold Fields to tender into an any and all fully financed hostile offer. Because the Supreme Court held that the original standstill agreement did not breach any fiduciary duty, the amendments, implemented only to cure a breach, were unnecessary. Accordingly, the analysis in the text focuses on the terms of the original standstill agreement.

[39] 535 A.2d at 1345.

Revlon's "sale" was that Newmont shifted control to management without its public shareholders receiving a premium.[40]

Perhaps as a result of its cryptic reasoning, *Ivanhoe Partners* did not resolve the issue of *Revlon*'s trigger. The two recapitalization cases that followed it were markedly less inclined to place decisive weight on transactional form. In Black & Decker Corp. v. American Standard, Inc.,[41] American Standard responded to a hostile offer by Black & Decker with a recapitalization plan that would have increased management's direct ownership interest in the company from 4.8% to 23.9%. This stake, together with an ESOP created as part of the plan, would have permitted management to control 54.5% of the company's stock. In reviewing this accumulation of voting power, 'the *Black & Decker* court first construed *Revlon* as being triggered when a target's board sponsors a transaction that results in a sale of control, during a control contest, regardless of the form of the transaction.[42]   After concluding that American Standard's recapitalization plan would "amount to a sale" of the company,[43] the court held that the plan's adoption triggered *Revlon*.

The *Black & Decker* opinion was soon followed by Robert M. Bass Group, Inc. v. Evans,[44] in which the Delaware Chancery Court reviewed an early phase of the same control contest that eventually led to the Delaware Supreme Court's decision in *Macmillan*. The recapitalization plan at issue

---

[40] In Chapter 17 and in Ronald Gilson & Reinier Kraakman, *Delaware's Intermediate Standard for Defensive Tactics: Is There Substance to Proportionality Review?*, 44 Bus.Law. 247 (1989), an explanation for the cursory treatment of the *Revlon* issue in *Ivanhoe Partners* was offered that would not foreclose treatment of management recapitalizations as triggering *Revlon*. The argument was that the Delaware Supreme Court thought the case was one in which Newmont management really was trying to avoid being caught between two potentially coercive offers. On the one hand, the Ivanhoe offer was a two-tier, potentially front-end loaded offer that the Court concluded "fit perfectly the mold of . . . a coercive device." 535 A.2d at 1342.

On the other hand, Consolidated Gold Fields, Newmont's largest shareholder with 26% of the outstanding stock, also posed a threat of coercion. Gold Fields held its shares subject to a 1983 standstill agreement that terminated if any other party acquired more than 9.9%. When Ivanhoe intentionally increased its holding to 9.95%, Gold Fields became free to "cancel the 1983 standstill agreement and acquire control of the company [presumably through market purchases], thus leaving the remaining shareholders without protection on the 'back end.'" *Id*.

As such, Newmont's defensive tactic -- financing a Gold Fields street sweep with a $33 per share special dividend that gave Gold Fields 49.7% of the outstanding stock but subject to a revised standstill agreement that limited Gold Fields' board membership to 40% -- could be justified as a careful effort to steer a path between the coercion threatened, explicitly or implicitly, by *both* Ivanhoe and Gold Fields.

As it turned out, in *Macmillan* the Delaware Supreme Court distinguished *Ivanhoe Partners* in precisely this way.

[41] 682 F.Supp. 772 (D.Del.1988).

[42] *Id*. at 780-2.

[43] *Id*. at 783.

[44] 552 A.2d 1227 (Del.Ch.1988).

in *Bass Group* would have shifted only 39.2% of the outstanding stock of a successor to the target company into management's hands: that is, a voting block significantly smaller than the 54.5% that management would have controlled under the *Black & Decker* plan.[45] Plaintiff's claim that this shift of stock triggered *Revlon* was never decided because the Chancery Court blocked the proposed recapitalization under *Unocal*. Nevertheless, the Court characterized the plan as a sale of control and broadly hinted that the plan would have been held to trigger *Revlon* if the question had been reached.[46] Thus, *Bass Group* not only supported the *Black & Decker* holding that a management recapitalization could trigger *Revlon*'s auctioneering duty, but it also suggested a critical extension of the position staked out by the *Black & Decker* opinion: The appropriate focus of the *Revlon* inquiry should be on whether a recapitalization results in the "transfer of effective control," regardless of whether it transfers voting control over an absolute majority of the company's outstanding stock.

So matters stood when the Delaware Supreme Court decided *Macmillan*.

The Delaware Supreme Court's *Macmillan* decision unmistakably resolved the tension between the apparently narrow formalism of *Ivanhoe Partners* and the substantive analysis of control shifts in *Bass Group*.[47] Following the Chancery Court's rejection of the management recapitalization in *Bass Group*, a bidding contest arose between sponsors of a management favored LBO and a hostile third party. In reviewing target management's conduct during that contest, the Supreme Court specifically endorsed the Chancery Court's dicta in *Bass Group*:

> At a minimum, *Revlon* requires that there must be the most scrupulous adherence to ordinary principles of fairness in the sense that stockholder interests are enhanced, rather than diminished, in the conduct of an auction for the sale of corporate control. This is so whether the "sale" takes the form of an active auction, a management buyout, or a "restructuring" such as that which the Court of Chancery enjoined in [*Bass Group*]. [Citation omitted.][48]

---

[45] The actual plan was somewhat more complicated than this figure suggests, since it would have split the target company into two entities and awarded management 39.2% of the equity in only one of these entities.

[46] In dicta, the court observed that "[s]uch a sale would arguably trigger duties under *Revlon*." 552 A.2d at 1243. This observation is all the more noteworthy because *Ivanhoe Partners* had previously stressed the importance of a 50% voting block, in contrast to the 39.2% block in *Bass Group*, for the purpose of determining when a control transaction might trigger *Revlon*. See Ivanhoe Partners v. Newmont Mining Corp., 535 A.2d 1334, 1343 (Del.1987).

[47] We will return to *Macmillan* later in this Chapter in assessing *Revlon*'s substantive obligations.

[48] 559 A.2d at 1285. *Macmillan* distinguished *Ivanhoe Partners* on its "special facts and circumstance. . . . Specifically, Newmont's management faced two potentially coercive offers." *Id.* at 1285 n.35.

In short, *Macmillan* clearly holds that *Revlon* is triggered when a recapitalization imposes a change in control. While the Court still speaks of the *Revlon*'s trigger as a "sale," a shift in control is the only feature common to the restructuring in *Bass Group*, the choreographed auction in *Macmillan*, and the original management buyout in *Revlon*.

b.   *The Implications of the Control Trigger in a Hostile Setting*

Given that the boundary between *Unocal* and *Revlon* is now fixed as a transaction that would result in a change in control, the remaining question that arises in the context of defending against a hostile takeover is: How much discretion should a board retain to propose a recapitalization without incurring *Revlon* obligations? The question has two forms, depending on whether a proposed recapitalization would result in a shift of control.

When a defensive management recapitalization *would* result in a change of control, the issue is whether invoking *Revlon* would also limit a board's discretion under the proportionality test to propose alternatives to a hostile offer. Even those who take the proportionality test seriously acknowledge that a board may appropriately offer an alternative transaction to shareholders who face an outside offer.[49] Yet, a management recapitalization would clearly trigger *Revlon*. Hence the question: Does the norm of evenhandedness among competing buyers, which *Revlon* requires in other contexts, conflict with a decision to offer shareholders the alternative of a management recapitalization?

The answer should focus on the position of the shareholders: As long as shareholders remain free to choose between alternatives, the board actually facilitates an auction -- and hence discharges its obligations under *Revlon* -- by offering shareholders an attractive alternative to an existing bid. The critical distinction is between the board's freedom to *offer* shareholders an alternative and the board's freedom to *impose* that alternative. Any recapitalization transaction can be cast either in a form that can be implemented on management's authority alone, as in *Black & Decker* and *Bass Group*, or in a form that requires shareholder approval, whether by tender or vote. For example, the recapitalization in *Black & Decker* could have been effected either through an issuer tender offer (as in AC Acquisitions Corp. v. Anderson, Clayton & Co.[50]), or through a charter amendment requiring shareholder approval. The key difference is the presence or absence of shareholder choice. If shareholders can choose between the recapitalization transaction and the hostile offer free of any form of pressure, then management's proposing the recapitalization should be

---

[49] See City Capital Assoc. v. Interco Inc., 551 A.2d 787, 790 (Del.Ch.1988); Gilson & Kraakman, *Delaware's New Intermediate Standard* (1989), *supra* note 40.

[50] 519 A.2d 103 (Del.Ch.1986).

permissible under both *Unocal* and *Revlon*. If, by contrast, the recapitalization is to be implemented without allowing the shareholders the opportunity to reject it, then it ought to trigger the board's *Revlon* obligations regardless of how unfair or coercive the outsider's offer might appear to be under *Unocal* analysis. Put differently, *Revlon* implies that a control transaction must be treated as a true alternative subject to shareholder choice, rather than as a routine defensive measure subject to balancing by the board against the coercive features of an outside offer under *Unocal*'s proportionality test.[51]

By contrast, when a proposed recapitalization would *not* result in a transfer of control, the corollary of the *Revlon* control rule in hostile transactions is that shareholders cannot demand to choose between management's proposed transaction and a hostile offer as a matter of right -- *Unocal*'s proportionality review applies. Here, the issue is whether *Revlon*'s control trigger allows the board too much flexibility to defeat a hostile offer. Why should a massive restructuring of the company in response to a hostile bid fail to give rise to a shareholder choice, regardless of whether it results in a shift of voting control?

One response might be that the target company may be able to equal or exceed the value of a hostile offer through a recapitalization. When the business plan underlying the hostile offer projects financial rather than operating gains -- for example, a post-acquisition strategy that contemplates increased leverage and the sale of some lines of business -- target management can duplicate the strategy by itself. Thus, Interco responded to what it perceived as a leveraged bust up takeover offer by proposing essentially to duplicate the bidders' strategy. It planned to borrow some $2 billion, to sell assets generating approximately one-half of its gross sales, and to distribute the proceeds -- together with subordinated debentures and preferred stock -- to its shareholders as a dividend. This dramatic restructuring, Interco claimed, would give shareholders the full profits that would otherwise have been shared with the bidder if the hostile offer had prevailed.[52]

---

[51] There is a more general approach to determining when management should be able to impose recapitalizations without shareholder approval. As developed in Chapter 16, the principle that explains why certain transactions require special approval procedures, including a shareholder vote, is the fact of a change in control. When management approves such a transaction, what economists call a final period problem is created. When parties expect to engage in a series of transactions, the expectation of future dealings creates an incentive for each side to treat the other fairly. Any cheating by a party in one transaction will be subject to retaliation by the other in the next transaction. In the last of the series of transactions, or when only a single transaction is contemplated, this incentive for fair dealing disappears. Because a control transaction is the final period in management's relation with shareholders, management's incentives with respect to a control transaction differ from management's incentives with respect to all other transactions, and special approval procedures are called for.

[52] See *City Capital Assoc., L.P. v. Interco, Inc.*, 551 A.2d 787 (Del.Ch.1988). As

Yet, the mere fact that a recapitalization plan might benefit shareholders relative to an outside offer is insufficient to distinguish Interco's plan from the proposed recapitalizations in *Black & Decker* and *Bass Group*, which now fall securely within *Revlon*'s reach. The critical reason that an Interco-style "non-management" recapitalization ought to escape *Revlon* (despite the enormous change that it works on the risk and return characteristics of shareholder investments) is that such a plan, which remains subject to review under *Unocal*'s proportionality test, leaves the company with incumbent management who remain vulnerable to a future takeover even if the offer at hand is defeated. As developed in Chapter 17, the threat of a future takeover bid is an integral aspect of meaningful proportionality review. Even if a company such as Interco can persuade a court that its proposed recapitalization is reasonable in relation to the threat posed by a hostile offer, management will be unlikely to maintain its independence indefinitely if its promise to create shareholder value proves to be empty. By contrast, a management recapitalization, like a management buyout, removes the company from the reach of the acquisitions market once and for all. Thus, unless shareholders can exercise a choice when the plan is proposed, they are unlikely to have a second chance.

4.   *Revlon*'s Substantive Obligations

Revlon described the consequences of its newly announced standard as shifting the responsibilities of the target board to "getting the best price for stockholders," a role the court characterized as that of "auctioneers."[53] Does the court's characterization of the target board's role require that a formal bidding process with the earmarks of an auction be organized in every case? Nowhere in its opinion does the *Revlon* court address whether a particular technique -- an auction -- is the only way by which the best price can be secured for the target company. Rather, the reference to the board as auctioneers is best understood as a metaphor that reflected the process in *Revlon*, which ultimately took a form that resembled an auction.

Looking past the auction metaphor, structuring a transaction to secure the highest price involves two parts: first, securing the information necessary to value the company;   and second, arranging the transaction so that the price secured approximates that value.

---

matters turned out, Interco's claim was mistaken, and shareholders would have been much better of with the terms of the hostile offer. See *Interco Could Be a Black Mark for Wasserstein*," Wall St.J., July 10, 1989, at p.C1, c.3.

[53] 506 A.2d at 182.

a.   *The Information Requirement*

An auction is one way of securing information about the company's value.   However, an auction may be costly to run and some potential acquirers may be reluctant to participate.   Moreover, in some circumstances the target board may believe it already knows the company's value and can itself assess any offer that it receives.   The board also can seek an opinion from its investment banker as to the range within which the company's value likely lies.   The board can "shop" the company: retain an investment banker to seek additional bids for the company.   Alternatively, the board may believe that the best evidence of value will come from vigorous one-on-one negotiations with only a single suitor.

In Barkan v. Amsted Industries, 567 A.2d 1279 (Del.1989), the Delaware Supreme Court stressed that the manner in which the target board of directors gathered information depended on the circumstances:

> . . . *Revlon* does not demand that every change in the control of a Delaware corporation be preceded by a heated bidding contest. *Revlon* is merely one of an unbroken line of cases that seek to prevent the conflicts of interest that arise in the field of mergers and acquisitions by demanding that directors act with scrupulous concern for fairness to shareholders.   When multiple bidders are competing for control, this concern for fairness forbids directors from using defensive mechanisms to thwart an auction or to favor one bidder over another.   When the board is considering a single offer and has no reliable grounds upon which to judge its adequacy, this concern for fairness demands a canvas of the market to determine if higher bids may be elicited. When, however, the directors possess a body of reliable evidence with which to evaluate the fairness of a transaction, they may approve that transaction without conducting an active survey of the market.   As the Chancellor recognized, the circumstances in which this passive approach is acceptable are limited.   "A decent respect for reality forces one to admit that . . . advice [of an investment banker] is frequently a pale substitute for the dependable information that a canvas of the relevant market can provide."   The need for adequate information is central to the enlightened evaluation of a transaction that the board must make.   Nevertheless, there is no single method that a board must employ to acquire such information.   Here, the Chancellor found that the advice of the Special Committee's investment bankers, when coupled with the special circumstances surrounding the negotiation and consummation of the MBO [management-sponsored leveraged buyout], supported a finding that Amsted's directors had acted in good faith to arrange the best possible transaction for shareholders.   Our own review of the record leads us to rule that the Chancellor's finding was well within the scope of his discretion.

Does this formulation sound less like an intermediate standard and more like the business judgment rule?   Recall that in *Trans Union*, decided before *Revlon* extended the intermediate standard of review to friendly transactions, the Delaware Supreme Court held the Trans Union board had breached the business judgment rule and the duty of care by accepting, and locking up, a friendly bid without first obtaining enough information to ascertain the company's intrinsic worth. Is the board process by which it secures the information necessary to assess a bid protected by the business judgment rule or subject to some form of the *Revlon* intermediate standard? Would the distinction matter so much if the court treated the extent of the duty to be informed as a function of the importance of the decision involved?

In Cinerama, Inc. v. Technicolor, Inc.,[54] the Chancery Court concluded that "plaintiff's claim that the board was insufficiently informed (because it had not conducted a *Revlon* auction, did not negotiate an effective post-agreement 'market check' mechanism, and was hurried and ill-advised) to meet its obligation of care, is a very close question." However, the court ultimately avoided resolving whether "the Technicolor directors failed to exercise due care, as in Smith v. Van Gorkom, and were not adequately informed, see *Revlon* . . ., when they agreed to a sale of Technicolor," because the plaintiff failed to show any injury as a result of the directors' belief -- that is, the price the target shareholders received was fair despite the breach. On appeal, the Delaware Supreme Court reversed, holding that proof of damages was not an element of a cause of action for breach of the duty of care, and that the Technicolor directors' conduct in selling the company had breached that duty.[55] In discussing the Technicolor board's obligations, the Supreme Court quoted with approval the Chancery Court's doctrinal formation of the issue:

> [T]he due care [*Trans Union*] theory and the *Revlon* theory do not present two separate legal theories justifying shareholder recovery. . . . [B]oth theories reduce to a claim that directors were inadequately informed (of alternatives or of the consequences of executing a merger and related agreements). An auction is one way to get information. A pre- or post-agreement market check mechanism is another, less effective but perhaps less risky, way to get information. A 'lock-up' is suspect because it impedes the emergence of information in that an alternative buyer that would pay (or would have paid) more is less likely to emerge once such an impediment is in place.[56]

Thus, whether the information requirement is one of due care to which the business judgment rule applies or subject to the *Revlon* intermediate standard, and whether the distinction matters, was unclear. We return to this issue in connection with determining *Revlon*'s trigger in the context of a friendly transaction, *infra*.

---

[54] 1991 WL 111134 (Del.Ch.).

[55] Cede & Co. v. Technicolor, Inc., 634 A.2d 345 (Del.1993).

[56] *Id*. at 369 n.37 (quoting Chancery Court opinion, citations omitted).

b. *Structuring the Transaction*

Revlon struck down lockup provisions that benefitted the management favored bidder. As discussed earlier, these provisions highlighted the inherent conflict of interest presented by friendly transactions. The Revlon board favored a bidder that intended to retain management in place and give them an equity interest in the post-transaction business. Yet the favoritism might have been necessary to secure a higher bid at all. *Revlon* stresses that lockup provisions are not per se illegal, but provides little guidance concerning how to tell good lockups from bad ones. In Mills Acquisition Co. v. Macmillan, Inc., the Delaware Supreme Court took up the application of the intermediate standard of review to structuring a transaction.

MILLS ACQUISITION CO. v. MACMILLAN, INC.
559 A.2d 1261 (Del.1989)

Before CHRISTIE, Chief Justice, and MOORE and HOLLAND Justices.

Moore, Justice. In this interlocutory appeal from the Court of Chancery, we review the denial of injunctive relief to Mills Acquisition Co., a Delaware corporation, and its affiliates Tendclass Limited and Maxwell Communications Corp., PLC, both United Kingdom corporations substantially controlled by Robert Maxwell.[1] Plaintiffs sought control of Macmillan, Inc. ("Macmillan" or the "company"), and moved to enjoin an asset option agreement -- commonly known as a "lockup" -- between Macmillan and Kohlberg Kravis Roberts & Co. ("KKR"), an investment firm specializing in leveraged buyouts. The lockup was granted by Macmillan's board of directors to KKR, as the purported high bidder, in an "auction" for control of Macmillan.

Although the trial court found that the conduct of the board during the auction was not "evenhanded or neutral," it declined to enjoin the lockup agreement between KKR and Macmillan. That action had the effect of prematurely ending the auction before the board had achieved the highest price reasonably available for the company. Even though the trial court found that KKR had received improper favor in the auction, including a wrongful "tip" of Maxwell's bid by Macmillan's chairman of the board and chief executive officer, and that Macmillan's board was uninformed as to such clandestine advantages, the Vice Chancellor nevertheless concluded that such misconduct neither misled Maxwell nor deterred it from submitting a prevailing bid.

Given our scope and standard of review under Levitt v. Bouvier, 287 A.2d 671 (Del.1972), we find that the legal conclusions of the trial court,

---

[1] Unless the context otherwise indicates, the plaintiffs will be referred to collectively as "Maxwell".

refusing to enjoin the KKR lockup agreement, are inconsistent with its factual findings respecting the unfairness of the bidding process. Our decision in Revlon, Inc. v. MacAndrews & Forbes Holdings, Inc., 506 A.2d 173 (Del.1986), requires the most scrupulous adherence to ordinary standards of fairness in the interest of promoting the highest values reasonably attainable for the stockholders' benefit. When conducting an auction for the sale of corporate control, this concept of fairness must be viewed solely from the standpoint of advancing general, rather than individual, shareholder interests. Here, the record reflects breaches of the duties of loyalty and care by various corporate fiduciaries which tainted the evaluative and deliberative processes of the Macmillan board, thus adversely affecting general stockholder interests. With the divided loyalties that existed on the part of certain directors, and the absence of any serious oversight by the allegedly independent directors, the governing standard was one of intrinsic fairness. Weinberger v. UOP, Inc., 457 A.2d 701, 710-11 (Del.1983). The record here does not meet that rigorous test, and the Court of Chancery failed to apply it. We take it as a cardinal principle of Delaware law that such conduct of an auction for corporate control is unsupportable. Accordingly, we reverse.

I

. . . Macmillan is a large publishing, educational and informational services company. It had approximately 27,870,000 common shares listed and traded on the New York Stock Exchange. In May, 1987, Macmillan's chairman and chief executive officer, Edward P. Evans, and its president and chief operating officer, William F. Reilly, recognized that the company was a likely target of an unsolicited takeover bid. They began exploring various defensive measures, including a corporate restructuring of the company. The genesis of this idea was a plan undertaken by another publishing company, Harcourt Brace Jovanovich, Inc., to defeat an earlier hostile bid by Robert Maxwell in May, 1987.[3] See *Macmillan I*, 552 A.2d at 1229. Indeed, Macmillan's management began exploring such a recapitalization or restructuring just one day after the public announcement of Harcourt's plan.[4] See 552 A.2d at 1229.

As Vice Chancellor noted in *Macmillan I*, for one year following the initial study of management's proposed restructuring plans:

---

[3] See British Printing & Communications Corp. v. Harcourt Brace Jovanovich, Inc., 664 F.Supp. 1519 (S.D.N.Y.1987).

[4] Evans and Reilly consulted the same lender and investment banker involved in the Harcourt restructuring, Morgan Guaranty & Trust Company and The First Boston Corporation, respectively. See *Macmillan I*, 552 A.2d at 1229. In February, 1988, a group of First Boston bankers formed their own firm, Wasserstein, Perella & Co., Inc. Wasserstein, Perella was similarly retained to represent Macmillan along with First Boston. After the retention of Wasserstein, Perella by management, it appears that First Boston's role was a mere formality, as they had little, if any, discernible involvement thereafter.

two central concepts remained constant. First Evans, Reilly and certain other members of management would end up owning absolute majority control of the restructured company. Second, management would acquire that majority control, not by investing new capital at prevailing market prices, but by being granted several hundred thousand restricted Macmillan shares and stock options.

Id. at 1229.

Management's plan was to "exchange" these options and shares granted by the company into "several million shares of the recapitalized company." See *id*. at 1229-30 & n.5. In addition, a Macmillan Employee Stock Option Plan ("ESOP") would purchase, with borrowed funds provided by the company, a large block of Macmillan shares. The then-existing independent ESOP trustee wold be replaced by Evans, Reilly, Beverly C. Chell, Vice President, General Counsel, and Secretary, and John D. Limpitlaw, Vice President - Personnel and Administration. *Id*. at 1230. This arrangement would have given these persons voting control over all of the unallocated ESOP shares.

At a meeting held on June 11, 1987, the Macmillan board authorized the above transactions. During the pendency of *Macmillan I*, the directors maintained that no relationship existed between the management-proposed restructuring and the June 11 approval of the ESOP transactions along with the grant of options and restricted shares to management. In rejecting this claim the Vice Chancellor observed that "[i]f the directors were unaware of the implications of their actions for the restructuring, it can only be because management failed appropriately to disclose those implications." *Id*. at 1230 n.7. This apparent domination of the allegedly "independent" board by the financially interested members of management, coupled with the directors' evident passivity in the face of their fiduciary duties, which so marked *Macmillan I*, continued unchanged throughout *Macmillan II*.

After the June 11 board meeting, management initiated various anti-takeover measures, including new lucrative severance contracts, known as "golden parachute" agreements, for several top executives in the event of a hostile takeover. Earlier, at the June 11 meeting, the board had approved generous five year "golden parachute" agreements for Evans and Reilly. The board also approved the adoption of a rights plan, commonly known as a "poison pill", from which the management-controlled ESOP was exempted. *Id*. at 1230-31 & n.9.

Until August, 1987, the restructuring plan contemplated a "one company" surviving entity. This concept was changed, however, to provide for the company to be split into two distinct and separately traded parts: the Information business ("Information") and the Publishing business ("Publishing"). *Id*. at 1231. Many "business related" reasons were advanced by management for the two company concept. It appears, however, that the real reason for this move was to greatly enhance management's control over the entities, thus making a hostile acquisition even more difficult. See *id*. at 1231 & n.10.

As initially planned, Information would trade two classes of common stock. One class, wholly owned by management, would be entitled to ten votes per share (constituting absolute voting control). *Id.* at 1231. The second class would have one vote per share and would be held by the public stockholders. The management owned shares were all to be deposited in a voting trust designating Evans as the sole voting trustee. Further, Information would hold a "blocking preferred" stock in Publishing (constituting 20% of Publishing's voting power). *Id.*

At the September 22, 1987 board meeting the directors were informed of the new two company restructuring concept, including its anti-takeover features and management's substantial voting and equity participation in Information. The board approved the plan without objection.[5] *Id.* at 1231-32.

On October 21, 1987, the Robert M. Bass Group, Inc., a Texas corporation controlled by Robert M. Bass, together with certain affiliates (hereafter collectively, "the Bass Group" or "Bass"), emerged as a potential bidder. By then, Bass had acquired approximately 7.5% of Macmillan's common stock. Management immediately called a special board meeting on October 29, where a rather grim and uncomplimentary picture of Bass and its supposed "*modus operandi*" in prior investments was painted by management. Bass was portrayed, among other things, as a "greenmailer." *Id.* at 1232. At the meeting, the previously adopted poison pill was modified to reduce the "flip-in" trigger from 30% to 15%. *Id.*

In its decisions the Macmillan board completely relied on management's portrayal of Bass. As it turned out, and the Vice Chancellor so found in *Macmillan I*, management's characterization of the Bass Group, including most if not all of the underlying "factual" data in support thereof, was "less than accurate." *Id.* at 1232 & n.15. Indeed, it was false. As the Vice Chancellor found: "[t]here is . . . no evidence that Macmillan management made any effort to accurately inform the board of [the true] facts. On the present record, I must conclude (preliminarily) that management's pejorative characterization of the Bass Group, even if honestly believed, served more to propagandize the board than to enlighten it."[7] *Id.* at 1232.

As the Bass Group increased its holdings in the company, the Macmillan board's executive committee, at the behest of management, examined two charts (initially) outlining the proposed restructuring. The first chart contemplated management's ownership in Information at 50.6%.

---

[5] In addition, the board granted options to management to purchase 202,500 shares of Macmillan at an exercise price of $74.24 per share. 552 A.2d at 1232.

[7] Further, the Vice Chancellor found that "[n]either management nor the board engaged in a reasonable investigation of the Bass Group, as required by *Unocal*." 552 A.2d at 1240. Management's characterization of Bass is belied by testimony to the contrary of some of the Macmillan managers themselves. Ironically, after Bass' interest in Macmillan became known, Evans himself had contacted Robert Bass and expressed an interest in joining Bass in his investment in Bell & Howell and other transactions. *Id.* at 1240 n.32.

The second chart, prepared two days later, increased Evans, Reilly and Chell's share to 60%. The committee studied other such charts at a later date, but according to the Vice Chancellor: "[a]ll restructuring proposals clearly contemplated that management would own an absolute majority of Information's stock." *Id.* at 1233.

At a regularly scheduled board meeting on March 22, 1988, the Macmillan directors voted to: (1) grant 130,000 more shares of restricted stock to Evans, Reilly, Chell and Charles G. McCurdy, Vice President - Corporate Finance; (2) seek shareholder approval of a "1988 stock option and incentive plan" and the issuance of "blank check" preferred stock "having disparate voting rights;" (3) increase the directors' compensation by some 25% per year; and (4) adopt a "non-Employee Director Retirement Plan."[8] *Id.*

Due to the significant financial interests of Evans, Reilly, Chell, McCurdy and other managers in the proposed restructuring, management decided in February or March to establish a "Special Committee" of the Board to serve as an "independent" evaluator of the plan. The Special Committee was hand picked by Evans, but not actually formed until the May 18, 1988 board meeting. See *id.* This fact is significant because the events that transpired between the time that the Special Committee was conceived and the time it was formed illuminate the actual working relationship between management and the allegedly "independent" directors. It calls into serious question the actual independence of the board in *Macmillan I and II.*

As the Vice Chancellor observed, starting in April, 1988, Evans and others in management interviewed, and for four weeks thereafter maintained intensive contact with, the investment banking firm of Lazard Freres & Co. ("Lazard"), which was to eventually become the Special Committee's financial advisor. *Id.* On April 14 representatives of Lazard met alone with Evans, and later with Evans, Chell and McCurdy. A few days later, Evans, Reilly, Chell, McCurdy and Samuel Bell, a Macmillan executive, again met with Lazard. All of these meetings involved extensive discussions concerning the proposed recapitalization. *Id.* . . .

On May 17, the day before the Macmillan annual stockholders' meeting, Evans received a letter from the Bass Group offering to purchase, consensually, all of Macmillan's common stock for $64 per share. The offer was left open for further negotiation. On May 18, the annual meeting was held at which the board recommended, and the shareholders approved, the

---

[8] Under this plan, all directors aged sixty years or older who had served on the Macmillan Board for at least five years (constituting seven of the eleven non-management directors) would be paid lifetime benefits equal to the directors' fees being paid at the time of "termination." In addition to the seven directors who would immediately qualify, three of the five members of the Special Committee who were considering the restructuring would also instantly qualify. Under this plan, as later amended, benefits also were to be paid to surviving spouses of board members. 552 A.2d at 1234.

previously mentioned 1988 Stock Option Plan and the "blank check" preferred stock. . . .

The Macmillan board convened immediately after the shareholders' meeting. Evans disclosed the Bass offer to the board. He then described the proposed restructuring, including the management group's planned equity position in Information. Thereafter the Special Committee was selected.[9] However, the Committee was not given any negotiating authority regarding the terms of the restructuring. Evans apparently designated himself to "negotiate" that matter with the board. . . .

The Special Committee remained dormant for one week following its formation, and met for the first time on May 24, 1988. Before its first meeting, Evans and Reilly again met with Lazard, allegedly the Special Committee's advisor, and Wasserstein, Perella, apparently to discuss the recapitalization plan. Evans, Reilly, Chell and McCurdy attended the May 24 Special Committee meeting, at which Lazard, as financial advisors, and the law firm of Wachtell, Lipton, Rosen & Katz were formally retained, having been invited to the meeting by Evans. Significantly, Evans and his management colleagues did not inform the Committee of their substantial prior discussions with Lazard over the preceding month. One of the outside directors, Thomas J. Neff, testified that if he had known of the activities between Lazard and management, it would have raised "serious doubts" concerning Lazard's independence. *Id.* at 1234-1235 & n.22. The restructuring plan, including management's proposed 55% ownership of Information, was presented to the Committee, which then directed Lazard to "evaluate" it further, along with the Bass offer.

Concurrent with the Special Committee meeting of May 24, Evans directed McCurdy to meet with John Scully, a Bass representative, that same day in Chicago. As the Vice Chancellor found, however, "Evans [had so] limited McCurdy's authority as to make it a foregone conclusion that the meeting would yield no meaningful result." *Id.* at 1235. In fact, the Vice Chancellor termed the meeting "little more than a charade", *Id.* at 1240, since McCurdy's only mission was to tell Scully that "Evans wanted the Bass Group to go away." *Id.* at 1235. . . .

The Special Committee met on May 28 to hear Lazard's presentation. Evans, Reilly, Chell and McCurdy attended. *Id.* at 1235 n.23. Lazard reported that management would ultimately own 39% of Information, instead of the previous 55%. This reduction occurred, ostensibly, to prevent the restructuring from being "regarded as a transfer of corporate control from the public shareholders to management." *Id.* at 1235. The Vice Chancellor found, however, that: "[d]ocuments internally generated by Macmillan reported that the management group would have effective control over

---

[9] The Special Committee consisted of Lewis A. Lapham, an old college classmate of Evans' father, (Chairman), James H. Knowles, Jr., Dorsey A. Gardner, Abraham L. Gitlow and Eric M. Hart. Hart failed to attend a single meeting of the Committee. 552 A.2d at 1234 n.20.

Information even with less than 50% of its stock." *Id.* at 1242-43.   In addition: "the conclusion that effective control will pass to management is consistent with the intent and historical evolution of the restructuring which, in every proposed permutation, had management owning over 50% of Information." *Id.* at 1243.

Macmillan's financial advisors valued the recapitalization at $64.15 per share. Lazard valued Macmillan at $72.57 per share, on a pre-tax basis, but advised the "independent" directors that it found the restructuring, valued at $64.15 per share, to be "fair." Lazard also recommended rejection of the $64 Bass offer because it was "inadequate." Wasserstein, Perella valued Macmillan at between $63 and $68 per share and made the same recommendations as Lazard concerning the restructuring and the Bass offer. All of these valuations will gain added significance in *Macmillan II.*

On the Special Committee's recommendation, the Macmillan board adopted the restructuring and rejected the Bass offer. The committee, however, had not negotiated any aspect of the transaction with management. *Id.* at 1236. . . .

The restructuring that was approved, and later preliminarily enjoined, treated the public shareholders and the management group differently. In exchange for their Macmillan shares, the public stockholders were to receive a dividend of $52.35 cash, a $4.50 debenture, a "stub share" of Publishing ($5.10) and a one-half share of Information ($2.20).   The management group, and the ESOP, would not receive the cash and debenture components. Instead, they would "exchange" their restricted stock and options for restricted shares of Information, representing a $39.2% stake in that company. *Id.*

The Information stock received by management could not be sold, pledged, or transferred for two years, and would not fully vest for five years. The management holders could, however, vote the shares and receive dividends. Management would also own 3.2% of Publishing. The ESOP would own 26% of Publishing.[13] *Id.*

The effect of all this would increase management's then-combined holdings of 4.5% in Macmillan to 39% in Information.   Additionally, management would receive substantial cash and other benefits from the transaction. See *id.* at 1237 n.28.

Following the board's public announcement on May 31, the Bass Group made a second offer for all Macmillan stock at $73 per share.   In the alternative, Bass proposed a restructuring, much like the one the board had approved, differing only in the respect that it would offer $5.65 per share

---

[13] Although the *Macmillan I* opinion did not further discuss this point, it appears that the combination of the ESOP and management holdings, along with the 20% "blocking preferred" that Information holds in Publishing, would give management effective control over Publishing as well.

more, and management would be treated the same as the public stockholders.[14]

Two days after the revised offer was announced, Lazard concluded that it could furnish an 'adequacy' opinion that would enable the Special Committee to reject the $73 per share cash portion of Bass' offer. They gave an oral opinion the following day, June 7, at a joint meeting of the Special Committee and the board that the Bass $73 cash offer, as distinguished from Bass' alternative restructuring proposal, was inadequate, given Lazard's earlier opinion that the "pre-tax break up" value of Macmillan was between $72 and $80 per share. *Id.* at 1237-38. These valuation ranges, obviously intended to accord with management's restructuring in *Macmillan I*, will assume an interesting significance in *Macmillan II*, when less than three months later, on August 25, these same advisors, at Evans' behest, found Maxwell's $80 all cash offer inadequate. . . .

On July 14, 1988, the Vice Chancellor preliminarily enjoined the Evans designed restructuring, and held that both of the revised Bass offers were "clearly superior to the restructuring." The Court further inferred that the only real "threat" posed by the Bass offers was to the incumbency of the board "or to the management group's expectation of garnering a 39% ownership interest in Information on extremely favorable terms."[16] *Id.* at 1241 & n.34.

Thus, *Macmillan I* essentially ended on July 14, 1988. However, it only set the stage for the saga of *Macmillan II* to begin that same day. It opened with Macmillan's senior management holding extensive discussions with KKR in an attempt to develop defensive measures to thwart the Bass Group offer. This included a management-sponsored buyout of the company by KKR. There is nothing in the record to suggest that this was done pursuant to board action. If anything, it was Evans acting alone in his own personal interest. . . .

On July 20, a most significant development occurred when Maxwell intervened in the Bass-Macmillan bidding contest by proposing to Evans a consensual merger between Macmillan and Maxwell at an all-cash price of $80 per share. This was $5.00 higher than any other outstanding offer for the company.[18] Maxwell further stated his intention to retain the company's

---

[14] The Vice Chancellor determined that "[t]here is no evidence that any member of the Board or the Special Committee questioned how a sale of 39% of Information would constitute a sale of the company if sold to the Bass Group, yet would not be if that same 39% interest is sold to the management group. The defendants have failed to explain that reasoning, and its logic continues to elude the Court." 552 A.2d at 1242.

[16] Consistent with the trial court's strong implication that any "threat" posed by the Bass offer was being used merely as a pretext, the court found that "management was . . . able to use the 'threat' posed by the Bass offers to '[avail] themselves of the takeover threat to increase their, and their employees' ownership interest in the company.'" 552 A.2d at 1243 & n.38 (citations omitted).

[18] Two days before the initial Maxwell bid, the Bass Group had raised its offer for the company to $75 per share. Although this final Bass offer remained open into September, the

management, and additionally, to negotiate appropriate programs of executive incentives and compensation.

Macmillan did not respond to Maxwell's overture for five weeks. Instead, during this period, Macmillan's management intensified their discussions with KKR concerning a buyout in which senior management, particularly Evans and Reilly, would have a substantial ownership interest in the new company. Upon execution of a confidentiality agreement, KKR was given detailed internal, non-public, financial information of Macmillan, culminating in a series of formal "due diligence" presentations to KKR representatives by Macmillan senior management on August 4 and 5, 1988.

On August 12, 1988, after more than three weeks of silence from the company, Maxwell made an $80 per share, all-cash tender offer for Macmillan, conditioned solely upon receiving the same nonpublic information which Macmillan had given to KKR three weeks earlier. . . . Notwithstanding the fact that on May 30 both Wasserstein, Perella and Lazard had given opinions that the management restructuring, with a value of $64.15, was fair, and on June 7 had advised the board that the company had a maximum breakup value of $80 per share, Wasserstein, Perella and Lazard issued new opinions on August 25 that $80 was unfair and inadequate. Accordingly, the Maxwell offer was rejected by the Macmillan board.

On August 30 a meeting was arranged with Maxwell at Evans' request at which Maxwell executed a confidentiality agreement, and was furnished with some, but not all, of the confidential financial information that KKR had received. At this meeting, Evans told Robert Maxwell that he was an unwelcome bidder for the whole company, but that a sale to Maxwell of up to $1 billion of Macmillan's assets would be considered. Undeterred, Maxwell indicated his intent and ability to prevail in an auction for the company, as "nobody could afford" to top a Maxwell bid due to the operational economies and synergies available through a merger of Maxwell's companies with Macmillan.

Nonetheless, on September 6, 1988, representatives of Macmillan and KKR met to negotiate and finalize KKR's buyout of the company. In this transaction Macmillan senior management would receive up to 20% ownership in the newly formed company. During this meeting, Evans and his senior managers suggested that they would endorse the concept and structure of the buyout to the board of directors, *even though KKR had not yet disclosed to Evans and his group the amount of its bid.* With this extraordinary commitment, KKR indicated that it would submit a firm offer by the end of the week -- September 9. Following this meeting with KKR, Macmillan's financial advisors were instructed by Evans to notify the six remaining potential bidders, during September 7 and 8, that "the process

entry of Maxwell into the fray, for all practical purposes, rendered the Bass bid academic.

seems to be coming to a close" and that any bids for Macmillan were due by Friday afternoon, September 9. . . .

In a September 8 meeting with Robert Maxwell and his representatives, Evans announced that the company's management planned to recommend a management-KKR leveraged buyout to the directors of Macmillan, and that he would not consider Maxwell's outstanding offer despite Maxwell's stated claim that he would pay "top dollar" for the entire company. Evans then declared that now he would only discuss the possible sale of up to $750 million worth of assets to Maxwell in order to facilitate this buyout. Furthermore, Evans flatly told Maxwell that senior management would leave the company if any other bidder prevailed over the management sponsored buyout offer. Following this meeting, Robert Maxwell expressed his concern to Evans that no lockup or other "break up" arrangements should be made until Macmillan had properly considered his proposal. Additionally, he volunteered to either negotiate his offering price or to purchase Information for $1.4 billion, subject to a minimal due diligence investigation.

On the morning of September 9, Maxwell representatives were granted a limited due diligence review with respect to certain divisions of the company. However, during these sessions Macmillan provided little additional material information to Maxwell. Indeed, throughout the bidding process, and despite its repeated requests Maxwell was not given complete information until September 25 -- almost two months after such data had been furnished to KKR.

In the late afternoon of September 9, Evans received another letter from Robert Maxwell, offering to increase his all-cash bid for the company to $84 per share. This revised offer was conditioned solely upon Maxwell receiving a clear understanding of which managers would be leaving Macmillan upon his acquisition of the company. However, Maxwell ended this correspondence with the statement:

> If you have a financed binding alternative proposal which will generate a greater present value for shareholders, I will withdraw my bid.

In their deliberations that weekend, Macmillan's advisors inferred from this remark that Maxwell was unwilling to bid over $84 per share for the company.

By 5:30 p.m. on September 9, two bidders remained in the auction: Maxwell, by virtue of his written $84 all-cash offer, and KKR, which had submitted only an oral bid to Macmillan's advisors. However, Macmillan representatives continued to negotiate overnight with KKR until an offer was reduced to writing on the next day, September 10, despite the bid deadline previously mandated by the company. In their written bid, KKR offered to acquire 94% of Macmillan's shares through a management participation, highly-leveraged, two-tier, transaction, with a "face value" of $85 per share and payable in a mix of cash and subordinated debt securities. Additionally, this offer was strictly conditioned upon the payment of KKR's expenses and an additional $29.3 million "break up" fee if a merger agreement between KKR and Macmillan was terminated by virtue of a higher bid for the company.

On September 10 and 11, Macmillan's directors met to consider Maxwell's all-cash $84 bid and KKR's blended bid of $85. Although Macmillan's financial advisors discounted KKR's offer at $84.76 per share, they nevertheless formally opined that the KKR offer was both higher than Maxwell's bid and was fair to Macmillan shareholders from a financial point of view. The Macmillan board, inferring from Maxwell's September 9 letter that he would not top a bid higher than $84 per share, approved the KKR offer and agreed to recommend KKR's offer to the shareholders. The Macmillan-KKR merger agreement was publicly announced the following day, accompanied by Macmillan's affirmation that it would take all action necessary to insure the inapplicability of its shareholder rights plan, i.e., "poison pill," to the KKR offer.

Subsequently, on September 15 -- and in seeming contradiction to his September 9 statement that he would not top his previous offer -- Maxwell announced that he was increasing his all-cash offer to $86.60 per share. Additionally, Maxwell asked the Court of Chancery to enjoin the operation of Macmillan's "poison pill" rights plan against the revised Maxwell offer.

After considering the increased Maxwell bid, on September 22 the Macmillan board withdrew its recommendation of the KKR offer to shareholders, and declared its willingness to consider higher bids for the company. The board therefore instructed its investment advisors to attempt to solicit higher bids from Maxwell, KKR or any other potential bidders, in an effort to maximize the company's value for shareholders. Additionally, the board directed that the shareholder rights plan be applied to all bidders in order to enhance the auction process.

On September 23, 1988, Wasserstein, Perella began establishing the procedures for submission of the Maxwell and KKR final bids. In partial deference to Maxwell's vocal belief that the auction would be "rigged" in KKR's favor, and in order to promote an appearance of fairness in the bidding process, a "script" was developed which would be read over the telephone to both KKR and Maxwell. According to this script, both bidders were called and advised on September 24 that "the process appears to be drawing to a close" and that any final amended bids were due by 5:30 p.m., September 26.

After receiving this information on September 24, Robert Pirie, Maxwell's financial advisor, once again expressed concern to Macmillan that KKR would be favored in the auction process, and would receive "break up" fees or a lockup agreement without Maxwell first being allowed to increase its bid. Perhaps as a result of this concern, Robert Maxwell stated unequivocally in a September 25 letter to Macmillan that he was prepared, if necessary, to exceed a higher competing offer from KKR.

KKR had further discussions with Macmillan's advisors during the afternoon of September 25. One of the primary topics was an agreement that

KKR's amended offer would include a "no-shop" clause. KKR's stated interpretation of this "blanket prohibition" was that disclosure by Macmillan of any element of KKR's bid, including price, would automatically revoke the offer. Macmillan's advisors thus knew that KKR would insist upon conditions that could hinder maximization of the auction process to the detriment of Macmillan's shareholders. . . .

By the auction deadline on that evening, both Maxwell and KKR had submitted bids. Maxwell made an all-cash offer, consistent with its previous bids, of $89 per share. Like its past bids, KKR submitted another "blended", front-loaded offer of $89.50 per share, consisting of $82 in cash and the balance in subordinated securities. However, this nominally higher KKR bid was subject to three conditions effectively designed to end the auction: (1) imposition of the "no-shop" rule, (2) the grant to KKR of a lockup option to purchase eight Macmillan subsidiaries for $950 million, and (3) the execution of a definitive merger agreement by 12:00 noon, the following day, September 27.

While Macmillan's financial analysts considered the value of KKR's bid to be slightly higher, they decided that the bids were too close to permit the recommendation of either offer, and that the auction should therefore continue. However, shortly after the bids were received, Evans and Reilly, who were present in the Macmillan offices at the time, asked unidentified financial advisors about the status of the auction process. Inexplicably, these advisors told Evans and Reilly that both bids had been received, informed them of the respective price and forms of the bids, and stated that the financial advisors were unable to recommend either bid to the board.[22]

Thereafter, in the presence of Reilly and Charles J. Queenan, . . . Evans telephoned a KKR representative and "tipped" Maxwell's bid to him. In this call, Evans informed KKR that Maxwell had offered "$89, all cash" for the company and that the respective bids were considered "a little close." After a few minutes of conversation, the KKR representative realized the impropriety of the call and abruptly terminated it.[23]

Meanwhile, Macmillan's financial advisors, apparently ignorant of Evans' "tip" to KKR, began developing procedures for a supplemental round of bidding. Bruce Wasserstein, the leading financial advisor to Macmillan management, who primarily orchestrated the auction process, developed a second "script" which was to be read over the telephone to both bidders. It stated:

---

[22] This epitomizes the problem of conducting an auction without board oversight, and under uncontrolled circumstances that gave Evans and Reilly, themselves interested bidders with KKR, complete and improper access to the process.

[23] In fairness to KKR even Maxwell concedes that but for the integrity of KKR's counsel, it is unlikely that Evans' tip would have been publicly disclosed. It also appears that counsel, who appeared in this action for the defendants, were unaware of the "tip" until it was disclosed by KKR.

We are not in a position at this time to recommend any bid. If you would like to increase your bid price, let us know by 10:00 p.m.

At approximately 8:15 p.m., Wasserstein first read this prepared text to a Maxwell representative, and then relayed the same message to KKR. However, the actual document in evidence, which purports to be the "script", significantly varies in what was said to KKR. Allegedly in response to questions from KKR, Wasserstein and other financial advisors impressed upon KKR "the need to go as high as [KKR] could go" in terms of price. Additionally, the Wasserstein "script" discloses the further statement:

To KKR: Focus on price but be advised that we do not want to give a lockup. If we granted a lockup, we would need: (1) a significant gap in your bid over the competing bid; (2) a smaller group of assets to be bought; and (3) a higher price for the assets to be bought.

At approximately 10:00 p.m., near the auction deadline of midnight, Pirie on behalf of Maxwell telephoned Wasserstein to inquire whether Macmillan had received a bid higher than the Maxwell offer. During the call, Pirie flatly stated that upon being informed that a higher bid had been received by Macmillan, Maxwell would promptly notify the company whether it would increase its standing offer. Pirie also said that if Maxwell had already submitted the highest bid for the company, he would not "bid against himself" by increasing his offer.

While Wasserstein could reasonably infer from this message that Maxwell intended to top any KKR offer, it is clear that Pirie wanted to know whether KKR had in fact submitted a higher bid. Wasserstein claims to have believed that such a revelation might violate KKR's "no-shop" condition, and would have terminated the KKR offer.[24] Therefore, he replied that if Maxwell had "anything further to say, tell us by midnight." Additionally, Wasserstein told Pirie to assume that Macmillan would not call Maxwell to inform them of a higher offer. After this conversation, and upon the advice of legal counsel, Wasserstein called Pirie back and reemphasized that he was not in a position to recommend a bid to the Macmillan board, and that Maxwell should submit their highest bid to the company by 12:00 midnight.

From the bulk of these conversations, Maxwell and Pirie reasonably, but erroneously, concluded that Wasserstein was attempting to force Maxwell to bid against itself, and that its offer was indeed higher than the competing KKR bid. Furthermore, the record is clear that Wasserstein, who later acknowledged this fact to the Macmillan board, knew that Pirie mistakenly believed that Maxwell was already the high bidder for the company. Yet, despite his responsibilities as "auctioneer" for the company, Wasserstein

---

[24] At oral argument the parties, including KKR, could not seriously claim that disclosing the mere existence of a higher bid would violate the "no-shop" clause. However, see n.21, *supra*, and n.31, *infra*.

never sought to correct Maxwell's mistaken belief that they prevailed in the auction. The cumulative effect of all this was that the Maxwell group did not increase their bid before the Macmillan board met on the next day, September 27.

At 11:50 p.m., September 26, ten minutes before the bid deadline, KKR submitted a final revised offer with a face value of $90 per share. Furthermore, the bid was predicated upon the same three previous conditions -- except that the revised lockup option, apparently reflecting the additional information relayed by Wasserstein in his special KKR "script," was reduced to include only four subsidiaries at a purchase price of $775 million.

In the early morning hours of September 27, after the midnight auction deadline, Macmillan negotiated with both parties over wholly different matters. Macmillan's advisors negotiated with Maxwell's representatives for several hours over the specific and unresolved terms of Maxwell's otherwise unconditional merger proposal. However, during these sessions Macmillan never suggested that Maxwell increase its bid. On the other hand, for almost eight hours Macmillan and KKR negotiated to increase KKR's offer. By the next morning, while only increasing its total bid by approximately $1.6 million, to $90.05 ($.05 per share), KKR extracted concessions from Macmillan which increased KKR's exercise price under the lockup by $90 million after adding three more Macmillan divisions to the group of optioned assets.

Significantly, the sale of the assets under the KKR lockup agreement was structured on a "cash" basis, which would immediately result in a $250 million current tax liability for Macmillan. Moreover, both KKR and Macmillan knew that this tax liability could have been avoided through an "installment" basis sale of the assets. Above all, they knew that it would produce a *de facto* financial "poison pill" which would effectively end the auction process.

On the morning of September 27, the Macmillan board met with its investment advisors to consider these competing bids. During the course of the meeting, chaired by Evans and with Reilly present, the company's financial advisors with Wasserstein as the lead spokesman (some directors said he presided), made presentations describing their communications with both Maxwell and KKR during the auction process. Wasserstein falsely claimed that the advisors had conducted "a level-playing field auction where both parties had equal opportunity to participate." Additionally, in answer to questioning, Wasserstein mistakenly assured the board that he had been the "only conduit of information" during the process and, falsely, that both parties had received *identical* information during the auction. Despite the obvious untruth of these assertions, Evans and Reilly remained silent, knowing also that Evans had clandestinely, and wrongfully, tipped Maxwell's bid to KKR.

Wasserstein then announced the results of the second round of the auction along with specific aspects of KKR's $90.05 "face amount" offer and Maxwell's $89 cash bid. Wasserstein, whose firm was originally retained as *management's* financial advisor, not the board's, then opined that the KKR offer was the higher of the two bids. The Lazard representative, who was retained as the financial advisor to the independent directors of the board, but throughout acquiesced in Wasserstein's predominant role, thereafter concurred in Wasserstein's assessment. Wasserstein additionally explained the ramifications of the conditions of KKR's offer, including the "deterrent" effect of the $250 million tax liability produced by the KKR lockup agreement.

However, through its deliberations on September 27, Macmillan's board, whether justified or not, was under the impression that the two bids were the product of a fair and unbiased auction process, designed to encourage KKR and Maxwell to submit their best bids.[25] The directors were not informed of Evans' and Reilly's "tip" to KKR on the previous day. Nor were they told of Wasserstein's extended "script" giving to KKR, but denying to Maxwell, additional information about the bidding process. Throughout the board meeting Evans and Reilly remained silent, deliberately concealing from their fellow directors their misconduct of tipping Maxwell's bid to KKR.

After these presentations, the Macmillan directors held extensive and closed discussions concerning the choices available to the board, including the possibility that Maxwell might increase its bid if the board "shopped" the KKR offer. Yet, as they believed that the risk of terminating the KKR offer outweighed the potential advantage of an increased Maxwell bid, the directors decided to accept the higher face value KKR proposal, and granted the KKR merger and lockup option agreements.

On the next day, Maxwell promptly amended its original complaint in the Court of Chancery, added KKR as a co-defendant, and among other things, sought to enjoin the lockup agreement, the break-up fees and expenses granted to KKR. . . .

On that same day, Robert Maxwell delivered a letter to Evans announcing that he had amended his cash tender offer to $90.25 per share, conditioned upon invalidation of the KKR lockup agreement. In his letter, Maxwell emphasized that he had previously stated his willingness to top any offer higher than his earlier $89 offer, and that he was nevertheless willing to purchase for $900 million the same four divisions which KKR originally proposed to purchase for $775 million.

On October 4, the Macmillan board met to consider both the revised Maxwell bid and Evans' September 26 "tip" to KKR. After some discussion and deliberation, the board rejected Maxwell's increased offer because it was conditioned on invalidating the KKR lockup. Furthermore, the board considered that Evans' "tip" to KKR was immaterial in light of the second round of bidding that occurred. Additionally, after consultation with counsel, the board concluded that their ignorance of this "tip", at the time

---

[25] Even though neither the Board as a whole, nor the allegedly "independent" directors, had taken any action to ensure such a process.

they approved the merger with KKR, was insufficient grounds for repudiating the lockup agreement.

After a hearing on Maxwell's motion for a preliminary injunction, on October 17, the Court of Chancery denied Maxwell's request to enjoin the lockup agreement, the break-up fees and expenses granted by the Macmillan board to KKR. In ruling for Macmillan, the trial court found that although KKR was consistently and deliberately favored throughout the auction process, Maxwell was not prevented from, or otherwise misled to refrain from, submitting a higher bid for the company. However, the court found that Macmillan's shareholders should have the opportunity to consider an alternative offer for the company, and therefore enjoined the operation of Macmillan's "poison pill" shareholder rights plan as a defensive measure to Maxwell's still open tender offer. In this appeal neither party has challenged that limited injunction. Thus, the sole issue before us is the validity, under all of the foregoing circumstances, of the asset lockup option granted pursuant to the KKR-Macmillan merger agreement with its attendant breakup fees and expenses.

II . . .

A

In denying relief to the plaintiffs, it is unclear what legal standards the trial court applied in reviewing defendants' conduct. . . . While it is apparent that the Court of Chancery seemingly attempted to evaluate this case under the relatively broad parameters of the business judgment rule, it nevertheless held that the relevant inquiry must focus upon the "fairness" of the auction process in light of promoting the maximum shareholder value as mandated by this Court in *Revlon*. In denying Maxwell's motion for an injunction, the Vice-Chancellor concluded that the auction-related deficiencies could be deemed "material" only upon a showing that they actually deterred a higher bid from Maxwell.

We have held that when a court reviews a board action, challenged as a breach of duty, it should decline to evaluate the wisdom and merits of a business decision unless sufficient facts are alleged with particularity, or the record otherwise demonstrates, that the decision was not the product of an informed, disinterested, and independent board. See Aronson v. Lewis, 473 A.2d 805, 812 (Del.1984); Pogostin v. Rice, 480 A.2d 619, 624 (Del.1984); Smith v. Van Gorkom, 488 A.2d 858, 872 (Del.1985). Yet this judicial reluctance to assess the merits of a business decision ends in the face of illicit manipulation of a board's deliberative processes by self-interested corporate fiduciaries. Here, not only was there such deception, but the board's own lack of oversight in structuring and directing the auction afforded management the opportunity to indulge in the misconduct which occurred. In such a context, the challenged transaction must withstand rigorous judicial scrutiny under the exacting standards of entire fairness. What occurred here cannot survive that analysis.

The Vice Chancellor correctly found that Evans and Reilly, as participants in the leveraged buyout, had significant self-interest in ensuring the success of a KKR bid. Given this finding, Evans' and Reilly's deliberate concealment of material information from the Macmillan board must necessarily have been motivated by an interest adverse to Macmillan's shareholders. Evans' and Reilly's conduct throughout was resolutely intended to deliver the company to themselves in *Macmillan I*, and to their favored bidder, KKR, and thus themselves, in *Macmillan II*. The board was torpid, if not supine, in its efforts to establish a truly independent auction, free of Evans' interference and access to confidential data. By placing the entire process in the hands of Evans, through his own chosen financial advisors, with little or no board oversight, the board materially contributed to the unprincipled conduct of those upon whom it looked with a blind eye.

. . .

III

The voluminous record in this case discloses conduct that fails all basic standards of fairness. While any one of the identifiable breaches of fiduciary duty, standing alone, should easily foretell the outcome, what occurred here, including the lack of oversight by the directors, irremediably taints the design and execution of the transaction.

It is clear that on July 14, 1988, the day that the Court of Chancery enjoined the management-induced reorganization, and with Bass' $73 offer outstanding, Macmillan's management met with KKR to discuss a management sponsored buyout. This was done without prior board approval. By early September, Macmillan's financial and legal advisors, originally chosen by Evans, independently constructed and managed the process by which bids for the company were solicited. Although the Macmillan board was fully aware of its ultimate responsibility for ensuring the integrity of the auction, the directors wholly delegated the creation and administration of the auction to an array of Evans' hand-picked investment advisors. It is undisputed that Wasserstein, who was originally retained as an investment advisor to Macmillan's senior management, was a principal, if not the primary "auctioneer" of the company. While it is unnecessary to hold that Wasserstein lacked independence, or was necessarily "beholden" to management, it appears that Lazard Freres, allegedly the investment advisor to the independent directors, was a far more appropriate candidate to conduct this process on behalf of the board. Yet, both the board and Lazard acceded to Wasserstein's, and through him Evans', primacy.

While a board of directors may rely in good faith upon "information, opinions, reports or statements presented" by corporate officers, employees and experts "selected with reasonable care," 8 Del.C. § 141(e), it may not avoid its active and direct duty of oversight in a matter as significant as the sale of corporate control. That would seem particularly obvious where insiders are among the bidders. This failure of the Macmillan board significantly contributed to the resulting mismanagement of the bidding process. When presumably well-intentioned outside directors remove themselves from the design and execution of an auction, then what occurred here, given the human temptations left unchecked, was virtually inevitable.

Clearly, this auction was clandestinely and impermissibly skewed in favor of KKR. The record amply demonstrates that KKR repeatedly received significant material advantages to the exclusion and detriment of Maxwell to stymie, rather than enhance, the bidding process.

As for any "negotiations" between Macmillan and Maxwell, they are noteworthy only for the peremptory and curt attitude of Macmillan, through its self-interested chief executive officer Evans, to reject every overture from Maxwell. In Robert Maxwell's initial letter to Evans of July 21, he proposed an $80 all-cash offer for the company. This represented a substantial increase over any other outstanding offer. Indeed, it equalled the highest per share price, which both Wasserstein, Perella and Lazard had previously ascribed to the value of the company on June 7, when the Evans sponsored restructuring was before the board. Now, not only was Maxwell ignored, but Evans convinced Wasserstein, Perella and Lazard, contrary to their June 7 opinions, ascribing a maximum value to the company of $80 per share, to declare Maxwell's August 12 bid of $80 inadequate.[28]   Not only did Macmillan's financial advisors dismiss all Maxwell offers for negotiations, but they also deliberately misled Maxwell in the final stage of the auction by perpetuating the mistaken belief that Maxwell had the high bid. Additionally, Maxwell was subjected to a series of short bid deadlines in a seeming effort to prevent the submission of a meaningful bid. The defendants have totally failed to justify this calculated campaign of resistance and misinformation, despite the strict duties of care and loyalty demanded of them. See *Revlon*, 506 A.2d at 181.

The tone and substance of the communications between Macmillan and Maxwell dispel any further doubt that Maxwell was seen as an unwelcome, unfriendly and unwanted bidder. Evans, a self-interested fiduciary, repeatedly stated that *he* would do everything to prevent Maxwell from acquiring Macmillan. Nonetheless, Robert Maxwell's response was a diplomatic, yet persistent, pursuit of Macmillan, emphasizing his desire to work with existing management and his intent to operate the company as a going concern. . . .

This continuing hostility toward Maxwell cannot be justified after the Macmillan board actually decided on September 10-11 to abandon any further restructuring attempts, and to sell the entire company. Although Evans had begun negotiations with KKR on July 14, the board's action in September formally initiated the auction process. Further discriminatory

---

[28] Yet, on May 30 these same advisors had found management's $64.15 restructuring to be fair.

treatment of a bidder, without any rational benefit to the shareholders, was unwarranted. The proper objective of Macmillan's fiduciaries was to obtain the highest price reasonably available for the company, provided it was offered by a reputable and responsible bidder.[29] *Revlon*, 506 A.2d at 182, 184. At this point, there was no justification for denying Maxwell the same courtesies and access to information as had been extended to KKR. *Id.* at 184. Without board planning and oversight to insulate the self-interested management from improper access to the bidding process, and to ensure the proper conduct of the auction by truly independent advisors selected by, and answerable only to, the independent directors, the legal complications which a challenged transaction faces under *Revlon* are unnecessarily intensified. See *Weinberger*, 457 A.2d at 709 n.7. Compare *Rosenblatt*, 493 A.2d 929, 937-40 (Del.1985), where an authentic independent negotiating structure had been established.

IV

In examining the actual conduct of this auction, there can be no justification for the telephonic "tip" to KKR of Maxwell's $89 all-cash offer following the first round of bidding held on September 26th. Although the defendants contend that this tip was made "innocently" and under the impression that the auction process had already ended, this assertion is refuted by the record. The recipient of the "tip", KKR, immediately recognized its impropriety. Evans' and Reilly's knowing concealment of the tip at the critical board meeting of September 27th utterly destroys their credibility. Given their duty of disclosure under the circumstances, this silence is an explicit acknowledgment of their culpability.

As the duty of candor is one of the elementary principles of fair dealing, Delaware law imposes this unremitting obligation not only on officers and directors, but also upon those who are privy to material information obtained in the course of representing corporate interests. See *Weinberger*, 457 A.2d at 710; Marciano v. Nakash, 535 A.2d 400, 406-407 (Del.1987); Brophy v. Cities Service Co., 70 A.2d 5, 7 (Del.1949). At a minimum, this rule dictates that fiduciaries, corporate or otherwise, may not use superior information or knowledge to mislead others in the performance of their own fiduciary obligations. The actions of those who join in such

---

[29] In reassessing the bid and the bidder's responsibility, a board may consider, among various proper factors, the adequacy and terms of the offer; its fairness and feasibility; the proposed or actual financing for the offer, and the consequences of that financing; questions of illegality; the impact of both the bid and the potential acquisition on other constituencies, provided that it bears some reasonable relationship to general shareholder interests; the risk of nonconsummation; the basic stockholder interests at stake; the bidder's identity, prior background and other business venture experiences; and the bidder's business plans for the corporation and their effects on stockholder interests. Cf. *Ivanhoe*, 535 A.2d at 1341-42; *Unocal*, 493 A.2d at 955-56; *Revlon*, 506 A.2d at 182-83.

misconduct are equally tainted. See e.g. Penn Mart Realty v. Becker, 298 A.2d 349, 351 (Del.Ch.1972).

Defendants maintain that the Evans-Reilly tip was immaterial, because it did not prevent Maxwell from submitting a higher bid in the second and final round of the auction on September 26th. However, this "immaterial" tip revealed both the price and form of Maxwell's first round bid, which constituted the two principal strategic components of their otherwise unconditional offer. With this information, KKR knew every crucial element of Maxwell's initial bid. The unfair tactical advantage this gave KKR, since no aspect of its own bid could be shopped, becomes manifest in light of the situation created by Maxwell's belief that it had submitted the higher offer. Absent an unprompted and unexpected improvement in Maxwell's bid, the tip provided vital information to enable KKR to prevail in the auction.

Similarly, the defendants argue that the subsequent Wasserstein "long script" -- in reality another form of tip -- was an immaterial and "appropriate response" to questions by KKR, providing no tactical information useful to KKR. As to this claim, the eventual auction results demonstrate that Wasserstein's tip relayed crucial information to KKR: the methods by which KKR should tailor its bid in order to satisfy Macmillan's financial advisors. It is highly significant that both aspects of the advice conveyed by the tip -- to "focus on price" and to amend the terms of its lock-up agreement -- were adopted by KKR. They were the very improvements upon which the board subsequently accepted the KKR bid on Wasserstein's recommendation. Nothing could have been more material under the circumstances. It violated every principle of fair dealing, and of the exacting role demanded of those entrusted with the conduct of an auction for the sale of corporate control.

V

Given the materiality of these tips, and the silence of Evans, Reilly and Wasserstein in the face of their rigorous affirmative duty of disclosure at the September 27 board meeting, there can be no dispute but that such silence was misleading and deceptive. In short, it was a fraud upon the board. See generally Nicolet v. Nutt, 525 A.2d at 149; Stephenson v. Capano, 462 A.2d at 1074.

Under 8 Del.C. § 141(e), when corporate directors rely in good faith upon opinions or reports of officers and other experts "selected with reasonable care", they necessarily do so on the presumption that the information provided is both accurate and complete. Normally, decisions of a board based upon such data will not be disturbed when made in the proper exercise of business judgment. However, when a board is deceived by those who will gain from such misconduct, the protections girding the decision itself vanish. Decisions made on such a basis are voidable at the behest of innocent parties to whom a fiduciary duty was owed and breached, and whose interests were thereby materially and adversely affected.[32] This rule is based on the unyielding principle that corporate fiduciaries shall abjure every temptation for personal profit at the expense of those they serve.[33]

VI

In *Revlon*, we addressed for the first time the parameters of a board of directors' fiduciary duties in a sale of corporate control. There, we affirmed the Court of Chancery's decision to enjoin the lock-up and no-shop provisions accepted by the Revlon directors, holding that the board had breached its fiduciary duties of care and loyalty.[34]

Although we have held that such agreements are not *per se* illegal, we recognized that like measures often foreclose further bidding to the detriment of shareholders, and end active auctions prematurely. *Revlon*, at 183-84; see also Thompson v. Enstar Corp., 509 A.2d 518 (Del.Ch.1984). If the grant of an auction-ending provision is appropriate, it must confer a substantial benefit upon the stockholders in order to withstand exacting scrutiny by the courts. Moreover, where the decision of the directors, granting the lock-up option, was not informed or was induced by breaches of fiduciary duties, such as those here, they cannot survive.

A

Perhaps the most significant aspect of *Revlon* was our holding that when the Revlon board authorized its management to negotiate a sale of the company:

> [t]he duty of the board had thus changed from the preservation of Revlon as a corporate entity to the maximization of the company's value at a sale for the stockholders' benefit. . . . [The board] no longer faced threats to corporate policy and effectiveness, or to the stockholders' interests, from a grossly

---

[32] In this context we speak only of the traditional concept of protecting the decision itself, sometimes referred to as the business judgment doctrine. *Revlon*, 506 A.2d at 180 n.10. The question of the independent directors' personal liability for these challenged decisions, reached under circumstances born of the board's lack of oversight, is not the issue here. However, we entertain no doubt that this board's virtual abandonment of its oversight functions in the face of Evans' and Reilly's patent self-interest was a breach of its fundamental duties of loyalty and care in the conduct of this auction. More than anything else it created the atmosphere in which Evans, Reilly and others could act so freely and improperly. . . .

[33] Although Wasserstein was not a Macmillan officer or director, it is bedrock law that the conduct of one who knowingly joins with a fiduciary, including corporate officials, in breaching a fiduciary obligation, is equally culpable. Thus, decisions based on the advice of such persons share the same defects as those discussed in n.32, *supra*.

[34] Following *Revlon*, there appeared to be a degree of "scholarly" debate about the particular fiduciary duty that had been breached in that case, i.e. the duty of care or the duty of loyalty. In *Ivanhoe*, 535 A.2d at 1345, we made it abundantly clear that *both* duties were involved in *Revlon*, and both had been breached.

inadequate bid. The whole question of defensive measures became moot. The directors' role changed from defenders of the corporate bastion to auctioneers charged with getting the best price for the stockholders at a sale of the company.

Id. at 182.

This case does not require a judicial determination of *when* Macmillan was "for sale."[35] By any standards this company was for sale both in Macmillan I and *II*. In any event, the board of directors formally concluded on September 11 that it would be in the best interests of the stockholders to sell the company.[36] Evidently, they reached this decision with the prospect of a KKR-management sponsored buyout in mind. Although Evans apparently made the decision to pursue a KKR buyout on July 14, the day the Court of Chancery enjoined his "restructuring", there is no evidence in the record that Evans had acted with board authority on that date.

What we are required to determine here is the scope of the board's responsibility in an active bidding contest once their role as auctioneer has been invoked under *Revlon*. Particularly, we are concerned with the use of lock-up and no-shop clauses.

At a minimum, *Revlon* requires that there be the most scrupulous adherence to ordinary principles of fairness in the sense that stockholder interests are enhanced, rather than diminished, in the conduct of an auction for the sale of corporate control. This is so whether the "sale" takes the form of an active auction, a management buyout, or a "restructuring" such as that which the Court of Chancery enjoined in *Macmillan I*. *Revlon* at 181-82. Under these special circumstances the duties of the board are "significantly altered". *Id*. at 182. The defensive aspects of *Unocal* no longer apply. *Id*. The sole responsibility of the directors in such a sale is for the shareholders' benefit. The board may not allow any impermissible

---

[35] This Court has been required to determine on other occasions since our decision in *Revlon*, whether a company is "for sale". Clearly not every offer or transaction affecting the corporate structure invokes the *Revlon* duties. A refusal to entertain offers may comport with a valid exercise of business judgment. Circumstances may dictate that an offer be rebuffed, given the nature and timing of the offer; its legality, feasibility and effect on the corporation and the stockholders; the alternatives available and their effect on the various constituencies, particularly the stockholders; the company's long term strategic plans; and any special factors bearing on stockholder and public interests. *Unocal*, 493 A.2d at 954-56. In *Ivanhoe* we recognized that a change in corporate structure under the special facts and circumstances of that case did not invoke *Revlon*. 535 A.2d at 1345. Specifically, Newmont's management faced two potentially coercive offers. In responding to such threats management's efforts were viewed as reasonable decisions intended to guide the corporation through the minefield of dangers directly posed by one bidder, and potentially by another. 535 A.2d at 1342-45. While it was argued that the transaction benefited management by strengthening its position, at most this was a secondary effect. . . .

[36] Macmillan informed this Court in a letter dated September 12, 1988, that the company was going to be sold. The letter was in connection with the pendency of an interlocutory appeal from the Court of Chancery's decision in *Macmillan I*.

influence, inconsistent with the best interests of the shareholders, to alter the strict fulfillment of these duties. *Id.* Clearly, this requires the intense scrutiny and participation of the independent directors, whose conduct comports with the standards of independence enunciated by us in Aronson v. Lewis, 473 A.2d at 816.

The Macmillan directors argue that a "blind auction" is a desirable means to fulfill their primary duty to the shareholders. That may be so, but it did not happen here. Only Maxwell was blind.

B

Turning to the lock-up, in *Revlon* we held that such an agreement is not *per se* unlawful under Delaware law. *Id.* at 183. We recognized its proper function in a contest for corporate control. Apparently, it has escaped some that in *Revlon* we distinguished the potentially valid uses of a lock-up from those that are impermissible:

> [W]hile those lock-ups which draw bidders into a battle benefit shareholders, similar measures which end an active auction and foreclose further bidding operate to the shareholders' detriment.

Id. at 183.

In this case, a lock-up agreement was not necessary to draw any of the bidders into the contest. Macmillan cannot seriously contend that they received a final bid from KKR that materially enhanced general stockholder interests. By all rational indications it was intended to have a directly opposite effect. As the record clearly shows, on numerous occasions Maxwell requested opportunities to further negotiate the price and structure of his bid. When he learned of KKR's higher bid, he increased his bid to $90.25 per share. Compare *Revlon* at 179, 184; *Hanson Trust*, 781 F.2d at 272. Further, KKR's "enhanced" bid, being nominal at best, was a *de minimis* justification for the lock-up. When one compares what KKR received for the lock-up, in contrast to its inconsiderable bid, the invalidity of the agreement becomes patent. Cf. *Revlon* at 184.

Here, the assets covered by the lock-up agreement were some of Macmillan's most valued properties, its "crown jewels."[37] Even if the lock-up is permissible, when it involves "crown jewel" assets careful scrutiny attends the decision. When the intended effect is to end an active auction, at the very least the independent members of the board must attempt to negotiate alternative bids before granting such a significant concession. See *Revlon* at 183. Maxwell invited negotiations for a purchase of the same four divisions, which KKR originally sought to buy for $775 million. Maxwell

---

[37] In the current takeover parlance, these are valuable assets or lines of business owned by a target company. The attempt is to sell them to third parties or place them under option at bargain prices as a device to defeat an unwanted takeover attempt. . . .

was prepared to pay $900 million. Instead of serious negotiations with Maxwell, there were only concessions to KKR by giving it a lock-up of seven divisions for $865 million.

Thus, when directors in a *Revlon* bidding contest grant a crown jewel lock-up, serious questions are raised, particularly where, as here, there is little or no improvement in the final bid. *Revlon* at 184, 187. The care and attention which independent directors bring to this decisions are crucial to its success.

C

As for the no-shop clause, *Revlon* teaches that the use of such a device is even more limited than a lock-up agreement. Absent a material advantage to the stockholders from the terms or structure of a bid that is contingent on a no-shop clause, a successful bidder imposing such a condition must be prepared to survive the careful scrutiny which that concession demands. *Id.* at 184.

VII

A

Directors are not required by Delaware law to conduct an auction according to some standard formula, only that they observe the significant requirement of fairness for the purpose of enhancing general shareholder interests. That does not preclude differing treatment of bidders when necessary to advance those interests. Variables may occur which necessitate such treatment.[38] However, the board's primary objective, and essential purpose, must remain the enhancement of the bidding process for the benefit of the stockholders.

We recognize that the conduct of a corporate auction is a complex undertaking both in its design and execution. See, e.g., MacAfee & Macmillan, *Auctions and Bidding*, 25 J.Econ.Lit. 699 (1987); Milgrom, *The Economics of Competitive Bidding: A Selected Survey*, in *Social Goals and Social Organization* 261 (Hurwicz, Schmeidler & Sonnenschein eds.1985). We do not intend to limit the broad negotiating authority of the directors to achieve the best price available to the stockholders. To properly secure that end may require the board to invoke a panoply of devices, and the giving or receiving of concessions that may benefit one bidder over another. See, e.g., In re J.P. Stevens & Co., Inc. Shareholders Litigation, 542 A.2d 770, 781-784 (Del.Ch.1988), *appeal refused*, 540 A.2d 1088 (Del.1988). But when

---

[38] For example, this Court has upheld actions of directors when a board is confronted with a coercive "two-tiered" bust-up tender offer. See *Unocal*, 493 A.2d at 956; *Ivanhoe*, 535 A.2d at 1342. Compare *Revlon* at 184.

that happens, there must be a rational basis for the action such that the interests of the stockholders are manifestly the board's paramount objective.

B

In the absence of self-interest, and upon meeting the enhanced duty mandated by *Unocal*, the actions of an independent board of directors in designing and conducting a corporate auction are protected by the business judgment rule. Thus, like any other business decision, the board has a duty in the design and conduct of an auction to act in "the best interests of the corporation and its shareholders." *Unocal*, 493 A.2d at 954-56; *Ivanhoe*, 535 A.2d at 1341-42.

However, as we recognized in *Unocal*, where issues of corporate control are at stake, there exists "the omnipresent specter that a board may be acting primarily in its own interests, rather than those of the corporation and its shareholders." *Id.* at 954. For that reason, an "enhanced duty" must be met at the threshold before the board receives the normal protections of the business judgment rule. *Id.* Directors may not act out of a sole or primary desire to "perpetuate themselves in office." *Id.* at 955.

As we held in *Revlon*, when management of a target company determines that the company is for sale, the board's *responsibilities* under the enhanced *Unocal* standards are significantly altered. *Id.* at 182. Although the board's *responsibilities* under *Unocal* are far different, the enhanced *duties* of the directors in responding to a potential shift in control, recognized in *Unocal*, remain unchanged. This principle pervades *Revlon*,[39] and when directors conclude that an auction is appropriate, the standard by which their ensuing actions will be judged continues to be the enhanced duty imposed by this Court in *Unocal*. . . .

When *Revlon* duties devolve upon directors, this Court will continue to exact an enhanced judicial scrutiny at the threshold, as in *Unocal*, before the normal presumptions of the business judgment rule will apply. However, as we recognized in *Revlon*, the two part threshold test, of necessity, is slightly different. *Id.* at 182.

At the outset, the plaintiff must show, and the trial court must find, that the directors of the target company treated one or more of the respective bidders on unequal terms. It is only then that the two-part threshold requirement of *Unocal* is truly invoked, for in *Revlon* we held that "[f]avoritism for a white knight to the total exclusion of a hostile bidder

---

[39] See, e.g., *Revlon* at 184 ("Thus, when a board ends an intense bidding contest on an insubstantial basis, and where a significant by-product of that action is to protect the directors against a perceived threat of personal liability . . . the action cannot withstand the enhanced scrutiny which *Unocal* requires of director conduct."). Further, "when bidders make relatively similar offers, or dissolution of the company becomes inevitable, the directors cannot fulfill their enhanced *Unocal* duties by playing favorites with the contending factions." *Id.*

might be justifiable when the latter's offer adversely affects shareholder interests, but . . . the directors cannot fulfill their enhanced *Unocal* duties by playing favorites with the contending factions." *Id.* at 184.

In the face of disparate treatment, the trial court must first examine whether the directors properly perceived that shareholder interests were enhanced. In any event the board's action must be reasonable in relation to the advantage sought to be achieved, or conversely, to the threat which a particular bid allegedly poses to stockholder interests. *Unocal* at 955.

If on the basis of this enhanced *Unocal* scrutiny the trial court is satisfied that the test has been met, then the directors' actions necessarily are entitled to the protections of the business judgment rule. The latitude a board will have in responding to differing bids will vary according to the degree of benefit or detriment to the shareholders' general interests that the amount or terms of the bids pose. We stated in *Revlon*, and again here, that in a sale of corporate control the responsibility of the directors is to get the highest value reasonably attainable for the shareholders. Beyond that, there are no special and distinct "Revlon duties". Once a finding has been made by a court that the directors have fulfilled their fundamental duties of care and loyalty under the foregoing standards, there is no further judicial inquiry into the matter.

For the foregoing reasons, the judgment of the Court of Chancery, denying Maxwell's motion for preliminary injunction, is REVERSED.

Macmillan states the doctrinal consequences of triggering *Revlon*:

> When *Revlon* duties devolve upon directors, this Court will continue to exact an enhanced judicial scrutiny at the threshold, as in *Unocal*, before the normal presumptions of the business judgment rule will apply. However, ... the two-part threshold test, of necessity, is slightly different.
>
> At the outset, the plaintiff must show . . . that the directors of the target company treated one or more of the respective bidders on unequal terms. It is only then that the two-part threshold requirement of *Unocal* is truly invoked, for in *Revlon* we held that "[f]avoritism for a white knight to the total exclusion of a hostile bidder might be justifiable when the latter's offer adversely affects shareholder interests, but . . . the directors cannot fulfill their enhanced *Unocal* duties by playing favorites with the contending factions."
>
> In the face of disparate treatment, the trial court must first examine whether the directors properly perceived that shareholder interests are enhanced. In any event the board's action must be reasonable in relation to the advantage sought to be achieved, or conversely, to the threat which a particular bid allegedly poses to stockholder interests.
>
> If on the basis of this enhanced *Unocal* scrutiny the trial court is satisfied that the test has been met, then the directors' actions necessarily are entitled to the protections of the business judgment rule. The latitude a board will have in responding to differing bids will vary according to the degree of benefit or detriment to the shareholders' general interests that the amount or terms of the

bids pose. We stated in *Revlon*, and again here, that in a sale of corporate control the responsibility of the directors is to get the highest value reasonably attainable for the shareholders. Beyond that, there are no special and distinct "Revlon duties".

The operational consequences of triggering *Revlon*, however are far less clear. Although *Revlon* and *Macmillan* speak of an obligation "to get the highest value reasonably attainable for the shareholders," the mere triggering of *Revlon* does not appear to alter the standard of review of board conduct. Only if the board favors one bidder must it justify its conduct as "reasonable in relation to the advantage sought. . . ." Absent favoritism then, only business judgment review applies, albeit, perhaps, of the *Trans Union-Technicolor* variety. One might therefore conclude that the terms of a company's sale will escape the heightened standard of review, despite the triggering of an intermediate standard whose very application is justified by the presence of a conflict of interest. The disarming of this conflict -- the presence of a conflict of interest yet the application of a measure of judicial review seemingly less rigorous than *Revlon*'s intermediate standard -- comes from recognizing other sources of review. The more casual *judicial* review implied by the business judgment rule[57] does not mean that a transaction escapes close scrutiny: In the absence of favoritism among potential bidders, less exacting judicial review invites more exacting *market* review.

Where the target's directors do not favor one bidder by erecting transaction barriers to competing bidders, the market can police the fairness of the sale even though its terms have been negotiated by a representative whom the court has recognized is subject to a conflict of interest. If the price is too favorable to the bidder, a competitive bid is likely to develop. Thus, *Macmillan*'s specification of business judgment review in the absence of favoritism may be best understood not as a statement that a designated conflict-of-interest transaction should escape heightened review but merely that it should receive "market review," in preference to judicial review, where market review is possible.

The situation changes, however, when market review of the transaction's terms has been short circuited. When a board favors a particular bidder through, for example, the provision of special access to nonpublic information, the grant of a lock-up, or the commitment to pay a break up or topping fee, the market's ability to police the terms of the transaction may be constrained. And precisely because favoritism erodes confidence in the market's review of the transaction, more rigorous judicial review -- an obligation to persuade the court that the advantage given was reasonable in relation to the benefit acquired -- is necessary.

Doctrinally, then, the *Macmillan* formulation of the intermediate standard poses two issues. First, under what circumstances will the board

---

[57] We take up whether *Trans Union* and *Technicolor* really reflect the judicial deference traditionally associated with the business judgment rule later in this Chapter.

be found to have so favored a bidder that judicial review should be substituted for market review? Second, where favoritism is present, what is the nature of the court's review?

(1) The Test of Favoritism: The Adequacy of Market Review

The rationale for preferring market review over judicial review is simply that the market is the best judge of a transactions's terms: if no higher bid is secured, then there is reason to believe that the allocation of the gain from the transaction between the bidder and the target shareholders is fair. Competition among bidders assures that the successful acquirer earns no more than a competitive return, with the balance of the transactional gain accruing to target shareholders.[58] Little need remains for court review. So understood, *Macmillan*'s criterion of favoritism -- "that the directors of the target company treated . . . the respective bidders on unequal terms" -- should focus on the adequacy of the market's review of the transaction's terms. Adequate market review renders judicial review unnecessary. Put in doctrinal terms, a favored bidder is thus one who has been sheltered from competition by the target's actions. So, for example, a formally structured auction, replete with bidding rules and an information package for potential bidders (as was the case in the RJR Nabisco transaction)[59] assures that there is no favoritism, and it is in this sense that commentators often refer to a *Revlon* "auction obligation." But a formal auction is not the only bidding process that assures adequate market review. The term auction therefore should not be understood as a literal description of the procedures that must be followed. Rather, it is best understood as a metaphor that evokes a sense of the confidence a court should feel that the procedures followed in a particular case have resulted in the substantive terms of the interested transaction being subjected to meaningful market review.

Two types of advantages may work in favor of one bidder in a competition to acquire the target. The first is positional and is characteristic -- indeed, inevitable -- in management buyouts; it results simply from the fact that the bidder in an MBO is affiliated with the target's management. The second is transactional and can appear in both MBOs and third party transactions; the board may protect a favored bidder from competition through such devices as lock-ups, no shop clauses, expense reimbursement

---

[58] See Chapter 8D for a summary of the empirical evidence concerning allocation of transactional gain between bidder and target shareholders. Additionally, the successful acquirer will retain the portion of the transactional gain that results from any unique resources contributed by the acquirer. For a helpful discussion of how both competition among bidders and the particular attributes of individual bidders affect the allocation of gain between the successful bidder and the target shareholders, see David Leebron, *Games Corporations Play: A Theory of Tender Offers*, 61 NYU L.Rev. 153 (1987).

[59] In re RJR Nabisco, Inc. Shareholders Litigation, [1988-89 Transfer Binder] Fed.Sec.L.Rep. (CCH) ¶ 93,923 (Del.Ch.1988).

provisions and breakup fees. The presence of either type of advantage can prevent adequate market review of a transaction's terms and, thus, trigger the substitution of judicial review for market review under *Macmillan*.

(a) Positional Advantages: Special Rules for MBOs

Management buyouts present an especially intense manifestation of the "omnipresent specter" of a conflict of interest to which *Unocal* referred. The nature of this conflict is set out in the following discussion.

Ronald Gilson
MARKET REVIEW OF INTERESTED TRANSACTIONS:
THE AMERICAN LAW INSTITUTE PROPOSAL ON
MANAGEMENT BUYOUTS
in *Leveraged Management Buyouts*
217-21 (Yakov Amihud ed.1989)

From the perspective of corporate governance, an MBO -- the acquisition, typically highly leveraged, of a corporation by an investment group that includes members of the target's senior management -- presents some troublesome characteristics. First, one must recognize from the outset that the claim of increased efficiency from MBOs is more difficult to analyze than the more general claim that third-party acquisitions lead to efficiency gains. An MBO simply cannot achieve either of the two most familiar sources of the efficiency gains commonly ascribed to acquisitions: synergy and displacement of inefficient management. Because an MBO makes no additional resources available to a target company, the absence of synergy is virtually tautological. Similarly, because a central characteristic of an MBO is to *retain* existing management, *displacement* of inefficient management is hardly a likely source of efficiency gains from the transaction.

That is not to say that there has been a shortage of explanations proffered for the source of the high premiums being paid in MBOs. But because of the very nature of the transaction, all of these explanations share a common characteristic. Since an MBO brings no new resources -- whether operating, financial or managerial -- to the target company, each of the potential sources of gain from the transaction is at least theoretically available to the target company even without an MBO.

So, for example, it is claimed that the gains from MBOs result from tax benefits, particularly a step-up in the basis of the target's depreciable assets and the deductibility of interest on the borrowed funds, available through the transaction. [As shown in Chapter 12,] however, in the period prior to the Tax Reform Act of 1986, an MBO was not the only way that these benefits could be achieved. The step-up in basis also was available (though to a lesser extent) through a sale and leaseback, and interest was deductible regardless of the use to which the borrowed funds were put. Thus, the tax hypothesis does not explain why target management would have chosen to achieve the tax gains through a control transaction, such as an MBO, rather than through a noncontrol transaction such as a sale and leaseback of appreciated assets or a leveraged recapitalization.

In turn, Michael Jensen argues that the obligation to service the debt associated with an MBO has the beneficial effect of eliminating management's opportunity to misinvest the target company's free cash flow. Again, however, precisely the same results can be achieved without a control transaction, as the success of defensive restructurings have demonstrated.

Finally, it is argued that the increase in the diversifiable risk borne by management after an MBO, as a result of both management's increased ownership and the increased risk to the manager's human capital associated with the company's increased leverage, provides a heightened incentive to managerial performance. But no claim is made that the increased incentive could not have been achieved -- for example, through stock options and self-leveraging -- without a control change.

A clear implication of this analysis is that management always has a choice of means to secure the gains claimed to be available through an MBO. Imagine that management discovers a favorable business strategy -- say increased after-tax cash flow through a step-up in the tax bases of depreciable assets -- that could be implemented in two ways. It could be implemented through a sale and leaseback, the gains from which management would participate in to the extent of its existing equity interest in the company. Alternatively, it could be implemented through an MBO, with the result that management would substantially increase its ownership and, therefore its share of the value created by the new strategy. Put this way, management's preference for implementing the new strategy through an MBO is not surprising. There is simply more in it for management with an MBO.

Nonetheless, it is too easy to treat management's preference for an MBO as simply an expression of greed. However implemented, the substance of the new strategy involves the company's borrowing the amount by which the market value of its depreciable assets exceeds their tax bases. Thus, by increasing the company's leverage, both strategies also increase the risk associated with the managers' undiversified human capital. A sale and leaseback causes the managers to bear this risk without compensation. In contrast, an MBO compensates management for the increased risk with the potential for an increased return.

Thus, one can understand the selection of an MBO rather than other means of securing a generic gain as a way by which management is compensated for altering the structure of the company in a fashion that results in gains for shareholders but, in the absence of increased managerial compensation, losses for management.

So considered, MBOs pose a familiar corporate governance problem. Many circumstances arise in which a transaction between management and the company may be more beneficial to both than an alternative transaction between the company and an unrelated third party. The governance problem is how to police the division of the gains from the interested transaction. In transactions with third parties, management acts on behalf of shareholders in negotiating the division of the gains. In MBOs, in contrast, no one negotiates on behalf of shareholders because management is on both sides of the transaction.

Based on the evidence reported by Steven Kaplan, an empirically inclined observer might be tempted to treat this inherent conflict of interest as just another example of lawyers creating a hypothetical problem which they then feel obligated to expend real resources to solve. Kaplan reports that the excess return earned by MBO investors, including management, is approximately the same as the excess return or premium earned by outside shareholders to take the company private -- the two groups come close to splitting the gains.[a] At first pass this allocation suggests that there is no need for careful scrutiny of the fairness of the division of gain from the transaction. What could be unfair about an equal sharing of the gains from MBOs between shareholders on the one hand and management and the investing group on the other? The problem, however, is that there is a second, substantially larger, body of empirical evidence suggesting that an equal division of the gain from MBOs may be dramatically unfair to shareholders.

Surveys of the division of gain between acquiring and target company shareholders in third-party transactions present a single consistent pattern: target shareholders earn a substantial multiple of the return earned by acquiring company shareholders. The puzzle thus presented by the two patterns of data is that in third-party offers "companies that are the targets of takeovers receive the bulk of the value created,"[14] whereas in MBOs the acquirer, which now includes target management, shares equally in the value created. While the data do not demonstrate that the acquirer gets a larger cut in an MBO than in the third-party transaction *because* management is on its side, neither do they demonstrate that the law's traditional concern over fair division in conflict of interest situations is unwarranted.

The logic of *Macmillan*'s singling out for judicial review under the intermediate standard those transactions where effective market review is not possible suggests an approach to dealing with MBOs. Unless the acquirer's inherent positional advantages in an MBO are neutralized, the favoritism test will be met, and the transaction should be reviewed under the intermediate standard.

---

[a] Steven Kaplan, *Sources of Value in Management Buyouts*, in *Leveraged Management Buyouts* 95 (Yakov Amihud ed.1988).

[14] Gregg Jarrell, James Brickley & Jeffry Netter, *The Market for Corporate Control: The Empirical Evidence Since 1980*, 3 J.Econ.Persp. 49, 53 (1988).

A management affiliated bidder making the initial bid for a target company starts with two important positional advantages over potential competitive bidders: better information and control over the transaction's timing. The management affiliated group, and its financing sources, have access to substantial nonpublic information about the target at essentially no cost. Moreover, even if a competitive bidder could independently develop similar information, the ability of the management affiliated group to choose the precise time of its offer, and to act first, puts any potential competitor at a substantial disadvantage.

This analysis suggests two minimal requirements that should be met before a court should be satisfied that a management affiliated bid is not by that reason alone improperly favored. First, competitive bidders should be allowed access to the non-public information that management possesses and has provided to its affiliates. Second, parties who undertake to review such information should be allowed a reasonable opportunity to evaluate it and prepare a competitive bid for the company.

Section 5.15 of the American Law Institute's Principles of Corporate Governance[60] reflects this understanding of the logic of *Revlon* and *Macmillan*.

§ 5.15 Transfer of Control in Which a Director or Principal Senior Executive Is Interested

(a) If directors or principal senior executives [§ 1.30] of a corporation are interested [§ 1.23] in a transaction in control [§ 1.38] or a tender offer that results in a transfer of control [§ 1.08] of the corporation to another person[§ 1.28], then those directors or principal senior executives have the burden of proving that the transaction was fair to the shareholders of the corporation unless (1) the transaction involves a transfer by a controlling shareholder [§ 1.10] or (2) the conditions of Subsection (b) are satisfied.

(b) If in connection with a transaction described in Subsection (a) involving a publicly held corporation [§ 1.31]:

(1) Public disclosure of the proposed transaction is made;

(2) Responsible persons who express an interest are provided relevant information concerning the corporation and given a reasonable opportunity to submit a competing proposal;

(3) The transaction is authorized in advance by disinterested directors [§ 1.15] after the procedures set forth in Subsections (1) and (2) have been complied with; and

(4) The transaction is authorized or ratified by disinterested shareholders [§ 1.16] (or, if the transaction is effected by a tender offer, the offer is accepted by disinterested shareholders), after disclosure concerning the conflict of interest [§ 1.14(a)] and the transaction [§ 1.14(b)] has been made;

---

[60] 1 American Law Institute, *Principles of Corporate Governance: Analysis and Recommendations* § 5.15 (1994) (cross-references are to the definitions in Part I of the Principles).

then a party challenging the transaction has the burden of proving that the terms of the transaction are equivalent to a waste or corporate assets [§ 1.42].

The Commentary to § 5.15 explains its operation

> Section 5.15 sets out governance rules that will allow the market for corporate control to operate as a realistic protection against non-arm's-length division of gains from a transaction in control of the corporation to which its directors or principal senior executives are parties. Section 5.15(b) provides a safe harbor for transactions that are subjected to an adequate market test of the fairness of their terms. Because a transaction that satisfies the requirements of § 5.15(b) will have been tested by the market, judicial review is limited to a waste standard. If the requirements of § 5.15(b) are not satisfied, there is no adequate market review of the fairness of the transaction. In that event, § 5.15(a) provides for judicial review of the fairness of the transaction, as is the case under Part V [Duty of Fair Dealing] for other transacting in which directors or principal senior executives have a personal interest.[61]

Absent exposure of transaction to the market, the management affiliated bidder enjoys a competitive advantage that should trigger judicial review of the terms of the transaction under the *Macmillan* formulation of the intermediate standard. However, the Delaware cases do not appear to single out MBOs for special treatment despite the heightened conflict of interest. In re Amsted Industries Inc. Litigation[62] provides a good example of procedures that blocked a satisfactory market review and that should give rise to more rigorous judicial review. There the court was called upon to approve a class action settlement that specified the terms by which the company would be acquired in an MBO. Although the Amsted board had created a special board committee to evaluate management's proposal for an MBO and an ESOP, it had made no effort to expose the terms of the MBO to the market before approving them. The existence of the proposal was public, but the board did not indicate that it would entertain competing proposals or offer any assurances that it would provide competitive bidders with the same information that it had released to the management bidder. Indeed, the board's only assurance about the price offered by the management group was the advice of its investment banker that, because of the tax advantages available to an ESOP, a non-ESOP buyer could not pay

---

[61] *Id.* at 363. The Commentary also notes that § 5.15 would not normally permit the target company to provide a lockup to a management affiliated bidder other than pursuant to a publicly announced intention to provide a lockup to the highest bidder.

Stephen Bainbridge has argued forcefully that the ALI approach slights the appropriate role for both independent directors and courts. See Stephen Bainbridge, *Independent Directors and the ALI Corporate Governance Project*, 61 Geo.Wash.L.Rev. 1034, 1068-81 (1993).

[62] 1988 WL 92736 (Del.Ch.1988), *aff'd*, 567 A.2d 1279 (Del.1989).

as high a price. On these facts, there was no meaningful market review of the transaction's terms and judicial review of the fairness of the transaction should be required.[63]

The auction metaphor does not require that management initiated MBOs be subjected to the procedures of a formal *RJR* style auction to assure adequate market review. In re Fort Howard Shareholders Litigation[64] provides a useful example of how the information and timing advantages of a management affiliated bidder may be dissipated (albeit, perhaps, barely) with a procedure quite different from a formal auction. There a special committee of the board chose to negotiate over a management buyout proposal without publicly disclosing that a sale of the company was under consideration. The negotiations led to board approval of a merger agreement that contemplated an initial tender offer commencing five business days following public announcement and remaining open for twenty five business days, a total of 30 business days and 43 calendar days. The agreement did not allow the company to actively solicit bids; however, the following procedure was described in the press release announcing the MBO:

> [T]he Special Committee directed the Company's management and the First Boston Corporation [the investment banker advising the Special Committee] to be available to receive inquiries from any other parties interested in the possible acquisition of the Company and, as appropriate, to provide information and, in First Boston's case in conjunction with the Special Committee, enter into discussions and negotiations with such parties in connection with any such indicated interest.

Although aspects of the procedures through which the transaction was negotiated are troublesome[65] and, again, the outcome might have been

---

[63] In *Amsted*, the Chancery Court approved the settlement, essentially a small increase in the price to be paid by the management affiliated acquirer, despite skepticism about the manner of sale, in large part because of the legal standard of review:

> Turning to the merits of the case, I admit I have found the case difficult. On balance, I have concluded in the exercise of my judgment, that the settlement is a fair one. In reaching that conclusion, I am most impressed with two facts. First, plaintiffs would have had to establish the gross negligence of the Special Committee (which I regard as a very dim prospect) or its lack of good faith.

1988 WL 92736, at *10. The court's treatment of the standard of review may reflect a confusion between the information requirement and the requirement concerning the structure of the transaction. Both the Chancery and Supreme Courts in *Amsted* treated review of the information requirement under the duty of care/business judgment rule analysis of *Trans Union* or the intermediate standard of *Revlon* as equivalent. Presumably application of the intermediate standard as a result of a finding or favoritism under *Macmillan* would have resulted in a different outcome. In affirming, the Supreme Court stressed its limited role in reviewing the trial court's approval of a settlement of litigation; however, the court gave no indication that it thought the Chancery Court had invoked the wrong substantive standard.

[64] 1988 WL 83147 (Del.Ch.1988).

[65] Chancellor Allen describes some areas of concern:

different had the court distinguished between MBOs and other transactions; *Fort Howard* does suggest that market review is feasible without the formal trappings of an auction.   To be sure, the time period and nature of information that must be provided will differ from transaction to transaction. For present purposes, however, the point is only that the information and timing advantages of a management affiliated bidder should be dissipated for an MBO not to cross *Macmillan*'s favoritism threshold, and that a variety of procedures will be adequate to achieve this end.

(b)   Positional Advantage: How Can You Tell if It's an MBO?

The discussion of positional advantage in the previous section implicitly assumed that it would be apparent whether a bidder is affiliated with target management.   In fact, this may not be the case.   In evaluating doctrinal solutions to a problem it must be remembered that the solution is not the last round in the game.   We also must anticipate the uncertainty that clever planners will predictably create as to when a bidder has such a positional advantage that the *Macmillan* favoritism threshold is crossed.

Suppose a leveraged buyout firm presents an acquisition proposal to the board of directors of a target company.   Suppose further that although no target director or senior executive has any connection with the buyout firm, it is apparent that the bidding firm does not itself have the capacity to manage the target if its proposal is successful.   Should the leveraged buyout firm be treated as an arm's length bidder, that is immune to more rigorous judicial review under *Macmillan* unless the target provides a transactional advantage, or should it be identified as a management affiliate whose positional advantage must be dissipated to avoid more rigorous judicial review?

A bright line rule might look to whether the buyout firm actually has promised members of target management an equity interest in the acquiring entity.   However, the expected precision of such a rule is likely to prove a mirage.   In the hypothetical, both target management and the buyout firm

---

It cannot, for example, be the best practice to have the interested CEO in effect handpick the members of the Special Committee. . . . Nor can it be the best procedure for him, in effect, to choose special counsel for the committee. . . . A suspicious mind is made uneasy contemplating the possibilities when the interested CEO is so active in choosing his adversary. The . . . decision to keep the management decision secret, in a sense, represents a decision to sell the Company to management if it would pay a fair price, but not to inquire whether another would pay a fair price if management would not do so. It implies a bias . . . that is a source of concern for a suspicious mind. Similarly the requested meeting between First Boston and Morgan Stanley. . . . [I]t is still odd for the Special Committee to risk infecting the independence of the valuation upon which it would necessarily place such weight, by requiring its expert to talk directly to Morgan Stanley.

1988 WL 83147 (Del.Ch.), slip opinion at 30-31.

need each other. Since the target company is likely to be acquired by someone once it is put in play, a buyout firm that may preserve target management's position is likely to be a favored acquirer from management's perspective. From the buyout firm's perspective, someone must run the business after the transaction and existing management is an obvious candidate. In such a setting, the bright line rule may be easily avoided by delaying discussion of target management's equity participation. Is either party's bargaining position significantly changed if the negotiation over target management's participation is delayed until after the transaction is completed? If not, the bright line rule has nothing on one side of the line; all transactions will be structured so that equity participation is discussed only after closing.

But does this analysis assume an implausible level of target management trust in the good faith of the buyout firm? If the buyout firm looks forward to doing similar transactions in the future, the need to maintain a reputation of dealing fairly with target management should ensure that the firm will live up to the terms that have been communicated, but not committed to, prior to closing. The bright line reduces to a range of gray.

If a bright line rule is illusory, then what? The only instance of a court confronting this problem is Chancellor Allen's opinion in In re J.P. Stevens & Co. Shareholders Litigation.[66] The background was a bidding contest for J.P. Stevens between a competitor of Stevens and an investment group. The latter, unlike Stevens' competitor, was not itself capable of operating Stevens' business, and had been formed for the purpose of the acquisition. The competitor complained that management's de facto affiliation with the investment group effectively transformed the group's bid into an MBO, which should have led the Stevens board to treat the two bids evenhandedly:

> Odyssey [the investment group] would be regarded by management as greatly to be preferred over West Point [the competitor] because Odyssey (a) had no real capacity to run Stevens, (b) had indicated that it wanted current management to stay on, and (c) had indicated a willingness to discuss equity participation by management. Thus, Odyssey, rather than being an arm's length bidder, as West Point is, appears in this version to be a white knight, favored by management and by a Special Committee that vibrates sympathetically to management's desires. Maybe this is true; it surely is plausible.[67]

While Chancellor Allen perceptively recognized the problem of evaluating target management's participation in the Odyssey bid,[68] his

---

[66] 542 A.2d 770 (Del.Ch.1988).

[67] *Id.* at 779.

[68] By comparison, the court in Cottle v. Storer Communication, Inc., 847 F.2d 570 (11th Cir.1988), approved ending a vigorous bidding contest by granting a crown jewels lock-up to KKR, despite the fact that the company's investment banker valued a competing bid by a company that itself would have operated the target at $2 per share higher. The court did not

resolution of the matter is troublesome. Despite quite open skepticism concerning the Stevens board's conduct,[69] Chancellor Allen concluded that

> in the end, plaintiffs' plausible story is not, in my opinion, sufficiently supported by the evidence at this time to permit the conclusion that it is reasonably likely that at trial it would be found that the Special Committee sought to promote the interests of management by advantaging Odyssey at the possible expense of shareholders.[70]

The outcome in *J.P. Stevens* seems to have been pre-determined by limiting judicial scrutiny to a choice between the business judgment and intrinsic fairness standards of review. In order to merit close scrutiny under the intrinsic fairness standard, Allen appears to have required the plaintiffs to meet the tough *Sinclair*[71] test of demonstrating that management was favored at the expense of shareholders. Otherwise, the business judgment rule applied. But if *Macmillan* is understood as requiring closer judicial scrutiny when a bidder enjoys a positional advantage, then the advisory criticisms of target board conduct in MBO transactions, offered in *Fort Howard, J.P. Stevens* and *Amsted* before ultimately approving the transaction, can be replaced by the intermediate standard. Chancellor Allen's skepticism over the conduct of the auction suggests a belief that Odyssey enjoyed a positional advantage. In a post-*Macmillan* world, that finding alone should suffice to cross the favoritism threshold.

---

appear to recognize the advantage of the KKR bid to target management.

[69] Chancellor Allen's description of the Stevens board's conduct displays his skepticism: For example, one is left with the suspicion that the need to reach a final decision may not have been so great as to require the Special Committee to decide by March 13th to sign a merger agreement, when another month might have resolved the antitrust question that presented the reason for preferring a lower offer. And if one is inclined to second guess board decisions, the decision to agree to a $1 per share break-up payment on March 13 seems a likely candidate for review. Odyssey had just submitted a proposal materially *lower* than West Point. If Odyssey really wanted to acquire the Company, how much leverage did it have, in those circumstances, to insist on a $17 million break-up fee? So the claim that the real purpose of that fee provision was to disadvantage West Point is not altogether hollow. And why did the Special Committee so easily accept Odyssey's threat to retract its March 28th $64 offer, if it was not accepted immediately? Would not the practicality of the matter suggest to the Special Committee that if Odyssey was willing to pay $64 on the 28th, it would be willing to do so a few days later.

542 A.2d at 779.

[70] *Id.* at 779-80.

[71] Sinclair Oil Corp. v. Levien, 280 A.2d 717 (Del.1971).

(c) Transactional Advantages

In almost all circumstances, the grant of a transactional advantage to a single bidder will cross *Macmillan*'s favoritism threshold. The purpose of devices like a lock up or break up fee is to advantage the recipient, and the purpose of more rigorous judicial review is to test the fairness of the transaction's terms when favoritism has prevented market review.

Yet, there is one circumstance in which advantaging a bidder should not trigger vigorous judicial review. Even a full and fair auction has to end sometime. Suppose the board determines that the auction technique most likely to maximize shareholder value is a single round of bidding. How can the board force the conclusion of the auction and insure that some bidders do not attempt to withhold their top bid until after other bidders have disclosed their positions? So long as the rules are clearly stated in advance, awarding a lockup to the auction's winner may be the only way to enforce the auction's terms. The key here is that techniques used to enforce the rules of an open contest for the target enhance rather than restrict market review.[72]

(2) Proportionality Review: Judicial Review of the Favoritism Trade

Once the favoritism threshold is crossed, *Macmillan* dictates active judicial review: The court must determine whether the benefit conferred upon the favored bidder "is reasonable in relation to the advantage" provided to the shareholders. At present, however, there is little guidance for how to think about the right trade off. We saw in *Revlon* the court's belief that an auction closing lockup was not reasonable in relation to a $1 price increase, but also saw that the outcome of not providing the lockup may have been a lower price. While we will return to this problem later in this Chapter in connection with the economics of auction design, for now some issues can at least be framed.

-- How should the procedures followed by the board in approving the favoritism affect a court's review of the substance of the tradeoff? Suppose the terms of the transaction were negotiated by a committee of independent directors with the benefit of separate legal and investment banking counsel. Can the court rely on the quality of the process as a proxy for the quality of the substance? Although *Macmillan* does not address this issue, the quality of the board's procedure does play an important role in the analogous area of judicial review of the terms of a minority freezeout under the entire fairness test of Weinberger v. UOP, Inc.[73]

---

[72] The economics are considered later in this Chapter.

[73] 457 A.2d 701 (Del.1983). See Chapter 22, *infra*.

-- Does the presence of an overt conflict of interest matter? Since the justification for the intermediate standard of review is the conflict of interest inherent in any sale, it is plausible that transactional advantages granted to a management affiliated bidder will be more carefully reviewed than similar favoritism toward a bidder in a true third-party transaction. If so, determining whether a bidder is affiliated with management takes on even more significance.

-- Are there any limits on the extent to which a bidder can be favored? Are there circumstances other than at the end of an even handed auction that the target can seek to prohibit further bidding against a favored acquirer?

-- Is it possible to do more than catalogue the factors a court might consider in reviewing the terms of the favoritism trade? Recall that the Delaware Chancery Court is a court of equity. Can the standard do more than ask whether, taking everything into account, the trade between the board and the favored bidder seemed sensible?

5. *Revlon's* Trigger in the Setting of a Friendly Transaction

The second setting in which a planner confronts the specter of triggering *Revlon's* application is in connection with a friendly transaction. Can a company agree to be acquired in what used to be the traditional manner -- that is, an agreement negotiated at arm's length calling for a form of transaction, like a merger or sale of assets, that would normally require shareholder approval -- without shopping the transaction or otherwise conducting an auction, and also protect it from competitive bidding by an effective lockup?

The planners' initial response to this problem took the form of a "merger of equals." Imagine that the boards of directors of two companies, which for sake of currency we can call Time and Warner, conclude that a friendly merger is in the best interests of both corporations. The transaction contemplates that the consideration for the merger will be voting stock rather than cash and that, following the merger, the shareholders of Warner, the disappearing company, will receive a substantial percentage -- perhaps as much as the 62% -- of the voting shares of Time, the surviving corporation.

The planner's dilemma is the application of *Revlon*. Because the boards of the two companies have determined that theirs is the best deal, neither board has any interest in causing the transactions to be shopped. However, if *Revlon* applies, both corporations will have an inchoate obligation to confirm that the implicit price reflected in the merger's exchange ratio is, in fact, the best price that can be obtained. The planner's fear, of course, is that *Revlon* might be read to imply that the discovery of an outside buyer willing to pay a price higher than the price implicit in the merger's exchange ratio would effectively terminate authority to pursue the original transaction, even though both boards of directors believed in good faith that the outsider's price was inferior to the value that the negotiated transaction would ultimately yield in the future.

Efforts to protect friendly competition have taken two forms. The first, more broadly based effort, has been the claim that *Revlon* does not apply to mergers of equals. The argument is essentially semantic. What triggered the shift in the board's obligation under *Revlon* was the "recognition that the company was for sale."[74] Only then did the board's duty change "from the preservation of Revlon as an entity to the maximization of the company's value at a sale for the stockholders' benefit."[75] However, a merger of equals, the argument goes, is not a "sale" but a consolidation of two companies, in which neither is the buyer nor the seller. The point of the argument is to alter the legal standard that would apply to the second form of protection for friendly deals -- the granting of lockups and break-up fees, privileged access to data and other means to favor a friendly bidder and discourage a competitive bidder. If *Revlon* applies, any effort to protect the favored transaction would be subject to *Macmillan's* formulation of the intermediate standard: the obligation would be on the board to show that it obtained a benefit reasonably related to the protection it provides to the preferred suitor.

a.   *Does a Merger of Equals Trigger Revlon?*

The argument that a merger of equals is not really a sale recalls the similar debate recounted in Chapter 13 over the availability of pooling of interest accounting in connection with an acquisition. An unfavorable accounting treatment follows when an acquisition at a price in excess of the market values of the target company's tangible assets is deemed to be a "purchase" of one company by the other: goodwill is created to the extent of the difference and the depreciable bases of tangible assets are increased to market value from their lower pre-transaction historical cost. As a result, the acquiring company's accounting earnings are reduced to reflect amortization of the good will and the now higher depreciation charges. By contrast, if the transaction is deemed a "pooling" of the two companies, "groups of stockholders combine their resources, talents, and risks to form a new entity to carry on in combination the previous businesses,"[76] with the consequence that the two financial statements may also be combined without reducing reported earnings. For twenty-five years, the accounting profession has wrestled with the distinguishing characteristics of a true pooling transaction; at the moment, APB No. 16 lists some ten factors. Yet, this result satisfies no one, precisely because it turns on the intrinsic meaning of the terms

---

[74] 506 A.2d at 182.

[75] *Id.*

[76] Accounting Principles Board Opinion No. 16, Paragraph 28 (reproduced in Chapter 13).

"pooling" and "purchase" rather than on the underlying issue of when historical costs are appropriately replaced with current costs for accounting purposes.[77]

Thus, the debate over *Revlon*'s application to a friendly merger threatened to come to a similar impasse if it remained focused on the intrinsic meaning of "sale" rather than on the substance at which the intermediate standard was directed. Chancellor Allen confronted this issue in Paramount Communications, Inc. v. Time, Inc. and declined the invitation to a semantic resolution.

PARAMOUNT COMMUNICATIONS, INC. v. TIME, INC.
Fed.Sec.L.Rep. (CCH) ¶ 94,514 (Del.Ch.1989)

ALLEN, Chancellor.

[The facts are set out in the case excerpt in Chapter 17.]

A

The legal analysis that follows treats the distinction that the Time board implicitly drew between current share value maximization and long-term share value maximization. . . . On the level of legal doctrine, it is clear that under Delaware law, directors are under no obligation to act so as to maximize the immediate value of the corporation or its shares, except in the special case in which the corporation is in a "Revlon mode." Mills Acquisition Co. v. Macmillan, Inc.; Ivanhoe Partners v. Newmont Mining, 535 A.2d 1334 (Del.1987); Revlon v. MacAndrews & Forbes Holdings, Inc., 506 A.2d 173 (Del.1986). See generally TW Services, Inc. v. SWT Acquisition Corp., (March 2, 1989). Thus, Delaware law does recognize that directors, when acting deliberately, in an informed way, and in the good faith pursuit of corporate interests, may follow a course designed to achieve long-term value even at the cost of immediate value maximization.

The legally critical question this case presents then involves *when* must a board shift from its ordinary long-term profit maximizing mode to the

---

[77] Ironically, the recent Time/Warner transaction raised not only the issue of whether a marriage of equals triggers the application of *Revlon*, but also the pooling/purchase controversy. The original merger transaction was designed to meet APB No. 16's requirements for pooling of interest accounting to avoid creating the substantial amounts of goodwill that would result if the transaction had to be accounted for as a purchase. Interestingly, the substance of the transaction ultimately proved a barrier to the desired accounting treatment. As a means of assuring that shareholders of both corporations would approve the merger, the transaction contemplated that the companies could exchange a substantial amount of their stock so as to place votes in friendly hands. If the exchange were carried out, however, it appears that Paragraph 46 of APB No. 16 would have prevented the transaction from being accounted for as pooling.

radically altered state recognized by the *Revlon* case in which its duty, broadly stated, is to exercise its power in the good faith pursuit of immediate maximization of share value. Surely, when as in *Revlon* itself and other cases construing its command, most notably *Macmillan*,[40] the board decides to enter a change in control transaction, it has elected to enter the Revlon zone. But it now appears resolved that a subjective disinclination to sell the company will not prevent that duty from arising where an extraordinary transaction including, at a minimum, a change in corporate control is involved:

> [*Revlon*'s requirements pertain] whether the "sale" takes the form of an active auction, a management buyout, or a "restructuring" such as that which the Court of Chancery enjoined in *Macmillan I*.

Mills Acquisition Co. v. Macmillan, Inc.
    Thus, more specifically, the first overarching question presented by these facts reduces legally to the inquiry whether the board was, on June 16, involuntarily in that special state -- what one can call, as a shorthand, the "Revlon mode" -- in which it was required to maximize immediate share value. . . . If the board was itself under no duty to choose to maximize current value, then the second overarching question must be addressed in terms of the legal questions presented. . . .

IV

Were the Time Directors Under an Obligation To Seek, in Good Faith, Only to Maximize Current Share Value on June 16?: Plaintiffs' Revlon Argument

A

    Plaintiff's first argument, restated most simply, is that the original merger agreement constituted an implicit decision by the board of Time to transfer control of the company to Warner, or more correctly its shareholders, and when the board decided to consider doing that, its duties changed from long-term management of the corporation for the benefit of the company's shareholders to the narrow and specific goal of present maximization of share value. That is, it entered a "Revlon mode." See Revlon v. MacAndrews & Forbes Holdings, Inc., 506 A.2d 173, 182 (Del.1986). The class action plaintiffs assert that any change in corporate

---

[40] See also In re J.P. Stevens & Co., Inc. Shareholders Litigation, 542 A.2d 770 (Del.Ch.1988); In re RJR Nabisco, Inc. Shareholders Litigation, Cons. C.A. No.10389 (Del.Ch.1989); In re Fort Howard Corp. Shareholders Litigation, Cons. C.A. No.9991 (Del.Ch.1988); In re Holly Farms Corp. Shareholders Litigation, Del.Ch., C.A. No.10350 (December 30, 1988), slip op. at 12.

control triggers this special duty. The individual shareholder plaintiffs urge a different theory as triggering the special Revlon duty. They contend that the original merger, if effectuated, would have precluded the Time shareholders from ever (that is, in the foreseeable future) realizing a control premium transaction, and thus, in its impact upon Time shareholders, the merger contemplated by the March 3 agreement would have implicitly represented the same loss of a control premium as would a change in control transaction with no premium. Thus, these plaintiffs assert that even if the stock for stock merger did not represent a change in control, the same duty to maximize current value should attach to it as to a "sale."

Plaintiffs, having purportedly shown that the board really was in a Revlon mode, then go on to argue that the board violated its Revlon duty by not seeking a *current* value maximizing transaction and by entering into a number of agreements that were intended to preclude or impede the emergence of current value maximizing alternatives. These agreements include the "dry up" fee payments, the Share Exchange Agreement and the restrictions on supplying information to or entering into discussions with anyone seeking to acquire control of Time.

Defendants respond first that the board did not consider that it was appropriate in March or thereafter to "sell" the company; the purpose of the original merger was quite the opposite in that it sought to preserve and improve the company's long-term performance. Second, defendants say that if something other than their subjective intention is relevant, it simply is not the case that the stock for stock merger they authorized represented a change in control. It is irrelevant in their view that some 62% of the equity of Time would be owned by former Warner shareholders after the merger, that Mr. Ross would serve as co-CEO or that half of the members of the enlarged board would be former Warner directors. There was no control block of Time shares before the agreement and there would be none after it, they point out. Before the merger agreement was signed, control of the corporation existed in a fluid aggregation of unaffiliated shareholders representing a voting majority -- in other words, in the market. After the effectuation of the merger it contemplated, control would have remained in the market, so to speak.

As to the individual plaintiffs' theory, defendants say it is flawed in law and in fact. Legally, they contend that a transaction that is otherwise proper cannot be deemed to trigger the radical "Revlon mode" obligations simply because it has the effect of making an attempted hostile takeover of the corporation less likely. All manner of transactions might have that effect and our cases, it is said, have explicitly rejected the notion that a would-be acquirer can compel a target to maintain itself in status quo while its offer proceeds.

Factually, defendants claim that this record does not establish a reasonable probability that the initial merger, if it had been consummated, would have precluded a future change in control transaction. The merged Time-Warner company would be large, it is true (a "private market" value approaching $30 billion, it is said), but recent history has shown that huge transactions can be done. While such a transaction would be rare, if a leveraged acquisition of both participants was feasible before the merger, one cannot say that a stock for stock consolidation of such firms would necessarily preclude an acquisition of it thereafter, or so defendants contend.

. . .

[I]n *Macmillan* our Supreme Court did indicate that a board may find itself in a Revlon mode without reaching an express resolve to "sell" the company:

> At a minimum, *Revlon* requires that there be the most scrupulous adherence to ordinary principles of fairness in the sense that stockholder interests are enhanced, rather than diminished, in the conduct of an auction for the sale of corporate control. *This is so whether the "sale" takes the form of an active auction, a management buyout, or a "restructuring" such as that which the Court of Chancery enjoined in Macmillan I. Revlon*, 506 A.2d at 181-82.

Id. at p. 56 (emphasis added).

Thus, I do not find it dispositive of anything that the Time board did not expressly resolve to sell the company. I take from *Macmillan*, however, and its citation of the earlier *Macmillan I* opinion in this court, that a corporate transaction that does represent a change in corporate control does place the board in a situation in which it is charged with the single duty to maximize current share value. I cannot conclude, however, that the initial merger agreement contemplates a change in control of Time. I am entirely persuaded of the soundness of the view that it is irrelevant for purposes of making such determination that 62% of Time-Warner stock would have been held by former Warner stockholders.

If the appropriate inquiry is whether a change in control is contemplated, the answer must be sought in the specific circumstances surrounding the transaction. Surely under some circumstances a stock for stock merger could reflect a transfer of corporate control. That would, for example, plainly be the case here if Warner were a private company. But where, as here, the shares of both constituent corporations are widely held, corporate control can be expected to remain unaffected by a stock for stock merger. This in my judgment was the situation with respect to the original merger agreement. When the specifics of that situation are reviewed, it is seen that, aside from legal technicalities and aside from arrangements thought to enhance the prospect for the ultimate succession of Mr. Nicholas, neither corporation could be said to be acquiring the other. Control of both remained in a large, fluid, changeable and changing market.

The existence of a block of stock in the hands of a single shareholder or a group with loyalty to each other does have real consequences to the financial value of "minority" stock. The law offers some protection to such shares through the imposition of a fiduciary duty upon controlling shareholders. But here, effectuation of the merger would not have subjected

Time shareholders to the risks and consequences of holders of minority shares. This is a reflection of the fact that no control passed to anyone in the transaction contemplated. The shareholders of Time would have "suffered" dilution, of course, but they would suffer the same type of dilution upon the public distribution of new stock. [Accordingly, the Chancellor held that *Revlon* obligations were not triggered by the Warner transaction.]

The Chancery Court's decision in *Time* leaves open a central question under the *Revlon* strand of the intermediate test. In the course of elaborating on *Macmillan*'s statement that the management recapitalizations in *Bass Group* triggered *Revlon*, the court emphasized that the key element was a change in control:

> The legally critical question this case presents then involves *when* must a board shift from its ordinary long-term profit maximizing mode to the radically altered state recognized by the *Revlon* case in which its duty, broadly stated, is to exercise its power in the good faith pursuit of immediate maximization of share value. Surely, when as in *Revlon* itself and other cases construing its commend, most notably *Macmillan*, the board itself decides to enter a change in control transaction, it has elected to enter the *Revlon* zone. But it now appears resolved that a subject disinclination to sell the company will not prevent that duty from arising when an extraordinary transaction including, at a minimum, a change in control is involved.

Yet, identifying *Revlon*'s trigger as a transaction that would result in a change in control does not end the inquiry. As the litigants in *Time* immediately pressed upon the Chancery Court, the next question is: What constitutes a change in control? Here, at least two rules are possible, either of which might be defended by plausible doctrinal and policy arguments: a "voting power" test and a "control block" test.

The voting power rule is a per se test of change in control based on how much a proposed transaction alters the existing voting power of the shareholders in a target company. Under such a rule, a transaction that allowed target shareholders to retain less than 60%, 70%, or even 80%, of their pre-existing voting power would be deemed to transfer control and trigger *Revlon* accordingly -- in much the same way that combination transactions trigger the voting and appraisal rights of shareholders in a constituent corporation who retain less than 80% of the voting power in the surviving entity under modern corporation statutes.[78] The basic rationale for the voting power test is that a shift of between 20%-40% of a corporation's voting shares significantly alters the ownership structure of the company in ways that are likely either to entrench a control group or to

---

[78] E.g., Calif.Gen.Corp.Code § 1201(b); Del.Gen.Corp.Law § 251(f)(3).

change the identify of the company's management. In addition, the voting power test would give *Revlon* a brightline boundary, and thus avoid the judicial and planning costs of case-by-case inquiry into the consequences of a large shift in voting power for continuing shareholders.

In contrast to a rule based only on changes in voting power, "change in control" might also be defined on a case-by-case basis by examining the consequences of shifts in voting power, just as the determination of whether a particular asset sale meets the statutory trigger of "substantially all" for a shareholder vote.[79] One logical focus of a case-by-case inquiry would be on whether a transaction shifted voting power to a coherent control group or to a diffuse aggregate of new shareholders who would be unable to exercise control. Chancellor Allen appears to have selected such a "control block" test in *Time*:

> If the appropriate inquiry is whether a change in control is contemplated, the answer must be sought in the specific circumstances surrounding the transaction. Surely under some circumstances a stock for stock merger could reflect a transfer of corporate control. But when, as here, the shares of both constituent corporations are widely held, corporate control can be expected to remain unaffected by a stock for stock merger. . . . [N]either corporation could be said to be acquiring the other. Control of both remained in a large, fluid, changeable and changing market.

From a doctrinal perspective, the case-by-case search for shifts of control blocks has the advantage of focusing directly on the entrenchment problem. It is only the creation of such a control block that restricts shareholders' opportunity to capture any additional acquisition premium for their shares in the market.[80] However, the price of a case-by-case focus on entrenchment is the difficulty of drawing meaningful lines. How restricted must be the shareholders' access to an acquisition premium before control has shifted? A continuum would begin at one extreme with transactions that made it impossible for shareholders to receive a subsequent premium, as when a recapitalization transaction eliminates the shareholders' equity interests. At the other extreme would be a transaction like Time's acquisition of Warner, which restricted shareholders access to a subsequent premium acquisition only because the greater size of the surviving entity discouraged future offers. Between the extremes are transactions like that in *Bass Group*, where the creation of a 39.2% block in management convinced both the Chancery and the Supreme Court that control had shifted, or the placement of a 15% stake with a white squire who could be expected to be friendly (more or less) to management's desire to remain independent.

---

[79] See Chapter 16.

[80] Theodore Mirvis first argued these points forcefully in his comments on an earlier draft of the Text. His analysis was especially prescient in light of Chancellor Allen's discussion of the change of control issue in *Time*.

Recognizing that the focus is properly on whether the transaction serves to entrench management, the problem, of course, is to know where to draw the line. How much entrenchment tips the balance and becomes a change in control?

Of course, one can always create a bright line rule For example, a change in control might be deemed to occur only when the transaction made it legally or factually *impossible* for shareholders to receive a subsequent premium offer. A transaction that eliminated the shareholders' equity interest, whether for cash or debt, would meet this test, but probably little else. However, it would appear from *Macmillan*'s favorable reference to *Bass Group* that something less than this extreme will suffice. Macmillan management would have held only a 39.2% block as a result of the transaction involved there; a subsequent offer that management approved would have still resulted in a premium to shareholders. Thus, impossibility cannot be the touchstone.

A more promising approach may be to look at the power of the newly established blockholder to prevent a hostile offer. If the focus is properly on entrenchment, then management's grant of blocking power to any party without shareholder approval should trigger *Revlon*. At least descriptively, this is what was at work in *Bass Group*. To be sure, a control block can be accumulated through private purchases, or by means of a non-management assisted street sweep, that would restrict shareholders' access to a future takeover premium no less than if management had facilitated the block's creation. But the difference is that without management participation, there is no entrenchment motive; management can act, for example, by invoking the poison pill, to protect the shareholders' interests.

In all events, a control block test is hardly a panacea. Precisely because the difference between an impossibility measure of a change in control and a blocking measure is management's ability effectively to entrench themselves, it was predictable that the litigants in *Time* would press this issue on the appeal to the Delaware Supreme Court.

PARAMOUNT COMMUNICATIONS, INC. v. TIME, INC.
571 A.2d 1140 (Del.1990)

HORSEY, Justice. . . . The Shareholder Plaintiffs first assert a *Revlon* claim. They contend that the March 4 Time-Warner agreement effectively put Time up for sale, triggering *Revlon* duties, requiring Time's board to enhance short-term shareholder value and to treat all other interested acquirors on an equal basis. The Shareholder Plaintiffs base this argument on two facts: (i) the ultimate Time-Warner exchange ratio of .465 favoring Warner, resulting in Warner shareholders' receipt of 62% of the combined company; and (ii) the subjective intent of Time's directors as evidenced in their statements that the market might perceive the Time-Warner merger as putting Time up "for sale" and their adoption of various defensive measures.

The Shareholder Plaintiffs further contend that Time's directors, in structuring the original merger transaction to be "takeover-proof," triggered *Revlon* duties by foreclosing their shareholders from any prospect of obtaining a control premium. In short, plaintiffs argue that Time's board's decision to merge with Warner imposed a fiduciary duty to maximize immediate share value and not erect unreasonable barriers to further bids. Therefore, they argue, the Chancellor erred in finding: that Paramount's bid for Time did not place Time "for sale"; that Time's transaction with Warner did not result in any transfer of control; and that the combined Time-Warner was not so large as to preclude the possibility of the stockholders of Time-Warner receiving a future control premium. . . .

The Court of Chancery posed the pivotal question presented by this case to be: Under what circumstances must a board of directors abandon an in-place plan of corporate development in order to provide its shareholders with the option to elect and realize an immediate control premium? As applied to this case, the question becomes: Did Time's board, having developed a strategic plan of global expansion to be launched through a business combination with Warner, come under a fiduciary duty to jettison its plan and put the corporation's future in the hands of its shareholders?

While we affirm the result reached by the Chancellor, we think it unwise to place undue emphasis upon long-term versus short-term corporate strategy. Two key predicates underpin our analysis. First, Delaware law imposes on a board of directors the duty to manage the business and affairs of the corporation. 8 Del.C. § 141(a). This broad mandate includes a conferred authority to set a corporate course of action, including time frame, designed to enhance corporate profitability.[12] Thus, the question of "long-term" versus "short-term" values is largely irrelevant because directors, generally, are obliged to charter a course for a corporation which is in its best interests without regard to a fixed investment horizon. Second, absent a limited set of circumstances as defined under *Revlon*, a board of directors, while always required to act in an informed manner, is not under any *per se* duty to maximize shareholder value in the short term, even in the context of a takeover. In our view, the pivotal question presented by this case is: "Did Time, by entering into the proposed merger with Warner, put itself up for sale?" A resolution of that issue through application of *Revlon* has a significant bearing upon the resolution of the derivative *Unocal* issue.

A

We first take up plaintiffs' principal *Revlon* argument, summarized above. In rejecting this argument, the Chancellor found the original Time-

---

[12] In endorsing this finding, we tacitly accept the Chancellor's conclusion that it is not a breach of faith for directors to determine that the present stock market price of shares is not representative of true value or that there may indeed be several market values for any corporation's stock. We have so held in another context. See *Van Gorkom*, 488 A.2d at 876.

Warner merger agreement not to constitute a "change of control" and concluded that the transaction did not trigger *Revlon* duties. The Chancellor's conclusion is premised on a finding that "[b]efore the merger agreement was signed, control of the corporation existed in a fluid aggregation of unaffiliated shareholders representing a voting majority -- in other words, in the market." The Chancellor's findings of fact are supported by the record and his conclusion is correct as a matter of law. However, we premise our rejection of plaintiffs' *Revlon* claim on broader grounds, namely, the absence of any substantial evidence to conclude that Time's board, in negotiating with Warner, made the dissolution or breakup of the corporate entity inevitable, as was the case in *Revlon*.

Under Delaware law there are, generally speaking and without excluding other possibilities, two circumstances which may implicate *Revlon* duties. The first, and clearer one, is when a corporation initiates an active bidding process seeking to sell itself or to effect a business reorganization involving a clear break-up of the company. See, e.g., Mills Acquisition Co. v. Macmillan, Inc., 559 A.2d 1261 (Del.1988). However, *Revlon* duties may also be triggered where, in response to a bidder's offer, a target abandons its long-term strategy and seeks an alternative transaction also involving the breakup of the company.[13] Thus, in *Revlon*, when the board responded to Pantry Pride's offer by contemplating a "bust-up" sale of assets in a leveraged acquisition, we imposed upon the board a duty to maximize immediate shareholder value and an obligation to auction the company fairly. If, however, the board's reaction to a hostile tender offer is found to constitute only a defensive response and not an abandonment of the corporation's continued existence, *Revlon* duties are not triggered, though *Unocal* duties attach.[14] See, e.g., Ivanhoe Partners v. Newmont Mining Corp., 535 A.2d 1334, 1345 (Del.1987).

The plaintiffs insist that even though the original Time-Warner agreement may not have worked "an objective change of control," the transaction made a "sale" of Time inevitable. Plaintiffs rely on the subjective intent of Time's board of directors and principally upon certain board members' expressions of concern that the Warner transaction *might* be viewed as effectively putting Time up for sale. Plaintiffs argue that the use

---

[13] As we stated in *Revlon*, in both such cases, "[t]he duty of the board [has] changed from the preservation of . . . [the] corporate entity to the maximization of the company's value at a sale for the stockholder's benefit. . . . [The board] no longer face[s] threats to corporate policy and effectiveness, or to the stockholders' interests, from a grossly inadequate bid." Revlon v. MacAndrews & Forbes Holdings, Inc., 506 A.2d 173, 182 (Del.1986).

[14] Within the auction process, any action taken by the board must be reasonably related to the threat posed or reasonable in relation to the advantage sought, see Mills Acquisition Co. v. Macmillan, Inc., 559 A.2d 1261, 1288 (Del.1988). Thus, a *Unocal* analysis may be appropriate when a corporation is in a *Revlon* situation and *Revlon* duties may be triggered by a defensive action taken in response to a hostile offer. Since *Revlon*, we have stated that differing treatment of various bidders is not actionable when such action reasonably relates to achieving the best price available for the stockholders. *Macmillan*, 559 A.2d at 1286-87.

of a lock-up agreement, a no-shop clause, and so-called "dry-up" agreements prevented shareholders from obtaining a control premium in the immediate future and thus violated *Revlon*.

We agree with the Chancellor that such evidence is entirely insufficient to invoke *Revlon* duties; and we decline to extend *Revlon*'s application to corporate transactions simply because they might be construed as putting a corporation either "in play" or "up for sale." See C[itron v. Fairchild Camera, 569 A.2d 53 (Del.1989)]; *Macmillan*, 559 A.2d at 1285 n.35. The adoption of structural safety devices alone does not trigger *Revlon*.[15] Rather, as the Chancellor stated, such devices are properly subject to a *Unocal* analysis. . . .

The Delaware Supreme Court appeared to reject the Chancery Court's adoption of *Macmillan*'s change of control test. While stating that the Chancellor's finding that a change in control had not occurred because control remained in the market was "correct as a matter of law," the court did not let the matter rest. It went on to "premise our rejection of plaintiffs' *Revlon* claim on different grounds, namely, the absence of any substantial evidence that Time's board, in negotiating with Warner, made the dissolution or breakup of the corporate entity inevitable, as was the case in *Revlon*." What does it mean for the court to premise its decision on "different grounds"? Must a transaction involve a dissolution or breakup to trigger *Revlon* even if control shifts? While the court qualifies its bidding contest or break-up trigger by the phrase "generally speaking and without excluding other possibilities," is the hedge sufficient to preserve the change of control test from the court's different grounds? Why would the court have sought different grounds if the change in control test was both correct and sufficient to resolve the case?

Is the active bidding or break-up standard coherent? Suppose in *Time* the transaction had been structured as a tender offer by Warner for 62% of the Time stock (the original merger transaction contemplated that Warner shareholders would end up with that percentage of Time's outstanding stock) and that the Time board approved the transaction. Could Time decline to cooperate with a higher competing bid because the bidding process was not active? What if the bidding process was not active because the lockups given

---

[15] Although the legality of the various safety devices adopted to protect the original agreement is not a central issue, there is substantial evidence to support each of the trial court's related conclusions. Thus, the court found that the concept of the Share Exchange Agreement predated any takeover threat by Paramount and had been adopted for a rational business purpose: to deter Time and Warner from being "put in play" by their March 4 Agreement. The court further found that Time had adopted the "no-shop" clause at Warner's insistence and for Warner's protection. Finally, although certain aspects of the "dry-up" agreements were suspect on their face, we concur in the Chancellor's view that in this case they were inconsequential.

Warner discouraged other bids? Keep in mind that the point of the substantive standard -- announced in *Macmillan* -- to be applied when *Revlon* does apply, is to determine when it is appropriate for active bidding to be cut off. Suppose instead that Time attempted a management buyout which did not contemplate the dissolution or breakup of the company. The Supreme Court's opinion in *Time* suggests that *Revlon* would not be triggered because the buyout would not contemplate the company's dissolution or breakup. Yet, *Macmillan* states specifically that *Revlon* is triggered by a management buyout. Finally, suppose that 62% of Time's stock was to be acquired by one person in a friendly transaction that did not contemplate Time's break up or dissolution. Would the Supreme Court then treat lockups that prevented competitive bidding as protected under the business judgment rule?

b. *Strategic Alliances: Paramount Again*

Time had a strategic vision in its acquisition of Warner, but so did Paramount in its pursuit of Time. Time would have given Paramount entry into the cable television industry, so it was not surprising that after losing the contest for Time, Paramount sought another means of entry. Mimicking what it saw as the winning strategy in *Time*, Paramount negotiated its acquisition by Viacom, a major cable television operator. The transaction's form, which carefully avoided both a breakup or a dissolution of Paramount, was clearly designed both to avoid what the Delaware Supreme Court appeared to have identified in *Time* as *Revlon*'s trigger, and to take advantage of that avoidance by providing Viacom significant lockups.

**PARAMOUNT COMMUNICATIONS, INC. v.
QVC NETWORK, INC.**

637 A.2d 34 (Del.1993)

VEASEY, Chief Justice. In this appeal we review an order of the Court of Chancery dated November 24, 1993 (the "November 24 Order"), preliminarily enjoining certain defensive measures designed to facilitate a so-called strategic alliance between Viacom Inc. ("Viacom") and Paramount Communications Inc. ("Paramount") approved by the board of directors of Paramount (the "Paramount Board" or the "Paramount directors") and to thwart an unsolicited, more valuable, tender offer by QVC Network Inc. ("QVC"). In affirming, we hold that the sale of control in this case, which is at the heart of the proposed strategic alliance, implicates enhanced judicial scrutiny of the conduct of the Paramount Board under Unocal Corp. v. Mesa Petroleum Co., 493 A.2d 946 (Del.1985), and Revlon, Inc. v. MacAndrews & Forbes Holdings, Inc., 506 A.2d 173 (Del.1986). We further hold that the conduct of the Paramount Board was not reasonable as to process or result.

QVC and certain stockholders of Paramount commenced separate actions (later consolidated) in the Court of Chancery seeking preliminary and permanent injunctive relief against Paramount, certain members of the Paramount Board, and Viacom. This action arises out of a proposed acquisition of Paramount by Viacom through a tender offer followed by a second-step merger (the "Paramount-Viacom transaction"), and a competing unsolicited tender offer by QVC. The Court of Chancery granted a preliminary injunction. . . .

The Court of Chancery found that the Paramount directors violated their fiduciary duties by favoring the Paramount-Viacom transaction over the more valuable unsolicited offer of QVC. The Court of Chancery preliminarily enjoined Paramount and the other individual defendants (the "Paramount defendants") from amending or modifying Paramount's stockholder rights agreement (the "Rights Agreement"), including the redemption of the Rights, or taking other action to facilitate the consummation of the pending tender offer by Viacom or any proposed second-step merger, including the Merger Agreement between Paramount and Viacom dated September 12, 1993 (the "Original Merger Agreement"), as amended on October 24, 1993 (the "Amended Merger Agreement"). Viacom and the Paramount defendants were enjoined from taking any action to exercise any provision of the Stock Option Agreement between Paramount and Viacom dated September 12, 1993 (the "Stock Option Agreement"), as amended on October 24, 1993. The Court of Chancery did not grant preliminary injunctive relief as to the termination fee provided for the benefit of Viacom in Section 8.05 of the Original Merger Agreement and the Amended Merger Agreement (the "Termination Fee").

Under the circumstances of this case, the pending sale of control implicated in the Paramount-Viacom transaction required the Paramount Board to act on an informed basis to secure the best value reasonably available to the stockholders. Since we agree with the Court of Chancery that the Paramount directors violated their fiduciary duties, we have AFFIRMED the entry of the order of the Vice Chancellor granting the preliminary injunction and have REMANDED these proceedings to the Court of Chancery for proceedings consistent herewith. . . .

I.   FACTS

. . . Paramount is a Delaware corporation with its principal offices in New York City. Approximately 118 million shares of Paramount's common stock are outstanding and traded on the New York Stock Exchange. The majority of Paramount's stock is publicly held by numerous unaffiliated investors. Paramount owns and operates a diverse group of entertainment businesses, including motion picture and television studios, book publishers, professional sports teams, and amusement parks.

There are 15 persons serving on the Paramount Board. Four directors are officer-employees of Paramount: Martin S. Davis ("Davis"),

Paramount's Chairman and Chief Executive Officer since 1983; Donald Oresman ("Oresman"), Executive Vice-President, Chief Administrative Officer, and General Counsel; Stanley R. Jaffe, President and Chief Operating Officer; and Ronald L. Nelson, Executive Vice President and Chief Financial Officer. Paramount's 11 outside directors are distinguished and experienced business persons who are present or former senior executives of public corporations or financial institutions.

Viacom is a Delaware corporation with its headquarters in Massachusetts. Viacom is controlled by Sumner M. Redstone ("Redstone"), its Chairman and Chief Executive Officer, who owns indirectly approximately 85.2 percent of Viacom's voting Class A stock and approximately 69.2 percent of Viacom's nonvoting Class B stock through National Amusements, Inc. ("NAI"), an entity 91.7 percent owned by Redstone. Viacom has a wide range of entertainment operations, including a number of well-known cable television channels such as MTV, Nickelodeon, Showtime, and The Movie Channel. Viacom's equity co-investors in the Paramount-Viacom transaction include NYNEX Corporation and Blockbuster Entertainment Corporation.

QVC is a Delaware corporation with its headquarters in West Chester, Pennsylvania. QVC has several large stockholders, including Liberty Media Corporation, Comcast Corporation, Advance Publications, Inc., and Cox Enterprises Inc. Barry Diller ("Diller"), the Chairman and Chief Executive Officer of QVC, is also a substantial stockholder. QVC sells a variety of merchandise through a televised shopping channel. QVC has several equity co-investors in its proposed combination with Paramount including BellSouth Corporation and Comcast Corporation.

Beginning in the late 1980s, Paramount investigated the possibility of acquiring or merging with other companies in the entertainment, media, or communications industry. Paramount considered such transactions to be desirable, and perhaps necessary, in order to keep pace with competitors in the rapidly evolving field of entertainment and communications. Consistent with its goal of strategic expansion, Paramount made a tender offer for Time Inc. in 1989, but was ultimately unsuccessful. See Paramount Communications, Inc. v. Time Inc., 571 A.2d 1140 (Del.1990) ("Time-Warner").

Although Paramount had considered a possible combination of Paramount and Viacom as early as 1990, . . . serious negotiations began taking place in early July [1993].

It was tentatively agreed that Davis would be the chief executive officer and Redstone would be the controlling stockholder of the combined company, but the parties could not reach agreement on the merger price and the terms of a stock option to be granted to Viacom. With respect to price, Viacom offered a package of cash and stock (primarily Viacom Class B nonvoting stock) with a market value of approximately $61 per share, but Paramount wanted at least $70 per share. . . .

[After a period of disagreement] the parties negotiated in earnest in early September, and performed due diligence with the assistance of their financial advisors, Lazard Freres & Co.; ("Lazard") for Paramount and Smith Barney for Viacom. On September 9, 1993, the Paramount Board was informed about the status of the negotiations and was provided information by Lazard, including an analysis of the proposed transaction.

On September 12, 1993, the Paramount Board met again and unanimously approved the Original Merger Agreement whereby Paramount would merge with and into Viacom. The terms of the merger provided that each share of Paramount common stock would be converted into 0.10 shares of Viacom Class A voting stock, 0.90 shares of Viacom Class B nonvoting stock, and $9.10 in cash. In addition, the Paramount Board agreed to amend its "poison pill" Rights Agreement to exempt the proposed merger with Viacom. The Original Merger Agreement also contained several provisions designed to make it more difficult for a potential competing bid to succeed. We focus, as did the Court of Chancery, on three of these defensive provisions: a "no-shop" provision (the "No-Shop Provision"), the Termination Fee, and the Stock Option Agreement.

First, under the No-Shop Provision, the Paramount Board agreed that Paramount would not solicit, encourage, discuss, negotiate, or endorse any competing transaction unless: (a) a third party "makes an unsolicited written, bona fide proposal, which is not subject to any material contingencies relating to financing"; and (b) the Paramount Board determines that discussions or negotiations with the third party are necessary for the Paramount Board to comply with its fiduciary duties.

Second, under the Termination Fee provision, Viacom would receive a $100 million termination fee if: (a) Paramount terminated the Original Merger Agreement because of a competing transaction; (b) Paramount's stockholders did not approve the merger; or (c) the Paramount Board recommended a competing transaction.

The third and most significant deterrent device was the Stock Option Agreement, which granted to Viacom an option to purchase approximately 19.9 percent (23,699,000 shares) of Paramount's outstanding common stock at $69.14 per share if any of the triggering events for the Termination Fee occurred. In addition to the customary terms that are normally associated with a stock option, the Stock Option Agreement contained two provisions that were both unusual and highly beneficial to Viacom: (a) Viacom was permitted to pay for the shares with a senior subordinated note of questionable marketability instead of cash, thereby avoiding the need to raise the $1.6 billion purchase price (the "Note Feature")' and (b) Viacom could elect to require Paramount to pay Viacom in cash a sum equal to the difference between the purchase price and the market price of Paramount's stock (the "Put Feature"). Because the Stock Option Agreement was not "capped" to limit its maximum dollar value, it had the potential to reach (and in this case did reach) unreasonable levels.

After the execution of the Original Merger Agreement and the Stock Option Agreement on September 12, 1993, Paramount and Viacom announced their proposed merger. In a number of public statements, the parties indicated that the pending transaction was a virtual certainty. Redstone described it as a "marriage" that would "never be torn asunder" and stated that only a "nuclear attack" could break the deal. ·Redstone also called Diller and John Malone of Tele-Communications Inc., a major stockholder of QVC, to dissuade them from making a competing bid.

Despite these attempts to discourage a competing bid, Diller sent a letter to Davis on September 20, 1993, proposing a merger in which QVC would acquire Paramount for approximately $80 per share, consisting of 0.893 shares of QVC common stock and $30 in cash. QVC also expressed its eagerness to meet with Paramount to negotiate the details of a transaction. When the Paramount Board met on September 28, it was advised by Davis that the Original Merger Agreement prohibited Paramount from having discussions with QVC (or anyone else) unless certain conditions were satisfied. In particular, QVC had to supply evidence that its proposal was not subject to financing contingencies. The Paramount Board was also provided information from Lazard describing QVC and its proposal.

On October 5, 1993, QVC provided Paramount with evidence of QVC's financing. The Paramount Board then held another meeting on October 11, and decided to authorize management to meet with QVC. Davis also informed the Paramount Board that Booz-Allen & Hamilton ("Booz-Allen"), a management consulting firm, had been retained to assess, *inter alia*, the incremental earnings potential from a Paramount-Viacom merger and a Paramount-QVC merger. Discussions proceeded slowly, however, due to a delay in Paramount signing a confidentiality agreement. In response to Paramount's request for information, QVC provided two binders of documents to Paramount on October 20.

On October 21, 1993, QVC filed this action and publicly announced an $80 cash tender offer for 51 percent of Paramount's outstanding shares (the "QVC tender offer"). Each remaining share of Paramount common stock would be converted into 1.42857 shares of QVC common stock in a second-step merger. The tender offer was conditioned on, among other things, the invalidation of the Stock Option Agreement, which was worth over $200 million by that point.[5] QVC contends that it had to commence a tender offer because of the slow pace of the merger discussions and the need to begin seeking clearance under federal antitrust laws.

Confronted by QVC's hostile bid, which on its face offered over $10 per share more than the consideration provided by the Original Merger Agreement, Viacom realized that it would need to raise its bid in order to remain competitive. Within hours after QVC's tender offer was announced, Viacom entered into discussions with Paramount concerning a revised

---

[5] By November 15, 1993, the value of the Stock Option Agreement had increased to nearly $500 million based on the $90 QVC bid.

transaction.   These discussions led to serious negotiations concerning a comprehensive amendment to the original Paramount-Viacom transaction. In effect, the opportunity for a "new deal" with Viacom was at hand for the Paramount Board. With the QVC hostile bid offering greater value to the Paramount stockholders, the Paramount Board had considerable leverage with Viacom.

At a special meeting on October 24, 1993, the Paramount Board approved the Amended Merger Agreement and an amendment to the Stock Option Agreement.   The Amended Merger Agreement was, however, essentially the same as the Original Merger Agreement, except that it included a few new provisions. One provision related to an $80 per share cash tender offer by Viacom for 51 percent of Paramount's stock, and another changed the merger consideration so that each share of Paramount would be converted into 0.20409 shares of Viacom Class A voting stock, 1.08317 shares of Viacom Class B nonvoting stock, and 0.20408 shares of a new series of Viacom convertible preferred stock. The Amended Merger Agreement also added a provision giving Paramount the right not to amend its Rights Agreement to exempt Viacom if the Paramount Board determined that such an amendment would be inconsistent with its fiduciary duties because another offer constituted a "better alternative."   Finally, the Paramount Board was given the power to terminate the Amended Merger Agreement if it withdrew its recommendation of the Viacom transaction or recommended a competing transaction.

Although the Amended Merger Agreement offered more consideration to the Paramount stockholders and somewhat more flexibility to the Paramount Board than did the Original Merger Agreement, the defensive measures designed to make a competing bid more difficult were not removed or modified. In particular, there is no evidence in the record that Paramount sought to use its newly-acquired leverage to eliminate or modify the No-Shop Provision, the Termination Fee, or the Stock Option Agreement when the subject of amending the Original Merger Agreement was on the table.

Viacom's tender offer commenced on October 25, 1993, and QVC's tender offer was formally launched on October 27, 1993. Diller sent a letter to the Paramount Board on October 28 requesting an opportunity to negotiate with Paramount, and Oresman responded the following day by agreeing to meet. The meeting, held on November 1, was not very fruitful, however, after QVC's proposed guidelines for a "fair bidding process" were rejected by Paramount on the ground that "auction procedures" were inappropriate and contrary to Paramount's contractual obligations to Viacom.

On November 6, 1993, Viacom unilaterally raised its tender offer price to $85 per share in cash and offered a comparable increase in the value of the securities being proposed in the second-step merger. At a telephonic meeting held later that day, the Paramount Board agreed to recommend Viacom's higher bid to Paramount's stockholders.

QVC responded to Viacom's higher bid on November 12 by increasing its tender offer to $90 per share and by increasing the securities for its second-step merger by a similar amount. In response to QVC's latest offer, the Paramount Board scheduled a meeting for November 15, 1993. Prior to the meeting, Oresman sent the members of the Paramount Board a document summarizing the "conditions and uncertainties" of QVC's offer. One director testified that this document gave him a very negative impression of the QVC bid.

At its meeting on November 15, 1993, the Paramount Board determined that the new QVC offer was not in the best interests of the stockholders. The purported basis for this conclusion was that QVC's bid was excessively conditional. The Paramount Board did not communicate with QVC regarding the status of the conditions because it believed that the No-Shop Provision prevented such communication in the absence of firm financing. Several Paramount directors also testified that they believed the Viacom transaction would be more advantageous to Paramount's future business prospects than a QVC transaction. Although a number of materials were distributed to the Paramount Board describing the Viacom and QVC transactions, the only quantitative analysis of the consideration to be received by the stockholders under each proposal was based on then-current market prices of the securities involved, not on the anticipated value of such securities at the time when the stockholders would receive them.[8]

The preliminary injunction hearing in this case took place on November 16, 1993. On November 19, Diller wrote to the Paramount Board to inform it that QVC had obtained financing commitments for its tender offer and that there was no antitrust obstacle to the offer. On November 24, 1993, the Court of Chancery issued its decision granting a preliminary injunction in favor of QVC and the plaintiff stockholders. This appeal followed.

II.   APPLICABLE PRINCIPLES OF ESTABLISHED DELAWARE LAW

The General Corporation Law of the State of Delaware (the "General Corporation Law") and the decisions of this Court have repeatedly recognized the fundamental principle that the management of the business and affairs of a Delaware corporation is entrusted to its directors, who are the duly elected and authorized representatives of the stockholders. 8 Del.C. § 141(a); Aronson v. Lewis, 473 A.2d 805, 811-12 (Del.1984); Pogostin v. Rice, 480 A.2d 619, 624 (Del.1984). Under normal circumstances, neither the courts nor the stockholders should interfere with the managerial decisions of the directors. The business judgment rule embodies the deference to which such decisions are entitled. *Aronson*, 473 A.2d at 812.

Nevertheless, there are rare situations which mandate that a court take a more direct and active role in overseeing the decisions made and actions taken by directors. In these situations, a court subjects the directors' conduct

---

[8] The market prices of Viacom's and QVC's stock were poor measures of their actual values because such prices constantly fluctuated depending upon which company was perceived to be the more likely to acquire Paramount.

to enhanced scrutiny to ensure that it is reasonable. The decisions of this Court have clearly established the circumstances where such enhanced scrutiny will be applied. *E.g.*, *Unocal*, 493 A.2d 946; Moran v. Household Int'l, Inc., 500 A.2d 1346 (Del.1985); *Revlon*, 506 A.2d 173; Mills Acquisition Co. v. Macmillan, Inc., 559 A.2d 1261 (Del.1989); Gilbert v. El Paso Co., 575 A.2d 1131 (Del.1990). The case at bar implicates . . . such circumstances: the approval of a transaction resulting in a sale of control. . . .

A.   The Significance of a Sale of Change[10] of Control

When a majority of a corporation's voting shares are acquired by a single person or entity, or by a cohesive group acting together, there is a significant diminution in the voting power of those who thereby become minority stockholders. Under the statutory framework of the General Corporation Law, many of the most fundamental corporate changes can be implemented only if they are approved by a majority vote of the stockholders. Such actions include elections of directors, amendments to the certificate of incorporation, mergers, consolidations, sales of all or substantially all of the assets of the corporation, and dissolution. 8 Del.C. §§ 211, 242, 251-258, 263, 271, 275. Because of the overriding importance of voting rights, this Court and the Court of Chancery have consistently acted to protect stockholders form unwarranted interference with such rights.

In the absence of devices protecting the minority stockholders,[12] stockholder votes are likely to become mere formalities where there is a majority stockholder. For example, minority stockholders can be deprived of a continuing equity interest in their corporation by means of a cash-out merger. *Weinberger*, 457 A.2d at 703. Absent effective protective provisions, minority stockholders must rely for protection solely on the fiduciary duties owed to them by the directors and the majority stockholder, since the minority stockholders have lost the power to influence corporate direction through the ballot. The acquisition of majority status and the consequent privilege of exerting the powers of majority ownership come at a price. That price is usually a control premium which recognizes not only the value of a control block of shares, but also compensates the minority stockholders for their resulting loss of voting power.

---

[10] For purposes of our December 9 Order and this Opinion, we have used the terms "sale of control" and "change of control" interchangeably without intending any doctrinal distinction.

[12] Examples of such protective provisions are supermajority voting provisions, majority of the minority requirements, etc. Although we express no opinion on what effect the inclusion of any such stockholder protective devices would have had in this case, we note that this Court has upheld, under different circumstances, the reasonableness of a standstill agreement which limited a 49.9% stockholder to 40% board representation. *Ivanhoe*, 535 A.2d at 1343.

In the case before us, the public stockholders (in the aggregate) currently own a majority of Paramount's voting stock. Control of the corporation is not vested in a single person, entity, or group, but vested in the fluid aggregation of unaffiliated stockholders. In the event the Paramount-Viacom transaction is consummated, the public stockholders will receive cash and a minority equity voting position in the surviving corporation. Following such consummation, there will be a controlling stockholder who will have the voting power to: (a) elect directors; (b) cause a break-up of the corporation; (c) merge it with another company; (d) cash-out the public stockholders; (e) amend the certificate of incorporation; (f) sell all or substantially all of the corporate assets; or (g) otherwise alter materially the nature of the corporation and the public stockholders' interests. Irrespective of the present Paramount Board's vision of a long-term strategic alliance with Viacom, the proposed sale of control would provide the new controlling stockholder with the power to alter that vision.

Because of the intended sale of control, the Paramount-Viacom transaction has economic consequences of considerable significance to the Paramount stockholders. Once control has shifted, the current Paramount stockholders will have no leverage in the future to demand another control premium. As a result, the Paramount stockholders are entitled to receive, and should receive, a control premium and/or protective devices of significant value. There being no such protective provisions in the Viacom-Paramount transaction, the Paramount directors had an obligation to take the maximum advantage of the current opportunity to realize for stockholders the best value reasonably available.

B. The Obligations of Directors in a Sale or Change of Control Transaction

The consequences of a sale of control impose special obligations on the directors of a corporation.[13] In particular, they have the obligation of acting reasonably to seek the transaction offering the best value reasonably available to the stockholders. The courts will apply enhanced scrutiny to ensure that the directors have acted reasonably. The obligations of the

---

[13] We express no opinion on any scenario except the actual facts before the Court, and our precise holding herein. Unsolicited tender offers in other contexts may be governed by different precedent. For example, where a potential sale of control by a corporation is not the consequence of a board's action, this Court has recognized the prerogative of a board of directors to resist a third party's unsolicited acquisition proposal or offer. See *Pogostin*, 480 A.2d at 627; *Time-Warner*, 571 A.2d at 1152; Bershad v. Curtiss-Wright Corp., 535 A.2d 840, 845 (Del.1987); *Macmillan*, 558 A.2d at 1285 n.35. The decision of a board to resist such an acquisition, like all decisions of a properly-functioning board, must be informed, *Unocal*, 493 A.2d at 954-55, and the circumstances of each particular case will determine the steps that a board must take to inform itself, and what other action, if any, is required as a matter of fiduciary duty.

directors and the enhanced scrutiny of the courts are well-established by the decisions of this Court. . . .

In the sale of control context, the directors must focus on one primary objective -- to secure the transaction offering the best value reasonably available for the stockholder -- and they must exercise their fiduciary duties to further that end. The decisions of this Court have consistently emphasized this goal. *Revlon*, 506 A.2d at 182 ("The duty of the board . . . [is] the maximization of the company's value at a sale for the stockholders' benefit."); *Macmillan*, 559 A.2d at 1288 ("[I]n a sale of corporate control the responsibility of the directors is to get the highest value reasonably attainable for the shareholders."); *Barkan*, 567 A.2d at 1286 ("[T]he board must act in a neutral manner to encourage the highest possible price for shareholders."). . . .

In pursuing this objective, the directors must be especially diligent. See *Citron v. Fairchild Camera and Instrument Corp.*, 569 A.2d 53, 66 (Del.1989) (discussing "a board's active and direct role in the sale process"). In particular, this Court has stressed the importance of the board being adequately informed in negotiating a sale of control: "The need for adequate information is central to the enlightened evaluation of a transaction that a board must make." *Barkan*, 567 A.2d at 1287. This requirement is consistent with the general principle that "directors have a duty to inform themselves, prior to making a business decision, of all material information reasonably available to them." *Aronson*, 473 A.2d at 812. See also *Cede & Co. v. Technicolor, Inc.*, 634 A.2d 345 (Del.1993); *Smith v. Van Gorkom*, 488 A.2d 858, 872 (Del.1985). Moreover, the role of outside, independent directors becomes particularly important because of the magnitude of a sale of control transaction and the possibility, in certain cases, that management may not necessarily be impartial. See *Macmillan*, 559 A.2d at 1285 (requiring "the intense scrutiny and participation of the independent directors").

Barkan teaches some of the methods by which a board can fulfill its obligation to seek the best value reasonably available to the stockholders. 567 A.2d at 1286-87. These methods are designed to determine the existence and viability of possible alternatives. They include conducting an auction, canvassing the market, etc. Delaware law recognizes that there is "no single blueprint" that directors must follow. *Id.* at 1286-87; *Citron*, 569 A.2d at 68; *Macmillan*, 559 A.2d at 1287.

In determining which alternative provides the best value for the stockholders, a board of directors is not limited to considering only the amount of cash involved, and is not required to ignore totally its view of the future value of a strategic alliance. See *Macmillan*, 559 A.2d at 1282 n. 29. Instead, the directors should analyze the entire situation and evaluate in a disciplined manner the consideration being offered. Where stock or other non-cash consideration is involved, the board should try to quantify its value, if feasible, to achieve an objective comparison of the alternatives.[14] In addition, the board may assess a variety of practical considerations relating to each alternative, including:

> [an offer's] fairness and feasibility; the proposed or actual financing for the offer, and the consequences of that financing; questions of illegality; . . . the risk of non-consum[m]ation; . . . the bidder's identity, prior background and other business venture experiences; and the bidder's business plans or the corporation and their effects on stockholder interests.

Macmillan, 559 A.2d at 1282 n.29. These considerations are important because the selection of one alternative may permanently foreclose other opportunities. While the assessment of these factors may be complex, the board's goal is straightforward: Having informed themselves of all material information reasonably available, the directors must decide which alternative is most likely to offer the best value reasonably available to the stockholders.

C. Enhanced Judicial Scrutiny of a Sale of Change of Control Transaction

Board action in the circumstances presented here is subject to enhanced scrutiny. Such scrutiny is mandated by: (a) the threatened diminution of the current stockholders' voting power; (b) the fact that an asset belonging to public stockholders (a control premium) is being sold and may never be available again; and (c) the traditional concern of Delaware courts for actions which impair or impede stockholder voting rights (see supra note 11). In *Macmillan*, this Court held:

> When *Revlon* duties devolve upon directors, this Court will continue to exact an enhanced judicial scrutiny at the threshold, as in *Unocal*, before the normal presumptions of the business judgment rule will apply.

559 A.2d at 1288. The *Macmillan* decision articulates a specific two-part test for analyzing board action where competing bidders are not treated equally:[16]

> In the face of disparate treatment, the trial court must first examine whether the directors properly perceived that shareholder interests were enhanced. In any event the board's action must be reasonable in relation to the

---

[14] When assessing the value of non-cash consideration, a board should focus on its value as of the date it will be received by the stockholders. Normally, such value will be determined with the assistance of experts using generally accepted methods of valuation. See In re RJR Nabisco, Inc. Shareholders Litig., Del Ch., C.A. No. 10389, Allen, C. (Jan. 31, 1989), reprinted at 14 Del.J.Corp.L. 1132, 1161 (1989).

[16] Before this test is invoked, "the plaintiff must show, and the trial court must find, that the directors of the target company treated one or more of the respective bidders on unequal terms." *Macmillan*, 559 A.2d at 1288.

advantage sought to be achieved, or conversely, to the threat which a particular bid allegedly poses to stockholder interests.

The key features of an enhanced scrutiny test are: (a) a judicial determination regarding the adequacy of the decisionmaking process employed by the directors, including the information on which the directors based their decision; and (b) a judicial examination of the reasonableness of the directors' action in light of the circumstances then existing. The directors have the burden of proving that they were adequately informed and acted reasonably.

Although an enhanced scrutiny test involves a review of the reasonableness of the substantive merits of a board's actions,[17] a court should not ignore the complexity of the directors' task in a sale of control. There are many business and financial considerations implicated in investigating and selecting the best value reasonably available. The board of directors is the corporate decisionmaking body best equipped to make these judgments. Accordingly, a court applying enhanced judicial scrutiny should be deciding whether the directors made *a reasonable* decision, not *a perfect* decision. If a board selected one of several reasonable alternatives, a court should not second-guess that choice even though it might have decided otherwise or subsequent events may have cast doubt on the board's determination. Thus, courts will not substitute their business judgment for that of the directors, but will determine if the directors' decision was, on balance, within a range of reasonableness.

D.   *Revlon* and *Time-Warner* Distinguished

The Paramount defendants and Viacom assert that the fiduciary obligations and the enhanced judicial scrutiny discussed above are not implicated in this case in the absence of a "break-up" of the corporation, and that the order granting the preliminary injunction should be reversed. This argument is based on their erroneous interpretation of our decisions in *Revlon* and *Time-Warner*

In *Revlon*, we reviewed the actions of the board of directors of Revlon, Inc. ("Revlon"), which had rebuffed the overtures of Pantry Pride, Inc. and had instead entered into an agreement with Forstmann Little & Co. ("Forstmann") providing for the acquisition of 100 percent of Revlon's outstanding stock by Forstmann and the subsequent break-up of Revlon.

---

[17] It is to be remembered that, in cases where the traditional business judgment rule is applicable and the board acted with due care, in good faith, and in the honest belief that they are acting in the best interests of the stockholders (which is not this case), the Court gives great deference to the substance of the directors' decision and will not invalidate the decision, will not examine its reasonableness, and "will not substitute our views for those of the board if the latter's decision can be 'attributed to any rational business purpose.'" *Unocal*, 493 A.2d at 949 (quoting Sinclair Oil Corp. v. Levien, 280 A.2d 717, 720 (Del.1971)). See *Aronson*, 473 A.2d at 812.

Based on the facts and circumstances present in *Revlon*, we held that "[t]he directors' role changes from defenders of the corporate bastion to auctioneers charged with getting the best price for the stockholders at a sale of the company." 506 A.2d at 182. We further held that "when a board ends an intense bidding contest on an insubstantial basis, . . . [that] action cannot withstand the enhanced scrutiny which *Unocal* requires of director conduct." *Id*. at 184.

It is true that one of the circumstances bearing on these holdings was the fact that "the break-up of the company . . . had become a reality which even the directors embraced." *Id* at 182. It does not follow, however, that a "break-up" must be present and "inevitable" before directors are subject to enhanced judicial scrutiny and are required to pursue a transaction that is calculated to produce the best value reasonably available to the stockholders. In fact, we stated in *Revlon* that "when bidders make relatively similar offers, or dissolution of the company becomes inevitable, the directors cannot fulfill their enhanced *Unocal* duties by playing favorites with the contending factions." *Id*. at 184 (emphasis added). *Revlon* thus does not hold that an inevitable dissolution or "break-up" is necessary.

The decisions of this Court following *Revlon* reinforced the applicability of enhanced scrutiny and the directors' obligation to seek the best value reasonably available for the stockholders where there is a pending sale of control, regardless of whether or not there is to be a break-up of the corporation. In *Macmillan*, this Court held:

> We stated in *Revlon*, and again here, that *in a sale of corporate control* the responsibility of the directors is to get the highest value reasonably attainable for the shareholders.

559 A.2d at 1288 (emphasis added). In *Barkan*, we observed further:

> We believe that the general principles announced in *Revlon*, in Unocal Corp. v. Mesa Petroleum Co., 493 A.2d 946 (Del.1985), and in Moran v. Household International, Inc., 500 A.2d 1346 (Del.1985) govern this case and every case in which *a fundamental change of corporate control* occurs or is contemplated.

567 A.2d at 1286 (emphasis added).

Although *Macmillan* and *Barkan* are clear in holding that a change of control imposes on directors the obligation to obtain the best value reasonably available to the stockholders, the Paramount defendants have interpreted our decision in *Time-Warner* as requiring a corporate break-up in order for that obligation to apply. The facts in *Time-Warner*, however, were quite different from the facts of this case, and refute Paramount's position here. In *Time-Warner*, the Chancellor held that there was no change of control in the original stock-for-stock merger between Time and Warner because Time would be owned by a fluid aggregation of unaffiliated stockholders both before and after the merger. . . .

Moreover, the transaction actually consummated in Time-Warner was not a merger, as originally planned, but a sale of Warner's stock to Time.

In our affirmance of the Court of Chancery's well-reasoned decision, this Court held that "The Chancellor's findings of fact are supported by the record *and his conclusion is correct as a matter of law*." 571 A.2d at 1150 (emphasis added). Nevertheless, the Paramount defendants here have argued that a break-up is a requirement and have focused on the following language in our *Time-Warner* decision:

> However, we premise our rejection of plaintiffs' *Revlon* claim on different grounds, namely, the absence of any substantial evidence to conclude that Time's board, in negotiating with Warner, made the dissolution or break-up of the corporate entity inevitable, as was the case in *Revlon*.
> Under Delaware law there are, generally speaking and *without excluding other possibilities*, two circumstances which may implicate *Revlon* duties. The first, and clearer one, is when a corporate *initiates an active bidding process seeking to sell itself* or to effect a business reorganization involving a clear break-up of the company. However, *Revlon* duties may also be triggered where, in response to a bidder's offer, a target abandons its long-term strategy and seeks an alternative transaction involving the breakup of the company.

Id. at 1150 (emphasis added) (citation and footnote omitted).

The Paramount defendants have misread the holding of *Time-Warner*. Contrary to their argument, our decision in *Time-Warner* expressly states that the two general scenarios discussed in the above-quoted paragraph are not the *only* instances where "*Revlon* duties" may be implicated. The Paramount defendants' argument totally ignores the phrase "without excluding other possibilities." Moreover, the instant case is clearly within the first general scenario set forth in *Time-Warner*. The Paramount Board, albeit unintentionally, had "initiate[d] an active bidding process seeking to sell itself by agreeing to sell control of the corporation to Viacom in circumstances where another potential acquirer (QVC) was equally interested in being a bidder.

The Paramount defendants' position that *both* a change of control *and* a break-up are *required* must be rejected. Such a holding would unduly restrict the application of *Revlon*, is inconsistent with this Court's decisions in *Barkan* and *Macmillan*, and has no basis in policy. There are few events that have a more significant impact on the stockholders than a sale of control or a corporate break-up. Each event represents a fundamental (and perhaps irrevocable) change in the nature of the corporate enterprise from a practical stand-point. It is the significance of *each* of these events that justifies: (a) focusing on the directors' obligation to seek the best value reasonably available to the stockholders; and (b) requiring a close scrutiny of board action which could be contrary to the stockholders' interests.

Accordingly, when a corporation undertakes a transaction which will cause: (a) a change in corporate control; *or* (b) a break-up of the corporate entity, the directors' obligation is to seek the best value reasonably available to the stockholders. This obligation arises because the effect of the Viacom-Paramount transaction, if consummated, is to shift control of Paramount from the public stockholders to a controlling stockholder, Viacom. Neither *Time-Warner* nor any other decision of this Court holds that a "break-up" of the company is essential to give rise to this obligation where there is a sale of control.

III. BREACH OF FIDUCIARY DUTIES BY PARAMOUNT BOARD

We now turn to duties of the Paramount Board under the facts of this case and our conclusions as to the breaches of those duties which warrant injunctive relief.

A. The Specific Obligations of the Paramount Board

Under the facts of this case, the Paramount directors had the obligation: (a) to be diligent and vigilant in examining critically the Paramount-Viacom transaction and the QVC tender offers; (b) to act in good faith; (c) to obtain, and act with due care on, all material information reasonably available, including information necessary to compare the two offers to determine which of these transactions, or an alternative course of action, would provide the best value reasonably available to the stockholders; and (d) to negotiate actively and in good faith with both Viacom and QVC to that end.

Having decided to sell control of the corporation, the Paramount directors were required to evaluate critically whether or not all material aspects of the Paramount-Viacom transaction (separately and in the aggregate) were reasonable and in the best interests of the Paramount stockholders in light of current circumstances, including: the change of control premium, the Stock Option Agreement, the Termination Fee, and coercive nature of both the Viacom and QVC tender offers, the No-Shop Provision, and the proposed disparate use of the Rights Agreement as to the Viacom and QVC tender offers, respectively.

These obligations necessarily implicated various issues, including the questions of whether or not those provisions and other aspects of the Paramount-Viacom transaction (separately and in the aggregate): (a) adversely affected the value provided to the Paramount stockholders; (b) inhibited or encouraged alternative bids; (c) were enforceable contractual obligations in light of the directors' fiduciary duties; and (d) in the end would advance or retard the Paramount directors' obligation to secure for the Paramount stockholders the best value reasonably available under the circumstances.

The Paramount defendants contend that they were precluded by certain contractual provisions, including the No-Shop Provision, from negotiating with QVC or seeking alternatives. Such provisions, whether or not they are presumptively valid in the abstract, may not validly define or limit the directors' fiduciary duties under Delaware law or prevent the Paramount directors from carrying out their fiduciary duties under Delaware law. To the extent such provisions are inconsistent with those duties, they are invalid and unenforceable. See *Revlon*, 506 A.2d at 184-85.

Since the Paramount directors had already decided to sell control, they had an obligation to continue their search for the best value reasonably available to the stockholders. This continuing obligation included the responsibility, at the October 24 board meeting and thereafter, to evaluate critically both the QVC tender offers and the Paramount-Viacom transaction to determine if: (a) the QVC tender offer was, or would continue to be, conditional; (b) the QVC tender offer could be improved; (c) the Viacom tender offer or other aspects of the Paramount-Viacom transaction could be improved; (d) each of the respective offers would be reasonably likely to come to closure, and under what circumstances; (e) other material information was reasonably available for consideration by the Paramount directors; (f) there were viable and realistic alternative courses of action; and (g) the timing constraints could be managed so the directors could consider these matters carefully and deliberately.

B.   The Breaches of Fiduciary Duty by the Paramount Board

The Paramount directors made the decision on September 12, 1993, that, in their judgement, a strategic merger with Viacom on the economic terms of the Original Merger Agreement was in the best interests of Paramount and its stockholders. Those terms provided a modest change of control premium to the stockholders. The directors also decided at that time that it was appropriate to agree to certain defensive measures (the Stock Option Agreement, the Termination Fee, and the No-Shop Provision) insisted upon by Viacom as part of that economic transaction. Those defensive measures, coupled with the sale of control and subsequent disparate treatment of competing bidders, implicated the judicial scrutiny of *Unocal, Revlon, Macmillan*, and their progeny. We conclude that the Paramount directors' process was not reasonable, and the result achieved for the stockholders was not reasonable under the circumstances.

When entering into the Original Merger Agreement, and thereafter, the Paramount Board clearly gave insufficient attention to the potential consequences of the defensive measures demanded by Viacom. The Stock Option Agreement had a number of unusual and potentially "draconian"[19] provisions, including the Note Feature and the Put Feature. Furthermore, the Termination Fee, whether or not unreasonable by itself, clearly made Paramount less attractive to other bidders, when coupled with the Stock Option Agreement. Finally, the No-Shop Provision inhibited the Paramount

---

[19] . . . We express no opinion whether a stock option agreement of essentially this magnitude, but with a reasonable "cap" and without the Note and Put Features, would be valid or invalid under other circumstances. . . .

Board's ability to negotiate with other potential bidders, particularly QVC which had already expressed an interest in Paramount.[20]

Throughout the applicable time period, and especially from the first QVC merger proposal on September 20 through the Paramount Board meeting on November 15, QVC's interest in Paramount provided the *opportunity* for the Paramount Board to seek significantly higher value for the Paramount stockholders than that being offered by Viacom. QVC persistently demonstrated its intention to meet and exceed the Viacom offers, and frequently expressed its willingness to negotiate possible further increases.

The Paramount directors had the opportunity in the October 23-24 time frame, when the Original Merger Agreement was renegotiated, to take appropriate action to modify the improper defensive measures as well as to improve the economic terms of the Paramount-Viacom transaction. Under the circumstances existing at that time, it should have been clear to the Paramount Board that the Stock Option Agreement, coupled with the Termination Fee and the No-Shop Clause, were impeding the realization of the best value reasonably available to the Paramount stockholders. Nevertheless, the Paramount Board made no effort to eliminate or modify these counterproductive devices, and instead continued to cling to its vision of a strategic alliance with Viacom. Moreover, based on advice from the Paramount management, the Paramount directors considered the QVC offer to be "conditional" and asserted that they were precluded by the No-Shop Provision from seeking more information from, or negotiating with, QVC.

By November 12, 1993, the value of the revised QVC offer on its face exceeded that of the Viacom offer by over $1 billion at then current values. This significant disparity of value cannot be justified on the basis of the directors' vision of future strategy, primarily because the change of control would supplant the authority of the current Paramount Board to continue to hold and implement their strategic vision in any meaningful way. Moreover, their uninformed process had deprived their strategic vision of much of its credibility. See *Van Gorkom*, 488 A.2d at 872; Cede v. Technicolor, 634 A.2d at 367; Hanson Trust PLC v. ML SCM Acquisition Inc., 781 F.2d 264, 274 (2nd Cir.1986).

---

[20] We express no opinion whether certain aspects of the No-Shop Provision here could be valid in another context. Whether or not it could validly have operated here at an early stage solely to prevent Paramount from actively "shopping" the company, it could not prevent the Paramount directors from carrying out their fiduciary duties in considering unsolicited bids or in negotiating for the best value reasonably available to the stockholders. *Macmillan*, 559 A.2d at 1287. As we said in *Barkan*: "Where a board has no reasonable basis upon which to judge the adequacy of an contemplated transaction, a no-shop restriction gives rise to the inference that the board seeks to forestall competing bids." 567 A.2d at 1288. See also *Revlon*, 506 A.2d at 184 (holding that "[t]he no-shop provision, like the lock-up option, while not *per se* illegal, is impermissible under the Unocal standards when a board's primary duty becomes that of an auctioneer responsible for selling the company to the highest bidder").

When the Paramount directors met on November 15 to consider QVC's increased tender offer, they remained prisoners of their own misconceptions and missed opportunities to eliminate the restrictions they had imposed on themselves. Yet, it was not "too late" to reconsider negotiating with QVC. The circumstances existing on November 15 made it clear that the defensive measures, taken as a whole, were problematic: (a) the No-Shop Provision could not define or limit their fiduciary duties; (b) the Stock Option Agreement had become "draconian"; and (c) the Termination Fee, in context with all the circumstances, was similarly deterring the realization of possibly higher bids. Nevertheless, the Paramount directors remained paralyzed by their uninformed belief that the QVC offer was "illusory." This final opportunity to negotiate on the stockholders' behalf and to fulfill their obligation to seek the best value reasonably available was thereby squandered.

IV. VIACOM'S CLAIM OF VESTED CONTRACT RIGHTS

Viacom argues that it had certain "vested" contract rights with respect to the No-Shop Provision and the Stock Option Agreement. In effect, Viacom's argument is that the Paramount directors could enter into an agreement in violation of their fiduciary duties and then render Paramount, and ultimately its stockholders, liable for failing to carry out an agreement in violation of those duties. Viacom's protestations about vested rights are without merit. This Court has found that those defensive measures were improperly designed to deter potential bidders, and that such measures do not meet the reasonableness test to which they must be subjected. They are consequently invalid and unenforceable under the facts of this case.

The No-Shop Provision could not validly define or limit the fiduciary duties of the Paramount directors. To the extent that a contract, or a provision thereof, purports to require a board to act or not act in such a fashion as to limit the exercise of fiduciary duties, it is invalid and unenforceable. Despite the arguments of Paramount and Viacom to the contrary, the Paramount directors could not contract away their fiduciary obligations. Since the No-Shop Provision was invalid, Viacom never had any vested contract rights in the provision.

As discussed previously, the Stock Option Agreement contained several "draconian" aspects, including the Note Feature and the Put Feature. While we have held that lock-up options are not *per se* illegal, no options with similar features have ever been upheld by this Court. Under the circumstances of this case, the Stock Option Agreement clearly is invalid. Accordingly, Viacom never had any vested contract rights in that Agreement.

Viacom, a sophisticated party with experienced legal and financial advisors, knew of (and in fact demanded) the unreasonable features of the Stock Option Agreement. It cannot be now heard to argue that it obtained vested contract rights by negotiating and obtaining contractual provisions from a board acting in violation of its fiduciary duties. As the Nebraska

Supreme Court said in rejecting a similar argument on ConAgra, Inc., v. Cargill, Inc., 382 N.W.2d 576, 587-88 (Neb.1986), "To so hold, it would seem, would be to get the shareholders coming and going." Likewise, we reject Viacom's arguments and hold that its fate must rise or fall, and in this instance fall, with the determination that the actions of the Paramount Board were invalid.

V. CONCLUSION

The realization of the best value reasonably available to the stockholders became the Paramount directors' primary obligation under these facts in light of the change of control. That obligation was not satisfied, and the Paramount Board's process was deficient. The directors' initial hope and expectation for a strategic alliance with Viacom was allowed to dominate their decisionmaking process to the point where the arsenal of defensive measures established at the outset was perpetuated (not modified or eliminated) when the situation was dramatically altered. QVC's unsolicited bid presented the opportunity for significantly greater value for the stockholders and enhanced negotiating leverage for the directors. Rather than seizing those opportunities, the Paramount directors chose to wall themselves off from material information which was reasonably available and to hide behind the defensive measures as a rationalization for refusing to negotiate with QVC or seeking other alternatives. Their view of the strategic alliance likewise became an empty rationalization as the opportunities for higher value for the stockholders continued to develop.

It is the nature of the judicial process that we decide only the case before us -- a case which, on its facts, is clearly controlled by established Delaware law. Here, the proposed change of control and the implications thereof were crystal clear. In other cases they may be less clear. The holding of this case on its facts, coupled with the holdings of the principal cases discussed herein where the issue of sale of control is implicated, should provide a workable precedent against which to measure future cases.

Note: **Where Are We After *QVC*?**

Change in Control as Revlon's Trigger. In *QVC*, the Delaware Supreme Court recanted the active bidding or breakup standard it appeared to have adopted in *Time*, returning instead to the change in control test proffered by the Chancery Court in *Time*. The Supreme Court met Paramount's understandable claim that its planners had dutifully followed *Time*'s "different ground" by commenting that Paramount's planners had "misread the holding of *Time-Warner*." The court points out that it had qualified the active bidding or breakup language in *Time* by the phrase "without excluding other possibilities." Is this the hat out of which the change in control rabbit reappeared? The court also notes that the Paramount board in fact, "albeit unintentionally, had 'initiated an active bidding process seeking to sell itself' by agreeing to sell control in circumstances where another potential bidder [QVC] was equally interested in being a bidder." Imagine a friendly transaction that does not involve a change in control. Is the fact that a third party appears who also wants to bid sufficient to meet the active bidding test even if the transaction otherwise does not meet the change in control test?

The same ambiguities that were associated with the Chancery Court's formulation of a change in control test in *Time* are also imbedded in the Supreme Court's formulation in *QVC*. The Supreme Court stresses that the sale of QVC to Viacom was, in effect, a sale to Redstone; control would no longer be in the market. Should the QVC board's obligations have been different if the favored bidder had been IBM? Casting the question in planning terms, should QVC have more freedom to protect a transaction with IBM than with Viacom?

The result of keying a planner's ability to protect a friendly transaction on the distribution of shareholdings in the favored acquirer may serve to privilege particular types of bidders. In high technology industries, successful companies are often controlled by the original founders and venture capital group. If such a company is the bidder in a friendly transaction, then the *QVC* change in control standard is seemingly triggered, reducing the planner's ability to protect the transaction. Is it sensible policy to make it more difficult for a target company to protect a friendly transaction with an entrepreneurial company like Microsoft, which is controlled by its founder Bill Gates, than a friendly transaction with IBM?

Does *Revlon's* trigger matter so much if *Revlon's* substance is understood as something other than the obligation to immediately conduct an auction of the target company? Recall that *Macmillan* treated the substantive effect of triggering *Revlon* as requiring the target board to show that what it received for favoring a bidder was reasonable in relation to the favoritism provided. *QVC* framed the standard as requiring the board to "realize for the stockholders the best value reasonably available." That standard can be applied as easily to evaluating the sale to a favored bidder of preferred stock that has the power to block a takeover, as to a sale of the company: the issue is not whether to force the target company's auction, but only whether the transaction requires more rigorous judicial review.[81] From this perspective, suppose the target of a hostile offer initiates a share repurchase the effect of which is to increase the holdings of its largest shareholder (who elects not to sell any shares) to an amount sufficient to block a freezeout

---

[81] For an interesting analysis that argues that the *QVC* formulation applies to all extraordinary corporate transactions, see Lawrence Cunningham & Charles Yablon, *Delaware Fiduciary Duty Law After QVC and Technicolor: A Unified Standard (and the End of Revlon Duties?)*, 49 Bus.Law. 1593 (1994). See also Robert Ragazzo, *Unifying the Law of Hostile Takeovers: Bridging the Unocal/Revlon Gap*, 35 Ariz.L.Rev. 989 (1993).

under the company's charter. Is it helpful to ask whether the company received reasonable value for favoring its largest shareholder by giving it blocking power? Does this inquiry differ from asking whether giving the largest shareholder blocking power realized the best value reasonably available? Can the *QVC* formulation apply to this transaction? See In re Unitrin Shareholders Litigation, 1994 WL 698483 (Del.Ch.).

The Boundary Between Revlon and the Business Judgment Rule. What standard of review applies to the target board's efforts to be adequately informed? If the duty to be informed is part of *Revlon*'s intermediate standard, then we confront the anomalous result that the extent of the target board's duty to be informed depends on whether the acquirer is controlled by a single individual or entity. Again, should review of the board's conduct depend on whether the acquirer is IBM or Microsoft? But how much difference is there between the business judgment rule and Revlon's intermediate standard? In *QVC* the court cites both *Trans Union* and *Technicolor* for the proposition that the board must be adequately informed in order to discharge its duty to shareholders. Both are pre-*Revlon* cases in which the court found that the board's failure to be adequately informed was not protected by the business judgment rule and violated the directors' duty of care. In note 17 of the *QVC* opinion the court states that the business judgment rule prohibits judicial inquiry into the reasonableness of board decisions. The QVC formulation, in contrast, expressly "involves a review of the reasonableness of the substantive merits of a board's actions. . . ."[82] Can we imagine circumstances where a court would conclude that directors were not reasonable, but the business judgment rule nonetheless bars the inquiry? To add just a little more confusion, recall that in *Amsted* the Supreme Court quoted with approval the following proposition: "[T]he due care theory and the Revlon theory do not present two separate legal theories justifying shareholder recovery. . . . [B]oth theories reduce to a claim that directors were inadequately informed. . . ."[83]

The Boundary Between Revlon and Unocal. Fraidin & Hanson, *supra*, stress the difference in rigor they perceive in the Delaware Supreme Court's application of the *Revlon* and *Unocal* strands of the intermediate standard. *Time*, they argue, shows great deference to a target board decision to reject all bidders by deployment of defensive tactics,[84] while *QVC* overrules a board's decision to favor a particular bidder. Why does the court react differently to a board's decision to just say yes rather than just say no?[85]

---

[82] 637 A.2d at 45.

[83] Cunningham & Yablon (1994), *supra* note 81, generously extract from the morass a single standard applicable to all extraordinary corporate transactions, regardless of whether *Revlon* is triggered.

[84] A different reading of *Time* is presented in Chapter 17, *supra*.

[85] Fraidin & Hanson (1994), *supra* note 14, at 1743-44.

One response is that a decision to block a takeover, presumably based on the belief that target shareholders receive the best value by the company remaining independent, is not irreversible. If independence does not prove to be the more valuable strategy, the price of the company's stock will further decline, encouraging a subsequent offer. Defending against a hostile offer at that time is less likely to be proportional to the threat of takeover.[86] In contrast, decisions which transfer control (or at least transfer the opportunity to block a future offer), may be effectively irreversible from the shareholders' perspective, and therefore will receive careful judicial review at the time of the transaction or not at all.

Unocal and *Revlon* must, however, meet at some point. Consider again the hypothetical of a target company defending against a hostile bid by a share repurchase that increases the holdings of its largest shareholder to a level that allows it to block a freezeout transaction. The repurchase may warrant enhanced scrutiny under *Unocal* because it blocks the hostile offer, and may be unreasonable in relation to the threat posed precisely because the defensive response is irreversible: the power to block a freezeout transaction is transferred not just with respect to the instant offer, but with respect to all future offers. The repurchase also may warrant enhanced scrutiny under *Revlon* because it irreversibly transfers an aspect of control. The transfer may not provide the best value reasonable available under the circumstances because the benefit received -- independence -- was not reasonably related to the favoritism granted: the power to block all future freezeout transactions.

Revlon's Substantive Obligations. *Revlon*'s trigger and the target board's satisfaction of the information requirement, are just preludes to review of target management's substantive obligations. As formulated in *Macmillan*, the target board in granting a lockup must determine that the company will receive a benefit reasonable in relation to the favoritism shown the preferred bidder. The problem is how reasonableness can be assessed.

The preferences given Viacom in *QVC* consisted of (i) a $100 million breakup fee, amounting to approximately 1.2% of Viacom's then $8.5 billion bid; (ii) an option to purchase approximately 19.9% of Paramount's common stock at the price bid by Viacom; and (iii) a no-shop provision subject to a fiduciary out with respect to offers not subject to a material financing contingency. What made these unreasonable? Courts in the past had approved breakup and similar fees amounting to 2% of the deal value as well as a topping fee of 25% of the increased consideration,[87] an arrangement roughly equivalent in relative magnitude to the stock lockup in *QVC*. To be sure, the stock lockup had no cap, and eventually had a value of $500 million when bidding reached $90 a share and a deal value exceeded

---

[86] See Gilson & Kraakman (1989), *Delaware's Intermediate Standard*, *supra* note 40.

[87] See Arthur Fleischer, Jr., Alexander Sussman & Henry Lesser, *Takeover Defenses* 987 (4th ed.1990).

$11 billion, but lockups without caps had been approved in other cases,[88] and its value in *QVC*, although it grew large in absolute magnitude, did have a relative cap -- its value was limited to approximately 20% of the value of subsequent bid increases.

Perhaps in the context of *QVC*, the Macmillan reasonable relation standard collapses into the information requirement. If the board did not make an informed decision that the lockups were reasonable in relation to the benefits achieved, the court would not itself determine lockups' wisdom in the first instance. Even with an objective standard, the court is still reviewing a board decision. If the board did not actually decide that the lockups were reasonable, the court has nothing to review, and the lockups should therefore be enjoined.

But that still leaves planners without guidance concerning when and to what extent lockups granted by adequately informed boards will be respected. Commentators have not so helpfully suggested that *QVC* limits lockups to "reasonable" amounts, and also warn that unusual terms, like the put and note provisions in *QVC*, increase the risk. Recast from a planner's perspective, the advice seems to be that provisions which actually promise to protect a friendly transaction may well not measure up. In this light, consider the answers to two questions provided by leading takeover lawyers Martin Lipton and Theodore Mirvis:

> *Question*: Is there any way to do a deal that is viewed as a sale of control without shopping or conducting an auction?
>
> *Answer:* Yes. If on the basis of well considered expert advice the board determines that it is more likely to get the best value reasonably available by not shopping or auctioning, then the board can authorize the transaction. In this situation, the board should . . . avoid any no-shop, lock-up option or bust-up fee provision that would impede a third party from competing.
>
> *Question*: If a company enters into a strategic merger that is not a sale of control in which the company gets a premium and a third party makes a hostile takeover for the company at a higher value to shareholders, can the company . . . continue . . . the merger and reject the hostile bid?
>
> *Answer*: Yes, in theory, but as a practical matter there may be so much pressure that the company will be forced into the auction mode and be forced to accept the highest bid.

Martin Lipton & Theodore Mirvis, *10 Questions and Answers Raised by Delaware's 'Paramount' Decision*, N.Y.L.J., Feb. 10, 1994. Do the lawyers' answers suggest that a target company cannot protect a friendly transaction from competing bids regardless of whether *Revlon* has been triggered?

Perhaps the continued lack of content in judicial and practitioner comment on the board's substantive obligations in structuring the target's sale

---

[88] See Fraidin & Hanson (1994), *supra* note 14, at 1761.

results from the absence of any clear conceptual framework for just how the target board should go about securing the "best value reasonably available." Lockups are required to be "reasonably" related to the benefits received because we apparently lack the tools to explain the connection between transaction structure and price received. In this regard, it is puzzling that neither judicial opinions nor newspaper accounts report that target companies or their advisers have made use of experts in the economics of auctions in structuring their transactions and the complex bidding rules that have been devised in *QVC* and other transactions such as the sale of RJR Nabisco.[89] The recent sales by the United States government of radio spectrum wave lengths, previously reserved for military use, to be used for personal communications services like pocket telephones, wireless computer networks and the like stand in sharp contrast. The value of the rights at issue has been estimated at $10.6 billion,[90] but the most unusual feature of the transaction was not its size, but that the rights were sold in an auction whose features were designed by the leading auction theorists in the world, who had been retained both by the government and by potential bidders.[91] Moreover, there is little doubt concerning the extent of the economist's influence.[92] What works for spectrum rights may also work for companies. The next section provides an introduction to the economics of auction design and its fit with the development of the law governing friendly transactions.

6.   An Introduction to the Economics of Auctions

QVC makes clear "that in a sale of corporate control the responsibility of the directors is to get the highest value reasonably attainable for the shareholders." This formulation of the board's responsibility meshes quite neatly with the goal of auction theory, a branch of microeconomics that seeks to understand what transaction structures maximize the revenue from an asset's sale. The economics of auctions thus focuses explicitly on how to accomplish the task that *Revlon*'s trigger imposes on target directors.

---

[89] See RJR Nabisco Litigation, Fed.Sec.L.Rep. (CCH) ¶ 94,194 (Del.Ch.1989) (1989 Transfer Binder). In *Macmillan*, Justice Moore did refer to two articles on auction theory in support of the proposition that "the conduct of a corporate auction is a complex undertaking both in its design and execution." 559 A.2d at 1287 (Preston McAfee & John McMillan, *Auctions and Bidding*, 25 J.Econ.Lit. 699 (1987); Paul Milgrom, *The Economics of Competitive Bidding: A Selected Survey*, in *Social Goals and Social Organization* 261 (Leonid Hurwicz, David Schmeidler & Hugo Sonnenschein eds.1985)). No use was made of the theory's content, however.

[90] See John McMillan, *Selling Spectrum Rights*, 8 J.Econ.Persp. 145 (1994).

[91] *Id.* at 146.

[92] "The FCC's adoption of a simultaneous multiple-round auction ahead of a sequential or a single-round-sealed-bid auction -- which are more conventional but arguably less effective for selling spectrum licenses -- was a triumph for game theory." *Id.* at 160.

Despite the striking correspondence between the target board's obligation and the goal of auction theory, we should temper our expectations concerning what auction theory can teach (an attitude consistent with auction theory's failure to penetrate transaction practice in takeovers) . Like much theory, it can specify precise outcomes only after making quite limiting assumptions. Once these assumptions are relaxed, outcome depends critically on context. But this too meshes neatly with the development of the legal standards against which target director performance is measured. The courts have recognized that different transaction structures may be appropriate in different circumstances. What is required is that the board's exercise of judgment in matching context to transaction structure be reasonable. As *Macmillan* put it, the board can favor a particular bidder only if what is received is reasonable in relation to the favoritism provided. This is where auction theory has the potential to contribute. By identifying links between context and transaction structure, auction theory may help directors construct revenue maximizing structures and, in turn, may help courts in evaluating whether particular structures are reasonably constructed to accomplish this end.

The following discussion provides an introduction to the economics of auctions.

R. Preston McAfee & John McMillan
AUCTIONS AND BIDDING
25 J.Econ.Lit. 699 (1987)

The Types and Uses of Auctions

. . . What are the types of auctions that are in use? Four basic types are used when a unique item is to be bought or sold: the English auction (also called the oral, open, or ascending-bid auction); the Dutch (or descending-bid) auction; the first-price sealed-bid auction; and the second-price sealed-bid (or Vickrey) auction.

The English auction is the auction form most commonly used for the selling of goods. In the English auction, the price is successively raised until only one bidder remains. This can be done by having an auctioneer announce prices, or by having bidders call the bids themselves. . . . The essential feature of the English auction is that, at any point in time, each bidder knows the level of the current best bid. Antiques and artwork, for example are often sold by English auction.

The Dutch auction is the converse of the English auction. The auctioneer calls an initial high price and then lowers the price until one bidder accepts the current price. The Dutch auction is used, for instance, for selling cut flowers in the Netherlands. . . .

With the first-price sealed-bid auction, potential buyers submit sealed bids and the highest bidder is awarded the item for the price he bid. The basic difference between the first-price sealed-bid auction and the English auction is that, with the English auction, bidders are able to observe their rival's bids and accordingly, if they choose, revise their own bids; with the sealed-bid auction, each bidder can submit only one bid. First-price sealed-bid auctions are used in the auctioning of mineral rights to U.S. government-owned land. . . .

Under the second-price sealed-bid auction, bidders submit sealed bids having been told that the highest bidder wins the item but pays a price equal not to his own bid but to the second-highest bid.

While this auction has useful theoretical properties, it is seldom used in practice. . . .

Two broad questions are prompted by the foregoing description of the use of auctions. First, why is an auction used rather than some other selling (or buying) procedure? Second, given the diversity of types of auctions, what determines which particular auctions form is chosen? In order to address these questions, some theoretical machinery is needed.

The Ability to Make Commitments

. . . Auction theory assume[s] that the organizer of the auction has the ability to commit himself in advance to a set of policies. He binds himself in such a way that all of the bidders know that he cannot change his procedures after observing the bids, even though it might be in his interest ex post to renege. . . .

Commitment matters because even as simple an institution as the first-price sealed-bid auction leaves the seller with a temptation to renege. As will be seen, the bidders submit bids that are functions of their valuations of the item for sale. Given the assumptions we shall make about the seller's knowledge, the seller is able to deduce from a bid the bidder's valuation of the item. Thus it would be in the seller's ex post interest to renege on his promise to charge a price equal to the highest bid; instead, he could offer the item at a price higher than the highest bid and yet slightly less than the highest valuation, and it would be in the interest of the bidder who has that valuation to accept this offer. Of course, if the bidders knew in advance that the seller might renege on his announced policy, they would not bid as hypothesized.

The advantage of commitment is that procedures can be adopted that induce the bidders to bid in desirable ways. . . . This follows from "the paradox that the power to constrain an adversary may depend on the power to bind oneself."[a] . . .

Nevertheless, it does not follow from that fact that one party has the ability to make commitments that he can extract all of the gains from trade. What limits his bargaining ability is the asymmetry of information: The

---

[a] Thomas Schelling, *The Strategy of Conflict* 22 (1960).

seller does not know any bidder's valuation of the item for sale. If the seller were able to observe bidders' valuations, he could offer the item to the bidder who values it the most at a price slightly below this bidder's valuation, threatening to refuse to sell it if this offer is rejected. Given that the seller has so committed himself, it is in the bidder's interest to accept this take-it-or-leave-it offer; the commitment makes the threat credible. When information is asymmetric, the seller's ability to extract surplus is more limited. The seller can exploit competition among the bidders to drive up the price; but usually the seller will not be able to drive the price up so far as to equal the valuation of the bidder who values the item the most, because the seller does not know what this valuation is. . . .

The Nature of the Uncertainty

Asymmetry of information is the crucial element of the auction problem. In the case of perfect information, the auction problem is easily solved: Given the ability to make commitments, the organizer of the auction extracts all of the gains from trade. Indeed, the reason a monopolist chooses to sell by auction rather than, say, simply posting a price is that he does not know the bidders' valuations

How the bidders respond to uncertainty depends on their attitudes toward risk. Thus one aspect of any particular bidding situation that the modeler must take into account is the bidders' risk attitudes. (The risk attitudes of the seller may also matter; however, we shall assume throughout that the seller is risk neutral).

Differences among the bidders' valuations of the item can arise for either of two distinct reasons. Which of these is relevant also affects how any particular bidding situation is to be modeled.

At one extreme, suppose that each bidder knows precisely how highly he values the item. . . . He does not know anyone else's valuation of the item; instead, he perceives any other bidder's valuation as a draw from some probability distribution. Similarly, he knows that the other bidders (and the seller) regard his own valuation as being drawn from some probability distribution. Differences among the bidders' evaluations reflect actual differences in their tastes. . . . Any one bidder's valuation is statistically independent from any other bidder's valuation. This is called the *independent-private-values model*. This model applies, for example to an auction of an antique in which the bidders are consumers buying for their own use and not for resale. . . .

At the other extreme, consider the sale of an antique that is being bid for by dealers who intend to resell it, or the sale of mineral rights to a particular tract of land. Now the item being bid for has a single objective value, namely the amount the antique is worth on the market, or the amount of oil actually lying beneath the ground. However, no one knows this true value. The bidders, perhaps having access to different information, have different guesses about how much the item is objectively worth. . . . This is called the *common-value model*.

Suppose a bidder were somehow to learn another bidder's valuation. If the common-value model describes the situation, learning someone else's valuation provides useful information about the likely true value of the item: The bidder would probably change his own valuation in the light of this. In contrast, if the independent-private-values model describes the situation, the bidder knows his own mind; learning about another's valuation will not cause him to change his own valuation (although he might, for strategic reasons, change his bid).

The independent-private-values model and the common-value model should be interpreted as polar cases: Real-world auction situations are likely to contain aspects of both simultaneously. For example, the bidders at an antiques auction may be dealers guessing about the ultimate market value of the item; but these dealers may differ in their selling abilities, so that the ultimate market value depends on which dealer wins the bidding. In the bidding for a government contract, there may be both inherent differences in the firms' production capabilities and a common element of technological uncertainty.

A general model that allows for correlations among the bidders' valuations and includes as special cases both the common-value model and the independent-private-values model was developed by Milgrom and Weber.[b] . . . The notion that bidders' valuations may to some extent be correlated is captured by the concept of *affiliation*. . . .

A further choice to be made by the modeler depends on the answer to the question: Are the bidders in some way recognizably different from each other? Is it appropriate to represent all bidders as drawing their valuations from the same probability distribution F, or should they be modeled as having different distributions? The former case will be described for the sake of brevity as the case of symmetric bidders and the latter as the case of asymmetric bidders. An example of an asymmetric bidding situation arises in government procurement when both domestic and foreign firms submit bids and, for reasons of comparative advantage, there are systematic cost differences between domestic and foreign firms.

Yet another modeling consideration arising from uncertainty is that the amount of payment can only be made contingent upon variables that are observable to both buyer and seller. In some circumstances, the only such variables are the bids. In other circumstances, however, there are other mutually observable variables. If these other variables are correlated with the item's true value, it might be in the seller's interest to make payment depend on these other variables as well as the bids. For example, in mineral-rights auction, royalties make the payment depend upon the amount of oil ultimately extracted as well as the winning bid.

---

[b] Paul Milgrom & Robert Weber, *A Theory of Auctions and Competitive Bidding*, 50 Econometrica 1089 (1982).

The auction model that is the easiest to analyze is based on the following four assumptions.

A1. The bidders are risk neutral.
A2. The independent-private-values assumption rule applies.
A3. The bidders are symmetric.
A4. Payment is a function of bids alone.

This model will be referred to as the benchmark model. . . .

The results to follow will describe bidding equilibria. Each bidder knows the rules of the auction that the seller has chosen and committed himself to. Bidder *i* knows his own valuation v_i (true valuation in the independent-private-values model, perceived valuation in the common-values model). Each bidder is assumed to know the number of bidders, their risk attitudes, and the probability distributions of valuations, and to know everyone else knows that he knows this, and so on. Based on what he knows, each bidder decides how high to bid. . . .

One result can be obtained immediately, regardless of which of the assumptions about risk attitudes and value correlations apply: *The Dutch auction yields the same outcome as the first-price sealed auction.* This is because the situation facing a bidder is exactly the same in each auction: The bidder must choose how high to bid without knowing the other bidders' decisions; if he wins, the price he pays equals his own bid. Because of this result, we do not need to analyze the Dutch auction in what follows.

The Benchmark Model: Comparing Auctions

Which of the four simple auction types (English, Dutch, sealed-bid first-price, sealed-bid second-price) should a seller choose? In what we are referring to as the benchmark model (defined by assumptions A1, A2, A3, and A4), this question has a surprising answer: It does not matter. Each of these auction forms yields on average the same revenue to the seller. At first glance, it may seem that this cannot be correct. For example, it might seem that receiving the highest bid, as in the first-price sealed-bid auction, must be better for the seller than receiving the second-highest bid, as in the second-price sealed-bid auction. The answer, of course, is that the bidders act differently in different auction situations; in particular, they bid higher in a second-price auction than in a first-price auction.

Consider first the English auction. When will the bidders stop bidding up the price in the English auction? The second-last bidder will drop out of the bidding as soon as the price exceeds his own valuation of the item. Thus the highest-valuation individual wins the bidding and pays a price equal to the valuation of his last remaining rival. Usually this will be strictly below his own valuation of the item: The successful bidder earns some economic rent in spite of the monopoly power of the seller. . . .

Consider now the second-price sealed-bid auction. In this, each bidder's equilibrium strategy is to submit a bid equal to his own valuation of the item. To see this, note that, because it is a second-price auction, the bidder's choice of bid determines only whether or not he wins; the amount he pays if he wins is beyond his control. Suppose the bidder considers lowering his bid below his valuation. The only case in which this changes the outcome occurs when this lowering of his bid results in his bid now being lower than someone else's and as a result this bidder now does not receive the item. Because he would have earned non-negative rents if he won, lowering his bid below his valuation cannot make him better off. Conversely, suppose he considers raising his bid above his valuation. The only case in which this changes the outcome occurs when some other bidder has submitted a bid higher than the first bidder's valuation but lower than his new bid. Thus raising the bid causes this bidder to win, but he must pay more for the item than it is worth to him; raising his bid above his valuation cannot make him better off. This argument shows that, like the English auction, the second-price auction results in a payment equal to the actual valuation of the bidder with the second highest valuation. . . .

[In a first-price sealed-bid auction,] the bidder estimates how far below his own valuation the next highest valuation is on average, and then submits a bid that is this amount below his own valuation. . . . Hence, on average, the price reached in a first-price sealed-bid auction is the same as in an English or a second-price auction.

The foregoing argument establishes the Revenue-Equivalence Theorem: *For the benchmark model, each of the English auction, the Dutch auction the first-price sealed-bid auction, and the second-price sealed-bid auction yields the same price on average.*

The Revenue-Equivalence Theorem does not imply that the outcomes of the four auction forms are always exactly the same. In an English or second-price auction, the price exactly equals the valuation of the bidder with the second highest valuation. In a first-price sealed-bid or Dutch auction, the price is the expectation of the second-highest valuation conditional on the winning bidder's own valuation. Only by accident, for particular highest and second highest valuations, will these two prices be equal. They are, however, equal on average. . . .

The Revenue-Equivalence Theorem is devoid of empirical predictions about which type of auction will be chosen by the seller in any particular set of circumstances. However, as will be seen, when assumptions that underlie the benchmark model are relaxed, particular auction forms emerge as being superior. . . .

What is the effect of increasing the amount of competition among the bidders? The more bidders there are, the higher on average is the valuation of the second-highest-valuation bidder. Hence: *Increasing the number of bidders increases the revenue on average of the seller.* . . .

This completes the analysis of the benchmark model. In the next four sections we examine the effects of changing the assumptions upon which the benchmark model is based.

Asymmetric Bidders: Price Discrimination

Instead of assuming that all bidders appear the same to the seller and to each other (assumption A3), suppose that the bidders fall into one of two recognizably different classes. (In this section we retain the other assumptions A1, A2, and A4) Thus, instead of there being a single distribution F from which the bidders draw their valuations, there are two distributions, $F1$ and $F2$. . . . For example, bidders at an antiques auction might be classifiable as either dealers or collectors, with the average demand price among dealers differing from that among collectors, or bidders for a government contract might be divided into domestic and foreign firms, with systematic production-cost differences. . . .

When bidders are asymmetric, the optimal auction is discriminatory, in the sense that there is a possibility that one bidder wins despite another bidder's having a higher valuation. . . .

Which type of bidder receives preferential treatment? The answer depends upon the relative shapes of the [bidders' distributions of expected values]. However, one special case is useful in aiding understanding. *If the distributions of valuations are identical except for their means, then the class of bidders with the lower average valuation are favored in the optimal auction.* There is a trade-off. By favoring the low-valuation type of bidders, the seller raises the probability of awarding the item to someone other than the bidder who values it the most and receiving a relatively low payment. The benefit from this policy, however, is that the favoritism forces the bidders from the higher-valuation class to bid higher than they otherwise would, driving up the price on average.

. . . For this policy to be workable, it must be the case . . . either that the seller can prevent the successful bidder from reselling the item to some other bidder or that the item being sold is inherently nontransferable. Arbitrage among the bidders, if it were possible, would sabotage any discriminatory selling scheme.

An important application of these results . . . occurs when a buyer has a sequence of projects: For example, a government offers a research-and-development contract followed by a production contract. The winner of the first auction reveals, by his winning, that he has a cost advantage. Thus *the buyer should discriminate against the incumbent in the second auction.*

Royalties and Incentive Payments

. . . It has been assumed so far that the seller is able to make payment depend upon only the bids. The bids give the seller some information about how highly the bidders value the item for sale. In many circumstances, however, the seller has, or can obtain, additional information about valuations. In this section, we maintain the assumptions, A1, A2, and A3 but relax the assumption A4 that payment can be a function only of bids. We show that it is in the seller's interest to condition the bidders' payments on any additional available information about the winner's valuation. . . .

For example, in an auction of oil rights to government-owned land, the government can observe, ex post, how much oil is actually extracted; this provides additional information on the true value of the tract. The payment by the successful bidder equals the amount he bids plus a royalty based on the amount of oil extracted. Publishing rights for books are sometimes auctioned, with payment to the author depending both on the bid and, via a royalty, on the book's ultimate sales. . . .

What is the reason for using royalties? [Assume that the seller can observe after the auction an attribute, like sales of a book or production from an oil lease, that is an indication of the winning bidder's valuation of the auctioned asset, and is outside the seller or buyer's control. In that event,] *the seller's expected revenue is an increasing function of the royalty rate.* The intuition behind this is that an increase in the royalty rate lessens the significance for the bidding of inherent differences in the bidders' valuation. [Because a part of the price then depends on something other than the bidders' values, the difference between the first and second highest valuations decreases and this] generates more aggressive bidding and therefore a higher expected revenue for the seller. . . . The royalty serves to transfer rents from the successful bidder to the seller.

If expected revenue . . . increases with the royalty rate, why are royalties not always set at 100 percent? One answer is that . . . the winning bidder, by his actions after the auction, often is able to affect the signal about his true valuation that the seller receives. There is a moral-hazard problem because the organizer of the auction cannot control what the winning bidder does afterward. This is the case in each of the examples above. The amount of oil extracted from a tract is decided by the extractor. Eventually, diminishing returns set in, and the higher the royalty rate, the less oil will be extracted. . . . The sales of a book vary with the amount of publicity the publisher chooses to give it. . . . Such moral-hazard considerations must be weighed against the effects on bidding competition in the choice of what royalty rate to set.

When there is a moral hazard, the optimal royalty is determined by trade-off. Increasing the royalty rate serves to increase the bidding competition and raise the bids, as already argued. But an increase in the royalty rate reduces the return to the winning bidder on his own actions after the auction: The royalty has the effect of transferring part of the benefit of these actions to the seller. Thus the higher the royalty rate, the less the ex post effort made by the winning bidder; this tends to lower the seller's expected revenue. *With moral hazard, the optimal royalty r is less than 100 percent*. Thus moral hazard results in the seller not making payment fully dependent on his ex post information. . . .

Making payments conditional on ex post observations of valuations serves not only to stimulate bidding competition; it also shifts risk from the bidders to the seller. If the bidders are risk averse while the seller is risk neutral, then some amount of risk shifting is mutually beneficial. *The more risk averse are the bidders relative to the seller, the higher is the optimal royalty rate.*

Risk-Averse Bidders

Auctions generally confront bidders with risk. Typically, a bidder obtains nothing and pays nothing if he loses, and earns positive rents if he wins. Thus if the bidders are risk averse, the extent of their aversion to risk will influence their bidding behavior. In this section we relax assumption A1 (that buyers are risk neutral), while maintaining the other assumptions of the benchmark model. We continue to assume that the seller is risk neutral and therefore wishes to maximize his expected earnings.

The seller can do at least as well as in the risk-neutral-bidders case, for if he sells the good using an English auction it remains the case that buyers will remain in the bidding so long as the price is less than their value. Thus, the seller can expect to earn at least as much when the buyers are risk averse as when they are not. Indeed, the seller can do strictly better, for *with risk-averse bidders, the first-price sealed-bid auction produces a larger expected revenue than the English or second-price auction.* The intuition behind this result is seen by examining the problem facing an agent in the first-price sealed-bid auction. If he loses, he gets nothing, while if he wins, he obtains a positive profit. Thus he is facing risk. By marginally increasing his bid, he lowers his profit if he wins, but increases the probability of this event. By smoothing his utility, he increases his expected utility (up to a point); but this also increases his payment to the seller. Thus the bidders' risk aversion works to the seller's advantage. . . .

Correlated Values

In many auctions, the uncertainty about each bidder's valuation of the item being sold does not result from inherent differences in the bidders' tastes, as has so far been assumed. Instead, it arises because each bidder, having access to different information, has a different estimate of the value of the item. In this section, we maintain assumptions A1, A3, and A4. We relax assumption A2, the independent-private-values assumption, and allow interactions among the different bidders' valuations.

Consider first the extreme case of the common-value auction, in which the bidders guess about the unique true value of the item. When the item being bid for has a common value, the phenomenon dramatically named the "winner's curse" can arise. Each bidder in sealed-bid auction makes his own estimate of the true value of the item. The bidder who wins is the bidder who makes the highest estimate. Thus there is a sense in which winning conveys bad news to the winner, because it means that everyone else estimated the item's value to be less. . . .

A . . . reasonable interpretation of the winner's curse is that sophisticated bidders, when deciding their bidding strategies, take into account the fact that winning reveals to the winner that his estimate of the item's value was the highest estimate; as a result, they bid more cautiously than if they adopted naive strategies. . . .

The rational bidder in a common-value sealed-bid auction avoids becoming a victim of the winner's curse by presuming that this own estimate of the item's value is higher than any other bidder's; that is, by presuming that he is going to be the winner. He then sets his bid equal to what he estimates to be the second-highest perceived valuation given that all the other bidders are making the same presumption. There is no cost to making this presumption when it is wrong, because losing bidders pay nothing. . . .

Consider now the more general model, that allows correlations among the bidders' valuations [the affiliated-value case], and of which the common-value model is a special case. Recall . . . that bidders' valuations are said to be affiliated if the fact that one bidder perceives the item's value to be high makes it likely that other bidders also perceive the value to be high. The essential difference between, on the one hand, the English auction and, on the other hand, the first-price sealed-bid, second-price, and Dutch auctions is that the process of bidding in the English auction conveys information to the bidders: The remaining bidders observe the prices at which the other bidders drop out of the bidding. It was shown for the independent-private-values auction that this extra information does not on average change the outcome, in the sense that the expected price reached is the same for each type of auction. When bidders' valuations are affiliated, in contrast, the bids in the English auction have the effect of partially making public each bidders' private information about the item's true value, thus lessening the effect of the winner's curse. As a result: *When bidders' valuations are affiliated, the English auction yields a higher expected revenue than the first-price sealed-bid auction, the second-price sealed bid auction, or the Dutch auction.* . . .

Sometimes the seller has independent information correlated with the item's value to any of the bidders. (For example, the government can do its own geological surveys before offering mineral rights for sale; the seller of a painting can obtain an expert's appraisal.) Should the seller conceal this information, or should he reveal it? *The seller can increase his expected revenue by having a policy of publicizing any information he has about the item's true value.* This is because the new information tends to increase the value estimates of those bidders who perceive the item's true value to be relatively low, causing them to bid more aggressively. . . .

Machiavellian Advice to a Monopolist

You are the seller of some good or service in the fortunate position of having no competitors. How should you design your selling methods so as to squeeze the last possible cent from your customers?

The first rule is to make your customers believe that, whatever pricing strategy you have chosen, you will not under any circumstances depart from it. Once you are visibly committed, all that prevents you from completely exploiting your customers is your lack of knowledge of exactly how high you can drive the price to any particular buyer without losing the sale.

Should you post a take-it-or-leave-it price, or should you hold an auction? If your production capacity is large, fixing a price maximizes your expected profits. The price you should charge, if you believe your customers' valuations of your product are approximately uniformly distributed, is the average of your unit production cost and the highest possible valuation (provided this exceeds the lowest possible valuation). On the other hand, if you have only one or a few units to sell, you should sell by auction.

What kind of auction should you choose? To answer this question, you must know whether your customers would be prepared to pay higher prices in exchange for your sheltering them from risk. You must also know whether differences among the bidders valuations of the item are due to inherent differences in their tastes [independent private values] or to their having made different guesses about the unique true value of the item [common value].

If your customers are no more reluctant to bear risk than you are and their different valuations reflect their different tastes, then your best selling device is any of the simple auction forms: English, Dutch, first-price sealed-bid, or second-price sealed-bid. . . .

If your customers prefer to avoid risk, then you are no longer indifferent among the simple auction forms; revenue will on average be higher from a first-price sealed-bid auctions than from an English auction.
. . .

If the bidders fall into several categories and you observe that there are systematic differences in valuations across categories, then you can exploit this to your advantage (provided you can somehow prevent resale by the winning bidder). You do this by discriminating in favor of bidders in the category with on average low valuations: You announce that you will accept a lower bid from a member of the favored category over a higher bid from a member of another category, provided the difference in bids is not too great.

If you can monitor the buyer's subsequent usage of the commodity, you should, by the use of a royalty scheme, require continuing payments from the buyer based on value in use: Royalties induce the bidding to be more competitive.

If the item you are selling has a unique true value, but the bidders have different imperfect estimates of this value, the English auction will on average yield more revenue for you than any of the other simple auction forms. You can encourage the bidders to raise their bids by having a policy of publicizing any information you yourself have about the item's true value.

. . . .

McAfee & McMillan list four assumptions on which they build their analysis of the revenue producing characteristics of different auction types: 1) that bidders are risk neutral; 2) that the asset being sold is one for which the bidders have independent private values; 3) that bidders are symmetric; and 4) that payment is a function of bids alone -- that is, the amount bid is not contingent on future events. A fifth assumption is also being made, although McAfee & McMillan do not make it explicit: that bidders have no investigation costs; that is, bidders do not need to incur costs to determine the value of the asset being sold. On these assumptions, the Revenue Equivalence Theorem makes the design of transactions irrelevant. All auction types generate the same result: the bidder that most highly values the asset wins the auction by bidding the smallest increment above the second highest bid. The winning bidder's profits are the difference between its valuation of the asset and the winning bid. When the five assumptions are relaxed, different transaction structures result in more or less revenue. The transaction planner's goal is to maximize the seller's revenue, which involves trying to shift a portion of the winning bidder's profit to the seller by causing the winning bidder to bid more than the asset's value to the second highest bidder.

Bidder Risk Neutrality. McAfee & McMillan argue that when bidders are risk averse, first price sealed-bid auctions produce more revenue because bidders bid more -- accept a lower expected profit -- to avoid the risk of losing. In an English auction, risk aversion makes no difference because a bidder will always know when it must bid another increment to remain in the contest. In a sealed bid transaction, a bidder must estimate what other bidders will offer and bid an increment above her estimate of the next highest bid (conditioned on her valuation being higher). A risk averse bidder will increase her bid to avoid the risk of losing (and further increase her bid if she believes that other bidders are risk averse and engaging in the same analysis).

Note that the success of this strategy depends on the bidders' belief that the seller in fact has committed to a one-round auction. If the bidders believed that they could bid again after the winner was announced, they would treat the auction as an English auction, bidding low until the winner is announced, and only then increasing their bid. Interestingly, target companies that have run formal auctions often have issued bidding rules that specify a first price sealed-bid auction, but also reserve the right to alter the rules at the discretion of the target board of directors, and have allowed subsequent bids.[92] If bidders believe the rules will be altered, the strategy of exploiting bidders' risk aversion by a first price sealed-bid auction will not work.

Why would target boards choose not to make the commitment necessary to the success of this strategy? Suppose the target did commit to a first price sealed-bid auction and then a bidder ignored the rules and made a higher bid after the winner was announced. Could the target directors sell the company to the winner in the face of a higher bid without breaching their obligation "to get the highest value reasonably attainable?" Because the target shareholders would still have to approve the transaction, whether by vote in the case of a merger or by tendering in the case of a tender offer, the target directors would have to promise the winner a lockup -- for example, a crown jewel option that would make the target less valuable to a rule ignoring subsequent bidder -- for its commitment to a one round sealed-bid auction to be credible. Could the target directors grant such an option? Should their decision be evaluated at the time the bidding rules are adopted (with the promise of a lockup to the winning bidder) or at the time of the rule breaking higher bid? Does *QVC*'s analysis of Viacom's rights in the lockups granted it by Paramount affect the analysis? As counsel to the target board in developing bidding rules, how would uncertainty about these issues affect your advice (and the target directors' actual ability to secure the highest value)?

Why would bidders in target company auctions be risk averse at all? One possibility is that a reputation for winning is valuable in subsequent transactions. This concern is said to have motivated KKR's bidding behavior in the auction for RJR Nabisco.[93]

Independent Private Value versus Common Value. Peter Cramton and Alan Schwartz argue that target directors maximize revenue by selling their companies by direct negotiation with a single bidder if the company would have a common value to all potential bidders.[94] To see this, suppose that all bidders could learn exactly what the company was worth, and that a first bidder offered less than that amount. As long as it was costly for a second bidder to learn the company's true value, no one else would enter. A potential bidder would know that the first bidder could bid the company's full value without incurring additional costs, so that a second bidder would expect to incur a loss on its investment in learning the company's value even if it won. As a result, no other bidder would enter and an auction would be impossible.

---

[92] See, e,g., In re RJR Nabisco, Inc., Shareholders Litigation, *supra*.

[93] See Burrough & Helyar (1990), *Barbarians at the Gate*, *supra* note 6.

[94] Peter Cramton & Alan Schwartz, *Using Auction Theory to Inform Takeover Regulation*, 7 J.L.Econ. & Org. 27 (1991).

What could a target company do to avoid (from its perspective) this unfortunate result? Suppose the first bidder underbid the company's value by more than the cost of a second bidder learning the company's value. If the target company agreed to reimburse the second bidder's investigation costs, then the target company could induce an auction that would increase the sale price by forcing the first bidder to increase its bid.

Cramton & Schwartz argue that an auction is undesirable in a common value setting even if bidders remain uncertain about the target company's value after investigation. So long as holding the auction is more costly than bilateral negotiations with a single bidder, they argue that the target may be best served by single bidder negotiations with the threat of an auction serving as a negotiating tool.[95] The wisdom of such a strategy, however, depends on how other potential bidders will interpret the breakdown of the initial negotiations. If the breakdown is interpreted as resulting from the bidder's discovery of unfavorable information about the target -- remember that in this case uncertainty remains about the target's value after a bidder's pre-offer investigation -- then the effectiveness of the threat is reduced and an auction becomes more attractive.[96]

In contrast to their position in a common value setting, Cramton & Schwartz conclude that auctions are desirable when the target's value differs among potential bidders. In their view, legal standards should then depend on whether most takeovers are common value or independent private value transactions. Takeovers that involve displacement of inefficient management or the breaking up of conglomerates are said to be common value because anyone can fire executives or sell divisions, while synergistic mergers are said to be independent private value. This suggests a tentative view that 1980s takeovers, characterized by bust-up transactions,[97] were common value transactions since the same post-acquisition strategy could be executed by any bidder. But does the fact that the same strategy is available to all bidders mean that each can execute it as effectively? For example, the 1980s

---

[95] *Id.* at 33-34.

[96] An early study, Peter Dodd, *Merger Proposals, Management Discretion and Stockholder Wealth*, 8 J.Fin.Econ. 105 (1980), finds that the stock price of target companies a party to a merger which the acquiring company terminates drops to a level below its price before the transaction was announced. From the shareholders' perspective, the negotiation strategy is further reduced to the extent that directors are disloyal, that is, they may be inclined to favor a particular bidder at the shareholders' expense, for example, a management offer of an MBO. Cramton & Schwartz acknowledge that the potential for the board to disregard shareholder interests in a negotiation counsels in favor of an auction. This is consistent with the analysis earlier in this Chapter of the special case of an MBO. Bainbridge (1993), *supra* note 61, and Jonathan Macey, *Auction Theory, MBOs and Property Rights in Corporate Assets*, 25 Wake Forest L.Rev. 85 (1990), argue that special structures like independent director committees are sufficient to police this conflict of interest, thereby allowing directors to be left free to determine whether bilateral negotiations or an auction is better in a particular case.

[97] See Chapter 9E, *supra*.

observed bidding contests between financial buyers -- typically LBO associations -- and operating buyers, typically a competitor of the target. Is this a common value or independent private value transaction? What if the acquisition strategy involved keeping the target's core business and selling off the rest, as in *Revlon*? More generally, any transaction has a mixture of common and independent private value components. The acquisition of a target company is the acquisition of a group of assets. Some assets, like cash or businesses that will be sold, are common value. Others, like businesses that will be retained and operated, are independent private value so long as the skills of alternative operating teams differ. So long as some significant portion of the assets is independent private value, would an auction dominate?

Bidder Symmetry. When all bidders are the same, McAfee & McMillan show that all should be treated the same. However, when bidders differ -- for example, when one bidder is a financial buyer and the other an operating buyer -- revenue may be increased by discriminating among buyers. From this perspective, the *Macmillan* formulation -- if one bidder is favored, the board must show that what the target company received was reasonable in relation to the favoritism provided -- can be understood as establishing bidder symmetry as the default rule, but allowing discrimination if the board can prove that discrimination maximizes revenue.

What kinds of discrimination increase the price received? Recall that the goal is to get the winning bidder to bid more than the second highest bidder's valuation. McAfee & McMillan suggest a strategy of favoring a lower valuing bidder (perhaps by providing a subsidy in the way of a stock lockup or a breakup fee), because that may force the highest valuing bidder to offer an amount closer to its actual valuation. Note that this argument differs from the standard argument in favor of lockups. Here the point is not to allow the favored bidder to win. If this happens, the net revenues to the target will be lower. Rather the goal is to force the highest valuing bidder into bidding more by increasing the second highest valuing bidder's valuation by the subsidy.

Contingent Payment. In McAfee & McMillan's analysis, making the price paid in part contingent on the future value of the asset being sold helps mitigate the winner's curse problem, and therefore encourages higher bids. Because more of bidders' information concerning the asset's value is common, the amount by which the winning bidder likely has overestimated the asset's value decreases.

While the winner's curse is a phenomenon of common value auctions, contingent payments as a response should still be relevant in the context of an acquisition since at least some elements of the target company's value will be common. One manifestation of this strategy may be a target bidding rule that a portion of the consideration be common stock of the post-acquisition entity.[98] Although framed in terms of allowing the target shareholders to participate in the future value of the target's assets, bidder payment in common stock also serves to make a portion of the purchase price contingent. Similar devices include explicit earn outs, where a portion of the purchase price depends explicitly on the post-acquisition performance of the target, and alphabet stock where the payment consists of a class of the acquirer's stock whose dividend is keyed only to the post-acquisition performance of the target.[99]

Positive Investigation Costs. McAfee & McMillan implicitly assume that bidders costlessly learn about the value of the asset being sold. Much changes when this assumption is relaxed. From the bidder's perspective, positive investigation costs -- in an acquisition, most importantly, due diligence -- reduce the price the bidder will pay. Indeed, some models indicate that the selling price will be reduced by the *sum* of the investigation costs of all bidders.[100]

The role of positive investigation costs has two implications for designing revenue maximizing transactions for the sale of targets. First, it will be to the target company's advantage to minimize the cost of bidder investigation. Thus, a target company should provide potential bidders as much information concerning the target's value as possible. Not only is the target the least cost producer of the information, but its central production avoids the duplicative costs of each bidder producing the same information.[101]

Second, bilateral negotiations may be preferable to an auction where investigative costs concerning the target's value are high. For example, imagine structuring the sale of an insurance company whose value depends heavily on the risks associated with its outstanding policies. Evaluating the target's outstanding policies is an expensive and time consuming process, involving a substantial investment of actuarial and accounting resources. Where an auction would require each bidder to incur these costs, a negotiated transaction that restricts entry to a single bidder, and thereby minimizes investigation costs, may generate more revenue than an auction.[102]

---

[98] See In re RJR Nabisco, Inc., Shareholders Litigation, *supra*.

[99] These devices, and the logic of their use in negotiated acquisitions, is considered in Chapter 27, *infra*.

[100] See Cramton & Schwartz (1991), *supra* note 94, at 34-35; Kenneth French & Robert McCormick, *Sealed Bids, Sunk Costs, and the Process of Competition*, 57 J.Bus. 417 (1984).

[101] Chapter 27, *infra*, analyzes techniques for reducing information costs in acquisitions. The effect also minimizes informational differences among buyers which, to the extent that a portion of the assets comprising the target are common value, reduces the impact of the winner's curse on bidders' behavior.

[102] See Macey (1990), *supra* note 96, at 88-90. McAfee & McMillan argue that increasing the number of bidders increases the revenue from an auction by increasing the likelihood that the valuation of the second highest bidder is close to that of the highest bidder. Where investigation costs are high, this effect is offset, with the result being a trade off

However, thoughtful transaction planning may substantially mitigate this problem. Suppose prior to conducting an auction the target secures a reinsurance policy[103] from a reputable company. The existence of the policy (and the size of the premium charged) both reduces the risk of the target's policy portfolio and credibly signals its quality. From this perspective, the reinsurance premium is the price of establishing an important element of the target company's value and operates to assure the cost is incurred only once. The point is that an important role exists for creativity in designing transaction structures that reduces bidder's investigation costs and therefore increases revenue from the target's sale.

Social Efficiency versus Revenue Maximization. A long standing debate concerns whether a well designed auction that maximizes the revenue from the sale also maximizes social efficiency. The target company maximizes revenue by reducing the winning bidder's profits, that is, by causing the winning bidder to pay a price closer to its value for the target than to the value of the second highest bidder. If an auction reduces the winning bidder's profits, it may also reduce potential acquirers' incentive to search for poorly performing targets. This, in turn, may reduce the extent to which the performance of management teams is monitored by the market and, ultimately, the overall efficiency of the economy. The public policy implication of this anti-auction position is to favor steps, like repealing the Williams Act and prohibiting poison pills, that increase the speed with which a tender offer can be completed and thereby reduce a target company's ability to initiate an auction. In contrast, the pro-auction position favors such things as regulatory waiting periods before a hostile tender offer can be completed that allow the target sufficient time to seek out competing bidders.

The initial round of the debate involved Easterbrook and Fischel, Gilson and Bebchuk.[104] It continued in an extended exchange between Bebchuk and Schwartz.[105] Merits aside, the development of Delaware law as

---

between the countervailing influence of number of bidders and investigation costs.

[103] A reinsurance policy is issued by another insurance company which, for a specified premium, agrees to assume a portion of the risks of the primary insurance company's portfolio.

[104] Frank Easterbrook & Daniel Fischel, *The Proper Role of a Target's Management in Responding to a Tender Offer*, 94 Harv.L.Rev. 1161 (1981); Ronald Gilson, *A Structural Approach to Corporations: The Case Against Defensive Tactics in Tender Offers*, 33 Stan.L.Rev. 819 (1981); Lucian Bebchuk, *The Case for Facilitating Competing Tender Offers*, 95 Harv.L.Rev. 1028 (1982); Frank Easterbrook & Daniel Fischel, *Auctions and Sunk Costs in Tender Offers*, 35 Stan.L.Rev. 1 (1982); Lucian Bebchuk, *The Case for Facilitating Competing Tender Offers: A Reply and Extension*, 35 Stan.L.Rev. 23 (1982); Ronald Gilson, *Seeking Competitive Bids Versus Pure Passivity in Tender Offer Defense*, 35 Stan.L.Rev. 51 (1982).

[105] See, e.g., Alan Schwartz, *Search Theory and the Tender Offer Auction*, 2 J.L.Econ. & Org. 229 (1986); Lucian Bebchuk, *The Case for Facilitating Competing Tender Offers: A Last (?) Reply*, 2 J.L.Econ. & Org. 253 (1986); Alan Schwartz, *Bebchuk on Minimum Offer*

described in this Chapter, and with respect to poison pills as described in Chapter 17, has been decidedly pro-auction.

Periods, 2 J.L.Econ. & Org. 271 (1986); Alan Schwartz, *The Fairness of Tender Offer Prices in Utilitarian Theory*, 17 J.Legal Stud. 165 (1988); Lucian Bebchuk, *The Sole Owner Standard for Takeover Policy*, 17 J.Legal Stud. 197 (1988); Alan Schwartz, *The Sole Owner Standard Reviewed*, 17 J.Legal Stud. 231 (1988).

CHAPTER 20: FEDERAL SECURITIES REGULATION OF FRIENDLY TRANSACTIONS

From the planner's perspective, the critical distinction between hostile and friendly transactions is the opportunity for cooperation between the acquiring and target companies. Cooperation, however, raises two matters of federal securities law that typically are not presented in hostile transactions.

The first results from greater flexibility in the consideration that can be used in a friendly acquisition. A hostile transaction must be cast as a tender offer, the only acquisition form available without the target company's cooperation. In a friendly offer, the full range of transaction forms -- mergers and sales of assets, and their triangular variations -- are available. Because the acquiring and target companies can cooperate to protect a friendly transaction, the delay associated with securing the shareholder vote required by these transaction forms may loom less large. More important, the reduced fear of delay also allows the use of the acquiring company's stock as consideration, even though the issuance of stock in an acquisition subjects the transaction to the Securities Act of 1933 ("1933 Act") which requires clearance from the SEC before the transaction can proceed. The application of the 1933 Act to acquisitions using stock as consideration is the first matter of federal securities law of special relevance to friendly transactions.

The second matter concerns disclosure. Friendly transactions are the result of a negotiating process. When must the acquiring and target companies disclose that negotiations are underway? Suppose rumors prompt inquiries to the target company? May the target company nonetheless disclaim knowledge because the negotiations are premature until agreement is actually reached? Because the disclosure of takeover negotiations can be expected to have a significant impact on the price of the target's stock, which in turn may adversely affect the negotiations, the question is important with respect to both transactional success and liability for nondisclosure.

Section A of this Chapter considers the application of the 1933 Act to acquisitions using stock as consideration. Section B then turns to disclosure obligations concerning preliminary negotiations.

A.   The Application of the Securities Act of 1933 to Acquisitions

Transaction planners seek to avoid an unwelcome regulatory structure by manipulating the transaction's formal characteristics to skirt the regulation's jurisdictional trigger. Regulators respond by choosing as jurisdictional triggers transactional characteristics that are costly to change. We have already seen one regulatory effort that encountered difficulty at this level -- the courts' problems with the de facto merger doctrine when the legislature defined in purely formal (and therefore easily avoidable) terms the jurisdictional trigger of those transactions subject to special decision rules.[1] The same problem arises when the regulators lack a clear idea of the substance of the transaction they seek to regulate. There are two parallel, and sometimes overlapping, patterns of federal securities regulation generally applicable to corporate acquisitions. The jurisdictional trigger of the Williams Act, which was the subject of Chapter 18, is the particular means of effecting an acquisition -- a tender offer. The jurisdictional trigger of the Securities Act of 1933, in contrast, is more general: The offer and sale of securities, whether in a corporate acquisition or otherwise. This difference in the specificity with which the jurisdictional trigger is described allows planners to choose which of the two regulatory patterns will govern their transaction. If the consideration used is cash, only the Williams Act applies; if the consideration includes securities to be issued by the acquirer, the 1933 Act applies.[2] Because differences in the two regulatory patterns have come to have very important transactional impacts, an acquirer's decision to offer cash or stock as consideration -- essentially the choice of how to finance its capital budgeting decision -- will be strongly influenced by considerations other than selecting the acquirer's optimal capital structure. In this section we review how this disparity in regulatory patterns came about, the resulting bias in transactional form it creates, and some partial efforts to ameliorate the problem.

That the federal securities regulation of corporate acquisitions currently lacks coherence is hardly surprising in light of its history. Prior to 1967, there was virtually no federal securities regulation of acquisitions at all. From the outset, the Securities and Exchange Commission took the position that a merger or sale of assets in which the consideration was the acquirer's securities was not an "offer" or "sale" of the securities within the meaning of the 1933 Act. Because the securities would be issued as a result of corporate acts authorized by a vote of the target company shareholders, the issuance was said to lack the individual volition by shareholders thought necessary under § 2(11) of the Securities Act.[3] As a result of this interpretation, and until the Williams Act was adopted, an exchange offer was the principal way in which a corporate acquisition could be subject to any federal securities regulation, because it fell outside the scope of Rule 133. For the planner, the combination of jurisdictional triggers made the application of the federal securities regulation to an acquisition entirely optional.

---

[1] See Chapter 16, *supra.*

[2] The Williams Act also applies if the transaction is cast as an exchange offer -- a tender offer in which the consideration is the acquirer's securities rather than cash. The proxy rules will apply to a cash merger or asset acquisition of a reporting company, but they can be effectively avoided by casting the first step of the acquisition in the form of a tender offer.

[3] The Commission's position was formalized in Rule 133 under the 1933 Act, adopted in Securities Act Release No. 3846 (Oct. 8, 1957). Following adoption of the Williams Act, solicitation of proxies with respect to the shareholder vote was subject to proxy regulation under § 14.

By 1972, federal securities regulation had been broadened to cover, with quite different levels of vigor, essentially all forms of acquisitions. The adoption of the Williams Act in 1967 brought cash tender offers under regulatory supervision, and the replacement of Rule 133 with Rule 145 (which specified that a "sale" did occur when securities were issued in an acquisition pursuant to the vote of target shareholders) in 1972 brought mergers and sales of assets in which the consideration was securities within the scope of the 1933 Act. This expansion of the reach of federal regulation, however, did not eliminate the differences in the patterns of regulation reflected in the Williams Act and the 1933 Act. These differences, made prominent by a change in the substantive character of the market for corporate acquisitions that we canvassed in the introduction to Chapter 19 -- the advent of unwanted competitive bids interfering with friendly (and hostile) transactions -- greatly increased the impact of the planner's strategic choice between the two regulatory patterns on the form in which a transaction was cast.

At this point in the development of federal securities regulation of acquisitions, which regulatory pattern applies to a transaction -- the Williams Act or the 1933 Act -- depends primarily on the form of consideration chosen by the planners. If the consideration chosen is cash, the natural transactional form is a tender offer, regulated by the Williams Act. For this purpose, the Williams Act's most important characteristic is that there is no waiting period. Once the disclosure requirements of the statute and Regulation 14D are met by filing with the SEC and otherwise disseminating the required information, the offer can commence without regulatory delay.[4] If, however, the consideration selected is stock, the transaction is subject to the 1933 Act, the most important characteristic of which is that no offer can be made until a registration statement is filed with the SEC[5] and no sale can be made -- the transaction cannot be closed -- until the SEC declares the registration statement effective. The time necessary for review and comment by the SEC staff, and for negotiating the revisions requested in the staff's letter of comments, results in significant delay.[6]

With a change in the market for corporate acquisitions, the timing difference between the Williams Act and the 1933 Act became critical. By the early 1980s, it was recognized that "we are in the midst of an era of intense competition for desirable acquisition candidates -- where auctions and

---

[4] In anything but an any or all offer, purchasing would have to await the end of the applicable proration period.

[5] Under Rule 145(b), the only information that may be disclosed about the transaction before the registration statement is filed is the identity of the parties and their businesses, the date of the shareholders' meeting, and a skeletal description of the transaction.

[6] James Freund & Richard Easton, *The Three-Piece Suitor: An Alternative Approach to Negotiated Corporate Acquisitions*, 34 Bus.Law. 1679, 1690 (1979), stated that review of a merger proxy statement (under Rule 145 the same as a registration statement) "can easily take a month before final clearance."

bidding contests are very much the 'in' thing. Just as third parties invade hostile takeover territory -- either invited in by the beleaguered target or simply attracted by the noise of the scuffle -- uninvited acquirers are likely to barge in on friendly situations."[7] If one contestant offers cash, while the other must use securities, the timing advantage to the more liquid bidder is substantial: Its entire twenty day cash tender offer can be completed and the contest ended before its opponent is in a position to move forward. Not surprisingly, both contested and friendly acquisitions were increasingly structured so that at least the first step of the transaction involved a cash tender offer.

This regulatory bias in favor of cash as consideration is difficult to justify and results from a regulatory regime that does not correspond to the transaction the planners have in mind. From the planners' perspective, what is at issue is an acquisition. If because of the accidents of history the regulatory regime treats an acquisition differently depending on whether cash or securities are used as the consideration then, subject to non-regulatory constraints, the planners will cast their transactions in the form least burdened by regulation. In this sense, the problem is similar to that raised by the de facto merger doctrine, only more troubling. In the de facto merger setting, the planners' strategic response involves only changing the form of the transaction; no costs are incurred by the parties or society other than the regulation's failure to achieve its purpose. If regulatory failure were the only cost associated with the strategic use of cash as consideration in order to avoid the delay the 1933 Securities Act imposes on the use of securities as consideration, little would be lost because there is little reason to differentiate between cash and securities for this purpose.[8] The problem, however, is that the planners' strategic response imposes another cost: The preference for the use of debt rather than equity financing. Is there any justification for a regulatory pattern that creates an incentive favoring a particular means of financing an acquisition?

One approach to eliminating the disparate treatment of acquisitions depending on the type of consideration used was set forth in Recommendation 12 of the SEC Advisory Committee on Tender Offers. Concluding that "the regulations applicable to exchange offers under the Securities Act are a major disincentive to using securities as consideration in a tender offer" and that

---

[7] *Id.*

[8] One might argue that shareholders receiving stock in a new corporation need more time to evaluate the transaction than one offered cash. Yet if the shareholder offered cash rejects the offer, he receives, in effect, stock in a new corporation if a sufficient number of other shareholders accept the offer. Moreover, even in a tender offer, target shareholders get twenty days, the minimum offer period under the Williams Act, to evaluate the offer. Finally, in light of the foregoing, is there any reason to believe that Commission staff review is more important when the consideration is stock than when it is cash?

"deterrence of exchange offers are not in the best interests of shareholders,"[9] the Committee recommended that:

> Bidders should be permitted to commence their bids upon filing of a registration statement and receive tenders prior to the effective date of the registration statement. Prior to effectiveness, all tendered shares would be withdrawable. Effectiveness of the registration statement would be a condition to the exchange offer. If the final prospectus were materially different from the preliminary prospectus, the bidder would be required to maintain, by extension, a 10 day period between mailing of the amended prospectus and expiration, withdrawal and proration dates. This period would assure adequate dissemination of information to shareholders and opportunity to react prior to incurring any irrevocable duties.[10]

The Commission has not acted on this recommendation.[11]

B.   Disclosure of Preliminary Negotiations

The negotiations that inevitably precede friendly acquisitions pose two critical questions concerning an issuer's disclosure obligations under federal securities law: 1) When must a target company disclose that it has begun preliminary negotiations for its acquisition; and 2) if a target company is not yet obligated to disclose, what can it say in response to direct inquiries concerning the existence of negotiations, or in response to indirect inquiries

---

[9] SEC Advisory Committee on Tender Offers, Report of Recommendations, reprinted in [Special Report No. 1028] Fed.Sec.L.Rep. (CCH) (July 15, 1983), at 20.

[10] *Id.* at 21.

[11] The historical distinction between the Williams Act and the 1933 Act, together with a lack of recognition of the differences between friendly and hostile transactions led to another anomaly -- substantial difference in the content and timing of disclosure to shareholders and the market depending on the nature of the consideration selected by the planner. See James Freund & Edward Greene, *Substance over Form S-14: A Proposal to Reform SEC Regulation of Negotiated Acquisitions*, 36 Bus.Law. 1483 (1981). A part of this anomaly was the subject of Advisory Committee Recommendation 11 which urged the extension of the Commission's efforts at integrating disclosure under the Securities and Exchange Act of 1934 and the Securities Act of 1933 to exchange offers. Advisory Committee Report (1983), *supra* note 9, at 21. The Commission has responded to this recommendation by the adoption Form S-4 under the 1933 which allows for substantial incorporation by reference of Exchange Act filings in registration statements filed with respect to securities to be issued in an acquisition. Securities Act Release No. 6578, [1985 Transfer Volume] Fed.Sec.L.Rep. ¶72,418 (April 23, 1985).

seeking an explanation for unusual activity in the target's stock?[12] Both the answers to these questions and their rationale have been subject to debate.

As the debate developed in the lower courts, one central outcome emerged. Disclosure was required only when there was a fair certainty that the transaction would -- not might -- take place. "[P]reliminary merger discussions are immaterial as a matter of law. . . . [But w]here an agreement in principle [to merge] has been reached a duty to disclose *does* exist." Greenfield v. Hublein, Inc., 742 F.2d 751, 756 (3d Cir.1983) (citations omitted, emphasis in the original), *cert. denied*, 469 U.S. 1214 (1985).[13] What was equally clear, however, was that the answer's expressed rationale was problematic.

As with disclosure of appraisals and other soft information discussed in Chapter 18, the rationale for nondisclosure was framed in the language of materiality, but the resolution appeared to turn on something very different indeed. Under the *TSC* materiality standard described in Flynn v. Bass Bros. Enterprises, 744 F.2d 978 (3rd Cir.1984) (reproduced in Chapter 18), is there any doubt that a reasonable shareholder "would consider it important" that a potential target company actually was engaged in negotiations concerning its acquisition? Thus, the lower courts stressed not that information concerning preliminary merger discussions was unimportant, but that the information is so uncertain that disclosure would do more harm than good:

> It does not serve the underlying purposes of the securities acts to compel disclosure of merger negotiations in the not unusual circumstances before us. . . . Such negotiations are inherently fluid and the eventual outcome is shrouded in uncertainty. Disclosure may in fact be more misleading than secrecy so far as investment decisions are concerned.

Reiss v. Pan American World Airways, 711 F.2d 11, 14 (2d Cir.1983).[14]

---

[12] The questions are critical because new information concerning the likelihood that a company will be the subject of a premium acquisition can be expected to have a significant impact on the price of its stock. However, the questions will also have relevance to acquiring companies, although the stock price reaction may be different. When acquiring companies announce unfavorable acquisitions, they suffer significant negative abnormal returns. See Mark Mitchell & Kenneth Lehn, *Do Bad Bidders Become Good Targets?*, 98 J.Pol.Econ. 372 (1990). In the case of a target company, pre-disclosure sellers of stock are adversely affected; in the case of an acquiring company, the injury falls on pre-disclosure buyers.

[13] Michaels v. Michaels, 767 F.2d 1185 (7th Cir.1985); accord Reiss v. Pan American World Airways, 711 F.2d 11 (2d Cir.1983); Staffin v. Greenberg, 672 F.2d 1196 (3d Cir.1982); Missouri Portland Cement Co. v. H.K. Porter, 535 F.2d 388 (8th Cir.1976); Susquehanna Corp. v. Pan American Sulphur Co., 423 F.2d 1075 (5th Cir.1970).

[14] Accord Michaels v. Michaels, *supra* note 13, at 1196 ("The need to protect shareholders from potentially misleading disclosure of preliminary merger negotiations . . . outweighs the rights of shareholders to have notice of corporate developments important to their investment decisions."); Staffin v. Greenberg, *supra* note 13, at 1206 ("The reason that preliminary merger discussions are immaterial as a matter of law is that disclosure of them may itself be misleading.").

This analysis seems to take a quite limited view of the ability of professional analysts to factor probabilistic information into their estimates of price. To be sure, particular individuals might misevaluate the significance of particular negotiations. But the lesson of the Efficient Capital Market Hypothesis, as developed in Chapter 5, is that the price of the target's stock would reflect the *market's* evaluation of the significance of the negotiations -- an aggregate of the individual assessments of market participants in which individual misassessments would be factored out. Just as with the question of the mandatory disclosure of appraisals, the claim that disclosure of accurate information is undesirable solely because it is probabilistic is difficult to take seriously.

The result, in contrast to the rationale, nonetheless warrants further consideration. The problem with disclosure of preliminary negotiations is that the act of disclosure itself may alter the probability that the transaction will ever take place. The court in Staffin v. Greenberg, 672 F.2d 1196, 1206 (3d Cir.1982), had a sense of what was at stake. Arguing that disclosure of preliminary negotiations would "do more harm than good to shareholders," *id.* at 1206, the court quoted a statement made during the Senate hearings on the legislation that became the Williams Act:

> Obviously, a company intending to make a tender offer strives to keep its plans secret. If word of the impending offer becomes public, the price of the stock will rise toward the expected tender price. Thus, the primary inducement to stockholders -- an offer to purchase their shares at an attractive price above the market -- is lost and the offerer may be forced to abandon its plans. . . .[15]

From this perspective, the difficulty associated with disclosure of preliminary negotiations is that different groups of shareholders are affected differently by disclosure, not that the information is so probabilistic as to be inherently misleading. Imagine two groups of target shareholders: One group, who because of personal reasons, will sell their shares in the target company during the period of negotiations before an agreement in principle is reached; and a second group, the remaining shareholders, who expect to hold their shares (at least until the negotiations have been resolved one way or the other). For the first group, disclosure of the preliminary negotiations is desirable regardless of the uncertainty of their outcome. Disclosure will cause some portion of the expected premium to be reflected in the target's stock price at that time. To that extent, the group of trading shareholders are

---

[15] Transcript, *Hearings before the Subcommittee on Securities of the Committee on Banking and Currency*, United States Senate, 90th Cong., 1st Sess., S. 510, p. 72 (statement of Mr. Calvin on behalf of the New York Stock Exchange, Inc.), quoted in Staffin v. Greenberg, *supra* note 13, at 1206. See SEC v. Gaspar, [Current Binder] Fed.Sec.L.Rep. (CCH) ¶ 92,004 at 90,980 (S.D.N.Y.1985) ("[L]eaks of tender offer plans are a threat to the entire transaction because of the potential disruption of the ordinary market characteristics of the target company's stock."); United States v. Newman, 664 F.2d 12, 17-18 (2d Cir.1981), *cert. denied*, 464 U.S. 853 (1983) (accord).

benefited by disclosure. The non-trading group of shareholders, however, will have been injured by disclosure to the extent that disclosure reduces the likelihood of a successful transaction. This group of shareholders, who by definition will not sell their shares until after the resolution of the negotiations, receives no benefit from having the market price early reflect the thereby lowered probability of a successful transaction. As the court in *Staffin* put it: "If the announcement is withheld until an agreement in principle on a merger is reached, the greatest good for the greatest number results." *Id.* at 1207.[16]

Whatever the underlying rationale for the agreement in principle rule, its application presents some mechanical difficulties. The first concerns how can one tell when in the course of negotiations an agreement in principle actually has been reached. In the context of the negotiations themselves, the issue may become circular: An agreement in principle exists at the point one is disclosed. Once the matter moves into a litigation context, however, the court must have a means to evaluate the claim that disclosure came too late. In Greenfield v. Hublein, Inc., *supra*, the court rejected an intent test -- had the parties reached an intent to merge -- in favor of focusing on whether agreement had been reached on the "price and structure" of the transaction. 742 F.2d at 756-57. Note that the stress on the price term is consistent with the similar stress in the SEC's automatic commencement rule for tender offers discussed in Chapter 18.

The second difficulty associated with a preliminary negotiations rule concerns what a party can say in response to an inquiry concerning indirect manifestations of the negotiations. The empirical evidence documents that there is typically a substantial increase in the price of, and the trading volume in, a potential target company's stock during the pre-disclosure negotiation period.[17] For an exchange listed stock, this can trigger an inquiry from the exchange seeking an explanation for the unusual activity in the company's stock. If the company does not know of any actual leakage of information concerning the negotiations, may it respond that "it is aware of no reason that would explain the activity in its stock" even though the only explanation it can imagine that would account for the trading activity is leakage of the ongoing negotiations? Compare Greenfield v. Hublein, Inc., *supra* (statement acceptable) with Schlanger v. Four-Phase Systems, Inc., 582 F.Supp. 128

---

[16] *Staffin* intertwines the two rationales for delaying when mandatory disclosure is required -- the misleading nature of the information and the substantive consequences of disclosure -- presenting first one and then the other, in alternating sentences, as if to avoid choosing between them (or, perhaps, because the difference between them was not recognized).

[17] Arthur Keown & John Pinkerton, *Merger Announcements and Insider Trading Activity: An Empirical Investigation*, 36 J.Fin. 855 (1981), found that the abnormal returns experienced by a target company in the 25 days *prior* to the public announcement of the transaction represented approximately half the total abnormal returns resulting from the transaction. Substantial increases in trading volume accompanied these returns. See Gregg Jarrell & Annette Poulsen, *Stock Trading Before the Announcement of Tender Offers: Insider Trading or Market Anticipation?*, 5 J.L.Econ. & Org. 225 (1989).

(S.D.N.Y.1984) (if go beyond "no comment," disclosure required). The Securities and Exchange Commission considered the issue itself in In the Matter of Carnation Co., Securities Exchange Release No. 22214 (July 8, 1985).[18] During a period in which Carnation was negotiating its acquisition by Nestle, S.A., and in connection with which Nestle had advised Carnation that it would terminate negotiations in the event of public disclosure, Carnation was asked to explain unusual activity in its stock and was asked directly about rumors of a Nestle takeover. The company representative responded by saying: "[T]o the best of my knowledge there is nothing to substantiate . . . [it]. We are not negotiating with anyone."[19] A public announcement of the acquisition of Carnation by Nestle followed two weeks later. The Commission concluded that "an issuer statement that there is no corporate development that would account for unusual market activity in its stock, made while the issuer is engaged in acquisition discussions, may be materially false and misleading."[20] In an unusual comment, the Commission went on to state its view that Greenfield v. Hublein "was wrongly decided."[21]

The *Four-Phase System* and SEC positions would allow the company not to disclose as long as all they say is no comment. But would not any observer recognize that a "no comment" response is, in fact, a statement that negotiations were in process. If there were no negotiations, the company would be free to issue a denial. Only if negotiations are underway is a "no comment" response required. From this perspective, the *Hublein* standard -- a denial is lawful unless the company has actual knowledge of the leaks that resulted in the increased activity -- may be best understood as a way to allow a company to avoid this implicit disclosure by telling a fib rather than a flat out lie.

The conflict among the lower courts and the SEC over the proper formulation of a target company's disclosure obligations during preliminary negotiations, as well as the pervasiveness of the problem, convinced the Supreme Court to take up the issue in Basic, Inc. v. Levinson. While the case directly dealt only with the second disclosure problem -- the target company's response to inquiries -- the court's discussion of materiality in this context is relevant as well to the question of when an affirmative disclosure obligation arises.[22]

---

[18] [1985 Transfer Binder] Fed.Sec.L.Rep. (CCH) ¶ 83,801.

[19] *Id.* at 87,594.

[20] *Id.* at 87,596.

[21] *Id.* at 87,596 n.8.

[22] *Basic* is also notable for the stance it takes on the relevance of the Efficient Capital Market Hypothesis in framing a presumption of reliance on market price for purposes of meeting the reliance requirement in a 10b-5 action. These portions of the opinion and the dissent are not reproduced.

BASIC, INC. v. LEVINSON
485 U.S. 224 (1988)

Justice BLACKMUN delivered the opinion of the Court.

This case requires us to apply the materiality requirement of § 10(b) of the Securities Exchange Act of 1934, and the Securities and Exchange Commission's Rule 10b-5, promulgated thereunder, in the context of preliminary corporate merger discussions. . . .

I

Prior to December 20, 1978, Basic Incorporated was a publicly traded company primarily engaged in the business of manufacturing chemical refractories for the steel industry. As early as 1965 or 1966, Combustion Engineering, Inc., a company producing mostly alumina-based refractories, expressed some interest in acquiring Basic, but was deterred from pursuing this inclination seriously because of antitrust concerns it then entertained. In 1976, however, regulatory action opened the way to a renewal of Combustion's interest. . . .

Beginning in September 1976, Combustion representatives had meetings and telephone conversations with Basic officers and directors . . . concerning the possibility of a merger. During 1977 and 1978, Basic made three public statements denying that it was engaged in merger negotiations.[4] On December 18, 1978, Basic asked the New York Stock Exchange to suspend trading in its shares and issued a release stating that it had been "approached" by another company concerning a merger. On December 19, Basic's board endorsed Combustion's offer of $46 per share for its common stock, and on the following day publicly announced its approval of Combustion's tender offer for all outstanding shares.

---

[4] On October 21, 1977, after heavy trading and a new high in Basic stock, the following news item appeared in the Cleveland Plain Dealer:

"[Basic] President Max Muller said the company knew no reason for the stock's activity and that no negotiations were under way with any company for a merger. He said Flintkote recently denied Wall Street rumors that it would make a tender offer of $25 a share for control of the Cleveland-based maker of refractories for the steel industry." App. 363.

On September 25, 1978, in reply to an inquiry from the New York Stock Exchange, Basic issued a release concerning increased activity in its stock and stated that

"management is unaware of any present or pending company development that would result in the abnormally heavy trading activity and price fluctuation in company shares that have been experienced in the past few days." Id. at 401.

On November 6, 1978, Basic issued to its shareholders a "Nine Months Report 1978." This Report stated:

"With regard to the stock market activity in the Company's shares we remain unaware of any present or pending developments which would account for the high volume of trading and price fluctuations in recent months." Id. at 403.

Respondents are former Basic shareholders who sold their stock after Basic's first public statement of October 21, 1977, and before the suspension of trading in December 1978. Respondents brought a class action against Basic and its directors, asserting that the defendants issued three false or misleading public statements and thereby were in violation of § 10(b) of the 1934 Act and of Rule 10b-5. Respondents alleged that they were injured by selling Basic shares at artificially depressed prices in a market affected by petitioners' misleading statements and in reliance thereon.

The District Court . . . held that, as a matter of law, any misstatements were immaterial: there were no negotiations ongoing at the time of the first statement and although negotiations were taking place when the second and third statements were issued, those negotiations were not "destined, with reasonable certainty, to become a merger agreement in principle."

The United States Court of Appeals for the Sixth Circuit . . . reversed the District Court's summary judgment, and remanded the case. 786 F.2d 741 (1986). The court reasoned that while petitioners were under no general duty to disclose their discussions with Combustion, any statement the company voluntarily released could not be "'so incomplete as to mislead.'" *Id.*, at 746, quoting SEC v. Texas Gulf Sulphur Co., 401 F.2d 833, 862 (2nd Cir.1968) (en banc), *cert. denied sub nom.*, Coates v. SEC, 394 U.S. 976 (1969). In the Court of Appeals' view, Basic's statements that no negotiations were taking place, and that it knew of no corporate developments to account for the heavy trading activity, were misleading. With respect to materiality, the court rejected the argument that preliminary merger discussions are immaterial as a matter of law, and held that "once a statement is made denying the existence of any discussions, even discussions that might not have been material in absence of the denial are material because they make the statement made untrue." 786 F.2d, at 749. . . .

We granted certiorari to resolve the split, see Part III, *infra*, among the Courts of Appeals as to the standard of materiality applicable to preliminary merger discussions. . . .

II

. . . The Court previously has addressed various positive and common-law requirements for a violation of § 10(b) or of Rule 10b-5. . . . The Court also explicitly has defined a standard of materiality under the securities laws, see TSC Industries, Inc. v. Northway, Inc., 426 U.S. 438 (1976), concluding in the proxy-solicitation context that "[a]n omitted fact is material if there is a substantial likelihood that a reasonable shareholder would consider it important in deciding how to vote." *Id.* at 449. Acknowledging that certain information concerning corporate developments could well be of "dubious significance," *id.* at 448, the Court was careful not to set too low a standard of materiality; it was concerned that a minimal standard might bring an overabundance of information within its reach, and lead management "simply to bury and shareholders in an avalanche of trivial information -- a result that is hardly conducive to informed decisionmaking." *Id*. at 448-449. It further explained that to fulfill the materiality requirement "there must be a substantial likelihood that the disclosure of the omitted fact would have been viewed by the reasonable investor as having significantly altered the 'total mix' of information made available." *Id*. at 449. We now expressly adopt the *TSC Industries* standard of materiality for the § 10(b) and Rule 10b-5 context.

III

The application of this materiality standard to preliminary merger discussions is not self-evident. . . . Where . . . [a corporate] event is contingent or speculative in nature, it is difficult to ascertain whether the "reasonable investor" would have considered the omitted information significant at the time.

A

Petitioners urge upon us a Third Circuit test for resolving this difficulty.[10] Under this approach, preliminary merger discussions do not become material until "agreement-in-principle" as to the price and structure of the transaction has been reached between the would-be merger partners. See Greenfield v. Heublein, Inc., 742 F.2d 751, 757 (3rd Cir.1984), *cert. denied*, 469 U.S. 1215 (1985). By definition, then, information concerning any negotiations not yet at the agreement-in-principle stage could be withheld or even misrepresented without a violation of Rule 10b-5.

Three rationales have been offered in support of the "agreement-in-principle" test. The first derives from the concern expressed in *TSC Industries* that an investor might be overwhelmed by excessively detailed and trivial information, and focuses on the substantial risk that preliminary merger discussions may collapse: because such discussions are inherently tentative, disclosure of their existence itself could mislead investors and foster false optimism. See Greenfield v. Heublein, Inc., 742 F.2d at 756; Reiss v. Pan American World Airways, Inc., 711 F.2d 11, 14 (2nd Cir.1983). The other

---

[10] See Staffin v. Greenberg, 672 F.2d 1196, 1207 (3rd Cir.1982) (defining duty to disclose existence of ongoing merger negotiations as triggered when agreement-in-principle is reached); Greenfield v. Heublein, Inc., 742 F.2d 751 (3rd Cir.1984) (applying agreement-in-principle test to materiality inquiry), *cert. denied*, 469 U.S. 1215 (1985). Citing *Staffin*, the United States Court of Appeals for the Second Circuit has rejected a claim that defendant was under an obligation to disclose various events related to merger negotiations. Reiss v. Pan American World Airways, Inc., 711 F.2d 11, 13-14 (2nd Cir.1983). The Seventh Circuit recently endorsed the agreement-in-principle as an agreement on price and structure). Flamm v. Eberstadt, 814 F.2d 1169 (7th Cir.), *cert. denied*, 484 U.S. 853 (1987). In some of these cases it is unclear whether the court based its decision on a finding that no duty arose to reveal the existence of negotiations, or whether it concluded that the negotiations were immaterial under an interpretation of the opinion in TSC Industries, Inc. v. Northway, Inc., *supra*.

two justifications for the agreement-in-principle standard are based on management concerns: because the requirement of "agreement-in-principle" limits the scope of disclosure obligations, it helps preserve the confidentiality of merger discussions where earlier disclosure might prejudice the negotiations; and the test also provides a usable, bright-line rule for determining when disclosure must be made. See Greenfield v. Heublein, Inc., 742 F.2d at 757; Flamm v. Eberstadt, 814 F.2d 1169, 1176-1178 (7th Cir.), *cert. denied*, 484 U.S. 853 (1987).

None of these policy-based rationales, however, purports to explain why drawing the line at agreement-in-principle reflects the significance of the information upon the investor's decision. The first rationale, and the only one connected to the concerns expressed in *TSC Industries*, stands soundly rejected, even by a Court of Appeals that otherwise has accepted the wisdom of the agreement-in-principle test. "It assumes that investors are nitwits, unable to appreciate -- even when told -- that mergers are risky propositions up until the closing." Flamm v. Eberstadt, 814 F.2d at 1175. Disclosure, and not paternalistic withholding of accurate information, is the policy chosen and expressed by Congress. . . . The role of the materiality requirement is not to "attribute to investors a child-like simplicity, an inability to grasp the probabilistic significance of negotiations," Flamm v. Eberstadt, 814 F.2d at 1175, but to filter out essentially useless information that a reasonable investor would not consider significant, even as part of a larger "mix" of factors to consider in making his investment decision. TSC Industries, Inc., v. Northway, Inc., 426 U.S. at 448-449.

The second rationale, the importance of secrecy during the early stages of merger discussions, also seems irrelevant to an assessment whether their existence is significant to the trading decision of a reasonable investor. To avoid a "bidding war" over its target, an acquiring firm often will insist that negotiations remain confidential, see, e.g., In re Carnation Co., Exchange Act Release No. 22214, 33 SEC Docket 1025 (1985), and at least one Court of Appeals has stated that "silence pending settlement of the price and structure of a deal is beneficial to most investors, most of the time." Flamm v. Eberstadt, 814 F.2d at 1177.[11]

We need not ascertain, however, whether secrecy necessarily maximizes shareholder wealth -- although we note that the proposition is at least disputed as a matter of theory and empirical research[12] -- for this case does not

---

[11] Reasoning backwards from a goal of economic efficiency, that Court of Appeals stated: "Rule 10b-5 is about *fraud*, after all, and it is not fraudulent to conduct business in a way that makes investors better off. . . ." Flamm v. Eberstadt, 814 F.2d at 1177.

[12] See, e.g., J. Robert Brown, Jr., *Corporate Secrecy, the Federal Securities Laws, and the Disclosure of Ongoing Negotiations*, 36 Cath.U.L.Rev. 93, 145-155 (1986); Lucian Bebchuk, *The Case for Facilitating Competing Tender Offers*, 95 Harv.L.Rev. 1028 (1982); Flamm v. Eberstadt, 814 F.2d at 1177, n.2 (citing scholarly debate). See also In re Carnation Co., Exchange Act Release No. 22214, 33 SEC Docket 1025, 1030 (1985) ("The importance of accurate and complete issuer disclosure to the integrity of the securities markets cannot be overemphasized. To the extent that investors cannot rely upon the accuracy and completeness

concern the *timing* of a disclosure; it concerns only its accuracy and completeness. We face here the narrow question whether information concerning the existence and status of preliminary merger discussions is significant to the reasonable investor's trading decision. Arguments based on the premise that some disclosure would be "premature" in a sense are more properly considered under the rubric of an issuer's duty to disclose. The "secrecy" rationale is simply inapposite to the definition of materiality.

The final justification offered in support of the agreement-in-principle test seems to be directed solely at the comfort of corporate managers. A bright-line rule indeed is easier to follow than a standard that requires the exercise of judgment in the light of all the circumstances. But ease of application alone is not an excuse for ignoring the purposes of the securities acts and Congress' policy decisions. Any approach that designates a single fact or occurrence as always determinative of an inherently fact-specific finding such as materiality, must necessarily be over- or underinclusive. In *TSC Industries* this Court explained: "The determination [of materiality] requires delicate assessments of the inferences a 'reasonable shareholder' would draw from a given set of facts and the significance of those inferences to him . . . ." 426 U.S. at 450. After much study, the Advisory Committee on Corporate Disclosure cautioned the SEC against administratively confining materiality to a rigid formula.[14] Courts also would do well to heed this advice.

B

The Sixth Circuit explicitly rejected the agreement-in-principle test, as we do today, but in its place adopted a rule that, if taken literally, would be equally insensitive, in our view, to the distinction between materiality and the other elements of an action under Rule 10b-5:

> When a company whose stock is publicly traded makes a statement, as Basic did, that 'no negotiations' are underway, and that the corporation knows of 'no reason for the stock's activity,' and that 'management is unaware of any present or pending corporate development that would result in the abnormally heavy trading activity,' information concerning ongoing acquisition discussions becomes material *by virtue of the statement denying their existence.* . . .

---

of issuer statements, they will be less likely to invest, thereby reducing the liquidity of the securities markets to the detriment of investors and issuers alike").

[14] "Although the Committee believes that ideally it would be desirable to have absolute certainty in the application of the materiality concept, it is its view that such a goal is illusory and unrealistic. The materiality concept is judgmental in nature and it is not possible to translate this into a numerical formula. The Committee's advice to the [SEC] is to avoid this quest for certainty and to continue consideration of materiality on a case-by-case basis as problems are identified." *Report of the Advisory Committee on Corporate Disclosure to the Securities and Exchange Commission* 327 (House Committee on Interstate and Foreign Commerce, 95th Cong., 1st Sess.) (Comm.Print 1977).

. . . In analyzing whether information regarding merger discussions is material such that it must be affirmatively disclosed to avoid a violation of Rule 10b-5, the discussions and their progress are the primary considerations. However, once a statement is made denying the existence of any discussions, even discussions that might not have been material in absence of the denial are material because they make the statement made untrue. 786 F.2d at 748-749 (emphasis in original).

This approach, however, fails to recognize that, in order to prevail on a Rule 10b-5 claim, a plaintiff must show that the statements were *misleading* as to a *material* fact. It is not enough that a statement is false or incomplete, if the misrepresented fact is otherwise insignificant.

C

Even before this Court's decision in *TSC Industries*, the Second Circuit had explained the role of the materiality requirement of Rule 10b-5, with respect to contingent or speculative information or events, in a manner that gave that term meaning that is independent of the other provisions of the Rule. Under such circumstances, materiality "will depend at any given time upon a balancing of both the indicated probability that the event will occur and the anticipated magnitude of the event in light of the totality of the company activity." SEC v. Texas Gulf Sulphur Co., 401 F.2d at 849. Interestingly, neither the Third Circuit decision adopting the agreement-in-principle test nor petitioners here take issue with this general standard. Rather, they suggest that with respect to preliminary merger discussions, there are good reasons to draw a line at agreement on price and structure.

In a subsequent decision, the late Judge Friendly, writing for a Second Circuit panel, applied the *Texas Gulf Sulphur* probability/magnitude approach in the specific context of preliminary merger negotiations. After acknowledging that materiality is something to be determined on the basis of the particular facts of each case, he stated:

Since a merger in which it is bought out is the most important event that can occur in a small corporation's life, to wit, its death, we think that inside information, as regards a merger of this sort, can become material at an earlier stage than would be the case as regards lesser transactions -- and this even though the mortality rate of mergers in such formative stages is doubtless high. SEC v. Geon Industries, Inc., 531 F.2d 39, 47-48 (2nd Cir.1976).

We agree with that analysis.[16]

---

[16] The SEC in the present case endorses the highly fact-dependent probability/magnitude balancing approach of *Texas Gulf Sulphur*. It explains: "The *possibility* of a merger may have an immediate importance to investors in the company's securities even if no merger ultimately takes place." Brief for SEC as *Amicus Curiae* 10. The SEC's insights are helpful, and we accord them due deference. See TSC Industries, Inc. v. Northway, Inc., 426 U.S., at 449, n.10.

Whether merger discussions in any particular case are material therefore depends on the facts. Generally, in order to assess the probability that the event will occur, a factfinder will need to look to indicia of interest in the transaction at the highest corporate levels. Without attempting to catalog all such possible factors, we note by way of example that board resolutions, instructions to investment bankers, and actual negotiations between principals or their intermediaries may serve as indicia of interest. To assess the magnitude of the transaction to the issuer of the securities allegedly manipulated, a factfinder will need to consider such facts as the size of the two corporate entities and of the potential premiums over market value. No particular event or factor short of closing the transaction need be either necessary or sufficient by itself to render merger discussions material.[17]

As we clarify today, materiality depends on the significance the reasonable investor would place on the withheld or misrepresented information.[18] The fact-specific inquiry we endorse here is consistent with the approach a number of courts have taken in assessing the materiality of merger negotiations. Because the standard of materiality we have adopted differs from that used by both courts below, we remand the case for

---

[17] To be actionable, of course, a statement must also be misleading. Silence, absent a duty to disclose, is not misleading under Rule 10b-5. "No comment" statements are generally the functional equivalent of silence. See In re Carnation Co., *supra*. See also New York Stock Exchange Listed Company Manual § 202.01, reprinted in 3 (CCH) Fed.Sec.L.Rep. ¶ 23,515 (premature public announcement may properly be delayed for valid business purpose and where adequate security can be maintained); American Stock Exchange Company Guide §§ 401-405, reprinted in 3 (CCH) Fed.Sec.L.Rep. ¶¶ 23,124A-23,124E (similar provisions).

It has been suggested that given current market practices, a "no comment" statement is tantamount to an admission that merger discussions are underway. See Flamm v. Eberstadt, 814 F.2d at 1178. That may well hold true to the extent that issuers adopt a policy of truthfully denying merger rumors when no discussions are underway, and of issuing "no comment" statements when they are in the midst of negotiations. There are, of course, other statement policies firms could adopt; we need not now advise issuers as to what kind of practice to follow, within the range permitted by law. Perhaps more importantly, we think that creating an exception to a regulatory scheme founded on a prodisclosure legislative philosophy, because complying with the regulation might be "bad for business," is a role for Congress, not this Court. See also *id.* at 1182 (opinion concurring in the judgment and concurring in part).

[18] We find no authority . . . for varying the standard of materiality depending on who brings the action or whether insiders are alleged to have profited. . . .

We recognize that trading (and profit making) by insiders can serve as *an* indication of materiality. . . . We are not prepared to agree, however, that "[i]n cases of the disclosure of inside information to a favored few, determination of materiality has a different aspect than when the issue is, for example, an inaccuracy in a publicly disseminated press release." SEC v. Geon Industries, Inc., 531 F.2d 39, 48 (2nd Cir.1976). Devising two different standards of materiality, one for situations where insiders have traded in abrogation of their duty to disclose or abstain (or for that matter when any disclosure duty has been breached), and another covering affirmative misrepresentations by those under no duty to disclose (but under the ever-present duty not to mislead), would effectively collapse the materiality requirement into the analysis of defendant's disclosure duties.

reconsideration of the question whether a grant of summary judgment is appropriate on this record.[20]

Basic extends the dominant tradition of analyzing an issuer's obligation to disclose or refuse comment on undisclosed merger negotiations in the language of materiality. One point emerges with clarity from *Basic*: The Supreme Court rejects the comparatively clear-cut "agreement in principle" (or "price and structure") rule adopted by several circuits prior to *Basic*. See, e.g., Greenfield v. Heublein, 742 F.2d 751 (3rd Cir.1984), *cert. denied*, 469 U.S. 1215 (1985); Flamm v. Eberstadt, 814 F.2d 1169 (7th Cir.) (Easterbrook, J.), *cert denied*, 484 U.S. 853 (1987). At some point, preliminary steps that may lead to the sale or merger of the company become material for the reasonable investor, and this point may occur well before the company has reached an agreement fixing the price and structure of the deal with its prospective transaction partner. In lieu of the agreement-in-principle test, the Court adopts the standard of materiality urged by the Securities and Exchange Commission -- in a mouthful, "a highly fact-dependent probability/magnitude balancing approach:"

> Generally, in order to assess the probability that the [corporate] event will occur, a factfinder will need to look to indicia of interest in the transaction at the highest corporate levels. . . . [W]e note by way of example that board resolutions, instructions to investment bankers, and actual negotiations between principals or their intermediaries may serve as indicia or interest. To assess the magnitude of the transaction to the issuer of securities allegedly manipulated, a factfinder will need to consider such facts as the size of the two corporate entities and of potential premiums over market value. No particular event or factor short of closing the transaction need be either necessary or sufficient by itself to render discussions material.

(footnote omitted).[23]

---

[20] The Sixth Circuit rejected the District Court's narrow reading of Basic's "no developments" statement, see n.4, *supra*, which focused on whether petitioners *knew* of any reason for the activity in Basic stock, that is, whether petitioners were aware of leaks concerning ongoing discussions. 786 F.2d at 747. See also Comment, *Disclosure of Preliminary Merger Negotiations Under Rule 10b-5*, 62 Wash.L.Rev. 81, 82-84 (1987) (noting prevalence of leaks and studies demonstrating that substantial trading activity immediately preceding merger announcements is the "rule, not the exception"). We accept the Court of Appeals' reading of the statement as the more natural one, emphasizing management's knowledge of *developments* (as opposed to leaks) that would explain unusual trading activity. See *id.* at 92-93; see also SEC v. Texas Gulf Sulphur Co., 401 F.2d at 862-863.

[23] The tradeoff between increasing the informational efficiency of the market by requiring disclosure and increasing the likelihood of a successful transaction by sanctioning nondisclosure that the Supreme Court rejected in *Basic* (along with the associated agreement-in-principle test), was retained by the Delaware Supreme Court in Arnold v. Society for

Basic suggests obliquely that the magnitude of an acquisition decision is likely to be very large for the selling corporation -- a matter of continued corporate existence (or perhaps more important for the shareholder, the prospect of receiving a premium over market).   Given this, when are preliminary negotiations likely to cross the materiality threshold?   Are discreet solicitations made to possible buyers, provided that they are approved "at the highest corporate levels," material events for a would-be seller?   Or must negotiations between the would-be seller and one or more possible buyers actually begin?   What would a reasonable investor say?

Putting aside the transaction planner's difficult task of applying *Basic*'s probability/magnitude balancing approach, the question remains: What consequences follow when negotiations or solicitations of interest cross the materiality threshold?

It is apparent from *Basic* that an issuer cannot *deny* or otherwise expressly misrepresent preliminary merger negotiations that have crossed the materiality threshold, just as corporate insiders cannot legally trade on information regarding material negotiations without disclosure. *Basic* affirms a single materiality test for all regulatory purposes under Rule 10b-5.

It is equally apparent, however, that an issuer does not have an affirmative duty to disclose preliminary merger negotiations, simply because these negotiations are material.   The Court takes great pains to stress that "this case does not concern the *timing* of a disclosure;   it concerns only its accuracy and completeness."   (Emphasis in original, footnote deleted).   The suggestion is that the issuer may delay the disclosure of any information about material merger negotiations for a valid business purpose, such as the risk that premature disclosure would jeopardize the deal, and respond to queries with silence or a statement of "no comment."

This is the SEC's position as expressed in *Carnation*.   To the objection that a "no comment" statement is tantamount to an admission, the Court responds that an issuer might make credible a statement of "no comment" by always issuing a "no comment" response to queries about merger or acquisition rumors.[24]

Savings Bancorp, 1994 Del. LEXIS 406 (Del.1994).   Considering the target board's fiduciary obligation under state corporate law to disclose all material facts in connection with shareholder approval of a control transaction, the court held that evaluating the materiality of a contingent bid "requires a careful balancing of the potential benefits of disclosure against the possibility of harm. . . . [S]peculative information which would tend to confuse stockholders" is not material.   In support of this proposition, the court referred to Delaware's adoption of the agreement-in-principle disclosure trigger in Bershad v. Curtiss-Wright Corp., 535 A.2d 840, 847 (Del.1987) ("Efforts by public corporations to arrange mergers are immaterial . . . as a matter of law, until the firms have agreed on the price and structure and the transaction.").   *Society for Savings* does not refer to *Basic*.

[24] See Ian Ayres, *Back to Basics: Regulating How Corporations Speak to the Market*, 77 Va.L.Rev. 945 (1991), for an analysis of *Basic* from the perspective of establishing the correct default rule concerning the honesty of issuer disclosure concerning preliminary negotiations.

Can *Basic* be understood, then, as an attempt to change the conventional overtones of the "no comment" statement in order to relieve companies of the need to fib to protect delicate negotiations? While the Court claims not to be advising issuers on policy toward commenting on merger rumors, it makes absolutely clear that the only safe way an issuer may be able to avoid confirming correct rumors is by refraining from denying incorrect rumors. Does such a policy serve the interests of disclosure on balance? Will this policy matter if savvy investors take issuer denials with a grain of salt in the first place?

In the end, *Basic* comes out squarely against fibbing and implies, without quite saying so, that corporations have the obligation of developing disclosure policies that preclude the need to fib in order to withhold sensitive information. However, *Basic* says very little about the first question with which we began: namely, when does a corporation have a duty to disclose merger negotiations? Could there be a valid business reason for nondisclosure even after the parties in merger negotiations have reached an agreement in principle?[25]

The same disclosure dilemma arises in a different context when the preliminary negotiations involve the target of an existing tender offer who is seeking a white knight. In that situation, the target's Schedule 14D-9 typically states that the target may, among a litany of alternatives, engage in negotiations looking toward an alternative transaction. Must the schedule be amended when the target enters actual, albeit preliminary, negotiations with a white knight? The SEC has emphatically taken the position that amendment is required. See In the Matter of Revlon, Inc., Exchange Act Release No. 23320 (June 16, 1986) Fed.Sec.L.Rep. (CCH) [1986 Transfer Binder] ¶ 84,006. Indeed, in this precise situation, the SEC began administrative enforcement proceedings under § 15c-4 of the Securities Exchange Act against the chief acquisitions attorney at Sullivan & Cromwell in connection with his role in Allied Stores Corp.'s decision not to amend its Schedule 14D-9 to disclose preliminary negotiations with Edward J. DeBartolo Corp. in the course of Allied's unsuccessful defense against a takeover by Campeau Corp. In the Matter of Allied Stores Corp. and George C. Kern, Fed.Sec.L.Rep. (CCH) [1987 Transfer Binder] ¶ 84,142 (June 29, 1987). Is there any reason to think that the preliminary negotiations are less material when they concern an initial bid than when they concern a competing bid? Review Rule 14d-9 and Schedule 14D-9 in Appendix A. Can the difference be justified by the language of the Rule and Schedule?

---

[25] See Jonathan Macey & Geoffrey Miller, *Good Finance, Bad Economics: An Analysis of the Fraud on the Market Theory*, 42 Stan.L.Rev. 1059 (1990), for an analysis of the issue from a property rights perspective -- nondisclosure or even outright lying about preliminary negotiations may make the market less efficient but allow the target corporation to maximize shareholder wealth.

CHAPTER 21: PARTIAL ACQUISITIONS THROUGH PRIVATE PURCHASE OF CONTROL

For a large number of publicly traded corporations, control does not rest in "a fluid aggregation of unaffiliated stockholders."[1] Rather, a dominant shareholder or group of shareholders own sufficient shares to exercise effective control. Data indicate that some 20% of all companies listed on the New York Stock Exchange, the American Stock Exchange, or traded over-the-counter have a least one nonofficer that owns more than 10% of the outstanding common stock,[2] and as of 1988, 663 exchange-listed firms had a majority shareholder.[3] In controlled corporations, the planning problem associated with a friendly transaction is quite different from that which we examined in Chapter 19. Because of concentrated share ownership, a friendly control transaction does not require protection against a competing bid. A competing bid cannot succeed without the approval of the controlling shareholder.

Centralization of decision making does not, however, eliminate the possibility of litigation. Traditionally, the conflict has been over which shareholders are allowed to participate in the sale of control, and how the premium paid for control is shared. The problem is posed by an acquisition of the controlling shareholder's shares at a premium, with minority shareholders being allowed to participate only at a lower price or not at all. The issue is whether the minority shareholders are entitled to share in the "control" premium, and the conflict is highlighted by the fact that the transaction could have been structured, without altering the substantive position of the *acquirer*, as a pro rata purchase with all shareholders participating equally. But if the transaction were structured in this way, the controlling shareholder would get less -- in total and per share. That, of course, is the source of the conflict.

More recently, litigation has arisen over precisely the opposite situation. Presumably, acquirers pay a control premium because of benefits associated with the ownership of control, as opposed to minority shares. Suppose an acquirer makes an offer to all shareholders at a price that represents an attractive premium over the price of minority shares, but the premium strikes the controlling shareholder as less than the capitalized value of maintaining

---

[1] Paramount Communications, Inc. v. Time, Inc., [1989 Transfer Binder] Fed.Sec.L.Rep. (CCH) ¶ 94,514 (Del.Ch.1989) (excerpted in Chapter 19, *supra*).

[2] Office of the Chief Economist, Securities and Exchange Commission, *A Survey of Partial Ownership of the Common Stock of Public Corporations* (unpublished paper, 1984). In a random sample of 240 New York Stock Exchange listed corporations, the board and top officers controlled at least 20% of the voting securities. Wayne Mikkelson & Megan Partch, *Manager's Voting Rights and Corporate Control*, 25 J.Fin.Econ. 263 (1989).

[3] Clifford Holderness & Dennis Sheehan, *The Role of Majority Shareholders in Publicly Held Corporations: An Exploratory Analysis*, 20 J.Fin.Econ. 317 (1988). See Harold Demsetz & Kenneth Lehn, *The Structure of Corporate Ownership: Causes and Consequences*, 93 J.Pol.Econ. 1155 (1985).

control. Can the controlling shareholder decline to sell her shares, thereby preventing the minority from receiving an attractive (to them) premium? Can the controlling shareholder offer to buy the minority's shares at a price lower than the controlling shareholder has rejected for her own shares?

Section A presents the traditional problem and its more recent incarnation. Perlman v. Feldmann is the classic formulation of the problem -- the controlling shareholder's power to sell at a premium -- but does not represent the direction the case law has taken. Mendel v. Carroll confronts the problem's more recent formulation -- the controlling shareholder's power to decline to sell at a premium. Section B examines the considerations bearing on the choice between alternative formulations of a rule governing sale of control at a premium: equal opportunity or unequal division. It also surveys the available empirical evidence.

A.   The Traditional Problem and Its More Recent Incarnation

PERLMAN v. FELDMANN
219 F.2d 173 (2d Cir. 1954)

Before CLARK, Chief Judge, and SWAN and FRANK, Circuit Judges.

CLARK, Chief Judge. This is a derivative action brought by minority stockholders of Newport Steel Corporation to compel accounting for, and restitution of, allegedly illegal gains which accrued to defendants as a result of the sale in August, 1950, of their controlling interest in the corporation. The principal defendant, C. Russell Feldmann, who represented and acted for the others, members of his family,[1] was at that time not only the dominant stockholder, but also the chairman of the board of directors and the president of the corporation. Newport, an Indiana corporation, operated mills for the production of steel sheets for sale to manufacturers of steel products, first at Newport, Kentucky, and later also at other places in Kentucky and Ohio. The buyers, a syndicate organized as Wilport Company, a Delaware corporation, consisted of end-users of steel who were interested in securing a source of supply in a market becoming ever tighter in the Korean War. Plaintiffs contend that the consideration paid for the stock included compensation for the sale of a corporate asset, a power held in trust for the corporation by Feldmann as its fiduciary. This power was the ability to control the allocation of the corporate product in a time of short supply, through control of the board of directors; and it was effectively transferred

---

[1] The stock was not held personally by Feldmann in his own name, but was held by the members of his family and by personal corporations. The aggregate of stock thus had amounted to 33% of the outstanding Newport stock and gave working control to the holder. The actual sale included 55,552 additional shares held by friends and associates of Feldmann, so that a total of 37% of the Newport stock was transferred.

in this sale by having Feldman procure the resignation of his own board and the election of Wilport's nominees immediately upon consummation of the sale.

. . . Jurisdiction below was based upon the diverse citizenship of the parties. Plaintiffs argue here, as they did in the court below, that in the situation here disclosed the vendors must account to the nonparticipating minority stockholders for that share of their profit which is attributable to the sale of the corporate power. Judge Hincks denied the validity of the premise, holding that the rights involved in the sale were only those normally incident to the possession of a controlling block of shares, with which a dominant stockholder, in the absence of fraud or foreseeable looting, was entitled to deal according to his own best interests. . . . Plaintiffs appeal from these rulings of law which resulted in the dismissal of their complaint.

The essential facts found by the trial judge are not in dispute. Newport was a relative newcomer in the steel industry with predominantly old installations which were in the process of being supplemented by more modern facilities. Except in times of extreme shortage Newport was not in a position to compete profitably with other steel mills for customers not in its immediate geographical area. Wilport, the purchasing syndicate, consisted of geographically remote end-users of steel who were interested in buying more steel from Newport than they had been able to obtain during recent periods of tight supply. The price of $20 per share was found by Judge Hincks to be a fair one for a control block of stock, although the over-the-counter market price had not exceeded $12 and the book value per share was $17.03. But this finding was limited by Judge Hincks' statement that "[w]hat value the block would have had if shorn of its appurtenant power to control distribution of the corporate product, the evidence does not show." It was also conditioned by his earlier ruling that the burden was on plaintiffs to prove a lesser value for the stock.

Both as director and as dominant stockholder, Feldmann stood in a fiduciary relationship to the corporation and to the minority stockholders as beneficiaries thereof. Pepper v. Litton, 308 U.S. 295 (1939); Southern Pac. Co. v. Bogert, 250 U.S. 483 (1919). His fiduciary obligation must in the first instance be measured by the law of Indiana, the state of incorporation of Newport. . . . Although there is no Indiana case directly in point, the most closely analogous one emphasizes the close scrutiny to which Indiana subjects the conduct of fiduciaries when personal benefit may stand in the way of fulfillment of trust obligations. In Schemmel v. Hill, 169 N.E. 678, 682, 683 (Ind.App.1930), McMahan, J., said:

> Directors of a business corporation act in a strictly fiduciary capacity. Their office is a trust. . . . When a director deals with his corporation, his acts will be closely scrutinized. Directors of a corporation are its agents, and they are governed by the rules of law applicable to other agents, and, as between themselves and their principal, the rules relating to honesty and fair dealing in the management of the affairs of their principal are applicable. They must not, in any degree, allow their official conduct to be swayed by their private

> interest, which must yield to official duty. In a transaction between a director and his corporation, where he acts for himself and his principal at the same time in a matter connected with the relation between them, it is presumed, where he is thus potential on both sides of the contract, that self-interest will overcome his fidelity to his principal, to his own benefit and to his principal's hurt.

And the judge added: "Absolute and most scrupulous good faith is the very essence of a director's obligation to his corporation. The first principal duty arising from his official relation is to act in all things of trust wholly for the benefit of his corporation."

In Indiana, then, as elsewhere, the responsibility of the fiduciary is not limited to a proper regard for the tangible balance sheet assets of the corporation, but includes the dedication of his uncorrupted business judgment for the sole benefit of the corporation, in any dealings which may adversely affect it. . . .

Although the Indiana case is particularly relevant to Feldmann as a director, the same rule should apply to his fiduciary duties as majority stockholder, for in that capacity he chooses and controls the directors, and thus is held to have assumed their liability. Pepper v. Litton, *supra*, 308 U.S. 295. This, therefore, is the standard to which Feldmann was by law required to conform in his activities here under scrutiny.

It is true, as defendants have been at pains to point out, that this is not the ordinary case of breach of fiduciary duty. We have here no fraud, no misuse of confidential information, no outright looting of a helpless corporation. But on the other hand, we do not find compliance with that high standard which we have just stated and which we and other courts have come to expect and demand of corporate fiduciaries. In the often-quoted words of Judge Cardozo:

> Many forms of conduct permissible in a workaday world for those acting at arm's length, are forbidden to those bound by fiduciary ties. A trustee is held to something stricter than the morals of the market place. Not honesty alone, but the punctilio of an honor the most sensitive, is then the standard of behavior. As to this there has developed a tradition that is unbending and inveterate. Uncompromising rigidity has been the attitude of courts of equity when petitioned to undermine the rule of undivided loyalty by the 'disintegrating erosion' of particular exceptions.

Meinhard v. Salmon, *supra*, 164 N.E. 545, 546 (N.Y.1928). The actions of defendants in siphoning off for personal gain corporate advantages to be derived from a favorable market situation do not betoken the necessary undivided loyalty owed by the fiduciary to his principal.

The corporate opportunities of whose misappropriation the minority stockholders complain need not have been an absolute certainty in order to support this action against Feldmann. If there was possibility of corporate gain, they are entitled to recover. In Young v. Higbee Co., 324 U.S. 204

(1945), two stockholders appealing the confirmation of a plan of bankruptcy reorganization were held liable for profits received for the sale of their stock pending determination of the validity of the appeal.   They were held accountable for the excess of the price of their stock over its normal price, even though there was no indication that the appeal could have succeeded on substantive grounds.   And in Irving Trust Co. v. Deutsch, 73 F.2d 121, 124 (2d Cir.1934), an accounting was required of corporate directors who bought stock for themselves for corporate use, even though there was an affirmative showing that the corporation did not have the finances itself to acquire the stock.   Judge Swan speaking for the court pointed out that:

> The defendants' argument, contrary to Wing v. Dillingham [239 F. 54 (5th Cir.1917)], that the equitable rule that fiduciaries should not be permitted to assume a position in which their individual interests might be in conflict with those of the corporation can have no application where the corporation is unable to undertake the venture, is not convincing. If directors are permitted to justify their conduct on such a theory, there will be a temptation to refrain from exerting their strongest efforts on behalf of the corporation since, if it does not meet the obligations, an opportunity of profit will be open to them personally.

This rationale is equally appropriate to a consideration of the benefits which Newport might have derived from the steel shortage.   In the past Newport had used and profited by its market leverage by operation of what the industry had come to call the "Feldmann Plan."   This consisted of securing interest-free advances from prospective purchasers of steel in return for firm commitments to them from future production.   The funds thus acquired were used to finance improvements in existing plants and to acquire new installations.   In the summer of 1950 Newport had been negotiating for cold-rolling facilities which it needed for a more fully integrated operation and a more marketable product, and Feldmann plan funds might well have been used toward this end.

Further, as plaintiffs alternatively suggest, Newport might have used the period of short supply to build up patronage in the geographical area in which it could compete profitably even when steel was more abundant. Either of these opportunities was Newport's, to be used to its advantage only. Only if defendants had been able to negate completely any possibility of gain by Newport could they have prevailed. It is true that a trial court finding states: "Whether or not, in August, 1950, Newport's position was such that it could have entered into 'Feldmann Plan' type transactions to procure funds and financing for the further expansion and integration of its steel facilities and whether such expansion would have been desirable for Newport, the evidence does not show." This, however, cannot avail the defendants, who -- contrary to the ruling below -- had the burden of proof on this issue, since fiduciaries always have the burden of proof in establishing the fairness of their dealings with trust property. . . .

Defendants seek to categorize the corporate opportunities which might have accrued to Newport as too unethical to warrant further consideration. It is true that reputable steel producers were not participating in the gray market brought about by the Korean War and were refraining from advancing their prices, although to do so would not have been illegal. But Feldmann plan transactions were not considered within this self-imposed interdiction; the trial court found that around the time of the Feldmann sale Jones & Laughlin Steel Corporation, Republic Steel Company, and Pittsburgh Steel Corporation were all participating in such arrangements. In any event, it ill becomes the defendants to disparage as unethical the market advantages from which they themselves reaped rich benefits.

We do not mean to suggest that a majority stockholder cannot dispose of his controlling block of stock to outsiders without having to account to his corporation for profits or even never do this with impunity when the buyer is an interested customer, actual or potential, for the corporation's product. But when the sale necessarily results in a sacrifice of this element of corporate good will and consequent unusual profit to the fiduciary who has caused the sacrifice, he should account for his gains. So in a time of market shortage, where a call on a corporation's product commands an unusually large premium, in one form or another, we think it sound law that a fiduciary may not appropriate to himself the value of this premium. Such personal gain at the expense of his co-venturers seems particularly reprehensible when made by the trusted president and director of his company. In this case the violation of duty seems to be all the clearer because of this triple role in which Feldmann appears, though we are unwilling to say, and are not to be understood as saying, that we should accept a lesser obligation for any one of his roles alone.

Hence to the extent that the price received by Feldmann and his co-defendants included such a bonus, he is accountable to the minority stockholders who sue here. Restatement, Restitution §§ 190, 197 (1937); Seagrave Corp. v. Mount, *supra*, 212 F.2d 389 (6th Cir.1954). And plaintiffs, as they contend, are entitled to a recovery in their own right, instead of in right of the corporation (as in the usual derivative actions), since neither Wilport nor their successors in interest should share in any judgment which may be rendered. . . .

Defendants cannot well object to this form of recovery, since the only alternative, recovery for the corporation as a whole, would subject them to a greater total liability.

The case will therefore be remanded to the district court for a determination of the question expressly left open below, namely, the value of defendants' stock without the appurtenant control over the corporation's output of steel. We reiterate that on this issue, as on all others relating to a breach of fiduciary duty, the burden of proof must rest on the defendants. Judgment should go to these plaintiffs and those whom they represent for any premium value so shown to the extent of their respective stock interests.

The judgment is therefore reversed and the action remanded for further proceedings pursuant to this opinion.

SWAN, Circuit Judge, dissenting. With the general principles enunciated in the majority opinion as to the duties of fiduciaries I am, of course, in thorough accord. But, as Mr. Justice Frankfurter stated in Securities and Exchange Comm. v. Chenery Corp., 318 U.S. 80, 85 (1943), "to say that a man is a fiduciary only begins analysis; it gives direction to further inquiry. To whom is he a fiduciary? What obligations does he owe as a fiduciary? In what respect has he failed to discharge these obligations?" My brothers' opinion does not specify precisely what fiduciary duty Feldmann is held to have violated or whether it was a duty imposed upon him as a dominant stockholder or as a director of Newport. Without such specification I think that both the legal profession and the business world will find the decision confusing and will be unable to foretell the extent of its impact upon customary practices in the sale of stock.

The power to control the management of a corporation, that is, to elect directors to manage its affairs, is an inseparable incident to the ownership of a majority of its stock, or sometimes, as in the present instance, to the ownership of enough shares, less than a majority, to control an election. Concededly a majority or dominant shareholder is ordinarily privileged to sell his stock at the best price obtainable from the purchaser. In so doing he acts on his own behalf, not as an agent of the corporation. If he knows or has reason to believe that the purchaser intends to exercise to the detriment of the corporation the power of management acquired by the purchase, such knowledge or reasonable suspicion will terminate the dominant shareholder's privilege to sell and will create a duty not to transfer the power of management to such purchaser. The duty seems to me to resemble the obligation which everyone is under not to assist another to commit a tort rather than the obligation of a fiduciary. But whatever the nature of the duty, a violation of it will subject the violator to liability for damages sustained by the corporation. Judge Hincks found that Feldmann had no reason to think that Wilport would use the power of management it would acquire by the purchase to injure Newport, and that there was no proof that it ever was so used. Feldmann did know, it is true, that the reason Wilport wanted the stock was to put in a board of directors who would be likely to permit Wilport's members to purchase more of Newport's steel than they might otherwise be able to get. But there is nothing illegal in a dominant shareholder purchasing from his own corporation at the same prices it offers to other customers. That is what the members of Wilport did, and there is no proof that Newport suffered any detriment therefrom.

My brothers say that "the consideration paid for the stock included compensation for the sale of a corporate asset," which they describe as "the ability to control the allocation of the corporate product in a time of short supply, through control of the board of directors; and it was effectively transferred in this sale by having Feldmann procure the resignation of his own board and the election of Wilport's nominees immediately upon consumation of the sale." The implications of this are not clear to me. If it means that when market conditions are such as to induce users of a corporation's product to wish to buy a controlling block of stock in order to be able to purchase part of the corporation's output at the same mill list prices as are offered to other customers, the dominant stockholder is under a fiduciary duty not to sell his stock, I cannot agree. For reasons already stated, in my opinion Feldmann was not proved to be under any fiduciary duty as a stockholder not to sell the stock he controlled.

Feldmann was also a director of Newport. Perhaps the quoted statement means that as a director he violated his fiduciary duty in voting to elect Wilport's nominees to fill the vacancies created by the resignations of the former directors of Newport. As a director Feldmann was under a fiduciary duty to use an honest judgment in acting on the corporation's behalf. A director is privileged to resign, but so long as he remains a director he must be faithful to his fiduciary duties and must not make a personal gain from performing them. Consequently, if the price paid for Feldmann's stock included a payment for voting to elect the new directors, he must account to the corporation for such payment, even though he honestly believed that the men he voted to elect were well qualified to serve as directors. He can not take pay for performing his fiduciary duty. There is no suggestion that he did do so, unless the price paid for his stock was more than its value. So it seems to me that decision must turn on whether finding 120 and conclusion 5 of the district judge are supportable on the evidence. They are set out in the margin.[1]

Judge Hincks went into the matter of valuation of the stock with his customary care and thoroughness. He made no error of law in applying the principles relating to valuation of stock. Concededly a controlling block of stock has greater sale value than a small lot. While the spread between $10 per share for small lots and $20 per share for the controlling block seems rather extraordinarily wide, the $20 valuation was supported by the expert testimony of Dr. Badger, whom the district judge said he could not find to be wrong. I see no justification for upsetting the valuation as clearly erroneous. Nor can I agree with my brothers that the $20 valuation "was limited" by the last sentence in finding 120. The controlling block could not by any possibility be shorn of its appurtenant power to elect directors and through them to control distribution of the corporate product. It is this "appurtenant power" which gives a controlling block its value as such block.

---

[1] "120. The 398,927 shares of Newport stock sold to Wilport as of August 31, 1950, had a fair value as a control block of $20 per share. What value the block would have had if shorn of its appurtenant power to control distribution of the corporate product, the evidence does not show."

"5. Even if Feldmann's conduct in cooperating to accomplish a transfer of control to Wilport immediately upon the sale constituted a breach of a fiduciary duty to Newport, no part of the moneys received by the defendants in connection with the sale constituted profits for which they were accountable to Newport."

What evidence could be adduced to show the value of the block "if shorn" of such appurtenant power, I cannot conceive, for it cannot be shorn of it.

The opinion also asserts that the burden of proving a lesser value than $20 per share was not upon the plaintiffs but the burden was upon the defendants to prove that the stock was worth that value. Assuming that this might be true as to the defendants who were directors of Newport, they did show it, unless finding 120 be set aside. Furthermore, not all the defendants were directors; upon what theory the plaintiffs should be relieved from the burden of proof as to defendants who were not directors, the opinion does not explain.

The final conclusion of my brothers is that the plaintiffs are entitled to recover in their own right instead of in the right of the corporation. This appears to be completely inconsistent with the theory advanced at the outset of the opinion, namely, that the price of the stock "included compensation for the sale of a corporate asset." If a corporate asset was sold, surely the corporation should recover the compensation received for it by the defendants. Moreover, if the plaintiffs were suing in their own right, Newport was not a proper party. . . .

I would affirm the judgment on appeal.

MENDEL v. CARROLL
651 A.2d 297 (Del.Ch.1994)

ALLEN, Chancellor. . . . [T]he stockholder plaintiffs in these consolidated actions seek an unprecedented remedy: an order requiring the board of directors of a Delaware corporation to grant an option to buy 20% of its stock to a third party for the primary purpose of diluting the voting power of an existing control block of stock. The order sought would direct the Board of Directors of Katy Industries, Inc. ("Katy") to grant to an affiliate of Pensler Capital Corporation (together with Pensler Capital Partners I.L.P., referred to here as "Pensler") an option to purchase up to 20% of Katy's outstanding common stock at $27.80 per share. The granting of such an option is a condition of an offer for a $27.80 per share cash merger extended by Pensler to Katy. The proposed merger is said by plaintiffs to be without other material conditions.

Katy's board of directors has declined to grant the option sought. The board took this position in the face of a claim by a group of related shareholders (the Carroll Family) that granting such an option would deprive them of their legitimate and dominant voice in corporate affairs, and would in the circumstances constitute a breach of fiduciary duty.

Plaintiffs' theory, stated most summarily, is that when the Katy board had earlier resolved to accept the terms of a $25.75 cash out merger proposed by the Carroll Family, the company was put up "for sale," and that as a result the board now has a single duty: to exercise its active and informed judgment in good faith effort to get the best available value for the stockholders. Plaintiffs contend that rejection of Pensler's $27.80 merger proposal is not consistent with that goal. They posit that granting the option sought is a necessary step for the board to satisfy its special duty (which plaintiffs call a "Revlon duty"), and thus it is obligated in these circumstances to do so.

The notable fact in this case is that at all relevant times a small group of Carroll Family members has controlled between 48% and 51% of Katy's voting stock. In fact, this group has coordinated its activities informally and through legal agreements. With a single exception, accounting for about 5% of the stock, this group has steadily taken the position that it would buy, but it would not voluntarily sell Katy stock. Thus, members of the Carroll Family early and continually announced active resistance to Pensler's proposal.

Following Pensler's September 1993 initial proposal, the Special Committee of the Katy Board withdrew its recommendation of the Carroll Merger. In December 1993 the Carroll Family withdrew its offer. To evidence its *bona fides* in withdrawing the offer, the Carroll Family further offered to execute a standstill agreement stating that it would not acquire additional Katy shares beyond some open market purchases certain family members had made in December.

The dilutive option sought by Pensler as a condition of its $27.80 offer is, of course, a means of overcoming the resistance of the Carroll shareholders. Exercise of the option sought would reduce the voting power of the Carrolls from their current level of 50.6% to approximately 40% and thus make feasible stockholder approval of the Pensler transaction. A Special Committee of the Katy board of directors, delegated to deal first with the Carroll Family proposal and then with Pensler, after obtaining advice from legal counsel, declined to recommend to the full board the granting of the dilutive option.

Plaintiffs filed this suit in February 1994, after the full board announced its intention to declare an extraordinary $14.00 per share dividend. In addition to the mandatory granting of a stock option, plaintiffs also seek an order: requiring the defendants to negotiate fairly with Pensler; prohibiting the voting of certain shares recently acquired on the market by certain members of the Carroll Family; prohibiting Katy from making certain payments; and prohibiting Katy from distributing the $14.00 special dividend authorized in March 1994 by the board of directors. On the last point, it is plaintiffs' contention that the special dividend is in fact an alternative to Pensler's value-maximizing proposal, and for that reason constitutes a violation of what they take to be the on-going special duties arising from the board's decision to approve the now withdrawn Carroll Family proposal.

For reasons that follow, I conclude that the board of Katy Industries is not under any special duty at this time to maximize the current value of the public shares or of the company's stock as a while. Thus, I reject the premise of the principal theory offered by plaintiffs to justify the strong relief they seek. More broadly, assuming that the radical step of granting stock for the primary purpose of affecting the outcome of a shareholder vote or tender could be justified under some set of circumstances, I can see here no overreaching or palpable breach of fiduciary duty by a controlling shareholder that might justify such a protective reaction. . . .

I

Katy is a New York Stock Exchange listed firm, founded in 1968 by Wallace E. Carroll, Sr. As a practical matter, control of Katy has always rested in the hands of Mr. Carroll, Sr. or his children. During periods relevant to this suit, the Carroll Family (defined here as Mr. Carroll, his three sons, his daughter Lelia Carroll Johnson and her former husband Philip, and affiliated trusts or other interests) has owned between 48% and 52% of Katy's outstanding common stock. Traditionally these interests were held in a coordinated way. In 1983, all of the Carroll Family Members entered into a Stock Purchase Agreement. That agreement granted a right of first refusal to other signatories with respect to all Katy stock owned, but contained no restrictions on the exercise of voting rights.

In August 1988, the Carroll Family's holdings of Katy stood at approximately 48%. At that time, the board of directors authorized the Company to repurchase up to 500,000 of the nine million shares outstanding. No shares, however, were acquired under that authority at that time.

Wallace Carroll, Sr. died in September 1990. In March 1991 Katy retained Dillon, Read & Co., Inc. to conduct a financial review of the company, and "to advise the board on a variety of financial alternatives available to [Katy]." Kurowski Aff. Ex. A. Among the Dillon, Read personnel assigned to that project was Mr. Sanford Pensler, now a principal in Pensler Capital Corp. In its August 1991 report Dillon, Read noted that "Katy appears to be awash in capital" and that "[i]t is unlikely the public markets will give full value to this collection of assets in its present configuration." Several strategic options were presented, including a "split off" of operating subsidiaries and the repurchase of "substantial amounts of equity." Dillon, Read noted that "investment in Katy's own shares appears to be very attractive."

In fact, Katy had already privately repurchased a substantial block of common stock in June 1991. It made another negotiated purchase in September, after receiving the investment bank's analyses. The June repurchase brought the Carroll Family's aggregate common stock ownership to over 50%; the September repurchase increased that aggregate interest to over 52%. Katy later repurchased another 5,800 shares in the market in April 1992.

A. The Family Buyout Proposal

Members of the Carroll Family retained Morgan Stanley & Co. to advise them with respect to their holdings in Katy. In June 1992 the Carroll Family publicly announced that it was reviewing its options concerning Katy. At that time Katy stock had been trading at about $16.00 per share. On September 1, 1992, the Carroll Family executed a Participation Agreement in which they agreed to act in concert in the acquisition of the publicly held shares of Katy.[5] On that same day, the Carroll Family offered to acquire all non-Carroll shares of Katy common stock at $22.00 per share.[6] In the intervening months the stock had risen to trade on the day prior to the announcement at $24.00 per share.

In presenting its proposal, the Carroll Family advised the board that it had no interest in selling any of its approximately 52.6% of Katy's common stock. In response to the offer, the board appointed a Special Committee comprised of directors who were apparently disinterested in the proposal. They retained the investment bank Goldman Sachs & Co., as well as the Dallas law firm Jenkens & Gilchrist, P.C., as counsel. After consideration, the Special Committee rejected the $22.00 offer as inadequate and attempted to negotiate a higher price with the Carroll Family. The Carroll Family offered $24.00 per share, but the Special Committee insisted on $26.00 per share. No agreement was reached and the Carroll Family withdrew its offer. The Special Committee was disbanded in December 1992.

On March 11, 1993, the Carroll Family made a new offer to purchase all outstanding non-Carroll Katy shares at $25.75 per share. In conjunction with the new offer, the Carroll Family amended the Participation Agreement to enable Barry Carroll and his affiliates to sell their 4.6% holding in Katy stock (hereinafter, "Barry Carroll's shares").[8] The Special Committee was reinstituted and advised of the treatment of Barry Carroll's shares. After Goldman Sachs indicated that it would render an opinion that $25.75 represented a price within a range of fair prices for the public stock, the Special Committee concluded that the new offer was in the best interests of

---

[5] The Participation Agreement generally provides that Carroll Family members: (i) will transfer shares only to a newly formed acquisition entity or to other family members; (ii) will vote in favor of a Carroll Merger and other measures to facilitate it; and (iii) will not solicit or vote in favor of any third party proposal.

[6] On September 2, 1992, six class action complaints were filed in this court, alleging that the $22.00 per share offer was grossly inadequate. . . .

[8] This fact is important to plaintiffs because they wish to establish that at this or some later point the "non-selling" members of the Carroll Family held less than 50% of Katy's voting stock. From this premise they then try to build an argument that "control" was at such time in the public shares and thus at the time of the March 15 acceptance by the board of the Family's $25.75 proposal, the transaction represented a change in corporate control as contemplated by Paramount Communications Inc. v. QVC Network Inc., 637 A.2d 34 (Del.1993), thus, in their theory triggering "Revlon duties." It is their view of the impact here of "Revlon duties" that leads to relief they seek.

Katy's shareholders, and recommended the offer to the full board. The board approved that offer on March 15, 1993, and authorized the officers of Katy to enter into a merger agreement with a Carroll Family-controlled entity on March 23. A proxy statement was mailed to shareholders on August 23, 1993.

B. A Rosecliff/Pensler Proposal Emerges

In a September 1, 1993 letter to Mr. Jacob Saliba, Katy's Chairman, a venture called Rosecliff Pensler Partners L.P. ("Rosecliff Pensler")[9] proposed to purchase, on a friendly basis only, all of Katy's outstanding shares for at least $29.00 per share, subject to completing due diligence, obtaining financing, and receiving necessary government approvals. On September 2, Barry Carroll wrote to Mr. Saliba that he thought the Rosecliff Pensler offer was attractive and should be pursued.

At a special meeting of the board of directors of September 17, 1993, representatives of the Special Committee advised the Board that Goldman Sachs had stated, in effect, that until the Rosecliff Pensler proposal could be more clearly defined and evaluated, the Special Committee could not rely upon Goldman's August 23, 1993 opinion concerning the fairness of the Carroll Family Merger. As a result, the Special Committee advised the full board that it was not then in a position to continue its endorsement of the Carroll Family Merger. At that meeting Philip Johnson reiterated that as shareholders the members of the Carroll Family were not interested in selling their shares; there was therefore no way in which a Rosecliff Pensler merger proposal could be effectuated; and thus no reason for Katy to permit Rosecliff Pensler to conduct a due diligence investigation.

Notwithstanding Mr. Johnson's position, the Katy board resolved at a further September 23, 1993 meeting to permit Rosecliff Pensler access to Company information on the same basis as it had been made available to the Carroll Family's advisors.

C. Steinhardt/Pensler Proposal

By mid-November 1993, Rosecliff Inc. appears to have lost interest in a Katy transaction, but Pensler found a new joint venturer in Steinhardt Enterprise Inc. On November 29, 1993, a new partnership of Pensler Capital Corporation and Steinhardt Enterprise Inc. ("Steinhardt Pensler") proposed to purchase all of Katy's outstanding shares at $28.00 per share, purportedly without financing or due diligence conditions. The offer was scheduled to expire on December 6, 1993.

Also on November 29, Barry Carroll advised Mr. Saliba and the board of directors that he would not sign another extension of the Participation

---

[9] Rosecliff Pensler was a partnership of Rosecliff, Inc. and Pensler Capital Corporation.

Agreement, scheduled to terminate on November 30, 1993, and that he intended to sell his shares pursuant to the 1983 Stock Purchase Agreement. The withdrawal of Barry Carroll's shares from the Participation Agreement left the Carroll Family, excluding Barry Carroll (hereinafter, the "Carroll Group"), with ownership of approximately 47.9% of Katy's outstanding common stock.

D. Carroll Family Market Purchases

On December 1, 1993, Philip Johnson wrote to Mr. Saliba that the Carroll Family was exercising its right to terminate the merger agreement.

Also on December 1, the Carroll Group (i.e., the family minus Barry Carroll and affiliates) filed a Schedule 13D amendment with the Securities and Exchange Commission disclosing that it intended to acquire additional shares of common stock "to establish the position of the [Carroll Group] as the holders, in the aggregate, of a majority of the outstanding Shares and thereby to assure the control of the Company by the members of the Carroll Family regardless of the level of Share holdings of Mr. Barry Carroll. . . ." The Carroll Group further stated that it had no present intention of engaging in any transaction to take Katy private. On December 2 and 3, 1993, Wallace Carroll, Jr. and Leila Carroll Johnson purchased shares in the market with the result that the Carroll Group's ownership rose again to 50.6% of the outstanding common stock of Katy.

E. Further Negotiations With Steinhardt/Pensler and the Requested Dilution of Carroll Group Control

On December 3, 1993, the Special Committee requested authority from the board to meet and negotiate with Steinhardt Pensler. After a spirited discussion during which Mr. Johnson reiterated that the Carroll Group was in no event interested in selling its Katy stock, and over the objection of certain directors, the board granted the permission requested.

On December 5, 1993, Steinhardt Pensler presented the Special Committee with a proposed Merger Agreement that contemplated a $28.00 per share cash merger and a proposed Stock Option Agreement. The Stock Option Agreement would grant Steinhardt Pensler an irrevocable option to purchase up to 1.8 million shares of authorized but unissued shares of Katy at a price equal to the merger consideration; it would also grant Steinhardt Pensler the right to put the shares to Katy if the shareholders subsequently failed to approve the merger. Both agreements would require Katy to indemnify Steinhardt Pensler and pay damages if the option was found to be improper.

On December 11, while the Special Committee and its legal and financial advisors were evaluating the offer, Steinhardt Pensler made another offer at a reduced price of $27.80, claiming that it had just learned that Goldman Sachs' fee arrangement with Katy was tied to the merger price.

On December 13, the Special Committee met with Steinhardt Pensler and its advisors. Later that same day, the Special Committee reported to the full board. The board then authorized the Special Committee to continue to meet and negotiate concerning the proposed Merger and Stock Option Agreements with Steinhardt Pensler. . . .

The Special Committee sent a revised draft of the proposed agreements to Steinhardt Pensler on December 14. . . . There was no timely response and, by its terms, the $27.80 Steinhardt Pensler offer expired on December 15, 1993.

Nevertheless, the two sides' representatives remained in contact regarding Steinhardt Pensler's financing and other matters through December 1993 and early January 1994. On January 18, 1994, the Special Committee reported to the full board that . . . Steinhardt Pensler . . . had access to capital sufficient for the commitment. Minor points arising from due diligence required further negotiation. The purchase price remained $27.80, but would rise to $28.00 if Goldman Sachs would cap its fee at $1 million. The legality of the grant of the dilutive option continued to be a crucial issue to the Special Committee. At the January 18 meeting, the board unanimously agreed, though it did not formally resolve that, without an opinion from the Special Committee's Delaware counsel, to the effect that the option would be valid and would not constitute a breach of duty, the Committee could not negotiate a merger agreement including such an option with Steinhardt Pensler.

F. Legal Opinions on the Dilutive Option

. . . The Special Committee now turned to [Delaware] counsel for advice on the question whether granting an option of the type sought would, in the circumstances, constitute a violation of the board's fiduciary duty to the Carroll Group as shareholders. The Special Committee's Delaware attorneys produced a thirty-two-page opinion analyzing the relevant facts and law, and essentially concluded that it was unclear whether granting the option would be legal.

Following the receipt of the inconclusive opinion of its counsel, the Special Committee made two recommendations at a January 28, 1994 special meeting of the full board. Given the uncertain validity of the option, the Special Committee first recommended that it was no longer in the best interests of Katy and its shareholders to pursue negotiations with Steinhardt Pensler. Second, the Special Committee recommended that the board appoint another committee to explore other methods to maximize shareholder value, including: (i) a self-tender by Katy; (ii) a Dutch auction of Katy; and/or (iii) a dividend in excess of $10.00 per share on Katy's common stock. In accordance with these recommendations, the board further established a new committee to consider strategies to enhance shareholder value.

On March 8, 1994, the new committee recommended that the board approve a special cash dividend of $14.00 per share of Katy common stock.

The board has endorsed that recommendation but has not yet declared such a dividend, pending outcome of this motion. . . .

IV

I turn then to the core issue: whether Katy's board of directors has or had a legal or equitable obligation [under *Revlon*] to facilitate a closing of Pensler's $27.80 cash merger proposal by granting the option that Pensler seeks. To provide an answer to such a question, particularly in the setting of a preliminary injunction application, does not require one to formulate an answer to the abstract question whether a board of directors could ever, consistent with its fiduciary obligations, grant an option to buy stock for the principal purpose of affecting the outcome of an expected shareholder action, such as an election, a consent solicitation, or a tender offer. Surely if the principal motivation for such dilution is simply to maintain corporate control ("entrenchment") it would violate the norm of loyalty. See Condec Corp. v. Lunkenheimer Co., 230 A.2d 769 (Del.Ch.1967); Canada Southern Oils, Ltd., v. Manabi Exploration Co., 96 A.2d 810 (Del.Ch.1953). Where, however, a board of directors acts in good faith and on the reasonable belief that a controlling shareholder is abusing its power and is exploiting or threatening to exploit the vulnerability of minority shareholders, I suppose . . . that the board might permissibly take such an action. See Unocal Corp. v. Mesa Petroleum Co., 493 A.2d 946 (Del.1985).

Here, of course, plaintiffs' core argument can be understood to be that the controlling shareholders *are* exploiting the vulnerability of the minority shares in a very particular way. The gist of plaintiffs' complaint is that the minority shareholders could get more cash for their stock in a Pensler cash deal than they would have gotten in the proposed $25.75 Carroll Group deal. Thus, plaintiffs would contend that the foregoing protective principle grounded in fiduciary obligation would apply to this situation, and that the board is, as a result, under a current obligation to take the radical step of intentionally diluting the control of the controlling block of stock.

In my opinion, this view is mistaken. I apprehend in the facts recited above no threat of exploitation or even unfairness towards a vulnerable minority that might arguably justify discrimination against a controlling block of stock. Plaintiffs see in the Carroll Group's unwillingness to sell at $27.80 or to buy at that price, a denial of plaintiffs' ability to realize such a price, and see this as exploitation or breach of duty. This view implicitly regards the $27.80 per share price and the Carroll Family Merger price of $25.75 as comparable sorts of things. But they are legally and financially quite different. *It is, for example, quite possible that the Carroll $25.75 price may have been fair, even generous, while the $27.80 Pensler price may be inadequate.* If one understands why this is so, one will understand one reason why the injunction now sought cannot be granted.

The fundamental difference between these two possible transactions arises from the fact that the Carroll Family already in fact had a committed block of controlling stock. Financial markets in widely traded corporate stock accord a premium to a block of stock that can assure corporate control. Analysts differ as to the source of any such premium but not on its existence. Optimists see the control premium as a reflection of the efficiency enhancing changes that the buyer of control is planning on making to the organization.[15] Others tend to see it, at least sometimes, as the price that a prospective wrongdoer is willing to pay in order to put himself in the position to exploit vulnerable others,[16] or simply as a function of a downward sloping demand curve demonstrating investors' heterogeneous beliefs about the subject stock's value.[17] In all events, it is widely understood that buyers of corporate control will be required to pay a premium above the market price for the company's traded securities.

The law has acknowledged, albeit in a guarded and complex way, the legitimacy of the acceptance by controlling shareholders of a control premium. See Cheff v. Mathes, 199 A.2d 555 (Del.1964); Hecco Ventures v. Sea-Land Corp., C.A. No. 8486 (Del.Ch.1986); Zetlin v. Hanson Holdings, Inc., 397 N.E.2d 387, 388-89 (N.Y.1979).[18]

The significant fact is that in the Carroll Family Merger, the buyers were not buying corporate control. With either 48% or 52% of the outstanding stock they already had it. Therefore, in evaluating the fairness of the Carroll proposal, the Special Committee and its financial advisors were in a distinctly different position than would be a seller in a transaction in which corporate control was to pass.

The Pensler offer, of course, was fundamentally different. It was an offer, in effect, to the controlling shareholder to purchase corporate control, and to all public shareholders, to purchase the remaining part of the company's shares, all at a single price. It distributed the control premium evenly over all shares. Because the Pensler proposed $27.80 price was a

---

[15] Frank Easterbrook & Daniel Fischel, *The Economic Structure of Corporate Law* (1991); Frank Easterbrook & Daniel Fischel, *Corporate Control Transaction*, 91 Yale L.J. 698 (1982).

[16] See Robert Hamilton, *Private Sale of Control Transactions: Where We Stand Today*, 36 Case W.Res.L.Rev. 248 (1985); see, e.g., Gerdes v. Reynolds, 28 N.Y.S.2d 622, 650-52 (N.Y.App.Div.1941).

[17] See Lynn Stout, *Are Takeover Premiums Really Premiums? Market Price, Fair Value, and Corporate Law*, 99 Yale L.J. 1235, 1244-52 (1990).

[18] The doctrine applicable to a sale of corporate control at a premium is far more complex than it may at first appear. Indeed one might conclude that courts afford it somewhat grudging recognition. A number of liability creating doctrines have been applied which have the effect of creating risks to the controlling shareholder who attempts to realize a control premium. These doctrines include negligence, see Harris v. Carter, 582 A.2d 222, 232-36 (Del.Ch.1990); Insuranshares Corp. v. Northern Fiscal Corp., 35 F.Supp. 22, 25-27 (E.D.Pa.1940); sale of corporate office, see Essex Universal Corp. v. Yates, 305 F.2d 572, 581-82 (2d Cir.1962) (Friendly, J., concurring); and sale of corporate opportunity, see Brown v. Halbert, 76 Cal.Rptr. 781, 791-94 (Cal.Ct.App.1969); Jones v. H.F. Ahmanson & Co., 460 P.2d 464, 476 (Cal.1969). See generally Einer Elhauge, *The Triggering Function of Sale of Control Doctrine*, 59 U.Chi.L.Rev. 1465 (1992).

price that contemplated not simply the purchase of non-controlling stock, as did the Carroll Family Merger, but complete control over the corporation, it was not fairly comparable to the per-share price proposed by the Carroll Group. . . .

To note that these proposals are fundamentally different does not, of course, mean that the board owes fiduciary duties in one instance but not in the other. That is not the case. But to describe the duty that corporate directors bear in any particular situation one must first consider the circumstances that give rise to the occasion for judgment. When the Katy board or its Special Committee evaluated the Carroll Family Merger, it was obligated to take note of the circumstance that the proposal was being advanced by a group of shareholders that constituted approximately 50% of all share ownership, and who arguably had the power to elect the board. In this circumstance, in my opinion, the board's duty was to respect the rights of the Carroll Family, while assuring that if any transaction of the type proposed was to be accomplished, it would be accomplished only on terms that were fair to the public shareholders and represented the best available terms from their point of view.

This obligation the board faces is rather similar to the obligation that the board assumes when it bears what have been called "Revlon duties," but the obligations are not identical. When presented with the controlling stockholders' proposal, the obligation of the Katy board was in some respects similar to that faced by a board when it elects to sell the corporation, because *if* the board were to approve a proposed cash-out merger, it would have to bear in mind that the transaction is a final-stage transaction for the public shareholders. Thus, the time frame for analysis, insofar as those shareholders are concerned, is immediate value maximization. The directors are obliged in such a situation to try, within their fiduciary obligation, to maximize the current value of the minority shares. In this respect the obligation is analogous to the board's duty when it is engaged in a process of "selling" the corporation, as for example in the recent Paramount Communications, Inc. v. QVC Network Inc., 637 A.2d 34 (Del.1994). But the duty is somewhat different because of the existence of the controlling Carroll Family block.

The Carroll Family made it clear throughout these events that, for the most part, its members were completely uninterested in being sellers in any transaction.[19] No part of their fiduciary duty as controlling shareholders requires them to sell their interest. See Bershad v. Curtiss-Wright Corp., 535 A.2d 840 (Del.1987); Jedwab v. MGM Grand Hotels, Inc., 509 A.2d 584 (Del.Ch.1986) (self-sacrifice not required). The board's fiduciary obligation to the corporation and its shareholders, in this setting, requires it to be a protective guardian of the rightful interest of the public shareholders.

---

[19] The fact that Mr. Barry Carroll parted company with his family does not appear to have affected the practical fact of control -- which of course is the predicate fact for the existence of a control premium.

But while that obligation may authorize the board to take extraordinary steps to protect the minority from plain overreaching, it does not authorize the board to deploy corporate power *against* the majority stockholders, in the absence of a threatened serious breach of fiduciary duty by the controlling stock.

To acknowledge that the Carroll Family has no obligation to support a transaction in which they would in effect sell their stock is not, of course, to suggest that they can use their control over the corporation to effectuate a self-interested merger at an unfair price. See Weinberger v. UOP, Inc., 457 A.2d 701 (Del.1983). There is nothing in the present record, however, that suggests to me that the $25.75 price the Carroll Group proposed to pay for the public shares was an inadequate or unfair price for the non-controlling stock. For the reasons stated above, the fact that Pensler was willing to pay more for all of the shares does not, logically, support an inference that the Carroll proposal for the non-controlling public shares was not fair.

Thus, while I continue to hold open the possibility that a situation might arise in which a board could, consistently with its fiduciary duties, issue a dilutive option in order to protect the corporation or its minority shareholders form exploitation by a controlling shareholder who was in the process or threatening to violate his fiduciary duties to the corporation,[20] such a situation does not at all appear to have been faced by the Katy board of directors.

In my opinion, far from "Revlon duties" requiring such action, the Katy board could not, consistent with its fiduciary obligations to all of the stockholders of Katy Industries, have issued the dilutive option for the purpose sought in this instance. Therefore, that the board considered the matter and declined to do so could in no event be considered to constitute a breach of duty to the minority shareholders.

V

The Carroll Group withdrew its proposed merger on December 1, 1993. Thereafter, on March 8, 1994, the board authorized the payment of an extraordinary $14.00 per share cash dividend. Plaintiffs seek to enjoin the payment of this dividend.

It is elementary that the declaration of dividends out of available corporate funds is a matter left to the discretion of the board of directors and that the declaration or payment of a dividend will be reviewed by a court only on the basis of fraud or gross abuse of discretion. See Gabelli & Co. v. Liggett Group, Inc., 479 A.2d 176, 180 (Del.1984) (quoting Eshelman v. Keenan, 194 A. 40, 43 (Del.Ch.1937) (Wolcott, C.)).

---

[20] In such an instance the board would bear a heavy burden to establish the justification for any steps purposely taken to affect the outcome of shareholder action. See Blasius Industries v. Atlas Corp., 564 A.2d 651 (Del.Ch.1988).

The only argument plaintiffs can advance in support of the position that the declaration and payment of the special dividend is "a gross abuse," is again predicated upon the assertion that "Revlon duties" require the board now to maximize the current value of the stock. The proposed dividend, they say, is inconsistent with a transaction with Pensler, and thus does not satisfy this Revlon duty. Concluding as I do above, it follows that plaintiffs have shown no gross abuse in the declaration of the special dividend, nor have plaintiffs shown any other ground for the grant of preliminary injunction at this time. Therefore the application will be denied.

It is so ordered.

Note: The Current State of the Law

In *Mendel*, Chancellor Allen describes how the *Perlman* equal opportunity principle failed to carry the day. The general rule allows a controlling shareholder to sell control at a premium without the obligation to allow other shareholders to participate, subject to a number of exceptions. The American Law Institute's Corporate Governance Project formulates the rule as follows:

§ 5.16 Disposition of Voting Equity Securities by a Controlling Shareholder to Third Parties

A controlling shareholder has the same right to dispose of voting equity securities as any other shareholder, including the right to dispose of those securities for a price that is not made proportinally available to other shareholders, abut the controlling shareholder does not satisfy the duty of fair dealing to the other shareholders if:

(a) The controlling shareholder does not make disclosure concerning the transaction to other shareholders with whom the controlling shareholder deals in connection with the transaction; or

(b) It is apparent from the circumstances that the purchaser is likely to violate the duty of fair dealing . . . in such a way as to obtain a significant financial benefit for the purchaser or an associate.[4]

As reflected in § 5.16, the potential for sellers of control at a premium to incur liability has been recognized in three circumstances.

1. *Be on the Lookout for Looters.* A number of cases assert the principle that a seller of control may be liable to minority shareholders when,

---

[4] American Law Institute, *Principles of Corporate Governance: Analysis and Recommendations* § 5.16 (1994).

following the sale, the purchaser loots or otherwise injures the corporation.[5] The efficacy of such a rule turns on the question of who is the cheapest cost avoider. Looting is undesirable and should be deterred in the manner that uses up the least resources subject, in all events, to the limit that the resources used to deter not exceed the benefits of reduced looting. One cost of deterrence is the number of otherwise desirable transactions which do not take place because of the potential liability of sellers. For this purpose, how clearly the rule specifies the seller's obligation is central. For example, must a seller investigate a buyer even in the absence of circumstances which would arouse suspicion?[6] How the rule is drawn -- whether there is a an absolute duty to investigate, the specificity of the statement of the circumstances which should lead a seller to forego the transaction -- bears substantially on the kind of transactions which will be deterred and, as a result, on the costs of imposing the rule in the first place:

> [O]ther things being equal, the more specific the prohibition, the less likely it is to deter socially desirable behavior not intended to be prohibited. Uncertainty concerning whether particular conduct is prohibited deters that conduct; precision, by reducing the uncertainty, reduces the unintended deterrence. The move toward specificity, however, is not costless. The more specific the prohibition, the more likely it is that undesirable conduct, which was intended to be prohibited and which would have been covered by a more general prohibition, will not be barred.[7]

Section 5.16 requires that something put the seller on notice of the buyer's nefarious plans. Here the critical issue is whether the fact of the control premium itself is sufficient to require inquiry by the seller. The ALI explicitly rejects inferring the potential for misconduct from the mere fact that a premium is paid.[8]

2. *Corporate Opportunity and Dealings with Minority Shareholders.* What if the purchaser first approaches the controlling shareholder in the shareholder's capacity as an officer or director, and proposes to acquire the

---

[5] E.g., Insuranshares Corp. v. Northern Fiscal Corp., 35 F.Supp. 22 (E.D.Pa.1940); DeBaun v. First Western Bank & Trust Co., 120 Cal.Rptr. 354 (Cal.App., 2d Dist.1975); Clagett v. Hutchinson, 583 F.2d 1259 (4th Cir.1978); McDaniel v. Painter, 418 F.2d 545 (10th Cir.1969).

[6] Compare Clagett v. Hutchinson, *supra* note 5 (circumstances must put seller on notice of possibility of fraud; sale at a premium is not alone enough), with Northway, Inc. v. TSC Industries, 512 F.2d 324, 342 (7th Cir.1975), *rev'd on other grounds*, 426 U.S. 438 (1976) (court "unable to read *Insuranshares* as holding that absent suspicious circumstances there is no duty to investigate prior to the transfer of a controlling interest").

[7] Ronald Gilson, *A Structural Approach to Corporations: The Case Against Defense Tactics in Tender Offers,* 33 Stan.L.Rev. 819, 883 (1981) (citations omitted). See Isaac Erlich & Richard Posner, *An Economic Analysis of Legal Rulemaking,* 3 J.Legal Stud. 257 (1974).

[8] American Law Institute (1994), *supra* note 4, Commentary to § 5.16 at 378.

target corporation in a transaction in which all shareholders can participate? May the controlling shareholder respond by suggesting a transaction in which only his shares are purchased at a higher price? Compare Brown v. Halbert, 76 Cal.Rptr. 781 (Cal.App.1969) (liability found), with Tyron v. Smith, 229 P.2d 251 (Or.1951) (no liability). The ALI rejects *Brown's* corporate opportunity approach as one of avoidable formalism: "[A] knowledgeable buyer could avoid the rule in such case simply by asking the controlling shareholder initially what price it would take for its shares."[9] However, in § 5.16(b), the ALI adopts an exception that tracks a narrower reading of *Brown*. In *Brown* the controlling shareholder advised minority shareholders to sell their shares at a lower price without disclosing that he had received a higher price. Section 5.16(b) does not require that an equal premium be paid to all shareholders, but only that the controlling stockholder disclose to minority shareholders the terms of his transaction.

3. *Sale of Office.* A final exception imposes liability on the selling shareholder when the premium is received for the sale of office rather than the sale of control. The issue is posed by a routine transactional corollary to the sale of shares by a controlling shareholder. As one of the conditions to the buyer's obligation to close the primary transaction, the directors resign seriatim, with each vacancy being filled by the buyer's designees. The result is that a board majority is transferred along with the sale of control, accelerating a process that otherwise might have taken until the next annual meeting (or the next two annual meetings if the board is staggered) to accomplish. A sale of office at a premium violates the director's fiduciary duty; a transfer of board control that parallels transfer of voting control merely facilitates an otherwise unobjectionable, and in all events inevitable, transfer. The case law distinguishes between the two characterizations based on the amount of stock held by the selling shareholder.[10]

The American Law Institute follows *Essex* in imposing liability only when the premium sale and associated transfer of board control is by a person that "owns significantly less than a majority of the voting stock. . . ."[11] The ALI does not elaborate on what might constitute "significantly less than a majority," but its favorable reference to *Essex* suggests the line is drawn somewhere below 28%.

4. *Federal and State Statutory Restrictions.* Rule 14d-10, adopted under §14d of the Williams Act, requires that a tender offer be open to all shareholders and that all shareholders receive the same price. Because of the

---

[9] American Law Institute (1994), *supra* note 4, Commentary to § 5.16 at 376.

[10] Compare Caplan v. Lionel Corp., 246 N.Y.S.2d 913 (App.Div.1964) (transfer of board control in connection with transfer of a 3% share block invalid) with Essex Universal Corp. v. Yates, 305 F.2d 572 (2d Cir.1962) (transfer of board control in connection with transfer of a 28% share block valid).

[11] American Law Institute (1994), *supra* note 4, Commentary to § 5.16 at 379.

private offering exception to the definition of a tender offer,[12] the rule does not apply to transactions in which the acquirer does not intend to purchase the minority shares. However, when the acquirer also wants to purchase the minority shares through a tender offer at a lower price, careful transactional planning in required.[13] Rule 10b-13 cuts off one obvious avoidance technique by prohibiting purchase of shares other than through a tender offer while the tender offer is pending; the controlling shares cannot be purchased outside the tender offer at the same time.

The approach taken to allow paying different prices for controlling and minority shares in a tender offer involves purchasing the controlling shares before commencing a tender offer and thereby triggering the application of Rules 10b-13 and 14d-10. Recall that under Rule 14d-2(d)'s safe harbor provision, a tender offer does not commence if an acquirer does not disclose the securities sought and the price to be paid. Suppose the premium purchase is completed before the announcement of a tender offer to minority shareholders at a lower price. Do Rules 10b-13 and 14d-10 apply? Can the acquirer protect against being left with too many minority shareholders (because the price offered is too low) by conditioning the closing of the transaction with the controlling shareholder on the success of the tender offer? For purposes of the application of Rules 10b-13 and 14d-10, is the premium acquisition made when the contract is entered into or when the contemplated transaction is closed? See W. R. Grace & Co., 1975 SEC No-Act. LEXIS 749 (April 17, 1975) (approving pre-tender offer contract and post-tender offer closing).

Section 14(f) of the Williams Act also imposes a disclosure requirement in connection with transfers of board control associated with transfers of voting control:

> (f) If, pursuant to any arrangements or understanding with the person or persons acquiring securities in a transaction subject to [§ 13(d) or 14(d)], any persons are to be elected or designated as directors of the issuer, otherwise than at a meeting of security holders, and the persons so elected or designated will constitute a majority of the directors of the issuer, then, prior to the time any such person takes office as a director, and in accordance with rules and regulations prescribed by the Commission, the issuer shall file with the Commission, and transmit to all holders of record of securities of the issuer who would be entitled to vote at a meeting for election of directors, information substantially equivalent to the information which would be required by the federal proxy rules to be transmitted if such person or persons were nominees for election as directors at a meeting of such security holders.

---

[12] See Chapter 18, *supra*.

[13] If the controlling shareholder can transfer a majority of outstanding stock, the acquiring company may forgo a followup tender offer in favor of a freezeout merger. Then state law restrictions are substituted for federal restrictions. See Chapter 22, *infra*.

Section 14(f) is limited to designations of a majority of directors. Would the disclosure obligations be different if one director less than a majority were subject to the arrangement? To what extent does the general obligation to disclose material facts under §§ 13(d) and 14(d) cover everything picked up by § 14(f)?[14]

State control share acquisition statutes also may affect private sale of control. As considered more fully in Chapter 23, a control share acquisition statute typically requires that an acquisition of shares that causes the purchaser to own more than a specified percentage of the outstanding stock, typically 20%, be approved by a vote of the majority of the outstanding stock held by disinterested shareholders. While minority shareholders might be reluctant to approve a transfer at a price higher than they will receive in an anticipated tender offer, the statutes typically exempt transactions approved by the existing board of directors. Is it a problem that the existing board of directors is under the control of the selling shareholder?

B.   Designing the Rule: Analysis and Empirical Results

Only recently have efforts been made to give substance to the competing claims of "fairness" that have dominated discussion of whether a controlling shareholder must share the premium associated with sale of control. We consider first the analytic framework underlying fairness claims, and then turn to the empirical evidence bearing on alternative analyses.

1.   Analytic Framework

William Andrews
THE STOCKHOLDER'S RIGHT TO EQUAL
OPPORTUNITY IN THE SALE OF SHARES
78 Harv.L.Rev. 505, 505-29 (1965)[*]

The right violated [in *Feldmann*] . . . is simply the right of all stockholders to have an equal opportunity to participate ratably in a sale of stock pursuant to an offer to purchase controlling shares at a favorable price.
. . .

The rule to be considered [to prevent that violation] can be stated thus: whenever a controlling stockholder sells his shares, every other holder of shares (of the same class) is entitled to have an equal opportunity to sell his shares, or a prorata part of them, on substantially the same terms. Or in terms of the correlative duty: before a controlling stockholder may sell his

---

[14] David Ratner, *Section 14(f): A New Approach to Transfers of Corporate Control*, 54 Cornell L.Q. 65 (1968), surveys the impact of § 14(f).

[*] Copyright © 1965 by the Harvard Law Review Association.

shares to an outsider he must assure his fellow stockholders an equal opportunity to sell their shares, or as high a proportion of theirs as he ultimately sells of his own. . . .

Now let us look briefly at what the rule means. First, it neither compels nor prohibits a sale of stock at any particular price; it leaves a controlling stockholder wholly free to decide for himself the price above which he will sell and below which he will hold his shares. The rule only says that in executing his decision to sell, a controlling stockholder cannot sell pursuant to a purchase offer more favorable than any available to other stockholders. Second, the rule does not compel a prospective purchaser to make an open offer for all shares on the same terms. He can offer to purchase shares on the condition that he gets a certain proportion of the total. Or he can even make an offer to purchase 51% of the shares, no more and no less. The only requirement is that his offer, whatever it may be, be made equally or proportionately available to all stockholders. . . .

The asserted right would prevent just what happened in *Feldmann*: a private sale by a controlling stockholder at a price not available to other stockholders. But there are two modes of compliance with the rule: either the purchaser can extend his offer to all stockholders, or the seller can offer participation in the sale to his fellow stockholders. A sale is prevented from taking place only when the purchaser is unwilling to buy more than a specified percentage of the shares, and the seller will sell only if he can sell out completely. Indeed, even under these circumstances it is an overstatement to say the rule would prevent a sale taking place, since the minority stockholders may consent to the sale. They may even sell to the purchaser at a lower price than what he pays the controlling stockholder, provided they are adequately informed of what is going on. Thus the rule only operates to prevent a sale when (1) the purchaser is unwilling to purchase more shares, (2) the seller insists on disposing of all his shares, and (3) the minority stockholders are unwilling to stay in the enterprise under the purchaser's control. . . .

2. Economic Analysis. -- The rule of equal opportunity prevents a purchaser, in a certain sense, from paying a premium for controlling shares. One way to evaluate the rule, therefore, is to examine the implications of the premium. Does the premium reflect factors that ought properly to enter into an evaluation of the controlling shares? Can the effects of different factors in producing a premium be separated from one another?

The assertion that a premium shows controlling shares to be worth more than noncontrolling shares has an important kernel of truth in it. But it needs to be analyzed in terms of the various reasons a purchaser might rationally have for paying a premium, in order to separate that kernel of truth from a considerable amount of chaff.

(a). -- We can begin with cases already discussed. Why were the purchasers in the looting cases, and in *Feldmann,* willing to pay a premium? In the looting cases the answer is simple -- the premium represents payment

for the opportunity to get into a position where the purchaser can steal from the corporation. The courts have recognized this motive, and have relied heavily on the premium paid to reach the conclusion that the sellers had adequate notice of the purchaser's intentions. . . .

Why was Wilport willing to pay a premium for Feldmann's stock? Again the answer is fairly obvious -- because it was willing to pay something extra in order to acquire power to control Newport's sales of steel. And again the court recognized this perfectly clearly when it spoke of the corporate product commanding a premium in the form of a premium price for stock. . . .

But different as it is from the corporation's standpoint, for the purchaser the significance of the premium is much the same in *Feldmann* as in the looting cases. In both situations the purchaser is paying a premium for an opportunity to profit from his investment in some other way than through dividends and appreciation in the value of his stock. In both situations the purchaser plans to use his position of control to create additional relationships between himself and the corporation, for his own profit and benefit, and the premium represents payment for that additional expectation of return on his investment. . . .

The *Feldmann* case is unique in that it involved a reasonably precise market price for the corporate product, but under rather artificial circumstances. Members of the purchasing syndicate were willing to play the game, paying the established price for Newport's product. But in this case the one clear thing was that the price established did not reflect the full amount the purchasers were willing to pay for a sure supply of steel. It might be impossible to say exactly what the purchasers would have paid, in an unrestrained market situation, for contracts that would have assured their requirements of steel, but clearly it would have been more than the prevailing market price. It was this premium for steel, forced by the peculiar circumstances of the case to take the form of a premium price for stock, for which the court required Feldmann to account.

As compared with other cases where the value to the purchaser of entering into extra-stockholder relations is not accurately gauged by some objective market figure -- all of the cases, for instance, where the purchaser makes himself a paid executive employee of the acquired corporation -- *Feldmann* is only unique for the rather graphic way it displays the relationship between what the corporation gets for its product (or pays for executive services) and what the controlling stockholder gets for his shares. In principle the case of a premium paid by a purchaser for the opportunity of making himself an executive employee, or of making a profit out of any other extra-stockholder relationship, is no different from that of a purchaser like Wilport who pays a premium in order to make himself a favored customer.

(*b*). -- The most important reason a purchaser might pay a premium for controlling shares, and one that has to be met squarely, is that an investment in controlling shares is a more promising, or at least a safer, investment than one in noncontrolling shares for the simple reason that it will enable the investor to implement what he believes to be the best policies in the management of his investment. . . .

This is the strongest part of any argument against a broad reading of *Feldmann*. It is the kernel of truth in the assertion that a premium paid for controlling shares only shows that controlling shares are inherently worth more than minority shares. It refutes any literal interpretation of the corporate asset theory by showing that control under some circumstances necessarily gives an element of value to some shares that it does not give to others. . . .

The rule of equal opportunity does not, however, prevent a purchaser from offering more per share if he acquires control, than if he does not. The rule tends to operate automatically to distinguish between a premium paid for the opportunity of entering into extra-stockholder relations, and one that reflects a change in investment appraisal resulting from a shift in control. This is one of the greatest advantages of the rule of equal opportunity over any corporate asset theory of control, and it needs to be set out and explored in some detail. . . .

The argument can be made first in relatively abstract terms. Assume that the only factors that would cause a particular purchaser to pay more for some shares than for others are the two so far discussed: (a) that he wants to enter into some advantageous extra-stockholder relationship with the corporation, which he can only achieve by gaining control; and (b) that he views the corporate stock as a better (safer or more profitable or both) investment if he is in control than if he is not. Assume further that the purchaser can be made to state the top price he would pay for any particular portion of the company's outstanding shares.

On these assumptions, if in a particular case the purchaser is only actuated by the second factor -- by a difference in investment appraisal associated with his acquisition of control -- then the only differential that will appear in his schedule of prices will be a differential between what he will pay per share if he does not achieve control, and what he will pay per share if he does achieve control. There will be no difference between his price per share for a bare controlling block, and his price per share for any larger amount. The return on his investment will be proportionate to the number of shares he owns; therefore he will be willing to pay in proportion to the number of shares he acquires; and his marginal price for supercontrol shares will be equal to what he would pay per share for a controlling block. For this purchaser, in this case, the rule of equal opportunity imposes no burden. The rule permits him to condition an offer to purchase at a particular price, on his achieving control. If he purchases a controlling block the rule only requires him to offer the same price per share for more shares, something he should be willing to do in any event.

On the other hand, if a purchaser is willing to pay more per share for a barely controlling block of shares than for a larger block -- still making the assumptions stated above -- this would show that he is actuated in part at least by the first factor, by the intention or expectation of enjoying some profit or advantage from entering into some extra-stockholder relationship with his newly acquired corporation. The measure of his investment appraisal with himself in control is the marginal price per share he would pay for shares in excess of those required to achieve control. If he is willing to pay more than that marginal price, for any number of shares, he must be paying for something other than the investment value of the shares. On the assumptions stated above, it must be an intention to derive a profit from some sort of extra-stockholder relationship. And that explanation fits the fact because the profit to be derived from an extra-stockholder relationship will be no greater on account of the purchase of supercontrol shares; therefore if a purchaser were motivated by an intention to derive that sort of profit, one would expect him to offer more per share for a controlling block than for supercontrol shares. . . .

Frank Easterbrook & Daniel Fischel
CORPORATE CONTROL TRANSACTIONS
91 Yale L.J. 698, 698-718 (1982)*

Transactions in corporate control often produce gains for the corporation. Substitution of one set of managers for another, for example, often produces gains because assets increase in value under better management, and would-be managers offer payments to shareholders to compete for the right to manage the firm's pool of assets. . . .

[D]evices for allocating corporate control pose a common problem because they sometimes involve an unequal division of the gains from the transaction. Shares in a control bloc, for example, may be sold at a price greater than that paid for the remaining shares; . . . one might argue that the gains should be distributed more widely. Such "sharing" arguments are popular among academic lawyers, and courts are beginning to apply these arguments to some corporate control transactions. We argue, in contrast, that those who produce a gain should be allowed to keep it, subject to the constraint that other parties to the transaction be at least as well off as before the transaction. Any attempt to require sharing simply reduces the likelihood that there will be gains to share.

Equal Treatment, Fiduciary Duty, and Shareholders' Welfare

Many scholars, and a few courts, conclude that one aspect of fiduciary duty is the equal treatment of investors. Their argument takes the following form: fiduciary principles require fair conduct; equal treatment is fair

---

* Reprinted by permission of The Yale Law Journal Company and Fred B. Rothman & Company.

conduct; hence, fiduciary principles require equal treatment. The conclusion does not follow. The argument depends upon an equivalence between equality and fair treatment, which we have questioned elsewhere. To say that fiduciary principles require equal (or even fair) treatment is to beg the central question -- whether investors would contract for equal or even roughly equal treatment.

Our analysis of this question requires that a distinction be drawn between rules that maximize value *ex ante* and actions that maximize the returns of certain investors *ex post*. A simple example illustrates the point. A corporation may choose to invest its capital in one of two ventures. Venture 1 will pay $100, and the returns can be divided equally among the firm's investors. Thus, if there are 10 investors in the firm, the expected value to each investor is $10. Venture 2 will pay $150, in contrast, but only if the extra returns are given wholly to five of the ten investors. Thus, five "lucky" investors will receive $20 apiece, and the unlucky ones $10. Because each investor has a 50% chance of being lucky, each would think Venture 2 to be worth $15. The directors of the firm should choose Venture 2 over Venture 1 because it has the higher value and because none of the investors is worse off under Venture 2.

Now consider Venture 3, in which $200 in gains are to be divided among only five of the ten investors with nothing for the rest. If investors are risk neutral, fiduciaries should choose Venture 3 over Venture 2 (despite the fact that some investors end up worse off under Venture 3), because the expected value to each investor is $20 under Venture 3 and only $15 under Venture 2.

In sum, if the terms under which the directors obtain control of the firm call for them to maximize the wealth of the investors, their duty is to select the highest-paying venture and, following that, to abide by the rules of distribution. If unequal distribution is necessary to make the stakes higher, then duty requires inequality. The *ex post* inequality under Ventures 2 and 3 is no more "unfair" than the *ex post* inequality of a lottery, in which all players invest a certain amount but only a few collect. The equal treatment of the investors going into Ventures 2 and 3, and the gains they receive from taking chances, make the *ex post* inequality both fair and desirable.

We hope that our analysis of Ventures 2 and 3 above are uncontroversial. If corporate control transactions sufficiently resemble Ventures 2 and 3, this analysis supplies a guide for analyzing the fiduciary duties of corporate managers. A class of control transactions resembles Ventures 2 and 3 if: (1) control changes and financial restructurings produce gains for investors to enjoy; (2) the existence or amount of the gain depends upon unequal distribution; and (3) shareholders would prefer the unequal distribution to a more equal distribution of smaller gains from an alternative transaction (or no transaction). We address these issues in the remainder of Part II and conclude by advancing a fiduciary principle under which managers always are free to engage in transactions resembling Venture 2.

For practical reasons, however, our principle prohibits transactions resembling Venture 3.

The Potential Gains from Control Transactions

It should be clear that managers do not always maximize the wealth of investors. . . . Managers may not work as hard as they would if they could claim a higher share of the proceeds -- they may consume excessive perquisites, and they may select inferior projects for the firm without bearing the consequences of their action. Corporate control transactions can reduce agency costs. . . .

The sale of a control bloc of stock, for example, allows the buyer to install his own management team, producing the same gains available from a tender offer for a majority of shares but at lower cost to the buyer. Because such a buyer believes he can manage the assets of a firm more profitably, he is willing to pay a premium over the market price to acquire control. The premium will be some percentage of the anticipated increase in value once the transfer of control is effectuated. If there were no anticipated increase in value, it would be irrational for the buyer to pay the premium. There is a strong presumption, therefore, that free transferability of corporate control, like any other type of voluntary exchange, moves assets to higher valued uses.

Of course, some control transactions do not produce gains. . . . At least for publicly-traded firms, the market offers information that distinguishes value-increasing control transactions from others in which looting or mismanagement may be in store. The information is contained in the price of a firm's shares. If the control change is associated with an increase in price, the investors apparently do not fear looting or other harm to the firm. If a syndicate acquires a control bloc of shares, and the price of the remaining shares *rises,* relative to the market as a whole, then the shareholders are betting on the basis of available information that the new controller will be better for their interests than the old.

The Gains May Depend on Unequal Division

In many cases the apportionment of the gain makes little difference to the success of the transaction. If the gain from taking over a corporation exceeds the cost incurred by the acquiror, he would be indifferent to who receives the premium that is necessary to obtain control. But a sharing requirement . . . may make an otherwise profitable transaction unattractive to the prospective seller of control. To illustrate, suppose that the owner of a control bloc of shares finds that his perquisites or the other amenities of his position are worth $10. A prospective acquiror of control concludes that, by eliminating these perquisites and other amenities, he could produce a gain of $15. The shareholders in the company benefit if the acquiror pays a premium of $11 to the owner of the controlling bloc, ousts the current managers, and makes the contemplated improvements. The net gains of $4 inure to each investor according to his holdings, and although the acquiror obtains the largest portion because he holds the largest bloc, no one is left out. If the owner of the control bloc must share the $11 premium with all of the existing shareholders, however, the deal collapses. The owner will not part with his bloc for less than a $10 premium. A sharing requirement would make the deal unprofitable to him, and the other investors would lose the prospective gain from the installation of better managers.

Investors Prefer the Fiduciary Principle That Maximizes Aggregate Gains

Do investors prefer a larger pie even if not everyone may have a larger slice in every case? We argue here that they do, for two reasons. First, their expected wealth is greatest under this interpretation of the fiduciary principle, and second, they may deal with any risk by holding diversified portfolios of investments.

Clearly, if control transactions produce gains, and if the gains depend on unequal allocation, then the expected wealth of the shareholders in the aggregate is maximized by a rule allowing unequal allocation. *All* share prices *ex ante* will be highest when the probability of a value-increasing transaction in the future is the greatest. Shareholders can realize this value at any time by selling their shares, or they can hold the shares and take the chance of gaining still more as a result of the unequal allocation of gains *ex post*.

This argument may seem to disregard the fact that many investors are risk averse -- they prefer a sure $10, say, to a one in ten chance of receiving $100. On the surface, therefore, it seems that investors might benefit from equal or fair division of gains notwithstanding the loss of some gains as a result. This argument, however, ignores the lessons of modern portfolio theory. By investing in many firms simultaneously, risk averse investors can reduce the risk of losses without extinguishing profitable-but-risky transactions.

The risks involved in corporate control transactions are diversifiable. . . . Indeed, there is a strongly negative correlation among the risks. An investor with a reasonably diversified portfolio would be on the winning side of some transactions and the losing side of others. For example, if shareholders of one corporation obtain little of the gain from a given merger, the shareholders of the other corporation obtain more. An investor holding a diversified portfolio with stock in both corporations is concerned with the total gain from the transaction, not with how the gain is allocated. Indeed, the investor with shares of both would see any expense in allocating the gain as pure loss. To the extent an unequal allocation raises the number and amount of gain transactions, therefore, investors with diversified portfolios would prefer to allow the unequal allocation to continue.

We have shown that the *ex post* inequality under Ventures 2 and 3, like the *ex post* inequality in a lottery, is not "unfair" if, *ex ante,* all investors have an equal chance to win and can eliminate risk through diversification. We now consider a potential objection to this reasoning. One might argue that this *ex ante* equality is absent in corporate control transactions because insiders systematically benefit at the expense of outsiders. Small shareholders, the argument runs, consistently will be frozen out, deprived of control premiums, and otherwise disadvantaged by insiders.

The argument loses its plausibility on close examination. One need not be wealthy to be on the "winning side" of a control transaction, and neither wealth nor status as an insider ensures being a winner. If corporation A purchases from corporation B a control bloc of shares in corporation C, a small (or outside) shareholder might participate in the gains by holding shares in any of the three firms.

There is no need for the small shareholder to identify these situations in advance. By holding a diversified portfolio containing the securities of many firms, the small shareholder can ensure that he will participate in the gains produced. All shareholders therefore have a chance of receiving the gains produced by corporate control transactions -- if not an equal chance, at least enough of a chance to allow diversification of the risk. There remain cases in which it is impossible for an investor to share in gains or diversify away the risk by holding stock in both firms. This would be true, for example, where one of the firms is privately held. The shareholder can minimize this non-diversifiable risk, however, by not investing in firms that are controlled by an individual or a privately-held firm.

Market Value as a Benchmark Under the Fiduciary Principle

In the circumstances we have discussed, shareholders unanimously prefer legal rules under which the amount of gains is maximized, regardless of how the gains are distributed. The ideal transaction is one like Venture 2 above, in which the gains are unequally distributed but all shareholders are at least as well off as they were before the transaction. Shareholders may also benefit from transactions in which the distribution of gains leaves some shareholders worse off than before the transaction -- as in Venture 3 -- but there are probably few such transactions. We cannot imagine why gains would depend on making some investors worse off, and we have not encountered any example of such a transaction. In a world of costly information, investors will view Venture 2 transactions very differently from Venture 3 transactions, which would raise all-but-insuperable difficulties in determining whether the transaction produced gain. One can imagine instances, of which looting is a good example, in which the person acquiring control pays a premium to some investor(s) in order to obtain control and obliterate the remaining claims, recouping the premium without putting resources to a more productive use. A requirement that all investors receive at least the market value of their positions prior to the transactions would be a useful rule-of-thumb for separating beneficial deals from potentially harmful ones. If every investor receives at least what he had before, and some receive a premium, the transaction *must* produce gains.

The requirement that everyone receive at least the value of his investment under existing conditions serves much the same function as the rule against theft. A thief *might* be able to put stolen resources to a better use than his victim, but if so then he can pay for those resources. Thus, a requirement of payment increases the likelihood that transactions are value-increasing. Moreover, the proscription of theft also reduces the incentive of property owners to take elaborate precautions against theft. For example, investors might resort to costly monitoring devices to reduce the chance of confiscation of their shares. When all transactions are consensual, these precautions become unnecessary. By prohibiting confiscation, therefore, the fiduciary principle reduces wasteful expenditures while simultaneously reducing the number of socially inefficient corporate control transactions.

The Fiduciary Principle in Operation

Sales of Control Blocs

Sales of controlling blocs of shares provide a good example of transactions in which the movement of control is beneficial. The sale of control may lead to new offers, new plans, and new working arrangements with other firms that reduce agency costs and create other gains from new business relationships. The premium price received by the seller of the control bloc amounts to an unequal distribution of the gains. For the reasons we have discussed, however, this unequal distribution reduces the costs to purchasers of control, thereby increasing the number of beneficial control transfers, and increasing the incentive for inefficient controllers to relinquish their positions.

Numerous academic commentators, however, argue for some form of sharing requirement. . . . This proposal would entitle the minority shareholders to sell their shares on the same terms as the controlling shareholder.

Both of these proposed treatments of the control premium would stifle transfers of control. If . . . minority shareholders may sell on the same terms as the controlling shareholder, bidders may have to purchase more shares than necessary, possibly causing the transaction to become unprofitable. Minority shareholders would suffer under either rule, as the likelihood of improvements in the quality of management declined.

The mountain of academic commentary calling for some type of sharing requirement has not been influential, and the legal treatment of control sales is largely along the lines of wealth maximization. Sales at a premium are lawful, and the controlling shareholder generally has no duty to spread the bounty. The rhetoric of the cases, however, is not uniform. In particular, the famous case of Perlman v. Feldmann suggests that the gains may have to be shared in some circumstances.

In *Perlman* the president and chairman (Feldmann) of the board of Newport Steel, a producer of steel sheets, sold his controlling bloc of shares for $20 per share at a time when the market price was less than $12 per share. The purchasers, a syndicate organized as Wilport Company, consisted of end-users of steel from across the country who were interested in a secure source of supply during a period of shortage attributable to the Korean War.

Because of the war, steel producers were prohibited from raising the price of steel. The "Feldmann Plan", adopted by Newport and some other steel producers, effectively raised the price of steel to the market-clearing price. Under the plan, prospective purchasers provided Newport and other steel producers with interest-free advances in exchange for commitments for future production. Newport had used those advances to replace equipment in order to expand and compete more effectively with other steel producers.

The Second Circuit held in *Perlman* that the seller of the control bloc had a duty to share the control premium with other shareholders. The court's holding that Feldmann could not accept the premium paid by Wilport without violating his fiduciary duty was based on a belief that the steel shortage allowed Newport to finance needed expansion via the "Plan", and that the premium represented an attempt by Wilport to divert a corporate opportunity -- to secure for itself the benefits resulting from the shortage. . . .

There are several problems with this treatment. Foremost is its assumption that the gain resulting from the "Plan" was not reflected in the price of Newport's stock. Newport stock was widely traded, and the existence of the Feldmann Plan was known to investors. The going price of Newport shares prior to the transaction therefore reflected the full value of Newport, including the value of advances under the Feldmann Plan. The Wilport syndicate paid some two-thirds more than the going price and thus could not profit from the deal unless (a) the sale of control resulted in an increase in the value of Newport, or (b) Wilport's control of Newport was the equivalent of looting. To see the implications of the latter possibility, consider the following simplified representation of the transaction. Newport has only 100 shares, and Wilport pays $20 for each of 37 shares. The market price of shares is $12, and hence the premium over the market price is $8 x 37 = $296. Wilport must extract more than $296 from Newport in order to gain from the deal; the extraction comes at the expense of the other 63 shares, which must drop approximately $4.75 each, to $7.25.

Hence, the court's proposition that Wilport extracted a corporate opportunity from Newport -- the functional equivalent of looting -- has testable implications. Unless the price of Newport's outstanding shares plummeted, the Wilport syndicate could not be extracting enough to profit. In fact, however, the value of Newport's shares rose substantially after the transaction. Part of this increase may have been attributable to the rising market for steel companies at the time, but even holding this factor constant,

Newport's shares appreciated in price.[43]   The data refute the court's proposition that Wilport appropriated a corporate opportunity of Newport.

It seems, then, that the source of the premium in *Perlman* is the same as the source of the gains for the shares Wilport did not buy: Wilport installed a better group of managers and, in addition, furnished Newport with a more stable market for its products.   The gains from these changes must have exceeded any loss from abolition of the Feldmann Plan.

<hr>

Although Andrews and Easterbrook & Fischel disagree as to the most desirable rule, they do not seem to disagree as to the standard by which the rules should be judged.   Both rules -- "equal opportunity" and "unequal division" -- are argued to be most beneficial to shareholders in general, an *ex ante* determination.   Further, both sides agree that control changes are potentially beneficial to all concerned.   The disagreement is over whether unequal division -- Feldmann keeping the entire premium -- is necessary to secure those benefits.   The resolution of the issue depends on the reason why a premium is paid at all.

Consider first a situation where the buyer is willing to pay a premium only because efficiency gains in the operation of the target company would result from replacing the current control holder, and where the current control holder derives no benefit from control not shared proportionately by other shareholders.[15]   In this admittedly unrealistic setting, it seems that an equal opportunity rule would be selected by shareholders.   As Andrews points out, the division of the premium would not affect the *purchaser's*

<hr>

[43] Charles Cope has computed changes in the price of Newport shares using the market model, well developed in the finance literature, under which the rate of return on a firm's shares is a function of the market rate of return, the volatility of the firm's price in the past, a constant, and a residual component that represents the consequences of unanticipated events. Increases in this residual reflect good news for the firm.   Cope found a significant positive residual for Newport in the month of the sale to Wilport. See Charles Cope, Is the Control Premium Really a Corporate Asset? (unpublished paper, 1981)

The raw price data are no less telling.   The $12 price to which the Perlman court referred was the highest price at which shares changed hands before the sale of control.   The average monthly bid prices for Newport stock during 1950 were:

July:	6-3/4
August:	8-1/2
September:	10-7/8
October:	12-1/2
November:	12-3/8
December:	12

The sale to the Wilport syndicate took place on August 31, 1950. This pattern of prices certainly does not suggest that the 63% interest excluded from the premium perceived any damage to Newport.

[15] For example, where the control holder provides goods or services to the company, only the market price is received.

incentives to make the acquisition. And to complete the argument, unequal division would not be necessary to convince the *holder* of control to sell. Although a control holder would like the right to take advantage of control by keeping the premium to himself, he would still sell even if unequal division were prohibited because, by definition, he has been offered a price higher than the market value of his shares. In this situation, then, an equal opportunity rule would not reduce the number of beneficial control transactions and, even considered *ex ante,* shareholders would choose such a rule in preference to one that allowed a controlling shareholder to exploit his strategic advantage.

Note, however, that even the conclusion in this strikingly artificial situation is not without qualification. What if the very existence of a control group has a positive benefit so that, all other things being equal, minority shareholders would prefer that there be a controlling shareholder? This hypothetical is in fact substantially less artificial than that which just supported the choice of an equal opportunity rule. As was stressed in the Gilson excerpt in Chapter 10, and by Easterbrook & Fischel, the separation of ownership and control imposes substantial agency and monitoring costs on shareholders. The creation of a control group reduces these costs by reducing the separation. The relation between the reduction in agency costs by forming a control group and a choice of a rule governing the division of a premium can be examined by considering the incentives associated with the formation of such a control group.

Assume a corporation characterized by a dispersal of share ownership such that, individually, no shareholder has "control." Further assume that a group of shareholders, whose holdings together would comprise control, are considering forming a coalition to exercise that control. If they do so, they would bear the costs of creating and maintaining the coalition,[16] but would share the resulting reduction in agency costs proportionately with shareholders who were not members of the coalition. But where a control coalition cannot capture all the benefits arising from their investment in creating control, it is predictable that fewer such coalitions, beneficial to all, would be created. To solve the incentive problem, minority shareholders then would be willing to cede to the control coalition a disproportionate amount of the gains resulting from the formation of the coalition by some means such as excess salaries, favorable transactions with the corporation, and the like -- that allowed the controlling coalition a private benefit, that is, a benefit not shared proportionately with other shareholders. Thus, minority shareholders would prefer a rule which left some room for self-dealing by a control coalition, but which limited the amount "stolen" by the holders of control below the per-share gain from the reduction in agency costs accruing to the minority shareholders. Where within this range the "price" of

---

[16] For an analysis of some of the costs of creating and maintaining a controlling coalition, see Larry Meeker & O. Maurice Joy, *Price Premiums for Controlling Shares of Closely Held Bank Stock,* 53 J.Bus. 297 (1980).

monitoring would be pegged is indeterminant. It would depend, in part, on the level of competition in the market for monitors (including substitutes for owner monitoring such as independent auditors) and, in part, on the skill at strategic bargaining possessed by each side.

If this analysis is correct, an equal opportunity rule for sale of control would be untenable. Once it is conceded that minority shareholders would allow a disproportionate return to members of the control coalition, then it follows that the control shares are, in fact, worth more than the minority shares. Controlling shareholders would require a higher price to sell their shares than would the holders of minority shares, and an equal opportunity rule would result in fewer control transactions.

The illustration can be taken a step further. Assume that, following the creation of the coalition, a third party wishes to acquire the corporation because of the potential for synergy. What rule would the minority choose in this setting? Surely an equal opportunity rule would not be chosen; the holders of control, already having been given a disproportionate share of the corporation's income because it was to the minority shareholders' advantage to encourage the formation of a control coalition, would not sell their shares except at a premium which reflected the capitalized value of that disproportionate share. Thus, in order to induce the control coalition to enter into a transaction that would be beneficial to the minority, the coalition must be allowed to keep at least that part of the premium which reflects the sum of (i) the value of their disproportionate share of income; plus (ii) their proportionate share of that part of the synergistic gain anticipated to result from the transaction that will accrue to the target.

At this point, a proponent of an equal opportunity rule might object that a standard of the sort suggested would be impossible in application. How could one so carefully limit the unequal division of the premium? The response, reflected in Easterbrook & Fischel's emphasis on market price, is that there is an obvious limit to the extent to which the minority would allow unequal division: The minority must get some of the premium from the synergistic aspect of the transaction. This limit, moreover, can be easily expressed. As long as the minority shares increase in price following the transaction, they have received some portion of the synergistic benefit in the transaction. On this basis, as Easterbrook & Fischel argue, minority shareholders would prefer a rule allowing precisely the transaction which occurred in Perlman v. Feldmann because there were positive abnormal returns associated with Newport stock following the transaction.

This analysis sheds light on the formulation of the legal rules governing changes in control. Einer Elhague has recently framed the debate between equal opportunity and unequal division rules as turning on comparative under- and overinclusion.[17] An equal sharing rule will deter all transactions that make minority shareholders worse off, but at the cost of overinclusion:

---

[17] Einer Elhauge, *The Triggering Function of Sale of Control*, 59 U.Chi.L.Rev.1465 (1992).

some transactions that would have made minority shareholders better off are deterred. An unequal division rule will assure that all beneficial transactions are undeterred, but at the cost of underinclusion: some transactions that make minority shareholders worse off nonetheless take place. Elhague argues that the legal rules governing sales of control at a premium can be understood as an effort to minimize overinclusion and underinclusion. The general rule of unequal division assures that beneficial transactions will go forward, but is subject to exceptions that are triggered when the risk of underinclusion -- of allowing transactions that make minority shareholders worse off -- is the highest. From this perspective, the critical question is relative not absolute: can we specify the circumstances when the private benefits taken by the new controlling shareholder are likely to increase, and when any increase in benefits will not be offset by increases in efficiency?[18]

Consider the existing exceptions to the unequal division rule in this light. When there is reason to believe that the buyer will loot the company, the private benefits to be taken by the buyer will exceed those taken by the seller without any likely offset from increased efficiency. The looting exception therefore reduces the underinclusion of the unequal division rule. The corporate opportunity exception also seems to fit. The manner in which the initial proposal is formulated -- to the corporation or to the controlling shareholder -- seems unrelated to the comparative honesty or efficiency of the would-be purchaser. Thus, no exception to the unequal division rule is called for. Does the analysis change when the seller negotiates with the minority shareholders on behalf of the buyer without disclosing his receipt of a higher price?

How does the sale of office exception fit in the analysis? Marcel Kahan (1993) argues that an equal opportunity rule will be less overinclusive -- that is, it will deter fewer efficient transfers of control -- the smaller the percentage of shares represented by the control block to be sold.[19] The reason is the availability of a market check on the reluctance of the blockholder to sell. Suppose the control block is small and the holder refuses to effect an efficient sale of control because the equal opportunity rule prevents her receipt of an unshared premium. Because the control block is small, the bidder can still make a tender offer for control to non-controlling shareholders whose shares, aggregated through the market for corporate control, can confer control on a buyer. So understood, the sale of office exception should shift from an unequal division rule to an equal sharing rule at the point when the control block is too small to block a hostile tender offer that, pursuant to Rule 14d-10, is made at the same price to all shareholders.

---

[18] See Lucian Bebchuk, *Efficient and Inefficient Sales of Corporate Control*, 109 Q.J.Econ. 957 (1994).

[19] Marcel Kahan, *Sales of Corporate Control*, 9 J.L.Econ. & Org. 368 (1993).

Perhaps this is what the ALI means by the triggering phrase "significantly less than a majority."[20]

Two implications arise from focusing on comparisons between the levels of private benefits to be taken by the control seller and the control buyer and their relative efficiency. First, as Clifford Holderness and Dennis Sheehan have stressed, "the identity of large-block shareholders, although ignored in the literature, is potentially important."[21] In general, one can imagine two very different kinds of controlling shareholders. One group has a *unidimensional* relation to their portfolio company -- that is, the controlling shareholder's only connection with the company is its shareholdings. A second group, in contrast, has a *multidimensional* relation to their portfolio company -- that is, in addition to the controlling shareholder's stock position, it also has an operational relation to the company, for example, as customer or supplier.

When the purchaser of control will have a unidimensional relation to the company, it is unlikely that the level of private benefits will materially increase from those taken by the seller of control. A unidimensional controlling shareholder has few channels by which to appropriate private benefits. The shareholder may cause the portfolio company to pay its representatives excessive directors' fees or otherwise secure perquisites, but this type of private benefit is both limited in amount and readily monitored by private shareholders because of securities law disclosure requirements.

In contrast, controlling shareholders with many operational ties to the company have many more channels through which to appropriate private benefits, some of which are more difficult for minority shareholders to detect, evaluate and challenge. For example, controlling shareholders in vertical relationships with the company can manipulate transfer pricing in ways that are difficult to detect and evaluate. Even if a controlling shareholder pays its supplier company a fair spot market price for the products it purchases, that price may be too low for an assured source of supply, but the existence of the assurance may be difficult to detect because it is likely implicit rather than explicit.

But while the purchaser of control whose relationship to the company will be multidimensional is more likely to increase the level of private benefits than a unidimensional purchaser (especially if the seller of control is unidimensional), the multidimensional purchaser also may have the promise of greater efficiency gains. To be sure, leveraged buyouts contemplate gains from the pure monitoring of a unidimensional relation, but securing gains from synergy requires a multidimensional relation.

---

[20] Elhauge (1992), *supra* note 17, reaches the same conclusion by a different route. The larger the control block, the larger will be the buyer's investment in the company and the smaller the private benefit from abusing control. Thus, sale of office does not suggest that the buyer is more likely to abuse control absent the more particularized showing necessary for the sale to looters exception. Elhauge (1992), *supra* note 17, at 1512-13.

[21] Holderness & Sheehan, (1988), *supra* note 3.

Second, the emphasis on the potential for different levels of private benefits to be taken by purchasers and sellers of control in turn emphasizes the importance of the underlying substantive law governing relations between controlling shareholders and their companies.   The more rigorous the substantive law, the less important are differences between controlling shareholders. This suggests that focusing so much academic attention on the equal opportunity aspect of Perlman v. Feldmann may be to allow the tail to wag the dog. Some of the energy might instead be devoted to formulating more effective fiduciary rules governing the manner in which controlling shareholders operate the company on an ongoing basis.

2. Empirical Results

As discussed earlier, the unequal division rule states a testable hypothesis: to be efficient, sales of control at a premium should result in increases in the value of minority shares. Perlman v. Feldmann provides a test case. Over the two months prior to the sale, during which negotiations were taking place, Newport's stock experienced abnormal returns of 32%. Over the entire year of the sale, abnormal returns were 77%.[22] Because market price measures the value of minority shares in a corporation that has a controlling shareholder,[23] these data show that minority shareholders benefitted from Feldmann's sale of control. Given the unusual circumstances of the steel industry at this time, one might object that these abnormal returns might have been caused by unusually positive stock market performance by the steel industry generally, rather than from Feldmann's sale of control. However, the positive abnormal returns persist when Newport's stock performance is adjusted by reference to the returns of the three largest U.S. steel producers: Newport's minority shareholders experienced industry adjusted abnormal returns of 13% in the week of the transaction's announcement, 34% over the two months of the negotiations, and 29% over the year of the sale.[24]

The experience of Newport's minority shareholders seems to generalize. In the same study, Barclay & Holderness collected a sample of 44 block trades of at least 5% of the stock of New York or American Stock Exchange listed companies that occurred between 1978 and 1982. The sample was

---

[22] Michael Barclay & Clifford Holderness, *The Law and Large Block Trades*, 35 J.L. & Econ. 265, 270 (1992).

[23] In that situation, only minority shareholders sell their shares over the market. See Ronald Lease, John McConnell & Wayne Mikkelson, *The Market Value of Differential Voting Rights in Closely Held Corporations*, 57 J.Bus. 443, 446 (1984).

[24] *Id.* at 270 n.7. Note that the year of the sale was a good one for the steel industry generally. While Newport experienced market adjusted returns of 77% for that period, industry adjusted returns were only 29%, indicating that the industry outperformed the market by roughly 48%.

limited to sales where the price paid for the block exceeded the post-announcement market price of minority stock (that is, the market price) and the company remained independent for at least a year after the sale.[25] Limiting the sample to trades at a price above post-announcement price presents the hardest case for the efficiency of an unequal distribution rule. Unless the buyer receives private benefits so that the value of the block shares exceeds the market price, the buyer loses money on the transaction. Despite the fact that the purchasers in the sample had to extract private benefits, minority shareholders experienced positive abnormal returns of 2.1% on the sale's announcement, 7.9% over the four month period beginning two months before announcement of the sale, and 15.7% over the 18 month period beginning 6 months before the trade.

Does this data demonstrate that an unequal division rule is more efficient than an equal opportunity rule? While data are consistent with that result, they do not establish it because the legal regime under which the sample purchases occurred did not impose a pure unequal division rule. Rather, as Mendel v. Carroll and § 5.16 of the ALI Corporate Governance Project show, the unequal division rule was qualified by three exceptions that more or less encouraged an equal opportunity rule in those circumstances where the risk to minority shareholders was greatest.

Some sketchy evidence exists concerning the impact of unidimensional as opposed to multidimensional controlling shareholders. In a recent study, Michael Barclay, Clifford Holderness and Jeffrey Pontiff examine a sample limited to multidimensional controlling shareholders in a quite special context: closed end mutual funds.[26] These are funds whose assets consist of marketable securities, but whose shares often trade at a discount to the market value of their underlying assets.[27] Controlling shareholders could convert these funds into open end funds which stand ready to redeem their shares at the market value of their underlying assets. Doing so would immediately eliminate the discount, thereby creating an immediate increase in value that the controlling and minority shareholders would share proportionately. A block holder would decline to "open-end" its fund only if the private benefits from control exceeded the blockholder's portion of the discount that would be eliminated by converting the fund.

The authors report evidence consistent with the presence of a controlling shareholder reducing minority shareholder wealth: the average discount for funds without controlling shareholders was 4.1%, while the average discount for funds with controlling shareholders was 14.2%. These controlling shareholders had multidimensional relations with their closed-end funds. Controlling shareholders served as investment advisers, financial researchers,

---

[25] The point of excluding companies that were subsequently taken over was to exclude sales that were perceived as a precursor to a premium offer for the minority stock.

[26] Michael Barclay, Clifford Holderness & Jeffrey Pontiff, *Private Benefits from Block Ownership and Discounts on Closed-End Funds*, 33 J.Fin.Econ. 263 (1993).

[27] Closed-end fund discounts are also discussed in Chapter 14, *supra*.

and stockbrokers for their funds; and relatives and associates of controlling shareholders were often employed by their funds.

To be sure, closed end funds are unusual creatures whose behavior cannot easily be generalized to operating companies. However, the data are sufficient to support the intuition that the opportunities for controlling shareholders to take private benefits differ depending on the character of their relation to their firm. Further research that divided the samples of previous studies along this dimension would be a useful addition to what we know about the impact of controlling shareholders.

CHAPTER 22: FREEZEOUT MERGERS

After a successful tender offer, whether hostile or friendly, or after a partial acquisition through the private purchase of control, an acquiring company inevitably will be left as the owner of a subsidiary with at least some minority shareholders. Whether because of sloth, lack of sophistication, or considered decision, some target company shareholders will not tender their shares. And in a private purchase of control, minority shareholders will not have had the opportunity to participate at all. An acquiring company's major post-acquisition corporate law concern is how the remaining target company shareholders must be treated. Can they be eliminated from further participation in the target company even if they object? Alternatively, if they are not eliminated from further participation in the target company, what standards govern their treatment by the acquiring company as the new majority shareholder?

Section A begins our analysis by considering why an acquiring company would want to freeze out minority shareholders following a successful tender offer in the first place: What is gained by eliminating minority shareholders that is worth the substantial premium that is typically paid? Section B examines the mechanical techniques by which freezeouts can be effected. Sections C and D trace the development of state and federal standards governing a controlling shareholder's power to freeze out minority shareholders. Section E then turns to the other side of the freezeout problem: The situation of minority shareholders in a target company who, because the acquiring company *declines* to freeze them out, are effectively "frozen in."

A. How Serious is the Acquiring Company's Problem?

It seems quite clear that acquiring companies, or at least those counseling acquiring companies, regard the flexibility to eliminate minority shareholders as crucial to their acquisition planning. Two experienced practitioners put the matter flatly: "The ability to squeeze out minority shareholders and thus obtain 100% of the equity of a corporation is a basic condition of the current market for corporations."[1] The starting point for analysis is to understand why this ability is thought to be so important. From a planning perspective, the need for the inquiry is apparent. The decision to freeze out a minority should be made by carefully comparing the costs and benefits of the minority's continued participation with the costs and benefits of freezing them out. From a policy perspective, the inquiry is equally

---

[1] Leo Herzel & Dale Colling, *Squeeze-Out Mergers in Delaware -- The Delaware Supreme Court Decision in Weinberger v. UOP, Inc.,* 7 Corp.L.Rev. 195, 196 (1984). For this reason, freezeout mergers were the focus of defensive planners' early efforts at designing defensive tactics. As described in Chapter 17, the original "flip-over" poison pill and some forms of shark repellent amendments were intended to deter hostile takeovers by making a freezeout merger more difficult. Chapter 23 tracks a similar strategy in state antitakeover legislation.

important. If the interests of the acquiring company and the remaining target shareholders ultimately must be balanced, we need to understand what each side has at stake.

1.   Discouraging Free-riders

One explanation for why it is important to acquirers to be able to freeze out minority shareholders focuses not on the post-acquisition consequences of minority shareholders' continued participation, but on the possibility that the tender offer will be less likely to succeed in the first place if target shareholders have the option of remaining shareholders in the target company following the offer. The idea is that when a tender offer is made, target shareholders will infer that the acquiring company must believe that the target company is worth more than the tender offer price or else it would not have made the offer. If this is correct, then target shareholders may respond strategically by not tendering, instead "free-riding" on the acquiring company's discovery of the target company's real value. If every target shareholder believes that her decision not to tender will not affect the offer's likelihood of success, no one will tender, no offer will succeed and, in anticipation of this behavior, no acquirer will make a bid and the market for corporate control will grind to a halt. Thus, the argument runs, the ability to freeze out non-tendering shareholders is necessary to discourage free-riding.[2]

The problem with the argument is that it focuses on only one method of discouraging free-riding. There are, however, alternatives. The empirical evidence canvassed in Chapter 21B concerning the ability of controlling shareholders to receive private benefits from the controlled corporation demonstrates that an acquiring company can allocate to itself a disproportionate share of the gains from post-acquisition transactions with its new subsidiary. This ability is itself a substantial barrier to free-riding even if minority shareholders cannot be frozen out. No matter how carefully the duty of loyalty is drawn, the costs of monitoring the numerous transactions between a parent company and a subsidiary with minority shareholders assures the parent at least some opportunity to structure transactions so as to favor itself. This irreducible friction serves to mitigate any free-rider problem because it makes it unattractive to remain a minority shareholder in a subsidiary. To the extent the duty of loyalty is less than carefully drawn, a subject of inquiry in Section A.4. of this Chapter, the incentive to free-ride is further reduced.

The available empirical evidence supports the idea that post-acquisition "self-dealing" by the acquiring company serves to discourage free-riding by target company shareholders. Michael Bradley examined the post-offer performance of target companies' stock following successful partial tender

---

[2] See Sanford Grossman & Oliver Hart, *Takeover Bids, the Free Rider Problem, and the Theory of the Corporation*, 11 Bell J.Econ. 42 (1980).

offers. For free-riding to be profitable, the value of the remaining target company stock would have to rise above the tender offer price. In fact, the post-offer price fell by 13%, leading Bradley to conclude that acquiring companies profit not by an increase in the value of the *target* company stock acquired, which would be shared by the remaining target shareholders, but through an increase in the value of the *acquiring* company's stock as a result of the ability to control target company resources.[3] The remaining shareholders, however, cannot share in this gain, so free-riding is impossible.

2.   Access to Target Company Assets

It is not uncommon for an acquiring company to be dependent on access to target company assets in order to pay off the debt incurred to finance the acquisition. If minority shareholders are not eliminated, the argument goes, then whether what is sought is the target company's existing cash, or the proceeds of post-acquisition sales of target company assets, the price of the acquiring company's access to those resources is the distribution of a proportionate amount to any remaining minority shareholders. That minority shareholders must participate proportionately in any distribution of target company assets does not, however, establish the desirability of freezing out the minority to eliminate their participation. The missing step in the argument is to compare the cost of freezing out the minority with the cost of alternative methods of gaining access to target company assets.

This balance does not necessarily favor a freezeout. Suppose an acquiring company has purchased through a tender offer 90% of the stock in a target company with a net book value of $500 million, including $50 million in cash. Further suppose that the acquiring company needs the target company's cash in order to repay its acquisition financing. One way of accomplishing this is to cause the target company to pay a $50 million dividend. This method would yield the acquiring company either $41.85 million or $45 million depending on whether it would be allowed to deduct 80% or 100% of the dividend in computing its taxable income:

---

[3] Michael Bradley, *Interfirm Tender Offers and the Market for Corporate Control*, 35 J.Bus. 345, 364, 365-68 (1980) (discussed in Chapter 14, *supra*); see Gregg Jarrell & Michael Bradley, *The Economic Effects of Federal and State Regulations of Cash Tender Offers*, 23 J.L. & Econ. 371, 381-82 (1980).

	80% Dividend Deduction[4] (in thousands)	100% Dividend Deduction[5] (in thousands)
Gross Dividend	$50,000	$50,000
Less: 10% to minority shareholders	(5,000)	(5,000)
Less: acquiring company tax on receipt of dividend	(3,150)	0
Net amount received by acquiring company	$41,850	$45,000

Estimating the cost of securing access to the target company's cash through a freezeout is more difficult because of the need to specify what price minority shareholders would be paid for their shares. We can, however, at least identify the factors to which the calculation is sensitive. In order for the acquiring company to have after-tax access to as much cash by means of a freezeout as it would have if it merely caused the target company to pay out a dividend, the freezeout price would have to be less than book value if the 100% dividend received deduction applied,[6] or less than 106.2% of book value if the 80% dividend received deduction applied.[7] The higher the premium that has to be paid the minority, the more favorable the dividend approach.

Two objections can be raised to this analysis. The first recognizes that the acquiring company is left in an apparently quite different position

---

[4] Under IRC § 243(c), a corporation that owns more than 20% of the voting power and value of a corporation is allowed to deduct 80% of the dividends received from that corporation. Assuming a 35% maximum corporate tax rate, the effective tax rate for the acquiring corporation is 7%, the rate used for the calculation in the text.

[5] A corporation can achieve a 100% dividend deduction under IRC § 243(a)(3) with respect to dividends from a member of its affiliated group under IRC § 1504(a). However, the 100% deduction applies only to earnings in years in which the dividend paying corporation was a member of the affiliated group -- i.e., the 100% deduction applies only to post-acquisition earnings.

[6] The book value of the remaining ten% would be $50 million, leaving the acquiring company with complete ownership of a subsidiary with a book value of $450 million following the freezeout. After the dividend, the acquiring company would have $45 million in cash from the dividend plus 90% of the remaining book value of $450 million, a total of $450 million. Note, however, that the freezeout would use up the target company's cash, thereby necessitating a refinancing, rather than a pay off, of the acquisition debt.

[7] If the 80% dividend received deduction applied, the acquiring company would have $41.85 million in cash from the dividend after tax plus 90% of the remaining book value of $450 million, a total of $446.85 million. If the freezeout price of the minority shares were 106.3% of the book value, the total price would be $53.15 million, leaving the acquiring company with complete ownership of a subsidiary with a book value of $446.85 million.

depending on which method of securing access to the target company's assets is chosen: If a dividend is paid, the acquiring company still only owns 90% of the company, while if the minority is frozen out the acquiring company then owns the entire company. The validity of this objection depends on what price is paid in the freezeout. Because a dividend reduces the value of the company, it can be seen as a down payment on the purchase of the minority shares. As a result, the objection is only valid if the purchase price that would be paid in the freezeout is lower than the implicit price reflected in the decrease in the market value of minority stock following the dividend. Put differently, 90% of a larger number may be more than 100% of a smaller number.

There is reason to believe that the freezeout price may be higher than the implicit price of allowing the minority to remain. Here the comparison is between the constraints on the acquiring company's ability to set a low price in the freezeout and the constraints on its ability to reduce the value of the minority's continuing interest through favoring itself in the ongoing conduct of the business. The availability of a statutory appraisal proceeding in a freezeout, as discussed in Section B of this Chapter, may well be more restrictive than judicial limits on self-dealing by the parent company in an affiliated group both because of lenient legal rules, and because it is expensive for minority shareholders to monitor effectively how much self-dealing actually takes place.[8]

The second objection to the claim that it may be more favorable to an acquiring company to gain access to the target company's assets by means of a dividend than by means of a freezeout is legal rather than financial: Would not the payment of a dividend solely because of the needs of the acquiring company violate the fiduciary duty owed minority shareholders by a majority shareholder? The Delaware Supreme Court considered precisely this point in the following case.

SINCLAIR OIL CORP. v. LEVIEN
280 A.2d 717 (Del.1971)

WOLCOTT, C.J., CAREY, J., and CHRISTIE, J., sitting.

WOLCOTT, Chief Justice. This is an appeal by the defendant, Sinclair Oil Corporation (hereafter Sinclair), from an order of the Court of Chancery, 261 A.2d 911 in a derivative action requiring Sinclair to account for damages sustained by its subsidiary, Sinclair Venezuelan Oil Company (hereafter Sinven), organized by Sinclair for the purpose of operating in Venezuela, as a result of dividends paid by Sinven, the denial to Sinven of industrial

---

[8] The legal rules governing the treatment of minority shareholders in an affiliated group are discussed in Section A.4 of this Chapter, *infra*.

development, and a breach of contract between Sinclair's wholly-owned subsidiary, Sinclair International Oil Company, and Sinven.[a]

Sinclair, operating primarily as a holding company, is in the business of exploring for oil and of producing and marketing crude oil and oil products. At all times relevant to this litigation, it owned about 97% of Sinven's stock. The plaintiff owns about 3,000 of 120,000 publicly held shares of Sinven. Sinven, incorporated in 1922, has been engaged in petroleum operations primarily in Venezuela and since 1959 has operated exclusively in Venezuela.

Sinclair nominates all members of Sinven's board of directors. The Chancellor found as a fact that the directors were not independent of Sinclair. Almost without exception, they were officers, directors, or employees of corporations in the Sinclair complex. By reason of Sinclair's domination, it is clear that Sinclair owed Sinven a fiduciary duty. Getty Oil Co. v. Skelly Oil Co., 267 A.2d 883 (Del.1970); Cottrell v. Pawcatuck Co., 116 A.2d 787 (Del.Ch.1955). Sinclair concedes this.

The Chancellor held that because of Sinclair's fiduciary duty and its control over Sinven, its relationship with Sinven must meet the test of intrinsic fairness. The standard of intrinsic fairness involves both a high degree of fairness and a shift in the burden of proof. Under this standard the burden is on Sinclair to prove, subject to careful judicial scrutiny, that its transactions with Sinven were objectively fair. Guth v. Loft, Inc., 5 A.2d 503 (Del.1939); Sterling v. Mayflower Hotel Corp., 93 A.2d 107 (Del.1952); Getty Oil Co. v. Skelly Oil Co., *supra*.

Sinclair argues that the transactions between it and Sinven should be tested, not by the test of intrinsic fairness with the accompanying shift of the burden of proof, but by the business judgment rule under which a court will not interfere with the judgment of a board of directors unless there is a showing of gross and palpable overreaching. Meyerson v. El Paso Natural Gas Co., 246 A.2d 789 (Del.Ch.1967). A board of directors enjoys a presumption of sound business judgment, and its decisions will not be disturbed if they can be attributed to any rational business purpose. A court under such circumstances will not substitute its own notions of what is or is not sound business judgment.

We think, however, that Sinclair's argument in this respect is misconceived. When the situation involves a parent and a subsidiary, with the parent controlling the transaction and fixing the terms, the test of intrinsic fairness, with its resulting shifting of the burden of proof, is applied. Sterling v. Mayflower Hotel Corp., *supra*; David J. Greene & Co. v. Dunhill International, Inc., 249 A.2d 427 (Del.Ch.1968); Bastian v. Bourns, Inc., 256 A.2d 680 (Del.Ch.1969), *aff'd per curiam* (unreported) (Del.1970). The basic situation for the application of the rule is the one in which the parent has received a benefit to the exclusion and at the expense of the subsidiary.

---

[a] The portion of the opinion concerning the denial of development and the breach of contract appears in Section A.4 of this Chapter, *infra*. Eds.

Recently, this court dealt with the question of fairness in parent-subsidiary dealings in Getty Oil Co. v. Skelly Oil Co., *supra*. In that case, both parent and subsidiary were in the business of refining and marketing crude oil and crude oil products. The Oil Import Board ruled that the subsidiary, because it was controlled by the parent, was no longer entitled to a separate allocation of imported crude oil. The subsidiary then contended that it had a right to share the quota of crude oil allotted to the parent. We ruled that the business judgment standard should be applied to determine this contention.   Although the subsidiary suffered a loss through the administration of the oil import quotas, the parent gained nothing.   The parent's quota was derived solely from its own past use. The past use of the subsidiary did not cause an increase in the parent's quota. Nor did the parent usurp a quota of the subsidiary. Since the parent received nothing from the subsidiary to the exclusion of the minority stockholders of the subsidiary, there was no self-dealing. Therefore, the business judgment standard was properly applied.

A parent does indeed owe a fiduciary duty to its subsidiary when there are parent-subsidiary dealings.   However, this alone will not evoke the intrinsic fairness standard.   This standard will be applied only when the fiduciary duty is accompanied by self-dealing -- the situation when a parent is on both sides of a transaction with its subsidiary. Self-dealing occurs when the parent, by virtue of its domination of the subsidiary, causes the subsidiary to act in such a way that the parent receives something from the subsidiary to the exclusion of, and detriment to, the minority stockholders of the subsidiary.

We turn now to the facts. The plaintiff argues that, from 1960 through 1966, Sinclair caused Sinven to pay out such excessive dividends that the industrial development of Sinven was effectively prevented, and it became in reality a corporation in dissolution.

From 1960 through 1966, Sinven paid out $108,000,000 in dividends ($38,000,000 in excess of Sinven's earnings during the same period). The Chancellor held that Sinclair caused these dividends to be paid during a period when it had a need for large amounts of cash. Although the dividends paid exceeded earnings, the plaintiff concedes that the payments were made in compliance with 8 Del.C. § 170, authorizing payment of dividends out of surplus or net profits. However, the plaintiff attacks these dividends on the ground that they resulted from an improper motive -- Sinclair's need for cash. The Chancellor, applying the intrinsic fairness standard, held that Sinclair did not sustain its burden of proving that these dividends were intrinsically fair to the minority stockholders of Sinven.

Since it is admitted that the dividends were paid in strict compliance with 8 Del.C. § 170, the alleged excessiveness of the payments alone would not state a cause of action. Nevertheless, compliance with the applicable statute may not, under all circumstances, justify all dividend payments. If a plaintiff can meet his burden of proving that a dividend cannot be grounded on any reasonable business objective, then the courts can and will interfere with the board's decision to pay the dividend.

Sinclair contends that it is improper to apply the intrinsic fairness standard to dividend payments even when the board which voted for the dividends is completely dominated. In support of this contention, Sinclair relies heavily on American District Telegraph Co. [ADT] v. Grinnell Corp., (N.Y.Sup.Ct.1969), *aff'd*, 33 A.D.2d 769, 306 N.Y.S.2d 209 (1969). Plaintiffs were minority stockholders of ADT, a subsidiary of Grinnell. The plaintiffs alleged that Grinnell, realizing that it would soon have to sell its ADT stock because of a pending anti-trust action, caused ADT to pay excessive dividends. Because the dividend payments conformed with applicable statutory law, and the plaintiffs could not prove an abuse of discretion, the court ruled that the complaint did not state a cause of action. . . .

We do not accept the argument that the intrinsic fairness test can never be applied to a dividend declaration by a dominated board, although a dividend declaration by a dominated board will not inevitably demand the application of the intrinsic fairness standard. Moskowitz v. Bantrell, 190 A.2d 749 (Del.1963). If such a dividend is in essence self-dealing by the parent, then the intrinsic fairness standard is the proper standard. For example, suppose a parent dominates a subsidiary and its board of directors. The subsidiary has outstanding two classes of stock, X and Y. Class X is owned by the parent and Class Y is owned by minority stockholders of the subsidiary. If the subsidiary, at the direction of the parent, declares a dividend on its Class X stock only, this might well be self-dealing by the parent. It would be receiving something from the subsidiary to the exclusion of and detrimental to its minority stockholders. This self-dealing, coupled with the parent's fiduciary duty, would make intrinsic fairness the proper standard by which to evaluate the dividend payments.

Consequently it must be determined whether the dividend payments by Sinven were, in essence, self-dealing by Sinclair. The dividends resulted in great sums of money being transferred from Sinven to Sinclair. However, a proportionate share of this money was received by the minority shareholders of Sinven. Sinclair received nothing from Sinven to the exclusion of its minority stockholders. As such, these dividends were not self-dealing. We hold therefore that the Chancellor erred in applying the intrinsic fairness test as to these dividend payments. The business judgment standard should have been applied.

We conclude that the facts demonstrate that the dividend payments complied with the business judgment standard and with 8 Del.C. § 170. The motives for causing the declaration of dividends are immaterial unless the plaintiff can show that the dividend payments resulted from improper motives and amounted to waste. The plaintiff contends only that the dividend payments drained Sinven of cash to such an extent that it was prevented from expanding.

The third objection may be more troublesome.   If the acquiring company's financing requires that the lender be given security interests in the target company's assets, a freezeout merger may be essential because the company's assets cannot be pledged to secure a controlling shareholder's debt. Nor can the problem be avoided by the controlling shareholder's target stock; the financing may violate margin rules. But even here there is an alternative. Suppose that after the acquisition the target company restructures by borrowing enough that, when the proceeds are paid out as a dividend, the acquiring company can pay off its lenders. Why would not this form of restructuring financing serve the same purpose? Would *Sinclair* block a refinancing done for the benefit of a controlling shareholder if the dividend was paid pro rata?

3.   Eliminating the Costs of Public Ownership

One reason for wanting to eliminate minority shareholders is simply that they cost too much. Issuers subject to reporting under § 13 of the Securities Exchange Act of 1934 are required to file with the Securities Exchange Commission, *inter alia,* a Form 10-K Annual Report, Form 10-Q Quarterly Reports, and Form 8-K Current Reports.   Additionally, those issuers registered under § 12 of the Act, essentially all companies whose securities are listed on a national securities exchange and all companies having total assets in excess of $3 million and a class of equity securities held of record by 500 or more persons, are also subject to the proxy solicitation rules of § 14.[9] Additional costs arise from the need to maintain transfer agents, stock exchange listings and the like. Of course, all of these obligations disappear with the elimination of minority shareholders.[10]

At least in absolute amounts, these costs appear to be non-trivial. Practitioners estimate that the out-of-pocket costs associated with public ownership of a company range generally from $60,000 to $200,000,[11] and from $150,000 to $400,000 for a company of a size that meets American Stock Exchange listing requirements.[12] Based on these figures, the present value of eliminating these costs, assuming capitalization as a perpetuity at

---

[9] There are also reporting requirements imposed by some state corporation laws. See, e.g., Cal.Corp.Code § 1501 (mailing of annual balance sheet and income statement and, for corporations with more than 100 shareholders, information concerning transactions with directors and officers).

[10] Under §§ 12(g)(4) and 15(d), all reporting and other obligations under §§ 13 and 14 of the Securities Exchange Act are lifted when the number of shareholders drops below 300.

[11] Carl Schneider, Joseph Manko & Robert Kant, *Going Public: Practice, Procedure and Consequences,* 27 Vill.L.Rev. 1 (1981). We have doubled the authors' estimates to take into account inflation in the cost of legal services.

[12] Arthur Borden, *Going Private -- Old Tort, New Tort, or No Tort?,* 49 NYU L.Rev. 987, 1007 (1974). We have also doubled these estimates.

10%, ranges from $600,000 to $4,000,000. Particularly when the target company is small, an acquiring company would find the opportunity to save amounts of this magnitude very attractive.

The larger the size of the target company, however, the less likely that these cost savings alone would be sufficient to justify paying the premium necessary to eliminate the target company's remaining minority shareholders. This can be seen by comparing the per share value of the savings with the per share premium that would be required in a freezeout. Because the costs of public ownership do not rise proportionately with the size of the company, we would expect that as the size of the target company increases, the likelihood that the cost of the premium will exceed the compliance savings also increases.

A final qualification concerning the claim that it is important to be able to freeze out minority shareholders in order to save the costs of public ownership is that it ignores the possibility that there also may be gains from public ownership. This idea finds some support in the increased frequency with which public ownership of a minority interest in a previously wholly-owned subsidiary is intentionally created either by a public offering or by spinning off some portion of the subsidiary's shares to the parent company's shareholders. The explanation for this seeming retrogression is that the market will value the subsidiary more highly when it has a public minority than when it is a wholly-owned subsidiary.[13] What assumptions about information costs would be necessary for this strategy to be consistent with the Efficient Capital Market Hypothesis?

4.   Capturing the Gains from Synergy

In an important sense, it is really not surprising that preventing free-riding, or having access to the target company's assets, or avoiding the costs of a regulatory regime, do not seem to explain why acquiring companies believe that freezing out minority shareholders is so central to their acquisition strategies. One lesson of Part II was that among the most persuasive explanations for how an acquiring company actually might make money through an acquisition is synergy -- that combining the acquiring and

---

[13] Gailen Hite & James Owers, *Security Price Reactions Around Corporate Spin-Off Announcements,* 12 J.Fin.Econ. 409 (1983); James Miles & James Rosenfeld, *The Effect of Voluntary Spin-Off Announcements on Shareholder Wealth,* 38 J.Fin. 1597 (1983); and Katherine Schipper & Abbie Smith, *Effects of Recontracting on Shareholder Wealth: The Case of Voluntary Spin-Offs,* 12 J.Fin. 437 (1983), all report positive abnormal returns to the parent company shareholders of about 3% in the two day period ending on the date of the Wall Street Journal announcement of the spinoff. Katherine Schipper & Abbie Smith, *A Comparison of Equity Carve-Outs and Equity Offerings: Share Price Effects and Corporate Restructuring,* 15 J.Fin.Econ. 153 (1986), report positive abnormal returns of 1.8% over the five day period around announcement of a public offering of a portion of the stock of a previously wholly-owned subsidiary.

target companies results in a post-acquisition value in excess of the sum of their pre-acquisition independent values. Most explanations for synergy, however, require that there be central control of the combined businesses in order to maximize overall value. But what if maximizing overall value causes the resulting gains to be shared unequally, that is, minority shareholders of one member of the affiliated group may not do as well as shareholders of the parent? For example, opportunities for new activities must be allocated among companies in the affiliated group. Can they be allocated to the most appropriate member of the group or must all members who have minority shareholders be allowed to participate?[14] Similarly, where synergy is intended to result from the merger of the constituent companies' administrative and support systems, there may be problems with allocating the costs and benefits in a way in which the minority shareholders of different affiliates participate equally. If equality is required by law but cannot be achieved -- either because inequality is necessary to achieving the synergy itself or because it is too expensive to create systems that measure and enforce equality -- then the ability to freeze out minority shareholders actually may be critical to an acquisition's success.

Under this analysis, the importance of freezing out minority shareholders is a function of the stringency of the legal standard governing review of the acquiring company's post-transaction conduct of the target company's business. As with the legal standard governing acquiring company access to target company assets, Sinclair Oil Corp. v. Levien, *supra*, which also involved claims both of unequal allocation of opportunities for new activities and of unequal allocation of the benefits of transactions between members of the affiliated group, is the classic statement of the governing law.

SINCLAIR OIL CORP. v. LEVIEN
280 A.2d 717 (Del.1971)

   . . . The plaintiff proved no business opportunities which came to Sinven independently and which Sinclair either took to itself or denied to Sinven. As a matter of fact, with two minor exceptions which resulted in losses, all of Sinven's operations have been conducted in Venezuela, and Sinclair had a policy of exploiting its oil properties located in different countries by subsidiaries located in the particular countries.

From 1960 to 1966 Sinclair purchased or developed oil fields in Alaska, Canada, Paraguay, and other places around the world. The plaintiff contends that these were all opportunities which could have been taken by Sinven. The Chancellor concluded that Sinclair had not proved that its denial of expansion opportunities to Sinven was intrinsically fair. He based this conclusion on the following findings of fact. Sinclair made no real effort to expand Sinven.

---

[14] Would a sharing requirement be consistent with Williamson's idea of achieving synergy by internalizing the allocative functions of the capital market? See Chapter 9B, *supra*.

The excessive dividends paid by Sinven resulted in so great a cash drain as to effectively deny to Sinven any ability to expand. During this same period Sinclair actively pursued a company-wide policy of developing through its subsidiaries new sources of revenue, but Sinven was not permitted to participate and was confined in its activities to Venezuela.

However, the plaintiff could point to no opportunities which came to Sinven. Therefore, Sinclair usurped no business opportunity belonging to Sinven. Since Sinclair received nothing from Sinven to the exclusion of and detriment to Sinven's minority stockholders, there was no self-dealing. Therefore, business judgment is the proper standard by which to evaluate Sinclair's expansion policies.

Since there is no proof of self-dealing on the part of Sinclair, it follows that the expansion policy of Sinclair and the methods used to achieve the desired result must, as far as Sinclair's treatment of Sinven is concerned, be tested by the standards of the business judgment rule. Accordingly, Sinclair's decision, absent fraud or gross overreaching, to achieve expansion through the medium of its subsidiaries, other than Sinven, must be upheld.

Even if Sinclair was wrong in developing these opportunities as it did, the question arises, with which subsidiaries should these opportunities have been shared? No evidence indicates a unique need or ability of Sinven to develop these opportunities. The decision of which subsidiaries would be used to implement Sinclair's expansion policy was one of business judgment with which a court will not interfere absent a showing of gross and palpable overreaching. Meyerson v. El Paso Natural Gas Co., 246 A.2d 789 (Del.Ch.1967). No such showing has been made here.

Next, Sinclair argues that the Chancellor committed error when he held it liable to Sinven for breach of contract.

In 1961 Sinclair created Sinclair International Oil Company (hereafter International), a wholly-owned subsidiary used for the purpose of coordinating all of Sinclair's foreign operations. All crude purchases by Sinclair were made thereafter through International.

On September 28, 1961, Sinclair caused Sinven to contract with International whereby Sinven agreed to sell all of its crude oil and refined products to International at specified prices. The contract provided for minimum and maximum quantities and prices. The plaintiff contends that Sinclair caused this contract to be breached in two respects. Although the contract called for payment on receipt, International's payments lagged as much as 30 days after receipt. Also, the contract required International to purchase at least a fixed minimum amount of crude and refined products from Sinven. International did not comply with this requirement.

Clearly, Sinclair's act of contracting with its dominated subsidiary was self-dealing. Under the contract Sinclair received the products produced by Sinven, and of course the minority shareholders of Sinven were not able to share in the receipt of these products. If the contract was breached, then Sinclair received these products to the detriment of Sinven's minority shareholders. We agree with the Chancellor's finding that the contract was breached by Sinclair, both as to the time of payments and the amounts purchased.

Although a parent need not bind itself by a contract with its dominated subsidiary, Sinclair chose to operate in this manner. As Sinclair has received the benefits of this contract, so must it comply with the contractual duties.

Under the intrinsic fairness standard, Sinclair must prove that its causing Sinven not to enforce the contract was intrinsically fair to the minority shareholders of Sinven. Sinclair has failed to meet this burden. Late payments were clearly breaches for which Sinven should have sought and received adequate damages. As to the quantities purchased, Sinclair argues that it purchased all the products produced by Sinven. This, however, does not satisfy the standard of intrinsic fairness. Sinclair has failed to prove that Sinven could not possibly have produced or someway have obtained the contract minimums. As such, Sinclair must account on this claim.

Finally, Sinclair argues that the Chancellor committed error in refusing to allow it a credit or setoff of all benefits provided by it to Sinven with respect to all the alleged damages. The Chancellor held that setoff should be allowed on specific transactions, e.g., benefits to Sinven under the contract with International, but denied an over all setoff against all damages claimed. We agree with the Chancellor, although the point may well be moot in view of our holding that Sinclair is not required to account for the alleged excessiveness of the dividend payments.

We will therefore reverse that part of the Chancellor's order that requires Sinclair to account to Sinven for damages sustained as a result of dividends paid between 1960 and 1966, and by reason of the denial to Sinven of expansion during that period. We will affirm the remaining portion of that order and remand the cause for further proceedings.

Understanding what the *Sinclair* standard means is especially important because, in the end, the acquiring company's strategic decision depends on how stringent the standard is perceived to be. If the standard is thought to interfere with maximizing the post-transaction value of the combined companies, then the ability to freeze out the minority is important because it results in an increased post-transaction value. If the standard is thought to be sufficiently lenient that it does not interfere with maximizing post-transaction value, then the ability to freeze out the minority may not be very important after all. Finally, if the standard is thought to be so lenient that it allows the acquiring company to "exploit" the minority through favorable post-transaction dealings between the acquiring company and the target company, then the ability to freeze out the minority shareholders simply may be beside the point because no acquiring company would ever do so. That is, if the freezeout price would be the minority shareholders' pro rata share of future cash flows while, if the minority shareholders were frozen in, they would receive less than their pro rata share, the acquiring company has little incentive to be rid of them.

This is an area where lawyers play a central role. The business decision -- to freeze out or not to freeze out -- depends on an analysis of judicial decisions. As a result, the client's perception of the importance of the ability to freeze out minority shareholders depends, in the end, on the substance and accuracy of the legal advice the client receives. The problem, however, is that there seems to be a conflict between the conventional wisdom concerning the rigor of the legal standard governing the acquiring company's post-transaction dealings with the target company, and the conventional wisdom that the ability to freeze out minority shareholders is critical to an acquisition's success.

The academic evaluation of the limitations imposed by the *Sinclair* standard is unambiguous.[15] Professor Eisenberg states this view clearly: "The checks on unfair dealing by the parent are few. In theory, of course, the fairness of the parent's behavior is subject to the check of judicial review; but in practice such review is difficult even where the courts have the will to engage in it, and they often lack the will."[16] On this basis, one would predict a low incidence of freezeout mergers; why freeze them when you can fleece them instead. This prediction, however, seems to be inconsistent with observed reality. As was stressed at the outset of this Chapter, practitioners clearly think it desirable to freeze out any minority shareholders remaining after a successful acquisition and it seems their advice is followed: Second-step transactions are, if not the rule, then at least a familiar phenomenon.

One explanation for this conflict may be an important difference in orientation between the academics and the practitioners. Although the academic literature may accurately describe the forest, the fact is that there remains some significant variation among the trees. Not only do the courts of some states reach quite different conclusions than do those of Delaware,[17] but even the Delaware courts occasionally reach surprising results.[18] From

---

[15] That is not to say, however, that evaluation of the desirability of the standard is as consistent as evaluation of its content. Compare William Cary, *Federalism and Corporate Law: Reflections Upon Delaware*, 83 Yale L.J. 663 (1974), with Frank Easterbrook & Daniel Fischel, *Corporate Control Transactions*, 91 Yale L.J. 698 (1982).

[16] Melvin Eisenberg, *The Structure of the Corporation* 309 (1976).

[17] Suppose the target company has a large net operating loss carryover for federal income tax purposes that could be used to offset the acquiring company's taxable income if the acquiring company causes the target company to join in the filing of a consolidated federal income tax return (which generally is allowable if the acquiring company owns 80% or more of the target company's stock). Must some portion of the savings resulting from filing the consolidated return be allocated to the target company so that minority shareholders benefit from the use of the target's "tax asset"? Delaware does not require an allocation. Meyerson v. El Paso Natural Gas Co., 246 A.2d 789 (Del.Ch.1967). California, in contrast, does require an allocation. Smith v. Tele-Communication, Inc., 184 Cal.Rptr. 571 (Cal.App.1982).

[18] For example, in TransWorld Airlines v. Summa Corp., 374 A.2d 5 (Del.Ch.1977),

the practitioner's perspective, it may make little difference that the forest is accurately described if an aberrant tree nonetheless falls on his client. And if the lawyer also has an independent reason to be more risk averse than his client, we may have an explanation for why, even if the academic characterization of the leniency of the *Sinclair* standard is accurate, practitioners still advise clients that it is critical to be able to freeze out any remaining target shareholders.

If clients had perfect information, there would be little reason for a lawyer to be more risk averse than her client with respect to the freezeout decision. Assuming the academic characterization of the *Sinclair* standard is correct, the lawyer simply would advise the client both of the limited reach of the restrictions on how post-acquisition transactions with the target company can be structured, and of the lawyer's estimate of the likelihood of an aberrant judicial result if such post-acquisition transactions were ever challenged. If on that basis the client then chose not to effect a freezeout and the aberrant result in fact occurred, the lawyer would not need to fear an unhappy client. A client with perfect knowledge would know that the unfavorable outcome was the result of bad luck, not bad legal advice -- the client would realize that the lawyer accurately predicted the probability distribution of the outcomes associated with not freezing out the remaining target shareholders, but that the actual outcome just ended up at the unfavorable tail of the distribution.

If a client does not have perfect information, however, the lawyer's level of risk aversion may turn out to differ quite substantially from that of his client. As a result, the lawyer may give quite different advice then he would to a better informed client.

Two important aspects of the lawyer-client relationship change as a result of the client's imperfect information. First, the uninformed client lacks the ability to recognize the quality of legal services, whether *ex ante,* in choosing a lawyer, or *ex post,* in evaluating the quality of the services actually rendered by a lawyer. This results in the second alteration in the lawyer-client relationship: The lawyer then has an incentive to invest in

---

TransWorld Airlines (TWA) claimed that its 78% majority shareholder, Hughes Tool Company, had delayed TWA's acquisition of first generation commercial jet aircraft by controlling negotiations over the kind and number of aircraft acquired and the manner in which the acquisition would be financed. The Court held that "by preventing TWA from making its own arrangements for the acquisition of jet planes, the defendants retained the capability of arranging the terms of such acquisitions so as to benefit themselves. . . . Thus, it is clear on the present record that the minority shareholders of TWA received nothing in exchange for the strictures imposed by defendants on plaintiff's operations and that such stockholders may have suffered injury as a result of the loss of TWA's freedom to compete." 374 A.2d at 10. This behavior was found to violate the *Sinclair* standard. In contrast, the Court held that the fact that the majority shareholder profited by leasing jet aircraft it had acquired to competitors of TWA until permanent financing had been arranged for their acquisition by TWA, did not violate the *Sinclair* standard. *Id.*

developing a reputation for quality as a means of attracting clients.[19] These two factors interact in a manner that suggests a significant difference in level of risk aversion between the client and the lawyer with respect to decisions like whether to freeze out minority shareholders.

In the context of the freezeout decision, the client's inability to evaluate the quality of the lawyer's services even after they have been rendered means that the client cannot determine whether the occurrence of an aberrant judicial result with respect to the validity of post-acquisition transactions reflects only the random bad luck of ending up on the unfavorable tail of a distribution the lawyer accurately described, or whether the lawyer misdescribed the distribution of possible outcomes in the first place. And in this circumstance, it is not at all surprising that a client may end up equating the quality of the lawyer's services with how favorable the outcome was to the client.[20] The result is that the lawyer bears the risk of the court's decision; she will be blamed for a bad result even if she was right.

Because the lawyer's investment in reputation is essentially an investment in human capital that cannot easily be diversified,[21] one of the few ways the lawyer can protect herself against the risk *she* bears when the *client* chooses a risky strategy -- one with both favorable and unfavorable outcomes -- is to shy away from recommending risky strategies to a client in favor of strategies whose outcome is more certain. This is not necessarily in the client's best interest, however, because the lawyer is better off with certainty *even if the risky alternative has a higher expected value for the client.*

Clients, of course, do not have perfect knowledge. Thus, clients may well select a lawyer based on the lawyer's reputation for quality rather than on direct investigation of the lawyer's skills, and may well equate the quality of the services rendered with the desirability of the result actually achieved. If this is correct, then we would predict that risk averse lawyers would give their clients more conservative advice -- in our setting, by recommending that minority shareholders be frozen out -- even though there may be a more attractive, but risky alternative available, that of exploiting minority shareholders through transactions favorable to the acquiring company.[22]

B.   The Mechanics of Freezeouts

---

[19] Ronald Gilson & Robert Mnookin, *Sharing Among the Human Capitalists: An Economic Inquiry into the Corporate Law Firm and How Partners Split Profits,* 37 Stan.L.Rev. 313, 363 (1985).

[20] *Id.* at 360 n.78.

[21] *Id.* at 324-29.

[22] What would happen if clients became better informed? One way this could happen is for the client's choice of a lawyer to be made by another lawyer, such as the client's general counsel. If, as seems to be the case, the influence and quality of general counsel increase, *id.* at 381-83, would this fact change the prediction of what advice outside counsel will give?

The most common technique for freezing out remaining target shareholders is a merger.[23] It will be recalled from Chapter 16 that the vote of shareholders owning the requisite number of shares to approve a merger, typically a majority, binds those shareholders who either vote against the merger or who do not vote at all. At least as far as the text of the corporation statute is concerned, these shareholders must either accept the consideration offered or exercise their appraisal rights. Moreover, where the acquiring company's initial offer has been sufficiently successful, even the shareholder vote may be dispensed with. The corporation statutes of most leading commercial states allow a majority shareholder with a high enough ownership -- Delaware and California, for example, require 90%[24] -- to approve a merger without a vote of the target company shareholders, although target shareholders may still exercise appraisal rights following notification of the transaction.[25]

The critical aspect of the freezeout transaction is not, however, whether a vote of the target company shareholders is required. So long as there is no supermajority requirement to approve the transaction, the shareholder vote may be an inconvenience, but will not be a barrier; the acquiring company typically will have the votes necessary to approve the transaction itself. Rather, it is the type of consideration that can be used in the merger that is central to the freezeout concept. In particular, the very notion of a freezeout requires that the minority shareholders be paid off in cash. Target shareholders who receive shares of the acquiring company are not truly gone and, what may be worse, the issuance of the shares carries with it the potential to dilute the earnings of the acquiring company.

Authorization of the use of cash as consideration in mergers is of comparatively recent origin. In 1925, Florida became the first state to authorize "the distribution of *cash,* notes on bonds, in whole or in part, in lieu of stock to stockholders of the constituent corporations of any of them."[26]

---

[23] For this purpose, the choice of merger form -- straight, triangular, or reverse triangular -- would be dictated by the concerns discussed in Chapter 16. In the past freezeouts also took the form of 1) dissolution freezeouts in which the plan of dissolution provides for the distribution of the company's productive assets to the majority shareholder and only cash or notes to the minority shareholders; 2) sale of assets freezeouts in which the majority shareholder purchases for cash or notes the productive assets of the company leaving the minority shareholders with an interest only in the proceeds of the sale; and 3) reverse stock split freezeouts in which the outstanding shares of the company are consolidated pursuant to a plan that sets a ratio such that no minority shareholder own as much as one full share of stock, and also provides for the compulsory exchange of fractional shares for cash. With respect to dissolution and sale of assets freezeouts, see William Cary & Melvin Eisenberg, *Cases and Materials on Corporations* 1517-30 (5th ed.1980). With respect to reverse stock split freezeouts, see Michael Lawson, *Reverse Stock Splits: The Fiduciary's Obligations Under State Law,* 63 Cal.L.Rev. 1226 (1975).

[24] Del.Gen.Corp.Law § 263; Cal.Corp.Code § 1110(b).

[25] See generally Note, *The Short Merger Statute,* 32 U.Chi.L.Rev. 596 (1965).

[26] Act of June 1, 1925, ch. 10096, § 36, 1925 Fla. Laws 134 (emphasis added), quoted in Elliot Weiss, *The Law of Take Out Mergers: A Historical Perspective,* 56 NYU L.Rev. 624,

Other states quickly followed suit, although some disagreement remains as to whether these early statutes really were intended to authorize freezeout transactions.[27] In any event, later action by the state legislatures definitively resolved the issue. In 1949, New York extended the reach of a public utility short-form merger statute that expressly authorized the use of cash to cover all corporations, and in 1961 authorized the use of cash in long-form mergers. Delaware authorized the use of cash in short-form mergers in 1957 and in long-form mergers in 1967, and the Model Act followed suit in 1968 and 1969, respectively.[28]

C.   State Law Limitations on Freezeout Mergers

The history of state law limitations on the ability of an acquiring company to freeze out minority shareholders is one of the most interesting -- and eventful -- stories in modern corporate law. It reflects, among other influences, the impact of political forces on judicial opinions, the opening shots of an ongoing debate over the appropriate role of the federal and state governments in setting corporate law standards, and the practical circumstances governing whether minority shareholders have any meaningful way to challenge their treatment in a freezeout transaction. The stage on which this historical drama took place was, not surprisingly, the Delaware courts. Interestingly, its plot has a circular quality. In some critical respects, the denouement -- the result of years of legal turmoil and thousands of pages of judicial opinions and legal commentary -- may be to have returned the characters to where they began, albeit having covered a good deal of ground in the interim.

1.   The History of the Conflict Over Freezeout Mergers

The drama's first act began with the statutory changes authorizing cash mergers described in the previous section. The action continued with their broad judicial construction. In Coyne v. Park & Tilford Distillers Corp.[29] and Stauffer v. Standard Brands, Inc.,[30] the Delaware courts explicitly rejected minority shareholders' objections to the use of short-form cash mergers to freeze them out. In *Stauffer,* the court set the terms of the later debate by rejecting the claim that oppressive treatment by the majority would

---

632 (1981). The discussion of the development of the use of cash as consideration in a merger draws heavily on Professor Weiss' excellent article.

    [27] Compare Weiss (1981), *supra* note 26, at 637-41, with Borden (1974), *supra* note 12, at 1026-27.

    [28] Weiss (1981), *supra* note 26, at 648.

    [29] 154 A.2d 893 (Del.Ch.1959).

    [30] 187 A.2d 78 (Del.Ch.1962).

be grounds for challenging the merger; where "the real relief sought is the recovery of the monetary value of plaintiff's shares . . . the statutory appraisal provisions [provide] an adequate remedy."   187 A.2d at 80.   While acknowledging the "ever-present power of equity to deal with illegality or fraud," *id.*, the court severely limited the reach of those terms:

> Indeed it is difficult to imagine a case under the short-form merger statute in which there could be such actual fraud as would entitle a minority to set aside the merger. This is so because the very purpose of the statute is to provide the parent corporation a means of eliminating the minority shareholder's interest in the enterprise.

Id. The *Stauffer* holding was extended to long-form mergers in David J. Breene & Co. v. Schenley Industries[31] Thus, the terms of the doctrinal debate, and at least its interim resolution, were quite clearly set. The issue was the exclusivity of the appraisal remedy -- could minority shareholders who objected to a freezeout challenge the merger itself, rather than merely contesting the adequacy of the price paid them, by invoking appraisal. The resolution was virtual exclusivity.

The drama's second act was ushered in by a shift in the tactics of plaintiffs seeking to challenge freezeout mergers and the concomitant growth of a political threat to the dominance of state law, particularly Delaware law, in this area. Plaintiffs' tactical shift followed what was by then a familiar pattern in corporate litigation: When state courts were unreceptive to claims of fiduciary breach, the federal courts, through resort to federal securities law, were sought as a more receptive forum. This effort reached its high point in the decision by the United States Court of Appeals for the Second Circuit in Green v. Santa Fe Industries[32] The Court there held that an allegation that a majority shareholder breached its fiduciary duty by effecting a freezeout of the minority "without any justifiable business purpose"[33] stated a claim under Rule 10b-5, even though plaintiffs had elected not to pursue the appraisal remedy that was available under Delaware law, and even though there was full and accurate disclosure concerning the merger to the minority shareholders.

At the same time as federal law was making litigation inroads into areas previously the exclusive domain of state law, political activity developed in response to the same perceived problem -- insufficient protection of shareholders, especially minority shareholders, under state law. This activity sought the same end as the litigation efforts -- "federalizing" areas of state corporate law -- but through Congressional, rather than judicial action. The legislative proposals generally contemplated some form of federal chartering of, or specification of minimum standards for, publicly held corporations, the

---

[31] 281 A.2d 30 (Del.Ch.1971).

[32] 533 F.2d 1283 (2d Cir.1976), *rev'd*, 430 U.S. 462 (1977).

[33] *Id.* at 1291.

terms of which would preempt more lenient state law. Again, Delaware law figured most prominently in the political debate. In an influential article, Professor William Cary accused the Delaware legislature and judiciary of pandering to corporate management by leading a "race to the bottom" in fiduciary standards.[34] In addition to castigating the substance of Delaware corporate law, Cary despaired of any likelihood of state judicial reform. Tracing the links between the Delaware legislature, judiciary and corporate bar, Cary concluded that "major participation in state politics and in the leading firms inevitably would align the Delaware judiciary solidly with Delaware legislative policy."[35]   This led Cary to propose a "Federal Corporate Uniformity Act" that would override state law on critical fiduciary issues.[36] His proposal did not stand alone.[37]

Act III began with the United States Supreme Court's reversal of the Second Circuit's decision in *Santa Fe*. From Delaware's perspective, the Supreme Court's opinion contained both good and bad news. The good news was that the Supreme Court slowed the expansion of federal securities law into state corporate law by construing Rule 10b-5 to require deception -- misrepresentation or nondisclosure -- for a violation. Significantly, that construction was based in part on a recognition of the historic dominance of state law in setting corporate fiduciary standards. The Court stated that "[a]bsent a clear indication of congressional intent, we are reluctant to federalize the substantial portion of the law of corporations that deals with transactions in securities, particularly where established state policies of corporate regulation would be overridden."[38]   The bad news was that the opinion could also be read as giving support to the political effort to displace state law by the adoption of federal chartering or minimum standards legislation. Citing Professor Cary's article, the Court also noted that "[t]here may well be a need for uniform federal fiduciary standards to govern mergers such as that challenged in this complaint. . . ."[39]

Against this background, the Delaware Supreme Court decided Singer v. Magnavox Co., which had been argued and was under submission at the time the *Santa Fe* opinion was issued.[40]

---

[34] Cary (1974), *supra* note 15.

[35] *Id.* at 692.

[36] *Id.* at 700-03.

[37] See, e.g., Ralph Nader, *The Case for Federal Chartering,* in *Corporate Power in America* 67 (1973); Donald Schwartz, *Federal Chartering of Corporations: An Introduction,* 61 Geo.L.J. 71 (1972); Donald Schwartz, *The Case for Federal Chartering,* 31 Bus.Law. 1125 (1976).

[38] 430 U.S. at 479.

[39] *Id.* at 479-80.

[40] For other suggestions that the Delaware Supreme Court's decision in *Singer* was influenced by political considerations, see, e.g., Herzel & Colling (1984), *supra* note 1; Robert Thompson, *Squeeze-Out Mergers and the "New" Appraisal Remedy,* 62 Wash.U.L.Q. 415, 420 (1984); Victor Brudney & Marvin Chirelstein, *A Restatement of Corporate Freezeouts,* 87 Yale L.J. 1354, 1354 n.2 (1978).

SINGER v. MAGNAVOX CO.
380 A.2d 969 (Del.1977)

Before HERMANN, C.J., DUFFY and McNEILLY, JJ.

DUFFY, Justice. In this action attacking a statutory corporate merger, plaintiffs appeal from an order of the Court of Chancery granting defendants' motion to dismiss the complaint for failure to state a claim upon which relief can be granted. 367 A.2d 1349 (Del.Ch.1976).

I

The litigation centers on a merger in July 1975 of The Magnavox Company (Magnavox) with T.M.C. Development Corporation (T.M.C.). Plaintiffs owned common stock of Magnavox at the time of the merger and they bring this class action for all persons who held such shares on the day before the merger. Defendants are: Magnavox, North American Philips Corporation (North American), North American Philips Development Corporation (Development), and individual members of Magnavox management who held their positions in July 1975. All corporations involved are chartered in Delaware. T.M.C. is a wholly-owned subsidiary of Development, which in turn is owned entirely by North American. Apparently, Development's only function was to assist North American in the acquisition of Magnavox.

II

The salient facts appear in the complaint and in a stipulation of the parties.[1] These develop the following scenario:

On August 21, 1974, North American incorporated Development for the purpose of making a tender offer for the Magnavox common shares. Prior to that time, North American and Magnavox were independent, unaffiliated corporations. On August 28, Development offered to buy all Magnavox shares at a price of $8 per share.

The tender offer included a statement informing Magnavox shareholders of Development's intention to acquire the entire equity interest in Magnavox, and advising them of the possible effects thereof, including: (1) delisting of present or future Magnavox shares by the New York Stock Exchange; (2) creation of an unfavorable market for the shares; (3) loss of information rights granted under Rules of the Exchange and under Federal securities law; and (4) depending on the number of shares acquired, the employment of other means of acquisition, particularly: ". . . through open market purchases,

---

[1] For the purpose of the motion to dismiss, the facts are taken as true. . . .

through a tender or exchange offer, or by any other means deemed advisable by it or whether to propose a merger, a sale or exchange of assets, liquidation or some other transactions. . . ."

The directors of Magnavox voted to oppose the offer on the grounds of price inadequacy, among other things, and so notified their shareholders by letter issued on August 30. The letter stated, in part, that the "Company was shocked at the inadequacy of the offer of $8 per share in relationship to a book value in excess of $11.00. . . ."

In September 1974, the respective managements of Magnavox, North American and Development compromised their differences over the terms of the tender offer. They agreed to terms which included an increase in the offer price to $9 per share and, at the request of North American and Development, two-year employment contracts for sixteen officers of Magnavox (including some of the individual defendants) at existing salary levels. As part of the agreement, Magnavox withdrew its opposition to the tender offer. As modified, the offer was thus not opposed by Magnavox and, in response thereto, Development acquired approximately 84.1% of Magnavox's outstanding common stock.

With Development firmly in control of Magnavox, the managements of those two companies, and of North American, then set about acquiring all equity interest in Magnavox through a merger. In May 1975, Development caused the creation of T.M.C. for that purpose.

The directors of Magnavox unanimously agreed to the merger with T.M.C. and scheduled a special stockholders meeting for July 24, 1975, to vote on the plan. At the time of this action, four of the nine Magnavox directors were also directors of North American, and three others each had an employment contract, referred to above, with Magnavox and an option to purchase five thousand of North American's common shares, effective on the date of merger. In June 1975, the shareholders of Magnavox were given notice of the meeting with a proxy statement advising on the book value ($10.16) and merger price ($9.00) of the shares, and they were told that approval of the merger was assured since Development's holding alone was large enough to provide the requisite statutory majority. The proxy statement also advised the shareholders of their respective options to accept the merger price or to seek an appraisal under 8 Del.C. § 262. . . .

The meeting was held in Delaware as scheduled, the proxies were voted here, stockholder approval was given, and the merger was accomplished. . .
.

Thereafter, plaintiffs filed a complaint in the Court of Chancery alleging that: (1) the merger was fraudulent in that it did not serve any business purpose other than the forced removal of public minority shareholders from an equity position in Magnavox at a grossly inadequate price to enable North American, through Development, to obtain sole ownership of Magnavox; (2) in approving the merger, at a cash price per share to the minority which they knew to be grossly inadequate, defendants breached their fiduciary duties to the minority shareholders. . . . Plaintiffs seek an order nullifying the merger and compensatory damages.

Defendants moved to dismiss the complaint on the ground that it fails to state a claim upon which relief may be granted, arguing that: (1) their actions are expressly authorized by 8 Del.C. § 251, and they fully complied therewith; (2) the exclusive remedy for dissatisfaction with the merger is an appraisal under 8 Del.C. § 262. . . .

The Court of Chancery granted the motion to dismiss, ruling that: (1) the merger was not fraudulent merely because it was accomplished without any business purpose other than to eliminate the Magnavox minority shareholders; (2) in any event, plaintiffs' remedy for dissatisfaction with the merger is to seek an appraisal. . . .

III

We turn, first, to what we regard as the principal consideration in this appeal; namely, the obligation owed by majority shareholders in control of the corporate process to minority shareholders, in the context of a merger under 8 Del.C. § 251, of two related Delaware corporations. It is, in other words, another round in the development of the law governing a parent corporation and minority shareholders in its subsidiary.

A

To state the obvious, under § 251 two (or more) Delaware corporations "may merge into a single corporation." Generally speaking, whether such a transaction is good or bad, enlightened or ill-advised, selfish or generous -- these considerations are beside the point. Section 251 authorizes a merger and any judicial consideration of that kind of togetherness must begin from that premise.

Section 251 also specifies in detail the procedures to be followed in accomplishing a merger. Briefly, these include approvals by the directors of each corporation and by "majority [vote] of the outstanding stock of" each corporation, followed by the execution and filing of formal documents. The consideration given to the shareholders of a constituent corporation in exchange for their stock may take the form of "cash, property, rights or securities of any other corporation." § 251(b)(4). A shareholder who objects to the merger and is dissatisfied with the value of the consideration given for his shares may seek an appraisal under 8 Del.C. § 262.

B

In this appeal it is uncontroverted that defendants complied with the stated requirements of § 251. Thus there is both statutory authorization for the Magnavox merger and compliance with the procedural requirements. But, contrary to defendants' contention, it does not necessarily follow that the merger is legally unassailable. We say this because, (a) plaintiffs invoke the fiduciary duty rule which allegedly binds defendants; and (b) Delaware case law clearly teaches that even complete compliance with the mandate of a statute does not, in every case, make the action valid in law.

The last stated proposition is derived from such cases as Schnell v. Chris-Craft Industries, 285 A.2d 437, 439 (Del.1971) (which involved advancement of the date of an annual meeting, accomplished in compliance with the relevant statute) wherein this Court said that ". . . inequitable action does not become permissible simply because it is legally possible;" and from Guth v. Loft, Inc., 5 A.2d 503, 511 (Del.1939), in which the Court, responding to an argument for a narrow examination of issues, said that "[t]he question [at issue] is not one to be decided on narrow or technical grounds, but upon broad considerations of corporate duty and loyalty." We apply this approach and reject any contention that statutory compliance insulates the merger from judicial review.

C

From this premise we must now analyze the encounter between the exercise of a statutory right and the performance of the alleged fiduciary duty. As we have noted, § 251, by its terms, makes permissible that which the North American side of this dispute caused to be done: the merger of T.M.C. into Magnavox. We must ascertain, however, what restraint, if any, the duty to minority stockholders placed on the exercise of that right.

Plaintiffs contend that the Magnavox merger was fraudulent because it was made without any ascertainable corporate business purpose and was designed solely to freeze out the minority stockholders. After a review of the cases, the Trial Court concluded that to the extent the complaint charges that the merger was fraudulent because it did not serve a business purpose of Magnavox, it fails to state a claim upon which relief may be granted. Our analysis leads to a different result, not on the basis of fraud but on application of the law governing corporate fiduciaries.

The statute is silent on the question of whether a merger may be accomplished only for a valid business purpose. . . . [T]he issue is one of first impression here. . . .

D

It is a settled rule of law in Delaware that Development, as the majority stockholder of Magnavox, owed to the minority stockholders of that corporation, a fiduciary obligation in dealing with the latter's property. Sterling v. Mayflower Hotel Corp., 93 A.2d 107, 109-10 (Del.1952). In that leading "interested merger" case, this Court recognized as established law in this State that the dominant corporation, as a majority stockholder standing on both sides of a merger transaction, has "the burden of establishing its entire fairness" to the minority stockholders, sufficiently to "pass the test of careful scrutiny by the courts." See 93 A.2d at 109, 110. The fiduciary obligation is the cornerstone of plaintiffs' rights in this controversy and the corollary, of course, is that it is likewise the measure of the duty owed by defendants.

Delaware courts have long announced and enforced high standards which govern the internal affairs of corporations chartered here, particularly when fiduciary relations are under scrutiny. It is settled Delaware law, for example, that corporate officers and directors, Guth v. Loft, Inc., *supra*, and controlling shareholders, Sterling v. Mayflower Hotel Corp., *supra*; Bennett v. Breuil Petroleum Corp., 99 A.2d 236 (Del.Ch.1953), owe their corporation and its minority shareholders a fiduciary obligation of honesty, loyalty, good faith and fairness. . . .

The classic definition of the duty was stated by Chief Justice Layton in *Guth*, where he wrote:

> . . . While technically not trustees, . . . [corporate directors] stand in a fiduciary relation to the corporation and its stockholders. A public policy, existing through the years, and derived from a profound knowledge of human characteristics and motives, has established a rule that demands of a corporate officer or director, peremptorily and inexorably, the most scrupulous observance of his duty, not only affirmatively to protect the interests of the corporation committed to his charge, but also to refrain from doing anything that would work injury to the corporation, or to deprive it of profit or advantage which his skill and ability might properly bring to it, or to enable it to make in the reasonable and lawful exercise of its powers. The rule that requires an undivided and unselfish loyalty to the corporation demands that there shall be no conflict between duty and self-interest. The occasions for the determination of honesty, good faith and loyal conduct are many and varied, and no hard and fast rule can be formulated. The standard of loyalty is measured by no fixed scale.

5 A.2d at 510. While that comment was about directors, the spirit of the definition is equally applicable to a majority stockholder in any context in which the law imposes a fiduciary duty on that stockholder for the benefit of minority stockholders. We so hold. . . .

Defendants concede that they owe plaintiffs a fiduciary duty but contend that, in the context of the present transaction they have met that obligation by offering fair value for the Magnavox shares. And, say defendants, plaintiffs' exclusive remedy for dissatisfaction with the merger is to seek an appraisal under § 262. We disagree. In our view, defendants cannot meet their fiduciary obligations to plaintiffs simply by relegating them to a statutory appraisal proceeding.[7]

At the core of defendants' contention is the premise that a shareholder's right is exclusively in the *value* of his investment, not its *form*. And, they

---

[7] See James Vorenberg, *Exclusiveness of the Dissenting Stockholder's Appraisal Right*, 77 Harv.L.Rev. 1189 (1964).

argue, that right is protected by a § 262 appraisal which, by definition, results in fair value for the shares. This argument assumes that the right to take is coextensive with the power to take and that a dissenting stockholder has no legally protected right in his shares, his certificate or his company beyond a right to be paid fair value[8] when the majority is ready to do this. Simply stated, such an argument does not square with the duty stated so eloquently and so forcefully by Chief Justice Layton in *Guth.*

We agree that, because the power to merge is conferred by statute, every stockholder in a Delaware corporation accepts his shares with notice thereof. See Federal United Corp. v. Havender, 11 A.2d 331, 338 (Del.1940). Indeed, some Delaware decisions have noted that to "the extent authorized by statute, . . . [mergers] are 'encouraged and favored.'" *Folk, supra* at 332. Beyond question, the common law right of a single stockholder to simply veto a merger is gone. *Id.* at 331. But it by no means follows that those in control of a corporation may invoke the statutory power conferred by § 251, a power which this Court in *Havender, supra,* said was "somewhat analogous to the right of eminent domain," 11 A.2d at 338, when their purpose is simply to get rid of a minority. On the contrary, as we shall ultimately conclude here, just as a minority shareholder may not thwart a merger without cause, neither may a majority cause a merger to be made for the sole purpose of eliminating a minority on a cash-out basis.

E

Plaintiffs allege that defendants violated their respective fiduciary duties by participating in the tender offer and other acts which led to the merger and which were designed to enable Development and North American to, among other things:

> [C]onsummate a merger which did not serve any valid corporate purpose or compelling business need of Magnavox and whose sole purpose was to enable Development and North American to obtain sole ownership of the business and assets of Magnavox at a price determined by defendants which was grossly inadequate and unfair and which was designed to give Development and North American a disproportionate amount of the gain said defendants anticipated would be recognized from consummation of the merger.

---

[8] That argument was rejected in Jutkowitz v. Bourns, Cal.Super.Ct. C.A. 000268 (Nov. 19, 1975), wherein the Court correctly summarized some of the values besides money which may be at stake in a "going-private" merger:

> Money may well satisfy some or most minority shareholders, but others may have differing investment goals, tax problems, a belief in the ability of . . . management to make them rich, or even a sentimental attachment to the stock which leads them to have a different judgment as to the desirability of selling out.

Cf. Bryan v. Brock & Blevins Co., 490 F.2d 563 (5th Cir.1974); Berkowitz v. Power/Mate Corp., 342 A.2d 566 (N.J.Super.1975).

Defendants contend, and the Court of Chancery agreed, that the "business purpose" rule does not have a place in Delaware's merger law. In support of this contention defendants cite: Stauffer v. Standard Brands, Inc., 187 A.2d 78 (Del.1962); Federal United Corp. v. Havender, *supra*; David J. Greene & Co. v. Schenley Industries 281 A.2d 30 (Del.Ch.1971); Bruce v. E.L. Bruce Co., 174 A.2d 29 (Del.Ch.1961); and MacCrone v. American Capital Corp., 51 F.Supp. 462 (D.Del.1943).

Each of these cases involved an effort to enjoin or attack a merger and each was unsuccessful. To this extent they support defendants' side of the controversy. But none of these decisions involved a merger in which the minority was totally expelled *via* a straight "cash-for-stock" conversion in which the only purpose of the merger was, as alleged here, to eliminate the minority. . . .

We hold the law to be that a Delaware Court will not be indifferent to the purpose of a merger when a freeze-out of minority stockholders on a cash-out basis is alleged to be its sole purpose. In such a situation, if it is alleged that the purpose is improper because of the fiduciary obligation owed to the minority, the Court is duty-bound to closely examine that allegation even when all of the relevant statutory formalities have been satisfied. . . .

Read as a whole, those opinions illustrate two principles of law which we approve: First, it is within the responsibility of an equity court to scrutinize a corporate act when it is alleged that its purpose violates the fiduciary duty owed to minority stockholders; and second, those who control the corporate machinery owe a fiduciary duty to the minority in the exercise thereof over corporate powers and property, and the use of such power to perpetuate control is a violation of that duty.

By analogy, if not *a fortiori,* use of corporate power solely to *eliminate* the minority is a violation of that duty. Accordingly, while we agree with the conclusion of the Court of Chancery that this merger was not fraudulent merely because it was accomplished without any purpose other than elimination of the minority stockholders, we conclude that, for that reason, it was violative of the fiduciary duty owed by the majority to the minority stockholders.

We hold, therefore, that a § 251 merger, made for the sole purpose of freezing out minority stockholders, is an abuse of the corporate process; and the complaint, which so alleges in this suit, states a cause of action for violation of a fiduciary duty for which the Court may grant such relief as it deems appropriate under the circumstances.

This is not to say, however, that merely because the Court finds that a cash-out merger was not made for the sole purpose of freezing out minority stockholders, all relief must be denied to the minority stockholders in a § 251 merger.[11] On the contrary, the fiduciary obligation of the majority to the

---

[11] Plaintiffs contend that a "business purpose" is proper in a merger only when it serves the interests of the subsidiary corporation; defendants contend, on the other hand, that if any such purpose is relevant, it is only that of the parent corporation. Since resolution of that

minority stockholders remains and proof of a purpose, other than such freeze-out, without more, will not necessarily discharge it. In such case the Court will scrutinize the circumstances for compliance with the *Sterling* rule of "entire fairness" and, if it finds a violation thereof, will grant such relief as equity may require. Any statement in *Stauffer* inconsistent herewith is held inapplicable to a § 251 merger. . . .

Accordingly, as to this facet of the appeal, we reverse.

It is fair to read *Singer* as having imposed greater limits on an acquiring company's ability to freeze out minority shareholders. Although Sterling v. Mayflower Hotel Corp., upon which the Court relied so heavily in *Singer*, had never been explicitly overruled, "[m]ost observers, however, believed that the *Stauffer* line of cases rendered the *Sterling* rule inapplicable to cash mergers, in which appraisal rights were available to dissenters."[41] The problem, however, was that it was impossible to tell from the *Singer* opinion just how significant the new limitations really were.

Singer's first limitation was that a merger could not be for the "sole purpose of freezing out minority shareholders."[42] But what additional purpose would be sufficient? On the one hand, if the additional purpose had to be that of the *target* company, so that the minority shareholders somehow were served by the transaction, then freezeout transactions might be impossible. On the other hand, if the additional purpose could serve the business interests of only the *acquiring* company, the limitation was a mirage. Presumably an acquiring company would always have a business purpose for -- an explanation for why it would gain from -- freezing out the minority. If there was no benefit to the acquiring company -- the freezeout really was for the "sole purpose of freezing out minority shareholders" -- why would it bother?

Even if a freezeout merger satisfied the business purpose requirement, *Singer* also required that the merger comply with "the *Sterling* rule of 'entire fairness.'"[43] But what would constitute "entire fairness"? If it was merely that the price paid had to be "fair," and plaintiffs in *Singer* did allege the price to be "grossly inadequate," then scrutiny for "entire fairness" might not be any different than the appraisal proceeding that had been available to those who objected to a merger prior to *Singer*.

Finally, *Singer* only briefly considered the remedy that would be available should the merger fail either the business purpose or the entire fairness requirements. The Court stated that in such event, it would "grant

---

question is not necessary to the disposition of this appeal, and since it was not central in the briefing and argument, we leave it to another day.

[41] Weiss (1981), *supra* note 26, at 655.

[42] 380 A.2d at 980.

[43] *Id.*

relief as equity may require."[44]　But if all equity required was a fair price, then how would the relief differ from that which would be forthcoming in an appraisal proceeding?　If, alternatively, the measure of damages was something other than would be forthcoming in an appraisal proceeding, what measure would be appropriate?　And, of course, if the measure of damages was different from the fair price determined by appraisal standards, then, in turn, "entire fairness" had to mean something more than just the fairness of the price.

These issues were addressed in a number of cases over the five years following *Singer*. The character of the business purpose necessary to support a freezeout merger was explored in Tanzer v. International General Industries,[45] decided less than a month following *Singer*.　In *Tanzer*, International General Industries, Inc. ("IGI"), the owner of 81% of the stock of Kliklok Corporation, accomplished the freezeout of the Kliklok minority by means of a long-form triangular cash merger.　Minority shareholders then challenged the merger, arguing that "a freeze-out merger imposed on a subsidiary corporation by a parent, and designed solely for the purpose of benefiting the parent, is impermissible under Delaware law."　379 A.2d at 1123.　The Court joined the issue directly:

> As we observed at the outset, *Singer* determines that a cash-out of minority stockholders, when that is the sole purpose of a merger, is a violation of a fiduciary duty owed to them by a majority stockholder.　In one sense, that may be said to be what is involved in the Kliklok merger because the minority were cashed out and it is not contended by defendants that Kliklok benefitted from the merger.　However, the real issue for decision centers around IGI's right to cause a merger "for a valid business reason" of its own, independent of any corporate interest of Kliklok.　In short, the question is whether the parent may cause a merger to be made solely for its own benefit, or whether that is a violation of fiduciary duty and actionable under Delaware corporation law.

Id. The Court's conclusion was straightforward.　So long as the freezeout served a *bona fide* purpose of the parent, the *Singer* business purpose test was met.　The Court stressed, however, as it had in *Singer,* that the *Sterling* test still had to be met, and remanded the case "for judicial scrutiny for 'entire fairness' as to all aspects of the transaction." *Id.* at 1125.　As in *Singer,* no clue was provided as to what "entire fairness" might consist of.[46]

---

[44] *Id.* at 980.

[45] 379 A.2d 1121 (Del.1977).

[46] Roland International Corp. v. Najjar, 407 A.2d 1032 (Del.1979), extended the *Singer* analysis to short-form mergers.　For these transactions, where the statute dispenses with even the requirement that the target shareholders approve the freezeout, it could be argued that the very purpose of the statute was to allow the minority to be eliminated.　Thus, for short-form mergers, further inquiry into "business purpose" should be unnecessary.　The Delaware Supreme Court declined to draw this distinction between long-form and short-form mergers.

Thus, after *Tanzer,* the *Singer* business purpose test seemed hardly burdensome; to be sure, a record concerning the parent's *bona fide* purpose would have to be created, but this would impose no more than a mechanical barrier to counsel planning the transaction. If *Singer* was to have any impact, it would have to come from the content of the entire fairness test. The problem was that little guidance was provided concerning what would render a merger entirely fair. What was clear, however, was the stakes: both the remedy and the procedure by which the remedy was obtained differed if the entire fairness test was not met.

Consider first the procedure. Suppose that even if a violation of *Singer* were found, the remedy would be to award minority shareholders the "fair value" of their shares determined in the same way as "fair value" would be determined in an appraisal proceeding. In this situation one could argue that *Singer* was simply beside the point. Minority shareholders end up in the same place with or without *Singer:* The value of their stock is appraised. The argument, however, ignores the reality of the litigation process.

Under Delaware § 262, a shareholder who wishes to invoke his appraisal rights must so notify the corporation prior to the vote on the freezeout transaction (§ 262(d)(1)) and must not vote in favor of it (abstention is sufficient). (§ 262(a)). Then, within 120 days after the merger, the shareholder must find a lawyer and commence an appraisal proceeding by petitioning the Court of Chancery (§ 262(e)). In the absence of a contingency fee, the shareholder must advance the costs and expenses, including expert witness fees, necessary to pursue the appraisal proceeding. Indeed, even a contingency fee would not entirely solve the problem of the expense of the proceeding. Unless the shareholder held a substantial number of shares, the potential reward would be too small to warrant the necessary investment of time and money by the lawyer. A solution would be to facilitate the lawyer's representation of a number of shareholders; however, it is difficult to aggregate plaintiffs in an appraisal proceeding. Because under the corporate statute each shareholder must individually perfect his appraisal rights, the universe of potential clients is not determined until after the shareholder meeting. As a result, shareholders who do not have a large enough investment to warrant hiring a lawyer in the first place may well have eliminated themselves as potential plaintiffs by voting in favor of the transaction.

It also declined to distinguish between types of freezeouts based on the circumstances of the particular transaction. Some commentators had argued persuasively that a second-step freezeout merger which followed a first-step tender offer should not be subject to the *Singer* test because it was really part of a single arms-length transaction that, by tendering in the first-step, target shareholders had already approved. On this analysis, there was no fiduciary duty and no self-dealing problem. See Brudney & Chirelstein (1978), *supra* note 40. The court held that *Singer* "applies to all majority shareholders, no matter how, nor how recently such majority was obtained." 407 A.2d at 1034 n.4.

The situation is not much better with respect to those shareholders who, by luck or design, remain eligible to exercise their appraisal rights. There is no procedural analogue to a class action that would allow a single lawyer to represent all eligible shareholders with respect to what are entirely common issues of law and fact -- the value of the shares -- and thereby both reduce the costs of the proceedings for shareholders and their counsel, and allow the aggregation of minority shareholders claims necessary to make a contingency fee an attractive investment for a lawyer.[47]

Under these circumstances, the best strategy for an acquiring company intent on freezing out the minority may be to "low-ball" -- to set the freezeout price *below* what it believes a court would determine to be fair value in an appraisal proceeding. Because of the procedural expense and difficulty of appraisal, and especially because the absence of a class action mechanism makes it impossible for lawyers to act, in effect, as surrogates for minority shareholders with respect to whether to invest in an appraisal proceeding, most shareholders will not dissent. As a result, many of the minority shares can be purchased for less than what would be the "appraisal" price. Thus, to the extent it can be anticipated that some shareholders will not seek appraisal, the acquiring company has an incentive to set the freezeout price too low.

The analysis changes radically if, instead of an appraisal proceeding, the entire fairness standard had been violated. Even though we have assumed that the substance of the remedy for such a violation would be the same as in an appraisal proceeding, the procedure is very different. Most important, the suit can be brought as a class action. Minority shareholders need take no affirmative action in order to participate, nor need they expend any resources to pursue the action. All the responsibility -- both for initiating the action and for its expenses -- is borne by the self-designated lawyer for the class who is compensated, one way or the other, out of the amount recovered. The lawyer then stands, in effect, as an independent investor who balances his estimate of the potential recovery to all shareholders against the cost of the proceeding and the uncertainty associated with its outcome. While the presence of transaction costs may still create some incentive for the acquiring

---

[47] Delaware § 262(j) does provide the potential for something of a class action with respect to those shareholders who do individually perfect their appraisal rights. The court is authorized to "order all or a portion of the expenses incurred by any stockholder in connection with the appraisal proceeding, including, without limitation, reasonable attorney's fees and the expenses of experts, to be charged pro rata against the value of all shares entitled to appraisal." If such an order could be obtained at the pre-trial stage, it at least would allow the designation of lead counsel and the avoidance of duplication of expense associated with a class action procedure.

company to "low-ball",[48] it is hardly of the magnitude of the incentive created by the mechanics of the appraisal proceeding.

Thus, even if the substance of the remedy for failing the entire fairness standard did not differ one whit from that which would be forthcoming in an appraisal proceeding, the availability of the class action mechanism to enforce a violation of *Singer* meant that substantially more shareholders could benefit from it. Whatever else it might have done, *Singer* operated, in effect, to provide the potential for class action appraisal.

The question that then remains is what valuation standard would be applied in such a class action appraisal. Some indication of the answer was provided in Lynch v. Vickers Energy Corp.[49] That case involved not a freezeout merger, but a tender offer by the existing majority shareholder. The minority shareholders who had accepted the offer subsequently sued, claiming that the majority shareholder had violated its fiduciary duty to the minority by not disclosing to them with "complete candor" all of the facts bearing on the tender offer. In particular, it was alleged that the majority shareholder withheld the fact that the company's net asset value had been estimated at an amount substantially in excess of that offered to the minority in the tender offer, and that management of the company had been authorized to make open market purchases of the company's stock at prices up to 25% higher than the tender offer price. Following the Delaware Supreme Court's decision in an earlier appeal that the nondisclosures had violated the majority shareholder's fiduciary duty, on remand the trial court held that the appropriate remedy was "a proceeding analogous to an appraisal hearing such as is provided in merger cases is appropriate here."[50] The appeal from the trial court's determination of the appropriate remedy thus presented the Delaware Supreme Court with the opportunity to resolve an issue analogous to that left open by *Singer:* If minority shareholders are eliminated from the corporation as a result of a breach of the majority shareholder's fiduciary duty, whether by a freezeout merger or by a misleading tender offer, was an appraisal standard the appropriate measure of relief?

---

[48] The advantages of a class action proceeding should not mask the conflict of interest problems that arise between the plaintiff's lawyer and the plaintiff class, especially with respect to settlement. Suppose the corporation has made a settlement offer of $25 per share and that the plaintiff's lawyer believes that if the matter goes to trial there is a 50% chance of receiving $40 per share and a 50% chance of receiving $15 per share. The plaintiff class might choose to go to trial because the expected value of the post-trial award, $27.50, exceeds the settlement offer. For the lawyer, however, the decision is more complex. To be sure, the lawyer, through the contingency arrangement, would share in the additional award; however, he would have to try the case in order to receive the additional fee, while the settlement could be achieved with no additional work. Thus, for the lawyer, the question is whether, at the margin, the additional fee is worth the time necessary to try the case. For an excellent discussion of such conflicts, see John Coffee, *The Unfaithful Champion: The Plaintiff as Monitor in Shareholder Litigation,* 48 Law & Contemp.Prob. 5 (1985).

[49] 429 A.2d 497 (Del.1981).

[50] 402 A.2d 5, 11 (Del.Ch.1979).

The Delaware Supreme Court rejected the appraisal standard. The court noted that because appraisal requires plaintiff's shares to be valued at the time of the transaction, it "has a built-in limitation, namely, gain to the corporation resulting from a statutory merger is not a factor in determining the value of the shares."[51] To avoid this limitation, the Court instead developed an alternative to the appraisal standard: The "monetary equivalent of rescission."[52] The value of plaintiff's stock would be determined not at the time of the transaction, as would be the case in appraisal, but at the time of judgment. This had the effect of giving the plaintiffs their share of the gain from the merger, which they would not have received in an appraisal.

A financially sophisticated plaintiffs' lawyer would see that this valuation standard gave minority shareholders (and the lawyer through her contingency fee) an option on the post-merger performance of the consolidated companies. The shareholder can accept the proffered consideration for the merger, but remain in the class challenging the merger's entire fairness. If the merger proves efficient, then the shareholder might get the higher post-transaction value contemplated by *Lynch* if the controlling shareholder does not carry the burden of proving the merger entirely fair. If not, then the litigation likely could be settled cheaply for attorneys' fees, thereby offsetting the option's cost to the lawyers. The provision of a free option to plaintiffs and a virtually free option to plaintiffs' lawyers made it very likely that any freezeout merger would be challenged.

At this point, the end of Act III of the drama, we knew the following with certainty. First, the appraisal remedy was not exclusive in freezeout mergers; minority shareholders could directly challenge the merger if it was for the sole purpose of freezing them out, or if it was not entirely fair. A credible reason why the freezeout benefitted the acquiring company would satisfy the business purpose test, but there was still no clear statement of what would satisfy the entire fairness test. Second, there was reason to believe that if either the business purpose test or the entire fairness test was violated, the remedy would not be limited to an appraisal standard; post-transaction gains would be taken into account. Finally, it was clear that, regardless of the measure of the remedy, minority shareholders were better off challenging the entire fairness of a freezeout merger than they would have been with a post-transaction appraisal hearing because of the differences between the two procedures; the *Singer* action could be brought as a class action.

2. The Current Framework of Review of Freezeout Mergers: Entire Fairness

---

[51] 429 A.2d at 501.

[52] *Id.*

The Delaware Supreme Court opened the final act of the drama with its decision in Weinberger v. UOP, Inc.

WEINBERGER v. UOP, INC.
457 A.2d 701 (Del.1983)

Before HERRMANN, C.J., McNEILLY, QUILLEN, HORSEY and MOORE, JJ., constituting the Court en banc.

MOORE, Justice. This post-trial appeal was reheard en banc from a decision of the Court of Chancery. It was brought by the class action plaintiff below, a former shareholder of UOP, Inc., who challenged the elimination of UOP's minority shareholders by a cash-out merger between UOP and its majority owner, The Signal Companies, Inc. Originally, the defendants in this action were Signal, UOP, certain officers and directors of those companies, and UOP's investment banker, Lehman Brothers Kuhn Loeb, Inc. The present Chancellor held that the terms of the merger were fair to the plaintiff and the other minority shareholders of UOP. Accordingly, he entered judgment in favor of the defendants.

Numerous points were raised by the parties, but we address only the following questions presented by the trial court's opinion:

1)   The plaintiff's duty to plead sufficient facts demonstrating the unfairness of the challenged merger;

2)   The burden of proof upon the parties where the merger has been approved by the purportedly informed vote of a majority of the minority shareholders;

3)   The fairness of the merger in terms of adequacy of the defendants' disclosures to the minority shareholders;

4)   The fairness of the merger in terms of adequacy of the price paid for the minority shares and the remedy appropriate to that issue; and

5)   The continued force and effect of Singer v. Magnavox Co., 380 A.2d 969, 980 (Del.1977), and its progeny.

In ruling for the defendants, the Chancellor re-stated his earlier conclusion that the plaintiff in a suit challenging a cash-out merger must allege specific acts of fraud, misrepresentation, or other items of misconduct to demonstrate the unfairness of the merger terms to the minority.[4] We approve this rule and affirm it.

The Chancellor also held that even though the ultimate burden of proof is on the majority shareholder to show by a preponderance of the evidence that the transaction is fair, it is first the burden of the plaintiff attacking the merger to demonstrate some basis for invoking the fairness obligation. We agree with that principle. However, where corporate action has been

---

[4] In a pre-trial ruling the Chancellor ordered the complaint dismissed for failure to state a cause of action. See Weinberger v. UOP, Inc., 409 A.2d 1262 (Del.Ch.1979).

approved by an informed vote of a majority of the minority shareholders, we conclude that the burden entirely shifts to the plaintiff to show that the transaction was unfair to the minority. See, e.g., Michelson v. Duncan, 407 A.2d 211, 224 (Del.1979). But in all this, the burden clearly remains on those relying on the vote to show that they completely disclosed all material facts relevant to the transaction.

Here, the record does not support a conclusion that the minority stockholder vote was an informed one. Material information, necessary to acquaint those shareholders with the bargaining positions of Signal and UOP, was withheld under circumstances amounting to a breach of fiduciary duty. We therefore conclude that this merger does not meet the test of fairness, at least as we address that concept, and no burden thus shifted to the plaintiff by reason of the minority shareholder vote. Accordingly, we reverse and remand for further proceedings consistent herewith.

In considering the nature of the remedy available under our law to minority shareholders in a cash-out merger, we believe that it is, and hereafter should be, an appraisal under 8 Del.C. § 262 as hereinafter construed. We therefore overrule Lynch v. Vickers Energy Corp., 429 A.2d 497 (Del.1981) (*Lynch II*) to the extent that it purports to limit a stockholder's monetary relief to a specific damage formula. See *Lynch II,* 429 A.2d at 507-08 (McNeilly & Quillen, JJ., dissenting). But to give full effect to § 262 within the framework of the General Corporation Law we adopt a more liberal, less rigid and stylized, approach to the valuation process than has heretofore been permitted by our courts. While the present state of these proceedings does not admit the plaintiff to the appraisal remedy per se, the practical effect of the remedy we do grant him will be co-extensive with the liberalized valuation and appraisal methods we herein approve for cases coming after this decision.

Our treatment of these matters has necessarily led us to a reconsideration of the business purpose rule announced in the trilogy of Singer v. Magnavox Co., *supra*; Tanzer v. International General Industries, 379 A.2d 1121 (Del.1977); and Roland International Corp. v. Najjar, 407 A.2d 1032 (Del.1979). For the reasons hereafter set forth we consider that the business purpose requirement of these cases is no longer the law of Delaware.

I

The facts found by the trial court, pertinent to the issues before us, are supported by the record, and we draw from them as set out in the Chancellor's opinion.

Signal is a diversified, technically based company operating through various subsidiaries. Its stock is publicly traded on the New York, Philadelphia and Pacific Stock Exchanges. UOP, formerly known as Universal Oil Products Company, was a diversified industrial company engaged in various lines of business, including petroleum and petro-chemical services and related products, construction, fabricated metal products, transportation equipment products, chemicals and plastics, and other products and services including land development, lumber products, and waste disposal. Its stock was publicly held and listed on the New York Stock Exchange.

In 1974 Signal sold one of its wholly-owned subsidiaries for $420,000,000 in cash. See Gimbel v. Signal Companies, Inc., 316 A.2d 599 (Del.Ch.), *aff'd*, 316 A.2d 619 (Del.1974). While looking to invest this cash surplus, Signal became interested in UOP as a possible acquisition. Friendly negotiations ensued, and Signal proposed to acquire a controlling interest in UOP at a price of $19 per share. UOP's representatives sought $25 per share. In the arm's length bargaining that followed, an understanding was reached whereby Signal agreed to purchase from UOP 1,500,000 shares of UOP's authorized but unissued stock at $21 per share.

This purchase was contingent upon Signal making a successful cash tender offer for 4,300,000 publicly held shares of UOP, also at a price of $21 per share. This combined method of acquisition permitted Signal to acquire 5,800,000 shares of stock, representing 50.5% of UOP's outstanding shares. The UOP board of directors advised the company's shareholders that it had no objection to Signal's tender offer at that price. Immediately before the announcement of the tender offer, UOP's common stock had been trading on the New York Stock Exchange at a fraction under $14 per share.

The negotiations between Signal and UOP occurred during April 1975, and the resulting tender offer was greatly oversubscribed. However, Signal limited its total purchase of the tendered shares so that, when coupled with the stock bought from UOP, it had achieved its goal of becoming a 50.5% shareholder of UOP.

Although UOP's board consisted of thirteen directors, Signal nominated and elected only six. Of these, five were either directors or employees of Signal. The sixth, a partner in the banking firm of Lazard Freres & Co., had been one of Signal's representatives in the negotiations and bargaining with UOP concerning the tender offer and purchase price of the UOP shares.

However, the president and chief executive officer of UOP retired during 1975, and Signal caused him to be replaced by James V. Crawford, a long-time employee and senior executive vice president of one of Signal's wholly-owned subsidiaries. Crawford succeeded his predecessor on UOP's board of directors and also was made a director of Signal.

By the end of 1977 Signal basically was unsuccessful in finding other suitable investment candidates for its excess cash, and by February 1978 considered that it had no other realistic acquisitions available to it on a friendly basis. Once again its attention turned to UOP.

The trial court found that at the instigation of certain Signal management personnel, including William W. Walkup, its board chairman, and Forrest N. Shumway, its president, a feasibility study was made concerning the possible acquisition of the balance of UOP's outstanding shares. This study was performed by two Signal officers, Charles S. Arledge, vice president (director of planning), and Andrew J. Chitiea, senior vice president (chief financial officer). Messrs. Walkup, Shumway, Arledge and Chitiea were all directors of UOP in addition to their membership on the Signal board.

Arledge and Chitiea concluded that it would be a good investment for Signal to acquire the remaining 49.5% of UOP shares at any price up to $24 each. Their report was discussed between Walkup and Shumway who, along with Arledge, Chitiea and Brewster L. Arms, internal counsel for Signal, constituted Signal's senior management. In particular, they talked about the proper price to be paid if the acquisition was pursued, purportedly keeping in mind that as UOP's majority shareholder, Signal owed a fiduciary responsibility to both its own stockholders as well as to UOP's minority. It was ultimately agreed that a meeting of Signal's executive committee would be called to propose that Signal acquire the remaining outstanding stock of UOP through a cash-out merger in the range of $20 to $21 per share.

The executive committee meeting was set for February 28, 1978. As a courtesy, UOP's president, Crawford, was invited to attend, although he was not a member of Signal's executive committee. On his arrival, and prior to the meeting, Crawford was asked to meet privately with Walkup and Shumway. He was then told of Signal's plan to acquire full ownership of UOP and was asked for his reaction to the proposed price range of $20 to $21 per share. Crawford said he thought such a price would be "generous", and that it was certainly one which should be submitted to UOP's minority shareholders for their ultimate consideration. He stated, however, that Signal's 100% ownership could cause internal problems at UOP. He believed that employees would have to be given some assurance of their future place in a fully-owned Signal subsidiary. Otherwise, he feared the departure of essential personnel. Also, many of UOP's key employees had stock option incentive programs which would be wiped out by a merger. Crawford therefore urged that some adjustment would have to be made, such as providing a comparable incentive in Signal's shares, if after the merger he was to maintain his quality of personnel and efficiency at UOP.

Thus, Crawford voiced no objection to the $20 to $21 price range, nor did he suggest that Signal should consider paying more than $21 per share for the minority interests. Later, at the executive committee meeting the same factors were discussed, with Crawford repeating the position he earlier took with Walkup and Shumway. Also considered was the 1975 tender offer and the fact that it had been greatly oversubscribed at $21 per share. For many reasons, Signal's management concluded that the acquisition of UOP's minority shares provided the solution to a number of its business problems.

Thus, it was the consensus that a price of $20 to $21 per share would be fair to both Signal and the minority shareholders of UOP. Signal's executive committee authorized its management "to negotiate" with UOP "for a cash acquisition of the minority ownership in UOP, Inc., with the intention of presenting a proposal to [Signal's] board of directors . . . on March 6, 1978". Immediately after this February 28, 1978 meeting, Signal issued a press release stating:

The Signal Companies, Inc. and UOP, Inc. are conducting negotiations for the acquisition for cash by Signal of the 49.5 per cent of UOP which it does not presently own, announced Forrest N. Shumway, president and chief executive officer of Signal, and James V. Crawford, UOP president.

Price and other terms of the proposed transaction have not yet been finalized and would be subject to approval of the boards of directors of Signal and UOP, scheduled to meet early next week, the stockholders of UOP and certain federal agencies.

The announcement also referred to the fact that the closing price of UOP's common stock on that day was $14.50 per share.

Two days later, on March 2, 1978, Signal issued a second press release stating that its management would recommend a price in the range of $20 to $21 per share for UOP's 49.5% minority interest. This announcement referred to Signal's earlier statement that "negotiations" were being conducted for the acquisition of the minority shares.

Between Tuesday, February 28, 1978 and Monday, March 6, 1978, a total of four business days, Crawford spoke by telephone with all of UOP's non-Signal, i.e., outside, directors. Also during that period, Crawford retained Lehman Brothers to render a fairness opinion as to the price offered the minority for its stock. He gave two reasons for this choice. First, the time schedule between the announcement and the board meetings was short (by then only three business days) and since Lehman Brothers had been acting as UOP's investment banker for many years, Crawford felt that it would be in the best position to respond on such brief notice. Second, James W. Glanville, a long-time director of UOP and a partner in Lehman Brothers, had acted as a financial advisor to UOP for many years. Crawford believed that Glanville's familiarity with UOP, as a member of its board, would also be of assistance in enabling Lehman Brothers to render a fairness opinion within the existing time constraints.

Crawford telephoned Glanville, who gave his assurance that Lehman Brothers had no conflicts that would prevent it from accepting the task. Glanville's immediate personal reaction was that a price of $20 to $21 would certainly be fair, since it represented almost a 50% premium over UOP's market price. Glanville sought a $250,000 fee for Lehman Brothers' services, but Crawford thought this too much. After further discussions Glanville finally agreed that Lehman Brothers would render its fairness opinion for $150,000.

During this period Crawford also had several telephone contacts with Signal officials. In only one of them, however, was the price of the shares discussed. In a conversation with Walkup, Crawford advised that as a result of his communications with UOP's non-Signal directors, it was his feeling that the price would have to be the top of the proposed range, or $21 per share, if the approval of UOP's outside directors was to be obtained. But again, he did not seek any price higher than $21.

Glanville assembled a three-man Lehman Brothers team to do the work on the fairness opinion. These persons examined relevant documents and information concerning UOP, including its annual reports and its Securities and Exchange Commission filings from 1973 through 1976, as well as its audited financial statements for 1977, its interim reports to shareholders, and its recent and historical market prices and trading volumes. In addition, on Friday, March 3, 1978, two members of the Lehman Brothers team flew to UOP's headquarters in Des Plaines, Illinois, to perform a "due diligence" visit, during the course of which they interviewed Crawford as well as UOP's general counsel, its chief financial officer, and other key executives and personnel.

As a result, the Lehman Brothers team concluded that "the price of either $20 or $21 would be a fair price for the remaining shares of UOP." They telephoned this impression to Glanville, who was spending the weekend in Vermont.

On Monday morning, March 6, 1978, Glanville and the senior member of the Lehman Brothers team flew to Des Plaines to attend the scheduled UOP directors meeting. Glanville looked over the assembled information during the flight. The two had with them the draft of a "fairness opinion letter" in which the price had been left blank. Either during or immediately prior to the directors' meeting, the two-page "fairness opinion letter" was typed in final form and the price of $21 per share was inserted.

On March 6, 1978, both the Signal and UOP boards were convened to consider the proposed merger. Telephone communications were maintained between the two meetings. Walkup, Signal's board chairman, and also a UOP director, attended UOP's meeting with Crawford in order to present Signal's position and answer any questions that UOP's non-Signal directors might have. Arledge and Chitiea, along with Signal's other designees on UOP's board, participated by conference telephone. All of UOP'S outside directors attended the meeting either in person or by conference telephone.

First, Signal's board unanimously adopted a resolution authorizing Signal to propose to UOP a cash merger of $21 per share as outlined in a certain merger agreement and other supporting documents. This proposal required that the merger be approved by a majority of UOP's outstanding minority shares voting at the stockholders meeting at which the merger would be considered, and that the minority shares voting in favor of the merger, when coupled with Signal's 50.5% interest would have to comprise at least two-thirds of all UOP shares. Otherwise the proposed merger would be deemed disapproved.

UOP's board then considered the proposal. Copies of the agreement were delivered to the directors in attendance, and other copies had been forwarded earlier to the directors participating by telephone. They also had before them UOP financial data for 1974-1977, UOP's most recent financial statements, market price information, and budget projections for 1978. In addition they had Lehman Brothers' hurriedly prepared fairness opinion letter finding the price of $21 to be fair. Glanville, the Lehman Brothers partner, and UOP director, commented on the information that had gone into preparation of the letter.

Signal also suggests that the Arledge-Chitiea feasibility study, indicating that a price of up to $24 per share would be a "good investment" for Signal, was discussed at the UOP directors' meeting. The Chancellor made no such finding, and our independent review of the record, detailed *infra*, satisfies us by a preponderance of the evidence that there was no discussion of this document at UOP's board meeting. Furthermore it is clear beyond peradventure that nothing in that report was ever disclosed to UOP's minority shareholders prior to their approval of the merger.

After consideration of Signal's proposal, Walkup and Crawford left the meeting to permit a free and uninhibited exchange between UOP's non-Signal directors. Upon their return a resolution to accept Signal's offer was then proposed and adopted. While Signal's men on UOP's board participated in various aspects of the meeting, they abstained from voting. However, the minutes show that each of them "if voting would have voted yes."

On March 7, 1978, UOP sent a letter to its shareholders advising them of the action taken by UOP's board with respect to Signal's offer. This document pointed out, among other things, that on February 28, 1978 "both companies had announced negotiations were being conducted."

Despite the swift board action of the two companies, the merger was not submitted to UOP's shareholders until their annual meeting on May 26, 1978. In the notice of that meeting and proxy statement sent to shareholders in May, UOP's management and board urged that the merger be approved. The proxy statement also advised:

> The price was determined after *discussions* between James V. Crawford, a director of Signal and Chief Executive Officer of UOP, and officers of Signal which took place during meetings on February 28, 1978, and in the course of several subsequent telephone conversations. (Emphasis added).

In the original draft of the proxy statement the word "negotiations" had been used rather than "discussions". However, when the Securities and Exchange Commission sought details of the "negotiations" as part of its review of these materials, the term was deleted and the word "discussions" was substituted. The proxy statement indicated that the vote of UOP's board in approving the merger had been unanimous. It also advised the shareholders that Lehman Brothers had given its opinion that the merger price of $21 per share was fair to UOP's minority. However, it did not disclose the hurried method by which this conclusion was reached.

As of the record date of UOP's annual meeting, there were 11,488,302 shares of UOP common stock outstanding, 5,688,302 of which were owned by the minority. At the meeting only 56%, or 3,208,652, of the minority shares were voted. Of these, 2,958,812, or 51.9% of the total minority, voted for the merger, and 254,840 voted against it. When Signal's stock was added to the minority shares voting in favor, a total of 76.2% of UOP's outstanding shares approved the merger while only 2.2% opposed it.

By its terms the merger became effective on May 26, 1978, and each share of UOP's stock held by the minority was automatically converted into a right to receive $21 cash.

II

A

A primary issue mandating reversal is the preparation by two UOP directors, Arledge and Chitiea, of their feasibility study for the exclusive use and benefit of Signal. This document was of obvious significance to both Signal and UOP. Using UOP data, it described the advantages of Signal of ousting the minority at a price range of $21-$24 per share. Mr. Arledge, one of the authors, outlined the benefits to Signal:[6]

Purpose Of The Merger

1) Provides an outstanding investment opportunity for Signal -- (Better than any recent acquisition we have seen.)
2) Increases Signal's earnings.
3) Facilitates the flow of resources between Signal and its subsidiaries -- (Big factor -- works both ways.)
4) Provides cost savings potential for Signal and UOP.
5) Improves the percentage of Signal's 'operating earnings' as opposed to 'holding company earnings'.
6) Simplifies the understanding of Signal.
7) Facilitates technological exchange among Signal's subsidiaries.
8) Eliminates potential conflicts of interest.

Having written those words, solely for the use of Signal, it is clear from the record that neither Arledge nor Chitiea shared this report with their fellow directors of UOP. We are satisfied that no one else did either. This conduct hardly meets the fiduciary standards applicable to such a transaction. While Mr. Walkup, Signal's chairman of the board and a UOP director, attended the March 6, 1978 UOP board meeting and testified at trial that he had discussed the Arledge-Chitiea report with the UOP directors at this meeting, the record does not support this assertion. Perhaps it is the result of some confusion on Mr. Walkup's part. In any event Mr. Shumway, Signal's president, testified that he made sure the Signal outside directors had this report prior to the March 6, 1978 Signal board meeting, but he did not testify that the Arledge-Chitiea report was also sent to UOP's outside directors.

Mr. Crawford, UOP's president, could not recall that any documents, other than a draft of the merger agreement, were sent to UOP's directors before the March 6, 1978 UOP meeting. Mr. Chitiea, an author of the report,

---

[6] The parentheses indicate certain handwritten comments of Mr. Arledge.

testified that it was made available to Signal's directors, but to his knowledge it was not circulated to the outside directors of UOP. He specifically testified that he "didn't share" that information with the outside directors of UOP with whom he served.

None of UOP's outside directors who testified stated that they had seen this document. . . . Even when queried at a prior oral argument before this Court, counsel for Signal did not claim that the Arledge-Chitiea report had been disclosed to UOP's outside directors. Instead, he chose to belittle its contents. This was the same approach taken before us at the last oral argument.

Actually, it appears that a three-page summary of figures was given to all UOP directors. Its first page is identical to one page of the Arledge-Chitiea report, but this dealt with nothing more than a justification of the $21 price. Significantly, the contents of this three-page summary are what the minutes reflect Mr. Walkup told the UOP board. However, nothing contained in either the minutes or this three-page summary reflects Signal's study regarding the $24 price.

The Arledge-Chitiea report speaks for itself in supporting the Chancellor's finding that a price of up to $24 was a "good investment" for Signal. It shows that a return on the investment at $21 would be 15.7% versus 15.5% at $24 per share. This was a difference of only two-tenths of one%, while it meant over $17,000,000 to the minority. Under such circumstances, paying UOP's minority shareholders $24 would have had relatively little long-term effect on Signal, and the Chancellor's findings concerning the benefit to Signal, even at a price of $24, were obviously correct. Levitt v. Bouvier, 287 A.2d 671, 673 (Del.1972).

Certainly, this was a matter of material significance to UOP and its shareholders. Since the study was prepared by two UOP directors, using UOP information for the exclusive benefit of Signal, and nothing whatever was done to disclose it to the outside UOP directors or the minority shareholders, a question of breach of fiduciary duty arises. This problem occurs because there were common Signal-UOP directors participating, at least to some extent, in the UOP board's decision-making processes without full disclosure of the conflicts they faced.[7]

---

[7] Although perfection is not possible, or expected, the result here could have been entirely different if UOP had appointed an independent negotiating committee of its outside directors to deal with Signal at arm's length. See e.g., Harriman v. E.I. DuPont de Nemours & Co., 411 F.Supp. 133 (D.Del.1975). Since fairness in this context can be equated to conduct by a theoretical, wholly independent, board of directors acting upon the matter before them, it is unfortunate that this course apparently was neither considered nor pursued. Johnston v. Greene, 121 A.2d 919, 925 (Del.1956). Particularly in a parent-subsidiary context, a showing that the action taken was as though each of the contending parties had in fact exerted its bargaining power against the other at arm's length is strong evidence that the transaction meets the test of fairness. Getty Oil Co. v. Skelly Oil Co., 267 A.2d 883, 886 (Del.1970); Puma v. Marriott, 283 A.2d 693, 696 (Del.Ch.1971).

B

In assessing this situation, the Court of Chancery was required to:

> examine what information defendants had and to measure it against what they gave to the minority stockholders, in a context in which 'complete candor' is required. In other words, the limited function of the Court was to determine whether defendants had disclosed all information in their possession germane to the transaction in issue. And by 'germane' we mean, for present purposes, information such as a reasonable shareholder would consider important in deciding whether to sell or retain stock. . . .
> Completeness, not adequacy, is both the norm and the mandate under present circumstances.

Lynch v. Vickers Energy Corp., 383 A.2d 278, 281 (Del.1977) (*Lynch I*). This is merely stating in another way the long-existing principle of Delaware law that these Signal designated directors on UOP's board still owed UOP and its shareholders an uncompromising duty of loyalty. The classic language of Guth v. Loft, Inc., 5 A.2d 503, 510 (Del.1939), requires no embellishment:

> A public policy, existing through the years, and derived from a profound knowledge of human characteristics and motives, has established a rule that demands of a corporate officer or director, peremptorily and inexorably, the most scrupulous observance of his duty, not only affirmatively to protect the interests of the corporation committed to his charge, but also to refrain from doing anything that would work injury to the corporation, or to deprive it of profit or advantage which his skill and ability might properly bring to it, or to enable it to make in the reasonable and lawful exercise of its powers. The rule that requires an undivided and unselfish loyalty to the corporation demands that there shall be no conflict between duty and self-interest.

Given the absence of any attempt to structure this transaction on an arm's length basis, Signal cannot escape the effects of the conflicts it faced, particularly when its designees on UOP's board did not totally abstain from participation in the matter. There is no "safe harbor" for such divided loyalties in Delaware. When directors of a Delaware corporation are on both sides of a transaction, they are required to demonstrate their utmost good faith and the most scrupulous inherent fairness of the bargain. Gottlieb v. Heyden Chemical Corp., 91 A.2d 57, 57-58 (Del.1952). The requirement of fairness is unflinching in its demand that where one stands on both sides of a transaction, he has the burden of establishing its entire fairness, sufficient to pass the test of careful scrutiny by the courts. Sterling v. Mayflower Hotel Corp., 93 A.2d 107, 110 (Del.1952); Bastian v. Bourns, Inc., 256 A.2d 680, 681 (Del.Ch.1969), *aff'd*, 278 A.2d 467 (Del.1970); David J. Greene & Co. v. Dunhill International Inc., 249 A.2d 427, 431 (Del.Ch.1968).

There is no dilution of this obligation where one holds dual or multiple directorships, as in a parent-subsidiary context. Levien v. Sinclair Oil Corp.,

261 A.2d 911, 915 (Del.Ch.1969). Thus, individuals who act in a dual capacity as directors of two corporations, one of whom is parent and the other subsidiary, owe the same duty of good management to both corporations, and in the absence of an independent negotiating structure (see note 7, *supra*), or the directors' total abstention from any participation in the matter, this duty is to be exercised in light of what is best for both companies. Warshaw v. Calhoun, 221 A.2d 487, 492 (Del.1966). The record demonstrates that Signal has not met this obligation.

C

The concept of fairness has two basic aspects: fair dealing and fair price. The former embraces questions of when the transaction was timed, how it was initiated, structured, negotiated, disclosed to the directors, and how the approvals of the directors and the stockholders were obtained. The latter aspect of fairness relates to the economic and financial considerations of the proposed merger, including all relevant factors: assets, market value, earnings, future prospects, and any other elements that affect the intrinsic or inherent value of a company's stock. Andrew Moore, *The "Interested" Director or Officer Transaction*, 4 Del.J.Corp.L. 674, 676 (1979); Charles Nathan & K.L. Shapiro, *Legal Standard of Fairness of Merger Terms Under Delaware Law*, 2 Del.J.Corp.L. 44, 46-47 (1977). See Tri-Continental Corp. v. Battye, 74 A.2d 71, 72 (Del.1950); 8 Del.C. § 262(h). However, the test for fairness is not a bifurcated one as between fair dealing and price. All aspects of the issue must be examined as a whole since the question is one of entire fairness. However, in a non-fraudulent transaction we recognize that price may be the preponderant consideration outweighing other features of the merger. Here, we address the two basic aspects of fairness separately because we find reversible error as to both.

D

Part of fair dealing is the obvious duty of candor required by *Lynch I, supra.* Moreover, one possessing superior knowledge may not mislead any stockholder by use of corporate information to which the latter is not privy. Lank v. Steiner, 224 A.2d 242, 244 (Del.1966). Delaware has long imposed this duty even upon persons who are not corporate officers or directors, but who nonetheless are privy to matters of interest or significance to their company. Brophy v. Cities Service Co., 70 A.2d 5, 7 (Del.Ch.1949). With the well-established Delaware law on the subject, and the Court of Chancery's findings of fact here, it is inevitable that the obvious conflicts posed by Arledge and Chitiea's preparation of their "feasibility study", derived from UOP information, for the sole use and benefit of Signal, cannot pass muster.

The Arledge-Chitiea report is but one aspect of the element of fair dealing. How did this merger evolve? It is clear that it was entirely initiated by Signal. The serious time constraints under which the principals acted were all set by Signal. It had not found a suitable outlet for its excess cash and considered UOP a desirable investment, particularly since it was now in a position to acquire the whole company for itself. For whatever reasons, and they were only Signal's, the entire transaction was presented to and approved by UOP's board within four business days. Standing alone, this is not necessarily indicative of any lack of fairness by a majority shareholder. It was what occurred, or more properly, what did not occur, during this brief period that makes the time constraints imposed by Signal relevant to the issue of fairness.

The structure of the transaction, again, was Signal's doing. So far as negotiations were concerned, it is clear that they were modest at best. Crawford, Signal's man at UOP, never really talked price with Signal, except to accede to its management's statements on the subject, and to convey to Signal the UOP outside directors' view that as between the $20-$21 range under consideration, it would have to be $21. The latter is not a surprising outcome, but hardly arm's length negotiations. Only the protection of benefits for UOP's key employees and the issue of Lehman Brothers' fee approached any concept of bargaining.

As we have noted, the matter of disclosure to the UOP directors was wholly flawed by the conflicts of interest raised by the Arledge-Chitiea report. All of those conflicts were resolved by Signal in its own favor without divulging any aspect of them to UOP.

This cannot but undermine a conclusion that this merger meets any reasonable test of fairness. The outside UOP directors lacked one material piece of information generated by two of their colleagues, but shared only with Signal. True, the UOP board had the Lehman Brothers' fairness opinion, but that firm has been blamed by the plaintiff for the hurried task it performed, when more properly the responsibility for this lies with Signal. There was no disclosure of the circumstances surrounding the rather cursory preparation of the Lehman Brothers' fairness opinion. Instead, the impression was given UOP's minority that a careful study had been made, when in fact speed was the hallmark, and Mr. Glanville, Lehman's partner in charge of the matter, and also a UOP director, having spent the weekend in Vermont, brought a draft of the "fairness opinion letter" to the UOP directors' meeting on March 6, 1978 with the price left blank. We can only conclude from the record that the rush imposed on Lehman Brothers by Signal's timetable contributed to the difficulties under which this investment banking firm attempted to perform its responsibilities. Yet, none of this was disclosed to UOP's minority.

Finally, the minority stockholders were denied the critical information that Signal considered a price of $24 to be a good investment. Since this would have meant over $17,000,000 more to the minority, we cannot conclude that the shareholder vote was an informed one. Under the circumstances, an approval by a majority of the minority was meaningless. *Lynch I*, 383 A.2d at 279, 281; Cahill v. Lofland, 114 A. 224 (Del.Ch.1921).

Given these particulars and the Delaware law on the subject, the record does not establish that this transaction satisfies any reasonable concept of fair dealing, and the Chancellor's findings in that regard must be reversed.

E

Turning to the matter of price, plaintiff also challenges its fairness. His evidence was that on the date the merger was approved the stock was worth at least $26 per share. In support, he offered the testimony of a chartered investment analyst who used two basic approaches to valuation: a comparative analysis of the premium paid over market in ten other tender offer-merger combinations, and a discounted cash flow analysis.

In this breach of fiduciary duty case, the Chancellor perceived that the approach to valuation was the same as that in an appraisal proceeding. Consistent with precedent, he rejected plaintiff's method of proof and accepted defendants' evidence of value as being in accord with practice under prior case law. This means that the so-called "Delaware block" or weighted average method was employed wherein the elements of value, i.e., assets, market price, earnings, etc., were assigned a particular weight and the resulting amounts added to determine the value per share. This procedure has been in use for decades. See In re General Realty & Utilities Corp., 52 A.2d 6, 14-15 (Del.Ch.1947). However, to the extent it excludes other generally accepted techniques used in the financial community and the courts, it is now clearly outmoded. It is time we recognize this in appraisal and other stock valuation proceedings and bring our law current on the subject.

While the Chancellor rejected plaintiff's discounted cash flow method of valuing UOP's stock, as not corresponding with "either logic or the existing law" (426 A.2d at 1360), it is significant that this was essentially the focus, i.e., earnings potential of UOP, of Messrs. Arledge and Chitiea in their evaluation of the merger. Accordingly, the standard "Delaware block" or weighted average method of valuation, formerly employed in appraisal and other stock valuation cases, shall no longer exclusively control such proceedings. We believe that a more liberal approach must include proof of value by any techniques or methods which are generally considered acceptable in the financial community and otherwise admissible in court, subject only to our interpretation of 8 Del.C. § 262(h), *infra*. See also D.R.E. 702-05. This will obviate the very structured and mechanistic procedure that has heretofore governed such matters.

Fair price obviously requires consideration of all relevant factors involving the value of a company. This has long been the law of Delaware as stated in *Tri-Continental Corp.*, 74 A.2d at 72:

> The basic concept of value under the appraisal statute is that the stockholder is entitled to be paid for that which has been taken from him, viz., his proportionate interest in a going concern. By value of the stockholder's proportionate interest in the corporate enterprise is meant the true or intrinsic value of his stock which has been taken by the merger. In determining what

figure represents this true or intrinsic value, the appraiser and the courts must take into consideration all factors and elements which reasonably might enter into the fixing of value. Thus, market value, asset value, dividends, earning prospects, the nature of the enterprise and any other facts which were known or which could be ascertained as of the date of merger and which throw any light on *future prospects* of the merged corporation are not only pertinent to an inquiry as to the value of the dissenting stockholders' interest, but *must be considered* by the agency fixing the value. (Emphasis added).

This is not only in accord with the realities of present day affairs, but it is thoroughly consonant with the purpose and intent of our statutory law. Under 8 Del.C. § 262(h), the Court of Chancery:

shall appraise the shares, determining their *fair* value exclusive of any element of value arising from the accomplishment or expectation of the merger, together with a fair rate of interest, if any, to be paid upon the amount determined to be the *fair* value. In determining such *fair* value, the Court shall take into account *all relevant factors* . . . (Emphasis added).

See also Bell v. Kirby Lumber Corp., 413 A.2d 137, 150-51 (Del.1980) (Quillen, J., concurring).

It is significant that § 262 now mandates the determination of "fair" value based upon "all relevant factors". Only the speculative elements of value that may arise from the "accomplishment or expectation" of the merger are excluded. We take this to be a very narrow exception to the appraisal process, designed to eliminate use of *pro forma* data and projections of a speculative variety relating to the completion of a merger. But elements of future value, including the nature of the enterprise, which are known or susceptible of proof as of the date of the merger and not the product of speculation, may be considered. When the trial court deems it appropriate, fair value also includes any damages, resulting from the taking, which the stockholders sustain as a class. If that was not the case, then the obligation to consider "all relevant factors" in the valuation process would be eroded. We are supported in this view not only by *Tri-Continental Corp.*, 74 A.2d at 72, but also by the evolutionary amendments to § 262.

Prior to an amendment in 1976, the earlier relevant provision of § 262 stated:

(f) The appraiser shall determine the value of the stock of the stockholders. . . . The Court shall by its decree determine the value of the stock of the stockholders entitled to payment therefor . . .

The first references to "fair" value occurred in a 1976 amendment to § 262(f), which provided:

(f) . . . the Court shall appraise the shares, determining their fair value exclusively of any element of value arising from the accomplishment or expectation of the merger. . . .

It was not until the 1981 amendment to § 262 that the reference to "fair value" was repeatedly emphasized and the statutory mandate that the Court "take into account all relevant factors" appeared [§ 262(h)]. Clearly, there is a legislative intent to fully compensate shareholders for whatever their loss may be, subject only to the narrow limitation that one can not take speculative effects of the merger into account.

Although the Chancellor received the plaintiff's evidence, his opinion indicates that the use of it was precluded because of past Delaware practice. While we do not suggest a monetary result one way or the other, we do think the plaintiff's evidence should be part of the factual mix and weighed as such. Until the $21 price is measured on remand by the valuation standards mandated by Delaware law, there can be no finding at the present stage of these proceedings that the price is fair. Given the lack of any candid disclosure of the material facts surrounding establishment of the $21 price, the majority of the minority vote, approving the merger, is meaningless.

The plaintiff has not sought an appraisal, but rescissory damages of the type contemplated by Lynch v. Vickers Energy Corp., 429 A.2d 497, 505-06 (Del.1981) (*Lynch II*). In view of the approach to valuation that we announce today, we see no basis in our law for *Lynch II*'s exclusive monetary formula for relief. On remand the plaintiff will be permitted to test the fairness of the $21 price by the standards we herein establish, in conformity with the principle applicable to an appraisal -- that fair value be determined by taking "into account all relevant factors" [see 8 Del.C. § 262(h), *supra*]. In our view this includes the elements of rescissory damages if the Chancellor considers them susceptible of proof and a remedy appropriate to all the issues of fairness before him. To the extent that *Lynch II,* 429 A.2d at 505-06, purports to limit the Chancellor's discretion to a single remedial formula for monetary damages in a cash-out merger, it is overruled.

While a plaintiff's monetary remedy ordinarily should be confined to the more liberalized appraisal proceeding herein established, we do not intend any limitation on the historic powers of the Chancellor to grant such other relief as the facts of a particular case may dictate. The appraisal remedy we approve may not be adequate in certain cases, particularly where fraud, misrepresentation, self-dealing, deliberate waste of corporate assets, or gross and palpable overreaching are involved. Cole v. National Cash Credit Ass'n, 156 A. 183, 187 (Del.Ch.1931). Under such circumstances, the Chancellor's powers are complete to fashion any form of equitable and monetary relief as may be appropriate, including rescissory damages. Since it is apparent that this long completed transaction is too involved to undo, and in view of the Chancellor's discretion, the award, if any, should be in the form of monetary damages based upon entire fairness standards, i.e., fair dealing and fair price.

Obviously, there are other litigants, like the plaintiff, who abjured an appraisal and whose rights to challenge the element of fair value must be preserved.[8] Accordingly, the quasi-appraisal remedy we grant the plaintiff here will apply only to: (1) this case; (2) any case now pending on appeal to this Court; (3) any case now pending in the Court of Chancery which has not yet been appealed but which may be eligible for direct appeal to this Court; (4) any case challenging a cash-out merger, the effective date of which is on or before February 1, 1983; and (5) any proposed merger to be presented at a shareholders' meeting, the notification of which is mailed to the stockholders on or before February 23, 1983. Thereafter, the provisions of 8 Del.C. § 262, as herein construed, respecting the scope of an appraisal and the means for perfecting the same, shall govern the financial remedy available to minority shareholders in a cash-out merger. Thus, we return to the well established principles of Stauffer v. Standard Brands, Inc., 187 A.2d 78 (Del.1962) and David J. Greene & Co. v. Schenley Industries, 281 A.2d 30 (Del.Ch.1971), mandating a stockholder's recourse to the basic remedy of an appraisal.

III

Finally, we address the matter of business purpose. The defendants contend that the purpose of this merger was not a proper subject of inquiry by the trial court. The plaintiff says that no valid purpose existed -- the entire transaction was a mere subterfuge designed to eliminate the minority. The Chancellor ruled otherwise, but in so doing he clearly circumscribed the thrust and effect of Singer. Weinberger v. UOP, 426 A.2d at 1342-43, 1348-50. This has led to the thoroughly sound observation that the business purpose test "may be . . . virtually interpreted out of existence, as it was in *Weinberger.*"[9]

The requirement of a business purpose is new to our law of mergers and was a departure from prior case law. See Stauffer v. Standard Brands, Inc., *supra*; David J. Greene & Co. v. Schenley Industries, *supra*.

In view of the fairness test which has long been applicable to parent-subsidiary mergers, Sterling v. Mayflower Hotel Corp., 93 A.2d 107, 109-10 (Del.1952), the expanded appraisal remedy now available to shareholders, and the broad discretion of the Chancellor to fashion such relief as the facts of a given case may dictate, we do not believe that any additional meaningful protection is afforded minority shareholders by the business purpose requirement of the trilogy of *Singer, Tanzer,*[10] *Najjar,*[11] and their progeny. Accordingly, such requirement shall no longer be of any force or effect.

---

[8] Under 8 Del.C. § 262(a), (d) & (e), a stockholder is required to act within certain time periods to perfect the right to an appraisal.

[9] Elliot Weiss, *The Law of Take Out Mergers: A Historical Perspective,* 56 NYU L.Rev. 624, 671, n.300 (1981).

[10] Tanzer v. International General Industries, 379 A.2d 1121, 1124-25 (Del.1977).

[11] Roland International Corp. v. Najjar, 407 A.2d 1032, 1036 (Del.1979).

The judgment of the Court of Chancery, finding both the circumstances of the merger and the price paid the minority shareholders to be fair, is reversed. The matter is remanded for further proceedings consistent herewith. Upon remand the plaintiff's post-trial motion to enlarge the class should be granted. . . . Reversed and Remanded.

Weinberger clearly eliminated one aspect of the restrictions on freezeout mergers. The requirement that the acquiring company demonstrate a business purpose for the transaction "shall no longer be of any force or effect." 457 A.2d at 715. This result, however, may have been one of the great anticlimaxes in corporate law history. Following *Tanzer*, "the Delaware chancellors reduced the business purpose test to a minor irritant requiring only a little imagination, proper planning, and rhetoric on the part of lawyers in formulating a business reason for the merger."[53] *Weinberger* merely announced a death that had occurred some time before. The real significance of *Weinberger* thus depends upon the substance of the entire fairness test and the consequences that flow from whether it is met. It is important to keep clearly in mind that the entire fairness test functions to determine the exclusivity of the appraisal remedy. If the transaction is found to be entirely fair, then appraisal is exclusive. Alternatively, if the transaction fails the entire fairness test, then a nonappraisal challenge can proceed. Intricately tied to evaluation of the substance of the entire fairness test is evaluation of the stakes: the procedural and remedial differences between appraisal and a challenge to the fairness of the merger.

3. Fair Price

We should start our consideration of fair price with a preliminary look at fair dealing. This, the court stressed, included how the transaction "was initiated, structured, negotiated, disclosed to the directors, and how the approvals of the directors and the stockholders were obtained." *Id.* In this regard, the court endorsed the use of procedural techniques -- like approval of the transaction by a majority of the minority shareholders and the appointment of an independent negotiating committee -- designed to sanitize approval of the transaction from the majority shareholder's controlling influence. Where such techniques are used, the burden of proof with respect to unfairness "entirely shifts to the plaintiff," making it more likely that the transaction will be found entirely fair, and the minority shareholders left to their appraisal rights. However, these procedures are not costless, since the price paid in the merger will be influenced by the bargaining power given the

---

[53] Herzel & Colling (1984), *supra* note 1, at 203.

minority. Thus, the incentive for a controlling shareholder to adopt such procedures depends on what they produce.

The most obvious benefit to the defendant from adopting arm's length procedures is the difference between a class action and appraisal. Even if both procedures result in the same court determined price, any increase over the merger price will have to be paid to fewer minority shareholders because the procedural difficulties in perfecting appraisal right will limit the number of shareholders entitled to the increment. But *Lynch* continued to hold out the potential of a free option in the form of recisionary relief. Does *Weinberger*'s new appraisal valuation apply in the absence of fair dealing? If all that is available to plaintiffs in a fairness challenge is the same measure of damage available in appraisal, then is *Weinberger* any more than a doctrinal exercise seeking to make up for the fact that the statutory appraisal procedure is fatally defective? Note that in Roland International Corp. v. Najjar, 407 A.2d 1032 (Del.1979), one of the decisions following closely on *Singer*, a dissenting Justice criticized the entire fairness exception to the exclusivity of appraisal as creating an "unnecessary damage forum." 407 A.2d at 1040, n.12 (Quillen, J. dissenting). Would the entire problem disappear if the Delaware legislature made a class procedure available in appraisal?[54]

Weinberger did make some effort to rationalize the measure of damages. The court specified a single measure of value -- "fair value based upon all relevant factors" and determined in light of "generally accepted techniques used in the financial community" -- that would be generally applicable both in an appraisal proceeding and in an action claiming violation of the entire fairness standard. This measure reflected two major changes in Delaware law. First, the court rejected the traditional Delaware "block" method of valuation that determined fair value by three different methods -- market value, asset value, and earnings value -- and then took an average of the three following an *ad hoc* weighting of each.[55] Second, the court took substantial liberty with the statutory language to allow valuation to take into account, and therefore to allow minority shareholders to share in, synergistic gains from the transaction. Recall that in *Lynch* the court crafted a monetary rescission remedy precisely because an appraisal remedy, as adopted by the Chancery Court, would have excluded the minority shareholders from participation in any synergistic gains; under the then terms of § 262, fair value was to exclude "any element of value arising from the expectation or accomplishment of the merger or consolidation." In *Weinberger*, the court construed that

---

[54] See American Law Institute, *Principles of Corporate Governance Project* (1994), Commentary to § 7.23 at 340-42 (limited effort to create class-like appraisal procedure).

[55] The Delaware block method of valuation is criticized in, e.g., Daniel Fischel, *The Appraisal Remedy in Corporate Law*, 1983 Am.B.Found.Res.J. 875, 890-93; and Elmer Schaeffer, *The Fallacy of Weighting Asset and Earnings Value in the Appraisal of Corporate Stock*, 55 S.Cal.L.Rev. 1031 (1982).

> language to be a very narrow exception to the appraisal process, designed to eliminate use of *pro forma* data and projections of the speculative variety relating to the completion of a merger. But elements of future value, including the nature of the enterprise, which are known or susceptible as proof as of the date of the merger and not the product of speculation, may be considered.

457 A.2d at 713.[56] Thus, having adopted the critical aspect of the *Lynch* measure of damages for both appraisal and non-appraisal proceedings, the court overruled *Lynch*, so as to maintain a single measure of damages. It thereby eliminated at least this pre-*Weinberger* basis for preferring one type of proceeding to the other.

That is not, however, to say that appraisal valuation is *exclusive*. The court is at pains to stress that it does

> not intend any limitation on the historic powers of the Chancellor to grant such relief as the facts of a particular case may dictate. The appraisal remedy we approve may not be adequate in certain cases, particularly where fraud, misrepresentation, self-dealing, deliberate waste of corporate assets, or gross and palpable overreaching are involved.

Id. at 714. Under these circumstances a non-appraisal damage remedy presumably would be available.

Cede & Co. v. Technicolor, Inc., 634 A.2d 345 (Del.1993), provides guidance on the extent to which the entire fairness standard contemplates a different damage measure than appraisal. *Cede* involved an arm's length two step acquisition in which a $23 per share tender offer, representing in excess of a 100% premium, was followed by a freezeout merger at the same price. Plaintiffs claimed that the target directors had violated their duty of care in accepting the terms of the transaction. The Chancery Court found that the target board had violated its duty of care by not sufficiently informing themselves before accepting the $23 per share offer. However, the Chancellor required proof of injury before imposing personal liability on directors for the violation: "[A]s in any case in which the gist of the claim is negligence, plaintiff bears the burden to establish that the negligence shown was the proximate cause of some injury to it. . . ." 634 A.2d at 368-9 (quoting Chancery Court opinion).[57] He found no liability because, despite the Technicolor board's negligence, the price received exceeded the fair value of Technicolor's shares in an appraisal proceeding.

The Supreme Court reversed, explicitly rejecting the Chancery Court's effort to avoid creating, in Justice Quillen's words, an "unnecessary damage forum." The court stated:

---

[56] Professor Fischel describes this portion of the court's opinion as "[i]n apparent disregard of the plain language of the appraisal statute." Fischel (1983), *supra* note 55, at 895.

[57] Technicolor directors were exposed to personal liability because the transaction pre-dated the adoption of § 102(b)(7) by the Delaware legislature. See Marshall Small, *Negotiating Delaware Merger Transactions*, 27 Rev.Sec. & Com.Reg. 29, 31 (1994).

We . . . find the [Chancery] court to have committed error under *Weinberger* in apparently capping Cinerama's recoverable loss under an entire fairness standard of review at the fair value of a share of Technicolor stock on the date of approval of the merger. Under Weinberger's entire fairness standard of review, a party may have a legally cognizable injury regardless of whether the tender offer and cash-out price is greater than the stock's fair value as determined for statutory appraisal purposes. See Weinberger, 457 A.2d at 714; Rabkin v. Phllip A. Hunt Chemical Corp., 498 A.2d 1099, 1104 (Del.1985) (appraisal not exclusive remedy).

634 A.2d at 367.

Determining the fair value of minority shares in the context of a freezeout merger raises in a different context the question of when minority shareholders should be allowed to participate equally in a control premium. Presumably the minority shares in a freezeout merger have less value than controlling shares by the amount of the control premium. In Mendel v. Carroll,[58] the Chancery Court explained why a controlling shareholder could appropriately decline an offer for its shares, even at a price higher than the price the controlling shareholder had offered for minority shares. Suppose the controlling shareholder then freezes out the minority. Is the measure of value a proportionate amount of the value of the entire company, thereby giving the minority a portion of the control premium, or merely the value of minority shares?

In Smith v. Shell Petroleum, Inc., 1990 WL 84218 (Del.Ch.1990), an appraisal proceeding, the court gave greater weight to stock market value than liquidation value when the existence of a majority shareholder made it apparent that the corporation would not be liquidated. While the court did not expressly note it, stock market value represents the value of minority shares, rather than a proportionate amount of the value of the entire company, because controlling shares do not trade.[59] Section 7.22(c) of the American Law Institute's Corporate Governance Project takes the opposite position, by requiring that, in effect, the control premium be shared in freezeout mergers: "If the transaction falls within . . . § 7.25, the court generally should give substantial weight to the highest realistic price that a willing, able, and fully informed buyer would pay for the corporation as an entity."[60] How does the ALI's position with respect to valuation in freezeout mergers correspond to the general principle, reflected in § 5.16 of the Corporate Governance Project, that a controlling shareholder can sell her shares at a premium without allowing the minority to participate?

---

[58] Excerpted in Chapter 21, *supra*.

[59] See Harry DeAngelo & Linda DeAngelo, *Managerial Ownership of Voting Rights: A Study of Public Corporations with Dual Classes of Stock*, 14 J.Fin.Econ. 33 (1985).

[60] American Law Institute (1994), *supra* note 54, § 7.22.

4.   Fair Dealing

KAHN v. LYNCH COMMUNICATION SYSTEMS, INC.
638 A.2d 1110 (Del.1994)

HOLLAND, Justice. [This] action, instituted by Kahn in 1986, originally sought to enjoin the acquisition of the defendant-appellee, Lynch Communication Systems, Inc. ("Lynch"), by the defendant-appellee, Alcatel U.S.A. Corporation ("Alcatel"), pursuant to a tender offer and cash-out merger.   Kahn amended his complaint to seek monetary damages after the Court of Chancery denied his request for a preliminary injunction. The Court of Chancery subsequently certified Kahn's action as a class action on behalf of all Lynch shareholders, other than the named defendants, who tendered their stock in the merger, or whose stock was acquired through the merger.

A three-day trial was held. . . .   Kahn alleged that Alcatel was a controlling shareholder of Lynch and breached its fiduciary duties to Lynch and its shareholders. According to Kahn, Alcatel dictated the terms of the merger; made false, misleading, and inadequate disclosures; and paid an unfair price.

The Court of Chancery concluded that Alcatel was, in fact, a controlling shareholder that owed fiduciary duties to Lynch and its shareholders. It also concluded that Alcatel had not breached those fiduciary duties. Accordingly, the Court of Chancery entered judgment in favor of the defendants.

Kahn raised three contentions in this appeal. Kahn's first contention is that the Court of Chancery erred by finding that "the tender offer and merger were negotiated by an independent committee," and then placing the burden of persuasion on the plaintiff, Kahn.   Kahn asserts the uncontradicted testimony in the record demonstrated that the committee could not and did not bargain at arm's length with Alcatel. Kahn's second contention is that Alcatel's Offer to Purchase was false and misleading because it failed to disclose threats made by Alcatel to the effect that if Lynch did not accept its proposed price, Alcatel would institute a hostile tender offer at a lower price. Third, Kahn contends that the merger price was unfair. . . .

This Court has concluded that the record supports the Court of Chancery's finding that Alcatel was a controlling shareholder. However, the record does not support the conclusion that the burden of persuasion shifted to Kahn. Therefore, the burden of proving the *entire* fairness of the merger transaction remained on Alcatel, the controlling shareholder. Accordingly, the judgment of the Court of Chancery is reversed. . . .

Facts

Lynch, a Delaware corporation, designed and manufactured electronic telecommunications equipment, primarily for sale to telephone operating companies. Alcatel, a holding company, is a subsidiary of Alcatel (S.A.), a French company involved in public telecommunications, business communications, electronics, and optronics. Alcatel (S.A.), in turn is a subsidiary of Compagnie Generale d'Electricite ("CGE"), a French corporation with operations in energy, transportation, telecommunications and business systems.

In 1981, Alcatel acquired 30.6% of Lynch's common stock pursuant to a stock purchase agreement. As part of that agreement, Lynch amended its certificate of incorporation to require an 80% affirmative vote of its shareholders for approval of any business combination. In addition, Alcatel obtained proportional representation on the Lynch board of directors and the right to purchase 40% of any equity securities offered by Lynch to third parties. The agreement also precluded Alcatel from holding more than 45% of Lynch's stock prior to October 1, 1986. By the time of the merger which is contested in this action, Alcatel owned 43.3% of Lynch's outstanding stock; designated five of the eleven members of Lynch's board of directors; two of three members of the executive committee; and two of four members of the compensation committee.

In the spring of 1986, Lynch determined that in order to remain competitive in the rapidly changing telecommunications field, it would need to obtain fiber optics technology to complement its existing digital electronic capabilities. Lynch's management identified a target company, Telco Systems, Inc. ("Telco"), which possessed both fiber optics and other valuable technological assets. The record reflects that Telco expressed interest in being acquired by Lynch. Because of the supermajority voting provision, which Alcatel had negotiated when it first purchased its shares, in order to proceed with the Telco combination Lynch needed Alcatel's consent. In June 1986, Ellsworth F. Dertinger ("Dertinger"), Lynch's CEO and chairman of its board of directors, contacted Pierre Suard ("Suard"), the chairman of Alcatel's parent company, CGE, regarding the acquisition of Telco by Lynch. Suard expressed Alcatel's opposition to Lynch's acquisition of Telco. Instead, Alcatel proposed a combination of Lynch and Celwave Systems, Inc. ("Celwave"), an indirect subsidiary of CGE engaged in the manufacture and sale of telephone wire, cable and other related products.

Alcatel's proposed combination with Celwave was presented to the Lynch board at a regular meeting held on August 1, 1986. Although several directors expressed interest in the original combination which had been proposed with Telco, the Alcatel representatives on Lynch's board made it clear that such a combination would not be considered before a Lynch/Celwave combination. According to the minutes of the August 1 meeting, Dertinger expressed his opinion that Celwave would not be of interest to Lynch if Celwave was not owned by Alcatel.

At the conclusion of the meeting, the Lynch board unanimously adopted a resolution establishing an Independent Committee, consisting of Hubert L. Kertz ("Kertz"), Paul B. Wineman ("Wineman"), and Stuart M. Beringer ("Beringer"), to negotiate with Celwave and to make recommendations concerning the appropriate terms and conditions of a combination with Celwave. On October 24, 1986, Alcatel's investment banking firm, Dillon,

Read & Co., Inc. ("Dillon Read") made a presentation to the Independent Committee. Dillon Read expressed its views concerning the benefits of a Celwave/Lynch combination and submitted a written proposal of an exchange ratio of 0.95 shares of Celwave per Lynch share in a stock-for-stock merger.

However, the Independent Committee's investment advisors, Thomson McKinnon Securities Inc. ("Thomson McKinnon") and Kidder, Peabody & Co., Inc. ("Kidder Peabody"), reviewed the Dillon Read proposal and concluded that the 0.95 ratio was predicated on Dillon Read's overvaluation of Celwave. Based upon this advice, the Independent Committee determined that the exchange ratio proposed by Dillon Read was unattractive to Lynch. The Independent Committee expressed its unanimous opposition to the Celwave/Lynch merger on October 31, 1986.

Alcatel responded to the Independent Committee's action on November 4, 1986, by withdrawing the Celwave proposal. Alcatel made a simultaneous offer to acquire the entire equity interest in Lynch, constituting the approximately 57% of Lynch shares not owned by Alcatel. The offering price was $14 cash per share.

On November 8, 1986, the Lynch board of directors revised the mandate of the Independent Committee. It authorized Kertz, Wineman, and Beringer to negotiate the cash merger offer with Alcatel. At a meeting held that same day, the Independent Committee determined that the $14 per share offer was inadequate. The Independent Committee's own legal counsel, Skadden, Arps, Slate, Meagher & Flom ("Skadden Arps"), suggested that the Independent Committee should review alternatives to a cash-out merger with Alcatel, including a "white knight" third party acquiror, a repurchase of Alcatel's shares, or the adoption of a shareholder rights plan.

On November 24, 1986, Beringer, as chairman of the Independent Committee, contacted Michiel C. McCarty ("McCarty") of Dillon Read, Alcatel's representative in the negotiations, with a counteroffer at a price of $17 per share. McCarty responded on behalf of Alcatel with an offer of $15 per share. When Beringer informed McCarty of the Independent Committee's view that $15 was insufficient, Alcatel raised its offer to $15.25 per share. The Independent Committee also rejected this offer. Alcatel then made its final offer of $15.50 per share.

At the November 24, 1986 meeting of the Independent Committee, Beringer advised its other two members that Alcatel was "ready to proceed with an unfriendly tender at a lower price" if the $15.50 per share price was not recommended by the Independent Committee and approved by the Lynch board of directors. Beringer also told the other members of the Independent Committee that the alternatives to a cash-out merger had been investigated but were impracticable.[3]   After the meeting with its financial and legal

---

[3] The minutes reflect that Beringer told the Committee the "white knight" alternative "appeared impractical with the 80% approval requirement"; the repurchase of Alcatel's shares would produce a "highly leveraged company with a lower book value" and was an alternative "not in the least encouraged by Alcatel"; and a shareholder rights plan was not viable because

advisors, the Independent Committee voted unanimously to recommend that the Lynch board of directors approve Alcatel's $15.50 cash per share price for a merger with Alcatel. The Lynch board met later that day. With Alcatel's nominees abstaining, it approved the merger.

Alcatel Dominated Lynch, Controlling Shareholder Status

This Court has held that "a shareholder owes a fiduciary duty only if it owns a majority interest in or *exercises control* over the business affairs of the corporation." Ivanhoe Partners v. Newmont Mining Corp., 535 A.2d 1334, 1344 (Del.1987) (emphasis added). With regard to the exercise of control, this Court has stated:

> [A] shareholder who owns less than 50% of a corporation's outstanding stocks does not, without more, become a controlling shareholder of that corporation, with a concomitant fiduciary status. For a dominating relationship to exist in the absence of controlling stock ownership, a plaintiff must allege domination by a minority shareholder through actual control of corporation conduct.

Citron v. Fairchild Camera & Instrument Corp., 569 A.2d 53, 70 (Del.1989) (quotations and citation omitted).

Alcatel held a 43.3% minority share of stock in Lynch. Therefore, the threshold question to be answered by the Court of Chancery was whether, despite its minority ownership, Alcatel exercised control over Lynch's business affairs. Based upon the testimony and the minutes of the August 1, 1986 Lynch board meeting, the Court of Chancery concluded that Alcatel did exercise control over Lynch's business decisions. . . . The record supports the Court of Chancery's factual finding that Alcatel dominated Lynch.

At the August 1 meeting, Alcatel opposed the renewal of compensation contracts for Lynch's top five managers. According to Dertlinger, Christian Fayard ("Fayard"), an Alcatel director, told the board members "[y]ou must listen to us. We are 43% owner. You have to do what we tell you." The minutes confirm Dertinger's testimony. They recite that Fayard declared, "you are pushing us very much to take control of the company. Our opinion is not taken into consideration."

Although Beringer and Kertz, two of the independent directors, favored renewal of the contracts, according to the minutes, the third independent director, Wineman, admonished the board as follows:

> Mr. Wineman pointed out that the vote on the contracts is a "watershed vote" and the motion, due to Alcatel's "strong feelings," might not carry if taken now. Mr. Wineman clarified that "you [management] might win the battle and lose the war." With Alcatel's opinion so clear, Mr. Wineman questioned "if management wants the contracts renewed under these circumstances." He

---

of the increased debt it would entail.

recommended that management "think twice." Mr. Wineman declared: "I want to keep the management. I can't think of a better management." Mr. Kertz agreed, again advising consideration of the "critical" period the company is entering.

The minutes reflect that the management directors left the room after this statement. The remaining board members then voted not to renew the contracts.

At the same meeting, Alcatel vetoed Lynch's acquisition of the target company, which, according to the minutes, Beringer considered "an immediate fit" for Lynch. Dertinger agreed with Beringer, stating that the "target company is extremely important as they have the products that Lynch needs now." Nonetheless, Alcatel prevailed. The minutes reflect that Fayard advised the Board: "Alcatel, with its 44% equity position, would not approve such an acquisition . . . it does not wish to be diluted from being the main shareholder in Lynch." From the foregoing evidence, the Vice Chancellor concluded:

> . . . Alcatel did control the Lynch board, at least with respect to the matters under consideration at its August 1, 1986 board meeting. The interplay between the directors was more than vigorous discussion, as suggested by defendants. The management and independent directors disagreed with Alcatel on several important issues. However, when Alcatel made its position clear, and reminded the other directors of its significant stockholdings, Alcatel prevailed. Dertinger testified that Fayard "scared [the non-Alcatel directors] to death." While this statement undoubtedly is an exaggeration, it does represent a first-hand view of how the board operated. I conclude that the non-Alcatel directors deferred to Alcatel because of its position as a significant stockholder and not because they decided in the exercise of their own business judgment that Alcatel's position was correct [citation omitted].

The record supports the Court of Chancery's underlying factual finding that "the non-Alcatel [independent] directors deferred to Alcatel because of its position as a significant stockholder and not because they decided in the exercise of their own business judgment that Alcatel's position was correct." The record also supports the subsequent factual finding that, notwithstanding its 43.3% minority shareholder interest, Alcatel did exercise actual control over Lynch by dominating its corporate affairs. The Court of Chancery's legal conclusion that Alcatel owed the fiduciary duties of a controlling shareholder to the other Lynch shareholders followed syllogistically as the logical result of its cogent analysis of the record.

Entire Fairness Requirement, Dominating Interested Shareholder

A controlling or dominating shareholder standing on both sides of a transaction, as in a parent-subsidiary context, bears the burden of proving its entire fairness. Weinberger v. UOP, Inc., 457 A.2d 701, 710 (Del.1983). See

Rosenblatt v. Getty Oil Co., 493 A.2d 929, 937 (Del.1985). The demonstration of fairness that is required was set forth by this Court in *Weinberger*:

> The concept of fairness has two basic aspects: fair dealing and fair price. The former embraces questions of when the transacting was timed, how it was initiated, structured, negotiated, disclosed to the directors, and how the approvals of the directors and the stockholders were obtained. The latter aspect of fairness relates to the economic and financial considerations of the proposed merger, including all relevant factors: assets, market value, earnings, future prospects, and any other elements that affect the intrinsic or inherent value of a company's stock. However, the test for fairness is not a bifurcated one as between fair dealing and price. All aspects of the issue must be examined as a whole since the question is one of entire fairness.

Weinberger v. UOP, Inc., 457 A.2d at 711 (citations omitted).

The logical question raised by this Court's holding in *Weinberger* was what type of evidence would be reliable to demonstrate entire fairness. That question was not only anticipated but also initially addressed in the *Weinberger* opinion. *Id.* at 709-10 n.7. This court suggested that the result "could have been entirely different if UOP had appointed an independent negotiating committee of its outside directors to deal with Signal at arm's length," because "fairness in this context can be equated to conduct by theoretical, wholly independent, board of directors." *Id.* Accordingly, this Court stated, "a showing that the action taken was as though each of the contending parties had in fact exerted its bargaining power against the other at arm's length is strong *evidence* that the transaction meets the test of fairness. *Id.* (emphasis added).

In this case, the Vice Chancellor noted that the Court of Chancery has expressed "differing views" regarding the effect that an approval of a cash-out merger by a special committee of disinterested directors has upon the controlling or dominating shareholders' burden of demonstrating entire fairness. One view is that such approval shifts to the plaintiff the burden of proving that the transaction was unfair. Citron v. E.I. DuPont de Nemours & Co., 584 A.2d 490, 500-02 (Del.Ch.1990); Rabkin v. Olin Corp., 1990 WL 47648, slip op. at 14-15 (Del.Ch.1990), *reprinted in* 16 Del.J.Corp.L. 851, 861-62 (1991), *aff'd*, 586 A.2d 1202 (Del.1990). The other view is that such an approval renders the business judgment rule the applicable standard of judicial review. In re TransWorld Airlines, Inc. Shareholders Litig., 1988 WL 111271, slip op. at 15-16 (Del.Ch.1988), *reprinted in* 14 Del.J.Corp.L. 870, 883 (1989).[4] See Cinerama, Inc. v. Technicolor, Inc., 1991 WL 111134, slip op. at 47-48 (Del.Ch.1991), *reprinted in* 17 Del.J.Corp.L. 551, 570-72 (1992),

---

[4] We note that the Court of Chancery opinion in *TransWorld Airlines, Inc.* did not cite *Rosenblatt*. See Citron v. E.I. DuPont de Nemours & Co., 584 A.2d 490, 501 n.15 (Del.Ch.1990).

aff'd in part and rev'd in part on other grounds sub nom. Cede & Co. v. Technicolor, Inc., 634 A.2d 345 (Del.1993).

"It is often of critical importance whether a particular decision is one to which the business judgment rule applies or the entire fairness rule applies." Nixon v. Blackwell, 626 A.2d 1366, 1376 (Del.1993). The definitive answer with regard to the Court of Chancery's "differing views" is found in this Court's opinions in *Weinberger* and *Rosenblatt.* In *Weinberger,* this Court held that because

> of the fairness test which has long been applicable to parent-subsidiary mergers, the expanded appraisal remedy now available to shareholders, and the broad discretion of the [Court of Chancery] to fashion such relief as the facts of a given case may dictate, we do not believe that any additional meaningful protection is afforded minority shareholders by the business purpose requirement of the trilogy of *Singer* [v. Magnavox Co., 380 A.2d 969 (Del.1977)], *Tanzer* [v. Int'l General Industries, 379 A.2d 1121 (Del.1977)], [Roland Int'l Corp. v.] *Najjar* [407 A.2d 1032 (Del.1979)], and their progeny. Accordingly, such requirement shall no longer be of any force or effect.

Weinberger v. UOP, Inc., 457 A.2d at 715 (citation and footnotes omitted). Thereafter, this Court recognized that it would be inconsistent with its holding in *Weinberger* to apply the business judgment rule in the context of an interested merger transaction which, by its very nature, did not require a business purpose. See Rosenblatt v. Getty Oil Co., 493 A.2d at 937. Consequently in *Rosenblatt,* in the context of a subsequent proceeding involving a parent-subsidiary merger, this Court held that the "approval of a merger, as here, by an informed vote of a majority of the minority stockholders, while not a legal prerequisite, shifts the burden of proving the unfairness of the merger entirely to the plaintiffs." *Id.*

Entire fairness remains the proper focus of judicial analysis in examining an interested merger, irrespective of whether the burden of proof remains upon or is shifted away from the controlling or dominating shareholder, because the unchanging nature of the underlying "interested" transaction requires careful scrutiny. See Weinberger v. UOP, Inc., 457 A.2d at 710 (citing Sterling v. Mayflower Hotel Corp., 93 A.2d 107, 110 (Del.1952)). The policy rationale for the exclusive application of the entire fairness standard has been stated as follows:

> Parent subsidiary mergers, unlike stock options, are proposed by a party that controls, and will continue to control, the corporation, whether or not the minority stockholders vote to approve or reject the transaction. The controlling stockholder relationship has the potential to influence, however subtly, the vote of [ratifying] minority stockholders in a manner that is not likely to occur in a transaction with a noncontrolling party.
>
> Even where no coercion is intended, shareholders voting on a parent subsidiary merger might perceive that their disapproval could risk retaliation of some kind by the controlling stockholder. For example, the controlling stockholder might decide to stop dividend payments or to effect a subsequent

cash out merger at a less favorable price, for which the remedy would be time consuming and costly litigation. At the very least, the potential for that perception, and its possible impact upon a shareholder vote, could never be fully eliminated. Consequently, in a merger between the corporation and its controlling stockholder -- even one negotiated by disinterested, independent directors -- no court could be certain whether the transaction terms fully approximate what truly independent parties would have achieved in an arm's length negotiation. Given that uncertainty, a court might well conclude that even minority shareholders who have ratified a . . . merger need procedural protections beyond those afforded by full disclosure of all material facts. One way to provide such protections would be to adhere to the more stringent entire fairness standard of judicial review.

Citron v. E.I. DuPont de Nemours & Co., 584 A.2d at 502.

Once again, this Court holds that the exclusive standard of judicial review in examining the propriety of an interested cash-out merger transaction by a controlling or dominating shareholder is entire fairness. Weinberger v. UOP, Inc., 457 A.2d at 710-11. The initial burden of establishing entire fairness rests upon the party who stands on both sides of the transaction. *Id*. However, an approval of the transaction by an independent committee of directors or an informed majority of minority shareholders shifts the burden of proof on the issue of fairness from the controlling or dominating shareholder to the challenging shareholder-plaintiff. See Rosenblatt v. Getty Oil Co., 493 A.2d at 937-38. Nevertheless, even when an interested cash-out merger transaction receives the informed approval of a majority of minority stockholders or an independent committee of disinterested directors, an entire fairness analysis is the only proper standard of judicial review. See *id*.

Independent Committees, Interested Merger Transactions

It is a now well-established principle of Delaware corporate law that in an interested merger, the controlling or dominating shareholder proponent of the transaction bears the burden of proving its entire fairness. Weinberger v. UOP, Inc., 457 A.2d 701, 710-11 (Del.1983). It is equally well-established in such contexts that any shifting of the burden of proof on the issue of entire fairness must be predicated upon this Court's decisions in Rosenblatt v. Getty Oil Co., 493 A.2d 929 (Del.1985) and 701 (1983). In *Weinberger*, this Court noted that "[p]articularly in a parent-subsidiary context, a showing that the action taken was as though each of the contending parties had *in fact* exerted its bargaining power against the other at arm's length is strong evidence that the transaction meets the test of fairness." 457 A.2d at 709-10 n.7 (emphasis added). Accord Rosenblatt v. Getty Oil Co., 493 A.2d at 937-38 & n.7. In *Rosenblatt*, this Court pointed out that "[an] independent bargaining structure, while not conclusive, is strong evidence of the fairness" of a merger transaction. Rosenblatt v. Getty Oil Co., 493 A.2d at 938 n.7.

The same policy rationale which requires judicial review of interested cash-out mergers exclusively for entire fairness also mandates careful judicial scrutiny of a special committee's real bargaining power before shifting the burden of proof on the issue of entire fairness. A recent decision from the Court of Chancery articulated a two-part test for determining whether burden shifting is appropriate in an interested merger transaction. Rabkin v. Olin Corp., 1990 WL 47648, slip op. at 14-15 (Del.Ch.1990), *reprinted in* 16 Del.J.Corp.L. 851, 961-62 (1991), *aff'd*, 586 A.2d 1202 (Del.1990). In Olin, the Court of Chancery stated:

> The mere existence of an independent special committee . . . does not itself shift the burden. At least two factors are required. First, the majority shareholder must not dictate the terms of the merger. Rosenblatt v. Getty Oil Co., 493 A.2d 929, 937 (Del.1985). Second, the special committee must have real bargaining power that it can exercise with the majority shareholder on an arms length basis.

Id., slip op. at 24-25, 16 Del.J.Corp.L. at 861-61.[6] This Court expressed its agreement with that statement by affirming the Court of Chancery decision in *Olin* on appeal.

Lynch's Independent Committee

In the case *sub judice,* the Court of Chancery observed that although "Alcatel did exercise control over Lynch with respect to the decisions made at the August 1, 1986 board meeting, it does not necessarily follow that Alcatel also controlled the terms of the merger and its approval." This observation is theoretically accurate, as this opinion has already stated. Weinberger v. UOP, Inc., 457 A.2d at 709-10 n.7. However, the performance of the Independent Committee merits careful judicial scrutiny to determine whether Alcatel's demonstrated pattern of domination was effectively neutralized so that "each of the contending parties had in fact exerted its bargaining power against the other at arm's length." *Id.* The fact that the same independent directors had submitted to Alcatel's demands on August 1, 1986 was part of the basis for the Court of Chancery's finding of Alcatel's domination of Lynch. Therefore, the Independent Committee's ability to bargain at arm's length with Alcatel was suspect from the outset.

The Independent Committee's original assignment was to examine the merger with Celwave which had been proposed by Alcatel. The record

---

[6] In *Olin*, the Court of Chancery concluded that because the special committee had been given "the narrow mandate of determining the monetary fairness of a non-negotiable offer," and because the majority shareholder "dictated the terms" and "there were no arm's-length negotiations," the burden of proof on the issue of entire fairness remained with the defendants. *Id.*, slip op. at 15, 16 Del.J.Corp.L. at 862. In making that determination, the Court of Chancery pointed out that the majority shareholder "could obviously have used its majority stake to effectuate the merger" regardless of the committee's or the board's disapproval, and that the record demonstrated that the directors of both corporations were "acutely aware of this fact." *Id.*, slip op. at 13, 16 Del.J.Corp.L. at 861.

reflects that the Independent Committee's adverse recommendation was not the pursuit of further negotiations regarding its Celwave proposal, but rather its response was an offer to buy Lynch. That offer was consistent with Alcatel's August 1, 1986 expressions of an intention to dominate Lynch, since an acquisition would effectively eliminate once and for all Lynch's remaining vestiges of independence.

The Independent Committee's second assignment was to consider Alcatel's proposal to purchase Lynch. The Independent Committee proceeded on that task with full knowledge of Alcatel's demonstrated pattern of domination. The Independent Committee was also obviously aware of Alcatel's refusal to negotiate with it on the Celwave matter.

Burden of Proof Shifted Court of Chancery's Finding

The Court of Chancery began its factual analysis by noting that Kahn had "attempted to shatter" the image of the Independent Committee's actions as having "appropriately simulated" an arm's length, third-party transaction. The Court of Chancery found that "to some extent, [Kahn's attempt] was successful." The Court of Chancery gave credence to the testimony of Kertz, one of the members of the Independent Committee, to the effect that he did not believe that $15.50 was a fair price but that he voted in favor of the merger because he felt there was no alternative.

The Court of Chancery also found that Kertz understood Alcatel's position to be that it was ready to proceed with an unfriendly tender offer at a lower price if Lynch did not accept the $15.50 offer, and that Kertz perceived this to be a threat by Alcatel. The Court of Chancery concluded that Kertz ultimately decided that, "although $15.50 was not fair, a tender offer and merger at that price would be better for Lynch's stockholders than an unfriendly tender offer at a significantly lower price." The Court of Chancery determined that "Kertz failed either to satisfy himself that the offered price was fair or oppose the merger."

In addition to Kertz, other members of the Independent Committee were Beringer, its chairman, and Wineman. Wineman did not testify at trial. Beringer was called by Alcatel to testify at trial. Beringer testified that at the time of the Committee's vote to recommend the $15.50 offer to the Lynch board, he thought "that *under the circumstances*, a price of $15.50 was fair and should be accepted" (emphasis added).

Kahn contends that these "circumstances" included those referenced in the minutes for the November 24, 1986 Independent Committee meeting: "Mr. Beringer added that Alcatel is 'ready to proceed with an unfriendly tender at a lower price' if the $15.50 per share price is not recommended to, and approved by, the Company's Board of Directors." In his testimony at trial, Beringer verified, albeit reluctantly, the accuracy of the foregoing statement in the minutes: "[Alcatel] *let us know* that they were giving serious consideration to making an unfriendly tender (emphasis added)."

The record reflects that Alcatel was "ready to proceed" with a hostile bid. This was a conclusion reached by Beringer, the Independent Committee's chairman and spokesman, based upon communications to him from Alcatel. Beringer testified that although there was no reference to a particular price for a hostile bid during his discussions with Alcatel, or even specific mention of a "lower" price, "the implication was clear to [him] that it probably would be at a lower price."

According to the Court of Chancery, the Independent Committee rejected three lower offers for Lynch from Alcatel and then accepted the $15.50 offer "after being advised that [it] was fair and after considering the absence of alternatives." The Vice Chancellor expressly acknowledged the impracticability of Lynch's Independent Committee's alternatives to a merger with Alcatel:

> Lynch was not in a position to shop for other acquirors, since Alcatel could block any alternative transaction. Alcatel also made it clear that it was not interested in having its shares repurchased by Lynch. The Independent Committee decided that a stockholder rights plan was not viable because of the increased debt it would entail.

Nevertheless, based upon the record before it, the Court of Chancery found that the Independent Committee had "appropriately simulated a third-party transaction, where negotiations are conducted at arms-length and there is no compulsion to reach an agreement." The Court of Chancery concluded that the Independent Committee's actions "as a whole" were "sufficiently well informed . . . and aggressive to simulate an arms-length transaction," so that the burden of proof as to entire fairness shifted from Alcatel to the contending Lynch shareholder, Kahn. The Court of Chancery's reservations about that finding are apparent in its written decision.

The Power to Say No, The Parties' Contentions, Arm's Length Bargaining

The Court of Chancery properly noted that limitations on the alternatives to Alcatel's offer did not mean that the Independent Committee should have agreed to a price that was unfair:

> The power to say no is a significant power. It is the duty of directors serving on [an independent] committee to approve only a transaction that is in the best interests of the public shareholders, to say no to any transaction that is not fair to those shareholders and is not the best transaction available. It is not sufficient for such directors to achieve the best price that a fiduciary will pay if that price is not a fair price.

(Quoting *In re First Boston, Inc. Shareholders Litig.,* 1990 WL 78836, slip op. at 15-16 (Del.Ch.1990).

The Alcatel defendants argue that the Independent Committee exercised its "power to say no" in rejecting the three initial offers from Alcatel, and that it therefore cannot be said that Alcatel dictated the terms of the merger or precluded the Independent Committee from exercising real bargaining power. Compare Rabkin v. Olin Corp., 1990 WL 47648, (Del.Ch.1990), *reprinted in* 16 Del.J.Corp.L. 851, 861-62 (1991), *aff'd*, 586 A.2d 1202 (Del.1990).[9] The Alcatel defendants contend, alternatively, that "even assuming that such a threat [of a hostile takeover] could have had a coercive effect on the [Independent] Committee," the willingness of the Independent Committee to reject Alcatel's initial three offers suggests that "the alleged threat was either nonexistent or ineffective." Braunschweiger v. American Home Shield Corp., 1991 WL 3920, (Del.Ch.1991), *reprinted in* 17 Del.J.Corp.L. 206, 219 (1992).

Kahn contends the record reflects that the conduct of Alcatel deprived the Independent Committee of an effective "power to say no." Kahn argues that Alcatel not only threatened the Committee with a hostile tender offer in the event its $15.50 offer was not recommended and approved, but also directed the affairs of Lynch for Alcatel's benefit in such a way as to make it impossible for Lynch to continue as a public company under Alcatel's control without injury to itself and its minority shareholders. In support of this argument, Kahn relies upon another proceeding wherein the Court of Chancery has been previously presented with factual circumstances comparable to those of the case *sub judice*, albeit in a different procedural posture. See American Gen. Corp. v. Texas Air Corp., 1987 WL 6337 (Del.Ch.1987), *reprinted in* 13 Del.J.Corp.L. 173 (1988).

In *American General*, in the context of an application for injunctive relief, the Court of Chancery found that the members of the Special Committee were "truly independent and . . . performed their tasks in a proper manner," but it also found that "at the end of their negotiations with [the majority shareholder] the Committee members were issued an ultimatum and told that they must accept the $16.50 per share price or [the majority shareholder] would proceed with the transaction without their input." *Id.*, 13 Del.J.Corp.L. at 181. The Court of Chancery concluded based upon this evidence that the Special Committee had thereby lost "its ability to negotiate in an arms-length manner" and that there was a reasonable probability that the burden of proving entire fairness would remain on the defendants if the litigation proceeded to trial. *Id.*, 13 Del.J.Corp.L. at 181.

Alcatel's efforts to distinguish *American General* are unpersuasive. Alcatel's reliance on *Braunschweiger* is also misplaced. In *Braunschweiger*, the Court of Chancery pointed out that "[p]laintiffs do not allege that [the management-affiliated merger partner] ever used the threat of a hostile

---

[9] Alcatel also points to the fairness opinions of two investment banking firms employed by the Committee, Kidder Peabody and Thomson McKinnon, and the involvement of independent legal counsel, Skadden Arps, in considering and rejecting alternatives to the Alcatel cash offers.

takeover to influence the special committee." Braunschweiger v. American Home Shield Corp., 17 Del.J.Corp.L. at 219. Unlike *Braunschweiger*, in this case the coercion was extant and directed to a specific price offer which was, in effect, presented in the form of a "take if or leave it" ultimatum by a controlling shareholder with the capability of following through on its threat of a hostile takeover.

Alcatel's Entire Fairness Burden Did Not Shift to Kahn

A condition precedent to finding that the burden of proving entire fairness has shifted in an interested merger transaction is a careful judicial analysis of the factual circumstances of each case. Particular consideration must be given to evidence of whether the special committee was truly independent, fully informed, and had the freedom to negotiate at arm's length. Weinberger v. UOP, Inc., 457 A.2d 701, 709-10 n.7 (Del.1983). See also American Gen. Corp. v. Texas Air Corp., 1987 WL 6337, (Del.Ch.1987), *reprinted in* 13 Del.J.Corp.L. 173 (1988). "Although perfection is not possible," unless the controlling or dominating shareholder can demonstrate that it has not only formed an independent committee but also replicated a process "as though each of the contending parties had in fact exerted its bargaining power at arm's length," the burden of proving entire fairness will not shift. Weinberger v. UOP, Inc., 457 A.2d at 709-10 n.7. See also Rosenblatt v. Getty Oil Co., 493 A.2d 929, 937-38 (Del.1985). . . .

The Court of Chancery's determination that the Independent Committee "appropriately simulated a third-party transaction, where negotiations are conducted at arm's-length and there is no compulsion to reach an agreement," is not supported by the record. Under the circumstances present in the case *sub judice*, the Court of Chancery erred in shifting the burden of proof with regard to entire fairness to the contesting Lynch shareholder-plaintiff Kahn. The record reflects that the ability of the Committee effectively to negotiate at arm's length was compromised by Alcatel's threats to proceed with a hostile tender offer if the $15.50 price was not approved by the Committee and the Lynch board. The fact that the Independent Committee rejected three initial offers, which were well below the Independent Committee's estimated valuation for Lynch and were not combined with an explicit threat that Alcatel was "ready to proceed" with a hostile bid, cannot alter the conclusion that any semblance of arm's length bargaining ended when the Independent Committee surrendered to the ultimatum that accompanied Alcatel's final offer. Rabkin v. Philip A. Hunt Chem. Corp., 498 A.2d 1099, 1106 (Del.1985).

Conclusion

Accordingly, the judgment of the Court of Chancery is reversed. This matter is remanded for further proceedings consistent herewith, including a redetermination of the entire fairness of the cash-out merger to Kahn and the other Lynch minority shareholders with the burden of proof remaining on Alcatel, the dominant and interested shareholder.

Note: Where Are We Left After *Lynch Communications*?

Meeting the Fair Dealing Component of Entire Fairness: What Do You Get? Under *Lynch Communications*, satisfying the fair dealing component of the entire fairness standard has a clear but limited effect: the burden of proving entire fairness shifts to the plaintiff. However, the court could have assigned greater consequence to the procedural character of the transaction. Satisfying the fair dealing component through genuine arm's length negotiations could have been treated as exorcising the taint of control from the transaction. The business judgment rule would then be the appropriate standard of review. The court justifies maintaining heightened review despite an independent negotiating structure by reference to the inherently coercive nature of the relationship: "The controlling shareholder relationship has the potential to influence, however subtly, the vote of a [ratifying] minority in a manner that is not likely to occur in a transaction with a noncontrolling party." But if satisfying the fair dealing component of entire fairness secures only a shift in the burden of proof, is it worth the effort? Does shifting the burden of proof significantly effect the remaining fair price component of entire fairness?

For example, in *Weinberger* the fair value of UOP minority stock apparently was somewhere in the range of $20 to $24. The court, however, seemed to think the "right" price was the top of the range: "[The Signal Report] shows that a return on the investment at $21 would be 15.7% versus 15.5% at $24 per share. This was a difference of only two-tenths of one%, while it meant over $17,000,000 to the minority. Under such circumstances, paying UOP's minority shareholders $24 would have had relatively little long-term effect on Signal. . . ." In arm's length negotiations, it is impossible to predict where in the range between the buyer's reservation price (the highest price the buyer will pay) and the seller's reservation price (the lowest price the seller will take) the deal will be struck. Perhaps the effect of shifting in the burden of proof as to fair price when the negotiating structure meets the fair dealing standard is to limit judicial inquiry to assuring that the price is within a range of reasonableness. This may be no small matter. In *Weinberger* the difference was $17 million.

What Procedures Establish Fair Dealing? The target board in *Lynch Communication* appeared to establish a genuinely independent negotiating committee; by rejecting three lower offers, the committee increased the price from $14.00 to $15.50 per share.[61] Nonetheless, the court concluded that "the ability of the Committee effectively to negotiate at arm's length was compromised by Alcatel's threats to proceed with a hostile tender offer if the $15.50 price was not approved by the Committee and the Lynch Board." The court raised the same concern with respect to a vote by a majority of the minority. Is it enough that the controlling shareholder does not explicitly threaten a hostile offer, or must the independent negotiating committee actually have the "power to say no" for the structure of the negotiating process to meet the fair dealing standard?[62] How can the power to say no be created? What about a standstill agreement that prohibited the controlling shareholder from acquiring additional shares for a period of time if the negotiations proved unsuccessful? Recall that Alcatel had been subject to an agreement that limited its holdings to 45% that had expired.

Why is the court so troubled by the threat of a hostile tender offer? Unlike a merger, shareholders cannot be forced to participate in a tender offer. Perhaps the concern is that the shareholders will feel coerced into tendering, as was the case with the target company self-tender in *Anderson, Clayton* discussed in Chapter 17. But in *Lynch Communications*, the court held that Alcatel already had control; other shareholders were a minority before a hostile offer, and those who thought the price too low and did not tender would be a minority after the offer. The hostile offer might have been an effective "negotiating" technique because shareholders would have tendered at a price closer to their reservation price. But what is wrong with that result? Suppose that the independent committee had the power to say no and Alcatel declined to go forward at a higher price. Could the minority shareholders then replace the negotiating committee and accept a lower price as still better than market price?

One cannot avoid the conclusion that the Delaware courts have yet to think through the complicated relationship between controlling and minority shareholders. Alcatel could have sold its control at a premium with little fear of liability for not sharing that premium with the minority. Alternatively, Alcatel could have retained control, enjoying the stream of private benefits whose capitalized value is reflected in the control premium and thereby freezing in minority shareholders. Or, in a tender offer, Alcatel could offer minority shareholders a way out at a price that would have to be above the

---

[61] This represented a 10.7% increase. In *Weinberger*, the difference between $24 and $21 per share was only approximately 14.3%, and that measure was to Signal's reservation price.

[62] The American Law Institute's Corporate Governance Project suggests that the power to say no is a necessary condition to giving credence to an independent negotiating structure: "[I]f the majority shareholder consummates the transaction over the objection of the independent negotiating committee, there will not have been arm's-length bargaining, and the committee's existence should not be given weight by a reviewing court." American Law Institute (1994), *supra* note 54, Commentary to § 7.25 at 388.

minority's reservation price to be successful. Why is the last alternative more suspect than the first two?[63]

Other Approaches to Exclusivity. Assessing the standards governing freezeouts requires something to which to compare it. Appraisal is the obvious candidate. Instead of creating what Justice Quillen called an "unnecessary damage forum," the court could have made explicit the implication of *Weinberger*'s elimination of the business purpose requirement: minority shareholders do not have a property right that allows them to remain participants in the corporation. From this perspective, *Weinberger* gives a controlling shareholder the power to eliminate the minority. The only question is the price. A statutory appraisal proceeding is specially designed to determine fair price. Appraisal could be exclusive.

The American Law Institute's Corporate Governance Project comes closer to making appraisal the exclusive means for challenging a freezeout merger. Provided that (i) minority shareholders are provided full disclosure and an adequate appraisal remedy; (ii) the merger is otherwise properly approved; and (iii) "the directors who approve the transaction . . . have an adequate basis, grounded on substantial objective evidence, for believing that the consideration offered to the minority shareholders . . . constitutes fair value for their shares . . . ," then appraisal is the exclusive remedy.[64] Does § 7.25 differ significantly from Delaware's entire fairness test? That directors must have an adequately grounded belief concerning fair value seems akin to the fair price component of the entire fairness test. On what basis would directors form this belief? Is this where a fair dealing component slips in?

So long as the acquiring company is not a controlling shareholder, both California and the American Law Institute's Corporate Governance Project treat appraisal as exclusive even if target directors have breached their duty of care .[65]

Entire Fairness as a Triggering Device. The entire fairness doctrine can be interpreted as what Einer Elhauge has called a triggering device; that is, a rule whose application determines whether another rule applies.[66] If entire fairness is met, appraisal is exclusive with the result that only the small number of shareholders who actually perfect their appraisal remedy can challenge the merger price under the appraisal standard. If entire fairness is not met, then the merger price can be challenged in a class action on behalf of all target shareholders (not just dissenters). Moreover, the possibility exists of a rescission remedy; if the value of the shares has risen following the

---

[63] At least in the tender offer alternative minority shareholders have a choice.

[64] American Law Institute (1994), *supra* note 54, § 7.25.

[65] See American Law Institute (1994), *supra* note 54, § 7.24; Steinberg v. Emplace, 729 P.2d 683 (Cal.1986). Compare Smith v. Van Gorkom, 488 A.2d 858 (Del.1985).

[66] Einer Elhauge, *The Triggering Function of Sale of Control*, 59 U.Chi.L.Rev. 1465 (1992).

transaction, a rescission remedy could result in damages in excess of the appraisal standard. Why should the entire fairness test determine who can challenge the transaction and the applicable measure of damages?

One explanation focuses on the character of shareholder choice. Making appraisal exclusive gives credence to a shareholder's decision to accept the offered consideration rather than dissent. That reliance seems appropriate if the fair dealing standard is met; the decision not to dissent then can be assumed to be based on the fairness of the process, rather than on the procedural difficulties and expense of appraisal. Alternatively, if the merger was not independently negotiated, then there is greater reason to believe that the inadequacies of the appraisal remedy drove a shareholder's decision to accept the offered consideration instead of dissenting. Then the remedy for failing entire fairness matches the wrong: the procedural trappings of appraisal are jettisoned and the challenge to the merger price proceeds as a class action -- that is, as if all shareholders had dissented.

What about the triggering function of entire fairness with respect to the measure of damages? Here the potential for damages in excess of the appraisal standard -- in effect, punitive damages -- reduces the incentive for a controlling shareholder to set the consideration low in the hope that few shareholders dissent and that a carefully constructed facade of independence will slip by the entire fairness test. If the only penalty for getting caught is paying the price that you should have paid in the first place, then why not try. The potential for a rescission remedy can balance the controlling shareholder's incentives. This analysis suggests focusing on the circumstances when non-appraisal damages are available. *Weinberger* describes the appraisal standard as potentially inadequate "where fraud, misrepresentation, self-dealing, deliberate waste of corporate assets, or gross and palpable overreaching are involved." Are these circumstances appropriate triggers?[67]

From this perspective, the triggering function of the entire fairness test ameliorates the incentives of the controlling shareholder. But what does it do to the incentives of the minority shareholders and their lawyers? As discussed earlier, the structure of the entire fairness/appraisal dichotomy creates a virtually free option that is acquired by filing a class action challenging the freezeout merger. It is therefore hardly surprising that every freezeout merger seems to be the subject of litigation. If every transaction will be challenged anyway, wouldn't the second best solution be to design a streamlined class oriented appraisal procedure (with an opt-out for

---

[67] See Cinerama, Inc. v. Technicolor, Inc., Civ.Ac. No. 8358, slip opinion at 26 (Del.Ch.1994) ("[R]ecissory damages should never be awarded against a corporate director as a remedy for breach of duty of care alone; that remedy may be appropriate where a breach of the directors' duty of loyalty has been found, but neither principle nor authority supports the awarding of rescission . . . against one who neither participates in the deal as a principal, nor is a co-conspirator of a principal or has a material conflict of interest of another sort.") (citations omitted).

shareholders who preferred the merger price) and make it exclusive? That approach might eliminate the incentive for the controlling shareholder to lowball, and at least minimize the option character of the minority shareholders' position, especially if a realistic possibility existed that the appraisal value could be lower than the merger price.

D.　Federal Law Limitations on Freezeout Mergers

The litigation effort to use federal securities law to supplement state law limits on freezing out minority shareholders, discussed in Section C of this Chapter, had an administrative law counterpart. Even before the decision of the Second Circuit in Green v. Santa Fe Industries[68] holding that a freezeout of minority shareholders without a business purpose violated Rule 10b-5, the Securities and Exchange Commission had begun to respond to criticism of freezeout transactions as unfair and to criticism of state law as unresponsive. In 1975, it issued for comment proposed Rule 13e-3 which would have authorized the Commission to block freezeout transactions it determined were "unfair."[69]

Rule 13e-3 as finally adopted in August 1979[70] did not directly prohibit of "unfair" freezeouts. Responding to comments that it lacked the authority to regulate the substance of these transactions, the Commission limited the Rule to specifying the required disclosure in connection with a freezeout transaction. At least part of the disclosure required, however, clearly seems to have a substantive intent. Item 8 of Schedule 13e-3 -- the disclosure schedule adopted with Rule 13e-3 -- requires the issuer to state whether it reasonably believes the transaction is fair or unfair to public shareholders. As Jennings, Marsh & Coffee have put it, "The Commission obviously thought that no one would say to the minority shareholders, 'I believe that this transaction is unfair to you.' If the issuer said, 'I believe this transaction to be fair,' and, in fact, it was not, the shareholders could bring an action under the rule on the theory that the issuer either did not believe its statement or was reckless in making it."[71]

The coverage and content of Rule 13e-3 is described in the Release which reported its adoption.

GOING PRIVATE TRANSACTIONS BY PUBLIC COMPANIES OR THEIR AFFILIATES
Sec.Exch.Act Rel. No.16075 (Aug. 2, 1979)

---

[68] 533 F.2d 1283 (2d Cir.1976), *rev'd*, 430 U.S. 462 (1977).

[69] Sec.Exch.Act Rel. No. 11231 (Feb. 6, 1975).

[70] Sec.Exch.Act Rel. No. 16075 (Aug. 2, 1979).

[71] Richard Jennings, Harold Marsh & John Coffee, *Securities Regulation* 777 (7th ed.1982).

Most of the commentators were opposed to the requirement in the 1977 proposals that a Rule 13e-3 transaction must be both substantively and procedurally fair to unaffiliated security holders. A number of these commentators expressed the view that the Commission does not have the authority to adopt such a requirement. They also maintained that, in the absence of an explicit legislative mandate to regulate the fairness of going private transactions, the Commission should, as a matter of policy, refrain from doing so because substantive regulation of corporate affairs is, in their view, a subject for state and not federal cognizance. It was noted in this regard that recent decisions by state courts indicate that state law provides protection to unaffiliated security holders if control persons act unfairly when taking a company private. The imposition of a federal fairness requirement was also criticized because it would, in their view, result in the staff making decisions concerning the fairness of a proposed transaction in connection with its review of registration statements, preliminary proxy materials and tender offer documents relating to going private transactions. These commentators believe that the staff would not have the resources and expertise to handle such a role.

The Commission believes that the question of regulation of the fairness of going private transactions should be deferred until there is an opportunity to determine the efficacy of the provisions of Rule 13e-3. Further developments in the remedies provided by state law for unfairness in going private transactions will also be important in this regard. In the interim, the Commission believes that the protection of investors will be enhanced substantially by the more meaningful disclosure, particularly with respect to the fairness of going private transactions, and the other protections afforded by Rule 13e-3.

Several commentators criticized the application of the 1977 proposals to transactions which in their view do not involve the potential for abuse and overreaching associated with the normal going private transaction. Thus, they were of the view that the following types of transactions, among others, should not be covered: (i) mergers following an any and all tender offer by a bidder who, as a result of the tender offer, becomes an affiliate if the same price were being paid in each transaction; (ii) exchange offers to holders of non-redeemable preferred stock or convertible debentures; (iii) transactions structured to create a holding company or reincorporate the entity in a new jurisdiction; and (iv) mergers with and exchange offers by affiliates in which unaffiliated security holders would receive common stock of the surviving entity. In response to these comments, exceptions for such transactions are now provided by paragraphs (g)(1) and (g)(2) of Rule 13e-3, assuming that the other conditions of those provisions are satisfied.

(a) Overview of Application of Rule 13e-3

. . . A Rule 13e-3 transaction is defined to mean any transaction or series of transactions involving one or more of the transactions specified in paragraph (a)(4)(i) which has either a reasonable likelihood or purpose of producing, directly or indirectly, any of the effects specified in paragraph (a)(4)(ii). The specified transactions are: (a) a purchase of any equity security by the issuer of such security or by an affiliate of such issuer; (b) a tender offer or request or invitation for tenders of any equity security made by the issuer of such class of securities or by an affiliate of such issuer; or (c) a solicitation or distribution subject to Regulation 14A or Regulation 14C in connection with certain corporate events. The corporate events include a merger, consolidation, reclassification, recapitalization, reorganization or similar corporate transaction by an issuer or between an issuer (or its subsidiaries) and its affiliates; a sale by the issuer of substantially all of its assets to its affiliate; or a reverse stock split of any class of equity securities of the issuer involving the purchase of fractional interests.

As proposed, the effects selected to trigger the application of Rule 13e-3 were entirely in the disjunctive. As noted by the commentators, this produced the unintended result of applying Rule 13e-3 to specified transactions which had the reasonable likelihood or purpose of causing, for example, a class of equity securities of the issuer to be subject to delisting from an exchange, even though the securities would have continued to be authorized to be quoted on an inter-dealer quotation system of a registered national securities association. As revised, Rule 13e-3 is triggered by a specified transaction which has either the reasonable likelihood or purpose of causing either (i) the termination of reporting obligations under the Exchange Act, by virtue of the class of securities being held of record by less than 300 persons, or (ii) the securities to be neither listed on any exchange nor authorized to be quoted on an interdealer quotation system of any registered national securities association. Accordingly, in the above illustration, delisting of a class of equity securities from an exchange would not trigger the application of Rule 13e-3 if the securities were nevertheless authorized to be quoted on an inter-dealer quotation system of a registered national securities association.

The tests of "a reasonable likelihood" or "a purpose" that the transaction or series of transactions will produce a specified effect operate as alternative standards. The tests are designed to operate independently; the presence of either will trigger the application of Rule 13e-3. In a given situation, however, both tests may be met. The tests would apply equally to issuers and affiliates of issuers. In resolving close questions as to the application of the tests, issuers and affiliates are encouraged to resolve such questions in favor of compliance with the more limited burdens imposed by the revised requirements of the rule.

Both tests were criticized by the commentators on the ground that they are overly subjective. However, a more objective standard would lend itself to circumvention through skillful planning. The Commission believes, moreover, that it is reasonable for the protection of investors to require the person who is engaging in a transaction which may have a specified effect to determine whether either or both of these tests are satisfied. In order to be effective, the disclosure required by Rule 13e-3 must be received by security holders before consummation of the transaction or the earliest transaction in a series of transactions having a specified effect. These tests ensure that this objective will be accomplished. . . .

If the requirements of a Rule 13e-3 transaction are present, the application of the rule would be triggered unless an exception is available. Accordingly, the second factor to be considered is the availability of the exceptions set forth in paragraph (g). The exceptions included in the 1977 proposals, *viz.* transactions by a holding company registered under the Public Utility Holding Company Act of 1935, certain solicitations by an issuer with respect to a plan of reorganization under Chapter X of the Bankruptcy Act, and redemptions, calls or purchases pursuant to the instruments creating or governing the class of equity securities involved, have been adopted essentially as proposed. Two new exceptions have also been added.

First, Rule 13e-3(g)(1) excepts second-step, clean-up transactions which occur within one year of a tender offer by or on behalf of a bidder who, as a result of such tender offer, became an affiliate, provided that the equal consideration, disclosure and other requirements of the rule are met. The Commission believes that if a transaction is structured to meet the conditions of that rule it may safely be viewed as a unitary transaction which is not within the purview of the purposes of Rule 13e-3.

Second, Rule 13e-3(g)(2) provides an exception for transactions, including recapitalizations, in which, *inter alia,* security holders are offered only an equity security which is either common stock or has essentially the same attributes as the equity security which is the subject of the Rule 13e-3 transaction. The Commission believes that such transactions are also outside the purpose of Rule 13e-3 since all holders of that class of security are on an equal footing and are permitted to maintain an equivalent or enhanced equity interest. . . .

(b) Filing Requirements

Under Rule 13e-3(d)(1), the issuer or affiliate engaging in a Rule 13e-3 transaction would be required to file a Rule 13e-3 Transaction Statement on Schedule 13E-3, including all exhibits thereto, with the Commission. The time for such an initial filing is set forth in General Instruction A to Schedule 13E-3. This instruction recognizes the variety of methods employed in such transactions. Consequently, the initial filing requirement for the proposed Schedule would depend on the type of Rule 13e-3 transaction involved. If the transaction involves the filing with the Commission of soliciting materials or an information statement pursuant to Regulations 14A or 14C, respectively, the Schedule 13E-3 would be filed concurrently with the filing of "Preliminary Copies" of such soliciting materials or information statement. If the transaction involves the filing of a registration statement under the Securities Act, the Schedule would be filed concurrently therewith. If the transaction involves a tender offer, the Schedule would be filed as soon as practicable on the date the tender offer is first published, sent or given to security holders of the class of equity securities which is the subject of the Rule 13e-3 transaction. In cases where the transaction does not involve a solicitation, an information statement, the registration of securities or a tender offer, as described above, the Schedule would be required to be filed with the Commission at least 30 days prior to the date of any purchase by the issuer or affiliate of any securities of the class of securities subject to the Rule 13e-3 transaction. If the Rule 13e-3 transaction involves a series of transactions, the issuer or affiliate would file a Rule 13e-3 Transaction Statement on Schedule 13e-3 at the specified time for the first transaction in such series and would promptly amend the schedule with respect to each subsequent transaction. . . .

A final amendment on Schedule 13E-3 disclosing the results of the Rule 13e-3 transaction would be required to be filed under Rule 13e-3(d)(3) promptly but not later than ten days after the termination of the transaction. If the Rule 13e-3 transaction is a tender offer governed by Rule 13e-4, the final amendment would be filed no later than ten business days after the termination of such tender offer. . . .

(d) Dissemination Requirements

Rule 13e-3(f) prescribes the methods of dissemination of the information required to be disclosed to the security holders of the class of equity securities which is the subject of the Rule 13e-3 transaction. The method of dissemination applicable to a Rule 13e-3 transaction depends on the type of transaction involved.

If the Rule 13e-3 transaction is a purchase as described in Rule 13e-3(a)(4)(i)(A) or a vote, consent or authorization or distribution of information statements, as described in proposed Rule 13e-3(a)(4)(i)(C) Rule 13e-3(f)(1) would apply. While the disclosure would be disseminated in accordance with the provisions of applicable Federal or state law, in no event would such dissemination occur later than 20 days prior to: any such purchase; any such vote; consent or authorization; or with respect to the distribution of information statements, the meeting date, or if corporate action is to be taken by means of the written authorization or consent of security holders, the earliest date on which corporate action may be taken. Thus, Rule 13e-3(f)(1)(i)(A) would provide for a 20 day waiting period during which a Rule 13e-3 transaction could not be effected. Moreover, Rule 13e-3(f)(1)(i)(B) requires that the disclosure be disseminated to persons who are record holders as of the date not more than 20 days prior to the date of dissemination. For example, if the vote on a Rule 13e-3 transaction will occur on August 30, the disclosure would be disseminated no later than August 10. If August 10 is the date of dissemination, the disclosure would be transmitted to persons who are listed as record holders as of date not earlier than July 21. . . .

(e) Schedule 13E-3

Schedule 13E-3 establishes specific disclosure requirements for Rule 13e-3 transactions. . . .

The most significant change in the items of the Schedule is with respect to disclosure of the fairness of the transaction. Item 8 requires the issuer or affiliate to state whether it reasonably believes the Rule 13e-3 transaction is fair or unfair to unaffiliated security holders. The issuer or affiliate is also required to provide a detailed discussion of the material factors upon which that belief is based. This discussion is required to address the extent to which the following factors were taken into account: (1) whether the transaction is structured so that approval of at least a majority of unaffiliated security holders is required; (2) whether the consideration offered to unaffiliated security holders constitutes fair value; (3) whether the majority of non-employee directors has retained an unaffiliated representative to act solely on behalf of unaffiliated security holders for the purposes of negotiating the terms of the transaction and/or preparing a report concerning the fairness of the transaction; (4) whether the Rule 13e-3 transaction was approved by a majority of the directors of the issuer who are not employees of the issuer; and (5) whether a report, opinion or appraisal of the type described in Item 9 of the Schedule[a] was obtained. In order to minimize meaningless, boilerplate responses an instruction specifies that conclusory statements are not considered sufficient disclosure in responding to this requirement.

These factors are based to a large extent on the considerations set forth in the Note to proposed Rule 13e-3(b) which rule would have required that the transaction be fair to unaffiliated security holders. The commentators were concerned that the factors chosen would conflict with the standards under state law for determining fairness. Since a substantive fairness requirement is not being adopted at this time, this concern is now inapplicable. Moreover, Instruction 1 to Item 8(b) of Schedule 13E-3 indicates that the factors which are important in determining the fairness of a transaction to unaffiliated security holders, and the weight which should be given to them in a particular context, will vary. The context in which this determination is made, of course, includes the applicable state law. Accordingly, accommodation with those requirements is assured.

In any event, the Commission believes that increased discussion of factors bearing upon fairness to unaffiliated security holders is necessary in view of the potential for abuse which exists in a Rule 13e-3 transaction. The absence of arms-length negotiations which is characteristic of going private transactions requires that unaffiliated security holders be furnished with detailed information so that they can determine whether their rights have been adequately protected.

---

[a] Item 9 covers any "report, opinion or appraisal relating to the consideration or the fairness of the consideration to be offered. . . ." Eds.

E.   The Parallel Problem: The Plight of the Frozen In Minority

Section A of this Chapter examined the claim that the ability to freeze out minority shareholders of a target company following a successful tender offer was critical to the acquiring company's decision to make the offer in the first place. Part of the evaluation consisted of evaluating the acquiring company's alternative to freezing out minority shareholders: freezing them in. The idea was that if a majority shareholder has substantial freedom to take a disproportionate part of the target company's future earnings, then an acquiring company's best strategy might well be simply to allow the remaining target shareholders to continue as an exploited minority. A fair reading of *Sinclair* suggested, consistent with the weight of the academic opinion, that an acquiring company does have substantial freedom to favor itself in its dealings with its controlled, but not wholly owned, subsidiaries. Indeed, in light of the substantial premiums typically paid to minority shareholders in freezeouts, the puzzle is to explain the fixation of American law with the plight of the shareholder who is frozen out, and its almost total disregard of the parallel plight of the shareholder who is "frozen in." Consider, for example, the December 1985 addition of § 912 to the New York Business Corporations Law. The new section essentially prohibits second-step transactions for a period of five years from the date the acquiring company first acquires 20% of the target company's stock, unless the entire acquisition was approved by the target's board of directors prior to the time the acquiring company's holdings reached 20%. Here the New York legislature has frozen in the minority for five years. Given the analysis in Section A, how would this protect minority shareholders? Could it plausibly act as a deterrent to the acquisition in the first place?

Actually, the puzzle is even more complicated. The result of the effort to protect frozen out shareholders, as expressed in *Weinberger,* may combine with the law's relative indifference to frozen in shareholders, as expressed in *Sinclair,* to give the acquiring company a valuable strategic option. *Weinberger* allows an acquiring company to freeze out the minority, with a liberalized appraisal standard to be sure, but leaves in place a structure that, by creating an option for plaintiffs' lawyers who challenge the transaction, virtually assures litigation. The leniency of the standards of *Sinclair,* in turn, provides the freeze in alternative to freezing out the minority shareholders. Finally, there is yet a third alternative -- freeze the minority shareholders in for now, but freeze them out later at the time acquiring company management thinks an appraisal proceeding will be most favorable to it. Given the availability of choices, an acquiring company could be expected in each case to choose the alternative most favorable to it.

In light of the difficulties in devising a system in which an acquiring company could not take advantage of minority shareholders through its choice of whether to freeze them out, or freeze them in, or both, a second best alternative commands attention. Instead of trying to ameliorate the problems associated with an acquiring company's strategic choice of how to treat minority shareholders, simply eliminate the choice. Some sense of how such a system might operate can be drawn from the British experience with an approach that essentially eliminates the acquiring company's option to freeze in minority shareholders -- the prohibition of partial offers.

Standards governing the substance of takeover activity in the United Kingdom are set forth in *The City Code on Take-overs and Mergers* which was written and is administered by an industry group, the Panel on Take-Overs and Mergers.[72]

The Code itself consists of ten general principles that specify basic standards of conduct which are then implemented by 38 rules that add procedural and substantive content to the principles. General Principle 10, together with Rules 9 and 36, represent the British approach to limiting an acquiring company's options with respect to the treatment of minority shareholders.

General Principle 10

ACQUISITION OF CONTROL

> Where control of a company is acquired by a person, or persons acting in concert, a general offer to all other shareholders is normally required; a similar obligation may arise when control is consolidated. . . .

General Principle 10 is given specific form by Rule 9 which requires in Rule 9.1 that any person (or group of persons acting in concert) who accumulates in one or more transactions 30% or more of the voting rights of a target company must offer to purchase all remaining target shares. Pursuant to Rule 9.5, the offer must be at the highest price paid for target shares by the acquiring person within the previous twelve months. Thus, once control is acquired -- whether by tender offer or otherwise -- the obligation to make an

---

[72] See generally Alexander Johnston, *The City Take-Over Code* (1980); Deborah DeMott, *Current Issues in Tender Offer Regulation: Lessons from the British,* 58 NYU L.Rev. 945 (1983). The Code was originally published in 1968 and was the product of a committee organized by the Bank of England and made up of representatives of the merchant banks, the stock exchanges and pension fund organizations. Johnston (1980), *supra* at 37-8. This exercise in self-regulation was openly recognized as a means to head off governmental regulation, as the introduction to the April, 1969, edition of the Code openly acknowledged: "It is generally accepted that the choice before the City in the conduct of Take-Overs and Mergers is either a system of voluntary self-discipline based on the Code and administered by the City's own representatives or regulation by law enforced by officials appointed by Government." M. Weinberg, *Takeovers and Mergers* 437 App. (3d ed.1971).

Self-discipline is also the principle method by which compliance with the Code is achieved. Although the Code does provide a mechanism by which complaints can be made, with decisions subject to an appeals process, the Panel has no independent authority to impose sanctions beyond public criticism. Johnston (1980), *supra* at 56-57; Weinberg (1971), *supra,* at 122, 126-29.

The fourth edition of the Code was published on July 8, 1993, and is reproduced in 4 Palmer's Company Law at D.001 (1993).

offer for all of the stock is triggered and minority shareholders are given a way out. The alternative of freezing in minority shareholders is thereby limited.

Rule 36, in turn, requires the Panel's consent before an acquiring company can make a partial offer for target company stock. Rule 36.2 states that consent for an offer for more than 30 but less than 100% of the target company's stock will not normally be granted if the offeror has made significant share acquisition in the prior twelve months. Finally, Rule 36.5 requires that an offer for more than 30% of the target's stock must be approved by a majority of the shares not held by the acquiring company.

This regulatory pattern significantly limits the ability of an acquiring company to exploit a remaining minority. First, Rule 36.5 means that shareholders cannot be made into a minority without majority consent.[73] Second, Rule 9 means that minority shareholders cannot be frozen in because a mandatory offer would be forthcoming even after an approved partial offer. Finally, even those who choose to remain minority shareholders by declining a mandatory Rule 9 offer may eventually get a second bite at the apple under § 430A of the Companies Act of 1985, which grants the remaining shareholders in a target, following the acquisition of 90% of the shares not previously held by the acquirer, the right to require that the acquirer purchase their shares.

The British approach to eliminating the opportunity for acquiring companies to exploit minority shareholders is not, however, without cost. By essentially prohibiting partial bids through the interaction of Rules 9 and 36, the benefits of acquisitions by acquirers without the capital to make complete acquisitions are foregone.[74] If capital markets are complete, however, might not these rules be avoided by means that do not raise the risk of minority shareholder exploitation? Suppose a company that had sufficient funds only for a partial acquisition borrowed the funds necessary for a complete acquisition with the commitment that it would sell off a portion of the target company's equity -- an "equity carve-out"[75] -- immediately following the acquisition. The proceeds from that sale would then be used to pay off the acquisition indebtedness. While the carve-out would itself create a minority, presumably purchasers would have chosen that condition and paid a price that reflected the risks inherent in their position. What assumptions about transaction costs in the capital market are necessary for this strategy to be available?

---

[73] The use of majority approval here highlights the difference in the American and British approaches. Recall that *Weinberger* recommended its use as a condition to freezing out the minority; Rule 27 uses it as a condition to creating a minority in the first place.

[74] DeMott (1983), *supra* note 72, at 986, and sources there cited.

[75] See Schipper & Smith (1986), *supra* note 13.

CHAPTER 23: STATE REGULATION OF TAKEOVERS

It was not surprising that state legislatures took an interest in the growth of hostile tender offers. Target companies are always "local" in the states in which their headquarters are located or in which they have substantial facilities. A takeover, with the potential for management restructuring, the relocation of executive offices, plant closings, the loss of jobs and the like, poses an obvious threat to local interests. From this perspective, state legislation that strengthens target management's hand in a hostile tender offer makes perfect sense: The interests of target management and the state correspond even if those of target management and target shareholders may not.[1] A state statute that reduces the likelihood of takeovers makes shareholders as a class worse off, and likely also has a negative impact on the national economy by reducing managerial incentives to maximize the efficiency of their enterprises. From the perspective of the state, however, its share of these costs would not outweigh its share of the benefits. The costs -- to shareholders and the overall economy -- are shared across the nation; the benefits, in contrast, are entirely local.[2]

Consistent with this cost-benefit analysis, state takeover laws spread widely. Virginia acted first in 1968,[3] some four months before the Williams Act was enacted by Congress. By 1979, every state except California that accounted for more than 1% of the national total of main offices or incorporation headquarters had adopted takeover legislation;[4] by 1994, the total number of states had reached 40.[5] A response to this movement was predictable. Acquiring companies had the incentive and resources to

---

[1] The coincidence may be more apparent than real. State antitakeover statutes protect constituencies other than management only when target management resists the takeover; no protection is provided against the impact of friendly transactions. Additionally, no state statute gives other constituencies, like labor, standing to challenge target management's approval of a takeover. Finally, as Roberta Romano notes, state antitakeover laws "are typically sponsored by the state chamber of commerce at the behest of a major local corporation that is the target of a hostile bid. Such laws are often rapidly enacted, sometimes over a few days in special emergency sessions. . . ." Roberta Romano, *The Genius of American Corporate Law* 57 (1993). Any inclination toward skepticism concerning the motives for such statutes is encouraged by the fact that the interests of other constituencies could be directly protected. A state could control the feared local impact of hostile takeovers directly by plant closing legislation or by contractual restrictions as a condition for local assistance to companies. Moreover, these efforts would protect local interests whether or not control of a company changes. Only a handful of states have adopted plant closing statutes with broad application. See Investor Responsibility Research Council, *State Takeover Laws* (1993).

[2] See Saul Levmore, *Interstate Exploitation and Judicial Intervention*, 69 Va.L.Rev. 563, 622-24 (1983); cf. Susan Rose-Ackerman, *Does Federalism Matter? Political Choice in Federal Republic*, 89 J.Pol.Econ. 152 (1981) (social choice approach to state-federal conflict).

[3] Va. Code § 13.1-528 to -541 (1978).

[4] Robert Smiley, *The Effect of State Securities Statutes on Tender Offer Activity*, 19 Econ. Inquiry 426, 432 (1981).

[5] See Investor Responsibility Research Center (1993), *supra* note 1.

challenge these statutes and the same cost-benefit analysis that explains their adoption suggests one of the legal bases for the challenge. Efforts by one state to benefit its economy at the expense of that of other states or of the nation call to mind the Commerce Clause. The second basis for challenge grew out of the Williams Act. If state takeover legislation could be shown to conflict with Congress' approach to takeover regulation, the Supremacy Clause would invalidate state efforts.

A. The Constitutionality of First Generation State Antitakeover Statutes

The first generation of state antitakeover statutes added a superstructure to the Williams Act foundation of disclosure and a waiting period. Typically, a state regulatory body was given the power to delay a takeover bid to hold hearings on the substantive fairness of its terms, and could block the offer altogether if the bid were found to fail the statutory fairness standard.[6] The constitutionality of these statutes was routinely challenged by acquiring companies and the ensuing litigation resulted in the invalidation of a large number of state takeover statutes on Commerce Clause and Supremacy Clause grounds.[7] After one abortive effort to resolve the federal-state conflict,[8] the Supreme Court first reached the merits of the conflict in the following case.

EDGAR v. MITE CORP.

457 U.S. 624 (1982)

Justice WHITE delivered an opinion, Parts I, II, and V-B of which are the opinion of the Court.[*]

The issue in this case is whether the Illinois Business Take-Over Act, Ill.Rev.Stat., ch. 121-1/2, ¶ 137.51 et seq. (1979), is unconstitutional under the Supremacy and Commerce Clauses of the Federal Constitution.

---

[6] Diane Wilner & Craig Landy, *The Tender Trap: State Takeover Statutes and Their Constitutionality*, 45 Ford.L.Rev. 1, 5-9 (1976), describe the characteristics of first generation statutes.

[7] A sampling of these cases is set out in Manning Warren III, *Developments in State Takeover Regulation: MITE and its Aftermath*, 40 Bus.Law. 671, 678 n.52 (1985).

[8] Great Western United Corp. v. Kidwell, 577 F.2d 1256 (5th Cir.1978) (Idaho takeover statute invalidated on Commerce Clause and Supremacy Clause grounds), *rev'd on other grounds sub. nom.*, Leroy v. Great Western United Corp., 443 U.S. 173 (1979).

[*] The Chief Justice joins the opinion in its entirety; Justice Blackmun joins Parts I, II, III, and IV: Justice Powell joins Parts I and V-B; and Justice Stevens and Justice O'Connor join Parts I, II, and V.

I

Appellee MITE Corp. and its wholly owned subsidiary, MITE Holdings, Inc., are corporations organized under the laws of Delaware with their principal executive offices in Connecticut. Appellant James Edgar is the Secretary of State of Illinois and is charged with the administration and enforcement of the Illinois Act. Under the Illinois Act any takeover offer[1] for the shares of a target company must be registered with the Secretary of State. Ill.Rev.Stat., ch. 121-1/2, ¶ 137.54.A (1979). A target company is defined as a corporation or other issuer of securities of which shareholders located in Illinois own 10% of the class of equity securities subject to the offer, or for which any two of the following three conditions are met: the corporation has its principal executive office in Illinois, is organized under the laws of Illinois, or has at least 10% of its stated capital and paid-in surplus represented within the State. ¶ 137.5-10. An offer becomes registered 20 days after a registration statement is filed with the Secretary unless the Secretary calls a hearing. ¶ 137.54.E. The Secretary may call a hearing at any time during the 20-day waiting period to adjudicate the substantive fairness of the offer if he believes it is necessary to protect the shareholders of the target company, and a hearing must be held if requested by a majority of a target company's outside directors or by Illinois shareholders who own 10% of the class of securities subject to the offer. ¶ 137.57.A. If the Secretary does hold a hearing, he is directed by the statute to deny registration to a tender offer if he finds that it "fails to provide full and fair disclosure to the offerees of all material information concerning the take-over offer, or that the take-over offer is inequitable or would work or tend to work a fraud or deceit upon the offerees. . . ." ¶ 137.57.E.

On January 19, 1979, MITE initiated a cash tender offer for all outstanding shares of Chicago Rivet & Machine Co., a publicly held Illinois corporation, by filing a Schedule 14D-1 with the Securities and Exchange Commission in order to comply with the Williams Act. The Schedule 14D-1 indicated that MITE was willing to pay $28 per share for any and all outstanding shares of Chicago Rivet, a premium of approximately $4 over the then-prevailing market price. MITE did not comply with the Illinois Act, however, and commenced this litigation on the same day by filing an action in the United States District Court for the Northern District of Illinois. The complaint asked for a declaratory judgment that the Illinois Act was pre-empted by the Williams Act and violated the Commerce Clause. In

---

[1] The Illinois Act defines "take-over offer" as "the offer to acquire or the acquisition of any equity security of a target company, pursuant to a tender offer. . . ." Ill.Rev.Stat., ch. 121-1/2, ¶ 137.52-9 (1979). "A tender offer has been conventionally understood to be a publicly made invitation addressed to all shareholders of a corporation to tender their shares for sale at a specified price." Note, *The Developing Meaning of "Tender Offer" Under the Securities Exchange Act of 1934*, 86 Harv.L.Rev. 1250, 1251 (1973) (footnotes omitted). The terms "tender offer" and "takeover offer" are often used interchangeably.

addition, MITE sought a temporary restraining order and preliminary and permanent injunctions prohibiting the Illinois Secretary of State from enforcing the Illinois Act.

Chicago Rivet responded three days later by bringing suit in Pennsylvania, where it conducted most of its business, seeking to enjoin MITE from proceeding with its proposed tender offer on the ground that the offer violated the Pennsylvania Takeover Disclosure Law, Pa.Stat.Ann., Tit. 70, § 71 et seq. (Purdon Supp.1982-1983). After Chicago Rivet's efforts to obtain relief in Pennsylvania proved unsuccessful, both Chicago Rivet and the Illinois Secretary of State took steps to invoke the Illinois Act. On February 1, 1979, the Secretary of State notified MITE that he intended to issue an order requiring it to cease and desist further efforts to make a tender offer for Chicago Rivet. On February 2, 1979, Chicago Rivet notified MITE by letter that it would file suit in Illinois state court to enjoin the proposed tender offer. MITE renewed its request for injunctive relief in the District Court and on February 2 the District Court issued a preliminary injunction prohibiting the Secretary of State from enforcing the Illinois Act against MITE's tender offer for Chicago Rivet.

MITE then published its tender offer in the February 5 edition of the Wall Street Journal. The offer was made to all shareholders of Chicago Rivet residing throughout the United States. The outstanding stock was worth over $23 million at the offering price. On the same day Chicago Rivet made an offer for approximately 40% of its own shares at $30 per share.[4] The District Court entered final judgment on February 9, declaring that the Illinois Act was pre-empted by the Williams Act and that it violated the Commerce Clause. Accordingly, the District Court permanently enjoined enforcement of the Illinois statute against MITE. Shortly after final judgment was entered, MITE and Chicago Rivet entered into an agreement whereby both tender offers were withdrawn and MITE was given 30 days to examine the books and records of Chicago Rivet. Under the agreement MITE was either to make a tender offer of $31 per share before March 12, 1979, which Chicago Rivet agreed not to oppose, or decide not to acquire Chicago Rivet's shares or assets. On March 2, 1979, MITE announced its decision not to make a tender offer.

The United States Court of Appeals for the Seventh Circuit affirmed sub nom. MITE Corp. v. Dixon, 633 F.2d 486 (1980). It agreed with the District Court that several provisions of the Illinois Act are pre-empted by the Williams Act and that the Illinois Act unduly burdens interstate commerce in violation of the Commerce Clause. We noted probable jurisdiction, 451 U.S. 968 (1981), and now affirm.

---

[4] Chicago Rivet's offer for its own shares was exempt from the requirements of the Illinois Act pursuant to Ill.Rev.Stat., ch. 121-1/2, ¶ 137.52-9(4) (1979).

II

The Court of Appeals specifically found that this case was not moot, 633 F.2d, at 490, reasoning that because the secretary has indicated he intends to enforce the Act against MITE, a reversal of the judgment of the District Court would expose MITE to civil and criminal liability[5] for making the February 5, 1979, offer in violation of the Illinois Act. We agree. . . .

Accordingly, the case is not moot.

III

We first address the holding that the Illinois Take-Over Act is unconstitutional under the Supremacy Clause. We note at the outset that in passing the Williams Act, which is an amendment to the Securities Exchange Act of 1934, Congress did not also amend § 28(a) of the 1934 Act.[6] In pertinent part, § 28(a) provides as follows:

> Nothing in this title shall affect the jurisdiction of the securities commission (or any agency or officer performing like functions) of any State over any security or any person insofar as it does not conflict with the provisions of this title or the rules and regulations thereunder. 48 Stat. 903.

Thus Congress did not explicitly prohibit States from regulating takeovers; it left the determination whether the Illinois statute conflicts with the Williams Act to the courts. Of course, a state statute is void to the extent that it actually conflicts with a valid federal statute; and

> [a] conflict will be found 'where compliance with both federal and state regulations is a physical impossibility . . .,' Florida Lime & Avocado Growers, Inc. v. Paul, 373 U.S. 132, 142-143 (1963), or where the state 'law stands as an obstacle to the accomplishment and execution of the full purposes and objectives of Congress.' Hines v. Davidowitz, 312 U.S. 52, 67 (1941); Jones v. Rath Packing Co., [430 U.S. 519,] 526, 540-541 [(1977)]. Accord, De Canas v. Bica, 424 U.S. 351, 363 (1976). . . .

[Ray v. Atlantic Richfield Co., 435 U.S. 151, 158 (1978).] Our inquiry is further narrowed in this case since there is no contention that it would be

---

[5] The Secretary of State may bring an action for civil penalties for violations of the Illinois Act., Ill.Rev.Stat., ch. 121-1/2, ¶ 137.65 (1979), and a person who willfully violates the Act is subject to criminal prosecution. ¶ 137.63.

[6] There is no evidence in the legislative history that Congress was aware of state takeover laws when it enacted the Williams Act. When the Williams Act was enacted in 1968, only Virginia had a takeover statute. The Virginia statute, Va.Code § 13.1-528 (1978), became effective March 5, 1968; the Williams Act was enacted several months later on July 19, 1968. Takeover statutes are now in effect in 37 States. Mark Sargent, *On the Validity of State Takeover Regulation: State Responses to MITE and Kidwell*, 42 Ohio St.L.J. 689, 690, n.7 (1981).

impossible to comply with both the provisions of the Williams Act and the more burdensome requirements of the Illinois law. The issue thus, is, as it was in the Court of Appeals, whether the Illinois Act frustrates the objectives of the Williams Act in some substantial way.

The Williams Act, passed in 1968, was the congressional response to the increased use of cash tender offers in corporate acquisitions, a device that had "removed a substantial number of corporate control contests from the reach of existing disclosure requirements of the federal securities laws." Piper v. Chris-Craft Industries, 430 U.S. 1, 22 (1977). The Williams Act filled this regulatory gap. The Act imposes several requirements. First, it requires that upon the commencement of the tender offer, the offeror file with the SEC, publish or send to the shareholders of the target company, and furnish to the target company detailed information about the offer.

The offeror must disclose information about its background and identity; the source of the funds to be used in making the purchase; the purpose of the purchase, including any plans to liquidate the company or make major changes in its corporate structure; and the extent of the offeror's holdings in the target company.

Second, stockholders who tender their shares may withdraw them during the first 7 days of a tender offer and if the offeror has not yet purchased their shares, at any time after 60 days from the commencement of the offer.

Third, all shares tendered must be purchased for the same price; if an offering price is increased, those who have already tendered receive the benefit of the increase.

There is no question that in imposing these requirements, Congress intended to protect investors. Piper v. Chris-Craft Industries, *supra*, at 35; Rondeau v. Mosinee Paper Corp., 422 U.S. 49, 58 (1975); S.Rep. No. 550, 90th Cong., 1st Sess., 3-4 (1967) (Senate Report). But it is also crystal clear that a major aspect of the effort to protect the investor was to avoid favoring either management or the takeover bidder. As we noted in *Piper*, the disclosure provisions originally embodied in S. 2731 "were avowedly pro-management in the target company's efforts to defeat takeover bids." 430 U.S., at 30. But Congress became convinced "that takeover bids should not be discouraged because they serve a useful purpose in providing a check on entrenched but inefficient management." Senate Report, at 3.[9] It also became apparent that entrenched management was often successful in defeating takeover attempts. As the legislation evolved, therefore, Congress disclaimed any "intention to provide a weapon for management to discourage takeover bids," Rondeau v. Mosinee Paper Corp., *supra*, at 58, and expressly embraced a policy of neutrality. As Senator Williams explained:

---

[9] Congress also did not want to deny shareholders "the opportunities which result from the competitive bidding for a block of stock of a given company," namely, the opportunity to sell shares for a premium over their market price. 113 Cong.Rec. 24666 (1967) (remarks of Sen. Javits).

"We have taken extreme care to avoid tipping the scales either in favor of management or in favor of the person making the takeover bids." 113 Cong.Rec. 24664 (1967). This policy of "evenhandedness," Piper v. Chris-Craft Industries, *supra*, at 31, represented a conviction that neither side in the contest should be extended additional advantages vis-a-vis the investor, who if furnished with adequate information would be in a position to make his own informed choice. We, therefore, agree with the Court of Appeals that Congress sought to protect the investor not only by furnishing him with the necessary information but also by withholding from management or the bidder any undue advantage that could frustrate the exercise of an informed choice. 633 F.2d, at 496.

To implement this policy of investor protection while maintaining the balance between management and the bidder, Congress required the latter to file with the Commission and furnish the company and the investor with all information adequate to the occasion. With that filing, the offer could go forward, stock could be tendered and purchased, but a stockholder was free within a specified time to withdraw his tendered shares. He was also protected if the offer was increased. Looking at this history as a whole, it appears to us, as it did to the Court of Appeals, that Congress intended to strike a balance between the investor, management, and the takeover bidder. The bidder was to furnish the investor and the target company with adequate information but there was no "inten[tion] to do . . . more than give incumbent management an opportunity to express and explain its position." Rondeau v. Mosinee Paper Corp., *supra*, at 58. Once that opportunity was extended, Congress anticipated that the investor, if he so chose, and the takeover bidder should be free to move forward within the time frame provided by Congress.

IV

The Court of Appeals identified three provisions of the Illinois Act that upset the careful balance struck by Congress and which therefore stand as obstacles to the accomplishment and execution of the full purposes and objectives of Congress. We agree with the Court of Appeals in all essential respects.

A

The Illinois Act requires a tender offeror to notify the Secretary of State and the target company of its intent to make a tender offer and the material terms of the offer 20 business days before the offer becomes effective. Ill.Rev.Stat., ch. 121-1/2, ¶¶ 137.54.E, 137.54.B (1979). During that time, the offeror may not communicate its offer to the shareholders. ¶ 137.54.A. Meanwhile, the target company is free to disseminate information to its shareholders concerning the impending offer. The contrast with the Williams Act is apparent. Under that Act, there is no precommencement notification requirement; the critical date is the date a tender offer is "first published or sent or given to security holders." 15 U.S.C. § 78n(d)(1). See also [Rule] 14d-2.

We agree with the Court of Appeals that providing the target company with additional time within which to take steps to combat the offer, the precommencement notification provisions furnish incumbent management with a powerful tool to combat tender offers, perhaps to the detriment of the stockholders who will not have an offer before them during this period.[10] These consequences are precisely what Congress determined should be avoided, and for this reason, the precommencement notification provision frustrates the objectives of the Williams Act.

It is important to note in this respect that in the course of events leading to the adoption of the Williams Act, Congress several times refused to impose a precommencement disclosure requirement. In October 1965, Senator Williams introduced S. 2731, a bill which would have required a bidder to notify the target company and file a public statement with the Securities and Exchange Commission at least 20 days before commencement of a cash tender offer for more than 5% of a class of the target company's securities. 111 Cong.Rec. 28259 (1965). The Commission commented on the bill and stated that "the requirement of a 20-day advance notice to the issuer and the Commission is unnecessary for the protection of security holders. . . ." 112 Cong.Rec. 19005 (1966). Senator Williams introduced a new bill in 1967, S. 510, which provided for a confidential filing by the tender offeror with the Commission five days prior to the commencement of the offer. S. 510 was enacted as the Williams Act after elimination of the advance disclosure requirement. As the Senate Report explained:

> At the hearings it was urged that this prior review was not necessary and in some cases might delay the offer when time was of the essence. In view of the authority and responsibility of the Securities and Exchange Commission to take appropriate action in the event that inadequate or misleading information is disseminated to the public to solicit acceptance of a tender offer, the bill as approved by the committee requires only that the statement be on file with the Securities and Exchange Commission at the time the tender offer is first made to the public. Senate Report, at 4.

Congress rejected another precommencement notification proposal during deliberations on the 1970 amendments to the Williams Act.[11]

---

[10] See n.11 and accompanying text, *infra.*

[11] H.R. 4285, 91st Cong., 2d Sess. (1970). The bill was not reported out of the Subcommittee. Instead, the Senate amendments to the Williams Act, which did not contain precommencement notification provisions, were adopted. Pub.L. 91-567, 84 Stat. 1497.

The Securities and Exchange Commission has promulgated detailed rules governing the conduct of tender offers. Rule 14d-2(b), requires that a tender offeror make its offer effective within five days of publicly announcing the material terms of the offer by disseminating specified information to shareholders and filing the requisite documents with the Commission.

B

For similar reasons, we agree with the Court of Appeals that the hearing provisions of the Illinois Act frustrate the congressional purpose by introducing extended delay into the tender offer process. The Illinois Act allows the Secretary of State to call a hearing with respect to any tender offer subject to the Act, and the offer may not proceed until the hearing is completed. Ill.Rev.Stat. ch. 121-1/2, ¶¶ 137.57A and B (1979). The Secretary may call a hearing at any time prior to the commencement of the offer, and there is no deadline for the completion of the hearing. ¶¶ 137.57.C and D. Although the Secretary is to render a decision within 15 days after the conclusion of the hearing, that period may be extended without limitation. Not only does the Secretary of State have the power to delay a tender offer indefinitely, but incumbent management may also use the hearing provisions of the Illinois Act to delay a tender offer. The Secretary is required to call a hearing if requested to do so by, among other persons, those who are located in Illinois "as determined by post office address as shown on the records of the target company and who hold of record or beneficially, or both, at least 10% of the outstanding shares of any class of equity securities which is the subject of the take-over offer." ¶ 137.57.A. Since incumbent management in many cases will control, either directly or indirectly, 10% of the target company's shares, this provision allows management to delay the commencement of an offer by insisting on a hearing. As the Court of Appeals observed, these provisions potentially afford management a "powerful weapon to stymie indefinitely a takeover." 633 F.2d, at 494.[12]   In enacting the Williams Act, Congress itself "recognized that delay can seriously impede a tender offer" and sought to avoid it. Great Western United Corp. v. Kidwell, 577 F.2d 1256, 1277 (5th Cir.1978); Senate Report, at 4.[13]

Otherwise the offeror must announce that it is withdrawing its offer. The events in this litigation took place prior to the effective date of Rule 14d-2(b), and because Rule 14d-2(b) operates prospectively only, see 44 Fed.Reg. 70326 (1979), it is not at issue in this case.

[12] Delay has been characterized as "the most potent weapon in a tender-offer fight." Donald Langevoort, *State Tender-Offer Legislation: Interests, Effects, and Political Competency*, 62 Cornell L.Rev. 213, 238 (1977). See also Herbert Wachtell, *Special Tender Offer Litigation Tactics*, 32 Bus.Law. 1433, 1437-1442 (1977); Diane Wilner & Craig Landy, *The Tender Trap: State Takeover Statutes and Their Constitutionality*, 45 Ford.L.Rev. 1, 9-10 (1976).

[13] According to the Securities and Exchange Commission, delay enables a target company to:

    (1) repurchase its own securities;

    (2) announce dividend increases or stock splits;

    (3) issue additional shares of stock;

    (4) acquire other companies to produce an antitrust violation should the tender offer succeed;

    (5) arrange a defensive merger;

    (6) enter into restrictive loan agreements; and

Congress reemphasized the consequences of delay when it enacted the Hart-Scott-Rodino Antitrust Improvements Act of 1976, Pub.L. 94-435, 90 Stat. 1397, 15 U.S.C. § 12 et seq.

> [I]t is clear that this short waiting period [the 10-day period for proration provided for by § 14(d)(6) of the Securities Exchange Act, which applies only after a tender offer is commenced] was founded on congressional concern that a longer delay might unduly favor the target firm's incumbent management, and permit them to frustrate many pro-competitive cash tenders. This ten-day waiting period thus underscores the basic purpose of the Williams Act -- to maintain a neutral policy towards cash tender offers, by avoiding lengthy delays that might discourage their chances for success. H.R. Rep. No. 94-1373, p. 12 (1976).[14]

As we have said, Congress anticipated that investors and the takeover offeror would be free to go forward without unreasonable delay. The potential for delay provided by the hearing provisions upset the balance struck by Congress by favoring management at the expense of stockholders. We therefore agree with the Court of Appeals that these hearing provisions conflict with the Williams Act.

C

The Court of Appeals also concluded that the Illinois Act is pre-empted by the Williams Act insofar as it allows the Secretary of State of Illinois to pass on the substantive fairness of a tender offer. Under ¶ 137.57.E of the Illinois law, the Secretary is required to deny registration of a takeover offer if he finds that the offer "fails to provide full and fair disclosure to the offerees . . . *or that the take-over offer is inequitable . . .*" (emphasis

---

(7) institute litigation challenging the tender offer.
Brief for Securities and Exchange Commission as *Amicus Curiae* 10, n.8.

[14] Representative Rodino set out the consequences of delay in greater detail when he described their relationship between the Hart-Scott-Rodino Act and the Williams Act:

> In the case of cash tender offers, more so than in other mergers, the equities include time and the danger of undue delay. This bill in no way intends to repeal or reverse the congressional purpose underlying the 1968 Williams Act, or the 1970 amendments to that act. . . . Lengthier delays will give the target firm plenty of time to defeat the offer, by abolishing cumulative voting, arranging a speedy defensive merger, quickly incorporating in a State with an antitakeover statute, or negotiating costly lifetime employment contracts for incumbent management. And the longer the waiting period, the more the target's stock may be bid up in the market, making the offer more costly -- and less successful. Should this happen, it will mean that shareholders of the target firm will be effectively deprived of the choice that cash tenders given to them: Either accept the offer and thereby gain the tendered premium, or reject the offer. Generally, the courts have construed the Williams Act so as to maintain these two options for the target company's shareholders, and the House conferees contemplate that the courts will continue to do so. 122 Cong.Rec. 30,877 (1976).

added).[15]   The Court of Appeals understood the Williams Act and its legislative history to indicate that Congress intended for investors to be free to make their own decisions. We agree. Both the House and Senate Reports observed that the Act was "designed to make the relevant facts known so that shareholders have a fair opportunity to make their decision." H.R. Rep. No. 1711, 90th Cong., 2d Sess., 4 (1968); S. Rep. at 3. Thus, as the Court of Appeals said, "[t]he state thus offers investor protection at the expense of investor autonomy -- an approach quite in conflict with that adopted by Congress." 633 F.2d, at 494.

V

The Commerce Clause provides that "Congress shall have Power . . . [t]o regulate Commerce . . . among the several States." U.S. Const., Art. I, § 8, cl.3. "[A]t least since Cooley v. Board of Wardens, 12 How. 299 (1852), it has been clear that 'the Commerce Clause . . . even without implementing legislation by Congress is a limitation upon the power of the States.' " Great Atlantic & Pacific Tea Co. v. Cottrell, 424 U.S. 366, 370-371 (1976), quoting Freeman v. Hewitt, 329 U.S. 249, 252 (1946). See also Lewis v. BT Investment Managers, Inc., 447 U.S. 27, 35 (1980). Not every exercise of state power with some impact on interstate commerce is invalid. A state statute must be upheld if it "regulates evenhandedly to effectuate a legitimate local public interest, and its effects on interstate commerce are only incidental . . . unless the burden imposed on such commerce is clearly excessive in relation to the putative local benefits." Pike v. Bruce Church, Inc., 397 U.S. 137, 142 (1970), citing Huron Cement Co. v. Detroit, 362 U.S. 440, 443 (1960). The Commerce Clause, however, permits only *incidental* regulation of interstate commerce by the States; direct regulation is prohibited. Shafer v. Farmers Grain Co., 268 U.S. 189, 199 (1925). See also Pike v. Bruce Church, Inc., *supra*, at 142. The Illinois Act violates these principles for two reasons. First, it directly regulates and prevents, unless its terms are satisfied, interstate tender offers which in turn would generate interstate transactions. Second, the burden the Act imposes on interstate commerce is excessive in light of the local interests the Act purports to further.

A

States have traditionally regulated intrastate securities transactions,[16]

---

[15] Appellant argues that the Illinois Act does not permit him to adjudicate the substantive fairness of a tender offer. Brief for Appellant 21-22. On this state-law issue, however, we follow the view of the Court of Appeals that ¶ 137.57.E allows the Secretary of State "to pass upon the substantive fairness of a tender offer. . . ." 633 F.2d 486, 493 (1980).

[16] For example, the Illinois blue-sky law, Ill.Rev.Stat., ch. 121-1/2, ¶ 137.1 et seq. (1979 and Supp.1980), provides that securities subject to the law must be registered "prior to sale

and this Court has upheld the authority of States to enact "blue-sky" laws against Commerce Clause challenges on several occasions.   Hall v. Geiger-Jones Co., 242 U.S. 539 (1917);   Caldwell v. Sioux Falls Stock Yards Co., 242 U.S. 559 (1917);   Merrick v. N.W. Halsey & Co., 242 U.S. 568 (1917).   The Court's rationale for upholding blue-sky laws was that they only regulated transactions occurring within the regulating States.

> The provisions of the law . . . apply to dispositions of securities *within* the State and while information of those issued in other States and foreign countries is required to be filed . . ., they are only affected by the requirement of a license of one who deals with them *within* the State.   . . .   Such regulations affect interstate commerce in [securities] only incidentally.

Hall v. Geiger-Jones Co., *supra*, at 557-558 (citations omitted).   Congress has also recognized the validity of such laws governing intrastate securities transactions in § 28(a) of the Securities Exchange Act, a provision "designed to save state blue-sky laws from pre-emption."   Leroy v. Great Western United Corp., 443 U.S. 173, 182, n.13 (1979).

The Illinois Act differs substantially from state blue-sky laws in that it directly regulates transactions which take place across state lines, even if wholly outside the State of Illinois.   A tender offer for securities of a publicly held corporation is ordinarily communicated by the use of the mails or other means of interstate commerce to shareholders across the country and abroad.   Securities are tendered and transactions closed by similar means. Thus, in this case, MITE Corp., the tender offeror, is a Delaware corporation with principal offices in Connecticut.   Chicago Rivet is a publicly held Illinois corporation with shareholders scattered around the country, 27% of whom live in Illinois.   MITE's offer to Chicago Rivet's shareholders, including those in Illinois, necessarily employed interstate facilities in communicating its offer, which, if accepted, would result in transactions occurring across state lines.   These transactions would themselves be interstate commerce.   Yet the Illinois law, unless complied with, sought to prevent MITE from making its offer and concluding interstate transactions not only with Chicago Rivet's stockholders living in Illinois, but also with those living in other States and having no connection with Illinois. Indeed, the Illinois law on its face would apply even if not a single one of Chicago Rivet's shareholders were a resident of Illinois, since the Act applies to every tender offer for a corporation meeting two of the following conditions: the corporation has its principal executive office in Illinois, is organized under Illinois laws, or has at least 10% of its stated capital and paid-in surplus represented in Illinois. Ill.Rev.Stat., ch. 121-1/2, ¶ 137.52-10(2) (1979).   Thus the Act could be applied to regulate a tender offer which would not affect a single Illinois shareholder.

---

in this State. . . ." ¶ 137.5.

It is therefore apparent that the Illinois statute is a direct restraint on interstate commerce and that it has a sweeping extraterritorial effect. Furthermore, if Illinois may impose such regulations, so may other States; and interstate commerce in securities transactions generated by tender offers would be thoroughly stifled. In Shafer v. Farmers Grain Co., *supra*, at 199, the Court held that "a state statute which by its necessary operation directly interferes with or burdens [interstate] commerce is a prohibited regulation and invalid, regardless of the purpose with which it was enacted." See also Hughes v. Alexandria Scrap Corp., 426 U.S. 794, 806 (1976). The Commerce Clause also precludes the application of a state statute to commerce that takes place wholly outside of the State's borders, whether or not the commerce has effects within the State. In Southern Pacific Co. v. Arizona, 325 U.S. 761, 775 (1945), the Court struck down on Commerce Clause grounds a state law where the "practical effect of such regulation is to control [conduct] beyond the boundaries of the state. . . ." The limits on a State's power to enact substantive legislation are similar to the limits on the jurisdiction of state courts. In either case, "any attempt 'directly' to assert extraterritorial jurisdiction over persons or property would offend sister States and exceed the inherent limits of the State's power." Shafer v. Heitner, 433 U.S. 186, 197 (1977).

Because the Illinois Act purports to regulate directly and to interdict interstate commerce, including commerce wholly outside the State, it must be held invalid as were the laws at issue in Shafer v. Farmers Grain Co. and *Southern Pacific*.

B

The Illinois Act is also unconstitutional under the test of Pike v. Bruce Church, Inc., 397 U.S., at 142, for even when a state statute regulates interstate commerce indirectly, the burden imposed on that commerce must not be excessive in relation to the local interests served by the statute. The most obvious burden the Illinois Act imposes on interstate commerce arises from the statute's previously described nationwide reach which purports to give Illinois the power to determine whether a tender offer may proceed anywhere.

The effects of allowing the Illinois Secretary of State to block a nationwide tender offer are substantial. Shareholders are deprived of the opportunity to sell their shares at a premium. The reallocation of economic resources to their highest valued use, a process which can improve efficiency and competition, is hindered. The incentive the tender offer mechanism provides incumbent management to perform well so that stock prices remain high is reduced. See Frank Easterbrook & Daniel Fischel, *The Proper Role of a Target's Management in Responding to a Tender Offer*, 94 Harv.L.Rev. 1161, 1173-1174 (1981); Daniel Fischel, *Efficient Capital Market Theory, the Market for Corporate Control, and the Regulation of Cash Tender Offers*,

57 Texas L.Rev. 1, 5, 27-28, 45 (1978);   H.R. Rep. No. 94-1373, p.12 (1976).

Appellant claims the Illinois Act furthers two legitimate local interests. He argues that Illinois seeks to protect resident security holders and that the Act merely regulates the internal affairs of companies incorporated under Illinois law. We agree with the Court of Appeals that these asserted interests are insufficient to outweigh the burdens Illinois imposes on interstate commerce.

While protecting local investors is plainly a legitimate state objective, the State has no legitimate interest in protecting nonresident shareholders. Insofar as the Illinois law burdens out-of-state transactions, there is nothing to be weighed in the balance to sustain the law. We note, furthermore, that the Act completely exempts from coverage a corporation's acquisition of its own shares. Ill.Rev.Stat., ch. 121-1/2, ¶ 137.52-9(4) (1979). Thus Chicago Rivet was able to make a competing tender offer for its own stock without complying with the Illinois Act, leaving Chicago Rivet's shareholders to depend only on the protections afforded them by federal securities law, protections which Illinois views as inadequate to protect investors in other contexts. This distinction is at variance with Illinois' asserted legislative purpose, and tends to undermine appellant's justification for the burdens the statute imposes on interstate commerce.

We are also unconvinced that the Illinois Act substantially enhances the shareholders' position. The Illinois Act seeks to protect shareholders of a company subject to a tender offer by requiring disclosures regarding the offer, assuring that shareholders have adequate time to decide whether to tender their shares, and according shareholders withdrawal, proration, and equal consideration rights. However, the Williams Act provides these same substantive protections, compare Ill.Rev.Stat., ch. 121-1/2, ¶¶ 137.59.C, D, and E (1979) (withdrawal, proration, and equal consideration rights), with [§§] 14(d)(5), (6), and (7) and [Rule] 14d-7 (1981) (same). As the Court of Appeals noted, the disclosures required by the Illinois Act which go beyond those mandated by the Williams Act and the regulations pursuant to it may not substantially enhance the shareholders' ability to make informed decisions. 633 F.2d, at 500. It also was of the view that the possible benefits of the potential delays required by the Act may be outweighed by the increased risk that the tender offer will fail due to defensive tactics employed by incumbent management. We are unprepared to disagree with the Court of Appeals in these respects, and conclude that the protections the Illinois Act affords resident security holders are, for the most part, speculative.

Appellant also contends that Illinois has an interest in regulating the internal affairs of a corporation incorporated under its laws. The internal affairs doctrine is a conflict of laws principle which recognizes that only one State should have the authority to regulate a corporation's internal affairs -- matters peculiar to the relationships among or between the corporation and its current officers, directors, and shareholders -- because otherwise a corporation could be faced with conflicting demands. See Restatement

(Second) of Conflict of Laws § 302, Comment *b*, pp.307-308 (1971). That doctrine is of little use to the State in this context. Tender offers contemplate transfers of stock by stockholders to a third party and do not themselves implicate the internal affairs of the target company. Great Western United Corp. v. Kidwell, 577 F.2d, at 1280, n.53; Restatement, *supra*, § 302, Comment *e*, p.310. Furthermore, the proposed justification is somewhat incredible since the Illinois Act applies to tender offers for any corporation for which 10% of the outstanding shares are held by Illinois residents, Ill.Rev.Stat., ch. 121-1/2, ¶ 137.52-10 (1979). The Act thus applies to corporations that are not incorporated in Illinois and have their principal place of business in other States. Illinois has no interest in regulating the internal affairs of foreign corporations.

We conclude with the Court of Appeals that the Illinois Act imposes a substantial burden on interstate commerce which outweighs its putative local benefits. It is accordingly invalid under the Commerce Clause.

The judgment of the Court of Appeals is affirmed.

Justice POWELL (concurring in part). I agree with Justice Marshall that this case is moot. In view, however, of the decision of a majority of the Court to reach the merits, I join Parts I and V-B of the Court's opinion.

I join Part V-B because its Commerce Clause reasoning leaves some room for state regulation of tender offers. This period in our history is marked by conglomerate corporate formations essentially unrestricted by the antitrust laws. Often the offeror possesses resources, in terms of professional personnel experienced in takeovers as well as of capital, that vastly exceed those of the takeover target. This disparity in resources may seriously disadvantage a relatively small or regional target corporation. Inevitably there are certain adverse consequences in terms of general public interest when corporate headquarters are moved away from a city and State.*

The Williams Act provisions, implementing a policy of neutrality, seem to assume corporate entities of substantially equal resources. I agree with Justice Stevens that the Williams Act's neutrality policy does not necessarily imply a congressional intent to prohibit state legislation designed to assure -- at least in some circumstances -- greater protection to interests that include but often are broader than those of incumbent management.

---

* The corporate headquarters of the great national and multinational corporations tend to be located in the large cities of a few States. When corporate headquarters are transferred out of a city and State into one of these metropolitan centers, the State and locality from which the transfer is made inevitably suffer significantly. Management personnel -- many of whom have provided community leadership -- may move to the new corporate headquarters. Contributions to cultural, charitable, and educational life -- both in terms of leadership and financial support -- also tends to diminish when there is a move of corporate headquarters.

Justice STEVENS (concurring in part and concurring in the judgment). [In Part I of his opinion, Justice Stevens concluded that the case was not moot.]

II

On the merits, I agree with the Court that the Illinois Take-Over Act is invalid because it burdens interstate commerce. I therefore join Part V of its opinion. I am not persuaded, however, that Congress' decision to follow a policy of neutrality in its own legislation is tantamount to a federal prohibition against state legislation designed to provide special protection for incumbent management. Accordingly, although I agree with the Court's assessment of the impact of the Illinois statute, I do not join its pre-emption holding.

Justice O'CONNOR (concurring in part). I agree with the Court that the case is not moot, and that portions of the Illinois Business Take-Over Act, Ill.Rev.Stat., ch. 121-1/2, ¶ 137.51 et seq. (1979), are invalid under the Commerce Clause. Because it is not necessary to reach the pre-emption issue, I join only Parts I, II, and V of the Court's opinion, and would affirm the judgment of the Court of Appeals on that basis.

[Justice MARSHALL, in an opinion joined by Justice BRENNAN, and Justice REHNQUIST in a separate opinion, would have found the case moot.]

The plethora of opinions in *MITE* made it somewhat difficult to specify the breadth of its invalidation of state efforts to regulate takeovers. Professor Loss points out that even though only the Chief Justice and Justice Blackmun joined Justice White in the preemption portion of the opinion, only Justice Stevens clearly stated that he disagreed with Justice White's position. The remaining Justices simply did not reach the issue.[9] Thus, Loss concludes that "the pre-emption issue is still altogether open, and even the Commerce Clause holding might be distinguished with respect to statutes, of narrower scope."[10]   Nonetheless, the federal courts generally treated *MITE* as invalidating all "first generation" state takeover statutes on Commerce Clause

---

[9] Louis Loss, *Fundamentals of Securities Regulation* 602-03 (1983). Justices Brennan, Marshall, Powell & Rehnquist thought the case moot; Justice O'Connor thought that the Court's Commerce Clause holding made it unnecessary to decide the pre-emption issue.

[10] *Id.* at 603.

grounds.[11] The critical issue confronting state legislatures after *MITE* was what room for state takeover regulation remained.

B.　The Constitutionality of Second Generation State Antitakeover Statutes

One approach to crafting a post-*MITE* statute would be to follow Professor Loss' suggestion and pare down a first generation statute to the point where a balance of the local benefits and the burdens on interstate commerce favor the validity of the statute. This could be accomplished by restricting the statute's application to only offers to in-state shareholders of companies closely connected with the state, and by eliminating pre-offer filing,[12] pre-offer hearings, and substantive review of the fairness of the terms of the offer.[13] However, most states concluded the game was not worth the candle. Recall that the state's interest in regulating the takeover process is to strengthen the hands of local management. If the scope of first generation statutes after *MITE* is limited to some expansion of required disclosure, perhaps to include a statement of the acquisition's impact on local interests,[14] target management is hardly empowered.

Any hope of protecting local companies in a fashion that would survive constitutional challenge thus required a new approach. After *MITE*, Ohio, Maryland, and Pennsylvania each adopted variants of such an approach.

The three statutes share a common theme. The Williams Act, and the first generation state statutes, treat tender offers as a unique type of transaction. In contrast, the three post-*MITE* statutory efforts recognize that a tender offer is only one way to make an acquisition; each statute is an effort to ameliorate problems facing target shareholders in tender offers that are not present in other acquisition techniques. The Ohio legislation, a control share acquisition statute, requires the approval of a majority of disinterested target company shareholders[15] before consummation of a

---

[11] See, e.g., Mesa Petroleum Co. v. Cities Service Co., 715 F.2d 1425 (10th Cir.1983) (Oklahoma statute); Telvest, Inc. v. Bradshaw, 697 F.2d 576 (4th Cir.1983) (Virginia statute); Martin-Marietta Corp. v. Bendix Corp., 690 F.2d 558 (6th Cir.1982) (Michigan statute); National City Lines, Inc. v. LLC Corp., 687 F.2d 1122 (8th Cir.1982) (Missouri statute). The *National City* court also relied upon pre-emption.

[12] The SEC's 1979 adoption of Rule 14d-2 made clear that state statutes that require public filings to be made a specified period prior to a bidder commencing an offer have been pre-empted because they conflict with the requirement of Rule 14d-2(b) that an offer commence within 5 business days after publication of the information typically required in a state filing. Securities Exchange Act Release No. 34-16623, *Interpretive Release Relating to Tender Offer Rules* (March 5, 1980), reprinted in 3 Fed.Sec.L.Rep. (CCH) ¶24,2841.

[13] See Cardiff Acquisitions, Inc. v. Hatch, 751 F.2d 917 (8th Cir.1984) (Upholding validity of Minnesota statute narrowly circumscribed by 1984 amendment in light of *MITE*).

[14] See Cardiff Acquisitions, Inc. v. Hatch, *supra* at 90,260.

[15] The exclusion of interested shareholders encompasses largely the acquiring company

tender offer, or an open market or private purchase, that would cause the acquiring company's holdings to exceed 20%, 33-1/3% or 50%.[16] The idea is to require the same kind of shareholder approval in tender offers as in other forms of acquisitions. Maryland approached the problem somewhat differently, focusing not on a tender offer at all, but on the subsequent second-step transaction that would freeze out non-tendering shareholders.[17] In effect the statute imposes a statutory fair price charter amendment[18] for Maryland corporations. Unless shareholders receive a fair price as calculated under the statutory formula, "business combinations," broadly defined to include mergers, sales of assets, liquidations and recapitalizations, with an "interested shareholder" must be approved by 80% of the outstanding shares and 66-2/3% of the shares held by disinterested shareholders.[19] Pennsylvania, in turn, created a statutory right of redemption, like the charter amendment of the same character,[20] that requires persons acquiring 30% or more of the stock of a Pennsylvania corporation to pay to the remaining shareholders the "fair value" of their shares.[21]

The strategy reflected in each of these three approaches is to cast the statute as part of the state's corporate law and, thus, no more in conflict with the Williams Act than the familiar requirement under state corporate law that target shareholders approve a statutory merger. Further buttressing the corporate law characterization of these statutes, none provide for a state administrative role; like the rest of state corporate law, it is self-administering. The explanation for this common emphasis on state corporate law is *MITE*'s treatment of the internal affairs doctrine: The conflict of laws principle that the state of incorporation has the authority to regulate a corporation's internal affairs. Justice White disposed of Illinois' reliance on this doctrine in the Commerce Clause balance by treating tender

---

and its affiliates.

[16] Ohio Rev.Code Ann. § 1701.831 (Page Supp.1984). See Gary Kreider, *Fortress without Foundation? Ohio Takeover Act II*, 52 U.Cin.L.Rev. 108 (1983). As of 1994, 27 states have adopted similar statutes. Investor Responsibility Research Center (1993), *supra* note 1.

[17] See Chapter 22, *supra*, for a discussion of second-step freezeout transactions.

[18] See Chapter 17, *supra*, for a discussion of fair price charter amendments.

[19] Md. Corps. & Ass'ns Code Ann. §§ 3-601 to 3-603 (Supp.1984). The board of directors retains some discretion with respect to whom the supermajority will apply, and the corporation can adopt a charter amendment electing not to be governed by the statute. See L.P. Scriggins & David Clarke, Jr., *Takeovers and the 1983 Maryland Fair Price Legislation*, 43 Md.L.Rev. 266 (1984). As of 1994, 27 states had adopted similar statutes. Investor Responsibility Research Center (1993), *supra* note 1.

[20] See Chapter 17, *supra*, for a discussion of right of redemption charter amendments.

[21] Pa.Stat.Ann. tit. 15, § 1910 (Purdon Supp.1984-85). As with the Ohio and Maryland statutes, the board of directors has significant discretion with respect to the application of the statute and a corporation may elect not to be covered by the statute by adopting a charter amendment. See William Newlin & Jay Gilmer, *The Pennsylvania Shareholder Protection Act: A New Approach to Deflecting Corporate Takeover Bids*, 40 Bus.Law. 111 (1984).

offers as an external matter: "Tender offers contemplate transfers of stock by stockholders to a third party and do not themselves implicate the internal affairs of the target company."[22]   How successful are the three statutes in invoking the internal affairs doctrine?   The three statutes do differ with respect to their placement on an internal-external continuum.   The Maryland statute concerns only intra-corporate transactions, like liquidations, or transactions to which the corporation is a party, like mergers.   The Pennsylvania statute, in contrast, creates an obligation between a third party and shareholders, and the Ohio statute imposes a pre-condition, albeit a shareholder vote, on precisely the "transfers of stock by stockholders to a third party" referred to by Justice White.[23]

Even if the internal affairs doctrine is successfully invoked, must it still be balanced against the impact of the statute on interstate commerce?   For example, would the weight of Delaware's interest in regulating the internal affairs of Delaware corporations be diminished by the fact that Delaware citizens own only a tiny portion of the shares of Delaware corporations?   If the weight of the internal affairs doctrine is not limited by the number of shareholders located within the state, what precisely is the state's interest in the matter?   Delaware could argue that it has an important local interest in remaining the leading state of incorporation for major corporations.[24]   To remain the leader, the argument would run, Delaware has to be able to offer laws at least as desirable as any other state.   If only more populous states (in which a larger percentage of shareholders reside and which therefore have a greater interest in the internal affairs of their corporations) could offer laws, like antitakeover provisions, that corporate management finds attractive, Delaware would be at a significant disadvantage.

From this perspective, giving weight to the internal affairs doctrine, and thereby allowing states to compete for the opportunity to "protect" non-resident shareholders, is the central legal underpinning for the existence of a market for corporate charters in which states compete for incorporation business.   The idea is that so long as a corporation can choose in which state to incorporate regardless of where it actually does business, and so long as the internal affairs doctrine assures that its choice will be respected, states seeking the revenue from incorporation will adopt laws that corporations find

---

[22] Justice White also noted that the Illinois statute applied to corporations chartered in other states and that Illinois could have "no interest in regulating the internal affairs of foreign corporations."   The application of each of the three statutes is limited to corporations chartered in that state.

[23] For an analysis of the application of the internal affairs doctrine to corporate control contests generally, and to the second generation statutes, see P. John Kozyris, *Corporate Wars and Choice of Law*, 1985 Duke L.J. 1

[24] For example, 55% of the top 200 American corporations by sales in 1981 were incorporated in Delaware.   Roberta Romano, *Law as a Product: Some Pieces of the Incorporation Puzzle*, 1 J.L.Econ. & Org. 225 (1985).   Over the period from 1960 to 1990, the percentage of Delaware's total tax collections that came from its corporate franchise tax ranged from 10.9% to 24.9%.   Romano (1993), *supra* note 1, at 7-8 (Table 1-1).

attractive. The competitive process would have no detrimental impact on interstate commerce because corporations would select the corporate statute most beneficial to its shareholders,[25] the great majority of whom will live in states *other* than the state of incorporation, thereby preventing any state from adopting a purely local perspective.

Does the argument that competition among states leads to the survival of the most efficient corporate laws, and therefore benefits rather than burdens interstate commerce, apply with respect to state regulation of takeovers? If, as argued in Chapter 17, management and shareholders have a conflict of interest with respect to takeovers, would not management select the state law that on this point served its interests rather than those of the shareholders?[26] And if the interests of the state and those of management coincide, then the argument, in the end, describes precisely the pattern with which we began this Chapter: States restricting takeovers to further their local economic interests, despite the costs imposed on the national economy.[27]

How do the second generation statutes fare with respect to pre-emption? If the Congressional purpose in the Williams Act was neutrality, with the intent of freezing the balance between offerors and target management where it stood in July, 1967, then virtually any subsequent state action affecting the success of tender offers would be suspect. If, alternatively, the

---

[25] Romano (1993), *supra* note 1, at Ch. 4, surveys this literature and the empirical literature addressing it.

[26] Five abnormal return studies have studied stock price reaction to companies changing their state of incorporation. Jeffry Netter & Annette Poulsen, *State Corporation Laws and Shareholders: The Recent Experience*, 18 Fin.Mgmt. 29 (1989); Michael Bradley & Cindy Schipani, *The Relevance of the Duty of Care Standard in Corporate Governance*, 75 Iowa L.Rev. 1 (1989); Romano (1985), *supra* note 24; Peter Dodd & Richard Leftwich, *The Market for Corporate Charters: "Unhealthy Competition vs. Federal Regulation,"* 53 J.Bus. 259 (1980); Allan Hyman, *The Delaware Controversy -- The Legal Debate*, 4 J.Corp.L. 368 (1979). The studies generally report positive abnormal returns on reincorporation, although these returns are somewhat ambiguous because of the potential for a conflicting information effect. Compare Lucian Bebchuk, *Federalism and the Corporation: The Desirable Limits on State Competition in Corporate Law*, 105 Harv.L.Rev. 1435 (1992), with Romano (1993), *supra* note 1, at 18-22. With respect to state antitakeover statutes, Romano (1985), *supra* note 24, looked at a sample of firms that reincorporated in another state explicitly to obtain takeover protection. Over a 99-day period before and after announcement of the reincorporation proposal, the sample earned positive but statistically insignificant returns of 1.3%. This result is subject to the same ambiguity as studies of adoption of shark repellent charter amendments and poison pills -- the substantive effect of the action may be offset by its information effect -- i.e., that management has a greater expectation of a hostile offer than the market previously thought. See Chapter 17, *supra*.

[27] How much of the constitutional problem confronting state legislative efforts results from the choice to control the local impact of corporate business decisions partially and indirectly by antitakeover statutes under the guise of shareholder protection? For a thoughtful analysis of the different Commerce Clause analysis that would apply to direct restriction of plant closings and other workplace restrictions, see Richard Buxbaum, *Federalism and Corporate Law*, 82 Mich.L.Rev. 1163, 1171-78 (1984).

Congressional purpose was to preserve shareholder autonomy, then might not the Maryland and Ohio statutes, by reducing the prisoners' dilemma pressure on individual shareholders to tender even when shareholders as a group would be better off not tendering, serve to further Congress' goal? If it is difficult to determine whether Congress had either goal in mind exclusively, then would the appropriate pre-emption analysis after *MITE* simply be to allow the states to try new approaches -- certainly less burdensome with respect to *both* goals than the first generation statutes struck down in *MITE* -- until Congress or the SEC make their intent more clear?[28]

Predictably, the constitutionality arguments in favor of second generation statutes sought to exploit *MITE*'s favorable reference to the internal affairs doctrine as a counterweight in the Commerce Clause balance. By and large, these statutes did not fare well in the lower Federal courts.[29] The tables turned, however, when the United States Supreme Court agreed to review the decision in CTS Corporation v. Dynamics Corporation of America, 794 F.2d 250 (7th Cir.), *prob. juris. noted*, 479 U.S. 810 (1986), invalidating on Commerce Clause and pre-emption grounds Indiana's control share acquisition statute.

CTS CORP. v. DYNAMICS CORP. OF AMERICA
481 U.S. 69 (1987)

Justice POWELL delivered the opinion of the Court.

This case presents the questions whether the Control Share Acquisitions Chapter of the Indiana Business Corporation Law, Inc. Code § 23-1-42-1 et seq. (Supp.1986), is pre-empted by the Williams Act, 82 Stat. 454, as amended, 15 U.S.C. §§ 78m(d)-(e) and 78n(d)-(f) (1982 ed. and Supp. III),

---

[28] A final issue with respect to the second generation statutes, now concerning their wisdom rather than their constitutionality, is also worth raising. These statutes typically allow individual companies to opt out of the statute. Regardless of whether the substance of the statutes is desirable, do they put the burden of initiating action to opt out on the wrong party? Assume that management will tend to protect itself from takeovers even if it is not in the shareholders' best interests. Would it be better to draft the statutes to authorize corporations to opt *into* the statutory scheme by charter amendment, rather than to opt *out* of it? If the statutes were structured this way, management would still be able to use corporate funds to propose the amendment and solicit votes in its favor, but shareholders would at least have the opportunity to reject it. As the statutes are actually structured, it is not in management's interests to propose the opt-out amendment so that, at best, a shareholder would have to overcome free rider problems and take the initiative to remove it. At worst, in some states the opt-out amendment could never be proposed because any charter amendment requires the prior approval of the board of directors.

[29] See, e.g., Fleet Aerospace Corp. v. Holderman, 637 F.Supp. 742 (S.D. Ohio), *aff'd*, 796 F.2d 135 (6th Cir.1986) (Ohio Control Share Acquisition Act); Terry v. Yamashita, 643 F.Supp. 161 (D.Haw.1986) (Hawaii Control Share Acquisition Act).

or violates the Commerce Clause of the Federal Constitution, Art. I, § 8, cl. 3.

I

A

On March 4, 1986, the Governor of Indiana signed a revised Indiana Business Corporation Law, Inc., Code § 23-1-17-1 et seq. (Supp.1986). That law included the Control Share Acquisitions Chapter (Indiana Act or Act). Beginning on August 1, 1987, the Act will apply to any corporation incorporated in Indiana, § 23-1-17-3(a), unless the corporation amends its articles of incorporation or bylaws to opt into the Act by resolution of its board of directors. § 23-1-17-3(b). The act applies only to "issuing public corporations." The term "corporation" includes only businesses incorporated in Indiana. See § 23-1-20-5. An "issuing public corporation" is defined as:

> a corporation that has:
>> (1) one hundred (100) or more shareholders;
>> (2) its principal place of business, its principal office, or substantial assets within Indiana; and
>> (3) either:
>>> (A) more than ten percent (10%) of its shareholders resident in Indiana;
>>> (B) more than ten percent (10%) of its shares owned by Indiana residents; or
>>> (C) ten thousand (10,000) shareholders resident in Indiana." § 23-1-42-4(a).[3]

The Act focuses on the acquisition of "control shares" in an issuing public corporation. Under the Act, an entity acquires "control shares" whenever it acquires shares that, but for the operation of the Act, would bring its voting power in the corporation to or above any of three thresholds: 20%, 33-1/3%, or 50%. § 23-1-42-1. An entity that acquires control shares does not necessarily acquire voting rights. Rather, it gains those rights only "to the extent granted by resolution approved by the shareholders of the issuing public corporation. § 23-1-42-9(a). Section 9 requires a majority vote of all disinterested[4] shareholders holding each class of stock for passage

---

[3] These thresholds are much higher than the 5% threshold acquisition requirement that brings a tender offer under the coverage of the Williams Act. See 15 U.S.C. § 78n(d)(1).

[4] "Interested shares are shares with respect to which the acquiror, an officer or an inside director of the corporation "may exercise or direct the exercise of the voting power of the corporation in the election of directors." § 23-1-42-3. If the record date passes before the acquiror purchases shares pursuant to the tender offer, the purchased shares will not be "interested shares" within the meaning of the Act; although the acquiror may own the shares on the date of the meeting, it will not "exercise . . . the voting power" of the shares.

of such a resolution.   § 23-1-42-9(b).   The practical effect of this requirement is to condition acquisition of control of a corporation on approval of a majority of the pre-existing disinterested shareholders.

The shareholders decide whether to confer rights on the control shares at the next regularly scheduled meeting of the shareholders, or at a specially scheduled meeting. The acquiror can require management of the corporation to hold such a special meeting within 50 days if it files an "acquiring person statement,"[6] requests the meeting, and agrees to pay the expenses of the meeting. See § 23-1-42-7. If the shareholders do not vote to restore voting rights to the shares, the corporation may redeem the control shares from the acquiror at fair market value, but it is not required to do so.   § 23-1-42-10(b). Similarly, if the acquiror does not file an acquiring person statement with the corporation, the corporation may, if its bylaws or articles of incorporation so provide, redeem the shares at any time after 60 days after the acquiror's last acquisition.   § 23-1-42-10(a).

B

On March 10, 1986, appellee Dynamics Corporation of America (Dynamics) owned 9.6% of the common stock of appellant CTS Corporation, an Indiana corporation. On that day, six days after the Act went into effect, Dynamics announced a tender offer for another million shares in CTS; purchase of those shares would have brought Dynamics' ownership interest in CTS to 27.5%. Also on March 10, Dynamics filed suit in the United States District Court for the Northern District of Illinois, alleging that CTS had violated the federal securities laws in a number of respects no longer relevant to these proceedings. On March 27, the Board of Directors of CTS, an Indiana corporation, elected to be governed by the provisions of the Act, see § 23-1-17-3.

Four days later, on March 31, Dynamics moved for leave to amend its complaint to allege that the Act is pre-empted by the Williams act, and

---

As a practical matter, the record date usually will pass before shares change hands. Under SEC regulations, the shares cannot be purchased until 20 business days after the offer commences. 17 CFR § 240.14e-1(a) (1986). If the acquiror seeks an early resolution of the issue -- as most acquirors will -- the meeting required by the Act must be held no more than 50 calendar days after the offer commences, about three weeks after the earliest date on which the shares could be purchased. See § 23-1-42-7. The Act requires management to give notice of the meeting "as promptly as reasonably practicable . . . to all shareholders of record as of the record date set for the meeting." § 23-1-42-8(a). It seems likely that management of the target corporation would violate this obligation if it delayed setting the record date and sending notice until after 20 business days had passed. Thus, we assume that the record date usually will be set before the date on which federal law first permits purchase of the shares.

[6] An "acquiring person statement" is an information statement describing, *inter alia*, the identity of the acquiring person and the terms and extent of the proposed acquisition. See § 23-1-42-6.

violates the Commerce Clause, Art. I, § 8, cl. 3. Dynamics sought a temporary restraining order, a preliminary injunction, and declaratory relief against CTS's use of the Act. On April 9, the District Court ruled that the Williams Act pre-empts the Indiana Act and granted Dynamics' motion for declaratory relief. 637 F.Supp. 389 (N.D.Ill.1986). Relying on Justice WHITE's plurality opinion in Edgar v. MITE Corp., 457 U.S. 624 (1982), the court concluded that the Act "wholly frustrates the purpose and objective of Congress in striking a balance between the investor, management, and the takeover bidder in takeover contests." 637 F.Supp. at 399. A week later, on April 17, the District Court issued an opinion accepting Dynamics' claim that the Act violated the Commerce Clause. This holding rested on the court's conclusion that "the substantial interference with interstate commerce created by the [Act] outweighs the articulated local benefits so as to create an impermissible indirect burden on interstate commerce." *Id.* at 406. The District Court certified its decisions on the Williams Act and Commerce Clause claims as final under Fed. Rule Civ.Proc. 54(b). *Ibid.*

CTS appealed the District Court's holdings on these claims to the Court of Appeals for the Seventh Circuit. Because of the imminence of CTS's annual meeting, the Court of Appeals consolidated and expedited the two appeals. On April 23 -- 23 days after Dynamics first contested application of the Act in the District Court -- the Court of Appeals issued an order affirming the judgment of the District Court. The opinion followed on May 28. 794 F.2d 250 (7th Cir.1986).

After disposing of a variety of questions not relevant to this appeal, the Court of Appeals examined Dynamics' claim that the Williams Act pre-empts the Indiana Act. The court looked first to the plurality opinion in Edgar v. MITE Corp., *supra*, in which three Justices found that the Williams Act pre-empts state statutes that upset the balance between target management and a tender offeror. The court noted that some commentators had disputed this view of the Williams Act, concluding instead that the Williams Act was "an anti-takeover statute, expressing a view, however benighted, that hostile takeovers are bad." *Id.* at 262. It also noted:

> [I]t is a big leap from saying that the Williams Act does not itself exhibit much hostility to tender offers to saying that it implicitly forbids states to adopt more hostile regulations. . . . But whatever doubts of the Williams' Act preemptive intent we might entertain as an original matter are stilled by the weight of precedent. *Ibid.*

Once the court had decided to apply the analysis of the *MITE* plurality, it found the case straightforward:

> Very few tender offers could run the gauntlet that Indiana has set up. In any event, if the Williams Act is to be taken as a congressional determination that a month (roughly) is enough time to force a tender offer to be kept open, 50 days is too much; and 50 days is the minimum under the Indiana act if the target corporation so chooses. *Id.* at 263.

The court next addressed Dynamics' Commerce Clause challenge to the Act. Applying the balancing test articulated in Pike v. Bruce Church, Inc., 397 U.S. 137 (1970), the court found the Act unconstitutional:

> Unlike a state's blue sky law the Indiana statute is calculated to impede transactions between residents of other states. For the sake of trivial or even negative benefits to its residents Indiana is depriving nonresidents of the valued opportunity to accept tender offers from other nonresidents.
>
> . . . Even if a corporation's tangible assets are immovable, the efficiency with which they are employed and the proportions in which the earnings they generate are divided between management and shareholders depends on the market for corporate control -- an interstate, indeed international, market that the State of Indiana is not authorized to opt out of, as in effect it has done in this statute. 794 F.2d at 264.

Finally, the court addressed the "internal affairs" doctrine, a "principle of conflict of laws . . . designed to make sure that the law of only one state shall govern the internal affairs of a corporation or other association." *Ibid.* It stated:

> We may assume without having to decide that Indiana has a broad latitude in regulating those affairs, even when the consequence may be to make it harder to take over an Indiana corporation. . . . But in this case the effect on the interstate market in securities and corporate control is direct, intended, and substantial. . . . [T]hat the mode of regulation involves jiggering with voting rights cannot take it outside the scope of judicial review under the commerce clause. *Ibid.*

Accordingly, the court affirmed the judgment of the District Court.

Both Indiana and CTS filed jurisdictional statements. We noted probable jurisdiction under 28 U.S.C. § 1254(2), 479 U.S. 810 (1986), and now reverse.

II

The first question in this case is whether the Williams Act pre-empts the Indiana Act. As we have stated frequently, absent an explicit indication by Congress of an intent to pre-empt state law, a state statute is pre-empted only

> 'where compliance with both federal and state regulations is a physical impossibility . . .,' Florida Lime & Avocado Growers, Inc. v. Paul, 373 U.S. 132, 142-143 (1963), or where the state 'law stands as an obstacle to the accomplishment and execution of the full purposes and objectives of Congress.' Hines v. Davidowitz, 312 U.S. 52, 67 (1941). . . .

[Ray v. Atlantic Richfield Co., 435 U.S. 151, 158 (1978).] Because it is entirely possible for entities to comply with both the Williams Act and the

Indiana Act, the state statute can be pre-empted only if it frustrates the purposes of the federal law.

A

Our discussion begins with a brief summary of the structure and purposes of the Williams Act. Congress passed the Williams Act in 1968 in response to the increasing number of hostile tender offers. Before its passage, these transactions were not covered by the disclosure requirements of the federal securities laws. See Piper v. Chris-Craft Industries, 430 U.S. 1, 22 (1977). The Williams Act, backed by regulations of the Securities and Exchange Commission (SEC), imposes requirements in two basic areas. First, it requires the offeror to file a statement disclosing information about the offer, including: the offeror's background and identity; the source and amount of the funds to be used in making the purchase; the purpose of the purchase, including any plans to liquidate the company or make major changes in its corporate structure; and the extent of the offeror's holdings in the target company.

Second, the Williams Act, and the regulations that accompany it, establish procedural rules to govern tender offers. For example, stockholders who tender their shares may withdraw them during the first 15 business days of the tender offer and, if the offeror has not purchased their shares, any time after 60 days from commencement of the offer. The offer must remain open for at least 20 business days. If more shares are tendered than the offeror sought to purchase, purchases must be made on a pro rata basis from each tendering shareholder. Finally, the offeror must pay the same price for all purchases; if the offering price is increased before the end of the offer, those who already have tendered must receive the benefit of the increased price.

B

The Indiana Act differs in major respects from the Illinois statute that the Court considered in Edgar v. MITE Corp., 457 U.S. 624 (1982). After reviewing the legislative history of the Williams Act, Justice WHITE, joined by Chief Justice BURGER and Justice BLACKMUN (the plurality), concluded that the Williams Act struck a careful balance between the interests of offerors and target companies, and that any state statute that "upset" this balance was pre-empted. Id. at 632-634.

The plurality then identified three offending features of the Illinois statute. Justice WHITE's opinion first noted that the Illinois statute provided for a 20-day pre-commencement period. During this time, management could disseminate its views on the upcoming offer to shareholders, but offerors could not publish their offers. The plurality found that this provision gave management "a powerful tool to combat tender offers." Id. at 635. This contrasted dramatically with the Williams Act; Congress had deleted express precommencement notice provisions from the Williams Act. According to the plurality, Congress had determined that the potentially adverse consequences of such a provision on shareholders should be avoided. Thus, the plurality concluded that the Illinois provision "frustrate[d] the objectives of the Williams Act." *Ibid*. The second criticized feature of the Illinois statute was a provision for a hearing on a tender offer that, because it set no deadline, allowed management "'to stymie indefinitely a takeover,'" *id.*, at 637 (quoting MITE Corp. v. Dixon, 633 F.2d 486, 494 (2nd Cir.1980). The plurality noted that "'delay can seriously impede a tender offer,'" 457 U.S., at 637 (quoting Great Western United Corp. v. Kidwell, 577 F.2d 1256, 1277 (5th Cir.1978) (per Wisdom, J.)), and that "Congress anticipated that investors and the takeover offeror would be free to go forward without unreasonable delay," 457 U.S. at 639. Accordingly, the plurality concluded that this provision conflicted with the Williams Act. The third troublesome feature of the Illinois statute was its requirement that the fairness of tender offers would be reviewed by the Illinois Secretary of State. Noting that "Congress intended for investors to be free to make their own decisions," the plurality concluded that "'[t]he state thus offers investor protection at the expense of investor autonomy -- an approach quite in conflict with that adopted by Congress.'" *Id.* at 639-640 (quoting MITE Corp. v. Dixon, *supra*, at 494).

C

As the plurality opinion in *MITE* did not represent the views of a majority of the Court,[8] we are not bound by its reasoning. We need not question that reasoning, however, because we believe the Indiana Act passes muster even under the broad interpretation of the Williams Act articulated by Justice WHITE in *MITE*. As is apparent from our summary of its reasoning, the overriding concern of the *MITE* plurality was that the Illinois statute considered in that case operated to favor management against offerors, to the detriment of shareholders. By contrast, the statute now before the Court protects the independent shareholder against both of the contending parties. Thus, the Act furthers a basic purpose of the Williams Act, "'plac[ing] investors on an equal footing with the takeover bidder,'" Piper v. Chris-Craft Industries, 430 U.S. at 30 (quoting the Senate Report accompanying the Williams Act, S.Rep. No. 550, 90th Cong., 1st Sess., 4 (1967)).

---

[8] Justice WHITE's opinion on the pre-emption issue, 457 U.S. at 630-640, was joined only by Chief Justice BURGER and by Justice BLACKMUN. Two Justices disagreed with Justice WHITE's conclusion. See *id.* at 646-647 (POWELL, J., concurring in part); *id.* at 655 (STEVENS, J., concurring in part and concurring in judgment). Four Justices did not address the question. See *id.* at 655 (O'CONNOR, J., concurring in part); *id.* at 664 (MARSHALL, J., with whom BRENNAN, J. joined, dissenting); *id.* at 667 (REHNQUIST, J., dissenting).

The Indiana Act operates on the assumption, implicit in the Williams Act, that independent shareholders faced with tender offers often are at a disadvantage. By allowing such shareholders to vote as a group, the Act protects them from the coercive aspects of some tender offers. If, for example, shareholders believe that a successful tender offer will be followed by a purchase of nontendering shares at a depressed price, individual shareholders may tender their shares -- even if they doubt the tender offer is in the corporation's best interest -- to protect themselves from being forced to sell their shares at a depressed price. As the SEC explains: "The alternative of not accepting the tender offer is virtual assurance that, if the offer is successful, the shares will have to be sold in the lower priced, second step." *Two-Tier Tender Offer Pricing and Non-Tender Offer Purchase Programs*, SEC Exchange Act Rel., No. 21,079 (June 21, 1984), [1984 Transfer Binder] CCH Fed.Sec.L.Rep. ¶ 83, 637, p.86,916 (footnote omitted) (hereinafter SEC Release No. 21-79). See Lowenstein, *Pruning Deadwood in Hostile Takeovers: A Proposal for Legislation*, 83 Colum.L.Rev. 249, 307- 309 (1983). In such a situation under the Indiana Act, the shareholders as a group, acting in the corporation's best interest, could reject the offer, although individual shareholders might be inclined to accept it. The desire of the Indiana Legislature to protect shareholders of Indiana corporations from this type of coercive offer does not conflict with the Williams Act. Rather, it furthers the federal policy of investor protection.

In implementing its goal, the Indiana Act avoids the problems the plurality discussed in *MITE*. Unlike the *MITE* statute, the Indiana Act does not give either management or the offeror an advantage in communicating with the shareholders about the impending offer. The Act also does not impose an indefinite delay on tender offers. Nothing in the Act prohibits an offeror from consummating an offer on the 20th business day, the earliest day permitted under applicable federal regulations. Nor does the Act allow the state government to interpose its views of fairness between willing buyers and sellers of shares of the target company. Rather, the Act allows *shareholders* to evaluate the fairness of the offer collectively.

D

The Court of Appeals based its finding of pre-emption on its view that the practical effect of the Indiana Act is to delay consummation of tender offers until 50 days after the commencement of the offer. 794 F.2d at 263. As did the Court of Appeals, Dynamics reasons that no rational offeror will purchase shares until it gains assurance that those shares will carry voting rights. Because it is possible that voting rights will not be conferred until a shareholder meeting 50 days after commencement of the offer, Dynamics concludes that the Act imposes a 50-day delay. This, it argues, conflicts with the shorter 20-business-day period established by the SEC as the minimum period for which a tender offer may be held open. We find the alleged conflict illusory.

The Act does not impose an absolute 50-day delay on tender offers, nor does it preclude an offeror from purchasing shares as soon as federal law permits. If the offeror fears an adverse shareholder vote under the Act, it can make a conditional tender offer, offering to accept shares on the condition that the shares receive voting rights within a certain period of time. The Williams Act permits tender offers to be conditioned on the offeror's subsequently obtaining regulatory approval. E.g., *Interpretive Release Relating to Tender Offer Rules*, SEC Exchange Act Rel. No. 34-16623 (Mar. 5, 1980), 3 CCH Fed.Sec.L.Rep. ¶ 24,2841, p.17,758, quoted in MacFadden Holdings, Inc. v. JB Acquisition Corp., 802 F.2d 62, 70 (2nd Cir.1986).[10] There is no reason to doubt that this type of conditional tender offer would be legitimate as well.[11]

Even assuming that the Indiana Act imposes some additional delay, nothing in *MITE* suggested that *any* delay imposed by state regulation, however, short, would create a conflict with the Williams Act. The plurality argued only that the offeror should "be free to go forward without *unreasonable* delay." 457 U.S. at 639 (emphasis added). In that case, the Court was confronted with the potential for indefinite delay and presented with no persuasive reason why some deadline could not be established. By contrast, the Indiana Act provides that full voting rights will be vested -- if this eventually is to occur --within 50 days after commencement of the offer. This period is within the 60-day maximum period Congress established for tender offers in 15 U.S.C. § 78n(d)(5). We cannot say that a delay within that congressionally determined period is unreasonable.

Finally, we note that the Williams Act would pre-empt a variety of state corporate laws of hitherto unquestioned validity if it were construed to pre-empt any state statute that may limit or delay the free exercise of power after a successful tender offer. State corporate laws commonly permit corporations to stagger the terms of their directors. See Model Business Corp. Act § 37 (1969 draft) in 3 Model Business Corp. Act Ann. (2d

---

[10] Although the SEC does not appear to have spoken authoritatively on this point, similar transactions are not uncommon. For example, Hanson Trust recently conditioned consummation of a tender offer for shares in SCM Corporation on the removal of a "lockup option" that would have seriously diminished the value of acquiring the shares of SCM Corporation. See Hanson Trust PLC v. ML SCM Acquisition, Inc., 781 F.2d 264, 272, and n.7 (2nd Cir.1986).

[11] Dynamics argues that conditional tender offers are not an adequate alternative because they leave management in place for three extra weeks, with "free rein to take other defensive steps that will diminish the value of tendered shares." Brief for Appellee Dynamics Corp. of America 37. We reject this contention. In the unlikely event that management were to take actions designed to diminish the value of the corporation's shares, it may incur liability under state law. But this problem does not control our pre-emption analysis. Neither the Act nor any other federal statute can assure that shareholders do not suffer from the mismanagement of corporate officers and directors. Cf. Cort v. Ash, 422 U.S. 66, 84 (1975).

ed.1971) (hereinafter MBCA); American Bar Foundation, Revised Model Business Corp. Act § 8.06 (1984 draft) (1985) (hereinafter RMBCA).[12] By staggering the terms of directors, and thus having annual elections for only one class of directors each year, corporations may delay the time when a successful offeror gains control of the board of directors. Similarly, state corporation laws commonly provide for cumulative voting. See MBCA § 33, ¶ 4; RMBCA § 7.28.[13] By enabling minority shareholders to assure themselves of representation in each class of directors, cumulative voting provisions can delay further the ability of offerors to gain untrammeled authority over the affairs of the target corporation. See Hochman & Folger, *Deflecting Takeovers: Charter and By-Law Techniques*, 34 Bus.Law. 537, 538-539 (1979).

In our view, the possibility that the Indiana Act will delay some tender offers is insufficient to require a conclusion that the Williams Act pre-empts the Act. The longstanding prevalence of state regulation in this area suggests that, if Congress had intended to pre-empt all state laws that delay the acquisition of voting control following a tender offer, it would have said so explicitly. The regulatory conditions that the Act places on tender offers are consistent with the text and the purposes of the Williams Act. Accordingly, we hold that the Williams Act does not pre-empt the Indiana Act.

III

As an alternative basis for its decision, the Court of Appeals held that the Act violates the Commerce Clause of the Federal Constitution. We now address this holding. On its face, the Commerce Clause is nothing more than a grant to Congress of the power "[t]o regulate Commerce . . . among the several States. . .," Art. I, § 8, cl. 3. But it has been settled for more than a century that the Clause prohibits States from taking certain actions respecting interstate commerce even absent congressional action. See, e.g., Cooley v. Board of Wardens, 12 How. 299 (1852). The Court's interpretation of "these great silences of the Constitution," H.P. Hood & Sons, Inc. v. Du Mond, 336 U.S. 525, 535 (1949), has not always been easy to follow. Rather, as the volume and complexity of commerce and regulation has grown in this country, the Court has articulated a variety of

---

[12] Every State except Arkansas and California allows classification of directors to stagger their terms of office. See 2 Model Bus. Corp. Act Ann. § 8.06, p.830 (3d ed., Supp.1986).

[13] "Cumulative voting is a means devised to protect minorities by providing a method of voting which assures to a minority, if it is sufficiently purposeful and cohesive, representation on the board of directors to an extent roughly proportionate to the minority's size. This is achieved by permitting each shareholder . . . to cast the total number of his votes for a single candidate for election to the board, or to distribute such total among any number of such candidates (the total number of his votes being equal to the number of shares he is voting multiplied by the number of directors to be elected)." 1 Model Bus.Corp. Act Ann. § 33, ¶ 4 comment (2d ed.1971). Every State permits cumulative voting. See 2 Model Bus. Corp. Act Ann. § 7.28, pp.675-677 (3d ed., Supp.1986).

tests in an attempt to describe the difference between those regulations that the Commerce Clause permits and those regulations that it prohibits. See, e.g., Raymond Motor Transportation, Inc. v. Rice, 434 U.S. 429, 441, n.15 (1978).

A

The principal objects of dormant Commerce Clause scrutiny are statutes that discriminate against interstate commerce. See, e.g., Lewis v. BT Investment Managers, Inc., 447 U.S. 27, 36-37 (1980); Philadelphia v. New Jersey, 437 U.S. 617, 624 (1978). See generally Regan, *The Supreme Court and State Protectionism: Making Sense of the Dormant Commerce Clause*, 84 Mich.L.Rev. 1091 (1986). The Indiana Act is not such a statute. It has the same effects on tender offers whether or not the offeror is a domiciliary or resident of Indiana. Thus, it "visits its effects equally upon both interstate and local business," Lewis v. BT Investment Managers, Inc., *supra*, 447 U.S. at 36.

Dynamics nevertheless contends that the statute is discriminatory because it will apply most often to out-of-state entities. This argument rests on the contention that, as a practical matter, most hostile tender offers are launched by offerors outside Indiana. But this argument avails Dynamics little. "The fact that the burden of a state regulation falls on some interstate companies does not, by itself, establish a claim of discrimination against interstate commerce." Exxon Corp. v. Governor of Maryland, 437 U.S. 117, 126 (1978). See Minnesota v. Clover Leaf Creamery Co., 449 U.S. 456, 471-472 (1981) (rejecting a claim of discrimination because the challenged statute "regulate[d] evenhandedly . . . without regard to whether the [commerce came] from outside the state"); Commonwealth Edison Co. v. Montana, 453 U.S. 609, 619 (1981) (rejecting a claim of discrimination because the "tax burden [was] borne according to the amount . . . consumed and not according to any distinction between in-state and out-of-state consumers"). Because nothing in the Indiana Act imposes a greater burden on out-of-state offerors than it does on similarly situated Indiana offerors, we reject the contention that the Act discriminates against interstate commerce.

B

This Court's recent Commerce Clause cases also have invalidated statutes that adversely may affect interstate commerce by subjecting activities to inconsistent regulations. E.g., Brown-Forman Distillers Corp. v. New York State Liquor Authority, 476 U.S. 573 (1986); Edgar v. MITE Corp., 457 U.S. at 642 (plurality of WHITE, J.); Kassel v. Consolidated Freightways Corp., 450 U.S. 662, 671 (1981) (plurality opinion of POWELL, J.). See Southern Pacific Co. v. Arizona, 325 U.S. 761, 774 (1945) (noting the "confusion and difficulty" that would attend the "unsatisfied need for uniformity" in setting maximum limits on train lengths);

Cooley v. Board of Wardens, *supra*, 12 How. at 319 (stating that the Commerce Clause prohibits States from regulating subjects that "are in their nature national, or admit only of one uniform system, or plan of regulation"). The Indiana Act poses no such problem. So long as each State regulates voting rights only in the corporations it has created, each corporation will be subject to the law of only one State. No principle of corporation law and practice is more firmly established than a State's authority to regulate domestic corporations, including the authority to define the voting rights of shareholders. See Restatement (Second) of Conflict of Laws § 304 (1971) (concluding that the law of the incorporating State generally should "determine the right of a shareholder to participate in the administration of the affairs of the corporation"). Accordingly, we conclude that the Indiana Act does not create an impermissible risk of inconsistent regulation by different States.

C

The Court of Appeals did not find the Act unconstitutional for either of these threshold reasons. Rather, its decision rested on its view of the Act's potential to hinder tender offers. We think the Court of Appeals failed to appreciate the significance of Commerce Clause analysis of the fact that state regulation of corporate governance is regulation of entities whose very existence and attributes are a product of state law. As Chief Justice Marshall explained:

> A corporation is an artificial being, invisible, intangible, and existing only in contemplation of law. Being the mere creature of law, it possesses only those properties which the charter of its creation confers upon it, either expressly, or as incidental to its very existence. These are such as are supposed best calculated to effect the object for which it was created. Trustees of Dartmouth College v. Woodward, 4 Wheat. 518, 636 (1819).

See First National Bank of Boston v. Bellotti, 435 U.S. 765, 822-824 (1978) (REHNQUIST, J., dissenting). Every State in this country has enacted laws regulating corporate governance. By prohibiting certain transactions, and regulating others, such laws necessarily affect certain aspects of interstate commerce. This necessarily is truer with respect to corporations with shareholders in States other than the State of incorporation. Large corporations that are listed on national exchanges, or even regional exchanges, will have shareholders in many States and shares that are traded frequently. The markets that facilitate this national and international participation in ownership of corporations are essential for providing capital not only for new enterprises but also for established companies that need to expand their businesses. This beneficial free market system depends at its core upon the fact that a corporation -- except in the rarest situations -- is organized under, and governed by, the law of a single jurisdiction, traditionally the corporate law of the State of its incorporation.

These regulatory laws may affect directly a variety of corporate transactions. Mergers are a typical example. In view of the substantial effect that a merger may have on the shareholders' interests in a corporation, many States require supermajority votes to approve mergers. See, e.g., MBCA § 73 (requiring approval of a merger by a majority of all shares, rather than simply a majority of votes cast); RMBCA § 11.03 (same). By requiring a greater vote for mergers than it required for other transactions, these laws make it more difficult for corporations to merge. State laws also may provide for "dissenters' rights" under which minority shareholders who disagree with corporate decisions to take particular actions are entitled to see their shares to the corporation at fair market value. See, e.g., MBCA § 80-81; RMBCA § 13.02. By requiring the corporation to purchase the shares of dissenting shareholders, these laws may inhibit a corporation from engaging in the specified transactions.[14]

It thus is an accepted part of the business landscape in this country for States to create corporations, to prescribe their powers, and to define the rights that are acquired by purchasing their shares. A State has an interest in promoting stable relationships among parties involved in the corporations it charters, as well as in ensuring that investors in such corporations have an effective voice in corporate affairs.

There can be no doubt that the Act reflects these concerns. The primary purpose of the Act is to protect the shareholders of Indiana corporations. It does this by affording shareholders, when a takeover offer is made, an opportunity to decide collectively whether the resulting change in voting control of the corporation, as they perceive it, would be desirable. A change of management may have important effects on the shareholders' interests; it is well within the State's role as overseer of corporate

---

[14] Numerous other common regulations may affect both nonresident and resident shareholders of a corporation. Specified votes may be required for the sale of all of the corporation's assets. See MBCA § 79; RMBCA § 12.02. The election of directors may be staggered over a period of years to prevent abrupt changes in management. See MBCA § 37; RMBCA § 8.06. Various classes of stock may be created with differences in voting rights as to dividends and on liquidation. See MBCA §15; RMBCA § 6.01(c). Provisions may be made for cumulative voting. See MBCA § 33, ¶ 4; RMBCA § 7.28; n.9 *supra*. Corporations may adopt restrictions on payment of dividends to ensure that specified ratios of assets to liabilities are maintained for the benefit of the holders of corporate bonds or notes. See MBCA § 45 (noting that a corporation's articles of incorporation can restrict payment of dividends); RMBCA § 6.40 (same). Where the shares of a corporation are held in States other than that of incorporation, actions taken pursuant to these and similar provisions of state law will affect all shareholders alike wherever they reside or are domiciled.

Nor is it unusual for partnership law to restrict certain transactions. For example, a purchaser of a partnership interest generally can gain a right to control the business only with the consent of other owners. See Uniform Partnership Act § 27, 6 U.L.A. 353 (1969); Uniform Limited Partnership Act § 19 (1916 draft), 6 U.L.A. 603 (1969); Revised Uniform Limited Partnership Act §§ 702, 704 (1976 draft), 6 U.L.A. 259, 261 (Supp.1986). These provisions -- in force in the great majority of the States -- bear a striking resemblance to the Act at issue in this case.

governance to offer this opportunity. The autonomy provided by allowing shareholders collectively to determine whether the takeover is advantageous to their interests may be especially beneficial where a hostile tender offer may coerce shareholders into tendering their shares.

Appellee Dynamics responds to this concern by arguing that the prospect of coercive tender offers is illusory, and that tender offers generally should be favored because they reallocate corporate assets into the hands of management who can use them most effectively.[15] See generally Frank Easterbrook and Daniel Fischel, *The Proper Role of a Target's Management in Responding to a Tender Offer*, 94 Harv.L.Rev. 1161 (1981). As indicated *supra*, at 1646, Indiana's concern with tender offers is not groundless. Indeed, the potentially coercive aspects of tender offers have been recognized by the Securities and Exchange Commission, see SEC Release No. 21079, p.86,916, and by a number of scholarly commentators, see, e.g., Michael Bradley & Michael Rosenzweig, *Defensive Stock Repurchases*, 99 Harv.L.Rev. 1377, 1412-1413 (1986); John Macey & Fred McChesney, *A Theoretical Analysis of Corporate Greenmail*, 95 Yale L.J. 13, 20-22 (1985); Lowenstein, 83 Colum.L.Rev., at 307-309. The Constitution does not require the States to subscribe to any particular economic theory. We are not inclined "to second-guess the empirical judgments of lawmakers concerning the utility of legislation," Kassel v. Consolidated Freightways Corp., 450 U.S. at 679 (BRENNAN, J., concurring in judgment). In our view, the possibility of coercion in some takeover bids offers additional justification for Indiana's decision to promote the autonomy of independent shareholders.

Dynamics argues in any event that the State has "'no legitimate interest in protecting the nonresident shareholders.'" Brief for Appellee Dynamics Corp. of America 21 (quoting Edgar v. MITE Corp., 457 U.S. at 644). Dynamics relies heavily on the statement by the *MITE* Court that "[i]nsofar as the . . . law burdens out-of-state transactions, there is nothing to be weighed in the balance to sustain the law." 457 U.S. at 644. But that comment was made in reference to an Illinois law that applied as well to out-of-state corporations. We agree that Indiana has no interest in protecting nonresident shareholders *of nonresident corporations*. But this Act applies only to corporations incorporated in Indiana. We reject the contention that Indiana has no interest in providing for the shareholders of its corporations the voting autonomy granted by the Act. Indiana has a substantial interest in preventing the corporate form from becoming a shield for unfair business

---

[15] It is appropriate to note when discussing the merits and demerits of tender offers that generalizations usually require qualification. No one doubts that some successful tender offers will provide more effective management or other benefits such as needed diversification. But there is no reason to *assume* that the type of conglomerate corporation that may result from repetitive takeovers necessarily will result in more effective management or otherwise be beneficial to shareholders. The divergent views in the literature -- and even now being debated in the Congress -- reflect the reality that the type and utility of tender offers vary widely. Of course, in many situations the offer to shareholders is simply a cash price substantially higher than the market price prior to the offer.

dealing. Moreover, unlike the Illinois statute invalidated in *MITE*, the Indiana Act applies only to corporations that have a substantial number of shareholders in Indiana. See Ind. Code § 23-1-42-4(a)(3) (Supp.1986). Thus, every application of the Indiana Act will affect a substantial number of Indiana residents, whom Indiana indisputably has an interest in protecting.

D

Dynamics' argument that the Act is unconstitutional ultimately rests on its contention that the Act will limit the number of successful tender offers. There is little evidence that this will occur. But even if true, this result would not substantially affect our Commerce Clause analysis. We reiterate that this Act does not prohibit any entity -- resident or nonresident -- from offering to purchase, or from purchasing, shares in Indiana corporations, or from attempting thereby to gain control. It only provides regulatory procedures designed for the better protection of the corporations' shareholders. We have rejected the "notion that the Commerce Clause protects the particular structure or methods of operation in a . . . market." Exxon Corp. v. Governor of Maryland, 437 U.S. at 127. The very commodity that is traded in the securities market is one whose characteristics are defined by state law. Similarly, the very commodity that is traded in the "market for corporate control" -- the corporation -- is one that owes its existence and attributes to state law. Indiana need not define these commodities as other States do; it need only provide that residents and nonresidents have equal access to them. This Indiana has done. Accordingly, even if the Act should decrease the number of successful tender offers for Indiana corporations, this would not offend the Commerce Clause.[16]

IV

On its face, the Indiana Control Share Acquisitions Chapter evenhandedly determines the voting rights of shares of Indiana corporations. The Act does not conflict with the provisions or purposes of the Williams Act. To the limited extent that the Act affects interstate commerce, this is justified by the State's interests in defining the attributes of shares in its corporations and in protecting shareholders. Congress has never questioned the need for state regulation of these matters. Nor do we think such regulation offends the Constitution. Accordingly, we reverse the judgment of the Court of Appeals.

---

[16] CTS also contends that the Act does not violate the Commerce Clause -- regardless of any burdens it may impose on interstate commerce -- because a corporation's decision to be covered by the Act is purely "private" activity beyond the reach of the Commerce Clause. Because we reverse the judgment of the Court of Appeals on other grounds, we have no occasion to consider this argument.

It is so ordered.

Justice SCALIA, concurring in part and concurring in the judgment.

I join Parts I, III-A, and III-B of the Court's opinion. However, having found, as those Parts do, that the Indiana Control Share Acquisitions Chapter neither "discriminates against interstate commerce," *ante*, at 1649, nor "create[s] an impermissible risk of inconsistent regulation by different States, *ante*, at 1649, I would conclude without further analysis that it is not invalid under the dormant Commerce Clause. While it has become standard practice at least since Pike v. Bruce Church, Inc., 397 U.S. 137 (1970), to consider, in addition to these factors, whether the burden on commerce imposed by a state statute "is clearly excessive in relation to the putative local benefits," *id.* at 142, such an inquiry is ill suited to the judicial function and should be undertaken rarely if at all. This case is a good illustration of the point. Whether the control shares statute "protects shareholders of Indiana corporations," Brief for Appellant in No. 86-97, p.88, or protects incumbent management seems to me a highly debatable question, but it is extraordinary to think that the constitutionality of the Act should depend on the answer. Nothing in the Constitution says that the protection of entrenched management is any less important a "putative local benefit" than the protection of entrenched shareholders, and I do not know what qualifies us to make that judgment -- or the related judgment as to how effective the present statute is in achieving one or the other objective -- or the ultimate (and most ineffable) judgment as to whether, given importance-level x, and effectiveness-level y, the worth of the statute is "outweighed" by impact-on-commerce z.

One commentator has suggested that, at least much of the time, we do not in fact mean what we say when we declare that statutes which neither discriminate against commerce nor present a threat of multiple and inconsistent burdens might nonetheless be unconstitutional under a "balancing" test. See Regan, *The Supreme Court and State Protectionism: Making Sense of the Dormant Commerce Clause*, 84 Mich.L.Rev. 1091 (1986). If he is not correct, he ought to be. As long as a State's corporation law governs only its own corporations and does not discriminate against out-of-state interests, it should survive this Court's scrutiny under the Commerce Clause, whether it promotes shareholder welfare or industrial stagnation. Beyond that, it is for Congress to prescribe its invalidity.

I also agree with the Court that the Indiana control shares Act is not pre-empted by the Williams Act, but I reach that conclusion without entering into the debate over the purposes of the two statutes. The Williams Act is governed by the antipre-emption provision of the Securities Exchange Act of 1934, which provides that nothing it contains "shall affect the jurisdiction of the securities commission (or any agency or officer performing like function) of any State over any security or any person insofar as it does not conflict with the provisions of this chapter or the rules and regulations thereunder."

Unless it serves no function, that language forecloses pre-emption on the basis of conflicting "purpose" as opposed to conflicting "provision." Even if it does not have literal application to the present case (because, perhaps, the Indiana agency responsible for securities matters has no enforcement responsibility with regard to this legislation), it nonetheless refutes the proposition that Congress meant the Williams Act to displace *all* state laws with conflicting purpose.   And if any are to survive, surely the States' corporation codes are among them.   It would be peculiar to hold that Indiana could have pursued the purpose at issue here through its blue-sky laws, but cannot pursue it through the State's even more sacrosanct authority over the structure of domestic corporations.   Prescribing voting rights for the governance of state-chartered companies is a traditional state function with which the Federal Congress has never, to my knowledge, intentionally interfered.   I would require far more evidence than is available here to find implicit pre-emption of that function by a federal statute whose provisions concededly do not conflict with the state law.

I do not share the Court's apparent high estimation of the beneficence of the state statute at issue here.   But a law can be both economic folly and constitutional.   The Indiana Control Shares Acquisition Chapter is at least the latter.   I therefore concur in the judgment of the Court.

Justice WHITE, with whom Justice BLACKMUN and Justice STEVENS join as to Part II, dissenting.

The majority today upholds Indiana's Control Share Acquisitions Chapter, a statute which will predictably foreclose completely some tender offers for stock in Indiana corporations.   I disagree with the conclusion that the Chapter is neither pre-empted by the Williams Act nor in conflict with the Commerce Clause.   The Chapter undermines the policy of the Williams Act by effectively preventing minority shareholders, in some circumstances, from acting in their own best interests by selling their stock.   In addition, the Chapter will substantially burden the interstate market in corporate ownership, particularly if other States follow Indiana's lead as many already have done.   The Chapter, therefore, directly inhibits interstate commerce, the very economic consequences the Commerce Clause was intended to prevent. The opinion of the Court of Appeals is far more persuasive than that of the majority today, and the judgment of that court should be affirmed.

I

The Williams Act expressed Congress' concern that individual investors be given sufficient information so that they could make an informed choice on whether to tender their stock in response to a tender offer.   The problem with the approach the majority adopts today is that it equates protection of individual investors, the focus of the Williams Act, with the protection of shareholders as a group.   Indiana's Control Share Acquisitions Chapter undoubtedly helps protect the interests of a majority of the shareholders in any corporation subject to its terms, but in many instances, it will effectively prevent an individual investor from selling his stock at a premium. Indiana's statute, therefore, does not "furthe[r] the federal policy of *investor* protection," *ante*, at 1646 (emphasis added), as the majority claims.

In discussing the legislative history of the Williams Act, the Court, in Piper v. Chris-Craft Industries, 430 U.S. 1 (1977), looked to the legislative history of the Williams Act and concluded that the Act was designed to protect individual investors, not management and not tender offerors: "The sponsors of this legislation were plainly sensitive to the suggestions that the measure would favor one side or the other in control contests; however, they made it clear that the legislation was designed solely to get needed information to the investor, the constant focal point of the committee hearings." *Id*. at 30-31. The Court specifically noted that the Williams Act's legislative history shows that Congress recognized that some "takeover bids . . . often serve a useful function." *Id*. at 30. As quoted by the majority, *ante*, at 1645, the basic purpose of the Williams Act is "'plac[ing] *investors* on an equal footing with the takeover bidder.'" *Piper, supra*, at 30 (emphasis added).

The Control Share Acquisitions Chapter, by design, will frustrate individual investment decisions. Concededly, the Control Share Acquisitions Chapter allows the majority of a corporation's shareholders to block a tender offer and thereby thwart the desires of an individual investor to sell his stock. In the context of discussing how the Chapter can be used to deal with the coercive aspects of some tender offers, the majority states, "In such a situation under the Indiana Act, the shareholders as a group, acting in the corporation's best interest, could reject the offer, although individual shareholders might be inclined to accept it." *Ante*, at 1646. I do not dispute that the Chapter provides additional protection for Indiana corporations, particularly in helping those corporations maintain the status quo. But it is clear to me that Indiana's scheme conflicts with the Williams Act's careful balance which was intended to protect individual investors and permit them to decide whether it is in their best interests to tender their stock. As noted by the plurality in *MITE*, "Congress . . . did not want to deny shareholders 'the opportunities which result from the competitive bidding for a block of stock of a given company,' namely, the opportunity to sell shares for a premium over their market price. 113 Cong.Rec. 24666 (1967) (remarks of Sen. Javits)." Edgar v. MITE Corp., 457 U.S. 624, 633, n.9 (1982).

The majority claims that if the Williams Act pre-empts Indiana's Control Share Acquisitions Chapter, it also pre-empts a number of other corporate-control provisions such as cumulative voting or staggering the terms of directors. But this view ignores the fundamental distinction between these other corporate-control provisions and the Chapter: Unlike those other provisions, the Chapter is designed to prevent certain tender offers from ever taking place. It is transactional in nature, although it is characterized by the State as involving only the voting rights of certain shares. "[T]his Court is not bound by '[t]he name, description or characterization given [a challenged statute] by the legislature or the courts of the State,' but will determine for itself the practical impact of the law." Hughes v. Oklahoma, 441 U.S. 322, 336 (1979). The Control Share Acquisitions Chapter will effectively prevent minority shareholders in some circumstances from selling their stock to a willing tender offeror. It is the practical impact of the Chapter that leads to the conclusion that it is pre-empted by the Williams Act.

II

Given the impact of the Control Share Acquisitions Chapter, it is clear that Indiana is directly regulating the purchase and sale of shares of stock in interstate commerce. Appellant CTS's stock is traded on the New York Stock Exchange, and people from all over the country buy and sell CTS's shares daily. Yet, under Indiana's scheme, any prospective purchaser will be effectively precluded from purchasing CTS's shares if the purchaser crosses one of the Chapter's threshold ownership levels and a majority of CTS's shareholders refuse to give the purchaser voting rights. This Court should not countenance such a restraint on interstate trade.

The United States, as *amicus curiae*, argues that Indiana's Control Share Acquisitions Chapter "is written as a restraint on the *transferability* of voting rights in specified transactions, and it could not be written in any other way without changing its meaning. Since the restraint on the transfer of voting rights is a restraint on the transfer of shares, the Indiana Chapter, like the Illinois Act [in *MITE*], restrains 'transfers of stock by stockholders to a third party.'" Brief for Securities and Exchange Commission and United States as *Amici Curiae* 26. I agree. The majority ignores the practical impact of the Chapter in concluding that the Chapter does not violate the Commerce Clause. The Chapter is characterized as merely defining "the attributes of shares in its corporations," *ante*, at 1652. The majority sees the trees but not the forest.

The Commerce Clause was included in our Constitution by the Framers to prevent the very type of economic protectionism Indiana's Control Share Chapter represents:

> The few simple words of the Commerce Clause -- 'The Congress shall have Power . . . To regulate Commerce . . . among the several States. . .' -- reflected a central concern of the Framers that was an immediate reason for calling the Constitutional Convention: the conviction that in order to succeed, the new Union would have to avoid the tendencies toward economic Balkanization that had plagued relations among the Colonies and later among the States under the Articles of Confederation. *Hughes, supra*, at 325-326.

The State of Indiana, in its brief, admits that at least one of the Chapter's goals is to protect Indiana corporations. The State notes that the Chapter permits shareholders "to determine . . . whether [a tender offeror] will liquidate the company or remove it from the State." Brief for Appellant in No. 86-97, p.19. The State repeats this point later in its brief: "The Statute permits shareholders (who may also be community residents or employees or suppliers of the corporation) to determine the intentions of any offeror concerning the liquidation of the company or its possible removal from the State." *Id.* at 90. A state law which permits a majority of an Indiana corporation's stockholders to prevent individual investors, including out-of-state stockholders, from selling their stock to an out-of-state tender offeror and thereby frustrate any transfer of corporate control, is the archetype of the kind of state law that the Commerce Clause forbids.

Unlike state blue sky laws, Indiana's Control Share Acquisitions Chapter regulates the purchase and sale of stock of Indiana corporations in interstate commerce. Indeed, as noted above, the Chapter will inevitably be used to block interstate transactions in such stock. Because the Commerce Clause protects the "interstate market" in such securities, Exxon Corp. v. Governor of Maryland, 437 U.S. 117, 127 (1978), and because the Control Share Chapter substantially interferes with this interstate market, the Chapter clearly conflicts with the Commerce Clause.

With all due respect, I dissent.

The question remaining after the Supreme Court's opinion in *CTS* was the amount of leeway the Court actually permitted the states and, in particular, Delaware to restrict hostile takeovers. Surely, all states could safely duplicate the Indiana statute, but that is not what Delaware and many other states chose to do. Note, for example, that if a Delaware statute were to follow the Indiana statute's jurisdictional focus on shareholders resident in the enacting state, it would apply to very few Delaware chartered corporations. The issue then, was how much latitude beyond the Indiana statute does *CTS* allow for states to reign in hostile takeovers?

To analyze this question, we must first ask: How far do the existing state statutes already go toward restricting hostile takeovers? It is fair to say that all three opinions in *CTS* shared the general view that the Indiana statute was an effective defensive technique. Yet, there is a persuasive argument that a control share acquisition statute may aid a hostile bidder far more than a target's management. And if this view is correct, then all states will have an interest in whether *CTS* will allow an anti-takeover statute that actually works. Because the power of the Indiana statute to deter takeovers reflects directly on the Court's grant of authority in *CTS*, consider the Indiana statute first.

Is a Control Share Acquisition Statute Effective? The possibility that a control share acquisition statute might not favor the management of a target company was raised by Roberta Romano some time before the *CTS* decision. Working through a decision tree analysis of shareholder choice under each of the three types of second generation statutes, Professor Romano concluded that "shareholders may tender more frequently under a control share acquisition statute than a fair price provision," and that acquirers would prefer an Indiana type statute to either a fair price statute like Maryland's, or a right of redemption statute like Pennsylvania's.[30] In fact, a stronger claim is also possible. A control share acquisition statute actually may work in favor of the acquirer.

The best case that a control share acquisition statute like Indiana's has a deterrent effect on hostile takeovers rests on the built-in 50 day delay before an acquirer can purchase shares under a hostile tender offer.[31] Delay imposes additional financing costs on the acquirer, and increases the chance that something fortuitous will occur -- perhaps an increase in interest rates or a change in industry conditions -- that will make the acquirer go away of its own accord. However, these seem a thin reed on which to build a pro-target argument, especially in light of the opportunities that the statute provides an acquirer.

The Supreme Court's opinion (and Justice White's dissent) treats the Indiana statute's mandate of a shareholder vote on a proposed transaction as a deterrent to making a tender offer. Interestingly, the central theme of defensive planners has been precisely the opposite: A successful defensive tactic is one that precludes shareholders from having the opportunity to accept a hostile offer, not one that grants them the right to accept one, whether individually or collectively. We have already seen that companies are reluctant to submit poison pill plans to shareholders for approval.[32] When real money is on the table, management is even less likely to win the votes of its institutional shareholders. Thus, one characterization of an Indiana type statute is that it gives acquirers exactly what they have always wanted -- the chance for the shareholders to decide whether to accept a premium over market for their shares.

A response to this argument is that an Indiana type statute at least assures that target management has an unbiased audience for its arguments that the hostile offer is not in the shareholders' best interests. In a typical tender offer, the response runs, the great majority of shares pass into the hands of arbitrageurs who, unlike "real" shareholders, will tender no matter what.[33] But it is not clear that a control share acquisition statute will

---

[30] Roberta Romano, *The Political Economy of Takeovers Statutes*, 73 Va.L.Rev. 111, 169 (1987).

[31] Although nothing in the Indiana statute prohibits the acquirer from purchasing shares before a shareholder vote, any shares purchased will be nonvoting. Thus, as the Supreme Court recognized in *CTS*, "[t]he practical effect of this requirement is to condition acquisition of control of a corporation on approval of a majority of the pre-existing disinterested shareholders." 481 U.S. at 73.

[32] See Chapter 17, *supra*.

[33] This analysis ignores the fact that the arbitrageurs could only have acquired their shares from "real" shareholders who, by selling into the market during the pendency of the offer, demonstrated that they favored the offer. See Ronald Gilson, *Just Say No to Whom?*, 25 Wake Forest L.Rev. 121 (1990).

change this. The risk that the shareholders will vote against the offer is not different in kind from the risks that arbitrageurs accept in the absence of a statute; a decision not to vote in favor of an offer is essentially the same as a decision not to tender. Thus, arbitrageurs can be expected to arbitrage the outcome of the shareholder vote. And just as in a tender offer where there is not a control share acquisition statute, the arbitrageurs will act as a loyal proxy for those from who they acquired their shares by voting in favor of the offer. Indeed, this kind of arbitrage could be prevented only by specifying a record date for voting at the special meeting on the proposed offer that predated the request for the meeting.[34]   Even assuming this were permissible, it still might not prevent arbitrage if sellers could provide a irrevocable proxy. Although this might be mechanically difficult for small market transactions, institutions would have no difficulty selling their shares in third market transactions in connection with which granting a proxy would be possible.

A second advantage that a 50 day delay might provide target management is the chance to undertake defensive tactics that might cause the acquirer to withdraw the offer before the vote. The problem with this idea, however, is that a court would be hard pressed to justify management action that had the effect of interfering with the shareholders' opportunity to approve an offer in a vote required by statute. Put in terms of the Delaware proportionality test[35], when a statute mandates a shareholder vote and effectively prohibits the offer unless the shareholders approve it, what possible threat could be reasonably related to precluding shareholders from voting in favor of the offer? Indeed, even an action like a restructuring that purported to give the shareholders greater value and which was allowed to proceed in *Interco* even though the court required the target's poison pill to be redeemed, might be problematic in the face of a control share acquisition statute. While *Interco* instructs us that the bidder generally has no right to insist that target management freeze the company pending the offer, a control share acquisition statute gives shareholders the right to decide whether to accept the offer by a shareholder vote. A separate line of cases restricts target management's ability to interfere with shareholder voting.[36]

In the end, there is substantial question whether a control share acquisition statute actually strengthens an acquirer's hand more than that of target management. Thus, the breadth of the license *CTS* gives the states is a matter of critical concern. If, as it appears, the real motivation of states is to deter hostile takeovers, something more effective than a control share acquisition statute is necessary.

---

[34] Pennsylvania and Ohio's extreme versions of a control share acquisition statute effect a temporal gerrymander of the electorate by excluding from the vote any shareholders who acquired their shares after the announcement of the intent to make an acquisition of control shares, thereby seeking to disenfranchise the arbitrageurs.

[35] See Chapter 17, *supra.*

[36] See Chapter 24, *infra.*

C.   The Constitutionality of the Delaware and Other Third Generation State Antitakeover Statutes

In terms of the impact of state antitakeover statutes on the operation of the market for corporate control, the critical question was how Delaware, which chartered upwards of 50% of major U.S. corporations, responded to *CTS*. Delaware did not prolong the suspense. The Supreme Court decided *CTS* on April 21, 1987. On April 24 -- three days later -- Delaware's Secretary of State asked the Corporate Law Section of the Delaware State Bar Association to consider the advisability of adopting a second-generation takeover statute in light of *CTS*.[37] By late May, 1987, a special subcommittee of the Corporate Law Section had drafted a control share acquisition statute similar to the Indiana statute, except that the Delaware draft -- unlike the Indiana statute -- would have reached all corporations chartered in Delaware regardless of the location of their shareholders. This initial effort, however, was met with withering criticism from a range of savvy critics, including some of the bar's top takeover lawyers. It was withdrawn almost as rapidly as it had been drafted, largely because the bar correctly suspected that, consistent with the analysis in the preceding section, a control share acquisition statute was more likely to aid acquirers than target managers.[38]

In place of the ill-starred control share acquisition draft, the Corporate Law Section -- and ultimately the State of Delaware -- turned to what has come to be termed a third generation "business combinations" statute, loosely modeled on an earlier New York statute. See N.Y.Bus.Corp.L. § 912 (McKinney 1987). The hallmark of all business combination statutes, including the new Delaware statute, Del.Gen.Corp.L. § 203, is the regulation of what acquirers can do in the second step of a two-step acquisition rather than the terms on which acquirers can assume control in the first step of the acquisition.

1.   The Delaware Business Combination Statute

DELAWARE GENERAL CORPORATION LAW

§ 203. Business Combinations With Interested Stockholders

(a) Notwithstanding any other provisions of this chapter, a corporation shall not engage in any business combination with any interested stockholder

---

[37] See D. Zarlin, *The Delaware Takeover Statute: Evolution and Implications* 1 (April 12, 1988).

[38] See Black, *Why Delaware is Wary of Anti-Takeover Law*, Wall St.J., July 10, 1987, at 20, col. 3.

for a period of 3 years following the date that such stockholder became an interested stockholder, unless (1) prior to such date the board of directors of the corporation approved either the business combination or the transaction which resulted in the stockholder becoming an interested stockholder, or (2) upon consummation of the transaction which resulted in the stockholder becoming an interested stockholder, the interested stockholder owned at least 85% of the voting stock of the corporation outstanding at the time the transaction commenced, excluding for purposes of determining the number of shares outstanding those shares owned (i) by persons who are directors and also officers and (ii) employee stock plans in which employee participants do not have the right to determine confidentially whether shares held subject to the plan will be tendered in a tender or exchange offer, or (3) on or subsequent to such date the business combination is approved by the board of directors and authorized at an annual or special meeting of stockholders, and not by written consent, by the affirmative vote of at least 66-2/3% of the outstanding voting stock which is not owned by the interested stockholder.

(b) The restrictions contained in this section shall not apply if:

(1) the corporation's original certificate of incorporation contains a provision expressly electing not to be governed by this section; . . .

(3) the corporation, by action of its stockholders, adopts an amendment to its certificate of incorporation or bylaws expressly electing not to be governed by this section, provided that, in addition to any other vote required by law, such amendment to the certificate of incorporation or bylaws must be approved by the affirmative vote of a majority of the shares entitled to vote. An amendment adopted pursuant to this paragraph shall not be effective until 12 months after the adoption of such amendment and shall not apply to any business combination between such corporation and any person who became an interested stockholder of such corporation on or prior to such adoption. A bylaw amendment adopted pursuant to this paragraph shall not be further amended by the board of directors;

(4) the corporation does not have a class of voting stock that is (i) listed on a national securities exchange, (ii) authorized for quotation on an inter dealer quotation system of a registered national securities association or (iii) held of record by more than 2,000 stockholders, unless any of the foregoing results from action taken, directly or indirectly, by an interested stockholder or from a transaction in which a person becomes an interested stockholder;

(5) a stockholder becomes an interested stockholder inadvertently and (i) as soon as practicable divests sufficient shares so that the stockholder ceases to be an interested stockholder and (ii) would not, at any time within the 3 year period immediately prior to a business combination between the corporation and such stockholder, have been an interested stockholder but for the inadvertent acquisition; or

(6) the business combination is proposed prior to the consummation or abandonment of and subsequent to the earlier of the public announcement or

the notice required hereunder of a proposed transaction which (i) constitutes one of the transactions described in the second sentence of this paragraph; (ii) is with or by a person who either was not an interested stockholder during the previous 3 years or who became an interested stockholder with the approval of the corporation's board of directors; and (iii) is approved or not opposed by a majority of the members of the board of directors then in office (but not less than 1) who were directors prior to any person becoming an interested stockholder during the previous 3 years or were recommended for election or elected to succeed such directors by a majority of such directors. The proposed transactions referred to in the preceding sentence are limited to (x) a merger or consolidation of the corporation (except for a merger in respect of which, pursuant to § 251(f) of the chapter, no vote of the stockholders of the corporation is required); (y) a sale, lease, exchange, mortgage, pledge, transfer or other disposition (in one transaction or a series of transactions), whether as part of a dissolution or otherwise, of assets of the corporation or of any direct or indirect majority-owned subsidiary of the corporation (other than to any direct or indirect wholly-owned subsidiary or to the corporation) having an aggregate market value equal to 50% or more of either that aggregate market value of all of the assets of the corporation determined on a consolidated basis or the aggregate market value of all the outstanding stock of the corporation: or (a) a proposed tender or exchange offer for 50% or more of the outstanding voting stock of the corporation. The corporation shall give not less than 20 days notice to all interested stockholders prior to the consummation of any of the transactions described in clauses (x) or (y) of the second sentence of this paragraph. Notwithstanding paragraphs (1), (2), (3) and (4) of this subsection, a corporation may elect by a provision of its original certificate of incorporation or any amendment thereto to be governed by this section, provided that any such amendment to the certificate of incorporation shall not apply to restrict a business combination between the corporation and an interested stockholder of the corporation if the interested stockholder became such prior to the effective date of the amendment.

(c) As used in this section only the term:

(1) 'affiliate' means a person that directly, or indirectly through one or more intermediaries, controls, or is controlled by, or is under common control with another person.

(2) 'associate,' when used to indicate a relationship with any person means (i) any corporation or organization of which such person is a director, officer or partner or is, directly or indirectly, the owner of 20% or more of any class of voting stock, (ii) any trust or other estate in which such person has at least a 20% beneficial interest or as to which such person serves as trustee or in a similar fiduciary capacity, and (iii) any relative or spouse of such person, or any relative of such spouse, who has the same residence as such person.

(3) 'business combination,' when used in reference to any corporation and any interested stockholder of such corporation, means:

(i) any merger or consolidation of the corporation or any direct or indirect majority-owned subsidiary of the corporation with (A) the interested stockholder, or (B) with any other corporation if the merger or consolidation is caused by the interested stockholder as a result of such merger or consolidation subsection (a) of this section is not applicable to the surviving corporation;

(ii) any sale, lease, exchange, mortgage, pledge, transfer or other disposition (in one transaction or a series of transactions), except proportionately as a stockholder of such corporation, to or with the interested stockholder, whether as part of a dissolution or otherwise, of assets of the corporation or of any direct or indirect majority-owned subsidiary of the corporation which assets have an aggregate market value equal to 10% or more of either the aggregate market value of all the assets of the corporation determined on a consolidated basis or the aggregate market value of all the outstanding stock of the corporation;

(iii) any transaction which results in the issuance or transfer by the corporation or by any direct or indirect majority-owned subsidiary of the corporation of any stock of the corporation or of such subsidiary to the interested stockholder, except (A) pursuant to the exercise, exchange or conversion of securities exercisable for, exchangeable for or convertible into stock of such corporation or any such subsidiary which securities were outstanding prior to the time that the interested stockholder became such, (B) pursuant to a dividend or distribution paid or made, or the exercise, exchange or conversion of securities exercisable for, exchangeable for convertible into stock of such corporation or any such subsidiary which security is distributed, pro rata to all holders of a class or series of stock of such corporation subsequent to the time the interested stockholder became such, (C) pursuant to an exchange offer by the corporation to purchase stock made on the same terms to all holders of said stock, or (D) any issuance or transfer or stock by the corporation, provided, however, that in no case under (B)-(D) above shall there be an increase in the interested stockholder's proportionate share of the stock of any class or series of the corporation of the voting stock of the corporation;

(iv) any transaction involving the corporation or any direct or indirect majority-owned subsidiary of the corporation which has the effect, directly or indirectly, or increasing the proportionate share of the stock of any class or series, or securities convertible into the stock of any class or series, of the corporation or of any such subsidiary which is owned by the interested stockholder, except as a result of immaterial changes due to fractional share adjustments or as a result of any purchase or redemption of any shares of stock not caused, directly or indirectly, by the interested stockholder; or

(v) any receipt by the interested stockholder of the benefit, directly or indirectly (except proportionately as a stockholder of such corporation) of any loans, advances, guarantees, pledges, or other financial benefits (other than those expressly permitted in subparagraphs (i)-(iv) above) provided by or through the corporation or any direct or indirect majority-owned subsidiary.

(4) 'control,' including the term 'controlling,' 'controlled by' and 'under common control with,' means the possession, directly or indirectly, of the power to direct or cause the direction of the management and policies of a person, whether through the ownership of voting stock, by contract, or otherwise. A person who is the owner of 20% or more of a corporation's outstanding voting stock shall be presumed to have control of such corporation, in the absence of proof by a preponderance of the evidence to the contrary. Notwithstanding the foregoing, a presumption of control shall not apply where such person holds voting stock, in good faith and not for the purpose of circumventing this section, as an agent, bank, broker, nominee, custodian or trustee for one or more owners who do not individually or as a group have control of such corporation.

(5) 'interested stockholder' means any person (other than the corporation and any direct or indirect majority-owned subsidiary of the corporation) that (i) is the owner of 15% or more of the outstanding voting stock of the corporation, or (ii) is an affiliate or associate of the corporation and was the owner of 15% or more of the outstanding voting stock of the corporation at any time within the 3-year period immediately prior to the date on which it is sought to be determined whether such person is an interested stockholder; provided, however, that the term 'interested stockholder' shall not include (x) any person who (A) owned shares in excess of the 15% limitation set forth herein as of, or acquired such shares pursuant to a tender offer commenced prior to, December 23, 1987 or pursuant to an exchange offer announced prior to the aforesaid date and commenced within 90 days thereafter and continued to own shares in excess of such 15% limitation or would have but for action by the corporation or (B) acquired said shares from a person described in (A) above by gift, inheritance or in a transaction in which no consideration was exchanged; or (y) any person whose ownership of shares in excess of the 15% limitation set forth herein is the result of action taken solely by the corporation provided that such person shall be an interested stockholder if thereafter he acquires additional shares of voting stock of the corporation, except as a result of further corporate action not caused, directly or indirectly, by such person. For the purpose of determining whether a person is an interested stockholder, the voting stock of the corporation deemed to be outstanding shall include stock deemed to be owned by the person through application of paragraph (B) of this subsection but shall not include any other unissued stock of such corporation which may be issuable pursuant to any agreement, arrangement or understanding, or upon exercise of conversion rights, warrants or options, or otherwise.

(6) 'person' means any individual, corporation, partnership, unincorporated association or other entity.

(7) 'voting stock' means stock of any class or series entitled to vote generally in the election of directors.

(8) 'owner' including the terms 'own' and 'owned' when used with respect to any stock means a person that individually or with or through any of its affiliates or associates:

(i) beneficially owns such stock, directly or indirectly; or

(ii) has (A) the right to acquire such stock (whether such right is exercisable immediately or only after the passage of time) pursuant to any agreement, arrangement or understanding, or upon the exercise of conversion rights, exchange rights, warrants or options, or otherwise; provided, however, that a person shall not be deemed the owner of stock tendered pursuant to a tender or exchange offer made by such person or any of such person's affiliates or associates until such tendered stock is accepted for purchase or exchange; or (B) the right to vote such stock pursuant to any agreement, arrangement or understanding; provided, however, that a person shall not be deemed the owner of any stock because of such person's right to vote such stock if the agreement, arrangement or understanding to vote such stock arises solely from a revocable proxy or consent given in response to a proxy or consent solicitation made to 10 or more persons; or

(iii) has any agreement, arrangement or understanding for the purpose of acquiring, holding, voting (except voting pursuant to a revocable proxy or consent as described in item (B) of clause (ii) of this paragraph), or disposing of such stock with any other person that beneficially owns, or whose affiliates or associates beneficially own, directly or indirectly, such stock.

(d) No provision of a certificate of incorporation or bylaw shall require, for any vote of stockholders required by this section, a greater vote of stockholders than that specified in this section.

(e) The Court of Chancery is hereby vested with exclusive jurisdiction to hear and determine all matters with respect to this section.

Section 2. The provisions of this Act are severable and any provision held invalid shall not affect or impair any of the remaining provisions of this Act.

SYNOPSIS

Section 203 is intended to strike a balance between the benefits of an unfettered market for corporate shares and the well documented and judicially recognized need to limit abusive takeover tactics. To achieve this end, the statute will delay for three years business combinations with acquirors not approved by the board unless the acquiror is able to obtain in his offer 85% of the stock as defined in the statute. This provision is intended to encourage a full and fair offer. Following the principles of corporate democracy, two-thirds of the stockholders other than the acquiror may vote or exempt a given business combination from the restrictions of the statute. Any corporation may decide to opt out of the statute within 90 days of enactment by action of its board or, at any time, by action of its stockholders. The effect of stockholder action in this regard is delayed for 12 months to avoid circumvention of the statute.

The statute is not intended to alter the case law development of directors' fiduciary duties of care and loyalty in responding to challenges to control or the burden or proof with regard to compliance with those duties. Nor is the statute intended to prevent the use of any other lawful defensive measure.

---

a.   *Section 203's Three-Year Freeze*

The operating mechanism of the new Delaware statute is contained in Subsections 203(a) and (c)(3): Any acquirer of more than 15% of the voting stock of a target company may be barred from engaging in a wide variety of transactions that fall into the general category of "business combination," construed broadly, between the acquirer and the target. The thrust of this proscription is to bar mergers, sales of assets, stock issuances, and other "self-dealing" transactions that would permit the acquirer to obtain direct access to the target's assets or to redistribute voting control over the target to the acquirer's favor.

The chief "abusive takeover tactics" against which the Delaware statute is directed are the usual suspects paraded before state legislatures: the unsavory trio of "two-tiered," "front-end loaded," and "bust-up" tender offers.[39] Curiously, however, the central operating mechanism of § 203 has very little to say about the structure of tender offers or acquirer's subsequent plans to liquidate target assets. Unlike the earlier New York statute on which it is modeled, § 203 does not bar an acquirer's plans for the liquidation or dissolution of a target firm after its acquisition of control; it covers only plans for a merger, consolidation, or sale of assets between the target and the acquirer or its affiliates. Thus, the statute provides no impediment at all to bust-up takeovers so long as the acquirer is acting as a pure middleman, selling off the target's component businesses to third parties. The real focus of § 203 is on transactions, such as freeze-out mergers, that might conceivably permit an acquirer to gain a non-pro-rata share of the value of a target's assets but -- and perhaps more to the point -- are also perceived as critical in financing transactions between leveraged acquirers and their lenders.

---

[39] See Norman Veasey, Jesse Finkelstein & Robert Shaughnessy, *The Delaware Takeover Law: Some Issues, Strategies and Comparisons*, 43 Bus.Law. 865, 871 (1988).

It would seem, then, that Delaware's regulation of takeover tactics is oddly indirect by comparison with control share acquisition statutes. Section 203 is aimed primarily against a *class of acquirers*, some of whom have been associated with "abusive" tactics in the past: namely, acquirers who rely on debt financing or who must, for other reasons, gain unencumbered access to target assets. Unlike control share acquisition statutes, moreover, § 203 makes no provisions for shareholders to vote their preferences about hostile tender offers. It is, by design, intended to be a preclusive statute when acquirers require asset-backed financing and cannot win the support of the target's board or exploit one of the exemptions built into the statute. In this same spirit, the Delaware legislature explicitly rejected the possibility of making § 203 an "opt-in" statute that would have permitted shareholders to vote on whether they wishes to be covered by the statute's protections.

Despite these mandatory features of § 203, however, the question of its effectiveness in deterring hostile takeovers remains an open issue. Although there is no suggestion that the Delaware statute might encourage acquisitions, as control share acquisition statutes might do, it is less clear precisely how much the statute will discourage hostile bids. There are two aspects to this issue: first, how difficult will it be for acquirers to exploit the exemptions built into § 203; and second, presuming that would-be acquirers cannot qualify for an exemption, how burdensome are they likely to find the three-year freeze on interested business combinations?

The § 203 Exemptions. Apart from the power of the target's board of directors to waive the statute's protections for the benefit of friendly acquirers, § 203 contains two primary exemptions that permit hostile acquirers to circumvent the three-year freeze on interested business combinations under certain circumstances. The first is the "85% ownership out" provision in subsection (a)(2): An acquirer escapes the statute if it obtains 85% of the target's voting stock *in the same transaction* in which it crosses the 15% "interested shareholder" threshold. The issue, then, is whether a hostile acquirer can raise its holdings from below 15% to above 85% of a target's voting stock in a single tender offer, excluding from the percentage calculation all shares held by the target's officer-directors or by employee stock ownership plans that do not "pass through" the decision to tender to their beneficiaries.[40]

The best answer may be: *hostile* acquirers have not easily met the 85% threshold in past offers, and it is not likely to become any easier after the passage of § 203. A 1985 study by the SEC's Office of the Chief Economist reports that on average hostile offers for all shares of target corporations have garnered only 75% of outstanding shares.[41] Although 16 of the 29 hostile offers in the study sample eventually did reach the 85% threshold, in

---

[40] See subsections (a)(2)(i) & (ii).

[41] See SEC Office of the Chief Economist, *The Economics of Any-and-All, Partial, and Two-Tier Tender Offers* (Table 9) (April 19, 1985).

five of these cases the bidder launched its offer after already obtaining well over 15% of the target's stock, a circumstance that would disqualify it from exemption under § 203.[42] While the task of a would-be acquirer is made to seem easier by Delaware's exclusion of shares held by officer-directors and some employee benefit plans from the calculations, this effect is offset by the inclusion of other shares held by outside directors and employees.

More to the point, it would seem to be child's play under § 203 for a Delaware corporation to arrange in advance for a blocking coalition by placing a small amount of stock (say 5% to 10% of outstanding shares) with a reliable outsider or a benefit plan that passes through the right to tender to employees.[43] The "ownership out," then, although ostensibly directed at partial offers, may well prove illusory even when acquirers make generous offers for all shares. If so, it might actually *discourage* bids for all shares.

The second major exemption offered by § 203 is the so-called "vote out" provision in subsection (a)(3). Under the vote out provision, an otherwise prohibited transaction is permitted under the statute if it is approved by the target's board of directors and authorized by an affirmative vote of 66.7% of all shares other than those held by the acquirer (the "interested stockholder"). Consider how the vote out provision is likely to work in practice. The acquirer cannot force a vote under this provision until it has made a tender offer, become an interested stockholder, and, presumably, assumed control of the board. Thus, an acquirer might attempt to capture, say, 51% of all shares after surmising that it could not reach the 85% threshold and qualify for the ownership out.[44] The 49% of public shares that remained after the acquirer's offer would presumably include all stock of managers and employees, as well as that of unresponsive and optimistic investors. The acquirer would have to win the votes of 67.7% of this reduced pool of shareholders. If 15% were simply nonresponsive -- a not unrealistic figure[45] -- the acquirer's actual threshold would approach

---

[42] See *id.*

[43] See Shamrock Holdings, Inc. v. Polaroid Corp., [1988-1989 Transfer Binder] Fed.Sec.L.Rep. (CCH) ¶ 94,176 (Del.Ch.1989), in which the Delaware Chancery Court upheld a plan by Polaroid to transfer 14% of its outstanding shares to an ESOP that provided for confidential voting of shares and thus was to be included in the 85% calculation for purposes of § 203(a)(2). This holding made it extremely unlikely that Shamrock -- the hostile bidder -- would have been able to reach the 85% exemption threshold. As a consequence, Shamrock's bid was dropped.

[44] Note that the vote out and ownership out exceptions suggest quite different strategies for a would-be acquirer. On its face, the ownership out exemption encourages acquirers to accumulate as many shares as possible. By contrast, the vote out exemption encourages acquirers to accumulate the minimum percentage of shares consistent with taking control of the board, in order to avoid concentrating a pro-management blocking coalition in a second-step vote.

[45] Proponents of the Delaware statute such as Veasey, Finkelstein & Shaughnessy (1988), *supra* note 39, at 874, posit that "up to 5%" of shareholders are totally nonresponsive to either tender offers or voting opportunities. Critics of the statute suggest much higher rates of nonresponsiveness, especially with respect to shareholder votes. Thus, a nonresponsiveness

82% of the voting shareholders in the reduced pool. This means, again, that a determined blocking coalition of 18% in the reduced pool (or 9% of the original, pre-offer pool) would prove more than adequate to defeat the acquirer's plans.

There are, however, a number of considerations that should bear on evaluation of these calculations. What incentives would an incumbent management group have to block an acquirer's plans *after* the acquirer has already assumed effective control of the board? Only money? How do the prospects of a second-step blocking coalition affect shareholder incentives to tender into the initial offer? Finally, how might the exemptive provisions of § 203 interact with "self-help" defensive tactics that targets might pursue; for example, a "flip-in" poison pill that would automatically increase the amount of voting equity after a successful tender offer?

b.   *Impact of the Three-Year Moratorium on Business Combinations*

Given that hostile acquirers could find it difficult, or at least very costly, to escape the Delaware statute's transactional freeze under the exemptive provisions, the question still remains: How much are acquirers likely to care? An acquirer can still tender for control of a target and simply operate it as a partially-held subsidiary for three years. Potential synergy gains are not precluded. Section 203, moreover, does not reach liquidations, dissolutions, or business combinations with disinterested third parties. Thus, nothing in the Delaware statute prevents a hostile acquirer from tendering for control of an apparently undervalued or discounted target and immediately liquidating its assets, providing that the proceeds of liquidation are distributed pro rata to shareholders.

Put another way, the issue is whether the § 203 freeze will deter hostile acquisitions or merely shift acquirer strategy -- deterring 100% ownership of targets for long-term investment while encouraging partially-held subsidiaries for investment purposes, and "bust-up" or liquidating acquisitions to exploit apparent undervaluation. Certainly portions of the Delaware bar, the SEC and at least two federal courts[46] believe that the § 203 freeze on interested business combinations will deter outright many hostile acquirers who cannot circumvent it. The chief reason proffered is, once again, the financing of leveraged acquirers: Without direct access to target assets, which for all practical purposes requires 100% ownership of the target and therefore a

---

rate of 15% in the reduced shareholder pool -- the equivalent of a 7.5% rate in the original pool -- might be an reasonable estimate of average nonresponsiveness. See RP Acquisitions Corp. v. Stately Continental, Inc., [CCH] Fed.Sec.L.Rep. ¶ 93,763 at 98,557 (D.Del.1988) (contrasting plaintiff's expert witness' estimate of 12.4% "dead shares" with the "generally accepted" estimate of 5.0%).

[46] See RP Acquisitions Corp. v. Stately Continental, Inc., *supra*, at 98,575; BNS Inc. v. Koppers Co., 458 F.Supp. 683, 469 (D.Del.1988).

freezeout transaction, creditors will assertedly not finance leveraged acquisitions.[47] The alternative reason proffered for expecting the § 203 moratorium to deter is that it will reduce the expected returns of many bidders by denying them the power to freeze out minority shareholders. For example, a prospective acquirer who expects significant synergy gains from merging a target with its own firm will be forced to share its gains with the target's minority shareholders if it cannot win 100% ownership of the target.

Query how far either of these obstacles are likely to block an otherwise attractive acquisition. Why must creditors assume a direct security interest in a target's assets, as opposed to accepting an acquirer's stock as collateral or accepting a commitment to liquidate the target? Further, might an acquirer who expected significant synergy gains from merging with a target manage to realize the bulk of these gains even without freezing out minority shareholders?[48] Consider in this regard Judge Easterbrook's opinion in Amanda Acquisition Corp. v. Universal Foods Corp., reproduced below.

2.   *CTS* and the Third Generation of Anti-Takeover Statutes

Until the Supreme Court returns to consider the Delaware statute or another of the business combination acts that follow the New York or Delaware models, the lower federal courts are left to arbitrate the constitutionality of the third generation statutes under the loose guidance of *CTS*. Although the federal courts have struck down anti-takeover legislation in several jurisdictions after *CTS*,[49] the current trend is to uphold the third generation statutes. The chief division among the courts concerns the question: How far does *CTS* go? Does it merely sanction "moderate" anti-takeover legislation, or does it implicitly allow even "takeover-proof" statutes so long as they do not run afoul of the SEC's rules and the competing regulatory claims of other jurisdictions, as did the first generation of takeover statutes?

In three decisions reviewing Delaware's § 203, the Delaware District Court has adopted the more limited view of the permissible scope of anti-takeover legislation, albeit in the context of upholding the Delaware statute.[50] The tenor of these decisions is best expressed by *BNS*, the lead case:

---

[47] See, e.g., *BNS Inc.*, 683 F.Supp. at 464.

[48] See Chapter 22A, *supra*.

[49] See, e.g., Hyde Park Partners, L.P. v. Connolly, [CCH] Fed.Sec.L.Rep. ¶ 93,619 at 97,792 (1st Cir.1988) (Massachusetts statute); RTE Corp. v. Mark IV Industries, [CCH] Fed.Sec.L.Rep. ¶ 93,789 at 98,722 (E.D.Wis.1988) (Wisconsin statute).

[50] See BNS, Inc. v. Koppers Corp., Inc., 683 F.Supp. 458 (D.Del.1988); RP Acquisitions Corp. v. Staley Continental, Inc., 686 F.Supp. 476 (D.Del.1988); City Capital Associates LTD v. Interco, Inc., 696 F.Supp. 1551 (D.Del.1988).

Section 203 is an exquisitely crafted legislative response to a variety of perceived problems. Were it less delicately constructed to remain within the sphere of constitutionality, the outcome of the Court's analysis might be quite different. But nothing prevents a state legislature from extending its power to the limits of constitutionality.[51]

To evaluate this conclusion, recall the two chief claims considered by *CTS* -- that the Indiana statute was pre-empted by the Williams Act and that it violated the Commerce Clause -- in conjunction with the heavier burden on acquirers imposed by the Delaware statute.

The core of the Supreme Court's pre-emption analysis in *CTS* concerned the congruence between the Williams Act's policy of investor protection and the Indiana statute's provision of a collective choice for shareholders to disarm a coercive offer. The Court stressed that the unconstitutional statute in *MITE*

> operated to favor management against offerors, to the detriment of shareholders. By contrast, the statute now before the Court protects the independent shareholder against both of the contending parties. Thus, the Act furthers a basic purpose of the Williams Act, "placing investors on an equal footing with the takeover bidder."

481 U.S. at 69 (citations omitted). The Williams Act, however, also contemplates that, whether individually or collectively, shareholders in the end will be allowed to make some sort of a decision concerning a tender offer. Yet an anti-takeover statute is effective precisely to the extent that the directors can preclude a shareholder decision. Whether a statute that precluded any shareholder decision at all would be protected under the Court's preemption analysis in *CTS* might thus raise serious questions. For example, the Court stressed that the Indiana statute allows "*shareholders* to evaluate the fairness of [an] offer collectively." (emphasis in the original). What if a state statute accorded tender offers the same treatment as mergers, so that shareholders could not vote unless the board of directors first approved an offer? Such a statute would be effective in giving target directors the power to preclude a takeover, but would it be consistent with the *CTS* Court's treatment of the purposes of the Williams Act? Certainly, the *BNS* court thought not in its analysis of the Delaware statute: "[T]he proposition that states may so heavily regulate hostile tender offers as to eliminate them altogether is untenable given the Supreme Court's interpretation of the goals of the Williams Act." 683 F.Supp. at 469. Thus, the question became "what *degree* of restriction of tender offers is unconstitutional" under a pre-emption analysis. *Id.* (emphasis added).

After reviewing the record, the *BNS* court concluded with praiseworthy candor that it simply lacked an empirical basis for upsetting the Delaware

---

[51] 683 F.Supp. at 473.

legislature's balancing of the costs and benefits of § 203. The benefits, according to the Court, arise entirely from the power that the statute vests in incumbent managers to protect shareholders by rejecting coercive hostile offers. 683 F.Supp. at 469, 472. The costs of the statute arise from the identical power when it is used by managers to defeat beneficial offers. *Id.* at 470, 472. And, in the court's view, the decisive factor that saved § 203 from constitutional defeat was the Legislature's assessment that the statute's exemptions, including the 8% ownership out and 65% vote out, would allow value enhancing hostile offers to proceed in the face of management's opposition. In the end, the *BNS* court's pre-emption analysis was a simple cost-benefit test:

> Notwithstanding § 203's possible injurious effects, because it benefits stockholders, and because the legislature presumably has balanced the countervailing effects and found the degree of stockholder protection to offset potential harm to stockholders, the Court concludes that the statute will be in all likelihood constitutional and not preempted. If the method Delaware has chosen to protect stockholders in fact on balance harms them, then at that time reconsideration of the statute's congruence with the Williams Act will be warranted.[52]

What forms of new evidence might persuade the Delaware District Court that the Legislature's assessment of the evidence was wrong? What if § 203 could be shown to favor partial tender offers over offers for all of a target's shares? Note in this regard that the Delaware District Court was *not* persuaded by the elaborate evidentiary submissions by acquirers in two subsequent challenges to § 203, which tended to show that acquirers would have an extraordinarily difficult time qualifying for the § 203 exemptions. See *RP Acquisition Corp.*, 686 F.Supp. at 482-86; *City Capital Associates*, 696 F.Supp. at 1554-55.

The alternative line of constitutional attack on state anti-takeover legislation rests on the Commerce Clause. In *CTS*, the Supreme Court's treatment of the Commerce Clause claim relied heavily on two variants of the internal affairs doctrine. Considering the traditional Commerce Clause attack that a statute subjects an activity to conflicting state regulation, the Court stressed that the internal affairs doctrine, by assuring only a single state's laws will apply, avoids the potential for conflict. Chalk up one for Delaware.

In response to the second claim that the Indiana statute violated the Commerce Clause by hindering takeovers, the Court stressed that states which create corporations also specify their internal rules, and therefore have an interest in the substance of those rules. "A State has an interest in promoting stable relationships among parties involved in the corporations it charters, as well as in ensuring that investors in such corporations have an

---

[52] 683 F.Supp. at 472.

effective voice in corporate affairs." 481 U.S. at 91. Countering the argument that Indiana lacked an interest in protecting nonresident shareholders whose only contact with Indiana was through Indiana incorporation, the Court stressed not only Indiana's interest in assuring that its corporations were not used unfairly, but also that

> unlike the Illinois statute invalidated in *MITE*, the Indiana Act applies only to corporations that have a substantial number of shareholders in Indiana. Thus, every application of the Indiana Act will affect a substantial number of Indiana residents, whom Indiana indisputably has an interest in protecting.

481 U.S. at 93. If this second justification were necessary for an anti-takeover statute to survive Commerce Clause attack, Delaware might seem to be in serious trouble. Yet, it did not figure importantly in any of the Delaware District Court opinions.

In the end, the *CTS* court did seem to employ a balancing test to decide the Commerce Clause issue with the balance heavily weighted toward Indiana's interest in regulation. The Supreme Court simply rejected the claim that the Indiana statute's purported reduction in the number of successful tender offers might create a Commerce Clause violation.

> [T]he very commodity that is traded in the 'market for corporate control' -- the corporation -- is one that owes its existence and attributes to state law. Indiana need not define these commodities as other States do; it need only provide that residents and nonresidents have equal access to them. This Indiana has done. Accordingly, even if the Act should decrease the number of successful tender offers for Indiana corporations, this would not offend the Commerce Clause.

Id. at 94.[53] Whether the Supreme Court would have been equally unimpressed if Indiana had drafted a statute that removed its corporations from the hostile takeover market entirely is another matter. In the hands of the Delaware District Court, the heavily weighted if indistinct balancing test that the Supreme Court seemed to deploy in *CTS* merged with the District Court's own balancing test under the Supremacy Clause to create a constitutional barrier to a preclusive anti-takeover statute. Thus, a marginally more restrictive, and therefore "protectionist," statute might have been held to "circumvent the policies of the Commerce Clause" even if Delaware's own statute did not. 450 F.Supp. at 473. In what way might Delaware, the state of incorporation for the majority of the Nation's large firms, have a "protectionist" interest in its corporate law? Note that what Delaware might wish to protect -- its corporate tax base -- differs dramatically from the likely protectionist interests of other states. See *id.* at 473 n.31.

---

[53] Thus, the Supreme Court would not have been impressed by recent studies showing that shareholders of corporations chartered in states that have adopted anti-takeover statutes have suffered statistically significant negative abnormal returns during windows surrounding key adoption dates. See Section E of this Chapter, *infra*.

Although the cumulative effect of the *BNS*, *RC Acquisition*, and *City Capital* cases is to put the Delaware statute safely out of constitutional danger, the balancing test articulated by these decisions remains the good news (such as it is) for proponents of an unobstructed market in corporate control. The one clear implication of a balancing test, whether it rests on a pre-emption theory or the Commerce Clause, is that a takeover-proof statute will not survive constitutional scrutiny. By contrast, the bad news for proponents of a free acquisitions market has always been the specter that one day an authoritative lower federal court would brush aside the Supreme Court's rhetorical effort in *CTS* to harmonize the Indiana takeover statute with the shareholder protection policies of the Williams Act in favor of the sterner language in *CTS* emphasizing the states' traditional power to regulate internal corporate affairs without reference to the securities market. That specter finally materialized in a most unlikely shape: A decision by the Seventh Circuit, which had struck down both the Illinois statute in *MITE* and the Indiana statute in *CTS*, written by Judge Frank Easterbrook, one of the most articulate proponents of an open takeover market.

AMANDA ACQUISITION CORP. v. UNIVERSAL FOODS CORP.
877 F.2d 496 (7th Cir.1989)

EASTERBROOK Circuit Judge. States have enacted three generations of takeover statutes in the last 20 years. Illinois enacted a first-generation statute, forbade acquisitions of any firm with substantial assets in Illinois unless a public official approved. We concluded that such a statute injures investors, is preempted by the Williams Act, and is unconstitutional under the dormant Commerce Clause. *MITE* Corp. v. Dixon, 633 F.2d 486 (7th Cir.1980). The Supreme Court affirmed that judgment under the Commerce Clause, Edgar v. MITE Corp., 457 U.S. 624, 643-46 (1982). Three Justices also agreed with our view of the Williams Act, *id.* at 634-40 (White, J., joined by Burger, C.J. & Blackmun, J.), while two disagreed, *id.* at 646-47 (Powell, J.), and 655 (Stevens, J.), and four did not address the subject.

Indiana enacted a second-generation statute, applicable only to firms incorporated there and eliminating governmental veto power. Indiana's law provides that the acquiring firm's shares lose their voting power unless the target's directors approve the acquisitions or the shareholders not affiliated with either bidder or management authorize restoration of votes. We concluded that this statute, too, is inimical to investors' interests, preempted by the Williams Act, and unconstitutional under the Commerce Clause. Dynamics Corp. of America v. CTS Corp., 794 F.2d 250 (7th Cir.1986). This time the Supreme Court did not agree. It thought the Indiana statute consistent with both Williams Act and Commerce Clause. CTS Corp. v. Dynamics Corp. of America, 481 U.S. 69 (1987). Adopting Justice White's view of preemption for the sake of argument, *id.* at 81, the Court found no inconsistency between state and federal law because Indiana allowed the bidder to *acquire* the shares without hindrance. Such a law makes the shares less attractive, but it does not regulate the process of bidding. As for the Commerce Clause, the Court took Indiana's law to be regulation of internal corporate affairs, potentially beneficial because it would allow investors to avoid the "coercion" of two-tier bids and other tactics. 481 U.S. at 83, 91-93. Justices White, Blackmun, and Stevens disagreed with the analysis under the Commerce Clause, *id.* at 99-101; only Justice White disagreed with the conclusion about preemption, *id.* at 97-99.

Wisconsin has a third-generation takeover statute. Enacted after *CTS*, it postpones the kinds of transactions that often follow tender offers (and often are the reason for making the offers in the first place). Unless the target's board agrees to the transaction in advance, the bidder must wait three years after buying the shares to merge with the target or acquire more than 5% of its assets. We must decide whether this is consistent with the Williams Act and Commerce Clause.

I

Amanda Acquisition Corporation is a shell with a single purpose: to acquire Universal Foods Corporation, a diversified firm incorporated in Wisconsin and traded on the New York Stock Exchange. Universal is covered by Wisconsin's anti-takeover law. Amanda is a subsidiary of High Voltage Engineering Corp., a small electronics firm in Massachusetts. Most of High Voltage's equity capital comes from Berisford Capital PLC, a British venture capital firm, and Hyde Park Partners L.P., a partnership affiliated with the principals of Berisford. Chase Manhattan Bank has promised to lend Amanda 50% of the cost of the acquisition, secured by the stock of Universal.

In mid-November 1988 Universal's stock was trading for about $25 per share. On December 1 Amanda commenced a tender offer at $30.50, to be effective if at least 75% of the stock should be tendered.[1] This all-cash, all-shares offer has been increased in stages to $38.00. Amanda's financing is contingent on a prompt merger with Universal if the offer succeeds, so the offer is contingent on a prompt merger with Universal if the offer succeeds, so the offer is conditional on a judicial declaration that the law is invalid. (It is also conditional on Universal's redemption of poison pill stock. For reasons that we discuss below, it is unnecessary to discuss the subject in detail.)

No firm incorporated in Wisconsin and having its headquarters, substantial operations, or 10% of its shares or stockholders there may "engage in a business combination with an interest stockholder . . . for 3

---

[1] Wisconsin has, in addition to § 180.726, a statute modeled on Indiana's, providing that an acquiring firm's shares lose their votes, which may be restored under specified circumstances. Wis. Stat. § 180.25(9). That law accounts for the 75% condition, but it is not pertinent to the questions we resolve.

years after the interested stockholder's stock acquisition date, unless the board of directors of the [Wisconsin] corporation has approved, before the interested stockholder's stock acquisition date, that business combination or the purchase of stock." Wis. Stat. § 180.726(2). An "interested stockholder" is one owning 10% of the voting stock, directly or through associates (anyone acting in concert with it). § 180.726(1)(j). A "business combination" is a merger with the bidder or any of its affiliates, sale of more than 5% of the assets to bidder or affiliate, liquidation of the target, or a transaction by which the target guarantees the bidder's or affiliate's debts or passes tax benefits to the bidder or affiliate. § 180.726 (1)(e). The law, in other words, provides for almost hermetic separation of bidder and target for three years after the bidder obtains 10% of the stock -- unless the target's board consented before then. No matter how popular the offer, the ban applies: obtaining 85% (even 100%) of the stock held by non-management shareholders won't allow the bidder to engage in a business combination, as it would under Delaware law. . . . Wisconsin firms cannot opt out of the law, as may corporations subject to almost all other state takeover statutes. In Wisconsin it is management's approval in advance, or wait three years. Even when the time is up, the bidder needs the approval of a majority of the remaining investors, without any provision disqualifying shares still held by the managers who resisted the transaction. § 180.726(3)(b).[3] The district court found that this statute "effectively eliminates hostile leveraged buyouts." As a practical matter, Wisconsin prohibits any offer contingent on a merger between bidder and target, a condition attached to about 90% of contemporary tender offers.

Amanda filed this suit seeking a declaration that this law is preempted by the Williams Act and inconsistent with the Commerce Clause. It added a pendent claim that the directors' refusal to redeem the poison-pill rights violates their fiduciary duties to Universal's shareholders. The district court declined to issue a preliminary injunction. 1989 U.S. Dist. LEXIS 2717 (E.D.Wis.1989). It concluded that the statute is constitutional and not preempted, and that under Wisconsin law (which the court believed would follow Delaware's) directors are entitled to prevent investors from accepting tender offers of which the directors do not approve.[4] . . .

---

[3] Acquirors can avoid this requirement by buying out the remaining shareholders at a price defined by § 180.726(3)(c), but this is not a practical option.

[4] The district court's explanation of its holding is more limited, because it said that the directors might have foreseen three "threats" in this all-cash, all-shares premium offer: a threat that the merger would not occur, leaving some investors locked into a minority position, a threat that the papers filed under the Williams Act "might" contain false information, and a "threat to the corporation itself" in the sense that Amanda might change Universal's business plans. Such "threats" are present in all tender offers. If they are enough to justify defensive tactics, then managers are entitled to "just say no" to tender offers. Nothing in this opinion endorses the district court's rationale concerning these "threats", which is in tension with recent Delaware cases. City Capital Associates L.P. v. Interco, Inc., 551 A.2d 787 (Del.Ch.1988); Grand Metropolitan, PLC v. Pillsbury Co., 1988 Del.Ch. LEXIS 158

II

Courts try to avoid constitutional adjudication. There is no escape for us today, however. . . . At oral argument counsel for Amanda said that if the statute is within Wisconsin's powers, then its offer is doomed. So starting with the statute holds out the prospect of avoiding some issues, while starting with private rights of action of directors' duties would not enable us to avoid the constitutional question. If we conclude that § 180.726 is within Wisconsin's power, the offer is defunct, and it would be unnecessary to decide whether targets have a private right of action to enforce the margin rules or whether Universal's directors had to redeem the poison pill. We begin, therefore, by considering whether Wis.Stat. § 180.726 conflicts with the Williams Act or the Commerce Clause.

A

If our views of the wisdom of state law mattered, Wisconsin's takeover statute would not survive. Like our colleagues who decided *MITE* and *CTS*, we believe that anti-takeover legislation injures shareholders.[5] *MITE*, 633 F.2d at 496-98 and 457 U.S. at 643-44; *CTS*, 794 F.2d at 253-55. Managers frequently realize gains for investors via voluntary combinations (mergers). If gains are to be had, but managers balk, tender offers are investors' way to go over managers' heads. If managers are not maximizing the firm's value -- perhaps because they have missed the possibility of

---

(Del.Ch.1988); MAI Basic Four, Inc. v. Prime Computer, Inc., 1988 Del.Ch. LEXIS 161 (Del.Ch.1988). In responding to a tender offer directors must exercise "the most scrupulous adherence to ordinary standards of fairness in the interest of promoting the highest values reasonably attainable for the stockholders' benefit." Mills Acquisition Co. v. Macmillan, Inc., 1989 Del.Ch. LEXIS 149, 4 (Del.1989). A policy denying investors the opportunity to accept a substantial premium, based on remote "threats", is not easy to square with the law of Delaware. See also Ronald Gilson & Reinier Kraakman, *Delaware's Intermediate Standard for Defensive Tactics: Is There Substance to Proportionality Review?*, 44 Bus.Law. 247, 256-60, 267-73 (1989).

[5] Because both the district court and the parties -- like the Williams Act -- examine tender offers from the perspective of equity investors, we employ the same approach. States could choose to protect "constituencies" other than stockholders. Creditors, managers, and workers invest human rather than financial capital. But the limitation of our inquiry to equity investors does not affect the analysis, because no evidence of which we are aware suggests that bidders confiscate workers' and other participants' investments to any greater degree than do incumbents -- who may (and frequently do) close or move plants to follow the prospect of profit. Joseph Grundfest, a Commissioner of the SEC, showed in *Job Loss and Takeovers*, address to University of Toledo College of Law, Mar. 11, 1988, that acquisitions have no logical (or demonstrable) effect on employment. See also Charles Brown & James Medoff, *The Impact of Firm Acquisitions on Labor*, in *Corporate Takeovers: Causes and Consequences* 9 (Alan Auerbach ed.1988); Roberta Romano, *The Future of Hostile Takeovers: Legislation and Public Opinion*, 57 U.Cin.L.Rev. 457 (1988); Steven Bradford, *Protecting Shareholders from Themselves? A Policy and Constitutional Review of a State Takeover Statute*, 67 Neb.L.Rev. 459, 529-34 (1988).

synergistic combination, perhaps because they are clinging to divisions that could be better run in other hands, perhaps because they are just not the best persons for the job -- a bidder that believes it can realize more of the firm's value will make investors a higher offer. Investors tender, the bidder gets control and changes things. Michael Bradley, Anand Desai & E. Han Kim, *Synergistic Gains from Corporate Acquisitions and Their Division Between the Stockholders of Target and Acquiring Firms*, 21 J.Fin.Econ. 3 (1988). The prospect of monitoring by would-be bidders, and an occasional bid at a premium, induces managers to run corporations more efficiently and replaces them if they will not.

Premium bids reflect the benefits for investors. The price of a firm's stock represents investors' consensus estimate of the value of the shares under current and anticipated conditions. Stock is worth the present value of anticipated future returns -- dividends and other distributions. Tender offers succeed when bidders offer more. Only when the bid exceeds the [value] of the stock (however investors compute value) will it succeed. A statute that precludes investors from receiving or accepting a premium offer makes them worse off. It makes the economy worse off too, because the higher bid reflects the better use to which the bidder can put the target's assets. (If the bidder can't improve the use of the assets, it injures itself by paying a premium.)

Universal, making an argument common among supporters of anti-takeover laws, contends that its investors do not appreciate the worth of its business plans, that its stock is trading for too little, and that if investors tender reflexively they injure themselves. If only they would wait, Universal submits, they would do better under current management. A variant of the argument has it that although smart investors are passive and will tender, even the smart investors then must tender to avoid doing worse on the "back end" of the deal. State laws giving management the power to block an offer enable the managers to protect the investors from themselves.

Both versions of this price-is-wrong argument imply: (a) that the stock of firms defeating offers later appreciates in price, topping the bid, thus revealing the wisdom of waiting till the market wises up; and (b) that investors in firms for which no offer is outstanding gain when they adopt devices so that managers may fend off unwanted offers (or states adopt laws with the same consequence). Efforts to verify these implications have failed. The best available data show that if a firm fends off a bid, its profits decline, and its stock price (adjusted for inflation and market-wide changes) never tops the initial bid, even if it is later acquired by another firm. Gregg Jarrell, James Brickley & Jeffry Netter, *The Market for Corporate Control: The Empirical Evidence Since 1980*, 2 J.Econ.Persp. 49, 55 (1988) (collecting studies); John Pound, *The Information Effects of Takeover Bids and Resistance*, 22 J.Fin.Econ. 207 (1988). Stock of firms adopting poison pills falls in price, as does the stock of firms that adopt most kinds of anti-takeover amendments to their articles of incorporation. Jarrell, Brickley & Netter, 2 J.Econ.Persp. at 58-65 (collecting studies). . . . Studies of laws similar to Wisconsin's produce the same conclusion: share prices of firms incorporated in the state drop when the legislation is enacted. Jonathan Karpoff & Paul Malatesta, *The Wealth Effects of Second Generation State Takeover Legislation* (Univ. of Wash. Grad. Sch. of Bus., working paper, 1988).

Although a takeover-*proof* firm leaves investors at the mercy of incumbent managers (who may be mistaken about the wisdom of their business plan even when they act in the best of faith), a takeover-*resistant* firm may be able to assist its investors. An auction may run up the price, and delay may be essential to an auction. Auctions transfer money from bidders to targets, and diversified investors would not gain from them (their left pocket loses what the right pocket gains); diversified investors would lose from auctions if the lower returns to bidders discourage future bids. But from the targets' perspective, once a bid is on the table an auction may be the best strategy. The full effects of auctions are hard to unravel, sparking scholarly debate.[6] For a planner, the most important impact of Rule 10b-13 is that it presents a further barrier to paying a control premium to a large shareholder. From this perspective, the Rule's critical feature is that it does not apply to purchases made before the commencement of a tender offer. Thus, so long as the acquisition of the controlling shares is made prior to the offer, neither § 14(d)(7) nor Rule 10d-13 prevent paying a controlling shareholder a higher price than will be paid in a subsequent tender offer.[7]

Devices giving managers some ability to orchestrate investors' responses, in order to avoid panic tenders in response to front-end-loaded offers, also could be beneficial, as the Supreme Court emphasized in *CTS*, 481 U.S. at 92-93. ("Could be" is an important qualifier; even from a perspective limited to targets' shareholders given a bid on the table, it is important to know whether managers use this power to augment bids or to stifle them, and whether courts can tell the two apart.)

State anti-takeover laws do not serve these ends well, however. Investors who prefer to give managers the discretion to orchestrate responses to bids may do so through "fair-price" clauses in the articles of incorporation and other consensual devices. Other firms may choose different strategies. A law such as Wisconsin's does not add options to firms that would like to give more discretion to their managers; instead it destroys the possibility of

---

[6] Compare Lucian Bebchuk, *Toward Undistorted Choice and Equal Treatment in Corporate Takeovers*, 98 Harv.L.Rev. 1693 (1985), and Ronald Gilson, *Seeking Competitive Bids versus Pure Passivity in Tender Offer Defense*, 35 Stan.L.Rev. 51 (1982), with Alan Schwartz, *Search Theory and the Tender Offer Auction*, 2 J.L.Econ. & Org. 229 (1986), and Sanford Grossman & Oliver Hart, *Takeover Bids, the Free-Rider Problem and the Theory of the Corporation*, 11 Bell J.Econ. 42 (1980). For the most recent round compare Alan Schwartz, *The Fairness of Tender Offer Prices in Utilitarian Theory*, 176 J.Legal Stud. 165 (1988), with Lucian Bebchuk, *The Sole Owner Standard for Takeover Policy*, 17 J. Legal Stud. 197 (1988), with Alan Schwartz, *The Sole Owner Standard Reviewed*, 17 J. Legal Stud. 231 (1988).

[7] This subject is also considered in Chapter 21.

divergent choices. Wisconsin's law applies even when the investors prefer to leave their managers under the gun, to allow the market full sway. Karpoff and Malatesta found that state anti-takeover laws have little or no effect on the price of shares if the firm already has poison pills (or related devices) in place, but strongly negative effects on price when firms have no such contractual devices. To put this differently, state laws have bite only when investors, given the choice, would deny managers the power to interfere with tender offers (maybe already *have* denied managers that power). See also Roberta Romano, *The Political Economy of Takeover Statutes*, 73 Va.L.Rev. 111, 128-31 (1987).

B

Skepticism about the wisdom of a state's law does not lead to the conclusion that the law is beyond the state's power, however, We have not been elected custodians of investors' wealth. States need not treat investors' welfare as their summum bonum. Perhaps they choose to protect managers' welfare instead, or believe that the current economic literature reaches an incorrect conclusion and that despite appearances takeovers injure investors in the long run. Unless a federal statute or the Constitution bars the way, Wisconsin's choice must be respected.

Amanda relies on the Williams Act of 1968, incorporated into § 13(d), (e) and 14(d)-(f) of the Securities Exchange Act of 1934, 15 U.S.C. § 78m(d), (e), 78n(d)-(f). The Williams Act regulates the conduct of tender offers. Amanda believes that Congress created an entitlement for investors to receive the benefit of tender offers, and that because Wisconsin's law makes tender offers unattractive to many potential bidders, it is preempted. See *MITE*, 633 F.2d at 490-99, and Justice White's views, 457 U.S. at 630-40.

Preemption has not won easy acceptance among the Justices for several reasons. First there is § 28(a) of the '34 Act, 15 U.S.C. § 78bb(a), which provides that "[n]othing in this chapter shall affect the jurisdiction of the securities commission . . . of any State over any security or any person insofar as it does not conflict with the provisions of this chapter or the rules and regulations thereunder." Although some of the SEC's regulations (particularly the one defining the commencement of an offer) conflict with some state takeover laws, the SEC has not drafted regulations concerning mergers with controlling shareholders, and the Act itself does not address the subject. States have used the leeway afforded by § 28(a) to carry out "merit regulation" of securities -- "blue sky" laws that allow securities commissioners to forbid sales altogether, in contrast with the federal regimen emphasizing disclosure. So § 28(a) allows states to stop some transactions federal law would permit, in pursuit of an approach at odds with a system emphasizing disclosure and investors' choice. Then there is the traditional reluctance of federal courts to infer preemption of "state law in areas traditionally regulated by the States", California v. ARC America Corp., 490

U.S. 93 (1989); see also, e.g., Hillsborough County v. Automated Medical Laboratories, Inc., 471 U.S. 707, 716 (1985); Air Line Pilots Ass'n v. UAL Corp., No. 88-3308 (7th Cir.1989), slip op. 14-15. States have regulated corporate affairs, including mergers and sales of assets, since before the beginning of the nation.

Because Justice White's views of the Williams Act did not garner the support of a majority of the Court in *MITE*, we reexamined that subject in *CTS* and observed that the best argument for preemption is the Williams Act's "neutrality" between bidder and management, a balance designed to leave investors free to choose. This is not a confident jumping-off point, though:

> Of course it is a big leap from saying that the Williams Act does not itself exhibit much hostility to tender offers to saying that it implicitly forbids states to adopt more hostile regulations, but this leap was taken by the Supreme Court plurality and us in *MITE* and by every court to consider the question since. . . . [W]hatever doubts of the Williams' Act preemptive intent we might entertain as an original matter are stifled by the weight of precedent.

794 F.2d at 262. The rough treatment our views received from the Court -- only Justice White supported the holding on preemption -- lifts the "weight of precedent."

There is a big difference between what Congress *enacts* and what it *supposes* will ensue. Expectations about the consequences of a law are not themselves law. To say that Congress wanted to be neutral between bidder and target -- a conclusion reached in many of the Court's opinions, e.g., Piper v. Chris-Craft Industries, 430 U.S. 1 (1977) -- is not to say that it also forbade the states to favor one of these sides. Every law has a stopping point, likely one selected because of a belief that it would be unwise (for now, maybe forever) to do more. Rodriguez v. United States, 480 U.S. 522, 525-26 (1987); Covalt v. Carey Canada Inc., 860 F.2d 1434, 1439 (7th Cir.1988). Nothing in the Williams Act says that the federal compromise among bidders, targets' managers, and investors is the only permissible one. See Daniel Fischel, *From MITE to CTS: State Anti-Takeover Statutes, the Williams Act, the Commerce Clause, and Insider Trading*, 1987 Sup.Ct.Rev. 47, 71-74. Like the majority of the Court in *CTS*, however, we stop short of the precipice. 481 U.S. at 78-87.

The Williams Act regulates the *process* of tender offers: timing, disclosure, proration if tenders exceed what the bidder is willing to buy, best-price rules. It slows things down, allowing investors to evaluate the offer and management's response. Best-price, proration, and short-tender rules ensure that investors who decide at the end of the offer get the same treatment as those who decide immediately, reducing pressure to leap before looking. After complying with the disclosure and delay requirements, the bidder is free to take the shares. *MITE* held invalid a state law that increased the delay and, by authorizing a regulator to nix the offer, created a distinct possibility that the bidder would be unable to buy the stock (and the holders to sell it) despite compliance with federal law. Illinois tried to regulate the process of tender offers, contradicting in some respects the federal rules. Indiana, by contrast, allowed the tender offer to take its course as the Williams Act specified but "sterilized" the acquired shares until the remaining investors restored their voting rights. Congress said nothing about the voting power of shares acquired in tender offers. Indiana's law reduced the benefits the bidder anticipated from the acquisition but left the process alone. So the Court, although accepting Justice White's views for the purpose of argument, held that Indiana's rules do not conflict with the federal norms.

CTS observed that laws affecting the voting power of acquired shares do not differ in principle from many other rules governing the internal affairs of corporations. Laws requiring staggered or classified boards of directors delay the transfer of control to the bidder; laws requiring super-majority vote for a merger may make a transaction less attractive or impossible. 481 U.S. at 85-86. Yet these are not preempted by the Williams Act, any more than state laws concerning the *effect* of investors' votes are preempted by the portions of the Exchange Act, 15 U.S.C. § 78n(a)-(c), regulating the process of soliciting proxies. Federal securities laws frequently regulate process while state corporate law regulates substance. Federal proxy rules demand that firms disclose many things, in order to promote informed voting. Yet states may permit or compel a super-majority rule (even a unanimity rule) rendering it all but impossible for a particular side to prevail in the voting. See Robert Clark, *Corporate Law* § 9.13 (1986). Are the state laws therefore preempted? How about state laws that allow many firms to organize without traded shares? Universities, hospitals, and other charities have self-perpetuating boards and cannot be acquired by tender offer. Insurance companies may be organized as mutuals, without traded shares; retailers often organize as co-operatives, without traded stock; some decently large companies (large enough to be "reporting companies" under the '34 Act) issue stock subject to buy-sell agreements under which the investors cannot sell to strangers without offering stock to the firm at a formula price; Ford Motor Co. issued non-voting stock for the family, thus preventing outsiders from gaining control (dual-class stock is becoming more common); firms issue and state law enforces poison pills. All of these devices make tender offers unattractive (even impossible) and greatly diminish the power of proxy fights, success in which often depends on buying votes by acquiring the equity to which the vote is attached. See Douglas Blair, Devra Golbe & James Gerard, *Unbundling the Voting Rights and Profit Claims of Common Shares*, 97 J.Pol.Econ. 420 (1989). None of these devices could be thought preempted by the Williams Act or the proxy rules. If they are not preempted, neither is Wis. Stat. § 180.726.

Any bidder complying with federal law is free to acquire shares of Wisconsin firms on schedule. Delay in completing a second-stage merger may make the target less attractive, and thus depress the price offered or even lead to an absence of bids; it does not, however, alter any of the procedures governed by federal regulation. Indeed Wisconsin's law does not depend in any way on how the acquiring firm came by its stock: open-market purchases, private acquisitions of blocs, and acquisitions via tender offers are treated identically. Wisconsin's law is no different in effect from one saying that for the three years after a person acquires 10% of a firm's stock, a unanimous vote is required to merge. Corporate law once had a generally-applicable unanimity rule in major transactions, a rule discarded because giving every investor the power to block every reorganization stopped many desirable changes. (Many investors could use their "hold-up" power to try to engross a larger portion of the gains, creating a complex bargaining problem that often could not be solved.) Wisconsin's more restrained version of unanimity also may block beneficial transactions, but not by tinkering with any of the procedures established in federal law.

Only if the Williams Act gives investors a right to be the beneficiary of offers could Wisconsin's law run afoul of the federal rule. No such entitlement can be mined out of the Williams Act, however. Schreiber v. Burlington Northern, Inc., 472 U.S. 1 (1985), holds that the cancellation of a pending offer because of machinations between bidder and target does not deprive investors of their due under the Williams Act. The Court treated § 14(e) as a disclosure law, so that investors could make informed decisions; it follows that events leading bidders to cease their quest do not conflict with the Williams Act any more than a state law leading a firm not to issue new securities could conflict with the Securities Act of 1933. See also Panter v. Marshall Fields & Co., 646 F.2d 271, 283-85 (7th Cir.1981); Lewis v. McGraw, 620 F.2d 192 (2d Cir.1980), both holding that the evaporation of an opportunity to tender one's shares when a defensive tactic leads the bidder to withdraw the invitation does not violate the Williams Act. Investors have no right to receive tender offers. More to the point -- since Amanda sues as a bidder rather than as investor seeking to sell -- the Williams Act does not create a right to profit from the business of making tender offers. It is not attractive to put bids on the table for Wisconsin corporations, but because Wisconsin leaves the process alone once a bidder appears, its law may co-exist with the Williams Act.

C

The Commerce Clause, Art. I § 8 cl. 3 of the Constitution, grants Congress the power "[t]o regulate Commerce . . . among the several States". For many decades the Court took this to be what it says: a grant to Congress with no implications for the states' authority to act when Congress is silent. See David Currie, *The Constitution in the Supreme Court: The First Hundred Years* 171-83, 222-36 (1985) (discussing cases); Martin Redish & Shane Nugent, *The Dormant Commerce Clause and the Constitutional Balance of Federalism*, 1987 Duke L.J. 569. Limitations came from provisions, such as the Contract Clause, Art. I § 10 cl. 1 ("No State shall . . . pass any . . . Law impairing the Obligation of Contracts"), expressly denying the states certain powers. The Contract Clause has been held to curtail states' authority over corporations, see Trustees of Dartmouth College v. Woodward, 17 U.S. (4 Wheat) 518 (1819), and it may have something to say about states' ability to limit the transferability of shares after they have been issued. See Henry Butler & Larry Ribstein, *State Anti-Takeover Statutes and the Contract Clause*, 57 U.Cin.L.Rev. 611 (1988). Broad dicta in Cooley v. Board of Wardens, 53 U.S. (12 How.) 299 (1852), eventually led to holdings denying states the power to regulate interstate commerce directly or discriminatorily, or to take steps that had unjustified consequences in other states. Meanwhile the Court began to treat the Contract Clause as if it said that "No State shall pass any *unwise* Law impairing the Obligation of Contracts," so that divergent clauses have become homogenized. Chicago Board of Realtors, Inc., v. Chicago, 819 F.2d 732, 742-45 (7th Cir.1987).

When state law discriminates against interstate commerce expressly -- for example, when Wisconsin closes its border to butter from Minnesota -- the negative Commerce Clause steps in. The law before us is not of this type; it is neutral between inter-state and intra-state commerce. Amanda therefore presses on us the broader, all-weather, be-reasonable vision of the Constitution. Wisconsin has passed a law that unreasonably injures investors, most of whom live outside of Wisconsin, and therefore it *has* to be unconstitutional, as Amanda sees things. Although Pike v. Bruce Church, Inc., 397 U.S. 137 (1970), sometimes is understood to authorize such general-purpose balancing, a closer examination of the cases may support the conclusion that the Court has looked for discrimination rather than for baleful effects. See Donald Regan, *The Supreme Court and State Protectionism: Making Sense of the Dormant Commerce Clause*, 84 Mich.L.Rev. 1091 (1986); Julian Eule, *Laying the Dormant Commerce Clause to Rest*, 91 Yale L.J. 425 (1982). At all events, although *MITE* employed the balancing process described in *Pike* to deal with a statute that regulated all firms having "contacts" with the state, *CTS* did not even cite that case when dealing with a statute regulating only the affairs of a firm incorporated in the state, and Justice Scalia's concurring opinion questioned its application. 481 U.S. at 95-96. The Court took a decidedly confined view of the judicial role: "We are not inclined 'to second-guess the empirical judgments of lawmakers concerning the utility of legislation,' Kassel v. Consolidated Freightways Corp., 450 U.S. [662] at 679 (BRENNAN J concurring in judgment)." 481 U.S. at 92. Although the scholars whose writings we cited in Part II.A conclude that laws such as Wisconsin's injure investors, Wisconsin is entitled to give a different answer to this empirical question -- or to decide that investors' interests should be sacrificed to protect managers' interests or promote the stability of corporate arrangements.

Illinois's law, held invalid in *MITE*, regulated sales of stock elsewhere. Illinois tried to tell a Texas owner of stock in a Delaware corporation that he could not sell to a buyer in California. By contrast, Wisconsin's law, like the Indiana statute sustained by *CTS*, regulates the internal affairs of firms incorporated there. Investors may buy or sell stock as they please. Wisconsin's law differs in this respect not only from that of Illinois but also from that of Massachusetts, which forbade any transfer of shares for one year after the failure to disclose any material fact, a flaw that led the First Circuit to condemn it. Hyde Park Partners, L.P. v. Connolly, 839 F.2d 837, 847-48 (1st Cir.1988).[9]

Buyers of stock in Wisconsin firms may exercise full rights as investors, taking immediate control. No interstate transaction is regulated or forbidden. True, Wisconsin's law makes a potential buyer less willing to buy (or depresses the bid), but this is equally true of Indiana's rule. Many other rules of corporate law -- supermajority voting requirements, staggered and classified boards, and so on -- have similar or greater effects on some persons' willingness to purchase stock. *CTS*, 481 U.S. at 89-90. States could ban mergers outright, with even more powerful consequences. . . . Wisconsin did not allow mergers among firms chartered there until 1947. We doubt that it was violating the Commerce Clause all those years. . . . Every rule of corporate law affects investors who live outside the state of incorporation, yet this has never been thought sufficient to authorize a form of cost-benefit inquiry through the medium of the Commerce Clause.

Wisconsin, like Indiana, is indifferent to the domicile of the bidder. A putative bidder located in Wisconsin enjoys no privilege over a firm located in New York. So too with investors: all are treated identically, regardless of residence. Doubtless most bidders (and investors) are located outside Wisconsin, but unless the law discriminates according to residence this alone does not matter. *CTS*, 481 U.S. at 87-88; Lewis v. BT Investment Managers, Inc., 447 U.S. 27, 36-37 (1980); Exxon Corp. v. Governor of Maryland, 437 U.S. 177 (1978). Every state's regulation of domestic trade (potentially) affects those who live elsewhere but wish to sell their wares within the state. A law making suppliers of drugs absolutely liable for defects will affect the conduct (and wealth) of Eli Lilly & Co., an Indiana firm, and the many other pharmaceutical houses, all located in other states, yet Wisconsin has no less power to set and change tort law than do states with domestic drug manufacturers. "Because nothing in the [Wisconsin] Act imposes a greater burden on out-of-state offerors than it does on similarly situated [Wisconsin] offerors, we reject the contention that the Act discriminates against interstate commerce." *CTS*, 481 U.S. at 88. For the same reason, the Court long ago held that state blue sky laws comport with the Commerce Clause. Hall v. Geiger-Jones Co., 242 U.S. 539 (1917); Caldwell v. Sioux Falls Stock Yards Co., 242 U.S. 559 (1917); Merrick v. N.W. Halsey & Co., 242 U.S. 568 (1917). Blue sky laws may bar Texans from selling stock in Wisconsin, but they apply equally to local residents'

---

[9] The name should ring a bell. Hyde Partners was trying to acquire High Voltage Engineering! As a result of the First Circuit's decision, it did. Now High Voltage as a parent of Amanda is trying to do to Universal what Hyde Park did to it. Ironies do not always come full circle, however.

attempts to sell. That their application blocks a form of commerce altogether does not strip the states of power.

Wisconsin could exceed its powers by subjecting forms to inconsistent regulation. Here, too, the Wisconsin law is materially identical to Indiana's. *CTS*, 481 U.S. at 88-89. This leaves only the argument that Wisconsin's law hinders the flow of interstate trade "too much". *CTS* dispatched this concern by declaring it inapplicable to laws that apply only the internal affairs of firms incorporated in the regulating state. 481 U.S. at 89-94. States may regulate corporate transactions as they choose without having to demonstrate under an unfocused balancing test that the benefits are "enough" to justify the consequences.

To say that states have the power to enact laws whose costs exceed their benefits is not to say that investors should kiss their wallets goodbye. States compete to offer corporate codes attractive to firms. Managers who want to raise money incorporate their firms in the states that offer the combination of rules investors prefer. Ralph Winter, Jr., *State Law, Shareholder Protection, and the Theory of the Corporation*, 6 J.Legal Stud. 251 (1977); Fischel, *supra*, 1987 Sup.Ct.Rev. at 74-84. Laws that in the short run injure investors and protect managers will in the longer run make the state less attractive to firms that need to raise new capital. If the law is "protectionist", the protected class is the existing body of managers (and other workers), suppliers, and so on, which bears no necessary relation to state boundaries. States regulating the affairs of domestic corporations cannot in the long run injure anyone but themselves. Professor Fischel makes the point, 1987 Sup.Ct.Rev. at 84:

> In the short run, states can enact welfare-decreasing legislation that imposes costs on residents of other states. . . . In the long run, however, states have no ability to export costs to non-resident investors. . . . States that enact laws that are harmful to investors will cause entrepreneurs to incorporate elsewhere.

The long run takes time to arrive, and it is tempting to suppose that courts could contribute to investors' welfare by eliminating laws that impose costs in the short run. See Gregg Jarrell, *State Anti-Takeover Laws and the Efficient Allocation of Corporate Control: An Economic Analysis of Edgar v. MITE Corp.*, 2 Sup.Ct.Econ.Rev. 111 (1983). The price of such warfare, however, is a reduction in the power of competition among states. Courts seeking to impose "good" rules on the states diminish the differences among corporate codes and dampen competitive forces. Too, courts may fail in their quest. How do judges know which rules are best? Often only the slow forces of competition reveal that information. Early economic studies may mislead, or judges (not trained as social scientists) may misinterpret the available data or act precipitously. Our Constitution allows the states to act as laboratories; slow migration (or national law on the authority of the Commerce Clause) grinds the failures under. No such process weeds out judicial errors, or decisions that, although astute when rendered, have become anachronistic in light of changes in the economy. Judges must hesitate for these practical reasons -- and not only because of limits on their constitutional competence -- before trying to "perfect" corporate codes.

The three district judges who have considered and sustained Delaware's law delaying mergers did so in large measure because they believed that the law left hostile offers "a meaningful opportunity for success". BNS, Inc. v. Koppers Co., 683 F.Supp. at 469. See also *RP Acquisition Corp.*, 686 F.Supp. at 482-84; *City Capital Associates*, 696 F.Supp. at 1555. Delaware allows a merger to occur forthwith if the bidder obtains 85% of the shares other than those held by management and employee stock plans. If the bid is attractive to the bulk of the unaffiliated investors, it succeeds. Wisconsin offers no such opportunity, which Amanda believes is fatal.

Even in Wisconsin, though, options remain. Defenses impenetrable to the naked eye may have cracks. Poison pills are less fatal in practice than in name (some have been swallowed willingly), and corporate law contains self-defense mechanisms. Investors concerned about stock-watering often arranged for firms to issue preemptive rights, entitlements for existing investors to buy stock at the same price offered to newcomers (often before the newcomers had chance to buy in). Poison pills are dilution devices, and so pre-emptive rights ought to be handy countermeasures.[11] So too there are countermeasures to statutes deferring mergers. The cheapest is to lower the bid to reflect the costs of delay. Because every potential bidder labors under the same drawback, the firm placing the highest value on the target still should win. Or a bidder might take down the stock and pledge it (or its dividends) as security for any loans. That is, the bidder could operate the target as a subsidiary for three years. The corporate world is full of partially owned subsidiaries. If there is gain to be had from changing the debt-equity ratio of the target, that can be done consistent with Wisconsin law. The prospect of being locked into place as holders of illiquid positions would cause many persons to sell out, and the threat of being locked in would cause many managers to give assent in advance, as Wisconsin allows. (Or bidders might demand that directors waive the protections of state law, just as Amanda believes that the directors' fiduciary duties compel them to redeem the poison pill rights.) Many bidders would find lock-in unattractive because of the potential for litigation by minority investors, and the need to operate the firm as a subsidiary might foreclose savings or synergies from merger. So none of these options is a perfect substitute for immediate merger, but

---

[11] Imagine a series of Antidote rights, issued by would-be bidding firms, that detach if anyone exercises flip-over rights to purchase the bidder's stock at a discount. Antidote rights would entitle the bidder's investors, *other than those who exercise flip-over rights*, to purchase the bidder's stock at the same discount available to investors exercising flip-over rights. Antidotes for flip-in rights also could be issued. In general, whenever one firm can issue rights allowing the purchase of cheap stock, another firm can issue the equivalent series of contingent pre-emptive rights that offsets the dilution.

each is a crack in the defensive wall allowing some value-increasing bids to proceed.

At the end of the day, however, it does not matter whether these countermeasures are "enough". The Commerce Clause does not demand that states leave bidders a "meaningful opportunity for success". Maryland enacted a law that absolutely banned vertical integration in the oil business. No opportunities, "meaningful" or otherwise, remained to firms wanting to own retail outlets. Exxon Corp. v. Governor of Maryland held that the law is consistent with the Commerce Clause, even on the assumption that it injures consumers and investors alike. A state with the power to forbid mergers has the power to defer them for three years. Investors can turn to firms incorporated in states committed to the dominance of market forces, or they can turn on legislators who enact unwise laws. The Constitution has room for many economic policies. "[A] law can be both economic folly and constitutional." *CTS*, 481 U.S. at 96-97 (Scalia, J., concurring). Wisconsin's law may well be folly; we are confident that it is constitutional.

AFFIRMED.

The Wisconsin business combination statute reviewed in *Amanda* is significantly tougher than the Delaware statute upon which it is modeled. There are no escapes built into Wisconsin's three-year ban on combinations: the ban applies even if a bidder obtains 100% of a target's outstanding stock, and some restrictions on combinations extend beyond the three-year post-acquisition period. There is not even an opt-out provision in the statute for companies wishing to avoid its strictures. In addition, Judge Easterbrook is fully persuaded of the economic folly of the Wisconsin statute. Why, then, did Judge Easterbrook write an opinion that SEC Commissioner Joseph A. Grundfest has observed, "may be sufficiently powerful to portend a trend that would leave the Williams Act, as a practical matter, no longer governing takeovers?"[54]

The more measured response of the Delaware District Court to the Delaware statute demonstrates that *Amanda*'s analysis of the preemption claim was hardly compelled by *CTS*. In *CTS*, after all, Justice Powell's majority opinion analyzed the preemption claim with the framework established by Justice White's plurality opinion in *MITE*. Although *CTS* noted that Justice White's view -- the view that the Williams Act mandates a neutral balance between acquirers and target management -- was not binding on the Supreme Court, *CTS* nonetheless applied that view to uphold the Indiana statute on the ground that it protected shareholders from coercion without unduly favoring management, and thus actually promoted the

---

[54] S. Sontag, *After Ruling, Stricter Laws on Takeovers?*, Nat'l L.J., July 10, 1989, at 24. Note that the SEC has vigorously opposed second- and third-generation anti-takeover statutes in federal courts.

Williams Act's substantive goals. By contrast, Judge Easterbrook in *Amanda* reads *CTS* to invite the lower courts to do something quite different from what the Supreme Court itself did in *CTS*: that is, to construct a new and extremely limited analysis of Congressional intent in promulgating the Williams Act. Under this new analysis, the Williams Act is said to be intended exclusively to regulate the process and terms of tender offers, while the states apparently remain wholly free to reconstruct the ground rules of corporate law in a fashion that makes hostile tender offers infeasible.

As a matter of original Congressional intent, is Judge Easterbrook's reading of the Williams Act persuasive? Presumably Congress regulated the process and terms of tender offers for a reason: to preserve shareholders' autonomy with respect to a third party offer. Given Congressional recognition of the benefits of tender offers, did Congress contemplate the states could eliminate them? If the answer to the preemption question is ambiguous, should Judge Easterbrook have approached the question as a blank slate, without reconciling his opinion with the actual analysis employed by the Supreme Court in *CTS*? Alternatively, if you believe with Judge Easterbrook that the implicit message of *CTS* is, "Do what you think we might like to do, not what we say," do you also believe that this is an appropriate form of deference to Supreme Court decisions by the lower federal courts?

Judge Easterbrook reconciles his own pro-takeover views with a broad grant of authority to the states to bar takeovers by relying upon long-run competition among the states to result in efficient corporate law and by dismissing amelioristic efforts by courts to improve upon state law as unwarranted interference destined to "dampen competitive forces." Does the past two decades of competition among the states in fashioning anti-takeover laws give grounds for optimism that the pressure of corporations choosing states of incorporation will eventually force state legislators to appreciate Judge Easterbrook's substantive views on takeover regulation? Recall Professor Romano's account of the moving political force behind the adoption of state antitakeover statutes. If corporations seek their enactment, who is left to stand against them? We consider the potential role for shareholders in the next section.

There are hints in *Amanda* that Judge Easterbrook may have hoped to spark new Congressional legislation that would explicitly preempt state anti-takeover statutes. One example is *Amanda*'s observation that "[our] Constitution allows the states to act as laboratories; slow migration (*or national law on the authority of the Commerce Clause*) grinds the failures under." *Id.* (emphasis added). Consider in this regard Professor Roberta Romano's conclusion after a study of data on public opinions about takeovers:

> The public opinion poll data reinforce the prediction that were Congress to act, it would not be able to internalize fully the costs of takeover regulation, and it would behave in a similar fashion to the states. Given public attitudes

toward and ignorance about takeovers, the policy recommendation of this Article is that advocates of preemption might best serve their cause by seeking to educate the public concerning the theoretical and empirical findings on the beneficial effects of takeovers and a competitive market for corporate control. Otherwise they will, in all likelihood, be sorely disappointed in the legislation that is produced.[55]

D.   Poison Pill, Long-Term Interest, and Expanded Constituency Statutes -- A Fourth Generation of Anti-Takeover Legislation?

Until quite recently, all anti-takeover legislation was centered on shareholders in the double sense that it was justified as a device for protecting shareholders from the perils of hostile offers, and it left undisturbed the great body of fiduciary doctrine establishing the primacy of shareholder interests in the management of the firm. During the past three years, however, a new generation of anti-takeover legislation has begun to drift free of these constraints by seeking to empower corporate boards to resist hostile takeovers, even (arguably) at the expense of shareholder interests.

The starting point for this novel strategy is explicit legislative approval of the poison pill defense in the form of a new provision authorizing the board to issue rights, options, and warrants without shareholder approval. Yet, the core of the strategy is a legislative reformation of the board's duties of care and loyalty that is designed to assure a target's board ample discretion to deploy and enforce its rights plan without judicial interference or the risk of personal liability in shareholder suits. Originally, such efforts to reformulate management's duties emphasized the board's discretion to consider the "long-term" interests of the corporation in addition to the "short-term" interests of the corporation and its shareholders. New York's 1988 statute, for example, stresses that the board may decide whether rights plans are to be "deployed, enforced or waived in the best long-term and short-term interests of the corporation and its shareholders considering, without limitation, the prospects for potential growth, development, productivity and profitability of the corporation." N.Y.Bus.Corp.Law § 505(a)(2)(ii) (1989). Such language is typical of the "long-term interest" statutes.

A number of recent statutes, however, not only include long-term interest provisions in formulating the director's duty of care, but also include a provision permitting the board to consider the effects of a takeover on constituencies other than shareholders. Some commentators have argued that these "expanded constituency" provisions merely make explicit the latent

---

[55] Roberta Romano, *The Future of Hostile Takeovers: Legislation and Public Opinion*, 57 U.Cin.L.Rev. 457, 504 (1988).

motivation behind most anti-takeover legislation by severing the link between shareholder welfare and takeover regulation.[56]

Once again, Indiana has been an anti-takeover pioneer. The following provisions of Indiana Senate Bill No. 255, enacted on February 23, 1989, illustrate the model extended constituency statute. (Indiana now has an anti-takeover cocktail on the books that includes the control share acquisition statute reviewed in *CTS*, a later business combination statute modelled on the Delaware act, and the entirely new extended constituency provision excerpted below.)

Indiana Senate Bill No. 255. . .

SECTION 2. IC 23-1-35-1 IS AMENDED TO READ AS FOLLOWS: § 1.

(a) A director shall, based on facts then known to the director, discharge the duties as a director, including the director's duties as a member of a committee:

(1) in good faith;

(2) with the care an ordinarily prudent person in a like position would exercise under similar circumstances; and

(3) in a manner the director reasonably believes to be in the best interests of the corporation. . . .

(d) A director may, in considering the best interests of a corporation, consider the effects of any action on shareholders, employees, suppliers, and customers of the corporation, and communities in which offices or other facilities of the corporation are located, and any other factors the director considers pertinent.

(e) A director is not liable for any action taken as a director, or any failure to take any action, unless:

(1) the director has breached or failed to perform the duties of the director's office in compliance with this section; and

(2)   The breach or failure to perform constitutes willful misconduct or recklessness.

(f) In enacting this article, the general assembly established corporate governance rules for Indiana corporations, including in this chapter, the standards of conduct applicable to directors of Indiana corporations, and the corporate constituent groups and interests that a director may take into account in exercising the director's business judgment. The general assembly intends to reaffirm certain of these corporate governance rules to ensure that the directors of Indiana corporations, in exercising their business judgment, are not required to approve a proposed corporate action if the directors in good faith determine, after considering and weighing as they deem appropriate the effects of such action of the corporation's constituents, that such action is not in the best interests of the corporation. In making such

---

[56] See, e.g., Lyman Johnson & David Millon, *Missing the Point About State Takeover Statutes*, 87 Mich.L.Rev. 846 (1989).

determination, directors are not required to consider the effects of a proposed corporate action on any particular corporate constituent group or interest as a dominant or controlling factor. Without limiting the generality of the foregoing, directors are not required to render inapplicable any of the provisions of IC 23-1-43, to redeem any rights under or to render inapplicable a shareholder rights plan adopted pursuant to IC 23-1-26-5, or to take of decline to take any other action under this article, solely because of the effect such action might have on a proposed acquisition of control of the corporation or the amounts that might be paid to shareholders under such an acquisition. Certain judicial decisions in Delaware and other jurisdictions, which might otherwise be looked to for guidance in interpreting Indiana corporate law, including decisions relating to potential change of control transactions that impose a different or higher degree of scrutiny on actions taken by directors in response to a proposed acquisition of control of the corporation, are inconsistent with the proper application of the business judgment rule under this article. Therefore, the general assembly intends:

> (1) to reaffirm that this section allows directors the full discretion to weigh the factors enumerated in subsection (d) as they deem appropriate; and

> (2) to protect both directors and the validity of corporate action taken by them in the good faith exercise of their business judgment after reasonable investigation.

(g) In taking or declining to take any action, or in making or declining to make any recommendation to the shareholders of the corporation with respect to any matter, a board of directors may, in its discretion, consider both the short term and long term best interests of the corporation, taking into account, and weighing as the directors deem appropriate, the effects thereof on the corporation's shareholders and the other corporate constituent groups and interests listed or described in subsection (d), as well as any other factors deemed pertinent by the directors under subsection (d). If a determination is made with respect to the foregoing with the approval of a majority of the disinterested directors of the board of directors, that determination was not made in good faith after reasonable investigation.

Legislation similar to the new Indiana statute has been adopted in twenty-six states.[57] As the Indiana legislation makes explicit, constituency provisions respond directly to the new judicial law of corporate takeovers in Delaware. In addition to authorizing directors to consider constituencies other than shareholders, the Indiana statute expressly rejects the intermediate standard of judicial review articulated by Unocal Corp. v. Mesa Petroleum Co., 493 A.2d 955 (Del.1985). Under the Indiana statute, a decision by a

---

[57] The statutes are compiled in ABA Committee on Corporate Laws, *Other Constituencies Statutes: Potential for Confusion*, 45 Bus.Law. 2253 (1990).

majority of disinterested directors to refuse to redeem a poison pill "shall conclusively be presumed to be valid unless it can be demonstrated that the determination was not made in good faith after reasonable investigation." § 2(g). This provision, of course, simply restricts judicial review of control decisions to the traditional business judgment rule.

The net effect of the constituency provisions may be to stop just short of legislating hostile takeovers out of existence by granting corporate boards virtually unreviewable discretion to reject takeover bids. Consider in this regard the following excerpt from an open letter to Governor Mario M. Cuomo from then SEC Commissioner Joseph A. Grundfest, regarding New York's subsequently enacted constituency provision:

Joseph Grundfest
LETTER TO THE HONORABLE MARIO M. CUOMO
June 6, 1989

. . . The most recent draft language of Bill No. 128 is, . . ., ambiguous. The bill's language is susceptible of an interpretation that would allow boards to consider interests of constituencies even if those interests bear no rational relationship, or are antithetical, to the interests of the corporation's stockholders. To the extent that Bill No. 128 is intended to reach this result, or to the extent that it can be so interpreted, Bill No. 128 sets New York on a dangerous and uncharted course that will not serve the interests the bill is intended to promote.

The danger of permitting board discretion in a manner that is not rationally related to stockholder interests is compounded by the fact that Bill No. 128 would clearly immunize directors from any accountability for the exercise of this broad and uncharted discretion. In particular, Bill No. 128 states that "[n]othing in this paragraph shall create a duty of any director to any person or entity to give or not give consideration to any such interests or effects." Put another way, Bill No. 128 can be read to give to boards the power to act in the interests of other constituencies, and against the interests of the corporation's stockholders, while immunizing the board from any responsibility to the very constituencies the board is purportedly defending.[9]

The grant of authority without accountability raises the real and present danger that boards will use Bill No. 128 as a fig leaf. Specifically, Bill No. 128 may allow boards to rationalize decisions that they could not otherwise support in the name of constituencies who are powerless to monitor or challenge the actions that are purportedly taken in their interest.

---

[9] This grant of authority without commensurate accountability raises serious questions about the motives of some of the Bill's supporters. It also highlights the extent to which the Bill may not operate as many of its drafters intend. See Ronald Gilson, *Just Say No to Whom?*, Stanford Law School, April 17, 1989 [subsequently published as "A Fight for the Right to 'Just Say No' to Hostile Tender Offers," Legal Times, June 26, 1989, p.19. Eds.]

Unfortunately, there is no shortage of real life situations in which boards could use this fig leaf to rationalize their behavior without any real regard for the constituencies in whose name they purport to act. Consider, for example, the position of certain large corporations and of the Business Roundtable with regard to recently enacted federal plant closing legislation. These organizations hotly opposed plant closing legislation on grounds that it would be harmful to corporations and to the national economy. At the same time, however, when the topic was takeovers, these organizations actively sought protectionist legislation on grounds that it was necessary in order to save jobs and prevent plant closings.

These conflicting positions on the need to regulate against plant closing are easily reconciled by the following observation: senior management may lose its job in a takeover but it encounters no such risk in a plant closing. Accordingly, management may be solicitous of employee concerns in a takeover context, where management jobs are on the line along with those of the corporation's employees, but totally ignore those concerns when management's tenure is not threatened. An incentive structure that provides unbridled, standardless, and effectively unreviewable discretion for boards to form such temporary, convenient, and self-serving loyalties to amorphous and ever-changing constituencies is a prescription for danger.

Put another way, Bill No. 128 may provide boards with a convenient means of promoting their own interests under the guise of serving the interests of some other constituency. By expanding the authority to consider other constituency interests without creating any accountability to those constituencies, Bill No. 128 will only exacerbate this situation and create further opportunities for such conduct.

Another danger of Bill No. 128 is that it will make principled judicial review of board decisions all but impossible. As a practical matter, if Bill No. 128 becomes law, and if it is interpreted to allow boards to abandon the requirement that their decisions be rationally related to stockholder interests, then courts may find it difficult to overturn any board decision, regardless of how arbitrary, capricious, or outrageous that decision may be.

In general, constituency statutes come in two varieties, depending on whether the statute explicitly authorizes directors to subordinate shareholder interests to those of other constituencies. In particular, Indiana, *supra*, and Pennsylvania[58] seem clearly to allow favoring other constituencies at the expense of shareholders. However, the great majority of statutes merely authorize directors to take the interests of other constituencies into account. Left ambiguous is whether these statutes were intended to change existing

---

[58] 15 Pa. Const. Stat. § 1721(e) (1990).

law. There was little doubt under existing law that the board of directors could take the interests of other constituencies into account, but only in determining the long-term interests of shareholders.

The American Bar Association's prestigious Committee on Corporate Laws recently reviewed this issue in the course of its ongoing stewardship over the Revised Model Business Corporations Act.

> The Committee has concluded that permitting -- much less requiring -- directors to consider [constituency] interests without relating such consideration in an appropriate fashion to shareholder welfare (as the Delaware courts have done) would conflict with directors' responsibility to shareholders and could undermine the effectiveness of the system that has made the corporation an efficient device for the creation of jobs and wealth.
>
> The Committee believes that the better interpretation of these statutes, and one that avoids such consequences, is that they confirm what the common law has been: directors may take into account the interests of other constituencies but only as and to the extent that the directors are acting in the best interests, long as well as short term, of the shareholders and the corporation.[59]

The American Law Institute's Corporate Governance Project endorses this interpretation of constituency statutes.[60]

Constituency statutes, like Indiana and Pennsylvania, that authorize directors to favor other constituents even at the expense of shareholders have attracted some academic supporters, who question the premise that increasing shareholder wealth, long-term or otherwise, is the sole function of the corporation.[61] To some extent, this commentary misses the point of the preferential role of shareholders in traditional corporate law. From this perspective, the goal of the corporation is to increase the wealth of all those whose circumstances depend on corporate performance -- corporate stakeholders in current parlance. The central role of shareholders in the traditional corporate structure is purely instrumental: Shareholders have a dominant position not because they are entitled to it in any normative sense, but because assigning them that role results in the greatest wealth creation. Thus, more is necessary to dislodge the shareholder-centered premise of corporate law than identifying other groups whose circumstances are tied to the corporation. One must also persuasively argue that a different configuration of decision-making authority results in greater wealth creation.

---

[59] Committee on Corporate Laws, *Other Constituencies Statutes: Potential for Confusion*, 45 Bus.Law. 2253, 2268-9 (1990).

[60] American Law Institute, *Principles of corporate Governance: Analysis and Recommendations*, Commentary to § 6.02 (1994).

[61] See, e.g., David Millon, *Redefining Corporate Law*, 24 Ind.L.Rev. 223 (1991); Lawrence Mitchell, *A Theoretical and Practical Framework for Enforcing Corporate Constituency Statutes*, 70 Tex.L.Rev. 579 (1992).

This effort, as much one of industrial organization as corporate governance, remains in its infancy.[62]

A practical question also arises with respect to expanding directorial authority to favor stakeholders over shareholders. So long as shareholders elect directors, the discretion of directors to disfavor shareholders ultimately depends on the Berle-Means phenomenon: Dispersed shareholders must be unable to use the electoral mechanism to replace disloyal directors. There is increasing reason to believe that shareholders are no longer so disabled. Suppose the board of directors of an Indiana corporation confronted with a favorable takeover bid declines to redeem its poison pill. The bidder then announces a proxy fight to replace the board of directors. The growing influence of institutional investors may render Indiana statutes toothless in the face of shareholders who can defend their interests through electoral activity rather than through litigation. This phenomenon is considered in Chapter 24, *infra*.

The potential power of institutions to diffuse the impact of state antitakeover statutes was demonstrated by the aftermath of Pennsylvania's adoption of the nation's most draconian antitakeover measures. SB 1310, enacted by the Pennsylvania legislature in early 1990, added a laundry list of antitakeover measures:

- A control share acquisition structure that excludes from the vote all shareholders who acquire their shares after announcement of an intent to acquire control shares.

- A "disgorgement" provision that requires any shareholder who announces an intent to acquire 20% of a corporation's voting shares or otherwise secure control (as through a proxy contest) to return to the corporation profits made on the sale of shares sold within 18 months after the triggering announcement that were acquired within 24 months before or 18 months after the triggering acquisition.[63]

- A severance pay requirement for employees terminated without cause following a shareholder approved control share acquisition.

- A declaration that no business combination transaction shall result in the termination of a collective bargaining agreement.

The statute also provided, however, a 90-day period following enactment during which a company could opt out of the statute's coverage by a board adopted bylaw. In response to a highly publicized effort by large institutions urging publicly traded companies to exercise this option, a

---

[62] See Ronald Gilson & Mark Roe, *Understanding the Japanese Keiretsu: Overlaps Between Corporate Governance and Industrial Organization*, 102 Yale L.J. 871 (1993).

[63] Query whether the Pennsylvania disgorgement provision falls within the internal affairs doctrine that *CTS* and *Amanda* thought provided constitutional shelter for state antitakeover statutes. Traditionally, sale of shares between shareholders was not part of a corporation's internal affairs. Does the preemption issue differ when the relevant federal legislation is the proxy regulation provisions of the Securities Exchange Act of 1934 rather than the tender offer provisions of the Williams Act?

substantial number of Pennsylvania companies chose to forgo the statute's coverage. Of 135 publicly traded Pennsylvania corporations with at least $10 million in market capitalization, 99 opted out of one or more of the statute's provisions.[64] More detailed information is available concerning the 63 Pennsylvania corporations listed on the New York or American Stock Exchanges. Their choices are shown in Table 23-1.

Data concerning the characteristics of those companies who did and did not opt out of some or all of the statute are confusing; they both support and conflict with standard agency accounts. Looking at Pound's sample of larger firms, those that did not opt out were more heavily protected by firm level defenses than firms that did. For example, only 25% of the opt-out firms had poison pill plans in place while 75% of those not opting out had such plans.[65] Consistent with an agency account of opt-out behavior, the market discounted the performance of firms that chose to remain covered by the statute; these firms had lower market valuation ratios measured by price to earnings or price to cash flow. Conversely, non-opt out firms had higher one-year stock returns,[66] and appear no different than opt out firms with respect to long-term accounting or operating performance.

Table 23-1
Opt-out Decisions by Pennsylvania Exchange Listed Corporations

Decision	# of Firms	Percent
Opting our of entire statute	18	28.6
Opting out of control share acquisition and disgorgement provisions[*]	21	33.3
Opting out of disgorgement provision only	3	4.8
Opting out of Control share provision only[*]	1	1.6
Not opting out of any provision	15	23.8
Unknown	5	7.9
Total	**63**	**100.00**

Source: Roberta Romano, *The Genius of American Corporate Law* (1993) (Table 4-2), at 69.

---

[64] John Pound, *On the Motives for Choosing a Corporate Governance Structure: A Study of Corporation Reaction to the Pennsylvania Takeover Law*, 8 J.L.Econ. & Org. 656 (1992).

[65] *Id.* The difference did not extend to other firm level defenses such as shark repellent amendments. Pound treats the difference as suggesting that firms not opting out had a penchant for defenses that did not require shareholder approval.

[66] Pound suggests the higher one-year stock returns may result from takeover speculation in the year preceding the opt-out decision. *Id.* at 669.

A difference does appear, however, with respect to ownership structure. Firms opting out of the statute have inside ownership twice as high as firms that chose to remain covered (13.8% versus 6.9%). However, there was no significant difference in institutional ownership.[67]

E.   The Valuation Consequences of State Takeover Statutes

State takeover statutes provided a wonderful opportunity for abnormal return studies. By measuring the returns to a portfolio of companies subject to a particular state takeover statute over the period of the statute's adoption, the statute's impact on shareholders could be tested: if the portfolio experienced positive abnormal returns, the takeover statute increased shareholder wealth; if the portfolio experienced negative abnormal returns, the takeover statute decreased shareholder wealth.   In practice, the application turned out to be more difficult than might have been expected; interpretive problems raised in Chapter 6 and encountered repeatedly in evaluating the effectiveness of defensive tactics in Chapter 17, made drawing clear conclusions difficult.

Surprisingly, the studies are in conflict over whether state takeover statutes resulted in any significant stock price effect. A number of these studies are summarized in Table 23-2 below.

The researchers differed in their choice of event windows and sample selection, so that the results, while different, are not necessarily comparable. Moreover, precisely because the legislative process does not lend itself to precise event dates -- legislation is often debated before it is formally introduced and may be certain of passage before the vote is taken and the Governor acts -- it is difficult to isolate the impact of the statute. Finally, it is difficult to control for confounding events. State legislation is often enacted in response to a hostile offer for a large local company whose performance may skew the sample.[68]

---

[67] *Id.*

[68] Jonathan Karpoff & Paul Malatesta, *State Takeover Legislation and Share Values: The Wealth Effects of Pennsylvania's Act 36* (Working Paper, Univ. of Wash.Sch. of Bus., June 1994), demonstrates the difficulty of abnormal return analysis of state antitakeover legislation. The authors find that when prior studies are corrected for firm size, non-synchronous trading, and stock return cross-sectional covariances, the evidence of negative returns from the Pennsylvania statute is substantially weakened. However, the authors also find that prior studies missed the date of the first news release concerning the statute. On this date, a sample of publicly traded Pennsylvania companies experienced statistically significant negative abnormal returns of 1.43%.

Table 23-2
Abnormal Return Studies of State Antitakeover Statute Adoption

Study[69]	State	Result
Schumann (1990)	New York	significant negative
Sidak & Woodward (1990)	New York, Indiana	significant negative
Ryngaert & Netter (1988)	Ohio	significant negative
Ryngaert & Netter (1990)	Ohio	significant negative
Romano (1987)	Connecticut Missouri Pennsylvania	no significant effect
Margotta, McWilliams & McWilliams (1990)	Ohio	no significant effect
Pugh & Jahera (1990)	Ohio, Indiana, New York, New Jersey	no significant effect
Jahera & Pugh (1990)	Delaware	positive not significant
Szewczyk & Tsetsekos (1991)	Pennsylvania	significant negative
Karpoff & Malatesta (1990)	Pennsylvania	significant negative

Karpoff and Malatesta (1989)[70] avoided these problems by measuring the announcement effects of all second-generation state takeover statutes enacted before 1988.[71] Over the entire sample, the authors find that

---

[69] Laurence Schumann, *State Regulation of Takeovers and Shareholder Wealth: The Case of New York's 1985 Takeover Statutes*, 19 Rand J.Econ. 557 (1990); J. Gregory Sidak & Susan Woodward, Corporate Takeovers, *The Commerce Clause, and the Efficient Anonymity of Shareholders*, 84 Nw.L.Rev. 1092 (1990); Michael Ryngaert & Jeffry Netter, *Shareholder Wealth Effects of the Ohio Antitakeover Law*, 4 J.L.Econ. & Org. 373 (1988); Michael Ryngaert & Jeffry Netter, *Shareholder Wealth Effects of the 1986 Ohio Antitakeover Law Revisited: Its Real Effects*, 6 J.L.Econ. & Org. 253 (1990); Romano (1987), *supra* note 30; Donald Margotta, Thomas McWilliams & Victoria McWilliams, *An Analysis of the Stock Price Effect of the 1986 Ohio Takeover Legislation*, 6 J.L.Econ. & Org. 235 (1990); Pugh & Jahera, *State Antitakeover Legislation and Shareholder Wealth*, 13 J.Fin.Res. 221 (1990); Jahera & Pugh, *State Takeover Legislation: The Case of Delaware*, 7 J.L.Econ. & Org. 410 (1990); Samuel Szewczyk & George Tsetsekos, *State Intervention in the Market for Corporate Control: The Case of Pennsylvania Senate Bill 1310*, 31 J.Fin.Econ. 3 (1992); Jonathan Karpoff & Paul Malatesta, *PA Law: State Antitakeover Laws and Stock Prices*, 46 Fin.Analysts J. 8 (July-Aug. 1990).

[70] Jonathan Karpoff & Paul Malatesta, *The Wealth Effects of Second-Generation State Takeover Legislation*, 25 J.Fin.Econ. 291 (1989).

[71] Although Delaware's takeover statute was adopted in 1988, it was proposed in 1987 and therefore was included in the sample.

announcement of a state takeover law is associated with a small (0.294%) but statistically significant decrease in shareholder wealth. Note, however, that because the companies in the sample cover 88% of all New York and American Stock Exchange firms, the 0.294% decline represents a loss of approximately $6 billion.

The authors also undertake an interesting cross-sectional analysis. State takeover statutes should have no influence on companies that already have firm level defenses like antitakeover charter amendments and poison pills. In contrast, state statutes serve as a substitute for firm level defenses for companies that have not built their own barriers. To test this hypothesis, the sample was divided into two subsamples: 1107 companies that had neither antitakeover charter amendments nor a poison pill prior to the adoption of a state statute and 368 companies that had firm level defenses. The data supported the hypothesis. The subsample with no firm level defenses experienced a statistically significant announcement period return of -0.388% (compared to -0.294% for the entire sample), while the subsample with prior defenses experienced a return of only -0.126%, which was not statistically significant.[72]

---

[72] This pattern was repeated in response to the 1990 enactment by Pennsylvania of the nation's most extreme antitakeover statute. See Szewczyk & Tsetsekos (1992), *supra* note 69; Karpoff & Malatesta (1994), *supra* note 68.

CHAPTER 24: PROXY FIGHTS AS ALTERNATIVES AND COMPLEMENTS TO TENDER OFFERS

Until 1965 or so, when Henry Manne "invented" the market for corporate control,[1] proxy fights were the principal means for changing control of a public company over the objection of the target's board of directors. A leading early example was the 1956 battle for control of Montgomery Ward, launched by Louis Wolfson to replace the aged CEO of Montgomery Ward, Sewell Avery.[2]

Proxy fights, though, have serious problems that made tender offers seem a better mousetrap. The gains from improved management flow pro rata to all shareholders, so a dissident who mounts a proxy fight will realize only a fraction of the gains from success. The dissident must, however, bear all of the costs of the effort if it loses. This collective action problem is inherent in fractional ownership, absent legal rules -- often proposed but never adopted -- that would require companies to reimburse a losing dissident's expenses.

Moreover, experience taught that proxy fights were hard to win. The managers had large built-in advantages, including the tendency of small shareholders to vote with the incumbent managers. If the dissidents appeared likely to win, the incumbents could sometimes stave off defeat by adopting some of the dissident platform. That was good for the other shareholders, but left the dissident to bear its own expenses. Precisely that result occurred during the Montgomery Ward battle. The incumbent directors quietly let it be known that if they were returned to office, Sewell Avery would soon retire. They won, and he resigned. Proxy fights also don't lend themselves to capturing the synergies, real or imagined, of common ownership, nor the benefits of tax consolidation.

Proxy fights never entirely disappeared. Contests for full or partial control averaged about 20 per year from the 1950s through 1980s with only random year to year variation.[3] But proxy fights occurred mostly at smaller companies. For large companies, the tender offer, or threat thereof, became much the preferred route. Indeed, as debt financing became increasingly available in the 1980s, a dissident who sought to mount a proxy fight faced a further obstacle in winning support. Other shareholders would be prone to tell the dissident: "If you think you can run the company better than the incumbents, put your money where your mouth is by buying my stock."

Several factors combined in the late 1980s and early 1990s to change the relative importance of tender offers and proxy fights as alternate means for changing corporate control. First, in response to a surge in defaults for

---

[1] Henry Manne, *Mergers and the Market for Corporate Control*, 73 J.Pol.Econ. 110 (1965).

[2] See Edmund Stephan, *Highlights of the Montgomery Ward Proxy Contest from a Lawyer's Viewpoint*, 11 Bus.Law. 86 (1955).

[3] See Ronald Schrager, *Corporate Conflicts: Proxy Fights in the 1980s* (Investor Responsibility Research Center 1986).

debt issued in leveraged acquisitions and recapitalizations, lenders tightened their standards. It is now harder to raise the funds needed to buy a target for cash. That difficulty also provides a response to the "put your money where your mouth is" argument. Once again, few people have or can borrow enough money to buy a big company.

Second, the increasing strength of legal obstacles to hostile takeovers, including the possibility that targets can "just say no," makes it essential for a hostile bidder to combine a takeover bid with a proxy fight, or at least make a bid at a time in the year that will let the bidder wage a proxy fight if the target refuses to negotiate. Shareholders who favor the bid are likely to support the bidder in a proxy fight. The target's board, facing this double-barreled threat, may agree to negotiate. If not, the bidder may succeed in kicking out the recalcitrant directors.

The combined proxy fight and tender offer was used successfully in, for example, the $6 billion takeover of NCR by AT&T in 1991 (the largest transaction of 1991), and the $3 billion take over of Great Northern Nekoosa by Georgia-Pacific in 1990. But 1992 was a quiet year for proxy fights, large and small.

A third possible factor is continued growth in the holdings of institutional investors, who now hold over half of all U.S. equities.[4] In theory, that should make it easier for a dissident to solicit favorable votes. Certainly, fewer *shareholders* are needed to form a majority of *shares*. The jury is still out, however, on the ease of persuasion, partly because many institutions are vulnerable to pressure to vote for incumbent managers, even if share price suffers thereby.[5] Perhaps because of such pressure, dissident success rates in proxy fights continue to be relatively low. Dissidents win outright in only about ⅓ of control contests, though they also receive minority representation or other partial success in about another ¼ of contests.[6]

In sum, proxy fights are again an important factor in hostile battles for corporate control, though the absolute number of fights remains small. Two distinct types of proxy fights must be evaluated: the proxy fight as an *adjunct* to a hostile tender offer; and the proxy fight as an *alternative* to a tender offer as a way to replace the target's managers.

As with tender offer defenses, some target directors will go to extraordinary lengths, courts permitting, to maintain their positions. Thus, the courts have had to consider what types of defensive tactics are permissible against a *proxy fight*, as opposed to a *tender offer*. The regulatory action has

---

[4] See Carolyn Brancato & Patrick Gaughan, *Institutional Investors and Capital Markets: 1991 Update* (Colum.L.Sch. Institutional Investor Project Sept. 12, 1991).

[5] Bernard Black, *Shareholder Passivity Reexamined*, 89 Mich.L.Rev. 520, 595-608 (1990), reviews the conflicts of interest faced by different institutions. See also James Heard & Howard Sherman, *Conflicts of Interest in the Proxy Voting System* (Investor Responsibility Research Center 1987).

[6] See Schrager (1986), *supra* note 3; Georgeson & Co., *Proxy Contest Study: October 1984 to September 1990* (Dec.1990); studies collected in Table 22-1, *infra*.

been largely in the courts, but in two recent proxy fights the Massachusetts and Pennsylvania state legislatures amended their corporate laws in midfight, to the (intended) disadvantage of the challenger.

The broad policy question raised by proxy fights is which, if any defensive tactics, should be allowed. To begin with, is there *any* legitimate role for proxy fight defenses? Recall Gilson's argument against tender offer defenses: Shareholders need preserve *some* way to circumvent directors' opposition to an acquisition. That argument also applies to proxy fights in a legal environment where tender offers are difficult to complete over the target's sustained opposition. A proxy fight may be the only way for shareholders to force a change in management, or bless a takeover, when the directors will not.

Doctrinally, one can replay in the proxy area the debate under *Unocal* over whether an all cash bid for all shares is a cognizable threat. Is the risk that the shareholders will vote out the incumbents a cognizable threat that justifies a defensive response? If so, how much of a threat does a proxy fight pose, for purposes of the *Unocal* requirement that the response be reasonable in relation to the threat posed?

If some defensive tactics are permissible in response to proxy fights, which ones, and by what standard(s) should their validity be judged? Should the limits on defensive tactics be stricter for a stand-alone proxy fight than for a combined proxy fight and tender offer? How is the boundary between stand-alone proxy fights and combined proxy fights and takeover bids to be policed? Suppose the proxy challenger is a frequent acquirer who denies having any present intention to make a tender offer (although things could always change). Which rules apply?

Should fewer defenses be permitted when a dissident seeks only minority representation on a company's board than when a dissident seeks control? For the many companies with staggered boards, only minority representation is available in a single campaign. A *Unocal* analysis -- balancing the threat to the corporation against the strength of the defense -- would suggest that target efforts to defeat bids for minority representation should be more narrowly circumscribed than efforts to defeat bids for majority control. Yet, as discussed below, this is not the way that the Delaware courts have thus far gone.

This chapter first reviews the empirical evidence on the value of proxy fights and the frequency of dissident success. We then canvass the array of proxy fight defenses, and the judicial and legislative responses to those defenses.[7]

---

[7] See generally Black (1990), *supra* note 5 (from which portions of this chapter are adapted); Randall Thomas, *Judicial Review of Defensive Tactics in Proxy Contests: When is Using a Rights Plan Right?* (working paper 1992); Norman Veasey, Gregory Varallo & Frederick Cottrell, *Delaware Developments in Proxy Contests*, Bank & Corp. Governance L.Rep. 1131 (1991); Irwin Warren & Kevin Abrams, *Evolving Standards of Judicial Review of Procedural Defenses in Proxy Contests*, 47 Bus.Law. 647 (1992); Note, *A Problem of Mixed*

A. The Empirical Evidence on the Value of Proxy Fights

The evidence on the value of takeovers to target shareholders should, for the most part, carry over to proxy contests conducted *as adjuncts to takeover bids*. One difference between takeovers without proxy fights and takeovers with an accompanying proxy fight involves the length of time needed to conduct a proxy fight. There is ample opportunity for a higher bidder to emerge, sometimes because management is looking for a white knight, and sometimes on its own. This may affect the takeover price, and the division of any gains between acquirer and target.

On average, as one might expect, proxy fights are targeted at poorly performing firms. Ikenberry & Lakonishok report that proxy fight targets earn negative CARs averaging −33.8% (significant at 99% confidence level), between 48 and 4 months preceding the contest announcement.[8] Accounting evidence confirms that proxy fight targets are poor performers. For example, during the 3 years preceding the contest, targets suffer a statistically significant decline in EBITD (earnings before interest, taxes, and depreciation) of 38% compared to a control sample matched by industry and size.[9]

Target shareholders earn positive abnormal returns when a proxy contest is *announced*. Table 22-1 collects the available studies. The last column shows, for those contests where dissidents sought majority control of the board, the percentage of contests where the dissidents won majority control, and the percentage where the dissidents obtained some board representation but not majority control.[10] The event window is measured relative to the date when the Wall Street Journal first reports the contest.

Motives: Applying Unocal to Defensive ESOPS, 92 Colum.L.Rev. 851 (1992); Note, *The Case for Heightened Scrutiny in Defense of the Shareholders' Franchise Right*, 44 Stan.L.Rev. 129 (1991).

This chapter focuses on the defensive tactics available to incumbent directors. But difficult questions can arise for dissidents as well. Suppose that a takeover bidder, having mounted a combined proxy fight/tender offer, wins at the polls. Do the bidder's nominees now have a fiduciary duty to the target's shareholders to negotiate (with the bidder) for a higher price? To seek out competing bids? See John Olson, *The Fiduciary Duties of Insurgent Boards*, 47 Bus.Law. 1011 (1992).

[8] David Ikenberry & Josef Lakonishok, *Corporate Governance Through the Proxy Contest: Evidence and Implications*, 66 J.Bus. 405 (1993).

[9] *Id.*

[10] Dissidents don't seek majority control in all proxy contests, often because they are precluded from doing so by a staggered board. When they seek control, they sometimes obtain control, sometimes obtain representation but not control, and sometimes win no seats. In Table 22-1, dissident success rates at obtaining *control* are computed as a fraction of the contests where the dissidents sought majority control; dissident success rates at obtaining *representation* are computed as a fraction of *all* contests.

Table 22-1
Target Returns When Proxy Fights are Announced[11]
(z-statistic or confidence level in parentheses)

Study	Sample Period	Sample Size	Event Window	Average CAR	Percent Dissident Success
Borstadt & Zwirlein (1992)	1962-86	142	(−60, resolution)	11.4% ($z = 5.83$)	34% control;
DeAngelo & DeAngelo (1989)	1978-85	60	(−1,0)	4.85% ($z = 10.83$)	38% control; 62% representation
Ikenberry & Lakonishok (1993)	1968-87	97	month 0	4.3% (99% confid.)	52% representation
Dodd & Warner (1983)	1962-78	96	(−60,0)	11.9% ($z = 5.09$)	25% control; 58% representation
Mulherin & Poulsen (1992)	1979-89	187	(−20,+5)	8.4% ($z = 10.52$)	56% representation

While shareholders treat proxy fight announcements as good news, event studies don't tell us where the value increase comes from. Efforts to understand the source of the stock price gains are complicated by a combination of many possible outcomes, limited sample sizes, and the need for long event windows to capture the resolution of the proxy fight, which reduces the power of statistical tests, and the various post-resolution outcomes. To name only some of the overlapping possibilities:

(i) the contest can be for all seats, some seats, or no seats;

(ii) the dissidents can gain control, gain some board seats but not control; or gain no board seats;

(iii) the proxy fight can be accompanied by a takeover bid or not;

(iv) a takeover can take place after the contest (say within 2 years) or not; and

(v) if no takeover takes place, the CEO can remain or be replaced.

The inference from the positive announcement period returns that proxy fights increase firm value is further complicated by evidence that shareholders are too optimistic when a proxy fight is announced, and that some of the shareholder market value gains are erased by the time the proxy fight is completed and the outcome is known. Table 22-2 collects studies of target CARs between the announcement date (denoted *AD*) and the day when the contest outcome is known (denoted *RD* for "resolution date").

---

[11] The studies reported in the table are: Lisa Borstadt & Thomas Zwirlein, *The Efficient Monitoring Role of Proxy Contests: An Empirical Analysis of Post-Contest Control Changes and Firm Performance*, Fin.Mgmt. 22 (Autumn 1992); Peter Dodd & Jerold Warner, *On Corporate Governance: A Study of Proxy Contests*, 11 J.Fin.Econ. 401 (1983); Harry & Linda DeAngelo, *Proxy Contests and the Governance of Publicly Held Corporations*, 23 J.Fin.Econ. 29 (1989); Ikenberry & Lakonishok (1993), *supra* note 8; J. Harold Mulherin & Annette Poulsen, *Proxy Contests, Shareholder Wealth and Operating Performance: An Analysis of the 1980s* (working paper 1994).

Table 22-2
Target Returns Between Proxy Fight Announcement and Resolution
(*z*-statistics in parentheses, where available)

Study	Sample Period	Sample Size	Event Window	Average Target CAR
DeAngelo & DeAngelo (1989)	1978-85	60	(AD+1, RD)	−12.8% (n.a.)
Dodd & Warner (1983)	1962-78	96	(AD+1, RD)	−4.3% ($z = -2.63$)
Ikenberry & Lakonishok (1993)[12]	1968-87	97	(month +1, month +4)	−5.3% (not signif.)
Mulherin & Poulsen (1992)	1979-89	187	(+6, RD)	−4.6% ($z = -1.67$)

The puzzle of negative drift between announcement and resolution is only deepened by evidence of further negative long-term drift after the proxy contest is completed. Table 22-3 collects the available studies of post-resolution target performance. These results do not appear to result from model misspecification. Ikenberry & Lakonishok uses several different asset pricing models, in an effort to control for the sensitivity of long-term returns to model specification, and find consistent results across different models. Nor does it appear that investors have learned the error of their ways. The announcement period gains are similar in early and more recent studies, and the negative drift persists in the more recent sample (1979-1989) used by Mulherin & Poulsen.

Table 22-3
Long-Term Returns to Proxy Fight Targets
(*z*-statistic or confidence level in parentheses, where available)

Study	Sample Period	Sample Size	Event Window	Average Target CAR
Borstadt & Zwirlein (1992)	1962-86	142	(month+1, month +24)	−7.4% ($z = -1.20$)
Ikenberry & Lakonishok (1993)	1968-87	97	(month +5, month +24)	−17.2% (95% confid.)
Mulherin & Poulsen (1992)	1979-89	187	(RD+1 day, RD + 1 year)	−4.0% ($z = -1.98$)

---

[12] Ikenberry & Lakonishok do not report resolution dates in their study. We chose their (+1 month, +4 months) window period (with the announcement month as month 0) as the most likely to approximate the time period between proxy fight announcement and resolution.

A natural question is whether the negative drift, both from announcement to resolution, and post-resolution, is concentrated in particular subsamples. Mulherin & Poulsen subdivide their sample into proxy fights where the target faces an accompanying takeover bid (either a preexisting bid or a bid made concurrent with the proxy fight announcement), and proxy fights with no accompanying takeover bid. They find reversal of the announcement gains only in their *no-accompanying-bid* subsample.

Within their *accompanying-bid* subsample, Mulherin & Poulsen find that firms that are subsequently acquired realize further gains after the proxy fight is announced, while firms that are not acquired suffer stock price losses, but the average return is near zero. This suggests that the dominant source of gains for this subsample is the prospect of a subsequent takeover. When the takeover fails, the target's stock drops, much as for takeover bids without an accompanying proxy fight.[13]

Another way to partition a proxy fight sample is by who wins. Surprisingly, post-resolution stock price losses occur only *when the dissidents win*! A similar pattern appears, though too weakly to be statistically significant, in the period from announcement to resolution. Table 22-4 shows the differences in post-resolution returns depending on who wins the proxy fight.

Table 22-4
Long-Term Returns to Proxy Fight Targets, Partitioned by Who Wins
(subsample size and *z*-statistic or confidence level in parentheses, if available)[14]

Study	Average Target CAR			
	Dissidents Win No Seats	Dissidents Win One or More Seats	Dissidents Win Control	Dissidents Don't Win Control
Borstadt & Zwirlein (1992)			−22.8% ($n = 320$) ($z = -2.23$)	−2.9% ($n = 110$) (not signif.)
Ikenberry & Lakonishok (1993)	−3.9% ($n = 45$) (not signif.)	−28.6% ($n = 50$) (99% confid.)	−41.6% ($n = 20$) (99% confid.)	
Mulherin & Poulsen (1992)[15]	1.2% ($n = 48$) ($z = -0.60$)	−13.6% ($n = 58$) ($z = -2.95$)		

---

[13] This is consistent with earlier evidence developed by DeAngelo & DeAngelo (1989), *supra* note 11, that proxy fight gains are concentrated in transactions where the proxy fight leads either to a takeover or to management turnover.

[14] The sample period and window period for each study is shown in Table 22-3.

[15] The results reported in the table are for Mulherin & Poulsen's *no-accompanying-takeover-bid* subsample. The authors do not partition their full sample based on dissident success.

The losses when dissidents win seats, in turn, are concentrated in those transactions where there is no subsequent takeover. A plausible explanation is that when the dissidents win, and find that they can engineer a successful turnaround, they are more likely to buy the target, to keep more of the gains for themselves. In contrast, if the target's prospects look doubtful, the dissidents won't buy any more shares.

An admittedly extreme case study illustrates this. In 1987, Elias Zinn and Victor Palmieri bought a toehold stake in Crazy Eddie, a consumer electronics discounter, and made a takeover bid for the whole company. After failing to receive satisfactory financial information from Crazy Eddie, they withdrew the takeover bid and launched a proxy fight instead. After winning control, they discovered that former management had cooked the books to the tune of about $50 million in missing inventory. Needless to say, Zinn and Palmieri decided not to acquire the rest of Crazy Eddie.[16]

The puzzle of weaker performance when dissidents win seats is present in the accounting data as well. It should come as no surprise that dissidents win seats when the target exhibits poor industry-adjusted performance in the pre-contest period. The target's poor performance is presumably what motivates shareholders to vote for the dissidents. Poor industry-adjusted performance persists, though, after the contest. For example, Mulherin & Poulsen report a 38% decline in EBIT from year -1 to $+3$ when dissidents win seats, for their no-accompanying-bid subsample.[17] And Ikenberry & Lakonishok report a 79% decline in EBITD from year 0 to year 5 when dissidents win seats. These results are either statistically insignificant or marginally significant, but the raw numbers are striking nonetheless.[18] Apparently, the dissidents aren't able to fix whatever ails the target.

Some of the post-fight decline in income may reflect a lag between when business problems appear and when they fully impact accounting income. Some may reflect survival bias, because dissidents are more likely to acquire firms whose performance improves. Some may reflect a greater incidence of divestitures when dissidents win seats -- Mulherin & Poulsen report only a 15% drop in operating income as a percentage of assets, compared to a 38% drop in raw operating income. But the accounting data may also explain the poor stock price performance of targets where dissidents win seats: At the time of the proxy fight, shareholders may expect more of the dissidents than they can deliver.

A third way to partition the data is by whether the CEO is replaced. Even though the incumbents retain control in most proxy fights, CEO turnover is more the norm than the exception. For example, Harry and Linda DeAngelo report that about 1/3 of the cases where incumbents retain control

---

[16] See, e.g., *SEC Charges Antar with Stock Manipulation*, Discount Store News, Sept. 25, 1989, at 5; Todd Vogel, *The Net Drops on Crazy Eddie*, Bus.Wk., Nov. 2, 1987, at 62. We thank Harold Mulherin for this anecdote.

[17] Mulherin & Poulsen (1994), *supra* note 11,

[18] Ikenberry & Lakonishok (1993), *supra* note 8.

are followed by sale of the target, and another 1/3 by resignation of the target's CEO, within three years after the proxy fight.[19]   Apparently, the proxy fight is a catalyst for internal change, perhaps because the board wants to avoid a repeat proxy fight a year or two hence. Unfortunately, the effort to estimate the effects of CEO turnover is complicated by the overlap between turnover without a takeover and turnover as an incident to a takeover. Mulherin & Poulsen find higher stock price returns when the CEO is replaced, but the differences are statistically significant only for their full sample, and not for their no-accompanying-bid subsample. Ikenberry & Lakonishok find higher returns when the CEO is replaced only when the dissidents win at least one seat, but they do not control for whether the CEO turnover accompanies a takeover.

Even if CEO replacement correlates with higher returns, that doesn't mean that dissidents should always try to replace the CEO. Proxy fight targets underperform their industry peers for several years preceding the contest, which suggests bad management. But sometimes, the problems may be unfixable. If so, there is no point in disrupting the firm by installing a new CEO. Such firms will suffer stock price losses as the news about their dire straits comes out, but replacing the CEO wouldn't have helped.

How might we untangle the surprising results discussed above, and determine whether (and when) proxy fights are good news for shareholders? There is no obvious explanation for the connection between dissident success and post-announcement losses. Nonetheless, it seems critical to distinguish (as only Mulherin & Poulsen do) between proxy fights with and without an accompanying takeover bid. When a takeover bid that accompanies a proxy fight fails, the target's stock price will drop, just as for failed takeover bids not accompanied by a proxy fight. It seems misleading to infer causation between the price drop and the proxy fight. In these situations, the takeover is the dog, and the proxy fight is the tail. The stock price drop when the takeover bid fails tells us very little about the effect of the proxy fight tail on shareholder wealth. A further important step, not taken by Mulherin & Poulsen, would be to further subdivide their no-accompanying-bid subsample into transactions with and without a subsequent takeover.

We must also be sensitive to the problems with inferring *causation* just because one observes *correlation* between an observable event, like a subsequent takeover or CEO change, and stock price returns. Often, the parties making the observable decision will have private information that is only gradually released into the market, partly by the announcement, or lack thereof, of a takeover or CEO change. Targets that are subsequently taken over may outperform targets that are not taken over, for reasons *independent* of the takeover. Similarly, targets where the CEO is not replaced may do worse than other targets for reasons independent of the CEO change, and

---

[19] DeAngelo & DeAngelo (1989), *supra* note 11.

targets where dissidents win seats may underperform other targets for reasons unrelated to the dissidents' actions after they win.

If the gains to target shareholders from proxy fights remain uncertain, the costs to incumbent managers are all to clear. We turn in the remainder of this chapter to consideration of the variety of tactics that incumbents use to try to retain their positions, and the judicial and legislative response.

B. Defensive Tactics I: Manipulating the Election Machinery

Corporate incumbents have substantial control over the technical details of proxy contests. For example, state corporate law and typical charter and bylaw provisions give incumbent directors substantial ability to delay or accelerate the shareholder meeting date, and the record date that establishes which shareholders are entitled to vote, fill vacancies on the board, establish advance notice provisions for director nominations or other shareholder proposals, etc.

The incumbents will often use this power to their own tactical advantage in a proxy contest. Courts must then decide which tactics to permit. The next case represents the high water mark of judicial willingness to limit the discretion of incumbent directors to manipulate the election machinery in the middle of a proxy contest.

BLASIUS INDUSTRIES v. ATLAS CORP.
564 A.2d 651 (Del.Ch.1988)

ALLEN, Chancellor. Two cases pitting the directors of Atlas Corporation against that company's largest (9.1%) shareholder, Blasius Industries, have been consolidated and tried together. Together, these cases ultimately require the court to determine who is entitled to sit on Atlas' board of directors. Each, however, presents discrete and important legal issues.

The first of the cases was filed on December 30, 1987. As amended, it challenges the validity of board action taken at a telephone meeting of December 31, 1987, that added two new members to Atlas' seven member board. That action was taken as an immediate response to the delivery to Atlas by Blasius the previous day of a form of stockholder consent that, if joined in by holders of a majority of Atlas' stock, would have increased the board of Atlas from seven to fifteen members and would have elected eight new members nominated by Blasius.

As I find the facts of this first case, they present the question whether a board acts consistently with its fiduciary duty when it acts, in good faith and with appropriate care, for the primary purpose of preventing or impeding an unaffiliated majority of shareholders from expanding the board and electing a new majority. For the reasons that follow, I conclude that, even though defendants here acted on their view of the corporation's interest and not selfishly, their December 31 action constituted an offense to the relationship between corporate directors and shareholders that has traditionally been protected in courts of equity. As a consequence, I conclude that the board action taken on December 31 was invalid and must be voided. . . .

I

Blasius Acquires a 9% Stake in Atlas.

Blasius is a new stockholder of Atlas. It began to accumulate Atlas shares for the first time in July, 1987. On October 29, it filed a Schedule 13D with the Securities Exchange Commission disclosing that, with affiliates, it then owed 9.1% of Atlas' common stock. It stated in that filing that it intended to encourage management of Atlas to consider a restructuring of the Company or other transaction to enhance shareholder values. It also disclosed that Blasius was exploring the feasibility of obtaining control of Atlas, including instituting a tender offer or seeking "appropriate" representation on the Atlas board of directors.

Blasius has recently come under the control of two individuals, Michael Lubin and Warren Delano, who after experience in the commercial banking industry, had, for a short time, run a venture capital operation for a small investment banking firm. Now on their own, they apparently came to control Blasius with the assistance of Drexel Burnham's well noted junk bond mechanism. Since then, they have made several attempts to effect leveraged buyouts, but without success. . . .

The prospect of Messrs. Lubin and Delano involving themselves in Atlas' affairs was not a development welcomed by Atlas' management. Atlas had a new CEO, defendant Weaver, who had, over the course of the past year or so, overseen a business restructuring of a sort. Atlas had sold three of its five divisions. It had just announced (September 1, 1987) that it would close its once important domestic uranium operation. The goal was to focus the Company on its gold mining business. By October, 1987, the structural changes to do this had been largely accomplished. Mr. Weaver was perhaps thinking that the restructuring that had occurred should be given a chance to produce benefit before another restructuring (such as Blasius had alluded to in its Schedule 13D filing) was attempted, when he wrote in his diary on October 30, 1987:

> 13D by Delano & Lubin came in today. Had long conversation w/MAH & Mark Golden [of Goldman Sachs] on issue. All agree we must dilute these people down by the acquisition of another Co. w/stock, or merger or something else.

The Blasius Proposal of a Leveraged Recapitalization or Sale.

Immediately after filing its 13D on October 29, Blasius' representatives sought a meeting with the Atlas management. Atlas dragged its feet. A meeting was arranged for December 2, 1987 following the regular meeting of the Atlas board. . . .

At that meeting, Messrs. Lubin and Delano suggested that Atlas engage in a leveraged restructuring and distribute cash to shareholders. In such a transaction, which is by this date a commonplace form of transaction, a corporation typically raises cash by sale of assets and significant borrowings and makes a large one time cash distribution to shareholders. The shareholders are typically left with cash and an equity interest in a smaller, more highly leveraged enterprise. Lubin and Delano gave the outline of a leveraged recapitalization for Atlas as they saw it.

Immediately following the meeting, the Atlas representatives expressed among themselves an initial reaction that the proposal was infeasible. On December 7, Mr. Lubin sent a letter detailing the proposal. In general, it proposed the following: (1) an initial special cash dividend to Atlas' stockholders in an aggregate amount equal to (a) $35 million, (b) the aggregate proceeds to Atlas from the exercise of option warrants and stock options, and (c) the proceeds from the sale or disposal of all of Atlas' operations that are not related to its continuing minerals operations; and (2) a special non-cash dividend to Atlas' stockholders of an aggregate $125 million principal amount of 7% Secured Subordinated Gold-Indexed Debentures. . . .

The proposal met with a cool reception from management. On December 9, Mr. Weaver issued a press release expressing surprise that Blasius would suggest using debt to accomplish what he characterized as a substantial liquidation of Atlas at a time when Atlas' future prospects were promising. He noted that the Blasius proposal recommended that Atlas incur a high debt burden in order to pay a substantial one time dividend consisting of $35 million in cash and $125 million in subordinated debentures. Mr. Weaver also questioned the wisdom of incurring an enormous debt burden amidst the uncertainty in the financial markets that existed in the aftermath of the October crash.

Blasius attempted on December 14 and December 22 to arrange a further meeting with the Atlas management without success. During this period, Atlas provided Goldman Sachs with projections for the Company. Lubin was told that a further meeting would await completion of Goldman's analysis. A meeting after the first of the year was proposed.

The Delivery of Blasius' Consent Statement.

On December 30, 1987, Blasius caused Cede & Co. (the registered owner of its Atlas stock) to deliver to Atlas a signed written consent (1) adopting a precatory resolution recommending that the board develop and implement a restructuring proposal, (2) amending the Atlas bylaws to, among other things, expand the size of the board from seven to fifteen members -- the maximum number under Atlas' charter, and (3) electing eight named persons to fill the new directorships. . . .

The reaction was immediate. Mr. Weaver conferred with Mr. Masinter, the Company's outside counsel and a director, who viewed the consent as an attempt to take control of the Company. They decided to call an emergency meeting of the board, even though a regularly scheduled meeting was to occur only one week hence, on January 6, 1988. The point of the emergency meeting was to act on their conclusion (or to seek to have the board act on their conclusion) "that we should add at least one and probably two directors to the board. . . ." A quorum of directors, however, could not be arranged for a telephone meeting that day. A telephone meeting was held the next day. At that meeting, the board voted to amend the bylaws to increase the size of the board from seven to nine and appointed John M. Devaney and Harry J. Winters, Jr. to fill those newly created positions. Atlas' Certificate of Incorporation creates staggered terms for directors; the terms to which Messrs. Devaney and Winters were appointed would expire in 1988 and 1990, respectively.

The Motivation of the Incumbent Board in Expanding the Board and Appointing New Members.

In increasing the size of Atlas' board by two and filling the newly created positions, the members of the board realized that they were thereby precluding the holders of a majority of the Company's shares from placing a majority of new directors on the board through Blasius' consent solicitation, should they want to do so. Indeed the evidence establishes that was the principal motivation in so acting.

The conclusion that, in creating two new board positions on December 31 and electing Messrs. Devaney and Winters to fill those positions the board was principally motivated to prevent or delay the shareholders from possibly placing a majority of new members on the board, is critical to my analysis . . . . If the board in fact was not so motivated, but rather had taken action completely independently of the consent solicitation, which merely had an incidental impact upon the possible effectuation of any action authorized by the shareholders, it is very unlikely that such action would be subject to judicial nullification. See, e.g., Frantz Manufacturing Co. v. EAC Industries, 501 A.2d 401, 407 (Del.1985); Moran v. Household International, 490 A.2d 1059, 1080 (Del.Ch.), aff'd, 500 A.2d 1346 (Del.1985). The board, as a general matter, is under no fiduciary obligation to suspend its active management of the firm while the consent solicitation process goes forward.

. . .

As noted above, on the 30th, Atlas received the Blasius consent which proposed to shareholders that they expand the board from seven to fifteen and add eight new members identified in the consent. It also proposed the adoption of a precatory resolution encouraging restructuring or sale of the Company. Mr. Weaver immediately met with Mr. Masinter. In addition to receiving the consent, Atlas was informed it had been sued in this court, but it did not yet know the thrust of that action. At that time, Messrs. Weaver and Masinter "discussed a lot of [reactive] strategies and Edgar [Masinter] told me we really got to put a program together to go forward with this consent . . . . [W]e talked about taking no action. We talked about adding one board member. We talked about adding two board members. We talked about adding eight board members. And we did a lot of looking at other and various and sundry alternatives. . . ."

They decided to add two board members and to hold an emergency board meeting that very day to do so. It is clear that the reason that Mr. Masinter advised taking this step immediately rather than waiting for the January 6 meeting was that he feared that the Court of Chancery might issue a temporary restraining order prohibiting the board from increasing its membership, since the consent solicitation had commenced. It is admitted that there was no fear that Blasius would be in a position to complete a public solicitation for consents prior to the January 6 board meeting.

In this setting, I conclude that, while the addition of these qualified men would, under other circumstances, be clearly appropriate as an independent step, such a step was in fact taken in order to impede or preclude a majority of the shareholders from effectively adopting the course proposed by Blasius.

. . .

The January 6 Rejection of the Blasius Proposal.

On January 6, the board convened for its scheduled meeting. At that time, it heard a full report from its financial advisor concerning the feasibility of the Blasius restructuring proposal. The Goldman Sachs presentation included a summary of five year cumulative cash flows measured against a base case and the Blasius proposal, an analysis of Atlas' debt repayment capacity under the Blasius proposal, and pro forma income and cash flow statements for a base case and the Blasius proposal, assuming prices of $375, $475 and $575 per ounce of gold.

After completing that presentation, Goldman Sachs concluded with its view that if Atlas implemented the Blasius restructuring proposal (i) a severe drain on operating cash flow would result, (ii) Atlas would be unable to service its long-term debt and could end up in bankruptcy, (iii) the common stock of Atlas would have little or no value, and (iv) since Atlas would be unable to generate sufficient cash to service its debt, the debentures contemplated to be issued in the proposed restructuring could have a value of only 20% to 30% of their face amount. . . . The board then voted to reject the Blasius proposal. . . .

II

Plaintiff attacks the December 31 board action as a selfishly motivated effort to protect the incumbent board from a perceived threat to its control of Atlas. Their conduct is said to constitute a violation of the principle, applied in such cases as Schnell v. Chris Craft Industries, 285 A.2d 437 (Del.1971), that directors hold legal powers subjected to a supervening duty to exercise such powers in good faith pursuit of what they reasonably believe to be in the corporation's interest. . . .

Defendants, of course, contest every aspect of plaintiffs' claims. They claim the formidable protections of the business judgment rule. See, e.g., Aronson v. Lewis, 473 A.2d 805 (Del.1983); Grobow v. Perot, 539 A.2d 180 (Del.1988).

They say that, in creating two new board positions and filling them on December 31, they acted without a conflicting interest (since the Blasius proposal did not, in any event, challenge their places on the board), they acted with due care (since they well knew the persons they put on the board and did not thereby preclude later consideration of the recapitalization), and they acted in good faith (since they were motivated, they say, to protect the shareholders from the threat of having an impractical, indeed a dangerous, recapitalization program foisted upon them). Accordingly, defendants assert there is no basis to conclude that their December 31 action constituted any violation of the duty of the fidelity that a director owes by reason of his office to the corporation and its shareholders.

Moreover, defendants say that their action was fair, measured and appropriate, in light of the circumstances. Therefore, even should the court conclude that some level of substantive review of it is appropriate under a legal test of fairness, or under the intermediate level of review authorized by Unocal Corp. v. Mesa Petroleum Co., 493 A.2d 946 (Del.1985), defendants assert that the board's decision must be sustained as valid in both law and equity.

III

One of the principal thrusts of plaintiffs' argument is that, in acting to appoint two additional persons of their own selection, including an officer of the Company, to the board, defendants were motivated not by any view that Atlas' interest (or those of its shareholders) required that action, but rather they were motivated improperly, by selfish concern to maintain their collective control over the Company. That is, plaintiffs say that the evidence shows there was no policy dispute or issue that really motivated this action, but that asserted policy differences were pretexts for entrenchment for selfish reasons. If this were found to be factually true, one would not need to inquire further. The action taken would constitute a breach of duty. Schnell v. Chris Craft Industries, 285 A.2d 437 (Del.1971); Guiricich v. Emtrol Corp., 449 A.2d 232 (Del.1982). . . .

On balance, I cannot conclude that the board was acting out of a self-interested motive in any important respect on December 31. I conclude rather that the board saw the "threat" of the Blasius recapitalization proposal as posing vital policy differences between itself and Blasius. It acted, I conclude, in a good faith effort to protect its incumbency, not selfishly, but in order to thwart implementation of the recapitalization that it feared, reasonably, would cause great injury to the Company.

The real question the case presents, to my mind, is whether, in these circumstances, the board, even if it is acting with subjective good faith (which will typically, if not always, be a contestable or debatable judicial conclusion), may validly act for the principal purpose of preventing the shareholders from electing a majority of new directors. The question thus posed is not one of intentional wrong (or even negligence), but one of authority as between the fiduciary and the beneficiary (not simply legal authority, *i.e.*, as between the fiduciary and the world at large).

IV

It is established in our law that a board may take certain steps -- such as the purchase by the corporation of its own stock -- that have the effect of defeating a threatened change in corporate control, when those steps are taken advisedly, in good faith pursuit of a corporate interest, and are reasonable in relation to a threat to legitimate corporate interests posed by the proposed change in control. See Unocal Corp. v. Mesa Petroleum Co., 493 A.2d 946 (Del.1985); Kors v. Carey, 158 A.2d 136 (Del.Ch.1960); Cheff v. Mathes, 199 A.2d 548 (Del.1964). Does this rule -- that the reasonable exercise of good faith and due care generally validates, in equity, the exercise of legal authority even if the act has an entrenchment effect -- apply to action designed for the primary purpose of interfering with the effectiveness of a stockholder vote? Our authorities, as well as sound principles, suggest that the central importance of the franchise to the scheme of corporate governance, requires that, in this setting, that rule not be applied and that closer scrutiny be accorded to such transaction.

1. *Why the deferential business judgment rule does not apply to board acts taken for the primary purpose of interfering with a stockholder's vote, even if taken advisedly and in good faith.*

A. *The question of legitimacy.*

The shareholder franchise is the ideological underpinning upon which the legitimacy of directorial power rests. Generally, shareholders have only two protections against perceived inadequate business performance. They may sell their stock (which, if done in sufficient numbers, may so affect security prices as to create an incentive for altered managerial performance), or they may vote to replace incumbent board members.

It has, for a long time, been conventional to dismiss the stockholder vote as a vestige or ritual of little practical importance. It may be that we are now witnessing the emergence of new institutional voices and arrangements that will make the stockholder vote a less predictable affair than it has been. Be that as it may, however, whether the vote is seen functionally as an unimportant formalism, or as an important tool of discipline, it is clear that it is critical to the theory that legitimates the exercise of power by some (directors and officers) over vast aggregations of property that they do not own. Thus, when viewed from a broad, institutional perspective, it can be seen that matters involving the integrity of the shareholder voting process involve consideration not present in any other context in which directors exercise delegated power.

B. *Questions of this type raise issues of the allocation of authority as between the board and the shareholders.*

The distinctive nature of the shareholder franchise context also appears when the matter is viewed from a less generalized, doctrinal point of view. From this point of view, as well, it appears that the ordinary considerations to which the business judgment rule originally responded are simply not present in the shareholder voting context.[2] That is, a decision by the board to act for the primary purpose of preventing the effectiveness of a shareholder vote inevitably involves the question who, as between the principal and the agent, has authority with respect to a matter of internal corporate governance. That, of course, is true in a very specific way in this case which deals with

---

[2] Delaware courts have long exercised a most sensitive and protective regard for the free and effective exercise of voting rights. This concern suffuses our law, manifesting itself in various settings. For example, the perceived importance of the franchise explains the cases that hold that a director's fiduciary duty requires disclosure to shareholders asked to authorize a transaction of all material information in the corporation's possession, even if the transaction is not a self-dealing one. See, e.g., Smith v. Van Gorkom, 488 A.2d 858 (Del.1985); In re Anderson Clayton Shareholders' Litigation, 519 A.2d 669, 675 (Del.Ch.1986).

A similar concern, for credible corporate democracy, underlies those cases that strike down board action that sets or moves an annual meeting date upon a finding that such action was intended to thwart a shareholder group from effectively mounting an election campaign. See, e.g., Schnell v. Chris Craft Indus., 285 A.2d 437 (Del.1971); Lerman v. Diagnostic Data, Inc., 421 A.2d 906 (Del.Ch.1980); Aprahamian v. HBO & Co., 531 A.2d 1204 (Del.Ch.1987).

The cases invalidating stock issued for the primary purpose of diluting the voting power of a control block also reflect the law's concern that a credible form of corporate democracy be maintained. See Canada S. Oils, Ltd. v. Manabi Exploration Co., 96 A.2d 810 (Del.Ch.1953); Condec Corp. v. Lunkenheimer Co., 230 A.2d 769 (Del.Ch.1967).

Similarly, a concern for corporate democracy is reflected (1) in our statutory requirement of annual meetings (Del.C. § 211), and in the cases that aggressively and summarily enforce that right. See, e.g., Coaxial Communications v. CNA Fin. Corp., 367 A.2d 994 (Del.1976); Speiser v. Baker, 525 A.2d 1001 (Del.Ch.1987), and (2) in our consent statute (Del.C. § 228) and the interpretation it has been accorded. See Datapoint Corp. v. Plaza Securities Co., 496 A.2d 1031 (Del.1985) (order); Allen v. Prime Computer, Inc., 538 A.2d 1113 (Del.1988); Frantz Mfg. Co. v. EAC Indus., 501 A.2d 401 (Del.1985).

the question who should constitute the board of directors of the corporation, but it will be true in every instance in which an incumbent board seeks to thwart a shareholder majority. A board's decision to act to prevent the shareholders from creating a majority of new board positions and filling them does not involve the exercise of the corporation's power over its property, or with respect to its rights or obligations; rather, it involves allocation, between shareholders as a class and the board, of effective power with respect to governance of the corporation. This need not be the case with respect to other forms of corporate action that may have an entrenchment effect -- such as the stock buybacks present in *Unocal, Cheff* or Kors v. Carey. Action designed principally to interfere with the effectiveness of a vote inevitably involves a conflict between the board and a shareholder majority. Judicial review of such action involves a determination of the legal and equitable obligations of an agent towards his principal. This is not, in my opinion, a question that a court may leave to the agent finally to decide so long as he does so honestly and competently; that is, it may not be left to the agent's business judgment.

2. *What rule does apply: per se invalidity of corporate acts intended primarily to thwart effective exercise of the franchise or is there an intermediate standard?*

Plaintiff argues for a rule of *per se* invalidity once a plaintiff has established that a board has acted for the primary purpose of thwarting the exercise of a shareholder vote. Our opinions in Canada Southern Oils, Ltd. v. Manabi Exploration Co., 96 A.2d 810 (Del.Ch.1953) and Condec Corp. v. Lunkenheimer Co., 230 A.2d 769 (Del.Ch.1967) could be read as support for such a rule of *per se* invalidity. *Condec* is informative.

There, plaintiff had recently closed a tender offer for 51% of defendants' stock. It had announced no intention to do a follow-up merger. The incumbent board had earlier refused plaintiffs' offer to merge and, in response to its tender offer, sought alternative deals. It found and negotiated a proposed sale of all of defendants' assets for stock in the buyer, to be followed up by an exchange offer to the seller's shareholders. The stock of the buyer was publicly traded in the New York Stock Exchange, so that the deal, in effect, offered cash to the target's shareholders. As a condition precedent to the sale of assets, an exchange of authorized but unissued shares of the seller (constituting about 15% of the total issued and outstanding shares after issuance) was to occur. Such issuance would, of course, negate the effective veto that plaintiffs' 51% stockholding would give it over a transaction that would require shareholder approval. Plaintiff sued to invalidate the stock issuance.

The court concluded, as a factual matter, that: ". . . the primary purpose of the issuance of such shares was to prevent control of Lunkenheimer from passing to Condec. . . ." 230 A.2d at 775. The court then implied that not even good faith dispute over corporate policy could justify a board in acting for the primary purpose of reducing the voting power of a control shareholder:

> Nonetheless, I am persuaded on the basis of the evidence adduced at trial that the transaction here attacked unlike the situation involving the purchase of stock with corporate funds [the court having just cited Bennett v. Propp, 187 A.2d 405, 409 (Del.1962), and Cheff v. Mathes, 199 A.2d 548 (Del.1964)] was clearly unwarranted because it unjustifiably strikes at the very heart of corporate representation by causing a stockholder with an equitable right to a majority of corporate stock to have his right to a proportionate voice and influence in corporate affairs to be diminished by the simple act of an exchange of stock which brought no money into the Lunkenheimer treasury, was not connected with a stock option plan or other proper corporate purpose, and which was obviously designed for the primary purpose of reducing Condec's stockholdings in Lunkenheimer below a majority. *Id.* at 777.

A *per se* rule that would strike down, in equity, any board action taken for the primary purpose of interfering with the effectiveness of a corporate vote would have the advantage of relative clarity and predictability. It also has the advantage of most vigorously enforcing the concept of corporate democracy. The disadvantage it brings along is, of course, the disadvantage a *per se* rule always has: it may sweep too broadly.

In two recent cases dealing with shareholder votes, this court struck down board acts done for the primary purpose of impeding the exercise of stockholder voting power. In doing so, a *per se* rule was not applied. Rather, it was said that, in such a case, the board bears the heavy burden of demonstrating a compelling justification for such action.

In Aprahamian v. HBO & Co., 531 A.2d 1204 (Del.Ch.1987), the incumbent board had moved the date of the annual meeting on the eve of that meeting when it learned that a dissident stockholder group had or appeared to have in hand proxies representing a majority of the outstanding shares. The court restrained that action and compelled the meeting to occur as noticed, even though the board stated that it had good business reasons to move the meeting date forward, and that action was recommended by a special committee. The court concluded as follows:

> The corporate election process, if it is to have any validity, must be conducted with scrupulous fairness and without any advantage being conferred or denied to any candidate or slate of candidates. In the interests of corporate democracy, those in charge of the election machinery of a corporation must be held to the highest standards of providing for and conducting corporate elections. The business judgment rule therefore does not confer any presumption of propriety on the acts of directors in postponing the annual meeting. Quite to the contrary. When the election machinery appears, at least facially, to have been manipulated those in charge of the election have the burden of persuasion to justify their actions. *Aprahamian*, 531 A.2d at 1206-07.

In Phillips v. Insituform of North America, Inc. (Del.Ch.1987), the court enjoined the voting of certain stock issued for the primary purpose of diluting the voting power of certain control shares. The facts were complex. After discussing *Canada Southern* and *Condec* in light of the more recent, important Supreme Court opinion in *Unocal*, it was there concluded as follows:

> . . . In applying the teachings of these cases, I conclude that no justification has been shown that would arguably make the extraordinary step of issuance of stock for the admitted purpose of impeding the exercise of stockholder rights reasonable in light of the corporate benefit, if any, sought to be obtained. Thus, whether our law creates an unyielding prohibition to the issuance of stock for the primary purpose of depriving a controlling shareholder of control or whether, as *Unocal* suggests to my mind, such an extraordinary step might be justified in some circumstances, the issuance of the Leopold shares was, in my opinion, an unjustified and invalid corporate act.

Thus, in *Insituform*, it was unnecessary to decide whether a *per se* rule pertained or not.

In my view, our inability to foresee now all of the future settings in which a board might, in good faith, paternalistically seek to thwart a shareholder vote, counsels against the adoption of a *per se* rule invalidating, in equity, every board action taken for the sole or primary purpose of thwarting a shareholder vote, even though I recognize the transcending significance of the franchise to the claims to legitimacy of our scheme of corporate governance. It may be that some set of facts would justify such extreme action.[5] This, however, is not such a case.

---

[5] Imagine the facts of *Condec* changed very slightly and coming up in today's world of corporate control transactions. Assume an acquiring company buys 25% of the target's stock in a small number of privately negotiated transactions. It then commences a public tender offer for 26% of the company stock at a cash price that the board, in good faith, believes is inadequate. Moreover, the acquiring corporation announces that it may or may not do a second-step merger, but if it does one, the consideration will be junk bonds that will have a value, when issued, in the opinion of its own investment banker, of no more than the cash being offered in the tender offer. In the face of such an offer, the board may have a duty to seek to protect the company's shareholders from the coercive effects of this inadequate offer. Assume . . . that just as the tender offer is closing, the board locates an all cash deal for all shares at a price materially higher than that offered by the acquiring corporation. Would the board of the target corporation be justified in issuing sufficient shares to the second acquiring corporation to dilute the 51% stockholder down so that it no longer had a practical veto over the merger or sale of assets that the target board had arranged for the benefit of all shares? It is not necessary to now hazard an opinion on that abstraction. The case is clearly close enough, however, despite the existence of the *Condec* precedent, to demonstrate, to my mind at least, the utility of a rule that permits, in some extreme circumstances, an incumbent board to act in good faith for the purpose of interfering with the outcome of a contemplated vote.

3. Defendants have demonstrated no sufficient justification for the action of December 31 which was intended to prevent an unaffiliated majority of shareholders from effectively exercising their right to elect eight new directors.

The board was not faced with a coercive action taken by a powerful shareholder against the interests of a distinct shareholder constituency (such as a public minority). It was presented with a consent solicitation by a 9% shareholder. Moreover, here it had time (and understood that it had time) to inform the shareholders of its views on the merits of the proposal subject to stockholder vote. The only justification that can, in such a situation, be offered for the action taken is that the board knows better than do the shareholders what is in the corporation's best interest. While that premise is no doubt true for any number of matters, it is irrelevant (except insofar as the shareholders wish to be guided by the board's recommendation) when the question is who should comprise the board of directors. The theory of our corporation law confers power upon directors as the agents of the shareholders; it does not create Platonic masters. It may be that the Blasius restructuring proposal was or is unrealistic and would lead to injury to the corporation and its shareholders if pursued. Having heard the evidence, I am inclined to think it was not a sound proposal. The board certainly viewed it that way, and that view, held in good faith, entitled the board to take certain steps to evade the risk it perceived. It could, for example, expend corporate funds to inform shareholders and seek to bring them to a similar point of view. See, e.g., Hall v. Trans-Lux Daylight Picture Screen Corp., 171 A. 226, 227 (Del.Ch.1934); Hibbert v. Hollywood Park, Inc., 457 A.2d 339 (Del.1982). But there is a vast difference between expending corporate funds to inform the electorate and exercising power for the primary purpose of foreclosing effective shareholder action. A majority of the shareholders, who were not dominated in any respect, could view the matter differently than did the board. If they do, or did, they are entitled to employ the mechanisms provided by the corporation law and the Atlas certificate of incorporation to advance that view. They are also entitled, in my opinion, to restrain their agents, the board, from acting for the principal purpose of thwarting that action. . . .

Note on the Boundary Between *Blasius* and *Unocal*

1. Were the actions of the Atlas board so bad? Consider that:

(i) Atlas had a staggered board, presumably adopted by shareholder vote, that was intended to ensure that a dissident could not obtain majority board representation in a single proxy fight. Blasius was trying to fit through a loophole that could have easily been closed before Blasius appeared on the scene, and probably would have been closed if Atlas had better (read: more expensive) legal advice.

(ii) Adding two directors to the staggered Atlas board bought the Atlas board a few months of time by forcing Blasius to wait until the next annual meeting to elect a majority of the Atlas board. After the board increase, Blasius could still elect 6 Atlas directors (out of 15) through its consent solicitation, and could elect three more at the next annual meeting. Atlas did not try to appoint 8 new directors, which would have prevented Blasius from obtaining a majority of the board seats at the next annual meeting.

(iii) Atlas' apparent intent -- to buy some time to consider alternatives, or perhaps to persuade the shareholders of its position -- is one that courts have blessed in permitting temporary use of a poison pill to block an any-and-all cash tender offer.

2. Chancellor Allen never clearly states the verbal formulation of the test that he applies. He describes two earlier cases as holding that "the board bears the heavy burden of demonstrating a compelling justification for [franchise-impairing] action." Is that the test -- "compelling justification"?

3. Chancellor Allen distinguishes *Unocal* as not involving the corporate franchise. He proceeds to apply very strict scrutiny to board action that has the primary purpose of impeding shareholder exercise of their voting rights. Is the distinction persuasive? Would the Delaware Supreme Court apply a similar, almost *per se* rule against director action that interferes with a shareholder vote?

4. *Blasius* involved a contest for board seats unaccompanied by a tender offer. When a dissident combines a tender offer with a proxy fight, the tension between the strict *Blasius* standard and the intermediate *Unocal* standard of review is enhanced. Whether a defensive action is scrutinized under *Blasius* or *Unocal* could well determine whether the action succeeds or falls.

Chancellor Allen confronted the problem of defining the boundary line between *Blasius* and *Unocal* in two decisions involving a bid by Stanley Stahl for Apple Bancorp. The first decision, on setting a meeting date, appears below. The second decision, on the circumstances under which a company can use a poison pill to impede a dissident's efforts to conduct a proxy fight, appears in the next section.

STAHL v. APPLE BANCORP (*Stahl I*)
579 A.2d 1115 (Del.Ch.1990)

ALLEN, Chancellor. On March 28, 1990 Stanley Stahl, who is the holder of 30% of the outstanding common stock of Apple Bancorp, Inc. ("Bancorp"), announced a public tender offer for all of the remaining shares of Bancorp's stock. Mr. Stahl had earlier informed Bancorp's board of an intention to conduct a proxy contest for the election of directors to the company's board. On April 10 Bancorp's board of directors elected to defer the company's annual meeting, which it had intended to call for mid-May, and announced it would explore the advisability of pursuing an extraordinary transaction, including the possible sale of the company. Mr. Stahl filed this action on April 12.

The complaint seeks an order requiring the directors of Bancorp to convene the annual meeting of the stockholders on or before June 16, 1990. The suit is not brought under Del.C. § 211 which creates a right in shareholders to compel the holding of an annual meeting under certain circumstances. Rather, the theory of the complaint is that the directors of Bancorp had intended to convene an annual meeting in May or June -- and had gone so far as to fix April 17 as the record date for the meeting -- but dropped that plan when it appeared that a proxy contest by plaintiff was likely to succeed. This change in plans is said, in the circumstances, to constitute inequitable conduct because it seeks to protect no legitimate interest of the corporation but is designed principally to entrench defendants in office. Defendants are the members of the board of directors of Bancorp. They answer the complaint by saying that in not scheduling the 1990 annual meeting in the Spring of the year as has been the practice, they are behaving responsibly in the best interests of the corporation and its shareholders. They claim that their decision to delay the annual meeting was not a response to a proxy contest by plaintiff but was a response to the announcement of plaintiff's tender offer which they conclude is coercive and at an inadequate price. . . .

I

. . . Mr. Stahl, who is Bancorp's largest shareholder, began acquiring shares of Apple Bank in 1986. Gradually he increased his holdings through open market purchases and privately negotiated transactions. . . . By November 7, 1989, he owned approximately 30.3% of the outstanding Bancorp shares. . . . On November 15, 1989, the company's board of directors met to consider what action, if any, should be taken with respect to Stahl's stock accumulation. Two proposals were suggested: negotiating a standstill agreement with Stahl and adopting a stock purchase rights plan (a "rights plan"). The board authorized the preparation of the rights plan.

On November 16, [Apple Bank CEO] McDougal informed Stahl of the board's intention to adopt a rights plan. McDougal suggested that one way of addressing the situation might be for Stahl to make a bid for the entire company at book value. Mr. Stahl indicated that he was unwilling to do so.

On November 17, the board adopted the rights plan. Stahl responded on November 22, 1989, by delivering to the company a proposal to be submitted to a vote at the next annual meeting of stockholders, calling for an amendment to the company's bylaws increasing the number of directors of the company from 12 to 21. In the proposal Stahl nominated 13 individuals (including himself) to be named to the board if his bylaw proposal were approved.[3] He nominated four individuals to be elected if his bylaw proposal were defeated. Later, Stahl stated in a Schedule 13D filing that he would solicit proxies in favor of his proposal and for the election of his nominees to the board. That filing also stated that, if elected, Stahl intended to recommend to the full board that the rights under the rights plan be redeemed and that the board evaluate the performance of management and make any changes it deemed necessary to improve overall management performance.

On March 19, 1990 the board fixed April 17, 1990 as the record date for determining the shareholders entitled to vote at the company's 1990 annual meeting. While no date for the annual meeting was fixed, it was anticipated that the meeting would be held in May 1990. Del.C. § 213 provides that the record date for an annual meeting shall not be less than 10 or more than 60 days before the date the meeting is held. Thus, the latest date at which an annual meeting could be held with an April 17 record date would be June 16.

On March 28, 1990, Stahl commenced a tender offer to purchase any and all outstanding shares of common stock of the company at $38 cash per share. The offer is conditioned upon the expansion of the company's board of directors to 21 members and the election of Stahl's 13 nominees to serve on the board. The offer is also conditioned upon the stock purchase rights being redeemed or Stahl otherwise being satisfied that the rights are invalid.

. . .

On April 9 and 10, the company's board of directors held a special meeting. The company's proxy solicitor informed the board that it was likely if the board did not present the stockholders with an economic alternative to Stahl's offer that Stahl would prevail in a proxy fight by a significant margin. The company received from its financial advisors a written opinion that Stahl's offer, which represented a 17% premium over the prior market price, was inadequate and unfair to the stockholders from a financial point of view. The financial advisors advised the board that greater value for the stockholders could be obtained through certain alternative strategies. They further advised the board that adequate exploration of those alternatives would require more time than was available before the meeting, if the record date stood at April 17.

The board resolved to recommend to Bancorp's stockholders that they reject Stahl's offer. It further resolved to withdraw the April 17 record date in order to allow itself more time to pursue alternatives to the Stahl offer. . . .

---

[3] Apple has a staggered board. Under the company's certificate of incorporation and bylaws, only 4 seats are open for election this year. Thus, in order for Stahl to gain majority control of the board, the bylaw proposal must be approved.

II

Stahl . . . claims that by requiring shareholders to submit matters to be voted upon at the annual meeting by November 1989 (which the board interpreted Bancorp's bylaws to do) and by fixing an April 17 record date, the defendants have initiated the proxy contest process. It is argued that the withdrawal of the record date . . . constitutes an impermissible manipulation of the corporate machinery having the effect of disenfranchising the company's stockholders and entrenching the incumbent directors. Stahl argues, citing Blasius Industries v. Atlas Corp., 564 A.2d 651 (Del.Ch.1988), that the board is required to present a compelling justification for its actions in rescinding the April 17 record date. This plaintiff asserts it cannot do.

Defendants . . . [argue] that no meeting date had been set, and under neither Del.C. § 211 nor Bancorp's bylaws, was one required until September of 1990. Thus, it is said, the board's withdrawal of the April 17 record date was not an action that impeded a shareholder vote. Defendants assert that unlike the actions struck down in *Blasius* and in Lerman v. Diagnostic Data, Inc., 421 A.2d 906 (Del.Ch.1980), the withdrawal of the April 17 record date did not render a shareholder vote ineffective, but simply delayed it.

Defendants [also] assert that the record date was withdrawn not as a response to a proxy contest by Stahl, but rather as a response to Stahl's tender offer. The appropriate standard for evaluating the board's action, say defendants, is that articulated in Unocal Corp. v. Mesa Petroleum Co., 493 A.2d 946 (Del.1985), *i.e.*, whether the board's withdrawal of the April 17 record date was a reasonable response to a reasonably perceived threat to corporate or shareholder interests. Defendants claim to have satisfied that standard. . . .

IV

Turning to the merits of plaintiff's claim that the directors' decision to postpone the annual meeting violated their fiduciary duties of loyalty owed to the corporation and its shareholders, one first confronts the question what is the appropriate legal standard against which the defendants' action is to be measured. Two approaches, which in the end become quite similar, are possible: the fiduciary duty analysis employed by cases [such as *Blasius*] dealing with board action designed to impact on the shareholder vote; or the modified business judgment test of *Unocal* and later cases which apply its test to board actions taken in the face of a threat to corporate control. The first approach is treated in this section of this opinion; the second in the next, concluding section.

Plaintiff contends that the deferral of the annual meeting and the rescission of the record date together constitutes a direct and intended interference with the exercise of the shareholders' right of franchise. . . . For the reasons that follow I am unable to accept plaintiff's argument. Explaining why this is so is helped by placing the "compelling justification" language of *Blasius*, which plaintiff invokes, into its larger doctrinal context.

It is an elementary proposition of corporation law that, where they exist, fiduciary duties constitute a network of responsibilities that overlay the exercise of even undoubted legal power. Thus it is well established, for example, that where corporate directors exercise their legal powers for an inequitable purpose their action may be rescinded or nullified by a court at the instance of an aggrieved shareholder. The leading Delaware case of Schnell v. Chris-Craft Industries, 285 A.2d 437 (Del.1971), announced this principle and applied it in a setting in which directors advanced the date of an annual meeting in order to impede an announced proxy contest.

Under this test the court asks the question whether the directors' purpose is "inequitable." An inequitable purpose is not necessarily synonymous with a dishonest motive. Fiduciaries who are subjectively operating selflessly might be pursuing a purpose that a court will rule is inequitable. Thus, for example, there was no inquiry concerning the board's subjective good faith in Condec Corp. v. Lunkenheimer Co., 230 A.2d 769 (Del.Ch.1967), where this court held that the issuance of stock for the principal purpose of eliminating the ability of a large stockholder to determine the outcome of a vote was invalid as a breach of loyalty. Nor was there such an inquiry in Canada Southern Oils, Ltd. v. Manabi Exploration Co., 96 A.2d 810 (Del.Ch.1953).

Lerman v. Diagnostic Data, Inc., 421 A.2d 906 (Del.Ch.1980), is a case that explicitly expresses the view that inequitable conduct does not necessarily require an evil or selfish motive. There the court held a bylaw invalid in the situation before it where that bylaw would have precluded a shareholder from mounting a proxy contest. The court referred to the fact that the bylaw "whether designedly inequitable or not, has had a terminal effect on the aspirations of Lerman and his group." 421 A.2d at 912.

Each of these cases dealt with board action with a principal purpose of impeding the exercise of stockholder power through the vote. . . . Consistent with these authorities, in *Blasius* and in Aprahamian v. HBO & Co., 531 A. 2d 1204 (Del.Ch.1987), this court held that action designed primarily to impede the effective exercise of the franchise is not evaluated under the business judgment form of review . . . [*Blasius*] admitted the possibility that in some circumstances such action might be consistent with the directors equitable obligations. It was suggested, however, that such circumstances would have to constitute "compelling justification," given the central role of the stockholder franchise.

Thus, *Blasius*' reference to "compelling justification" reflects only the high value that the prior cases had placed upon the exercise of voting rights and the inherently particularized and contextual nature of any inquiry concerning fiduciary duties. Neither it nor *Aprahamian* represent new law.

Thus the fundamental question when the motion is evaluated under these cases may be expressed as whether the defendants have exercised corporate power inequitably. In answering that question, it is necessary to ask, in the context of this case, whether they have taken action for the purpose of impairing or impeding the effective exercise of the corporate franchise and, if they have, whether the special circumstances are present (compelling justification) warranting such an unusual step.

. . . [I] need not inquire into the question of justification in this instance, for I cannot conclude that defendants have taken action for the primary purpose of impairing or impeding the effective exercise of the corporate franchise. I reach this conclusion . . . on the narrow ground that the action of deferring this company's annual meeting where no meeting date has yet been set and no proxies even solicited does not impair or impede the effective exercise of the franchise to any extent. To speak of the effective exercise of the franchise is to imply certain assumptions concerning the structure and mechanism that define the vote and govern its exercise. Shares are voted at meetings; meetings are generally called as fixed in bylaws. While the refusal to call a shareholder meeting when the board is not obligated to do so might under some imaginable circumstance breach a fiduciary duty, such a decision does not itself constitute an impairment of the exercise of the franchise that sparked the close judicial scrutiny of *Schnell, Blasius*, etc.

In no sense can the decision not to call a meeting be likened to kinds of board action found to have constituted inequitable conduct relating to the vote. In each of these franchise cases the effect of the board action -- to advance (*Schnell*) or defer (*Aprahamian*) a meeting; to adopt a bylaw (*Lerman*); or to fill board vacancies (*Blasius*) -- was practically to preclude effective stockholder action (*Schnell, Blasius, Lerman*) or to snatch victory from an insurgent slate on the eve of the noticed meeting (*Aprahamian*). Here the election process will go forward at a time consistent with the company's bylaws and with Del.C. § 211. Defendant's decision does not preclude plaintiff or any other Bancorp shareholder from effectively exercising his vote, nor have proxies been collected that only await imminent counting. . . .

[Having concluded that the *Blasius* standard did not apply, Chancellor Allen analyzed whether the Apple Bancorp board's response passed muster under the *Unocal* standard -- defensive responses must be reasonable in relation to the threat posed. He concluded, without difficulty, that the board's response met that standard.]

Note: Understanding *Stahl I*

1. Why didn't Stanley Stahl attempt the faster route, used by Blasius, of soliciting written consents, at least to expand the Apple Bancorp board from 12 to 21 and elect 9 of his own nominees? One likely answer: Apple Bancorp had probably abolished shareholder power, available under Del.C. § 228 *unless the charter otherwise provides*, to act by written consent.

2. If it was reasonable, under *Unocal*, for the Apple Bancorp board to delay its annual meeting for months while it searched for alternatives to Stahl's bid, it would seem equally reasonable for the Atlas board to delay Blasius' ability to obtain majority board control until Atlas' next annual meeting. From this perspective, Chancellor Allen's distinction between deferring a meeting not yet called (*Stahl I*) and interfering with a consent solicitation already begun in order to delay a control transfer (*Blasius*) seems a triumph of form over substance, and an invitation to corporate planners not to fall into the trap in which Atlas found itself.

3. For additional cases testing board power to accelerate or postpone a meeting date in the middle of a proxy contest, see Terrell, *Can Stockholders' Annual Meetings Be Postponed in the Midst of a Proxy Contest*, 4 Insights: Corp. & Sec.L. Advisor 12 (Oct.1990) (collecting Delaware cases); ER Holdings Inc. v. Norton Co., 735 F.Supp. 1094 (D.Mass.1990), *aff'd mem.*, 907 F.2d 142 (1st Cir.1990) (allowing deferral of meeting date).

4. Given the decision in *Stahl I*, potential dissidents can reduce the target board's ability to delay calling a meeting by not announcing a proxy fight until the last minute, *after* the target has established a meeting date. The incumbents could respond to the threat of a last-minute proxy fight by adopting a bylaw requiring advance notice of director nominations. If *Stahl I* had come out the other way, that would invite a different planning response by corporate managers: They would not establish a record date until the last possible minute, the better to smoke out a potential dissident.

5. The Delaware Supreme Court's first opportunity to address the *Blasius* doctrine came recently, in Stroud v. Grace. *Stroud* involved the validity of a bylaw adopted by Milliken Enterprises, a privately held company controlled by the Milliken family. The bylaw established qualifications for directors, and let the board decide that a nominee was not qualified *at the shareholders' meeting*, when it was too late to propose a substitute nominee. Vice-Chancellor Hartnett invalidated the bylaw, relying on *Blasius*.

The Delaware Supreme Court reversed. It held that neither *Unocal* nor *Blasius* were implicated, since the company faced no threat to control and the bylaw had been approved by shareholder vote. The Court could have easily stopped there, and upheld the bylaw under the business judgment rule. Instead, it took the opportunity to expound on the scope of *Blasius*, and it's relationship to the intermediate standard of review established by *Unocal*.

STROUD v. GRACE
606 A.2d 75 (Del.1992)

MOORE, Justice. This appeal arises out of a series of disputes between Milliken Enterprises, Inc. ("Milliken"), a privately-held Delaware corporation, and certain shareholders, mostly members of the Stroud branch of the Milliken family (the "Strouds"). Plaintiffs brought individual and derivative claims against Milliken and its board of directors ("defendants"), alleging that the board breached its fiduciary duties by recommending certain charter amendments to its shareholders (the "Amendments"). The Strouds also . . . challenged the validity of the amendments and a by-law ("By-law 3") which established the procedure for nominating candidates to Milliken's board of directors.

The Court of Chancery *sua sponte* granted summary judgment for the defendants on all of Stroud's claims but upheld Stroud's attack on By-law 3. . . . [T]he trial court assessed Stroud's challenge to the validity of the Amendments and By-law 3 under the "compelling justification" standard of *Blasius Industries v. Atlas Corp.*, 564 A.2d 651 (Del.Ch.1988). The Vice Chancellor found that the Amendments were fair, but that By- law 3 was unreasonable on its face because it potentially prevented the shareholders from nominating their candidates for the board of directors.

We . . . reject an analysis under the heightened *Blasius* standard. While we generally agree with the broad principles articulated in *Blasius*, we find that the Amendments and By-law 3 did not merit such close judicial scrutiny. The board did not act when its control was threatened, and an overwhelming majority of Milliken's fully-informed shareholders approved the Amendments. Finally, we reverse the trial court's invalidation of By-law 3. We reiterate that Delaware courts should exercise caution when invalidating corporate acts based upon hypothetical injuries and without giving due deference to established principles of Delaware law regarding corporate governance.

I

. . . Milliken is a privately-held Delaware corporation. It is one of the largest and most successful textile businesses in the world. Most of Milliken's 200 shareholders are direct descendants of its founder, Seth Milliken. The Milliken board has ten members. Four directors, Roger Milliken, Chief Executive Officer, Gerrish Milliken, a retired Vice President, Minot Milliken, Vice President, and Dr. Thomas Malone, President, are all members of the Milliken family or employees of the corporation. The remaining six directors are otherwise unaffiliated with the company. Roger, Gerrish, and Minot Milliken own or control, through various trusts, over 50% of Milliken's preferred and common shares.

The current controversy arose after the death in 1985 of Mrs. W.B. Dixon Stroud, Roger and Gerrish's sister. As a result of her death, certain Milliken shares were released from a trust under the control of Roger, Gerrish and Minot to the Strouds, who now own or control close to 17% of Milliken's shares. . . .

Soon after Mrs. Stroud's death, Roger proposed that the Milliken shareholders enter into a General Option Agreement ("GOA"). The GOA gave the Milliken family and then Milliken itself, a right of first refusal to purchase any shares offered to unrelated persons. The GOA recited that it was intended to keep the company in private hands and to prevent the dissemination of confidential data. Almost 75% of Milliken's shareholders executed the GOA. Only the Strouds and a few others did not do so. . . .

[Thereafter, the Milliken board unanimously proposed] charter and by-law amendments which were recommended to the shareholders for their approval at the [1989] annual meeting. . . . The most controversial aspects of the Amendments are charter Article Eleventh (c) and By-law 3. Article Eleventh (c) established a new method of qualifying directors for membership on Milliken's board. By-law 3 established the procedure for nominating board candidates. By-law 3 required the shareholders to submit a notice of their candidates to the board, specifying their qualifications under Article Eleventh (c), well in advance of the annual meeting. By-law 3 also empowered the board to disqualify a shareholder's nominee at any time even at the annual meeting. . . . The Amendments were approved at the meeting by 78% of the shares entitled to vote.

. . . [Plaintiffs argue] that the board breached its duty of care and loyalty in approving and recommending the Amendments. They also argued that the Amendments were unfair to Milliken's shareholders by effectively entrenching Roger, Gerrish and Minot Milliken's control of the board. The Strouds then moved for summary judgment. With one exception, the trial court *sua sponte* granted summary judgment in defendants' favor. The Vice Chancellor granted summary judgment in favor of the Strouds by ruling that By-law 3 was unfair to Milliken's shareholders. . . .

IV

In the absence of fraud, a fully informed shareholder vote in favor of even a "voidable" transaction ratifies board action and places the burden of proof on the challenger. See Bershad v. Curtiss-Wright Corp., 535 A.2d, 840, 846 (Del.1987); *Van Gorkom*, 488 A.2d at 890. The fact that controlling shareholders voted in favor of the transaction is irrelevant as long as they did not breach their fiduciary duties to the minority holders. *Unocal Corp. v. Mesa Petroleum Co.*, 493 A.2d 946, 958 (Del.1985); *Bershad*, 535 A.2d at 845. There is no proof whatever of any such breach in this case. . . .

VI

Since there was no breach of any fiduciary duty in connection with the shareholder vote at the 1989 annual meeting, a fully informed majority of the shareholders adopted the Amendments and effectively ratified the board's action. This shifts the burden of proof to the Strouds to prove that the transaction was unfair. They have utterly failed in that regard. . . .

The Strouds' attack on the Amendments and the defendants' cross-appeal of the trial court's invalidation of By-law 3 both challenge the analytical framework employed by the Court of Chancery in resolving their respective claims. The choice of the applicable "test" to judge director action often determines the outcome of the case.

A

The Vice Chancellor, relying on Blasius Industries v. Atlas Corp., 564 A.2d 651 (Del.Ch.1988), and Aprahamian v. HBO & Co., 531 A.2d 1204 (Del.Ch.1987), examined the Amendments under an "intrinsic fairness" test. While the trial court concluded that the board had not breached its fiduciary duty, it nonetheless stated that:

> Because . . . the critical Charter and By-law amendments affect the Milliken shareholders' franchise, particularly their right to nominate directors, the validity of these amendments must be reviewed for their intrinsic fairness rather than considered pursuant to the business judgment rule.

. . . [W]e conclude that it was error to apply *Blasius* here.

B

In Schnell v. Chris-Craft Industries, 285 A.2d 437, 439 (Del.1971), this Court recognized that management may not inequitably manipulate corporate machinery to perpetuate "itself in office" and disenfranchise the shareholders. The crux of *Schnell* is that:

> [I]nequitable action does not become permissible simply because it is legally possible. *Id.*

Schnell's broad holding spawned an entirely new line of Court of Chancery decisions. Lerman v. Diagnostic Data, Inc., 421 A.2d 906 (Del.Ch.1980); *Aprahamian*, 531 A.2d at 1208; *Blasius*, 564 A.2d at 659-60; Centaur Partners, IV v. National Intergroup, 582 A.2d 923, 927 (Del.1990); Stahl v. Apple Bancorp, 579 A.2d 1115, 1122-23 (Del.Ch.1990).

C

While we accept the basic legal tenets of *Stahl* and *Blasius*, certain principles emerge from those cases which are inextricably related to their specific facts. Almost all of the post-*Schnell* decisions involved situations where boards of directors deliberately employed various legal strategies either to frustrate or completely disenfranchise a shareholder vote. As *Blasius* recognized, in those circumstances, board action was intended to thwart free exercise of the franchise. There can be no dispute that such conduct violates Delaware law.

The stringent standards of review imposed by *Stahl* and *Blasius* arise from questions of divided loyalty, and are well-settled. See Gilbert v. El Paso Co., 575 A.2d 1131, 1144 (Del.1990); Paramount Communications v. Time, Inc., 571 A.2d 1140, 1153-54 (Del.1990); Mills Acquisition Co. v. MacMillan, 559 A.2d 1261, 1287 (Del.1989); *Unocal*, 493 A.2d at 954-56.[3] After reviewing the record in this case, we conclude that a *Blasius* analysis in connection with the validity of the Amendments and By-laws was inappropriate.

D

Clearly, the Milliken board did not face any threat to its control. Roger, Gerrish and Minot Milliken effectively owned or controlled a majority interest in the corporation. Furthermore, most of the other shareholders had executed the GOA. Thus, it cannot be said that the "primary purpose" of the board's action was to interfere with or impede exercise of the shareholder franchise.

---

[3] Board action interfering with the exercise of the franchise often arose during a hostile contest for control where an acquiror launched both a proxy fight and a tender offer. Such action necessarily invoked both *Unocal* and *Blasius*. We note that the two "tests" are not mutually exclusive because both recognize the inherent conflicts of interest that arise when shareholders are not permitted free exercise of their franchise. See, e.g., Shamrock Holdings, Inc. v. Polaroid Corp., 559 A.2d 278, 285-86 (Del.Ch.1989) (*Blasius* represents "specific expression" of *Unocal* test); cf. Stahl v. Apple Bancorp (Del.Ch.1990) [*Stahl II*; excerpted later in this chapter]. *Gilbert* should nonetheless resolve any ambiguity. It clearly holds that a reviewing court must apply *Unocal* where the board "adopts any defensive measure taken in response to some threat to corporate policy and effectiveness which touches upon issues of control." *Gilbert*, 575 A.2d at 1144. This does not render *Blasius* and its progeny meaningless. In certain circumstances, a court must recognize the special import of protecting the shareholders' franchise within *Unocal*'s requirement that any defensive measure be proportionate and "reasonable in relation to the threat posed." *Unocal*, 493 A.2d at 955. A board's unilateral decision to adopt a defensive measure touching "upon issues of control" that purposefully disenfranchises its shareholders is strongly suspect under *Unocal*, and cannot be sustained without a "compelling justification." See, e.g., In re Time Inc. Shareholder Litigation, 1989 WL 79880 (Del.Ch.1989), *aff'd*, 571 A.2d 1140 (Del.1990) ([Chancellor Allen] refused to apply *Blasius* to assess board's initial decision to withdraw merger proposal requiring shareholder vote in favor of proposal not requiring vote because board acted within its broad statutory authority).

More fundamentally, the Vice Chancellor ruled, and we agree, that a fully- informed majority of Milliken's shareholders ratified the Amendments. Therefore, the factual predicate of unilateral board action intended to inequitably manipulate the corporate machinery is completely absent here. Cf. *Centaur Partners*, 582 A.2d at 927. Milliken's shareholders, unlike those in both *Blasius* and *Aprahamian*, had a full and fair opportunity to vote on the Amendments and did so. The result of the vote, ceding greater authority to the board, does not under the circumstances implicate *Unocal* or *Blasius*.

In sum, after finding that the shareholder vote was fully informed, and in the absence of any fraud, waste, manipulative or other inequitable conduct, that should have ended the matter on basic principles of ratification.

VIII

Finally, we turn to the defendants' cross-appeal regarding validity of Milliken's By-law 3. That provision establishes, in part, the procedure for nominating candidates to Milliken's board. By-law 3 initially requires all board candidates to meet the qualifications mandated in Article Eleventh (c). By-law 3, § (d), requires a shareholder proposing a board candidate to include in his or her notice of nomination:

> ... [T]he proposed nominee's name, the principal occupation or employment of each such nominee, the nominee's written consent to nomination and to serving as a director if elected, *information establishing such nominee's fulfillment of any qualification requirements set forth in the Corporation's Certificate of Incorporation*, and such additional information with respect to such person as the Board of Directors may reasonably request. (Emphasis added)

... The most controversial subsection of By-law 3 concerns the board's ability to determine a candidate's qualifications under Article Eleventh (c) at any time before the election up to and including the annual meeting. By-law 3 subsection (f) provides:

> The Board of Directors, or if not feasible, the officer of the Corporation or other person *presiding at the meeting of stockholders shall determine any questions concerning whether nominations have been made in accordance with the provisions of this By-law 3 and whether such person has met the qualification requirements, if any, set forth in the Corporation's Certificate of Incorporation.* If such a determination is so made, the officer of the Corporation or other person presiding at the meeting of stockholders shall so declare to the meeting and shall declare that any such nomination shall be disregarded. (Emphasis added).

The trial court, applying *Blasius*, held that By-law 3 was "unreasonable and unfair, on its face." The Vice Chancellor noted that By-law 3 precluded the shareholders from knowing exactly what information to include in their notice of nomination "[b]ecause the . . . criteria are not defined in Article Eleventh and are dependent on a determination by incumbent directors. . . ." The Vice Chancellor found that the board could effectively disenfranchise voters because subsection (f), when read in conjunction with the subsection limiting the shareholders' right to submit its notice of nomination not less than 14 days before the election, gave the directors the unfettered discretion to disqualify the shareholders' candidates without recourse. . . .

There was no basis to invalidate By-law 3 upon some hypothetical abuse. . . . [Indeed], the board respected W.B. Dixon Stroud, Jr.'s nominees and circulated a list of his candidates to the shareholders prior to the 1989 annual meeting. The shareholders overwhelmingly rejected Stroud's nominees. That is not an injury. It is a reality flowing from a proper turning of the wheels of corporate democracy -- and nothing more -- a point which the plaintiffs totally and repeatedly missed throughout this litigation. . . . It is not an overstatement to suggest that every valid by-law is always susceptible to potential misuse. Without a showing of abuse in this case, we must reverse the trial court's decision and uphold the validity of By-law 3.[5] The validity of corporate action under By-law 3 must await its actual use.

Notes on *Stroud v. Grace*

1. Does it make sense to limit the heightened scrutiny of *Blasius* to situations involving control, as *Stroud* seems to? Suppose, to change the facts of *Blasius* slightly, that (i) Atlas' charter allowed a maximum of 11 directors, and Blasius had sought to add four new directors to the board, who would constitute a minority even if elected; and (ii) Atlas, on learning of Blasius' consent solicitation, added four new members to its board to forestall Blasius' efforts. Should that change in facts affect the outcome? Should it affect the standard of review? In either case, the Atlas board is thwarting a shareholder effort to elect directors.

2. How broad is the holding in *Stroud*? Would the court have reached the same result, do you think, if the board had adopted By-law 3 without shareholder approval? If the board had adopted By-law 3 without shareholder approval after a dissident had announced plans to run for the board? If the bylaw, adopted after a dissident announced plans to run, was drafted to exclude the dissident's nominees?

3. The Delaware Supreme Court clearly means to discourage efforts to challenge corporate charter provisions and by-laws *on their face*, rather than as applied in a particular situation. How broadly does the opinion sweep?

---

[5] Our decision does not leave plaintiffs without a remedy. They can always file an action in the Court of Chancery under Del.C. § 225 if they want to contest the board's actual conduct in relation to any future corporate election of a Milliken director.

Suppose that a board adopts a by-law that gives the incumbent directors the power to disapprove any nominee for election, at any time up to the annual meeting, if "the incumbent directors, in their sole discretion, think that it would be inadvisable for the nominee to serve on the board." Such a by-law would discourage an election campaign, if only because it adds to the risk and potential litigation cost of the proxy campaign. Would such a by-law survive an "on its face" challenge in light of *Stroud?* Should it?

4.   Can a company, through charter amendment, eliminate a shareholder's voting rights if the shareholder either owns *or solicits proxies from* holders of more than 20% of the voting shares (thus prohibiting a conventional proxy contest)? How could a dissident run for election to the board of such a company?[20]

C.   Defensive Tactics II: Applying a Poison Pill

Poison pills have several strong implications for proxy fight tactics. First, a flip-in poison pill can stop a single shareholder from owning more than the threshold percentage for triggering the pill's dilutive effects -- often as low as 10%. That limits a dissident's ability to buy votes by buying the accompanying shares, even without intent to buy all or a majority of the outstanding shares.

A recent study by Randall Thomas and Kenneth Martin reports that dissidents who run proxy contests at firms with low-threshold poison pills own significantly less stock than dissidents who run proxy contests at firms with high-threshold poison pills or with no poison pills. Anecdotal evidence confirms that companies sometimes adopt poison pills, or reduce pill thresholds, to prevent an already known dissident from buying more shares. Despite this dampening effect, average dissident holdings are about 10% even for firms with poison pills. This suggests that universal use of a pill with a 10% threshold would significantly affect dissident ability to accumulate stock.[21]

---

[20] A 1992 control contest for Van Dorn Co. presented this fact pattern. The dissident shareholder chose not to challenge the charter provision in court under Ohio law. Instead, the dissident advised other large shareholders of his intent to nominate a competing slate of directors from the floor at Van Dorn's annual meeting, and invited other shareholders to attend Van Dorn's annual meeting and vote in person. The dissident was careful *not* to solicit anyone's support. See *Van Dorn Dissidents Win Board Seat, Spur Sale with Unorthodox Proxy Tactics,* Corp.Control Alert 1 (Nov.1992).

[21] Randall Thomas & Kenneth Martin, *The Impact of Rights Plans on Proxy Contests: Reevaluating Moran v. Household Finance* (working paper, July 1993). John Pound, *Proxy Contests and the Efficiency of Shareholder Oversight,* 20 J.Fin.Econ. 237 (1988), finds a significant positive correlation between dissident holdings and dissident success rates. Thomas & Martin find a positive but statistically insignificant correlation, and Schrager (1986), *supra* note 3, ch. 4, finds essentially zero correlation. These relatively weak results may reflect the sample selection bias problems that plague any attempt to infer, from a sample of *proxy contests that actually took place,* what factors predict proxy contest success. These problems are discussed later in this chapter.

Second, a typical pill defines beneficial ownership broadly to include the right to vote shares, except pursuant to a revocable proxy given in response to a public solicitation that complies with SEC rules. The company's board of directors, hardly a disinterested body, determines a shareholder's beneficial ownership.

The broad definition of beneficial ownership puts even shareholders who stay below the threshold percentage at risk of inadvertently triggering a pill. Dissidents must be careful to comply with the SEC's proxy rules and other relevant rules, such as the Schedule 13D filing requirements, lest the proxies they receive count toward the pill's threshold percentage. The judicial remedy for violating the proxy rules or the 13(d) rules is often only corrective disclosure. The pill dramatically escalates the cost of a violation, or a decision to test the outer limits of the SEC's broad definitions of solicitation, proxy, or 13(d) group.

Third, poison pills treat a shareholder group as a single person in determining whether the pill has been triggered. They define "group" at least as broadly as the SEC's definition in Rule 13d-5(b)(1): "two or more persons who agree to act together for the purpose of acquiring, holding, *voting*, or disposing of equity securities." (Emphasis added.) The courts have also construed the group concept broadly. A group can be formed informally, without written documentation, and its existence can be proven by circumstantial evidence.[22]

Targets will predictably push use of poison pills to the furthest reaches that the courts will allow. The key questions for the courts are: (i) is there any lower limit on the trigger percentage; and (ii) can companies use a poison pill to prevent the formation of a *voting* group, formed solely to pursue a voting initiative. So far, no court has directly addressed the first question, but nothing in *Moran v. Household International*, 500 A.2d 1346 (Del.1985), or subsequent decisions upholding the use of poison pills suggests that the 20% threshold in Household International's pill is a lower limit. Only Chancellor Allen has directly addressed the second question, in *Stahl II*.

STAHL v. APPLE BANCORP (*Stahl II*)
Fed.Sec.L.Rep. (CCH) ¶ 95,412 (Del.Ch.1990)

ALLEN, Chancellor. [The factual background for the case is contained in *Stahl I*]

Stanley Stahl, a 30.6% shareholder of defendant Apple Bancorp, Inc. ("Bancorp"), is presently extending a tender offer for any and all shares of that company's stock at $38 cash per share. He is also conducting a proxy

---

[22] On the informal nature of a group, see, e.g., Wellman v. Dickinson, 682 F.2d 355, 363 (2d Cir.1982); SEC v. Savoy Indus., 587 F.2d 1149, 1163 (D.C.Cir.1978), *cert. denied*, 440 U.S. 913 (1979).

contest to increase the size of Bancorp's board and elect a majority of new members who would be committed to redeeming rights issued pursuant to the company's recently adopted poison pill stock rights plan. Closing of the tender offer is conditioned upon Mr. Stahl's slate prevailing in the proxy contest.

The amended complaint in this matter challenges a series of steps taken by the board of directors of Bancorp that impede Mr. Stahl's ability to acquire control of the company including the adoption of the "flip-in/flip-over poison pill" stock rights plan. . . . Mr. Stahl has moved for summary judgment declaring that:

> 1. No person shall be deemed to be the "beneficial owner," within the meaning of the Rights Plan, of shares of [Bancorp] stock owned by any other person solely by reason of any agreement, arrangement or understanding with such other person for:
>
> a) the formation of and membership on a committee for the purpose of promoting or opposing any stockholder resolution or for nominating or electing a slate of nominees to the Board of Directors of [Bancorp] and/or service on such a slate of nominees and/or agreement to a slate of director nominees;
>
> b) entry into revocable voting agreements or the granting or solicitation of revocable proxies with respect to the foregoing; and/or
>
> c) the sharing of expenses and the indemnification against expenses and liabilities by any such other person with respect to expenses incurred or conduct occurring during the time such other person is a nominee or a member of such committee. . . .

. . . No one has argued contract interpretation. Rather both sides have assumed the language [of the rights plan] covers the activities in question and for purposes of his motion so will I.

I

In order to determine whether rights under the stock rights plan have become exercisable it is necessary to have a definition of ownership or of the relationship between a stockholder and stock that is pertinent. The stock rights plan in issue, as do most such plans, reflects the concept of Rule 13d-5 in defining that relationship broadly. For purposes of the triggering mechanisms of the stock rights plan a shareholder is deemed to own any shares:

> (iii) which are beneficially owned, directly or indirectly, by any other person with which such person or any such person's affiliates has any agreement, arrangement or understanding . . . for the purpose of acquiring, holding, voting or disposing of any securities of the [company].

The plan, however, exempts from this definition of "agreement, arrangement or understanding" to vote [the Company's securities] any agreement, etc., that "arises solely from a revocable proxy or consent given in response to a public proxy or consent solicitation." It is assumed by both parties (and thus not an issue for the court on this motion) that Mr. Stahl is precluded [by the rights plan] from entering into an agreement with other shareholders (if those shareholders own .7% of Bancorp's stock) to serve on the same slate of directors in opposition to the management slate; from agreeing to indemnify (or be indemnified by) other shareholders in connection with running for office; and from asking for and receiving permission to use the name of another stockholder for purposes of endorsing his slate, even if there were no irrevocable proxy given or other promises made.

In other words Stahl contends, and the company agrees, that the *in terrorem* effect of the beneficial ownership definition upon him is to isolate him; to prevent him from reaching agreements with other shareholders (whether revocable or not) that would not direct the voting of stock, but that would otherwise concern the election contest. Mr. Stahl does not contend that a definition preventing him from entering into contracts, agreements or understandings that *bind* another to vote for his slate or that *bind* another not to vote in favor of the management nominees would be invalid. The formation of blocks of committed (legally bound) shares, he implicitly concedes, involves circumstances and considerations closely analogous to those arising from the existence of a large single shareholder, which considerations have been held to present threats justifying the rights that poison pill plans contemplate. But agreements that broadly *relate* to the vote but that do not bind other shareholders (such as agreements of the kind specified above) cannot, he says, be seen as presenting a sufficient risk to justify the direct imposition on the fairness of the proxy contest that, he asserts, the broad definition of beneficial ownership in the rights plan entails.

The board responds that the restrictions on Mr. Stahl's proxy contest activities are minimal. It correctly points out that the restriction does not directly infringe upon Mr. Stahl's ability to present a slate and to communicate with shareholders; nor does it impair the shareholders' ability to vote for Mr. Stahl's slate at the meeting. The board reminds us that similar provisions were upheld in Moran v. Household International, 500 A.2d 1346 (Del.1985), and it asserts that enforcement of this isolating definition does serve an important corporate interest. The board contends that it is not faced with a simple proxy contest, but with a cash tender offer for all shares at what it reasonably believes to be an unfair price. It is currently exploring economic alternatives to this low offer but it is doing so under a handicap: the existence of Mr. Stahl's 30% block of stock itself creates a disincentive for other bidders to invest the time and resources necessary to bring a competing proposal forward. The board contends that if Mr. Stahl is able to reach agreements with other shareholders (such as agreements to run on the same slate) this disincentive will be increased. If Stahl gets stronger by whatever means, the board gets weaker in dealing with him. Thus, the argument runs, it is in the corporation's interest to isolate him and do what can legitimately be done to weaken his current prospects for success in the proxy contest. Perception of a weakened state, it is asserted, will encourage

others to bid and will encourage Stahl to bargain, when that time comes. . .
.

<h2 style="text-align:center">II</h2>

As indicated above, the relief sought in the amended complaint and in the motion before the court appears to be a judicial declaration that the beneficial ownership provision of Bancorp's stock rights plan cannot validly be applied to agreements or understandings that *direct the voting of shares but are unconditionally revocable* or agreements that relate to the proxy contest *but do not legally bind any person to vote* in one way or another.

There is a strong normative argument that might be offered in support of such a position. While corporate elections are not perfectly parallel to civic elections (one can, for example, accumulate votes by buying shares), notions of what a fair election means and entails do inescapably carry over to some extent from one setting to the other. It is troubling in either context if the side in control of the levers of power employs them with respect to an election to coerce its opposition to restrict its legitimate electioneering activities. One need not assume bad faith on the part of incumbents to foresee in such a situation the prospects for unfairness; honest men seeking their (disputable) vision of what is best, if not bound-in by rules, are capable of gross impositions. Thus, it offers cold comfort that the law will assume that directors are acting in good faith. Where the franchise is involved a special obligation falls upon courts to review with care action that impinges upon legitimate election activities.

In *Moran v. Household International. . .*, the stockholder argued:. . .

> that the "20% trigger" effectively prevent[ed] any stockholder from first acquiring 20% or more shares before conducting a proxy contest and further, *it prevent[ed] stockholders from banding together into a group to solicit proxies if, collectively, they own[ed] 20% or more of the stock.* . . . 500 A.2d at 1355 (emphasis added).

The Supreme Court quoted the Vice Chancellor's ruling on this point:
. . .

> On the evidence presented *it is highly conjectural* to assume that a particular effort to assert shareholder views in the election of directors or revisions of corporate policy will be frustrated by the proxy feature of the Plan. Household's witnesses, Troubh and Higgins described recent corporate takeover battles in which insurgents holding less than 10% stock ownership were able to secure corporate control through a proxy contest or the threat of one. *Id.* (emphasis added).

The Supreme Court then found that:

There was sufficient evidence at trial to support the Vice Chancellor's finding that *the effect upon proxy contests will be minimal. Id.* (emphasis added).

Having concluded that the impact on proxy contests would be minimal, the court rejected the contention that the rights plan would impermissibly burden a proxy contest. The Supreme Court's determination that the flip-over pill considered in *Moran* involved acceptable ("minimal") effects on proxy contests, points us first to the recognition that validity of stock rights must be assessed at the time of the corporate action creating them; validity of corporate securities cannot rise or fall on future contingencies once issued. . . . *Moran* held that there was only "conjecture" and "speculation" to support the conclusion that the effects of the pill were other than "minimal" on proxy contests in that instance. . . .

The thrust of the Supreme Court's reasoning in *Moran* was simply that the restrictions imposed by the stock rights plan on a proxy contest were immaterial to conducting a proxy fight effectively. In adopting the stock rights plan here, it has not been shown that the Bancorp board could not have reasonably concluded similarly. If it did the restrictions here at issue should be valid, as were those in *Moran*, unless the kinds of revocable voting agreements or other agreements not covering the voting of stock that are our focus, can be said to require or deserve the same treatment received by revocable proxies, which the Supreme Court in *Moran* in effect exempted from the language of the rights plan. See 500 A.2d at 1355. But while the kinds of agreements we consider now are the same as revocable proxies in that they are revocable, they may be different in many particulars of practical significance. The most salient difference, however, arises from the fact that an exemption for revocable proxies from the beneficial ownership definition is mandated by the Supreme Court's "immateriality" test. The acceptance of proxies is the essence of a proxy contest. A prohibition on accepting them beyond the triggering point could never be immaterial; it would be fatal to a proxy contestant's position. But voting agreements or understandings of the type here in question plainly could be (and in this instance probably are) immaterial in the sense that a shareholder may put forth a slate of candidates and communicate her position to others, and others may vote for that slate without restriction.

. . . [G]iven the fact that the summary judgment record does not permit me to say that the Bancorp board could not have reasonably concluded that the restrictions here addressed would not materially impair the ability of the shareholders to turn out the existing board, I cannot now conclude that the provision of the stock rights plan that defines beneficial ownership constitutes an invalid provision beyond the board's power to adopt.

III

[Stahl also argues] that it was a breach of fiduciary duty for the board to "retain the challenged provisions of the Rights Plan." Thus, this argument does not address the validity of the provision, but implicitly assumes the validity of it and seeks an order that it be amended (or judicially nullified) in the light of present circumstances. This argument is founded upon the undoubtedly correct premise that a board has a continuing duty to assess the impact of its stock rights plan upon the corporation and its stockholders and, to the extent it has legal power to do so, amend the plan or redeem the rights, when and if its fiduciary duty to the corporation dictates.

Plaintiff contends that, whether viewed under the enhanced business judgment test of Unocal Corp. v. Mesa Petroleum Co., 493 A.2d 946 (Del.1985), or under the non-business judgment test that this court has applied where corporate action is directed specifically towards affecting the exercise of the franchise, Blasius Industries v. Atlas Corp., 564 A.2d 651 (Del.Ch.1988); Aprahamian v. HBO & Co., 531 A.2d 1204 (Del.Ch.1987), the board's failure to now modify the reach of the beneficial ownership definition cannot be justified.

I pass rather quickly over the question what legal test structures the court's inquiry here. As the earlier opinion in this case relating to the calling of the annual meeting tried to show, these tests are structurally similar and may, as there, be functionally similar as well. Under either test the board bears a burden to justify its actions. The burden will be greater when the board action is directed specifically and primarily towards the voting process, because that process is the way in which the board itself derives power and thus is of central concern to the corporation and to the corporation law.

In this instance choice of a form of judicial review between these formulations is probably not decisive of anything. In all events, *Unocal* offers the appropriate framework for determination of the issues posed in this instance. In *Moran*, the Supreme Court directs our attention to *Unocal* in connection with claims of breach of fiduciary duty for failure to redeem a poison pill. For that reason alone it is presumptively the standard to employ. 500 A.2d at 1357. Moreover the approach taken in *Blasius*, *Aprahamian* and other cases is appropriate when board action appears directed primarily towards interfering with the fair exercise of the franchise (*e.g.*, moving a meeting date; adopting a bylaw regulating shareholder voting, etc.). The stock rights plan may or may not have that effect, but it does not represent action taken for the primary purpose of interfering with the exercise of the shareholders' right to elect directors.

Unocal's structure and content need not be revisited here. The gist of the enhanced review is a judicial judgment concerning the reasonableness of the action taken in light of the threat to which it responds. Thus, where it is applicable, *Unocal* requires a judicial judgment finely focused upon the particulars of the case. . . .

I conclude in these circumstances, that the position of the board to leave in place and enforce the beneficial ownership term of the stock rights plan is reasonable in relation to the threat posed by the Stahl offer at this time. See Paramount Communications. v. Time, Inc., 571 A.2d 1140, 1153 (Del.1989). The motion for summary judgment will therefore be denied.

Note: Understanding Stahl II

1. Note Chancellor Allen's sleight of hand in interpreting *Moran* to control whether a board has the power to adopt a definition of beneficial ownership that impairs a dissident's chances in a proxy fight. *Moran* involved a *facial* challenge to a first-generation flip-over pill in its entirety. The Delaware Supreme Court was concerned about the pill's *potential* impact on a proxy fight, but found that a material impact on proxy contests had not been shown. That did not preclude careful scrutiny of the provisions of the much more potent flip-in pill used by Apple Bancorp, to assess how those provisions would affect an actual, ongoing proxy contest. Indeed, *Moran* seems to invites careful scrutiny of a poison pill *as applied* in a particular proxy contest.

Chancellor Allen declines the invitation. Instead, he treats the question almost as one of business judgment, holding that "it has not been shown that *the Bancorp board could not have reasonably concluded*" that the pill would have an immaterial impact on a proxy fight (emphasis added). The Apple Bancorp board did not even have to show that they had *in fact* reached that conclusion. Contrast this with the *Unocal* standard, where the court must decide whether a defensive response was *in fact* reasonable in relation to the threat posed, not whether the target's board *thought* the response was reasonable or, weaker yet, *could reasonably have thought* the response was reasonable.

2. What happened, one is tempted to ask, to Chancellor Allen's bold rhetoric in *Blasius* about the need for a "compelling justification" for the board to interfere with shareholder power to elect directors? After *Stahl II* and *Stroud v. Grace*, how large is the sphere of shareholder voting power specially protected by *Blasius*?

3. Poison pills necessarily affect proxy fights by limiting the stake that any shareholder can own. Should corporate law permit poison pills to be drafted in ways that have a further effect on a proxy fight, material or otherwise? Chancellor Allen assumes that the answer is yes, but this does not follow directly from *Moran*, where the challenge was to the poison pill as a whole, not to a particular provision that affected proxy contests. An affirmative answer is scarcely obvious as a matter of corporate theory. If boards can adopt poison pills, without shareholder approval, with provisions whose principal impact is on proxy contests, doesn't that undermine the legitimacy of director power? In *Blasius*, Chancellor Allen develops the common argument that the legitimacy of director power derives from

shareholder ability to choose the directors. Isn't that argument equally powerful here?[23]

4. Recall the Delaware Supreme Court's statement in *Stroud* that *Blasius* is a "specific expression" of the more general *Unocal* test. Similarly, Chancellor Allen states in *Stahl II* that the *Blasius* test is "structurally similar and may, as [in *Stahl I*], be functionally similar" to the *Unocal* test. If so, how much difference does it make whether *Blasius* applies or not? How much special justification do target directors need for actions that interfere with the shareholder franchise?

D. Defensive Tactics III: ESOPs and Other Tainted Votes

The procedural maneuvers explored above, and the obstacles to joint action created by a poison pill, form only part of the incumbents' arsenal in a proxy contest. In many proxy contests, corporate managers will receive votes from shares they don't personally own, for reasons unrelated to the merits of the proposal. The managers can often increase in mid-contest the number of votes in their pocket, should the need arise. First, managers can put pressure on institutional investors to vote promanager for reasons unrelated to the merits of the proposal.

Second, under New York Stock Exchange (NYSE) rules, stockbrokers who hold shares in street name for their clients can vote those shares on routine matters unless the client gives them voting instructions at least 10 days before the meeting. They can't vote client shares if they know of a contest, nor on a merger or other matter "which may affect substantially the rights or privileges of such stock."[24] Operating under this vague standard, the NYSE lists in a weekly bulletin the matters on which member firms may vote client shares. Brokers invariably vote client shares promanager.

Usually, this rule simply pads the affirmative vote on routine matters. But the NYSE staff has more than once authorized a promanager vote despite a well-publicized proxy fight. Even when the NYSE instructs brokers not to vote client shares on a particular matter, enforcement is nonexistent, and anecdotal evidence suggests that brokers sometimes vote when they shouldn't.

Third, commercial banks, which also hold stock as nominees, can vote client shares on *any* matter, subject only to the bank's fiduciary duty to its clients. Banks, like broker-dealers, routinely vote promanager.

Fourth, company proxy cards invariably provide that shareholders who simply sign the card have voted for the managers' choice on all issues

---

[23] Compare the skepticism expressed in dictum by Vice Chancellor Jacobs, in Henley Group v. Santa Fe Southern Pacific Corp., 1988 WL 23945 (Del.Ch.1988), about whether a poison pill could be used to obstruct joint efforts directed at a proxy contest. In *Henley*, Santa Fe Southern Pacific, fearing an adverse decision, amended its pill to permit such joint efforts, before Henley's challenge reached Vice Chancellor Jacobs.

[24] New York Stock Exchange, *Listed Company Manual* ¶ 402.06(D).

presented. Some shareholders simply sign and return the card, never having read the proxy statement.

Fifth, the managers tabulate the ballots, or at least appoint the tabulators. Even if the tabulators are basically honest,[25] the complex system of proxy voting, where shareholders vote through layers of record holders, and votes can be repeatedly cast and revoked, produces many ballots that can be either counted or thrown out as irregular, and some where the number of votes cast is unclear. The tabulators must exercise discretion, and experience teaches that they exercise that discretion in the managers' favor more often than not.[26]

Sixth, managers can put blocks of stock in friendly hands, even in mid-contest. Polaroid, for example, recently defeated a hostile bid by issuing a 14% block to an employee stock ownership plan (ESOP) and selling a large block of voting preferred stock to Corporate Partners, a white squire fund, on terms highly favorable to Corporate Partners. A mid-contest issuance is likely to be upheld, the cases suggest, if the transaction is at arms-length and the voting power is reasonably related to the price paid for the stock.[27]

Finally, managers can vote some shares that they don't own. Corporate pension plans usually own at least some stock in the sponsoring company. Company managers usually can ensure that these shares are voted promanager; some vote the shares themselves. Contrast this with the usual rule that treasury shares and shares held by subsidiaries can't vote. Similarly, ESOP trustees, who are often company managers, can vote unvested ESOP shares. Unvested ESOP shares were an important factor in the 1990 Lockheed proxy fight. Moreover, some companies have standstill agreements with large shareholders under which the shareholder agrees to vote promanager on all or at least some matters.

ESOPs are of special interest to target managers who would like to stuff the ballot box in a proxy fight. White squires cannot always be found, and are potentially dangerous. The white squire must have the power to vote as

---

[25] Some aren't. See, e.g., Committee for New Management of Guar. Bancshares v. Dimeling, 772 F.Supp. 230 (E.D.Pa.1991) (election judge, who had close ties to the incumbents, abused discretion in throwing out large proxy given to dissidents).

[26] Blasius Indus. v. Atlas Corp., 564 A.2d 651 (Del.Ch.1988), provides a good example. The tabulators chose a procedure for interpreting multiple ballots by record holders that they had been orally told was incorrect by a representative of Independent Election Corp. of America, which handles voting for many record holders. The chosen procedure swung the vote in the managers' favor. The court (in a portion of the opinion not excerpted in this chapter) upheld the tabulators' choice as reasonable.

[27] Compare, e.g., Shamrock Holdings v. Polaroid Corp., 559 A.2d 278 (Del.Ch.1989); British Printing & Communication Corp. v. Harcourt Brace Jovanovich, Inc., 664 F.Supp. 1519 (S.D.N.Y.1987) (upholding sale of stock to investment bank); and Gelco Corp. v. Coniston Partners, 811 F.2d 414 (8th Cir.1987) (same), with, e.g., Unilever Acquisition Corp. v. Richardson-Vicks, Inc., 618 F.Supp. 407 (S.D.N.Y.1985) (enjoining dividend of supervoting stock which loses most of its votes upon transfer); Packer v. Yampol, C.A.No. 8432 (Del.Ch.1986) (enjoining sale of supervoting stock to CEO).

it sees fit on director elections, if the stock placement is to survive judicial scrutiny. It can be counted on to vote promanager this time, but the future carries the risk that the white squire will change hats. Employees are safer, as long as they think a pro-incumbent vote will safeguard their jobs.

For ESOPs, the current practice is to give employees a small number of vested shares immediately, and then bind the ESOP trustees to vote the much larger number of unvested shares in the same proportion as the vested shares.[28] Employees almost always vote promanager, at least in the ESOP's early years, when employees own few vested shares and the expected benefit of greater security of employment far exceeds the gain from a higher price for their vested stock.

Incumbents can, however, to go too far in giving employees an incentive to vote promanager, and protecting them against a fall in stock price if they do so. In the next case, NCR crossed the line in establishing a leveraged ESOP as part of its defense against AT&T, in the largest hostile takeover battle of 1991:

NCR CORP. v. AMERICAN TELEPHONE AND TELEGRAPH CO.
761 F.Supp. 475 (W.D.Ohio 1991)

RICE, District Judge. . . . Following an expedited discovery period, a trial on the question of whether NCR Corporation's [employee stock ownership plan (ESOP)] is valid and enforceable (or the converse) was held on March 11 and 12, 1991. . . . [T]he court hereby makes the following Findings of Fact and Conclusions of Law.

FINDINGS OF FACT

*   *   *

C. *American Telephone and Telegraph Company's Tender Offer and Subsequent Proxy Contest*

16. Beginning in mid-November, 1990, AT&T made unsolicited proposals to NCR to purchase all of NCR's outstanding common stock in exchange for AT&T stock. . . .

19. NCR has a "staggered" Board, with one-third of the seats up for election at each regular annual meeting. Therefore, under normal circumstances, a proxy contestant, even with the support of a majority of shares, must wait two years to gain control of the Board. . . .

---

[28] Earlier efforts to have company managers serve as ESOP trustees and have discretion to vote unvested shares foundered on the rock of fiduciary duty under ERISA. See Donovan v. Bierwirth, 680 F.2d 263 (2d Cir.1982).

21. Under the terms of NCR's Charter, a "supermajority" vote of 80% of all *outstanding* voting shares is required to replace a majority of Directors at a special meeting. Since it is necessary to obtain 80% of the outstanding shares, as opposed to 80% of the shares actually voted, shares not voted at a special meeting are the functional equivalent of votes for the incumbent Board. . . .

D. *Adoption of the NCR ESOP*

26. [NCR considered adopting an ESOP as a takeover defense in 1986 and 1988, but rejected the idea both times.] NCR began reconsidering the concept of establishing an ESOP in December, 1990. Once again, the ESOP was discussed in the context of a takeover defense, not as an employee benefits option. . . .

39. At the February 20, 1991, Board meeting, [NCR Chief Financial Officer John] Giering made a detailed presentation of the proposed ESOP. In conjunction with this presentation, the Directors were given "Board books," which basically reflected the materials sent to them over the previous month.

40. The Board books do not contain a great deal of substantive information regarding the specifics of the proposed ESOP. Rather, most pages simply contain a number of "bullets," evidently signifying general areas of interest or topics of conversation. There are a number of graphs comparing the proposed plan with the current benefits package, and various charts showing the general economic impact of the ESOP on the company. Some general articles on ESOPs are reproduced, but there is no comparison of the proposed ESOP to working models at other companies. Following Giering's presentation, the Board voted unanimously to adopt the proposal. . . .

E. *The NCR ESOP's Size and Voting Impact*

45. On February 20, 1991, nine days before the record date of March 1 [for NCR's shareholder meeting], NCR authorized the issue of 5,509,641.873 shares of preferred stock to State Street Bank and Trust Company as ESOP Trustee at a price of $90.75 per share, for an aggregate price of $500 million.

46. The NCR preferred stock initially is convertible into eight-tenths of a share of common stock at a conversion price of $113.4375 per share of common stock. This price represents a conversion premium of 25% over the closing of NCR common stock the day before the transaction was submitted to the Board for approval.

47. Under the terms of the preferred stock, the approximately 5,500,000 newly issued shares are entitled to one vote per share even though each preferred share is convertible into only eight-tenths of a share of common stock. This preferential treatment of the voting power of the NCR convertible preferred stock vis-a-vis the common shares is referred to by the NCR Board as "heavy voting."

48. The ESOP provides for an initial allocation of one share of preferred stock for each of the approximately 24,000 salaried employees who are eligible to participate in the ESOP. This step was taken in advance of the March 1 record date for the upcoming special meeting, notwithstanding that the period in which employees are entitled to elect whether to participate in the ESOP did not begin until March 4, three days after the record date. . . .

52. Through the ESOP, NCR has vested voting power over the entire 5,500,000 share block of NCR preferred stock, including approximately 5,476,000 shares that have not yet been allocated to anyone, in approximately 24,000 employees who have been given one share each. The Trustee is obligated by the "pass-through" or "mirrored" voting provisions of the ESOP to vote the entire block of unallocated shares in the same proportion as [the allocated] employee shares voting at any NCR shareholders meeting.

53. Since the power to vote the 5,500,000 preferred shares is divided among the holders of 24,000 shares, the pass-through voting procedure vests each of the shares held by NCR's current employees with the equivalent of 229 votes.

54. Since the ESOP in question is a leveraged ESOP, all shares were issued at once. The 5,500,000 share block puts about 8% of the outstanding NCR voting stock into employee hands. At the same time, this large issue dilutes [the ownership interest of the already] outstanding common stock . . . .

57. James Ahstrom, an ESOP specialist with First Boston Corporation, testified, and the Court so finds, that unleveraged ESOPs enjoy substantial tax advantages not available to leveraged ESOPs. Specifically, a corporation which has an unleveraged ESOP may deduct depreciation. If NCR's stock rises in the manner predicted by NCR's financial advisors, NCR will have foregone potentially hundreds of millions of dollars in tax savings by leveraging its ESOP.

58. Testimony also established that the same objectives of providing incentive to employees by vesting them with partial ownership and by tying their compensation to the growth of the company may be achieved with equal success through an unleveraged ESOP. . . .

G. *The Issuance of the Preferred Stock*

66. The only consideration NCR received for the issuance of 5,500,000 shares of convertible preferred stock to the ESOP Trustee was the Trustee's $500 million non-recourse promissory note due in 2016. . . .

68. The contract documents by which the ESOP was implemented require NCR to provide the Trustee with sufficient funds to permit the Trustee to turn around and pay NCR the amounts of principal and interest due from time to time upon the note. In effect, NCR agreed to pay itself principal and interest upon the $500 million note, using the Trustee as a conduit for such payments, throughout the 25-year life of the ESOP.

69. An ESOP transaction in which the issuer receives only the trustee's non-recourse promissory note in exchange for the issuance of stock differs in substance from the conventional leveraged ESOP financed by a bank loan guaranteed by the issuer. In the case of bank financing, cash flows into the corporation that can be used to generate additional earnings. In contrast, in a case where the corporation simply issues stock in exchange for a promissory note, the existing shareholders' interest is diluted without any enrichment of the corporation.

70. The customary practice when a new series of securities is issued is for the purchaser or receiver to demand a legal opinion stating the securities are validly issued. In Maryland, such legal opinions customarily contain language indicating that the securities are "validly issued, full paid, and nonassessable."

71. The Trustee's outside legal counsel requested both Charles Russ, NCR's general counsel, and NCR's Maryland counsel, Piper & Marbury, to render such an opinion. Although both offered legal opinions, neither opinion contained the words "validly issued, full paid, and nonassessable."

72. The legal opinions were obtained after negotiations. While it is not uncommon for parties to negotiate over the language of legal opinions, Lowell Bowen, an expert on Maryland corporate law, described the terms "validly issued, full paid, and nonassessable" as being "irreducible minimums." . . .

H. *Economic Incentives for Preferred Shareholders to Vote for NCR*

78. The holders of NCR preferred stock are the beneficiaries of a unique "reset" provision. Under this provision, if the price of NCR common stock drops (for example, should AT&T withdraw its tender offer), the conversion formula for the ESOP preferred stock will be "reset" in order to compensate for the lower common stock value. The preferred shares, currently convertible into eight-tenths of a share of common stock, will

actually become convertible into more than one share of common stock. No such "downside" protection is available to holders of NCR common stock. . . .

81. If AT&T withdraws its tender offer, the price of NCR stock is expected to fall as much as twenty or thirty points. If that occurs, the preferred shares will be reset, diluting the common stock even further.

82. The holders of NCR preferred stock have no downside risk. Preferred shareholders have downside protection at all times because of a perpetual "floor" at the $90.75 purchase price that is built into the terms of the preferred. At any time during the life of the plan when a share of preferred stock can be redeemed, the holder of the preferred stock may elect to receive either (i) the fair market value of the shares of common stock into which the preferred stock is convertible, plus any dividends which have accrued over the years, or (ii) the issue price of $90.75 per share. Thus, while common holders are subject to full market risk, an ESOP participant is guaranteed a minimum payment of $90.75 per preferred share, regardless of however low the price of NCR common stock may drop.

83. If [AT&T drops its offer and], after falling, [NCR's] stock price ultimately rises again, common shareholders will have suffered an interim loss in value. In contrast, under such circumstances, preferred shareholders will actually have obtained a benefit from the interim downturn in market price because of the operation of the reset provision. Therefore, preferred shareholders have an economic incentive to vote against AT&T's nominees at the special meeting. . . .

87. Even if AT&T were to raise its tender offer price [above the current level of $90 per share], the 25% "redemption premium" built into the preferred stock operates so that the holders of the preferred will gain no value; the preferred stock is indifferent to increases in prices below $ 123.08 per share. By contrast, if AT&T were to raise its price, the common stock will, in turn, benefit dollar for dollar. . . .

88. In short, the economic incentives built into the terms of the preferred shares would cause most rational preferred shareholders who understood the terms and provisions of those shares to vote for the incumbent NCR Directors and against AT&T at the special meeting.

I. *The ESOP's Effect on the Outcome of the Special Meeting*

. . . 102. . . . [T]he ESOP has the effect of placing a substantial block of stock into "friendly" hands. . . . NCR needs only garner 20% of the vote at the special meeting to avoid replacement of its Directors. Since the Board and management hold approximately 2% of the outstanding shares, and the

ESOP accounts for approximately 8%, roughly half of the votes necessary to forestall AT&T's attempt to control the Board appear to be a "lock" for NCR.

103. ... [T]he 80% target, which is realistically attainable for AT&T absent the ESOP, is, for all practical purposes, an unreachable goal if preferred shares created by the ESOP are allowed to vote.

J. *Information Not Presented to or Discussed by the Board*

104. When a new series of stock is issued, it is customary for a corporation to obtain a "fairness opinion," stating, in essence, that the issue is fair to current shareholders.

105. No fairness opinion was sought or received in connection with the issue of the convertible preferred stock. Although at least some Board members are familiar with the concept of a fairness opinion, the desirability of obtaining one was never even discussed.

106. The Board was not informed that NCR's senior benefits professionals would not recommend the plan if the "primary criteria were benefits related."

107. The dividend on the preferred stock is about two percentage points higher than that on common shares, a situation which [First Boston ESOP specialist] Ahstrom characterized as a "transfer of wealth" from common holders to holders of preferred stock. . . .

109. The Board was told that one of the assumptions upon which the ESOP was based was that NCR stock would grow at an average rate of 11% per year throughout the 25-year life of the plan. Board members were not shown the annual breakdown prepared by Goldman, Sachs, which estimated that the stock would realize huge growth in the next few years and experience negative growth during the final years of the plan, thus resulting in a final average of 11%. . . .

111. Although the Board was told in the Board book that the ESOP shares "are considered outstanding" if issued in exchange for the Trustee's note, the Directors were not told that, at the very least, there was a substantial legal doubt that this was true under Maryland law, and that neither NCR's Maryland counsel nor NCR's general counsel was willing to give the customary legal opinion certifying that the shares were validly issued.

112. The Directors were similarly not informed by management that the stock certificates were not in the customary form in that they lacked the legend indicating that payment has been made.

113. Unaware of potential problems with Maryland law, the Board could not have known that the possibility of the ESOP later being refinanced through a bank loan had been jeopardized by the absence of customary opinions that lending institutions generally require.

114. For the same reason, the Directors could not have known that a proper listing application could not be made to the New York Stock Exchange for the common shares into which the ESOP preferred is convertible. No such application was made, in apparent violation of the Stock Purchase Agreement and the Exchange's Listed Company Manual, and there is no evidence that the Board was ever so informed.

115. The Board was not advised that the tax and accounting benefits that had made ESOPs more attractive financing devices until the end of 1989 had been repealed.

116. The Board was not advised that the terms of the ESOP preferred were extremely unusual, and that no other ESOP preferred has the combination of terms contained in the NCR ESOP. A Duff & Phelps summary of some 60 ESOPs, although contained in Goldman Sachs' files, was neither given to the Directors nor summarized for them.

117. The Board was presented only with a leveraged ESOP proposal, not an unleveraged one as well. The Board was either unaware of or simply did consider the fact that the same employee benefits and incentives could be conferred and created through an unleveraged ESOP in which (i) the company would retain hundreds of millions of dollars of potential tax deductions which a leveraged ESOP sacrifices; (ii) the company could keep control over share allocations on an annual basis instead of attempting to estimate benefits needs 25 years into the future; and (iii) there would accordingly be no risk of overfunding. . . .

OPINION

[The court first concludes that this case is governed by Maryland law.]

B. *NCR's Business Judgment Justification*

"In Maryland, as elsewhere, directors of a corporation occupy a fiduciary relationship to the corporation and its stockholders." Martin Marietta Corp. v. Bendix Corp., 549 F.Supp. 623, 633 (D.Md.1982). . . . The heart of the fiduciary duty imposed upon directors of publicly-held corporations is the obligation to "act in a manner they reasonably believe to be in the best interests of the corporation." *Id.* This duty is plainly composed of two separate elements, one subjective and the other objective. A director may take no action on behalf of a corporation unless he or she is of the belief that such action is in the corporation's best interest. However, the second condition implicit in the director's fiduciary duty is that his or her belief be reasonable.

Applying the first prong of this test to the facts of the case at bar, the Court has difficulty in believing that NCR's outside Directors adopted the ESOP with the subjective belief that they were acting in a manner harmful to the corporation or its common shareholders. NCR's ten outside Directors are both accomplished and respected in their various fields, are independent of NCR's management, and would appear to have little to gain by acting improperly. . . .

This, however, does not automatically entitle NCR to judgment in this case. As the court noted in *Martin Marietta*, a board's belief that it acts properly must be reasonable. The business judgment rule serves to uphold the decisions of a board which acts "*on an informed basis*, in good faith and in the honest belief that the action taken was in the best interests of the company." Aronson v. Lewis, 473 A.2d 805, 812 (Del.1984) (emphasis added). See also Smith v. Van Gorkom, 488 A.2d 858 (Del.1985). Any decision undertaken on the basis of insufficient knowledge is inherently unreasonable. "Under the business judgment rule there is no protection for directors who have made an unintelligent or unadvised judgment." *Van Gorkom*, 488 A.2d at 872. . . .

In the present case, the record is rife with references to information which was readily available but which was either not presented to the outside Directors by management or, if it was presented, was apparently not duly considered by the Board. While there is no one topic or subject which, if not fully discussed and evaluated by a board of directors, will cause a transaction to become *per se* invalid, the totality of the circumstances in this case indicates that the NCR Board, in approving management's ESOP plan, acted manifestly without an adequate body of knowledge.

[The court justified this conclusion by reviewing various information that wasn't presented to the board, questions that the board failed to ask, and alternatives that the board failed to consider.]

C. *Invalidity of the ESOP Under the Primary Purpose Test*

In the seminal case of Cummings v. United Artists Theatre Circuit, Inc., 204 A.2d 795, 806 (Md.1964), the Maryland Court of Appeals declared that

> where a good corporate purpose is being furthered and is the principal motivation for an action by a board of directors, the fact that the consummation of such transaction may have some effect on the control of the corporation is immaterial and the agreement will stand or fall depending on whether it is fair to the corporation.

The import of the *Cummings* holding was later expounded upon by the court in Mountain Manor Realty v. Buccheri, 461 A.2d 45, 53 (Md.App.1983):

> Whatever the law may be elsewhere, it seems fairly clear that in Maryland stock issuances which have the effect of consolidating or perpetuating management control are not necessarily invalid. They are, instead, to be examined under a sort of balancing test; assuming that the transaction is legal in all other respects . . . the court must look to see if there was any legitimate business purpose for the transaction other than the self-interest of the directors. If it finds such a purpose, under *Cummings* it would then have to determine whether that independent purpose was a primary or principal one, or whether, conversely, the primary object was merely to manipulate control.

The court concluded:

> If the court finds that the transaction was, on the whole, motivated by a legitimate corporate purpose, it should declare the sale [of stock] to be valid; if it finds to the contrary -- that the purpose of the transaction was primarily one of management's self-perpetuation and that purpose outweighed any other legitimate business purpose -- it should declare the sale to be invalid. *Id.*

. . . Under the above referenced test, the Court must make an initial determination of whether the NCR ESOP has "the effect of consolidating or perpetuating management control." There is little doubt that it does. . . .

The next determination is whether the ESOP serves any legitimate corporate purpose. Quite apart from their perceived utility as a defense to hostile takeover attempts, ESOPs are a common form of employee compensation. They serve the purpose of giving salaried employees a stake in the company's future, thereby presumably providing those employees with added incentive to put forth their best efforts. Robert Allen, AT&T's Chief Executive Officer, stated in his deposition that he believes "that ownership in any company has characteristics of incentive or has the potential of providing incentive to employees." . . .

Since the ESOP has the effect of perpetuating management control, but also serves a valid purpose, the Court must embark upon the balancing test referred to in *Mountain Manor*. Upon weighing the facts, the evidence, taken as a whole, overwhelmingly demonstrates that the primary purpose of the ESOP is to entrench NCR management, in contravention of the principles of corporate democracy. The Court bases this determination upon a series of factors, none of which, standing alone, is dispositive, but which, in the aggregate, allow for no other conclusion.

1. *Timing*

The timing of the ESOP is, in and of itself, enough to raise an inference that it was motivated by a desire to perpetuate management control. The

ESOP concept, which had been abandoned over a year earlier as unfeasible, was suddenly resurrected in the face of AT&T's tender offer, and in spite of intervening tax law and accounting rule changes which made the concept far less attractive as a means of benefitting employees. . . .

In its haste to get all the pieces in place by the record date, the finance department outraced the employee benefits department, resulting in the enrollment period opening before informational booklets and software had been made available to workers. In addition, NCR was willing to settle for [an unsatisfactory] legal opinion regarding the validity of the stock issue under Maryland [law] which calls into question its ability to refinance the ESOP at a later date.

2. *Size*

The enormous size of the initial stock issue also reveals its true purpose. Despite the fact that NCR had no firm indication of what employee response would be to the ESOP, over five and a half million shares were issued for 24,000 current salaried employees. NCR sacrificed thousands, if not millions, of dollars in future tax benefits and left itself without the ability to adjust the plan to meet actual benefits needs. All this was done for the sole purpose of creating a sizable voting block of shares in time for a meeting crucial to the continued survival of the company as an independent entity.

NCR's own benefits people are of the opinion that the size of the ESOP is not benefits related. Moreover, the vast majority of the shares are not allocated to employees. Unallocated shares of stock are not likely to provide much of an incentive to employees to work harder. The same objectives of giving salaried employees a stake in NCR's future could have been just as effectively and much less expensively achieved through a smaller ESOP, either leveraged or unleveraged.

3. *Mirrored Voting*

Closely related to the size of the ESOP is the fact that the ESOP has a mirrored voting provision which allows each employee to, in effect, cast 229 votes at the election. However, from a compensation standpoint, the same employee who votes 229 shares receives a benefit based only upon his one allocated share. If the primary purpose of the ESOP is to provide employees with better benefits, there is no need for the mirrored voting procedure. . . .

4. *Context of ESOP Discussions*

Director Bowen stated at trial that all discussions that the Board undertook in late 1990 and early 1991 took place in the context of the AT&T tender offer, an understandable state of affairs. Both he and Exley admitted that the ESOP idea resurfaced as one of a range of possible defenses to the takeover attempt.

However, that is only part of the story. Even though there was no apparent threat of a takeover attempt in 1986 or in 1988-89, NCR's interest in ESOPs during those time periods was similarly limited to their use as a defensive measure. At no time was an ESOP ever proposed as a means of employee compensation or as a tool to provide greater incentive to workers, even during the years 1988 and 1989, when the favorable tax and accounting treatment of ESOPs motivated numerous other companies to establish them.

5. *Lack of Personnel or Employee Benefits Department Input or Support*

The testimony establishes that employee benefit changes usually had their genesis in either the personnel or the employee benefits departments. However, the finance committee took the lead in investigating and structuring the ESOP. The employee benefits people did not have a great deal of input when it came to putting together the final proposal. Indeed, the Board showed surprisingly little interest in the opinion of the benefits department. Although McElwain, the ranking employee benefits person at NCR, was present at the February 1991 Board meeting, he did not give a presentation, nor did the Board direct questions to him. The evidence also demonstrates that the benefits department was not in favor of the ESOP. . . .

6. *Structure of the Preferred Stock*

Finally, the economic incentives built into the preferred stock cannot be ignored. These incentives pit the interests of preferred shareholders against those of common shareholders. Moreover, the preferred stock is structured in a manner which virtually assures that no rational holder, fully apprised of the terms and conditions of the preferred stock, will vote against the incumbent Board at the special meeting. . . .

The Court's determination that the NCR Board acted with the primary purpose of "rigging" the vote at the special meeting is sufficient to invalidate the transaction under the applicable law of Maryland. However, the parties have also thoroughly briefed this case under the law of Delaware. . . . On the chance that Maryland would follow pertinent Delaware case law, the Court emphasizes that the same result is mandated by that body of authority.

The courts of Delaware recognize that "the business judgment rule is available to directors acting in response to a takeover threat." Shamrock Holdings v. Polaroid Corp., 559 A.2d 278, 286 (Del.Ch.1989) (*Polaroid II*). However, because of the "omnipresent specter that a board may be acting primarily in its own interests," two requirements must be satisfied before the business judgment rule will be applied. The directors must establish "reasonable grounds for believing that a danger to corporate policy and effectiveness existed because of another person's stock ownership" and the defensive measure chosen by the board must be "reasonable in relation to the threat posed." *Id.* at 286-87 (citing Unocal Corp. v. Mesa Petroleum Co., 493 A.2d 946, 954-55 (Del.1985)). . . .

[I]t is unlikely that the ESOP was a rational response to [any danger posed by the AT&T bid]. First, as referenced above, the Board did not exercise informed judgment in its decision to adopt the ESOP. Moreover, the ESOP itself appears hastily thrown together and unfair to common shareholders, both to an extreme. . . .

No fairness opinion was sought. A [nonstandard] legal opinion regarding the validity of the offer was quickly negotiated. The benefits people were not consulted to any significant degree. The stock issue was authorized nine days before the record date. Shares were distributed before the enrollment period began to employees who might not even choose to participate in the ESOP. The enrollment period commenced before informational booklets and software had been made available.

The Board either was not acting upon full information, or it failed to deliberate upon serious matters. There was a general unfamiliarity with the changes in tax laws and accounting rules. There was no conception of how the plan would be received by employees. . . . The views of McElwain and other benefits department representatives were not considered. In sum, the ESOP was not the result of careful planning.

In addition to presenting 24,000 employees with an immediate, irrevocable choice of benefit plans, the ESOP appears unfair to common shareholders. . . . The preferred stock has the benefit of heavy voting, as well as a reset provision which negates the risk of market fluctuations. The preferred stock carries a higher dividend, and is dilutive of the common. Finally, it creates a potential conflict of interest between the two classes of stock. . . . Since the leveraging was internal, no new capital flows into the company. NCR is locked into a large ESOP which cannot be adjusted to meet actual needs. Significant tax advantages were lost by the decision to leverage the plan.

Finally, NCR contends that the decision in Shamrock Holdings v. Polaroid Corp., 559 A.2d 257 (Del.Ch.1989) (*Polaroid I*) supports its position. This argument need not long detain the Court.

In *Polaroid I*, the court held that where, as here, the board of directors fails to act in an informed capacity, "the business judgment rule will not be applied and the transaction at issue will be scrutinized to determine whether it is entirely fair." 559 A.2d at 271. In that case, Polaroid established an ESOP which the court determined to be "partly defensive." The nine million shares of stock allocated to the ESOP caused a dilution of about 5%.

The Polaroid ESOP had a mirrored voting provision which allowed the independent trustee to vote unallocated shares in proportion to shares actually voted, similar to the NCR plan. Through the use of mirrored voting, Polaroid employees gained the right to vote 14% of the company's stock. Since Delaware law requires an 85% "supermajority" vote to replace an entire slate of directors, the proxy contestant found itself with only a 1% margin for error. The court, however, found that, on the whole, the plan was fair.

The fatal flaw in NCR's argument, of course, is that, in addition to having all the above referenced characteristics present in the Polaroid plan, the NCR ESOP has additional features which make the Polaroid plan pale in comparison. First, while the Polaroid plan was found to be "partly" defensive, the NCR plan was adopted with the overwhelming purpose of thwarting AT&T's tender offer. Employee benefits were not a primary concern.

Second, Polaroid financed its ESOP with a $285 million bank loan, thus realizing an influx of capital. It further financed the project by immediately cutting employee salaries and reducing the pay scale. Polaroid employees, therefore, shouldered part of the financial burden. Here, the ESOP was internally leveraged, and NCR employees contribute nothing toward the cost of the plan. The preferred shares have a dividend two percent higher than common stock, representing a further transfer of wealth from common shareholders to preferred.

. . . NCR preferred shares enjoy heavy voting and are protected from market fluctuations by a price "floor" and a reset provision, features absent in the Polaroid ESOP. Finally, despite the fact that NCR has no direct control over the votes cast by employees, the economic incentives inherent in the ESOP preferred stock assure NCR of employee loyalty at the ballot box. Accordingly, the Court cannot conclude that, even under the lenient standards of *Polaroid I*, the NCR ESOP may be characterized as fair.

Based upon the above, the Court concludes that AT&T has met its burden of proof on its Counterclaim of demonstrating that the primary purpose of the NCR ESOP was not benefits related but, rather, was an attempt by NCR management to impede corporate democracy and to perpetuate its control of the company. Accordingly, the ESOP is invalid and unenforceable. . . .

Note on Ballot Box Stuffing

1. Judge Rice, applying Maryland law, evaluated the NCR board's decision to adopt an ESOP in the middle of AT&T's proxy fight/tender offer under two standards: the business judgment rule and a "primary purpose" test similar to the early Delaware case of Cheff v. Mathes.[29] Under current Delaware law, what would the standard of review have been?

2. There are some traditional corporate law problems associated with leveraged ESOPs like NCR's. NCR's ESOP paid for its stock with a note. Under most corporate statutes, an unsecured note (or one secured only by the stock purchased) is not valid consideration for the purchase of stock. That

---

[29] 199 A.2d 548 (Del.1964).

is why neither NCR's outside counsel nor its in-house general counsel would give the standard opinion that the ESOP stock was validly issued.

The consideration problem can be avoided by having the ESOP borrow the funds necessary to pay for the stock from a bank. But when the transaction is funded in this way, the unallocated ESOP stock begins to resemble treasury stock. Typically, the company is required to guarantee the ESOP loan, and all dividends paid on the unallocated stock (or any proceeds from the sale of the stock or liquidation distributions) are used to pay down the loan. Thus, all the economic attributes of the stock belong to the company, with only the voting rights being transferred to the ESOP. The result is similar to the company giving a proxy with respect to treasury stock and separately borrowing funds. Under state corporate law, treasury stock cannot be voted. No case, as yet, addressed the validity of votes cast by a leveraged ESOP in this situation.

3. If *NCR* shows the limits on ballot box stuffing by directors, Polaroid's successful 1989 defense against a combined tender offer/proxy fight by Shamrock Holdings shows that the incumbents can do quite a lot of stuffing. Polaroid (i) placed 14% of the company's stock in an ESOP (to prevent Shamrock from using the exception to the Delaware antitakeover statute conditioned on the bidder acquiring 85% of the outstanding stock in the offer); (ii) Polaroid delayed the record date for its annual meeting to allow the sale of a large block of voting preferred stock to Corporate Partners, a "white squire" fund organized by Lazard Freres & Company; (iii) announced a $1.1 billion stock buyback at a substantial premium, in which the ESOP planned to sell its stock and then use the proceeds to purchase more Polaroid stock at the lower post-buyback price. The final stake held by ESOP, Corporate Partners, and management would have topped 30%. That would make a Shamrock-led proxy fight futile. Chancellor Berger upheld the defenses.[30] Soon thereafter, Shamrock abandoned its bid.[31]

4. More generally, if the board can convince a reviewing court that it had an ordinary business purpose for issuing shares, unrelated to diluting an unwanted shareholder's interest, neither heightened scrutiny under *Blasius* nor intermediate review under *Unocal* will be invoked. The transaction will be reviewed under the business judgment rule, and is thus almost certain to survive judicial challenge.[32]

5. The usual challenge to board action involves the board taking steps to dilute the interest of a *unwanted* shareholder, to *prevent* a change in control. Under what circumstances might it be appropriate for a board to

---

[30] See Shamrock Holdings v. Polaroid Corp., 559 A.2d 257 (Del.Ch.1989) (*Polaroid I*); Shamrock Holdings v. Polaroid Corp., 559 A.2d 278, 286 (Del.Ch.1989) (*Polaroid II*).

[31] See Norris, *The Polaroid Defense: A Potential Classic*, N.Y. Times, Feb. 24, 2989, at D1, col.4. Lilli Gordon & John Pound, *ESOPs and Corporate Control*, 27 J.Fin.Econ. 525 (1990), document the increased use of leveraged ESOPs as takeover defenses following Polaroid's success in warding off Shamrock.

[32] See, e.g., Glazer v. Zapata Corp., 1993 WL 193523 (Del.Ch.1993) (Allen, J.)

dilute the interest of a long-time controlling shareholders, to *facilitate* a change in control? In Mendel v. Carroll,[33] Chancellor Allen rejected a claim that the board of directors of Katy Industries had an obligation to dilute the voting power of the Carroll family, which controlled slightly over 50% of Katy's stock, to enable an unsolicited merger proposal by Pensler Capital, opposed by the Carroll family, to go forward. The Carrolls had proposed their own buyout, at a lower price than the Pensler proposal, and had withdrawn their offer rather than match Pensler's offer.

Chancellor Allen left for another day the possibility that a board could take such a "radical step" to protect the minority against "overreaching or palpable breach of fiduciary duty by a controlling shareholder." But where no overreaching or breach of fiduciary duty could be found, he concluded not only that the board didn't have to dilute the majority shareholder, but that it *couldn't* -- to do so would be a breach of fiduciary duty owed to the majority shareholder.

Note on the Independence of Investment Bankers

1. Why is Goldman Sachs' 25-year scenario for NCR's future stock price -- a rapid rise in the next few years, then slower growth, and finally a decline in price late in the period -- impossible? Hint: What is the relationship between present value and expected future value?

2. Why would Goldman offer such a ridiculous scenario? One possible reason: The predicted fast growth in the next few years helped to justify NCR's refusal to sell at a price below $125 per share. But long-term growth much faster than 11% apparently wasn't plausible. So Goldman's investment bankers compromised, and apparently didn't notice that their overall scenario violated basic principles of corporate finance.

Or maybe Goldman did notice, and that's why they wouldn't give a fairness opinion. It's standard practice to obtain an investment banker's fairness opinion in circumstances like this. NCR's counsel (Weil, Gotshal & Manges, an experienced takeover firm) almost surely explored obtaining a fairness opinion on the issuance of the ESOP shares. NCR's failure to obtain, or even formally request, a fairness opinion suggests that Goldman informally advised Weil Gotshal, in effect: "We can't deliver a clean opinion, so don't ask."

3. The quality of Goldman's advice brings to mind an old joke about accountants. A CEO needed to find a new accounting firm. He called in partners from a number of different firms for an interview and asked each a single question: "How much is two plus two?"

The losing response: "Four."

---

[33] Del.Ch. June 17, 1994 (Allen, Ch.).

The winning response: "What answer did you have in mind?"[34]

E.   Defensive Tactics IV: Putting a Price on Success

Can managers plant bombs of various sorts that will explode if a dissident wins a proxy fight? Can they, for example, adopt employee benefit plans in which benefits are triggered by a change of control, and then define change of control to include a successful proxy fight? Can they issue securities -- poison preferred or poison debt -- that have put rights, or a reduced price for conversion into common, if a dissident wins?

The next article describes the Time-Warner poison preferred. Should issuance of such a security like this be considered a breach of the duty of loyalty? If so, how should the court deal with the rights of the holders of the offending security, if they have bought at arms-length?

Joseph Grundfest, CATCH-22 TIME
6 Banking & Corp. Governance L.Rep. 1 (1991)

Catch 22 is one of the great classics of modern American literature. *Paramount Communications v. Time, Inc.* is one of the great classics of modern corporate law. Great literature and great corporate law usually have little in common, and when literary and judicial classics exhibit deep thematic similarities, my initial impulse is either to celebrate the law or to mourn the state of modern fiction.

In this case, however, the Delaware courts' unintended sequel to Joseph Heller's masterpiece provides reason to mourn the state of the law. Instead of capturing the stark realism that underscores Heller's work, the courts may have emulated *Catch-22*'s Kafkaesque sense of irrational impossibility and introduced it into the world of corporate law. *Catch-22* has great virtue as a work of fiction. As a model for corporate law, however, I am not so sure.

The Catch-22 In *Time*

In *Catch-22*, the protagonist, John Yossarian, decides that flying bombing missions over Germany is a bit dangerous for his blood. So he tells Doc Daneeka, the unit's physician, that he intends to go crazy. That, Yossarian thinks, should definitely get him grounded.

---

[34] For discussion of the business pressures on investment bankers that make fairness opinions, even when delivered, often echo the advice of the winning accounting firm, see Lucian Bebchuk & Marcel Kahan, *Fairness Opinions: How Fair Are They and What Can Be Done About It*, 1989 Duke L.J. 27 (1989); William Carney, *Fairness Opinions: How Fair Are They and Why We Should Do Nothing About It*, 70 Wash.U.L.Q. 523 (1992).

No such luck, explains Daneeka. You see, once you've flown enough dangerous missions over Germany, you have to be crazy to keep flying dangerous missions over Germany. But to get out of flying these missions, you have to ask to be relieved on grounds that you're crazy. But if you ask to be grounded you can't be crazy because "anyone who wants to get out of combat isn't really crazy."

There it is. Catch-22. To Yossarian its "spinning reasonableness" had "an elliptical precision about its perfect pairs of parts that was graceful and shocking, like good modern art" Yossarian was deeply moved by the absolute simplicity of Catch-22, "and let out a respectful whistle."

Well, if Yossarian liked Catch-22, he'd love *Time*. Without recounting the lawsuit in detail, Time's shareholders thought their board of directors was "crazy" to turn down Paramount's bid of $200 for each Time share so that Time could pursue a tender offer for Warner Communications. The shareholders also objected to the board's preventing them from directly considering Paramount's bid. So the shareholders complained to Delaware's courts. After due deliberation, the courts explained -- and here I paraphrase -- that the board [may] well be crazy but, because it was the board, it had every right to be crazy as long as it was honestly and diligently crazy -- particularly if it was in pursuit of a chronic vision held in the form of a business plan. The courts, you see, recognize that they aren't very good at deciding who is or isn't crazy in the business world; they're much better at deciding who is or isn't honest or diligent, so they leave it at that.[9]

What then are the stockholders to do? As Delaware's Supreme Court explicitly reasoned in *Unocal*, "[if the stockholders are displeased with the actions of their elected representatives, the powers of corporate democracy are at their disposal to turn the board out."[10] But unbeknownst to the courts, in order to vote out Time's board the shareholders would have to inflict on themselves a potentially massive dilution with serious adverse financial consequences for their own portfolios. To do that, the shareholders would have to be crazy. . . .

---

[9] Delaware courts are genteel places in which the word "crazy" is occasionally thought, but never written or spoken. Lawyers instead speak of breaches of the duty of care, or breaches of the duty of loyalty. They might also speak of violations of fiduciary obligations, or of defensive measures that are unreasonable in relation to the threat posed, or of the broad deference provided under the business judgment rule. No matter. Boiled down to simple English, the plaintiffs in leading takeover cases are often calling the defendants crazy, the defendants are often calling the plaintiffs crazy, and the judges are generally trying to stay out of competition with psychoanalysts by avoiding the need to decide whether anyone is crazy. Most particularly, the courts seek to avoid the dangerous though entertaining comparative exercise of determining whether plaintiffs are crazier than defendants, or vice versa. To illustrate the point, § 401(c) of the ALI's Principles of Corporate Governance Project suggests that a director's duty of care is satisfied if he in good faith makes a decision that he rationally believes . . . is in the best interest of the corporation." And the opposite of "rational" is . . . ? Yossarian would understand.

[10] Unocal Corp. v. Mesa Petroleum Co., 493 A.2d 946, 959 (Del.1985).

This dilution stems from event-risk provisions built into several series of securities issued by Time Warner. . . . Consider, for example, the event risk built into Time Warner's Series C 8-¾% Convertible Exchangeable Preferred Stock ("Series C Preferred"). Time Warner has a staggered 24-member board of directors with eight directors standing for election each year. The event-risk provision in the Series C Preferred is triggered by, among other things, the election of "individuals who would constitute a majority of the members of the Board of Directors elected at any meeting of stockholders or by written consent . . . and the election or nomination . . . of such directors was not approved by a vote of at least a majority of the directors in office immediately prior to such election." Translated into English, if five of the eight directors elected at an annual meeting are not to the liking of the incumbent board, then the event-risk provision is triggered despite the fact that the dissidents have only 20.83% of the votes on the board and cannot control the corporation. . . .

Just what does the "event-risk" provision do if it kicks in? The event-risk provision operates by changing the rate at which the Series C Preferred is convertible into Time Warner Common. Absent the triggering of an event-risk provision, each Series C share is convertible into five shares of Time Warner common stock. This ratio is called the "Common Stock Conversion Rate" ("CSCR"). If incumbent directors lose five seats in any election, then the CSCR is adjusted upward (but never downward) according to the following formula . . .

$$\text{New CSCR} = \$1,000/[\text{Current Market Price}]$$

. . . So there you have it. If the common is trading at $102 per share, its high on February 12, 1991, the old conversion ratio of 5 almost doubles to 9.80 ($1,000/$102). However, if the common is trading at its 1990 low of 66-⅛ . . ., the old conversion rate of 5 more than triples to 15.12 ($1000/$66.125).

Apparently, the lower Time's common stock price immediately before the election the greater the increase in the dilution that results from a successful proxy contest. Therein lies the double Catch-22 hidden in Time's event-risk protection. Simply put, the lower the price of Time's common shares, the greater the incentive stockholders have to oust the board through a proxy contest. But the lower the price the greater the dilution imposed on the voting common stockholders in the event they are able to capture even a powerless fifth of the board. Thus, the more you want to get rid of the board because of the company's low stock price the more painful it is to get rid of the board because of the company's low stock price.

Voila: a mathematical manifestation of Catch-22 elegantly strewn across several paragraphs of an intricately drafted certificate of designation. . . . I can hear Yossarian whistling in the distance. . . . All the while, [Time-Warner's general counsel claims] that the sole purpose of these provisions has nothing to do with their consequences for the operation of a proxy contest for seats on Time Warner's board. . . .

The Land Beyond Time

Simply describing the Catch-22 embedded in Time Warner's capital structure is not, however, the end of the story. The courts have it within their power to prevent the massive dilution that would accompany an "upsetting" challenge to Time-Warner's board. The question, however, is whether the courts would ever step in and prevent Time Warner's board from triggering its Catch-22 simply because it lost all or part of a staggered board election. Without attempting to be exhaustive in cataloguing arguments that might be made in the course of a lawsuit raising the issue, some brief observations are useful.

Defenders of Time Warner's event-risk provisions might draw an analogy to the approach used by Delaware courts in their poison pill analysis. After all, in *Moran v. Household International*,[25] Delaware's Supreme Court permitted the adoption of a poison pill as a proper exercise of business judgment, but observed that the decision to trigger the pill would have to be judged separately. Thus the "ultimate response to an actual takeover bid must be judged by the Directors' actions at that time, and nothing we say here [about the validity of the pill's adoption] relieves them of their basic fundamental duties to the corporation and its stockholders."[26]

Couldn't Time Warner's event-risk provision be judged similarly? Couldn't it be argued that the adoption of the event-risk provision was reasonable on the advice of investment bankers, and that the decision to trigger the dilution caused by the event-risk provision would have to be judged later, depending on the facts and circumstances existing at that time?

There are several responses to this line of reasoning, but for openers consider just one fundamental difference between Household's poison pill and Time Warner's event-risk provision. The effect of Household's pill on proxy contests was found to be "minimal," and the court observed that "the key variable in proxy contest success is the merit of an insurgent's issues, not the size of his holdings.[27] In contrast, the effect of Time Warner's event-risk provision is overwhelming and strikes at the heart of the proxy process.

If Time Warner's shareholders do not know as of the date of the meeting whether the board will declare the insurgents hostile -- thereby triggering the dilution -- then every vote will be cast under the threat of retribution by a spurned board. Further, unless the stockholders are informed early enough in the campaign as to whether the board will pull the trigger if

---

[25] 500 A.2d 1346 (Del.1985).

[26] Id. at 1357.

[27] Id. at 1355.

the insurgents win, the entire campaign will be conducted under a dark and foreboding cloud. . . .

At this stage, however, matters get truly dicey. How does the board decide whether to pull the trigger on the event-risk dilution provisions? Will the incumbent board interview insurgent directors in order to determine whether to pull the trigger or not? Will the incumbent board reach its position by evaluating the campaign run by the insurgents? Will the incumbents refuse to approve any insurgents that fail to run a campaign to the incumbents' liking? By what standards will incumbent board members, whose policies may be in the process of being repudiated by the stockholders, decide that shareholders have "properly" repudiated their views by supporting the insurgents? How will courts review these inherently self-interested decisions?

Most fundamentally, what are board members doing in a position where they even have to think of passing on the substantive merits of their electoral opponents? Aren't the stockholders the ones to judge "the merits of the insurgents' issues"? More bluntly, when did Delaware's legislature adopt a provision allowing approval by an incumbent board as a condition of grace for the election of an insurgent slate? These questions are all much tougher than the ones typically encountered in the poison pill context because there the board has a presumption of legitimacy -- it was, after all, duly elected. Here, however, the structural affront is to the electoral process that provides legitimacy to the board itself.

Note: Poison Securities

There is no direct holding on the validity of change-of-control provisions such as Time-Warner's. But in a recent case, excerpted below, Chancellor Allen went out of his way to criticize a board of directors for including similar provisions in an employee benefit plan.

SUTTON HOLDING CORP. v. DESOTO, INC.
Fed.Sec.L.Rep. (CCH) ¶ 96,012 (Del.Ch.1991)

ALLEN, Chancellor. Sutton Holding Corp. is a substantial (8.9%) shareholder of DeSoto, Inc. that is currently engaged in a proxy contest to elect a slate of directors at DeSoto's forthcoming May 20, 1991 annual meeting. It here claims that an effective and open election is being thwarted by the defendants, who constitute the majority of the current board of directors of the Company, and seeks a declaratory judgment that, it says, will have the effect of clarifying matters that may importantly affect the outcome of the voting contest.

As the case is now structured it revolves around the question whether election of the challenger slate would constitute a "change in control" as that term is used in the Company's two pension plans.

On December 11, 1987, DeSoto amended its two existing pension plans to insert a "change in control" provision. This provision provides that for a period of five years following a "change in control" the Company may not terminate the plans, nor may it amend them in a manner that would reduce benefits to the beneficiaries under the plans. Section 10.4(d) of the plans reads as follows:

> A "Change in Control" shall be deemed to have occurred at such time as (1) without the prior approval of two-thirds of the Whole Board and a majority of the Continuing Directors (but not less than one Continuing Director), any New Substantial Stockholder becomes a Beneficial Owner, directly or indirectly, of 35 percent or more of the voting power of the Voting Stock of the Company; or (2) one-third or more of the Board consists of members not nominated for membership by the Company or the Board. . . . For purposes of this subsection 10.4(d), a person shall be considered a Beneficial Owner of Voting Stock which such person has a proxy (other than a proxy solicited by or on behalf of the Company or the Board) to vote for the election of directors of the Company.

Provisions in corporate instruments that are intended principally to restrain or coerce the free exercise of the stockholder franchise are deeply suspect. Blasius Industries v. Atlas Corp., 564 A.2d 651 (Del.Ch.1988). The shareholder vote is the basis upon which an individual serving as a corporate director must rest his or her claim to legitimacy. Absent quite extraordinary circumstances, in my opinion, it constitutes a fundamental offense to the dignity of this corporate office for a director to use corporate power to seek to coerce shareholders in the exercise of the vote. It is not surprising that the attempt to do so should be made. As long as there have been elections there have been those who seek to gain unfair advantage in them (and those, who like some lawyers today, can suggest and guide that effort). But courts must remain sensitive to the risk and alert to act when they legitimately can to thwart it. Thus, I suppose (but cannot on this [limited] record hold) that adoption of this 1987 provision constituted a breach of the duty of loyalty that the members of the DeSoto board at that time owed to the company and its shareholders.

When the DeSoto board injected this provision in the Company's pension plans, its dominant motivation was doubtlessly not to create a valuable economic right in plan beneficiaries. Provisions of this sort -- like so-called poison pill stock rights plans -- are designed to deter a change in control, not to create useful rights in the event they are triggered. But by inserting this provision, even if its creation constituted a violation of the loyalty that the board owed to the corporation and its shareholders, the directors, at the least, created litigable claims by plan beneficiaries to rights [under the Employee Retirement Income Security Act of 1974 (ERISA)]. . . .

The provision is critically important now. At the moment, the excess funding of the Company's pension plans (on a per share basis) equals about 50% of the Company's share price on the New York Stock Exchange. The existing board has resolved to terminate the pension plans and to distribute that excess funding to the Company's shareholders. It has been delayed in doing so.

The challenger slate has announced a similar intention, but . . . the election of that slate might constitute a "change in control" under the plans. The occurrence of a change in control would mean that the pension plans could not be terminated (and the excess funding distributed to shareholders) for a period of five years. . . .

Promptly upon filing of the complaint, the defendants, however, announced that they had no wish to impede the free choice of the shareholders in the election and that they did not oppose the relief sought. Indeed, after the action was filed, the DeSoto board on April 26th, adopted a resolution that provided as follows:

> RESOLVED, that to the fullest extent permitted by the DeSoto Salaried Employees' Pension Plan and the DeSoto Hourly Employees' Pension Plan, and to the fullest extent consistent with applicable law, including without limitation all applicable fiduciary conduct rules, any election of Sutton Holding Corp. nominees to the DeSoto Inc. Board of Directors at 1991 annual meeting of the stockholders of the Company and/or the accumulation of proxies for the purpose of such election shall not be deemed to constitute a "Change in Control" for purposes of the plans.[6]

. . . In this action Sutton now seeks a declaratory judgment that the April 26th DeSoto resolution is "valid, binding and effective." . . . [That judgment], however, would do little good if the determination did not "bind" the plan beneficiaries, for it is they who might arguably assert rights arising out of "change in control." . . .

This court . . . is capable of affording a part, but only a part, of the judicial process necessary to address the problem of uncertainty that threatens the integrity of the forthcoming election of directors of DeSoto. It could do so by requiring the defendants to postpone for a short period, say sixty to ninety days, the forthcoming annual meeting of DeSoto shareholders. Such a delay could only be justified if plaintiff (derivatively) undertakes to commence and promptly requests expedited treatment of a defendant class declaratory judgment action against plan beneficiaries, seeking an adjudication of the questions necessary to determine whether the DeSoto board has, consistently with federal law, exempted the plaintiff's slate of candidates from the change in control provisions of the Company's pension plans.

---

[6] In adopting this resolution the Board declined to actually "nominate for membership" (Plan § 10.4) the challenger slate.

Should plaintiff seek to adjudicate such questions of law in an action in which pension plan beneficiaries would be bound by the judgments entered, then it would appear to me that an order requiring the board to postpone the annual meeting for the period mentioned might be justified. The board could have little objection to such a procedure as it has taken the position that it desires to do all that it can do legally to remove the "coercive" features of the present situation . . . .

Note on *Sutton Holding*

Chancellor Allen's return in this case to the bold language of *Blasius* is in marked contrast to his efforts in *Stahl I* and *Stahl II* to downplay the difference between *Blasius* and *Unocal*. What might explain the difference? One possibility is that *Sutton Holding*, like *Blasius* and unlike the *Stahl* cases, involved a proxy fight not complicated by a simultaneous tender offer. Was Chancellor Allen emboldened because the dictum in *Sutton Holding* wasn't reviewable by the pro-incumbent Delaware Supreme Court?

F.   Defensive Tactics V: Appealing to the State Legislature

The analysis thus far of defensive tactics in proxy fights has focused on the courts, who must apply general common law doctrines like the duty of care and the duty of loyalty, and general corporate statutes that weren't written with proxy fights specifically in mind. The recent wave of antitakeover legislation did not, however, leave proxy fights alone.

Most states have antitakeover laws that restrict shareholder voting power to some degree. A few have recently adopted laws that sharply restrict shareholder power. This may reflect an emerging trend in the 1990s, as the states, with hostile takeovers fading and institutional voting power growing as a threat to local companies and their managers, turn their attention to proxy contests. This section surveys the principal types of statutes.

From a shareholder voting perspective, freeze laws are the least troublesome of the major types of antitakeover laws. These statutes prohibit mergers and other business combinations with an "interested shareholder" for three to five years after the shareholder acquires stock above a threshold level, usually 10-15% of the outstanding shares. They provide a reason for shareholders not to buy large blocks, but don't otherwise greatly affect shareholder voting[35] Disclosure laws, adopted by 21 states, require a shareholder or group that owns more than a threshold percentage (typically 5%) to file a disclosure form with the state in addition to the Schedule 13D

---

[35] See, e.g., Del.C. § 203; N.Y.Bus.Corp.Law § 912.

federal filing. These laws add modestly to the disclosure and litigation risk burden created by the 13(d) Rules.[36]

Control share laws, adopted in at least 27 states, have a greater chilling effect on shareholder action. They typically deprive a person or group that acquires a 20% stake from voting any shares over the 20% threshold unless the other shareholders vote to restore voting rights at a special shareholder meeting.[37] The 20% holder must pay the company's expenses for holding the special meeting. Some statutes also prohibit acquisition of shares over the 20% threshold without the consent of the other shareholders;[38] some limit which shareholders can vote to restore voting rights in an effort to make a favorable vote harder to obtain.[39]

Control share laws typically adopt the broad 13(d) definition of "group," which covers voting groups. Thus, a shareholder consortium can't cross the 20% threshold. Some states exclude voting power obtained through a proxy solicitation governed by the Proxy Rules, but others don't. Without this exclusion, a shareholder proponent could arguably lose voting rights if she gains more than 20% support, which -- Catch 22 -- will happen for any successful proposal.

Committee or New Management of Guaranty Bancshares Corp. v. Dimeling[40] illustrates the problems that control share laws can pose for dissidents. The Pennsylvania control share law at issue in *Dimeling* exempted voting power that arose from revocable proxies or consents that were limited to "the specific matters described in such proxy or consent."[41] The dissident proxy card let the named proxies vote for the dissident directors *and*, as is standard practice, on "such other business as may properly come before the meeting." Dissidents want this authority in case the incumbents, at the meeting, propose a postponement of the meeting or another procedural tactic. Its use to vote on substantive matters would violate the proxy rules. No other business came before the meeting, and the dissidents won the election.

The reviewing court threw out the election results on the grounds that the dissidents' use of an overbroad proxy had cost them their voting power, and ordered a new election. Yet, without this discretionary power, the incumbents could have achieved the same result -- a new election -- by moving to postpone the meeting for several months, and voting their own proxies (which conveyed equivalent discretionary power) in favor of postponement.[42]

---

[36] See, e.g., N.Y.Bus.Corp.Law §§ 1600-1614.

[37] See, e.g., NASAA-ABA Model Control Share Act, 20 Sec.Reg. & L.Rep. (BNA) 708 (1988), Ind.C. §§ 23-1-42-1 to -11.

[38] See, e.g., Ohio C. § 1701.831(A).

[39] See, e.g., Ohio C. § 1701.1(Z)(3)(CC)(2); 15 Pa.Stat. §§ 2562-2563.

[40] 772 F.Supp. 230 (E.D.Pa.1991).

[41] 15 Pa.Stat. § 2563.

[42] With the benefit of perfect hindsight, the dissidents could have redrafted their proxy card to grant authority to vote for their director nominees, and on a laundry list of the most obvious

A few states have recently adopted more extreme antishareholder laws. Massachusetts, for example, recently required public companies to have staggered boards. Employees also receive "tin parachute" severance benefits if terminated within one year after a proxy fight. A new Pennsylvania "disgorgement" law requires any shareholder or group who acquires a 20% stake in a Pennsylvania company, or discloses that it "may seek to acquire control . . . through any means," to disgorge any profits from selling shares for 18 months thereafter, if the shares were bought up to 24 months before the attempt. "Control" is defined using the broad SEC definition, which covers both actual control and the *power* to exercise control, even if that power isn't used. Thus, a shareholder effort to nominate and elect directors may foreclose liquidity for 18 months, *even if the effort fails.*[43] Pennsylvania also has a "cash-out" law that requires any person or group which acquires 20% voting power in a public company to offer to buy all other shares at a court-determined fair price. The law has no exception for voting power obtained by soliciting proxies. In theory, anyone who receives 20% support in an election contest must offer to buy out all other shareholders![44]

Many states combine multiple antitakeover laws. For example, Pennsylvania has freeze, disclosure, control share, and tin parachute laws in addition to the disgorgement and cash-out laws discussed above; Ohio has freeze, disclosure, control share, and disgorgement laws. Some laws nominally apply to companies incorporated elsewhere that meet specified nexus requirements. These laws are probably unconstitutional, but the need to challenge them adds to a shareholder's litigation burden.

In sum, state antitakeover laws further burden the process of shareholder collective action. They affect all types of shareholder action, and make it especially hard for shareholders to nominate and elect directors, even to a minority of board seats. Moreover, if shareholders gain power at the polls, the states -- acting out of some combination of concern for employees and communities and accession to managers' lobbying and campaign contributions -- may act to preserve the managers' autonomy. The states can: change structural rules (e.g., require a staggered board; allow managers to adopt flip-in poison pills; reduce the vote needed to adopt a manager proposal); create roadblocks for active shareholders; or cut back shareholder rights, such as power to call a special meeting or act by written consent.

---

procedural tactics that the managers might use at the meeting. This is less satisfactory than discretionary power though, because the incumbents may think of some trick that one has missed, and because the laundry list will itself require explaining to shareholders who are used to the standard language.

[43] 15 Pa.Stat. §§ 2573-2574; see also Ohio C. § 1707.043 (18-month disgorgement period; limited exception for bona fide attempt to acquire control).

[44] 15 Pa.Stat. §§ 2541-2548; see also Me.Stat. tit. 13-A, § 910 (cash-out law with 25% threshold). Pennwalt Corp. v. Centaur Partners, 710 F.Supp. 111 (E.D.Pa.1989) holds that the Pennsylvania cash-out law is triggered by execution of shareholder consents to call a special shareholder meeting.

Note on Antitakeover Statutes and Proxy Fights

The Massachusetts law mandating a staggered board and providing tin parachute benefits was adopted as an emergency response to a combined tender offer/proxy fight launched by BTR plc for Norton Industries, which did not have a staggered board defense already in place. The Pennsylvania disgorgement law was adopted in response to a combined tender offer/proxy fight by the Belzberg family for Armstrong World Industries. These laws suggest that state legislatures are not drawing hard distinctions between control transfers effected through a tender offer, and control transfers effected through a proxy fight. What implication for judicial efforts to distinguish between the two?

Should a statute such as the Pennsylvania control share law that (as interpreted in *Dimeling*) limits the use of revocable proxies, be considered to be implicitly preempted by Exchange Act § 14(a), or the proxy rules adopted thereunder by the SEC? If not, does the SEC have the power to explicitly preempt such state statutes, if it so chooses?[45]

Note on the Factors that Affect Dissident Success Rates

Management supporters have claimed that proxy contest defenses are not too strong, and proxy regulation not too strict, by pointing to evidence of dissident success in the face of existing defenses and regulation.[46] Does this claim withstand analysis? How would one expect the defensive tactics discussed in this chapter to affect the (i) the frequency of proxy fights; and (ii) dissident success rates?

The effect of defensive tactics on the *frequency* of proxy fights is clear: Strong defenses should lead to fewer contests. The infrequency of control contests suggests the difficulty of the endeavor under the best of circumstances; stronger defenses can only further reduce the already small number of proxy fights for control.

In contrast, it isn't clear what effect, if any, strong defenses should have on dissident success rates *in the contests that still take place*. The problem is one of *sample selection bias*: Firms that undergo proxy contests are a

---

[45] For an argument that the answer to both questions is no, see Stephen Bainbridge, *Redirecting State Takeover Laws at Proxy Contests*, 1992 Wis.L.Rev. 1072. Our own view is that there is no implicit preemption, but the SEC has some preemptive *power*. The Commission could, for example, adopt a rule that "no proxy shall be deprived of its effect because it conveys the power, consistent with the proxy rules, to vote the proxy on new matters that arise after the proxy is distributed to shareholders."

[46] See, e.g., Robert Rosenbaum, *Foundations of Sand: The Weak Premises Underlying the Current Push for Proxy Reform*, 17 J.Corp.L. 163 (1991) (Mr. Rosenbaum represented the Business Roundtable in its efforts to oppose proxy rules changes, adopted by the SEC in 1992, which were intended to reduce regulatory obstacles for shareholder proxy campaigns).

severely biased sample of all firms. *Once a contest has begun*, stronger defenses improve the incumbents' chances of success. But *ex ante*, dissidents will take the available defenses into account in deciding whether to begin a contest. They will only incur the multimillion dollar expense of a proxy fight if they believe, taking all factors into account, that they have a substantial chance of success. If defenses are strong, other factors must be favorable to compensate for the strong defenses. Indeed, the *greater* the costs of the process, including litigation costs, the greater the expected gains must be before a dissident will incur those costs. Thus, if the cost of waging a proxy contest increases, that increase must be offset by either a higher probability of success, or larger expected gains if successful.

More generally, sample selection bias will plague any effort to find a correlation between the existence of a factor (whether a poison pill, a high level of dissident stock ownership, a high level of institutional stock ownership, or whatever) that plausibly affects dissidents' chances, and actual outcomes in the proxy contests that take place, or to infer causation if a correlation is found.

Randall Thomas & Kenneth Martin report a *positive* correlation, in a regression analysis, between dissident success rate in a proxy contest and the existence of a poison pill defense. They attribute this to the badly run firms that make good targets being more likely to adopt poison pills. This is plausible, but the observed results could also reflect dissidents insisting on a higher chance of success to compensate for the cost of expected litigation over use of the pill, or weak incumbents adopting pills once a contest is imminent.[47]

---

[47] Thomas & Martin (1993), *supra* note 21.

PART IV: NON-CORPORATE LAW PLANNING CONCERNS

In this Part we continue study of the public ordering aspect of private transactions: The task of structuring a transaction to minimize the cost of the variety of regulatory systems that may touch on it. Part III began this survey by examining the influence of corporate and securities law considerations on the structure of hostile and friendly corporate acquisitions. Our focus here is on the influence of other regulatory regimes. Chapter 25 considers two areas of pre-transaction government review of acquisitions: the Hart-Scott-Rodino Antitrust Improvements Act of 1976, which imposes a regime of pre-transaction notification whose burden differs significantly depending on the form in which a transaction is cast; and the Exon-Florio Amendment, providing for pre-transactional executive department review of acquisitions that implicate the national security. Chapter 26 then focuses on a more general problem: The successor liability of the acquiring company. Here the concern is whether the form in which the transaction is cast does -- or should -- affect the acquiring company's ability to select which of the target company's liabilities and contractual obligations it assumes.

CHAPTER 25: PRE-TRANSACTION GOVERNMENT REVIEW: HART-SCOTT-RODINO AND EXON-FLORIO

A. The Hart-Scott-Rodino Act

In the early 1970s, a concern was being raised about the effectiveness of § 7 of the Clayton Act, the principal federal antitrust restriction on corporate acquisitions.[1] The concern was not substantive -- that the measure of whether an acquisition violated the statute was too lenient or too strict -- though there was plenty of those criticisms also. Rather, it was that when courts ultimately found a violation, the relief awarded did not restore competition to pre-acquisition levels. Two studies of the relief obtained following successful government Clayton Act prosecutions concluded that in the overwhelming percentage of cases, relief was ineffective.[2] The principal explanation for this phenomenon was the government's difficulty in obtaining a preliminary injunction preventing the transaction while its legality was resolved.[3] Where preliminary relief was not obtained, divestiture could come as much as 10 years after the complaint was filed,[4] and rarely took place at all.[5] The difficulties in recreating an viable independent competitor after two firms had been merged for years were substantial. The failure to obtain preliminary relief was partly due to the Antitrust Division of the Justice Department and the Federal Trade Commission, the federal government's two antitrust enforcement arms, lacking an effective means of securing the information about a proposed acquisition necessary to establish that a preliminary injunction was appropriate.[6]

---

[1] 15 U.S.C. § 18. Section 7 provides that no corporation "shall acquire, directly or indirectly, the whole or any part of the stock . . . [or] the whole or any part of the assets of another corporation . . . , where in any line of commerce in any section of the country, the effect of such acquisition may be substantially to lessen competition, or to tend to create a monopoly."

[2] Malcolm Pfunder, Daniel Plaine & Anne Marie Whittemore, *Compliance with Divestiture Orders under Section 7 of the Clayton Act: An Analysis of Relief Obtained*, 17 Antitrust Bull. 19 (1972); Kenneth Elzinga, *The Antimerger Law: Pyrrhic Victories?*, 12 J.L. & Econ. 43 (1969).

[3] "In most cases where preliminary injunctions were denied and divestiture was subsequently ordered, the divestiture which was ordered did not prove to be an adequate remedy." Pfunder, Plaine & Whittemore (1972), *supra* note 2, at 117.

[4] Stephen Axinn, Blaine Fogg & Neal Stoll, *Acquisitions Under the Hart-Scott-Rodino Antitrust Improvements Act* § 3 (1984).

[5] In the Pfunder, Plaine & Whittemore sample of 103 cases, the ordered divestiture never took place at all in 8 cases, and in 4 others there was a substantial reduction in the scope of divestiture.

[6] Private parties fared even worse with respect to preliminary relief. In their cases, the public interest and balance of equities factors consistently were found lacking. It seemed that courts believed that only the government could represent the public interest. Consistent with this problem, no private party had ever obtained divestiture relief, as opposed to damages, under § 7 of the Clayton Act.

It was against this background that Congress enacted the Hart-Scott-Rodino Antitrust Improvements Act of 1976, which added a new § 7A to the Clayton Act, excerpted below.

HART-SCOTT-RODINO ANTITRUST IMPROVEMENTS ACT
(Clayton Act § 7A, 15 U.S.C. § 18a)

(a) **Filing**. Except as exempted pursuant to subsection (c), no person shall acquire, directly or indirectly, any voting securities or assets of any other person, unless both persons (or in the case of a tender offer, the acquiring person) file notification pursuant to rules under subsection (d)(1) of this section and the waiting period described in subsection (b)(1) of this section has expired, if --

(1) the acquiring person, or the person whose voting securities or assets are being acquired, is engaged in commerce or in any activity affecting commerce;

(2)(A) any voting securities or assets of a person engaged in manufacturing which has annual net sales or total assets of $10,000,000 or more are being acquired by any person which has total assets or annual net sales of $100,000,000 or more;

   (B) any voting securities or assets of a person not engaged in manufacturing which has total assets of $10,000,000 or more are being acquired by any person which has total assets or annual net sales of $100,000,000 or more; or

   (C) any voting securities or assets of a person with annual net sales or total assets of $100,000,000 or more are being acquired by any person with total assets or annual net sales of $10,000,000 or more; and

(3) as a result of such acquisition, the acquiring person would hold --

   (A) 15% or more of the voting securities or assets of the acquired person, or

   (B) an aggregate total amount of the voting securities and assets of the acquired person in excess of $15,000,000.

In the case of a tender offer, the person whose voting securities are sought to be acquired by a person required to file notification under this subsection shall file notification pursuant to rules under subsection (d) of this section.

(b) **Waiting period; publication; voting securities**

(1) The waiting period required under subsection (a) of this section shall --

   (A) begin on the date of the receipt by the Federal Trade Commission and the Assistant Attorney General in charge of the Antitrust Division of the Department of Justice . . . of --

      (i) the completed notification required under subsection (a) of this section, or

(ii) if such notification is not completed, the notification to the extent completed and a statement of the reasons for such noncompliance,

from both persons, or, in the case of a tender offer, the acquiring person; and

(B) end on the thirtieth day after the date of such receipt (or in the case of a cash tender offer, the fifteenth day), or on such later date as may be set under subsection (e)(2) or (g)(2) of this section.

(2) The Federal Trade Commission and the Assistant Attorney General may, in individual cases, terminate the waiting period specified in paragraph (1) and allow any person to proceed with any acquisition subject to this section, and promptly shall cause to be published in the Federal Register a notice that neither intends to take any action within such period with respect to such acquisition.

(3) As used in this section --

(A) The term "voting securities" means any securities which at present or upon conversion entitle the owner or holder thereof to vote for the election of directors of the issuer or, with respect to unincorporated issuers, persons exercising similar functions.

(B) The amount or percentage of voting securities or assets of a person which are acquired or held by another person shall be determined by aggregating the amount or percentage of such voting securities or assets held or acquired by such other person and each affiliate thereof.

(c) **Exempt transactions.** The following classes of transactions are exempt from the requirements of this section --

(1) acquisitions of good or realty transferred in the ordinary course of business;

(2) acquisitions of bonds, mortgages, deeds of trust, or other obligations which are not voting securities;

(3) acquisitions of voting securities of an issuer at least 50% of the voting securities of which are owned by the acquiring person prior to such acquisition;

(4) transfers to or from a Federal agency or a State or political subdivision thereof;

(5) transactions specifically exempted from the antitrust laws by Federal statute;

(6) transactions specifically exempted from the antitrust laws by Federal statute if approved by a Federal agency, if copies of all information and documentary material filed with such agency are contemporaneously filed with the Federal Trade Commission and the Assistant Attorney General;

(7) transactions which require agency approval under [§ 18(c) of the Federal Deposit Insurance Act (12 U.S.C. §1828(c)), or § 3 of the Bank Holding Company Act of 1956 (12 U.S.C. §1842)];

(8) transactions which require agency approval under [§ 4 of the Bank Holding Company Act of 1956 (12 U.S.C. §1843), §§ 403 and 408(e) of the National Housing Act (12 U.S.C. §1726 and §1730(a), or § 5 of the Home Owners' Loan Act of 1933 (12 U.S.C. §1464)], if copies of all information and documentary material filed with any such agency are contemporaneously filed with the Federal Trade Commission and the Assistant Attorney General at least 30 days prior to consummation of the proposed transaction;

(9) acquisitions, solely for the purpose of investment, of voting securities, if, as a result of such acquisition, the securities acquired or held do not exceed 10% of the outstanding voting securities of the issuer;

(10) acquisitions of voting securities, if, as a result of such acquisition, the voting securities acquired do not increase, directly or indirectly, the acquiring person's per centum share of outstanding voting securities of the issuer;

(11) acquisitions, solely for the purpose of investment, by any bank, banking association, trust company, investment company, or insurance company, of (A) voting securities pursuant to a plan of reorganization or dissolution; or (B) assets in the ordinary course of its business; and

(12) such other acquisitions, transfers, or transactions, as may be exempted under subsection (d)(2)(B) of this section.

(d) **Commission rules**. The Federal Trade Commission, with the concurrence of the Assistant Attorney General and by rule in accordance with § 553 of title 5, United States Code, consistent with the purposes of this section --

(1) shall require that the notification required under subsection (a) of this section be in such form and contain such documentary material and information relevant to a proposed acquisition as is necessary and appropriate to enable the Federal Trade Commission and the Assistant Attorney General to determine whether such acquisitions may, if consummated, violate the antitrust laws; and

(2) may --

(A) define the terms used in this section;

(B) exempt, from the requirements of this section, classes of persons, acquisitions, transfers, or transactions which are not likely to violate the antitrust laws; and

(C) prescribe such other rules as may be necessary and appropriate to carry out the purposes of this section.

(e) **Additional information; waiting period extensions**

(1) The Federal Trade Commission or the Assistant Attorney General may, prior to the expiration of the 30-day waiting period (or in the case of a cash tender offer, the 15-day waiting period) specified in subsection (b)(1) of this section, require the submission of additional

information or documentary material relevant to the proposed acquisition, from a person required to file notification with respect to such acquisition under subsection (a) of this section prior to the expiration of the waiting period specified in subsection (b)(1) of this section, or from any officer, director, partner, agent, or employee of such person.

(2) The Federal Trade Commission or the Assistant Attorney General, in its or his discretion, may extend the 30-day waiting period (or in the case of a cash tender offer, the 15-day waiting period) specified in subsection (b)(1) of this section for an additional period of not more than 20 days (or in the case of a cash tender offer, 10 days) after the date on which the Federal Trade Commission or the Assistant Attorney General, as the case may be, receives from any person to whom a request is made under paragraph (1). . . .

(f) **Preliminary injunctions; hearings**. If a proceeding is instituted or an action is filed by the Federal Trade Commission, alleging that a proposed acquisition violates [§ 7 of this Act or § 5 of the Federal Trade Commission Act], or an action is filed by the United States, alleging that a proposed acquisition violates such [§ 7 or § 1 or 2 of the Sherman Act], and the Federal Trade Commission or the Assistant Attorney General . . . files a motion for a preliminary injunction against consummation of such acquisition pendente lite . . ., the chief judge of such district court shall immediately notify the chief judge of the United States court of appeals for the circuit in which such district court is located, who shall designate a United States district judge to whom such action shall be assigned for all purposes.

(g) **Civil penalty; compliance; power of court**

(1) Any person, or any officer, director, or partner thereof, who fails to comply with any provision of this section shall be liable to the United States for a civil penalty of not more than $10,000 for each day during which such person is in violation of this section. Such penalty may be recovered in a civil action brought by the United States. . . .

The requirement that pre-transaction information concerning an acquisition be given to the enforcement agencies, the creation of a waiting period to provide the time necessary to evaluate the information received, and the specification in § 7A(f) that a government motion for preliminary injunction be given priority in federal court, were designed to improve the likelihood that an acquisition likely to violate the Clayton Act would be prevented from ever taking place.[7] This, in turn, would reduce the need to

---

[7] The Act also imposes non-trivial penalties. Section 7A(g) provides for a fine of up to $10,000 a day for noncompliance.

resort to post-acquisition divestiture relief, believed to be generally ineffective at restoring competition.

As is apparent, the principal terms of the Act itself are quite skeletal. Although jurisdictional limits are specified, no effort was made to provide definitions for the terms used or otherwise to flesh out the detail of how the Act would apply to a transaction whose metamorphic character has been repeatedly stressed in previous Chapters. This detail is provided by an extraordinary set of Rules[8] developed by the FTC pursuant to the direction of § 7A(d). These Rules and an accompanying Statement of Bases and Purposes, taking up over 100 pages of the Federal Register when adopted,[9] represent an advanced evolutionary form of the regulator's craft. The problem was, simultaneously, (i) to cast a net broad enough that planners could not avoid the Act merely by altering the formal characteristics of the transaction, yet at the same time to treat some forms of transactions differently when their substance warranted it; (ii) to provide sufficient detail that planners could structure their transactions with some certainty of how the Act would apply; and (iii) to avoid conflict with the terms of the other bodies of regulation, principally the federal securities laws, that also would apply to the same transactions.

From the perspective of a transaction planner, the starting point for analysis of the Act is to recognize that, despite the legislative intent and the Act's codification as part of the Clayton Act, it is *not* an antitrust statute. The substantive content of the antitrust laws changed not one whit as a result of its passage.[10] For the planner, the task is to understand how the Act and the Rules, independently and in their interaction with federal securities regulation, influence the optimal transaction forms and acquisition strategies.

B.   An Overview of the Hart-Scott-Rodino Act and Rules

The Hart-Scott-Rodino (HSR) Act requires that a pre-acquisition filing be made if the persons who are parties to the transaction, and the assets or stock acquired in it, are of the requisite size. The size-of-person requirement is satisfied if one party to the transaction has sales *or* assets of $100 million or more and the other party, if engaged in manufacturing, has sales *or* assets

---

[8] 16 C.F.R. §§ 801-803.

[9] See 43 Fed.Reg. 33,450-35,562 (1978). Charitably, it has been the practice of the Federal Trade Commission staff to provide advice on compliance with the Act and Rules in any given or hypothetical case without requiring disclosure of the identity of the principal.

[10] Titles I and III of the Act also were directed at improving enforcement rather than changing substantive standards. Title I expanded the authority of the Antitrust Division to use the Civil Investigative Demand authorized by the Antitrust Civil Process Act, 15 U.S.C. §§ 1311-1314, prior to the commencement of an action. Title III amended § 4 of the Clayton Act, 15 U.S.C. §§ 15(c-h) to give state attorneys general a damage action on behalf of state citizens.

of $10 million or, if not engaged in manufacturing, has assets of $10 million.[11] Under the statute, the size-of-transaction test is satisfied if, as a result of the transaction, the acquiring person will hold 15% of the voting stock or assets of the acquired person or voting stock or assets with a value in excess of $15 million.[12] The Rules, however, first substantially expand, then even more substantially contract, and finally entirely reshape the events that trigger a filing obligation under the Act.

The expansion results from the treatment of "creeping acquisitions" in § 801.13. The problem is to identify which transactions are to be taken into account in determining whether the size-of-transaction test is met. In statutory terms, the question is posed in terms of what stock or assets are held "as a result of" the acquisition. In substance, however, the inquiry is

---

[11] § 7A(a)(2). To implement the size-of-person test the drafter of the Rules had to define the term "person" in a way that prevented planners from using a small related entity, distantly controlled by the "real" acquirer, to avoid the Act. This effort provides a good example of how complicated it is to fully anticipate all available planning options. The Rules proceed by defining three terms in § 801.1(a): Person, entity and ultimate parent entity. An "ultimate parent entity" is an entity which is not controlled by any other entity. A "person" is an ultimate parent entity *and* all   other entities, including natural persons, any type of organization, *and* any group however organized, which it controls. Thus, the size-of-person test is measured against, the aggregate size of an entire group of related entities. Some indication of the resulting complexity -- keep in mind that the term control is also subject to a complex definition in § 801.1(b) and that the notion of when a group exists is itself complex -- can be seen from an example. In the following diagram, the percentages and arrows represent ownership interests, UPE stands for ultimate parent entity, and Mr. and Mrs. A are husband and wife. Assume entity S-1 is making an acquisition. Who is the acquiring person (assuming, as provided in § 801.1(c), that the ownership of one spouse is imputed to the other)? The answer is that there are *four* chains of acquiring persons: 1) S-1, P, UPE-1, and X; 2) S-1, Mrs. A, and S-2; 3) S-1, P, and UPE-2; and 4) S-1, Mr. A, and S-2; and the size of each link in each chain must be aggregated with that of each other link in the chain to determine the size of the acquiring person. Figure it out.

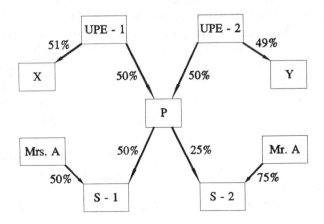

---

simply another variation of the familiar step transaction doctrine from tax law: Can the regulatory apparatus be avoided by dividing one transaction into a number of "separate" transactions? The thrust of the Rules is to eliminate this response from the planner's repertoire. For stock acquisitions, § 801.13(a) provides that all stock of the acquired party that will be held by the acquiring person after the transaction is held "as a result of" the acquisition. Thus, a succession of entirely separate stock acquisitions will trigger a filing obligation when the aggregate of the transactions meet the size-of-transaction test. Asset acquisitions are also subject to aggregation, but in a much more limited way. Section 801.13(b) treats assets acquired within the 180 days preceding the execution of the contract, agreement in principle, or letter of intent with respect to the current transaction, as acquired "as a result of" the current transaction, but only for purposes of the $15 million test. There is no asset aggregation for purposes of the 15% test.

From the perspective of the drafter of the Rules, what explains the different treatment of creeping stock, as opposed to creeping asset, acquisitions? Keep in mind that a planner's ability to manipulate the form of the transaction for regulatory purposes is constrained by the non-regulatory costs associated with the manipulation. What costs are imposed by acquiring a target company's stock over a period of time rather than in one transaction? Is your answer different with respect to acquisitions of a target's assets? Changes in stock ownership affect only the ownership of the target. Changes in the ownership of the target's assets change the company's productive capability which may have real competitive consequences. Thus, the existence of real consequences to the target company from having to operate without the assets disposed of for at least 180 days makes a creeping asset acquisition a less likely planning vehicle for regulatory avoidance.

The contraction in the Act's coverage results from the exemption from the filing and waiting period requirements contained in § 802.20. Under § 7A(a)(3) of the Act, an asset acquisition is covered if it represents 15% of the acquired person's assets *or* if the assets acquired have a value in excess of $15 million. Thus, even a small asset acquisition measured in dollar value is subject to the Act if it meets the percentage-of-assets requirement. Section 820.20(a) recognizes that some acquisitions that meet the percentage-of-assets requirement of the Act are simply too small to have an anticompetitive effect. For example, if a $100 million person acquired 15% of the assets of a $10 million person, the Act is triggered by an acquisition of only $1.5 million in assets.[13] This problem is met by exempting from the Act all asset acquisitions of less than $15 million. A somewhat broader exemption is provided for small stock acquisitions. First, acquisitions of more than 50% of an acquired person's stock are exempted from the Act if the acquired person has both sales and earnings of less than $25 million and if the stock

---

[13] Statement of Background and Purposes, Background Information to § 802.20, 43 Fed.Reg. 33,490 (1978).

acquired is valued at less than $15 million. Second, acquisitions of less than 50% of an acquired person's stock are exempt, regardless of the size of the person, if the stock acquired is valued at less than $15 million.[14] The § 802.20 exemption can have significant transactional importance. Because of the exemption, "it may be possible to obtain *de facto* control of many smaller publicly held companies without filing and observing the pre-acquisition waiting period."[15]

Finally, the Rules change the structure of the Act by introducing the concept of "notification thresholds." These are defined in § 801.1(h) as:

> (h) *Notification threshold.* The term "notification threshold" means:
>
> (1) Fifteen percent of the outstanding voting securities of an issuer, or an aggregate total amount of voting securities and assets of the acquired person valued in excess of $15 million;
>
> (2) Fifteen percent of the outstanding voting securities of an issuer, if valued in excess of $15 million;
>
> (3) Twenty-five percent of the outstanding voting securities of an issuer; or
>
> (4) Fifty percent of the outstanding voting securities of an issuer.

The concept is implemented by the exemption provided in § 802.21 which generally relieves acquisitions of the Act's filing and waiting periods obligations if "[t]he acquisition will not increase the holdings of the acquiring person to meet or exceed a notification threshold greater than the greatest notification threshold met or exceeded in [an] earlier acquisition." The exemption's operation is explained in the Statement of Bases and Purposes to § 802.21 and illustrated in the examples set forth following § 802.21.

Background Information to § 802.21

The language of the act indicates that Congress contemplated agency review of stock acquisitions not only at the 15% or $15 million level, but also at additional, higher levels of ownership. Further review is desirable because holdings that may be innocuous at low levels may pose antitrust concerns at higher levels. Section 801.13 construes the phrase "as a result of" to fulfill this congressional purpose.

However, this principle would not justify notification and a waiting period prior to every acquisition above the 15% or $15 million level. The delay and expense of repeated filings would be extremely burdensome to reporting persons and would present too substantial an administrative burden

---

[14] As with implementation of all of the Act, the determination of the value of stock and assets is quite complex. See Timothy Tomlinson, *Premerger Notification under Hart-Scott-Rodino: Valuation of Assets and Voting Securities*, 26 UCLA L.Rev. 1321 (1979).

[15] Axinn, Fogg & Stoll (1984), *supra* note 4, at 274.6-.7.

for the enforcement agencies. Nor would such notifications serve any enforcement purpose. Percentage holdings varying by a few percentage points will in most cases have equivalent antitrust significance, and periodic review at the levels of the notification thresholds, or within the timing constraints of § 802.21, should be sufficient. The rule insures that the agencies learn of appreciable increases in holdings by imposing the reporting requirements at the prescribed notification thresholds, and insures that the agencies learn of changed circumstances by imposing the reporting requirement in any event after 5 years. Of course, in a particular case an acquisition exempted by the rule may prove to have antitrust significance, and the fact that the acquisition was exempt under this (or any other) rule does not preclude either agency from challenging the acquisition.[16]. . .

Hart-Scott-Rodino Examples
(from 16 C.F.R. § 802.21)

1. Corporation *A* acquires 15% of the voting securities of Corporation *B* and both "*A*" and "*B*" file notification as required. Within five years of the expiration of the original waiting period, "*A*" acquires additional voting securities of *B* but not in an amount sufficient to meet or exceed 25% of the voting securities of *B*. No additional notification is required.

2. In example 1, "*A*" continues to acquire *B*'s securities. Before "*A*'s*" holdings meet or exceed 25% of *B*'s outstanding voting securities, "*A*" and "*B*" must file notification and wait the prescribed period, regardless of whether the acquisition occur within five years after the expiration of the earlier waiting period.

3. In example 2, suppose that "*A*" and "*B*" file notification at the 25% level and that, within 5 years after expiration of the waiting period, "*A*" continues to acquire voting securities of *B*. No further notification is required until "*A*" plans to make the acquisition that will give it 50% ownership of *B*. (Once "*A*" holds 50%, further acquisitions of voting securities are exempt under § 7A(c)(3)).

The combination of the notification threshold and aggregation concepts is a clever resolution of a problem inherent in the Act. As written, the Act requires filing when an acquiring person's stake hits 15%. Absent some creative interpretation, however, compliance with the filing and waiting period requirements at that time eliminates any obligation for further filings when the acquiring person later increases its stake. Literally, the acquiring person would not hold 15% of the acquired person's stock "as a result of"

---

[16] See § 7A(i).

the later, in contrast to the earlier, acquisition. The result would be that the later acquisition, when control shifted and the potential for an anticompetitive effect arose, would not be subject to the Act. The aggregation principle in § 801.13(a) meets this problem by treating all stock held by an acquiring person as held as a result of *any* acquisition. The notification threshold concept avoids the potential problem created by the solution -- that the acquisition of even a small number of shares by an acquiring person that already held 15% always would trigger the filing and waiting period requirements.

C.   Length of Waiting Period and Impact on Transactional Form

In the end, the importance of the Act and Rules to the planner is how they impact on the selection of the optimal transaction form. For this purpose, the critical aspect of the regulation is the waiting period. Preparing and filing the information required may be expensive and may tip the Justice Department or the FTC to an upcoming transaction with which they should be concerned; however, the costs of complying with these obligations would warrant little effort in avoidance. Standing alone, they do not affect the planner's real strategic concern: Causing the transaction to be completed as quickly as possible so as to minimize the possibility of defensive conduct in unfriendly transactions, or of competitive bids whether the transaction is friendly or unfriendly. This concern is affected only when the Act's principal impact on a potential transaction is considered: The delay associated with the waiting period.

In specifying the waiting period applicable to different forms of transactions, the Act and Rules draw two important distinctions, one dealing with the length of the waiting period, and the second dealing with the date on which the waiting period begins to run. Sections 7A(b)(1) and 7A(e) of the statute establish the length of the waiting period. Both distinguish between cash tender offers and all other transactions. For cash tender offers, § 7A(b)(1) sets the initial waiting period at 15 days, and § 7A(e) limits to 10 days the extension of the waiting period that results from a request for additional information from the enforcement agency. For all other acquisitions, the initial waiting period is 30 days and the extension following a request for additional information is 20 days. The justification for this distinction is set forth in the legislative history of the Act quoted by Justice White in his opinion in Edgar v. MITE Corp.[17] Congressman Rodino, speaking with respect to the shorter waiting period for cash tender offers, noted that "[i]n cash tender offers, more so than in other mergers, the equities include time and the danger of undue delay."[18] In this regard, the

---

[17] 457 U.S. 624 (1982).

[18] 122 Cong.Rec. 30,877 (1976). The legislative history of the shorter waiting period for cash tender offers is set out in detail in Axinn, Fogg & Stoll (1984), *supra* note 4, at 51-56.

Act maintains, in direction, if not precisely in magnitude, the timing difference between cash tender offers and transactions where the consideration is the acquiring company's securities created by the jurisdictional boundaries of the Williams Act and the Securities Act of 1933.

Section 7A(b)(1) of the Act also distinguishes between cash tender offers and other acquisition forms with respect to the date on which the waiting period begins to run. For all transactions except cash tender offers, the waiting period commences on the date when both the acquiring and the acquired persons have filed their reports. For cash tender offers, the waiting period commences when the acquiring person files its report. Although the Act carves out only cash tender offers for special treatment with respect to commencement of the waiting period, the problem at which the statutory distinction is directed has broader application. In setting different waiting period lengths, the Act properly focused on the type of consideration used in the transaction because that distinction determined a parallel timing difference under the federal securities law; to do otherwise would have negated a seemingly important difference in treatment under a regulatory structure applicable to the same range of transactions. The distinction between types of transactions with respect to the commencement of the waiting period, however, has nothing to do with the meshing of the Act with other bodies of regulation. Rather, it is intended to solve a problem associated not with the form of the transaction, but with whether the transaction is friendly or unfriendly. If the transaction is friendly, then there is no difficulty in the waiting period commencing only after both parties make the required filing because target management, by definition, is cooperative. But when the transaction is hostile, the effect of delaying the commencement of the waiting period until the target company has filed its report would be to give the target company the ability to substantially delay the acquisition, simply by not making the required filing, at the cost of no more than $10,000 a day in penalties. Where the daily fees of the target company's lawyers in takeover litigation can run substantially in excess of that amount, the price of delay might not appear excessive to a hard pressed target.

The Act's distinction with respect to the commencement of the waiting period thus is best understood as intending to distinguish between friendly and hostile transactions, using the cash tender offer as a shorthand definition of an unfriendly transaction. Although the shorthand definition may be somewhat overinclusive -- some cash tender offers are friendly transactions[19] -- the more serious problem is that it is significantly underinclusive. Some hostile transactions -- for example, an exchange offer -- take a form other than a cash tender offer, and under the terms of the Act, the waiting period for these transactions will not begin until the acquired

---

[19] See the excerpt from James Freund & Richard Easton, *The Three-Piece Suitor: An Alternative Approach to Negotiated Corporate Acquisitions*, 34 Bus.Law. 1679 (1979) in Chapter 19, *supra*.

person makes its filing. As a result, "an apathetic or hostile issuer could frustrate the transaction merely by neglecting to file notification."[20] The Rules attempt to remedy this statutory shortcoming in § 801.30 which "extends to analogous types of transactions the treatment accorded tender offers"[21] with respect to the commencement of the waiting period.[22] The result is to distinguish between acquisitions of securities from third parties and acquisitions of securities from the issuer. The waiting period for the former commences with the filing by the acquiring person; only when the issuer is a party to the transaction does commencement await the filing by both parties.[23]

The terms of the waiting period dictate the transactional impact of the Act. For our purposes, however, the critical concern is not simply whether the Act imposes a delay. Rather, it is whether the Act's waiting period has planning implications: Can a timing advantage be secured by casting a transaction in one form or another? Most generally, the application of the Act's waiting period reinforces the bias in favor of cash consideration created by the Williams Act. An acquiring person making a cash tender offer will be free to begin purchasing shares 15 to 25 days before an acquiring person whose proposed transaction, whether an exchange offer or a merger, involves the issuance of securities. In an acquisition market in which an acquirer must anticipate the possibility of a competitive bid whether the initial transaction is friendly or hostile, the bias in favor of cash, and in favor of a two step transaction when the use of some stock as consideration is anticipated, is substantial.

The Act does more, however, than reinforce existing biases. With respect to the two most important forms of unconventional transactions -- securing control through private purchases or open market purchases -- the Act may significantly impair their attractiveness.

We can examine the Act's impact on efforts to take control of a company through privately negotiated stock purchases by seeing how the Act would have applied to the transaction involved in Wellman v. Dickinson[24] -

---

[20] Statement of Bases and Purpose, § 801.30 -- Tender Offers and Acquisitions of Voting Securities from Third Parties, 43 Fed.Reg. 33,483 (1978).

[21] *Id.*

[22] The principal transactions covered by § 801.30 are "exchange offers, open-market purchases, private purchases, and conversions of non-voting securities." The central theme of the list is to include all "transactions that may be initiated by the acquiring person without the agreement of the acquired person." *Id.*

[23] Although the acquired person's filing need not be made in order for the waiting period to commence in a § 801.30 transaction, § 801.30(b)(2) does impose an obligation on the acquired person to make the filing within 15 days (10 days in a cash tender offer) after receiving notice from the acquiring person. Section 803.5 in turn requires that the acquiring person's filing in a § 801.30 transaction include an affidavit that the acquiring person has notified the acquired person of the transaction.

[24] 475 F.Supp. 783 (S.D.N.Y.1979), *aff'd,* 682 F.2d 355 (2d Cir.1982), *cert. denied,* 460 U.S. 1069 (1983), reprinted in Chapter 18, *supra.*

- the purchase by Sun Company, in a single day, of 34% of the voting stock of Becton, Dickinson & Company from some 30 institutions and individuals.[25]   The Act's requirement that one party be involved in commerce and the size-of-person test were clearly satisfied. What is the relevant transaction for purposes of the size-of-transaction test? If each of the purchases involved less than 15% of the outstanding Becton, Dickinson stock, when would the Act's filing and waiting period requirements be triggered? Recall that § 801.13(a) provides that all stock held by an acquiring person is deemed acquired in each acquisition of additional stock.

Once the filing requirement is triggered, who must file as the acquired person: Becton, Dickinson or each of the individual sellers? If the sellers were required to file, a substantial coordination problem could be created. In this regard, consider the following example in Rule 801.2(b):

> 1. Assume that person "Q" will acquire voting securities of corporation X held by "P" and that X is not included within person "P." Under this section, the acquired person is the person within which X is included, and is not "P."[26]

The most critical strategic issue is the length of the waiting period that would apply to the transaction.[27] Under the Act, all acquisitions other than a cash tender offer have a 30-day waiting period, with the possibility of a 20-day extension if the enforcement agency requests additional information. For cash tender offers, the waiting period is only fifteen days with the possibility of a ten day extension. Is the *Wellman* transaction a cash tender offer for purposes of the Act? The possibility of a clever planner crafting a transaction that was a cash tender offer for purposes of Hart-Scott-Rodino, and thereby subject only to the shorter waiting period, but not a tender offer for purposes of the Williams Act, was eliminated by the Rules' cross reference to the Williams Act for a definition of a tender offer.[28] Thus, a planner is put to a choice: The price of the shorter waiting period under Hart-Scott-Rodino is compliance with the Williams Act.

How one makes this choice depends on the importance of the extra 15 days of initial waiting period, given that there will be a minimum 15 day

---

[25] The Act did not, in fact, apply to the transaction in *Wellman*. Although the Act became law on September 30, 1976, a Federal Trade Commission transitional rule exempted all acquisitions completed prior to the adoption of the FTC Rules on September 5, 1978. The *Wellman* transaction took place in January, 1978, and therefore was exempt.

[26] In the examples to the Rules, persons are designated by letters within quotation marks and entities are designated by letters without quotation marks.

[27] When the waiting period would commence is not in doubt. Because the transaction is one "in which voting securities are to be acquired from a holder or holders other than the issuer," § 801.30 provides that the waiting period is commenced by the acquiring person's filing.

[28] Rule 801.1(g) defines a tender offer as "any offer to purchase voting securities which is a tender offer within the meaning of § 14 of the Securities Exchange Act."

period in practically all events.[29]   Answering this question, in turn, requires resolution of two additional inquiries.   As a threshold matter, can the transaction even be mechanically accomplished in light of the waiting period? If so, do any benefits of a *Wellman* type transaction survive the imposition of any waiting period?

With respect to the threshold inquiry, the planner's principal concern is that the acquiring company be able to enter into a binding purchase contract with the seller prior to the expiration of the waiting period so that it does not have to tip its hand to other potential sellers before it has completed its purchasing activity.[30]   One approach would be to enter into binding purchase contracts the closing of which are conditioned on compliance with the Act.   By entering into such a contract, does one "acquire" the security within the meaning of the Act?   Under the Rules, the answer depends on whether the contract transfers beneficial ownership of the stock.[31]   What provisions should be included in the contract concerning such matters as voting and dividend rights pending the closing of the transaction?

Assuming that the contract could be drafted to avoid the passage of beneficial ownership until the expiration of the waiting period, would the transaction still be worth doing?   The point of the transaction's structure, after all, is to be able to pressure the institutions to make a decision and tender quickly.   Would the pressure imposed be reduced if the purchases could not be closed for 30 days?   This problem, of course, would not be present in connection with private purchases entered into as part of a negotiated transaction as described by Freund & Easton (1979).[32]   There the point was only to discourage competitive bidders by securing a significant stock holding before public disclosure.   So long as the contracts were conditioned *only* on the running of the waiting period, the impact on competitive bidders should be the same.

The technique of acquiring a significant ownership position by means of open market purchases fares worse under the Act's regulatory regime than do private acquisitions.   Recall that open market purchases could not be carried out if the Williams Act applied because it would be mechanically

---

[29] The Rules provide for early termination of the initial or subsequent waiting periods upon the discretion of the FTC or Justice Department. This discretion is subject to judicial review. See Heublein, Inc. v. FTC, 539 F.Supp. 123 (D.Conn.1982).

[30] The enforcement agencies are obligated to keep filings under the Act, including the identity of the parties, confidential throughout the process until an injunction is sought or early termination of the waiting period is granted.

[31] Technically, neither the statute nor the rules define the term "acquire." Section 801.1(c) defines "holds" to mean "beneficial ownership" and § 801.13 uses the word "held" in the phrase "held by the acquiring person as a result of the acquisition." Taken together, one holds securities as a result of an acquisition when one acquires beneficial ownership of them. It should follow that one acquires securities when one becomes the beneficial owner of them. Accord Axinn, Fogg & Stoll (1984), *supra* note 4, at 82-83.

[32] See Freund & Easton (1979), *supra* note 19.

impossible to comply with the proration, withdrawal and length of offer requirements. A similar problem arises under Hart-Scott-Rodino. If Hart-Scott-Rodino applies, the open market purchase cannot be consummated until the 30-day waiting period has run but, unlike in private purchases, there is no way in which open market purchases can be conditioned on the expiration of the waiting period. Thus, the Act effectively reduces to $15 million the amount of stock an acquiring company can purchase without any public disclosure. This may have a much more significant impact on acquiring company strategy than simply making it impossible to secure working control through a campaign of large open market purchases. One of the means by which an initial bidder can protect itself against the risk of losing the target to a competitive bidder, and thereby losing its investment in discovering the target in the first place, is to take a position in the target's stock as a hedge. So long as the hedge was purchased before disclosure of the first offer caused the price of the target's stock to rise, the gain on its sale to the winning bidder would offset the loss on the investment in information. The effect of the Act is to cap the size of the hedge possible and, as a result, to increase the risk of a competitive bidder that the initial bidder actually must bear. To that extent, the Act reduces the incentives to make an initial bid to the detriment of target shareholders.[33]

This final point -- that the Act may reduce the absolute number of acquisitions to the detriment of target shareholders and, perhaps, the economy as a whole, poses an interesting issue concerning the Act's overall value. If the problems which led to the Act could be solved without imposing costs beyond the simple transaction costs of compliance such as filling out the notification form, the overall value of the Act would be subject to little debate. The problem, however, is that the Act does impose other costs. Most importantly, the effect of the waiting period is to reduce the incentive to make acquisitions. This is especially troublesome because the Act is terribly overinclusive from the perspective of preserving competition.

---

[33] The potential acquiring company could file under the Act with respect to anticipated open market purchases with the intent of not beginning to purchase until the waiting period had expired. The problem, however, is that under § 801.30 the waiting period will not commence until the target company is notified of the information specified in § 803.5, including the amount of securities intended to be purchased. So long as the target company made this information public prior to the expiration of the waiting period, the market price of the target's stock would rise in anticipation and, by reducing the potential profit from reselling the stock to a higher bidder, to that extent reduce the value of the hedge.

The practical application of the Act creates an additional disincentive to identifying a takeover target when a competitive bid is possible. The first filing under the Act requires the FTC or the Antitrust Division to learn about the two companies and their competitive overlap. A subsequent filing by a competitive bidder requires study of only that company; the target has already been analyzed. As a practical matter, the request for additional information often issues only to buy the enforcement agencies more time to analyze the information they have, as much as to acquire more information. Thus, the initial bidder -- the first filer -- is taxed with the time to learn about the target and, often, with an additional waiting period and document production cost.

The disincentive created does not depend on whether an acquisition has the potential to be anticompetitive; it applies equally to conglomerate and horizontal acquisitions. Is it possible to balance in any meaningful way the cost of discouraging some perfectly desirable acquisitions against the gains from avoiding later failures in obtaining effective divestiture by facilitating the issuance of a preliminary injunction? Would it be helpful to know how many times the Department of Justice and the FTC have sought pre-transaction preliminary injunctions in transactions where notification was filed?[34] One way in which the overinclusive nature of the statute could be ameliorated is through the authority of the Federal Trade Commission and the Assistant Attorney General in charge of the Antitrust Division under § 7A(b)(2) of the Act to terminate the waiting period prior to its expiration "in individual cases" if neither intends to take any action. Would the adoption

---

[34] In 1983, neither the Antitrust Division nor the FTC sought a single preliminary injunction in a merger case, although the Antitrust Division did inform parties on four occasions that it would challenge the transaction unless it were restructured to eliminate competitive overlap or abandoned. In each case the parties complied.

Also interesting is the percentage of reportable transactions in which either enforcement agency made a request for additional information:

> 1979 - 12.9%
> 1980 - 9.0%
> 1981 - 7.5%
> 1982 - 4.3%
> 1983 - 4.3%

Seventh Annual Report to Congress Pursuant to § 201 of the Hart-Scott-Rodino Antitrust Improvements Act of 1976, 3 (1984). This data is subject to differing interpretations. The Report itself states:

> [T]his persistent downward trend may in part reflect a beneficial deterrent effect to the premerger notification program. Because the program enables the enforcement agencies to detect and challenge virtually all sizeable anticompetitive acquisitions before they are consummated, businesses may be increasingly avoiding transactions that approach the line of illegality.
>
> The drop in the second request issue rate since 1981 may also reflect the impact of the Justice Department's 1982 Merger Guidelines and the Federal Trade Commission's contemporaneous Statement Concerning Horizontal Mergers. These documents have provided business decision makers with a better understanding of the types of transactions that are likely to be challenged as well as the factors the enforcement agencies will consider in making their decisions. With this knowledge, business decision makers can more easily avoid transactions of questionable legality. In addition, because of these documents, parties involved in transactions that appear to raise antitrust issues have been better able to identify areas of concern and have, on several occasions, voluntarily provided information addressing these concerns. Thus, the agencies have been able to resolve some concerns without resorting to a second request.

In contrast, FTC Commissioner Pertschuk, in a separate statement concerning the Seventh Annual Report, challenged the Report's evaluation of the data. In response to the above-quoted analysis, Commissioner Pertschuk noted that "the number of acquisitions during 1983 [was] a nine-year high and the number of large mergers [was] an all time high" and went on to state that he "simply cannot accept the [Report's] Panglossian vision of what is actually happening."

of a rule specifying the circumstances under which requests for early termination would be allowed reduce the disincentive to make acquisitions that do not pose antitrust problems? Would the statutory phrase "in individual cases" limit the extent to which a rule might authorize blanket early termination in specified categories of acquisitions?

A final point concerning the impact of the Act concerns its interaction with the presence of a poison pill in a hostile offer. Recall from Chapter 18 that a poison pill in large measure eliminated the strategic effect of the William's Act's application: The delay imposed by the Williams Act is exceeded by the time the courts will allow the target company before requiring it to redeem its pill. Similarly, the delay imposed by Hart-Scott-Rodino is exceeded by the time given the target by its poison pill. In general, the strategic impact of public regulatory structures has been effectively diluted by the private regulation of the poison pill.

Note: Avoiding the Waiting Period by Making the Acquisition Through a Partnership

Given their extraordinary complexity, the Federal Trade Commission's Premerger Notification Rules were remarkably free of gaps through which transaction planners could avoid compliance. One gap, however, proved to be a serious problem. Under the Rules, it was possible to fall outside the coverage of the Act simply by using a partnership as an acquisition vehicle. Once recognized, it became a favorite means by which an acquirer could prolong the period in which stock could be acquired without public disclosure, So, for example, this approach was used in unsuccessful efforts by T. Boone Pickens to acquire Phillips Petroleum Co., by Carl Icahn to acquire USX Corp., and by Sir James Goldsmith to acquire Goodyear Tire and Rubber Co.[35] The Federal Trade Commission explained the problem and its proposed solution in the following 1987 release.

Federal Trade Commission
PREMERGER NOTIFICATION:
REPORTING AND WAITING PERIOD REQUIREMENTS
52 Fed.Reg. 7095 (1987)

Control of Partnerships and Other Entities
That Have Not Issued Voting Securities

There have been widely publicized instances in which acquisitions were structured to be made by partnerships rather than corporations, and were not

---

[35] See Linda Blumkin, *FTC Moves to Close Often-Used Loophole in Pre-Merger Rules*, Legal Times, July 6, 1987, at 16.

reported under the act, even though the partnerships were owned and operated principally by one person, and that person was a competitor of the acquired person. That result is inconsistent with the treatment of corporations that are dominated by one person, and with the objectives of the act and the rules.

Acquisitions by partnerships can avoid premerger review as a result of two principles of premerger reporting: one, a formal rule for calculating assets of an entity, 16 C.F.R. 801.11(e), and the other, a Premerger Notification Office informal interpretation that a partnership is its own "ultimate parent entity" (that is, a partnership is not controlled by its partners). Section 801.11(e) directs that an entity without a balance sheet not include, in determining its size, any assets that are contributed to the entity for the purpose of making an acquisition. Thus, for example, if a partnership is formed to buy a $1 billion company and the partners contribute $1 billion in cash, the acquisition of the company by the partnership is not reportable. The partnership does not meet the $10 million minimum size criterion of § 7A(a)(2) of the act because § 801.11(e) directs the partnership not to count the $1 billion that will be used to pay for the acquisition. The informal interpretation deems the acquisition to have been made by the partnership itself, which has no other assets, rather than its partners, who may well have other assets.

Of course, if the partnership were employed in the acquisition "for the purpose of avoiding the obligations to comply with the requirements of the act," its existence would be disregarded and the obligations of the act would be determined by applying the act and the rules to the substance of the transaction.[a] For example, some persons might be tempted to make an acquisition through a partnership for the purpose of delaying their premerger notification to the antitrust agencies until they were required by the Federal securities laws to announce their acquisition publicly. If a partnership were used for the purpose of delaying or avoiding reporting, § 801.90 would attribute the acquisitions to the partners individually. They would be required to comply with the obligations of the act personally prior to consummating the transaction.

The Commission now proposes to require partners, rather than partnerships, to report transactions in certain other circumstances. It proposes to accomplish this result by amending the rule defining control, § 801.1(b), to provide that a partnership or other unincorporated entity will be deemed to be controlled by any person who owns 50% or more of the entity. Thus, a partner who met the statutory $10 million minimum size criterion and owned 50% or more of the partnership would be required to report acquisitions made by the partnership. The rule would be analogous to the circumstances in which a corporation is deemed to be controlled by one or

---

[a] 16 C.F.R. § 801.90.

more of its shareholders. It would thereby abolish the overly general presumption that partnerships are always independent entities.

This change would mean, in the example of the acquisition of the $1 billion company discussed above, the transaction could be reportable if one of the partners was entitled to 50% or more of the firm's profits (or, upon dissolution, of its assets), and that partner's total assets of net annual sales were $10 million or more. That controlling partner, or its parent, would become the "ultimate parent entity" pursuant to § 801.1(a)(3). It would therefore be deemed to be the person making the acquisition.

This proposed attribution of control to persons owning such large economic interests in entities that do not issue voting securities seems to be a more appropriate way to apply the premerger notification procedures. As matters currently stand, for example, a person can make a purchase through a limited partnership in which it is the general partner and 95% beneficial owner. If, pursuant to § 801.11(e), the partnership does not meet the size-of-person criteria of § 7A(a)(2), and the partnership was not created for the purpose of avoiding compliance with the act, the transaction would not be reportable because the partnership is deemed to be its own ultimate parent entity. It seems more appropriate for such transactions to be reportable by any person that dominates the acquiring entity. That is what the proposed rule seeks to do.

In the past, the Premerger Notification Office has not deemed partnerships to be controlled. Section 801.1(b) provides, in part, that control exists if one person can "designate a majority of the directors of a corporation, or in the case of unincorporated entities, of individuals exercising similar functions." The Commission staff has declined to equate partners with "individuals exercising similar functions" to "directors of a corporation." This interpretation was adopted principally because the variable structure of partnerships made it too difficult to specify an objective set of criteria by which to attribute control. For example, partnerships can provide for equal operating authority for all partners or can restrict those rights in any of a number of ways. However, in formulating the acquisition vehicle proposal[b] the Commission developed the concept of attributing control of unincorporated entities on the basis of beneficial interests. While not perfect, this concept, which relies on the entitlement to profits or to assets in the event of dissolution, seems an adequate indicator of control where one person has a right to 50% or more of the profits or is entitled to 50% or more of the assets upon dissolution. At the very least, it seems unlikely that such an entity would be permitted to continue its existence if it operated in any way that was adverse to the wishes of the 50% owner. Consequently, quite apart from any concern about intentional avoidance of

---

[b] This was an earlier Commission proposal to deal with the problem in which each partner was treated as acquiring the same proportion of the target company as its interest in the partnership. See 50 Fed.Reg. 38,742 (1985). Eds.

the act's obligations, the Commission considers this proposal to be an appropriate supplement to its existing definition of control.

The 50% beneficial ownership requirement would parallel in important respects the treatment of corporations under the existing control rule. Although effective or working control of a corporation can exist as a practical matter with a smaller percentage of shares, § 801.1(b) deems a corporation to be a controlled entity only if one person owns "50% or more of the outstanding voting securities" or has a right "presently to designate a majority of the board of directors." While this 50% requirement understates actual control of many corporations, the rule is clear and easily determinable. It is also arguably overinclusive because one corporation with two 50% owners is deemed to have two ultimate parent entities. Nevertheless, this arguable overinclusiveness correctly reflects the joint control that generally exists in such circumstances. In the Commission's experience, this requirement that both controlling entities file has not prevented persons from fulfilling the premerger notification requirements. . . . In formulating the 50% ownership criterion, consideration was given to whether other indicators of control should be included. . . .

[S]ome consideration was given to adopting a rule that would attribute assets of unincorporated entities to all owners, even if they held only a minority interest. This would have been similar to the coverage of the previously proposed acquisition vehicle rule. The Commission does not feel such a proposal is warranted at this time. In the Commission's experience, partnership vehicles that had any potential for anticompetitive consequences have been dominated by a single person or by two persons holding equal rights. Accordingly, the Commission believes it is sufficient at present to extend the scope of the premerger notification program to an unincorporated entity only if at least one person is entitled to either 50% of its profits, or, upon dissolution, of its assets. However, should competitively significant transactions escape reporting obligations under the proposed new rule because no person controlled the partnerships undertaking those acquisitions, the Commission would reconsider the acquisition vehicle approach.

Although the amendment to § 801.1(b) narrowed the gap, it did not close it completely. A partnership in which no partner owns 50% of the profits or assets remains free of the Rules. Also, the acquisition of less than 100% of a partnership has been treated as not reportable.[36] Thus, a transaction by which a partnership with no 50% owner acquired a company, followed by the acquisition of control of the partnership by one of the partners, remains outside the Rules unless treated as an avoidance device under § 801.90.

---

[36] See 52 Fed. Reg. 20058, 20061 (1987).

In the commentary adopting the amendment to §801.1(b), the Commission noted that it was considering Rule revisions that would require reporting the acquisition of control of a partnership. This comment was pursued some two years later when the Commission issued an advance notice of proposed rulemaking and requested comments on five alternative means to attack the remaining issues concerning partnership reporting.[37]

Efforts to avoid the pre-notification requirements by means of a partnership is an example of a more general phenomenon: Structuring the form of the transaction to fall outside the terms of the regulations without altering its substance.[38]

Note: The Effectiveness of Hart-Scott-Rodino from an Antitrust Perspective

The principal policy issue implicated by pre-transaction review is balancing the cost of deterring some desirable acquisitions against the benefit of avoiding prolonged post-acquisition antitrust litigation and assuring effective divestiture. Johnson & Parkman (1991)[39] provides some help with respect to one side of the balance by measuring the impact of the Act on post-acquisition antitrust litigation. The hypothesis is that because the Act allows the government to obtain detailed information concerning the transaction before it is consummated, the acquiring firm will be less able to prolong post-transaction litigation in order to retain the target company's cash flow as long as possible and, perhaps, even to defeat divestiture entirely. To test this hypothesis, the authors divided a sample of all acquisitions with respect to which an antitrust complaint was filed between 1965 and 1985 into two subsamples: those cases filed before and after the Act became effective on September 5, 1978. The average duration of litigation concerning an acquisition was then compared.

The Act seems to have had a desirable effect. For all firms, duration of litigation fell by more than 50%, from 837 days in the pre-HSR period to 399 days in the post-HSR period. Looking only at acquisitions that had been completed before a complaint was filed, the decrease in litigation duration was even greater (from 969 days in the pre-HSR period to 415 days in the post-HSR period).

---

[37] 54 Fed. Reg. 7960 (1989).

[38] For an effort by the individual who coordinated the original drafting of the Hart-Scott-Rodino rules to interpret § 801.90 (avoidance transactions), see Malcolm Pfunder, *Transactions or Devices for Avoidance of Premerger Notification Obligations: Toward an Administrable and Enforceable Interpretation of 16 C.F.R. § 801.90*, 58 Antitrust L.J. 1031 (1990).

[39] Ronald Johnson & Allen Parkman, *Premerger Notification and the Incentive to Merge and Litigate*, 7 J.L.Econ. & Org. 145 (1991).

D. Exon-Florio: Presidential Review of Acquisitions by Foreigners Affecting National Defense

Section 5021 of the Omnibus Trade and Competitiveness Act of 1988 (The Exon-Florio Amendment) adds § 721 to the Defense Production Act.[40] This Act, like Hart-Scott-Rodino, creates a process of pre-acquisition review. Unlike Hart-Scott-Rodino, Exon-Florio does not require court action; the President is granted broad power to review and suspend or prohibit any acquisition by a foreign person of a company engaged in interstate commerce in the United States. Exercise of this power by the President requires findings that the foreign acquirer "might take action that threatens to impair the national security,"[41] and that other provisions of the law do not "provide adequate and appropriate authority for the President to protect the national security" in connection with the particular transaction.[42] The legislation suggests five factors that the President *may* take into account in his review:

(1) domestic production needed for projected national defense requirements,
(2) the capability and capacity of domestic industries to meet national defense requirements, including the availability of human resources, products, technology, materials, and other supplies and services,
(3) the control of domestic industries and commercial activity by foreign citizens as it affects the capability and capacity of the United States to meet the requirements of national security,
(4) the potential effects of the proposed or pending transaction on sales of military goods, equipment, or technology to any country [to which sales of military equipment and technology is limited for various reasons], and
(5) the potential effects of the proposed or pending transaction on United States international technological leadership in areas affecting United States national security.[43]

The President has delegated his authority under the Act to the Committee on Foreign Investment in the United States (CFIUS), composed of the Secretaries of State, Treasury, Defense, Commerce, the Attorney General, the U.S. Trade Representative, the Chairman of the Council of Economic Advisers, and the Director of the Office of Management and Budget. To date, the President and the Committee have shown restraint in the exercise of the authority conferred by the Act. On only a handful of occasions has the President blocked transactions, typically where there was concern over the transfer of weapons technology.[44]

---

[40] 50 U.S.C.App. § 2170.

[41] § 721(d).

[42] § 721(e)(2).

[43] § 721(f)(1-5)

[44] See Marc Greidinger, *The Exon-Florio Amendment: A Solution in Search of a Problem*, 6 Am.U.J. Int'l L. & Pol. 111, 118-19 (1991) (discussing the two interventions prior to 1991).

The Treasury Department's Office of International Investment has published regulations governing the review of proposed foreign acquisitions under the Act.[45]   The regulations establish a three-stage review of transactions falling within the Exon-Florio Amendment, and sets forth a broad conception of the scope of the transactions subject to review.

The review process begins with the voluntary filing of a notice with the CFIUS by any party to a covered transaction. The filing triggers a 30-day period during which CFIUS determines whether an investigation is warranted, which is followed by a 45-day period in which any investigation must take place, and a 15-day period following the investigation during which the President may act.

REGULATIONS PERTAINING TO MERGERS, ACQUISITIONS, AND TAKEOVERS BY FOREIGN PERSONS
(31 C.F.R. § 800)

Subpart B: Definitions

§ *800.201 Acquisition.* The term *acquisition* is used within these regulations to refer collectively to an acquisition, merger, or takeover. It includes, without limitation:

(a) The acquisition of a person by:
    (1) The purchase of its voting securities, or
    (2) The conversion of its convertible voting securities,
    (3) The acquisition of its convertible voting securities if that involves the acquisition of control, or
    (4)   The acquisition and the voting of proxies, if that involves the acquisition of control.

(b) The acquisition of a business, including any acquisition of production or research and development facilities operated prior to the acquisition as part of a business, if there will likely be a substantial use of:
    (1) The technology of that business, excluding technical information generally accompanying the sale of equipment or,
    (2) Personnel previously employed by that business.

(c) A consolidation. . . .

§ *800.204 Control.* The term *control* means the power, direct or indirect, whether or not exercised, and whether or not exercised or exercisable through the ownership of a majority or a dominant minority of the total

---

[45] Regulations Pertaining to Mergers, Acquisitions, and Takeovers by Foreign Persons, 54 Fed.Reg. 29744 (1989).

outstanding voting securities of an issuer, or by proxy voting, contractual arrangements or other means, to determine, direct, or decide matters affecting an entity; in particular, but without limitation, to determine, direct, take, reach or cause decisions regarding:

(1) The sale, lease, mortgage, pledge or other transfer of any or all of the principal assets of the entity, whether or not in the ordinary course of business;

(2) The dissolution of the entity;

(3) The closing and/or relocation of the production or research and development facilities of the entity;

(4) The termination or non-fulfillment of contracts of the entity; or

(5) The amendment of the Articles of Incorporation or constituent agreement of the entity with respect to the matters described at (1) through (4) above. . . .

Subpart C -- Coverage

§ 800.301　Transactions that are acquisitions under § 721.

(a) § 721 [the Exon-Florio Amendment] applies to acquisitions:

(1) Proposed or pending on or after the effective date

(2) By or with foreign persons

(3) Which could result in foreign control of persons engaged in interstate commerce in the United States.

(b) Transactions that are acquisitions under § 721 include, without limitation:

(1) Proposed or completed acquisitions by or with foreign persons which could or did result in foreign control of a U.S. person, irrespective of the actual arrangements for control planned or in place for that particular acquisition.

> *Example 1.* Corporation A, a foreign person, proposes to purchase all the shares in Corporation X, which is organized in the United States and engages in interstate commerce in the United States. Under applicable law, Corporation A will have the right to elect directors and appoint other primary officers of Corporation X, and those directors will have the right to reach decisions about the closing and relocation of particular production facilities, and the termination of contracts. They also will have the right to propose (for approval by Corporation A as a shareholder) the dissolution of Corporation X and the sale of its principal assets. For purposes of § 721, the proposed acquisition of Corporation X by Corporation A could result in control of a U.S. person (Corporation X) by a foreign person (Corporation A).

> *Example 2.* Same facts as in Example 1, except that Corporation A plans to retain the existing directors of Corporation X, all of whom are U.S. nationals. Although, under these plans, Corporation A may not in fact exercise control over Corporation X (because the directors as U.S. nationals may exercise that

control), the acquisition of Corporation X by Corporation A still would result in foreign control over a U.S. person for purposes of § 721.

(2) A proposed acquisition by or with a foreign person, which could result in foreign control of a U.S. person, including, without limitation, an offer to purchase all or a substantial portion of the securities of a U.S. person.

> *Example.* Corporation A, a foreign person, makes an offer to purchase all the shares in Corporation X, a U.S. person. That acquisition is "proposed" and subject to § 721.

(3) Proposed or completed acquisitions even by entities organized in the United States, if those entities are "foreign persons," and if those acquisitions could or did result in a different foreign interest controlling the U.S. person to be acquired.

> *Example 1.* Corporation X is organized and operates in the United States. Its shares are held by a foreign person. While Corporation X is a "U.S. person," it is also a "foreign person" within the meaning of § 721, because control over it is or could be exercised by a foreign person. Its acquisition of a U.S. person is subject to § 721 because that acquisition could result in control by Corporation X (a "foreign person") of a U.S. person.

> *Example 2.* Same facts as Example 1, except that Corporation Y, a foreign person, seeks to acquire Corporation X from its existing shareholder. That proposed acquisition is subject to § 721 because it could result in control of Corporation X (in this context a "U.S. person") by a different foreign person (Corporation Y).

(4) Proposed or completed acquisitions by or with foreign persons which involve acquisitions of businesses and could or did result in foreign control of businesses located in the United States.

> *Example 1.* Corporation A, a foreign person, proposes to buy a branch office business in the United States of Corporation X, which is a foreign person. For purposes of these regulations, the branch office business of Corporation X is a United States person to the extent of its business activities in the U.S., and the proposed acquisition of the business in question is subject to § 721.

> *Example 2.* Corporation A, a foreign person, buys a branch office business located entirely outside the United State of Corporation Y, which is incorporated in the United States. The branch office business of Corporation Y is not deemed to be a United States person, and the acquisition is not subject to § 721.

> *Example 3.* Corporation A, a foreign person, makes a start-up or "greenfield" investment in the United States. That investment involves such activities as

separately arranging for the financing of and the construction of a plant to make a new product, buying supplies and inputs, hiring personnel, and purchasing the necessary technology. The investment may involve the acquisition of shares in a newly incorporated subsidiary. Corporation *A* will not have acquired the "business" of a U.S. person, and its greenfield investment is not subject to § 721.

(5) Joint ventures in which a United States person and a foreign person enter into contractual or other similar arrangements, including agreements on the establishment of a new entity, but only if a United States person contributes an existing identifiable business in the United States and a foreign interest would gain control over that existing business by means of the joint venture.

Example 1. Corporation *A*, a foreign person, and Corporation *X*, a United States corporation, form a separate corporation, JV Corp., to which Corporation *X* contributes an identifiable business in the United States. There is no foreign interest which does or could exercise control over Corporation *X*. Under the Articles of Agreement of JV Corp., Corporation *A* through its shareholding in JV Corp. may elect a majority of the Board of Directors of JV Corp. The formation of JV Corp. could result in foreign control of a U.S. person and is an acquisition subject to § 721.

Example 2. Same facts as in Example 1, except that Corporations *A* and *X* each own 50% of the shares of JV Corp. and, under the Articles of Incorporation of JV Corp. both *A* and *X* have veto power over all decisions by JV Corp. identified under § 800.204(a) (1) through (5). The formation of JV Corp. is not an acquisition subject § 721.

Example 3. Corporation *A*, a foreign person, and Corporation *X*, a United States person, form a separate corporation, JV Corp., to which Corporation *A* contributes funding and managerial and technical personnel, while Corporation *X* contributes certain patents and equipment that do not under these circumstances constitute an identifiable business. The formation of JV Corp. is not an acquisition subject to § 721. . . .

[The descriptions below of subparts D-F are taken from the notice of proposed rulemaking for the regulations.[a] Eds.]

Subpart D: Notice

§ *800.401.* This section establishes a voluntary system of notice. If a proposed transaction consists of an acquisition in which a foreign person controls or could control a U.S. person, then the transaction falls within §

---

[a] *Department of the Treasury, Notice of Proposed Rulemaking: Regulations Pertaining to Mergers, Acquisitions, and Takeovers by Foreign Persons*, 54 Fed.Reg. 29744 (1989).

721, and either party to the transaction -- even if the proposed acquisition is "hostile" -- may submit notice of the transaction in accordance with the procedures in § 800.401. Once such notice is given, the Committee may also request information from the non-notifying party. Although the regulations create a voluntary notice scheme, it is important to note that if a transaction comes under § 721 and neither party, nor a Committee agency, submits notice to the Committee, it remains indefinitely subject to divestment should the President subsequently make the required findings as described in § 800.601(b).

Notice will only be accepted from parties. . . . Therefore, notice from third parties, such as shareholders, would not constitute notice under these regulations. However, any person, including non-parties, may informally contact the committee regarding a particular transaction. Since such informal contacts would not constitute notice, they would not commence the running of the thirty-day notice period under § 721.

In addition to notice from the parties to a transaction, these regulations also provide for notice by an agency that is a member of the Committee. . . .

§ *800.402.* This section describes the information that must be submitted in order to constitute sufficient notice under § 721. Paragraph (h) provides that the Staff Chairman retains the right to reject voluntary notices that do not comply with the section. As provided in paragraph (g), parties are required to advise the Committee of any developments that are material to the Committee's review of the proposed transaction. The Committee has the right to reject any notice at any time if, after the notice has been submitted, there is a material change in the transaction that has been notified. The Committee would view such a material change as giving rise to a new transaction that may warrant a separate notice to the Committee.

§ *800.403.* This section provides that the 30-day period following notice from parties is deemed to begin on the first calendar day following receipt of notice by the Committee Staff Chairman. . . .

Subpart E: Committee Procedures: Review and Investigation

§§ *800.501-800.504.* Subpart E sets forth Committee procedures for conducting its initial 30-day review and 45-day investigation. As provided in § 800.501, the Committee may examine three questions: (1) Is there an acquisition which could result in foreign control of a U.S. person? (2) Is there credible evidence to support a belief that such foreign control could threaten to impair the national security? and (3) Are no other provisions of law adequate to protect the national security? If the Committee's initial review leads it to believe that no national security concerns are raised by the transaction, the Committee will conclude its action under § 721, and the Staff

Chairman will notify the parties accordingly. In such cases, no investigation will be undertaken, and no further action is available under § 721.

If, on the other hand, the Committee's initial review leads it to believe an investigation is warranted, the Committee will begin an investigation of the transaction no later than 30 days after the date the review period began. The Committee may ask the parties to provide additional information, and may schedule meetings for the parties to discuss the transaction with the Committee. This investigation period shall end no later than 45 days after it commences. Upon completing the investigation, the Committee shall make a recommendation to the President, unless the Committee is unable to reach a unanimous decision, in which case it will submit a report to the President that sets forth the differing views. . . .

Subpart F: Presidential Action

§ *800.601*. Subpart F concerns the Standards and nature of Presidential action under § 721. Section 800.601(a) reiterates the statutory time frame and requirements for Presidential action. As provided in § 800.601(c), Presidential action may include divestment with respect to a concluded transaction, as well as other appropriate relief. Section 800.601(d) makes clear that all authority available to the President under § 721(c), including divestment authority, remains available indefinitely, at the discretion of the President, for all acquisitions concluded after August 23, 1988, except for those which the Committee has decided not to investigate or with respect to which the President has determined not to exercise his authority. This authority extends to transactions that have not been the subject of a voluntary or agency notice. However, as provided in paragraph (d), divestment remains available for non-notified transactions only if the purpose for which divestment is sought is based on circumstances existing at the time the transaction was concluded.

The President's authority includes the ability to obtain divestment relief before the completion of a Committee review or investigation where a proposed acquisition is or may be completed after notice has been given, but before the close of the 15-day period for Presidential action. . . .

Paragraph (e) provides for Committee action in the event parties to an acquisition have submitted false or misleading information, or have omitted material information. In such cases, the Committee can reopen the investigation, revise its recommendation to the President, and accept a new or resubmitted agency notification. Moreover, the President may take appropriate temporary action, and revise actions earlier taken.

Note: The Impact of Exon-Florio

The impact of the Exon-Florio Amendment depends both on its breadth of coverage and on how aggressively CFIUS uses its power. The regulations define expansively the critical terms *acquisition* and *control* and, hence, produce an expansive reach for the statute.

How does the Exon-Florio Amendment apply when, in connection with a loan to a United States corporation, a foreign lender takes a security interest in assets which, if transferred to a foreign person, would be covered? Is review triggered by the creation of the security interest or only by an effort to enforce it?

CHAPTER 26: SUCCESSOR LIABILITY
OF THE ACQUIRING COMPANY

The survey of alternative acquisition techniques in Chapter 16 disclosed substantial differences in the protections provided shareholders and creditors by different techniques. A statutory merger provides the most protection. Shareholders of both the acquiring and target companies typically have voting and appraisal rights. In turn, creditors of the target company are protected because the surviving company in a merger assumes as a matter of law all of the target's liabilities, including unknown or contingent liabilities. Because these protections are costly, planners responded by casting their transactions in an alternative form which provided fewer protections. The alternative most often chosen is a purchase of the target company's assets. When the transaction is cast in this form, acquiring company shareholders lose their vote, in many jurisdictions target shareholders lose their appraisal rights, and, in all jurisdictions, the general rule is that the acquiring company is responsible for only those liabilities of the target company that it expressly agrees to assume. Creditors of the target company then run the post-acquisition risk that the target company, now a shell holding only the consideration received in the transaction, quickly will dissolve, leaving creditors unpaid and without other recourse. It was predictable that in precisely those circumstances in which the planners thought it advantageous to eliminate the protections given shareholders and creditors in a statutory merger, those denied the protections would complain. Chapter 16 examined the de facto merger doctrine -- the claim by *shareholders* that they are entitled to just those protections planners sought to eliminate by choosing a particular form of acquisition. This Chapter considers the parallel doctrine of successor liability -- the claim by *creditors* of the target company that the acquiring company should be deemed to have assumed their claims, as would have been the case if the transaction had been structured as a merger rather than as a sale of assets.

It is helpful at the outset to identify more precisely those target company creditors whose claims are particularly vulnerable to reduction in value as a result of the form in which an acquisition is cast. Although corporate law does not give traditional lenders, such as bondholders or banks, a vote on acquisitions as a means of protecting their interests,[1] they can, and often do, protect themselves against this risk by contracting for a veto over major corporate changes like acquisitions.[2] The borrowing company will be willing to provide such protection in order to secure a lower interest rate -- one that does not reflect the risk of a future acquisition structured to disadvantage creditors. Moreover, neither the contracting nor monitoring costs associated with this form of creditor protection are likely to be significant. The marginal

---

[1] See Chapter 16, *supra.*

[2] See American Bar Foundation, *Commentaries on Model Debenture Indenture Provisions* 290-301 (§ 801) (1971); Clifford Smith & Jerold Warner, *On Financial Contracting: An Analysis of Bond Covenants*, 7 J.Fin.Econ. 117, 126-27 (1979).

costs of contracting for the protection are low because negotiations already will be under way concerning the loan itself, and monitoring the debtor's behavior for violations of the contractual restrictions should not be burdensome given the specialized character of these types of lenders. Finally, state corporate law substantially restricts the ability of target shareholders to disadvantage this class of creditors by absconding with the proceeds of an asset sale by promptly dissolving the target corporation. State law typically requires that known debts, obviously including debts of this character, must either be paid or otherwise adequately provided for as a condition to dissolution.[3]

Trade creditors, in contrast, will not be protected by elaborate contractual provisions because the costs of contracting and monitoring are too high given the typical size of the debt and the character of the creditor. They are not, however, unprotected. Just like specialized lenders, trade creditors must be paid prior to dissolution because their debts are known. Thus, even though the acquiring company does not assume their debt, the consideration paid to the target company remains subject to it. Moreover, because trade credit is typically short term, creditors often will have sufficient notice of a sale of assets that would increase the debtor's default risk that they can protect themselves simply by declining further business with the debtor or by altering their terms of trade.

Contingent unknown creditors -- those who are not yet aware that they may have a claim against the target company -- are in a radically different position. They cannot protect themselves by a tailored contractual provision because their claims typically do not arise out of a negotiated contract. And precisely because the claim is contingent and unknown, the dissolution of the target company can deprive the potential creditor of its only potential defendant. State corporate statutes commonly require either that only known debts and claims be paid or provided for as a condition to dissolution, or provide for a post-dissolution period in which creditors can bring suit. If suit is not brought within this period, because the claim is still unknown, it is cut off.[4]

---

[3] See, e.g., Cal.Corp.Code § 2004. Some states provide a two or more year post-dissolution period in which claims can be brought. See, e.g., Rev. Model Bus.Corp. Act §§ 14.01, 14.07; Del.Code Ann. tit. 8, § 278; Mass.Gen.Laws Ann., C. 156B, § 102, Cal.Corp. Code § 2011(a). This approach provides effectively identical protection for known creditors.

[4] See, e.g., Michael Green, *Successor Liability: Supermajority of Statutory Reform to Protect Products Liability Claimants*, 72 Cornell L.Rev. 17 (1986); Note, *The Post-Dissolution Products Liability Claim Problem: A Statutory Versus a Judicial Solution*, 38 Syracuse L.Rev. 1279 (1987); Note, *Recognizing Products Liability Claims at Dissolution: The Compatibility of Corporate and Tort Law Principles*, 87 Colum.L.Rev. 1048 (1987); George Wallach, *Products Liability: A Remedy in Search of a Defendant -- The Effect of a Sale of Assets and Subsequent Dissolution on Product Dissatisfaction Claims*, 41 Mo.L.Rev. 321 (1976). Delaware's 1987 amendments to the dissolution provisions of its corporate law partially alleviate this problem. Sections 280-82 provide a mechanism by which a dissolving corporation can "make such provision sufficient to provide compensation for claims . . . that

The prototype of such a contingent creditor -- and the major concern of planners with respect to the successor liability of an acquiring company -- is the future products liability plaintiff. First, potential products liability claims are often large enough to get the attention of planners; there is sufficient incentive for planners to devote their attention to avoiding them. Second, defective or unsafe products can create claims far in the future. The effects of chemicals and drugs may take years to appear; even a mundane product like a ladder can cause injuries in the future when someone falls off of it years after it was manufactured. Thus, there is both an incentive for planners to structure their transaction to avoid these future liabilities and, because the dissolution statutes effectively protect only known creditors, a real potential for tort victims to be left uncompensated. In the absence of successor liability, a tort victim simply may have no available defendant because the manufacturer of the product that caused the injury will have ceased to exist before the victim was injured.

In this Chapter we begin by examining the doctrine of successor liability in its most prominent manifestation: What is the effect of an acquisition on the target company's as yet unasserted products liability claims? Section A first considers the traditional rules governing successor liability and attempt to understand the real nature of the problem at which successor liability is directed. Section B then evaluates the different approaches courts have used to expand the doctrine of successor liability, largely in response to the problem of products liability claims and Sections C and D suggest an alternative -- an internalization approach to successor liability. Next, Section E examines what room remains for planners to limit the acquiring company's liability for the target company's potential products liability claims. Finally, Section F briefly surveys three other areas of potential successor liability -- labor union contracts, pension fund obligations, and environmental claims.

A. "Buy Assets -- Sell Stock": Traditional Distinctions Between Acquisition Techniques

The traditional expression of the acquisition planner's decision rule is to buy assets and sell stock. The principal explanation for the preference was the problem of contingent and unknown liabilities: In an asset acquisition one assumed only those liabilities specified in the contract, while in a stock acquisition (or a merger) all liabilities, including contingent and unknown liabilities, became the responsibility of the acquiring company. Thus, an

---

have not arisen, but that, based on facts known to the corporation . . . are likely to arise . . . prior to expiration of an applicable statute of limitations." Del.Gen.Corp.Law § 281(b). If the corporation chooses to seek judicial approval of the amount set aside, and the court approves, directors are freed from liability to creditors in connection with dissolution distributions. For a careful analysis of the statutory framework and a conclusion that the amount provided for future claims was insufficient, see In re Rego Co., 1992 LEXIS 205 (Del.Ch.).

acquiring company would like to buy assets and leave unwanted liabilities to target shareholders; symmetrically, target shareholders would like to sell stock (or merge) and thereby be relieved of them.

This formulation of the decision rule obscures the real nature of the problem. As expressed, the traditional decision rule posits a conflict between the acquiring company and the target company -- one or the other ends up holding the liability bag. The real problem associated with the successor liability doctrine becomes apparent only after it is realized that, if the acquiror and target cooperate, neither need end up with the unwanted liabilities. Suppose a target company has a value of $5 million if future products liability claims are ignored, but both it and the acquiring company believe that it is subject to $2 million of such claims. In this event, the target company is worth $3 million if it is subject to the products liability claims. The choice of the acquisition technique does not alter this valuation one bit. If the acquisition is structured as a sale of assets so that the acquiring company does not assume the future products liabilities claims, it will be willing to pay $5 million -- the value of the assets it receives -- but the target company will still be worth only $3 million because its assets, albeit now consisting of only the $5 million consideration, remain subject to $2 million in future products liabilities claims. If, alternatively, the acquisition is structured as a merger so that the acquiring company assumes the future products liability claims, it will pay only $3 million. The target shareholders, however, will retain all of the consideration because the consideration is no longer subject to the future claims. Thus, the acquiring and target companies end up in precisely the same position whether assets are bought or stock is sold. To be sure, one or the other party ends up bearing the future liabilities, but that party is compensated for it. As well, the future products liability claimants end up no worse off as a result of the transaction; either way the transaction is structured, $5 million in assets are subject to their claims, just as before the transaction took place.

This analysis does not, however, demonstrate that planners cannot improve the position of the acquiring and target companies. If we assume that the traditional rule governing dissolution prevails -- that a company can liquidate without provision for unknown contingent claims like future products liability claims and that shareholders cannot later be charged with these claims even to the extent of their liquidation distributions -- then both the acquiring company and the target company will want the transaction structured in precisely the same way. If the transaction is structured as an asset acquisition following which the target company is dissolved, the value of the target company's assets is increased by $2 million. This result follows from the combination of the dissolution rule and the ability of the acquiring company to specify which liabilities it will assume in an asset acquisition. The assets are worth $5 million to the acquiring company in an asset acquisition because they will not be subject to the future products liability claims. If the target company promptly liquidates, before the future claims are made, its shareholders get to keep all of the consideration. The target company is thus worth $2 million dollars more because structuring the transaction as a sale of assets and a dissolution eliminates $2 million dollars in liabilities. Although the target and acquiring companies may disagree about how this windfall should be shared, they *will* agree that the transaction should be structured so as to create it. An accurate statement of the decision rule then is buy assets, liquidate the target, and cut off the future products liability claimants.[5]

The doctrine of successor liability is thus directed at the ability of planners to use a corporate acquisition to externalize products liability risks -- to leave the victims uncompensated and thereby allow manufacturers to make product safety decisions without taking into account the costs of defective products. So understood, it is hardly surprising that the doctrine historically took a quite restrictive form. Prior to the rapid development of products liability law, few circumstances posed the risk of large contingent future liabilities. In this setting, successor liability doctrine imposed the target company's liabilities on the acquiring company in an asset acquisition under the following four circumstances:

(1) the acquiring company explicitly or implicitly agreed to assume the target company's liabilities;

(2) the acquiring company was a mere continuation of the target company;

(3) the target company's transfer of assets was fraudulent in that its only purpose was to escape liability for its debts; or

(4) the transaction constituted a de facto merger.[6]

From a planning perspective, only one of the four elements is of special concern. The first -- contractual assumption -- is of little interest in a planning setting. There has never been any doubt that an acquiring company *could* assume the target company's contingent future liabilities; the successor liability doctrine takes on planning significance only to the extent it limits the acquiring company's ability *not* to assume them. The second and third elements -- mere continuation and fraud on creditors -- do have some general planning implications; however, they are directed not at arm's length transactions, but merely at contrivances without substance independent of the impact on creditors. In this sense, they are corporate law restatements of the traditional prohibitions on fraudulent conveyances reflected in the Uniform

---

[5] See Mark Roe, *Mergers, Acquisitions, and Tort: A Comment on the Problem of Successor Corporate Liability*, 70 Va.L.Rev. 1559, 1565 (1984); David Phillips, *Products Liability of Successor Corporations: A Corporate and Commercial Law Perspective*, 11 Hofstra L.Rev. 249, 264 (1982).

[6] See, e.g., Jerry Phillips, *Product Line Continuity and Successor Corporation Liability*, 58 NYU L.Rev. 906, 908-12 (1983); Ann Rae Heitland, *Survival of Products Liability Claims in Asset Acquisitions*, 34 Bus.Law. 489, 489-90 (1979).

Fraudulent Conveyance Act.[7] That leaves the de facto merger element as the focus of traditional successor liability doctrine.

This result is entirely understandable. For a court faced with a creditor's claim that the form of an arms-length acquisition should be disregarded and the creditor given the same protections as if the acquisition had been cast in a different form, the obvious analogy was the de facto merger doctrine. The difficulty, however, was that the analogy, although facially accurate, was empty. First, as we saw in Chapter 16, the de facto merger doctrine that developed in response to shareholder claims itself lacked a coherent core. There was no clear statement of the circumstances when the planner's choice would be respected and of those when it would be disregarded. Thus, the analogy served not to answer the successor liability question, but merely to move the uncertainty down one level. Second, and more important, the analogy did not recognize that target shareholders, for whom the de facto merger doctrine was created, and target creditors, for whom the successor liability doctrine was created, are in quite different situations. Although the same transactional trigger -- the planner's selection of an asset acquisition instead of a merger -- creates the problem in both cases, there is no a priori reason to think that the solution, or even the mode of analysis, should be the same in both.

B.   Judicial Responses to Products Liability Claims

By the time the products liability onslaught hit the courts, it was increasingly clear that the traditional formulation of the successor liability doctrine provided little guidance concerning how to deal with products liability claims against a target company that no longer existed. Plaintiffs, of course, had no difficulty deciding where to turn; they sued the acquiring company, the only deep pocket in sight. The courts, however, faced a more complicated choice in deciding how to respond to these new claims. They could have stayed within the traditional vocabulary of the successor liability doctrine, trying to add products liability content to the empty vessel of de facto merger analysis. Alternatively, the courts could forge a new approach to the problem in recognition of the fact that when plaintiffs were tort victims

---

[7] Uniform Fraudulent Conveyance Act, 7A Unif.L.Ann. (1978); see Robert Clark, *The Duties of the Corporate Debtor to its Creditors*, 90 Harv.L.Rev. 505 (1977) (relationship between Uniform Fraudulent Conveyance Act and corporate law principles); D. Phillips (1982), *supra* note 5, at 261-64. It is possible to treat the mere continuation element as the equivalent of de facto merger, see J. Phillips (1983), *supra* note 6, at 909, but the better reading treats it as a species of non-arms length contrivance. For example, the California Supreme Court has held that proof of mere continuation requires "a showing of one or both of the following factual elements: (1) no adequate consideration was given for the predecessor corporation's assets and made available for meeting the claims of its unsecured creditors; (2) one or more persons were officers, directors, or stockholders of both corporations." Ray v. Alad Corp., 560 P.2d 3, 7 (Cal.1977).

instead of target shareholders, the traditional formulation of the successor liability doctrine, and especially reliance on the de facto merger concept, were simply beside the point. Both approaches were tried.

1. Expanding Traditional Doctrine to Cope With Products Liability

KNAPP v. NORTH AMERICAN ROCKWELL CORP.
506 F.2d 361 (3d Cir.1974), *cert. denied,* 421 U.S. 965 (1975)

Before ALDISERT, ADAMS and ROSENN, Circuit Judges.

ADAMS, Circuit Judge. The principal question here is whether it was error to grant summary judgment on the ground that one injured by a defective machine may not recover from the corporation that purchased substantially all the assets of the manufacturer of the machine because the transaction was a sale of assets rather than a merger or consolidation.

I

Stanley Knapp, Jr., an employee of Mrs. Smith's Pie Co., was injured on October 6, 1969, when, in the course of his employment, his hand was caught in a machine known as a "Packomatic." The machine had been designed and manufactured by Textile Machine Works (TMW) and had been sold to Mrs. Smith's Pie Co. in 1966 or 1967.

On April 5, 1968, TMW entered into an agreement with North American Rockwell whereby TMW exchanged substantially all its assets for stock in Rockwell. TMW retained only its corporate seal, its articles of incorporation, its minute books and other corporate records, and $500,000. in cash intended to cover TMW's expenses in connection with the transfer. TMW also had the right, prior to closing the transaction with Rockwell, to dispose of land held by TMW or its subsidiary. Among the assets acquired by Rockwell was the right to use the name "Textile Machine Works." TMW was to change its name on the closing date, then to distribute the Rockwell stock to its shareholders and to dissolve TMW "[a]s soon as practicable after the last of such distributions."

The accord reached by Rockwell and TMW also stipulated that Rockwell would assume specified obligations and liabilities of TMW, but among the liabilities not assumed were: "(a) liabilities against which TMW is insured or otherwise indemnified to the extent of such insurance or indemnification unless the insurer or indemnitor agrees in writing to insure and indemnify [Rockwell] to the same extent as it was so insuring and indemnifying TMW."

Closing took place pursuant to the agreement on August 29, 1968. Plaintiff sustained his injuries on October 6, 1969. TMW was dissolved on

February 20, 1970, almost 18 months after the bulk of its assets had been exchanged for Rockwell stock.

Plaintiff filed this suit against Rockwell in the district court on March 22, 1971. He alleged that his injuries resulted from the negligence of TMW in designing and manufacturing the machine and that Rockwell, as TMW's successor, is liable for such injuries. Rockwell joined plaintiff's employer, Mrs. Smith's Pie Co., as a third-party defendant.[3]

Rockwell moved for summary judgment in the district court on June 19, 1973. On September 6, 1973, the district court granted the motion, ruling that Rockwell had neither merged nor consolidated with TMW, that Rockwell was not a continuation of TMW, and that Rockwell had not assumed TMW's liability to Knapp. . . .

II

Both parties agree that this case is controlled by the following principle of law:

> The general rule is that "a mere sale of corporate property by one company to another does not make the purchaser liable for the liabilities of the seller not assumed by it." . . . There are, however, certain exceptions to this rule. Liability for obligations of a selling corporation may be imposed on the purchasing corporation when (1) the purchaser expressly or impliedly agrees to assume such obligations; (2) the transaction amounts to a consolidation or merger of the selling corporation with or into the purchasing corporation; (3) the purchasing corporation is merely a continuation of the selling corporation; or (4) the transaction is entered into fraudulently to escape liability for such obligations.

Shane v. Hobam, Inc., 332 F.Supp. 526, 527-528 (E.D.Pa.1971) (citations omitted) (decided under New York law).

In light of this language, Knapp contends that the transaction in question "amounts to a consolidation or merger of [TMW] with or into the purchasing corporation [Rockwell]" or, alternatively, that Rockwell is a "continuation" of TMW. Although the TMW corporation technically continued to exist until its dissolution approximately 18 months after the consummation of the transaction with Rockwell, TMW was, Knapp argues, a mere shell during that period. It had none of its former assets, no active operations, and was required by the contract with Rockwell to dissolve itself "as soon as

---

[3] On July 13, 1972, after Rockwell had denied responsibility for any liability TMW may have had to Knapp, Knapp sued TMW in a Pennsylvania state court to recover for his injuries. That suit was barred, however, either by the two year statute of limitations on personal injury actions [12 Pa.Stat.Ann. § 31] or by the statute requiring that suits against a dissolved corporation be commenced within two years of the date of dissolution [15 Pa.Stat.Ann. § 2111 (Supp.1974)].

practicable." Knapp urges in effect that the transaction between TMW and Rockwell should be considered a de facto merger. . . .

III

In a diversity case, the federal court must apply the rule of law which would govern if suit were brought in a court of the forum state. . . .

No prior cases decided under Pennsylvania law have addressed the problem presently before this Court. However, when courts from other jurisdictions have considered similar questions, they have ascertained the existence *vel non* of a merger, a consolidation or a continuation on the basis of whether, immediately after the transaction, the selling corporation continued to exist as a corporate entity and whether, after the transaction, the selling corporation possessed substantial assets with which to satisfy the demands of its creditors.

Thus, in Bazan v. Kux Machine Co.,[12] the plaintiff was injured in 1966 by a machine purchased by his employer from Kux Machine Co. in 1961. In 1963, after the sale of the machine to plaintiff's employer but prior to the accident, Kux sold to the Wickes Corporation the bulk of Kux's assets, retaining only its accounts receivable, its prepaid insurance and its real estate. Wickes acquired Kux' tangible personal property, licenses, trademarks, patents, good will, and the exclusive right to use the name "Kux Machine." Kux, after changing its name, remained in existence for ten months before dissolving as required by the contract with Wickes. The court held that the transaction was not a merger, consolidation or continuation. It reasoned that Kux continued to exist for a substantial period after the exchange, that the transaction was a cash sale rather than an exchange of stock, and that none of the owners or management of the seller acquired any interest in the buyer.

Similarly, in McKee v. Harris-Seybold Co.[13] the court held that there had been no merger or consolidation between the alleged tortfeasor and the purchaser of its assets. The plaintiff was injured in 1968 by a paper-cutting machine manufactured in 1916 by the Seybold Machine Co. In 1926, Seybold agreed to sell its assets to Harris Automatic Press Co. In exchange, Harris agreed to give Seybold cash plus common stock in Harris, and to assume certain of Seybold's liabilities. Harris acquired all the assets of Seybold including its good will and the exclusive use of the name "Seybold Machine Co." Seybold agreed to change its name and not to engage in any manufacturing activities. Seybold continued to exist under a different name for one year after the exchange. Prior to the consummation of the transaction Harris assigned its interest in the contract to a new corporation formed for the purpose. The new corporation was later renamed the Harris-Seybold Co. The court held that Harris-Seybold was not liable for the plaintiff's injuries

---

[12] 358 F.Supp. 1250 (E.D.Wis.1973).

[13] 264 A.2d 98 (N.J.Super.L.Div.1970) *aff'd per curiam*, 288 A.2d 585 (N.J.Super.1972).

because there had been no merger or consolidation between the Harris and Seybold corporations. Nor, the court ruled, was Harris or Harris-Seybold a continuation of Seybold. After observing that this was not an exchange for securities alone, the court stressed that "[t]he identity of the [Seybold] corporation and of its stockholders as an integral part of the corporate identity was not eradicated by the transfer." 264 A.2d at 104. . . . The court's analysis was that "[i]f the vendor corporation receives the consideration for the transfer, as opposed to those situations where the stockholders directly receive the same, and that corporation is thereby kept alive, there seems to be nothing in the nature of a merger or consolidation." *Id.* . . .

This cluster of cases[16] illustrates the significance which the decisions from other jurisdictions accord to corporate theory and the continued existence of the corporate entity. The adequacy of the consideration received by the selling corporation has also been given great weight in deciding the existence of a sale as contrasted with a merger or continuation. . . . [T]he court emphasized in *McKee, supra,* that the selling corporation had received substantial value for its assets, and that there was no hint the selling corporation was being denuded of assets with which it might satisfy the claims of its creditors. The district court for the District of Colorado, in Kloberdanz v. Joy Mfg. Co.,[17] stated that "the emphasis should be on whether the sale was a bona fide one involving the payment of money or property to the selling corporation whereby it can respond [in damages] in actions like the present one."

In Jackson v. Diamond T. Trucking Co.,[18] the court found the purchasing corporation to be a continuation of the selling corporation because the "purchaser" took all the assets of the "seller" in return for nominal consideration only. Similarly, in Ruedy v. Toledo Factories Co.[19] and Hoche Productions v. Jayark Films Corp.,[20] the courts concluded that the transactions were mergers after the "selling" corporations were left without appreciable assets to satisfy the claims of their creditors.

---

[16] See also Forest Laboratories v. Pillsbury Co., 452 F.2d 621 (7th Cir.1971); West Texas Refining & Dev. Co. v. Commissioner of Internal Revenue, 68 F.2d 77 (10th Cir.1933); Kloberdanz v. Joy Mfg. Co., 288 F.Supp. 817 (D.Colo.1968); Copease Mfg. Co. v. Cormac Photocopy Corp., 242 F.Supp. 993 (S.D.N.Y.1965); J.F. Anderson Lumber Co. v. Myers, 206 N.W.2d 365 (Minn.1973); Schwartz v. McGraw-Edison Co., 14 Cal.App.3d 767 (1971); Buis v. Peabody Coal Co., 190 N.E.2d 507 (Ill.App.1963).

[17] 288 F.Supp. 817, 820 (D.Colo.1968).

[18] 241 A.2d 471 (N.J.Super.L.Div.1968).

[19] 22 N.E.2d 293 (Ohio App.1939).

[20] 256 F.Supp. 291 (S.D.N.Y.1966).

IV

The cases discussed above, all decided under the law of jurisdictions other than Pennsylvania, may suggest that the arrangement between Rockwell and TMW should be considered a sale rather than a merger or a continuation, since TMW did not officially terminate its corporate existence for 18 months after the exchange, and throughout that period possessed valuable assets with which to respond to tort claims similar to the one now advanced. However, a number of considerations indicate the insubstantiality of the continued existence of TMW, including the brevity of the corporation's continued life, the contractual requirement that TMW be dissolved as soon as possible, the prohibition on engaging in normal business transactions, and the character of the assets TMW controlled. Although each of these factors was present in one or more of the above cases, the present appeal is unique in combining all these elements. In addition, the better-reasoned result would be to conclude that, for the purpose of determining liability to tortiously injured parties, the Rockwell-TMW transaction should be treated as a merger, thereby subjecting Rockwell to liability for injuries caused by defective products distributed by TMW prior to the transaction.

We must, of course, apply the rule we believe a Pennsylvania appellate tribunal would adopt if the case arose in the state courts. In resolving issues relating to the recognition of a cause of action in favor of an injured party, the Pennsylvania courts have emphasized the public policy considerations served by imposing liability on the defendant rather than formal or technical requirements. . . .

In Farris v. Glen Alden Corp.,[24] a shareholder of Glen Alden sought to enjoin a meeting of Glen Alden shareholders called to approve a "reorganization agreement" with List Industries. Plaintiff asked that the meeting be enjoined because management had failed to inform the shareholders that the purpose of the meeting was the approval of a merger and that the shareholders had a right to dissent from the merger and obtain a valuation of their stock. Management responded that the shareholders had no valuation rights because the transaction did not conform to the statutory merger procedures and therefore was not a merger, but a sale of assets to which valuation rights did not apply. Pursuant to the plan of reorganization, Glen Alden was to acquire all the assets of List except a small amount of cash reserved for payment of expenses in connection with the transaction. In exchange, Glen Alden was to assume all List's liabilities and to issue stock to List that List would distribute to its stockholders. List was then to dissolve and Glen Alden to change its name to List Alden.

The Court expressed the view in *Farris* that because of the complexities of modern corporate reorganizations,

---

[24] 143 A.2d 25 (Pa.1958).

it is no longer helpful to consider an individual transaction in the abstract and solely by reference to the various elements therein determine whether it is a "merger" or a "sale". Instead, to determine properly the nature of a corporate transaction, we must refer not only to all the provisions of the agreement, but also to the consequences of the transaction and to the purposes of the provisions of the corporation law said to be applicable. [143 A.2d at 28]

The rationale of dissenting shareholders' rights, the Court stated, is to allow shareholders to treat their membership in the original corporation as terminated when the corporation, in combining with another, "lose[s] its original nature." The List-Glen Alden agreement, the Court held, fundamentally altered the relationship between Glen Alden and its shareholders, and therefore the provisions relating to dissenting shareholders' rights should apply.

The present case, like *Farris*, involves a transaction which resembles a merger but does not possess all the formal characteristics of one. It seems appropriate to infer from *Farris* that in deciding whether to treat such an arrangement as a merger the Pennsylvania courts would consider the purposes which would be served by imposing liability on Rockwell for the tortious conduct of TMW.[27]

In the present case, Knapp is confronted with the melancholy prospect of being barred from his day in court unless Rockwell is held subject to suit. And quite significantly, if Knapp had been injured more than two years after the dissolution of TMW, Knapp would never have had any opportunity to recover at law, since under Pennsylvania law a dissolved corporation is subject to suit for only two years after the date of dissolution.

Denying Knapp the right to sue Rockwell because of the barren continuation of TMW after the exchange with Rockwell would allow a formality to defeat Knapp's recovery. Although TMW technically existed as an independent corporation, it had no substance. The parties clearly contemplated that TMW would terminate its existence as a part of the transaction. TMW had, in exchange for Rockwell stock, disposed of all the assets it originally held, exclusive of the cash necessary to consummate the transaction. It could not undertake any active operations. . . . Most significantly, TMW was required by the contract with Rockwell to dissolve "as soon as practicable."

On the other hand, Rockwell acquired all the assets of TMW, exclusive of certain real estate that Rockwell did not want, and assumed practically all of TMW's liabilities. Further, Rockwell required that TMW use its "best efforts," prior to the consummation of the transaction, to preserve TMW's business organization intact for Rockwell, to make available to Rockwell

---

[27] Although the facts of the present case are admittedly a step beyond those in *Farris*, in view of the legislative intent deduced by the Pennsylvania courts in the field of dissenting shareholders' rights, it might be contended that the Pennsylvania Supreme Court would find that the legislature intended to permit tort liability in cases like the one *sub judice*.

TMW's existing officers and employees, and to maintain TMW's relationship with its customers and suppliers. After the exchange, Rockwell continued TMW's former business operations.

If we are to follow the philosophy of the Pennsylvania courts that questions of an injured party's right to seek recovery are to be resolved by an analysis of public policy considerations rather than by a mere procrustean application of formalities, we must, in considering whether the TMW-Rockwell exchange was a merger, evaluate the public policy implications of that determination.

In resolving, where the burden of a loss should be imposed, the Pennsylvania Supreme Court has considered which of the two parties is better able to spread the loss. . . .

[N]either Knapp nor Rockwell was ever in a position to prevent the occurrence of the injury, inasmuch as neither manufactured the defective device. As between these two parties, however, Rockwell is better able to spread the burden of the loss. Prior to the exchange with Rockwell, TMW had procured insurance that would have indemnified TMW had it been held liable to Knapp for his injuries. Rockwell could have protected itself from sustaining the brunt of the loss by securing from TMW an assignment of TMW's insurance. There is no indication in the record that such an assignment would have placed a burden on either Rockwell or TMW since TMW had already purchased the insurance protection, and the insurance was of no continuing benefit to TMW after its liability to suit was terminated by Pennsylvania statute. Rockwell has adduced no explanation, either in its brief or at oral argument, why it agreed in the contract not to take an assignment of TMW's prepaid insurance. Rockwell therefore should not be permitted to impose the weight of the loss upon a user of an allegedly defective product by delaying the formal dissolution of TMW. In the absence of contrary controlling decisions by the Pennsylvania courts, we conclude that the state judiciary would adopt the rule of law that appears to be better reasoned and more consistent with the social policy set forth in recent Pennsylvania cases.

The judgment of the district court will therefore be reversed and the case remanded for further proceedings consistent with this opinion.

ROSENN, Circuit Judge, concurring. The majority holds that, under certain circumstances, a corporation which acquires substantially all the assets of another corporation may be held liable for injuries caused by defective products manufactured by the other corporation before the date of acquisition. In the present case, they conclude that, even though the transaction was structured as a sale of assets, it should be "treated as a merger" for the purpose of imposing tort liability. Although I concur in the result reached by the majority, I wish to clarify the basis upon which I would impose such liability. . . .

In the present day of complex corporate reorganizations and acquisitions, the intrinsic nature of a transaction cannot be ascertained merely from the form in which it is structured. Courts therefore must examine the substance of the transaction to ascertain its purpose and true intent. . . .

The Pennsylvania Supreme Court has had occasion to examine the rights of dissenting shareholders when a transfer of the business operations of one corporation to another is effectuated by sale rather than by utilization of the statutory procedures provided for merger. Farris v. Glen Alden Corp., *supra.* . . .

If, in protecting dissenting shareholders, a court should scrutinize a corporate transaction to ascertain the presence of certain attributes of merger relevant to the enforcement of appraisal rights, it should do no less in protecting tort claimants. Both dissenting shareholders under § 805 and tort claimants under § 803 are the intended beneficiaries of protective legislation. Although a transaction should be scrutinized to protect both shareholders and tort claimants, a court should search for somewhat different attributes of merger for purposes of imposing tort liability. This difference in relevant attributes stems from the distinct relationships to the corporation of the persons whom the legislature has sought to protect. While dissenting shareholders need protection against alteration of their investment rights, tort claimants need protection against attempts by ongoing businesses to avoid liability through transfer of their operations to another legal entity.

I believe that, where a corporation purchases substantially all the assets of a second corporation, the legislature intended to impose the second corporation's tort liabilities on the acquiring corporation at least if the following attributes of merger are present:

(1) an ongoing business, including its name and good will, is transferred to the acquiring corporation; and

(2) the corporation whose assets are acquired is dissolved after distribution to its shareholders of the consideration received from the acquiring corporation.

In the present case, TMW transferred to Rockwell almost all its assets, retaining only its corporate records and a limited amount of cash to effectuate the transaction. The "Agreement and Plan of Reorganization" specifically provided for the transfer of TMW's business "as a going concern," including good will, the exclusive right to use the name "Textile Machine Works," and the "permits or licenses to conduct [TMW's] business as now carried on." TMW also agreed to change its name and dissolve. . . .

In addition, this transaction has another characteristic of a statutory merger. The consideration given for TMW's assets was Rockwell stock, which in turn was to be distributed to TMW's shareholders on TMW's liquidation and dissolution. Thus, TMW shareholders became shareholders in Rockwell just as if they had exchanged their shares directly with Rockwell under the statutory merger procedure. . . .

While I recognize the rightful prerogative of a corporation to rearrange its business or go out of business entirely, there is also a practical and reasonable basis for construing this transaction as a merger. Were we in the circumstances of this case to absolve of liability a corporation which acquires a functioning business by purchasing substantially all the assets of another corporation, many injured parties would be unable to maintain products liability actions after the former corporate owner of the business has been dissolved. Although by statute Pennsylvania corporations are amenable to suit for two years after dissolution, a defect in a product manufactured by a dissolved corporation may not come to light until long after the two-year period. Because the statute of limitations generally does not begin to run until the defect is discovered, such an action probably would not be time-barred.

In imposing liability for the torts of the acquired corporation, I realize that the acquiring corporation was not a party to any tortious act and had no connection with the acquired corporation at the time the allegedly defective product was manufactured. The acquiring corporation, however, is in a position both before and after the acquisition to take necessary measures for its protection against potential products liability claims.

Knapp and a number of other cases explicitly stretched, but did not quite break, the bounds of traditional successor liability doctrine in an effort to accommodate the public policy underpinnings of products liability and the corporate law origins of the de facto merger and mere continuation elements.[8] These opinions are laudable in that they clearly recognized that it was the products liability aspect of the cases that made them difficult. The problem, however, is understanding the scope of their holdings. The opinions reflect an uneasy mix of (a) seeing how closely the transaction fits the traditional de facto merger mold; and (b) policy analysis focusing on the usual reasons for imposing strict products liability, including the acquiring company's ability to spread the loss, to insure, and to improve the product in the future. There is nothing in *Knapp* that explains how one "balances" in a particular case the power of products liability policy against the extent to which the facts deviate from those usually necessary to finding a de facto merger -- we do not learn how much policy buys how much deviation. For example, the transaction in *Knapp* did meet one of the traditional requirements of the de facto merger doctrine: The consideration received by the target company was stock.[9] Would the result in *Knapp* have been different if the consideration had been cash?

In Turner v. Bituminous Casualty Co., *supra*, the court imposed successor liability despite the fact that the consideration was cash rather than stock, listing the following elements of a "prima facie case" for successor

---

[8] See, e.g., Cyr v. B. Offen & Co., 501 F.2d 1145 (1st Cir.1974) (expansion of mere continuation exception); Turner v. Bituminous Casualty Co., 244 N.W.2d 873 (Mich.1976) (expansion of de facto merger analysis).

[9] See, e.g., Kloberdanz v. Joy Mfg. Co., 288 F.Supp. 817 (D.Colo.1968); McKee v. Harris-Seybold Co., 264 A.2d 98 (N.J.Super.1970), *aff'd*, 288 A.2d 585 (N.J.Super.1972).

liability: (1) a basic continuity of the enterprise of the target company, including a retention of key personnel, assets, and general business operations; (2) dissolution of the target company after distribution of the consideration; (3) assumption by the acquiring company of those liabilities necessary to the continuation of the target company's business; and (4) the acquiring company held itself out as the effective continuation of the target company. *Turner*, 244 N.W.2d at 883-84. Under this quasi-traditional analysis, would the result in *Turner* have been different if the acquiring company manufactured the product line acquired under its own name rather than under the name of the target company?

2.   The Product Line Theory of Successor Liability

In light of the analytic difficulty of balancing the public policy favoring products liability against the traditional corporate law limits on successor liability, it was not surprising that other courts soon developed an entirely new doctrine of successor liability designed especially for products liability cases. Indeed, it is entirely possible that the efforts in *Knapp* and Cyr v. B. Offen & Co., *supra*, to stretch traditional doctrine rather than discard it were artifacts of the limits of diversity jurisdiction: Federal courts required under Erie Railroad v. Tompkins[10] to apply state law can stretch existing doctrine but are limited in their freedom to announce entirely new doctrine in the face of contrary state precedent.[11]

RAMIREZ v. AMSTED INDUSTRIES
431 A.2d 811 (N.J.1981)

CLIFFORD, J. This products liability case implicates principles of successor corporation liability. We are called upon to formulate a general rule governing the strict tort liability of a successor corporation for damages caused by defects in products manufactured and distributed by its predecessor. The Appellate Division, in an opinion reported at 408 A.2d 818 (N.J.Super.1979), devised the following test, based essentially on the holding of the Supreme Court of California in Ray v. Alad Corp., 560 P.2d 3 (Cal.1977):

> [W]here, as in the present case, the successor corporation acquires all or substantially all the assets of the predecessor corporation for cash and continues

---

[10] 304 U.S. 64 (1938).

[11] The requirement that federal courts apply state law has been an explicit factor in the decision of some federal courts to reject any broadening of successor liability. See Leannais v. Cincinnati, Inc., 565 F.2d 437 (7th Cir.1977) (applying Wisconsin law); Travis v. Harris Corp., 565 F.2d 443 (7th Cir.1977) (applying Ohio and Indiana law).

essentially the same manufacturing operation as the predecessor corporation the successor remains liable for the product liability claims of its predecessor. ---

In affirming the judgment below we adopt substantially this test for determining successor corporation liability in the factual context presented.

I

On August 18, 1975 plaintiff Efrain Ramirez was injured while operating an allegedly defective power press on the premises of his employer, Zamax Manufacturing Company, in Belleville, New Jersey. The machine involved, known as a Johnson Model 5, sixty-ton punch press, was manufactured by Johnson Machine and Press Company (Johnson) in 1948 or 1949. As a result of the injuries sustained plaintiffs filed suit against Amsted Industries, Inc. (Amsted) as a successor corporation to Johnson, seeking to recover damages on theories of negligence, breach of warranty and strict liability in tort for defective design and manufacturing. After discovery had been completed, Amsted moved for summary judgment on the ground that the mere purchase of Johnson's assets for cash in 1962 did not carry with it tort liability for damages arising out of defects in products manufactured by Johnson. The trial court granted summary judgment for Amsted, holding that there is no assumption of liability when the successor purchases the predecessor's assets for cash and when the provisions of the purchase agreement between the selling and purchasing corporations indicate an intention to limit the purchaser's assumption of liability. That holding was consistent with the traditional rule governing the liability of successor corporations. See McKee v. Harris-Seybold Co., 264 A.2d 98 (N.J.Super..L.Div.1970), *aff'd*, 288 A.2d 585 (N.J.Super.App.Div.1972).

On their appeal to the Appellate Division plaintiffs argued that a corporation that purchases the assets of a manufacturer and continues the business of the selling corporation in an essentially unchanged manner should not be allowed to use exculpatory contractual language to avoid liability for contingent personal injury claims arising out of defects in the predecessor's product. The Appellate Division agreed and reversed the trial court. Although it recognized that the purchase agreement manifested a clear intent to negate any assumption of liability by Amsted for contingent product claims, the court below took notice of "[t]he recent trend towards a rule imposing liability on the successor corporation without regard to the niceties of corporate transfers where the successor has acquired and has continued the predecessor's commercial activity in an essentially unchanged manner." 408 A.2d 818. Taking cognizance of New Jersey's position "in the vanguard" advancing the principle of enterprise liability and the philosophy of spreading the risk to society for the cost of injuries from defective products, the Appellate Division reasoned that the result in this troublesome area of products liability law should not be controlled by the form of the corporate transfer nor by exculpatory language in the purchase agreement. *Id.* at 408

A.2d 818. It concluded that because Amsted ultimately acquired all or substantially all the assets of Johnson and continued essentially the same manufacturing operation, Amsted could not as a matter of law avoid potential liability for injuries caused by defects in the Johnson product line, notwithstanding an intervening ownership by an intermediate corporation. *Id.* at 408 A.2d 818. It therefore remanded the cause for trial. We granted Amsted's petition for certification. 412 A.2d 804 (N.J.1980).

II

. . . As indicated above, the machine that caused the injury was manufactured in 1948 or 1949 by Johnson Machine and Press Company of Elkhart, Indiana. In 1956 Johnson transferred all of its assets and liabilities to Bontrager Construction Company (Bontrager), another Indiana corporation. Johnson transacted no business as a manufacturing entity following its acquisition by Bontrager, but Bontrager did retain a single share of Johnson common stock in order to continue the Johnson name in corporate form. Bontrager's primary activity then became the manufacture of the Johnson press line.

By purchase agreement dated August 29, 1962, Amsted acquired all of the assets of Bontrager, including all the Johnson assets that Bontrager had acquired in 1956, plus the one share of Johnson stock. The purchase price was $1,200,406 in cash.[2] The assets purchased by Amsted in the 1962 transaction included the manufacturing plant in Elkhart, which had been operated by Johnson prior to its transfer to Bontrager in 1956. Amsted also required all of Bontrager's inventory, machinery and equipment, patents and trademarks, pending contracts, books and records, and the exclusive right to adopt and use the trade name "Johnson Machine and Press Corporation." Bontrager further agreed to "use its best efforts to make available" to Amsted the services of all of its present employees except its three principals, who covenanted not to compete with Amsted for a period of five years.

In addition, the August 1962 agreement provided that Amsted would assume responsibility for certain specified debts and liabilities necessary to an uninterrupted continuation of the business. Included, however, was the following reservation:

> It is understood and agreed that Purchaser shall not assume or be liable for any liability or obligations other than those herein expressly assumed by Purchaser.

---

[2] Although as noted by the Appellate Division, 408 A.2d at 818 "[t]he fate of Bontrager is not revealed by the present record," other courts analyzing the very same corporate transaction have determined that Bontrager distributed the cash proceeds of the transaction to its shareholders and dissolved its inert corporate existence not long thereafter. See Korzetz v. Amsted Industries, Inc., 472 F.Supp. 136, 144 (E.D.Mich.1979); Ortiz v. South Bend Lathe Co., 46 Cal.App.2d 842, 846, 120 Cal.Rptr. 556, 558 (Dist.Ct.App.1975).

. . . Thus it is clear that Amsted expressly declined to assume liability for any claims arising out of defects in products manufactured by its predecessors.

Following the 1962 acquisition Amsted manufactured the Johnson press line through its wholly-owned subsidiary, South Bend Lathe, Inc. (South Bend I), in the original Johnson plant in Elkhart. . . .

In September 1965 South Bend I, the Amsted subsidiary that had been manufacturing the Johnson product line, was dissolved and its assets and liabilities were assumed by Amsted.   The manufacturing business was operated by Amsted until June 1975, at which time the business was sold to a newly-formed Indiana corporation also named South Bend Lathe, Inc. (South Bend II).   As part of this transaction Amsted agreed to indemnify South Bend II for any losses arising out of machinery manufactured and sold prior to the date of closing.   Amsted acknowledges that by virtue of this indemnity agreement, it is responsible for the defense against and payment of any liability claims against South Bend II arising out of any defects in the Johnson product line.

III

Amsted urges this Court to judge its potential liability for defective Johnson products on the basis of the traditional analysis of corporate successor liability. . . .

In recent years, however, the traditional corporate approach has been sharply criticized as being inconsistent with the rapidly developing principles of strict liability in tort and unresponsive to the legitimate interests of the products liability plaintiff. Courts have come to recognize that the traditional rule of nonliability was developed not in response to the interests of parties to products liability actions, but rather to protect the rights of commercial creditors and dissenting shareholders following corporate acquisitions, as well as to determine successor corporation liability for tax assessments and contractual obligations of the predecessor. Turner v. Bituminous Cas. Co., 244 N.W.2d 873, 878 (Mich.1976); see Cyr v. B. Offen & Co., Inc., 501 F.2d 1145, 1152 & n.12 (1st Cir.1974).

Strict interpretation of the traditional corporate law approach leads to a narrow application of the exceptions to nonliability, and places unwarranted emphasis on the form rather than the practical effect of a particular corporate transaction.   The principal exceptions to nonliability outlined in *McKee*, *supra*, condition successor liability on a determination of whether the transaction can be labeled as a merger or a de facto merger, or whether the purchasing corporation can be described as a mere continuation of the selling corporation. Traditionally, the triggering of the "de facto merger" exception has been held to depend on whether the assets were transferred to the acquiring corporation for shares of stock or for cash -- that is, whether the stockholders of the selling corporation become the stockholders of the purchasing corporation. Under a narrow application of the *McKee* exception of de facto merger no liability is imposed where the purchasing corporation paid for the acquired assets principally in cash. *Id.*

In like manner, narrow application of *McKee's* "continuation" exception causes liability *vel non* to depend on whether the plaintiff is able to establish that there is continuity in management, shareholders, personnel, physical location, assets and general business operation between selling and purchasing corporations following the asset acquisition. Where the commonality of corporate management or ownership cannot be shown, there is deemed to have been no continuation of the seller's corporate entity..

When viewed in this light, narrow application of the *McKee* approach to corporate successor liability is indeed inconsistent with the developing principles of strict products liability and unresponsive to the interests of persons injured by defective products in the stream of commerce. The Supreme Court of Michigan has offered this insight:

> To the injured persons the problem of recovery is substantially the same, no matter what corporate process led to transfer of the first corporation and/or its assets. Whether the corporate transaction was (1) a traditional merger accompanied by exchange of stock of the two corporations, or (2) a de facto merger brought about by the purchase of one corporation's assets by part of the stock of the second, or (3) a purchase of corporate assets for cash, the injured person has the same problem, so long as the first corporation in each case legally and/or practically becomes defunct. He has no place to turn for relief except to the second corporation. Therefore, as to the injured person, distinctions between types of corporate transfers are wholly unmeaningful. [Turner v. Bituminous Cas. Co., *supra*, 244 N.W.2d at 878.]

We likewise refuse to decide this case through a narrow application of *McKee*. The form of the corporate transaction by which Amsted acquired the manufacturing assets of Bontrager should not be controlling as to Amsted's liability for the serious injury suffered by plaintiff some thirteen years after that transaction. We therefore must consider the alternative approaches to successor corporation liability that have been adopted by other reviewing courts in an effort to arrive at the standard most consistent with the principles underlying the New Jersey law of strict products liability.

IV

In an effort to make the traditional corporate approach more responsive to the problems associated with the developing law of strict products liability several courts have broadened the *McKee* exceptions of "de facto merger" and "mere continuation" in order to expand corporate successor liability in certain situations. See, e.g., Knapp v. North American Rockwell Corp., 506 F.2d 361 (3rd Cir.1974); *Cyr, supra, Turner, supra.*

The "mere continuation" exception was first expanded by a federal court applying New Hampshire law in Cyr v. B. Offen & Co., Inc., *supra.* . . .

The *Cyr* court based the justification for its holding on the public policy considerations underlying strict products liability. It recognized that the successor corporation, not being the original manufacturer, is not the specific legal entity that placed the defective product in the stream of commerce or made implied representations as to its safety. Nonetheless, there were several other policy justifications for imposing strict products liability on the successor. The first was in essence the risk-spreading approach:

> The very existence of strict liability for manufacturers implies a basic judgment that the hazards of predicting and insuring for risk from defective products are better borne by the manufacturer than by the consumer. The manufacturer's successor, carrying over the experience and expertise of the manufacturer, is likewise in a better position than the consumer to gauge the risks and the costs of meeting them. The successor knows the product, is as able to calculate the risk of defects as the predecessor, is in position to insure therefor and reflect such cost in sale negotiations, and is the only entity capable of improving the quality of the product. [*Id.* at 1154.]

The court also reasoned that the successor corporation, having reaped the benefits of continuing its predecessor's product line, exploiting its accumulated good will and enjoying the patronage of its established customers, should be made to bear some of the burdens of continuity, namely, liability for injuries caused by its defective products.

Perhaps the most significant decision expanding the "mere continuation" exception to the traditional rule of corporate successor nonliability is Turner v. Bituminous Cas. Co., 244 N.W.2d 873 (Mich.1976). The defendant in *Turner* contended that where manufacturing assets are acquired by a purchasing corporation for cash rather than for stock, there is no continuity of shareholders and therefore no corporate successor liability. However, the court looked upon the kind of consideration paid for assets as but "one factor to use to determine whether there exists a sufficient nexus between the successor and predecessor corporations to establish successor liability." It reasoned that there was no practical basis for treating a cash purchase of corporate assets any differently from an acquisition of assets for stock, concluding that "[i]t would make better sense if the law had a common result and allowed products liability recovery in each case."

Accordingly, the *Turner* court held that in applying the "mere continuation" exception to situations involving the sale of corporate assets for cash, continuity of shareholders between selling and purchasing corporations is not a relevant criterion for the purposes of determining successor liability for injury caused by defective products. Rather, it adopted a less stringent version of the "mere continuation" exception in the sale-of-assets-for-cash context, jettisoning the criterion of continuity of shareholders and emphasizing continuity of the enterprise of the predecessor corporation. Applying the rule it had adopted to the record before it, the court concluded that all relevant elements of continuation were present.

In the instant case plaintiffs contend that Amsted can be held responsible for liability arising out of defective Johnson products based upon *Turner's* expanded "continuation" approach. To support this line of attack they rely on Korzetz v. Amsted Industries, Inc., 472 F.Supp. 136 (E.D.Mich.1979). In *Korzetz*, a federal court in Michigan applied the *Turner* analysis to the very same corporate succession involved in the instant case (Johnson to Bontrager to Amsted), and determined that Amsted could be held liable for injuries caused by presses manufactured by Johnson well before Amsted acquired the Johnson assets from Bontrager. . . .

We agree with plaintiffs that under *Turner*, which simply expands the "continuation" exception to the traditional *McKee* approach, Amsted may be held to be the mere continuation of Johnson for the purpose of imposing corporate successor liability for injuries caused by defective Johnson products. However, the Appellate Division actually based its decision below and its ultimate test of successor corporation liability not on the *Turner* analysis but rather on the so-called "product line exception" developed by the California Supreme Court in Ray v. Alad Corp., 560 P.2d 3 (Cal.1977).

There are fundamental practical and analytical differences between *Turner's* expanded "mere continuation" exception and *Ray's* "product line" approach. *Turner* merely broadens the inroads into the traditional principles of corporate successor nonliability expressed in *McKee* and related cases, while *Ray* completely abandons the traditional rule and its exceptions, utilizing instead the policies underlying strict liability in tort for injuries caused by defective products. Whereas the *Turner* variation on continuation of the enterprise contemplates such factors as the ownership and management of the successor's corporate entity, its personnel, physical location, assets, trade name, and general business operation, the *Ray* test is concerned not with the continuation of the corporate entity as such but rather with the successor's undertaking to manufacture essentially the same line of products as the predecessor.

Because we believe that the focus in cases involving corporate successor liability for injuries caused by defective products should be on the successor's continuation of the actual manufacturing operation and not on commonality of ownership and management between the predecessor's and successor's corporate entities, and because the traditional corporate approach, even as broadened by *Turner* and its progeny, renders inconsistent results,[3] we adopt substantially *Ray*'s product line analysis.

V

In Ray v. Alad Corp., *supra*, the plaintiff was injured in a fall from a defective ladder on which he had been working. One year prior to plaintiff's injury the manufacturer of the ladder, Alad Corporation (Alad I), had sold to Lighting Maintenance Corporation its assets, stock in trade, trade name and goodwill. As part of the transaction Alad I agreed to dissolve its corporate existence as soon as practical and to assist the purchasing corporation in the organization of a new business entity under the name of Alad Corporation (Alad II). The principal stockholders of Alad I agreed not to compete with Alad II for forty-two months and to render nonexclusive consulting services during that period. The principal stockholder of Alad I was employed as a salaried consultant for the initial five months of Alad II's organization. Once in operation Alad II continued to manufacture the same line of Alad I ladders, under the same name, using the same equipment, employees and customer lists. No contractual provisions were made for the assumption of liability by Alad II for defects in products manufactured or sold by Alad I prior to the asset acquisition. The injured plaintiff in *Ray* sued Alad II on the theory of strict liability in tort.

The California Supreme Court reversed a trial court's summary judgment in favor of Alad II. It determined that none of the four stated exceptions to the general rule of nonliability under the traditional corporate law approach was sufficient basis for imposing liability on the purchasing corporation, Alad II. Nevertheless, the court determined that a special departure from that traditional approach was called for by the policies underlying strict tort liability for injuries caused by defective products. Rather than adopt the expanded "mere continuation" exception to the corporate law approach as developed in *Cyr*, *supra*, and *Turner*, *supra*, the *Ray* court abandoned the traditional analysis. It developed instead the

---

[3] For example, in Hernandez v. Johnson Press Corp., 388 N.E.2d 778 (Ill.App.Ct.1979), an Illinois appellate court applied the *Turner* analysis to the very same corporate genealogy as involved herein, and determined that there was no de facto merger between Johnson and Amsted. The court's findings of fact, however, indicate that the plaintiff presented a shamefully weak record, as the court was unable to point to facts indicating continuity of management, personnel, physical location, assets and general business operation. 388 N.E.2d at 780. In *Korzetz, supra*, *Turner*'s continuity rationale was applied to the identical factual situation and the court found "strong and convincing evidence of continuity of enterprise" from Johnson to Amsted, emphasizing continuity of personnel, physical location, assets, trade name, sales contract, customer lists, and general business operations. 472 F.Supp. at 144. While the record in the present case clearly supports the *Korzetz* court's result, the point is that the *Turner* analysis lends itself to inconsistency and ambiguity. *Ray*'s product line analysis, focusing primarily on the continuation of the general business operations, not only can be applied with greater consistency, but better reflects the underlying policy in New Jersey that liability for defective products attaches to the manufacturing enterprise.

following formulation, which has since come to be known as the "product line" approach to successor corporation liability for injuries caused by defective products:

> We . . . conclude that a party which acquires a manufacturing business and continues the output of its line of products under the circumstances here presented assumes strict tort liability for defects in units of the same product line previously manufactured and distributed by the entity from which the business was acquired.

The *Ray* court offered a three-fold justification for its imposition of potential liability upon a successor corporation that acquires the assets and continues the manufacturing operation of the predecessor:

> (1) The virtual destruction of the plaintiff's remedies against the original manufacturer caused by the successor's acquisition of the business, (2) the successor's ability to assume the original manufacturer's risk-spreading role, and (3) the fairness of requiring the successor to assume a responsibility for defective products that was a burden necessarily attached to the original manufacturer's good will being enjoyed by the successor in the continued operation of the business.

In our view these policy considerations likewise justify the imposition of potential strict tort liability on Amsted under the circumstances here presented. First, the plaintiff's potential remedy against Johnson, the original manufacturer of the allegedly defective press, was destroyed by the purchase of the Johnson assets, trade name and good will, and Johnson's resulting dissolution. It is true that there was an intermediate transaction involved, namely, the acquisition of the Johnson assets by Bontrager in 1956. But the acquisition of these assets by Amsted in 1962 directly brought about the ultimate dissolution of Bontrager's corporate existence. Accordingly, the Bontrager acquisition destroyed whatever remedy plaintiff might have had against Johnson, and the Amsted acquisition destroyed the plaintiff's potential cause of action against Bontrager. What is most important, however, is that there was continuity in the manufacturing of the Johnson product line throughout the history of these asset acquisitions.

Second, the imposition of successor corporation liability upon Amsted is consistent with the public policy of spreading the risk to society at large for the cost of injuries from defective products. The progressive character of New Jersey decisional law in the area of strict products liability is well known, and its development need not be retraced here. See Suter v. San Angelo Foundry and Machine Co., 406 A.2d 140 (N.J.1979). . . .

In essence, Amsted contends that because it had no physical control over the allegedly defective Johnson press when it was placed into the stream of commerce, it is not the maker of the product who put it in the channels of trade. But to argue that a successor corporation can not be liable for injuries arising out of defects in certain products because it is not the same corporate entity that actually manufactured or distributed those products is to beg the underlying question involved in downstream corporate liability cases in the products liability context. No one asserts that Amsted was responsible for actually placing the allegedly defective press into the commercial stream. This was done by Johnson, the original manufacturer. But the injured plaintiff obviously cannot look to Johnson for a recovery of the damages occasioned by the accident involving the defective press. Rather, he looks to a viable successor corporation that continued to manufacture and sell the line of products that injured him. Strict liability for injuries caused by defective products placed into the stream of commerce is "an enterprise liability" one that continues so long as the defective product is present on the market. The successor corporation that continues the manufacturing enterprise of its predecessor may not have had the means available for avoiding the risk of placing a defective product into the stream of commerce initially, but it does have the means available for avoiding the risk of harm caused by its predecessor's defective products still present on the market.

As stated by Justice Schreiber for the Court in *Suter, supra*:

> Strict liability in a sense is but an attempt to minimize the cost of accidents and to consider who should bear those costs. See the discussion in Calabresi & Hirschoff, *Toward a Test for Strict Liability in Torts*, 81 Yale L.J. 1055 (1972), in which the authors suggest that the strict liability issue is to decide which party is the "cheapest cost avoider" or who is in the best position to make the cost-benefit analysis between accident costs and accident avoidance costs and to act on that decision once it is made. *Id.* at 1060. Using this approach, it is obvious that the manufacturer rather than the factory employee is "in the better position both to judge whether avoidance costs would exceed foreseeable accident costs and to act on that judgment." *Id.*

Similarly, because the manufacturer transfers to its successor corporation "the resources that had previously been available to [the manufacturer] for meeting its responsibilities to persons injured by defects in [products] it had produced," Ray v. Alad, *supra*, the successor rather than the user of the product is in the better position to bear accident-avoidance costs. By the terms of the 1962 purchase agreement with Bontrager, Amsted acquired the Johnson trade name, physical plant, manufacturing equipment, inventory, records of manufacturing designs, patents and customer lists. Amsted also sought the continued employment of the factory personnel that had manufactured the Johnson presses for Bontrager. "With these facilities and sources of information, [Amsted] had virtually the same capacity as [Johnson] to estimate the risks of claims for injuries from defects in previously manufactured [presses] for purposes of obtaining [liability] insurance coverage or planning self-insurance."

Amsted was in the same position as its predecessors to avoid the costs and to spread the risk of accident injuries to users of defective Johnson power presses.

Third, the imposition upon Amsted of responsibility to answer claims of liability for injuries allegedly caused by defective Johnson presses is justified as a burden necessarily attached to its enjoyment of Johnson's trade name, good will and the continuation of an established manufacturing enterprise. See Ray v. Alad, *supra*. Through acquisition of the Johnson trade name, plant, employees, manufacturing equipment, designs and customer lists, and by holding itself out to potential customers as the manufacturer of the same line of Johnson power presses, Amsted benefited substantially from the legitimate exploitation of the accumulated good will earned by the Johnson product line. Public policy requires that having received the substantial benefits of the continuing manufacturing enterprise, the successor corporation should also be made to bear the burden of the operating costs that other established business operations must ordinarily bear. By acquiring all of the Johnson assets and continuing the established business of manufacturing and selling Johnson presses, Amsted "became 'an integral part of the overall producing and marketing enterprise that should bear the cost of injuries resulting from defective products.' "

VI

Defendant contends that the imposition of strict products liability on corporations that purchase manufacturing assets for cash will have a chilling -- even a crippling -- effect on the ability of the small manufacturer to transfer ownership of its business assets for a fair purchase price rather than be forced into liquidation proceedings. Business planners for prospective purchasing corporations will be hesitant to acquire "a potential can of worms that will open with untold contingent products liability claims." In order to divest itself of its business assets, the small manufacturing corporation will be forced to sacrifice such a substantial deduction from a fair purchase price that it would lose the ability to net a sum consistent with the true worth of the business assets.

These contentions raise legitimate concerns. We do not look upon them as "cassandrian arguments," see *Turner, supra*.

However, in light of the social policy underlying the law of products liability, the true worth of a predecessor corporation must reflect the potential liability that the shareholders have escaped through the sale of their corporation. Thus, a reduction of the sale price by an amount calculated to compensate the successor corporation for the potential liability it has assumed is a more, not less, accurate measure of the true worth of the business.

Furthermore, a corporation planning the acquisition of another corporation's manufacturing assets has certain protective devices available to insulate it from the full costs of accidents arising out of defects in its predecessor's products. In addition to making adjustments to the purchase price, thereby spreading the potential costs of liability between predecessor and successor corporations, it can obtain products liability insurance for contingent liability claims, and it can enter into full or partial indemnification or escrow agreements with the selling corporation. True, the parties may experience difficulties in calculating a purchase price that fairly reflects the measure of risk of potential liabilities for the predecessor's defective products present in the market at the time of the asset acquisition. Likewise do we acknowledge that small manufacturing corporations may not find readily available adequate and affordable insurance coverage for liability arising out of injuries caused by the predecessor's defective products. However, these concerns, genuine as they may be, cannot be permitted to overshadow the basic social policy, now so well-entrenched in our jurisprudence, that favors imposition of the costs of injuries from defective products on the manufacturing enterprise and consuming public rather than on the innocent injured party. In time, the risk-spreading and cost avoidance measures adverted to above should become a normal part of business planning in connection with the corporation acquisition of the assets of a manufacturing enterprise.

VII

Defendant further asserts that it is unfair to impose on it liability for defects in a predecessor's product manufactured and placed into the stream of commerce twenty eight years and two corporate transactions before the accidental injury occurred. This argument, however, goes essentially to a question of repose, namely, whether there should be a limitation on the time period during which a party may bring suit for injury arising out of a defective product. As the Appellate Division correctly concluded, only the legislature is authorized to establish a limitation on the period during which suit may be commenced against a manufacturer, its successor, or seller of allegedly defective products. . . . With the expanded potential liability of successor corporations for injuries arising out of defects in their predecessors' products, legislative response may be in order with respect to product liability claims. . . .

IX

Under today's determination the *McKee* approach is no longer the standard to be applied in determining the liability of a successor corporation for injuries caused by a defective product manufactured and placed in the stream of commerce by a predecessor. Rather, we hold that where one corporation acquires all or substantially all the manufacturing assets of another corporation, even if exclusively for cash, and undertakes essentially the same manufacturing operation as the selling corporation, the purchasing corporation is strictly liable for injuries caused by defects in units of the same product line, even if previously manufactured and distributed by the selling corporation or its predecessor. The social policies underlying strict products liability in New Jersey are best served by extending strict liability to a successor corporation that acquires the business assets and continues to manufacture essentially the same line of products as its predecessor, particularly where the successor corporation benefits from trading its product line on the name of the predecessor and takes advantage from its accumulated good will, business reputation and established customers. . . . Affirmed.

The product line approach to successor liability generally has met a favorable response from the commentators and from some states,[12] but a number of states have refused to follow the lead of New Jersey and California.[13]   Although it is easy enough to cheer the rejection of the traditional successor liability doctrine because it gave no weight to the public policy underlying products liability law, the attractiveness of the product line approach depends on the persuasiveness of the justifications for it.   The *Ramirez* court offers four justifications, each of which warrants attention.

The court first notes that in the absence of successor liability, the plaintiff will have no one to sue because the actual manufacturer of the defective press dissolved following the acquisition. The point is accurate, but why does it dictate *successor* liability in contrast to no liability or liability on the part of the entire industry?[14]

The court then stresses the successor's ability to assume the original manufacturer's risk-spreading role: To help spread "the risk to society at large for the cost of injuries from defective products." Again, however, does the justification meet its goal? Would not imposing liability on almost any entity or group of entities, including the entire industry or even the federal

---

[12] See, e.g., Charles Cantu & David Goldberg, *Products Liability: An Argument for Product Line Liability in Texas*, 19 St. Mary's L.J. 621 (1988); J. Phillips (1983), *supra* note 6; Note, *Intermediate and Successor Corporations Strictly Liable Under Product Line Standard*, 12 Seton Hall L.Rev. 327 (1982); Note, *Successor Liability for Defective Products: A Tort Exception to a Corporate Rule*, 10 Hofstra L.Rev. 831 (1982); Note, *Postdissolution Product Claims and the Emerging Rule of Successor Liability*, 64 Va.L.Rev. 861 (1978).

[13] See, e.g., Niccum v. Hydra Tool Corp., 438 N.W.2d 96 (Minn.1989); Stratton v. Garvey Int'l, Inc., 676 P.2d 1290 (Kan.App.1984); Tucker v. Paxson Machine Co., 645 F.2d 620 (8th Cir.1981) (applying Missouri law); Rhynes v. Branick Mfg. Corp., 629 F.2d 409 (5th Cir.1980) (applying Texas law); Leannais v. Cincinnati, Inc., *supra* (applying Wisconsin law); Travis v. Harris Corp., *supra* (applying Ohio and Indiana law); Bernard v. Kee Mfg. Co., 394 So.2d 552 (Fla.App.1981); Domaine v. Fulton Iron Works, 395 N.E.2d 19 (Ill.App.1979); cf. Andrews v. John E. Smith's Sons, Co., 369 So.2d 781 (Ala.1979) (rejecting product line theory, but accepting a modified de facto merger analysis). William Fletcher, *Cyclopedia of the Law of Private Corporations*, ¶ 7123.07 (rev.perm.ed. & 1993 Supp.) provides a listing of the states that have accepted and rejected the product line approach.

[14] Industry-wide liability might be argued by analogy to Sindell v. Abbott Laboratories, 26 Cal.3d 588, 607 P.2d 924, *cert. denied*, 449 U.S. 912 (1980), in which the court allowed victims of DES to sue all DES manufacturers when the victims could not prove which manufacturer was associated with a victim's injury. There, industry wide liability was created to protect victims against the absence of a defendant; in the successor liability setting, industry liability would serve the same purpose.

government, serve to spread the risk equally as well as imposing liability on the successor?

The court's next justification does at least focus on a factor peculiar to the successor. The court notes that one justification for products liability is to place the cost of accidents on the "cheapest cost avoider" so that the optimum investment in safety is undertaken. Because the acquiring company presumably will continue to manufacture the product that caused the injury, placing the costs on it will guide it in evaluating the safety of the product's design. Is it necessary, however, to impose successor liability to accomplish this? Suppose instead of having liability imposed on it, the successor merely was told that a court had determined that the current design of the product was defective. Would not the fact that the successor would be liable for all injuries due to the products that *it* manufactured be sufficient for it to determine the optimal investment in safety? Indeed, might not imposing the costs of prior defects on the successor cause it to invest too much in safety? A second problem with this justification is that it imposes a limit on successor liability doctrine that the court does not acknowledge and may not even recognize. If the justification for successor liability is to influence the successor's decision about how it manufactures the product in question, then should successor liability be imposed where the successor did not continue to manufacture the product?[15] Note that the other justifications considered thus far are not affected by whether the successor continues to manufacture the product.[16]

The final justification offered by the court also applies uniquely to the successor. The court stressed that because the successor "benefited substantially from the legitimate exploitation of the accumulated goodwill" of the original manufacturer, it is only fair that it bear the costs associated with that goodwill. The goodwill to which the court referred is presumably the manufacturer's reputation for a quality product; the idea is that one should not be able to rely on that reputation without having to bear the cost when its reputation proves incorrect.[17] The difficulty with this analysis is that the successor already bears this cost. The successor paid for the manufacturer's goodwill in the acquisition. The effect of revelation of the defective product is to reduce the value of the goodwill; certainly the successor would not have paid as much for the manufacturer's reputation had it known it was not

---

[15] See Gee v. Tennaco, Inc., 615 F.2d 857 (9th Cir.1980) (applying California law).

[16] If the product line that caused the injury is purchased, does it make any difference if the selling company remains in business manufacturing other products? See Kline v. Johns-Manville, 745 F.2d 1217 (9th Cir.1984) (applying California law). What if the defendant is a distributor rather than the manufacturer of the defective product? See Kaminski v. Western MacArthur Co., 220 Cal.Rptr. 895 (1985) (extend Ray v. Alad to distributors).

[17] This justification also contains its own limitation. What if the successor company made substantial efforts to disclose that it, and not the predecessor, now manufactures the product line acquired? See Kline v. Johns-Manville, *supra* note 16.

justified.[18]   The successor thus bears the cost of the defective product through the reduction in the value of the asset it purchased. What is added by imposing the additional cost of liability to the victim?

There is a common thread to the difficulties encountered with all of the court's justifications for successor liability. Grounded as they are in the public policy of products liability, each of them makes sense as applied to the original manufacturer. None, however, explains why the public policy underlying products liability dictates *successor* liability. And if products liability policy does not solve the problem, then perhaps we were too facile in applauding the courts turn away from corporate law analysis -- i.e., analysis focusing on the character of the particular transaction. This approach to making sense out of the doctrine of successor liability is considered in the next section.

C.   An Internalization Approach to Successor Liability

In Section A of this Chapter we saw that the issue really posed by the doctrine of successor liability was whether the acquiring company and the target company would be allowed to structure the acquisition transaction to serve their *joint* goal of cutting off -- externalizing in the vocabulary of products liability -- contingent future products liability claims. The goal of products liability policy is to insure that the manufacturer takes into account -- internalizes -- the cost of injuries caused by the product in making decisions about product safety. From this perspective, the function of successor liability is straightforward. Imposing liability on any future purchaser of the manufacturer's business means that the manufacturer must take the cost of future products liability claims into account currently because it will always bear them. If it continues to operate the business, it will bear the costs directly through products liability litigation; if it sells the business, it will bear the costs indirectly through a reduction in the price a purchaser will be willing to pay for the business. Thus, the point of successor liability is not to cause the *successor* to bear the costs of the predecessor's defective products, but as a tool to insure that the *predecessor* bears the cost.[19] In the

---

[18] See D. Phillips (1982), *supra* note 5, at 255-56; Note, *Imposing Strict Liability Upon a Successor Corporation for the Defective Products of its Corporate Predecessor: Proposed Alternatives to the Product Line Theory of Liability*, 23 Bos.Col.L.Rev. 1397, 1421-22 (1982).

[19] Alan Schwartz, *Products Liability, Corporate Structure and Bankruptcy: Toxic Substances and the Remote Risk Relationship*, 14 J.Legal Stud. 689 (1985); Roe (1984), *supra* note 5. D. Phillips (1982), *supra* note 5, reaches the same conclusion by examining comparable commercial law doctrines. In particular, he notes that the § 6-106 of the Uniform Commercial Code, dealing with bulk sales, imposes a duty on the purchaser in a bulk sale "to assure that such consideration [paid for the business] is applied so far as necessary to pay those debts of the transferor." *Id.* at 265-66. Both applications build on the Coase Theorem's insight that, as long as the parties are in a bargaining relationship, it makes no difference on which party liability is initially imposed; the parties will reallocate the burden by contract in the most

absence of internalization, there is an incentive to operate the company in a manner that maximizes current profits at the expense of future injuries because the company can be sold free of claims so long as the sale takes place in time.[20] Moreover, the absence of internalization may lead not only to unreasonably dangerous operations, but inefficient operations as well. A rule of predecessor liability but no successor liability means that externalization can be accomplished only by selling the company. Thus, an incentive is created to sell the company even if management of the acquiring company is less efficient.[21]

This analysis suggests a rule of absolute successor liability. Does such an internalization approach to products liability provide sufficient guidance concerning the types of transactions which would be subject to an absolute successor liability rule? For example, in light of the court's reliance in *Ramirez* on the successor's ability to make the product line safer, a powerful argument can be made that the product line approach would not impose liability on a successor company if it did not continue to produce the particular product line. How would such a case come out under an internalization approach?[22] Are there other differences in result between an internalization approach and the various judicial approaches to the problem?

D.   Limits on an Internalization Approach to Successor Liability

An internalization approach to successor liabilities is subject to a number of objections. One raises the issue of its fairness; the remainder concern its feasibility.

1.   The Fairness of an Internalization Approach

An acquiring company on whom successor liability is imposed based on an internalization approach might well object on the simple basis of fairness. It did not manufacture the product which caused the injury -- as the court stated in *Ramirez*: "No one asserts that Amsted was responsible for actually placing the allegedly defective press into the commercial stream." It is correct that the acquiring company has the means to make the product safer in the future. But that effort to link liability if not to the past conduct of the successor, at least to the possibility of its future action, is a sham. An internalization approach contemplates absolute successor liability; even if the defect that caused the injury has already been corrected, so that no future

---

efficient way. For an accessible introduction to Coasean analysis, see A. Mitchell Polinsky, *An Introduction to Law and Economics* 11-14 (1983).

[20] See Schwartz (1985), *supra* note 19.

[21] Roe (1984), *supra* note 5, at 1565.

[22] See D. Phillips (1982), *supra* note 5, at 270-71.

action by the successor was necessary, successor liability would still be imposed. Finally, and perhaps most troubling from the perspective of an "innocent" successor, a morally culpable defendant does exist: The individuals who, as shareholders of the target company, presumably reaped the benefits of having placed the unsafe product into commerce. Even conceding the overall validity of an internalization approach, the successor would object that the desired internalization could be effected by imposing liability on the morally culpable party rather than on a stranger. Imposing personal liability on the former shareholders of a dissolved company to the extent of dissolution distributions also forces the target company to internalize the costs of expected products liability claims. Because the goal of internalization can be satisfied by imposing liability on either the successor or the former shareholders, the argument concludes, simple fairness dictates that it be placed on the parties who actually caused, or benefitted from, the harm.

The short response to this concern is that imposing liability on the former shareholders of a dissolved company is not feasible. Precisely because products liability claims may arise long after the dissolution of the target company, it would be difficult and expensive to discover the identity of the former shareholders, trace the proceeds if, as can be expected, the passage of time has allowed the proceeds to move to new holders by gift, inheritance and the like, and to bring multiple actions against multiple defendants in order to recover an amount sufficient to cover plaintiff's damages. To the extent that these transaction costs reduce the likelihood that actual, as opposed to theoretical, liability will be imposed on the former shareholders, the extent of internalization achieved is reduced.

Does the principle of matching culpability and liability warrant this reduction in internalization, especially when imposition of successor liability on the acquiring company does not determine the incidence of that liability? The point of successor liability is not to impose liability on the successor, but to use the successor as a tool to impose liability -- through bargaining over the acquisition price -- on the target company. The acquiring company may still object that there is something morally offensive about using it as a tool to get at the culpable party, but that type of liability strategy is not unusual. For example, the Securities Act of 1933 imposes near identical liability for misrepresentations in a registration statement on the issuer and on the underwriter, despite the fact that the underwriter does not retain the proceeds of the offering. Liability is imposed on the underwriter to give it an incentive to police the issuer -- in essence, to use the underwriter as an enforcement tool.[23]

---

[23] Reinier Kraakman, *Corporate Liability Strategies and the Costs of Legal Controls*, 93 Yale L.J. 857 (1984), provides a thoughtful analysis of this type of liability strategy.

2.   Strategic Responses to an Internalization Approach

A second, and more telling, criticism of successor liability as a means to force internalization of expected products liability costs is that it will not work; that is, it will not be sufficient to achieve the desired internalization. It has been repeatedly stressed in prior Chapters that planners and regulators are engaged in a multi-round strategic game. If planners can reformulate their transactions to avoid new regulation, then nothing has been gained. Thus, the case for successor liability is compromised if planners can devise techniques other than selling the company by which to externalize the future costs of products liability. Two such techniques come to mind: A piecemeal sale of assets followed by dissolution; and bankruptcy.

At least on the surface, a piecemeal sale of assets followed by dissolution will serve to externalize future products liability claims. First, as has been stressed, distributions in dissolution generally are not subject to recapture from former shareholders if previously unknown liabilities arise. Second, successor liability is unworkable in a true piecemeal sale of assets because there simply is no successor. To be sure, if the company is sold division by division or product line by product line, successor liability could be applied on that basis. But if the sale is truly piecemeal, so that no aspect of the business is sold as a going concern, successor liability would be quite difficult to apply.

What practical limitations constrain the use of piecemeal sales of assets to avoid forced internalization through successor liability? It is important to keep in mind that a planner does not have an entirely free hand in manipulating transaction form to avoid regulatory constraints; the alteration in transaction form may have real non-regulatory costs. A piecemeal sale of assets has the potential of imposing a very substantial non-regulatory cost: the loss of the company's goodwill, the difference between the company's going concern value and its liquidation value. Thus, avoiding internalization by means of a piecemeal sale of assets will be desirable only when the present value of the future products liability claims, eliminated by the sale, exceed the value of the company's goodwill, also eliminated by the sale.

The necessary relation between future products liability claims and goodwill may exist where, in anticipation of the availability of a piecemeal sale, the owners of the company treat their ownership as an option and systematically underinvest in product safety. If they are lucky -- they end up on the "safe" side of the probability distribution of future injury caused by their product -- they can sell the business as a going concern and reap the benefits of their goodwill even in the face of successor liability. If they are unlucky and end up with a product that looks like it will cause substantial injury, they can sell the assets piecemeal. In option terms, they get the upside, the potential victims bear the downside. This situation, however, is only one manifestation of the general problem created by limited liability for shareholders. So long as shareholders' responsibility for injuries inflicted by the company's products cannot exceed their investment in the company, there is an incentive to underinvest in safety and insurance. To that extent, products liability risks are externalized.[24] Successor liability thus does not solve the problem of asset insufficiency that is associated with limited liability generally,[25] but it does narrow the extent to which externalization is possible. Put differently, the planner's freedom of action is substantially constrained.[26]

The second means of avoiding successor liability -- bankruptcy -- is really a variation on the piecemeal sale theme. A piecemeal sale of assets followed by dissolution functions as an informal bankruptcy liquidation: A company resorts to it only if it is worth more in pieces than as a going concern, *or* if the process cuts off the claims of enough creditors -- future products liability claimants -- that the loss of goodwill is outweighed. It follows that a formal bankruptcy liquidation may also be a means of avoiding successor liability. If future products liability plaintiffs are not treated as creditors for purposes of bankruptcy -- in technical terms, if they are not holders of *claims* under § 726 of the Bankruptcy Act -- then they are excluded from any distribution to creditors.[27] Thus a formal as well as an

---

[24] Schwartz (1985), *supra* note 19; Christopher Stone, *The Place of Enterprise Liability in the Control of Corporate Conduct*, 90 Yale L.J. 1 (1980).

[25] Schwartz (1985), *supra* note 19; Kraakman (1984), *supra* note 23, at 868-76.

[26] In situations where asset insufficiency allows externalization of risks, the use of liability as an indirect technique of controlling conduct gives way to direct regulation with specified standards and penalties and imprisonment for violations. See Steven Shavell, *Liability for Harm Versus Regulation of Safety*, 13 J.Legal Stud. 357 (1984). While this approach has its own limitations, it does avoid the critical problem posed by the alternative of eliminating limited liability altogether: The need to balance the benefits from eliminating externalization against the cost of the reduction in capital market efficiency that would result from eliminating limited liability. See Paul Halpern, Michael Trebilcock & Stuart Turnbull, *An Economic Analysis of Limited Liability in Corporation Law*, 30 U.Toronto L.J. 117 (1980); Frank Easterbrook & Daniel Fischel, *Limited Liability and the Corporation*, 52 U.Chi.L.Rev. 89 (1985). Recent analyses of the capital market impact of limited liability generally have discounted the relationship between limited liability and capital market efficiency, making a proportionate liability regime a conceivable alternative. See Henry Hansmann & Reinier Kraakman, *Toward Unlimited Shareholder Liability for Corporate Torts*, 100 Yale L.J. 1879 (1991); David Leebron, *Limited Liability, Tort Victims and Creditors*, 91 Colum.L.Rev. 1565 (1991). In response, Joseph Grundfest has argued that responses by the capital market to a regime where shareholders had proportionate liability for the corporation's debts would dissipate the incentive effect through arbitrage strategies. Joseph Grundfest, *The Limited Future of Unlimited Liability: A Capital Markets Perspective*, 102 Yale L.J. 387 (1992).

[27] Thomas Jackson, *The Logic and Limits of Bankruptcy Law: The Implications of Collective Action and Discharge Policy* ch. 4 (1986). Professor Jackson points out that, in addition to facilitating some amount of externalization, a rule barring future products liability plaintiffs from participating as creditors in the bankruptcy proceeding has the perverse effect of leading to a liquidation even though the company is worth more as a going concern. If the plaintiffs do not hold "claims", then whatever we call what they do have is not discharged in bankruptcy; any reorganized company would remain subject to them. Thus, existing creditors may well prefer to liquidate, thereby getting 100 % of a smaller pie, rather than share a larger pie, the reorganized company, with an additional group of claimants. If the future products liability plaintiffs were treated as having claims, so that they could not be excluded from

informal bankruptcy liquidation has the potential to allow some externalization.

What if substantially all of the assets of the bankrupt company were sold in the bankruptcy proceeding as a going concern rather than piecemeal? Would successor liability extend to a purchaser from the trustee in bankruptcy? Should the answer depend on whether future products liability victims are treated as having "claims"?[28]

3. Uncertainty and the Failure of Internalization

An additional objection to an internalization approach goes to its very heart. Suppose that the defect that caused the injuries in question was not foreseeable at the time the product was designed or produced. A rule that imposes successor liability for injuries caused by this type of defect will not cause the predecessor to take the expected costs of future liability into account in making design or production decisions; by definition, costs that cannot be anticipated cannot be internalized.[29] What is the effect of imposing successor liability with respect to unforeseeable product defects? One response to the objection that successor liability was unfair to the successor was that the successor did not bear the incidence of the liability; the successor is merely a convenient place to put initial liability because the successor will shift the liability to the target company through bargaining. Can this liability shifting work if neither the successor nor the predecessor can anticipate, even probabilistically, the potential for future liability? From the perspective of the acquiring company, where successor liability for unforeseeable defects exists, an acquisition takes on something of the character of a game of Russian roulette, but played without any knowledge of the number of chambers in the cylinder, nor the number of bullets that

---

participation in the bankrupt's assets, existing creditors would make the socially correct choice: To maintain the company as a going concern through reorganization because that maximizes the size of the pie. These issues are at the heart of the controversy over the role of asbestos victims in the Johns-Manville bankruptcy. See In re UNR Industries, Inc. 725 F.2d 1111 (7th Cir.1984); In re Johns-Manville Corp., 36 B.R. 743 (S.D.N.Y.1984). See generally Mark Roe, *Corporate Strategic Reaction to Mass Tort*, 72 Va.L.Rev. 1 (1986); Mark Roe, *Bankruptcy and Tort*, 84 Colum.L.Rev. 846 (1984); Note, *The Manville Bankruptcy: Treating Mass Tort Claims in Chapter 11 Proceedings*, 96 Harv.L.Rev. 1121 (1983).

[28] See Thomas Jackson, *Translating Assets and Liabilities to the Bankruptcy Forum*, 14 J.Legal Stud. 73, 94-97 (1985). California, a product line state, has not applied the doctrine to bankruptcy sales. See Stewart v. Telex Communications, Inc., 1 Cal.Rptr.2d 669 (Cal.App.1991); Nelson v. Tiffany Industries, Inc., 778 F.2d 533 (9th Cir.1985). New Jersey, also a product line state, has applied the doctrine to bankruptcy sales. See Wilkerson v. C.O. Porter, 237 N.J.Super. 282 (L.Div.1989); Goncalves v. Wire Technology, 253 N.J.Super. 327 (L.Div.1991); Pacius v. Thermtroll Corp., 259 N.J.Super. 41 (L.Div.1992). See generally David Kott & Walter Effross, *Forgive Us Our Predecessions: Bankruptcy Sales and the Product Line Exception*, 4 Prod.Liab.L.J. 123 (1993).

[29] Schwartz (1985), *supra* note 19.

have been inserted. Under these circumstances, a rule of absolute successor liability would prevent anything but a piecemeal transfer of the predecessor's assets.[30]

Is the problem in this situation with an internalization approach to successor liability, or with the basic products liability rule that imposes liability on the predecessor in the first place?[31] If the problem lies with the initial imposition of products liability, and if that result is treated as given, as it might be in judicial consideration of a case that raised only the successor liability issue, how should the internalization approach be applied? One choice would be to recognize that internalization is impossible with respect to unforeseeable risks, and, as a result, that the justification for successor liability was not present. The internalization approach thus would define its own limits: Successor liability would not be imposed when internalization would be impossible. An alternative would be to opt for consistency -- to impose successor liability whenever the predecessor would have been liable -- even though an internalization approach would not require it. Would this result benefit future products liability claimants on an *ex ante* basis? If the anticipation of successor liability for unforeseeable claims prevents the company from being sold at all, so that no successor will exist, claimants are left with recourse only to the original company, subject to a piecemeal sale of assets and bankruptcy.[32] Which way are products liability claimants better off?

How easily could a court determine whether or not a particular risk was or should have been foreseeable? Could a court determine with any accuracy whether a reasonable person would have done more research, and thereby would have discovered the product defect that later caused injury? If this type of determination is subject to error, then what will be the impact on behavior? Will it result in too much research or not enough?

If it is difficult to determine long after the fact whether a particular risk was foreseeable at the time the product was designed, would a statute of limitations -- measured from the date the product was purchased rather than the date of injury -- serve as a more certain proxy for foreseeability? The idea would be that a successor would always know at least the period of exposure, if not its size. Are there some risks -- for example, with respect to toxic substances -- where the injury is foreseeable but nonetheless would not occur for a significant period of time?

---

[30] See Roe (1984), *supra* note 5, at 1573-74.

[31] See Schwartz (1985), *supra* note 19.

[32] Professor Roe reports that "GAF, a co-defendant in the massive asbestos litigation, recently attempted to sell a chemical division to Allied Corporation. The two firms were reported to have reached preliminary agreement about the transfer, but the deal collapsed with Allied claiming it could not be assured it would not be subject to GAF's potentially large asbestos liability." Roe (1984), *supra* note 5, at 1561.

E.   Planning for Successor Liability for Future Products Claims

What are the planning implications of the expansion of successor liability for future products liability claims?[33] One clear message is that an acquiring company must make a substantial investment in investigating the potential for future liability with respect to products previously manufactured by the target. To be sure, this has always been necessary because, in estimating the target company's future cash flows, the acquiring company has to estimate the likelihood of future liability with respect to *post*-acquisition production, an estimate that would depend heavily on past experience. Now, however, the estimate not only would help set the price, it would also help set the bounds of any contractual protection the acquiring company might seek from the target company concerning the maximum amount of future liability.

Up to this point, we have not considered the character of the actual negotiations between the acquiring company and the target company that would cause the target to internalize products liability costs. Wouldn't the target have an incentive to understate the potential for future liability? And to the extent that the target company succeeds in fooling the acquiring company, the incidence of successor liability then remains on the successor. We consider in Chapter 27 the contractual techniques that an acquiror can use to protect against the target's understatement of future risk.

Assuming that an internalization approach to successor liability limits the planner's ability to avoid future product liability entirely, and further assuming that the target company has provided as much contractual protection as possible, can anything be done to protect against disaster? Suppose that both the acquiring company and the target company greatly underestimate the potential of future liability, perhaps because the particular jurisdiction imposes both primary and successor liability for products liability even if the risk was unforeseeable. Here the need for protection is critical; as suggested above, in the absence of protection, the acquisition becomes a game of Russian roulette. In the past, disaster insurance was provided either by making a triangular acquisition, so that the target company remained a wholly owned subsidiary of the acquiring company, or, particularly in a close corporation, achieving the same result by simply buying all of the target company's outstanding stock.[34] The advantage sought was limited liability. Although the assets of the target company would remain subject to future products liability claims, the parent's assets would be shielded because, as a shareholder, the parent's liability would be limited.[35]

---

[33] For reviews, see John Arness, Anthony Sutin & Teresa Plotkin, *Preventing Successor Liability for Defective Products: Safeguards for Acquiring Corporations*, 67 Wash.U.L.Q. 535 (1989).

[34] In a public company, an exchange offer would be unlikely to garner 100% of the target's outstanding shares, thereby requiring recourse to a triangular technique in any case.

[35] See, e.g., Heitland (1979), *supra* note 6.

As yet, the momentum of products liability law has not breached the parent-subsidiary boundary, at least when the subsidiary has not been systematically stripped of its assets. Thus, the rule governing parent liability for the torts of its subsidiary has remained largely a creature of corporate law, technical and restrictive much as was the original successor liability doctrine.[36] Does an internalization approach require treating the parent company as the successor in this setting? Have future products liability plaintiffs been made worse off by the acquisition? Prior to the transaction, the doctrine of limited liability imposed on the plaintiff the risk that the target company's assets would be insufficient to pay the plaintiff's claim at the time of judgment; after the transaction, the plaintiff is subject to the identical risk. In both cases, the claim is protected by the same amount of assets. An argument that an internalization approach should make it easier to pierce the corporate veil following an acquisition would require demonstrating that the acquisition -- the target's shift from an independent company to a subsidiary -- increases the risk of asset insufficiency.

Would it be enough to show that the parent generally has an incentive to keep the subsidiary undercapitalized and to try to increase the risks of all creditors? Do not these incentives also exist for shareholders of an independent company? Could it be shown that externalization is easier to accomplish in a parent-subsidiary relationship? Suppose the comparison was between the pre-acquisition behavior of a publicly held company and its post-acquisition behavior as a wholly owned subsidiary. Would the existence of separation with respect to the public company, so that all shareholders desired to maximize the value of the company,[37] distinguish that situation from the sole shareholder setting of the parent-subsidiary, where what would be maximized would be the value of the parent's entire portfolio, not the value of the subsidiary alone?[38]

Insurance is a final method of dealing with the risk of successor products liability. "Claims made" insurance, a policy that covers any claims

---

[36] See, e.g., C.M. Corp. v. Oberer Development Corp., 631 F.2d 536 (7th Cir.1980); Note, *Piercing the Corporate Veil: The Alter Ego Doctrine Under Federal Common Law*, 95 Harv.L.Rev. 853 (1982).

[37] See Chapter 4, *supra*.

[38] For example, below market rate loans from parent to subsidiary, overattribution of corporate overhead to the subsidiary, diversion of profitable opportunities to the parent, and transfer pricing favorable to the parent are available to divert assets in the subsidiary setting in a way not possible for a publicly held company (although they would be available to a privately held company). Additionally, the parent-subsidiary relationship may eliminate some of the collateral costs of increasing the risk to creditors. Dividends to individuals, likely a significant portion of the publicly held company's shareholders, are taxed at ordinary income rates. Dividends to a corporation that owns 20% or more of the voting power and value of the payor corporation are subject to an 80% dividend deduction under IRC § 243, which reduces the effective rate to 7%. For dividends paid by a wholly-owned subsidiary to a member of its affiliated group, there is no tax at all. Thus, the cost of moving assets out of the company, and out of the grasp of creditors, is reduced.

made while the policy is in force, regardless of when the product was manufactured, and "tail" coverage, covering claims with respect to products no longer manufactured, are helpful.[39] The problem, however, is that such insurance may not be available at all, or only at an unacceptable price. An important part of what is typically referred to as the products liability crisis is that such insurance is unavailable to large numbers of manufacturers.[40]

F.   Other Areas of Successor Liability

Future products liability claims are not the only target company obligations that pose the risk of successor liability. Obligations relating to the target company's collective bargaining agreements, its pension plans and environmental compliance obligations also raise the problem in important ways. Where, for example, an acquisition is motivated by synergy, the imposition on the acquiring company of a duty to bargain with the target company's union may interfere with the changes in production techniques, plant location or employment levels necessary to achieve the contemplated synergy. The importance of successor liability for target company pension fund obligations is even more straightforward: Liability for underfunding can be as high as 30% of the combined net worth of the acquiring company and its affiliates. Finally, the cost of environmental cleanup may exceed the combined net worth of all the companies involved.

1.   Successor Liability Under Collective Bargaining Agreements

The acquisition of a target company subject to a collective bargaining agreement raises the question of whether, and to what extent, the acquiring company succeeds to the target's collective bargaining obligations.[41] As with future products liability claims, issues of public policy -- in this case the policy of discouraging labor strife embodied in the National Labor Relations

---

[39] For a general discussion of products liability insurance coverage, see Michael Kadens, *Practitioner's Guide to Treatment of Seller's Products Liabilities in Asset Acquisitions*, 10 U.Tol.L.Rev. 1, 32-44 (1978).

[40] See United States Dept. of Commerce Interagency Task Force on Product Liability, Final Report VI 2-13 (1977).

[41] The area has generated a substantial literature. See, e.g., Edward Rock & Michael Wachter, *Labor Law Successorship: A Corporate Law Approach*, 92 Mich.L.Rev. 203 (1993); Keith Hylton & Maria Hylton, *Rent Appropriation and the Labor Law Doctrine of Successorship*, 70 B.U.L.Rev. 821 (1990); William DuRoss, *Increasing the Labor-Related Costs of Business Transfers and Acquisition -- The Spectre of Per Se Liability for New Owners*, 67 Wash.U.L.Q. 375 (1989); Johnathan Silver, *Reflections on the Obligations of a Successor Employer*, 2 Cardozo L.Rev. 545 (1981); Charles Morris & William Gaus, *Successorship and the Collective Bargaining Agreement: Accommodating Wiley and Burns*, 59 Va.L.Rev. 1359 (1973).

Act -- have led to the development of a doctrine of successor liability peculiar to the context. Unlike in the products liability context, however, the issue is not limited to the single matter of monetary responsibility for damages. In the collective bargaining context, successor liability is possible with respect to four different target obligations: Does the acquiring company succeed

(1) to the target's recognition of a union and obligation to bargain with it?[42]

(2) to the target's obligations under the collective bargaining agreement with the union?[43]

(3) to the target's contractual obligation to arbitrate grievances?[44]

(4) to the target's obligations to remedy past unfair labor practices?[45]

Both the federal courts' analysis of these questions and the answers reached differ depending on which issue is considered. However, all four pose interesting contrasts to the performance of state courts in developing the doctrine of successor liability with respect to products liability[46] and, in all events, the answers to these questions may be critical to the success of an acquisition. As already noted, whether the acquiring company succeeds to some or all of the collective bargaining obligations of the target company may determine whether the synergy anticipated from the transaction can be accomplished or whether a reduction in wages, in order to make the company more competitive, is possible.

Historically, the federal courts have dealt with these issues in terms that recall the state courts' development of the de facto merger doctrine. Successorship depended on the finding of "a substantial continuity of identity in the business enterprise"[47] as evidenced by a litany of factors including whether a majority of the post-acquisition employees had been employees of the target, and whether, after the acquisition, the same business operations were continued, the same supervisors were employed, the same methods of production were maintained, and the same products or services were manufactured.[48] At the same time, however, the Supreme Court has stressed that no simple tallying of the factors is possible. In Howard Johnson Co., Inc. v. Detroit Local Joint Executive Board, 417 U.S. 249, 262 n.9 (1974), the Court stated:

---

[42] See NLRB v. Burns Int'l Security Serv., 406 U.S. 272 (1972).

[43] See *id.*

[44] See John Wiley & Sons v. Livingston, 376 U.S. 543 (1964); Howard Johnson Co., Inc., v. Detroit Local Joint Executive Bd., 417 U.S. 249 (1974).

[45] See Golden State Bottling Co. v. NLRB, 414 U.S. 168 (1973).

[46] The status of an acquiring company employer with respect to the target company's collective bargaining obligations is a matter of federal law under the National Labor Relations Act. Products liability remains an issue of state law. See Section C of this Chapter, *supra.*

[47] John Wiley & Sons, 376 U.S. at 551.

[48] See generally, Frederick Slicker, *A Reconsideration of the Doctrine of Employer Successorship -- A Step Toward a Rational Approach*, 57 Minn.L.Rev. 1051 (1973).

The question of whether Howard Johnson [the acquirer] is a "successor" is simply not meaningful in the abstract. Howard Johnson is of course a successor employer in the sense that it succeeded to operation of a restaurant and motor lodge formerly operated by the [target]. But the real question in each of these successor cases is, on the particular facts, what are the legal obligations of the new employer to the employees of the former owner. . . . The answer to this inquiry requires analysis of the interests of the new employer and the employees and of the policies of the labor laws in light of the facts of each case and the particular legal obligation at issue, whether it be the duty to recognize and bargain with the union, the duty to remedy unfair labor practices, the duty to arbitrate, etc. There is, and can be, no single definition of "successor" which is applicable in every legal context. A new employer, in other words, may be a successor employer for some purposes and not for others.

Without excluding the possibility that unique labor law considerations dictate the result with respect to one or more of the four central issues, it is interesting to see how each would be evaluated under an internalization approach to successor liability. Recall that under this approach, successor liability is justified to prevent the acquiring and target companies from combining to externalize risks on creditors -- like future products liability claimants -- who cannot protect themselves. Thus, contract creditors who can negotiate the terms of their relationship directly with the target company and, as a result, can force the target company to take into account the cost to them of an unexpected termination of the contract, generally are not protected by the successor liability doctrine. In contrast, where creditors cannot themselves negotiate with the target company, as with future products liability claimants, an internalization approach to the successor liability doctrine imposes liability on the successor so that the successor acts as a surrogate for the interests of the creditors in its negotiations with the target.

Under an internalization approach, might not the Supreme Court's fragmentation of the problem of successorship in labor law be wrong? In any case in which a successorship issue is raised, the target company and the union were, by definition, already in a contractual relationship out of which a contract determining their rights and responsibilities -- the collective bargaining agreement -- was negotiated. One matter that could have been negotiated was what would happen if the company were sold; the successorship issue could have been resolved by contract in a labor setting just as the successorship issue is resolved by contract in a bond indenture. Indeed, it appears that a significant number of collective bargaining agreements do contain a successorship clause.[49] And where such a contract

---

[49] BNA, *Basic Patterns of Union Contracts* 8 (8th ed.1975), reports that 22% of a sample of collective bargaining agreements contained a successorship clause. See Note, *The Efficacy of Successorship Clauses in Collective Bargaining Agreements*, 79 Geo.L.Rev. 1549, 1568 (1991). One such clause provided that:

exists, the courts have held that a pending acquisition of the target can be enjoined unless the acquiring company satisfies the contract.[50]

In light of the opportunity for the union to bargain with respect to successorship, what reason is there to create *any* labor law successor liability doctrine? When some unions bargain for successor protection and others do not, one inference is that the unions which did not secure a successorship clause chose to take the consideration the employees' bargaining position could command in a different currency. For example, a decision to give up a successorship clause in favor of higher wages is, in effect, a decision to prefer current benefits to future benefits. Unless we believe that the union systematically applied an erroneously high discount rate to future benefits, why as a matter of federal labor policy should we override the union's choice of the timing of benefits?[51]

One explanation for such a bias might be that labor unions, like any other representative organization, are subject to agency costs: Those representing employees in the bargaining may pursue the goals of some subgroup of employees rather than what makes the entire group of affected employees best off. From this perspective, a union bias against the future may be perfectly understandable. In negotiating a successorship clause, the union represents two groups of potentially different employees: present employees, who will benefit from higher current wages; and future employees, who will be present when the company is acquired and who would be benefitted by a successorship clause. Only if it is certain that the two groups will be identical can there be confidence that the union will apply the correct discount rate. The higher the turnover in the particular workforce,

---

This agreement shall be binding upon the successors and assigns of the parties hereto, and no provisions, terms or obligations herein contained shall be affected, modified, altered or changed in any respect whatsoever by consolidation, merger, sale, transfer or assignment of either party hereto or affected, modified, altered or changed in any respect whatsoever, by any change of any kind of the legal status, ownership or management of either party hereto.

11 *Collective Bargaining Agreement Negotiations and Contracts* (BNA) 70:182 (1981) (Fairchild Republic Co. and United Auto Workers). Examples of other clauses can be found in International Union, UMWA v. Eastover Mining, 603 F.Supp. 1038 (W.D.Va.1985); Marley-Waylain Co. v. Local 101, Sheet Metal Workers' Int'l Assn., 88 Lab.Arb. (BNA) 978 (1987).

[50] Local Lodge No. 1266, IAM, v. Panoramic Corp., 668 F.2d 276 (7th Cir.1981). However, the successorship clause will not subject an acquiring company to the terms of the target company's collective bargaining agreement unless the acquiror assumes the contract or is deemed a successor under the successorship doctrine. Howard Johnson Co. v. Detroit Local Joint Executive Bd., *supra*, at 258 n.3. Therefore, knowledge of a pending sale by the union is critical to securing injunctive relief. An effective successorship clause requires a pre-transaction notice provision. See Note, *The Efficacy of Successorship Clauses in Collective Bargaining Agreements, supra* note 49. See generally Jules Crystal & Richard Brodecki, *Are Successors and Assigns Clauses Really Binding?*, 38 Labor L.J. 547 (1987).

[51] Cf. Thomas Jackson, *Fresh-Start Policy in Bankruptcy Law*, 98 Harv.L.Rev. 1393 (1985) (individual discharge under federal bankruptcy law justified by systematic biases in consumer decision making).

the greater the likelihood that the makeup of the two groups of employees will differ, and the greater the likelihood that the union will honor the preference of current employees, whose vote is required to approve the contract, for higher current wages even if the joint welfare of both groups of employees would be maximized by trading current wages for a successorship clause.[52]

There may be circumstances in other labor related areas where an internalization approach might favor successor liability. For example, suppose a company that systematically engaged in employment discrimination sought, as with products liability claims, to cut off future employment discrimination claims by selling its assets and dissolving. Subject to the requirement that the claims be foreseeable, the imposition of successor liability in this circumstance would serve to force the target to internalize the costs of employment discrimination.[53]

From a planning perspective, what elements of the litany of factors the courts have described as relevant to successorship are subject to control? Would it be worthwhile to try to minimize the number of target employees who are hired? If so, does the successorship doctrine protect employees?

In Fall River Dyeing & Finishing Corp. v. NLRB, 482 U.S. 27 (1987), the Supreme Court returned to the successorship issue for the first time in 13 years. The Court noted that the danger of an acquirer and target externalizing the costs of a collective bargaining agreement was a relevant concern in the successorship area. "[W]ith the wide variety of corporate transformations possible, an employer could use a successor enterprise as a way of getting rid of a labor contract and of exploiting the employees' hesitant attitude towards the union to eliminate its continuing presence." *Id.* at 39. However, the puzzle in understanding the Court's finding that the conditions of successorship had been met is that case presented no danger of externalization.

Most important, *Fall River* did not involve an acquisition. Rather, it involved the re-creation of an operating business from the pieces of a failed, and thereafter liquidated, company. Justice Powell's description of the facts in his dissent is shorter, but not inconsistent with that of the majority:

. . . On February 12, 1982, a financially troubled Sterlingwale [the predecessor] ceased operations and indefinitely laid off its production workers,

---

[52] See Douglas Leslie, *Labor Bargaining Units*, 70 Va.L.Rev. 353 (1984) (development of a collective goods model of labor unions).

[53] The requirement in the case law that the successor employer have notice of the claims of employment discrimination could be read as a foreseeability requirement. See Wiggins v. Spector Freight Systems, 583 F.2d 882 (6th Cir.1978). *Wiggins*, however, has been read to exonerate a successor if charges had not been filed with the EEOC at the time the acquisition took place. Rabidue v. Osceola Refining Co., 584 F.Supp. 419, 424 (E.D.Mich.1984). Under an internalization approach, all that is necessary is that the employment discrimination claims be foreseeable on a probabilistic basis; they need not be certain. What incentive would a bright line rule like that of *Rabidue* create?

retaining only a skeleton crew to ship out the remaining orders and liquidate the inventory. . . . Attempts to obtain new financing to keep the business afloat were unsuccessful. Sterlingwale commenced its liquidation by making an assignment for the benefit of creditors, and then hired a professional liquidator to sell the remaining assets at a public auction. By mid- to late-summer of 1982, all business activity had ceased and the company permanently closed its doors.

Petitioner Fall River Dyeing & Finishing Corp. [the successor] was incorporated at the end of August 1982. It bought most of Sterlingwale's machinery, furniture, and fixtures. It also bought a portion of the Sterlingwale inventory at the public auction.

482 U.S. at 55.

Under an internalization approach, Fall River would not be a successor employer. Failure and piecemeal liquidation is not a promising device to externalize the costs. As discussed in Section C.2, *supra*, externalization through a piecemeal sale of assets, as in a liquidation, is desirable to the liquidating company only when the costs of the collective bargaining agreement that would be avoided exceed the value of the company's good will -- that is, the difference between its value as a going concern and the value of its assets through a piecemeal sale. In the context of a failed company, however, there is no good will and, for the same reason, there are no costs to externalize -- the collective bargaining agreement has no cost when the company has gone out of business. Thus, the effect of the decision is only to make it less likely that a new employer will arise from the ashes of the old. In whose interest is this result?

What, then, pushed the Court toward the conclusion that Fall River Dyeing was a successor employer? Seemingly motivate by visions of industrial peace, the Court stressed that "[i]f the employees find themselves in essentially the same jobs after the employer transition and if their legitimate expectations in continued representation by their union are thwarted, their dissatisfaction may lead to industrial unrest." 482 U.S. at 43. In this case, because the new employer was in the same business as the old, the actual jobs of the employees did not change. The Court found this of "particular significance." *Id.* Put somewhat differently, the Court held that if enough former employees are rehired following a piecemeal liquidation, a bargaining relationship will be imposed, but if enough former employees are left unemployed, the resurrection of the business can proceed without the union (unless, of course, the new business is successfully organized). This seems like an odd prescription for industrial peace.

Did anything prevent the parties to the collective bargaining agreement in *Fall River* from negotiating over what would happen if the company's assets were sold, whether as a going concern or piecemeal? What provisions could the predecessor employer and the union have put in their contract that would have covered piecemeal liquidation? Could a severance pay arrangement be devised that turned workers' expectations of continued employment under the contract into a creditors' claim that would participate in liquidation distributions? Would this approach assure that the predecessor internalized all costs?[54]

At the state level, Massachusetts became the first state to impose successorship as a matter of state law. Mass.Gen.L.Ann.C. 149 § 20E (effective July 19, 1989) requires that a post-acquisition company remain subject to any collective bargaining agreement covering Massachusetts employees that was in effect at the time control of the employer shifted. Delaware and Pennsylvania have adopted similar provisions. Del.Gen.Corp. Law § 706; Pa.Bus.Corp. Law tit. 15, ch. 25I. Massachusetts and Pennsylvania have also required severance payments for employees fired after an acquisition. Mass.Gen.L.Ann.C. 149 § 183; Pa.Bus.Corp. Law tit. 15, ch. 25I, §§ 2581-83.

A final consideration from a planning perspective is whether the imposition of successor liability can be avoided by restructuring the transaction. Subject to the uncertainty created by *Fall River*, a piecemeal sale of assets would seem to work to avoid successor liability; however, it would be subject to the same non-regulatory costs as were noted with respect to products liability claims. Is anything gained if the target company is first put into bankruptcy and the acquisition is made as part of a plan of reorganization? In NLRB v. Bildisco & Bildisco, 465 U.S. 513 (1984), the Supreme Court held that a debtor could reject a collective bargaining

---

[54] For a detailed evaluation of the impact of a bargaining relationship on a court's role in imposing outcomes with respect to matters that the parties could have bargained over, see Stewart Schwab, *Collective Bargaining and the Coase Theorem*, 72 Cornell L.Rev. 245 (1987).

Rock & Wachter (1993), *supra* note 41, have developed an interesting approach to the successorship problem that is consistent with a general internalization approach, but also draws on labor economics to contextualize the analysis. In their approach, the problem in the successorship setting is the acquirer's incentive to avoid the costs of the target company's collective bargaining agreement while retaining the benefits of the target's internal labor market -- the web of explicit and implicit contracts and relationship specific investments made by the company and employees that govern the actual work relationship. From this perspective, the authors suggest that existing successorship doctrine implicitly poses just the right question: "The obligations of the surviving firm turn on whether or not the firm reestablishes or retains the [internal labor market] of the old firm." *Id.* at 237.

How does one know the substantive content of a company's internal labor market in order to tell whether it has been reestablished or retained? For example, Rock & Wachter conclude that the *Fall River* facts should establish successorship because a majority of the liquidated company's workers were subsequently employed doing similar work, despite the piecemeal liquidation. This subsequent employment posed the risk that the new employer was appropriating a larger share of the value of the liquidated target's internal labor market. To what extent does this analysis pose the same problem presented in Chapter 15 by the claim that the gains from acquisitions generally result from breaches of the target's implicit contracts with employees? Efforts to explicitly enforce implicit contracts make defining the terms of the implicit contracts very important. Does their existing bargaining relationship allow the union and target company to solve the problem with a successorship clause -- in effect, committing the union and company to bargain over the division of the gains from selling the internal labor market?

agreement under § 365 of the Bankruptcy Reform Act[55] "if the debtor can show that the collective-bargaining agreement burdens the estate, and that after careful scrutiny, the equities balance in favor of rejecting the labor contract." 465 U.S. at 526. The Court's decision was widely viewed as an invitation to otherwise healthy companies to enter bankruptcy in order to shed their collective bargaining agreements.[56] After a tortured legislative process that coincided with Congressional efforts to resurrect bankruptcy court jurisdiction after the Supreme Court had held a significant portion of it unconstitutional,[57] Congress responded to *Bildisco* by adding § 1113 to the Bankruptcy Act. Under § 1113, a trustee can reject a collective bargaining agreement, but the section requires that the court make the presumably more stringent finding that the equities "clearly" favor rejection and that "all of the affected parties are treated fairly and equitably."[58] Assuming that the trustee retains relative freedom to reject collective bargaining agreements,[59] how likely is it that, for companies that are not in serious financial trouble, the advantages of rejecting a collective bargaining agreement will outweigh the collateral costs of bankruptcy?

2. Successor Liability With Respect to Defined Benefit Pension Plan Obligations

Successor liability with respect to the target company's defined benefit pension plan obligations is both an important and an interesting issue.[60] Its importance derives from the size of the stakes; in the worst case scenario, the acquiring company's liability could reach 30% of the aggregate net worth of the company and its affiliates. The subject's interest derives from the fact that successor liability for pension plan obligations is an anomaly in two respects. First, in contrast to the common law development of the standards for successor liability for products liability and collective bargaining obligations, successor liability for pension fund obligations is determined by

---

[55] 11 U.S.C. § 365 (1982) (Trustee, subject to court's approval, may assume or reject any executory contract of the debtor.).

[56] See James White, *The Bildisco Case and the Congressional Response*, 30 Wayne L.Rev. 1169, 1181-82 (1984) (available on Westlaw).

[57] Marathon Pipeline Co. v. Northern Pipeline Co., 458 U.S. 50 (1982).

[58] § 1113(d)(1)(A).

[59] See White (1984), *supra* note 56, at 1201-02 (§ 1113 somewhat more restrictive than *Bildisco* test but less restrictive than pre-*Bildisco* law.).

[60] A defined benefit pension plan is one that promises the employee a fixed benefit on retirement. In contrast, a defined contribution plan promises the employee only the money that has been contributed to the employee's account augmented or diminished by investment performance since its contribution. In a defined benefit plan, the company bears the risk that the plan will have insufficient funds to pay the benefits; in a defined contribution plan, such a shortfall is impossible. Because pension liability, and therefore successor liability, focuses on this shortfall, our concern here is only with defined benefit plans.

statute, part of the complex legislative scheme adopted by the Employment Retirement Income Security Act of 1974 (ERISA),[61] as amended by the Multiemployer Pension Plan Amendments Act of 1980,[62] and as influenced by the detailed requirements governing the federal income tax treatment of pension funds under the Internal Revenue Code (IRC). Second, the manner in which Congress resolved the successor liability issue stands in stark contrast to the manner in which the courts have dealt with successor liability for products liability and collective bargaining obligations. With respect to pension plan obligations, Congress chose to forgo successor liability in favor of what may be called predecessor liability. This manner of dealing with the problem provides a useful counterpoint in understanding the bases for the internalization approach developed earlier in this Chapter.

An acquisition poses the risk of three general categories of liability with respect to the target company's defined benefit pension plan:[63]

   (1) liability under ERISA and the IRC to fund already vested benefits under the plan:

   (2) liability under ERISA if the plan is terminated; and

   (3) liability under the IRC for back income taxes if the plan retroactively loses its qualification for special tax treatment.

With respect to each of these categories of liability, the obligation of the acquiring company is determined by the form of the transaction. If the acquisition is structured as a merger, the acquiring company assumes all obligations of the target company, including pension obligations, as a matter of state law. If the transaction is structured as a stock acquisition, the assets of the target remain subject to its pension obligations and, at least for purposes of termination liabilities, the assets of the acquiring company and all members of its affiliated group also may become subject to the liabilities. Finally, and most importantly from planning a perspective, if the transaction is structured as a sale of assets, the traditional rule is retained: The acquiring

---

[61] 29 U.S.C. §§ 1001-1381 (1982).

[62] Pub.L. No. 96-364, 94 Stat. 1208 (1980).

[63] What follows is a general description of an enormously complicated problem. Although the successor liability problem can be described straightforwardly, the manner in which the size of the liability is calculated, and the details of the rules governing the precise circumstances in which the liability is created, are extraordinarily complex and beyond the scope of this Chapter. For more detailed discussions of some of these issues, see, e.g., Linda Griffey, Joan Brophy & Susan Curtis, *Employee Benefit Plans in Corporate Acquisitions, Dispositions and Mergers in Acquiring or Selling the Privately Held Company 1994* (PLI, 1994); Linda Laarman & D. Hildebrandt, *Plan Terminations and Mergers*, 357 Tax Management Portfolios (1983); Richard Reichler, *Handling Significant Benefit Plans in Mergers and Acquisitions*, in *Business Acquisitions* 831 (John Herz & Charles Baller eds., 2d ed.1981); Harold Novikoff & Beth Polebaum, *Pension Related Claims in Bankruptcy Code Cases*, 40 Bus.Law. 373 (1985); Herbert Krueger, *Corporate Transactions -- Retirement Plan Issues*, 61 Taxes 147 (1983); Bruce Miller, *The Employee Benefit Aspects of Acquisitions and Divestitures: The Liabilities*, 4 Corp.L.Rev. 99 (1981); Ronald Kladder, *Asset Sales after MPPAA -- An Analysis of ERISA § 4204*, 39 Bus.Law. 101 (1983).

company succeeds to only those of the target company's liabilities, including pension obligations, as are expressly assumed in the acquisition agreement.

Liability for unfunded vested benefits -- benefits already earned by plan participants but for which employer contributions have not yet been made -- has two aspects. The first is a tax liability. Under IRC § 412 and ERISA § 302, an employer has the obligation to meet minimum annual funding standards. If the standards are not met, IRC § 4791(a) imposes an annual 5% excise tax on the accumulated funding deficiency and, if the deficiency is not eliminated during a specified correction period, IRC § 4791(b) imposes an excise tax equal to 100% of the remaining accumulated funding deficiency. The Internal Revenue Code does not impose liability on the acquiring company in an asset acquisition for excise taxes owed by the target;[64] as a result, there are no limits short of a sham transaction attack on a planner's efforts to use an asset acquisition to avoid assuming excise taxes owed by the target company.

The second aspect of liability for unfunded vested benefits is the obligation ultimately to pay the benefits. If the pension plan is assumed by the acquirer, the funding and payment obligations are, of course, also assumed. If the acquiring company does not assume the pension plan, because the acquisition is in the form of a sale of assets and the acquisition agreement does not provide for assumption, the target company retains liability for unfunded vested benefits. The problem, however, is that a target company typically goes out of business following a sale of its assets. This results in a termination of the plan with the consequence that, under Title IV of ERISA, the Pension Benefit Guaranty Corporation (PBGC) guarantees the payment to employees of certain vested plan benefits. If the assets of the plan are insufficient to pay the benefits guaranteed by the PBGC -- if the plan is underfunded -- the target company is liable to the PBGC for 100% of the plan's unfunded benefit liabilities whether vested or nonvested.[65] Of critical importance to the acquiring company, no successor liability attaches to the acquiring company if the target's assets are insufficient to satisfy the PBGC's claim.[66]

A second form of termination liability arises when the target company is a member of a multiemployer pension plan. Under the MPPAA, an employer who withdraws from a multiemployer pension plan is immediately

---

[64] Successor liability will exist only where imposed by applicable state law such as the Uniform Fraudulent Conveyances Act or a bulk sales act. Miller (1981), *supra* note 63, at 114-16.

[65] ERISA § 4062(b)(1)(A).

[66] ERISA § 4062(d); PBGC Opinion Letter 78-10 (June 21, 1978). Two qualifications are necessary. If the transfer was a subterfuge to shield target company assets, liability may attach to the transferee. Additionally, the PBGC has a lien against the target company's assets to secure payment of the target's liability to the PBGC. From the acquiring company's perspective, the critical date is that on which the PBGC files a claim similar to that filed with respect to a federal tax lien. Property acquired from the target before the filing is not subject to the lien. See Miller (1981), *supra* note 63, at 110.

liable for a portion of the plan's unfunded vested benefits. An acquisition of the target company operates as a withdrawal unless the acquisition is a merger,[67] or unless in a sale of assets the acquiring company assumes the target's obligations under the plan and posts a bond or sets up an escrow to secure against liability for future withdrawals.[68] As with liability for termination of a single employer plan, the acquiring company has no successor obligation in a sale of assets unless there has been an explicit assumption.[69]

The final category of liability is the target company's obligations for back taxes if a plan is retroactively disqualified because of an acquisition. This will have the effect of making unavailable the income tax deduction taken by the target in previous years for contributions to the plan.[70] The standards which determine disqualification are complex;[71] however, for our purpose the important point is that in an asset acquisition no successor liability is imposed for deficiencies resulting from retroactive disqualification.[72]

The common thread that joins each category of potential liability is the fact that the planner's decision to cast the transaction as a sale of assets, so that the acquiring company does not assume the target's liabilities, will be respected. That result, quite different from the results encountered earlier in this Chapter, poses a question. If successor liability is necessary to force internalization of future products liability costs, why is it not necessary with respect to future pension costs? Recall that what allowed externalization of future products liability costs was the target company's ability to dissolve under state corporate law and thereby cut off future claims. Because pension obligations are known -- the amount of future claims can be determined actuarially -- they must be paid or adequately provided for prior to dissolution; externalization in this sense is not possible. Indeed, in some circumstances, ERISA imposes "predecessor liability" on the target company with respect to obligations explicitly assumed by the acquiring company. In connection with both liability arising from the termination of a single employer pension plan,[73] and liability arising from withdrawal from a multiemployer pension plan,[74] the target company remains secondarily liable

---

[67] ERISA § 4218.

[68] ERISA § 4204.

[69] See generally Kladder (1983), *supra* note 63.

[70] An assessment would be possible with respect to all years for which the statute of limitations, under IRC § 6501(a) generally three years after the filing of a return, has not run.

[71] See Reichler (1981), *supra* note 63, at 837-42.

[72] The liability could create a federal tax lien. Prior to the filing of the lien, however, an acquirer would be protected in the same manner as discussed earlier with respect to excise taxes owed by the target.

[73] Miller (1981), *supra* note 63, at 112-13.

[74] ERISA § 4204.

if the acquiring company fails to discharge the assumed obligation.[75]   But why would Congress worry about predecessor liability if a successor has already assumed the predecessor's obligations? So long as the liability is not externalized, because the successor has assumed it, what does predecessor liability add?

Might not ERISA be concerned with the risk of underfunding being externalized not to employees -- they are protected by the guarantee of the PBGC -- but to the PBGC itself? The PBGC is essentially an insurance company to which companies that maintain covered plans pay premiums. If a company can avoid potential liability by shifting the obligation to a riskier company, perhaps one with a net worth below what would have been the target's obligation, the risk to that extent has been externalized to the PBGC.[76] The maintenance of predecessor liability thus functions to protect the PBGC.

It is a mistake, however, to overestimate the planning flexibility that the absence of successor liability provides.[77]   Quite often there will be substantive reasons for the acquiring company to assume the target's pension liabilities.[78]   In this situation, ERISA eliminates one of the planning techniques that remains available with respect to future products liability claims despite the expansion of successor liability. The acquiring company's assets can be shielded from the target company's future products liability claims, even if the target's assets cannot be, either by acquiring the stock of the target and keeping it as a separate subsidiary, or by casting the transaction in triangular form. Under ERISA, a parent's liability for the pension obligations of its subsidiary is *not* limited; the net worth of all businesses

---

[75] In the multiemployer setting, ERISA § 4204(a)(1)(C) requires that the contract of sale explicitly provide for secondary liability, and § 4204(a)(3) requires that a bond be posted or an escrow created if the target is to be liquidated before its secondary liability terminates.

[76] See Jeremy Bulow, Myron Scholes & Peter Menell, *Economic Implications of ERISA*, in *Financial Aspects of the U.S. Pension System* 37 (Zvi Bodie & John Shoven eds.1984) (right to terminate PBGC insured plan as put option).

[77] For discussion of the ability to use bankruptcy to cut off pension fund obligations, see Novikoff & Polebaum (1985), *supra* note 63. Upholsterers' International Union Pension Fund v. Artistic Furniture of Pontiac, 920 F.2d 1323 (7th Cir.1990), demonstrates the potential interaction of common law and statutory successor liability rules. There the court concluded that labor law successor principles would impose liability on an asset acquiror for contributions due under a multiemployer pension plan if on remand the trial court found that the acquiror knew of the pension liability before the acquisition. While the court's emphasis on the acquiring company's knowledge was consistent with an internalization approach, its use of common law successorship principles in the context of the Multiemployer Pension Plan Amendments of 1980 was a little puzzling. The court explained that a significant factor in imposing successor liability was the need for "vindication of an important statutory policy," and that "Congressional policies underlying ERISA and the Multiemployer Pension Plan Amendments Act of 1980 are at least as important as the NLRA. . . ." *Id.* at 1327. The court does not mention the consistent statutory pattern of predecessor liability for pension liabilities, which might have led to an inquiry into what the statutory policy actually was.

[78] See Krueger (1983), *supra* note 63, at 152-54.

under "common control" as determined under IRC §§ 414(b) and (c) are subject to liability to the PBGC.[79]

The message to planners is that investigation and contractual protection is critical here. That the liability cannot be externalized means that, for this item, the acquiring and target companies will be engaged in distributive bargaining. Thus, allocation of the burden of pension liability by, for example, the manner in which the purchase price is calculated and by contractual representations, warranties and indemnification, requires consideration of techniques of private, rather than public ordering. This is the subject of Part V.

3.   Successor Liability With Respect to Environmental Claims

The expanding range of federal and state statutes which impose liability on corporations for harms caused to the environment is a third area in which the application of successor liability doctrines is critical to acquisition planning. Because current projections of the total costs of cleaning up improperly managed waste sites range up to $700 billion,[80] whether an acquiring company will inherit the target company's environmental liabilities is potentially the most significant application of successor liability doctrine.

To date, the major focus concerning successorship has been on liabilities imposed under the Comprehensive Environmental Response, Compensation and Liability Act of 1980 ("CERCLA").[81] CERCLA's primary function is to assign liability for cleanup costs of hazardous waste sites which pose threats to public health and the environment. The Environmental Protection Agency may either direct responsible parties to eliminate the danger[82] or clean up the site itself under its response authority using money from the Superfund.[83] The EPA may then bring cost recovery actions against any responsible party in order to replenish the Superfund.[84]

---

[79] Not surprisingly given the stakes, the precise contours of the phrase "common control" has generated a substantial amount of litigation. See, e.g., Pension Benefit Guaranty Corp. v. Dickens, 535 F.Supp. 922 (D.C.Mich.1982); Pension Benefit Guaranty Corp. v. Ouimet Corp., 630 F.2d 4 (1st Cir.1980), *cert. denied* 450 U.S. 914 (1981); Pension Benefit Guaranty Corp. v. Anthony Co., 575 F.Supp. 953 (N.D.Ill.1983).

[80] David Sommerfield, *Going Bare*, Institutional Investor 99,102 (Mar.1990).

[81] See 42 U.S.C. § 9601-9675 (1989), as amended by the Superfund Amendments and Reauthorization Act of 1986 (SARA). The other major federal statutes creating civil liability for environmental damage are the Resources Conversation and Recovery Act, 42 U.S.C. § 6901 et.seq. (1989); the Federal Water Pollution Control Act, 33 U.S.C. § 1251 et.seq. (1989); the Clean Air Act, 42 U.S.C. § 7401 et.seq. (1989); the Federal Insecticide, Fungicide and Rodenticide Act, 7 U.S.C. § 136 et.seq. (1989); the Safe Drinking Water Act, 42 U.S.C. § 300f et.seq. (1989); and the Toxic Substances Control Act, 15 U.S.C. § 2601 et.seq. (1989).

[82] 42 U.S.C.A. § 9606 (1989).

[83] 42 U.S.C.A § 9604 (1989).

[84] 42 U.S.C.A. § 9607(a) (1989).

CERCLA identifies four categories of people as liable for releases or threatened releases of hazardous substances from facilities. Potentially responsible parties include (1) current owners and operators of hazardous waste facilities or vessels (2) past owners and operators of hazardous waste facilities (3) persons who arranged for the disposal of hazardous substances (generators) and (4) transporters of hazardous substances[85]. This extremely wide definition of potentially responsible parties means that the issue of CERCLA liability for successor corporations will need to be considered in virtually every corporate acquisition, since a target corporation may have liability not only for conduct that has long since ceased, but for conduct of its own predecessors.

For the acquisition planner, potential CERCLA liabilities of the target company raise three primary issues: (a) whether the acquiring company will be held liable as a successor corporation even if it acquires only the target company's assets and does not assume its environmental liabilities; (b) whether the parties can allocate potential CERCLA liability between them by way of indemnity, warranty or otherwise; and (c) whether transaction planning can in any event help shield at least the acquiring company's assets, from the target company's liability. The resolution of these questions is complicated by the fact that CERCLA is a federal statute, hence the courts must determine both whether the traditionally state corporate law doctrine of successorship should apply at all and, if so, whether its content should be determined by particular state laws or by development of a federal common law.

a.　*CERCLA Liability for Successor Corporations*

Although CERCLA does not itself explicitly address whether an acquiring company succeeds to a target company's statutory liability, the courts now seem to have reached a consensus view that liability does extend to successor corporations in some circumstances. Smith Land & Improvement Corp. v. The Celotex Corporation[86] and Louisiana-Pacific Corp. v. Asarco, Inc.[87] found the statutory language ambiguous, but concluded that the legislative history demonstrated Congressional expectation that the courts would develop a federal common law to supplement the statute, a result followed by virtually every court that has subsequently considered the issue.[88] The courts have disagreed, however, on the

---

[85] *Id.*

[86] 851 F.2d 86 (3rd Cir.1988).

[87] 909 F.2d 1260 (9th Cir.1990).

[88] See, e.g. Merritt Fox, *Corporate Successor under Strict Liability: A General Economic Theory and the Case of CERCLA*, 26 Wake Forest L.Rev. 183 (1991); Lynda Oswald & Cyndy Schipani, *CERCLA and the "Erosion" of Traditional Corporate Law Doctrine*, 86 Nw.L.Rev. 259 (1992). '

appropriate sources to guide developing federal law. Both *Smith Land* and *Louisiana-Pacific* looked to traditional state corporate law principles of successor liability, in particular the general rule that asset acquisitions do not give rise to successor liability unless one of the familiar four exceptions are satisfied.[89] In contrast, Anspec Company, Inc. v. Johnson Controls, Inc.,[90] interpreted the statutory language to unambiguously impose successor liability in appropriate circumstances. CERCLA imposes liability on "persons," 42 U.S.C. § 9607 (a), defined to include "corporations." The court concluded that the term corporation, which is not defined by the statute, includes corporate successors. Basing CERCLA's application to successors on the statutory language invites a court to bypass the state law limits on the traditional four circumstances when successor liability attaches despite an asset acquisition in favor of a more expansive standard said to be consistent with CERCLA's special remedial concerns. Following this analysis, United States v. Distler[91] and United States v. Carolina Transformer Co.[92] applied a "substantial continuity" or "continuity of business enterprise" test of successorship paralleling that used in labor cases,[93] which focuses on whether "the business of both employers were the same . . ., the employees of the new company were doing the same job, and . . . the new company produced the same product for essentially the same customers." *Caroline Products*, 739 F.Supp. at 1039.

The EPA has also advocated an expanded notion of successor liability under CERCLA. In a 1984 Memorandum, the EPA announced that it would hold an acquiring corporation liable for the environmental torts of a target corporation if the acquirer continues substantially the same business operations as the predecessor.[94]

How would an internalization approach apply to successor liability under CERCLA? Recall from Section C.3 that internalization fails when neither the predecessor not the successor can anticipate the probability of future liability. Under CERCLA, a target company can have liability based on past ownership or operation of hazardous waste facilities, even if the hazardous substances were released when the land in question was owned by someone else. Liability can also attach pursuant to the application of successor liability to the target's predecessors. Thus, while any acquisition poses a risk of CERCLA successor liability, it may be very difficult to assess the probability

---

[89] See Section A of this Chapter, *supra*.

[90] 922 F.2d 1240 (6th Cir.1991).

[91] 741 F.Supp. 637 (W.D.Ky.1990).

[92] 739 F.Supp. 1030 (E.D.N.C.1989).

[93] See also United States v. Mexico Feed and Seed Co., 764 F.Supp. 902 (E.D.Mo.1990); United States v. Western Processing Co., 751 F.Supp. 902 (W.D.Wash.1990).

[94] EPA Memorandum, *Liability of Corporate Shareholders and Successor Corporations for Abandoned Sites Under the Comprehensive Environmental Response, Compensation and Liability Act (CERCLA)*, Courtney Price, Assistant Administrator for Enforcement and Compliance Monitoring (June 13, 1984).

and the size of the risk,[95] thereby interfering with the purchase price adjustment that is at the heart of internalization.

b. Indemnification of CERCLA Liabilities

Given the uncertainty as to an acquiring company's liability for the target's CERCLA liabilities, whether the acquiring and target companies can allocate the risk of such liability between themselves is very important to a transaction planner. The confusion in this area stems from the terms of CERCLA itself. Section 107 (e) (1) of CERCLA provides: "No indemnification, hold harmless, or similar agreement or conveyance shall be effective to transfer from the owner or operator of any vessel or facility or from any person who may be liable for a release or threat of release under this section, to any other person the liability imposed under this section. Nothing in this subsection shall bar any agreement to insure, hold harmless, or indemnify a party to such agreement for any liability under this section."[96]

As many courts have noted, this inartfully drafted provision seems internally consistent. The first sentence of § 107(e)(1) appears to prohibit indemnification agreements under all circumstances, while the second sentence of § 107(e)(1) appears to permit indemnification under all circumstances.

Mardan Corp. v. C.G.C. Music, Ltd.,[97] resolved the confusion by distinguishing between liability to the government and liability under risk shifting contracts among private parties. The first sentence of § 107(e)(1) was interpreted as assuming that "all responsible parties will be fully liable to the government regardless of the indemnification contracts they have entered into." *Id.* at 1459. The second sentence was then construed to allow potentially responsible parties to contract among themselves to distribute the incidence of liability. However, if the party to whom the liability is shifted pursuant to the second sentence defaults, the first sentence assures that the government retains the original defendant. Thus, contractual risk allocation through the acquisition agreement[98] remains viable under CERCLA. A majority of courts have followed this approach.[99]

---

[95] See Fox (1991), *supra* note 88, at 218.

[96] 42 U.S.C. § 9607(e)(1).

[97] 804 F.2d 1454 (9th Cir.1986).

[98] See Chapter 27, *infra*.

[99] Some controversy remains over whether liability can be contractually shifted if all parties to the contract face liability under CERCLA. If liability is shifted to a party who does not itself face liability, the risk-shifting agree functions merely as private insurance. Where all parties face liability, then risk shifting can be seen as interfering with the statutory liability scheme. See Note, *Misconceptions of Contractual Indemnification Against CERCLA Liability: Judicial Abrogation of the Freedom to Contract*, 42 Cath.U.L.Rev. 179 (1992).

c. *Issues of Transaction Planning*

If an acquiror cannot entirely avoid the target company's past environmental liability by purchasing assets, can it at least shield its own assets from the target company's future liabilities? This inquiry is important precisely because the size and likelihood of CERCLA liability are difficult to estimate. Transactionally, a liability shield might be erected by acquiring the target company's stock, or its assets in a triangular acquisition, with the result in either event that the target becomes a wholly owned subsidiary.

In general, courts have applied traditional corporate law veil-piercing doctrine in determining parent responsibility for subsidiary CERCLA liability relating to pre-acquisition behavior.[100] For post-acquisition violations, however, some courts have imposed direct liability on the parent, as opposed to vicarious liability for a subsidiary's behavior, through CERCLA's imposition of liability on an "operator" of a hazardous waste facility.[101] The two approaches may differ in that inquiry into whether a parent is an operator should focus on actual exercise of control over those aspects of the target's activities relevant to CERCLA's purpose. In contrast, more formal matters typically said to be relevant to a veil-piercing inquiry, like central insurance, accounting, and books and records, should be of little significance. An alternative route to the same result, paralleling that used in CERCLA successor doctrine, focuses on the statutory term "person." In a complex corporate structure, which person's behavior did Congress seek to influence by CERCLA's remedial structure? This approach would impose liability on the party -- perhaps the parent -- who controlled the policy decisions relative to CERCLA compliance.

A third approach to imposing liability on a parent corporation for its subsidiary's environmental torts (and crimes) is old fashioned agency law. A parent corporation can use a subsidiary corporation as its agent, in which even it will have responsibility as a principal for its agent's liability creating actions. This approach was used successfully in the criminal prosecution of Exxon Corporation for the acts of its subsidiary corporation, Exxon Shipping, in connection with the Valdez oil spill.[102]

---

[100] See, e.g., Joslyn Mfg. Co. v. T.L. James & Co., Inc., 893 F.2d 80 (5th Cir.1990), *cert. denied*, 498 U.S. 1108 (1991). See George Dent, Jr., *Limited Liability in Environmental Law*, 26 Wake Forest L.Rev. 151 (1991).

[101] See United States v. Kayser-Roth Corp., 910 F.2d 24 (lst Cir.1990).

[102] See United States v. Exxon Corp., No. A90-015CR (D.Ala.1990) (distinguishing agency approach from veil-piercing in denying motion to dismiss indictment).

PART V. PRIVATE ORDERING ASPECTS OF CORPORATE ACQUISITIONS

We began this book in Chapter 1 with the goals of understanding the relationship between what business lawyers do in a transaction and the value of the transaction, of developing analytical techniques that identify what activities have the potential for creating value, and of exploring professional approaches that make business lawyers better at achieving this potential. In Parts III-IV we pursued these goals in connection with the public ordering aspects of business transactions -- the influence of various regulatory regimes on the structure of a transaction. Now in Part V we turn to the private ordering aspects of business transactions -- matters bearing on transactional structure that would be important even in a world with *no* regulation and that are equally important in a world where regulation imposes liability on one party, but allows the parties to alter the incidence of liability by contract. Passing now the easier task of structuring a transaction to minimize the cost of regulation, how else can a business lawyer help private parties order their relationship in a way that increases the value of the transaction? Chapter 27 focuses on this question in the context of a corporate acquisition agreement.

CHAPTER 27: THE CORPORATE ACQUISITION AGREEMENT: THE PRIVATE ORDERING ROLE OF BUSINESS LAWYERS[1]

[Read the form of corporate acquisition agreement in Appendix C.]

A business transaction typically involves the transfer of a capital asset from one party to another. In a corporate acquisition, the asset is generally an entire business; in a loan agreement, the asset is the borrower's promise to repay the loan plus interest; in a real estate transaction, the asset is a piece of real estate; in a joint venture, the asset is a fractional interest in the joint venture. The critical issue in these and many other types of business transactions is the value of the asset to be transferred. Asset pricing theory specifies that the asset to be transferred will be priced based on (i) the expected cash flows associated with the asset; and (ii) the discount rate appropriate to those cash flows, which depends on the expected systematic risk associated with the cash flows.

If both sides to the transaction had perfect information about the value of the asset -- in other words, if the market in which the asset was traded were strong form efficient -- there would be little role for business lawyers to play in the transaction. The parties could correctly price the asset without legal assistance. They would still need lawyers to write down exactly what was being transferred, when, and on what conditions, but this work would be, from the parties' perspective, principally a transaction cost. They would have little ability to increase the value of the transaction. Absent regulatory-based explanations, the fees charged by business lawyers would *decrease* the net value of the transaction.

The matter, of course, cannot be left there. Simple principles of survivorship strongly suggest a more positive role for business lawyers. Identifying it, or at least establishing its absence, requires another look at capital asset pricing theory.

Like many economic models, capital asset pricing theory can be derived only after a number of important simplifying assumptions are made. The reason for such assumptions in economic models is straightforward enough: Reality is too complicated and admits of too many interactions to be modeled. The assumptions function to eliminate those complications not critical to understanding the relationship under study. To be sure, when one makes these assumptions, the examined relationship no longer corresponds exactly to the real-world relationship, curiosity about which originally gave rise to the inquiry. The value of the model, however, rests not on how well it describes reality, but on whether it allows us better to understand it. And as has been the case with capital asset pricing theory, the effect of relaxing

---

[1] This Chapter draws heavily on Ronald Gilson, *Value Creation by Business Lawyers: Legal Skills and Asset Pricing*, 94 Yale L.J. 239 (1984).

the assumptions can also be modeled once the structure of the simple relationship is understood.

The difference between the simple world of capital asset pricing theory and the complex world in which transactions actually take place provides the focus for developing a hypothesis concerning the potential for a business lawyer to increase a transaction's value. In the world described by capital asset pricing theory's simplifying assumptions, the lawyer has no function. What happens, however, when we relax the assumptions on which capital asset pricing theory is based? Is there a value creating role for the business lawyer in this less orderly world?

At this point we need to look more carefully at the assumptions on which capital asset pricing theory is built. Of particular importance to our inquiry are four:

1. All investors have a common time horizon -- i.e., they measure the return to be earned from the asset in question over the same period of time.

2. All investors have the same expectations about the future, in particular, about the future risk and return associated with the asset in question.

3. There are no transaction costs.

4. All information is costlessly available to all investors.[2]

These assumptions, of course, do not describe the real world. Investors do not have the same time horizons; indeed, it is often precisely because they do not -- for example, an older person may wish to alter the composition of his portfolio in favor of assets whose pattern of returns more closely match his remaining life span -- that a transaction occurs in the first place. Similarly, investors do not have homogeneous expectations; the phenomenon of conflicting forecasts of earnings or value even among reputed experts is too familiar for that assumption to stand. Transaction costs, of course, are pervasive. Finally, information is often one of the most expensive and poorly distributed commodities.[3] In short, the world in which capital assets are priced and transactions actually carried out differs in critical respects from the world of perfect markets in which capital asset pricing theory operates.

For a business lawyer, however, the unreality of these perfect market assumptions is not cause for despair. Rather, it is in the very failure of these

---

[2] These assumptions are common to both the CAPM and the Arbitrage Pricing Model (APM). See Stephen Ross, *The Current Status of the Capital Asset Pricing Model*, 33 J.Fin. 885 (1978). Thus, the distinctions between the two are not critical for purposes of this analysis.

There are additional assumptions not listed in the text which are necessary to derive the two-parameter CAPM, such as the ability to borrow and to lend at the same rate, no differential taxes, risk aversion, normal distribution of returns, and risk measured by standard deviation, not all of which are necessary to derive the APM. These, however, can be relaxed without invalidating the approach. See Chapter 4, *supra*.

[3] See Chapter 5B, *supra*.

assumptions to describe the real world that the potential for value creation by lawyers is to be found. When markets fall short of perfection, incentives exist for private innovations that improve market performance. As long as the costs of innovation are less than the resulting gains, private innovation to reduce the extent of market failure creates value. It is in precisely this fashion that opportunity exists for business lawyers to create value.

A.   A Hypothesis Concerning Value Creation: Business Lawyers as Transaction Cost Engineers

The basic assumptions on which capital asset pricing theory is built can be reduced to the simple statement that there are no costs of transacting; there are neither informational disparities between the parties, nor any of the more traditional forms of transaction costs. In such a setting, even one unfamiliar with capital asset pricing theory hardly would be surprised that assets would be correctly priced. In this Coasean world, private outcomes are always optimal,[4] and capital asset pricing theory is no more than the inevitable result of the investor's ability costlessly and thoroughly to diversify his portfolio in a frictionless world. The accuracy of capital asset prices, however, is reduced to the extent there are deviations from capital asset pricing theory's perfect market assumptions. For assets to be correctly priced, the real-world deviations from these assumptions must be constrained. This insight is the first step toward a hypothesis explaining how business lawyers might create value.

The next step, then, is to focus on the mechanisms which reduce real-world deviations from capital asset pricing theory's central assumptions. From this perspective, the variance between assumption and reality is, in effect, a form of market failure. Our concern here is with the character of the market response to that failure. Just as competitive conditions create incentives that encourage reduction of production costs, the market also encourages private efforts to reduce transaction costs. A service that reduces a good's costs -- transaction or otherwise -- will earn a positive return. To

---

[4] See, e.g., Guido Calabresi, *Transaction Costs, Resource Allocation and Liability Rules -- A Comment*, 11 J.L. & Econ. 67, 68 (1968) ("[A]ll misallocations . . . can be remedied by the market, except to the extent that transactions cost money. . . ."); Carl Dahlman, *The Problem of Externality*, 22 J.L. & Econ. 141, 142 (1979) ("[I]f there were no costs of transacting, then the potential Pareto improvement could be realized by costless bargaining between self-interested economic agents.") Such a world, of course, is quite unfamiliar. George Stigler puts the point nicely:

> If this [world] strikes you as incredible on first hearing, join the club. The world of zero transaction costs turns out to be as strange as the physical world would be with zero friction. Monopolies would be compensated to act like competitors, and insurance companies and banks would not exist.

George Stigler, *The Law and Economics of Public Policy: A Plea to the Scholars*, 1 J.Legal Stud. 1, 12 (1972).

the extent that private economizing successfully reduces transaction costs, the deviation between the real world in which assets are transferred and the frictionless world of the capital asset pricing theory is minimized.   The continued presence of a voluntary social convention -- for example, the pervasive use of business lawyers -- raises an inference that it is a cost-saving, in our terms value-creating, phenomenon.[5]

Formulating a hypothesis about how business lawyers create value, however, requires more than establishing the importance of private innovation as an important method of reducing transaction costs. Two steps are necessary: The specification of precisely how business lawyers can reduce transaction costs, and the tie between their activities and transaction value.

It is useful at this point to return to the idea that a business transaction is the transfer of a capital asset in which the central aspect of the transaction is the asset's valuation. And the role of the business lawyer is precisely as Vonnegut described it in Chapter 1: To look "for situations where large amounts of money are about to change hands." The lawyer places himself strategically in the transfer of valuable assets so as to control the process. He will survive economically -- be allowed to take a little of the treasure before passing it on -- as long as the gains to the parties exceed his fees. Completing the hypothesis of how business lawyers create value now requires only specifying from where these gains come.

This suggests that the tie between legal skills and transaction value is the business lawyer's ability to create a transactional structure that reduces transaction costs and therefore results in more accurate asset pricing. Put in terms of capital asset pricing theory, the business lawyer acts to constrain the extent to which conditions in the real world deviate from the theoretical assumptions of capital asset pricing. The hypothesis about how business lawyers can create value is simply this: Lawyers function as *transaction cost engineers*, devising efficient mechanisms that bridge the gap between capital asset pricing theory's hypothetical world of perfect markets and the less-then-perfect reality of effecting transactions in this world. Value is created when the transactional structure designed by the business lawyer allows the parties to act, *for that transaction*, as if the assumptions on which capital asset pricing theory is based were accurate.

The central role of transaction cost economizing in private ordering is, by now, no longer surprising.[6] What has received less attention is the link

---

[5] For a discussion of the use of evidence of survival in economic theory, see Michael Jensen, *Organization Theory and Methodology*, 58 Acct.Rev. 319, 331-33 (1983).

[6] Oliver Williamson put the matter aptly: "The overall object of the exercise essentially comes down to this: for each abstract description of a transaction, identify the most economical governance structure -- where by governance structure I refer to the institutional framework within which the integrity of a transaction is decided." Oliver Williamson, *Transaction-Cost Economics: The Governance of Contractual Relations*, 22 J.L. & Econ. 233, 234-234 (1979).

between capital asset pricing theory and transaction cost economics, and the institutional framework in which transaction cost economizing takes place. The hypothesis -- the business lawyer as transaction cost engineer -- thus asserts the dual claim that skilled structuring of the transaction's form can create transaction value *and* that business lawyers are primary players at the game. In the next section, we evaluate both the positive and normative implications of the hypothesis using a standard corporate acquisition agreement as the text. If the hypothesis is correct, the traditional contractual approaches reflected in the agreement should be explainable by their relation to one or more of the perfect market assumptions on which capital asset pricing theory is based. And if major elements of a corporate acquisition agreement can be understood by reference to their impact on these assumptions, then this discovery would constitute substantial empirical evidence of business lawyers' potential to create value. Moreover, we would not only better understand the function of different portions of the agreement, but also be better able to draft and negotiate them.

B.   The Acquisition Agreement

1.   An Overview of the Acquisition Agreement

Acquisition agreements have become forms, not in the sense of becoming boilerplate -- enormous amounts of time still are spent on their negotiation -- but in the sense that the general contents of the agreement have by now become pretty much standardized.[7] This is not to say that the distributive consequences of acquisition agreements are likely to be the same. Rather, it is that the problems confronted and the mechanics of the solutions

---

[7] James Freund, a leading practitioner in the mergers and acquisition area, makes this point explicitly: "[M]ost agreements utilized in the mergers and acquisition field do manage to cover pretty much the same ground and contain relatively similar provisions. I'll go further; there are abundant instances of nearly identical words, phrases and clauses, suggesting that respectful plagiarism is indeed the order of the day." James Freund, *Anatomy of a Merger: Strategies and Techniques for Negotiating Corporate Acquisitions* 140 (1975) (footnote omitted). The similarity can also be seen by comparing a number of agreements contained in form books. See *Business Acquisitions* 55-60, 84-165, 240-343 (Paul Gaynor, 2d ed.1981); California Continuing Education of the Bar, *Drafting Agreements for the Sale of Businesses* (1971) [hereinafter cited as *Drafting Agreements*]; California Continuing Education of the Bar, *Drafting Agreements for the Sale of Business -- Supplement* (1983) [hereinafter cited as *Drafting Agreements Supp.*]; *4 West's Legal Forms* (P. Lieberman 2d ed.1982).

Freund also captures something of the process by which the pattern of practice develops: "I freely confess, in small point, to having lifted from the drafts of my friends and adversaries a number of valuable nuggets for further utilization." Freund, *supra* at 140 n.2. The existence of commercial form books, as well as the conscious practice of law firms to create and urge the use of in-house form files, *id.* at 140-141, also reflect the systematization of the process.

adopted are similar, even if the impact of the specific application of the solution to the parties will differ from transaction to transaction. The form of agreement set forth in Appendix C, to which reference will be made throughout this discussion, was selected for use not because it is necessarily the best the profession can offer or even a recommended form, but because it is typical and because it illustrates some of the points we will consider.

A description of the subject necessarily precedes an examination of the functional significance of its parts. A skeletal outline of the form of a typical agreement provides a representative picture.

Description of the Transaction.   The initial, and usually most straightforward, portion of the agreement provides an overall description of the transaction. The parties are identified, the structure of the transaction -- for example, a purchase of stock or assets, or some triangular variation -- is described, and details concerning such matters as the timing and location of the closing of the transaction are set forth.

Price and Terms of Payment.   The next portion of the agreement typically focuses on the price to be paid and the medium and timing of payment. The text is most straightforward when the medium of payment is cash and the entire amount is to be paid on closing.[8]   But where the transaction contemplates other than immediate payment of the entire purchase price, the document inevitably becomes a great deal more complicated. For example, at the time the agreement is prepared, it may be possible to describe the purchase price only by reference to a formula because its amount depends on the performance of the business over some period following the agreement's execution.[9]   As discussed shortly, the need to specify the appropriate performance measure and to protect against manipulation of the indicia of performance makes for a more expansive discussion in the document. Similarly, when the medium of payment is other than cash, the need to address valuation issues -- for example, if the consideration will be shares of the acquirer's stock, how the effects of pre-closing changes in the market price of the stock will be shared -- also expands the document's text.[10]   Of course, if the timing of the payment will

---

[8] There are complications, however, even in an all-cash transaction. For example, if the purchase price is not literally to be paid in cash, but by the transfer of bank funds, then specification of the character of the funds to be provided -- e.g., Clearinghouse Funds, same-day funds -- can affect the availability of overnight investment, the interest on which can be a substantial amount in a major transaction.

[9] If the period extends beyond the closing of the agreement, as well as beyond its execution, the technique is commonly referred to as a contingent-price formula or simply as an "earnout." This technique is considered in detail in Section B.2 of this Chapter, *infra*.

[10] Suppose that the acquisition agreement provides that the consideration for the purchase of the target's assets will be one million shares of the acquirer's common stock that, at the time of the agreement's execution, trade for $50 per share -- a $50 million transaction. If the price of the acquirer's stock changes during the post-execution/pre-closing period, however,

be delayed -- for example, if the medium of payment will be the acquirer's note -- the agreement must cover what is, in effect, an additional transaction: a loan from the target to the acquirer.[11]

Representations and Warranties. The next major portion of the agreement consists of representations and warranties made by the target and, typically to a much lesser extent, by the acquirer.[12] These provisions consist of a series of detailed statements of fact concerning the relevant business. The target commonly will warrant, *inter alia*, the accuracy of its financial statements; the absence of any liabilities for taxes or other matters accruing after the date of its most recent audited financial statements including, most importantly, the absence of contingent liabilities; the ownership and condition of various assets of importance to the operation of the target's business; the existence of litigation against the target, whether actual or threatened; and the extent to which the target's operations are unionized.[13] Thoroughly done, this portion of the acquisition agreement paints a detailed picture of the target -- the capital asset that is being acquired.

Covenants and Conditions. The two final steps in the survey of the major portions of a typical acquisition agreement result from the fact that many acquisition transactions contemplate a significant gap between the date

---

the value of the transaction will change accordingly. Thus, the acquisition agreement typically will allocate the risk of such price fluctuation between the parties. There is typically not a parallel problem with movements in the price of the target's stock because the potential for arbitrage will cause its value to be a function of the value of the acquirer's stock unless there is a possibility either that the transaction will not occur, or that a higher offer for the target will be made. In those cases, the price of the target's stock would likewise reflect these possibilities through the action of risk arbitraguers.

[11] Thus, matters such as the interest rate, security, payment schedule, and acceleration terms all must be negotiated just as in a transaction involving *only* a loan. Where the note is big enough (a rather frequent occurrence in the increasingly common divestiture transaction where the subject of the acquisition is a division of a larger company), the transaction may make the divesting company one of the acquirer's major creditors with the same need for protection as other major lenders. As a result, one would expect the acquisition agreement to contain the same type of detailed operating covenants as a standard institutional loan agreement.

[12] The asymmetry between the extent of the acquirer's and target's representations and warranties results from the different character of their roles in the transaction. At the extreme, in an all-cash transaction that is both executed and closed at the same time, the only fact concerning the acquirer that will be of interest to the target is that the check be good. As the time between execution and closing grows, and as the character of the consideration moves from cash to a form like stock or debt, the value of which depends on the future performance of the acquirer, the target begins to take on some of the attributes of an acquirer and the asymmetry in the extent of representations and warranties is reduced.

[13] See *Drafting Agreements, supra* note 7, at 53-182; *Drafting Agreements Supp., supra* note 7, at 45-64; Freund (1975), *supra* note 7, at 248-53; Jere McGaffey, *Buying, Selling, and Merging Businesses,* 37-41 (1979); Howard Weinreich, *Contract of Sale,* in *1 Business Acquisitions* 145, 170-86 (John Herz & Charles Baller eds., 2d ed.1981).

on which the acquisition agreement is signed and the date on which the transaction is closed. Whether delay is caused by regulatory necessity, such as the requirement that a proxy statement seeking the approval of the transaction by the target's shareholders be filed and reviewed by the Securities and Exchange Commission, by regulatory convenience, such as the need for an Internal Revenue Service ruling as to the income tax consequences of the transaction, or simply by the acquirer's need for additional time to complete its investigation of the target,[14] the temporal gap between execution and closing requires contractual bridging. This is accomplished by two complementary techniques: *Covenants* governing the operation of the business during the gap period, and *conditions* which, if not satisfied, relieve a party of its obligation to complete the transaction. Typically these two techniques combine with the representations and warranties to operate as a unit, providing a hierarchy of obligations and the potential for a hierarchy of remedies if one or more of the other party's obligations are not met.[15] Thus a covenant may require that the target maintain working capital above a specified level pending closing. At the same time, the target also may have warranted that working capital was, and at closing will be, above the specified level, and the acquirer's obligation to close the transaction may be conditioned generally on the accuracy of the

---

[14] The critical role of the investigation that occurs in the post-agreement/pre-closing period is illustrated by the course of the transaction in which American Express Co. purchased Investors Diversified Services, Inc. ("IDS"), the principal subsidiary of Alleghany Corp. On July 13, 1983, American Express announced the transaction, at a purchase price of $1.01 billion in American Express common stock. *Alleghany to Sell Most of Its Assets for $1.01 Billion*, Wall St.J., July 13, 1983, at 3, col.1. By August 12, 1983, the intensive investigation of IDS by American Express had raised doubts about whether American Express would actually proceed with the transaction. *Some Officials at American Express Fear Problems if IDS Purchase Goes Through*, Wall St.J., August 12, 1983, at 3, cols.2-3. These doubts proved correct when, on August 17, 1983, American Express announced that it would not proceed with the acquisition of IDS "after a review of the company disclosed potential problems in absorbing it." *American Express Abandons Plan to Buy Alleghany Assets After Operations Check*, Wall St.J., Aug. 17, 1983, at 3, cols.2-3. Abandonment proved only temporary as by late September American Express and Alleghany had renegotiated the transaction at a price of $773 million, some $237 million lower than the original price. *Alleghany to Sell IDS to American Express Co.*, Wall St.J., Sept. 27, 1983, at 2, col.2.

Available data suggest that the cancellation of a friendly acquisition by the acquirer after initial announcement of the transaction is not an isolated phenomenon. According to one study of all announced mergers among New York Stock Exchange listed companies from 1971 through 1977, 36% were canceled by the acquirer prior to their consummation. Peter Dodd, *Merger Proposals, Management Discretion and Stockholder Wealth*, 8 J.Fin.Econ. 105 (1980). Thus, the acquirer's post-announcement investigation seems to be of major importance.

There also are other non-regulatory reasons for a delay between execution of an agreement and the closing of the transaction. For example, where the seller's lease or contract rights require consent for assignment or assumption, these must be secured during the period.

[15] The importance of the interaction of these elements of the agreement is thoughtfully canvassed in Freund (1975), *supra* note 7, at 153-61.

target's representations and warranties as of the date of closing, on the target's satisfaction of all covenants during the pre-closing period, and, specifically, on the required level of working capital at the closing date. A failure to maintain adequate working capital will then constitute both a breach of warranty and a violation of a covenant, as well as providing the acquirer with a number of justifications for not completing the transaction.[16]

In formal terms, then, the acquisition agreement is simply a more complicated version of what one would expect in any sales agreement: It states the form and terms of the transaction, describes the asset to be transferred, and specifies the manner in which the asset will be preserved pending the completion of the transaction. The possibility that this contractual structure has the potential to create value, however, arises not from a formal overview, but from the manner in which different elements of the agreement respond to the problem of constraining the effect of real world deviations from capital asset pricing theory's perfect market assumptions. For this purpose, it is necessary to focus attention directly on the assumptions themselves, particularly the assumptions that all investors have homogeneous expectations, that they share a common time horizon, that information is costlessly available to all, and that there are no other transaction costs. It is in response to the potential impact of this unholy host that the hypothesis holds out the potential for a value-creating role for business lawyers.

2. The Failure of the Homogeneous-Expectations Assumption: The Earnout Response

a. *Conceptual Analysis*

We can begin with the assumption that can be most clearly examined from this perspective: The assumption that all investors have homogeneous expectations. The critical place in asset pricing theory of the assumption that all investors share the same beliefs about the future risk and return associated with owning the asset in question, in our case a business, is obvious: As long as we all agree about the future income stream associated with owning that business and about the systematic risk associated with that income, there is no reason to expect potential buyers and sellers of the business to disagree about its price. But it is also obvious that buyers and sellers often *do not* share common expectations concerning the business future.

---

[16] Having alternative and, indeed, cumulative remedies for a particular event can be of substantial benefit to an acquirer. For example, the failure of a condition would provide only an excuse not to close. A breach of warranty or a violation of a covenant would additionally give rise to a damage action for expenses if the decision were made not to close and, depending on the terms of the agreement, perhaps a damage action for the reduced value of the target even if the acquirer went forward with the acquisition. See Freund (1975), *supra* note 7, at 287-89; Sue Ann Dillport, *Breaches and Remedies*, in 2 *Business Acquisitions* 1249 (John Herz & Charles Baller eds., 2d ed.1981).

Imagine a negotiation between the presidents of an acquirer and a target concerning the price at which the transaction will take place. Imagine further that the negotiations have progressed to the point where agreement has been reached on an abstract, but nonetheless important, pricing principle, that the appropriate way to value the target's business is $1 in purchase price for each $1 in annual sales.[17]   The critical nature of the homogeneous-expectations assumption should be apparent.   Even after agreement on a valuation principle, the parties will agree on price *only* if they share the same expectations about the target's future sales.   The problem, of course, is that they will not. The negotiating dance that results is familiar to practitioners.

Now suppose that the acquirer's president, having done his homework, believes that there is a 50% chance the target will do $10 million in sales next year and a 50% chance that it will do only $5 million. The expected value of the alternatives is $7.5 million[18] which the acquirer's president offers as the purchase price that the agreed-upon valuation principle dictates. The president of the target, not surprisingly, has different expectations. He is much more optimistic about the probabilities associated with next year's sales. His homework suggests an 85% chance of $10 million in sales and only a 15% chance of sales as low as $5 million. These figures yield an expected value, and a purchase price under the agreed valuation principle, of $9.25 million.[19] The result is inaccurate pricing at best and, because of the resulting conflict over the purchase price, at worst no transaction at all if the parties are unable to resolve their differences.

It is important to emphasize at this point that the problem that "kills" our hypothetical deal is not distributional conflict -- disagreement over sharing the gains from the transaction. The distributional principle in the form of a valuation formula has already been approved. Rather, the problem is an example of the failure of the homogeneous-expectations assumption: The parties simply have different expectations concerning the future performance of the business. If this problem could be solved, a deal could

---

[17] The example could be restated directly in the terms of capital asset pricing theory without much difficulty. Suppose that we could establish the systematic risk associated with the target's business. This would allow us to determine the return which the market deems necessary to bear such risk. The purchase price would then represent the capitalized value of that return. The issue in doubt would remain, as in the text, whether the target's future performance would generate the necessary results. The application of capital asset pricing theory to capital budgeting is examined in Chapter 4D, *supra*.

[18] The calculation is:

$10 million X	.50	=	$5.0 million
5 million X	.50	=	$2.5 million
			$7.5 million

[19] The calculation is:

$10 million X	.85	=	$8.50 million
5 million X	.15	=	$0.75 million
			$9.25 million

be made. Tautologically, the value of the transaction would be increased. And if the hypothesis about what business lawyers do is correct, a particularly inviting opportunity then exists for value creation by a business lawyer. The lawyer can increase the value of the transaction if he can devise a transactional structure that creates homogeneous expectations.

As the hypothesis predicts, there is a familiar remedy, commonly called an "earnout" or "contingent price" deal, for this failure of the homogeneous-expectations assumption. It is intended, as a prominent practitioner has put it, to "bridge the negotiating gap between a seller who thinks his business is worth more than its historical earnings justify and a purchaser who hails from Missouri."[20] The solution that business lawyers resort to for this problem is one that economists refer to as state-contingent contracting.[21] Its central insight is that the difference in expectations between the parties as to the probabilities assigned to the occurrence of future events will ultimately disappear as time transforms a prediction of next year's sales into historical fact. If determination of the purchase price can be delayed until next year's sales are known with certainty, the deal can be made. The solution, therefore, is to formulate the purchase price as an initial payment, here $7.5 million, to be followed by an additional payment at the close of the next fiscal year equal, in this case, to $1 for each $1 of sales in excess of $7.5 million. The problem of non-homogeneous expectations is avoided by making the failure irrelevant. Only uncertainty concerning the future forced the parties to rely on expectations about the future; the earnout solution allows the purchase price to be set after that uncertainty has been resolved. That is, each party is allowed to act *as if* his expectation was shared by the other. In effect he bets on the accuracy of his expectation, with a settling up only after the uncertainty has been eliminated and the parties really do have homogeneous beliefs concerning the matter.

The business lawyer's traditional response to failure of the homogeneous-expectations assumption can thus create value by allowing a transaction to go forward that might otherwise not have occurred. But the technique's potential for value creation is greater than just allowing the deal to be made; it also may increase the total value of the deal beyond that which would have resulted even if the parties were capable of compromising their differences. Recall that under capital asset pricing theory the value of the business turns on both the expected return -- the weighted average of the possible sales for the next year in our hypothetical -- and the systematic risk associated with that return. The effect of the contingent price arrangement is to reduce the acquirer's risk by transforming the price from a function of

---

[20] Freund (1975), *supra* note 7, at 205.

[21] See Kenneth Arrow, *Essays in the Theory of Risk-Bearing* 121-43 (1971); Oliver Williamson, *Markets and Hierarchies: Analysis and Antitrust Implications* 21-23 (1975). The idea is that a contract will specify a different result for each possible outcome of an uncertain future event. The result called for by the contract is thus contingent on the actual outcome of the uncertain event -- i.e., which "state" of the world actually occurs.

expected -- risky -- returns to one of certain returns. Thus, the acquirer should be willing to pay a higher price per unit of sales because there is no risk associated with that return.[22]

Thus far, the hypothesis about what business lawyers do and how they create value seems confirmed. At least with respect to the failure of the homogeneous-expectations assumption, business lawyers create a transactional structure which bridges the gap between the perfect market assumptions of capital asset pricing theory and the imperfect reality of transacting.

b.   *Regulatory Constraints*

Despite the potential value of an earnout in mitigating the parties' differing expectations, regulatory constraints significantly limit the manner in which the technique can be implemented and, in some cases, make its use undesirable. These limitations result from the impact of an earnout on the tax and accounting treatment of the transaction.

The critical tax constraints apply to transactions that are intended to qualify as reorganizations.[23] For an acquisition to qualify as any of the forms of reorganization, the selling shareholders must receive all or a significant portion of their consideration in the form of the acquiring company's voting stock. The issue posed by an earnout arrangement is whether the contingent right to receive voting stock if the conditions of the earnout are met counts as voting stock.[24] The Internal Revenue Service has established guidelines specifying the circumstances under which it will issue a ruling that an earnout will be treated as voting stock.[25] For planning purposes, the most important of the ruling requirements are:

(1) At least 50% of the maximum number of shares issuable in the transaction must be issued at the outset.

---

[22] The target also benefits because the target is inevitably better informed than the acquirer about its prospects and, as a result, is better able to "price" the risk associated with its future sales. Thus, the target is likely to be the best risk bearer. This need not, however, always be the case. Where the target is more risk averse than the acquirer, as frequently may be the case in the acquisition of a privately held company by a publicly held company, and where the target's future depends on information to which the acquirer has better access -- the potential for synergy comes to mind as an example -- it becomes more difficult to determine the party best able to price and bear the risk.

[23] The general requirements for qualification as a reorganization are reviewed in Chapter 12A.1, *supra*.

[24] For example, in a *B* reorganization the consideration must be solely voting stock. If the shareholders' rights under the earnout are not treated as voting stock, the entire transaction will not qualify as a reorganization.

[25] Rev.Proc. 77-37, § 3.03, 1977-2 CB 568, as amplified by Rev.Proc. 84-42, 1984-20 IRB 12.

(2) The earnout must terminate and all stock earned must be issued within five years after the closing of the transaction.

(3) The right to receive earnout stock cannot be assignable.

The prohibition of assignable interests in earnout shares has a critical impact on the use of the earnout technique in the acquisition of public companies. Despite the attraction of the technique as a response to divergent beliefs about the future of the target company's business, it may well be difficult to persuade public shareholders to accept an entirely illiquid investment. In response to a different problem, Ness & Indoe, suggest as an alternative to an earnout the issuance of a voting convertible preferred stock whose conversion ratio is adjusted to increase the number of shares into which the preferred may be converted if the target's post-acquisition earnings reach specified levels.[26] Ness & Indoe report that the Internal Revenue Service has ruled that adjustment of the conversion rate to implement an earnout will not result in the shareholders being treated as having received a taxable stock dividend under IRC § 305(c). Would this approach also serve to avoid the restriction on making rights under an earnout nontransferable?

Where the earnout is created in connection with a taxable transaction, the critical issue is whether a cash basis shareholder must report the value of the earnout right as income in the year the transaction closes despite the fact that actual payment pursuant to the earnout is both deferred and contingent. Prior to the amendments to IRC § 453 by the Installment Sales Revision Act of 1980,[27] installment sales treatment was not available for contingent payments; the Internal Revenue Service required immediate valuation and recognition. Under the regulations adopted under § 453 following amendment, earnout payments can be reported on the installment basis.

The constraint imposed on the use of an earnout by accounting rules results from the earnout's impact on the availability of the pooling of interests method of accounting for the acquisition. Under Paragraph 47-g of Accounting Principles Board Opinion No. 16, the pooling of interests method cannot be used if the transaction contemplates the issuance of contingent stock in an earnout.[28] Despite the evidence that the manner of accounting for an acquisition does not effect the post-acquisition price of the acquiring

---

[26] Theodore Ness & William Indoe, *Tax Planning for Dispositions of Business Interests* 6-29, 30 (1985). The solution was directed at the problem of how to avoid original issue discount under IRC § 1274, or imputed interest under IRC § 483, caused by an earnout's deferral of the receipt of consideration. An alternative approach to this problem is to issue the stock at the outset, but place it in escrow subject to forfeiture if the earnout conditions are not met. The Internal Revenue Service has ruled that, so long as shareholders are allowed to vote and receive dividends on the escrowed stock, no stock released from escrow will be treated as imputed interest or original issue discount. Rev.Rul. 70-120, 1970-1 CB 124. For an example of such an approach see Section II.B of the form of acquisition agreement in Appendix C.

[27] Pub.L.No. 96-471, 94 Stat. 2,247 (1980).

[28] Accounting Principles Board Opinion No. 16 is excerpted in Chapter 13, *supra*.

company's stock, the adoption of APB Opinion No. 16 in 1970 resulted in a sharp reduction in the use of earnouts.[29] In the 1980s, however, earnouts enjoyed something of a renaissance, although in a quite different form, when for other reasons the market for corporate control was not conducive to the all stock transactions that would satisfy APB Opinion No. 16's conditions for pooling. One example was the structure of General Motors' acquisition of Electronic Data Systems Corp. EDS shareholders received cash plus shares of a new GM Class E common stock whose dividend level was tied to the post-acquisition performance of EDS. GM used a similar structure for its acquisition of Hughes Aircraft Corp., and Eli Lily & Cos. used a publicly traded contingent payment right in its acquisition of Hybritech Inc.[30]

3.   The Failure of the Common-Time-Horizon Assumption: Conduct of the Business During the Earnout Period

The failure of a second assumption -- this time that investors measure risk and return over the same period -- provides an additional opportunity for business lawyers to create value. This can be seen most easily by pursuing discussion of the earnout solution just considered. The earnout concept responds to the failure of the homogeneous-expectations assumption. Efforts to make the concept operational, however, highlight the absence of a common time horizon and the resulting potential for strategic, opportunistic behavior. Where the parties do have different time horizons, each has an incentive to maximize value in the period relevant to the other party. This conflict reduces the value of the transaction.[31]

Consider first what behavior we would expect during the earnout's one-year measuring period if the target's original management were allowed to run the company for that time. From the target's perspective, the earnout formula reduces to one year the relevant period over which asset value is to be determined; at the end of that year the target's shareholders will receive whatever payment is due under the earnout formula. At least for them, the asset will cease to exist. To the target's shareholders, therefore, the asset is worth only what it can earn for them in a year's time. Their goal is to maximize value over that short period. The acquirer, in contrast, is concerned with the value of the business over a much longer period: The

---

[29] See Freund (1975), *supra* note 7, at 205. See Chapter 13, *supra*.

[30] See Robert Herz & Edward Abahoonie, *Alphabet Stocks and CPUs: Innovative but Complex*, 21 Mergers & Acquisitions 24 (Nov./Dec.1986).

[31] We are taking some liberties in our treatment of this assumption. The requirement that investors maximize end-of-period wealth results in a one-period model that avoids difficult statistical problems associated with compounding returns over multiple periods. See Robert Merton, *An Intertemporal Capital Asset Pricing Model,* 41 Econometrica 867 (1973). In the absence of an impersonal market, as in a corporate acquisition, a shift to a multi-period setting, where buyers and sellers may maximize over different periods, also causes serious strategic problems. These, rather than the statistical problems, are the object of concern here.

entire time it expects to operate the target's business. Accordingly, the acquirer's behavior will differ substantially from that which would be dictated by the target's short-term orientation.

Returning to the terms of the hypothetical earnout formula -- an additional $1 in purchase price for each $1 in sales over $7.5 million -- the target would maximize sales during the one-year measuring period. For example, prices might be cut and advertising expenditures substantially increased, even if these actions meant that the company actually suffered a loss. In contrast, the acquirer, which would ultimately bear the loss because it continues to own the company after the one year period, has a very different interest. And the conflict is not merely the result of a poorly specified earnout formula. Stating the formula in terms of profits rather than sales, thus eliminating the target's incentive to maximize sales at the expense of the acquirer's long term interest in earnings, would be a possible improvement. But even then the different time horizons would create an incentive for the target's management to behave opportunistically. Short-term profits could be maximized by eliminating research and development expenditures, cutting maintenance, and, in general, deferring expenses to later periods.

This failure of the common-time-horizon assumption reduces the value of the transaction. So long as the acquirer anticipates that the target's management will behave opportunistically -- which hardly requires a crystal ball -- it will reduce its offer accordingly. The business lawyer then has the opportunity to create value by devising a transaction structure that constrains the target's ability to maximize the value of the business over a period different from that relevant to the acquirer.[32] The typical earnout agreement responds to precisely this challenge.

---

[32] The problem is not avoided if the acquirer undertakes to operate the business. Rather, the opportunity to behave strategically merely shifts to the acquirer. From its perspective, value is maximized by deferring sales or earnings to the following year, thereby reducing the purchase price of the business. This behavior, of course, would be anticipated by the target and, unless the behavior were prohibited by contract, would alter the terms on which it would be willing to sell the business.

One might argue that if the acquirer could fully anticipate the target's opportunistic behavior in setting the purchase price, no potential for value creation would exist because the net purchase price to the acquirer -- the reduced purchase price plus the cost of the target's opportunistic behavior -- would remain the same, i.e., it would be a zero-sum game. In fact, the game is negative-sum in the absence of a transactional structure that responds to the failure of the common-time-horizon assumption. First, it is likely to be quite difficult to estimate the cost of allowing the target to behave opportunistically: The lack of precision results in greater risk for the acquirer and a lower value for the transaction. Second, the target's or acquirer's short-run behavior may result in a *decrease* in the value of the business. For example, if research and development is deferred, opportunities may be lost that cannot be recovered. Although the acquirer may not be cheated -- the price of the business would be reduced to reflect the reduction in value -- the business would be worth more to both parties if a transactional structure could be designed that prevents value-reducing behavior.

Stated most generally, a complete earnout formula is a complicated state-contingent contract, that, by carefully specifying in advance the impact on the purchase price of all events that might occur during the earnout period, substantially reduces the incentives and opportunity for the parties to behave strategically. Actually creating such a formula, however, poses difficult problems of design and drafting. Consider, for example, the following issues.

How do you eliminate the perverse incentives caused by an earnout formula that specifies either sales or earnings as the sole measure of success? Put differently, how do you prevent the existence of the earnout from influencing the outcome of a business decision that poses a short run tradeoff between sales and earnings? The acquisition agreement in Appendix C confronts this problem in Section II.B by requiring both sales growth *and* an increase in profits as a percentage of sales. How effectively does that combination constrain strategic behavior? Could a cut in the research and development budget of a research oriented company serve to increase profits as a percentage of sales without, at least in the short run, adversely affecting sales growth? How do you determine which variables bearing on the target company's operation must be specified in the formula to prevent their manipulation? Could sensitivity analysis[33] (together with a good spread sheet program) help answer this question?

How long should the earnout period be? From the target's perspective, a multi-year period may be preferable to avoid the impact of a single unpredictable event adversely affecting the target company's chances under a one year earnout. Additionally, a multi-year period reduces the influence of the existence of the earnout on operating decisions. If the target will get a number of bites at the apple, the acquirer has less incentive to influence the target's operations so as to reduce the target's chance of success in any one year; an effort to reduce the target's chance of success over a number of years likely poses too great a risk of damaging the target in a way that will not disappear after the earnout is over.

The choice of a multi-year period, however, raises other issues. For example, are the years independent or cumulative? If the earnout is not met in one year, must the deficit be made up before the earnout can be met in a subsequent year? Is the portion of the earnout not made in one year lost forever, or may it be made up in subsequent years? If the earnout formula is exceeded in one year, does the excess carry over to give the target a head start in the next period?

How does the acquisition agreement in Appendix C handle these problems? Note that under Section II.B. nothing cumulates until the end of the third year at which point the trigger for release of the remainder of the earnout is meeting the sales and earnings requirements for the third year *plus* the appropriate earnings percentage of whatever sales were in the first two

---

[33] See Chapter 6A, *supra.*

years. What kind of a compromise between the acquirer and the target does this resolution suggest?

How are earnings defined for purposes of the formula? Most importantly, is there a way to segregate the earnings of what constituted the pre-acquisition target company? Even though the acquisition agreement in Appendix C contemplates that the target will remain a separate subsidiary, the agreement anticipates the possibility that additional operations may be added or some removed; Section II.B.2.e defines the relevant earnings as those of the "business operations which constituted the Target on the date of closing."

Assuming that the business of the target can be segregated, how will earnings be computed? Is it sufficient simply to refer to earnings "computed in accordance with generally accepted accounting principles consistently applied?" Would this definition include non-operating gains? If there are assets that the target does not need to conduct its business, should gain on their sale count toward the earnout? Suppose that the consideration paid is greater than the book value of the target's assets, and that Accounting Principles Board Opinion No. 16 requires that the acquisition be accounted for as a purchase. Will earnings be reduced by the higher depreciation associated with the increase in asset value resulting from purchase accounting? Does GAPP resolve how large an overhead or central office allocation can be charged against the target's earnings?

Who gets to run the business during the earnout period? If it is target management, under what circumstances can the acquirer intervene? After all, the purpose of making the acquisition was not just to facilitate the earnout; one can easily imagine that competitive conditions could put the acquirer in a position where it had to take action even though it would interfere with the operation of the earnout.

Finally, who should bear the risk of industry-wide changes that influence target company performance? If target company shareholders are more risk averse than the acquiring company, the risk can be shifted to the acquiring company by measuring performance, at least in part, relative to other companies in the industry. Pay out would be in part keyed to performing better than the target's competitors.[34]

A thoroughly specified earnout formula is thus extraordinarily complex and, in any event, cannot entirely eliminate the potential for strategic behavior. To be fully effective, a formula would have to specify not only the complete production function for the business, but all possible exogenous events that might occur during the earnout period and the impact of such

---

[34] This approach is a familiar technique in devising incentive contracts; the point is to minimize the risk necessary to create the incentive. See Paul Milgrom & John Roberts, *Economics, Organization and Management* Ch.7 (1991). The employment contract of the head of Salomon Brothers, Inc., reflects this approach. The individual's rewards are based in part on Salomon Brothers' absolute performance relative to its competitors. See Michael Siconolfi, *Salomon's Chief Stands to Hit the Jackpot*, Wall St.J., May 5, 1994, p.C1.

events on the formula. Neither, of course, is possible. Moreover, the cost of detailed contracting -- not just in lawyers' fees, but in the time and goodwill of the parties -- will be substantial and in many cases prohibitive. There will be times, then, where the gain in transaction value resulting from ameliorating the failure of the homogeneous-expectations or common-time-horizons assumptions will be outweighed by the cost of the cure. But this possibility merely constrains, rather than eliminates, the potential for value creation by business lawyers. That transaction costs are, at some level, irreducible hardly diminishes the value of efforts to keep costs at that level. It is value creation of the sort that reflects what clients may mean by the comment that a particular lawyer has good "judgment," to know when the game is not worth the candle.[35]

4. The Failure of the Costless-Information Assumption: Representations, Warranties, Indemnification, and Opinions

Perhaps the most important assumption of all is that information is costlessly available to all parties. Its central importance derives in part because it is, in a sense considered shortly, a *master* assumption that controls the other assumptions we have considered, and in part because it is in response to its failure that business lawyers have been most creative.

The relation between the costless-information assumption and the homogeneous-expectations assumption illustrates the central role for information problems in our analysis. For our purposes, information is data that can alter the parties' beliefs about the price of an asset. But it is also useful to characterize information in terms of a second attribute: To distinguish between the "hard" information of known "facts" and the "soft" information of forecasts and predictions.

This fact/forecast dichotomy rests on the simple difference between the fixed past and the uncertain future, a distinction that can be illustrated by reference to a hypothetical fully informed trader.[36] Imagine a trader who has

---

[35] There has been a spate of continuing education programs emphasizing the cost-effective use of lawyers. See, e.g., Ronald Gilson & Robert Mnookin, *The Cost Effective Use of Counsel: Strategies for Controlling Your Company's Legal Costs* (June 24, 1982); Ronald Gilson & Robert Mnookin, *Reducing the Cost of Outside Counsel: Strategies for Controlling Your Company's Legal Costs* (June 5, 1981). A central theme in this movement is that the quality of legal services cannot be evaluated in the abstract, but only in a particular context. Thus, careful and detailed contract drafting or litigation discovery is "good" work *only* if the matter warrants the expense. In this sense, clients increasingly seem to be equating a lawyer's judgment with the wisdom of knowing when not to "over-lawyer" a transaction or lawsuit. Cf. Steven Shavell, *The Design of Contracts and Remedies for Breach*, 99 Q.J.Econ. 121 (1984) (costs of contracting must be incorporated into a model for determining optimal contractual provisions).

[36] The discussion of the character of information that follows in the text is based on Ronald Gilson & Reinier Kraakman, *The Mechanisms of Market Efficiency,* 70 Va.L.Rev.

knowledge of all past events -- "hard" information because it concerns events that have already occurred -- relevant to pricing an asset. Even so thoroughly endowed a trader would still lack a type of information critical to asset pricing. Because asset value ultimately depends on predictions of *future* earnings, hard information about *past* events alone is insufficient for accurate pricing. Soft information -- forecasts of future events -- is also necessary.

The homogeneous-expectations assumption considered earlier is thus really an assumption that all parties have the same soft information. Understanding the relation between soft and hard information then should also disclose the relation between the homogeneous-expectations assumption and the costless-information assumption. The critical point is that our forecasts of the future are based, in significant part, on our knowledge of the past; if we know, for example, that high interest rates adversely affected performance of a company in the past, our prediction of future performance will be substantially influenced by that fact. Changes in hard facts will change soft projections.

So understood, a major part of the reason for the failure of the homogeneous-expectations assumption -- potential acquirers and targets have different soft facts -- is that they base their expectations on different hard facts.[37] In this sense, the costless-information assumption might be rephrased as the assumption of *homogeneous retrospection.* The assumption of homogeneous *expectations* would require that the parties share common soft facts; that of homogeneous *retrospection* would require common hard facts. And if acquisition of hard facts is not only costly, but differentially so, the impact on asset pricing is clear: There will be greater disagreement about the price of an asset, and the resulting pattern of prices will be suboptimal.

The business lawyer's response to the failure of the homogeneous-expectations assumption has been to devise a structure -- state-contingent pricing -- which does not *eliminate* the parties' differences in expectations, but merely reduces the *impact* of the disagreement. Because the disagreement in significant measure results from differences in hard information held by the parties, efforts to constrain the extent of the conflict in expectations (in contrast to efforts to minimize the impact of the conflict) respond to the failure of the costless-information assumption. And because these differences result from differential information costs for the acquirer and target, if business lawyers do function to alleviate failures of the perfect market assumptions underlying capital asset pricing theory, we would then expect the typical corporate acquisition agreement to contain provisions

---

549, 560-64 (1984), reprinted in Chapter 5, *supra.*

[37] There also may be differences in forecasting ability, because of differences in training or in inherent ability of the forecasters, even given identical hard facts.

designed to reduce the extent of information asymmetry -- information differences between the acquirer and target.[38]

The portion of the acquisition agreement dealing with representations and warranties -- commonly the longest part of a typical acquisition agreement and the portion that usually requires the most time for a lawyer to negotiate[39] -- has as its primary purpose to remedy conditions of asymmetrical information in the least-cost manner. To understand the way in which the device of representations and warranties operates to reduce information asymmetry between the acquirer and the target, it is helpful to distinguish between the costs of acquiring new information and the costs of verifying previously acquired information.

a.   *Costs of Acquiring Information*

During the negotiation, the acquirer and target will face different costs of information acquisition for two important reasons. First, as a simple result of its prior operation of the business, the target will already have large amounts of information concerning the business that the acquirer does not have, but would like to acquire. Second, there usually will be information that neither party has, but that one or both would like and which one or the other can acquire more cheaply. The question is then how both of these situations are dealt with in the acquisition agreement so as to reduce the informational differences between the parties at the lowest possible cost.

At first, one might wonder why any cooperative effort is necessary. Assuming that the target did not affirmatively block the acquirer's efforts to acquire the information the acquirer wanted (and the target already had), nothing would prevent the acquirer from independently acquiring the desired information. Similarly, assuming both parties had the opportunity to acquire the desired new information, nothing would prevent both parties from independently acquiring it.

Actually, however, it is in the target's best interest to make the information that the target already has available to the acquirer as cheaply as possible. Suppose the target refused to assist the acquirer in securing a particular piece of information that the target already had. If the information

---

[38] If information costs were not different, then the parties would hold the same facts and, subject to the conditions of the previous note, reach the same predictions. To be sure, they would still be less accurate than if information were costless, but then the role of the business lawyer would be to lower the cost of information generally, rather than, as the discussion will emphasize, to reduce the cost differential between the parties. While the lawyer can accomplish this with respect to particular types of information, this function is likely to be best performed by a different professional -- the accountant.

[39] James Freund observes: "There are no known statistics on the subject, but I'm willing to bet my briefcase that lawyers spend more time negotiating 'Representations and Warranties of the Seller' than any other single article in the typical acquisition agreement." Freund (1975), *supra* note 7, at 229.

could have either a positive or negative value on the acquirer's evaluation of the worth of the business, a rational acquirer would infer from the target's refusal to cooperate that the information must be unfavorable. Thus, the target has little incentive to withhold the information.[40] Indeed, the same result would follow even if the information in question would not alter the acquirer's estimate of the value of the business, but only increase the certainty with which that estimate was held.[41] Once we have established that the target wants the acquirer to have the information, the only issue that remains is which party can produce it most cheaply. The total price the acquirer will pay for the business is the sum of the amount to be paid to the target and the transaction costs incurred by the acquirer in effecting the transaction. To the extent that the acquirer's information costs are reduced, there simply is more left over for division between the acquirer and the target.

Precisely the same analysis holds for information that neither party has yet acquired. The target could refuse to cooperate with the acquirer in its acquisition. To do so, however, would merely increase the information costs associated with the transaction to the detriment of both parties.

There is thus an incentive for the parties to cooperate both to reduce informational asymmetries between them and to reduce the costs of acquiring information either believes necessary for the transaction. As a result, we would expect an acquisition agreement to contain provisions for three kinds of cooperative behavior concerning information acquisition costs. First, the agreement would facilitate the transfer of information the target already has to the acquirer. Second, the agreement would allocate the responsibility of producing information that neither the target nor the acquirer already has to the party who can acquire it most cheaply, thereby both avoiding duplication

---

[40] See Sanford Grossman, *The Informational Role of Warranties and Private Disclosure About Product Quality,* 24 J.L. & Econ. 461, 479 (1981); Sanford Grossman & Oliver Hart, *Disclosure Laws and Takeover Bids,* 35 J.Fin. 323 (1980). The analysis becomes more complicated, however, if disclosure imposes other kinds of costs on the target -- for example, disclosure of some accounting data might provide to competitors insights into the target's future strategy, and disclosure of product information might allow competitors more easily to duplicate the target's product. Where there are such proprietary costs to disclosure, the signal conveyed by nondisclosure becomes "noisy": Nondisclosure may mean that the information kept private is negative; less ominously, it may mean that disclosure of the information would be costly. The result would be an equilibrium amount of nondisclosure. Robert Verrecchia, *Discretionary Disclosure,* (Working Paper No. 101, Center for Research in Security Prices, Aug.1983). While Verrecchia's argument has important insights for the issue of voluntary disclosure in the setting of organized securities markets, it is much less relevant in the acquisition setting. There the opportunity for face-to-face bargaining allows the use of techniques such as confidentiality agreements, see *3 Business Acquisitions, supra* note 7, at 399-401 (form of confidentiality agreement), that can substantially reduce such proprietary disclosure costs and, as a result, reduce the noise associated with failure to disclose.

[41] In other words, the new information would not alter the mean estimate of value but would reduce the variance associated with the distribution of possible values.

of costs and minimizing those that must be incurred. Finally, the agreement would try to control overspending on information acquisition by identifying not only the type of information that should be acquired, but also how much should be spent on its acquisition.

(1) Facilitating the Transfer of Information to the Acquirer

In the course of negotiating an acquisition, there is an obvious and important information asymmetry between the acquirer and the target. The acquirer will have expended substantial effort in selecting the target from among the number of potential acquisitions considered at a preliminary stage and, in doing so, may well have gathered all the available public information concerning the target. Nonetheless, the target will continue to know substantially more than the acquirer about the business. Much detailed information about the business, of interest to an acquirer but not, perhaps, to the securities market generally, will not have been previously disclosed by the target.[42]

It is in the target's interest, not just in the acquirer's, to reduce this asymmetry. If the target's private information is not otherwise available to the acquirer at all, the acquirer must assume that the undisclosed information reflects unfavorably on the value of the acquirer's business, an assumption that will be reflected to the target's disadvantage in the price the acquirer offers. Alternatively, even if the information could be gathered by the acquirer (a gambit familiar to business lawyers is the target's statement that it will open all its facilities to the acquirer, that the acquirer is welcome to come out and "kick the tires," but that there will be no representations and warranties), it will be considerably cheaper for the target, whose marginal costs of production are very low,[43] to provide the information than for the acquirer to produce it alone. From the acquirer's perspective, the cost of acquiring information is part of its overall acquisition cost; amounts spent on information reduce the amount left over for the target.

This analysis seems to account for the quite detailed picture of the target's business that the standard set of representations and warranties presents. Among other facts covered by Section III of the acquisition agreement in Appendix C, the identity, location and condition of the assets

---

[42] For example, the potential for synergy between the target's business and that of a particular potential acquirer will become of interest to the market only at the point where the possibility of the acquisition comes to the market's attention.

[43] The costs are still *not* zero. While the information exists, there are still costs associated with finding out where within the target's organization the information is located, putting it in a form that is useful to the acquirer, and verifying it. As a result, even some information that already exists may not be worthwhile to locate and transmit. See Section B.4.a.(3) of this Chapter, *infra* (limitations on for what, and how hard, to look). Additionally, there will be situations where a third party will be able to produce the information even more cheaply than the target. See Section B.4.a.(2) of this Chapter, *infra* (lawyers' opinions).

of the business are described;[44]   the nature and extent of liabilities are specified;[45]   and the character of employee relationships -- from senior management to production employees -- is described.[46] This is information that the acquirer wants and the target already has; provision by the target minimizes its acquisition costs to the benefit of both parties.

What remains puzzling, however, is the apparent failure by both business lawyers and clients to recognize that the negotiation of representations and warranties, at least from the perspective of information acquisition costs, presents the occasion for cooperative rather than distributive bargaining.[47] Reducing the cost of acquiring information needed by either party makes both better off. Yet practitioners report that the negotiation of representations and warranties is the most time-consuming aspect of the transaction; it is termed "a nit-picker's delight, a forum for expending prodigious amounts of energy in debating the merits of what sometimes seem to be relatively insignificant items."[48] And it is not merely lawyers who are seduced by the prospect of combat; acquirers also express repugnance for a "three pound acquisition agreement"[49] whose weight and density owe much to the detail of the article titled "Representations and Warranties of the Target." As a result, targets' lawyers are instructed to negotiate ferociously to keep the document -- especially the representations and warranties -- short. Increased information costs needlessly result. Indeed, a business lawyer's inability to explain the actual function of these provisions can often cause the acquirer incorrectly to attribute the document's length to its own lawyer's preference for verbosity and unnecessary complexity. This failure to explain can prevent recognition of value creating activity even when it occurs.

---

[44] See *Drafting Agreements, supra* note 7, at 81-94 (warranties disclosing identity and condition of real property and leases; compliance with zoning; composition, condition, and marketability of inventory; personal property and condition; accounts receivable and collectability; trade names, trademarks, and copyrights; patent and patent rights;   trade secrets; insurance policies; and employment contracts).

[45] See *id.* at 76-81, 94-96, 118 (warranties concerning undisclosed liabilities, tax liabilities, compliance with laws, accuracy of financial statements, and pending or threatened litigation).

[46] See *id.* at 93 (disclosure of all employment, collective bargaining, bonus, profit-sharing, or fringe benefit agreements).

[47] We will put off for the moment the question of what happens when one of the target's representations and warranties turns out to be incorrect. The issue of indemnification for breach of warranty will be taken up in connection with the verification function. See Section B.4 of this Chapter, *infra*.

[48] Freund (1975), *supra* note 7, at 229.

[49] *Id.* at 233.

(2) Facilitating the Production of Previously Nonexistent Information

A similar analysis applies when the acquirer needs information that the target has not already produced. For example, the acquirer may desire information about aspects of the target's operation that bear on the opportunity for synergy between its own business and that of the target and that, prior to the negotiation, the target had no reason to create. Alternatively, the acquirer may be interested in the impact of the transaction itself on the target's business; whether the target contracts can be assigned or assumed; whether, for example, the transaction would accelerate the target's obligations. Like the situation in which the acquirer has already produced the information desired by the target, the only issue here should be to minimize the acquisition cost of the information in question.

While the analysis is similar to the situation in which the target had previously produced the information, the result of the analysis is somewhat different. Not only will the target not always be the least-cost information producer, but there will also be a substantial role for third-party information producers. Returning to the synergy example, a determination of the potential for gain from the combination of the two businesses requires information about both. The particular character of the businesses, as well as the skills of their managers, will determine whether such a study is better undertaken by the target, which knows its own business but will be required to learn about the acquirer's business or by the acquirer, which knows about its own business and is in the process of learning about the target's.[50]

The more interesting analysis concerns the potential role for third-party information producers. This can be seen most clearly with respect to information concerning the impact of the transaction itself on the target's business. As between the acquirer and the target, the target will usually be the least-cost producer of information concerning the impact of the transaction on, for example, the target's existing contracts. Although there is no reason to expect that either party routinely will have an advantage in interpreting the contracts, it is predictable that the target can more cheaply assemble the facts on which the interpretation will be based. The real issue, however, is not whether the target is the lower-cost producer out of a group

---

[50] The least-cost producer typically will be the acquirer. Although the acquirer will already know something about the target, the target will have had little reason to learn about the acquirer's business prior to initiation of negotiations. As a result, the amount that still must be learned about the other party's business in order to evaluate the potential for synergy is likely to be smaller for the acquirer than for the target. This yields a prediction that should be subject to empirical testing. If this hypothesis is correct, we would expect to find few representations and warranties by the target that could be understood to speak to conditions directly related to the manner in which the two entities could be combined. The *absence* of a representation by the target, of course, leaves the information-production function with the acquirer.

of candidates artificially limited to the target and acquirer. Rather, the group of candidates must be expanded to include third parties.

The impact of including third-party information production in the analysis can be seen by examining the specialized information production role for lawyers in acquisition transactions. Even with respect to the production of information concerning the target's assets and liabilities, the area where our prior analysis demonstrated the target's prominence as an information producer, there remains a clear need for a specialized third party. Production of certain information concerning the character of the target's assets and liabilities simply requires legal analysis. For example, the target will know whether it has been cited for violation of environmental or health and safety legislation in the past, but it may require legal analysis to determine whether continued operation of the target's business likely will result in future prosecution.

The need for third-party assistance is even more apparent with respect to information about the impact of the transaction itself on the target's business. Again, however, much of the information requires legal analysis; there exists a specialized information-production role for third parties. For example, it will be important to know whether existing contracts are assignable or assumable: The continued validity of the target's leasehold interests will depend on whether a change in the control of the target operates -- as a matter of law or because of the specific terms of the lease -- as an assignment of the leasehold,[51] and the status of the target's existing liabilities, such as its outstanding debt, will depend on whether the transaction can be undertaken without the creditor's consent.

In both cases, the target's lawyer appears to be the lowest-cost producer of such information.[52] As a result, we would expect the typical acquisition agreement to assign lawyers this information-production role. And it is from this perspective that important elements of the common requirement of an "Opinion of Counsel for the Target" are best understood.

Any significant acquisition agreement requires, as a condition to the buyer's obligation to complete the transaction, that the acquirer receive an opinion of target's counsel with respect to a substantial number of items.[53]

---

[51] For example, would a general clause prohibiting assignment of a lease by a corporate tenant prohibit the sale of all the tenant's stock, or a merger of the tenant, or even the dissolution of the tenant and the succession to the tenancy by the tenant's shareholders? See 1 Milton Friedman, *Friedman on Leases* 244-52 (2d ed.1983).

[52] The target's lawyer will likely have been involved in the original preparation of the documents and, as a result, will have much better information concerning their contents and the context in which they were negotiated.

[53] See Section VI.C. of the acquisition agreement in Appendix C. There is a substantial practical literature concerning opinions of counsel. See Arnold Jacobs, *Opinion Letters in Securities Matters: Text -- Clauses -- Law* (1983); Frank Babb, James Barnes, Phillip Gordon & Evan Kjellenberg, *Legal Opinions to Third Parties in Corporate Transactions,* 32 Bus.Law. 553 (1977); George Bermant, *The Role of the Opinion of Counsel -- A Tentative Reevaluation,* 49 Cal.St.B.J. 132 (1974); Committee on Corporations of the Business Law Section of the

Consistent with our analysis, most of the matters on which legal opinions are required reflect the superiority of the target's lawyer as an information producer. For example, determination of the target's proper organization and continued good standing under state law, the appropriate authorization of the transaction by target, the existence of litigation against the target, the impact of the transaction on the target's contracts and commitments, and the extent to which the current operation of the target's business violates any law or regulation, represent the production of information which neither the acquirer nor the target previously had, by a third party -- the lawyer -- who is the least-cost producer.[54]

Just as was the case in our examination of the function of representations and warranties, this focus on the information production role for lawyers' opinions also provides a nonadversarial approach to resolving the conflict over their content. Because reducing the cost of information necessary to the correct pricing of the transaction is beneficial to both acquirer and target, determination of the matters to be covered by the opinion of counsel for the target[55] should be in large measure a cooperative, rather than a competitive, opportunity. Debate over the scope of the opinion, then, should focus explicitly on the cost of producing the information. For example, where a privately owned business is being sold, the target may retain special counsel to handle the acquisition transaction, either because the company has had no regular counsel prior to the transaction, or because its regular counsel is not experienced in acquisition transactions. In this situation, recognition of the informational basis of the subject matter usually covered by legal opinions not only suggests that a specialized third-party producer is appropriate, but also provides guidance about *whose* third party should actually do the production.

State Bar of California, *Report of the Committee on Corporations Regarding Legal Opinions in Business Transactions,* 14 Pac.L.J. 1001 (1983) [hereinafter cited as California State Bar Report]; Committee on Developments in Business Financing, *Legal Opinions Given in Corporate Transactions,* 33 Bus.Law. 2389 (1978); James Fuld, *Legal Opinions in Business Transactions -- An Attempt to Bring Some Order Out of Some Chaos,* 28 Bus.Law. 915 (1973); Special Comm. on Legal Opinions on Commercial Transactions, N.Y. County Lawyers' Association, *Legal Opinions to Third Parties: An Easier Path,* 34 Bus.Law. 1891 (1979).

[54] The opinion of counsel also serves an important verification function. See Section B.4.b.(2) of this Chapter, *infra.*

[55] Typically there will be occasions that call for an opinion of *acquirer's* counsel as well. See Section VII.C. of the acquisition agreement in Appendix C. Consistent with an information-cost analysis, the scope of the opinion of acquirer's counsel increases as information about the acquirer becomes important to pricing the transaction. This would be the case, for example, where the two parties are so close in size that the transaction is really a merger, or where the consideration to be given by the seller is the acquirer's stock. In virtually all transactions, the opinion of the acquirer's counsel will be required with respect to the impact of the transaction itself, such as proper authorization of the transaction by the acquirer.

From this perspective, target's counsel typically will be the least-cost producer of the information in question. Past experience with the target will eliminate the need for much factual investigation that would be necessary for someone who lacked a prior professional relation to the target. Similarly, target's counsel may well have been directly involved in some of the matters of concern -- such as the issuance of the securities which are the subject of an opinion concerning the target's capitalization, or the negotiation of the lease which is the subject of an opinion concerning the impact of the transaction on the target's obligations. Where the target has retained special counsel for the transaction, however, the production-cost advantage in favor of target's counsel will be substantially reduced, especially with respect to past matters. In those cases, focus on the cost of information production provides a method for cooperative resolution of the frequently contentious issue of the scope of the opinion.[56]

(3) Controls Over What Information to Look for and How Hard to Try

Emphasis on the information-production role of the target's representations and warranties and the opinion of counsel for the target leads to the conclusion that determination of the least-cost information producer provides a cooperative focus for negotiating the content of those provisions. The same emphasis on information production also raises a related question. The demand for information, as for any other good, is more or less price elastic.   Information production is costly even for the most efficient producer, and the higher the cost, the less the parties will choose to produce. Thus, some fine tuning of the assignment of information-production roles would seem to be necessary. We would expect some specific limits on the kind of information required to be produced. And we would also expect some specific limits on how much should be spent even for information whose production is desired.

Examination of an acquisition agreement from this perspective identifies provisions which impose precisely these kinds of controls. Moreover, explicit recognition of the function of these provisions, as with our analysis of representations and warranties and opinions of counsel, can facilitate the negotiation of what traditionally have been quite difficult issues.

---

[56] The role of information-producer also may be played by another third-party specialist: The public accountant. The accountant typically also renders an opinion concerning the transaction -- the cold comfort letter -- and easily can be imagined having an information-production role. The common presence of an internal accounting staff within the seller, however, is persuasive evidence that the transactional function of the public accountant is one of verification. See Section B.4.b.(2) of this Chapter, *infra*. Whether or not there is also an information-production role for the public accountant depends on the comparative information-production costs of the public accountant and the target's internal accounting staff.

Consider first the question of limiting the type of information that must be produced in light of the cost of production. To put the problem in context, we can focus on the standard representation concerning the target's existing contracts. The acquirer's initial draft typically will require the target to represent that an attached schedule lists "all agreements, contracts, leases, and other commitments to which the target is a party or by which any of its property is bound." In fact, it is quite unlikely that the acquirer really wants the target to incur the costs of producing all the information specified. In a business of any significant size, there will be a large number of small contracts -- for office plant care, coffee service, postal meters, and the like -- the central collection and presentation of which would entail substantial cost. Moreover, to the extent these contracts are all in the normal course of the target's business, the information may have little bearing on the pricing of the transaction. As a result, it would be beneficial to both parties to limit the scope of the target's search.

It is from this perspective that the function of certain common qualifications of the representations and warranties of the target are best understood. The expected response of a target to a representation as to existing contracts of the breadth of that described above would be to qualify the scope of the information to be produced: To limit the obligation to only *material* contracts.[57] If the contracts themselves are not important, then there is no reason to incur the cost of producing information about them. Variations on the theme include qualifications based on the dollar value of the contracts,[58] or on the relationship of the contracts to "the ordinary course of business."[59]

A second common form of qualification -- a limit on the information costs to be incurred -- is best understood as an instruction concerning how hard to look for information whose subject matter cannot be excluded as unimportant ahead of time. Here the idea is to qualify not the object of the inquiry, but the diligence of the search.[60] Consider, for example, the common representation concerning the absence of defaults under disclosed contracts.[61] While it might involve little cost to determine whether the target, as lessee, has defaulted under a lease, it may well be quite expensive to

---

[57] See Freund (1975), *supra* note 7, at 272-74.

[58] See Section III.A.(16) of the acquisition agreement in Appendix C.; 3 *Business Acquisitions, supra* note 7, at 96-97 ("Set forth as Schedule G hereto are complete and accurate lists of the following: (i) all arrangements of the Seller, except for purchase and sales order that involve future payments of less than $250,000. . . .").

[59] See *Drafting Agreements, supra* note 7, at 94 ("Neither corporation nor subsidiary is a party to, nor is the property of either bound by . . . any agreement not entered into in the ordinary course of business . . . except the agreements listed in Exhibit -. . . .").

[60] This analysis, and that concerning the object of the inquiry, applies as well to the role of third-party information producers.

[61] See Section III.A.(16) of the acquisition agreement in Appendix C.; *Drafting Agreements, supra* note 7, at 94 ("There is no default or event that with notice or lapse of time, or both, would constitute a default by any party to any of these agreements.").

determine whether the lessor is in default. In that situation, the acquirer might consider it sufficient to be told everything that the target had thought appropriate to find out for its own purposes, without regard to the acquisition, but not to require further investigation.

This type of qualification, limiting the representation to information the target already has and requiring no further search, is the domain of the familiar "knowledge" qualification. In form, the representation concerning the existence of breaches is qualified by the phrase "to target's knowledge." In function, the qualification serves to limit the scope of the target's search to information already within its possession; no new information need be sought.[62]

Recognizing the function of the knowledge qualification also raises another question concerning the variation in form that the qualification takes in typical acquisition agreements. In fact, the knowledge qualification -- the limit on how hard the target must search for information -- comes in a variety of forms. Often within the same agreement one will see all of the following variations:

"to target's knowledge";[63]
"to the best of target's knowledge";[64]

---

[62] James Freund identifies another function for representations and warranties that suggests a different role for the knowledge qualification. Freund points out that an unqualified representation serves, in effect, as an insurance policy. Thus, an unqualified representation may be made even though the target is aware of a possibility that the representation is incorrect, because the parties have determined that the target should bear the risk and the absolute representation serves to allocate that risk to the target. Freund (1975), *supra* note 7, at 247-48. From an information perspective, however, Freund's point is part of an approach to dealing with the problem of information asymmetry. Suppose both the acquirer and the target are aware that certain of the target's trade secrets may be subject to a misappropriation claim, and that such a claim, if successful, would reduce the value of the target's business by $1,000,000. It would hardly be surprising if the acquirer and the target had different estimates of the probability of a successful misappropriation claim; after all, the target has vastly more information concerning the circumstances in which the trade secrets were developed than does the acquirer. Suppose further that the acquirer, based on its information, estimates the probability of liability at .5, and therefore argues that the purchase price should be reduced by $500,000. The target, however, based on its information, estimates the probability at only .15, which would justify only a $150,000 reduction in the purchase price. The effect of the target's making an unqualified warranty concerning ownership of trade secrets is to allocate the risk of liability to the seller, the party with the best information and, therefore, the party best able to price the risk. From the acquirer's perspective, the risk has been eliminated. From the target's perspective, $350,000 has been gained: The expected value of the purchase price -- total price less expected liability -- is $350,000 higher than if the acquirer's estimate was used. Thus, unqualified representations and warranties can serve, as Freund perceptively suggests, as insurance policies. However, the determination of which party should be the insurer turns on the determination of which party has better information and, as a result, is better able to price the risk.

[63] See Sections III.A.(14), (15), and (25) of the acquisition agreement in Appendix C.

[64] See *id.* at Sections III.A.(10), (13), and (16).

"to the best of target's knowledge and after diligent investigation."[65]

What seems to be at work, at least implicitly, is the creation of a hierarchy of search effort that must be undertaken with respect to information of different levels of importance.[66]

This result is perfectly consistent with a view of the business lawyer as a transaction cost engineer, and with a view of representations and warranties as a means of producing the information necessary to pricing the transaction at the lowest cost. However, it also raises the question of whether explicit recognition of the information-cost function of these qualifications might not facilitate the design of more effective cost reduction techniques. Although this is not the occasion to detail the changes in the form of acquisition agreements that might result from conscious attention to issues of information cost, it seems quite clear that once we understand more precisely what it is we are about, we should be able to do a more effective job.

Consider, for example, the qualifications that we have just discussed concerning how hard the target must look. Given our understanding of their purpose, the problem of limiting the scope of the target's investigation might be better approached explicitly, rather than implicitly through a variety of undefined adjectives. If, for example, the concern is whether the lessor of a real estate lease, under which the target is the lessee, has breached the lease, as in Section III.A.(10) of the acquisition agreement in Appendix C, why not specify the actual investigation the target should make? Do we want the target to go directly to the lessor to secure a statement by the lessor as to the lessor's satisfaction of its obligations?[67] Different levels of cost obviously are associated with the different inquiries; specificity about the desired level of cost, however, should allow further minimization of information costs. To make the point in a slightly different way, is it possible to say with any assurance which of the forms of qualification listed above imposes an obligation to inspect the premises, but no obligation to inquire directly of the lessor?

---

[65] See *id.* at Section VI.C.(v).

[66] This proposition -- that different forms of qualification reflect the different levels of intended search effort -- also may be subject to empirical evaluation. If one of the parties to an acquisition agreement is a reporting company under the Securities Exchange Act, its Form 10K Annual Report typically would contain the agreement as an exhibit. Thus, one could gather a substantial sample of acquisition agreements to analyze whether there was a pattern to the types of information subject to qualification and to the form of qualification used.

[67] If information is too costly to produce, the issue shifts to who is best able to price and bear the risk, again information-cost issues.

b.   *Costs of Verifying Information*

Problems of information cost do not end when the information is acquired. Even if cooperative negotiation between the acquirer and target minimizes the costs of reducing the informational asymmetry confronting the acquirer, another information-cost dilemma remains: How can the acquirer determine whether the information it has received is accurate? After all, the target, who has probably provided most of the information, has a clear incentive to mislead the acquirer into overvaluing the business.

Just as the market provides incentives that offset a target's inclination to withhold unfavorable information, the market also provides incentives that constrain a target's similar inclination to proffer falsely favorable information. If, before a transaction, an acquirer can neither itself determine the quality of the target's product nor evaluate the accuracy of the target's representations about product quality, the acquirer has no alternative but to treat the target's product as being of low quality, regardless of the target's protestations.[68] To avoid this problem, a high quality target has a substantial incentive to demonstrate to an acquirer that its representations about the quality of its business are accurate and can be relied upon. And because it is in the target's interest to keep all information costs at a minimum, there is also an incentive to accomplish this verification in the most economical fashion.

Verification techniques, then, are critical means of reducing total information costs. Like efforts to reduce acquisition costs, verification techniques can be implemented both by the parties themselves and through the efforts of third parties. It is helpful to consider each approach to verification separately.

(1)   Economizing by the Parties

Perhaps the cheapest verification technique is simply an expectation of future transactions between the acquirer and target. When the target's misrepresentation in one transaction will be taken into account by the acquirer in decisions concerning future transactions, whether by reducing the price to reflect lowered expectations, or, at the extreme, by withdrawing

---

[68] In the absence of some method by which the seller of a high quality product can demonstrate to potential buyers that its product is in fact of high quality, the seller may have no incentive to provide a high quality product at all. If a buyer cannot tell a good product from a bad one, all products will be treated, and priced, as if they were of low quality. The result is the standard "lemon problem": Poor quality products drive higher quality products from the market. See George Akerlof, *The Market for "Lemons": Quality Uncertainty and the Market Mechanism,* 84 Q.J.Econ. 488, 489-90 (1970); Grossman (1981), *supra* note 40; Charles Wilson, *The Nature of Equilibrium in Markets with Adverse Selection,* 11 Bell J.Econ. 108 (1980).

patronage altogether, the target will have little incentive to mislead.[69] In a corporate acquisition, however, the target has no expectation of future transactions; for the target, a corporate acquisition is, virtually by definition, a one-shot transaction. Thus, the expectation of future transactions is simply not available as a constraint on the target's incentive to misrepresent the information provided.[70]

Nonetheless, the insight gleaned from understanding how an expectation of future transactions serves to validate a target's information can be used to create an inexpensive verification techniques that will work even in the one-period world of a corporate acquisition. The expectation technique works because of the existence of additional periods; the insight is simply to devise what Oliver Williamson has called a "hostage" strategy,[71] i.e., an artificial second period in which misrepresentations in the first period -- the acquisition transaction -- are penalized. If any of the target's information turns out to be inaccurate, the target will be required to compensate the acquirer; in effect, the target posts a bond that it has provided accurate information. This technique has the advantage of being quite economical: Beyond the negotiating cost involved in agreeing to make the acquirer whole, there is no cost to the target *unless* the information proves inaccurate.[72]

This technique is among the most common approaches to verification that appear in corporate acquisition agreements. The target verifies the accuracy of the information it has provided through its representations and

---

[69] The expectation of future transactions can serve as a means to facilitate low-cost verification even if the seller has no reason to believe that it will deal with a particular buyer again. So long as any discrepancy between the represented and actual quality of a seller's product can be easily communicated to potential buyers by a buyer who has been misled, a seller can effectively signal to potential buyers that it is a high quality producer -- that the disclosed information concerning product quality is correct -- by making investments in form-specific capital, like reputation and advertising, that would be lost if the seller's product turned out to be of lower quality than represented. See Benjamin Klein & Keith Leffler, *The Role of Market Forces in Assuring Contractual Performance,* 89 J.Pol.Econ. 615 (1981).

[70] Final-period problems of the sort described in the text may still be present even in the unusual situation when the target in an acquisition transaction in fact can be anticipated to engage in future transactions. Suppose a target is engaged in a divestiture program, trying to shed previously acquired businesses that have not worked out. While a misrepresentation in a particular transaction may make it more expensive for a target to verify the quality of its information in a subsequent transaction, the extent of the constraint is limited for a number of reasons. First, the misrepresentation may not become known before the target has completed the divestiture program, after which point the target can no longer be penalized through future transactions. In this sense, a final period may be long enough to shelter a number of transactions. Second, the transactions may not be of equal magnitude. A successful misrepresentation in a particularly large transaction may more than offset the resulting penalty with respect to a number of small transactions.

[71] Oliver Williamson, *Credible Commitments: Using Hostages to Support Exchange,* 73 Am.Econ.Rev. 519 (1983).

[72] Williamson provides a number of other examples of how this approach has been used. *Id.* at 532-33. Additional examples can be found in Charles Knoeber, *An Alternative Mechanism to Assure Contractual Reliability,* 12 J.Legal Stud. 333, 337-38, 342-43 (1983).

warranties by agreeing to indemnify the acquirer if the information turns out to be wrong, i.e., if a breach of representation or warranty occurs.[73]   And the hostage metaphor rings especially true because the target's promise to indemnify the acquirer is frequently backed by the acquirer's or a neutral third party's retention of a portion of the consideration as a fund to assure the target's performance of its indemnification obligation.[74]

Emphasis on verification costs also highlights that indemnification, like the target's representations and warranties, ultimately works principally to the target's advantage.   As long as the target recognizes that the perceived quality, as well as the amount, of the information provided by the target will be reflected in the price the acquirer is willing to pay, the subject provides the opportunity for cooperative, rather than merely distributive, bargaining.[75]

The common appearance of target indemnification against inaccuracies in the information contained in the target's representations and warranties is persuasive evidence of the information-cost basis for the technique.   But it is also true that use of the technique is not universal.   There are a significant number of acquisitions containing no contractual provision for indemnification.   Even more troubling, its presence or absence follows a predictable pattern: Indemnification is typically used if the target is a private company, but not if the target is a public company.[76]   A complete information-cost explanation for indemnification in acquisition agreements thus also must explain why indemnification provisions are rarely, if ever, used when the target is a public company.   And the range of possible explanations is limited in an important respect: There is no reason to believe that the need for verification is any less significant when the target is a public

---

[73] See Section V of the acquisition agreement in Appendix C.

[74] See Section II and the Escrow Agreement of the acquisition agreement in Appendix C; Freund (1975), *supra* note 7, at 363-88; Weinreich (1981), *supra* note 13, at 191-194 (discussion of escrow arrangements).

The negotiation of indemnification and "hold back" funds is quite complicated. See Freund (1975), *supra* note 7, at 383-84. Nonetheless, the common elements out of which a solution is built -- for example, "baskets" that require a minimum amount before any claim can be made and "cut-offs" that limit claims to breaches discovered during a specified period -- have become standard.

[75] It is hard to know what to make of the anecdotal evidence that can be marshalled in response to the claim that indemnification presents a target with the opportunity for cooperative bargaining. Practicing business lawyers will recount that the price is set by the clients long prior to the negotiation over whether there will be indemnification; as a result, they may argue that the presence or absence of provisions for indemnification have *no* effect on the price of the transaction. Evaluation of the argument requires information about the expectations of the acquirer when the price was negotiated and about whether price and other provisions were negotiated at the same time by sophisticated clients. In any event, the core of the argument is that understanding the function of such provisions can make for different and better results.

[76] See Freund (1975), *supra* note 7, at 160. Indemnification is absent if the acquisition agreement states that the target's representations and warranties do not survive the closing of the transaction. See Weinreich (1981), *supra* note 13, at 187.

rather than a private company. The real task is to identify the alternative means of verification that are available in the acquisition of a public company and to understand why their comparative cost advantage does not extend to private companies.

Two significant differences seem to account for the absence, in the acquisition of public companies, of the dominant verification technique in acquisitions of private companies. First, less costly verification techniques are available in the public setting but unavailable in a private transaction. Second, the indemnification technique is more costly to implement in a public than in a private transaction.

Consider first the verification techniques that are available to public, but not to private, companies as alternatives to indemnification. One, which functions to reduce the incentives of the target's management to provide misleading information in the first place, is not an innovative contractual technique that cleverly alters incentives. Rather it simply reflects that the differences in transactional setting and in the cast of characters between the acquisition of a public and private company result in different incentives with respect to the provision of inaccurate information by the target. Here the critical players are the target's management, who will negotiate the transaction and actually provide the information whose verification is required. And the central point is that the managers' incentives to provide accurate information differ critically depending on whether the target is privately or publicly owned. Where the target is private, management is typically dominated by the principal shareholders who also will receive the lion's share of the proceeds from the acquisition. The transaction enables these individuals to diversify their previously undiversified portfolio. Prior to the transaction, most of their wealth was tied up in their private company;[77] after the transaction, their wealth has been transformed into either cash or the publicly traded stock of the acquirer, either of which allows portfolio diversification. To be sure, these owner-managers will also have an undiversifiable *human* capital investment in the company they manage, and this investment may remain after the transaction through a post-acquisition employment relationship. But this benefit will constitute so small a portion of the total benefits from the transaction that the owner-managers will see the transaction as a one-time event that presents the incentives to mislead associated with any final period situation.

Separation of ownership and management in public companies puts management of a publicly held target in a quite different position. Even if these employee-managers have some ownership position in the target as a

---

[77] The critical financial characteristic of private corporations is that the absence of a public market prevents their owners from achieving optimally diversified portfolios by selling off a portion of the ownership of the private company. As a result, the company may well be worth more to a publicly held acquiring company, whose shareholders can optimally diversify, than to the private owners of the company. See Eugene Fama & Michael Jensen, *Organizational Forms and Investment Decisions,* 14 J.Fin.Econ. 101, 103-07 (1985).

result of stock option or bonus plans, their principal investment in the company is typically their human capital. As a result, a post-acquisition employment contract is of much greater importance both in absolute terms and, because their human capital investment cannot be diversified, in relative terms as well. These factors combine to create an interesting verification technique. For the employee-managers, the acquisition transaction is a two-period rather than a single-period game. During the first period, in which the actual transaction takes place, the employee-managers provide the acquirer with information bearing on the target's value. However, their compensation from the transaction, post-transaction employment contracts, unlike the compensation of the shareholders of the target, comes not in the first period but later, as payments are received under the employment contracts. These second-period payments serve as a bond of the accuracy of the information provided by the employee-managers in the first period: If misrepresentations are discovered, their employment can be terminated.[78] Precisely because post-transaction employment is substantially less valuable to owner-managers, this verification technique is simply not available to private companies[79] which, as a result, must rely on indemnification.

Some evidence supports this explanation of the different transactional structures found in the acquisitions of public and private companies. A familiar type of company is neither truly public nor truly private. Such a company is public in that its stock is freely traded on a national securities exchange or in the over-the-counter market, but private in that there is a single dominant shareholder, or group of shareholders, whose own situation

---

[78] Management buyouts, see Chapter 11, *supra*, are an extreme example of this verification technique: Management demonstrates to the third parties (or their lenders) who are putting up the bulk of the investment the accuracy of the information provided, including, most importantly, projections of post-transaction cash flows, by making a substantial personal investment in the post-transaction company.

[79] This analysis suggests that "golden parachute" employment arrangements create a perverse incentive in addition to the anti-takeover motive discussed in Chapter 17, *supra*. Golden parachute arrangements are commonly justified as reducing the conflict of interest between employee-managers and shareholders with respect to acquisition offers by providing a benefit to management that offsets the loss of management's control if an acquisition takes place. But it also has been recognized that too high a payoff under the arrangement creates a moral hazard: The employee-manager may be better off if an acquisition takes place even on terms that make the shareholders worse off. The conflict of interest has not been eliminated; it has merely been reshaped. Golden parachute arrangements thus can interfere with the verification technique of reducing information costs. The engine that drives the technique is the risk that the value of the employee-manager's most important asset -- his post-transaction employment relationship -- will be reduced if he is discovered to have made misrepresentations to the acquirer. But that risk can be eliminated, and the effectiveness of the information-cost reducing technique impaired, if the manager acquires a hedge -- another asset that will increase in value as a result of the same event that causes the decrease in the value of the employment relationship. A golden parachute arrangement provides precisely such a hedge. It pays off only on post-transaction termination, precisely the event that reduces the value of the manager's employment relationship. Golden parachutes, then, should increase an acquirer's verification costs even in friendly transaction.

is much closer to that of the owner-managers in the prototypical private company than to that of the employee-managers in a truly public company. Because the operative factor in the analysis is the character of the managers' portfolios -- the public/private distinction is only the common shorthand characterization -- one would expect acquirers of these quasi-public companies to treat them more like private than public companies. This prediction appears to be correct. The literature treats the situation of a public company with a dominant shareholder as an exception to the general rule that indemnification is not appropriate in the acquisition of a public company: An explicit agreement by the dominant shareholder of a quasi-public company to indemnify the acquirer for breaches of representations and warranties is a quite familiar transactional structure.[80]

The second verification technique that is uniquely available in the acquisition of a public company results from the continuing disclosure obligations imposed by the Securities Exchange Act of 1934[81] only on public companies. In the course of compliance with its regulatory obligations, the target will previously have disclosed substantial amounts of the information covered by the representations and warranties contained in the acquisition agreement. The critical point, however, is not that the information was previously produced -- we have already seen that the target is typically the least-cost information producer -- but that it was produced subject to a powerful verification technique. Material misrepresentations and omissions in disclosures made pursuant to the 1934 Act requirements subject both a company and its management to potential civil and criminal penalties.[82] This potential liability serves further to bond the accuracy of the representations made by employee-managers and, thus, further to reduce both the incentives and the opportunity to mislead the acquirer. In this sense, the 1934 Act serves to collectivize the verification problem.[83]

---

[80] See Section V of the acquisition agreement in Appendix C; Freund (1975), *supra* note 7, at 161, 365.

[81] 15 U.S.C. § 78m. The obligation to file periodic quarterly and annual reports under § 13 of the Securities Exchange Act, 15 U.S.C. § 78m (1982), is triggered either by registration pursuant to § 12, 15 U.S.C. § 78l (1982), or by the filing of a registration statement under the Securities Act of 1933, pursuant to § 15(d), 15 U.S.C. § 78o(d) (1982).

[82] In addition to standard civil remedies, § 32(a), 15 U.S.C. § 77ff(a) (1982), provides for fines of up to $10,000 and imprisonment for up to five years (although § 32(b), 15 U.S.C. § 77ff(b) (1982), reduces the maximum penalty for failure to file, as opposed to filing an inaccurate report for companies whose reporting obligation arises under § 15(d), 15 U.S.C. § 79o(d) (1982)).

[83] The idea of legislation serving as a collective response to problems of verification cost is developed in Gilson & Kraakman (1984), *supra* note 36, at 605. It should be stressed that employee-managers are likely to be quite risk averse with respect to incurring such penalties. The simple fact is that most of the benefits from "successful" violations go to the shareholders, while the costs of getting caught are borne more than proportionally by the managers, absent an effective indemnification arrangement. For a comprehensive analysis of the impact of managers' attitudes toward risk on corporate compliance with regulatory obligations, see Reinier Kraakman, *Corporate Liability Strategies and the Costs of Legal*

The operation of these two verification techniques in the acquisition of a public company thus goes a long way toward explaining why indemnification, the central verification technique in the acquisition of a private company, is not observed in the public setting. An additional point should also be made, however, bearing not on the availability of alternatives to indemnification as a means of verification, but on the differential costs of using indemnification in acquisitions of public, as opposed to private, companies. An indemnification arrangement is costly to administer. If a claim of breach of warranty arises, it must be resolved. This resolution, whether by litigation or some alternative method of dispute resolution such as arbitration, is expensive. Moreover, there are significant collective action problems: Someone must act on behalf of the target in responding to the acquirer's claim. Where the target is privately held, the collective action problem is minimal; the shareholder group is small enough that it can play that role directly. Where the target is publicly held, however, the collective action problem is quite real. Dispersal of ownership among numerous shareholders dilutes the incentive for any single shareholder to monitor the indemnification process; a collective solution is required to overcome the free-rider problem. Thus, a trustee, typically a commercial bank, is appointed.[84] The cost of this arrangement includes not merely the amount the trustee must be paid, but also the dilution of incentives to oppose an acquirer's claim that results from the inevitable divergence in interests between the target's shareholders and the appointed trustee.[85]

In short, an information-cost approach to the problem of verification explains a good deal about the presence or absence of indemnification provisions in acquisition agreements. But the range of verification techniques available is not limited to those involving participation only by the acquirer and target. Just as with the production of the information in the first place, there are verification techniques that depend upon participation by third

---

Controls, 93 Yale L.J. 857 (1984).

[84] Freund (1975), *supra* note 7, at 387.

[85] The agreement with the trustee typically holds the trustee harmless from claims by the target's shareholders, as long as the trustee has acted in good faith. See the Escrow Agreement in Appendix C. Additionally, the trustee's fee is usually fixed, although all costs -- especially attorney's fees in the event of litigation -- are reimbursed. The result is that the trustee bears a significant portion of the cost of resisting, through the extra work for its personnel, while the target's shareholders receive all the benefits. The divergence in interests creates a clear bias on the part of the trustee in favor of early settlement.

Just as was the case with respect to the differential impact of post-acquisition employment on the incentives of target management to misrepresent depending on whether the target is publicly or privately held, the intermediate case of a publicly held company with a dominant shareholder is more like the privately held company than the publicly held company with respect to the need for a third party to monitor the indemnification process. The concentration in holdings represented by the dominant shareholder overcomes the free-rider problem inherent in diverse public ownership. Again, the result is to suggest a greater role for indemnification in this setting.

parties. And these also help to demonstrate the information-cost basis for additional provisions of the typical agreement.

(2)   Third-Party Verification Techniques

Regardless of whether the target is a public or private company, there is a common limit on the effectiveness of all of the verification techniques discussed thus far; the possibility of misleading statements remains. Consider first the limits on the verification techniques associated with the sale of a public company: Senior management may not expect their misrepresentations to be discovered at all; they may be far enough along in their careers that they expect to retire before discovery; golden parachute agreements may have reversed senior management's incentives; and, ultimately, the possibility remains that the particular misleading disclosure, or failure to disclose, masks information which is so damaging that senior management is better off with misleading disclosure even in the face of possible future penalties.[86]

Even the more direct verification technique associated with the sale of a private company -- indemnification arrangements backed by the withholding of a portion of the purchase price -- will not be completely effective. The indemnification obligation often is limited to an amount lower than the purchase price.[87] Moreover, the obligation is typically limited in time; a contractual statute of limitations limits the period in which claims for indemnification may be asserted.[88] If the reduction in value resulting from complete disclosure exceeds the limit on indemnification, then indemnification operates not as bond, but as bait; a piece of the proceeds is given up in order to increase the net take. Most troubling to a potential

---

[86] The analysis can be generalized. Most unfavorable disclosure reduces the value of the target by shifting the acquirer's estimate of the probable distribution of future earnings. For the target, the disclosure calculus compares the certain reduction in value that results from disclosure (the acquirer's expected value is lowered), with the penalty for making a misrepresentation of non-disclosure discounted by the possibility that the actual result will still fall on a part of the probability distribution that exceeds the acquirer's uncorrected expected value, and by the possibility that the misrepresentation or nondisclosure will remain undetected. From this perspective, for example, the decision by senior management of National Telephone Co. not to disclose the company's violation of its loan agreements may be understandable. See In re Carter, [1981 Transfer Binder] Fed.Sec.L.Rep. (CCH) ¶ 82,847 (S.E.C.Admin.). Alternatively, the size of the penalties that can be imposed may be bounded because of bankruptcy or retirement or, as in the Equity Funding scandal, see Dirks v. SEC, 463 U.S. 646 (1983), because the fraud is so large as to dwarf the potential penalties, i.e., the penalties are insufficient to eliminate the final period problem by creating an artificial second round.

[87] It is not uncommon to limit the target's total exposure for indemnification to the amount of the purchase price that has been withheld as a hostage. Freund (1975), *supra* note 7, at 385-86.

[88] *Id.* at 386.

acquirer, the balance of incentives facing owner-managers of a private target favors misrepresentation or nondisclosure in precisely those situations where the information in question would result in the greatest downward adjustment in the purchase price. Verification fails in the situation where it is most needed.

Ultimately, all of these verification techniques are imperfect because they do not entirely eliminate the potential for opportunism inherent in one-time transactions. The techniques examined -- indemnification, employment contracts, liability under the Securities Exchange Act -- reduce final-period problems by adding an artificial second round to the transaction. For this reason, all share a common limit on their effectiveness: If the gain from cheating in the first round can exceed the penalties if caught in the second -- whether because the probability of detection is less than 1.0, or because the financial risk borne by the target in the second round is too low, since the solutions to other kinds of problems conflict with what would be the optimal resolution of the verification problem[89] -- the acquirer lacks the assurance that the information provided by the target can be entirely trusted.

At this point, further efforts at verification by the acquirer or target are unlikely to be successful.[90] A critical role is thus created for third parties to

---

[89] One response might be that any reluctance by the target to take full advantage of available verification techniques -- for example, by attempting to limit its indemnification obligation to an amount less than the total proceeds to be received -- would be understood by the acquirer as a signal that the target's information was inaccurate, and would result in an equivalent reduction in the offered purchase price, thereby eliminating any gain to the target from the gambit. The problem, however, is that the information content of the signal -- in the example, the target's desire to put a ceiling on the indemnification obligation -- is noisy. If reasons other than the inaccuracy of the information could explain why the target might want to limit indemnification, then the acquirer will have difficulty sorting out how much of a price reduction is warranted. See Verrecchia (1983), *supra* note 40. For example, the target might want to limit the indemnification obligation because of a fear that the acquirer will behave opportunistically with respect to claims of breach, i.e., if the business performs poorly after the transaction, the acquirer may claim that the poor performance resulted from facts that were not disclosed -- the buyer's probability distribution of future performance was skewed because of misleading disclosure -- rather than from the mere bad luck of ending up on an unfavorable portion of an accurately disclosed probability distribution. Alternatively, the target may want to keep the size of the holdback low, even though this may be seen by the acquirer as an effort to limit the "real" exposure for indemnification and, therefore, as a negative signal about the accuracy of the information, in order to allow desirable diversification of what had previously been an undiversifiable investment. Where there is this kind of noise surrounding a signal, it can be expected that a full discount will not occur: That is, there will be some equilibrium amount of misleading disclosure. *Id.* at 18.

The noisiness of the signal of inaccuracy also suggests that some of the costs to target's management from misleading disclosure are not scale related. If any misrepresentation signals that the information provided is inaccurate, but without providing guidance as to the extent of the problem, there will be a greater incentive to tell only the "big lie." Put differently, there may be economies of scale in misrepresentation.

[90] The target has already pledged all of its assets -- both tangible physical property and the intangible values associated with the reputations of its managers -- so little else can be done in the absence of inventive means to reduce the noise associated with the target's signals.

act to close the verification gap left by the target's residual final-period problems. Suppose one could discover what can be called a reputational intermediary: Someone paid to verify another party's information.[91] When residual final-period problems prevent a target from completely verifying the information it provides, a third party can offer *its* reputation as a bond that the target's information is accurate. The value of the transaction then increases because information costs are reduced, and the reputational intermediary is paid some portion of the increase as compensation for the pledge of its reputation.

The third party's role will be successful, however, only if there are no final-period problems associated with its verification. The intermediary is paid only because its reputation renders it trustworthy in circumstances when a party to the transaction could not be trusted. Unlike the target, the intermediary expects future transactions in which it again will pledge its reputation. If the intermediary cheats in one transaction -- by failing to discover or disclose seller misrepresentations[92] -- its reputation will suffer and, in a subsequent transaction, its verification will be less completely believed. The result will be a smaller increase in the value of the subsequent transaction because of the intermediary's participation and, in turn, a lower payment to the intermediary.[93] And as long as the intermediary will be penalized in subsequent periods for cheating in this period, there will be no final-period problems to dilute the intermediary's signal of accuracy.[94]

Cf. Anjan Thakor, *An Exploration of Competitive Signaling Equilibria with "Third Party" Information Production: The Case of Debt Insurance*, 37 J.Fin. 717 (1982) (problem of additional verification when issuer of debt has already pledged its assets to repay).

[91] The concept of a reputational intermediary is developed in Gilson & Kraakman (1984), *supra* note 36, at 604-07, 618-21.

[92] The intermediary can cheat in two quite different ways. First, the intermediary may discover that the target's information is misleading, but because of payments received from the target, may not disclose to the acquirer. In this setting it is the acquirer who is being cheated. Second, the intermediary may simply shirk its responsibilities to investigate the accuracy of the target's information. In this setting both the acquirer and target are being cheated, the acquirer because it has been misled about the accuracy of the target's information by the behavior of the intermediary, and the target because it has paid for verification that was not actually performed, with the resulting risk that it will be blamed by the acquirer for future failures of the business. The latter conclusion is limited to cases where the loss to the target resulting from the risk of future blame exceeds the gain to the target from the nondisclosure.

[93] The intermediary may pledge more than its reputation depending on whether it also incurs liability if the target's information behind which it has stood proves inaccurate. The liability standards with respect to lawyers are considered *infra*. For discussion of liability for accountants acting as reputational intermediaries, see T.J. Filflis, *Current Problems of Accountants' Responsibilities to Third Parties*, 28 Vand.L.Rev. 31 (1975); Samuel Gruenbaum & Marc Steinberg, *Accountants' Liability and Responsibility: Securities, Criminal and Common Law*, 13 Loy.L.A.L.Rev. 247 (1980).

[94] To say that there are *no* final-period problems is something of an overstatement. The analysis is really an application of the insight that when product quality is difficult to determine ex ante, as here with the verification role of an intermediary, but easy to determine ex post, as here when the passage of time will demonstrate whether the target's information

In fact, lawyers and accountants commonly play the role of reputational intermediary. And once we think of them as being in the business of selling -- more accurately, renting -- their reputations,[95] a number of examples readily come to mind in which this phenomenon seems to be at work. Practicing lawyers will recall instances when, having been advised that they were to represent their client in a transaction with an unfamiliar party on the other side, their initial question to their client concerned the identity of the other side's lawyers. Implicit in the question is that the identity of the lawyer conveys information about the lawyer's client; i.e., a reputable business lawyer would not risk his reputation by representing an untrustworthy client.[96] Similarly, it is a common occurrence for companies about to make an initial public offering to switch to a Big Six auditor.[97] Since the previous auditing firm apparently satisfied *management's* need for information, the discovery of systematic switching when the company is, in effect, to be sold to the public, strongly suggests a reputational explanation.[98]

It is from this perspective that an important part of the role for lawyers and accountants described in the acquisition agreement can best be understood. As already discussed, acquisition agreements commonly require that an opinion of the target's counsel be delivered to the acquirer as a condition to the acquirer's obligation to complete the transaction. It is also common further to condition the acquirer's obligation on receipt of an opinion of the target's independent accountant -- the "cold comfort" letter.[99] While we cannot examine here the entire range of third-party opinions given in acquisition transactions, a particular opinion often required of the target's lawyer and the accountant's cold comfort letter most prominently highlight the reputational intermediary role played by both professionals.

---

was inaccurate, the provider of the good or service will make investments in firm-specific capital -- like reputation -- that will be devalued if actual quality turns out to be lower than that represented. Cf. Linda DeAngelo, *Auditor Size and Audit Quality,* 3 J.Acct. & Econ. 183 (1981) (value of audit depends on size of investment in firm-specific assets made by particular auditor; larger accounting firms offer a more believable signal of accuracy to third parties than smaller firms).

[95] The role of lawyers as reputational intermediaries is developed in Ronald Gilson & Robert Mnookin, *Sharing Among the Human Capitalists: An Economic Inquiry into the Corporate Law Firm and How Partners Split Profits,* 37 Stan.L.Rev. 313 (1985).

[96] See Gilson & Mnookin (1985), *supra* note 95, at 366-68.

[97] Charles Carpenter & Robert Strawser, *Displacement of Auditors When Clients Go Public,* 131 J.Acct. 55 (June 1971); cf. DeAngelo (1981), *supra* note 94 (verification-based explanation for phenomenon).

[98] The reputational role of public accountants generally is discussed in a substantial literature, with particular emphasis on the need for and function of the independence requirement. See George Benston, *The Market for Public Accounting Services: Demand, Supply and Regulation,* 2 Acct.J. 2 (1979); DeAngelo (1981), *supra* note 94; Ross Watts & Jerold Zimmerman, *Agency Problems, Auditing, and the Theory of the Firm: Some Evidence,* 26 J.L. & Econ. 613 (1983); Robert Wilson, *Auditing: Perspectives from Multi-Person Decision Theory,* 58 Acctng.Rev. 305 (1983).

[99] See Freund (1975), *supra* note 7, at 301-04.

The opinion commonly requested from the target's lawyer that "we are not aware of any factual information that would lead us to believe that the agreement contains an untrue statement of a material fact or omits to state a fact necessary to make the statements made therein not misleading,"[100] and the cold comfort opinion typically requested of the target's accountant to the effect that there have been no changes in specified financial statement items since the last audited financial statements,[101] share a common conceptual underpinning that is reputationally based. The central characteristic of both opinions is that neither alters the total *quantity* of information that has been produced for the buyer. Rephrased, the lawyer's statement is simply that a third party who has been intimately involved in the *target's* production of information for the acquirer does not believe the target has misled the acquirer. It is quite clearly the *lawyer's* reputation[102] for diligence and honesty -- that is intended to be placed at risk.[103] Similarly, the cold comfort

---

[100] See Bermant (1974), *supra* note 53, at 190; *California State Bar Report, supra* note 53, at 1012.

[101] Prior to 1971, the language of the accountants' cold comfort letter was quite similar to that of the lawyers' opinion: Based on a limited review, nothing had come to their attention that gave them reason to believe that there had been any material adverse change in the company's financial position. This correspondence changed with the issuance of Statement on Auditing Procedures No. 48 (October, 1971), codified as American Institute of Certified Public Accountants, Statements on Auditing Standards § 630 (1973), which limits the letter to identifying decreases in the amounts of specified items -- such as net current assets, net sales and net assets. See Freund (1975), *supra* note 7, at 302-03.

[102] There is also a small risk of liability based on the rendering of an incorrect opinion. The standards for the imposition of liability to third parties based on incorrect legal opinions are discussed in, e.g., *California State Bar Report, supra* note 53, at 1006-07; James Fuld, *Lawyers' Standards and Responsibilities in Rendering Opinions*, 33 Bus.Law. 1295 (1978). It is also interesting that the legal profession has developed ethical prohibitions barring misrepresentation of facts by lawyers. See *Model Rules of Professional Conduct* ¶ 4.1 (1983) (a lawyer shall not knowingly make a false statement of material fact to a third person or fail to disclose a material fact when nondisclosure would be equivalent to a material misrepresentation). This prohibition may be best understood as an effort to extend a reputational role to lawyers generally, by reducing the incentives for a lawyer to free ride -- by making misrepresentations to help a client -- because he did not bear the full cost of the reduction in the profession's reputation that would result from his action.

[103] The importance of the lawyer's reputation in shaping the character of the expected opinion can be clearly seen in the familiar debate over from whom the acquirer will accept an opinion on behalf of the target. For example, acquirers will frequently object to receiving the opinion of the target's in-house counsel with respect to certain items. Identifying the matters for which the acquirer will or will not accept the opinion of the target's in-house counsel is a good way to distinguish those aspects of the opinion of counsel that serve primarily an information-production function from those that serve primarily a verification function. In-house counsel will often have a cost advantage with respect to the information-production function because of their more intimate knowledge of their client. With respect to the verification function, however, the ability to serve as a reputational intermediary requires a sufficient diversity of clients such that a penalty will be imposed in future dealings if the intermediary cheats. See Gilson & Mnookin (1985), *supra* note 95, at 368. As a result, opinions that serve a verification function are largely limited to outside

letter adds no new facts to those that have already been produced by means of the target's representations and warranties; the accountant's letter adds only the imprimatur of a respectable third party by attesting to the accuracy of the information produced by the target.

The care with which both of these third-party opinions are qualified further demonstrates their information-verification function. The lawyer's opinion typically will state explicitly that the firm has made no independent investigation of the facts -- i.e., that it has engaged in no information production concerning the accuracy of the information provided by the target.[104]   The accountant's opinion, in turn, will set out in detail the procedures that were undertaken, and stress that they are far more limited than what would be required for an audit.[105]

C.   Normative Implications: How to Create Value

In Section B of this Chapter, we examined the central elements of a typical corporate acquisition agreement for evidence that business lawyers do serve as transaction cost engineers, and that this function has the potential for creating value. If business lawyers do act to bridge the gap between the perfect market assumptions of capital asset pricing theory and the drastically less-than-perfect market conditions of the world in which transactions actually take place, this activity should be visible from examination of a by now standardized document -- the acquisition agreement -- that creates the structure for the transfer of a significant capital asset. From this perspective, the traditional contractual approaches reflected in the agreement should act to ameliorate the failure of one or more of the key perfect market assumptions.

We found, consistent with the transaction cost engineer hypothesis, that important elements of the acquisition agreement serve to remedy failures of the perfect market assumptions on which capital asset pricing theory is based. Earnout or contingent pricing techniques respond to the failure of the

---

counsel, while those that serve an information-production function are often accepted from in-house counsel.

Similarly, where the target's counsel wishes to deliver the opinion of another lawyer, as with respect to a matter governed by the law of a foreign jurisdiction, the acquirer often will require either that the target's counsel nonetheless render his opinion, albeit with explicit reference to reliance on the supplemental opinion, or give the opinion that the acquirer is justified in relying on the supplemental opinion. See Freund (1975), *supra* note 7, at 310-11. Here the underlying assumption seems to be that an out-of-state lawyer is not likely to be a repeat player in the acquirer's state and, thus, has not really put his reputation at stake. This analysis would suggest that when a "national" firm renders a foreign law opinion, the acquirer would not require a covering opinion by the target's counsel.

[104] See *California State Bar Report, supra* note 53, at 1012.

[105] See American Institute of Certified Public Accountants, Statement on Auditing Standards ¶ 630 (1973).

homogeneous-expectations assumption; controls over operation of the target's business during the period in which the determinants of the contingent price are measured respond to the failure of the common-time-horizon assumption; and the panoply of representations and warranties, together with provisions for indemnification and other verification techniques, respond to the failure of the costless-information assumption.

The next step is to emphasize the normative implications of identifying how a business lawyer can create value. The discussion of the acquisition agreement in Sections A and B of this Chapter highlighted a variety of ways in which recognition of the business lawyer's transaction cost engineering role and its theoretical underpinnings can make devising and negotiating responses to market imperfections easier and more effective. For example, understanding the function of the different elements of the agreement exposed the cooperative character of some matters -- like warranties and indemnification -- that traditionally have been considered as involving only distributive bargaining. Similarly, understanding the function of the variety of knowledge qualifications found in typical representations and warranties suggests a more effective way of achieving that end.

An additional value to understanding the theoretical underpinnings of transactional structure should also be stressed. Theory is an extremely efficient way of conveying and storing information. Suppose a client asks a lawyer to represent him in a transaction. One way the lawyer might analyze the transaction is first to categorize it -- as a corporate, or real estate, or venture capital deal -- and then look to alternative structural techniques commonly used in the relevant category. More prosaicly, the lawyer would look in the index to his firm's form file under the heading of the category of the particular transaction. Because this approach treats each technique as unique to a category -- solutions used in venture capital deals -- it requires the lawyer to learn and retain an amount of information equal to the sum of the techniques available in each category. A transaction cost engineering approach to the analysis defines structural techniques in a way -- as responses to failures of perfect market assumptions -- that they are applicable to all categories of transactions. One thus analyzes a transaction by, for example, first locating the inevitable information-cost problem and then selecting an information-cost technique to solve it, rather than by pigeonholing the transaction and then limiting the techniques considered to those traditionally associated with a particular category. Not only does this approach make it easier to teach new lawyers how to analyze a transaction, but it also facilitates creative responses to new forms of transactions that do not fit within traditional categories.

A final point should also be stressed. We have focused in this Chapter on bringing capital asset pricing theory to bear on the general structure of the acquisition agreement. It can also have significant value in shaping the substance of the transaction itself. Suppose the seller of a business agrees to take an installment note as part of the consideration to be received. In the absence of a market for that note, so that it can be sold and the proceeds invested in a diversified portfolio, capital asset pricing theory tells us that the seller bears more than systematic risk; he bears the unsystematic, firm specific, risk that the buyer will default. If that risk can be eliminated, the value of the installment note to the seller will be increased; the lawyer will have created value. How should the seller's lawyer determine what kind of security best protects the seller against the risk of default? Understanding that the problem is one of portfolio diversification facilitates design of an appropriate transactional structure. The seller in the first instance holds a portfolio composed of a single asset: The buyer's note. The analytic problem is devising additional assets that can be added to the portfolio so as to cause its value to be invariant to the buyer's default.

The importance of understanding the opportunity for business lawyers to create value by acting as transaction cost engineers is underscored by recognition that this function is not traditionally "legal," nor are there any special requirements peculiar to lawyers necessary to play this role. One need not be able to recite ancient Latin incantations to bless the union of the parties' interests through exchange.[106] The fact is that formal distinctions between professions which protected the lawyer's central role in transactional structuring have been and are likely to continue to break down.[107] There has been a substantial growth in competition for transactional responsibility -- not among lawyers, although that, to be sure, has also grown -- but with other professions. Increasingly, other institutions, like investment banking and public accounting firms, are recognizing that the role of transaction cost engineer, long dominated by the legal profession,[108] is contestable. Even if the imprimatur of a lawyer remains necessary to convince a client that all bases have been touched, lawyers can be employed by investment banking and accounting firms without fear of being charged with unlawful practice. In a competitive market, those who are best succeed. Bringing theory to bear on practice can make business lawyers better at what they do.

---

[106] One might, however, need a license; legislation providing that only a lawyer can provide a specified service may result in lawyers providing the service even though non-lawyers could also provide it. See Deborah Rhode, *Policing the Professional Monopoly: A Constitutional and Empirical Analysis of Unauthorized Practice Prohibitions,* 34 Stan.L.Rev. 1 (1981). Yet the very fact that non-lawyers could provide the service belies the fact that it is peculiarly legal. In any event, such restrictive licensing regimes have not been the basis for direct protection of the lawyer's role as transaction cost engineer.

[107] James Freund has noted this blurring of professional roles in an acquisition setting:
There is a great intermeshing of disciplines in connection with a merger negotiation. My experience is that everyone else involved -- accountants, businessmen, investment bankers -- contributes ideas that could be termed "legal," while the lawyer himself is frequently pointing out considerations that could be considered "accounting" or "business" or "financial."
Freund (1975), *supra* note 7, at 4-5.

[108] See Gilson (1984), *supra* note 1, at 296-300.

APPENDIX *A*

SELECTED PROVISIONS OF THE SECURITIES EXCHANGE ACT OF 1934 AND RELATED REGULATIONS

Table of Contents

EXCHANGE ACT §§ 13(d), (e), (f) and (g)

(d)(1) Any person who, after acquiring directly or indirectly the beneficial ownership of any equity security of a class which is registered pursuant to section 12 of this title, or any equity security of an insurance company which would have been required to be so registered except for the exemption contained in section 12(g)(2)(G) of this title, or any equity security issued by a closed-end investment company registered under the Investment Company Act of 1940, is directly or indirectly the beneficial owner of more than 5 per centum of such class shall, within ten days after such acquisition, send to the issuer of the security at its principal executive office, by registered or certified mail, send to each exchange where the security is traded, and file with the Commission, a statement containing such of the following information, and such additional information, as the Commission may by rules and regulations prescribe as necessary or appropriate in the public interest or for the protection of investors—

(A) the background, and identity, residence, and citizenship of, and the nature of such beneficial ownership by, such person and all other persons by whom or on whose behalf the purchases have been or are to be effected;

(B) the source and amount of the funds or other consideration used or to be used in making the purchases, and if any part of the purchase price is represented or is to be represented by funds or other consideration borrowed or otherwise obtained for the purpose of acquiring, holding, or trading such security, a description of the transaction and the names of the parties thereto, except that where a source of funds is a loan made in the ordinary course of business by a bank, as defined in section 3(a)(6) of this title, if the person filing such statement so requests, the name of the bank shall not be made available to the public;

(C) if the purpose of the purchases or prospective purchases is to acquire control of the business of the issuer of the securities, any plans or proposals which such persons may have to liquidate such issuer, to sell its assets to or merge it with any other persons, or to make any other major change in its business or corporate structure;

(D) the number of shares of such security which are beneficially owned, and the number of shares concerning which there is a right to acquire, directly or indirectly, by (i) such person, and (ii) by each associate of such person, giving the background, identity, residence, and citizenship of each such associate; and

(E) information as to any contracts, arrangements, or understandings with any person with respect to any securities of the issuer, including but not limited to transfer of any of the securities, joint ventures, loan or option arrangements, puts or calls, guaranties of loans, guaranties against loss or guaranties of profits, division of losses or profits, or the giving or withholding of proxies, naming the persons with whom such contracts, arrangements, or understandings have been entered into, and giving the details thereof.

(2) If any material change occurs in the facts set forth in the statements to the issuer and the exchange, and in the statement filed with the Commission, an amendment shall be transmitted to the issuer and the exchange and shall be filed with the Commission, in accordance with such rules and regulations as the Commission may prescribe as necessary or appropriate in the public interest or for the protection of investors.

(3) When two or more persons act as a partnership, limited partnership, syndicate, or other group for the purpose of acquiring, holding, or disposing of securities of an issuer, such syndicate or group shall be deemed a "person" for the purposes of this subsection.

(4) In determining, for purposes of this subsection, any percentage of a class of any security, such class shall be deemed to consist of the amount of the outstanding securities of such class, exclusive of any securities of such class held by or for the account of the issuer or a subsidiary of the issuer.

(5) The Commission, by rule or regulation or by order, may permit any person to file in lieu of the statement required by paragraph (1) of this subsection or the rules and regulations thereunder, a notice stating the name of such person, the number of shares of any equity securities subject to paragraph (1) which are owned by him, the date of their acquisition and such other information as the Commission may specify, if it appears to the Commission that such securities were acquired by such person in the ordinary course of his business and were not acquired for the purpose of and do not have the effect of changing or influencing the control of the issuer nor in connection with or as a participant in any transaction having such purpose or effect.

(6) The provisions of this subsection shall not apply to—

(A) any acquisition or offer to acquire securities made or proposed to be made by means of a registration statement under the Securities Act of 1933;

(B) any acquisition of the beneficial ownership of a security which, together with all other acquisitions by the same person of securities of the same class during the preceding twelve months, does not exceed 2 per centum of that class;

(C) any acquisition of an equity security by the issuer of such security;

(D) any acquisition or proposed acquisition of a security which the Commission, by rules or regulations or by order, shall exempt from the provisions of this subsection as not entered into for the purpose of, and not having the effect of, changing or influencing the control of the issuer or otherwise as not comprehended within the purposes of this subsection.

(e)(1) It shall be unlawful for an issuer which has a class of equity securities registered pursuant to section 12 of this title, or which is a closed-end investment company registered under the Investment Company Act of 1940, to purchase any equity security issued by it if such purchase as in contravention of such rules and regulations as the Commission, in the public interest or for the protection of investors, may adopt (A) to define acts and practices which are fraudulent, deceptive, or manipulative, and (B) to prescribe means reasonably designed to prevent such acts and practices. Such rules and regulations may require such issuer to provide holders of equity securities of such class with such information relating to the reasons for such purchase, the source of funds, the number of shares to be purchased, the price to be paid for such securities, the method of purchase, and such additional information, as the Commission deems necessary or appropriate in the public interest or for the protection of investors, or which the Commission deems to be material to a determination whether such security should be sold.

(2) For the purpose of this subsection, a purchase by or for the issuer or any person controlling, controlled by, or under common control with the issuer, or a purchase subject to control of the issuer or any such person, shall be deemed to be a purchase by the issuer. The Commission shall have power to make rules and regulations implementing this paragraph in the public interest and for the protection

of investors, including exemptive rules and regulations covering situations in which the Commission deems it unnecessary or inappropriate that a purchase of the type described in this paragraph shall be deemed to be a purchase by the issuer for purposes of some or all of the provisions of paragraph (1) of this subsection.

(3) At the time of filing such statement as the Commission may require by rule pursuant to paragraph (1) of this subsection, the person making the filing shall pay to the Commission a fee of <sfr>1/50<efr> of 1 per centum of the value of securities proposed to be purchased. The fee shall be reduced with respect to securities in an amount equal to any fee paid with respect to any securities issued in connection with the proposed transaction under section 6(b) of the Securities Act of 1933, or the fee paid under that section shall be reduced in an amount equal to the fee paid to the Commission in connection with such transaction under this paragraph.

(f)(1) Every institutional investment manager which uses the mails, or any means or instrumentality of interstate commerce in the course of its business as an institutional investment manager and which exercises investment discretion with respect to accounts holding equity securities of a class described in section 13(d)(1) of this title having an aggregate fair market value on the last trading day in any of the preceding twelve months of at least $100,000,000 or such lesser amount (but in no case less than $10,000,000) as the Commission, by rule, may determine, shall file reports with the Commission in such form, for such periods, and at such times after the end of such periods as the Commission, by rule, may prescribe, but in no event shall such reports be filed for periods longer than one year or shorter than one quarter. Such reports shall include for each such equity security held on the last day of the reporting period by accounts (in aggregate or by type as the Commission, by rule, may prescribe) with respect to which the institutional investment manager exercises investment discretion (other than securities held in amounts which the Commission, by rule, determines to be insignificant for purposes of this subsection), the name of the issuer and the title, class, CUSIP number, number of shares or principal amount, and aggregate fair market value of each such security. Such reports may also include for accounts (in aggregate or by type) with respect to which the institutional investment manager exercises investment discretion such of the following information as the Commission, by rule, prescribes—

(A) the name of the issuer and the title, class, CUSIP number, number of shares or principal amount, and aggregate fair market value or cost or amortized cost of each other security (other than an exempted security) held on the last day of the reporting period by such accounts;

(B) the aggregate fair market value or cost or amortized cost of exempted securities (in aggregate or by class) held on the last day of the reporting period by such accounts;

(C) the number of shares of each equity security of a class described in section 13(d)(1) of this title held on the last day of the reporting period by such accounts with respect to which the institutional investment manager possesses sole or shared authority to exercise the voting rights evidenced by such securities;

(D) the aggregate purchases and aggregate sales during the reporting period of each security (other than an exempted security) effected by or for such accounts; and

(E) with respect to any transaction or series of transactions having a market value of at least $500,000 or such other amount as the Commission, by rule, may determine, effected during the reporting period by or for such accounts in any equity security of a class described in section 13(d)(1) of this title—

    (i) the name of the issuer and the title, class, and CUSIP number of the security;

    (ii) the number of shares or principal amount of the security involved in the transaction;

    (iii) whether the transaction was a purchase or sale;

    (iv) the per share price or prices at which the transaction was effected;

    (v) the date or dates of the transaction;

    (vi) the date or dates of the settlement of the transaction;

    (vii) the broker or dealer through whom the transaction was effected;

    (viii) the market or markets in which the transaction was effected; and

    (ix) such other related information as the Commission, by rule, may prescribe.

(2) The Commission, by rule or order, may exempt, conditionally or unconditionally, any institutional investment manager or security or any class of institutional investment managers or securities from any or all of the provisions of this subsection or the rules thereunder. . . .

(4) In exercising its authority under this subsection, the Commission shall determine (and so state) that its action is necessary or appropriate in the public interest and for the protection of investors or to maintain fair and orderly markets or, in granting an exemption, that its action is consistent with the protection of investors and the purposes of this subsection. In exercising such authority the Commission shall take such steps as are within its power, including consulting with the Comptroller General of the United States, the Director of the Office of Management and Budget, the appropriate regulatory agencies, Federal and State authorities which, directly or indirectly, require reports from institutional investment managers of information substantially similar to that called for by this subsection, national securities exchanges, and registered securities associations, (A) to achieve uniform, centralized reporting of information concerning the securities holdings of and transactions by or for accounts with respect to which institutional investment managers exercise investment discretion, and (B) consistently with the objective set forth in the preceding subparagraph, to avoid unnecessarily duplicative reporting by, and minimize the compliance burden on, institutional investment managers. Federal authorities which, directly or indirectly, require reports from institutional investment managers of information substantially similar to that called for by this subsection shall cooperate with the Commission in the performance of its responsibilities under the preceding sentence. An institutional investment manager which is a bank, the deposits of which are insured in accordance with the Federal Deposit Insurance Act, shall file with the appropriate regulatory agency a copy of every report filed with the Commission pursuant to this subsection.

(5)(A) For purposes of this subsection the term "institutional investment manager" includes any person, other than a natural person, investing in or buying and selling securities for its own account, and any person exercising investment discretion with respect to the account of any other person.

    (B) The Commission shall adopt such rules as it deems necessary or appropriate to prevent duplicative reporting pursuant to this subsection by two or more institutional investment managers exercising investment discretion with respect to the same amount.

(g)(1) Any person who is directly or indirectly the beneficial owner of more than 5 per centum of any security of a class described in subsection (d)(1) of this section shall send to the issuer of the security and shall file with the Commission a statement setting forth, in such form and at such time as the Commission may, by rule, prescribe—

(A) such person's identity, residence, and citizenship; and

(B) the number and description of the shares in which such person has an interest and the nature of such interest.

(2) If any material change occurs in the facts set forth in the statement sent to the issuer and filed with the Commission, an amendment shall be transmitted to the issuer and shall be filed with the Commission, in accordance with such rules and regulations as the Commission may prescribe as necessary or appropriate in the public interest or for the protection of investors.

(3) When two or more persons act as a partnership, limited partnership, syndicate, or other group for the purpose of acquiring, holding, or disposing of securities of an issuer, such syndicate or group shall be deemed a "person" for the purposes of this subsection.

(4) In determining, for purposes of this subsection, any percentage of a class of any security, such class shall be deemed to consist of the amount of the outstanding securities of such class, exclusive of any securities of such class held by or for the account of the issuer or a subsidiary of the issuer.

(5) In exercising its authority under this subsection, the Commission shall take such steps as it deems necessary or appropriate in the public interest or for the protection of investors (A) to achieve centralized reporting of information regarding ownership, (B) to avoid unnecessarily duplicative reporting by and minimize the compliance burden on persons required to report, and (C) to tabulate and promptly make available the information contained in any report filed pursuant to this subsection in a manner which will, in the view of the Commission, maximize the usefulness of the information to other Federal and State agencies and the public.

(6) The Commission may, by rule or order, exempt, in whole or in part, any person or class of persons from any or all of the reporting requirements of this subsection as it deems necessary or appropriate in the public interest or for the protection of investors.

REGULATIONS 13D–G

Rule 13d–1.   Filing of Schedule 13D and 13G

(a) Any person who, after acquiring directly or indirectly the beneficial ownership of any equity security of a class which is specified in paragraph (d), is directly or indirectly the beneficial owner of more than 5 percent of such class shall, within 10 days after such acquisition, send to the issuer of the security at its principal executive office, by registered or certified mail, and to each exchange where the security is traded, and file with the Commission, a statement containing the information required by Schedule 13D. Six copies of the statement, including all exhibits, shall be filed with the Commission.

(b)(1) A person who would otherwise be obligated under paragraph (a) to file a statement on Schedule 13D may, in lieu thereof, file with the Commission, within 45 days after the end of the calendar year in which such person became so obligated, six copies, including all exhibits, of a short form statement on Schedule 13G and send one copy each of such schedule to the issuer of the security at its principal executive office, by registered or certified mail, and to the principal national securities exchange where the security is traded: *Provided,* That it shall not be necessary to file a Schedule 13G unless the percentage of the class of equity security specified in paragraph (d) of this section beneficially owned as of the end of the calendar year is more than 5 percent: *And provided further,* That:

(i) Such person has acquired such securities in the ordinary course of his business and not with the purpose nor with the effect of changing or influencing the control of the issuer, nor in connection with or as a participant in any transaction having such purpose or effect, including any transaction subject to Rule 13d–3(b);   and

(ii) Such person is:

(A) A broker or dealer registered under section 15 of the Act;

(B) A bank as defined in Section 3(a)(6) of the Act;

(C) An insurance company as defined in Section 3(a)(19) of the Act;

(D) An investment company registered under Section 8 of the Investment Company Act of 1940;

(E) An investment adviser registered under Section 203 of the Investment Advisers Act of 1940;

(F) An employee benefit plan, or pension fund which is subject to the provisions of the Employee Retirement Income Security Act of 1974 ("ERISA") or an endowment fund;

(G) A parent holding company, provided the aggregate amount held directly by the parent, and directly and indirectly by its subsidiaries which are not persons specified in Rule 13d–1(b)(ii)(A) through (F), does not exceed one percent of the securities of the subject class;

(H) A group, provided that all the members are persons specified in Rule 13d–1(b)(1)(ii)(A) through (G);   and

(iii) Such person has promptly notified any other person (or group within the meaning of Section 13(d)(3) of the Act) on whose behalf it holds, on a discretionary basis, securities exceeding five percent of the class, of any acquisition or transaction on behalf of such other person which might be reportable by the person under Section 13(d) of the Act. This paragraph only requires notice to the account owner of information which the filing person reasonably should be expected to know and which would advise the account owner of an obligation he may have to file a statement pursuant to Section 13(d) of the Act or an amendment thereto.

(2) Any person relying on Rules 13d–1(b)(1) and 13d–2(b) shall, in addition to filing any statements required thereunder, file a statement on Schedule 13G, within ten days after the end of the first month in which such person's direct or indirect beneficial ownership exceeds ten percent of a class of equity securities specified in Rule 13d–1(c) computed as of the last day of the month, and thereafter within ten days after the end of any month in which such person's beneficial ownership of securities of such class, computed as of the last day of the month, increases or decreases by more than five percent of such class of equity securities. Six copies of

such statement, including all exhibits, shall be filed with the Commission and one each sent, by registered or certified mail, to the issuer of the security at its principal executive office and to the principal national securities exchange where the security is traded. Once an amendment has been filed reflecting beneficial ownership of five percent or less of the class of securities, no additional filings are required by this paragraph (b)(2) unless the person thereafter becomes the beneficial owner of more than ten percent of the class and is required to file pursuant to this provision.

(3)(i) Notwithstanding paragraphs (b)(1) and (2) and Rule 13d–2(b), a person shall immediately become subject to Rules 13d–1(a) and 13d–2(a) and shall promptly, but not more than 10 days later, file a statement on Schedule 13D if such person:

(A) Has reported that it is the beneficial owner of more than five percent of a class of equity securities in a statement on Schedule 13G pursuant to paragraph (b)(1) or (b)(2), or is required to report such acquisition but has not yet filed the schedule;

(B) Determines that it no longer has acquired or holds such securities in the ordinary course of business or not with the purpose nor with the effect of changing or influencing the control of the issuer, nor in connection with or as a participant in any transaction having such purpose or effect, including any transaction subject to Rule 13d–3(b); and

(C) is at that time the beneficial owner of more than five percent of a class of equity securities described in Rule 13d–1(c).

(ii) For the ten day period immediately following the date of the filing of a Schedule 13D pursuant to this paragraph (b)(3), such person shall not: (A) Vote or direct the voting of the securities described in paragraph (b)(3)(i)(A); nor, (B) Acquire an additional beneficial ownership interest in any equity securities of the issuer of such securities, nor of any person controlling such issuer.

(4) Any person who has reported an acquisition of securities in a statement on Schedule 13G pursuant to paragraph (b)(1) or (b)(2) and thereafter ceases to be a person specified in paragraph (b)(1)(ii) shall immediately become subject to Rules 13d–1(a) and 13d–2(a) and shall file, within ten days thereafter, a statement on Schedule 13D, in the event such person is a beneficial owner at that time of more than five percent of the class of equity securities.

(c) Any person who, as of December 31, 1978, or as of the end of any calendar year thereafter, is directly or indirectly the beneficial owner of more than 5 percent of any equity security of a class specified in paragraph (d) and who is not required to file a statement under paragraph (a) by virtue of the exemption provided by Section 13(d)(6)(A) or (B) of the Act, or because such beneficial ownership was acquired prior to December 20, 1970, or because such person otherwise (except for the exemption provided by Section 13(d)(6)(c) of the Act) is not required to file such statement, shall, within 45 days after the end of the calendar year in which such person became obligated to report under this paragraph, send to the issuer of the security at its principal executive office, by registered or certified mail, and file with the Commission a statement containing the information required by Schedule 13G. Six copies of the statement, including all exhibits, shall be filed with the Commission.

(d) For the purpose of this regulation, the term "equity security" means any equity security of a class which is registered pursuant to Section 12 of that Act, or any equity security of any insurance company which would have been required to be so registered except for the exemption contained in Section 12(g)(2)(G) of the Act, or any equity security issued by a closed-end investment company registered under the Investment Company Act of 1940; *Provided,* Such term shall not include securities of a class of non-voting securities.

(e) For the purpose of Sections 13(d) and 13(g), any person, in determining the amount of outstanding securities of a class of equity securities, may rely upon information set forth in the issuer's most recent quarterly or annual report, and any current report subsequent thereto, filed with the Commission pursuant to this Act, unless he knows or has reason to believe that the information contained therein is inaccurate. . . .

Rule 13d–2.   Filing of Amendments to Schedules 13D or 13G

(a) *Schedule 13D.* If any material change occurs in the facts set forth in the statement required by Rule 13d–1(a), including, but not limited to, any material increase or decrease in the percentage of the class beneficially owned, the person or persons who were required to file such statement shall promptly file or cause to be filed with the Commission and send or cause to be sent to the issuer at its principal executive office, by registered or certified mail, and to each exchange on which the security is traded an amendment disclosing such change.   An acquisition or disposition of beneficial ownership of securities in an amount equal to one percent or more of the class of securities shall be deemed "material" for purposes of this rule; acquisitions or dispositions of less than such amounts may be material, depending upon the facts and circumstances. Six copies of each such amendment shall be filed with the Commission.

(b) *Schedule 13G.* Notwithstanding paragraph (a) of this rule, and provided that the person or persons filing a statement pursuant to Rule 13d–1(b) continues to meet the requirements set forth therein, any person who has filed a short form statement on Schedule 13G shall amend such statement within forty-five days after the end of each calendar year if, as of the end of such calendar year, there are any changes in the information reported in the previous filing on that Schedule; *Provided, however,* that such amendment need not be filed with respect to a change in the percent of class outstanding previously reported if such change results solely from a change in the aggregate number of securities outstanding. Six copies of such amendment, including all exhibits, shall be filed with the Commission and one each sent, by registered or certified mail, to the issuer of the security at its principal executive office and to the principal national securities exchange where the security is traded. Once an amendment has been filed reflecting beneficial ownership of five percent or less of the class of securities, no additional filings are required unless the person thereafter becomes the beneficial owner of more than five percent of the class and is required to file pursuant to Rule 13d–1.

NOTE: For persons filing a short form statement pursuant to Rule 13d–1(b), See also Rule 13d–1(b)(2), (3) and (4).

Rule 13d–3.   Determination of Beneficial Owner

(a) For the purposes of section 13(d) and 13(g) of the Act a beneficial owner of a security includes any person who, directly or indirectly, through any contract, arrangement, understanding, relationship, or otherwise has or shares:

(1) *Voting power* which includes the power to vote, or to direct the voting of, such security; and/or,

(2) *Investment power* which includes the power to dispose, or to direct the disposition, of such security.

(b) Any person who, directly or indirectly, creates or uses a trust, proxy, power of attorney, pooling arrangement or any other contract, arrangement, or device with the purpose or effect of divesting such person of beneficial ownership of a security or preventing the vesting of such beneficial ownership as part of a plan or scheme to evade the reporting requirements of section 13(d) or 13(g) of the Act shall be deemed for purposes of such section to be the beneficial owner of such security.

(c) All securities of the same class beneficially owned by a person, regardless of the form which such beneficial ownership takes, shall be aggregated in calculating the number of shares beneficially owned by such person.

(d) Notwithstanding the provisions of paragraphs (a) and (c) of this rule:

(1)(i) A person shall be deemed to be the beneficial owner of a security, subject to the provisions of paragraph (b) of this rule, if that person has the right to acquire beneficial ownership of such security, as defined in Rule 13d–3(a) within sixty days, including but not limited to any right to acquire: (A) through the exercise of any option, warrant or right; (B) through the conversion of a security; (C) pursuant to the power to revoke a trust, discretionary account, or similar arrangement; or (D) pursuant to the automatic termination of a trust, discretionary account or similar arrangement; *Provided, however,* any person who acquires a security or power specified in paragraphs (A), (B) or (C), above, with the purpose or effect of changing or influencing the control of the issuer, or in connection with or as a participant in any transaction having such purpose or effect, immediately upon such acquisition shall be deemed to be the beneficial owner of the securities which may be acquired through the exercise or conversion of such security or power. Any securities not outstanding which are subject to such options, warrants, rights or conversion privileges shall be deemed to be outstanding for the purpose of computing the percentage of outstanding securities of the class owned by such person but shall not be deemed to be outstanding for the purpose of computing the percentage of the class by any other person.

(ii) Paragraph (i) remains applicable for the purpose of determining the obligation to file with respect to the underlying security even though the option, warrant, right or convertible security is of a class of equity security, as defined in Rule 13d–1(c), and may therefore give rise to a separate obligation to file.

(2) A member of a national securities exchange shall not be deemed to be a beneficial owner of securities held directly or indirectly by it on behalf of another person solely because such member is the record holder of such securities and, pursuant to the rules of such exchange, may direct the vote of such securities, without instruction, on other than contested matters or matters that may affect substantially the rights or privileges of the holders of the securities to be voted, but is otherwise precluded by the rules of such exchange from voting without instruction.

(3) A person who in the ordinary course of business is a pledgee of securities under a written pledge agreement shall not be deemed to be the beneficial owner of such pledged securities until the pledgee has taken all formal steps necessary which are required to declare a default and determines

that the power to vote or to direct the vote or to dispose or to direct the disposition of such pledged securities will be exercised, provided that:

(i) The pledgee agreement is bona fide and was not entered into with the purpose nor with the effect of changing or influencing the control of the issuer, nor in connection with any transaction having such purpose or effect, including any transaction subject to Rule 13d–3(b);

(ii) The pledgee is a person specified in Rule 13d–1(b)(ii), including persons meeting the conditions set forth in paragraph (G) thereof; and

(iii) The pledgee agreement, prior to default, does not grant to the pledgee:

(A) The power to vote or to direct the vote of the pledged securities; or

(B) The power to dispose or direct the disposition of the pledged securities, other than the grant of such power(s) pursuant to a pledge agreement under which credit is extended subject to Regulation T and in which the pledgee is a broker or dealer registered under section 15 of the Act.

(4) A person engaged in business as an underwriter of securities who acquires securities through his participation in good faith in a firm commitment underwriting registered under the Securities Act of 1933 shall not be deemed to be the beneficial owner of such securities until the expiration of forty days after the date of such acquisition.

Rule 13d–4.   Disclaimer of Beneficial Ownership

Any person may expressly declare in any statement filed that the filing of such statement shall not be construed as an admission that such person is, for the purposes of section 13(d) or 13(g) of the Act, the beneficial owner of any securities covered by the statement.

Rule 13d–5.   Acquisition of Securities

(a) A person who becomes a beneficial owner of securities shall be deemed to have acquired such securities for purposes of Section 13(d)(1) of the Act, whether such acquisition was through purchase or otherwise. However, executors or administrators of a decedent's estate generally will be presumed not to have acquired beneficial ownership of the securities in the decedent's estate until such time as such executors or administrators are qualified under local law to perform their duties.

(b)(1) When two or more persons agree to act together for the purpose of acquiring, holding, voting or disposing of equity securities of an issuer, the group formed thereby shall be deemed to have acquired beneficial ownership, for purposes of Sections 13(d) and 13(g) of the Act, as of the date of such agreement, of all equity securities of that issuer beneficially owned by any such persons.

(2) Notwithstanding the previous paragraph, a group shall be deemed not to have acquired any equity securities beneficially owned by the other members of the group solely by virtue of their concerted actions relating to the purchase

of equity securities directly from an issuer in a transaction not involving a public offering, provided that:

(i) All the members of the group are persons specified in Rule 13d–1(b)(1)(ii);

(ii) The purchase is in the ordinary course of each member's business and not with the purpose nor with the effect of changing or influencing control of the issuer, nor in connection with or as a participant in any transaction having such purpose or effect, including any transaction subject to Rule 13d–3(b);

(iii) There is no agreement among, or between any members of the group to act together with respect to the issuer or its securities except for the purpose of facilitating the specific purchase involved; and

(iv) The only actions among or between any members of the group with respect to the issuer or its securities subsequent to the closing date of the non-public offering are those which are necessary to conclude ministerial matters directly related to the completion of the offer or sale of the securities.

Rule 13d–6.   Exemption of Certain Acquisitions

The acquisition of securities of an issuer by a person who, prior to such acquisition, was a beneficial owner of more than five percent of the outstanding securities of the same class as those acquired shall be exempt from section 13(d) of the act, *provided that:*

(a) The acquisition is made pursuant to preemptive subscription rights in an offering made to all holders of securities of the class to which the preemptive subscription rights pertain;

(b) Such person does not acquire additional securities except through the exercise of his pro rata share of the preemptive subscription rights; and

(c) The acquisition is duly reported, if required, pursuant to section 16(a) of the Act and the rules and regulations thereunder. . . .

Schedule 13D.   Information to be Included in Statements Filed Pursuant to Rule 13d–1(a) and Amendments Thereto Filed Pursuant to Rule 13d–2(a)

* * *

GENERAL INSTRUCTIONS

* * *

C. If the statement is filed by a general or limited partnership, syndicate, or other group, the information called for by Items 2-6, inclusive, shall be given with respect to (i) each partner of such general partnership; (ii) each partner who is denominated as a general partner or who functions as a general partner of such limited partnership; (iii) each member of such syndicate or group; and (iv) each person controlling such partner or member. If the statement is filed by a corporation or if a person referred to in (i), (ii), (iii) or (iv) of this Instruction is a corporation, the information called for by the above mentioned items shall be given with respect to (a) each executive officer and director of such corporation; (b) each person controlling such corporation; and (c) each executive officer and director of any corporation or other person ultimately in control of such corporation.

Item 1. Security and Issuer

State the title of the class of equity securities to which this statement relates and the name and address of the principal executive offices of the issuer of such securities.

Item 2. Identity and Background

If the person filing this statement or any person enumerated in Instruction C of this statement is a corporation, general partnership, limited partnership, syndicate or other group of persons, state its name, the state or other place of its organization, its principal business, the address of its principal business, the address of its principal office and the information required by (d) and (e) of this Item. If the person filing this statement or any person enumerated in Instruction C is a natural person, provide the information specified in (a) through (f) of this Item with respect to such person(s).

    (a) Name;

    (b) Residence or business address;

    (c) Present principal occupation or employment and the name, principal business and address of any corporation or other organization in which such employment is conducted;

    (d) Whether or not, during the last five years, such person has been convicted in a criminal proceeding (excluding traffic violations or similar misdemeanors) and, if so, give the dates, nature of conviction, name and location of court, any penalty imposed, or other disposition of the case;

    (e) Whether or not, during the last five years, such person was a party to a civil proceeding of a judicial or administrative body of competent jurisdiction and as a result of such proceeding was or is subject to a judgment, decree or final order enjoining future violations of, or prohibiting or mandating activities subject to, federal or state securities laws or finding any violation with respect to such laws; and, if so, identify and describe such proceedings and summarize the terms of such judgment, decree or final order; and

    (f) Citizenship.

Item 3. Source and Amount of Funds or Other Consideration

State the source and the amount of funds or other consideration used or to be used in making the purchases, and if any part of the purchase price is or will be represented by funds or other consideration borrowed or otherwise obtained for the purpose of acquiring, holding, trading or voting the securities, a description of the transaction and the names of the parties thereto. Where material, such information should also be provided with respect to prior acquisitions not previously reported pursuant to this regulation. If the source of all or any part of the funds is a loan made in the ordinary course of business by a bank, as defined in Section 3(a)(6) of the Act, the name of the bank shall not be made available to the public if the person at the time of filing the statement so requests in writing and files such request, naming such bank, with the Secretary of the Commission. If the securities were acquired other than by purchase, describe the method of acquisition.

Item 4. Purpose of Transaction

State the purpose or purposes of the acquisition of securities of the issuer. Describe any plans or proposals which the reporting persons may have which relate to or would result in:

(a) The acquisition by any person of additional securities of the issuer, or the disposition of securities of the issuer;

(b) An extraordinary corporate transaction, such as a merger, reorganization or liquidation, involving the issuer or any of its subsidiaries;

(c) A sale or transfer of a material amount of assets of the issuer or of any of its subsidiaries;

(d) Any change in the present board of directors or management of the issuer, including any plans or proposals to change the number or term of directors or to fill any existing vacancies on the board;

(e) Any material change in the present capitalization or dividend policy of the issuer;

(f) Any other material change in the issuer's business or corporate structure, including but not limited to, if the issuer is a registered closed-end investment company, any plans or proposals to make any changes in its investment policy for which a vote is required by section 13 of the Investment Company Act of 1940;

(g) Changes in the issuer's charter, bylaws or instruments corresponding thereto or other actions which may impede the acquisition of control of the issuer by any person;

(h) Causing a class of securities of the issuer to be delisted from a national securities exchange or to cease to be authorized to be quoted in an inter-dealer quotation system of a registered national securities association;

(i) A class of equity securities of the issuer becoming eligible for termination of registration pursuant to Section 12(g)(4) of the Act; or

(j) Any action similar to any of those enumerated above.

Item 5. Interest in Securities of the Issuer

(a) State the aggregate number and percentage of the class of securities identified pursuant to Item 1 (which may be based on the number of securities outstanding as contained in the most recently available filing with the Commission by the issuer unless the filing person has reason to believe such information is not current) beneficially owned (identifying those shares which there is a right to acquire) by each person named in Item 2. The above mentioned information should also be furnished with respect to persons who, together with any of the persons named in Item 2, comprise a group within the meaning of Section 13(d)(3) of the Act;

(b) For each person named in response to paragraph (a), indicate the number of shares as to which there is sole power to vote or to direct the vote, shared power to vote or to direct the vote, sole power to dispose or to direct the disposition. Provide the applicable information required by Item 2 with respect to each person with whom the power to vote or to direct the vote or to dispose or direct the disposition is shared;

(c) Describe any transactions in the class of securities reported on that were effected during the past sixty days or since the most recent filing on Schedule 13D (§ 240.13d–101), whichever is less, by the persons named in response to paragraph (a).

Instruction. The description of a transaction required by Item 5(c) shall include, but not necessarily be limited to: (1) the identity of the person covered by Item 5(c) who effected the transaction; (2) the date of the transaction; (3) the amount of securities involved; (4) the price per share or unit; and (5) where and how the transaction was effected.

(d) If any other person is known to have the right to receive or the power to direct the receipt of dividends from, or the proceeds from the sale of, such securities, a statement to that effect should be included in response to this time and, if such interest relates to more than five percent of the class, such person should be identified. A listing of the shareholders of an investment company registered under the Investment Company Act of 1940 or the beneficiaries of an employee benefit plan, pension fund or endowment fund is not required.

(e) If applicable, state the date on which the reporting person ceased to be the beneficial owner of more than five percent of the class of securities.

Instruction. For computations regarding securities which represent a right to acquire an underlying security, see Rule 13d–3(d)(1) and the note thereto.

Item 6. Contracts, Arrangements, Understandings or Relationships With Respect to Securities of the Issuer

Describe any contracts, arrangements, understandings or relationships (legal or otherwise) among the persons named in Item 2 and between such persons and any person with respect to any securities of the issuer, including but not limited to transfer or voting of any of the securities, finder's fees, joint ventures, loan or option arrangements, puts or calls, guarantees of profits, division of profits or loss, or the giving or withholding of proxies, naming the persons with whom such contracts, arrangements, understandings or relationships have been entered into. Include such information for any of the securities that are pledged or otherwise subject to a contingency the occurrence of which would give another person voting power or investment power over such securities except that disclosure of standard default and similar provisions contained in loan agreements need not be included.

Item 7. Material to Be Filed as Exhibits

The following shall be filed as exhibits: Copies of written agreements relating to the filing of joint acquisition statements as required by Rule 13d–1(f) (§ 240.13d–1(f)) and copies of all written agreements, contracts, arrangements, understandings, plans, or proposals relating to: (1) The borrowing of funds to finance the acquisition as disclosed in Item 3; (2) the acquisition of issuer control, liquidation, sale of assets, merger, or change in business or corporate structure, or any other matter as disclosed in Item 4; and (3) the transfer or voting of the securities, finder's fees, joint ventures, options, puts, calls, guarantees of loans, guarantees against loss or of profit, or the giving or withholding of any proxy as disclosed in Item 6. . . .

Rule 13e–1.   Purchase of Securities by Issuer Thereof

When a person other than the issuer makes a tender offer for, or request or invitation for tenders of, any class of equity securities of an issuer subject to section 13(e) of the Act, and such person has filed a statement with the Commission pursuant to Rule 14d–1 and the issuer has received notice thereof, such issuer shall not thereafter, during the period such tender offer, request or invitation continues, purchase any equity securities of which it is the issuer unless it has complied with both of the following conditions:

(a) The issuer has filed with the Commission eight copies of a statement containing the information specified below with respect to the proposed purchases:

(1) The title and amount of securities to be purchased, the names of the persons or classes of persons from whom, and the market in which, the securities are to be purchased, including the name of any exchange on which the purchase is to be made;

(2) The purpose for which the purchase is to be made and whether the securities are to be retired, held in the treasury of the issuer or otherwise disposed of, indicating such disposition; and

(3) The source and amount of funds or other consideration used or to be used in making the purchases, and if any part of the purchase price or proposed purchase price is represented by funds or other consideration borrowed or otherwise obtained for the purpose of acquiring, holding, or trading the securities, a description of the transaction and the names of the parties thereto; and

(b) The issuer has at any time within the past 6 months sent or given to its equity security holders the substance of the information contained in the statement required by paragraph (a).

Provided, however, That any issuer making such purchases which commenced prior to July 30, 1968, shall, if such purchases continue after such date, comply with the provisions of this rule on or before August 12, 1968.

Rule 13e–3.   Going Private Transactions by Certain Issuers or Their Affiliates

(a) *Definitions.* Unless indicated otherwise or the context otherwise requires, all terms used in this section and in Schedule 13E–3 shall have the same meaning as in the Act or elsewhere in the General Rules and Regulations thereunder. In addition, the following definitions apply:

(1) An "affiliate" of an issuer is a person that directly or indirectly through one or more intermediaries controls, is controlled by, or is under common control with such issuer. For the purposes of this section only, a person who is not an affiliate of an issuer at the commencement of such person's tender offer for a class of equity securities of such issuer will not be

deemed an affiliate of such issuer prior to the stated termination of such tender offer and any extensions thereof;

(2) The term "purchase" means any acquisition for value including, but not limited to, (i) any acquisition pursuant to the dissolution of an issuer subsequent to the sale or other disposition of substantially all the assets of such issuer to its affiliate, (ii) any acquisition pursuant to a merger, (iii) any acquisition of fractional interests in connection with a reverse stock split, and (iv) any acquisition subject to the control of an issuer or an affiliate of such issuer;

(3) A "Rule 13e–3 transaction" is any transaction or series of transactions involving one or more of the transactions described in paragraph (a)(3)(i) of this section which has either a reasonable likelihood or a purpose of producing, either directly or indirectly, any of the effects described in paragraph (a)(3)(ii) of this section;

(i) The transactions referred to in paragraph (a)(3) of this section are:

(A) A purchase of any equity security by the issuer of such security or by an affiliate of such issuer;

(B) A tender offer for or request or invitation for tenders of any equity security made by the issuer of such class of securities or by an affiliate of such issuer; or

(C) A solicitation subject to Regulation 14A of any proxy, consent or authorization of, or a distribution subject to Regulation 14C of information statements to, any equity security holder by the issuer of the class of securities or by an affiliate of such issuer, in connection with: a merger, consolidation, reclassification, recapitalization, reorganization or similar corporate transaction of an issuer or between an issuer (or its subsidiaries) and its affiliate; a sale of substantially all the assets of an issuer to its affiliate or group of affiliates; or a reverse stock split of any class of equity securities of the issuer involving the purchase of fractional interests.

(ii) The effects referred to in paragraph (a)(3) of this section are:

(A) Causing any class of equity securities of the issuer which is subject to section 12(g) or section 15(d) or the Act to be held of record by less than 300 persons; or

(B) Causing any class of equity securities of the issuer which is either listed on a national securities exchange or authorized to be quoted in an inter-dealer quotation system of a registered national securities association to be neither listed on any national securities exchange nor authorized to be quoted on an inter-dealer quotation system of any registered national securities association.

(4) An "unaffiliated security holder" is any security holder of an equity security subject to a Rule 13e–3 transaction who is not an affiliate of the issuer of such security.

(b) *Application of Section to an Issuer (or an Affiliate of Such Issuer) Subject to Section 12 of the Act.*

(1) It shall be a fraudulent, deceptive or manipulative act or practice, in connection with a Rule 13e–3 transaction, for an issuer which has a class of equity securities registered pursuant to Section 12 of the Act or which is a

closed-end investment company registered under the Investment Company Act of 1940, or an affiliate of such issuer, directly or indirectly

(i) To employ any device, scheme or artifice to defraud any person;

(ii) To make any untrue statement of a material fact or to omit to state a material fact necessary in order to make the statements made, in light of the circumstances under which they were made, not misleading; or

(iii) To engage in any act, practice or course of business which operates or would operate as a fraud or deceit upon any person.

(2) As a means reasonably designed to prevent fraudulent, deceptive or manipulative acts or practices in connection with any Rule 13e–3 transaction, it shall be unlawful for an issuer which has a class of equity securities registered pursuant to Section 12 of the Act, or an affiliate of such issuer, to engage, directly or indirectly, in a Rule 13e–3 transaction unless:

(i) Such issuer or affiliate complies with the requirements of paragraphs (d), (e) and (f) of this Section; and

(ii) The Rule 13e–3 transaction is not in violation of paragraph (b)(1) of this section.

(c) *Application of Section to an Issuer (or an Affiliate of Such Issuer) Subject to Section 15(d) of the Act.*

(1) It shall be unlawful as a fraudulent, deceptive or manipulative act or practice for an issuer which is required to file periodic reports pursuant to Section 15(d) of the Act, or an affiliate of such issuer, to engage, directly or indirectly, in a Rule 13e–3 transaction unless such issuer or affiliate complies with the requirements of paragraphs (d), (e) and (f) of this section.

(2) An issuer or affiliate which is subject to paragraph (c)(1) of this section and which is soliciting proxies or distributing information statements in connection with a transaction described in paragraph (a)(3)(i)(A) of this section may elect to use the timing procedures for conducting a solicitation subject to Regulation 14A (Rules 14a–1 to 14a–103) or a distribution subject to Regulation 14C (Rules 14c–1 to 14c–101) in complying with paragraphs (d), (e) and (f) of this section, *provided,* That if an election is made, such solicitation or distribution is conducted in accordance with the requirements of the respective regulations, including the filing of preliminary copies of soliciting materials or an information statement at the time specified in Regulation 14A or 14C, respectively.

(d) *Material Required to Be Filed.* The issuer or affiliate engaging in Rule 13e–3 transaction shall, in accordance with the General Instructions to the Rule 13e–3 Transaction Statement on Schedule 13E–3:

(1) File with the Commission eight copies of such schedule, including all exhibits thereto;

(2) Report any material change in the information set forth in such schedule by promptly filing with the Commission eight copies of an amendment on such schedule; and

(3) Report the results of the Rule 13e–3 transaction by filing with the Commission promptly but no later than ten days (ten business days if Rule 13e–4 is applicable) after the termination of such transaction eight copies of a final amendment to such schedule.

(e) *Disclosure of Certain Information.*

(1) The issuer or affiliate engaging in the Rule 13e–3 transaction, in addition to any other information required to be disclosed pursuant to any other applicable rule or regulation under the federal securities laws, shall disclose to security holders of the class of equity securities which is the subject of the transaction, in the manner prescribed by paragraph (f) of this section, the information required by Items 1, 2, 3, 4, 5, 6, 10, 11, 12, 13, 14, 15 and 16 of Schedule 13e–3, or a fair and adequate summary thereof, and Items 7, 8 and 9 and include in the document which contains such information the exhibit required by Item 17(e) of such Schedule. If the Rule 13e–3 transaction involves (i) a transaction subject to Regulation 14A or 14C of the Act, (ii) the registration of securities pursuant to the Securities Act of 1933 and the General Rules and Regulations promulgated thereunder, or (iii) a tender offer subject to Regulation 14D or Rule 13e–4 such information shall be included in the proxy statement, the information statement, the registration statement or the tender offer for or request or invitation for tenders of securities published, sent or given to security holders, respectively.

(2) If any material change occurs in the information previously disclosed to security holders of the class of equity securities which is the subject of the transaction, the issuer or affiliate shall promptly disclose such change to such security holders in the manner prescribed by paragraph (f) (iii) of this section.

(3) Any document transmitted to such security holders which contains the information required by paragraph (e)(1) of this section shall:

(i) set forth prominently the information required by Items 7, 8 and 9 of the Rule 13e–3 Transaction Statement on Schedule 13E–3 in a Special Factors section to be included in the forepart of such document; and

(ii) set forth on the outside front cover page, in capital letters printed in bold face roman type at least as large as ten point modern type and at least two points leaded, the statement in paragraph (e)(3)(ii)(A) of this section, if the Rule 13e–3 transaction does not involve a prospectus, or the statement in paragraph (e)(3)(ii)(B) of this section, if the Rule 13e–3 transaction involves a prospectus, and in the latter case such statement shall be used in lieu of that required by Item 501(c)(5) of Regulation S–K.

(A) THIS TRANSACTION HAS NOT BEEN APPROVED OR DISAPPROVED BY THE SECURITIES AND EXCHANGE COMMISSION NOR HAS THE COMMISSION PASSED UPON THE FAIRNESS OR MERITS OF SUCH TRANSACTION NOR UPON THE ACCURACY OR ADEQUACY OF THE INFORMATION CONTAINED IN THIS DOCUMENT. ANY REPRESENTATION TO THE CONTRARY IS UNLAWFUL.

(B) NEITHER THIS TRANSACTION NOR THESE SECURITIES HAVE BEEN APPROVED OR DISAPPROVED BY THE SECURITIES AND EXCHANGE COMMISSION. THE COMMISSION HAS NOT PASSED UPON THE FAIRNESS OR MERITS OF THIS TRANSACTION NOR UPON THE ACCURACY OR ADEQUACY OF THE INFORMATION CONTAINED IN THIS PROSPECTUS. ANY REPRESENTATION TO THE CONTRARY IS UNLAWFUL. . .

(f) *Dissemination of Disclosure.*

(1) If the Rule 13e–3 transaction involves a purchase as described in paragraph (a)(3)(i)(A) of this section or a vote, consent, authorization, or distribution of information statements as described in paragraph (a)(3)(i)(C) of this section, the issuer or affiliate engaging in the Rule 13e–3 transaction shall:

(i) Provide the information required by paragraph (e) of this section: (A) in accordance with the provisions of any applicable federal or state law, but in no event later than 20 days prior to: any such purchase; any such vote, consent or authorization; or with respect to the distribution of information statements, the meeting date, or if corporate action is to be taken by means of the written authorization or consent of security holders, the earliest date on which corporate action may be taken: *Provided, however,* That if the purchase subject to this section is pursuant to a tender offer excepted from Rule 13e–4 by paragraph (g)(5) of Rule 13e–4, the information required by paragraph (e) of this section shall be disseminated in accordance with paragraph (e) of Rule 13e–4 no later than 10 business days prior to any purchase pursuant to such tender offer, (B) to each person who is a record holder of a class of equity security subject to the Rule 13e–3 transaction as of a date not more than 20 days prior to the date of dissemination of such information;

(ii) If the issuer or affiliate knows that securities of the class of securities subject to the Rule 13e–3 transaction are held of record by a broker, dealer, bank or voting trustee or their nominees, such issuer or affiliate shall (unless Rule 14a–3(d) or 14c–7 is applicable) furnish the number of copies of the information required by paragraph (e) of this section that are requested by such persons (pursuant to inquiries by or on behalf of the issuer or affiliate), instruct such persons to forward such information to the beneficial owners of such securities in a timely manner and undertake to pay the reasonable expenses incurred by such persons in forwarding such information; and

(iii) Promptly disseminate disclosure of material changes to the information required by paragraph (d) of this section in a manner reasonably calculated to inform security holders.

(2) If the Rule 13e–3 transaction is a tender offer or a request or invitation for tenders of equity securities which is subject to Regulation 14D or Rule 13e–4, the tender offer containing the information required by paragraph (e) of this section, and any material change with respect thereto, shall be published, sent or given in accordance with Regulation 14D or Rule 13e–4, respectively, to security holders of the class of securities being sought by the issuer or affiliate.

(g) *Exceptions.* This section shall not apply to:

(1) Any Rule 13e–3 transaction by or on behalf of a person which occurs within one year of the date of termination of a tender offer in which such person was the bidder and became an affiliate of the issuer as a result of such tender offer *provided* that the consideration offered to unaffiliated security holders in such Rule 13e–3 transaction is at least equal to the highest consideration offered during such tender offer and *provided further,* That:

(i) If such tender offer was made for any or all securities of a class of the issuer;

          (A) Such tender offer fully disclosed such person's intention to engage in a Rule 13e–3 transaction, the form and effect of such transaction and, to the extent known, the proposed terms thereof; and

          (B) Such Rule 13e–3 transaction is substantially similar to that described in such tender offer; or

          (ii) If such tender offer was made for less than all the securities of a class of the issuer:

          (A) Such tender offer fully disclosed a plan of merger, a plan of liquidation or a similar binding agreement between such person and the issuer with respect to a Rule 13e–3 transaction; and

          (B) Such Rule 13e–3 transaction occurs pursuant to the plan of merger, plan of liquidation or similar binding agreement disclosed in the bidder's tender offer.

    (2) Any Rule 13e–3 transaction in which the security holders are offered or receive only an equity security *provided,* That:

          (i) such equity security has substantially the same rights as the equity security which is the subject of the Rule 13e–3 transaction including, but not limited to, voting, dividends, redemption and liquidation rights except that this requirement shall be deemed to be satisfied if unaffiliated security holders are offered common stock;

          (ii) such equity security is registered pursuant to section 12 of the Act or reports are required to be filed by the issuer thereof pursuant to section 15(d) of the Act; and

          (iii) if the security which is the subject of the Rule 13e–3 transaction was either listed on a national securities exchange or authorized to be quoted in an inter-dealer quotation system of a registered national securities association, such equity security is either listed on a national securities exchange or authorized to be quoted in an inter-dealer quotation system of a registered national securities association.

    (3) Transactions by a holding company registered under the Public Utility Holding Company Act of 1935 in compliance with the provisions of that Act;

    (4) Redemptions, calls or similar purchases of an equity security by an issuer pursuant to specific provisions set forth in the instrument(s) creating or governing that class of equity securities; or

    (5) Any solicitation by an issuer with respect to a plan of reorganization under Chapter X of the Bankruptcy Act, as amended, if made after the entry of an order approving such plan pursuant to section 174 of that Act and after, or concurrently with, the transmittal of information concerning such plan as required by section 175 of the Act.

Rule 13e–100.   **Schedule 13E–3 Transaction Statement Pursuant to Section 13(e) of the Securities Exchange Act of 1934 and Rule 13e–3 Thereunder**

* * *

GENERAL INSTRUCTIONS

* * *

C. If the statement is filed by a general or limited partnership, syndicate or other group the information called for by Items, 2, 3, 5, 6, 10, and 11 shall be given with respect to: (i) each partner of such general partnership; (ii) each partner who is denominated as a general partner or who functions as a general partner of such limited partnership; (iii) each member of such syndicate or group; and (iv) each person controlling such partner or member. If the statement is filed by a corporation or if a person referred to in (i), (ii), (iii) or (iv) of this Instruction is a corporation, the information called for by the above mentioned items shall be given with respect to: (a) each executive officer and director of such corporation; (b) each person controlling such corporation; and (c) each executive officer and director of any corporation ultimately in control of such corporation. . . .

E. The information required by the items of this statement is intended to be in addition to any disclosure requirements of any other form or schedule which may be filed with the Commission in connection with the Rule 13e–3 transaction. To the extent that the disclosure requirements of this statement are inconsistent with the disclosure requirements of any such forms or schedules, the requirements of this statement are controlling.

F. If the Rule 13e–3 transaction involves a transaction subject to Regulation 14A of the Act, the registration of securities pursuant to the Securities Act of 1933 and the General Rules and Regulations promulgated thereunder, or a tender offer subject to Regulation 14D or Rule 13e–4, the information contained in the proxy or information statement, the registration statement, the Schedule 14D–1, or the Schedule 13E–4, respectively, which is filed with the Commission shall be incorporated by reference in answer to the items of this statement or amendments thereto; this statement shall include an express statement to that effect and a cross reference sheet showing the location in the proxy or information statement, the registration statement, the Schedule 14D–1 or the Schedule 13E–4 of the information required to be included in response to the items of this statement. If any such item is inapplicable or the answer thereto is in the negative and is omitted from the proxy or the information statement, the registration statement, the Schedule 14D–1, or the Schedule 13E–4, a statement to that effect shall be made in the cross reference sheet.

G. If the Rule 13e–3 transaction involves a proxy or an information statement subject to Regulation 14A or Regulation 14C and if preliminary copies of such materials have been incorporated by reference into this statement pursuant to Instruction F of this statement, this Schedule 13E–3 shall be deemed to constitute "Preliminary Copies" within the meaning of Rule 14a–6(e) and Rule 14c–5 and shall not be available for public inspection before an amendment to this statement containing definitive material has been filed with the Commission.

H. Amendments disclosing a material change in the information set forth in this statement may omit any information previously disclosed in this statement.

Item 1. Issuer and Class of Security Subject to the Transaction

(a) State the name of the issuer of the class of equity security which is the subject of the Rule 13e–3 transaction and the address of its principal executive offices.

(b) State the exact title, the amount of securities outstanding of the class of security which is the subject of the Rule 13e–3 transaction as of the most recent practicable date and the approximate number of holders of record of such class as of the most recent practicable date.

(c) Identify the principal market in which such securities are being traded and, if the principal market is an exchange, state the high and low sales prices for such securities as reported in the consolidated transaction reporting system or, if not so reported, on such principal exchange for each quarterly period during the past two years. If the principal market is not an exchange, state the range of high and low bid quotations for each quarterly period during the past two years, the source of such quotations and, if there is currently no established trading market for such securities (excluding limited or sporadic quotations); furnish a statement to that effect.

(d) State the frequency and amount of any dividends paid during the past two years with respect to such class of securities and briefly describe any restriction on the issuer's present or future ability to pay such dividends.

Instruction. If the person filing this statement is an affiliate of the issuer, the information required by Item 1(d) should be furnished to the extent known by such affiliate after making reasonable inquiry.

(e) If the issuer and/or affiliate filing this statement has made an underwritten public offering of such securities for cash during the past three years which was registered under the Securities Act of 1933 or exempt from registration thereunder pursuant to Regulation A, state the date of such offering, the amount of securities offered, the offering price per share (which should be appropriately adjusted for stock splits, stock dividends, etc.) and the aggregate proceeds received by such issuer and/or such affiliate.

(f) With respect to any purchases of such securities made by the issuer or affiliate since the commencement of the issuer's second full fiscal year preceding the date of this schedule, state the amount of such securities purchased, the range of prices paid for such securities and the average purchase price for each quarterly period of the issuer during such period.

Instruction. The information required by Item 1(f) need not be given with respect to purchases of such securities by a person prior to the time such person became an affiliate.

Item 2. Identity and Background

If the person filing this statement is the issuer of the class of equity securities which is the subject of the Rule 13e–3 transaction, make a statement to that effect. If this statement is being filed by an affiliate of the issuer which is other than a natural person or if any person enumerated in Instruction C to this statement is a corporation, general partnership, limited partnership, syndicate or other group of persons, state its name, the state or other place of its organization, its principal business, the address of its principal executive offices and provide the information required by (e) and (f) of this Item. If this statement is being filed by an affiliate of the issuer who is a natural person or if any person enumerated in Instruction C of this statement is a natural person, provide the information required by (a) through (g) of this Item with respect to such person(s).

(a) Name;

(b) Residence or business address;

(c) Present principal occupation or employment and the name, principal business and address of any corporation or other organization in which such employment or occupation is conducted;

(d) Material occupations, positions, offices or employments during the last 5 years, giving the starting and ending dates of each and the name, principal business and address of any business corporation or other organization in which such occupation, position, office or employment was carried on;

(e) Whether or not, during the last 5 years, such person has been convicted in a criminal proceeding (excluding traffic violations or similar misdemeanors) and, if so give the dates, nature of conviction, name and location of court, and penalty imposed or other disposition of the case;

(f) Whether or not, during the last 5 years, such person was a party to a civil proceeding of a judicial or administrative body of competent jurisdiction and as a result of such proceeding was or is subject to a judgment, decree or final order enjoining further violations of, or prohibiting activities subject to, federal or state securities laws or finding any violation of such laws; and, if so, identify and describe such proceeding and summarize the terms of such judgment, decree or final order;

Instruction. While negative answers to Items 2(e) and 2(f) are required in this schedule, they need not be furnished to security holders.

(g) Citizenship(s).

Item 3. Past Contacts, Transactions or Negotiations

(a) If this schedule is filed by an affiliate of the issuer of the class of securities which is the subject of the Rule 13e–3 transaction:

(1) Briefly state the nature and approximate amount (in dollars) of any transaction, other than those described in Item 3(b) of this schedule, which has occurred since the commencement of the issuer's second full fiscal year preceding the date of this schedule between such affiliate (including subsidiaries of the affiliate and those persons enumerated in Instruction C of this schedule) and the issuer: *Provided, however,* That no disclosure need be made with respect to any transaction if the aggregate amount involved in such transaction was less than one percent of the issuer's consolidated revenues (which may be based upon information contained in the most recently available filing with the Commission by the issuer unless such affiliate has reason to believe otherwise) (i) for the fiscal year in which such transaction occurred or (ii) for the portion of the current fiscal year which has occurred, if the transaction occurred in such year; and

(2) Describe any contacts, negotiations or transactions which have been entered into or which have occurred since the commencement of the issuer's second full fiscal year preceding the date of this schedule between such affiliate (including subsidiaries of the affiliate and those persons enumerated in Instruction C of this schedule) and the issuer concerning: a merger, consolidation or acquisition; a tender offer for or other acquisition of securities of any class of the issuer; an election of directors of the issuer; or a sale or other transfer of a material amount of assets of the issuer or any of its subsidiaries.

(b) Describe any contacts or negotiations concerning the matters referred to in Item 3(a)(2) which have been entered into or which have occurred since the commencement of the issuer's second full fiscal year preceding the date of this schedule (i) between any affiliates of the issuer of the class of securities which is the subject of the Rule 13e–3 transaction; or (ii) between such issuer or any of its affiliates and any person who is not affiliated with the issuer and who would have a direct interest in such matters. Identify the person who initiated such contacts or negotiations.

Item 4. Terms of the Transaction

(a) State the material terms of the Rule 13e–3 transaction.

(b) Describe any term or arrangement concerning the Rule 13e–3 transaction relating to any security holder of the issuer which is not identical to that relating to other security holders of the same class of securities of the issuer.

Item 5. Plans or Proposals of the Issuer or Affiliate

Describe any plan or proposal of the issuer or affiliate regarding activities or transactions which are to occur after the Rule 13e–3 transaction which relate to or would result in:

(a) An extraordinary corporate transaction, such as a merger, reorganization or liquidation, involving the issuer or any of its subsidiaries;

(b) A sale or transfer of a material amount of assets of the issuer or any of its subsidiaries;

(c) Any change in the present board of directors or management of the issuer including, but not limited to, any plan or proposal to change the number or term of directors, to fill any existing vacancy on the board or to change any material term of the employment contract of any executive officer;

(d) Any material change in the present dividend rate or policy or indebtedness or capitalization of the issuer;

(e) Any other material change in the issuer's corporate structure or business;

(f) A class of equity securities of the issuer becoming eligible for termination of registration pursuant to Section 12(g)(4) of the Act; or

(g) The suspension of the issuer's obligation to file reports pursuant to Section 15(d) of the Act.

Item 6. Source and Amounts of Funds or Other Consideration

(a) State the source and total amount of funds or other consideration to be used in the Rule 13e–3 transaction.

(b) Furnish a reasonably itemized statement of all expenses incurred or estimated to be incurred in connection with the Rule 13e–3 transaction including, but not limited to, filing fees, legal, accounting and appraisal fees, solicitation expenses and printing costs and state whether or not the issuer has paid or will be responsible for paying any or all of such expenses.

(c) If all or any part of such funds or other consideration is, or is expected to be, directly or indirectly borrowed for the purpose of the Rule 13e–3 transaction,

(1) Provide a summary of each such loan agreement containing the identity of the parties, the term, the collateral, the stated and effective interest rates, and other material terms or conditions; and

(2) Briefly describe any plans or arrangements to finance or repay such borrowings, or, if no such plans or arrangements have been made, make a statement to that effect.

(d) If the source of all or any part of the funds to be used in the Rule 13e–3 transaction is a loan made in the ordinary course of business by a bank as defined by Section 3(a)(6) of the Act and Section 13(d) or 14(d) is applicable to such transaction, the name of such bank shall not be made available to the public if the person filing the statement so requests in writing and files such request, naming such bank, with the Secretary of the Commission.

Item 7. Purpose(s), Alternatives, Reasons and Effects

(a) State the purpose(s) for the Rule 13e–3 transaction.

(b) If the issuer or affiliate considered alternative means to accomplish such purpose(s), briefly describe such alternative(s) and state the reason(s) for their rejection.

(c) State the reasons for the structure of the Rule 13e–3 transaction and for undertaking such transaction at this time.

(d) Describe the effects of the Rule 13e–3 transaction on the issuer, its affiliates and unaffiliated security holders, including the federal tax consequences.

Instructions. (1) Conclusory statements will not be considered sufficient disclosure in response to Item 7.

(2) The description required by Item 7(d) should include a reasonably detailed discussion of the benefits and detriments of the Rule 13e–3 transaction to the issuer, its affiliates and unaffiliated security holders. The benefits and detriments of the Rule 13e–3 transaction should be quantified to the extent practicable.

(3) If this statement is filed by an affiliate of the issuer, the description required by Item 7(d) should include but not be limited to, the effect of the Rule 13e–3 transaction on the affiliate's interest in the net book value and net earnings of the issuer in terms of both dollar amounts and percentages.

Item 8. Fairness of the Transaction

(a) State whether the issuer or affiliate filing this schedule reasonably believes that the Rule 13e–3 transaction is fair or unfair to unaffiliated security holders. If any director dissented to or abstained from voting on the Rule 13e–3 transaction, identify each such director, and indicate, if known, after making reasonable inquiry, the reasons for each dissent or abstention.

Instruction. A statement that the issuer or affiliate has no reasonable belief as to the fairness of the Rule 13e–3 transaction to unaffiliated security holders will not be considered sufficient disclosure in response to Item 8(a).

(b) Discuss in reasonable detail the material factors upon which the belief stated in Item 8(a) is based and, to the extent practicable, the weight assigned to each such factor. Such discussion should include an analysis of the extent, if any, to which such belief is based on the factors set forth in instruction (1) to paragraph (b) of this Item, paragraphs (c), (d), and (e) of this Item, and Item 9.

Instructions. (1) The factors which are important in determining the fairness of a transaction to unaffiliated security holders and the weight, if any, which should be given to them in a particular context will vary. Normally such factors will include, among others, those referred to in paragraphs (c), (d) and (e) of this Item and whether the consideration offered to unaffiliated security holders constitutes fair value in relation to:

(i) current market prices

(ii) historical market prices

(iii) net book value

(iv) going concern value

(v) liquidation value

(vi) the purchase price paid in previous purchases disclosed in Item 1(f) of Schedule 13e–3

(vii) any report, opinion, or appraisal described in Item 9 and

(viii) firm offers of which the issuer or affiliate is aware made by any unaffiliated person, other than the person filing this statement, during the preceding eighteen months for (A) the merger or consolidation of the issuer into or with such person or of such person into or with the issuer, (B) the sale or other transfer of all or any substantial part of the assets of the issuer or (C) securities of the issuer which would enable the holder thereof to exercise control of the issuer.

(2) Conclusory statements, such as "The Rule 13e–3 transaction is fair to unaffiliated security holders in relation to net book value, going concern value and future prospects of the issuer" will not be considered sufficient disclosure in response to Item 8(b).

(c) State whether the transaction is structured so that approval of at least a majority of unaffiliated security holders is required.

(d) State whether a majority of directors who are not employees of the issuer has retained an unaffiliated representative to act solely on behalf of unaffiliated security holders for the purposes of negotiating the terms of the Rule 13e–3 transaction and/or preparing a report concerning the fairness of such transaction.

(e) State whether the Rule 13e–3 transaction was approved by a majority of the directors of the issuer who are not employees of the issuer.

(f) If any offer of the type described in instruction (vii) to Item 8(b) has been received, describe such offer and state the reason(s) for its rejection.

Item 9. Reports, Opinions, Appraisals and Certain Negotiations

(a) State whether or not the issuer or affiliate has received any report, opinion (other than an opinion of counsel) or appraisal from an outside party which is materially related to the Rule 13e–3 transaction including, but not limited to, any such report, opinion or appraisal relating to the consideration or the fairness of the consideration to be offered to security holders of the class of securities which is the subject of the Rule 13e–3 transaction or the fairness of such transaction to the issuer or affiliate or to security holders who are not affiliates.

(b) With respect to any report, opinion or appraisal described in Item 9(a) or with respect to any negotiation or report described in Item 8(d) concerning the terms of the Rule 13e–3 transaction:

(1) Identify such outside party and/or unaffiliated representative;

(2) Briefly describe the qualifications of such outside party and/or unaffiliated representative;

(3) Describe the method of selection of such outside party and/or unaffiliated representative;

(4) Describe any material relationship between (i) the outside party, its affiliates, and/or unaffiliated representative, and (ii) the issuer or its affiliates, which existed during the past two years or is mutually understood to be contemplated and any compensation received or to be received as a result of such relationship;

(5) If such report, opinion or appraisal relates to the fairness of the consideration, state whether the issuer or affiliate determined the amount of consideration to be paid or whether the outside party recommended the amount of consideration to be paid.

(6) Furnish a summary concerning such negotiation report, opinion or appraisal which shall include, but not be limited to, the procedures followed; the findings and recommendations; the bases for and methods of arriving at such findings and recommendations; instructions received from the issuer or affiliate; and any limitation imposed by the issuer or affiliate; and any limitation imposed by the issuer or affiliate on the scope of the investigation.

Instruction. The information called for by subitem 9(b)(1), (2) and (3) should be given with respect to the firm which provides the report, opinion or appraisal rather than the employees of such firm who prepared it.

(c) Furnish a statement to the effect that such report, opinion or appraisal shall be made available for inspection and copying at the principal executive offices of the issuer or affiliate during its regular business hours by any interested equity security holder of the issuer or his representative who has been so designated in writing. This statement may also provide that a copy of such report, opinion or appraisal will be transmitted by the issuer or affiliate to any interested equity security holder of the issuer or his representative who has been so designated in writing upon written request and at the expense of the requesting security holder.

Item 10. Interest in Securities of the Issuer

(a) With respect to the class of equity security to which the Rule 13e–3 transaction relates, state the aggregate amount and percentage of securities beneficially owned (identifying those securities for which there is a right to acquire) as of the most recent practicable date by the person filing this statement (unless such person is the issuer), by any pension, profit sharing or similar plan of the issuer or affiliate, by each person enumerated in Instruction C of this Schedule or by any associate or majority owned subsidiary of the issuer or affiliate giving the name and address of any such associate or subsidiary.

Instructions. 1. For the purpose of this Item, beneficial ownership shall be determined in accordance with Rule 13d–3 under the Exchange Act.

2. The information required by this paragraph should be given with respect to officers, directors and associates of the issuer to the extent known after making reasonable inquiry.

(b) Describe any transaction in the class of equity securities of the issuer which is the subject of a Rule 13e–3 transaction that was effected during the past 60 days by the issuer of such class or by the persons named in response to paragraph (a) of this Item.

Instructions. 1. The description of a transaction required by Item 10(b) shall include, but not necessarily be limited to: (i) the identity of the person covered by Item 10(b) who effected the transaction; (ii) the date of the transaction; (iii) the amount of securities involved; (iv) the price per security; and (v) where and how the transaction was effected.

2. If the information required by Item 10(b) is available to the person filing this statement at the time this statement is initially filed with the Commission, the information shall be included in the initial filing. However, if the information is not available to such person at the time of such initial filing, it shall be filed with the Commission promptly but in no event later than seven days (or 2 business days with respect to a tender subject to Regulation 14D or 10 business days with respect to a tender offer subject to Rule 13e–4 [§ 240.13e–4]) after the date of such filing and, if material, disclosed to security holders of the issuer pursuant to Rule 13e–3(e), and disseminated to them in a manner reasonably calculated to inform security holders.

Item 11. Contracts, Arrangements or Understandings With Respect to the Issuer's Securities

Describe any contract, arrangement, understanding or relationship (whether or not legally enforceable) in connection with the Rule 13e–3 transaction between the person filing this statement (including any person enumerated in Instruction C of this schedule) and any person with respect to any securities of the issuer (including, but not limited to, any contract, arrangement, understanding or relationship concerning the transfer or the voting of any of such securities, joint ventures, loan or option arrangements, puts or calls, guaranties of loans, guaranties against loss or the giving or withholding of proxies, consents or authorizations), naming the persons with whom such contracts, arrangements, understandings or relationships have been entered into and giving the material provisions thereof. Include such information for any of such securities that are pledged or otherwise subject to a contingency, the occurrence of which would give another person the power to direct the voting or disposition of such securities, except that disclosure of standard default and similar provisions contained in loan agreements need not be included.

Item 12. Present Intention and Recommendation of Certain Persons With Regard to the Transaction

(a) To the extent known by the person filing this statement after making reasonable inquiry, furnish a statement of present intention with regard to the Rule 13e–3 transaction indicating whether or not any executive officer, director or affiliate of the issuer or any person enumerated in Instruction C of this statement will tender or sell securities of the issuer owned or held by such person and/or how such securities, and securities with respect to which such person holds proxies, will be voted and the reasons therefor.

Instruction. If the information required by Item 12(a) is available to the person filing this statement at the time this statement is initially filed with the Commission, the information shall be included in the initial filing. However, if the information is not available to such person at the time of such initial filing, it shall be filed with the Commission promptly but in no event later than seven days (or two business days with respect to a tender offer subject to Regulation 14D or ten business days with respect to a tender offer subject to Rule 13e–4) after the date of such filing and, if material, disclosed to security holders of the issuer pursuant to Rule 13e–3(e), and disseminated to them in a manner reasonably calculated to inform security holders.

(b) To the extent known by the person filing this statement after making reasonable inquiry, state whether any person named in paragraph (a) of this item has made a recommendation in support of or opposed to the Rule 13e–3 transaction and the reasons for such recommendation. If no recommendation has been made by such persons, furnish a statement to that effect.

Item 13. Other Provisions of the Transaction

(a) State whether or not appraisal rights are provided under applicable state law or under the issuer's articles of incorporation or will be voluntarily accorded by the issuer or affiliate to security holders in connection with the Rule 13e–3 transaction and, if so, summarize such appraisal rights. If appraisal rights will not be available under the applicable state law, to security holders who object to the transaction, briefly outline the rights which may be available to such security holders under such law.

(b) If any provision has been made by the issuer or affiliate in connection with the Rule 13e–3 transaction to allow unaffiliated security holders to obtain access to the corporate files of the issuer or affiliate or to obtain counsel or appraisal services at the expense of the issuer or affiliate, describe such provision.

(c) If the Rule 13e–3 transaction involves the exchange of debt securities of the issuer or affiliate for the equity securities held by security holders of the issuer who are not affiliates, describe whether or not the issuer or affiliate will take steps to provide or assure that such securities are or will be eligible for trading on any national securities exchange or an automated inter-dealer quotation system.

Item 14. Financial Information

(a) Furnish the following financial data concerning the issuer:

(1) Audited financial statements for the two fiscal years required to be filed with the issuer's most recent annual report under sections 13 and 15(d) of the Act;

(2) Unaudited balance sheets and comparative year-to-date income statements and statements of changes in financial position and related earnings per share amounts required to be included in the issuer's most recent quarterly report filed pursuant to the Act;

(3) Ratio of earnings to fixed charges for the two most recent fiscal years and the interim periods provided under Item 14(a)(2); and

(4) Book value per share as of the most recent fiscal year end and as of the date of the latest interim balance sheet provided under Item 14(a)(2).

(b) If material, provide pro forma data disclosing the effect of the Rule 13e–3 transaction on:

(1) The issuer's balance sheet as of the most recent fiscal year end and the latest interim balance sheet provided under Item 14(a)(2);

(2) The issuer's statement of income, earnings per share amounts, and ratio of earnings to fixed charges for the most recent fiscal year and the latest interim period provided under Item 14(a)(2); and

(3) The issuer's book value per share as of the most recent fiscal year end and as of the latest interim balance sheet date provided under Item 14(a)(2).

Item 15. Persons and Assets Employed, Retained or Utilized

(a) Identify and describe the purpose for which any officer, employee, class of employees or corporate asset of the issuer (excluding corporate assets which are proposed to be used as consideration for purchases of securities which are disclosed in Item 6 of this schedule) has been or is proposed to be employed, availed of or utilized by the issuer or affiliate in connection with the Rule 13e–3 transaction.

(b) Identify all persons and classes of persons (excluding officers, employees and class of employees who have been identified in Item 15(a) of this Schedule) employed, retained or to be compensated by the person filing this statement, or by any person on behalf of the person filing this statement, to make solicitations or recommendations in connection with the Rule 13e–3 transaction and provide a summary of the material terms of such employment, retainer or arrangement for compensation.

Item 16. Additional Information

Furnish such additional material information, if any, as may be necessary to make the required statements in the light of the circumstances under which they are made, not materially misleading.

Item 17. Material to Be Filed as Exhibits

Furnish a copy of:

(a) Any loan agreement referred to in Item 6 of this Schedule;

Instruction. The identity of any bank which is a party to a loan agreement need not be disclosed if the person filing the statement has requested that the identity of such bank not be made available to the public pursuant to Item 6 of this schedule.

(b) Any report, opinion or appraisal referred to in Items 8(d) or 9 of this schedule;

(c) Any document setting forth the terms of any contract, arrangements or understandings or relationships referred to in Item 11 of this schedule; and

(d) Any disclosure materials furnished to security holders in connection with the transaction pursuant to Rule 13e–3(d).

(e) A detailed statement describing the appraisal rights and the procedures for exercising such appraisal rights which are referred to in Item 13(a) of this schedule.

(f) If any oral solicitation of or recommendations to security holders referred to in Item 15(b) are to be made by or on behalf of the person filing this statement, any written instruction, form or other material which is furnished to the persons making the actual oral solicitation or recommendation for their use, directly or indirectly, in connection with the Rule 13e–3 transaction. . . .

Rule 13e–4.   Tender Offers by Issuers

(a) *Definitions.* Unless the context otherwise requires, all terms used in this section and in Schedule 13E–4 shall have the same meaning as in the Act or elsewhere in the General Rules and Regulations thereunder. In addition, the following definitions shall apply:

(1) The term "issuer" means any issuer which has a class of equity security registered pursuant to section 12 of the Act, or which is required to file periodic reports pursuant to section 15(d) of the Act, or which is a closed-end investment company registered under the Investment Company Act of 1940.

(2) The term "issuer tender offer" refers to a tender offer for, or a request or invitation for tenders of, any class of equity security, made by the issuer of such class of equity security or by an affiliate of such issuer.

(3) The term "business day" means any day, other than Saturday, Sunday or a federal holiday, on which the principal office of the Commission at Washington, D.C. is scheduled to be open for business. In computing any time period under this section, the date of commencement of the issuer tender offer shall be included.

(4) The term "commencement" means the date an issuer tender offer is first published, sent or given to security holders.

(5) The term "termination" means the date after which securities may not be tendered pursuant to an issuer tender offer.

(6) The term "security holders" means holders of record and beneficial owners of securities of the class of equity security which is the subject of an issuer tender offer.

(7) The term "security position listing" means, with respect to the securities of any issuer held by a registered clearing agency in the name of the clearing agency or its nominee, a list of those participants in the clearing agency on whose behalf the clearing agency holds the issuer's securities and of the participants' respective positions in such securities as of a specified date.

(b)(1) It shall be a fraudulent, deceptive or manipulative act or practice, in connection with an issuer tender offer, for an issuer or an affiliate of such issuer, in connection with an issuer tender offer:

(i) to employ any device, scheme or artifice to defraud any person;

(ii) to make any untrue statement of a material fact or to omit to state a material fact necessary in order to make the statements made, in the light of the circumstances under which they were made, not misleading; or

(iii) to engage in any act, practice or course of business which operates or would operate as a fraud or deceit upon any person.

(2) As a means reasonably designed to prevent fraudulent, deceptive or manipulative acts or practices in connection with any issuer tender offer, it shall be

unlawful for an issuer or an affiliate of such issuer to make an issuer tender offer unless:

(i) such issuer or affiliate complies with the requirements of paragraphs (c), (d), (e) and (f) of this section; and

(ii) the issuer tender offer is not in violation of paragraph (b)(1) of this section.

(c) *Material Required to Be Filed.* The issuer or affiliate making the issuer tender offer shall, in accordance with the General Instructions to the Issuer Tender Offer Statement on Schedule 13E–4.

(1) File with the Commission ten copies of such schedule, including all exhibits thereto, prior to or as soon as practicable on the date of commencement of the issuer tender offer;

(2) Report any material change in the information set forth in such schedule by promptly filing with the Commission ten copies of an amendment on such schedule;

(3) Report the results of the issuer tender offer by filing with the Commission no later than ten business days after the termination of the issuer tender offer ten copies of a final amendment to such schedule.

(d) *Disclosure of Certain Information.*

(1) The issuer or affiliate making the issuer tender offer shall publish, send or give to security holders in the manner prescribed in paragraph (e)(1) of this section a statement containing the following information:

(i) the scheduled termination date of the issuer tender offer and whether it may be extended;

(ii) the specified dates prior to which, and after which, persons who tender securities pursuant to the issuer tender offer may withdraw their securities pursuant to paragraph (f)(2) of this section;

(iii) if the issuer tender offer is for less than all the securities of a class, the exact dates of the period during which securities will be accepted on a pro rata basis pursuant to paragraph (f)(3) of this section and the manner in which securities will be accepted for payment and in which securities may be withdrawn; and

(iv) the information required by Items 1 through 8 of Schedule 13E–4 or a fair and adequate summary thereof.

Provided, however, That if the issuer tender offer involves the registration of securities pursuant to the Securities Act of 1933 and the General Rules and Regulations promulgated thereunder, any prospectus relating to such securities shall include all of the information, not otherwise required to be included therein, required by this paragraph.

(2) If any material change occurs in the information previously disclosed to security holders, the issuer or affiliate shall disclose promptly such change in the manner prescribed by paragraph (e)(2) of this section. . . .

(3) If an issuer or an affiliate publishes, sends or gives the issuer tender offer to security holders by means of a summary publication in the manner prescribed in paragraph (e)(1)(iii) of this section, the summary advertisement shall not contain a transmittal letter pursuant to which securities which are sought in the issuer tender offer may be tendered, and shall disclose only the following information:

(i) the identity of the issuer or affiliate making the issuer tender offer;

(ii) the amount and class of securities being sought and the price being offered;

(iii) the information required by paragraphs (d)(1)(i)-(iii) of this section;

(iv) a statement of the purpose of the issuer tender offer;

(v) appropriate instructions for security holders regarding how to obtain promptly, at the expense of the issuer or affiliate making the issuer tender offer, the statement required by paragraph (d)(1) of this section; and

(vi) a statement that the information contained in the statement required by paragraph (d)(1) of this section is incorporated by reference.

(e) *Dissemination of Tender Offers.*

(1) The issuer or affiliate making the issuer tender offer will be deemed to have published, sent or given the issuer tender offer to security holders if such issuer or affiliate complies fully with one or more of the following methods of dissemination. Depending on the facts and circumstances involved, and for purposes of paragraphs (e)(1)(i) and (e)(1)(iii) of this section, adequate publication of the issuer tender offer may require publication in a newspaper with a national circulation or may require only publication in a newspaper with metropolitan or regional circulation or may require publication in a combination thereof.

(i) *Dissemination of Cash Issuer Tender Offers by Long-Form Publication:* By making adequate publication in a newspaper or newspapers, on the date of commencement of the issuer tender offer, of the statement required by paragraph (d)(1) of this section.

(ii) *Dissemination of Any Issuer Tender Offer by Use of Shareholder and Other Lists:*

(A) By mailing the statement required by paragraph (d)(1) of this section to each security holder whose name appears on the most recent shareholder list of the issuer;

(B) By contacting each participant named on the most recent security position listing of any clearing agency within the possession or access of the issuer or affiliate making the tender offer, and making inquiry of each such participant as to the approximate number of beneficial owners of the securities for which the issuer tender offer is made which are held by such participant;

(C) By furnishing to each such participant a sufficient number of copies of the statement required by paragraph (d)(1) of this section for transmittal to the beneficial owners; and

(D) By agreeing to reimburse promptly each such participant for reasonable expenses incurred by it in forwarding such statement to the beneficial owners.

(iii) *Dissemination of Certain Cash Issuer Tender Offers by Summary Publication:*

(A) If the issuer tender offer is not subject to Rule 13e–3, by making adequate publication in a newspaper or newspapers, on the date of commencement of the issuer tender offer, of a summary advertisement containing the information required by paragraph (d)(3) of this section; and

(B) By mailing or otherwise furnishing promptly the statement required by paragraph (d)(1) of this section and a transmittal letter to any security holder who requests either a copy of such statement or a transmittal letter.

(2) If a material change occurs in the information published, sent or given to security holders, the issuer or affiliate shall disseminate promptly disclosure of such change in a manner reasonably calculated to inform security holder of such change.

(f) *Manner of Making Tender Offer.*

(1) The issuer tender offer, unless withdrawn shall remain open until the expiration of at least fifteen business days from its commencement.

(2) The issuer or affiliate making the issuer tender offer shall permit securities tendered pursuant to the issuer tender offer to be withdrawn

(i) at any time until the expiration of ten business days from the commencement of the issuer tender offer;

(ii) if not yet accepted for payment, at any time until the expiration of seven business days from the date another tender offer for securities of the same class is first published, sent or given to security holders, pursuant to Section 14(d)(1) of the Act or otherwise; and

(iii) if not yet accepted for payment after the expiration of forty business days from the commencement of the issuer tender offer.

(3) The issuer of affiliate making the issuer tender offer shall accept tendered securities as nearly as practicable on a pro rata basis (disregarding fractions) according to the amount of securities tendered by each security holder if the amount of securities tendered within ten business days (or such longer period as may be specified) from the commencement of the issuer tender offer exceeds the amount of securities that will be accepted. The provisions of this paragraph shall also apply to securities tendered within ten business days (or such longer period as may be specified) from the date notice of an increase in the consideration offered to security holders, as described in paragraph (f)(4) of this section, is first published, sent or given to security holders; *Provided, however,* That this provision shall not prohibit the issuer or affiliate making the issuer tender offer from

(i) accepting all securities tendered by persons who own, beneficially or of record, an aggregate of not more than a specified number which is less than one hundred shares of such security and who tender all their securities, before prorating securities tendered by others, or

(ii) accepting by lot securities tendered by security holders who tender all securities held by them and who, when tendering their securities, elect to have either all or none accepted, if the issuer or affiliate first accepts all securities tendered by security holders who do not so elect;

(4) In the event the issuer or affiliate making the issuer tender increases the consideration offered after the issuer tender offer has commenced, such issuer or affiliate shall pay such increased consideration to all security holders whose tendered securities are accepted for payment by such issuer or affiliate.

(5) The issuer or affiliate making the tender offer shall either pay the consideration offered, or return the tendered securities, promptly after the termination or withdrawal of the tender offer.

(6) Until the expiration of at least ten business days after the date of termination of the issuer tender offer, neither the issuer nor any affiliate shall make any purchases, otherwise than pursuant to the tender offer, of:

(i) any security which is the subject of the issuer tender offer, or any security of the same class and series, or any right to purchase any such securities; and

(ii) in the case of an issuer tender offer which is an exchange offer, any security being offered pursuant to such exchange offer, or any security of the same class and series, or any right to purchase any such security.

(g) This section shall not apply to:

(1) Calls or redemptions of any security in accordance with the terms and conditions of its governing instruments;

(2) Offers to purchase securities evidenced by a scrip certificate, order form or similar document which represents a fractional interest in a share of stock or similar security;

(3) Offers to purchase securities pursuant to a statutory procedure for the purchase of dissenting security holders' securities;

(4) Any tender offer which is subject to section 14(d) of the Act; or

(5) Offers to purchase from security holders who own an aggregate of not more than a specified number of shares that is less than one hundred: *Provided, however,* That the offer is made to all record and beneficial holders (other than participants in an issuer's plan, as that term is defined in Rule 10b–6(c)(4) under the Act, if the issuer elects not to extend the offer to such participants) who own that number of shares as of a specified date prior to the announcement of the offer; or

(6) Any other transaction or transactions, if the Commission, upon written request or upon its own motion, exempts such transaction or transactions, either unconditionally, or on specified terms and conditions, as not constituting a fraudulent, deceptive or manipulative act or practice comprehended within the purpose of this section.

Rule 13e–101.   Schedule 13E–4. Tender Offer Statement Pursuant to Section 13(e)(1) of the Securities Exchange Act of 1934 and Rule 13e–4 Thereunder.

* * *

GENERAL INSTRUCTIONS

* * *

C. If the statement is filed by a general or limited partnership, syndicate or other group, the information called for by Items 2–5, inclusive, shall be given with respect to (i) each partner of such general partnership; (ii) each partner who is denominated as a general partner or who functions as a general partner of such limited partnership; (iii) each member of such syndicate or group; and (iv) each person controlling such partner or member. If the statement is filed by a corporation, or if a person referred to in (i), (ii), (iii) or (iv) of this Instruction is a corporation, the information called for by Items 2–5, inclusive, shall be given with respect to (a) each executive officer and director of such corporation; (b) each person controlling such corporation; and (c) each executive officer and director of any corporation ultimately in control of, such corporation.

D. Upon termination of the tender offer, the person filing this statement shall promptly, but in no event later than ten business days after the termination of the tender offer, file a final amendment to Schedule 13E–4 disclosing all material changes in the information set forth in such statement and stating that the tender offer has terminated, the date of such termination and the results of such tender offer.

E. Amendments disclosing a material change in the information set forth in this statement may omit information previously disclosed in this statement.

Item 1. Security and Issuer

(a) State the name of the issuer and the address of its principal executive office;

(b) State the exact title and the amount of securities outstanding of the class of security being sought as of the most recent practicable date; the exact amount of such securities being sought and the consideration being offered therefor; whether any such securities are to be purchased from any officer, director or affiliate of the issuer, and the details of each such transaction; and

(c) Identify the principal market in which such securities are being traded and, if the principal market is an exchange, state the high and low sales prices for such securities as reported in the consolidated transaction reporting system or, if not so reported, on such principal exchange for each quarterly period during the past two years. If the principal market is not an exchange, state the range of high and low bid quotations for each quarterly period during the past two years, the source of such quotations, and if there is currently no established trading market for such securities (excluding limited or sporadic) furnish a statement to that effect.

(d) State the name and address of the person filing this statement, if other than the issuer, and the nature of the affiliation between such person and the issuer.

Item 2. Source and Amount of Funds or Other Consideration

(a) State the source and total amount of funds or other consideration for the purchase of the maximum amount of securities for which the tender offer is being made.

(b) If all or any part of such funds or other consideration is, or is expected to be borrowed, directly or indirectly, for the purpose of the tender offer:

(1) Provide a summary of each such loan agreement or arrangement containing the identity of the parties, the term, the collateral, the stated and effective interest rates, and other material terms or conditions relative to such loan agreement; and

(2) Briefly describe any plans or arrangements to finance or repay such borrowings, or if no such plans or arrangements have been made, make a statement to that effect.

Item 3. Purpose of the Tender Offer and Plans or Proposals of the Issuer or Affiliate

State the purpose or purposes of the tender offer, and whether the securities are to be retired, held in the treasury of the issuer, or otherwise disposed of, indicating such disposition, and any plans or proposals which relate to or would result in:

(a) The acquisition by any person of additional securities of the issuer, or the disposition of securities of the issuer;

(b) An extraordinary corporate transaction, such as a merger, reorganization or liquidation, involving the issuer or any of its subsidiaries;

(c) A sale or transfer of a material amount of assets of the issuer or any of its subsidiaries;

(d) Any change in the present board of directors or management of the issuer including, but not limited to, any plans or proposals to change the number or the term of directors, to fill any existing vacancy on the board or to change any material term of the employment contract of any executive officer;

(e) Any material change in the present dividend rate or policy, or indebtedness or capitalization of the issuer;

(f) Any other material change in the issuer's corporate structure or business, including, if the issuer is a registered closed-end investment company, any plans or proposals to make any changes in its investment policy for which a vote would be required by Section 13 of the Investment Company Act of 1940;

(g) Changes in the issuer's charter, bylaws or instruments corresponding thereto or other actions which may impede the acquisition of control of the issuer by any person;

(h) Causing a class of equity security of the issuer to be delisted from a national securities exchange or to cease to be authorized to be quoted in an inter-dealer quotation system of a registered national securities association;

(i) A class of equity security of the issuer becoming eligible for termination of registration pursuant to Section 12(g)(4) of the Act; or

(j) The suspension of the issuer's obligation to file reports pursuant to Section 15(d) of the Act.

Item 4. Interest in Securities of the Issuer

Describe any transaction in the class of subject security that was effected during the past 40 business days by the issuer or the person filing this statement, by any person referred to in Instruction C of this schedule or by any associate or subsidiary of any such person, including any executive officer or director of any such subsidiary.

Instructions. 1. The description of a transaction required by this Item shall include, but not necessarily be limited to: (1) the identity of the person covered by this Item who effected the transaction; (2) the date of the transaction; (3) the amount of securities involved; (4) the price per security; and (5) where and how the transaction was effected.

2. If the information required by this Item is available to the person filing this statement at the time this statement is initially filed with the Commission, the information should be included in the initial filing. However, if the information is not available to such person at the time of such initial filing, it shall be filed with the Commission promptly but in no event later than ten business days after such date of the filing and, if material, should be disclosed to security holders of the issuer in a manner reasonably calculated to inform security holders.

Item 5. Contracts, Arrangements, Understandings or Relationships With Respect to the Issuer's Securities

Describe any contract, arrangement, understanding or relationship relating, directly or indirectly, to the tender offer (whether or not legally enforceable) between the person filing this statement (including any person enumerated in Instruction C of this schedule) and any person with respect to any securities of the issuer (including, but not limited to, any contract, arrangement, understanding or relationship concerning the transfer or the voting of any such securities, joint ventures, loan or option arrangements, puts or calls, guaranties of loans, guaranties against loss, or the giving or withholding of proxies, consents or authorizations) naming the persons with whom such contracts, arrangements, understandings or relationships have been entered into and giving the material provisions thereof. Include such information for any of such securities that are pledged or otherwise subject to a contingency, the occurrence of which would give another person the power to direct the voting or disposition of such securities, except that disclosure of standard default and similar provisions contained in loan agreements need not be included.

Item 6. Persons Retained, Employed or to Be Compensated

Identify all persons and classes of persons employed, retained or to be compensated by the person filing this statement, or by any person on behalf of the person filing this statement, to make solicitations or recommendations in connection with the tender offer, and provide a summary of the material terms of such employment, retainer or arrangement for compensation.

Item 7. Financial Information

(a) If Material, furnish the following financial data of the issuer:

(1) Audited financial statements for the two fiscal years required to be filed with the issuer's most recent annual report under Sections 13 and 15(d) of the Act;

(2) Unaudited balance sheets and comparative year-to-date income statements and statements of changes in financial position and related earnings per share amounts required to be included in the issuer's most recent quarterly report filed pursuant to the Act;

(3) Ratio of earnings to fixed charges for the two most recent fiscal years and the interim periods provided under Item 7(a)(2); and

(4) Book value per share as of the most recent fiscal year end and as of the date of the latest interim balance sheet provided under Item 7(a)(2).

(b) If material, provide pro forma data disclosing the effect of the tender offer on:

(1) The issuer's balance sheet as of the most recent fiscal year end and the latest interim balance sheet provided under Item 7(a)(2);

(2) The issuer's statement of income, earnings per share amounts, and ratio of earnings to fixed charges for the most recent fiscal year and the latest interim period provided under Item 7(a)(2); and

(3) The issuer's book value per share as of the most recent fiscal year end and as of the latest interim balance sheet date provided under Item 7(a)(2).

Item 8. Additional Information

If material to a decision by a security holder whether to sell, tender or hold securities being sought in the tender offer, furnish information including, but not limited to, the following:

(a) Any present or proposed contracts, arrangements, understandings or relationships between the issuer and its executive officers, directors or affiliates (other than any contract, arrangement or understanding required to be disclosed pursuant to Item 5 of this schedule);

(b) Any applicable regulatory requirements which must be complied with or approvals which must be obtained in connection with the tender offer;

(c) The applicability of the margin requirements of Section 7 of the Act and the regulation promulgated thereunder;

(d) Any material pending legal proceedings relating to the tender offer, including the name and location of the court or agency in which the proceedings are pending, the date instituted, the principal parties thereto and a brief summary of the proceedings and the relief sought; and

Instruction. In connection with sub-item(d), a copy of any document relating to a major development (such as pleadings, an answer, complaint, temporary restraining order, injunction, opinion, judgment or order) in a material pending legal proceeding should be furnished promptly to the Commission on a supplemental basis.

(e) Such additional material information, if any, as may be necessary to make the required statements, in light of the circumstances under which they are made, not materially misleading.

Item 9. Material to be Filed as Exhibits

Furnish a copy of:

(a) Tender offer material which is published, sent or given to security holders by or on behalf of the person filing this statement in connection with the tender offer;

(b) Any loan agreement referred to in Item 2 of this schedule.

(c) Any document setting forth the terms of any contract, arrangements, understandings or relationships referred to in Items 5 or 8(a) of this Schedule;

(d) Any written opinion prepared by legal counsel at the request of the person filing this statement and communicated to such person pertaining to the tax consequences of the tender offer;

(e) In an exchange offer where securities of the issuer have been or are to be registered under the Securities Act of 1933, any prospectus filed with the Commission in connection with the registration statement; and

(f) If any oral solicitation of security holders is to be made by or on behalf of the person filing this statement, any written instruction, form or other material which is furnished to the persons making the actual oral solicitation for their use, directly or indirectly, in connection with the tender offer. . . .

Rule 13f–1.   **Reporting by Institutional Investment Managers of Information With Respect to Accounts Over Which They Exercise Investment Discretion**

(a) Every institutional investment manager which exercises investment discretion with respect to accounts holding section 13(f) securities, as defined in paragraph (c) of this section, having an aggregate fair market value on the last trading day of any month of any calendar year of at least $100,000,000 shall file a report on Form 13F with the Commission within 45 days after the last day of such calendar year and within 45 days after the last day of each of the first three calendar quarters of the subsequent calendar year.

(b) For the purposes of this rule, "investment discretion" has the meaning set forth in section 3(a)(35) of the Act. An institutional investment manager shall also be deemed to exercise "investment discretion" with respect to all accounts over which any person under its control exercises investment discretion.

(c) For purposes of this rule "section 13(f) securities" shall mean equity securities of a class described in section 13(d)(1) of the Act that are admitted to trading on a national securities exchange or quoted on the automated quotation system of a registered securities association. In determining what classes of securities are section 13(f) securities, an institutional investment manager may rely on the most recent list of such securities published by the Commission pursuant to section 13(f)(3) of the Act. Only securities of a class on such list shall be counted in determining whether an institutional investment manager must file a report under this rule and only those securities shall be reported in such report. Where a person controls the issuer of a class of equity securities which are "section 13(f) securities" as defined in this rule, those securities shall not be deemed to be "section 13(f) securities" with respect to the controlling person, provided that such person does not otherwise exercise investment discretion with respect to accounts with fair market value of at least $100,000,000 within the meaning of paragraph (a) of this section. . . .

Schedule 13G.　Information to Be Included in Statements Filed Pursuant to 13d–1(b) and Amendments Thereto Filed Pursuant to 13d–2(b)

* * *

Item 1(a). Name of Issuer
Item 1(b). Address of Issuer's Principal Executive Offices
Item 2(a). Name of Person Filing
Item 2(b). Address of Principal Business Office or, if None, Residence
Item 2(c). Citizenship
Item 2(d). Title of Class of Securities
Item 2(e). CUSIP No.

Item 3. If This Statement Is Filed Pursuant to Rules 13d–1(b), or 13d–2(b), Check Whether the Person Filing Is a

(a) [ ] Broker of Dealer registered under Section 15 of the Act
(b) [ ] Bank as defined in section 3(a)(6) of the Act
(c) [ ] Insurance Company as defined in section 3(a)(19) of the Act
(d) [ ] Investment Company registered under section 8 of the Investment Company Act
(e) [ ] Investment Adviser registered under section 203 of the Investment Advisers Act of 1940

(f) [ ] Employee Benefit Plan, Pension Fund which is subject to the provisions of the Employee Retirement Income Security Act of 1974 or Endowment Fund; see Rule 13d–1(b)(1)(ii)(F)

(g) [ ] Parent Holding Company, in accordance with Rule 13d–1(b)(ii)(G) (Note: See Item 7)

(h) [ ] Group, in accordance with Rule 13d–1(b)(1)(ii)(H)

Item 4. Ownership

If the percent of the class owned, as of December 31 of the year covered by the statement, or as of the last day of any month described in Rule 13d–1(b)(2), if applicable, exceeds five percent, provide the following information as of that date and identify those shares which there is a right to acquire.

(a) Amount Beneficially Owned:

_____

(b) Percent of Class:

_____

(c) Number of shares as to which such person has:
    (i) sole power to vote or to direct the vote _____
    (ii) shared power to vote or to direct the vote _____
    (iii) sole power to dispose or to direct the disposition of _____
    (iv) shared power to dispose or to direct the disposition of _____

Instruction. For computations regarding securities which represent a right to acquire an underlying security see Rule 13d–3(d)(1).

Item 5. Ownership of Five Percent or Less of a Class

If this statement is being filed to report the fact that as of the date hereof the reporting person has ceased to be the beneficial owner of more than five percent of the class of securities, check the following [ ].

Instruction. Dissolution of a group requires a response to this item.

Item 6. Ownership of More than Five Percent on Behalf of Another Person

If any other person is known to have the right to receive or the power to direct the receipt of dividends from, or the proceeds from the sale of, such securities, a statement to that effect should be included in response to this item and, if such interest relates to more than five percent of the class, such person should be identified. A listing of the shareholders of an investment company registered under the Investment Company Act of 1940 or the beneficiaries of employee benefit plan, pension fund or endowment fund is not required.

Item 7. Identification and Classification of the Subsidiary Which Acquired the Security Being Reported on By the Parent Holding Company

If a parent holding company has filed this schedule, pursuant to Rule 13d–1(b)(ii)(G), so indicate under Item 3(g) and attach an exhibit stating the identity and the Item 3 classification of the relevant subsidiary. If a parent holding company has filed this schedule pursuant to Rule 13d–1(c), attach an exhibit stating the identification of the relevant subsidiary.

Item 8. Identification and Classification of Members of the Group

If a group has filed this schedule pursuant to Rule 13d–1(b)(ii)(H), so indicate under Item 3(h) and attach an exhibit stating the identity and Item 3 classification of each member of the group. If a group has filed this schedule pursuant to Rule 13d–1(c), attach an exhibit stating the identity of each member of the group.

Item 9. Notice of Dissolution of Group

Notice of dissolution of a group may be furnished as an exhibit stating the date of the dissolution and that all further filings with respect to transactions in the security reported on will be filed, if required, by members of the group, in their individual capacity. See Item 5.

Item 10. Certification

The following certification shall be included if the statement is filed pursuant to Rule 13d–1(b):

> By signing below I certify that, to the best of my knowledge and belief, the securities referred to above were acquired in the ordinary course of business and were not acquired for the purpose of and do not have the effect of changing or influencing the control of the issuer of such securities and were not acquired in connection with or as a participant in any transaction having such purposes or effect. . . .

EXCHANGE ACT §§ 14(d), (e) and (f)

(d)(1) It shall be unlawful for any person, directly or indirectly, by use of the mails or by any means or instrumentality of interstate commerce or of any facility of a national securities exchange or otherwise, to make a tender offer for, or a request or invitation for tenders of, any class of any equity security which is registered pursuant to section 12 of this title, or any equity security of an insurance company which would have been required to be so registered except for the exemption contained in section 12(g)(2)(G) of this title, or any equity security issued by a closed-end investment company registered under the Investment Company Act of 1940, if, after consummation thereof, such person would, directly or indirectly, be the beneficial owner of more than 5 per centum of such class, unless at the time copies of the offer or request or invitation are first published or sent or given to security holders such person has filed with the Commission a statement containing such of the information specified in section 13(d) of this title, and such additional information as the Commission may by rules and regulations prescribed as necessary or appropriate in the public interest or for the protection of investors. All requests or invitations for tenders or advertisements making a tender offer or requesting or inviting tenders of such a security shall be filed as a part of such statement and shall contain such of the information contained in such statement as the Commission may by rules and regulations prescribe. Copies of any additional material soliciting or requesting such tender offers subsequent to the initial solicitation or request shall contain such information as the Commission may by rules and regulations prescribe as necessary or appropriate in the public interest or for the protection of investors, and shall be filed with the Commission not later than the time copies of such material are first published or sent or given to security holders. Copies of all statements, in the form in which such material is furnished to security holders and the Commission, shall be sent to the issuer not later than the date such material is first published or sent or given to any security holders.

(2) When two or more persons act as a partnership, limited partnership, syndicate, or other group for the purpose of acquiring, holding, or disposing of securities of an issuer, such syndicate or group shall be deemed a "person" for purposes of this subsection.

(3) In determining, for purposes of this subsection, any percentage of a class of any security, such class shall be deemed to consist of the amount of the outstanding securities of such class, exclusive of any securities of such class held by or for the account of the issuer or a subsidiary of the issuer.

(4) Any solicitation or recommendation to the holders of such a security to accept or reject a tender offer or request or invitation for tenders shall be made in accordance with such rules and regulations as the Commission may prescribe as necessary or appropriate in the public interest or for the protection of investors.

(5) Securities deposited pursuant to a tender offer or request or invitation for tenders may be withdrawn by or on behalf of the depositor at any time until the expiration of seven days after the time definitive copies of the offer or request or invitation are first published or sent or given to security holders, and at any time after sixty days from the date of the original tender offer or request or invitation, except as the Commission may otherwise prescribe by rules, regulations, or order as necessary or appropriate in the public interest or for the protection of investors.

(6) Where any person makes a tender offer, or request or invitation for tenders, for less than all the outstanding equity securities of a class, and where a greater number of securities is deposited pursuant thereto within ten days after copies of the offer or request or invitation are first published or sent or given to security holders than such person is bound or willing to take up and pay for the securities taken up shall be taken up as nearly as may be pro rata, disregarding fractions, according to the number of securities deposited by each depositor. The provisions of this subsection shall also apply to securities deposited within ten days after notice of an increase in the consideration offered to security holders, as described in paragraph (7), is first published or sent or given to security holders.

(7) Where any person varies the terms of a tender offer or request or invitation for tenders before the expiration thereof by increasing the consideration offered to holders of such securities, such person shall pay the increased consideration to each security holder whose securities are taken up and paid for pursuant to the tender offer or request or invitation for tenders whether or not such securities have been taken up by such person before the variation of the tender offer or request or invitation.

(8) The provisions of this subsection shall not apply to any offer for, or request or invitation for tenders of, any security—

(A) if the acquisition of such security, together with all other acquisitions by the same person of securities of the same class during the preceding twelve months, would not exceed 2 per centum of that class;

(B) by the issuer of such security; or

(C) which the Commission, by rules or regulations or by order, shall exempt from the provisions of this subsection as not entered into for the purpose of, and not having the effect of, changing or influencing the control of the issuer or otherwise as not comprehended within the purposes of this subsection.

(e) It shall be unlawful for any person to make any untrue statement of a material fact or omit to state any material fact necessary in order to make the statements made, in the light of the circumstances under which they are made, not misleading, or to engage in any fraudulent, deceptive, or manipulative acts or practices, in connection with any tender offer or request or invitation for tenders, or any solicitation of security holders in opposition to or in favor of any such offer, request, or invitation. The Commission shall, for the purposes of this subsection, by rules and regulations define, and prescribe means reasonably designed to prevent, such acts and practices as are fraudulent, deceptive, or manipulative.

(f) If, pursuant to any arrangement or understanding with the person or persons acquiring securities in a transaction subject to subsection (d) of this section or subsection (d) of section 13 of this title, any persons are to be elected or designated as directors of the issuer, otherwise than at a meeting of security holders, and the persons so elected or designated will constitute a majority of the directors of the issuer, then, prior to the time any such person takes office as a director, and in accordance with rules and regulations prescribed by the Commission, the issuer shall file with the Commission, and transmit to all holders of record of securities of the issuer who would be entitled to vote at a meeting for election of directors, information substantially equivalent to the information which would be required by subsection (a) or (c) of this section to be transmitted if such person or persons were nominees for election as directors at a meeting of such security holders. . . .

REGULATION 14D

Rule 14d–1. **Scope of and Definitions Applicable to Regulations 14D and 14E**

(a) *Scope.* Regulation 14D shall apply to any tender offer which is subject to section 14(d)(1) of the Act, including, but not limited to, any tender offer for securities of a class described in that section which is made by an affiliate of the issuer of such class. Regulation 14E shall apply to any tender offer for securities (other than exempted securities) unless otherwise noted therein.

(b) *Definitions.* Unless the context otherwise requires, all terms used in Regulation 14D and Regulation 14E have the same meaning as in the Act and in Rule 12b–2 promulgated thereunder. In addition, for purposes of sections 14(d) and 14(e) of the Act and Regulations 14D and 14E, the following definitions apply:

(1) The term "bidder" means any person who makes a tender offer or on whose behalf a tender offer is made: *Provided, however,* That the term does not include an issuer which makes a tender offer for securities of any class of which it is the issuer;

(2) The term "subject company" means any issuer of securities which are sought by a bidder pursuant to a tender offer;

(3) The term "security holders" means holders of record and beneficial owners of securities which are the subject of a tender offer;

(4) The term "beneficial owner" shall have the same meaning as that set forth in Rule 13d–3: *Provided, however,* That, except with respect to Rule 14d–3, Rule 14d–9(d) and Item 6 of Schedule 14D–1, the term shall not include a person who does not have or share investment power or who is deemed to be a beneficial owner by virtue of Rule 13d–3(d)(1);

(5) The term "tender offer material" means:

(i) The bidder's formal offer, including all the material terms and conditions of the tender offer and all amendments thereto;

(ii) The related transmittal letter (whereby securities of the subject company which are sought in the tender offer may be transmitted to the bidder or its depositary) and all amendments thereto; and

(iii) Press releases, advertisements, letters and other documents published by the bidder or sent or given by the bidder to security holders which, directly or indirectly, solicit, invite or request tenders of the securities being sought in the tender offer;

(6) The term "business day" means any day, other than Saturday, Sunday or a federal holiday, and shall consist of the time period from 12:01 a.m. through 12:00 midnight Eastern time. In computing any time period under section 14(d)(5) or section 14(d)(6) of the Act or under Regulation 14D or Regulation 14E, the date of the event which begins the running of such time period shall be included *except that* if such event occurs on other than a business day such period shall begin to run on and shall include the first business day thereafter; and

(7) The term "security position listing" means, with respect to securities of any issuer held by a registered clearing agency in the name of the clearing agency or its nominee, a list of those participants in the clearing agency on whose behalf the clearing agency holds the issuer's securities and of the participants' respective positions in such securities as of a specified date.

Rule 14d–2.   Date of Commencement of a Tender Offer

(a) *Commencement.* A tender offer shall commence for the purposes of section 14(d) of the Act and the rules promulgated thereunder at 12:01 a.m. on the date when the first of the following events occurs:

(1) The long form publication of the tender offer is first published by the bidder pursuant to Rule 14d–4(a)(1);

(2) The summary advertisement of the tender offer is first published by the bidder pursuant to Rule 14d–4(a)(2);

(3) The summary advertisement or the long form publication of the tender offer is first published by the bidder pursuant to Rule 14d–4(a)(3);

(4) Definitive copies of a tender offer, in which the consideration offer by the bidder consists of securities registered pursuant to the Securities Act of 1933, are first published or sent or given by the bidder to security holders; or

(5) The tender offer is first published or sent or given to security holders by the bidder by any means not otherwise referred to in paragraphs (a)(1) through (a)(4) of this section.

(b) *Public Announcement.* A public announcement by a bidder through a press release, newspaper advertisement or public statement which includes the information in paragraph (c) of this section with respect to a tender offer in which the consideration consists solely of cash and/or securities exempt from registration under section 3 of the Securities Act of 1933 shall be deemed to constitute the commencement of a tender offer under paragraph (a)(5) of this section *except that* such tender offer shall not be deemed to be first published or sent or given to security holders by the bidder under paragraph (a)(5) of this section on the date of such public announcement if within five business days of such public announcement, the bidder either:

(1) Makes a subsequent public announcement stating that the bidder has determined not to continue with such tender offer, in which even paragraph (a)(5) of this section shall not apply to the initial public announcement; or

(2) Complies with Rule 14d–3(a) and contemporaneously disseminates the disclosure required by Rule 14d–6 to security holders pursuant to Rule 14d–4 or otherwise in which event:

(i) The date of commencement of such tender offer under paragraph (a) of this section will be determined by the date of information required by Rule 14d–6 is first published or sent or given to security holders pursuant to Rule 14d–4 or otherwise; and

(ii) Notwithstanding paragraph (b)(2)(i) of this section, section 14(d)(7) of the Act shall be deemed to apply to such tender offer from the date of such public announcement.

(c) *Information.* The information referred to in paragraph (b) of this section is as follows:

(1) The identity of the bidder;

(2) The identity of the subject company; and

(3) The amount and class of securities being sought and the price or range of prices being offered therefor.

(d) *Announcements Not Resulting in Commencement.* A public announcement by a bidder through a press release, newspaper advertisement or public statement which only discloses the information in paragraphs (d)(1) through (d)(3) of this section concerning a tender offer in which the consideration consists solely of cash and/or securities exempt from registration under section 3 of the Securities Act of 1933 shall not be deemed to constitute the commencement of a tender offer under paragraph (a)(5) of this section.

(1) The identity of the bidder;

(2) The identity of the subject company; and

(3) A statement that the bidder intends to make a tender offer in the future for a class of equity securities of the subject company which statement does not specify the amount of securities of such class to be sought or the consideration to be offered therefor.

(e) *Announcement Made Pursuant to Rule 135.* A public announcement by a bidder through a press release, newspaper advertisement or public statement which discloses only the information in Rule 135(a)(4) concerning a tender offer in which the consideration consists solely or in part of securities to be registered under the Securities Act of 1933 shall not be deemed to constitute the commencement of a tender offer under paragraph (a)(5) of this section: *Provided,* That such bidder files a registration statement with respect to such securities promptly after such public announcement.

Rule 14d–3.   Filing and Transmission of Tender Offer Statement

(a) *Filing and Transmittal.* No bidder shall make a tender offer if, after consummation thereof, such bidder would be the beneficial owner of more than 5 percent of the class of the subject company's securities for which the tender offer is made, unless as soon as practicable on the date of the commencement of the tender offer such bidder:

(1) Files with the Commission ten copies of a Tender Offer Statement on Schedule 14D–1, including all exhibits thereto;

(2) Hand delivers a copy of such Schedule 14D–1, including all exhibits thereto:

(i) To the subject company at its principal executive office; and

(ii) To any other bidder, which has filed a Schedule 14D–1 with the Commission relating to a tender offer which has not yet terminated for the same class of securities of the subject company, at such bidder's principal executive office or at the address of the person authorized to receive notices and communications (which is disclosed on the cover sheet of such other bidder's Schedule 14D–1);

(3) Gives telephonic notice of the information required by Rule 14d–6(e)(2)(i) and (ii) and mails by means of first class mail a copy of such Schedule 14D–1, including all exhibits thereto:

(i) To each national securities exchange where such class of the subject company's securities is registered and listed for trading (which may be based upon information contained in the subject company's most recent Annual Report on Form 10–K filed with the Commission unless the bidder has reason to believe that such information is not current) which telephonic notice shall be made when practicable prior to the opening of each such exchange; and

(ii) To the National Association of Securities Dealers, Inc. ("NASD") if such class of the subject company's securities is authorized for quotation in the NASDAQ interdealer quotation system.

(b) *Additional Materials.* The bidder shall file with the Commission ten copies of any additional tender offer materials as an exhibit to the Schedule 14D–1 required by this section, and if a material change occurs in the information set forth in such Schedule 14D–1, ten copies of an amendment to Schedule 14D–1 (each of which shall include all exhibits other than those required by Item 11(a) of Schedule 14D–1) disclosing such change and shall send a copy of such additional tender offer material or such amendment to the subject company and to any exchange and/or the NASD, as required by paragraph (a) of this section, promptly but not later than the date such additional tender offer material or such change is first published, sent or given to security holders.

(c) *Certain Announcements.* Notwithstanding the provisions of paragraph (b) of this section, if the additional tender offer material or an amendment to Schedule 14d–1 discloses only the number of shares deposited to date, and/or announces an extension of the time during which shares may be tendered, then the bidder may file such tender offer material or amendment and send a copy of such tender offer material or amendment to the subject company, any exchange and/or the NASD, as required by paragraph (a) of this section, promptly after the date such tender offer material is first published or sent or given to security holders.

Rule 14d–4.   Dissemination of Certain Tender Offers

(a) *Materials Deemed Published or Sent or Given.* A tender offer in which the consideration consists solely of cash and/or securities exempt from registration under section 3 of the Securities Act of 1933 shall be deemed "published or sent or given to security holders" within the meaning of section 14(d)(1) of the Act if the bidder complies with all of the requirements of any one of the following sub-paragraphs: *Provided, however,* That any such tender offers may be published or sent or given to security holders by other methods, but with respect to summary publication, and the use of stockholder lists and security position listings pursuant to Rule 14d–5, paragraphs (a)(2) and (a)(3) of this section are exclusive.

(1) *Long-Form Publication.* The bidder makes adequate publication in a newspaper or newspapers of long-form publication of the tender offer.

(2) *Summary publication.*

(i) If the tender offer is not subject to Rule 13e–3, the bidder makes adequate publication in a newspaper or newspapers of a summary advertisement of the tender offer; and

(ii) Mails by first class mail or otherwise furnishes with reasonable promptness the bidder's tender offer materials to any security holder who requests such tender offer materials pursuant to the summary advertisement or otherwise.

(3) *Use of Stockholder Lists and Security Position Listings.* Any bidder using stockholder lists and security position listings pursuant to Rule 14d–5 shall comply with paragraphs (a)(1) or (a)(2) of this section on or prior to the date of the bidder's request for such lists or listing pursuant to Rule 14d–5(a).

(b) *Adequate Publication.* Depending on the facts and circumstances involved, adequate publication of a tender offer pursuant to this section may require publication in a newspaper with a national circulation or may only require publication in a newspaper with metropolitan or regional circulation or may require publication in a combination thereof: *Provided, however,* That publication in all editions of a daily newspaper with a national circulation shall be deemed to constitute adequate publication.

(c) *Publication of Changes.* If a tender offer has been published or sent or given to security holders by one or more of the methods enumerated in paragraph (a) of this section, a material change in the information published, sent or given to security holders shall be promptly disseminated to security holders in a manner reasonably designed to inform security holders of such change; *Provided, however,* That if the bidder has elected pursuant to Rule 14d–5(f)(1) of this section to require the subject company to disseminate amendments disclosing material changes to the tender offer materials pursuant to Rule 14d–5, the bidder shall disseminate material changes in the information published or sent or given to security holders at least pursuant to Rule 14–5.

Rule 14d–5. Dissemination of Certain Tender Offers by the Use of Stockholder Lists and Security Position Listings

(a) *Obligations of the Subject Company.* Upon receipt by a subject company at its principal executive offices of a bidder's written request, meeting the requirements of paragraph (e) of this section, the subject company shall comply with the following sub-paragraphs.

(1) The subject company shall notify promptly transfer agents and any other person who will assist the subject company in complying with the requirements of this section of the receipt by the subject company of a request by a bidder pursuant to this section.

(2) The subject company shall promptly ascertain whether the most recently prepared stockholder list, written or otherwise, within the access of the subject company was prepared as of a date earlier than ten business days before the date of the bidder's request and, if so, the subject company shall promptly prepare or cause to be prepared a stockholder list as of the most recent practicable date which shall not be more than ten business days before the date of the bidder's request.

(3) The subject company shall make an election to comply and shall comply with all of the provisions of either paragraph (b) or paragraph (c) of this section. The subject company's election once made shall not be modified or revoked during the bidder's tender offer and extensions thereof.

(4) No later than the second business day after the date of the bidder's request, the subject company shall orally notify the bidder, which notification shall be confirmed in writing, of the subject company's election made pursuant to paragraph (a)(3) of this section. Such notification shall indicate (i) the approximate number of security holders of the class of securities being sought by the bidder and, (ii) if the subject company elects to comply with paragraph (b) of this section, appropriate information concerning the location for delivery of the bidder's tender offer materials and the approximate direct costs incidental to the mailing to security holders of the bidder's paragraph (g)(2) of this section.

(b) *Mailing of Tender Offer Materials by the Subject Company.* A subject company which elects pursuant to paragraph (a)(3) of this section to comply with the provisions of this paragraph shall perform the acts prescribed by the following subparagraphs.

(1) The subject company shall promptly contact each participant named on the most recent security position listing of any clearing agency within the access of the subject company and make inquiry of each such participant as to the approximate number of beneficial owners of the subject company securities being sought in the tender offer held by each such participant.

(2) No later than the third business day after delivery of the bidder's tender offer materials pursuant to paragraph (g)(1) of this section, the subject company shall begin to mail or cause to be mailed by means of first class mail a copy of the bidder's tender offer materials to each person whose name appears as a record holder of the class of securities for which the offer is made

on the most recent stockholder list referred to in paragraph (a)(2) of this section. The subject company shall use its best efforts to complete the mailing in a timely manner but in no event shall such mailing be completed in a substantially greater period of time than the subject company would complete a mailing to security holders of its own materials relating to the tender offer.

(3) No later than the third business day after the delivery of the bidder's tender offer materials pursuant to paragraph (g)(1) of this section, the subject company shall begin to transmit or cause to be transmitted a sufficient number of sets of the bidder's tender offer materials to the participants named on the security position listings described in paragraph (b)(1) of this section. The subject company shall use its best efforts to complete the transmittal in a timely manner but in no event shall such transmittal be completed in a substantially greater period of time than the subject company would complete a transmittal to such participants pursuant to security position listings of clearing agencies of its own material relating to the tender offer.

(4) The subject company shall promptly give oral notification to the bidder, which notification shall be confirmed in writing, of the commencement of the mailing pursuant to paragraph (b)(2) of this section and of the transmittal pursuant to paragraph (b)(3) of this section.

(5) During the tender offer and any extension thereof the subject company shall use reasonable efforts to update the stockholder list and shall mail or cause to be mailed promptly following each update a copy of the bidder's tender offer materials (to the extent sufficient sets of such materials have been furnished by the bidder) to each person who has become a record holder since the later of (i) the date of preparation of the most recent stockholder list referred to in paragraph (a)(2) of this section or (ii) the last preceding update.

(6) If the bidder has elected pursuant to paragraph (f)(1) of this section to require the subject company to disseminate amendments disclosing material changes to the tender offer materials pursuant to this section, the subject company, promptly following delivery of each such amendment, shall mail or cause to be mailed a copy of each such amendment to each record holder whose name appears on the shareholder list described in paragraphs (a)(2) and (b)(5) of this section and shall transmit or cause to be transmitted sufficient copies of such amendment to each participant named on security position listings who received sets of the bidder's tender offer materials pursuant to paragraph (b)(3) of this section.

(7) The subject company shall not include any communication other than the bidder's tender offer materials or amendments thereto in the envelopes or other containers furnished by the bidder.

(8) Promptly following the termination of the tender offer, the subject company shall reimburse the bidder the excess, if any, of the amounts advanced pursuant to paragraph (f)(3)(iii) over the direct costs incidental to compliance by the subject company and its agents in performing the acts required by this section computed in accordance with paragraph (g)(2) of this section.

(c) *Delivery of Stockholder Lists and Security Position Listings.* A subject company which elects pursuant to paragraph (a)(3) of this section to comply with the provisions of this paragraph shall perform the acts prescribed by the following subparagraphs.

(1) No later than the third business day after the date of the bidder's request, the subject company shall furnish to the bidder at the subject

company's principal executive office a copy of the names and addresses of the record holders on the most recent stockholder list referred to in paragraph (a)(2) of this section and a copy of the names and addresses of participants identified on the most recent security position listing of any clearing agency which is within the access of the subject company.

(2) If the bidder has elected pursuant to paragraph (f)(1) of this section to require the subject company to disseminate amendments disclosing material changes to the tender offer materials, the subject company shall update the stockholder list by furnishing the bidder with the name and address of each record holder named on the stockholder list, and not previously furnished to the bidder, promptly after such information becomes available to the subject company during the tender offer and any extensions thereof.

(d) *Liability of Subject Company and Others.* Neither the subject company nor any affiliate or agent of the subject company nor any clearing agency shall be:

(1) Deemed to have made a solicitation or recommendation respecting the tender offer within the meaning of section 14(d)(4) based solely upon the compliance or noncompliance by the subject company or any affiliate or agent of the subject company with one or more requirements of this section;

(2) Liable under any provision of the Federal securities laws to the bidder or to any security holder based solely upon the inaccuracy of the current names or addresses on the stockholder list or security position listing, unless such inaccuracy results from a lack of reasonable care on the part of the subject company or any affiliate or agent of the subject company;

(3) Deemed to be an "underwriter" within the meaning of section (2)(11) of the Securities Act of 1933 for any purpose of that Act or any rule or regulation promulgated thereunder based solely upon the compliance or noncompliance by the subject company or any affiliate or agent of the subject company with one or more of the requirements of this section;

(4) Liable under any provision of the Federal securities laws for the disclosure in the bidder's tender offer materials, including any amendment thereto, based solely upon the compliance or noncompliance by the subject company or any affiliate or agent of the subject company with one or more of the requirements of this section.

(e) *Content of the Bidder's Request.* The bidder's written request referred to in paragraph (a) of this section shall include the following:

(1) The identity of the bidder;

(2) The title of the class of securities which is the subject of the bidder's tender offer;

(3) A statement that the bidder is making a request to the subject company pursuant to paragraph (a) of this section for the use of the stockholder list and security position listings for the purpose of disseminating a tender offer to security holders;

(4) A statement that the bidder is aware of and will comply with the provisions of paragraph (f) of this section;

(5) A statement as to whether or not it has elected pursuant to paragraph (f)(1) of this section to disseminate amendments disclosing material changes to the tender offer materials pursuant to this section; and

(6) The name, address and telephone number of the person whom the subject company shall contact pursuant to paragraph (a)(4) of this section.

(f) *Obligations of the Bidder.* Any bidder who requests that a subject company comply with the provisions of paragraph (a) of this section shall comply with the following sub-paragraphs.

(1) The bidder shall make an election whether or not to require the subject company to disseminate amendments disclosing material changes to the tender offer materials pursuant to this section, which election shall be included in the request referred to in paragraph (a) of this section and shall not be revocable by the bidder during the tender offer and extensions thereof.

(2) With respect to a tender offer subject to section 14(d)(1) of the Act in which the consideration consists solely of cash and/or securities exempt from registration under section 3 of the Securities Act of 1933, the bidder shall comply with the requirements of Rule 14d–4(a)(3).

(3) If the subject company elects to comply with paragraph (b) of this section,

(i) The bidder shall promptly deliver the tender offer materials after receipt of the notification from the subject company as provided in paragraph

(ii) The bidder shall promptly notify the subject company of any amendment to the bidder's tender offer materials requiring compliance by the subject company with paragraph (b)(6) of this section and shall promptly deliver such amendment to the subject company pursuant to paragraph (g)(1) of this section;

(iii) The bidder shall advance to the subject company an amount equal to the approximate cost of conducting mailings to security holders computed in accordance with paragraph (g)(2) of this section;

(iv) The bidder shall promptly reimburse the subject company for the direct costs incidental to compliance by the subject company and its agents in performing the acts required by this section computed in accordance with paragraph (g)(2) of this section which are in excess of the amount advanced pursuant to paragraph (f)(2)(iii) of this section; and

(v) The bidder shall mail by means of first class mail or otherwise furnish with reasonable promptness the tender offer materials to any security holder who requests such materials.

(4) If the subject company elects to comply with paragraph (c) of this section,

(i) The subject company shall use the stockholder list and security position listings furnished to the bidder pursuant to paragraph (c) of this section exclusively in the dissemination of tender offer materials to security holders in connection with the bidder's tender offer and extensions thereof;

(ii) The bidder shall return the stockholder lists and security position listings furnished to the bidder pursuant to paragraph (c) of this section promptly after the termination of the bidder's tender offer;

(iii) The bidder shall accept, handle and return the stockholder lists and security position listings furnished to the bidder pursuant to paragraph (c) of this section to the subject company on a confidential basis;

(iv) The bidder shall not retain any stockholder list or security position listing furnished by the subject company pursuant to paragraph (c) of this section, or any copy thereof, nor retain any information derived from any such list or listing or copy thereof after the termination of the bidder's tender offer;

(v) The bidder shall mail by means of first class mail, at its own expense, a copy of its tender offer materials to each person whose identity appears on the stockholder list as furnished and updated by the subject company pursuant to paragraphs (c)(1) and (c)(2) of this section;

(vi) The bidder shall contact the participants named on the security position listing of any clearing agency, make inquiry of each participant as to the approximate number of sets of tender offer materials required by each such participant, and furnish, at its own expense, sufficient sets of tender offer materials and any amendment thereto to each such participant for subsequent transmission to the beneficial owners of the securities being sought by the bidder;

(vii) The bidder shall mail by means of first class mail or otherwise furnish with reasonable promptness the tender offer materials to any security holder who requests such materials; and

(viii) The bidder shall promptly reimburse the subject company for direct costs incidental to compliance by the subject company and its agents in performing the acts required by this section computed in accordance with paragraph (g)(2) of this section.

(g) *Delivery of Materials, Computation of Direct Costs.*

(1) Whenever the bidder is required to deliver tender offer materials or amendments to tender offer materials, the bidder shall deliver to the subject company at the location specified by the subject company in its notice given pursuant to paragraph (a)(4) of this section a number of sets of the materials or of the amendment, as the case may be, at least equal to the approximate number of security holders specified by the subject company in such notice, together with appropriate envelopes or other containers therefor; *Provided, however,* That such delivery shall be deemed not to have been made unless the bidder has complied with paragraph (f)(3)(iii) of this section at the time the materials or amendments, as the case may be, are delivered.

(2) The approximate direct cost of mailing the bidder's tender offer materials shall be computed by adding (i) the direct cost incidental to the mailing of the subject company's last annual report to shareholders (excluding employee time), less the costs of preparation and printing of the report, and postage, plus (ii) the amount of first class postage required to mail the bidder's tender offer materials. The approximate direct costs incidental to the mailing of the amendments to the bidder's tender offer materials shall be computed by adding (iii) the estimated direct costs of preparing mailing labels, of updating shareholders lists and of third party handling charges plus (iv) the amount of first class postage required to mail the bidder's amendment. Direct costs incidental to the mailing of the bidder's tender offer materials and amendments thereto when finally computed may include all reasonable charges paid by the subject company to third parties for supplies or services, including costs attendant to preparing shareholder lists, mailing labels, handling the bidder's materials, contacting participants named on security position listings and for postage, but shall exclude indirect costs, such as employee time which is devoted to either contesting or supporting the tender offer on behalf of the subject company. The final billing for direct costs shall be accompanied by an appropriate accounting in reasonable detail.

Rule 14d–6.   Disclosure Requirements With Respect to Tender Offers

(a) *Information Required on Date of Commencement.*

(1) *Long-Form Publication.* If a tender offer is published, sent or given to security holders on the date of commencement by means of long-term publication pursuant to Rule 14d–4(a)(1), such long-form publication shall include the information required by paragraph (e)(1) of this section.

(2) *Summary Publication.* If a tender offer is published, sent or given to security holders on the date of commencement by means of summary publication pursuant to Rule 14d–4(a)(2),

(i) The summary advertisement shall contain and shall be limited to, the information required by paragraph (e)(2) of this section; and

(ii) The tender offer materials furnished by the bidder upon the request of any security holder shall include the information required by paragraph (e)(1) of this section.

(3) *Use of Stockholder Lists and Security Position Listings.* If a tender offer is published or sent or given to security holders on the date of commencement by the use of stockholder lists and security position listings pursuant to Rule 14d–4(a)(3).

(i) Either (A) the summary advertisement shall contain, and shall be limited to the information required by paragraph (e)(2) of this section, or (B) if long form publication of the tender offer is made, such long form publication shall include the information required by paragraph (e)(1) of this section; and

(ii) The tender offer materials transmitted to security holders pursuant to such lists and security position listings and furnished by the bidder upon the request of any security holder shall include the information required by paragraph (e)(1) of this section.

(4) *Other Tender Offers.* If a tender offer is published or sent or given to security holders other than pursuant to Rule 14d–4(a), the tender offer materials which are published or sent or given to security holders on the date of commencement of such offer shall include the information required by paragraph (e)(1) of this section.

(b) *Information Required in Summary Advertisement Made After Commencement.* A summary advertisement published subsequent to the date of commencement of the tender offer shall include at least the information specified in paragraphs (e)(1)(i)–(iv) and (e)(2)(iv) of this section.

(c) *Information Required in Other Tender Offer Materials Published After Commencement.* Except for summary advertisements described in paragraph (b) of this section and tender offer materials described in paragraphs (a)(2)(ii) and (a)(3)(ii) of this section, additional tender offer materials published, sent or given to security holders subsequent to the date of commencement shall include the information required by paragraphs (e)(1) and may omit any of the information required by paragraphs (e)(1)(v)–(viii) of this section which has been previously furnished by the bidder in connection with the tender offer.

(d) *Material Changes.* A material change in the information published or sent or given to security holders shall be promptly disclosed to security holders in additional tender offer materials.

(e) *Information to Be Included.*

(1) *Long-Form Publication and Tender Offer Materials.* The information required to be disclosed by paragraphs (a)(1), (a)(2)(ii), (a)(3)(i)(B) and (a)(4) of this section shall include the following:

(i) The identity of the holder;

(ii) The identity of the subject company;

(iii) The amount of class of securities being sought and the type and amount of consideration being offered therefor;

(iv) The scheduled expiration date of the tender offer, whether the tender offer may be extended and, if so, the procedures for extension of the tender offer;

(v) The exact dates prior to which, and after which, security holders who deposit their securities will have the right to withdraw their securities pursuant to section 14(d)(5) of the Act and Rule 14d–7 and the manner in which shares will be accepted for payment and in which withdrawal may be effected;

(vi) If the tender offer is for less than all the outstanding securities of a class of equity securities and the bidder is not obligated to purchase all of the securities tendered, the period or periods, and in the case of the period from the commencement of the offer, the date of the expiration of such period during which the securities will be taken up pro rata pursuant to Section 14(d)(6) of the Act or Rule 14d–8, and the present intention or plan of the bidder with respect to the tender offer in the event of an over subscription by security holders;

(vii) The disclosure required by Items 1(c); 2 (with respect to persons other than the bidder, excluding sub-items (b) and (d); 3; 4; 5; 6; 7; 8; and 10 of Schedule 14D–1 or a fair and adequate summary thereof; *Provided, however,* That negative responses to any such item or sub-item or Schedule 14D–1 need not be included; and

(viii) The disclosure required by Item 9 of Schedule 14D–1 or a fair and adequate summary thereof. . . .

(ix) If the financial statements are prepared according to a comprehensive body of accounting principles other than those generally accepted in the United States, the summary financial information shall be accompanied by a reconciliation to generally accepted accounting principles of the United States.

(2) *Summary Publication.* The information required to be disclosed by paragraphs (a)(2)(i) and (a)(3)(i)(A) of this section in a summary advertisement is as follows:

(i) The information required by paragraph (e)(1)(i) through (vi) of this section;

(ii) If the tender offer is for less than all the outstanding securities of a class of equity securities, a statement as to whether the purpose or one of the purposes of the tender offer is to acquire or influence control of the business of the subject company;

(iii) A statement that the information required by paragraph (e)(1)(vii) of this section is incorporated by reference into the summary advertisement;

(iv) Appropriate instructions as to how security holders may obtain promptly, at the bidders expense, the bidder's tender offer materials; and

(v) In a tender offer published or sent or given to security holders by the use of stockholders lists and security position listings pursuant to Rule 14d–4(a)(3), a statement that a request is being made for such lists and listings and that tender offer materials will be mailed to record holders and will be furnished to brokers, banks and similar persons whose name appears or whose nominee appears on the list of stockholders or, if applicable, who are listed as participants in a clearing agency's security position listing for subsequent transmittal to beneficial owners of such securities.

(3) *No Transmittal Letter.* Neither the initial summary advertisement nor any subsequent summary advertisement shall include a transmittal letter (whereby securities of the subject company which are sought in the tender offer may be transmitted to the bidder or its depository) or any amendment thereto.

Rule 14d–7.   Additional Withdrawal Rights

(a) *Rights.* In addition to the provisions of section 14(d)(5) of the Act, any person who has deposited securities pursuant to a tender offer has the right to withdraw any such securities during the following periods:

(1) At any time until the expiration of fifteen business days from the date of commencement of such tender offer; and

(2) On the date and until the expiration of ten business days following the date of commencement of another bidder's tender offer other than pursuant to Rule 14d–2(b) for securities of the same class, *Provided,* That the bidder has received notice or otherwise has knowledge of the commencement of such other tender offer and, *Provided further,* That withdrawal may only be effected with respect to securities which have not been accepted for payment in the manner set forth in the bidder's tender offer prior to the date such other tender offer is first published, sent or given to security holders.

(b) *Computation of Time Periods.* The time periods for withdrawal rights pursuant to this section shall be computed on a concurrent, as opposed to a consecutive basis.

(c) *Knowledge of Competing Offer.* For the purposes of this section, a bidder shall be presumed to have knowledge of another tender offer, as described in paragraph (a)(2) of this section, on the date such bidder receives a copy of the Schedule 14D–1 pursuant to Rule 14d–2 from such other bidder.

(d) *Notice of Withdrawal.* Notice of withdrawal pursuant to this section shall be deemed to be timely upon the receipt by the bidder's depositary of a written notice of withdrawal specifying the name(s) of the tendering stockholder(s), the number or amount of the securities to be withdrawn and the name(s) in which the certificate(s) is (are) registered, if different from that of the tendering security holder(s). A bidder may impose other reasonable requirements, including certificate numbers and a signed request for withdrawal accompanied by a signature guarantee, as conditions precedent to the physical release of withdrawn securities.

Rule 14d–8.   Exemption From Statutory Pro Rata Requirements

Notwithstanding the pro rata provisions of Section 14(d)(6) of the Act, if any person makes a tender offer or request or invitation for tenders, for less than all of the outstanding equity securities of a class, and if a greater number of securities are deposited pursuant thereto than such person is bound or willing to take up and pay for, the securities taken up and paid for shall be taken up and paid for as nearly as may be pro rata, disregarding fractions, according to the number of securities deposited by each depositor during the period such offer, request or invitation remains open.

Rule 14d–9.   Solicitation/Recommendation Statements With Respect to Certain Tender Offers

(a) *Filing and Transmittal of Recommendation Statement.* No solicitation or recommendation to security holders shall be made by any person described in paragraph (d) of this section with respect to a tender offer for such securities unless as soon as practicable on the date such solicitation or recommendation is first published or sent or given to security holders such person complies with the following sub-paragraphs.

(1) Such person shall file with the Commission eight copies of a Tender Offer Solicitation/Recommendation Statement on Schedule 14D–9, including all exhibits thereto; and

(2) If such person is either the subject company or an affiliate of the subject company,

(i) Such person shall hand deliver a copy of the Schedule 14D–9 to the bidder at its principal office or at the address of the person authorized to receive notices and communications (which is set forth on the cover sheet of the bidder's Schedule 14D–1 filed with the Commission; and

(ii) Such person shall give telephonic notice (which notice to the extent possible shall be given prior to the opening of the market) of the information required by Items 2 and 4(a) of Schedule 14D–9 and shall mail a copy of the Schedule to each national securities exchange where the class of securities is registered and listed for trading and, if the class is authorized for quotation in the NASDAQ interdealer quotation system, to the National Association of Securities Dealers, Inc. ("NASD").

(3) If such person is neither the subject company nor an affiliate of the subject company.

(i) Such person shall mail a copy of the schedule to the bidder at its principal office or at the address of the person authorized to receive notices and communications (which is set forth on the cover sheet of the bidder's Schedule 14D–1 filed with the Commission); and

(ii) Such person shall mail a copy of the Schedule to the subject company at its principal office.

(b) *Amendments.* If any material change occurs in the information set forth in the Schedule 14D–9 required by this section, the person who filed such Schedule 14D–9 shall:

(1) File with the Commission eight copies of an amendment on Schedule 14D–9 disclosing such change promptly, but not later than the date such material is first published, sent or given to security holders; and

(2) Promptly deliver copies and give notice of the amendment in the same manner as that specified in paragraph (a)(2) or paragraph (a)(3) of this section, whichever is applicable; and

(3) Promptly disclose and disseminate such change in a manner reasonably designed to inform security holders of such change.

(c) *Information Required in Solicitation or Recommendation.* Any solicitation or recommendation to holders of a class of securities referred to in section 14(d)(1) of the Act with respect to a tender offer for such securities shall include the name of the person making such solicitation or recommendation and the information required by Items 1, 2, 3(b), 4, 6, 7 and 8 of Schedule 14D–9 or a fair and adequate summary thereof: *Provided, however,* That such solicitation or recommendation may omit any of such information previously furnished to security holders of such class of securities by such person with respect to such tender offer.

(d) *Applicability.*

(1) Except as provided in paragraphs (d)(2) and (e) of this section, this section shall only apply to the following persons:

(i) The subject company, any director, officer, employee, affiliate or subsidiary of the subject company;

(ii) Any record holder or beneficial owner of any security issued by the subject company, by the bidder, or by any affiliate of either the subject company or the bidder; and

(iii) Any person who makes a solicitation or recommendation to security holders on behalf of any of the foregoing or on behalf of the bidder other than by means of a solicitation or recommendation to security holders which has been filed with the Commission pursuant to this section or Rule 14d–3.

(2) Notwithstanding paragraph (d)(1) of this section, this section shall not apply to the following persons:

(i) A bidder who has filed a Schedule 14D–1 pursuant to Rule 14d–3;

(ii) Attorneys, banks, brokers, fiduciaries or investment advisers who are not participating in a tender offer in more than a ministerial capacity and who furnish information and/or advice regarding such tender offer to their customers or clients on the unsolicited request of such customers or clients or solely pursuant to a contract or a relationship providing for advice to the customer or client to whom the information and/or advice is given.

(e) *Stop-Look-and-Listen Communications.* This section shall not apply to the subject company with respect to a communication by the subject company to its security holders which only:

(1) Identifies the tender offer by the bidder;

(2) States that such tender offer is under consideration by the subject company's board of directors and/or management;

(3) States that on or before a specified date (which shall be no later than 10 business days from the date of commencement of such tender offer) the subject company will advise such security holders of (i) whether the subject company recommends acceptance or rejection of such tender offer; expresses

no opinion and remains neutral toward such tender offer; or is unable to take a position with respect to such tender offer and (ii) the reason(s) for the position taken by the subject company with respect to the tender offer (including the inability to take a position); and

 (4) Requests such security holders to defer making determination whether to accept or reject such tender offer until they have been advised of the subject company's position with respect thereto pursuant to paragraph (e)(3) of this section.

 (f) *Statement of Management's Position.* A statement by the subject company's of its position with respect to a tender offer which is required to be published or sent or given to security holders pursuant to Rule 14e–2 shall be deemed to constitute a solicitation or recommendation within the meaning of this section and section 14(d)(4) of the Act.

Rule 14d–100. Schedule 14D–1. Tender Offer Statement Pursuant to Section 14(d)(1) of the Securities Exchange Act of 1934

* * *

GENERAL INSTRUCTIONS

* * *

 C. If the statement is filed by a partnership, limited partnership, syndicate or other group, the information called for by Items 2–7, inclusive, shall be given with respect to: (i) each partner of such partnership; (ii) each partner who is denominated as a general partner or who functions as a general partner of such limited partnership; (iii) each member of such syndicate or group; and (iv) each person controlling such partner or member. If the statement is filed by a corporation, or if a person referred to in (i), (ii), (iii), or (iv) of this Instruction is a corporation, the information called for by the above mentioned items shall be given with respect to: (a) each executive officer and director of such corporation; (b) each person controlling such corporation; and (c) each executive officer and director of any corporation ultimately in control of such corporation. A response to an item in the statement is required with respect to the bidder and to all other persons referred to in this instruction unless such item specifies to the contrary.

 D. Upon termination of the tender offer, the bidder shall promptly file a final amendment to Schedule 14D–1 disclosing all material changes in the items of that Schedule and stating that the tender offer has terminated, the date of such termination and the results of such tender offer.

 E. If the bidder, before filing this statement, has filed a Schedule 13D with respect to the acquisition of securities of the same class referred to in Item 1(a) of this statement, the bidder shall amend such Schedule 13D and may do so by means of this statement and amendments thereto, including the final amendment required to be filed by Instruction D: *Provided,* That the bidder indicated on the cover sheet of this statement that it is amending its Schedule 13D by means of this statement.

 F. The final amendment required to be filed by Instruction D shall be deemed to satisfy the reporting requirements of section 13(d) of the Act with respect to all securities acquired by the bidder pursuant to the tender offer as reported in such final amendment.

  G. For purposes of this statement, the following definitions shall apply:

    (i) The term "bidder" means any person on whose behalf a tender offer is made; and

    (ii) The term "subject company" means any issuer whose securities are sought by a bidder pursuant to a tender offer.

Item 1. Security and Subject Company

  (a) State the name of the subject company and the address of its principal executive offices;

  (b) State the exact title and the number of shares outstanding of the class of equity securities being sought (which may be based upon information contained in the most recently available filing with the Commission by the subject company unless the bidder has reason to believe such information is not current), the exact amount of such securities being sought and the consideration being offered therefor; and

  (c) Identify the principal market in which such securities are traded and state the high and low sales prices for such securities in such principal market (or, in the absence thereof, the range of high and low bid quotations) for each quarterly period during the past two years.

Item 2. Identity and Background

  If the person filing this statement or any person enumerated in Instruction C of this statement is a corporation, partnership, limited partnership, syndicate or other group of persons, state its name, the state or other place of its organization, its principal business, the address of its principal office and the information required by (e) and (f) of this Item. If the person filing this statement or any person enumerated in Instruction C is a natural person, provide the information specified in (a) through (g) of this Item with respect to such person(s).

  (a) Name;

  (b) Residence or business address;

  (c) Present principal occupation or employment and the name, principal business and address of any corporation or other organization in which such employment or occupation is conducted;

  (d) Material occupations, positions, offices or employments during the last 5 years, giving the starting and ending dates of each and the name, principal business and address of any business corporation or other organization in which such occupation, position, office or employment was carried on;

  Instruction. If a person has held various positions with the same organization, or if a person holds comparable positions with multiple related organizations, each and every position need not be specifically disclosed.

  (e) Whether or not, during the last 5 years, such person has been convicted in a criminal proceeding (excluding traffic violations or similar misdemeanors) and, if so, give the dates, nature of conviction, name and location of court, and penalty imposed or other disposition of the case;

Instruction. While a negative answer to this sub-item is required in this schedule, it need not be furnished to security holders.

(f) Whether or not, during the last 5 years, such person was a party to a civil proceeding of a judicial or administrative body of competent jurisdiction and as a result of such proceeding was or is subject to a judgment, decree or final order enjoining future violations of, or prohibiting activities subject to, federal or state securities laws or finding any violation of such laws; and, if so, identify and describe such proceeding and summarize the terms of such judgment, decree or final order; and

Instruction. While a negative answer to this sub-item is required in this schedule, it need not be furnished to security holders.

(g) Citizenship(s).

Item 3. Past Contracts, Transactions or Negotiations With the Subject Company

(a) Briefly state the nature and approximate amount (in dollars) of any transaction, other than those described in Item 3(b) of this schedule, which has occurred since the commencement of the subject company's third full fiscal year preceding the date of this schedule, between the person filing this schedule (including those persons enumerated in Instruction C of this schedule) and:

(1) the subject company or any of its affiliates which are corporations: *Provided, However,* That no disclosure need be made with respect to any transaction if the aggregate amount involved in such transaction was less than one percent of the subject company's consolidated revenues (which may be based upon information contained in the most recently available filing with the Commission by the subject company, unless the bidder has reason to believe otherwise) (i) for the fiscal year in which such transaction occurred or, (ii) for the portion of the current fiscal year which has occurred, if the transaction occurred in such year; and

(2) the executive officers, directors, or affiliates of the subject company which are not corporations if the aggregate amount involved in such transaction or in a series of similar transactions, including all periodic installments in the case of any lease or other agreement providing for periodic payments or installments, exceeds $40,000.

(b) Describe any contacts, negotiations or transactions which have occurred since the commencement of the subject company's third full fiscal year preceding the date of this schedule between the bidder or its subsidiaries (including those persons enumerated in Instruction C of this schedule) and the subject company or its affiliates concerning: a merger, consolidation or acquisition; a tender offer or other acquisition of securities; an election of directors; or a sale or other transfer of a material amount of assets.

Item 4. Source and Amount of Funds or Other Consideration

(a) State the source and the total amount of funds or other consideration for the purchase of the maximum number of securities for which the tender offer is being made.

(b) If all or any part of such funds or other consideration are or are expected to be, directly or indirectly, borrowed for the purpose of the tender offer:

(1) Provide a summary of each loan agreement or arrangement containing the identity of the parties, the term, the collateral, the stated and effective interest rates, and other material terms or conditions relative to such loan agreement; and

(2) Briefly, describe any plans or arrangements to finance or repay such borrowings, or if no such plans or arrangements have been made, make a statement to that effect.

(c) If the source of all or any part of the funds to be used in the tender offer is a loan made in the ordinary course of business by a bank as defined by section 3(a)(6) of the Act, the name of such bank shall not be made available to the public if the person filing the statement so requests in writing and files such request, naming such bank, with the Secretary of the Commission.

Item 5. Purpose of the Tender Offer and Plans or Proposals of the Bidder

State the purpose or purposes of the tender offer for the subject company's securities. Describe any plans or proposals which relate to or would result in:

(a) An extraordinary corporate transaction, such as a merger, reorganization or liquidation, involving the subject company or any of its subsidiaries;

(b) A sale or transfer of a material amount of assets of the subject company or any of its subsidiaries;

(c) Any change in the present board of directors or management of the subject company including, but not limited to, any plans or proposals to change the number or the term of directors or to fill any existing vacancies on the board;

(d) Any material change in the present capitalization or dividend policy of the subject company;

(e) Any other material change in the subject company's corporate structure or business, including, if the subject company is a registered closed-end investment company, any plans or proposals to make any changes in its investment policy for which a vote would be required by section 13 of the Investment Company Act of 1940;

(f) Causing a class of securities of the subject company to be delisted from a national securities exchange or to cease to be authorized to be quoted in an inter-dealer quotation system of a registered national securities association; or

(g) A class of equity securities of the subject company becoming eligible for termination of registration pursuant to section 12(g)(4) of the Act.

Item 6. Interest in Securities of the Subject Company

(a) State the aggregate number and percentage of the class represented by such shares (which may be based on the number of shares outstanding as contained in the most recently available filing with the Commission by the subject company unless the bidder has reasons to believe such information is not current), beneficially owned (identifying those shares for which there is a right to acquire) by each person named in Item 2 of this schedule and by each associate and majority-owned subsidiary of such person giving the name and address of any such associate or subsidiary.

(b) Describe any transaction in the class of securities reported on that was effected during the past 60 days by the persons named in response to paragraph (a) of this item or by any executive officer, director or subsidiary of such person.

Instructions: 1. The description of a transaction required by Item 6(b) shall include, but not necessarily be limited to: (1) the identity of the person covered by Item 6(b) who effected the transaction; (2) the date of the transaction; (3) the amount of securities involved; (4) the price per share; and (5) where and how the transaction was effected.

2. If the information required by Item 6(b) of this schedule is available to the bidder at the time this statement is initially filed with the Commission pursuant to Rule 14d–3(a)(1), such information should be included in such initial filing. However, if such information is not available to the bidder at the time of such initial filing, it shall be filed with the Commission promptly but in no event later than two business days after the date of such filing and, if material, shall be disclosed in a manner reasonably designed to inform security holders. The procedure specified by this instruction is provided for the purpose of maintaining the confidentiality of the tender offer in order to avoid possible misuse of inside information.

Item 7. Contracts, Arrangements, Understandings or Relationships With Respect to the Subject Company's Securities

Describe any contract, arrangement, understanding or relationship (whether or not legally enforceable) between the bidder (including those persons enumerated in Instruction C to this schedule) and any person with respect to any securities of the subject company (including, but not limited to, any contract, arrangement, understanding or relationship concerning the transfer or the voting of any of such securities, joint ventures, loan or option arrangements, puts or calls, guaranties of loans, guaranties against loss, or the giving or withholding of proxies) naming the persons with whom such contracts, arrangements, understandings or relationships have been entered into and giving the material provisions thereof. Include such information for any of such securities that are pledged or otherwise subject to a contingency, the occurrence of which would give another person the power to direct the voting or disposition of such securities, except that disclosure of standard default and similar provisions contained in loan agreements need not be included.

Item 8. Persons Retained, Employed or to Be Compensated

Identify all persons and classes of persons employed, retained or to be compensated by the bidder, or by any person on the bidder's behalf, to make solicitations or recommendations in connection with the tender offer and describe briefly the terms of such employment, retainer or arrangement for compensation.

Item 9. Financial Statements of Certain Bidders

Where the bidder is other than a natural person and the bidder's financial condition is material to a decision by a security holder of the subject company whether to sell, tender or hold securities being sought in the tender offer, furnish current, adequate financial information concerning the bidder, *Provided,* That if the bidder is controlled by another entity which is not a natural person and has been formed for the purpose of making the tender offer, furnish current, adequate financial information concerning such parent.

Instructions. 1. The facts and circumstances concerning the tender offer, particularly the terms of the tender offer, may influence a determination as to whether disclosure of financial information is material. However, once the materiality requirement is applicable, the adequacy of the financial information will depend primarily on the nature of the bidder.

In order to provide guidance in making this determination, the following types of financial information will be deemed adequate for purposes of this item for the type of bidder specified: (a) financial statements prepared in compliance with Form 10 as amended for a domestic bidder which is otherwise eligible to use such form; and (b) financial statements prepared in accordance with Item 17 of Form 20–F for a foreign bidder that is otherwise eligible to use such form.

2. If the bidder is subject to the periodic reporting requirements of sections 13(a) or 15(d) of the Act, financial statements contained in any document filed with the Commission may be incorporated by reference in this schedule solely for the purposes of this schedule, *Provided*, That such financial statements substantially meet the requirements of this item; an express statement is made that such financial statements are incorporated by reference; the matter incorporated by reference is clearly identified by page, paragraph, caption or otherwise; and an indication is made where such information may be inspected and copies obtained. Financial statements which are required to be presented in comparative form for two or more fiscal years or periods shall not be incorporated by reference unless the material incorporated by reference includes the entire period for which the comparative data is required to be given.

3. If the bidder is not subject to the periodic reporting requirements of the Act, the financial statements required by this item need not be audited if such financial statements are not available or obtainable without unreasonable cost or expense and a statement is made to that effect disclosing the reasons therefor.

Item 10. Additional Information

If material to a decision by a security holder whether to sell, tender or hold securities being sought in the tender offer, furnish information as to the following:

(a) Any present or proposed material contracts, arrangement, understandings or relationships between the bidder or any of its executive officers, directors, controlling persons or subsidiaries and the subject company or any of its executive officers, directors, controlling persons or subsidiaries (other than any contract, arrangement or understanding required to be disclosed pursuant to Items 3 or 7 of this schedule);

(b) To the extent known by the bidder after reasonable investigation, the applicable regulatory requirements which must be complied with or approvals which must be obtained in connection with the tender offer;

(c) The applicability of anti-trust laws;

(d) The applicability of the margin requirements of section 7 of the Act and the regulations promulgated thereunder;

(e) Any material pending legal proceedings relating to the tender offer including the name and location of the court or agency in which the proceedings are pending, the date instituted, the principal parties thereto and a brief summary of the proceedings; and

Instruction. In connection with this sub-item, a copy of any document relating to a major development (such as pleadings, an answer, complaint, temporary restraining order, injunction, opinion, judgment or order) in a material pending legal proceeding should be promptly furnished to the Commission on a supplemental basis.

(f) Such additional material information, if any, as may be necessary to make the required statements, in light of the circumstances under which they are made, not materially misleading.

Item 11. Material to Be Filed as Exhibits

Furnish a copy of:
(a) Tender offer material which is published, sent or given to security holders by or on behalf of the bidder in connection with the tender offer;
(b) Any loan agreement referred to in Item 4 of this schedule;

Instruction. The identity of any bank which is a party to a loan agreement need not be disclosed if the person filing the statement has requested that the identity of such bank not be made available to the public pursuant to Item 4 of this schedule.

(c) Any document setting forth the terms of any contracts, arrangements, understandings or relationships referred to in Item 7 or 10(a) of this schedule;
(d) Any written opinion prepared by legal counsel at the bidder's request and communicated to the bidder pertaining to the tax consequences of the tender offer;
(e) In an exchange offer where securities of the bidder have been or are to be registered under the Securities Act of 1933, the prospectus containing the information to be included therein by Rule 432 of that Act;
(f) If any oral solicitation of security holders is to be made by or on behalf of the bidder, any written instruction, form or other material which is furnished to the persons making the actual oral solicitation for their use, directly or indirectly, in connection with the tender offer. . . .

Rule 14d–101. Schedule 14D–9

* * *

Item 1. Security and Subject Company

State the title of the class of equity securities to which this statement relates and the name and the address of the principal executive offices of the subject company.

Item 2. Tender Offer of the Bidder

Identify the tender offer to which this statement relates, the name of the bidder and the address of its principal executive offices or, if the bidder is a natural person, the bidder's residence or business address (which may be based on the bidder's Schedule 14D–1 filed with the Commission).

Item 3. Identity and Background

(a) State the name and business address of the person filing this statement.

(b) If material, describe any contract, agreement, arrangement or understanding and any actual or potential conflict of interest between the person filing this statement or its affiliates and: (1) the subject company, its executive officers, directors or affiliates; or (2) the bidder, its executive officers, directors or affiliates.

Instruction. If the person filing this statement is the subject company and if the materiality requirement of Item 3(b) is applicable to any contract, agreement, arrangement or understanding between the subject company or any affiliate of the subject company and any executive officer or director of the subject company, it shall not be necessary to include a description thereof in this statement, or in any solicitation or recommendation published, sent or given to security holders if such information, or information which does not differ materially from such information, has been disclosed in any proxy statement, report or other communication sent within one year of the filing date of this statement by the subject company to the then holders of the securities and has been filed with the Commission: *Provided,* That this statement and the solicitation or recommendation published, sent or given to security holders shall contain specific reference to such proxy statement, report or other communication and that a copy of the pertinent portion(s) thereof is filed as an exhibit to this statement.

Item 4. The Solicitation or Recommendation

(a) State the nature of the solicitation or the recommendation. If this statement relates to a recommendation, state whether the person filing this statement is advising security holders of the securities being sought by the bidder to accept or reject the tender offer or to take other action with respect to the tender offer and, if so, furnish a description of such other action being recommended. If the person filing this statement is the subject company and a recommendation is not being made, state whether the subject company is either expressing no opinion and is remaining neutral toward the tender offer or is unable to take a position with respect to the tender offer.

(b) State the reason(s) for the position (including the inability to take a position) stated in (a) of this Item.

Instruction. Conclusory statements such as "The tender offer is in the best interest of shareholders," will not be considered sufficient disclosure in response to Item 4(b).

Item 5. Persons Retained, Employed or to Be Compensated

Identify any person or class of persons employed, retained or to be compensated by the person filing this statement or by any person on its behalf, to make solicitations or recommendations to security holders and describe briefly the terms of such employment, retainer or arrangement for compensation.

Item 6. Recent Transactions and Intent With Respect to Securities

(a) Describe any transaction in the securities referred to in Item 1 which was effected during the past 60 days by the person(s) named in response to Item 3(a) and by any executive officer, director, affiliate or subsidiary of such person(s).

(b) To the extent known by the person filing this statement, state whether the persons referred to in Item 6(a) presently intend to tender to the bidder, sell or hold securities of the class of securities being sought by the bidder which are held of record or beneficially owned by such persons.

Item 7. Certain Negotiations and Transactions by the Subject Company

(a) If the person filing this statement is the subject company, state whether or not any negotiation is being undertaken or is underway by the subject company in response to the tender offer which relates to or would result in:

(1) An extraordinary transaction such as a merger or reorganization, involving the subject company or any subsidiary of the subject company;

(2) A purchase, sale or transfer of a material amount of assets by the subject company or any subsidiary of the subject company;

(3) A tender offer for or other acquisition of securities by or of the subject company; or

(4) Any material change in the present capitalization or dividend policy of the subject company.

Instruction. If no agreement in principle had yet been reached, the possible terms of any transaction or the parties thereto need not be disclosed if in the opinion of the Board of Directors of the subject company such disclosure would jeopardize continuation of such negotiations. In such event, disclosure that negotiations are being undertaken or are underway and are in the preliminary states will be sufficient.

(b) Describe any transaction, board resolution, agreement in principle, or a signed contract in response to the tender offer, other than one described pursuant to Item 3(b) of this statement, which relates to or would result in one or more of the matters referred to in Item 7(a)(1), (2), (3) or (4).

Item 8. Additional Information to Be Furnished

Furnish such additional information, if any, as may be necessary to make the required statements, in light of the circumstances under which they are made, not materially misleading.

Item 9. Material to Be Filed as Exhibits

Furnish a copy of:

(a) Any written solicitation or recommendation which is published or sent or given to security holders in connection with the solicitation or recommendation referred to in Item 4.

(b) If any oral solicitation or recommendation to security holders is to be made by or on behalf of the person filing this statement, any written instruction, or other material which is furnished to the persons making the actual oral solicitation or recommendation for their use, directly or indirectly, in connection with the solicitation or recommendation.

(c) Any contract, agreement, arrangement or understanding described in Item 3(b) or the pertinent portion(s) of any proxy statement, report or other communication referred to in Item 3(b). . ..

REGULATION 14E

Rule 14e–1.   Unlawful Tender Offer Practices

As a means reasonably designed to prevent fraudulent, deceptive or manipulative acts or practices within the meaning of section 14(e) of the Act, no person who makes a tender offer shall:

(a) Hold such tender offer open for less than twenty business days from the date such tender offer is first published or sent or given to security holders: *Provided, however,* That this paragraph shall not apply to a tender offer by the issuer of the class of securities being sought which is not made in anticipation of or in response to another person's tender offer for securities of the same class.

(b) Increase the offered consideration or the dealer's soliciting fee to be given in a tender offer unless such tender offer remains open for at least ten business days from the date that notice of such increase is first published, sent or given to security holders: *Provided, however,* That this paragraph shall not apply to a tender offer by the issuer of the class of securities being sought which is not made in anticipation of or in response to another person's tender offer for securities of the same class.

(c) Fail to pay the consideration offered or return the securities deposited by or on behalf of security holders promptly after the termination or withdrawal of a tender offer.

(d) Extend the length of a tender offer without issuing a notice of such extension by press release or other public announcement, which notice shall include disclosure of the approximate number of securities deposited to date and shall be issued no later than the earlier of (i) 9:00 a.m. Eastern time, on the next business day after the scheduled expiration date of the offer or (ii), if the class of securities which is the subject of the tender offer is registered on one or more national securities exchanges, the first opening of any one of such exchanges on the next business day after the scheduled expiration date of the offer.

Rule 14e–2.   Position of Subject Company With Respect to a Tender Offer

(a) *Position of Subject Company.* As a means reasonably designed to prevent fraudulent, deceptive or manipulative acts or practices within the meaning of section 14(e) of the Act, the subject company, no later than 10 business days from the date the tender offer is first published or sent or given, shall publish, send or give to security holders a statement disclosing that the subject company:

(1) Recommends acceptance or rejection of the bidder's tender offer;

(2) Expresses no opinion and is remaining neutral toward the bidder's tender offer; or

(3) Is unable to take a position with respect to the bidder's tender offer.

Such statement shall also include the reason(s) for the position (including the inability to take a position) disclosed therein.

(b) *Material Change.* If any material change occurs in the disclosure required by paragraph (a) of this section, the subject company shall promptly publish, send or give a statement disclosing such material charge to security holders.

Rule 14e–3.   Transactions in Securities on the Basis of Material, Nonpublic Information in the Context of Tender Offers

(a) If any person has taken a substantial step or steps to commence, or has commenced, a tender offer (the "offering person"), it shall constitute a fraudulent, deceptive or manipulative act or practice within the meaning of section 14(e) of the Act for any other person who is in possession of material information relating to such tender offer which information he knows or has reason to know is nonpublic and which he knows or has reason to know has been acquired directly or indirectly from (1) the offering person, (2) the issuer of the securities sought or to be sought by such tender offer, or (3) any officer, director, partner or employee or any other person acting on behalf of the offering person or such issuer, to purchase or sell or cause to be purchased or sold any of such securities or any securities convertible into or exchangeable for any such securities or any option or right to obtain or to dispose of any of the foregoing securities, unless within a reasonable time prior to any purchase or sale such information and its source are publicly disclosed by press release or otherwise.

(b) A person other than a natural person shall not violate paragraph (a) of this section if such person shows that:

(1) The individual(s) making the investment decision on behalf of such person to purchase or sell any security described in paragraph (a) or to cause any such security to be purchased or sold by or on behalf of others did not know the material, nonpublic information; and

(2) Such person had implemented one or a combination of policies and procedures, reasonable under the circumstances, taking into consideration the nature of the person's business, to ensure that individual(s) making investment decision(s) would not violate paragraph (a), which policies and procedures may include, but are not limited to, (i) those which restrict any purchase, sale and causing any purchase and sale of any such security or (ii) those which prevent such individual(s) from knowing such information.

(c) Notwithstanding anything in paragraph (a) to the contrary, the following transactions shall not be violations of paragraph (a) of this section:

(1) Purchase(s) of any security described in paragraph (a) by a broker or by another agent on behalf of an offering person; or

(2) Sale(s) by any person of any security described in paragraph (a) to the offering person.

(d)(1) As a means reasonably designed to prevent fraudulent, deceptive or manipulative acts or practices within the meaning of section 14(e) of the Act, it shall be unlawful for any person described in paragraph (d)(2) of this section to communicate material, nonpublic information relating to a tender offer to any other person under circumstances in which it is reasonably foreseeable that such communication is likely to result in a violation of this section *except* that this paragraph shall not apply to a communication made in good faith:

(i) To the officers, directors, partners or employees of the offering person, to its advisors or to other persons, involved in the planning, financing, preparation or execution of such tender offer;

(ii) To the issuer whose securities are sought or to be sought by such tender offer, to its officers, directors, partners, employees or advisors or to other persons, involved in the planning, financing, preparation or execution of the activities of the issuer with respect to such tender offer; or

(iii) To any person pursuant to a requirement of any statute or rule or regulation promulgated thereunder.

(d)(2) The persons referred to in paragraph (d)(1) of this section are:

(i) The offering person or its officers, directors, partners, employees or advisors;

(ii) The issuer of the securities sought or to be sought by such tender offer or its officers, directors, partners, employees or advisors;

(iii) Anyone acting on behalf of the persons in paragraph (d)(2)(i) or the issuer or persons in paragraph (d)(2)(ii); and

(iv) Any person in possession of material information relating to a tender offer which information he knows or has reason to know is nonpublic and which he knows or has reason to know has been acquired directly or indirectly from any of the above.

Rule 14f–1.   Change in Majority of Directors

If, pursuant to any arrangement or understanding with the person or persons acquiring securities in a transaction subject to section 13(d) or 14(d) of the Act, any persons are to be elected or designated as directors of the issuer, otherwise than at a meeting of security holders, and the persons so elected or designated will constitute a majority of the directors of the issuer, then, not less than 10 days prior to the date any such person take office as a director, or such shorter period prior to that date as the Commission may authorize upon a showing of good cause therefor, the issuer shall file with the Commission and transmit to all holders of record of securities of the issuer who would be entitled to vote at a meeting for election of directors, information substantially equivalent to the information which would be required by Items 5(a), (d), (e), and (f), 6 and 7 of Schedule 14A of Regulation 14A to be transmitted if such person or persons were nominees for election as directors at a meeting of such security holders. Eight copies of such information shall be filed with the Commission.

APPENDIX *B*

SELECTED PROVISIONS OF THE
DELAWARE GENERAL CORPORATION LAW
SUBCHAPTER IX. MERGER OR CONSOLIDATION

Table of Contents

§ 251   Merger or consolidation of domestic corporations.

(a) Any 2 or more corporations existing under the laws of this State may merge into a single corporation, which may be any 1 of the constituent corporations or may consolidate into a new corporation formed by the consolidation, pursuant to an agreement of merger or consolidation, as the case may be, complying and approved in accordance with this section.

(b) The board of directors of each corporation which desires to merge or consolidate shall adopt a resolution approving an agreement of merger or consolidation. The agreement shall state: (1) The terms and conditions of the merger or consolidation; (2) the mode of carrying the same into effect; (3) in the case of a merger, such amendments or changes in the certificate of incorporation of the surviving corporation as are desired to be effected by the merger, or, if no such amendments or changes are desired, a statement that the certificate of incorporation of the surviving corporation shall be its certificate of incorporation; (4) in the case of a consolidation, that the certificate of incorporation of the resulting corporation shall be as is set forth in an attachment to the agreement; (5) the manner of converting the shares of each of the constituent corporations into shares or other securities of the corporation surviving or resulting from the merger or consolidation and, if any shares of any of the constituent corporations are not to be converted solely into shares or other securities of the surviving or resulting corporation, the cash, property, rights or securities of any other corporation or entity which the holders of such shares are to receive in exchange for, or upon conversion of such shares and the surrender of any certificates evidencing them, which cash, property, rights or securities of any other corporation or entity may be in addition to or in lieu of shares or other securities of the surviving or resulting corporation; and (6) such other details or provisions as are deemed desirable, including, without limiting the generality of the foregoing, a provision for the payment of cash in lieu of the issuance or recognition of fractional shares, interests or rights, or for any other arrangement with respect thereto, consistent with § 155 of this title. The agreement so adopted shall be executed and acknowledged in accordance with § 103 of this title. Any of the terms of the agreement of merger or consolidation may be made dependent upon facts ascertainable outside of such agreement, provided that the manner in which such facts shall operate upon the terms of the agreement is clearly and expressly set forth in the agreement of merger or consolidation.

(c) The agreement required by subsection (b) of this section shall be submitted to the stockholders of each constituent corporation at an annual or special meeting for the purpose of acting on the agreement. Due notice of the time, place and purpose of the meeting shall be mailed to each holder of stock, whether voting or nonvoting, of the corporation at his address as it appears on the records of the corporation, at least 20 days prior to the date of the meeting. The notice shall contain a copy of the agreement or a brief summary thereof, as the directors shall deem advisable. At the meeting, the agreement shall be considered and a vote taken for its adoption or rejection. If a majority of the outstanding stock of the corporation entitled to vote thereon shall be voted for the adoption of the agreement, that fact shall be certified on the agreement by the secretary or assistant secretary of the corporation. If the agreement shall be so adopted and certified by each constituent corporation, it shall then be filed and shall become effective, in accordance with § 103 of this title. It shall be recorded in the office of the recorder of the county of this State in which the registered office of each such constituent corporation is located; or if any of the constituent corporations shall have been specially created by a public act of the General Assembly, then the agreement shall be recorded in the county where such corporation had its principal place of business in this State. In lieu of filing and recording the agreement of merger or consolidation required by this section, the surviving or resulting corporation may file a certificate of merger or consolidation, executed in accordance with § 103 of this title, which states:

(1) The name and state of incorporation of each of the constituent corporations;

(2) That an agreement of merger or consolidation has been approved, adopted, certified, executed and acknowledged by each of the constituent corporations in accordance with this section;

(3) The name of the surviving or resulting corporation;

(4) In the case of a merger, such amendments or changes in the certificate of incorporation of the surviving corporation as are desired to be effected by the merger, or, if no such amendments or changes are desired, a statement that the certificate of incorporation of the surviving corporation shall be its certificate of incorporation;

(5) In the case of a consolidation, that the certificate of incorporation of the resulting corporation shall be as set forth in an attachment to the certificate;

(6) That the executed agreement of consolidation or merger is on file at the principal place of business of the surviving corporation, stating the address thereof; and

(7) That a copy of the agreement of consolidation or merger will be furnished by the surviving corporation, on request and without cost, to any stockholder of any constituent corporation.

(d) Any agreement of merger or consolidation may contain a provision that at any time prior to the filing of the agreement (or a certificate in lieu thereof) with the Secretary of State, the agreement may be terminated by the board of directors of any constituent corporation notwithstanding approval of the agreement by the stockholders of all or any of the constituent corporations. Any agreement of merger or consolidation may contain a provision that the boards of directors of the constituent corporations may amend the agreement at any time prior to the filing of the agreement (or a certificate in lieu thereof) with the Secretary of State, provided that an amendment made subsequent to the adoption of the agreement by the stockholders of any constituent corporation shall not (1) alter or change the amount or kind of shares, securities, cash, property and/or rights to be received in exchange for or on conversion of all or any of the shares of any class or series thereof of such constituent corporation, (2) alter or change any term of the certificate of incorporation of the surviving corporation to be effected by the merger or consolidation, or (3) alter or change any of the terms and conditions of the agreement if such alteration or change would adversely affect the holders of any class or series thereof of such constituent corporation.

(e) In the case of a merger, the certificate of incorporation of the surviving corporation shall automatically be amended to the extent, if any, that changes in the certificate of incorporation are set forth in the agreement of merger.

(f) Notwithstanding the requirements of subsection (c) of this section, unless required by its certificate of incorporation, no vote of stockholders of a constituent corporation surviving a merger shall be necessary to authorize a merger if (1) the agreement of merger does not amend in any respect the certificate of incorporation of such constituent corporation, (2) each share of stock of such constituent corporation outstanding immediately prior to the effective date of the merger is to be an identical outstanding or treasury share of the surviving corporation after the effective date of the merger, and (3) either no shares of common stock of the surviving corporation and no shares, securities or obligations convertible into such stock are to be issued or delivered under the plan of merger, or the authorized unissued shares or the treasury shares of common stock of the surviving corporation to be issued or delivered under the plan of merger plus those initially issuable upon conversion of any other shares, securities or obligations to be issued or delivered under such plan do not exceed 20% of the shares of common stock of such constituent corporation outstanding immediately prior to the effective date of the merger. No vote of stockholders of a constituent corporation shall be necessary to authorize a merger or consolidation if no shares of the stock of such corporation shall have been issued prior to the adoption by the board of directors of the resolution approving the agreement of merger or consolidation. If an agreement of merger is adopted by the constituent corporation surviving the merger, by action of its board of directors and without any vote of its stockholders pursuant to this subsection, the secretary or assistant secretary of that corporation shall certify on the agreement that the agreement has been adopted pursuant to this subsection and, (1) if it has been adopted pursuant to the first sentence of this subsection, that the conditions specified in that sentence have been satisfied, or (2) if it has been adopted pursuant to the second sentence of this subsection, that no shares of stock of such corporation were issued prior to the adoption by the board of directors of the resolution approving the agreement of merger or consolidation. The agreement so adopted and certified shall then be filed and shall become effective, in accordance with § 103 of this title. Such filing shall constitute a representation by the person who executes the agreement that the facts stated in the certificate remain true immediately prior to such filing.

§ 252   Merger or consolidation of domestic and foreign corporations; service of process upon surviving or resulting corporation.

(a) Any 1 or more corporations of this State may merge or consolidate with 1 or more other corporations of any other state or states of the United States, or of the District of Columbia if the laws of the other state or states, or of the District permit a corporation of such jurisdiction to merge or consolidate with a corporation of another jurisdiction. The constituent corporations may merge into a single corporation, which may be any 1 of the constituent corporations, or they may consolidate into a new corporation formed by the consolidation, which may be a corporation of the state of incorporation of any 1 of the constituent corporations, pursuant to an agreement of merger or consolidation, as the case may be, complying and approved in accordance with this section. In addition, any 1 or more corporations existing under the laws of this State may merge or consolidate with 1 or more corporations organized under the laws of any jurisdiction other than 1 of the United States if the laws under which the other corporation or corporations are organized permit a corporation of such jurisdiction to merge or consolidate with a corporation of another jurisdiction.

(b) All the constituent corporations shall enter into an agreement of merger or consolidation. The agreement shall state: (1) The terms and conditions of the merger or consolidation; (2) the mode of carrying the same into effect; (3) the manner of converting the shares of each of the constituent corporations into shares or other securities of the corporation surviving or resulting from the merger or consolidation and, if any shares of any of the constituent corporations are not to be converted solely into shares or other securities of the surviving or resulting corporation, the cash, property, rights or securities of any other corporation or entity which the holders of such shares are to receive in exchange for, or upon conversion of, such shares and the surrender of any certificates evidencing them, which cash, property, rights or securities of any other corporation or entity may be in addition to or in lieu of the shares or other securities of the surviving or resulting corporation; (4) such other details or provisions as are deemed desirable, including, without limiting the generality of the foregoing, a provision for the payment of cash in lieu of the issuance or recognition of fractional shares of the surviving or resulting corporation or of any other corporation the securities of which are to be received in the merger or consolidation, or for some other arrangement with respect thereto consistent with § 155 of this title; and (5) such other provisions or facts as shall be required to be set forth in certificates of incorporation by the laws of the state which are stated in the agreement to be the laws that shall govern the surviving or resulting corporation and that can be stated in the case of a merger or consolidation. Any of the terms of the agreement of merger or consolidation may be made dependent upon facts ascertainable outside of such agreement, provided that the manner in which such facts shall operate upon the terms of the agreement is clearly and expressly set forth in the agreement of merger or consolidation.

(c) The agreement shall be adopted, approved, certified, executed and acknowledged by each of the constituent corporations in accordance with the laws under which it is formed, and, in the case of a Delaware corporation, in the same manner as is provided in § 251 of this title. The agreement shall be filed and recorded and shall become effective for all purposes of the laws of this State when and as provided in § 251 of this title with respect to the merger or consolidation of corporations of this State. In lieu of filing and recording the agreement of merger or consolidation, the surviving or resulting corporation may file a certificate of merger or consolidation, executed in accordance with § 103 of this title, which states:

(1) The name and state or jurisdiction of incorporation of each of the constituent corporations;

(2) That an agreement of merger or consolidation has been approved, adopted, certified, executed and acknowledged by each of the constituent corporations in accordance with this subsection;

(3) The name of the surviving or resulting corporation;

(4) In the case of a merger, such amendments or changes in the certificate of incorporation of the surviving corporation as are desired to be effected by the merger, or, if no such amendments or changes are desired, a statement that the certificate of incorporation of the surviving corporation shall be its certificate of incorporation;

(5) In the case of a consolidation, that the certificate of incorporation of the resulting corporation shall be as is set forth in an attachment to the certificate;

(6) That the executed agreement of consolidation or merger is on file at the principal place of business of the surviving corporation and the address thereof;

(7) That a copy of the agreement of consolidation or merger will be furnished by the surviving corporation, on request and without cost, to any stockholder of any constituent corporation;

(8) If the corporation surviving or resulting from the merger or consolidation is to be a corporation of this State, the authorized capital stock of each constituent corporation which is not a corporation of this State; and

(9) The agreement, if any, required by subsection (d) of this section.

(d) If the corporation surviving or resulting from the merger or consolidation is to be governed by the laws of the District of Columbia or any state or jurisdiction other than this State, it shall agree that it may be served with process in this State in any proceeding for enforcement of any obligation of any constituent corporation of this State, as well as for enforcement of any obligation of the surviving or resulting corporation arising from the merger or consolidation, including any suit or other proceeding to enforce the right of any stockholders as determined in appraisal proceedings pursuant to § 262 of this title, and shall irrevocably appoint the Secretary of State as its agent to accept service of process in any such suit or other proceedings and shall specify the address to which a copy of such process shall be mailed by the Secretary of State. In the event of such service upon the Secretary of State in accordance with this subsection, the Secretary of State shall forthwith notify such surviving or resulting corporation thereof by letter, certified mail, return receipt requested, directed to such surviving or resulting corporation at its address so specified, unless such surviving or resulting corporation shall have designated in writing to the Secretary of State a different address for such purpose, in which case it shall be mailed to the last address so designated. Such letter shall enclose a copy of the process and any other papers served on the Secretary of State pursuant to this subsection. It shall be the duty of the plaintiff in the event of such service to serve process and any other papers in duplicate, to notify the Secretary of State that service is being effected pursuant to this subsection and to pay the Secretary of State the sum of $50 for the use of the State, which sum shall be taxed as part of the costs in the proceeding, if the plaintiff shall prevail therein. The Secretary of State shall maintain an alphabetical record of any such service setting forth the name of the plaintiff and the defendant, the title, docket number and nature of the proceeding in which process has been served upon him, the fact that service has been effected pursuant to this subsection, the return date thereof, and the day and hour service was made. The Secretary of State shall not be required to retain such information longer than 5 years from his receipt of the service of process.

(e) Subsection (d) of § 251 of this title shall apply to any merger or consolidation under this section; subsection (e) of § 251 of this title shall apply to a merger under this section in which the surviving corporation is a corporation of this State; subsection (f) of § 251 of this title shall apply to any merger under this section.

§ 253 Merger of parent corporation and subsidiary or subsidiaries.

(a) In any case in which at least 90% of the outstanding shares of each class of the stock of a corporation or corporations is owned by another corporation and 1 of the corporations is a corporation of this State and the other or others are corporations of this State, or any other state or states, or the District of Columbia and the laws of the other state or states, or the District permit a corporation of such jurisdiction to merge with a corporation of another jurisdiction, the corporation having such stock ownership may either merge the other corporation or corporations into itself and assume all of its or their obligations, or merge itself, or itself and 1 or more of such other corporations, into 1 of the other corporations by executing, acknowledging and filing, in accordance with § 103 of this title, a certificate of such ownership and merger setting forth a copy of the resolution of its board of directors to so merge and the date of the adoption; provided, however, that in case the parent corporation shall not own all the outstanding stock of all the subsidiary corporations, parties to a merger as aforesaid, the resolution of the board of directors of the parent corporation shall state the terms and conditions of the merger, including the securities, cash, property, or rights to be issued, paid, delivered or granted by the surviving corporation upon surrender of each share of the subsidiary corporation or corporations not owned by the parent corporation. If the parent corporation be not the surviving corporation, the resolution shall include provision for the pro rata issuance of stock of the surviving corporation to the holders of the stock of the parent corporation on surrender of any certificates therefor, and the certificate of ownership and merger shall state that the proposed merger has been approved by a majority of the outstanding stock of the parent corporation entitled to vote thereon at a meeting duly called and held after 20 days' notice of the purpose of the meeting mailed to each such stockholder at his address as it appears on the records of the corporation if the parent corporation is a corporation of this State or state that the proposed merger has been adopted, approved, certified, executed and acknowledged by the parent corporation in accordance with the laws under which it is organized if the parent corporation is not a corporation of this State. A certified copy of the certificate shall be recorded in the office of the recorder of the county in this State in which the registered office of each constituent corporation which is a corporation of this State is located. If the surviving corporation exists under the laws of the District of Columbia or any state or jurisdiction other than this State, subsection (d) of § 252 of this title shall also apply to a merger under this section.

(b) If the surviving corporation is a Delaware corporation, it may change its corporate name by the inclusion of a provision to that effect in the resolution of merger adopted by the directors of the parent corporation and set forth in the certificate of ownership and merger, and upon the effective date of the merger, the name of the corporation shall be so changed.

(c) Subsection (d) of § 251 of this title shall apply to a merger under this section, and subsection (e) of § 251 of this title shall apply to a merger under this section in which the surviving corporation is the subsidiary corporation and is a corporation of this State. References to "agreement of merger" in subsections (d) and (e) of § 251 of this title shall mean for purposes of this subsection the resolution of merger adopted by the board of directors of the parent corporation. Any merger which effects any changes other than those authorized by this section or made applicable by this subsection shall be accomplished under § 251 or § 252 of this title. Section 262 of this title shall not apply to any merger effected under this section, except as provided in subsection (d) of this section.

(d) In the event all of the stock of a subsidiary Delaware corporation party to a merger effected under this section is not owned by the parent corporation immediately prior to the merger, the stockholders of the subsidiary Delaware corporation party to the merger shall have appraisal rights as set forth in § 262 of this title.

(e) A merger may be effected under this section although 1 or more of the corporations parties to the merger is a corporation organized under the laws of a jurisdiction other than 1 of the United States; provided that the laws of such jurisdiction permit a corporation of such jurisdiction to merge with a corporation of another jurisdiction.

§ 254 Merger or consolidation of domestic corporation and joint-stock or other association.

(a) The term "joint-stock association" as used in this section, includes any association of the kind commonly known as a joint-stock association or joint- stock company and any unincorporated association, trust or enterprise having members or having outstanding shares of stock or other evidences of financial or beneficial interest therein, whether formed by agreement or under statutory authority or otherwise, but does not include a corporation, partnership or limited liability company. The term "stockholder" as used in this section, includes every member of such joint-stock association or holder of a share of stock or other evidence of financial or beneficial interest therein.

(b) Any 1 or more corporations of this State may merge or consolidate with 1 or more joint-stock associations, except a joint-stock association formed under the laws of a state which forbids such merger or consolidation. Such corporation or corporations and such 1 or more joint-stock associations may merge into a single corporation, or joint-stock association, which may be any one of such corporations or joint-stock associations, or they may consolidate into a new corporation or joint-stock association of this State, pursuant to an agreement of merger or consolidation, as the case may be, complying and approved in accordance with this section. The surviving or resulting entity may be organized for profit or not organized for profit, and if the surviving or resulting entity is a corporation, it may be a stock corporation or a nonstock corporation.

(c) Each such corporation and joint-stock association shall enter into a written agreement of merger or consolidation. The agreement shall state: (1) The terms and conditions of the merger or consolidation; (2) the mode of carrying the same into effect; (3) the manner of converting the shares of stock of each stock corporation, the interest of members of each nonstock corporation, and the shares, memberships or financial or beneficial interests in each of the joint-stock associations into shares or other securities of a stock corporation or membership interests of a nonstock corporation or into shares, memberships, or financial or beneficial interests of the joint-stock association surviving or resulting from such merger or consolidation, and, if any shares of any such stock corporation, any membership interests of any such nonstock corporation, or any shares, memberships or financial or beneficial interests in any such joint-stock association are not to be converted solely into shares or other securities of the stock corporation or membership interest of the nonstock corporation or into shares, memberships, or financial or beneficial interests of the joint-stock association surviving or resulting from such merger or consolidation, the cash, property, rights or securities of any other corporation or entity which the holders of shares of any such stock corporation, membership interests of any such nonstock corporation, or shares, memberships or financial or beneficial interests of any such joint-stock association are to receive in exchange for, or upon conversion of such shares, membership interest or shares, memberships or financial or beneficial interests, and the surrender of any certificates evidencing them, which cash, property, rights or securities of any other corporation or entity may be in addition to or in lieu of shares or other securities of the stock corporation or membership interests of the nonstock corporation or shares, memberships, or financial or beneficial interests of the joint-stock association surviving or resulting from such merger or consolidation; and (4) such other details or provisions as are deemed desirable, including, without limiting the generality of the foregoing, a provision for the payment of cash in lieu of the issuance of fractional shares where the surviving or resulting entity is a corporation. There shall also be set forth in the agreement such other matters or provisions as shall then be required to be set forth in certificates of incorporation or documents required to establish and maintain a joint-stock association by the laws of this State and that can be stated in the case of such merger or consolidation. Any of the terms of the agreement of merger or consolidation may be made dependent upon facts ascertainable outside of such agreement, provided that the manner in which such facts shall operate upon the terms of the agreement is clearly and expressly set forth in the agreement of merger or consolidation.

(d) The agreement required by subsection (c) of this section shall be adopted, approved, certified, executed and acknowledged by each of the stock or nonstock corporations in the same manner as is provided in § 251 or § 255 of this title, respectively, and in the case of the joint-stock associations in accordance with their articles of association or other instrument containing the provisions by which they are organized or regulated or in accordance with the laws of the state under which they are formed, as the case may be. Where the surviving or resulting entity is a corporation, the agreement shall be filed and recorded and shall become effective for all purposes of the laws of this State when and as provided in § 251 of this title with respect to the merger or consolidation of corporations of this State. In lieu of filing and recording the agreement of merger or consolidation, where the surviving or resulting entity is a corporation it may file a certificate of merger or consolidation, executed in accordance with § 103 of this title, which states:

(1) The name and state of domicile of each of the constituent entities;

(2) That an agreement of merger or consolidation has been approved, adopted, certified, executed and acknowledged by each of the constituent entities in accordance with this subsection;

(3) The name of the surviving or resulting corporation;

(4) In the case of a merger, such amendments or changes in the certificate of incorporation of the surviving corporation as are desired to be effected by the merger, or, if no such amendments or changes are desired, a statement that the certificate of incorporation of the surviving corporation shall be its certificate of incorporation;

(5) In the case of a consolidation, that the certificate of incorporation of the resulting corporation shall be as is set forth in an attachment to the certificate;

(6) That the executed agreement of consolidation or merger is on file at the principal place of business of the surviving corporation and the address thereof; and

(7) That a copy of the agreement of consolidation or merger will be furnished by the surviving corporation, on request and without cost, to any stockholder of any constituent entity.

Where the surviving or resulting entity is a joint-stock association, the agreement shall be filed and recorded and shall be effective for all purposes when filed in accordance with the laws regulating the creation of joint-stock associations.

(e) Sections 251(d), 251(e), 251(f), 259 through 262 and 328 of this title shall, insofar as they are applicable, apply to mergers or consolidations between corporations and joint-stock associations; the word "corporation" where applicable, as used in those sections, being deemed to include joint-stock associations as defined herein. Where the surviving or resulting entity is a corporation, the personal liability, if any, of any stockholder of a joint- stock association existing at the time of such merger or consolidation shall not thereby be extinguished, shall remain personal to such stockholder and shall not become the liability of any subsequent transferee of any share of stock in such surviving or resulting corporation or of any other stockholder of such surviving or resulting corporation.

(f) Nothing in this section shall be deemed to authorize the merger of a charitable nonstock corporation or charitable joint-stock association into a stock corporation or joint-stock association if the charitable status of such nonstock corporation or joint-stock association would be thereby lost or impaired, but a stock corporation or joint-stock association may be merged into a charitable nonstock corporation or charitable joint-stock association which shall continue as the surviving corporation or joint-stock association.

§ 255 Merger or consolidation of domestic nonstock corporations.

(a) Any 2 or more nonstock corporations of this State, whether or not organized for profit, may merge into a single corporation, which may be any 1 of the constituent corporations, or they may consolidate into a new nonstock corporation, whether or not organized for profit, formed by the consolidation, pursuant to an agreement of merger or consolidation, as the case may be, complying and approved in accordance with this section.

(b) The governing body of each corporation which desires to merge or consolidate shall adopt a resolution approving an agreement of merger or consolidation. The agreement shall state: (1) the terms and conditions of the merger or consolidation; (2) the mode of carrying the same into effect; (3) such other provisions or facts required or permitted by this chapter to be stated in a certificate of incorporation for nonstock corporations as can be stated in the case of a merger or consolidation, stated in such altered form as the circumstances of the case require; (4) the manner of converting the memberships of each of the constituent corporations into memberships of the corporation surviving or resulting from the merger or consolidation; and (5) such other details or provisions as are deemed desirable. Any of the terms of the agreement of merger or consolidation may be made dependent upon facts ascertainable outside of such agreement, provided that the manner in which such facts shall operate upon the terms of the agreement is clearly and expressly set forth in the agreement of merger or consolidation.

(c) The agreement shall be submitted to the members of each constituent corporation who have the right to vote for the election of the members of the governing body of their corporation, at an annual or special meeting thereof for the purpose of acting on the agreement. Due notice of the time, place and purpose of the meeting shall be mailed to each member of each such corporation who has the right to vote for the election of the members of the governing body of his corporation, at his address as it appears on the records of the corporation, at least 20 days prior to the date of the meeting. The notice shall contain a copy of the agreement or a brief summary thereof, as the governing body shall deem advisable. At the meeting the agreement shall be considered and a vote by ballot, in person or by proxy, taken for the adoption or rejection of the agreement, each member who has the right to vote for the election of the members of the governing body of his corporation being entitled to 1 vote. If the votes of two thirds of the total number of members of each such corporation who have the voting power above mentioned shall be for the adoption of the agreement, then that fact shall be certified on the agreement by the officer of each such corporation performing the duties ordinarily performed by the secretary or assistant secretary of a corporation. The agreement so adopted and certified shall be executed, acknowledged and filed, and shall become effective, in accordance with § 103 of this title. It shall be recorded in the office of the recorder of the county in this State in which the registered office of each such constituent corporation is located; or if any of the constituent corporations shall have been specially created by public act of the General Assembly, then the agreement shall be recorded in the county where such corporation had its principal place of business in this State. The provisions set forth in the last sentence of subsection (c) of § 251 shall apply to a merger under this section, and the reference therein to "stockholder" shall be deemed to include "member" hereunder.

(d) If, under the certificate of incorporation of any 1 or more of the constituent corporations, there shall be no members who have the right to vote for the election of the members of the governing body of the corporation other than the members of that body themselves, the agreement duly entered into as provided in subsection (b) of this section shall be submitted to the members of the governing body of such corporation or corporations, at a meeting thereof. Notice of the meeting shall be mailed to the members of the governing body in the same manner as is provided in the case of a meeting of the members of a corporation. If at the meeting two thirds of the total number of members of the governing body shall vote by ballot, in person, for the adoption of the agreement, that fact shall be certified on the agreement in the same manner as is provided in the case of the adoption of the agreement by the vote of the members of a corporation and thereafter the same procedure shall be followed to consummate the merger or consolidation.

(e) Subsection (e) of § 251 shall apply to a merger under this section.

(f) Nothing in this section shall be deemed to authorize the merger of a charitable nonstock corporation into a nonstock corporation if such charitable nonstock corporation would thereby have its charitable status lost or impaired; but a nonstock corporation may be merged into a charitable nonstock corporation which shall continue as the surviving corporation.

§ 256   Merger or consolidation of domestic and foreign nonstock corporations; service of process upon surviving or resulting corporation.

(a) Any 1 or more nonstock corporations of this State may merge or consolidate with 1 or more other nonstock corporations of any other state or states of the United States, or of the District of Columbia if the laws of such other state or states or of the District permit a corporation of such jurisdiction to merge with a corporation of another jurisdiction. The constituent corporations may merge into a single corporation, which may be any 1 of the constituent corporations, or they may consolidate into a new nonstock corporation formed by the consolidation, which may be a corporation of the state of incorporation of any 1 of the constituent corporations, pursuant to an agreement of merger or consolidation, as the case may be, complying and approved in accordance with this section. In addition, any 1 or more nonstock corporations organized under the laws of any jurisdiction other than 1 of the United

States may merge or consolidate with 1 or more nonstock corporations of this State if the surviving or resulting corporation will be a corporation of this State, and if the laws under which the other corporation or corporations are formed permit a corporation of such jurisdiction to merge with a corporation of another jurisdiction.

(b) All the constituent corporations shall enter into an agreement of merger or consolidation. The agreement shall state: (1) The terms and conditions of the merger or consolidation; (2) the mode of carrying the same into effect; (3) the manner of converting the memberships of each of the constituent corporations into memberships of the corporation surviving or resulting from such merger or consolidation; (4) such other details and provisions as shall be deemed desirable; and (5) such other provisions or facts as shall then be required to be stated in a certificate of incorporation by the laws of the state which are stated in the agreement to be the laws that shall govern the surviving or resulting corporation and that can be stated in the case of a merger or consolidation. Any of the terms of the agreement of merger or consolidation may be made dependent upon facts ascertainable outside of such agreement, provided that the manner in which such facts shall operate upon the terms of the agreement is clearly and expressly set forth in the agreement of merger or consolidation.

(c) The agreement shall be adopted, approved, certified, executed and acknowledged by each of the constituent corporations in accordance with the laws under which it is formed and, in the case of a Delaware corporation, in the same manner as is provided in § 255 of this title. The agreement shall be filed and recorded and shall become effective for all purposes of the laws of this State when and as provided in § 255 of this title with respect to the merger of nonstock corporations of this State. Insofar as they may be applicable, the provisions set forth in the last sentence of subsection (c) of § 252 of this title shall apply to a merger under this section, and the reference therein to "stockholder" shall be deemed to include "member" hereunder.

(d) If the corporation surviving or resulting from the merger or consolidation is to be governed by the laws of any state other than this State, it shall agree that it may be served with process in this State in any proceeding for enforcement of any obligation of any constituent corporation of this State, as well as for enforcement of any obligation of the surviving or resulting corporation arising from the merger or consolidation and shall irrevocably appoint the Secretary of State as its agent to accept service of process in any suit or other proceedings and shall specify the address to which a copy of such process shall be mailed by the Secretary of State. In the event of such service upon the Secretary of State in accordance with this subsection, the Secretary of State shall forthwith notify such surviving or resulting corporation thereof by letter, certified mail, return receipt requested, directed to such corporation at its address so specified, unless such surviving or resulting corporation shall have designated in writing to the Secretary of State a different address for such purpose, in which case it shall be mailed to the last address so designated. Such letter shall enclose a copy of the process and any other papers served upon the Secretary of State. It shall be the duty of the plaintiff in the event of such service to serve process and any other papers in duplicate, to notify the Secretary of State that service is being made pursuant to this subsection, and to pay the Secretary of State the sum of $50 for the use of the State, which sum shall be taxed as a part of the costs in the proceeding if the plaintiff shall prevail therein. The Secretary of State shall maintain an alphabetical record of any such service setting forth the name of the plaintiff and defendant, the title, docket number and nature of the proceeding in which process has been served upon him, the fact that service has been effected pursuant to this subsection, the return date thereof, and the day and hour when the service was made. The Secretary of State shall not be required to retain such information for a period longer than 5 years from his receipt of the service of process.

(e) Subsection (e) of § 251 of this title shall apply to a merger under this section if the corporation surviving the merger is a corporation of this State.

§ 257   Merger or consolidation of domestic stock and nonstock corporations.

(a) Any 1 or more nonstock corporations of this State, whether or not organized for profit, may merge or consolidate with 1 or more stock corporations of this State, whether or not organized for profit. The constituent corporations may merge into a single corporation, which may be any 1 of the constituent corporations, or they may consolidate into a new corporation formed by the consolidation, pursuant to an agreement of merger or consolidation, as the case may be, complying and approved in accordance with this section. The surviving constituent corporation or the new corporation may be organized for profit or not organized for profit and may be a stock corporation or a nonstock corporation.

(b) The board of directors of each stock corporation which desires to merge or consolidate and the governing body of each nonstock corporation which desires to merge or consolidate shall adopt a resolution approving an agreement of merger or consolidation. The agreement shall state: (1) The terms and conditions of the merger or consolidation; (2) the mode of carrying the same into effect; (3) such other provisions or facts required or permitted by this chapter to be stated in a certificate of incorporation as can be stated in the case of a merger or consolidation, stated in such altered form as the circumstances of the case require; (4) the manner of converting the shares of stock of a stock corporation and the interests of the members of a nonstock corporation into shares or other securities of a stock corporation or membership interests of a nonstock corporation surviving or resulting from such merger or consolidation, and, if any shares of any such stock corporation or membership interests of any such nonstock corporation are not to be converted solely into shares or other securities of the stock corporation or membership interests of the nonstock corporation surviving or resulting from such merger or consolidation, the cash, property, rights or securities of any other corporation or entity which the holders of shares of any such stock corporation or membership interests of any such nonstock corporation are to receive in exchange for, or upon conversion of such shares or membership interests, and the surrender of any certificates evidencing them, which cash, property, rights or securities of any other corporation or entity may be in addition to or in lieu of shares or other securities of any stock corporation or membership interests of any nonstock corporation surviving or resulting from such merger or consolidation; and (5) such other details or provisions as are deemed desirable. In such merger or consolidation the interests of members of a constituent nonstock corporation may be treated in various ways so as to convert such interests into interests of value, other than shares of stock, in the surviving or resulting stock corporation or into shares of stock in the surviving or resulting stock corporation, voting or nonvoting, or into creditor interests or any other interests of value equivalent to their membership interests in their nonstock corporation. The voting rights of members of a constituent nonstock corporation need not be considered an element of value in measuring the reasonable equivalence of the value of the interests received in the surviving or resulting stock corporation by members of a constituent nonstock corporation, nor need the voting rights of shares of stock in a constituent stock corporation be considered as an element of value in measuring the reasonable equivalence of the value of the interests in the surviving or resulting nonstock corporations received by stockholders of a constituent stock corporation, and the voting or nonvoting shares of a stock corporation may be converted into voting or nonvoting regular, life, general, special or other type of membership, however designated, creditor interests or participating interests, in the nonstock corporation surviving or resulting from such merger or consolidation of a stock corporation and a nonstock corporation.   Any of the terms of the agreement of merger or consolidation may be made dependent upon facts ascertainable outside of such agreement, provided that the manner in which such facts shall operate upon the terms of the agreement is clearly and expressly set forth in the agreement of merger or consolidation.

(c) The agreement required by subsection (b) of this section, in the case of each constituent stock corporation, shall be adopted, approved, certified, executed and acknowledged by each constituent corporation in the same manner as is provided in § 251 of this title and, in the case of each constituent nonstock corporation, shall be adopted, approved, certified, executed and acknowledged by each of said constituent corporations in the same manner as is provided in § 255 of this title. The agreement shall be filed and recorded and shall become effective for all purposes of the laws of this State when and as provided in § 251 of this title with respect to the merger of stock corporations of this State.   Insofar as they may be applicable, the provisions set forth in the last sentence of subsection (c) of § 251 of this title shall apply to a merger under this section, and the reference therein to "stockholder" shall be deemed to include "member" hereunder.

(d) Subsection (e) of § 251 of this title shall apply to a merger under this section, if the surviving corporation is a corporation of this State; subsection (d) of § 251 of this title shall apply to any constituent stock corporation participating in a merger or consolidation under this section; and subsection (f) of § 251 of this title shall apply to any constituent stock corporation participating in a merger under this section.

(e) Nothing in this section shall be deemed to authorize the merger of a charitable nonstock corporation into a stock corporation, if the charitable status of such nonstock corporation would thereby be lost or impaired; but a stock corporation may be merged into a charitable nonstock corporation which shall continue as the surviving corporation.

§ 258   Merger or consolidation of domestic and foreign stock and nonstock corporations.

(a) Any 1 or more corporations of this State, whether stock or nonstock corporations and whether or not organized for profit, may merge or consolidate with 1 or more other corporations of any other state or states of the United States or of the District of Columbia whether stock or nonstock corporations and whether or not organized for profit, if the laws under which the other corporation or corporations are formed shall permit such a corporation of such jurisdiction to merge with a corporation of another jurisdiction. The constituent corporations may merge into a single corporation, which may be any 1 of the constituent corporations, or they may consolidate into a new corporation formed by the consolidation, which may be a corporation of the place of incorporation of any 1 of the constituent corporations, pursuant to an agreement of merger or consolidation, as the case may be, complying and approved in accordance with this section. The surviving or new corporation may be either a stock corporation or a membership corporation, as shall be specified in the agreement of merger required by subsection (b) of this section.

(b) The method and procedure to be followed by the constituent corporations so merging or consolidating shall be as prescribed in § 257 of this title in the case of Delaware corporations. The agreement of merger or consolidation shall also set forth such other matters or provisions as shall then be required to be set forth in certificates of incorporation by the laws of the state which are stated in the agreement to be the laws which shall govern the surviving or resulting corporation and that can be stated in the case of a merger or consolidation. The agreement, in the case of foreign corporations, shall be adopted, approved, executed and acknowledged by each of the constituent foreign corporations in accordance with the laws under which each is formed.

(c) The requirements of subsection (d) of § 252 of this title as to the appointment of the Secretary of State to receive process and the manner of serving the same in the event the surviving or new corporation is to be governed by the laws of any other state shall also apply to mergers or consolidations effected under this section. Subsection (e) of § 251 of this title shall apply to mergers effected under this section if the surviving corporation is a corporation of this State; subsection (d) of § 251 of this title shall apply to any constituent stock corporation participating in a merger or consolidation under this section; and subsection (f) of § 251 of this title shall apply to any constituent stock corporation participating in a merger under this section.

(d) Nothing in this section shall be deemed to authorize the merger of a charitable nonstock corporation into a stock corporation, if the charitable status of such nonstock corporation would thereby be lost or impaired; but a stock corporation may be merged into a charitable nonstock corporation which shall continue as the surviving corporation.

§ 259   Status, rights, liabilities, of constituent and surviving or resulting corporations following merger or consolidation.

(a) When any merger or consolidation shall have become effective under this chapter, for all purposes of the laws of this State the separate existence of all the constituent corporations, or of all such constituent corporations except the one into which the other or others of such constituent corporations have been merged, as the case may be, shall cease and the constituent corporations shall become a new corporation, or be merged into 1 of such corporations, as the case may be, possessing all the rights, privileges, powers and franchises as well of a public as of a private nature, and being subject to all the restrictions, disabilities and duties of each of such corporations so merged or consolidated; and all and singular, the rights, privileges, powers and franchises of each of said corporations, and all property, real, personal and mixed, and all debts due to any of said constituent corporations on whatever account, as well for stock subscriptions as all other things in action or belonging to each of such corporations shall be vested in the corporation surviving or resulting from such merger or consolidation; and all property, rights, privileges, powers and franchises, and all and every other interest shall be thereafter as effectually the property of the surviving or resulting corporation as they were of the several and respective constituent corporations, and the title to any real estate vested by deed or otherwise, under the laws of this State, in any of such constituent corporations, shall not revert or be in any way impaired by reason of this chapter; but all rights of creditors and all liens upon any property of any of said constituent corporations shall be preserved unimpaired, and all debts, liabilities and duties of the respective constituent corporations shall thenceforth attach to said surviving or resulting corporation, and may be enforced against it to the same extent as if said debts, liabilities and duties had been incurred or contracted by it.

(b) In the case of a merger of banks or trust companies, without any order or action on the part of any court or otherwise, all appointments, designations, and nominations, and all other rights and interests as trustee, executor, administrator, registrar of stocks and bonds, guardian of estates, assignee, receiver, trustee of estates of persons mentally ill and in every other fiduciary capacity, shall be automatically vested in the corporation resulting from or surviving such merger; provided, however, that any party in interest shall have the right to apply to an appropriate court or tribunal for a determination as to whether the surviving corporation shall continue to serve in the same fiduciary capacity as the merged corporation, or whether a new and different fiduciary should be appointed.

§ 260 Powers of corporation surviving or resulting from merger or consolidation; issuance of stock, bonds or other indebtedness.

When 2 or more corporations are merged or consolidated, the corporation surviving or resulting from the merger may issue bonds or other obligations, negotiable or otherwise, and with or without coupons or interest certificates thereto attached, to an amount sufficient with its capital stock to provide for all the payments it will be required to make, or obligations it will be required to assume, in order to effect the merger or consolidation. For the purpose of securing the payment of any such bonds and obligations, it shall be lawful for the surviving or resulting corporation to mortgage its corporate franchise, rights, privileges and property, real, personal or mixed. The surviving or resulting corporation may issue certificates of its capital stock or uncertificated stock if authorized to do so and other securities to the stockholders of the constituent corporations in exchange or payment for the original shares, in such amount as shall be necessary in accordance with the terms of the agreement of merger or consolidation in order to effect such merger or consolidation in the manner and on the terms specified in the agreement.

§ 261 Effect of merger upon pending actions.

Any action or proceeding, whether civil, criminal or administrative, pending by or against any corporation which is a party to a merger or consolidation shall be prosecuted as if such merger or consolidation had not taken place, or the corporation surviving or resulting from such merger or consolidation may be substituted in such action or proceeding.

§ 262   Appraisal rights.

(a) Any stockholder of a corporation of this State who holds shares of stock on the date of the making of a demand pursuant to subsection (d) of this section with respect to such shares, who continuously holds such shares through the effective date of the merger or consolidation, who has otherwise complied with subsection (d) of this section and who has neither voted in favor of the merger or consolidation nor consented thereto in writing pursuant to § 228 of this title shall be entitled to an appraisal by the Court of Chancery of the fair value of his shares of stock under the circumstances described in subsections (b) and (c) of this section. As used in this section, the word "stockholder" means a holder of record of stock in a stock corporation and also a member of record of a nonstock corporation; the words "stock" and "share" mean and include what is ordinarily meant by those words and also membership or membership interest of a member of a nonstock corporation.

(b) Appraisal rights shall be available for the shares of any class or series of stock of a constituent corporation in a merger or consolidation to be effected pursuant to § 251, § 252, § 254, § 257, § 258, § 263 or § 264 of this title:

(1) Provided, however, that no appraisal rights under this section shall be available for the shares of any class or series of stock which, at the record date fixed to determine the stockholders entitled to receive notice of and to vote at the meeting of stockholders to act upon the agreement of merger or consolidation, were either (i) listed on a national securities exchange or designated as a national market system security on an interdealer quotation system by the National Association of Securities Dealers, Inc. or (ii) held of record by more than 2,000 stockholders; and further provided that no appraisal rights shall be available for any shares of stock of the constituent corporation surviving a merger if the merger did not require for its approval the vote of the stockholders of the surviving corporation as provided in subsection (f) of § 251 of this title.

(2) Notwithstanding paragraph (1) of this subsection, appraisal rights under this section shall be available for the shares of any class or series of stock of a constituent corporation if the holders thereof are required by the terms of an agreement of merger or consolidation pursuant to §§ 251, 252, 254, 257, 258, 263 and 264 of this title to accept for such stock anything except:

a. Shares of stock of the corporation surviving or resulting from such merger or consolidation;

b. Shares of stock of any other corporation which at the effective date of the merger or consolidation will be either listed on a national securities exchange or designated as a national market system security on an interdealer quotation system by the National Association of Securities Dealers, Inc. or held of record by more than 2,000 stockholders;

c. Cash in lieu of fractional shares of the corporations described in the foregoing subparagraphs a. and b. of this paragraph; or

d. Any combination of the shares of stock and cash in lieu of fractional shares described in the foregoing subparagraphs a., b. and c. of this paragraph.

(3) In the event all of the stock of a subsidiary Delaware corporation party to a merger effected under § 253 of this title is not owned by the parent corporation immediately prior to the merger, appraisal rights shall be available for the shares of the subsidiary Delaware corporation.

(c) Any corporation may provide in its certificate of incorporation that appraisal rights under this section shall be available for the shares of any class or series of its stock as a result of an amendment to its certificate of incorporation, any merger or consolidation in which the corporation is a constituent corporation or the sale of all or substantially all of the assets of the corporation. If the certificate of incorporation contains such a provision, the procedures of this section, including those set forth in subsections (d) and (e) of this section, shall apply as nearly as is practicable.

(d) Appraisal rights shall be perfected as follows:

(1) If a proposed merger or consolidation for which appraisal rights are provided under this section is to be submitted for approval at a meeting of stockholders, the corporation, not less than 20 days prior to the meeting, shall notify each of its stockholders who was such on the record date for such meeting with respect to shares for which appraisal rights are available pursuant to subsection (b) or (c) hereof that appraisal rights are available for any or all of the shares of the constituent corporations, and shall include in such notice a copy of this section. Each stockholder electing to demand the appraisal of his shares shall deliver to the corporation, before the taking of the vote on the merger or consolidation, a written demand for appraisal of his shares. Such demand will be sufficient if it reasonably informs the corporation of the identity of the stockholder and that the stockholder intends thereby to demand the appraisal of his shares. A proxy or vote against the merger or consolidation shall not constitute such a demand. A stockholder electing to take such action must do so by a separate written demand as herein provided. Within 10 days after the effective date of such merger or consolidation, the surviving or resulting corporation shall notify each stockholder of each constituent corporation who has complied with this subsection and has not voted in favor of or consented to the merger or consolidation of the date that the merger or consolidation has become effective; or

(2) If the merger or consolidation was approved pursuant to § 228 or § 253 of this title, the surviving or resulting corporation, either before the effective date of the merger or consolidation or within 10 days thereafter, shall notify each of the stockholders entitled to appraisal rights of the effective date of the merger or consolidation and that appraisal rights are available for any or all of the shares of the constituent corporation, and shall include in such notice a copy of this section. The notice shall be sent by certified or registered mail, return receipt requested, addressed to the stockholder at his address as it appears on the records of the corporation. Any stockholder entitled to appraisal rights may, within 20 days after the date of mailing of the notice, demand in writing from the surviving or resulting corporation the appraisal of his shares. Such demand will be sufficient if it reasonably informs the corporation of the identity of the stockholder and that the stockholder intends thereby to demand the appraisal of his shares.

(e) Within 120 days after the effective date of the merger or consolidation, the surviving or resulting corporation or any stockholder who has complied with subsections (a) and (d) hereof and who is otherwise entitled to appraisal rights, may file a petition in the Court of Chancery demanding a determination of the value of the stock of all such stockholders. Notwithstanding the foregoing, at any time within 60 days after the effective date of the merger or consolidation, any stockholder shall have the right to withdraw his demand for appraisal and to accept the terms offered upon the merger or consolidation. Within 120 days after the effective date of the merger or consolidation, any stockholder who has complied with the requirements of subsections (a) and (d) hereof, upon written request, shall be entitled to receive from the corporation surviving the merger or resulting from the consolidation a statement setting forth the aggregate number of shares not voted in favor of the merger or consolidation and with respect to which demands for appraisal have been received and the aggregate number of holders of such shares. Such written statement shall be mailed to the stockholder within 10 days after his written request for such a statement is received by the surviving or resulting corporation or within 10 days after expiration of the period for delivery of demands for appraisal under subsection (d) hereof, whichever is later.

(f) Upon the filing of any such petition by a stockholder, service of a copy thereof shall be made upon the surviving or resulting corporation, which shall within 20 days after such service file in the office of the Register in Chancery in which the petition was filed a duly verified list containing the names and addresses of all stockholders who have demanded payment for their shares and with whom agreements as to the value of their shares have not been reached by the surviving or resulting corporation. If the petition shall be filed by the surviving or resulting corporation, the petition shall be accompanied by such a duly verified list. The Register in Chancery, if so ordered by the Court, shall give notice of the time and place fixed for the hearing of such petition by registered or certified mail to the surviving or resulting corporation and to the stockholders shown on the list at the addresses therein stated. Such notice shall also be given by 1 or more publications at least 1 week before the day of the hearing, in a newspaper of general circulation published in the City of Wilmington, Delaware or such publication as the Court deems advisable. The forms of the notices by mail and by publication shall be approved by the Court, and the costs thereof shall be borne by the surviving or resulting corporation.

(g) At the hearing on such petition, the Court shall determine the stockholders who have complied with this section and who have become entitled to appraisal rights. The Court may require the stockholders who have demanded an appraisal for their shares and who hold stock represented by certificates to submit their certificates of stock to the Register in Chancery for notation thereon of the pendency of the appraisal proceedings; and if any stockholder fails to comply with such direction, the Court may dismiss the proceedings as to such stockholder.

(h) After determining the stockholders entitled to an appraisal, the Court shall appraise the shares, determining their fair value exclusive of any element of value arising from the accomplishment or expectation of the merger or consolidation, together with a fair rate of interest, if any, to be paid upon the amount determined to be the fair value. In determining such fair value, the Court shall take into account all relevant factors. In determining the fair rate of interest, the Court may consider all relevant factors, including the rate of interest which the surviving or resulting corporation would have had to pay to borrow money during the pendency of the proceeding. Upon application by the surviving or resulting corporation or by any stockholder entitled to participate in the appraisal proceeding, the Court may, in its discretion, permit discovery or other pretrial proceedings and may proceed to trial upon the appraisal prior to the final determination of the stockholder entitled to an appraisal. Any stockholder whose name appears on the list filed by the surviving or resulting corporation pursuant to subsection (f) of this section and who has submitted his certificates of stock to the Register in Chancery, if such is required, may participate fully in all proceedings until it is finally determined that he is not entitled to appraisal rights under this section.

(i) The Court shall direct the payment of the fair value of the shares, together with interest, if any, by the surviving or resulting corporation to the stockholders entitled thereto. Interest may be simple or compound, as the Court may direct. Payment shall be so made to each such stockholder, in the case of holders of uncertificated stock forthwith, and the case of holders of shares represented by certificates upon the surrender to the corporation of the certificates representing such stock. The Court's decree may be enforced as other decrees in the Court of Chancery may be enforced, whether such surviving or resulting corporation be a corporation of this State or of any state.

(j) The costs of the proceeding may be determined by the Court and taxed upon the parties as the Court deems equitable in the circumstances. Upon application of a stockholder, the Court may order all or a portion of the expenses incurred by any stockholder in connection with the appraisal proceeding, including, without limitation, reasonable attorney's fees and the fees and expenses of experts, to be charged pro rata against the value of all the shares entitled to an appraisal.

(k) From and after the effective date of the merger or consolidation, no stockholder who has demanded his appraisal rights as provided in subsection (d) of this section shall be entitled to vote such stock for any purpose or to receive payment of dividends or other distributions on the stock (except dividends or other distributions payable to stockholders of record at a date which is prior to the effective date of the merger or consolidation); provided, however, that if no petition for an appraisal shall be filed within the time provided in subsection (e) of this section, or if such stockholder shall deliver to the surviving or resulting corporation a written withdrawal of his demand for an appraisal and an acceptance of the merger or consolidation, either within 60 days after the effective date of the merger or consolidation as provided in subsection (e) of this section or thereafter with the written approval of the corporation, then the right of such stockholder to an appraisal shall cease. Notwithstanding the foregoing, no appraisal proceeding in the Court of Chancery shall be dismissed as to any stockholder without the approval of the Court, and such approval may be conditioned upon such terms as the Court deems just.

(l) The shares of the surviving or resulting corporation to which the shares of such objecting stockholders would have been converted had they assented to the merger or consolidation shall have the status of authorized and unissued shares of the surviving or resulting corporation.

§ 263 Merger or consolidation of domestic corporation and limited partnership.

(a) Any 1 or more corporations of this State may merge or consolidate with 1 or more limited partnerships, of this State or of any other state or states of the United States, or of the District of Columbia, unless the laws of such other state or states or the District of Columbia forbid such merger or consolidation. Such corporation or corporations and such 1 or more limited partnerships may merge with or into a corporation, which may be any 1 of such corporations, or they may merge with or into a limited partnership, which may be any 1 of such limited partnerships, or they may consolidate into a new corporation or limited partnership formed by the consolidation, which shall be a corporation or limited partnership of this State or any other state of the United States, or the District of Columbia, which permits such merger or consolidation, pursuant to an agreement of merger or consolidation, as the case may be, complying and approved in accordance with this section.

(b) Each such corporation and limited partnership shall enter into a written agreement of merger or consolidation. The agreement shall state: (1) The terms and conditions of the merger or consolidation; (2) the mode of carrying the same into effect; (3) the manner of converting the shares of stock of each such corporation and the partnership interests of each such limited partnership into shares, partnership interests or other securities of the entity surviving or resulting from such merger or consolidation, and if any shares of any such corporation or any partnership interests of any such limited partnership are not to be converted solely into shares, partnership interests or other securities of the entity surviving or resulting from such merger or consolidation, the cash, property, rights or securities of any other corporation or entity which the holders of such shares or partnership interests are to receive in exchange for, or upon conversion of such shares or partnership interests and the surrender of any certificates evidencing them, which cash, property, rights or securities of any other corporation or entity may be in addition to or in lieu of shares, partnership interests or other securities of the entity surviving or resulting from such merger or consolidation; and (4) such other details or provisions as are deemed desirable, including, without limiting the generality of the foregoing, a provision for the payment of cash in lieu of the issuance of fractional shares or interests of the surviving or resulting corporation or limited partnership. Any of the terms of the agreement of merger or consolidation may be made dependent upon facts ascertainable outside of such agreement, provided that the manner in which such facts shall operate upon the terms of the agreement is clearly and expressly set forth in the agreement of merger or consolidation.

(c) The agreement required by subsection (b) of this section shall be adopted, approved, certified, executed and acknowledged by each of the corporations in the same manner as is provided in § 251 of this title and, in the case of the limited partnerships, in accordance with their limited partnership agreements and in accordance with the laws of the state under which they are formed, as the case may be. The agreement shall be filed and recorded and shall become effective for all purposes of the laws of this State when and as provided in § 251 of this title with respect to the merger or consolidation of corporations of this State. In lieu of filing and recording the agreement of merger or consolidation, the surviving or resulting corporation or limited partnership may file a certificate of merger or consolidation, executed in accordance with § 103 of this title, if the surviving or resulting entity is a corporation, or by a general partner, if the surviving or resulting entity is a limited partnership, which states: (1) The name and state of domicile of each of the constituent entities; (2) that an agreement of merger or consolidation has been approved, adopted, certified, executed and acknowledged by each of the constituent entities in accordance with this subsection; (3) the name of the surviving or resulting corporation or limited partnership; (4) in the case of a merger in which a corporation is the surviving entity, such amendments or changes in the certificate of incorporation of the surviving corporation as are desired to be effected by the merger, or, if no such amendments or changes are desired, a statement that the certificate of incorporation of the surviving corporation shall be its certificate of incorporation; (5) in the case of a consolidation in which a corporation is the resulting entity, that the certificate of incorporation of the resulting corporation shall be as is set forth in an attachment to the certificate; (6) that the executed agreement of consolidation or merger is on file at the principal place of business of the surviving corporation or limited partnership and the address thereof; (7) that a copy of the agreement of consolidation or merger will be furnished by the surviving or resulting entity, on request and without cost, to any stockholder of any constituent corporation or any partner of any constituent limited partnership; and (8) the agreement, if any, required by subsection (d) of this section.

(d) If the entity surviving or resulting from the merger or consolidation is to be governed by the laws of the District of Columbia or any state other than this State, it shall agree that it may be served with process in this State in any proceeding for enforcement of any obligation of any constituent corporation or limited partnership of this State, as well as for enforcement of any obligation of the surviving or resulting corporation or limited partnership arising from the merger or consolidation, including any suit or other proceeding to enforce the right of any stockholders as determined in appraisal proceedings pursuant to § 262 of this title, and shall irrevocably appoint the Secretary of State as its agent to accept service of process in any such suit or other proceedings and shall specify the address to which a copy of such process shall be mailed by the Secretary of State. In the event of such service upon the Secretary of State in accordance with this subsection, the Secretary of State shall forthwith notify such surviving or resulting corporation or limited partnership thereof by letter, certified mail, return receipt requested, directed to such surviving or resulting corporation or limited partnership at its address so specified, unless such surviving or resulting corporation or limited partnership shall have designated in writing to the Secretary of State a different address for such purpose, in which case it shall be mailed to the last address so designated. Such letter shall enclose a copy of the process and any other papers served on the Secretary of State pursuant to this subsection. It shall be the duty of the plaintiff in the event of such service to serve process and any other papers in duplicate, to notify the Secretary of State that service is being effected pursuant to this subsection and to pay the Secretary of State the sum of $50 for the use of the State, which sum shall be taxed as part of the costs in the proceeding, if the plaintiff shall prevail therein. The Secretary of State shall maintain an alphabetical record of any such service setting forth the name of the plaintiff and the defendant, the title, docket number and nature of the proceeding in which process has been served upon him, the fact that service has been effected pursuant to this subsection, the return date thereof, and the day and hour service was made. The Secretary of State shall not be required to retain such information longer than 5 years from his receipt of the service of process.

(e) Sections 251(d)-(f), 259-261 and 328 of this title shall, insofar as they are applicable, apply to mergers or consolidations between corporations and limited partnerships.

§ 264 Merger or consolidation of domestic corporation and limited liability company.

(a) Any 1 or more corporations of this State may merge or consolidate with 1 or more limited liability companies, of this State or of any other state or states of the United States, or of the District of Columbia, unless the laws of such other state or states or the District of Columbia forbid such merger or consolidation. Such corporation or corporations and such one or more limited liability companies may merge with or into a corporation, which may be any one of such corporations, or they may merge with or into a limited liability company, which may be any 1 of such limited liability companies, or they may consolidate into a new corporation or limited liability company formed by the consolidation, which shall be a corporation or limited liability company of this State or any other state of the United States, or the District of Columbia, which permits such merger or consolidation, pursuant to an agreement of merger or consolidation, as the case may be, complying and approved in accordance with this section.

(b) Each such corporation and limited liability company shall enter into a written agreement of merger or consolidation. The agreement shall state:

(1) The terms and conditions of the merger or consolidation;

(2) The mode of carrying the same into effect;

(3) The manner of converting the shares of stock of each such corporation and the limited liability company interests of each such limited liability company into shares, limited liability company interests or other securities of the entity surviving or resulting from such merger or consolidation, and if any shares of any such corporation or any limited liability company interests of any such limited liability company are not to be converted solely into shares, limited liability company interests or other securities of the entity surviving or resulting from such merger or consolidation, the cash, property, rights or securities of any other corporation or entity which the holders of such shares or limited liability company interests are to receive in exchange for, or upon conversion of such shares or limited liability company interests and the surrender of any certificates evidencing them, which cash, property, rights or securities of any other corporation or entity may be in addition to or in lieu of shares, limited liability company interests or other securities of the entity surviving or resulting from such merger or consolidation; and

(4) Such other details or provisions as are deemed desirable, including, without limiting the generality of the foregoing, a provision for the payment of cash in lieu of the issuance of fractional shares or interests of the surviving or resulting corporation or limited liability company. Any of the terms of the agreement of merger or consolidation may be made dependent upon facts ascertainable outside of such agreement, provided that the manner in which such facts shall operate upon the terms of the agreement is clearly and expressly set forth in the agreement of merger or consolidation.

(c) The agreement required by subsection (b) shall be adopted, approved, certified, executed and acknowledged by each of the corporations in the same manner as is provided in § 251 of this title and, in the case of the limited liability companies, in accordance with their limited liability company agreements and in accordance with the laws of the state under which they are formed, as the case may be. The agreement shall be filed and recorded and shall become effective for all purposes of the laws of this State when and as provided in § 251 of this title with respect to the merger or consolidation of corporations of this State. In lieu of filing and recording the agreement of merger or consolidation, the surviving or resulting corporation or limited liability company may file a certificate of merger or consolidation, executed in accordance with § 103 of this title, if the surviving or resulting entity is a corporation, or by an authorized person, if the surviving or resulting entity is a limited liability company, which states:

(1) The name and state of domicile of each of the constituent entities;

(2) That an agreement of merger or consolidation has been approved, adopted, certified, executed and acknowledged by each of the constituent entities in accordance with this subsection;

(3) The name of the surviving or resulting corporation or limited liability company;

(4) In the case of a merger in which a corporation is the surviving entity, such amendments or changes in the certificate of incorporation of the surviving corporation as are desired to be effected by the merger, or, if no such amendments or changes are desired, a statement that the certificate of incorporation of the surviving corporation shall be its certificate of incorporation;

(5) In the case of a consolidation in which a corporation is the resulting entity, that the certificate of incorporation of the resulting corporation shall be as is set forth in an attachment to the certificate;

(6) That the executed agreement of consolidation or merger is on file at the principal place of business of the surviving corporation or limited liability company and the address thereof;

(7) That a copy of the agreement of consolidation or merger will be furnished by the surviving or resulting entity, on request and without cost, to any stockholder of any constituent corporation or any member of any constituent limited liability company; and

(8) The agreement, if any, required by subsection (d) of this section.

(d) If the entity surviving or resulting from the merger or consolidation is to be governed by the laws of the District of Columbia or any state other than this State, it shall agree that it may be served with process in this State in any proceeding for enforcement of any obligation of any constituent corporation or limited liability company of this State, as well as for enforcement of any obligation of the surviving or resulting corporation or limited liability company arising from the merger or consolidation, including any suit or other proceeding to enforce the right of any stockholders as determined in appraisal proceedings pursuant to the provisions of § 262 of this title, and shall irrevocably appoint the Secretary of State as its agent to accept service of process in any such suit or other proceedings and shall specify the address to which a copy of such process shall be mailed by the Secretary of State. In the event of such service upon the Secretary of State in accordance with this subsection, the Secretary of State shall forthwith notify such surviving or resulting corporation or limited liability company thereof by letter, certified mail, return receipt requested, directed to such surviving or resulting corporation or limited liability company at its address so specified, unless such surviving or resulting corporation or limited liability company shall have designated in writing to the Secretary of State a different address for such purpose, in which case it shall be mailed to the last address so designated. Such letter shall enclose a copy of the process and any other papers served on the Secretary of State pursuant to this subsection. It shall be the duty of the plaintiff in the event of such service to serve process and any other papers in duplicate, to notify the Secretary of State that service is being effected pursuant to this subsection and to pay the Secretary of State the sum of $50 for the use of the State, which sum shall be taxed as part of the costs in the proceeding, if the plaintiff shall prevail therein.   The Secretary of State shall maintain an alphabetical record of any such service setting forth the name of the plaintiff and the defendant, the title, docket number and nature of the proceeding in which process has been served upon him, the fact that service has been effected pursuant to this subsection, the return date thereof, and the day and hour service was made.   The Secretary of State shall not be required to retain such information longer than 5 years from his receipt of the service of process.

(e) Sections 251(d)-(f), 259-261 and 328 of this title shall, insofar as they are applicable, apply to mergers or consolidations between corporations and limited liability companies.

APPENDIX C
FORM OF ACQUISITION AGREEMENT

PLAN OF REORGANIZATION

Table of Contents

PREAMBLE

This Agreement, made as of this _____ day of _____, 19__, between Acquiring Corp., a Delaware corporation (hereinafter called "Acquiring"), Target Corp., a California corporation (hereinafter called "Target"), and Controlling Shareholder, a California resident (hereinafter called the "Shareholder"):

WITNESSETH:

WHEREAS, Target is a corporation duly organized, validly existing and in good standing under the laws of the State of California; and

WHEREAS, Acquiring is a corporation duly organized, validly existing and in good standing under the laws of the State of Delaware; and

WHEREAS, Acquiring will form a California corporation (hereinafter "Subsidiary") which shall be a wholly-owned subsidiary of Acquiring; and

WHEREAS, if the conditions for the merger contemplated herein are satisfied, Subsidiary will be merged into Target pursuant to Section 368(a) of the Internal Revenue Code of 1954, as amended; and

WHEREAS, the respective Boards of Directors of Acquiring and Target deem it advisable for the general welfare and advantage of the respective corporations and their respective shareholders that, subject to the terms and conditions herein contained and in accordance with the applicable laws of the State of California, Subsidiary merge (hereinafter sometimes called the "Merger") with and into Target, with Target being the surviving corporation (hereinafter sometimes called the "Surviving Corporation");

NOW, THEREFORE, in consideration of the premises and the mutual agreements, provisions, covenants and grants herein contained, the parties hereto hereby agree that if the conditions for the Merger contained herein are satisfied prior to the Merger, Subsidiary shall be merged into Target in accordance with the applicable laws of the State of California, and that the terms and conditions of the Merger and the mode of carrying it into effect are and shall be as hereinafter set forth:

I.   Computation of Target's Net Worth and Acquiring's Net Worth

A.   Acquiring shall cause a certified public accounting firm (the "Accountants") of its own selection, at its own expense, to audit the financial position of Target as of December 31, 19__. This audit shall be of the financial position of Target prior to giving effect to the sale of certain assets of Target constituting its "Southward Division," although all other references herein give effect to such sale having been consummated. In connection therewith, Acquiring and its representatives, and the Accountants, may make such investigation of the properties, books and records of Target and its legal and financial condition as Acquiring or the Accountants shall deem necessary and/or advisable to familiarize Acquiring and Subsidiary with said properties and other matters; such investigation shall not, however, affect the Shareholder's and Target's representations and warranties hereunder. The Shareholder and Target agree to permit Acquiring and said other parties to have full access to all premises occupied by and to all the books and records of Target, and the officers and employees of Target will be instructed to furnish them with such financial and operating data and other information with respect to the business and properties of Target as they shall from time to time reasonably request. The Shareholder and Target shall deliver to Acquiring unaudited interim financial statements of Target as they are prepared and shall cause such other reasonable financial information of Target to be prepared and delivered to Acquiring at any time during the term of this Agreement as Acquiring may request; provided, however, that the Shareholder and Target shall not be required to cause such interim financial information to be prepared more frequently than once each month. At any time during the term of this Agreement, but not more frequently than once each three months, Acquiring may, in its sole discretion and at its own expense, cause a firm of independent certified accountants to audit the financial position of Target.

B. The audit of the financial position of Target as of December 31, 19__, to be conducted by the Accountants, shall be conducted in accordance with generally accepted accounting principles consistently applied. A balance sheet (the "Balance Sheet") setting forth Target's financial position as of December 31, 19__, shall be prepared based on the audit, and certified by the Accountants, without exception. The Balance Sheet, so prepared, shall be a final determination of the financial position of Target as of the date thereof, and shall be conclusive for purposes of determining Target's Net Worth. Target's Net Worth shall be the amount of the shareholders' equity of Target as of December 31, 19__.

C. For purposes of this Agreement, Acquiring's Net Worth shall mean the amount of its stockholders' equity as of December 31, 19__, as presented on its unaudited financial statements as filed with the Securities and Exchange Commission on Form 10–Q. For purposes of this Agreement, Acquiring's Book Value Per Share shall be that quotient resulting from dividing Acquiring's Net Worth by the number of shares of Acquiring Common Stock which are issued and outstanding on December 31, 19__.

D. When Target's Net Worth and Acquiring's Net Worth and Book Value Per Share have been computed as provided in this Agreement, the Shareholder, Target and Acquiring shall execute Exhibit I to be attached hereto, acknowledging said Net Worth figures and Acquiring's Book Value Per Share.

II.   Terms of Merger

Subject to this Agreement being consummated and to the terms and conditions herein stated:

A. At the Closing, all of the common stock of Target shall be converted as a result of the Merger into shares of Acquiring's Common Stock. The number of shares of Acquiring's Common Stock which Shareholder will receive as a result of the Merger will be equal to the amount computed by dividing Target's Net Worth by Acquiring's Book Value Per Share and adding 15,000 shares thereto. The shares of Acquiring Common Stock which are so computed to be due to Shareholder are hereinafter identified as the "Merger Shares."

B. (1) The Shareholder hereby agrees that at the Closing, upon receipt of the Merger Shares, he will immediately deposit 15,000 of such Merger Shares into escrow for a period ending no later than 42 months after the Closing at which time the escrowed Merger Shares then remaining in escrow will be returned to him.

(2) The Shareholder agrees to enter into an escrow agreement substantially in the form of the escrow agreement attached hereto as Appendix

A (hereinafter the "Escrow Agreement"), with National Bank (hereinafter "Depository"), which Escrow Agreement will provide that the 15,000 escrowed shares will be held subject to the following provisions:

(a) If during the first four full fiscal quarters of Target succeeding the Closing ("Year One"), the business operations which constituted Target on the date of the Closing (hereinafter the "Operations") shall experience net sales equal to or in excess of 115% of those experienced by the Operations in the twelve full months (the "Base Year") immediately preceding Year One and have pretax earnings (after elimination of all non-operating gains and losses) equal to or in excess of 3.4% of net sales, then 5,000 shares of Acquiring Common Stock placed in escrow by the Shareholder shall be released from the escrow and delivered to the Shareholder within 90 days of the end of Year One.

(b) If during the first four fiscal quarters of Target following Year One ("Year Two"), the Operations experienced net sales equal to or in excess of 132% of those experienced by the Operations in the Base Year, and pretax earnings (after elimination of non-operating gains and losses) equal to or in excess of 4.2% of such net sales, then 5,000 shares of Acquiring Common Stock placed in escrow by the Shareholder shall be released from the escrow and delivered to the Shareholder within 90 days of the end of Year Two.

(c) If during the four fiscal quarters of Target following Year Two ("Year Three"), the Operations shall experience net sales equal to or in excess of 152% of those experienced by the Operations in the Base Year, and pretax earnings (after elimination of non-operating gains and losses) equal to or in excess of 4.8% of such sales, then 5,000 shares of Acquiring Common Stock placed in escrow by the Shareholder shall be released from the escrow and delivered to the Shareholder within 90 days after the end of Year Three.

(d) Notwithstanding subsections II.B.(2)(a)—(c) above, in the event that any Merger Shares received by the Shareholder at the Closing remain in escrow after the end of Year Three, all of such shares shall be released from the escrow and delivered to the Shareholder within 90 days after the end of Year Three, if the Operations shall experience net sales in Year Three equal to or in excess of 152% of those experienced by the Operations in the Base Year, and the aggregate pretax earnings (after elimination of non-operating gains and losses) of the Operations in the Years One, Two and Three shall equal or exceed the sum of (i) 3.4% of the Year One's net sales, (ii) 4.2% of Year Two's net sales and (iii) 4.8% of Year Three's net sales.

(e) Those escrowed Merger Shares which are not released from escrow and delivered to Shareholder pursuant to Sections II.B.(2)(a) through II.B.(2)(d) shall be returned to Acquiring 42 months following the Closing. Prior to such date all voting and dividend rights in the escrowed Merger Shares shall belong to Shareholder, as stated in the Escrow Agreement. Dividends, whether in cash, stock or other securities or property (other than Acquiring Common Stock) paid on, or in respect of the escrowed Merger Shares, shall be retained by Shareholder. Dividends in Acquiring Common Stock and Acquiring Common Stock issued as a result of a stock split shall be delivered by

Shareholder to the Depository to be held in escrow and distributed with the Acquiring Common Stock in respect of which it was issued.

(f) It is agreed that until the end of Year Three, Acquiring shall not charge any general or administrative expenses of Acquiring to the Surviving Corporation nor shall it be reimbursed by the Surviving Corporation for any expenses other than those directly incurred on the Surviving Corporation's behalf; *provided, however,* Acquiring shall be entitled to reasonable interest on any loans or advances made to the Surviving Corporation.

C. When this Agreement and the transaction contemplated hereby shall have been adopted, approved, executed, and an agreement of Merger filed in accordance with the laws of the State of California, the separate existence of Subsidiary shall cease and it shall be merged into Target. The date on which the Merger is effected shall be known as the "Closing Date".

D. The laws which are to govern the Surviving Corporation are the laws of the State of California. The Articles of Incorporation of Target as in effect on the Closing Date (unless otherwise set forth in the Agreement of Merger) shall be the Articles of Incorporation of the Surviving Corporation from and after the Closing, subject always to the right of the Surviving Corporation to amend its Articles of Incorporation in accordance with the laws of the State of California.

E. The Bylaws of Target in effect immediately prior to the Closing Date shall be and remain the Bylaws of the Surviving Corporation until the same shall be altered, amended or repealed as provided therein or as provided by law.

F. The directors and officers of Target on the Closing Date shall be the directors and officers of the Surviving Corporation immediately following the Merger.

G. On, or prior to, the Closing Date, Acquiring will issue and deliver the Merger Shares to Subsidiary to be delivered to Shareholder upon surrender by the Shareholder to Acquiring of the certificates theretofore representing all of the outstanding shares of the common stock of Target.

H. At the Closing, all of the common stock of Subsidiary shall be converted as a result of the Merger into 100 shares of Target common stock.

I. In the event that, subsequent to the date of this Agreement but prior to the Closing, the outstanding shares of Acquiring Common Stock shall have been, without consideration, increased, decreased, changed into or exchanged for a different number or kind of shares of securities through reorganization, recapitalization, reclassification, stock dividend, stock split, reverse stock split, or other like changes in Acquiring's capitalization, then an appropriate and proportionate adjustment shall be made in the number and kind of shares to be issued to the Shareholder on the Closing Date and to be placed in escrow by the Shareholder.

III.   Warranties, Representations and Agreements of the Shareholder and Target

A. Target and the Shareholder jointly and severally represent, warrant and agree as follows:

(1) Target is a corporation duly organized, validly existing and in good standing under the laws of the State of California, with the power to own its

property, to carry on its business as now being conducted, and to enter into and carry out the terms of this Agreement.

(2) Target is not qualified to do business as a foreign corporation in any jurisdiction; and neither the character of the properties owned and leased by Target, nor the nature of the business conducted by Target makes qualification as a foreign corporation in any other jurisdiction necessary.

(3) The Shareholder is the lawful owner of, and has good and marketable title to, all of the outstanding capital stock of Target, free and clear of any mortgages, pledges, claims, liens, charges or encumbrances, or other rights in third persons to purchase any shares thereof.

(4) The authorized capital stock of Target consists of _____ shares of common stock, $1 par value, of which _____ shares are issued and outstanding, and no shares are held as treasury stock. All of the issued and outstanding shares of Target have been duly authorized and validly issued and are fully paid and non-assessable. There are no outstanding options, warrants, rights, calls, commitments, conversion rights, plans or other agreements of any character providing for the purchase of any authorized but unissued shares of the capital stock of Target. Prior to the Closing, Target will not issue any capital stock or authorize any increase in the number of shares of its authorized capital stock or issue any options, warrants, calls, commitments or rights to subscribe for or purchase any of its securities. Copies of the Articles of Incorporation, Bylaws and all minutes of Target are contained in the minute books of Target and such minute books and all stock books of Target will be delivered to Acquiring at the Closing.

(5) Each balance sheet delivered to Acquiring pursuant to this Agreement shall reflect all claims, debts or liabilities of Target which should be reflected thereon in accordance with generally accepted accounting principles. Without the prior written consent of Acquiring other than in the ordinary course of business or as otherwise permitted herein, Target will not incur, prior to the Closing, any indebtedness for money borrowed or incur any liabilities.

(6) All of Target's inventories, except for quantities deemed not to be material, of finished foods, work in process, raw materials and supplies are current, usable and merchantable and are not excessive or out of balance, are in the physical possession of Target and will be valued on the Balance Sheet and all financial statements furnished to Acquiring pursuant to this Agreement at the lower-of-cost-or-market (cost being computed on a "First-in, First-out" basis).

(7) Since November 30, 19__, Target has not issued, or declared or paid any dividend on, or declared or made any distribution on, or authorized the creation or issuance of, or effected any split-up or any recapitalization of any of its capital stock of any class, or, directly or indirectly, redeemed, purchased or otherwise acquired any of its outstanding stock or authorized or made any change in its Articles of Incorporation or agreed to take any such action and, prior to the Closing, Target will take no such action.

(8) Target has filed all requisite Federal income, payroll and excise tax returns and all appropriate state and local income, sales, payroll, personal property and franchise tax returns required to be filed by it and has paid all taxes and assessments (including interest or penalties) owned by it to the extent that such taxes and assessments are due. To the extent any subsequent tax

liabilities have accrued but have not become payable, the full amounts thereof have been reflected as liabilities on the books and in the financial statements of Target as of the date of their accrual. In addition, Target has paid all taxes which would not require the filing of returns and which are required to be paid and which otherwise would be delinquent.

(9) Target does not own any real property. Except as noted on Schedule A,[a] Target has good and marketable title to all of its personal property, free and clear of all encumbrances, liens and charges of every kind and character. None of the personal property of Target is subject (i) to a contract for sale, except inventory to be sold in the ordinary course of business, or (ii) to mortgages, pledges, liens, encumbrances, security interests or charges of any kind of character except as herein disclosed or as set forth in Schedule A. Except as set forth on Schedule A, all buildings, structures, appurtenances, machinery and equipment owned or leased by Target are in good operating condition and in a state of good maintenance and repair, ordinary wear and tear excepted. There is no real or personal property currently used in the Operations which is not either leased or owned by Target, and all property owned or leased by Target is in its possession.

(10) Set forth on Schedule B hereto is a list of all leases under which Target holds any real or personal property. Each lease set forth in such schedule is in full force and effect, all rents and additional rents due to date on each such lease have been paid; in each case the lessee has been in peaceable possession since the commencement of the original term of such lease and neither Target nor, to the best of its knowledge, any lessor is in default thereunder; no waiver, indulgence or postponement of the lessee's obligations thereunder has been granted by the lessor, or of the lessor's obligations by lessee; and there exists no event, occurrence, condition or act which, with the giving of notice, and lapse of time or the happening of any further event or condition would become a default by the lessee (or to the best of Target's knowledge any lessor) under any such lease. Target has not violated any of the terms or conditions under any such lease and all of the covenants to be performed by the lessee and lessor under each such lease have been fully performed.

(11) Set forth on Schedule C hereto is a true and correct list of all obligations for indebtedness and all obligations not incurred in the ordinary course of business stating the origin of the obligation, amount owed and the terms of payment.

(12) Set forth on Schedule D hereto is a true and correct list of all policies of insurance on which Target is named as the insured party, including the amounts thereof, in force as at the date hereof, and such policies are in full force and effect. Target will continue to maintain

---

[a] The disclosure schedules referred to in this agreement have been omitted. Eds.

the coverage afforded by such policies in full force and effect up to and including the Closing Date.

(13) Set forth on Schedule E is a true and correct listing of all trade secrets, technical information, patents, patent rights, applications for patents, trademarks, trade names, copyrights, processes or formulae owned, possessed, licensed or used by Target in its business. Except as set forth in such schedule, none of such trademarks or trade names have been registered in, filed in, or issued by any governmental office. Except as noted on such schedule, to the best of Shareholder's and Target's knowledge, no such trademark or trade name infringes on others. Except as noted on such schedule, no such trademark or trade name is licensed by Target to, or used by Target, pursuant to a license from, any other person, firm or corporation in the United States or elsewhere. Except as set forth in Schedule E, Target has full right, title and ownership to its corporate name and to any and all other names under which it does business. Target possesses valid rights to use all trademarks, trade names, and licenses now used or necessary to conduct its business as presently being conducted.

(14) Except as set forth in Schedule F hereto, there are no actions, suits or proceedings which have been served on Target or to Target's knowledge, threatened against or which affect Target, at law or in equity, by or before any Federal, state or municipal court or other governmental department, commission, board, bureau, agency or instrumentality. Target is not subject to any material liability by reason of a violation of any order, rule, or regulation of any Federal, state, municipal or other governmental agency, department, commission, bureau, board or instrumentality to which it is subject. To the best information and belief of the Shareholder, there exists no event, condition or other circumstance (relating particularly to the business of Target as contrasted with matters relating to its industry or of a regional, national or international character) which immediately or with a lapse of time will materially adversely affect the business of Target as presently conducted.

(15) Except as set forth in Schedule G hereto, Target does not have any collective bargaining agreements with employees, employment agreements, compensation plans, employees' pension or retirement plans or pension trust, employees' profit sharing or bonus or stock purchase plans or any other similar agreements or plans (formal or informal). To the knowledge of Target and Shareholder, no party is in violation of any of the provisions of such agreements or plans. Target has not had any work stoppage due to concerted action by any of its employees and to the best of its knowledge none is threatened or contemplated. Between the date hereof and the Closing, Target will not, without the written consent of Acquiring, except in the ordinary course of business and consistent with prior practices, make or agree to make any increase in the rate of wages, salaries, bonuses, or other

remuneration of any employee or employees, or become a party to any employment contract or arrangement with any of its officers or employees, or become a party to any contract or arrangement with any officers or employees providing for bonuses or profit sharing payments, severance pay or retirement benefits.

(16) Set forth in Schedule H hereto is a true and correct list of all outstanding contracts, agreements or understanding to which Target is a party, except (i) those referred to elsewhere in this Section II, (ii) any contract, agreement or understanding involving an aggregate expenditure of less than $5,000 and (iii) purchase commitments for Target inventory which Target expects to sell within 30 days of receipt in the ordinary course of business. Neither Target nor to the best of its knowledge any other party to any such contract, agreement or understanding is in default under the terms of any such contract, agreement or understanding. Between the date hereof and the Closing, Target will not, without the written consent of Acquiring, make any changes or modifications in any such contracts, agreements or understanding, which result in an increase of Target's obligations by more than $2,000 for each such agreement or surrender any rights thereunder, or make any further additions to its property or further purchases of equipment except such changes or modifications, each in an amount less than $5,000, as are in the ordinary course of business or are necessary or appropriate to maintain its properties and equipment and except for the replacement of any trucks as are necessary or appropriate. Target is not a party to any continuing contract for the future purchase of materials, supplies or equipment in excess of the requirements for its business as now being conducted. Neither Target nor the Shareholder is subject to, or is a party to, any mortgage, lien, lease, agreement, contract, instrument, order, judgment or degree or any other restriction of any kind or character which would prevent the continued operation of the business of Target after the Closing on substantially the same basis as theretofore operated.

(17) Neither Target nor the Shareholder is subject to any order, judgment or decree with respect to Target's business or any of Target's assets or property, or to any charter, bylaw, mortgage, lease, agreement, instrument, order, judgment or decree which would prevent the consummation of any of the transactions contemplated hereunder, or compliance by Target or the Shareholder with the terms, conditions and provisions hereof.

(18) All outstanding accounts receivable (trade or other) of Target as will be set forth in the Balance Sheet and in Target's books and records, and in any other financial statements prepared by Target pursuant to the terms of this Agreement will be collectible, except to the extent of the reasonable reserve for bad debts to be set forth on said Balance Sheet, books and records, or other financial statements.

(19) Since December 31, 19__, the business, properties, or condition, financial or otherwise, of Target has not been materially adversely affected in any way as a result of any legislative or regulatory change, revocation of any license or right to do business, fire, explosion, accident, casualty, labor trouble, flood, drought, riot, storm, condemnation, or act of God or other public force or otherwise (whether or not covered by insurance).

(20) The copies of all leases, instruments, agreements or other documents that have been or will be delivered to Acquiring or Subsidiary pursuant to the terms of this Agreement are and will be complete and correct as of the date delivered and as of the Closing. Except as set forth in Schedule I, the execution and delivery of this Agreement and the other agreements which are to be executed pursuant to this Agreement (all such agreements, including this Agreement, are sometimes collectively referred to as the "Executed Agreements"), and the performance of the obligations thereunder do not on the date hereof and will not hereafter violate any of the terms or provisions of any leases, instruments, agreements or other documents to which Target is a party and none require the consent of any third party to the transactions contemplated hereby.

(21) Target has maintained its books of account in accordance with generally accepted accounting principles applied on a consistent basis.

(22) In the negotiations leading up to the transactions contemplated by this Agreement, neither the Shareholder nor Target has retained or utilized the services of any broker or finder.

(23) During the period from the date hereof to and including the Closing, Target will conduct its business solely in the usual and ordinary manner and will refrain from any transaction not in the ordinary course of business or except as otherwise permitted herein unless the prior written consent of Acquiring to such transaction has been obtained.

(24) All actions and proceedings required by law to be taken either by Target or the Shareholder at or prior to the Closing in connection with the Executed Agreements and the transactions provided for therein shall be duly and validly taken on or prior to the Closing.

(25) To the knowledge of the Shareholder, no information necessary to make any of the representations and warranties herein contained not materially misleading has been withheld from or has not been disclosed to, Acquiring.

(26) The only officers and directors of Target are:

Name/Position
President and Director
Vice President, Secretary and Director
Vice President, Sales
Treasurer and Director

Assistant Secretary and Director

Director

(27) Target will give Acquiring written notice of all meetings (or actions in writing without a meeting) of Target's Board of Directors and/or its shareholder held (or taken) prior to the Closing at least ten days prior to such meeting (or the taking of actions without a meeting). The notice herein provided shall disclose the purpose of the meeting or the proposed action in writing without a meeting. Acquiring may at its discretion waive the ten days' notice requirement of this subsection. Target shall allow a representative of Acquiring to attend, as an observer, any meeting of its Board of Directors or of its shareholders. Promptly after preparation of the minutes for any of the above-described meetings or actions, Target shall cause a copy of such minutes to be forwarded to Acquiring.

(28) Target does not have any subsidiaries or affiliates or own any interest in any other business, corporation, joint venture, partnership or proprietorship.

B. The Shareholder covenants, warrants and represents both as of the date hereof and as of the Closing Date, as follows:

(1) That, except as required in connection with his employment by Target, he will not disclose or use at any time any secret, confidential or proprietary information or knowledge pertaining to the business affairs of Target.

(2) That he has no claim against Target except for current salary, and claims disclosed in Schedule J attached hereto.

(3) That he has full power, right and authority to enter into this Agreement and agrees to vote his shares of Target common stock in favor of the transactions contemplated by this Agreement.

(4) Shareholder recognizes that among the intangible assets of Target is its goodwill. Until the Closing, Shareholder will utilize his best efforts to keep Target's business intact, to keep available to the Surviving Corporation the services of Target's present officers and employees, and to preserve for the Surviving Corporation the goodwill of Target's suppliers and customers and the goodwill of others with whom Target has business relations. Shareholder agrees that, for a period of three (3) years following the Closing Date, he will not, without the written consent of Acquiring or as an employee of Target, on his own behalf or as a partner, officer, executive, employee, agent, consultant, director, trustee, or shareholder (except as a shareholder of not more than 5% of the outstanding securities of a publicly held corporation) carry on a business of the type conducted by Target on the Closing Date or engage in any business which would be competitive with such business within any county in any state in which Target has carried on its business and so long as Target continues a like business therein.

IV.   Warranties, Representations and Agreements of Acquiring

Acquiring represents, warrants and agrees as follows:

A. Acquiring is a corporation duly organized, validly existing and in good standing under the laws of the State of Delaware and has the corporate power to own its property and to carry on its business as now being conducted by it.

B. As of November 30, 19__, the authorized capital stock of Acquiring consisted of _____ shares of Common Stock, par value $1 per share, and _____ shares of Preferred Stock, par value $1 per share.

C. The Merger Shares when issued and delivered pursuant to this Agreement will be duly authorized, validly issued, fully paid and nonassessable Common Stock of Acquiring listed on the American Stock Exchange (or listed subject to notice of issuance), free and clear of all preemptive rights, and other claims, liens or encumbrances whatsoever.

D. All actions and proceedings required by law to be taken by Acquiring and Subsidiary at or prior to the Closing Date in connection with the Executed Agreements and the transactions provided for therein shall have been duly and validly taken on or prior to the Closing Date.

E. Acquiring's Board of Directors has approved the transactions contemplated by this Agreement.

F. Acquiring shall apply for a tax ruling at its expense that no gain will be realized as a result of the Merger or as a result of the release of shares from the escrow referred to in Article II.

G. In the event the Merger is not consummated, all written information furnished to Acquiring or its representatives with respect to Target shall be returned to Acquiring, and Acquiring shall keep confidential all non-public information obtained pursuant to the terms of this Agreement.

H.(1) Acquiring will at any time or times during the three years immediately following the Closing Date, upon the written request of the Shareholder and at his expense, file as soon as practicable a Registration Statement pursuant to the Securities Act of 1933 (the "Act"), and all requisite registrations or qualifications under any state securities laws, covering the sale by such Shareholder of all or part of the Acquiring Common Stock to be issued to him hereunder (and any additional shares distributed thereon in any stock dividend or stock split), and shall use its best efforts to have such Registration Statement made effective in order to permit a sale of such Common Stock upon terms of an offering to be supplied to Acquiring in writing. The Shareholder shall promptly pay and reimburse Target for all costs and expenses (or, if any other shareholder of Acquiring shall join in such registration as provided in subsection (3) below, each "selling shareholder" participating in such registration shall pay and reimburse Acquiring for his proportionate share of all costs and expenses) related to such registration (including legal, accounting and printing expenses), without regard to whether the Registration Statement is made effective or the proposed sale of Acquiring Common Stock is carried out.

(2) Acquiring agrees to notify the Shareholder in writing prior to the filing of any Registration Statement (including any Registration Statement filed pursuant to the provisions of subsection H(1)) during the three years immediately following the Closing Date. If so requested by the Shareholder within ten (10) days after receipt of such notice as aforesaid, Acquiring shall include in such registration all or such part of the shares of Target Common Stock received by the Shareholder hereunder as the Shareholder may request.

(3)(a)   The covenants and obligations of Acquiring under subsections H(1) and/or H(2) are subject to the following conditions:

(i) Acquiring shall not be required to file more than one Registration Statement during any period of twelve consecutive calendar months.

(ii) The Shareholder shall deliver to Acquiring a statement in writing that he bona fide intends to sell the shares of Common Stock which he proposes to include in the Registration Statement.

(iii) The Shareholder shall cooperate with Acquiring in the preparation of the Registration Statement to the extent required to furnish information concerning the Shareholder therein.

(iv) With respect to any Registration Statement relating to any shares of Common Stock of the Shareholder, the Shareholder will indemnify Acquiring and each person, if any, who controls Acquiring within the meaning of the Act, in writing, in form and substance acceptable to counsel for Acquiring, against all expenses, claims, damages or liabilities to which Acquiring may become subject, under the Act or otherwise, insofar as such expenses, claims, damages or liabilities arise out of or are based upon any untrue statement or alleged untrue statement of any material fact contained in any Preliminary Prospectus, the Registration Statement, the final Prospectus or any amendment or supplement thereto, or arise out of or are based upon the omission or alleged omission to state therein a material fact required to be stated therein or necessary to make the statements therein not misleading, in each case to the extent, but only to the extent, that such untrue statement or alleged untrue statement or omission or alleged omission was made therein in reliance upon and in conformity with written information furnished to Acquiring by the Shareholder expressly for use in the preparation thereof.

(v) With respect to any Registration Statement relating to any shares of Common Stock of Shareholder, Acquiring will indemnify the Shareholder, each Underwriter of the shares of the Shareholder, and each person, if any, who controls the Shareholder or any such Underwriter within the meaning of the Act, in writing, in form and substance acceptable to counsel for Target, the Shareholder and such Underwriters, against all expenses, claims, damages or liabilities to which the Shareholder, any such Underwriter, or any such controlling person may become subject, under the act or otherwise, insofar as such expenses, claims, damages or liabilities arise out of or are based upon any untrue statement or alleged untrue statement of any material fact contained in any Preliminary Prospectus, the Registration Statement, the final Prospectus or any amendment or supplement thereto, or arise out of or are based upon the omission or alleged omission to state therein a material fact required to be stated therein or necessary to make the statements therein not misleading; provided, however, that (X) Acquiring shall not be liable to the Shareholder (or any controlling person of the Shareholder) in any such case to the extent that such expenses, claims, damages or liabilities arise out of or are based upon any untrue statement or alleged untrue statement or omission or alleged omission made therein in reliance upon and in conformity with written information furnished to Acquiring by such Shareholder expressly for use in the preparation thereof, and (Y) Acquiring shall not be liable to any Underwriter (or any controlling person of such Underwriter) in any such case to the extent that such expenses, claims, damages or liabilities arise out of or are based upon any untrue statement or omission or alleged omission made therein in reliance upon and in conformity with written information furnished to Acquiring by such Underwriter expressly for use in the preparation thereof.

Any such Underwriter, as a condition to obtaining the indemnity agreement referred to in this subparagraph (v), shall be required to indemnify Acquiring on the same terms as provided in the previous subparagraph (iv) in the case of the Shareholder in respect of the written information furnished by such Underwriter which is referred to in clause (Y) of the preceding paragraph.

(b) The covenants and obligations of Acquiring under subsection H(2) are subject to the following conditions:

(i) Acquiring shall not be required to include any of the Common Stock if, by reason of such inclusion, Acquiring shall be required to prepare and file a Registration Statement on a form other than that which Acquiring otherwise would use.

(ii) Acquiring shall not be required to include any Common Stock in such Registration Statement if any managing underwriter with respect to the Common Stock then being offered by Acquiring shall in good faith object to the inclusion therein of the Common Stock of the Shareholder.

(iii) The Shareholder shall offer and sell his Common Stock pursuant to such Registration Statement and the Prospectus forming a part thereof upon such terms and conditions and at such times as shall be agreed upon and consented to by any managing underwriter with respect to the Common Stock offered by Acquiring pursuant to such Registration Statement.

(iv) In the event that by reason of such inclusion of the Common Stock of the Shareholder in any Registration Statement the effective date of such Registration Statement is unduly delayed, Acquiring may thereupon amend any such Registration Statement and remove therefrom any of the Common Stock owned by the Shareholder previously included therein.

(v) Without regard to whether the Registration Statement relating to the proposed sale of any Common Stock of Acquiring is made effective or the proposed sale of such Common Stock is carried out: (x) if the Shareholder shall propose to sell Common Stock received by the Shareholder hereunder in conjunction with the proposed sale of Common Stock by Acquiring, then Acquiring shall pay the Shareholder's portion of the fees and expenses in connection with such Registration Statement, including without limitation, legal, accounting, and printing fees and expenses; except that the Shareholder shall pay his pro rata portion of the registration fees under the Act and the state securities laws, all of the underwriting discounts and commission with respect to the Common Stock of the Shareholder included in the Registration Statement, and all of the fees and expenses of counsel to the Shareholder, (y) if the Shareholder shall propose to sell any Common Stock of Acquiring received by the Shareholder hereunder in conjunction with the sale of such Common Stock by any other shareholder of Acquiring, each selling shareholder shall pay his proportionate share of all costs and expenses related to such registration (including legal, accounting and printing expenses), each such shareholder paying a percentage of such costs and expenses equal to the percentage of such shareholder's interest in the net proceeds of the sale of all of the Common Stock which are offered for sale in such registration.

V.   Agreements and Indemnification

Target, and the Shareholder, jointly and individually, agree as follows:

A. The Shareholder agrees that, notwithstanding any investigation of the business and assets of Target made by or on behalf of Acquiring prior to the Closing, he will indemnify and hold harmless Target and Shareholder from and against any "Loss," which with respect to Target and Shareholder shall mean any claims, liabilities, losses, costs or damages, net of any taxes and future tax benefits or other recoverable sums, and actual expenses (including without limitation reasonable counsel fees incurred in litigation or otherwise) arising out of or sustained by Target or Shareholder directly or indirectly due to (i) breach of any warranty, representation or agreement of

Target or Shareholder contained in this Agreement, or in any Certificate, Schedule, Exhibit, Appendix or writing attached hereto or required by this Agreement, or (ii) any liability, debts, claim, tax penalty, or loss of Target arising out of any transaction prior to the Closing Date which was required to be disclosed and was not fully disclosed pursuant to this Agreement, or (iii) any cost or expense which may be incurred by Target or Shareholder in curing any breach of warranty contained in the Executed Agreements.

B. The Shareholder and Target agree that (i) any expense incurred, settlement made or judgment paid by Acquiring or Target after December 31, 19__ which arose out of any action or inaction prior to January 1, 19__ (including those which are described in Exhibit F hereto) or which occurred at any time on or after January 1, 19__ and prior to the Closing (x) as to which it is probable that a claim will be asserted and (y) which was not disclosed to Acquiring as required by Sections VI.B. shall be a "Loss" as to which Target is indemnified under Section V.A. above; and (ii) any expense incurred, settlement made or judgment paid by Target or Acquiring after December 31, 19__ which arose out of any action or inaction of Target which occurred after December 31, 19__ shall not be a "Loss" as to which Acquiring is indemnified under Section V.A. above, unless such action or inaction occurred prior to the Closing Date, it is probable that a claim will be asserted with respect thereto, and Target has failed to disclose the facts surrounding such an event to Acquiring by the Closing Date.

C. In the event a claim is made against Target or Subsidiary in respect of which they are (or either of them is) indemnified hereunder, Target or Subsidiary shall notify the Shareholder of such claim. In case any action is brought against Target, Subsidiary or Acquiring and Acquiring shall notify the Shareholder of the commencement thereof, the Shareholder shall assume the defense thereof with counsel satisfactory to Acquiring. Acquiring shall have the right to employ separate counsel in any such action and participate in the defense thereof but the fees and expenses of such counsel shall be at the expense of Acquiring unless the Shareholder has authorized the employment of such counsel. The Shareholder shall have the right to settle any such action or judgment based on any such action and in such event the Shareholder shall pay the amount of such settlement. If the Shareholder shall fail to promptly defend such action, Acquiring may do so with attorneys of its own selection and the Shareholder shall be responsible and pay any settlement or judgment effected by Acquiring and attorneys' fees. Notwithstanding anything contained herein to the contrary, the Shareholder shall not be required to pay the first $25,000 of Losses (as defined in this Article V.).

VI.   Conditions to Acquiring's and Subsidiary's Obligation to Close

The obligations of Acquiring and Subsidiary to consummate the transactions herein contemplated shall be subject to the fulfillment on or prior to the Closing Date of the following:

A. (1) Target must have: (i) realized pretax earnings (after elimination of non-operating gains and losses) or at least the lesser of 2.2% of net sales or $220,000 in the six-month period preceding July 1, 19__; or (ii) not incurred a loss in the first quarter of 19__ and realized pretax earnings (after elimination of non-operating gains and losses) of at least the lesser of 2.2% of net sales or $220,000 in the six-month period preceding September 30, 19__; or (iii) realized pretax earnings (after elimination of non-operating gains and losses) of 1% of net sales in calendar year 19__; and have informed Acquiring in writing at least two weeks prior to the end of each of the above-referenced periods during which Target believes that it might satisfy the pretax earnings condition referred to above as to such period and given written notice to Acquiring of having met one of the earnings goals outlined in this Section VI.A.(1) within thirty (30) days of having first reached one of such goals (which notice hereby agrees to give).

(2) Notice from Target (for purposes of this Section VI.A.) shall include a balance sheet and statement of earnings of Target, which Acquiring, at its election may have audited by a firm of independent certified accountants in the same manner and subject to the same requirements as provided in Section I hereof. In the event Acquiring should desire to perform an audit, the conclusions of the firm of certified public accountants selected by Acquiring to perform such audit as to whether the conditions set forth in this Section VI.A. have been met shall be conclusive and binding on the parties hereto. Provided that the conditions set forth in Sections VI and VII are met or waived, the Closing shall occur upon 72 hours notice from Target to Acquiring, but no later than ninety (90) days after receipt by Target of notice from Acquiring that the conditions of this Section VI.A. have first been met, or thirty (30) days from the delivery to Target and Acquiring of the above-referenced audit, whichever shall occur first.

(3) Notwithstanding the foregoing, in the event of Shareholder's death or permanent disability, the Closing will occur no later than one hundred twenty (120) days after receipt by Acquiring of notice of such death or evidence reasonably satisfactory to Acquiring of such permanent disability.

B. Contemporaneously with giving notice to Acquiring, Target shall have provided Acquiring with revised Schedules dated as of the last day of the applicable period referred to in Section VI.A.(1) hereof (the "Revised Schedules"), with material changes through such date duly noted, and the Revised Schedules shall not contain any disclosures which would constitute a violation of this Agreement unless any such disclosures have been approved in writing by Acquiring.

C. Acquiring shall have received from _____, counsel for Target and the Shareholder, a favorable opinion, dated the Closing Date, to the effect that (i) is a corporation duly organized and existing in good standing under the laws of the State of California; (ii) Target has the corporate power to carry on its business as then being conducted and, to the knowledge of such counsel, is not required to be qualified as a foreign corporation in any jurisdiction in which the character of the properties owned and/or leased by it or the nature of the business conducted by it makes such qualification necessary; (iii) the authorized and outstanding capital stock of Target is as represented in this Agreement, and all the issued shares have been duly and validly authorized and issued and are fully paid and non-assessable; (iv) neither the execution of this Agreement nor the consummation of the transactions contemplated herein will conflict with any provision of the Articles of Incorporation or Bylaws of Target or to the best of such counsel's knowledge (after having made due investigation with respect thereto), conflict with or result in a breach of any indenture, mortgage, deed of trust or other agreement to which Target or Shareholder is a party and which violation would have a material adverse effect on Target; (v) to the knowledge of such counsel (after having made due investigation with regard thereto), there are no outstanding options or agreements on the part of Target or the Shareholder to issue or sell any capital stock of Target; (vi) this Agreement, the Merger Agreement, the Escrow Agreement and the Employment Agreement have been duly executed and delivered to the extent required by Target and the Shareholder and, assuming valid execution by Target and Subsidiary, each of this Agreement, the Merger Agreement and the Employment Agreement is the legal, valid and binding obligation of Target and the Shareholder to the extent executed by it or him and all corporate action required pursuant to the terms of this Agreement has been taken; (vii) to the knowledge of such counsel, Target is not engaged in or threatened with any legal action or other proceeding, except such legal actions or proceedings as are disclosed on the Revised Schedules, nor has Target been charged with any presently pending violation of any Federal, state or local law or administrative regulation, which would materially adversely affect the financial condition, business, operations, prospects, properties or assets of Target; (viii) no stock transfer taxes are applicable to the transactions provided herein; (ix) all other actions and proceedings required by law, or any of the Executed Agreements, to be taken by Target or the Shareholder at or prior to the Closing Date in connection with the Executed Agreements and the transactions provided for therein have been duly and validly taken; (x) upon filing the Merger Agreement with the California Secretary of State, the Merger will be effective under and in compliance with the laws of the State of California; and (xi) as to such other matters incident to the transactions contemplated hereby as Acquiring may reasonably request at or prior to the Closing.

D. No action or proceeding before a court or any other governmental agency or body shall have been instituted or threatened to restrain or prohibit the Merger contemplated hereby.

E. The representations and warranties of Target and the Shareholder (and any written statement, certificate or schedule furnished pursuant to or in connection with this Agreement) shall have been correct when made and the information contained in the Revised Schedules shall be true on and as of the Closing Date with the same effect as though all such information had been given to Acquiring on and as of such date and each and all of the actions of Shareholder and to be performed on or before the Closing Date pursuant to the terms hereof shall have been duly performed; and Shareholder and Target shall have provided Acquiring with a certificate to that effect.

F. The Shareholder shall have entered into an Employment Agreement with Target in substantially the form attached hereto as Appendix B and executed an investment letter in substantially the form attached hereto as Appendix C.[b]

G. Target and the owner of the building currently leased by Target in _____, California shall have entered into a lease in substantially the form of the existing lease covering that property, except that: (i) the original term shall end five years after the Closing Date; (ii) Lessee shall have a five year option to renew at same basic rent; and (iii) Lessee shall, if Lessor desires to sell the premises, have the option to purchase the premises for $1.2 million. Lessor shall give Lessee written notice of such desire and Lessee shall have 15 days to exercise the option and an additional 30 days to consummate the transaction and to pay the purchase price.

H. All consents, if any, to the consummation of the transactions contemplated herein required in order to prevent a breach of or a default under the terms of any agreement to which Target or the Shareholder is a party or is bound shall have been obtained.

I. The parties shall have complied with all Federal and state securities laws applicable to the transactions contemplated by this Agreement.

J. The Shareholder shall have executed on the Closing Date a general release of all claims which such Shareholder may have to the date thereof against Target, Subsidiary and Acquiring, except claims for current salary, and rights and claims under this Agreement, the Employment Agreement, the lease referred to in Section VI.G., and claims disclosed to Acquiring prior to the Closing Date and consented to in writing by Acquiring.

K. Acquiring shall have received on the Closing Date certificates of good standing, qualification and tax certificates from the State of California.

L. Acquiring shall have received on the Closing Date certificates representing all the issued and outstanding shares and all treasury shares of Target.

---

[b] Appendices B and C have been omitted. Eds.

M. Acquiring shall have received on the Closing Date the corporate minute books, seals and stock transfer books of Target and its predecessors (if any) certified by the corporate secretary of Target (in form and substance acceptable to Acquiring) as complete, true and correct.

N. Acquiring shall have received at the Closing copies of minutes of meetings of the shareholders and the Board of Directors of Target, certified by the corporate secretary of Target, unanimously approving and authorizing the Merger and the other transactions contemplated by this Agreement.

VII.   Conditions to Target's Obligation to Close

The obligation of the Shareholder and Target to consummate the transactions herein contemplated shall be subject to the fulfillment on or prior to the Closing of the following conditions:

A. The Shareholder shall have received from _____, counsel for Acquiring, a favorable opinion, dated the Closing Date, in form and substance satisfactory to Target, the Shareholder and their counsel, to the effect that (i) Acquiring is a corporation duly organized, validly existing and in good standing under the laws of the State of Delaware and it has the corporate power to own its property and to carry on its business as it is now being conducted; (ii) Subsidiary is a corporation duly organized, validly existing and in good standing under the laws of the State of California; (iii) the shares of Acquiring Common Stock to be issued and delivered to the Shareholder pursuant to this Agreement have been duly and validly authorized and issued and upon consummation of the transactions contemplated herein will be fully paid and non-assessable; (iv) this Agreement and the transactions contemplated herein have been duly authorized by the Board of Directors of Acquiring and Subsidiary and, assuming valid execution by the Shareholder and Target, this Agreement is a valid and binding obligation of Acquiring and Subsidiary in accordance with its terms; (v) the Merger Shares have been listed, or approved for listing subject to official notice of issuance, on the American Stock Exchange; and (vi) the issuance of the Merger Shares is exempt from registration under the Act pursuant to Section 4(2) thereof.

B. The representations and warranties made by Acquiring herein shall have been correct when made, and shall be deemed to have been repeated at the Closing Date and shall be true and correct as of such date.

C. No action or proceeding before a court or any other governmental agency or body shall have been instituted or threatened by an agency of the United States Government to restrain or prohibit the Merger contemplated hereby.

D. Shareholder shall have received a favorable tax ruling covering the matters referred to in Section IV.F.

E. The parties shall have complied with all Federal and state securities laws applicable to the transactions contemplated by this Agreement.

F.   The Book Value Per Share of Acquiring Common Stock (determined in the same manner as set forth in Section I.C., but using up-dated information) as of the end of Acquiring's most recent financial quarter prior to the Closing Date shall not be less than Acquiring's Book Value Per Share on December 31, 19__.

VIII.   Closing

The Closing shall be held on the Closing Date at the office of Acquiring or its counsel.   At the Closing, Acquiring, Target and Subsidiary shall consummate the Merger contemplated by this Agreement by filing an Agreement of Merger complying with the laws of the State of California relating to the merger of domestic corporations.   At the Closing the Shareholder shall receive the Acquiring Shares to which he is entitled pursuant to Section II. hereof.

IX.   Termination

This Agreement may be terminated and abandoned prior to the Closing Date:

A.   By mutual written consent of Acquiring, Target and the Shareholder.

B.   By Acquiring if, by the Closing Date, the conditions set forth in Sections V and VI hereof shall not have been met or waived.

C.   By Target or the Shareholder if, by the Closing Date, the conditions set forth in Sections V and VII hereof shall not have been met or waived.

D.   By any party hereto if the Closing Date contemplated herein shall not have occurred on or before March 1, 19__.

X.   Additional Representations of Shareholder

The Shareholder hereby acknowledges:

A.   That in his opinion he has such knowledge and experience in financial and business matters, and particularly the business conducted by Acquiring, that he is capable of evaluating the risks of the investment in Acquiring Common Stock contemplated by this Agreement.

B.   That he is able to bear the economic risk of the investment in Acquiring Common Stock contemplated by this Agreement.

C.   That the Merger Shares which Shareholder may receive are for his own account and not on behalf of other persons;

D.   That Acquiring has furnished to Shareholder a copy of its annual report for the fiscal year ended _____, 19__ on Form 10-K, its quarterly report for the quarter ended _____, 19__ on Form 10-Q, its proxy statement dated _____, 19__, all as filed with the Securities and Exchange Commission, and its 19__ Annual Report to Stockholders and a description of Acquiring Common Stock. Acquiring has made available, and does hereby agree to continue to make available, any additional information which the Shareholder may wish to obtain to the extent Acquiring possesses such information or can acquire it without unreasonable effort or expense necessary to verify the accuracy of any information contained in the above-referenced documents and descriptions.

E.   That he has been informed that he must continue to bear the economic risk of the investment in Acquiring Common Stock contemplated herein for an indefinite period because the Merger Shares will not have been registered under the Securities Act of 1933 and therefore will be subject to the restrictions set forth in subsection F below and cannot be sold unless they are subsequently registered under the Securities Act of 1933 or an exemption from such registration is available.

F.   That the certificates representing the Merger Shares will contain a legend stating that the Acquiring Common Stock has not been registered under the Securities Act of 1933 and cannot be sold absent registration under such Act or an exemption therefrom and that stop transfer instructions will be given to the transfer agent for Acquiring prohibiting such transfer agent from transferring the Acquiring Common Stock without compliance with the provisions of the Securities Act of 1933.

G.   That he will be required as a condition to receiving his Acquiring Common Stock at the Closing (and thereafter) to execute an investment letter in the form of the letter attached hereto as Appendix C.

XI.   Notices

Any notices or communication required or permitted hereunder shall be sufficiently given if sent by first class mail, postage prepaid, and if to the Target or the Shareholder addressed to: _____, California with a copy to _____, Attention: _____. If to Acquiring or Subsidiary addressed to it at _____, marked for the attention of _____, with a copy thereof to _____, Attention: _____.

XII.   Heirs, Legal Representatives and Assigns

This Agreement and the rights of the parties hereunder may not be assigned and shall be binding upon and shall inure to the benefit of the parties hereto and their heirs, legal representatives and successors.

XIII.   Entire Agreement

This Agreement and the Schedules, Exhibits and Appendices attached hereto and to be attached hereto, and the documents delivered pursuant hereto constitute the entire agreement and understanding between Acquiring, Subsidiary, Target and the Shareholder and supersede any prior agreement and understanding relating to the subject matter of this Agreement. No change, amendment, termination or attempted waiver of any of the provisions hereof shall be binding on Acquiring, Subsidiary, Target or Shareholder unless in writing and signed by the President or other senior officer of Acquiring, Subsidiary, or Target, as the case may be, and if such change affects the Shareholder, then if signed by the Shareholder. Unless specifically otherwise herein provided or agreed to by Acquiring, Subsidiary, Target and the Shareholder in writing, no modification, waiver, termination, rescission, discharge or cancellation of this Agreement shall affect the right of Acquiring, Subsidiary, Target or the Shareholder to enforce any claim whether or not liquidated, which accrued prior to the date of such modification waiver, termination, rescission, discharge or cancellation of this Agreement, and no waiver of any provision or of any default under this Agreement shall affect the rights of Acquiring, Subsidiary, Target or the Shareholder thereafter to enforce said provision or to exercise any right or remedy in the event of any other default, whether or not similar.

XIV.   Counterparts

This Agreement may be executed simultaneously in two or more counterparts, each of which shall be deemed an original and all of which together shall constitute but one and the same instrument.

XV.   Expenses

Whether or not the transactions herein contemplated shall be consummated, Acquiring, Subsidiary and the Shareholder will each pay their own fees, expenses and disbursements and their counsels in connection with the subject matter of this Agreement or any of the Executed Agreements and any amendments thereto and all other costs and expenses incurred by it or him in performing and complying with all conditions to be performed by it or him under this Agreement or any of the Executed Agreements. Target will pay the fees, expenses and disbursements incurred by it and its counsel in connection with the subject of this Agreement or any of the Executed Agreements and any amendments thereto and all other costs and expenses incurred by it in performing and complying with all conditions to be performed by it under this Agreement, and any of the Executed Agreements.

XVI. Further Assurances

Upon reasonable request from time to time, the Shareholder shall execute and deliver all reasonably required documents and do all other acts which may be reasonably requested by Acquiring to implement and carry out the terms and conditions of the transaction contemplated by this Agreement, all such actions to be performed without further consideration, but at the expense of Acquiring, unless arising out of the default of the Shareholder. Except as prohibited by law, the Shareholder shall be required to furnish evidence against himself.

XVII. Miscellaneous

A. Any party hereto may waive any provision contained in this Agreement for its benefit and such waiver shall not affect any of the other provisions hereof.

B. The singular shall include the plural and the plural shall include the singular; any gender shall include all other genders—all as the meaning and context of this Agreement shall require.

C. This Agreement shall be governed and regulated and the rights and liabilities of all parties hereto shall be construed in accordance with the laws of the State of California.

IN WITNESS WHEREOF, the undersigned parties have set their hands as of the day and year first above written.

ESCROW AGREEMENT

AGREEMENT made as of this _____ day of _____, 19__, by and among _____ ("_____"), _____, a California resident ("Shareholder"), and _____ ("Depository") hereinafter referred to as "ESCROW AGREEMENT".

Preliminary Statement

Acquiring Corp. ("Acquiring") and the Shareholder have entered into a Plan of Reorganization for the conversion of all of the issued and outstanding shares of Target Corp., a California corporation ("Target") into shares of Acquiring's common stock, par value $1 ("Acquiring Common Stock"), dated _____ __, 19__ (the "Acquisition Agreement"), which Acquisition Agreement is incorporated herein by reference and made a part hereof. The parties have agreed that Shareholder will deposit certain of the

Acquiring Common Stock received pursuant to the Acquisition Agreement (the "Merger Shares") in escrow in accordance with the provisions of Section II of the Acquisition Agreement.

NOW, THEREFORE, in consideration of the mutual covenants, representations and promises of the parties to this Escrow Agreement, the parties hereto agree as follows:

1. Deposit of Shares. Shareholder will deliver to the Depository that portion of the Merger Shares referred to in Section II.B. of the Acquisition Agreement (i.e., 15,000 shares) at the time a place of Closing (as defined in the Acquisition Agreement).

Such shares as are delivered to Depository (the "Escrow Shares") shall be held and distributed by Depository as provided herein and in Section II of the Acquisition Agreement. The Escrow Shares will have attached thereto a stock power duly executed in blank by Shareholder, with signature guaranteed by a bank or trust company having an office or correspondent in New York City or by a broker or by a firm of brokers having membership in the New York Stock Exchange, in proper form to permit the transfer of the Shares represented thereby on the books of Acquiring.

The Escrow Shares shall continue to be registered in the name of Shareholder unless they are transferred to _____ in accordance with the terms of this Escrow Agreement.

For purposes of this Escrow Agreement:

(a) "Year One" is the four fiscal quarters of 19__ ending on _____. The "Base Year" is the twelve full months immediately preceding Year One. "Year Two" is the first four fiscal quarters of 19__ following Year One. "Year Three" is the first four fiscal quarters of 19__ following Year Two.

(b) The "Target Operations" are the business operations which constituted Target immediately prior to the Closing.

(c) "Pretax Earnings" are the pretax earnings of the Operations after elimination of all non-operating gains and losses, as computed by the public accounting firm which is the public accounting firm of _____ at the time of such computation (the "Accounts"). "Net Sales" are the net sales of the Operations (as determined by the Accountants) for the time period in question. Acquiring, Shareholder and Depository hereby agree that, for purposes of this Escrow Agreement, determinations of Net Sales and Pretax Earnings, as computed by the Accountants, shall be final and binding.

2. The Term of the Escrow. The Depository (or its nominee) agrees to accept delivery of the certificates representing the Escrow Shares subject to the provisions of this Escrow Agreement, and to hold and distribute said shares during the period of this Escrow Agreement, all as herein provided.

3. Delivery and Distribution of Escrow Shares. Within sixty days from the end of each Year (Year One, Year Two or Year Three), as appropriate, the Accountants shall compute and deliver to the Shareholder, Acquiring and to the Depository, a statement showing the Net Sales and the Pretax Earnings of the Operations for such Year. Within thirty days from the date of the receipt of such statements from the Accountants, the Depository shall distribute and deliver to Shareholder the number of Escrow Shares (if any) to which Shareholder may be entitled pursuant to this Escrow Agreement, and upon termination of this Escrow Agreement, the Depository shall distribute all of the Escrow Shares remaining in escrow and deliver same to Shareholder or Acquiring all in accordance with the following provisions:

(a) If during Year One the Target Operations shall experience Net Sales equal to or in excess of 115% of those experienced by the Target Operations in the Base Year and have Pretax Earnings equal to or in excess of 3.4% of such Net Sales, then 5,000 of the Escrow Shares shall be delivered to Shareholder.

(b) If during Year Two the Target Operations experience Net Sales equal to or in excess of 132% of those experienced by the Operations in the Base Year, and have Pretax Earnings equal to or in excess of 4.2% of such Net Sales, then 5,000 of the Escrow Shares shall be delivered to Shareholder.

(c) If during Year Three the Target Operations experience Net Sales equal to or in excess of 152% of those experienced by the Target Operations in the Base Year, and have Pretax Earnings equal to or in excess of 4.8% of such Net Sales, then 5,000 of the Escrow Shares shall be delivered to Shareholder.

(d) Notwithstanding Sections 3(a) through 3(c) above, in the event that any Escrow Shares remain in escrow after the end of Year Three, all remaining Escrow Shares shall be delivered to the Shareholder if the Target Operations shall experience Net Sales in Year Three equal to or in excess of 152% of those experienced by the Target Operations in the Base Year, and the aggregate Pretax Earnings of the Target Operations in the Years One, Two and Three shall equal or exceed the sum of (i) 3.4% of Year One's Net Sales (ii) 4.2% of Year Two's Net Sales, and (iii) 4.8% of Year Three's Net Sales. Those Escrow Shares which are not released from escrow and delivered to Shareholder pursuant to Sections 3(a) through 3(d) shall be returned to Acquiring 42 months following the Closing.

4. Dividends and Other Distributions: Voting. Shareholder shall be entitled to retain all dividends, whether in cash, shares or other securities or property paid or distributed on or in respect of the Escrow Shares other than dividends payable in Common Stock. Shareholder agrees to deliver to Depository to be held in escrow subject to the term of this Escrow Agreement, all dividends in Acquiring Common Stock and all Acquiring

Common Stock issued as a result of a stock split, together with stock powers duly executed in blank by Shareholder, with signature guaranteed by a bank or trust company having an office or correspondent in New York City or by a broker or by a firm of brokers having membership in the New York Stock Exchange, in proper form to permit the transfer of the Shares represented thereby on the books of Acquiring. All such shares shall be distributed by Depository in the same manner as the Escrow Shares in respect of which it was issued.

5. Fees and Expenses. Acquiring shall bear and pay all expenses and charges of the Depository incurred in connection with this Escrow Agreement upon demand by the Depository.

6. Limitation of Depository's Liability. The Depository shall incur no liability in respect of any action taken or suffered by it in reliance upon any notice, direction, instruction, consent, statement or other paper or document believed by it to be genuine and duly authorized, nor for anything except its own willful misconduct or gross negligence. The Depository shall not be responsible for the validity or sufficiency of any shares or other securities which may be delivered to it hereunder. In all questions arising under this Escrow Agreement, the Depository may rely on the advice of counsel, and for anything done, omitted or suffered in good faith by the Depository shall not be liable to anyone.

Without limiting the generality of the foregoing provisions, the Depository shall be entitled to completely rely on the statements delivered to it by the Accountants and/or on the certification and direction of the President or any Vice-President of Acquiring, and shall not be liable for any error, misstatement, misinformation or misdirection in the Statements of the Accountants or the certification or direction of the President or any Vice-President of Acquiring.

7. Notices. All notices, instructions and other communications required or permitted to be given hereunder or necessary or convenient in connection herewith shall be in writing and shall be deemed to have been duly given if delivered personally or mailed first-class, postage prepaid, registered or certified mail, as follows:

If to the Depository:

If to Shareholder:

If to _____ :

With copy to:

or to such other addresses as the Depository, Shareholder or shall designate in writing delivered to each other.

8. General. This Agreement shall be governed by and construed in accordance with the laws of the State of _____ and shall be binding upon and inure to the benefit of the parties hereto and their respective heirs, executors, administrators or other legal representatives, and their respective successors.

9. Additional Documents. Acquiring and the Shareholder agree to execute all other documents reasonably required by the Depository, in keeping with the meaning and intent of this Escrow Agreement and the Acquisition Agreement.

IN WITNESS WHEREOF, the parties hereto have set their hands as of the day and year first above written.

INDEX

References are to Pages.